good life

M000200913

Tom
Snowball
11/16/ 95

SLOW FOOD GUIDE TO THE WINES OF THE WORLD

1900 wineries
5000 tasting notes
150 Top Wines

Slow Food Editore

Slow Food Guide to the Wines of the World

First Edition

Edited and designed by Slow Food Editore
Via della Mendicità Istruita, 14, 12042 Bra (Cuneo)
Tel. (0172)426207 - Fax 421293

ISBN 88-86283-00-8

The author and publishers will be grateful for any information that will assist them in keeping
future editions up to date. Although all reasonable care has been taken in the preparation of this
book, neither the publishers nor the authors can accept any liability for any consequences
arising from the use thereof or from the information contained herein.

Art Design: Studio Maremmani Gualzetti (Milano)
Typeset by: Slow Food Editore (Bra) & Carma (Milano)
Printed and bound in Italy by: Rotolito Lombarda (Pioltello - Mi)

Conceived, directed and produced by the
International *Slow Food* Movement

original Italian edition
Editor-in-Chief: Carlo Petrini
Coordination: Federica Colla, Mavi Negro, Gigi Piumatti, Carmen Wallace
Paging & Maps: Maurizio Burdese
Production: Antonio Attorre, Roberto Burdese, Federica Colla, Maria Mancuso, Vittorio Manganelli, Mavi Negro, Giovanni Ruffa, Gigi Piumatti, Piero Sardo, Carmen Wallace
Translations: Susanna Bunzel, Marta Del Zanna, Marcella Leone, Claudio Micca, Serenella Pinca, Leila Pruneti, Irene Sardo

English edition
Senior Editors: Richard Baudains, Tom O'Toole, Carmen Wallace
Assistant Editors: Geoffrey Anscombe, Nick Mason, Laura Pragnall, James Lawther, Kylie Sharp, Rupert Volheim, Giles Watson
Translators: Cecilia Castellini, Christie Cardelio, Laura Kramer, Jill Norris, Kylie Sharp, Giles Watson, Kim Wicks

National Coordinators:
    Argentina, Chile, Uruguay: Miro Popic
    Australia: Huon Hooke
    Austria: Wolfgang Obermaier
    CIS, South Africa: David Molyneux-Berry, MW
    France: Roger Feuilly, Tim Johnston
    Germany: Jens Priewe
    Italy: Antonio Attorre, Giovanni Ruffa, Gigi Piumatti
    Mexico: Giorgio De'Angeli
    New Zealand: Bob Campbell, MW
    Portugal: Guillermo Campos
    Slovenia: Giulio Colomba
    Spain: Carlos Delgado
    Switzerland: Peter Osterwalder, Holger Zwink
    USA: Bob Thompson
    Bulgaria, Czech Rep. & Slovakia, Cyprus, Greece, Hungary, India, GB, Israel, Lebanon, Morocco, Romania, Turkey, Zimbabwe: Nicolas Belfrage, MW

Contributors: Antonio Attorre, Isabelle Bachelard, Paolo Battimelli, Richard Baudains, Fiona Beeston, Nicolas Belfrage, Gerhard Benz, Peter Blaha, Juan Bureo, Bob Campbell, Guillermo Campos, Daniele Cernilli, Roberto Checchetto, Etienne Clerq, Giulio Colomba, Giorgio De'Angeli, Carlos Delgado, Markus Del Monego, Gilles Dupuis, Roger Feuilly, Andrea Gabbrielli, Huon Hooke, Tim Johnston, Frank Kämmer, Rudolf Knoll, Joachim Krieger, James Lawther, Fernando Laudao, Pierre Leblanc, Carlo Leidi, Carlo Macchi, William Madcock, Vittorio Manganelli, Gianni Mantoanello, Nicolas Mason, Giacomo Mojoli, David Molyneux-Berry, Jean-Christophe Piquet, Laura Pragnall, Wolfgang Obermaier, Peter Osterwalder, Nereo Pederzolli, Jim Pithbury, Gigi Piumatti, Miro Popic, Jens Priewe, Nanni Ricci, Maurizio Rossi, Michel Renard, Venancio Romero, Giovanni Ruffa, Sandro Sangiorgi, Bartolomé Sanchez, Piero Sardo, Heiko Schapitz, Gunter Schimdt, Martin Schimdt, Paul Smith, Diego Soracco, Claudia Stern, Eckard Supp, Bob Thompson, Sylvain Vérut, Evaristo Valderrama, Guido Zublena, Holger Zwink

Table of Contents

Foreword

Introduction

Once it was cool to be cool. Now it is slow to be slow. For those who have not met the purposeful snail of Arcigola Slow Food, a word of introduction.

Carlo Petrini is the Pavarotti of food and wine; his "sotto voce" is your "mezzo forte", his sips your swallows, his nibbles your bites. When McDonalds opened in Rome he smelt sacrilege. Revolted by the idea of fast food, he founded Slow Food. You do not snatch at life's great pleasures; you savour them. In a world where homogenization is running out of control, you relish what is particular, original, indigenous – and if Brussels has its way – will probably soon be illegal.

Petrini is the champion of the authentic, however awkward. At his table you eat dishes of transcendental simplicity; plates that smell of home. His guides encourage the kind of food which Michelin stars try to smother out of existence.

Slow Food's *Guide to Daily Wines* is already an Italian classic. Now we have the snail's eye view of the world's best wines: deliberately unhomogenized, the work of seventy-some disciples whose palates palpitate to regional rhythms.

The philosophy of the snail applies to wine like this: wine is a product of the soil, its flavour the flavour of a place, its quality the quality of the person who makes it. Thus a good Bordeaux cannot be a good Burgundy, a good Barolo a good Chianti, or a good New Zealand wine a relevant comparison to one from the Napa valley. You will prefer one to the other, because anybody given two glasses can state a preference.

But the secret of enjoyment (let alone understanding) is seeing the virtues of each in its turn.

The snail rejects as 'fast' the illiberal practice of giving wines scores like students in exams. The snail rejects all political correctness. It lives for today, and for the future of our todays: may they be as slow a summer afternoons, as the crust in the sleeping port, as the purposeful snail picking his way across the dewy vineyard.

Hugh Johnson

Introduction

Foreword

This first edition of the *Slow Food Guide to the Wines to the World* is the work of many hands. The editorial team was adamant from the start that the wines featured in the book should be selected and described, wherever possible, by authors based in the world's great wine-producing areas. Underlying the decision is respect for hands-on local knowledge and, above all, for taste buds and judgements of local wine professionals. Who better to write about wines than the people who actually live and work where they are made?

Recruiting a small army of native contributors from five continents, setting up a network of national co-ordinators and establishing a common working language with them proved to be no mean feat. No less complicated, given the wide cross-section of tasters involved, was the job of devising the criteria for evaluating the wines. We deliberately avoided the hair-splitting of the commonly used 100-points scale and finally opted, instead, for a system which groups the 5,000-plus wines in the Guide into three broad categories. The ratings are indicated by the grape-bunch symbol. 'One bunch' wines are exemplary of their type and generally outstanding representatives of the grape varieties and traditions of their zones of origin. The standard is high. Many winerys are represented in the Guide by only one or two (maximum five) of the products from larger, often reliable and well-made ranges. 'Two bunches' indicate wines with the features of international premium quality: exceptional character, balance and concentration and wide international appeal. Finally, the 'three-bunch' symbol is reserved for 150 Top Wines of the world, chosen after repeated tasting and long, passionate debate at both regional and national levels. The Top Wines selection, like all subjective classifications, will inevitably divide opinion. We hope it will stimulate discussion and promote general interest in wine.

The Guide aims to talk about wine in a concise, straightforward and informative way which will increase enjoyment and understanding. The 1,250 pages of this book present the infinite diversity of the world's wines and the fascinating differences between producing nations. They also bring to life the human side of wine-making, the personalities and philosophies of the men and women behind the great wines of the world.

The Guide has been produced and will be distributed world-wide under the auspices of Slow Food, the growing Italian-based wine and food association with affiliated groups in 18 countries.

We are convinced that the trend towards 'internationalization' in the wine trade is a sign of consumer demand, not only in relatively young wine-drinking countries, but also in those with conservative, nationalistic traditions such as France, Italy and Spain. Hence the need for a truly international, up-to-date reference book, which gives a comprehensive overview of the fantastically rich panorama of the world's wines, and is published in all the major European languages. (by June 1993, the book will be available in French, German and Spanish as well as English and the original Italian.) We hope that the Slow Food Guide will bring wine-drinkers everywhere closer in touch with the fast-developing, exciting world of wine.

Carlo Petrini

How to Use the Guide

Entries are arranged in alphabetical order by country, region and winery or producer name. Australia, France, Germany, Italy, Spain and the USA are divided by wine region.

Types of Wines

🍇 White

🍇 Rosé

🍇 Red

Rating System

The 'grape bunch' symbol is used to indicate the color of the wine; the number of bunches represents the quality rating assigned by the contributor.

🍇 An exemplary wine of its type with outstanding local character

🍇🍇 An international premium quality wine

🍇🍇🍇 A Top Wine, considered one of the 150 best wines in the world

Price Levels

The 'ex-cellar', or direct from the producer, bottle prices, are calculated in US dollars and are intended only as an approximate guide.

① up to $ 9.99

② $ 10.00 - $ 14.99

③ $ 15.00 - $ 24.99

④ $ 25.00 or more

Publisher's note:
Imported wines, in the United States, for example, typically arrive on the retail shelf through a 'three tier system': importer, wholesaler, retailer. Each tier usually practises a 33%-50% markup. A wine bought by an importer 'ex-cellar' from the producer at $5.00 is sold to the wholesaler for $7.50; the wholesaler sells to the retailer at $10.00; the retailer buys the wine and puts it on the shelf for the consumer at $15.00. Thus, the wine that cost $5.00 'ex-cellar' becomes a $15.00 bottle of wine.
The British import market, amongst others, is often more direct. Retail prices may vary considerably between importing countries depending on import duties, tax and the distribution system. For the purposes of this guide, the only common parameter possible is the 'ex-cellar' bottle price.

Top Wines

AUSTRALIA

Cabernet Sauvignon Cyril Henschke 1988	Henschke
Cabernet Sauvignon John Riddoch 1988	Wynns Coonawarra Estate
Chardonnay Eileen Hardy 1989	Hardy
Chardonnay Margaret River Art Series 1986	Leeuwin Estate
Grange Hermitage Bin 95 1986	Penfolds
Rhine Riesling 1990	Petaluma
Sauternes Australian Botrytis Semillon 1987	De Bortoli
Shiraz 1990	Craiglee

AUSTRIA

Muskat Ottonel Beerenauslese Zwischen den Seen 1988	Kracher
Riesling Ried Dürnsteiner Kellerberg Smaragd 1990	Franz Xaver Pichler
Ruster Furmint Ausbruch Ried Satz 1989	Robert Wenzel
Ruster Ruländer Ausbruch 1981	Peter Schandl

CHILE

Cabernet Sauvignon Antiguas Reservas Maipo 1986	Cousiño-Macul
Cabernet Sauvignon Colchagua 1990	Los Vascos
Cabernet Sauvignon Don Melchor Reserva Privada 1987	Concha y Toro

FRANCE

Alsace Riesling Clos Saint Urbain Rangen de Thann 1989	Zind Humbrecht
Alsace Riesling Vendanges Tardives 1990	Weinbach
Bandol 1989	Château de Pibarnon
Bandol Cuvée Spéciale La Tourtine 1989	Domaine Tempier
Bonnezeaux Château La Chapelle 1990	Château de Fesles
Bourgueil Cuvée Vaumoreau 1990	Pierre-Jacques Druet
Chablis Montée de Tonnerre 1990	François et Jean Marie Raveneau
Champagne 1986	Pol Roger
Champagne Clos du Mesnil 1983	Krug
Champagne Vieilles Vignes Françaises 1985	Bollinger
Châteauneuf-du-Pape 1989	Château de Beaucastel
Château Chalon 1985	Jean Macle
Chevalier-Montrachet 1989	Domaine Leflaive
Chinon Clos de la Dioterie 1989	Charles Joguet
Condrieu Coteau de Chery 1991	André Perret
Cornas 1989	Auguste Clape
Côte Rôtie 1989	Bernard Burgaud
Côte Rôtie La Mouline 1988	Etienne Guigal
Coteaux d'Aix-en-Provence Les Baux 1989	Domaine de Trévallon
Hermitage 1990	Jean-Louis Chave
Jurançon Vendanges Tardives 1990	Domaine Cauhapé
Madiran Cuvée Prestige Château Montus 1989	Alain Brumont
Margaux 1989	Château Margaux
Meursault Perrières 1990	Domaine des Comtes Lafon
Meursault Perrières 1990	Jean-François Coche-Dury

Top Wines

Pauillac 1989	Château Pichon-Longueville
Pauillac 1989	Château Pichon Longueville Comtesse de Lalande
Pauillac 1989	Château Latour
Pauillac 1989	Château Mouton-Rothschild
Pessac-Léognan 1988	Château Pape-Clément
Pessac-Léognan 1989	Château de Fieuzal
Pessac-Léognan 1989	Château Haut-Brion
Pomerol 1988	Vieux Château Certan
Pomerol 1989	Pétrus
Pomerol 1989	Château Trotanoy
Quarts de Chaume 1990	Château Bellerive
Romanée-Conti 1989	Domaine de La Romanée-Conti
Saint-Emilion 1989	Château Ausone
Saint-Emilion 1989	Château Cheval Blanc
Saint-Estèphe 1990	Château Montrose
Saint-Estèphe 1989	Cos d'Estournel
Saint-Julien 1989	Château Ducru-Beaucaillou
Saint-Julien 1989	Château Léoville Las-Cases
Saumur-Champigny Cuvée Le Bourg 1990	Clos Rougeard
Sauternes 1986	Château d'Yquem
Sauternes 1989	Château Suduiraut
Sauternes-Barsac 1990	Château Climens
Savennières-Coulée de Serrant 1990	Nicolas Joly
Volnay Clos de la Bousse d'Or 1990	Domaine de la Pousse d'Or
Volnay Les Champans 1989	Domaine de Montille
Vosne-Romanée Les Suchots 1988	Jacques Confuron-Cotetidot
Vouvray Réserve Moelleux 1990	Domaine du Clos Naudin

GERMANY

Assmannshäuser Höllenberg Spätburgunder Spätlese *** trocken 1990	
	August Kesseler
Berncasteler Doctor Riesling Auslese 1989	
	Wwe. Dr. H. Thanisch
Brauneberger Juffer Sonnenuhr Riesling Auslese Lange Goldkapsel 1990	
	Fritz Haag
Haardter Bürgergarten Riesling Spätlese trocken 1991	
	Müller-Catoir
Ihringer Winklerberg Spätburgunder Auslese *** trocken 1990	
	Dr. Heger
Iphöfer Julius-Echter-Berg Riesling Spätlese 1990	
	Hans Wirsching
Julius-Echter-Berg Riesling Spätlese trocken 1990	
	Juliusspital
Kiedricher Gräfenberg Riesling Trockenbeerenauslese 1991	
	Robert Weil
Leiwener Laurentiuslay Riesling Auslese trocken 1990	
	St.Urbanshof

Top Wines

Maximin Grünhäuser Abtsberg Riesling Auslese Nr. 96 1990
C. von Schubert´sche Gutsverwaltung
Niersteiner Brudersberg Riesling Spätlese trocken 1990
Freiherr Heyl zu Herrnsheim
Oberhäuser Brücke Riesling Auslese 1991
Hermann Dönnhoff
Essinger Osterberg Grauburgunder Eiswein 1989
Winfried Frey
Schloßgut Diel Riesling Auslese Goldkapsel No. 4 1990
Schlossgut Diel
Saarburger Rausch Riesling Eiswein 1989
Zilliken Forstmeister Geltz Erben
Wehlener Sonnenuhr Riesling Auslese Lange Goldkapsel 1990
Joh. Jos. Prüm
Weissburgunder Tafelwein trocken 1990
Wolfgang Geissler
Würzburger Stein-Harfe Riesling Auslese 1990
Bürgerspital zum Heiligen Geist

ITALY

Acininobili 1989	Maculan
Arte 1990	Domenico Clerico
Barbaresco Bricco Asili 1989	Ceretto
Barbaresco Sorì San Lorenzo 1988	Gaja
Barbera d'Alba 1989	Paolo Scavino
Barolo Bricco Bussia Vigna Colonnello 1988	Aldo Conterno
Barolo Cerequio 1988	Roberto Voerzio
Barolo Riserva Monfortino 1985	Giacomo Conterno
Brunello di Montalcino Riserva Poggio all'Oro 1985	Banfi
Brunello di Montalcino Riserva Poggio al Vento 1985	Tenuta Col d'Orcia
Cabernet Sauvignon Collezione De Marchi 1988	Isole e Olena
Chardonnay 1990	Ronco del Gnemiz
Chianti Classico Riserva Anfiteatro 1988	Vecchie Terre di Montefili
Chianti Classico Riserva Ducale Etichetta Oro 1988	Tenimenti Ruffino
Chianti Classico Riserva Vigneto Rancia 1988	Fattoria di Felsina
Chianti Classico Vigneto Bertinga 1988	Castello di Ama
Collio Chardonnay 1990	Gravner
Duca Enrico 1987	Duca di Salaparuta
Isonzo Sauvignon Vieris 1990	Vie di Romans
La Vigna di Sonvico 1990	La Barbatella
Le Pergole Torte 1988	Fattoria di Montevertine
Sassicaia 1988	Tenuta San Guido
Solaia 1988	Marchesi Antinori
Trebbiano d'Abruzzo 1988	Edoardo Valentini
Vigna Arborina 1989	Elio Altare
Vintage Tunina 1990	Vinnaioli Jermann

Top Wines

NEW ZEALAND
Cabernet/Merlot Coleraine 1990   Te Mata
Pinot Noir 1990   Martinborough
Sauvignon Blanc 1991   Cloudy Bay

PORTUGAL
Barca Velha 1981   Ferreira
Quinta de Vargellas Vintage Port 1978   Taylor, Fladgate & Yeatman

SOUTH AFRICA
Cabernet Sauvignon Stellenryck 1987   The Bergkelder
Edelkeur 1988   Nederburg
Pinotage 1989   Kanonkop
Rust en Vrede 1988   Rust en Vrede
Vintage Reserve Port 1989   Boplaas

SPAIN
Clos de L'Obac 1989   Clos de l'Obac
Jerez Oloroso Bailen   Osborne
Jerez Palo Cortado Sibarita   Pedro Domecq
Jerez Pedro Ximénez Noé   González Byass
Jerez Amontillado Escuadrilla   Emilio Lustau
Manzanilla Pasada San León   Herederos de Argüeso
Navarra Viña Magaña Merlot Reserva 1985   Magaña
Penedés Gran Coronas Mas La Plana 1983   Torres
Ribera de Duero Pesquera Janus Reserva Especial 1982   Alejandro Fernández
Ribera de Duero Vega Sicilia Unico 1982   Vega Sicilia
Rioja Barón de Chirel Reserva 1986   Herederos del Marqués de Riscal
Rioja Imperial Gran Reserva 1981   C.V.N.E.
Rioja Prado Enea Reserva 1981   Muga
Rioja Reserva 904 1981   La Rioja Alta

USA
Anderson Valley Gewürztraminer 1990   Lazy Creek
Carneros Pinot Noir 1989   Etude
Dry Creek Valley Zinfandel 1990   Nalle
Napa Valley Cabernet Sauvignon 1987   Mt Veeder
Napa Valley Cabernet Sauvignon Hillside Select 1987   Shafer
Napa Valley Cabernet Sauvignon Reserve 1987   Chappellet
Napa Valley Chardonnay 1990   Trefethen
Napa Valley Reserve 1987   Clos Duval
Napa Valley Zinfandel 1989   Frog's Leap
Russian River Valley Pinot Noir 1989   Dehlinger
Russian River Valley Pinot Noir Rochioli 1989   Williams & Selyem
Santa Barbara Pinot Noir 1989   Sanford
Sonoma Valley California Chardonnay 1990   Kistler
Sonoma Valley Zinfandel Jack London 1989   Kenwood Winery
Yakima Valley Merlot David Lake 1989   Columbia Winery

The Number of Entries per Country

Europe

Austria 40
Bulgaria 5
Confederation of Independent States 9
Czech Republic & Slovakia 4
France 672
Germany 187
Great Britain 5
Greece..10
Hungary 6
Italy...366
Portugal 27
Romania..3
Slovenia 10
Spain...198
Switzerland...25

The Americas

Argentina 14
Chile 14
Mexico...3
United States of America 152
Uruguay 2

Africa

Morocco...1
South Africa 40
Zimbabwe...1

Asia

Cyprus 2
India..1
Israel 1
Lebanon 1
Turkey..1

Oceania

Australia 80
New Zealand..20

ARGENTINA

Argentina is a huge wine producing country with a potential surface area of 2.7 million square kilometers suitable for growing all types of grape varieties and for producing any style of wine. The first people to make wine in Argentina were Spanish settlers who arrived around the middle of the 16th century and benefitted from the winemaking skills of the Jesuit and Franciscan missionaries. The Mendoza and San Juan provinces were planted primarily with Mexican and Peruvian grape varieties and a few from Spain like the Pedro Ximènez. However, the wine industry did not really take off until the middle of the 19th century with the arrival of the first Italian and Spanish immigrants who brought with them their traditions and culture including that of wine. They devised new irrigation systems to supply water to the land, until then abandoned, and increased the vineyard area. Production doubled when the Mendoza region became linked by rail to the capital and therefore the Atlantic Ocean. The rapid growth resulted in production of a large volume of low quality wine, a situation that did not start to change until the mid 1900s.

Today the most important wine provinces in terms of surface area are Mendoza (63.1%), San Juan (26.3%), La Rioja (5.6%), Rìo Negro (2.5%) and Salta (1.3%). A number of different grape varieties are grown of French and other origins. Malbec (70%) is the most planted red varietal but Merlot, Cabernet Sauvignon, Cabernet Franc, Pinot Noir, Syrah, Nebbiolo, Tannat, Bonarda, Lambrusco, Barbera, Sangioveto and Verdot are also grown. The whites include Chardonnay, Chenin Blanc, Sauvignon, Sémillon, Tocay, Riesling, Torrontés, Pedro Ximénez, Saint Jeannet, Pinot Gris, Moscatel and Ugni Blanc.

Argentinians have consumed entirely domestic wines for over 400 years exporting only musts for fermentation, mainly to distant markets. Argentinian wine producers have therefore traditionally been more concerned with quantity rather than quality. At one stage over 350,000 hectares were planted in vineyards and in 1967 wine production reached a record high of 2,080 million liters. In 1968 per capita consumption was 87.5 liters. Today the situation has changed considerably. There are 250,000 hectares under vine, production has decreased to 1,440 million liters and consumption has shrunk to nearly 45 liters per head.

Exporting Argentinian wines is a relatively new trend which began around 1970 with the export of Trapiche from Bodegas Penaflor. Over the last five years only 40 of the country's 1,800 most important wineries have started making special cuvées to enter the difficult international market.

In summary, the style of Argentina's wines was set essentially by the first Italian and Spanish immigrants, who upon their arrival in Argentina aimed at a vast and cheap production. Faced with the challenge of the international market the situation is changing although there are still no precise laws regulating appellation of origin as in Europe. Supervision and controls are currently being carried out by the producers who want to improve the image and quality of their wines. Argentinian wines are destined to improve within a very short time but they need to be more realistically priced as at present prices are higher than those of their South American competitors.

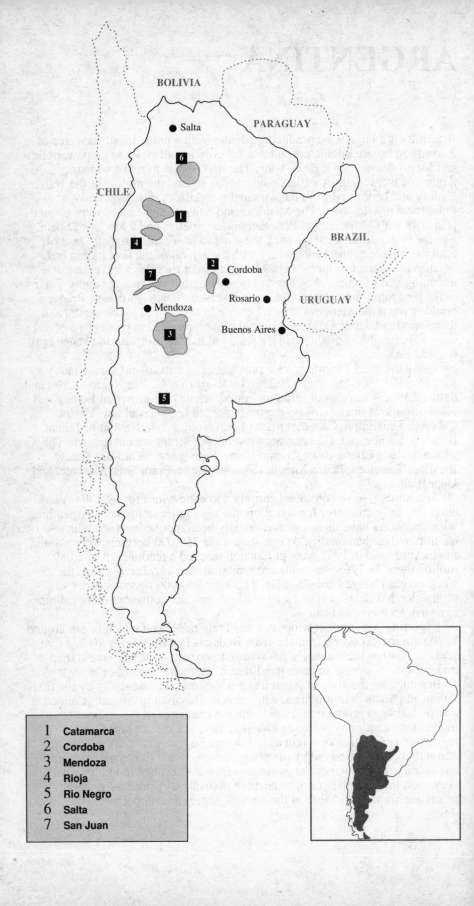

ARGENTINA

BOLIVIA

PARAGUAY

● Salta

6

CHILE

1

4

BRAZIL

2

● Cordoba

7

Rosario ●

URUGUAY

● Mendoza

Buenos Aires ●

3

5

1	**Catamarca**
2	**Cordoba**
3	**Mendoza**
4	**Rioja**
5	**Rio Negro**
6	**Salta**
7	**San Juan**

Bodega Banyuls

Corrientes 2548 - 2° D
1046 Buenos Aires
Tel/Fax (1) 476977

The term Banyuls brings to mind the Pyrenees mountains and one of the greatest fortified dessert wines of France. The South American Banyuls, however, has little connection with this. Under the management and supervision of the French enterprise, Cave Joseph Banyuls, the Argentinian Banyuls produces premium and table wines which are completely different from the French. The winery is located in the province of Mendoza, the country's main wine district and was one of the first to claim regional identity for its wines. Other producers from Lujàn de Cuyo, one of Mendoza's main sub-regions, followed suit and are currently establishing a regional appellation system. Mendoza wines will soon therefore be identified by regional names such as Barrancas, Cruz de Piedra, Vistalba and Russell. Whites at this winery are marketed under the Banyuls label while the reds are sold under the labels Pontigny and Close des Nobles even though the producer's official name still appears on the label.

Banyuls Vino Fino Blanco
Origen Barrancas 1991
Made from 100% Chenin Blanc the wine has a pale yellow-green color and is medium-bodied with fruity aromas and floral overtones. On the palate it is soft, light, well-balanced and of medium persistence.

Pontigny Russel Superior 1990
A Cabernet Sauvignon and Malbec blend which has a lively clear color. Intense with fruity aromas and typical herbaceous overtones on the nose it is light and pleasant on the palate. This is an easy drinking, excellent value for money wine.

Clos de Nobels
Cabernet Sauvignon Origen Agredo 1980
Clear, bright cherry-red color with brick tones. It has intense aromas that fully reveal its varietal nature, elegant with oak-aged spicy overtones. On the palate it is balanced with a good finish.

Bodega Valentín Bianchi

Comandante Torres 500
6500 San Rafaél, Mendoza
Tel. (627) 28393
Fax (627) 24782

The Bodega Valentín Bianchi is undoubtedly one of the best known Argentinian wineries. Heavily marketed locally, this family-run winery has been based in the Mendoza district for several generations. As a subsidiary of Seagram's it was one of the first to export Argentinian wine. It produces a range of Argentina's most popular wines from sparkling méthode champenoise to contemporary varietal wines and large volumes of every-day table wine. Bodega Bianchi currently has 400 hectares under vine, planted mainly with European varieties used for premium wines. Grapes for its domestic table wines are bought. A conservative and hierarchical company in the old Italian tradition it is run by members of the Bianchi family with Alcides Bianchi as managing director, Enzo Bianchi as manager-winemaker and Valentin Bianchi as chief winemaker. The wines themselves could also be described as traditional since the company does not have marketing problems and are not interested in innovation. In Argentina the name Bianchi guarantees convential, classic wines.

Valentín Bianchi Elsa's Vineyard
Chenin Blanc 1990

This is the winery's most modern white. Pale yellow in color with greenish shadows it has fruity aromas with clear apple nuances. On the palate it is full and crisp with a pleasantly bitter finish.

Valentín Bianchi Elsa's Vineyard
Malbec 1988
A typical Argentinian red reminiscent of good, traditional Burgundy. It has red fruit and berry aromas and is smooth, pleasant and round, suitable for every-day drinking. Good value for money.

Valentín Bianchi Elsa's Vineyard
Cabernet Sauvignon 1987

A powerful and straightforward Cabernet with dry plum and spicy aromas, typical of this varietal when grown in a warm climate. It has good structure, an accentuated astringency with a slightly bitter, lingering finish.

Bodega Luigi Bosca e Hijos

San Martín 2045
5507 Luján de Cuyo, Mendoza
Tel. (61) 980437
Fax (61) 249395

This is a small winery with a sound reputation located in the country's most privileged wine district. The Bosca family originate from the Piedmont in Italy where records show they produced wine as far back as 1831. In 1867 Domenico Bosca moved to Argentina and set up a company to import the family's Italian wines. The difficulty of competing with the local wines led Domenico to produce wines locally. In 1904 his son Alfredo registered the name and set up in Lujàn de Cuyo in the province of Mendoza, considered by most to be Argentina's best wine area. In a country where a producer's worth was measured in terms of liters, Bosca developed an important line of premium varietal wines that have already won numerous medals, proportionally more than any other winery. Together with other producers (Leonzio Arizù and Horacio Lopez) Bodega Bosca was one of the first to establish regulations for the province's wines prior to the government regulating what varieties could be grown and where. Since 1987 Luigi Bosca has entered the international market exporting 35% of total production.

Luigi Bosa Sauvignon Blanco
Orogen Maipu 1991
This is one of Argentina's few good whites. Modern, 100% varietal and fruity it has a pale straw-yellow color with greenish nuances. The nose is floral with herbaceous overtones and the palate soft, full and fresh with a clean lingering finish.

Luigi Bosca Pinot Noire
Origen Maipu 1986
A great Burgundy-style wine made on the other side of the world. It has a bright garnet-red color with new oak aromas and spicy overtones. Fat, well-structured with slight tannic astringency it is very pleasant with a full finish.

Luigi Bosca
Cabernet Sauvignon Origen Maipu 1980
A full-bodied red made according to old Italian tradition which is aged in oak for seven years. It has an intense red color and combines evolved aromas with fruity flavors. It is full and structured with a good finish.

Bodegas y Viñedos Humberto Canale

Martín Garciá 320
1165 Buenos Aires
Tel. (1) 265001
Fax (1) 278664

These wines come from the cold part of the country almost on the edge of the world. At a latitude of 40° south Rio Negro is the world's most southerly wine region. The climate is cold and dry with mild summers that dictate harvests in late autumn. Humberto Canale wines are the most typical of this Patagonian area. The winery ranks third in the country with nearly 9,000 hectares under vine. It was founded in 1913 introducing viticulture to an area more traditionally known for fruit cultivation. Canale has always been family run, and for some time has undertaken to make premium wines. A third of the total production is devoted to traditional French varietals which have produced some excellent results. The whites have been particularly successful especially the Sémillon, Riesling and near native Torrontés. Humberto Canale are reserving a greater portion of wines for export, encouraged by the international awards obtained regularly since 1987. The winery also produces a second label, Diego Murillo.

Humberto Canale
Semillon Blanc Río Negro 1990
A white wine made to meet Argentinian tastes. It has a dull yellow color with medium aromas. On the palate it is pleasant, fresh and full with a slightly bitter finish.

Humberto Canale Intimo
Cabernet Sauvignon Río Negro 1984
An interesting Cabernet Sauvignon with a dash of Merlot made in a typically cold and dry climate. It has an intense ruby-red color with fruity aromas. A little lean it has an astringent finish.

Arnaldo Etchart

Nicaragua 4994
1414 Buenos Aires
Tel. (1) 728148
Fax (1) 7751141

This company has long been a major
exporter of grape products and produces a
fairly large volume of table wines for local
consumption. Lately, however, the Bodegas
Arnaldo Etchart have introduced some
wines.that meet international standards. The
winery owns 18,000 hectares of vineyards,
over 300 in the province of Salta and over 50
in the province of Mendoza, yielding grapes
used exclusively to make estate wines. The
most popular wine is made from Torrontés, a
variety originally from Galicia and today
commonly found throughout Argentina,
particularly in the province of Salta. The
winery's northern vineyards are planted with
Cabernet Sauvignon, Pinot Noir,
Chardonnay, Chenin, Riesling, Sauvignon
and Gewurztraminer. Varieties grown in
Mendoza include Cabernet Sauvignon and
Malbec. The winery is advised by French
oenologist Michel Rolland. Etchart's best
wines come from the Salta vineyards and are
marketed under the Cafayate label, the name
of its original region of production. All the
wines represent good value for money in
particular the table wines.

Etchart State Cafayate   🍇 ①
Chardonnay Salta 1991
This is a pale gold Chardonnay with amber tints
with intense varietal aromas and yeasty
overtones. It is fresh, full and persistent on the
palate with a warm alcoholic finish.

Etchart State Cafayate   🍇 ①
Torrontés Salta 1990
Cafayate in the northern region of Salta is
practically a regional appellation for Torrontés.
The wine has a light straw-yellow color with
greenish reflections and fruity flavors. On the
palate it is savoury, full, and captivating and
typical of the grape variety.

Finca Flichman

Corrientes 1891 - Piso 4°
1045 Buenos Aires
Tel. (1) 409860
Fax (1) 112480

Established at the beginning of the century
by Sammy Flichman this winery is now one
of the most important in the country and one
of the bigger wine exporters. Wines are made
exclusively from estate owned vineyards
situated in Mendoza's Barrancas valley.
Owned for three generations by the Flichman
family it is now part of a large and powerful
Argentinian commercial group which has
modernized techniques and markedly
improved wine quality. Managing director
Roberto Luka is a great professional. Th
winery has won numerous international
awards including a gold medal for Caballera
de la Cepa at Vinexpo in 1987. Finca
Flichman has a range of over 15 wines
including a Merlot Nouveau which is not of
great interest. Only 12% of the production
goes towards premium wines for export. The
ordinary table wines are among the most
acceptable in their category.

Caballero de la Cepa   🍇 ①
Chardonnay Mendoza 1990
This 100% Chardonnay has a bright yellow color
with a green tint. It has fruity, citrus aromas and
on the palate is fresh and balanced with a good
fruity finish.

Flichman Privado Tinto 1987   🍇 ①
This wine is a blend of Malbec and Cabernet
Sauvignon which has been oak-aged for 18
months. It has a garnet-red color with balsamic
aromas and vanilla notes. On the palate it is full
and balanced and is a classic Argentinian wine.

Caballero de la Cepa Tinto   🍇🍇 ①
Medalla de Oro 1983
This is a classic Cabernet Sauvignon from a
great vintage and is one of the winery's best. It
has a bright, cherry-red color with brick tones
and a ripe, characterful nose. This is a round,
elegant wine with a persistent and complex
finish.

Javier Edmundo Navarro Correas

Ave. Corrientes 2554 - Piso 1B
1046 Buenos Aires
Tel. (1) 480245
Fax (1) 485171

This is one of Mendoza's oldest and most artisanal wineries. It was founded in 1798 by Juan de Dios Correas and in 1852 managed by Javier Navarro Correas. Since then it has remained in the hands of the same family. One of Javier Navarro Correas' sons was one of Argentina's first oenologists. The estate vineyards are located in Mendoza's Maipù district. The family owns five properties, all planted with vines, and three wineries two of them equipped with modern French machinery from Gasquet. Production capacity exceeds 6 million liters per year, but under the guidance of oenologist Wilma Gutierrez quality is strictly controlled and yields limited. All premium wines are sold in numbered bottles. Navarro Correas owns vineyards planted with two varieties unusual for Mendoza, Pinot Noir and Petite Sirah. Prices are quite high compared to the country's average, but are well justified since Correas are amongst Argentina's top 15 wineries. The winery also produces a sparkling méthode champenoise under the supervision of French champagne house Deutz.

Navarro Correas Riesling 1991   🍇 ①
This is undoubtedly the winery's best white. It has a bright straw-yellow color with fragrant aromas and exotic fruit nuances. In the mouth it is soft, balanced and fresh with an elegant and full finish.

Navarro Correas   🍇🍇 ①
Pinot Noir 1986
Good intense ruby-red color closely resembling Burgundy. It has traightforward, clean, evolving aromas. The wine is harmonious and full in the mouth with medium-intensity and a clean finish. Production stands at 90,000 bottles.

Navarro Correas   🍇🍇 ①
Colección Privada Cabernet Sauvignon 1984
A limited-production wine made from a Cabernet Sauvignon, Cabernet Franc and Merlot blend and aged in French oak for four years. It has a bright cherry-red color with hints of brick at the rim. The body is full and powerful and the wine aromatic with a good finish.

Viñedos y Bodegas José Orfila

Salguero 1242
1177 Buenos Aires
Tel. (1) 8626868
Fax (1) 3251733

This small century-old winery has always made excellent premium wines and good table wines and represents excellent value for money. Its founder, José Orfila, always believed that good wine was made in the vineyards and not in the cellar. Today his nephews follow this example without neglecting the wine-making process. They have modernised the winery and produced excellent wines that won awards and praise at Vinexpo in 1989 and in Canada in 1990. The 180 hectares of estate vineyards are planted with Cabernet Sauvignon, Malbec, Merlot, Chardonnay, Sauvignon Blanc, Chenin Blanc and Riesling and only these are used for production. The best wines are marketed under the Cautivo label and include an excellent Cabernet Sauvignon and an extremely interesting Chardonnay-Riesling blend. Table wines are marketed under the Château Arlanc label. In a country with over 1,800 producers that make a range of different wines José Orfila ranks among the top twenty. Its standing owes much to the efforts made to limit production and concentrate on quality rather than quantity.

Viñas de Orfila Chardonnay 1990   🍇 ①
A Chardonnay that is an example of a good local product with definite varietal flavors, balanced acidity and a dry, ample, persistent finish.

Cautivo de Orfila   🍇 ①
Cabernet Sauvignon 1981
A traditional Bordeaux blend of 80% Cabernet Sauvignon and 20% Merlot which won a medal at Vinexpo. It has a cherry-red color with a brick edge. The intense, elegant aromas reveal aging in wood and and on the palate the wine is complex, balanced and has a pleasant dry finish.

Bodega San Telmo

Marcelo T. de Alvear 590 - Piso 2°
1058 Buenos Aires
Tel. (1) 3118759
Fax (1) 3111981

Established in 1973 when the first vines were planted San Telmo is Argentina's youngest and most technically advanced winery. Its wines have only recently appeared on the market. Although not very well-known in Argentina, San Telmo deserves to be mentioned for its modern views on quality. Only four grape varieties are grown, producing the same number of varietal wines: Cabernet Sauvignon, Malbec, Chardonnay and Chenin Blanc. San Telmo strongly believes in the importance of good vineyard management and in conscientious winemaking methods. Managing director Sigfrido Alonso confirms they are looking to the future and aim to do everything in the best possible way. The winery owns 230 hectares in Cruz de Piedra, Maipù and Mendoza and only plants vines grown in its own nurseries. Only grapes harvested from the winer's own vineyards are used. San Telmo differs from Argentina's other producers in that it has made premium wines since its conception. A regular production of good quality wines should not be far away. Locally San Telmo is commercialized under the label Cuesta del Madera.

San Telmo
Chardonnay Mendoza 1990
The Argentinian answer to straight Chardonnay. It has a bright, straw-yellow color with greenish hints and good fruity aromas. On the palate it is savoury and light with a grassy finish.

San Telmo
Malbeck Mendoza 1985
This is a successful attempt at producing a wine from 100% Malbec. It has medium-intensity, fruity aromas, good texture, balanced acidity and an ample finish. A good value for money wine.

San Telmo
Cabernet Sauvignon Mendoza 1984
This is a 100% Cabernet Sauvignon made in a modern style with the aid of modern technology. The color is bright cherry-red and the wine has a floral, herbaceous aroma. It is full on the palate with a slightly acid finish.

Santa Ana

San Martin 579 P.B.
1004 Buenos Aires
Tel. (1) 3932471
Fax (1) 3932793

With a production of 3,000 hectoliters the company prides itself on being South America's largest producer. Most of the wines are made from grapes bought from several of the region's producers and only a small percentage from the estate owned vineyards. Santa Ana's wine making history goes back to 1891 so it has helped form Argentina's wine industry. Taking advantatge of favorable prices the winery has exported wines since 1946. It produces a full range of drink products, from premium wines for exportation and sparkling méthode champenoise to cider and apple brandy. The table wines are among the best in the country, while export wines have won several awards notably in 1912 at the International Exposition in Paris and more recently at Vinexpo in Bordeaux. The winery adapted rapidly to modern technology and the needs of the international market. However, it may need to revise its philosophy on quality remembering that great wines are obtained by supervising all phases of production including the cultivation of the grapes themselves. At present Santa Ana produces good but not yet excellent wines.

Santa Ana Cepas Privadas
Chardonnay Mendoza 1989
A modern white made from 100% Chardonnay with the help of modern technology. It has intense primary aromas, good balance and nice floral notes on the finish.

Selección Santa Ana
Vino Fino Blanco 1989
This is a Spanish-style white made from a Pedro Ximénez (60%) and Torrontés blend. It has a bright pale yellow color and intense fruity aromas. On the palate it is pleasant, soft and fresh with a. full and persistent finish .

Seleccioón Santa Ana
Vino Fino Tinto 1989
Probably the most "Italian" Argentinian wine which is perhaps a little obscure for most palates. A Lambrusco (70%) and Barbera blend which matures rapidly it has a pale ruby-red color and intense, fresh, lingering aromas.

Santa Ana Privadas
Mendoza Cabernet Sauvignon 1984
This is a typical Argentinian wine which is 100% varietal and oak-aged at length before being bottled. It has a bright red color of medium intensity with full, ripe aromas confirmed on the palate. It conforms exactly to national tastes

Bodega y Viñedos Suter

Casilla de Correos 80
San Rafaél, Mendoza
Tel/Fax (42) 21076

In a country like Argentina where grape growing was developed essentially by Spanish and Italian immigrants it is unusual to find a Swiss influence. The winery was established at the beginning of the century in a Swiss colony 250 kilometers south of Mendoza at San Rafaél. Here Otto Suter planted his first Pinot vines and later Swiss Riesling and French Malbec and Merlot. Today the winery is run by his two nephews Alberto and Carlos who manage a warehouse that can store up to 15 million liters of wine. About 5 million bottles of premium wine are bottled each year, made from grapes grown on 280 hectares of estate owned vineyards. The grape varieties include Chenin Blanc, Chardonnay, Cabernet Sauvignon, Merlot and Malbec. Wines are sold under the label Bodegas Suter in both Argentinian and foreign markets. In Argentina the group also markets wine under other labels including Valle Hermoso and Coto de Caza from Vinas del Cazador.

Suter San Rafaél Chenin Blanc 1990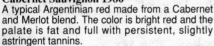
This is a white made from non-traditional grapes. It has a bright, pale golden yellow color and intense floral aromas. On the palate it is soft, full and fresh. This is a good regular drinking wine.

Bodega Suter JS
Cabernet Sauvignon 1986
A typical Argentinian red made from a Cabernet and Merlot blend. The color is bright red and the palate is fat and full with persistent, slightly astringent tannins.

Michel Torino Hns. Bodega La Rosa

Av. Rivadavia 2358 - Piso 5°
1034 Buenos Aires
Tel. (1) 9515819
Fax (1) 9539799

This is one of the few Argentinian wineries run by a woman. Maria Luisa Cambolive Michel Torino de Cornejo Costas is a descendant of David Michel who founded the winery in 1892 with his brother Salvador. La Rosa is located in the north of the country, in the Salta province, and is one of the area's most modern and representative wineries though not the largest. Among Argentina's wine provinces, Salta is only fifth in terms of production averaging 183,000 hectoliters per year which represents only 1.3% of Argentina's total production. La Rosa is located at an altitude of 1,700 meters on sandy soil in the Cafayate valley which is said to have the best microclimate in the area. Unlike other Argentinian wine regions, the most frequently grown varieties are the traditional Torrontés, Chenin Blanc, Barbera, Malbec and Merlot. Michel Torino's Torrontés is of a singular style and one of the best in the country.

Michel Torino
Torrontés de Don David 1991
This is one of the country's most prestigious wines and is made from 100% Torrontés, traditionally a Spanish variety that over the centuries has become truly Argentinian. It has a bright, clean pale yellow color and fruity aromas. In the mouth it is soft, delicate, low in alcohol and has a pleasant finish.

Michel Torino Tinto Viejo 1989
This is a young red for Argentinian tastes and is made from an interesting blend of Malbec, Barbera and Merlot. It has a pale ruby-red color and red-fruit and floral aromas. On the palate it has a good texture and a full finish although slightly astringent. This is a wine for everyday drinking.

Michel Torino
Cabernet de Don David 1987
This is the winery's most important red. A Cabernet with typical varietal aromas and oak nuances it is ripe, balanced in the mouth and has a complex, oaky finish.

Industrial y Agrícola Pascual Toso

Alberdi 808
5519 San José, Gaymallén, Mendoza
Tel. (61) 380213-72
Fax (61) 380283

Do not be surprised if you find a certain Piedmontese touch in this winery's wines. Pascual Toso was orginally from Canale in the Piedmont and when he came to Argentina in 1890 to build his first winery he brought with him Piedmontese traditions and wine-making techniques. His heirs continue this style, but fortunately have slowly modernized the winery, although wines are still aged in the same old oak barrels. Hopefully these too will soon be replaced. Only grapes from the estate owned vineyards in Las Barrancas in the region of Maipù, in the south of Mendoza are used. Pascual Toso is a medium quality winery but constantly improving. The Cabernet Sauvignon and Malbec are among Argentina's best quality reds. The winery also makes one of Argentina's best sparkling méthode champenoise which is sold locally as Champagne since Argentinian law does not place a restriction on the use of this name.

Champagne Extra Toso   🍇 ①
This is one of Argentina's best sparkling méthode champénoise wines made from Chardonnay and Chenin. The color is yellow with greenish tones. It has a good bubble, intense varietal aromas and honey nuances. It is well-structured and harmonious.

Pascual Toso Malbec Mendoza 1989   🍇 ①
Made from a predominantly Malbec blend it has a ruby-red color and polished intense aromas. On the palate it is soft, structured and full and is an excellent value for money wine.

Pascual Toso   🍇🍇 ①
Cabernet Sauvignon Mendoza 1988
A Cabernet that is clearly a cut above the country's average. It has a garnet-red color with orange tones and an intense bouquet with bell-pepper nuances. It is full, fat and tannic in the mouth with a clean and restrained aftertaste. This is a wine that needs a little time in the bottle.

Trapiche Saica

Av. Juan B. Justo 1015
1425 Buenos Aires
Tel (1) 7725091
Fax (1) 7758814

In describing Trapiche Saica one must first mention Bodegas Penaflor. Penaflor is one of the largest wine companies in the world, second only to Gallo in the United States. It is a real wine giant which harvests 25,000 tonnes of grapes every year and has a production capacity of 980,000 liters of wine per day and warehouse capacity for over 1,800 million liters This empire was founded at the beginning of the twentieth century by an Italian immigrant, Angelo Antonio Pulenta. Fortunately Penaflor's wines do not leave Argentina for they are inexpensive and lack character. In 1973 Penaflor decided to enter the premium wine market for export purposes and purchased Trapiche, a winery founded in 1883 and considered one of the best in Argentina. This has allowed Penaflor to obtain what is possibly Argentina's most important line of wines of an international standard. Worthy of mention are the Malbec, Merlot, Pinot Noir, Chardonnay, Cabernet Sauvignon and Torrontés wines. They cost between five and ten dollars per bottle and are prestigious wines of guaranteed quality.

Trapiche Mendoza   🍇 ①
Chardonnay Reserva 1990
This wine is part of a single varietal selection made for the North American market rather than for the domestic one. It has clear varietal aromas of apple with floral nuances and is light and fresh on the palate with a clean dry finish. The same wine aged in new oak for four months is marketed under the Oak Cask label.

Trapiche Mendoza   🍇🍇 ①
Malbec Reserva 1988
This is one of Argentina's best wines and is a good interpretation of the Malbec variety. It has a bright, cherry-red color and fruity, plummy aromas. On the palate it is full, well-structured and ample with a clean finish. It is excellent value for money.

Trapiche Mendoza   🍇🍇 ①
Cabernent Sauvignon Oak Cask Reserva 1986
A special selection of Cabernet aged six months in French oak barrels. This is a full-bodied, elegant wine with fruity cherry aromas and herbaceous, bell-pepper nuances. It has balanced tannins and a sustained finish. It is well-priced.

AUSTRALIA

The first Australian vineyard was planted in 1788 in the Sydney area by Captain Arthur Phillip of the British Navy, Australia's first governor. The new continent's viticulture developed slowly, and it took several decades, and the praise-worthy work of several European pioneers, to understand which areas were most suited to vines and which varietals were most suited to Australia's climate and soils. Viticulture was a consolidated reality by the second half of the 1800s, although it was primarily based on British tastes and needs. For a long time production concentrated on quantity rather than quality, and only at the beginning of the 1960s was the land's potential used to advantage. Today Australian wine is going through testing times, with an export boom on one hand and stagnant domestic sales on the other. The wine itself has never been better, but the recession has reduced the market for premium products. Exports have been absorbing an ever-increasing volume of premium wine, becoming the producers' primary hope. Exports are increasing at a rate of 35% per year, with 7.2 million cases in 1991 (18% of total production of 40 million cases).

Although per capita consumption has decreased, Australians are drinking better than ever, thanks to new wine-making techniques and to a generation of trained winemakers. Furthermore, the shift of grape growing from the traditional, hotter regions to cooler climates, the emergence in the '70s of Padthaway and other regions for premium whites, and the constant increase in the number of wineries in Coonawarra, have allowed the production of large quantities of fine wines at relatively low production costs.

Small wineries with a limited production (more than 600 in Australia) multiplied in the '70s and '80s in the cooler regions such as southern Victoria, the south-west of Western Australia, the southern and higher areas of South Australia and Tasmania. Great changes have concurrently taken place in the large wine companies which, perhaps spurred by the smaller ones, have also improved wine quality through vineyard site selection and high-tech winemaking. Although Australian wines have at times been accused of being too modern and lacking character, no one has ever said they are badly made. The standard of wine-making, second to none, is backed up by an active and skilled research organization, the Australian Wine Research Institute and by two viticulture and enology schools, the Adelaide University Roseworthy Campus and the Charles Sturt University, Wagga Campus. They have revolutionized wine-making technology to such an extent that,where once it was only Australian winemakers who went to France to train, nowadays many young European technicians come to work the vintage in Australian wineries.

Australian wine is predominantly characterized by fruit: the continent's abundant sunshine and warmth ensure smooth aromas of ripe fruit in both white and red wines, which may be excessive for some palates, but are highly appreciated by the British, Scandinavians and other Europeans in general.

Chardonnay, the varietal which is seemingly taking over the world, is prolific in Australia, currently representing 11% of total white wine production, without counting the numerous plantings which are about to come into production. Until recently Riesling was the most widely planted white varietal, and Sémillon's reputation is higher in Australia than any other country. The Portuguese Verdelho is being used increasingly to make delicate and aromatic dry whites for early consumption, and Sauvignon Blanc is becoming more popular. For reds, Shiraz is omnipresent, so common that it is actually looked down upon, lacking the status it enjoys in France. In the late 1980s winemakers began to recognize the great personality and quality of the best Shiraz wines (such as Penfolds' Grange Hermitage), and have since paid more attention to this varietal. Today, the list of excellent Shiraz wines is long and getting longer, and it is particularly encouraging to see that the Barossa Valley is re-evaluing its old vineyards, which have never been touched by phylloxera; many vines are over a hundred years old, still capable of producing superb wines. Historically Shiraz was used like Sémillon, for all wine types, from the most inexpensive "bag-in-a-box" wine to important ageworthy classics (so-called 'softpacks', incidentally, account for 65% of Australian wine production). Before the wine boom of the '70s, there was very little Cabernet Sauvignon and virtually no Chardonnay, and the market was dominated by Shiraz, Sémillon and Riesling. The arrival of Chardonnay in the mid '70s inevitably stole the limelight from Sémillon and Riesling, just as Cabernet Sauvignon did from Shiraz. Whereas in the past the classic red blend had been Shiraz-Cabernet, today it is more likely to be Cabernet-Merlot, or less frequently Cabernet Sauvignon-Cabernet Franc-Merlot. Pinot Noir plantings increased in the '70s and '80s, but its wines have not had the same immediate success: although ductile, it has proven to be unpredictable, yielding wines that range from light rosés to overwhelmingly concentrated reds. Some hard-working passionate producers have however obtained heartening results, particularly in the cooler climates of southern Victoria and Tasmania. Today Australian wines are on the whole more polished, fresher, fruitier and less alcoholic with less astringent tannins. They are lighter, more suited to modern consumption, with less need for cellaring.

Each of Australia's six states produce wine: Southern Australia (51% of the nation's total production), New South Wales (30%), Victoria (18%), with smaller vineyards in Western Australia and Tasmania producing limited quantities of excellent wines. Queensland's viticulture is tiny, but already yielding good results. In total, the country has 33 distinct wine regions and about 7,000 vineyards for a total of 60,000 hectares concentrated on the southern and eastern coasts, since most of Australia's inland is desert. The range of climates and soils is vast.

While many of the smaller producers use only grapes from their own vineyards, Australians have always blended grape varietals. Many companies, especially the larger ones, blend grapes from several regions to achieve consistency of style and quality, and thanks to modern transportation it is not unusual to see blends of Hunter-Coonawarra or Hunter-McLaren Vale, or even of Hunter Valley (New South Wales), Goulburn Valley (Victoria) and Margaret River (Western Australia), involving three states and thousands of kilometers by truck. In South Australia there is much blending between Coonawarra, McLaren Vale, Clare, Langhorne Creek and the Barossa Valley, a practice allowed as there is no denomination of origin. In Tasmania, Mudgee and Margaret River there are local denomination schemes which guarantee regional authenticity, but this model has little future in Australia.

11

The wine industry, with an eye on exports, has however recently set up a Label Integrity Program (LIP) which, through control and inspection, requires producers to substantiate any claims made on labels, such as vintage, varietal, region, vineyard, etc. The LIP scheme will help protect the integrity of Australian wines and safeguard their future export potential, which is believed to be enormous.

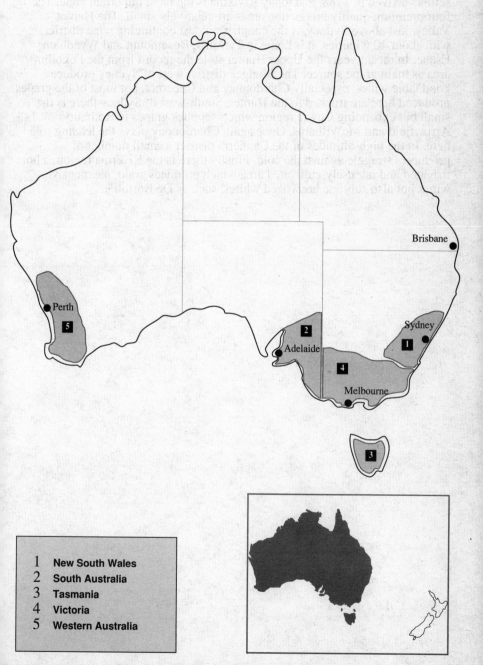

Brisbane

Sydney

Perth

Adelaide

Melbourne

1
2
3
4
5

1   **New South Wales**
2   **South Australia**
3   **Tasmania**
4   **Victoria**
5   **Western Australia**

AUSTRALIA

New South Wales

New South Wales is the nation's oldest wine state, with 12,000 hectares of vineyards (20% of Australia's total) and almost 30% of total production. Vines were first planted at Sydney when the original white (European?) settlers arrived in 1788, and today Riverina is the most important zone. The four premium quality production areas are relatively small. The Hunter Valley, just above Sydney, is the country's oldest continuing wine district, with about 40 wineries. It is home to Tyrrell's, Rosemount and Wyndham Estate. In recent years the Upper Hunter stole the record from the Pokolbin area as main grape source. The Mudgee district west of Sydney produces good table wines, especially Chardonnay and Cabernet, but most of the grapes produced here are trucked to the Hunter. South-west of Sydney there is the small but expanding Cowra region which supplies grapes to Rothbury, Arrowfield and McWilliams. Once again Chardonnay plays the leading role here. In the high-altitudes of the Canberra district a small number of producers struggle against the cold. Finally there is the Riverina region, a hot irrigated and intensely-cultivated area which produces good, inexpensive wines but also sublime botrytized whites, such as De Bortoli's.

Allanmere

Allandale Road, Allandale via
Pokolbin 2321
Tel. (049) 307387

Dr. Newton Potter and wife Virginia started
Allanmere in 1984, rapidly showing that lack
of vineyard ownership was no obstacle to
quality. Most of their grapes are bought from
the Talga vineyard, close by in the Lower
Hunter, and trained winemaker Geoff
Broadfield works magic in the winery. The top
Chardonnay is named Durham, after the
Potters' English home. It's their best wine,
although the reds are also excellent,
including the Cabernet Sauvignon which is
one of the few successful examples of this
varietal from the district. Trinity White and
Trinity Red are creative three-way varietal
blends which have succeeded both in quality
and in capturing the public's imagination. Dr.
Potter is a diabetic and it's a point of health
as much as honor that there is never any
residual sugar in his wines. Unfortunately for
the Hunter Valley, the Potters - who came to
wine late in life - find the work too much
strain and the business is on the market.
Lack of vineyards is hindering a sale, despite
superb wine quality and the high reputation of
the label.

Durham Chardonnay 1990   ♟ ♟ ③
The pick of the Chardonnay crop and the best
oak give a very stylish Chardonnay with some
individuality. Full, soft and well-rounded with
beguiling peach, fig and smoky characteristics.
Winner of some top show awards.

Trinity White 1990   ♟ ②
A fine seafood wine, with low-key grassy and
gooseberry aromas, a fresh tangy unwooded
palate with crisp dry acidity. Made from
Chardonnay, Sémillon and Sauvignon Blanc
grapes.

Cabernet Sauvignon 1988   ♟ ②
More Hunter Valley red than Cabernet, showing
forward development and already some
complex, mature regional flavors. Rich and
supple with earthy, leathery flavors and it is
beginning to develop the classic Bordeaux
cigarbox character.

Trinity Red 1988   ♟ ②
There is some richness and concentration in this
Cabernet Sauvignon, Merlot and Shiraz blend.
Complex regional overtones fill the bouquet with
meaty, nutty, roasted and oaky nuances. The
palate is generous and mouth-filling. Already
drinks well.

Brokenwood

McDonalds Road
Pokolbin 2321
Tel. (049) 987559
Fax (049) 987893

Brokenwood embraces the Hunter Valley
tradition of inter-regional blending, but
ironically its best wines, the Hermitage
(Shiraz) and Cabernet Sauvignon, are 100%
from its own Graveyard Vineyard. Bottled
separately since 1986, they are wines of
enormous profundity with great cellaring
potential while many other Hunter reds have
slackened their standards in recent years.
They spring from spindly, low-yielding vines
planted on poor clay soil that was once
gazetted for a parish cemetery (although
never used as such). Begun as the weekend
hobby of a trio of Sydney lawyers,
Brokenwood is now a highly professional
business owned by a syndicate of 20.
Regular releases now comprise a deliciously
fruity blend of McLaren Vale Sauvignon
Blanc and Hunter Sémillon, a fresh, crisp and
appealingly grassy unoaked Sémillon, an
elegant Cabernet Sauvignon blended from
Coonawarra and the Hunter (and
occasionally a third region), a Pinot Noir from
the Yarra Valley, a Hunter Hermitage-
Cabernet , and a standard Hunter
Chardonnay. Botrytized Sémillon sweet table
wine occasionally appears and there is also a
rich, nutty Graveyard Chardonnay.

Graveyard Chardonnay 1991   ♟ ③
A serious, austere style showing plenty of nutty
and spicy high quality French oak and a lean,
dry palate which will be likely to fill out and
gather richness with a few years' bottle age.

Sauvignon Blanc Semillon 1991   ♟ ②
Blended from McLaren Vale Sauvignon and
Hunter Sémillon, a delicious lime an gooseberry
flavored unoaked dry white, fresh and crisp with
lively acidity and pungent fruitiness.

Graveyard   ♟ ♟ ③
Cabernet Sauvignon 1990
Every bit as profound as the Hermitage, a big,
muscular wine with firm tannic structure
supporting deep currany Cabernet and French
oak flavors. Firm finish promises long aging
potential. And 1990 is reputedly a bad year in
the Hunter!

Graveyard Hermitage 1990   ♟ ♟ ③
Meagre yields give a very concentrated, 20-year
Shiraz, one of the Hunter's best. Almost
impenetrable purple color, powerful nutty
American oak and varietal aromas of plum and
spice. Great depth and weight of concentrated
flavor fill the mouth and assertive tannins bring a
long, firm finish.

De Bortoli

De Bortoli Road
Bilbul 2680
Tel. (069) 635344
Fax (069) 635382

The enterprising De Bortoli family started out in the Riverina near Griffith, producing basic inexpensive bottle and cask wine as well as a great Botrytis Sémillon Sauternes which has been delighting lovers of sweet whites for a decade. In the late '80s they bought the Yarra Valley winery as a going concern and greatly expanded the plantings. Immaculate estate-grown Chardonnay, Cabernet Sauvignon, Shiraz and Pinot Noir appear under the elegant Yarra label and are good value for money. Under a slightly cheaper label, Windy Peak, Yarra winemakers Steven Webber and David Ellis turn out larger quantities of wines blended from the Yarra and southern Victoria, including commendable Rhine Riesling, Chardonnay and Cabernet-Shiraz. An impressively designed and built tasting and sales complex features an excellent restaurant serving northern Italian food, which is run by Webber's wife Leanne De Bortoli. De Bortoli has quickly emerged as a leading force in the Yarra, while the Griffith operation is possibly the fastest growing Australian winery in recent years, directed by Leanne's brother Darren and father Deen.

Yarra Valley Chardonnay 1991   ♛♛ ②
Produced with barrel and malolactic fermentation with all the trimmings but remains fruit-dominant with delicate, fresh green-fig and peach flavors and fine balance. The more impressive because 10,000 cases were made.

Yarra Valley   ♛ ②
Cabernet Sauvignon 1990
A lighter style, lean but elegant with sweet mulberry, cherry fruit and toasted oak aromas leading into a tight-structured palate with a firm, lightly tannic finish.

Yarra Valley Pinot Noir 1990   ♛ ②
Typical Yarra Pinot. Although the color is fairly light there is plenty of eight with a fine harmony of varietal flavors, very clean sweet strawberry and cherry aromas that perhaps lack a little complexity. Fresh acidity.

Yarra Valley Shiraz 1989   ♛ ②
Soft, mulberry style red laced with black pepper and spice and built for early drinking. Elegant sweet flavors make an attractive, stylish wine.

Sauternes Australian   ♛♛♛ ④
Botrytis Semillon 1987
Several contract grape growers at Bilbul near the winery leave some of their Sémillon grapes very late in April/May each year when they reach high botrytis infection. Several pickings are made and the ideal Baume is 24°. The juice is fermented in new French oak barriques in coolrooms and allowed to reach its own level of sweetness. The wine is aged for about 12 months more in the same barrels, and bottle-aged for several years before release. A number of Riverina wineries make similar styles but De Bortoli is the leader, carrying more oak and living longer than any other. The '87, harvested at 24° Baume in a high botrytis year, is deep gold in color with extravagant honey, citrus peel, dried apricot aromas tied in with vanilla and nuttiness from the oak. Noticeable volatile acidity is part and parcel of the style. The palate has luscious depth and complexity of flavor and sweetness.

Huntington Estate

Cassilis Road
Mudgee 2850
Tel. (063) 733825
Fax (063) 733730

Former Sydney solicitor Bob Roberts "went bush" in the early 1970s and immediately started producing some of N.S.W.'s finest red wines. These days he and his wife Wendy indulge their twin loves of music and wine with regular concerts in their acoustically-excellent winery, attracting the very finest musicians. Roberts has yet to make a very interesting white wine, but his reds are sublime, fleshy, rich and smooth. They include Shiraz, Cabernet-Shiraz, Cabernet Sauvignon and Cabernet-Merlot and are classified variously as FB (full-bodied) or MB (medium-bodied) with a 'bin number', a peculiarly Australian way of designating the cuvée. They are usually soft and supple enough to drink young, but also age extremely well. The wines have a low profile but a devoted core of followers. Seldom seen in liquor stores, they are mainly sold ex-winery to mailing list customers, and through a sprinkling of restaurants.

Semillon 1991 ♿ ②
A classic, dry, delicate young Sémillon which shows fresh, crisp, lightly grassy aroma, good subtlety, balance and finesse. No oak has been used. Can be enjoyed young for its freshness and fruit or aged for up to a decade as it develops toasty, nutty complexities.

Shiraz Bin FB7 1989 ♿ ②
The pick of Huntington's current offering, an outstanding, concentrated Shiraz with deep, rich color and spicy, nutty, earthy bouquet. The palate has a sensuous, fleshy richness, chunky construction and silky texture. A great Australian Shiraz from a top Mudgee vintage.

Cabernet Sauvignon Bin FB 29 1988 ♿ ②
This wine's dominant character is a mintiness which evokes aniseed and eucalyptus aromas. Very good depth of sweet, developed fruit on the palate, with typical supple but definite tannin and overall smoothness.

Shiraz Cabernet Sauvignon ♿ ②
Bin FB 12 1987
Complex cigarbox maturing bouquet with a slight barnyard overtone. A soft, smooth, rich, full-bodied red with loads of character.

Lake's Folly

Broke Road
Pokolbin 2321
Tel. (049) 987507

Dr. Max Lake led a stampede of small-scale 'weekend winemakers' to the Hunter Valley in 1963 and started the trend of planting Cabernet Sauvignon in this area where it had all but died out. His powerful personality also drew attention to the area and to his wines,which took on cult status. Lake has long since left the winemaking to son Stephen, who has refined and developed the styles. The vineyard is on an excellent site, a south-facing slope of the red volcanic soil so prized in the Hunter for red wines. Lake's Folly's most famous wine, a Cabernet Sauvignon, is boosted by a fraction of Petit Verdot, Lake's secret ingredient. The style is medium-weight, elegant, brilliantly balanced and somewhat exotic in character. Stephen Lake's Chardonnays are towards the lighter, earlier-harvested, more reserved end of the style spectrum, and mature well with age. The wines are sometimes found not to live up to their high reputation, though at least it is easier to find them nowadays.

Chardonnay 1988 ♿ ③
A delicate but structured style starting to show some development, with strong 'sur lie' and malolactic overtones which lead into a complex toasted nut bouquet. The palate is lean and tautly structured with some austerity.

Cabernet 1990 ♿ ③
A very complex red which opens with some reductive smells and breathes to reveal interesting flavors of red-currant, cherry and raspberry with a gamey overlay. The color and body are lighter than normal, oak is underplayed, and there is great elegance and length. An intriguing, individual style.

McWilliam's

Winery Road
Hanwood 2680
Tel. (069) 630001
Fax (069) 630002

This large family company, whose origins dateback to 1877, is Riverina-based but most of its premium wines come from the Mount Pleasant winery in the Hunter Valley, where Phillip Ryan makes some of the area's most long-living, classic Sémillon and Shiraz. Particularly remarkable is Elizabeth, a bottle-aged unoaked Sémillon released after seven years aging. Its complex aromas of honey, nuts and toast are derived from its lengthy bottle-age. In the 1940s and '50s Mount Pleasant was the home of legendary winemaker Maurice O'Shea, and today most of the wines continue O'Shea's traditions. The reds, quaintly named after vineyard blocks such as Old Paddock, Old Hill and Rose Hill, are earthy, sensuous and complex, and age well. Chardonnay is fresher, full-bodied, rich with peach and butter flavors.

Mount Pleasant Elizabeth 1984 ♥♥ ②
From a line of mature Hunter Sémillons whose low prices totally belie their great depth of character. The '84, from a cooler year, combines toast, nutty mellow complexities with crisp freshness, and a dry savory finish that lingers long.

Mount Pleasant Sauternes 1978 ♥ ③
Made from non-botrytized Sémillon and Trebbiano grapes, aged in old oak for many years. Deep golden hue, lovely honeysuckle bouquet, sweet honey and vaguely citrus flavors without great lusciousness.

Show Series ♥ ④
Liqueur Muscat MCW11
This old blend has luscious toffee, vanilla and raisin flavors with rancio derived from lengthy wood-aging. Dark and treacly, luscious and powerful. To sip with chocolates.

Barwang Cabernet Sauvignon 1990 ♥ ②
The youthful color still contains purple tints, echoing the freshness in the gentle cherry fruit aromas and supple, berry flavored, lightly tannic palate with clean varietal suggestions.

Barwang Shiraz 1989 ♥ ②
From a newly-acquired property at Young, New South Wales, comes this elegant Shiraz whose spicy varietal nature is starting to mellow into a soft, round but lively wine with gentle tannins.

Rosemount Estate

Rosemount Road
Denman 2328
Tel. (065) 472467
Fax (065) 472742

Established in the Upper Hunter Valley in 1969, Rosemount was successful from the outset and grew so rapidly that it soon had to buy grapes from other Australian districts. It recently purchased the venerable Ryecroft of McLaren Vale which will neatly augment the main winery. Still owned by the former coffee grower Bob Oatley and his family, Rosemount is highly successful in the U.S. and U.K., where its inexpensive, value-for-money yellow diamond label Chardonnay has been a big hit. There are other Chardonnays above it, which in ascending order of character, weight and complexity are Show Reserve, Giants Creek and Roxburgh. Rosemount's talented, hard-working winemaker Philip Shaw also excels in a straight Sauvignon grape Fumé Blanc, floral Rhine Riesling, sappy and remarkably weighty Pinot Noir and a Coonawarra Cabernet Sauvignon that is among the more structured of its kind.

Roxburgh Chardonnay 1989 ♥♥ ④
Rosemount's flagship, individual vineyard wine. The '89 has a strongly oaky and peachy fruit nose. On the palate full bodied, soft, rich and quite complex with peach and cedary oak flavor pervading. Age may improve the balance, but it will always be very oaky.

Show Reserve Chardonnay 1989 ♥♥ ③
Complex, Burgundy-influenced Chardonnay with rather strong flavors of smoky bacon, buttery malolactic and dusty, sweaty lees-influenced overtones. Rich, chunky sweet-fruit palate with dry finish of grainy tannins. Somewhat feral, but very interesting.

Kirri Billi Coonawarra ♥ ③
Cabernet Sauvignon 1989
In a very similar style to the Show Reserve, shy and unforthcoming with subdued currant and attractive oak aromas. Big, firm palate structured with gripping tannins. Cellar for five years or more.

Show Reserve Coonawarra ♥ ③
Cabernet Sauvignon 1989
Regularly one of the most substantial Cabernets from Coonawarra. The '89 looks like a solid long-term proposition with a shy nose, deep latent dark-berry flavors and firm astringency. A little tough now, much better in four to five years.

Kirri Billi Coonawarra ♥♥ ③
Merlot 1988
Seldom does unblended Merlot make such a complete wine in Australia. This has a cedary, smoky bouquet and plump, savory flavors on palate. Pentiful fruit and good structure should enable it to age well although it is a superb drink now.

Rothbury Estate

Broke Road
Pokolbin 2321
Tel. (049) 987555
Fax (049) 987870

Started in the early 1970s producing just one dry white (Sémillon) and one red (Shiraz), after many changes of course Len Evans' winery has eventually found a successful formula by specializing in Chardonnay, grown both in the Hunter and the newly-emerging Cowra district. Sémillon, both the pure unoaked styles and black-label Individual Paddock bottlings, are still the best wines, deliciously fresh and fruity when young, and gloriously rich and toasty honeyed when mature at about 15 years. Reserve Hunter Chardonnays are full-bodied, opulently fruity with sophisticated oak treatment. Len Evans' own Evans Family Chardonnays, from his own small Hunter vineyard, are also superb, with more structure and reserve than many of their peers. Rothbury's reds, since 1988 characterized by a new, more accessible style with depth yet softness, now encompass Pinot Noir, Shiraz and Cabernet Sauvignon but the Hunter mainstay, Shiraz, is the best of them. Since 1991 a Sauvignon Blanc with superb gooseberry aroma is the first wine produced from the estate's vines at Marlborough in New Zealand.

Barrel Fermented Chardonnay 1991 🍇 ②
Rothbury produces several Chardonnays, and this one is the second-top priced, made from Hunter grapes grown on the Brokenback vineyard. Typical house style: soft, broad, tending fat, with sweet, ripe peach and fig-jam taste and long, warm finish. Rich, quite oaky, up-front, to be drunk young.

Semillon 1991 🍇 ②
Quite light for what was undoubtedly a great Hunter vintage, unusual greenish, herbal flavor and delicate structure, but judging by Rothbury's track record it will develop into a very good wine with time.

Reserve Syrah 1989 🍇🍇 ③
An excitingly bold Shiraz debuts this new Rothbury label. It is a quantum leap up from the standard Shiraz, with dense hue, concentrated nose and palate of peppermint and coconut. On the palate big, strong, rustic and tannic, rather tough at present, but with undoubtedly great cellaring potential.

Shiraz 1989 🍇 ②
Intense, packed with flavor, firm tannic structure and a spicy vanilla bouquet of varietal Shiraz and oak. Lively, deep and youthful, should repay over a decade of cellaring.

Tyrrell's

Broke Road
Pokolbin 2321
Tel. (049) 987509
Fax (049) 987723

Murray Tyrrell took over the family property and in thirty years transformed it into a leading medium-large winery, with a full range of wines from inexpensive to premium, including Vat 47 Chardonnay, which many consider Australia's best. Fermentation in French barriques and great care in the winery contribute in producing a sophisticated, rich and velvety wine which Tyrrell compares unashamedly with Puligny Montrachet but "at a fraction of the price". The reds - Hunter Sémillon and Hermitage (Shiraz) - are highly traditional regional styles, complex but rather rustic with leather and tar overtones. The whites are soft with toasty flavors that mature into wonderfully complex, golden, honeyed, nutty wines. Vats 1 and 18 are Sémillon, Vat 47 is Chardonnay from the sandy soils of the Lower Hunter Valley, Vats 5, 9 and 11 are Hermitage and Vat 6 is Pinot Noir from red volcanic soils. The unique Futures selection provides mature Sémillon and Shiraz for restaurant sales. Sparkling Pinot Noir Brut is powerfully varietal, , without any concessions to delicacy. Vat 70 Quirindi Cabernet and Vat 5 Shiraz-Merlot are excellent reds. 'Old Winery' is a second label of above-average wines at lower prices.

Vat 63 Chardonnay Semillon 1991 🍇🍇 ②
This half and half blend is exceptional in '91, showing wonderfully intense straw Sémillon aromas and the extra richness and depth of Chardonnay on the palate. Dry with a very long aftertaste.

Vat 1 Semillon 1991 🍇🍇 ②
An outstanding year for whites in the Hunter has produced a classic Vat 1, showing intense straw and lanolin varietal fruit aromas and a fresh, dry, harmonious flavor with a slight tone of grassiness and lemony finish.

Vat 47 Chardonnay 1990 🍇🍇 ③
From a cool, wet year this wine is a triumph: comparatively fine and subtle but with profound flavor and beguiling complexity of lemon, grapefruit, honey and passionfruit tones.

Vat 1 Semillon 1986 🍇🍇 ③
Tyrrell's Vat 1 is among the best Hunter Sémillons, especially after a few years' cellaring. Superbly developed with a toasted bread, resin and lanolin bouquet, lean, bone-dry and lemony on the palate.

Vat 9 Dry Red 1991 🍇🍇 ②
One of Tyrrell's classic wines, the top Shiraz of the year. From a great year, brilliant purple-red hue, spicy meaty regional Hunter aroma and deep, rich, chocolate and spice flavour.

South Australia

South Australia is the country's most important wine-producing state, with 25,000 hectares of vineyards (42% of the total) and production of 200 million hectoliters (51%). The first vineyards were planted in the 1840s and 1850s by German immigrants who had escaped from religious persecution in Silesia. They settled in the Barossa Valley, and many of their descendants carry on their work today. The state is made up of seven main regions. The Barossa Valley houses most of the best-known wineries, including Penfolds, Orlando, Seppelt, Wolf Blass and Yalumba. It is a warm, low-altitude region known for its Shiraz, Cabernet Sauvignon and Riesling and is a major processing center for grapes from other regions. The Adelaide Hills has a cool climate and grows a variety of grapes. The Clare Valley to the north is known for its Riesling. The Southern Vales to the south is home to Hardy's and 50 other wineries, while Langhorne Creek, further south, supplies red grapes to the Barossa wineries. To the south-west Coonawarra has become one of Australia's most important regions for reds and Padthaway is known as a premium white wine producer.

Tim Adams

Warenda Road
Clare 5453
Tel/Fax (088) 422429

Tim Adams worked for the Leasingham winery in Clare and currently works part-time at Eaglehawk, but over the past few years has attracted more than passing interest for his own wines. He owns only a few rows of Sémillon vines next to the winery and purchases the rest from personally-selected local growers who can deliver the high quality he demands. Witness the Aberfeldy Shiraz, a great selection from a vineyard of the same name, with more body and concentration than his standard Shiraz, itself a wine worthy of all respect. All the wines, from an excellent floral Riesling and subtly-oaked Sémillon, to the ripe Cabernet and peppery minty Shiraz, fully deserve their black label. The 1990 botrytized Sémillon earns a special mention for excellence. These wines are all hand-crafted in small quantities in the Clare Valley and are sold at better than reasonable prices.

Rhine Riesling 1991 � ☆ ②
A lively and fresh wine with mouth-filling fruity flavors of dried fruit and apple, penetrating but soft acidity, finishing with hints of grapefruit. Dry but pleasant; drinks well young but should be lovely in a few years time.

Semillon 1991 ☆ ②
Two-thirds barrel fermented, revealing a lemon/nutty wood nose which will blend further with the wine with a year or two in bottle. Excellent on the palate, slightly grassy with peppermint nuances.

Botrytis Semillon 1991 ☆ ③
A sweet wine of great character and balance. Exuberant pineapple, fig, vanilla and honey blend with a subtle touch of oak and masterful balance of sugar and fruit. More elegant than many of its overpowering peers.

Shiraz 1990 ♦ ②
Softer than the Aberfeldy, an early drinker with potential to age well. Ripe cherry aromas with spice and liquorice nuances. Smooth, silky and fleshy on the palate. Top value for money.

Aberfeldy Shiraz 1988 ♦♦ ③
Adams' top-line red, made from the grapes of a single vineyard planted in 1904. Very intense purple-red color; deep spicy and plummy Shiraz aromas blend with mint and violets. A fleshy wine, softly tannic and rich. Develops quite slowly, but should age well for many years. A classic Clare Shiraz.

Wolf Blass

Sturt Highway
Nuriootpa 5355
Tel. (085) 621955
Fax (085) 622156

"No wood, no good" was the battle-cry of this German migrant who in 1969 took Australian wine by storm, merging in 1990 with Mildara. A change in style is currently underway: the character of his wines now meet changing new tastes. As colorful and flamboyant as its labels, Blass grew steadily in the 70s and 80s. Today Wolf Blass no longer owns the company, but is still involved in marketing. Blass's color-coded labels were a stroke of genius. The reds are led by the superbly complex Black Label, the increasingly fine Grey Label and the Brown Label Hermitage (the only red which is not a Cabernet Sauvignon or Shiraz). Others are the more commercial Yellow Label and the down-market Red Label. The best white is the excellent Gold Label Clare Rhine Riesling, followed by a pleasant Chardonnay, the commercial but good Yellow Label Rhine Riesling and the White Label Sémillon; lastly the wooded varietal blend Classic Dry White. Blass has always been an uninhibited blender of regions and varieties.

Gold Label Rhine Riesling 1990 ☆ ②
Made entirely from Clare Valley grapes, this is Blass's top Riesling. It has a volume of fruit on the nose and palate, with lush lime/lemon and slightly herbal tones. Balanced, with a dry finish, a superb early drinker.

Brown Label Classic Shiraz 1988 ♦ ③
More than a definitive varietal Shiraz. An attempt to enrich a full, soft red wine with American oak. Full-bodied, fleshy, richly textured, will last until 1998.

Grey Label ♦ ③
Cabernet Sauvignon Shiraz 1988
The Black Label's younger brother, with less power but more style. This 1988 is very elegant as winemaker John Glaetwer has shortened skin-contact and improved oak quality .

Show Reserve ♦♦ ③
Cabernet Sauvignon Shiraz 1987
An incredible adventure by Blass into Coonawarra, with amazing results. A great red which combines oak fermentation and maturation in casks with Coonawarra's complex fruit.

Black Label ♦♦ ④
Cabernet Sauvignon Shiraz Merlot 1986
Blass's top red, always aged at least six years. Made with grapes from South Australia's four best wine regions. The '86 is rich, full-bodied and smooth, cedary, with supple tannins and a big finish.

Bowen Estate

Penola-Naracoorte Road, Coonawarra
Penola 5277
Tel. (087) 372229

Coonawarra is very much a red wine region and Doug Bowen is very much a red wine maker. Although he makes a good Chardonnay and a passable Rhine Riesling, his true love - and strength - lies with his classically elegant Cabernet Sauvignon and spicy Shiraz. The Bowen Estate was established in 1972 without the razzamatazz and million-dollar investments which usually accompany a new winery. Doug and his wife Joy have gradually built up their property and with it a new stone winery. Their estate is the result of sheer hard work and their success is well-deserved. There is no fancy PR machine here, and even if there were, the reserved laconic but good-humored Bowen wouldn't know how to make it work. A personal following is very important in the wine business and Bowen, who is also a trained wine maker, has always had a group of devotees who would walk on hot coals for a bottle of his red. His estate has a reputation as being the best small winery in Coonawarra, an estate in the true sense of the word since all grapes are from the estate's own vines.

Shiraz 1990
A magnificent Coonawarra Shiraz, with sumptuous depth of spicy fruit, oak and nut. Rich and intense on the palate, with lively astringency and marvellous persistence. An excellent vintage for one of the district's best Shiraz. Should age for 20 years.

Cabernet Merlot 1989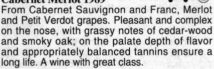
From Cabernet Sauvignon and Franc, Merlot and Petit Verdot grapes. Pleasant and complex on the nose, with grassy notes of cedar-wood and smoky oak; on the palate depth of flavor and appropriately balanced tannins ensure a long life. A wine with great class.

Grant Burge

Jacobs Creek
Tanunda 5352
Tel. (085) 633700
Fax (085) 632807

The Burge family is among the oldest and most important winemaking families in the Barossa Valley. Fifth generation winemaker Grant Burge set up a business of his own in 1988 after his previous winery was absorbed by Mildara. At a time in which large wineries were selling vineyards, Burge was buying. and managed to acquire a substantial property. Today his vineyards produce more than he needs for his own young and rapidly-growing label. Some of his vines are very old, such as the Shiraz vineyard in Filsell originally planted in 1928 and which today supplies the grapes for the Meshach Shiraz. Meshach is a prestigious red named after one of Grant's ancestors, Meshach Burge, who lived to be 99. Red-grape yields are limited (from 80 to 120 tons per hectare), and the result is a rich, ripe, smooth and pleasant red, typical of the Barossa Valley. Whites are flavorsome, from floral Riesling and fruity White Frontinac, to rich, oaky Chardonnay and Sémillon. Grant Burge is a shrewd businessman and excellent winemaker - he surely has a great future.

Wood-matured Semillon 1991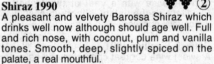
Full, soft, fruity wine with more subtle oak than previous vintages. Young, abounds with soft lemon and peach flavors. Drinks well now.

Shiraz 1990
A pleasant and velvety Barossa Shiraz which drinks well now although should age well. Full and rich nose, with coconut, plum and vanilla tones. Smooth, deep, slightly spiced on the palate, a real mouthful.

Cabernet Sauvignon 1989
A cooler than average year gave polish to this wine. Nicely modulated fruit, oak and tannin, balanced and suave. Its deep hue and quality cedar-wood complete the picture.

Meshach Shiraz 1988
The grapes come from 60 year-old vines and although not very fleshy, the wine is striking because of the silky richness and gentle, subtly-oaked voluptuous texture and flavor. A premium vintage for this red, the winery's flagship.

Chapel Hill

Chapel Hill Road
McLaren Vale 5171
Tel. (08)3238429
Fax (08) 3239245

Pam Dunsford gained her experience making wine in the Southern Vales for 15 years before becoming Chapel Hill's winemaker in 1989. Her arrival has had a strong impact on the winery, mediocre until that point. A perfect vintage in 1990 put the icing on the cake, and today Chapel Hill is on the rise. The '90 reds have deservedly won awards in various competitions. The Reserve Shiraz is outstanding, made with grapes from three carefully-selected vineyards with mature vines: Betty Harris's Elysium, Lloyd Light's Bakers Gully and Blewitt Springs. Dunsford herself admits it's impossible to always make reds as rich and powerful as the '90s. As for whites, since Southern Vales Chardonnay usually lacks finesse, Dunsford believes the challenge is to control that generous flavor, to stop it getting too big and blowsy, resulting in rich wines, best drunk young. The Southern Vales is not a good Riesling district, therefore the grapes come from Eden Valley, the best Riesling area in Australia.

Reserve Chardonnay 1991 ♈ ②
The district yields unmistakable full-bodied whites as well as reds. This Chardonnay may lack finesse but abounds in flavor and body. Strong hazel-nut and peach aromas with obvious oak and a very long finish. A wine for grilled meat.

Cabernet Sauvignon 1990 ♈ ②
Big, generous, warm red with silky texture, plum and chocolate flavors, enriched by unmistakable Cabernet blackcurrant. A grilled meat wine.

Reserve Shiraz 1990 ♈♈ ③
A magnificient wine from a great year for McLaren Vale. Exuberant flavors without the excessive Port overtones which threaten this region. Thick purple hue with concentrated chocolate, vanilla, spice and coconut aromas. Robust flavors with smooth tannins. Great now, will be sensational in 10 years' time.

Grosset

King Street
Auburn 5451
Tel. (088) 492175
Fax (088) 492292

Jeffrey and Cate Grosset run one of Clare Valley's smallest yet finest wineries. Grapes are partly purchased, but the rest come from estate-owned or estate-managed vineyards. A new vineyard, called Gaia, is located in the Valley's highest region and produces a Cabernet Sauvignon/Merlot blend, named after the Greek goddess of the earth, the guardian of the productive cycle. The Grossets are very concerned with nature's balance and believe in limiting chemical interference in their work. The Clare Valley is dry and relatively disease-free. The estate's Chardonnay is made 20% with grapes from the Piccadilly Valley (Adelaide Hills) to enhance its varietal character. Jeffrey Grosset, who has worked for larger wineries such as Lindemans, is a Riesling purist and makes two classically delicate styles from the Watervale and Polish Hill sub-regions. All Grosset wines are subtle, restrained and extremely refined. They may be a bit coarse when young, needing patient cellaring.

Polish Hill Noble Riesling 1991 ♈♈ ③
Made with a 30% botrytized Riesling, refined with tight and restrained perfumes and clear polished citrus and vanilla tones. Goes well with an orange tart.

Semillon 1991 ♈♈ ③
In typical Grosset style: refined, slow-aging, with subtle oak (it is fermented in Vosges barriques), pale in color. Strikingly intense flavor. Currently a food wine, will be richly rewarded with cellaring.

Watervale Rhine Riesling 1991 ♈♈ ③
A sensational wine, of limited production, from a classic producer. The Riesling floral aroma is intense, with a steely dry palate and fresh crisp acidity. The citrus flavors will increase with age. Can be cellared for up to 15 years.

Chardonnay 1990 ♈♈ ③
Restrained but intensely aromatic and delicately structured Chardonnay which gains further finesse from the 20% Adelaide Hills grapes. Crisp, clean acidity with good grip and finish. Complex bouquet of apple, butter and bread. Should cellar well..

Gaia 1989 ♈ ③
Grosset's Cabernet/Merlot blend usually follows the house style rather than Clare Valley's slightly masculine character, but the 1989 is full-bodied, with tannin and authority. Liquorice, mint and berry aromas. Needs to cellar 2 to 3 years, then can be drunk for 10.

Hardy

Reynell Road
Reynella 5161
Tel. (08)3812266
Fax (08) 3811968

Hardy is one of Australia's largest wine groups, with Leasingham in the Clare Valley, Houghton in Western Australia and the Chateau Reynella label. The group, which still belongs to the Hardy family, also owns La Baume in France and has a share in Tuscany's Barone Ricasoli. In ascending order of quality, Hardy's Australian labels are: the cheaper Bird Series, Nottage Hill, Siegersdorf, the Hardy Collection and the excellent Eileen Hardy. Wines are worth their price at all levels, but the Hardy Collection and Eileen Hardy are their very best. The Eileen Hardy Chardonnay, made from a Padthaway vineyard with carefully tended but not trained vines, is among the most complete in Australia. The delicate Classique Cuvée, a méthode champenoise made from Pinot Noir and Chardonnay, crowns a full range of sparkling wines. The excellent McLaren Vale fortified wines are led by an incredible Shiraz Vintage Port, among the country's best of its kind. Hardy is based in the old homestead of Chateau Reynella surrounded by old vineyards that produce Chateau Reynella Stony Hill Cabernet, but the best whites and some of the reds come from Padthaway. David O'Leary takes care of the reds, Tom Newton of the whites and Geoff Weaver is chief winemaker.

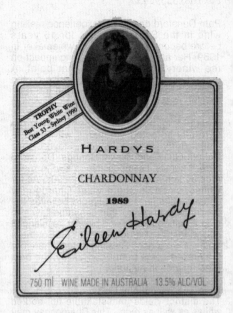

Siegersdorf Rhine Riesling 1991   ①
Market-leader among mid-priced Rieslings, made with Padthaway grapes, offers value for money. The '91 is a good vintage; stone-fruit aromas, light body lots of fruit and slightly sweet initial impact with a clear, smooth finish.

Collection Chardonnay 1990   ②
An outstanding Chardonnay in the $12 price range. Passionfruit aromas give away its Padthaway origins. Subtle aged cedar-wood overtones, rather complex, medium-bodied, with a pleasant dry finish.

Chateau Reynella Stony Hill Cabernet Sauvignon 1989   ②
Concentrated and complex, a red of great character. The bouquet speaks of mint, vanilla, chocolate and earthy aromas. In the mouth rich and fleshy, with powerful tannins, berries and mint. An outstanding wine that recalls the great Reynellas of the '60s.

Chateau Reynella Stony Hill Shiraz 1989   ②
Robust and slightly old-fashioned Shiraz, laden with aromas of ripe sweet cherries, plum jam, mint and eucalyptus. Rich and powerful on the palate with tannins that finely set on edge, promises a long cellar life.

Eileen Hardy   ③
Chardonnay 1989
Prolific award-winner, flagship wine, named in memory of the family's matriarch. Grapes are grown in Hardy's large Padthaway vineyard, where vines are trellised, trained and pruned to give lower yields of concentrated grapes. Winemakers Geoff Weaver and Tom Newton are Chardonnay experts, employing the most sophisticated methods to craft a wine of maximum complexity and richness. Barrel fermentation, quality oak, malolactic, pomace-aging and oxidizing techniques are all elements that help give birth to this wine. Full of subtle shadings, rich and complex, greatly balanced. Ripe notes accompany the typical fruit of Padthaway wines, distinctive melon, peach and tropical fruit aromas.

Henschke

Moculta Road
Keyneton 5353
Tel. (085) 648223
Fax (085) 648294

It is difficult not to be enthusiastic about Henschke, whose reds are amongst the best in Australia. Stephen Henschke trained at Geisenheim in Germany and in 1980, together with his wife Prue, took over the family winery, thus becoming a fifth generation winemaker of his line. The Henschke vineyards are among the best and oldest in South Australia, and their reds fully achieve the grapes great potential. One of Australia's most sought-after wines is the Hill of Grace, made from a vineyard of gnarled and century-old Shiraz vines, a concentrated rich wine made in small quantities from low yields. Close in terms of prestige and character is Mount Edelstone, made from another old Shiraz vineyard. Of the same class is the Cyril Henschke Cabernet Sauvignon made by Stephen in memory of his father who died in 1979. The pick of the whites is the outstanding Rhine Riesling grown in Keyneton, but the future of the whites probably lies in Lenswood, a cool hilly location from which Henschke is already making a very fine Chardonnay, an excellent Riesling and a promising Pinot Noir.

Lenswood Chardonnay 1990   🍇 ③
Exceptionally complex Chardonnay from a new, higher-altitude vineyard. Has a strong oak component but the fruit is up to the challenge with clear peach, hazel-nut and cedar-wood aromas and peach and pineapple flavors. Concentrated with a very long finish.

Rhine Riesling 1990   🍇🍇 ②
A remarkable Eden Valley Riesling, among the best from this winery. Fresh and sustained citrus aromas follow through to a spicy, tangy palate flavor with lots of fruit and vivacity. Should age well.

Mount Edelstone 1989   🍇 ②
Made from an old Shiraz vineyard, this wine is perhaps more polished than Hill of Grace and of similar quality. Toasted coconut oak and a twist of mint tickle the nose. In the mouth not as full as the glorious '88, but refined, intense and firmly structured.

Hill of Grace 1988   🍇🍇 ④
1988 was a great year for all Henschke reds. This vineyard's century-old Shiraz vines yielded a concentrated wine whose potential is still to be seen. It has ripe plum and cedar aromas coupled with deep complex spice and hazel-nut flavors of great length. An outstanding wine, an Australian classic.

Cyril Henschke   🍇🍇🍇 ③
Cabernet Sauvignon 1988
Henschke's fame was built on Mount Edelstone and Hill of Grace, but this Cabernet, named after Stephen's father and made only after his death in 1979, is in the same league although its pedigree is shorter. The grapes come from the family vineyard and Eden Valley growers. The '88 includes 5% Merlot. Crushing is light and many whole grapes go into the traditional concrete vats where fermentation takes place. With two to three degrees Baumé remaining the wine is drained off the skins and placed in barrels for a touch of oak. There is no fining and minimal filtration. Henschke says his best reds come from warm years like 1988. This Cabernet is full-bodied and concentrated, rich and fleshy with a ripe aroma of toast and berries - blackberry and blackcurrent. In the mouth a slightly astringent tannin gives a dry clean finish. A serious, powerful wine whose cellar future is at least 20 years.

Hollick

Racecourse Road
Coonawarra 5263
Tel. (087) 372318
Fax (087) 372952

One of the more successful small wineries to open in Coonawarra at the beginning of the '80s was that of Ian Hollick, a former viticulturist with Mildara. With two vineyards on some of the region's best red soil Hollick has made some fine reds in particular a fine and leafy Cabernet Merlot followed by a peppery and liberally-oaked Wilgha Shiraz. In 1988 respected winemaker Pat Tocaciu and his family joined Hollick, and one of his first moves was to make Ravenswood, a red made from straight Cabernet Sauvignon grapes, harvested from the property's finest vines. It is definitely Hollick's best wine, a Cabernet of great intensity and elegance. The whites are also among the best in the region: the Rhine Riesling, which many experts consider ill-suited to Coonawarra, has won many show trophies and even the Chardonnay has its own reserved style of charm. Tocaciu's abililty with sparkling wines is revealed above all in a Pinot Noir-Chardonnay blend, the Cuvée Cornel.

Chardonnay 1991　　　🍷 ②
Typical of this winery, a restrained, nearly shy wine, attractively subtle, discreet but complex character. A 40% malolactic fermentation in oak gives it smoky, hazelnut and melon flavors.

Rhine Riesling 1991　　　🍷 ②
An excellent Riesling with soft floral aromas, traces of toast and good varietal flavors. In the mouth full, smooth, dry; lingers nicely.

Botrytis Riesling 1990　　　🍷 ②
The delicate and refined style of botrytized wine becomes subtly refreshing, with good balance of sweetness and appealing citrus aromas.

Cabernet Merlot 1990　　　🍷🍷 ②
All the concentration and depth that the great 1990 Coonawarra vintage gave to it best reds. Intense red-purple hue, concentrated grape aromas without the grassy scents of some earlier years. Full-bodied and well-balanced, possibly Hollick's finest yet.

Ravenswood　　　🍷🍷 ③
Cabernet Sauvignon 1989
One of Hollick's most succesful reds and one of Coonawarra's best wines, with concentration from the vineyard's best lowest-yielding vines. Leaner than the swashbuckling '88 but traditionally regional, with superb cedarwood, berry and new oak aromas. Has a 10 to 15 years aging potential.

Katnook

Penola-Naracoorte Road
Coonawarra 5263
Tel. (087) 372394
Fax (087) 372397

The Coonawarra Machinery Company is the district's largest vineyard owner and sells most of its grapes to other wineries. Its own wines are produced after a careful selection by winemaker Wayne Stehbens. The up-market Katnook label is expensive but usually very good, with a full-bodied, nearly opulent Chardonnay, a very intense Sauvignon Blanc, an occasionally good Rhine Riesling and Gewürztraminer and an interesting, increasingly-complex Cabernet Sauvignon. The second label is called Riddoch Estate since the Katnook winery comprises part of the original property of John Riddoch, founder a century ago of Coonawarra's wine industry. The first Katnook wines were made in 1979, but Cabernets tended to suffer the excessively vegetative character which at the time penalized Coonawarra. With time the wines have improved remarkably, although pricing remains a problem in today's depressed market. The whites can age well, and the Riddoch Estate Cabernet-Shiraz is usually good, lighter but elegant.

Sauvignon Blanc 1991　　　🍷 ③
Clean and fresh gooseberry aromas of considerable intensity and good depth, lively on the palate. Slightly overpowering acidity, well tamed when paired with the right foods.

Chardonnay 1990　　　🍷🍷 ③
One of Katnook's best wines, made with all the most modern winemaking techniques. The oak and barrel-fermentation characters are integrated with intense fruit and a buttery touch. A powerful and impressive wine.

Rhine Riesling 1986　　　🍷 ③
A wine that shows the benefits of combining bottle-age with top-quality grapes. Lovely, restrained and ripe bouquet, soft on the palate, good persistence.

Cabernet Sauvignon 1987　　　🍷 ③
Bottle-age is starting to give polished elegance to this medium-bodied Cabernet, with slightly leafy, currant and toasted-oak tones. Full and quite complex in the mouth, drinks well with beef.

Tim Knappstein

2 Pioneer Avenue
Clare 5453
Tel. (088) 422600
Fax (088) 423831

Tim Knappstein, whose family used to own Leasingham, set out on his own in 1976 after purchasing the old Enterprise brewery, a beautiful stone building in the town of Clare. Wolf Blass owns the winery, but the vineyards belong to Knappstein, including 25 hectares situated high in the Adelaide Hills near Stafford Ridge and Henschke's Lenswood. Knappstein has always made some of Clare Valley's best Rhine Riesling and Gewürztraminer. He was the first in Australia to market a Fumé Blanc (from Sauvignon Blanc grapes) in 1980, but has never been satisfied with Clare Valley Chardonnay. Therefore since 1991 he has added Lenswood Chardonnay for fruit and finesse. The first wood-aged Sémillon, the 1990, is superb, the Lenswood Chardonnay is more reserved and refined. Knappstein grows 75% of his grapes in Clare at an altitude of approximately 450 meters in the highest part of the region where the clay topsoil is red to brown. The vines, irrigated to maintain their vigor during summer draughts, yield a rich and well-structured Cabernet Sauvignon and a softer, rounder Cabernet Merlot.

Gewurztraminer 1991   ☙ ②
Refined, delicate, dry wine with dried fruit overtones and typical varietal aromas. Medium-bodied with a pleasant fresh finish.

Lenswood Semillon 1991   ☙ ②
Made from grapes grown in the cool Adelaide Hills, this wine features a pungent herbaceous note typical of cooler climates, contrasting with citrus aromas and the slightest trace of oak. Full and deep on the palate, decidedly intriguing with a dry finish.

Rhine Riesling 1991   ☙ ②
Intense and pungent lime aromas are echoed on the palate, full flavor is underscored by a light but pleasant tannin grip.

Cabernet Sauvignon 1988   ☙ ☙ ②
A better, more balanced vintage than the lighter '89. Sweet raspberry and cherry aromas are laced with mint. Flavor is full and tannic, with a firm dry finish. Three or four years of aging will build complexity.

Leasingham

7 Dominic Street
Clare 5453
Tel. (088) 422555
Fax (088) 423293

This century-old winery has produced some of Clare Valley's greatest Rieslings and Cabernet-based reds. After hard times in the '80s, it was purchased by the Hardy group in 1987. Since then the winery has changed image. The equipment was updated and long-standing winemaker Chris Proud was replaced by Richard Rowe. In five years quality production and simple but effective marketing have restored Leasingham to the prestigious position it occupied in the '60s. There are two brands, the Domaine, good value for price, and the more demanding Hutt Creek. The Domaine range includes five typical Clare wines: Shiraz and Cabernet-Malbec (structured, rich, flavorsome and deeply-colored reds) and the well-made Rhine Riesling, wood-aged Sémillon and Chardonnay. To the amazement of on-lookers, during the mid-1980s Leasingham eliminated some of its older vineyards, a decision that time has proven right and which has been fully rewarded. Leasingham is still the largest winery in Clare and although it buys grapes from many growers the wines are all 100% Clare.

Domaine Chardonnay 1991   ☙ ①
Possibly Clare's most successful yet least expensive Chardonnay. The '91 has intense fruit flavors and a pleasant dry finish. Not particularly complex on the palate, reveals peach and caramel aromas with oak undertones and its softness makes it highly drinkable.

Domaine Rhine Riesling 1990   ☙ ①
Traditional Clare style, without yeast or botrytis aromas. Soft, floral, fine and dry, shows its true colors only after 4 or 5 years, reaching its peak at 15.

Domaine Cabernet Sauvignon Malbec 1990   ☙ ①
A traditional blend (80% plus 20%) gives a soft, round, full-bodied wine with depth of color and subtly balanced oak. Plum, cherry, mint and vanilla aromas. A rich wine, satisfying on the palate, with long aging potential.

Domaine Shiraz 1989   ☙ ①
Rich and full yet soft and round. Great depth of color and full, ripe bouquet with chocolate and vanilla tones. Generous depth of palate which fills the mouth and lingers at length.

Leconfield

Penola-Naracoorte Road
Coonawarra 5263
Tel. (087) 372326
Fax (087) 372285

Sydney Hamilton, member of a distinguished South Australian winemaking family, was 76 years old when he decided to plant a new vineyard on quality Coonawarra red soil in 1974. His first wines included some excellent Cabernet Sauvignons, but after a great 1980 the wines did not fulfill their early promise. In 1981 Sydney sold the estate to his nephew, Richard Hamilton, whose namesake ancestor is said to have been the first to make wine in South Australia. Then in 1990 the expert Ralph Fowler, formerly at Tyrrell's, Hungerford Hill and Cassegrain, took over winemaking. Leconfield's '90 and '91 Cabernet Sauvignons and Cabernet-Merlots were excellent, a sign that the winery is back on track. The vineyards are quite old, and unlike most in Coonawarra are pruned and harvested manually. These practices, together with low yields, give excellent aromatic complexity and great tannin structure, in an area used to mechanized, high-yield viticulture and consequently lighter wines.

Chardonnay 1991 ✿ ②
A major improvement on the '90, greater complexity with abundant oak and deep, lively fresh fruit flavors. Ralph Fowler's vast experience with Chardonnay is clearly evident.

Cabernet Merlot 1990 ✿✿ ③
A great Coonawarra vintage: a full-bodied and powerful blend with intense ripe berry flavors and cleverly handled oak that elegantly fuses with a toasty note. Cedar and dry tannin finish. Continues the improvement signalled by the '89.

Cabernet Sauvignon 1990 ✿ ②
Typical Cabernet flavors of leaves, tobacco and berry are present in this medium-bodied red, much more so than in the Merlot blend. Also has less oak and is highly drinkable.

Peter Lehmann

Samuel Road off Para Road
Tanunda 5352
Tel. (085) 632500
Fax (085) 633402

Peter Lehmann worked for a few years with Saltram. He left when Seagram took over, taking with him a number of Barossa and Eden Valley growers, and created a new winery in Tanunda. Chief winemaker Andrew Wigan and various assistants left with Lehmann who is well-respected in the valley by both growers and staff. His son Doug runs twin winery Basedows. Winemaking standards have always been high although great wines have seldom been found at Lehmann's. The situation has improved recently and several outstanding wines have gained recognition for Lehmann. After many years of experience with over 100 growers Peter Lehmann has identified special parcels of Chardonnay, Shiraz and Cabernet Sauvignon resulting in out-of-the-ordinary wines. The Cellar Collection is the top label and includes wines with extra bottle-age or wines that have special cellar potential. Old Redemption is a great and rare old Tawny Port.

Chardonnay 1991 ✿ ②
Those who love rich, opulent, oaky Chardonnays will surely appreciate this wine. Australian winetasting judges have, awarding it several prizes. Quite complex and expansive when young when it is probably at its best.

Noble Semillon 1990 ✿ ③
A sweetly opulent, oak-matured botrytized Sémillon with vanilla and honey aromas. Good acidity gives life to this rich, caramel and golden-colored dessert wine.

Cabernet Malbec
Merlot Shiraz 1989 ✿ ③
A wine that clearly reveals oak combined with rich Barossa Valley fruits. Pleasant spice and chocolate complexity - clover, nutmeg and berry aromas, long lingering flavor.

Clancy's Gold Preference 1989 ✿ ②
This inexpensive and ready to drink Shiraz, Cabernet Sauvignon and Merlot blend has caught the Australian public's attention. Medium-bodied, soft and juicy, with sweet vanilla, fruit and oak flavors.

Vintage Port AD 2006 1985 ✿ ②
The name refers to the expected date of maturity. Lehmann is a Port expert and this wine has true Port vintage structure: intense color, great depth of sweet spicy fruit and powerful tannin and alcohol structure.

Charles Melton

Krondorf Road
Tanunda 5352
Tel. (085) 633606

Those who accuse Australian wines of lacking character should get to know Charlie Melton and his wines. The wine business rewards eccentric and creative characters, and Charlie is one of them. After training at Saltram and Peter Lehmann he set out on his own in 1984 and began making quality wines. Together with a few other producers in Krondorf Road, a sub-region of the Barossa Valley, he was able to restore the valley's credibility after a crisis in the early 1980s. Melton has transformed Shiraz, Barossa's most important varietal, into a rich chocolaty essence and has shown that even the unfashionable Grenache varietal, through low-yield cultivation on poor soil, can give rich and structured wines. His flagship wine is the Nine Popes, made from a concentrated blend of Shiraz and Grenache and at times Mataro (Mourvèdre) that wins over lovers of great reds. The Shiraz is rich in aromas, whereas the Pinot-Hermitage follows the Hunter Valley style. The sparkling red made from Shiraz grapes is also excellent. Melton harvests the grapes from a few hectares of old vines around the winery, the rest come from old, low-yielding vineyards.

Rose of Virginia 1991 ①
A summer rosé made from Grenache grapes: light but better quality than rosés found in Australian supermarkets, with greater depth and a touch of tannin. Delicately sweet.

Nine Popes 1990 ②
Intensely colored Shiraz-Grenache blend that recalls good Gigondas. Concentrated, robust and full-bodied on the palate, rich aromas and supple tannins. Shows what dry soil and low-yields can do for Barossa Grenache.

Shiraz 1990 ②
This fascinating Rhone-style Shiraz has an unforgettable gamey, pepper and spice bouquet, with green-leaf tones and great complexity. Powerful and deep on the palate, with many nuances and a leathery touch. With time it will reveal even more secrets.

Cabernet Sauvignon 1989 ②
Quite lively berry and herbal aromas ,with a hint of oak. On the palate gentle and fresh but deep.

Pinot Hermitage 1988 ②
A nod towards the traditional Hunter Valley style, well-made. Complex earth, mushroom and faint tar bouquet. Soft, elegant and savoury palate.

Geoff Merrill

Pimpala Road
Reynella 5161
Tel. (08) 3816877
Fax (08) 3222244

Geoff Merrill's walrus moustache and larrikin ways are as famous as his wines. If strong character and extrovert behaviour were essential in obtaining success in the wine industry, Merrill would definitely have a big advantage over common mortals. Although not a formally qualified winemaker he gained experience in South Africa and South Australia and was chief winemaker at Hardy's Chateau Reynella before setting out on his own. His main label, Geoff Merrill, features an elegant Cabernet Sauvignon made from Coonawarra and local grapes, and a wooded Sémillon-Chardonnay blend. His second label is Mount Hurtle, named after the old stone winery that he restored himself. This colorful label also features a Cabernet and a Sémillon-Sauvignon Blanc blend, as well as an interesting Grenache rosé. All wines rely heavily on purchased grapes and are therefore influenced more by winemaking techniques than by the McLaren Vale region. The Southern Vales are dotted with small wineries run by straightforward winemakers who cater well for the intense regional tourist trade, and Mount Hurtle, with its landscaped lawns and wildlife, is no exception. Merrill is a very sociable and open person, just like his wines.

Mount Hurtle Sauvignon Blanc 1990 ②
Not one of those herbaceous and thin examples of Sauvignon Blanc. This MacLaren Vale wine shows mint and floral notes, a good full palate with generous sweet fruit aromas and green nuances.

Semillon Chardonnay 1988 ③
A structured wine that improves with bottle-age. Deep yellow color with ripe hazelnut and resin aromas, and abundant use of oak. Full and ripe aromas on the palate with an oak and tannin finish.

Mount Hurtle Grenache 1991 ①
A rosé by another name, warm pink color with fresh berry aromas, particularly raspberry. The highly perfumed, smooth and fruity impact is balanced by lively fresh acidic finish.

Cabernet Sauvignon 1987 ③
This vintage yielded a lighter wine, with mint, coconut and cherry aromas. Needs to age to allow its fruit and oak components to come together. Medium-bodied and well-made, without much aging potential.

Mildara

Penola-Naracoorte Road
Coonawarra 5263
Tel. (087) 363380
Fax (087) 363307

Mildara is a glorious winery that owns the Krondorf, Yellowglen and Balgownie brands and recently merged with Wolf Blass. Today, all of Mildara's premium reds are made in Coonawarra. Alexanders, a Bordeaux-style blend, had to struggle to match great Coonawarrra wines, but succeeded with an excellent '88. The white label Cabernet Sauvignon and the Jamieson's Run (mostly Shiraz) are excellent value for money and widely available. Mildara strongly supports minimal pruning and its wines are almost always good. Winemaker Gavin Hogg opts for an early harvest, consequently reds are rather light, elegant with fruit and berry flavors. Among the whites, Jamieson's Run Chardonnay is lightly-oaked, fruity and soft, of great appeal whilst the Krondorf Show Chardonnay is more complex and weighty. Yellowglen is the premium sparkling wine brand (Cuvée Victoria is the most important) and the Cabernet and Shiraz-based Balgownie reds are rich, full-bodied and minty, in keeping with the traditional central Victoria style.

Krondorf Show Reserve ♈ ③
Chardonnay 1991
This formerly rustic wine has been refined to suit changing tastes. The '91, considered an excellent year for this label, is medium-bodied and dry, with fig, passionfruit and oak aromas. With age it should gain charm and complexity.

Cabernet Sauvignon 1990 ♈♈ ②
Coonawarra's best "white label" in recent years, with great depth and weight. Cherry, currant and smoky oak aromas are intense, with good body in the mouth.

Church Hill Cabernet Merlot 1990 ♈ ①
An inexpensive red worth more than its price thanks to a 60% Coonawarra component. Smoke, leaf and toast aromas are supported by deep, supple and sweet fruit, and a surprisingly strong tannin framework.

Jamieson's Run Shiraz Blend 1990 ♈ ②
Tasted directly from the barrel this wine definitely makes a grand impression. The great '90 season has given it outstanding depth and weight, rich harmony of spice, plum and cherry flavors with substantial texture and harmony.

Alexanders 1988 ♈ ③
Deep, intensely colored wine with concentrated currant Cabernet aromas and ripe oak. Powerful and rich aromas with the harmony and elegance that characterize this winery's style.

Mitchell

Hughes Park Road, Skillogalee Valley
Sevenhil via Clare 5453
Tel. (088) 434258
Fax (088) 434340

Jane Mitchell and her winemaker Neil Pike produce one of Clare's finest Rhine Rieslings, with intense floral aromas and great fullness of flavor. Jane Mitchell is interested in the region's well-known characteristics and wants distinctive Clare character and structure. She has stopped making Chardonnay as she has so far been unimpressed with the results. Most of the vineyards are at Watervale, a premium sub-region with limestone-based soils that yield some of the area's finest Rieslings. Many of these have aged beautifully as witnessed by the amazing 1980, 1982 and 1984. The Shiraz is more peppery than most in the district and was named Peppertree Shiraz because by coincidence it comes from a vineyard with a pepper tree in the center. The winery was founded in 1975 and 16 years of experience have taught Jane to harvest the Shiraz at 12.5 to 13.5 degrees (Baumé), which gives the wine a full range of flavors, from pepper to spices through to cherry and plum. The Cabernet Sauvignon can also be very good.

Semillon 1991 ♈ ②
An excellent white from a very successful year. Lemon flavors and subtle ripe wood nuances. Lean and dry, excellent with fish or chicken.

Watervale Rhine Riesling 1991 ♈ ②
This Riesling's fresh ester aromas recall those of passionfruit. The flavor is intense and fresh yet soft and smooth. A superb example of pure Clare Riesling style, absolutely typical of this district. Should mellow like the excellent '80, '82, '84 and '86 which have greatly contributed to Mitchell's reputation in Clare.

Peppertree Shiraz 1990 ♈ ②
This vineyard is famous for its clearly peppery wines. The Peppertree Shiraz is full, soft and chunky with vanilla and chocolate aromas and lively tannin grip.

Cabernet Sauvignon 1988 ♈ ②
The warm, smooth and fleshy style is developing soft earth overtones. Mint plays an important role in the bouquet, with a touch of spice.

Mountadam

High Eden Road
High Eden Ridge 5235
Tel. (085) 641101
Fax (085) 641064

Adam Wynn is one of Australia's most inspired winemakers, and is as articulate about his philosophy as he is adept at expressing it in his wine. His father David built Wynns Coonawarra Estate and sold it in the 1970s when he and Adam, fresh from the University of Bordeaux, chose a new location for Mountadam on a windy peak with poor, shallow soil. Very low yields, concentrated flavors and Adam's own very personal yet French-influenced style, combined with modern winemaking techniques, yield some outstanding wines. The Rhine Riesling is unique but the rich and fleshy Pinot Noir (the '88 is outstanding), the Cabernet-based blend called The Red and the botrytized Riesling are sensational. To date, however, the major output has been Chardonnay, very popular in Australia and well-received in the USA and Japan. It is made in classic Burgundian style employing barrel fermentation, lees stirring, full malolactic fermentation and low doses of sulfur. A sparkling wine made from Pinot Noir and Chardonnay is improving.

Chardonnay 1990   🍇 ③
A wine of character rather than subtly, with Burgundy as role model. The '90 is an unusual style for Mountadam, with quince aromas and flavors that mix with toasted oak. Harmonious and intense, with a long finish.

Noble Riesling 1990   🍇 ③
The low alcohol content (10.5°) and moderate sugar level indicate mild botrytis, resulting in a rather restrained style. Clean citrus flavors and aromas amalgamate with a sweet overtone and appealing elegance.

Pinot Noir Chardonnay   🍇 ③
Methode Champenoise 1987
Honey, flower and coconut scents tickle the nose. Rich concentrated flavors of fruit, hazelnut complexity with a touch of oak fill the palate.

The Red 1989   🍷 ③
The first vintage of this new Cabernet Sauvignon-Merlot blend bursts with ripe fruit flavors and aromas. Typical exuberant Australian style rather than an attempt to resemble Bordeaux.

Pinot Noir 1989   🍷 ③
A Pinot with a powerful aroma of dried prunes. Original in depth and intensity of flavor, lacking the varietal charm of the best Pinots. Good but not in the same class as the magical '88.

Orlando

Sturt Highway
Rowland Flat 5350
Tel. (085) 213111
Fax (085) 213100

Australia's second largest winery with a complete range of wines that are good value for money. Orlando was founded in 1847 by the Gramp family, early German settlers of the Barossa Valley, and now belongs to the French company Pernod-Ricard. It has grown to include wineries in Griffith (Wickham Hill), Rutherglen (Morris) and Hunter Valley (Wyndham Estate, Saxonvale, Richmond Grove) but the center of production remains its original site in Rowland Flat. Orlando was once known primarily for its whites, particularly the Riesling, but today under the dirction of Robin Day it is equally strong in reds. The vineyards are concentrated in the Eden Valley, Barossa and Riverland although most grapes are purchased, primarily from Padthaway and Coonawarra. The Saint range offers top quality with St. Helga Eden Valley Riesling, St. Hugo Coonawarrra Cabernet Sauvignon, St. Hilary Chardonnay and St. Hewitt Pinot Noir. At the top there is the excellent Flaxmans Eden Valley Traminer, a Steingarten Riesling, the Lawson Shiraz and the exceptional Jacaranda Ridge Coonawarra Cabernet. At the lower price level there is the RF range with well-priced Cabernet Sauvignon, Chardonnay and Rhine Riseling. Lastly, there is the omnipresent Jacobs Creek.

St Helga Eden Valley   🍇 ①
Rhine Riesling 1991
Appealing lime and floral Riesling aromas join with a fresh bread-dough nuance. Light and lively on the palate with young and clean flavors and the right acidity. Best when young, recent vintages tend to develop strong pineapple flavors with age.

St Hilary Chardonnay 1989   🍇 ②
A fleshy, wood-aged wine made from a blend of McLaren Vale, Padthaway and Coonawarra grapes. Color is intense with ripe buttery aromas and flavors. Soft and full, has reached peak maturation.

Jacaranda Ridge Coonawarra   🍷 ④
Cabernet Sauvignon 1988
Orlando's flagship red has hit a peak in '88. Concentrated and full-bodied, with an enveloping oak and cedarwood bouquet. Intense and sweet vanilla flavors, berry aromas finish with a persuasive tannin backbone.

St Hugo Coonawarra   🍷🍷 ③
Cabernet Sauvignon
The St Hugo style is fresh enough to enjoy now, but should improve with extended cellaring. More savoury and complex than typical Coonawarra, with oak and fungal complexity and dry tannin finish. A superb wine, already developing tobacco aromas.

Penfolds

Tanunda Road
Nuriootpa 5355
Tel. (085) 620389
Fax (085) 621669

Penfolds was founded in 1844 by a doctor who was interested in wine as a tonic for his patients, developed by his family and sold in 1976. Today Penfolds is a key brand in S.A. Brewing's market share, and makes Australia's most famous wine, Grange Hermitage as well as wine of every style and price. Grange Hermitage is at the top of Penfolds' range, a wine of monumental structure and power that lives up to 30 years, unbeaten since 1951. Other wines include Magill Estate, an elegant Shiraz from the original Grange vineyard at Magill, Bin 707 Cabernet Sauvignon, Bin 389 Cabernet Shiraz, St Henri Claret, Bin 28 Kalimna, Bin 128 Coonawarra and Koonunga Hill. American oak, Shiraz grapes and the Kalimna vineyards are the three key elements that create the overtly oaky, rich and savoury character of Penfolds reds. John Duval and his assistant winemakers buy grapes from various areas: McLaren Vale, Langhorne Creek, Clare, the Barossa and Eden Valleys, the Hunter, Victoria and Riverlands, but primarily from Barossa. Other estate vineyards are located in Coonawarra, Padthaway, Eden Valley and Clare. Oak is also a fundamental element in Penfolds' finest whites, a rich toasty Chardonnay and an elegant Sémillon Chardonnay.

The Clare Estate Chardonnay 1991 ②
An unusual but appealing Chardonnay, with lime-juice, pineapple and tropical fruit flavors, toasted nuances from subtle use of oak. On the palate intense, lively and elegant.

Bin 28 Kalimna 1989 ②
A magnificently generous old-school Shiraz. Earth and fruit aromas with liquorice and blackberry flavors and a touch of mint. Key words are concentration and richness, power and impact, unexpected in such a reasonably-priced wine.

Bin 707 Cabernet Sauvignon 1988 ③
A massive, powerfully structured wine made to last. The clear hazelnut, coconut and vanilla nuances from American oak barrels set it apart from other Cabernets. Full, chocolaty Barossa flavors with strong tannin grip. Penfolds' number two, after the Grange, for the past twenty years .

St Henri Claret 1987 ③
Traditionally made without new or small barrels, St Henri has become an alter-ego of the more robust and oaky Grange Hermitage. Typically a red to drink rather than smell, with Shiraz dry grass and chocolate flavors and strong, mature, savoury palate.

Grange Hermitage Bin 95 1986 ④
Deservedly Australia's most celebrated red wine, made since 1951 from Shiraz grapes grown on old, low-yielding Kalimna vines and other Barossa growers' vineyards. Fermentation is critical. The skins are submerged beneath heading-down boards and the juice is periodically pumped out to a holding tank and back through a heat exchanger, aerating as it goes, giving maximum extraction. Fermentation is completed in new 240 liter American oak barrels, a technique that adds extra aromas and flavors. The wine then remains two years in the same oak, with regular racking and topping. The Grange style is consistent thanks to Barossa's climate and to the decision to blend grapes from several different vineyards. The Grange lives at least 30 years and the '86, a top vintage, will be no exception. A massive wine, loaded with rich concentrated spicy fruit, coconut and vanilla oak and gripping tannin. Should not be opened for a few years and will reach its peak well after the year 2000.

SOUTH AUSTRALIA
AUSTRALIA

Penley Estate

McLeans Road
Coonowarra 5263
Tel. (08) 2312400
Fax (08) 2310589

Kym Tolley, a descendant of Penfolds founder Dr. Christopher Rawson Penfold, combined the surnames of two famous winemaking families to create the name Penley Estate. After 17 years as winemaker at Penfolds he established his own brand in 1988. Vines planted that year in Coonawarra will not contribute to Penley wines for a few years and until then Tolley, who considers himself an artist fulfilling a creative need, uses purchased grapes. "Making wine is like starting with a blank canvas," he says,"you start from nothing and develop something special." His best wine to date is the 1989 Cabernet Sauvignon, followed by the 1989 Shiraz Cabernet. Both wines are made from Coonawarra grapes, full-bodied and ripe, with oak reminiscent of Penfolds' finest reds. The 1989 and 1990 Chardonnays are stylish McLaren Vale and Coonawarra blends. In the same range are the Coonawarra Shiraz and a sparkling wine, both expensive but well-presented. Penley Estate has started on the right foot with these excellent wines which have performed well in competitions.

Chardonnay 1990

Fruity, pure McLaren Vale style. Elegant, full-flavored wine with deep buttery, peach and honey aromas. Fine and smooth on the palate, with good texture.

Cabernet Sauvignon 1989

Kym Tolley has succeeded in capturing more body than most Coonawarra Cabernets. Mulberry, currant, mint and cedarwood flavors mingle in a complex and multi-faceted wine of great concentration and stature,with long aging potential.

Shiraz Cabernet 1989
An elegant red, with herbaceous berry fruit aromas coupled with toasty oak. Savoury and well modulated on the palate, with crisp acidity and good tannin backbone.

Petaluma

Spring Gully Road
Piccadilly 5151
Tel. (08) 3394122
Fax (08) 3395253

Winemaker Brian Croser has an enormous influence on the Australian wine scene. He made his first Petaluma vintage in 1977 as a wine science lecturer having studied at Davis University in California. While planting vineyards and building a winery in the Adelaide Hills he worked as a consultant. Petaluma is a medium sized producer and arguably makes the best Clare Valley Rhine Riesling as well as one of Australia's finest and most restrained Chardonnays (gradually using more Adelaide Hills grapes) and an elegant Coonawarra Cabernet Sauvignon-Merlot. All are made from estate-owned vineyards. The sparkling Croser, one of Australia's best and most prestigious méthode champenoise, is made from a maze of small parcels in the steepest parts of the Adelaide Hills. It is bottle-fermented and aged at least two years on lees in the Bridgewater Mill, a beautifully restored stone building that also houses a restaurant. Bridgewater Mill is also the name of the group's second label (with partners Len Evans and Bollinger) of less expensive but often impressive wines. Croser, who also owns the Argyle vineyard in Oregon, is president of the Federation of Australian Winemakers and a wine judge.

Chardonnay 1990   🍇🍇 ③
The first wine made exclusively with Adelaide Hills grapes and also the best. Hazelnut and melon flavors are intense and deliciously refined. The oak, barrel fermentation, malolactic and lees-age give it the final touches. Should develop great complexity with five or six years in bottle.

Croser 1988   🍇🍇 ③
For many experts, the house's most elegant sparkling wine, made exclusively from a single vineyard. The '88 is fine, fresh, fruit-dominated and lightly yeasty with a round start and dry finish. The Pinot Noir varietal is matched with a creamy mousse.

Tiers Pinot Noir 1989   🍇 ②
Brian Croser is still feeling his way with this wine, made from Petaluma's original Adelaide Hills vineyard. Good complexity of nuances, with earth, floral and strawberry aromas. Smooth and round on the palate with dry tannins.

Coonawarra 1988   🍇🍇 ③
The Cabernet Sauvignon dominates the Merlot in this wine, the best of its line to date. Clean, purple-hued, anaerobically-made with concentrated berry fruit. May seem straightforward when young, but will undoubtedly mature into a great wine.

PETALUMA

1990 RHINE RIESLING

750ml

PRODUCE OF AUSTRALIA BOTTLED AT PICCADILLY SA

Rhine Riesling 1990   🍇🍇🍇 ②
The grapes were grown in Petaluma's Hanlon Hill vineyard on the Clare Valley's highest slopes, on brown sandy loam with a limestone sub-layer. A long, cool dry autumn allowed the grapes to remain on the vines at length, obtaining 12-12.5° (Baumé), which Brian Croser calls the Australian dry late-harvest style. Vines are irrigated to prevent the negative effects of drought, but yields are not high. Grapes are hand-picked, trucked to the Adelaide Hills winery and crushed. Must is clarified and fermented cool in steel tanks. Both the juice and wine are strictly protected from the air at every stage. The '90 was nearly perfect, recalling the 1980 made under similar conditions. The superb floral, fruit and bread-dough aromas combine with great finesse with the primary citrus flavors of Clare Riesling. The finish is dry but not austere. A wine that will last 20 years and reach its peak in the year 2000.

Rockford

Krondorf Road
Tanunda 5352
Tel. (085) 632720
Fax (085) 633787

Robert O'Callaghan is a real traditionalist. From the ancient vines that yield his concentrated wines to the old basket press in which he crushes his Shiraz and the winery he painstakingly built out of local stone, O'Callaghan maintains his little Barossa Valley corner old-style. Nostalgia sells well, especially when combined with superior quality, and Rockford's 1886 Vine Vale Riesling, Basket Press Shiraz and Dry Country Grenache are evocative titles. His sparkling burgundy, deeply-colored and concentrated in flavor is called Black Shiraz. Few regions in the world can boast significant areas of century-old non-grafted and non-irrigated vines like those of the Barossa Valley, and O'Callaghan respects their unique qualities. He owns small plots of vines but was moved to buy the one hectare Vine Vale Riesling vineyard to save it from the bulldozer. Most of his grapes are bought from 27 carefully selected small growers.

1886 Vine Vale Riesling 1991 ① ①
Century-old vines produce a soft, bone-dry and full-flavored Riesling, with great aroma and finesse. Senses are tickled by softly floral, yeasty, doughy and buttery nuances.

Eden Valley Riesling 1990 ① ①
A semi-sweet and more commercial style than Vine Vale, with understated aroma and mature developed notes. Attractive depth with floral and slighty honeyed flavor. For every-day drinking.

Black Shiraz NV ③
A magnificient example of an obscure Australian style, known as sparkling burgundy. Barrel-aged before bottling for its second fermentation, deeply colored with spicy plum fruit aromas and flavors of Shiraz. Its frothy mousse mixes with sweet and soft tannins.

Basket Press Shiraz 1989 ②
One of the great, concentrated Barossa Shiraz made with grapes from old vineyards. The '89 is fleshy, solid, dense and full-flavored with spice, berry, hazelnut and vanilla aromas. Immense depth yet amazingly balanced and harmonious. Seems to equal the '88 despite a modest year.

Cabernet Sauvignon 1988 ②
The winemaker's skills are not restricted to his famous Shiraz. This Cabernet is superb, deeply colored with powerful, lively berry and leafy aromas. Complex fruit and tannin flavors, promises to age well.

Saltram

Angaston Road
Angaston 5353
Tel. (085) 638200
Fax (085) 642876

Saltram dates back to 1859 and in the 1960s and 1970s was home to Barossa doyen Peter Lehmann until it was bought by Seagram in 1979. Within a few years it markedly reduced its enormous dimensions, giving up large-scale production of cheap bottled and cask wines to aim at the more prestigious premium market. The most successful range is the Classic consisting of quality wines around the AUS$10 price range: Chardonnay, Sauvignon Blanc, Sémillon, Riesling and reds. The Mamre Brook range is a cut above with complex cedary Chardonnay and a Cabernet Shiraz which became a classic with Peter Lehmann. The top range is the Pinnacle: full-bodied tannic reds created to last, structured and opulent Chardonnay, round and delicate Sauvignon Blanc, floral Barossa Riesling, and an excellent botrytized Pinnacle Coonawarra Riesling, particulary the '82. Mr Pickwick's Particular Port is a very old Tawny, one of Australia's finest. Saltram also makes Stonyfell Metala from Cabernet and Shiraz grapes grown on a century-old Langhorne Creek vineyard. The 1986 is exceptional while the 1987 is not as interesting.

Classic Chardonnay 1990 ① ①
Excellent value for money (AUS$8-9). Pleasant fresh peach and melon aromas with lightly handled oak. The balance is unquestionable.

Pinnacle Chardonnay 1989 ③
Deep yellow color with a complex and powerful fruity bouquet of hazelnut and oak. A savoury, ripe wine, enlivened by crisp acidity.

Mamre Brook Chardonnay 1988 ③
A complex Chardonnay with evident oak. Deep yellow color with cedarwood and sandalwood aromas mixed with ripe and slightly buttery flavors. Dry and full on the palate with yet again strong oak flavors, which may not appeal to everyone.

Pinnacle Coonawarra
Cabernet Sauvignon 1984 ③
Complex wine which benefits from age, appealing dried herb and walnut overtones united with raspberry and currant aromas. A classy wine with smoothly balanced tannin. Ready to drink even now.

Mr Pickwick's Particular Port ④
A Tawny Port of great age and character. Bursting with oak and Madeira complexity, concentrated and powerful on the palate, yet mellow with a very long aftertaste and pleasantly dry finish.

Seppelt

Seppeltsfield via
Tanunda 5352
Tel. (085) 28028
Fax (085) 628333

Seppelt is one of the oldest names in the Australian wine industry, dating back to 1851 when migrant Joseph Seppelt established the spectacular Seppeltsfield estate. The winery, which has recently been restored, plays a key role in the S.A. Brewing group, but Great Western is Seppelt's main winery. Here they have created a reputation as Australia's leading sparkling winemaker, with inexpensive Imperial Reserve, excellent Salinger, Vintage Brut and Fleur de Lys, made from the three Champagne varietals. Seppeltsfield also houses the largest cellar of fortified wines in the southern hemisphere. The superb Tawny Port blend relies on extremely old base wines. DP90 and Para are the finest and every year the century-old Para Liqueur Ports are released with a price of around AUS$ 2000 a bottle. Seppelt also has a wide range of excellent table wines. Great Western Hermitage excelled in 1985 and 1986. Dorrien Cabernet, a single-vineyard Barossa, is only sold in top years.

Partalunga Rhine Riesling 1991   ♥ ②
Unusually pungent and spicy aromas, with plenty of fruit and a pleasant acidic balance. This line comes from a new Adelaide Hills vineyard and is emerging as Seppelt's leading Riesling.

Fleur de Lys Pinot Noir   ♥ ②
Chardonnay Brut 1989
A youthful, fresh and fruity sparkling wine with a light yeasty influence but plenty of lively flavors. Not too rich but soft on the finish. Top value for money.

Jean Trouette Vintage Brut 1988   ♥ ③
Pinot Noir and Chardonnay aromas dominate over yeasty overtones, with fresh, refined nuances of butter, toast and hazelnut that lead into a fresh and creamy palate.

Great Western Vineyards   ♥♥ ③
Hermitage 1986
Very rich, ripe and complex Shiraz with a toasty bouquet, tickled with mint and spice on the palate. Outstanding aging potential, as shown by the best vintages: '64, '67, '71 and '85.

Seppeltsfield Show   ♥♥ ④
Tawny Port DP90
Arguably Australia's finest Tawny Port. Light and dry with an average life of over 20 years. The depth of its maderized character, its complexity and concentration and the length of its finish are absolutely spellbinding.

St Hallett

St Hallett's Road
Tanunda 5352
Tel. (085) 632319
Fax (085) 632901

Several years ago wine-marketer Bob McLean bought a share of Carl Lindner's winery, founded in 1944, and gave it a new surge of life by improving both quality and image with the help of winemaker Stuart Blackwell. Extra income is generated by crushing, pressing and extracting grape juice under contract for larger wineries, while McLean attempts to intensify St. Hallett sales. The best-known wine is the Old Block Shiraz, made from vines 90 to 130 years old. Together with Penfolds' wines, it has educated palates of consumers and winemakers, encouraging other wineries to use old ungrafted and unirrigated Barossa Shiraz vines, many untrellised, which give low yields of small, intensely flavored berries. The Cabernet Merlot is a delicate ready-to-drink red, the Chardonnay is big and somewhat oaky while the Sémillon-Sauvignon Blanc is crisp, grassy and refreshing.

Chardonnay 1991   ♥ ②
Elegant and rich style, deep yellow color with hazelnut and butter aromas. Full-bodied, rich, soft and doughy with near-solid texture and viscosity. Possibly St. Hallett's best Chardonnay to date.

Semillon Sauvignon Blanc 1991   ♥ ②
A light-bodied, dry, early-drinking white with crisp pineapple and cashew-nut aromas. Soft and lean on the palate, with tropical fruit, lively acidity and a firm dry finish.

Cabernet Merlot 1990   ♥ ②
A wine of great charm, for early consumption or short-term cellaring. The '90 has leafy berry aromas and flavors, with soft tannins and a smooth, delicate palate.

Old Block Shiraz 1989   ♥♥ ②
All of the 13 source vineyards are over 60 years old. Excellent blackberry, coconut and spice aromas with touches of new oak. Concentrated warmth and richness, powerful and closed. At AUS$16 one of the most affordable old-vine reds available.

Stafford Ridge

2 Gilpin Lane
Mitcham 5062
Tel. (08) 2722105

Geoff Weaver was a winemaker at Hardy's for 17 years, initially in charge of whites and later chief winemaker. In 1980 he planted his own small vineyard, Stafford Ridge, high in the Adelaide Hills at Lenswood. It had been Weaver's dream for years to plant vines in the most suitable district to pursue the objective of growing grapes free of the natural commercial restraints imposed by working within a large company. He chose an area where the climate is cool, ideal for delicate, intensely varietal whites such as Sauvignon Blanc, Chardonnay and Riesling, but less suited to reds which to date lack body but are nevertheless interesting. Located at an altitude of 540 meters, the soil is well-drained podsolic loam over clay, and by Australian standards the vines are very closely planted (2,600 per hectare) and trained upwards to expose the grapes. The Chardonnay is oak-fermented and lees-aged for one year. With the Chardonnay and Cabernet-Merlot, Weaver aims for subtle oak, purely in a supporting role. The Sauvignon Blanc is much fruitier.

Sauvignon Blanc 1991   ❦ ❦ ②
Shows all the stylish aromas and fruit intensity of the cool Adelaide Hills. Pale color, a slightly restrained gooseberry and herbaceous varietal aroma. Intense and varietal, yet gentle on the palate.

Chardonnay 1989   ❦ ❦ ③
The fantastic complexity of this Burgundy-like wine makes it a success of rare perfection. Charming floral, honey toasted hazelnut, butter and spice notes display all the winemaker's imagination. The palate is a lesson on how to control power.

Wendouree

Wendouree Road
Clare 5453
Tel. (088) 422896

When Roly Birks left Wendouree to retire it could have marked the end of a legend. Fortunately the winery fell into the hands of Tony and Lita Brady, a jovial and modest couple who wish to preserve this little national treasure - an ageless winery founded in 1895, with old-fashioned techniques that modern companies have long since forgotten. Their finest wines are the Shiraz from 1919 vineyards on red loam over limestone (2.9 tons of small berries per hectare); a Cabernet Sauvignon from 1971 vines planted on red loam over limestone (5 tons per hectare) and a Cabernet-Malbec from 60% Cabernet Sauvignon vineyards dated 1896, 1920 and 1975 that yield 1.8 to 5 tons per hectare. The 40% Malbec component is from 1896, 1920 and 1940 vineyards that yield between 2.5 to 5 tons per hectare. Three other reds are produced: Shiraz-Mataro (Syrah-Mourvèdre), Shiraz-Malbec and 100% Malbec. All wines come from estate-grown grapes and are made and bottled on site.

Cabernet Malbec 1990   ♥ ♥ ③
The almost impenetrable color hides a powerful wine, with concentrated mint and eucalyptus aromas and tannic berry and mint flavors. With age it will become exceptional.

Malbec 1990   ♥ ②
A structured red, rich in extracts, with vanilla and berry aromas and a herbaceous Malbec varietal overlay. Soft and clean chocolate, vanilla and berry flavors. For current drinking, but will live at least until the year 2010.

Shiraz 1990   ♥ ③
Another full-bodied red, soft and gentle, smooth and mouth-filling, not as complex as the wines described above. A strong vanilla essence prevails with a touch of chocolate and a soft tannin sensation. Pleases now, but will improve with age.

Shiraz Malbec 1990   ♥ ②
Very full-bodied and rich in extracts, needs to age to soften and mellow. Great depth of concentrated aromas, sumptuous blackberry and plum flavors with hints of violets and spices.

Shiraz Mataro 1990   ♥ ②
Lighter and more elegant in color and flavor than most Wendouree wines, yet good depth of peppery spiced flavor and a steely tannin finish. Will improve with five or six years in bottle.

Wirra Wirra

McMurtrie Road
McLaren Vale 5171
Tel. (08) 3238414
Fax (08) 3238596

Wirra Wirra is owned by Greg Trott and his cousin Roger. In 1969 they rebuilt an old 1894 property and its superb stone winery maintaining the "old world" style on the inside and placing all modern machinery in the rear. Most grapes come from nearby estate-owned vineyards, the rest is supplied by other premium district growers. The Chardonnay is rich, with strong woody influences, at its best with three or four years age. When young, the Sémillon-Sauvignon Blanc has pleasant melon and berry flavors, but matures into a full wine with hazelnut overtones that can age up to 10 years. The Cabernet Sauvignon is full-bodied, dense with notes of cocoa in true regional style, while Church Block is softer, to drink young and is very popular with restaurants. The Rhine Riesling is McLaren Vale's best. The Cousins is a fine Pinot-Chardonnay méthode champenoise made at Petaluma's Bridgewater Mill. All wines have more finesse than usual for the area.

Sauvignon Blanc 1991   ♈ ②
Good weight and depth of flavors, with tropical fruit and subtle hazelnut aromas (although there is no wood aging). Dry and refreshing flavors and lingering finish.

McLaren Vale Chardonnay 1990   ♈ ♈ ③
Rich, full-bodied Chardonnay boasting excellent intensity and complexity of flavors. Good harmony of peach, butter, yeast and toast from barrel-fermentation. An amazing finish.

Wood-matured Semillon   ♈ ②
Sauvignon Blanc 1990
Soft, full blend with slightly resinous oak touches that make it a bit astringent. An unusual style that will mature into a rich, ripe and golden wine.

Church Block   ♈ ②
Cabernet Shiraz Merlot 1990
Big, solid yet not very complex with honest quality of ripe grape aromas. Structure and persistence are acceptable. Needs four to five years in bottle.

The Angelus   ♈ ③
Cabernet Sauvignon 1990
A fresh and youthful Cabernet, needs a few years in bottle. Intense purple hue, rather raw, undeveloped fruity aromas and flavors that show the very sweet and ripe fruit.

Wynns Coonawarra Estate

Memorial Drive
Coonawarra 5263
Tel. (087) 363266
Fax (087) 363202

A magnificient building with stone pediment built in 1891 by Coonawarra's founder John Riddoch houses the region's largest and most important winery, now owned by S.A. Brewing. The expansion of vineyards, contrary to tradition, led to a marked improvement in the quality of Wynns wines, particularly since the introduction in 1982 of a new production philosophy that gets the most from the grapes by using new oak barrels and selecting the best grapes. The 1982 vintage also produced the first John Riddoch Cabernet Sauvignon made from the oldest and lowest-yielding vines planted on terra rossa soil and now regarded as one of Australia's greatest reds. Black Label Cabernet Sauvignon and White Label Hermitage (Shiraz) have also improved and although quantities are large their release is eagerly awaited every year, particularly after recent price reductions. The Rhine Riesling, also inexpensive and produced in large quantities, is good value for money and the Chardonnay is one of the most competitively priced early drinking wines available. Also good are the Cabernet Hermitage and Pinot Noir. Since 1986 the talented Peter Douglas is in charge of winemaking and has added his own personal touch to a line of reds, the district's best for intensity and texture.

Hermitage 1990 ♥ ①
From the best vintage in recent years, this breathtaking Shiraz is purple-colored and powerful with spicy, peppery and plum aromas. On the palate deep, strong yet velvety. It needs two or three years but can age up to 15. Destined for greatness.

Black Label ♥♥ ②
Cabernet Sauvignon 1989
Not from one of the best vintages but this full-bodied and currant flavored wine doesn't lack anything. Rich, toasty berry aroma with variegated, concentrated flavors. John Riddock selection was not made in 1989 and all grapes went into this wine.

Cabernet Hermitage 1989 ♥ ①
Not a wine for contemplation but for early drinking. It is a soft honest red with light herbaceous flavors, not suited to long aging.

John Riddoch ♥♥ ③
Cabernet Sauvignon 1987
Concentration is the key word in color, aroma and flavor. Intense super-ripe blackcurrant and blackberry fruit with supple tannins. Full-flavored and fleshy texture. Ready to drink now but should keep improving for at least 15 years, becoming a Coonawarra classic.

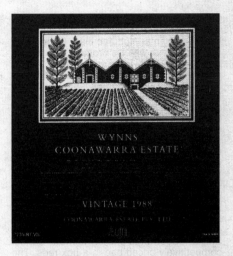

John Riddoch ♥♥♥ ③
Cabernet Sauvignon 1988
The grapes are machine-harvested from low-vigour vines planted on lean terra rossa soil where the limestone sub-layer shows through. Yields are low and the grape flavor is the most concentrated among the large Wynns vineyards. Peter Douglas uses 100% Cabernet Sauvignon since the Merlot would dilute its strength. Musts are fermented in closed stainless-steel tanks with a submerged cap and frequent pumping to obtain maximum extraction. The wine then spends 24 months in new French or American oak barriques. This wine is made only in the best years, and was not bottled in 1983 or 1989. An initial selection takes place after fermentation and continues in smaller barrels. The '88 follows the sumptuous, concentrated and vigorous style of the '87. It has a bright purple color and aromas of blackcurrant jam, crème de cassis and toasted oak with great depth of flavor that mellows into a tannic, lingering finish. Goes well with sharp cheeses.

Yalumba

Eden Valley Road
Angaston 5353
Tel. (085) 642423
Fax (085) 642549

The Hill-Smiths, owners of Yalumba for 129 years, consider wine and horseracing the heritage of an aristocratic clan. Robert Hill-Smith, together with his brother Sam, bought out the rest of the family and is now managing director. From the estate vineyards in Pewsey Vale, Heggies and Hill Smith Estate they have developed a strong collection of good wines: Rhine Riesling, Cabernet, botrytis Riesling, Sauvignon Blanc, Chardonnay. New vigour has been given to the house's flagship wines, Signature Series Chardonnay (by white winemaker Alan Hoey) and Cabernet-Shiraz (by red winemaker Brian Walsh). The market is strong for its sparkling wines, from the inexpensive and popular Angas Brut to exceptional Yalumba D. Yalumba hit the jackpot with its new, lower-premium brand Oxford Landing, an outstanding Chardonnay. Galway Vintage Shiraz-Cabernet is one of Australia's most competitively priced bag-in-a-box reds. The winery also produces excellent Tawny and Vintage Ports and Brandy.

Hill Smith Estate   ♀ ②
Sauvignon Blanc 1991
Strong vegetal aromas and flavors, appealing pleasant wine when young but rapidly loses freshness. Light-bodied therefore best consumed now.

Family Reserve Rhine Riesling 1990 ♀ ②
Light and delicate with floral aromas. Lean, clear flavors with a dry finish. Should improve with up to five years cellaring.

Hill Smith Estate Chardonnay 1990 ♀ ②
A new addition, charming, elegant, medium-priced Chardonnay that shows honey and hazelnut complexity with soft and rich fullness on the mouth and well aromatized oak. Does not need further aging.

Yalumba D   ♀♀ ③
Methode Champenoise 1988
The best of its line, combines flavor, depth and richness with elegance. Ripe and slightly toasty aromas with varietal Pinot Noir overtones. Fine mousse and a lingering, dry and balanced finish.

The Menzies   ♥ ②
Cabernet Sauvignon 1988
Typical of the softer, open-knit Coonawarra Cabernet, with leaf and mulberry aromas. Medium bodied on the palate with soft tannins. Develops delicate cedary nuances in the mouth. Ready to drink.

Price levels

①   up to $ 9.99

② $ 10.00 - $ 14.99

③ $ 15.00 - $ 24.99

④ $ 25.00 or more

The 'ex-cellar', or direct from the producer, bottle prices, are calculated in US dollars and are intended only as an approximate guide

Tasmania

This island, to the south of the continent, is Australia's smallest state in terms of population, surface area and viticulture, with only 200 hectares of vineyards and a production of 766 tonnes of grapes in 1990-91. The wine industry is based on a multitude of vineyards with few hectares and there is no mass production of low quality or fortified wines since everything is aimed at a premium market. The climate is rather cold therefore the successful varietals are the ones that ripen first, such as Chardonnay. Great hope lies in Pinot Noir which, in this climate, should give excellent results although to date high yields and inappropriate clones have caused problems. Even Riesling, Gewürztraminer and Pinot Gris can be excellent. Oddly enough Shiraz is not cultivated, but Cabernet Sauvignon -which becomes too herbaceous in the Pipers River district - has produced some good wines in West Tamar, the East Coast and Huon Valley. The sparkling wines could turn out to beTasmania's biggest success: Heemskerk Jansz is made in collaboration with Louis Roederer and both Taltarni and Domaine Chandon produce in Tasmania base wines for their champagne method sparklers, and other projects are underway.

Freycinet

Tasman Highway
Bicheno 7215
Tel. (002) 578384
Fax (002) 578454

Most of Tasmania's wineries are tiny and fairly new, and Freycinet is no exception. The vineyard, owned by Geoff Bull and his family, was planted in 1980 and is located on the east coast, far from the island state's three main wine regions. The coastal climate is maritime and relatively dry, with a long growing season that can extend into May and even June. Soils are podsolic from decaying granite with a friable clay subsoil and drainage is good due to a sloping aspect. The vineyard overlooks a peninsula and national park, both called Freycinet. Geoff Bull, helped by roving consultant Gary Baldwin, makes the wines, the most impressive being a pungent Chardonnay and the 1990 version is loaded with exciting tropical fruit aromas. Tasmanian Cabernets can often be rather herbaceous, but Freycinet's '89 is ripe and well structured. Pinot Noir is Tasmania's pet grape, and Freycinet's '90 is deeply colored and flavored with intensity and purity of varietal character. These are some of the most attractive and competently made wines in the island state.

Chardonnay 1990 ❦ ③
A sensational wine with fantastic, aromatic, lifted tropical fruit nose enhanced by cashew nut and vanilla nuances. The palate is concentrated with pungent fruit-dominant flavors which are thoroughly captivating, although perhaps not everyone's idea of classic Chardonnay.

Pinot Noir 1990 ❦ ③
Exceptional depth of color and flavor from a region which should be perfect for Burgundian varietals. Complex aromas of sweet cherry, oak and slightly gamey. On the palate very good flavor intensity and tannin give a strong finish and very long aftertaste.

Cabernet Sauvignon 1989 ❦ ③
Impressive depth of color and flavor from such a cold climate, with surprisingly gripping tannins. Stylish toasty oak embellishes the flavors of currants and violets. Well structured and balanced.

Heemskerk

Pipers Brook 7254
Tel. (003) 827133
Fax (003) 827242

The vineyard was the creation of Graham Wiltshire, who recently departed almost 25 years after he established Heemskerk in partnership with the Fesq and Haselgrove families. Recently the Champagne house Louis Roederer became a partner for the production of a long-awaited sparkling wine called Jansz. The first, 'Cuvée 89', was launched in late 1991 and met with a very mixed reception. Some sections of the media did not find the style to their liking and it was also rejected in wine shows, although the retail trade and other critics embraced it enthusiastically. This product has undoubtedly been affected by the very marginal climate of the main vineyard at Pipers River, a region where reds have strong varietal characters and the whites excessive acidity. A new vineyard of 20 hectares was therefore planted at Rebecca in the warmer, neighboring West Tamar region. The retention of talented young Roederer winemaker Jean-Baptiste Lecaillon should also help lift quality and consistency, as proven by the 1990 Pinot Noir, arguably the best Pinot yet made in the Pipers River region.

Chardonnay 1990 ❦ ③
A very delicate Chablis-style white with lean yet firm structure, a slightly austere palate with a grassy note in the honey-like aroma. From a cool year, should reward cellaring.

Jansz Cuvée 89 ❦ ③
The first product of the Heemskerk-Louis Roederer joint venture has light straw color, nutty and toasted bread aromas and a youthful, lean and dry but pleasingly balanced palate showing well-judged liqueuring.

Pinot Noir 1990 ❦ ❦ ③
A peak Pinot year for Heemskerk. Classic dark-cherry and strawberry ripe Pinot Noir scents with some new oak and an attractive gamey aspect make this a most alluring wine, its depth of sweet fruit and roundness setting it apart from other vintages.

Pipers Brook Vineyards

Bridport Road
Piper's Brook 7254
Tel. (003) 827197
Fax (003) 827226

Andrew Pirie, owner of the highest-profile Tasmanian winery, has partly succeeded in his quest to produce elegant and fine wines in a cool Burgundy-like climate. Chardonnay has proved to have both finesse and longevity, while some see Riesling as the vineyard's main triumph. Pinot Noir has big potential and some superb wines have been produced, while the Cabernet Sauvignon-based blend, labelled Opimian since 1990, are persistently herbaceous and lack charm, suggesting that the region is too col for some varietals. A selection of the best parts of the vineyard, where sunlight and warmth are maximal, produces a premium Chardonnay cuvée called Summit. Full Burgundy treatment - barrel and malolactic fermentation, lees contact - is employed on all Chardonnay. Soils in all three vineyards are fertile, deep red-brown of volcanic origin. Vines are close-planted to reduce vigor. Barrel fermented Sauvignon Blanc is very good and Pinot Gris, made in tiny quantities, is exciting. The second label, Tasmania Wine Company, includes good value Sémillon and Pinot Noir.

Chardonnay 1991 ☙☙ ③
A very good vintage for one of Australia's finest, most subtle cool-climate Chardonnays. Intense yet restrained fruit flavors of melon and grapefruit, with the customary deftly handled oak, spicing the wine rather than dominating. Will be long-lived.

Pinot Gris 1991 ☙ ②
A rare and exciting wine. Vinified in barrel and put through malolactic fermentation. Rich, smoky, spicy, nutty and toasty aromas with fine oak and delicate buttery overtones. A subtle, complex dry white and a good successor to the '90.

Riesling 1991 ☙☙ ②
A great Australian Riesling. The pure flavors of well ripened grapes have been captured with high fidelity: intense lime and citrus with superb balance and a long, fresh aftertaste. Destined for a long life.

Tasmania Wine Company ☙ ②
Chardonnay 1991
Very good depth of flavor and character for an inexpensive wine. Hints of spice, sweet peach and butter. Not oak-matured and not intended for cellaring.

Pinot Noir 1990 ❦ ③
Sweet ripe cherry, strawberry aromas dressed up with spicy oak, giving a complex perfume. Good length and weight of flavor with lively acid tartness, suggesting it will benefit from brief cellaring.

Entries are arranged in alphabetical order by country, region and winery or producer name.

Victoria

No region has undergone such a rapid and intense viticultural expansion as
Victoria. With less than 20 wineries in the early 1960s, by 1990 they had
become 169 spread across a vast range of climates and soils, making Victoria
into Australia's most exciting wine state. And the number is still growing.
Wineries are mostly small, the largest being Seppelt, Brown Brothers and
Mitchelton, not counting the enormous Lindemans and Mildara on the
northern border. In total there are 19,000 hectares of vines (32% of the
national total) which give 18% of Australia's wine. The vineyards'scattered
distribution makes regional grouping very difficult; in any case the main
premium-quality regions are in the south, with the Yarra Valley and
Mornington Peninsula near Melbourne, and Geelong a little further west. All
grow excellent Chardonnay, Pinot Noir, Cabernet and Merlot. Richer and
fuller wines are produced at Bendigo, Heathcote, Great Western, Pyrenees
and Goulburn Valley while cooler Macedon gives delicate table wines and
sparkling cuvées. The warm north-eastern regions (Rutherglen, Milawa,
Glenrowan) produce great fortifieds and full-bodied reds, while the north-
eastern highlands have some fine whites.

Baileys

Taminick Gap Road
Glenrowan 3675
Tel. (057) 662392
Fax (057) 662596

The awesome quality of Bailey's fortified wines, particularly liqueur Muscat and Tokay, is legendary in Australia and the Winemaker's Selection labels are at the pinnacle of their style. The red wines inspire perhaps an even more devoted following: they are very robust, tannic and have been described as ferruginous. Winemaker Steve Goodwin is sticking with traditional styles in reds and fortifieds, although the reds, particularly the Classic Hermitage (Shiraz) are more refined than in the past , benefitting from some new barriques and less-heavy extraction in the vinification. Goodwin puts a lot of effort into white table wines with mixed results; in truth, Glenrowan's hot, dry climate is not the right locality for fine white wines. Baileys' strengths remain its solid, rich reds that demand flavorsome food, and wonderfully luscious Muscat and Tokay. The latter come in various price gradings which coincide with degrees of wood-age and concentration, but all of this historical winery's products are good value for money.

Winemakers Selection 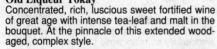 ⍩⍩ ④
Old Liqueur Tokay
Concentrated, rich, luscious sweet fortified wine of great age with intense tea-leaf and malt in the bouquet. At the pinnacle of this extended wood-aged, complex style.

Classic Hermitage 1989 ⍩ ②
A rich, smooth, full-bodied red with aromas of nuts and dried herbs. Excellent depth and fullness on the palate without excessive tannin, although it will live and improve for many years. Less extractive than warm-year Baileys reds.

Classic Cabernet Sauvignon 1988 ⍩ ②
Enormous, eucalyptus and mint scented wine which may lack elegance but makes up for it by generosity of flavour and tannins.

Winemakers Selection ⍩⍩ ④
Old Liqueur Muscat
Burnished amber color, enormously complex raisiny Muscat nose showing very aged rancio character. Very sweet, spicy, luscious palate of great concentration. Classic example of aged Australian dessert Muscat.

Bannockburn

Midland Highway
Bannockburn 3331
Tel. (052) 811363
Fax (052) 811349

The commitment of supermarket owner Stuart Hooper and winemaker Gary Farr knows no bounds. The first vines were planted in 1974 near Geelong, in a cool southerly climate, on low-yielding clay-based riverside soils. The winery was fitted out with every latest technical innovation and Gary Farr travelled to Burgundy for successive vintages to gain experience making Pinot Noir at Domain Dujac. This learning produced invaluable benefits, so much so that Bannockburn makes one of the leading Australian Pinot Noirs in a bigger style than most, as well as a complex Chardonnay. Young Burgundy winemakers regularly spend a 'stage' at Bannockburn, and the French influence extends to Sauvignon Blanc, as a winemaker from Sancerre also worked at the winery. Viticulture is also Gallic, with close-spacing of vines and very low yields, as are the vinification methods which give high concentrations and high color and tannin levels.Farr also makes two less consistent reds; Shiraz and Cabernet Sauvignon.

Chardonnay 1990 ⍩⍩ ③
A serious Burgundy pretender, loaded with barrel-ferment and lees-aged complexities giving nutty, toasty overtones to the fine, well-structured base fruit. It is emerging as one of this country's stand-out Chardonnays.

Sauvignon Blanc 1990 ⍩ ②
With more than a tilt at Sancerre, this is Bannockburn's best Sauvignon to date. Chalky, flinty Loire-like aromas without herbaceousness lead into a full, quite rich palate which has very appealing flavor and long aftertaste. A most unusual Australian Sauvignon Blanc.

Pinot Noir 1990 ⍩⍩ ③
The grape that carved winemaker Gary Farr's reputation produced a slightly lighter wine in 1990 than the usual big and quite tannic style. Still shows the complex cherry smoky and slightly earthy characteristics imparted by the vineyard.

Cabernet Sauvignon 1988 ⍩ ②
Fresh purply color and youth, intense smoky blackcurrant flavors and smooth fruit with just a touch of astringency.

Shiraz 1988 ⍩⍩ ②
Oak plays a minor role here, with spicy and dark-berry Shiraz fruit dominatng a fresh, youthful wine. The palate is smooth with sweet ripe fruit and no excess tannin. Enjoyable now, it will keep well for at least a decade.

Best's

Concongella Vineyards
Great Western 3377
Tel. (053) 562250
Fax (053) 562430

Viv Thomson's family has owned the 125-year-old Best's Concongella Vineyards since 1920, successive generations establishing deserved renown for their table wines, particularly the Hermitage from Shiraz grapes. Great Western is historically one of Australia's most revered Shiraz regions thanks largely to Seppelt across the road, but Best's has fared just as well in a more understated style. The wines are never big, but often peppery and spicy in cool years and redolent of sweet, ripe cherries in warmer years. Great Western is an old gold-mining village in the Great Dividing Range, but the hills are not very high and the summers are only moderately cool. The oldest vineyards are planted on very poor, grey, powdery silt flats beside the Concongella Creek where frost is a problem and yields very low. Since the late '70s an excellent, tropical-fruit styled Chardonnay has come from an irrigated hillside vineyard free from frost and drought. Since the late 1980s newer plantings of Cabernet Sauvignon and Merlot have yielded the vineyard's first Cabernet-based wine. A new tradition is therefore being established at this staunchly traditional winery which offers some of Victoria's best value-for-money table wines.

Great Western Chardonnay 1991 ☙ ③
A distinctive style, smelling of melon, tropical fruits and peach with perfumed oak and a touch of smokiness. Follows the house style of refined, complex wines which age well.

Great Western Rhine Riesling 1990 ☙ ②
Very fine, fresh, 'bread dough' estery and citrusy floral aromas combine in a style of great finesse which has seen a general improvement in recent years.

Great Western Hermitage 1990 ❦ ②
Medium to full in body, stylish, intense Shiraz smelling of spices, violets and plums. The American oak is subtly handled and the tannins are smooth and easygoing. A typically elegant Best's Shiraz. A 10-year keeper.

Great Western Hermitage 1989 ❦ ②
A lighter style for Best's, from a troubled year, but the wine is softly spicy, lightly tannic, well structured and has good balance. Probably best drunk young.

Great Western ❦ ③
Cabernet Sauvignon 1988
Stylish, elegant wine with attractive soft purity of berry flavors, subtle oak, and fine-grained tannins. A recently introduced line which shows much promise.

Chambers Rosewood

Corowa-Rutherglen Road
Rutherglen 3685
Tel. (060) 329641

Bill Chambers runs a winery that time forgot in a tumbledown iron shed that must be much as his grandfather left it, yet his liqueur Muscats (from red Frontignac grapes) and Tokays (from Muscadelle) are arguably the best in Rutherglen and therefore, Australia. Labelled simply Old Muscat or Old Tokay, they are sublime, sweet, luscious wood-aged fortifieds of a style and quality unmatched in the world. They sell at over AUS$100 and are exceedingly rare. Chambers has blending stocks over 100 years old, and would rather keep putting the price up than see the reserves of aged wines depleted.The "Special" Muscats and Tokays are not as old but only slightly less great, while the standard "Liqueur" Muscats and Tokays are quite young, fruity, fresh and inexpensive. Chambers buys some grapes from the Lakeside vineyard nearby, and his own vineyards contain some relics from Rutherglen's golden past: Gouais, Alicante Bouchet, Blue Imperial (Cinsaut) and Chasselas. The white table wines are not of great interest; the reds are better, with a good, reasonably priced Cabernet Sauvignon.

Old Liqueur Tokay ☙☙ ④
Dark color with green to gold nuances, wonderfully complex aged tea-leaf, malt aromas showing great depth of very old material which explodes on the palate and lingers for ages in the finish. Slightly less sweet than the muscats but wonderfully luscious nonetheless.

Cabernet Sauvignon 1987 ❦ ①
A deep, savoury, full-bodied wine with pencil shavings of oak and plenty of long, smooth tannin, more elegant than the typical Rutherglen red, with attractive balance. Unfortunately these very inexpensive wines are underrated.

Old Liqueur Muscat ❦❦ ④
Sheer ambrosia. The epitome of the Rutherglen Muscat style, unique, very old and very great. Dark amber/garnet color, fantastic concentration, lusciousness and complexity, exploding with toffee, raisin and vanilla flavors. Carries a rose-like perfume that sets it apart from its neighbors.

Coldstream Hills

Lot. 6, Maddens Lane
Coldstream 3770
Tel. (059) 649388
Fax (059) 649389

The speed of Coldstream Hills' rise from a standing start in 1985 has exceeded that of any other winery, assisted no doubt by the high profile of its managing director and winemaker, the newspaper columnist and author James Halliday. Halliday is a Burgundy lover and specializes in Pinot Noir and Chardonnay, both of which have done very well in Gault & Millau Wine Olympiads. Grape sourcing has moved from 100% other Yarra Valley sources to 30% estate-grown in the Coldstream vineyards perched on a steep north-facing hill on the eastern side of the valley. They provide all grapes for the Reserve wines and a high proportion of the standard labels, the balance coming from two contracted growers. Chardonnay style is restrained, building complexity with bottle age. Pinot Noir is arguably Australia's best, with sappy cherry scents and overt new oak. Reserve labels of both are especially good (the '88 and '87 Miller Vineyard Pinots are outstanding), while Cabernet Sauvignon and Cabernet-Merlot are superb in an ultra-modern smooth, fruity style. The second label is Steel's Range.

Reserve Chardonnay 1991 ♈♈ ③
This could turn out to be the best Coldstream Chardonnay yet, but these wines need time. Initially shy and austere with refined melon and nutty aromas in the maker's typical style, it has excellent concentration and all the makings of a great bottle in five to seven years.

Pinot Noir 1991 ♈ ②
Just a whisker behind the Reserve, the standard bottling shows just how good '91 was for Yarra Pinot. A little less oak, more yielding in youth, this is also a superb Pinot, typical of the region, and already drinks well.

Reserve Pinot Noir 1991 ♈♈ ③
1991 was even better for Pinot than '90, producing a sensational Reserve wine. New oak is very much a part of the Coldstream style, adding a cedary overtone to the classic dark-cherry, smoky fruit. The most concentrated, powerful and impressive Pinot yet from this leading producer.

Cabernet Merlot 1990 ♈♈ ③
Roughly equal parts of Cabernet Sauvignon and Merlot. From an outstanding season in the Yarra, this smacks of fresh cherry, plum and currant Cabernet fruit offset by oak. Lean, fine and elegant, very gentle and deceptively drinkable now, although it will undoubtedly age well.

Key to the symbols

Types of Wines

♈ White

▣ Rosé

♈ Red

Rating System

♈
An exemplary wine of its type with outstanding local character

▣▣
An international premium quality wine

♈♈♈
A Top Wine, considered one of the 150 best wines in the world

The 'grape bunch' symbol is used to indicate the color of the wine; the number of bunches represents the quality rating assigned by the contributor

Price levels

① up to $ 9.99

② $ 10.00 - $ 14.99

③ $ 15.00 - $ 24.99

④ $ 25.00 or more

The 'ex-cellar', or direct from the producer, bottle prices, are calculated in US dollars and are intended only as an approximate guide

Entries are arranged in alphabetical order by country, region and winery or producer name.

Craiglee

Sunbury Road
Sunbury 3429
Tel. (03) 7441160
Fax (03) 7447905

Craiglee was a famous name last century, and immaculate bottles of 1872 vintage are still being drunk around Melbourne by the very fortunate. The vineyard, just an hour's drive north of Melbourne, went out of production from the 1930s until the Carmody family replanted it in 1976. The most famous wine today is Shiraz, which in the best years (1990, '86, '88) can be rich and explosively flavored, with lifted pepper and spice aromas and well-structured, firm palate. All grapes come from the estate's low-yielding vines planted on grey loamy soils at Sunbury, a satellite town of Melbourne. Winemaker Pat Carmody Jr. believes in full-bodied wines, and his Shiraz and Cabernet Sauvignon both fit that description. Chardonnay is also well-made, rich and unctuous, with subtlety yet depth, the oak component not overstated. The tasting/salesroom is an old bluestone building which once served as the winery. Today the wines are made in a less glamorous, but more functional, corrugated iron shed.

Shiraz 1988 🍇🍇 ②
Deep, bright red-purple color, soft nose with lots of pepper and spice. Very intense flavor, soft, rich and multi-layered with subtle oak and excellent chewy tannins. A textured wine of great harmony, outgunned only by the '90.

Shiraz 1990 🍇🍇🍇 ②
A leader among the trendy new cool-climate pepper/spice Shirazes of southern Victoria. Grown on Craiglee's own vines planted in 1976 on deep, rich, alluvial riverside soils where watering is not usually needed and yields are seven to ten tonnes per hectare. The wine is fermented in steel tanks and aged mainly in American oak, a maximum of 20% new, and some older French. The 1990 vintage is a big, concentrated, solid wine. Scents of peppercorns, cloves and dark berries pervade the nose while the palate is enormously deep, full-flavored, tannic and complete. The finish is very long and the overall impression is of a very satisfying drink. It should age well for at least a decade. Although the vineyard is too young to have much of a track record, the previous planting, which went out of production in the late 1920s, produced reds of extraordinary longevity.

Dalwhinnie

Taltarni Road
Moonambel 3478
Tel. (054) 672388
Fax (054) 672237

Architect Ewan Jones and his family started
Dalwhinnie, next door to the high-profile
Taltarni, in 1976 and his first wines were
made at Yellowglen by Ian Home. In the mid
1980s the Jones developed their own winery
and Ewan's son David took over as
winemaker, with some help from another
local winery, Mount Avoca. Dalwhinnie's
wines are all from its own vineyard, at 360
meters on the slopes of the eucalyptus-
dotted Pyrenees Range, where the soils are
old, weathered quartz-based clay and gravel,
yielding small crops (7 tonnes per hectare) of
concentrated fruit. Hence the red wine style
is rich and chunky, with very intense flavor,
big structure and firm tannins. These wines -
especially the great '88s - promise to be long-
lived and demand cellaring. Made from
Shiraz and Cabernet Sauvignon, kept
separate, they are very typical of the district,
often showing definite mint and eucalyptus
notes. Chardonnay is also big and rich, laden
with peach, creamy flavors and a toasty
character deriving from barrel fermentation.

Chardonnay 1990   ❦ ③
A very big wine, concentrated and oaky with
massive fruit, high alcohol and considerably
long finish.

Moonambel Cabernet 1990   ❦ ❦ ③
The region produces big reds with abundant
tannin and extract and this is no exception.
Dense purple-red color, intense aromas and
mouth-puckering tannins will soften into a rich
bottle of red given time.

Moonambel Shiraz 1990   ❦ ③
A gloriously concentrated Shiraz of full-bodied
richness and supple tannin. Spices, berries and
a hint of vanilla, a solid and very appealing wine
to drink now although it surely has a
distinguished future.

Delatite

Stoneys Road
Mansfield 3722
Tel. (057) 752922
Fax (057) 752911

At an altitude of 475 meters, close to the
Victorian snowfields, Delatite is a chilly
climate for growing grapes. The harvest
comes late (Riesling in late April) and the
grapes are high in acidity, giving the white
wines finesse and bite. Established by the
Ritchie family as a sideline on their cattle and
sheep property in 1969, Delatite has become
much more than a hobby, with all members
of the family deeply involved. Roseworthy-
trained Rosalind Ritchie and her brother
David make the wines and father Robert
looks after the vines, producing grapes of
such delicacy that Pinot Noir is in demand for
Domaine Chandon's sparkling wines. The
alpine air seems to permeate the wines,
among which the Rhine Riesling and
Gewürztraminer stand out, reserved, delicate
whites which need a couple of years age to
show their true colors. Chardonnay is also
subtle and a sparkling Demelza is well worth
trying. Reds from Cabernet Sauvignon, Pinot
Noir and Malbec are deeply colored,
extremely fruity and flavorsome in the riper
years. The top-line red is Devil's River, a rich
blend of Cabernet Sauvignon and Merlot.

Chardonnay 1991   ❦ ③
Light yellow, reserved, fine Chardonnay with low
intensity, nutty, lightly peachy and vanilla
aromas with lightly handled oak. Good now but
should be much improved in a year or two.

Rhine Riesling 1991   ❦ ②
Like the Traminer, pale-colored, delicate and
backward. A Riesling in the classic Australian
style, dry with citrus and floral flavors of great
poise. Needs several years to develop
character. Long life-span. The '90 is similarly
fine, reserved and promises much for the future.

Dead Man's Hill Gewurztraminer 1990 ❦ ②
Very restrained, slow-developing cool-climate
wine. Pale color with subtle floral aromas, a
delicate, fresh, soft tasting wine of finesse and
balance which will grow into a top wine after four
or five years.

Devil's River 1990   ❦ ③
From Merlot, Cabernet Sauvignon and Franc
and Malbec grapes, a wine that opens with
exuberant young fruit. Secondary aromas are
those of dark berry, spices and mint. Smooth on
the palate with gentle tannins.

Pinot Noir 1989   ❦ ②
This wine is acquiring an interesting gamey
aspect with age, adding to the lively berry
fruitiness. The vineyard's trademark -
eucalyptus and mint - is a slight distraction from
the innate charm of the grape.

Diamond Valley

Kinglake Road
St Andrews 3761
Tel. (03) 7101484
Fax (013) 7101369

Pinot Noir is the Holy Grail for many Yarra Valley growers. Winemaker David Lance, who with his wife Cathy owns this tiny estate, makes one of the finest and manages to do so consistently, even though his "estate" wine comes from only a hectare of vines. The 1990 vintage is highly decorated and arguably the best yet, giving light-bodied, ethereal, wonderfully perfumed and extremely complex wines for Pinot purists. The '91 wine, from a dry year, is very big and concentrated. A second Pinot, made from bought-in grapes and sold under a blue label, is lighter and involves some carbonic maceration. The attention given to Pinot tends to eclipse the winery's other wines, which are all good: a fine, light-bodied Chardonnay, an aromatic Rhine Riesling, an elegant Cabernet "Bordeaux blend" and a spicy melange of odd varietals called White Diamond. Winemaker David Lance, a PhD in chemistry, worked in Melbourne's biggest brewery before embarking full-time in wine, planting Diamond Valley in 1976.

Estate Chardonnay 1990 ❦ ③
Very fine, restrained, backward in development but already shows great character. Subtly oaked, allowing the grapefruit and melon fruit flavors full expression. A fine thread of acidity gives firmness.

Estate Pinot Noir 1991 🍇 ③
From a very low-yielding year this is an atypical style: quite massive, concentrated and powerful with tannin and a long spicy aftertaste. Destined to make history.

Estate Pinot Noir 1990 🍇🍇 ③
The most awarded Pinot Noir ever in Australian competitions, this wine is the essence of the Yarra Valley, fairly lightly colored with wonderful perfume, fruit dominant and lightly wooded, with a surpassingly fine palate. At its best now.

Domaine Chandon

Greenpoint, Maroondah Highway
Coldstream 3770
Tel. (03) 7391110
Fax (03) 7391095

Domaine Chandon Australia, a wholly-owned subsidiary of Louis Vuitton Moët Hennessy, has been selling wine for just four years but is already among the top Australian sparkling producers. Its policy of sourcing grapes from many regions is unique and even when its own vineyards have reached full bearing will continue buying most of its crush because of the need for complexity, blending options and insurance against bad seasons in the Yarra Valley. Hence the Cuvée Brut 89-1, based on the generally poor 1989 vintage, is arguably the best blend yet. Manager Tony Jordan and winemaker Wayne Donaldson source about 50% of the intake from various sites in the Yarra.The rest comes from Coonawarra, Geelong, Mansfield, Mornington Peninsula, Nagambie and the Strathbogie Ranges. Dr. Jordan was for several years a consultant enologist, regularly servicing clients all over Australia and New Zealand, and draws on this vast experience in his present role. The blending is assisted by Richard Geoffroy of Moët & Chandon, but otherwise the Aussies are given free rein. Aside from the Cuvée Brut, which is Pinot Noir, Chardonnay and sometimes a little Meunier, there are occasional Blancs de Noirs and Blancs de Blancs, as well as recently disgorged editions.

Cuvée 89-1 ❦ ❦ ③
Based on the 1989 vintage, with more than 20% reserve wines. Vigorous mousse gives creamy mouth-feel. Delicate, fresh, clean style with light yeastiness and apple fruit with a trace of herbaceousness. Needed a year or so in bottle to develop character.

Blanc de Noirs Cuvée 88-3 ❦ ③
100% Pinot Noir grapes, faintly pink colored sparkling wine with slightly candied, nutty/smoky Pinot Noir aromas. Dry on the tongue with a slightly rounded finish.

Dromana Estate

Harrisons Road
Dromana 3936
Tel. (059) 873800
Fax (059) 810714

Garry Crittenden was a horticulturist and managed nurseries before planting grapevines on the cool, maritime Mornington Peninsula. He is one of the most respected cool-climate viticulturists in Australia and in demand as a consultant, a luxury his energetic promotion of Dromana Estate leaves little time for. The small vineyard shows intelligent planning and management. Crittenden avoided from the outset the region's prevalent herbaceous characters by planting on poorer soils, avoiding the rich volcanic earth on the higher ridges and with clever control of irrigation (a necessity here) and vine canopy he makes some of the most successful wines on the peninsula. Chardonnay is fine and subtly oaked, Cabernet-Merlot is irresistably berryish and varietal, Sauvignon Blanc is bracing and fruity, and Pinot Noir is the essence of the grape. Second label Schinus Molle is even more keenly sought-after in the U.K. than at home. Crittenden is that combination needed but seldom found in small wineries: an expert grape grower, winemaker, taster and promoter, with the result that his wines have a deservingly high profile.

Chardonnay 1991   ♀ ♀ ③
Chardonnay is the grape that impresses most on the Mornington Peninsula. A superbly subtle, restrained style within the Australian context. The oak is nicely underplayed. Fine melon and grapefruit aromas with a suggestion of gooseberry. Great depth and intensity yet very refined. Crittenden's best yet.

Schinus Molle Sauvignon Blanc 1991 ♀ ②
A fruit-accented style in which herbaceousness has largely been tamed and replaced with gooseberry and melon flavors of lightness and delicacy. It has become a hit in the U.K.

Schinus Molle Pinot Noir 1991   ♀ ②
Excellent value in this lower price range. Delicious spicy, sappy, strawberry elements to the bouquet. Very good intensity, weight and grip.

Pinot Noir 1990   ♀ ③
A young Pinot Noir yet it already has earthy and gamey aromas with fruit aspects (strawberry and cherry). Still has high-fidelity varietal character which may build more complexity with a little more age.

Cabernet Merlot 1989   ♀ ③
Ultra-modern wine which bursts out of the glass with blackberry, currant and leafy/tobacco aromas laced with oak. May lack a degree of 'stuffing', but the flavor intensity is hard to beat and tannins are soft and light.

Giaconda

Wangaratta Road
Beechworth 3747
Tel/Fax (057) 270246

Rick Kinzbrunner was an engineer before he felt the call of the vine. He worked in wineries in Napa Valley, Bordeaux and New Zealand before settling on his own patch of land in the eastern highlands of Victoria, in 1981. In low-fertility clay-gravel-granitic soils, his tiny vineyard produces roughly equal parts Pinot Noir, Chardonnay and a Cabernet Sauvignon-Franc-Merlot blend. Yields per hectare are low, 5 to 7.5 tonnes. The results are voluptuous and exotic Chardonnay, sappy and individualistic Pinot Noirs, arguably the most successful in Victoria outside the southern coastal regions. The Bordeaux red blend is often overlooked because the others are so impressive, but it can also be very good although the 1989, from a lighter year, was declassified into a second label called Enigma. Kinzbrunner has developed a cult following and his wines sell out quickly each year. He has almost completed a new winery and house, built sturdily of stone, on the hill overlooking his vines and a beautiful panorama of the western side of the Great Dividing Range.

Chardonnay 1990   ♀ ♀ ③
A rich, velvety, smooth wine laden with fig, peach and nutty/cedary aromas. Obvious Burgundy influence shows, with barrel-fermentation and interventionist winemaking characteristics. An outstanding Chardonnay with a lot of personality.

Cabernet Sauvignon Merlot 1990   ♀ ③
The least exciting of the three; but a good full-bodied yet supple blend (60% Cabernet Sauvignon, 30% Merlot, 10% Cabernet Franc) showing deep color with currants and violets in the bouquet.

Pinot Noir 1990   ♀ ♀ ③
Rick Kinzbrunner means to make a wine with some strength and succeeds: an expressive spice and ripe-cherry aroma coupled with deep, powerful flavor and firm tannin on the finish take you straight to the Côte de Nuits.

Jasper Hill

Drummonds Lane
Heathcote 3523
Tel. (054) 332528

Deep, rich, red volcanic Cambrian soil is the secret of Ron and Elva Laughton's Jasper Hill vineyards. The dry growing season would normally prohibit grape growing without irrigation if the vines chanced to be on the surrounding grey clay soil, but thanks to the rare properties of the red soil, un-watered vines thrive and produce small but superb crops of Shiraz grapes. Ron Laughton was a Melbourne food technologist before opting for the country life in 1979. He bought two vineyards, the smaller (planted to the unlikely combination of Shiraz and Cabernet Franc) he named Emily's Paddock after one daughter; the second, larger plot, planted to Shiraz and Rhine Riesling, he named Georgia's Paddock after his other daughter. The grapes are kept separate and the wines, beautifully and creatively labelled, are called simply Georgia's Paddock and Emily's Paddock. They are rich, concentrated, fleshy wines of superb fruit character and suppleness. The Rhine Riesling is bottled as a single varietal and can also be very good.

Rhine Riesling 1991   🍷 ②
The fastidious Ron Laughton makes classic, steely-dry Riesling which ages well. Big toast/citrus peel nose with some early development, with a fine, crisp, well-structured palate that demands food.

Georgia's Paddock Shiraz 1990   🍷 ③
A sumptuous wine with concentrated, chewy flavors of great length and allure. A meaty aspect to the pepper and spice nose does not mar: the wine has fascinating complexity of character, tannin and structure for long life.

Emily's Paddock   🍷🍷 ③
Shiraz/Cabernet Franc 1990
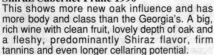
This shows more new oak influence and has more body and class than the Georgia's. A big, rich wine with clean fruit, lovely depth of oak and a fleshy, predominantly Shiraz flavor, firm tannins and even longer cellaring potential.

Lindemans

Nangiloc Road, Karadoc via
Mildura 3500
Tel. (050) 240303
Fax (050) 240324

The group's main winery is at Karadoc on the Murray River, where mainly quaffing wine is made, but also the popular Bin 65 Chardonnay. Premiums are made at the Hunter Valley and Coonawarra wineries. Mature Lindemans Hunter River Sémillon (also labelled Chablis or White Burgundy) is one of Australia's great wines. Shiraz, labelled Hunter River Burgundy or Steven Vineyard, is an excellent aging red. The Coonawarra red trio, Limestone Ridge (Shiraz-Cabernet Sauvignon), St. George (Cabernet Sauvignon) and Pyrus (Bordeaux blend), come from individual company vineyards. Huge 570 hectare Padthaway vineyard produces outstanding Chardonnay and respectable Sauvignon Blanc. Padthaway Verdelho, Riesling and Cabernet can impress. The Leo Buring brand offers a good quality/price rapport in Cabernet, Chardonnay, Sauvignon and Riesling. Its Reserve Bin Rieslings from the '70s were Australia's best at that time and have aged beautifully.

Bin 65 Chardonnay 1991   🍷 ①
For a 330,000 case brand selling for AUS$6 to $7, this is extraordinary quality. Full, soft and rich with floral, fruity perfumes and good complexity on the palate.

Padthaway Chardonnay 1991   🍷 ②
Lindemans' winemaker Greg Clayfield pushes fine French oak to the limit in this wine, coming up regularly with a complex style that smells of toasted nuts and nectarines and tastes rich, dry and long. One of Australia's leading Chardonnays.

Leo Buring Eden Valley   🍷🍷 ④
Rhine Riesling DWC 17 1973
Lindemans used to cellar these along the same lines as their Hunter Sémillons and results are equally spectacular. Full yellow color, toasted bread, nutty, honey and lime complexities delight the nose and tongue.

Hunter River   🍷🍷 ④
Chablis Bin 3875 1970
A traditional Hunter Valley style, dry and unwooded, which has matured into a wine of great personality and deep golden hue. Prolific award-winner.

St George Cabernet Sauvignon 1988 🍷 ③
From a ripe Coonawarra year comes this full-bodied, lean and tautly structured Cabernet with nutty oak and restrained berry flavors.

Mitchelton

Mitchellstown via
Nagambie 3608
Tel. (057) 942710
Fax (057) 942615

With its unusual "witch's hat" tower, housing a restaurant with views over the vineyards and the Goulburn River, Mitchelton is an impressive place to visit. The best wines are under the arty Classic Release labels, the least, under the Thomas Mitchell brand, are very good value for money. All wines are reliable, well-made and well-priced. Mitchelton was established by the legendary Seppelt winemaker Colin Preece in the early 1970s on fertile loamy flats beside the Goulburn River. A Cabernet and Chardonnay, stylish and modern in packaging and taste, have been named after him. Marsanne is a Goulburn Valley specialty and winemaker Don Lewis crafts a fine unwooded version for Thomas Mitchell and an oaky one for Mitchelton. Rhine Riesling is arguably Victoria's best - certainly its most consistent - and one of Australia's best. Reds have in recent years been rather one-dimensional, but lately have become more complex and satisfying.

Rhine Riesling 1991　　　　🍷 ①
This is well up to the maker's usual high standard. Intense, lively passionfruit and lime flavors finish dry despite a touch of sweetness. Fresh acidity will soften with a little age.

Classic Release Semillon 1985　　🍷 ③
Magnificent aged Sémillon, as good as a top Hunter Valley Semillon, smelling of vanilla, straw and toasted bread. Dry palate with great depth, length and finesse. Oak, usually obvious in this wine, is nicely underplayed here.

Print Series Shiraz 1990　　　🍇 ③
Winner of a celebrated show trophy for one-year-old reds, this wine represents a great leap forward for the maker. Intense red, robust, concentrated, full with plenty of oak, sweet fruit and underplayed pleasant tannins. Should age well.

Reserve Cabernet Sauvignon 1989　🍇 ②
One of the best reds ever made by Mitchelton, with deep color, oak and leafy-berry Cabernet fruit showing on the nose. On the palate there is masses of sweet, ripe currant flavor with supple tannins. More complexity than past Mitchelton reds.

Reserve Shiraz 1989　　　　🍇 ②
A well crafted, elegant red with a lifted, perfumed nose of ripe fruit laced with a sprinkle of spice. Young, fresh and lively on the palate, will probably drink at its best over the next two or three years.

Morris

Mia Mia Road
Rutherglen 3685
Tel. (060) 267303
Fax (060) 267445

Rutherglen is famous for its fortified wines Liqueur Muscat and Liqueur Tokay, made respectively from red Frontignac and Muscadelle. Morris's are outstanding, wonderfully unctuous and luscious, matured in large old oak barrels for long periods, blends that comprise various wines stretching back over several generations of the Morris family. The pinnacle of quality is the magnificent Old Premium range, at AUS$35 a bottle ridiculously cheap considering their age and quality. The winery has been run by a Morris since its beginning in 1859 and still today, despite being purchased by Orlando in the 1970s, Mick Morris is allowed free rein. The reds remain distinctively north-east Victorian in style; Cabernet Sauvignon and Shiraz are traditional, full-blooded with abundant ripe flavors and tannins, while wood-aged Sémillon and Chardonnay are good in an up-front, forward style, strong character and presence, and are among the region's best. An excellent botrytized Sémillon comes from the Orlando winery at Griffith. Specialty red varietals are the unusual Blue Imperial (Cinsaut) and Durif.

Old Premium Liqueur Tokay　🍷🍷 ④
Sister wine of the Muscat and just as good. Powerful, concentrated malt and toffee flavors of great depth. Lots of rancio from extended wood age and the lusciousness one expects of the leading exponents of this style, although tannin and acidity help to dry the finish.

Cabernet Sauvignon 1989　　🍇 ②
The lighter years often yield more elegant wines in Rutherglen, the home of thumping big reds. This is full-bodied nevertheless, smelling of spicy, chestnut and bayleaf regional character, with a chunky, fleshy full palate.

Sparkling Shiraz Durif 1980　🍇 ②
A traditional Australian red bubbly style known as Sparkling Burgundy. Dense color, concentrated plum and spice fruit flavor, sweetness and soft tannin combine with bubbles to give a wonderful drink. Superb now, but several years of age will only improve it.

Old Premium Liqueur Muscat　🍇 ④
Very dark amber color reflecting great age. Very concentrated raisiny Muscat flavors with rancio and dense, chewy, weighty, luscious palate flavors of great age and complexity. One of the oldest and greatest Australian dessert Muscats.

Mount Langi Ghiran

Vine Road
Buangor 3375
Tel. (053) 543207
Fax (053) 543277

Geisenheim-trained Trevor Mast made wine at Best's for 12 years before moving full-time to Langi Ghiran (Aboriginal for 'home of the black cockatoo') in 1987 in partnership with Melbourne businessman Ian Menzies. The vineyard is on the southerly slope of a forested granite hill about 30 kms from Great Western. The region is noted for Shiraz but the 'Langi Shiraz' from this vineyard is more full-bodied and more intensely spicy than anything from Great Western proper. It is an arresting style, strongly built and promising to age long-term with aromas of black pepper dominating the young wine, but there is no lack of fruit or structure. The '88 and '89 could rival the highest fliers from the Rhone Valley. Cabernet Sauvignon is also good in a similarly full-bodied style. Other products include a Rhine Riesling, to date not very successful, Chardonnay and Pinot, big and well-colored but lacking varietal charm.

Circa 1990   ♥ ②
A new label for a Shiraz, Cabernet, Pinot Noir blend, intended as a softer red for earlier drinking, but there is nothing light about it. Coffee, oak, sweet ripe berries and spices, with Shiraz uppermost. Elegant wine on the palate with the trademark tannic finish.

Langi Shiraz 1990   ♥ ♥ ②
Possibly the best yet under this label, deep purplish color and full-bodied, powerful palate. Perhaps has less crushed black pepper aroma, but more currants, cherries, mint and spices. Chunky texture. Should be very long-lived, at least 15 years.

Cabernet Sauvignon 1989   ♥ ②
The fame of the vineyard is with Shiraz, but Cabernet is right up there. Cedary perfumed oak and curranty fruit with a streak of the pepper found in the Shiraz. Again a structured wine for long keeping.

Mount Mary

Coldstream West Road
Lilydale 3140
Tel. (03) 7391761
Fax (03) 7390137

To label Dr. John Middleton as unconventional would be an understatement. As a winemaker he is positively eccentric, reclusive, with no time for competitions of any kind, exhibitions, promotions or public relations; yet his wines are among the most highly-prized by enthusiasts and highly collectable. Mount Mary 'Cabernets' (a blend of Cabernet Sauvignon and Franc, Merlot, Malbec and Petit Verdot) is a masterpiece of elegance. Pinot Noir is similarly polished with all the charm and finesse one hopes for in this varietal. Both are long-lived. The Chardonnay however, which enjoys similar cachet, mystifies many experienced tasters, seeming to lack fruit, but reportedly ages well. Middleton aims for international styles and his whites (the other is a white Bordeaux blend of Semillon, Sauvignon Blanc and Muscadelle) could never be described as typically Australian.

Chardonnay 1991   ♥ ③
Tightly structured Chardonnay with delicacy and refinement on the palate. Quite un-Australian Chardonnay aroma, reflecting high solids content in the juice and extended contact with lees. Lean, lemony, honeyed palate without obvious fruit or oak. Built for long aging.

Sauvignon 1990   ♥ ♥ ③
A Sémillon, Sauvignon Blanc and Muscadelle blend resembling white Bordeaux. Totally lacks herbaceousness, and while the bouquet is subdued there is a tonne of body and concentrated flavors linger long and dry. Very individual style.

Quintet 1990   ♥ ♥ ③
The name reflects the five Bordeaux grapes employed. Outstanding wine from a top year, fresh purple hues, perfumed curranty nose of great charm. Superb wine with tremendous depth of fruit, stellar harmony and gentle tannin.

Cabernets 1989   ♥ ♥ ③
A triumph from a lesser year in the Yarra Valley. Perfumed, cool-climate Cabernet flavors with mint, cassis and crushed leaves. Not a big wine, yet elegant and intense with unobtrusive tannin and lots of charm.

Pinot Noir 1989   ♥ ♥ ③
A great Yarra Valley Pinot. Medium-light purple-red with lovely complex perfume of strawberry, cherry and slightly gamey aromas. Quite full-bodied, rich and deep with tight, lively structure. Mouth-coating tannins and complex flavors linger long on the finish.

St Huberts

Maroondah Highway
Coldstream 3770
Tel. (03) 7391421
Fax (03) 7391015

Big changes here, with winemaker Brian Fletcher leaving for Evans & Tate following the absorption of St Huberts and Baileys into the new public company, Rothbury Wines Ltd, in 1992. Planted in 1966 near the location of Hubert DeCastella's 19th century vineyard of the same name, which had an overseas reputation in its day, the present vineyard does not seem a prime location, being low-lying and damp, but with increased vineyard effort and inspired winemaking, the results are impressive. Yields are not low (15 tonnes per hectare for Cabernet Sauvignon and 13.3 for Chardonnay), but the quality is there. Chardonnay is fruit-driven, peachy and supple (1991, '90 and '88 stand out), while Pinot Noir is of a lightish weight, but with good intensity of fruit and excellent character. Cabernet-Merlot is elegant, smooth, berry-flavored, typical of straight Cabernet Sauvignon. Rhine Riesling often has botrytis, hence the dessert styles are better than dry table wines. Roan, the group's second label, is not all from Yarra Valley.

Chardonnay 1991   🍇🍇 ③
Subtly oaked despite four months in new French barriques, this is St Huberts' best Chardonnay to date. Loaded with melon and peach flavors with tropical hints, the palate is very fine and fruit-dominant. A simply delicious wine.

Cabernet Merlot 1990   🍇🍇 ②
The epitome of Yarra Valley elegance, bursting with leafy and blackcurrant Cabernet flavors: fresh, lively and clean. Soft, well-modulated tannins make it easy to drink now, but long cellaring is also indicated.

Cabernet Sauvignon 1990   🍇🍇 ③
From a top vintage, achieves concentration matched in its region only by Yarra Yering. Intense purple color, great power of berry, spicy fruit and smooth, supple tannins, creating an almost luscious effect. Needs five years and will profit from 20.

Pinot Noir 1990   🍇 ②
A Pinot with typical Yarra valley finesse. Good depth of color, ripe cherry and nutty aromas together with cedary new oak giving a stylish perfume. Sweet strawberry flavors with light tannin and superb balance. Probably best drunk young.

Taltarni

Taltarni Road
Moonambel 3478
Tel. (054) 672218
Fax (054) 672306

This sister winery to Napa Valley's Clos du Val is managed by Bordelais Frenchman Dominique Portet. Initial impact was with blockbuster reds from Shiraz and Cabernet Sauvignon, but impressive whites are now being made (a wooded Fumé Blanc and unwooded Sauvignon Blanc, both dry and from the same varietal), as well as a clutch of continually improving sparkling wines. These include a faintly pink Brut Taché, a Brut Royale, standard non-vintage Cuvée Brut, and creamy Blanc de Blancs. Planted on loam of volcanic origin, the Taltarni vineyards are the sole grape source. Winemakers are Portet and long-serving assistant, Greg Gallagher. Red wines are undoubtedly the winery's forte, bigger and more tannic than most Australian reds although they have softened in recent vintages. 1988 is a peak year for all reds. French Syrah is deep and peppery/spicy, Cabernet Sauvignon has powerful blackberry and smoky flavors, firm structure and grip. Both have outstanding aging potential.

Fumé Blanc 1991   🍇 ③
A leading Fumé Blanc, made 100% from Sauvignon grapes with subtle oak treatment, resulting in a gooseberry flavored and only faintly herbaceous style of rewarding palate depth, exemplary structure and great charm.

Blanc de Blancs Non-vintage Cuvée   🍇 ③
A fine, creamy Chardonnay cuvée whose subtle flavors, persistent frothy mousse and dry aftertaste put it among the more serious Australian style sparkling wines.

Cabernet Sauvignon 1988   🍇🍇 ②
Perhaps the best Cabernet yet from Taltarni, the '88 is a 20-year wine, built with structure and power. Profound blackcurrant flavor with obvious oak and mouth-puckering tannin. Avoids both herbaceousness and regional eucalyptus notes.

French Syrah 1988   🍇🍇 ②
Super Shiraz with deep, rich, spicy and cherry-plum flavors that intertwine with a twist of licorice. Tannins are rich and smooth. A serious, concentrated mouthful which should develop beautifully in the cellar.

Cabernet Sauvignon 1984   🍇 ③
Reissued from the cellar reserve stocks, superbly mellow, supple, cedary, elegant. Is starting to reach its prime.

Yarra Ridge

Glenview Road
Yarra Glen 3755
Tel. (03) 7301022
Fax (03) 7301131

Former solicitor Louis Bialkower was a late starter, planting in 1983, but made up for lost time. He is now the Yarra's second-largest producer, and all his wines (except Griffith botrytis Sémillon) are from local grapes. Bialkower has drive and enthusiasm, rapidly achieving market penetration by increasing output with grapes from two other Yarra vineyards. Yields have always been high, but Bialkower's open mind led him to try several modern trellising systems to improve quality without sacrificing yields. For example, the Geneva Double Curtain method works well on Pinot Noir, which is then thinned-out from 20 tonnes per hectare to 10. Trials with six Pinot clones gave results of interest to many other growers. Chardonnay is on U-trellis to achieve better grape exposure. Others in the valley who put their Chardonnay in expensive, top-quality French oak are irritated that Bialkower uses cheap American at a fraction of the price, but the wine sells well and reaps show awards.

Chardonnay 1991   ℬ ②
A delicate, light-bodied Chardonnay in which fruit and oak stand without malolactic fermentation characteristics. Pineapple and coconut adorn the nose, on the palate there is good depth of fine, peachy fruit and a long, balanced finish.

Sauvignon Blanc 1991   ℬ ②
A strong 'peapod' green-picked herbaceous flavor and vivacious tartness have given this distinctive wine good backbone and bracing freshness.

Cabernet Sauvignon 1990   ♥ ②
Made to be approachable early, this has attractive cherry and currant aromas coupled with distinct American oak. On the palate quite full-bodied and rich, with good length and some keeping potential.

Pinot Noir 1990   ♥ ②
Lightish color and a fine fragrance of strawberry lead into a delicately structured, subtle Pinot of lighter body but good intensity.

Yarra Yering

Briarty Road
Coldstream 3770
Tel. 059/649267

Dr. Bailey Carrodus is a shy, reclusive man who uses some bizarre methods to make sublime red wines. A model vineyard, planted in 1969 on grey silty loam with bands of gravel, produces very modest yields of top-class grapes, and their concentration shows in the wines. Labelled simply Dry Red No. 1 (a Bordeaux blend, with Petit Verdot) and Dry Red No. 2 (Rhône blend, including Viognier), they are densely colored, packed, tannic and intense, aging slowly and capable of long cellaring. The No. 1, the best of the two, achieves a depth and dimension seen nowhere else in the Yarra Valley; it is fermented in a flock of small epoxy-lined boxes allowing easy one-man handling. Pinot Noir is frighteningly priced but often very good. Underhill Shiraz, from a neighboring 4 hectare vineyard bought in 1988, is spicy but lighter, whereas Chardonnay and Dry White No. 1 are much less interesting than the reds. In 1989, a cold, wet year when others made ordinary wines, Carrodus's reds were excellent, albeit at the softer end of the Yarra Yering spectrum.

Chardonnay 1990   ℬ ③
A light-bodied, lean, austere style without much fruit but compact nutty flavors with touches of peach and vanilla. Complex and lingering.

Pinot Noir 1990   ♥♥ ④
Quite full-bodied for this varietal, with soft plum aromas and without strong oak influences. Soft, rich flavors with good tannins and length. Subtly powerful rather than ostentatious. Expensive at AUS$50.

Dry Red Wine No. 1 1989   ♥♥ ③
There is no hint of a cold, rainy year in this wine. Dense color, big, strong rich Cabernet nose with gorgeous depth of sweet currant and ripe berry flavors on palate. Lush, intense, concentrated and soft.

Dry Red Wine No. 2 1989   ♥ ③
A success from a poor vintage, this Shiraz-based red has a relatively light color with an intriguing combination of black pepper, nettle/vegetal and sweet cherry aromas. Light-bodied but intense, it is fresh, clean and elegantly structured. Probably not for long keeping.

Western Australia

Australia's most remote production zones are in the west, approximately 4,000 kms. from Sydney. Although far from all major markets the premium quality of the state's wines has helped overcome this barrier. Since the early 1970s the "new" Margaret River and Mount Baker wine regions have produced the state's - and in some cases Australia's - most interesting single-varietal wines. With only 2,000 hectares of vines and 11,000 tonnes of grapes in 1990-91, Western Australia produces less than 1% of the national total, yet its wines are much more significant than these figures suggest. The Swan Valley and the area surrounding Perth have been producing wine for over 160 years, but the boom of the '60s led new entrepreneurs to venture into the south's cooler climates to grow vines which give dry whites and quality reds. Margaret River was the first Australian wine region to be scientifically selected for wine production, in the mid 1960s, and immediately attained fame, initially with Cabernet Sauvignon and later with Chardonnay. The isolated Lower Great Southern, 350 kms. south of Perth, has not attracted the same attention, but its wines are still interesting.

Alkoomi

Wingenballup Road
Frankland 6396
Tel. (098) 552229
Fax (098) 552284

Sheep farmers Merv and Judy Lange found the lure of the grape stronger than that of wool, and sold their flock to devote their energies to Alkoomi, which is aboriginal for "a place we chose". The Langes chose Riesling, Cabernet Sauvignon and Shiraz, and shrewdly too since their first efforts in the early 1970s produced astonishingly good wines that have also matured well. Alkoomi now has a resident woman winemaker, the Roseworthy College-trained Kim Hart. Frankland is a cool region by Australian standards, and the soils are gravelly and low in fertility. Typically in Australia, although the grapes ripen in late autumn, there is not usually a rain problem, allowing a trouble-free harvest of ripe grapes. Riesling ripens with high acidity and low pH, giving a classic Australian dry, steely structured, floral scented style of abundant flavor. Excellent Chardonnay and Sauvignon Blanc are also produced, but the reds, of which Merv Lange is an avowed fan, are the winery's forte: deeply colored, full-bodied, with plenty of grip and masses of fruit without precluding elegance, wines that deserve a wider audience.

Chardonnay 1991   ☖☖ ②
An unusual aromatic Chardonnay, with an exciting and slightly perplexing combination of tropical pineapple, lime, honey and gooseberry flavors. Intense fruity palate with great youthful charm. Interesting to follow its development.

Classic White 1991   ☖ ②
Cleverly blended Sémillon (70%), Chardonnay and Sauvignon Blanc with interesting honey and citrus tones, plenty of flavor, not quite bone-dry, and finishing clean. Inexpensive sipping wine and good value. for money.

Rhine Riesling 1991   ☖☖ ②
Another superb '91 white from Alkoomi. Traces of yeast esters linger on the aroma with passionfruit tropical flavors threaded with crisp acidity promising long life. Age will confer toast and lime-citrus flavors over the next decade.

Sauvignon Blanc 1991   ☖ ②
The '91 harvest brought greater volume of flavor than normal; while the aroma is fresh and herbaceous with gooseberry overtones, the palate has excellent depth of sweet fruit, finishing dry with some richness without losing delicacy.

Classic Red 1988   ☗ ②
Mainly Shiraz with Merlot, Cabernet Sauvignon and Malbec. Intense and dominated by spicy Shiraz flavor with clean berry fruit and a trace of black pepper. Big finish, with firm dry tannins and long flavor. Surpasses the (more expensive) Cabernet of the same vintage.

Cape Mentelle

Wallcliffe Road
Margaret River 6285
Tel. (097) 573266
Fax (097) 573233

David Hohnen, trained at Fresno University in California, planted his first vines in 1976 and quickly placed Cape Mentelle in the premium league. Rapid growth through the '80s, including the establishment of Cloudy Bay in New Zealand, necessitated a partner and Champagne Veuve Clicquot is now the majority shareholder. Hohnen built the great name of Cape Mentelle on reds: a rich, punchy Cabernet Sauvignon, and intensely spicy Shiraz (which has a little Grenache blended in) and Australia's best Zinfandel, big and strong. While the reds have always been excellent, an increasing share of the spotlight is now on whites. A rich and unctuous, buttery/peachy Chardonnay and a delightfully crisp, tropical fruit style Sémillon-Sauvignon Blanc have won the hearts and palates of Australians in recent years. The ripe, opulent Chardonnay and solid cassis/leafy Cabernet are typical examples of Margaret River's classic varietals.

Semillon Sauvignon Blanc 1991   ☖☖ ②
The best vintage so far on a steeply improving upward curve. Captivating gooseberry, pineapple and citrus aromas and a lush, juicy taste. Best while young and fresh.

Chardonnay 1990   ☖☖ ③
A full-bodied, rich style employing barrel fermentation, malolactic and lees stirring. Silky, voluptuous and endowed with great complexity of peachy, buttery, honied flavors. The archetypal "red drinker's white".

Cabernet Sauvignon 1990   ☗☗ ③
A serious, full-bodied style crafted for long cellaring. Color is dark purple-red, aroma is deep in currants and other dark berries, mint and crushed leaves, with low-key oak. Flavor is full and intense, layered and velvety. Needs four years but could partner beef now.

Shiraz 1990   ☗☗ ②
Blended with Grenache and matured only in large vats, this wine is purple and bitingly peppery in youth with massive raw spicy fruit, great structure and fullness, ending in a blast of tannin which demands four or five years in the cellar.

Zinfandel 1989   ☗ ②
The best example of this varietal in Australia, but there's little competition. Made in a boots-and-all style, with very high alcohol (14.5%), extractive tannins and quite an aggressive nature. A hefty wine which needs strong cheddar or grana.

Capel Vale

Lot 5, Capel North West Road
Sterling Estate, Capel 6271
Tel. (097) 272439
Fax (097) 912452

One of a group of small Western Australian wineries opened by doctors, Capel Vale was started by radiologist Dr. Peter Pratten in a little-known region just north of Margaret River but on sandier soils. Planting commenced in 1979 and Pratten has managed to turn out impressive white wines for most of the intervening years, with a popular Sémillon-Sauvignon Blanc blend, Chardonnay and Rhine Riesling at the top. The reds have been overshadowed somewhat, although do occasionally hit the heights. There is a spicy Shiraz, a Cabernet Sauvignon and a Cabernet-based blend named Baudin after an early French explorer of the West Australian coast. Grapes are brought in from Margaret River and the Lower Great Southern to supplement the Capel fruit, and most of the wines are blended from more than one region, but always based on Capel. hence the Riesling benefits from the finesse of Mount Barker fruit and the Shiraz is spiced up by cooler-grown grapes. Pratten has had some changes of winemaker but now Rob Bowen, one of the state's top enologists, is at the helm and this move can bring nothing but good to Capel Vale.

Chardonnay 1991 ⅋ ③
10% Mount Barker, 70% barrel fermented, with 30% having undergone malolactic fermentation. A top Capel Chardonnay: toasty, nutty spiced aromas in tandem with tropical fruit. Excellent depth and complexity of palate, very lingering.

Rhine Riesling 1991 ⅋ ②
One-third Mount Barker fruit, light yellow with delicate floral Riesling nose of straw and estery overtones. Intense and delicate, an excellent Riesling.

Baudin 1989 ❦ ③
Has 50:50 Merlot and Cabernet Sauvignon from Capel, Margaret River and Mount Barker. A more serious, solid style with firmer structure and longer cellar potential. Reserved aromas of violets, deep and concentrated, a little tough now but two or three years should allow it to open up.

Cabernet Sauvignon 1989 ❦ ②
Grown at Capel, Mount Barker and Margaret River. Quite up-front style with leafy, tobacco and smoky plum overtones. The chunky sweet, silky smooth palate has subtle oak and good depth. Drink now till at least 1999.

Shiraz 1989 ❦ ②
Rich purple colored wine with aromas of coconut, chocolate, vanilla and plum. Full, ripe, supple and rich with grainy tannins. Drink now and for six to seven years.

Chateau Xanadu

Railway Terrace, off Wallcliffe Road
Margaret River 6285
Tel. (097) 572581
Fax (097) 573389

Xanadu was set up by local doctors John Lagan and Eithne Sheridan, currently assisted by their son Conor, the manager, and Juerg Muggli, chief winemaker. The whites, particularly Chardonnay, are the strength at Xanadu, with their extraordinary intensity of tropical aroma and flavor: pineapple, mango and passionfruit spring to mind. Some accuse them of being excessively aromatic and not resembling Chardonnay, but there is no doubt they have powerful personality and plenty of flavor. In a region noted for herbaceous whites, Xanadu's Sémillon and Sauvignon Blanc are both strongly aromatic, grassy yet with floral and stone-fruit overtones, crisp and lively with good balance. The reds are perhaps not as good as the whites, although the sumptuous '89 reserve Cabernet Sauvignon is outstanding. John Lagan is proudly Irish with a sense of fun, and celebrates the start of each harvest with a party laden with Celtic ritual. The label carries a line from Coleridge's famous poem about Xanadu, Kubla Khan: "For he on honey-dew hath fed, and drunk the milk of paradise", and the sense of poetry and wine flow happily together.

Sauvignon Blanc 1991 ⅋ ②
A rather extravagant wine, pungently fruity and quite grassy with a soft, sweetly aromatic palate. Begs to be drunk young.

Chardonnay 1990 ⅋ ③
A distinctive Chardonnay style, quite extraordinary to the uninitiated. Fruit-driven and subtly oaked, highly aromatic, slightly herbaceous, but with pungent tropical fruit aromas and a very fruity palate. Striking when young - its future is uncertain.

Semillon 1990 ⅋ ②
A very grassy herbaceous style, more reminiscent of Sauvignon Blanc than Sémillon, with crisp, lively, unoaked flavor of commendable depth and interest.

Cabernet Sauvignon 1989 ❦ ②
A Perth Show trophy-winner, had less time in oak than the Reserve. A less-complex wine with minty aromas, soft sweet fruit and easy drinkability.

Reserve Cabernet Sauvignon 1989 ❦ ③
Had extended time (18 months) in all-new oak. Toasty oak, rich, multi-layered flavor, tannic but supple. Sumptuous wine with complexity and length.

Cullen

Caves Road, Willyabrup via
Cowaramup 6284
Tel. (097) 555277
Fax (097) 555550

The formidable Cullen women run one of
Margaret River's best and most original
wineries, which has come a long way since
its beginnings in 1971. Diana established the
vineyards with her husband Kevin, a local
doctor, and made the wines until recently
when daughter Vanya stepped in. Another
daughter, Shelley, is involved in sales and
marketing. The whites have always been
good, while the reds have improved markedly
in recent years, particularly the Cabernet-
Merlot and reserve Cabernet Sauvignon ('88
is exceptional) which have become much
more complex. The soils at Cullen's are
different to most of the district, being poor,
shallow ironstone-based, and the reds used
to be tougher than those of their neighbors.
No such complaint with the smooth late '80s
Cabernets. Chardonnay is archetypal
Margaret River: full-bodied, rich, complex and
profound with flavors that linger on and on.
The Cullens never liked the herbaceous local
style of Sauvignon Blanc and strove to avoid
those characteristics in their wines, first with
obvious oak and now with more subtle wood,
as well as barrel and malolactic fermentation
and lees contact developing an interesting
and individual style. Their Botrytis Sauvignon
Blanc can also be good.

Chardonnay 1990   🍇🍇 ③
Cullens go for broke with this wine, giving it the
full Burgundian treatment, including barrel and
malolactic fermentation together with lees-aging,
resulting in a creamy-rich, complex and full-
bodied Chardonnay with smoky grilled nuts,
vanilla and buttery flavors.

Sauvignon Blanc 1990   🍇 ③
The Cullens dislike the herbaceousness that
usually manifests in this varietal, going to some
lengths (including 10 months in wood) to avoid
it. Perfumes of lime, peppermint and flowers
dominate this substantial dry wine of length and
strength.

Cabernet Merlot 1989   🍷 ③
Toasty oak and smoky, curranty Cabernet
flavors of velvety softness and structure. Easy to
like young, but with a good 10 years'
improvement in it.

Reserve Cabernet Sauvignon   🍷🍷 ③
Merlot 1988
Vanya Cullen gave this rare selected Cabernet
an extra year in oak, producing a concentrated
wine of profound and complex flavor. Toasted
oak, tobacco leaf, smoky and curranty. Massive
structure, wonderfully rich and should repay
long cellaring.

Evans & Tate

Metricup Road
Willyabrup 6284
Tel. (097) 556244
Fax (09) 2961148

Evans & Tate started in a small way in the
Swan Valley in 1971 and although the major
source for grapes has long since moved
down south to Margaret River, all the grapes
are still processed at the Swan Valley winery.
There are visitors' tasting and sales facilities
in both places. The first wine to bring the
company fame was Gnangara Shiraz, a soft
early-drinking and inexpensive red made
from Swan Valley grapes. Today the flagship
wines are an extremely complex, rich
Margaret River Chardonnay and ripe, chunky
Margaret River Merlot.. Next on the ladder
are a very good two-vineyards Chardonnay
and Cabernet Sauvignon from Margaret
River, a region which also produces a fine
unwooded Sémillon and a blended white
Margaret River Classic. Owners John and
Toni Tate bought out their partners, the
Evans family, in 1983 and their son Franklin
joined later as marketing manager. The Tates
are a serious, hard-working family and their
brand is one of the quiet achievers of
Western Australia. They won a government
award for small business in 1988 and have
scored numerous medals at wine shows.
Since the beginning all wines have been
made by Bill Crappsley who was recently
replaced by Brian Fletcher.

Margaret River Semillon 1991   🍇🍇 ③
30% barrel fermented, outstanding regional
style which has better depth and strength of
flavor than usual. Clean, fresh cashew nut,
herbaceous and melon/lemon aromas with
excellent palate fullness and length. Best
enjoyed young.

Margaret River Chardonnay 1990 🍇🍇 ③
This winery's top-line Chardonnay, malolactic
butterscotch aromas feature strongly in a softly
structured, sweetly-flavored, big mouthful of
wine.

Two Vineyards Chardonnay 1990   🍇 ③
Fruit flavors of pineapple and cashew nut
dominate this attractive wine. It has good length
and a degree of richness.

Margaret River   🍷 ③
Cabernet Sauvignon 1988
A serious red with some early-drinking appeal, a
rich blend of toasty, oaky and cassis-like flavors
underlined by supple tannin. Typical of the
region, with drinkability as well as cellar
potential.

Goundrey

Muir Highway
Mount Barker 6324
Tel. (098) 511777
Fax (098) 511997

Goundrey Wines was begun by Mike and Alison Goundrey in 1970, and is now a large and rapidly growing unlisted public company which has swallowed several small local vineyards. In the late '80s a new winery was built on Langton, the name now used on a second, less expensive label while the Goundrey Windy Hill label is reserved for the top wines. The cool, southerly West Australian climate of Mount Barker gives some of the finest Rhine Riesling in Australia, as well as tightly-structured Chardonnay, tangy Sauvignon Blanc and intensely flavored reds from Cabernet Sauvignon and Shiraz. Despite a succession of winemakers since Claudio Radenti, winemaker of the past two years, left, Goundrey has managed a line of excellent varietal table wines. Economic and seasonal factors have slowed the expected rapid rate of Goundrey's growth, but a marketing agreement with Japanese distributor Hokuriku should ensure a foot in the Japan market.

Windy Hill Chardonnay 1991 � ②
Dry, slightly austere Chardonnay which needs bottle-age and promises to develop slowly. Attractive fruit of good depth with lemony oak and a slight volatile lift. Fine, crisp and intense.

Windy Hill Rhine Riesling 1991 ☐ ②
Clean peach and stone fruit aromas, excellent depth of fruit on the palate, nicely balanced with a touch of sweetness and a hint of Botrytis characterize this wine of beautiful drinkability.

Windy Hill Sauvignon Blanc 1991 ☐ ③
Tightly focused style with controlled grassiness and good strength, assisted by a steely spine of acidity. Excellent with fish.

Windy Hill ☐ ③
Cabernet Sauvignon 1988
This label consistently offers big, rich wines packed with flavor and tannin, with strong charred oak overtones. The '88 has an unusual stalky aspect, but also good color, rich sweet-fruit flavors of some complexity and good texture on the palate.

Houghton

Dale Road
Middle Swan 6055
Tel. (09) 2745100
Fax (09) 2745372

Houghton, of the BRL Hardy group, is by far the largest producer in Western Australia, with a proud history stretching back to 1836. The winery is located in the Swan Valley near Perth, a popular destination for tourists who catch a paddle boat up the Swan River. Winemakers Peter Dawson and Paul Lapsley take grapes from company vineyards and growers in the Swan Valley, as well as the eastern states for the Wildflower Ridge series. Houghton White Burgundy, first made in 1937 by Jack Mann who served for 42 vintages, is one of Australia's biggest selling brands. It is based on Chenin Blanc and Tokay (Muscadelle) with minor additions of Chardonnay, Sémillon and Verdelho. Its quality is backed by Show Reserve stocks of the same wines, which are aged for seven or eight years and re-issued with labels glittering with medals. The Houghton label is however the most profitable arm for the Hardy wine group, thanks to an excellent Cabernet Sauvignon rosé, a delicate Verdelho from Gingin and Frankland, a Rhine Riesling from the zone of Frankland and a lively Sémillon from Margaret River. Under the Moondah Brook label Houghton produces good Verdelho and Chenin Blanc.

Semillon 1991 ☐ ②
Crisp, simple citric herbaceous style typical of Margaret River although it is actually a blend of grapes from this area and from the region of Frankland to the south.

White Burgundy 1991 ☐ ①
One of Australia's biggest selling table wines. Fresh flavor resembling melons and a subtle touch of oak. Very pleasant drinking, balanced and straightforward with a dry finish.

Moondah Brook Verdelho 1990 ☐ ②
Full-flavored specialty grape of Western Australia. The 1990 was typical of the varietal, with perfumed and slightly spicy nose and delicious musky fruit on a soft palate. Best drunk young.

Show Reserve ☐ ③
White Burgundy 1984
The most awarded white wine in Australian shows in 1990. Fully mature, golden hued, richly complex and yet fresh with a honeyed, toasty bouquet and flavor.

Rosé 1991 ☐ ①
Made from early-picked Cabernet Sauvignon, grown in warm-climate vineyards, vivid purple-red hue when young, a crisp, fresh leafy Cabernet aroma, and clean, almost dry finish.

Howard Park

Lot 11, Little River Road
Denmark 6333
Tel. (098) 481261
Fax (098) 482064

John Wade first made his mark at Wynns
Coonawarra Estate and moved to the West in
1985. Astutely perceiving the potential of the
Mount Barker region when most of western
Australia's attention was focused on
Margaret River, Wade went down south to
make wine. First he worked for Alkoomi, then
Goundrey; now he is firmly entrenched at
Plantagenet where he makes their wines as
well as those of many small vineyards.
Selected grapes from some of those
vineyards are blended to produce John and
Wendy Wade's own Howard Park wines,
which were first produced in 1986. There are
only two, a Rhine Riesling which Wade
attempts - and usually succeeds - in making
as a classically dry, fine, austere style for
lengthy aging, and a very serious Bordeaux-
like Cabernet Sauvignon made using
prolonged skin contact. Both are made with
great care, and will be long-lived wines.

Rhine Riesling 1991   🍇 ③
Superbly intense lemon and lime aromas of
great purity, happily lacking the Botrytis that
tinged recent vintages. The flavor is wonderfully
lime-juicy, fine and long. Virtually dry with
pleasant acidity on the finish. Great now, should
mellow into a classic over a decade or so.

Cabernet Sauvignon 1989   🍇 ③
Howard Park's Cabernets are built for cellaring,
and the '89 is the best yet. Vanilla and coffee
over blackcurrant, earth and small-berry fruit
scents, concentrated and very undeveloped
flavor, big tannic grip and classic Bordeaux
structure.

Price levels

①   up to $ 9.99

② $ 10.00 - $ 14.99

③ $ 15.00 - $ 24.99

④ $ 25.00 or more

*The 'ex-cellar', or direct from the
producer, bottle prices, are calculated in
US dollars and are intended only as an
approximate guide*

Leeuwin Estate

Gnarawary Road
Margaret River 6285
Tel. (097) 576253
Fax (097) 576364

Begun in 1974 with no expense spared, early advice from Robert Mondavi, and a breathtaking pricing policy, Leeuwin Estate has silenced its critics by almost invariably coming up with the goods. Proprietor Denis Horgan became involved full-time with the winery as managing director, with winemaker Bob Cartwright and vineyard manager John Brocksopp as key players. While the recession has caused many price cuts, Leeuwin Art Series Chardonnay remains out front at AUS$ 39 and no vintage justified the price better than the current '86. Its release at six years old is normal and serves to remind that it is one of Australia's most ageworthy Chardonnays. Cabernet Sauvignons are occasionally superb ('79 Reserve, '82, '87) but often are more herbaceous than those of their neighbors. Sauvignon Blanc is soft, complex yet grassy, Rhine Riesling is Margaret River's most successful and Pinot Noir is an enigma, showing early promise but not always living up to it in bottle. Leeuwin's second label, Prelude, is for younger wines at lower prices. The Chardonnay and Pinot Noir are very good.

Art Series Sauvignon Blanc 1991   🍇 ③
Pale-colored and intensely herbaceous aroma, rather expensive Sauvignon with fresh, delicate, simple young varietal flavor on the palate, as well as good structure. Devotees of the full-on pungent style will love it.

Prelude Chardonnay 1991   🍇🍇 ②
A sneak preview of the wine which will later be released as Art Series at a higher price, hence the name. Superb wine with the maker's typical fine, nutty melon and tropical fruit flavors and well harmonized oak.

Art Series Rhine Riesling 1990   🍇 ②
A remarkably rich, full-flavored Riesling which does not sacrifice finesse. Very good white with the ripeness of pure Riesling, floral aromas and rich soft flavor.

Art Series Cabernet Sauvignon 1986 🍇 ③
An enormous red wine with seemingly contradictory attributes of a dusty peppery herbaceous aroma and fleshy, concentrated, massive palate flavor with gripping tannins. Tobacco, berries and earth aromas are buried in this dense wine. Needs long cellaring.

Art Series Margaret River Chardonnay 1986   🍇🍇🍇 ④
The best-selling release under this label in recent years despite its high price. Arguably Australia's greatest Chardonnay, produced with fastidious care by Bob Cartwright and John Brocksopp from Leeuwin's own vineyards on gravelly soils at the southern end of Margaret River. Deliberate lack of irrigation strictly limits the yields to around 3.5 tons per hectare, resulting in concentrated wine of great flavor. The Chardonnay undergoes the full Burgundy treatment: barrel fermentation, lees contact, 50% malolactic fermentation and the best oak money can buy. Strict barrel selection ensures that only the best wines go into the blend. The wine is five years old before release, but because of its unusually tight structure it does not fatten with age. Well outside the Australian mainstream, it is fine and firm but exceptionally complex, with tropical fruit, toasted nut, honey and butter nuances plus a hallmark twist of gooseberry.

Moss Wood

Metricup Road, Willyabrup via
Cowaramup 6284
Tel. (097) 556266
Fax (097) 556303

Together with Cullens and Vasse Felix, the
Moss Wood winery, which was established in
1969 by Dr. Bill Pannell, was a pioneer of
Margaret River. Wine was superb from the
outset and soon assumed cult status. Pannell
sold out to his winemaker Keith Mugford, who
has guided Moss Wood since 1978. Best-
known is the Cabernet Sauvignon,
distinctively different from its neighbors, silky
smooth, voluptuously rich and high in extract,
yet carries the regional trademark of
blackcurrants with a leafy overlay, together
with skilfully handled oak. The vines, which
produce all the grapes processed by the
winery, are on deep gravelly loam soils with
a clay base, giving good moisture retention
during the typically dry growing season. Pinot
Noir is a special interest of both Pannell and
Mugford, but it is the most variable and least
successful of the wines, although
occasionally it is very good (1981
exceptional). The Cabernet is the leader: in
top years (for example the 1980) a superb
reserve wine is made by barrel aging for an
extra year. Sémillon, both wooded and
unwooded, is the region's best, while
Chardonnay is complex, Burgundian and
rare.

Chardonnay 1991   ❦ ③
The '91 benefits from breathing. It opens with an
unusual character, developing strong smoky
buttery aromas. Has attractive softness, rich,
sweet fruit, subtle oak and interesting
complexities from sophisticated winemaking.

Semillon 1991   ❦❦ ③
Fresh and delicate as a young wine, but will put
on weight with several years' aging. A fine, well-
made wine without oak and showing low-
intensity but attractive straw toast aromas and
flavors. The palate is dry and balanced, delicate
enough to drink with oysters.

Cabernet Sauvignon 1989   ❦ ③
Quite typical of the house style, smells of rich
currant and berry fruit with earthy, herbaceous
and violet traces. The palate is soft, sweet and
rich with high extract and a velvety feel.
Sumptuous Cabernet.

Pinot Noir 1989   ❦ ③
Winemaker Keith Mugford tries hard with this
varietal but has so far failed to match the
brilliance of the great 1981. This '89 has an
attractive, developed, earthy, mossy, sous-le-
bois nose and a sappy, lean palate that shows
high alcohol and some stalk influence.

Pierro

Caves Road, Willyabrup via
Cowaramup 6284
Tel. (097) 556220
Fax (097) 556308

Dr. Michael Peterkin makes one of Australia's
most complex Chardonnays at this tiny,
model vineyard established quite recently in
the heartland of Margaret River. Peterkin
uses much closer vine spacing than is usual
in Australia, vertical shoot positioning and
applies water sparingly in summer to
compensate for the lack of rain during the
growing season. On light sandy loam soil
with a friable clay base he achieves small
yields of premium quality grapes. The vines,
on a west-facing slope, are sheltered from
wind - a common local problem - by forest.
Winemaking has changed radically from the
anaerobic, high-tech methods Peterkin
originally used, and today Chardonnay is
fermented in barrique, without being overly
protected against oxidation, aged on lees and
undergoes malolactic fermentation. It's a
formidable wine that promises to age well.
Sémillon-Sauvignon Blanc blend is also very
fine, flowery, subtly oaked and a delight to
drink young. Pinot Noir is constantly
improving and evolving, but needs a little fine
tuning. The second label, Fire Gully, has a
dry white blend of merit alongside a lighter-
weight Pinot.

Fire Gully Dry White 1991   ❦ ②
Fresh citrus, grassy aromas dominate this blend
under Pierro's cheaper second label. Crisp,
clean, slightly herbaceous and very attractive
when young.

Semillon Sauvignon Blanc 1991   ❦ ②
Restrained melon, floral and tropical fruit flavors
triumph over the region's usual grassy
herbaceousness in this deliciously fine, fruity
blend.

Chardonnay 1990   ❦❦ ③
The specialty of this tiny winery is a refined
Chardonnay which has more Burgundy-like
complexity than most. Aromas are smoky,
toasty, nutty, spicy and buttery, reflecting heavy
winemaker intervention. The palate is dry and
supremely fine but has wonderful depth of
flavor.

WINE OF AUSTRALIA

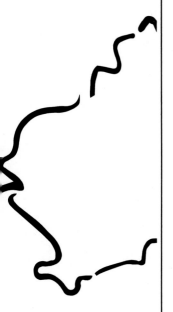

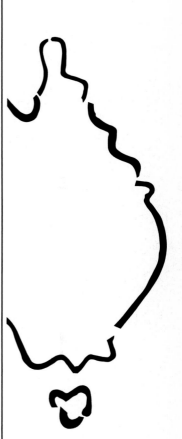

"Quietly Sensational"

Contact: Hazel M. Murphy
Fifth Floor
Australia House
Strand
London WC2B 4LA
Telephone: 071-438 8259
Fax: 071-836 4250

Campania has always been a land of world-renowned wines. F[...]
Faustiniano, and Caleno were considered the greatest wines [...]
world, their praises sung by Horace, Virgil, Cato, and Pliny the [...]
such as *Vitis hellinica*, *Animea gemina*, *Vitis apiana*, and vulpin[...]
originally brought to this southern Italian region by the Greek[...]
descendants are known as aglianico, asprinio, biancolella, [...]
falanghina, fiano, forastero, greco, and piedirosso. And many o[...]
are grown exclusively in Campania. These varieties fully [...]
potential here thanks to a mild climate, volcanic soils, low yield[...]
winemaking techniques. The quality wines produced have [...]
aromas and characteristics. But most of all, they are truly uniq[...]
Campania's centuries-old tradition.

Campania, An Ancient Tra[...]

The DOC wines of Campania[...]

- Ischia
- Taurasi
- Capri
- Lacryma Christi del Vesuvio
- Aglianico del Taburno
- Castel San Lorenzo

- Greco di Tufo
- Solopaca
- Fiano di Avell[...]
- Cilento
- Falerno del M[...]

soon to become DOC wines

Asprinio di Aversa, Guardiolo, Sant'Agata dei C[...]

REGIONE CAMPANIA
Assessorato Agricoltura - Se.S.I.R.C.A.

Plantagenet

Albany Highway
Mount Barker 6324
Tel. (098) 511150
Fax (098) 511839

Tony Smith, who can trace his ancestry to the Plantagenets, migrated from England in search of adventure and decided to farm in the wilds of remote Western Australia. He soon turned his hand to viticulture after seeing early Agriculture Department trials, and today his winery is the largest in the south, with winemaker John Wade handling the grapes of 21 other vineyards. Spicy, pungent Shiraz, classically styled Cabernet Sauvignon and crisp Rhine Riesling stood out early, but fine peachy Chardonnay may be the flagship. Very good Chenin Blanc and Sauvignon Blanc are also produced, as well as a popular medium-dry Frontignac and light red called Fleur. A second, unwooded Chardonnay, blended with grapes from outside Mount Barker, is less-expensive. The vineyard was established in 1968 and the early reds have proved their ability to mature well in bottle.

Mount Barker Chardonnay 1991 🍷🍷 ③
Emerging as one of Australia's top Chardonnay labels, the '91, from an outstanding season, is sensational. Wonderfully pungent and fruit dominant, with complexity and yet great elegance.

Rhine Riesling 1990 🍷 ②
Delicate floral Riesling aromas and a fine, dry palate. An example of what Mount Barker can achieve in a good year, while the 1989 and '91 both display the marked effects of Botrytis.

Cabernet Sauvignon 1988 🍷 ③
This vintage shows a richness not usually apparent in Mount Barker Cabernet. The aromas are of cassis and coffee-like oak which follow through to the palate, which has deep, accessible berry flavors with soft tannins.

Pinot Noir 1988 🍷 ③
A complex; forward and seemingly quite mature Pinot which tastes good now and probably should not be cellared. Light bodied but has considerable Pinot charm.

Shiraz 1988 🍷 ②
From a much more successful vintage than '89, this delightfully spicy, plummy Shiraz is full of classic varietal flavor with a soft, round palate which is also lively, crisp and snappy.

Wignalls

Chester Pass Road
Albany 6330
Tel. (098) 412848

Bill Wignall, a veterinarian, turned part of his cattle farm over to vines in 1982. Wisely, he chose not to build a winery but asked the skilful John Wade to make the wines at nearby Plantagenet. Although some distance from other vineyards in the Mount Barker region, Wignalls is setting high standards in cool-climate estate-grown table wines, especially Pinot Noir, which is considered by some to be among the top in the country and has garnered several important awards. Its style is very fine, with low tannin and only medium color depth, but intense varietal fruit of a sappy, cherry, plum and slightly herbal nature which should get even better as the vines mature. Chardonnay is also excellent in a fine, subtle style and the tiny quantities of Sauvignon Blanc are also exciting. The vineyard is closer to the sea than others in the Lower Great Southern, with a more maritime climate giving less diurnal temperature variation. Bill's wife Pat is involved in the business and son Robert manages the vineyard.

Sauvignon Blanc 1991 🍷🍷 ②
Delicious ripe style which boasts gooseberry and lime aromas with a lightly grassy aspect. On the palate the lush fruit blossoms with freshness, verve and a degree of complexity not usually found in this varietal.

Chardonnay 1990 🍷🍷 ③
Complex Burgundian style with delicacy and yet showing honeysuckle, floral, and butterscotch aromas. Superb Chardonnay, with richness as well as finesse.

Pinot Noir 1990 🍷🍷 ③
The '90 is typical of this vineyard's style and its best yet. Earthy and gamey development over ripe cherry and sappy notes with a slightly herbaceous aspect. The palate is medium-light in weight but has good intensity and length.

AUSTRIA

The annual volume of wine produced in Austria has varied considerably since 1970. 1.1 million hectoliters were produced in 1985 as compared to 4.9 million in 1982, with an average of 2.8 million per year. The vineyards cover about 58,000 hectares, which is about half that of Germany. The nation is divided into four regions: Burgenland, Lower Austria (Niederösterreich), Styria (Steirmark) and Vienna (Wien).

According to statistics, Austrians consume about 35 liters each per year, totalling 2.5 million hl. As in most countries, the trend is moving away from ordinary quality products, and the demand for fine wines is healthier than ever.

Austria's climate, being close to the northern limit for growing classic varieties, is excellent for producing fruity, racy white wines with firm acidity (7 to 9 g/lt at harvest time depending on variety) and which, at the upper quality level, attain natural alcohol levels of 10.5-13.5°. There are considerable climatic differences between Austria's wine-growing areas, which account for the great variety in wine styles. Average hours of sunshine vary from 1,805 per year measured at Gumpoldskirchen and 1,956 at Klöch, with average rainfall between 461 mm at Retz and 854 mm at Klöch, while average temperatures are 19°C in summer and 0.5°C in winter.

The most important white grape varieties in Austria are Grüner Veltliner, which covers 36% of the vineyard area, followed by Müller Thurgau (9%), Welschriesling (8.5%), Pinot Blanc (3%), Neuburger (3%) and Riesling (2.5%). Muscat Ottonel, Traminer and Pinot Gris each account for about 1%. Among the reds, Zweigelt leads with a modest 6%, followed by Blauer Portugieser (5.5%), Blaufränkisch (5%) and St Laurent (1%). Other international varieties are grown on a much smaller scale, though are held in high esteem by wine-lovers and include Chardonnay, Sauvignon Blanc and Gelber Muskateller (a variety of Muscat which, in Austria, produces racy, dry wines). The classic French red varieties Cabernet Sauvignon, Cabernet Franc, Merlot and Pinot Noir are also on the increase and have to date produced excellent wines.

To fully understand Austria's wine scene, it is important to understand its classifications which are primarily based on the varietals, specific must weights, harvest methods and production zones. Austria's wine-growing regions are subdivided into vineyard areas and "Qualitätsweine" may only come from one specific vineyard area. For Lower Austria they are: Donauland-Carnuntum, Kamptal-Donauland, Thermenregion, Wachau and Weinviertel. Burgenland is made up of Neusiedlersee, Neusiedlersee-Hügelland, Mittelburgenland and Südburgenland, while Styria is divided into Südsteiermark, Süd-Ostststeiermark and Weststeiermark. Vienna is not subdivided.

The quality classifications are based on grape variety and the sugar content of the grapes, or in other words, their degree of ripeness. Other criteria such as origin and how the grapes were harvested are also considered, though origin does not feature as prominently in quality classifications as it does in other countries. A 1990 Riesling Kabinett, for example, can come from anywhere, though on the label and, hopefully, in restaurant wine lists the place of origin, producer and much more will be clearly stated.

The Austrian Wine Law is very similar to the German system, which means it differs from the French AOC or the Italian DOC laws. Wines with the designation "Qualitätsweine" are generally made from single varieties though there are, of course, exceptions which are well worth seeking out. There are three quality categories which, in ascending order, are Qualitätswein, Kabinett and Prädikatswein. The latter is again subdivided into six levels based on the percentage of sugar in the grapes and, thus, their ripeness. This is expressed in degrees 'Babo', ie $1° = 1\%$ of sugar in the grapes. The following is a brief scale for quality wines from all wine-growing regions:
1) Qualitätswein must attain at least 15°, which would result in about 10.5° alcohol. The sugar content and, thus, the potential alcohol, can only be increased by adding sugar, a method called chaptalization, to a maximum of 4.5 kg per 100 liters to reach 19° for whites and 20° for red wines;
2) Kabinett wines are not allowed to be chaptalized and must attain at least 17°;
3) for Prädikatsweine the minimum sugar level must be at least 19° and chaptalization is also forbidden. The subdivisions are as follows, again in ascending order: Auslese at least 21°, Eiswein at least 25° and the grapes must be frozen when they go into the press, Beeren-Auslese at least 27° and Trocken-Beeren-Auslese at least 30°. In the last three cases there is so much sugar in the juice that the wine could never ferment out to dryness.
Altogether not a particularly simple system, indeed. In certain areas (especially the Wachau) growers have introduced their own classifications, which in the Danube valley between Melk and Krems are Steinfeder, Federspiel and Smaragd. More and more producers now use the simple Qualitätswein designation for all dry wines, even if they are entitled to higher status, as most consumers have come to expect Spätlese and Auslese to be sweet. An alternative is to feature the word "trocken" (dry) on the labels, though for sweet wines, all are used.
Austria's strength lies definitely with its white wines, which the climatic conditions endow with a very individual style of fruitiness. The national variety, Grüner Veltliner, covers more than a third of Austria's vineyard area which is, of course, far too much. The wines it produces range from the thin and acidic through to absolute international top quality. In recent years two aspects have emerged with this vine. First, by reducing yields per vine to a minimum it can produce wines of quality hitherto undreamed of and, secondly, very concentrated wines from this variety can keep well and improve in bottle for 10 to 20 years, outstripping even the best Rieslings. This brings us to another characteristic of good Austrian white wines: their longevity. This is a quality of Wachau wines, in particular, which come from valley and hillside vineyards along the Danube between Melk and Krems. Riesling and Veltliner wines from here are among Austria's finest.

For purity of vibrant fruit and perfume, the Wachau's nearest competitor is Southern Styria (Südsteiermark), which performs well with international varieties such as Welschriesling, Pinot Blanc, Chardonnay, Sauvignon Blanc, Gelber Muskateller. Just east of Wachau, Lower Austria (Niederösterreich) is also well-known. The small areas bordering onto the Wachau have earned a high reputation, especially the vineyards around the town of Krems and

Langenlois, in Kamptal, Manhartsberg-Vorland, Wagram and small 'oasis' areas in the Weinviertel. Nonetheless, the most decisive element is, as always, the grower's attitude towards quality.

The Thermenregion wine-growing area extends southwards from Vienna with its center around the town of Gumpoldskirchen. Its main varieties are Zierfandler and Rotgipfler along with many others; there is no point in looking for Veltliner here, and Riesling is also rare. Although this part of Austria is best known for dry, elegant white wines, its most notorious is a striking dessert wine called Spätrot-Rotgipfler Auslese, with long aging potential. Certain areas, including the vineyards around Soos and Tattendorf, are specialized in producing red wines.

East of Vienna is the wine-growing area Carnuntum which, due to illogical regulations, is joined to the Donauland area to the west of the capital. It forms a single wine-growing region called Donauland-Carnuntum.

Vienna was already a bustling, wine-growing city in pre-Roman times. Indeed the Viennese love of wine shows through in the fact that there are still 700 ha of vineyard within the city limits - a small wonder in the face of urban sprawl! The times when the yearly adult consumption reached 350 lt (more than a bottle a day, per person) in the 16th century are long gone. Today, however, there are hundreds of "Heurigen" that are happy to serve their wines in a very relaxed, informal atmosphere. Often the wine can be very good indeed. The Heurigen are a much loved, integral part of Viennese life-style. Among the wines made in Vienna, the whites are without a doubt the best.

Burgenland is divided into four, distinct wine-growing areas. In the north, lake Neusiedlersee, on the border with Hungary, is the source of Austria's great sweet wines. The two denominations are Neusiedlersee and Neusiedler Hügelland (the hill zone of the lake). Here, once the conditions are right, the noble mold Botrytis Cinerea turns berries into raisins at incredible speed to produce some of the world's most unique dessert wines. In addition to sweet wines, this area also produces excellent dry whites, mainly from international varieties like Welschriesling and Pinot Blanc. Many other types are made, as well as fruity red wines from Zweigelt, Blaufränkisch, Pinot Noir and, more recently, Cabernet Sauvignon.

To the south, still within sight of the lake, lies Mittelburgenland which has specialized in Blaufränkisch. The microclimate, together with heavy, clayey soils with high water retention, produces deep, full red wines with pure fruit flavors. Cabernet Sauvignon is on the increase here and does very well when blended with Blaufränkisch. Farther south Eisenberg completes the picture. Here, too, Blaufränkisch reigns and in the mineral-rich soils produces very unique wines.

Austria's wines have improved enormously over the past ten years, mainly due to the efforts of small estates. A major factor has been the number of young people with international training who have taken over at many estates. Now, with few exceptions, the best wines tend to come from small producers with a maximum of 12-15 ha of estate-vineyard. To date, Germany has been Austria's best customer abroad for top quality wines, but many of the most famous wines sell quickly every year, only weeks after release. For this reason, you need luck as well as money to be able to enjoy them!

CZECH REP. & SLOVAKIA

GERMANY

SWITZERLAND

ITALY

SLOVENIA

HUNGARY

Wien

Graz

Lower Austria
1 **Donauland-Carnuntum**
2 **Thermenregion**
3 **Kamphal-Donauland**
4 **Wachau**
5 **Weinviertel**
Vienna
6 **Wien**
Burgenland
7 **Mittelburgenland**
8 **Neusiedlersee**
9 **Neusiedlersee-Hügelland**
10 **Südburgenland**
Stiria
11 **Südsteiermark**
12 **Süd-Oststeiermark**
13 **Weststeiermark**

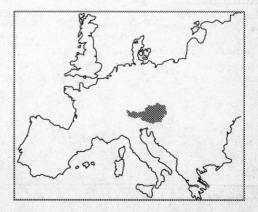

Weingut Leo Alzinger

3601 Unterloiben 11
Tel. (02732) 59125
Fax (02732) 77900

Leo Alzinger, who in the early 1980s was still supplying the Loiben cooperative, switched to estate bottling and marketing in record time to become one of the top names in the Wachau region. Now, along with F.X. Pichler and Emmerich Knoll, also from Loiben, he forms a trio constellation which has made the town of Dürnstein into the Wachau's wine Mecca. At first his wines were often closed, hard and unapproachable in their youth, demanding plenty of patience from curious wine enthusiasts, but recent years have seen them become increasingly more subtle and harmonious. After the 1990 vintage, which produced opulent, big wines, the 1991s from a more difficult growing season also turned out to be excellent. Indeed, some regard the 1991s as his most successful yet, especially the Rieslings from the Steinertal, Loibenberg and Dürnsteiner Hollerin sites which attained almost 13° alc. His Veltliners from the Hochstrasse, Mühlpoint and Steinertal vineyards are also very impressive.

Grüner Veltliner Smaragd ☷ ②
Cuvée 1991
A soft, grapey aroma, very elegant and sweet on the palate, gentle and very fruity, an extremely attractive Veltliner with good aging potential.

Grüner Veltliner Smaragd Ried ☷ ②
Loibner Steinertal 1991
On the nose typically ripe and fruity, very rich and harmonious and already very elegant in spite of its youth.Will peak in about ten years without losing its fruit..

Riesling Smaragd Ried ☷☷ ②
Loibner Berg 1991
Clear, pure and fruity Riesling with gooseberry overtones, very complex and complete. On the palate firm, long-lasting and full. A great Wachau Riesling with plenty of development ahead.

Weingut Wilhelm Bründlmayer

Zwettler Strasse 23
3550 Langenlois
Tel. (02734) 2172
Fax (02734) 3748

This is a traditional family estate with a large vineyard area by Austrian standards. Sites like Zöbinger Heiligenstein have scaled the heights in recent years due to the efforts of Bründlmayer Junior, Willi. The spirit of innovation comes natural to him, such as the introduction of the Bordeaux 'lyre' vine training system which enables the leaves and grapes to absorb more sunlight. Grüner Veltliner and Riesling have always been specialities of this Langenlois estate and since the mid 1980s barrique-fermented Chardonnay has earned them international acclaim, along with Pinot Gris which is also made as a cuvée with Pinot Blanc. For red wines, Bründlmayer has long been a Pinot Noir pioneer, though since the introduction of other red varieties his barrique cuvées like the supple Cuvée Cécile (made from Pinot Noir and Merlot) or the tougher, more tannic Cuvée Vincent (made from Cabernet Sauvignon and Cabernet Franc) have stolen the limelight.

Chardonnay 1990 ☷ ③
Barrique-fermented, mainly in Austrian oak, it is very flowery and fresh and only starting to develop. It has aromas of toast, dried fruit and vanilla, while on the palate it is juicy and round with plenty of body to balance its vibrant acidity. Excellent aging potential.

Grau- und Weissburgunder ☷ ②
Ried Langenloiser Spiegel 1990
A cuvée of Pinot Gris and Pinot Blanc, very rich and concentrated with excellent aging potential. Although very approachable now, its firm acidity and muscular structure will not attain full harmony for several years to come.

Riesling Kabinett Ried ☷☷ ②
Zöbinger Heiligenstein 1990
From one of Austria's best Riesling vineyards. Deep yellow in color, pure varietal aromas, full, mature, almost unctuous and very long. A Riesling of top international class, very elegant, of great character with the substance to last at least another 15-20 years.

Ruländer 1990
Fine, very supple and not too heavy, with a fruity impact on the palate. Perfectly made, delicate and ready to drink now. One of the best Austrian Pinot Gris.

Weingut Feiler-Artinger

Hauptstrasse 3
7071 Rust
Tel. (02685) 237
Fax (02685) 312

Feiler Artinger, formed by the merger of three estates, has become one of the standard-bearers of the Free City of Rust, a town not exactly lacking in excellent wine estates. Wine-maker Hans Feiler has an uncompromising concept of quality and has intuitively grasped the means of harnessing the attributes of varying terrains with their microclimates and grape varieties to produce a range of superb wines. The estate's tradition lies mainly with its sweet dessert wines from Ruster Ausbruch through to Trocken-Beeren-Auslese. In 1991 the Ausbruch wines attained acidity levels hitherto unknown at Rust, adding a new quality dimension to the wines. As a result the 1991 Prädikatsweine are very fine with a rare balance of fruit, body, sweetness and class. Although Rust is much less famous for its dry whites, Hans Feiler is equally successful and without doubt one of the town's best producers. The microclimate here enables him to make Chardonnay, Sauvignon Blanc, Pinot Blanc and Neuburger from fully ripe grapes even in ordinary vintages. Another example of his versatility is the very fine Cuvée Solitaire, one of Austria's top reds.

Ruster Chardonnay Auslese 1991
Pure aromas characterized by subtle nutty flavors. Wonderful lively acidity and balance. A dessert wine of great style, not as sweet and heavy as the Ausbruch wines, fruitier and lacking the latter's intense botrytis flavor.

Ruster Sauvignon
Blanc Kabinett 1991
Typical Sauvignon fruit, medium weight, racy. Pleasantly low in alcohol (11°) considering its structure, with the racy acidity typical of 1991. Very pleasant and well-balanced.

Ruster Ausbruch Pinot
Cuveé 1988
Nuances of toast and hints of vanilla, coffee and milk-chocolate. Very rich pure elements. Great complexity on the palate characterized by the very skilled use of barrique, with fruit and oak in perfect harmony. Very elegant with enough concentration to last for decades.

Cuvée Solitaire Blaufränkisch
Kabinett 1989
Subtle plum and cherry aromas with accentuated vanilla overtones, deep and smoky. A very compact wine already showing breed but will repay a few years' aging.

Freie Weingärtner Wachau

3601 Dürnstein 107
Tel. (02711) 371
Fax (02711) 37113

Wilhelm Schwengler, the long-serving director of this cooperative, together with his member growers has managed to turn this estate into the best of its kind in Austria, placing it among the elite of Wachau wine producers. The 'Independent Wine Growers' have remained faithful to their principles: the vineyard area has not been extended and grapes are delivered to five different press houses spread around the Wachau. This makes it possible to carry out strict selections during the harvest according to variety, site and quality. The number of crus which genuinely express different soils and microclimates has increased on a yearly basis. In 1991, 12 different Grüner Veltliners, a Riesling and two Neuburger wines attained the top Wachau classification 'Smaragd'. Wilhelm Schwengler has worked with determination to defend the traditional Neuburger variety as well as earning recognition for attaining high quality on the right-hand bank of the Danube at Rossatz and in neighboring villages.

Grüner Veltliner Smaragd
Terrassen Herrschaft Spitz 1991
Honey-sweet nuances, interplay of hay and pure Veltliner fruit. Opulent on the palate, denoting fully ripe grapes. Unctuous and noble with a strong, ripe acid backbone, very harmonious and complex. Will keep for over 20 years.

Riesling Smaragd
Terrassen Thal Wachau 1991
Pure Riesling fruit with pineapple and gooseberry aromas; typical Wachau breed, very concentrated, full-bodied with masses of fruit. A convincing follow-up to the excellent series of Rieslings from this site. Along with the Rieslings from Ried Kellerberg and Spitzer Bürgerspitalstiftung, it is a continuously great wine.

Veltliner Smaragd
Terrassen Herrschaft Thal Wachau 1990
Round and deeply fruity, peppery and at the same time velvety and intense, interwoven with almost Riesling-like fruit, very fine and striking. Proof that this kind of Veltliner quality need not fear comparison with Riesling. At its best when aged.

Weingut Engelbert Gesellmann

Lange Gasse 65
7301 Deutschkreutz
Tel. (02613) 360
Fax (02613) 8544

Engelbert Gesellmann has behaved rather like a rebel among Burgenland's family estates, and when it comes to coaxing the ultimate degrees of quality from his Mittel-Burgenland vineyards, he is no blind adherer to handed-down tradition. In this vein he was one of the pioneers in planting the new-comers Cabernet Sauvignon and Chardonnay, and in using barriques. But, there again, his ideas and aims were different right from the start. His humble manner makes it difficult to guess at first glance that he has proven himself to be one of the most reliable and innovative among Mittel-Burgenland's producers in recent years. His skill is manifested in wines such as a very fine barrique-aged Chardonnay, or the excellent Opus Eximium, a cuvée of St Laurent, Pinot Noir, Blaufränkisch and Cabernet Sauvignon, aged in four different types of oak. 1988 was the first release and although very good it has been overshadowed by successive vintages, which have shown an increasing degree of refinement. In addition to reds he adds the finishing touch to his range with sweet wines.

Scheurebe Eiswein 1989　　
Very exotic aromas with clear melon and passionfruit flavors. A full and perfumed dessert wine, intensely spiced, concentrated and extremely 'firey' due to its high alcohol content. An unusual yet appealing style of Eiswein. A true rarity.

Blaufränkisch 1990　　
Ruby-red, with intense fruity, smoky aromas. Medium weight and delicate showing impressive elegance and a lengthy finish. A very nice red wine with good structure and harmony between fruit and acidity.

Cabernet Sauvignon 1989　　🍇 ③
Clear cassis and not at all 'green' in character. Ripe and generous. On the palate peppery and spicy, not too heavy but sustained by a harmonious tannic backbone. One of Austria's best Cabernets.

Opus Eximium Cuvée Nr.2 1989　　🍇 ①
Cherry and dark berry aromas, unique and balanced, an elegant cuvée even if a little overpowered by oak. Harmonious and muscular, will last well past the turn of the century.

Weingut Alois Gross

Ratsch 10
8461 Ehrenhausen
Tel. (03453) 2527
Fax (03453) 2728

Alois Gross belongs to the "Junge Wilde" (wild youth) generation, a group of active and ambitious growers who have recently raised the quality of Styrian wines to new heights. His 1990 Sauvignon Blanc from the Nussberg vineyard was perhaps the best of this vintage in which Sauvignon excelled all over Austria, while in 1991 it was the turn of his Pinot Blanc (Weissburgunder) from the Kittenberg site to excel on a national level. Two heavy hailstorms and very unfavorable weather during the growing season make this a surprising achievement. One of Alois Gross' specialties is his Altsteirischer Rebsatz, from a very old vineyard planted with ten different varieties, all harvested, crushed and vinified together. Another rarity is Roter Riesling, not related to the familiar white Riesling, which makes a meaty but rather neutral wine. Another interesting wine is Pinot Gris which, when the grapes are ripe enough, is partly matured in barriques.

Gelber Muskateller 1991　　🍇 ①
Light yellow color, fresh, grapey aromas with traditional Muscat spice. The ideal summer wine, light (only 10.5° alc), lively, 'spritzig' and refreshing.

Morillon Kabinett　　
Ried Nußberg 1991
A well-built Chardonnay (called Morillon in these parts), racy with accentuated fruit, fairly concentrated, long on the finish but a relatively simple wine which will not benefit from further aging.

Weißburgunder Kabinett　　
Ried Kittenberg 1991
Subtle and understated aromas, very pure and delicate. Elegant and surprisingly concentrated for a 1991 Pinot Blanc, showing plenty of finesse.

Sauvignon blanc　　
Ried Nußberg 1990
Sweet and ripe aromas of white asparagus and cassis, soft and lush, incredibly rich on the palate with sweet fruit, though not totally dry. A brilliant explosion of fruit, unique and evocative.

Weingut Franz Hirtzberger

Kremserstrasse 8
3620 Spitz
Tel. (02713) 2209
Fax (02713) 2405

Franz Hirtzberger has recently attracted attention for three reasons: the excellent quality of his wines, their record-breaking prices and the work done in recultivating traditional Wachau sites. The latter was an expensive project to erect new stone walls to terrace the steep Singerriedl site. It was obviously worth the effort as his top quality Rieslings come from here and the very steep, terraced Hochrain vineyard. When it comes to fine Veltliners with strong personality, the Honivogl and Rotes Tor sites are an absolute guarantee. He has also begun focusing on Neuburger, an old Austrian variety which to date has performed best at Spitz. Very typical is what an inspired journalist once described as their 'cool breath', a combination of soft and fruity aromas from the microclimate at Spitz. At night cool breezes descend from the forests on Mount Jauerling. The enormous difference between day and night-time temperatures furthers the powerful aromas. A staunch supporter of the traditional Wachau style, Franz was one of the founders of "Vinea Wachau", to protect the region's wines. A highly respected, traditional estate, both in the Wachau and in Austria.

Grüner Veltliner
Federspiel Rotes Tor 1990
Intense aromas with smoky flavors. Aromatic, complex and ripe, full-bodied, complex rather than fruity. Very delicate and pleasantly light.

Grüner Veltliner Smaragd
Ried Honivogl 1990
Brilliant golden yellow, rich in body and finesse. Perfectly balanced with 13.3° alc. Has all the prerequisites to become a great Veltliner.

Neuburger Smaragd
Ried Burgberg 1990
Succulent scent of walnuts, rich with fruit. Powerful and full-bodied, though a little austere and smoky due to aging in large new-oak casks. An important contribution to preserve the image of Wachau Neuburger.

Riesling Federspiel
Ried Hochrain 1990
Concentrated, aromatic Riesling with exotic pineapple and peach nuances; the deep scent of maturity is beginning to take the place of pure fruit. Very nice, showing complexity, a little hard now but will improve with age. Unique among Wachau wines.

Riesling Smaragd
Ried Singerriedel 1990
A monument to Wachau's wine culture: golden yellow and clings to the glass. An original aroma reminiscent of porcini mushrooms, strawberry, pineapple, opulent and 'firey'. Develops quickly in the glass. A powerful wine (13.5° alc). Pure Riesling fruit lurks behind the big muscular structure. Very fine.

Weingut Haus Iby

Kirchengasse 4a
7312 Horitschon
Tel/Fax (02610) 2292

At first Anton Iby, director of a local company which makes technical products, had little time for the family estate until he was angered by the disastrously low prices obtained for the 1982 vintage which caused many growers to dump their grapes. Beginner's luck turned into regular success, motivating him to contemplate giving up his former profession to become a wine-grower. The vineyards are looked after by his hard-working wife Joanna. One of his pet ideas has been to bottle age Blaufränkisch for several years, to release it only when it has begun to show true class. This has resulted in a series of reserve wines, very full-bodied and concentrated, cask-aged for 16 months, after which they mature for several years in bottle before release. In spite of very low-key marketing Iby's wines have found their way into numerous top restaurants.

Blaufränkisch
Jahrgangsreserve 1990
Concentrated and complex fruit, not quite as sweet as the Hockäcker of the same vintage. By "Jahrgansreserve" Iby refers to a wine with exceptionally long potential for development. Matured in cask for 16 months.

Blaufränkisch Ried Hochäcker 1990
Hochäcker is the name of one of the best Horitschon vineyards. Deep, classic fruit, round, harmonious and long. Very good potential for development and more complete than the 1991.

Horitschoner Blaufränkisch 1990
Barrique-aged. Elegant aroma, very fruity, medium-weight though fine with finesse. A very successful example of an aging method not traditional in Burgenland.

Weingut Hans Igler

Lange Gasse 49
7301 Deutschkreutz
Tel. (02613) 365
Fax (02613) 79116

Apart from his status as "grandseigneur" among producers in Mittel-Burgenland, Hans Igler, together with Anton Kollwentz and Moser's Malteser Weingut, has been the first in Austria to focus on red wines. Back in 1983 he was the first in Burgenland to successfully age Blaufränkisch in new barriques at a time when malolactic fermentation was practically unknown in Austria. He was one of the first to plant Cabernet Sauvignon on a commercial basis (after Schlumberger in Vöslau) and to produce a red wine cuvée. His Blaufränkisch and Cabernet blend is called 'cuvée Vulcano'. The criticism, that his wines are light and hard is only true in rare cases, as even here there have been small disappointments alongside great successes. With the help of his son-in-law Igler now makes his best reds ever. Even though Deutschkreutz makes slightly lighter wines than those from neighboring Horitschon they make up for this by their silky elegance. It is much to his credit that Hans Igler, the senior leader in Mittel-Burgenland, is always ready to come to the aid of his junior colleagues with advice and practical help.

Deutschkreutzer ♥ ③
Cabernet Sauvignon Ried Kart 1990
Dark ruby-red, with very intense ripe fruit aromas; pure Cabernet Sauvignon, firm, mellow and supple, sweet, complex and long. Of international class and proof of Burgenland's potential to produce top quality from this variety.

Deutschkreutzer Cuvée Vulcano 1990 ♥ ②
Beautiful ruby-red, intense and ripe on the nose, elegant and harmonious. Very subtle use of barrique with well-integrated oak. A very compact wine with great aging potential.

Blaufränkisch Ried Hochberg 1989 ♥ ①
Refined and fresh aromas with grape-seed and almond flavors, understated and elegant. Medium-weight and harmonious, a classic Blaufränkisch.

Weingut Johanneshof Familie Reinisch

Am Raiffeisenplatz 6
2523 Tattendorf
Tel. (02253) 18423
Fax (02253) 81924

Hans Reinisch's estate is located in the part of the Thermenregion which is specialized in red wine. He has become the rising star among producers of great red wines in Austria, and the word 'great' is no exaggeration. His success can be attributed to painstaking attention in the vineyard, extensive investment in the winery together with the experience and know-how gathered during his many trips abroad, making Johanneshof one of the top names for red wines in the country. Few producers are as skilled as Reinisch when it comes to choosing the right kind of oak and just the right degree of toasting for barriques. As a result his 1988 cuvée made from Cabernet and Merlot has achieved cult status, and every Austrian wine-lover would like a bottle in his cellar. He has also focused on white wines in recent years, and his 1990s have brought remarkable improvement. He also produces what is probably Austria's best 'nouveau' wine from the early-ripening Blauer Portugieser.

Alter Rebstock 1990 ♥ ①
A cuvée of St Laurent, Blaufränkisch and Zweigelt, matured in traditional oak casks. Good fruit on the nose, powerful and long.

Merlot 1990 ♥ ③
The first attempt at making Merlot as a 100% varietal. Very fruity and mature in aroma, good weight, succulent and still very young (tasted in spring 1992) though already elegant, complex and extraordinarily long. A very promising start.

Cabernet Sauvignon Merlot 1989 ♥ ③
Subtle and complex bouquet reminiscent of grass and red berries though rather closed at the moment with the fruit still overlayed by tannin. Weighty and succulent promising good potential for further development in bottle.

Pinot Noir Ried Mitterfeld 1989 ♥ ②
A beautiful aroma of ripe Pinot with understated oak nuances, needs to breathe for several hours to show its best. Powerful, well-packed fruit on the palate with plentiful reserves for further development.

Weingut Emmerich Knoll

3601 Unterloiben 10
Tel. (02732) 79355

As far back as the 1979 vintage Emmerich Knoll set new standards for the Wachau Riesling culture. His wines are very individual and easy to tell apart from those of his colleagues. Knoll's flair is most noticeable in his very succulent, full-bodied Rieslings and Veltliners, which in good vintages seem almost over-ripe and opulent. Bad vintages, it seems, do not exist in this estate and the recipe is quite simple: Knoll's heart is in the vineyard, where he gives almost every vine individual attention. In this way he manages to compensate for the vicissitudes of the growing season, which in unfavorable years entails drastically reducing yields. Knoll aims at preserving the natural characteristics of his wines imparted by soil and microclimate and, therefore, intervenes as little as possible during wine-making. His long-lasting Rieslings from the Dürnsteiner Schütt and opulent Veltliners from the Loibenberg sites are legendary. The only novelty to emerge from this fundamentally conservative estate in recent years has been an unusually fruity Chardonnay which, as may be expected, is made in the traditional way without new oak.

Riesling Federspiel   ℗ ②
Ried Loibenberg 1991
A very pleasant, fruit accentuated aroma combining pure grapes and pepper, a distinguishing characteristic of all Knoll's wines. Good weight and acid backbone. An elegant wine, drinking well now but which will profit from further bottle aging.

Grüner Veltliner Smaragd   ℗ ②
Ried Loibner Schütt 1990
Full-bodied, concentrated, very elegant: a classic Veltliner which continues a decade long series of superb wines. To enjoy it at its best it needs cellaring for several years.

Riesling Smaragd   ℗℗ ②
Ried Dürnsteiner Schütt 1990
Yellow peach and apricot aromas, compact, and concentrated. Intense Riesling aromas linger on the palate; meaty and harmonious, lively and of great class. Very persistent, with plenty of development ahead. It would be a shame to drink it young.

Riesling Smaragd   ℗ ②
Ried Loibenberg 1990
Loibenberg is a vineyard which stretches across Dürnstein to the limits of the Wachau, close to Ried Pfaffenberg, with its primitive-rock and loess soils. Ripe on the nose, with extremely refined Riesling aromas. Full-bodied and fruity, already accessible and ready to drink.

Type of Wines

℗℗℗   White

▦   Rosé

🍇   Red

Weinlaubenhof Weingut
Alois Kracher

Apetlonerstraße 37
7142 Illmitz
Tel. (02175) 24202

Vineyards on the eastern side of Lake Neusiedl in the Pannonian Plain around the town of Illmitz have long been famous for their ability to produce world-class dessert wines from botrytis-stricken grapes. The town has reaped numerous awards for its Beeren-Auslese and Trocken-Beeren-Auslese wines, though nobody has achieved more recognition than the Kracher family. What has set this estate apart more than anything is the spirit of innovation and the development of an individual style, typical of young Alois Kracher's strategic thinking. While the wines called "Zwischen den Seen", or between the Lakes, are made in the traditional maner and express the regional character of "Seewinkel", as the flat, eastern side of the lake is called, the 'Nouvelle Vague' range are made in a more international style, with higher alcohol and aged in barrique. Kracher's most successful sweet wines are made from Welsch Riesling, Bouvier and Traminer, though also from the less prestigious Sämling (Scheurebe) vine. He has recently planted Riesling which will undoubtedly make superb sweet wines due to its high acidity and finesse. However, his dry wines should not go unmentioned and here, too, his methods are aimed at developing an international style, with long skin maceration before pressing and prolonged lees contact after fermentation.

Sämling 88   🍇 ③
Beerenauslese Zwischen den Seen 1989
Sweet with enormous complexity of aromas, which follows through to the palate. Very long, a classic Illmitz wine combining tremendous opulence with delicacy.

Traminer Ausbruch   🍇🍇 ③
Nouvelle Vague 1989
Elegant interplay of coconut and rose aromas. Alcohol, richness and the sweet vanilla character deriving from new oak are gradually merging to produce a nobly harmonious wine with great potential for further development. Promises to become a truly great dessert wine.

Welschriesling Trockenbeeren-   🍇🍇 ③
auslese Zwischen den Seen 1988
Made from extremely ripe grapes, fat, weighty and powerful it is the incaranation of botrytis, very typcal of Illmitz, the 'Botrytis Capital'. Very long bottle aging will produce further finesse: to be enjoyed in thimble-size portions!

Muskat-Ottonel   🍇🍇🍇 ③
Beerenauslese Zwischen den Seen 1988
Magnificent color, deep gold shot with amber and orange. On the nose the Muscat Ottonel aromas still hold their own against those of botrytis. Very striking on the palate, combining the aromatic character of the grape with the honeyed intensity of botrytis, supple, complex, sweet in spite of 15° alcohol! When botrytis runs rampant in the vineyards, it tends to introduce its own flavors into the young wine which can become very dominant, leading to piercing taste sensations, overpowering the varietal character of the grape. Open-minded producers like Alois Kracher have come to the conclusion that the secret of making great dessert wines lies in preserving primary fruit aromas in spite of botrytis. In this wine the Muscat Ottonel comes through perfectly. Those who are lucky enough to have this wine in their cellars should keep it for another 15-20 years.

Weingut Hermann und Martha Krutzler

7474 Deutsch-Schützen 84
Tel. (03365) 2242

Promotional literature describes the quaintly sleepy Southern Burgenland (Süd-Burgenland) as 'Idyllic Wineland'. The main varieties grown here are Blaufränkisch and Welschriesling. The steep slopes of the Eisenberg mountain which forms a south-facing arena for vines, and sites around Deutsch-Schützen are excellent for growing red varieties, although in the past the area's true potential was seldom evident due to excessively high vineyard yields and careless or wrong vinification methods. In the meantime Hermann and Martha Krutzler have thrown new light onto the region, producing excellent, characterful Blaufränkisch and Zweigelt with the help of their sons Erich and Reinhold. The inimitable, earthy-spicy bouquet, the "goût de terroir" is found only here in Eisenberg and Deutschsützen sites. Its nuances of iron and truffle induce a very individual in character, though with increasing maturity the earthiness begins to yield. The best Blaufränkisch receives a small dose of Cabernet Sauvignon, though never more than 15°, to enrich it with more concentration and tannin. It is a very successful combination and yet another example of how traditional Austrian and international varieties go well together. There are no immediate plans to make a varietal Cabernet.

Blauer Zweigelt Ried Weinberg 1990 🍇 ①
This mass-producing variety only yielded 45 hl/ha resulting in a concentrated, complex and potentially elegant wine. Ruby-red and rich in aromas, its earthy-spicy character make it a very unique wine. Already drinking well, it will keep for several years.

Blaufränkisch Alter Weingarten 1990 🍇 ①
Elegant almond aroma on the nose, mature and delicate with fine, raspberry fruit on the palate, generous and fine with lots of soft tannin on the finish.

Blaufränkisch 🍇 ②
Cabernet Sauvignon 1989
Spicy on the nose with a nuance of black truffle and cassis, complex, mature and rich, a big and unique barrique-aged red wine with a long future ahead.

Blaufränkisch Ried Weinberg 1989 🍇 ①
Deep ruby-red, with herbaceous spicy aromas and clear minerally nuances, medium weight, bitter tannins; on the whole still a little rustic though with good potential for improvement over the next few years.

Weingut Josef Leberl

Hauptstraße 91
7051 Großhöflein
Tel. (02682) 34853

"My time has still to come" was Josef Leberl's standard response when his wines evoked even the slightest criticism. It was always gentle, well-meant criticism, as for about 10 years now his wines have ranked among Burgenland's best. Together with his neighbor and hero Anton Kollwenz, he has been a pioneer in improving red wine vinification, an area in which much was learned during the 1980s. He is probably his own severest critic and has tried hard to put more muscle and elegance into is sometimes rather light reds, modelling them on Bordeaux. With the 1990 and 1991 vintages he made an important stride forwards, partly due to investment in modern fermenting equipment and partly due to more of his own vineyards coming into production, making the business free from the necessity to buy in grapes. Occasionally, when climatic conditions permit, he makes sweet wines up to Trocken-Beeren-Auslese level. His 1988 Sauvignon Blanc Beeren-Auslese and Sämling Eiswein have become legendary, and the 1991 Auslese, high in alcohol and still in cask is a sweet wine which Leberl expects to do more than stand up to Sauternes.

Sämling Auslese 1990 🍇🍇 ②
Refreshing, almost exotic scent of kiwi and pineapple, very intense on the nose with great delicacy. More fruit than botrytis and very good interplay between sweetness and acidity. An excellent sweet wine in the Auslese class and the perfect match for goose liver. Another five to ten years' aging is almost a must.

Blaufränkisch 1990 🍇 ①
Very fruity, firm and elegant. The barrique flavor has been carefully dosed. A fine Blaufränkisch typical of Leberl's house style. Ready for drinking in five to eight years.

Cabernet Sauvignon 1990 🍇 ③
Beautiful deep ruby-red, on the nose youthful and slightly herbaceous, medium-bodied, still restrained at the time of tasting, but already very elegant. Best to wait until 1995.

Zweigelt 1990 🍇 ②
Oak-aged, very intense and spicy on the nose, tightly knit with smoky flavors and intense fruit on the palate. Interesting balance between the wine and oak, which will take another two or three years to become better integrated.

Kommende Mailberg des Malteser Ritterordens

Mailberg 2024
c/o Lenz Moser-3495 Rohrendorf bei Krems
Tel. (02732) 85541
Fax (02732) 85900

When Laurenz Moser took over the Castle of the Order of the Knights of Malta estate in the 1960s, he gained a wide scope for experimentation. Ecological wine-growing was practiced here on a large scale and, true to his pioneering spirit, Moser started using barriques as long ago as 1978 Red wines have greatly contributed to the estate's reputation, especially the Cabernet Sauvignon and Merlot cuvée and their Pinot Noir. Among whites Chardonay and Sauvignon Blanc enhance the local production which otherwise is dominated by Grüner Veltliner. The latest addition to the range is a sparkling wine made from Veltliner. Altogether their innovative spirit and continuous strive to improve quality both in the winery and vineyards leave hope for tasting increasingly better Malteser wines in years to come. Their reds have already become a yardstick by which other estates measure their success.

Grüner Veltliner Ried   ☙ ①
Hundsschupfen Kommende Mailberg 1990
Bright yellow colour, with a clear varietal nose, complex and ripe. Fruity and lively on the palate, marvellously balanced, very soft thanks to the ripeness of the grapes. The best vintage from this vineyard since 1979. A wine that perfectly embodies the area's typical Veltliner style.

Blauburgunder   🍇 ②
Kommende Mailberg 1989
Typical Pinot aromas with soft and delicate almondy nuances. Very mellow, tannins are still hidden, an elegant Pinot Noir requiring further bottle-aging.

Cabernet Sauvignon Merlot   🍇 ②
Kommende Mailberg 1989
Very elegant and fresh though still very closed. Wild berry aromas with a nuance of vanilla, complex and subtle; full-bodied, boding well for interesting future development.

Weingut Mantlerhof

Hauptstraße 50
3494 Brunn im Felde
Tel. (02735) 8248

Josef Mantler's vineyards are planted on terraces of loess soils which were deposited by the wind during the ice age and are very unique in Europe. They are a dominant characteristic of the vinescape around Gedersdorf and produce very opulent, ripe Grüner Veltliner wines, while Rieslings are suppler and more open than their Wachau counterparts. Mantlerhof owes its solid reputation to consistently high quality and also to a grape variety which the present owner's father cultivated with care, the Roter Veltliner. It is unrelated to the Grüner Veltliner and not a red variety as the name implies. Due to its unreliable behavior many growers have abandoned it and as a result it has become rare. Being a mass producing vine, the prerequisite for attaining high quality is short pruning and severe reduction in yields by thinning out the grapes. In good years Roter Veltliner produces meaty wines with unmistakable spice and is one of Austria's most expressive varieties. Those who have been fortunate enough to taste mature Mantlerhof wines will attest to their longevity. We fondly remember the 1954, 1959 and 1961.

Chardonnay Erste Lage 1991   ☙ ②
Traditional aging without new oak. Fruity acidity, fresh, firm, racy and stimulating with a touch of class. A successful version of the increasingly popular 'Chardonnay, yes - barrique, no' trend in Austria.

Grüner Veltliner Erste Lage   ☙ ②
Ried Spiegel 1991
The first yield from a newly planted vineyard. Muscular, concentrated with a good acid backbone. A worthy successor to the great Mantlerhof Veltliners from the Spiegel site.

Roter Veltliner   ☙ ②
Qualitätswein 1988
The estate's standard-bearer. Smoky, powerful, strong and warm with plenty of alcohol, full and lush. Power, botrytis flavors and acidity are slowly melting into one. Potential to age for decades.

Grüner Veltliner Auslese   ☙ ②
Ried Spiegel 1986
The last vintage before the vineyard was uprooted. A powerful wine with 15.3 % alcohol, and a few grams of residual sugar. Intense yellow colour, bouquet characterized by botrytis. Extremely full-bodied and substantial; sweet thanks to weight of body and residual sugar. An extraordinary Veltliner with well defined botrytis and great potential.

Franz Mayer

Heiligenstädter Pfarrplatz 2
1190 Wien
Tel. (0222) 373361
Fax (0222) 374714

Many tourists believe the connection between Vienna and wine to be limited to the anonymous liquid served without too much ceremony in Heurigen, the typical cellars-cum-wine taverns of the Austrian capital. However, Franz Mayer has proved that it can be much more than this. His legendary Heurige called Mayer am Pfarrplatz is not not so much a tourist spot as a meeting place for prominent people and a point of reference for discerning wine lovers. The cellar is also well-stocked with numerous mature vintages and it is still possible to buy an 1983 or a 1973. Franz Mayer is fundamentally a wine-producer and owns Vienna's largest wine estate which has all its vineyards within the city limits. Under the direction of his son-in-law, Mario Galler, the estate produces varietals such as Grüner Veltliner, Riesling, Traminer, Sauvignon Blanc, Pinot Blanc (Weissburgunder) and Chardonnay. They also make a traditional wine called Gemischter Satz, from an old vineyard planted with several varieties, all harvested and vinified together. The best sites are Ried Alsegg at Wien-Dornbach, Ried Nussberg plus the Preussen site, which in 1991 produced an amazing Riesling.

Alter Satz Nußberger Kabinett 1991 ♈ ①
Made from Riesling, Binot Blanc, Neuberger, Spätrot-Rotgipfler and Grüner Veltliner, all harvested and fermented together. Very complex due to number of varieties, dry and very good with food.

Chardonnay Spätlese 1990 ♈ ③
Rye bread and slightly earthy and metallic on the nose. Harmonious in spite of high alcohol with a sweet, fruity character, good weight and will develop further.

Nußberger Traminer Auslese ♈ ③
Kaiser Probus 1990
Reddish reflections produced by this grape variety which turns pinkish-red when ripe. Typical Traminer spice well-evident on the nose, full, rich and long.

Rheinriesling Kabinett ♈ ②
Ried Nußberger Preußen 1991
Light yellow, rich on the nose, sweet with all the characteristics of ripe grapes. On the palate strong and harmonious. Very young but already signs of developing elegance. The best Ried Preussen Riesling made in recent years.

Weingut Ludwig Neumayer

Inzersdorf 22
3130 Herzogenburg
Tel. (02782) 2985

Ludwig Neumayer, together with his brother, Karl, decided to produce premium wines in 1985, the year that the Austrian wine market was violently shaken by the adulterated wines scandal. He could not have chosen a better year, since 1985 produced excellent wines from a very low-yielding harvest. The Neumayer brothers suddenly emerged from anonymity, and from one year to the next the well-known wine region near St Pölten, previously known for mass production of ordinary wines, finally had its very own premium producer. Their success continued the following year with the excellent 1986 dry whites, well-balanced with high-alcohol (over 14%), and this small estate soon found itself ranked among the best in Austria. Their most interesting wines are full-bodied Pinot Blancs (Weissburgunder), Chardonnays, and Grüner Veltliners, especially from the excellent Zwirch vineyard. It is still too early to evaluate (after only two vintages) the Riesling which was recently planted on limestone soil in Inzersdorf which imparts a 'chalky' flavor to the wine. Future plans include planting Sauvignon Blanc which currently is very popular among Austrian consumers.

Chardonnay ♈ ②
Der Wein vom Stein 1991
An unoaked Chardonnay with 13 percent alcohol. Opulent on the palate with good fruit and weight. Long on the finish. Potentially a very elegant wine - needs time.

Riesling Der Wein vom Stein 1991 ♈ ②
Not a particularly complex wine but clean and elegant; on the palate fresh, pleasant and uncomplicated. A wine to be drunk over the next five to six years.

Weißburgunder ♈ ②
Der Wein vom Stein 1991
Subtle, delicate, typical varietal aroma; full, good weight with lively acidity, and firm, ripe structure. Already drinking well and promises to improve with bottle age.

Weingut Josef Nigl

Priel 8
3541 Senftenberg
Tel. (02719) 2609

This estate is located on the plateau that dominates the valley of Krems, a calm and secluded area not easily discovered by tourists. The primative rock on which the terraced vineyards are planted and the climate, characterized by considerable temperature differences between night and day, combine to create growing conditions similar to those of the Wachau. This probably explains the fresh, fruity character of the Veltliners and Rieslings from the Pellinge, Hochäcker and Rammeln sites. The trend was set by young grower and wine-maker, Martin Nigl, with his 1988 Ried Hochäcker Rieslings, comparable to any of the best of the Wachau. Since then this small estate's wines have found their way into Austria's finest resturants. The extremely full and elegant 1990 and 1991 Rieslings have proved worthy successors. Apart from the Senftenberg sites, Nigl's family owns more vineyards near the city of Krems, including the excellent Kremsleiten and Weinzierlberg. They also make other interesting products, like the sparkling wine made from pas dosé Grüner Veltliner and a pleasant round Riesling grappa.

Kremser Grüner   ♀ ②
Veltliner Spätlese 1991
A complex wine, showing the finesse Veltlliner can attain when made from sufficiently ripe grapes.The high alcohol (13.4°) is well-integrated. Opulent, long, ready to drink in ten years.

Riesling Ried Kremsleiten   ♀ ③
Privat 1991
Sweet and intense bouquet. On the palate still restrained but full-bodied with high alcohol, full and long. Has the potential to age at length, should not be opened for another three or four years.

Kremstaler Urgesteinsriesling   ♀ ②
Ried Rammeln 1990
A wine that was not fully fermented out, leaving about 4 g/lt of residual sugar, and, therefore, by Austrian law must be labelled as "halbtrocken". Typical Riesling aromas, appealing, very subtle with a hint of sweetness.

Riesling Spätlese   ♀ ♀ ③
Ried Hochäcker 1990
Concentrated nose. Opulent and complex on the palate with an explosion of fruit. Intense and harmonious, 'firey' on the finish. A very nice Riesling with a long future ahead.

Weingut Nikolaihof, Familie Saahs

Nikolaigasse 77
3512 Mautern in der Wachau
Tel. (02732) 82901
Fax (02732) 76440

The owner of this estate, Nikolaus Saahs, is thought of as a wine-growing pioneer and a traditionalist. Though this is partly true, it is not the whole story. The apparent contradiction in terms arises from the way the estate developed. On the one hand he was already making excellent Riesling and Veltliner as far back as 1977, at a time when most of today's top producers had not even dreamed of this kind of quality. On the other, he used an old wood beam press for years and still swears by fermentation in wood, followed by prolonged cask aging. Tradition has always featured prominently at Nikolaihof. Nevertheless, helped by his wife, Cristine, a courageous assistant in building the estate's reputation, Nikolaus Saahs was the first to react to the rise of wine culture worldwide: he introduced packaging which reflected the quality of the contents without going in the 'designer' direction, prices were adapted to international levels, and he was very active in finding suitable sales partners in export markets. The best sites are Im Weingebirge and Vom Stein on the right hand bank of the Danube in the Wachau, as well as Steiner Hund on the left bank belonging to the town of Krems and the Kamptal-Donauland region. Since 1988 Saahs has made a cuvée of various white varieties called Cuvée Elisabeth. Made from perfectly ripe grapes, Nikolaihaof wines are very long-lasting, easily aging 10-20 years when kept in a cool cellar.

Riesling Spätlese   ♀ ③
Ried Steiner Hund 1991
Deeply spicy on the nose and powerful on the palate. Fantastic interplay of fruit flavors, full of charm and finesse. The Hund site produces long lasting wine which need to breathe before serving.

Riesling Smaragd   ♀ ♀ ③
Im Weingebirge 1990
Elegant aromas, characterized by berry flavors laced with apple and peach; round and appealing on the palate where light residual sugar (just over 4 grams) is well-integrated. A wine which will peak after five or even ten years in bottle.

Riesling Smaragd Vom Stein 1990 ♀ ♀ ③
Perfumed and complex, concentrated with racy acidity. Firm and ripe Riesling, full of nuances from the aroma through to the finish. Great potential for further development.

Weingut Anita und Hans Nittnaus

Untere Haupstraße 49
7122 Gols
Tel. (02173) 2248

Ecological wine-growing, low yields and white wine fermentation in stainless steel tanks are normal standards for Hans Nittnaus and most other Austrian producers who aim at making premium-quality wines. He is typical of the new generation of ambitious wine-growers who measure their success by international standards. He is very intent on pointing out that the best sites at Gols are not in the flat plain to the east of Lake Neusiedl called Seewinkel. He first attracted attention with his meticulously-vinified dry white wines. Even the most experienced tasters would have difficulty in recognizing his characterful, complex Rieslings and Sauvignon Blancs as Austrian. But the area still needs to work hard at creating an image for this kind of quality. In recent years he has also produced muscular red wines, especially from Blaufränkisch and Cabernet Sauvignon and made his breakthrough with the superb 1990s. Genuine skill manifests itself when a producer manages to make good wines in ordinary vintages, as in 1991, when Nittnaus made a very weighty and concentrated Blaufränkisch.

Sauvignon Blanc
Ried Altenberg 1991
A wonderful Sauvignon Blanc, non grassy but rich;good extracts with racy, crisp acidity; international in style yet with typical 'terroir' character.

Ausbruch 1989
Made from Welschriesling, Sauvignon Blanc and Pinot Gris. Very high in alcohol at 15.5°, sweet and held together by a very strong backbone of acidity. Opulent on the palate, enormous intensity of fruit and botrytis aromas. Drink well after the year 2000.

Comondor Qualitätswein 1990
Made from 60% Cabernet Sauvignon and 40% Blaufränkisch, aged for one year in new oak. Dark ruby-red, with the aroma of ripe Cabernet. On the palate sweet, full-bodied, complex and long. Great cellaring potential.

Pannobile Qualitätswein 1990
A cuvée made from 60% St Laurent, 30% Cabernet Sauvignon and 10% Blaufränkisch, aged for 12 months in oak. Dark ruby-red, refined and delicate on the nose, full-bodied but not heavy; very elegant.

Cabernet Sauvignon
Qualitätswein 1989
Still closed, powerful and austere with berry and cassis aromas. Tannic, weighty, warm with well-integrated oak. Great aging potential.

Weingut Roman Pfaffl

Haupstraße 24
2100 Stetten
Tel. (02262) 46323
Fax (02262) 62246

This estate developed from humble beginnings on the outskirts of Vienna and made its first hit with superb Veltliner wines. Formally an insider tip, Pfaffl has become one of the rising stars on the Austrian wine scene. The increasing demand for his wines has enabled him to gradually add new sites to the estate. In addition to the original Veltliner, Welschriesling and Zweigelt varieties, he now produces Sylvaner, Chardonnay and Cabernet. The first Chardonnay vintage came from the neighboring village Münichsthal where Pfaffl has recently bought a vineyard in a superb site. In this vein the estate's vineyard area is set to double in the near future. Pfaffl, a self-made-man, is a quiet but very active quality fanatic who has managed to come up with concentrated wines full of character on a regular basis without availing himself of modern technology. When the new winery, now under construction, is finished we can look forward to even finer wines from this estate.

Grüner Sylvaner Kabinett 1991
A level of acidity unusual for this variety has produced a very attractive Sylvaner. Experience dictates that it is best drunk young.

Grüner Veltliner
Rieden Hundsleiten & Sandtal 1991
Deep, very ripe fruit on the nose. On the palate quite opulent, a characteristic of the very good 1991 vintage for Veltliner. Full with a long finish.

Zweigelt 1989
A complex aroma of cherries and roses and very slightly tarry; sweet fruit and supple, soft nuances of red berries. A weighty barrique-aged red with accentuated vanilla on the finish. Fine, almost Pinot Noir character.

Weingut Franz Xaver Pichler

3601 Oberloiben 27
Tel. (027328) 85375

This estate's incredible rise to fame during the 1980s made an enormous impact on wine culture in the Wachau not to mention the whole of Austria. Since at least the 1984 vintage Franz Pichler has progressively improved his products from year to year and now, after a series of sensational wines - first Riesling and Veltliner, followed by the trend-setter Gelber Muskateller and finally Sauvignon Blanc - he can rightly be acclaimed as Austria's N° 1 wine-grower. His powerful Grüner Veltliners from the Loibenberg, Von den Terrassen and Mühlpoint sites have converted many doubters to the intrinsic qualities of Austria's main grape variety. His Rieslings from Dürnsteiner Kellerberg as well as from the Steinertal and Oberhauser sites are superb and always sold out even before the grapes are picked. He seems to succeed in everything, though he insists there is no secret recipe: "You have to make hundreds of decisions every year and always have to start from scratch as the problems are always new. If I don't make any mistakes, then the wine is good."

Grüner Veltliner Smaragd M 1991 ᵽ ᵽ ᵽ ③
The 'M' stands for Monument. Pichler carried out a rigorous grape selection for this wine, made from minute yields. Very concentrated, powerful (13.8° alc), ripe and opulent with an exotic dimension of fruit. A superb wine to admire even more in years to come.

Grüner Veltliner Smaragd ᵽ ᵽ ②
Ried Loibner Berg 19 Terrassen 1991
A selection of grapes from 19 terraces of the Loibner Berg site. Deep, pure fruit on the nose, very concentrated, weighty and ripe - a 'sleeping lion'. Promises to develop great finesse and improve until well beyond the year 2000.

Riesling Smaragd ᵽ ᵽ ③
Ried Loibner Steinertal 1991
Intense Riesling nose, pure concentrated fruit. Fantastic sweet fruit and succulent on the palate with perfectly interwoven fruity acidity. Finesse, harmony and elegance in excess. Already superb in its youth.

Sauvignon Blanc Smaragd 1991 ᵽ ②
Impressive bouquet, ripe Sauvignon aromas with nuances of paprika and cassis. In spite of its power, very fine and long. Finesse derives from very ripe fruit.

Riesling Smaragd ᵽ ᵽ ᵽ ③
Ried Dürnsteiner Kellerberg 1990
Golden yellow shot with green, brilliant and so full in extract that it clings to the glass. Complex and soft on the nose with nuances of rose and pineapple. Powerful on the palate, a combination of power and fruit hitherto unknown in these parts, fantastic weight, great viscosity but still very elegant in spite of the enormous structure. Already very attractive in its youth. Probably the best wine ever produced in the Wachau, which wine freaks can dig deep into their pockets for. This is the climax of several vintages of fine Kellerberg Rieslings. The quality factors? Soils based on primary rock, the microclimate, the fantastic growing season and Pichler's undeniable genious in caring for the vines and subsequently in making the wine. This is a milestone in the Wachau's wine culture.

Weingut Familie Pitnauer

2464 Göttlesbrunn 9-10
Tel. (02162) 8249
Fax (02162) 82497

Wine-lovers have only recently started to take notice of the wine-growing region Carnuntum, to the east of Vienna, and it was Hans Pitnauer, along with a small number of other excellent estates, who first drew attention to its wines. Here, as in so many cases, it was the change-over from the old to the young generation which brought about the rapid upward turn. Building on the foundations established by his father, the innovative Hans Pitnauer constantly searched for ideas and comparisons both elsewhere in Austria and abroad in order to raise the image of his family's estate. After a phase of experimentation, he found his own style by using various varieties of oak for barrique-ageing. The climatic influence of the Pannonian Plain, which produces a similar average temperature as that on the west bank of Lake Neusiedl, enables him to produce very vigorous Pinot Blancs as well as full red wines with an alcohol content of around 13°. His red wines made from Zweigelt (a successful Austrian crossing) are very interesting, which he labels under the name of a rare bird called "Bienen-Fresser" (bee-eater). The monarchistic-sounding cuvée Franz Josef is named after his father and grandfather, who were respectively Franz and Josef, and is kept for three years before release.

Chardonnay Kabinet ♛ ②
Ried Hagelsberg 1990
Intense fruit, still slightly overpowered by the oak. It has enough richness and body to peak in two to three years. Not too heavy in spite of its power. Very promising.

St. Laurent Ried Hagelsberg 1990 ♛ ①
Aroma still quite youthful with cherry overtones, ripe and complex. Full and succulent on the palate, with soft acidity and tannins. A full red with a good future, typical of a varietal known for the longevity of its wines.

Zweigelt Qualitätswein ♛ ①
Ried Bärenreisser Bienenfresser 1990
Intense cherry aroma, still somewhat rough and youthful. Subtle smoky flavours, fresh and tart. An appealing and succulent red, its velvety character is reminiscent of good Pinot Noir. An excellent example of this varietal's qualitative potential.

Franz Josef Barrique Selection 1989 ♛ ②
Rather oaky, medium-weight red wine with the fruit still hidden behind the oak. Airing brings forth interesting nuances and elegance. It wins through elegance rather than power, though still not for early drinking. Should peak in a few years.

Weingut Reinhold Polz und Söhne

Grassnitzberg 54
8471 Spielfeld
Tel. (03453) 2301
Fax (03453) 4180

Brothers Erich and Walter Polz run this Styrian estate which has achieved one of the fastest rises to fame in recent years. After continuously improving their products with each successive vintage they have made a significant contribution towards the newly achieved prestige enjoyed by Southern Styrian (Südsteirmark) wines. Together with those from the Wachau, Southern Styria's whites have become synonymous with purity of fruit and vibrant flavors. The climax of a dramatic upward spiral in quality were the two stunning vintages 1989 and 1990, though they even managed to make excellent wines from the difficult 1991 growing season. Their best wines come from steep sites close to the Slovenian border called Hochgrassnitzberg and Obegg, with their warm soils composed of eroded shells. Their Morillon (Chardonnay) and Sauvignon Blanc from the Hochgrassnitzberg site have made wine history nation-wide as well as in Southern Styria. Their other products like Pinot Blanc, Pinot Gris, Traminer and Muskateller are also well worth trying. New developments include barrique-aged whites and experiments with Blaufränkisch and Cabernet Sauvignon. Newly planted vineyards of their own will shortly come into production, assuring continued excellence in this corner of Southern Styria.

Weißburgunder Kabinett 1991 ♛ ②
Subtle apple and orange aromas, fruity and compact, a full-bodied Pinot Blanc, deeply fruity, lightly structured and already well-developed.

Morillon Kabinett ♛ ♛ ③
Ried Hochgraßnitzberg 1990
Very fine nose reminiscent of bread and apricots; an explosion of fruit on the palate, apricot, melon and also slightly smoky; an excellent Chardonnay typical of the superb vintage.

Ruländer Kabinett 1990 ♛ ②
Fermented in a large, new oak cask. Aroma of red berries, massive and lightly toasty. Smoky and slightly chocolatey on the palate, great charm and elegance, 'firey' and long.

Sauvignon Blanc 1990 ♛ ②
Deep, elegant nose. Powerful, concentrated and racy; compact fruit, elegant and complex. Weighty, making it seem a little sweet, with a long finish and much finesse.

Weingut Franz Prager

3610 Weißenkirchen 48
Tel. (02715) 2248
Fax (02715) 2532

The Prager estate has long been among the best in the Wachau with an enormous quality potential, given the size of its vineyard area. From the early 1980s onwards little was heard of this traditional producer until they made a comeback in 1989. This was partly due to son-in-law and dedicated wine-grower Anton Bodenstein, who has modified their wine-making methods. His efforts have resulted in a series of very good wines. While the Rieslings from the excellent 1990 vintage from the legendary sites Steinriegl and Achleiten are difficult to beat, the have also made good progress with their 1991 Veltliners, especially from the sites Hinterkirchen and Hinter der Burg. Their first Chardonnay vintage, 20% fermented in new barriques, also bodes well for the future. Other plans are to make dessert wines whenever the growing season permits. When talk turns to the best wines of the Wachau, it is difficult to ignore Prager.

Grüner Veltliner Smaragd   ❦ ②
Ried Weißenkirchner Steinriegl 1991
Pleasant aroma, a firm and delicate Veltliner. Complex, harmonious with plenty of fruit. Although a wine for laying down, it is already accessible. Not quite as much weight as the 1990 Achleiten.

Riesling Smaragd   ❦ ③
Ried Weißenkirchner Steinriegl 1991
Tart spice on the nose, peachy fruit dormant in the background. Succulent flavor and power in excess. The small proportion of unfermented sugar - typical of the very ripe 1990 vintage - is not yet fully integrated. Fat, powerful and long.

Grüner Veltliner Smaragd   ❦ ❦ ③
Ried Weißenkirchner Achleiten 1990
Deep, slightly exotic fruit and the very typical nuance of cherry; velvety and supple, full and very succulent; an excellent Veltliner which will benefit from further aging.

Riesling Smaragd   ❦ ❦ ③
Ried Weißenkirchner Steinriegl 1990
Very spicey, with peach nuances, succulent and robust. The considerable residual sugar, from the vintage's very ripe grapes, is not yet well-integrated; rich and lingering.

Weingut Sattlerhof

Sernau 2
8462 Gamlitz
Tel. (03453) 2556
Fax (03453) 4454-4

Wilhelm Sattler left the Wachau in the 1970s to take over his parents-in-laws' estate in Southern Syria, which has made wine since 1887. He began making dry, acidulous wines reflecting the natural growing conditions of the area, which was nothing short of a revolutionary step at a time when chaptalization and deliberately making wines sweet for were the norm. In the meantime, practically all his colleagues in the area have gradually recognized he was right. The result has been a very fast rise of Southern Styria into the top division among Austria's wine-growing regions. Sattler Senior is looked upon as leader in the development of Sothern Styria's wine culture and Sattlerhof as the most successful in the whole region. The Sattlers have always anticipated trends. This does not mean they follow the fashions; in fact, they are usually one step ahead of the competition. They were the first to respond to the trend for light, fresh wines, producing a Welschriesling with only 10° alcohol and were also the first to market a dry Muskateller. While making products like these has become quite normal, at that time they were a break with tradition. They also realized the potential of making Sauvignon Blanc and Chardonnay (called Morillon in Styria) the leading varieties. Together with Klevner (Styrian for Pinot Blanc), they are the estate's main varieties. Since 1990 they have introduced a premium range called Prämiumweine.

Morillon Prämium 1991   ❦ ②
Very fine nose with a multitude of nuances. Medium-weight, concentrated and complex on the palate, very elegant and long. Delicate, very good.

Sauvignon Blanc Prämium 1991   ❦ ③
Very pure, deep Sauvignon fruit with nuances of cassis and complexity. Although the vintage produced lightly-structured wines it is concentrated and long with sweet richness and finesse. Very elegant due to the interplay of concentrated fruit and firm, fruity acidity.

Gelber Muskateller   ❦ ❦ ②
Kabinett Prämium 1990
Grapy and concentrated with deep spice reminiscent of cinnamon and nutmeg. Opulent, youthful and striking. Classy with almost an excess of fruit: a superb example of this variety.

Morillon Kabinett Prämium 1990   ❦ ❦ ③
Multi-layered, subtle bouquet with apple, orange, pepper, tobacco and many more aromas. Concentrated fruit and volume, sweet richness and very long. Has reserves for several years' bottle aging.

Weingut Peter Schandl

Haydngasse 3
7071 Rust
Tel. (02685) 265
Fax (02685) 36012

The Schandl family has been at Rust since 1741 and own vineyards in every significant site around the town. The most important varieties grown are Welschriesling, Neuburger, Pinot Gris, Traminer, Pinot Blanc, Blaufränkisch, Pinot Noir, Cabernet Sauvignon and Cabernet Franc. Peter Schandl was one of the first to grow Cabernet around Lake Neusiedl and is a great red wine enthusiast. However, this estate's great wines are Ruster Ausbruch and Trocken-Beeren-Auslese. The conditions for producing these wonderfully sweet dessert wines from grapes shrivelled by the noble mold Botrytis Cinerea - humidity, sun and wind, though each at the right time - are perfect at Rust. Schandl has a very ecological approach to wine-growing: organic fertilizers, growing vetch and rape between the vines and avoiding herbicides has long been normal practice for him. The results more than confirm he is right.

Ruster Riesling Kabinett 1991   ♀ ①
Full, straw yellow, very unique nose combining classic Riesling aromas with the breath of ripeness and sweet fruit typical of Rust. Very individual, dry on the palate but finishes sweet and has nice acidity to support the fruit. A delicious wine.

Ruster Ruländer Ausbruch 1989   ♀♀ ③
Gold and amber. Very young on the nose with an accentuated botrytis aroma. Well balanced and delicate on the palate, sweet and classy, supple, interwoven with nice acidity. Generous as an Ausbruch should be, with honey aromas. Already very elegant though only at the start of a long life.

Ruster Blaufränkisch 1990   ♀ ①
Dark color and very concentrated, grapey, well-integrated fruit. Full-bodied, plump, generous - a classic Blaufränkisch with sweet richness and, for the uninitiated, very interesting to compare with the style of other growing areas like Mittel-Burgenland.

Ruster Ruländer   ♀♀♀ ④
Ausbruch 1981
Dark amber, with such great viscosity that it clings to the glass. Very complex on the nose, full of nuances in which botrytis no longer has the upper hand, yielding to roasted, coffee-like aromas. On the palate richly sweet, evolved and soft, it lingers for several minutes in the mouth. After over a decade of maturity, the wine has just started to show the first signs of development, becoming nicely woven, more harmonious, noble with unbeatable finesse. The great complexity of this Ausbruch is seldom found in younger wines. In spite of the minute quantity produced, perhaps because the wine world has not yet discovered it. Surprisingly, it is still available at the winery. Ruster Ausbruch cannot be made every year; the important factors are sunny days in late summer, the humidity from the lake and a warm wind to dry out the grapes in the morning.

Weingut Rosi Schuster

Hauptstraße 59
7011 Zagersdorf
Tel. (02687) 8111

Zagersdorf, where this estate's vineyards are located, has produced the oldest evidence of wine-growing in Austria in the discovery of 2,700 year-old seeds from white grapes. However, today the town is best known for its tannic, concentrated reds while white wines play a secondary role. The most typical are those of the Schuster estate, which in their youth are ink-like in color, with a typical, piquant note of morello charry. The tannic background accompanied by soft acidity deriving from malolactic fermentation makes it easy to recognize them in blind tastings. Franz Schuster, a teacher at the Eisenstadt wine-growing school has managed to combine theory with practice to the best advantage. Contrary to the once accepted theory, he believes in intervening as little as possible during wine-making. He was one of the first to understand the advantages of malolactic fermentation and practiced it with his own wines. Alongside Blaufränkisch, the predominant variety in the estate, since 1988 he has made a cuvée CMB mainly from Cabernet Sauvignon and Merlot with a small percentage of Blaufränkisch. They have recently started to produce white wine from St. Margareten, Rosi Schuster's home town, including a pleasant, clean Welschriesling and a very ripe Chardonnay from the vineyard's first production.

Blaufränkisch Classique 1990 ♥ ①
Embodies the traditional wine-making style without barriques. Over-ripe grapes on the nose with an aroma of blackberries and black cherries. Plenty of depth, accentuated fruit, succulent, rich and tannic. Typical Zagersdorf Blaufränkisch.

CMB 1990 ♥ ③
A barrique-aged cuvée made from Cabernet Sauvignon, Merlot and Blaufränkisch, characterized by ivy and black olive aromas with the Merlot component the dominating feature. Still quite closed, compact and vigorous. Harmonious, savoury, bone dry and long.

Pinot Noir 1990 ♥ ②
Its bouquet is rich in nuances, appealing and intense; the aroma hints at the tannin-accentuated style. Firm, compact promising finesse though still rather tough and needs time.

Weingut Sonnhof

Rudolfstraße 37-39
3550 Langenlois
Tel. (02734) 2116
Fax (02734) 2116-11

The three Jurtschitsch brothers have divided up responsibilities at Sonnhof: Edwin is in charge of the vineyards, Paul, the winery and Karl, of marketing. They have developed it into one of the best-known quality estates in Austria without abandoning certain principles, like working the most important sites at Langenlois on ecological lines. The slim to medium-weight, fruity white wine style has become their trademark. Many of these very charming, pleasant wines have become immensely popular in restaurants, like the light Grüve Veltliner or the Grüner Veltliner Langenloiser Hahnkreuz. The fuller, longer-lasting and more complex wines are the Weissburgunder (Pinot Blanc), Grüner Veltliner from the Steinhaus site and the Kamptaler Riesling, as well as their conventionaly-named, barrique-aged Chardonnay Classic which they have produced since 1988. They also made a smashing hit with their first release of Sauvignon Blanc. Among the reds the cuvée Rotspon is the estate's most prestigious, made from Pinot Noir and Zweigelt (a cross between Blaufränkisch and St Laurent). They also make an interesting Merlot 'blanc de noirs', a white wine made from red grapes.

Chardonnay Classic Klassifizierte ♥ ②
Lage 1991
Greenish yellow. Very clean, varietal Chardonnay nose, concentrated, confirmed on the palate. Powerful, almost fat, with a fine thread of racy acidity and very ripe fruit. Will peak in two to three years.

Grüner Veltliner Erste Lage 1991 ♥ ②
Very open, pleasant Veltliner bouquet, clean, supple, medium weight, vary harmonious, round, charming and perfectly developed. Its clear fruit makes it a very appealing young wine.

Sauvignon blanc Klassifizierte ♥ ③
Lage 1991
Clear, pure Sauvignon fruit, very appealing with volume, balance and firm acidity which suits it well. Combines pure fruit flavor with richness and finesse.

Weingut Johann Stadlmann

Wiener Straße 41
2514 Traiskirchen
Tel. (02252) 52343
Fax (02252) 56332

Johann Stadlmann's estate is to the south of Vienna at Traiskirchen. During the 1980s, thanks to his hard work and determination, he became the N° 1 producer of white wines in the Thermen-Region. He was also one of the first to go against popular taste and stick to making dry wines, thereby contributing considerably to express the area's natural identity. The very favorable microclimate and chalky soils on the slopes of the Anninger mountain produce fully ripe grapes every year, resulting in full and harmonious tasting whites. Stadlmann is especially fond of Zierfandler, the rare native variety which only performs well in this area. In the sites Igeln and Mandl-Höh he makes striking dessert wines as well as dry wines from this variety. The same goes for the almost equally rare Rotgipfler, the second most important regional variety, while his very fruity and delicate varietal wines from Pinot Blanc and Riesling are always made dry. The fast disappearing Sylvaner is also occasionally found here. Stadlmann's white wines embody the individuality of the area at a very high quality level and are very different in style to wines from Lower Austria or Burgenland. The keeping quality of his Kabinett and Spätlese wines is also remarkable: Mandl-Höh Auslese is a wine to last for generations.

Weißburgunder Pfaffstättner ♈ ①
Untere Höfen 1991
According to the sugar content of the grapes this is a dry Spätlese. Great delicacy of aroma, complex, intense, round and long. A classic "vin de garde", with all the prerequisites for a long life.

Zierfandler Auslese ♈ ♈ ②
Ried Mandl-Höh 1991
Intense on the nose, pure fruit. Sweet and very well-balanced with a fine interplay between sweetness and acidity. Has potential to keep for over 20 years - a great dessert wine.

Rotgipfler Auslese ♈ ♈ ②
Ried Tagelsteiner 1990
Fine raisiny nose, smoky and piquant. Elegant apple aromas on the palate, intensely fruity and succulent; a dessert wine with muscle and aging potential. Sugar and alcohol perfectly balanced.

Zierfandler Ausbruch ♈ ♈ ④
Ried Mandl-Höh 1990
Golden yellow, deep, honey-sweet nose; very delicate on the palate, perfect harmony, very concentrated fruit and very long on the finish. A milestone in area's long sweet wine tradition. Kept in a cool cellar will last for well over 20 years.

Weingut Georg Stiegelmar

Untere Hauptstraße 60
7122 Gols
Tel. (02173) 2203 - 2748
Fax (02173) 3323

Georg Stiegelmar is in many ways the wine-growing pioneer in the district around Lake Neusiedl and one of the most highly respected in the whole of Burgenland. Even though his daredevil manner and many successes have not endeared him to everybody, today the 50 year-old has plain and simply made it. The road to becoming the most famous wine-grower in the Neusiedlersee area is paved with a series of innovative wines which, in most cases, he was the first to make: a "blanc de noirs" (a white wine made from red grapes), a "Strohwein" (made by laying out grapes on straw mats until they become slightly raisined) and a "Maszlasch" (a sweet wine made by the Tokaj method). He was also a pioneer in working with barriques and in reintroducing the traditional technique of fining wine with egg white, a practice which, until recently, was not explicitly allowed in Austria and therefore forbidden. He was also quick to respond to the trend back to planting vineyards with mixed varieties as well as the international trend towards making white wine cuvées. His son, Axel, spent part of his training period abroad and for a few years now has been helping to coordinate the estate's various activities. An old cask cellar has recently been converted into a magnificent barrique cellar. Axel has been responsible for the red wine Cuvée Anniversaire, which was composed for his father's 50th birthday. Red wines are also Stiegelmar's strength, even if saying so does an injustice to their dry and especially sweet wines. A stop at Stiegelmar's "Heurige" is a must for any wine-lover visiting the area.

Chardonnay Qualitätswein 1989 ♈ ♈ ③
Buttery, creamy and fat on the nose; fine fruit and already well-integrated oak. A full and extremely attractive Chardonnay which has caused a sensation in Austrian wine circles.

Cabernet Sauvignon 1989 ♈ ③
Pure, fine fruit; elegant in style with much charm and already very pleasant to drink, reflecting Stiegelmar's philosphy of making wines for which "you don't have to wait an eternity to enjoy".

Pinot Noir 1989 ♈ ③
Generally one of Stiegelmar's most interesting reds. Muscular, concentrated fruit, meaty, soft and supple. The oak is very well-integrated and the wine should continue to develop for several years.

Weingut Helmut Taubenschuss

Kramergasse 2
2170 Poydorf
Tel. (02552) 2589

This estate is located in the extreme north-east of the Weinviertel on the "Brunnerstrasse", as the vineyard area along the road between Vienna and Brunn is called, and has long enjoyed the position as leader in these parts. The Taubenschuss family made their reputation mainly with their very reliable Veltliner wines. Limiting vineyard yields by short pruning and dramatically thinning out the grapes is normal practice in this estate, while so many others merely talk about it. The plump Veltliners with a breath of "goût de terroir" are at their most expressive from the Maxendorf, Weisser Berg and Blauer Treu sites. Another cornerstone of their success are Pinot Blanc (Weissburgunder) and Chardonnay which attain Spätlese level almost every year. They are also experimenting with barriques. In contrast to the usual white wines of the area Taubenschuss have proved that theirs can improve with bottle age.

Grüner Veltliner Kabinett ♥ ①
Ried Weißer Berg 1991
Clear, delicate fruit, characteristic of classic Veltliner. Succulent, dry and well-knit; slim but surprisingly concentrated and long on the finish.

Chardonnay Spätlese 1990 ♥ ②
Nose of dried fruit, youthful and lively, concentrated and vigorous. Fruit and acidity are slowly beginning to harmonize; has good prerequisites for becoming perfectly round and powerful with maturity.

Weißburgunder Spätlese 1990 ♥ ②
Youthful Pinot Blanc with a soft hint of walnut; piquant and supple though still needs time to come together. Sweet fruit and volume on the palate, might even beat the legendary 1986. Proves what can be achieved in the Brunnerstrasse area by the right viticultural methods.

Weingut Edina und Manfred Tement

Zieregg 13
8461 Berghausen
Tel. (03453) 4101

The untimely death of his father forced Manfred Tement to take over the family estate straight from school, a challenge which he mastered brilliantly in spite of his youth. Having nobody to turn to he developed his own ideas on viticulture and wine-making. This turned out to be a blessing for the wines, as it soon became clear that the wine-maker was not adhering blindly to handed down traditions. They were perfectly clean, reductive and fresh, their pure, deep fruit giving the sensation of biting into fresh grapes, setting them apart from others and making it easy to spot them in blind tastings. One of Tement's strengths is the production of very light, delicate wines with accentuated finesse. His Welschrieslings are exemplary representatives of this much sought-after type of digestible, low alcohol but still characterful style, and he is often said to make the best wines of this kind of wine in Austria. Recently he has been concentrating on getting more body into his wines by adapting viticultural methods to produce a higher degree of ripeness in the grapes. He has experimented intensively on the wine-making side with international methods, such as malolactic fermentation for whites and various forms of barrique aging to make more expressive, better structured wines. His 1989s and 1991s show the benefits of this while still remaining true to their Southern Styrian origin.

Morillon - Weißburgunder ♥ ♥ ③
Ried Zieregg 1990
Very fruity and elegant on the nose, full and subtle, absolutely round, harmonious and fine. Gains in stature from the Chardonnay element. In character a classic Southern Styrian; this brilliance of fruit is difficult to match elsewhere.

Sauvignon blanc Kabinett Rieden ♥ ②
Graßnitzberg und Zieregg 1990
Pure cassis on the nose, clear as a whistle and fresh. Sweetly rich and peppery, great finesse and vigour. Harmonious, racy and complex with concentrated, brilliant fruit. A text-book example of what Southern Styrian Sauvignon is all about.

Weißburgunder Ried Zieregg 1989 ♥ ③
Golden yellow. A little botrytis evident on the nose, vigorous and strong in alcohol; sweetly rich though the varietal character is overpowered by botrytis. With this kind of assertive expression, a true rarity with very good potential for future development.

Weingut Ernst Triebaumer

Raiffeisenstraße 9
7071 Rust
Tel. (02685) 528
Fax (02685) 6431

In the early 1980s Ernst Triebaumer came up with extremely impressive, ripe wines; the vineyards were never a problem but he spent years of experimenting and learning on the wine-making side. His 1985s pointed the way, while his 1986 Marientaler Blaufränkisch was an enormous success, at that time unequalled in Austria and became one of the country's most sought-after reds. In addition to Mariental, the Öberwald site regularly produces very ripe fruit. His love of viticulture has led him to try out varieties like Gamay, Terrano, Nebbiolo and Sangiovese. However, Cabernet Sauvignon and Merlot have gone well beyond the experimentation phase and produced the first wine in 1989. The Merlot especially has proven very successful. His Sauvignon Blanc and Chardonnay are also very impressive dry whites. It goes without saying that he also produces the sweet wines for which Rust is renowned and at a very high quality level.

Weißburgunder Auslese
Ried Öden 1991
Wonderful golden yellow. On the nose very compact, pure fruit accentuating the ripe sweetness. Delicate, vigorous and sweet on the palate, very harmonious with great potential. An excellent sweet wine with a very firm acid backbone (10 g/lt with 13.5° alc).

Ruster Ausbruch 1989
Powerful, rich with lots of botrytis; stunning on the palate with opulent sweetness in spite of its 17.7° alcohol which is noticeable but does not disturb the overall harmony. An Ausbruch of this stature is extremely rare.

Blaufränkisch
Ried Mariental 1990
On the nose very concentrated and full, elegant with sweet, clear fruit. Powerful on the palate with firm tannin but still soft, supple, complex and long. A worthy successor in a line of superb wines going back to 1985.

Cabernet Sauvignon Merlot 1990
Deep, concentrated. Rich fruit which marries well with the ripe volume of flavor. Very vigorous and well-knit. When the vines become mature this wine is bound to reach a high international standard. Drink after 1995.

Weingut Paul Triebaumer

Neue Gasse 18
7071 Rust
Tel. (02685) 6135

At the beginning of the 1980s, Paul Triebaumer was slightly over-shadowed by his more famous brother, Ernst. This was unfortunate, as he has repeatedly shown his ability to produce wines in a very different style all of his own. He is a Pinot Noir specialist, a very difficult variety in Austria, though Paul Triebaumer's from the Turner site are among the country's finest. He also attains excellent results with Blaufränkisch, especially from the Pandkräftn vineyard. In 1992 he also made a Nebbiolo from vines planted experimentally in 1987. This highlights the family's joy in experimenting, though they have even greater hopes for Syrah, a variety which son Günter learned to appreciate during his practical studies in South Africa. With white wine Paul is perhaps a little ahead of his brother, and his Chardonnay and Pinot Blanc are very reliable with crystal clear fruit. The Triebaumers are also staunch upholders of Rust's traditional sweet wines, especially Ausbruch and Trocken-Beeren-Auslese. The 1981 Neuburger Trocken-Beeren-Auslese from the Turner vineyard, kept in wood for six years, can take its place alongside the absolute best of its kind. Their Keltenwein (Celtic Wine) a dry, fresh white is also much more than a curiosity, and, according to Paul Triebaumer, it is made in a completely natural way using pre-Roman methods.

Ruster Muskateller
Beerenauslese Ried Pandkräftn 1991
Rich golden yellow; full Muskateller fruit on the nose, superb, subtle and great finesse. On the palate a whole range of flavors, though dominated by the aromatic Muskateller fruit. The high alcohol (14.5°) is perfectly integrated. A perfectly balanced wine.

Ruster Ausbruch Neuburger
Ried Turner 1989
After two years in cask it has developed a perfect Ausbruch nose reminiscent of wallnuts and rye bread; smoky and caramelly. Strong alcohol is balanced by good acidity but slightly dominates over the fruit. Very firm and compact, will keep for decades. A truly great dessert wine.

Ruster Ausbruch Neuburger 1981
Cask-aged for six years. Dark amber in color, tremendous viscosity in the glass; smoky nose, some maturity, and the botrytis aroma is well-integrated. Very concentrated on the palate, sweet, fantastically rich with finely interwoven acidity and rare finesse. An extraordinary wine with all the virtues of a great Ruster Ausbruch.

Pinot Noir Kabinett
Ried Turner 1989
Very evocative nose with a gush of aromas of raspberry, roasted almonds and a nuance of botrytis in the background. Spans a whole spectrum of flavors, well-knit and deeply fruity with just a hint of new oak. Austria's best Pinot Noir?

Weingut Familie Umathum

Sankt Andräer-Straße 7
7132 Frauenkirchen
Tel/Fax (02172) 2173

The young, self-confident Josef Umathum has been one of Austria's sudden hits. Since 1985 he has caused a lot of excitement in Austria with a variety of very different wines. Most have been reds, of such elegance as had never been seen before around Lake Neusiedl apart from Georg Stiegelmar's. The most amazing thing about his career is the way he has managed to raise the quality of his wines from year to year, an astonishing feat considering the jump from the excellent1990 to the poor 1991 vintage. His philosophy of ecological wine-growing together with investment in very efficient fermentation equipment have largely contributed to his success, though the most decisive element is Umathum's flair, intuition plus a clear idea of style and how to achieve it, both in the vineyard and in the cellar. With white wines, with the possible exception of Willi Bründlmayr, there is nobody who can match him for dry Pinot Gris. His Pinot Cuvée, a mix of Chardonnay, Pinot Blanc and Pinot Gris is always a round, very fruity, powerful and succulent white which, a few years ago hardly anybody thought possible in this area. Among the reds his Cuvée Hallebühl has been the star, aged in new oak for almost two years and made from Blaufränkisch and Cabernet, though the structure comes from Zweigelt, an Austrian crossing of Blaufränkisch and St Laurent and this wines main component. His St Laurent has also been taken for a Pinot Noir from Côte des Nuits.

Pinot Cuvée Kabinett 1991 ❦❦ ②
A cuvée of Pinot Blanc, Pinot Gris and Chardonnay. Smoky and firm aromas of meadow flowers and toast, full and meaty in flavor, well-balanced and long. Disproves that white wines must come from single varieties.

Beerenauslese 1989 ❦❦ ③
A dessert wine made from Welschriesling and Pinot Gris, aged in small new oak barrels. Amber and gold, deeply colored; enormously rich on the palate, compact and multi-layered complexity. Powerful on the palate, very sweet in spite of 14° alcohol, lively acidity and very, very long finish.

Ried Hallebühl 1990 ❦ ③
Lovely ruby red; elegant, already developed on the nose with morello cherry and a very nice hint of Cabernet. Medium-weight and thus elegant, complex and long.

St. Laurent vom Stein 1990 ❦ ③
Ruby red, typically soft and elegant St Laurent fruit. Well-knit but not a heavy wine. Promises to develop great elegance. Open, soft and supple with great length. Very well made.

Weingut Franz und Martina Weninger

Florianigasse 11
7312 Horitschon
Tel. (02610) 2531
Fax (02610) 216550

Franz Weninger has influenced wine-growing in Mittel-Burgenland in many ways: on the one hand as largest vineyard owner in the area and on the other, through his courage and spirit of innovation. He took time to study various techniques of growing and making red wines including differing methods of barrique-aging. Although during this phase he was often accused of offering a chaotic range of too many different wines he carried on with determination. His reward is a high degree of expertise, a virtue which is expressed in the wines. Mittel-Burgenland, with its main variety, Blaufränkisch, does not produce wines with the same degree of ripeness and generosity as vineyards around Lake Neusiedl. However, the heavy, clayey, cold soils retain water, and, therefore, in hot, very dry years they can produce superb red wines. Wines from Horitschon vineyards are characterized by a fine spiciness which can seem austere and unpleasant when they are young, but the Blaufränker mellow with bottle age, becoming similar to Pinot Noir. On the subject of Pinot Noir, trials with this variety and Cabernet have been in progress for several years and the first results are very encouraging.

Blaufränkisch Kabinett ❦ ①
Ried Hochacker 1990
Dark ruby red. Very characteristic Blaufränkisch fruit with appealing depth. Full-bodied, accentuated fruit, harmonious. A text-book example of Blaufränkisch aged in traditional, large casks.

Tinavera Blaufränkisch 1990 ❦ ①
Very dark. Vigorous, deep Blaufränkisch fruit, youthful aromas. Good weight, tough and long. Still very closed but has good reserves to age into a very harmonious wine.

Veratina Cuvée 1990 ❦ ②
Dark ruby-red, delicately spiced and intense, well-knit but still closed, with firm acidity hinting at future elegance. Should not be drunk before 1995/96.

Cabernet Sauvignon 1988 ❦ ②
Barrique-aged. Fresh hay and redcurrant aromas still slightly overpowered by new oak. On the palate smoky and still rather restrained, a little too light in body.

Weingut Robert Wenzel

Haupstraße 29
7071 Rust
Tel. (02685) 28

Robert Wenzel is the great master craftsman of Rust's sweet Ausbruch wines, though his skill in making noble dessert wines often distracts attention form the excellent dry white and red wines which he also produces, like most other estates at Rust. His dry Sauvignon Blanc and Furmint are a veritable enrichment in Burgenland's wine spectrum in the way they beautifully embody the region's rich, harmonious style. He is also a driving force behind the renaissance of historic local varieties such as Gelber Muskateller and Gelber Furmint, though Sauvignon Blanc is another variety on which he plans to focus and it has been present in his vineyards for over 40 years. In addition, like his ancestors he of course concentrates on Rust's traditional sweet wines. This entails observing the weather conditions during the growing season to recognise the arrival of a 'sweet wine year' well in advance of the harvest. First of all, the harmony between sun, summer rain, followed by warm autumn rain and sunshine, then the all important mist from the lake, all of which combine to produce the right conditions for the appearance of noble rot. Wenzel's sweet wines, whether they be Beeren-Auslese, Ausbruch or Trocken-Beeren-Auslese are among Austria's finest and can take their place alongside the world's greatest sweet wines.

Ruster Ausbruch Cuvée 1990 🍇🍇 ③
Delicate aroma of quince and flowers. Only a hint of botrytis on the palate; fresh aroma of honey and citrus fruits. Original and at the same time classic.

Ruster Ausbruch 🍇 ④
Riesling x Sylvaner 1989
Riesling x Sylvaner = Müller Thurgau. Full golden yellow with intense fruit aromas combined with rich botrytis; very sweet on the palate and relatively low in alcohol (11.9°).

Blauburgunder Beerenauslese 1989 🍇 ③
A red dessert wine is very rare around Lake Neusiedl. Very light color due to botrytis. In the first instance the varietal character is evident on the nose, then becomes quickly overpowered by the botrytis. Magnificent on the palate, powerful with high alcohol. Very individual.

Ruster Furmint Ausbruch 🍇🍇🍇 ④
Ried Satz 1989
Golden orange in color, enormous viscosity as it sticks to the side of the glass. Very accentuated fruit in spite of the concentrated botrytis aroma. Fat, powerful and interlaced with firm acidity. In spite of the high alcohol (14.9°) still very sweet. Perfectly embodies the centuries-old style of Ruster Ausbruch with a magnificent balance between sweetness, acidity and richness. Its life expectancy will only become evident after several decades. An absolutely great wine in the tradition of Lake Neusiedl's sweet botrytis wine culture. Ruster Ausbruch's history goes back to 1681, when the town supplied 500 buckets to the court at Vienna as part of a deal to buy its status as a free city and Robert Wenzel continues to make it in its original form. The Furmint vine is one of its original main components which, thanks to Wenzel, has been rescued from oblivion.

Barbara und Friedrich Wieninger

Stammersdorfer Straße 72
1210 Wien
Tel. (0222) 394106
Fax (0222) 398671

As elsewhere in Vienna, the wine from the Danube's left bank is mainly consumed as jug wine in the city's "Heurigen", small taverns which serve their own wines. This is part of the city's tradition and should remain so. However, in recent years good Heurigen have begun serving quality wine alongside their simple, though often delicious, jug wine. Thanks to the fanaticism of young Friedrich Wieninger, this family has become a very dynamic standard-bearer for high quality in the city. Along with like-minded colleagues like wine-growers Herbert Schilling and Leo Breyer, Weninger has often shown that wines from Bisamberg have nothing to fear from comparison with the much better known Döbling sites. In the Bisamberg vineyards on the Danube's left bank Pinot Blanc and Chardonnay seem to be the most successful varieties, that if the grower and wine-maker is as talented as Wieninger. He gained his know-how and knowledge through resolute studies as well as experience gained working in California and makes all his wines in a clean, fruity, fresh style. Concentration adds the necessary finesse. In the production of red wines (Cabernet in particular) and especially in the use of barriques Wieninger has set new standards in the Austrian capital.

Riesling Kabinett 1991 🍇 ②
Very harmonious, delicate, already completely open and appealing. Not a wine for meditation - pleasant and enjoyable.

Chardonnay Kabinett 1990 🍇🍇 ③
After about a year in medium-toasted Allier and Nevers barriques the cocoa aroma of oak has married well with the subtle, fresh fruit. A compact, muscular and complex Chardonnay with an almost perfect symbiosis of fruit and oak. Great future.

Blauburgunder 1990 🍇 ②
Light ruby. Soft, elegant Pinot Noir spice and a hint of new oak behind. On the palate medium-weight, nice fruit and elegant in spite of its youth. Not an opulent wine but very good Pinot which needs another 4 - 5 years in bottle.

Cabernet Sauvignon Kabinett 1988 🍇 ③
Elegant, young nose in which the varietal fruit and oak are well mixed; very well dosed oak. Morello cherry aroma, complex; opens up with airing. Vigorous and still subtle on the palate. Very full, sweet fruit with soft wood in the background.

Rating System

🍇 An exemplary wine of its type with outstanding local character

🍇🍇 An international premium quality wine

🍇🍇🍇 A Top Wine, considered one of the 150 best wines in the world

The 'grape bunch' symbol is used to indicate the color of the wine; the number of bunches represents the quality rating assigned by the contributor

BULGARIA

Of all the old Comecon countries, Bulgaria is probably the best equipped to deal with the new realities of the Eastern European wine world: the loss of a market willing to take huge quantities of mediocre plonk and the collapse of the state system. The main reason is simple. Bulgaria, alone, already has an established market in the West, notably in Britain. In fact, the U.K.'s best selling red from any country in 1990 was a Bulgarian wine and total exports to Britain today are around the two million case mark. Another reason is that Bulgaria, having been occupied for five centuries by teetotalling Turks, had little wine culture to feel nostalgic about and was quite prepared to go along with the massive state programs set up from the early 1940s on for the industrial production of large volumes of good if rarely inspiring wine. Grape farms tended under socialism to be just part of larger agricultural cooperatives -mainly extended areas on plains for ease of management - and even now that the whole system has been shaken by the introduction of the 1991 Land Reform Act, giving peasants the right to reclaim historic property, most farmers realise that it is in their long-term interest to pull together. As for wineries, they are for the most part massive, very well equipped and rationally planned in the best socialist tradition.

Vines (around 150,000 hectares) are planted in all parts of Bulgaria, which geographically is roughly on a parallel with central Italy, while production is in the area of 3,000,000 hectoliters annually. Grape varieties are a mixed bag of native and western European strains, but Bulgarians, since the 2nd World War have gone farther than most in planting the international varieties. Thus, Cabernet Sauvignon is the most widely planted red variety, with Merlot a strong second and the native Gamza (Hungary's Kadarka) only third. On the white side, Chardonnay, Sauvignon, Welschriesling and Ugni Blanc rub shoulders with Rkatsiteli, Misket and Dimiat.

Bulgaria also possesses an intelligent system of quality classification, starting at the most basic level with Country Wines and Varietals, or Vin de Pays, which are non-vintage, through Reserve and Special Reserve to, at the top, Controliran wines - some 20 or more whose characteristics are precisely defined in the manner of AOC.

Just what will happen in the transitional periods now facing the Bulgarian wine industry is not clear - it will be three to five years at least before it becomes so. There are, of course, dangers in the break-up of the monolith. For example, growers could sell outside their area or even outside the country to circumvent very low prices, leaving the huge wineries underemployed and unable to meet demands or forced to increase prices to the point that demand falls. But Bulgaria's experience of Western markets should, at least, give her a useful head-start over her competitors.

BULGARIA

ROMANIA

EX YUGOSLAVIA

● Varna

● Sofia

GREECE

TURKEY

1	The Balkans
2	Southern Bulgaria
3	Western Bulgaria
4	Eastern Bulgaria
5	Northern Bulgaria

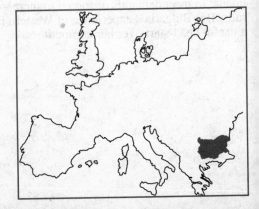

Vinprom Haskovo

Haskovo
Tel. 383 1771
Fax 383 1760

Vinex Preslav

Preslav
Tel. 538 2127
Fax 538 2336

Perhaps more than others in Eastern Europe this establishment is in the throes of radical change, for which reason information on the current situation is difficult to obtain. Although founded as recently as 1944 the Haskovo winery, in the south of Bulgaria, has developed a reputation for producing excellent red wines, being particularily famous for its various Merlots (Sakar, Haskovo and Stambolovo). The proportion of red to white is in fact five to one, the other important variety being Cabernet Sauvignon. Sakar Mountain Cabernet, in particular, has gained itself something of a reputation in Britain. The region, being quite southerly, tends to be hot, in compensation for which high training and thick canopies are employed in the 5,500 hectares under vine. Production is in the region of 175,000 hectoliters per year. The best reds are aged in American oak barriques, the rest in large oak barrels and glass-lined concrete.

Stambolovo Merlot
Spécial Réserve 1986
This wine, aged up to two years in new oak barriques, has a medium deep, mature colou, good berry fruit on the nose and a discreetly oaky, pleasantly soft-fruit palate. There is a certain finesse if something of a lack of concentration. The style is similar to Rioja, for which it has often been taken.

Most of the production in this zone is of white wine, the climate being relatively cool thanks to its Entre-deux-Mers situation between the Danube to the north and the Black Sea to the east. The main grape variety for quality if not quantity is Chardonnay, for which the Preslav complex, with establishments at Khan Krum and Novi Pazar, has gained something of a reputation in the West. Of the two establishments, the better-known is Khan Krum, where the first cold sterile bottling line in Bulgaria was installed in 1979. It has a capacity of 3 million bottles a year. All picking is by hand (partly by dictate of the terrain), and the best grapes are placed in small containers. Care is taken to minimize oxidation between vineyard and winery and only 60% of the press goes into the best quality wines. Fermentation is either temperature controlled by refrigeration units or cold water or in barrel using small American oak barriques, often new. The best wine is also barrique-aged.

Preslav Chardonnay
Controliran 1991
Though tasted at a different time, the note is uncannily similar to the 1990. There is a faint but distinctive varietal bouquet on nose, fair concentration and typicity on palate. It is clean enough but lacks any special character. One feels that, with a little more effort, a much better wine could be produced.

Novi Pazar Chardonnay
Controliran 1990
A dry white of rather faint varietal character of the nose. Clean, to be sure, but of medium concentration at best, fair typicity. Correct but not special - the quality level of a lesser Mâcon.

Khan Krum Chardonnay 1987
Though aged for a few months in barrique this dry white presents no obvious oakiness on nose or palate (probably a good thing). There is, however, a certain biscuity-savoury character, with some of Chardonnay's famous butter; but rather attenuated. The wine lacks concentration, while having good typicity. Considering the reputation, somewhat disappointing.

Vinprom Russe

Russe
Tel. 822 0011
Fax 827 2581

Russe is the name of Bulgaria's fourth largest city and of one of its principal wine-producing zones. Apart from the main winery in Russe, which handles white wine production and bottling, there are cellars also at Dve Mogilli and Bjala (two) specialising in the production of reds. The winery owns no vineyards but processes the grapes of some 3,000 hectares of vineyards in the region. Production figures, with the collapse of the Comecon market, are said to be unreliable. Main varieties are Rkaziteli (white), Cabernet Sauvignon, Merlot, Muscat and Riesling, plus various others. Bulgaria was certainly Eastern Europe's most advanced wine-producing nation under the ancien regime, and both technique and technology at Russe bear this out. Only the first pressing is used for quality table wines. Fermentation is carried out in stainless steel with cooling by water (22° C maximum) and the wines are of a good commercial style.

Welschriesling Misket 🍇 ①
Made from Italian Riesling and Misket, it is a medium-dry white with a light, straw color, a rather non-descript nose and a certain sweetness on the palate, with reasonable balancing acidity. Ultimately, a wine for the mass market, with little character.

Yantra Valley 🍇🍇 ②
Cabernet Sauvignon Controliran 1987
A claret-like, Bordeaux-style red wine of surprising youthfulness despite a mature colou. There is a whiff of blackcurrant on the nose and a wealth of sweet fruit on the palate, lowish tannin, also a slightly low acidity. Very drinkable yet quite refined wine.

Vini Sliven

Sliven
Tel. 442 8342
Fax 442 2388

The district of Sliven, in the south-eastern foothills of the Balkans, accounts for some 20% of all Bulgarian wine production (there are over 10,000 hectares under vine). The winery at Sliven itself is the largest in the land. Up to 500,000 hectoliters were being produced before the market for industrial wine went awry, much of it of the good commercial variety. There is also a small amount of higher quality wine including some Special Reserves which seemed to one expert to have, at first tasting, an unusual finesse. In both quantity and quality terms Cabernet Sauvignon is the most important grape. Indeed, it is estimated that up to 1/3 of all Bulgarian Cabernet passes through the winery, despite the fact that 60% of production is white (mainly the ubiquitous Rkatziteli). Some good Merlot, as well as a bit a Pinot Noir and Chardonnay, is also produced.

Merlot Pinot Noir 1990 🍇 ①
A dry red wine of attractive, youthful, ruby-purple hue. It has ripe cherry fruit on the nose, is soft and easy-drinking, having lots of juicy fruit cut by a touch of tannin and a hint of bitterness on finish. Mild on the acid, it slips down easily.

Cabernet Sauvignon 🍇🍇 ①
Korten Région 1988
This dry red wine has a deepish ruby color with little sign of age. There is an upfront, clean, blackcurranty nose, rich fruit and good balancing acidity, with little astringency despite the presence of some tannin. A wine well made to a popular formula, though not without seriousness.

Vinprom Suhindol

Suhindol
Tel. 610 8797
Fax 610 8697

The town of Suhindol is situated between the Danube and the Balkan Mountains in rolling countryside ideal for red wine grapes. Production is limited to between six to eight tons per hectare (Barolo levels or lower), which accounts for the typicity of both the Cabernet and Merlot wines of this zone. The other main variety, the local Gamza, makes a wine which, with age, develops the spicy character of Southern Rhône. The Suhindol complex controls about 1,500 hectares of vineyard (among other agricultural products) and makes about 100,000 hectoliters of wine a year, most of it Cabernet Sauvignon, for which it has established in a short time a massive following in the West. Amazingly, Suhindol Cabernet was the number one best selling red wine in Great Britain in 1990, a statistic which underlines Bulgaria's huge lead over other emerging wine nations of Eastern Europe in their new search for markets in the West. Let's hope it doesn't give rise to complacency, since there is plenty of room still for improvement.

Gamza Suhindol 1988　　　　🍷 ①
The Gamza of Bulgaria is apparently the Kadarka of Hungary's "Bulls Blood". Here the color is not deep but medium-light, there is a herby (thyme/origan) nose, slightly scented and tomatoey fruit. It is a touch more tannic than Cabernets, also more individualistic and interesting.

Cabernet Sauvignon Reserve 1985 🍷 🍷 ①
A dry red wine of medium deep ruby color, little sign of aging. The fruity style of Cabernet, blackcurranty rather than herbaceous, brings to mind Chile. There is plenty of soft fruit and charm, yet the wine does not lack backbone. Great value.

Vinenka Sabernet Reserve 1985　　🍷 ①
A dry red wine of medium-light color and considerable brightness of bouquet. There is evolved berry fruit and good balancing acidity. You wouldn't call it complex, nor particularly varietal, but it is mature and very drinkable.

CHILE

Chile was exporting wine to Europe as far back as the end of the 16th century. Spanish settlers planted the first vineyards in the mid 1500s, and within 50 years Jesuit and Franciscan missionaries had established an important and solid wine production and sent in large part to Spain. Chilean wines soon became a great threat to Andalusian production and in 1602 King Phillip III forbade the planting of new vineyards in South America. Fortunately this law was not respected but in 1680 the Spanish crown was forced to prohibit the importation of these so-called 'wines of the Indies'. Two centuries later Latin America gained independence, and with it began the New World's wine revolution. The new ruling class were land-owners interested in wine. In 1850 they started sending their sons to France to seek the advice of wine experts on how to build Bordeaux-style wineries and how to substitute local and Spanish grape varieties for the finer Bordeaux and Burgundy varieties. The result is that today Chile's most common varieties are Cabernet Sauvignon, Merlot, Pinot Noir, Malbec (also known in Chile as Cot), Sauvignon Blanc, Riesling, Moscatel and recently even Chardonnay.

Viticulture spread without difficulty, particularly as Chile is practically the only country in the world that has never been affected by phylloxera. In the central-northern regions, in the provinces of Atacama and Coquimbo, areas where rainfall is practically nil, grape-growing is possible only with irrigation. The resulting wines are strong with a low acidity and primarily used for distilling. The central area includes the Aconcagua vineyards and the valley of Maipo, the most versatile and presitigious production region for great reds. Further south vines continue to be grown, although conditions are extreme. Along the Pacific, the central-southern region of Secano is suited to white varietals.

For many years Chilean reds were generally soft and slightly maderized and the whites very tart with high oxidation levels. Only towards the end of the 1970s did a second wine-making revolution take place. The arrival of Miguel Torres in 1979 changed both the concept and strategy of Chilean wines, leading to a vast improvement in quality. The owners of Canepa and Concha y Toro were the first to modernize their wineries by using stainless steel, temperature control and French and American oak barrels. In 1988 Eric de Rothschild, owner of Château Lafite, again altered the course of the history of Chilean wines by purchasing 50% of the Los Vascos winery and by making wines according to the best of French traditions.

Chile's per capita wine consumption has, however, shrunk from 59 lt in 1973 to 30 lt in 1988, and many wineries have closed or replaced vines with other crops. Vineyards have shrunk from 110,000 to 60,000 ha in 1991 and today Chile produces about 300 million lt of wine annually. Exports are on the increase, and in 1991 it exported 66 million lt. This figure is expected to rise to 100,000,000 lt for 1992, one third of the total production.

The quality of Chilean wine is constantly improving. Some reds, especially the Cabernet Sauvignon, are among the best in the world. The recent popularity of Chilean wines does not seem to decline and quality will probably continue to get better despite a few problems that can not be ignored. First of all, there is no legislation in Chile with regards to a Appellation Contrôlée system. It is also not obligatory to show the vintage on the label. The only attempt at defining origin that has been made is a kind of geographic classification of the vineyards, with different production zones identified among the various rivers that flow from the Andes, from the Aconcagua in the north to Talca in the south. There are no labeling regulations so the same wine can be marketed under different names and, worse still, the same label can be placed on bottles containing different wines. Luckily, a few serious producers have individually established their own control systems which are indicated on the label.

Nonetheless, Chilean wine continues to improve and will certainly be able to reach even higher levels of quality when legislation for standards and origin is finally introduced.

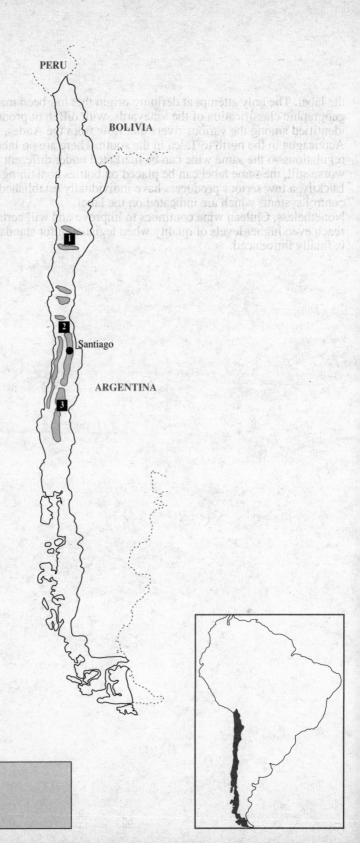

PERU

BOLIVIA

1

2

Santiago

ARGENTINA

3

1   North
2   Central
3   South

Viña Caliterra

Ave. Nueva Costanera 3759
Santiago
Tel. (2) 2422985
Fax (2) 2422987

Viña Caliterra was created in 1989 out of a joint venture between Viña Errazuriz-Panquehue from Aconcagua and Franciscan Vineyards of the Napa Valley, California. It makes excellent wines for export only. Viña Caliterra uses grapes from a small property in Curicò and the rest are bought locally and from Maipo (considered one of the most prestigious Chilean wine districts). The winery produces Californian-style wines for the United States market. Augustin Huneus, one of the owners of Franciscan Vineyards, is originally from Chile but moved to California 20 years ago. His aim is to place premium Chilean wines at the same level as top Californian and French wines. Viña Caliterra's wines are marketed in the United States by Franciscan Vineyards. Winemakers Greg Upton and Jonathan Rodwell, both Californians, are in charge of wine-making. The wines have a modern fruity style and character that meets the needs of the market. They represent excellent value for money. Caliterra's Sauvignon Blanc and Chardonnay are ranked among the country's best.

Caliterra Chardonnay Curicó 1991   ❦ ①
Those who like Californian wines will appreciate this excellent American-style Chardonnay at a third of the price. It has green fruit aromas and is clean and bright. On the palate it is harmonious with a herbaceous finish.

Caliterra Cabernet Sauvignon   ❦❦ ①
Maipo 1989
A great wine with an intense purple-red color. It has concentrated berry aromas and is still evolving. On the palate it is big, powerful and tannic. This is a wine that will improve greatly with age.

Viña Canepa José Canepa

Luis Thayer Ojeda 236 - Piso 6°
Santiago
Tel. (2) 2331311
Fax (2) 2316391

Viña Canepa is one of Chile's best wineries. Founded in 1930 by José Canepa it was one of the first to use stainless steel in winemaking at the end of the 1970s and is currently one of Chile's most modern wineries. The grapes come from estate-owned vineyards located in Maipo near Santiago and further south in Lontuè and Curicò. Some grapes are also bought from growers in the same areas. Varietals grown are Sauvignon Blanc, Sémillon, Cabernet Sauvignon, Cabernet Franc, Malbec and more recently Chardonnay, Riesling, Gewurztraminer and Pinot Noir. Viña Canepa, which is well established on the local market, is increasing exports thanks to an entrepreneurial and far-reaching policy. Viña Canepa's whites, especially the Sauvignon Blanc, are fruity, youthful and fresh and are among the best in the country. Many of the company's wines are marketed under other brands such as Domaine Caperana, Hacienda St. Georges and Canepa Estate, but all are registered as Canepa and indicate the region of origin and in most cases the variety. Among Chilean wines they offer some of the best value for money.

Canepa Sauvignon Blanc   ❦ ①
Maipo 1991
This is an excellent, modern-style wine. It has a bright, lemon-yellow color and intense primary aromas with notes of banana. On the palate it is full with a good lingering finish.

Cabernet Sauvignon Malbec   ❦ ①
Maipo 1989
Made from a Malbec and Cabernet Sauvignon blend, this wine is fruity, fresh and powerful. A modern wine, it is suited to all occasions and is undoubtedly among the best of its kind for the price.

Canepa Finísimo   ❦❦ ①
Cabernet Sauvignon Maipo 1985
This is one of Chile's finest wines and the winery's best. It is a typical Cabernet Sauvignon, deep cherry-red in color with brick tones. It has medium intensity, a direct bouquet and is loaded with herbaceous aromas. On the palate it is full with lingering tannic notes and a lengthy ample finish.

Viña Concha y Toro

Fernando Lazcano 1220
Santiago
Tel. (2) 5567882
Fax (2) 5568425

Founded in 1883, Concha y Toro is today Chile's largest wine producing company and the market leader. Ninety percent of its production is consumed domestically yet it is also Chile's leading exporter in terms of volume. It owns vineyards in Santa Isabel, Puente Alto and Pirque in the Maipo valley, Rapel near Curicò and further south in Mulchén. The winery's transformation began in the 1980s with the introduction of new technology and in 1987 with the use of the first French oak barrels. It regularly seeks the advice of Bordeaux oenologists including, it is said, Emile Peynaud. Under the guidance of winemaker Goetz von Gersdorf the company has started to produce varietal whites, reducing the production of Sémillon, which is popular in Chile, and increasing that of Sauvignon Blanc and Chardonnay. The export wines are among Chiles' best, with quality labels such as Don Melchor, Marqués de Casa Concha and Casillero del Diablo. In Japan the wines are marketed under the Châtau Mercian brand. Concha y Toro is also an important shareholder in the wineries Tocornal, Subercaseaux and Santa Emiliana which exports to the United States under the Walnut Crest label.

Chardonnay Marqués de Casa Concha Maipo 1990
An intense, bright, golden-yellow color, this is a wine for those who love Chardonnay with strong oaky flavors. On the palate it is unctuous, full, polished and big with a slightly bitter finish.

Casillero de Diablo Cabernet Sauvignon Pirque 1984
This is one of the most popular reds for domestic consumption. It has a strong red to brick color and forward aromas with an herbaceous note and an astringent finish. This is a typically Chilean wine made in a traditional way.

Don Melchor Reserva Privada Cabernet Sauvignon Maipo 1987
This is one of the world's great Cabernet Sauvignons made in a typical Bordeaux style although on the other side of the world. It is the first vintage that has been aged for 18 months in French oak (Allier and Nevers). It was racked four times and spent 15 months in bottle before release. It has a good intense dark cherry to red color with brick tones and characteristic oak aromas softened by fruit, vanilla and chocolate flavors. It has a complex powerful structure, lingering and loaded with tannin, and on the palate is aromatic with a good long finish. It still needs time to develop, peaking around 1996-98, when it should fully reveal its magnificient potential.

Viña Cousiño Macul

Huérfanos 979 Of. 704
Santiago
Tel. (2) 6956515
Fax (2) 331520

This Chilean winery most resembles a Bordeaux estate. It was founded in 1554 by early Spanish settlers who planted their vineyards where Viña Cousiño Macul is currently located. This is at the foot of the Andes in the Maipo valley, in a privileged position dominated by the city of Santiago. In 1856 the company was bought by Matias Cousiño, and since then has remained under family control. The first French varieties were planted in 1860 and included Cabernet Sauvignon vines from Pauillac and Margaux and Sauvignon and Sémillon from Martillac in the Graves area. Some Riesling from the Rheingau and Pinot Noir from Burgundy were planted later. Over the last few years Viña Cousino Macul has become one of Chile's most prestigious wine-making companies. It uses only grapes from estate-owned vineyards and carefully controls yields. Under the guidance of winemaker Jaime Rios, a graduate from Bordeaux University, and thanks to the use of the latest technology, this company's wines are constantly improving and should remain among Chile's best.

Gran Vino Doña Isidora
Riesling 1991
A good Chilean Riesling for current drinking. It has a pale yellow color with greenish tints and fruity herbal aromas. On the palate it is full, balanced and pleasing with a clean restrained finish.

Gran Vino Chardonnay 1990
Made from 100% Chardonnay this is one of the company's latest wines. It is well made and has a bright straw-yellow color with intense fruity aromas. On the palate it is harmonious and has a spicy flavor.

Gran Vino Don Matías
Cabernet Sauvignon 1988
This is a typical example of Cabernet Sauvignon made to please local tastes. It has an intense ruby-red color with typical aromas. It is a wine with character having soft fruit with typically varietal tannins and hard finish.

Antiguas Reservas
Cabernet Sauvignon Maipo 1986
This is the flagship wine of this company. Cousino Macul produced some of Chile's best wines long before its competitors started catching up. and thanks to new technology they still continue to lead the field. Antiguas Reservas comes from the first Cabernet Sauvignon vines planted in Chile, on estate-owned vineyards located in extremely adaptable regions. It has a bright ruby color with brick tones and oaky berry-fruit aromas. It is a wine of outstanding character, intense and ripe and loaded with tannins. It has a complex, full finish in true Bordeaux style and a promising future.

Viña Errazuriz Panquehue

Ave. Nueva Costanera 3759
Santiago
Tel/Fax (2) 2422987

About a century ago this estate was probably the largest privately owned winery in the world. It had 700 hectares all owned by Rafael Errazuriz Urmeneta, son of Maximiliano Errazuriz Valdivieso who founded the winery in 1870. At one time Viña Errazuriz owned two underground cellars designed by Bordeaux architects. One of these original cellars still houses the winery which has been enthusiastically run since 1983 by the young Eduardo Chadwick. Errazuriz Panquehue owns two vineyards, one in the valley of Aconcagua, north of Santiago, and the other further south in the Mataquito valley. The valley of Aconcagua, with its well-drained limestone soil, cold winters and extremely dry summers is well suited to Cabernet Sauvignon. The winery's whites come from the Mataquito valley vineyards which have cold, rainy winters and mild summers, more suitable for varieties such as Sauvignon Blanc and Sémillon. The wines are made almost exclusively from grapes grown on estate-owned vineyards.

Sauvignon Blanc Maule 1991
A modern white made to meet international tastes the wine has a pale yellow color with greenish tints and is fruity and aromatic. It is fresh, easy drinking and has a fairly lingering finish.

**Doña Leonor Mataquito
Sauvignon Sémillon 1990**
This is a white made in a Chilean style from a Sémillon and Sauvignon Blanc blend. It has been aged six months in American oak and twelve in the bottle. The color is a bright golden yellow and on the palate it is dry, full and lingering with a slightly hard but polished finish.

**Don Maximiliano Aconcagua
Cabernet Sauvignon 1989**
This is a wonderful red wine that improves each year. It is made from 100% Cabernet Sauvignon and has a limited production. The nose reveals secondary aromas of berry fruit and on the palate it is clean, concentrated, complex and loaded with tannins. This is a powerful wine to keep.

Mitjans

Juan Mitjans 200
Santiago
Tel. (2) 2382511
Fax (2) 2382383

The most important producer of spirits in the country, Mitjans established a foothold in the wine industry with the purchase 40 years ago of a winery. The company has also recently established other production facilities that produce and commercialize a number of different wines under labels that change according to the target market. Founded in 1903 by Juan Mitjans the company purchased Viña Valdivieso in 1950, an old family-run winery originally established in 1872 and the oldest and most important producer of sparkling méthode champenoise. It was also one of the first wineries to plant Chardonnay and Pinot Noir in Chile. Mitjans owns very little land but buys both grapes and must which are processed in one of the four fully-equipped wineries. Its main export brand is Saint Morillon while table wines are marketed under the Casa de Piedra label. Mitjans also bottles wine for other companies under their labels.

Champaña Valdivieso Grand Brut
Labelled as Champagne as the local law allows it this is an excellent sparkling méthode champenoise made from Chardonnay and Pinot Noir grapes. It has a pale yellow color, elegant bead and persistent mousse. It is Chile's most prestigious sparkling wine.

Saint Morillon Merlot 1989
This is a good red made from a varietal seldom used in this country. It has a cherry-red color with purple tints. It is clean on the nose with an elegant aroma of spices and good length on the palate. It is still developing.

**Saint Morillon
Cabernet Sauvignon Reserva Especial 1987**
With its garnet red color this is a Cabernet Sauvignon with a penetrating rich aroma of berry fruit with herbaceous and vanilla notes. On the palate it is complex, balanced and harmonious. A wine that represents good value for money.

Viña Montes-Discovery Wines

Ave. Apoquindo 3507
Las Condes, Santiago
Tel/Fax (2) 2467649

Montes represents one of the oddest partnerships in Chilean viticulture. Here a combination of good wine-making skills and commercial talent have come together to create quality wines even though the estate owns virtually no vineyards. Aurelio Montes was for years winemaker at one of the country's largest wine producers. He then decided to set up on his own in an old abandoned winery called Viña Nogales. Of the wines produced 80% are made from purchased grapes, but Montes knows how to buy intelligently as the results prove. The commercial ability of his North American partner Douglas Murray soon had all the leading US wine magazines.writing about their wines. Viña Montes specialises in Cabernet Sauvignon and Merlot bottled under its own label but other brands include Villa Montes and Discovery Wines. They also produce wines for other clients.

Sauvignon Blanc Curicó 1991
This 100% Sauvignon Blanc is fruity, fresh and light with a clean but not lingering finish. This is the winery's most convincing white.

Cabernet Sauvignon Curicó 1989
A pleasing, modern version of Cabernet for current consumption this wine is loaded with fruit and has spicy aromas. It is well balanced, herbaceous, easy drinking and is excellent value for money.

Cabernet Sauvignon
Curicó Alpha 1988
This is a Cabernet to please North American tastes. It is well balanced and has primary and tertiary aromas of oak and berries. It is firm, polished, has a long finish and is one of the winery's best.

Viña San Pedro

Ave. Vicuña Mackenna 3600
Santiago
Tel. (2) 2382131
Fax (2) 2381747

The winery was established in 1865 in the Lontuè district in Molina south of Santiago on land planted with vines as far back as 1701. The first French varieties including Cabernet Sauvignon, Merlot and Sauvignon Blanc were planted in the middle of the 18th century. In 1907 French oenologist Pacottet developed the world's first system of temperature control for cooling musts. In the mid 1980s, owned by the Spanish company Banesto, the winery began a process of modernization which has made it Chile's second most important producer and exporter of wine. Under the guidance of winemaker Fernando Torres they are experimenting with new varietals such as Chardonnay, Merlot and Syrah. The wines which best represent this winery are Castillo Molina, an excellent Cabernet Sauvignon and Gato de Oro. The two best known commercial brands are Gato Negro and Gato Bianco. Through Vinex the group also makes Las Encinas and Santa Helena.

Las Encinas Vino Blanco Seco
This is an unusual non-vintage wine which is made to resemble Sherry although it is made from 100% Sémillon. It is golden-yellow in color and reveals old oxidised aromas. It is warm and dry on the palate and has a very individual style.

San Pedro Merlot Lontué 1989
An excellent pure Merlot with a bright intense red color. It has sweet fruity aromas, great texture and is harmonious and full with a spicy finish. Good value for money.

Castillo de Molina Lontué
Cabernet Sauvignon 1986
This is a typical Cabernet Sauvignon made the traditional way to meet Chilean tastes. It has a deep garnet-red color with brick tones, intense aromas with a dominance of oaky wood. It is complex and powerful and resembles a Rioja.

Viña Santa Carolina

Rodrigo de Araya 1431
Santiago
Tel. (2) 2382855
Fax (2) 2380307

Santa Carolina ranks among the five largest wineries in Chile. Founded in 1870, the original building was declared a national monument for its architectural design. The wines are good but not quite good enough to deserve such an honor. The company owns vineyards in Maipo and Rapel and five wineries in close proximity with a production capacity of nearly 20 million lt. The current owners proudly display a long list of awards and medals, from Paris in 1889 to Barcelona in 1989 and 1990. Santa Carolina wines are greatly appreciated by Chileans and have a particular taste given by the small barrels in which they are aged. These are made from a local, rather rustic wood called "raulì". One wonders what the results would be if better quality oak was used? Today, although the reds are outstanding, the whites are mostly oxidized and woody, suitable for local palates but far from modern tastes. The winery traditionally ranks its wines with stars, gold indicating the top of the line. Among these the Special Reserva Cabernet Sauvignon is excellent, whereas the Chardonnay still has room to improve.

Chardonnay Reserva 1990   ☷ ①
A good Chardonnay although probably overrated by the awards it has won. Two years in rauli casks have, in this case, given the wine a certain polish; intense straw-yellow, with characteristic bouquet and good balance. A well-made wine that can improve in bottle.

Sauvignon Blanc Reserva 1990   ☷ ①
The winery's first great success with white; this varietal Sauvignon Blanc won a gold medal in Bordeaux in 1991. Quite tart with clear citrus aromas, easy-drinking, not very complex, pleasing.

Cabernet Sauvignon Merlot   ☷ ①
Valle San Fernando 1989
A typical Bordeaux blend, 75% Cabernet Sauvignon and 25% Merlot, bright red color, intense, medium-bodied and well-balanced with individual character, best as a good every-day table wine, well-priced.

Special Reserve   ☷☷ ①
Cabernet Sauvignon Estrella de Oro 1982
Beautiful bright brick-red color, intense aromas and notes of game and fruit. Balanced, tannic wine, harmonious, great texture. Lengthy and complex finish, good maturation.

Viña Santa Rita

Gertrudis Echeñique 49
Santiago
Tel. (2) 2289166
Fax (2) 481406

Viña Santa Rita is one of Chile's largest wineries, ranked second in terms of quantity with Viña San Pedro. Founded in 1883, it was owned by the same family until 1980 when it was purchased by an international consortium. With an investment of over 6 million dollars, the vineyards and 18th century cellars have been modernized. Stainless steel vats for the temperature controlled fermentation of white wines were installed in 1986. The winery is a leading producer of table wines and makes wines for export which have gained international recognition. Reds aged in large barrels made from local wood are aimed at the local market, whereas wine for export is aged in American or French oak. Under the direction of winemaker Klaus Schroeder the company is developing an entrepreneurial export policy aimed at meeting the tastes of international consumers. The wines are undoubtedly well made, with only a third produced from estate-owned vineyards, but lack real character.

Chardonnay 120 Maipo 1991   ☷ ①
A bright, fresh, clean Chardonnay with intense fruity aromas and spicy flavors. In the mouth it is full, balanced, fresh with a big polished finish. A very reasonably priced wine.

Sauvignon Blanc 120 Maipo 1991   ☷ ①
A good example of how to make varietal Sauvignon Blanc. Delicate green fruit aromas, intense and appetizing, soft in the mouth, fresh and balanced with a big lingering finish. Good value for money.

Cabernet Sauvignon 120   ☷☷ ①
Maipo 1988
An excellent Cabernet with aromas of small black berry fruit and oak. Fleshy, moderately tannic, still evolving. One of the best values on the market.

Cabernet Sauvignon   ☷☷ ①
Medalla Real Maipo 1988
A limited reserve that reveals complexity and great class. Polished oaky aromas, fruity background, powerful wine with great tannic structure, yet delicate. Will improve with age.

Viña Tarapaca ex Zavala

Ave. Tobalada 9092 La Florida
Santiago
Tel. (2) 2851735
Fax (2) 2851271

Ask Chileans which is the country's best winery and they will definitely mention Tarapaca ex Zavala. This may be true, according to local tastes, since it has made Chile's top wines for years. Today, despite the introduction of new wine-making processes, temperature control and stainless steel, the wines are rich and tannic and more representative of the old style of wine-making. Viña Tarapaca is currently owned by an international consortium and has the best land in the Maipo valley, very close to Cousino Macul. The land is ideal for planting Cabernet Sauvignon, Pinot Noir and Malbec. If the current owners decide to update the cellar and keep the land they will soon produce wines of a superior quality. However, if they choose to sell the land for building and seek other land further south, the result will be mass production, but not quality.

Gran Reserva Tarapaca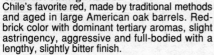
Cabernet Sauvignon 1982
Chile's favorite red, made by traditional methods and aged in large American oak barrels. Red-brick color with dominant tertiary aromas, slight astringency, aggressive and full-bodied with a lengthy, slightly bitter finish.

Miguel Torres

Panamericana Sur km 195
Curicó
Tel. (75) 310455
Fax (75) 312355

Cultivation of the vine in Chile was introduced in 1500 by the Spanish and 470 years later a Spaniard, Miguel Torres, helped revolutionize Chilean wine-making. The Torres family have been making wines in the Penédes area of Spain since the 17th century. In 1979 Miguel Torres purchased some vineyards in Chile, thus changing the history of Chilean wine. He introduced the most avant-garde technology; stainless steel, temperature controlled fermentation, etc, and thanks to his family's century-old grape-growing and wine-making tradition and to the excellent Chilean conditions, started making wines of international quality. These wines were aimed at export markets rather than local consumption. Success was immediate, and other producers soon started following his example. Thanks to Miguel Torres Chilean wine currently occupies a priviliged position. His innovations ranged from new vine-growing methods to bottling procedures giving the Chilean wine industry a new impetus. For marketing purposes he placed more importance on white wines, with excellent results. The winery, managed by Javier Garcia-Berro, currently exports 70% of total production.

Don Miguel riesling 1991
An authentic Alsatian-styled wine made on the other side of the world from Riesling and Gewurztraminer grapes. Delicate and pleasing, floral aromas, very drinkable.

Santa Digna Sauvignon Blanc 1991
The first modern wine made in Chile for the international market. A 100% varietal with light straw-yellow color and greenish tints. The palate is fruity, fresh, youthful, full and persistent.

Brut Nature
A limited production méthode champenoise wine made from 75% Chardonnay and 25% Pinot Noir. Bright, pale yellow color with intense floral aromas, polished and with a persistent mousse.

Santa Digna
Cabernet Sauvignon 1988
A classic Cabernet, aged 15 months in American oak. Dark cherry-red color with brick tones, intense varietal aroma and spicy, vanilla and chocolate bouquet. Firm, polished on the palate, excellent value for money.

Viña Undurraga

Lota N° 2304, Providencia
Santiago
Tel. (2) 2326687
Fax (2) 2341834

Undurraga is a legendary name in the Chilean wine industry. Like many wineries in the country it has had its ups and downs, alternating from good to bad. Once a model winery, Undurraga was subjected to family problems and disputes among heirs and due to this the quality of the wines suffered. Today the winery seems to finally be on the right track in terms of quality, thanks to solid technical guidance and the presence of an English group which between 1976 and 1990 has invested more than 6 million dollars to relaunch the company. The original winery's beautiful colonial mansion, founded in the 19th century in the Maipo valley, was completely restored; everything is new except the land and the vineyards. Under the direction of Chilean winemaker Francisco Ureta Cortés, 70% of annual production is exported. Since 1985 the wines are 100% varietal. There is an excellent Merlot and a Cabernet Sauvignon which improves each year. Viña Undurraga was one of the first Chilean companies to export to Europe and the U.S; wines are therefore readily available in these markets. Check the label carefully and don't be sceptical due to the very low prices - you will not be disappointed.

Cabernet Sauvignon Maipo 1988 🍇 ①
A wine with characteristic varietal aromas of berry fruits, cherries and blackberries with an oaky overlay. On the palate it is full with soft tannins and great finish. Comes close to the Reserve and is excellent value at half the price.

Réserve Sélection 🍇 ①
Cabernet Sauvignon Maipo 1987
Excellent Cabernet, bright cherry-red color with brick rim. Concentrated, intense aromas of fruit and spice. Big, powerful on the palate, round, maintaining a strong tannic structure. A wine to keep.

Price levels

①   up to $ 9.99

② $ 10.00 - $ 14.99

③ $ 15.00 - $ 24.99

④ $ 25.00 or more

The 'ex-cellar', or direct from the producer, bottle prices, are calculated in US dollars and are intended only as an approximate guide

Viña Los Vascos

Isidora Goyenechea 3156
Las Condes, Santiago
Tel. (2) 2326633
Fax (2) 2314373

Viña Los Vascos was established in 1750, but its real growth only began recently when, in November 1988, Eric de Rothschild bought a 50% share in the company that once belonged to the Eyzaguire family. This first French investment in a Chilean company is yielding incredible results. Everything that could be improved was quickly changed, and stainless steel, French oak barrels, temperature controlled fermentation were introduced. New cultivation methods maximized Ceneten valley's excellent microclimates. The winery's vineyards are currently planted to Cabernet Sauvignon (79%), Sauvignon Blanc (15%), Chardonnay (5%) and Merlot (1%). Gilbert Rokvam, Chateau Lafite's technical director, visits the company regularly and says that Viña Los Vascos wines are Lafite made in Chile. Fernando Ureta, Los Vascos' Chilean winemaker, prefers to say that Viña Los Vascos are Chilean wines made the French way. He aims at producing Chile's best wine, and he will succeed since the winery has been improving since 1988. All labels that appear after 1990 are made exclusively under Rothschild's total responsability and control.

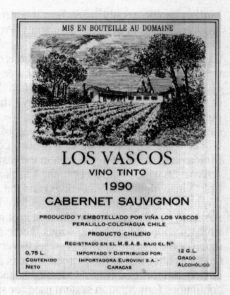

Sauvignon Blanc Colchagua 1990

Impeccably made, 100% Sauvignon Blanc; bright, light straw-yellow color, intense ripe fruit aromas and herbaceous bouquet. On the palate fresh, full with a nice clean dry finish.

Cabernet-sauvignon Colchagua 1989

The 1989 is a typical Bordeaux Cabernet with a fruity background and gamey notes, powerful yet delicate. It has a red-berry color and is loaded with fruit extract. Cassis and tobacco bouquet, delicate aftertaste with a hint of new oak.

Cabernet Sauvignon Colchagua 1990

When talking about this wine remember its vintage date. The investment in this winery in 1988 by the Rothschild group has led to constant qualitative improvements that now place this Cabernet Sauvignon among the world's great wines. The 1990, tasted before being released onto the international market, is loaded with concentrated fruit and spice aromas. Beautiful, intense garnet red color, balanced, complex, refined and elegant, recalls great Bordeaux. Still developing, it will start to reveal its greatness in 1994. A wine to buy now and keep for a few years; undoubtedly one of the best value for money wines around.

CONFEDERATION OF INDEPENDENT STATES

Little is known or published about the former Soviet Union's wine industry, which is quite significant in terms of quantity. Production is around 40 million hl per year, thus, it is the third largest producer in the world. For many years, the producers themselves were largely kept anonymous due to the state system. Most wines were bottled in Moscow regardless of their area of production, with the obvious disadvantages that such distances involved when the level of technology was not of the most advanced and, particularly, when personnel motivation was virtually non-existent. However, there are certain wineries of outstanding merit, and these suggest that, with the necessary support of outside technology, significant results will be achieved in the future. Wine is produced all around the Black Sea, from Moldavia in the west to Georgia in the east, and even further south and east in Azerbaijan which borders both the Caspian Sea and Iran. In fact, presumibly the first "vitis vinifera" vines evolved and the first wine produced in Iran. Throughout this huge region which encompasses Moldavia, the Ukraine, the Crimea, Georgia, Armenia and Azerbaijan production is of red and white, mainly dry natural strength wine and sparkling wines. There are a number of sweet red wines and much of the sparkling wine is sweet to very sweet, and this includes reds as well. On the south coast of the Crimea, there is a unique area which is famous for its dessert and fortified wines. Odessa, located in the Ukraine, is famous for its continuous fermentation system used for sparkling wine production.

CRIMEA

The southern coast of Crimea is one of the most impwortant wine regions of the former Soviet Union. It is home to the Magarach Institute, which founded in 1829, remains the former USSR's foremost viticultural and winemaking research center. The majority of the wines produced in this rather narrow, yet long strip of coastal land, bounded on the one side by the Crimean mountains and, on the other, by the Black Sea, is of the dessert variety. Nearly all are fortified. The result is a wide variety of wines, ranging from the traditional European classics of the last century (or earlier) to some quite remarkable wines, which in their own way are unique and of world class. Generally speaking, most of the wineries live on a hand-to-mouth basis and available vintages will be recent, usually between two to four years-old (most wines spend one to three years in large old wood). Most wine producing areas are basically associated with a winery which takes its name from the area, a local town or perhaps imPortant site: for example, Massandra (a hamlet and the Tsar's winery), Alupka (a famous palace) or Ai-Danil (a village). This is the basic form of appellation. Wines that are produced from a number of different sites are given a more general name such as "South Coast' Muscat. All the wineries detailed here are located on the south coast of the Crimea and with only one exception they all come under the control of Massandra. The structure of the "Soviet" industry is very different to that seen in the "West" and should be seen in such context.

Publisher's note:
Due to the political and economic turmoil and changes taking place in wine producing countries in the former Soviet Union, it has been difficult, if not impossible, in some cases, to obtain current profile information or sample their wines for review. Nonetheless, we wish to provide the reader with a general overview of Crimea's most important wine producers.

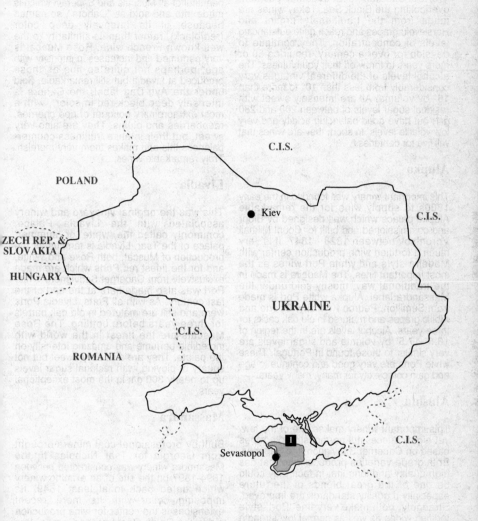

POLAND

ZECH REP. &
SLOVAKIA

HUNGARY

ROMANIA

C.I.S.

C.I.S.

● Kiev

C.I.S.

UKRAINE

C.I.S.

C.I.S.

Sevastopol ● **1**

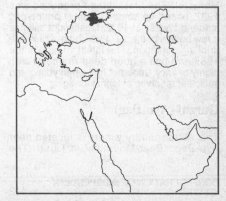

1   Crimea

Ai-Danil (Saint Daniel

One of the most important villages, has an outstanding reputation of top-quality "Tokay", Pinot Gris and Muscat. Before the revolution it was noted for making some of the finest red "Ports". Situated in a beautiful position, overlooking the Black Sea, Tokay wines are made from the traditional Furmint and Harslevelu grapes and reach quite outstanding levels of concentration. They continue to develop for over a century, requiring 50 or more years to throw off their youthfulness. The alcohol levels of the different vintages vary considerably from less than 10° to more than 16° by volume. All are intensely sweet with residual sugar levels of between 200 and 280 g/1t but have good balancing acidity and very low volatile levels. In short, they are wines that will live for centuries.

Alupka

This important winery was founded in the early 1800s to supply wine for the remarkable Alupka palace which was designed by Bloor and commissioned and built for Count Mikhail Vorontsov between 1828 - 1847. It is very much a fortified wine production center with Madeira-style and white Port wines as the most important lines. The Madeira is made in the traditional way, mostly sold under the Massandra label. Alupka white Port is made from Sémillon, Pedroo Krymsky, Oporto and Albillo grapes and matured in old oak casks for three years. Alcohol levels are in the region of 16.5°-17.5° by volume and sugar levels are very similar to those found in Portugal. These white Ports are very good and continue to age and gain complexity for many, many years.

Alushta

This important winery makes one of the few, yet highly successful normal strength wines based on Cabernet Sauvignon and Saperavi. Both grape varieties produce wine that has high quality and long life. In fact, they could be one of the great blends of the future especially if quality standards are improved. Strangely, both make very fine 'Port' style fortified wines as well as normal low strength wines. The actual blend is usually 50% Cabernet Sauvignon, 30% Saperavi and 20% Morastel. The first vintage produced was 1937, based on some Cabernet prototypes made at Livadia in 1932. Massandra still has a few bottles of the 1974 which are still in fine drinking condition. The latest vintage is the 1987 and has a good deep red color with plenty of juicy Cabernet fruit when young and sufficient reserves of tannin for aging.

Gurzuf (Ayu-Dag)

This extraordinary winery is located near Ayu-Dag, "Bear Mountain" in Tartar. The forested mountain juts out into the Black Sea and resembles a bear on all fours, drinking from the sea. A site of early man dating from the 6th to 5th centuries BC and nearby evidence prove that Muscat grapes were grown here at least 2000 years ago. A major center for growing Rose Muscat, the most beautiful of all Muscats and Saperavi which is made into and sold as "Cahors", so named because of its intensely deep color (red/black), rather than its similarity to the well-known French wine. Rose Muscat is very perfumed and increases in intensity with age, perhaps not quite so fine as those produced at Livadia but still remarkable. Sold under the Ayu-Dag label, the Cahors is intensely deep black-red in color , with a most extraordinary bouquet of ripe cherries, raspberries and plums. They are also very sweet, but their intense fruitiness counter-balances this and makes them very moreish. Truly remarkable wines.

Livadia

This was the original vineyard and winery associated with the Livadia Palace, commonly called the 'white' or 'summer' palace of the Tsar. Livadia is famous for the production of Muscat, both Rose and White, and for the finest red Ports which are made exclusively from Cabernet Sauvignon. White Port was also made here at the end of the last century. As with all Ports, Livadia Ports were and still are matured in old oak barrels for three years before bottling. The Rose Muscats are the finest in the world with incredible perfume and amazing intensity on the palate. They are also very sweet but not sugary or cloying, with residual sugar levels up to nearly 300 g/lt in the most exceptional years.

Massandra

Built by professional coal miners brought from Georgia for Tsar Nicholas II, the Massandra winery was constructed between 1894-1897 on the site of an existing winery which dated back to at least 1849. Its imposing cellar with its more recent extensions is the center for wine production along the South Coast of the Crimea. It is responsible for bottling and distributing all the wine sent into it from its members, which include independent co-operatives as well as traditional wineries. The technical staff work closely with the Magarach Institute and there has been some significant updating of equipment. A large number of wines are sold under the Massandra label, although today no wines are actually made there. They do, however, mature a significant number of the wines produced on the South Coast and are guardians of "the Collection" which is the greatest cellar of outstanding, rare old vintage wine in the USSR and possibly in the world. It is a unique collection of century-old wines, including bottles set aside when 10 years old, representing the cream of the country's production. Started by Prince Lev Golitzin while he was in charge of the winery, the Collection was conserved and enriched until his death in 1951. Protected throughout the most turbulent of times, in 1941, to avoid possible looting by German invaders, the entire collection was moved to secret locations. It was returned to its original site shortly before the Yalta Conference of February 1945. Some of these fabulous old wines can be found around the world as a number were sold by Sotheby's at auction in London in 1990 an 1991. Otherwise they can only be purchased directly from Massandra on a bottle by bottle basis. The oldest and rarest vintages are no longer available for sale but form part of a 'national heritage'. The oldest wine in the collection is the 1776 Sherry (a true Spanish Sherry). Some three million bottles are in store, but the annual production of the wineries under Massandra's control is over 13 million bottles.

Novy Svet

The Novy Svet, or 'New World', winery was established by Prince Golitzin in the second half of the 19th century, in a very barren area of the south coast of the Crimea. Golitzin was a brilliant linguist who had been trained in Roman law at the Sorbonne (Paris), and later at Moscow university. His greatest passion was wine and he soon began to develop a number of new styles for the Tsar after a number of false starts. He was responsible for developing the early dessert and fortified wine styles and also had great success with Russian 'champagne' which is what Novy Svet still concentrates on producing. Golitzin also started the Massandra Collection which was a reference 'library' of old wines to see how the various wine styles developed with age in the hope of improving quality standards. Much of the extraordinary collection still exists today. Although the winery at Novy Svet is extremely difficult to reach, it is well worth a visit just to see the old limestone cellars where some of the Massandra collection was hidden during World War 2. Novy Svet produces one of the best Russian champagne which when drunk without any "dosage" is remarkably similar in style to true Champagne. However, most of its production is sweetened up for the market and a substantial amount is exported to Germany. Although production techniques could certainly be improved, the actual Novy Svet product is very interesting. Brut to very sweet styles are made.

Sudak (Surozh)

Sudak is located further to the east than Novy Svet, in an arid and rather hot area noted for producing white Port from Kokour grapes. This white variety has been growing in this area for over 200 years. It is either made into a white Port or a dessert wine that is remarkable in its youth. Its luscious bouquet smells of honey, figs, apricots and strawberries but develops with age to a pronounced sponge cake aroma which often includes chocolate! Vintage that might be available are the 1958 and 1965. The wines are now all sold under the Surozh label (Surozh was the old name for Sudak). Massandra has a 1936 white Port which came from his area but which is called Su-Dag, a local village which in Tartar means water mountain or mountain river. The white port usually has a strength of around 17° and ages well. The climate in this area must be very similar in some respect to the Douro valley.

Tavrida

Tavrida, the old word for Crimea, is one of the country's main state-owned wine companies. Located near Frunzenskoye, between Alushta and Gurzuf, it supplies large quantities of grapes to the Massandra consortium for its range of wines. Perhaps its best known wine is the Black Muscat, which is only grown in the Crimea (within the USSR), mainly at Travrida. The Black Muscat is not a true Muscat, but is a variety, better-known as Alicante, that came from Spain or Portugal. It is known locally as Kaliabsky and is often blended with a little Aleatico. The wine is very sweet but lacks the sheer beauty of the true Muscats. The wines which are relatively low in alcohol, that is below 12.5° by volume, are sweet (220-280 g/lt residual) and display marked coffee aromas.

CYPRUS

The wine industry of the Mediterranean's third largest island has seen better days. In the early 1970s annual production was in excess of 1,000,000 hectoliters. Today, it is just over half that, and sinking fast. Why? Until Britain joined the Common Market (as one called it then) there was a great thirst in the country for a product called Cyprus Sherry, which for the most part bore as much resemblance to the Spanish original as a mass-produced hamburger does to a proper meal. Actually, unlike most hamburgers, at its best it was not a bad product, only it did not resemble Sherry.

The loss of the U.K. market was a classic illustration of the "don't put all your eggs into one basket" dictum. And then, to add to the misery, there were political troubles - Turks invading, partition, inevitable loss of the tourist trade. Things went downhill both at home and abroad.

Cyprus is a hot country and until the arrival of modern technology, it was not really possible to produce decent table wines. Thus the large-producer syndrome that existed 20 years ago has not only not disappeared, but intensified, since the equipment necessary for producing good wines of the type the international consumer is prepared to drink is only within the reach of the financially muscular. In such a context, growers remain growers and producers remain powerful - even, indeed more so, in a shrinking market.

There is at least one healthy sign on the Cyprus wine-scene: nobody seems to be experimenting with Cabernet Sauvignon, Chardonnay or even French barrique. The indigenous Mavro (or Mavron) still accounts for the vast majority of plantings of red grapes, with Xynisteri, a rather neutral variety, yet not without quality, supreme among whites.

Cyprus can boast one great and historic wine, Commandaria, which is made from raisined grapes of true Cypriot origin (as far as one can determine). There is something marvellous and mysterious about tasting a wine which to all intents and purposes has stayed the same over the centuries. One can only hope that world taste does not become so modern (which after all is in itself an utterly relative concept) as to deprive these golden oldies of a market, resulting, like the endangered species one hears so much about, in their extinction.

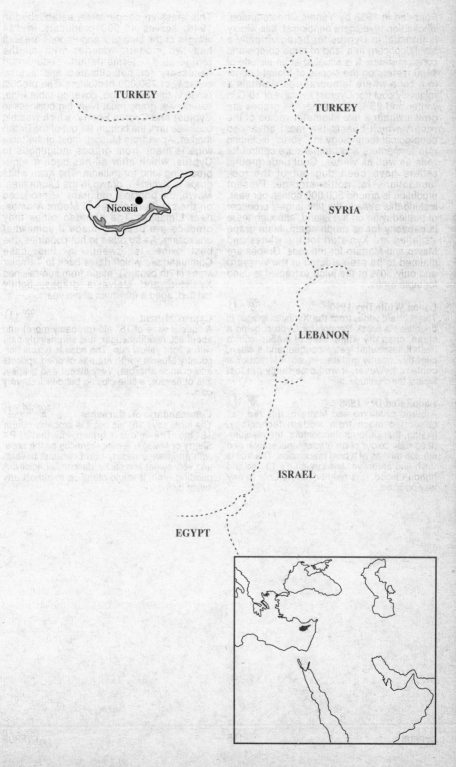

Laona Arsos Model Winery

Chrysalia Court - P.O. Box 465
206 Makarios Ave., Limassol
Tel. (051) 63763
Fax (051) 66233

Founded in 1988 by Yannis Christodoulou, whose son is resident oenologist, this winery is unusual in Cyprus for being virtually a family concern in a land of huge co-ops and conglomerates. It is situated at an altitude of 1100 meters on the slopes of Mount Laona, in a zone where temperatures maintain a relatively cool (for Cyprus) average of 10°C in winter and 25°C in summer. All grapes are grown within a five kilometer radius of the winery which boasts the most advanced oenological technology in Cyprus, including roto-fermenters and temperature control for reds as well as whites. Cool underground cellars have been dug out of the rock foundations for bottle storage. Present prodution is around 500,000 bottles per year, making this already the fifth largest producer of bottled wine on the island, although there is capacity for as much again. Main grape varieties are Xynisteri for the whites and Mavro and Mattaro for the reds. Grapes are claimed to be pre-selected in the vineyard and only 50% of the juice extracted is used for table wines.

Laona White Dry 1990   ❦ ①
This 12° alc wine, from the Xynisteri grape, is doubtless a break-through for Cyprus, being a clean, crisp dry white, pale of colour, with a fresh if somewhat feeble bouquet and a clean, slightly creamy palate. In an international context, however, it would certainly get lost amidst the multitude.

Laona Red Dry 1988   ❦ ①
A blend of Mavro and Mattaro, this red has benefitted much from modern technology, having, thanks to rotofermentors, the medium-deep ruby colour of an efficient maceration and the soft tannins of a brief maceration. The fruit is fresh and attractive, and though it's 13° alc and aged in wood, it is neither too rich nor in any way oxidized.

Sodap Ltd.

P.O. Box 6314
Limassol
Tel. (051) 36405
Fax (051) 364013

This massive cooperative, established in 1948, serves 10,000 producers in 144 villages of the Limassol and Paphos areas. It has two modern wineries with all the refrigerated fermentation equipment necessary for hot climates and a total capacity of 750,000 hectoliters. The product range is fairly vast, too, covering table wine, eau-de-vie, grape must (very big business in Cyprus) and Cyprus Sherry, which was big business until the bottom fell out of the British market. Apart from Muscat, most of the table wine is made from grapes indigenous to Cyprus, which after all has been a wine-producing land for millenia. The main white grape is Xynisteri, grown in the Laona area. Mavro, the principal red grape, is produced on the southern slopes of Mount Afames, near Limassol. The branded wines they produce are decently made if somewhat unexciting. As so often in hot countries, the best wine is sweet, in this case Commandaria which dates back to Templar times (17th century), made from sun-raisined Xynisteri and Malvasia grapes, lightly fortified, aged a minimum of ten years.

Cyprus Muscat   ❦ ①
A liqueur wine of 15° alc (probably more) and about 8% residual sugar, it is surprisingly pale with a light yellow hue. The nose is typical hot-country Muscat - with aromas of dried apricots and orange sherbet. Very sweet and grapey, lots of flavour, a little cloying but delicious very cold.

Commandaria St. Barnabas   ❦❦ ②
The label says 15° alc but it is probably nearer 18° alc. The colour is brown, like that of PX Sherry or Malaga. A mite marmitey on the nose, with an intense raisiny-burnt caramel flavour, and very sweet and sticky, despite fair acidity. A pudding wine, it would stand up to almost any sweet dish.

THE CZECH REPUBLIC AND SLOVAKIA

Wine has never been an important product of this land famous for its beer (Pilsen) and what was produced was almost entirely for home consumption. In fact, Czechoslovakia (as it was called until it split into two halves) is a net importer of wine, in particular the Czech side consisting of Bohemia and Moravia. Nevertheless, approximately 40,000 hectares of farmland are planted to the vine, with 1,500,000 hectoliters of wine produced, representing not insignificant figures. Something over half of all production is in Slovakia, with the rest mainly from Moravia and a little from Bohemia.

On the whole, the quality of these wines in recent times, in the days of the commissars, has been pretty second-rate, not to say poor. Yet there is no reason why Slovakia and Moravia should not be able to produce good wines. They lie on a parallel with Alsace, and 40% of the vineyards are on slopes similar to those of Alsace and Burgundy, the remainder being planted in rolling country. Grape varieties include, among whites (two thirds of the total), Pinots Blanc and Gris, Gewürztraminer, Muscat and Sauvignon, as well as the more common Rizling Vlassky, Müller Thurgau, Gruner Veltliner and Silvaner. Among reds the most important varieties are Frankovka and St. Laurent, with small but significant amounts of Cabernet Sauvignon, Pinot Noir and Zweigeltrebe.

Whether Slovakia and Moravia have it in them to become producers of high quality wines remains to be seen. At the moment the best efforts are going into the production of good value supermarket wines selling at by Western standards, distinctly low prices. Obviously this is just the first step. We will know more when in the new free market system it is finally sorted out who controls what and whether there is a will and ability to make the kind of very considerable capital investment in equipment and personnel which is needed.

GERMANY

GERMANY

POLAND

● Prague

1

2 ● Ostrava

3

● Bratislava

C.I.S.

AUSTRIA

HUNGARY

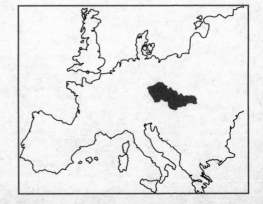

Vino-Produkt s.p. Bratislava
ul. Baronka 1
835 02 Bratislava, Slovakia
Tel. 728 5224
Fax 728 4228

Malokarpatsky Vinarsky Podnik, Pezinok
Za drahou 21
902 20 Pezinok, Slovakia
Tel 704 2051
Fax 704 3767

Vino Nitra s.p. Nitra
Lyrova 1
949 89 Nitra-Luziansky, Slovakia
Tel 87 416 009
Fax 419 122

These three groups, each with their own satellites, account for almost all of the wine production of Slovakia (about 750,000 hectoliters per year). At the time of writing, the system is undergoing a radical review, so as far as organisation is concerned, it is impossible to say today what will be true tomorrow. From one point of view, however, they may be considered together, since they have been taken in hand by a group lead by Oldrich Pospisil, a Liverpool-based Czech plastic surgeon with a mission to raise the image of his country's wine industry, and Angela Muir, a London-based Master of Wine. When Angela first arrived in the summer of 1990 she found large volumes of wine which had been made to a distinctly mediocre standard (if indeed they were not faulty) for the now defunct Russian market. Problems included a chemical approach to stabilisation, a mechanical attitude to racking and handling, inadequate hygiene and a total absence of pride in the product. There was also insufficient capital for investment in equipment. Nitra had a decent bottling line, Pezinok a functional refrigeration plant, while Bratislava was the administrative center (no longer). There was, however, underlying it all, excellent raw material which Angela Muir felt could in future be harnessed to make wines of good commercial quality and better. About 10% - if that - of the existing wines were good enough to propose to the international (specifically British) market, and that is what the group has been relying on until present. Pinot Blanc, Rizling Vlassky, Gewürztraminer, Irsay Oliver (a clone of Muscat) among whites, Pinot Noir, Frankovka and St. Laurent among reds are the ones that have so far met with commercial approval - at very low prices, it must be said. Hope for the future resides in the fact that, with the undemanding markets of the East closed and the highly competitive ones to the West beckoning, the end of state control and organisation and with a bit of enthusiasm and care the quality

will rise to meet its potential. It will be interesting to see what comes out of the 1992 vintage.

Gewurztraminer Pezinok 1991   🍇 ①
A clean, quite fruity, dry white somewhat lacking in varietal perfume but having a fresh fruitiness and the typical soft acidity of the grape variety. Agreeable and easily drinkable, if not particularily expressive.

Rizling Vlassky Pezinok 1991   🍇 ①
White wine just off-dry, with a 8 g/lt residual sugar but a lean, crisp finish. The bouquet is unusually penetrating and the sappy fruit unusually expressive for this normally rather plodding grape variety.

Irsay Oliver Nitra 1990   🍇 ①
A dry, white wine with unmistakable peachy-grapey aroma of Muscat. The aromas persisted in the mouth, but the lowish acidity let it down at the end, and it faded quickly. This again was a slightly aging tank sample.

Pinot Blanc Nitra 1990   🍇 ①
Among the only samples available for tasting from the Nitra winery was this slightly aging dry white from tank. The color was yellowing, but there was a typical appley yeastiness on the nose. It was surprisingly, perhaps slightly excessively soft, considering the normally rather acidic style of the grape.

Frankovka Saint Laurent Bratislava/Racca   🍷 ①
A dry red wine with a luminous ruby color and a "ripe beetroot juice" nose, according to Angela Muir. It has lots of fresh, zingy fruit, an uppish acidity and some tannin. This tank sample will have 8 g/lt residual sugar when bottled.

Saint Laurent Pezinok 1991   🍷 ①
This native Czechoslovakian red grape, which also rejoices in the name Vavrinecke, produces wine of deep color and a rather vegetal aroma but with plenty of fruit which seems almost sweet, though it is technically dry. This is a fresh, eminently drinkable red which should do well commercially in the West.

Pinot Noir Bratislava 1989   🍷🍷 ①
This dry red wine has good Pinot Noir type, with a tomatoey/vegetal bouquet. On the palate one senses gentle, slightly perfumed fruit, well-balanced acidity, and some tannin. Wine of a certain complexity, having very good varietal character, especially considering the low price.

Zemedelské Druzstuvo Jiskra

Ceikovice 60615 (o Kres Hodnin)
Tel. 9520516

It is hard to say what the future holds in store for this state-run winery situated in an ex-Templar friars monastry with seventh century cellars still intact. The cooperative stands alone in maintaining the reputation of an important viticultural part of what was once Czechoslovakia. It oversees the vineyard operations and wine-making for associated growers with a total surface area of 180 hectares. Most of the vineyards are situated at an average altitude of 500 meters in the milder region of Moravia near the Austrian border. With some Slovakian white wines (but generally those of a higher level) - Sauvignon, Müller Thurgau, Neuburgské, Rulandské, Mojar - Irsay Oliver of Ceikovice maintains good quality in a country where the quality of wine produced is unjustly undervalued. And this despite a few antiquated winery techniques (no temperature controlled fermentation apart from the natural use of cool cellars) and the unfortunate habits of a vast majority who drink the wines before maturity. The reds on the other hand are not quite up to scratch, at least with the 1991 vintage that we tasted. They had a pleasant bouquet but lacked texture and body. Stanislav Hriba (who moonlights with his own small winery) greets visitors at the cooperative. A new hospitality center provides fairly spartan accommodation, with one bath for every other room, but it is clean and friendly and very modestly priced.

Mopr 1991   🍇 ①
Made from a native grape, this dry Muscat has an elegant, semi-sweet flavor, a medium-body and a considerably long finish. Nice with pâté or aged cheese, or simply for sipping.

Müller Thurgau 1991   🍇 ①
Medium straw yellow in color with green highlights, it has a pleasant, dry backbone, a slightly salty aftertaste and good local character. Lingering finish.

Neuburgské 1991   🍇 ①
This well-balanced Pinot has lots of pleasant floral notes and fresh fruit on the nose, while being crisp on the palate with a long finish.

Sauvignon 1991   🍇 ①
Pale brilliant straw yellow in color, an intense bouquet turns into a herbaceous/grassy, slightly bitter flavor. Full-bodied and long enough on the finish, presumably it could improve with two or three years aging.

Rating System

🍇   An exemplary wine of its type with outstanding local character

     An international premium quality wine

🍇🍇🍇   A Top Wine, considered one of the 150 best wines in the world

The 'grape bunch' symbol is used to indicate the color of the wine; the number of bunches represents the quality rating assigned by the contributor

FRANCE

France, a land of great wines, continues to uphold her tradition of outstanding quality and to maintain a firm hold on her undisputed leadership of world wine culture. Gourmets and connoisseurs all over the world face the pleasurable task of testing their palates against the products of French viticulture. For such individuals, the great wine regions of France conjure up the legendary labels which for generations have provided both enjoyment and a topic for endless discussion. It is respect, scholarship and the continuous study of the culture of wine which in France, more than anywhere else in the world, have over the centuries been built into a solid tradition. In practical terms, wine culture involves over one million French wine-growers spread over most of the rural areas of the "Hexagon", as the French call their country, and is intimately linked to the strong regional traditions of gastronomy.

In a country that has always produced wine, the roots of tradition run deep. Indeed, the foundation and growth of the unitary French state over the last four centuries has enhanced the prestige of the wines of France to the point of assuming world leadership. A flourishing trade in French wine has undoubtedly supported this overwhelmingly strong position. In the 17th century, the wine routes from Bordeaux, Champagne, Burgundy and the Loire Valley already criss-crossed the whole of Europe with London providing a particularly discriminating and attentive market. These trade routes have since been developed and expanded and there are now few countries around the world that do not have a ready market for French wines.

Food culture in general is inarguably deep rooted in France. One has only to think of authors such as Grimod de la Reynière, who in the early 19th century published the "Almanach des Gourmands" which, based on information gathered from every corner of France, selected and described all that was best in food at the time. In the wine world, the Bordeaux Chamber of Commerce at the behest of Emperor Napoleon III classified the châteaux of the Médoc and Sauternes/Barsac in 1855 thus initiating one of the earliest and most effective marketing operations ever. Today, the 1855 classification is still the subject of discussion and re-assessment. These two examples are significant for the dates at which they took place for no other country in the world at the time would have even considered cataloguing and classifying its foods and wines.

It is no surprise that over the last 50 years, the wines, vineyards and growers of France have been the focus of attention of journalists, vintners and connoisseurs around the world. Dozens upon dozens of guides and articles, and comparative tastings by the thousands have scrutinized the wines of France. This kind of exposure not only helps in consolidating the trade market but also in encouraging growers and merchants to improve their product and tighten up self-regulation.

France now boasts more than 1,000,000 ha (around 2,500,000 acres) under vine with an average annual production of about 70,000,000 hl (over 1,900 million US gallons). Domestic consumption has for many years been in slow but apparently irreversible decline. The 120 lt per capita annual consumption of the 1960s has fallen to the present level of 80 lt. This trend of course also affects other traditional European wine producers and consumers, such as

Italy, Spain and Portugal. It is a natural result of new consumer models and the profound social changes that have taken place since World War II. Strong international demand means that exports amount to several million hectoliters. This is more than the substantial quantities of wines imported, chiefly for blending purposes. Of course, this gap widens enormously if measured in monetary terms.

Statistics (production figures, per capita consumption, imports and exports, etc.) are meaningful if considered globally. They risk, however, being obscure unless accompanied by a more detailed analysis of the production of the various regions and the three categories of wine admitted by French legislation. For example, there is no comparison between the yields per hectare of the great regions of Burgundy and Bordeaux and the huge volumes of the Midi. Such differences are regulated by a solid body of legislation, the appellation d'origine, which sets precise standards for the growers in each region.

The three distinct categories of French appellation d'origine are: Appellation d'Origine Contrôlée, Vin Délimité de Qualité Supérieure and Vins de Pays. The first category is the most exclusive and is regulated by laws which take into account the growers' proposals. They are subjected to the scrutiny of a national institute (INAO) and are rendered legally binding by the Ministry of Agriculture. About 22% of French wines belong to this category. A very small number of wines fall into the second category, with its VDQS label, while an increasing percentage is made up of Vins de Pays. These wines have less stringent controls, are generally attractively priced, and range in style from the unpretentious to the more serious, and include the now fashionable "varietal" wines.

The regulations concerning appellation d'origine are among the most advanced in the world. They restrict the growers to using those varieties which are most suitable for the terrain and micro-climate of their own particular region and, as a result, have endowed wines with a strong local character. On the whole, French wine laws have enforced a more serious approach from the producers, to the benefit of both the domestic and non-domestic consumers. Yields per hectare, blending, authorized vine varieties and the irrigation ban are all rigorously regulated to conserve a vast heritage. The association between variety and region has enabled highly characteristic wines to emerge from each individual wine-growing area. Syrah and Grenache make one think immediately of the wines of the Rhône, from the legendary Hermitage to sumptuous Châteauneuf-du-Pape and the wonderful Tavel rosé.

France has also exported her own grape varieties to vineyards all over the world, creating an international taste which has contributed to the ever more widespread planting of French grape varieties. Two in particular have conquered the world: Chardonnay and Cabernet Sauvignon. From California to Chile, South Africa to New Zealand and Australia to France's neighboring Italy and Spain, they have expressed their great potential more than any other language in the world. Pinot Noir, Sauvignon Blanc, Chenin Blanc and Merlot have also established themselves firmly in many wine-growing areas. Pinot Noir, which together with Chardonnay make up the élite of the wines of

Burgundy, is a difficult grape to grow. Despite all its complications, however, Pinot Noir is today, perfectly at home in New World countries like Australia, New Zealand and California.

Back on French soil the grape varieties Sémillon and Sauvignon unite to make the great Sauternes, easily distinguished for its much-prized botrytis, or noble rot, character. The aromatic Gewürztraminer, Pinot Blanc and Sylvaner are at home in Alsatian soil. Gamay and Carignan grapes may be little-known abroad but in France are widespread. Gamay is the grape used to make the beloved Beaujolais or, in November, the Beaujolais Nouveau, which is as eagerly anticipated by the French bistrots as the rest of the world. The latter, Carignan, is the most widely cultivated variety in France. Grown mainly in the south, it is responsible for the production of a vast amount of wine and is also quite commonplace in neighboring Spain. The ampelographic heritage of France is far more complicated than we could possibly explain, and it is on this heritage that so many rare and great wines have been founded.

In this guide, France is sub-divided into 12 viticultural regions, each containing various appellations d'origine. Within these appellations, we have described and tasted wines from 673 cellars, châteaux or domaines, representing over a third of the producers in the entire guide.

Burgundy and Bordeaux are the most important sections, not only for historical reasons but also because of their international reputations. Although the quality of Burgundy is a constant point of discussion the wines of the Côtes d'Or and great Chablis continue to be irresistibly fascinating and many of these wines are permanently in the international "hit parade." Thanks also to her rich and varied cuisine, Burgundy is a mecca for gourmets and wine lovers as well as for most of the world's leading wine producers. Pinot Noir and Chardonnay, for the more noble wines, and Gamay and Aligoté for the more modest, are the two varietal pairings which dominate the region. The cataloguing by quality of the various crus (designated vineyards) is, together with the famous pyramid of appellations, the most typical characteristic of the wines of Burgundy and the perhaps impossible dream of many other wine-growing areas.

If many wine lovers imagine Burgundy to be rich, generous and rustic, then Bordeaux, in contrast, evokes aristocracy, distinction and nobility. The world's largest concentration of high quality wines is produced around the city of Bordeaux and along the banks of the Dordogne, the Garonne and the Gironde estuary. The four main regions, Graves, Libournais, Médoc and Sauternes, all boast appellations and wines which are often masterpieces. It was in this region that modern enology found an environment in which to research and study the problems of wine-making. The doyen of this new era of wine is Professor Emile Peynaud, celebrated wine consultant, author and former director at the University of Bordeaux. No surprise that the wines of Bordeaux should take the lion's share of places in the list of the World's Top Wines compiled for this guide. Bordeaux quality is a serious affair and the result of many years patient work.

Another legendary region is Champagne, with its wine of the same name which has been the joy of connoisseurs for over two centuries. At its best

Champagne made by the méthode champenoise from a blend of grapes and wines and then aged for a time on its lees in the cool, chalk cellars of Champagne can be one of the world's greatest wines. However, not all producers follow the good practices necessary to produce fine Champagne. There has recently been a feeling that standards have dropped, particularly in relation to price. The Champenois have taken significant steps to rectify this problem but the future will require great care in order to find the right balance between price and quality.

The region offering great value for today's market is the Rhône Valley, having made miraculous progress in the past ten years in terms of quality. Both the northern region of the Rhône Valley, with Cornas, Hermitage, Saint-Joseph, Crozes-Hermitage and Côte Rôtie, as well as the southern, where Châteauneuf-du-Pape reigns supreme and Gigondas, Tavel and good Côtes du Rhône are found, have witnessed a momentous renaissance of quality. There has been a marked increase of new growers who produce good wines at relatively modest prices. The Rhône Valley is rapidly becoming another mecca for wine professionals and enthusiasts.

The wine areas of Provence, Languedoc and Roussillon have developed in a similar way but to a lesser extent. The Midi comprises over 30% of France's vineyards and for years has meant almost exclusively "vin ordinaire." Today, as we have already mentioned, there is new investment and, above all, a new approach to the issue of quality with prices that are, for the time being at least, fair and highly competitive. The quality and variety of wines being produced, particularly in the Languedoc and Roussillon, has improved dramatically making this one of France's most exciting wine regions.

Flanking the country's east and west, Alsace and the Loire are the home of principally white wine. Alsatian wines are generally crisper and more aromatically scented while the Loire wines are more delicate and elegant. Muscadet, Savennières, Chinon, Vouvray, Pouilly-Fumé and Sancerre are just some of the appellations of the Loire. The vineyards run parallel to France's longest river, with the majority located along the northern stretch which runs from Pouilly-sur-Loire and Sancerre in the east to Nantes and the Atlantic Ocean.

Another swiftly developing region is the South West. A huge area embracing different climates and widely differing types of wine, this historically old wine-making region is an area to follow closely and this guide gives it ample space. Finally, we also include three other regions, Jura, Savoie and Corsica. There are but a few entries but all have excellent reputations and have the highest quality standards.

In all the regions listed and, indeed, in every wine-growing area of France, there are road signs which invite passers-by to taste and buy a few bottles of wine. These, too, are representative of the commercial and promotional spirit which animates French vignerons. Direct selling to the local market and tourist trade represents for many small producers a substantial part of their income. The most important export markets are Great Britain and the United States, the Benelux countries, Germany and Switzerland. Of course, demand for great wines is always relentless.

The most demanding challenge facing the new generation of growers is that of guaranteeing good wines at a fair price. The arrival of good Australian, Italian, Spanish and Californian wines should stimulate the extraordinary expertise of both vignerons and négociants to conquer new markets and consolidate their domestic position. France benefits enormously from its long-established policies of international wine marketing and promotion which can count on connoisseurs and enthusiasts all over the globe.

The wines featured in this guide naturally have been tasted, appellation by appellation. The rigorous selection process adopted for this first edition indeed may have left out some deserving, good-quality producers just as some selections may appear debatable. It must be borne in mind, however, that they are included as a result of careful tasting and discussion. Alongside the great names in this guide, there are some small producers ranking in excellence and worthy of inclusion. Indeed, these growers represent the spirit of France, a country that has never rested on its laurels but has constantly kept up with changing times, marrying the new to its own inimitable tradition.

France
Appellations in the Guide

Bordeaux

Bordeaux
  Bordeaux
Bourgeais Blayais
  Premières Côtes de Blaye
  Premières Côtes de Bourg
Entre-Garonne-et-Dordogne
  Loupiac
  Premières Côtes de
Bordeaux
  Sainte-Croix-du-Mont
Graves
  Graves
  Pessac-Léognan
Libournais
  Canon-Fronsac
  Côtes de Castillon
  Côtes de Francs
  Fronsac
  Lalande de Pomerol
  Pomerol
  Saint-Emilion
Médoc
  Haut-Médoc
  Listrac
  Margaux
  Médoc
  Moulis-en-Médoc
  Pauillac
  Saint -Julien
Sauternais
  Barsac
  Cérons
  Sauternes

Bourgogne

Auxerrois
  Chablis
Beaujolais
  Beaujolais
  Beaujolais-Villages
  Chiroubles
  Côte de Brouilly
  Fleurie
  Juliénas
  Morgon
  Saint-Amour
Côte Chalonnaise
  Givry
  Mercurey
  Rully
Côte de Beaune
  Aloxe-Corton
  Auxey-Duresses
  Beaune
  Blagny
  Chassagne-Montrachet
  Chorey-lès-Beaune
  Ladoix
  Meursault
  Monthélie

Pernand-Vergelesses
Pommard
Puligny-Montrachet
Saint-Aubin
Saint-Romain
Santenay
Savigny-lès-Beaune
Volnay
Côte de Nuits
  Chambolle-Musigny
  Fixin
  Gevrey-Chambertin
  Marsannay
  Morey-Saint-Denis
  Nuits-Saint-Georges
  Vosne-Romanée
  Vougeot
Mâconnais
  Mâcon
  Mâcon-villages
  Puilly-fuissé
  Saint-Véran

Languedoc Roussillon

Languedoc
  Corbières
  Costières de Nîmes
  Coteaux du Languedoc
  Faugères
  Fitou
  Minervois
  Saint-Chinian
  Vins de Pays de l'Hérault
Roussillon
  Banyuls
  Collioure
  Côtes du Roussillon
  Maury
  Muscat de Rivesaltes
  Rivesaltes

Loire

Anjou Saumur
  Anjou
  Anjou-Villages
  Bonnezeaux
  Coteaux de L'Aubance
  Coteaux du Layon
  Quarts de Chaume
  Saumur-Champigny
  Savennières
Nantais
  Fiefs Vendéens
  Muscadet
Touraine
  Bourgueil
  Cheverny
  Chinon
  Jasnières
  Montlouis
  Saint-Nicolas-de-Bourgueil

Touraine
Vouvray
Vins du Centre
  Côtes Roannaises
  Menetou-Salon
  Pouilly-Fumé
  Reuilly
  Saint-Pourçain
  Sancerre

Provence

Bandol
Bellet
Cassis
Coteaux d'Aix
Coteaux Varois
Côtes de Provence
Palette

Côtes-du-Rhône

North
  Château-Grillet
  Condrieu
  Cornas
  Côte Rôtie
  Crozes-Hermitage
  Hermitage
  Saint-Joseph
  Saint-Péray
South
  Châteauneuf-du-Pape
  Coteaux du Tricastin
  Côtes du Lubéron
  Côtes du Rhône
  Côtes du Rhône-Villages
  Gigondas
  Muscat de Beaumes-de-
Venise
  Tavel
  Vacqueyras

Sud-Ouest

Bergerac
Buzet
Cahors
Côtes de Duras
Côtes du Frontonnais
Gaillac
Irouléguy
Jurançon
Madiran
Pécharmant
Saussignac
Tursan
Vins de Marcillac
VdP des Côtes de Gascogne
VdP de Haute-Garonne

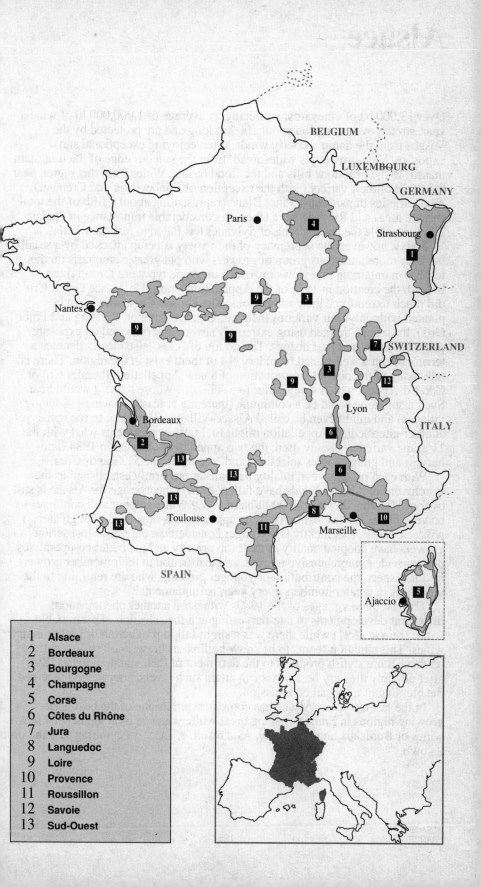

BELGIUM

LUXEMBOURG

GERMANY

Paris

Strasbourg

4

1

9

3

Nantes

9

9

7 SWITZERLAND

3

12

9

Bordeaux

Lyon

ITALY

6

2

6

13

13

13

Toulouse

8

10

13

11

Marseille

SPAIN

Ajaccio

5

1	Alsace
2	Bordeaux
3	Bourgogne
4	Champagne
5	Corse
6	Côtes du Rhône
7	Jura
8	Languedoc
9	Loire
10	Provence
11	Roussillon
12	Savoie
13	Sud-Ouest

Alsace

Over 13,000 ha of vineyards, producing an average of 1,000,000 hl of wine a year, stretch over an region about 100 km long and are protected by the Vosges from the damp westerly winds, often enjoying exceptional sun exposure. Vine-growing is widespread, from the silicous edge of the mountain massif, to the limestone hills and the flood basins. Wines from this region bear the name of their variety (with the exception of Edelzwicker and Crémant). Two varieties in particular, Pinot Blanc (representing about a fifth of the total surface area) and Riesling have taken on considerable importance in the last 20 years while the productiong of Sylvaner has fallen to less than 19%.

Today, however, the supremacy of the variety is being attacked by a small but ever more numerous group of growers who put greater emphasis on the terrain, maintaining that views in Alsace on grape types are far too fixed. Indeed, the creation in 1975 of the Appellation Contrôlée Alsace Grand Cru did much to reinforce their convictions. The Grands Crus, which can be planted with only four varieties (Muscat, Gewürztraminer, Riesling and Pinot Gris), have been defined using extremely severe criteria based on exposure, geology, yields and past history. The notion of "clos" also clearly denotes a territory with a well-traced boundary; 14 of them exist in the region. There is talk today of the possible introduction of a new Appellation, Premier Cru or Côtes d'Alsace, which would refer to a sub-zone whose name it would bear. Such a sub-zone could be a commune (there are at least 110 wine-producing villages) and might even be called Alsace-Villages. However, to recognize yet another intermediate Appellation might fuel further arguments what with the 11 grape varieties already used, the two appellations created in 1984 (late-harvest and grains nobles selection) and, above all, the 51 Grands Crus.

With each passing year, quality becomes more firmly established as the watchword of Alsace. Yields have fallen, even if the average for Alsace is still over of 80 hl/ha, down from 90 hl/ha in 1989. While sulphur still continues to be very present it has lost much of its appeal and is now used with greater wisdom. Sugar, too, luckily is no longer considered a cure-all. Most serious growers have adopted quality as their top priority and the better co-operatives now provide comprehensive training and instruction to their member growers. In this respect, the contribution of younger growers, who are returning to the vineyards in greater numbers every year, is fundamental.

The last three vintages of the 1980s witnessed another phenomenon: important developments in late-harvesting and the selection of grain noble wines (rare in 1991) while there was a slight fall in production of premium dry wines. This situation seems to be snow-balling, as growers often concentrate on these more stylish products to the detriment of their standard wines. But, after all, only the very best wines can attain such levels, after having received the blessing of a special commission.

In the last ten years, Alsace has come forward as one of the best wine-growing regions in France, making great white wines to rival the better-known wines of Bordeaux and Burgundy. As a result, Alsace, is beginning to stand on its own.

Excellent cuisine.

Excellent cuisine (continued).

illy, a glorious conclusion to your finest meals (and we
recommend it even after your worst). *illy. The perfect espresso.*

TRENTINO D.O.C.

Fine Wines, Sparkling Wine & Grappa from Trentino, Italy

VITICULTURE IS WIDESPREAD IN THE MOUNTAINOUS REGION OF TRENTINO, IT IS NOT ONLY A CENTURIES-OLD TRADITION BUT A VITAL ECONOMIC REALITY. ANNUAL PRODUCTION AVERAGES 120.000 TONNES OF GRAPES AND, WITH THE EMPHASIS ON QUALITY, 71% OF THE 8734 GROWING HECTARES (21.500 ACRES APPROXIMATELY) HAVE D.O.C. STATUS.
TRENTINO WINES, TOGETHER WITH THE WINES OF ALTO ADIGE, HAVING THE HIGHEST D.O.C. PERCENTAGE IN ITALY.

VINES ARE A FUNDAMENTAL COMPONENT OF THE TRENTINO LANDSCAPE DOTTED WITH THE TRADITIONAL "PERGOLA" GROWING SYSTEM BLENDING GRACEFULLY WITH THE NATURAL ENVIRONMENT OF STEEP SLOPES AND HIGH MOUNTAINS.

TRENTINO'S REMARKABLE VARIATION IN TOPOGRAPHY AND CLIMATE CREATES VERY DISTINCTIVE GROWING CONDITIONS AND THE CAREFULLY SELECTED VINES GROW UP TO AN ALTITUDE OF 600 METERS ABOVE SEA LEVEL.

THE CLIMATE IS PARTICULARLY SUITABLE FOR GRAPE PRODUCTION AND WIDE TEMPERATURE VARIATIONS IN THE PRE-HARVEST PERIOD ENHANCE THE CHARACTERISTIC BOUQUET OF TRENTINO WINES.

DIVERSITY OF POSITION, EXPOSURE, SLOPE AND SOIL RESULT IN DIFFERENT GROWING CONDITIONS IN EACH OF THE PRODUCING AREAS AND DICTATES THE CHOICE OF SUITABLE VINES. THESE PRODUCE A FULL RANGE OF WHITES, REDS, ROSES'S AND DESSERT WINES IN ADDITION TO SPUMANTI AND GRAPPA.

THE RICH RESULTS OF TRENTINO PRODUCTION ARE CLASSIFIED UNDER TWO D.O.C. DENOMINATIONS, **"TEROLDEGO ROTALIANO"** AND **"TRENTINO"** WITH ITS TWENTY VARIETAL APPELLATION: CHARDONNAY, PINOT BIANCO, BIANCO, PINOT GRIGIO, NOSIOLA, MÜLLER THURGAU, RIESLING ITALICO, RIESLING RENANO, TRAMINER AROMATICO, LAGREIN, PINOT NERO, MARZEMINO, MERLOT, CABERNET, CABERNET FRANC, CABERNET SAUVIGNON, ROSSO, MOSCATO GIALLO, MOSCATO ROSA, VINO SANTO.

ATTENTIVE QUALITY CONTROL AND CONSTRUCTIVE IMPROVEMENT SUGGESTED BY THE AGRICOLTURAL INSTITUTE OF SAN MICHELE, ONE OF THE LEADING SCHOOLS OF OENOLOGY IN EUROPE, HAS GUIDED TRENTINO ON THE ROAD TO QUALITY PRODUCTION.
SEVERAL CONSORTIA HAVE ALSO BEEN SET UP, SUCH AS "THE INSTITUTE TRENTO METODO CLASSICO" FORMED TO PROTECT TRENTINO PRODUCTION OF SPUMANTE BY ENSURING CONSTANT QUALITY CONTROL TO THE CONSUMER AND "THE INSTITUTE TUTELA GRAPPA DEL TRENTINO" WHICH SUPERVISES ENDLESS RESEARCH IN GRAPPA PRODUCTION AND ENSURE ATTENTIVE CARE AT ALL STAGES OF PRODUCTION. IT IS HOWEVER THE RESPONIBILITY OF THE WINE GROWERS ASSOCIATION, **THE COMITATO VITIVINICOLO**, TO ADVISE AND CO-ORDINATE THE VARIOUS WINE-GROWING PRODUCERS ACTIVITIES.

FOR INFORMATION IN THE UK, PLEASE CONTACT

**TRENTINO D.O.C.
93 HANGLETON ROAD
HOVE BN3 7GH
PHONE 0273 418100
FAX 0273 418858**

Domaine Lucien Albrecht

9, Grand-Rue
68500 Orschwihr
Tel. 89769518
Fax 89762022

The Albrechts are the heirs of a family which has lived in Orschwihr, in the southern part of Alsace, since 1772. Jean and Lucien own at least 30 ha around the village, but they also produce several wines from grapes they buy in (including an excellent Pinot Blanc). The Albrecht cellar offers a full line of Alsatian appellation wines and is well-known to local restaurateurs. These two wizards of wine look after their vineyards with the same care they take in the cellar, using low temperature fermentation and careful grape selections from particular areas, such as the riesling from the Himmelreich Clos, for which they have the exclusive. The 18th century Albrecht cellar produces excellent late-harvest wines and botrytis-selections, beginning with the Grand Cru Pfingstberg, pride and joy of the house. Facing south-west, it produces a great Riesling as well as Tokay, Pinot Gris and Gewürztraminer. The Albrechts were, in fact, among the first to produce this wine and each year continue to play their part in improving the quality of Alsatian wines.

Pinot Blanc 1991   ☏ ①
All the quality of Alsace is apparent in this very delicate wine, which promises much for the future. Full-flavored, fruity and well-balanced, it could be drunk now or within the next two years.

Riesling Clos Himmelreich 1991   ☏ ②
This special Albrecht wine, made from a selection of grapes picked from the Himmelreich Clos, lives up to its reputation. Though dry and pleasantly refreshing now, it still needs a little more time to be at its best.

Sylvaner 1991   ☏ ①
A clean, supple wine with good natural alcohol content. A refreshing acidity predominates, without becoming too aggressive. The delicate nose gives hints of honey. It's ready now.

Riesling Grand   ☏☏ ②
Cru Pfingstberg 1990
From a great vintage for Riesling comes this wine with outstanding aromatic power, with mineral and citrus notes. A fine, ripe-grapey texture. Well-rounded and opulent on the palate, it has a surprisingly lively finish.

Barmès-Buecher

23-30, rue Sainte-Gertrude
68920 Wettolsheim
Tel. 89808292
Fax 89793080

This village to the south of Colmar, where vine and mountain meet, has witnessed the happy union of two wine-growing families in the persons of Geneviève Buecher and François Barmès. Their rich and opulent wines come from an estate of 14 ha with 35 year-old vines and a loess/limestone soil. There are two Grands Crus, Hengst, which faces south, and Steingrubler, sited at 280-300 mt and known since 1487. Gewürztraminer, Muscat and Riesling grapes are often picked super-ripe in these two vineyards. Geneviève and François have a different approach from that of their parents. Fewer chemicals used on the vines, which are pruned well back, while the harvesting is done by hand and is highly selective. Yields are kept low, averaging 60-70 hl/ha but no more than 30-40 hl/ha for the Grands Crus or even lower for the late-harvest wines from the older vineyards. Since 1988, "grains nobles" selection has produced Gewürztraminer, Riesling and Tokay-Pinot Gris: wines worth sampling several years from now.

Pinot Blanc 1990   ☏ ①
This is a fine example of this cru, with its faint bouquet of bananas and honey. Elegant and refreshing. The considerable acidity helps to balance the finish, although some residual sugar is still detectable.

Riesling Réserve Personnelle 1990   ☏ ②
With a yield of 45 hl/ha, this reserve shows good soil character. It is refreshing both to the nose and on the palate, and there is a faint hint of menthol. Very well-balanced finish.

Gewurztraminer   ☏☏ ④
Sélections de Grains Nobles 1988
Yellow-gold in color, it has a delicious grapey aroma joined later by honey, grapefruit, figs, quince and candied fruit. On the palate, these elements come together perfectly to give rise to a voluptuously enveloping sensation. Although the sugar is quite nice here, it is a super rich wine, to be laid down for the future.

Domaine Jean-Claude Beck

16, rue Irma-Mersiol
67650 Dambach-la-Ville
Tel. 88924729
Fax 88926118

A true Alsatian who loves his land, Jean-Claude Beck is a young man in charge of an eight ha family estate that dates back to the 16th century. With vines spread over three communes (Dambach, Epfig and Dieffenthal), he takes pride in producing distinctive cuvées from each. Since 1986, he has been dividing his Riesling into four selections: Premier, from the granite sands of Dambach; Nuit Blanche, produced from sandy loamy soil; and Pierre à Feu, from Epfig, and its loess-clay soil along the pebbly banks of the Rhine. The latest Cuvée Maude was created in 1990 from vines planted 40 years ago in the Dieffenthal granite soil. No more than 100 cases a year are produced. Jean-Claude dislikes high yields and with good reason. His vineyards are nearly all (80%) sited on well-exposed slopes and Jean-Claude well remembers his father's not wanting to abbandon them to keep working the horses! Jean-Claude also owns some old Gewürztraminer vines in the Fronholz area and vineyards at Grand Cru Frankenstein, where his Riesling and Tokay-Pinot Gris grapes produce wines with cellaring potential.

Gewürztraminer 1990   ⚜ ②
This is an archetypal example of a wine from this varietal. It has everything: the depth, the fruit, the spiciness and that indefinable touch of sensuality.

Riesling   ⚜⚜ ③
Grand Cru Frankstein 1990
A typical classy Riesling from this region. The grapes were harvested at peak ripeness giving a depth of exceptional fullness. Flowery notes prevail in the bouquet. On the palate, the wine is lively with good acidity, clean and elegantly refreshing. This wine will age without any problem.

Riesling Maude 1990   ⚜ ②
A full-bodied wine from the magnificent Dieffenthal area from vines more than 45 years old. The bouquet is spicy and smoky, the flavor well-rounded, the finish long.

Riesling Nuit Blanche 1990   ⚜ ②
In need of a name for a cuvée from sand and loam terrain, Jean-Claude Beck and his wife decided, after staying up all night thinking the problem over, to call it Nuit Blanche (Sleepless Night). A lovely Riesling, faultless.

Beyer

2, rue de la Première-Armée
68240 Eguisheim
Tel. 89414105
Fax 89239363

The grace and beauty of this lovely town and its flowers are undeniable. Undeniably much of the credit for this goes to the Beyer family. The versatile and loquacious mayor he is, Léon Beyer, is an indefatigable promoter of the wines of Alsace like Jean Pierre Haeberlin of the Auberge d'Ill, négociant and vintner. Jean Pierre is an outstanding personalité who has taken Alsace's best wines to the world's best restaurants. Léon owns 20 ha of vines, some in the Grand Cru Eichberg, but he was never much of an enthusiast of the Grands Crus, preferring his own labels, especially the well-known Cuvée des Ecaillers. Marc, Léon's son, continues the family tradition as a widely respected taster. The Beyer family tends, on the one hand, towards wines with cellaring potential, often very mature, and also, on the other, to elegant wines appreciated by restauranteurs. The last four vintages have provided good examples of this policy as has the 1991, which was not damaged by the frost. The Beyers also excel in producing special cuvées and late-harvest wines which shine in great vintages, such as 1971, 1976 and 1983. But, then again, anything labelled Beyers automatically carries a guarantee of good quality.

Pinot Blanc 1991   ⚜ ①
In the classic Beyer style, it has a refreshing fragrance containing hints of lemon and honey and the finish is reasonably long, considering the vintage.

Riesling Cuvée Particulière 1990   ⚜⚜ ③
A lovely, bright yellow color, minerally nose with hints of slight super-ripening. Mostly made from grapes from the Grand Cru Pfingstberg, this Riesling is fresh and elegant on the palate, despite being somewhat full-bodied. A wine for laying down.

Gewürztraminer   ⚜⚜ ③
Vendanges Tardives 1989
A wine of unusually elegant appearance, with a spicy bouquet and a dry flavor (with aromas of candied fruit), it is rich in texture, full-bodied and well-balanced on the palate, with a long finish which promises some good ageing. Very generous.

Blanck-Domaine des Comtes de Lupfen

32, Grand-Rue
38240 Kientzheim
Tel. 89762356
Fax 89471645

The Blancks are as well known in wine circles all over Alsace as they are in this small walled town. Marcel is a jovial type and one of wine's personalities (former president of the regional branch of the I.N.A.O.), but it is his son who today defends the honor of the family's Grands Crus, Altenberg, Furstentum, and Patergarten as well as Schlossberg, first listed of Alsace's classified Grands Crus The Blancks were pioneers in bringing the Appellation to the highest levels. This large domaine with 27 ha of vines (nine of which are in Grands Crus) planted on gravel, sand, granite, loam and limestone lies at the foot of the Sigolsheim necropolis. The Blancks aim to achieve a balance between the character of the variety and that of the terrain. Harvesting is done by hand and vinification is carried out under inert gas at low temperatures in glass-lined steel vats. The wines are cellar-aged before going onto the market. The Blancks' professional approach produces "grains nobles" selections of quite breathtaking quality.

Riesling Grand Cru Furstentum 1990 ❦ ③
A typical Riesling which remains true to its roots. This wine has everything: the typical minerally note, regional character, full-bodied depth and fresh acidity.

Riesling Grand Cru Schlossberg 1990 ❦ ③
The oldest of the classified Grands Crus, here the wine becomes a bonafide institution. It is, of course, still young and tight, but one can already make out its magnificent structure and rest assured that it will develop in the years to come.

Domaine Emile Boeckel

2, rue de la Montagne
67140 Mittelbergheim
Tel. 88089102-88089191
Fax 88089188

The medieval town of Mittelbergheim is nestled on top of a hill, shrouded in misleadingly austere splendour. The sober Renaissance-age stone houses conceal a townfolk ever ready to pour their wines in good company. The old Boeckel house with its great courtyard, turret, and timbered façade is in the local style and stands right in the center of the town. The domaine boasts 20 ha, eight of which are Grands Crus in the Kirchberg, Muenchberg, Wiebelsberg and Zotzenberg area. The latter is a slope with a high limestone content and is the family's crown jewel. The vineyard produces a stupendous Sylvaner Vielles Vignes, to rival the sublime Riesling. With several centuries of winemaking experience in his blood, the bright-eyed 57 year-old Emile Broeckel takes infinite pains over his crus while also managing his flourishing business. A Riesling from sandy terrain, a deliciously thirst-quenching Sylvaner and a late-harvest Gewürztraminer all prove that Boeckel wines are of the highest quality and made with enormous talent.

Sylvaner Zotzenberg 1991 ❦ ①
Born of time-worn vines, this full and elegant wine is unusually light and refreshing. The bouquet is part animal-like and part flowery. Soft and elegant on the palate, it has a considerably long finish.

Riesling Grand Cru Wedelsberg 1990 ❦ ②
A great vintage, fulfilling all expectations The fruity nose is followed by an extremely elegant body, a delicate fullness on the palate and a finish worthy of the variety. A Riesling which is just dry enough, well-balanced and refreshing.

Domaine Lucien et Charles Brand

71, rue de Volxheim
Ergersheim
67120 Molsheim
Tel. 88381771

Alsace is changing with the new generation of growers who, while not turning their backs on the work of their predecessors, do not hesitate to take their own initiatives. 36 year-old oenology school graduate Charles Brand has followed enthusiastically in his father's footsteps although puts less emphasis on the commercial side of the business. Located not far from Strasburg in a lovely wine-growing village, the estate is comprised of 7 ha of loess and limestone soil vineyards. A sturdy six-footer, Charles is an expert on "geology of the terrain" - which predominates over variety in the older vintages - as well as on vinification. What are his preferences? The Lower Rhine style for drier wines, where residual sugar is restricted to the bare minimum, but also wines which express the "goût de terroir" - like the Kepferberg grown on deep, marly soil - rather than their varietal character. There is also a Crémant d'Alsace brut from Rimlerpfad which bears a good resemblance to the better crus of Champagne. Keep your eye on this up and coming grower.

Gewürztraminer Kepferberg 1989 ☙ ②
For the time being, the varietal qualities are predominant over the special characteristics imparted by the cru. The bouquet gives off hints of roses and spices. Very dry on the palate, velvety and rich, it has a well-balanced finish and no residual sugar.

Crémant d'Alsace du Rimlerpfad ☙ ②
It has a lovely color with bright straw highlights and lively bubbles just as fine is its perlage. Clean and crisp on the nose and elegant and honest on the palate. Pleasant lingering finish.

Joseph Cattin et fils

68420 Voegtlingshoffen
Tel. 89493021
Fax 89492602

Rest asured, there will be no war between the Cattins. In fact, the only battle fought ever by these two families, rivals since the 17th century, is a battle over quality. In the midst of it all is a unique character, reigning like an emperor over the vines, with his motto "Always imitated, never equalled". Jacky Cattin is always ready to defend the South of the Route du Vin. Jacky cultivates 23.5 ha of loess and limestone soil, with a modest foothold in the Grand Cru Hatschbourg (not to mention an extremely well-structured Gewürztraminer and some top quality "grains nobles" selections), well positioned on a sunny, even, well-drained slope. He is a serious winemaker who prefers well-rounded, full-flavored fragrant wines. There is an excellent Crémant d'Alsace, with good structure (one third Tokay-Pinot Gris) and an attractive, persistent perlage - enough to make Champagne envious. Jacky expects great things of the Tokay-Pinot Gris he planted in 1991 at Hagelberg on a slope abandoned years ago. We shall make an appointment for the next edition of this guide - or perhaps a little later.

Gewürztraminer ☙ ②
Grand Cru Hatschbourg 1989
Finally a varietal wine with a more mineral expression than of flowers. The bouquet is less discreet and offers a spicy note over an aroma of honey and citrus. The finish contains no hint of heaviness.

Crémant d'Alsace ☙ ②
Rich, elegant color and a bouquet with a yeasty side. Full-flavored with delicate perlage, it is a very successful wine, easily comparable to some Champagnes.

Cave Vinicole de Pfaffenheim

5, rue du Chai
68250 Pfaffenheim
Tel. 89496108
Fax 89497165

Pfaffenheim is a co-operative winery which is as successful with its lesser wines as it is with the more noble. The old 18th century press standing in front of the cellars in no way clashes with the latter's modernity. Growers from over 200 ha of vineyards bring all their fruit to Pfaffenheim and they have good reason to be proud. Alex Heinrich, the manager and guru, is a model of commercial energy and the head cellarman Michel Kueny is always in search of the very best in quality. The winery possesses three Grands Crus covering the whole range (Hatschbourg, Goldert and Steinert), but it also has a selection of four limited zones and eight cuvées denominated great vintages. The wines made feature a blend of Pinot Blanc, Sylvaner, Tokay-Pinot Gris and Chasselas which produces a noteworthy Edelzwicker, a Pinot Blanc from Scneckenberg which was extremely successful in 1989 an 1990, excellent Rieslings, and a Tokay-Pinot Gris which has fascinated one of France's great chefs, Bernard Loiseau. The late-harvests and "grains nobles" selections are of a high standard. All in all, a leading winery.

Edelzwicker   ℘ ①
A blend of Pinot Blanc, Sylvaner and Tokay-Pinot Gris grapes, with 10% Chasselas. An excellent drinking wine.

Pinot Blanc Schneckenberg 1990   ℘ ①
Made with grapes from vines growing next to the Grand Cru Steinert, this Pinot Blanc has a fine, clean hue and a bouquet with hazelnut notes and a slightly smoky feel. On the palate, it has a pleasant, fresh character with good acidity and balance.

Tokay Pinot Gris   ℘℘ ③
Cuvée Rabelais 1989
This cuvée is always hard to get hold of, since nearly all of it goes to Bernard Loiseau, traditionally decorated with Michelin 's three-stars, who has practically made this wine into his own private special reserve. The nose initially offers animal-like nuances, followed by pears and flowers, most elegant on the whole. On the palate it is extremely fruity, with a freshness that reveals some residual sugar and has yet to reach full maturity. Best kept for a few years still.

Gewürztraminer   ℘℘ ④
Sélection de Grains Nobles 1988
Simply extraordinary. With its rich bouquet with notes of roses, lemon and super-ripe fruit, it has an impressive body, supple on the palate. Refreshing and full of zip, despite its high alcohol content. A near perfect example of its genre.

Cave Vinicole de Turckheim

16, rue des Tuileries
68230 Turckheim
Tel. 89270625
Fax 89273533

Busy as a beehive, this winery, founded in 1955, is untiring in its promotion of Alsace and her wines. In what Léonard Humbrecht, leading light of Alsatian wine, considers the most beautiful town in the region, with its paved square, characteristic houses, costumed Singer of the Hours, fortified gates and much else besides, we find a co-operative with a range of fine wines. Indeed, its products are to be found in three of the five Michelin three-star restaurants in Paris and at all the best tables in Alsace. The experience of 280 members comes together with modern technology (pneumatic presses, up to 20 selections per variety and controlled-temperature fermentation) to make wine from 300 ha including many Grands Crus (Brand, Hengst, Ollwiller, Schlossberg, Schoenenbourg, Sommerberg, Sporen and Wineck). These are growers who favor low yields, wines to lay down, Pinot Noir aged in new barriques which will stand comparison with many Burgundies, a Riesling Cru Sporen which is quite perfect, superb late-harvests, and a Klevner to drink until your thirst is quenched. Jean-Paul Ritzenhaler, the manager, will tell you all about it, passionately.

Pinot Blanc   ℘ ①
Côte du Val Saint-Grégoire 1990
This Pinot Blanc, from the south-facing granite terrain of the Vallée Haute, is a triumph of fruit. Well-rounded on the palate, with hints of pear appearing through overtones of acacia. Very soft finish.

Riesling Grand Cru Brand 1990   ℘℘℘ ③
Grown on a granite slope, this cru has enjoyed this year's exceptional sunshine, which has helped to make it one of the appellation's best. Superbly delicate and complex nose, with toasted aromas. Surprisingly fresh, excellently structured and with spicy hints in the finish.

Muscat Heimbourg 1989   ℘ ②
Rich in freshness, with hints of ripe fruit which lend fullness on the palate. A luscious wine with substantial body which finishes on a vegetal note. To be drunk as an aperitif.

Pinot Noir 1990   ♥ ②
Vinified in the traditional manner, as in Burgundy, but in new barriques, this cru has an intense garnet color and a delicate bouquet with liquorice and toasty notes. Soft on the palate, it maintains its aromatic qualities well.

Deiss

15, Route du Vin
68750 Bergheim
Tel. 89736337
Fax 89733267

Hard-working, rigorous, proud and bursting with personality, Jean-Michel Deiss runs a tight ship and has one motto: terrain, variety and vintage. Obstinate and unswerving, he is one of the rising stars of Alsace, with his 20 ha under cultivation. Jean-Michel is a top oenologist who is not easily contented, a stickler for lower and lower yields and selective vinification, zone by zone. He loves Riesling, offering no less than a dozen types. The 1990 Rieslings are very successful, particularly the Grand Cru Grasberg which will be sublime in 20 years. Jean-Michel is also a skilled maker of Pinot Blanc and is an owner in Grand Cru Altenberg (above all with a Tokay-Pinot Gris) as well as in Schoenenberg at Riquewihr, where he tests his skills on a Pinot Noir Burlenberg aged in new wood, comparable to a great Burgundy. Jean-Michel is also utterly reliable when it comes to late-harvest wines or "grains nobles" selections.

Pinot Blanc 1991   🍇 ①
A white wine made with an artist's touch, from top-knotch fruit. All is enhanced by a powerful fruity fragrance.

Riesling   🍇🍇 ③
Grand Cru Grasberg 1990
The cru finds perfect expression in this truly great wine, which offers an attractive nose of citrus fruits and flowers, an unexpected freshness, perfectly balanced structure, excellent acidity and a powerful finish. A wine to cellar and to leave in peace for a few years.

Pinot Noir Burlenberg 1990   🍷🍷 ②
"It was a Pinot Noir year", Jean-Michel Deiss confesses, with no sense of inferiority towards Burgundy. True enough, his new oak-aged Pinot Noir could easily match some of the great blue-blood Côte de Nuits.

Domaine Jean-Pierre Dirler

13, rue d'Issenheim
68500 Bergholtz
Tel. 89769100
Fax 89768597

The little Alsatian-style courtyard possesses great charm. Jean-Pierre Dirler and his wife, Marthe, welcome you with the penetrating gaze of those who wish to size the visitor up. Under the austere, outward appearance, however, lies passion. The estate dates from 1871 and extends over 7 ha with 40% in Grands Crus (Kessler, Saering and Spiegel) where Jean-Pierre proves his skills as an extraordinary grower, allowing low yields and making careful selections. He has endeavored to cultivate sylvaner in Kessler and Kitterlé, in an effort to show to the that the often under-rated grape can indeed do wonderful things, when cultivated on good soil, with care. Jean-Pierre is a firm believer in letting the cru express itself in its purest form, letting the man's touch only intervening for last, to enhance the final result. This is precisely his technique when ageing his Pinot Noir in new oak barrels, or when he manages to produce a magnificent Riesling or other equally extraordinary "grains nobles" selections. Yesterday, Jean-Pierre was virtually unheard-of; today, he is a rising star.

Riesling Grand Cru Saering 1990   🍇🍇 ②
The vines are still young but as many as three selections have been made for this wine so that the final quality of the grapes is exceptional. The bouquet is intense with all-embracing flowery overtones. On the palate, the wine is robust but elegant. Well-balanced, with almost perfect acidity.

Sylvaner Cuvée Vieilles Vignes 1990   🍇 ①
Made from grapes from the Grands Crus Kessler and Kitterlé at Guebewiller, this cuvée offers an amazingly fresh Sylvaner with a very rich texture. There is apricot, pear, and the typical varietal fragrance in the bouquet. Good acidity and a long finish of great charm, with vaguely mineral notes.

Gewürztraminer   🍇🍇 ③
Vendanges Tardives Spiegel 1989
A cru wine made with painstaking perfectionism, it has a charming bouquet with overtones of lemon, mango, mint ,and roses. On the palate, it does not yet express its full potential, but the extracts are certainly there, as it is rich, well-balanced and clean-tasting. Worth waiting a few years to drink.

Pinot Noir 1990   🍷🍷 ②
Tronçais oaks contributes much to the success of this wine, although very subtle on the nose. Enhances the wine's complexity, body and structure, without disguising the kirsch and wild cherry on the palate. Some secondary tannins, not too over-powering, come towards the finish.

Dopff & Irion

Château de Riquewihr
68340 Riquewihr
Tel. 89479890
Fax 89479890

Created by the merger of the Dopff and Irion family estates, the winery has been active since the 16th century. Its headquarters are in the Riquewihr castle, in a small medieval village to the north-west of Colmar, where the owners manage other business interests together with the cultivation of 27 ha of vineyards. Purchases are made in the form of grapes (two thirds of the total, from 30 loyal growers) with the rest directly in wine. The estates wines are marketed under the Château de Riquewihr label and are made from grapes grown within the commune. A minimal quantity of carbon dioxide is used in vinification and, in contrast to past practice, residual sugar is avoided. Different vineyards growing the same grape type are labelled individually, one per type: Les Murailles for the riesling, Les Maquisards for the tokay-pinot gris, Les Amandiers for the muscat, and Les Sorcières for the gewürztraminer. Dopff & Irion also have vines in two Grands Crus: Sporen, where Tokay-Pinot Gris and Gewürztraminer have been planted, and Schoenenberg, which produces mMuscat and Riesling suitable for ageing. Interesting experiments are also being carried out in the ageing of Tokay-Pinot Gris in oak barrels.

Gewürztraminer Les Sorcières 1990 ♈ ③
A young wine with a pale color, its nose is well-developed, strongly varietal and well-balanced between flowers (roses) and spices (pepper). Dry on the palate, frank with a good, fresh, minty finish. Ready to drink.

Tokay Pinot Gris ♈ ③
Grand Cru Sporen 1988
Yellow-gold in color, with a nose of ripe fruit, mingled with straw. Full-flavored on the palate, well-balanced and of good length. A wine that is ready to drink from a great vintage for its genre.

Maison Faller Robert et fils

36, Grand-Rue
68150 Ribeauvillé
Tel. 89736047
Fax 89733480

The town holds a magnificent fair on the first Sunday in September. It is called "Pfifferdaj", or "the minstrels' festival", and commemorates the generosity of a certain Lord of Ribeaupierre who gave a minstrel a "louis d'or" (gold coin) after breaking his instrument. The town is also the home of the Faller family, a family which needs no introduction, having been active (and universally respected) in the world of wine since 1967. A leading member of the Confrérie de Saint-Étienne, Jean-Baptiste is a 55 year-old patriarch with a crown of white hair and the air of a jolly friar and one of the nicest wine-people of the region. He will gladly talk to you about his wine, the area he lives in and good places to eat, both well-known and not so well-known, welcoming you to his home in town. The fairly anonymous façade hides a charming "old Alsace" decor, with antique furniture and beautiful etchings of the vineyards. Jean-Baptiste favors wines for ageing and owns 12 ha, three of which are in Grands Crus (Geisberg and Kirchberg). He rents out a few more hectares, buying back the grapes, and makes a very fruity, full-bodied Riesling, a superb late-harvest Gewürztraminer as well as a delicious, straightforward Sylvaner, for easy drinking anytime.

Sylvaner 1991 ♈ ①
Fairly elegant fruit with a fresh, delicate palate. A Sylvaner which need not be ashamed of its origins.

Riesling Grand Cru Gaisberg 1990 ♈ ③
Lovely yellow color, tending towards amber. Dry fruity nose with real fullness on the palate and a full body, brought together in a well-balanced whole.

Gewürztraminer ♈ ③
Grand Cru Kirchberg 1988
An extremely pleasant wine with a fascinating bouquet containing notes of spices and roses. The palate is rich and full with an exceptionally long finish.

Serge Fend

3, rue des Tilleuls
67520 Marlenheim
Tel. 88875140
Fax 88876456

At 35 years of age, this "enfant prodige" of oak-aged Pinot Noir is also capable of making wine from the other varieties on his estate. Serge Fend has six ha of vineyards on loam and limestone soil near the celebrated Hostellerie du Cerf run by the great Husser family in the first commune along the Route du Vin (or the last, depending on which way you are coming from). In this industrious town (which puts on its party clothes every year on the 15th August to take part in the "Our friend Fritz's Wedding" at Erckmann-Chatrian) we pay a visit to Serge as one would a close friend, who receives us in person for a tasting (by appointment only). We sample a Pinot Noir - with ageing potential, a favorite of Burgundy enthusiasts - but we also taste some good Rieslings and Gewürztraminers, some from Grand Cru Steinklotz, which are both attractively drinkable and priced. The late-harvest version of Gewürztraminer proves an excellent aperitif, with its delicate, spicy fruit.

Riesling 1990 ☙ ①
A classic Riesling, where flowery notes mingle with outstanding freshness. Fresh on the palate, with moderate acidity and a lively finish. Very agreeable to drink now.

Pinot Noir 1990 ☙ ②
Nothing better than this cru, skillfully made in oak barrels, to take Burgundy enthusiasts moreby surprise. The tannins have not yet fully mellowed, but the nose, with its notes of ripe red fruit, is sumptuous. Its body and structure on the palate seduce at first sip.

Pierre Frick

5, rue de Baer
68520 Pfaffenheim
Tel. 89496299
Fax 89497378

Alsace needed a hard-line ecologist. Pierre Frick was born into a family who has been cultivating vines for twelve generations, using environment-friendly methods on the nine ha. property since 1970. He converted to "biodynamics" (a farming method which avoids the use of synthetic chemicals or fertilizers) in 1981 thus taking a further step towards a better appreciation of the rhythms of the land and the influence of external agents upon it. Pierre's motto now is to accept the natural course of things. Of course, he would never contemplate the use of sulphur or chaptalization (the use of added sugar). Instead, he would much rather tell you about nettle tea and the other infusions he uses on his vines. It is Pierre's pleasure to take you in hand and convert you to his methods, as he pours you a minerally Riesling which shows good grape character, an elegant Muscat, pleasantly refreshing Pinot Blancs, or any one of his botrytis selections, which make him one of the leading winemakers in the region.

Riesling Lerchenberg 1991 ☙ ①
Unchaptalized, like all of Pierre Frick's wines, this is a wine of typical varietal character. The nose is very minerally, with a light muscat finish. Full on the palate, with both balance and length.

Pinot Blanc 1991 ☙ ①
A highly characteristic Pinot with a lovely fruity fragrance. Fresh on the palate, with a soft texture and a slightly smoky finish.

Gewürztraminer ☙ ☙ ④
Sélection de Grains Nobles 1989
This cru is a splendid concentration of aromas of ginger and honey. Made from super-ripe grapes, harvested at just the right moment, it is a tiny miracle which places its maker in the top rank.

Paul Ginglinger

8, place Charles de Gaulle
68420 Eguisheim
Tel. 89414425
Fax 89249488

Dominated by the Schlossberg and the Trois Châteaux, Eguisheim was the home of Pope Leo XI. Today, Paul Ginglinger, defender of the Grands Crus, lives here. His family moved to the outskirts of this town of circular, flower-lined streets in 1810. Ginglinger favors low yields and selection by sub-zone, as in the case of his Gewürztraminer from vines on loess and limestone soil, protected from the west wind by its warm, dry micro-climate. Paul's careful selections result in wines of great solidity from the Eichberg and Pfersigberg vineyards. Grown from over 12 ha of vineyards, all of his wines have structure and character, like the marvellous Klevner from 60% Auxerrois and 40% Pinot Blanc and a Riesling which, like the previous wine, comes from the loam and limestone soil. Paul's Eichberg Muscat generally leaves an impression of great freshness while the Pinot Blanc is the epitome of a drinking wine which should not be hidden away in the cellar.

Riesling Grand Cru Pfersigberg 1990 ⚜ ②
Elegant appearance with a fine, intense bouquet containing marked flowery and fruity notes. Full-flavored, rich in extracts with outstanding concentration and balance. Finish of exceptional length.

Gewürztraminer ⚜ ③
Vendages Tardives 1989
A jewel of extraordinarily captivating elegance. Yellow-gold in color with a bouquet in which fruit is combined with mineral notes on a background of white peach and super-ripe grapes. Complex structure with a long, long finish.

Rémy Gresser

2, Rue de l'École
67140 Andlau
Tel. 88089588
Fax 88085599

The red-clay roofs, the grey-stone walls, the main door of the 12th century church with its magnificent Romanesque sculptures, venerated by the inhabitants of Andlau, are among the curiosities to be found in this village whose outline rises up over the Route du Vin. A man not to miss is a grower called Rémy Gresser, holder of several offices: Vice-President of the Grands Crus Commission; President of the Young Growers 15 years ago; of the village grape-pickers today; and - the one of which he is proudest - President of the Confraternity of the Hospitallers of Andlau. On his 10 ha, Rémy makes wine from the whole range of cru varieties and also owns parcels in the Grands Crus of Muenchberg, Wiebelsberg and Kastelberg. Wise and reasonable (when he has to moderate one of his passionate outbursts), Rémy goes to similar extents for each of his wines. From the soft and honest Sylvaner to the finest "grains nobles" selections and the Pinot Noir Brandhof (for which he confesses a special interest), this young grower's wines are to be followed, for Rémy is not lacking in ambition.

Sylvaner 1991 ⚜ ①
Good freshness, good acidity and moderate fruit make up a pleasant, satisfyingly thirst-quenching wine. An honest Sylvaner for which the producer can be proud.

Riesling Muenchberg 1990 ⚜ ②
From chalky soil, this Grand Cru from an exceptional year for Riesling has rather minerally, intense fragrances and good body on the palate, with a crisp, clean finish.

Pinot Noir Brandhof 1990 🍇 ②
From chalky soil on south-south-east facing hills, this wine is the result of a lengthy maceration and wood ageing in both barrels and barriques. Deep red in hue, the nose has a faint note of wood and the palate reveals well-rounded tannins.

Domaine Pierre Hering

6, rue du Docteur Sultzer
67140 Barr
Tel. 88089007
Fax 88080854

Pierre Hering can see his vineyards from his house at the edge of town. He has been renting the Folie Marco estate, which belongs to the commune since 1959, land locked among the houses on loamy and chalky soil at the foot of the Kirchberg. The estate has a unique sheltered micro-climate which has been noted since the 17th century. Sylvaner is cultivated here over 1.5 ha on very old vines which are pruned right back with stupendous results. Half of the rest of Pierre's vines (10 ha in total) are in the Grand Cru Kirchberg, yielding Riesling and a fine Gewürztraminer. His late-harvests are often powerful without being exceedingly heavy. All Pierre's wines are aged in wooden barrels and are generally bottled after about a year. This gives them a certain Lower-Rhine character, rather undeveloped when young and of outstanding complexity when aged. Prices are very reasonable.

Gewürztraminer Grand Cru 🍇🍇 ②
Kirchberg Clos Gaensbronnel 1990
From a vineyard in the Grand Cru Kirchberg right behind the producer's house. Yellow-gold in color with characteristic, delicate fragrances of rose and pepper. The varietal nature is also apparent in the palate, which is delicate and well-structured. A classic Lower Rhine wine.

Riesling 🍇🍇 ②
Grand Cru Kirchberg 1990
The complexity of the cru may be sensed right from the delicate spicy fragrance. The flavor is strikingly well-rounded and the body, full. A serious Riesling, for ageing. It will keep its flowery characteristics for four or five years before going over to the more mineral side and finally developing the charcteristic aroma of petrol after at least 12 years.

Sylvaner Clos de la Folie Marco 1990 🍇 ①
Delicate and light on the nose, a very elegant wine, considering the variety. Full and satisfying flavor, rich with a slight hint of mineral. A really enthralling, fascinating wine which is excellent value for money.

Gewürztraminer 🍇🍇 ②
Vendanges Tardives 1989
Golden in color with a delicate, botrytized bouquet. Intense fragrances of candied grape over a full, rich flavor, free of any heaviness. A late-harvest with little residual sugar, to lay down. An excellent product of a well-balanced vintage.

Heywang

17, rue Principale
67140 Heiligenstein
Tel. 88089141
Fax 88089553

Pinot Blanc and Klevner are often confused because the Klevner grape is also known as Pinot Blanc. The Heiligenstein Klevner (which is a communal Appellation like Ottrott red wine or Marlenheim rosé), however, is defined by special legislation and restricted to a specific geographical area. An ancient Alsatian variety which dates from the 18th century, it was first cultivated by Ehret Wantz and celebrated its 250th anniversary in 1922. This Klevner is the forerunner of the ungrafted traminer, also called savagnin rose, from the Jura and today is produced exclusively by the winemakers in the commune of Heiligenstein. Something of a rarity, it unites the animal-like fragrance of Tokay to the fruit of a Gewürz. Best drunk with gusto as an aperitif or sipped on a hot afternoon in the shade of a vine-layed garden gazebo. Jean Heywang, who was head cellarman at Klipfel for five years, is the acknowledged master of Klevner. His five ha estate produces all the varieties of this cru. Heywang really knows his trade and is also capable of presenting a marvellous Sylvaner, grown on loam and limestone.

Sylvaner 1991 🍇 ①
From grapes grown on clay and limestone soil, this white wine has a great future ahead of it. The nose is quite pleasant, but, best of all, it has that considerable freshness: something to look for in the varietal.

Klevner d'Heiligenstein 1990 🍇 ②
A fruity nose of unusual elegance, evoking Gewürztraminer at first and then the more animal-like aromas of Tokay-Pinot Gris. Good body, perfect balance and refreshing acidity. A wine which will age with no trouble at all.

Hugel et fils

3, rue de la Première Armée
68340 Riquewihr
Tel. 89479215
Fax 89490010

What a lovely family they are! Jean Hugel is a wonderful "raconteur", full of stories and anecdotes. The region should erect a monument to him for the special legislation done to benefit late-harvest and "grains nobles" selection wines. His elder son, Georges, who looks after the business-side, is a perfect foil while André, the younger son, turns his hand to anything. His own sons, Étienne and Marc, the 12th generation of the family since 1639, also lend a hand. The Hugels have 25 ha of vines (45% Riesling, 45% Gewürztraminer, 8% Tokay-Pinot Gris and 2% Pinot Noir, with an average vine age being 28 years old). Most vineyards are situated on the glorious slopes of Sporen and Schoenenbourg, but they also buy in the equivalent of the production of a further 115 ha. All vinification takes place in the winery at Riquewihr, where some of the bottles are over a hundred years old. Harvesting is done by hand, vinification by controlled temperatures and the bottles are cellared at least 30 months before release. The Hugels are always ready to sing the praises of their Alsace and the wines they make reflect their personalities: serious and beyond reproach.

Riesling 1990   ☆ ②
An exceptional year in which the Hugels could not fail to produce a wonderful cuvée. From loam and chalk soil, this Riesling has the typical varietal aroma, a full flavor on the palate and a perfect balance.

Riesling   ☆☆ ④
Vendanges Tardives 1988
An excellent wine considering that it is among the first tries at late-harvest wines. The 1988 vintage will not be available until 1993, but we suggest you book now. The ripe-grapey bouquet is magnificent, as are the flowery fragrances and the beautifully rounded flavor. The finish is equally eloquent.

Pinot Noir 1989   ☆ ②
Previous generations of Hugels will no doubt be turning in their graves as this wine bears few of the family's traditional hallmarks. However, one must admit that the new generation of Hugels, Étienne and Marc, have been successful in their efforts.

André Kientzler

50, rue de Bergheim
68150 Ribeauvillé
Tel. 88736710

Kientzlers have been making wine from native Alsace grapes on their 10 ha estate for five generations. Despite his high standing as a famed oenologist, André has a serious reputation and remains dynamic and good-natured. In support of low yields and long ageing, he is one of the "éminences grises" of the Geisberg, whose loam and limestone soil produces great Rieslings, especially ageing character, like one particular Riesling from the south-facing 1.5 ha of the Grand Cru Geisberg. Needless to say, do not overlook the other wines, like the very drinkable Kirchberg Muscat, a delicate Pinot Blanc, the late-harvests and "grains nobles" selections which produce quite superb wines to lay down as if they were treasure chests. Everything produced here is worth a detour and a few words of reverent praise, including the unpretentious Chasselas, a lively, pleasant table wine, and the Auxerrois, more subtle and well-rounded.

Auxerrois 1990   ☆ ①
A small triumph of freshness, delicacy and finesse, this Auxerrois is outstandingly well-balanced. The bouquet reveals hints almost of over-ripeness while the fruit, a little on the candied side, dominates the flavor. A lovely wine, well-rounded and full of fascination. Excellent drinking.

Riesling 1990   ☆ ②
Full-flavored, elegant and with good flowery fragrance. The flavor is slightly minerally, with good intensity. The acidity, which is well-balanced for its structure, suggests that this wine will age well. The finish has a freshness all its own.

Riesling   ☆☆ ④
Sélection de Grains Nobles 1990
From vines on the Grand Cru Geisberg, on which André Kientzler is a great specialist, this wine has an aromatic richness, a fullness on the palate, and a balance which come near to perfection. There is not a shadow of heaviness nor any hint of excess alcohol to upset the pleasure it gives.

Domaine Klipfel

6, avenue de la Gare
67140 Barr
Tel. 88089485
Fax 88085318

Guy and André Lorentz deserve a medal for such a well-stocked cellar, full of fine vintage wines. It is a great privilege to taste a stupendously fresh 1959 Sylvaner, or a 1943 or 1961 Gewürztraminer from the Zisser estate, wines which prove (if any proof were needed) that Alsatian wines can age wonderfully. Granted the quality is there, the Lorentzes run a flourishing business and own 40 ha of vineyards in the Grands Crus Kastelberg and Kirchberg and in the famous Freiberg area. They are certainly one of the most up and coming wineries in the area. In the cellar are 3,000 hl worth of wooden barrels dating back to the turn of the century, but they also have 7,000 hl of capacity in glass-lined cement vats, 1,500 hl of stainless steel vats, 1,600 square m of underground ageing rooms and an efficient bottling system. Not long ago, the Lorentzes started making wine from pinot noir in small oak barrels from Burgundy. For their other wines, however, they prefer the traditional method of using medium-large wooden barrels until the wine is transferred to steel vats under nitrogen. They are also keen promoters of wine tourism and their museum is a must for visitors to the area: especially to meet the friendly Lorentz family.

Riesling   🍇🍇 ②
Grand Cru Kirchberg 1990
This wine is concentrated, with an intense range of floral aromas. A stupendous fresh acidity counterbalances the alcohol and a surprising lengthy finish gives off a minerally note.

Tokay Pinot Gris Freiberg 1990   🍇🍇🍇 ②
A sumptuous wine. The nose is already inebriating on its own, with oriental aromas of spice and musk. On the palate, the richness of the acidity offsets the alcohol. The finish is very complex; a wine worth laying down, which should develop in due time.

Gewürztraminer   🍇🍇 ④
Sélection de Grains Nobles Clos Zisser 1989
In the Grand Cru Kirchberg, the abundant sunlight guarantees excellent results every time and this vintage is no exception. The nose is eloquent with its overtones of ripe grapes and candied fruit. The palate, with the traces of botrytis, is voluptuous and full of promise for the future.

Rouge de Barr 1990   🍇 ②
Fine bright ruby color. Fresh bouquet of red fruit with muscat fragrances. The palate reveals an elegant, delicate and extremely supple body, with a very harmonious finish.

Jean-Marie Koehly

64, rue du Général de Gaulle
67600 Kintzheim
Tel. 88620977
Fax 88827049

The courtyard aviary in the castle, with the eagles and the other breeds of day and night birds, the stork-breeding center and the mountain, where 300 Atlantic Barbary apes live, are not the only attractions of this village, situated at the foot of Haut-Koenigsbourg. There is also a family of winegrowers worth getting to know. The Koehlies were the first to plant Pinot Noir at Rodern in 1922. Their ten hectares of vineyards have a splendid view to the south-west over the castle of Haut-Koenigsbourg, which was rebuilt by Kaiser Wilhelm II. Almost as if they wanted to prove their ancestors right after all, the Koehlies are endeavoring to produce a Pinot Noir with lots of body - and they are succeeding. Rather than looking for lightness or fruit in their wines, they aim for a certain fullness and a firm structure, achieved by extending maceration well past the usual limits. The Koehlies use oak barrels with inarguably good results in terms of balance, fragrance, harmony and enhanced ageing potential.

Pinot Noir 1989   🍇🍇 ②
This oaked Pinot Noir is better than those usually produced in the region and may help to relaunch the variety. Limpid in appearance, the fragrance of red berries is all-pervading and the structure of the wine is well-balanced, with fine, elegant tannins which guarantee a sure future.

Kreydenweiss

12, rue Deharbe
67140 Andlau
Tel. 88089583
Fax 88084116

Tucked away in this village of the green Andlau valley, between the plains and the mountains, lies a poet, countryman and grower. An outstanding figure among the new generation of Alsatian winemakers, Marc Kreydenweiss has for 13 years been at the head of a 13 ha family estate, with its three centuries of history. A fervent supporter of the importance of the cru, which he privileges over variety, he does not hesitate to make his position clear on his labels. For ten years, Marc has been harvesting by hand, picking grapes at their peak, and practising low yields and prolonged vinification in oak barrels. Grapes are not stripped from the bunch and fermentation is temperature-controlled, as Kreydenweiss is wary of residual sugar. Moreover, until bottling, his wines remain "sur lies", or "on the lees", imparting a rich, fat smoothness. Marc's Grands Crus Muenchberg, Wiebelsberg and Kastelberg of Riesling and Tokay-Pinot Gris resemble their producer, as does the Kritt Sylvaner, vinified in oak barriques, or the Muscat from the Rebgarten vineyard. The magnificent late-harvests and "grains nobles" which found their best expression in 1989 and 1990 are along the same lines - sophisticated wines with a distinctive, elegant flavor and a vibrant soul.

Pinot Blanc Kritt 1990   🍷 ①
If all Alsatian wines could have the same charm of those served in the bistrots of Paris after the war, they would once again be universally respected. This wine, with its pleasantly complex bouquet, has a strong fragrance of pears. Fresh finish on a clean, round palate.

Riesling   🍷🍷 ③
Grand Cru Kastelberg 1990
This wine, mineral and flowery on the nose with hints of citrus coming through, is highly successful. Exceptionally good density on the palate, pleasantly dry; inarguably a wine with class. Very long finish.

Tokay Pinot Gris   🍷🍷 ④
Sélection de Grains Nobles 1989
There is no need to look any further; this cru is without doubt one of the true wonders of Alsatia. Of rare richness and balance which nears perfection. A splendid wine on the palate with an absolutely exceptional finish.

Gewürztraminer Kritt 1988   🍷🍷 ③
The ultimate expression of a wine from century-old glacier deposit soils. It has a magnificent bouquet of exotic and candied fruit, with hints of roses, a beautifully balanced full-body and texture and pleasant fresh acidity.

Maison Kuentz-Bas

14, route du Vin
68420 Husseren-les-Châteaux
Tel.89493024
Fax 89492339

Christian Bas and Jean Weber are two spirited young cousins who own and manage this winery founded in 1795, when the Valais grower, Joseph Kentz, came to live in the village. The 12 ha estate on south-south-east facing loam and limestone soil (with a small proprotion in the "grands crus" of Eichberg and Pfersigberg). It is particularly suited to Gewürztraminer, but all the classic local varieties may be found. Bas and Weber do not live in the past. Every year, together with a jury of Parisian journalists, they award the Lauréades trophy to young chefs. They use a traditional method of vinification which privileges low yields and allows the fruit to express itself to its fullest. More recently, they have been paying particular attention to wines produced from super-ripe grapes, with interesting results like the late-harvest cuvée Caroline and the "grains nobles" selection cuvée Jérémy. Residual sugar is sometimes excessive ,but the overall production standard is high. Wines are put on the market only after two years in the cellar and the bottle.

Pinot Blanc 1991   🍷 ①
This cuvée offers a fine nose, excellent fruit and a robust palate, not, however, without its freshness.

Riesling Vendanges Tardives   🍷🍷 ④
Cuvée Caroline 1989
A cuvée named after Christian Bas's daughter. It has the characteristic varietal fragrances, in which flowers predominate over citrus. Residual sugar is well-balanced and the finish is fresh and lingering.

Gewürztraminer   🍷 ③
Grand Cru Pfersigberg 1988
A lovely, yellow color. The nose is of great finesse, dominated by mineral and fumé tones. Full and rich on the palate, the finish is particularly long, promising nice ageing.

Seppi Landman

20, rue de la Vallée
68750 Soultzmatt
Tel. 89470933

Seppi Landman is a giant of a man specializing in late-harvest wines and "grains nobles" selections. Unknown only a few years ago, he has shaken up the cushy world of the great Alsatian growers. Seppi has a style and ideas all his own when it comes to achieving his objectives: low yields, careful selections and an ideal relationship with the cru (magnificent terrain, like that of Zinnkoepflé in Soultzmatt, with its fossil/limestone compostion). Sometimes fortune smiles on him, as it does on all great players. When on 26th October, 1990, his harvest of first choice Riesling grown in the Grand Cru Zinnkoepflé was superb. Unfortunately, the second selection got rained out when heavy rains began fallling on Nov. 2nd and lasted throughout the month. Seppi grumbled and, even more so, as temperatures fell to minus 7° C for two nights in the beginning of December. Then, of course, it snowed. At that point, Seppi got a brilliant idea and decided to follow his neighbors on the other side of the Rhine: he made what turned out to be an exceptional Eiswein with 14° potential alcohol. That particular vintage proved to be very rewarding for Landman (and luckily a treat for us, too).

Riesling Vendanges Tardives   ❦❦❦ ④
Grand Cru Zinnkoepflé 1990
A combination of exceptional climatic conditions and the skills of a grower who loves to take risks. It is a Riesling sold with the qualification "vendages tardives" because, unlike Germany, France does not recognize the category Eiswein. The bouquet opens with the grapey aroma of figs and blackcurrants. The body is exceptionally full on the palate (with 14° potential alcohol in the grapes) and the finish is very fresh and clean.

Gewürztraminer Sélections de   ❦❦❦ ④
Grains Nobles Grand Cru Zinnkoepflé 1988
Amber yellow in appearance with an outstandingly elegant bouquet comprising hints of rose, nuts and spices. This cru is exceptionally rich and opulent in texture with a never-ending aromatic finish.

Riesling   ❦❦ ③
Grand Cru Zinnkoepflé 1988
Rather unusual in its varietal aroma of wild flowers, this wine is full-bodied, rich and concentrated on the palate, finishing with an extremely elegant, dry flavor. A very well-balanced wine with a structure that will allow it to age for a long time to come.

Gustave Lorentz

35, Grand' Rue
68750 Bergheim
Tel. 89736308
Fax 89733049

The Lorentzes have been firmly established in this winemaking village, both as merchants and as growers, for almost 150 years. They own 32 ha of vines on loam and limestone soil on the sunny slopes of Altenberg and Kanzlerberg (12 ha). The double doors and ancient well of their house on the Grand' Rue seem eternal, as does the flourishing cellar of more than 1,500,000 bottles. A well-matched trio of serious wine people head this small empire. The patriarch is Charles Lorentz; the number two is his energetic 30 year-old son, who has studied at Beaune and the third is the oenologist, Auguste Baffrey, almost clairvoyant in his winemaking skills. What do we find as a result? Excellent value for money all through the range of quality Alsatian wines: from the simple Sylvaners to the Rieslings. The Grands Crus of Altenberg and Kanzlerberg de Bergheim often produce marvellous wines and, if you keep asking, you might get a legendary late-harvest 1983 Riesling, or perhaps a 1985, or, better still, a sublime Gewürztraminer.

Pinot Blanc 1991   ❦ ①
A fine, dry wine with good length which leaves a pleasant fresh taste in the mouth. The careful vinification is a hallmark of the producer.

Gewürztraminer   ❦ ②
Cuvée Particulière 1989
A spicy, animal-like fragrance, typical of the variety. On the palate, this wine is full-bodied, rich, concentrated and balanced. Final aroma of apricot.

Gewürztraminer   ❦❦ ④
Sélection de Grains Nobles 1988
A wine from 30 to 80 year-old vines in the Grand Cru Altenberg. Deep gold in color, the bouquet offers a veritable explosion of aromas (spices, roses, apricot, quince). On the palate, it is full-bodied, with perfect balance. Should be kept well into the next century.

Hubert Metz

57, route du Vin
67650 Blienschenwiller
Tel. 88924306
Fax 88926208

Hubert Metz is hardly one of those growers to seek out attention from the mass-media; indeed he is relatively unheard of. Nevertheless, in this village up against the foothills facing the Vosges, he is a boon for the Alsatian wine production. At 42, friendly and articulate, he seems to be omnipresent in his lovely, old cellar with its carved barrels, known as the "tithe cellar". Painstakingly overseeing operations in his 9 ha estate where loam and sandstone predominate, Hubert has a penchant for the Grand Cru Winzenberg, recently classified at Blienschenwiller, where he grows Gewürztraminer, and prefers a drier, cleaner and more direct approach to vinification, avoiding excess residual sugar. His Riesling Cuvée de la Dîme is notable and his special Pinot Noir (from a hectare of old vines on clay and granite/sandy soil and macerated for 12 days) has fine, soft tannins, harmoniously incorporated into a real richness of flavor. It is a perfect Lower Rhine wine to compare with Upper Rhine neighbors, but find out for yourselves, before it becomes too fashionable.

Riesling Cuvée de la Dîme 1990 ℘ ②
Every vintage from the Metz cellar is commendable and the 1990 is no exception. Ever drier rather than sweetish, this cuvée is rich and elegant, and pleasantly full-bodied on the palate with good depth and a promising finish.

Gewürztraminer ℘ ②
Grand Cru Winzenberg 1989
A wine of appealing finesse, dry and with no superfluous residual sugar. Scents of roses, spices and nuts. Balanced on the palate, full-bodied and with good aromatic length.

Pinot Noir Vieilles Vignes 1990 ℘ ②
A lovely, garnet color with all-pervading fruit (cherry, wild cherry and kirsch). Dense, concentrated, vigorous structure with an exquisitely delicate finish.

Jos Meyer et fils

76, rue Clémenceau
68920 Wintzenheim
Tel. 89270198
Fax 89270398

When he was elected "Winemaker of the year" in 1990 by Gault-Millau, Jean Meyer didn't let it go to his head. This able merchant also has a grower's soul, inherited from the previous generations of Meyers, who have always put quality before quantity. Jean, however, has ideas of his own. He takes great care during bottling, only after wood ageing in 60 hl barrels which date from the last century. Moreover, he does not blend wine from the upper part of the barrel with wine from the lower, but transfers the contents of each barrel into two separate waiting barrels, filtering slowly to achieve greater evenness in the wine. In this way, Jean obtains two similar, but not identical products. Wine from the lower part of the barrel is bottled first and gets longer ageing while wine from the upper part is closer to its best and is put on the market earlier. Another instance of Jean's original approach is his spring cuvée, a more drinkable Pinot Blanc. The Pinot Blanc H, from ancient vines on Hengst, is suitable for laying down and will surprise many a taster. All of the above will be charmingly illustrated by Jean, a man who genuinely spreads happiness wherever he goes.

Pinot Blanc ℘ ②
Cuvée de Printemps 1991
To drink for the fun of it. A delicious, free and easy wine without any pretensions. Fresh, light and vivacious, on a background of spices and flowers.

Gewürztraminer ℘℘ ②
Cuvée des Folastries 1990
Fresh nose with pleasing notes of roses. Fruit is all-pervading on the palate. Moderately rounded and almost dry, with an outstandingly elegant persistence of flavor which promises excellent prospects for ageing.

Pinot Blanc H Vieilles Vignes 1990 ℘ ③
From the Grand Cru Hengst, this cuvée - which will age for several years despite its Pinot Blanc origins - is a real delight. Nose of white flowers with animal tones, rich palate of fragrant grape but not without roundness. The finish is endless.

Riesling Grand Cru Hengst 1990 ℘℘ ③
Luminous color and a complex nose which brings together white flowers, apricots and honey with mildly mineral notes. A wine with a particularly rich palate, very full-bodied and a long finish. Wait a few years before tasting.

Mittnacht-Klack

8, rue des Tuileries
68340 Riquewihr
Tel. 89479254
Fax 89478950

A historic pearl of the Alsatian wine world, Mittnacht-Klack has remained intact since the 16th century, with its merry Protestant outlook, and certainly deserves a visit. The winery is discreetly off the beaten path, situated away from the town center, and tends to be overlooked by the press. Mittnacht-Klack owns a total of 9.5 ha of vineyards at Hunawihr, Kientzheim, Ribeauvillé and Zellenberg as well as in the Grands Crus of Rosacker, Schoenenbourg, Sporen and the Oberberg and Clos Saint Ulrich areas. Jean Mittnacht is a highly qualified expert who boasts typical wines like a Riesling, of course, (Riquewihr is almost the "capital" of Riesling) which ages well, thanks to the loam and limestone soil which imparts the fragrance known in Alsace as petrol-schmagen, well-rounded, elegantly seductive late-harvest wines, super-concentrated botrytis selections, skillfully showing the winemaker's good judgement, a well-made Muscat (the latter two types come from the Muelhforst area), a Gewürztraminer to lay down and, lastly, a generally well-developed Tokay-Pinot Gris. The dynamic Annie Mittnacht, nicknamed "Klack", passionately defends them all.

Muscat Muelhforst 1990   ♥ ②
The aromatic sensations offered by this cru are still moderate. Good structure and with a fragrant charm on the palate. Lowish acidity combines well with a richness of alcohol. A rather short but interesting finish.

Frédéric Mochel

56, rue Principale
67130 Traenheim
Tel. 88503867
Fax 88505619

The carefully looked-after press in the courtyard dates from 1669, and the caveau, or "cellar" is laid out with Teutonic tidiness. The Route du Vin begins just around the corner and the nearby village of Marlenheim is home to the Auberge du Cerf, where the Husser family celebrate the cru wines. The nearby Mossig vineyard boasts the Grand Cru Altenberg de Bergbeiten. Frédéric Mochel pours his wines with all the pride and precision of a skilled and passionate artesan. He uses wood in the traditional fashion (one of his barrels dates from the early 19th century) and controls temperatures. Frédéric's wines deserve to be cellared and are sure to be worth the wait. His 8 ha estate pays tribute to his skill as a winemaker, offering a Muscat, a marvellously thirst-quenching Pinot Blanc, and, from the earlier vintages, a Riesling Grand Cru Altenberg Cuvée Henriette which is a veritable explosion of fragrances with fruit marrying happily with other, more flowery notes and, finally, the Gewürztraminer Altenberg, usually of exceptional length with a rich, spicy nose. A "vigneron d'élite".

Riesling 1990   ♥ ②
Pale yellow in color with greenish tinges and a simple, sincere bouquet characteristic of the variety. A classic wine in its flowery, fruity style to be drunk young for its agreeable balance.

Riesling Grand Cru Altenberg   ♥ ②
de Bergbieten Cuvée Henriette 1990
From 45 year-old vines growing on loam, loess and limestone, a wine with complex fragrances of sun-warmed straw and honey. Round, rich and with a good, lingering finish. Wait a few years before drinking.

Tokay Pinot Gris 1990   ♥ ②
Clear, golden color, well-developed, rich nose and good consistency on the palate with lovely fruit and good length. Not outstandingly complex but captivating, with a refreshing balance. Beautifully drinkable.

Domaine Muré

Clos Saint-Landelin
68250 Rouffach
Tel. 89496219
Fax 89497485

René Muré comes from a winegrowing family active since 1648 and has been sole owner since 1935 of the 16 ha in the Clos Saint-Landelin (classified Grand Cru Vorbourg). It is a stoney hill of Jurassic limestone with a magnificent south-facing prospect and one of the driest micro-climates in the region, together with some steep slopes requiring terrace cultivation. In his splendid cellar with its ancient barrels and 13th century press, this convinced exponent of systematic malolactic fermentation (known locally as the "Muré method") produces round, soft wines, never lacking in rich fruit and power. The Gewürztraminer Grand Cru Vorbourg needs at least two or three more years; the Pinot Noir is oaked. The Gewürztraminer Grand Cru Zinnkoepflé and the Tokay-Pinot Gris from the Clos Saint-Landelin are the pride of the cellar, together with its "grains nobles" selections.

Riesling Sélection de 🍇🍇 ④
Grains Nobles Clos Saint-Landelin 1990
The color of fine gold is the hallmark of this superb quality cru, which will give exceptional drinking pleasure in years to come. Outstanding concentration and an extremely interesting aromatic complexity which features an exciting marriage of candied citrus and flowers.

Tokay Pinot Gris 🍇🍇 ③
Vendages Tardives 1990
Inebriating and with its typical spicy range of aromas, this Tokay is the perfect expression of its vintage. The over-ripened grapes have permitted the production of a high-alcohol wine which is by no means without elegance.

Pinot Noir 1990 🍇 ②
Aged in small oak casks, a wine with an intense ruby hue and a palate which still bears traces of oak, good rich, dense texture and a slight astringent note. It needs a little more time.

Domaine Ostertag

87, rue Finkwiller
67680 Epfig
Tel. 88855134
Fax 88855895

André Ostertag may love living in the city of Strasburg, but he visits his vineyards every single day of the year. This unique, young man won a Fondation de la Vocation award and yet has the air of a poet, proud of his grass-root traditions. On taking over the family estate of 10 ha in Epfig and Nothalten with 1.5 ha in the Grand Cru Muenchberg, André brought his own contribution to the house style with his own distinctions between mineral and fruit, his Latin approach to cru and Germanic approach to variety. The spirit of his wines (among the best in Alsace) may be seen in the label design, but it is also in André's every glance and gesture: from the low yields, the pre-fermentation maceration, the approach to non-filtration, the use of barriques to a myriad other details. A man to get to know.

Sylvaner Vieilles Vignes 1991 🍇🍇 ②
"Bâtonné" in the best Burgundy style, this vintage, unlike the 1990, has undergone a slight filtration. The soft fermentation has rendered it untypical in comparison with the usual treatment of the variety. The bouquet is very fruity, with hints of citrus, the palate full with rich, round, glycerine extracts; fresh, thirst-quenching, lively and agreeably drinkable.

Riesling Fronholz 1990 🍇🍇 ③
A quintessential Alsatian wine for its elegance. The Latin and Germanic schools pool together, in its aromas, extracts and structure. Tactful use of oak, here, for the fermentation, which oddly enough many of the best Alsatian producers do not generally like. Above all a tribute to the great skill of the winemaker.

Tokay Pinot Gris 🍇🍇 ③
Muenchberg Vendanges Tardives 1990
A cru which has spent 11 months in barriques and yet the fruit is not over-oaked. The fragrances are spicy and flowery, on a background of vanilla. A well-developed body with a good balance between acidity and alcohol; super-ripening of the grapes here was crucial for the vintage. A wine with great ageing potential.

Pinot Noir Fronholz 1990 🍇🍇 ③
Oak aged for ten months or so, this is a wine from low-yield vines (45 hl/ha) with a lovely, deep ruby hue and hints of wild cherry, cherry and kirsch. Good concentration of fruit on the palate, rich in extracts, with a slightly toasty finish of considerable elegance.

André Pfister

53, rue Principale
67310 Dalenheim
Tel. 88506632
Fax 88506749

This modern young grower's estate is located about 20 km from Strasburg on a bend in the Route du Vin near Marlenheim. André is a dynamic and expert winemaker who will win you over with charm. He welcomes you in his lovely, flower-filled courtyard with rare courtesy and talks about his wines with never-failing enthusiasm. One part of his six ha has a chalky terrain with lime sub-soil and the other is in the Grand Cru Engelgarten. This advocate of low yields offers high-quality Rieslings and Gewürztraminers, but it is his Tokay-Pinot Gris, however, which is legendary, for its utter lack of heaviness or excess sugar and its dry, animal-like bouquet, beautifully suited to accompany sweetbreads or game. André's uncomplicated Pinot Blanc is fruity and graceful when young but full of potential for ageing. Marvellously fresh, its washes down easily, especially in the lovely Alsatian "weinstuben".

Pinot blanc 1991   ℗ ①
Simplicity is often the essence of quality. André proves the point with this fruity, dry, thirst-quenching wine of good texture, made by a master craftsman.

Riesling   ℗ ②
Grand Cru Engelgarten 1990
A Grand Cru wine (whose name means "Garden of Angels") of real strength. The bouquet is rich with the fragrance of ripe grapes. The palate is well-rounded and the acidity foretells excellent ageing.

Rolly-Gassman

2, rue de l'Église
68590 Rorschwihr
Tel. 89736328
Fax 89733306

The closely-knit Rolly-Gassman family firmly believes in giving their wines time. Louis, the head of the family, is one of those jolly-looking people who know that nature has needs and rights that humankind must respect. Although they have no stakes in the Grands Crus, their wines deserve such a title. Their 25 ha vineyards at the foot of Haut-Koenisbourg produce a notable range of wines, while the winery's future is in the good hands of the two daughters of the family, both in their early 1920s and studying viticulture. The estate's vines are treated like family treasures; yields are kept at a more than acceptable level; the grapes are only hand-picked at full ripeness, and fermentation is natural. Last but not least, the Rolly-Gassmans have the patience to cellar their wines before release and keep a full range of older vintages.

Auxerrois 1990   ℗ ①
A cuvée which has aged in new barriques and is of rare elegance, although the wood is not overwhelming. It has a fairly intense color and pleasant bouquet, with flowery notes on the palate. Very long finish.

Gewürztraminer 1990   ℗℗ ③
The Rolly-Gassmans have always favored the use of carbon dioxide. This cuvée is no exception as the gas is immediately detectable. An agreeable nose of roses and exotic fruit, full, supple palate with residual sugar, which will provide support in the future.

Sylvaner Réserve   ℗ ②
Rolly-Gasmann 1990
Fruit, the whole fruit, and nothing but the fruit: pure and simple. It's the kind of Sylvaner to drink every single day of the week, especially under a shady pergola with good friends.

Muscat Moenchreben 1989   ℗℗ ③
The varieties (Muscat Ottonel and Muscat d'Alsace) predominate, with a range of fragrances from apricot to quince, from roses to spices, as well as mineral notes. Pleasantly full on the palate with a good, rich texture and a particularly fresh finish.

Tokay Pinot Gris   ℗℗ ④
Sélection de Grains Nobles 1989
The typical varietal character is obvious on the nose, with a slightly undeveloped meaty toastiness. Pear and exotic fruit predominate on the palate. Nice acidity/sugar balance. A somewhat honeyed finish nonetheless leaves a fresh palate. A fine, full-bodied wine to lay down for a good few years.

Martin Schaetzel

3, rue de la 5ème Division Blindée
68770 Ammerschwihr
Tel. 89471139
Fax 89782977

Once the construction industry began losing its charm, 39 year-old Jean Schaetzel whole heartedly turned to his uncle's business and became a wine-grower, having gained experience in Dijon and Macon. He did not do things by halves, either. With his fertile vineyards at Ammerschwihr, he aims for low yields and manages a four ha estate, one quarter of which is on Kaefferkopf, with great wisdom. Jean likes subtle, easy-to-drink wines, but his production also has the complexity to age well. Generally oaked-style wines, they are often good buys for the money. Jean's Riesling and Gewürztraminer, produced on the muddy and silicous Kaefferkopf, and a Pinot Noir Cuvée Mathieu in barrique, which every year has a distinctively seductive fragrance of wild cherry, are among his best wines. He also produces an unusual Auxerrois aged in new barriques which is of outstanding character.

Auxerrois 1991 🍇 ②
Aged in new oak barriques, a wine with a pleasant oaky, vanilla nose. A successful, thirst-quenching, easy-drinking white.

Riesling Kaefferkopf 🍇 ②
Cuvée Nicolas 1990
1990 was a particularly good year for Riesling and Jean Schaetzel was particularly successful with this cuvée, which expresses the variety magnificently. Powerful but also elegant.

Gewürztraminer 🍇🍇 ②
Cuvée Isabelle 1989
Thanks to the diverse selections made and single-vineyard vinification, this elegant cuvée is an unqualified success. Complex nose of flowers and spices. Full-flavored on the palate with a finish of great finesse.

Pinot Noir Cuvée Mathieu 1990 🍇 ②
Aged in barriques, a wine with an intense purple color, fruity nose and a well-rounded palate with a background of pleasingly soft tannins. It finishes with aromas of wild cherry.

Domaine Edgard Schaller et fils

1, rue du Château
68630 Mittelwihr
Tel. 89479028
Fax 89490266

In this winemakers' village considered Alsace's "Midi," there is a friendly young grower with curly, blond hair named Patrick Schaller. Normally outgoing and rather loud-mouthed, Patrick becomes dead serious when it comes to wine. He has quickly made a reputation for himself as "The" specialist of Alsatian sparkling wines and makes one of the best Crémants d'Alsace (accounting for half of his sales), standing up to the better Champagnes. This is no surprise, as Patrick is a graduate of the École Champenoise at Avise. He has eight ha. on loam and limestone soil, part on the Grand Cru Mandelberg, or the "Almond hill", on a particularly sunny slope which favors early ripening. His Mandelberg Rieslings and Muscats also have lots of charm and fruit. There's a happy marriage of Science and Poetry here: wines to love wholeheartedly.

Crémant d'Alsace 1990 🍇🍇 ②
It has very fine bubbles, a clean, subtle bouquet and excellent length. Have fun comparing it with some of the wines from Avise, Dizy or thereabouts.

Riesling 🍇 ②
Grand Cru Mandelberg 1990
A bouquet of great finesse with excellent potential reminiscent of acacia and exotic fruit. Lovely acidity and a balance which promises well for the future.

Domaine Schlumberger

100, rue Théodore Deck
68500 Guebwiller
Tel. 89742700
Fax 89748575

A glass of Schlumberger wine is not just our average wine but a lesson in 183 years of wine-history. The Schlumberger family has been cultivating its unique, 140-ha steep sloped and terraced vineyard since 1810, back when horses plowed the lands. Owners of the single largest private estate in Alsace, the Schlumbergers are able-bodied and skilled producers, with all their grapes undergoing vinification in wood and carefully aged wines, with exactly the same passion reserved for their four Grands Crus, Kessler, Kitterlé, Saering and Spiegel. Wine-making is Eric Beydon-Schlumberger's job, meanwhile his wife painstakingly explains the house philosophy to incoming visitors and buyers. In their case, no superlative is ever good enough. The yields are very low (25 hl/ha - among the lowest in Alsace). Schlumbergers wines are famous for being full but delicate, robust but marvellously well-balanced. They are the perfect expression both of variety and cru. An exceptional family.

Gewürztraminer   🍇🍇 ④
Vendanges Tardives Cuvée Christine 1989
The complex and seductive nose is still rather undeveloped but it opens up some with breatheing, with spices (cinnamon, cumin, saffron) and dried and candied fruit. Well-rounded, delicate and elegant on the palate, with superb concentration and marvellous alcohol/acidity/sugar balance. Good, clean finish. For special occasions.

Riesling Grand Cru Saering 1989 🍇🍇 ③
Unobtrusive notes of petrol and a firm, elegant bouquet with citrus overtones. Well-rounded palate with good texture and refreshing acidity which pairs well with the alcohol. Excellent length.

Tokay Pinot Gris Kitterlé 1989   🍇🍇 ③
Yellow-gold color with an intense, complex nose, slightly toasty with gentle hints of spices. Considerable aromas of super-ripe grapes, quince and toastiness on the palate. Good varietal character, with unusual balance and fresh texture (with residual sugar well integrated). Will age for a few years yet.

Roland Schmitt

Bergbeiten
35-50 rue des Vosges
67520 Marlenheim
Tel. 88382072

Roland Schmitt won't let Marlenheim's enslavement to Pinot Noir intimidate him. In fact, with his 7.5-ha estate (family-owned since the beginning of the 17th century) Roland is determined to demonstrate that the Lower Rhine can indeed produce wines to rival those made by Upper Rhine's legendary Mochel and Pfister winemakers. It is true that people here - as most French, in general - continue to insist that the best wines are made in the South. But from the Grand Cru Altenberg de Bergbeiten - with its 2.1 ha of sunny vineyards, old vines, and the loess terrain and gravel-rich topsoil, which allows warm air to circulate - Roland produces some exceptional Gewürztraminers and Rieslings. Schmitt loves well-balanced wines in which strength and delicacy are perfectly paired, without a trace of residual sugar to ruin the palate. To top it all off, his wines are very affordable.

Riesling 1990   🍇 ①
Delicate, elegant and full-bodied, this wine combines strength with charm and elegance. Of pleasantly refershing acidity, too.

Gewürztraminer   🍇 ②
Grand Cru Altenberg de Berbieten 1989
A wine which will age well. The nose is not yet fully developed and the fruity aromas blend, for the time being, with more flowery overtones. It is well-rounded on the palate, with rich grapey flavor. Clean, with a good lingering finish.

Robert Schoffit

27, rue des Aubépines
68000 Colmar
Tel. 89244114

Traditional vigneron Robert Schoffit started out with a 2.5 ha estate on the edge of town towards Sundhoffen in the legendary Rangen de Thann vineyard. Robert now has 13 ha and still greets his visitors with the skeptical air of a country-dweller, almost putting them through a test-tasting before confiding with any hospitality. His son Bernard has recently qualified at the Dijon school of enology and explains the difficulties of the job. They can only harvest by hand, as the terraces are difficult to get to, the slopes are very steep (up to 70° hills) and the yields are, of course, extremely small. A late-harvest selection of Tokay-Pinot Gris, for instance, yields less than 20 hl/ha. Furthermore, the growing conditions encourage botrytis to develop rapidly, thus creating wines that have a honeyed, late-harvest style. But, the Schoffit family also takes great pleasure in making (on the Harth at Colmar) a splendidly drinkable Chasselas, a rich Gewürztraminer and a great Riesling. They are truly a wonderful family.

Pinot Blanc 1990   ♈ ①
The 1990 vintage was spectacularly successful, more so, in our opinion, than its successor. Pleasing toasty aromas of menthol and honey on a body not weighed down with residual sugar. Very soft on the palate with a full finish.

Riesling Grand Cru Rangen   ♈ ♈ ③
Clos Saint-Théobald 1990
Schoffit has achieved good results with this Riesling from his Rangen adventure. Obtained from ripe grapes in perfect condition, it offers a rich, aromatic nose dominated by exotic fruit on a mineral background. Very delicate texture with a hint of honey. A late-harvest of outstanding quality.

Tokay Pinot Gris   ♈ ♈ ③
Vendanges Tardives 1990
A magnificent wine with a gold color which plays all the notes on a scale of animal, spice, candied fruit and quince notes. Body rich in alcohol but achieving balance thanks to the unparallelled skill of the winemaker. Exceptionally full-flavored on the palate with an elegant, almost dry finish which lasts and lasts. Comparable, with no reserve, to a great Burgundy.

Albert Seltz

21, rue Principale
67140 Mittelbergheim
Tel. 88088177
Fax 88085272

The Selz family has lived in the same lovely old house since 1576 and harvest all seven varieties of Alsatian grapes on their 10 ha estate, buying in the grapes from another seven ha. They export two thirds of what they produce. Father Pierre, 63, has handed over to son Albert, 30, who supervises work on the loam and limestone soil of the estate. Albert considers himself to be heir of the family tradition but approaches his work in his own way, keeping yields low and preferring elegance and sophistication to strength and excess residual sugar. His Gewürztraminers are always a careful balance between fullness, sugar and acidity. Albert's treasure is the Sylvaner Vieilles Vignes Zotzenberg, neither racked nor filtered, of an incomparable freshness, bone dry and uncompromising, but he is equally successful with his masterful Rieslings, grands crus and late-harvest wines.

Gewürztraminer Zotzenberg 1990   ♈ ②
A yellow-gold cuvée with a spicy nose and good body on the palate, testifying to a successful balance of extract, sugar and acidity. A lovely wine worthy of thsi family of vintners.

Sylvaner Vieilles Vignes   ♈ ②
Zotzenberg 1990
The sylvaner variety is not deemed worthy of the name Grand Cru but this example is surely more than good enough. It has a wonderfully fresh nose with hints of vanilla and quince, while the acidity perfectly balances the fruit and a well-rounded finish.

Sick-Dreyer

17, route de Kientzheim
68770 Ammerschwihr
Tel. 89471131
Fax 89473260

Passionately advocating quality wines in the region, the Dreyers have carried down the tradition of high-quality Alsatian wine for generations. Joseph Dreyer founded the Confrérie de Saint-Étienne and his son Pierre gone on to found the Association of Friends of Ammerschwihr and Kaefferkopf, an area of loam and limestone soil which gives its wines a distinctive flavor. It has not yet been recognized as a Grand Cru by the I.N.A.O., although the application is being processed. Pierre now runs the family business enthusiastically with his uncle, Robert Sick, who looks after the administration. They have 13 ha of vineyards, with a penchant for a two ha. piece of property at Kaefferkopf. Winemaking is done in the traditional manner, with a preference for dry wines. The Cuvées named after Pierre's father and grandfather are always successful, with the grapes often harvested at super-ripeness. The range also features excellent Rieslings, Gewürztraminers and others.

Riesling Kaefferkopf 1990   ℗ ①
Lively, with good acidity and not without elegance, this wine is subject to bone-dry vinification. It has a fresh, clean finish, which sets a good example for many other Rieslings.

Gewürztraminer Kaefferkopf 1989   ℗ ②
How could the driving spirit behind the Friends of Ammerschwihr and Kaefferkopf fail to get this wine right. Beautifully full, with pleasant spicy fruit and rich texture, this is an archetypal Gewürz of good "terroire" character; also, an excellent value (and flavor) for the money.

Jean-Bernard Siebert

Le Moulin
67120 Wolxheim
Tel. 88384392

The town of Wolxheim, located about 20 km from Strasburg, is not generally much of a tourist attraction, and its winemakers are not terribly media-conscious. Jean-Bernard Siebert is no exception, although he is a favorite of the Hussers at the Auberge du Cerf restaurant in Marlenheim. Fashion has passed Wolxheim by and, fortunately, the prices show it. Jean-Bernard is determined in his quest to cultivate a vineyard at the foot of the Horn, a small holding in the Grand Cru Altenberg. Anyone can knock on the door of this producer and be welcomed as if they were an old friend, insisting that one try his Wolxheim Riesling, the Tokay-Pinot Gris or the Gewürztraminer Grand Cru Altenberg. Often, there are some pleasant surprises. Jean-Bernard is a man of few words and lets his marvellous wines do the talking. Well-rounded and lively, full-bodied and well-balanced, they boast both structure and length. Be sure to pay a visit to this serious grower and admire his model winery.

Riesling Réserve 1990   ℗ ①
Clear in color, with a slightly vegetal nose, concentrated fruit and a moderately rich palate. In short, a well-balanced wine with good acidity and a backbone of vigorous alcohol.

Gewürztraminer   ℗ ②
Grand Cru Altenberg de Wolheim 1988
A lovely yellow-gold color with a nose of intense peach and mint fragrances. Well-rounded palate with fruit well in evidence. Long finish.

Maison Pierre Sparr

2, rue de la Première Armée
68240 Sigolsheim
Tel. 89782422

Hospitality is only one of the aces up the sleeve of the Sparr family, with father and sons René, Charles, Bernard and Pierre, who come from a winemaking dynasty dating from 1680. Their establishment is at the foot of the necropolis for those who fell during the Liberation and here they make wine from grapes bought in from 120 ha of vineyards as well as from the 30 ha or so they own on loam and limestone and sandy soil over Grands Crus like Mambourg at Sigolsheim. Pierre Sparr, the family oenologist, produces cru-dedicated wines of great quality, Brand at Turckheim and Schlossberg at Kientzheim, as well as on the alluvial terrain of Hardt at Colmar. This allows the Sparrs to offer a highly diversified range of wines which goes from easier-drinking wines like Pinot Blanc and Sylvaner to the magnificent late-harvests and "grains nobles" selections (sold in half bottles). Vinification is invariably carried out with care and expertise by experts: quite possibly the secret of the company's success.

Tokay Pinot Gris
Grand Cru Mambourg 1990
Made from very ripe grapes, athis is cru with pleasant fullness and a mineral, spicy nose. Rich fruit and palate with a very well-rounded finish.

Tokay Pinot Gris Prestige 1989
Its nose is full of the aromas of super-ripe fruit, tending towards acacia. Full and gentle on the palate. Spices predominate on the finish, while the wine remains well-rounded and delicate.

Fernand Stentz

40, Route du Vin
68420 Husseren-les-Châteaux
Tel. 89493004

Fernand Stentz's vineyards are located at the highest altitude in Alsatia. The 50 year-old brother-in-law of the great Jean Schillinger (two Michelin stars at Colmar), Fernand treads his own Pinot Noir grapes to make wines of great character. At present, he is working only five ha. of loam-and-limestone and loess-and-limestone terrain - including 0.4 ha of Reisling in the Grand Cru Pfersigberg which overlooks the village - in the communes of Eguisheim, Oberschmorwihr and Husseren-les-Châteaux. The Pinot Noir is made from grapes left on the stem which are then vinified in oak barrels. The cellar is located at the crossroads between the Route du Vin and the Route des Cinque Châteaux. Of course, production is limited and the quantities available are very small, but there's always hope for a sample tasting and a spare bottle.

Riesling
Grand Cru Pfersigberg 1990
A very exclusive production. Even in its youth, it is a wine with elegant fragrances of fresh mint, revealing almond and musk. Should be at its peak in three or four years.

Pinot Noir 1990
The grapes, which are not de-stemmed, are trodden in the time-honored fashion to produce a proud, intensely red wine which opens to an incomparable bouquet of blackcurrant. Order it at once, if there's still any left.

Thomann Frères

Domaine du Manoir
56, rue de la Promenade
68040 Ingersheim
Tel. 89272369

When your hillsslope at a steep 30°, or even 60,° angles, your neighbors raise their eyebrows with sceptisism and everything seems to be conspiring against you, it takes a certain courage to become a grower. But, two self-taught brothers have managed to do just that. Christoph and Jean Thomann showed the locals that you can leave teaching or banking and go back to the land with good results. Christoph and Jean rolled up their sleeves and ploughed 12 ha of the most daunting terrain. Their back-breaking labors have produced some glorious results. In fact, the Letzenberg vineyard supplies top quality grapes to make one of the most sophisticated Rieslings in Alsace. The brothers rely on the expert advice of Alex Schaeffer, an I.N.R.A. oenologist with an untiring intent for quality. Naturally, grapes are only hand-picked, and low yields are "de rigueur" for these two enthusiasts who have become fine vignerons.

Riesling Letzenberg 1990 ❦ ②
Green with youth, fruity and flowery, all at the same time. The primary fragrances nicely mix with aromas of lemon, acacia, white flowers amd bergamot. Genuinely outstanding acidity. With its considerably fresh acidity, this is a well-made Riesling with a clean, aristocratic finish.

Gewürztraminer Letzenberg 1988 ❦ ②
Best to wait a few more years before drinking. It has its own distinct personality, which nonetheless carries the hallmarks of its variety. There are roses, peonies and lemon, on the nose, with faint mineral notes. It has a good backbone and a very long finish.

Domaine Trimbach

15, route de Bergheim
68150 Ribeauvillé
Tel. 89736030
Fax 89738904

The close-knit Trimbach family can trace its wine-making history in the area since 1626. Today, they produce a range of wines typical of the area on their 20 ha or so estate and can afford to ignore the Grand Cru Appellation on the label, focusing more on the artwork instead. The production philosphy is inarguably more traditional, rather than trendy, putting out wines with real ageing potential: only hand-picking , rigorous selections, no malo-lactic fermentation, no residual sugar and no use of the barrique (except for one late-harvest Pinot Blanc). These aristocrats of the vineyard are firm believers in long fermentation and cellar ageing rather than instant marketing and plainly prefer elegance and finesse to high yields and corner-cutting. Their Riesling from the Saint-Hune vineyard, with its lingering mineral notes and complex structure, is a wonder. The Cuvée Frédéric-Emile, from loam and limestone soil classified as Grands Crus Geisberg and Osterberg with evident petrol overtones in the great years (try the 1971, if you want proof), is their flagship. The Gewürztraminer Cuvée Seigneurs de Ribeaupierre and the Tokay-Pinot Gris Réserve Personnelle are still rather undeveloped and require ageing, but anything with the Trimbach signature on the label will be a pleasure to drink.

Riesling ❦ ❦ ③
Cuvée Frédéric-Emile 1990
A wine from loam and limestone terrain with two distinct aspects, one mineral and the other floral. Good complexity. Great concentration of fragrances on a background of exotic fruit. Excellent finesse and density on the palate. Quite dry on the finish but of outstanding length.

Tokay Pinot Gris ❦ ②
Réserve Personnelle 1990
Incomparable simplicity and freshness as the variety takes a bow here. The nose is still somewhat undeveloped, but the fruit and gamey aromas are underlying. The complex finish is not lacking in elegance.

Gewürztraminer ❦ ②
Cuvée des Seigneurs de Ribeaupierre 1989
A Trimbach cru through and through. Very spicy on the nose, with a marvellously concentrated texture and a superbly long finish. This is what a master vigneron can do, year in, year out.

Vonville

4, place des Tilleuls
67530 Ottrott
Tel. 88959108

Jean-Charles Vonville lives in a village which weaves between the vineyards and the Vosges. A jovial, strong-willed young grower, he is one of Alsace's leading aces in red wine-making, in this case obtained from the sandy hills around Ottrott. Situated in the shadow of Mont Saint-Odile, the village is proud of its vineyards almost exclusively planted with the local favourite, pinot noir. Jean-Charles favours long maceration and will not be tempted by the easy way out of making a rosé from his Pinot. The stainless-steel vat wines are drinkable enough but seem a little flat. They are wines which have a ripe fruit flavour on the palate, fairly ruby red in color. Light in body, they are not without concentration. The special cuvées, oaked for two years, are worth waiting for, since still slightly tannic from the barrel: an unusual wine to sample for yourself.

Rouge d'Ottrott Cuvée Spéciale 1990 ❦ ②
The first vines planted in Alsace for the production of red wine were imported from Burgundy by Benedictine monks. Indeed, this oaked Pinot has a typical Burgundian-style nose, with cherries and wild cherries on the nose. The body is very rich, the finish long and elegant, indicating a wine of breeding.

Key to the symbols

Types of Wines

❦ White

❦ Rosé

❦ Red

Rating System

❦ An exemplary wine of its type with outstanding local character

❦❦ An international premium quality wine

❦❦❦ A Top Wine, considered one of the 150 best wines in the world

The 'grape bunch' symbol is used to indicate the color of the wine; the number of bunches represents the quality rating assigned by the contributor

Price levels

① up to $ 9.99

② $ 10.00 - $ 14.99

③ $ 15.00 - $ 24.99

④ $ 25.00 or more

The 'ex-cellar', or direct from the producer, bottle prices, are calculated in US dollars and are intended only as an approximate guide

Entries are arranged in alphabetical order by country, region and winery or producer name.

Domaine Weinbach

25, route du Vin
68240 Kaysersberg
Tel. 8941321
Fax 89473818

Pride of the Weinbach estate (23 ha, with parcels in the Grands Crus Furstentum and Schlossberg), the Clos des Capucins was sold to the brothers Jean-Baptiste and Théodore Faller in 1898. Théodore's son, Théo, has a deep passion for wine, helping the estate grow to what it is today, now managed by his charming and persuasive wife, Colette, who painstakingly seeks out perfection. The vineyards are situated on the low flood banks by the Weiss river in a microclimate whose temperatures which reach 35°C in summer, with mild autumns whose morning mists encourage botrytis. The Weinbachs cultivate all grape types, with a penchant for Muscat, Gewürztraminer, Riesling and Tokay-Pinot Gris, best suited to the soil type and composition. The grapes are pressed lightly and the must fermented in huge tartar-caked oak barrels, avoiding the malolactic fermentation. Colette won't hear of using new barrels! Wines are then filtered with fossil flour, aged back in the same barrels and bottled from April to June. From a straightforward Sylvaner to the late-harvest wines and his "grains nobles" selections, Weinbach's wines are clean, with crisp, fresh fruity bouquets and a fresh acidity that guarantees good bottle aging.

Riesling Cuvée Théo 1991   🍇 ②
A granite-terrain cuvée with a lovely golden-yellow color. Dry on the nose, as is typical of the variety, with a hint of grapefruit, citrus and grapes and warm toasty notes. Dense body, which amalgates well on the palate. A wine of bite and breeding, sustained by excellent acidity and an extremely fresh finish.

Sylvaner 1991   🍇🍇 ①
A superior cru from old vines which works wonders at any time of the day. Its formidable freshness derives from the flowery scents of candied quince and green apple. A remarkable wine and truly amazing value for money.

Gewürztraminer   🍇🍇 ④
Sélection de Grains Nobles 1990
Extraordinary richness in golden vestments. A stupendous explosion of fragrances which contains notes of honey, vanilla and almond. The highly botrytized background is outstanding, extremely dense with an almost perfect structure. Absolutely no heaviness whatsoever on the palate, with a fabulous equilibrium between acidity and residual sugar. Sumptuous finish.

Riesling   🍇🍇🍇 ④
Vendanges Tardives 1990
Color and clarity absolutely superb, elegant and pure. Already tasted from the barrel in 1991 and again the following year, this Schlossberg cuvée continues to amaze. The aromatic expression is an explosion of pears and honey, the rich aroma of candied fruit, citrus and passion fruit which combine with discreet flowery notes to reveal immense complexity. The acidity - in this case, frankly in a class of its own - opens up the possibility of prolonged aging. Crisp, unbelievably clean finish. A wine for the 21st century to save for the most special of occasions

Wolfberger

6, Grand' Rue
68240 Eguisheim
Tel. 89222020
Fax 89234709

The Wolfberger co-operative brings together 800 vignerons who supply almost all of their grapes. It covers a total surface area of about 1,200 ha., which is approximately 10% of the total area under vines in Alsace. In addition, wineries such as Jux, Kuhri and Willm as well as the Dambach and Wuenheim cellars also take part. The co-operative policy aims to produce top-quality products but maintains a discreet respect for the more old-fashioned traditions. For example, the old Hungarian-oak oval barrels made by Fruhinsholz Co. of Schiltigheim are still towering in the cellar; meanwhile the cellar masters use some of the most sophisticated machinery available. The state-of-the-art press, which is microprocessor-controlled, can handle up to 700 tonnes of grapes a day. Wolfberger makes a complete range of appellation wines, from the unpretentious, easy-drinking Sylvaner to the award-winning grands cuvées, not to mention the oaked Tokay-Pinot Gris and a Pinot Noir that would put many a Burgundian vigneron to shame. Last, but not least, the Crémant, with its distinctive character, and the splendid distilled spirits. Pierre Hussher is a dynamic chairman of the co-operative and Roland Guth, the expert oenologist.

Riesling Grand Cru Hengst 1990   ♥ ②
It is still a little undeveloped on the nose but the fruity/grassy notes of the varietal, with a slightly over-ripe flavour, show through underneath. The characteristic petrol-schmagen aroma, as they say in Alsace, is very evident here. A full-bodied wine with good structure.

Sylvaner 1991   ♥ ①
There is a pleasant hint of honey, with a mushroom background. Firm flavor and clean finish. A nice thirst-quencher.

Pinot Noir Cuvée Prince Hugo 1989   ♥ ②
A fine wine which will be drunk avidly, it has a lovely fragrance of ripe fruit on a background of wild cherries. The palate reveals a certain fullness of flavour, with happily integrated tannins and a nice fresh finish.

Entries are arranged in alphabetical order by country, region and winery or producer name.

Domaine Zind-Humbrecht

34, rue du Maréchal Joffre
68920 Wintzenheim
Tel. 89270205
Fax 89272258

"1991 may not go down in history in Alsace, but it certainly will for our winery", whisper Léonard Humbrecht and his son, Olivier. It was a difficult year for many vignerons, particularly those with high yields, who rely on anti-botrytis treatments. The Humbrechts, to the contrary, had an average yield of 37 hl/ha, with grapes with good sugar. They are great vignerons. Much credit for the initial Grands Crus goes to Léonard, who has now replanted Rangen and, today, dedicates himself wholeheartedly to Windsbuhl, rewarding him with some marvellously fat and well-balanced Tokay- Pinot Gris in 1990. His latest project is a Chardonnay, aimed to rival the great white wines of Burgundy. But, something's always cooking at this estate, otherwise laid out like patchwork puzzle across some of the best and sunniest vineyards, towns, and growing areas in Alsace. More recently, in 1992, according to blue prints drawn by the architect Yves Pircher, the new Turckheim cellar was installed, going completely underground in porous cement, similar to the cellars of Margaux.

Gewürztraminer Heimbourg Vendanges Tardives 1990
Yellow-gold in color, with a bouquet of flowers and candied fruit, the rich and delicate concentration of fruit, indicating exceptionally ripe and healthy grapes. The structure and never-ending finish confer a rare fascination to this wine. It would be a crime not to let this wine age in peace.

Tokay Pinot Gris Clos Jebsal Vendanges Tardives 1989
This delicate variety is vinified by the Humbrechts with a master's skill. The bouquet is of citrus, animal-like and candied quince. Powerful and concentrated on the palate, with a remarkable balance of acidity and sugar. Stunningly fresh, botrytis and honey-like aromas show though especially on the finish, nonetheless leaving a clean palate.

Pinot Noir Herrenweg 1990
The more or less declared intent of this élite Pinot Noir is to rival the Grands Crus of Burgundy. Intense color, clean nose, with aromatic notes of berries like cassis and blackberry. Stunningly concentrated with a simply perfect balance of acidity and alcohol. Wonderfully light and captivating finish.

Riesling Clos Saint Urbain Rangen de Thann 1989
Nobody thought it was even feasible, but Léonard Humbrecht has certainly brought it back to life. The Rangen de Thann slope is absolutely exceptional. Amazingly enough, it is practically vertical (at 68°), plummeting down to the cool waters of the Thur river. This remarkable producer has always had the gift of obtaining extraordinary results and here he's done it again. Harvesting almost always start late, as the pickers virtually go through hell, bending over to gather the precious bunches that make up the tiny yield (25-30 qu/ha). The wine that crowns their efforts is quite simply stupendous. The bouquet is inebriating, on a background first of mineral, only to become lime blossoms and exotic candied fruit. Powerful, rich concentration with a brilliant complexity and the typical flavors of the cru - the Rangen vulcanic rock shows through. A truly great wine, worthy of some ageing before being drunk.

Bordeaux

No other wine region in the world, past or present, has the fame and prestige of Bordeaux. The climatic conditions and nature of the terrain, together with long-established skills in the growing, making and marketing of wine have, over the centuries, built Bordeaux into a legend. The history of the city and its surrounding region is marked by the alternating fortunes of its wines and the enormous wine-related economic interests which have ensured prosperity for many generations. The Gironde, estuary of the Garonne and the Dordogne, the slow and muddy watercourse which links Bordeaux to the Atlantic, has been likened to a gigantic wine funnel.

In the Middle Ages, Bordeaux rose to become the undisputed capital of the wine trade, thnaks to its strategic position, which enabled it to control all river traffic on the Gironde, Dordogne and Garonne, and the privileges that came from the long period of English domination (from the 12th to the 14th century). The British passion for the wine of Bordeaux dates from that period. Bordeaux wines were exported in huge quantities not only to England but also, thanks to the good offices of the Dutch, to the German and Scandinavian Hanseatic cities. The English, however, have never lost their taste for Claret, as wine from Bordeaux is called generically. Wars, famines and revolutions have swept across France and Europe, but the wine merchants of Bordeaux, a formidable breed of entrepreneurs, have always survived despite them.

Bordeaux first pulled off its most stunning marketing coup in 1855, when Napoleon III° gave the Bordeaux Chamber of Commerce the task of drawing up a classification on the grounds of merit of the great wines of Bordeaux. The 'wine agents' guild' who actually wrote this classification of the Grand Crus of the Gironde were mainly assigning official status to exisiting lists based on the daily tariffs. Nonetheless, it was a supreme effort, which had to overcome and confront petty jealousies, protests as well as inevitable boycotts. Over the years the original classification has become obsolete in some respects, but it has served to confer prestige on the whole region. It remains a standard from which to judge the wine quality. Today, after some minor modifications and the addition of the Saint-Emilion and Pomerol zones (that were not included in 1855), the original classification is still an important part of the heritage of Bordeaux. It is important to remember, however, that the vineyard boundaries of the classified châteaux have changed over the years, and exchanges, leases, sales and inheritance have altered the original ownership patterns. The classification has never precisely laid down the cru areas, something which has been done, for instance, in Burgundy. Ranking in the classification is historical and related to the prestige of the producer. It is a spur to owners to maintain a certain level of quality for a demanding market and a host of connoisseurs. The fabulous run of 1980s vintages has confirmed the general high standard of quality achieved throughout the whole Bordeaux region and has also enabled a number of committed younger winemakers to come forward.

Entries in this guide follow the geographical division of the region on which are based the Appellations d'Origine Contrôlée. Apart from the two zones of Bourgeais-Blayais and Entre-Garonne-et-Dordogne, which have a limited number of albeit important chateaux, the great wines of Bordeaux are produced in four districts: Médoc, Libournais, Graves and Sauternes. In inverse proportion to its reputation, the Médoc is very small, covering a narrow strip of gravelly terrain along the left bank of the Gironde. The best wines of this area bear the names of the four most famous communes, namely Margaux, Saint-Julien, Pauillac and Saint-Estèphe. Also included in the Médoc are the lesser known Moulis and Listrac. Margaux is the most extensive of the Appellations with hundreds of hectares of vines and is capable of producing the most delicate wines in the region, as the flagship wine, Château Margaux, amply demonstrates. The list of other really outstanding wines to add to this name is, however, lamentably short, despite the excellent results obtained by châteaux like Palmer, Angludet Monbrison, Labégorce-Zédé and Cantenac-Brown under the management of Jean-Michel Cazes. The guide gives thorough coverage to Saint-Julien, Paulliac, Saint-Estèphe and the rest of the Médoc.

Behind the first rank of superb châteaux in these areas, there is an army of excellent and reliable producers. Paulliac, in particular, stands out for its robust, full-flavored wines which are more powerful than the elegant Margaux and Saint-Julien, however with less structure than those two authentic giants, Saint-Emilion and Pomerol. It should also be said that relatively unknown producers at Canon-Fronsac, Fronsac, Côtes de Francs and Côte de Castillon have been making excellent wines recently. Saint-Emilion, on the other hand, has been turning out some very commercial ones. The best crus of this appellation are divided into two zones, each with its own terrain. One part is on the plateau around the city where a shallow top soil covers the limestone underneath and the other, with stoney clay/soil, borders on Pomerol. The wines from the plateau are more subtle and 'feminine' (Ausone and Belair stand out) while the lowland wines, including Cheval Blanc and Figeac, have more body and depth. In Pomerol the rarity of some the amazing wines from tiny vineyards makes the district more similar to Burgundy or the Rhône than the nearby Médoc. Merlot accounts for 75% of the grapes grown in Pomerol, the rest being Cabernet Franc with a very little Cabernet Sauvignon. These varieties, together with the soils of gravelly sand and clay, give well-rounded, full-bodied wines which age sooner than those of the Médoc. The Graves, which includes Pessac-Léognan, is not easy to generalize about as the quality of the terrain is very different from the hinterland and growing conditions are considerably more difficult. Finally, we have the Sauternais district with Barsac, Cérons and Sauternes. This area has taken full advantage of the opportunities in the last decade to produce a series of stupendous vintages. The general standard of winemaking here remains very high.

The next few years are sure to be difficult for the entire Bordeaux region. Supermarket shelves in Europe and other countries everywhere are brimming with a wide range of quality wines at relatively more accessible prices. There are outstanding Italian, Spanish and American competitors ready to attack both Bordeaux's traditional and new markets. Whatever happens, though, we can rely on the traditional ability of the merchants of Bordeaux to open up new outlets for fine and premium wines and on the new generation of growers to continue to produce tomorrow's legends.

Château de Rabouchet

33220 Sainte-Foy-La-Grande
Tel. 57464681
Fax 57461719

Christian Fournier has interests in a number of estates. He has shares in Château Canon and Château Franc-Grace-Dieu at Saint-Emilion, Château Broustet at Barsac and Château de Birot in the Côtes-de-Bordeaux, but Chateau de Rabouchet is the one he has fallen in love with. Christian was destined to buy a vineyard, as he has been designing and building cellars for over 20 years: in the Bordeaux region alone he has completed more than 150. His 19 ha vineyard is on a single parcel on the first slopes overlooking Sainte-Foy. Enjoying excellent sunlight on clay and limestone soil, the estate is planted with Merlot (50%), Cabernet Franc (25%) and Cabernet Sauvignon (25%). In the future, Christian intends to review the percentage of Cabernet Sauvignon and replace it with Merlot and Cabernet Franc, which are more suited to the soil. The cellar is modern with temperature-controlled equipment and the property is run by Hervé des Garets, who looks after the vines, Paul Cazenave, a head cellarman who learned his trade at Château Canon, and Gilles Pauquet, an oenologist who also looks after Château Cheval Blanc. Rabouchet is definitely a property worth keeping an eye on.

Château de Rabouchet 🍇 ①
Bordeaux 1989

Lovely deep ruby color with a slightly vanillae bouquet containing notes of berries, blackcurrant, raspberry and cassis. Concentrated and very dense on the palate, with firm, supple tannins. Good acidity and balance.

Château de Sours

33750 Saint-Quentin-de-Baron
Tel. 57241081
Fax 57241083

Founded in the 17th century, Château de Sours was entirely rebuilt by the Counts of Richemont in 1740. Today, it is a large, comfortable farmhouse with a walled courtyard. Records of vines on the property date back to 1790. The present owner, an ambitious young Scot Esme Johnstone, grows about 25 ha of Merlot and Cabernet for the production of red wine as well as 6 ha of Sémillon for dry white. The Johnstones bought Chateau de Sours in 1990, though they already had experience in the wine trade, being one of the founders of a large chain of wine warehouses in England. On arrival he secured the services of the well-known Libourne-based consulting enologist, Michel Rolland, for his red wines and those of Hugh Ryman, a young Australian and Bordeaux-trained Briton, for his whites. In addition, Esme modernized the cellar and re-discovered a vast gallery of limestone caves for ageing and storing wines. The estate produces about 80,000 bottles of red, 35,000 of white and some 25,000 of an amusing rosé with a stunning pink capsule. All the wines are of good sound quality, the red being the most interesting.

Château de Sours Bordeaux 1989 🍇 ①

Beautifully luminous, rich color. Soft, clean and fruity on the nose. Softness is also the predominating characteristic in the mouth. Very round and easy to drink, with plenty of red fruits on the finish.

BORDEAUX/BORDEAUX
BORDEAUX
FRANCE

159

BORDEAUX/BORDEAUX
BORDEAUX
FRANCE

Château Méaume

33230 Maransin
Tel. 57494104
Fax 57690270

Château Méaume stands in rolling countryside some 15 km from Pomerol and Saint-Emilion. Perhaps more of a comfortable country house than a real château as such, this property was bought in 1980 by the present British owners, Sue and Alan Johnson-Hill. Enchanted by the French countryside and the way of life, up until then the couple had lived in Hong Kong and were used to the hustle and bustle of the Hong Kong business world. Alan quickly set himself to work on the land and today the château produces about 200,000 bottles of Bordeaux Supérieur. The winery has be refurbishing since the Johnson-Hills took over. New temperature-controlled equipment has been installed, and the old chais turned into a cellar for the oak-aging. Alan renews 15% of his barriques every year. While the techniques used at Méaume are very up to date, the 30 ha of vines are cultivated in the traditional fashion, and no chemical weed-killers are used on the property. 80% of the vineyards are planted with Merlot, 15% Cabernet Franc and 5% Cabernet Sauvignon, which probably explains why the wines of Château Méaume are so wonderfully drinkable.

Château Méaume
Bordeaux Supérieur 1989
Good rich, deep red color. A bouquet of light red fruits with slightly green, herbaceous notes. Soft in the mouth, well-balanced and very clean. A pleasant wine, well-made and very easy to drink.

Château Charron

33390 Saint-Martin-la-Caussade
Tel. 56315021
Fax 56748872

A small star in the galaxy of Germain vineyards (whose leading light is the Grand Cru Classé Saint-Emilion Château Yon Figeac), this estate dominates the Blaye area, occupying 26 ha of rich clay and limestone, south-facing terrain on the lovely Saint-Martin-la-Caussade hills. The grapes are picked by hand for white wine (70% sémillon and 30% Sauvignon) and by machine for the red (80% Merlot and 20% Cabernet Sauvignon). There are about 6,000 vines per ha, the plants being on average 25 years-old. Nowadays, throughout the Blayais white wine production has fallen in favor of red, but Château Charron carries on the old tradition. The vigorous red with its rustic elegance ages very well as you might expect from a château which is busy every single day of the year at some aspect of winemaking whether it be in the vineyard or in the cellar, always immaculately clean and efficient. A wine to rediscover.

Château Charron
Premières Côtes de Blaye 1991
Aging in new oak barrels gives this wine a certain elegance and appeal in addition to being excellent value for money. The balance between fruit and wood is remarkable. Very rich on the palate, with a pleasantly refreshing finish.

Château Charron
Premières Côtes de Blaye 1990
A fine, ruby red color and an intensely nose with lots of ripe, red fruits. Mouthwatering and rich on the palate with somewhat rough tannins backed by solid fruit. The overall sensation is one of considerable softness before the finish, not in the least astringent. The ideal wine to drink young.

Château Haut Bertinerie

33620 Cubnezais
Tel. 57687074
Fax 57680103

The Côtes de Blaye, like neighboring Côtes de Bourg, has an unfortunate association with dull, lack-luster wines. However, this is not due to any lack of potential, something that Daniel Bantegnies is amply demonstrating with his Château Bertinerie. Not only is he making an excellent red Premières Côtes de Blaye but easily the finest white, too. His 33 ha of vines are gradually being converted to lyre pruning, so they can be more efficiently cultivated. The 40 year-old vines are all traditional Bordeaux types; Sauvignon Blanc and Merlot on deep clay whilst the Muscadelle, Sémillon and Cabernet on flinty and limestone clays, all on south-facing slopes which are sheltered from hail. Main wines include two whites, two reds and a Claret. Château Bertinerie Blanc Sec is macerated on the skins, tank fermented and aged on the lees whilst Haut Bertinerie Blanc is fermented and aged in entirely new oak casks. The Château Bertinerie red is classicly vinified and aged in one year old casks; the more expensive Haut Bertinerie is aged in 90% new oak for a year. The lavish use of materials demonstrates Monsieur Bantegnies' commitment to prove that Blaye is no back-seat appellation.

Château Haut Bertinerie
Premières Côtes de Blaye 1991
Bright, rich, pale straw color with a fresh, clean nose and pleasant oak nuances. Fine with floral fresh honeysuckle fruit flavors and despite the oak it has a good balance. Drink within the next twelve months.

Château Haut Bertinerie
Premières Côtes de Blaye 1990
Good rich color with rich and stylish with ripe black fruits and class. Full on the palate with good black ripe wild fruits, good structure and well-balanced. A touch of liquorice on the finish.

Château Le Roc de Cambes

33710 Bourg-sur-Gironde
Tel. 57247057
Fax 57744211

Château Le Roc de Cambes is an exception in the Côtes de Bourg appellation where wines are ususally diluted and ubiquitous with high yields taken off fertile soils. At Le Roc de Cambe, however, vigorous pruning to keep yields low and concentration high. François Mitjavile bought the property in 1988, and his wife owns Château Le Tertre-Rôteboeuf which she inherited in the early 1980s. Between them they have already produced wine at Rôtebouef that the press have heralded. Mitjavile has even been compared to the likes of Guigal for his winemaking genius. Such opinions are always open to debate, but the wines made at Le Roc de Cambes wine are very good, bench-mark for the appellation. There are 9.5 ha of 30 year-old vines, with 35% Merlot, 25% each of Malbec and Cabernet Franc as well as 15% Cabernet Sauvignon. The vineyard sits at the bottom of a southfacing limestone clay amphitheatre cooled by breezes off the wide Gironde. Grapes are hand-picked and destemmed but not crushed on arrival. The three to four week vinification takes places at carefully controlled but quite high temperatures. The wine is aged for 16-20 months in barriques (either new or one year-old). Fining is carried out in tank just before bottling and the wine is filtered only when absolutely necessary.

Château Le Roc de Cambes
Côtes de Bourg 1989
Young, plummy ruby with ripe cherries and plum jam and a surprising level of toasty oak on the nose. The oak is very forward with a strong tannin and acidic backbone backed by ripe cherry and chocolate fruit.

Château Le Roc de Cambes
Côtes de Bourg 1988
Deep brilliant plum ruby, the nose is warm and smooth with flesh and leather characters. In the mouth the fruit is very soft and warm with an easy and round structure and a considerable presence of alcohol on the finish.

BOURGEAIS BLAYAIS/1ERES COTES DE BLAYE
BORDEAUX
FRANCE

161

BOURGEAIS BLAYAIS/1ERES COTES DE BOURG
BORDEAUX
FRANCE

Château du Cros

33410 Loupiac
Tel. 56629931
Fax 56621259

It was probably the English who recognised the real value of Château du Cros before anyone else. In 1274, Edward II (at that time the King of Aquitaine) ordered Sir Guilhem Arnaud to build a castle on the hill at Loupiac. The English non longer benefit from its defensive position, simply the light, honeyed aromas of its botrytized wines from the limestone and clay vineyards around the castle. Michel Boyer's family has owned the 41 ha of vines since 1921 and produces a very fine Loupiac from 48 year-old plantings of Sauvignon, Muscadelle and Sémillon, this last accounting for a good 70% of the white grapes. 5 ha are for Merlot and Cabernet Franc for an AOC Bordeaux red. There is also a dry white from oak-aged Sauvignon, but it is the luscious, botrytis-affected Loupiac that has made Château du Cros the leading property here. Morning mists and warm afternoons encourage botrytis to spread and the pickers go through the vines as many as four times to select the best. The grapes are then crushed and the thick must goes into small tanks to be vinified by each separate picking and each parcel of wines. The wine is aged for 18 months in cask, a third of which are replaced yearly. Boyer also owns and manages Château de Lucques at Barsac and Château Haut-Mayne in Graves.

Château du Cros Loupiac 1989   ❦ ②
Bright, pale gold color, good depth with a sweet, round nose; in the mouth it is sweet, perhaps lacks acidity but has good length. Not particularly botrytized but has good richness and sweetness, not cloying.

Domaine du Noble

33410 Loupiac
Tel. 56629936/1478
Fax 56769131

The three Dejean brothers run this 12 ha property which earned a good reputation under their father, Pierre. Their vines are for the most part 40 year old Sémillon planted on two hills, one of gravelly and the other of a heavier, limestone clay. The vines seem to be regularly blessed with a good dose of botrytis and during the harvest, the picker-srun through the vines several times under Dominique Dejean's expert guidance to select the best grapes. Patrick, the brother in charge of making the wines, displays plenty of versatility from vintage to vintage in his techniques. Philippe, the third brother, is now owner of the Premier Cru Classé Rabaud Promis across the river at Sauternes. Once in decline, the cru is rapidly making up for lost time. The 1988 Domaine du Noble was vinified in temperature-controlled stainless steel and aged in cask for 16 months while the 1989 and 1990 were aged for 18-24 months. With such adaptability, the Dejean family and the Domaine du Noble will continue to produce excellent buys, much underrated, too.

Domaine du Noble Loupiac 1990   ❦ ②
Bright, rich yellow-gold color with a quite botrytized, stylish nose and a fruity sweetness. It is a sweet, buttery, creamy wine, somewhat acidic and very full-flavored. A touch of bitter-sweet orange together with the characteristic botrytis rounds everything off.

Domaine de Chastelet

33360 Quinsac
Tel. 56208602
Fax 56726583

Once you have wasted your time grubbing around for the hidden treasure amongst Domaine de Chastelet's 8.5 ha of vineyards, go back to the "Cave" for some refreshing Claret from the estate or some excellent red Premières Côtes de Bordeaux. The domaine was founded by a pirate who is supposed to have buried his plunder here but probably spent it to the castle instead. The current owner is now Pierre Estanson, a qualified oenologist, whose father Jean bought the property. Most of the grapes go into the making of the reds, with 50% Merlot, 20% each Cabernet Franc and Sauvignon with some petit verdot and Malbec. The plantings are on average 38 years-old on gravelly, limestone clay. The grapes, de-stalked and crushed, and go on to ferment and macerate in temperature-controlled stainless steel and cement vats; after malolactic fermentation, the wine is racked into Allier, Nièvre and Vosges oak casks, a quarter to a third of which are replaced every year.

Domaine de Chastelet 🍇 ①
Premières Côtes de Bordeaux 1989
A good example of this great value Appellation. Super rich, deep, dark colored, the nose is rich, quite tight and structured. In the mouth again very rich despite having a tough, rustic style; this wine has plenty of ripe layered fruit and is reasonably well-balanced.

Domaine de Chastelet 🍇 ①
Premières Côtes de Bordeaux 1988
Quite a rustic style, but a very honest wine which certainly shows the differences between the two. The 1988 also has a lovely deep dark color, with rich, tight fruit on the nose, without the ripeness of the 1989. Very clean with good fruit, with a sensation of structured toughness. A really well-made wine that needs food to lift the fruit.

Château du Juge

Route de Branne
33410 Cadillac
Tel. 56621777
Fax 56621759

Pierre Dupleich is an amusing man with a permanent twinkle in his eye. Together with his wife, Chantal, he produces some of the very best value dry white wine in France today. Historically, Cadillac has always been known for its sweet whites, made from Sémillon and Sauvignon grapes in the style of Sauternes, just across the Garonne. The sweet wine crisis of the late 1950s and early 1960s, however, drove growers to plant red grapes and today, nearly half Pierre Dupleich's wine is red. He makes some 80,000 bottles of Premières Côtes de Bordeaux plus 90,000 bottles of dry white Bordeaux. Just recently, with the rekindling of the fashion for sweet wines, Pierre has begun to make a perfectly drinkable style of Cadillac. Domaine du Juge has belonged to Chantal Dupleich's family since 1880, when it was acquired by M. Mathelot, one of the founding fathers of Cadillac wines. It was he who dedicated his life to putting together the 35 ha property. Mathelot would have been proud of the wines coming out of his cellar today. Furthermore, this is one of France's rare areas that has been little affected by fashions and trends and prices have remained stable.

Château du Juge 🍇 ②
Bordeaux Blanc Sec 1991
From Sémillon and Sauvignon grapes, a wine with a lovely light, bright, pale color. Fresh crispy-crunchy fruit on the nose, with traces of apple. Clean, dry and again very fresh on the palate with a good balance of fruit and acidity. A perfect aperitif for a hot summer's day.

*ENTRE-GARONNE-ET-DORDOGNE/1ERES COTES
DE BORDEAUX
BORDEAUX
FRANCE*

163

*ENTRE-GARONNE-ET-DORDOGNE/1ERES COTES
DE BORDEAUX
BORDEAUX
FRANCE*

Château Reynon

33410 Cadillac
Tel. 56629651
Fax 56621489

According to Denis Dubourdieu, "technology is like a yo-yo". This observation, like his philosophy in general is accented by a sharp sense of the relativity of all things. An agricultural specialist and enologist, he did much to increase awareness and use of the "maceration pelliculaire" technique (for white wines) during the 1960s. He had realized from his studies on fermentation that the skins contained elements of aromas that could be imparted to the juice. The aim was to make wines that could age better and highlight the "terroir". Denis still has reservations about those who use the method as a selling point and speaks of "partisan" opinions when it comes to the biological aspects of winemaking. In fact maceration on the skins was already practiced by winemakers who used slow crushing. Furthermore, the method is no good to wine regions which are either too cold or too hot. Indeed, this expert, who still consults for many properties around the Bordeaux region, has none of the airs of a "guru" !

Château Reynon   ❦ ❦ ②
Premières Côtes de Bordeaux 1990
Pale straw yellow in color, it has a floral bouquet, with herbaceous notes and yeast. The palate has fresh flavors with round notes of ripe melon and a fleshy, savoury Sauvignon finish. A wine of great finesse.

Château Lousteau-Vieil

Sainte-Croix-du-Mont
33410 Cadillac
Tel. 56620141
Fax 56631182

Château Lousteau-Vieil has 15 ha of the best vineyards in the hilly Appellation of Sainte-Croix-du-Mont, just over the river Garonne from Sauternes and Barsac. Although there are few properties producing wines from this commune that are up to the standard of much Sauternes, the reason is probably commercial rather than due to any lack of potential. Lousteau-Vieil fortunately is well known and widely sold and can afford to make wine without compromise demonstrating at the same time that good Sainte-Croix-du-Mont has superb structure and can age as well as many of its better known rivals across the Garonne. Rémy Sessacq, whose family have owned the property since 1843, makes the wine using a high proportion (a quarter) of Muscadelle to give the wine extra sweet perfume. The botrytis is normally evident in the misty fall mornings and like all good 'sticky' estates in the area, numerous pickings allow the syrupy concentration to make superb wine. Lousteau-Vieil is fermented in tank and aged at least 18 months in new oak casks. The 70,000 bottles made in most years are available all over the world and credit should go to the Sessacq family for keeping Sainte-Croix-du-Mont firmly on the map.

Château Lousteau-Vieil   ❦ ②
Saint-Croix-du-Mont 1989
Lovely yellow-gold color and clean on the nose with notes of citrus and honey. Fresh and well-rounded on the palate, agreeably sweet, with a long, honeyed finish. A good example of Ste Croix du Mont.

ENTRE-GARONNE-ET-DORDOGNE/1ERES COTES
DE BORDEAUX
BORDEAUX
FRANCE
164
ENTRE-GARONNE-ET-DORDOGNE/SAINTE-CROIX-
DU-MONT
BORDEAUX
FRANCE

Château d'Archambeau

Illats
33720 Podensac
Tel. 56625146
Fax 56624798

"He does everything himself", says Madame Dubordieu of her husband Jean-Philippe, the owner and manager of a property which has belonged to the family for over a century. Jean-Philippe concentrates on producing fat, full traditional white Graves, as well as a good red wine from half Cabernet Sauvignon and half Merlot. The 30 ha of vineyards on gravelly clay and chalk soil are planted with particularly ancient 60 year-old Sémillon and Sauvignon Blanc vines, whose grapes are hand picked and sorted before vinification. The white must undergoes a 24-hour maceration before fermentation, so that the cap of skins that comes to the surface can be removed. It is then fermented in casks, a fifth of them new, and is also aged in the same casks which are regularly cleaned. The wines may be "bâtoné", or stirred up with the remaining skins and yeasts, if necessary, and are fined and blended in stainless steel tanks before being filtered and bottled. The red wines are fermented in temperature-controlled stainless steel vats and then aged for a year, half in vats and half in the wood. He fines with egg whites and filters before bottling, for a total production of about 1,000 cases a year.

Château d'Archambeau Graves 1990 ♉ ②
Vibrant straw color with aromas of fresh tropical fruit and of light vanilla. The wood is well-married by the firm structure and the palate ends on a long almost decadently honeyed and fragrant note.

Château de Chantegrive

33720 Podensac
Tel. 56271738
Fax 56272942

25 years ago Château Chantegrive did not exist, and it has only been with the perseverance and patience that Franÿoise and Henri Lévêque have gradually bought up small parcels of vineyards and built the cellars for winemaking and aging. Today they have about 90 ha on gravelly terraces in the communes of Cérons, Podensac, Illats and Virelade. Over half their estate produces white wine; 25,000 bottles of a sweet Cérons wine, 200,000 of dry Graves and another 200,000 of red Graves. The dry white is of particular interest, especially the Cuvée Caroline, (50,000 bottles made a year) which can be remarkable. This cuvée is obtained with equal parts of Sémillon and Sauvignon Blanc grapes, fermented in new oak and left on "lies fine" for 7-8 months before bottling. The reds, made from 60% Cabernet and 40% Merlot, ferment in stainless steel and then age in oak barrels (one third of which are replaced each year) for 18 months. A small amount of red, the Cuvée Édouard, is aged entirely in new oak. Even if not perhaps of exceptional quality, the reds are extremely drinkable and generally ready after 3-4 years in bottle.

Cuvée Caroline Graves 1990 ♉ ♉ ②
Bright, very pale color. Sauvignon is well-marked on the nose but the new oak predominant. On the palate, the fruit is very fresh, ripe and crunchy. Clean, with good length. With its solid acid balance, a wine to be kept for a couple of years.

Château Chantegrive Graves 1989 ♉ ②
A bright rich red color. A soft and fruity nose. The palate abbounds with elegant, ripe red fruit and it is extremely drinkable and well-made.

GRAVES/GRAVES
BORDEAUX
FRANCE

165

GRAVES/GRAVES
BORDEAUX
FRANCE

Château Le Bonnat

Saint-Selve
33650 Labrède
Tel. 56647786
Fax 56641888

Château Le Bonnat makes elegantly stylish wines, which is hardly surprising as it is owned and run by the same team behind Château de Fieuzal. Headed by Gérard Gribelin and Fieuzal's technical director Michel Dupuy, they bought Bonnat in 1987. The 27 ha property has already established itself as one of the best Graves estates having paid particular attention to quality. 15 ha are devoted to equal shares of Merlot and Cabernet Sauvignon. The rest are planted with mostly Semillon and Sauvignon with some Muscadelle. The parcels are on three slightly different gravel outcrops. Although a fair proportion of the vines are young, the wines already show plenty of concentration. They follow a carefully temperature-controlled vinification in tank and go on to age in 40-60% new Tronçais oak, the red for 18 months and the white for nine. The red wine is regularly racked off into clean casks, whilst the white wine remains on its lees. Both are fined before being bottled in heavy glass bottles with long corks. The winemaking team from Château de Fieuzal are already saying that a cellaring of 10-20 years is recommended for the red Le Bonnat, which makes one ponder on its final potential. As the price of Fieuzal's wine has skyrocketed, the Le Bonnat white Graves is a refreshing alternative.

Château Le Bonnat Graves 1990 ❦ ③
Pale bright yellow in color, the nose is fruity, but the wood is still quite perceptible. Rich, luscious fruit on the palate, full-flavored and well-rounded, with plenty of acidity on the finish, providing some freshness. A really delicious wine to drink in 1993/94.

Château Le Bonnat Graves 1990 ❦ ③
Super rich, deep color, extremely intense red on the edges with a hard, but fresh nose of red fruits. Fruit again on the palate, ripe and round, full-bodied but with very drinkable balance. With five years in bottle, this will be a true delight.

Château Le Bonnat Graves 1989 ❦❦ ③
Rich color, plenty of depth, it has a soft, fleshy appeal and really pleasant aromas of ripe red fruit. Lots of fruit in the mouth, with not much acidity and very round tannins. A very agreeable wine, truly in the style of the 1989s.

Château Magneau

12, chemin Maxime Ardurats
33650 Labrède
Tel. 56202027
Fax 56203995

Château Magneau produces a seductively creamy white Graves from a blend of 15% Muscadelle, 40% Semillon and 45% Sauvignon. Since 1980 when Henri Ardurats and his son Jean-Louis invested in the latest technology for their winery, they have been able to obtain optimum results with their white wines which are made from grapes off 20 of their 30 ha vineyard. The fruit is carefully crushed on arrival at the "chai", and the juice is chilled down to to settle over a couple of days. The fermentation is controlled at a low 16-18°C in the large stainless steel tanks. The wines stay in tank, being cold stabilized in December and bottled in the February following the harvest. The Ardurats also make an oak-fermented white called Cuvée Julie from roughly a third each of their three varieties which ages for six months on their lees undergoing regular "bâtonnage" before bottling around May. The other ten hectares of vines are given over to the cultivation of Cabernet Sauvignon and Merlot, but the strength of this property definitely lies in its delectable whites.

Château Magneau Graves 1991 ❦ ②
Very pale yellow in color, clean and bright. The nose is crisp and fruity with a nice touch of softness. Again fruity and crisp, clean and well-rounded on the palate. Very well-made, drinkable and very typical of the better wines of this region.

Château Magneau ❦ ②
Cuvée Julien Graves 1990
Warm, clean, bright clean colored, the nose is richer with a light, well-married and discreet tough of wood. Well-rounded on the palate; the oak again comes through in a way which will please those who like this style of wine.

Château Magneau Graves 1989 ❦ ②
Star bright, rich red, of good depth, the nose is soft, round and slightly minty. Very soft, plump and full on the palate, with plummy fruit, typical of the vintage. Not a wine to keep for long. Solid but very, very drinkable, while the fruit is still very much alive.

GRAVES/GRAVES
BORDEAUX
FRANCE

166

GRAVES/GRAVES
BORDEAUX
FRANCE

Château Rahoul

33640 Portets
Tel. 56670102
Fax 56670288

For a number of years Château Rahoul was owned by the Australian entrepreneur and winewriter Len Evans. This might explain why all of the plantings for white wine production are Sémillon, an occurence that is quite rare outside Australia. Alain Thienot, the present owner, has not changed this idea. The wine is not aged in traditional Aussie style in concrete tanks but is lavishly fermented and aged in new oak barrels. Indeed, not much is typical about Château Rahoul. Three quarters of the 20 ha are given over to plantings of four-fifths Merlot and one fifth Cabernet Sauvignon, giving the red wines considerable fleshy weight. All the grapes are gathered in small plastic bins to avoid maceration and fermentation starting in the vineyard and the maceration in vats is punctuated by regular "pigeage manuelle". Both red and white wines are aged in casks in air-conditioned comfort and the final results, 72,000 bottles of red and 24,000 bottles of white, have a particularly dedicated and steady following.

Château Rahoul Graves 1989 ⑬
A pale lemon-yellow in color, the nose is certainly rich! Heavy, buttery oakiness dominates the citrus, petrol fruit and mineral aromas to the point of being overblown. Full-flavored with a long oaky finish .

Château Rahoul Graves 1989 ③
A rich, deep color with an ruddy rim, there's lots of smoky cherry on the nose and a minerally yet full palate of woody cherry jam. The finish is a little aggressive and alcoholic which suggests it will be best enjoyed young.

Château Respide-Medeville

33210 Toulenne
Tel. 56762844
Fax 56762843

Château Respide-Medeville is owned by the remarkable Christian Medeville, who is much better-known for his very special Château Gilett (a Sauternes aged for 25 years in glass-lined tanks, before Monsieur Medeville deems it ready for bottling. Given the figure he must impose for Gilette as a result, it is probably a relief for him to have another, relatively straightforward property to look after as well. The 15 ha of Respide-Medeville lie on a gravelly outcrop near the village of Toulenne in the Graves. Two thirds of the wine is red, 60% Cabernet Sauvignon and 40% Merlot. The white is unusual, too, with its makeup of 12% Muscadelle (giving a more grapey, ripe melon and floral character), 50% Sauvignon and 38% Sémillon. It is vinified and aged for 8 months in new oak. During the first two months, the wines are "bâtonés" or stirred to circulate the yeasts and bacteria in the barrels. For the red wine the grapes are destalked and fermented in stainless steel for about three weeks. The wine is then aged in cask for a year. Although Respide-Medeville is not the finest wine of the appellation, it is certainly a well-made and most enjoyable wine.

Château Respide-Medeville Graves 1990 ⑫
Pale, very bright lemon in color, it has a lively, crisp oak-tinged nose and well-balanced fruit. The fruit is clean and mouth-filling as it reaches the palate with the lots of oak and good structure and an acid balance behind the wood. Still needs a few months to round out to its best.

Château Respide-Medeville Graves 1989 ②
Rich, deep dark, the nose has good layered smokey oak fruit. Rich on the palate, with aromas of blackcurrant fruit predominates with a good structure. All the really good features of the vintage with really ripe grapes and fruit tannins.

GRAVES/GRAVES
BORDEAUX
FRANCE

167

GRAVES/GRAVES
BORDEAUX
FRANCE

Clos Floridène

c/o Château Reynon Beguey
33410 Cadillac
Tel. 56629651
Fax 56621489

Denis Dubordieu produces his superb white Bordeaux and a good red Premières Côtes de Bordeaux from Château Reynon and the 17 ha of Clos Floridène (bought in 1982) in the Graves. Some normal red varieties are grown, but the most important plantings are 12 ha of Sauvignon, Sémillon and Muscadelle. Most of the vines are still quite young, 5-25 years old. The grapes are hand-picked, destalked and crushed as soon as they reach the cellar at Château Reynon. The must is macerated on the skins for 24 hours, a technique which appears to be a Dubordieu family favorite. air-conditioned cellars. The wine is kept in the same casks, only being "bâtoné" until the spring when it is blended and fined in tanks before being filtered and bottled. The red, a wine made predominantly of Cabernet Sauvignon, is vinified in stainless steel and aged for 15 months in cask having been both fined and filtered before bottling.

Clos Floridène Graves 1990
A very rich yellow-gold color, with a clean spicy nose with a touch of oak. Rich, buttery, powerful and long on the palate with the same well-blended oaky spicy flavors. A wine that does wonders with food.

Domaine du Moulin à Vent

33720 Landiras
Tel. 56625066
Fax 56624122

Paulette Labuzan is a dedicated agrobiologist. She is very proud of the fact that the only chemical to come into contact with her vineyard is a little sulphur dioxide, which she uses to clean the barrels and equipment for her red and white Graves, as well as a little sweet Graves Supérieure from 12 ha of vines. The plantings are on average 25 years-old, and all the Bordelais varieties are used. Yields vary widely depending on the the vintage and the parts of the vineyard that have no vines remain fallow for some years to allow the gravelly soil to recuperate. The vinification of the carefully nurtured grapes is traditional and simple with a long maceration for the red and a light pressing of the white grapes before fermentation. All the wines age in Alliers oak casks and are never filtered. Madame Labuzan has diligently pursued these principles since 1963 and, in line with most organic producers, makes very concentrated and well developed wines.

Domaine du Moulin à Vent
Graves 1990
Rich and full in every respect. Dark rich colored, with concentrated round, ripe fruit and blackcurrant on the nose. On the palate round, again, with soft, ripe smokey fruit; very accessible for enjoyable drinking, with good length.

GRAVES/GRAVES
BORDEAUX
FRANCE

168

GRAVES/GRAVES
BORDEAUX
FRANCE

Clos Tourmillot

33210 Langon
Tel. 56630252

Clos Tourmillot is a small 7-ha property just outside Langon at the southern end of the Graves Appellation. Monsieur Marc Bélis, who lives in a charming Girondin house, is on the point of retiring but is busy passing on his knowledge to the family so that the estate he bought 30 years ago will continue to produce top red and white Graves for years to come. The soils are particularly gravelly, and 4 ha are planted with 40% Merlot, 60% Cabernet Sauvignon whilst the other three are planted with similar proportions of Sauvignon and Semillon. The cellar is simply equipped with stainless steel and concrete tanks, all temperature-controlled. Monsieur Bélis does not believe his wines should be wood aged and concentrates on carefully aging them in tank and gently clarifying them with regular rackings. Both red and white spend about 18 months in tanks, in separate lots, before being fined, filtered, blended and bottled. The 20,000 bottles of red wine are labelled Clos Tourmillot whilst the 18,000 bottles of white, Domaine Tourmillot. Climatic conditions permitting, a tiny quantity of sweet, botrytized wine is occasionally made and labelled under the Graves Supérieures Appellation. Like the other wines, this enjoys Monsieur Bélis' refreshing policy of using no oak during aging.

Clos Tourmillot Graves 1989
Very deep, dark red color. Clean nose, dry and rather spicy with hints of red fruit. The palate has a delicate, fleshy and blackcurrant flavor with good balance and a lovely long finish. Fairly typical of the vintage and extremely pleasant to drink with enough body to age for another three to five years.

Château Carbonnieux

33850 Léognan
Tel. 56870828
Fax 56875218

At one time Château Carbonnieux was owned by the fathers of the Abbey of Sainte-Croix in Bordeaux, who with a keen eye for foreign markets, sent the Islamic king of Turkey some Carbonnieux labelled as mineral water. The Sultan was thrilled and exclaimed "If French mineral water is so good, why do they bother to make wine ?" This is unlikely to be a reflection on the concentration of white Carbonnieux today, particularly as the already widely respected wine is now being made according to the 'Denis Dubourdieu method'. Carbonnieux is one of the largest estates in the Graves with 75 ha and its present owners, Toni Perrin and family, own about one quarter of the plantings in the Léognan appellation. The vines are roughly split between white and red wine production. The red, which is rapidly improving, is 60% Cabernet Sauvignon, 30% Merlot and 10% Cabernet Franc. The white is two-thirds Sauvignon Blanc and one third Sémillon, with a small percentage of Muscadelle harvested in two runs. After pressing, the must remains on the skins for 24 hours before fermentation and aging, in new oak casks. The recent results of this technique have further contributed to the reputation of Carbonnieux wines and to their success in even more exotic markets than his predecessors.

Château Carbonnieux
Pessac-Léognan 1989
Pretty, star bright and a clean fruity nose with a touch of oak, well-married and round. Crisp and fruity on the palate, but again there is oak and soft roundness. Excellent drinking now but will probably improve over another 12 months.

Château Carbonnieux
Pessac-Léognan 1989
Good, medium red with a clean, light nose with soft fruits and oak. It is round in the mouth, soft and quite medium-bodied. Excellent drinking now but capable of aging for some tikme yet.

GRAVES/GRAVES
BORDEAUX
FRANCE

169

GRAVES/PESSAC-LEOGNAN
BORDEAUX
FRANCE

Château de Fieuzal

33850 Léognan
Tel. 56647786
Fax 56641888

Chateau Fieuzal was once owned by La Rochfoucald, famous for his severe maximes. The property was abandoned during the revolution but was bought back to life by Alfred de Griffon who sold it in 1892 to the negociant Jean Ricard. In the 1900s Fieuzal wines were so prized, they were being pulled out of the Vatican Cellars for the papal table. Today the winery is directed by Gerard Gribelin, and he must be pleased as Fieuzal has acquired a fine reputation. The 42 ha of vineyards are on the undulating land south of Léognan on poor sandy/gravel soils; the vines average 35 years-old and flourish under such stress. The red grapes are 60% Cabernet Sauvignon, 30% Merlot with a little Cabernet Franc and Petit Verdot, whilst the white are half Sauvignon, half Sémillon. The cellars are modern and well-equipped with temperature-controlled steel tanks. Red grapes are destalked and tank-fermented after which the wine is racked off into oak casks, of which half are replaced every year. The barrel aging lasts for about 18 months during which time the wine is fined with egg whites. The white wine follows a simple vinification and is aged in new oak. The results are certainly powerful, big wines with plenty of fruit to support so much wood.

Château de Fieuzal   ♈ ♈ ④
Pessac-Léognan 1989
Rich, bright color with hints of light yellow-gold. The nose has all the glycerine richness, oaky aromas and Sauternes notes. The palate has magnificent richness, truly stylish honeyed tones and great acidity that gives a long, clean and dry finish. One of the great white wines of France and, despite its high price-tag, still relatively unknown.

Château de Fieuzal   ♥ ♥ ④
Pessac-Léognan 1990
Lovely deep, dark concentrated in color, the nose has lots and lots of layered ripe, rich fruit. More ripe fruit in the mouth, full and rounded, with distinct hints of blackberries, quite wild and briary. Plenty of tannins give this wine a good structure. Delicious.

Château de Fieuzal   ♥ ♥ ♥ ④
Pessac-Léognan 1989
This Château de Fieuzal has lots of richness from the extracts, as marked by its distinctive intense hue and confirmed on the elegant fruity nose. Good deep, dark, rich color. On the nose it is extremely ripe with marked red fruits. In the mouth it is a very well-structured wine with great richness, depth of flavors and the ripe fruit marries perfectly with the oak. A fine example of the artistry of the enologist Monsieur Gérard Gribelin. This wine has a richness to its style that one does not expect in the Graves and is, in fact, much more Médocain. It remains, however, one of the truly great wines of the region of Bordeaux.

GRAVES/PESSAC-LEOGNAN
BORDEAUX
FRANCE

170

GRAVES/PESSAC-LEOGNAN
BORDEAUX
FRANCE

Château de France

33850 Léognan
Tel. 56647539
Fax 56647213

The estate of Château de France covers 32 ha of vines extending over the highest of the four terraces formed by the Garonne at flood level. It was bought in 1971 by Bernard Thomassin, who thoroughly rennovated and modernized the property. 29 ha of the vineyards are planted with red varieties and three with whites, which produced their first vintage in 1988. The vines stand on gravel with a percentage of clay in the sub-soil, which sometimes imparts a spongy character to the terrain. The estate borders on that of Fieuzal and enjoys excellent growing conditions and sunlight once the morning mists have disappeared. Château de France's red varieties follow the classic pattern of 40% Merlot and 60% Cabernet Sauvignon while the whites feature a surprisingly high proportion of Muscadelle (20%) along with the Sauvignon Blanc (60%) and Sémillon (20%). All wines are aged in cask, half of which are new wood for red wines meanwhile all are new for the white, aged three to six months. All recent vintages have been surprisingly good. With a name like Château de France, "noblesse oblige".

Château de France   🍇 ③
Pessac-Léognan 1989
Rather dark and intense in color, the nose has toasty, autumn leaves aromas with hints of videts. Robust and somewhat hard on the palate but with good, concentrated tannins which are working away to soften and round out. Acidity is good and firm, and the finish, very fresh, with a spicy background and finish.

Château de France   🍇 ③
Pessac-Léognan 1988
Deep garnet-red, with fragrances of spices and ripe red fruit (particularly jammy mulberry) on a floral smokey background. Fleshy on the palate with soft tannins and a supple oaky finish.

Château de Rochemorin

Martillac
33650 Labrède
Tel. 57845207
Fax 57749859

Another jewel in the crown of André Lurton, Château de Rochemorin is making a name for itself in an appellation crowded with big names that are increasingly fashionable. One of the earliest residents of Rochemorin (or Moor's rock) in the 17th century was Montesquieu. After a period in the doldrums, Lurton nurtured the property back to life, completely replanting it with Cabernet Sauvignon, Sémillon, Merlot and Sauvignon. The cellar confirms his style with their impressive ranks of insulated stainless steel vats, rows of immaculate barrels and everything kept spotlessly clean. As with Château La Louvière, the white grapes are picked by hand and the red are machine harvested. All the red must and half of the white ferments in the vat while the remaining white ferments in new oak. The white wine goes on to age for six months in cask while the red spends a year in 30% new oak. All wines are fined with egg whites and filtered before bottling. Such uncompromising winemaking is now providing some very rewarding results.

Château de Rochemorin   🍇 ②
Pessac-Léognan 1990
Pale, light yellow color, its nose has fresh appley fruit and light woody and vanilla aromas. The palate has clean fruitiness, very direct yet soft and really well-balanced.

Château de Rochemorin   🍇 ②
Pessac-Léognan 1988
A wine with a lovely, bright rich red color and a clean, ripe, stylich fruit on the nose. Evolved and well-balanced, it is pleasant to drink now although the structure and length ensure a good future.

GRAVES/PESSAC-LEOGNAN
BORDEAUX
FRANCE

171

GRAVES/PESSAC-LEOGNAN
BORDEAUX
FRANCE

Château Haut-Bailly

33850Léognan
Tel. 56647511
Fax 56645360

Turning out some superb wines at the moment, Château Haut-Bailly belongs to Jean Sanders and has 20 ha of vineyards of the traditional red varieties, predominantly planted on typically sandy gravel soil. The vines are on average more than 30 years-old. Monsieur Sanders and his father Daniel have done much to turn Haut-Bailly into such a formidable wine. It is vinified in the traditional manner but with the prudent use of technological progress. The tanks are either cement or stainless steel and are all temperature-controlled and the 18-21 day maceration period is carried out at relatively low temperatures maintained throughout. The wines are aged for about 18 months in new Nevers oak casks. The second wine, La Parde de Haut-Bailly, itself a really delicious wine, absorbs a third of the production, keeping the quality of the 120,000 bottles of the main wine very high. Haut-Bailly's strength is that the wines are particularly elegant and approachable when young.

Château Haut-Bailly
Pessac-Léognan 1989
Garnet color with a brick rim, the nose is warm and jammy with molasses and big new oak on the palate. Already signs of a crumbling backbone and low acidity show this wine has youthful character rather than cellaring potential.

Château Haut-Bailly
Pessac-Léognan 1988
Concentrated, mahogany red in color, the nose has notes of dried figs, prunes and spice. Powerfully structured, with jammy fruits and big tannins for this property's usually softer style. An excellent wine to see out the century.

Bordeaux Appellations in this Guide

Bordeaux
Bordeaux

Bourgeais-Blayais
Premières Côtes de Blaye
Premières Côtes de Bourg

Entre-Garonne-et-Dordogne
Loupiac
Premières Côtes de Bordeaux
Sainte-Croix-du-Mont

Graves
Graves
Pessac-Léognan

Libournais
Canon-Fronsac
Côtes de Castillon
Côtes de Francs
Fronsac
Lalande de Pomerol
Pomerol
Saint-Emillon

Médoc
Haut-Médoc
Listrac
Margaux
Médoc
Moulis-en-Médoc
Pauillac
Saint-Estèphe
Saint-Julien

Sauternais
Barsac
Cérons
Sauternes

GRAVES/PESSAC-LEOGNAN
BORDEAUX
FRANCE
172
GRAVES/PESSAC-LEOGNAN
BORDEAUX
FRANCE

Château Haut-Brion

33600 Pessac
Tel. 56982817

Château Haut-Brion's history is long and illustrious, with many famous people involved. The 17th-century English writer, Samuel Pepys, was clear in his praise for "Ho Bryen". The famous stones, left by the glacial melting waters of the Pyrenées allow the 55% Cabernet Sauvignon, 20% Cabernet Franc and 25% Merlot plantings to have excellent drainage and to retain the sun's heat on summer's cool nights. The 44 ha of vines were replanted one hectare a year, and no grapes from vines that are under eight years-old are used in the great wine. The grapes ripen relatively quickly thanks to the more southerly position of the appellation and the heat-retaining stones. Consequently, the vintages are much more consistent. The winery is superbly equipped, having been the first to use stainless steel tanks for temperature-controlled fermentation in the 1960s. In addition to the great red wine, Château Haut-Brion also produces one of Bordeaux's rarest and most expensive great whites from half Sémillon, half Sauvignon grapes aged in new oak. The second wine, Bahans Haut-Brion, is also of excellent quality. The château has been owned by the Dillon family since 10935, but they also more recently purchased La Mission Haut-Brion. Inarguably, both châteaux are sure to remain at the forefront of the world's great estates.

Château Haut-Brion   🍇🍇 ④
Pessac-Léognan 1989
Clean, bright and pale. A rich, ripe mineral character, with the mature aromas and fullness of a sweet wine. On the palate, it has a tremendous rich, ripe fruit and richness rarely seen in a Graves, powerful and very long. It will drink well for a number of years: more like a Hermitage or a Burgundy than a Bordeaux.

Château Haut-Brion   🍇🍇 ④
Pessac-Léognan 1988
A good, rich deep color. Tighter and tougher than the 1989 on the nose, without the fatness. Perhaps it is only a little closed as of yet. Rich fruit and freshness on the palate, elegant and very stylish, with lots of good tannins. A wine which will indeed age at length.

Château Haut-Brion   🍇🍇🍇 ④
Pessac-Léognan 1989
Fermented at controlled temperatures for about 15 days, a wine which is the result of a cuvée of the very best of the year's production. Aged for 30 months in new oak casks and fined with egg whites before bottling. Big, deep, bright red color with with lovely depth and great structure. Very ripe Cabernet Graves-style fruit on the nose, with notes of black currants and raspberries, it has the ripeness and fleshiness of the vintage but has acquired a really good backbone of smart oak wood that is very well-married into the wine. It will keep for sometime but would also be drinkable soon, since the tannins are so round and smooth.

GRAVES/PESSAC-LEOGNAN
BORDEAUX
FRANCE

173

GRAVES/PESSAC-LEOGNAN
BORDEAUX
FRANCE

Château La Louvière

33850 Léognan
Tel. 57845207
Fax 57749859

André Lurton owns three large properties in the Graves as well as a couple of smaller ones, all of which run from yet another property at Château Bonnet in Entre-Deux-Mers. Louvière, although never classified, can be considered one of the best estates in Pessac-Léognan, with a reputation that has been carefully built over the years thanks to the quality if its wines, particularily the whites. 48 of the 62 ha grow traditional red and white varieties. The white are 85% Sauvignon Blanc and 15% Sémillon while the red are 70% Cabernet Sauvignon, 20% Merlot and 10% Cabernet Franc, all grown on gravelly soil. The white grapes are picked by hand and the red by machine. Emphasis at La Louvière is very much on spotless modern machinery together with traditional methods. The reds ferment in stainless steel vats and then age in oak barriques half of which are replaced every year. The whites, on the other hand, ferment entirely in new oak, where they then age for six months. All the wines are fined with egg white and filtered before bottling. The second wine, L' de La Louvière, is made from grapes off the younger vines.

Château La Louvière
Pessac-Léognan 1990
A very attractive wine, ideal accompaniment with fish. Starbright but pale straw-yellow, the nose is rich, oaked but beautifully floral with ripe fruit. The fruit also comes out on the palate, in all its richness, softness and depth, without being overpowered by the wood.

Château La Louvière
Pessac-Léognan 1989
Rich and full, round and soft. Being ripe and warm also in the mouth, it is a wine which will mature fast and, as long as it retains the soft fruitiness, will be a pleasure to drink.

Château La Louvière
Pessac-Léognan 1988
A wine with a lovely, much more elegant style, with rich, very well-defined fruit on the nose and depth of color. Full-bodied, refined and elegant again on the palate, with lovely length and a good backbone.

Château La Mission Haut-Brion

33600 Pessac
Tel. 56983373

Some of the most impressive winemaking technology can be seen in the "chai" at La Mission Haut-Brion. Bought in 1983, it was built up by the Dillons, who also own Château Haut-Brion, where the first stainless steel tanks to be ever used were installed in 1961. La Mission is naturally blessed with a similar soil to Haut-Brion's; the vines, therefore, produce very concentrated fruit. As the two are so close to each other, comparison is inevitable. If Haut-Brion is the greater wine, La Mission is certainly not far behind and, if La Mission does not match Haut Brion in the greatest years, it often can surpass it in more difficult ones. Vinification of the 50% Cabernet Sauvignon, 40% Merlot and 10% Cabernet Franc grapes is still classically Bordelais, with a carefully controlled fermentation followed by a long maturation in new oak. A little white is also made at La Mission, under the Laville Haut-Brion label. Before the Dillons, it used to be aged in used or older casks, but now only new oak is used. With a marked difference in styles between the two, both have produced some superb wines. The Dillons also own the 6-ha La Tour Haut-Brion estate, once La Mission's second wine. The grapes are still vinified there and make a bit coarser but still well-made 'little brother'.

Château La Mission Haut-Brion
Pessac-Léognan 1990
A lovely, elegant wine with an inviting color. The nose has a good concentration of berries and plums while the palate reveals a fullness of sweet, ripe fruit. Not quite up to the 1989, but it should be kept for a few years.

Château La Tour Haut-Brion
Pessac-Léognan 1990
A stylish wine with great balance, rich and full on the nose, it is certainly capable of holding its own against its 'big brother' La Mission.

Château La Mission Haut-Brion
Pessac-Léognan 1989
A wine of great personality, with a deep bright color, a nose rich in ripe fruit and nuts and spices on the palate. Powerful and concentrated, with the soft tannins typical of the vintage.

GRAVES/PESSAC-LEOGNAN
BORDEAUX
FRANCE

174

GRAVES/PESSAC-LEOGNAN
BORDEAUX
FRANCE

Château Larrivet-Haut-Brion

53, avenue de Cadaujac
33850 Léognan
Tel. 56657551
Fax 56645347

Château Larrivet-Haut-Brion lies about 15 km
to the south-west of Bordeaux, just outside
Léognan. At the end of the last century, it
was a large domain with a castle, park and
50 ha of vines. However, by the mid-1930s,
war and the depression had meant that much
of the vines had been pulled up and production had all but ground to a halt. In 1987, the
château was purchased by the Societé
Andros and is now directed by Philippe Ger-
voson and Francis Boutemy. Thanks to these
two, the estate once again produces some
first class wines. Today, there are about 45
ha of vines yielding 210,000 bottles of red
Graves (the estate's finest product) from
almost equal proportions of Cabernet Sauvignon and Merlot under the Pessac-Léognan
Appellation and 60,000 bottles of white Graves from equal quantities of Sémillon and
Sauvignon under the same label. The white
is fermented in new Allier and Troncais
casks, then bottled the spring later. The red
ferments in stainless steel and cement vats
on the skins for up to 21 days, depending on
the vintage. The wine goes into wood after
three months and ages for a year before bottling. One quarter of the barriques are
renewed each year and the wine is fined with
egg whites before bottling.

Château Larrivet-Haut-Brion
Pessac-Léognan 1990
Deep, rich color and full, ripe fruit with good con-
centration and black fruit length on the palate.
An extremely well-balanced wine.

Château Larrivet-Haut-Brion
Pessac-Léognan 1989
Another good red with a fine color, rich and
deep, if slightly less elegant on the nose than
the previous wine. On the palate, however, it is
very long and stylish, quite typical of the vintage.

Château Larrivet-Haut-Brion
Pessac-Léognan 1988
The color is again very rich and deep. Instinctively well-made on the nose, although the ripe
fruit aromas are slightly overpowered by the
oak. The elegance comes back again on the
palate and finishes with good length.

Château Les Carmes Haut-Brion

197, avenue Jean Cordier
33600 Pessac
Tel. 56482872
Fax 56931071

Les Carmes Haut-Brion, like its two illustrious
neighbors, is constantly under threat from
that burgeoning blight of suburbia, in this
case of Bordeaux itself. Les Carmes has
remained practically unchanged from when
the barefooted Carmelite friars settled up
until its acquisition by the present owners, the
Chantecailles, who are descendants of the
original family who purchased in 1850. The
terrain is typical Pessac with the large pebbles left by the meltingwaters off the the gla-
ciers in the Pyrenees, during the Ice Age.
The vineyards lie in a small valley which slopes down to the stream called Peugue, and
the 4 ha of vines have kept an unusual
legacy of varieties used by the Carmelites.
They used 50% Merlot, 40% Cabernet Franc
and only 10% Cabernet Sauvignon in their
wines. The winemaking is now supervised by
Philippe Chantecaille and his son-in-law,
Didier Furt, who have done much to elevate
the quality. All vats are of stainless steel and
temperature-controlled, and the casks are
renewed by a third each year. Long and initially violent fermentation, enhanced by 18
months wood maturation, gives big structured, robust wines which are powerful but elegant. Chantecaille and Furt's efforts can only
be judged on the 1,500 cases of their wine
made each year.

Château Les Carmes Haut-Brion
Pessac Léognan 1989
Bright, rich color, evolved at the edges. Good
balance on the nose, with notes of soft jam, with
flavors of sweet, ripe red fruits, like jam and
mint, on the palate. Perhaps not exceptional but
pleasant and eminently drinkable.

GRAVES/PESSAC-LEOGNAN
BORDEAUX
FRANCE

175

GRAVES/PESSAC-LEOGNAN
BORDEAUX
FRANCE

Château Olivier

33850 Léognan
Tel. 56647331
Fax 56645423

Owner of this 200-ha estate, Jean-Jacques de Bethmann is a dynamic entrepreneur. Sections of the estate's castle date back to the 12th century and are of considerable architectural importance. In 'real' life, so to speak, Jean-Jacques runs a financial consulting service for businesses; as a vigneron, he has flanked himself with capable helpers such as Christian Dubile (in charge of the vineyards) and enologists Guy Guimberteau and Denis Dubordieu, respectively for the red and white wines. Evidently, Jean-Jacques pays great heed to their advice, as the wines seem to be improving steadily. His 40 ha plot is planted with vines on a south-facing slope just outside Bordeaux. In 1985, de Bethmann and his collaborators embarked on a project to upgrade the vineyard and the cellar. The program included increasing density planting (from 8,000 to 10,000 vines/ha), severe pruning, more rigorous bunch selection at harvest, longer fermentation (from 10 up to 30 days) for the reds and lower temperature-vinification for whites, and renew the oak casks by a third every year. These ideas are now bearing fruit in the current vintages.

Château Olivier Pessac-Léognan 1990 ♀ ③
Sure enough, it pays to make quality wines. The commitment to progress at Château Olivier has created a white with a very elegant pale-color and intense fruity aromas of lemon on a luscious peary background. The fruit is full, well-defined and dense and the finish, full of finesse.

Château Olivier ♥♥ ③
Pessac-Léognan 1990
A particularly successful vintage,with a full-bodied richness which represents excellent value for money. The floral nose also has strawberry fruit aromas and spiciness; the flavors are concentrated on a palate with excellent underlying tannins and a lovely, slightly minty finish.

Château Pape-Clément

216, avenue du Docteur Marcel Pénord
33600 Pessac
Tel. 56070411
Fax 56073670

Château Pape-Clément would appear to be one of the least likely places in which to produce wines of quality, besieged as it is by the sprawling suburbia of Bordeaux. It is, in fact, on first sight, a most unlikely place to make great wine. The name of the estate is drawn from one of its former owners, Bertrand de Goth, Bishop of Bordeaux, who was made Pope in 1305 and chose Clement V for his name. The estate remained the property of the Church until it was confiscated during the Revolution in February 1791. The present owners bought the château in 1939. Today Léo Montagne is very fortunate to have the highly skilled and likable Bernard Pujol directing his property. There are 30 ha of Cabernet Sauvignon (60%) and Merlot (40%) producing 130,000 bottles of red wine and only 2 ha of Sauvignon, Sémillon and Muscadelle for the white. The vines are planted in the sandy, gravelly soil typical of the region. Much has been done recently to improve the cellar, including a series of stainless steel vats installed just as all casks have been replaced. All this effort has been amply rewarded, according to the outstanding wines made in recent years. A pleasant, well-made wine called Clémentin is made from the younger vines off those lots judged not to be up to the "Château" label.

Château Pape-Clément
Pessac-Léognan 1990
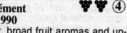
Rich, intense color, broad fruit aromas and upfront oak. Lovely ripe and juicy, red fruit on the palate with a balance and a finish which are quite exceptional.

Château Pape-Clément
Pessac-Léognan 1989
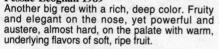
Another big red with a rich, deep color. Fruity and elegant on the nose, yet powerful and austere, almost hard, on the palate with warm, underlying flavors of soft, ripe fruit.

Château Pape-Clément
Pessac-Léognan 1988
Superbly, dark and rich in color, with extraordinary depth. Powerful, distinctive nose, still rather closed. Behind the first impression it hides luscious aromas of ripe cherries and tabacco, buried in an elegant bouquet. On the palate, there is a flavor of rich, fresh fruit with plenty of tannin. With its great structure but also outstanding balance and elegance, this is the wine which truly marks the return of Pape-Clément, flaunting all château's potential and grandeur. It has the body that will enable it to last well into the next century, and yet, with its apparently very mature, round tannins, it could also be impressively drunk young. A wine which sets the Pessac-Léognan Appellation into a class all its own, high above the rest of the Graves.

GRAVES/PESSAC-LEOGNAN
BORDEAUX
FRANCE

177

GRAVES/PESSAC-LEOGNAN
BORDEAUX
FRANCE

Domaine de Chevalier

33850 Léognan
Tel. 56641616
Fax 56641818

Famous for its particular style of Graves and its exceptional performances even in mediocre vintages, Domaine de Chevalier has many followers around the world. Indeed, no effort is spared to produce the best possible wines. Four hectares of vineyards, for the Sémillon and Sauvignon Blanc, are protected by 200 heaters (a more common sight in in Chablis or Champagne). The 27 ha of red, mainly Cabernet Sauvignon, are planted on a sandy/gravel soils with gravel/clay subsoils. All are carefully tended, and the grapes picked with what the young owner Olivier Bernard calls 'Draconian precision'. The white wine ferments and ages for 18 months in oak casks, one third of which are replaced every year; it does not undergo malolactic fermentation and the sediment is left to lie on the bottom. The red ferments in stainless steel at a high but short 32°C to extract maximum color and structure. After malolactic fermentation, it is blended before finally being put into small oak casks, half of which are replaced every year. Recent vintages of the reds have gone against the trend for early-drinking wines and are actually bigger, more robust and slower maturing. The white can have a richness and concentration which bring to mind a great white Burgundy.

Domaine de Chevalier   ④
Pessac-Léognan 1989
Bright, yellow in color with greenish highlights, it has a strong varietal Sémillon nose, meanwhile the freshness of Sauvignon stands out on the palate. The fruit is rich and powerful, assuring exceptional aging potential. One of the great whites of Bordeaux.

Domaine de Chevalier   ④
Pessac-Léognan 1990
Good things come to those who have the patience to wait. Full and rich both on the nose and on the palate, this grand wine has an outstanding fruit character and an impressive structure.

Domaine de Chevalier   ④
Pessac-Léognan 1989
Rich fruit and oak are well-balanced, the nose, fine and elegant. Soft on the palate, despite the relatively marked tannins, slightly rough and scrapey on the finish. A fine example of the finesse of Graves reds.

Domaine de Grandmaison

33850 Léognan
Tel. 56647537
Fax 56645524

The vineyards of the Domaine de Grandmaison are sandwiched between those of Châteaux Olivier, Carbonnieux and La Louvière on the edge of the Pessac-Léorgan Appellation. The estate belongs to Jean Bouquier, whose father purchased it in 1939, and began to produce wines in the late 1950s. When Jean inherited it in 1970, there were few vines left, but over the years he has replanted. Today he produces a fresh, clean Pessac-Léognan white as well as a good red. The estate covers 23 ha, 14 of which are planted with Merlot and Cabernet Sauvignon, and 3 with Muscadelle, Sémillon and Sauvignon Blanc (60%). All lie on the gravelly/limestone clay of Léognan. The Grandmaison cellar is well-equipped and the red undergoes fermentation in stainless steel before aging in oak (one-quarter new) for 18 months. As for the delicious white, one fifth is fermented and aged in new oak for 6 months, the rest in stainless steel, the two cuvées being blended before bottling. Grandmaison vines' average 14 years-old, which means that Bouquier's 100,000 bottles will surely become even better than they already are.

Domaine de Grandmaison   ②
Pessac-Léognan 1990
Light and bright in color, the nose is clean, fresh, and quite typical Sauvignon in style, even in the mouth, with all its fruity freshness with a certain mineral quality, finishing dry and clean. Not a powerful wine but elegant and charming.

GRAVES/PESSAC-LEOGNAN
BORDEAUX
FRANCE

178

GRAVES/PESSAC-LEOGNAN
BORDEAUX
FRANCE

Château Canon de Brem

33126 Fronsac
Tel. 57517896
Fax 57517979

Under the ownership of Jean-Pierre Moueix, Château Canon de Brem is one of the most highly reputed wineries in the Libournais Appellation of Canon-Fronsac. In reality, it is part of the Château La Dauphine group, which Jean-Pierre Moueix owns. The estate was built around the year 1750 by Victor Louis, the architect who also designed the Grand Théâtre at Bordeaux. Canon-Fronsac, as an Appellation, represents the very best of the Fronsac zone has to offer. Since he bought this Château, Jean-Pierre has shown that he is capable of producing really excellent wines. The 4 ha of vines lie on classic limestone soil planted 60% to Merlot and the remainder to Cabernet Franc; in either case, most of the vines are at least 25 years-old. All grapes are picked by hand and vinified in the traditional method with fermentation which lasts 14 to 21 days in cement vats before going on to aging for 20 months in cask. Every year half of the barriques are replaced. The wine is racked every three months and fined with egg whites before bottling.

Château Canon de Brem
Canon-Fronsac 1989
An intense ruby color, its fruity, delicate bouquet is redolent of ripe red fruit with more than a hint of wood. Warm and rich on the palate, with ripe fruit. It opens with delicate fruit aromas, meanwhile the palate develops a concentrated meatiness, with good length. Wait a couple of years to drink, before the fruit develops too far but after the tannins have had time to round out a little.

Château Cantegrive

Terrasson-Monbadon
33370 Puisseguin
Tel. 26521474
Fax 26522402

Formerly the property of the Barton et Guestier merchants, Château Cantegrive was purchased in June 1990 by the Boyard brothers, who have been active in Champagne since 1927 and are also owners of the Château Gasquerie in the Côtes de Francs appellation. Château Cantegrive, although in Puisseguin, is technically a Côtes de Castillon AOC. The soil tends to be muddy clay on the surface with a limestone subsoils; the vineyards, on the average 28 years-old, are planted to 65% Merlot, 15% Cabernet Franc and 20% Cabernet Sauvignon and enjoy a favorable maritime climate due to the nearby oceanside. The harvesting is done by hand and every parcel is separately vinified. The bunches are carefully selected before crushing and de-stalking. Placed in temperature-controlled vats, they then undergo a fairly long maceration to extract the rich aromas and structure. A further selection of the cuvées is done for the final blending, which are then aged in the wood. These are wines with a great future ahead.

Château Cantegrive
Côtes de Castillon 1990
Open on the nose with fruit of good intensity which blends into pleasing aromas of blackcurrant and violets on a background of wood. A wine which will age gracefully in the bottle for a good few years.

LIBOURNAIS/CANON-FRONSAC
BORDEAUX
FRANCE

179

LIBOURNAIS/COTES DE CASTILLON
BORDEAUX
FRANCE

Château de Pitray

33350 Gardegan
Tel. 57406338
Fax 57406624

Château de Pitray is the most representative estate of the Côtes de Castillon appellation. The 100 ha estate, 29 ha of which are vineyards, belongs to the Countess Pierre-Édouard de Borgne and are managed by the skilled winemaker Pierre Chilbery. The south-facing vines lie on the clay and limestone terrain typical of the Plateau de Gardegan, which is similar to that of the western sub-zone of Saint-Emilion. Two thirds of the vines are Merlot and the rest, Cabernet Franc, with a small percentage of Malbec, which is locally referred to as Pressac. Winemaking is kept traditional, as the grapes are de-stemmed and macerated at controlled temperatures for a period of 15-20 days, then the unfinished wine spends 18 months in the vat before being bottled. The system, in conjunction with the full-bodied varietal character of Merlot, has helped Pitray to earn its excellent reputation, despite the unrenowned location.

Château de Pitray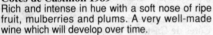
Côtes de Castillon 1989
Rich and intense in hue with a soft nose of ripe fruit, mulberries and plums. A very well-made wine which will develop over time.

Château Puygueraud

Société Thienpont de Berlaère
33570 Saint-Cibard
Tel. 57406104
Fax 57406708

Georges Thienpoint bought this property in 1946 and pulled up the vines to diversify production and started rearing livestock. At the end of the 1970s, the soil had recovered and was ready to be replanted with low-yielding root-stock. Clones were chosen with great care and the vine density adjusted to the nature of the terrain. Tradition coupled with the skills acquired by Georges at the Vieux Château Certan, also owned by the family, did the rest. Today, 20 ha are cultivated with 40% Merlot, 30% Cabernet Sauvignon and another 30% Cabernet Franc on clay and chalk soil with a subsoil of limestone, clay and loess. Vinification is supervised by Nicolas Thienpoint, one of Georges' sons, and sales are managed by Dominique and François, another two of his 13 children. Grape bunches are selected at harvest, destalked and pressed in the winery's cellars. Fermentation lasts about three weeks and takes place in stainless steel vats at 32°-34°C in order to extract the maximum from the grapes, with frequent racking. Aging is carried out in vats and oak barriques, one quarter of which are new, for a period of 18-24 months; bottling is done without filtering. Nicolas Thienpoint is also the owner of Château Claverie (which is also in Côtes de Francs), with 7.5 ha of vineyards on which he produces one of the best wines in the appellation.

Château Puygueraud
Côtes de Francs 1989
Rich in color and in bouquet, with lovely ripe fruit. Well-rounded and soft on the palate with plenty of red berries. Good texture, with firm tannins and a solid structure.

Château Puygueraud
Côtes de Francs 1988
Perhaps not as firm as the 1989, but considerably fresher, both on the nose and in the mouth. Soft on the palate with tar notes which precede a surprisingly powerful structure, with well-marked tannins. Elegant and well-balanced.

LIBOURNAIS/COTES DE CASTILLON
BORDEAUX
FRANCE

180

LIBOURNAIS/COTES DE FRANCS
BORDEAUX
FRANCE

Château Fontenil

15, cours des Girondins
33500 Libourne
Tel. 57511094
Fax 57250554

Anyone who knows anything about winemaking in the Bordeaux region will certainly have heard of Michel Rolland, owner of Château Le Bon Pasteur, the man with the magic touch with the exciting top properties in Libournais. His latest venture is to have brought the Fronsac appellation back to life almost single-handedly. In 1986, he and his wife Dany bought 7 ha of vineyards largely planted to Merlot, with 15% Cabernet Sauvignon, to create Château Fontenil. The soil is shallow limestone clay and the vines are around 30 years-old, carefully pruned to ensure low yields. They hand-pick as late as possible, to ensure quality grapes and optimum ripeness. Rolland's cellar techniques (fairly high temperature-controlled fermentation for three to four weeks) are as well-known as his skilled use of new oak. 30% of the wine ages in vats, the rest in small wooden barrels, one third of which are replaced every year. In spite of its short winemaking history, Château Fontenil is already recognized as one of the most interesting producers in the Fronsac Appellation.

Château Fontenil Fronsac 1990   🍇🍇 ③
Really lovely, deep, rich color. The nose is rich and concentrated with ripe fruit and smokey smart oak; those same flavors return on the palate, together with fragrances of mint, in a soft balance with outstanding structure.

Château Fontenil Fronsac 1988   🍇🍇 ③
Rich in color, it seems to have evolved quite rapidly. Round red fruits on the nose, soft and complex. Harmonious, with good strength, with fruit freshness and good length. Delicious drinking now or in a few years' time.

Château La Rivière

La Rivière
33216 Saint-Michel-de-Fronsac
Tel. 57249801
Fax 57249439

La Rivière must be a mystery - a mystery as unfathomable as its cellars buried 18 m under solid rock, as impressive as its 47 ha of vineyards, and as formidable as the choice of vintages presently released (from the 1979s on up to the1989s). One thing is certain: Jacques Borie's wines have all the elegance to surpass many a Bordeaux Crus Classés in blind tastings. Inexperienced tasters, perhaps? Certainly not, not when you know that this wine is the result of a determined quality effort and the use of modern technology to obtain an impeccable crop of healthy grapes. Half of the vineyard is over 50 years-old and nine tenths is south-facing. The harvest takes place when the grapes are super-ripe and they then pass through a system of heat-treatment to eliminate the grey mould. As for the musts, they are partially concentrated to eliminate excess water in the grapes and fermetation lasts for at least a month. Aging is also unique, just as the smart use of oak (12-16 months) is limited to used casks. Jacques Borie is a man of character, used to taking on wine writers and throwing himself against all preconceptions. He has, by no means, finished surprising us.

Château La Rivière 1990   🍇🍇 ②
A wine of great texture, clean and with outstanding concentration. Almost black in color with a relatively closed nose. The remarkable tannin structure prevails on the palate. These are still green and hard but of such complexity as to allow the wine to maintain its lively fruit for many years to come without fading, even well into the next century.

Château La Rivière 1987   🍇 ②
This vintage was generally underrated and, at best, was considered only mediocre. Such was hardly the case with this wine. Ideal for drinking now, it is amazingly soft and has an aromatic backbone of spice and vanilla fragrances.

LIBOURNAIS/FRONSAC
BORDEAUX
FRANCE

181

LIBOURNAIS/FRONSAC
BORDEAUX
FRANCE

Château Villars

33141 Saillans
Tel. 57843217
Fax 57843125

This magical château is the work of one man: Jean-Claude Gaudrie. The building enjoys a wonderful view overlooking the vines. It may not be awestrikingly beautiful, but it is carefully looked after, as are the vineyards and the cellar. The Gaudries have been working here on an estate of 29 ha, 18 of which have been vineyards for six generations. 70% Merlot, 20% Cabernet Franc and 10% Cabernet Sauvignon grow on clay and limestone soils. The climate has a strong maritime influence from the ocean, with cool, wet winters and hot, dry summers. Wine with the Villars label is the product of 100% de-stemmed vinification and uncompromising bunch selection. Only grapes from vines of an average age of 35 years are used while the rest goes to produce the second label wines Château Moulin Haut Villars and Château Maluat. Jean-Claude Gaudrie loves traditional vinification, which takes place in closed cement vats, temperature-controlled during the entire operation. After fermenting for three to four weeks, aging in barriques (one third of which are replaced every year) takes from 10-14 months, depending on the year. This is a wine which will age in the bottle for one or two decades.

Château Villars Fronsac 1990 ♥♥ ③
With an explosive bouquet with a whole kaleidoscope of aromas, from truffles, to coffee and cedarwood, it has great body and richness with delicate, elegant tannins, with a voluptuous and exceptionally long finish. An excellent result given the year, which confirms both the improvements in the area and the talent of the producer.

Château Villars Fronsac 1988 ♥♥ ③
Lovely deep ruby-red in color, at first it is a little closed on the nose with a slight note of wood. The palate is full and fleshy with tannins still well in evidence but nevertheless delicate. Subtle and elegant, balanced, although the finish is a little rugged. Drink in a few years' time.

Château La Croix de Chenevelle

33500 Lalande de Pomerol
Tel. 57519993
Fax 57740063

Château La Croix de Chenevelle is a relatively small 10-ha estate situated on chalky, gravelly soil in the heart of Lalande de Pomerol. Thanks to careful fermentation techniques, Chevenelle is a prime example of what the area can produce at its best. The 25 years-old vines are mainly Merlot, with only 10% Cabernet Franc. Grapes are subjected to a typical traditional fermentation process. Hand-picked and de-stemmed, they ferment for 15-25 days in cement and stainless steel vats, all temperature-controlled. Bernard Levrault and his assistants skillfully blend the first press must and the various cuvées after a tasting which takes place before the wine is transferred into wooden barrels, 20-35% of them new, for the aging stage of the process. Monsieur Levrault comes from a family which has been making wine for four generations. Thus he prefers not to filter his wines but believes in racking and clarification with egg white. His approach may be straightforward and unassuming but nonetheless provides us 500 cases of excellent, sound wine every year.

Château La Croix de Chenevelle ♥♥ ② Lalande de Pomerol 1989
Attractive bright deep ruby, the nose is beautifully rich with spicey, dark plum jam, chocolate and dried fruits. All the richness of the fruit explodes on the palate, with a soft but excellent structure and a long finish.

LIBOURNAIS/FRONSAC
BORDEAUX
FRANCE

182

LIBOURNAIS/LALANDE DE POMEROL
BORDEAUX
FRANCE

Château Tournefeuille

33500 Néac
Tel. 57511861
Fax 57510004

Of the great wineries neighboring with Tournefeuille, Pétrus is probabily the most famous. The owners of the estate, the Sautarel brothers, Jacques and André, joke that they are "three generations of 'sauterelles', or locusts, on these lands". They continue to manage their 18 ha of vineyards situated on a stunning clay and gravel slope with considerable traces of iron. Although the two are highly respected in the restaurant world, particularly by Jean-Marie Amat, who has always recommended their wines in his restaurant at Bouliac, they do not neglect their own buyers. More importantly, thanks to their fierce sense of loyalty to their roots and local traditions, they have maintained a keen sense of proportion and manage to sell their wines at affordable prices. This offshoot of a sub-Appellation of Pomerol is produced with real care. The harvest is done by hand, and temperature controls are highly efficient, allowing regulation of the entire fermentation process; wood aging is carried out in wooden casks for 24 months. After all this, you may have to wait five years to drink the wine, but it will be worth it.

Château Tournefeuille 1989   🍇 ③
One of the Appellation's most successful wines, this vintage particularly needs to wait a few years before drinking. Deep in color with a tight, closed nose, so far, with a rich texture on a gamey, animal-like background. Tannins still well in evidence.

Château Tournefeuille 1988   🍇 ③
Garnet red in color with lovely aromas of ripe berries, the palate is well-rounded and silky with tannins already well-blended and a finish without even a hint of aggressiveness. Drink now.

Château Belle Brise

40, chemin de la Béquille
33500 Pomerol
Tel. 57511682

Hidden by age-old trees, the peaceful and charming 2.5 ha Lafage estate is to be found at the end of a path running alongside the railroad tracks The barrel rooms and cellars are in what used to be the old arsenal of Libourne. The vines lie on muddy, sandy soil, where they enjoy good sunlight, and the château is named after breezes which swift across from the nearby Dordogne and Isle rivers. Nothing is left to chance to ensure that the grapes are of the very best quality. After the catastrophic frosts of 1956, the vineyards were completely replanted, with 70% Merlot, 25% Cabernet Franc and 5% Cabernet Sauvignon. Yields are kept deliberately low as Michel Lafage looks first and foremost for roundness and concentration in his grapes and fermentation lasts only a very short time. About 10,000 bottles a year are produced of a wine that is put on the market only after 36 months of cellaring: the seal of top-quality wine.

Château Belle Brise Pomerol 1990   🍇 ②
When barrel-tasted, it was still opaque in appearance. Good depth on a rich texture, full of character, with an almost old-fashioned "goût de terroir" nature. Excellent prospects for aging.

Château Belle Brise Pomerol 1989   🍇 ③
Fine ruby color, the nose has faint hints of prune. Very velvety on the palate. Rich, concentrated body and good tannins with no astringency. A fine wine to lay down.

Château Belle Brise Pomerol 1988   🍇 ③
Already developed, with an orangey color. Rich in texture with elegant, voluptuous tannins and great intensity over delicate, seductive aromas. May be drunk now.

LIBOURNAIS/LALANDE DE POMEROL
BORDEAUX
FRANCE

183

LIBOURNAIS/POMEROL
BORDEAUX
FRANCE

Château Bonalgue

28, rue Trocard
33500 Libourne
Tel. 57512056
Fax 57512828

Lying to the north-east of Libourne, the house on this 6-ha estate, with its magnificent position and sandy gravel soil, is surrounded by a park in which two splendid century-old fir trees stand proudly. Owned today by the outgoing, well-known Libourne merchant, Pierre Bourotte, it was built by one of Napoleon's officers, Antoine Rabion, on his return from Egypt when he inherited the estate in 1798. The coat of arms and standards of the former owner may still be seen in the bas-reliefs on the gable. The varieties grown are 75% Merlot and 25% Bouchet (Cabernet Franc). Vinification is done with great care, half of the wine passing into oak casks (half of which are new) while the rest goes into vats (two fifths) and one year-old barriques (three fifths). Pierre Bourotte also looks after other properties, namely Château Les Hautes Tuileries at Lalande de Pomerol and Château du Courlat at Lussac-Saint-Emilion.

Château Bonalgue Pomerol 1989   🍇 ④
Intense purple color, with fragrances of briary undergrowth and truffles. A wine with good balance between delicacy of tannins and richness of texture. A vintage which demonstrates the desire to make the most elegant of wines while maintaining the unique qualities of the "terroir".

Château Bonalgue Pomerol 1988   🍇 ④
A very ripe, forward wine which bears the hallmark of its gravel and sandy soil. Aromas of ripe fruit and game unfold invitingly. Good tannins, with a well-rounded palate and balanced finish.

Château Clinet

33750 Saint-Germain-du-Puch
Tel. 56301001
Fax 56301145

At the height of her glory, after a series of fabulous vintages, Château Clinet suddenly changed hands. Jean-Michel Arcaute threw in the towel in 1991 and left GAM Audy the keys to the château and its gravel soiled vineyards planted with Merlot (75%), Cabernet Sauvignon (15%) and Cabernet Franc (10%). In the meantime, Arcaute decided to invest with the well-known enologist, Michel Rolland, amongst others, a considerable sum of money in Hungarian vineyards, as the trade barriers and markets of Eastern Europe were opening up. It is still too early to say whether the new owners will take the château further along the road to success that their predecessor mapped out with such skill. There are, however, some definite and reassuring signs. While Jean-Michel Arcaute is no longer "King of the Castle", he appears to have stayed on to supervise vinification. It is equally reassuring to note that the estate prefers not to make officially any "en primeur" offers for the '91 vintage. So everything seems to be going in the right direction at Château Clinet, a magnificent property which has everything it needs to stay right at the top of the class in Pomerol for years to come.

Château Clinet 1990   🍇🍇 ④
A wine of wonderful texture and a truly exceptional quality of extracts. This vintage has rare softness with notes of violet and a voluptuous palate with tannins of great delicacy and infinite length. Pure pleasure !

Château Clinet 1989   🍇🍇 ④
Made with only 75% Merlot, this wine offers a deep red color, almost black, and a dense, powerful concentration on a background of red fruit (loads of ripe cherries) and spices. Big in structure, with a long distinguished finish.

LIBOURNAIS/POMEROL
BORDEAUX
FRANCE

184

LIBOURNAIS/POMEROL
BORDEAUX
FRANCE

Château de May-de-Certan

33500 Pomerol
Tel. 57514153
Fax 57518851

Situated in the south-eastern part of the clay and sand Pomerol plateau, the estate was created by a noble family of Scottish origin, the de Mays, who settled in France in the Middle Ages and arrived in Guyenne at the end of the 16th century. At that time, the entire property of Certan was handed over to them by royal decree. The vineyard is, in fact, one of the oldest in the region. Today, Odette Barreau-Badar, a tiny bundle of energy, and her son Jean-Luc, who qualified at the viticultural school of Château La Tour Blanche, look after the cultivation of a 5 ha vineyard planted mainly with Merlot, of course, but also with Bouchet, Cabernet Sauvignon and Malbec. Harvesting always takes place as late as possible in order to obtain the maximum concentration from the grapes. After a long, slow fermentation, the wines are aged in casks (one third new) for up to 20 months, depending on the characteristics of the vintage. The family also owns Château Poitou in the Lussac-Saint-Emilion appellation, which produces a good-quality wine.

Château de May-de-Certan
Pomerol 1990
Wonderful development in prospect for this sumptuous cuvée, which is a magnificent expression of its vintage. Dense ruby-red in color, it has a characteristic nose of truffles and an outstanding "goût de terroir". Meaty consistency and closely knit texture. An aristocratic wine sure to please to many wine-lovers.

Château de May-de-Certan
Pomerol 1989
Generous and at the same time mellow. Concentrated, slightly grassy, nose on an aftertaste of truffles and wild game. Good firm acidity, typical of the wine. The tannins are still a touch bitter and robust but are beginning to mellow into a dense body, showing hints of spice on the finish.

Château de May-de-Certan
Pomerol 1988
Magnificent black-cherry in color, it has a velvety smooth palate of captivating concentration and complexity. The tannins, very delicate on the finish, emphasize this wine's aging potential. An excellent result.

Château de Sales

33500 Pomerol
Tel. 57510492
Fax 57232391

This property has been owned by the De Lambert family since 1490 and is the largest in Pomerol, with its 47.5 ha of vines on fine, sandy gravel with clay deposits and iron. The vineyard is planted with classic 70% Merlot, 15% Cabernet Sauvignon and 15% Cabernet Franc. Henri de Lambert's son, Bruno, who has a degree in enology and ampelography from the University of Bordeaux, has been managing the vineyard for over 15 years. At Château de Sales, quality comes first. Every year, wines from the different varieties and plots are tasted, only 60% being selected to become Château de Sales (there is also a second wine, Château Chantalouette, and in some years, such as 1987, everything is sold as generic Pomerol). Two-thirds of the harvest is mechanized but the vines are otherwise cultivated in the traditional fashion. Fermentation is temperature-controlled in cement vats after total de-stemming and lasts for about three weeks. Aging is two-thirds in barrels and one-third in the vat, with a switch between the two every three months on racking. The wood is not new, although one fifth of the casks are replaced every year. Excessive tannin in new wood goes against the production policy of producing well-rounded, soft wines.

Château de Sales Pomerol 1989 ♥ ③
A delicious, built-to-last wine, with fragrant and round aromas that is open and generous on the nose with a palate of blackberries and harmonious tannins which are delicate and sweet, revealing great elegance.

Château de Sales Pomerol 1988 ♥ ③
A wine of breeding with great charm, with hints of spice and ripe fruit on the nose. Palate of extraordinary roundness and beautifully structured fruit. A full, delicate finish is totally dominated by the fruit.

LIBOURNAIS/POMEROL
BORDEAUX
FRANCE

185

LIBOURNAIS/POMEROL
BORDEAUX
FRANCE

Château Gazin

33500 Pomerol
Tel. 57510705
Fax 57516996

Château Gazin is an estate to be envious of, with its 23 ha of vines (80% Merlot, 15% Cabernet Franc and 5% Cabernet Sauvignon) in a single plot that is wedged into the splendid clay and gravel plateau between Pétrus and Château L'Évangile. The terrain is one of the five or six best in the appellation. The château itself, property of the Bailliencourt family for generations, was built in the 18th century where the ancient hospital of the Knights of Malta once stood. Nicolas de Bailliencourt now manages the large estate, which is third in vineyard size in the Appellation, after Château Nénin and Château de Sales. Vinification follows the traditional formula and aging takes about 18 months in oak casks, one third of which are replaced every year. In 1989 and 1990, the proportion of Merlot in the final "mélange" reached 95% while the creation of a second wine, l'Hospitalet de Gazin, enabled indispensable selection to be carried out. Given its soils and its resources, this château should reach the very top position among crus of the appellation. To be quite frank, this does not always happen although the quality in some years appears more in line with expectations.

Château Gazin Pomerol 1991　　🍇 ④
In a difficult year, Château Gazin has done rather well. Good concentration on the nose while the palate is nicely full with a balance which will improve with aging. A wine worth waiting for.

Château Gazin Pomerol 1990　　🍇 ④
A very deep red in color with ripe red fruit on the nose and all the typical varietal character of Merlot. On the palate, the cru is beautifully expressed, with tannins still hard but beginning to mellow out. The finish, with a slight note of wood, has good length.

Château L'Enclos

1, L'Enclos
33500 Pomerol
Tel. 57510462

This estate belongs to one of the oldest, established families in Pomerol, the Carteau family, whose ancestors held important governmental posts in the 17th century. The château was built at the end of the last century and is protected from inquisitive eyes by a thick screen of trees. The 10.5 ha of vines are spread over slopes on the plateau on the west side of Pomerol where the the soil is sandy gravel on top with mixed iron-rich clay underneath. They are planted mostly with Merlot and Cabernet Franc and Malbec for the remaining 20%. Vinification is kept traditional, and the wines age in the wood (one quarter being replaced every year). Ever since a bottle of Château L'Enclos 1947 was served to Queen Elizabeth II at the Royal court of Holland in 1958, the estate has proudly been the regular suppliers to the Dutch court. They feel sure this bears testament to the quality and consistency of Pomerol.

Château L'Enclos Pomerol 1989　　🍇 ④
A potent wine which has a good balance between fruit concentration and tannin. A complex nose with cherry aromas, that tend towards kirsch and toastiness, offers a long-lasting finish.

Château L'Enclos Pomerol 1988　　🍇 ④
Another rich, dark colored wine, with aromas which recall scents of tobacco on a rich body. The tannins are already well-blended and the wine is round, of real finesse, with a clean finish.

LIBOURNAIS/POMEROL
BORDEAUX
FRANCE

186

LIBOURNAIS/POMEROL
BORDEAUX
FRANCE

Château L'Évangile

33500 Pomerol
Tel. 57511530

No introductions are needed for this château situated at the top of the Pomerol plateau. Château L'Évangile has a solid reputation and its wines are always among the best from the Appellation. No small wonder, either, when the estate borders with Pétrus to the north and Chaval Blanc straight cross to the south. Owned by the Ducasse family since 1862, the estate passed in 1990 into the hands of Baron Eric de Rothschild, who holds two thirds of the shares. Madame Ducasse remains a dynamic co-owner at 89 years-old and continues to look after operations. The wines are always of consistent quality thanks to the soil of the 13.25 ha planted with two thirds Merlot and one third Bouchet. The terrain is of almost equal proportions of pure clay with iron-bearing soil underneath and gravel and sandy areas which contribute towards an aristocratic wine, austere and of incomparable finesse. The wine is aged in oak barrels (one third of which are replaced every year) and bottled at between 18 to 24 months after fermentation.

Château L'Evangile
Pomerol 1990
Better in structure than the preceding year, and rich in violet fragrances. The bouquet is already developed and the palate, sumptuous with a dense body and a chewy meatiness. With great finesse on the finish, this is one most successful crus of the Appellation.

Château L'Evangile
Pomerol 1989
This wine's cherry stone aromas tend towards kirsch and scents of leather. It was a fine vintage, with rather elegant tannins. A wine of great complexity with a light liquorice finish. A brilliant future lies ahead.

Château L'Evangile
Pomerol 1988
Rich and very concentrated in texture, its aromatic intensity slowly unfurls itself. Although the tannins may seem rather harsh and austere, the elegance and body are definitely present.

Château La Conseillante

Société Civile des Héritiers Nicolas
33500 Pomerol
Tel. 57511532
Fax 57514239

Owned by the Nicolas family since 1871, Château La Conseillante stretches over 12 ha on the edge of the Saint-Emilion Appellation, on that part of the Pomerol plateaux which slopes gently downhill. The particular clay and gravel soil contains iron-bearing elements in the subsoil, and, in this respect, resembles the Saint-Emilion Premier Cru. The vineyard is also very characteristic in its planting pattern, too. Naturally, Merlot takes the lion's share of the estate (65%), but the percentages of Cabernet Franc (30%) and Malbec (5%) are especially high. As a result, the wine has a singular freshness and richness. Fermented in temperature-controlled stainless steel vats, Château La Conseillante then spends 20 months or so in new oak barriques, replaced every year with others bought traditionally from three different coopers. The collection of old vintages is remarkable and undoubtedly unique in Pomerol. For decades, two barriques of every vintage have been held back, thus building up over the years a faithful record of the château. A benchmark winery for the entire Appellation.

Château La Conseillante
Pomerol 1990
Dark, very deep color. The bouquet has medium intensity but this is a wine of outstanding density with tannins of unusual richness which express its origins. The fullness on the palate is also noteworthy. Wait for several years before drinking.

Château La Conseillante
Pomerol 1989
A marvellous success. The density of the fruit and the richness of the tannins are well-blended. the aromas are intense and fruity, with a background of cherry, with a note of toastiness. Full on the palate with a very complex finish. A great and very enjoyable wine, as good as the 1985.

LIBOURNAIS/POMEROL
BORDEAUX
FRANCE

187

LIBOURNAIS/POMEROL
BORDEAUX
FRANCE

Château La Croix

37, rue Pline-Parmentier
33500 Libourne
Tel. 57514186
Fax 57517683

The name Janoueix is closely linked to the history of Libourne, because the family occupies a position of privilege in both the wine trade and in winemaking. It is to Marie-Antoinette Janoueix-Estrade, the first lady of Pomerol, that we owe the renowned quality of Château La Croix. Her son, Jean-François, now plays a significant role as well as being a member of the Société des Amis de Saint-Jacques-de-Compostelle (the château wall bears a cross indicating the route of the pilgrimage, in which Jean-François himself took part, and inviting the faithful to knock on the door and ask for hospitality). The 12 ha of the estate are on a single plot on the southern slope of Pomerol hill. They are planted with 60% Merlot, 25% Cabernet Franc and 15% Cabernet Sauvignon on gravelly and sand-and-gravel soil that has an iron-rich substratum. The wines are consistently delicate and elegant. The Janoueix family also owns land in Saint-Emilion, including Château Haut-Sarpe, a Grand Cru Classé.

Château La Croix Pomerol 1990   🍷 ④
It was a warm year, but vinification was carried out with such skill that this wine is beautifully balanced in its sugar and alcohol. Lovely structure on pleasant tannins which preserve the fruity aromas of the wine.

Château La Croix Pomerol 1989   🍷 ④
An intense red color, mineral aromas typical of the "goût de terroir", a subtle nose, with the tannins not yet well-blended. A balanced, complete and complex wine that lives up to its reputation.

Château La Croix Pomerol 1988   🍷 ④
A fascinating, aristocratic and well-balanced wine. Deep red in color, with the fragrances of ripe fruit harmonizing elegantly with a solid, well-knit texture. Excellent aging potential.

Château La Croix de Gay

33500 Pomerol
Tel. 57511905
Fax 57741562

The Pomerol producers' association was founded by an ancestor of the Raynaud family. Still today, the château is an important part of the local heritage. It is, indeed, true that the 12 ha of vines on gravel and clay/gravel soil have exceptionally favorable positions on the Pomerol plain. And, it is also true that father, mother, daughter and son look after the estate, even if Alain, the son, is a practises medicine, as well. 80% of the vineyard is devoted to Merlot and 20% Cabernet Franc and Cabernet Sauvignon, all harvested by hand. Fermentation takes place in closed vats with frequent racking and continuous temperature-control by means of a cooling system. The wines are aged in casks, one third of which are replaced every year. The Raynauds also make a wine for a few select customers from a plot of old vines called La Fleur de Gay. Although the Raynauds are well-known and widely respected, success has not gone to their heads as their wines continue to be accessible and considered excellent value for money.

Château La Croix de Gay   🍷🍷 ③
Pomerol 1990
A ruby color and aromas which open out with strawberry, cherry and kirsch. Elegantly well-rouned on the palate, with a juicy extract and agreeably spiced finish. To be laid down for a few more years yet.

Château La Croix de Gay   🍷🍷 ④
Pomerol 1989
A rich and delicate wine of impressive structure yet delicate on the palate, with hints of truffle and liquorice and a slightly woody finish which allows the vanilla to come through. Open around the end of the century.

LIBOURNAIS/POMEROL
BORDEAUX
FRANCE

188

LIBOURNAIS/POMEROL
BORDEAUX
FRANCE

Château La Pointe

33500 Pomerol
Tel. 57510211
Fax 57514233

This impressive stretch of property lies, as its name suggests, on a "point" of vineyards. The château is a splendid construction in the 'Directoire' style dating from the 18th century, situated in a park of tall, old trees. Stéphane d'Arfeuille, whose family also owns a property in Saint-Emilion, is in charge of the estate while his father is a merchant in Libourne. The vineyard is one of the most important in the appellation with 21.5 ha producing around 100,000 bottles a year. The soil is very mixed, with iron-bearing elements and clay in the sub-soil and sandy and gravelly strata above. Three quarters of the vines are Merlot with the rest Cabernet Sauvignon (20%) and Noir de Pressac (5%). The harvests are traditional with reduced yields since 1985. Fermentation is in stainless steel vats. The wines are aged in oak casks (with about one third being replaced every year) and vinification lasts up to 20 months. La Pointe was one of the first French estates to use and go by the Château name, in 1868, and continues to live up to the title today.

Château La Pointe Pomerol 1990 🍷 ③
With slight notes of leaves, not a complex wine but one with a good structure. Rounded and with delicate tannins that are nevertheless a touch astringent. A good solid Pomerol to drink now.

Château La Pointe Pomerol 1989 🍷 ③
A rather charming ruby color with a nose offering hints of tomatoes, vegetables and wood. A nice texture but slightly lacking in depth. Agreeable, however, with a somewhat rustic style all its own.

Château Lafleur

33500 Pomerol
Tel. 57844403

Don't hesitate to ask anyone in Pomerol If you do not know the way to one of the most picturesque vineyards in the appellation. Marie Robin is well-known around these parts. She and her sister Thérèse (who has since passed away) ,took over their parents' estate at the end of World War 2. The single plot, 4 ha vineyard is crisscrossed by two intersecting paths. Jacques Guinaudeau, their nephew, has a big say in the care of the vines and in winemaking. The gravelly soil with traces of clay is treated with great respect, being fertilized solely with cow manure, Bordeaux-mixture and sulphur. Fermentation takes place in cement vats and the wine is aged only partially in new barrels. A second wine called Les Pensées de Lafleur has been made since 1987, from the newer plantings of the vineyard.

Château Lafleur Pomerol 1989 🍷🍷 ③
Very dark in color, almost opaque. A nose marked by aromas of briary undergrowth and truffles. A palate with gamey, animal-like scents on a very concentrated body in which the tannins are complex and meaty.

Château Lafleur Pomerol 1988 🍷🍷 ③
A wine with a good structure and real potential. Delicate and velvety in texture, the subtle nose has notes of autumn leaves, spices and leather. The palate offers soft, well-blended tannins, with a lovely, slightly floral finish.

Les Pensées de Lafleur Pomerol 1988 🍷 ④
Rather dark in color, like its big brother Lafleur. Toasty-oak scents on the nose. The palate is full and the wine can age for some time yet.

LIBOURNAIS/POMEROL
BORDEAUX
FRANCE

189

LIBOURNAIS/POMEROL
BORDEAUX
FRANCE

Château Lafleur-Gazin

33500 Pomerol
Tel. 57511866

Located along the road which leads from Libourne to Lussac, leaving Gazin to the north and Lafleur to north-east, Château Lafleur-Gazin has belonged to the Borderie family for several generations. The vineyard is almost 8 ha, planted with two thirds Merlot and the rest Cabernet Franc, and lies on the north-eastern boundary of the plateau. Production is a shade under 30,000 bottles a year, and most of the sales are guaranteed by Jean-Pierre Moueix. The Borderie family takes care of the vineyard and the making and aging of the wine. The vineyard is divided up into two types of soil. On the edge of the plateau, we find clayey, sandy soil while at the foot of the hill, the terrain is exclusively sandy and is mainly planted with Cabernet Franc. In most cases, Lafleur-Gazin wines are full, generous Pomerols.

Château Lafleur-Gazin ♟ ④
Pomerol 1989
Dark in color, the nose is rather young and undeveloped, especially where Cabernet Franc is still marked. The tannin is strong on the palate and the wine will only balance out in quite a few more months' time.

Château Lafleur-Gazin ♟♟ ④
Pomerol 1988
The Cabernet Franc, still strong with its spicy varietal fragrances, is beginning to round out thanks to the Merlot, here with its ripe fruit aromas. The tannins are slowly harmonizing and the rich structure is coming into balance so that it can gain finesse and elegance.

Château La Fleur Pétrus

33500 Pomerol
Tel. 57517696
Fax 57517979

The 9 ha of this estate belong to Jean-Pierre Moueix , 'for a change'. Although they are in the immediate vicinity of Pétrus, they produce somewhat different styles of wines compared to those of the neighboring vineyards which still rank high for the Appellation's standards. Soil plays a crucial role here. In the case of its legendary neighbor-winery, clay is important to a substantial degree, but here the deep gravel produces lighter wines which focus on finesse rather than concentration and boldness. Moreover, the Cabernet Franc, comprising 20% of the vines here (and only 5% at Pétrus), against 80% Merlot, plays a more important role at La fleur. Occasionally Pétrus does not even use its Cabernet Franc at all. The vines here are 30 years-old on average, as opposed to 45 at Pétrus. On the other hand, the Château La Fleur Pétrus can call on all the technical and human resources of the Moueix company, which looks after the growing, harvest, vinification, aging and marketing of its wines. Needless to say, the wine is carefully crafted; after aging in oak (one third new) and bottling at between 18 and 24 months, the results are quite superb.

Château La Fleur Pétrus ♟♟ ④
Pomerol 1990
Fine, intense ruby color. Fairly closed nose which nonetheless bursts with aromas of black cherries and raspberries together with vanilla. The palate is full with a lovely fresh body. A good wine for the future, to bring in the new century.

Château La Fleur Pétrus ♟♟ ④
Pomerol 1989
Very intense and dark in color. The nose offers a lovely range of fragrances of super-mature fruit. Very soft on the palate, dense, highly concentrated body with young, closed tannins. Wonderfully balance and structured. A very appealing wine, with exceptional aging potential.

Château La Fleur Pétrus ♟♟ ④
Pomerol 1988
From grapes of outstanding quality, this is a near perfect example of what a great Pomerol can do. The color is elegant, the bouquet is of ripe fruit and spices, the palate is meaty. Refined tannins and a mouthfilling, long finish complete the picture of a very successful wine.

LIBOURNAIS/POMEROL
BORDEAUX
FRANCE

190

LIBOURNAIS/POMEROL
BORDEAUX
FRANCE

Château La Grave Trigant de Boisset

54, quai du Priourat
33500 Libourne
Tel. 57517896

Submerged in a lush green area, the château is situated on an 8 ha of property in the north-western part of the plateau on the border of Lalande. It has belonged to Christian Moueix since 1971. The original name of the château, La Grave, derives from the abundance of a gravel sub-soil particularly suited to Cabernet Franc. The modest yields give a production of 80% Merlot and 20% Cabernet Franc. Production is of about 40,000 bottles a year. Naturally, vinification is in the hands of the Jean-Pierre Moueix company, with the quality-oriented production philosophy that has always distinguished the firm. Wine is aged in new barriques in proportions that vary from year to year. In addition, recent vintages have had full benefit of the aging of the vines. The wine is soft and aristocratic. Much is exported to Great Britain, where it is especially well-liked.

Château La Grave Trigant de Boisset
Pomerol 1989
As rich in color as it is in body, a wine which is still undeveloped on the nose. Complex, yet soft, with light woody aromas. Not to be drunk for some time yet.

Château La Grave Trigant de Boisset
Pomerol 1988
A robust, rich wine with a significant percentage of Cabernet which gives it a further touch of austerity. On the nose, toastiness mingles with spices and vanilla. Lovely harmonious finish, with no aggressive tannin.

Château Latour à Pomerol

33500 Pomerol
Tel. 57517896
Fax 57517979

The estate dates back to the last century and the name of the château comes from the small tower which can be seen through the shadey curtain of trees. There is no link between this Latour and the château of the same name in the Médoc, which is explains why the geographical name was added. Jean-Pierre Moueix's company has rented the property from Mme. Lacoste, who also owns a part of Pétrus. With a surface area of almost 8 h. in two plots (in 1971, the Clos des Grandes Vignes was added to these), the vineyard enjoys two perfectly complementary types of soil. On the plateau, the gravel lies on a sunny hump; otherwise, all around the château, there is clay with an iron-rich sub-soil. The grape types are 80% Merlot and 20% Cabernet Sauvignon. Fermentation, in cement vats, can last 20 days and aging of the wines is carried out in oak barrels (with a third being replaced every year). Even though Latour à Pomerol is nowhere near Pétrus, its cru wines resemble them more than any other winery. But after all, with the Moueix family involved, what more could one expect.

Château Latour à Pomerol
Pomerol 1990
Very dark garnet in color. The nose is rich in grapey aromas which tend to mulberry and spices. Tannins reveal the great quality of the raw material and are magnificent, still closed but well-defined and clean. A wine which promises well and will bring Château Latour to the highest level.

Château Latour à Pomerol
Pomerol 1988
Color is quite superbly star-bright and limpid. The nose shows aromas which mingle cocoa with liquorice and autumn leaves. The palate is very full-bodied, with a lovely balance throughout, with an exceptionally long finish. It will age well beyond the end of the this century.

Château Latour à Pomerol
Pomerol 1985
The different types of soil found on the estate unite to impart a unique character with this lovely, very rich wine. Eextremely concentrated in texture, as the tannins are very well integrated. Finesse and elegance are the twin pillars of this wine.

LIBOURNAIS/POMEROL
BORDEAUX
FRANCE

191

LIBOURNAIS/POMEROL
BORDEAUX
FRANCE

Château Le Bon Pasteur

33500 Pomerol
Tel. 57511094
Fax 57250554

Michel Rolland made his debut in winemaking in one of the great vintages of the century (1947) and today is one of the most sought-after enologists of the region. His knowledge is now used as much on both banks of the Garonne, as one would expect. He also works in South America, where the seasons are reversed as the harvests take place during the European spring, and in Hungary, where Rolland has invested and makes marvellous Tokaj. The 7-ha estate vineyards are situated on the edge of the Saint-Emilion appellation and have belonged to the Rolland family since the 1920s. Rolland is, in fact, one of two grandsons of the founders. The estate is a sort of privileged experimental laboratory and 'window' onto the world for winemakers everywhere. Unlike many of his colleagues, since the early 1980s Rolland actually practices what he preaches, getting rid of mechanical pickers as well as avoiding picking the Merlot too early and short fermentation. Here, every parcel is harvested (and fermented) separately in order to preserve their unique character until final blending. Among the most seductive Pomerol wines made.

Château Le Bon Pasteur ④
Pomerol 1990
Beautiful dark purple in color from late-harvest Merlot grapes with an exceptional sugar content, it the end product of incomparable, skillful winemaking. Immense lush body and elegant tannins which will combine magnificently with time. Wait to drink for a good few years.

Château Le Bon Pasteur ④
Pomerol 1988
Intense in color, still rather gripping and tannic, but still one can fortell a good softness on a background of ripe red fruit and mature grapes. The finish has a faint hint of wood with a scent of vanilla.

Château Le Gay

33500 Pomerol
Tel. 57511243

Unusual and reserved. That is how the two Robin sisters had to be, if they were to be true to their father's motto "Quality over Quantity". Shunning the temptation of higher yields, these two unrepentant spinsters have always defended old-fashioned methods of fermentation and "clean" vine cultivation with unfailing seriousness and devotion. Thérèse died in 1985, but together they were also owners of Château Lafleur. Today, their nephew, Jacques Guineaudeau, looks after the vines entrusted to him by Marie Robin. The 8-ha estate (with vines averaging over 30 years old) is to the north of the Pomerol plateau in the immediate neighborhood of Pétrus on soil with a gravel surface that is planted to half Merlot, half Cabernet Franc. The wines are very consistent, year in year out, but already bear the imprint of Jacques' ideas (see Château Lafleur). All wines produced are marketed and distributed by the Jean-Pierre Moueix firm, with which the Robin sisters have always been on excellent terms.

Château Le Gay Pomerol 1990 ♛♛ ④
Dark purple color. Nose as yet undeveloped. Palate full and soft. A wine of incredible richness which is marvellously balanced on somewhat rustic tannins. An example of old-fashioned winemaking which will age for a long, long time.

Château Le Gay Pomerol 1989 ♛ ④
Dark red in color. Aromas of ripe red fruit. Good structure on already well-blended tannins. Very rich and warm palate, with lots of depthoin the finish.

LIBOURNAIS/POMEROL
BORDEAUX
FRANCE

192

LIBOURNAIS/POMEROL
BORDEAUX
FRANCE

Château Mazeyres

33500 Libourne
Tel. 57246515
Fax 57246674

Built on the remains of an ancient Gallo-Roman villa, Château Mazeyres is one of the most charming estates in the Libournais. The 9 ha of vineyards are planted with Merlot (70%) and Cabernet Franc (30%), with an average age of 25 years-old, on gravel and sand soil. Owned by the Querre family, established merchants in Libourne for the three generations, like many other properties in the Libournais, the château and its vineyards changed hands in 1989. They now belong to the Caisse de Retraite de la Société Générale (pension fund of one of France's most important banks). Consdiearble projects to upgrade the winery are underway and aim to bring the estate up to the highest standards of the appellation. Michel Querre is still in charge and, for the time being, winemaking follows its tried and tested course. The grapes are totally de-stemmed before temperature-controlled fermentation, which lasts three weeks. Aging is 80% in barriques, of which one third are replaced every year, and takes place in the cellars of a 16th-century convent. Château Mazeyres is a member-winery of the Cercle Pomerol Prestige and is a fascinating example of the Appellation at its very best.

Château Mazeyres Pomerol 1990 🍇 ③
Rich, deep color and a bouquet with sweetish notes of mint, typical of Merlot. A very well-made wine which combines a soft fruity style with chocolatey aromas. Long, clean finish.

Château Mazeyres Pomerol 1989 🍇 ③
Deep rich hue with a warm, soft fruity nose. Well-rounded, rich and fleshy on the palate with good strength and balance. To drink within the next two years.

Château Montviel

Grand Moulinet
33500 Pomerol
Tel. 57515063

Catherine and Yves Péré-Vergé purchased the estate in 1985. Before then, it had belonged to the Brieux family for four generations and was called the Bellevue-Montviel. It is a fair to say that the château's future is now in good hands. Catherine is director at the Cristallerie d'Arques, for whom Dany, Michel Rolland's wife designed the famous "enologist" wine glass. Yves, in contrast, is a surgeon who comes originally from the South-West. Certainly these two have the means to put their policies into practice, and, indeed, they have already begun replanting on some plots and given the go-ahead to a build a barrel room and cellar, not to mention restore parts of the château. Fundamental to the quality of their wine is also the dual composition of the soil, with gravelly sand from the erosion of the ancient terrace of the Pomerol plateau and the clayey soil in the Cline zone (60% Merlot, 30% Cabernet Franc and 10% Cabernet Sauvignon and noir de Pressac). All grapes are picked by hand, picking the Merlot for last, when they are super-ripe. Fermentation lasts up to four weeks while aging is exclusively in new barrels for Merlot and partially so for Cabernet Franc. Keep and eye on this one.

Château Montviel Pomerol 1990 🍇 ③
Still dark in color with an undeveloped nose which nonetheless confirms its complexity with notes of liquorice, very ripe red fruit and prunes. Concentrated body with the tannins still closed up. A wine with a great future.

Château Montviel Pomerol 1988 🍇 ③
The color is already well-developed and the nose is dominated by aromas of dried fruit. Delicate and elegant in texture. Warm and spicy on the palate. Has all the fine features of an aristocratic Pomerol.

LIBOURNAIS/POMEROL
BORDEAUX
FRANCE

193

LIBOURNAIS/POMEROL
BORDEAUX
FRANCE

Château Petit Village

33500 Pomerol
Tel. 56732400
Fax 56592642

Although the origins of the name Château Petit Village are unknown, the château itself stands behind an impressive wrought-iron gate. Perhaps its roots lie in the first inhabited settlement in the area or perhaps it got the name from the way its buildings are laid out for they do resemble a "small village". The 11 ha of vines are in a single plot which borders on Château La Conseillante and Vieux Château Certan in a spot called Catusseau on the highest part of the plateau. Jean-Michel Cazes of Château Lynch Bages has managed Petit Villages for the AXA group since 1989. The vine stock is 75% Merlot with the rest equal parts of Cabernet Franc and Cabernet Sauvignon. Harvesting is traditional, and fermentation takes place in stainless steel vats. The wines are aged in oak barrels, half of which are replaced every year. Experiments aimed at determining the influence of different woods on the wine are a long-standing feature of the Château's aging policy. Approximately 50,000 bottles of consistently good wines are produced each year.

Château Petit Village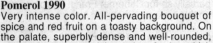
Pomerol 1990
Very intense color. All-pervading bouquet of spice and red fruit on a toasty background. On the palate, superbly dense and well-rounded, with perfect, chewy, rich tannins. A wine which will prove to be a long-aging Pomerol.

Château Petit Village
Pomerol 1989
A slightly less dark ruby color than normally found in the appellation. A very attractive wine with hints of toasty wood. Good body fullness and structure, with the elegance of a Médoc. Perhaps slightly lacking in Pomerol character. A note of wood is evident in the finish but without being aggressive.

Château Rêve d'Or

33500 Pomerol
Tel. 57511192
Fax 57518770

The Château Rêve d'Or is a family-run business founded in 1886 by Pierre Vigier. Today, it is still run by the whole Vigiers family (father, mother and children Pierrette, Maurice and Alain), who welcome visitors with a rare and genuine sense of hospitality. Seven hectares of vineyards are spread over various plots on iron-rich sand and gravel soil that flank both sides of the "route nationale 89" at the junction with the secondary road to go to Grand Moulinet. The vines are 70% Merlot and 30% Cabernet Sauvignon, averaging 40 years of age. Traditions are respected in this château, with the soil around the vines still being tilled, Bordeaux mixture still in use and the grapes picked by hand. No insecticides or pesticides are used. Many would be surprized to hear just how low the yields are. Winemaking equipment, however, is modern, as the cellars have recently been rebuilt. Fermentation takes place in temperature-controlled stainless steel vats. Aging is carried out in oak casks, roughly one third of which are replaced every year. A exemplary Pomerol with a perfect "goût de terroir".

Château Rêve d'Or
Pomerol 1989
Elegant and bright in color. Hints of wood, with light floral scents, and aromas of undergrowth. A really lovely concentrated palate and a supple finish with clean tannins. A well-made wine which will improve with age.

Château Rêve d'Or
Pomerol 1988
Limpid garnet color and a nose proffering hints of truffle followed by lively fruit. Well-rounded and supple on the palate with genuine freshness. An earthy, authentic Pomerol.

LIBOURNAIS/POMEROL
BORDEAUX
FRANCE

194

LIBOURNAIS/POMEROL
BORDEAUX
FRANCE

France
Appellations in the Guide

Bordeaux

Bordeaux
  Bordeaux
Bourgeais Blayais
  Premières Côtes de Blaye
  Premières Côtes de Bourg
Entre-Garonne-et-Dordogne
  Loupiac
  Premières Côtes de
Bordeaux
  Sainte-Croix-du-Mont
Graves
  Graves
  Pessac-Léognan
Libournais
  Canon-Fronsac
  Côtes de Castillon
  Côtes de Francs
  Fronsac
  Lalande de Pomerol
  Pomerol
  Saint-Emilion
Médoc
  Haut-Médoc
  Listrac
  Margaux
  Médoc
  Moulis-en-Médoc
  Pauillac
  Saint -Julien
Sauternais
  Barsac
  Cérons
  Sauternes

Bourgogne

Auxerrois
  Chablis
Beaujolais
  Beaujolais
  Beaujolais-Villages
  Chiroubles
  Côte de Brouilly
  Fleurie
  Juliénas
  Morgon
  Saint-Amour
Côte Chalonnaise
  Givry
  Mercurey
  Rully
Côte de Beaune
  Aloxe-Corton
  Auxey-Duresses
  Beaune
  Blagny
  Chassagne-Montrachet
  Chorey-lès-Beaune
  Ladoix
  Meursault
  Monthélie

Pernand-Vergelesses
Pommard
Puligny-Montrachet
Saint-Aubin
Saint-Romain
Santenay
Savigny-lès-Beaune
Volnay
Côte de Nuits
  Chambolle-Musigny
  Fixin
  Gevrey-Chambertin
  Marsannay
  Morey-Saint-Denis
  Nuits-Saint-Georges
  Vosne-Romanée
  Vougeot
Mâconnais
  Mâcon
  Mâcon-villages
  Puilly-fuissé
  Saint-Véran

Languedoc Roussillon

Languedoc
  Corbières
  Costières de Nîmes
  Coteaux du Languedoc
  Faugères
  Fitou
  Minervois
  Saint-Chinian
  Vins de Pays de l'Hérault
Roussillon
  Banyuls
  Collioure
  Côtes du Roussillon
  Maury
  Muscat de Rivesaltes
  Rivesaltes

Loire

Anjou Saumur
  Anjou
  Anjou-Villages
  Bonnezeaux
  Coteaux de L'Aubance
  Coteaux du Layon
  Quarts de Chaume
  Saumur-Champigny
  Savennières
Nantais
  Fiefs Vendéens
  Muscadet
Touraine
  Bourgueil
  Cheverny
  Chinon
  Jasnières
  Montlouis
  Saint-Nicolas-de-Bourgueil

Touraine
Vouvray
Vins du Centre
  Côtes Roannaises
  Menetou-Salon
  Pouilly-Fumé
  Reuilly
  Saint-Pourçain
  Sancerre

Provence

Bandol
Bellet
Cassis
Coteaux d'Aix
Coteaux Varois
Côtes de Provence
Palette

Côtes-du-Rhône

North
  Château-Grillet
  Condrieu
  Cornas
  Côte Rôtie
  Crozes-Hermitage
  Hermitage
  Saint-Joseph
  Saint-Péray
South
  Châteauneuf-du-Pape
  Coteaux du Tricastin
  Côtes du Lubéron
  Côtes du Rhône
  Côtes du Rhône-Villages
  Gigondas
  Muscat de Beaumes-de-
Venise
  Tavel
  Vacqueyras

Sud-Ouest

Bergerac
Buzet
Cahors
Côtes de Duras
Côtes du Frontonnais
Gaillac
Irouléguy
Jurançon
Madiran
Pécharmant
Saussignac
Tursan
Vins de Marcillac
VdP des Côtes de Gascogne
VdP de Haute-Garonne

Château Trotanoy

33500 Libourne
Tel. 57517896
Fax 57597979

A lovely estate, surrounded by ancient trees, in the western part of the little Pomerol plain, it has belonged to Jean-Marie Moueix, the owner of Château Pétrus, since 1953. The vineyard, in a single plot, gets plenty of sunshine and managed to survive the terrible frosts of 1956 unscathed. There are 8 ha of vines averaging 35 years of age on a gravel and deep clay soil. During the summer, the ground is so hard that it lives up to its ancient name "Trop ennoye", which means "too hard to work". The vines are mainly Merlot (80%) while the remainder is made up of Cabernet Franc, Cabernet Sauvignon and Noir de Pressac. The grapes are hand picked at perfect ripeness and the fermentation is long. Aging is done in new barriques, waiting to bottle for a full 24 months. Annual output is about 30,000 bottles. The hard work on the land and the exploits of a remarkable team in the cellar guarantee Trotanoy one of the leading places in the appellation's 'honor roll'. Things particularily changed when Jean-Pierre Moueix took the helm in the 1980s. The château's products regularly score higher in the numerous blind tastings than many more famous wines.

Château Trotanoy Pomerol 1990 🍷🍷 ③
Intense ruby with elegant and complex aromas of ripe red fruit and a slightly woody hint. On the palate, the initial impression is soft, with fine-grained tannins but certainly no lack of richness in the texture.

Château Trotanoy 🍷🍷🍷 ④
Pomerol 1989
Intense, dark color with a truly staggering bouquet of ripe blackcurrant, with strong, well-knit new oak. Richness and power are again apparent on the palate, where fruit reigns. Produced in a hot year, it is already well-developed despite its tannins and like many 1989 wines will develop fairly rapidly and prove to be above all outstandingly drinkable. Also of interest here is the fact that, despite the aging in 100% new casks and the high proportion of Merlot, it has managed to tame the wood and achieve a fine balance and great finesse. Grand in structure and extremely well-made, it is thought by many to be the best Château Trotanoy since 1982.

LIBOURNAIS/POMEROL
BORDEAUX
FRANCE

196

LIBOURNAIS/POMEROL
BORDEAUX
FRANCE

Clos du Clocher

35, quai du Priourat
33500 Libourne Cedex
Tel. 57516217
Fax 57512828

Clos du Clocher's six hectares of vinearyds are 300 yards away from the church and Pétrus in the heart of the Pomerol plateau. With a clay and gravel soil, they are planted with Merlot (70%) and Cabernet Franc (30%) vines of an average of 25 years of age. The estate has belonged to the Audy family since 1924 and is managed today by Pierre Bourotte. His nephew (and the great-nephew of Jean-Baptiste Audy) international rugby player, Jean-Baptiste Lafont, is sure to attract new customers every year. Michel Rolland oversees winemaking at Clos du Clocher, as he does at all the family's other estates including Château de Brondeau in Bordeaux Supérieur, Château du Curlat at Lussac-Saint-Emilion, Château Les Hauts Conseillants at Lalande de Pomerol and Château Bonalgue at Pomerol. The result is an estate of admirable consistency which has established itself as one of the classic Pomerols. Vinification is traditional, filtration light and aging is in barriques, half of which are replaced every year. There is a second wine, Château Mauregard-la-Croix, which allows the quality of Clocher to be safeguarded. A bench-mark wine.

Clos du Clocher Pomerol 1990 ♥♥ ④
A perfectly classic wine with lots of promise for evolution. Elegant purple in color, with a complex nose of autumn leaves, slightly raisined fruit and plums. Great finesse and elegance on the palate with full-bodied, densely fruity. A hint of vanilla on the finish.

Clos du Clocher Pomerol 1988 ♥♥ ④
A fine bright red color with a nose revealing considerable wood. Good depth on the palate with well-knit tannins and an admirably long-lasting finish.

Price levels

①   up to $ 9.99

② $ 10.00 - $ 14.99

③ $ 15.00 - $ 24.99

④ $ 25.00 or more

The 'ex-cellar', or direct from the producer, bottle prices, are calculated in US dollars and are intended only as an approximate guide

LIBOURNAIS/POMEROL
BORDEAUX
FRANCE

197

LIBOURNAIS/POMEROL
BORDEAUX
FRANCE

Pétrus

33500 Pomerol
Tel. 57517896
Fax 57517979

The label rather blandly states "Grand Vin". Better yet, it should read "Très Grand Vin". However, those same initials might inadverently mislead to the French TGV high-speed train. Indeed, time tells all at Pétrus, which looks more like a modest, doll-house château, without the flashy, luxurious appeal. Quite the contrary, in fact, as the makers behind Pétrus (namely Lacoste, Moueix, Berrouet, Veyssière and Gillet) are no great believers in doing things in a hurry. Special care is taken during harvest time, when over 100 pickers are brought in under precise timing, always in the afternoon only. De-stemming is kept to a limit, meanwhile fermentation lasts for about 25 days; the wine ages in new oak for 24 to 30 months. The 11.5 ha estate is planted with vines averaging 45 years of age (the vines were not removed after the devastating frost of 1956), 95% Merlot (with 5% Bouchet which is not always used) is situated on the highest part of the plateau with excellent sunlight. It also boasts superb soils, the upper clay layers resting on an iron-rich substratum. Yields are strictly limited with production fixed at about 40,000 bottles, for which the international market pays lavishly. France itself only keeps a small portion of the total as Pétrus, for better or worse, has become more a legend than a wine.

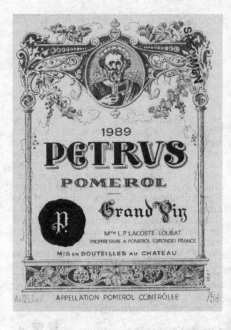

Pétrus Pomerol 1990   🍇🍇 ④
Almost black in color with a very closed nose, despite the initial orange scents. Extremely rich in texture, dense and concentrated, still rough on the edges, showing powerful oak, neither harsh nor coarse. Seemingly well-balanced and a little less alcoholic than the 1989. The tannins are still tight but, on the whole, it is a wine of great depth.

Pétrus Pomerol 1988   🍇🍇 ④
Bottled in August 1990, it impresses on impact with its dark, almost black color and its vanilla, coffee, spice and toasty aromas. A bouquet of rare complexity, although not yet fully developed. The tannin structure is well in evidence with remarkable acidity to support the rich body. Outstandingly smooth on the finish. A great wine to cellar, easily lasting well into the next century.

Pétrus Pomerol 1985   🍇🍇 ④
Great elegance combined with remarkable body and concentration. Purple in color. On the nose, there are aromas of very ripe fruit over scents of violet, vanilla and spices which blossom magnificently on the palate. The tannins are marvellously knit, as the wine is already ready to drink.

Pétrus Pomerol 1989   🍇🍇🍇 ④
From perfectly mature grapes, this is a wine of quite exceptional breadth and richness of structure. On the nose, hints of briary undergrowth and truffles with gamey scents that lead up to a true kaleidoscope of aromas. A velvety softness in the mouth, of incomparable elegance, with a finish that perfectly expresses the varietal Merlot character together with all the potential of the "terroir". Rather low acidity with a spectacular finish of an absolutely awesome length. A great Pomerol from an outstanding vintage, the like of which has not been seen for many years at Pétrus. However, one can only build a cathedral once in a century and, even so, not every century!

LIBOURNAIS/POMEROL
BORDEAUX
FRANCE

198

LIBOURNAIS/POMEROL
BORDEAUX
FRANCE

Vieux Château Certan

33500 Pomerol
Tel. 57511733
Fax 57253508

Vieux Château Certan is an old-age agricultural farm, that converted to viticulture in the 18th century. It is also the most ancient cru in Pomerol. The vineyard is a single plot located in the most beautiful part of the little plateau on quaternary gravel with a sub-soil of iron-rich clay. Bought in 1924 by George Thienpont, who was then a wine merchant in Etikhove, Belgium, the château is still managed by his heirs. Output is about 60,000 bottles a year, but there is also a second wine, La Gravette de Certan. The 13.5 ha of vines (on the average 35 years-old) grow 50% Merlot, 25% Cabernet Franc, 20% Cabernet Sauvignon and 5% Malbec, which are rather unusual proportions for Pomerol. After traditional harvesting, submerged-cap fermentation takes place in open wood vats and lasts from two to three weeks. The wines age for 18-22 months in oak casks, half of which are replaced yearly. The range of varieties gives the wine a rather tannic, firmly-structured character, especially when young. As a result, it often has less appeal than other, more famous crus in the appellation and may be drunk at its fullest only after prolonged bottle-aging. After 10 or 15 years, it is a match for its famous neighbor Pétrus.

Vieux Château Certan
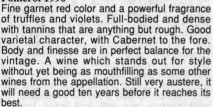
Pomerol 1990
Fine garnet red color and a powerful fragrance of truffles and violets. Full-bodied and dense with tannins that are anything but rough. Good varietal character, with Cabernet to the fore. Body and finesse are in perfect balance for the vintage. A wine which stands out for style without yet being as mouthfilling as some other wines from the appellation. Still very austere, it will need a good ten years before it reaches its best.

Vieux Château Certan
Pomerol 1989
An intense color and a fragrance of juicy, ripe fruit. Rich fruit again on the palate together with superb balance, even if the vintage lacks the backbone the 1988. had It does have, however, great elegance with clean fruit and well-knit wood. This wine will probably mature more quickly than the 1988, becoming very agreeable indeed, thanks to its fine fruit.

Vieux Château Certan
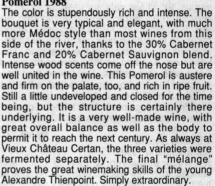
Pomerol 1988
The color is stupendously rich and intense. The bouquet is very typical and elegant, with much more Médoc style than most wines from this side of the river, thanks to the 30% Cabernet Franc and 20% Cabernet Sauvignon blend. Intense wood scents come off the nose but are well united in the wine. This Pomerol is austere and firm on the palate, too, and rich in ripe fruit. Still a little undeveloped and closed for the time being, but the structure is certainly there underlying. It is a very well-made wine, with great overall balance as well as the body to permit it to reach the next century. As always at Vieux Château Certan, the three varieties were fermented separately. The final "mélange" proves the great winemaking skills of the young Alexandre Thienpoint. Simply extraordinary.

LIBOURNAIS/POMEROL
BORDEAUX
FRANCE

199

LIBOURNAIS/POMEROL
BORDEAUX
FRANCE

Château Ausone

33330 Saint-Emilion
Tel. 57247094 - 57247026
Fax 57246711

The property takes its name from the 4th-century poet Ausonius. Together with the neighboring Cheval Blanc estate, it is considered one of the most important in Saint-Emilion. It has been in the hands of one family since 1770 and today is jointly owned by Madame Jean Dubois-Chalon and her nephew, Alain Vauthier. According to "régisseur", Pascal Delbeck, Château Ausone's strength lies in the micro-climate created by the easterly and south-easterly position of the vineyards. Four fifths of the 7 ha are planted on the steep southern slopes of St. Emilion; the rest are on the St. Martin plateau. The soil is a mixture of clay, limestone and "molasse". The vines (half Merlot and half Cabernet Franc) are 35 years-old on average. Grapes from each parcel are fermented separately using natural yeasts. Small oak vats are used for alcoholic fermentation with the wine passing to stainless steel vats for its malolactic. Aging takes 20 months in new oak in the naturally cool cellars carved out of the limestone. The wines are handled as little as possible and fined with egg whites. Only wine that has reached required quality standard is bottled under the Château Ausone label, the remainder being sold in bulk to the négociant trade. Production averages 27,000 bottles.

Château Ausone 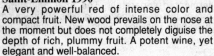 ④
Saint-Emilion 1990

A very powerful red of intense color and compact fruit. New wood prevails on the nose at the moment but does not completely diguise the depth of rich, plummy fruit. A potent wine, yet elegant and well-balanced.

Château Ausone ❦❦❦ ④
Saint-Emilion 1989

Magnificent rich, dense and deep in color. The nose has rich, ripe, well-rounded fruit with spicy wood. On the palate, it has all the concentration of very ripe red fruit, a truly great structure and the toastiness of wood (this is a wine which was aged in 100% new oak). Thanks to the limited yields of 1989 harvest as well as bunch selection at picking which together favored only the very best fruit, it has an amazing concentration of aromas. It is certainly one of the finest wines ever produced in the Appellation and a magnificent example of the enourmous potential of Château Ausone. A wine which will comfortably cross the threshold of the next century and will fool many tasters, especially those used to the Ausone style of the 1960s, or even earlier, when the château's wines only faintly resembled this 1989.

LIBOURNAIS/SAINT-EMILION
BORDEAUX
FRANCE

200

LIBOURNAIS/SAINT-EMILION
BORDEAUX
FRANCE

Château Beauséjour

Héritiers Duffau-Lagarrosse
33330 Saint-Emilion
Tel. 57247161
Fax 57744840

Château Beauséjour has been in the same family since 1847. It used to be part of a single estate known as Château Beau-Séjour Bécot, which split up in 1869. Since then, Château Beauséjour has remained the property of the descendants of the Duffau-Lagarrosse family. Jean-Michel Dubos has been manager since 1984. The vineyards lie in the eastern part of Saint-Emilion, near Château Canon and Beau-Séjour Bécot. The 7 ha of vines face south or south-west and are 55% Merlot, 30% Cabernet Franc and 15% Cabernet Sauvignon. They are ploughed and treated with organic fertilizers. No chemicals have been used for 10 years. The bunches are thinned out in July and August, the harvest being delayed as long as possible. The grapes are de-stemmed, gently crushed and then fermented for three to five weeks in stainless steel and cement vats. The wine then ages in oak barrels, half of them new, for up to 14 months. In difficult years, such as 1984, part of the wine is downgraded to the second label, Château Croix de Mazerat. 80% of the annual output of 35,000 bottles goes for export. Recent vintages are very suitable for long cellaring.

Château Beauséjour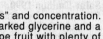
Saint-Emilion 1990
A very big wine of "gras" and concentration. Dark purple in color, marked glycerine and a nose which is rich in ripe fruit with plenty of depth. A powerful red with an excellent texture and up-front fruit and a very evident tannic structure.

Château Beauséjour
Saint-Emilion 1989
This is a very tight knit concentrated wine with a more elegance than the 1990. The rich fruit is offset by dense, yet fine tannins. Overall a rich and balanced wine of subdued power.

Château Belair

33330 Saint-Emilion
Tel. 57247094
Fax 57246711

Château Belair is one of the oldest properties in Saint-Emilion. It was bought in 1916 by Jean Dubois-Challon and is owned today by his widow, Madame Dubois-Challon, who is also the co-owner of Château Ausone. Since 1975 Pascal Delbeck has been the amiable and talented "régisseur". Compared to neighboring Château Ausone, the vines have a more southerly exposure are planted on level ground, rather than the "côtes" slopes. The 13-ha vineyard did not suffer during the 1956 frosts so the vines (65% Merlot, the rest Cabernet Franc) average 35 years of age. Winemaking is meticulous, with unique techniques inspired by Pascal Delbeck. The hand-picked grapes are loaded into a machine that destalks and gently crushes them before dispatching them into stainless steel vats via a conveyor belt. Pumping of any sort is avoided at all costs with even the "remontage" accomplished by gravity. Malolactic fermentation is carried out in stainless steel vats and finally the wine is blended for aging in barriques (65% new). The wood from these barrels comes from forests in the Nièvre and Sarthe and is seasoned on location. Annual production hovers around 55,000 bottles.

Château Belair Saint-Emilion 1990
A full purple color is backed by a rich fruitcake nose with notes of orange zest, raisin and spice. There is plenty of depth and intensity with a fresh lively acidity. The palate has the same expression of fruit and the overall impression is one of balance and finesse.

LIBOURNAIS/SAINT-EMILION
BORDEAUX
FRANCE

201

LIBOURNAIS/SAINT-EMILION
BORDEAUX
FRANCE

Château Boutisse

Saint-Christophe-des-Bardes
33330 Saint-Emilion
Tel. 57247446
Fax 57246440

Château Boutisse is about 5 km east of the town of Saint-Emilion, near the village of Saint-Christophe-des-Bardes and although some distance from the epicenter of Grands Crus Classés, the vines are on high ground. They grow on a very old Aquitanian limestone soil where quartz pebbles are visible. The estate was purchased in 1975 by Jean-François Carrille, who also owns others in the area. Since then, the vines have been completely replaced and restoration work continues on the house and other facilities, including some old bread ovens. Jean-Louise Faure is the cellarmaster and has turned out some consistently excellent products over recent years. The 15 ha are planted with 65% Merlot and 35% Cabernet Franc; the average age of them being 25 years. Fermentation takes place in stainless steel vats at controlled temperatures. The grapes are gently crushed, and the wine ages in vats and oak barrels for 12 to 16 months, when finally it is clarified with egg white and bottled. The average production of Château Boutisse is around 80,000 bottles.

Château Boutisse
Saint-Emilion 1988
A wine with an frank, appealing style of great drinkability. Medium to full ruby color and a bouquet of soft red fruits with a hint of strawberry. The palate is soft and aromatic, with a slight herbaceous flavor and good acidity. The tannins are present but not intrusive.

Château Cadet-Bon

33330 Saint-Emilion
Tel. 57744320
Fax 57246641

Château Cadet-Bon was bought in 1986 by Bernard Gans and his wife, Marceline, who have since invested time and money in improving the buildings and equipment including the construction of a new "chai" for fermentation. Over recent years, there has been a marked improvement in the quality of the château's wines. The consulting enologist is Lucien Guillemet, the technical director of Château Giscours. Château Cadet-Bon's 6 ha are on clay and limestone slopes to the north of Saint-Emilion and are planted with 70% Merlot and 30% Cabernet Franc. The average age of the vines is 25 years. Grapes are harvested by hand and each parcel vinified separately. Fermentation takes place in stainless steel vats at a controlled temperature of 30°-32°C. Interestingly enough, the wine is pumped over every hour for a short period of time which allows for a shorter length of "cuvaison". The wine then ages in oak barrels, one third of which are replaced every year, for 8-11 months. A second label, Vieux Moulin du Cadet, has been introduced to leave the best cuvées for Cadet-Bon, of which 30,000 bottles a year are produced.

Château Cadet-Bon ♈ ③
Saint-Emilion 1990
Full, dense ruby in color, full and dense. Quite an opulent wine with rich red fruit, good zesty acidity, firm tannins and well-integrated oak. A smoky, minerally taste on the palate overlays the fruit. Good depth on the finish with considerable tannins.

Château Cadet-Piola

33330 Saint-Emilion
Tel. 57744769
Fax 57746969

In the first (1868) edition of Cocks and Feret's guide to Bordeaux, Château Cadet-Piola was already mentioned. The name of the estate comes from the acquisition in 1856 of the Domaine Cadet by the Piola family, who added their own surname to the original name. Since 1952, the property has been in the hands of the Jabiol family (who also own Faurie-de-Sauchard), with Alain Jabiol running the show. The estate lies to the north of Saint-Emilion at the highest point of the flat land and the côtes. 7 ha. of vines are completely surrounded by an ancient stone wall and are planted with 51% Merlot, 28% Cabernet Sauvignon, 18% Cabernet Franc and 3% Malbec, known locally as noir de Pressac. The vines are 25 years-old on average. The grapes are harvested manually after rigorous selection and de-stemmed, before fermenting in cement and glass-fibre vats for 18-21 days. They then spend 4 months in vats before ageing for 15-18 months in oak barrels, half of which are new. Ageing takes place in cellars carved out of the limestone, which guarantees a cool, constant temperature. Château Cadet-Piola wines (about 36,000 bottles a year) are by nature robust and need time to show their best.

Château Cadet-Piola
Saint-Emilion 1989
The wine is slightly austere at present but with plenty of depth and character. It has a lovely ruby color and typical plummy Merlot fruit. Rich on the palate with a slightly dusty, brackeny edge and a prominent tannic structure. A traditional style of Saint-Emilion.

Château Canon

33330 Saint-Emilion
Tel. 57247079
Fax 57246800

Jacques Canon was the commander of a pirate ship before he retired to become a winemaker just outside the town of Saint-Emilion in 1760 on the estate which today bears his name. The 18 ha. of vineyard are planted on the same clay slope from which much of the stone used to build Saint-Emilion was extracted. 55% of the vines, averaging 35 years old, are Merlot and 45% are Cabernet Franc. They yield particularly concentrated grapes and it is for this reason that the texture of Château Canon is truly outstanding, enhanced by the long fermentation in wooden vats and ageing for two years in barriques. The Fournier family has owned the château since 1919 but it is only since 1972, when Eric Fournier took over, that the quality has become consistent. About 80,000 bottles a year are produced and these are increasingly hard to get hold of. Château Canon is one of the best wines in the Appellation.

Château Canon
Saint-Emilion 1989
Deep dark purple ruby. The nose together is powerfully oaked with plenty of rich ripe blackcurrant fruit. The palate has a strong tannic structure, well backed by full fruit that dominates the finish.

Château Canon
Saint-Emilion 1988
Similar in color to the 1989 but more intense. The nose is of tightly woven layers of blackcurrant, black treacle and spice. The palate is full and well-balanced between fruit and tannins and carries through on the long finish.

LIBOURNAIS/SAINT-EMILION
BORDEAUX
FRANCE

203

LIBOURNAIS/SAINT-EMILION
BORDEAUX
FRANCE

Château Cap de Mourlin

33570 Montagne-Saint-Emilion
Tel. 57746206
Fax 57745934

Château Cap de Mourlin is situated on the sandy slopes of the northern part of Saint-Emilion and for more than 500 years it has belonged to the Capdemourlin family. In the 70s, the two branches of the family grew and bottled separately under the same label but with the different names of Jean and Jacques Capdemourlin. They were reunited under Jacques (who also owns the Château Balestard la Tonnelle) in 1982 when he bought out his aunt, Mme Jean Capdemourlin. There are 14 ha. of vines (average age - 37 years), 60% Merlot, 25% Cabernet Franc, 12% Cabernet Sauvignon and 3% Malbec. They stand on clay, loess and limestone soil with a sandy surface. The grapes are de-stemmed for fermentation and then macerate for 12-15 days. A hydraulic press is used before the wine is transferred into oak barrels, of which one third are replaced each year, for ageing. Bottling is carried out on average 18-24 months after the harvest. Annual output is about 72,000 bottles.

Château Cap de Mourlin
Saint-Emilion 1989
A wine with a medium garnet color and a rich fruity nose that shows good vinosity. It is sweet and fleshy on the palate with a generous layer of flavor and fine tannins.

Entries are arranged in alphabetical order by country, region and winery or producer name.

LIBOURNAIS/SAINT-EMILION
BORDEAUX
FRANCE
204
LIBOURNAIS/SAINT-EMILION
BORDEAUX
FRANCE

Château Cheval Blanc

33330 Saint-Emilion
Tel. 57247070
Fax 57246901

Château Cheval Blanc is the most famous name in Saint-Emilion and, many would say, the greatest. The style and character of its wines are due to the situation of its vineyards, the grape mix and a scrupulous attention to detail. The château's 37 ha. lie in the north-western part of the Saint-Emilion zone on the border with Pomerol, a little off the beaten track compared to the majority of the estates which are huddled around the town. Instead of on limestone slopes, the vines stand on a fertile terrace with a sandy, pebbly base. The other factor which makes Cheval Blanc unique is the original range of varieties. Cabernet Franc dominates with 66%, then comes Merlot with 33% and Malbec with 1%. Fermentation takes place in vats at controlled temperatures and then the wine is aged in new barriques for 20 months. The end result may be seen in the very deep color of the wines and savoured in the intensity of the bouquet and the rich fullness of the palate. Production, from a yield of 35 hl/ha., is 144,000 bottles a year. Originally, the estate was part of Figeac but since 1832 it has belonged to the Fourcaud-Laussac family. Pierre Lurton is the present manager.

Château Cheval Blanc
Saint-Emilion 1988
The color is rich and bright. The nose is perhaps slightly closed but fresher than the 1989. Not a wine of great complexity but with excellent firm tannins and long, soft, well-rounded fruit. Given a little time, it will become a great wine.

Château Cheval Blanc
Saint-Emilion 1989
This Premier Grand Cru has a lovely intense red hue with a nose which is perhaps a little undeveloped and unpolished at the moment but is nonetheless rich in fruit. On the palate, there are complex flavors of ripe fruit with notes of spices and toasty wood, great concentration and good tannins. All the signs are that this will become a quite exceptional wine in the next eight to ten years. It is the epitome of the Cheval Blanc style. One third Merlot grapes confers delicate fruit and roundness while two thirds Cabernet Franc, planted in gravelly terrain, ensure robust structure. It is partly this mélange which makes Cheval Blanc stand out from neighboring estates but also the unswerving attention to detail, both in the vineyard and in the cellar.

LIBOURNAIS/SAINT-EMILION
BORDEAUX
FRANCE

205

LIBOURNAIS/SAINT-EMILION
BORDEAUX
FRANCE

Château Couvent des Jacobins

33330 Saint-Emilion
57247066

The Couvent des Jacobins cellars are in the town center at Saint-Emilion, right opposite the post office, partly housed in a fourteenth-century monastery one of whose walls is actually a section of the city wall. The estate is managed by Alain and Rose-Noëlle Joinaud-Borde. Rose-Noëlle's grandfather bought Couvent des Jacobins in 1902 and for the past twelve years, the couple have been restoring and improving the buildings and cellars. The 9.5 ha. of vines lie along the route du milieu which goes from the area north of Saint-Emilion towards Château Grand-Mayne. They are planted with two thirds Merlot and the rest Cabernet Franc and Cabernet Sauvignon on soil composed mainly of limestone and clay, with sandy and iron-bearing deposits. Vines are on average 40 years old. Vinification is in the traditional manner with no filtering and clarification only just before bottling. Fermentation takes place in stainless steel and cement vats while ageing is in oak barrels, one third of which are new. Wines produced from the newer plants are sold under a second label, Château Beau-Mayne.

Château Couvent des Jacobins
Saint-Emilion 1989
A wine with more elegance than power. Ruby red color of medium intensity, with ripe fruit flavors including a note of strawberry and vanilla. There is a sweet ripe impact on the palate and good acidity with a good tannic strucutre.

Château Curé-Bon-la-Madeleine

33330 Saint-Emilion
Tel. 57544320
Fax 57246641

It will be interesting over the next few years to follow the progress of this estate, which was acquired in 1992 by Bernard Gans, also the owner of Château Cadet-Bon. M. Gans, whose family hails from the Dordogne, had attempted to buy the property in 1986 but bought Cadet-Bon when talks fell through. To judge by developments at Cadet-Bon, progress at Château Curé-Bon-le-Madeleine should be considerable for this is a gem of an estate on the limestone plain to the south-east of the town, near properties like Ausone, Belair and Canon. The soil is chalk and clay with a thin top layer. The vineyards comprise 4 ha., of which 80% is planted with Merlot and 20% with Cabernet Franc, while the vines are 30 years of age on average. Up to the present day, vinification has always been traditional, producing good, but not outstanding, wines. Bernard Gans plans to give the cellar up-to-date equipment like that at Château Cadet-Bon. Today, wines are aged in oak of which in future no more than one third will be new. Château Curé-Bon-le-Madeleine produces an average of 20,000 bottles a year.

Château Curé-Bon-la-Madeleine
Saint-Emilion 1988
Light ruby with purple tints. A heady bouquet with vinous, plummy fruit and a palate which begins with a sweet note of fruit, a slightly rustic mushroomy middle and tannic finish. A well-structured, sinewy style of wine that lacks a little flesh and a certain amount of charm.

LIBOURNAIS/SAINT-EMILION
BORDEAUX
FRANCE

206

LIBOURNAIS/SAINT-EMILION
BORDEAUX
FRANCE

Château Figeac

33330 Saint-Emilion
Tel. 57247226
Fax 57744574

Château Figeac, like its neighbor Château Cheval Blanc, is on the Pomerol - Saint-Emilion border and indeed in the eighteenth century, it extended over about 200 ha. and included the present Cheval Blanc as well as several other estates. In the nineteenth century, while still remaining an important property it shrank to 37 ha.. In the hands of the Manoncourt family since 1892, since 1947 it has been run by Thierry Manoncourt whose son-in-law Eric d'Aramon has been assisting him since 1988. The vines (average age - 35 years) are planted on the characteristic gravelly terrain found in the area. 70% of them are equal parts Cabernet Franc and Cabernet Sauvignon with Merlot making up the remainder. Soil and variety produce a characteristic style for which the wines have always enjoyed a solid reputation. Alcoholic and malolactic fermentation both take place in open, temperature-controlled, wooden vats. Stainless steel, on the other hand, is used for the fermentation of the second wine, Grange Neuve de Figeac. Château Figeac ages only in new oak barrels for 18 to 20 months in splendid underground cellars.

Château Figeac Saint-Emilion 1988 ♥ ④
The influence of Cabernet prevails in this wine. The color is an intense purple, with smoky red berry aromas on the nose. Firm on the palate, with vanilla and chocolate flavors indicating the influence of the new oak. A firm, solid wine, without the Merlot opulence that will be for very long keeping.

Château Gueyrosse

33500 Libourne
Tel. 57510263

Château Gueyrosse lies on a plain where red gravel mixes with sand on the outskirts of Libourne and has the river Dordogne at its back. The 15 riverside ha. have belonged to the same family since 1850. The present owner and winemaker is the bearded Yves Delal, at present helped out by his daughter Samuelle. The same family also owns another excellent Saint-Emilion estate, Domaine Chante Alouette Cormeil. The 5 ha. of Château Gueyrosse are planted with 60% Merlot, 20% Cabernet Sauvignon and 20% Cabernet Franc, the vines being on average 25 years old. Yves Delal believes in low yields, so the vines are carefully pruned to give 30 to 45 hl/ha. for an annual output of about 24,000 bottles. Fermentation lasting 4-6 weeks takes place in cement vats where the wine remains for another four months before spending 12 to 18 in two year-old oak barrels. Château Gueyrosse wines, never filtered and clarified only with egg white, are made to age well.

Château Gueyrosse ♥♥ ④
Saint-Emilion 1990
A superb, very firm, dense purple color. Very closed but with a firm raisin-like character and evident fruit. Hard, dry and tarry on the palate with an aggressively tannic structure. Plenty of concentration, but the wine is a little over extracted for maximum finesse.

LIBOURNAIS/SAINT-EMILION
BORDEAUX
FRANCE

207

LIBOURNAIS/SAINT-EMILION
BORDEAUX
FRANCE

Château L'Angélus

33330 Saint-Emilion
Tel. 57247139
Fax 57246856

This important Cru Classé tries hard to keep pace with its great neighbors and indeed both the reception rooms and the cellars have just been magnificently renovated. The vines are south-facing and therefore enjoy excellent sunlight, extending for 25 ha. over terrain which varies from clay to chalk to muddy clay to muddy sand. Merlot is the principal variety (about 50%), then Cabernet Franc (45%) and Cabernet Sauvignon (5%). Harvesting is done by hand and fermentation takes place in cement and stainless steel vats, with a maceration which lasts for three to four weeks. Ageing is in barriques (which are 60% new) and can last from fourteen to sixteen months. The new wood-and-Merlot combination, the Cabernet Franc and, above all, a rigorous selection aimed at producing the best wine possible have allowed L'Angélus to present one stupendous year after another since 1988. The appearance of a second wine under the nicely musical name of Carillon ("Bells") de L'Angélus has contributed to the enhancement of the main Château L'Angélus label.

Château L'Angélus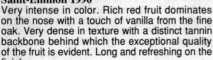
Saint-Emilion 1990
Very intense in color. Rich red fruit dominates on the nose with a touch of vanilla from the fine oak. Very dense in texture with a distinct tannin backbone behind which the exceptional quality of the fruit is evident. Long and refreshing on the finish.

Château L'Angélus
Saint-Emilion 1989
A lovely, appealing color with a note of new oak on the nose over complex aromas of ripe fruit, mint and spice. Great long finish. A wine to lay down until the beginning of the next century.

Château L'Arrosée

33330 Saint-Emilion
Tel. 57247047

The vines of this Grand Cru Classé are on the slopes leading down to the route nationale at the foot of the hills to the south-west of the town. According to Franÿois Rodhain, the owner of Château L'Arrosée, the micro-climate in this bowl produces early ripening while the terrain, which goes from chalky to silicous, gives the estate's wines their hallmark balance and character. Another important factor is the role of Cabernet Sauvignon in the blend (35%), to which are added Merlot (45%) and Cabernet Franc (20%). The 10 ha of the château have belonged to the Rodhain family since 1910 but it is only in the last five years that it has really made a name for itself. Grapes are picked as late as possible and fermented in the traditional fashion. De-stemming and soft-crushing are effected using special equipment brought from Burgundy. Fermentation in cement vats last from three to five weeks and the wine is then aged in oak. In 1987, a second label was produced, Les Coteaux de l'Arrosée, and it is likely that this will also happen in 1991 but with the name changed to Les Roches de l'Arrosée. The estate produces an average of 48,000 bottles a year, sold exclusively en primeur to the merchants of Bordeaux.

Château L'Arrosée
Saint-Emilion 1990
A steady, concentrated color leads to a Cabernet Sauvignon nose. The aroma is very stylish with notes of bilberry and cassis. On the palate there are heaps of ripe fruit on the impact and throughout, together with fine tannins. A red with more elegance than power, almost Médoc in style.

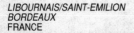
LIBOURNAIS/SAINT-EMILION
BORDEAUX
FRANCE

208

LIBOURNAIS/SAINT-EMILION
BORDEAUX
FRANCE

Château La Clotte

33330 Saint-Emilion
Tel. 57246685

This delightful, tiny and very old estate is just outside the Saint-Emilion city walls to the south-east of the town. Until a short time ago, it was managed by Jean-Pierre Moueix but the owners, the Chailleau heirs, have taken over again and winemaking is now supervised by the dynamic young Nelly Moulierac, a member of the family. The 4 ha. of vines stand on both sides of the côtes on terrain which is basically clay-and-limestone and sand. Merlot accounts for 80% of the vine stock, the other 20% Cabernet Franc. The average age of the plants is 50 years but some are even older and there is a replanting program planned. The harvest lasts two days. The various grape varieties are fermented together in cement vats where they usually stay for a month. Thereafter, the wines age in oak barrels, 10% of which are new, for up to 18 months. Nelly Moulierac intends to equip the cellar soon with temperature-control equipment and there are other improvements in the pipeline. Château La Clotte only produces 15,000 bottles and most of these are distributed by Jean-Pierre Moueix.

Château La Clotte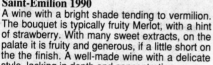
Saint-Emilion 1990
A wine with a bright shade tending to vermilion. The bouquet is typically fruity Merlot, with a hint of strawberry. With many sweet extracts, on the palate it is fruity and generous, if a little short on the the finish. A well-made wine with a delicate style, lacking in depth and concentration.

Château La Dominique

33330 Saint-Emilion
Tel. 57514460
Fax 57516304

Well worth a detour, as the Michelin guide might say. This estate owns 21 ha 18 of which are planted with vines with an average age of 23 years. It lies on the north-western edge of the town on rich clay terrain with traces of iron and a sand and gravel topsoil. Bordering on one side with Château Cheval Blanc, its quality is easily comparable. In 1975, the property was bought by Clément Fayat, a Libourne builder. It is planted manily with Merlot (80%) and the yields are very low. Over the last ten years, they have not exceeded 35 hl/ha. A second wine was created in 1986, Château Saint-Paul-de-Dominique, allowing an improvement in quality of the main wines. Maceration in stainless steel vats can last for up to five weeks, the wine being pumped over the cap twice a day and the temperature being controlled. Such techniques, under the careful guidance of Étienne Priou, produce wines of rare concentration. Since 1969, Clément Fayat has owned a "cru bourgeois" in the Haut Médoc, Château Clément-Pichon, and in 1984, he also acquired Prieur de la Commanderie, a promising Pomerol.

Château La Dominique
Saint-Emilion 1990
Lovely in color with a very elegant nose with aromas of ripe plums, truffles and spice. Rich and long on the palate. The exceptional concentration is due to grapes of quite outstanding quality. An excellent wine for its vintage.

Château La Dominique
Saint-Emilion 1988
The nose is dominated by the oak. On the palate, the toasted flavors are still rather closed and lack roundness, but the wine, which will develop over time, already shows good balance.

LIBOURNAIS/SAINT-EMILION
BORDEAUX
FRANCE

209

LIBOURNAIS/SAINT-EMILION
BORDEAUX
FRANCE

Château La Gaffelière

33330 Saint-Emilion
Tel. 57247215
Fax 57246524

A Premier Grand Cru which has been in the Malet-Roquefort family for four centuries. Since 1976, the same family has also owned the excellent Château Tertre Daugay, another Grand Cru Classé on the southern side of Saint-Emilion. The 22 ha of Château La Gaffelière lie in a single plot on clay/chalk and sandy/chalk soil, with plantings of 66% Merlot and 33% Cabernet Franc and Cabernet Sauvignon. The plants are on average 40 years-old with a density of 5,800 vines/ha; yields are about 35 hl/ha. A second wine is made from the younger vines (up to 15 years of age) under the Clos La Gaffelière label. Harvesting is manual and the bunch selection, strict; after thorough de-stemming, each variety gets fermented separately for three-weeks in temperature-controlled stainless steel vats. The wine is topped up each week and racked once every three months. It is aged in 100% new oak barrels for 18-20 months. Bottling takes place after clarification with egg whites, without undergoing any mechanical filtration. A rising star.

Château La Gaffelière
Saint-Emilion 1990
A lovely purple color for a fleshy, chewy, well-rounded wine with aromas of spices. Generous and full-bodied. Firm, silky tannins and a classy finish. A great wine to lay down, worth waiting a few years for.

Château La Gaffelière
Saint-Emilion 1988
Bright color with an elegant bouquet and aromas of wood and spice. Good balance, with all the components already well-integrated. To drink in two or three years' time.

Château Larcis-Ducasse

33330 Saint-Emilion
Tel. 57247084

Château Larcis-Ducasse is a very traditional but quite charming estate which produces wines for laying down of outstanding structure. It belongs to an energetic eighty three-year-old, Madame Hélène Gratiot-Alphandéry, who has been commuting backwards and forwards for over 50 years from Paris, where she teaches at the Sorbonne, to keep an eye on her estate. Her son, Jacques Olivier, who also lives in Paris, is the director at present while Philippe Dubois is the manager. The château's 11 ha. are on the côtes to the south, right by Château Pavie, on the border between the communes of Saint-Emilion and Saint-Laurent-des-Combes. The limestone and clay soil is planted with 65% Merlot, 25% Cabernet Franc and 10% Cabernet Sauvignon. Harvesting is done by hand and the de-stemmed grapes are gravity-fed into cement vats, where they stay for fifteen days to a month. An old vertical press is used to extract a second pressing, which is added according to the needs of the particular vintage. The unfiltered wines age for 12 to 18 months in oak barrels - never more than one quarter new - for a total annual production which never exceeds 60,000 bottles.

Château Larcis-Ducasse
Saint-Emilion 1989
Bright, full ruby color. The bouquet of ripe fruit with a smoky edge, a little on the austere side. Solid tannic structure on the palate, tightly knit with good concentration.

Château Larcis-Ducasse
Saint-Emilion 1988
Again a full color is full and solid structure. A more developed bouquet of ripe fruit, with a touch of lime-blossom. The tannins are hard and dense, but there is perhaps just a little less concentration than in the 1989.

LIBOURNAIS/SAINT-EMILION
BORDEAUX
FRANCE

210

LIBOURNAIS/SAINT-EMILION
BORDEAUX
FRANCE

Château Larmande

33330 Saint-Emilion
Tel. 57247141
Fax 57744280

Château Larmande has always enjoyed a good reputation. In 1991, it was acquired by Mondiale Assurances, an insurance company based in Lille, in the north of France. The property had previously belonged to the Méneret-Capdemourlin family since the turn of the century. Thanks to Mondiale's policy of investment, the Château is taking on a hi-tech look, with new premises for ageing and modern equipment in the cellar. 22 ha. of vines stand on the lower slopes to the north of Saint-Emilion, where the soil is a mixture of limestone, clay and sand. The vine stock is 65% Merlot, 25% Cabernet Franc and 10% Cabernet Sauvignon with an average age of 25 years, but there is also a miniscule plot of pre-phylloxera Cabernet Franc planted in 1875. The bunches are thinned in summer, harvested manually and selected in the cellar. Fermentation is in stainless steel vats and the wine ages for 14 to 16 months in oak barrels, half of which are new. Present production under the management of Mark Doworkin is around 90,000 bottles, in addition to the second-label Le Cadet de Larmande wines.

Château Larmande　　　　　🍇 ③
Saint-Emilion 1990
A very polished, 'modern' style with a lovely purple color and the influence of new oak is apparent. A combination of ripe fruit and vanilla on the nose, with an almost chocolatey, toffe aspect. The fruit is soft and sweet on the palate with fine tannins. Quite stylish.

Château Laroze

33330 Saint-Emilion
Tel. 57511131
Fax 57511036

The history of Château Laroze goes back almost 400 years, but the same Meslin family still looks after its 30 ha of vineyards planted on sandy soil with a ferrous sub-soil, the vines enjoy a steady climate influenced by the Atlantic. Guy Meslin, the son and winemaker of the family, has been the catalyst behind a minor revolution. In 1992 the entire property was turned over to organic cultivation methods, after having seen the success of experiments on one third of the estate in 1991. Now an integrated part of their production philosophy, they avoid using all unnatural products, additives and chemical fertilizers. According to the family, soil ecology is what strengthens the natural defence system of the vines, together with natural aids. "This is the agriculture of the future", says Guy Meslin, "It enhances both plant and environment, as well as providing greater satisfaction for the grower and the consumer". Harvesting is by hand, with careful bunch selection of only the ripest fruit, with as little foreign plant material as possible. Look out for this winery in the future.

Château Laroze Saint-Emilion 1989　🍇 ②
A very rich color and an intense, full bouquet with a grassy note. Soft and round on the palate with a gamey hint and well-developed fruit. A no-nonsense red wine, very drinkable and one which will be even more agreeable after aging for a short while longer.

LIBOURNAIS/SAINT-EMILION
BORDEAUX
FRANCE

211

LIBOURNAIS/SAINT-EMILION
BORDEAUX
FRANCE

Château Magdelaine

33330 Saint-Emilion
Tel. 57517896
Fax 57517979

When the famous Libourne wine merchant, Jean-Pierre Moueix, bought this property in 1925, it was in a sad state of neglect. Since that date, however, the vines have been in large measure replanted and in 1989, a new chais was opened. Other projects are still under way. The château can call on the expertise of the Moueix group and oenologist Jean-Claude Berrouet and cellarman Franÿois Yessière turn out wines of elegance and breeding. Château Magdelaine lies to the south of Saint-Emilion and has Château Belair and Château Canon as its neighbors. Half of the plants are on the Saint-Martin plain and the other half are on the côtes. The average age is 35 years and a small lot, still worked with horses, was planted in 1920. The 10.5 ha. are 90% Merlot, with the rest Cabernet Franc. Fermentation is in cement vats at a computer-controlled temperature of between 30°C and 32°C and lasts for three weeks. The wine is blended and vin du presse, extracted as at Ausone with an old vertical press, is added to the final mélange. It ages in oak barrels (50% new) for up to 20 months and about 48,000 bottles are produced each year.

Château Magdelaine 🍇 ④
Saint-Emilion 1990
A very fine wine with a bright, full ruby color and a rich concentrated aroma of crystallized fruit. Flattering on the palate, with the same aromatic quality, good acidity, firm but fine-grained tannins and a long finish. A rich and well-balanced wine.

Château Pavie

33330 Saint-Emilion
Tel. 58247202
Fax 57246399

Château Pavie is the largest estate on the Saint-Emilion côtes, with its 37 ha. on the Côte Pavie to the south-east of the town. Like the other two estates in the area, Château Pavie-Decesse and La Clusière, it belongs to the Consorts Valette company. The presence of Jean Paul Valette, manager since 1967, has been crucial for the improvements in the quality of Pavie and of the other estates. Vine stock at Pavie averages 45 years of age but there are some plants which are more than a hundred years old and date from the pre-phylloxera era. The terrain is essentially limestone and clay with 7 ha. of sandy clay at the foot of the slopes. The varieties are 55% Merlot, 25% bouchet (or Cabernet Franc) and 20% Cabernet Sauvignon. Grapes are harvested by hand and completely de-stemmed. Fermentation is in cement vats using natural yeasts and lasts from 10 to 15 days, followed by a further period of maceration. Wines are aged in oak barrels, of which about 40% are new. The ageing cellars date back to the twelfth century and at one point you can actually see the roots of the vines growing overhead. Average annual production is about 180,000 bottles.

Château Pavie 🍇 ③
Saint-Emilion 1990
A very deep, dark purple color, unusual for a St. Emilion. A firm and powerful style of wine that will be for long keeping. Lots of sweet, ripe extract with a dense tannic structure. Very good length with notable depth on the palate. A very fine wine.

LIBOURNAIS/SAINT-EMILION
BORDEAUX
FRANCE

212

LIBOURNAIS/SAINT-EMILION
BORDEAUX
FRANCE

Château Rolland-Maillet

15, cours des Girondins
33500 Libourne
Tel. 57511094
Fax 57250554

Michel Rolland is today considered the 'God father' of Libourne enology. In all truth, however, he is more frequently concerned with Pomerol than Saint-Emilion. Both avid vine and wine buffs, he and his wife, Dany, are one of the most famous couples in the world of viticulture. Dany is more softspoken but ever-present in the laboratory where she tends the classic Grand Cru wines as if they were her own children. Michel's advice is sought all over the world - from the shores of the Atlantic to the most remote corners of Argentina. But, it is here on the 3.5 ha of vineyards at Corbin that he makes a classic Merlot-dominated Saint-Emilion. The long maceration and aging, which lasts from 12 to 15 months in one to two year-old casks, produces predictable and dependable results. The wines have abundant tannin and are fleshy and silky, wth perfectly balanced ripe fruit.

Château Rolland-Maillet
Saint-Emilion 1988
Deep ruby color, with an open and powerful nose containing notes of ripe plums and cherry jam. The palate is robust and fleshy, rich in Merlot fruit, with forward but soft tannins.

Château Troplong-Mondot

33330 Saint-Emilion
Tel. 57247072
Fax 57744115

In the 18th century, the vineyards that now belong to Château Troplong-Mondot were connected with those of Château Pavie, since both originally belonged to the Abbey of Sèze. The château and its vineyard were purchased by Raymond Troplong, President of the Senate, in 1850 and later passed on to Alexandre Valette. Christine Valette, great-granddaughter of Alexandre, has managed this magnificent estate since 1980. It overlooks the commune of Saint-Emilion. The 30 ha of vineyards stretch across a 100 m hill top in Mondot and mainly grow Merlot, with 15% Cabernet Sauvignon and 15% Cabernet Franc. They are undoubtedly one of the largest Grands Crus classés in the Appellation. Harvesting is always done by hand and de-stemming is thorough. Aging takes place in barriques, half of which are replaced every year. More recently, Christine Valette's enthusiasm has been coupled with Michel Rolland's keen supervision to create a second wine, which has now become one of the most sought-after Saint-Emilions. The 100,000 bottles of the premium label and the 30,000 of the second sell like hot cakes.

Château Troplong-Mondot 1990
The nose has yet to open but nonetheless shows a clear aroma of strawberry. The tannins are fine, and the wine is vigorous on the palate, fleshy, with a very well-balanced structure. The finish is very big and powerful.

Château Troplong-Mondot 1988
Bright ruby color, stylish complex bouquet and a concentration of fruit in which roasted hazelnuts and almonds may be picked out. Exceptionally rich structure and a finish which shows elegant scents of wood.

LIBOURNAIS/SAINT-EMILION
BORDEAUX
FRANCE

213

LIBOURNAIS/SAINT-EMILION
BORDEAUX
FRANCE

Château Trottevieille

33330 Saint Emilion
Tel. 56247134-56000070
Fax 56522954

Château Trottevieille is different from the other Saint-Emilion premiers Grands Crus Classés in being situated on the plateau to the east of the town. Bought in 1950 by the Bordeaux merchant Borie-Manoux, it belongs in practice to Philippe Castéja and Jacques Combescot has been head cellarman since 1983. The building used to be a Carthusian monastery and the walled vineyard comprises 50% Merlot, 45% Cabernet Franc and 5% Cabernet Sauvignon. The average age of the vines is between 50 and 60 years, although there is one hectare of ungrafted pre-phylloxera plants. The 10 ha are east-facing on limestone and clay terrain with pebbles on the surface. The soil is tilled and only organic fertilizers are used. The grapes are picked by hand then de-stemmed and fermented in cements vats for about three weeks. After this, the wine ages in oak barrels, 80% of which are new. It is bottled under the characteristic black-and-gold Château Trottevieille label. The average yield is 47 hl/ha and the annual production of around 60,000 bottles is sold exclusively by Borie-Manoux.

Château Trottevieille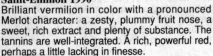
Saint-Emilion 1990
Brilliant vermilion in color with a pronounced Merlot character: a zesty, plummy fruit nose, a sweet, rich extract and plenty of substance. The tannins are well-integrated. A rich, powerful red, perhaps a little lacking in finesse.

Château Yon Figeac

33330 Saint-Emilion
Tel. 56315021
Fax 56748872

Today, Bernard Germain manages more than 200 ha of land which is made up of 11 vineyards. His latest purchase was the Roches-Neuves estate, one of the best Saumur-Champignys. Inarguably, however, Château Yon Figeac is his pride and joy among them all. It is a Grand Cru Classé which extends over about 25 ha of sandy slopes with iron-bearing sub-soil and is planted with 80% Merlot and 20% Cabernet Franc. Wines are made in the old-fashioned style, so much so that still today Bernard Germain refuses to use an automatic temperature-regulation system. It's not that he lacks the means, but because Bernard would rather that a wine maintain its soul and personality. This is why, although there is a temperature-control system, Bernard prefers to set it himself without the aid of sophisticated software. Aging is 80-90% in new oak barriques while none of the other barriques is more than a year old - after that period, the barriques are distributed among the other estates to improve the quality of the wines produced there.

Château Yon Figeac
Saint-Emilion 1990
Made with 80% Merlot and 20% Cabernet Franc, a Grand Cru to which the Germain family dedicate an obsessive degree of attention. The color, the nose, the fruit, the structure, the aromatic balance and indeed everything in this wine contributes to enhance the magnificent "goût de terroir" and the master skills of the winemakers. A wine with a great, long future ahead of it and of unbeatable value for money.

Château Yon Figeac
Saint-Emilion 1988
A soft wine, perhaps too much so, where the notes of ripe red fruit are well in evidence. The texture is elegant, with firm tannins and lots of fruit. On the palate, it is of great depth and harmony. The finish contains a hint of liquorice. Splendid for drinking now.

LIBOURNAIS/SAINT-EMILION
BORDEAUX
FRANCE
214
LIBOURNAIS/SAINT-EMILION
BORDEAUX
FRANCE

Clos Fourtet

33330 Saint-Emilion
Tel. 57247090
Fax 57744652

An estate in an excellent position in the north-eastern sub-zone of Saint-Emilion. It was acquired in 1948 by Franÿois Lurton and is run today by his sons. André also manages Château La Louvière in the Graves and Lucien is active at Brane-Cantenac and Durfort-Vivens at Margaux as well as Château Climens at Barsac. Tony Ballu, originally from Champagne, is the manager at Clos Fourtet. The 19 ha of clay and limestone on the Saint-Martin plateau are planted with 70% Merlot, 20% Cabernet Franc and 10% Cabernet Sauvignon. The underground cellars are breath-taking, extending for all of 14 ha. on three levels. Submerged-cap fermentation takes place in stainless steel vats, lasting for 20-30 days. After blending the various components, ageing takes place in oak for 12-15 months. Since 1984, grapes obtained from the younger vines have produced a second wine, Domaine de Martialis. This initiative, together with the care taken in the vineyard and cellars, has considerably enhanced the quality of Clos Fourtet's 55,000 bottles a year over the course of the 80s.

Clos Fourtet Saint-Emilion 1989 🍷 ③
A wine of a bright, full hue and fruit fragrances with a just a hint of leather, vanilla and raw sausage. The palate is soft textured and supple with plenty of depth of fruit. Already very drinkable. It is quite fine but lacks just a little punch.

Château Beaumont

Cussac-Fort-Médoc
33460 Margaux
Tel. 56589229
Fax 56589094

Château Beaumont lies about 3 km from the Gironde, halfway between Saint-Julien and Margaux. The estate spreads over 105 ha, of which two thirds are planted with Cabernet Sauvignon and the rest with Merlot, and a very little Cabernet Franc and verdot. The plants are on average 15 years old and grow on a low hill of typically stony terrain. On being harvested, the grapes are brought to the cellar and selected by hand before being de-stemmed and left to macerate in stainless steel vats at a controlled temperature for over three weeks. Wines are aged in oak barrels, one third of which are new, for 16 months before being lightly filtered and bottled. Beaumont has two second-label wines, Château Moulin d'Arvigny and Les Tours de Beaumont, which together make up about one third of the 60,000 bottles produced each year by the estate. In 1986, Beaumont was taken over by the Grands Millésimes de France, which also owns the fine Grand Cru Classé, Château Beychevelle, at Saint-Julien. Château Beaumont wines are very elegant, beautifully made and, while not Bordeaux wines of the very highest standard, still enjoy an excellent repuatation all round the world.

Château Beaumont
Haut-Médoc 1989
Deep, brilliant ruby in color, the nose is ripe, with plenty of bramble jelly and new oak. The palate is fleshy and forward with lots of vanilla and blackcurrant fruit with hints of cedar and cigars. Not a wine to keep too long.

LIBOURNAIS/SAINT-EMILION
BORDEAUX
FRANCE

215

MEDOC/HAUT-MEDOC
BORDEAUX
FRANCE

Château Hanteillan

Cissac
33250 Pauillac
Tel. 56593531
Fax 56593151

In 1809, Château Hanteillan was acquired by Madame Antoinette Rose de Lapeyrière. She and her daughter were the first women to own the property. In 1972, the charming and well-known Catherine Blasco and her family took over the château. There are 83 ha of vineyards, planted with the classics in the ratio of 39% Merlot, 57% Cabernet Sauvignon and Cabernet Franc and 4% Malbec and Petit Verdot. The soil is clay and limestone witha a gravelly topsoil; the vines average an age of 15 years. Despite an up-to-date battery of 35 stainless steel temperature control vats, fermentation is in the traditional manner, the average length of maceration being four weeks. Aging lasts for 12 months, with rotation of the wine every four barriques (one third) and vat (two-thirds). Catherine Blasco also produces another wine from her younger vines, Château Laborde, also an AC Haut-Médoc. This wine is aged exclusively in vats and, for obvious reasons, does not have the same characteristics as the Château Hanteillan, which is fuller and more elegant.

Château Hanteillan
Haut-Médoc 1989
Full and intense color, bright red on the rim. The nose is well-rounded, fruity and warm although still a little undeveloped. Soft on the palate, too, with good strength and balance. A wine with an attractive style, rich in fruit.

Château Hanteillan
Haut-Médoc 1988
A wine with a good, attractive color. The nose is very fruity and evolving in aromatic complexity. Pleasant to drink now, it is round and full-bodied on the palate. Very appealing and stylish, with lots of fruit.

Château La Lagune

33290 Ludon Médoc
Tel. 56304407
Fax 56300537

Before attempting to cultivate Cabernet Sauvignon at Château Vignelaure in the Coteaux d'Aix-en-Provence, George Brunet had taken over the management of La Lagune and in a few short years, had made it one of Haut-Médoc's outstanding estates. On buying the property from Champagne Ayala, he equipped the cellar with the best technology of the day. Recently, the cellar has been modernized again and quality continues to be superb under the dynamic direction of Jeanne Boyre who, with her no-nonsense management style, has worked wonders for women in the world of wine. There are 70 ha of vineyard, planted with 55% Cabernet Sauvignon and 45% Merlot and Cabernet Franc. The plants are about 30 years old, because Brunet replanted much of the estate in the late 1950s. Wines ferment for about 20 days in temperature-controlled stainless steel vats before ageing for 18 to 22 months in Allier barriques, nearly all of which are replaced every year. Lots considered below the standard for Grand Cru are used for the second label, Ludon Pomies Agassac.

Château La Lagune
Haut-Médoc 1989
Another deep ruby wine, the blast of rich, decadent plummy black cherry fruit with a hefty dose of new oak is almost too much to take. The structure on the palate is soft but very big; a very rewarding wine even now. It will last purely on the power of its fruit.

Château La Lagune
Haut-Médoc 1986
Dark ruby right up to the rim, this is a particualrily big La Lagune, with a big nose of cedary, tabacco toastiness and ripe plum fruit. The tannin on the palate is powerful but well-matched by the long-lasting and opulent fruit.

MEDOC/HAUT-MEDOC
BORDEAUX
FRANCE

216

MEDOC/HAUT-MEDOC
BORDEAUX
FRANCE

Château Liversan

Saint-Sauveur
33250 Pauillac
Tel. 56595707
Fax 56595959

Château Liversan has a 50-ha vineyard on a gravel outcrop at Saint-Sauveur, only three km. from the center of Pauillac. The estate was purchased in 1984 by Prince Guy de Polignac, who was for many years the manager of the Pommery company in Champagne. In pursuit of wines to compete with the neighboring Grands Crus Classés, the prince modernized and improved cellar and estate on a large scale. There is a high proportion of Merlot (38%) in the wine, although half is Cabernet Sauvignon and the rest Cabernet Franc and petit verdot. The grapes are de-stemmed and then fermented separately, plot by plot, in temperature-controlled stainless steel vats. The wine is aged in oak barrels, one third of which are replaced every year. The 180,000 bottles produced each year are good value for money, as indeed is the second-label wine, Château Fonpiqueyre, made from the grapes - around 30% of the total production - judged to be lower quality. The prince and his son Henri-Melchior do not make the best wine in the area, but their commitment has been rewarded by the high quality of recent vintages at Liversan.

Château Liversan Haut-Médoc 1989 ♥ ③
The depth of color in this wine would suggest a far more austere style than the blackcurranty, toasty nose and soft plum and blackcurrant palate than this Liversan exudes, with great style and length.

Château Peyrabon

Saint-Sauveur
33250 Pauillac
Tel. 56595710
Fax 56595945

"Peyrabon" means "good stones" and the vineyard is in fact on gravel soil lying 5 km to the north of Pauillac at Saint-Saveur. The estate is managed by Jacques Babeau, whose father René bought it in 1958. There are 53 ha of vines, 5 of which are actually in the Pauillac Appellation right next to some of the most famous estates in the world. Grapes from these plots are separately fermented and sold under the La Fleur Peyrabon label. Most of the vine stock is Cabernet Sauvignon with one quarter Cabernet Franc and one Merlot, scattered over 48 different plots around the Médoc. The fruit is handled in the traditional fashion in temperature-controlled cement vats and ageing (18-24 months depending on the vintage) is in barrels of French oak. Babeau's wines are absolutely reliable. The quality is always high and the style, rich and compact. They sell well, mainly in Belgium, Luxemburg and Switzerland.

Château Peyrabon Haut-Médoc 1989 ♥ ②
The nose is closed but quite clean. The color is deep, rich red. In the mouth, good rich, ripe fruits with nice acidity, good, soft and well-balanced. A good example of the 1989 as it is already quite accessible. Yet, judging from the nose, it is clear that this wine will surely improve with cellaring.

MEDOC/HAUT-MEDOC
BORDEAUX
FRANCE

217

MEDOC/HAUT-MEDOC
BORDOLESE
FRANCIA

Château Ramage La Batisse

Saint-Sauveur
33250 Pauillac
Tel. 56595724
Fax 56595414

Château Ramage La Batisse is one of the Saint-Sauveur estates which are hard on the heels of the great names from the surrounding communes. It is owned by the insurance company MACIF, which bought it in 1986 and delegated Pierre Chevrier to run it. The Mannoyeur family had completely overhauled the estate and the company in 1963, leaving it in excellent shape. There are 65 ha of plants on gravel and sand, half of them Cabernet Sauvignon, one third Merlot and the rest Cabernet Franc and petit verdot. As a result of the massive replanting of the 1960s, most of the plants are about 25 years old. Harvesting is exclusively manual, the grapes being selected, de-stemmed and placed in enamelled steel vats. Each variety is fermented separately and then blended before going into Allier wood barrels, half of which are new. After ageing for 12-16 months, the wines are again blended, clarified with egg white, filtered and bottled. Although some is sold en primeur, most of the 200,000 bottles will be kept in the cellar for two years. A further 100,000 bottles of the second-label wine, Château Tourteran, follow the same procedure. Good quality wines at an attractive price.

Château Ramage La Batisse
Haut-Médoc 1988
Mid-weight ruby in color. The nose is oaky but a little shy, with hints of cassis. The palate is lean, with developed blackcurrant fruit with cedary scents. Gritty tannins give the wine a rather austere end.

Château Sociando-Mallet

33180 Saint-Seurin-de-Cadourne
Tel. 56593657
Fax 56597088

In the words of Monsieur Gautreau, "a nobleman named Sociando gave his name to this land in about 1630, a woman named Mallet added hers about 1850 and Jean Gautreau bought it in 1969, when it and its 7 ha of vines were in ruins". Since then, Gautreau has worked ceaselessy to improve the quality of the estate and the château on the banks of the river, just north of Saint-Estèphe. Today, the reputation of Château Sociando-Mallet is growing. There are 50 ha of vines, with an average age of 25 years, on stony clay and limestone soil. 60% is Cabernet Sauvignon, 10% Cabernet Franc, 25% Merlot and 5% petit verdot. The de-stemmed grapes are fermented in stainless steel and cement vats at a controlled temperature for three to four weeks. Ageing then continues in new barrels of Allier, Nièvre and Vosges oak. The second wine of the estate, La Demoiselle de Sociando-Mallet, is aged in barriques in their second year. Jean Gautreau is particularly skilled at matching wine and wood and, although they are not cheap, the 270,000 bottles of Château Sociando-Mallet and the 80,000 bottles of La Demoiselle de Sociando-Mallet are of a high standard and bear comparison with almost any other wine in the Médoc.

Château Sociando-Mallet
Haut-Médoc 1989
Deep, dark, rich intense color. The nose shows dense blackcurrant and ripe fruit, with liquorice, and well-married cigar box and oak. The fruit is concentrated, seductive and spicy on the palate, with an excellent structure and finish.

Château Sociando-Mallet
Haut-Médoc 1988
A dark plummy ruby color. Powerful cassis, liquorice and violets with the new oak assail the nose. The palate is massive and concentrated with a structure to give it a good 15-20 years' life.

MEDOC/HAUT-MEDOC
BORDEAUX
FRANCE

218

MEDOC/HAUT-MEDOC
BORDEAUX
FRANCE

Château Tour du Haut Moulin

Cussac-Fort-Médoc
33460 Margaux
Tel. 56589110
Fax 56589930

This 35 ha estate does not possess a real château, only a fine country house. On the other hand, it has what counts: the terrain. Its gravel slopes are bounded by the famous Fort-Médoc and the Garonne estuary, which is a guarantee of quality. As it lies between Saint-Julien and Margaux, Cussac ought to have obtained the Appellation Saint-Julien, but this was only granted to about 30 ha. Laurent Poitou is the successor of four generations of famous growers. His son, also called Laurent, and the enologist, Michel-Bernard Couasnon, look after the winemaking while his daughter Béatrice is in charge of sales. The wine is made by blending, mainly Cabernet Sauvignon with a little Merlot and Petit Verdot, right at harvest. Fermentation takes three or four weeks in cement vats and aging (from 10 to 15 months) is in the oak, one third of which is new. The estate does not produce wines that are ready to drink at once and in good years they should age for up to ten years. Recent vintages are amongst the best of the Crus Bourgeois.

Château Tour du Haut Moulin
Haut-Médoc 1989
Bright ruby color. Forward nose, round on the palate. Perfectly balanced with good fruit extract. The tannins are quite tough but are already well-integrated. The finish is rather woody and very long, with good prospects for the future.

Château Tour du Haut Moulin
Haut-Médoc 1987
The outstanding fruit in this wine perfectly reflects the blend of Cabernet Sauvignon, Merlot and Petit Verdot grapes. A good example of a wine to drink young.

Château Ducluzeau

33250 Saint-Julien-Beychevelle
Tel. 56590520
Fax 56592737

Château Ducru-Beaucaillou is the guiding spirit behind this tiny 4.5 ha property. It has belonged to the Borie family for more than a century and is lovingly looked after by Jean-Eugène Borie and the Ducru-Beaucaillou duo, François-Xavier Borie and head cellarman René Lusseau. If the the blend of 90% Merlot and 10% Cabernet Sauvignon grapes appears very unusual for the AC, it is because Listrac tends to produce wines which are hard and rustic if the proportion of varieties is otherwise. Elegance is paramount here, an elegance sustained by top class fruit and constant care and attention to detail in the vineyard and cellar. The grapes are picked by hand at optimal ripeness. Temperature-controlled fermentation lasts on average more than three weeks at controlled temperatures and aging is in oak barrels from Ducru-Beaucaillou (one third of which are replaced every year) for a maximum of 18 months.

Château Ducluzeau Listrac 1990 ③
The Borie style is apparent in all the estate's products. The quality of the grapes, the careful fermentation and the ageing in barriques. Merlot gives this wine a beautiful aromatic range of ripe fruit, a mouthfilling palate with gentle tannins and a soft oaky finish.

MEDOC/HAUT-MEDOC
BORDEAUX
FRANCE

219

MEDOC/LISTRAC
BORDEAUX
FRANCE

Château Cantenac-Brown

33460 Margaux
Tel. 56883007
Fax 56887425

Anyone who tasted Château Cantenac-Brown wines in the 1960s or 1970s will remember how hard, tannic and generally poorly structured they used to be. Today, Cantenac-Brown wines are hardly recognizable as coming from the same château that produced those modest wines 30 years ago. The estate, which now belongs to the AXA insurance group, has been entrusted to the capable hands of Jean-Michel Cazes, who has already done much to improve the quality of Château Pichon-Baron at Pauillac. The 19th century, Tudor-style Château Cantenac-Brown has 32 ha of vines planted on stony soil to the south of the village of Margaux, with two thirds Cabernet Sauvignon and one third Cabernet Franc and Merlot. Since 1987, the cellar has been completely re-equipped and now boasts 24 huge temperature-controlled stainless steel vats where all the grapes are fermented. The richer, more concentrated wines are blended to make Château Cantenac-Brown wines while the rest go to produce second-label Château Canuet. Cantenac ages for 12-15 months in oak barrels. In 1855, the wine was considered a "troisième cru", and it is certainly regaining much of its original style. The 12,000 cases produced each year are still sold at reasonable prices.

Château Cantenac-Brown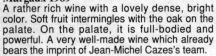
Margaux 1989
A rather rich wine with a lovely dense, bright color. Soft fruit intermingles with the oak on the palate. On the palate, it is full-bodied and powerful. A very well-made wine which already bears the imprint of Jean-Michel Cazes's team.

Château d'Angludet

33460 Cantenac
Tel. 56887141

Chairman of the Bordeaux Union des Grands Crus, Peter Siche has owned this 80-ha estate, 33 of which are planted with vines, since 1961. The property also features a superb Médoc-style house and one of the loveliest parks in Bordeaux. The great viticulturalist, Jules Jadouin, re-established the vineyard on splendid sand and gravel outcrops and planted it mainly with Cabernet Sauvignon. The estate is also crossed by two watercourses running through its woods and fields. Here, one can walk in the footsteps of the 12th century "Chevalier d'Angludet". During the French Revolution, on the other hand, the château was the headquarters of the local militia. In addition, Peter Sichel is also the co-owner together with the Mahler-Bresse family of wine merchants of the Château Palmer estate. The strong point of d'Angludet wines is their finesse and natural elegance. They are soft, rather than tannic, and of good complexity. This is a wine which ages in oak (one third new) for 12 months and is worthy of comparison with the best wines of Margaux.

Château d'Angludet
Margaux 1991
A deep ruby color and a nose which is, for the time being, forceful and direct. Fine complexity of aromas on a background of violets. Attractive fragrance and silkiness, but also unusually concentrated extracts, much richer than those of the preceding vintage. An excellent wine to lay down, indeed not to do so would be a crime.

Château d'Angludet
Margaux 1988
A wine of great natural balance and elegance. The estate aims above all for round, soft tannins something it has undoubtedly achieved in this vintage. The nose is dominated by fruit, but there are also scents of vanilla and autumn leaves. The mid-palate has a rich, open texture. The finish is slightly oaky and very long-lasting.

MEDOC/MARGAUX
BORDEAUX
FRANCE

220

MEDOC/MARGAUX
BORDEAUX
FRANCE

Château Labégorce Zédé

Soussans
33460 Margaux
Tel. 56887131
Fax 56887254

The wines of Labégorce Zédé are quite simply astonishing. From a back-seat position in the end of the 1970s, the château has clawed its way back towards the front rank of an Appellation which is full of great names. It even looks as if Château Labégorce Zédé will be able to compete on equal terms with the greatest of them in the very near future. One of the reasons for the comeback is Luc Thienpoint, a Belgian, who is a member of the same family which owns the Vieux Château Certan and the châteaux Puygueraud and Claverie in Côtes de Franc. Thienpoint bought the estate in 1970, replacing a third of the vines. Today he has 27 ha in the commune of Margaux on gravel soil half in Cabernet Sauvignon, one third in Merlot and the rest in Cabernet Franc and Petit Verdot. Fermentation takes place in stainless steel containers at controlled temperatures in immaculate cellars. Aging is in wood barrels (35%-40% of which are new) for 12-14 months. The wines have met widespread and enthusiastic approval and the 180,000 bottles produced every year are in great demand as, indeed, is the second-label wine, Domaine Zédé and even Z de Zédé, a simple Bordeaux. To judge by wines from recent vintages, one can expect this estate to reach exceptional heights in the next ten years.

Château Labégorce Zédé
Margaux 1990
Superbly rich in color with an intense bouquet well-married oak with ripe lyered fruits show. Very concentrated, but still elegant, on the palate with lots of new oak tannins on the finish. A well-balanced wine, despite the heavy oak. With some years in bottle it will show the true style of Margaux.

Château Labégorce Zédé
Margaux 1989
Elegant aromas of ripe fruit combined with the vanilla, oaky flavors from the wood. On the palate, rich in fruit, very elegant and remarkably fresh for this vintage. This will make a fine bottle in a few years thanks to the excellent balance of fruit/acidity/tannins.

Château Labégorce Zédé
Margaux 1988
Beautiful, deep and intense. The nose is evolving and has started to develop a delicious soft leathery elegance and texture. Rich, ripe and intensely soft, elegant fruit, with truly remarkable length. A great examply of this fine vintage. Not perhaps the power or plumpness of the 1989 but true Margaux elegance.

MEDOC/MARGAUX
BORDEAUX
FRANCE

221

MEDOC/MARGAUX
BORDEAUX
FRANCE

Château Margaux

33460 Margaux
Tel.56887028-56883559
Fax 56883132

With its park and tall columns, Château Margaux is singly one of the loveliest châteaux in the Médoc and its wine, amongst the top wines of the world. Much of the credit must go to the late André Mentezelopoulos who, with his wife Laura and daughter Corinne, bought the property from the Ginestets in 1978. Prior to their arrival, the estate had suffered a painful decline. Consequently, an enormous amount of money and effort was needed to restore château and vineyards to their former splendor. Today, there are about 78 ha of vines, planted 75% in Cabernet Sauvignon and 20% Merlot with the remaining 5% Cabernet Franc and Petit Verdot. All of this goes to produce 350,000 bottles a year of red wine. Always attentive to quality, at Château Margaux the grapes are picked by hand, still using the great oak vats for fermentation with maceration for three weeks. The wine then spends 18 to 24 months in new oak barriques, many of which are made on location. The cellar-master Jean Grangerou and the dynamic, unassuming director Paul Pontallier supervise every stage of production and aging. In addition to the Grand Vin du Château Margaux, the château also produces a second wine, Pavillon Rouge, made with grapes from the younger vines and wine eliminated from the final selection of the "Chateau" wine. Since the 1st World War, there has always been a white made at the château, and today some 40,000 bottles of Pavillon Blanc are made from 12 ha of Sauvignon Blanc. The white is barrel-fermented and bottled after 6-7 months oak-aging. A crisp Sauvignon, 'Graves-style' when young, it develops complexity with four or five years in bottle.

Château Margaux Margaux 1990 🍇🍇 ④
Very rich and dense in colour with great intensity. The bouquet is of ripe fruit, very clean with smart oak. In the mouth again lots of fruit, a touch of tar and plenty of fine fruit tannins behind. A very elegant wine, truly superb.

Le Pavillon Rouge 🍇🍇 ③
Margaux 1988
Fine in color, rich and deep. The nose is typical, clean quite lean, elegant style, with lots of fruit rather hard, closed and oaky right now. In mouth again closed at the moment but good rich fruit and lots of finesse. This is a great example of what a good second wine should be like and will make a delicious bottle of wine in its own right in 8-10 years.

Château Margaux 🍇🍇🍇 ④
Margaux 1989
A deep rich color, ruby depths. Nose has completly ripe powerful intense blackcurrant fruit and in the moth rather a massive powerful wine for Margaux, with lots of very smart oak and good tannic structure. A wine which is typical of the Château Margaux style over the last few years and, while not perhaps as great as the 1986. It has amazing concentration of fruit and has acquired a backbone that is rare for the vintage. This is an outstanding example of the proper marriage of modern cellar technology when it is intelligently harnessed to 'draconian', quality-oriented growing methods. It is only by this method of bringing the highest quality fruit into the winery and transforming it with the same attention to quality that one can achieve wines of the consistency of Château Margaux.

MEDOC/MARGAUX
BORDEAUX
FRANCE

222

MEDOC/MARGAUX
BORDEAUX
FRANCE

Château Monbrison

33460 Arsac
Tel. 56588004
Fax 56588533

Château Palmer

33460 Margaux
Tel. 56887272

Sadly, the sprited figure behind Château Monbrison, Jean-Luc Vonderheyden, who was gun-collector and wine-lover, died just last year, in 1992. Many connoisseurs regard his 1990 as being one of the best wines of the last ten years. The château may have been orphaned, but Laurent Vonderheyden, who has taken over in Jean-Luc's place, is well-aware of his responsibilities. The estate comprises 25 ha, of which 21 are planted, standing on one of the loveliest hills in the Médoc. The gravel soil is well-drained and capable of maintaining this Cru Bourgeois at past levels since the necessary determination and equipment are not lacking. Fermentation is in enamelled stainless steel vats and lasts for about three weeks. The fermentation temperature (30°-32°C) is constant, thanks to a cooling system and the wine is pumped over the cap twice a day. It then spends 15 to 18 months in oak one third of the barriques being replaced every year. All recent vintages have been totally successful, including those of the second-label wine, Château Cordet. Château Monbrison has also twice won the "Coupe des Crus Bourgeois" organized by Gault-Millau (1988 and 1990).

Château Monbrison   🍇🍇 ②
Margaux 1989
Intense purple color. Bouquet of ripe fruit, with a vanilla scent. Rich and full-bodied on the palate with a good structure. Although produced in considerable quantity, this wine maintains all the elegance of a Margaux.

Château Monbrison   🍇🍇 ②
Margaux 1988
Intense aromas of ripe fruit, with an agreeable freshness which may also be found in the rich, deep colour. The tannins harmonize well with the wood on the palate into an outstandingly elegant tasting experience. A fine example of a Margaux, concentrated and very fine.

The superbly presented Château Palmer bottles, with its distinctive black and gold label, do not detract at all from their actual contents. Château Palmer is one of the finest, most concentrated wines in the Médoc. The estate belongs to three different companies (Sichel, Bouteiller and Malher-Besse), but credit for the quality of the wine goes to the Chardon family, who have looked after the château for many years. The 42 ha property is, surprizingly, 40% Merlot, which perhaps explains the rich style of this wine. The vineyards are managed in the traditional fashion, and winemaking is conducted similarly. Château Palmer finally set aside the old faithful, hand-operated de-stemmer in 1982. The grapes ferment for 15-25 days in wooden vats and then age for about 18 months in oak casks, one third of which are new. Clarification is effected solely by fining with egg white and racking. In the past, the entire year's production has at times been judged unsuitable for the Château Palmer label and sold unbottled wholesale. This happened in 1963 and again in 1968. A second wine was created in 1983, Réserve du Général, to take up a good part of the inferior-quality cuvées. Standards at Château Palmer are therefore as high as ever and the 1855 classification as a "troisième cru" certainly understates its true market standing.

Château Palmer Margaux 1989   🍇🍇 ④
Almost inky in its depth, an impenetrable purple-ruby. The nose is tightly knit as yet, with violets, blackberries and plum jellies, with coffee and a solid presence of new oak. The palate is surprisingly fat, with little acidity but with firm if not hard tannins and abundant alcohol mercifully outweighed by the rapidly developing fruit.

MEDOC/MARGAUX
BORDEAUX
FRANCE

223

MEDOC/MARGAUX
BORDEAUX
FRANCE

Château Prieuré-Lichine

33460 Margaux
Tel. 56883628
Fax 56887893

The story of Château Prieuré-Lichine is the story of a man who became one of the fathers of the modern wine trade thanks to his vision and foresight. Alexis Lichine arrived from Russia at an early age with his parents to become one of wine's most tireless ambassadors, above all in the United States. He also found time to dedicate to what was Château Prieuré-Cantenac when he bought it in 1951. The property became Château Prieuré-Lichine in 1953. Alexis is no longer with us, but today his son Sasha carries on his work. The Lichine family buys and sells plots with great care, chosing more promising sites to replant vineyards. As a result, the property is spread over a large number of small plots, all of outstanding quality. The total is now at about 71 ha with 54% Cabernet Sauvignon, 37% Merlot and 9% Cabernet Franc and Petit Verdot. The grapes are fermented in stainless steel at controlled temperatures with an unusually long 25-day fermentation to achieve the maximum extract. A small quantity of the second pressing is added before the wines age for 18 months in Allier oak barrels, 50%-70% of which are new. They are clarified with egg white and lightly filtered before bottling. Any wine not considered to be of Prieuré-Lichine standard is used for the second label, Château de Clairefont.

Château Prieuré-Lichine   🍷 ③
Margaux 1989
A ruby red-colored wine with attractive black and red currants fruits well-combined with the strength of the new oak. The almost severely alcoholic palate is tempered by the richness of the fruit and the softness of the tannins.

Château Tayac

Soussans
33460 Margaux
Tel. 56883306

Monsieur Favin bought Château Tayac in 1960 and before his sad death in 1988, he set the estate on solid ground. He created a company with the other members of the family and convinced the husband of one of his two daughters to learn the art of winemaking inside out. In 1988, Guy Portet debuted with his first wine despite having had no knowledge of the process only a few short years before. Château Tayac possesses 35 ha under vines with two thirds Cabernet Sauvignon and the rest Merlot with a little Petit Verdot. The soil is typical Margaux gravel. Monsieur Favin built the house and the cellars in the 1960s, installing mainly cement vats with some stainless steel. Controlled-temperature fermentation lasts about 21 days. After malolactic fermentation, the wines are blended and pass into Nièvre barrels (30%-40% new) where they age for 18 months. There follows fining using egg white and light filtering before bottling. The resulting wines are elegant and stylish even when young. About 200,000 bottles are produced annually, including a second label, Château Tayac La Rosa.

Château Tayac Margaux 1990   🍷 ③
Pretty bright, ruby-red with a rich, elegant nose with ripe fruit. Again, rich, powerful and well-extracted fruit on the palate. A well-structured wine of good length, perhaps a bit overblown and not enough Margaux elegance.

MEDOC/MARGAUX
BORDEAUX
FRANCE

224

MEDOC/MARGAUX
BORDEAUX
FRANCE

Château La Tour de By

33340 Bégadan
Tel. 56415003
Fax 56413610

Château La Tour de By is a well-known Cru Bourgeois often found on wine lists both in France and abroad. Its red wines are, while not really outstanding, very good indeed. They are produced on 73 ha planted in the typical Médoc fashion or rather two-thirds Cabernet Sauvignon, a little over a quarter Merlot and the rest Cabernet Franc and Petit Verdot. Vinification is also in the traditional Médoc style with a three-to-four week fermentation followed by malolactic fermentation and 10 days' rest in vats before passing the wine into oak barrels, 20% of which are new. Only four egg whites per barrique are used for fining and there is no filtering. The outstanding enologist, Boissenot, and the owner-manager, Marc Pages, are responsible for the success of Château La Tour de By. 500,000 bottles a year are produced, and they have won so many medals and trophies in the past that for the time being, the château's wines are no longer being entered for competitions.

Château La Tour de By Médoc 1989
Deep dark, almost opaque. The nose is tight with only a hint of oaky, inky blackcurrant and pepper fruit. The palate is almost fiercely tannic, tempered only by the treacley nature of the fruit.

Château Lacombe-Noaillac

Jau-Dignac-Loirac
33590 Saint-Vivien-de-Médoc
Tel. 56094255
Fax 56095849

Château Lacombe-Noaillac is on the northern edge of the Médoc in the commune of Jau-Dignac-Loirac. Since 1979, the estate has belonged to the thirty-seven year-old Jean-Michel Lapalu and his father, who also manages the neighboring Château Patache d'Aux, a very well known cru bourgeois. At the time of the purchase, the estate had been neglected since the end of the Second World War and much effort was required to restore the vineyards to productivity. Jau-Dignac-Loirac lies with the estuary of the Gironde on one side and the Atlantic Ocean on the other. It is a position which enjoys a temperate climate, escaping the coldest winter weather and the most intense heat of summer. The Lapalus today have about 28 ha. of vines, most of which (60%) are planted with Cabernet Sauvignon. The remainder comprises Merlot with a small quantity of Petit Verdot and Cabernet Franc. The wine ferments in stainless steel barrels and then ages for a year, partly in vats and partly in oak barrels. The vines at Château Lacombe-Noaillac are young and the quality of the grapes is improving every year. Keep an eye on Jean-Michel Lapalu's wines for the future.

Château Lacombe-Noaillac
Médoc 1990
A fresh deep color. The nose is a bit tough and quite closed. In the mouth it shows good, fresh, clean fruit with ripe concentrated blackcurrant and good length.

Château Lacombe-Noaillac
Médoc 1989
Good, deep, rich color. The nose has a faintly herbaceous character and soft fruits. In the mouth it is round, soft, very ripe and well-balanced. Typical of the vintage.

MEDOC/MEDOC
BORDEAUX
FRANCE

225

MEDOC/MEDOC
BORDEAUX
FRANCE

Château Les Ormes-Sorbet

33340 Couquèques
Tel. 56415378
Fax 56413842

Château Les Ormes-Sorbet lies in the village of Couquèques in the northern Médoc. It has always been noteworthy and has been in the same family for eight generations. Owner Jean Boivert uses his skills in winemaking while his wife looks after public relations and runs the estate. The château's 23 ha of vineyards are planted with two-thirds Cabernet Sauvignon and one third Merlot, turning out some of the most agreeable wines in the Médoc. The vineyards, including small plots of Petit Verdot, are spread out over limestone, sand and gravel terrains and give exceptional grapes. Boivert's vinification techniques are straightforward and make careful use of modern technology. The de-stemmed grapes ferment in stainless steel at controlled temperatures before aging in oak casks, one third of which are replaced every year, for 18-24 months. The wine is clarified with egg whites and filtered. The château produces 100,000 bottles a year and continue to be reasonable priced. They have a good following both in France and abroad.

Château Les Ormes-Sorbet 🍇🍇 ③
Médoc 1988
Intense, deep color with an elegant, soft nose which is already quite well-developed. The palate starts out with rich fruit, later balancing out well into a pleasing finish. A typical Boisvert wine, elegant and fruity. Excellent value for money.

Château Potensac

Ordonnac
33340 Lesparre
Tel. 56592526
Fax 56591833

Michel Delon looks after Château Potensac as well as managing and making the excellent Cru Classé of Saint-Julien Château Léoville-Las-Cases and its second label, Clos du Marquis. The château stands on the northern edge of the Médoc in the village of Ordonnac a few kilometres to the north-west of Saint-Estephe. It has belonged to the Delon family for more than two hundred years. The vineyards stand on 50 ha of clay and gravel soil. The vines are on average 30 years-old, just over half being Cabernet Sauvignon, a quarter Merlot and the rest Cabernet Franc. The wines are de-stemmed on their arrival in the cellar, where they ferment for 15-18 days with regular racking. The wine is aged for 18-20 months in oak (the barrels are either new or two years-old) and is clarified with egg white in the traditional manner. Rightfully, the château has a particularly good reputation. Château Potensac wines are of a quality standard not easy to find outside the Grands Crus.

Château Potensac Médoc 1989 🍇 ②
With its intense purple hue, this is a wine with an exceptional texture. On the nose, it discloses notes of berries and spices, cedar and liquorice. The palate is powerful, with ripe fruit, tannins and alcohol all in evidence. A long, flavorful finish.

Château Potensac Médoc 1986 🍇 ②
The bouquet contains grassy notes of Cabernet which combine well with the wood. Full-flavored and juicy on the palate with hints of cassis knit into soft tannins give this wine genuine elegance.

MEDOC/MEDOC
BORDEAUX
FRANCE

226

MEDOC/MEDOC
BORDEAUX
FRANCE

Château Tour Haut-Caussan

Blaignan
33340 Lesparre-Médoc
Tel. 56090077
Fax 56090624

The Courrian family has lived in the area since 1634, but it was only in 1877 that the grandfather of the present owner, Philippe's grandfather, bought this 35-ha estate lying around an 18th century mill, which Philippe restored in 1981 with the help of Patrick Eymerick. Today, the whole family works on the château. Daughter Véronique, 27, looks after business relations and son Fabien, 23, works in the vineyards and winery. There are 18 ha planted with equal parts of Cabernet Sauvignon and Merlot, producing an average of 10,000 cases a year. No chemical herbicides are used as it is the Courrians' passionate conviction that the quality of the wine depends on the way the vines are treated. Fermentation is carried out in cement vats at controlled temperatures between 28°-32°C, depending on the variety and its quality. After a fairly lengthy fermentation, aging is in oak barrels (with one third replaced every year) for 18 months, during which time the wine is racked eight times and clarified with egg white. The results are excellent: one of the best Médocs, with one of the best value-for-money ratings.

Château Tour Haut-Caussan
Médoc 1989
Intense hue with a fruity nose containing a note of tar. Rich on the palate. Rather warm, with notes of ripe fruit and rich in extract. A good example of its year, soft and with already well-rounded tannins.

Château Tour Haut-Caussan
Médoc 1988
The bouquet, while still rather undeveloped, is sharp and clean with hints of spices and fruit. A little rough on the palate due to its powerful structure and immature tannins but beginning to balance out in aromas and body.

Château Bel-Air Lagrave

Grand-Poujeaux
33480 Moulis-en-Médoc
Tel. 56580189

For those of us who cannot afford to drink Grands Crus every evening, Château Bel-Air Lagrave is an alternative from one of those less well-known sub-zones well-worth investigating. A Cru Bourgeois, its 12.5 ha of carefully tended vines produce about 600 cases of wine a year. Madame Bacquey is an owner with a keen eye on quality. The vines are pruned short and no chemical preparations are used. The hand-picked grapes are de-stemmed before going on to temperature-controlled fermentation in vats which have recently been improved to extract the fruit while maintaining the structure. The wine is made from 60% Cabernet Sauvignon, 35% Merlot and 5% Petit Verdot. After malolactic fermentation, it ages in oak barrels, one third of which are replaced every year, during which period the wine is clarified with egg white and regularly racked. In the search for quality, which she extends to her other two estates at Château La Closerie du Grand-Poujeaux and Château Haut-Franquet, Madame Bacquey keeps a reserve of past Bel-Air Lagrave vintages, from 1970 on.

Château Bel-Air Lagrave
Moulis-en-Médoc 1985
A Claret-style of red that the British love. Intense red with shades of brick, the nose shows cooked fruit and cherry jam. Tannins and acidity prevail over fruit on the palate and the length is outstanding.

MEDOC/MEDOC
BORDEAUX
FRANCE

227

MEDOC/MOULIS-EN-MEDOC
BORDEAUX
FRANCE

Château Brillette

33480 Moulis-en-Médoc
Tel. 56582209
Fax 56888226

Madame Berthault lived in Paris until her husband died in 1981. As they had bought this estate five years earlier, Madame Berthault decided to move to Bordeaux to look after the business herself. Château Brillette is still comparatively little known, but its wine is rapidly proving as much of a revelation as its dynamic owner. The property is fairly extensive and only half (35 ha) is used to grow grapes. At 40% Merlot, 50% is Cabernet Sauvignon and 10% Cabernet Franc and Petit Verdot, the vineyards have an average age of 25 years and are laid out for mechanical harvesting. After de-stemming, the grapes ferment for three weeks at controlled temperatures of about 25°C, according to the variety and zone of origin. They are only blended just before going into Allier oak barrels, one third of which are replaced every year. The wines age for roughly 15 months, being clarified with egg white and filtered before bottling. Annual output is of 150,000 bottles as well as another 30,000 bottles of a second.label wine, Château Berthault-Brillette, which is proving encouragingly successful on the export market.

Château Brillette
Moulis-en-Médoc 1989
Pretty red, with mid-reds on the edge. Full, rich, fruity fragrances with all the soft ripeness of the year. In the mouth again soft, ripe fruit but also with a good structure and length with well-married oak, very good balance.

Château Brillette
Moulis-en-Médoc 1985
Bright red in appearance, still evolving. The nose is rich, soft and surprisingly elegant. A very pleasant wine on the palate, dominated by a sensation of outstanding softness.

Château Chasse-Spleen

33480 Moulis-en-Médoc
Tel. 56580237

Unfortunately, the highly talented Madame Bernadette Villars died tragically early in 1993. She had managed Château Chasse-Spleen since 1976 and had earned the greatest respect around the wine world for her untiring work both at Chasse-Spleen but also at her other two estates, Château Haut-Bages Libéral at Pauillac and Château La Gurgue at Margaux. The latter two are more prestigious, but nonetheless Château Chasse-Spleen has been turning out excellent wines for many years. Five km to the north-west of Margaux just outside the village of Grand-Poujeaux, the château's 25-year old vines flourish on a well-drained outcrop of gravel which extends over about 70 ha. A little over half of the varieties are Cabernet Sauvignon with about one third Merlot and the rest, Petit Verdot. The grapes are de-stemmed and fermented in stainless steel and cement vats. The wines are then aged for about two years in the wood. They are not filtered, merely clarified with egg white. About 350,000 bottles are produced each year, of which 80,000 are Ermitage de Chasse-Spleen, the second-label wine made from younger vines, with a fruity character for those who like an easy-to-drink wine. Today, Château Chasse-Spleen is only classified as a Grand Bourgeois Exceptionnel, but it would beyond any doubt be reclassified to a higher ranking in any Médoc review.

Château Chasse-Spleen
Moulis-en-Médoc 1990
What concentration! Black purple with a rich ruby rim. Sharply-defined aromas with notes of tar, toastiness and abundant fruit. The palate is rich, with good structure and length, hinting at a wine exploding with richness in the future.

Château Chasse-Spleen
Moulis-en-Médoc 1989
A wine of great concentration both in its appearance, a purple so deep as almost to be black, and on the nose, which is intense and complex with notes of cedar, toasty wood, mulberries and other berries. The palate is rich, chewy, full-bodied and powerful, with soft tannins, just the right level of acidity and lavish fruit, especially on the finish.

MEDOC/MOULIS-EN-MEDOC
BORDEAUX
FRANCE   228

MEDOC/MOULIS-EN-MEDOC
BORDEAUX
FRANCE

Château Poujeaux

33480 Moulis-en-Médoc
Tel. 56580296
Fax 56580125

The Thiel family has owned the well-respected Château Poujeaux since 1921. The 52 ha of vines are trained for machine harvesting and are half Cabernet Sauvignon, one third Merlot with some Cabernet Franc and Petit Verdot, on average 25 years-old. Grapes are de-stemmed on their arrival in the cellar, and they are then fermented in temperature-controlled vats. The Allier and Limousin barrels in which the wine is aged for from 12 to 18 months are replaced every three years. Egg white is used for fining, and there is no filtering. About a quarter of total production is sold as a second wine, La Salle de Poujeaux. Although it is not one of the better-known estates in the Moulis Appellation, Château Poujeaux is very consistent and is certainly not far behind its illustrious neighboring vineyards. This château has always had its admirers, including that great wine-lover, the late president of the French Republic, Georges Pompidou.

Château Poujeaux
Moulis-en-Médoc 1989
Toasted aromas, mulberries and spices are to the fore both on the nose and on the palate, well-structured, if a little lacking in acidity. An attractive and classic Claret, with a nice round finish, to drink over the next ten years.

Château Bernadotte

Saint-Sauveur
33250 Pauillac
Tel. 56595704
Fax 56595484

The château takes its name from Germain Bernadotte, great-grandfather of Napoleon's troublesome General Bernadotte, later King of Sweden. Ironically, the estate was purchased in 1976 by Curt Eklund, a Swede. At the time, the 7.5-ha property was in decline. Eklund took it in hand and restored it, rebuilding cellars and chais which are now impeccably equipped. He also employed the great Jacques Boissenot, who is active at Ducru-Beaucaillou and Grand-Puy-Lacoste as well. Most of the vines were planted at the end of the 1970s and are two-thirds Cabernet Sauvignon, one third Merlot with a small quantity of Petit Verdot. 50% of the harvest is carried out mechanically, and all the grapes are selected on arrival in the cellar. The must ferments for two to three weeks in stainless steel vats at controlled temperatures then the wine ages for two years in new barrels in three different varieties of Massif Central oak. There are 45,000 bottles of the Château Bernadotte produced every year. It is not always the easiest of wines to find, but it is worth the money asked for it.

Château Bernadotte Pauillac 1990 ♥ ③
A well-balanced red, very well-made and elegant. Slightly leaner than the '89, with a fairly intense fragrance of black fruits. Full on the palate, where well-rounded tannins are in evidence.

Château Bernadotte Pauillac 1989 ♥ ③
Plenty of rich oak aromas on the nose, combining with an elegant bouquet of fruit. Full, ripe and elegant on the palate with the fruit well sustained by a powerful structure aided by the wood. A good example of 1989 Pauillac, complete and beautifully balanced.

MEDOC/MOULIS-EN-MEDOC
BORDEAUX
FRANCE

229

MEDOC/PAUILLAC
BORDEAUX
FRANCE

Château d'Armailhacq

33250 Pauillac
Tel. 56592020
Fax 56596054

The 50-ha Château d'Armailhacq estate has changed its name three times since 1933. When Baron Philippe de Rothschild bought it, it was called Château Mouton-d'Armailhacq. Later on, he called it Château Mouton-Baron-Philippe then he changed it to Château Mouton-Baronne-Philippe, in memory of his wife who had died in Nazi Germany during World War 2. Baron Philippe died in 1988 and his daughter, the ex-actress Philippine de Rothschild took over the management of the wine interests in 1992. She then gave the property its separate identity as Château d'Armailhacq. Despite all these changes, the wines have continued to be excellent, especially in recent years. The château stands next door to Château Mouton-Rothschild, and its wines share many of that estate's characteristics, including the marked oakiness, great depth and powerful fruit. Winemaking is carried out in the traditional Médoc fashion, the grapes being de-stemmed and then fermented at length in controlled-temperature cement vats. The wines contain a slightly higher percentage of Merlot than Mouton and spend more or less the same time (about 24 months) in cask, although in this instance only a third of these are replaced every year.

Château d'Armailhacq Pauillac 1989 🍇 ③
Soft all over, the nose is warm with velvety notes of plum jam and a sweet, spicy note of new oak. The fruit is rich and full-bodied on the palate, the tannins soft, the alcohol hefty and the finish soft.

Château Duhart-Milon

33250 Pauillac
Tel. 56592297

Château Duhart-Milon is next to Château Lafite on the northern edge of the commune of Pauillac on an outcrop of the Jaille de Breuil, which works miracles for Cos d'Estrournel. Monsieur Duhart appears to have been one of those 17th-century pirates who chose this area to take up viticulture and a more respectable way of life. The estate was classified as a "quatrième cru" in 1855 and went through a period of serious decline during almost the whole of the first half of the century. It began to work its way back again by the end of the 1970s with an elegant and powerful wine once the vines from the replantings launched by Domaine Barons de Rothschild began to bear fruit. The Rothschilds bought Duhart-Milon in 1962 and re-equipped the cellar with stainless steel fermentation vats. The wines are about three-fifths Cabernet Sauvignon and one fifth Merlot and Cabernet Franc, and age in oak barrels (30%-40% of which are new) for about one and a half years. A second wine, Moulin de Duhart, takes up those cuvées which do not make the final selection for the Château Duhart-Milon, of which 200,000 bottles are produced each year. Recent vintages have been particularly good.

Château Duhart-Milon Pauillac 1988 🍇 ③
Vibrant ruby in color with a lovely minty, black cherry and tabacco bouquet. The palate is fat and round, with good structure and a long fruit dominated finish.

MEDOC/PAUILLAC
BORDEAUX
FRANCE

230

MEDOC/PAUILLAC
BORDEAUX
FRANCE

Château Grand-Puy-Ducasse

Quai Antoine Ferchaud
33250 Pauillac
Tel. 56592141
Fax 56792357

Château Grand-Puy-Ducasse is a difficult wine to sum up. Fairly straightforward and without great individuality, yet it is of excellent quality. This paradox is the Cruse family's obsession, and they are doing all they can to make the wine even more interesting. The 1990 is lovely and represents a step in the right direction, confirming that Château Grand-Puy-Ducasse is a wine to keep an eye on. The 39 ha are planted with 61% Cabernet and 39% Merlot on coarse gravel in the Pauillac Appellation. The grapes are fermented in a leisurely fashion in temperature-controlled stainless steel vats after having been de-stemmed and soft-crushed. The wine ages for a year in barrels, 30% of which are new. The second-label wine, Château Artigues Arnaud, is made in almost exactly the same way but with grapes from younger plants. Each year, 180,000 bottles of Grand-Puy and 50,000 of Artigues are produced. Grand-Puy-Ducasse fully deserves its "cinquième cru" status and sooner or later will realize its potential to the fullest.

Château Grand-Puy-Ducasse
Pauillac 1990
Slightly toasty aromas and a fullness of fruit on the palate behind an impressive tannic structure. Well-rounded and austere finish.

Château Grand-Puy-Ducasse
Pauillac 1989
Intense and rich in color with a nose of medium intensity which has not yet fully developed. Ripe fruit on the elegant and powerful palate with a very long finish. A wine in a solid, full style.

Château Grand-Puy-Lacoste

33250 Pauillac
Tel. 56590666
Fax 56592737

In 1978, the 83 year-old Raymond Dupin, worried about the future of his beloved Château Grand-Puy-Lacoste, decided to sell it to the Borie family, who lived on the other side of his estate at Ducru-Beaucaillou. During negotiations, not only was a case of Ducru-Beaucaillou 1955 exchanged for one of Grand-Puy-Lacoste 1953, but it was also agreed that François-Xavier Borie would go to work alongside the elderly Dupin for five years to learn all about Grand-Puy-Lacoste. Sadly, Dupin died two years later and today, François Xavier and his wife, Marie-Hélène, supervise 50 ha of impeccable vineyards. The cellar is well-equipped and François is helped out by his father's head cellarman at Ducru. Together, they make 200,000 bottles a year of one of the most interesting wines in Pauillac. The average age of the winemaking team at this château is 35. They are, in fact, younger than their own vines. The grapes are picked by hand, de-stemmed and fermented separately by variety. The wine is aged in barriques (of which 30%-50% are new) for 18 months. The results are excellent and the spirit in which the Bories are running this estate is being rewarded by the increasing recognition accorded to Grand-Puy-Lacoste.

Château Grand-Puy-Lacoste
Pauillac 1989
Rich, fruity nose and intense color. A full-bodied wine on the palate, with good structure, dense fruit and a long, nice tannic finish. An extremely agreeable bottle of wine.

Château Grand-Puy-Lacoste
Pauillac 1988
The bouquet, as is the case with many 1988s, is still rather harsh and undeveloped. On the palate there is great fullness of fruit, although it has not emerged entirely while the tannins are still rough. This will be a great wine by the end of the century.

MEDOC/PAUILLAC
BORDEAUX
FRANCE

231

MEDOC/PAUILLAC
BORDEAUX
FRANCE

Château Haut-Bages-Libéral

33250 Pauillac
Tel. 5691188

It was the Cruse family who really turned Château Haut-Bages-Libéral around and brought it out of obscurity to become one of the most interesting producers in Pauillac. The vineyards were completely replanted in the 1970s and now produce excellent grapes. A large part of the 23-ha estate on the fine gravel at Bages borders Latour on one side. Unfortunately, the Cruses had to sell the château before the results of their efforts became apparent. The estate was purchased by a large company which made use of the skills of Bernadette Villars of Château Chasse-Spleen to make a successful Cabernet Sauvignon which is sumptuously rich and delicately fruity. Fermentation is ultra-modern in an impressive series of 200-hl stainless steel temperature-controlled vats. Wines are aged for 18 to 24 months in the wood and clarified with egg white. Château Haut-Bages-Libéral's production is fairly limited for the Médoc, only 10,000 cases a year of a truly excellent wine.

Château Haut-Bages Libéral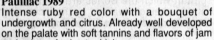
Pauillac 1989
Intense ruby red color with a bouquet of undergrowth and citrus. Already well developed on the palate with soft tannins and flavors of jam and spices. A wine to drink young.

Château Haut-Batailley

33250 Pauillac
Tel. 56590520
Fax 56592737

One of the crucial elements in the improvement and success of any Médoc château is the human factor. This is especially true of Château Haut-Batailley, which is managed by Jean-Eugène Borie of Château Ducru-Beaucaillou on behalf of his sister, Madame Brest-Borie. Monsieur Borie and his son François-Xavier are well-known for their laudable efforts at Ducru-Beaucaillou and Grand-Puy-Lacoste. Château Haut-Batailley has 20 ha of good vines, 30 years-old on average, two-thirds of which are Cabernet Sauvignon. Winemaking is in the classic tradition. All the grapes are de-stemmed, before long maceration in temperature-controlled stainless steel vats. The wine ages for 18-20 months in wood barrels, which are replaced according to the vintage, and the wines are fined with eggwhite. The entire production, including the second wine, La Tour l'Aspic, is sold through Bordeaux wine merchants. Château Haut-Batailley, classified as a 'cinquième cru' in 1855, is at present very well-made and, despite the hefty percentage of Cabernet Sauvignon, it is a wine that seems to mature fairly quickly.

Château Haut-Batailley ❦❦ ③
Pauillac 1989
Brilliant ruby color and a complex bouquet of red fruit, liquorice and spice. On the palate the ripe fruit is in perfect harmony with the already soft tannins, which give a velvety texture. The finish is long and deliciously balanced.

MEDOC/PAUILLAC
BORDEAUX
FRANCE

232

MEDOC/PAUILLAC
BORDEAUX
FRANCE

Château La Bécasse

21, rue Édouard de Pontet
Pauillac 33250
Tel. 56590714

Château La Bécasse is an unusual estate for the Médoc. It was created only recently, in 1966, by Georges Fonteneau, who bought up 18 small plots, often bordering on vineyards belonging to famous châteaux like Lynch-Bages or Pichon Longueville Comtesse de Lalande. The Fonteneau family were, however, hardly newcomers to winemaking. Georges' father, René, had been cooper at Saint-Julien and his grandfather, in addition to being the manager of Château Ducru-Beaucaillou, had owned some vineyards at Saint-Julien from which he had produced a wine called Cru de la Bécasse. It was, therefore, natural that the name of the property should be changed to Château La Bécasse when they purchased vineyards at Pauillac. Today Georges and his son, Roland, produce 25,000 bottles of Pauillac a year from 4 ha of Cabernet Sauvignon, Merlot and Cabernet Franc. The grapes are harvested by hand, fermented in stainless steel vats with 21 days' maceration and aged for 18 months in oak with one third of the barrels being replaced every year. The wine is not filtered but merely clarified with egg white. Château La Bécasse wines are usually robust and well-made, perhaps not stunning but always very good value for money.

Château La Bécasse Pauillac 1988 🍇 🍇 ③
A rich and attractive color and intense nose with fresh aromas of red fruit. The flavor is mouthfilling, fruity and tannic, somewhat closed and harsh at the moment but well-balanced and with good length.

Château La Bécasse Pauillac 1986 🍇 ③
Fine, deep, rich color. the bouquet is full and clean and the palate is marked by the rather delicate flavor of fruit. Good balance between tannins and acidity.

Château Lafite-Rothschild

33250 Pauillac
Tel. 56731818
Fax 56592683

Château Lafite is a legendary name which is heir to a heritage of traditional winemaking both in the vineyard and in the winery. The vines themselves (100 ha with an average vine age of 80 years) are 70% Cabernet Sauvignon, 20% Merlot and the remainder Cabernet Franc. Yields are extremely kept low, the harvesting done by hand and the wines fermented partly in stainless steel vats and partly in old wood casks, for 18-25 days. Wines are aged in the splendid new cellars in barrels of new wood, made on site by Lafite's own coopers. The wine is clarified with egg white and the blends are the result of a rigorous selection of the various barriques. A second-label, Le Moulin des Carruades, is used for wines not considered to be good enough and for those from the young vines. As far as the excellent production is concerned (600,000 bottles), the price is certainly high, but this wine always represents a fine investment. For a time the image of Château Lafite was somewhat tarnished by the less than exciting outcome of occasional blind tastings. The truth is that when young these wines do not show well; also Lafite needs time in bottle for its true character to express itself. They have a lighter, more elegant style that happens to go against the current trend for high extract, powerful Pauillacs.

Château Lafite-Rothschild
Pauillac 1988
A wine of considerable strength compared to the normal Lafite style. The nose is classic, with blackcurrant, cedar, charred oak and violets. The palate is robust, with vigorous tannins backed by fruit exploding with aromas of chocolate and mint with mineral notes. The finish is magnificently rich, albeit still with a little harshness.

MEDOC/PAUILLAC
BORDEAUX
FRANCE

233

MEDOC/PAUILLAC
BORDEAUX
FRANCE

Château Latour

33250 Pauillac
Tel. 56590051
Fax 56592349

The 47 ha of vineyard in the Château Latour's "enclos", or walled park, are planted on soil which is largely composed of egg-sized quartz pebbles some of which the Marquis of Ségur, once the owner not only Château Latour but also Château Lafite and Château Calon-Ségur, had polished and sewn onto a splendid waistcoat, prompting Louis XV to call him "the richest man in my kingdom". The British company, Allied Lyons, now owns most this historic château at present. The vines (40 years-old on average) stand closer together than is usual in the Médoc so the yield is low and the grapes are very concentrated. Old plants are not replaced by substituting the entire plot but "à jardinage", or one at a time. Four-fifths of the plantings are Cabernet Sauvignon, hence the massive, long-lived, heavy-structured wine. The "chai" was re-equipped in 1964, bringing in stainless steel vats for fermentation. Aging is in new casks for two years and any casks not considered good enough for Château Latour are used for a second label, Les Forts de Latour, or are declassified as generic Pauillac. The annual production of 130,000 bottles of Les Forts de Latour also uses grapes from 14 ha of vineyard lying outside L'Enclos together with grapes from younger vines, which are harvested separately. This particularly rigorous style of winemaking ensures that both wines maintain impeccable quality. The 220,000 bottles produced each year richly deserve the reputation they enjoy around the world.

Château Latour Pauillac 1990 ❦ ❦ ④
A rich red in color, shading into crimson. Great abundance of fruit both on the nose and on the palate with concentrated flavors and an excellent acid-tannin balance. A wine out of the top drawer, which will only begin to give of its best after at least 10 to 15 years.

Les Forts de Latour Pauillac 1985 ❦ ❦ ④
Brilliant ruby red colour, with pinkish tones round the edges. The nose has sweet, fruity aromas with extremely elegant hints of menthol. Rich, well-rounded and soft on the palate, with delicate tannins. An elegant wine with a long finish. Delicious and ready to drink, it shows the rich style of this vintage. A great example of a second-label wine.

Château Latour Pauillac 1989 ❦ ❦ ❦ ④
The colour is stupendously dark and intense and the bouquet has a wealth of rich, velvety fruit which is evident again on the palate, where flavors of ripe blackcurrant dominate the still-developing tannins. A wine without perhaps the immediate impact of a Mouton or the finesse of a Margaux, it remains nevertheless one of the great Bordeaux of 1989 and an excellent Latour. It is a big, powerful wine with a rich texture well-integrated in extracts and acidity. A veritable iron fist in a velvet glove! This Château Latour can happily be laid down until the end of the century. It has all the features of a great Pauillac with the power and character to take its rightful place in the annals of its historic château.

Château Lynch-Bages

33250 Pauillac
Tel. 56732400
Fax 56292642

Classified as a fifth growth in 1855, today Château Lynch-Bages would in all probability be placed in the second category in a new ranking. It belongs to the tireless Jean-Michel Cazes and lies in the southern sub-zone of Pauillac, spread over 85 ha of gravel soil planted with Cabernet Sauvignon, Merlot and Cabernet Franc. The vineyards, with an average age of 35 years, provide excellent grapes. Less concentrated fruit, together with the harvest from younger vines, goes to make the second-label wine, Château Haut-Bages-Averous. Production amounts to 84,000 bottles of the second label and 420,000 of the premier label wine. The Lynch-Bages winery is modern with an appealing use of wood. The "chais" and tasting room are centered around a grass courtyard, with a Californian atmosphere. Wines ferment in stainless steel and then age in oak barrels for 12-15 months. Château Lynch-Bages is never a cheap wine but one can be certain that every bottle, even from a lesser vintage, represents the very best of the Médoc. Since 1987, a small quantity of white wine has also been produced from 4.5 ha. of Sauvignon Blanc, Sémillon and Muscadelle. For the time being, only 20,000 bottles are produced, but when Monsieur Cazes is involved, we can always expect surprises.

Château Lynch-Bages ④
Pauillac 1989
A wine with a magnificent rich, deep, silky appearance. Powerful, concentrated aromas of ripe berries with a hint of liquorice and aniseed. The palate has an outstanding texture and a range of elegant fruit which is complex, soft and ripe. The whole is supported by a tannins and acidity which bespeak a great wine.

Château Lynch-Bages ④
Pauillac 1988
Superbly rich in color with an elegant nose of ripe fruit, especially blackcurrant. Mouthfilling palate with liquorice to the fore and an underlying hint of autumn leaves. Excellent balance with outstanding strength and length. A great wine, which ought to feature in every connoisseur's cellar.

Château Lynch-Bages Pauillac 1987 🍇 ④
The appearance of this wine is already well developed, the aromas are clean, open and rounded. The same impression is left on the palate. A wine which is ready to drink with pleasure and satisfaction.

Rating System

🍇   An exemplary wine of its type with outstanding local character

🍇🍇   An international premium quality wine

🍇🍇🍇   A Top Wine, considered one of the 150 best wines in the world

The 'grape bunch' symbol is used to indicate the color of the wine; the number of bunches represents the quality rating assigned by the contributor

MEDOC/PAUILLAC
BORDEAUX
FRANCE

235

MEDOC/PAUILLAC
BORDEAUX
FRANCE

Château Mouton-Rothschild

33250 Pauillac
Tel. 56592020
Fax 56596054

Château Mouton-Rothschild is style. Perhaps only a dozen wines in the world equal its beauty, richness and power. Mouton's closest match is perhaps the herculean Latour, which whilst undeniably the same caliber and perhaps greater nobility, lacks Mouton's sheer vivacity and opulence, particularily when young. Much credit must go to the stylish and hardworking branch of the Rothschild family who has owned the château since 1853. Baron Philippe de Rothschild, who was at the helm from 1922 to 1988, did more than anyone to improve the quality and style of his wine. On the one hand, he made Mouton infinitely collectable by commissioning legendary labels from legends of the art world. On the other hand, in 1924, he laid down stringent and unheard of maxim that a wine must be bottle on the property to ensure its quality. Whilst failing to precipitate an overall re-classification of the Médoc estates he did achieve what he regarded as a correction of judgement when Mouton was promoted to a First Growth in 1973, the year Picasso put his name to the unfortunate vintage. Over the last few years the wine has become very consistent, a particular feat when 85% of the plantings are Cabernet Sauvignon. The 93-ha vineyards are planted on typically Pauillac gravel soil are vinified for as long as possible to achieve maximum extract. Mouton is well-known for its heavy but well-combined oakiness which it acquires during its two years in new casks.

Château Mouton-Rothschild   🍷🍷 ④
Pauillac 1990
An extremely intense color and a nose with hints of toasty oak, beautifully highlighted by clean, highly concentrated fruit. Good structure on the palate, with copious elegant, ripe fruit. Perhaps without the strength of the 1989, but with an elegance and texture which augur well for the future.

Château Mouton-Rothschild   🍷🍷🍷 ④
Pauillac 1989
Obtained from a selection of the estate's best grapes from vines at least 10 years old after unhurried fermentation and ageing for two years in barriques of new oak, this is a wine which is rich, deep and of great intensity in appearance. The bouquet is overwhelming with its notes of spice and berries, including blackcurrant. The first impression on the palate is that of exceptional fruit, followed by substantial tannins, already ripe and soft. Finally, it is the strength and depth of the flavors which reveal the true character of the wine. As it is already a pleasure to drink, many will do so now, well before the wine has reached full maturity. But whenever you do decide to drink it, you can be sure of having savoured an extraordinary Pauillac.

Château Pibran

1, rue Édouard-de-Pontet
33250 Pauillac
Tel. 56591443

Most of the Château Pibran vineyards are to be found in a valley near Château Mouton-Rothschild. The rather rich soil of the sub-zone gives the wine an even fuller-bodied flavor than that of its neighbors. In the past, this has led to the wine's having a reputation for being heavy, dark and difficult but all this changed when the AXA insurance giant bought the estate and put Jean-Michel Cazes in charge. The estate vineyards (60% Cabernet Sauvignon, 25% Merlot, 15% Cabernet Franc and Petit Verdot) extend over 9.5 ha. and give sufficient grapes to produce 10,000 bottles of wine a year. Slow fermentation takes place in temperature-controlled vats and the wine is the aged in the typical Cazes fashion in oak barrels for 12-15 months, with regular racking and clarification using egg whites. Cazes has only been in charge for a short time but the quality of the wine has improved beyond all expectations, and even the 1987, not generally considered a good vintage, produced flattering results.

Château Pibran Pauillac 1990　🍷🍷 ③
Both on the nose and on the palate, intense ripe fruit, dry tannins and outstanding structure and strength are in evidence. The concentration and style of this 1990 demonstrate not only the quality of the vintage but also the progress this château has made.

Château Pibran Pauillac 1989　🍷🍷 ③
Another rich, full-bodied wine but soft on the nose and frank and concentrated on the palate, where it proves to be both full and long. Without doubt, this is a powerful, direct red wine, excellent for drinking young but not without the texture characteristic of the 1990.

Bordeaux Appellations in this Guide

Bordeaux
Bordeaux

Bourgeais-Blayais
Premières Côtes de Blaye
Premières Côtes de Bourg

Entre-Garonne-et-Dordogne
Loupiac
Premières Côtes de Bordeaux
Sainte-Croix-du-Mont

Graves
Graves
Pessac-Léognan

Libournais
Canon-Fronsac
Côtes de Castillon
Côtes de Francs
Fronsac
Lalande de Pomerol
Pomerol
Saint-Emillon

Médoc
Haut-Médoc
Listrac
Margaux
Médoc
Moulis-en-Médoc
Pauillac
Saint-Estèphe
Saint-Julien

Sauternais
Barsac
Cérons
Sauternes

MEDOC/PAUILLAC
BORDEAUX
FRANCE

237

MEDOC/PAUILLAC
BORDEAUX
FRANCE

Château Pichon-Longueville

33250 Pauillac
Tel. 56731717
Fax 56731729

Château Pichon-Longueville lived for many years in the shadow of its illustrious neighbors Château Latour and Château Pichon-Lalande. In 1987, it was acquired by the AXA insurance group, which has aimed to give it an identity of its own by appointing as manager the dynamic Jean-Michel Cazes, owner of Château Lynch-Bages and Château Les Ormes-de-Pez. Cazes has made momentous strides in putting Pichon Baron back amongst its better known second growth neighbors. He has built a new, circular, warehouse known locally as the 'blockhouse', upgraded the entire winemaking process and has totally rennovated the château building itself. The 50 ha of vines (35 years-old on average) are carefully looked after. Three quarters of the vine stock is Cabernet Sauvignon and the rest Merlot, with a very small amount of Petit Verdot and Malbec, planted on gravel soil. Both alcoholic and malolactic fermentation take place in stainless steel at controlled temperatures, then the wines spend 12-15 months in the wood. Only the most concentrated wines are chosen for the Château Pichon-Longueville label, the rest going for the second wine, Les Tourelles de Longueville. The 1988, 1989, 1990 and even the 1987 have outstanding style, but all the château's wines (in all, about 25,000 cases a year) are immensely powerful but elegantly made.

Château Pichon-Longueville   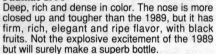 ④
Pauillac 1990
Deep, rich and dense in color. The nose is more closed up and tougher than the 1989, but it has firm, rich, elegant and ripe flavor, with black fruits. Not the explosive excitement of the 1989 but will surely make a superb bottle.

Château Pichon-Longueville   🍷🍷🍷 ④
Pauillac 1989
A wine with a depth and intensity of color which are quite incredible. The aromas are complex and concentrated, already disclosing hints of tar together with cool notes of mint. On the palate, the structure is powerful with flavors of smallblack berries, outstanding personality and excellent length. A great Pauillac which shows that the combination of investment in modern technology and the intelligent use of human resources can produce results which are simply exceptional. The progress made by this château in just three years is stunning and the potential of its wine seems unlimited. A true work of art.

MEDOC/PAUILLAC
BORDEAUX
FRANCE
                238
MEDOC/PAUILLAC
BORDEAUX
FRANCE

Château Pichon-Longueville
Comtesse de Lalande

33250 Pauillac
Tel. 56591940
Fax 56592978

One of the most striking châteaux in the Médoc, with its sparkling towers and soaring chimneys. The 75 ha of vineyards are spread out around the château on a series of gravelly plateaux between Château Latour and Château Pichon-Baron, on the far side of the road which links Pauillac to Saint-Julien. Before the death of Baron Joseph de Pichon-Longueville in 1850, the Richou Lalande and Pichon Baron estates were one. Since 1975, this estate has been owned by May-Eliane, daughter of Édouard Miailhe, from whom she inherited it in 1978. It has been very much thanks to the strength of character of May-Eliane de Lencquesaing that Pichon-Lalande has maintained such high standards, which perhaps deserve better than the classification of "deuxième cru". Pichon-Lalande wines are characterized by a softness and elegance due, at least in part, to the high percentage of Merlot in the vineyards (35%, the remainder being Cabernet Sauvignon, Cabernet Franc and Petit Verdot). The winemaking skills of the manager, Monsieur Godin, play an important part, as does the presence of Jean-Michel Cazes, a "wizard" of the Médoc, who tends to add "vine de presse" (the more tannic and astringent second pressing) thus perfectly controlling the structuring of his wines. Apart from the 350,000 bottles of Château wine, Pichon-Lalande also produces an excellent second wine, Réserve de la Comtesse, made from the young vines as well as certain vats not used for the final Château selection.

Château Pichon-Longueville 🍷🍷 ④
Comtesse de Lalande Pauillac 1986
The fragrance is wonderfully rich, with abundant ripe fruit, an excellent structure and a fantastic finish. The Cabernets are really beginning to make their presence felt in this wine.

Château Pichon-Longueville 🍷🍷 ④
Comtesse de Lalande Pauillac 1985
Rich color, superbly concentrated. The fragrance is of sweet, ripe fruit and the flavor is well-rounded and full, of great richness but fresh and well-balanced. A mature and fruity wine with fine structure.

Château Pichon-Longueville 🍷🍷🍷 ④
Comtesse de Lalande Pauillac 1989
A magnificently intense and dark color. The bouquet is outstandingly complex, with plenty of classy, chewy, ripe fruit which is found again on the palate, succulent and smooth, with an excellent structure on the background and a stunning finish. This wine's balance is quite unexpectedly fine as the Cabernets are really beginning to give of their best. At first, it seemed as if the wine had a delicate, softer side but, as Godin explains, Pichon-Lalande often has such a tendency when it is still in the barrique. It begins its life as pure first-pressing must with the second pressing being added drop by drop during the first year of ageing. This procedure allows a degree of control over the final structure of the wine and undoubtedly brings out its intrinsic characteristics. Perhaps this wine will not last forever, but it will give great satisfaction.

MEDOC/PAUILLAC
BORDEAUX
FRANCE

239

MEDOC/PAUILLAC
BORDEAUX
FRANCE

Château Pontet-Canet

33250 Pauillac
Tel. 56590404
Fax 56592663

Guy Teresson and his son, Alfred, are brave men. With passionate faith, they have dedicated themselves to re-establishing the declining reputation of the two châteaux Pontet-Canet and Lafon-Rochet. Pontet-Canet has 75 ha in one of the world's greatest winegrowing regions, right next door to Château Mouton-Rothschild. It used to make and sell mediocre wines that did not even come from its own vineyards. The estate began to bottle its own production when the Tesserons took over in the early 1970s. By the end of the 1980s, quality standards had already risen noticeably and Pontet-Canet was once again among the best producers in the area. All the right ingredients are there. The vines average 27 years-old and are planted in 68% Cabernet Sauvignon, 20% Merlot and 12% Cabernet Franc. The cellar is well-equipped and maintained. Moreover, with the second label, Les Hauts de Pontet, it has ensured that only the best of the harvest is used for the Château Pontet-Canet wines. The 1989 shows that this production policy is proving to be worthwhile.

Château Pontet-Canet Pauillac 1989 🍇 ③
Deep, rich color and a nose typical of the vintage. Soft and ripe with red fruit and a touch of the characteristic Pauillac liquorice. On the palate the wine is rich in ripe fruit, well-rounded and open. A pleasant, fruity red wine, to drink in the next three or four years.

Château Calon-Ségur

33180 Saint-Estèphe
Tel. 56593008
Fax 56597151

Château Calon-Ségur takes its name from a small river vessel called a "calon", which was used to transport wood from one side of the Gironde to the other in the Middle Ages. Once upon a time, the present Saint-Estèphe area was known as Les Calones. At the beginning of the 18th century, the Marquis of Ségur married a member of the family which owned not only this estate but also the châteaux of Latour and Lafite. The current manager of Calon-Ségur is Philippe Capbern Gasqueton, who took over from his uncle Édouard Gasqueton in 1962. The 94 ha of vines stand on gravel terrain. The average age is 35 years and the stock is half Cabernet Sauvignon, one quarter Cabernet Franc and one quarter Merlot. As is traditional in the area, the grapes are de-stemmed and then fermented for about two weeks in vats. In some years, must from a delicate second pressing is added to that from the first. Aging goes on for 24 months in oak barrels and the wine is clarified with egg white. After a period of inconsistent production, Château Calon-Ségur has managed in recent years to confound its critics for the vintages of the 1980s were quite simply outstanding, in the pure Saint-Estèphe style.

Château Calon-Ségur 🍇 ③
Saint-Estèphe 1990
Purple-red in color, with an as yet rather undeveloped nose which promises great things to come. Already, there are hints of cedar, blackcurrant, spices and wood. The palate is deep and rich, with lively tannins that are well-integrated with the fruit. A wine which will be great in a few years, if not 20 or so.

Château Cos d'Estournel

33180 Saint-Estèphe
Tel. 56731550
Fax 56597259

Château Cos d'Estournel rises majestically above high ground at the southern edge of Saint-Estèphe, opposite Château Lafite. It was built at the beginning of the 19th century, thanks to a devoted Louis-Gaspard d'Estournel, who was heir to one of the small plots of vineyard which cover the Cos hill. He put together other plots and created a great estate. Having a special affinity for India, d'Estournel began to restore his château in an oriental style. He did not have sufficient funds to complete the project and was forced to sell. In 1853, d'Estournel died broken hearted, two years before Château Cos was to gain its status of "deuxième cru". The owners who came after him maintained the prestige and quality of the wine and then in 1917, the property was acquired by Fernand Ginestet, whose grandson, Bruno Prats, has now taken over management. The terrain has a particularly gravelly nature and grows 60% Cabernet Sauvignon, with the rest Merlot and some Cabernet Franc. The Merlot tends to impart style and elegance in the Cos wine. The grapes are hand-picked and then de-stemmed, crushed and fermented in stainless steel at controlled temperatures. Production techniques, blending of varieties, aging and barrels, vary considerably from year to year and annual production of Cos d'Estournel ranges from 180,000 to 400,000 bottles, depending on how much wine goes for the second wine, Château de Marbuzet.

Cos d'Estournel
Saint-Estèphe 1991
This barrel-sampled wine turned out to be one of the vintage's stars. Very rich in color and a typical Cos nose with strong oakiness (it is aged in 90% new oak). The full-bodied palate is rich in fruit and of great strength and concentration. The estate, in fact, produced 30% less wine, given the difficult year.

Cos d'Estournel
Saint-Estèphe 1990
One of the most intense colors of the year, a nose rich in berries, which are present again on the palate and with a firm, yet somewhat rough, tannin backbone. In time, it will balance fruit acidity and tannins and will age well.

Cos d'Estournel
Saint-Estèphe 1989
This 1989 was a huge success and certainly has a very long and distinguished future ahead of it. A wine which shows its richness in color, which is intense and deep. On the nose, there is a real concentration of berries (especially cassis), with wood well in evidence. On the palate, the fruit is partially masked by the tannins, which are developing, but it is nonetheless ripe and of outstanding concentration. The oak is rather prominent but perfectly webbed into the texture of the wine. The body, which is full and powerful, will mellow out and guarantee superb aging.

MEDOC/SAINT-ESTEPHE
BORDEAUX
FRANCE

241

MEDOC/SAINT-ESTEPHE
BORDEAUX
FRANCE

Château Cos Labory

33180 Saint-Estèphe
Tel. 56593022
Fax 56597352

Cos Labory shares a pebble-strewn outcrop called Jalle du Breuil with the neighboring Cos d'Estournel and with Château Lafite on the far side of the road in Pauillac. For a while, it belonged to the London forwarding agent, Martyns, who also owned Cos d'Estounel. Today, under the ownership of the Audoy family, the quality of the wine is improving appreciably. Both the 1988 and the 1989 have color, structure and lots of fruit, contrary to the somewhat pale and tart wines of the past. All this is despite the fact that Bernard Audoy claims there have been no substantial changes in winemaking techniques. Nonetheless, an estate which a few short years ago barely merited the "cinquième cru" classification now makes excellent wines. Winemaking is traditional, with de-stemming, fermentation in cement and stainless steel vats for about 25 days and aging in barriques, half of which are new. Clarification with egg white is practiced as is some filtration. Traditional techniques like these work to make many illustrious wines, including those of Château Cos Labory, an estate to watch for in the next few years.

Château Cos Labory   🍇 ③
Saint-Estèphe 1989
A very well-made wine, without perhaps the class of the great Saint-Estèphes but indisputably attractive. Rich in appearance with fragrances of spices, ripe fruit and tar. Good strength and full on the palate.

Château Cos Labory   🍇🍇 ③
Saint-Estèphe 1988
An excellent example of a Saint-Estèphe, with good Cabernet character. Elegant on the nose and frank on the palate. Still a little closed but with power and a firm structure which promise a great future.

Château de Pez

33180 Saint-Estèphe
Tel. 56593007

Château de Pez has many unusual, if not unique, features. Once part of the Ormes de Pez estate, it is today one of the few properties with all its 23 ha in a single plot around the château itself. Cabernet Franc accounts for over 70%, with the rest being split between Cabernet Sauvignon and Merlot. Today, the Dusson brothers produce 144,000 bottles a year on the estate. Robert and Bernard-Franÿois Dusson's parents bought Château de Pez in 1920. Since then the Dusson family has unfailingly turned out wines with a vigorous, full-bodied style. The grapes are picked by hand and winemaking techniques are very traditional, with a long fermentation (three weeks) in wood. Wines are aged for 18 months in barrels (half of which are replaced every year) although in some special cases, like the 1990, they are given a little extra time. Fining with egg white but no filtering gives a product with the depth and concentration to age for many, many years.

Château de Pez Saint-Estèphe 1989   🍇 ③
Rich aromas of berries, with a generous grassy note of liquorice well-integrated with the wood. The palate has all the characteristics of the best Saint-Estèphes, being soft and full with a weight and structure which will enable the wine to age for a long time to come.

MEDOC/SAINT-ESTEPHE
BORDEAUX
FRANCE

242

MEDOC/SAINT-ESTEPHE
BORDEAUX
FRANCE

Château Haut-Marbuzet

33250 Pauillac
Tel. 56593054
Fax 565 97087

Winemaking is still very much a traditional art at Château Haut-Marbuzet. The grapes are de-stemmed and then fermented for a whole month in cement vats (practically obsolete nowadays) before being pressed. The free run wine is in some years enriched with the second, more tannic, pressing. The wine is not filtered, merely fined with egg white, and then aged in new oak for 18 months. This technique used by the owner and enologist Henri Dubosq is a luxury that only few great producers can afford. The wine made in this way is so extraordinarily full-bodied and rich in fruit that it can handle heavy-handed owk aging. Henri Dubosq also makes a second wine, Château Chambert-Marbuzet, which comes from a vineyard of 17 ha inside his 62-ha estate. The second label is aged in oak, half of which is new and the rest two years-old. The composition of the wines reflects that of the vine stock, with Cabernet Sauvignon dominating and small quantity of Cabernet Franc and Merlot. The terrain is somewhat gravelly and the plants are 35 years-old on average. Henri's two sons are studying enology. Hopefully they will continue to use their father's uncompromising techniques and ensure the Château's ongoing quality.

Château Haut-Marbuzet　　🍇 ③
Saint-Estèphe 1990
A wine of great concentration, with an abundance of rich fruit on both the nose and the palate. Aromas of black berries and a hint of tar. Powerful and firmly structured, it is a wine will need time to mellow in texture and to smooth the rough edges.

Château Haut-Marbuzet　　🍇 ③
Saint-Estèphe 1989
Very rich and deep in color, with intense new wood on the nose. Mouthfilling, with soft hints of liquorice and menthol. Still a little rough, but time and bottle-age will bring out the best of this fine wine.

Château Lafon-Rochet

33250 Pauillac
Tel. 56593206
Fax 5651605

When the Médoc began to enjoy increasing commercial success during the 1980s, little was left untried in the region's estates. Château Lafon-Rochet, like so many others, was restored to past glory by new owners, in this case the Tesserons, who ensured that it once again lived up to its 1855 classification of "quatrième cru". Guy Tesseron has re-equipped the cellar and the grapes from the 40 ha are no longer harvested by machine, because Guy believes that hand-picked fruit gives a better-quality wine. The de-stemmed grapes ferment in temperature-controlled stainless steel vats, where malolactic fermentation is completed before blending and aging in barrels for a year. About 30% of the barrels are new, the wine being fined and racked regularly into new barrels. A second wine, Château Lafon, is made from the fruit of the younger vines but is made and aged in the same way as the premier-label wine, being bottled a little earlier. The Tesserons' main efforts are devoted to their most important estate, Château Pontet-Canet, but Château Lafon-Rochet also seems to be on the road to success, judging by their last few vintages.

Château Lafon-Rochet　　🍇🍇 ③
Saint-Estèphe 1989
Very intense color and a complex bouquet of berries, green pepper and toasty wood. The palate discloses opulent fruit and mouthfilling tannins, lending the wine an impressive structure and a long finish.

MEDOC/SAINT-ESTEPHE
BORDEAUX
FRANCE

243

MEDOC/SAINT-ESTEPHE
BORDEAUX
FRANCE

Château Le Crock

Domaines Cuvelier
33180 Saint-Estèphe
Tel. 56864925
Fax 56865718

Château Le Crock is owned and managed by Didier Cuvelier, who has done so much in recent years to breathe life into the moribund Château Léoville-Poyferré. The success of Le Crock as a typical, well-made Saint-Estèphe "cru bourgeois" is due to its high-energy owner and the talented enologist Jacques Boissenot, responsible for many of the great wines of the Médoc. The Cuveliers have owned Château Le Crock since 1903, together with the smaller, nearby La Croix Saint-Estèphe. Altogether, there are 33 ha of vines, with an average age of 30 years. 61% of the vineyards are planted with Cabernet Sauvignon, 25% Merlot and 13% Cabernet Franc, with a tiny 1% Petit Verdot. The vineyards stand on a stony outcrop, with very little clay. It all goes to produce a wine which, after a long maceration and 18-20 months' aging in barrels one third of which are replaced every year, is solidly built and rich in concentrated fruit, needing time to express its potential to the full.

Château Le Crock
Saint-Estèphe 1989
Outstanding texture, with a fragrance of ripe blackcurrant and apple, blending with the soft aromas of the new wood. The palate is tannic but not rough, the fruit lively and the finish well-rounded and clean. To be drunk in the next few years.

Château Les-Ormes-de-Pez

c/o Château Lynch-Bages
33250 Pauillac
Tel. 56732400
Fax 56592642

Château Les-Ormes-de-Pez has belonged to the Cazes family for about 50 years and enjoys a fine and well-deserved reputation for its consistently excellent wines. Jean-Michel Cazes, grandson of the Jean-Michel Cazes who acquired the property, is a winemaking and estate management legend. In addition to supervising the production of at least six other estates on the left and right banks of the Garonne for the insurance group AXA, Cazes produces 15,000 cases of Les-Ormes-de-Pez a year and 35,000 cases of another wine, Château Lynch-Bages. The Les-Ormes-de-Pez vineyards extend over 32 ha, divided into two parcels, on sandy gravel and clay in the middle and northern parts of the territory of the commune of Saint-Estèphe. The vines are 30 years-old on average, with 55% Cabernet Sauvignon, 10% Cabernet Franc and 35% Merlot, this last being responsible for the fleshy, succulent style of the wine. Fermentation takes place in temperature-controlled stainless steel vats, lasting about 18 days before the transfer into wood two months after harvest. Ageing continues for 12-15 months, the wines being clarified with egg white. The end result is one of the Médoc's most enjoyable wines, unjustly underrated up to now.

Château Les-Ormes-de-Pez
Saint-Estèphe 1989
A wine of great strength, that will need a couple of years to express its full potential. The nose is rich, with ripe fruit, candied orange peel and tar, while the palate is fleshy and mature.

Château Les-Ormes-de-Pez
Saint-Estèphe 1988
Intense and deep in color, with a nose of rich, well-defined fruit. Body and structure amalgamate well on the palate. An elegant wine, without being overly ripe like the the previous year. It should develop well and burgeon into a great bottle of wine around the year 2000.

MEDOC/SAINT-ESTEPHE
BORDEAUX
FRANCE

244

MEDOC/SAINT-ESTEPHE
BORDEAUX
FRANCE

Château Lilian-Ladouys

33180 Saint-Estèphe
Tel. 56597196
Fax 56593597

Château Lilian-Ladouys is a new Saint-Estèphe estate build around a property which was very famous at the turn of the century. Christian and Lilian Thiéblot produced their first wine in 1989 from a vineyard originally of 75 ha which today has 48 planted with vines on average 30 years-old. Merlot comprises 37% of the total stock, in line with the general trend in Saint-Estèphe to use this variety to offset the force of the Cabernet. The remaining vines are 58% Cabernet Sauvignon and 5% Cabernet Franc. The estate lies in the middle of the commune's territory where the terrain slopes gently down to the river. It is very stony, with sand and chalky clay. The bunches are selected on conveyor belt before de-stemming. Different varieties and lots are separately fermented in temperature-controlled stainless steel vats for 25-30 days. The best batches are selected for Château Lilian-Ladouys and aged in Allier oak casks, at least 70% of which are new. The Thiéblots avoid filtering and believe that clarification with egg white and regular racking suffice. The wines already have an interesting style, with firm structure and good prospects.

Château Lilian Ladouys
Saint Estèphe 1991
An attractively bright red color. Clean, full-bodied and fruity on the nose. Well-rounded and balanced on the palate. The initial fruit is followed by a sensation of good tannin and acidity. A wine with medium-term prospects for aging, well-made and perfectly acceptable for its vintage.

Château Lilian Ladouys
Saint Estèphe 1990
Very rich, dark, deep and youthful in color. Full on the nose, rather oaky but well-rounded. On the palate, the first sensation is of ripe, chewy fruit. In the aftertaste, there are considerable wood tannins, good structure and fine length.

MEDOC/SAINT-ESTEPHE
BORDEAUX
FRANCE

245

MEDOC/SAINT-ESTEPHE
BORDEAUX
FRANCE

Château Montrose

33180 Saint-Estèphe
Tel. 56593012
Fax 56593848

The Charmolüe family has owned Château Montrose since 1889 and are now approaching their fifth generation on the property. Today, Jean-Louis Charmolüe has about 65 ha, lying to the south of Saint-Estèphe at the very northern edge of the Médoc. He produces about 230,000 bottles of Château Montrose as well as about 90,000 bottles of a generally excellent second wine, La Dame de Montrose. The vine stock is largely Cabernet Sauvignon and Cabernet Franc, with 25% Merlot. Harvesting is done by hand and the grapes ferment in stainless steel and oak vats, with 25 days' maceration. Aging is in barriques of Allier oak for about 18 months. One third of the barrels are replaced every year, the wine being racked every three months and clarified with egg white in the traditional Bordeaux manner. Under Jean-Louis Charmolüe, Château Montrose has witnessed considerable improvements in the quality of its wines over the last ten years. Perhaps this was helped by the fact that there were a plentiful amount of vintages in the 1980s when the Cabernet grape was able to reach full maturity.

Château Montrose
Saint-Estèphe 1989
🍇🍇 ③
A massively solid, full-bodied wine with a fragrance of very ripe black cherries. On the palate, it has well-rounded tannins and great concentration of fruit, giving the wine an agreeable softness over a very firm structure.

Château Montrose
Saint-Estèphe 1988
🍇🍇 ③
Intense, dark and regally rich in color. Still a little undeveloped on the nose and almost harsh on the palate despite good fruit. A Claret through and through, to lay down.

Château Montrose
Saint-Estèphe 1990
🍇🍇🍇 ③
Dense and rich in color, its bouquet is brimming with lots of fresh, ripe red fruit. The nose tends once again, at this stage, to red berries, on a rich, mouthfilling texture. Exceptional balance of tannins and acidity. Outstanding length. This wine is a great example of the finesse of the true Claret style of this vintage but is also a fine example of the remarkable wines produced at Château Montrose. This is a wine which may be laid down for 25-30 years. Like the 1989, so far its structure lies hidden under the typically fruity character common to both vintages, but this is a wine which will develop and open again once the tannins have finally mellowed.

MEDOC/SAINT-ESTEPHE
BORDEAUX
FRANCE
246
MEDOC/SAINT-ESTEPHE
BORDEAUX
FRANCE

Château Phélan-Ségur

33180 Saint-Estèphe
Tel. 56593009
Fax 56593004

In the mid-1980s, when Bordeaux was celebrating a series of outstanding vintages to ship to its eager markets, Château Phélan-Ségur was going through a very difficult period. In 1983, the 66 ha of vines were sprayed with a chemical that contaminated the wine, which then had to pulled from the shelves. It took over two years for the 30 year-old plants to recover. The 1984 and 1985 vintages were never made, and, in the meantime, the estate was sold to Xavier Gardinier. Thanks to his hard work the Château has not only survived but is producing some interesting wines. The varieties are largely Cabernet Sauvignon, with 30% Merlot and 10% Cabernet Franc on sandy gravel soil overlooking the Gironde just outside the village of Saint-Estèphe. 30,000 bottles of Château Phélan-Ségur a year are produced. together with 60,000 of a second wine, Frank-Phélan. The cellar is well-equipped, with stainless steel vats for fermentation. Wines age for 12-18 months in barriques, one third of which are replaced every year. Gardinier has recently produced four really good vintages, and Phélan-Ségur seems set to take a place among the top Bordeaux.

Château Phélan-Ségur
Saint-Estèphe 1990
Rich and deep in color, it is still rather closed and undeveloped on the nose. The palate has ripe, fruity blackcurrants and good balance. Not yet at its best and a little short in the finish.

Château Phélan-Ségur
Saint-Estèphe 1989
A very typical Saint-Estèphe. Medium-intense color, round but still tannic palate with a touch of mint in the finish. In need of bottle-age.

Château Phélan-Ségur
Saint-Estèphe 1988
A balanced, well-built red wine which has all the best qualities of a top-class Claret. An example of a good vintage with an additional touch of elegance. A wine worth waiting a few years for.

Château Pomys

Leyssac
33180 Saint-Estèphe
Tel. 56593226
Fax 56593524

The vineyard of this excellent "cru bourgeois", once as famous as Cos d'Estournel, has been painstakingly reorganized. Today it is a single plot cultivated skillfully by François Arnaud, who is the guiding light of the viticulturalists' union. His wines, made by traditional Médoc methods, are rich and tannic, perfect expressions of Cabernet grown on these soils. Best left alone when young, these "vins de garde" are unusually dense and full of promise for the future. Patience will be rewarded after a few years' bottle age. The splendid results of recent years have made Château Pomys, with its full, almost rustic color, one of the best examples of the AC and one of the most promising estates for the future. Château Saint-Estèphe is the second wine.

Château Pomys Saint-Estèphe 1990
A year in which the grapes ripened perfectly, with higher acidity than average, to produce an outstanding wine. The color is dark and deep. The nose is open and elegant. Powerful, still immature and tannic on the palate where fruit dominates in a finish of good length.

Château Pomys Saint-Estèphe 1989
Rich aromas of toasty wood and fruit, with an intense, deep color. A slightly rustic-style Saint-Estèphe, typical of the producer, and one which will probably develop and mellow with a few years' bottle age.

Château Pomys Saint-Estèphe 1988
Fine ruby color and an oaky nose on a background of gingerbread. Good structure on the palate, with well-developed tannins and a finish dominated by mineral flavors.

MEDOC/SAINT-ESTEPHE
BORDEAUX
FRANCE

247

MEDOC/SAINT-ESTEPHE
BORDEAUX
FRANCE

Château Tronquoy-Lalande

33180 Saint-Estèphe
Tel. 56355300-56593024
Fax 56355329

Tronquoy-Lalande is a 'real man's' Saint-Estèphe which has always had a reputation for its big, brawny and traditional wines. However, the percentage of Merlot in the blend has recently dramatically increased, giving the wine a more rounder style, albeit still well-structured and powerful. Château Tronquoy-Lalande is managed by Arlette Castéja, who took over after her husband's tragic death in 1973. She has struggled hard to put the estate, which belongs to the Dourthe brothers, on an even keel. The Dourthes are also sole distributors of the 90,000 bottles produced every year. Dourthe's enologist to Tronquoy-Lalande, Monsieur Couasnon makes very consistent wines using equal quantities of Cabernet Sauvignon and Merlot from the 17 ha of the estate. The vine stock, which includes a small quantity of Petit Verdot, is 25 years-old on average and grows on typically stony clay to the north of Château Montrôse. After a long, temperature-controlled fermentation, the wines spend a year in barriques, one third of which are replaced every year. Clarification is done by the classic Bordeaux methods, regular racking and fining with egg white. The results are generally of a high standard.

Château Tronquoy-Lalande 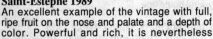 ③
Saint-Estèphe 1989
An excellent example of the vintage with full, ripe fruit on the nose and palate and a depth of color. Powerful and rich, it is nevertheless beginning to soften.

Domaine Castaing

Saint-Julien-Beychevelle
33250 Pauillac
Tel. 56592560

Domaine Castaing is a relatively unknown property in Saint-Julien whose proprietor, Jean-Jacques Cazeau, carefully makes wine in his own personal style and sell it all with ease. The vineyards were largely planted in the 1950s, although some are more than 70 years-old. The varieties are Cabernet Sauvignon (50%), Merlot (40%) and Cabernet Franc and Petit Verdot (10%) with very low and unpredictable yields, given the age of the vines, planted on stony terrain and on the black soil typical of a small area of Saint-Julien. The grapes are selected on harvesting and fermented in temperature-controlled cement and stainless steel vats. All the wine spends some time in oak (12 months on average), despite the fact that there are only about thirty barriques in the cellar, one third of which are replaced every year. Monsieur Cazeau, being a lober of tradition and coming from a long line of vignerons, is a traditionalist who does not believe in filtering. His tiny production reflects an individualism rare in the area.

Domaine Castaing ❦ ②
Saint-Julien 1986
Very rich and intense in color, with wild berry aromas. The palate is powerful with considerable tannic sinew and abundant concentration of fruit in the finish.

MEDOC/SAINT-ESTEPHE
BORDEAUX
FRANCE

248

MEDOC/SAINT-JULIEN
BORDEAUX
FRANCE

Château Branaire-Ducru

33250 Saint-Julien-Beychevelle
Tel. 56592586
Fax 56591626

Château Branaire-Ducru stands right opposite Château Beychevelle, on the other side of the Route du Vin. The present owners bought the 50-ha estate in 1988 and have entrusted its management to the very able Philippe Dhalluin. He is the man behind the success of the "cru bourgeois" Château Beaumont. The same thing seems to be happening at Branaire-Ducru, after a mediocre period in the mid 1980s. The 1989, 1990 and 1991 vintages have already shown that the château is capable of producing extraordinarily classy and vigorous wines, even in difficult years. The vine stock is 75% Cabernet Sauvignon, 22% Merlot and 3% Petit Verdot. The grapes are selected and de-stemmed, and then ferment in stainless steel vats before spending 12-18 months in barriques, 50% of which are replaced every year. Egg white is used for clarification and light filtration is carried out before bottling. Annual production is about 26,000 cases. On the basis of the last three vintages and the quality of the second wine, Château Duluc, prospects for this estate are definitely most interesting.

Château Branaire-Ducru
Saint-Julien 1990
A fine example of the progress made over the last few years by this estate. The wine is well-balanced, rich, clean and lively on the nose, and with great fruit on the palate.

Château Branaire-Ducru
Saint-Julien 1989
Deep intense color, with as yet undeveloped aromas. The initial impact on the palate is soft, with full, round fruit, while the finish is long and elegant. An excellent 1989, with sufficient structure to support the rich extracts.

Château Capdet

Rue de la Loi
33250 Saint-Julien-Beychevelle
Tel. 56591492

Château Capdet is a rather unusual estate. Gérard Capdet and his sister Annick have little more than half a hectare of vineyard, about half of which are Cabernet Sauvignon and half Merlot, both on average 50 years-old. These low-yielding vines produce barely enough wine for the 2,500-bottle average annual output but it is a wine made with 'une veritable passion'. Unfortunately, it is not easy to get hold of. The precious grapes are de-stalked and fermented in wooden vats. After malolactic fermentation, the various cuvées are blended and then transferred to barriques to age for two years. During this time, the wine is cleaned in the traditional manner by racking and fining with egg white, never by filtering. The powerful wine is not filtered and bottled at the château. One is unlikely to find any Capdet as it is mysteriously snapped up by ever faithful private clients and restaurants within France.

Château Capdet 1988
A Saint-Julien with the distinctive light and velvety character of the Appellation. A lovely garnet red color and a delicate nose of strawberry and cinnamon. The palate is soft and delicately toasty at first, with well-defined fruit, before a finish with a hint of kirsch.

MEDOC/SAINT-JULIEN
BORDEAUX
FRANCE

249

MEDOC/SAINT-JULIEN
BORDEAUX
FRANCE

Château Ducru-Beaucaillou

33250 Saint-Julien-Beychevelle
Tel. 56590520
Fax 56592737

When the wine press talks of a reclassifying the Grand Cru châteaux of the Médoc, one of the first names for elevation to first growth status is Ducru-Beaucaillou. In terms of price, prestige and demand, this is already universally considered to be one of the world's truly outstanding wines. Jean-Eugène Borie inherited the estate from his father in the 1950s and since then, he has worked tirelessly not only for Ducru but also for the entire Saint-Julien Appellation. The vineyards of Ducru-Beaucaillou are planted with Cabernet Sauvignon (65%), Merlot (25%), Cabernet Franc and Petit Verdot over an area of 50 ha famous for the depth of its 'beautiful pebbles". Borie, who works alongside his son, Xavier, lives over the "shop", as he calls the cellar. The grapes are harvested very late then de-stemmed before fermenting slowly in cement vats. Aging is in barrels which are 20-50% new for 12 to 18 months, depending on the vintage. The wine is not filtered, only fined with egg white. Ducru-Beaucaillou is not only the slowest developer but also the longest lived of all the Saint-Juliens. Annual production is of about 240,000 bottles, plus a small quantity of second wine, called Lacroix, sold exclusively through the shipper Lebegue.

Château Ducru-Beaucaillou 🍇 ④
Saint-Julien 1988
Rich and deep color, slightly young, unevolved aromas and a fresh note of spices with a touch of toasty oak on the palate. Austere texture. A wine for the future.

Château Ducru-Beaucaillou 🍇🍇 ④
Saint-Julien 1986
The color testifies to the richness of the fruit, which is again evident on the nose. Elegant palate, very tannic but with good intensity and balance. A truly classic wine from a good vintage, typical of Ducru.

Château Ducru-Beaucaillou 🍇🍇🍇 ④
Saint-Julien 1989
The color is majestic. The nose has great concentration but also all the finesse of ripe fruit. There is the same impressive richness of extract on the palate, together with great elegance. A classic example of the excellent Ducru-Beaucaillou, a wine which makes up in elegance what it might lack in structure. This is however a solid Saint-Julien and while agreeably drinkable, has tannins which guarantee a great future. In contrast to the wines of Léoville or Pichon, many recent vintages of Ducru-Beaucaillou, like this 1989, have a slight tendency to lack personality when tasted young and it is only after a lengthy sojourn in the cellar that the wine's true characteristics become apparent. Experience proves that it is a wine well worth waiting for.

MEDOC/SAINT-JULIEN
BORDEAUX
FRANCE

250

MEDOC/SAINT-JULIEN
BORDEAUX
FRANCE

Château Gruaud-Larose

33250 Saint-Julien-Beychevelle
Tel. 56314444
Fax 56313003

Even though at the time of going to press uncertainty surrounds the future of the Cordier empire, it is unlikely that a change of ownership will affect the quality of Château Gruaud-Larose, a huge estate with remarkably high standards. The 84 ha of vineyards are located on a stony plateau to the west of Château Beychevelle and are planted with 63% Cabernet Sauvignon, 25% Merlot, 8% Cabernet Franc and 4% Petit Verdot (average age, 25-30 years). The grapes are de-stemmed before fermentation, which takes place in glass-fibre vats. After malolactic fermentation, the wines are blended, with the addition of 6-8% of second-pressing wine. Cuvées not considered up to the standards of the Château label are used for the second wine, Sarget de Gruaud-Larose. Both wines age in oak, with one third of the barrels replaced every year, for 20-22 months. Gruaud-Larose is one of the most dependable, top quality "deuxième cru" wines in the Médoc.

Château Gruaud-Larose
Saint-Julien 1989
A wine with superb body, rich color, fine bouquet and excellent flavor. Typical Gruaud aromas of toasted wood with hints of chocolate and game, and power which also comes over on the palate.

Château Gruaud-Larose
Saint-Julien 1988
Very concentrated and direct on the nose, with well-defined aromas of tobacco and cedar as well as the Gruaud-Larose gamey and chocolate notes. The highly concentrated fruit is well supported on the palate by a solid tannic texture. A wine which will amaze future generations of tasters.

Château Lagrange

33250 Saint-Julien-Beychevelle
Tel. 56592363
Fax 56592609

The Japanese drinks group, Suntory, purchased this château in 1983. Since then, it has completely refurbished the otherwise neglected property. Lagrange used to be the biggest estate in the Médoc, with as much as 200 ha under cultivation at the end of the 19th century. In 1983, only 56 were in production but under the careful management of Marcel Ducasse, replanting has brought the total to 113 ha, with an output of about 600,000 bottles. 40% of production is sold under the name Château Lagrange with the rest being sold as Les Fiefs de Lagrange, the second label. The varieties are typical of the Médoc, two thirds Cabernet Sauvignon and the remainder Merlot with the exception of a small quantity of Petit Verdot. Grapes are hand-picked and fermented in temperature-controlled stainless steel vats. Blending takes place after malolactic fermentation, after which the wines are transferred to barriques, half of which are new, for 16-20 months. Marcel Ducasse has done a splendid job. If Lagrange is not yet one of the great Saint-Juliens, it is well on its way.

Château Lagrange
Saint-Julien 1990
Solid, deep and rich in color. The nose is elegant, with hints of ripe fruit which are also present on the full, well-rounded palate. A wine with a tender heart but nonetheless well-built with good tannins. It is still a little lacking in suppleness but has good concentration and will certainly develop well.

Château Lagrange Saint-Julien 1989
Lovely full, intense color. Still a little undeveloped and harsh on the nose, but the palate promises a velvety softness. A wine rich in fruit with a tannic finish still lacking complete balance.

MEDOC/SAINT-JULIEN
BORDEAUX
FRANCE

251

MEDOC/SAINT-JULIEN
BORDEAUX
FRANCE

Château Langoa-Barton

33250 Saint-Julien-Beychevelle
Tel. 56590605

A "troisième cru" which has belonged to the Barton family since 1821 and represents, together with de Rothschild, the only family name to be found in the 1855 classification. Behind the great green gates, the magnificent 17th-century Carthusian monastery preserved in original style by the architect Rigby A. Lee is scrupulously maintained by Anthony Barton, an Irishman born in County Kildare and one of Bordeaux's great gentlemen. The rooms of the château, filled with the family heirlooms, glow with an awra of calm strength and serenity. The wine produced here on an 20-ha estate is more 'feminine', in Anthony Barton's opinion, than that of the family's other property, Château Léoville-Barton (a "deuxième cru classé"). Whatever the case, both wines are well on their way to becoming Grands Crus. Here at Château Langoa-Barton, great wine is venerated as an art form.

Château Langoa-Barton
Saint-Julien 1990
Aged, like the estates other wines, in the new cellar which bears Thomas Barton's name. Dark ruby color, nose of great elegance and intensity with a hint of blackcurrant in the fruit and an almost mineral quality. A wine with a pronounced tannic structure; rich and without astringency right to the finish.

Château Langoa-Barton
Saint-Julien 1989
A lovely dark color from grapes of outstanding quality. Complex nose which tends to cedar with faint smoky overtones. Smooth on the palate with still undeveloped tannins and an elegant structure. The finish is delicate, and the wine will peak in about three or four years.

Château Langoa-Barton
Saint-Julien 1988
An attractive dark color with hints of blue, again the result of fierce selection in the vineyard. Aromas of super-ripeness and discreet notes of wood on the nose. The lovely tannins are already integrated on a round and fleshy palate. The finish bodes well for the future.

Lady Langoa Saint-Julien 1988
A second wine, but still a top quality product which is drinking well now, while the château's more prestigious crus are still unready. Fine in structure, with an elegant nose and a well-rounded, sensuous palate.

Château Léoville-Barton

33250 Saint-Julien-Beychevelle
Tel. 56590605

Thomas Barton, the age-old figure behind this Bordeaux-based this Irish family, was known to his friends as French Tom. His grandson, Hugh, purchased Léoville-Barton on 25 May, 1826. Ever since he took over the estate 1983, the good name of the family has been upheld by Anthony Barton. Having recently recived an offer to sell Léoville-Barton for a fantastic sum of money, Anthony replied that one would have to be mad to turn down such an offer. Of course, the middleman thought that the deal had been struck by then. When he suggested they get down to business, Barton exclaimed "No, after all, I am mad"! This madman has worked since 1984 with an energetic manager, Michel Raoult, and has upgraded the equipment, increased the area under vines (now 40 ha) and acquired new wooden and stainless steel vats. The old barrique cellar has been renovated and a new one, capable of holding 1,600 barriques, has been built. Despite the tragic loss of his son Thomas (his daughter Lilian also works on the estate), Anthony Barton continues to live up to the family motto "Fide et Fortitudine", with faith and courage.

Château Léoville-Barton
Saint-Julien 1990
Rigorous bunch selection makes this a great wine. The color is very intense, almost blue-tinted. The fragrances of berries blend with flowery, violet notes. Rich, complete body and a perfect balance of alcohol and acidity. Great structure with marked tannins well-integrated, with the fresh and candied fruit flavors.

Château Léoville-Barton
Saint-Julien 1988
Deep in color with a marked tendency towards shades of blue. The aromas are of unusual complexity on a background of elegant toasted oak and ripe fruit. The structure on the palate is rich and deep, with vigorous tannins, and great breeding. The finish is satisfyingly long. Clearly needs more time to develop.

Château Léoville-Barton
Saint-Julien 1987
One of the best wines of its vintage in the whole Médoc. Garnet color. Well-defined fragrances of spice over a cocoa background. The body is elegant on the palate with agreeably developed tannins while the finish has hints of oaky vanilla.

MEDOC/SAINT-JULIEN
BORDEAUX
FRANCE

252

MEDOC/SAINT-JULIEN
BORDEAUX
FRANCE

Château Léoville-Las-Cases

33250 Saint-Julien-Beychevelle
Tel. 56592526
Fax 56591833

Travelling north along the busy D2, as one leaves the village of Saint-Julien one comes to the daunting gateway of the Château Léoville-Las-Cases, a "deuxième cru classé". The estate is managed by Michel Delon, owner of Château Potensac and one of the wine market's top experts. Most of the 95-ha vineyard is in the "clos" that shares a border with Château Latour. The vine stock, on gravel soil, is on average 35 years-old, having been largely replanted in the 1950s. The most concentrated grapes go towards the Château-label wine while the grapes from the younger plants make the excellent second wine, Clos du Marquis, which accounts for one fifth of total production. Two thirds of the varieties are Cabernet Sauvignon, with 19% Merlot, 13% Cabernet Franc and a small quantity of Petit Verdot. The de-stemmed grapes ferment for 15-20 days at 28°C in a combination of cement, oak and stainless steel vats. Aging is in oak barrels for 18-20 months, depending on the vintage. Las Cases' quality shows right through even on lesser vintages, like the 1987 that Monsieur Delon cunningly held back until 1990 before releasing at a reasonable price - at a time when reason was impossible to find in the Médoc.

Clos du Marquis   🍇🍇 ③
Saint-Julien 1988
A deep, full red in color with a nose that is still a little closed but fresh and fruity. The palate offers a wealth of clean fruit and satisfying structure. A wine which will need another four or five years before it is ready. Unlike nearly every other second wine, this Clos du Marquis could, in a blind tasting, happily bear comparison with a premier-label Saint Julien.

Grand vin de Léoville   🍇🍇🍇 ④
du Marquis de Las-Cases Saint-Julien 1988
An intense red color with typically rich, elegant aromas. The palate is still undeveloped with prominent flavors of firm fruit but also with good balance. Perhaps closer to the traditional idea of a drinking wine than the 1989 and certainly a bottle with a great future, thanks to its formidable tannins.

Grand Vin de Léoville   🍇🍇🍇 ④
du Marquis de Las-Cases Saint-Julien 1989
A wine of a truly majestic color, rich and intense, with a nose still a little undeveloped and hard but with an enormously rich, superb palate, wonderful balance and impressive length. One of the best wines of the vintage in which the ripe and complex fruit and soft tannins typical of the year are complemented by the character of the wood and the structure of a Léoville-Las-Cases at its outstanding best. Most certainly a wine to lay down. Monsieur Delon and his team carried out long, painstaking research for this, as for so many other of their wines, to obtain a Grand Cru Classé with the precise characteristics of Saint Julien, that would be superior in structure and sheer class compared to the wines of neighboring communes. Year after year, it is a wine to tuck away in the cellar. When the reclassification of the Médoc finally takes place, it will deservedly achieve the rank of Premier Grand Cru Classé, together with Latour, Margaux, Mouton Rothschild, Lafite and Haut-Brion.

MEDOC/SAINT-JULIEN
BORDEAUX
FRANCE

253

MEDOC/SAINT-JULIEN
BORDEAUX
FRANCE

Château Léoville-Poyferré

33250 Saint-Julien-Beychevelle
Tel. 56590830
Fax 56596009

Baron Poyferré bought Château Léoville-Poyferré, one quarter of the original Léoville estate, after the French revolution. In the 1920s, wine from this château was regarded as the best of the three Léoville products, but, unfortunately, since then it has lapsed. It was not until 1979, when Didier Cuvelier decided to take an active interest in the management of Léoville-Poyferré, that the turn-around came. Since then, the wines have made constant progress, and their modest price makes them excellent value for money. The vines are an average 25 years-old and grow on 60 ha of gravel and sandy soil. Two thirds of the varieties are Cabernet Sauvignon and one quarter Merlot, with a little Cabernet Franc and Petit Verdot. Enologist Jacques Boissenot oversees the traditional methods used in winemaking, with aging in oak barrels lasting 20-24 months. 50-75% of the barrels are replaced each year. A further 20 ha produce the grapes for a second wine, Château Moulin-Riche, which is also of good quality. The whole estate has considerable potential, although it has still to show that it can equal the complexity of the neighboring Château Léoville-Las-Cases.

Château Léoville-Poyferré
Saint-Julien 1990
A wine characterized by fresh, rich fruit both on the nose, where there is also an elegant note of wood, and on the palate, where it is warm and full-bodied. Excellent balance and excellent prospects for laying down.

Château Léoville-Poyferré
Saint-Julien 1989
Without the elegance of the 1990 but perhaps fuller and richer in fruit. Well-rounded and soft on the palate, also showing great power and depth with a vanillaed note of oak. A great bottle.

Château Léoville-Poyferré
Saint-Julien 1988
A slightly paler color than the subsequent vintages but still of a rich red. Excellent structure, clean and dry in the finish after a soft, well-rounded initial impact. A wine which will age well.

Château Saint-Pierre

33250 Saint-Julien-Beychevelle
Tel. 56590818
Fax 56591618

Like many other estates, the property of Château Saint-Pierre was divided for many years as a result of the French laws on inheritance. It was united again in 1920. The owner, Alfred Martin, busy making his fortune as a cooper, installed himself in the cellar while his son Henri who preferred to devote himself to viticulture built up Château Gloria, a very successful Saint-Julien. Henri then bought Saint-Pierre in 1982 and since then has combined both châteaux in a single estate. Classified as a fourth growth in 1855, like many other wines in the lower categories, it is very similar in quality to its nominal superiors. The estate extends over 17 ha which are largely planted with Cabernet Sauvignon, with only 20% Merlot and 10% Cabernet Franc. The grapes are fermented in the brand-new Château Gloria cellar and age for from 13 to 18 months, half in large oak barrels and half in new barriques. The wine, which then spends some time in vats, provides 5,000 cases of a very well-built Saint-Julien.

Château Saint-Pierre
Saint-Julien 1989
Ruby color with shades of purple and a nose of berries and toasted oak. The palate is very rich with full fruit to sustain the ample tannins of the new oak.

MEDOC/SAINT-JULIEN
BORDEAUX
FRANCE
254
MEDOC/SAINT-JULIEN
BORDEAUX
FRANCE

Château Talbot

33250 Saint-Julien-Beychevelle
Tel. 5624280
Fax 56422880

Most English Claret-lovers will have at least a few bottles of Château Talbot hidden away. Whether their success in Britain over the years has more to do with its worth as a wine or as a rich topic of conversation around its split English and French past, and John Talbot, Earl of Shrewsbury, is very debatable. Classified in 1855 as a fourth growth, today Château Talbot produces a quality wine definitily beyond this status from the grapes grown on its single, 107-ha vineyard. Often compared to the nearby Château Gruaud-Larose because the same winemaking techniques are used, Château Talbot produces a Saint-Julien which is more noteworthy for its elegance than for its power, the result of more Merlot grapes, which are backed by Cabernet Sauvignon and small quantities of Cabernet Franc and Petit Verdot. Wines age for 18 months in oak barriques, one third of which are replaced every year, are racked regularly and are fined with egg white. Annual production is about 600,000 bottles, including the second wine, Connétable. Jean Cordier, the present owner, has begun to experiment with a white wine, turning out 48,000 bottles from Sauvignon grapes under the label Le Caillou Blanc.

Château Talbot Saint-Julien 1989 🍇🍇 ③
A deep ruby color with intense aromas of blackcurrant, mulberries and green pepper. The palate has flavors of red fruit jam, chocolate and spices with robust tannins.

Domaine du Jaugaret

33250 Saint-Julien-Beychevelle
Tel. 56590971

Jean-François Fillastre learned to make wine when he was a youngster working alongside his father and grandfather. The Fillastre family has owned this 7-ha property since 1654 and growing and winemaking techniques have been handed down almost unchanged from generation to generation. The vineyard (only about one hectare is cultivated) is looked after by Jean-François, his two brothers, his sister and their respective families. The vine stock is two-thirds Cabernet Sauvignon and one-third Merlot, with a little malbec. The plants have an average age of over 50 years and give very low yields. The grapes are carefully selected and de-stemmed before the must goes into wooden vats for a fermentation lasting three to four weeks.A small quantity of the press is wine used in the final blend, which is aged for three years in Allier oak barrels, only 15-20% of which are replaced each year. Fillastre cleans his wines using only regular racking and fining with egg white. The 3-4,000 bottles produced every year are quickly snapped up and this is no surprise, considering that this Saint-Julien beautifully combines the best of the old and new Médoc styles.

Domaine du Jaugaret 🍇 ③
Saint-Julien 1989
Transparent, fairly light but brilliant. Powerful nose with a strong hint of oak. The palate is well-rounded, with flavors of mint and good fruit. Reasonably elegant, despite its slightly rustic character, it is an exception to the modern-style wines generally produced in the zone.

MEDOC/SAINT-JULIEN
BORDEAUX
FRANCE

255

MEDOC/SAINT-JULIEN
BORDEAUX
FRANCE

Château Broustet

33720 Barsac
Tel. 57247079
Fax 57246800

Eric Fournier, who makes the rich and powerful Château Canon wine at Saint-Emilion, also makes one of the most attractive wines in Barsac, in a light floral style. Château Broustet is a Deuxième Cru of 16 ha which produces a mere 24,000 bottles a year from Sémillon grapes (63%), Sauvignon (25%) and Muscadelle (12%), which are on average 40 years-old. The yields are typically low because of the painstaking selection of the most botrytized grapes with the most concentrated juice. Fermentation takes place at controlled temperatures in stainless steel vats. The wine is then aged in barrels which are only one third new, a fact which explains the elegant style. Although not quite on a par with the great Château Climens, Broustet is without doubt amongst the half dozen other leading and top quality Barsac châteaux, and its prices over recent vintages have suffered the consequences of this.

Château Broustet Barsac 1988 ☙ ③
Yellow-gold color with a nose strongly characterized by the fragrance of lemon marmalade, biscuits and peaches, typical of botrytis. The pleasant fruit is supported on the palate by lively acidity and a moderate level of alcohol.

Château Caillou

33720 Barsac
Tel. 56271638
Fax 56270960

Château Caillou was classified as a Deuxième Cru in 1855. Its vineyards are situated just north of Château Climens and south of Château Coutet in the commune of Barsac. The varieties are Sémillon (90%) and Sauvignon (10%), planted on sandy and stony clay and limestone soil (the name "Caillou" means stone). Owned by the Bravo family for three generations since 1909, the estate produces robust, yet sophisticated wines. This feature is largely explained by the winemaking methods, which are a little unusual. The must is fermented in stainless steel-covered vats and then the wines spend the winter in cement. At the end of this period, part of the wine goes into barrels and the rest remains in the cement for six months before being transferred to barriques for two years' aging. Jean-Bernard Bravo produces 35,000 bottles of Barsac, 6,000 bottles of Vin Sec de Château Caillou under the Bordeaux Appellation and finally 5,000 bottles of La Private Cuvée du Château Caillou, a wine which was once able to be sold as Crème de Tête and which represents the very best of the year's production.

Château Caillou Barsac 1988 ☙ ③
An excellent example of the brilliant, flavorful Barsac style. The lemon yellow color is most attractive and the nose is magnificently fragrant with hints of orange blossoms and pineapple. Elegant and fresh on the palate, a wine with a long, refreshing finish.

SAUTERNAIS/BARSAC
BORDEAUX
FRANCE

256

SAUTERNAIS/BARSAC
BORDEAUX
FRANCE

Château Cantegril

33720 Barsac
Tel. 56271584
Fax 56271899

As well as owning and managing the magnificent Château Doisy-Daëne, Pierre Dubordieu and his son, Denis, run the Château Cantegril. It was not classified as a Grand Cru in 1855, but it did share part of its estate with the Deuxième Cru, Château Mirat (which sadly no longer makes wine) until 1882, when a court ruled that the two should be separated. Today, Cantegril has 20 ha planted on sandy, clay and limestone Barsac terrain. 70% of the varieties are Sémillon, with the rest Sauvignon and Muscadelle. The harvest is carefully executed in stages to obtain the best quality from the ripe, botrytized grapes. Vinification is carried out in exactly the same manner as at Doisy-Daëne, with generous use of new oak, aging for 24 months and light clarification with egg whites. About 50,000 bottles a year of excellent quality Barsac with a distinct personality are produced, much of it for sale to the restaurants of Paris.

Barsac Château Cantegril 1990   ❦ ❦ ③
Brilliant yellow-gold, with a delicate and complex nose that has scents of honey, orange, almonds and tropical fruit. On the palate, it is subtle and rich with pineapple, oranges and fruit cocktail flavors that last a long time.

Price levels

①   up to $ 9.99

② $ 10.00 - $ 14.99

③ $ 15.00 - $ 24.99

④ $ 25.00 or more

The 'ex-cellar', or direct from the producer, bottle prices, are calculated in US dollars and are intended only as an approximate guide

SAUTERNAIS/BARSAC
BORDEAUX
FRANCE

257

SAUTERNAIS/BARSAC
BORDEAUX
FRANCE

Château Climens

33720 Barsac
Tel. 56271533
Fax 56272104

Brigitte Lurton-Belondrade seems to have a considerable following for the beauty of her eyes, as much as the beauty of her wines. They are small masterpieces which seem to be ever closer to the lofty pedestal occupied by Château d'Yquem. Climens is the quintessence of Barsac, intense, delicate and firmly structured, exquisitely refreshing and therefore somewhat different from the pure concentration and intensity of Yquem. Mentioned for the first time as a vineyard in 1640, Château Climens has passed from one illustrious owner to another over the centuries, until Lucien Lurton acquired it in 1971. The 25 ha produce about 50,000 bottles a year of a fragant gold liquid. Almost all the vine stock is Sémillon (only 2% Sauvignon) and the average age is 25 years. The vines stand on reddish sand and chalky clay, benefiting from the morning mists frequent in the area which are ideal for botrytis. The grapes are harvested in four stages and naturally the last are the best in terms of concentration. Fermentation and aging are in oak barrels, with the sugars halting fermentation and oxidization naturally. In some years, the estate produces a second wine, Les Cyprès de Climens which while not having the intensity and concentration of Château Climens, does preserve its finesse and elegance.

Château Climens Barsac 1988 🍇🍇 ④
Rich, bright color and an elegant, delicate nose which is fresh, with hints of candied orange peel. Quite fantastic on the palate, with opulent fruit, full of power and depth. A great bottle which will happily keep for the next generation.

Château Climens Barsac 1990 🍇🍇🍇 ④
The result of fanatical selection of the grapes (Sémillon with a small percentage of Sauvignon Blanc) affected by botrytis and harvested in several runs to pick only the richest and most concentrated bunches. The very best of Barsac. The rich and brilliant yellow-gold color is rich and enticing. The aromas are unbelievably concentrated, subtle and of great complexity as is typical of Château Climens. On the palate, the wine is full of honeyed fruit and is fine, long and intense. Perfectly balanced, despite its sheer power of personality and the sweetness of its fruit. This is a very rewarding wine to drink. It could convert even the more sceptical wine-drinkers to the pleasures of sweet wine.

SAUTERNAIS/BARSAC
BORDEAUX
FRANCE

258

SAUTERNAIS/BARSAC
BORDEAUX
FRANCE

Château Coutet

33720 Barsac
Tel. 56271546
Fax 56270220

Château Coutet, originally owned by the Lur-Saluces family, shares its style of architecture with Château d'Yquem and the design of its label with Château Filhot. The estate is currently run by the Costantins on behalf of the new owner, Monsieur Baly, who is from Alsace. In addition to the main sweet wine, there is a small quantity of a second wine known as La Chartreuse de Coutet and a dry white wine. Very occasionally about a thousand bottles of the legendary Cuvée Madame appear, an immensely rich sweet wine made exclusively from the best grapes of great vintages. Vinification at Coutet is very traditional. After fermentation, the wine is aged in oak barrels, one quarter of which are replaced every year. Clarification with egg whites is carried out before bottling and filtering is done only if absolutely necessary. Classified as a Premier Cru in 1855, Château Coutet produces about 90,000 bottles each year from its outstanding 38 ha of limestone terrain planted with Sauvignon and Muscadelle (27%).

Château Coutet Barsac 1989   ☙ ☙ ④
Rich, bright lemon yellow color with intense aromas of wood and honey, with hints of petrol. The wine has an excellent balance between sweetness and acidity, and between fruit and structure, despite the considerably high alcohol.

Château Coutet Barsac 1988   ☙ ☙ ④
Paler than the 1989, an elegant wine with the intense botrytis character that is very evident on the nose. On the palate, it has all the sweet opulence of marmalade and cream, with a long, long finish.

Château Doisy-Daëne

33720 Barsac
Tel. 56271584
Fax 56271859

Pierre Dubourdieu owns the "deuxième cru" of Château Doisy-Daëne, an estate which produces a wine with a mature, fleshy character from 14 ha of Sémillon, used alone to produce the AC Barsac, Sauvignon and Muscadelle (which are used for a dry Doisy-Daëne in the Graves style). The terrain here is sand and clay on a limestone sub-soil, and the vine stock averages 35 years of age. The grapes are picked in as many as eight runs during the harvest and the wine is then fermented and aged in barrels for 24 months. It is clarified with egg white and filtered before bottling. The 50,000 bottles are cellared before release. Pierre and his son Denis have rebuilt the estate after having bought Château Doisy Dubroca. Since the early 1980s, their efforts have been rewarded by excellent wines, the most refined of which was the 1983.

Château Doisy-Daëne Barsac 1989   ☙ ④
In a year where many of these wines were overblown and alcoholic, this wine is rich and up-front with its marmalade and honey botrytis fruit, but admirably well-balanced with good acidity and a long, clean finish.

Château Doisy-Daëne   ☙ ☙ ④
Barsac 1988
Rich gold in color, this wine is very much botrytis dominated on the nose with lots of over-ripe tropical fruits. The palate is beautifully structured, refreshing but very bisquity and pinapply.

SAUTERNAIS/BARSAC
BORDEAUX
FRANCE

259

SAUTERNAIS/BARSAC
BORDEAUX
FRANCE

Château Gravas

33720 Barsac
Tel. 56271520
Fax 56272983

Pierre Bernard became a legend in France when he fell into a vat of the family Sauternes, an episode which he claims had a positive effect on him. The Bernard family have been making wine at Château Gravas since 1740 and their philosophy is simple. All factors are taken into consideration, but in the end, the wine itself dictates the various operations in the cellar. The vine stock is mainly Sémillon growing on chalky clay in the commune of Barsac. The grapes are harvested in five separate selections and are then fermented and aged apart, to be blended just before bottling. After crushing in a horizontal press, the must ferments first in stainless steel and then in barrels for three to four weeks. The wine is then aged in barriques for a period which is decided according to the individual circumstances. Bernard's two children are very busy, not only at Château Gravas but also at Château Duc d'Armauton in the Graves at a family property of 18 ha which produces 100,000 of both red and white Graves wine every year. About half is exported to Australia.

Château Gravas Sauternes 1988 ❦❦ ④
Rather pale in color with a fresh and delicate botrytis nose with scents of orange blossoms, pineapple and marmalade. Very soft on the palate with notes of almonds and honey, a superb texture, good body but also good fresh acidity in the finish.

Château Nairac

33720 Barsac
Tel. 56271616
Fax 56272650

The Nairacs were a powerful Huguenot family who built this property in 1786. The château was ranked as a "deuxième cru" in 1855 but sadly fell in decline until it was bought by Nicole Tari-Heeter and her American husband, Tom, in 1971. Today, it ranks high among Barsac estates. Production is carefully monitored, and if the wine fails to come up to the required quality standards, it is sold off wholesale. Grapes from the different selections are crushed in a hydraulic vertical press and ferment in new oak barrels at controlled temperatures. They age in the wood for about 30 months, during which time they may be blended before the final 'mélange', two months before bottling. Madame Tari-Heeter is not an admirer of filtration and limits herself to regular racking, pointing out that her wines require at least a dozen years before they begin to approach maturity. Undoubtedly the structure that comes from 90% Sémillon growing on well-drained sandy gravel and limestone terrain gives Nairac wine a capacity for aging which is out of the ordinary.

Château Nairac Barsac 1990 ❦❦ ④
The sweet and very rich fruit of this wine gives the nose aromas with notes of pineapple well to the fore. The palate is very elegant and firm, with good length.

SAUTERNAIS/BARSAC
BORDEAUX
FRANCE

260

SAUTERNAIS/BARSAC
BORDEAUX
FRANCE

Château Piada

33720 Podensac
Tel. 56271613
Fax 56272630

Château Piada is a small property in Barsac which once belonged to the Lur-Salaces family and is now the property of the enthusiastic Jean Lalande who acquired it in 1940. There are 10 ha of vineyard, nine tenths of which are planted with Sémillon. The vines, planted on stony clay and lime soils, are an average 30 years-old. The grapes from younger vines are used for the dry Bordeaux Clos du Roi while the botrytized grapes, harvested in several different selections and particularly concentrated, go for the premier-label wine. After crushing, the must goes into oak barrels, one quarter of which are replaced every year. The wines are then blended, racked into clean barrels and left to age for a year before they are fined with bentonite, filtered and bottled. After cellaring for a further six months or so, the 20,000 bottles are ready to be sold. They are generally of a high quality and, unlike many Sauternes, are reasonably priced.

Château Piada Barsac 1988   ⚜ ③
Lemon yellow color, with a very clean nose of fruit and honey. On the palate, it is soft and ripe with a good balance between acidity, wood and fruit.

Château Prost

c/o Château de Cérons
33720 Cérons
Tel. 56270113
Fax 56272277

Château Prost is run by its owners, Jean and Suzanne Perronat, who bought the property 30 years ago, together with their son Xavier. The same family has also owned the famous Château de Cérons for over 150 years as well as other smaller estates in the Graves and at Loupiac. Château Prost has 11 ha of vineyards, 80% of which are planted with Sémillon, 10% with Sauvignon Blanc and 10% Muscadelle, on gravelly limestone and clay terrain in the commune of Barsac. The grapes are harvested over the course of six or seven pickings and each selection is subjected to separate vinification. Soft-pressing of the concentrated, sun-dried grapes lasts over 24 hours after which the free-run juice is placed in new barrels of Allier oak to ferment. The wines age in barriques for 18-24 months, during which period they are cleaned by means of regular racking. Before bottling they are blended in stainless steel vats and lightly filtered. To improve the quality of Château Prost still further, the Perronats cellar the wine for two years before release (at a reasonable price). Further proof of their commitment to quality.

Château Prost Barsac 1989   ⚜ ③
Straw-yellow color with golden highlights. Luscious fragrant marmalade, oranges and acacia blossoms on the nose. The fruit is mouthfilling with flavors of honey and almonds, well-balanced by the acidity. Long lasting finish.

SAUTERNAIS/BARSAC
BORDEAUX
FRANCE

261

SAUTERNAIS/BARSAC
BORDEAUX
FRANCE

Château de Cérons

33720 Podensac
Tel. 56270113
Fax 56272217

Jean Perronat is the owner of Château de Cérons, the largest estate in the Appellation of the same name together with the Grand Enclos du Château de Cérons, which is also part of the same property. Perronat, who also owns Château Prost near Barsac, uses similar vinification techniques to those employed at Sauternes and Barsac. The 20 ha are planted mainly with Sémillon and are harvested in several selections to make maximum use of the "noble rot" which is very common in the area. Sauvignon Blanc and Muscadelle make up the rest of the vine stock, as the three varieties are separately vinified. The grapes are crushed in pneumatic presses for about 24 hours to obtain the maximum extracts possible and the free-run juice is fermented and aged in new Allier oak barrels. It is lightly fined, blended and bottled about two years after the harvest. Only about 40,000 bottles a year of this wine are made, from botrytized grapes. It is an excellent example of its type.

Château de Cérons Cérons 1988   🍇 ③
Straw-yellow with golden reflections. A nose of apricots, almonds and butter. On the palate, it has flavors of honey and fruit. A delicate wine. Without great depth but quite attractive, with good length.

Château Haura

33720 Illats
Tel. 56625338

Madame Jacqueline Leppert, an energetic 80 year-old, and her son, Bernard, are the present owners of this estate which has belonged to the same family for 400 years. Château Haura has 15 ha under cultivation with traditional varieties including 80% Sémillon, 10% Sauvignon blanc and 10% Muscadelle. Soils are the stony sand on limestone characteristic of the plateau on the lefthand bank of the Garonne which comprises the Cérons Appellation. Yields are consistently low, around 30 hl/ha but in 1991, but after the frost, they dropped to 12-14 hl/ha. Winemaking equipment is shared with Château Hillot, a red Graves that also belongs to the Lepperts. Fermentation and aging take place in a combination of oak vats and barrels. New wood is not used because of the prohibitive cost. Wine which is not up to the Château Haura standard is sold wholesale and only the best lots are given the Château label. In 1982, a special Cuvée Madame was made, limited to 200 lt, using botrytized grapes selected in the course of a single day. As elsewhere in the region, 1988, 1989 and 1990 were very successful years.

Château Haura Cérons 1990   🍇 ②
A wine with a great wealth of fruit on the palate and crisp, clean flowery fragrances. Superbly balanced with a pleasantly sweet finish which does not cloy.

Grand Enclos
du Château de Cérons
33720 Cérons
Tel. 56270153
Fax 56270886

Château Clos Haut-Peyraguey

33210 Langon
Tel. 56766153
Fax 56766965

The Grand Enclos du Château de Cérons is a large walled vineyard which produces the best wine in this commune with its stony terrain. The vines are four-fifths Sémillon and one fifth Sauvignon, with 35 year-old plants on average which give very concentrated fruit. The grapes often attract botrytis cinerea, which thrives in the morning mists of the left-hand bank of the Garonne. Olivier Lataste is the latest in the Lataste family's long winemaking history to have made wine here since the 16th century. The sun-dried grapes, rich in sugar, are soft-pressed and the free-run juice ferments and ages in new oak. Two years in barrique give the wine a singularly rich character despite the sub-zone generally held to be lighter than the neighboring Barsac. The Grand Enclos, like many Cérons, is largely absorbed by the French domestic market.

Grand Enclos du Château de Cérons 🍷 ③
Cérons 1988
Gold-straw shade. The nose is of wild honey with hints of botrytis and citrus. The palate has rich fruit, is sweet but not cloying with fresh acidity to balance out the finish.

In 1879, the Peyraguey estate in the commune of Bommes, classified as a Premier Cru in 1855, was split in two following the death of the owner. Today, Jacques Pauly and his wife, Jacqueline, manage Château Clos Haut-Peyraguey, which has kept the status of a Premier Cru. Its 15 ha of vines on the sandy, gravelly terrain around the château, are 83% Sémillon, and the rest Sauvignon and Muscadelle. The 35 year-old vines produce enough grapes to make about 36,000 bottles of wine a year. A further 10 ha produce grapes for a second wine, the "cru bourgeois" Sauternes Château Haut-Bommes. Grapes for the Château Clos Haut-Peyraguey are picked with extreme care, and only the best are selected. After crushing, the must ferments in barrels or temperature-controlled stainless steel vats, depending on the climatic conditions. Aging for 18-22 months is in barriques, one quarter of which are replaced every year to give an intense, creamy, flowery wine of great subtlety.

Château Clos Haut-Peyraguey 🍷 ③
Sauternes 1989
Marked by a complex and elegant bouquet of almond blossoms, honeysuckle and apricots, this is a wine with delicate structure and good balance of fruit, alcohol and acidity. The finish is long and lingering.

SAUTERNAIS/CERONS
BORDEAUX
FRANCE

263

SAUTERNAIS/SAUTERNES
BORDEAUX
FRANCE

Château d'Yquem

33210 Sauternes
Tel. 56632105
Fax 56768369

Château d'Yquem is legendary, in the opinion of many the best wine in the world. Like all great wines, it is the result of the combination of natural factors and meticulous winemaking. The estate is vast and stands on the hill on top of which sits the château itself. There are 104 ha planted with four-fifths Sémillon and one fifth Sauvignon. Every year, about 3 ha of the older plants are uprooted with the dual purpose of resting the soil and making way for new plants. The terrain consists of sandy clay and gravel on a deep bed of limestone. It is carefully drained by means of a system installed in 1880. The 150-strong team of pickers works with unrelenting care for six to eight weeks. The Lur-Saluces family has never compromised on winemaking methods. The famous "one-glass-per-plant" yield is terribly low and the costs of fermentation and aging for three and a half years in new oak barrels are prohibitive. The astronomic prices fetched by Château d'Yquem should not raise any eyebrows. Legends do not come cheap!

Château d'Yquem
Sauternes 1983
🍇🍇 ④

A rich gold color, intense, brilliant and incredibly concentrated. The bouquet is big and broad with powerful notes of botrytis, honey and melon. The palate is outstandingly concentrated and complex and despite all the sweet honeyed aromas has a fresh clean acidity which lends the wine superb balance. The lingering finish goes on forever. Serve with a dessert of honey and vanilla or a fruit salad of strawberries, muscat grapes and pineapple. All the flavors of the dessert will thus be present in the wine and vice versa. Magnificent!

Château d'Yquem
Sauternes 1986
🍇🍇🍇 ④

A stunning, brilliant golden-yellow color, already very intense although the wine is still young. The bouquet is intense and complex, rich in the aromas of delicate red fruit as well as vanilla and with crisp, elegant aromas of botrytis, perhaps more evident than in the '83. An absolutely typical example of the Yquem style which bursts onto the palate with opulent exotic aromas and a creamy sweetness, smooth consistency and a quite fantastic aromatic length. This wine is simply a work of art, totally amazing in its long-lasting richness on the nose and palate, with a balance which will continue to give drinking satisfaction well into the next century. Slightly less powerful than the 1983 but of extraordinary subtlety. Yet another demonstration of Yquem's superiority over all other wines of its type.

SAUTERNAIS/SAUTERNES
BORDEAUX
FRANCE

264

SAUTERNAIS/SAUTERNES
BORDEAUX
FRANCE

Château de Fargues

33210 Fargues
Tel. 56631605

Of all the Sauternes estates, Château de Fargues is the one most justifiably comparable to the great Château d'Yquem. It has been the property of the Lur-Saluces family since the 15th century and its wine is made by the same oenologists, using the same techniques. The estate is not in the immediate neighborhood of its famous 'cousin' but in the easternmost commune of Fargues. The wine itself, blind-tasted, is evidence of the quality demanded by Count Alexandre de Lur-Saluces. However, to consider Fargues merely a cheaper and more commercial version of Château d'Yquem would be a mistake. Fargues has 12 ha of vines compared to the 104 of Yquem, but the vineyard techniques are the same and yields are even up to 30% lower than the already low yields of Yquem (with its "one glass of wine from every vine"). The difference between the two wines shows the importance of "terroir". Fargues is very similar to Yquem when young but personality comes out in three to four years' aging. Some consider it better than Yquem. Fargues is a more subtle wine and needs six months less in casks than Yquem's three and a half years, but the relatively low price makes it a fantastic buy.

Château de Fargues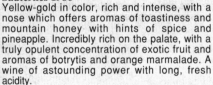
Sauternes 1986
Yellow-gold in color, rich and intense, with a nose which offers aromas of toastiness and mountain honey with hints of spice and pineapple. Incredibly rich on the palate, with a truly opulent concentration of exotic fruit and aromas of botrytis and orange marmalade. A wine of astounding power with long, fresh acidity.

Château de Malle

33210 Preignac
Tel. 56623686
Fax 56768240

Château de Malle was created by Jacques de Malle, President of the Bordeaux parliament in the early 17th century. The estate was passed on by marriage to the Lur-Saluces family who have lived there for seven generations. Today, it is run by the Countess de Bournazel following the death of her husband Pierre, grandson of the last Lur-Saluces, who had managed it until his death in 1985. De Malle is one of the loveliest estates in the Bordeaux region, with splendid architecture and marvellous gardens. The wines live up to this image and certainly deserve their classification as a "deuxième cru". The vineyards extend over 55 ha of gravel and clay terrain in the eastern part of the Appellation, in the sub-zone of Preignac. Three quarters of the varieties are Sémillon, the remainder being Sauvignon with only 2% Muscadelle. The botrytized grapes are carefully selected and fermented then aged in oak barrels for about 30 months. As well as producing about 15,000 cases of Sauternes, there is also a Château de Sainte-Hélène, a dry white Graves called M and a red Graves called Les Tours de Malle. All wines have a good name, thanks to the untiring efforts of the Countess.

Château de Malle Sauternes 1989 ⚇ ③
A yellow-gold color with hints of wood. The nose has aromas of honey, apricot and new oak. Sweet on the palate, with a finish dominated by vanilla and honey.

SAUTERNAIS/SAUTERNES
BORDEAUX
FRANCE

265

SAUTERNAIS/SAUTERNES
BORDEAUX
FRANCE

Château de Rayne-Vigneau

33210 Bommes
Tel. 56626163
Fax 56792357

Château de Rayne-Vigneau is a wellknown Premier Cru estate in the commune of Bommes that borders with Château d'Yquem. For many years, the wines failed to justify their classification, but the most recent vintages have followed the Bordeaux trend where potential is never left idle; the 1990 is particularly rich and elegant. The Cruse family own the property, in addition to some of the most prestigious estates in Bordeaux. The vineyards extend over about 80 ha, two thirds of which are planted with Sémillon and one third with Sauvignon. The vines average 25 years-old planted on sand and gravel over a subsoil of clay. The grapes are picked in successive pickings and ferment in separate lots, some in oak casks others in temperature-controlled vats. The wines age in barriques, half of which are new. Like all Sauternes estates, production varies considerably according to the vintage, ranging from 45,000 to 150,000 bottles. A second wine, Clos d'Albeilly, is made from the grapes of younger vines, as well as a dry Sauvignon called Le Sec de Rayne-Vigneau. Whether the wines have regained their original quality is still debatable, but the improvement thus far is noticeable.

Château de Rayne-Vigneau
Sauternes 1990
A rich and elegant wine of a bright pale yellow color. The nose is very fresh with delicious notes of citrus and sweet-bitter orange marmalade. The palate shows rich, very sweet flavors, succulent with fine balance and great length.

Château Doisy-Védrines

33720 Barsac
Tel. 56271513
Fax 56272676

Classified as a "deuxième cru" and situated near Château Climens and Château Coutet, Château Doisy-Védrines belonged to the Védrines family from the early 17th century until 1850, when it was acquired by the Castéja family who still own it today. Pierre Castéja produces an Appellation Sauternes although his 27 ha are, in fact, in the commune of Barsac. The terrain is well-drained, chalky clay and the predominant variety is Sémillon, together with one fifth Sauvignon. The plants are 30 years-old on average. The harvesters make six runs through the vineyard in the fall. The Sauvignon and Sémillon are fermented separately after being soft-crushed in a pneumatic press. The must is then fermented in controlled-temperature stainless steel vats for about three weeks and aged in Allier barriques for 18 months. Racking is carried out every three months. Clarification is with egg white or gelatine, and the wine is filtered before bottling. With the tiny yields, production is only about 60,000 bottles a year, but Monsieur Castéja managed only 17,000 bottles in 1991.

Château Doisy-Védrines
Sauternes 1989
Very deep golden yellow. A fatty wine with intense, well-rounded marmalade and honey aromas. The palate is typical of botrytized grapes and the finish pleasantly dry, without excessive sweetness.

SAUTERNAIS/SAUTERNES
BORDEAUX
FRANCE

266

SAUTERNAIS/SAUTERNES
BORDEAUX
FRANCE

Château Filhot

33210 Sauternes
Tel. 56766109
Fax 56766791

It was the Marquis of Lur-Saluces who completed the beautiful château after the French Revolution, after the original work begun by M. Filhot, president of the Bordeaux parliament who first used the name Sauternes for the sweet wines of this area. Today, under the direction of Count Henri de Vaucelles, Filhot is an estate of 300 ha, one fifth of which are under vines. The gravel terrain yields about 100,000 bottles a year of excellent Sauternes, using an unusually high 40% of Sauvignon Blanc grape. In 1855, Filhot was awarded the rank of "deuxième cru". Its wines have always had a light, aromatic, citrus style, rather delicate in comparison to the more opulent, sweet styles of other châteaux. Harvested in several runs, the Sémillon, Sauvignon Blanc and small percentage of Muscadelle grapes are fermented in 50-hl temperature-controlled vats. The wine ages from 30 to 44 months, spending a maximum of 6 in the wood, which is new only in poorer years. The subject of some criticism for lack of consistency during the 1970s, Filhot now appears to be producing fine, fresh wines with excellent structure whenever the notoriously fickle area allows.

Château Filhot Sauternes 1989   ℗ ③
The 1989 is very fat and rich in fruit with lots of pineapple and stewed fruit on the nose, full, fat and very sweet on the palate. The color is a nice golden hue. Have well-chilled on its own.

Château Gilette

33210 Preignac
Tel. 56762844
Fax 56762843

Little-known and perhaps undervalued, Château Gilette is many things and most lof all wonderful. Christian Médeville's family have owned these 4.5 ha of vines, with Sémillon as the principal variety, since the 18th century, but the wine has never been included in the classification of the crus. The estate is run in a traditional fashion, with tcareful pickings going on for several weeks during the misty autumn harvest. The stabilized must is not fermented in oak but in temperature-controlled stainless steel vats with the addition of selected yeasts, hence the start of Château Gilette's uniqueness. Legend has it that once one Médeveille, having made his wine, found the market for it so depressed that he decided not to bottle it until prospects improved. He waited for 25 years, keeping the wine in glass-lined tanks. Today, Gilette wines still spend 20 years in fibre-glass, during which time they develop a truly unique elegance and style. There are two cuvées produced, the Doux and the richer Crème de Tête; both appear on the wine lists of the world's best restaurants at high (but totally justified) prices. Don't be shy if you come across a 1970 or 1971, the latest available vintages.

Château Gilette Crème de Tête   ℗ ④
Sauternes 1971
Clear, bright color with pale yellow-gold reflections. The nose and palate are on the lightish side. The flavor is delicious and concentrated, of ripe, chewy apricots and vanilla. Outstandingly fresh for a wine of its age and such balance.

Château Gilette Crème de Tête   ℗ ℗ ④
Sauternes 1970
Unbelievably rich and intense in appearance: pure, sparkling gold. The nose is very full and complex with notes of vanilla and light toastiness. Well-rounded and soft on the palate with a considerable butterscotch aftertaste. Such power. A complete wine, without being too much.

Château Gilette Crème de Tête   ℗ ℗ ④
Sauternes 1955
Superb in color, it has the deep, sparkling, rich hue of old gold. Elegant on the nose, with typical botrytized bouquet and essence of vanilla, honey and apricot. Stupendous butterscotch sweetness on the palate, well-rounded and with low, lingering acidity on a fabulous finish which just goes on and on.

SAUTERNAIS/SAUTERNES
BORDEAUX
FRANCE

267

SAUTERNAIS/SAUTERNES
BORDEAUX
FRANCE

Château Guiraud

33210 Sauternes
Tel. 56766101
Fax 56766752

Château Guiraud used to be the sort of wine you would find on the well-thumbed wine lists of second-rate London clubs, only achivieving distinction by ageing idly in their cellars. However in 1981, the estate was acquired by an energetic Canadian, Hamilton Narby, from the Seagram empire. Since that time, the elegant 'black and gold label' wine has gained an excellent reputation. The property itself is vast, covering 105 ha of gravel-soil vineyards in the commune of Sauternes, where it is the only Premier Cru apart from Château d'Yquem. Narby is firmly convinced that his wine has the potential to compete with its illustrious rival and intends to invest in the technology required to prove his point. 85 ha provide the grapes for the sweet wine and most of the rest goes for the production of G, a very complex dry white Bordeaux. The rotted grapes for Château Guiraud are picked during numerous runs and after being crushed they are fermented and aged in oak barrels. The Château wine is two thirds Sémillon and one third Sauvignon Blanc; G is conversely made from two thirds Sauvignon and one third Sémillon.

Château Guiraud Sauternes 1989
A yellow-gold color of medium intensity with aromas of peach jam, the palate is generous and rich, with the flavors of fruit still crisply defined, again with more peaches overtones. An excellent fresh finish.

Château Haut-Bergeron

33210 Preignac
Tel. 56632476
Fax 56632331

Château Haut-Bergeron is an estate with a long family tradition. Monsieur Robert Lamothe, whose family has owned the property for 200 years, makes just one wine, a magnificently rich Sauternes. He is aided by his two daughters and his wife, who keeps a tight grip on the administration. Vineyard and cellar techniques are typically 'Sauternais' and helped by the fact that many of the 90% Sémillon are very old. The oldest were planted in 1898 and yield a tiny amount of fruit. The wine is aged in barrels of Tronçais wood, four fifths of which are replaced each year. The finished Haut-Bergeron wine is always of the very highest standard. Lamothe and his neighbors go to arduous lengths for the Appellation, but he is nonetheless very aware of competition. He is particularly complimentary about the abilites of many of the Australians who make sweet wines but, at the same time, is quick to point out that they will never match the magic of his left bank home.

Château Haut-Bergeron   ℘ ③
Sauternes 1990
A well-built wine with a superb rich, yellow-gold color. The bouquet of peaches, apricot and honey is voluptuous and the sweetness exquisitely balanced by a note of acidity on the finish.

Château Lafaurie-Peyraguey

33120 Bommes
Tel. 56314444
Fax 56313003

Château Lafaurie-Peyraguey is a owned by
the Bordeaux wine négociants Cordier and,
as with all the firm's properties, this Premier
Cru Sauternes' future is somewhat in the air
at the moment. The quality is at the present
particularly good, thanks to Cordier's decision
to repair Lafaurie-Peyraguey's flagging
reputation in the late 1970s. The Cordier
family have actually owned the property since
1917. The Byzantine-style château buildings
look out over 30 ha of Sémillon, Sauvignon
and Muscadelle vines, with an average age
of 30 years. Careful and numerous pickings
ensure that the grapes are always
concentrated. The must is then fermented in
barrels at a constant 18°C temperature, after
which the wine is aged from 24 to 30 months
in barriques, one third of which are replaced
every year. Over the last decade, Château
Lafaurie-Peyraguey has achieved quite
outstanding levels of excellence and is today
one of the richest and most interesting
Sauternes available.

Château Lafaurie-Peyraguey ꙮ ꙮ ③
Sauternes 1988
A real example of what Sauternes and Barsacs
should be about. Intense botrytis and honey on
the nose while the palate is delicate, not
obviously sweet against the level of fine fruit and
fresh acidity. A long, lingering biscuity finish.

Château Pascaud-Villefranche

33720 Barsac
Tel. 56271609
Fax 56272707

Château Pascaud-Villefranche is a tiny but
excellent Barsac estate. The Pascaud family
have owned 7 ha of vineyards on clay-and-
chalk terrain for three generations and
produce about 18,000 bottles a year of
Sauternes Appellation. The vines are
typically four-fifths Sémillon with the balance
made up with Sauvignon and Muscadelle. All
botrytized grapes are, of course, hand-picked
during several selections and then pressed.
The juice is chilled to 1°C to stabilize it before
fermentation in temperature-controlled
stainless steel vats. The wines are aged for
18 to 24 months, ten of which are spent in
three year-old oak barrels. By regularly
racking the wines and lightly filtering them,
Pascaud achieves a final end result of
brilliant golden color, with great
concentration. He is enormously proud of the
wine just as he is of the mighty Château
Suduiraut where both he and his sons work.

Château Pascaud-Villefranche ꙮ ③

Sauternes 1988
Brilliant yellow-gold in color with delicate
fragrances of almond blossom, orange flower
and honeyed biscuit. Fine and elegant on the
palate, the sweetness is pleasantly tempered
with the acidity. A clean, uncloying finish.

SAUTERNAIS/SAUTERNES
BORDEAUX
FRANCE

269

SAUTERNAIS/SAUTERNES
BORDEAUX
FRANCE

Château Rabaud-Promis

33210 Bommes
Tel. 56766738
Fax 56766310

Although classified as a 'first growth' in 1885, Château Rabaud-Promis did not deserve this position for many years, until recently when it was taken over by Philippe Déjean. His wife's family bought the estate in 1974. Déjean's own family are the proprietors of the Domaine de Noble at Loupiac, and, indeed, Philippe still helps his two brothers there. However, if he is to make a name for himself, it must be at Rabaud-Promis, where the wines are suddenly improving considerably. The vines are mainly Sémillon, with some Sauvignon and a little Muscadelle and are planted on 33 ha of gravel and clay in the commune of Bommes. Only the most concentrated fruit goes to make Château Rabaud-Promis. In more difficult years, such as 1991, about two thirds of the wine is downgraded and sold off as Domaine de l'Estremade or Château Bequet in order to maintain the Rabaud-Promis quality standards at the highest levels. Fermented and aged in oak barrels, one third of which are replaced every year, the wine is lightly clarified and filtered. Bottling takes place at the beginning of spring, about 15 months after the harvest and recent vintages have shown what a turnaround Monsieur Déjean has brought to the property.

Château Rabaud-Promis
Sauternes 1988
A wine with an unexpected initial impact. The nose is intensely rich, with aromas of opulent botrytis, vanilla and peach jam. On the palate, there is a marvellous balance of acidity and sweetness with a rich complexity of outstanding length.

Château Raymond-Lafon

33210 Sauternes
Tel. 56632102
Fax 56631958

Château Raymond-Lafon was built in 1850 and so the wine was not showing its true potential by the time of the 1855 classification. There is no doubt that today they would be classed as Premiers Crus. Apart from a dull patch in the middle of this century, Raymond-Lafon has consistently produced majestic wines , never more so than since 1972 when the Meslier family took over. Former manager of Château d'Yquem, just up the road, from 1963 to 1989, Pierre Meslier really understands the importance of quality. He has managed to bring the plantings at Raymond-Lafonat up from 1.5 ha to 15. Four fifths of the varieties are Sémillon and the rest, Sauvignon. The harvests are highly selective and long (in 1985, the last of the 'tries' was in December). The grapes are first crushed in a vertical press and then in a hand-press. The must ferments for three to five weeks in a cellar heated to 20°C and then ages in new oak barriques for three years with racking every three months. Pierre and Francine Meslier run the estate with their three children, Marie-Françoise, Charles-Henry and Jean-Pierre.

Château Raymond-Lafon
Sauternes 1989
A very complete wine. A lovely yellow-gold and a powerful nose, with a hint of alcohol. The palate is ripe, full-bodied, concentrated and extraordinarily fresh, with notes of exotic fruit and a lingering finish.

Château Raymond-Lafon
Sauternes 1988
Without quite the weight of the 1989, it is magnificently well-balanced on the palate, showing great richness and complexity, with a subtle note of mint and outstanding freshness. Very concentrated on the nose with a lovely attractive color.

Château Rieussec

33210 Fargues
Tel. 56622071
Fax 56762782

In 1985, Albert Veuilley, the owner of a supermarket chain, sold his stake in the Château Rieussec to the Domaines Barons de Rothschild, who also own Château Lafite and Château Duhart-Milon. Rieussec is undoubtedly one of the most outstanding Sauternes estates and capable of producing a very high-class wine from the fruit of its 66 ha of Sémillon, Sauvignon and Muscadelle, grown in the classic 'Sauternais' proportions. Recently, however, the results have been uneven with wines at times lacking structure despite their high alcohol. In better years, like 1983 and 1990, Rieussec reasserts itself by producing a stunning wine, even better than those of its prestigious neighbors. Rieussec is not frighteningly expensive, either, so the wines represent a good buy for early drinking. The unevenness is perhaps due to the change of ownership, as it is certainly not a question of lack of investment. The cellar is superbly equipped with temperature-controlled stainless steel vats and modern presses. The second wine, the dry white "R" de Rieussec (Appellation Bordeaux sec) is a honeyed white of toasty elegance with a hint of botrytis that drinks well when young.

Château Rieussec Sauternes 1988 ♈ ♈ ④
Golden straw-yellow color with an intense honey-and-citrus nose of quite enchanting elegance. The palate is equally sophisticated and deeply layered. An unexpected result from a property that of late had an almost overly rich, marmalade style.

Key to the symbols

Types of Wines

♈ White

▨ Rosé

♈ Red

Rating System

♈
An exemplary wine of its type with outstanding local character

▨▨
An international premium quality wine

♈♈♈
A Top Wine, considered one of the 150 best wines in the world

The 'grape bunch' symbol is used to indicate the color of the wine; the number of bunches represents the quality rating assigned by the contributor

Price levels

①   up to $ 9.99

② $ 10.00 - $ 14.99

③ $ 15.00 - $ 24.99

④ $ 25.00 or more

The 'ex-cellar', or direct from the producer, bottle prices, are calculated in US dollars and are intended only as an approximate guide

Entries are arranged in alphabetical order by country, region and winery or producer name.

SAUTERNAIS/SAUTERNES
BORDEAUX
FRANCE

271

SAUTERNAIS/SAUTERNES
BORDEAUX
FRANCE

Château Suduiraut

33210 Preignac
Tel. 56632729
Fax 56630700

in the heart of Sauternes, just down the hill from the vines of Château d'Yquem are those of Château Suduiraut. Planted on sandy, limestone/clay soils, they recieve plenty of the vital morning mists from the nearby river Ciron, which helps fuel the advent of noble rot. In June 1992, Château Suduiraut was bought by the AXA insurance group, which has done so much for Bordeax wines, particularly in the Médoc. The change of ownership and consequent investment are bound to have had a positive effect on the château, which has been producing excellent Sauternes for ten years. As in all the large estates in the zone, both the vineyards and the cellar are carefully supervised. Six or seven pickings of bunches are needed to harvest the best quality, botrytized grapes and the yields of the 87-ha property are very low. The vines are four-fifths Sémillon and one fifth Sauvignon Blanc. The must is fermented and aged in wooden barrels (one third of which are new) for two and a half years. This vast estate managed by Pierre Pascaud produces only 12,000-15,000 cases of wine a year, each of exceptional quality.

Château Suduiraut   ♟ ♟ ④
Sauternes 1990
Made from grapes harvested during several runs beginning on 28th September, this wine is typical of Suduiraut's recent vintages. Power and elegance are harmoniously combined in the nose, with botrytis prevailing over an austere sweetness and volume. The weight on the palate is balanced by complexity and excellent length.

Château Suduiraut   ♟ ♟ ♟ ④
Sauternes 1989
The product of a selection of the best botrytized grapes on the estate and a subsequent blend of the most successful cuvées, this 1989 has a wonderful rich yellow-gold color. The aromas are immensely concentrated, and on the palate there is all the strength and depth of the fruit, supported by firm acidity and highlighted by the wood, two elements which guarantee beyond all doubt that this wine will have a long life span. With its 15° alc and 7° of residual sugar, this is true monster of a wine which will have to wait for several decades before it will attain its moment of true perfection.

Château Thibaut

33210 Fargues
Tel. 56630561

Information about this estate is almost as hard to come by as the wines. The owner, 46 year-old Jacques Latournerie, is every bit the down to earth vigneron. However, where verbosity may be in short supply, there is certainly no lack of winemaking skill at this domaine. Château Thibaud's tiny production is in line with the size of the estate and the necessarily small yields. On average, 20-25 hl/ha are obtained from the 6 ha of vines and in the difficult 1991 vintage, yields fell to 12 hl/ha. The vineyards, like the wines themselves, are 80% Sémillon with 15% Sauvignon blanc and 5% Muscadelle. The oldest plants are 60 years-old and a portion of the estate is replanted every year. The harvest lasts for 15 to 20 days, with five or six runs. Oak vats and barrels are used for fermentation and aging and usually it is three years after harvest before the wine is bottled. No new wood is used, but in certain years Jacques Latournerie does use one year-old barriques.

Château Thibaut Sauternes 1988   🍇 ③
Attractive and bright with a nose which features rich notes of botrytis as well as honey and bitter marmalade. Very rich on the palate, rather fat and buttery sweet with barley sugar flavors but good acidity providing freshness and balance.

SAUTERNAIS/SAUTERNES
BORDEAUX
FRANCE

273

SAUTERNAIS/SAUTERNES
BORDEAUX
FRANCE

Bourgogne

Montrachet, Romanée-Conti and Gevrey-Chambertin are some of the names from Bourgogne which send a thrill of pleasure down the spine of wine-lovers all over the globe. It must be said, however, that for some years now the quality of the wines from Bourgogne has been uneven and unpredictable.

The area generally known as Bourgogne is made up of five very different sub-regions which change considerably in from north to south.

1) In the extreme north is the area known as the Yonne: home of the great white wines of Chablis, with their excellent aging potential. The northerly location and the chalky soil give the wine a unique vivacity and mineral-like character. The reds are less important but are surprisingly good.

2) A good hour's drive to the south is the Côte d'Or with its south-east facing hills which produce some of Bourgogne's greatest and most renowned wines. It is a 70 km-long strip of land which varies in width from a few hundred meters to about 20 km. The northern half, the Côte de Nuits, which runs from Marsannay to Corgoloin, produces red wines that can age beautifully. The Côte de Beaune, just to the south around the peaceful city of Beaune, carries on to Chagny. It is equally famous for its red wines and dry whites which have become the world's benchmarks for Pinot Noirs and Chardonnays.

3) The Côte Chalonnaise is a hilly continuation of the Côte de Beaune, the richer soil yielding red and white wines which, while not as delicate, are full of personality.

4) Further south still is the Mâcon, an area full of potential that produces some stunning white wines at very affordable prices. The exception is Pouilly-Fuissé which can produce wonderful wines which can cost as much as any other white Bourgogne. The Gamay reds of the Mâcon are uneven but can nonetheless provide good wines for drinking immediately.

5) The last area of Bourgogne is far more Lyonnais than Burgundian. The granite hills of the Beaujolais are a paradise for Gamay. Beaujolais and Beaujolais-Villages wines are traditionally drunk young, yet some crus like Juliénas and Moulin-à-Vent age well, if carefully made.

Viticulture in Bourgogne has a long history. Some of the parcels of vines which are famous today already existed in their present form, and enjoyed excellent reputations, in the Middle Ages. The monks of the various religious orders are to be given credit for the first classification, particularly the Benedictines of Cluny and the local Cistercians, followers of Bernard of Chiaravalle at the Abbey of Côteaux. The most important achievement of the monks was the foundation of the Clos de Vougeot which epitomizes the great crus of Bourgogne. This clos also amply demonstrates the disastrous effect Napoleonic inheritance laws have had on the small parcels. There are now over 80 families who own vines in the tiny Clos de Vougeot. As a result of this sub-division of the land and the classification of the various crus, today most winemakers are obliged to produce several different wines.

In ascending order of quality, there are four basic wine denominations: Appellation Régionales which are given to the most basic wines like Bourgogne Aligoté and Bourgogne Rouge; Village names which are given to wines from vineyards deemed to be of an exceptional standard around well-known communities, like Meursault and Pommard; finally, the very best sites have been judged to be Grand Cru or Premier Cru, an analysis that has been done over the years row by row across the vineyards. With the exception of Chablis, it is not necessary for a Grand Cru to indicate the name of the commune to which it belongs. They are simply called, for example, Le Chambertin, Le Montrachet or La Romanée.

There are four different grape varieties in Bourgogne, two of them 'noble', Pinot Noir for red wines and Chardonnay for whites, and two humbler grapes, the white Aligoté and the red Gamay. Gamay is the basis for Beaujolais and Mâcon Rouge.

Not all Burgundies live up to the region's reputation. Many wines have an intense, vibrant color, with beautifully defined fruit and are velvety and structured on the palate, but others are pale, thin and insipid or coarse and alcoholic, dominated by stewed, vegetal characteristics, the results of over-cropping, over-chaptalization, re-acidification or just careless winemaking. The wines we have selected show what conscientious vignerons and négociants can do with Bourgogne's terroir and heritage. Their vines are carefully tended, chemical fertilizers are avoided, yields are low, long maceration is practiced and fermentation is carefully temperature-controlled . Finally, it should be noted that Bourgogne's vintages are extremely variable but recently the region has enjoyed a series of outstanding harvests, such as the exceptional 1990.

Bourgogne Appellations in this Guide

Auxerrois	**Côte de Beaune**	**Côte de Nuits**
Chablis	Aloxe-Corton	Chambolle-Musigny
	Auxey-Duresses	Fixin
Beaujolais	Beaune	Gevrey-Chambertin
Beaujolais	Blagny	Marsannay
Beaujolais-Villages	Chassagne-Montrachet	Morey-Saint-Denis
Chiroubles	Chorey-lès-Beaune	Nuits-Saint-Georges
Côte de Brouilly	Ladoix	Vosne-Romanée
Fleurie	Meursault	Vougeot
Juliénas	Monthélie	
Morgon	Pernand-Vergelesses	**Mâconnais**
Saint-Amour	Pommard	Mâcon
	Puligny-Montrachet	Mâcon-Villages
Côte Chalonnaise	Saint-Aubin	Pouilly-Fuissé
Givry	Saint-Romain	Saint-Véran
Mercurey	Santenay	
Rully	Savigny-lès-Beaune	
	Volnay	

Hervé Azo

Milly
89800 Chablis
Tel. 86424356
Fax 86424979

Lying far off the beaten tourist track, the tiny winemaking village of Milly is a jewel, as indeed is the Azo family residence with its ever vigilant stone dogs. During the 1970s, M. Azo, who comes originally from Brittany, left Paris and the world of advertising to settle here. Initially he rented a vineyard, but now he owns 15 ha including some of the Premier Cru Vau-de-Vey. His vines (which are an average of about 15 years old) are treated exclusively with organic fertilizers and are harvested manually. Azo has recovered from the damage caused by the heavy frosts in 1985 and is now producing wines (his Petit-Chablis in particular) which have won the praise of his fellow growers. Production is very limited, but it is worth keeping a sharp eye out for these wines.

Petit Chablis 1990
Round, attractively fleshy and always very smooth; a supreme wine for drinking. This Petit Chablis is in the front rank of an Appellation where good wines are increasingly hard to find.

Chablis Vau-de-Vey
Premier Cru 1989
Pale in color, but verging on gold. The nose is still light although the honeyed aromas are beginning to open out. Good depth on the palate with notes of candied fruit. A wine which still needs time to develop.

Domaine Collet et fils

15, avenue de la Liberté
89800 Chablis
Tel. 86421193
Fax 86424743

At night, the front of the Collet cellar is illuminated by powerful neon lights, doubtless so that the fake parking meters placed there can be easily seen. During the daytime, the Collet family is out in the 20 ha of vineyards they own, 13 of which are in various crus (Montmains, Vaillons and Valmur). Today, Gilles Collet, the third generation of the family after father Jean and grandfather Marius, runs the business. He is a powerfully built and dynamic, direct man and the undisputed head of the estate. Fermentation takes place in stainless steel vats and second-hand barrels of solid Bercy wood and some of the cru wines go on to age in new barriques. The wines tend to be rather robust, for the Collets often chaptalize, but they have good aging potential and prices are still very reasonable in comparison with others in the area.

Chablis Montmains
Premier Cru 1989
Pale color and an undeveloped nose. It will be several years before this wine is ready. The alcohol is still dominant but the flowery finish is well-balanced.

Chablis Valmur Grand Cru 1989
Lovely golden color. The nose is still rather tight but it does give hints of mint and leaves. A fresh wine on the palate, with no aggressive wood and an elegant finish.

Chablis Vaillons Premier Cru 1985
A wine which has taken its time to develop. Today, it is in excellent condition, with aromas of spice and apple and even some aniseed, all beautifully knit. A wine with good freshness and a honeyed, mineral finish.

AUXERROIS/CHABLIS
BOURGOGNE
FRANCE

276

AUXERROIS/CHABLIS
BOURGOGNE
FRANCE

René et Vincent Dauvissat

8, rue Emile Zola
89800 Chablis
Tel. 86421158

Dauvissat is a very common surname in Chablis, but René is the Dauvissat 'par excellence'. His cellar is a shrine dedicated from time immemorial to the greatest vineyards of Chablis. René's family, today under the guiding hand of his son Vincent, is regarded with great respect. Grandfather Robert, who died in 1973, left his mark by gradually perfecting the aging of his wines in oak and we should not forget that Robert's own grandfather was a cooper. The Dauvissat's nine hectares on the left bank of the river are tended with great care and adaptability. Yields are low and the wines are never rushed onto the market. The Grands Crus (Les Preuses and Les Clos) and Premiers Crus (Sécher, Vaillons and legendary La Forest) are all transformed into liquid gold by these masterful winemakers. It is easy to understand why their wine is so hard to find.

Chablis La Forêst Premier Cru 1991
The winemaker's skill is crucial in the amazing success of this cuvée which will certainly become a bench-mark for the vintage. The bouquet plays variations on a theme of honey, the texture is dense and very representative of the vineyard. Prominent acidity and a finish with a range of perfectly matched flavors.

Chablis Les Clos Grand Cru 1990
A wine with an outstanding "goût de terroir" which is a credit to the vintage and the winemaker. Fabulously complex nose and a rich, highly concentrated texture. It has a much higher alcohol content than the previous year, yet it has lovely freshness, thanks to its firm acidity.

Chablis Vaillons Premier Cru 1990
Limpid, pure and clean color. Flinty and mineral-like with honeyed aromas. Great freshness on the palate despite the high alcohol content. A landmark wine, not to be opened before the end of the century.

Chablis Les Clos Grand Cru 1989
A wine that we must wait for. The barrel has done its job, but the oak does not dominate. The nose has hints of pepper on a background of vanilla and the palate is rich and full with a well defined "goût de terroir".

Domaine Daniel Defaix

14, rue Auxerroise
89800 Chablis
Tel. 86421444
Fax 86424856

It is over four centuries since the Defaix family established itself here. Daniel, the friendly, "thirty-something" son of Etienne Defaix, is a determined character who refuses to stoop to modernization, high yields or to the degradation, as he sees it, of selling his beloved Chablis prematurely. Indeed, for many years he has been supplying the Vatican, an institution which knows the value of patience. The Defaix estate includes 24 ha in the Léchet, Les Lys (which once belonged to the French crown) and Vaillons Premiers Crus and to which Daniel gives a personal touch. Above all, he loves to wait. This is particularly apparent in his shop "Le Monde du Vin" in the center of town, where this artist of rare and fine wine only sells bottles which have reached full maturity, or rather, their peak, for Daniel Defaix is a specialist who stamps the seal of quality on everything he sets his hand to.

Chablis Vaillons Premier Cru 1986
Bright yellow color with a light nose where delicate flowers overlay flint. Good structure with a fresh, slightly mineral palate and excellent acidity. A wine which will be superb in two or three years time.

Chablis Les Lys Premier Cru 1985
Dark yellow in color. Light aromas of toastiness on the nose with hints of lime and wood which persist well on the mineral palate, which is also fleshy, well-rounded and fresh. A rich structure with a finish of roasted almonds.

Chablis Vaillons Premier Cru 1985
A wine with a lovely golden color, toasted bread on the nose and chewy, well-rounded and well-structured fruit on the palate. Supported by only moderate acidity and therefore a wine to drink now.

AUXERROIS/CHABLIS
BOURGOGNE
FRANCE

277

AUXERROIS/CHABLIS
BOURGOGNE
FRANCE

Jean-Paul Droin

14 bis, rue Jean-Jaurès
89800 Chablis
Tel. 86421678
Fax 86424209

There are still winemakers in Chablis with something to sell. Jean-Paul Droin, who comes from an old family of winemakers, is one of these. His estate covers 20 ha, including 3.7 in Grands Crus and 9 in Premiers Crus, and he is much talked about, not just because of his magnificent vaulted cellar with its neatly lined-up barrels, but also because he is a firm believer in low yields and was one of the first to ferment and age his wine in new oak. Indeed, at first he perhaps used too much new wood but now follows a more moderate line, not using it at all for example for the Premier Cru Fourchame and in general Droin's wines no longer have that strong nose of Tronçais oak. Now, the wood adds a genuine touch of complexity. Most of his wines are aged in barrels of different ages, but the Grands Crus only ever see new barriques. A really fine example of adaptable winemaking.

Chablis 1990   ❦ ②
Fermented and aged in vats, this is classic Chablis and is not without complexity. Good balance, a full palate and a crisp finish.

Chablis Grenouilles   ❦❦ ③
Grand Cru 1990
In 1990, Jean-Paul Droin managed to obtain 14.6° natural alcohol from his Grand Cru. He fermented it in his own unique way, initially in new barrels and then in vats. There was no malolactic fermentation and this is, or will be, one of Droin's great wines. It expresses the Chardonnay variety well, with vivacity and a palate of inimitable fullness. There is a slight hint of wood in the finish.

Chablis Montée de Tonnerre   ❦❦ ③
Vieilles Vignes Premier Cru 1989
An intense yellow color and a nose of delicious vanilla wood over a flowery background. Rich, ripe and full-bodied on the palate with a long-lasting finish.

Ghislaine et Jean-Hugues Goisot

30, rue Bienvenu-Martin
89530 Saint-Bris-le-Vineux
Tel. 86533515
Fax 86536203

When you call one of your wines Cuvée du Corps du Garde, there has to be a good reason. In this case, it is to be found in the famous medieval cellars under the town center where Ghislaine and Jean-Hugues Goisot live (they should not be confused with their namesakes, Marie-Claude and Hugues, or Serge and Arnaud Goisot). Carved out of the living rock, the cellars were indeed the headquarters of an 11th-century corps of guards. The Goisots have always stood up for this area on the left bank of the Yonne where they own a 16.5 ha property on limestone soil with a vineyard of an average age of 25-30 years. They have smallholdings in the Saint-Bris, Bourgogne Aligoté, Bourgogne Saint-Bris Blanc and Bourgogne Saint-Bris Rouge Appellations. Ghislaine and Jean-Hugues have always put quality first both in cultivation and vinification (carried out with advice from the enologist Véronique Vallenot) and in the barrique aging where nothing is left to chance. Furthermore, not only do the Goisots make superb wines, but they also have exquisite old-world manners which makes one look for their label that much harder.

Saint-Bris Sauvignon 1991   ❦ ①
Despite the frosts which decimated the year's production, the Goisots managed to make a small quantity of Sauvignon, with prominent varietal aromas of blackcurrant leaves, pepper, rose and mint. The palate is full and chewy, with an elegant finish.

Bourgogne Aligoté 1990   ❦ ①
A lovely pale yellow in color with a straightforward nose with full flowery fruit. Good texture on the palate with a clean finish and no excess alcohol.

Bourgogne   ❦ ②
Cuvée du Corps de Garde 1989
The initial impact on the nose is a magnificent explosion of cherry, plum and pepper. Intense color, with powerful yet elegant tannins and a rich body which bodes well for the future.

AUXERROIS/CHABLIS
BOURGOGNE
FRANCE

278

AUXERROIS/CHABLIS
BOURGOGNE
FRANCE

Domaine Grossot

Fleys
89800 Chablis
Tel. 86424464
Fax 86421331

Corinne and Jean-Pierre Grossot moved to the village of Fleys in 1979. These two young experts in Chablis cultivate a 15-ha property with 20 year-old vines which enjoys a semi-continental climate on clay-and-chalk marl. Their generic Chablis is wonderfully successful; the 1990 is a fine example and may be tasted in their vaulted underground cellar. Their carefully made wines include five Premiers Crus: Côtes-de-Troëmes, Fourchaume, Les Fourneaux, Mont-de-Milieu and Vaucoupin. The harvest is part manual and part mechanical and alcoholic fermentation takes place at controlled temperatures. Malolactic fermentation is only partial, depending on the vintage. The wine is stored partly in glass-lined vats and partly in barrels of Tronçais or Nièvre oak. The oak-aged wine is blended after about six months with vat-aged wine in a proportion which varies from year to year. Wines are only bottled 10-15 months after the harvest and results are often quite exceptional.

Chablis 1990   ❦ ②
Aged in the wood, this wine discloses fragrances of quince and acacia honey on the nose. The body is rich and impressive while the palate is lively and sinewy. A crisp finish, with a lingering aftertaste of hazelnut.

Chablis Vaucoupin   ❦ ❦ ③
Premier Cru 1990
A Premier Cru made from the grapes of old vines which is a veritable paragon of a Chardonnay. This is to some extent thanks to the fruit, which is exceptionally rich in 1990. The nose is already developed and convincing with hints of acacia honey and citrus. Fleshy on the palate, with good length and an outstandingly elegant finish.

Domaine de l'Eglantière

4, Grande Rue
Château de Maligny - 89800 Chablis
Tel. 86474449
Fax 86475549

Jean Durup, whose family has lived in Maligny for five centuries, is Chablis' greatest supporter in Paris. You can often see him at Goumard-Prunier while he chats amiably about his favorite wine. It is also true that he is the largest property-owner in the region with no less than 155 ha around the 12th-century Château de Maligny. For the last ten years, together with his enologist Michel Poitout, he has been bringing his own style to Chablis. His wines never see wood either in fermentation or during aging for Jean Durup ferments in glass-fiber or enamel-lined cement vats to preserve the natural freshness and bouquet of the wine. With yields of about 50 hl/ha, systematic use of yeasts and controlled temperatures which never exceed 25°C, Durup's wines are modern in style. From his Petit Chablis to his Chablis Premier Cru Vau-de-Vey, and including his other Premier Cru, Fourchaume, Jean Durup makes wines of rare elegance. He needs only to make his mark in a Grand Cru, where he has no plots at all. Perhaps one day his dream will come true.

Chablis Château de Maligny   ❦ ❦ ③
Forchaume Premier Cru 1990
Straw-yellow in color with flecks of green. The nose has a fine range of fragrances with minerals over a background of citrus (lemon marmalade and grapefruit). Great texture on the palate, perfect balance and a long, lingering fruity finish.

Chablis   ❦ ③
Domaine de l'Eglantière 1990
Although a generic Chablis, this is a wine of remarkable quality. The nose has delicate but ripe fruit, the palate is full and well-rounded with a good, firm structure. The finish is satisfyingly long.

AUXERROIS/CHABLIS
BOURGOGNE
FRANCE

· 279

AUXERROIS/CHABLIS
BOURGOGNE
FRANCE

Domaine de la Maladière

14, rue Jules-Rathier
89800 Chablis
Tel. 86421251- (1) 69311787
Fax 86421914- (1) 69311788

The first impression of this estate is made by the large white house, the modern cellars and the stores where the barriques are proudly lined up. The property comprises 50 ha of vineyards - and buys in the grapes from another 50, all of which are an average of 15 years old, planted on limestone clay loess and fossilized oyster shells. A good-humored, self-confident patriarch is in charge and when William Fèvre begins to talk about his wine, he is easily moved to poetry. He makes wine from Valmur, Les Lys, Bourgos and many other crus with their golden color, delicate lemon, ripe apple and hazelnut aroma, their fresh and elegant acacia flavor and their iodine and oyster mineral odors. Fèvre's methods include manual harvesting as late as possible, with several selections to check the progress of botrytis, crushing the grapes in their bunches and temperature-controlled fermentation in barriques or vats to preserve the aromas of exotic fruit and vegetation. These are wines which have the chewiness of great Chardonnays and should be drunk at least 18 months after bottling.

Chablis Champ Royaux 1990
The name on the label of this wine does not refer to a vineyard but was invented by William Fèvre to denote a blend of grapes from different zones, some of which are Premiers Crus. The 1990 vintage, with its lovely pale straw-yellow color, has a nose which prominently features almond and lemon on a light iodine background with a good finish.

Chablis Bougros
Grand Cru 1989
Golden-yellow in color. The bouquet is delicate and complex, with hints of jam, flowers, autumn leaves and minerals. On the palate, the wood is apparent (the wine is aged in new barriques) but this does not detract from the overall elegance. The fruit is mouthfilling and the acidity well-balanced. Rich texture, classically "Chardonnay", in a wine which will age comfortably for some years yet.

Domaine Laroche

L'Obédiencerie - 22, rue Louis-Bro
89800 Chablis
Tel. 86421430
Fax 86421908

The history of the Laroche family, which has been active in the area for five generations, is intricately linked to the history of the Appellation. Michel Laroche is an enologist who began managing the company in 1967 when he had just six hectares. At the time, Chablis was going through its blackest period; demand was much lower than it is today and growers could not always fight off the spring frosts. Laroche, however, was a firm believer in the future of Chablis and today his estate extends over about 100 ha, including 6 Grands Crus and 30 Premier Crus. After having attempted to expand into the Côte d'Or, M. Laroche wisely fell back on Chablis and his wines are all superbly made, from the Chablis Saint-Martin to the Grand Cru Blanchots Vieilles Vignes. In 1991, he decided to turn his back on large yields and easy triumphs to experiment with his finest plot in Blanchots. The very ripe grapes were manually harvested and aged in barrels for six months with no filtration before bottling. The results have been encouraging.

Chablis Saint-Martin
Vielles Vignes 1990
Brilliant in color with the typically clean fragrances of Chardonnay, both soft and elegant. Rich in fruit on the palate; a characteristically varietal wine, but not in the classic Chablis mould.

Chablis Vaillons Premier Cru 1990
Straw-yellow in color with tinges of green. The nose reveals great intensity of fruit. On the palate it is clean with a pleasantly acidic note. A well-rounded and rich Chardonnay, to drink within the next two or three years.

AUXERROIS/CHABLIS
BOURGOGNE
FRANCE

280

AUXERROIS/CHABLIS
BOURGOGNE
FRANCE

Louis Michel et fils

9, boulevard de Ferrières
89800 Chablis
Tel. 86421024
Fax 86421747

The Michels have been growers for five generations and know all there is to know about vines and wines. Their 20 ha of vines (all about 25 years old) grow on chalky clay, where Louis Michel and his son, Jean-Loup, apply their philosophy of low yields: 50 hl/ha for the Premiers Crus (La Forêt, Montée de Tonnerre, Montmains and Vaillons) and 45 hl/ha for the Grands Crus (Les Clos, Grenouilles and Vaudésir). Part of the harvest is gathered in mechanically, where the ground is not too steep. The harvest is followed by automatic crushing, 12-hour static clarification and fermentation at a controlled temperature of 18-20°C before aging in stainless steel vats. The Michels maintain that wood has a rather inelegant effect on Chardonnay. The whole process takes place in an immaculately clean cellar. Michel wines, especially the Grands Crus, are made for aging and do not give their best when young. It is best to wait patiently for a few years so that they can realize their full potential.

Chablis Grenouilles Grand Cru 1990 ♥ ②
An outstanding example of the cru. The nose has plenty of honey and minerals and is still a little undeveloped, but the palate is crisp and clean. Wait for a few years before drinking.

Chablis Montée de Tonnerre ♥ ②
Premier Cru 1989
The nose, initially very flowery, fades into minerals with a touch of honey. Full, fleshy palate with notes of almond. Great length.

Gilbert Picq et fils

3, route de Chablis
89800 Chichée
Tel. 86421830
Fax 86421770

The Picqs owned no vines at all when they were selling their produce on the local wholesale market, but things changed completely when they decided to start bottling in 1981. Today, they have 12 ha, 2 of which are Premier Cru (Vosgros), and yield an average of 50,000 bottles a year. A real success for a family which makes excellent wines, with Didier in the cellar and his brother Pascal looking after the vineyards under the watchful eye of their father, Gilbert. Winemaking is traditional, with no chaptalization and with fermentation in vats for the generic Chablis, the Vieilles Vignes (from vines with an average age of 40 to 45 years old) and the Premier Cru. For the Vieilles Vignes, there is also a cru made solely in barriques, half of which are new. Another positive sign is the assistance of Véronique Vallenot, the enologist, who has a fine reputation in the area and with whose help the Picqs won a bronze medal at Mâcon for their Vieilles Vignes 1990.

Chablis Vieilles Vignes 1990 ♥ ②
A product which has put the name Picq into the first rank of the Appellation's best wines. The harvest reached a level of 13.5° alc so this is a wine which combined all the qualities of a Chablis of breeding without chaptalization or wood.

Chablis Vosgros Premier Cru 1990 ♥ ②
Lovely color and a wholly typical nose. The palate has good structure and is delicate and elegant with a fresh floweriness. A well-balanced wine which finishes on a clean, fresh, supple note.

Chablis 1989 ♥ ①
Clear, lemon yellow and green in appearance, with a fruity, mineral nose and a palate which sustains its flinty flavor well. Good freshness in the finish.

AUXERROIS/CHABLIS
BOURGOGNE
FRANCE

281

AUXERROIS/CHABLIS
BOURGOGNE
FRANCE

François et Jean-Marie Raveneau

9, rue Chiché
89800 Chablis
Tel. 86421746
Fax 86424555

François Raveneau and his son Jean-Marie, like their wines, are very hard to find. You may try telephoning or visiting them personally, but they often have so little stock you most probably won't find what you want. The only way to be sure of savoring Raveneau's wines is to book a table at one of the famous, inevitably expensive restaurants that serve them. The reward is a wine that leaves the most demanding connoisseurs lost for words. Raveneau's wines are models of perfection, born on a pocket-sized estate, with only seven hectares spread over the Grands Crus of Blanchot, Les Clos and Valmur and Premier Crus of Butteaux, Chapelot, Montée-de-Tonnerre and Vaillons on fossil-rich clay and limestone. Thanks to manual harvests, low yields, classic winemaking and a transfer to old oak barrels before the final blending, the Raveneaus have attained the quintessence of what a Chablis should be. It should only be drunk when it is ready, several years after bottling, and with the greatest respect.

Chablis   🍇🍇 ④
Montée de Tonnerre Premier Cru 1985
Just right and without blemishes, a supremely successful vintage for this Premier Cru. The nose immediately presents its crisp fragrances of honey and flint. The palate is full and fleshy, while the finish is of the usual outstanding length.

Chablis   🍇🍇 ④
Vaillons Premier Cru 1985
Delicate in color. A nose which compliments the minerality of the cru with gentle floral character. The palate is mouthfilling and concludes with an explosion of fierce intensity.

Chablis   🍇🍇 ④
Valmur Grand Cru 1985
The transfer to the barrel has made this Chablis a superb wine to lay down. Almost oily on the palate, but with no flaws. It is beautifully structured and very fresh on the finish. A very aristocratic wine.

Chablis   🍇🍇 ④
Butteaux Premier Cru 1983
Stunning, extraordinary, incisive, unique - these are some of the more moderate adjectives that spring to mind for this wine. Its color is of an unparalleled limpidity and purity. The nose opens on notes of honey and acacia while the palate is well-rounded and fleshy with great depth. The length is truly remarkable and is far from having peaked. Proof, if proof were needed, that a Chablis can be on a par with a great Bourgogne.

Chablis   🍇🍇🍇 ③
Montée de Tonnerre Premier Cru 1990
Welcome to Chablis! All those years of hearing of the classic Chablis color, crystalline bright with hints of green, and here it is! The nose of this wine is exceptionally subtle, even shut down, with just a touch of buttery toffee and damp, raw wool, not giving more than the slightest impression of its true character yet to come. In the mouth it is bone-dry, crisp with fresh fruit and a really hard, flinty style so clean and long that one can already feel its true potential. This is a real wine with lots of bite; very tight with clean fruit that is definitely not immediately to everyone's taste. This is surely a wine that will live up to the reputation of the many great Raveneau wines; a wine of modest immediate appeal which will offer extraordinary rewards to those who have the patience and cellars to keep it for five to seven years.

Pierre-Marie et Martine Chermette

Domaine du Vissoux
69620 Le Vissoux-Saint-Vorand
Tel. 74717942
Fax 74718426

In the south of Beaujolais on the hills to the west of Villefranche, Pierre-Marie and Martine Chermette are making some of the most distinctive and authentic wines in the whole region. On an estate of about 15 ha planted mainly with Gamay, Domaine du Vissoux produces three wines: about 40,000 bottles of classic Beaujolais; 7,000 of white Beaujolais from Chardonnay grapes (rare in the region); and another 40,000 bottles of a remarkable Beaujolais Cuvée Traditionelle. This last wine was first produced in 1986 and constitutes an attempt to re-launch an old-fashioned red wine, made without added sulphur or yeasts during fermentation, little or no chaptalization and with special care over the selection of the ripest grapes during the harvest. Despite the wine's quality, the Vissouxs had great difficulty selling it at first, but today this deliciously thirst-quenching red is one of the few Beaujolais that can be found in many of the capital's best restaurants, wine bars and wine merchants.

Beaujolais Cuvée Traditionelle 1991
A lovely bright ruby-red color with a fresh and fruity nose with inviting hints of strawberry. Lively and uncomplicated on the palate while also being well-rounded and delicate. Unremarkable in its structure, it is nevertheless a wine of a good texture as it has been neither clarified not filtered.

Georges et François Duboeuf

Boîte Postale 12
71570 Romanèche-Thorins
Tel. 85355113
Fax 85355658

Mention the word Beaujolais and the name of George Duboeuf springs to mind. In the short period since 1964 Duboeuf has built up an international reputation for his wines. Whether you like them or not, with his extraordinary energy and vision Georges Duboeuf has done wonders for the Beaujolais region on a worldwide scale. The company, which he runs like a small family business with his wife and son François, produces a staggering 25 million bottles a year, 60% of which are Beaujolais and Mâconnais with the rest made up of Côtes du Rhônes and varietal and generic table wines. The key to Duboeuf's success lies in the attention to technical details and the care with which his products are selected and bottled. In fact, Georges began his career by equipping himself with France's first mobile bottling unit and he continues to take it round hundreds of small estates from Bandol to Beaune. Duboeuf, as a result, is a guarantee of quality the world over.

Saint Véran 1991
Pale yellow in color, limpid and bright. Clean and fresh on the nose with the flowery characteristics typical of Chardonnay. There is a good balance on the palate between fruit and acidity, making this wine pleasant and very drinkable.

Fleurie 1991
The color is agreeably intense and brilliant and the nose is typical of Fleurie, with all the fruit and freshness of Gamay. Frank on the palate and easy to drink, yet with a good texture.

Moulin à Vent 1990
Aged in oak, a wine with a rich deep color and toasty notes on the nose. Good richness of fruit, more in the Pinot Noir style than in that of Gamay. The palate, too, is rich in wood but well-balanced by the strength of the wine. The aging potential is more reminiscent of a Côte de Beaune than a Beaujolais.

BEAUJOLAIS/BEAUJOLAIS
BOURGOGNE
FRANCE

283

BEAUJOLAIS/BEAUJOLAIS
BOURGOGNE
FRANCE

Jean-Marc Meunier

69640 Ville-sur-Jarnioux
Tel. 74038635
Fax 74038775

Jean-Marc Meunier is a native of Villefranche-sur-Saône with a family tradition of winemaking, an "enfant du pays" who has worked since boyhood in the vineyards, growing, pruning and harvesting vines. On the steep slopes in the heart of Pierres Dorées, the harvest is of course manual. Until a few years ago, Meunier sold some of his produce to a merchant who needs no introduction, Georges Duboeuf, but today he keeps the grapes from his 19 ha exclusively for his own wines. Fermentation is in temperature-controlled stainless steel vats with a four-day maceration. Jean-Marc is an enthusiastic producer of wines to drink young. His red wine has been enjoying success for some time both in Paris and elsewhere. Every year, on the third Thursday of November, his Beaujolais "primeur" makes its appearance. Meunier also makes a Beaujolais rosé and a white. He likes his "primeur" fresh, young, crisp, frank and a little bit cheeky. Just like Jean-Marc himself.

Beaujolais 1991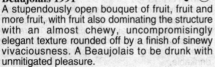
A stupendously open bouquet of fruit, fruit and more fruit, with fruit also dominating the structure with an almost chewy, uncompromisingly elegant texture rounded off by a finish of sinewy vivaciousness. A Beaujolais to be drunk with unmitigated pleasure.

Jean-Charles Pivot

Montmay
69430 Quincié-en-Beaujolais
Tel. 74043032
Fax 74890070

His brother Bernard Pivot is the popular presenter of France's top literary television program, but behind the cedars of the family estate at Montmay Jean-Charles is one of those quiet winemakers who are landmarks on the enological map of the region. The secret of Jean-Charles' success is a vineyard which he looks after with an ecologist's zeal, aware that mistakes have been made in the past. He uses a tool of his own invention, the "backsaver" (a sort of seat) for pruning the vines. There are 12 ha of clay and sandy soil spread over Quincié and Le Perréon, two of them with vines of over 90 years-old. In fact, much of the success of his Beaujolais "primeur" is due to the fact that he uses grapes from old vines. Pivot is also thrifty with yeasts, yields are moderate and there is little chaptalization. His Beaujolais-Villages is the wine to choose, though, if given the chance. It is always full-bodied and well-balanced, quite able to age for a couple of years, and vintage after vintage, the texture continues to improve.

Beaujolais-Villages 1991 ♥ ②
Bright color and a nose with hints of cherry and plum, the varietal fruit also revealing its ripeness. Very drinkable on the palate, agreeable and well-rounded, with soft, developed tannins. A sort of archetypal Beaujolais in a fragrant, lighter version. A wine that is excellent to drink straight away, or which may be laid down for a few years.

Beaujolais-Villages 1990 ♥ ②
The 1990 presents a less complex structure than the 1989. It is still, however, a Beaujolais made in the proper manner, rich in extracts, soft and velvety. Well-balanced in its components, a very attractive wine with a long finish.

BEAUJOLAIS/BEAUJOLAIS
BOURGOGNE
FRANCE

284

BEAUJOLAIS/BEAUJOLAIS-VILLAGES
BOURGOGNE
FRANCE

André Desmures

Chatenay
69115 Chiroubles
Tel. 74042342

With slopes of up to one in three on sandy, stony soils from crumbling granite, and the risk of frosts from the north, Chiroubles is certainly not the cru most favored by Mother Nature in the region. André Desmures has been cultivating six hectares since 1969 and, despite the steep slopes, he has never failed to plough in the vineyard, often using special equipment. Bearing in mind the quality of the grapes and the climatic conditions during the harvest, in difficult years several selections are necessary. Desmures is against high yields and keeps them down to 35-50 hl/ha. He avoids the use of added yeasts or chaptalization while knowing very well that his customers in a blind tasting will always opt for a wine with a higher alcohol content. Fermentation is in cement vats and takes from 5-12 days, depending on the type of wine. Desmures makes only one cuvée but bottling is spread over two periods: one at Easter for a fruity Chiroubles and another in September to obtain more rounded wines.

Chiroubles 1990
A spring bottling which offers a limpid ruby color, a delicate aroma of strawberries, a dense and well-balanced palate and a very respectable finish.

Chiroubles 1990
Bottled in September, a wine with a hint of strawberry in the bouquet. The structure and length are substantial, although there is a slight touch of alcohol in the finish.

Chiroubles 1989
Also bottled in September, this wine has a deep purple color and a fragrance of spices and violets. An uncomplicated, soft, well-balanced and attractive wine.

Daniel Guillet

La Chaize
69460 Odenas
Tel. 74034806

At the foot of Mont de Brouilly with its superb view over Dombes, Mont d'Or and Beaujolais, we find a quiet grower who produces a Gamay, or rather a Brouilly, of a kind one would like to find more often in the bars of Lyons. Daniel Guillet is a tenant on the famous Château de la Chaize estate, which takes its name from Louis XIV's confessor, and consigns half his harvest to the château. In 1990, Daniel produced a firm Brouilly, ready for drinking now but which will be better still in 1993. Yields are minimal (about 45 hl/ha) and chaptalization is very limited; from its natural 11.8° the wine was brought up to 13°. The vines cover 9.8 ha and are an average age of 40 years old. Winemaking is simple, with no pressing, and fermentation lasts from eight to ten days for Brouilly, or five to seven for the "vin nouveau".

Beaujolais-Villages 1991
A wine with appeal thanks to its freshness, fruit, roundness and length. A good classic Appellation wine.

Brouilly 1990
Fine garnet color. The nose releases hints of slightly candied red fruit (strawberry and raspberry) while the palate has the cru's typical roundness and fruit. A good, powerful but well-balanced texture.

BEAUJOLAIS/CHIROUBLES
BOURGOGNE
FRANCE

285

BEAUJOLAIS/COTE DE BROUILLY
BOURGOGNE
FRANCE

Domaine Berrod

Le Vivier
69820 Fleurie
Tel. 74041363
Fax 74698619

René Berrod, with his daughter and two sons, cultivates an extensive property whose vines average over 50 years old on granite-based soil. The southwest facing estate enjoys earlier ripening than the rest of the commune and the harvest can commence as much as fifteen days earlier if the sun has been particularly generous. Berrod is careful to select fully ripened grapes and moreover has extended fermentation from 8 to 10 days for the Fleurie, to extract the maximum fruit. Fermentation takes place in stainless steel or cement vats at temperatures of 25-32°C which are checked on a daily basis. The two cuvées are both firmly stamped with their crus. One, La Madonne, is all fruit while the other, Les Roches du Vivier, has a more determined character. Bottling usually takes place in May but is sometimes moved to make allowances for production or market demands.

Fleurie La Madonne 1990 🍇 ②
Superbly rich with the typical Gamay color, a wine which still has a slightly hard and undeveloped nose. Good fruit on the palate, well-balanced with good length. Its special structure gives it another dimension when compared to other Beaujolais and one which will allow it to develop like a Givry or Santenay. Lay down for three years before drinking.

Moulin-à-Vent Fût de Chêne 1990 🍇 ②
A fine intense color and a slightly rustic nose, rich in fruit with a note of wood. Rich on the palate but still a little undeveloped. Good depth of aromas and length. A wine which should improve over the next two years with fruit able to sustain the tannins.

André Métrat

La Roilette
69820 Fleurie
Tel. 74041235

André Métrat thinks there are too many wines to be drunk young in Beaujolais. He prefers to give his wines enough structure to age comfortably and confesses that he prefers Fleurie with some bottle-age. Métrat's four-hectare property borders on the Appellation of Moulin-à-Vent with granite, clay and sandstone soils which give his wines an easily recognizable tannin content. Fermentation takes place in stainless steel and cement vats, normally for 8-10 days, but this can be extended and allowed to run at a higher temperature for poorer vintages. Each year, there are two bottlings, one at Easter and the other three months later, after aging in tank and Allier barrels for 2-4 years. Time spent in the oak is carefully calculated and involves only 10% of the total in case the wood should dominate the wine. Yields are moderate and chaptalization is in proportion to the quality of the harvest. André Métrat avoids easy ways out and produces wines which are a credit to their Appellation.

Fleurie 1991 🍇🍇 ①
A cuvée from old vines which is exceptionally concentrated, thanks to the low yield. Pepper and capsicum are present on the nose, the tannins are undeveloped but well-rounded, with a touch of astringency and a powerful finish. A wine which is very representative of its vintage.

Fleurie 1990 🍇 ②
Bottled at Easter, this cuvée discloses moderate aromas of red fruit and good roundness, even though the finish seems a little dry.

Fleurie 1990 🍇🍇 ②
A wine from the second bottling with smoky aromas from the wood, skilfully used here. There is good balance between the body, the fruit and an almost perfect finish. Beautifully made.

René Gonon - Jean-Marc Monnet

Les Bucherats
69840 Juliénas
Tel. 74044101-74044546

It is a long time since the Canard Enchaîné, the satirical magazine, made Juliénas famous thanks to its cartoonist Henri Monnier. Monnier was a friend of Victor Peyret, a famous wine merchant whose name was associated with the annual prize awarded to the public figure who best "described" Juliénas. René Gonon still remembers those days. He owns a property of little more than three hectares which is farmed by his tenant, Jean-Marc Monnet who, at 32, is too young to remember the time when Juliénas featured in the Canard Enchaîné. Here we find the same wine under two different labels since the tenant-farmer gives part of his crop as rent to his landlord. Gonan and Monnet belong to two different generations but are united in their efforts to make superb Juliénas from the two sites of Les Bucherats and Les Mouilles. These two wines are everything a Juliénas should be.

Juliénas 1991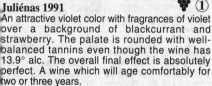
An attractive violet color with fragrances of violet over a background of blackcurrant and strawberry. The palate is rounded with well-balanced tannins even though the wine has 13.9° alc. The overall final effect is absolutely perfect. A wine which will age comfortably for two or three years.

Domaine Calot

69910 Villié Morgon
Tel. 74042055
Fax 74697293

If you ever come across a bottle of François and Jean Calot's Morgon Vieilles Vignes in a blind tasting, chances are that the sheer intensity and rustic power of the wine would take you away from an area where light, carbonic maceration wines are the norm. Morgon is, of course, an exceptional village and the Calots are one of the most traditional producers there. They have a large vineyard for Beaujolais with 11 ha of Gamay vines that are on average 25 years old, planted on the village's granite soil. The Calots are one of the area's important "producteurs greffes" or growers of young nursery vines for replanting. Their knowledge of viticulture is one of the main reasons for the excellent quality of their wines as they take conservative yields from their carefully tended plantings. The concentrated fruit is vinified very traditionally in cement tanks at relatively high temperatures with a long maceration to extract maximum color and character. The wines are aged in a mixture of cement vats and oak "foudres" and are not filtered. The 75,000 bottles or so produced annually are a fine example of the high standard Gamay is actually attaining.

Morgon Vieilles Vignes 1990 ②
An intense ruby color, shading into eggplant round the edges. Very powerful on the nose, still gamey but delicate. There are flavors of black cherry, chocolate and truffle on the palate as well as syrupy, almost leathery, notes. The tannins are soft, like a highly extracted old style Bourgogne.

BEAUJOLAIS/JULIENAS
BOURGOGNE
FRANCE

287

BEAUJOLAIS/MORGON
BOURGOGNE
FRANCE

Domaine de la Chanaise

69910 Villié-Morgon
Tel. 74691020
Fax 74691665

Dominique Piron is a go-ahead, forward-looking young man, full of ideas. He works on two estates: Domaine de la Chanaise, a 13-ha property chiefly in the Morgon Appellation, with a little Régnié and Beaujolais, and the Combiaty estate with 8 ha of Appellation Brouilly. He has recently set up the Les Vins Dominique Piron company, which buys-in grapes to make Primeur, Beaujolais, Morgon and Mâcon Blanc and manages the vineyards. All the company labels are characterized by the typical colors of the crus' soils with ochre for the soil of Régnié, blue for the rock of the Mont de Brouilly and purple for the granite of Morgon. Winemaking is very traditional with a fermentation which lasts 5 to 12 days, depending on the wine. For Morgon, each plot is harvested, fermented and aged separately until the spring, with 5-10% being put into oak barrels for a period of 6-8 months. The blending is done late and the cuvées containing more fruit are blended with those of greater richness. Dominique Piron also belongs to an association of roughly a dozen growers who are committed to solving some of the area's problems, particularly chaptalization.

Morgon
Domaine de la Chanaise 1991
"Ah ! Morgon!" the most knowledgeable tasters around these parts will say at once and indeed this de la Chanaise is chewy, vigorous and perfectly mouthfilling. A lovely garnet red color. The nose is all peppery fruit and hazelnuts. The tannins are splendidly soft on the palate and the structure is well-balanced and crisp.

Brouilly
Domaine de Combiaty 1990
A wine with good structure and frank aromas of fruit (raspberry and strawberry). Good concentration on the palate, with tannins which are slowly mellowing out. Drink now.

Domaine de la Rose du Py

69910 Villié-Morgon
Tel. 74042497
Fax 74691271

"The terroir will express itself. I'm here to get the best out of the grapes". Jean Foillard's falsely naïve declaration highlights two of nature's gifts. The 9 ha of vines which lie on the shale slopes of the Py giving the wine its unique liquorice aroma are on average 60 years old. The resulting low yields produce wines of great concentration, thanks to skilful fermentation and aging. Carbonic maceration, usually in stainless steel vats, is carried out without the addition of yeasts at controlled temperatures for 15-24 days. The wines age in Bourgogne barrels from Domaine de La Romanée-Conti and Henri Jayer and bottling takes place in spring. Blending is determined by the quality of the various barrels and there are two cuvées for sale, the best from the oldest vines which is not filtered and contains no sulfites (otherwise present in tiny quantities). Jean bottles separately when a lot of wine is of exceptional quality, so while his philosophy is of extreme simplicity, it is easy to see that his winemaking leaves absolutely nothing to chance.

Morgon Jean Foillard 1991
Bright red in color with a scarlet tinge, a clean, fresh nose of Gamay grapes with good complexity and ripeness. The freshness of the variety is still apparent on the palate of this very drinkable wine, perhaps not as rich as the '89 or the '90, but still with good length.

Morgon Jean Foillard 1989
Rich, full and intense in color, with a sweet nose full of concentrated, fairly characteristic, fruit. The rich palate confirms the presence of the fruit. Agreeable, well-balanced length and roundness. Rather unusual in that there is such a rich concentration of fruit. A remarkable wine.

BEAUJOLAIS/MORGON
BOURGOGNE
FRANCE

288

BEAUJOLAIS/MORGON
BOURGOGNE
FRANCE

Marcel Lapierre

Les Chênes
69910 Villié-Morgon
Tel. 74032389
Fax 74041440

Marcel Lapierre cultivates eight hectares of Morgon and half a hectare of Beaujolais (for vin nouveau) with vines averaging 35 years old, although some plants are as old as 45 years. He uses the most natural methods he can, tilling the vineyards, banning all chemical fertilizers and herbicides and keeping yields low, while being almost fanatically strict in his vinification. The perfectly ripened, healthy grapes are carefully selected on harvesting and then placed in temperature-controlled oak vats for carbonic maceration. No sulphur, chaptalization or added yeasts are used. Fermentation takes from two to three weeks and then the wines are aged in barrels that are up to about five years old. At the end of February, clarification is carried out using egg whites and bottling follows three months later using a devise invented by Lapierre himself which ensures an even and natural flow of wine into the bottles. The vintage is put on the market under two different labels, one just his basic Morgon and the second from grapes from a single plot. This rare wine is then divided into two. One part is neither filtered nor sulphured and the other is given a light treatment of both. These Morgons are of a flower-filled potency and have much in common with more illustrious Bourgogne wines.

Morgon 1991 🍇🍇 ①
No sulphur and no filtration was used to produce this unusually limpid color. The aroma releases definite notes of blackcurrant. The tannins are silky and delicate while the finish is long and lingering.

Morgon 1990 🍇🍇 ②
Once again, a wine which has not been filtered or treated with sulphur. The color is deep and the aromas are more peppery and spicy than the preceding wine. The tannins are already well tied in and the palate is aromatic and finishes long.

Domaine Savoye

Les Micouds
69910 Villié-Morgon
Tel. 74042192

Pierre Savoye is a grower with nerves of steel and his feet firmly on the ground. His 14-ha estate has been handed down from father to son since 1852 and lies on the hill with crumbling shale soil called "blue stone" or even "rotten rock" by the locals. From the point of view of environment and climate, the Côte de Py, where Pierre has 1.5 ha, is certainly one of the best sites to give Morgon delicacy and structure. The unique geological accident also gives the wine that unmistakable mineral flavor, rapidly hidden by the unbelievable fragrances of kirsch. Harvesting on the slopes of this famous hill has to be done manually and the bunches are kept whole. The wine is then fermented in closed vats at controlled temperatures. Best results are obtained after a couple of years in the bottle.

Morgon Côte de Py 1990 🍇 ②
A pleasant bright red in color with an unmistakably and typical nose which offers a fine range of red fruit. On the palate, there is a good balance between the harmonious tannins, and strength, acidity and exceptional freshness. The finish is just a little spicy.

BEAUJOLAIS/MORGON
BOURGOGNE
FRANCE

289

BEAUJOLAIS/MORGON
BOURGOGNE
FRANCE

Domaine des Pierres

2, route de Juliénas
71570 La Chapelle-de-Guinchay
Tel. 85367070
Fax 85338231

From 1965 to 1979, George Trichard was a tenant of a former Minister of Economy and Finance, Edouard Balladur. He then bought from Balladur six hectares of vines for himself while one of the minister's friends has bought the pretty house on the estate. The friend is Helmar Pieroth, a wine merchant and himself an ex-minister, and thus history repeats itself. This kind of continuity perhaps explains the loyalty to Trichard of two of the world's best sommeliers, Jean-Luc Pouteau and Jean-Claude Jambon, who won the world championship title in 1983 and 1986 respectively. Today the estate is made up of 10 ha. of Beaujolais -Villages on land squeezed in between the crus of Chénas and Saint-Amour on rather lean soil (shale and stones) at an elevation of 240-400 m. Yields are moderate at about 56 hl/ha and the vines, with an average age of 45 years, enjoy a favorable micro-climate. The grapes are picked by hand and go through a semi-carbonic vinification with the Saint-Amour and Chénas being fermented in whole bunches. Aging is in oak barrels and cement vats. 80% of the Beaujolais-Villages is sold as "primeur".

Saint-Amour 1991

A red wine beautifully made from grapes picked by hand. The nose reveals aromas of smoked wood and a meaty element which mingles with plum and pepper while the palate discloses a well-balanced structure with good, soft tannins and a long, well-integrated finish.

A. & P. de Villaine

71150 Bouzeron
Tel. 85912050
Fax 85870410

Aubert de Villaine is something of a personality in Bourgogne. He is co-owner of the famous Romanée-Conti on the Côte d'Or and throws himself just as passionately into the management of this more modest estate on the Côte Chalonnaise. Indeed, he has been working actively for the official recognition of the Aligoté de Bouzeron and Bourgogne Côte Chalonnaise Appellations. 18 ha, or more than half of this estate, is dedicated to the cultivation of Aligoté, well suited to the "terroir" of Bouzeron, a village to the south of Chagny. To maintain the characteristic freshness of the variety, fermentation is carried out in vats and aged for a very short time in huge barrels. On the other hand, the Chardonnay from the Appellations of the Côte Chalonnaise and Rully is aged in small barrels. His Pinot Noir vines, which are an average age of 15 years old, are still young and Aubert de Villaine has no compunction about using the "saignée" method of vinification for his reds and rosés. His rosé is full-bodied and very attractive and the red La Digoine is remarkable for its firmness and concentration.

Bourgogne Côte Chalonnaise
Les Clous 1990

The golden color does not mask the time spent in the wood. The nose is open, powerful and pleasantly characteristic with notes of honey and wood. Not a vivacious wine but full-bodied and serious, reminiscent of a fleshy Mercurey. Ready for drinking.

Bourgogne Côte Chalonnaise
La Digoine 1990

Ruby red color of medium intensity with flecks of blue. The nose reveals a rare purity of fruit. Blackcurrant, bilberry, all the red berries and even fresh figs can be distinguished on the palate in a well-balanced whole. The rustic touch typical of Côte Chalonnaise is marked and adds to the overall charm of the wine. A really lovely product, to be drunk young at cellar temperature.

BEAUJOLAIS/SAINT-AMOUR
BOURGOGNE
FRANCE

290

BOURGOGNE/COTE CHALONNAISE
BOURGOGNE
FRANCE

René Bourgeon

71640 Jambles
Tel. 85443585

René Bourgeon is a researcher as well as a grower. Not content with being in constant contact with Michel Rolland, the grand master of Bordeaux enologists, he has made countless research trips both in France and abroad. René will be the happiest man in the world when he can make his first Givry Blanc from the two hectares of Clos de la Brûlée, which he now rents exclusively. He also has eight hectares of Pinot Noir and is in favor of low yields and thinning out the density of the plantings. In making his red Givry, René practices "maceration pelliculaire" lasting 8 to 10 days after de-stalking the grapes and cold-macerating the must at 2°C. The vats gradually warm up, allowing all the natural yeasts to survive. Alcoholic fermentation takes 10-12 days and clarification is deliberately slow, so that the wine can settle before going into barriques, 20% of which are new. Malolactic fermentation takes place in summer and the wine is not disturbed again (it is only racked once) before being bottled in spring. Bourgeon wines have good structure and strong color. They should only be opened after three or four years in the bottle.

Givry 1989
A delicate bright red color with a rich, fresh nose redolent of Pinot grapes, sweet and clean. Well-rounded on the palate with ripe fruit and a well-balanced cool, pungent acidity. A couple of years in the bottle will work further wonders.

Domaine Joblot

4, rue Pasteur
71640 Givry
Tel. 85443017
Fax 85443672

In the heart of Côte Chalonnaise, Jean-Marc Joblot is a young grower who is preparing to take his place in the charmed circle of the great names of Bourgogne. He runs a 14-ha estate lying entirely in the Premiers Crus of Givry, a small commune producing above all a red wine which was one of the many to have found favor with King Henry IV. Joblot is not content merely to make wine. As he himself points out, his concern is the vineyard and he limits the yields of his vines, which are on average 20 years old. "For twelve years, our work has consisted above all in obtaining grapes of the highest quality. Today, we pursue three objectives - concentration, balance and purity". The new wood here does not serve to make up for any failing. It is merely the finishing touch to a well-integrated whole. Some vintages even earn the right to age exclusively in new Allier oak. Clos de la Servoisine is a superb Givry, both white and red, but the pride of the estate is the red Clos du Cellier aux Moines, an aristocratic wine perfect for laying down.

Givry Clos de la Servoisine 1990
A lovely bright red in color with a nose that is absolutely typical of Joblot wines, rich and clean with forward fruit. The palate discloses an excellent sweet concentration of Pinot Noir and is very attractive, with much character. A fine example of the vintage.

Givry Clos du Cellier aux Moines ♥♥ ③ Premier Cru 1990
Obtained from one of the best crus in the Appellation, a wine with a superbly rich color and good concentration of fruit on the nose. The fruit continues on the palate, where there is also a pleasantly supple hint of wood as well as natural tannins. A really pleasant wine.

COTE CHALONNAISE/GIVRY
BOURGOGNE
FRANCE

291

COTE CHALONNAISE/GIVRY
BOURGOGNE
FRANCE

Château de Chamirey

71640 Mercurey
Tel. 85452222
Fax 85452449

This vast Côte Chalonnaise estate owned by the Devillard family has 25 ha of Pinot Noir and 10 of Chardonnay. The Château itself is an elegant 18th-century building surrounded by vineyards spread over 10 plots, all classified as Premiers Crus, including Clos du Roi, Clos l'Evêque, La Mission, Les Ruelles and Les Sazenays. About one third of the estate's production is white wine and two thirds red. Part of the white ferments in new oak barrels, the remainder starts its fermentation in vats and finishes in barrels. Aging lasts for 10-12 months. For red wines, fermentation takes place both in stainless steel vats (with auto-"pigeage") and in open wooden vats. Maceration takes about 12 days and is followed by 14-18 months aging in oak barrels, one third of which are new. Château de Chamirey is distributed by the well-known négociant Antonin Rodet. Thanks to the efforts of the company chairman, Bertrand Devillard, this is a château whose products are constantly improving.

Mercurey 1990
A clear, straw-yellow color. Crisp nose of ripe fruit and roasted almonds. Uncomplicated, racy palate which is moderately fleshy. To be drunk young.

Mercurey 1990
Intense ruby color flecked with violet. The nose is impressive but rather undeveloped. Powerful initial impact with a well-balanced palate, fleshy and of good length. A Mercurey from a great vintage, which will need bottle-age.

Mercurey 1989
Fine ruby color. The nose bursts into the aromas of red berries (mulberries and blackcurrants) and sloes. Bilberries dominate on the palate and the tannins are a little hard. Rustic in style, as befits a Mercurey. Needs a year or two more in the bottle.

Domaine Michel Juillot

B.P. 10
71640 Mercurey
Tel. 8542727
Fax 8542552

The Juillots have documents to prove that they were already cultivating vines as early as 1404 and Michel Juillot, at 53, is a worthy representative of the thirty-sixth generation. Mercurey has in Michel a traditionalist with a spirit of enquiry (he advises the Fontodi estate in Tuscany). He also produces a Corton and a Corton-Charlemagne in the Côte de Beaune. Here, Michel has 30 ha, 75% Pinot Noir and 25% Chardonnay, on clay-and-limestone soil where the 25 year-old vines stand 230-270 m above sea level. It is his interest in barrels, however, which makes Michel particularly fascinating. His come from the Vosges and he chooses their 'toast' with particular care to suit the wines he is making and the conditions of the vintage. Harvesting is manual, with systematic de-stemming, while fermentation is in open vats with "pigeage" one to three times a day. Fermentation lasts for 12-16 days, there is no clarification and the wines are only filtered when it is absolutely necessary. Michel Juillot also avoids chaptalization. His son is already working with him while his daughters are both growers, one at Givry, the other at Montagny. What a wonderful family!

Mercurey Les Champs Martins
Premier Cru 1990
Softness is the principal characteristic of this wine, which comes from a vineyard of only one hectare. Butter on the nose with flowers and tobacco. Good, juicy body on the palate with good concentration. Well-balanced finish with a slightly toasty note.

Mercurey Clos de Tonnerre
Premier Cru 1989
Very intense color and a nose that is still a little undeveloped, perhaps woody, even though the wine is not aged in new barriques. Notes of autumn leaves and pepper, soft, delicate and supple tannins and a very elegant finish. An excellent wine which still needs time to age.

COTE CHALONNAISE/MERCUREY
BOURGOGNE
FRANCE

292

COTE CHALONNAISE/MERCUREY
BOURGOGNE
FRANCE

Henri et Paul Jacqueson

En Chèvremont
71150 Rully
Tel. 85912591
Fax 85871492

The Jacqueson family has lived on Côte de Chalon for centuries. Henri founded the present estate and today manages the nine hectares jointly with his son Paul. They produce red and white wines in almost exactly equal measures. The Jacquesons are considered to be among the best growers in the Chalonnais and bottle and sell all their wines under their own label. In addition to a small plot of excellent Aligoté, they grow white grapes in two vineyards in Rully (classified as Premiers Crus), Gresigny and La Pucelle. The latter has recently been replanted but the rest of the vine stock has an average age of 20 years. The wines are aged for 11 months, half in vats and half in barriques, one quarter of which are replaced every year. The property's greatest achievement is without doubt the red Rully Premier Cru, Les Clouds, a complex wine which needs to be laid down for at least five years to give its best. The other Rully Premier Cru, Les Chaponnières, and the Mercurey Premier Cru, Les Nauges, tend to mature more rapidly. All the wines are fermented in open vats for 15-18 days, and the wine is pumped over the cap two or three times a day. They are bottled after a year's aging in oak barrels, one quarter of which are replaced every year.

Mercurey Les Nauges
Premier Cru 1990
A lovely deep, bright red color and a nose with good fruit, although the concentration is slightly inferior to that of the Rully. On the palate, the fruit is a little firmer and fuller. The finish is clean and well-rounded. After three or four years in the cellar, this will be a very enjoyable bottle.

Rully Les Clouds
Premier Cru 1990
A wine with a red color as intense at the edges as it is in the middle of the glass. The nose is sweet and slightly grassy Pinot Noir. Good concentration of fruit on the palate and pleasing balance. Typical, rich and with excellent structure.

Domaine de la Renarde

Rue de la République
71150 Rully
Tel. 85871012

The speciality of this estate, which celebrated its fiftieth birthday in 1992, is Crémant de Bourgogne. It is a product which is beautifully made thanks to the careful techniques used at the well equipped cellars. Credit must also go to the legislation which in 1975 obliged Bourgogne's growers to observe production regulations almost identical to those of Champagne. Jean-François Delorme has taken over from his father and is now in charge of the business. His brothers have recognized that he is an authentic Crémant genius. This opinion is confirmed by the excellent results he achieves both when making a white wine from black grapes or when he uses white grapes (50% Chardonnay and 50% Aligoté). However, this dynamic grower, who is also mayor of Rully and exports 40% of his production, is not limited merely to Crémant. His cellar also provides an interesting range of still wines typical of the Côte Chalonnaise. The vineyards are expanding and in recent years have gone from 44 to 65 ha (18 of them in a single plot) over several Appellations - Bourgogne, Côte Chalonnaise, Bouzeron, Givry, Mercurey, Montagny and Rully.

Crémant de Bourgogne
Blanc de Blancs
A racy wine, moderately sparkling with a very fine mousse. On the palate, the structure is not outstandingly full but is very elegant. A classic aperitif.

Rully Les Varot 1989
Bright, almost luminous color. The nose is dominated by ripe berries, with obvious cherries and strawberries. Elegant structure, good sinew and a soft, clean finish.

Givry Clos du Cellier aux Moines
Premier Cru 1988
The grapes come from vine stock which is barely 20 years old. The color is a lovely bright garnet while the nose reveals wild cherry and vanilla. The richness of the structure is apparent on the palate together with a balance which will allow the wine to age for some years in the bottle.

COTE CHALONNAISE/RULLY
BOURGOGNE
FRANCE

293

COTE CHALONNAISE/RULLY
BOURGOGNE
FRANCE

Domaine Comte Senard

21420 Aloxe-Corton
Tel. 80264165
Fax 80264599

This estate is best known for its Corton Clos du Roi, Corton and Corton-Bressandes and the house and cellars sit in the middle of Senard's two-hectare "monopole" of Corton Clos des Meix tucked in among the Aloxe-Corton Premier Cru Les Valozières (3 ha). Not content with running his father's estate, Philippe Senard has a further six hectares under his management. This new vineyard added another two thirds to the area he cultivated, increasing his parcels in Chorey-lès-Beaune, Beaune and above all Savigny-lès-Beaune, with 1.5 ha in the Premier Cru Les Vergelesses. Senard has never made light or simple wines, but his products have had an added dimension since 1988. Every aspect has been re-thought, with the help of the Lebanese enologist Guy Accad. Starting in the vineyards by lowering yields and trying to pronounce the character of the various "terroirs". They fed the soils with 'oligo-elements' which allow the vines to draw on the poor nutrients in the highly oxygenated soil. Meanwhile, in the cellar the wines now undergo cold maceration before fermenting slowly up to a maximum temperature of 25°C, to preserve their aromas. Senard has gone back to aging the wines for two years in wood and abandoned clarification and filtration with the result that color, density and bottle-age potential have all improved. A step back has in fact proved to be the way forward and Senard is now producing some of the region's finest wines.

Aloxe-Corton 1990 ③
Pure raspberry red color with light flecks of blue. The nose is undeveloped and characterized by new wood but offers aromas of berries (mulberry and bilberry) with a hint of citrus. Wood dominates the initial impact on the palate, giving way to dense fruit. A wine which comes from a great vintage, with powerful yet supple tannins.

Corton Clos des Meix Monopole ④
Grand Cru 1990
Intense color with bluish tints and an incredibly concentrated nose which offers an unusual aroma of orange blossom. The wood, although somewhat masked, is present on the palate. There are also the classic aromas of red berries to be savored while all the depth and balance of this Grand Cru shine through. The tannins are present but are attractively sweet. Everything contributes to make this a great wine for drinking in the 21st century.

Jean-Pierre Diconne

Rue Velle
21190 Auxey-Duresses
Tel. 80212560

Jean-Pierre Diconne has settled at Auxey-Duresses, between Volnay and Meursault, and looks after a small property of 6.5 ha. His production is more or less equally divided between whites (Aligoté, Auxey-Duresses and Meursault) and reds (Auxey-Duresses, Côte de Beaune-Villages, Bourgogne and Passetoutgrain). Winemaking is completely traditional: the grapes are crushed but not de-stemmed and cold macerate for three or four days after treatment with sulphur. The grapes ferment in vats for ten days or so with daily "pigeage". The temperature can reach 35°C and sometimes Diconne uses the "saignée" method to encourage the concentration of the great wines and to give added delicacy to the others. With the exceptions of the Aligotés and Passetoutgrains, all the wines are aged in barrels, up to 20% of which are replaced every year. The white wines complete their fermentation in wood and stay there until they are bottled, up to 16 months later. These are wines of great concentration and delicacy, to lay down for three to eight years.

Auxey-Duresses 1990 ②
A wine with a lovely clear color and the clean, pure nose of young Chardonnay. The initial impact is crisp and lean, gaining in depth a few moments later. The palate is well-rounded with the Appellation's typical vivacity and a pleasant mineral note in the finish.

Auxey-Duresses 1990 ②
A fairly intense ruby red color. Aromas of cherry and ripe fruit. The palate features well-balanced tannins, discreet but nonetheless evident, and finishes with excellent length again on hints of cherry. A very attractive, fresh wine.

Leroy

Chemin départemental 973
21190 Auxey-Duresses
Tel. 80212110
Fax 80216381

Leroy is known as the "gardien des millésimes" partly because it sells concentrated, well-aged wines and partly thanks to Lalou Bize-Leroy, long-time owner of half the Domaine de La Romanée-Conti and a much respected local figure. She sold out of DRC in 1992 but far from running down her empire, Mme Bize-Leroy has expanded it. She was already the owner of the d'Auvenay estate at Auxey-Duresses, Meursault and Puligny-Montrachet, but felt she could not be sure of sufficient supplies of quality wine. Therefore, when in 1988 she had the opportunity to buy the Charles Noëllat property at Vosne-Romanée and then the Rémy estate at Gevrey-Chambertin, she did not need to be asked twice. With the aid of André Porcheret, a former master cellarman at the Hospices de Beaune, Lalou has introduced biodynamic cultivation methods for the vines. She has replanted with carefully selected clones and keeps yields low and fermentation long, refrigerating the vats where the wine is protected by carbon gas right from the beginning of the fermentation process and then slowly allowing the must to rise to 30-32°C. All her wines, including the eight Grands Crus, are sold at extremely high prices when young and, paradoxically, at relatively low prices when they are ready for drinking.

Richebourg Grand Cru 1989 🍇🍇 ④
This 7.7-ha vineyard only yielded 25 hl/ha for this unchaptalized wine. The nose is undeveloped, the palate pure fruit and superbly sinewy. A wine which will be ready for drinking in about ten years' time.

Vosne-Romanée 🍇🍇 ④
Les Beaux Monts Premier Cru 1988
A wine from the Noëllat property. The 2.6 ha parcel, first planted in 1903, produced 19.28 hl/ha from vines now averaging 50 years-old. Dark in color with flecks of blue, the full nose has absorbed the new wood and the palate is very structured. A wine for the future.

Nuits-Saint-Georges 🍇🍇 ④
Les Boudots Premier Cru 1964
An impressive mahogany color, intense and showing less age than one would expect. A complex, well-developed lovely gamey nose. Full-bodied initial impact with hints of talcum powder. The structure is still tannic but the finish is clean and long. Superb class.

Mazis-Chambertin 🍇🍇 ④
Grand Cru1959
Intense, faintly brown color. Very full nose, well-rounded and complex. The palate is delicate, more flowers and fruit than animal. Perfectly balanced on the palate and an exquisite texture which lingers endlessly with inimitable delicacy.

Domaine Michel Prunier

Route départementale 973
21190 Auxey-Duresses
Tel. 80212105
Fax 80216473

We owe the Prunier family a great deal when it comes to character and quality in the Appellation of Auxey-Duresses Blanc. Although it lacks the reputation of the great wines in the area, it is very well made. Michel Prunier started out with less than a single hectare of vines inherited from his father. Since then, he has become one of the most respected growers in the area with his efforts to produce wines rich in fruit and concentration, both at Auxey-Duresses and in the Appellations of Beaune and Volnay. Today, Michel has eight hectares of vineyards in several plots with chalky soil over clay-and-limestone subsoil. The vines are 65% Pinot Noir, 25% Chardonnay and 10% Aligoté. Harvesting is manual and the winemaking traditional, with 50% de-stemming and a fermentation which lasts for an average of 8-10 days at controlled temperatures. Aging in barriques (25-35% new for the Premiers Crus) lasts for 12-18 months for a relatively modest total production of about 26,000 bottles, which deserve to be left to age quietly in the cellar.

Auxey-Duresses 1990 🍇 ③
The ripe fruit and concentration in this wine are the result of moderate yields. An elegant and very soft wine with aromas of honey and fruit on the nose. Good body on the palate over a slightly hard background. Lovely balance.

Auxey-Duresses 1990 🍇 ③
Fine color and concentration, with aromas of ripe red berries and dominating blackcurrants. The wood is still present on the palate but the texture is delicate, with pleasant tannins. A wine with character.

COTE DE BEAUNE/AUXEY-DURESSES
BOURGOGNE
FRANCE

295

COTE DE BEAUNE/AUXEY-DURESSES
BOURGOGNE
FRANCE

Maison Camille Giroud

3, rue Pierre Joigneaux
21200 Beaune
Tel. 80221265
Fax 80224284

A long-established company which every year buys a few hundred barrels of wines, mainly in the Côte de Beaune, from small producers with very old vines and very low yields. The wines are aged for over two years in old barriques with minimal use of sulphur, which makes them unusually pure and easy to digest. Indeed, these wines are looked after with extreme care, protected from the air, racked only twice and lightly filtered before bottling. Bernard and François Giroud run the company their grandfather founded and sell a limited number of older vintages at prices which defy competition. They are held in particularly high regard by the best of the present generation of growers, such as Pascal Marchand at Pommard and Dominique Lafon at Meursault, who are always ready to sell them a barrel or two of their finest produce as the Girouds' aging methods are renowned. But the Giroud brothers have no desire to invent anything new. They believe that they are continuing a worthwhile commercial tradition. The Giroud catalogue contains 60-80 wines from various crus and vintages, which are listed only when they become ready for drinking.

Beaune Les Teurons 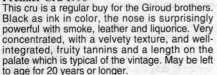 Premier Cru 1990
This cru is a regular buy for the Giroud brothers. Black as ink in color, the nose is surprisingly powerful with smoke, leather and liquorice. Very concentrated, with a velvety texture, and well-integrated, fruity tannins and a length on the palate which is typical of the vintage. May be left to age for 20 years or longer.

Savigny-lès-Beaune
Les Marconnet Premier Cru 1990
This wine has that concentrated black color that only old vines can produce. Rarely will you find a Savigny as powerful and smooth as this or with such ripe spiciness and toastiness.

Nuits-Saint-Georges
Les Hauts-Pruliers Premier Cru 1966
Mahogany in color, with a compact nose of musk, game, spice and truffle. A wine which has conserved all the freshness and fruit of its younger days while acquiring additional hints of musk. There is no trace of over-aging. Surprisingly long on the palate.

Maison Louis Jadot

5, rue Samuel-Legay
21200 Beaune
Tel. 80221057

Everybody talks about his Meursaults, like the Premier Cru Les Charmes, but it is from the Appellations around Beaune that the Louis Jadot company offers exceptionally good wines. This is because André Gagey, who has owned the company since 1954, has found that his son Pierre-Henri is a managing director capable of allowing cru and variety to speak for themselves. He therefore encourages his growers to select severely and harvest late, to de-stem, to ferment at controlled temperatures and to limit yields to a maximum of 35 hl/ha. Pierre-Henri is not enamored with primary aromas and recommends allowing wines to develop. He looks for purity in his Pinot Noir expressed through the richness of the extracts, preferring soft, sweet tannins to harder ones. One can see this in all the wines whether it be the Clos-des-Couchereaux, Beaune Premier Cru, the Pommard Premier Cru Les Arvelets, or the company's exclusive Clos-des-Ursules, Beaune Premier Cru, which enjoys an excellent exposure on its 2.5 ha. These and many more are to be found in the immense Jadot cellar which contains more than 5,000 barrels.

Meursault Les Charmes Premier Cru 1990
220 barriques carefully lined up in the huge cellar contained this Premier Cru with a lovely light straw-yellow color and a very delicate, if still undeveloped, nose. The palate is fresh and racy, with good structure. The finish is clean and frank. A wine which is ready to drink.

Beaune Clos-des-Couchereaux
Premier Cru 1990
Made with grapes from a two-hectare vineyard, the nose is all red fruit, autumn leaves, musk and mushrooms. The structure is rich, thanks to the exceptional quality and ripeness of the fruit, with elegant tannins and a truly rare freshness. The palate is complex and has good body, with a good balance of acidity and tannins. A lovely wine.

COTE DE BEAUNE/BEAUNE
BOURGOGNE
FRANCE

296

COTE DE BEAUNE/BEAUNE
BOURGOGNE
FRANCE

Domaine Joseph Matrot

21190 Meursault
Tel. 80212013
Fax 80212964

In contrast to many Bourgogne estates, the 18 ha of this property have remained more or less intact since Joseph Matrot bought them at the beginning of the century. Today, his grandson Thierry strives constantly to improve quality. The 12 ha of Chardonnay provide an interesting range of whites in the Appellations of Meursault and Puligny-Montrachet, while the 4.3 ha of Pinot Noir produce an Auxey-Duresses, the Blagny Premier Cru La Pièce Sous Le Bois and the Premier Cru Volnay Santenots. Today there are 35 ha, all on clay and limestone soil. Matrot is a firm believer in wines which express the "terroir" rather than masking its characteristics behind wood. For this reason he never uses new barrels for his white wines. After fermenting in the used wood for three weeks and aging "sur lies" for ten months, the whites are bottled before the following harvest to conserve their freshness and fruit. The reds, on the other hand, are made traditionally in open vats, and spend 11 months in barriques, 10% of which are new. This careful style of winemaking is certainly reflected in the wines.

Meursault 1990   ♉ ♉ ③
Bright yellow gold in color with flecks of green. Superbly concentrated aromas of honey, almond and grape. The palate has magnificent structure, subtlety and elegance, with firm, delicate acidity and well-balanced fruit, with citrus and hazelnut in the finish, and considerable length.

Meursault Les Charmes   ♉ ♉ ④
Premier Cru 1990
Pale gold in color and still a little undeveloped on the nose. Rich and buttery on the palate with a good lemony acidity which explodes in the finish with hazelnuts and almonds. Great structure, but needs time to express its full potential.

Blagny La Pièce Sous Le Bois   ③
Premier Cru 1990
Deep ruby red color. The nose has typical Pinot Noir fruit, with a hint of wood. On the palate, it is delicious, earthy and spicy with a hint of cherry and game. The marriage of fruit and wood is particularly good and it finishes superbly.

Domaine Jean-Noël Gagnard

21190 Chassagne-Montrachet
Tel. 80213168
Fax 80213307

Gagnards have lived in Chassagne-Montrachet for more than a century. The inheritance laws have gradually broken up the family vineyard into tiny parcels which often bear the names of various spouses. Jean-Noël Gagnard is a member of the committee which checks the yields from Grand Cru vineyards and has recently been joined by his daughter in their own vineyard. His pride and joy, from an estate which extends over 8.5 ha, is Bâtard-Montrachet, where he has a 36.4 are parcel acquired by his parents, the Gagnard-Coffinets. Jean-Noël also has plots in the red and white Premiers Crus of Chassagne-Montrachet Les Caillerets, Le Clos Saint-Jean, La Maltroie and Morgeot. Most of their production goes to select private customers who come to buy them knowing that they are some of the finest wines in the area.

Bâtard-Montrachet   ♉ ♉ ④
Grand Cru 1989
Intense pale yellow color with a flowery, nutty nose of multi-layered complexity that slowly opens out. The palate is rich and limey with plenty of structured Chardonnay fruit. It promises to age well with its beautifully balanced structure, excellent acidity and captivating concentration.

Chassagne-Montrachet Morgeot   ♉ ④
Premier Cru 1988
Intense and vibrant pale gold, the nose of flowers and hazelnut opens out slowly but is intense and fine. The palate is rather warm, but not lacking in zesty freshness or structure and this is another wine that can only benefit from some age.

Chassagne-Montrachet Morgeot   ④
Premier Cru 1989
Bottled after aging for 18 months in oak, this wine is already open and appealing. The color is an intense ruby and has a delicate cherry and spice nose. The tannins are already well integrated and the texture on the palate is elegant and fine, but the structure and intensity of fruit betray the fact that time will make this an even greater wine.

COTE DE BEAUNE/BLAGNY
BOURGOGNE
FRANCE

COTE DE BEAUNE/CHASSAGNE-MONTRACHET
BOURGOGNE
FRANCE

297

Marquis de Laguiche - Maison Joseph Drouhin

7, rue de l'Enfer
21201 Beaune
Tel. 80246888

The history of France has unfolded on the 2.06 ha of Montrachet which have belonged to the Laguiche family since 1776. The same family also owns the Château de Chaumont, in Saône-et-Loire, whose 17th-century stables can hold up to 99 horses. Members of this noble family have covered themselves in "gloire" both in diplomacy and in battle and Alexandre Dumas recounts that the Three Musketeers enjoyed their hospitality. Today, the Joseph Drouhin company makes and sells all their wines from this historic vineyard. Their enologist, Laurence Jobard, oversees vinification with a keen attention to detail. She is herself a grower at Pommard on her family estate and since 1989 has also been active in Provence at Domaine de la Mascaronne. These Montrachets from the Marquis of Laguiche's property have always been the subject of much attention, to the point that Maurice des Ombiaux compared its bouquet to a "Magnificat under the vault of a Gothic cathedral". Without being quite so lyrical, we can assure you that it is a truly great wine.

Montrachet Grand Cru 1990   ℞ ℞ ④
The nose is still very tight, but like most of the 1990s betrays the hidden power and intensity that will eventually develop. The palate is rich with honey, toast, acacia and lime blossom. A wine of great elegance and perfect balance which will be at its best in three or four years, perhaps under a Gothic arch.

Bernard Morey et fils

3, rue de Morgeot
21190 Chassagne-Montrachet
Tel. 80213213
Fax 80213972

The 1.5 ha of the south-east facing Les Embazées (or Embassées) vineyard occasionally worries Bernard Morey. His grapes are sometimes so super-ripe they lack sufficient acidity to guarantee good freshness. Morey puts the must, after the grapes have been crushed and refrigerated to 15°C, into barrels, one quarter new, without clarification. The must then ferments at 15-20°C and malolactic fermentation takes place while the wine is still "sur lies". There is one "bâtonnage" a week until fermentation is complete. Bottling is only done around mid - August, after blending. M. Morey has such an aversion to bad quality wood that he is toying with the idea of buying it himself and seasoning it in the open air for two or three years. Morey's concern over oak does credit to one of the best growers in the area, whose 10 ha cover many of the most prized crus.

Chassagne-Montrachet   ℞ ②
Premier Cru Les Embazées 1990
This tiny plot at the edge of the Appellation, also called Bois de Chassagne, gives a wine with a highly attractive, fresh bouquet on a background of toastiness. The wood is beautifully knit on the ripe palate, with a slightly honeyed and very concentrated finish. Ready to drink.

Domaine Marc Morey et fils

3, rue Charles Paquelin
21190 Chassagne-Montrachet
Tel. 80213011
Fax 80219020

It is difficult to make sense of the many branches of the Morey family in Chassagne and Meursault, but this estate is run by Bernard Mollard-Morey, son-in-law of Marc, whose father was one of the earliest in-house bottlers in the 1930s. A third of the wines produced on this 8.75-ha property are white and include a simple but very good Saint-Aubin Blanc. Fermentation of the Chardonnay grapes starts in temperature-controlled steel vats and finishes in 25%-30% new Allier and Vosges barriques where the wine stays for one year. 90% of the Pinot Noir grapes are de-stemmed and they all ferment for about 12 days at carefully-controlled temperatures. The wines age for 15-18 months in barrels (up to 25% of which are new). The house style tends towards forward wines which are ready to drink after five years. It is however necessary to wait longer for the Bâtard-Montrachet and the Chassagne-Montrachet Les Caillerets.

Chassagne-Montrachet 1991   🍇 ②
Pale gold in color. A very young nose, still bearing the signs of recently-completed fermentation with lots of bread-dough and flowery fruit under rough new oak. In the mouth the initial impact is clean and uncomplicated. Well-made, but difficult to judge so young.

Chassagne-Montrachet   🍇🍇 ③
Premier Cru Virondot 1990
Pale straw-yellow in color, with a winey nose, already very expressive with discreet wood and plenty of pure fruit. The palate is beginning to develop fascinating aromas of exotic fruit, vanilla and spices. The "terroir" really shows through with fine concentration.

Chassagne-Montrachet   🍇🍇 ③
Premier Cru Les Chenevottes 1989
Well-developed, characteristic notes of butter and hazelnut. The clean palate is rather undeveloped but has obvious power with typically marked acidity and a great future. The structure is impeccable with no trace of heaviness on the finish .

Chassagne-Montrachet 1991   🍇 ②
A wine with a beautiful bluish ruby color which is very tight and undeveloped on the nose. The palate is fruity and vigorous at first with marked acidity and agreeable wood, albeit a little heavy. Intense structure which will mellow out with time.

Domaine Michel Niellon

21190 Chassagne-Montrachet
Tel. 80213095

Michel Niellon has a fairly large property at Chassagne, the reputed home of the best white wines in the world. Niellon has vines in most of these legendary vineyards including 11.9 ares planted in 1926 on Bâtard-Montrachet at the feet of Montrachet and 22.73 ares planted between 1962 and 1968 in Chevalier-Montrachet. The soil is that classic sandy clay and chalk. Niellon also produces red Chassagne in the Premier Cru of Clos Saint-Jean and a variety of white Premiers Crus from Les Chenevottes and Les Vergers to the north of the village and at La Maltroie to the south. While selling off part of his production to négociants, Michel Niellon keeps the best wines for himself and has recently offered excellent vintages which are soon ready to drink.

Bâtard-Montrachet 1986   🍇 ④
A fine pale straw-yellow color with a powerful nose. Fleshy on the palate with a regal generosity and good acidity. The fruit on the finish is so fresh and concentrated it easily balances the hefty alcohol.

Chevalier-Montrachet   🍇🍇 ④
Grand Cru 1986
Pale gold in color. The nose is all candied fruit, wood and flowers. The palate is fleshy, with alcohol unmistakably dominant but well balanced out by good acidity. Opulent and firm but fresh on the finish.

COTE DE BEAUNE/CHASSAGNE-MONTRACHET
BOURGOGNE
FRANCE

299

COTE DE BEAUNE/CHASSAGNE-MONTRACHET
BOURGOGNE
FRANCE

Domaine Ramonet

21190 Chassagne-Montrachet
Tel. 80213088

Ramonet was a world-famous, magical name even before its appearance on the wine-lists of the greatest restaurants in France, yet Pierre, André, Noël, Jean-Claude and Michaël are not mentioned in the first International Who's Who of Wine. That, however, is the least of their worries for they are people who keep their feet firmly on the ground. The vineyards are their life and their talk is the talk of growers who have always worked hard and are not trying to put on airs and graces. They live modestly and are still puzzled by the interest shown by the enthusiasts who come to visit them from all over the world. Their 17-ha estate includes a tiny vineyard at Puligny for Montrachet (25.9 ares) which they bought in 1978 and from which they produce only two 225-l barriques, or about 600 bottles, every year. They also have parcels in the white Chassagne-Montrachet Premiers Crus of Cailleret, Morgeot and Ruchottes as well as in red Premiers Crus of Boudriotte, Clos Saint-Jean and Morgeot. Finally, they also have holdings bought in 1955 in Bâtard-Montrachet and Bienvenues-Bâtard-Montrachet. This is indeed a family rich beyond the dreams of avarice because the Montrachet parcel alone is worth over a million dollars at today's prices.

Montrachet Grand Cru 1985   🍷🍷 ④
If you are not quite sure what you can get from ripe Chardonnay, come and learn from the Ramonets. Their hard work in the vineyard has produced a cuvée of enormous complexity. On the nose, on the palate and in the finish, it has a veritable explosion of aromas and flavors of lemon, almond and mint among many, many others. A wine of rare elegance.

Montrachet Grand Cru 1983   🍷🍷 ④
Great memories never dim. First tasted in the company of the late Alain Chapel at Mionay, this wine began with one revelation and finished with another. It has spicy notes of honey and citrus on the balmy nose while the generous palate releases vanilla and lime. The rich alcohol content (14.5°) and the elegantly aristocratic finish guarantee at least two decades of comfortable aging in the bottle.

Domaine Tollot-Beaut et fils

21200 Chorey-lès-Beaune
Tel. 80221654
Fax 80221261

Perhaps because of its unusually large size for Bourgogne (22 ha), the Tollot-Beaut estate has always been family-run. Jacques, François and Alain Tollot manage the property with skill and passion, carefully nurturing wines from 14 Appellations which range from ordinary Aligoté to Grands Crus. They cultivate seven hectares, with the largest parcel in the Appellation of Chorey-lès-Beaune, which gives wines for drinking young. They also have a large parcel in Aloxe-Corton, half of which is in Premier Crus and which gives wines for laying down. The harvest from the tiny parcels at Chorey, Savigny and Bourgogne is blended into an excellent Bourgogne Blanc, much favored by restaurateurs for its youthful zest. The Tollots ferment in open vats and macerate for 8-12 days. All their wines are aged in wood, with varying proportions of new oak. The Tollot style tends towards delicate, rather than powerful wines but the Grands Crus are chewy, complex and deserve to be laid down. The Corton and Corton-Bressandes are two such wines as are the 4-5 barrels of Corton-Charlemagne Blanc, made from old vines with an average age of over 40 years.

Beaune Clos du Roi   🍷🍷 ②
Premier Cru 1990
Intense color with faint violet tinges. Clear aromas of raspberry, blackcurrant and toasty wood on the nose. The palate is full-bodied and well-balanced, right from the initial impact. Still a little undeveloped, the structure is firmer than that of the Savigny. Perfect fruit, with fresh, elegant length in the finish. An excellent result which will age well.

Chorey-lès-Beaune 1990   🍷 ②
Lovely, delicate, youthful color of ruby and strawberry red. The nose is typical Pinot with plenty of raspberry and cherry. No great impact on the palate, but a wine with attractive fruit and elegance.

Savigny-Les-Beaune   🍷🍷 ②
Les Lavières Premier Cru 1990
Splendid ruby color of medium intensity. Aromas of red fruit and cherry with a discreet hint of wood. All the fascination of Savigny with typically outstanding length on the palate. There is an elegant aroma of blackcurrant on the finish. A wine which will develop body and length.

Aloxe-Corton 1988   🍷🍷 ③
Bright, youthful color. The palate is complex and gamey. The fruit is frank and uncomplicated with a surprisingly powerful structure . A wine which will need time to mellow out and age.

Chevalier père et fils

Buisson
21550 Ladoix-Serrigny
Tel. 80264630
Fax 80264147

Claude Chevalier has been working with his father Georges for about 20 years on this estate with nearly 11-hectares in Ladoix and Aloxe-Croton. Four fifths of their wine is red, but the greatest and best-known of their wines is a white Charlemagne. The Chevaliers are rather traditional in outlook and take good care of their vines. The red grapes are de-stemmed and ferment for about 8 days, with twice daily "pigeage". The cement vats are easy to look after and make few demands on the refrigeration system. Bottling is done after 18 months in barrel, during which time the wine is racked only twice. White wines ferment in the vat and are immediately transferred to wood. The Grands Crus spend some time in new barriques, one fifth of which are replaced every year. The estate includes 3 ha in Ladoix, 1.5 ha in a single plot in Aloxe-Corton and above all 1.5 ha in Corton and Corton Rognet. These last two are austere wines which need time, like the Ladoix white Les Gréchons.

Ladoix 1990
A pale straw-yellow color with a slight nose of new wood. The fruit is more evident on the palate, but it is not fleshy or full, with the typical austerity of this Appellation.

Bourgogne Passetoutgrain 1990
The color is an attractively full pink. The nose is all fresh red fruit while the palate is straightforward and agreeable. The finish is crisp and aromatic. The Gamay is particularly well handled here and lacks the hardness it often acquires from the "terroir" of the Côte d'Or.

Ladoix Le Clou d'Orge Premier Cru 1989
Cherry in color with faint hints of mahogany. The nose is complex and delicate, with burnt wood and fruit. The subtly softening aromas make it attractive with round, fruity tannins. A successful vintage which is now coming into its own.

Corton Le Rognet Grand Cru 1986
A younger, more intense color than the Ladoix, and one which does not pale at the edge. The nose is powerful and characteristic of the cru with flowers, earth and white truffle. The palate is slight at first and then full and generous with a velvety texture, good structure and fruit that returns agreeably on the finish over chewy tannins.

Domaine Michel Mallard et fils

Route Nationale
21550 Ladoix-Serrigny
Tel. 80264064
Fax 80264749

Michel Mallard's wines are well-known to Parisians, who have been enjoying them for years at the Tour d'Argent as well as in old bistrots like La Cloche des Halles and l'Henri IV. His 14-ha estate produces Aligoté de Bourgogne and Ladoix Blanc, but above all it produces red wines like Passetoutgrain, Aloxe-Corton, Corton and Ladoix, including the Les Joyeuses Premier Cru (1.3 ha), a much more serious wine than its name would suggest. Michel uses a computerized monitoring system for vinification which allows him to regulate temperatures with great accuracy, 25-27°C for the reds and 16-18°C for the whites. The reds undergo a 12-15 day maceration and age for about 15 months in barriques, 20-25% of which are new. The commune of Ladoix, the first village you come to in the Côte de Beaune after leaving the Côte de Nuits, is still under-rated and like all the good growers who live there, Michel Mallard sells wines which are excellent value for money.

Ladoix Les Joyeuses Premier Cru 1989
A superb wine with a lovely dark ruby color, typical of outstanding young Bourgogne. The nose is simple and correct, with concentrated red fruit (raspberry and redcurrant) and biscuits. A well-balanced wine on the palate with prominent fruit, good body and a finish of very fruity tannins. There is no excess alcohol in the structure and this wine has a long future ahead of it.

Ladoix 1985
The garnet color has pretty flecks of mahogany. The open nose is full of ripe fruit and autumn leaves. The palate is well-developed and, while not of outstanding depth, is soft and lingering with good consistency.

COTE DE BEAUNE/LADOIX
BOURGOGNE
FRANCE

301

COTE DE BEAUNE/LADOIX
BOURGOGNE
FRANCE

Jean-François Coche-Dury

9, rue Charles Giraud
21190 Meursault
Tel. 80212412

If Jean-François Coche-Dury's wines had to be summed up in a single word, it would be "reserved", which perfectly describes Jean-François himself. He is a man who works for the future with discipline and meticulous care, refusing to make (while not condemning) "Meursaults which go onto the market after only 11 or 12 months". Jean-François' own brand of perfectionism has led him to buy directly his Allier oak barrels to be sure that they are properly seasoned. The grapes of the Premiers Crus, which he harvests at their absolute peak, are only a small proportion of the nine hectares he cultivates. Both crushing and clarification are kept to a minimum. Fermentation takes place in barrels, one sixth of which are replaced annually, and the cap is broken up only for the first three months. Malolactic fermentation is slow and goes ahead at its own pace, finishing after 8-10 months. Bottling takes place an average of 20 months after the harvest and there is no filtration.

Meursault 1990

A very clear green-gold color with a bright, limpid appearance. There are aromas of fresh green apple and creamy vanilla accompanied by a little toastiness. The flavor reveals a solid structure with lively acidity which leaves the mouth fresh and clean. The flavor of apple returns with a rather strong aroma of almond skins. The agreeable vanilla flavor is due to the 20% new wood and the delicious fresh fruit. A wine which is more racy than austere, with good length for a straight Meursault, and very typical of the vintage.

Bourgogne 1990

Despite having been in the bottle for a year, the color is still a youthful bright cherry red. The aroma is pure fruit and warm wood together with hints of leather. This fruit is also present on the palate with fruits of the forest which mingle outstandingly well with the 30% new wood. It has full fruit, consistent tannins and pleasing length. An uncompromising wine which is a credit to the Appellation.

Meursault Perrières
Premier Cru 1990

The same pale green-gold color as the Meursault 1990 but with a much more sophisticated bouquet which is still giving little away at this stage of its development with a touch of vanilla and toasty oak, hardly surprising as it was only bottled in May 1992. The palate is still undeveloped although it discloses great sweetness and concentration of fruit with wood and a pleasing creaminess, together with the taste of apple we found in the Meursault. The structure is extremely seductive but there is little of the wine's real character and potential for the time being, just sheer concentration. Harmonious, free of rough edges, with subtle acidity and a finish of almonds, this is a wine with all the hallmarks of excellence.

COTE DE BEAUNE/MEURSAULT
BOURGOGNE
FRANCE
302
COTE DE BEAUNE/MEURSAULT
BOURGOGNE
FRANCE

Domaine Darnat

20, rue des Forges
21190 Meursault
Tel. 80212330
Fax 80216462

Henri Darnat is one of a kind in Meursault. He has only recently taken to growing, for it is only six years since his father died and he took over the four hectares of the estate. He has sole rights to Clos Richemont, a sloping vineyard with wonderful sunlight where the vines stand on lean soil. Work in winter and spring aerates the soil and builds up the strength of the vines. Henri has no qualms about harvesting 4 or 5 days after other growers and leaves the grapes for 9-12 hours to settle in the vats after crushing. Then they go into large, young barrels (1-3 years old). Once fermentation is over (and the must has undergone a light "bâtonnage"), he opens the doors of his cellar under the old city hospital which keeps the temperature at between 0°C and 5°C. After malolactic fermentation, the Clos Richemont, clarified and racked, is bottled in the spring. Only the 10% of the production bound for the French market is not filtered.

Meursault Clos Richemont Premier Cru 1990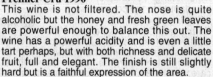
This wine is not filtered. The nose is quite alcoholic but the honey and fresh green leaves are powerful enough to balance this out. The wine has a powerful acidity and is even a little tart perhaps, but with both richness and delicate fruit, full and elegant. The finish is still slightly hard but is a faithful expression of the area.

Meursault Clos Richemont Premier Cru 1989
Slight presence of alcohol and wood. The nose is laden with lime and wood with plenty of honey and an astringency on the palate which does not obscure the delicacy and concentration of the fruit. Absolutely typical long, concentrated finish.

Meursault Clos Richemont Premier Cru 1988
A vintage with a delicate nose of flowers and fruit (rhubarb and rose petals) with roundness and grip on the palate. Will continue to age for some years to come.

Bernard Delagrange

10, rue du 11 Novembre
21190 Meursault
Tel. 80212272
Fax 80216593

This ancient feudal residence, carved from the rock in the 14th and 15th centuries, still has unusual two-storey cellars dating from that period. It was already producing wine in the days when it belonged to Charles the Bold and today the expert hands of Bertrand Delagrange carry on the tradition. The Delagranges have been growers for several generations, a heritage of which Bertrand (well into his seventies) is very conscious. His 23 ha of vines are on clay and limestone soil and are an average of 20 years old. They produce enough grapes to make 120,000-150,000 bottles a year, ranging from straightforward Aligoté to various Volnays and a remarkable white Meursault Charmes Premier Cru and complex red Meursault Le Clos. Bernard remains a fervent supporter of traditional methods, aging his reds for 18 months in oak and indeed keeps all his white wines in barrel for at least a year. M. Delagrange is also a passionate enthusiast for older vintages, but then all his wines deserve to age for a few years before being tasted.

Volnay Clos du Village 1990
Pale ruby color with well-developed Pinot nose. On the palate there is plenty of fruit but without great finesse: good for a Villages.

Volnay Les Caillerets Premier Cru 1990
Intense ruby color with a frank nose which is still relatively undeveloped. Fine initial impact with all the fruit of Volnay. Extremely elegant on the palate, with a delicate structure and good length.

COTE DE BEAUNE/MEURSAULT
BOURGOGNE
FRANCE

303

COTE DE BEAUNE/MEURSAULT
BOURGOGNE
FRANCE

Jean-Michel Gaunoux

1, rue de Leignon
21190 Meursault
Tel. 80212202

Jean-Michel Gaunoux is a sportsman who plays to win and the game he really wants to win is that of making his Pommards. It should not be too difficult either; he has a total of sic hectares including two hectares of Pinot Noir right under Les Épenots, perfectly placed to really express the "terroir". His yields from the 30-35 year old vines are often lower than the Appellation's limits (which average 40 hl/ha) and the grapes are picked at peak ripeness. To extract the maximum color from the grapes, the bunches are placed in temperature-controlled stainless steel vats and fermented for 15-20 days in the completely renovated cellar. M. Gaunoux has no hesitation in using the "saignée" method when the harvest is good with the aim of obtaining good concentration. The wines are aged in relatively new barrels (one to three years old) for about 18 months. Jean-Michel thinks that clarification is to be avoided as it takes more away from the wine than light filtration. He prefers to use traditional methods with modern equipment. Both his whites (Meursaults) and his reds are in fact very reliable.

Pommard Les Perrières 1990　🍇 ③
A rich deep red in color. The nose is of ripe and candied fruit, pepper and capsicum as well as a slightly grassy. The tannins are rather dominant on the palate but are clean, full and delicate. The finish is powerful with the overall richness of the vintage.

Pommard Les Perrières 1989　🍇 ③
The alcohol is quickly overwhelmed by aromas of leather and dry tobacco. Solid initial impact and impressive texture on a palate which is full-bodied and not without freshness. A well-structured wine with a little way to go yet.

Pommard Les Perrières 1988　🍇 ③
Intense in color, well-rounded on the palate with a faint note of astringency. The tannins are still a little hard but the structure shows quality. Still needs time.

Patrick Javillier

7, impasse des Acacias
21190 Meursault
Tel. 80212787
Fax 80212939

Patrick Javillier demands a lot from his Meursault; "goût de terroir", delicacy and richness of fruit as well as character and good aging qualities. Each plot in his 3.5-ha estate is individually vinified. The vines in the vineyards of Narvaux and the Casse-Tête grow on poor soil with the underlying rock very near the surface and produce his most mineral, powerful and concentrated wines which also need most time to age (a minimum of five years). Les Tillets produces a more delicate wine, whilst Les Cloux and the Clos du Cromin are good but altogether less fine. All Javillier wines are fermented and aged "sur lies" (with "bâtonnage") in oak barrels which are replaced every five years. New wood is limited to about 15-20% as, according to Patrick, its over-use can damage young wines. Bottling generally takes place in September, sometimes without filtration (especially in the case of Narvaux and Casse-Tête) where the wine has settled on its own or been clarified. Patrick Javillier maintains that there are no absolute truths or dogmas in winemaking. Technique, he believes, should be adapted to the conditions.

Bourgogne Cuvée des Forgets 1990　🍇 ②
Easily confused with a Meursault in blind tastings, which shows that this wine, with its sparkling bright color, has been made with great care. Unfiltered, it is of rare complexity with a structure that superbly expresses Chardonnay. A perfect example of what can be done with Bourgogne's stupendous soil.

Meursault Les Casse-Tête
Premier Cru 1990　🍇🍇 ③
The advantages of aging in oak are particularly clear in this wine. Toasty oak is superbly built into the fruit and visible in the yellow-gold color. The aromas of acacia are accompanied by minerals. The balance between acidity and supple alcohol is perfect.

Meursault Les Tillets
Premier Cru 1989　🍇🍇 ③
A wine with a beautiful golden color and a very intense nose of vanilla and honey. On the palate it is both powerful and aromatic, dense and deep, with a rich extract which will last for many more years in the cellar. A wine of overwhelming charm and excitement.

COTE DE BEAUNE/MEURSAULT
BOURGOGNE
FRANCE
304
COTE DE BEAUNE/MEURSAULT
BOURGOGNE
FRANCE

Domaine des Comtes Lafon

Clos de La Barre
21190 Meursault
Tel. 80212217

The Lafons have been active in Meursault for more than a century but had always run the risk of seeing their name disappear from the labels as almost all of their harvest was grown by tenants and then sold on to négociants. In 1956 Count René Lafon took over and started the business and its 13 ha of vines, which are now run by the young Bruno and Dominique Lafon. Dominique, whilst at Beaune's enological college, met André Ostertag, a young grower from Alsace, and they became such great friends that Dominique finally admitted that it was possible to grow great wine outside Bourgogne. The Lafon vines are up to 70 years old and are dotted around Volnay, Montrachet and above all Meursault. Quality is the only objective. Yields are kept low (25-35 hl/ha for both red and white wines), pruning is severe, little fertilizer is used and chaptalization is carried out only if absolutely necessary. The wine is fermented in entirely new barrels in the case of the grands and Premiers Crus and in one year-old barrels in the case of other wines. White wines are aged "sur lies" for 18 months. The wines are fined but not filtered before they are bottled. In short, these wines are made with quite exceptional commitment to quality.

Meursault Clos de la Barre 1990 🍇🍇 ④
The winemaker has left his indelible mark on this impressive-looking Meursault. The nose is lemon, lime and honey while the palate has a background of hazelnuts, a rich, fleshy body free of alcoholic heaviness and a long, supple finish. All the characteristics of a typical Meursault, but this one is a Clos de la Barre.

Montrachet Grand Cru 1990 🍇🍇 ④
You will have to wait until the end of the century for this wine. A pale, elegant hue of outstanding richness and a full body, this is a fleshy white wine which is still undeveloped on the nose but nonetheless exudes refinement and distinction.

Volnay Les Santenots du Milieu 🍇🍇 ④
Premier Cru 1990
A master stroke which takes Dominique Lafon right to the top of the list of great Burgundian winemakers. He has harvested grapes of a stunning quality, the like of which is seen perhaps once or twice a century. They contain over 14° natural alcohol and far from being over-ripe have a beautiful balance of acidity. The fruit is fantastically layered and complex in a wine which will age without difficulty.

Meursault -Perrières 🍇🍇🍇 ④
Premier Cru 1990
If winemaking is an art, this bottle is a masterpiece by Dominique Lafon. As soon as you lift the glass to your nose, you know that this is a Meursault, but above all it is a Meursault-Perrières. The cru is beautifully represented by the aristocratic nose and exemplary vinification. Fleshy on the palate, with a rich body absolutely free of heaviness. The balance between alcohol and acidity is perfect. A great wine and, as André Ostertag says, one born of a special encounter between a man, a variety and a "terroir".

COTE DE BEAUNE/MEURSAULT
BOURGOGNE
FRANCE

305

COTE DE BEAUNE/MEURSAULT
BOURGOGNE
FRANCE

Domaine Michelot

31-33, rue de la Velle
21190 Meursault
Tel. 80212317
Fax 80216362

"Even if you can always feel the winemaker's personal touch, it is the terroir that really stands out", says Bernard Michelot, whose wines grace the grandest tables in France. Easy to say when your "terroir" is 22 ha of magnesium rich limestone-clay in ten Climats and Premiers Crus of Meursault. Les Grands Charrons, a one-hectare plot close to the Goutte d'Or, stands on well-drained soil where the grapes are always picked ripe, or even over-ripe, before being gently crushed by a pneumatic press. The must ferments in barrels which are one to four years old, without clarification, and has five or six "bâtonnages" before being racked and blended in May. The wines are bottled in September, as Bernard does not want them to be overwhelmed by wood. For similar reasons, his wines were not chaptalized at all in 1989-1991 as nature had already made sufficient provision. An honest, hard-working family with a consistently fine Meursault.

Meursault   ⅋ ③
Les Grands Charrons 1991
A highly seductive wine despite its rustic appearance. The nose reveals very delicate aromas of honey, almond, hazelnut and lemon. The initial impact on the palate is frank and clean, with excellent length. All of this is to the credit of the winemaker. The finish has a faint hint of alcohol which is quickly smoothed over by the overall freshness of the wine.

Meursault   ⅋ ③
Les Grands Charrons 1988
A very correct wine with delicate aromas of honey. The palate holds notes of muscat grapes and is clear, with good acidity. Will need time to reach its full potential.

Domaine Jacques Prieur

2, rue des Santenots
21190 Meursault
Tel. 80212385
Fax 80212919

The Prieur estate has long been famous but had a difficult period during the 1980s. Previously managed by Martine Prieur, the property has now passed to the serious and ambitious négociant, Antonin Rodet, who in turn has handed distribution over to the giant Laurent-Perrier. The dynamic Bertrand Devillard should help the estate to make up lost ground. He is Rodet's right-hand man and capable of doing justice to the vineyards, 15 ha in Côte de Beaune and Côte de Nuits including 8 Grands Crus and 6 Premiers Crus. The white wines are put into oak barrels right from the start of fermentation and stay there for a year. The Pinot Noir is de-stemmed and fermented in open vats for two weeks, with "pigeage" three times a day and aging in new barrels for 18 months. The largest parcels on the estate are to be found at Puligny-Montrachet Les Combettes (white), Meursault Clos de Mazeray (red and white), Beaune Clos de la Féguine and Clos Vougeot (both red). It is, however, the Grands Crus that are most anxiously awaited - Chambertin, Chambertin-Clos de Bèze and Musigny and, for white wine, Chevalier-Montrachet and Montrachet. Look out: the Prieur estate is poised for a comeback.

Chambertin Grand Cru 1989   ⅋⅋ ④
An intense color with bluish tints. The nose has typical notes of liquorice. The initial impact on the palate seems rather weak but it then firms up. A great wine, still relatively undeveloped, which is at present only hinting at great things to come.

Musigny Vieilles Vignes   ⅋ ④
Grand Cru 1989
A parcel of 0.75 ha which produces a wine with a dark, violet-flecked color. The nose at the moment is dominated by very toasty wood. The palate is impressive, with wood and alcohol prevalent, and does not yet give off its best. It will be at least ten years before this wine is fully developed.

COTE DE BEAUNE/MEURSAULT
BOURGOGNE
FRANCE
306
COTE DE BEAUNE/MEURSAULT
BOURGOGNE
FRANCE

Domaine Roulot

1, rue Charles Giraud
21190 Meursault
Tel. 80212165
Fax 80216436

After starting out as an actor, Jean-Marc Roulot has become more and more drawn to viticulture. It has to be said that it was not an easy choice for him to make. His father, Guy, was a genuine character and on his sudden death, he was brilliantly replaced by the young Ted Lemon, and American-Burgundian enologist who is currently managing the Woltner estate in California. Today, Jean-Marc has taken charge of the 12 ha of 25-35 year-old vines with skill and enthusiasm. While he produces two good quality red wines, a Bourgogne and an Auxey-Duresses, Jean-Marc's estate is best-known for its whites, from the simple Bourgogne to the Premiers Crus Meursaults like Les Tillets or Les Luchets whose value for money has been noted by restaurateurs. Roulot wines are delicate, rather than powerful, and are typified by their perfect cleanness (they are made in an immaculate cellar). The wood (20-30% new) is not dominating but does give an important contribution. The wines are aged "sur lies", until malolactic fermentation is complete, to preserve the freshness and elegance of the wines. Indeed these characteristics have become the property's hallmarks.

Bourgogne Chardonnay 1991 🍇 ②
Recently bottled, a wine with a delicate golden color and a very youthful nose. Rich in fresh, young fruit, there is also a slight hint of yeast. Good structure on the palate, with sweet fruit and the vanilla of new wood. Needs time. Excellent value for money.

Meursault Les Luchets 1990 🍇🍇 ③
Vibrant gold color with flecks of green. Typical Meursault nose, slightly vegetal with hints of honey. Rich and full, it bursts onto the palate with a concentration of honey and ripe fruit. Splendid texture and the delicate acidity which characterized the 1990 vintage. Excellent length.

Meursault Les Perrières 🍇🍇 ④
Premier Cru 1990
An almost luminous green-gold in color. Complex nose with intense aromas of honey and walnut. Absolutely stunning on the palate, strong and elegant with honey, butter and caramel enveloping a remarkable texture. Excellent balance and length. A truly great wine.

Auxey-Duresses 1990 🍇 ②
Dark ruby red in color, as befits a 1990. The nose is pure Pinot, with stewed prunes and strawberries. The palate is clean and full of raspberries. An honest, fruity example, not too long and with hard tannins. In time, this should become a very attractive wine.

Domaine Bouzerand-Dujardin

Place du Monument
21190 Monthélie
Tel. 80212008

Xavier Bouzerand was the first grower in the village of Monthélie, between Volnay and Meursault, to sell his wines in bottles. Having taken over his grandfather's estate, in 1990 he joined up with the young, enthusiastic grower Ulrich Dujardin. Bouzerand has seven hectares of vines, five of which he owns outright, mainly in the commune of Monthélie, with small plots in the communes of Beaune, Meursault and Auxey-Duresses. The Monthélie Appellation makes provision exclusively for red wines, but the Bouzerand-Dujardin duo has planted a few hectares with white varieties and will soon start making white wine here. With Ulrich Dujardin's arrival, quality can be expected to improve even further. A first sign is the new techniques in the vineyard. No fertilizers or herbicides are used and cultivation is now biodynamic. Vinification is traditional with one or two refinements like totally de-stemming the Pinot Noir and putting it through a cold maceration before fermentation with pigeage several times a day. The whites that they already produce are fermented in barrique after the must has been stabilized. The lesser known Appellations, which are mostly sold straight to an eager private clientele, are superb value.

Auxey-Duresses 1989 🍇 ②
A very concentrated wine which will age well for several years. Gold in color with greenish tints which bring out its youth. The nose is crisp and clean with ripe fruit. Good initial impact on the palate, mellow and well-balanced, with character and personality.

Monthélie 1989 🍇 ②
A pale ruby red in color with initially undeveloped aromas which later develop into ripe Pinot Noir. The palate is fresh and soft. A wine to drink young.

COTE DE BEAUNE/MEURSAULT
BOURGOGNE
FRANCE

307

COTE DE BEAUNE/MONTHELIE
BOURGOGNE
FRANCE

Domaine Bonneau du Martray

Pernand-Vergelesses 21420
89, rue de l'Université - 75007 Paris
Tel. (1) 42257122
Fax (1) 45614604

Not many growers can claim to own only vineyards in Grands Crus, but the Le Bault de la Morinière family can. They inherited the estate about 20 years ago and are fortunate enough to have all their property in a single plot. Notwithstanding a couple of hectares of red Corton, the estate's fame is based on its relatively vast parcel of white Corton-Charlemagne, which is situated on the hill facing south and south-east in the part of the property which borders onto the Hospices de Beaune. M. Le Bault de la Morinière has taken considerable steps to combat soil erosion by reconstructing the retaining walls and by carrying out ground stabilization and drainage operations. He has also maintained the average age of the vines at about 40 years, replanting at least seven different clones, and keeps yields to 40-50 hl/ha. Small 17-hl stainless steel vats are now in operation for the initial fermentation at a maximum temperature of 18-20°C. Maturation continues for 12 months in barriques, one third of which are replaced every year. The wines are complex and need some age. They require at least seven years in the cellar before they can be appreciated to the full.

Corton-Charlemagne ♈♈ ④
Grand Cru 1989
Pale gold color and still undeveloped on the nose. Strong and intense. Full-bodied on the palate but the alcohol is still predominant at this stage and it is difficult to distinguish the body, which comes out in the finish. Need to wait.

Corton-Charlemagne ♈♈ ④
Grand Cru 1987
The color is beginning to mature but the wine is still young in appearance. The aroma gives a first impression of what is to come, with lovely notes of flowers and straw. The initial impact is more aromatic than powerful but is followed by good structure on the palate. A good, if not great, Charlemagne.

Corton Grand Cru 1989 ♈ ③
Very light in color and with a delicate nose of wood which is also present on the palate, where it dominates the beautifully pure fruit. The whole is harmonious and will develop well. This Corton has an elegant, rather than powerful, style.

Domaine Dubreil-Fontaine

21240 Pernand-Vergelesses
Tel. 80215543
Fax 80215169

If your father was Pierre Dubreil, known as Popaul, one of the area's personalities and town-mayor for 38 years, and you yourself were a town councillor, then you would have one overriding duty to your community: to become one of the top growers in the area. And this is indeed the case with Bernard Dubreil. If you make your way along the winding streets of Pernand, you can find him and his formidable secretary, Madame Goris, right at the top of the village. His 20-ha property, on principally limestone clay soil, is planted with 75% Pinot Noir, 20% Chardonnay and 5% Aligoté, which allow him to make just about every permitted wine-type. Tradition reigns supreme when it comes to winemaking, without Dubreil allowing it to become a religion. The grapes are picked by hand, the whites are fermented in barriques and the reds in open wooden vats at controlled temperatures, and de-stemming is partial or total, depending on the harvest. The quality of the wines, which are to be found on the best wine lists in France, is unquestionably superb.

Bourgogne Aligoté 1990 ♈ ②
The appearance alone is seductive and the nose is rich in fruit with forward lemons and limes. The finish is long, supple and very elegant.

Pernand-Vergelesses ♈♈ ③
Ile-de-Vergelesses Premier Cru 1989
Garnet red in color, with a nose which releases intense aromas of roasted coffee on a background of wild cherries. The palate is chewy, mouthfilling and elegant, over a meaty, chewy texture with delicate tannins. A very agreeable wine.

Savigny-lès-Beaune ♈ ③
Les Vergelesses Premier Cru 1989
An attractive wine, ready for drinking rather early. Well-rounded and full bodied, it is delicate on the palate and with a finish which discloses great richness of fruit.

COTE DE BEAUNE/PERNAND-VERGELESSES
BOURGOGNE
FRANCE   308

COTE DE BEAUNE/PERNAND-VERGELESSES
BOURGOGNE
FRANCE

Domaine Laleure-Piot

21420 Pernand-Vergelesses
Tel. 80215237

On this 14-ha estate, Jean-Marie Laleure-Piot and his son Frédéric (an ex-student of the Thono-les-Bains hotel and catering college) make some of the best wines in the Côte de Beaune and the Côte de Nuits. Their 10 ha of red varieties and 4 of white include plots of Corton-Bressandes, Corton-Charlemagne, Pernand-Vergelesses (the most northerly Appellation in the Côte de Beaune), Savigny and others in Bourgogne Aligoté and Chorey-lès-Beaune. Their wines generally have a good structure and are vinified in a very traditional manner, whether they are simple Pernands or Premiers Crus. For a few years now, particularly in the better vintages, their white Pernand has been very similar in character to Corton-Charlemagne, which they also produce. Their range of wines is appreciated by connoisseurs and restaurateurs alike.

Pernand-Vergelesses 🍇 ③
Ile-de-Vergelesses Premier Cru 1990
Although this wine is still rather undeveloped, aromas of oak are already present on the nose. On the palate, the flavors are firm with a dominant note of blackcurrant. Enormous aging potential.

Savigny-lès-Beaune 🍇 ③
Les-Vergelesses Premier Cru 1990
The wood is still dominant but intense notes of blackcurrant can already be found. The palate is dense with tannins which are beginning to knit harmoniously. A good wine to lay down.

Jean-Marc Boillot

Route d'Autun
21630 Pommard
Tel. 80249757
Fax 80249480

Boillot is a common surname amongst growers in this part of the Côte de Beaune. Jean-Marc Boillot first made a name for himself away from the family estate while working as head cellarman at Olivier Leflaive, and he has done much to contribute to Leflaive's success. Today, Jean-Marc runs one of the most beautiful properties in the area, with vines at Bâtard-Montrachet, in four Puligny-Montrachet Premiers Crus (Les Combettes, Les Truffières, Les Champs-Canet and Les Refferts), at Meursault, at Beaune with the Premier Cru Les Montrevenots, in the Volnay Premiers Crus Les Ronceraies and Les Poutures and in three Pommard Premiers Crus, Les Saussilles, Les Jarollières and Les Rugiens. White wines are aged "sur lies" in barrels with regular "bâtonnage". For some years, the reds have been undergoing brief cold maceration before fermentation, which lasts for more than two weeks. Both reds and whites achieve a very high concentration of structure and fruit.

Puligny-Montrachet 1990 ③
With 13.5° natural alcohol obtained thanks to the limited yield, this is an exceptional wine with a nose of honey and ferns. A body and a depth of flavor that herald a long future career.

Beaune Les Montrevenots   ③
Premier Cru 1990
An attractive bluish red color and fascinating aromas of wild cherry and blackcurrant. Good concentration of flavor, mouthfilling texture and superb aromatic length. Will be ready to drink in five or six years' time.

Pommard Les Rugiens 🍇🍇 ④
Premier Cru 1990
There are only three large barrels of this monument to richness and concentration. Black in color and with a nose where new wood mingles with truffle. The density is on a par with a great Hermitage but, unfortunately, the grower sells it by the thimbleful.

Volnay Les Poutures ③
Premier Cru 1990
A small hill near Clos des Ducs which produces wines of particularly high tannin content. In 1990, the natural alcohol in the grapes (14°) added exceptional smoothness. A Premier Cru to lay down for at least 25 years.

COTE DE BEAUNE/PERNAND-VERGELESSES
BOURGOGNE
FRANCE

309

COTE DE BEAUNE/POMMARD
BOURGOGNE
FRANCE

Domaine Coste-Caumartin

Rue du Parc
21630 Pommard
Tel. 80224504
Fax 80226522

The estate has been in existence since 1780, but it is only a few years since the two Sordet brothers, Jérôme and Antoine, began to bottle and sell the wine. They have a dozen hectares, most of which are in Pommard, and thus grow red varieties. There are 3.7 ha at Pommard, 1.6 ha of the Premier Cru Les Frémiers and 1.8 ha of the Premier Cru Les Boucherottes, to which they have sole rights. They also produce a Bourgogne Blanc, mostly from a three-hectare vineyard at Saint-Roman. Winemaking is traditional, with the reds fermenting in wooden barrels for 12-14 days with regular "pigeage". The temperature is carefully regulated and reaches 33°C. Bottling takes place after 14-16 months in barriques, about 20% of which are replaced annually. The white wines begin fermentation in stainless steel vats and finish with about a year in barriques. They are racked swiftly so as not to leave them on the lees. There are no older vintages yet to judge this estate's potential by, so this is a grower to keep an eye on in the future.

Saint-Romain 1991
In the barrel, this is a pale, frank and straightforward wine. It has the typical aromas of Chardonnay and is a wine of spirit and charm.

Pommard 1991
A violet color in the barrel and an intense nose with an agreeable toasty note. The initial impact is lively and is followed by a good structure. A vintage which will be ready sooner rather than later.

Pommard Les Boucherottes
Premier Cru 1990
This is from one of the brothers' "monopoles", a wine with a broad, fruity nose with much charm and softness. A 1990 which will be ready to drink very quickly.

Pommard Les Frémiers
Premier Cru 1990
The tiny yields from this vintage have produced a dense, violet wine with an intense nose offering raisiny depth. Good tannins and body, which will age well. Lovely finish.

Domaine des Epeneaux

Place de l'Eglise
21630 Pommard
Tel. 80247050
Fax 80227237

Count Armand's cellar at Pommard produces a unique wine, the Clos des Epeneux, a 5.28-ha Premier Cru in a single plot most of which is in Petits-Epenots and the rest in Grands-Epenots. The estate's fortunes have taken a turn for the better since the arrival of a new manager, Pascal Marchand, a thirty year-old from Québec who fell in love with Bourgogne when he was working for Jacques Germain and Bruno Clair. The property's small size and its concentration in a single "climat" allows the vines to be looked after with exceptional care. Paul Marchand uses no herbicides and since 1986 has been replanting the vineyards with clonally selected grafts and thinning the bunches to obtain yields which at 35 hl/ha are well below the maximum allowed by law. After de-stemming, the must ferments in vats for about 15 days, having been cold-macerated for 3 or 4 days. Yeasts and sugar are only added if necessary. The wine is then transferred to new barrels, where malolactic fermentation commences. It is aged for three years before being bottled. The wines fully reflect the characteristics of Pommard. A red which will improve with age.

Pommard Clos des Epeneaux
Premier Cru 1989
An excellent wine which will improve further with bottle-age. The dark color has violet tints and the nose is developed with aromas of cherry, raspberry and faint hints of toastiness. Good structure on the palate, delicate, with well-rounded, soft tannins.

Pommard Clos des Epeneaux
Premier Cru 1988
Intense color with an outstanding nose with lots of immediate spicy oak. A complex nose of cherry and blackcurrant mingling with cocoa and tobacco. Rich, warm and firmly structured on the palate with lovely fruit in the finish. A Pommard with elegance and strength from an excellent vintage. Definitely one to lay down.

COTE DE BEAUNE/POMMARD
BOURGOGNE
FRANCE

310

COTE DE BEAUNE/POMMARD
BOURGOGNE
FRANCE

Domaine Jean Monnier et fils

20, rue du 11 Novembre
21190 Meursault
Tel. 80212256
Fax 80212965

Even though the property itself lies in Meursault, the Jean Monnier estate produces more red wine than white. It includes over a hectare of red Meursault and has exclusive rights to three hectares in the magnificent Pommard-Epenots "climat", Clos de Côteaux, which used to belong to the monks of the abbey of that name. The Monnier family has made wine in Meursault for more than two centuries but it was the grandfather of Jean-Claude, the present manager, who laid the foundations of its reputation for quality. The vineyard today extends over 17 ha with Premiers Crus at Pommard (Premiers and Argillières), at Beaune (Montrevenots) and at Meursault (Charmes and Genevrières) as well as Villages Appellations at Puligny-Montrachet and Meursault (Clos de Cromin, La Barre and Les Chevalières). There are also five hectares planted for red and white Bourgogne and Aligoté. Winemaking is traditional with wood aging for all the wines. 25-35% of the barrels are replaced every year. Jean-Claude Monnier's wines are characterized by great purity of fruit and a rare balance, which allow them to be enjoyed when young.

Meursault Les Genevrières Premier Cru 1989

Crystal-clear with a pale gold color, the very discreet nose reveals honey, beeswax and toastiness. Richer on the palate than the Chevalières, it has a much more robust structure but lacks something in elegance. Sumptuous fruit and toastiness dominate the finish.

Meursault Les Chevalières 1989

The delicate gold color is enhanced by faint flecks of green. The nose is delightfully intense, revealing a fresh aroma of fruit, almonds and honey. Still very youthful, the flavor is delicately sculpted and brimming with honey and walnuts. Delicious without being oily, it has beautiful balance and length.

Beaune Les Montrevenots Premier Cru 1989

The color is less intense than one might expect in a Bourgogne Pinot. The nose is dominated by wood and discloses hints of roasted coffee, caramel and toasty wood. The same aromas emerge on the palate together with a flavor of fresh, tart fruit and of leather. A pleasant wine with medium body.

Pommard-Epenots
Clos des Côteaux Premier Cru 1988

Very representative of its cru. Again a color of medium intensity which is beginning to develop. The nose is slight with gamey, earthy hints. The palate is attractive with a solid structure and very well-knit wood.

Louis Carillon et fils

21190 Puligny-Montrachet
Tel. 80213034/80213075
Fax 80219002

The Carillons have been growing vines at Puligny since the 16th century. Jacques and François, with their father Louis, run a 12-ha estate in the Côte de Beaune, most of it in the "climats" of Puligny and Chassagne. Some of the wine is still sold to local négociants and most of the rest goes for export. Techniques are fairly traditional, with 14-20 day fermentation for the reds and aging for a year in barriques before bottling. 10 to 20% of the barrels are replaced every year. The cellar's mainstay is straight Puligny-Montrachet, with five hectares of vineyards, but the really great bottles come from the Premiers Crus Les Combettes, Les Champ-Canet, Les Perrières, Les Referts and Les Champs-Gains as well as from a small parcel in the Grand Cru Bienvenues-Bâtard-Montrachet. Although they only represent one third of production, red wines are not neglected. As well as Bourgogne and Côtes de Beaune Villages, the Chassagne and Mercurey (from the Côte Chalonnaise) are wines of good structure which should not be drunk for at least three years.

Bienvenue-Bâtard-Montrachet
Grand Cru 1990

Clear gold in color, this wine is much less developed than the others, which is quite normal for a Grand Cru at this stage of its development. There are hints of coconut, butter and vanilla on the nose and extraordinary strength on the palate, with excellent balance between the components of delicate acidity, lemon and buttery fruit. The wine's huge potential is only just apparent, needing time to emerge.

Puligny-Montrachet 1990

Beautiful pale gold color with a nose of quite incredible intensity with honeyed, yeasty fruit. The flavor is superb, with intense fruit again and honey with sweet, juicy tropical fruit on a background of outstanding acidity.

Puligny-Montrachet
Les Perrières Premier Cru 1990

Bottled six months after the Puligny-Montrachet, the nose offers younger fruit together with hints of coconut and caramel. It has the same pale gold color, with flecks of green. The palate is rich, with a concentrated, buttery taste of wood and vanilla and a touch of coconut in the finish. Stupendous, bearing in mind the short time it has spent in the bottle so far.

COTE DE BEAUNE/POMMARD
BOURGOGNE
FRANCE

311

COTE DE BEAUNE/PULIGNY-MONTRACHET
BOURGOGNE
FRANCE

Domaine Leflaive

Place des Marroniers
21190 Puligny-Montrachet
Tel. 80213013

Domaine Leflaive, with its wonderfully delicate but long-lived white Burgundies, is one of the most prestigious names on the Côte d'Or. The origins of the estate date back to 1735, but it was Joseph and Vincent Leflaive who really built up this great domaine. Today, the estate is in the hands of a company whose shares are held by 27 members of the Leflaive family. It is actually run, however, by Olivier Leflaive (who also owns his own négociant firm) and his cousin Anne-Claude, while Pierre Moray is the "maître de chais". The property's 22 ha. are planted almost exclusively with Chardonnay. There are 7 ha.of Grands Crus (Chevalier-Montrachet, Bâtard-Montrachet, Bienvenues-Bâtard-Montrachet and, since 1991, Le Montrachet); 8 in Premiers Crus (Les Pucelles, Les Combettes, Clavaillon, Les Chalumaux and Les Folatières); and there are a further 7 ha. suitable for Puligny-Montrachet and Bourgogne Blanc. Yields for the Grands Crus are around 37 hl/ha while they reach 50 hl/ha in the Premiers Crus. Annual production is of around 120,000 bottles. The grapes are picked by hand and crushed in a pneumatic press. Alcoholic and malolactic fermentation takes place in 228 l barriques, with 40% new wood used for the Grands Crus. The wines age for a year in wood and then go into stainless steel six months before bottling.

Bâtard-Montrachet ♛ ♛ ④
Grand Cru 1990
Yellow-gold color with greenish tints. On the nose still undeveloped, but delicate with hints of flowers and appetizing fruit. A very fresh wine with dominating oak. Rich and concentrated, full of sweet fruity vanilla and butter with a warm toastiness emerging on the palate to give way to delicious walnut flavors in the finish.

Puligny-Montrachet ♛ ♛ ④
Les Pucelles Premier Cru 1990
Crystal-clear in appearance with a green-flecked golden color. The nose is by no means forward, but of great depth. A vaguely flowery nose, where the intense honey predominates. The palate opens explosively with honey again and butter. It is full-bodied and sumptuous with the flavors growing more intense the longer the wine lingers in the mouth. Glorious, never-ending finish of walnuts while the perfectly married wood stays discreetly in the background.

Chevalier-Montrachet ♛ ♛ ♛ ④
Grand Cru 1989
Another limpid, brilliant wine with a youthful golden color and a much more complex bouquet than those of other wines tasted in 1990. Rich and highly representative of the vintage, it contains honey and hazelnuts, flowery notes and juicy tropical fruit. The flavor is of extraordinary richness. Fleshy and opulent, it opens with aromas of pineapple and other exotic fruit which bring to mind papaya followed by a marked aromatic note which lasts through to the finish. It is so high in glycerine and full as to seem almost heavy. The wood remains almost completely hidden, so overwhelming is the fruit and aromas of nuts. Stupendous structure, perhaps lacking the elegance of the '90, but of quite stunning length. A superb wine.

Olivier Leflaive

1, place du Monument
21190 Puligny-Montrachet
Tel. 80212765
Fax 80213394

This estate is Bourgogne's new star. The Leflaives were already in Puligny in 1717, but it is only since the 42 year-old Olivier arrived that the property has taken off and produced wines so attractive they are to be seen on the tables of the great and the good. Olivier has spared no effort or expense to achieve his goal. He has rediscovered the vineyard's potential together with Claude Bourguignon, a well-known microbiologist, and the enologist Frank Grux, who used to supervise the Roulot estate. The result is that the wines from the 8.5-ha estate, with its roughly 30 year-old vines on clay-and-limestone soil, have acquired complexity and chewiness with a much more correct aging in the wood and biodynamic cultivation techniques as well as must from grapes acquired through Leflaive's commercial operations. Growing 40% Chardonnay, 40% Pinot Noir and 20% Aligoté, with yields that have been reduced, the estate offers white wines from Côte Chalonnaise and Côte de Beaune together with red wines from Côte de Beaune and Côte de Nuits. These wines are often sublime, with aging prospects which stretch beyond the end of the century.

Bienvenues-Bâtard-Montrachet 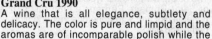 ③
Grand Cru 1990
A wine that is all elegance, subtlety and delicacy. The color is pure and limpid and the aromas are of incomparable polish while the body is rich and well-balanced with an endless finish. The hallmarks of a great white wine.

Meursault Narvaux 1989 ♈♈ ③
Yellow-gold color, a nose with sweet aromas and a palate of rich body and concentration which distinguish one of the best wines in the Appellation. The finish is of outstanding complexity, powerful and long. To be laid down for several years before drinking.

Domaine Etienne Sauzet

21190 Puligny-Montrachet
Tel. 80213210

The Sauzets are always spoken of with respect at Puligny. The family patriarch, Etienne, who died in 1975, did much for the reputation of Puligny wines and his grandchildren are carrying on the tradition. Thanks to parcels in the Grands Crus of Bâtard-Montrachet and Bienvenues-Bâtard-Montrachet as well as Puligny Premiers Crus such as Champ-Canet, Les Combettes, Les Perrières, Les Referts and La Truffière, this is one of the most famous estates in Bourgogne. Today, the manager is a forty year-old golfer who comes from Creusot and whose athletic build, relaxed manners and 'savoir faire' have gained him entry to the turn-of-the-century family residence; Gérard Bourdot married the estate when he married Jeanine Boillot in 1974 for she is one of the heirs to the property. Since then, Gérard has worked tirelessly to introduce new vinification techniques, to increase the proportion of new barrels used for aging and to focus the marketing once again on the domestic French market.

Bâtard-Montrachet ♈♈ ④
Grand Cru 1988
Without doubt a perfect expression of its climat. Brilliant hue. The nose has slightly candied fruit with a flowery and vegetal side. The power of this wine is apparent on the aristocratically elegant palate. A very promising wine from a difficult vintage.

Puligny-Montrachet ♈♈ ④
Les Combettes Premier Cru 1988
A very successful wine with genuine fullness. The nose is frank, with aromas of almonds and honey. Good softness on the palate with a generous texture which reflects the "terroir". Enough acidity to age for some time yet.

Puligny-Montrachet ④
Les Perrières Premier Cru 1985
Straw gold color with a rich nose, a voluptuous palate and a very long finish endow this wine with unusual balance. The subtle aromas range from vegetal and flowery fruit. The palate is of surprising freshness over a full, dense texture. Outstandingly long finish with an elegant background.

COTE DE BEAUNE/PULIGNY-MONTRACHET
BOURGOGNE
FRANCE

313

COTE DE BEAUNE/PULIGNY-MONTRACHET
BOURGOGNE
FRANCE

Marc Colin

Gamay - Saint-Aubin
21190 Meursault
Tel. 80213043
Fax 80219004

Marc Colin was very young when he found himself in charge of the family estate but he has proved that Saint-Aubin can, if properly cultivated, achieve better results than many more prestigious communes. M. Colin's wines are often as good as Chassagne-Montrachets and are half the price. Marc also has parcels at Chassagne, among which are the excellent Premiers Crus Les Champs Gain and Les Caillerets and the Grand Cru Le Montrachet, where he produces two priceless barriques. The domaine has 13 ha, half of which it owns and the other half it rents. There are no special techniques apart from scrupulous, unfailing attention to both vineyards and cellar. Marc Colin uses well-tried methods with low yields, fairly lengthy fermentation and a moderate proportion of new wood (10-20%, with the exception of Le Montrachet where he uses 100%). The whites receive a "bâtonnage" every ten days. The purity and aging potential of these wines is well-known so it is not always easy to find them, unless you go directly to the grower.

Saint-Aubin Premier Cru
La Châtenière 1990
Strong color and a nose which offers generous aromas of flowers and fruit. Good, spirited initial impact and a finish that is rich and well-balanced.

Chassagne-Montrachet 1989
Rather pale color with very attractive aromas of flowers and nuts. An austere palate dominated by an acidity which promises well for the future. A wine which will certainly develop and which has just the right Chassagne characteristics.

Montrachet Gran Cru 1989
Tapped from the barrel, this is a rather turbid, but dense, wine. The nose is also noteworthy for its density and delicacy while the extremely powerful palate has remarkable breadth and fruit. A great bottle in the year 2000.

Saint-Aubin En Créots
Premier Cru 1989
A wine of great charm with its youthful color and nose of red fruit and freshly turned soil. The palate is full, well-rounded, complex and long. This kind of quality really questions the ability of winemakers using much more prestigious material.

Santenay 1989
Lovely density of color and a nose of pure redcurrant, with toasty notes. The palate is classically tender and elegant, with well-defined fruit and enough body to age well.

Alain Gras

21190 Saint-Romain-le-Haut
Tel. 80212783
Fax 80216556

Alain Gras impresses with his frankness and honesty, qualities which are mirrored in his wines. His estate is not large, only 2.5 ha of Chardonnay at Saint-Romain and another 3.5 of Pinot Noir at Saint-Romain and Auxey-Duresses. His vines are about 25 years old and stand on hard chalky terrain which gives his wines their characteristic mineral-like nature, with a flinty note. As he wishes to bring out the Saint-Romain style, Alain highlights the purity of the fruit by avoiding the use of wood with his white wines and limiting his reds to 20% new oak. The white spends ten months in stainless steel before being bottled and is best drunk within five years. The reds stay somewhat longer in the wood, but nevertheless manage to preserve their freshness and primary aromas.

Saint-Romain Blanc 1991
Pale gold color with fresh, fruity aromas. The fruit and mineral components are well-balanced on the palate. A slight hint of yeast adds to the complexity of a wine which will develop splendidly in the future.

Saint-Romain Rouge 1991
A cherry red color of medium intensity. The nose has plenty of butter, pepper and spices. The palate contains the typical mineral elements of Saint-Romain. Perhaps a little rustic, it is nonetheless firm with generous fruit and hints of game and oak.

COTE DE BEAUNE/SAINT-AUBIN
BOURGOGNE
FRANCE

314

COTE DE BEAUNE/SAINT-ROMAIN
BOURGOGNE
FRANCE

Vincent Girardin

Rue Narosse
21590 Santenay
Tel. 80206429
Fax 80206488

Vincent Girardin is a young grower who has come a long way in just ten years. His father left him a quarter of the 12 ha which used to make up the property and he has managed to get back to the original 12 ha area by renting some other parcels. Vincent has restructured the estate several times to improve quality by buying, renting, selling, uprooting and replanting vineyard after vineyard. His approach to winemaking begins with a 4-5 day cold-maceration and a first fermentation of about 14 days with completely de-stemmed grapes. In some cases, when the skins and stems are very ripe, some bunches are left on the stem. Another feature of Vincent's style with red wines is the absence of filtration or clarification. The white wines ferment in barriques, with the temperature held at around 22°C. Clarification is carried out only if suspended matter is present in the wine. In addition to Santenay, Savigny-lès-Beaune and Chassagne-Montrachet, the estate also has a plot in the tiny Maranges Appellation, a name which is little-known at present but which is destined to produce wines on a par with the others in the future.

Santenay 1990 ℣ ③
An excellent Santenay. A pale yellow-gold color with intense nose of toast and vanilla oak. The palate is rich, with striking ripe fruit and excellent weighty structure and complexity.

Savigny-lès-Beaune ℣℣℣ ③
Les Vermots Dessus 1990
Golden straw color with a complex nose that is much lighter and has more delicate fruit than the Santenay. The palate is well structured, delicate and finishes with marked acidity: very refreshing.

Maranges Clos des Loyères ❦❦ ③
Premier Cru Vieilles Vignes 1990
A wine of extraordinary concentration, this Marange comes from the oldest vines on the estate. Intense red color, this is a wine that is powerful and concentrated rather than elegant or fine.

Santenay Clos de la Confrérie ❦❦ ③
Monopole 1990
A red which exemplifies the characteristics of Santenay: intense color, complex nose, delicate palate, fruity and with good structure and balance.

Santenay Les Gravières ❦❦ ③
Premier Cru 1990
A fine example of pure Pinot Noir. The nose is complex fruits of the forest while the palate is full-bodied and delicate with a clean, fruity aftertaste.

Domaine Jessiaume père et fils

10, rue de la Gare
21590 Santenay
Tel. 80206003
Fax 80206287

This property came into being around 1850 and comprises 14 ha, more than half in Santenay and 5 of these (a vast area for Bourgogne) in the Les Gravières Premier Cru. The remainder is spread over Premiers Crus situated in the Auxey-Duresses, Les Ecusseaux, Volnay-Brouillard and Beaune-Cent-Vignes Appellations. The estate's pride and joy is the collection of old vintages of Santenay Les Gravières. There are examples from 1908, 1913, 1915, 1928, 1929 and 1949 still on sale and all of superb quality. Marc and Pascal Jessiaume, who run the property with their father, harvest fairly early and employ a winemaking technique which takes account of both tradition and technological innovation. The grapes are still crushed with the feet to make sure the process is as gentle as possible and the must is fermented in wooden vats for about 15 days, with "pigeage" three times a day, all done at controlled temperatures. The white wines are also good. Unlike the reds, they are made exclusively in new wood, whether they are crus or ordinary wines such as Aligoté.

Bourgogne Aligoté 1990 ℣ ①
A classic Aligoté with a straw-yellow color. The crisp aromas are braced by toasty oak. Racy, supple and direct on the palate, with good refreshing acidity.

Santenay Les Gravières ❦ ②
Premier Cru 1989
Moderately intense color with violet tones. The nose is clean and characteristic, with notes of blackcurrant and red fruit. The palate is typically elegant, structured and winey.

Santenay Les Gravières ❦❦ ④
Premier Cru 1949
A Santenay Premier Cru which carries its years lightly. The ruby color has the orange tints characteristic of aging and the complex nose of autumn leaves. The structure is full-bodied, mouthfilling and soft, with a long, lingering finish.

COTE DE BEAUNE/SANTENAY
BOURGOGNE
FRANCE

315

COTE DE BEAUNE/SANTENAY
BOURGOGNE
FRANCE

Simon Bize et fils

21420 Savigny-lès-Beaune
Tel. 80215057
Fax 80215817

The wines of Savigny have long been famous and the Bize family has done much to enhance their reputation. Although Simon continues to work, it is his son Patrick who manages operations now. He is a serious young man who takes great care of every detail, often experimenting with methods and containers and assiduously tasting competitors' wines both from France and from abroad. The estate is on the large side for the region (20 ha) and Patrick can afford to ferment the grapes from his various plots separately. Three quarters of production is red wine from two sub-zones of Savigny, Les Bourgeots and Grands Liard, and four Premiers Crus, Fourneaux, Marconnettes, Vergelesses and Guettes, the top of the estate's range. Recently, a parcel in Aloxe-Corton, Suchot, has been added. The Chardonnay whites, Bourgogne and Savigny, are less demanding. The Bize style is one of great elegance with wines that are both dense and delicate. To be tasted carefully.

Bourgogne Les Champlains 1990 ♥ ♥ ②
A splendid, radiantly bright yellow color, lying somewhere between gold and lemon. The nose is frank and fresh, with hints of new oak mingling perfectly with flowery aromas. The palate is both well-rounded and fresh, with notes of almond. Has much of the cru's length and attractiveness.

Savigny-lès-Beaune ♥ ③
Les Bourgeots 1990
A very youthful ruby red color with a complex nose of fruit and earth together with discreet, elegant oak. The full palate epitomizes all the elegance of Savigny - concentrated aromas, a finish of violets and discreet tannins.

Savigny-lès-Beaune ♥ ♥ ③
Les Vergelesses Premier Cru 1990
Rather opaque color with prevailing wood overtones which are in no way excessive. The palate is intense and velvety, without yet having achieved the attractiveness of the Les Bourgeots. We shall have to wait until the tannins of this great vintage mellow out and its aromas are more clearly differentiated.

Domaine Chandon de Briailles

S.C.E. du Manoir
21420 Savigny-lès-Beaune
Tel. 80215231
Fax 80215915

The Chandon de Briailles estate is one of the few Burgundy properties to boast a real château, in this case a superb Louis XIV folly surrounded by a park. The estate is skilfully managed by the Countess de Nicolay, a dynamic and enthusiastic woman who is constantly striving to raise quality standards even further. To that end, fermentation has been extended to three weeks, with eight days at 30°-32°C. Yields are less than 40 hl/ha and the grapes are only partially destemmed. Aging is in barriques, of which 20% to 50% are new, depending on the cru, and lasts for 18-20 months. There are 13 ha, with parcels at Savigny-lès-Beaune (the Premiers Crus Aux Fourneaux and Les Lavières), Aloxe-Corton and Pernand-Vergelesses. The largest plot is the Premier Cru Ile-de-Vergelesses at Pernand (3.75 ha), a small proportion of which is planted with white varieties. The red wine is solid and complete, offering the best value for money on the estate. The Corton, Corton-Bressandes and Corton Clos du Roi Grands Crus are wines of impressive structure for laying down, as is the rare Corton Blanc.

Corton Grand Cru 1990 ♥ ♥ ④
The bouquet is a little less intense than that of the 1989. There is a delicate aroma of pear on the pleasantly rounded palate. The follow-through is, for the time being, somewhat lacking in spirit, but this cru needs time to develop and give its best.

Corton Grand Cru ♥ ♥ ④
Bressandes 1990
A lovely dark, bluish color. Delicate aromas of violets and a spirited initial impact with a full-bodied and velvety follow-through and impressive structure. Outstanding balance, thanks to the perfect ripeness of the grapes.

Corton Grand Cru ♥ ♥ ④
Clos du Roi 1990
Splendidly intense color. Delicate aroma and sharp initial impact. Good body and elegance on the palate. A complete wine which will age stupendously.

Pernand-Vergelesses ♥ ♥ ③
Ile de Vergelesses Premier cru 1990
Dark, vivacious color and a very pure aroma of red berries. Excellent concentration on the palate with great delicacy and outstanding length. A great success for the estate and for the vintage.

COTE DE BEAUNE/SAVIGNY-LES-BEAUNE
BOURGOGNE
FRANCE

316

COTE DE BEAUNE/SAVIGNY-LES-BEAUNE
BOURGOGNE
FRANCE

Domaine du Marquis d'Angerville

21190 Volnay
Tel. 80216175

The name d'Angerville can be found on the wine lists of the greatest restaurants both in France and abroad. The vine stock on the 13 ha of brown, chalky soil comprises 12 ha of Pinot Noir and 1 ha of Chardonnay. The plants have always been carefully looked after here and today they are the responsibility of Jacques, Marquis d'Angerville, member of the mutual assistance association of the French nobility and a former Chairman of the Comité Interprofessionel des Vins de Bourgogne. The estate has parcels in the Premiers Crus of Angles, Caillerets, Champans, Clos des Ducs, Fremiets, Lormeau, Piture and Taille-Pieds in the Volnay Appellation as well as in Pommard at Les Combes and in Meursault with the Premier Cru Santenots. Production overall has some of the most moderate yields in the Appellation. Tradition reigns supreme here, both when it comes to the harvest, which is de-stemmed, and to the winemaking. Fermentation and aging, too, are exclusively in the oak. Such - they maintain here - is the price of quality.

Volnay Clos des Ducs 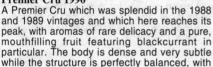 Premier Cru 1990
A Premier Cru which was splendid in the 1988 and 1989 vintages and which here reaches its peak, with aromas of rare delicacy and a pure, mouthfilling fruit featuring blackcurrant in particular. The body is dense and very subtle while the structure is perfectly balanced, with rich, satisfyingly soft tannins.

Volnay Les Taille-Pieds Premier Cru 1990
Thanks to the exceptional quality of the grapes harvested in 1990, it was perhaps easier than at other times to make a great wine, but when the result is so typical of the cru, so concentrated and of such perfect balance then some of the credit must also go to the winemaker.

Domaine Jean Boillot et fils

Rue des Angles
21190 Volnay
Tel. 80216190
Fax 80219984

Few estates are broken up into as many parcels as the Domaine Boillot. Henri, Jean's son, runs 13 ha spread over six communes from Nuits-Saint-Georges to Puligny-Montrachet by way of Savigny-lès-Beaune, Beaune, Volnay and Meursault. The property produces some lovely white Premiers Crus at Puligny-Montrachet (Clos de la Mouchère, to which they have exclusive rights, and Les Pucelles) and at Meursault (Genevrières). These are fermented "sur lies" in new barrels, with "bâtonnage" until the end of malolactic fermentation, an approach which gives them great concentration. In the case of red wines, the grapes are de-stemmed and vinified half in traditional barrels and half in rotating self-crushing vats - the long-term effect of which on the wine has yet to be seen - with a fermentation lasting about 15 days. Aged in new barrels for at least a year, the red, like the white, is bottled after being clarified. The Boillot estate is best-known for its Volnay Premiers Crus, Les Fremiets, Les Chevrets and, above all, Les Caillerets.

Puligny-Montrachet Clos de la Mouchère Premier Cru Monopole 1989
Bright gold color and a bouquet which is almost heavy, with aromas of vanilla coming from 70% new wood. Powerful on the palate, the longer it rests in the mouth, the more concentration it develops with an attractive toasty note all the way through and firm acidity to bind everything together. More remarkable for its structure than for its elegance, it still needs time to mellow. At present, the oak is a little overwhelming.

Beaune Les Epenotes Premier Cru 1989
A typical Burgundy Pinot, with a color of medium intensity. The bouquet is subtle with hints of strawberry. On the palate, it is lively, elegant, long and very attractive with a delicious note of sweet fruit and well-blended oak. Hints of coffee emerge in the finish together with faint overtones of walnut kernels and wood. A very complex wine, despite its delicate texture.

Volnay Les Chevrets
Premier Cru 1989
A warm wine with just the right amount of tannins to balance the fruit and wood. A lovely ruby color, deep and youthful, with aromas of cherry, chocolate and coffee. A little on the full-bodied side, partly owing to the wood which is not fully assimilated, the palate, too, has touches of chocolate and coffee. Dense in structure, with sweet fruit aromas of cherry pips and satisfactory length.

COTE DE BEAUNE/VOLNAY
BOURGOGNE
FRANCE

317

COTE DE BEAUNE/VOLNAY
BOURGOGNE
FRANCE

Domaine de la Pousse d'Or

21190 Volnay
Tel. 80216133
Fax 89212997

Pousse d'Or seems to be a name with a history going back almost a thousand years. The estate is currently run by the nephew of the main owner, Gérard Potel, who is a superb winemaker as well as an enologist and an agricultural engineer. The entire 13-ha estate is classified Premier Cru and is spread over Pommard (Les Jarollières), Santenay (Clos Tavannes and Les Gravières) and, above all, Volnay, with Les Caillerets and three exclusive sub-zones, Clos de la Bousse d'Or (not Pousse), Les Caillerets Clos des 60 Cuvées and Clos d'Audignac. Fermentation is carried out in open vats and takes 12 to 20 days, the wine being pumped over the cap four times a day. Grapes are de-stemmed in proportions which vary from year to year, crushing is light and aging is in oak barrels for 15-18 months. Volnays and Pommards have from 20% to 30% new wood. The Pousse d'Or style has great intensity of aroma and an appeal which is apparent after only a short time in the cellar, despite the fact that these wines will age admirably for 10 to 15 years. At that point, Pousse d'Or wines are ready to enhance the best that the kitchen has to offer.

Santenay Les Gravières
Premier Cru 1990
Richer in color than a Santenay. The bouquet is of autumn leaves and pepper, with a gamey note. The same flavors are present again on the palate, together with lively acidity. Gamay gives way to aromas of cherries and other red fruit in the pleasant, lingering finish.

Volnay Les Caillerets
Premier Cru 1990
A wine of extraordinary intensity in appearance, with a spicy note of oak. The flavor is so dense as to make it difficult to identify its component elements. Sumptuously fruity, fleshy, spicy and perfectly balanced, with amazing length.

Volnay Clos de la Bousse d'Or
Premier Cru 1989
Although not quite as concentrated as the 1990, the color is impressively deep. There is a discreet animal and cherry aroma and a fresh, lively flavor with medium fruit. Already very enjoyable, this also is a wine to lay down.

Volnay Clos de la Bousse d'Or ♥♥♥ ④
Premier Cru 1990
A wine with a rich, deep, truly magnificent color. The bouquet is extremely complex, with aromas of game and vegetal notes, followed by ripe black berries, rich earthiness and spices. The concentrated earthy taste of Gamay comes back on the palate with notes of coffee, spices and oak. A wine of rare intensity and richness of flavor with a very long finish - a work of art. A red which is ready for drinking now, although some might think it sacrilegious to do so for this is a wine which will age happily for many years to come.

COTE DE BEAUNE/VOLNAY
BOURGOGNE
FRANCE

318

COTE DE BEAUNE/VOLNAY
BOURGOGNE
FRANCE

Domaine de Montille

21190 Volnay
Tel. 80216267
Fax 80428578

The 7-ha Montille estate has belonged to the same family since before the Revolution and Hubert de Montille, the present owner, is one of the most highly respected figures in Burgundy. The property in Volnay is at Mitans and in the Premiers Crus of Champans and Taille-Pieds and produces wines which are models of elegance. The Pommard Premiers Crus, Pézerolles and above all Les Rugiens, are powerful and at the same time delicate. During the week, Hubert de Montille is a lawyer in Dijon and at the weekend, he is a grower in Volnay. His philosophy is to interfere as little as possible with grape and wine. Yields are low, at 35 to 40 hl/ha, and the grapes are totally de-stemmed on harvesting. They are left to ferment for at least three weeks and age for up to 24 months, with a maximum 20% new wood. Hubert de Montille does not make alcohol a priority and chaptalization is kept to the bare minimum necessary to maintain the balance of the wine. The alcohol content is around 12°. Wines age in wood and can appear very hard during the early years of bottle-aging. They are slightly clarified but not filtered and often need 5-10 years to give their best. When they do mature, however, they are monuments to the reputation of Burgundy and the Côte de Beaune.

Volnay Les Champans Premier Cru 1989

The deep red color of Pinot Noir, but very bright and with a slight shading of pale rose. Complex nose, which is nonetheless fresh and fruity with agreeable hints of ripe red cherries. A delicious, even thirst-quenching, wine, which is unusual for Burgundy reds of this type. A light, brilliant style with clean aromas of fresh fruit and none of the excessive alcohol of heavily chaptalized wines. Above all, it has remarkable, refreshing elegance. A great wine, characteristic of vintages where delicacy and fruit have the better of strength and structure. A beautiful example of the multi-faceted complexity of Pinot Noir and a winemaking style which aims for elegance and freshness.

COTE DE BEAUNE/VOLNAY
BOURGOGNE
FRANCE

319

COTE DE BEAUNE/VOLNAY
BOURGOGNE
FRANCE

Michel Rossignol

Rue de l'Abreuvoir
21190 Volnay
Tel. 80216290
Fax 80216031

There are many Volnay growers whose surname is Rossignol and since 1964 Michel Rossignol has managed a property which used to be known as Rossignol-Boillot. It was Michel's father who bottled here for the first time in 1929. Besides Volnay (Villages and the Premier Cru Les Petures), the other wines produced are Beaune Premier Cru Les Teurons, the Monthelie Premier Cru Les Champs-Fulliot and also Côte de Beaune - not to be confused with Côte de Beaune Villages. There are so few wines with the Côte de Beaune Appellation because it overlaps with the Beaune Appellation and only nine partially-cultivated hectares are in the Côte de Beaune. Grapes are de-stemmed after the harvest and begin fermentation after a short period of maceration. Yeasts are added during fermentation. This traditional approach to winemaking explains the house style, which tends towards delicacy rather than structure. An elegant, soft wine but not one to lay down.

Côte de Beaune 🍷 ②
Clos des Pierres Blanches 1991
Ruby color of medium intensity with a delicate, lively, fruity nose. A pleasant, light wine which does not lack charm.

Volnay Les Petures 🍷🍷 ③
Premier Cru 1991
A fine example of Volnay with an intense color. The aromas are complex and full with a slight peppery note in the finish. The palate is rounded and well-balanced, with good structure and elegance.

Domaine Ghislaine Barthod

Ruelle du Lavoir
21220 Chambolle-Musigny
Tel. 80628016

This is the former Barthod-Noëllat estate which was originally founded by Marcel Noëllat in 1929 and then taken over by his son-in-law Gaston Barthod. Since 1986, Marcel's grand-daughter Ghislaine has been running the property. Since she rents her father's vine stock, the wine is sold under the label Barthod-Noëllat. The 6.3 ha lie entirely within the Chambolle-Musigny Appellation, with some generic labels (Bourgogne Aligoté, Rouge and Passetoutgrain), Chambolle-Musigny (sub-zone Aux Beaux Bruns) as well as Premiers Crus. Among these are Les Cras, at Bonnes-Mares, Les Véroilles above Bonnes-Mares and Les Charmes, with parcels in all three sub-zones of Charmes. Ghislaine Barthod works virtually on her own, with just her parents to help her. The grapes are totally de-stemmed and fermented for 15-18 days in wooden vats. Aging is in the wood (20% of which is replaced every year) and the wines are partially filtered. Ghislaine has never seen a vintage like 1990, which appears to have an ideal balance. Her 1990 wines are absolutely correct and their dense body and their structure guarantee an excellent future.

Chambolle-Musigny 🍷🍷 ③
Les Charmes Premier Cru 1990
Dark in color, with flecks of red. Excellent aroma, barely sweetened by the new wood. A very well-made wine, with good length of bouquet and burgeoning maturity.

Chambolle-Musigny 🍷🍷 ③
Les Véroilles Premier Cru 1990
Lovely violet color. The nose is undeveloped but the palate impresses with its softness. A very well-made wine which combines tannic structure with elegance.

Chambolle-Musigny 🍷 ③
Les Charmes Premier Cru 1989
A dark wine which needs to breathe before it releases its aroma of cherries. Lower in alcohol than the 1990, but with good structure. A wine which will develop quickly.

Chambolle-Musigny 🍷🍷 ④
Les Cras 1989 Premier Cru
Dark and very young in appearance. Intense aroma of red berries, with an earthy note. All the richness of a great wine right from the start on the palate. The soft texture is very attractive. Moderate length. Les Cras needs at least three years to start developing.

COTE DE BEAUNE/VOLNAY
BOURGOGNE
FRANCE

320

COTE DE NUITS/CHAMBOLLE-MUSIGNY
BOURGOGNE
FRANCE

Domaine Comte Georges de Vogüe

Rue Sainte Barbe
21220 Chambolle-Musigny
Tel. 80628625
Fax 80628238

One of the most famous and oldest estates in Burgundy, dating back to 1450, which has remained in the same family for 17 generations. Since 1766, it has borne the name Vogüe. The property's fame rests on the quality and importance of the crus it owns. There are 18.2 ha of vineyards, of which only two are in communes, while the remaining 16.2 are in the Grand Cru Musigny, the Petit Musigny, in Bonnes-Mares to the south of Chambolle-Musigny and in the Premier Cru Les Amoureuses at Chambolle-Musigny. Since 1986 the estate has been owned and run by a group of youngsters who have taken over from the old manager, Alain Roumier, and today almost the entire production is bottled. The best grapes, from vines which are between 25 and 60 years-old, are used for Musigny, always labelled Vieilles Vignes. Some of the grapes are de-stemmed and fermentation, which lasts about a month, is in the wood at controlled temperatures. Aging is in barriques (of which a maximum of 40% are new) and lasts 18 months. The resulting wines are of great character with excellent aging potential. In addition to the reds, four hectares of Chardonnay have been planted, a very unusual occurrence in the Musigny zone.

Musigny Vieilles Vignes Grand Cru 1989
An intense color with violet tints. The nose is delicate and complex with an agreeable note of wood. Rich and intense on the palate, a wine with soft and mouthfilling tannins of great fascination, elegant and lingering. Frank in the finish, without excessive alcohol. A product which reflects in every respect the persuasive characteristics of the cru.

Bonnes-Mares Grand Cru 1989 ♥♥ ④
A medium-dark color with tinges shading into violet. A wine of character and strength, with intense aromas and distinct notes of ripe fruit. The palate has outstanding structure and good length. A fine example of the cru.

Jacques-Frédéric Mugnier

Château de Chambolle-Musigny
21220 Chambolle-Musigny
Tel. 80628539
Fax 80628736

Frédéric Mugnier is now comfortably settled into the family estate he bought in 1985. One can easily understand why, when one realizes that of the four hectares he owns, 1.13 produce Musigny, 0.33 ha produce Bonnes-Mares, 0.5 ha Chambolle-Musigny Premier Cru Les Amoureuses and the rest Premier Cru Les Fuées. Frédéric's father and grandfather rented their vineyards or sold their wine wholesale and Frédéric, whose background is not in wine, still moves cautiously. He adds no yeasts and has slightly lowered the fermentation temperature (to 32°C-34°C), preceding fermentation with 4-5 days' maceration at 15°C-16°C but without the help of large doses of sulphur dioxide, which he dislikes. Fermentation lasts at least 15 days and the wines age for a minimum of 18 months in 25% new barrels. Since 1988, the wines have been classics of their Appellation, uniting elegance and power but without coming into the category of wines which are excessively soft or rich in wood.

Bonnes-Mares Grand Cru 1990 ♥♥ ④
Still very undeveloped on the nose, and very rigid in its form and structure. The hard tannins will mellow out only after a long period of bottle-age.

Chambolle-Musigny Les Amoureuses Premier Cru 1990 ♥♥ ④
Very similar to Musigny in its aromas with a little more delicacy and lightness. A very successful product of the vintage in a cru of legendary elegance.

Chambolle-Musigny Les Fuées Premier Cru 1990 ♥♥ ③
A slightly brighter color than the Les Amoureuses with a pleasant nose of violets and raspberries. Seriously well-balanced and with good tannins, but attractive in its aromaticity and length. Confirmation of the successful vintage at Chambolle.

Musigny Grand Cru 1990
One of the great wines of the last 25 years. Outstanding intensity of color and a very expressive nose with flowery notes prevailing (dog-rose and violets). All the delicacy and complexity one could wish for from this Grand Cru.

COTE DE NUITS/CHAMBOLLE-MUSIGNY
BOURGOGNE
FRANCE

321

COTE DE NUITS/CHAMBOLLE-MUSIGNY
BOURGOGNE
FRANCE

Domaine Georges Roumier

21220 Chambolle-Musigny
Tel. 80628637
Fax 80628355

Founded in the 1920s, this estate has an excellent reputation which it has always lived up to. Christophe Roumier is in charge of a lovely property of 13.8 ha of red varieties, with the exception of 0.2 ha of Corton Charlemagne. He keeps up a tradition of fermentation in open vats, breaking up the cap and pushing it under the surface of the wine daily. Fermentation is at controlled temperatures and lasts 14 to 23 days, depending on the vintage. The wine is then immediately placed in barrels, 10% to 30% of which are new, depending on the cru. Bottling takes place after clarification with egg whites and normally there is no filtration. The vineyards are divided between the Bourgogne Appellation, the Chambolle-Musigny Premier Cru Les Amoureuses, the Morey-Saint-Denis Premier Cru Clos de la Bussière and the Grands Crus of Clos-Vougeot, Bonnes-Mares and Musigny. The wines are concentrated with yields of 24 to 40 hl/ha and will age comfortably for at least 15 years.

Bonnes-Mares Grand Cru 1990 🍷🍷 ④
Moderately intense in color. Extremely delicate nose with a superb touch of orange peel. Right from the initial impact, the class of the Grand Cru is obvious in the stupendous elegance and intensity. Given structure by the wood and the vintage, this is definitely a wine to lay down.

Chambolle-Musigny 1990 🍷 ③
Medium ruby color. Pure, simple nose with the wood still in evidence. The initial impact is well-defined and fruity. Good balance between acidity and body. Fine depth of bouquet, braced by the new wood. Will be at its best in two years' time.

Morey-Saint-Denis 🍷🍷 ④
Clos de la Bussière Premier Cru 1990
The color is tinged with blue. The nose is delicate but a little undeveloped. The initial impact is subtle and full of character and the follow-through well-rounded, beautifully made and typical of Morey. Lovely concentration of wild berries (bilberries), with a mineral note and a very long finish.

Pierre Gelin

2, rue du Chapitre
21220 Fixin
Tel. 80524524
Fax 80514780

This estate, the largest in the village of Fixin, was created in the 1930s. Historically, it became famous for the interest which Napoleon showed in the property and indeed there is a statue on the estate by François Rude to "The Emperor Awakening to Immortality". Today, both the Gelins and the Molins are dedicated to quality, with Jacqueline in the vineyards, Marie-Odile, always ready to welcome visitors, André, President of the local Fixin wine union, and Stephen, the grower-poet. It is a quality which extends from the exclusive Premiers Crus, Clos Napoléon and Clos du Chapitre, right down to the small regional Appellations which they always make so well, including Chambertin-Clos de Bèze and Mazis-Chambertin. These are growers whose skill is evident in everything they do. A bench-mark.

Fixin Premier Cru 🍷🍷 ③
Clos Napoléon 1990
A distinct violet purple in appearance, this is a wine which in its first flush of youth reveals a bouquet redolent of spices and candied fruit. Good structure on the palate, with rich, delicate tannins and a rare density and strength. Certainly a wine which will age comfortably for a very long time.

Mazis-Chambertin 1988 🍷 ③
Coming from vines with an average age of 40 years, a wine with a black cherry color and a very intense aroma of toast and spices on a background of candied fruit. Well-rounded and full-bodied, the finish has a slightly bitter note.

COTE DE NUITS/CHAMBOLLE-MUSIGNY
BOURGOGNE
FRANCE

322

COTE DE NUITS/FIXIN
BOURGOGNE
FRANCE

Alain Burguet

18, rue de l'Eglise
21220 Gevrey-Chambertin
Tel. 80343635
Fax 80585045

There are no Grands Crus or Premiers Crus on this estate. Alain Burguet, unlike most of his colleagues in the region, only produces one Appellation, Gevrey-Chambertin. It has to be said, however, that half of his vine stock is now 50 years old and that his Vieilles Vignes tends to be of a concentration one would like to find more often in Premiers Crus or in Charmes. And concentration is the key word when talking about this Gevrey for two reasons: the first is the low yields (30-35 hl/ha) which are a consequence of the age of the plants, and the second is the care that goes into winemaking and aging. Alain Burguet is not a man to do things in a hurry. His fermentation takes a long time and the cap is regularly broken up. After malolactic fermentation, Burguet lets his wines age for one or two years in the barrel, with only 5% new wood, before bottling them. The resulting wines are full-bodied, with excellent structure thanks to their tannins, which require aging in the bottle and need to be allowed to breathe before serving. The ripeness of the grapes from recent vintages has given Burguet's wines exceptional density in comparison with the notional quality level of the Appellation.

Gevrey-Chambertin Vieilles Vignes 1990
Intense ruby red in color, characteristic of the vintage. The nose is undeveloped but superbly clean. Excellent concentration right from the initial impact, with the mature tannins balanced by the fruit. A great wine with a great future, with the cru well to the fore.

Gevrey-Chambertin Vieilles Vignes 1989
Medium intensity of color with a faint tinge lent by bottle-age. After being allowed to breathe, the nose is very complex and the palate is crisp from the start with good fruit and structure. Pleasing aromas of blackcurrant are left on the nose.

Gevrey-Chambertin Vieilles Vignes 1988
A wine with a bright, intense, youthful color, frank and still to develop on the nose. The palate is full-bodied, generous and well-balanced. Well-rounded tannins with agreeable acidity and sufficient structure to age well.

Bruno Clair

5, rue du Vieux-Collège
21160 Marsannay-la-Côte
Tel. 80522895
Fax 80521814

Bruno Clair has settled in the area of the former Clair-Daü estate, with 18 ha spread over 20 different crus ranging from the humble Aligoté to the most noble Gevrey-Chambertin Clos Saint-Jacques. His talent lies in his marvellous knowledge of the "terroir", where 100 year-old wines grow alongside others in the first flush of youth, for example, Marsannay Blanc, which he has recently replanted, and his 1992 harvest of Chambolle-Musigny. Clair does not try to push Nature. The vines are cultivated in the traditional manner with manual harvesting and yields kept low (as little as 30 hl/ha in the best plots). The grapes are partially de-stemmed and then fermented in wooden vats. Aging is in barrels, one quarter of which are new. The product range is decidedly impressive, from the La Dominode Premier Cru at Savigny-lès-Beaune to the Morey-Saint-Denis by way of Marsannay Les Grosses Têtes, Vosne-Romanée and Chambertin-Clos-de-Bèze. An excellent job.

Marsannay 1989
This particular rosé saved the Appellation, which lies in an excellent position at the foot of the Côte de Nuit slopes, when it was threatened by the expansion of Dijon. A lovely pale color with just the right hint of orange. Vinous, well-rounded and powerfully scented, a wine which goes well with food.

Chambertin-Clos-de-Bèze Grand Cru 1990
Dark in color with a clean nose, currently still lacking in development. The fruit is evident right from the initial impact and opens out into intense raspberry notes in the finish. Superbly well-made.

Gevrey-Chambertin Les Cazetiers Premier Cru 1990
Pleasingly complex nose, with notes of roasted almonds and red fruit. Lovely, elegant structure with a delicious liquorice finish. Typical of the cru. A wine which will age into the medium term.

Marsannay Les Longeroles 1990
From deep clay soil at mid-slope, a wine with superb notes of red and black berries. Elegant on the palate, with pure fruit and a very fresh finish. A magnificent example of Pinot Noir, to be drunk young.

Savigny-lès-Beaune La Dominode Premier Cru 1990
Vine stock dating from 1902 gives the wine a dark color and immense concentration of fruit. A hugely elegant Savigny, to lay down several years before drinking.

COTE DE NUITS/GEVREY-CHAMBERTIN
BOURGOGNE
FRANCE

323

COTE DE NUITS/GEVREY-CHAMBERTIN
BOURGOGNE
FRANCE

Domaine Fourrier

7, route de Dijon
21220 Gevrey-Chambertin
Tel. 80343399
Fax 80341623

Jean-Claude Fourrier inherited this estate from his great-uncle Joseph Pernot, whose wines were very famous in the 1960s, and which he himself is about to hand over to his children, Jean-Claude and Isabelle. The nine hectares are in good locations, mainly in Gevrey-Chambertin, but also in Morey-Saint-Denis (with two or three parcels in the Premier Cru Clos Sorbès), Chambolle-Musigny and Vougeot (Premier Cru Les Petits Vougeots). The Fourriers dislike productive clones, selling grapes from these wholesale. Fermentation is relatively brief at 10-15 days, giving wines which are scented and elegant, developing rather quickly in spite of the age of the plants. The Fourriers tend to favor fruit over structure and de-stem their grapes. Aging is in barriques, only a very small proportion of which are new, and lasts 22 months. Chemical fertilizers are no longer used and nowadays the cellar concentrates on light wines for drinking young - very different from those made by great-uncle Joseph.

Gevrey-Chambertin 1990
A lovely red color with violet tinges. From plants situated at the northern edge of the commune, this is a wine with the complexity and structure typical of the neighboring Brochon crus. Good body and a very crisp finish.

Griotte-Chambertin
Grand Cru 1990
This small parcel of 25 ares is the estate's only Grand Cru. The wine has a ruby color with bluish tints. The aroma of Pinot Noir is frank and well in evidence together with notes of waxed wood and red fruit. On the palate, the fruit is concentrated, soft and velvety thanks to the light tannins, but the finish is lacking a little in length.

Gevrey-Chambertin
Premier Cru 1988
A blend of several parcels of Premier Cru, each too small to be vinified separately. A fine ruby color and a well-balanced wine which is only now beginning to blossom. Impressively intense and outstandingly long aromas.

Domaine Geantet-Pansiot

3-5, route de Beaune
21220 Gevrey-Chambertin
Tel. 80343237

Vincent Geantet has been managing the 11-ha family estate since 1980. Most of the property is in the commune of Brochon (7 ha, lying to the north of Gevrey-Chambertin) and several different types of Gecrey-Chambertin are produced. As well as the generic Bourgogne Appellations, the other wines are Gevrey-Chambertin Premiers and Grands Crus and a pleasant Marsannay. The grapes are totally de-stemmed and then undergo three days' cold-maceration before fermenting for a period which varies from 10 to 12 days. The wine is pumped over the cap three times a day during fermentation. Vincent is happy to let the temperature rise to 36°C-37°C, but at the same time refrigerates a tank which serves as a yeast store. The yeasts are used to lengthen the fermentation period. Bottling takes place in the month of May after 18 months in barriques, one third of which are replaced every year. The vine stock dates from 1902-1978 with the respectable average age of 40 years. The finest clonal selections are used for new planting. The 1990 and 1991 wines are concentrated thanks to very low yields and are emblematic of the domaine's continuous improvement.

Charmes-Chambertin
Grand Cru 1990
These 45 ares of Grand Cru are the estate's pride and joy. The wine is a fine violet red in appearance and the initial impact is very impressive, being both full-bodied and restrained at the same time. Lovely soft tannins, with the fruit coming back perfectly on the finish. A great bottle with a wonderful future.

Gevrey-Chambertin
Vielles Vignes 1990
Just bottled, the aroma is a far from being developed yet. The initial impact is frank and then the fruit takes over. Good structure to guarantee a bright future.

Gevrey-Chambertin
Le Poissenot Premier Cru 1990
This plot on the very top of the slope to the left of Clos-Saint-Jacques was replanted in 1969. Biscuity aromas together with red berries. On the palate, the first impact overwhelms the delicacy of the wine but then the fruit is crisp and lingering.

Gevrey-Chambertin
Vieilles Vignes 1989
Lovely gamey aroma with notes of strawberry and mulberry. Less concentrated than the 1990 with a full-bodied and fruity palate. Above all, a fine finish, with no trace of heaviness.

Domaine Philippe Leclerc

13, rue des Halles
21220 Gevrey-Chambertin
Tel. 80343072

It would be difficult to find another grower and winemaker quite as passionate as Philippe Leclerc. In the truest Burgundy tradition, he inherited his estate and the eight hectares are spread across various Gevrey-Chambertin Appellations including Bourgogne, Villages and three Premiers Crus, all planted solely with Pinot Noir. Leclerc's wines are made in the most natural manner possible using traditional techniques. They spend a minimum of two years in the wood before being considered ready for bottling. The Premiers Crus are aged in 100% new wood while Villages and Bourgogne have 50% and 30% respectively. The 45 year-old plants stand on clay-and-limestone soil, giving an average annual production of 40 hl/ha. The yields and the new wood impart good structure and aging potential. Philippe Leclerc's trademark is his faithfulness to his uncompromising philosophy. Much patience is indicated before opening one of his bottles.

Bourgogne 1990   🍷 ②
A medium-intensity cherry red color with a seductive nose of spices and vanilla. The fruit is prominent on the palate. Delicate and with a good balanced of texture and wood with a full and lingering finish. Excellent value for money.

Gevrey-Chambertin 1990   🍷🍷 ③
A very deep cherry red color and the typical Gevrey-Chambertin nose, intense and gamey with notes of red fruit. Fleshy on the palate with rich fruit (cherries) and elegant wood. While not over-burdened with tannins, it will nonetheless require time before it reaches its peak.

Gevrey-Chambertin   🍷🍷 ④
Les Cazetiers 1990 Premier Cru
Deep cherry red color, this is the most "feminine" of Leclerc's three Premiers Crus. A little unforthcoming, almost shy, on the nose, it is rich and sumptuous on the palate where it opens out soft and full into subtle, ripe fruit and almost chewy wood. A voluptuous, harmonious wine with great strength.

Joseph Roty

24, rue Maréchal de Lattre de Tassigny
21220 Gevrey-Chambertin
Tel. 80343897

Joseph Roty belongs to the tenth generation of a family of Gevrey-Chambertin growers. A difficult man to get to know, passionate, introverted and talkative at the same time, he is interested in anything to do with vines and is most opinionated. He grafts by himself, using neither clones nor chemical fertilizers, and hoes and tills by hand, replacing the plants a few at a time. Winemaking begins with cold-maceration, and Joseph is very much opposed to additional yeasts. Fermentation lasts for a month with a maximum 25°C, the wine being left on the skins in barriques of which one sixth to one third are new. Bottling is only done at the two equinoxes with no clarification or filtration for either white or red wines. The end result is a range of great reds with good alcohol and aging potential. 90% is usually booked by exporters, restaurateurs and loyal customers, despite the relatively high prices. As well as a vineyard at Marsannay, the estate also has three Premiers Crus at Gevrey-Chambertin, Les Champs Chenys, Les Fontenys and Le Clos Prieur, and the Grands Crus Mazis, Griottes and Charmes-Chambertin. Now that his son is working with him, they will expand the estate.

Charmes-Chambertin   🍷🍷 ④
Grand Cru 1990
70% of the original old vines, planted in 1881, are still producing. The color is black and the aroma, intense with hints of liquorice. Superbly rich with a very concentrated body and exceptional length. A wine with a great future.

Gevrey-Chambertin   🍷🍷 ③
Les Champs Chenys Premier Cru 1990
'Poor Man's Charmes-Chambertin' is situated directly above Charmes-Chambertin on soil where nothing is easy to grow. This gives rise to a very concentrated wine with a delicate aroma and a well-balanced palate, compact in texture, with excellent length. A great Premier Cru.

Gevrey-Chambertin   🍷🍷 ④
Les Fontenys Premier Cru 1990
This cru yields Roty's favorite wines. Undeveloped aromas but very delicate, with powdery notes. The palate is full and the body dense. Definitely needs time to age.

Griottes-Chambertin   🍷🍷 ④
Grand Cru 1990
Planted after the last war. Dark in color with a pure aroma of red berries. The initial impact is gripping and full. The tannins are intense and the wood straightforward. Remarkable concentration. Drink in a few years' time.

COTE DE NUITS/GEVREY-CHAMBERTIN
BOURGOGNE
FRANCE

325

COTE DE NUITS/GEVREY-CHAMBERTIN
BOURGOGNE
FRANCE

Domaine Armand Rousseau

21220 Gevrey-Chambertin
Tel. 80343055
Fax 80585025

The Rousseau estate is one of Burgundy's monuments. Armand Rousseau, who put the property together piece by piece, was one of the first owner-producers to bottle his own wine in the 1930s. His son Charles, an enologist, has managed the enterprise since 1959 and is now helped by his son Eric. The outstanding feature of this 14-ha estate is that it comprises more than three-quarters Grands Crus. These include large parcels in Chambertin (1.95 ha) and Chambertin-Clos-de-Bèze (1.19 ha) while the Charmes-Chambertin, Clos de la Roche and Clos de Ruchottes (in Ruchottes-Chambertin) plots are splendid crus of over one hectare each. The Clos-Saint-Jacques, to which they have exclusive rights, is a Premier Cru which comes close to the level of the Grands Crus. Fermentation takes place in open stainless steel vats, lasting 12 to 15 days at a high 30°C to extract the color of the grape. All wines are aged in barriques (20 to 24 months) and lightly filtered. For the Grands Crus, the barrels are totally replaced every year and they are one quarter replaced in the case of the other wines. Having gone through a somewhat disappointing period in the 1970s, the estate is once again in top shape, with vines now averaging 35 to 55 years-old.

Chambertin-Clos-de-Bèze ♥♥ ④
Grand Cru 1989
Never before has this Rousseau wine been so dark and full-bodied. The classic liquorice aromas of the cru can barely be distinguished. The aromatic and tannic intensity of the cuvée ensure an excellent long-term future.

Chambertin Grand Cru 1989 ♥♥ ④
Slightly paler in color than the Clos-de-Bèze with less developed but more elegant aromas. The palate is of a similar density and flavor, albeit with a smaller range of overtones. The tannins are a little harder but show class. Wait at least 15 years for this one.

Clos-de-la-Roche ♥♥ ④
Grand Cru 1989
Color of moderate intensity with well-developed aromas of new leather and spices. Soft, with generous alcohol and rich in glycerine, it is not markedly acidic on the palate. The full-flavored tannins would suggest to drink soon.

Gevrey-Chambertin ♥♥ ④
Le Clos Saint-Jacques Premier Cru 1989
Dark ruby with aromas of lovely vanilla and spice from the new oak with raisiny overtones typical of the vintage. A rich, flavorful wine with a finish of outstanding elegance and unusual balance for its vintage.

Domaine Tortochot

12, rue de l'Eglise
21220 Gevrey-Chambertin
Tel. 80343068

Both in its size (11 ha) and in its winemaking methods, the Tortochot estate is a classic Côtes de Nuits property. The vineyards are for the most part in the commune of Gevrey-Chambertin in the Villages Appellation, in two Premiers Crus (Lavaux-Saint-Jacques and Les Champeaux) and three Grands Crus (Mazis-Chambertin, Charmes-Chambertin and Chambertin). The remainder of the property is in Moray-Saint-Denis and Clos de Vougeot. Half of the estate's production is still sold unbottled on the local market; this enables the wines for bottling to be rigorously selected. Gabriel Tortochot, chairman of the local commune's growers' association for the past 20 years, is a well-known figure at Gevrey. He ferments in the traditional manner (12 to 15 days in open vats) but at controlled temperatures. All his wines are aged for two years in oak barriques with those used for the Grands Crus being replaced every year. The style of Gabriel's wines is more remarkable for its delicacy than for its strength with Pinot Noir's berry aromas present in the purest form. There is no trace of heaviness to cloud the elegance, but these wines nonetheless possess all the structure necessary to ensure a long life in the cellar.

Gevrey-Chambertin ♥♥ ③
Champerrier Vieilles Vignes 1990
An intense color with tinges of blue. Frank, gamey nose of ripe fruit and blackcurrant. Very well-balanced on the palate with excellent structure and the discreet tannins of the vintage. A 1990 to drink while still relatively young.

Gevrey-Chambertin ♥♥ ③
Champerrier Vieilles Vignes 1989
Very intense, youthful ruby color and superb aromas of Pinot, flowers and fruit (raspberry, redcurrant and cherry) on the nose. Uncomplicated on the palate yet with a fascinating softness. A typical Gervey, soft, lingering and ready for drinking in 7 or 8 years.

Gevrey-Chambertin ♥♥ ③
Champerrier Vieilles Vignes 1988
A wine with a youthful, if pale, color and a nose of undeveloped aromas which are nevertheless frank and elegant. On the palate, the fruit bursts out in a delicate flavor of exceptional length. The fine balance will enable this wine to age for some time yet.

COTE DE NUITS/GEVREY-CHAMBERTIN
BOURGOGNE
FRANCE   326

COTE DE NUITS/GEVREY-CHAMBERTIN
BOURGOGNE
FRANCE

Jean Fournier

29/39, rue du Château
21160 Marsannay-la-Côte
Tel. 80522438
Fax 80527740

Fourniers have lived in Marsannay since the
time of Louis XI, so it will come as no
surprise that Jean Fournier, an inexhaustible
font of local lore, is chairman of the
Marsannay Appellation in the northernmost
part of the Côtes de Nuits near Dijon. The
zone seems to have been able to defend
itself against the invasion of Dijon's middle
classes in search of rustic peace through its
recent nomination as an Appellation d'Origine
Contrôlée. Today, the vineyards are at last
increasing in value, the négociants are taking
an interest and the vignerons are replanting.
Jean Fournier could not fail to note this
phenomenon and so began to extend his
estate by a hectare in 1991, looking out in the
meantime for further parcels to acquire. He
inherited 2.5 ha from his father in 1960 and
possesses about 14 ha all told, mainly in the
Marsannay zone, with small parcels in
Bourgogne Aligoté and Gevrey-Chambertin.
All his wines are excellent value for money
and excellent drinking.

Bourgogne Aligoté 1990   🍇 ①
It is said rather too often that Aligoté is the
Muscadet of the Burgundy region, but here is
the proof that this is a wine which deserves to
age. A lovely pale gold color, a frank nose, good
acidity and a finish of well-sustained aromas.

Marsannay Blanc 1990   🍇 ②
Bright color with a highly aromatic nose where
the prevailing menthol balances out the flowery
component. On the palate, the wine offers
attractive oak and has sufficient acidity to age
outstandingly well.

Marsannay Rouge Clos du Roi 1990 🍇 ②
A wine well worthy of the Côtes de Nuits which
might bring to mind a Gevrey with its deep color,
its aromas of black-cherry shading into mulberry
and blackcurrant, and its finish of lovely, delicate
tannins. A wine of breeding to drink in the next
two or three years.

Domaine Dujac

Rue de la Bussière
21220 Morey-Saint-Denis
Tel. 80343258
Fax 80518976

Unlike Burgundian producers of families with
centuries-old, winemaking traditions, Jacques
Seysses is a first-generation grower. Since
1968, the former Parisian has built up a 11.5
ha estate (three-quarters of which is
Chardonnay) between Morey-Saint-Denis,
Chambolle-Musigny and Gevrey-Chambertin.
Jacques' approach is simple and consists in
making as few interventions as possible - no
de-stemming, no added yeasts, no filtration,
soft-crushing and limited racking.
Fermentation lasts for 16-20 days at no more
than 30°C, with the cap regularly broken up
and pushed under the wine, followed by 15-
16 months' aging in barrels of Allier oak
(100% new for the Grands Crus). Although
the plants are only 20 years-old on average,
the wines are pure and intense with the Pinot
Noir showing all its delicacy and the cru its
generosity. In addition to the Grands Crus
Clos-Saint-Denis and Clos-de-la-Roche,
there is the superb Gevrey-Chambertin
Premier Cru, Aux Combettes. Having
inspired a new generation of Burgundies,
Jacques Seysses is on to a new adventure
with Vins de Pays at a new estate in
Provence.

Clos-de-La Roche   🍇🍇 ④
Grand Cru 1990
Very deep ruby red and intense aromas of
cherry, black berries, cinnamon and game. Rich,
complex and strong on the palate with nice
balance and sufficient tannins to sustain the
fruit. Fills the mouth wonderfully, enhanced by
the delicate flavor of oak. Outstanding length
with intense spices and cherry.

Clos-Saint-Denis Grand Cru 1989 🍇🍇 ④
Medium intense color with aromas of delicious
red fruit, spices and violets. The depth and
complexity marry perfectly with the delicacy and
elegance. The hint of wood is very faint. A real
thoroughbred which finishes on notes of autumn
leaves, coffee, violets and possesses surprising
length.

Gevrey-Chambertin   🍇🍇 ④
Aux Combottes Premier Cru 1989
Medium color and a nose with hints of toasty
wood, hazelnuts and cherries with great
delicacy. The palate is rich and full-bodied, yet
elegant. Highly scented, with the typical nutty
aromas of the vintage beautifully marrying the
wood. Subtle in texture, persistent with lean
tannins.

Morey-Saint-Denis 1989   🍇🍇 ③
Fairly light in color, with goood fruit aroms
developing into autumn leaves. Well-rounded
and subtle, with a delicious aroma of strawberry
and raisins. Good acidity and unobtrusive
tannins. Pleasant length for a Villages.

COTE DE NUITS-MARSANNAY
BOURGOGNE
FRANCE

327

COTE DE NUITS/MOREY-SAINT-DENIS
BOURGOGNE
FRANCE

Jean-Paul Magnien

5, ruelle de l'Eglise
21220 Morey-Saint-Denis
Tel. 80518310

Jean-Paul Magnien runs this small property, created by his grandfather, which including rented parcels has only 4.5 ha. Since it lies over three different communes with many different Appellations ranging from Passetoutgrain to Grand Cru, the quantities produced of each individual wine are sometimes very small. This was even truer than usual in 1991, when frost and hail slashed the yields of some plots to as little as 16 hl/ha. The Premiers Crus here are Les Façonnières, Monts-Luisants, Clos Baulet and Guenchers at Morey-Saint-Denis and Les Sentiers at Chambolle-Musigny. The tiny parcels in Grands Crus are at Charmes-Chambertin and Clos-Saint-Denis. Jean-Paul began selling bottled wine in 1976 and since then has built up a small group of faithful customers. He is not fond of alcohol and is pleased that in recent vintages he has often been able to avoid chaptalization. He ferments in open oak vats for 15 days or so, regularly breaking the cap and pushing it under the wine. For aging, he uses 20% new barrels for the first year and barrels more than five years-old for the second. Vines average 20 years-old, but some in Les Athées are 55.

Morey-Saint-Denis 🍇🍇 ③
Les Façonnières Premier Cru 1991
Impresses with its concentration, superior to that of most 1991s. The nose is very pure and the structured palate is full of clean fruit. A bright future awaits.

Clos-Saint-Denis 🍇🍇🍇 ④
Grand Cru 1990
An intense red color with flecks of blue. Excellent, clean aroma of fruit at its purest. The well-blended wood is evident only in the delicacy it adds to the full-bodied and complete palate. Fine softness and agreeable hints of pepper on the finish. Outstanding length and a guaranteed future. The 12.2° alcohol is obtained without chaptalization.

Morey-Saint-Denis 🍇 ③
Les Façonnières Premier Cru 1990
Magnificent color. The aroma is undeveloped as yet, with a herbaceous note. The palate is very frank and impresses with its density and seriousness. The fruit comes back attractively in the finish, with no trace of heaviness from the alcohol.

Morey-Saint-Denis 🍇 ③
Les Façonnières Premier Cru 1989
A lovely dark red. The nose is slightly vegetal, opening up when allowed to breathe and disclosing delicious hints of red fruit. Good structure on the palate, with a very fresh finish.

Domaine Ponsot

21, rue de la Montagne
21220 Morey-Saint-Denis
Tel. 80343246
Fax 80585170

The Ponsot estate was one of the first in the region to sell bottled wine in the 1930s. Jean-Marie Ponsot, who manages the property with his son, sells his entire production to a small number of faithful customers. Jean-Marie has a strong personality and has been mayor of his commune for several years. A real Burgundy character, he played a prominent part in the selection and dissemination of Pinot Noir clones, many of which came from his own vineyards. The estate has about eight hectares of vines in excellent locations, with a large proportion of Grands Crus, the largest being Clos-de-la-Roche at three hectares. In addition to this, there are other Grands Crus at Les Charmes in Chambolle-Musigny and Les Monts Luisants at Morey-Saint-Denis, where a rather original white wine is produced. The chief virtue of these wines is the delicacy of their aromas, but they are also only moderately alcoholic. These are the qualities which Ponsot values, sometimes to the point of sacrificing concentration, and they are obtained despite the fact that he does not usually use de-stemming or filtration.

Chapelle-Chambertin 🍇🍇
Grand Cru 1989
Very intense color. Extremely pure aromas, well worthy of a Grand Cru. The palate is rich and at the same time delicate but with a crisp, alcohol-free finish.

Griotte-Chambertin 🍇🍇🍇
Grand Cru 1989
A very pleasant nose of pure Pinot fruit of the highest quality. The wood is still present on the palate, which has vanilla notes but is as yet less than totally convincing in terms of concentration.

Latricières-Chambertin 🍇🍇
Grand Cru 1989
Intense color. Superb nose, rich and complex. The perfectly blended wood is not overwhelming. A wine whose charm is beginning to come out thanks to its outstanding softness.

Morey-Saint-Denis 🍇🍇
Clos-de-la-Roche 1989
Very different from the Chambertins. Nose of very ripe red fruit. The initial impact on the palate is soft; the light structure barely comes through. The balance, on the other hand, is superb, the texture subtle and the delicacy quite remarkable. The Clos-de-la-Roche style features great attractiveness and elegance.

Clos-de-la-Roche Grand Cru 1987 🍇🍇🍇 ④
A very delicate nose with hints of tea and toastiness. The palate is soft with delicate flavors and fine length. Already perfect for drinking.

Domaine de l'Arlot

Premeaux
21700 Nuits-Saint-Georges
Tel. 80610192
Fax 80610422

Domaine de l'Arlot is one of Burgundy's most prestigious names. It was initially the property of the Viénot family, and later belonged to the Belins who in 1987 sold it to the French insurance group AXA. AXA owns several châteaux amongst which is the famous Château Pichon-Longueville Baron in the Bordeaux region. Their Burgundy property comprises 13 ha of vines in some of the best-known Premiers Crus of Nuits-Saint-Georges and Vosne-Romanée as well as some less important vineyards in neighboring communes. Although in an area planted almost entirely with red varieties, Domaine de l'Arlot features a one-hectare vineyard called Clos d'Arlot planted with Chardonnay and Pinot Gris. Since the change of ownership, under the management of the dynamic Jean-Pierre de Smet there have been profound changes with large investments to achieve the quality objectives AXA budgets for when it takes over an estate. The Arlot star is once again in the ascendant as are the traditionally-made wines, produced for aging in the cellar. Harvesting is done by hand with selection of the best grapes. The wine is bottled without filtration after aging for about 18 months in barriques, at least half of which are new.

Nuits-Saint-Georges 🍇🍇 ③
Clos-des-Forêts Premier Cru 1990
This is the first vintage in which the change of ownership has really made its presence felt. An attractive ruby color of medium intensity with flecks of violet in appearance, indicative of youth. The aroma is very vinous and wooded with the fruit barely distinguishable. The palate is sustained and lingering with a pleasingly elegant finish. An excellent interpretation of the cru and not without intensity and personality. To be tasted again in a few years' time.

Robert Chevillon

68, rue Félix Tisserand
21700 Nuits-Saint-Georges
Tel. 80623488
Fax 80611331

Robert Chevillon and his two children manage 22 Premiers Crus at Nuits-Saint-Georges in addition to making, like most Burgundians, Aligoté, Bourgogne Blanc, Bourgogne Rouge and Passetoutgrain. When the estate was founded in 1926, it had only three hectares, but it has grown over the generations to the present eight. Robert has a huge plot (six hectares) in the Premier Cru Les Saint-Georges, which may be considered the Nuits-Saint-Georges Grand Cru. Winemaking is carried out in the traditional manner, with one third new barriques every year. Bottling takes place after 18 months of aging in wood and light filtration. The main characteristic of Chevillon wines is to enhance the cru of origin to the full. This policy is successful as almost all the estate's production is sold "en primeur", especially abroad. Do be careful, though, for Chevillon is quite a common surname in Nuits-Saint-Georges. Before you buy the bottle, be sure to check the first name too.

Nuits-Saint-Georges 🍇🍇 ③
La Roncière Premier Cru 1991
A superb flowery nose with exuberant gamey notes and a rather soft, mouth-filling palate. A wine which strongly characteristic of the cru.

Nuits-Saint-Georges 🍇🍇 ③
Les Vaucrains Premier Cru 1991
Dark in color and an intense nose of violets with lovely mineral hints. The palate is dense, considering the vintage, but this is made possible by the low yields of the 60 year-old vines.

Nuits-Saint-Georges 🍇🍇 ③
La Roncière Premier Cru 1989
Fine ruby color with violet tonalities. Well-developed nose where the fruit is beginning to appear, without the exuberant tones of the 1991. Powerful and well-rounded on the palate, given time it will come into its own. The beautiful finish is typical of the zone.

COTE DE NUITS/NUITS-SAINT-GEORGES
BOURGOGNE
FRANCE

329

COTE DE NUITS/NUITS-SAINT-GEORGES
BOURGOGNE
FRANCE

Domaine Gavignet Bethanie

18, rue Félix Tisserand
21700 Nuits-Saint-Georges
Tel. 80611604
Fax 80612007

Somewhat unusual for Burgundy, this estate is woman's territory. Christian Gavignet looks after the cellar while five women, including his wife and their two young daughters, tend the 10 ha of estate-vineyards in Côtes de Nuits-Villages and Nuits-Saint-Georges. The sub-zone Les Athées is the largest parcel while the Premiers Crus Aux Damodes and Les Poulettes are the pride of the property. Traditionally, the estate also produces Aligoté and Passetoutgrain and has recently replanted the Clos des Huguette in the Hautes Côtes de Nuits. The remainder of the vines average 30 to 40 years-old. As far as winemaking goes, Christian relies on the enologist Guy Accad. The wines undergo cold-maceration for a few days before fermenting for three weeks to one month, depending on the vintage. The result is the complete extraction of both color and fruit. Wines age for 12 to 18 months in barriques which are replaced only in minimal part each year. So far, they still use filtration but are likely to stop in the near future.

Bourgogne Aligoté 1990 🍇 ①
Obtained after light maceration on the skins, this is a more open and fleshier wine than its Appellation would suggest. Excellent value for money.

Nuits-Saint-Georges Les Poulettes 🍇🍇 ③
Premier Cru 1990
This Premier Cru is the natural extension of the equally famous Roncières and Perrières. Still in the barrel, its concentration of color and texture are nonetheless impressive. The fruit is evident in good structure and delicacy.

Côte de Nuits-Villages 1989 🍇 ②
Color with violet tinges and a nose with hints of wild berries. Soft on the palate with a fresh finish. A wine of greater elegance than the zone can usually claim.

Nuits-Saint-Georges 🍇🍇 ②
Les Athées 1989
An intense color tinged with violet. The nose is extremely concentrated with superb mineral notes. A fine expression of the Nuits Cru where structure outshines delicacy.

Nuits-Saint-Georges Les Poulettes 🍇🍇 ③
Premier Cru 1988
Dark color and intense aromas of flowers and redcurrant. The initial impact is spirited, with remarkable tannins and ideal balance. The finish is very attractive.

Domaine Henri Gouges

7, rue du Moulin
21700 Nuits-Saint-Georges
Tel. 80610440
Fax 80613284

In the years between the wars, Henri Gouges did much to defend Burgundy. His Premiers Crus at Nuits-Saint-Georges, Porets, Pruliers, Vaucrains, Chaignots and Saint-Georges were bench-marks for the region's winemakers. More recently, the quality has failed to live up to its reputation, but today Henri's nephew, Christian Georges, and cousin, Pierre, have painstakingly brought the estate back to its former glory. One works in the cellar, while the other looks after the vineyard. The vines stand in grass, and all treatment is with homeopathic products. Replanting is done using only 50% productive clones; yields never exceed 35 hl/ha. For experimental purposes, the estate is lucky enough to possess 3.5 ha in a single lot in Clos des Porets. Christian Gouges ferments in cement vats and has masterminded an efficient system for breaking up the cap and pumping the wine over it. Fermentation itself lasts for 15-20 days, the wines being aged in the wood, thereafter, for two winters and one summer. Each year, only 10%-20% of the barriques are replaced, to ensure that the oak never dominates the cru.

Nuits-Saint-Georges 🍇🍇 ③
La Perrière Premier Cru 1991
White Nuits are a rarity. The chalky soil to which the name refers is, however, suitable for white varieties, which here develop mineral notes and plenty of elegance.

Nuits-Saint-Georges 🍇 ③
Les Saint-Georges Premier Cru 1991
A vintage which brought out all the delicacy of the Pinot Noir variety. In the barrel, a wine with an intense color. The moderate oak-aging allows the primary aromas to come through; marked acidity enhances the varietal characteristics of the grape. An interesting, almost floral-iris finish.

Nuits-Saint-Georges 🍇🍇 ③
Clos de Porets Premier Cru 1990
The 1990 is a superb vintage but, according to Christian, not a typical one. Thinned grapes and drought gave the wine great concentration; dense in color; original hints of eucalyptus on the nose. Intense and full of character, with highly concentrated aromas with lots of violets. Impressive tannins.

Nuits-Saint-Georges 🍇🍇 ③
Les Saint-Georges Premier Cru 1987
Christian Gouges is extremely fond of this vintage, 70% was hit by hail before flowering, and which proved so difficult to vinify. Orange-colored, the nose is complex with notes of fruit, mineral, toastiness and spices. The flavor tends towards autumn leaves and is strikingly correct and delicate. Well worth waiting for.

COTE DE NUITS/NUITS-SAINT-GEORGES
BOURGOGNE
FRANCE
330

COTE DE NUITS/NUITS-SAINT-GEORGES
BOURGOGNE
FRANCE

Domaine Jayer-Gilles

Route de Corgoloin
21700 Magny-les-Villiers
Tel. 80629179
Fax 90629977

Robert Jayer has settled in the Hautes Côtes de Nuits, far away from the more famous Appellations. The 11-ha estate was formed from the merger of his father's vines (Nuits-Saint-Georges Premier Cru Les Damodes and Grand Cru Echézeaux) with those of his father-in-law in the Hautes-Côtes as well as generic Appellations. Robert Jayer learned much during his apprenticeship at Romanée-Conti. He manages a vine stock of between 20 and 70 years of age and prunes short to limit the yields. In his vast cellar, recently built and impeccably maintained, he gives all his Appellations the same care and attention, whether simple Bourgognes or Grands Crus. The white wines are fermented partly in vats and partly in new barrels with no regulation of the temperature which is, however, in excess of 20°C to obtain good concentration. The reds are cold-macerated for 5 or 6 days before being fermented for about 15 days. Since 1984, both white and red wines have been aged in barriques for 15 months before bottling. The end-product has great personality and is very suitable for laying down. The only drawbacks are the stiff prices, and the speed at which wines are snapped up.

Bourgogne Aligoté 199   ❦ ①
A very surprising Aligoté. Highly-scented, fruity, supple and very, very drinkable.

Haute Côte de Nuits 1990   ❦ ❦ ③
Made from 100% Pinot Blanc, a well-rounded and attractive wine, very characteristic with aromas of earth and fresh walnut. Austere, lingering and well-balanced on the palate. A white wine to lay down.

Côte de Nuits-Villages 1990   🍇 🍇 ③
Intense, violet color. The wood is still present on the nose but the palate has a fine balance between acidity and tannins. Less rustic than the equally excellent Haute Côte de Nuits red wine.

Echézeaux Grand Cru 1990   🍇 🍇 ④
A wine of a violet hue, moderately bright with hints of toasty wood on the nose. The palate is austere, dense and lingering. A great bottle for the cellar.

Nuits-Saint-Georges   🍇 🍇 ④
Les Hauts Poirets Premier Cru 1990
A beautiful example of Nuits, which expresses to the full the characteristics of the grape varieties of the zone. Delicate, complex aromas with impressive structure and balance.

Dominique Laurent

2, rue Jacques Duret
21700 Nuits-Saint-Georges
Tel. 80613162
Fax 80623242

This young pastry-chef from Vézoules has such a passion for wine that he was able to convince some of the most sought-after producers in France, including Guigal, Lafon, Raveneau and Ramonet, to let him have some of their best crus to put on sale in his shop. By 1987, he was hooked and although he didn't have a franc to his name, he settled in Nuits-Saint-Georges and started up as a négociant before going on to produce his 'ideal wine'. He began by aging a few selected wines in the traditional fashion, racking by hand, sulphite treatments restricted to the barriques themselves and bottling without clarification or filtration. These wines were selected both for style and concentration, as good as anything produced after World War 2. Little by little, he has managed to reassure his initially alarmed creditors and to increase his output from the 12 barriques of 1988 to the 70 of 1990. He believes that the wine, which comes from a number of prestigious crus, and the carefully selected wood need at least a year to get to know each other and his 1990 wines achieve a powerful aroma and body that are rarely found in today's Burgundies.

Bourgogne 1990   🍇 🍇 ①
From a Pommard made with grapes from exceptionally old vines, a wine with a lively color which perfectly develops the typical aromas of the cru (chestnuts, truffles and rain-soaked earth) over an incredibly dense texture one would like to find in other prestigious wines from the zone.

Gevrey-Chambertin   🍇 🍇 ④
Clos Saint-Jacques Premier Cru 1990
A monumental wine for color, aromatic intensity, strength of structure and clarity of flavor. Today, its appeal lies in its lovely toasty new wood, but it can be laid down for several decades. At peak maturity, it will offer a splendidly complex bouquet worthy of the greatest Côtes de Nuits.

Monthélie 1990   🍇 🍇 ③
Incredibly dark in color. The aromas of violets and spices are similar to those of a great Clos des Chênes at Volnay. Sumptuous texture and depth on the palate typical of a vintage in which the Pinot Noir variety naturally produced 14° alc.

Bourgogne Cuvée N°1 1988   🍇 🍇 ②
Aged in fine-quality new wood, this is a generic Bourgogne of surprising delicacy and complexity. It is a product from the north of the Côte de Nuits, very similar in aromas and structure to a good Gevrey-Chambertin Villages.

COTE DE NUITS/NUITS-SAINT-GEORGES
BOURGOGNE
FRANCE

331

COTE DE NUITS/NUITS-SAINT-GEORGES
BOURGOGNE
FRANCE

Alain Michelot

6, rue Camille Rodier
21700 Nuits-Saint-Georges
Tel. 80611446
Fax 80613508

Alain Michelot is best known for his great Nuits-Saint-Georges wines, which may be found on many of the most exclusive tables in France, but he also owns plots in Morey-Saint-Denis. His estate covers a total of 7.6 ha, including seven Premiers Crus more or less equally distributed between Nuits (Chaignots, Richemone and Champs-Perdrix) and Prémeaux (Saint-Georges, Vaucrains, Cailles and Porets Clos de Porets). Alain manages to achieve a very respectable average age in his stock by replanting as the vines need replacing with the overall aim of maintaining a planting pattern of 10,000-11,000 plants per hectare. The grapes are totally de-stemmed and cold-macerated before fermenting for about three weeks, with a temperature that never exceeds 32°C. Wines are aged for 18 months in barriques, one third of which are replaced every year, and then lightly filtered but not clarified. Alain Michelot's wines impress with their alcohol as well as with their balance and aging potential. According to Alain, their softness is due to the low temperature maintained during the final stages of fermentation.

Nuits-Saint-Georges 🍇🍇 ③
Les Chaignots Premier Cru 1991
Dark, tending to violet color and an intense, elegant nose of wild berries. It has the soft tannins of the vintage but is not lacking in structure.

Nuits-Saint-Georges 🍇 ③
Les Vaucrains Premier Cru 1991
This 70-are parcel was replanted in two phases during the 1970s and 1980s. Despite the young age of the plants, the wine already has a lovely aroma of violets although the palate does not have quite the same depth.

Nuits-Saint-Georges 🍇🍇 ④
Les Cailles Premier Cru 1990
An extremely intense, complex nose with notes of liquorice and violets. Fine breadth on the supple, elegant palate. A cru which lies somewhere between a Saint-Georges and a Porets.

Nuits-Saint-Georges 🍇🍇 ④
Les Champs-Perdrix Premier Cru 1990
In this great vintage, the 50 year-old vines produced a highly concentrated wine of remarkable length. The bouquet opens out into overtones which highlight the distinctive features of the cru. A great Nuits to tuck away in the cellar.

Domaine Pernin-Rossin

Vosne-Romanée
21700 Nuits-Saint-Georges
Tel. 80610741
Fax 80613413

With his eight hectares in the communes of Nuits-Saint-Georges and Vosne-Romanée, André Pernin is a small grower but he is by no means just any old grower. The wines crafted by this perfectionist risk disappointing the newcomer to the appreciation of great wine, but their obvious potential is without exception enormous. Older vintages are always satisfying and expectations rise with the passage of time. Pernin insists on absolutely perfect grapes and thanks to this policy, his cellars offer some outstanding Nuits-Saint-Georges - if you get there before they have all been sold! The La Richemone '82 may justifiably be considered the archetypal wine of the Appellation, with its gamey and spicy notes over a very elegant background of supple tannins and a finish which releases engaging hints of toastiness.

Chambolle-Musigny 🍇🍇 ④
Premier Cru 1989
The color is very intense while the nose is still undeveloped, although it discloses ripe fruit. The texture is rich, with tannins still prominent Remarkable, almost stunning, concentration. The finish contains a delicate gamey note.

Nuits-Saint-Georges 🍇🍇 ④
La Richemone Premier Cru 1988
A wine which lives up to its Appellation in every respect. Intense cherry-red in color with a nose that for the time being is barely sketched out, although a gamey note is evident. The chewy, concentrated tannins are elegant on the palate. In the finish, there is the promise of a secure future, but not a single trace of alcohol.

COTE DE NUITS/NUITS-SAINT-GEORGES
BOURGOGNE
FRANCE
332
COTE DE NUITS/NUITS-SAINT-GEORGES
BOURGOGNE
FRANCE

Domaine Daniel Rion et fils

Prémeaux
21700 Nuits-Saint-Georges
Tel. 80623128
Fax 80611341

This property was founded in 1955 by Daniel Rion on only two hectares of vineyards located in the commune of Vosne-Romanée. Today, it has 18 ha spread over 14 Appellations in six villages of the Côtes de Nuits and produces almost 100,000 bottles a year. The Rions - father and children Christophe, Olivier and Patrice - offer very representative wines which are among the best in Burgundy, both with their Grand Cru Clos Vougeot (0.73 ha) and with their unpretentious Bourgogne Pinot Noir, whose vines stand at the foot of the hills. Patrice is a graduate of the school at Beaune and looks after vinification, having also set up another property at Chambolle-Musigny (Chambolle-Musigny Le Cras and Bourgogne Les Bons Batons). This latter vineyard is planted 75% Pinot Noir and is looked after without recourse to risky chemical treatments. Fertilizers are biological and fermentation is in covered vats with careful regulation of the temperature and a maceration of about 15 days. Aging is in oak barriques, 20%-40% of which are new depending on the Appellation, and the filtration before bottling is very light.

Bourgogne Aligoté 1989 🍇 ②
From plants of more than 20 years old, in this Vieilles Vignes Burgundy the Rions have produced a small miracle of concentration and strength. With its apricot aromas, it is attractively fresh and easy to drink.

Nuits-Saint-Georges 🍇🍇🍇 ④
Clos-des-Argillières Premier Cru 1989
A wine which will age beautifully, so much so that it is a sin to drink it now. From grapes grown on clayey soil, its aromas are well-defined and the palate is decidedly elegant, although still a little earthy. The texture is very concentrated. A wine whose delicacy will seduce all lovers of Burgundy.

Vosne-Romanée Les Chaumes 🍇🍇 ④
Premier Cru 1988
A classically representative cru wine with marvellous intensity of bouquet and an aroma of wet straw. Full-flavored on the palate, this is a wine which will need a few years to mature if justice is to be done to its potential. A wine to lay down.

COTE DE NUITS/NUITS-SAINT-GEORGES
BOURGOGNE
FRANCE

333

COTE DE NUITS/NUITS-SAINT-GEORGES
BOURGOGNE
FRANCE

Jacques Confuron-Cotetidot

10, rue de la Fontaine
21700 Vosne-Romanée
Tel. 80610339

It would be difficult to find a more typical Burgundy. Jacques Confuron, short, tubby and ruddy-cheeked, is from a long line of Vosne-Romanée growers. He lives simply, enjoys hard work and is not averse to the pleasures of the table. His wines are full of personality and models of purity - the kind of Burgundy which is getting harder and harder to find these days. Jacky, as he is known, began to work in his father's vineyard at the age of 15 and since then has never taken a single day's holiday. His wife Bernadotte works with him on the eight hectares of their estate, which is spread over the Côtes de Nuits at Clos-Vougeot, Vosne-Romanée Les Suchots, Echézeaux, Nuits-Saint-Georges and Chambolle-Musigny. Confuron is a traditionalist and never takes the easy way out. He has always refused to use herbicides on his property and continues to hoe his vineyards. He is equally strict in his adherence to traditional methods in the cellar as they represent the only guarantee, in his opinion, of obtaining wines of character. Indeed, tradition reigns at all stages of Confuron's winemaking and he is helped in this by Guy Accad, the enologist, to whom some of the merit for the success of these wines must surely go.

Nuits-Saint-Georges Premier Cru 1990

A powerful wine with an intense color, produced in a generous vintage. Overall yields were on average 45 hl/ha. This Nuits-Saint-Georges is made from very ripe Pinot Noir grapes which gave a natural alcohol content of a little over 13°. Impressive structure and a splendidly velvety texture. To leave in the cellar for at least ten years.

Vosne-Romanée Les Suchots Premier Cru 1988

1988 was a lean vintage and the Confurons, who always prune their plants right back, obtained an even lower yield than other growers in the zone. This explains the quite extraordinary concentration of ripe-fruit aromas, lingering on the palate into the finish, which the wine presents. Pinot Noir here achieves its ultimate expression, voluptuous, succulent, of great delicacy and solid tannic structure, with every aspect enhanced by the traditional winemaking methods. Those who can restrain themselves from drinking it now will find that this 1988 will be at its peak around the year 2000.

COTE DE NUITS/VOSNE-ROMANEE
BOURGOGNE
FRANCE

334

COTE DE NUITS/VOSNE-ROMANEE
BOURGOGNE
FRANCE

Domaine René Engel

Place de la Mairie
21700 Vosne-Romanée
Tel. 80611054
Fax 80623973

At the Domaine René Engel, there is a genuine desire to open the doors of Burgundy to the world. The family has always made great efforts to promote the region and its wines and René himself was in 1936 a founder-member of the Confrérie des Tastevins. His grandson Philippe has decided to dedicate all his energies to producing the best wines possible from his seven hectares in the prestigious Appellations of Echézeaux, Grands Echézeaux and Clos Vougeot, where the 45 year-old plants stand on the renowned chalky Côte de Nuits soil. Since taking over management of the property in 1981, Philippe has changed the style of the wines considerably in an attempt to render them more approachable when young while respecting the characteristics of the cru. Winemaking methods are still traditional, with crushing aimed at preserving the best of the fruit's quality. 50% new wood for certain cuvées give a little extra something to those wines which have sufficiently good structure to sustain the contribution. A family with immense respect for its own winemaking history and one which strides purposefully and proudly towards the future.

Clos Vougeot Grand Cru 1990 🍇🍇 ④
An intense, deep ruby red color with echoes of violets on the nose. The most attractive of the Engel wines, with a palate which is an explosion of fruit and warm toasty oak. Full-bodied and well-blended, a wine with an outstanding, ethereal power and very feminine elegance.

Grands-Echézeaux Grand Cru 1990 🍇🍇 ④
Another wine with a deep color and a discreet nose of game and spices. Less immediately attractive on the palate than the Clos Vougeot but more complex, full-bodied and seductive, with a structure of breeding. The palate combines coffee, pepper and vanilla, with an elegant, delicate finish. A truly great wine.

Vosne-Romanée 1990 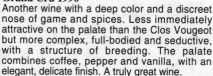 ②
Intense in color and with a beautiful bouquet of cherries, wood and spices with a faint gamey note. The palate has highly concentrated fruit well balanced out by the wood. Full-bodied structure, with a finish of coffee and autumn leaves.

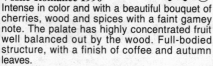

Domaine Jean Grivot

6, rue de la Croix-Romanée
21700 Vosne-Romanée
Tel. 80610595
Fax 80613299

Since 1990, Etienne Grivot has been officially in charge of the 14.5-ha family estate where he had already been working since 1982. The property consists almost entirely of Premiers Crus and Grands Crus at Chambolle-Musigny, Vosne-Romanée and Nuits-Saint-Georges and its wines sell at a very brisk pace. Etienne's first priority is quality, primarily achieved through meticulous vineyard management. Fertilizers are used sparingly, missing vines are carefully replanted and only fully ripe grapes are harvested, almost late-harvested, regardless of their acidity. Vinification techniques are aimed at making wines with good balance. There is no clarification, little filtration and the estate's wines are built to last. Etienne is almost obsessive about temperature, which he regulates to bring out a wealth of extracts without losing the primary aromas. He detests over-gamey aromas, which indicate the beginnings of decline. A true Burgundian and lover of the Pinot Noir variety, he goes for delicate bouquets of fruit and flowers, precisely those which you will find in his wines.

Vosne-Romanée Les Beaux-Monts 🍇🍇 ③
Premier Cru 1991
A Romanée for the cellar which needs at least a dozen or so years to reach its peak. Lovely color and a nose with distinct aromas of red berries. The palate is very full with fine, mature tannins. Crisp, lingering finish.

Nuits-Saint-Georges La Roncière 🍇 ④
Premier Cru 1990
Located in between the Premiers Crus of Porrets and Pruliers, this La Roncière produces a wine which lacks the breadth of the Boudos but which is nonetheless interesting with its gamey notes. Has a balance which will last.

Richebourg Grand Cru 1990 🍇🍇 ④
A wine with everything, from its full bouquet to its huge aftertaste. Entry, structure and fruit are in perfect balance. Pity there only six barriques (1,800 bottles) left.

Vosne-Romanée 1990 🍇🍇 ③
Exceptional and quite unrepeatable as the cru enjoyed extremely favorable weather conditions. The late-harvest reaches as much as 13.7° alc. Rich extracts, with superb concentration. The aromas are attractive and on the palate the wine has formidable texture, with very elegant tannins.

Vosne-Romanée Les Rouges 🍇🍇 ④
Premier Cru 1990
This cru located above Echézeaux has a dark color and a nose which has yet to develop but explodes on the palate with its structure. Fabulous length and freshness. The tannins are soft for the vintage but well to the fore.

COTE DE NUITS/VOSNE-ROMANEE
BOURGOGNE
FRANCE

335

COTE DE NUITS/VOSNE-ROMANEE
BOURGOGNE
FRANCE

Domaine de La Romanée-Conti

21700 Vosne-Romanée
Tel 80610457
Fax 80610572

The 1.8-ha vineyard in the heart of Côtes de Nuits, whose boundaries have remained unchanged for four centuries by the name of La Romanée-Conti, is the source of legends. It was the subject of controversy in the 1950s, when the vines had to be replanted, but La Romanée-Conti very soon re-established its reputation and its aura of nobility. This historical, world-famous wine is only a tiny part of this same-named estate. The property also has six Grands Crus for red wine in the communes of Flagley-Echézeaux and Vosne-Romanée, La Tâche (the largest at 6.06 ha and one to which the estate has sole rights), Richebourg, Romanée-Saint-Vivant, Grand-Echézeaux and Echézeaux as well as two Grands Crus for white wine, Montrachet and Bâtard-Montrachet. The last, along with the Villages Appellations and the Premiers Crus, is not sold directly by the estate. From the vine selection to the non-filtered, vacuum bottling, nothing is left to chance in the effort to make great wines with huge aging potential. There is minimal grape de-stemming, fermentation is slow and aging takes place in new oak barriques. Human intervention is inevitable although they like to say that "the wines make themselves". There is also selection by vintage, thus no Romanée-Conti was made in 1950 and no Echézeaux in 1965. The wines are sold within about three years, in cases which vary in composition depending on the harvest of the crus, with the addition of a bottle of La Romanée-Conti. The estate belongs to two families and is co-managed by their representatives, Aubert de Villaine and Henry-Frédéric Roch, the latter having succeeded Marcelle (known as Lalou) Bize-Leroy in 1992. All the estate's wines are hard to come by and very expensive. Do not miss the chance to taste them, should you be so lucky.

La Tâche Grand Cru 1990   ④

A vintage likely to be long-cherished as the best. Sumptuous color and an admirable nose which unites an elegant spicy side with an aromatic explosion over background of violets. All this is wrapped in a texture of unbelievable richness, unparalleled in the vintages which led up to it.

Richebourg Grand Cru 1988   ᵂ ᵂ ④

Dark ruby color. The tannins are still rich and all-pervading, almost hard. The alcohol still covers the fruit but an intense subtlety can still be made out, together with great purity and a clean dense body which makes this wine exceptional. Drink at the dawn of the third millennium now approaching.

SOCIÉTÉ CIVILE DU DOMAINE DE LA ROMANÉE-CONTI
PROPRIÉTAIRE A VOSNE-ROMANÉE (COTE-D'OR) FRANCE

ROMANÉE-CONTI
APPELLATION ROMANÉE-CONTI CONTROLÉE

6.723 Bouteilles Récoltées

BOUTEILLE Nº
ANNÉE 1990   LES ASSOCIÉS-GÉRANTS

Mise en bouteille au domaine

La Romanée-Conti   ᵂ ᵂ ᵂ ④
Grand Cru 1990

One always expects miracles from this tiny plot of land and once again the miracle has happened, thanks to Nature and to human skill. The 1990 vintage gave a yield of 32 hl/ha and is the finest to be harvested since the vine stock was replanted at the end of the last war. These plants gave their first fruit in 1952 and the 1990 vintage is now able to stand comparison with the years between the two world wars. For the time being, the delicacy of the barely hinted at aromas is enhanced by the oak, the body has enormous concentration and the aftertaste on the palate is quite movingly exquisite.

Domaine Mugneret

5, rue des Communes
21700 Vosne-Romanée
Tel. 80610157
Fax 80613308

Dr. Georges Mugneret, who died in 1988, was a well-known personality in Burgundy. His daughter, Marie-Christine, has given up her pharmacy for enology and she is the one who is now following in her father's footsteps on the family estate. The main wines, Vosne-Romanée, Échézeaux, Nuits-Saint-Georges Premier Cru and Ruchottes-Chambertin, are divided into two lines under different labels, for reasons related to problems of inheritance. Fermentation is preceded by 48 hours' cold-maceration, with minimal use of sulphite. Yeasts prepared at the University of Dijon are then added. Marie-Christine thinks they are ideal for the local Pinot Noir. Fermentation is retarded, reaching 32°C and bottling takes place after 18 months' aging in barriques. The wine is racked two or three times, clarified with egg whites and lightly filtered only if absolutely necessary. The nine hectares of vineyards are still worked by tenants, which means that only half of the harvest is returned to the estate. The system has the advantage of allowing comparison between different methods of vinification for the same grapes. There is no doubt that Marie-Christine has taken the opportunity to learn much.

Nuits-Saint-Georges
Aux Chaignots Premier Cru 1990
Freshly bottled. Dark in color with violet tinges and an undeveloped aroma of flowers. Very intense on the palate, with the impressive structure typical of the 1990 vintage, somewhat unusual for a Nuits.

Ruchottes-Chambertin
Grand Cru 1990
An intense violet-tinted color. Concentrated and rich in alcohol, with evident softness which is already very attractive.

Nuits-Saint-Georges
Aux Chaignots Premier Cru 1989
Beautiful ruby in color, the bouquet is developed, with hints of fruit and elegant oak. Extremely pleasing sinew on the palate, with tannins to the fore. Outstanding length. Generally reflects the Nuits style. To lay down.

Ruchottes-Chambertin
Grand Cru 1989
This great vintage is still rather young. Impressive structure and marked acidity. Everything points to an outstanding bottle, but not for another eight years.

Château de La Tour

Clos-de-Vougeot
21640 Vougeot
Tel. 80628613

Rising impressively in the distance as you approach, Château de La Tour, despite its turrets, spiral staircases, halls and massive medieval-style oak tables, was actually built at the end of the last century. It is the only estate to lie within the walls of the celebrated Clos built by the monks of Côteaux. Out of the total 50 ha of the Clos (which belong to about 70 different owners) the grapes are actually harvested over 5.6 ha. The estate is managed by two sisters, Jacqueline Labet and Nicole Déchelette. The former, with her son François, takes the leading role in a property which, until the arrival of the enologist Guy Accad, did an honest enough job but little more. Accad has left his mark by transforming winemaking and the wines produced now are of great delicacy with the fruit, and nothing but the whole fruit, taking precedence. Château de La Tour is already one of the outstanding names in the Appellation, a position which the future can only confirm.

Clos-de-Vougeot
Grand Cru 1990
Intense color. The nose, while still undeveloped, discloses aromas where blackcurrant features strongly. The body on the palate is unmistakable, the tannins soft and seductive. Very suitable for the cellar.

Clos-de-Vougeot
Grand Cru 1989
Dark purple color. Remarkable concentration. A nose of mulberry, blackcurrant and cherry. The palate is powerful, with light tannins. The finish is of fine length and exceptional softness.

Clos-de-Vougeot
Grand Cru 1988
Dark ruby color. Cherry is prominent on the nose, with a slightly peppery note. On the palate, the wine's rich alcohol is confirmed along with delicate and well-balanced tannins. A lovely wine which will age for many years to come.

COTE DE NUITS/VOSNE-ROMANEE
BOURGOGNE
FRANCE

337

COTE DE NUITS/VOUGEOT
BOURGOGNE
FRANCE

Domaine du Vieux-Sorlin

La Roche Vineuse
71960 Mâcon
Tel. 85366209
Fax 85366645

Having found one's way with difficulty around this village of winemakers, one comes to the six-hectare estate of Olivier and Corinne Merlin, an enthusiastic young couple who took up viticulture in 1987. Olivier, who is in his thirties, has no family links with wine. He served his apprenticeship, so to speak, first at a cooperative in the Jura region and then during a two-year spell in the Napa Valley in California. The style of his wines undoubtedly reflects his past experience for he favors moderate pruning, manual harvesting, low yields (always lower than those permitted by the Appellation), separate fermentation of vineyard lots and maturing on the skins, with a consequent need for light filtration. The results are there for all to see - and taste. Olivier's white Mâcons have much more depth than the majority of the wines from the Appellation, while his Bourgognes also show promise. Olivier Merlin and Jean Manciat are without doubt the guiding stars in the younger generation of Mâconnais growers.

Mâcon La Roche Vineuse 1990   ♀♀ ①
Matured in oak barrels, partly on the skins, this Chardonnay has excellent aging potential thanks to its good acidity and excellent concentration. Over a background of aromas which lies halfway between flowers and muscat grapes, the palate has good depth and alcohol while the finish is pleasingly toasty, with just the right proportion of oak.

Bourgogne Pinot Noir 1990   ♀ ①
A good, rich ruby color and an intense nose of red berries. The palate is full-bodied over rich tannins and is nicely delicate. A wine which will age comfortably.

Mâcon La Roche Vineuse 1990   ♀♀ ①
A Mâcon which can stand comparison with many a Burgundy. Very agreeable extracts and a nose which yields a sumptuous range of berry-fruit fragrances. The palate is frank and concentrated, with crisp, positive tannins and the finish lingers on notes of pepper and chocolate to great effect.

Jean Manciat

557, rue des Gérards, Levigny
71850 Charnay-les-Mâcon
Tel. 85343550
Fax 85343550

To be born into a winemaking family, is to be singled out by destiny. To study at the Beaune enological school with Etienne Grivot, Dominique Lafon and André Ostertag is a further stroke of good fortune. Jean Manciat was lucky enough to be blessed in both respects, although he himself did not at first feel particularly drawn to viticulture. Today, at 33 years of age, he manages a five-hectare estate, 30% of whose vine stock is over 40 years old. Since 1988, he has produced a Mâcon-Villages Vieilles Vignes with yields of less than 50 hl/ha. He also obtains a fabulous Vieilles Vignes Tradition from a parcel of less than one hectare. Jean's parents use to sell all their production to wholesalers. Jean has re-planted Chardonnay, keeping a third of the property for Gamay and Pinot Noir and his first bottling was the '86 vintage. He has taken the estate from yields of an average 100 hl/ha to less than 60, going over to careful clonal selection and Guyot pruning - the style used in the Côte d'Or. Jean Manciat's commitment to quality is beginning to bear fruit.

Mâcon-Villages Franclieu 1990   ♀ ②
Obtained from 10-12 year-old plants, rather pale in color. The nose is fresh and fruity, with notes of citrus. The palate is nicely rounded. A wine which offers excellent value for money.

Mâcon-Villages   ♀♀ ②
Vieilles Vignes 1990
Vinified in stainless steel vats, a wine with no contribution from the wood but much from the 40 year-old vines which produced the grapes. The nose is splendidly fresh, with no lack of complexity, and mingles citrus with notes of toastiness. Very rounded on the palate, and with remarkable acidity which guarantees its aging potential. A lingering finish.

Mâcon-Villages   ♀♀ ③
Vieilles Vignes Tradition 1990
Very rarely does tasting hold such marvellous surprises in store. This Cuvée Tradition from a tiny plot could be mistaken for a Meursault. Almost iridescent in color, it has a supremely subtle nose and a lively, fresh palate, well-rounded and meaty with stupendous concentration and superb balance. The length is stunning, with the wood never intrusive.

MACONNAIS/MACON
BOURGOGNE
FRANCE

338

MACONNAIS/MACON-VILLAGES
BOURGOGNE
FRANCE

Domaine René Michel et ses fils

Cray
71260 Clessé
Tel. 85369427
Fax 85369963

Five generations of vignerons have worked around this area. René Michel and his sons, Denis and Jean-Pierre, are continuing a family tradition. Their 10-ha estate today produces about 50,000 bottles of very special white Mâcon Clessé as well as 1,200 bottles of a rare red Mâcon Clessé from some Gamay stock. All the plants are old (around 50 years) and they grow on the typical clay and limestone soil of a south east-facing slope. Harvesting is manual for the white grapes and after crushing, almost all of the must ferments slowly in temperature-controlled stainless steel vats. A very small quantity is transferred to Allier and Tronçais wood barrels before bottling. The Michels mature all of their wines for two to three years to show their customers how important it is to give the rich, toasty Mâcon style enough time to develop.

Mâcon Clessé 1990 ℘ ②
Lovely, brilliantly limpid appearance. The nose is clean and slightly pungent with a note of apple. Fresh, dry and crisp on the palate with the characteristic aromas of Chardonnay and good, pleasingly harmonious acidity. A very agreeable wine and very good drinking.

Gilbert Mornand

71260 Clessé
Tel. 85369409

The Mornand family has been contributing to viticulture in southern Burgundy for several generations. It has owned this estate since 1880 with Gilbert Mornand taking over from his father in 1955. He produces a Mâcon Clessé Le Clos du Château and a small quantity of Crémant de Bourgogne. The property comprises five hectares of Chardonnay in the commune of Clessé near a sub-zone called Quintaine, one of the finest in the Mâconnais. The vine stock has an average age of 45-50 years and stands on chalky, south east-facing soil which yields about 60 hl/ha. A horizontal press is used for crushing the grapes and fermentation takes place in the wood. The wine passes a further six months in 40- to 60-hl pre-used barrels. Not all of Gilbert Mornand's production is bottled on-site as some is sold wholesale.

Mâcon Clessé ℘ ②
Le Clos du Château 1991
A wine which expresses the best of the fruit, from its pale gold color to its aromas of tropical fruit, where pineapple is to the fore. The palate is fresh and fruity, with a lively touch of acidity. A straightforward but well-balanced white wine.

MACONNAIS/MACON-VILLAGES
BOURGOGNE
FRANCE

339

MACONNAIS/MACON-VILLAGES
BOURGOGNE
FRANCE

Jean Thévenet

Quintaine
71260 Clessé
Tel. 85369403
Fax 85369925

Jean Thévenet and his wife Marie-Thérèse manage two properties with a total area of 15 ha, producing various cuvées of Mâcon Clessé and a Mâcon Viré. Domaine de la Bongran has been handed down from father to son for several generations and Bernard took it over from his father in 1973. The wines are all made from Chardonnay grapes obtained from 40 year-old stock on sunny chalk slopes in the Quintaine sub-zone, in the commune of Clessé. Crushing in a pneumatic press is followed by slow fermentation, part in temperature-controlled stainless steel vats, part in wooden barrels. The Mâcon Clessé - of which 40,000 bottles are produced annually - is sold under the label Cuvée Tradition. In outstanding vintages, a limited quantity of Cuvée Le Vroutée is obtained from Chardonnay grapes which have been mildly attacked by botrytis and a Cuvée Botrytis, a Chardonnay with a Sauternes style, from fruit that the "noble rot" has fully consumed. The six hectares of the Domaine Emilian Gillet are a recent addition, acquired with the aim of increasing production. The Thévenet family cultivates this estate as tenants, making wine using exactly the same techniques as at Domaine de la Bongran. Total production amounts to 10,000 bottles of Mâcon Clessé and 18,000 of Mâcon Viré.

Mâcon Clessé Quintaine ☗☗ ③
Domaine de Bongran Cuvée Tradition 1989
A white Mâcon of very good quality, owing little to the Appellation. It has the richness and delicately flowery nose with aromas of honey typical of a good Meursault. The color is rich and bright, with flecks of gold. The nose brings to mind acacia honey with its flowery, ripe notes of Chardonnay. The depth, roundness and unbelievable length all come back on the palate. A very well-balanced and original wine.

Mâcon Viré Quintaine ☗ ②
Domaine Emilian Gillet 1989
A lovely bright, clear color. The bouquet is rich and clean but with a more opulent side to its nature which reminds one of honey. The rich, sweet fruit is very noticeable on the palate together with the spicy aromas typical of Chardonnay. The finish is long, with a slight note of residual sugar. A wine with a declared alcohol content of 14°. It has all the body needed to accompany the most robust fish dishes, including those which require sauces.

Château de Fuissé

71960 Fuissé
Tel. 85356144
Fax 85356734

Much snobbery and "winemanship" has attached itself to Château de Fuissé, queen of southern Burgundy. It is featured on most of the world's most prestigious wine maps and its Vieilles Vignes is as expensive as the wines of such famous Appellations as Chassagne-Montrachet and Meursault. In defence of Château de Fuissé, it must be said that its products are completely different, very 'Burgundian' and of outstanding consistency. Jean-Jacques Vincent, owner of the 25 ha of vineyards, is a hard worker whose efforts are directed at maintaining the same high level of quality in the wine vintage after vintage. The result is that loyal customers are never in short supply. Château de Fuissé is obtained only from plants of more than 15 years-old while the Vieilles Vignes comes from even older vine stock. Fermentation and aging is in the wood, with one fifth of the barrels replaced every year. Great care is taken when matching the kind of oak used to the vintage. The cellar temperature is carefully controlled at every stage of both winemaking and aging, which usually takes around ten months. Château de Fuissé also produces other good-quality wines, including Mâcon-Villages, Saint-Véran and Pouilly-Fuissé Cuvée Première, from the younger vines on the estate.

Château de Fuissé ☗☗ ④
Vieilles Vignes 1988
A bright straw-yellow color, with notes of melted butter, tropical fruit and vanilla. The palate shows aromas of ripe grapefruit, quince and citrus. A wine of good structure and excellent length.

MACONNAIS/MACON-VILLAGES
BOURGOGNE
FRANCE

340

MACONNAIS/POUILLY-FUISSE
BOURGOGNE
FRANCE

Domaine Corsin

Les Coreaux
71960 Fuissé
Tel. 85358369
Fax 85358664

The Corsin family has been making excellent Mâcon wines in the cool cellars at Davayé for several generations. Today, Gilles and his brother Jean-Jacques, helped by their father André, manage 9.5 ha of Chardonnay in three different Appellations on soil types which range from the clay and limestone of Puoilly-Fuissé, to the pure chalk slopes of Saint-Véran. They make four wines: a straightforward Mâcon-Villages and a sincere, uncomplicated Saint-Véran cuvée, both of which are bottled after spending five to seven months in vats; a Saint-Véran Vieilles Vignes; and a Pouilly-Fuissé. Two thirds of the Saint-Véran is aged in the vat, the remainder spending six to eight months in two to five year-old Vosges and Allier oak barriques. The Puoilly-Fuissé is half aged in the vat and half in barriques, replaced in rotation over a five-year cycle. All the estate's wines are full-bodied and tend to have a rather high alcohol content, as the traditional winemaking techniques employed in their production would lead one to expect.

Pouilly-Fuissé 1990   ❦ ❦ ③
A brilliant golden straw-yellow color. A sturdy, full-bodied and inviting wine. Hints of toastiness and butter emerge on the nose together with a profusion of rich notes of herbs, ripe fruit, mango and quince. The palate is fully developed, rich and long, with good structure.

Domaine Guffens-Heynen

71960 Vergisson
Tel. 85358422
Fax 85358272

This domaine is the creation of Belgian-born Jean-Marie Guffens and his wife Mainke Heynen. It is the archetypal designer cellar, producing small quantities of "hand-crafted" wines from an estate of only three hectares Two thirds of the property is given over to Chardonnay, which is used to produce three different Pouilly Fuissé cuvées and 4,500 bottles of Mâcon-Pierreclos. The vine stock ranges in age from 4 to 80 years, with most of the fruit from the younger plants being used for the Pouilly-Fuissé Les Croux (about 1,200 bottles), perhaps the most characteristic of the entire Appellation. The La Roche cuvée (3,000 bottles) is obtained from grapes grown on chalky soil and is the Guffens-Heynen wine with most structure. The Clos des Petits Croux comes from 40 year-old plants growing at a higher elevation and is made in very limited quantities. The craftsman's approach to winemaking is evident everywhere. The grapes are crushed very gently with a 17th-century vertical press and the first-pressing must goes into the various cuvées. Fermentation is in wooden barrels, one third of them new, with the addition of yeasts. Wines are not filtered before bottling. Last but by no means least, Jean-Marie Guffens produces a Mâcon-Pierreclos red from extremely old Gamay plants. No wine is sold direct from the cellar.

Pouilly-Fuissé La Roche 1988   ❦ ❦ ③
An intense golden yellow color with a very delicate nose. The ripe fruit yields aromas of exotic fruit, butter and toastiness in a beautifully integrated whole. Lemon, resin and pineapple are in evidence on the palate, supported by good body and structure.

MACONNAIS/POUILLY-FUISSE
BOURGOGNE
FRANCE

341

MACONNAIS/POUILLY-FUISSE
BOURGOGNE
FRANCE

Domaine des Deux Roches

71960 Davayé
Tel. 85358329
Fax 85358612

Henry Collovray, his son Christian and his two brothers-in-law, Jean-Luc Terrier and Alain Martinot, own about 20 ha in the commune of Davayé, to the west of Mâcon, near the famous castle of Solutré, much loved by François Mitterand, and close to the less well-known fortress of Vergisson. The estate is particularly renowned for its Saint-Véran, a white wine made from Chardonnay plants growing on clay and limestone slopes, but it also produces a Mâcon-Villages white and a Mâcon red. Winemaking is carried out in a new cellar, most of the white wines being vinified in stainless steel vats. Several cuvées are sold as Saint-Véran and one, the Vieilles Vignes with its gold label, is obtained from plants with an average age of 50 years. Half is fermented in new oak barrels. The oak tends to make its presence felt, but wine from the better vintages can comfortably age for three or four years. The Les Terres Noires cuvée, which comes from 2.5 ha of 30 year-old vine stock, is the most delicate as only 20% is vinified in new barriques. The Terrier-Collovray-Martinot team produces wines which are generally very well-balanced across the whole of their range, including their early cuvées of Saint-Vran or Mâcon-Villages.

Saint-Véran 🍷🍷 ③
Les Terres Noires 1990
A lovely clear, bright color. Delicate and rather flowery Chardonnay aroma. Agreeably fruity, with good acidity which gives the wine real freshness. Faint aftertaste of oak. A fairly fleshy wine of good complexity and balance. A year or two more in the bottle will enhance it still further.

MACONNAIS/SAINT-VERAN
BOURGOGNE
FRANCE

342

MACONNAIS/SAINT-VERAN
BOURGOGNE
FRANCE

Champagne

There is no wedding, birthday, christening or otherwise festive occasion of practically any kind which cannot be enhanced with a bottle of Champagne. The famed wine comes from the most northerly of France's winegrowing regions, extending over five départements from Aisne to Seine-et-Marne by way of Haute-Marne and Aube. The Marne is the key département with the two capitals of Champagne, Épernay and Reims. Six areas can be distinguished among the hills and valleys of Champagne. 50 km of vineyards are situated at the highest elevations in the south in the Aube département, on marly-chalk often subject to spring frosts; the Congy-Sézanne sub-region is an extension of the famous Côte des Blancs stretching to Villenauxe-la-Grande; the chalky-clay sloped vineyards of the Marne Valley; the stable-climated Côte de Blancs overlooking the city of Epernay; the Montagne de Reims that gently slopes above the latter for 20 km; lastly, the Basse Montagne, surrounding the Montagne de Reims.

Champagne country is truly enchanting. There are 30,000 ha of vines with a further 5,000 ha potentially available. The most noteworthy characteristic of the Champagne region is that the vignerons are largely growers who sell their harvest to the great cellars, which then make and bottle the wine. The main varieties are Chardonnay, Pinot Noir and Pinot Meunier, which are blended in varying proportions in most cuvées. This situation has led to a system of ranking the various vineyards by commune. The Grands Crus are given a classification of 100%, the Premiers Crus range from 99% to 90% and the others go from 89% to 80%. The percentage is linked to the price of grapes per kilogram. The price established for the vintage is paid in full for grapes from Grands Crus 99% to 90% of the full price is paid for grapes from Premiers Crus, and so on. Some of the most important communes are Ambonnay, Bouzy, Louvois, Mailly-Champagne, Sillery and Verzenay et Verzy in Montage de Reims with Aÿ et Mareuil-sur-Aÿ in the Vallée de la Marne and Avize, Cramat, Oger and Le Mesnil-sur-Oger in the Côte des Blancs.

Stocks are of extreme importance for the quality of the wine and in mid-1991, 765 million bottles of Champagne lay in the cellars of the region. 1991 was one of the five great vintages enjoyed since 1983. Eight of the last eleven have been worthy of mention with the 1988, 1989 and 1990 considered particularly outstanding.

However, it is whispered abroad that Champagne is not what it used to be. Champagne's "Parliament", the Committée Interprofessionale des Vins de Champagne (CIVC), which brings together vignerons, négociants and government officials, acknowledged in September 1992 that the boom years of the 1970s and 1980s were over. The optimistic CIVC 1990 sales forecast for 1992 of 350 million bottles was put back in the drawer, reduced to tatters by the Gulf War and recession.

Until recently, the price of grapes used to reach levels as high as 30 FF/kg, or even 40 FF where no advance contract had been concluded. After the collapse of Champagne sales, grape prices fell to a more reasonable 24 FF/kg (the same as the asking price in 1989), in the hope that this would encourage an increase in overall Champagne consumption. 1989 was in fact a record year, with 250 million bottles sold, 38% being for export markets. In 1991, the figure was much lower. The 210 million bottles sold reflected a 34% fall in sales in Great Britain, for instance, and substantial declines elsewhere. The trend appears to be continuing. In fact, 1992 statistics show that there was a 5% decrease in sales witessed in the first six months and a 10% decrease in exports. This recession has struck hard for an industry which has grown from 13,000 growers in 1970 to 15,700 in 1992.

This unique situation is also generated in part by the fragmentation of the region's vineyards. They are often passed down through generations by inheritance, causing the average size of the estates to shrink. In deed, more than 8,000 growers own less than one hectare of vines; this has led to an increase in price levels which has not necessarily been offset by quality improvements.

Indeed, quality has become a watchword in a region that for many years monopolized the market of sparkling wines. Today, both in France and in other winegrowing countries, there are many kinds and styles of sparkling wines available. Quality standards are constantly improving, and the prices are generally much lower than those of Champagne. In Champagne itself, there is always surprise when the fall in quality of the local product is mentioned. The impressive investments in technology over the last ten years are pointed out, although critics assert that the new technology has served only to rationalize production, not to improve the quality of the wine.

The "Quality Charter" signed at the famous September 1992 meeting was the first important step towards rectifying the situation. The decision to increase to 160 kg the weight of grapes needed to obtain a single hectoliter of must means that the juice is purer and concentration greater. Will this be enough? The vineyards have already been exploited to their limit, often forcing excessive yields. Today, an intelligent control of yields and vineyard management is called for in Champagne.

We are confident that the opulent and prosperous years have not permanently spoiled the renowned long-term vision of the true makers of Champagne, without a doubt one of the richest 'Eldorado' wine areas of the world.

Besserat de Bellefon

19, avenue de Champagne
51202 Épernay Cedex
Tel. 26595100
Fax 26595119

Besserat de Bellefon, or "B de B" as they say in Champagne, was established in Aÿ by Edmond Besserat in 1843. Today, the B de B label can be seen on the tables of the world's finest restaurants. The cellar was acquired, after a difficult period of transition, by the Burtin-Mora family group, who have consistently made quality their number one priority. One of the most famous products of the house is the Crémant Cuvée des Moines, which takes its name from the Benedictine monks who were once very prominent in the area. The cuvée was created for a bet by Victor Besserat in the 1920s and today this Crémant is a great source of pride for the cellar, together with for example the Brut Grande Tradition and the Grande Cuvée B de B. Cuvée des Moines is of an unbelievable lightness, thanks to "dosage" with almost one third less sugar than normal, which gives the wine its creamy mousse. Now that Marie-Laurence Mora has taken over the firm, B de B is assured of a great future.

Besserat de Bellefon   🍾🍾 ④
Cuvée des Moines
This wine, which embodies the house style, is obtained from the grapes of three different vineyards. Mousse and perlage are delicate and ethereal, giving an incomparably light Champagne which makes a delightful aperitif. The aroma is subtle and the flavor lingers on the palate for just the right length of time.

Besserat de Bellefon   🍾🍾 ④
Grande Cuvée Blanc de Blancs
One of the cellar's leading products and one which over the years has proved to be a consistently perfect balance of white and black grapes. Elegant and delicate, it is a wine with a beautifully clean aroma which features flowery notes.

Besserat de Bellefon Brut   🍾🍾 ④
Grande Tradition
A quite marvellous aperitif. Outstanding freshness on the palate, a wine with all the drinkability of a perfect non-vintage brut.

Billecart-Salmon

40, rue Carnot
51160 Mareuil-sur-Aÿ
Tel. 26526022
Fax 26526466

The art of producing great Champagne lies in making a successful non-vintage brut as the house's most basic cuvée. The Billecart-Salmons do this superbly and as a result many of France's greatest chefs buy it for their own-label Champages. Despite being small, Billecart-Salmon is a member of the Syndicat des Grandes Marques. Production is around 500,000 bottles a year and almost all the grapes are bought in, 95% from Crus Classés. The cellar is one of the few which is still family-run, today's generation being the sixth to run the company, since it was founded in 1818 by Nicolas-François Billecart. Billecart-Salmon has always been managed strictly in accordance with the heritage of Champagne, as handed down in monastic texts and oral tradition. There is no rush to expand at Billecart-Salmon. Stocks are maintained at good levels, with four vintages waiting to be sold in the cellars. The winemaking is of the highest standard and the results are cuvées of great purity offering refined elegance to a clientele of connoisseurs.

Billecart-Salmon Brut   🍾 ④
A classic, easy-to-drink cuvée. Good appearance with plenty of ripe fruit. Crisp and fresh flavor on the palate, without being immature, and a finish of great purity.

Billecart-Salmon   🍾🍾 ④
Blanc de Blancs 1985
This blend of three 100% classed growths has an attractively clear color and lingering mousse with delicate bubbles and a harmonious aroma which brings to mind lemon and flowers. A great wine, with character and a powerful bouquet.

Billecart-Salmon   🍾🍾 ④
Cuvée N.F.-Billecart 1985
A wine dedicated to the founder of the house could only be superb. The nose unfolds agreeably ripe, almost toasty quinces and pears while the palate is full-bodied with a crisp entry sustained by an elegant and stylish finish. A truly great Champagne which demonstrates all Denis-Rolland Billecart-Salmon's skills.

Boizel

14, rue de Bernon
51205 Épernay Cedex
Tel. 26552151
Fax 26543183

For some years now, this cellar, run by Evelyne Roques-Boizel, has been making steady progress towards the ranks of the great. Cellars and other facilities were purchased in 1986, a temperature-regulation system was installed in 1989, an enological laboratory was set up in 1990 and a new "cuverie" was built in 1992, all going to show that hardly a year goes by without some major improvement in this family-run business. Fate has been unkind to Boizel, but the cellar has always reacted positively to misfortune. 1972 was particularly tragic for the company with the death of both René Boizel and of his son Eric. Evelyne, who has degrees in history, archaeology and museum studies, is married to Christophe Roques, who himself has a degree in physics and electronics as well as a passion for computers. The future is clearly mapped out and since 1983 Evelyne has been the only woman to run one of the great names of Champagne while her husband looks after purchasing and production, which reached a total of 1,800,000 bottles in 1991. Prospects are good for quality is the only priority at Boizel.

Boizel Blanc de Blancs   ♈ ③
A wine of breeding. Created from 100% Chardonnay, the Boizel Côtes des Blancs cuvée can be recognized by its Second Empire-style label, but it also stands out for its finesse and elegance, supported by lovely texture and fine length on the palate.

Boizel Joyau de France 1985   ♈ ♈ ④
This cuvée first saw the light of day in 1969. Its aromas are in perfect harmony, the blend of 65% Pinot Noir and 35% Chardonnay having just the right balance of body and alcohol. The rich, complex nose is already well developed and the finish leaves an agreeable final note of freshness on the palate.

Boizel Rosé Brut   🏵 ③
This blend of 50% Pinot Noir, 40% Pinot Meunier and 10% Chardonnay is a little jewel. With its tawny gold-flecked hue, its elegant bouquet and its wonderfully delicate finish, this is a quite beautifully made rosé.

Key to the symbols

Types of Wines

♈ White

🏵 Rosé

♥ Red

Rating System

♈
An exemplary wine of its type with outstanding local character

🏵🏵
An international premium quality wine

♥♥♥
A Top Wine, considered one of the 150 best wines in the world

The 'grape bunch' symbol is used to indicate the color of the wine; the number of bunches represents the quality rating assigned by the contributor

Price levels

① up to $ 9.99

② $ 10.00 - $ 14.99

③ $ 15.00 - $ 24.99

④ $ 25.00 or more

The 'ex-cellar', or direct from the producer, bottle prices, are calculated in US dollars and are intended only as an approximate guide

Entries are arranged in alphabetical order by country, region and winery or producer name.

Bollinger

16, rue Jules-Loubet
51160 Aÿ
Tel. 26552131
Fax 26548559

The house of Bollinger owns about 150 ha of vineyards with an average rating of 98% on the cru ranking system which supply about 70% of its requirements. Founded on the 6th of February, 1829, Bollinger is unique in the world of Champagne and is also one of the few independent family-run firms still active. It is managed by Christian Bizot, nephew of Mme Jacques Bollinger, memories of whom, riding her bicycle through the vines, are still very much alive. To demonstrate its notoriety, Bollinger in exceptional years makes a hand-disgorged cuvée Vieilles Vignes Françaises from a small parcel of ancient, ungrafted, pre-Phylloxéra vines. Only 2,000 bottles are ever made in a vintage. Throughout the range, only the best musts are used and later pressings are sold off. Much of the fermentation is carried out in small 205 lt barrels, and most of the wines are kept in magnums sealed with corks and not crown-caps. The Bollinger approach to marketing is admirable. Vintage cuvées go onto the market after an average five years in the cellars, which i s often much later than most other Champagnes. It is no surprise then that Bollinger offers wines of rare quality.

Bollinger Grande Année 1985 🍇 🍇 ④

Crystal clear and a superb golden color. The nose opens out gradually showing strength and a background of rich, well-rounded aromas redolent of autumn leaves. Fresh and lively on the palate, with just the right dosage. Beautiful structure and a lovely lingering finish with a faint hint of hazelnut.

Bollinger R.D. 1982 🍇 🍇 ④

R.D. stands for "récemment dégorgé". Rich in yeasts and incomparably fresh, with the structure and body of Pinot Noir. A well-balanced wine with a very clean finish and excellent length.

Bollinger 🍇 🍇 🍇 ④
Vieilles Vignes Françaises 1985

A unique Champagne: a credit to the Appellation and to French winemaking in general. This masterpiece is obtained from vines planted before the arrival of phylloxera. Made exclusively from Pinot Noir, the wine proffers a nose which reveals the secret of perfection: the Bollinger flavor in all its purity with a stylish sweet note which brings to mind croissants and honey. The balance between potency and elegance is struck with a precision that is rarely if ever achieved in other wines. Silky aromas in the background. The density on the palate is quite incredible while the never-ending finish is austere yet frank. A genuinely great, unsurpassable wine which stands alone on a pinnacle of tasting pleasure.

Deutz

18, rue Jeanson
51160 Aÿ
Tel. 28551511
Fax 28540121

A book dedicated to Deutz in 1988 called the firm a symbol of Champagne. Founded in 1838 by Pierre-Hubert Geldermann, the company has seen five generations create, enhance and add their own contributions to a wine which Schiller said "bubbled and sprayed up to heaven". Deutz fully deserves such praise and today, after many trials and tribulations, the company, still family-run, belongs to the élite of Champagne. The present chairman, André Lallier, makes full use of this hard-won heritage. Rahter uncommunicative and parsimonious, Lallier is content to be patient and rely on the family and traditions handed down from father to son. He has a rare authenticity and independence increasingly hard to find in Champagne. The end result is that the 40 ha of the family vineyards produce a range which, from the humblest wines to the prestigious Cuvée William Deutz, bears the hallmark of outstanding winemaking skill.

Deutz Brut ♟♟ ④
This base wine, always a guaranteed success, has an attractive, outstandingly clear, appearance as well as being delicious. Solid structure and perfect body, but nonetheless elegant. Splendidly fresh and well-rounded flavor.

Deutz Blanc de Blancs 1985 ♟♟ ④
The transparent bottle is quite delightful and is protected from UVA rays thanks to special packaging. The bottle reflects the stupendous clarity of the wine, with its crisp, clean aromas and outstanding freshness. Sinewy at first on the palate, it melts gently away beautifully.

Deutz Cuvée William Deutz 1985 ♟♟ ④
Presented in old-fashioned bottles, this prestigious cuvée has a golden color. Complex yet fresh on the nose with hints of toast and gingerbread. The elegant liquorice finish has a lovely lingering aroma.

Duval-Leroy

69, avenue de Bammental
51130 Vertus
Tel. 26521075
Fax 26521293

Run by the same family since 1859 and with more than a quarter of its supply of grapes coming from its own estates (120 ha), Duval-Leroy has leapt into second place in Champagne production in the space of a few years. Production (200,000 bottles in 1970) has risen to 4 million bottles a year and the cellar stocks of 12 million bottles could put some of the great names to shame. Investment is a constant factor in company policy at Duval-Leroy (over 30,000,000 FF since 1988). The vineyards enjoy an exceptionally favorable position in the heart of the Côte des Blancs. Grapes destined for the Fleur de Champagne cuvée, which has been produced since the end of the last century, come from parcels classed 95% on the cru ranking system. Duval-Leroy is also an expert in making wine from the Pinot Noir produced in the village of Vertus. The result is a still wine with the Appellation Coteaux Champénois. Last but not least, Duval-Leroy is a company that puts quality first, employing both a first and a second pruning as well as cold maturation, which has been practiced since 1988 in collaboration with the Oenological Institute of Bordeaux and the Reims Faculty of Science.

Fleur de Champagne Brut ♟ ④
A wine of unvarying quality from a blend of 70% Chardonnay and 30% Pinot Noir. A brut with a frank and forthcoming entry, a mouthfilling flavor, fine perlage and a finish which opens out beautifully.

Cuvée des Roys 1985 ♟♟ ④
Obtained from 100% Grand Cru Champagne grapes and aged for at least 5 years, this generous cuvée of 95% Chardonnay d'Avize and Cramant with 5% Verzenay Pinot Noir has an agreeably flowery and very slightly honeyed nose. The fresh, complex entry leads into a satisfyingly long finish.

Coteaux Champénois Vertus ♟ ④
Only a few thousand bottles of this stylish, light, fruity Vertus are made every year. Aged in oak for a year and then matured in bottle for another 12 months. A wine of real freshness.

Gosset

69, rue Jules-Blondeau
51160 Aÿ
Tel. 26551416
Fax 26515588

Gosset is one of the smallest négociants in Champagne. The Gossets have been active in the legendary village of Aÿ for four centuries and an ancestor, Pierre Gosset, was mayor of the town in 1584, before Champagne began to be made. The story of the family is intimately connected with the story of the town and it is the black grapes of Aÿ and crus around Avenay, Bouzy, Dizy, Hautvilliers, Louvois and Mareuil which go into Gosset wines. Gosset also regularly buys grapes from the Montagne de Reims (Ecueil, Rilly and Verzenay), from the crus of the Côte des Blancs (Avize, Grauves and Le Mesnil) and from those of the Marne Valley (Chatillon, Cumières and Venteuil). One third of total requirements come from vineyards owned by the Gosset company. Considerable stocks are held, with the result that Gosset can sell consistently well-balanced, beautifully matured wines of irreproachable quality year after year. Grosset's customers also benefit from the house policy of storing all bottles purchased horizontally until the client requires delivery. Only then is the wine finished, with "remuage", "dégorgement" and corking done when the customer is ready. Class will always tell !

Brut Réserve　　　　　　🍾 ④
This straight cuvée has a certain maturity, like all the other Grosset cuvées. Good balance between power and delicacy.

Grande Réserve　　　　　🍾 ④
A rather elegant blend of three vintages: 1985 reserve wines; and 1986 and 1987 single-vineyard wines. Rich nose with full body and good structure. Well-balanced finish.

Grand Millésime 1982　　🍾🍾 ④
The style of bottle dates from the 17th century, and the vintage is famous. Lingering mousse in a blend of two thirds Chardonnay, from about 20 different crus, and one third Pinot Noir. Good structure, yet of great elegance. A well-balanced wine with lots of character.

Jacquart

5, rue Gosset
51066 Reims Cedex
Tel. 26072020
Fax 26071207

Jacquart is a name which prompts a series of statistics worthy of the Guinness Book of Records. A cooperative enterprise, Jacquart is the sixth-largest producer in Champagne with 1,000 ha of vine stock spread over 45 crus in the Côte des Blancs, Montagne de Reims and the Marne Valley. The 7 ha Jacquart premises in the heart of Reims has cellars on three separate levels going down as far as 18 m below ground where the temperature, winter and summer, is a constant 12°C. Crushing is actually carried out at the 154 harvest sites. There is a whole range of 10 to 1,000 hl vats with a total capacity of 120,000 hl. The two "remuage" cellars hold 1,200,000 bottles, production is in excess of 10 million bottles a year and the aging cellars can hold up to 27 million bottles. What is the secret of Jacquart's success? Much of the credit must go to Christian Doisy, the general manager, who promoted Jacquart by sponsoring the Los Angeles Olympics, the Mozart Train and even a European Cup Final. But the success of Jacquart is also due to the superb winemaking and aging techniques which are used for everything from the traditional Champagne brut to the most prestigious cuvées. Constant quality is assured.

Brut Sélection　　　　　🍾 ③
A wine with no hidden surprises. Sinewy, with good structure and balance. Obtained from 50% Chardonnay and 50% black grapes, this is essentially a wine to drink as an aperitif.

Cuvée Nominée 1985　　🍾🍾 ④
This blend of prestigious crus is presented in a diamond-cut bottle. The wine is generous and has good body while still being elegant. The delicate bubbles rise quickly to the surface of the glass. Full on the palate with a lingering finish.

Cuvée Mosaïque 1986　　🏵 ④
Stylish and rich in elegant aromas on a background of black berries and rose-flavored sweets. A gold-tinged cuvée which has good body and a fresh palate with a velvety finish.

Jacquesson et fils

68, rue du colonel Fabien
51200 Dizy
Tel. 26556811
Fax 26510625

This company, dating from 1798, was famous in the 19th century, and with discretion, modesty and above all much hard work it has managed to get back on the road to success. The present managers, Jean-Hervé and Laurent Chiquet, are doing their utmost to keep the flag of tradition flying high in Champagne. The 25 ha of Jacquesson vineyards in the crus of Avize, Aÿ, Dizy and Hautvilliers provide half of the grapes the company requires. Jacqueson also still employs a technique now rare in Champagne, making the cuvée 'Signature Millesime' in 75 hl oak casks solely with grapes from its own vineyards. The cuvée is a blend of 50% Chardonnay d'Avize with 25% each Aÿ and Dizy Pinot Noir. Yields are low (about 6 kg/ha in 1985). All the wines are aged for at least five years. Everything that the Jacquesson company bottles, from Perfection Brut, Blanc des Blancs, vintage Perfection Brut to Rosé Brut is of an elegance which comes close to perfection. And, in this case, perfection is not too strong a word.

Jacquesson Blanc de Blancs   ♀♀ ④
With its 18% 1987 vintage Chardonnay d'Avize and 82% of the 1988 vintage, this Cuvée Blanc des Blancs has an almost flowery nose, outstanding finesse and tremendous elegance. Matured in 50hl oak barrels, this is a wine with a wonderfully fresh finish.

Jacquesson Perfection Brut   ♀ ③
Clean, crisp and delightfully fresh, this non-vintage brut is an exemplary, irreproachably drinkable Champagne.

Jacquesson Cuvée   ♀♀ ④
Signature 1985
The low yield (6,600 kg/ha) produced only a little over 20,000 bottles and 1,179 magnums of this blend of 25% Pinot Noir d'Aÿ, 25% Dizy Pinot Noir and 50% Chardonnay d'Avize. It is one of the finest cuvées in the whole of Champagne. Full on the palate with just a faint hint of wood, the balance is near to perfection.

Entries are arranged in alphabetical order by country, region and winery or producer name.

Krug

5, rue Coquebert
51051 Reims Cedex
Tel. 26844420
Fax 26844449

Krug Champagne is known all over the world
so let us describe the makers themselves,
the Krug brothers. Henri is the more retiring.
He works in the cellar but also joins his 25
year-old son, Olivier, (who represents the
sixth generation of Krugs) out in the
vineyards to savor the smells of wild
mushrooms and wood. Rémi, who has a
degree in economics from Paris, promotes
the Krug name around the globe. Henri and
Rémi are both moved by the same spirit
which inspired Johann-Joseph in 1843 when
he founded the company. It is only by using
the best raw materials that one can obtain
the best results and any other approach
merely serves to jeopardize the good name
of the company. Today, Krug owns two
vineyards, at Mesnil-sur-Oger and Aÿ, and
uses grapes from the best crus in the Marne
département. After pressing, only the first
2,050 lt obtained from 4,000 kg of grapes are
used. The first fermentation is exclusively in
small Argonne oak barrels, a unique touch
which gives the wine the Krug imprint. With
stocks to cover sales for six to eight years,
the Krugs are well aware that "quality knows
how to wait". Indeed, the whole devoted Krug
team is well aware that some things just
cannot be hurried.

Krug Grande Cuvée   🍾 ④
Straw-yellow in color with a fine mousse, a wine
with a delicate nose, rich and well developed.
Rich, too, on the palate where it has a creamy,
almost caramel, sweetness and fresh acidity
which lingers into the long finish.

Krug   🍾🍾 ④
A stupendous pale pink color with an
outstandingly delicate mousse. A wine with an
old-fashioned personality, one might almost say,
such is the body, the definite hint of bottle-age
and the length of this really special Champagne.
The style is reminiscent of an old white
Burgundy.

Krug Clos du Mesnil 1983   🍾🍾🍾 ④
Incredibly light, pale starbright color for its age
with fine bubbles. The nose is fine and fresh and
in the mouth again it is fine and light with great
acidity, making the whole ipression one of clean,
dry, elegance. This is certainly a quite
remarkable Champagne that strikes one by its
freshness and youthfulness. A superb, stylish
Blanc de Blancs from 1.87 ha of Chardonnay at
Mesnil-sur-oger, all vinified in oak barrels and
really demonstrating the unique style that is
Krug.

Lanson

12, boulevard Lundy
51056 Reims Cedex
Tel. 26785050
Fax 26785099

A lovely old-fashioned and reassuring residence in boulevard Lundy is where we find former osteopath François-Xavier Lanson, heir, with his wife, Laurence, to the house of Lanson through the actual owners the Marne et Champagne group. The group was looking for an export label to bring it up to the level of the great houses of Champagne. In 1991, the Lanson label gave them the opportunity, although it could not offer any vineyards of its own. With the help of Allied Lyons, who came in as Marne et Champage shareholders, Lanson is gaining ground in export markets thanks to its increasingly successful sales team. Thanks are also due to tha fact that the company has maintained its traditional relationships with growers. Lanson sells almost 8,000,000 bottles a year and continues to preserve its unique style through the efforts of its team, from the cellar manager Vincent Malherbe to the production manager Gérard Germain, all of whom are certain that they are going in the right direction.

Lanson Black Label   ♚ ④
About 6 million bottles a year of this straight cuvée are produced. It is obtained from a blend of 60% black grapes and 40% white. The resulting wine is fresh and harmonious.

Lanson Brut 1985   ♚♚ ④
A very warm summer in Champagne contributed to this finely balanced blend of half Chardonnay and half Pinot Noir grapes. The nose has a vague hint of toasted bread while the consistent aromas on the palate are reminiscent of white flowers. The finish has exceptional purity.

Lanson Noble Cuvée 1985   ♚ ④
White grapes dominate this cuvée, with 60% Chardonnay against 40% Pinot Noir. The supreme expression of the house style, which here unites elegance and fruit with a slightly flowery finish.

Laurent-Perrier

Avenue de Champagne
51150 Tours-sur-Marne
Tel. 26589122
Fax 26589510

Bernard de Nonancourt, "Le Magnifique", is not only a "cavalier of sparkling wine", as he has been called, but also a hero of the Resistance who made his mark at Vercors and the Eagle's Nest at Berschtesgaden with General Leclerc's Second Armoured Division. Could he make a poor Champagne? No, he certainly could not. Since he took over Laurent-Perrier in 1949 and settled into the big white house, he has seen Laurent-Perrier Champagne poured at the noblest of christenings, making Fouquet's motto "Quo non ascendam" his own. Bernard de Nonancourt looks after 100 ha of vineyards with the help of a dedicated staff. The grapes from these, together with some bought from the best outside growers, go to make several different cuvées of an elite Champagne. Laurent-Perrier has over 30,000,000 bottles stored in chalk cellars, guaranteeing the continuing quality of a Champagne whose quality has never been in doubt.

Laurent-Perrier Brut L.P.   ♚ ③
A house which excels at making the best wines could not make a bad cuvée. This non-vintage brut is sheer drinking pleasure. Good balance and an attractive aroma with a hint of hazelnut. Genuinely full on the palate.

Laurent-Perrier Cuvée Ultra-Brut ♚♚ ③
A cuvée of extraordinary finesse, the peak of Champagnes "pas dosée". Crystal clear, with an outstanding, slightly toasty nose, an incomparably soft wine on the palate with a mouthfilling finish.

Laurent-Perrier Grand Siècle   ♚♚ ④
Laurent-Perrier also markets a 1985 vintage Grand Siècle but this is the finest of the wines produced by the company. A great prestige Champagne of rare elegance, evident power, remarkable depth and a vanilla finish.

Laurent-Perrier   ♚♚ ④
Grand Siècle Alexandra 1982
Elegant, well-rounded, powerful and fruity. These few words admirably sum up the cuvée dedicated to Alexandra, Bernard de Nonancourt's daughter. Delicate mousse and a perfect balance contribute to a wine fit for the gods.

Leclerc-Briant

67, rue Chaude-Ruelle
51200 Épernay
Tel. 26544533
Fax 26544959

Pascal Leclerc is a man who will not let you down. One day in the 10th arrondissement in Paris, he happened to be passing the 'bistrot à vin' L'Enchotte. He liked the look of the place and its owner so much that he started to recommend it. Leclerc is also in the Guinness Book of Records for his pyramids of champagne flutes. But in his chalk "caves" (the deepest in Champagne), he is a perfectionist of the most traditional kind. His wines fully reflect the customary practices of the region. The Leclerc-Briant estate was created in 1872 and comprises 30 ha of vineyards. The cuvées of 50% Pinot Noir, 30% Chardonnay and 20% Pinot Meunier are always superb, but there are also other projects under way. Biodynamics is one, for only organic products, manure and peat, are used as fertilizers. In rather Burgundian fashion, at the end of 1992, special, evocatively named single-parcel wines were launched, like Les Chèvres Pierreuses, Le Pont à la Vanelle, Les Crayères, Le Clos Nito, Le Bois des Jots and Les Houssettes. All of which goes to show just how unusual a Champagne producer Leclerc-Briant is.

Cuvée Réserve Brut 🍇 ③
A classic Champagne of outstanding quality. A blend of Pinot Noir (70%) and Chardonnay (30%) with a beautiful mousse and a heady bouquet. The finish is fresh and long.

Cuvée Divine 1985 🍇🍇 ④
Half Chardonnay and half Pinot Noir harvested on the Coteaux de Cumières and de Hautvillers, this cuvée has a remarkably full bouquet on a background of honey sustained by the full-bodied palate. The bubbles linger, and the finish is long and elegant.

Brut Rosé 🍇 ③
Fine structure from the 100% Pinot Noir which comes out clearly together with aromas that are almost Burgundian, this cru has a chewy body and a liquorice finish of moderate length.

Moët et Chandon

20, avenue de Champagne
51205 Épernay Cedex
Tel. 26547111
Fax 26548423

1993 is the 250th anniversary of Moët et Chandon, which belongs to the Louis Vuitton Moët Hennessy group. The estate receives over 200,000 visitors a year and produces the best-selling Champagne in the world. One bottle of Champagne in four is Moët et Chandon, far ahead of its nearest competitor. The company owns over 500 ha of vineyards as well as the rights to one of Champagne's great legends, the name of the cellarer monk Dom Pérignon. No launch, sporting victory or social event would be complete without the Moët star. Everybody, at least once in their lives, should take the miniature railway through the "caves" 40 m below ground level to see the fabulous towers of bottles, a total of 90,000,000 of them. Moët et Chandon also moves with the times. In 1985, an experimental grafting center was set up. The research sector was further developed during the 1980s with the building of temperature-controlled cellars and automatic computer-operated storage systems. Consistent quality is the basis of Moët et Chandon's success from the straight non-vintage to the Brut Impérial, up to the superb Dom Pérignon.

Brut Impérial 🍇 ④
This classic cuvée has moderate balance and fruit and gives of its best on tasting. The bubbles are perfect, the power and body excellent. A Champagne drunk all over the world which tastes even better from a magnum.

Dom Pérignon 1985 🍇🍇 ④
The legendary Dom Pérignon cuvée was launched in the United States in 1936, only becoming available in France after the war, in 1949. The 1985 lives up to the Dom Pérignon tradition. It has absolutely everything; depth, elegance, finesse and power. The Chardonnay gives it great freshness, with just a hint of 'croissant', and remarkable body on the palate. A selection of the firm's best cuvées.

Brut Impérial 1988 🍇 ④
A Champagne with an attractive salmon-pink color and a well-developed bouquet supported by aromas of wild berries. Well-rounded and supple, it has a fairly dense yet fresh structure which comes back in the finish with citrus characters .

Moncuit

11, rue Persault-Maheu
51190 Le Mesnil-sur-Oger
Tel. 26575265
Fax 26579789

Confidentiality is the first word to come into one's mind when talking about Moncuit, a Champagne which gives much pleasure to its famous and not so famous admirers. The reason for the faithful following enjoyed by Pierre Moncuit's Champagne is to be found in the 20 ha of vineyards classed 100% owned by the estate in the very heart of the Côte des Blancs, although grapes from Mesnil-sur-Oger are also used. Today, Pierre's grandchildren Nicole and Yves have taken over, Nicole looking after winemaking and Yves being in charge of sales. This new generation has decided not to sell any of the harvest. All grapes picked in 1990 were vinified on the estate. Any of the vintages available from the 1980 to the 1986 and any of the wines, whether the "Réserve" or the straight "Hughes de Coulmet", can be confidently selected in the knowledge that the wine will be well-balanced, with a consistent freshness and elegance year after year and will have a powerful bouquet from the Côte des Blancs Chardonnay. A connoisseur's wine.

Pierre Moncuit 🍇🍇 ③
Blanc de blancs 1985
A mature and concentrated wine made in the old-fashioned way. There is a good percentage of Chardonnay which expresses the "terroir" perfectly. The bouquet has white flowers, fresh butter, almonds and fresh country bread while the palate reveals all the power of the wine while not lacking either finesse or freshness. A wine which will age for a few years yet.

Pierre Moncuit Cuvée Réserve 🍇 ③
A wine that is above all light, with full, concentrated aromas of fresh citrus, hazelnuts and croissant. The mousse is extremely delicate and the powerful finish ends on a mineral note.

Mumm

29, rue du Champ-de-Mars
51053 Reims Cedex
Tel. 26495969
Fax 26404613

This famous house was founded in 1827 and used to be located in the wonderfully named rue de la Grosse Bouteille. Mumm has 220 ha of vineyards, some in Grands Crus on the typically chalky soil of the region, planted 60% in Pinot Noir and 40% in Chardonnay. The Cordon Rouge has been shipped all over the world since it was lauched in 1875, symbolizing a cuvée that requires the contribution of all three Champagne varieties and no less than 40 parcels of vines. Known in every corner of the globe, the celebrated "Red Ribbon" was the darling of artistic and literary circles at the turn of the century and in 1927 at the inauguration of La Coupole restaurant in Montparnasse, its legendary status was assured when Mac Orlan, Derain, Carco, Braque, Maillol and Foujita among others drank glass after glass of Mumm Champagne. After that memorable occasion, René Lalou promoted the label in grand style. It was, in due course, acquired by the Canadian group, Seagram.

Mumm de Mumm 1982 🍇🍇 ④
Very pale and bright in color with fine, straight bubbles. Crisp and very refreshing aromas which are well-developed; the bouquet is essentially elegant with foward freshness. The sensation of attractive freshness returns on the palate with its well-rounded entry and sinewy acidity leading to a clean, dry finish.

Joseph Perrier

69, avenue de Paris
51005 Châlons-sur-Marne
Tel. 26682951-26681604
Fax 26705716

Founded in 1825 by Joseph Perrier and sold in 1888 to the Pithois family, this cellar, one of the few in Châlons, has remained in the family since then. The Joseph Perrier vineyards are in some of the best sites in Champagne at Cumières, Damery and Hautvillers. These provide about one third of the grapes required. The rest are bought in from the Côte des Blancs and from as far away as the Montagne de Reims so that 20 or so crus go to make Joseph Perrier cuvées. After harvesting, the grapes are pressed in the field. The must is then transported to Châlons-sur-Marne where ancient Roman galleries carved out of the chalk were converted at the end of the 19th century into three km of cellars. Here the wine is transformed into Champagne. Joseph Perrier has a considerable reserve stock and produces a non-vintage Champagne obtained from 35% Blanc de Blancs and 65% Blanc de Noir with a 1-1.5% dosage. A new 'cuvée-prestige' has recently been launched (1982 vintage) from a blend of Grands Crus of Pinot Noir and Chardonnay with an old-fashioned bottle whose design dates from over a century ago. Superb.

Cuvée Royale Blanc de Blancs   🍾 ④
The bubbles of this pale green-flecked wine are extremely delicate. Fruity and vivacious on the palate, the finish is never-ending. An ideal way to start a meal.

Cuvée Joséphine 1982   🍾 ④
A deliciously fruity bouquet with a hint of flowers as well as notes of plums and toasty, smoky oak. Full-bodied and elegant, there is an agreeable hint of dried grapes. The finish is very stylish.

Perrier-Jouët

26, avenue de Champagne
51200 Épernay
Tel. 26552053
Fax 26545455

People around these parts tend to judge a company by the quality of its ordinary, non-vintage brut and Perrier-Jouët, with its 110ha mainly in the Cramant area, has everything it needs to ensure an excellent reputation locally. The vine stock, on chalky soil, comprises about 40% Chardonnay on the Côte des Blancs with the remainder Pinot Meunier and Pinot Noir and the company makes full use of both traditional skills and its knowledge of the 'terroir'. The Perrier-Jouët story is inextricably linked to the story of the Belle Époque bottle, known as Fleur de Champagne in the United States. Created by Gallé, a glassblower of the Nancy school, at the beginning of the century, the bottle was rediscovered in the Perrier-Jouët cellars in 1965. Decorated with delicate, white anemones and enamelled, gold-laced roses, the bottle contains a wine of outstanding quality whose characteristics are reminiscent of the Belle Époque - a little extravagant, graceful and with an unmistakeable elegance. The legend lives on thanks also to the Belle Époque Pierre-Jouët house, a superb jewel in the crown of France's artistic heritage. Works by Majorelle, Guimard and Rodin are on exhibition together with mementos of Sarah Bernhardt, André Gide, Rostand and many others. A fascinating place to visit.

Grand Brut   🍾 ④
A golden color and rather unforthcoming bouquet, but the powerful structure explodes on the palate. Good balance and excellent length.

Belle Epoque 1985   🍾 🍾 ④
A fine wine with good structure and body. The high percentage of Chardonnay also gives the wine finesse. Very complex, with notes of charred oak and toasted bread. On the palate, elegance mingles with the freshness of the finish.

Philipponnat

13, rue du Pont
51160 Mareuil-sur-Aÿ
Tel. 26526043
Fax 26526149

The first thing that comes into one's mind when the name Philipponnat is mentioned is the Clos des Goisses. This vineyard comprises a single south-facing plot on a one-in-three hillside along the "Côte de Noirs" path opposite Marne. The vines of this exceptional property sink their roots deep into the chalk, which lies under a 50 cm layer of top-soil. Since 1935, the property has belonged to the Philipponnat company, controlled since 1987 by Marie Brizard. Remuage at Philipponnat is always done by hand on the traditional "pupitres". Dégorgement is also by hand, and each vintage ages for six years before being put on the market. The 11ha estate, of which the Clos des Goisses accounts for 5.5 ha, provides 25% of grape requirements. Philipponnat can produce their 'everyday' Champagne, called Royal Réserve Brut, by blending various different vintages, obtained from 70% Pinot Noir and Pinot Meunier with 30% Chardonnay. A company which can make the very best will certainly also be able to make a good standard product.

Royal Réserve Brut
This blend of Pinot Noir (50%), Chardonnay (33%) and Pinot Meunier (17%) produces a pale gold-colored wine with a floral bouquet which remains fresh on the palate.

Clos des Goisses 1985
From a dozen or so separately harvested parcels, it lives up to its reputation. Gold in color with a particularly fine mousse, the bouquet is a little mineral and develops a wide range of fruity notes on a background of flowers with citrus, plum, redcurrant and nettles. Velevety and lingering, this is a Champagne to lay down.

Rating System

An exemplary wine of its type with outstanding local character

An international premium quality wine

A Top Wine, considered one of the 150 best wines in the world

The 'grape bunch' symbol is used to indicate the color of the wine; the number of bunches represents the quality rating assigned by the contributor

Pol Roger

1, rue Heri-Lelarge
51206 Épernay
Tel. 26554195
Fax 26552570

Pol Poger is a master of the art of perfection. Triumphing at blind tastings all over France today, the wines had always been known abroad (it was Winston Churchill's favorite Champagne) but used to be underrated at home. Exports remain strong, (60% of the turnover), but Christian de Billy and Christian Pol Roger, direct descendants of the founder Pol Roger from 1849, have adjusted their marketing. The estate has 85 ha of vineyards on the Côte des Blancs, 50% of the total in Grands Crus or Premiers Crus. Production is 1,400,000 bottles a year and five years' stock is held to back up the policy of quality first. Pol Roger is a connoisseur's wine. The non-vintage Cuvée Brut, made from 20-30% of the reserve wines from the 3 or 4 most recent vintages, is a marvel of consistency and speaks volumes for Pol Roger's technique and taste. The prestige cuvée, PR, with equal parts of Blanc de Noirs and Blanc de Blancs, is stunning every year and the 1985 comes from 6 crus classed 100%. The wines undergo a first fermentation in vats and then a second in the bottle. Non-vintage wines age for three years and vintage Champagnes, for five or six. Pol Roger has always been a great Champagne and now, sadly for some of us, it has been discovered by the French.

Pol Roger Brut   🍾🍾 ④
A non-vintage brut from Pinot Blanc grapes from the Montagne de Reims together with Côte des Blancs Chardonnay and Marne Valley Pinot Meunier. This sand-colored wine with its delicate mousse and floral, ripe red-berry bouquet, its well-balanced structure and lingering aromatic finish, has great style and class.

Blanc de Chardonnay 1985   🍾🍾 ④
A vintage from Chardonnay grapes with more than 10° potential alcohol and 9 g/lt acidity. The grapes were harvested in five Côte de Blancs Grands Crus, which gives the wine its lovely pale, gold color, a lingering mousse and aromas of spring flowers, hazelnut and white peaches. An outstandingly fresh finish.

Réserve Spéciale P.R. 1985   🍾🍾 ④
From equal parts of Pinot and Chardonnay grapes from six Grands Crus classed 100%. The balance of acidity and alcohol in this prestigious reserve is wonderful. Golden amber color, with lovely mousse and clarity, the bubbles rise smoothly up the glass. With a floral, fruity nose, the palate has firm concentration and a full-flavored, well-rounded and never-ending finish.

Pol Roger 1986   🍾🍾🍾 ④
Contrary to widespread expectations, 1986 will not be a mediocre vintage. Not, at least, at Pol Roger, where after excellent flowering and a difficult summer, particularly at the beginning of September, yields were limited. This wine is obtained from 60% Pinot Noir and 40% Chardonnay from around 20 Grands Crus, including Le Mesnil, Oger and Vertus for Chardonnay and Aÿ, Hautvillers, Mareuil and Bouzy for Pinot. It is Pinot which gives the wine body, power, depth and aging potential while Chardonnay brings finesse, elegance and nobility. Exquisitely harmonious and fresh with a creamy mousse, the structure has great breeding and a stylish, almost sensuous, finish. This is the epitome of Champagne at its peak. It is hardly surprising that people talk about Pol Roger's 'seductive simplicity'. It would be nice to find the quality more often in the wines of Champagne.

Louis Roederer

21, boulevard Lundy
51053 Reims Cedex
Tel. 26404211
Fax 26476651

Alexander II, Czar of all the Russias, was the most celebrated admirer of Cristal, the splendid Champagne that was created in 1876, practically at his explicit request. Today, ordinary mortals as well as the crowned and anointed, can drink the prestige cuvée of this company founded in 1833. Louis Roederer grows a high proportion of its grape requirements. It has an estate of 180 ha, of which 75 ha are planted in Chardonnay and 130 are in Grands Crus classed 100%. Remaining requirements come from vineyards that Roederer controls. Overall, the grapes used are classed 98%. This explains in part the Roederer miracle but much credit must also go to the quality standards imposed by Jean-Claude Rouzand, who manages this family-run company. Quality is apparent in the 7,000 hl of reserve wines kept in an impressive array of 60 hl "foudres", waiting for blending into non-vintage Champagne. Another 1,200 hl of "tête de cuvée" wines age in barriques for 4 years. At Roederer, this is the price for quality.

Brut Premier   ❦❦ ④
Every year, this non-vintage brut achieves a remarkable standard of quality thanks to the blend in which Pinot Noir is prevalent (roughly two thirds). A great wine: elegant, stylish, well-rounded and of incomparable freshness.

Cristal 1985   ❦❦ ④
This blend of selected cuvées has excellent ageing prospects. Chardonnay and Pinot Noir are here blended in almost exactly equal proportions. A wine with marvellous balance, where body blends seamlessly with fruit.

Salon

5, rue de la Brèche d'Oger
51190 Le Mesnil-sur-Oger
Tel. 26565165
Fax 26577929

Salon possesses only one hectare of 20 year-old vines on the chalky soil of Mesnil-sur-Oger, planted in 100% Chardonnay. The climate is northerly. Only one wine is produced, the 'Cuvée S', and it is not made every year. Since the beginning of the century, only 21 vintages have been considered worthy of the Salon label, which is to Champagne what Rolls-Royce is to motor cars. It was Aimé Salon, a Paris furrier, who in the 1920s wanted to create a special wine for his friends and thus was born a single-vineyard Blanc de Blancs to be produced solely in great vintages. This rigorously exclusive policy has been consistently applied and continues to be followed by Bernard de Nonancourt's Laurent-Perrier, who have owned the property since 1988. The hand-picked grapes, the traditional wooden press, the fermentation in stainless steel vats before transfer to oak barrels (with no malolactic), the long aging on the yeasts (7-10 years) and the bottle-aging for around 12 years all denote quality. A bottle of Salon is a rare delight to be found on the world's most exclusive tables. The mysterious magic of Salon never fades.

Cuvée S 1982   ❦❦ ④
This Blanc de Blancs from a single parcel at Mesnil-sur-Oger is quite extraordinary. Golden color, with a compact, delicate mousse and a lingering 'crown'. The bouquet is powerful with hints of butter, almonds, spices and citrus. The wine's elegant texture emerges accompanied by a slightly peppery, vanilla note. The finish is incredibly long with a mineral purity that is almost too perfect. When will the next wine be ready?

Jacques Selosse

22, rue Ernest-Valle
51190 Avize
Tel. 26575356
Fax 26577822

Most unusual, this Champagne is produced on 5 ha of Chardonnay classed as 100% Grand Cru which Corinne and Anselme Selosse tend with all the love that the family inheritance deserves. The Selosses do not take a conservative approach to winemaking. Fermentation is in the large barrels and small oak casks, some new, which line the Selosse cellar in impressive fashion. The wines are then aged on the yeasts for four years. The Selosses aim for rich, substantial wines which are still elegant, wines which have just the right note of wood. All Selosse wines require bottle-aging and in fact are only put on the market after several years in the cellar (the 1989, for example, will be available in 1995). Dégorgement takes place at the last possible moment and the date of the operation is noted on the back label of the bottle. While we are waiting for the 1989, we can amuse ourselves with the Extra-Brut, a blend of the vintages from 1985 to 1987 and a wine with remarkable length.

Grand Cru Blanc de Blancs   🍇 🍇 ③
Fermented in oak, this wine was tasted in September 1992, having been disgorged on 5th September 1991. The bubbles are delicate and the aroma of wood is very elegant. The balance and exceptional purity on the palate, which leads to a crisp finish, are outstanding. A stylish, indeed thirst-quenching Champagne which is ready to drink now.

Grand Cru Extra-Brut   🍇 🍇 ③
Aged in barrels and casks, 17% of which are new oak from the Vincent Leflaive company, this is an Extra-Brut, "pas dosée", obtained from a blend of 100% Chardonnay from three different vintages. This is a substantial Champagne which conveys its sinew and body with the first sip. The long finish promises well for the future.

Taittinger

9, place Saint-Nicaise
51100 Reims
Tel. 26854535
Fax 26501430

A visit to the Cathedral and the basilica of Saint-Rémy is a must at Reims. The other obligatory trip is to to the ancient cellars of a company which has been active for more than 250 years: Taittinger. After the Great War, Taittinger took over the company Forest et Fourneax (founded in 1734) with its entire stock and a particularly fine Grand Cru vineyard used for making a wine known as "des Comtes-de-Champagne". The Comte was Thibaut V, a crusader who stayed in the Gallo-Roman chalk galleries and in the remains of the 13th-century chapel and the 15th-century crypt of the abbey of Saint-Nicaise on the way back from the Holy-Land. The 250 ha of vineyards are exemplary and extend over 30 different crus, providing 40-45% of the production requirements of the estate. Extreme care is taken both over the traditionally made non-vintage brut (often a little on the hard side) and special wines, such as the Taittinger Collection in its bottles decorated by Vasarely. All Tattinger wines are lovingly made, with a real elegance balanced by controlled power. Taittinger also owns the Carneros estate in the Napa Valley.

Brut Réserve   🍇 ④
A classic non-vintage Champagne with a pale color. Moderate bouquet but the palate is full-bodied and winey. The finish, too, is long.

Comtes de Champagne 1985   🍷🍷 ④
A wine for great occasions. Strong color, more reddish than rosé with a fine fruity bouquet of red fruit, citrus and vanilla and a hint of oak. Toasty notes emerge on the palate to leave a pleasant sensation, free of heaviness. Only the price (around 500FF) might discourage one from sampling it.

George Vesselle

16, rue des Postes
Bouzy 51150
Tel. 26570015
Fax 26570920

There are Vesselles everywhere in Bouzy so why mention this one rather than any of the others? One good reason is that George Vesselle has been mayor of Bouzy for 25 years and is almost a symbol of the town. Another reason is that Vesselle, the son of a humble country family, has never lost his taste for the good things in life, one of the greatest of which, he claims, is the wine of his home town. George has about 17.5 ha of vineyards, all classified as Grands Crus, planted with 90% Pinot Noir and 10% Chardonnay. But George has not restricted himself to the production of his own wine. For 20 years, until 1991, he headed Mumm Vignobles et Recherches, where he contributed to introducing the use of helicopters in Champagne, developing a planting machine, clonal selection and invitro cultivation in collaboration with Professor Claude Martin, Director of the Vegetable Physiopathological Laboratory of the Dijon INRA. Vesselle has always been a producer of Champagne and claims that Champagne has been made in Bouzy since the town came into existence.

Bouzy Cuvée Véronique Sylvie   🍇 ④
This wine is made of an "assemblage" of old wines up to about ten years old which and is regarded by the house as a kind of Cuvée Prestige. The nose is delicately spicey with full fresh fruit that come through on the palate and long finish.

Bouzy 1988   🍇 ③
This wine is a reference point for others. It has a rich, bright ruby color and is made entirely of Pinot Noir from the Côteaux Champenois which amply shows itself on both nose and palate. It should be served slightly cool and the balance is excellent with a finesh of lovely finesse.

Veuve Clicquot-Ponsardin

1, place des Droits-de-l'Homme
51100 Reims
Tel. 26402542
Fax 26406017

The largest chalk tunnelsin Champagne, dating from Gallo-Roman times, are to be found here, winding for a total 24 km, 18 of which are used to cellar the precious bottles of Champagne. At 25 m below ground level, the temperature maintains a constant 10°C, and the stocks of 32 million bottles of Champagne are kept here under ideal conditions. The name Veuve Clicquot is inextricably bound up with the history of Champagne and of France. It was in 1772 that Jean Clicquot, a magistrate of the city of Reims, met Louis XV who had come to the city to be crowned. It was a widow of the family, Nicole (whose maiden name was Barbe-Ponsardin) who was to make the company famous. She first used the technique of "remuage" to make her Champagne clear and limpid. She also exported the famous yellow label all over the world, to London, Berlin and St. Petersburg. Today, Veuve-Clicquot is sold in more than 150 countries. The company also owns 150 ha of vineyards in the Grands Crus of Montagne de Reims, Vallée de la Marne and Côte des Blancs which puts it in one of the most enviable positions in Champagne.

La Grande Dame 1985   🍇🍇 ④
From vineyards classified 100%, this fine cuvée is the quintessence of power. The floral bouquet is very forthcoming and elegant, slightly spicy flavors develop on the palate. Full-bodied and with excellent structure, the aromatic finish lingers on and on.

Vintage Réserve 1985   🍇🍇 ④
Two thirds Pinot and one third Chardonnay bring this elegant cuvée with its golden color to life. There are stylish aromas of dried fruits, apricots and croissant on the nose. A harmonious, well-rounded wine of perfect balance which finishes on a velvety sensation of fruit.

Corse

History, tourism and wine have found themselves living side by side on this magical island, and the experience has not always been an easy one. History arrived in the form of returning former residents from Algiers, who planted vineyards particularly on the plains where yields have always been high. Tourism has served to soak up much of local wine production, and it is always difficult to find quality wine at the end of August. All this has tended to exclude those producers whose aim is quality. However, the third element of our original trio is emerging today in a trend to develop native Mediterranean varieties and improve general quality standards. This trend should continue, given the commitment of a good number of producers who are investing and adapting to the extremes of the Corsican climate with its sun-drenched hills and slopes and the beneficial maritime influence. The trend towards quality is making progress despite the constant decrease in the total area of vines, which in 15 years has passed from more than 25,000 ha to less than 10,000 ha, and in the number of growers too, which has fallen from just over 1,800 to the 800 of 1990.

As so often happens, Paris has led the way in promoting Corsican wines. Prices are at least 40% higher in Paris than in Corsica, where there is no value added tax. This has not stopped the island's eight Appellations from being freely available in the wine bars and restaurants of the capital city.

The Corsican Appellations include Ajaccio, which produces mainly red wines, and Patrimonio, the oldest of the island's Appellations. Then come the five Vin de Corse-Villages Appellations, according to the name of the areas where they are produced: Calvi, mentioned by Sénèque; Coteaux du Cap Corse, with a multitude of small vineyards; Figari, the most southerly Appellation in France; Porto Vecchio, with its small vineyards perched on the hillsides; and Sartène, much appreciated by Napoleon. Finally, there is the regional Appellation Vin de Corse which is produced principally on the Gulf and the east coast, where Aléria, the home of Corsican viticulture, is to be found.

The most famous wines are those produced from three important noble varieties. For rosé and red wines, there is Nielluccio (known as Sangiovese in Tuscany) and Sciaccarello or Schiuchitajolu (literally crunchy under the teeth), which is highly thought of in Ajaccio and the south-east of the island. For white wines, there is Vermentinu (or Malvoisie de Corse) which is Provençal Rolle. In addition, interesting experimental wines are being made with Muscat and Cinsaut using either sun-dried grapes or partially fermented musts muted with spirit. As far as winemaking techniques are concerned, the diffidence of vignerons with regard to any of the modernization and technology so popular on the mainland is striking. Industrial yeasts, low temperatures, new wood and chemical herbicides are all shunned and yields are naturally reasonable.

The above observations allow us to be moderately optimistic about the future of Corsican wines, or at least the future of the Appellation d'Origine Contrôlée wines (less than 15% of the vineyards). Efforts will have to be made to keep increasing sales under control and to promote the sale of wines for laying down. The first step has been taken but many others must follow.

Clos Capitoro

Pisciatella - Route de Sartène
20166 Porticcio
Tel. (95) 251961
Fax (95) 251933

Jacques Bianchetti is 38 years-old and belongs to the fifth generation of growers in his family. He cultivates the vineyards that his grandfather completely replanted after phylloxera. Corsican enology owes a great deal to Jacques' grandfather as it was he who taught his neighbors how to graft the American vines. The Bianchetti's have a marked preference for concentrated red wines from completely de-stemmed 70% Sciaccarello grapes. Grenache grapes give the wine strength and color and they should not be drunk for at least two or three years. The white wines are fermented at a moderately low temperature (19°C) to conserve their depth and avoid their becoming too high in glycerine. This is the only estate on the island which produces good naturally sweet wines from Grenache, when the climate permits, from Vermentinu and from Sciaccarello Rosé; clean, uncomplicated wines with good body that are always a pleasure to drink.

Clos Capitoro 1990   🍇 ①
Agreeable, almost mineral bouquet with a background of Mediterranean white-flower aromas. Full-flavored on the palate. Hint of astringency in the finish.

Clos Capitoro 1989   🍷 ②
This blend of Sciaccarello and Grenache is still a little rustic. Very concentrated, with hints of liquorice on the nose and good length on the palate. Needs a few years before it will be ready for drinking.

Domaine Péraldi

Chemin du Stiletto
20167 Mezzavia
Tel. (95) 223730
Fax (95) 209291

This estate of Count Guy Tyrel de Poix on the Mezzavia coast has belonged to the same family for decades. Its 40 ha overlook the Gulf of Ajaccio, although they lie within the boundaries of the city itself. The vines are traditional for the area with Sciaccarello being the dominant variety (40% of the total). The rest is 40% Nielluccio, Malvoisie and small quantities of Cinsaut and Grenache and 20% Carignan. The grapes are hand picked and carefully selected. Fermentation takes place in temperature-regulated cellars, each variety being vinified separately at controlled temperatures. Yields rarely exceed 35 hl/ha and every parcel is carefully analyzed by computer. This helps to explain why the estate's products have a solid presence on the international market and can command high prices. The superb Cuvée Clos du Cardinal is a pure Sciaccarello. This variety gives virtually no color at all and the comparison with Pinot Noir is obvious. Interesting experiments with the maceration of white grapes on the skins are being carried out.

Cuvée Clos du Cardinal 1989   🍷 ②
Obtained from 100% Sciaccarello, this cuvée has a clear, very light red color. The bouquet is slightly spicy with hints of jam on a background of ripe red berries. Very concentrated and firm, this is a well-built and rather tannic wine. The finish, however, is very elegant.

Domaine de Torraccia

20137 Lecci de Porto Vecchio
Tel. (95) 714350
Fax (95) 715003

Until 1964, Christian Imbert ran an estate in the endless bush of Chad. Now, his property comprises 110 ha lying between the mountains and the sea to the north of Porto Vecchio. Imbert has completely cleared and broken up the soil and planted 43 ha of steep, south-east facing granite sand with traditional Corsican varieties (Sciaccarello and Nielluccio) just when the Corsicans themselves were beginning to lose interest in them. Imbert has been totally accepted by the locals, becoming a "singer of the tradition" who even speaks Corsican. Picturesque details aside, Corsicans should be genuinely grateful to Imbert. He has made Corsican wines acceptable once again in the French capital, where they had long been forgotten. Imbert uses no chemical fertilizers or herbicides, the grapes are picked by hand and aging is first in barrels and then in the bottle, "where the truth of the wine is hidden", as he himself is wont to say.

Domaine de Torraccia
Porto Vecchio Blanc 1991
A wine of great aromatic potential. Quite a surprise, considering the vintage. Bright yellow color and a burgeoning honey aroma which fills the palate.

Domaine de Torraccia
Réserve Oriu 1989
Rich and warm with great fruit and body. Obtained from a blend where Nielluccio grapes dominate, this is a wine with real freshness and a lingering aromatic finish.

Côtes du Rhône

Over the last ten years, the Rhône Valley has proved how good its wines can be. In the early 1970s, when prices were low and agriculture was going through a period of crisis, young people were deserting family-run properties "en masse" to go first to university and then to well-paid jobs in the cities. With the arrival of the wine boom of the early 1980s, many of these youngsters, dissatisfied with their urban employment, returned to their family estates. This input of new blood has had especially significant consequences for the region.

Today, the Rhône Valley makes some of France's top quality and best value premium wines. It is also a region with one of the widest range of wine types in the world. Here we find the great, full-bodied reds of Appellations like Côte Rôtie, Hermitage and Cornas in the north or Gigondas and Châteauneuf-du-Pape in the south as well as the legendary white wine Condrieu and the vigorous white Hermitage. In between, there is a huge range of delicious red and white wines, from the sensual, sweet Muscats of Beaumes-de-Venise to the full, thirst-quenching rosés of Tavel and Listrac. Attention to quality appears to be spread uniformly over the whole of the Côtes du Rhône region, both among the cooperatives (the more enterprising of which have instituted a bonus system for quality-conscious growers) and private estates.

The most northerly of the principal Appellations is Côte Rôtie, with its excellent quality red wines. Over the last decade, a new generation of dynamic young growers has totally transformed this Appellation.

To the south of Ampuis, vineyard expansion around the town of Condrieu has resulted in an increase in production of 500% over the last ten years. Viognier has become fashionable and the increase in the area planted in this variety from the Ardèche to Gard and the Languedoc is one of the negative repercussions of Condrieu's commercial success. Another unfortunate side-effect is the situation at the legendary Château Grillet, the smallest Appellation d'Origine Contrôlée in the world, where quality has slipped badly. One hopes that things will improve.

Saint-Joseph seems to have achieved consistency, with less and less difference in style between wines produced in the northern zone of the Appellation and the intense, full-bodied wines of Mauves, traditionally the heart of Saint-Joseph.

Hermitage is the most famous Rhône cru and perhaps also one of the most ancient. For many years, there was little to report from the magnificently sited hill on the eastern bank of the river, but now change is in the air and the Chapoutier estate in particular is making encouraging moves to reintroduce the very highest quality standards to the Appellation. Recent Chapoutier wines have been remarkable and the friendly rivalry with Jaboulet has re-emerged.

To the west of Valence, on the other side of the river Rhône, the lazy little town of Cornas, where the amicable and gentlemanly Auguste Clape continues to make his stupendously full, intense wines, has remained much the same over the years. Also at Cornas, Jean Lionnet and the charming Jean-Luc Colombo are making great strides with methods which combine modern technology with the use of barriques. The wine made at Saint-Péray is nearly all consumed locally, south of Cornas.

The Crozes-Hermitage Appellation, which includes 11 villages around Tain l'Hermitage, has developed rapidly in the last decade and produces wines of improving quality.

During the 1980s, the Gigondas Appellation came out with a series of outstanding wines which are also excellent value for money.

As far as Châteauneuf-du-Pape is concerned, the progress made in the late 1970s with the installation of ultra-modern technology did not produce the improvement in quality one might have expected during the 1980s. There are, of course, exceptions. Both Château de Beaucastel and Paul Avril's Clos des Papes have made a series of splendid vintages. The last ten years have also witnessed the return of traditional varieties like Mourvèdre and Counoise, which are starting to give excellent results.

The Beaumes-de-Venise Appellation is noted for its naturally sweet wines obtained from Muscat grapes. Beaumes-de-Venise is also one of the 16 communes which have the privilege of adding Côtes du Rhône-Villages to the Appellation on the label of their wines. The same is true of Rasteau, which has Côtes du Rhône-Village status for its best red table wines and the Rasteau Appellation for its Grenache-based Vin Doux Naturel. Village red wines from Rasteau are often stylish and easy drinking. It is likely that Cairanne will soon have its own Appellation like Vacqueyras, which achieved this distinction in 1989.

The Côtes du Rhône-Village Appellation, which allowed 16 communes to add the word Villages to their labels, was replaced in 1984 by a more complicated system under which 54 communes can use the name Villages without specifying the commune of origin. The new Côtes du Rhône-Villages wines, however, often lack the style and character of the original AOC.

Côtes du Rhône is the base Appellation of the Rhône Valley and is applied to more than 2 million hl of wine a year, from vin ordinaire sold unbottled or in plastic containers to good-quality wines which are excellent value for money. This is perhaps the category which has derived the greatest benefit from the introduction of modern technology, not because there are now more outstanding wines but simply because the bad wines of the past have virtually disappeared from circulation.

Other zones in the Rhône Valley where delicious wines can be found at attractive prices are Coteaux du Tricastin, Côtes du Ventoux and the slopes of Lubéron, not forgetting the sparkling wines of Clairette de Die.

The future of the Rhône Valley will depend on the stability of its quality and price levels. Producers in what is today indisputably one of the best wine regions in the whole of France will have to be careful not to fall into the trap of markedly increasing prices as such a move would cut them out of a market which is going through a period of recession. But while there are wines with the quality and value for money offered by many Gigondas or Croze-Hermitages, the Côtes du Rhône run no risk of drifting back into the obscurity of not so many years ago.

Château Grillet

42410 Verin
Tel. 74595156

Château Grillet is France's smallest Appellation Contrôlée with only 3.5 ha of powdery, mica-rich granite soil formed into terraces. The estate is very difficult to cultivate because the precious soil is washed away with every rainfall and has to be brought back to the vineyard manually. Viognier, a difficult, delicate grape, is the sole variety permitted. The harvest in this natural vine-clad amphitheater lasts only three days. After fermentation the wine remains on its lees in casks for 18 months. Malolactic fermentation takes place at the beginning of the spring. The legendary name of Château Grillet is much sought-after and the 10,000 bottles produced each year are not enough to satisfy demand, despite their price. However, this enviable commercial situation seems insufficient to guarantee the future of the château. Labor costs are high and the owner, André Neyret-Gachet, claims that if he did not have an income from his other business activities then Château Grillet alone would certainly not provide him with a living. It is for this reason that he has extended the vineyard over the last 20 years. While any great wine has its critics, the general consensus seems to be that Château Grillet deserves its elevated reputation, despite its fantastic potential.

Château Grillet 1989 🍇 ④
A clear, gold-tinged yellow. The nose is not yet fully developed and the rounded, full-flavored palate is a little astringent, leaving the mouth dry.

Château Grillet 1988 🍇 ④
Another wine with a pale, bright color. The nose is complex but not entirely clean and the rich texture on the palate also has a rather unattractive vein of astringency. One expects rather better from such a prestigious producer, particularly at this price.

Yves Cuilleron

Les Prairies
42410 Chavanay
Tel. 74870237
Fax 74870562

The young and initially rather shy Yves Cuilleron lives a solitary existence in a large and modest-looking farmhouse on the main road in the center of Chavanay. Cuilleron took over the management of a five-hectare vineyard from his uncle in 1987, and in the last few years has extended the property to 15 ha with six in Condrieu, six devoted to red Saint-Joseph, six to white Saint-Joseph and a little over one hectare in Côte Rôtie. At present, the estate produces around 40,000 bottles a year with 10% of production for export. A good half is sold directly to private customers. Currently very little wine is made from the vineyard in Côte Rôtie as the vines are too young. Only 1,000 bottles were produced in 1990, but the potential of the wine is enormous. Yves Cuilleron is a man who likes to leave his own personal mark on his products and this is certainly the case with the Condrieu Les Eguets 1991, obtained from a tiny production of Viognier selected in the course of two pickings at the end of October with its 14° alcohol and 25 grams of residual sugar. It may not be to everyone's taste, but this is a wine with lots of personality.

Saint-Joseph 1991 🍇 ②
A lovely bright, clean, pale color. The nose is very fresh and fruity with lively apple aromas. Apple is again present on the palate, which has good length. A very well-made wine, with citrus notes which lend freshness to the finish.

Condrieu Les Eguets 1991 🍇🍇 ③
Attractively rich, bright color. The nose has attractive sweetness and hints of almond and apricot peel. Apricot flavors return on the very clean palate which is remarkably fresh, despite its 14° alcohol, and almost spicy. A fine, highly concentrated wine.

Saint-Joseph 1990 🍇 ②
Typically intense, invitingly rich and lively Syrah color. The nose is dominated by lovely rich, clean fruit with gamey aromas in the background which follow through on the palate. Long fresh fruit flavors and good balance. Superior to the previous vintage and a fine example of Cuilleron's abilities.

CHATEAU GRILLET
COTES DU RHONE NORTH
FRANCE

366

CONDRIEU
COTES DU RHONE NORTH
FRANCE

Jean-Yves Multier

Château du Rozay
69420 Condrieu
Tel. 74878880
Fax 74878913

Jean-Yves Multier lives in a beautiful, slightly tumbledown château above Condrieu looking out over the hills and the Rhône Valley. His grandfather Claude bought the château and its estate in 1896. After the First World War, the domaine, which had previously employed 50 vineyard workers, fell into a period of neglect which lasted until the 1970s. Paul Multier, Jean-Yves' father, started the reconstitution of the domaine at the end of the 1970s. The vineyards until then had been looked after by his friend, Georges Vernay, who for nine years bottled and sold the wine under the Château du Rozay label. Today, Jean-Yves Multier has about four hectares of vines of which three are planted to Viognier at Condrieu. The majority of the vines are on well-sited slopes which include the Coteau du Chéry. Two versions of Condrieu are produced: one is a standard A.O.C., from yields of about 35 hl/ha, and the other is the more stylish and concentrated Château du Rozay, from vines which yield only 20 hl/ha. Jean-Yves also produces a light and pleasant 100% Syrah Côtes du Rhône. At only 31, Jean-Yves has been managing the estate for eight years already and the quality of his wines is constantly improving. Definitely an estate to watch.

Condrieu 1991   🍇 ③
Bright, very pale color. Clean and fragrant on both nose and palate, although the wine is a shade lightweight in the mouth and lacks something in concentration and acidity. Should improve with bottle age as it has all the elegance of Viognier from Condrieu.

Condrieu Château du Rozay 1991   🍇 ④
Pale, clean and bright. Stylish nose, fairly light and mineral. The palate has depth and elegance but lacks acidity. Concentration is better than average for Condrieu, which testifies to the progress made by Multier.

Côtes du Rhône Appellations in this Guide

North
Château-Grillet
Condrieu
Cornas
Côte Rôtie
Crozes-Hermitage
Hermitage
Saint-Joseph
Saint-Péray

South
Châteauneuf-du-Pape
Coteaux du Tricastin
Côtes du Lubéron
Côtes du Rhône
Côtes du Rhône-Villages
Gigondas
Muscat de Beaumes-de-Venise
Tavel
Vacqueyras

CONDRIEU
COTES DU RHONE NORTH
FRANCE

367

CONDRIEU
COTES DU RHONE NORTH
FRANCE

André Perret

Verlieu
42410 Chavanay
Tel. 74872474
Fax 74870526

Until the early 1960s, André Perret's grandfather sold his Condrieu to the Cave Cooperative in Tain l'Hermitage. It was only after 1983, when the young André produced his first white and then the following year a red, that the Perret name began to acquire the reputation it enjoys today. Half of the eight-hectare domaine is planted to Viognier for Condrieu and the rest in Syrah and Marsanne for red and white Saint-Joseph. Perret produces about 25,000 bottles a year, of which 10,000 are Condrieu. The soil is granite-based, a factor which, together with the dry summer weather, the age of many of the vines (25 years or more) and the nature of the Viognier variety, keeps the yields for his Condrieu very low. Perret produces two Condrieu cuvées, Clos Chanson and Coteau de Chéry. The wines ferment slowly at low temperatures, one third in oak and two thirds in stainless steel. The wines undergo malolactic fermentation and in certain years the grapes are given a few hours skin contact. Wines are aged in barrel or tank for at least one year before bottling. As well as his extraordinary Condrieu, André Perret also makes some noteworthy Saint-Josephs, both red and white.

Condrieu Clos Chanson 1991　🍇 ③
Very pale clear color, the wine has full aromas with an agreeable hint of freshness. Good body on the palate, and at this point in its evolution it is slightly bitter in the finish. There is good length and complexity.

Saint-Joseph 1990　🍇 ②
Splendid deep, inviting color. Peppery Syrah fruit on the nose with the typically gamey character of Saint-Joseph. On the palate the impact is fruity, but the wine is still undeveloped with a hint of oak on the finish. Excellent structure which will round out with a few months in bottle.

Saint-Joseph Les Grizières 1990　🍇🍇 ②
The wine has a deeply rich color and bouquet. Notes of concentrated blackberry juice on the nose and on the palate deep flavors of blackcurrant and blackberry with quite outstanding length. A fine example of a classic Saint-Joseph.

Condrieu
Coteau de Chery 1991　🍇🍇🍇 ③
A wonderful rich, bright color. The nose is richer and more stylish than the Clos Chanson. Deliciously full on the palate, with a very marked but exceptionally elegant flavor of peach kernel and apricot skins. A classic example of a great Condrieu and a supreme expression of the Viognier variety. While 1991 was not the greatest of vintages, growers who picked before the rain arrived produced excellent wines which have more elegance and balance than those of hotter vintages.

CONDRIEU
COTES DU RHONE NORTH
FRANCE

368

CONDRIEU
COTES DU RHONE NORTH
FRANCE

Georges Vernay

1, rue Nationale
69420 Condrieu
Tel. 74595222
Fax 74566098

There was a time when Georges Vernay was the only grower to defend the reputation of Condrieu as one of France's great white wines. Today, the Appellation has no need of publicity. The vineyard area has grown from about 11 ha at the end of the 1960s to more than 80 ha and no self-respecting young grower in Côte Rôtie is without a few rows of Viognier. Georges Vernay is a man of stature with a firm handshake and an outgoing manner. He and his 34 year-old son, Luc, cultivate seven hectares planted to Viognier for Condrieu and two hectares in Syrah for Côte Rôtie planted at Semons Tupin and Ampuis. The remainder of their 14-ha estate is planted to Syrah, which produces an uncomplicated Côtes du Rhône, and Viognier grown at an elevation of over 300 meters which does not have the right to the Condrieu Appellation but produces a 100% Viognier called Vin de Pays des Collines Rhodaniennes. Vernay's leading wine is the Condrieu Coteaux du Vernon, which ferments in ten year old, 2,000 lt oak barrels at 15-16°C for three weeks and is aged for ten months in oak barrel. Luc's arrival has done much for the quality of the red wines and the Côte Rôtie, in particular, is making great progress.

Viognier
Vin de Pays des Collines Rhodaniennes 1991
A bright, very pale color and a clean, fresh nose with rich fruit which is mirrored on the palate. A straightforward Viognier with good balance and length, which does full justice to the quality of the vineyards from which it comes.

Condrieu
Coteaux du Vernon 1990
Pale yellow color of exceptional brilliance. It is outstanding on the nose, with striking notes of peach. Complex and very stylish on the palate with the fruity flavor of apricot and peach kernel typical of a great Viognier. It has good length and depth.

Côte-Rôtie 1990
Lovely deep rich color. The nose has hints of ink and mineral, together with ripe black Syrah fruit and notes of smoky oak and game. The ripe fruit comes back on a palate of medium depth which is well-built and has good balance and length.

Thierry Allemand

Cornas
07310 Saint-Peray
Tel. 75404793

Although his mother is from Cornas, Thierry Allemand is the first member of the family to have taken up viticulture. A traditionalist, he learned his art from his friend Robert Michel who encouraged him to purchase his first two hectares of vineyard on the granite coteaux in 1982. Over half his Syrah vines are of a very respectable age. Allemand makes only one wine, vinified in temperature-controlled polyester tanks. Maceration of the whole bunches of grapes lasts for about 15 days, during which time the must is pumped over and the grape cap plunged down. The wine is then aged in a mixture of stainless steel tanks, wooden vats and second-hand Burgundy barrels. Thierry Allemand is terrified of "disturbing" his wine. It is racked only twice during the whole 12-month aging process and only very lightly fined with egg whites. Most of the 7,000 bottles of inky-dark Cornas made each year are sold in Paris, although the Americans are hammering hard on his door.

Cornas 1989
Vibrant ruby color with slight brick-red tint, this wine looks delicate in comparison with its neighbors. The bouquet has a stylish aroma of strawberry jam and sweet spices. The palate is full, well-developed, opulent and long but is not for aging.

CONDRIEU
COTES DU RHONE NORTH
FRANCE

369

CORNAS
COTES DU RHONE NORTH
FRANCE

Guy de Barjac

07130 Cornas
Tel. 75403203

Guy de Barjac looks a little out of place in rural Cornas. He has the contemplative expression of a Shakespearean actor, speaks a number of languages and has a cigarette perpetually hanging from his lips. The de Barjac family has, however, had vineyards in Cornas since the 15th century, and Guy too has fallen victim to the charms of these granite slopes. Rather than modernize the winery, de Barjac chose to enlarge his holding to two hectares by planting in the "climats" of Les Chaillots and La Barjasse. He tends the vines, which range in age from 12 to 70 years old, almost single-handedly. Guy has conserved all the old wooden fermentation vats and has lengthened the fermentation time to produce a wine with more extract and structure. The grapes are not de-stemmed before crushing and sulfur is only used when absolutely necessary. He regularly punches down the grape cap with bare feet in traditional Burgundian fashion. The wines are then aged in old wooden barrels for about 18 months. Clarification is left exclusively to the cold Ardèchois winter, the reason why this very typical traditional Cornas always leaves a thick deposit at the bottom of the bottle.

Cornas 1989

Bright but opaque ruby-red color. It has an austere undeveloped nose. This wine will not be ready to drink for some years yet. Dense, rustic and vigorous with a pronounced aroma of black cherries and spices.

CORNAS
COTES DU RHONE NORTH
FRANCE

370

CORNAS
COTES DU RHONE NORTH
FRANCE

Auguste Clape

07130 Cornas
Tel. 75403364

The quietly anonymous village of Cornas harbors a great vigneron and his family. Auguste Clape is still the undisputed king of this Appellation and is now assisted by his son Pierre-Marie who in 1988, at the age of forty, returned to work on the family domaine. Their house on the main road is the picture of discretion, but behind the closed door and in the most modest of cellars one of the greatest wines in the Rhône Valley is produced. The five-hectare domaine consists of four hectares in Appellation Cornas and another hectare in Appellation Côtes du Rhône. All the wines are produced from Syrah, with the exception of a small quantity of Saint-Péray and white Côtes du Rhône made from Marsanne. The vines have an average age of between 50 and 60 years and are planted on friable, dry, south/south-east facing granite slopes. Auguste Clape picks the grapes by hand and ferments them (with the stems) in traditional fashion in cement vats, with maceration lasting for about 12 days. Before bottling the wine ages unhurriedly for a year in the cellar in old wooden barrels for this is a wine which has no need of new wood. Clape's Cornas is an aristocrat which gives its best after eight or ten years in bottle and has the potential to age for at least twenty.

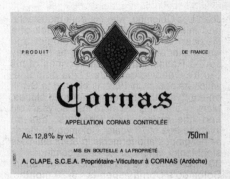

Cornas 1990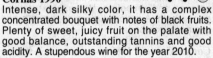
Intense, dark silky color, it has a complex concentrated bouquet with notes of black fruits. Plenty of sweet, juicy fruit on the palate with good balance, outstanding tannins and good acidity. A stupendous wine for the year 2010.

Cornas 1989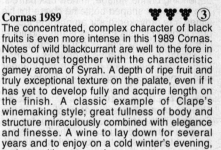
The concentrated, complex character of black fruits is even more intense in this 1989 Cornas. Notes of wild blackcurrant are well to the fore in the bouquet together with the characteristic gamey aroma of Syrah. A depth of ripe fruit and truly exceptional texture on the palate, even if it has yet to develop fully and acquire length on the finish. A classic example of Clape's winemaking style; great fullness of body and structure miraculously combined with elegance and finesse. A wine to lay down for several years and to enjoy on a cold winter's evening, perhaps with game or cheese.

CORNAS
COTES DU RHONE NORTH
FRANCE

371

CORNAS
COTES DU RHONE NORTH
FRANCE

Jean-Luc Colombo

Pied-de-la-Vigne
07130 Cornas
Tel. 75402447
Fax 75401649

Jean-Luc Colombo, with his dark moustache and mischievous eyes, has the look of a Mexican bandit. He is an enologist and winemaker and wine producers as far away as the Roussillon use the services of his Centre Oenologique. His 17-ha domaine, which he bought in 1987, is planted to Syrah on south/south-east facing terraced slopes. Many of the vines are more than 50 years old and one parcel, Les Chaillots, has an average age of 70 years. Colombo de-stems all his grapes and ferments in 50 hl stainless steel tanks, where maceration continues for 30 days. After the malolactic fermentation, Colombo's Cornas spends 15-20 months, depending on the vintage, in new oak barrels. The Bordeaux shaped bottle he chose for his wines has provoked a stir among the locals, but Colombo insists that this is the traditional Cornas shape. As well as a fine Cornas Les Ruchets, Jean-Luc also produces Cornas Colline de Laure, with grapes from younger vines, and an excellent Cotes-du-Rhône.

Cornas Les Ruchets 1990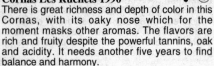

There is great richness and depth of color in this Cornas, with its oaky nose which for the moment masks other aromas. The flavors are rich and fruity despite the powerful tannins, oak and acidity. It needs another five years to find balance and harmony.

Marcel Juge

Place de la Salle des Fêtes
07130 Cornas
Tel. 75403668
Fax 75403005

Cornas is certainly not a village lacking in character. The vignerons all have their own ideas about how the wine should be made, which possibly explains why one of France's greatest Appellations is fighting for survival. Marcel Juge, now in his sixties, is a proponent of the "feminine" style of Cornas and produces three beautifully made cuvées from his three hectares of Syrah vines. These plantings, which on average are 40 years old, are divided equally between the granite slopes and the richer soil at the foot of the hills. Following a fairly brief fermentation in open vats, the wine spends at least 18 months in used oak barrels. Juge's labelling of the three cuvées causes a certain amount of confusion: his ordinary Cornas comes from vines at the foot of the hills, the Cuvée C from the Coteaux and the Cuvée SC from the best vineyards with later picking and more concentrated grapes. It is not known whether "SC" stands for Super Cuvée, Special Cuvée or Sélection Coteaux, a situation Juge is happy to encourage. In the meantime he continues to make about 15,000 bottles of consistently good wine.

Cornas Cuvée C 1990

Deep, dark color and a typically earthy, rich, dark nose with a note of tar. Splendid palate with rich, well-rounded, fruit flavors and hints of aniseed and chocolate. Velvety texture and good length. A typical Juge wine, smooth and beautifully polished.

Cornas Cuvée C 1989

Dark and deep in appearance with a rich bouquet and very elegant sweet fruit. The palate has rounded, delicate flavors which are well balanced by the other components to give good length, but without the freshness of the 1990.

Cornas Cuvée C 1988

A paler red color which is beginning to evolve. Aromas of sweet cooked fruit are confirmed on the smooth and stylish palate. While the body is not outstanding, this is an elegant wine with remarkable balance and length.

CORNAS
COTES DU RHONE NORTH
FRANCE

372

CORNAS
COTES DU RHONE NORTH
FRANCE

Jean Lionnet

07130 Cornas
Tel. 75403601
Fax 75810062

Lionnets have been making wine at Cornas for about 400 years. The latest in the family line, Jean, produces about 15,000 bottles a year from extremely old Syrah vines on ten hectares of granite soil on the steep slopes which surround the village. He also makes 6,000 bottles of Saint-Péray and a similar quantity of good Syrah Côtes du Rhône from the younger vines and plantings on the lower slopes. Lionnet uses the consultancy services of enologist Jean-Luc Colombo. The winery and cellars are particularly smart for a producer in Cornas. The stainless steel tanks are temperature-controlled and all the wines are fermented and stored at low temperatures. About 60% of the red wine is aged in cask, one fifth new, for the time necessary to achieve the right balance. The other 40% is aged in tank and blended to the wood aged prior to bottling. In good vintages, Lionnet's best wines are sold under the Domaine de Roche Pertuis label and provide eloquent proof of how good Cornas can be.

Saint-Péray 1991   ❦ ②
The wine has a pale, bright color and is fresh and clean on the nose with citrus notes. Light on the palate, where the creamy, fresh fruit is again in evidence. A delicious wine, obtained from 20% Roussanne and 80% Marsanne vines more than 40 years old.

Côtes du Rhône 1991   ❦ ②
Wonderful deep, rich color. Sweet ripe fruit on the nose and the palate, where all the delicately gamey character of Syrah emerges on the finish. Aged half in wood and half in stainless steel, this is an instantly attractive, well-made wine.

Cornas   ❦❦ ③
Domaine de Rochepertuis 1990
Intense, bright color. Still quite closed, although there is already well-defined fruit on the nose. Incredibly concentrated, well-balanced and exceptionally long. The 20% of new oak is unobtrusive thanks to the rich texture of the wine.

Cornas   ❦❦ ③
Domaine de Rochepertuis 1989
Another wine with an intense, deep color. The oak component is very evident but does not obscure the concentration of the wine. A rich, chewy wine with powerful, gamey aromas and outstanding length and complexity. A bottle to lay down for ten years or more.

Robert Michel

Grande-Rue
07130 Cornas
Tel. 75403870
Fax 75405857

Robert Michel produces excellent Cornas from his seven hectares, most of which are located on rocky granite slopes overlooking the village where his deep, cool cellar is to be found. The vines have an average age of 40 years although the grapes that go to make La Geynale, a cuvée obtained from a single vineyard at the top of the slope, are from 70 year-old plants. Two other cuvées are also produced, Le Coteau and Le Pied-de-Coteau, the latter produced from grapes grown on the heavier alluvial soils at the foot of the slopes. Michel uses traditional techniques. After fermentation in cement vats, the wines remain in tank for six months before going into used Vosges casks, bought from friends in Chambolle-Musigny and Mercurey in Burgundy. Robert Michel does not believe in filtration but fines using egg whites. He is a small producer with boundless enthusiasm and travels widely in search of new ideas. Some of the La Geynale 1990 was, for example, aged in an acacia cask.

Cornas Coteau 1990   ❦ ③
Intense, rich color and typical Syrah nose, with a distinct smoky note. The palate has characteristic rich, wild fruit, is of attractive length and is well balanced with aromas of chocolate and raspberry in the finish. Needs five years in bottle to give its best.

Cornas La Geynale 1990   ❦❦ ③
Even richer in color than the Coteau. A little undeveloped on the nose, with a hint of smoky bacon. The palate has complex, succulent, concentrated fruit which lingers on the finish. A dense, slightly rustic wine which a few years in the cellar will bring to a splendid peak.

CORNAS
COTES DU RHONE NORTH
FRANCE

373

CORNAS
COTES DU RHONE NORTH
FRANCE

Domaine Barge

Route de Bauchoney
69420 Ampuis
Tel. 74561390
Fax 74561098

The father-and-son team of Pierre and Gilles
Barge are still working side by side, yet
fiscally they are independent. Their vineyards
are mostly on the Côte Brune. Gilles'
grandfather was the first Barge to bottle
under the family name in 1929 and Gilles
continues to make wine in a traditional style.
At least half his vines are over 40 years old
and planted on the most precipitous
schistous slopes. He uses a little Viognier in
the wine to add a touch of finesse, and
makes it with whole bunches of grapes
vinified for 15 to 20 days in wooden vats.
After malolactic fermentation, the wine ages
in a mixture of vat and barrels for at least two
years. Having tried various clarifying
techniques in the past, Gilles now trusts in
the winter cold, neither fining nor filtering. As
well as making a tiny quantity of Condrieu,
never seen for sale, Gilles will undoubtedly
one day direct his attention to his father's
vines, which are extremely old and rich in
fruit concentration. In the meantime, the
energetic Pierre produces and ages his own
wines with more or less the same methods
as Gilles, although he is perhaps not entirely
in agreement with his son over the use of
Burgundy barrels. Together, they produce
slightly more than 27,000 bottles a year.

Côte Rôtie Gilles Barge 1989   🍇🍇🍇 ③
Intense, full color, with a royal crimson edge.
Attractive nose with ripe fruit to the fore and a
hint of oak. Rich and ripe on the palate, with
good structure and balance and notes of wild
berries. A truly great wine from a stupendous
vintage.

Côte Rôtie Gilles Barge 1988   🍇🍇 ③
Rich, intense color with bitter chocolate and
raspberry on the nose. Fine structure on the
palate, where the flavors of chocolate and
raspberry are again present. Slightly acidic and
tannic, a wine which gives its best if decanted.
Very good length and fresh fruit.

Key to the symbols

Types of Wines

🍇 White

🍇 Rosé

🍇 Red

Rating System

🍇   An exemplary wine of its
type with outstanding local
character

🍇🍇   An international premium
quality wine

🍇🍇🍇   A Top Wine, considered one
of the 150 best wines in the
world

*The 'grape bunch' symbol is used to
indicate the color of the wine; the
number of bunches represents the quality
rating assigned by the contributor*

Price levels

①   up to $ 9.99

② $ 10.00 - $ 14.99

③ $ 15.00 - $ 24.99

④ $ 25.00 or more

*The 'ex-cellar', or direct from the
producer, bottle prices, are calculated in
US dollars and are intended only as an
approximate guide*

**Entries are arranged in
alphabetical order by country,
region and winery or producer
name.**

COTE ROTIE
COTES DU RHONE NORTH
FRANCE

374

COTE ROTIE
COTES DU RHONE NORTH
FRANCE

Bernard Burgaud

Le Champin
69420 Ampuis
Tel. 74561186
Fax 74561303

The young and ruddy-cheeked Bernard Burgaud is perhaps the rising star of the Appellation Côte Rôtie. Until Bernard took over the four hectares of Syrah which belong to the Burgaud family, his father used to sell most of the production in bulk. Bernard began to bottle his Côte Rôtie seriously in 1984 and today he produces 10,000 to 15,000 bottles a year for tables as far away as Australia, Japan and the United States. The winery is directly beneath the family home, high on the hillside up the winding narrow road which leads to the other side of the Côte Brune. Most of the vines are on steep slopes overlooking the town of Ampuis, but he does have vines on the plateau above. The de-stemmed grapes ferment in open vats with the cap plunged down to extract the maximum color from the skins. The best cuvées are then selected for bottling after 15 months aging in casks, 20% of which are new. The rest is sold in bulk to the négociants. It is the process of meticulous selection, as well as hard and intelligent work in the vineyards and winery, that has enabled Bernard to produce a series of excellent vintages of Côte Rôtie, even in mediocre years like 1987.

Côte Rôtie 1990　🍇🍇 ③
Fabulous dark, immensely rich color. The rich, powerful, fairly grassy bouquet brings to mind ripe wild black fruits. Full and fruity on the palate, with aromas of blackcurrant followed by good acidity and length. A hint of liquorice and aniseed in the finish.

Côte Rôtie 1988　🍇🍇 ③
Once again the color is intense and extremely concentrated. The bouquet is warm and beginning to evolve towards the typical aromas of the variety. Closed on the palate but starting to show the gamey character of Syrah. Less powerful and fruity than the 1989 or 1990, it has outstanding elegance and will develop well thanks to good acidity and tannins.

Côte Rôtie 1989　🍇🍇🍇 ③
Yet again, a wine with an exceptionally full, deep, intense color tinged with purple and mauve. The bouquet is sumptuous with a strong suggestion of blackcurrant leaves. Immensely rich on the palate, an irresistibly chewy, ripe wine with all the blackcurrant concentration of ripe Syrah, supported by satisfying acidity and tannins. A full-bodied wine with superb aging potential. The charm of this Côte Rôtie lies in its exceedingly attractive fruit, but its structure is such that it can comfortably be laid down until the beginning of the next century.

COTE ROTIE
COTES DU RHONE NORTH
FRANCE

375

COTE ROTIE
COTES DU RHONE NORTH
FRANCE

Domaine Clusel-Roch

Verenay
69420 Ampuis
Tel. 74561595
Fax 74561974

Just to the north of Ampuis are a cluster of houses known as Verenay. It is here that a young couple, Gilbert Clusel and Brigitte Roch, have established themselves amongst the top flight of Côte Rôtie producers. With almost 3.5 ha in the Côte Rôtie Appellation and half a hectare on the Coteau de Chéry at Condrieu, they produce about 12,500 bottles a year. Gilbert Clusel inherited his land and skills from his father, who produced robust, concentrated wines but never with the style and consistency that Gilbert and Brigitte have recently achieved. The standard cuvée of Côte Rôtie is produced from partially de-stemmed grapes which are fermented for 12-15 days and which then undergo malolactic fermentation and aging for 18 months in oak barrels. There is also a special cuvée made with grapes from vines grown on the steep slopes known as Les Grandes Places. This is aged in 50% new oak and 50% first-year barrels and needs time in the bottle to mellow out. The Condrieu is fermented two thirds in stainless steel and the rest in barrel. Like all wines made from Viognier it tends to be inconsistent but the best vintages produce quite excellent results.

Côte Rôtie 1990 🍷🍷 ③
Attractive, rich and intense color with a peppery, ripe Syrah nose. The palate is very full and round with an outstanding concentration of fruit. This is a very well-made wine with good length and structure.

Côte Rôtie 🍷🍷 ③
Les Grandes Places 1990
Incredibly intense, deep color. The nose is tough, very extracted and closed. It is full-bodied on the palate with the same concentration of black fruits and gamey aromas and wonderful length. A great wine which will need a few years to reach full maturity, but well worth waiting for.

Côte Rôtie 1989 🍷🍷 ③
A perfect Syrah with an exceptionally concentrated color. Still rather undeveloped, it is immensely rich and ripe on the palate, with aromas of succulent fruit and the juice of wild berries. The length is quite staggering. A wine which can be drunk now while the fruit is still at its peak or later when it has evolved and softened.

Marius Gentaz-Dervieux

Ampuis
69420 Condrieu
Tel. 74561083

It has always been difficult to get hold of a bottle of the exquisite Côte Rôtie produced by Marius Gentaz-Dervieux and from now on it will become even harder. He has recently reduced his vineyard to just over 4,000 square meters of his oldest vines in the heart of the Côte Brune. Gentaz is one of the most highly regarded growers in the commune. His very stylish and concentrated traditional wines always contain a modest proportion of highly scented Viognier which is grown, oddly enough, on the heavier soils of his tiny Côte Brune holding. The whole bunches of Syrah are fermented in cement vats with the cap submerged. Maceration lasts from 18 to 21 days. Gentaz detests new wood and uses a battery of ancient barrels to age his wines for an average of 18 months. True wine-lovers are already lamenting the day when one of the Appellation's legends will finally give it all up.

Côte Rôtie Côte Brune 1989 🍷🍷 ③
Dark ruby color tinged with violet. Much leaner on the nose than the 1988 but still gamey with unmistakable notes of chocolate and smokey bacon. The palate is well structured making the wine less approachable at this stage. Flavors of bitter chocolate and black cherries emerge in the finish.

Côte Rôtie Côte Brune 1988 🍷🍷 ③
Very opaque ruby color. The bouquet has a powerful overtone of smokey bacon which slightly veils the notes of raspberry and spice. Velvety, fresh and juicy on the palate, this wine melts in the mouth. The big structure promises well for the future making this a potentially long-lived Côte Rôtie.

COTE ROTIE
COTES DU RHONE NORTH
FRANCE

376

COTE ROTIE
COTES DU RHONE NORTH
FRANCE

Gérin

Rue de Montmain - Verenay
69420 Ampuis
Tel. 74561556

Jean-Michel Gérin's family are not
newcomers to the Côte Rôtie Appellation as
there have been Gérins in Ampuis for five
generations. Jean-Michel's father was a
senator and mayor of the town and created
something of a sensation in the 1970s when
he sold part of his estate to American
investors. Today Jean-Michel Gérin and his
wife Monique have broken away from the old
Domaine Gérin, which is now owned by a the
famous Beaujolais négociant Georges
Duboeuf and the Michelin three star chef
Georges Blanc. Jean-Michel and Monique
produced their first wine in 1987, but only
since 1990 have they had their own
company. They own about eight hectares of
vines mostly on the steep slopes of Ampuis
which are used for the Côte Rôtie. Included
in the total are just under two hectares of
Viognier on the Coteau de la Loye in
Condrieu and some Syrah vines that make a
generic Côtes du Rhône. One hectare of their
Côte Rôtie vines is located on the
south/south-east facing vineyard known as
Les Grandes Places. They make a special
cuvée from this parcel which is planted with
95% Syrah and 5% Viognier. The Gérins look
set to play an important part in the small
group of young Côte Rôtie growers who are
determined to develop this great Appellation.

Côte Rôtie
Les Grandes Places 1989
Unusually intense, dark deep color.
Concentrated and powerful on the nose, with
the oak aromas nicely integrated. On the palate
there is good structure, vigorous and dense, but
also rich in fruit. The 20 months of new oak
aging is evident.

COTE ROTIE
COTES DU RHONE NORTH
FRANCE

377

COTE ROTIE
COTES DU RHONE NORTH
FRANCE

Etienne Guigal

69420 Ampuis
Tel. 74561022
Fax 74561876

No one has done more for an Appellation, or indeed for an entire winemaking region, than Marcel Guigal. When his father Etienne left Vidal Fleury in 1946, where he had been cellarmaster for 22 years, no one imagined the incredible impact that this family would have on the world of wine. Etienne laid down the company guidelines and Marcel has achieved an almost unparalleled success for the name Guigal, developing the great single vineyard wines. La Mouline was first produced in 1966, La Landonne was created in 1978 and the latest arrival, La Turque, was introduced in 1985. Through intelligent winemaking and a sophisticated use of oak barrels, Marcel Guigal has developed such a highly individual style that even his detractors admit that he has achieved a quality admired by wine lovers the world over. Today the Guigals produce around 200,000 bottles of wine from grapes grown in their own Côte Rôtie vineyards and from purchased grapes and wines. Their range includes an outstanding Condrieu from Viognier grapes, red and white Hermitage, Châteauneuf-du-Pape, Gigondas, a rather old-fashioned Tavel Rosé, generic white and red Côtes du Rhône and, of course, the Côte Rôties.

Gigondas 1989 ♥♥ ②
Dark color and a very spicy bouquet of ripe fruit. The palate has plenty of ripe fruit with a cigar-box flavor and good length and balance. The use of 33% Mourvèdre shows in the structure. An excellent example of Gigondas.

Côte Rôtie Brune et Blonde 1988 ♥♥ ③
A rich Syrah-deep red color. The bouquet is powerful but stylish, laced with elegant traces of oak. Liquorice is evident on the palate together with well-integrated oak. The fruit is full and ripe and the wine has great depth of aroma and length.

Côte Rôtie La Landonne 1988 ♥♥ ④
Extraordinarily intense, rich and complex color. The bouquet has a powerful gamey, meaty note over a background of rich fruit. Great depth of flavor on the palate with powerful fruit and an even more imposing structure than either La Mouline or La Turque. A big wine to lay down and forget about for 10-15 years.

Côte Rôtie La Turque 1988 ♥♥ ④
Once again, the color is stunning. The rich bouquet has aromas of black berries and sweet liquorice. Enormous concentration of ripe fruit on the palate, but without the full-bodied sweetness of La Mouline or the structure of La Landonne. A very dense wine which buries the aromas of new wood in the depth of its structure. Quite exceptional, particularly when one remembers that the vines were only planted in 1981.

Côte Rôtie La Mouline 1988 ♥♥♥ ④
Rich, deep, intense color with a sweet nose of rich, ripe Syrah tempered by an extra roudness contributed by the 10% Viognier used in this wine. A truly complete wine on the palate with a series of sweet, sensuous aromas combined with the full, ripe, intense flavors of the fruit. A wine of impressive length and an elegance to which the Viognier seems to bring an extra dimension. Despite having spent more than 30 months in new oak, the wood is well integrated. It is one of the world's great wines which adds rare elegance to a beautifully balanced range of flavors. It may be drunk young to savor all the velvety softness of the fruit or aged in the bottle until it has evolved the rich leathery character of a mature La Mouline.

COTE ROTIE
COTES DU RHONE NORTH
FRANCE

378

COTE ROTIE
COTES DU RHONE NORTH
FRANCE

Domaine Jamet

Le Vallin
69420 Ampuis
Tel. 74561257

The Jamets live on the plateau a few kilometers behind the vineyards that overlook Ampuis. Joseph Jamet managed the estate for many years but recently his sons Jean-Luc and Jean-Paul have taken over the original four hectares and are extending the property, building a new cellar to cope with the increased production. The original vine stock is almost entirely Syrah with just 1% Viognier and is located on good sites along the slopes of Ampuis. Following the harvest, the grapes are gently crushed before they ferment for 15 days at controlled temperatures in stainless steel vats. The wine is then aged in Allier oak barrels, but the Jamets, whose modern approach to winemaking never excludes tradition, use only a small percentage of new wood. Bottling takes place 20 months later and the resulting wines are powerful and fruity with smokey, ripe strawberry and violet aromas. At present, 20,000 bottles a year are produced but the new vineyards will considerably increase this figure, making this estate's stunning Côte Rôtie more available.

Côte Rôtie 1989   🍇🍇 ③
Very dark, shading to purple round the edges, a wine with a concentrated bouquet with notes of raspberry fruit and smokey oak. Again very concentrated on the palate with elegant, powerful tannins, raspberry fruit concentration, good acidity and excellent structure and length.

Côte Rôtie 1988   🍇🍇 ③
Purple-red color with a rich bouquet which seems more complex than the powerful 1989. Abundant aromas of game, leather, raspberry and spices. Layers of mouthfilling, sweet berry flavors on the palate which combine with spicy, smokey, gamey notes. Velvety-rich, stylish texture and a voluptuously long finish.

René Rostaing

Le Port
69420 Ampuis
Tel. 74561200
Fax 74566256

René Rostaing is a particularly serious manager who began producing Côte Rôtie from only two hectares. Today, having acquired family vineyards from Albert Dervieux and Marius Gentaz-Dervieux, he owns six hectares with vines of around 50 years old. This includes some Viognier and a parcel of Syrah on La Landonne, although this wine has no connection with the Guigal single-vineyard wine. Rostaing is a careful winemaker who uses traditional methods, many no doubt learned from his father-in-law Albert Dervieux. He ferments in open cement vats and allows a long maceration to obtain maximum concentration. He adds a little of the "vin de presse" to the wine. Rostaing ages his wines for two to three years in Allier oak barrels of various sizes. There is no filtration or fining, the wine is merely racked three times. The reds Rostaing obtains are powerful with particularly good structure and benefit from a little new oak. Perhaps the best of all Rostaing's wines is the Côte Blonde. With a sizeable holding in these famous vineyards he must be a contented man. He exports much of his wine.

Côte Rôtie Côte Blonde 1990   🍇🍇 ③
Intense purple color and a very concentrated bouquet with an abundance of toasty, ripe black-cherry jam aromas. Dense and deep on the palate, this wine has a velvety softness and an almost unctuous fruit which lingers at length in the mouth. A wine of great style.

COTE ROTIE
COTES DU RHONE NORTH
FRANCE

379

COTE ROTIE
COTES DU RHONE NORTH
FRANCE

J. Vidal-Fleury

69420 Ampuis
Tel. 74561018
Fax 74561919

Vidal-Fleury is one of the legendary names of the Rhône Valley, but its recent history demonstrates just how precarious the future for the northern Rhône can be as the wines become popular and commercially exploited. Joseph Vidal-Fleury died in 1976 and since no one could be found to replace him, the estate was sold in 1985 to Marcel Guigal, the extraordinary winemaker whose father learned his skills at Vidal-Fleury in the 1940s. The Guigals are keen to keep the two businesses apart, although 1985 saw the first vintage of Côte Rôtie La Turque (E.Guigal), made from one of Vidal-Fleury's prime parcels of vines in the heart of the Côte Brune. Today Monsieur Rochias manages the property and although Guigal's winemaking techniques have been introduced and many of the vineyards produce excellent grapes, the wines are not what they once were. It would be unfair to say the wines are not good, but one thing is certain: this great house has yet to achieve its full potential.

Côte Rôtie La Chatillonne 1988 🍇 ③
Dark purple color with tinges of violet. The bouquet is very mature with notes of leather and blackcurrant, which dominate the palate where elegant tannins are also evident. This wine, obtained entirely from the Côte Blonde, is stupendous now but will unfortunately rapidly lose its attraction.

Saint-Joseph 1989 🍇 ②
Good rich, deep color. Marked peppery bouquet which is rich and a little warm but with good Syrah character. Slightly overpowering on the palate and lacks a little freshness, although it possesses all the character it needs to evolve in the bottle over the next year or more.

Vacqueyras 1989 🍇 ②
Intense color and a warm, fruity bouquet which bears the hallmark of spicy, sunny Grenache. Complex on the palate with the warm, spicy fruit of a Mediterranean wine. It has good length and balance.

Cave des Clairmonts

Beaumont-Monteux
26600 Tain l'Hermitage
Tel. 75846191
Fax 75845698

This winery groups six different families and is in effect a mini cave cooperative. Established in 1972, it produced its first wine in 1973 and now releases about 100,000 bottles of red Crozes-Hermitage and 15,000 of white Crozes-Hermitage every year. This is by no means the total production for the estate comprises over 90 ha of Appellation Contrôlée vineyards and a little over eight hectares of vines which produce Vin de Pays de la Drome. The estate sells a large volume of wine in bulk to merchants and serves a large private clientele which buys both bottled and unbottled wines. The winery itself is in a large building with Cave des Clairmonts printed in massive letters above the entrance; it is well-equipped and highly functional, although it would be difficult to describe it as pleasing to the eye. Jean-Michel Borja and his wife Sylviane, who run the cellar with an eye to quality, comprise one of the families who own a share of the business. The red Crozes-Hermitage is their best wine and although it may not be the quality of a Graillot or a Pochon, there are very few wines in the Rhône Valley today that can match it for value.

Crozes-Hermitage 🍇 ①
Cave des Clairmonts 1989
Intense, dark red color with good depth. Full-bodied and sweet on the nose with black fruit aromas. The palate has a fruity blackberry concentration. A very well-made and well-balanced wine which shows off all the style of Syrah in a warm year.

COTE ROTIE
COTES DU RHONE NORTH
FRANCE

380

CROZES-HERMITAGE
COTES DU RHONE NORTH
FRANCE

Domaine des Entrefaux

GAEC de la Syrah - Chanos-Curson
26600 Tain l'Hermitage
Tel. 75073338
Fax 75073527

Charles Tardy and Bernard Ange are brothers-in-law who left the Tain Cooperative in 1979 to merge their respective estates. Today, with their wives and Charles' son François, who joined the estate in 1990, they produce 1,000 hl of red Crozes-Hermitage and 200 hl of white. The 25 ha of vineyards are planted 80% with Syrah and 20% with Marsanne and Roussanne, and are located half on clay and chalk and half on alluvial soils. The wines are vinified in the traditional manner in impeccable cellars. Temperatures are controlled and the wine is pumped over the cap twice a day. Alcoholic fermentation takes two weeks and once malolactic fermentation is completed, the wines are racked and fined with egg whites. The wines are then aged partly in oak barrels and partly in stainless steel vats. The wines are generally bottled in March after aging for 12 months. The reds are usually amongst the best in the Appellation with the characteristic fruit and spice of Syrah, and the whites are fresh and fruity.

Crozes-Hermitage 1991
Very clear, pale color. Dry, flowery, walnut bouquet of great finesse. An extremely drinkable wine, perhaps a little lacking in length but clean-tasting with the typical walnut aromas of Marsanne. Drink young.

Crozes-Hermitage 1991
Very dark with purple and mauve tinges. The bouquet is redolent of wild black berries, typical of succulent, fresh, ripe Syrah. Wild berries are again in evidence on the palate. A wine whose modesty of structure makes it eminently drinkable.

Crozes-Hermitage 1990
Red color of attractive intensity. The bouquet is richer than that of the 1991 and characterized by the moderately peppery and spicy aroma of Syrah. The palate is slightly closed at the moment but has the same Syrah character, with meaty flavors and a long finish.

Alain Graillot

Les Chênes Verts
26600 Pont-de-l'Isère
Tel. 75071793
Fax 75072431

In 1985 Alain Graillot gave up his job as marketing manager with a large pharmaceutical company to settle in Tain l'Hermitage. A few weeks before the harvest, he rented some cellars and bought some grape and with the help of his friend Jacques Seysses (of Domaine Dujac in Morey-Saint-Denis in Burgundy) and a young Australian winemaker, he produced his first wine. Encouraged by his instant success, Alain bought a cellar and vineyards and has become one of the best-known growers in the Appellation Crozes-Hermitage. His domaine now consists of 18 ha of vineyards with an average age of 20 years on alluvial gravel and sand planted to Syrah, with the exception of half a hectare of Roussanne and two hectares of Marsanne. The grapes are hand-picked and not de-stemmed and are vinified in a traditional fashion. There is a long fermentation and the must is frequently pumped over the must. Aging generally takes a year and is carried out partly in cement vats and at least 50% in one to four year-old oak barrels. White wines are vinified at controlled temperatures. Alain Graillot also produces a small quantity of red Saint-Joseph from two hectares of vineyard, and Hermitage from a small parcel of vines located on the Les Greffieux part of the hill.

Crozes-Hermitage 1990
Extraordinarily intense color. The bouquet is redolent of game and rich, ripe fruit. Very well made, clean and fresh. The palate is pure Syrah with typical peppery aromas. Well-rounded, with good balance despite the tannins. A great wine and very, very drinkable.

Crozes-Hermitage
La Guiraude 1988
The rich, dark color is still very young. The bouquet brings to mind wild fruit and pepper, with notes of ripe blackcurrant and mint. Rich fruit also on the palate, where the wine is still firm with a hardish finish. Rather more austere than the normal cuvée, lacking the explosive aroma of the Syrah variety.

CROZES-HERMITAGE
COTES DU RHONE NORTH
FRANCE

381

CROZES-HERMITAGE
COTES DU RHONE NORTH
FRANCE

Domaine du Pavillon

Les Chassis - Mercurol
26600 Tain l'Hermitage
Tel. 75082447
Fax 75082447

Stephane Cornu was one of the winemakers at Jaboulet, but in 1990 he decided to make use of the family vineyard and created the Domaine du Pavillon. Cornu's first wine was a 1989 red Crozes-Hermitage, which he bought and aged in new oak barrels before bottling in Bordeaux-shaped bottles. Since then, Domaine du Pavillon has been made with machine-picked Syrah grapes which Cornu grows on the family's nine-hectare property. The vines, with their average age of 18 years, do not yield more than 40 hl/ha. Cornu ferments the whole bunches in cement vats and allows a three week maceration to produce color and extract. As was the case with the 1989, successive vintages have been aged in new Allier oak for three to four months. The style is full and rich and somewhat oaky. In the short history of the domaine, Cornu has created a truly individual Crozes-Hermitage.

Crozes-Hermitage 1990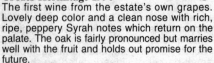
The first wine from the estate's own grapes. Lovely deep color and a clean nose with rich, ripe, peppery Syrah notes which return on the palate. The oak is fairly pronounced but marries well with the fruit and holds out promise for the future.

Étienne Pochon

Château Curson
26600 Chanos Curson
Tel. 75073460
Fax 75073027

The name Pochon is not new to the Crozes-Hermitage region since Etienne's grandfather was one of the first members of the Tain l'Hermitage Cooperative. In 1983, having finished his studies, Etienne took over the running of part of the family estate and in 1987 he left the Cooperative to found Château Curson. He made his first wines in 1988 and today produces about 36,000 bottles of red Crozes-Hermitage and 9,000 bottles of white. There are 12 ha of vineyards of which 3.5 are planted to Marsanne and Roussanne with the rest in Syrah. The principal wine is sold under the Château Curson label. Grapes are 100% de-stemmed. The white grapes, where possible, remain on the skins for four to eight hours before fermentation which takes place at low temperatures in stainless steel vats and oak barrels. The wine then ages until February on fine lees, when the vats and barrels are blended. Bottling takes place in April. The red wines ferment in stainless steel at relatively high temperatures and the wine is then aged in barrel for 15 months. A second label, Domaine Pochon, offers red and white wines of a different style which are slightly less complex than the Château wines but no less well-made and good value.

Crozes-Hermitage
Château Curson 1991
Very clear color with lemon-yellow tinges. The nose is rich and lingering. Rich, elegant fruit on the palate with good length. The oak is well integrated and the finish has fresh acidity. 20% Roussanne adds an element of complexity to the wine.

Crozes-Hermitage
Domaine Pochon 1991
Clear, moderately rich color. Clean, fresh and complex bouquet. The palate is forthcoming with good balance. Still needs to age for a few months,but undoubtedly has excellent potential.

Crozes-Hermitage
Château Curson 1990
Attractively intense color. Rich, ripe fruit on the nose with a hint of vanilla from the wood. Very concentrated fruit flavors on the palate with splendid length. A very good wine with a different style from the Domaine, perhaps a little less fresh, but superior in complexity and enhanced by the oak.

Crozes-Hermitage
Domaine Pochon 1990
Very correct, intense, dark color, with peach and plum jam on the nose. The palate has the superb flavor of fresh, dark Syrah fruit. Pleasantly long, this is a juicy, full-bodied wine with excellent balance. A very successful example of Crozes at its best.

CROZES-HERMITAGE
COTES DU RHONE NORTH
FRANCE

382

CROZES-HERMITAGE
COTES DU RHONE NORTH
FRANCE

Michel Chapoutier

18, avenue du Dr. Paul Durand
26600 Tain l'Hermitage
Tel. 75082865
Fax 75088170

Chapoutier is the oldest family firm in Tain l'Hermitage. Active since 1808, the last three generations have been headed by Marius, Marc and Max, and today it is Marius' great-grandson, Michel, who manages the company. Chapoutier is also one of the largest producers in the Rhône with a huge range of owned and rented vineyards which extend from Côte Rôtie, Saint-Joseph, Hermitage and Crozes-Hermitage in the north, to Châteauneuf-du-Pape in the south. Vinification is traditional with the Syrah grapes being de-stemmed and fermented in closed wooden vats for two to three weeks. The wines then age in barrels for 18 months and are regularly racked, but neither filtered nor fined. The white wines are made from Marsanne grapes which are crushed and settled for 24 hours before being fermented in temperature-controlled vats and wooden barrels. The wines are subsequently blended then aged in wood until they are considered ready for bottling. Michel Chapoutier has now called upon the services of local enologist Jean-Luc Colombo and in recent vintages the wines have shown a marked improvement in quality.

Hermitage Chante Alouette 1990   ♈ ④
Rich, bright color with a long, intense nutty nose. The palate is buttery, well-rounded, big and again long. A fairly typical wine of this style with low acidity and excellent body.

Hermitage La Sizeranne 1990   ♈♈ ④
Deep color and intensely concentrated bouquet of black berries. Rich on the palate with attractively ripe, dense, sweet Syrah fruit - almost "primeur" in style. A well-made wine with good structure.

Côtes du Rhône Appellations in this Guide

North
Château-Grillet
Condrieu
Cornas
Côte Rôtie
Crozes-Hermitage
Hermitage
Saint-Joseph
Saint-Péray

South
Châteauneuf-du-Pape
Coteaux du Tricastin
Côtes du Lubéron
Côtes du Rhône
Côtes du Rhône-Villages
Gigondas
Muscat de Beaumes-de-Venise
Tavel
Vacqueyras

HERMITAGE
COTES DU RHONE NORTH
FRANCE

383

HERMITAGE
COTES DU RHONE NORTH
FRANCE

Domaine Jean-Louis Chave

37, Avenue de Saint-Joseph
07300 Mauves
Tel. 75082463
Fax 75071421

Few great wineries are as well-camouflaged behind such a modest façade as this one, located on the busy road that runs through the Rhône Valley. Gérard Chave is not an easy man to visit simply because he has no wine left to sell. His production is regularly reserved in advance by a faithful clientele of export clients, Michelin-starred restaurants and private customers. The Chave family is one of the oldest winemaking families in the Rhône with a history dating back to the 15th century. Today, Gérard Chave is one of the largest landowners on the hill of Hermitage with 15 ha planted two-thirds with Syrah and the rest with Marsanne and Roussanne. Vinification faithfully follows tradition. Fermentation is in open vats and the grape cap is plunged down twice a day. Aging, which lasts 18 months, is in barrels of varying size. The different parcels of grapes are vinified separately and a crucial date in the Chave calendar is the final blending day. The Hermitage white is fermented in stainless steel tanks and in barrels, then aged in oak barrels and 15 hl oak vats for 18 months. Chave also produces minuscule quantities of a delightful red Saint-Joseph and a "vin de paille" which was once thought to be the classic style for a white Hermitage.

Hermitage 1990
Lovely bright, clear, lemon-yellow color. The immensely rich nose is nutty with plenty of creamy fruit. The palate is rich, nutty and well-balanced. A deliciously full-flavored wine from Marsanne grapes with 15% Roussanne.

Saint-Joseph 1990 ②
Attractively bright, intense red with a hint of purple and rich, concentrated ripe Syrah nose. Stylish fruit dominates the palate, which has outstanding balance. Truly exquisite.

Hermitage 1989 ④
Dark color, but without the concentration of the 1990. Rich, ripe fruit on the nose, with notes of candied peel. Ripe fruit again on the palate which is starting to close up and is hard on the finish.

Hermitage 1988 ④
Superb deep, rich color. Inviting, elegant bouquet in the Syrah style, with mineral notes. Juicy, rich fruit on the palate with attractive length and great structure. A wine to drink after the 1989 while waiting for the 1990.

Hermitage 1990 ④
Rich and complex with a magical concentration of fruit and a stupendous, outstandingly deep color. The palate is striking in its density of flavors with a structure which despite the volume of the wine leaves a lasting impression of finesse. This is an extraordinary Hermitage of exceptional complexity, but by no means lacking in elegance. A wine to lay down until the temptation to taste it becomes too strong to resist. Only 35,000 bottles of this superb red wine, which will continue to improve for many years, were produced. It is the embodiment of Gérard Chave's winemaking skills, which over the last few years have reached top form. Today, he consistently makes some of the finest wines in all of France.

HERMITAGE
COTES DU RHONE NORTH
FRANCE

384

HERMITAGE
COTES DU RHONE NORTH
FRANCE

Maison Delas Frères

Saint-Jean-de-Muzols
07300 Tournon-sur-Rhône
Tel. 75086030
Fax 75085367

The purchase of Delas by Champagne Deutz in 1977 seems to have put a little metaphorical fizz back into the wines. The reds in particular are less heavy than they once were and today are honest, if a little technical. The house of Delas produces large quantities of ordinary Southern Rhône wines, but their best wines from Cornas, Hermitage, Côte Rôtie and Condrieu are a more serious proposition. In the cellar at Saint-Jean-de-Muzols, winemaker Antoine Fuchs employs up-to-date techniques to make both white and red wines. The latter, partially de-stemmed, ferment at controlled temperatures for about 15 days and age for 12-16 months in wood. They are fined with egg whites. The red Hermitage La Marquise de la Tourette comes from five hectares of vines in Les Bessards and four in l'Hermite, two of the best sites on the hill. The estate vineyards also provide the Marsanne and Roussanne grapes for a Hermitage white. Delas have one and a half hectares in Cornas, from which they produce the Chante Perdrix, and four hectares on the Côte Brune for their Côte Rôtie Seigneur de Maugiron. The 40,000 bottles of La Marquise de la Tourette produced annually are especially noteworthy, but all the Delas wines have character and finesse.

Hermitage ♥ ④
Marquise de la Tourette 1988
Dark, rich color and fruity nose typical of ripe Syrah, with earthy, mushroomy aromas. Rich and fruity once again on the palate, which is well-rounded and fresh with good structure and balance. A well-made wine which, though not a giant, will be a thoroughly satisfying bottle in a few years time.

Paul Jaboulet Aîné

26600 Tain l'Hermitage
Tel. 75846893
Fax 75845614

In the 1980s, the old traditional family firm of Paul Jaboulet Aîné moved its cellars from Tain l'Hermitage to a more modern installation at La Roche Glun. Together with Guigal and Chapoutier, this 1834 estate is probably the best-known in the whole Rhône Valley. The vineyards and winery are presently managed by Philippe Jaboulet, while the outgoing Gérard looks after sales. The company owns 25 ha of vines in Hermitage and 45 in Crozes-Hermitage. They produce a range of wines from the Rhône Valley including a good-quality Vacqueyras and Muscat de Beaumes-de-Venise, but it is above all the red Hermitage La Chapelle and Crozes-Hermitage Domaine de Thalabert which have made the Jaboulet name. The estate also produces a white Hermitage, Le Chevalier de Sterimberg, and a white Crozes-Hermitage, Mule Blanche, both from Marsanne and Roussanne grapes, which are clean and well-made but a little lacking in personality. The Crozes-Hermitage Domaine de Thalabert is a stylish wine and the La Chapelle may be counted among the great Hermitage wines (the 1961 is legendary) although opinion on current examples is divided.

Crozes-Hermitage ♥ ♥ ②
Domaine de Thalabert 1988
Very rich, dark red color with a bouquet of sweet raspberry jam, spices and game. The palate is ripe and rich with a good tannic structure to go with the spicy Syrah fruit.

Hermitage La Chapelle 1988 ♥ ④
Opaque, dark, ruby color. The spice and chocolate notes on the nose are matched by a slightly stalky character. The palate is very full-bodied and mature with sweet, spicy fruit and a long, warm finish.

HERMITAGE
COTES DU RHONE NORTH
FRANCE

385

HERMITAGE
COTES DU RHONE NORTH
FRANCE

Marc Sorrel

26600 Tain l'Hermitage
Tel. 75071007
Fax 75087588

Marc Sorrel studied engineering and only became involved in the family vineyard in 1983 when the health of his legendary father Henri began to fail. Marc is now one of Hermitage's leading producers with just under three hectares of his own vines and another three and a half hectares rented. He also rents parcels of Marsanne and Roussanne in Crozes-Hermitage on the white clay soils of Bouvate and Les Reines. Since 1985 Sorrel has produced the remarkable red Le Gréal, a blend of the best wines from his Le Méal and Les Greffieux vineyards. The remaining Syrah grapes go into the "regular" Hermitage. The whole bunches are fermented for about 15 days and after malolactic fermentation the wine goes into second-hand Meursault barrels. Le Gréal ages for two years and the Hermitage for 18 months. Neither wine is filtered or fined. The excellent single vineyard white Hermitage Les Rocoules is produced from 90% Marsanne with a little Roussanne to add finesse. Vinification takes place initially in barrels from Meursault and the wine is then transferred to tank for the malolactic and then back into casks to age for six to nine months. All Sorrel wines are in great demand, particularly from the British market.

Hermitage Le Gréal 1989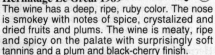
The wine has a deep, ripe, ruby color. The nose is smokey with notes of spice, crystalized and dried fruits and plums. The wine is meaty, ripe and spicy on the palate with surprisingly soft tannins and a plum and black-cherry finish.

Domaine du Chêne

Le Pecher
42410 Chavanay
Tel. 74872734
Fax 74870270

Domaine du Chêne was founded in 1985 by Marc and Dominique Rouvière and today comprises nine hectares of vines on the best slopes in Condrieu as well as vines in Saint-Joseph near Chavanay, at the northern edge of the Appellation. The Rouvières have a pragmatic but carefully thought-out approach and have no qualms about using new wood and modern technology. In addition to aging their dry Condrieu in new oak casks for several months, they also produce a "vendange tardive" Condrieu, the Cuvée Julien, made from selected grapes and vinified at low temperature in stainless steel tanks. The white Saint-Joseph, made from Marsanne, is also fermented at low temperatures and aged in new oak casks for several months. The style is fresh, zesty and a little resinous. There are also two cuvées of red Saint-Joseph made from four hectares of Syrah, the normal cuvée and the Cuvée Anaïs. The latter is produced from the grapes of old vines and slowly macerated before aging in oak casks for a year. All the Rouvière wines, especially the red Saint-Joseph, have won awards and the future looks bright for this young domaine.

Saint-Joseph Cuvée Anaïs 1990
A modern-style red, very clean but also with very full-bodied fruit. Very intense color and a bouquet of pure exotic Syrah. The palate is very agreeable, with good concentration. The flavor is slightly herbaceous, but with a well-rounded and velvety finish. A really delicious Saint-Joseph.

HERMITAGE
COTES DU RHONE NORTH
FRANCE

386

SAINT-JOSEPH
COTES DU RHONE NORTH
FRANCE

Laurent Courbis

07130 Châteaubourg
Tel. 75403212
Fax 75402539

Laurent Courbis has only recently taken over this property from his father Maurice, an unforgettable figure with his beret, flashy sunglasses and Gitanes cigarette perennially hanging from his lips, who was also mayor of Châteaubourg. Laurent has modernized the cellars, but his Saint-Joseph and small quantity of Cornas are still made traditionally. The domaine extends over 13 ha, four of which are planted with 95% Marsanne and a little Roussanne. The remainder is, of course, Syrah, planted on a mixture of limestone, clay and sandy granite soils at the southern edge of the extended Saint-Joseph Appellation. Less than two hectares are in Cornas. All the grapes ferment in temperature-controlled stainless steel tanks. The Syrah from the Saint-Joseph vineyards macerates for 15 days, while the Cornas requires a week longer. All the red wines age in wooden vats for about 18 months. The white is kept in tank until the spring following the harvest, when it is bottled. Courbis' overall production is limited: 50,000 bottles of red Saint-Joseph , 20,000 bottles of white Saint-Joseph and 8,500 bottles of Cornas, most of which is sold locally.

Saint-Joseph 1990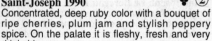
Concentrated, deep ruby color with a bouquet of ripe cherries, plum jam and stylish peppery spice. On the palate it is fleshy, fresh and very drinkable.

Pierre Coursodon

Place du Marché
07300 Mauves
Tel. 75081829
Fax 75087572

Pierre Coursodon is the fourth generation to work the family vineyards in Saint-Joseph. The domaine consists of ten hectares mostly planted to Syrah with an additional 1.5 ha of Marsanne. The vineyards are located on steep terraces of shale and granite soil facing south and south-east. Vinification is traditional, the Syrah being fermented in open oak vats for up to three weeks and then left to age in oak barrels of various shapes and sizes for about 18 months. Small quantities of two red wines are also produced from very old vines. These are Paradis Saint-Pierre and l'Olivaie which, while interesting, often lack the explosive fruit typical of Syrah which one finds in the generic cuvées. For white wines, the must is settled for 12 hours after crushing and then ferments at 18-20°C. It is bottled after malolactic fermentation to preserve the freshness of the fruit. There is also a small quantity of white wine fermented in oak and bottled slightly later.

Saint-Joseph 1990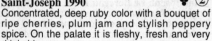
A typical Syrah with intense color and sweet, rich bouquet which is characterized by notes of wild black fruit. The palate is full-flavored and well-rounded, juicy and with good depth. A great example of a concentrated Mauves Saint-Joseph with its wild fruit character.

SAINT-JOSEPH
COTES DU RHONE NORTH
FRANCE

387

SAINT-JOSEPH
COTES DU RHONE NORTH
FRANCE

Pierre Gaillard

Chez Favier
42520 Malleval
Tel. 74871310
Fax 74871766

"Gaillard" in French means a strapping young man, a description which suits the 37 year-old Pierre Gaillard. He lives up on the hills overlooking the Rhône river above Chavanay and enjoys an excellent reputation for his red and white Saint-Joseph. He produces these from Syrah, Marsanne and Roussanne planted on precipitous granite slopes in the north of this large Appellation. Gaillard acquired his nine hectares over the last ten years, having previously worked for Vidal-Fleury and Guigal. As apprenticeships go, few can be better. One of the advantages of only having recently started the business is that the Gaillard cellars are better equipped than most in the area. White grapes remain on the skins for ten hours before fermentation (20% in new oak barrels). The wines then age for six months on lees, are stirred regularly, and undergo malolactic fermentation. Reds ferment in open vats with regular "pigeage" before being aged in Allier and Nièvre oak barrels for a year. As well as Saint-Joseph, Gaillard also produces a Côte Rôtie and a 100% Viognier Côtes du Rhône made in the same way as the white Saint-Joseph.

Côte Rôtie 1990　🍇 ③
Very rich in appearance with an attractive bouquet. Agreeably well-rounded on the palate, full of stylish fruit aromas. Good balance and although lacking the complexity of a great Côte Rôtie, this is a classy and very drinkable wine.

Saint-Joseph 1990　🍇🍇 ②
A good rich Syrah color with a bouquet characterized by wild black-fruit and blackcurrant concentration. Very fresh and lively on the palate with aromas of robust Syrah fruits, good structure and a hint of pepperiness. The finish is very clean and lingering in this exemplary Saint-Joseph.

Bernard Gripa

5, avenue Ozier
07300 Mauves
Tel. 75081496
Fax 75070691

Bernard Gripa is the grandson of one of three brothers whose surnames are all spelled differently due to a clerical error on their birth certificates. Bernard makes Saint-Joseph with grapes from his well-sited six-hectare domaine above Mauves. Two-thirds of the production is from Syrah vines and one-third Marsanne. The average age of the vines is 35 years, and in the case of the parcel called Le Berceau this rises to 65 years. The slope is so steep that a sledge and pulleys are used to transport the grapes down from the vineyard. White grapes are fermented for two to three weeks in temperature-controlled stainless steel vats. The wine is filtered and fined before bottling in the spring. Whole bunches of red grapes go into huge wooden vats and during fermentation the cap is submerged by punching down with a wooden baton. In some vintages, free-run juice is blended with the second pressing and the wine then ages for a year in barrels, some of which are new. Red wines are also filtered and fined before bottling. Bernard Gripa also produces a still white wine from the grapes of his one-hectare vineyard of Marsanne and Roussanne at Saint-Péray.

Saint-Joseph Le Berceau 1990　🍇🍇 ②
Bright intense purple color with plenty of extract. The bouquet is intense and concentrated with aromas of ripe blackcurrants and redcurrants with a hint of caramel and game. The palate is sweet and fleshy with a creamy texture. The finish is long with a lingering aroma of wild berries.

SAINT-JOSEPH
COTES DU RHONE NORTH
FRANCE

388

SAINT-JOSEPH
COTES DU RHONE NORTH
FRANCE

Domaine Jean-Louis Grippat

La Sauva
07300 Tournon-sur-Rhône
Tel. 75081551

The Grippat family originally hails from Saint-Péray, and Jean-Louis Grippat still has winemaking cousins there and in Mauves (see Bernard Gripa) down the road from Tournon. The Grippats have only recently built a new cellar which is spacious without being showy. Here the red wines are vinified in the traditional manner in open oak vats and the grape cap is plunged down twice a day. The white wines are fermented at low temperatures in stainless steel. The Grippats continue to use their old cellars to age part of the red wine production in oak for 12 to 16 months. Jean-Louis has recently been joined by his daughter Sylvie and together they produce about 20,000 bottles of red and 8,000 bottles of white Saint-Joseph, as well as 1,500 of red Hermitage and 4,000 of white Hermitage. Both reds are produced from pure Syrah while the whites are made from Marsanne. Jean-Louis has 6.5 ha in Saint-Joseph and 1.5 ha in Hermitage at Les Murets, traditionally an area for white wine. This perhaps helps to explain why Jean-Louis, a modest but highly professional winemaker, makes such elegant wines.

Hermitage 1990   🍷 🍷 ③
A bright wine with a slightly fuller color than the Saint-Joseph. The bouquet is clean and concentrated and the palate rich and vigorous and at the same time well-rounded and clean with aromas of nuts and peach stone. The finish is long with excellent freshness.

Saint-Joseph 1990   🍷 🍷 ②
Bright, pale yellow color. The bouquet of elegant fruit is fresh and clean. The impact on the palate has good freshness, a lot of fruit and excellent balance. All the characteristics of an exceedingly well-made wine.

Hermitage 1990   🍇 🍇 ②
Lovely deep, rich color. The nose is rich, soft but with powerful Syrah aromas. The palate is full-bodied and firmly structured, a wine with very elegant balance despite its youth. The finish is long and well-defined. Will improve over the next five years, but is already a pleasure to drink.

Saint-Joseph 1990   🍇 🍇 ②
Full color and an extremely delicate bouquet with a wealth of juicy fruit notes and a hint of grassy blackcurrant. Full-bodied with an outstandingly rich palate and very easy to drink, thanks to its moderate tannins and good depth of flavor. A delicious wine to drink over the next three years.

Clos de L'Arbalastrier

32, avenue de Saint-Joseph
07300 Mauves
Tel. 75071060

Although this is one of the most traditional wines made in the Appellation Saint-Joseph, it is also one of the most controversial. Dr. Emile Florentin has as many critics as he does fans. He has owned Clos de l'Arbalastrier since 1957, but is still a "Parisian" in the eyes of his neighbors. All the members of his family have a medical background and lend a hand in running the estate which produces 20,000 bottles of organically-produced wines. The Syrah (80%) and Marsanne (20%) vines are planted in the Clos, next to the cellars where the wine is made. The soil of the five hectares of vines is stony and well-drained and the old plants give excellent fruit. Dr. Florentin's son Dominique, a doctor in Valence, is the winemaker and vinification techniques are old-fashioned. Both reds and whites ferment in wooden vats and then age for three years in barrels without filtration or fining. These wines are made with scrupulous care and attention, but need to be laid down for a long time to lose their harsh edges and to mellow fully.

Saint-Joseph 1989   🍇 ②
Opaque straw color with greenish tinges and not very bright. A wine with a complex, full bouquet, slightly mature and with notes of pine, resin and orange peel. Rich and well-rounded on the palate with aromas of sandalwood and citrus. A very individual wine.

SAINT-JOSEPH
COTES DU RHONE NORTH
FRANCE

389

SAINT-JOSEPH
COTES DU RHONE NORTH
FRANCE

GAEC du Biguet

Toulaud
07130 Saint-Péray
Tel. 75404944

Despite its glorious past, the situation today is far from being a happy one for many of the growers in Saint-Péray. The suburban sprawl of Valence and a changing market for sparkling wines is putting the producers under great pressure, and it is only with much effort that Saint-Péray manages to stay alive. One of the area's greatest champions is Jean-Louis Thiers, who owns some of the finest vineyards in the Appellation on the steep granite slopes above Toulaud. Jean-Louis' six hectares are planted with Marsanne (with the exception of a tiny parcel of Syrah at Cornas) and from this variety he produces about 25,000 bottles a year, three-quarters of which is méthode champenoise sparkling Saint-Péray and the rest still wine. Both wines are fermented in temperature-controlled stainless steel tanks and the still wine bottled in the spring after the malolactic fermentation. The sparkling wine is bottled much earlier having first been dosed with cane sugar and selected yeasts from the Champagne district. Thiers exports a good proportion of his wine to Great Britain, America, Japan and Belgium and is particularly proud of Saint-Péray's unique identity. Thanks to his firmness of purpose and to the quality of his wines, the Appellation will hopefully continue to survive.

Saint-Péray Nature 1990   ♈ ②
Clean, bright and clear with a sweet, fresh and very flowery bouquet. Fresh fruitiness and crispness are the main characteristics on the palate of this soft wine which is dry and well-made with good balance.

Saint-Péray Mousseux   ♈ ②
Lovely clear color and a delicate bead. The bouquet is fresh and yeasty. Full and stylish on the palate, it is perhaps lacking a little in acidity but is nonetheless very clean. It could be an agreeable alternative to Champagne, particularly considering the reasonable price.

Bosquet des Papes

Route d'Orange
84230 Châteauneuf-du-Pape
Tel. 90837233
Fax 90835052

Domaine Bosquet des Papes was established in 1966 when the Boirons built their cellar at the foot of the hill leading to the Palais des Papes, in an area known as Bosquet. Today the Boirons own 26 ha of vineyards made up for the most part of tiny parcels of Grenache together with Mourvèdre, Syrah and a little Cinsaut and Vaccarèse for the red wines, and Clairette, Grenache Blanc and Bourboulenc in almost equal proportions for white wines. Red wine is made in a traditional manner for the region. The grapes are not de-stemmed and ferment slowly for about three weeks in cement vats. Aging lasts for 18 to 24 months in large oak barrels. Maurice Boiron also produces a small quantity of white wine in a modern style: cold fermentation, blocking of the malolactic fermentation and bottling in spring to preserve the aroma of the fruit. It is his red wines, however, which are often outstanding in a robust and heady style - definitely not suited to those who enjoy light wines.

Châteauneuf-du-Pape 1989   ♈ ♈ ③
Rich, dark color. The bouquet is spicy and a little rustic. The palate is still very fruity and spicy with lots of tannins, but these are dominated by the body and the finish is remarkably long. The length and depth of the aromas will enable this wine to age in the bottle for at least 3-5 years.

Châteauneuf-du-Pape 1988   ♈ ③
A rich, evolving red color. The bouquet, which is spicy and full-bodied with no hard edges, is full of elegant fruit and is beginning to evolve towards notes of leather. The palate is full of spicy flavor with attractive length. Already mature, this is a wine to drink within the next two years.

Château de Beaucastel

84350 Courthezon
Tel. 90707060
Fax 90702524

Beaucastel is one of the two largest estates in the region with 100 ha of vineyards, 70 of which are in Appellation Châteauneuf-du-Pape. The remaining 30 are in Appellation Côtes du Rhône and supply the grapes for the generic Coudoulet de Beaucastel. The property dates back to the 16th century and the Perrin family has owned it since the beginning of this century. It is presently run by the Perrin brothers François and Jean-Pierre. Beaucastel is one of the few estates still to cultivate all 13 grape varieties authorized for the Appellation. The harvest is manual, the red grapes being selected, then de-stemmed before fermenting in enamel tiled tanks for around 12 days. On their way to the vats the grapes are heated to 80°C and then cooled to 20°C in order to extract color and flavor and reduce sulfur levels. Each variety is vinified separately and the final blend varies from year to year. Besides the red Châteauneuf-du-Pape, which is aged for a year in oak vats and fined but not filtered, 12,000 bottles of white Châteauneuf are also produced. There are two cuvées, one a classic blend of Grenache Blanc, Bourboulenc and Roussanne and the other made from 100% Roussanne. This is an extraordinary wine and one of the few white Châteauneuf-du-Papes which improves with age. Beaucastel is at present at the summit when it comes to Châteauneuf-du-Pape. Also worth investigation are the red and white Coudoulet de Beaucastel.

Châteauneuf-du-Pape 1990 ♟♟ ③
Very clear, bright color with gold tints. The bouquet is nutty and fresh but with a slight sensation of warmth which returns on the palate. A well-rounded, full-flavored and juicy wine with spicy, peppery aromas and good length. This is a wine which bears no relation to traditional white Châteauneuf-du-Pape and needs another five years to be at its best.

Châteauneuf-du-Pape 1988 ♟♟ ③
Very dark in appearance with a dense, very concentrated bouquet of grape aromas, fruity but not over-ripe. Tannins are well to the fore and the balance is very attractive. A classic wine with a hint of dry extract from the tannins and a rather harder style than the 1989.

Châteauneuf-du-Pape 1986 ♟ ④
Dark red color. Agreeable fruit and spicy bouquet. The flavor on the palate is already gamey with a concentration of black fruit and a warm note of green pepper and mint. A solid, fairly tough wine which will improve over the next four to eight years.

Châteauneuf-du-Pape 1989 ♟♟♟ ④
The appearance of this superb wine is quite stupendous: intense, very concentrated and dark. The bouquet is unassuming at first, with gamey notes in evidence, and it is only after several hours that all the complexity of the fruit comes through. The palate is rich and full, with black fruit aromas dominating and an exceptional concentration. The depth of flavor and the never-ending finish have supreme balance. This is undoubtedly a great wine which needs a minimum of five years to develop but can be laid down for many more.

CHATEAUNEUF-DU-PAPE
COTE DU RHONE SOUTH
FRANCE

391

CHATEAUNEUF-DU-PAPE
COTE DU RHONE SOUTH
FRANCE

Château Fortia

84230 Châteauneuf-du-Pape
Tel. 90837225
Fax 90835103

As "father" of the Appellation Contrôlée system, Baron Pierre Le Roy de Boiseaumarie was a perfectionist all his life, a trait he passed on to his son Henri who now manages Château Fortia. The estate lies to the east of the town, between Paul Avril's house and the Château des Fines Roches. It produces some of the finest red Châteauneufs, including the extraordinary 1978 which still has plenty of concentrated fruit and the ability to age for a while yet. The vines grown in the two stony vineyards, which on average are 40 years old,.are mostly Grenache, but there is also 15% Syrah, 8% Mourvèdre and 8% of other authorized varieties. About 10% of the domaine is given over to the production of traditional white wine. The reds are vinified in cement and, with the exception of the tannin-rich Mourvèdre, are not de-stemmed. After malolactic fermentation, the wines are left to age in 50 hl oak vats for 18 to 24 months. The Baron considers that light filtration and fining with egg whites are necessary to stabilize what is often one of the best aging wines in the Appellation.

Châteauneuf-du-Pape 1989 ☙ ②
Deep, rich color and a bouquet of great depth containing a profusion of pepper and spice aromas. The flavor is agreeably velvety with fleshy, raspberry fruit. A relatively straightforward wine, but also very full-flavored.

Château La Nerthe

Route de Sorgues
84200 Châteauneuf-du-Pape
Tel. 90837011
Fax 90837969

This is one of the most beautiful and historically most famous properties in the Rhône Valley. The château was built in 1736 and in 1785 there is evidence to show that the wines of La Nerthe were shipped as far afield as Boston. It was at La Nerthe that Commandant Ducos, the owner of the property at the time of the phylloxera epidemic, classified the different grape varieties of the region (ten of these are still cultivated today). La Nerthe's fortunes then went into decline and during the Second World War, when the Luftwaffe was stationed at the château, very little wine was produced. In 1985 the property was acquired by the Paris wine merchant Richard in association with the Beaujolais firm of David & Foillard. Alain Dugas was appointed as manager and much building, replanting and renovation has since taken place. There are 90 ha of vineyards, planted to Grenache, Syrah, Mourvèdre and Cinsaut for red varieties and Bourboulenc, Roussanne, Clairette and Grenache Blanc for the whites. The wines are of an excellent standard, despite a tendency to over-use new wood, and quality is improving steadily. This is definitely a property to keep an eye on.

Châteauneuf-du-Pape 1991 ☙ ②
Brilliant pale-gold color. Still undeveloped on the nose, which is a little short with a dusty note. The palate is very fresh with citrus and sweet fruit aromas and a good length. The wine is a little too heavy, but with enough depth to make this a fairly classic white Châteauneuf-du-Pape.

Châteauneuf-du-Pape ☙ ③
Cuvée des Cadettes 1990
Looks big and full-bodied in the glass and has a rich bouquet of ripe fruit overlayed by new oak. A powerful wine with perhaps not the body or fruit to carry the oak. Needs time to find a satisfying balance.

Châteauneuf-du-Pape 1989 ☙ ③
Lovely bright red color. The bouquet has fresh fruit with a hint of raspberry jam. Full-flavored and well-rounded, this is a wine which lingers on the palate displaying the juicy, fresh aroma of Grenache grapes. Extremely drinkable, but not a wine to lay down.

CHATEAUNEUF-DU-PAPE
COTE DU RHONE SOUTH
FRANCE

392

CHATEAUNEUF-DU-PAPE
COTE DU RHONE SOUTH
FRANCE

Château Mont Redon

84230 Châteauneuf-du-Pape
Tel. 90837275
Fax 90837720

In spite of its long history, Château Mont-Redon owes its name as a winery solely to Henri Plantin who bought the property in 1921 when it comprised less than three hectares. His grandsons Jean Abeille and Didier Fabre today produce 350,000 bottles a year of Châteauneuf on 95 ha of excellent stony soil. Mont-Redon is by far the largest estate in the Appellation and maintains high quality standards thanks to excellent vineyards and a superbly equipped cellar. The grapes, which are two-thirds Grenache and the remainder mainly Mourvèdre, Syrah and Cinsaut, are crushed and partly de-stemmed then fermented, using only natural yeasts, for two to three weeks. The wine then ages in large oak vats for 14-36 months according to the characteristics of the vintage. The white wine is cool-fermented and made from 40% Grenache Blanc, 25% Bourboulenc and a small percent of Clairette, Roussanne and Picpoul. Malolactic fermentation is blocked to preserve acidity and all wines are filtered. Mont-Redon also produces 100,000 bottles of Côtes du Rhône. Exports account for 70% of the production with the wines traveling as far as Bermuda and Hong Kong.

Châteauneuf-du-Pape 1991   🍇 ③
A lovely clear, bright color with no signs of oxidation. The bouquet is rich and clean with notes of almond and apricot. Full and clean on the palate with considerable body and attractive length.

Châteauneuf-du-Pape 1989   🍇 ③
Stupendous dark color. The nose is a little dusty and earthy. Fairly rich on the palate, but a little woody with powdery tannins. A rich wine with plenty of body and power which has yet to evolve - it needs time to smooth out the rough edges.

Châteauneuf-du-Pape 1988   🍇🍇 ③
Good deep, rich, bright color. The nose is rich and the fruit beginning to show. Elegant and well-rounded on the palate with aromas of spicy, ripe, juicy fruit. Good structure and outstanding length. Slightly less rich than the 1989, but with better balance and excellent texture. It will age well.

Domaine Durieu

10, avenue Baron Le Roy
84230 Châteauneuf-du-Pape
Tel. 90372814
Fax 90377605

In an Appellation where the winemaking families have histories which would fill a whole library of books, it is quite a relief to find a new arrival, particularly one who is quality-conscious. Paul Durieu makes an excellent style of Châteauneuf which is neither modern nor traditional, in his long, dark 18th-century cellars underneath the town of Châteauneuf-du-Pape. He has acquired 21 ha of vines dotted around the different communes of the Appellation. Mostly Grenache is planted but there is a reasonable proportion of Syrah, Counoise and Cinsaut. He also grows Roussanne, Bourboulenc, Clairette, Picpoul and Grenache Blanc for his modern-style white Châteauneuf. The red grapes are carefully selected and overripe or underripe grapes discarded. Fermentation lasts about 12 days and the wines age in both large oak barrels and tank. Durieu adopts almost exactly the same techniques for his growing production of Côtes du Rhône and Côtes du Rhône Villages and achieves a vibrant, velvety style, spicy at first with a full, rich follow-through. This is a happy marriage of old and new.

Châteauneuf-du-Pape 1990   🍇 ②
Lovely deep color and a spicy bouquet with full, clean fruit notes. On the palate the impact is spicy with an agreeably rich and well-balanced flavor of fruit. An excellent example of an above-average Châteauneuf-du-Pape with all the stylish, warm characteristics of elegant Grenache. At its best over the next four years.

CHATEAUNEUF-DU-PAPE
COTE DU RHONE SOUTH
FRANCE

393

CHATEAUNEUF-DU-PAPE
COTE DU RHONE SOUTH
FRANCE

Domaine Font de Michelle

14, impasse des Vignerons
84370 Bedarrides
Tel. 90330022
Fax 90332027

Brothers Michel and Jean Gonnet are
admirers of the Châteauneuf style pioneered
by their father Etienne Gonnet and uncle
Henri Brunier. A bottle of the red Domaine
Font de Michelle has that subtle, velvety
lightness which deceives the palate and leads
one to under-estimate the 14° alcohol. The
rarer white wine is on occasion the most floral
in the Appellation. Winemaking techniques
are very similar to those at Brunier's Vieux
Télégraphe as are the percentages of the
varieties used for the red wine - two-thirds
Grenache and one-third Syrah, Mourvèdre,
Cinsaut and various others. These, along
with the white varieties, are grown on 29 ha of
stony, uneven soil. 80% of the red grapes are
fermented in whole bunches in temperature-
controlled stainless steel tanks. The skins are
pressed in a pneumatic press, and the
various varieties and wines are blended
before going into large barrels where they
age for 6 to 12 months. Surprisingly, the
Gonnets have recently begun to experiment
with Allier-oak casks, but one hopes that
market pressure and the desire to export
does not persuade them to alter this attractive
example of a soft, fleshy Châteauneuf.

Châteauneuf-du-Pape 1991   ❦ ③
Very clear, bright color. There are notes of
butter and ginger on the nose over an alcohol-
rich base. Fresh, rich and very clean flavor in a
modern style. Rich in fruit and very long with a
high alcohol content.

Châteauneuf-du-Pape 1990   ❦ ③
Lovely deep color. Intense warm bouquet of
jammy fruit with the same aroma on the palate
accompanied by a sweet spiciness. This is a
very easy style of wine that lacks complexity but
is pleasantly attractive.

Domaine de Marcoux

3, chemin du Clos
84230 Châteauneuf-du-Pape
Tel. 90346743
Fax 90518453

Twenty-four of this estate's 28 ha have 40 to
60 year-old vines, and the remaining four-
hectare parcel has 95 year-old vines.
Grenache is planted to 80% and the rest
comprises 10% Mourvèdre, 5% Syrah and
5% Muscardin, Vaccarèse and Terret Noir.
The property, which is run by Philippe
Armenier, offers the full range of soil types to
be found at Châteauneuf-du-Pape: large
smooth stones which retain the heat of the
day to release it at night, sand, gravel,
limestone and clay. Since 1990, one third of
the estate has been cultivated using organic
methods. Grapes for the red wines are hand-
picked and rigorously selected. After
malolactic fermentation and filtration, they go
into wooden barrels for 6-12 months
depending on the vintage. The red wines
themselves are rich and full-bodied,
especially the Cuvée Vieilles Vignes which
since 1989 has been so concentrated that it
brings to mind vintage Port. The white is
obtained from two hectares of Clairette,
Bourboulenc and Grenache Blanc. It is bottled
in December with no malolactic fermentation
in order to maintain freshness. It has a high
alcohol content and tends to lack complexity.

Châteauneuf-du-Pape 1990   ❦❦ ③
Both the color and the bouquet are rich and
deep. The nose is spicy and the flavor clean and
once again spicy, reminiscent of ripe fruit, with
stylish tannins and good balance. The final
impression is of fruit, spice and pronounced
alcohol. A wonderful wine for cold days.

Châteauneuf-du-Pape 1989   ❦❦ ③
Once again a lovely dark color and a nose
which is both fresh and powerful. The palate is
well-rounded, big and fruity, with black cherries
and figs to the fore. It is a more powerful wine
than the 1990, with tannins a little harsh in the
finish but good length.

Châteauneuf-du-Pape   ❦❦ ③
Vieilles Vignes 1989
Unbelievable density of color, almost opaque.
Heady, potent bouquet, similar to that of vintage
Port. The flavor is characterized by a wide range
of sweet fruit preserves, with opulent texture,
good tannins and length. A massive wine
without the freshness of the standard cuvée, but
with remarkable concentration of flavor.

CHATEAUNEUF-DU-PAPE
COTE DU RHONE SOUTH
FRANCE
                                    394

CHATEAUNEUF-DU-PAPE
COTE DU RHONE SOUTH
FRANCE

Clos du Mont-Olivet

15, avenue Saint-Joseph
84230 Châteauneuf-du-Pape
Tel. 90837246

Joseph Sabon's three sons, Jean-Claude, Pierre and Bernard, are keeping the old Châteauneuf style of winemaking alive. Their 35 ha of small parcels of vines are located all over the Appellation on excellent stony soil. The vines are very old - 50 years or more - and most are Grenache, with small quantities of Cinsaut, Syrah, Mourvèdre and other varieties. The cellar lies beneath the family house and has a bare minimum of equipment, with bottling being entrusted to the Reflets de Châteauneuf-du-Pape next door. The resulting wines are serious, traditional and surprising. The wine undergoes malolactic fermentation and is then transferred to oak barrels for aging. Among the final blends are one filtered wine, one unfiltered and a wine aged in small oak casks. The Sabons also produce a white Châteauneuf-du-Pape, Clos du Mont-Olivet, from grapes harvested very early which is often rather alcoholic and a little green. This small defect does not, however, detract from the Sabons' standing as producers of exceptionally fine red wines.

Châteauneuf-du-Pape 1990   🍇🍇 ③
A wine with a remarkable structure which will be in spectacular form in five years time. The color is deep and rich, and the bouquet full, clean and fruity with notes of quince jelly. Superb balance, with a deliciously fresh aroma of black cherries and outstanding length on the palate. Serve with roast red meat or game.

Domaine de Nalys

84230 Châteauneuf-du-Pape
Tel. 90837252
Fax 90835115

Domaine de Nalys currently belongs to an insurance company, but the style of its wines was created by the previous owner, Dr. Philippe Dufays, considered by many as the "father" of carbonic maceration. The winemaker today is the youthful Monsieur Pelissier who produces about 260,000 bottles a year of red and white wine from the 52 ha located to the north-east of the town. All 13 authorized varieties are still grown, although half the red grapes are Grenache. The vines are old and include about 20% white varieties - Grenache Blanc, Bourboulenc, Clairette and Roussanne. It is without doubt the Domaine de Nalys whites which create the greater interest. These are simply vinified in temperature-controlled stainless steel vats and bottled early to maintain the freshness of what is one of the most elegant wines in the Appellation. Carbonic maceration is used to produce the red wines which are aged for about 12 months in cement or oak vats. The resulting wine is light and fragrant, very soft and easy to drink but without the solid structure of the more traditional wines of the area.

Châteauneuf-du-Pape 1990   🍇 ②
Obtained from several different grape varieties, this wine confirms the house style created by Philippe Dufays. Fresh, fruity and attractive with plenty of personality.

Châteauneuf-du-Pape 1990   🍇 ②
Moderately clear, bright red color with pink edges. A very fragrant, fruity wine with faint musky overtones. On the palate the wine is soft and fruity. An easy to drink and instantly attractive wine.

CHATEAUNEUF-DU-PAPE
COTE DU RHONE SOUTH
FRANCE

395

CHATEAUNEUF-DU-PAPE
COTE DU RHONE SOUTH
FRANCE

Clos des Papes

13, avenue de Pierre de Luxembourg
84230 Châteauneuf-du-Pape
Tel. 90837013
Fax 90835087

Customers of this well-known domaine have
included Presidents Charles de Gaulle and
Pompidou. The 32 ha are planted with most
of the varieties authorized by the Appellation,
including Roussanne, Bourboulenc, Clairette,
Grenache Blanc and Picpoul which is used in
the production of the 15,000 bottles a year of
wonderful, but expensive, white Châteauneuf-
du-Pape. It is the red Châteauneuf-du-Pape,
however, that makes up the lion's share of
production and the 100,000 bottles made
annually are held in high esteem all over the
world. The red grapes are carefully selected
before going into the vats and are de-
stemmed only in particularly difficult years.
Fermentation is long to extract the maximum
of color and tannins. The wine is then aged in
45 hl vats after having been fined with egg
whites. Bottling takes place in the spring or
autumn and the wine, which is not filtered,
merits aging for some years. The dynamic
and innovative Paul Avril runs the estate
assisted by his son who has been gaining
experience working in the Yarra Valley in
Australia and in Provence with the Ott
brothers.

Châteauneuf-du-Pape 1991   🍇🍇 ③
Very clear and bright appearance. The rich
bouquet is warm with alcohol but also contains
fresh notes of pear and apricot. The palate is full
and fruity with a hint of almonds and is well-
rounded, elegant and has a good finish.

Châteauneuf-du-Pape 1990   🍇🍇 ②
Deep, dark color. The nose of this excellent
wine has intense aromas of spices and ripe fruit.
The palate perfectly complements the bouquet
and the wine has balance, concentration and
great length.

Châteauneuf-du-Pape 1989   🍇🍇 ②
Deep, rich color. The bouquet is typically spicy
with notes of ripe black fruit. The palate has a
spicy, crystalized fruit concentration and is long
on the finish. Despite the fullness of the body,
this is a very elegant wine.

Châteauneuf-du-Pape 1988   🍇🍇 ③
Wonderful rich red. The nose is reminiscent of
spice, black pepper and fruits. Soft, spicy fruit
texture on the palate with good balance and
length. A great wine from a classic vintage.

Domaine de la Roquette

84230 Châteauneuf-du-Pape
Tel. 90330031
Fax 90331847

The Brunier family bought Domaine de la
Roquette from Réné Laugier in 1986. Today,
Henri Brunier's two sons, Frédéric and
Daniel, run the estate with the intention of
taking it into the very front rank of
Châteauneuf-du-Pape properties. The estate
has 30 ha planted with 70% Grenache, 20%
Syrah and 10% Mourvèdre, as well as a
small parcel reserved for white varieties.
Winemaking techniques are modern, in line
with those used by many other properties in
the area. In the well-equipped cellar, the red
grapes are not de-stemmed but crushed and
vinified in temperature-controlled stainless
steel tanks. After malolactic fermentation, the
wine goes into cement vats for the first year's
aging. This is followed by six months in
wooden vats before bottling and a further six
months evolution in the bottle prior to
release. The Domaine de la Roquette
produces about 127,000 bottles a year of
which 7,000 are white Châteauneuf-du-Pape.
Both white and red wines are very good
modern style wines which will probably
improve further under the careful supervision
of the Bruniers.

Châteauneuf-du-Pape 1990   🍇 ③
Lovely deep, bright red color. The bouquet is a
little warm with notes of plums and jammy fruit.
On the palate there are aromas of spicy fruit and
mint. A wine which lacks a little structure, but
one which demonstrates the progress made by
the domaine.

*CHATEAUNEUF-DU-PAPE
COTE DU RHONE SOUTH
FRANCE*
396
*CHATEAUNEUF-DU-PAPE
COTE DU RHONE SOUTH
FRANCE*

Domaine du Vieux Télégraphe

Route de Châteauneuf-du-Pape
84370 Bedarrides
Tel. 90330031
Fax 90331847

Hypolite Brunier established Domaine du Vieux Télégraphe in 1900 on the site of Chappe's experimental tower. When sales of bottled wines began to increase in the late 1970s, Hypolite's grandson Henri decided to bottle more wine under the Domaine de la Vieux Télégraphe label, reducing the sale of wines to the négociants. He also modernized the cellars and adopted new winemaking techniques. Henri Brunier's intelligent use of modern technology has enabled Vieux Télégraphe to become one of the most important estates in the Appellation producing a less robust, cleaner style of wine. The 60 ha of vines, with an average age of 40 years, are located on stony terrain with a sandy clay subsoil. The red wine is obtained from two-thirds Grenache and a little Syrah and Mourvèdre. The varieties are fermented separately for 12 days in temperature-controlled stainless steel vats. After malolactic fermentation, the wines evolve in stainless steel until blending, after which they spend 12 months in oak vats. A white Châteauneuf-du-Pape is also produced from Clairette, Grenache Blanc, Bourboulenc and Roussanne grapes.

Châteauneuf-du-Pape 1990 🍇 ②
Intense, full color and a rich nose with aromas of warm, ripe, spicy fruit. The same flavors are in evidence on the palate, which is well-rounded and already very approachable. A wine to enjoy on a cold winter's evening with game or a strong cheese.

Châteauneuf-du-Pape 1988 🍇 ②
Dark color with a pink edge. Perfumed, rich bouquet with sweet, spicy notes. Full on the palate with warm aromas of red fruit and a hint of thyme. A good finish and great balance.

Domaine de Grangeneuve

26230 Roussas
Tel. 75985022
Fax 75985109

Odette and Henri Bour fled Algeria in 1964 and moved to Roussas in the Drôme to plant vines. Today they have over 100 ha, most of which constitute the Domaine de Grangeneuve in the Appellation Tricastin. The cellar, which was modernized in 1974, produces a light, fruity rosé and red wines fermented in temperature-controlled cement and stainless steel vats. Grapes used for the rosé macerate on the skins for 12 hours before the juice is run off and vinified. Syrah, Grenache, Cinsaut and Mourvèdre grapes are used to make the Cuvée Classique and Cuvée Spéciale red wines, the latter being produced only in the best vintages. Fermentation is carried out by variety and blending takes place at the end of winter. There is also a Cuvée Prestige made from 100% Syrah as the Bours believe that this noble local variety can produce by itself an outstanding wine with abundant character. All Grangeneuve wines are filtered to ensure stability and are very well-made and extremely drinkable.

Coteaux du Tricastin 1990 🍇 ①
Light but bright color and a very juicy, clean, spicy nose. The wine is soft and well-rounded on the palate with spicy fruit and good balance. An extremely drinkable wine to serve cool in summer or at room temperature in the winter months.

CHATEAUNEUF-DU-PAPE
COTE DU RHONE SOUTH
FRANCE

397

COTEAUX DU TRICASTIN
COTE DU RHONE SOUTH
FRANCE

Domaine Saint-Luc

26790 La Baume de Transit
Tel. 75981151
Fax 75981922

In the middle of Domaine Saint-Luc's 16 ha of
Syrah and Grenache there is an attractive
farmhouse built round a courtyard. It is the
home of Ludovic Cornillon and his wife
Elianne which also functions as a "chambres
d'hôte." Elianne is a superb cook and Ludovic
tends the vines and makes the wines, most of
which are red Coteaux du Tricastin and Côtes
du Rhône together with a small quantity of
white and rosé. Winemaking techniques are
very straightforward and traditional but
include the use of temperature-controlled
stainless steel vats for fermentation and
enamel-lined cement vats for malolactic
fermentation. Ludovic Cornillon produces two
Tricastins which are his best wines: the
Cuvée Syrah, which is aged for a year in 30%
new Allier oak barrels, and a blend of
Grenache and Syrah matured in old barrels.
He started up the domaine by himself and
produces about 40,000 bottles a year of
Tricastin in these enviably attractive rural
surroundings.

Coteaux du Tricastin 1991   ❦ ①
Obtained from Grenache Blanc and
Bourboulenc grapes, this is a pale, fruity,
aromatic wine with good acidity. One of the
most interesting wines from the Coteaux du
Tricastin.

Coteaux du Tricastin 1990   🍇 ①
40% Syrah and 60% Grenache are blended for
this intense, purple-red wine. Heady with fine
structure and balance, it is an excellent example
of this particular blend.

Coteaux du Tricastin   🍇 ②
Cuvée Syrah 1989
Cornillon is a great believer in Syrah, and when
you taste this wine you have to admit that there
is much to be said for this opinion. Intense,
complex bouquet with notes of vanilla, cassis,
red-berry jam and tobacco. The first impression
on the nose is superb, the palate is elegant and
has good texture. The 1991, tasted from the
barrel, also promises well.

Château La Canorgue

84480 Bonnieux
Tel. 90758101
Fax 90758298

Jean-Pierre Margan's estate is half a mile
from Bonnieux, along the Pont-Julien road,
and owes its name to the many underground
conduits, often carved out of the rock, which
the Romans constructed to ensure their
water supply. From the terrace of the château
there is a splendid view of the Lubéron, the
Ventoux and the neighboring château of the
Marquis de Sade. The Margans took over the
estate in 1976 and since then have been
collecting awards by the sackful in national
competitions. This success serves to
demonstrate just how consistent their wines
have become. The 22-ha property (70%
planted with red varieties) has a privileged
soil which is treated organically following the
guidelines of the "Nature et Progrès" organic
organization. Yields are rarely above 40
hl/ha. Fermentation in stainless steel vats is
traditional and the red wines then spend four
to eight months in wood. Rosés and whites
are fermented at low temperatures and
bottled in the spring to preserve the best of
their aroma and freshness. These are wines
which provide a bench-mark for this new
Appellation.

Côtes du Lubéron 1990   🍇 ②
Deep rich color and fully revealed nose of ripe
red fruit. On the palate, the spicy flavors and
powerful, but not aggressive, tannins culminate
in a rounded and well-balanced finish. A
delicious wine to drink now while the fruit is still
attractively prominent.

Côtes du Lubéron 1989   🍇 ②
Very rich color shading into violet. The nose is
agreeably fruity with aromas of herb and mint.
Lovely dense, well-integrated structure and a
fine, lingering finish.

Clos Murabeau

Murabeau
84120 Pertuis
Tel. 90770026

It required genuine passion and dedication to take in hand this 20-ha property and bring it back to life in such a short space of time. The publisher Jean-Claude Lattès moved to this former Riquetti estate to write a new chapter in the story of a village where wine has rich historical and literary associations. It was here that Count Gabriel-Honoré, better known as Mirabeau, was elected as the representative of the Tiers Etat after a youth spent in pursuit of a series of turbulent love affairs. He campaigned actively for a constitutional monarchy which was never to be established. Another famous admirer of the wines of Clos Murabeau was the nationalist writer Maurice Barrès. In order to preserve the spirit of this historic literary past, Jean-Claude Lattès has dedicated each vintage to a literary personality. Names of some of the dedications are Jorge Amado, Edmonde Charles-Roux, Pierre Perret and José Sarney. It is a marketing initiative like any other which neither adds to, nor detracts from, the quality of the wines. Previously a simple Vin de Pays, the Côtes du Lubéron was accorded Appellation Contrôlée status on 26 February 1988.

Côtes du Lubéron 1990
A splendid result which proves how well Ugni Blanc adapts to the local "terroir." The nose is slightly flowery and the palate full with good concentration and a very clean finish. A well-made wine.

Côtes du Lubéron 1989
A robust red from good-quality grapes. Intense fruit on the nose, including blackcurrant and cherry. The palate is full and young with prominent tannins. A wine to lay down in anticipation of a pleasant surprise.

Domaine du Vieux Chêne

Rue Buisseron
84850 Camaret
Tel. 90372507
Fax 90377684

Jean-Claude and Dominique Bouche's father used to take his grapes to the Serignan cooperative and it wasn't until the end of the 1970s that these young brothers built their own winery, producing their first Domaine du Vieux Chêne wine in 1978. Today the brothers have gone their separate ways, Dominique running the recently-established Domaine Bouche while Jean-Claude continues to run Domaine du Vieux Chêne, ably assisted by his wife Béatrice. The couple possess about 50 ha of vines, most of which are located on the "Plan du Dieu," a broad, rocky plain to the east of Orange where the mistral blows in winter and the heat in summer is unbearable. Jean-Claude and Béatrice produce 65,000 bottles of red Côtes du Rhône, 6,700 of red Côtes du Rhône-Villages, 4,000 of Côtes du Rhône rosé and 6,700 of white Côtes du Rhône-Villages. Vinification consists of a minimum of crushing of the fruit followed by long fermentation on the skins. The resulting wines are soft, round and aromatic. The Cuvée de la Haie aux Grives is the cellar's best wine, but all the Vieux Chêne wines are extremely good.

Côtes du Rhône
La Haie aux Grives 1991
An excellent example of what a good winemaker can do with a mediocre vintage. Intense, bright red color with a well-defined bouquet laced with the aromas of fresh, ripe red fruit. The palate is clean and fruity, with good balance and length. A very agreeable wine for a reasonable price.

COTES DU LUBERON
COTE DU RHONE SOUTH
FRANCE

399

COTES DU RHONE
COTE DU RHONE SOUTH
FRANCE

Domaine des Grands Devers

84600 Valréas
Tel. 90351598
Fax 90374956

René Sinard has made a name for himself as a winegrower from next to nothing. He has 14 ha of Grenache, six of Syrah and two of Carignan, all located on the clay and chalk soil of the wild, hilly area between Coteaux du Tricastin and Nyons. The latter, according to the French, is the best place in the world for olive oil. The micro-climate is relatively cool and produces wines that for the Rhône Valley are relatively elegant and refined. The Côtes du Rhône Enclave des Papes is made almost exclusively from Syrah and the Côtes du Rhône-Villages Valréas largely from Grenache. Both wines are vinified in whole bunches in cement tanks for 12 to 18 days. They age in cement and are bottled after 18 months as intense, concentrated wines of great style.

Côtes du Rhône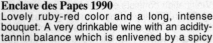
Enclave des Papes 1990
Lovely ruby-red color and a long, intense bouquet. A very drinkable wine with an acidity-tannin balance which is enlivened by a spicy note of green pepper.

Côtes du Rhône Syrah 1990
Acidity, tannins and alcohol had not yet found their point of balance when we tasted this wine, but bottle-age will do wonders. A wine to lay down and watch as it develops.

Côtes du Rhône-Villages
Valréas 1990
1990 was a good vintage but failed to reach the heights of 1989. This wine's present freshness and drinkability should not lead one to under-estimate its aging potential.

Côtes du Rhône-Villages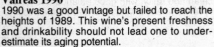
Valréas 1989
A wine of great elegance with a nice balance of flavor and aroma. The attractive bright red color, the intense fruity nose with a faint hint of spice on the palate and the marvelously dry finish make this an excellent example of Côtes du Rhône-Villages.

Domaine des Moulins

30650 Saze
Tel. 90317043

André Payan's domaine is located in the village of Saze in the Gard département, west of the Côtes du Rhône-Villages Appellation. The cellar is neat and tidy reflecting the personality of its owner for André Payan has not gone for eye-catching interior design but for functional, carefully thought-out architecture which puts a premium on insulation and ease of cleaning. His 30 ha of vines are also immaculately planted with equal quantities of Syrah and Grenache, as well as a little Cinsaut and Carignan. Roughly a quarter of the vines are more than 50 years old with the remainder averaging around 25 years. All are located on limestone and clay soil. The wines are typically made in cement vats with maceration which lasts about a fortnight. The majority of the wine (about 17,000 bottles) is Appellation Côtes du Rhône with a further 13,000 bottles of a highly prized Côtes du Rhône-Villages. The wines are not filtered and may leave a deposit, but they are are velvety smooth, in sharp contrast to the spicier, more alcoholic wines made to the east in the Vaucluse.

Côtes du Rhône-Villages 1990
Splendid intense color with dark red round the edges. Powerful, fruity nose and nice balance on the palate. A stylish, fruity, easy-drinking wine, like so many products of the Gard.

Côtes du Rhône-Villages 1989
A more intense color and a full-bodied, fruity, fresh, clean bouquet. The palate also has elegant fruit. A well-made, full-bodied wine with a long, clean finish.

COTES DU RHONE-VILLAGES
COTE DU RHONE SOUTH
FRANCE

400

COTES DU RHONE-VILLAGES
COTE DU RHONE SOUTH
FRANCE

Domaine Pelaquié

7, rue du Vernet
30290 Saint-Victor-la-Coste
Tel. 66500604
Fax 66503332

Young Luc Pelaquié's grandfather Joseph made his first wine at Domaine Pelaquié in 1924. Luc, who inherited the property with his brother Emanuel in 1976, is by far the best producer of Côtes du Rhône-Villages wines from Laudun. The brothers own 75 ha of vines located on sandy clay soil. Luc makes red and white Laudun, a Lirac rosé and a small quantity of rosé from Grenache and Cinsaut at Tavel. The reds are produced from equal proportions of Syrah, Mourvèdre and Carignan harvested mechanically and de-stemmed before crushing and fermentation. The red wines age for 12-15 months and are filtered before bottling. Grapes for the whites and rosés are picked manually and pressed in a pneumatic bladder press. The temperature for fermentation is held at a constant 17°C for eight days and the wines are filtered before bottling which takes place at the beginning of spring. Pelaquié has also planted three hectares of Viognier which is used in the final blend and gives extra aroma and weight to the wine.

Côtes du Rhône-Villages   🍇 ①
Laudun 1991
Very pale, clean, star-bright color. The nose is fresh and floral and the palate well-rounded and fruity. The style is fresh, fruity and easy-to-drink, with no hard edges.

Domaine Rabasse-Charavin

Quartier de La Font d'Estevenas
84290 Cairanne
Tel. 90307005
Fax 90307442

Corinne Couturier is the tiny, outgoing and immediately likable owner of Domaine Rabasse-Charavin. The domaine is located just outside the picturesque village of Cairanne, which stands like a mound in a sea of vines, and has been in the Couturier family for five generations. Couturier's 65 ha of vines, mainly Grenache with a little Syrah, Mourvèdre, Cinsaut and Carignan, range in age from 30 to 70 years and grow on limestone clay soils. The domaine's wines include Côtes du Rhône-Villages from Cairanne, traditionally-made Rasteau and a generic Côtes du Rhône. The grapes are vinified in cement vats in whole bunches and then matured in old, large barrels. A little of the "vin de presse" is added to the free-run juice and the wines are lightly fined with egg whites but never filtered. The Rasteau and Cairanne, especially the Cuvée d'Estevenas, are fine examples of the area's potential.

Côtes du Rhône-Villages   🍇 ②
Cairanne 1990
Good bright red color. Spicy and rounded on the nose with good sweet fruit. The palate is rich and full of fruit and has a long, stylish, finish. A wine to drink over the next three years, preferably at a cool temperature.

Côtes du Rhône-Villages   🍇🍇 ②
Cairanne Cuvée Estevenas 1990
Light, bright color, more intense than the other two wines. The bouquet is an explosion of ripe fruit as is the full, ripe, mellow palate. Quite warm but good depth of fruit and a lingering finish.

Côtes du Rhône-Villages   🍇 ②
Rasteau 1990
Produced from 40% Mourvèdre, this wine has a rich, red color and spicy fruit aroma. The fruit is evident once again on the palate which has good length, balance and structure, and firm tannins in the finish.

COTES DU RHONE-VILLAGES
COTE DU RHONE SOUTH
FRANCE

401

COTES DU RHONE-VILLAGES
COTE DU RHONE SOUTH
FRANCE

Marcel Richaud

Route de Rasteau
82490 Cairanne
Tel. 90308525
Fax 90307112

Marcel Richaud's father was a grower who took his grapes to the local cooperative. Marcel started on his own in 1974 when he rented 14 ha and slowly began to buy parcels, one at a time, until he finally took over his father's vineyards as well. Today he produces 1,000 hl of wine, 600 hl of which is Appellation Côtes du Rhône-Villages Cairanne. Marcel now has 25 ha with an average age of 50 years which are planted 50% in Grenache, 25% in Syrah and 15% in Mourvèdre. The remaining 10% is made up of Grenache Blanc, Marsanne and Roussanne. All the vineyards are located on limestone and clay slopes or terraces. The climate is Mediterranean with dry summers and the influence of the "mistral" which blows down the valley from the north. The harvest is manual, the grapes destined for Villages wines being collected in small crates to protect the berries. Red grapes are vinified in whole bunches at strictly controlled temperatures after being gently crushed. The wines are fined, lightly filtered and bottled in spring before the heat of the summer. Marcel prefers to bottle his wines young to maintain freshness, but he then ages them in bottle for a year before they are released.

Côtes du Rhône-Villages
Cairanne 1991
Lovely bright, deep red-mauve color. The bouquet is distinctly the style of southern Grenache - gamey, warm and spicy with good concentration. The palate is rich and surprisingly fresh with ripe fruit and a touch of Syrah spice.

Côtes du Rhône-Villages
Cairanne 1990
Rich, bright color and a warm, clean, spicy bouquet with the typical aromas of Grenache. The palate is also spicy, full-bodied and round with good plum fruit and moderate tannins. A very clean, well-balanced wine.

Côtes du Rhône-Villages
Cairanne Cuvée l'Ebrescade 1989
A more intense color than the Cairanne 1990, with a nose that is richer and has more intensity. It has spicy, herbal (rosemary and thyme) flavors on the palate with ripe fruit and good length. This is a robust wine to serve with red meat and game.

Domaine Sainte-Anne

Les Cellettes
30200 Banglos-sur-Cèze
Tel. 66827741
Fax 66827457

Domaine Sainte-Anne represents a milestone in recent French viticultural history as it was one of the first estates to produce excellent wines from local southern varieties outside the traditionally "noble" regions. A style was created and imitators look on enviously as Guy Steinmaier and his family, who bought the property in 1965, continue to add to their achievements. There are 25 ha of red varieties, mainly Syrah, Mourvèdre, Grenache and Cinsaut, as well as two hectares of Marsanne, Roussanne and Bourboulenc and three hectares of Viognier. The vines are located on well-drained gravel and limestone soils perched above Saint-Gervais on the right bank of the broad southern Rhône basin. The grapes are hand-picked and ferment at controlled temperatures in the well-equipped winery. The Syrah, used in the Cuvée Syrah, Côtes du Rhône-Villages and Côtes du Rhône, is the only variety to spend a year in wood. All wines are fined and filtered and have the concentration to age well. Steinmaier is making a name for himself with his Cuvée Viognier, but his interesting blends of Marsanne, Roussanne and Bourboulenc are also becoming increasingly and deservedly better-known.

Côtes du Rhône-Villages
Cuvée Notre Dame des Cellettes 1989
Stupendous depth of color. The bouquet is very concentrated and rich in ripe black fruit. Great concentration of powerful fruit on the palate together with depth and a long, flavorsome finish. A delicious example of a full-bodied yet elegant Rhône from the Gard, to serve with white meat and poultry.

COTES DU RHONE-VILLAGES
COTE DU RHONE SOUTH
FRANCE   402

COTES DU RHONE-VILLAGES
COTE DU RHONE SOUTH
FRANCE

Caves Michel Faraud

Domaine de Cayron
84190 Gigondas
Tel. 90658746
Fax 90658881

Michel Faraud produces a Gigondas which is powerful, robust and in a certain sense, rustic. While many of the region's wines, despite their potential for further aging, are drinkable at four years, Faraud's wines take longer to come round. Following the same techniques his father Georges used, Michel vinifies the whole bunches of grapes for two weeks in cement vats. The wine is then transferred to 60 hl vats to age for 18 to 24 months. The final blend comprises two-thirds Grenache and the remainder Syrah, Cinsaut and Mourvèdre. The pressed juice is added to the free-run juice to obtain a wine of remarkable concentration and structure which is neither fined nor filtered. More than half of the 50,000-bottle annual production goes in export, in particular to discerning customers in the United States, Northern Europe and Canada.

Gigondas 1988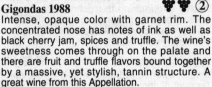
Intense, opaque color with garnet rim. The concentrated nose has notes of ink as well as black cherry jam, spices and truffle. The wine's sweetness comes through on the palate and there are fruit and truffle flavors bound together by a massive, yet stylish, tannin structure. A great wine from this Appellation.

Domaine de Font-Sane

84190 Gigondas
Tel. 90658636-90658431
Fax 90658171

The rugged peaks of the Dentelles de Montmirail form a natural backdrop to the village of Gigondas. Monsieur Peysson and his daughter Véronique, the winemaker at the domaine, have 14 ha of vineyards which are located at between 160 and 400 meters altitude, high enough to escape the humidity of the plain. Indeed their north and north-east facing vineyards are located in some of France's most beautiful countryside. Most of the vineyard area is planted with Grenache with one fifth Syrah and a small percentage of Cinsaut. The vines are around 40 years old and grow on stony sand, limestone and clay. Yields per hectare are low and the concentrated fruit is fermented in cement vats for 8-12 days before aging in wood. The base cuvée matures in great oak barrels for 6-8 months, while the cuvée Futée ages for 8-12 months in new wood. The Peyssons also produce a Côtes de Ventoux red from pure Grenache which is fermented and aged in cement. Gigondas from Domaine de Font-Sane may not be the Appellation's most full-bodied wine, but it is certainly among the most elegant.

Gigondas 1989
A wine that is representative of the domaine style without excessive body, but full of style and fruit and very well-made. Dark, bright color with a discreet bouquet of plummy fruit. Well-rounded and spicy on the palate with Grenache sweetness and juiciness.

Gigondas Cuvée Futée 1988
Intense color shading to pink round the edge. The bouquet has a marked note of wood and the fruit seems quite evolved. Meaty with notes of spice on the palate. The wine has softened nicely and should be at its best in a year or so.

GIGONDAS
COTE DU RHONE SOUTH
FRANCE

403

GIGONDAS
COTE DU RHONE SOUTH
FRANCE

Domaine Les Pallières

84190 Gigondas
Tel. 90658507

Until he passed away a couple of years ago, Christian Roux used to help his brother Pierre run the Domaine Les Pallières. Their father Hilarian Roux was the first to estate-bottle his Gigondas at the end of the last century, and today Pierre carries on the family tradition. Production stands at 100,000 bottles a year of one of the finest and most robust red Gigondas, as well as 3,500 bottles of heady and somewhat rare Gigondas rosé. The quality should come as no surprise because the Roux family has been making wine here for more than 250 years. The estate comprises 25 ha of Grenache, Syrah, Mourvèdre and Cinsaut vines, many of which are more than half a century old. They are located on the steep limestone clay slopes of the majestic Dentelles de Montmirail. Mechanized harvesting is illegal in Gigondas so the grapes are hand-picked and crushed before fermenting in cement containers for 15-18 days. The wine ages for a minimum of 18 months in old oak vats and then goes into bottle where it usually matures for a further year before it is sold. Pierre Roux undoubtedly produces some of the best wines in the southern Rhône.

Gigondas 1988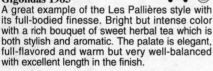
Brilliant red color of moderate intensity evolving at the edges. The sweet aroma of Grenache is evident on the nose, together with a strong note of aromatic herbs. The palate is sweet, round and herbal with good length. The finish is a little dry and tannic in the typical Les Pallières style. A wine which needs time to mellow.

Gigondas 1986
Clear, bright color, quite evolved. Full bouquet with notes of mint and spicy fruit. The palate is sweet and very elegant. A wine with good balance which is ready for drinking straightaway. The time spent in old oak casks has softened the wine nicely.

Gigondas 1985
A great example of the Les Pallières style with its full-bodied finesse. Bright but intense color with a rich bouquet of sweet herbal tea which is both stylish and aromatic. The palate is elegant, full-flavored and warm but very well-balanced with excellent length in the finish.

Domaine Raspail-Ay

Le Colombier
84190 Gigondas
Tel. 90658301
Fax 90658955

The estate was created around 1860 by Eugène Raspail and won its first award at the 1867 Exposition Universelle in Paris. Today Dominique Ay and his father François own and manage the 18-ha property producing about 40,000 bottles, mainly of red wine but including a few bottles of Gigondas rosé. The vineyard is planted with 65% Grenache, 16% Syrah and the remainder is split between Mourvèdre, Cinsaut and Clairette. The vines have an average age of 25 years and are located on the limestone terrain of the gentle slopes to the south of Gigondas. Grapes for the red wine are de-stemmed and fermented in stainless steel for three weeks before being transferred into large barrels for 18 to 24 months. The wine is bottled without fining or filtration and is usually among the region's best. Robust, full-bodied and powerful, it is a classic Gigondas. The rosé, like most of those from the region, tends to be a little heavy and lacking in freshness, but when consumed cold in summer, under the shade of the trees by the village bistrot, it can be absolutely delicious.

Gigondas 1990
Bright, intense red color with a clean, spicy bouquet of ripe plums. Good body and fruit with faint spice on the palate. A Gigondas with lots of tannin and backbone. An excitingly robust wine which combines finesse with balance.

Gigondas 1989
Another wine with a deep dark color and attractive red edge. Still a little hard and undeveloped, it is delicious on the palate, spicy-rich, chewy with a gamey character. The finish is exceptional. An outstanding wine with a great future which will age and improve for many years.

Gigondas 1988
Bright, pale red color. The nose is well-rounded and spicy with mineral notes. The palate is firm with good body and attractive mint aromas. Although lighter than the 1989 and 1990, this is a wine with pleasing balance which lingers on the palate.

GIGONDAS
COTE DU RHONE SOUTH
FRANCE

404

GIGONDAS
COTE DU RHONE SOUTH
FRANCE

Domaine de Saint-Gayan

84190 Gigondas
Tel. 90658633
Fax 90658510

Roger Meffre is one of the driving forces in the Rhône Valley and is also active nationally as regional representative of the Institut National des Appellations d'Origine (INAO). The Meffre family has lived here since the beginning of the 15th century. Roger has planted half the vines on the 32-ha estate, but his son Jean-Pierre continues to cultivate some that were planted by his great-grandfather François, some of which were re-grafted by his grandfather Gustave more than 50 years ago. Today, the Meffres produce around 100,000 bottles a year of Gigondas, Rasteau and red, white and rosé Côtes du Rhône, as well as 3,000 bottles of Châteauneuf-du-Pape. The Meffre Gigondas is produced from Grenache and Syrah, with a little Mourvèdre and Clairette added. These are traditional wines from grapes lightly crushed and not de-stemmed which macerate slowly and which are gently pressed. Aging lasts for about a year in older oak barrels as the wines are tannic and do not need the influence of new wood. The end result is a great wine for laying down which will age for 15 years without difficulty.

Gigondas 1988
Intense color with a powerful, well-knit spicy bouquet with notes of rosemary and thyme. Very full-bodied on the palate, rich in fruit and tannins with considerable alcohol. Still undeveloped and slightly astringent finish which will evolve over the next two or three years.

Rasteau 1988
Again dark deep color and a fruity, spicy bouquet with hints of plums and ripe figs. The palate has considerable depth of flavor and although still undeveloped and tough, underneath there is plenty of full fruit. When the Mourvèdre (30% of the blend) has mellowed this will be one of the best value-for-money wines in France.

Gigondas 1986
Brilliantly rich cherry-red color. Elegant spicy fruit emerges sweet and ripe on the nose while herbaceous aromas dominate the full-flavored palate. Good structure and length. A very consistent, vigorous wine, perfect for drinking now or to lay down for a few years yet.

Domaine de Coyeux

Boîte Postale 7
84190 Beaumes-de-Venise
Tel. 90629796
Fax 90650187

If you are looking for a particularly stunning view of the entire southern Rhône Valley, climb up through the Muscat vineyards of the Domaine de Coyeux in the Dentelles de Montmirail, just above Beaumes. Yves and Catherine Nativelle bought the 80-ha estate with its 20 year old vines in 1977. Today they make an incredibly full and unctuous wine; it would be a mistake to compare it to Domaine Durban (the Appellation's other exciting product) since the Coyeux is as opulent and decadent as Durban is stylish and fragrant. At Coyeux, grapes are picked over the course of several stages and pressed in full bunches. The must ferments at low temperatures (from 6-10°C) in stainless steel vats for seven to nine days when fermentation is halted with a dose of 5-7% alcohol. The end product, blended and bottled in the month of February following the vintage, has an alcohol content of about 15° and over 110 gm/lt of residual sugar. It is then aged for 18 months in bottle before release. Coyeux Muscat was very fashionable in Paris in the late 1980s, and although quality has remained excellent the wine has suffered an inexplicable decline in popularity, particularly in France.

Muscat
de Beaumes-de-Venise 1989
An invitingly rich, bright gold color. The nose confirms the first impression of opulence with fleshy, well-rounded notes and a sweet hint of caramel. Full and vigorous on the palate, a wine better appreciated with a fruit dessert than as an aperitif. The finish is extremely long in the classic Beaumes style.

GIGONDAS
COTE DU RHONE SOUTH
FRANCE

405

MUSCAT DE BEAUMES-DE-VENISE
COTE DU RHONE SOUTH
FRANCE

Domaine de Durban

84190 Beaumes-de-Venise
Tel. 90629426
Fax 90650185

Bernard Leydier owns 20 ha of Muscat à Petit Grains Dorés which produce grapes that easily exceed the minimum of 252 gm/lt of residual sugar required by law for Muscat de Beaumes-de-Venise. The pale color and fragrant, generous style of the Domaine de Durban have earned it a faithful following among lovers of mouthfilling, ripe, opulent wines. The domaine is located in the hills above Beaumes-de-Venise from where it enjoys a breath-taking panorama and excellent sunlight. The wines are made to the highest standards, fermenting at very low temperatures until they reach 5° of alcohol, at which point Leydier adds pure alcohol to kill the yeasts. They are kept at a low temperature until bottled in the spring and sold almost immediately to customers all over the world. Domaine de Durban Beaumes-de-Venise is best drunk young when its vigor and freshness are at a peak.

Muscat ♙ ♙ ②
de Beaumes-de-Venise 1991
Clear and brilliant with a fresh aroma of sweet, flowery Muscat. The flavors are grapey, sweet, fragrant, very well-defined and in no way cloying, with a clean finish. An uncomplicated wine which unlike similar wines, does not tire the palate.

Château d'Aquéria

S.C.A. Jean Olivier
30126 Tavel
Tel. 66500456
Fax 66501846

Château d'Aquéria has been producing wine for many years, but it has been managed with particular skill since 1920 when it was bought by Jean Olivier, whose grandchildren run the estate today. Most of the 58 ha are devoted to the production of Tavel rosé, which is made with Grenache, Cinsaut, Clairette, Mourvèdre and Bourboulenc. The vines, tended with painstaking care, are located on a terrain covered with large pebbles which help to supply the heat necessary for the grapes to ripen. The grapes are hand-picked and placed in vats to macerate for 12 hours to extract the rich color of a rosé "saigné." Fermentation follows in temperature-controlled tanks at 18°C. The wine then remains in the tanks for two to three months before being bottled. About 320,000 bottles are produced annually, including a red Lirac and a small quantity of a rare white Lirac of great finesse. Château d'Aquéria's Tavel rosé is still today one of the very best rosés made in France.

Tavel 1990 ▩ ②
Full, florid rosé color. The nose is peppery with a note of strawberry jam. A wine with the personality to stand comparison with many reds. The palate is surprisingly refreshing, but the alcohol and spice come through in the finish.

MUSCAT DE BEAUMES-DE-VENISE
COTE DU RHONE SOUTH
FRANCE

406

TAVEL
COTE DU RHONE SOUTH
FRANCE

Domaine de la Mordorée

30126 Tavel
Tel. 66500075
Fax 66504739

Christophe Delorme, a retired clothes-merchant, first bottled his father's Domaine de la Mordorée in 1987. While their 30 ha are largely devoted to the production of 90,000 bottles of Côtes du Rhône, their real passion is for the Tavel rosé and red Lirac. The grapes for the rosé, mostly Grenache with some Syrah, Mourvèdre, Cinsaut and Clairette, are de-stemmed and macerated for 12 hours. The juice is then chilled and run off the skins which are then pressed, the juice being added only to assist color. Fermentation takes place in temperature-controlled stainless steel tanks and only natural yeasts are used. The wine is then fined, lightly filtered and stored in tank until bottling. The Lirac is made from equal quantities of de-stemmed Syrah, Grenache and Mourvèdre vinified in stainless steel. After a long fermentation and maceration the wine is aged for five to six months in tank and casks, 25% of which are new. The wine is not fined but lightly filtered. The Delormes at present only make 15,000 bottles a year of Lirac, but a further ten hectares which they recently planted in the Appellation should help augment the production.

Tavel 1991
Superb, bright pink rosé color with a fruity nose. On the palate the wine is fruity, clean and robust. This is a heavier style of Tavel that should be served well chilled.

Lirac 1990
Deep, rich, concentrated color with a rich, ripe fruit nose. Good soft, round, depth of flavor on the palate with plenty of ripe fruit and good length. This is a big wine for drinking now.

Domaine des Amouriers

Les Garrigues
84260 Sarrians
Tel. 90658322
Fax 90658413

The Domaine des Amouriers derives its name from the "mûriers", or brambles, which grow around the property. The domaine was first planted as a vineyard in 1940 by Jocelyn Chudzikiewicz's grandfather, a Pole who had emigrated to France. It now consists of 12 ha in three Appellations: Vacqueyras, Côtes du Rhône and Vin de Pays de Vaucluse. The Vacqueyras is produced from Grenache, Cinsaut and Syrah vines planted on poor, well-drained limestone clay soils. The grapes are hand-picked and fermented separately in whole bunches in concrete vats for 10-15 days. The various lots are blended before aging for 15-18 months in epoxy-lined cement and glass-lined steel tanks. No wood is used and the wines are neither fined nor filtered. The resulting wine is a big, traditional Vacqueyras with plenty of extract.

Côtes du Rhône 1990
As many as four varieties are needed to produce this wine: Grenache, Syrah, Cinsaut and Carignan. It is an honest wine with character and has good structure, balance and tannins.

Vacqueyras 1990
A wine whose depth demonstrates the potential of the Appellation and which will improve with a little age in bottle. The tannins are for the moment a little aggressive, but should integrate well given a little time. This is a wine to lay down.

TAVEL
COTE DU RHONE SOUTH
FRANCE

407

VACQUEYRAS
COTE DU RHONE SOUTH
FRANCE

Domaine Le Clos de Cazaux

84190 Vacqueyras
Tel. 90658583
Fax 90658394

Lucette Archimbaud's grandfather was the first grower to bottle wine in the Vacqueyras Appellation. Today she and her husband Maurice Vache produce about 25,000 bottles a year of Vacqueyras, a little white Côtes du Rhône and a tiny quantity of Gigondas. There are two cuvées of Vacqueyras: the Cuvée des Templiers (the Knights Templar once owned the estate) produced from 90% Syrah, and the Cuvée Saint-Roch which has a softer style and comes from 90% Grenache. There is also a small proportion of Mourvèdre planted in the 40-ha limestone chalk vineyard which is exposed to the gusts of the mistral wind which helps dry out the land. The grapes ferment for seven to eight days in concrete vats. The wine is then pressed out and aged for two years in concrete tanks. The Gigondas comes from a steeply sloping vineyard high up in the Dentelles de Montmirail and is made in the same way as the other wines. The wines are generally robust and powerful with a tendency at times to be a little too alcoholic. They are great wines to serve with game on a cold winter's evening.

Vacqueyras
Cuvée des Templiers 1989
Lovely, intense red color, warm and spicy although still undeveloped. The palate is compact with warm aromas of fruit, spices and liquorice. The wine is tough and alcoholic, but with good flavor and length. The cooler vintages from this domaine are more balanced.

Price levels

①   up to $ 9.99

② $ 10.00 - $ 14.99

③ $ 15.00 - $ 24.99

④ $ 25.00 or more

The 'ex-cellar', or direct from the producer, bottle prices, are calculated in US dollars and are intended only as an approximate guide

VACQUEYRAS
COTE DU RHONE SOUTH
FRANCE

408

VACQUEYRAS
COTE DU RHONE SOUTH
FRANCE

Jura

Jura is a little off the beaten track with respect to France's better-known winegrowing regions. It has a harsh continental climate with very cold winters and hot summers, frequently punctuated by heavy thunderstorms. The area under vines lies at an elevation of between 250 and 500 m. above sea-level and comprises roughly 1,400 ha in total. Yields are low, particularly in Château-Châlon, and production amounts to about 5 million bottles a year.

The 1991 vintage witnessed a disaster of immense proportions when on 21st April, frost damaged most of the vine stock. In many cases, it proved impossible to produce any wine at all that year.

The majority of plants in the region belong to one of two kinds of varieties: the classic varieties of nearby Burgundy (Chardonnay and Pinot Noir); and the local ones (Poulsard, Trousseau and Savagnin). Fine red and white wines are obtained as well as excellent rosés and Jura's pride and joy, Vin Jaune, the best examples of which are produced in the Château-Châlon Appellation. It is a white wine aged by the grower for at least six years with a complexity of bouquet and palate that is hard to find elsewhere. Obtained from a mere 30 ha of vineyards, Vin Jaune can comfortably be laid down for decades. The variety from which this enological jewel is obtained is Savagnin which is very similar to Traminer in its characteristics, and it achieves the outstanding results of Vin Jaune thanks to the slow and beneficial process of oxidization that takes place during its long evolution in wood.

The Jura region's Appellations d'Origine Contrôlée (AOC) are: Arbois, which alone accounts for about 3 million bottles a year of mainly white wine and is the largest appellation; Château-Châlon, the most prestigious, with an average production which does not exceed 85,000 bottles; Côtes de Jura, the appellation which is most difficult to characterize and includes wines of all types; and finally l'Étoile with its excellent white wines, both still and sparkling.

Caveau de Bacchus

39600 Montigny-les-Arsures
Tel. 84661102

With his aristocratic features and white beard, Lucien Aviet is a hearty trencherman who enjoys arguing with his old schoolfriend and fellow-grower Jacques Tissot over winetastings. Lucien himself produces wine from a 5.7-ha estate divided up between 12 different parcels, some containing plants as much as 70 years-old. For the most part he offers two cuvées: the Cuvée des Géologues and the Cuvées des Docteurs. Both are made with particular attention to the soil type, which is sometimes marl and gravel, sometimes gravel and sometimes only marl. Winemaking is strictly traditional with separate fermentation in wood for each variety after a selection which takes into account the different parcels of origin. Maceration lasts three weeks and aging takes place in wood barrels. These wines will age for two to four years and even more. Wine from the Poulsard variety may be drunk young while the Trousseau, thanks to its 30 year-old plants, is suitable for laying down. There is also a very interesting Chardonnay.

Arbois Chardonnay 🍇🍇 ②
Cuvée des Docteurs 1989
Elegant pale color with a bouquet of walnut and candied figs. Fleshy but stylish on the palate with moderate acidity. Classy finish.

Arbois Trousseau 🍇 ②
Cuvée des Géologues 1989
Made in honor of the world's geologists, who have apparently been encouraging its sale by word-of-mouth, this is a dark cru from four different soil types. Red berries (cassis) are particularly to the fore on the nose while the palate is fleshy and the finish has good length.

Château d'Arlay

38140 Arlay
Tel. 84850422
Fax 84481796

Renaud de Laguiche is one of wine's, and winemaking's, gentlemen. With his tortoise-shell glasses, country attire complete with leather boots and his clear, elegant manner of expressing his passionate love for wine, he is constantly aware that the product is born of its 'terroir'. De Laguiche's own estate comprises 27 ha of clay and chalk soil which he allows to express itself to the full. Herbicides are no longer used and tilling is once again practiced, Philippe Chatillon, a full-time eonologist, has joined the staff and harvesting, vinification and aging are all carried out in the traditional fashion. Yields, too, are low with only 22 hl/ha obtained for the Vin Jaune '82. Renaud also experiments and in 1991 he launched a cuvée of Pinot Noir (only 10,000 bottles) from lyre-pruned vines. The wine was fermented in a single vat, with eight months in the wood, and was neither filtered or fined. Apart from a superb Vin Jaune, the Cuvée Corail is equally remarkable. This is obtained from a cocktail of five red and white varieties. Château d'Arlay is a historic building and the park inside the ruins of the ancient fortress of the Princes of Orange is the venue in summer for artistic events, exhibitions and concerts. A final note: Renaud de Laguiche's passion for birds of prey has led to the creation, in the park itself, of the first aviary for these creatures in the region .

Arbois Vin Jaune 1983 🍇🍇 ④
Fermented in glass-lined barrels, this vintage has a strong yellow color. The splendid bouquet is scented with walnut. The wine is almost oily on the palate and is particularly full-bodied. The finish is elegant and fresh with a hint of lemon in the background. A wine which will age and age.

Côtes du Jura 1989 🍇 ②
Lovely garnet-red color. Obtained from Pinot Noir, this wine is slightly oaky on the nose and full on the palate. Good balance and a satisfyingly long finish.

Château de l'Étoile

39570 L'Étoile
Tel. 84473307
Fax 84249352

The Vandelles are now into their fourth generation since Auguste Vandelle bought the estate in 1883 from a crown jeweller during the Second Empire. Bernard Vandelle looks after the commercial side today while Georges is the technically-minded Vandelle, who uses a helicopter to keep a watchful eye on the vineyards. As well as these two family-members, the entire Vandelle tribe of grandparents to wives and children takes an active part in the running of the property. And it is thanks to people like the Vandelles that the l'Étoile Appellation (the name comes from the shape of a local fossil) has emerged from obscurity. The château is little more than a pile of ruins so nowadays visitors are made welcome in the mansion or the other, more modern residence to talk about these 22 ha of clay-and-chalk soil and their vine stock of 70% Chardonnay with the remainder Savagnin and Poulsard. This is fertile soil which gives higher yields - about 40 hl/ha - than the neighboring Château-Châlon and the fine white, red, rosé and sparkling crus are made in the traditional manner.

Côtes-du-Jura Chardonnay 1989

This monovarietal Melon - the local name for Chardonnay - has taken full advantage of the opulence of its vintage. The flavors of walnut, candied peel, nuts, chicory and spices, the full aromas and the finish which allows the cru to speak for itself make tasting this wine a very rewarding experience.

L'Etoile Vin Jaune 1983

Classic appearance, flecked with green and a nose redolent of walnut. Excellent structure. Fleshy on the palate, with an agreeably lingering finish. Will certainly age for a few more years, perhaps quite a few more.

Domaine Michel Faudot

Mesany
39600 Arbois
Tel. 84661356-84662320

Young Michel has already a respectable place on the Jeunet family wine list at their Le Paris restaurant in Arbois, where he is one of the most popular producers. Serious, hard-working and modest, Michel makes his cuvées with rare skill. The plants on his 8-ha estate have an average age of 25 years and while two-thirds of the stock is red varieties (Trousseau, Poulsard and Pinot Noir), the Chardonnay is his favorite with its old vines on their gravelly soil. The yields of Chardonnay are restricted to 40 hl/ha as are those of Michel's Savagnin, which always gives cuvées with good aging potential. During the exclusively manual harvest, selection is rigorous. Grapes for the red wines are totally de-stemmed, those for white only partially. Maceration is brief but the wine goes on to age slowly in capacious vats before evolving further in the bottle for 12 months. The excellent end results are typical of their producer.

Arbois 1990

A blend of Poulsard and Pinot Noir which is outstandingly successful. Brilliant color and aromatic notes which are redolent of Burgundy. Fine body on the palate.

Arbois Trousseau 1990

The very concentrated grapes give this wine a festive air. The variety comes through strongly in the lovely dark red color and produces an impressively full-bodied and well-rounded sensation on the palate. The finish is a riot of red fruit.

Domaine Florian Frachet

39190 Maynal
Tel. 84489756

Florian Frachet is emblematic of a new generation of growers who have realized just how much the local terroir has to offer. Florian had always wanted to be a vigneron and his dream came true in 1984. Today he owns 4.3 ha of vineyards located on mainly chalk-and-clay terrain which also includes heavier marl plots where his old vines are to be found. From these 50-60 year-old plants, Frachet obtains an excellent monovarietal Chardonnay Côtes du Jura which is fermented in stainless steel vats before aging for a minimum of 24 months in 600-l. tuns, a wine which is symbolic of the Appellation's resurgence. Frachet's Pinot Noir-based red wines macerate for 8 to 15 days. The quantity of wine (100-150 hl), obtained from younger plants, which the domaine sells unbottled each year, is steadily diminishing. Stocks of red wine are low because the excellent 1990 vintage was damaged by frost and the '91 yielded a mere 10 hl/ha, but Florian Frachet is not a man who gives up easily. He knows that sooner or later the weather will be kind to him and his vines.

Côtes du Jura Chardonnay 1990 ♔ ②
Old vines have produced here an outstanding result: splendid delicate yellow color, a bouquet of honey, a fresh, full-bodied palate and an elegant finish.

Côtes du Jura Pinot Noir 1990 ♔ ②
This cuvée is the result of a 10-day maceration and despite having caught a mild frost at the end of May, has a rich bouquet of red fruit on a background of cherry and raspberry. Good structure.

Domaine Jean-Claude Gallois

14, rue Nécy
39600 Arbois
Tel. 84661287

The ancient city walls of Arbois have echoed for many years to the noise of the wine trade, and there are well-known landmarks to bear this out, such as the Pasteur family residence and the museum of vine and wine. There is also someone who has immortalized Arbois on his labels. Jean-Claude Gallois is, with his air of solemnity, one of the newest vignerons and also a passionate student of local history. His bottles carry the names of medieval locations he has discovered in ancient texts. His cuvées, therefore, have names like Tour de Raisins, which is obtained from old Chardonnay, also known as Melon d'Arbois, and fermented in oak barrels. Or Faubourg Danjoutin, or Tiercelines from low-yielding young Nature, the old name for Savagnin. Jean-Claude is, however, more than just a local historian; his Arbois Trousseau is excellently made, having fermented for six weeks and then been blended with the second pressing.

Arbois Cuvée des Tiercelines 1990 ♔ ②
The young Savagnin vines here bring off a small miracle in preserving the character of the variety without turning into Vin Jaune. The nose has notes of butter while the palate is stylish and fresh, with a lingering flavor of pear and green apple.

Arbois Trousseau 1990 ♔ ②
Slow maceration here produces a wine with a bright color. Hints of red fruit are accompanied by notes of pepper. The body is powerful and the tannins are unobtrusive with a very elegant finish on the palate.

Frédéric Lornet

L'Abbaye
39600 Montigny-lès-Arsures
Tel. 84374495

As well as being one of the up-and-coming growers of the region, Frédéric Lornet is also one of the favorites of Jean-Paul Jeunet, Arbois' great chef. Frédéric is articulate and plain-speaking and a man who belives that patience is the supreme virtue. For a long time he worked in the shadow of his father, but today he is totally independent, working confidently and consistently towards his goal of quality. Thus it is that his Chardonnay, from plants that are more than 30 years old, is aged "sur lies" for a year. The Arbois Trousseau, which comes from 40 year-old vines, never yields more than 30 hl/ha and ferments for 20 days. Frédéric is in favor of a certain measure of complexity; he prefers fleshy wines to an abundance of tannins and his products are rich in fruit, which makes them very suitable for laying down. He took the frost damage of 1991 very philosophically, regarding it as Nature's way of exacting tribute. This philosopher of the vineyard knows that next year, Nature will be kinder.

Arbois Chardonnay 1989   🍇 ②
The color is almost leathery and the nose has ripe aromas with honey and walnut to the fore. The first impression on tasting is of lively vivacity with flowery notes in the background. Sensations of freshness and youth follow.

Arbois Trousseau 1989   🍇 ②
Dark appearance. The producer here deliberately sought maximum concentration of the fruit (cassis and raspberry). A big wine, with tannins which do not intrude. Will age for some years yet.

Jean Macle

Rue de la Roche
39210 Château-Châlon
Tel. 84852185

Château-Châlon is undoubtedly the star of the Jura region. The vineyards are located on black marl terrain at the foot of the steep peaks which tower over the ancient township. Jean Macle, former president of the Château-Châlon consortium to which more than two-thirds of local growers belong, is the Appellation's leading light. It is obvious as soon as you meet this calm 50 year-old, with his proud bearing and reputation for having brought the Appellation back to first-rank status, that here is someone special. With the sole exception of improved health and safety practice, Jean makes wine in the traditional way, just as his forebears did: sulfur is scarcely used, yields at 20 to 35 hl/ha according to the soil type are low and his Savagnin plants grow on slopes, 60% of which are located at between 270 and 400 m above sea-level. Moreover, Jean is adamant that six years should be the compulsory minimum for aging in the barrel. It is only on these conditions, he maintains, that Château-Châlon will mature for a century or more, that Nature will give of her best, that the thin veil of saccharomyces baynus yeasts will lend the wine the characteristic "yellow" taste, and that the aromas of walnut, truffle, almond, resin, hawthorn and earth will develop. Macle is perfectly capable of downgrading his wine in a poor vintage, as was the case in '74, '80 and '84. If we also take into account the terrible frost of 1991, then we begin to understand why he has to restrict sales to six bottles per customer. For a wine that will last forever, six bottles is better than none at all.

Château-Châlon 1985   ♀♀♀ ④

This Vin Jaune is to the Jura what Yquem is to the Sauternais. The region's leading grower is something of a 'fundamentalist' when it comes to Château-Châlon, but one who puts his fruit before all else. The powerful bouquet is redolent of white and yellow flowers, truffle, toastiness, apricot, spices, almond and walnut. The exceptional depth of the nose continues on the palate where the flavors are equally complex, with an incredible breadth of aromas and quite staggering length. A concentrated wine with near-perfect balance despite the natural Savagnin acidity which gives the wine its incomparable freshness. Make a date with your grandchildren to taste this masterpiece at the end of the next century!

Domaine de Montbourgeau

39570 L'Étoile
Tel. 84473296

The 64 ha of the L'Étoile ("Star") Appellation could not possibly shine any brighter. The town, whose name derives from the small five-pointed fossils found locally, produces only 2,000 hl of wine. The Gros family has lived here since 1920 and today the young enologist Nicole Deriaux, née Gros, and her husband Marc run the property while Nicole's father, Jean Gros, watches over them affectionately. The 8 ha of this estate, with its verdant setting, are planted 80% to Chardonnay with the rest to Savagnin, on chalky terrain containing gray and blue marl. Étoile wines are either monovarietal Chardonnay, or a blend of Chardonnay with 15% Savagnin, and their production starts in stainless steel vats with natural yeasts while aging is carried out in oak barrels. The cellar also produces a dessert wine from ripe bunches of Savagnin grapes placed on trellises to dry in the sun. An interesting and unusual wine.

Arobis Vin Jaune 1985   🍇 🍇 ④
Already shading into gold. On the nose, the wine maintains all its promise with delicate aromas of quince, pepper and spices. The palate reveals the wine's richness, with walnut dominating the aromas, although nicely balanced by white truffle. A great wine which will be talked about for many generations to come.

L'Etoile Vin de Paille 1989   🍇 🍇 ③
Obtained from super-ripe Chardonnay and Savagnin left on trellises to dry and sweeten, this is a wine of great concentration with aromas of dried fruit (date and apricot) and candied peel (cherry and plum). Juicy on the palate while losing nothing in finesse, the balance of alcohol and fruit is sublime and the finish lingering.

Domaine Pierre Overnoy

Pupillin
39600 Arbois
Tel. 84661460

Pierre Overnoy is an ecologist with a vaguely romantic approach and an elegant shock of white hair. He is, in short, one of those growers without whom life would be a little duller for he speaks his mind when other people keep quiet. Pierre's current campaign is for the re-instatement of the original name of one of the Jura varieties, Plousard instead of Poulsard as it is called today. Overnoy's harsh Jura accent articulately defends his opinions on such subjects as the use of tilling instead of chemical herbicides, Bordeaux mixture instead of chemicals and a ban on sulfur, tartaric acid and filtration. After his 2.25-ha estate has been harvested, the grapes are de-stemmed and selected by hand and then fermented slowly for up to a month and a half. They remain "sur lies" until they are bottled. Overnoy produces no more than 100,000 bottles a year and parts with them only very reluctantly, so it is fair to say that those who have the privilege of tasting his wines are a very lucky few among the world's wine-lovers.

Arobis Pupillin Chardonnay 1988   🍇 ②
This bottle of monovarietal Chardonnay is decorated with a stylish wax seal and has a bouquet which, though still closed, is of walnut and hazelnut. Firm and racy on the palate with a finish of outstanding intensity.

Arobis Pupillin Plousard 1989   🍷 ②
Although classed as a rosé, this wine is actually a wonderful red color. The aromas are of cherry and wild cherry, the structure is truly delicate and the palate is voluptuous. Good length of aroma in the finish.

Domaine Jacques Puffeney

Saint-Laurent
39600 Montigny-lès-Arsures
Tel. 84661089

Located in the upper part of a picture-postcard village and with barrels piled high all around, Jacques Puffeney's cellar looks attractively rural. This bearded grower has more than 30 years' experience behind him as well as a family which has been making wine for three centuries, and he is not a man given to confidences. He likes to talk wine with you before he lets you in on what he is thinking. Jacques' six hectares are on marl terrain, divided up into about 15 plots where bright colors like wine-red and green abound. The estate is planted about one-third in Savagnin, one-third in Poulsard and the remainder in Chardonnay and Trousseau. Jacques' passions are: the preservation of traditional Jura varieties; picking by hand; rigorous selection of the fruit; traditional fermentation in oak barrels; the aging of red wines for a few years with periodic checks to drink them at their best; and for white wines, freshness obtained by systematic malolactic fermentation. To sum up, Puffeney is a serious grower who has never let his clients down.

Arois Savagnin 1987 ♔ ②
Deep yellow color with a herbaceous nose over a background of acacia bark. Good structure and concentration with a chewy note and a finish of fine aromatic freshness.

Arbois Poulsard 1990 ▧ ②
Obtained from old vines, this cru has a slightly peppery nose on a background of spices. The texture is very elegant, with good density on the palate. Will age happily for a good few years.

Domaine Rolet

39600 Montigny-les-Arsures
Tel. 84660005-84660889
Fax 84374741

There seem to be Rolets everywhere, and between Arbois and Montigny you are very likely to come across one or other branch of the family . M. Rolet is the guardian of the family tradition and his son and daughter guarantee that the next generation will carry the torch with love and passion. Their 60-ha estate, on its clay-and-chalk and marl slopes planted with the traditional Poulsard, Trousseau and Pinot for reds and Chardonnay and Savagnin for whites, is the second-largest in the Jura after Henri Maire's. It is, more importantly, one of the top estates for quality with modern equipment and tried and tested technology. Vinification is done separately by variety, at low temperatures in the case of white wines, in a cellar where fermentation is continuously monitored and only the natural yeasts are used. Aging lasts for up to 24 months in large barrels and barriques. Vins Jaunes, of course, remain in the vat for a minimum of six years. Although severely put to the test by the frosts of 1991, when yields were lower than 5 hl/ha, the Rolets have excellent stocks and there is no fear of their wine running out.

Côtes du Jura Chardonnay 1989 ♔ ②
Deep yellow color and a bouquet of fresh walnut and lime-blossom. Good structure, rather fleshy with a very fresh finish of almonds.

Arbois Vin Jaune 1983 ♔ ♔ ④
A monovarietal Savagnin that has been neither topped up nor racked. Aromas of mushrooms, particularly morel, are prominent in the bouquet while the palate has great depth and almost infinite length. A wine of excellent structure which will age well into the next century, perhaps right to the end.

Arbois Tradition 1989 ♔ ②
A very successful blend of Pinot Noir, Poulsard and Trousseau with inviting reflections of lively color. The red fruit of the nose comes through a base of spicy aromas and the wine is robust on the palate.

Jacques Tissot

39, rue de Courcelles
39600 Arbois
Tel. 84661427
Fax 84662483

Jacques Tissot is known to everyone in the region for his passionate love of viticulture and is one of those rare collectors of old vintages. He started off with 20 ares and today can boast 25 ha His son Philippe is ready to take over from him and to add a touch of modernity to the estate. Not that Philippe's father ever produced wines that could in any way be considered run-of-the-mill, but the time had come to impose a little rationalization on proceedings. Now that their cellar next to Louis Pasteur's vineyard has been completely renovated and re-named Les Bruyères, the two Tissots feel that the future is just beginning. One has to share their optimism when one sees the ultra-modern cellar and remembers that the grapes are picked entirely by hand, vinification is rigorously traditional and aging is in wooden vats. Here one can also find a perfectly executed traditional method of dessert wine production, with the grapes being naturally dried for several months. A marvel to behold !

Arbois Chardonnay 1990 ♈ ②
Intense yellow color and a bouquet which exalts the variety with notes of green walnut. Good texture.

Arbois Poulsard 1989 ♈ ②
Bright red color with red fruit and spicy, peppery notes on the nose. Full-bodied and concentrated with excellent length on the palate.

Key to the symbols

Types of Wines

♈ White

🍇 Rosé

♈ Red

Rating System

♈
An exemplary wine of its type with outstanding local character

🍇🍇
An international premium quality wine

♈♈♈
A Top Wine, considered one of the 150 best wines in the world

The 'grape bunch' symbol is used to indicate the color of the wine; the number of bunches represents the quality rating assigned by the contributor

Price levels

① up to $ 9.99

② $ 10.00 - $ 14.99

③ $ 15.00 - $ 24.99

④ $ 25.00 or more

The 'ex-cellar', or direct from the producer, bottle prices, are calculated in US dollars and are intended only as an approximate guide

Entries are arranged in alphabetical order by country, region and winery or producer name.

Languedoc and Roussillon

Languedoc and Roussillon is a compact winegrowing region, the hottest in France, which extends over a good portion of the South and South-west. Traditionally, Languedoc and Roussillon has played a major part in the life of the average French family by providing a large proportion of the wine which appeared daily on the country's tables. Unfortunately, just as the traditional "baguette" has suffered at the hands of mass production, so too has the quality of Languedoc and Roussillon wine, and with the collapse of wine consumption over the last 20 years from almost 55 million lt a year to only 41 million in 1990, many vineyards have been abandoned or uprooted. Recently, however, the exorbitant prices reached by vineyards in the classic zones of Bordeaux and Burgundy have pushed would-be investors south, and the resulting injection of new energy and capital has revitalized the region. In addition to French investors, there are also Australian and American firms with interests in the region which is undoubtedly a healthy sign.

There have been many changes over the last ten years, especially in the Languedoc. After much research, what used to be a sea of Carignan, Aramon and similar varieties has been replaced by grape types such as Grenache, Syrah and Mourvèdre for Appellation d'Origine Contrôlée wines with Cabernet Sauvignon, Chardonnay and, more recently, the universally fashionable Viognier for Vins de Pays. Another important factor in the general improvement has been the emergence of a new breed of growers who realize that low yields are crucial for high quality production, a phenomenon which is spreading to Corbières, Fitou and Minervois. Particularly at Corbières, it seems that eastern producers are once again focussing on quality and the sub-region has started to organize, with promotional initiatives and much more freely available information on local wines and vineyards than in the past. Finally, it must be mentioned that estates like Mas de Daumas Gassac have given many other producers something to think about. If similarly expensive wines serve only to promote interest in traditional methods and a more thoughtful approach to winemaking, then they will have rendered the consumer an immense service.

Many fine fortified Vins Doux Naturels are made in the Appellations of the South, such as those from the glorious seafaring town of Banyuls or the delicious, opulently juicy Muscats of both Rivesaltes and Saint-Jean de Minervois. With all the health worries over alcohol and legislation against alcohol abuse, fortified wines have seen their market drastically reduced, but it is also true that there have never been so many examples of top quality wines of this type on the market as there are today.

Given its geography and climate, the entire Languedoc and Roussillon region ought to be able to produce some of the best wines in France, but apart from the need for one or two exceptional producers to lead the way, the area is perhaps still paying for its past reputation as a producer of heavy, alcohol-rich wines with no character. Once this reputation has been finally laid to rest, the future will be decidedly brighter for Languedoc and Roussillon producers.

Château Bel-Évêque

11430 Gruissan
Tel. (1) 45040025
Fax (1) 45042370

Château Bel-Évêque is a 50-ha estate to the south-east of Narbonne, near the Étang de l'Ayrolle, a stone's throw from the Mediterranean. The actor Pierre Richard bought the château in 1986 and since then he has set up a program to improve the quality of the wine. Long-term projects include the restructuring of the cellars, but the bulk of investment until now has been devoted to the vineyards. The original eight hectares on chalky marl in the Corbières Appellation have been extended to the present 17, with an increase in the area planted with Syrah, Grenache and Mourvèdre. The Corbières red, with an annual production of 56,000 bottles, is obtained from 45% Carignan from vines over 40 years old together with 30% Grenache, 15% Syrah and 10% Mourvèdre. The varieties are fermented separately using carbonic maceration then blended and aged in vats for 12 months and for 6 in oak barrels, 10% of which are new. The wine is then matured in the bottle for at least three months prior to being sold. The estate also produces 8,000 bottles of rosé from Grenache (35%), Cinsaut (30%), Syrah (20%) and Mourvèdre (15%) grapes.

Château Bel-Evêque Corbières 1989 ![grape] ①
Deep, bright and very rich color which hints at the character of the wine itself which on the nose is spicy with juicy fruit and subtle hints of well-integrated oak. Mouthfilling fruit which lingers on into the extremely long finish. Good structure in what is an outstanding wine, taking into account the fact that it is a first vinification. An estate to keep an eye on.

Château Grand Moulin

Jean-Noël Bousquet
11200 Luc-sur-Orbieu
Tel. 68274080
Fax 68274761

Jean-Noël Bousquet has always believed in Corbières as a top-quality wine region. He created his own estate by ploughing up virgin soil and, in 1988, by buying the all but abandoned Château Grand Moulin. He has achieved very impressive results in a very short time. The vineyards are located on stony chalk soil and their Mediterranean conditions are tempered by a micro-climate which makes the sub-zone one of the driest in Corbières. The 50 ha of vines have an average age of 30 years and are planted in the various grape types permitted in the Appellation, that is Syrah, Mourvèdre, Grenache, Cinsaut and Carignan for red and rosé wines in addition to one hectare of Grenache Blanc and one of Macabeo for white. Château Grand Moulin produces 120,000 bottles of Tradition rosé, red and white, 4,000 bottles of white fermented in oak as well as 12,000 bottles of red fermented in wood, all Appellation Corbières. The Carignan is fermented using carbonic maceration while the other red varieties are de-stemmed and fermented traditionally. The Macabeo spends four hours "sur lies" at a controlled temperature.

Corbières 1991
Very bright pale pink color and a nose with very clean, flowery aromas. The palate is fresh, dry, fruity and well-rounded.

Corbières 1991 ![grape] ①
Beautifully rich color and a nose of ripe, elegant, spicy aromas. The same notes return on the palate, where the wine also has good structure and balance. A frank, easy-to-drink wine which confirms the quality standards of the cellar.

CORBIERES
LANGUEDOC
FRANCE

419

CORBIERES
LANGUEDOC
FRANCE

Château Les Ollieux Romanis

Montséret
11200 Lézignan-Corbières
Tel. 67394239
Fax 67761499

Château Les Ollieux Romanis stands on the site of an ancient Roman villa, and there is also a Medieval priory to be found in the history of this estate, but it was only in 1826 that it began to be exploited as a wine-growing enterprise. Jacqueline Bories and her lawyer husband François bought the property in 1980 and since then they have done much to improve quality. After renovating the cellars, in 1983 they initiated a re-planting program with 15 of the total 55 ha in Syrah, Grenache and Mourvèdre while a further 15 are being planted with white varieties. The vines grow on stony, chalk-rich soil and the grapes, hand-picked, are transported to the cellars on an unusual rail system which dates back to the turn of the century. The red Corbières are obtained from old Carignan, Grenache Noir, Syrah and Mourvèdre vines, fermented separately in wood using carbonic maceration. The wine is not filtered but aged in wood and stainless steel. The rosé is obtained from Grenache Gris, Cinsaut and Syrah.

Corbières 1989   🍇🍇 ②
Medium-intensity garnet purple color. Wild berries dominate the bouquet where there are also notes of leather, eucalyptus and grass. The entry on the palate is crisp and firm, the fruit has good texture and the tannins and concentration are satisfying.

Château de Campuget

Départementale 403
30129 Manduel
Tel. 66202015
Fax 66206057

The terrain of this vast, 350-ha estate is a mixture of round pebbles and sandy clay like that at Châteauneuf-du-Pape and, typical to the region, the land is divided between viticulture (155 ha) and orchards (195 ha). The estate comprises two distinct companies, L'Amarine and Château de Campuget, but both retain their own distinct personality under the management of Yves du Tremblay. New vines become part of the Appellation only when they are seven years-old (one quarter of the vine stock is over 50 years-old) and the varieties are fermented separately. L'Amarine white is made from 20% Grenache Blanc and 80% Roussanne. The red, Cuvée de Bernis, from equal parts of Grenache and Syrah from old vines, is aged in one to three year-old Burgundy barriques for 10 months. The Campuget white is obtained from 20% Grenache Blanc, 30% Clairette and 50% Marsanne and Roussanne, while the traditional red is similar to the l'Amarine red but without the wood. Each cuvée has its own personality, and the wines maintain a laudably consistent quality from one year to the next. Also worthy of mention are the experimental plantings of Chardonnay, Merlot, Sémillon, Cabernet Franc and Sauvignon.

Costières de Nîmes Domaine de   🍇 ①
l'Amarine Cuvée de Bernis 1989
An attractive, well-made and easy-to-drink wine. The rich, deep color is inviting. The nose if fruity and velvety and the palate confirms the full-bodied, ripe, juicy fruit. Words are superfluous for this is a wine which speaks for itself.

CORBIERES
LANGUEDOC
FRANCE

420

COSTIERES DE NIMES
LANGUEDOC
FRANCE

Domaine de l'Hortus

34270 Valflaunes
Tel. 67553120
Fax 67553803

Jean Orliac is an agricultural engineer who started out by renting five hectares of vineyards and went on from there to put together, over the last 15 years, an estate of about 30 ha on land where vines and olives have been cultivated since time immemorial. The landscape is wild and beautiful, but the area has been inhabited since the prehistoric cave was first occupied. There are also two castles from the 12th and 13th centuries. Domaine de l'Hortus has 18 ha planted in Mourvèdre, Syrah, Grenache and young Viognier, all located on rocky slopes of the chalky red Mediterranean soil. Production amounts to about 90,000 bottles of red wine, 3,000 bottles of rosé and soon there will also be Viognier-based white. Red wines are fermented traditionally for 14 days while the rosés are obtained by the "méthode saignée". Jean Orliac also produces a small quantity of a quite outstanding red wine, half from Mourvèdre, which is aged for 12 months in Allier-oak barrels. But anyone who can get the best out of the best can also make an excellent base wine, so the estate's real forte is the AOC cuvée.

Coteaux du Languedoc
Pic Saint-Loup 1990
Invitingly intense color with a fruity nose of berries and the typical Syrah note of pepper. Good fruit and concentration on the palate, frank, clean and very drinkable. Very well-balanced.

Domaine de l'Hortus
Grande Cuvée Pic Saint-Loup 1991
Color even more intense than the AOC cuvée with a full nose featuring an intense note of menthol. The palate has well-defined hints of mulberries and blackcurrants, attractive concentration and good balance. A wine whose supreme drinkability is in no way compromised by a slight lack of structure.

Mas Julien

Jonquières
34150 Gignac
Tel. 67966004
Fax 67966050

Mas Julien is the pride and joy of Olivier Julien, who owns 15 ha of vineyards in the Coteaux du Languedoc, in the district of Jonquières, planted on two very different soil types, one shale and the other chalk and clay. Julien is convinced that the combination of these two terrains is absolutely necessary for the production of a well-balanced wine. He grows Grenache, Cinsaut and Syrah in more or less equal proportions as well as Carignan and Mourvèdre. The vines are 25 years old on average and the grapes, hand-picked and selected by vineyard and variety, go into one of the two cuvées of red wine produced by the estate. Les Depierre is a pure and simple blend of grapes from the two soil types, while Les Cailloutis is a version with more structure and extract obtained from better-quality grapes which is aged for about 18 months in wooden vats and barrels. Mas Julien rosé is a "vin saigné". The grapes are gently crushed in order to obtain just the right shade of color before they go on to ferment at low temperatures. The resulting wine is fresh, flowery and very drinkable. Julien produces about 250,000 bottles a year, including a small quantity of white wine.

Coteaux du Languedoc
Les Depierre 1990
Intense color and a nose rich in fruit, spice and pepper. The palate is full-bodied and fleshy with excellent texture and a delicious note of pepper in the finish. A very successful product which goes to show just how far this region has come.

Coteaux du Languedoc
Les Caillouitis 1989
Bright, intense deep red and a fruit-rich nose with gamey notes which has already started to evolve. Rounded on the palate, with ripe flavors full of berries and a slightly viscous note. Full-bodied and powerful.

COTEAUX DU LANGUEDOC
LANGUEDOC
FRANCE

421

COTEAUX DU LANGUEDOC
LANGUEDOC
FRANCE

Gilbert Alquier et fils

Faugères
34600 Bédarieux
Tel. 67230789
Fax 67953051

The estate crest tells us that the Alquiers have been growers since 1893. Gilbert obtains a very traditional range of wines from his 30 ha, planted 45% in Syrah, 15% in Mourvèdre and the remaining 40% in equal parts of Grenache and Carignan. The vines are 40-50 years old on average and Gilbert makes sure that yields are kept low. The slopes where the plants are located have the hard, shale soil typical of the zone. The grapes are completely de-stemmed when they are picked and then undergo slow fermentation and maceration at about 25°C. The wines then age for 14 months in wooden barrels to become Faugères, one of the most powerful and robust products of the entire Appellation. Alquier obtains about 120,000 bottles a year, which all contribute to the growing and well-deserved interest in this excellent wine region.

Faugères 1990 ♥ ②
Deep ruby red color which hints at the wine's youth. The bouquet is toasty and rich in new wood with further notes of red fruit, leather and violets. Well-rounded and smooth on the palate, the structure is straightforward but very inviting.

Château de Grézan

34480 Laurens
Tel. 67902746
Fax 67902901

Château de Grézan is a large estate whose vineyards comprise almost the whole of the Appellation of Faugères. The 120 ha boast a wide range of varieties including Grenache, Syrah, Mourvèdre, Carignan, Cinsaut, Cabernet Sauvignon, Merlot, Gamay, Pinot Noir, Chardonnay and others. The plants are located on slate-bearing shale which takes full advantage of the Mediterranean climate. The red grapes are picked mechanically, crushed in a pneumatic press and fermented traditionally with slow, temperature-controlled maceration. Three cuvées are made: Château de Grézan and Château de Laurens, both AOC Faugères and the Commanderie de Saint-Jean, a Vin de Pays. Most of the Faugères, of course, comes from Grenache, Syrah and Mourvèdre, which together make up about half of the vine stock. The owners, Lubac, Fardez and Pujol, call their product a "development of mass-production wine" which seems to us to be an over-critical definition of their very well-made wines.

Faugères Château de Grézan 1990 ♥ ②
Intense color and on the nose the powerful, spicy aromas which are characteristic of the South. The palate, too, is fruity and spicy. Makes up in power for what it lacks in elegance. A wine for a cold winter's evening which warms like a good fire.

FAUGERES
LANGUEDOC
FRANCE

422

FAUGERES
LANGUEDOC
FRANCE

Château des Estanilles

34480 Lenthéric-Cabrerolles
Tel. 67902925
Fax 67901099

It is not easy to find a bottle of Château des Estanilles as almost all of the estate's production is distributed throughout France by post and often advance demand exceeds the year's supply. Michel Louison established his vine stock 15 years ago on 14 ha of sloping, pebbly shale terrain outside the village of Lenthéric in the Faugères Appellation. Today he has 24 ha of Syrah, Mourvèdre, Grenache, Cinsaut, Viognier, Roussanne, Marsanne and other varieties. As well as producing a traditional Faugères red and a surprisingly good rosé, Louison also makes a Cuvée Syrah and a Cuvée Prestige from Mourvèdre, Grenache and Syrah, both of which are very highly thought of. Syrah is vinified in stainless steel at controlled temperatures and aged for 13 months in oak barrels, one third of which are replaced every year. Mourvèdre and Grenache for the Cuvée Prestige age in vats, while the Syrah goes into wood and is blended in at a later stage. Louison has no difficulty either in producing an excellent white in his well-equipped cellar. The recent discovery that Viognier grows well on his slopes has led him to the conclusion the Faugères true vocation may well be to produce top-quality white wines.

Faugères Cuvée Syrah 1988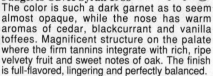
The color is such a dark garnet as to seem almost opaque, while the nose has warm aromas of cedar, blackcurrant and vanilla toffees. Magnificent structure on the palate where the firm tannins integrate with rich, ripe velvety fruit and sweet notes of oak. The finish is full-flavored, lingering and perfectly balanced.

Domaine du Fraïsse

1 bis, Chemin-de-Ronde
34480 Autignac
Tel. 67902340
Fax 67901020

When Jacques Pons inherited the family vineyards in the early 1970s, he had two causes for concern. The first was the generally low standing of the region's wines and the second was the fact that grapes grown on the "garrigue", the rocky hill slopes around the estate, were of superior quality to his own. With this in mind, Pons began to re-organize the property by exchanging parcels on low ground for others on the slopes and by purchasing virgin plots on the "garrigue" where he established new vineyards. In 1982 the sub-zone was assigned to the Faugères Appellation and today Domaine du Fraïsse comprises 20 ha of Appellation vineyards and another 20 of Vin de Table vine stock. The Appellation vineyards are planted in 48% Carignan, but this variety is gradually giving way to Syrah and Grenache, which today represent about 24% each of the total stock. There is also a small percentage of Cinsaut. Pons has also started to plant premium varieties on the muddy low ground with the intention of making varietal wines. A Merlot has already been produced and 1992 was the first vintage for Chardonnay. The 100,000 bottles of Faugères are produced by carbonic maceration. The varieties are fermented separately and then blended. Production of Faugères rosé is around 20,000 bottles.

Faugères 1989
Powerful and full-bodied in every respect, starting with the impenetrably dark red color. The nose is warm and sweet with a southern personality reminiscent of Port. On the palate, the warmth and sweet fruit are juicy and mouthfilling. Not a wine to drink if you are thirsty as it will go straight to your head!

FAUGERES
LANGUEDOC
FRANCE

423

FAUGERES
LANGUEDOC
FRANCE

Château de Nouvelles

11350 Tuchan
Tel. 68454003
Fax 68454921

Robert Daurat-Fort makes an exceptional Fitou at Château de Nouvelles, an estate where an ancient Roman settlement has come to light. At present the property comprises 88 ha of vine stock, on average 40 years old, located on various different soil types, clay, shale and sand. Over half of the estate's production comes from Carignan, Grenache, Syrah and Mourvèdre while the remainder is accounted for by the naturally sweet Muscat de Rivesaltes wine obtained from Grenache or Muscat grapes. Grapes for Fitou are fermented separately by variety with one fifth undergoing carbonic maceration and the rest fermenting at controlled temperatures in stainless steel where the wine is regularly pumped over the cap to obtain maximum extract. Wines are then blended and go into wood. The Muscat also receives careful attention as does the Rivesaltes red, which is unfortunately unfashionable at the moment. Both of these wines are fermented at controlled temperatures after a period of maceration on the skins in stainless steel vats.

Muscat de Rivesaltes   ♈ ②
Bright gold color with a rich, full, sweet bouquet of typical Muscat aromas. Well-rounded, fleshy and full-bodied as is characteristic of the variety. The ideal wine to serve with a fruit salad in summer or to savor on its own around four o'clock in the afternoon with a good biscuit.

Fitou 1985   ♈ ②
A wine with lots of personality, as you can see at once from the dark red color. The nose has all the ripe, spicy aromas which are typical of the South with an additional hint of plums and figs. Fruit returns on the powerful, mouthfilling palate, which has excellent length. The perfect accompaniment for roast meats and soft cheeses.

Château Fabas

11800 Laure-Minervois
Tel. 68781782
Fax 68782261

Château Fabas is a fortified farmhouse dating from the Middle Ages which today has 155 ha, 44 of which are planted with Grenache, Syrah, Cinsaut, Mourvèdre and Carignan together with a few white varieties. The soil is clay and chalk on a substratum of marl and the vines are on average 18 years old. The owner, Jean-Pierre Ormières, concentrates his energies on the production of 200,000 bottles of red Minervois in three different styles. Tradition is a soft, meaty wine to be drunk young and fresh while the Alexandre and Reservée cuvées are matured in wood and have good aging potential. All Fabas wines are made with meticulous care from partially de-stemmed grapes which are slowly fermented at controlled temperatures in a series of cement and glass-lined steel containers. Aging takes place in an air-conditioned cellar where the wines stay in wood for at least 12 months. Jean-Pierre's technically impeccable approach is apparent in his Minervois, some of which are quite exquisite.

Minervois Cuvée Alexandre 1990   ♈ ②
Bright red color with an elegant, spicy nose containing a hint of pepper in the classic southern style. The palate is rounded, soft and drinkable with subtle hints of fruit jam.

FITOU
LANGUEDOC
FRANCE

424

MINERVOIS
LANGUEDOC
FRANCE

J. et H. Madalle

Rue de Béziers
34490 Saint-Nazaire-de-Ladarez
Tel. 67896264
Fax 67895979

German and Jacques Madalle are vignerons whose wines reflect the regional spirit and their own honest endeavors. Theirs is an approach based on time, patience and hard work, which they apply to their 17-ha estate at the foot of the Haut Languedoc mountain in arid, south-facing shale countryside. The vines are 25 years old on average and the varieties are the traditional ones for the region: Carignan, Cinsaut, Grenache, Syrah and Mourvèdre. The grapes are hand-picked, in the case of the Cuvée des Schistes (one of the three cuvées produced) over the course of several careful selections. Fermentation takes place in enamelled vats, lasting 6 to 10 days according to variety. The 40,000 bottles of Tradition produced every year are obtained from a blend of all the varieties. The Cuvée des Schistes, vinified without the use of wood, is 80% Syrah with Grenache and Mourvèdre, while the Clos de la Boutarelle, obtained from 40% Mourvèdre and Grenache with the remainder Syrah, matures for eight months in old wood. 120,000 bottles each of the last two cuvées are produced.

Domaine Madalle Saint Chinian 1990 🍇 ①
An extraordinarily deep, dark, rich red. The bouquet is already a little evolved and while not absolutely clean is pleasantly spicy and sunny. The flavor on the palate is the full, sweet, ripe taste of southern grapes. A well-rounded wine with something a little reminiscent of Port in the palate.

Domaine du Bosc

Vias 34450
Tel. 67217358
Fax 67216838

Pierre Bésinet's energy and dynamism have done much to promote viticulture in the Hérault area. As well as founding Cante Cigale, a property he runs with two of his neighbors, he has also set up Domaine du Bosc, an estate which has won praise and recognition from all over the world, particularly for its fine range of headily-scented white wines. There are 55 ha of vineyards on volcanic soil planted with Sauvignon, Chardonnay, Marsanne, Grenache Blanc, Viognier and Muscat vines from which Bésinet obtains a range of varietal wines. All the musts spend a certain length of time on the skins in the vat before they are stabilized and fermented at low temperatures. Domaine du Bosc wines are clean and fresh and bring out the character of their variety to the full, from the intense grape aroma of Muscat to fleshy, opulent Grenache Blanc and herbaceous Sauvignon Blanc with its aromas of cedar and lemon.

Marsanne 1990 🍇 ②
A classic expression of the marvels of which Marsanne is capable. Pale straw-yellow with a delicate nose of fennel and other herbs as well as a note of pine. Refreshing acidity on the palate and moderate alcohol to accompany the dense fruit.

SAINT CHINIAN
LANGUEDOC
FRANCE

425

VINS DE PAYS D'HERAULT
LANGUEDOC
FRANCE

Mas de Daumas Gassac

Aniane 34150
Tel. 67577128
Fax 67574103

Mas de Daumas Gassac is an estate that has created a good deal of debate. Its customers are among the world's most prestigious consumers of wine, but there are people who say that its excellently-made Vin de Pays owes rather too much to astute marketing and that it is above all disgracefully expensive. The 24 ha of vineyards are located on terrain of glacial origin which was first identified in the late 1960s by Professor Enjalbert. He considers the soil type ideal for viticulture and the first wines were produced in 1978. Today the owners, the Guibert de la Vaissière family, produce about 70,000 bottles of red wine, 20,000 bottles of white and the same number of sparkling rosé. The varieties used are quite fascinating: the red is 80% Cabernet Sauvignon plus equal parts of Cabernet Franc, Merlot, Syrah, Malbec, Tannat and Pinot Noir while the whites are obtained from Chardonnay, Viognier and Petit Manseng (a Pyrenean variety generally used for sweet wines) with 5% Roussanne, Marsanne and Bourboulenc. Vinification techniques at Mas owe their inspiration to the great Émile Peynaud. Red wines are made with the Médoc method while the hard-to-find, expensive white spends five days on the skins before fermenting at controlled temperatures. All the wines are very good, the whites in particular, so it is worth encouraging one's friends to purchase a few!

Blanc de Raisins Blancs 1991   🍇 ③
Magnificently rich, bright color with an opulent, clean nose dominated by Muscat and Viognier. The full-flavored aromatic characteristics of Muscat seem for the moment to be prevalent on the palate, too, while the acidity is still a little suppressed. An interesting wine with considerable power.

Mas de Daumas Gassac 1990   🍇 ③
Superbly intense, deep color with full-bodied fruity aromas. The palate is firm and well-rounded, with remarkable extract and power. A very well-made wine whose acidity and tannins confer genuine personality.

Haute Vallée du Gassac 1989   🍇🍇 ③
Another red with a super-concentrated color. Intense and complex on both nose and palate, a wine of great structure with plenty of fruit, tannins and length which will age comfortably. A "new" wine which in many ways echoes the style of older, traditional Appellations.

Cave L'Étoile

26, avenue du Puig-del-Mas
66650 Banyuls-sur-mer
Tel. 68880010
Fax 68881510

The modest-looking l'Étoile cellar is the best and most consistent of the three cooperatives in this tiny Catalan port. While the Colliure still has much to prove in our opinion, the quality of the Banyuls wine is guaranteed, with its special "rancid" aroma which lies somewhere in between green walnut and bitter orange, in addition to an impressive range of oriental aromas. The manager, Jean-Paul Ramio, is a local boy and contributing member of the cooperative who successfully blends authenticity with seriousness. Tastings here are unforgettable and may include prodigies like the Sélect Vieux 1974, one of the most expensive wines in Banyuls. It all takes place in an atmosphere of cosy chaos in the midst of old barrels, old-fashioned fat-bellied bottles and demijohns lined up under the sun on the roof. The cellar was founded in 1921 and has 55 members who cultivate 180 ha which include some of the best land in the cru. Annual production is 165,000 bottles.

Rimatge 1989   🍇 ②
This vintage-style wine is excellent value for money. The nose has pine, fig and plum aromas while the palate is fleshy but not excessively so. Lay this one down.

Hors d'Age Doux Paillé   🍇🍇 ③
With its old-gold color, this is the most elegant, complex wine the cellar produces. The nose has figs, caramel, dates, vanilla, candied pear and a whole range of other evocatively sweet aromas. The sensual, subtle palate has great finesse and excellent length. A wine for connoisseurs but still at a very reasonable price.

Domaine du Mas Blanc

9, avenue du Général de Gaulle
66650 Banyuls-sur-mer
Tel. 68883212

Founded by Doctor André Parcé, a local celebrity, this cellar's 20 ha of vineyards in Collioure and Banyuls produce 12,000 and 35,000 bottles a year, respectively. His son Jean-Michel has gradually taken over management of the estate. Vats are equipped with automatic crushing equipment, systematic de-stemming; careful selection of the fruit; barriques and vats of different ages are lined up in an air-conditioned cellar and old barrels are employed together. These elements allow aging to be carried out zone by zone for the still reds (Piloums and Cosprons Levant) or the blends according to vintage or degree of dryness by blocked fermentation. Some of these blends feature on the wine lists of France's greatest restaurants. The reds are outstanding, such as the Cosprons '88 with its aromas of tea, coffee, leather and tobacco or the '86 with its great personality and splendid body. The high point of the range of naturally sweet products is the "solera" method wine, the result of a unique pyramid system of aging which could theoretically last forever. In fact, the earliest barrel still in use dates from 1925. It is, however, in the vintage Banyuls (Rimage in Catalan), that the talent of the Parcé father-and-son team really shines.

Rimage Cuvée La Coume 1989 🍷🍷 ②
This cuvée comprises 3,520 numbered bottles of satisfyingly bright-colored wine with an intense nose, good concentration, a hint of wood and a touch of alcohol. Full-bodied, sinewy and fleshy on the palate. A bottle to lay down until the components have had time to integrate.

Rimage 1985 🍷🍷 ③
A dark-colored Banyuls with an intense nose, full, fleshy palate and good structure. Outstanding length which leaves an impression of breeding and distinction. A great wine.

Domaine de la Rectorie

54, avenue du Puig-del-Mas
66650 Banyuls-sur-mer
Tel. 68881345
Fax 68881855

Brothers Marc and Thierry Parcé are cousins of Jean-Michel, the owner of Mas Blanc. They are city boys who have moved successfully back to the land their ancestors used to cultivate. The Parcés run a 23-ha estate which produces 80,000 bottles a year on shale soil and greet visitors in and elegant 1930s villa. Their wine is made in unassuming cellars near l'Étoile with Thierry, the younger brother, in charge of operations. Thierry is always ready to experiment in accordance with the characteristics of each vintage and one of the results of his efforts is the lovely '91 Collioure Rosé from Grenache, Carignan and Mourvèdre grapes which at 13.5° is powerful, meaty, peppery and very long. The red Collioures aged in the bottle sell like hot cakes, and if you can still find a case of the 1990 second bottling blended from Grenache, Mourvèdre and Carignan, then grab it! A first bottling containing Syrah is put on sale first and the '91 in this version is concentrated and tannic, promising well for the future. The same principle is used for Banyuls with a "young" version known as Parcé Frères and another version aged for a year in old barrels called Léon Parcé, in honor of the brothers' grandfather. Thierry and Marc also make drier Banyuls.

Cuvée Léon Parcé 1991 🍷🍷 ③
A still closed Banyuls with a dark color, but the wine's great class can be made out despite the lack of evolution. On the palate, the class is confirmed and notes of plum, mulberry and bitter orange come through. Superbly well-balanced with excellent length. A collector's wine.

Cuvée Parcé Frères 1991 🍷🍷 ②
Good rich color. Discreet, serious yet elegant smoky aromas. This Banyuls is sweet on entry but develops eloquently on the palate and has good tannins. Fine length. A wine to put away in the cellar until after the year 2000.

BANYULS
ROUSSILLON
FRANCE

427

BANYULS
ROUSSILLON
FRANCE

Château de Jau

66600 Cases-de-Pène
Tel. 66389010
Fax 66389133

This superb estate at the foot of the Cathar castles houses a modern art foundation and an open-air restaurant which is open during the summer. The Dauré family, Bernard, Sabine and their daughter Estelle, run this large property with 134 ha of vineyards from which they obtain the typical wines of the region, including a very light and drinkable Vin de l'Eté, a Côtes du Roussillon white with an impressive entry, a remarkable Villages red and an increasingly elegant and bright Muscat de Rivesaltes which is deliciously chewy on the palate, especially the '91 when the alcohol content was kept to the minimum of 15°. The modern, clean vat cellar, the pneumatic press, total de-stemming, carbonic maceration of Carignan and the air-conditioned cellar all contribute to the success of the 725,000 bottles produced every year. The Daurés cultivate 48 ha on the coast overlooking the stupendous bay of Paulilles in the Collioure and Banyuls Appellations, the last-mentioned of which is sold under the label Robert Doutres, the name of a friend of the family. The 60% Grenache and 40% Syrah of the Collioure rosé undergo a brief maceration on the skins. The red, which has a high proportion of Mourvèdre, is aged for 11 months in one and two year-old barriques.

Collioure Clos de Paulilles Rosé 1991 🏆 ①
Garnet color with an elegant peppery aroma over discreet notes of red berries. Strong on the palate and the fruit makes its presence felt. A fairly light rosé whose moderate length is amply compensated by stupendous balance and a captivating style.

Collioure 🍷🍷 ②
Clos de Paulilles Rouge 1989
Lovely appearance. Complex nose with hints of green coffee beans, mulberry, toastiness and spices. Soft on the palate, well-balanced and long with well-integrated tannins. To drink in three years' time.

Domaine La Tour Vieille

3, avenue du Mirador
66190 Collioure
Tel. 68824220
Fax 68823842

Christine Campadieu, a Banyuls girl whose father is an enologist, married Vincent Cantié from Collioure whose father salted anchovies for a living. The match has produced some very attractive bottles of wine (about 25,000 to 30,000 a year) obtained from two sub-zones which were once rivals despite coming under the same Appellation. Their 12 ha are equally divided between Collioure and Banyuls, with Banyuls producing the better wines. The couple still have an excellent Banyuls 1985, the Cuvée Francis Cantié named after Vincent's grandfather, which has the characteristic dark, brown-flecked appearance and "rancid" aroma of this wine. Fleshy, well-balanced and attractive on the palate, where it lingers invitingly, this Banyuls goes superbly with chocolate. As far as the Collioure is concerned, apart from a bright, lively rosé, there is still some way to go. Two cuvées are made, each corresponding to a particular locality and a special blend of grapes which completes the basic Grenache Noir with a touch of old Carignan. The Puig Ambeille, with 30% Mourvèdre, is the more promising under its heavy layer of tannins. The Puig Oriol, with 30% Syrah, has lighter tannins with a peppery flavor. Keep an eye on the promising Banyuls '88.

Banyuls Vintage 1990 🍷🍷 ②
Dense purple color and flavors of liquorice, tea and spices. The palate is frank and well-defined with good balance and depth. There is just the right note of spices and candied peel. A great wine to lay down, if the length on the palate is anything to go by.

COLLIOURE
ROUSSILLON
FRANCE

428

COLLIOURE
ROUSSILLON
FRANCE

Cellier des Templiers

Route du Mas Reig
66650 Banyuls-sur-mer
Tel. 68883159
Fax 68880084

Located on the high plains of Banyuls, the Cellier is the visible part of a huge enterprise comprising many business activities specializing in sales to large distribution chains, wine merchants and catering companies. This "hypermarket", which uses solar-powered air-conditioning for its cellars, brings together various wineries and estates and vinifies at least 70% of the Collioure and Banyuls crus, more than 3 million bottles a year. Many of these are laid down for leisurely aging. The enologist, Pierre Campadieu, has a huge number of barriques for his Collioures, some of which, like the well-known Abbaye de Valbone and the Château Reig, sell out within a month. Winemaking techniques are by and large traditional except for the old Carignans, up to 20% of which undergo carbonic maceration. For the Banyuls, aging is still in immense tuns. A part of these wines is placed out-doors in large barrels to enhance their typically "rancid" flavor. For special cuvées of old vintages - the '79 is the oldest currently available - AOC Banyuls Grand Cru, which requires a minimum of 30 months aging in wood, is widely used.

Cuvée Haute Tradition 1990   🍇 ②
A generic red of attractive appearance. The wood (from 6 months in new oak) is moderately elegant and lends aromas of cinnamon, bay-leaf and vanilla to the nose. The palate is fresh with plenty of Grenache Noir and the moderate length is rounded off by a lovely raspberry finish. Drink in two years.

Collioure Rouge   🍇 ②
Domaine du Roumani 1990
A moderately intense Collioure, red in appearance. Austere nose, still closed, with hints of wood tar. Fleshy, well-balanced palate with very attractive body and pleasing length. Drink within the next five years.

Château de Cazenove

66300 Trouillas
Tel. 68216633
Fax 68216633

With an average annual production of 2,400 hl, one third of which is bottled and sold locally while the rest is sold wholesale, this old property is committed to relaunching the Aspres sub-zone, considered by some to be of little interest. Jacques Montès is easy to get on with and knowledgeable. He is in the process of gradually handing over the management of the 50-ha estate to his sons Etienne and Emanuel. The precious advice of Jean-Luc Colombo and Albéric Mazoyer, the two stars of the Côtes du Rhône, is starting to bear tangible fruit for white wines from the '92 vintage as well as for the reds, particularly the Côtes du Roussillon where a blend of Grenache and Carignan with a little Syrah is worth mentioning for the way in which it marries a classic style with an innovative approach. De-stemming is systematic and the grapes are fermented with a maceration which in 1991 lasted for 14 days, the wines reaching as much as 13.5° alcohol. Another blend, macerated for three weeks, has a majority of Syrah with 20% Carignan and 20% Grenache Noir. There is also a Muscat de Rivesaltes in preparation in addition to a white Côtes du Roussillon from Malvoisie, Grenache Blanc and old Macabeo.

Côtes du Roussillon 1991   🍇🍇 ①
This wine obtained from Grenache and Carignan, which we tasted from the barrel, has a very intense color. The nose is still very closed but the finesse and promise of future complexity are clear. Alcohol, earth, spices and dried fig are already in evidence. A powerful, tannic wine with stamina which lingers on the palate and has a faint rustic hint in the finish.

COLLIOURE
ROUSSILLON
FRANCE

429

COTES DU ROUSSILLON
ROUSSILLON
FRANCE

Domaine Gauby

Le Fradjal
66600 Calce
Tel. 68643519-68642340

Ghislaine and Gérard Gauby are fast becoming stars in this tiny village of 130 inhabitants on the Corbières spurs. Leaving sweet wines to the cooperative, they concentrated on their first real red wine in 1988. Their great wine at the moment is a '90 Villages from half Grenache and Carignan from plants over 80 years old blended with Mourvèdre and Syrah thinned out before the grapes took on color to limit the yield to 30 hl/ha, de-stemmed by hand and fermented for 21 days. Aged for a year in one-third new barriques, this wine is a jewel which won the approval of a very severe jury at the annual Saint-Bacchus festival at Perpignan. The other Gauby reds are not without their attractions, whether it be the straightforward Vin de Pays or the excellent Côtes du Roussillon from grapes left on the stem, which is neither filtered nor fined and where the much-berated Carignan plays a significant role. Production is not, however, limited to red wines; the 45 ha of chalky soil, part of it shale-bearing, also provides a singular dry Muscat and a magnificent Vin de Pays from old Macabeo vines, Carignan Blanc and Grenache, part of which ferments in new barrels. It is the presence of Grenache Blanc excludes this wine from the Appellation d'Origine Contrôlée.

Vieilles Vignes 1991   ℗ ①
The color of old gold, with aromas of toastiness and flowers. Well-rounded on entry, with a lovely fresh structure, a wine which is well-balanced on the palate despite its alcohol content and has a lingering finish.

Côtes du Roussillon 1990   ℗℗ ①
An attractive dark color and discreet notes of oak on the nose. Dense on the palate, with a lovely structure which makes this a very drinkable wine.

Rouge Villages 1990   ℗℗ ①
Luminous color and subtle, invitingly oaky aroma where hints of leather and fruit are in evidence.

Domaine du Mas Crémat

66600 Espira-de-l'Agly
Tel. 68389206
Fax 68389223

A hint of Côte d'Or on the spurs of Corbières for a thoroughly admirable product. Jean-Marc and Catherine Jeannin - Catherine's parents run the Mongeard-Mugneret estate at Vosne Romanée - recently left the Côtes de Nuits to take over a 25-ha property on black shale in the Agly Valley, a very promising sub-zone just above Rivesaltes. At present they produce about 50,000 bottles, with 30% going to the local market. They make rather more white wine than red and produce no sweet wines for the time being. There are two kinds of white: the Vin de Pays, a splendid dry Muscat, and a Côtes du Roussillon obtained from very old vines of Macabeo and Grenache Blanc. A parcel of Vermentino (Rolle) was recently established. The red grapes are completely de-stemmed and vinified in the traditional fashion, with no carbonic maceration,and with a 12-day fermentation in enamelled stainless steel vats. The Côtes du Roussillon includes 30% Syrah and 10% Mourvèdre. Syrahs are aged in one year-old barriques for at least eight months.

Côtes du Roussillon Blanc 1991   ℗ ①
A wine with a luminous golden yellow color and a nose with elegant aromas of toastiness and mint. The palate is full-bodied, fleshy and mouthfilling. Outstanding body and superb fruit.

Domaine Sarda-Malet

Mas Saint-Michel - 12, chemin de Sainte-Barbe
66000 Perpignan
Tel. 68567238
Fax 68564760

We are grateful to Max and Suzy Malet for being among the first to believe in something a little different from the rather simplistic image of Roussillon wines that had come to be commonplace. In 1985 they began their adventure with aging in barrels in the manner of the great châteaux of Bordeaux. Now that they have acquired some experience, they are continuing with white wines, including a small quantity of Roussanne and Marsanne fermented in new barrels and noting this on the label with the initials SM. They also make a Muscat with a long, well-balanced, almost late-harvest style and a Rivesaltes, including a version which includes wines over 20 years old where there are powerful notes of toastiness. There are two red cuvées: one, the white label, is for wines which have undergone a brief maceration and are ready to drink; the other, the black label, is aged for 12 months in one-quarter new barriques, and is for wines to lay down to fully appreciate the contribution of Grenache Noir (50%) and equal parts of Syrah and Mourvèdre. The estate extends over 50 ha to the north of Perpignan and produces 180,000 bottles a year.

Côtes du Roussillon Blanc 1991 ☙ ①
Clear, pale color. The nose is ethereally light with tiny hints of spices and juniper. Discreet freshness on the palate with notes of peach and honey. Drink young.

Côtes du Roussillon Rouge 1989 ☙☙ ②
This "black label" wine, with a moderately intense color, is fruity despite its powerful tannins; fortunately, these are not excessively hard. The finish is of liquorice. Taste again in a couple of years' time when the tannins have mellowed out.

Mas Amiel

66460 Maury
Tel. 68290102
Fax 68291782

These breathtakingly beautiful shale terraces are 30 km. from Perpignan, in an arid valley between Fenouillèdes and the Corbières spurs in the shadow of the Cathar castles. In total, there are 155 ha in two parcels entirely devoted to sweet wines, above all the Appellation Maury, but also a Muscat de Rivesaltes that is perhaps a little lacking in finesse. The estate is planted 90% in Grenache Noir, a variety which is perfectly at home in the hot, dry climate. The yard is an unforgettable sight, with over 3,000 70-l demijohns of low-yield wine stored in the open air to acquire the classic "rancid" flavor. The crushed grapes are stabilized with 96° alcohol and then macerate for 15 to 30 days, depending on the end-product desired, before going into old vats in a Corinth-grape scented cellar. Charles Dupuy, the owner, and his manager Jérémie Gark pay particular attention to their bottles; for the Vintage wine, they use an Italian-designed long-necked bottle while other products, including the superb '86 reserve and the '82 special production, are bottled in more traditional containers.

Maury Vintage 1991 ☙ ②
Ripe cherry, near-black color. Aromas of dried grape, caramel, cassis and bilberry. The sweet entry is followed up by a full, tannic and moderately firm palate. May be drunk young and cool (10°C) while the fruit is at its best or left in the cellar to mature for ten years or so.

Maury Vintage 1985 ☙☙ ③
Beautiful deep color. The bouquet is intense and complex, but still closed. Again, the first impression on the palate is sweet, but with outstanding balance. Great finesse, which lends the wine elegance and admirable length. A wine to drink in a comfortable armchair with a good cigar.

*COTES DU ROUSSILLON
ROUSSILLON
FRANCE*

431

*MAURY
ROUSSILLON
FRANCE*

Domaine Laporte

Château Roussillon, route de Canet
66000 Perpignan
Tel. 68500653
Fax 68667752

Raymond Laporte is a fine young enologist who has chosen to focus on the Appellation after a phase of making monovarietal wines, to the exclusion of all else. The success of his dry Muscat Vin de Pays from old Muscat d'Alexandrie vines is one result of this change of direction. A thirst-quenching wine, it is produced by fermenting the uncrushed grapes and bottling early. Laporte's Syrah-based rosé is equally attractive with its light, pleasant style. His other wines, all monovarietal, are a Cabernet, a Merlot to drink all through the meal and a Grenache Blanc under the Blanc de Blanc label, as the variety is excluded from the Appellation d'Origine Contrôlée. Laporte's Côtes de Roussillon, where Syrah is dominant, lacks something in structure and concentration, but this situation will improve over the next few years as Raymond, who is assisted on the estate by his charming sister Bernadette, has the humility and intelligence to listen carefully to benevolent criticism. It is, however, Raymond's masterpiece, the Muscat de Rivesaltes, which will continue to win awards. The Muscat grapes, all of the Petits Grains variety, undergo light maceration on the skins and are then gently crushed and the must removed from the lees at low temperatures.

Muscat de Rivesaltes 1991   🍷 🍷 ②
Brilliant appearance and a bouquet of lemon blossom with a faint liqueur stickiness on the palate. Invitingly fleshy and full with aromas of citrus and excellent length, this is one of the best Muscats of the moment. Not to be missed!

Domaine Cazes

4, rue Francisco Ferrer
66600 Rivesaltes
Tel. 68640826
Fax 68646979

The dynamic Cases brothers, André and Bernard, produce 700,000 bottles a year on their 150 ha on the terraces of Rivesaltes and the Roussillon plain. Half is Vin de Pays and a quarter naturally sweet wines, but their wide range of products goes from barrique-fermented Chardonnay to a complex, elegant Côtes du Roussillon-Villages with aromas of candied strawberry, kirsch, coffee and vanilla, not forgetting the speciality of the house, one of the most stylish and consistent Muscats de Rivesaltes around. The bulk of Cazes sales is provided by their highly popular Canon du Maréchal, an easy-to-drink Vin de Pays which comes in both a red version, based mainly on Merlot, and a dry white Muscat-based version. The name commemorates Maréchal Joffre, a native of Rivesaltes. The Cazes are superlative technicians who have won a host of awards, such as the Saint-Bacchus Trophy. Their cellars feature pneumatic presses and they have long been enthusiastic users of air-conditioning and other refrigeration equipment. Cazes Muscat de Rivesaltes is as good drunk as an aperitif as it is served with dessert. Based on a blend of 20% Muscat Petits Grains and 80% Muscat d'Alexandrie, it is a wine obtained by bringing together the end-results of different vinification techniques.

Rivesaltes Vieux 1980   🍷 ②
A Rivesaltes the color of seasoned oak with a nose of sun-dried grapes and dried figs. Well-balanced and sweet on the palate with hints of jam and a long finish. Will improve with another couple of years in the bottle, but this wine has sufficient texture to evolve for at least a decade.

Rivesaltes   🍷 🍷 ③
Cuvée Aimé Cazes 1973
An old-gold Rivesaltes to delight the most demanding connoisseur. The still-evolving nose is hard to define, going from nutmeg to candied lemon peel through fig, curry and pistachio. Beautifully smooth on the palate. A wine worth spending many hours getting to know.

MUSCAT DE RIVESALTES
ROUSSILLON
FRANCE

432

RIVESALTES
ROUSSILLON
FRANCE

Cave Les Vignerons de Rivesaltes

1, rue de la Roussillonnaise
66600 Rivesaltes
Tel. 68640663
Fax 68646469

This huge cooperative serves an area of 2,000 ha and produces a range of 30 wines, many attractively-priced monovarietal white Vins de Pays including Chardonnay, Sauvignon, Muscat and Malvoisie. The peach-and-honey Malvoisie '91 is an excellent example, made from fully ripened grapes by the cooperative's enologist Fernand Baixas. It is a fleshy, dense wine which those in search of something different might be tempted to lay down. The other speciality of the cooperative is the Muscat de Rivesaltes which is on sale in practical half-bottles. Light and modern in style, it goes perfectly with a piece of Roquefort or Stilton. Like the Cazes Muscat, the Les Vignerons product undergoes a light maceration on the skins and is invitingly young, fresh and fruity. The Côtes du Roussillon '91 rosé is also an interesting, well-made wine, one version of which has spent a few days fermenting in barriques and then fermented only in vats, is the more lively and less demanding. Besides two stylish reds aged in oak, one from the Rombeau property, also worthy of mention are the good, no-nonsense red wines which are exported in large quantities thanks to their very competitive prices and excellent presentation.

Côtes du Roussillon 🍇 ①
Cuvée Pierre de la Fabrègue 1990
A red Côtes du Roussillon from the Rombeau property with good color and fairly intense oak aromas accompanied by cocoa, oak bark, spices and prunes which combine with a certain elegance. Lively and forthright on the palate at present, this is a wine to lay down for 3 to 5 years.

Cuvée Arnaud de Villeneuve 1990 🍇 ②
A Village red with a charred-oak entry which leads into more stylish and concentrated notes. Initially soft, the palate allows the fine tannins and length to come invitingly through. May be drunk immediately or laid down for five years.

Languedoc and Roussillon Appellations in this Guide

Languedoc
Corbières
Costières de Nîmes
Coteaux de Languedoc
Faugères
Fitou
Minervois
Saint-Chinian
Vins de Pays de l'Hérault

Roussillon
Banyuls
Collioure
Côtes du Roussillon
Maury
Muscat de Rivesaltes
Rivesaltes

RIVESALTES
ROUSSILLON
FRANCE

433

RIVESALTES
ROUSSILLON
FRANCE

Loire

When you mention the Loire, most people immediately think of the royal châteaux of Chambord and Chenonceaux, the renowned cheese Crottin de Chavignol and the dry white wines Sancerre and Muscadet. These, however, are only a small portion of the wide range of marvellous wines, most of which are unknown outside of France, produced in the Loire Valley.

The Loire is France's longest river running for 1,000 km from the Massif Central in central southern France to the Atlantic Ocean with 80,000 ha of vineyard in close proximity. The river itself has made the fortune of the wines. Until the 19th century, river traffic between Tours and Nantes enabled the wines to reach England The inhabitants of Paris used to embark on barges at Orléans to go downriver to acquire supplies of the wines of Touraine and Anjou.

The Loire is sub-divided into four large sub-regions for wine: Central Loire, including Sancerre and Pouilly-Fumé; Touraine, including the generic Appellation, the white-wine Appellations of Montlouis and Vouvray and the red Appellations Chinon, Bourgueil and Saint-Nicolas-de-Bourgueil; Saumur/Anjou, including the important Anjou Appellation, the fashionable Saumur-Champigny and the famous sweet white wines of Coteaux du Layon; Pays Nantais, noted for Muscadet.

The unifying element in such a diverse range of micro-climates, varieties and soil types is the northerly position of the Loire Valley. Whether they are sweet or dry, red, white or rosé, still or sparkling, Loire wines are always uniquely fresh with a natural acidity which sets them apart from the products of the warmer vineyards of Southern Europe and the New World.

The most widely cultivated grape varieties in the Loire are Sauvignon, which reaches its peak in France on the chalky slopes of Sancerre, and Gamay, which produces excellent thirst-quenching reds to drink young. The better growers in Sancerre, dissatisfied with their pinkish-colored red wine made from Pinot Noir, have studied the techniques used in Burgundy to obtain some really interesting wines. Cabernet Franc, popular in Bordeaux, is also the main red variety in Touraine and Anjou. Traditionally in most Appellations, for example Chinon and Bourgueil, vinification is carried out by grape variety and in the best vintages, such as the exceptional 1989, the best producers obtained superb results with immense aging potential. Chenin Blanc is another of the Loire's noble varieties and nowhere else on earth does it produce such stylish, elegant wines. In 1989 and 1990, Chenin in Vouvray and Coteaux du Layon produced wines that are universally acclaimed as being among the four greatest vintages of the century, opulent sweet whites to rival the best Sauternes with the potential to age for 50 to 100 years. In colder vintages, Chenin is also capable of producing fresh, classy dry or demi-sec white wines. Here and there in the Loire some interesting local varieties can also be found, such as Fief Gris, a first cousin of Sauvignon, Romorantin, introduced into Touraine by Francis I, and Groslot de Luynes. All of these, if correctly treated, are capable of producing interesting Vins de Pays with distinctive personalities. The Loire's post-war image is finally changing and the days when négociants used to sell enormous quantities of semi-sweet rosés are over. The new generation of growers have studied winemaking techniques and know the importance of a well-equipped cellar and of sheer hard work in the production of wines with an unmistakeable regional character. Few have followed the trend popular elsewhere for aging wines in oak. Leading producers are now shifting their attention from the cellar to the vineyard in search of a biodynamic approach to cultivation which balances soil type, substratum and vine variety.

Soil types range from chalk-based to volcanic, from shale-bearing to sandy, and much remains to be done despite the fact that the same family has often been growing vines on the land for centuries. The present generation is trying a new approach and producing outstanding wines at prices that are still attractive. Now is the time for wine-lovers to take another look at the Loire.

Gérard Depardieu

Château de Tigné
49540 Tigné
Tel. 41596859
Fax 41596851

When that most Gallic of French actors, Gérard Depardieu, bought Château de Tigné, he did not do so for the sake of acquiring a hobby or merely to enjoy the impressive 11th-century towers. He did so because he genuinely loves wine and he had seen the potential latent in the estate's 30 ha. Depardieu's highly capable enologist Dominique Polleau, a native of Tigné, is a born vigneron as well as mayor of the town. To work with someone who wants to rediscover traditional wine styles is for Dominique a dream come true. There are no rows of gleaming new stainless steel vats here, nor are there enologists striving to avoid risks at all costs. Paramount here is the desire to get the very best out of the "terroir" and the grapes without the use of chemicals. To obtain the right tannins, red wines are subjected to slow maceration in a style which has now gone out of fashion. The Cuvée Cyrano 1990, already sold out, was aged for 18 months in old oak and bottled without filtration. The resulting wine is attractively rustic, warm and full-bodied, the kind of wine that Rabelais might have enjoyed and certainly the sort of wine that Depardieu himself drinks with the greatest of pleasure.

Anjou Blanc 1989   🍇 ①
Straw-yellow with elegant aromas of good intensity and a generous body. A wine with tons of personality, from Chenin Blanc grapes.

Anjou Rouge 1990   🍇 ②
A full-bodied, rustic red wine with an intense garnet color which brings to mind a classic Cahors. Rich fruit with aromas of berries alongside other more pungent, earthier notes. The tannins in the finish suggest that this wine should be allowed to mature in the bottle for a year or two more.

Domaine des Hautes Ouches

Linières
49700 Brigné-sur-Layon
Tel. 41593051

It was hard work tasting the 1990 Anjou reds as almost all the wines had the intense color which indicates that the producer has tried to extract as much as possible from a very ripe vintage. As a result, some of the wines were coarse with harsh tannins ruining the palate while others were bland, although technically perfect. This could not be said of Hautes Ouches wines, whose character makes them a real delight to taste. It is a pleasure that more and more wine-lovers are discovering now that Joël Lhumeau has extended his vineyards and opened up new outlets for his products, which are still sold at very competitive prices. He belongs to the third generation of a family of growers and began his career with three hectares in 1962. Today, Joël is the owner of 42 ha and has never used the services of a consultant enologist, but has always maintained an open mind and a willingness to experiment in his own individual fashion with up-to-date techniques. His sons, who have studied enology and business studies, all work in the family firm. It will be interesting to see what new directions the estate takes when they take over.

Anjou Rouge 1990   🍇 ①
Rich red color and a nose with the typical peppery aroma of Cabernet Franc. A full-bodied, complex wine with a faint hint of charred oak and liquorice. Ready to drink now.

ANJOU SAUMUR/ANJOU
LOIRE
FRANCE

436

ANJOU SAUMUR/ANJOU
LOIRE
FRANCE

Dominique Polleau

Domaine de l'Errue
49540 Tigné
Tel. 41594158
Fax 41596851

Dominique Polleau is a busy man. Not only does he manage his own 20-ha estate, but he also finds time to be mayor of Tigné. When the local château with its neglected vineyard was put up for sale, a possible buyer came to taste the mayor's wines to see whether the soil was capable of producing decent wines. The buyer was so captivated that he bought the château and then asked Dominique to be his enologist. The buyer in question was Gérard Depardieu and he and Dominique get on famously. Both hate 'technical' wine and know how to combine the latter's discipline and sensitivity for the cru with the former's outgoing, inspirational approach. Dominique had a very strict upbringing - his father made him help out in the vineyard when he was a small child - but he has also inherited an extraordinary passion, which he has passed on to his own son. His wines may not be outstandingly commercial but they are authentic, genuine, loyal to tradition and shaped by the experience of past generations.

Anjou Rouge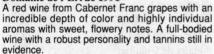
Domaine de l'Errue 1991
A red wine from Cabernet Franc grapes with an incredible depth of color and highly individual aromas with sweet, flowery notes. A full-bodied wine with a robust personality and tannins still in evidence.

Domaine Richou Père et Fils

Chauvigné
49610 Mozé-sur-Louet
Tel. 41787213
Fax 41787605

The Richou family has been producing wine since 1550. Today the tradition of generation after generation of vignerons is maintained by Didier Richou, an extremely enthusiastic individual with an insatiable curiosity for anything to do with wine. He even worked with one of the very first growers in Minnesota. In 1979, Didier joined his father on the 30-ha estate and today he produces eight different wines ranging from dry and sweet whites to reds, some ready for drinking and some with good aging potential. Didier's energies during his first ten years on the estate have been directed towards a series of experiments which have led him to abandon the rather rustic, old-fashioned traditional winemaking style to go for wines with a more attractive personality. Now that the winemaking has been sorted out, he is concentrating on the vineyard. Didier is enthralled by the topography of the land and the nature of the schistous and volcanic soil on his estate and is approaching his studies with the spirit of a true pioneer.

Coteaux d'Aubance
Les Trois Demoiselles 1990
Obtained from botrytized Chenin grapes, partly fermented in new barriques, this is a sweet white wine with the color of old gold and a nose of honey and oak. The palate is complex and powerful.

Anjou Villages Rouge 1990
A wine with good structure from Cabernet Franc grapes. The bright red color is flecked with violet and the nose has ripe fruit and a stupendous concentration of aromas thanks to the low yield and very ripe grapes. Tannins still very much to the fore. A wine which will benefit enormously from a few more years in the bottle.

ANJOU SAUMUR/ANJOU
LOIRE
FRANCE

437

ANJOU SAUMUR/ANJOU-VILLAGES
LOIRE
FRANCE

Mark Angeli

La Sansonnière
49380 Thouarcé
Tel. 41540808
Fax 41540010

Mark Angeli is the new-comer to the region. If he carries on the way he has been up until now, then growers will soon be standing in line to get his advice. Mark's secret, though, is not to be found in a new hi-tech cellar. Even if he had wanted one he could not have afforded it from the proceeds of the sale of his small construction company in Aix-en-Provence. Mark's obsession with wine grew from a contract he had with a family which produced wine in Sauternes. Once Mark had tasted such nectar, there was no going back. He sold his business, signed up for a course on wine at La Tour Blanches in Sauternes and spent a dispiriting year in search of a vineyard in a sweet wine region. The day after he arrived in Coteaux du Layon, he found what he was looking for. Mark's first vintage was 1990, when he made 600 bottles of an extraordinary Bonnezeaux. He aims to make concentrated wines with good aging potential and he is convinced that top-quality juice can only be obtained through biodynamic cultivation and the use of old vertical presses. He might just be right.

Anjou Blanc Cuvée Christine 1991 ℣ ①
A refreshing white wine with loads of personality fermented in oak and bottled with no added sulfites. Pale golden yellow with a complex bouquet where orange peel is prominent. A fine result from Chenin grapes, despite the difficult vintage.

Coteax du Layon 1991 ℣ ℣ ①
Chenin grapes give this wine its golden color and a nose with a subtle, lingering aroma of plum jam and apricots. Sweet on the palate but with a frank, dry finish. Surprisingly concentrated for the vintage.

Bonnezeaux Cuvée Mathilde 1990 ℣ ℣ ④
Obtained from botrytized grapes carefully selected from old vines and aged for 18 months in oak. A bright gold wine with an aromatic bouquet of almost oriental complexity featuring apricots and dried figs. Sweet palate nicely complemented by fresh acidity and considerable weight.

Loire Appellations in this Guide

Anjou Saumur
Anjou
Anjou-Villages
Bonnezeaux
Coteaux de l'Aubance
Coteaux du Layon
Quarts de Chaume
Saumur-Champigny
Savennières
Nantais
Fiefs Vendéens
Muscadet
Touraine
Bourgueil
Cheverny
Chinon
Jasnières
Montlouis
Saint-Nicolas-de-Bourgueil
Touraine
Vouvray
Vins du Centre
Côtes Roannaises
Menetou-Salon
Pouilly-Fumé
Reuilly
Saint-Pourçain
Sancerre

Château de Fesles

49380 Thouarcé
Tel. 41541432
Fax 41540610

When the Boivins bought Château de Fesles in the middle of the last century, phylloxera was devastating the entire region. The large number of abandoned vineyards put up for sale meant they were able to put together a unique 12-ha estate which today produces by far the most elegant and opulent wines in Bonnezeaux. Jacques Boivin was working with his father as long ago as the 1960s, but it was in 1980, when he inherited the 33-ha property, that things started to change and the estate's reputation rose with the new quality standards he imposed. In 1991 Gaston Lenôtre, the internationally famous chef and director of a restaurant and catering chain, bought the château leaving Jacques Boivin to manage the estate. In 1992, a brand-new cellar and store were built. Didier Coutenceau, a leading Loire enologist, is working on the Anjou reds and Jacques Boivin assures his faithful customers that his Bonnezeaux can only continue to improve.

Bonnezeaux 🍷🍷🍷 ④
La Chapelle 1990
Obtained from Chenin vines planted near Jacques Boivin's house on the site of an old chapel. The bunches and indeed individual grapes attacked by noble rot are carefully selected as these are the only ones suitable for the production of the finest of the estate's sweet wines. In 1990, fermentation of La Chapelle was partly in stainless steel vats and partly in one year-old barriques purchased from Château d'Yquem. The second version is labelled La Chapelle Barrique, a wine with delicate hints of oak and a faint exotic note. Both wines are extremely attractive, the first being a more traditional expression of the cru. Pale gold in color, the nose has subtle aromas of honey and flowers. An elegant, opulent wine with great balance between its firm structure and complex aromas. It will be at its best in about 20 years.

ANJOU SAUMUR/BONNEZEAUX
LOIRE
FRANCE
439
ANJOU SAUMUR/BONNEZEAUX
LOIRE
FRANCE

Domaine de Terrebrune

Place du Champ de Foire
49380 Thouarcé
Tel. 41540199
Fax 41540906

René Renou inherited not just his father's vineyards but also his energy and initiative. Clear-headedly, he realized that a fragmented property would not permit him to produce the wines he wanted to and that he was not going to have time to pursue three careers, as grower, producer and négociant. As a result, René and his two partners founded the Domaine de Terrebrune in 1986, merging their estates, buying other vineyards and establishing a clear division of responsibility. Today Alain Bouleau manages the 54-ha estate, Patrice Laurendeau runs the cellar and René looks after the commercial side of the business. The property produces the entire range of Anjou wines: reds, dry and demi-sec rosés as well as both sweet and dry white wines, but beyond any doubt the estate's most prestigious wines are those from the nine meticulously groomed hectares at Bonnezeaux. For the Cuvée Spéciale, the botrytized grapes are picked over the course of several weeks and individually selected again in the cellar. Painstaking craftsmanship of this order would simply not have been practical if René had decided to go it alone.

Bonnezeaux 1990   🍇 ③
1990 was the kind of vintage sweet wine producers dream about. This exceptional cuvée was obtained from selected Chenin grapes, about 80% of which were botrytized. Yellow gold with aromas of honey and spice, this is a complex, full-bodied and powerful wine.

Domaine de Haute-Perche

9, chemin de la Godelière
49610 Sainte-Mélaine-sur-Aubance
Tel. 41577565
Fax 41459251

In 1966 Christian Papin moved a full three kilometers from where he was brought up having bought with his wife a nine-hectare vineyard entirely planted in hybrids. These they uproooted and replaced. Thanks to their hard work and abundant enthusiasm, the property has grown to 30 ha, a third of which produces white wines. Christian is always eager to learn and works in close collaboration with the government-sponsored Technical Insitute of Wine (ITV) and carries out experiments for the Institute on the estate. At the moment, Christian is following the progress of three vats of dry white wine that have undergone skin contact, a procedure which he uses habitually for the marvellously scented sweet wines he obtains from five hectares in the Coteaux de l'Aubance. Making sweet white wine is what interests Papin most of all. His red wines are beautifully made but lack the flair of the whites.

Coteaux de l'Aubance   🍇 🍇 ②
Sélection de Grains Nobles 1990
One of the best sweet whites of the Appellation from a cuvée obtained exclusively from selected botrytized grapes. Magnificent intense yellow gold with aromas of apricot and candied peel. A smooth Chenin-based wine with excellent balance of texture and freshness.

Anjou Villages 1990   🍇 🍇 ①
Made from Cabernet Franc with a small proportion of Cabernet Sauvignon. Intense red color with a nose of ripe grapes. Velvet-smooth on the palate with enough tannins to age for several years.

Victor e Vincent Lebreton

Domaine de Montgilet
49610 Juigné-sur-Loire
Tel. 41919048
Fax 41546428

Victor remembers the days when at the age of five he used to help his father in the vineyard with the horse-drawn plough that they used to plant new vines. Things have changed and the estate has doubled in area since he and his brother took over in 1986. They no longer sell their wine wholesale, and since sweet wines came back into fashion they have rediscovered the art of late-harvesting. Most of their rivals would agree that in 1990, the brothers produced one of the best Coteaux de l'Aubance in the region from their four-hectare vineyard. The Lebretons obtained the highest natural sugar content possible from the completely botrytized grapes, except for a small quantity which were harvested early to give the wine acidity and balance. The remainder of the estate extends over 24 ha planted in the Anjou and Anjou-Villages Appellations. The latter is planted for the most part with Cabernet Franc on shale soil which in the best vintages produces intense, concentrated wines which require at least two years aging in bottle to mellow out the tannins.

Coteaux de l'Aubance   ☙☙ ④
Cuvée Prestige 1990
Victor Lebreton is one of the up-and-coming producers in the region and in 1990 he produced this opulent white wine from botrytized Chenin grapes, partially fermented in oak. Intense yellow-gold color with elegant aromas of honey and a full, fruity palate. A special treat for lovers of sweet wine which is splendid now but which will mature comfortably for 50 years or more.

Domaine Cady

Valette
49190 Saint-Aubin-de-Luigné
Tel. 41783369
Fax 41786779

In the early 1970s, the Cady family Cabernets were a little on the coarse side. They refused to admit that red wine needs malolactic fermentation and used to make a rosé from their Cabernet grapes! Philippe Cady has managed the 21-ha estate, which has been in the family since 1927, since 1980. He still talks about those days with a wry smile for the Cadys have made a lot of progress. The Gamay bears the imprint of a stay in Beaujolais and in fact undergoes the carbonic maceration typical of "vin nouveau". The Cabernet is in contrast often riper and ages well. The pride and joy of the family is the Coteaux du Layon, from a stony shale and clay based terrain on hill slopes. The grapes are picked over the course of several rigorous weeks and the wine is often made entirely from fruit attacked by botrytis cinerea, ensuring an exuberantly aromatic nose and intense flavors. In 1990, the phenomenal Cuvée Anatole Pierre achieved 15° alcohol and 110 gm/lt residual sugar.

Coteaux du Layon 1990   ☙ ①
Pale color from a very favorable vintage. A semi-sweet wine with 13° alc and 50 gm residual sugar. An elegant sweet Chenin which finishes with a note of bitter almonds.

Coteaux du Layon St. Aubin   ☙ ③
Cuvée Anatole Pierre 1990
The most highly botrytized grapes available were used for this cuvée with its lovely yellow-gold color and classic aromas of noble rot. A beautifully aromatic, delightfully old-fashioned wine.

ANJOU SAUMUR/COTEAUX DE L'AUBANCE
LOIRE
FRANCE

441

ANJOU SAUMUR/COTEAUX DU LAYON
LOIRE
FRANCE

Château des Rochettes

49700 Concourson-sur-Layon
Tel. 41591151

"Nobody ever has a glass of wine in the afternoon, which is a pity since it's the only time of the day to taste the elegant demi-sec rosés from Layon," complains Jean-Louis Douet, who inherited his estate from his father in 1980. Nowadays he produces complex reds with good aging potential on half of the 25-ha property, but the family skill at making sweet wine has not been lost. The other half of the property is in the Coteaux du Layon and its Chenin vines have produced some exceptional wines over the last ten years, particularly in 1990. Douet usually vinifies grapes from different "tries" separately and blends them later on. In 1990, the harvest of botrytized grapes went on for more than two months and the wines from the three separate pickings turned out to be very different from each other. Jean-Louis therefore decided to bottle them separately for the first time and the result is an interesting array of three opulent wines with different aging potentials. Jean-Louis maintains that sweet rosés can be as elegant as whites and he intends to demonstrate this at the next great vintage.

Coteaux du Layon ⚜⚜ ②
Cuvée Diane 1990
A golden wine with 14° alc and 96 gm residual sugar, powerful but perfectly balanced. The nose is still closed but the pleasantly fresh acidity on the palate ensures that this wine will age for at least half a century. Wait at least ten years before tasting.

Coteaux du Layon ⚜⚜ ②
Cuvée Sophie 1990
Jean-Louis Douet will only sell this wine to customers who promise not to open it for at least five years. A full-bodied wine with an intense yellow color and complex flavors of honey (70 gm residual sugar) with a touch of mint on the finish.

Coteaux du Layon ⚜⚜ ②
Sélection de Grains Nobles 1990
A cuvée from the first botrytized Chenin grapes picked. Rich and honeyed, this is an opulent, thoroughly delicious wine.

Anjou Rouge 1990 ⚜ ①
The Douets have always loved the wines of Bordeaux and this explains why their red is made with a high percentage of Cabernet Sauvignon (50%). Still tannic, it will need a few years bottle-age to bring out the typical Cabernet fruit.

Philippe Delesvaux

Domaine de la Pierre-Saint-Maurille
Rue des Grands-Crus
41190 Saint-Aubin-de-Luigné
Tel. 41781871

Philippe Delesvaux, a Parisian with a biology degree, was about to go into research when three job offers made him think twice. He decided that he really had no intention of spending the rest of his life in a white coat doing research on horses, pig pathology or worms and returned instead to the estate in the Coteaux du Layon where he had once picked grapes. There he decided that what he really wanted to do was make wine. Having started out in 1983 with three hectares of old vines, he carried out the first late harvest of Chenin in 1985 and today Philipppe is an authority on the subject. He absolutely refuses to chaptalize his white wines, preferring to offer a dry version, if need be. The Delesvaux vineyards have since grown to 9.5 ha, including two hectares of Cabernet Franc. Today he is assisted by his wife who is also from Paris. Until 1992, she was director of the local school but she too fell victim to the fascination of wine.

Coteaux du Layon ⚜⚜ ②
Saint Aubin 1991
1991 was not a great vintage, but there were exceptions like this white wine from Chenin grapes, a nectar which Philippe Delesvaux managed to produce only in very small quantities. Full-bodied and concentrated, it has aromas of apricots and a dry, elegant finish.

ANJOU SAUMUR/COTEAUX DU LAYON
LOIRE
FRANCE

442

ANJOU SAUMUR/COTEAUX DU LAYON
LOIRE
FRANCE

Domaine des Hauts Perrays

GAEC Fardeau-Robin
49290 Chaudefonds-sur-Layon
Tel. 41780438

Winemaking is nothing new to the Robin family. They have been producers in the Coteaux du Layon since 1670. Although wine has always been part of the Robin way of life, this did not stop Jean-Louis Robin from studying the subject before he inherited the 25-ha estate in 1969. Today Jean-Louis is in charge of vinification while his brother-in-law Michel Fardeau looks after the vineyards. The two of them produce dry Chenins using skin contact when it is felt that the wine might otherwise be too hard and closed. The Anjou reds are obtained from 70% Cabernet Franc and 30% Cabernet Sauvignon. The most valuable parcel in the estate is the half hectare at Rochefort with 90 year-old vines. Grapes from this parcel are always vinified and bottled separately. In 1990, the grapes were harvested in five separate "tries" over a period of several weeks and only the grapes attacked by noble rot were selected. The resulting wine is honeyed and incredibly intense. The other star of the 1990 vintage was bottled under the name Cuvée 23. It is a luscious wine which takes its name from the incredibly high natural sugar content which gives 15° alc and the equivalent of another 8° alc of unconverted sugar (for a total of 136 g. residual sugar).

Coteaux du Layon   ♀♀ ③
Clos du Cochet 1990
Obtained from botrytized grapes in three separate pickings from vines over 60 years old. The intense yellow-gold color presages the typically rich, honeyed aromas of botrytis to the point that this wine could be mistaken for a great Sauternes. It is the fresh note of acidity in the finish which marks this out as a true product of Layon.

Coteaux du Layon Cuvée 23 1990   ♀♀ ④
From the same vineyard as the preceding wine but made only with grapes from the third picking, this is Chenin botrytized to the full. The intense gold color is delightful and the nose is even more closed than that of the Clos du Cochet, but the aging potential here is enormous. Concentrated, with aromas of apricot and honey, the structure is outstanding and the flavor is absolutely delicious.

Pierre-Yves Tijou

Domaine de la Soucherie
49750 Beaulieu-sur-Layon
Tel. 41783118
Fax 41784829

Pierre-Yves Tijou's family have been involved with wine since before the French Revolution and gained notoriety by being the first to resume producing wine in Anjou after phylloxera had destroyed the region's vineyards. In 1968, Pierre-Yves took over the estate which today has 35 ha under vine, including those bought by his father in the 1950s. Recent acquisitions include the Clos des Perrières, a 1.5-ha parcel in Savennières, an Appellation which Pierre-Yves has always wanted to produce. In 1989 and 1990, natural sugar content was on the high so demi-sec wines were produced, a decision which was easier to take for someone who is used to making sweet wines than it would have been for a native of Savennières, where the traditional style is dry white. The most important part of the Domaine de la Soucherie is the four-hectare parcel with vines more than a century old. They were planted in the last century at the time when the Tijou family laid its claim to fame.

Coteaux du Layon Chaume 1990   ♀♀ ②
Chenin from this vineyard gives fuller, more unctuous wines than elsewhere. Yellow-gold color and a honey-sweet palate balanced beautifully by the acidity.

Coteaux du Layon   ♀♀ ②
Vieilles Vignes 1990
The color of old gold and splendidly rich and honeyed, this is a superbly balanced wine with a delightful citrus freshness on the finish. With its 14.5° alc and 65 gm. of residual sugar, it is a powerful wine. Ready to drink now but will also age for a long time to come.

ANJOU SAUMUR/COTEAUX DU LAYON
LOIRE
FRANCE

443

ANJOU SAUMUR/COTEAUX DU LAYON
LOIRE
FRANCE

Domaine des Baumard

8, rue de l'Abbaye
49190 Rochefort-sur-Loire
Tel. 41787003
Fax 41788382

Florent Baumard's grandfather possessed a
few vines which initially provided the wine he
served at his modest café in Rochefort, but
he soon began to cultivate his vines full-time.
His son Jean followed in his footsteps, and
after completing his studies in mathematics
and literature wanted nothing more than to
produce fine wine. He studied enology in
Bordeaux and Burgundy, then taught the
subject for ten long years in Angers until he
had saved enough to buy a vineyard in the
Appellation of his dreams, Quarts de
Chaume. Today the family owns 30 ha
spread over several Appellations. When the
market for sweet wine went into decline, Jean
Baumard was one of the first in the region to
switch to sparkling wine made by the
méthode champenoise which remained a
mainstay of the estate for many years. Then,
in 1968, Jean bought 15 ha in Savennières.
He was the first owner from the other side of
the Loire to take an interest in what at that
time was an unfashionable Appellation.
Today it is the Savennières which keeps the
property in the black and enables it to
produce top-quality wines in the Baumard
style.

Quarts de Chaume 1990   White White (4)
This Chenin-based sweet white wine is golden
yellow with an intense honeyed nose, almost
Muscat-like. The palate is opulent and, while
perhaps lacking a touch of acidity on the finish,
is nonetheless of great power.

Savennières Trie Spéciale 1990   White (3)
The Baumards know how to make sweet wines
and when botrytis started to spread in
Savennières they decided to late-harvest and
produce a sweet wine. For the time being the
character of the vintage prevails over the cru.
The wine has 15° alc and is rich and spicy.

Anjou Clos de la Folie 1989   Red (1)
Very intense red color with ripe fruit and new
wood on the nose. Again, rather untypical of the
region. Very classy with a full body and soft
texture from the Cabernet Franc grapes.

Key to the symbols

Types of Wines

White   White

Rosé   Rosé

Red   Red

Rating System

White
An exemplary wine of its
type with outstanding local
character

Rosé Rosé
An international premium
quality wine

Red Red Red
A Top Wine, considered one
of the 150 best wines in the
world

*The 'grape bunch' symbol is used to
indicate the color of the wine; the
number of bunches represents the quality
rating assigned by the contributor*

Price levels

(1)   up to $ 9.99

(2) $ 10.00 - $ 14.99

(3) $ 15.00 - $ 24.99

(4) $ 25.00 or more

*The 'ex-cellar', or direct from the
producer, bottle prices, are calculated in
US dollars and are intended only as an
approximate guide*

**Entries are arranged in
alphabetical order by country,
region and winery or producer
name.**

Château Bellerive

49190 Rochefort-sur-Loire
Tel. 41783366

Jacques Lalanne obtains one of the most stylish and refined white wines of the Loire from a steeply sloping vineyard which leads down to the river Layon. Jacques' father owned the vineyard before him but never had the time to produce any wines of interest as he was a highly successful négociant who bought and sold the only Loire wines for which there was a market in the 1950s - semi-sweet rosés. Jacques studied at art college and probably expected to end up in the world of advertising. However, in 1972 at the age of 28, he decided to take charge of the vineyard and restore it to its former glory. His only formal wine training amounted to three days in the local wine school. Over the years he has worked at perfecting the quality of his Quarts de Chaume. His battle for quality is in part won before the grapes are completely ripe when, at the beginning of summer, he painstakingly goes through the vineyard and selects four to six bunches per vine and discards the rest. Jacques Lalanne has never had to use his advertising skills to promote his wine since quality speaks for itself.

Quarts de Chaume 1990 ♟♟ ♟♟ ♟♟ ④
Unlike the neighboring Appellations of Bonnezeaux and Coteaux du Layon, Quarts de Chaume had little noble rot in 1990 and the Chenin grapes were largely sun-dried and raisin-like. Over a period of several weeks, Jacques Lalanne picked only the ripest berries of each bunch to ferment, as is his custom, in used 200 to 600 l second-hand casks. Lalanne never uses new wood. The resulting wine is an intense yellow gold with a magnificently elegant bouquet featuring notes of verbena and vanilla on a ripe, full-flavored background. The opulent richness of the 14.8° alc and 88 gm residual sugar are fully evident on the palate, which finishes on a firm, fresh note. Yet another milestone from Lalanne which will age comfortably for 50 years or more. His 1989 from botrytized grapes will probably age even longer, but there are no more bottles on the market.

ANJOU SAMUR/QUARTS DE CHAUME
LOIRE
FRANCE

445

ANJOU SAMUR/QUARTS DE CHAUME
LOIRE
FRANCE

Château de Suronde

49380 Chavagnes-les-Eaux
Tel. 41541406
Fax 41784214

Pascal Laffourcade is a busy man. Not only is he the owner of a huge estate which makes up half of the Quarts de Chaume Appellation, but he is also the proprietor of Anjou Vinicole, a wholesale wine-merchants specializing in the wines of the Loire. He manages to look after both interests very capably and indeed recently expanded his vineyard holdings into the increasingly popular Savennières Appellation. Pascal vinifies three distinct types of wine: exceptional sweet whites from 21 ha in Quarts de Chaume and 1.5 ha in Bonnezeaux; reds from 17 ha in Anjou; and dry Savennières from 13 ha in that Appellation. To those who criticize producers from the left bank of the Loire who cross the river to make Savennières in a different style, Laffourcade replies: "If we crossed the river it was because we realized that the wines had great potential - if treated differently!" Pascal thinks that a carefully chosen team makes all the difference. His enologist, for example, has worked in the best châteaux in Bordeaux and thanks to his scrupulous care, Suronde wines today are of exemplary elegance.

Quarts de Chaume 1990   ♟ ♟ ④
The Chenin grapes were picked over the course of a whole month to ensure that only the ripest berries would go into this wine. There was no botrytis in 1990, but this wine still has raisiny aromas together with apricots, marmalade and elegant notes of wax. A soft-textured wine ideal for laying down.

Savennières 1990   ♟ ♟ ③
A yellow-gold wine with stupendous flowery aromas from late-harvest Chenin grapes. Excellent balance on the palate with honeyed sweetness and a fresh finish.

Jean-Claude Bourdin

Rue des Martyrs
49730 Turquant
Tel. 41381183

Jean-Claude Bourdin might have been a market gardener like his father, but destiny decided instead that a wine-producing uncle who lived on the far side of the Loire should nominate him as his heir. Thus it was that in 1959, at the age of 19, Jean-Claude started out in the world of wine, following in the footsteps of his highly experienced relative. The 1959 vintage is one Jean-Claude will always remember because it was an outstanding year for the sweet white wines of Saumur and he would have to wait three full decades until 1989 to witness another like it. In the interim, Jean-Claude put into practice all he had learnt from his uncle about traditional winemaking including the long, slow fermentation in used barriques which produces classic wines, unaffected by the whims of fashion, at prices which are far from being exorbitant. Although Jean-Claude makes dry whites, dry and demi-sec rosés and red wines under the Anjou, Saumur, Saumur-Champigny and Coteaux de Saumur Appellations, none of the above can rival the sublime purity of his sweet whites from 1989 and 1990 vintages. In time there are sure to be other great vintages, when botrytis cinerea once again transforms the grapes on Jean-Claude's estate.

Coteaux de Saumur 1990   ♟ ♟ ②
This estate is one of the last few remaining where Chenin is planted on the chalky soil for many producers have now planted Cabernet Franc to meet the growing demand for Saumur-Champigny reds. This sweet white 1990 is made from particularly highly botrytized grapes. The nose has concentrated fruit with elegant mineral notes. Vinified in the traditional style, it is a wine which will age in the bottle for 50 years.

Château de Chaintre

49400 Dampierre-sur-Loire
Tel. 41529054
Fax 41529992

Gaël de Tigny had just graduated in the United States when he inherited, among other things, a beautiful 17th-century house and a unique 20-ha vineyard in the heart of Saumur-Champigny's best red wine producing region. It might sound incredible today, but when Gaël settled in Chaintre in 1962, the Appellation was primarily a producer of rosés, almost all of which were sold in bulk. For 20 years Gaël worked hard in his quiet, modest way to bring the Appellation out of the decline into which it had fallen. By 1970, half of the wine made on his estate was red and ten years later customers were no longer asking for Breton, the local name for Cabernet Franc, but Saumur-Champigny. The Appellation had finally made a name for itself. By 1980 Château de Chaintre reds featured regularly among the best Champignys and Gaël de Tigny moved on to new challenges. The property is now managed by the Englishman Krishna Leister, but Gaël keeps closely in touch noting that the Appellation that used to make attractive drinkable wines, runs the risk of taking itself too seriously and turning out wines which are far too imposing..

Saumur-Champigny 1990　　🍇🍇 ②
The domaine's policy is to make wines which need no more than a year's bottle-age before they are drinkable, but 1990 produced a generous, tannic wine which will definitely need a little longer to evolve.

Saumur-Champigny 1989　　🍇🍇 ②
Another exceptional vintage for the Château de Chaintres which has produced here a deep, concentrated wine with a very fruity palate. A couple of years bottle-age will mellow out the tannins to perfection.

Domaine de l'Enchantoir

Chavannes
49260 Le Puy-Notre-Dame
Tel. 41522633

François Guyard is a busy man with his 40 ha of arable land and 32 ha of vines. Despite all the work, he is good company and a good host while his attractive Saumur is available at very reasonable prices. François' father was the local mayor and never had enough time to look after the estate so François learnt his trade at the side of his father's faithful foreman, who worked on the property for well over 45 years. Today he is assisted by Mme. Blain, a well-known local enologist who has clear ideas about her role. She has no desire to "mother" Saumur producers, merely to help them obtain the very best from their wines. With her help, François vinifies not just Saumur red and white here on the border between Saumur and Anjou, but also a range of Anjou wines as well as a Vin de Pays from Gamay grapes.

Saumur Blanc 1990　　　🍇 ①
Pale straw yellow with a fruity bouquet and medium texture on the palate. A technically correct Chenin-based wine but without the personality of the Enchantoir red.

Saumur Rouge 1990　　　🍇 ①
Lovely intense red with an elegant aroma of red berries and a prominent hint of mulberry. Rich fruit on the palate. A well-made Cabernet Franc with soft tannins and moderate length.

ANJOU SAUMUR/SAUMUR-CHAMPIGNY
LOIRE
FRANCE

447

ANJOU SAUMUR/SAUMUR-CHAMPIGNY
LOIRE
FRANCE

Didier Pichot

Domaine du Bois Ménard
6, rue des Vignes
79100 Tourtenay - Thouars
Tel. 49677709

30 km south of Saumur there is a hill with the same chalky soil as Saumur itself. This explains why the remote village of Tourtenay may legally call its wines Appellation Saumur. The situation is even more unique when one takes into account that there is only one producer - Didier Pichot. Didier and his brother knew that they were destined to work on their father's 120 ha arable farm, but Didier also knew that he would one day inherit the last remaining five hectares of vines in the village. He therefore decided to study winemaking, the subject which most intrigued him. He has been able to improve quality considerably while continuing to use the traditional techniques his father used before him. The Pichot cellar is carved out of the chalky hillside and enjoys a year-round temperature of 11°C, which ensures that the wine ferments slowly in its large oak vats. Didier Pichot has doubled the area under vines but maintains that ten hectares is more than enough for one man to look after and attempt to produce good wine.

Saumur Blanc 1990

It is no easy task to find good quality Saumur whites, but this 1990 from Chenin grapes grown on chalk soil is soft-textured with an attractive bouquet.

Méthode Traditionelle Non Vintage

A non-vintage méthode champenoise sparkling wine of considerable personality. Bright appearance and a bouquet with notes of fruit and pepper. The palate is firm and dry . A refreshing wine at a refreshing price.

Domaine des Roches Neuves

56, boulevard Saint-Vincent
49400 Varrains
Tel. 41529402
Fax 41524930

Roches Neuves is one of the best-known estates in the Appellation, thanks, in great part, to the exuberant personality of Denis Duveau, now in Chile, who owned the domaine until 1991. As he was on the point of leaving France, he had his greatest vintage ever, the 1990. A 15-ha family domaine cannot just be abandoned to its own fate and so Denis found a suitable successor in Thierry Germain. Denis has promised him that he will come back for at least the first three vintages of Thierry's management to help his new friend settle in. Although he is only in his mid-twenties, Thierry already has a wealth of wine experience. He has his father's bubbling energy and desire to succeed but had no desire to join him on the 100-ha estate in Bordeaux. Thierry preferred a more "down-to-earth" environment and in its new owner, Roches Neuves has found someone who will uphold its enviable reputation. The Clos Prieur 1991, partly Thierry's work, is a magnificent product. He has also decided to limit yields further.; we can therefore expect even more concentration in the first "all-Germain" vintage, the 1992.

Saumur-Champigny
Clos Prieur 1990

This cuvée is largely produced from the domaine's younger vines, 10 to 15 years old, which are planted on gravel and chalk soils in the communes of Chacé and Varrains. An intensely colored, attractively fruity, soft wine. Ready to drink now.

Saumur-Champigny
Terres Chaudes 1990

A wine from Cabernet Franc grapes which will age for at least 20 years. Intense red color, almost black. Generous fruit with notes of plum on the nose. Excellent, velvety texture with a crisp, tannic finish.

Saumur-Champigny
La Marginale 1989

This is a small cuvée and is a-typical for the region. The wine is made from selected grapes from the best two parcels in the Terres Chaudes, macerated for three weeks and then aged for 18 months in new 600 l casks. Oak dominates the nose for the time being but with time the typical varietal aromas will emerge.

ANJOU SAUMUR/SAUMUR-CHAMPIGNY
LOIRE
FRANCE   448

ANJOU SAUMUR/SAUMUR-CHAMPIGNY
LOIRE
FRANCE

Clos Rougeard

15, rue de l'Église
49400 Chacé
Tel. 41529265

The Foucault brothers make a sumptuous Saumur-Champigny. Their recipe is by no means a simple one, particularly since they do not divide up the various tasks. Both work in the cellar and both work in the vineyard. Long before it became fashionable to age in oak, Charlie and Bernard came to the conclusion that their wine had sufficient character to support the oak, and so began the practice of slow aging in oak barrels acquired from the greatest estates in France. The Foucaults aim to get the maximum extract from their grapes. They fine with egg white and avoid filtration. Furthermore, they have a few rows of old Chenin vines and in 1990 the botrytized grapes were fermented in new wood (including two acacia-wood barrels) to see if the aromas of the variety would integrate with the wood. The result is a perfectly balanced sweet wine. At a time when Saumur-Champigny wines often suffer from a policy of seeking high yields and the systematic addition of yeasts, Clos Rougeard continues to work in the traditional manner, without chemical herbicides or fertilizers which might compromise the wine's ability to do justice to the cru.

Saumur-Champigny   ②
Clos Rougeard 1990
Produced from a 4.5-ha vineyard with a yield of under 50 hl/ha and bottled in spring 1992, this is the most supple of Clos Rougeard's wines. It was aged for 18 months in oak barrels and has a lovely range of aromas and excellent concentration.

Saumur-Champigny   🍷 ②
Cuvée Les Poyeux 1989
A splendidly robust cuvée with fine structure thanks to an exceptionally sunny vintage. The Cabernet Franc, with its almost peppery liquorice flavor, emerges beautifully on the palate. This is Saumur-Champigny at its very best.

Saumur-Champigny   🍷🍷🍷 ③
Cuvée Le Bourg 1990
The grapes from this one-hectare vineyard were treated like VIP's. Many of the vines date from 1895 and the yields never exceed 30 hl/ha. Unfortunately, this is the last vintage to be produced from such a high proportion of old vines as many died from the frost in 1991. Aged for 24 months in new barriques, this wine combines the elegance of Bordeaux with the personality of Cabernet Franc. Drunk young, it is more reminiscent of a Bordeaux than of a Loire wine, but after seven or eight years the terroir begins to take over from the vanilla oak flavors. This last historic Le Bourg demonstrates the heights that Saumur-Champigny can reach. To be tasted again in 50 years time.

ANJOU SAUMUR/SAUMUR-CHAMPIGNY
LOIRE
FRANCE

449

ANJOU SAUMUR/SAUMUR-CHAMPIGNY
LOIRE
FRANCE

Philippe Vatan

Le Hureau
49400 Dampierre-sur-Loire
Tel. 41676040
Fax 41504335

Philippe Vatan is the son of a vigneron, which is no doubt why he took his degree in agronomy specializing in...apples ! At the age of 35, when the family had not made wine for seven years and were selling the grapes to the négociants, he took the 18-ha domaine in hand. Assisted by Didier Coutanceau, the most fashionable enologist in the region, he carefully vinified a dry white, a red and in 1989 and 1990, a sweet white. His experience in the orchard has proved very useful in the vineyard for he has adopted state-of-the-art methods of vine cultivation. He also continues to cultivate his 30 ha of orchards even though it is now obvious that wine will always come first. Despite the fashion for Saumur-Champigny, Philippe has wisely kept three hectares of Chenin Blanc which were planted in 1949 on a tufa plateau overlooking the Loire, a location and soil type particularly suited to white grapes. Philippe Vatan, who is lucky enough to have a solid family background, a good education and desire for perfection in everything he undertakes, has all it takes to become the star of the Appellation.

Coteaux-de-Saumur 1990 ♀♀ ②
The result of careful selection of Chenin grapes from old vines in an exceptional vintage, the wine has a honeyed sweetness and fresh acidity. A wine with superb aging potential.

Saumur Blanc 1990 ♀ ①
This dry white wine was partially vinified by skin contact, softening the often hard Chenin style. Fleshy on the palate and with good fruit, a wine with excellent length as well as outstanding freshness.

Saumur-Champigny 1990 ♥ ①
A splendidly bright color from an excellent vintage. Full-bodied and concentrated with mouthfilling fruit, this is a wine to drink at around 12°C to enhance its characteristic fruit-cake flavor.

Domaine du Closel

Place du Mail
Savennières 49170
Tel. 41728100

Madame de Jessey lived the tranquil life of a director's wife in the north of France until 1961 when her aunt asked her to take over the running of the family's 15-ha domaine in the heart of Savennières. Her husband could not leave his job, but Madame de Jessey didn't hesitate one minute, knowing that she could nonetheless rely on her husband to deal with the financial side of the business. She threw her energy into the domaine and has never looked back since. She followed all the wine courses possible and has learned to extract the best from the domaine's exceptional terroir. She is in the vineyard almost every day of the year, and in particular during the harvest when she leads the pickers through the vineyard in search of the ripest grapes. Savennières is lucky to have kidnapped Madame de Jessey, who in her uncle's footsteps has become the dynamic president of the Appellation.

Savennières 1990 ♀♀ ①
Madame de Jessey recalls that when this vintage was fermenting the wine must smelt of exotic fruit. Golden colour with a honeyed spicey, peppery nose. The wine is fairly supple giving immediate pleasure.

Nicolas Joly

Château de la Roche-aux-Moines
49170 Savennières
Tel. 41722232
Fax 41722868

Nicolas Joly used to work for a merchant bank in New York and then was transferred to London. There he met his future wife, a young German lady who thought she was going to marry a successful banker, not an earthy "paysan." Nicolas soon abandoned city life to settle on the family estate, Coulée de Serrant, which according to Curnonsky, the widely respected food critic of the 1920s, produced one of the five best white wines in France. The Coulée de Serrant's seven-hectare vineyard is perhaps the prettiest domaine in the whole Loire region. Its Chenin vines are located on shale slopes overlooking the majestic river. Nicolas Joly is of the opinion that terroir is the key factor in a wine and since 1981, when Nicolas moved back to the property, the vines have been cultivated without chemicals using biodynamic methods. Some commentators recognize Nicolas' skill as a grower of superb-quality fruit, but criticize his winemaking ability. The 1990 vintage proves them wrong in no uncertain terms and if the Coulée de Serrant continues along its chosen path, it will very soon take its place once again at the pinnacle of French white wine production.

Savennières Beycherelle 1990   🍇🍇 ②
Nicolas Joly cleared one of the domaine's steepest slopes to recreate a vineyard for the first time in 40 years. The Chenin planted on this virgin slatey soil gives vibrant dry wines.

Savennières La Bergerie 1990   🍇 ①
Obtained from a 1.75-ha vineyard flanked by cypress trees which is planted in Chenin Blanc and biodynamically cultivated. A fresh wine to drink young.

Clos de la   🍇🍇🍇 ④
Coulée de Serrant 1990
Nicolas Joly has no need of special tricks when it comes to winemaking. His secret is the quality of the Chenin Blanc grapes which ferment naturally without additional yeast. After aging in wood, the wine is not fined, merely lightly filtered. In the case of the 1990, which Nicolas puts on a par with the superb 1947, the estate started harvesting 15 days before other producers in the region with the intention of obtaining a very dry white. The color is intense golden yellow. The first impression on the nose is only moderately intense, but the bouquet then opens out in crisp mineral aromas mingling with notes of lime-blossom. The palate has stupendous texture with its 13° of natural alcohol and a superb concentration of aromas. Soft and clean-tasting, this Coulée de Serrant is a genuine masterpiece and a unique expression of its terroir. A wine which may comfortably be laid down for 40 to 50 years.

ANJOU SAUMUR/SAVENNIERES
LOIRE
FRANCE

451

ANJOU SAUMUR/SAVENNIERES
LOIRE
FRANCE

Pierre et Yves Soulez

Château de Chamboureau
49170 Savennières
Tel. 41772004
Fax 41772778

The Soulez brothers run a large business comprising four domaines with a total area of 28 ha in the most prestigious Appellations of Anjou. They include Château de Chamboureau and Château de la Bizolière with part of the famous Clos du Papillon all in Savennières, five hectares in La Roche-aux-Moines and a recent acquisition of 3.5 ha in Quarts de Chaume. Yves is in charge of the cellar, where he seeks to maintain a classic style of production. In 1991, he aged the wine for a short period in oak barrels instead of in stainless steel vats. His brother Pierre returned to the family estate in 1982 after a period working in Africa, where he carried out research on tropical fruits. Despite his inquisitive mind, Pierre too aims to remain faithful to tradition while accepting the cost-effectiveness of mechanical harvesting. In 1989 and 1990 the brothers produced exceptional wines and put their experience acquired with sweet Quarts de Chaume wine to good use in the vinification of the unusually rich Savennières grapes.

Savennières   ☙ ②
Château de Chamboureau 1990
A brilliant golden yellow with inviting, slightly toasty, aromas. A luscious sweet white wine from Chenin grapes with flavors of crystallized fruit and a slightly bitter finish. Ready for drinking.

Savennières   ☙ ☙ ③
Roche aux Moines 1990
Intense golden color with a typically crisp Savennières mineral nose. A firm, powerful wine with opulent texture.

Ferme des Ardillers

85320 Mareuil-sur-Lay
Tel. 51972010

The wines of Mareuil were once appreciated by Cardinal Richelieu. There followed a period during which they were all but neglected until Georges Jallerat of the Grand Monarque in Chartres rescued them from obscurity, and the efforts of many Mareuil growers were finally rewarded. Ferme des Ardillers is managed by two young enthusiasts, Jean Mourat, a qualified enologist, and Jean Larzelier, who has successfully cultivated vines that most people would have given up on. The 30-ha estate is located 50 km from the coast and is planted with Gamay, Pinot, Cabernet Franc and Cabernet Sauvignon for reds and Chardonnay and Chenin for white wines. The soil type is clay and silica studded with sandstone, quartz, shale and blue granite. The climate is maritime and the sunshine, while only moderate, is sufficient to guarantee that the fruit ripens fully. The wines are easy to like and easy to drink.

Fiefs Vendéens   ☙ ①
Tête de Cuvée Mareuil 1990
Lovely intense red color with aromas of red berries and moorland. Concentrated texture on the palate, full-bodied and fresh with a rustic note. Well-defined finish of great elegance. Drink now.

ANJOU SAUMUR/SAVENNIERES
LOIRE
FRANCE

452

ANJOU SAUMUR/FIEFS VENDEENS
LOIRE
FRANCE

Guy Bossard - Domaine de l'Écu

La Bretonnière
44430 Le Landreau
Tel. 40064091
Fax 40064679

There are still those in Muscadet who are content to produce a fresh, easy-to-drink white wine to wash down oysters by the dozen, but Guy Bossard is not one of them. This hard-working perfectionist with his biting sense of humor is rarely happy with the great wines he makes. He will, however, admit to having had some great years since he started working on the family estate in 1985 and maintains that the 1985, 1989 and 1990 are all vintages that should not be uncorked for at least 15 years. This is, in fact, one of Bossard's qualities. He makes Muscadets for laying down and leaves no aspect of production to chance. Bossard comes from a family of growers who also have a long tradition as orchard farmers, and he, therefore, goes to great lengths to look after his vines in the best possible manner. He even uses a horse instead of a tractor in those vineyards where the plants are particularly delicate. Bossard uses no chemicals on his estate and the grapes are picked by hand before being gently crushed. With a little bottle-age, these firm, solid and bone dry Muscadets develop a distinctive mineral flavor of which Guy Bossard is very proud.

Muscadet 1990   ❦ ①
Guy Bossard is an oddball who has set out to prove that Muscadet can produce great dry white wines. His 1990 has a delicious mineral flavor and plenty of body and power. It may be drunk in the next two years but has the potential to age for much, much longer.

Léon Boullault et fils

Château La Touche
44330 Route du Puiset-Doré - Vallet
Tel. 40339530
Fax 40362685

Léon Boullault would probably never have become a producer had it not been for supermarkets. His wholesale textile business got into difficulty when many of the small traders in the Nantes area closed down. For this reason, when his father-in-law died in 1962 leaving the family estate without anyone to run it, Léon decided to become a vigneron. He was not an absolute beginner for he had worked in the vineyard once a week since 1945. At a time when growers were changing to chemical products, Léon Boullault continued to use exclusively organic fertilizers because he firmly believes that "terroir" plays a major role in creating a wine's personality. Boullault was also one of the first to try to convince the market that the right Muscadet crus can be wines with aging potential. Some growers and consumers have recently come round to his way of thinking. Today, the Boullault estate extends over 38 ha and is run by Léon's two sons.

Muscadet Cuvée Choisie 1991   ❦ ①
Obtained from Muscadet grapes and aged in wood, this is a full-flavored, frank wine with good body which will age comfortably for several years.

NANTAIS/MUSCADET
LOIRE
FRANCE

453

NANTAIS/MUSCADET
LOIRE
FRANCE

André-Michel Brégeon

Les Guisseaux
44190 Gorges-Clisson
Tel. 40069319
Fax 40069591

André-Michel Brégeon is a cheerful, hard working character who began his working life at the age of seven in his father's vineyard. When his father retired in 1975, he took over the three hectare property, and since then has been producing splendid Muscadets, proving that in good vintages the wine can reach superb levels of quality. On the estate, which has now expanded to 10 ha, André-Michel always vinifies in what he calls the simplest way. His theory has it that to obtain a top quality wine, you need a complete absence of oxygen as well as good soil, low yields (35 hl/ha) and manually-harvested grapes. With this in mind, Brégeon never ages his wines in wood and always blends during the harvest. It is at this point that he decides which of his 30 separate parcels will be harvested, crushed and then fermented together without additional yeasts.

Muscadet 190 ❦ ①
Pale straw-yellow with attractive aromas of ripe fruit. A wine with a personality of its own. Good structure and a forthright, full-flavored, fresh palate.

Louis Métaireau

La Févrie
44690 Maisdon-sur-Sèvre
Tel. 40548192
Fax 40548783

Louis Métaireau has done a lot for Muscadet in his own way, particularly abroad. His wine, bottled with imaginatively designed labels, is probably the most expensive of its kind but restaurateurs are willing to stand in line to get hold of it. Louis has never had a high opinion of Muscadet's image and has developed his business almost single-handedly. However, he has not been quite alone for he has created what can only be described as a unique, exclusive cooperative. For 30 years, he and four other growers who represent 98 ha of Muscadet vineyards have been meeting once a month and tasting each others' wines. Wines which fail the test are sold wholesale and those which pass are divided into four separately labeled categories. The Number One label wines are "top quality, elegant and fresh, with good structure." Such a wine might come from one of the estates or from all four. All in all, an unusual but effective method of guaranteeing quality to the consumer.

Muscadet Number One 1990 ❦ ①
Pale straw-yellow and a subtle nose that leads into a satisfyingly full-bodied palate. The aromas are elegant with a deliciously chalky mineral note. A perfect wine to make you think again if you imagined that all Muscadets were nondescript and a little too acid.

NANTAIS/MUSCADET
LOIRE
FRANCE

454

NANTAIS/MUSCADET
LOIRE
FRANCE

Maison Sauvion

Le Cléray
44330 Vallet
Tel. 40362255
Fax 40363462

Jean Sauvion is no newcomer to wine for his estate has been in the family for three generations. When he joined his father in the late 1960s, he set up a trading company like hundreds of others in France, but he soon realized that he would never be able to do more than bottle honest table wines. It was at this point that he thought very carefully about the role of the négociant and reached a simple, original conclusion. Quality wine can never be blended wine. In 1978, Jean invested in a mobile bottling plant and began to bottle directly from the producers' own vats. He made a further step forward when he started to print the name and village of the producer on the label of Sauvion wines in a series known as Les Découvertes. It was Jean's way of proving that there are quality wines in Muscadet which come from a whole range of different crus. Jean also manages 30 ha of Sauvion family vineyards, where he carries out small scale experiments. The Sauvions have been innovating and improving the quality of their Muscadets for 30 years and their reward has been a constant growth of interest in their wines.

Muscadet Cardinal Richard 1991   ❦ ①
This cuvée is another of Jean Sauvion's original ideas. A few years ago, he started to organize a tasting where a panel of experts was asked to select the most elegant Muscadet in a range of wines from various producers. The winner is given the Cardinal Richard label. The 1991 is a light, fresh, attractively fruity wine.

Muscadet Château du Cléray 1990   ❦ ①
This Muscadet from the Sauvion family's own vineyards is partly aged in oak but inviting flowery notes dominate the wood. A forward, ample wine with a rich palate.

Yannick Amirault

La Coudraye
37140 Bourgueil
Tel. 47977807
Fax 47979478

The neighboring villages of Bourgueil and Saint-Nicolas-de-Bourgueil are in the habit of reviving the "guerres picrocholines," so dear to Rabelais, in order to establish which one is superior. However, there is one grower who tries not to get involved in this story of local rivalry. Yannick Amirault has vineyards in both appellations. He has no doubts as to which is the better zone, preferring Les Malgagnes at Saint-Nicolas-de-Bourgueil. Amirault has a particularly weak spot for this parcel he inherited from his grandfather, a skillful vigneron who passed on his knowledge to his grandson. Yannick did not lose heart in 1991 when the vintage produced barely ripe grapes. He vinified his must to extract the best possible results and the color and aromas he obtained were quite outstanding. In 1989, he experimented by not filtering a selection from a gravel and sand vineyard. The resulting wine was so extraordinarily successful that the technique was applied to the entire 1990 vintage.

Bourgueil Les Graviers   ❦ ①
Vieilles Vignes 1990
A classic Cabernet Franc with the typical aromas of green pepper and liquorice. The palate has generous fruit and a tannic note on the finish.

Saint-Nicolas-de-Bourgueil   ❦ ①
Les Malgagnes Vieilles Vignes 1990
Deep purple red with intense, elegant aromas where hints of ripe cherry develop over gamey notes. Good structure and excellent aging potential.

NANTAIS/MUSCADET
LOIRE
FRANCE

455

TOURAINE/BOURGUEIL
LOIRE
FRANCE

Jean-Yves Billet

Domaine des Forges
Place des Tilleuls
37140 Restigné
Tel. 47973287

Jean-Yves Billet always wanted to be a pilot but he was destined to be a grower. Both his father and his mother come from families which have made Bourgueil wine for four generations. Jean-Yves has an inquisitive nature and boundless energy which has enabled him to shake off some of the traditions he inherited. When he took over the seven hectares of vineyards (now 16 ha) in 1963, the estate sold all its wine unbottled to négociants and restaurateurs. Jean-Yves himself rode a horse around the property. Only two years later, the wine was being bottled after a meticulous vinification. Later still, Jean-Yves acquired a mechanized grape-harvester and today his new cellar gleams with stainless steel. Two different soil types allow Billet to produce wines with very different characteristics. The vines planted in gravel give light, fruity wines to be drunk young while those planted in tufa yield more tannic wines, sold under the Cuvée Les Bézards label. Finally, as president of the Bourgueil Appellation, Jean-Yves Billet is absolutely committed to improving the quality standards of the region's wines.

Bourgueil Rosé 1991 🏵 ①
Fairly intense pink color with attractively fruity aromas. Well-balanced, dry and light, this rosé is a perfect complement at table and a valid alternative to the rosés of the South of France, which tend to have a higher alcohol content.

Bourgueil Cuvée Les Bézards 1990 🍇 ①
Bright color and an inviting nose of liquorice and soft red fruit. A medium bodied wine which finishes on a firm tannic note. Delicious to drink now but with the potential to age for several years.

Marc Delaunay

Domaine de la Lande
37140 Bourgueil
Tel. 47978073
Fax 47979565

Marc Delaunay is one of those charming, old-fashioned growers who have remained close to their roots. He started work on the family estate in 1955 at the age of 15. When he got married ten years later, he took on a more important role in the management of the property, deciding to uproot the orchards and concentrate on wine. Today, Delaunay owns 10 ha of Cabernet Franc, most of which is located on the highest, and best, slopes in Bourgueil. He vinified his wines in great wooden vats for a very long time, treading some of the grapes himself. But he has recently acquired some stainless steel tanks equipped with automatic treading devices and these have helped him to make the kind of wine he has always dreamt of making. Marc's son François also works on the estate and shares his father's outlook. When François was learning how to make wine, he did not go to one of the châteaux in Bordeaux, like most of his contemporaries. He served his apprenticeship in a cellar in the nearby village of Chinon.

Bourgueil Cuvée Prestige 1990 🍇 ①
A delicious, classic Bourgueil from Cabernet Franc grapes. Marc Delaunay and his son represent the very best of the Loire winemaking tradition. It is a pity there are so few growers like them left.

TOURAINE/BOURGUEIL
LOIRE
FRANCE

456

TOURAINE/BOURGUEIL
LOIRE
FRANCE

Pierre-Jacques Druet

Le Pied-Fourrier
37140 Benais
Tel. 47973734
Fax 47974640

In viticultural terms, Pierre-Jacques Druet might be considered a sort of "defrocked priest." He is an enologist turned vigneron who has abandoned technology and put his trust entirely in his own skills. Enology for Pierre-Jacques is not the be all and end all of winemaking. He believes that only through long experience and hard work in the vineyard can an intimate knowledge of wine be acquired. Pierre-Jacques started out with no family estate or fortune behind him but as luck would have it his progress was swift. By the time he was 30, he judged that his experience and savings were sufficient to start out on his own and he began scouring France from one end to the other in search of his ideal vineyard. He wanted a location which could match the great châteaux for quality and the more modest estates for price. Then he came across a collection of old vines in the pretty village of Bourgueil, in the sector known as Benais, noted for its wines since the Middle Ages. In his very first vintage, 1980, Pierre-Jacques won a gold medal. Today, he produces one of the best red wines in the Loire. His Bourgueils are complex and aristocratic, avoiding the common fault in today's wines of being too easy to drink. Druet is a craftsman and he passionately believes that.his Cuvée Vaumoreau with its superb aging potential will last for 50 years or maybe 100 years in better vintages.

Bourgueil Les Cent Boissélées 1990 🍇 ①
This fine Bourgeuil was made to slake thirsts but its intense color and full texture give it an added dimension. Drink in the next year or two.

Bourgueil Grand Mont 1989 🍇🍇 ②
The house style tends towards concentrated, tannic wines with plenty of character and this Grand Mont, named after the vineyard from which it is obtained, is just such a wine, thanks to the exceptional vintage. Wise connoisseurs will wait for twenty years before tasting.

Bourgueil 🍇🍇🍇 ④
Cuvée Vaumoreau 1990
Pierre-Jacques Druet's latest creation is a prestigious cuvée from 80 year-old vines which many other growers would have uprooted on account of their tiny yields. The quality of the fruit is quite exceptional. The resulting wine is very concentrated, often being mistaken for an elegant Bordeaux in blind tastings, and was aged for more than two years in 600 hl. barrels. The natural alcohol content is 13.7° but is well balanced by the structure and complexity of flavors of the wine. If drunk within the next 10 years, this wine should be decanted at least two hours before serving but it will only be at its peak in fifty years' time. A 100% Cabernet Franc, this cuvée is as expensive as a great Bordeaux and is sold by the bottle, not the case, because of the extremely limited quantity available.

TOURAINE/BOURGUEIL
LOIRE
FRANCE

457

TOURAINE/BOURGUEIL
LOIRE
FRANCE

Domaine de la Désoucherie

Cour-Cheverny
41700 Contres
Tel. 54799008

It is not so many months since the wines of Cheverny were finally recognized as an Appellation d'Origine Contrôlée. The moment marked the end of a 20 year battle waged by 80 growers who were determined to rise out of the VDQS classification. While overall progress has been made, it is also fair to say that yields are still often too high and winemaking is not always as carefully done as it might be. That is not the case with the wines of Christian Tessier. Christian was destined for a career in the police but decided instead to take over his father's 15 ha estate. At the age of 45, he is now one of the region's leading lights. "There used to be a bit of everything here, including hybrids. The only way to make quality wine was to start from scratch." Christian re-planted the estate with traditional varieties, including Romorantin, a white variety related to the Melon de Bourgogne or as it is better known the Muscadet grape. One third of the property is planted in Pinot Noir. Normally in this region, Pinot Noir produces uninteresting wines but not when Christian Tessier makes them. His secret is to limit yields, pump the wine over the cap in the Bordeaux manner twice a day and age partly in old oak barrels.

Cheverny Romorantin 1990   🍇 ①
Pale straw-yellow and fruity aromas with notes of lemon. An unusual white wine for one based on Romorantin with a complex palate and a clean, fresh finish.

Cheverny Pinot Noir 1991   🍇 ①
Light red color with the classic aromas of the variety. It combines warm, peppery, complex flavors while remaining refreshingly lightweight.

Philippe Alliet

L'Ouche-Mondé
37500 Cravant-les-Coteaux
Tel. 47931762

Philippe Alliet has happy childhood memories of playing in the vineyard of his grandfather, who passed on a love of the countryside to his young grandchild. When the old man finally retired Philippe, who had studied viticulture and enology, was more than ready to take over the six hectare property. Philippe is a keen gardener as well as a vigneron and looks after the vines, planted on pebble-strewn alluvial soil, with the same painstaking care shown in the splendid vegetable gardens of the nearby Château de Villandry. Alliet is a highly skilled winemaker. In 1983, at the age of 26, he visited Bordeaux for the first time, returning with a number of second-hand barrels from some of the top châteaux and a determination to extract the maximum color and substance from his fermenting must. Since then, Philippe has perfected his own personal approach to winemaking, combining the traditions of Chinon and Bordeaux. Today, he makes a wine with perfect structure which he neither filters nor fines.

Chinon Cuvée Prestige 1990   🍇🍇 ①
A wine aged in used barrels (one to four vintages) whose elegance is not undermined by the influence of the wood.

Chinon Cuvée Traditionelle 1990 🍇🍇 ①
This is the first vintage for which Philippe has decided to make two separate bottlings. The wine is partly aged in 5 to 10 year old Bordeaux barrels. The oak is therefore barely perceptible while the concentrated Cabernet Franc fruit is splendidly in evidence.

TOURAINE/CHEVERNY
LOIRE
FRANCE

458

TOURAINE/CHINON
LOIRE
FRANCE

Bernard Baudry

Coteau de Sonnay
37500 Cravant-les-Coteaux
Tel. 47931579
Fax 47984444

Bernard Baudry fell under the spell of wine during the five years he spent working with Jacques Puissais, the Loire's philosopher-enologist. Born on a beautiful estate in Chinon and a former student of Beaune school of enology, Baudry had had plenty of contact with the world of wine. At the age of 29, he was on the point of leaving the Loire to become a wine consultant in the Rhône when he unexpectedly changed his mind. He had inherited a house at Chinon together with two hectares of vine stock. There was not enough to support his family but he told himself he could always rent some more land. In a few short years, he proved himself to be one of the most talented winemakers in Chinon, earning the admiration of other growers. In 1982, he extended his estate significantly and today he has 25 ha, 40% of which is planted with old vines. Bernard Baudry produces three red wines from vines of varying age. The Haies-Martel is made from young vines of 8 to 12 years of age, the Bernard Baudry from 30 to 35 years and Les Grézeaux from 35 to 60 years.

Chinon 1990　　　　　　　🍇🍇 ①
A structured, complex, full-bodied wine. Very similar to Les Grézeaux but not aged in Bordeaux barrels so the Chinon character is expressed to the full. For purists of the cru.

Chinon　Les Grézeaux 1990　🍇🍇 ①
Aged partly in used oak barrels, this is a delicious wine with soft tannins well to the fore. The oak and fruit will require another five years to integrate perfectly.

Chinon Les Haies Martels 1990　🍇🍇 ①
The grapes come from gravely, sandy soil and give a fruity, light wine to drink young. The 1990 is particularly concentrated, especially if the young age of the vines is taken into account.

Jean-Marie Dozon

Domaine Dozon
Le Rouilly
37500 Ligré
Tel. 47931767

Jean-Marie Dozon is an agronomist. He first worked as a consultant for a rice growing cooperative in Niger and then moved on to Morocco, where he looked after a 100,000 ha oak forest. In 1973, he decided to return to the famous Clos du Saut au Loup, the 13 ha vineyard which surrounds the family domaine. Wine lovers who usually buy their Chinon at Cravant, the largest commune in the appellation, find Ligré wines harder and more suitable for laying down, thanks to the heavier, clay soil. This is exactly the type of wine which Jean-Marie likes. He does his best to extract a little extra tannin and body from some of his cuvées to enable them to be aged in the bottle for a good number of years. In total, the Dozon estate extends over 23 ha and produces a range of red wines which go from the light and fruity to the more tannic and full-bodied. The tannic Cuvée des Fabrices is a wine for connoisseurs.

Chinon Clos du Saut au Loup　🍇 ②
Cuvée Laure 1990
The grapes come from the 13 ha of the original Dozon family estate and the wine is pumped over the cap twice a day during fermentation. A cuvée aged in 300 lt barrels which produces a complex, mature wine, rich in fruit and with a long finish.

Chinon Clos du Saut au Loup　🍇 ②
Cuvée Prestige 1990
This wine was going to be part of the Cuvée Laure but then Dozon decided to bottle it separately as it had such a distinctive personality. Aged in new barriques and not filtered, it is a tannic, complex wine with a sophisticated bouquet and pleasingly unobtrusive oak.

Chinon Cuvée des Fabrices 1990　🍇 ①
From Cabernet Franc grapes cultivated on clay and chalk soil. An agreeably tannic wine whose relatively brief maceration allows the fruit to assert itself to the full. Drink young.

TOURAINE/CHINON
LOIRE
FRANCE

459

TOURAINE/CHINON
LOIRE
FRANCE

Charles Joguet

Clos de la Dioterie
37220 Sazilly - L'Ile-Bouchard
Tel. 47585553
Fax 47585222

Charles Joguet abandoned the countryside in the 1960s to go and live among the artists of Montparnasse and exercise his own talents as a painter. After his father's death, he returned to Chinon on a regular basis to help his mother and the family vineyards gradually began to fascinate him more and more. Père Taffoneau, one of the great characters of Chinon viticulture, taught him the art of winemaking and today Charles himself is the 'guru' of Chinon. He still spends his weekends at his Paris atelier. Joguet produces uniquely deep, intense wines which are beyond the whims of fashion. It would be a long process to list all the revolutionary practices introduced by this reluctant subversive. He was the first in Chinon to sell his wine bottled; he was the first to separate his cuvées and sell them labeled as being from young or old vines; with the help of his partner Jacques Puissais, he invented a machine for punching down the grape cap in order to extract maximum substance during maceration. He revitalized a neglected vineyard, the Chêne Vert, abandoned yet renowned as far back as the eleventh century. Finally, with the support of the INAO, he has planted some ungrafted vines to revive a sublime expression of French viticulture which will allow us to taste at last a pre-phylloxera Chinon.

Chinon Jeunes Vignes 1991 ♥ ①
An excellent wine from a poor vintage. Joguet's talent is once again evident in this light, attractive, fruity red.

Chinon Franc de Pied 1990 ♥♥ ③
There are very few bottles of this wine made from ungrafted Cabernet Franc vines planted on an experimental one hectare plot. A powerful wine with quite outstanding balance and concentration. A unique and memorable wine.

Chinon ♥♥♥ ③
Clos de la Dioterie 1989
This extraordinary Chinon, unfortunately available only in limited quantities, comes from a two and a half hectare vineyard. Part of its secret lies in the Cabernet Franc vines, one third of which are over 80 years old, but it is Charles Joguet's magic touch that really sets it apart. The ripest bunches were individually selected before being de-stemmed and trodden mechanically in a device designed by Joguet himself in collaboration with the famous Loire enologist Jacques Puissais. The wine then spent 18 months in old Bordeaux barriques. According to Joguet, the 1989 is the best wine he has ever made and is capable of aging for 30 years. The color is stupendously intense while the palate has great concentration and a perfect balance between ripe fruit and aromas of black olives and cloves. It has a soft, velvety texture with a powerful finish and a note of tannin. Decant a few hours before serving. The cellar has unfortunately sold out all its stocks of this wine.

TOURAINE/CHINON
LOIRE
FRANCE

460

TOURAINE/CHINON
LOIRE
FRANCE

Guy Lenoir

Clos des Roches
5, rue des Roches
37420 Avoine
Tel. 47588959

Guy Lenoir is a busy 69 year old. He has been a hairdresser in his native village of Avoine all his working life, except for a three year apprenticeship in nearby Chinon. He has also always made wine. His father owned a three and a half hectare walled vineyard in the village and another two hectares nearby. Guy is very proud of always having made his own wine. He has never taken his grapes to the cooperative and in any case his father would never have allowed it. Guy follows rigorously traditional techniques but does admit one twentieth century intrusion. Five years ago, he invented a device to do the laborious job of punching down the cap on the fermenting wine. The wine is aged in large wooden vats and is neither fined nor filtered. Guy bottles only when he deems the wine ready, which might be after a wait of several years. The Clos des Roches is listed at Les Roches, the hotel and restaurant that Guy and his wife ran for more than thirty years (now managed by their son Alain), as well as at one of the best restaurants in France, Jean Bardet's Relais et Château in Tours.

Chinon Clos des Roches 1989 🍇 ①
An unfiltered red wine of medium intensity from Cabernet Franc grapes. The aromas are rustic and fruity, dominated by blackcurrant. The palate has lots of personality and a soft, tannic finish. An old-fashioned wine with a very individual character.

Joël Gigou

4, rue des Caves
72340 La Chantré-sur-le-Loir
Tel. 43444872
Fax 43444215

Joël Gigou was born in Jasnières, one the less familiar Loire appellations. The region produces dry white Chenin-based wines which generally require decades of bottle-age before they begin to reveal the attractiveness that lies behind their acidity. The wait is well worthwhile. Jasnières vineyards extend over less than 50 ha of a superb south-facing chalk slope overlooking the Loir, a tributary of the Loire. Instead of working with his father, who has always sold his wine wholesale, Joël set up on his own in 1974 with just four and a half hectares. When he started out, he knew virtually nothing about wine-making but he is today beyond any doubt the producer who has done most for the quality and reputation of the appellation. 1989 and 1990 were extraordinary years. Noble rot spread throughout Gigou's vines and he staggered the harvest to select only botrytized grapes, something that had never before been done in the area. In addition, he surprised his neighbors by producing a marvellously concentrated oak-aged Gamay under the Coteaux du Loir appellation and proved that the local variety Pineau d'Aunis can produce not only rosés but also top-quality red wines.

Jasnières 🍇🍇 ②
Cuvée Clos Saint Jacques 1990
Obtained from late-harvested Chenin grapes, a splendidly unique wine. Concentrated with subtle aromas of lime-blossom. Full-bodied palate with a note of honey and a crisp, dry finish. A wine with plenty of personality, to drink young.

Jasnières 🍇 ③
Sélection de Raisins Nobles 1990
A cuvée from 95% botrytized grapes. A sweet wine of great opulence which will probably turn out to be the vintage of the century at Jasnières. Has the potential to age in the bottle for fifty years.

Coteaux du Loir 🍇 ①
Cuvée Cénomane 1990
Ruby red color and interesting herbal, rose-scented nose. The palate is complex and well-balanced. Elegant tannins. A Gamay-based wine which has nothing in common with a Beaujolais.

TOURAINE/CHINON
LOIRE
FRANCE

461

TOURAINE/JASNIERES
LOIRE
FRANCE

Domaine Delétang et fils

19, route d'Amboise
37270 Saint-Martin-le-Beau
Tel. 47506725
Fax 47502646

Olivier Delétang studied enology in Champagne before returning to the family property. However, his love affair with sparkling wine came to an end as soon as he had tried his hand at making demi-sec and sweet wines. He began by making four different kinds of white wine, from dry to sweet, including a sparkling wine, but as the years went by, he found it more and more difficult to resist the temptation to vinify his grapes separately in accordance with their vineyard of origin and degree of ripeness. In 1990, he produced a total of two dry wines, one demi-sec and six sweet wines from his 23 ha estate. When Olivier started helping his father, the property consisted solely of vines in the village of Saint-Martin-le-Beau. Later on, they acquired Les Batisses, a parcel at Montlouis which gives more elegant and complex wines than the seductively aromatic products of Saint-Martin-le-Beau. Despite his passion for sweet wines, Olivier has not totally lost his interest in sparkling wines. He takes great care with his méthode champenoise production, selecting the driest, most full-bodied wines to produce a pétillant wine with less pressure (bubbles) than a classic méthode champenoise which he considers much finer.

Montlouis Les Batisses Grande 🍇🍇 ③ Réserve Tries 1990
A Chenin-based wine with 110 g of residual sugar which also has an attractive note of acidity. Will age for 50 years, thanks to a vintage which at Montlouis was more balanced than the exceptional 1989.

Montlouis Les Petits Boulay Grande 🍇 ③ Réserve Tries 1990
The first vintage in which the super-ripe Chenin grapes from this section of the vineyard were vinified separately. The resulting wine is honeyed and flowery, with the flavor of quince.

Claude Levasseur

38, rue des Bouvineries
37270 Montlouis-sur-Loire
Tel. 47508453
Fax 47451485

It is worth spending a little time with Claude Levasseur, not just for the pleasure of tasting his beautifully clean wines, but also to listen to his wonderful way of expressing himself. Claude speaks pure, almost regal, French. As far as wines are concerned, Claude has a special touch there, too, thanks to the five generations of his family which have made wine in the commune of Montlouis. In 1962 at the age of 23, Claude left the family estate to go and live on his father-in-law's property a few kilometers away. At first, with no customers of his own, he sold everything to négociants but slowly he built up a solid core of faithful buyers, mainly through local fairs. The customers appreciated his ability to combine finesse and freshness, almost unique in Montlouis. Claude's sweet wines are never cloying or over unctuous and are almost demi-sec in style. Finally, despite the spectacular success of his wines, Claude has not allowed the praise to go to his head. He still sells his wines at very moderate prices.

Montlouis Cuvée Réserve 1990 🍇🍇 ③
Deep golden yellow with aromas of apricot and honey on the nose and a sweet uncloying palate. From Chenin grapes, a wine more notable for its elegance than its body.

Montlouis Demi-sec 1989 🍇🍇 ②
Levasseur's great strength is his ability to produce consistently fresh, racy wines. This demi-sec is an attractive combination of flowery aromas and the rich texture of botrytized grapes. A very classy wine.

TOURAINE/MONTLOUIS
LOIRE
FRANCE

462

TOURAINE/MONTLOUIS
LOIRE
FRANCE

Christian Prud'homme

Domaine de la Taille aux Loups
37270 Husseau
Tel. 47395080
Fax 47384560

Christian Prud'homme likes a challenge. He is not particularly fond of Merlot and Cabernet Sauvignon which he considers easy to grow. In the early 1980s, while he was still working at Château Mouton-Rothschild and was looking for a property in the Médoc, he settled on Château de Tressan, partly because 75% of the vineyard, lying in the Margaux and Moulis appellations, was planted with the unusual Petit Verdot variety. In 1988 on a visit to the vineyards of Montlouis, Christian realized that they were under-rated and had the potential to produce sweet white wines of a much superior quality. He also liked the idea of working with the Chenin grape as it is one of the varieties he classifies as "difficult" and that "reflects the hard work you need to put into it." Christian therefore decided to invest in the zone and bought an eight hectare estate. He at once started to question the modern traditions of Montlouis. He stopped fertilizing the soil and refused to make sparkling wines. He limited yields and paid particular attention to the harvest. Christian's slow fermentation and aging takes place in second-hand Yquem barrels. All these innovations have upset the locals but the results show that Christian is right.

Montlouis Cuvée des Loups 1990 ❦ ③
The quality and style of this wine is based on low yields (25 hl/ha), fermentation with no additional yeasts, very little sulphur and aging in oak barrels. The botrytized grapes used for this cuvée come from vines over 60 years old and give the wine intense aromas which might be mistaken for Sauternes. The Chenin character comes through in the fresh acidity of the finish.

Domaine de Saint-Jérôme

7, quai Albert-Baillet
37270 Montlouis-sur-Loire
Tel. 47450775

Jacky Supligeau interrupted a four hundred year old family tradition when he abandoned viticulture for professional cycling. However, his passion for the vine followed him all round France on his punishing training runs. When he was fifteeen, an inheritance allowed him to buy his first plot of vines and from that moment on, he knew that he would go back to winemaking when his cycling days were over. He set about buying land in his free time, building up an estate of 247 small parcels acquired from about thirty different owners. By the age of 25, he had 15 ha in a single parcel on one of the best slopes in the appellation. Jacky's first vintage, 1979, suffered from frost. The following year, it snowed during the grape harvest and in 1981 the harvest was extremely limited. It would have taken much more than this to discourage a man who spent his youth cycling up and down the local hills. Jacky learnt his trade from the old notebooks of a great-uncle, Armel Supligeau, and from Claude Levasseur. This seems to have been an ideal introduction to the art of making outstanding Montlouis wine and Jacky Supligeau is certainly a young man to watch.

Montlouis Cuvée Numérotée 1990 ❦ ❦ ②
Unfortunately, only 4,200 bottles of this intense yellow-gold wine with its honey and beeswax nose and generous, rich palate were produced. The Chenin grapes, although not botrytized, were picked when very ripe. The ripest berries were then selected from each bunch to go into this delicious cuvée.

TOURAINE/MONTLOUIS
LOIRE
FRANCE

463

TOURAINE/MONTLOUIS
LOIRE
FRANCE

Joël et Clarisse Taluau

Chevrette
37140 Saint-Nicolas-de-Bourgueil
Tel. 47977879
Fax 47979560

Joël Taluau is an enthusiastic, go-getting producer who really knows his trade. Those who think that all wine must age in wooden barrels should try one or two of Joël's reds in a blind tasting. Taluau wines are completely different from the usual run-of-the-mill products fermented and aged in stainless steel despite the fact that they are made with the same technique. Thanks to slow maceration, Joël manages to obtain red wines full of personality that are similar to wines made by traditional methods. When Joël inherited the property from his father, it looked as if he too was destined to grow apples for a living. In 1970, however, he decided to devote himself to his real interest and uprooted the orchard to make way for vines. Today he owns 14 ha of vines at Saint-Nicolas-de-Bourgueil and produces wines that he bottles under three different labels, according to the age of the vines. Since 1991, he has also been bottling wine from two hectares he owns at Bourgueil, which is separated from the Saint-Nicolas appellation by a narrow path. Wine from this parcel is called Cuvée du Domaine.

Saint-Nicolas-de-Bourgueil
Domaine de Chevrette 1990
A fairly tannic cuvée with an intense purple color that will need to age in the bottle for at least five years before its green pepper and red berry bouquet begins to open out.

Saint-Nicolas-de-Bourgueil
Jeunes Vignes 1990
Intense red with classic liquorice aromas and a crisp, fresh palate. A pleasant, highly drinkable wine to enjoy young.

Saint-Nicolas-de-Bourgueil
Vieilles Vignes 1990
Although not aged in wood, this wine can comfortably be laid down for 20 to 45 years. Intense, elegant nose, this is a wine that espresses beautifully both the Cabernet Franc variety and the personality of its cru.

Jean-Maurice Beaufreton

12-18, Le Grand-Verger
37230 Luynes
Tel. 47556413

Located 15 km from Tours, the fourteenth century château of Luynes majestically overlooks the Loire from a lofty hill halfway between the vineyards of Vouvray and Bourgueil. This is an area which has been exporting wine to England and the Netherlands since the twelfth century. After the phylloxera epidemic during the last century, half of the 1,200 ha under vine were abandoned. This calamity was followed by the First World War, when 80 locals lost their lives. The drift to the towns at the end of the Second World War completed the process with the result that the appellation lost nearly all its growers. Jean-Marc Beaufreton is one of the few that have hung on. He is very much attached to his old vines and continues to produce concentrated wines of great character on his five hectare estate rather than move over to the middle-of-the-road products one so often finds in Touraine. Jean-Marc's grandfather used to sell his wine unbottled to Champagne producers and they certainly did not use it to make Touraine! Today, Jean-Marc proudly and meticulously turns out an excellent méthode champenoise that often scores above Champagnes in blind tastings.

Touraine Rosé
Méthode Champénoise Brut
Obtained largely from a local variety, Cinq-Mars-La-Pile Groslot (named after a nearby village), this delicate, dry rosé has a distinctive note of Muscat grapes on the nose.

Touraine Rouge 1989
There is nothing secret about how this wine is made. The low yields of 40 hl/ha ensure that it has a full-bodied texture, good structure and an attractively rustic appeal. Best decanted if drunk young but it will age for at least five years.

TOURAINE/SAINT-NICOLAS-DE-BOURGUEIL
LOIRE
FRANCE
464
TOURAINE/TOURAINE
LOIRE
FRANCE

Charles Guerbois

Domaine des Acacias
41700 Chémery
Tel. 54718153
Fax 54717598

When Charles Guerbois decided to take over his grandfather's abandoned vineyard on the Loire in 1981, he knew absolutely nothing about wine so he took an intensive course in the subject at the best wine bars in Paris. "It's the perfect place to meet the most interesting producers," he says. He spoke to the best growers in Sancerre about the problems and potential of Sauvignon and discussed Gamay with vignerons from the Beaujolais but he had still never worked in a cellar or a vineyard. Charles learned by experience. Today his estate extends over 23 ha and he planted most of the vines himself. Every vintage has its own little quirks and Charles is not a man to try to iron them out. In 1989, he experimented with late-harvesting half a hectare of Sauvignon grapes and the resulting wine is full of personality, robust and aromatic with 14° of natural alcohol and 80 g of residual sugar. Charles foresaw that 1990 would be a red wine vintage so he macerated part of his Gamay grapes for a month in a refrigerated vat. The wine he made is called Delirium, a real collector's item.

Touraine Domaine des Acacias 1991 ☖ ①
Straw-yellow color and an elegantly floral and aromatic nose. Full, generous palate, despite the difficult vintage. If only there were more Sauvignons as good as this in Touraine !

Touraine ☖ ☖ ②
Delirium Caroli Bellum Silva 1990
Charles Guerbois likes unusual wines and offbeat labels. His Delirium is obtained from late-harvested Gamay grapes that have undergone carbonic maceration. The resulting wine is more reminiscent of a soft northern Rhône red than a Loire. Quite delicious and absolutely unique.

Domaine de la Charmoise

Henry Marionnet
41230 Soings
Tel. 54987073
Fax 54987566

Henry Marionnet is a man who likes the challenge of something new. He might have continued to make a modest Touraine, growing a little asparagus on the side like his father before him but his insatiable curiosity and spirit of adventure got the better of him. Long before the fashion for unchaptalized wines, Marionnet was making an exquisitely light Gamay Nature with a bouquet rich in fruit that is eagerly awaited every year. It proved more difficult to reduce the percentage of sulphur but Henry succeeded brilliantly with the 1990 vintage. There is not a single gram of sulphur in the Gamay Première Vendage, so-called because it is made "as wine used to be made at the beginning of time." Henry's adventures extend beyond red wines for he has also re-though Sauvignon. He selects the best parcels and harvests when the grapes are fully ripe, but not over-ripe, and his dry white wine is unique. Henry planted a hectare of ungrafted vines in 1992 and he is hoping that these Gamay vines, which he cultivates in the traditional style with goblet pruning, will survive long enough to recreate the taste of nineteenth century wines.

Touraine M de Marionnet 1990 ☖☖ ☖ ②
There are no grassy notes here, only inviting flowery aromas. A dry, aromatic, full-bodied Sauvignon Blanc that could almost be mistaken for an Alsatian wine. An original product which restores the variety's prestige.

Touraine ☖ ①
Gamay Première Vendange 1990
Marionnet has managed to transform the taste of Gamay. On the nose, this wine strikingly resembles Pinot Noir. Slightly peppery on the palate with no added sugar or sulphur, it is a typically drinkable light, fruity wine. Unfortunately, it is only produced in outstanding vintages.

TOURAINE/TOURAINE
LOIRE
FRANCE

465

TOURAINE/TOURAINE
LOIRE
FRANCE

Le Clos-Neuf des Archambaults

Jean-François Dehelly
37800 Sainte-Maure-de-Touraine
Tel. 47654870

Jean-François Dehelly makes a wine that is unlike his neighbors. He is the first to admit, however, that he can afford to do so as he only has a one and a half hectare vineyard to look after. He de-stems by hand and has chaptalized his wine only once in his life, in 1984 when he added sugar for the equivalent of one degree of alcohol. He uses so little sulphur that he is almost tempting disaster. Jean-François is a curious mixture of risk taker and solid common sense whose wines do not come into any of the modern categories. He used to be a company director in Paris and commuted every weekend to his estate in the Chinon area. Today at nearly 90 years of age he has finally made his dream come true and bought a few hectares to enlarge his property. A gentleman farmer whose family wine traditions go back over three hundred years, Jean-François only drinks vintage wine at table and criticizes today's trend towards alcohol rich wines. He claims that wines today are merely standardized products and that clonal selection has led to excessive yields even when pruning is rigorous. Can anyone honestly contradict him ?

Touraine Jeunes Vignes 1990   ♈ ①
Very concentrated color with plenty of extract despite the relatively low alcohol content. Plenty of character and a well-defined note of acidity. More expensive than most Touraines.

Jacky Preys et fils

Domaine de la Pierre à Feu
41130 Meusnes
Tel. 54710034
Fax 57713491

Jacky Preys is the proprietor of 70 ha of Sauvignon, Chardonnay, Pineau d'Aunis, Gamay, Cot, Cabernet Franc, Pinot Noir and Fié Gris. While he was looking around for more land to buy to meet growing demand, he came across an unusual parcel of Sauvignon. At first, he was going to uproot the two hectares of old vines but then he decided to give them a stay of execution in order to produce one vintage. When Jacky tasted the delicious succulent pink grapes from the century old vines he realized that they were not Sauvignon. He decided to keep the plants, which were identified by Onivins as some of the last surviving examples of Fié Gris, a cousin of Sauvignon grown in the Loire and the Vienne in the eighteenth century. Since then, Jacky has carefully vinified the grapes separately. In 1990, they yielded 9,000 bottles and in 1991, they miraculously escaped frost damage to produce 7,000 bottles. Fié Gris cuttings taken by Onivins will provide clones of the variety in a few years. But for Jacky Preys' tenacity, the variety would have disappeared and the world would have lost for ever a delicious curiosity.

Touraine Fié Gris 1990   ♈ ①
The grapes were picked when very ripe, at the end of October, and vinified without chaptalization or filtration. Pale straw-yellow with a fruity nose, this is a less aggressive wine than Sauvignon. Full-bodied, attractively dry and with a personality all of its own.

TOURAINE/TOURAINE
LOIRE
FRANCE

466

TOURAINE/TOURAINE
LOIRE
FRANCE

Clos Roche Blanche

41110 Mareuil-sur-Cher
Tel. 54751703
Fax 54751702

Catherine Roussel's parents were vignerons and when her father died, she decided to run the 15 ha family estate with her mother. The two have wisely kept their old vines, despite their low yields and today Catherine cultivates her four hectares of old Cot vines, also known as Malbec, with particular care. She has carried out experiments with the various clonal selections of Cot available and she is proud of having kept her old vines, which give marvellous grapes. Her Cot-based Touraine is the estate's premium wine. Didier Barouillet, her partner and winemaker, is a Parisian who has always loved the property. He has not missed a harvest in seven years. Didier openly admits to having made mistakes in the cellar in his early days but with experience has come wisdom and even creativity. For once, an outsider has contributed new techniques to winemaking.

Touraine Cot 1991 ♥ ①
Tangible proof that the under-rated Touraine Cot variety can produce a wine that is far from ordinary. Fermented at low temperatures to avoid extracting too much tannin, this is a particularly spicy wine for the Loire. The estate also makes a limited quantity of the same wine aged in old Bordeaux barrels and bottled without filtration.

Touraine 1990 ♥ ①
Produced from one third Gamay, one third Cabernet Franc and one third Cot. Vibrant dark red color with new wood evident on the nose and briefly dominating the fruit on the palate. A fine result for Touraine and the vintage.

Didier Champalou

7, rue du Grand Ormeau
37210 Le Portail - Vouvray
Tel. 47526449
Fax 47526799

It is rather unusual for a husband and wife both to be interested in wine. Generally, the wife has the ungratifying task of looking after the office work while the husband makes wine. This is not the case with Catherine Champalou, who left her family at the age of 15 to study at a wine college. There she met her future husband whose parents, like her own, were growers. Both Catherine and her husband knew that they wanted their own estate. In 1982, Catherine started planting their first hectare at Vouvray while Didier worked on a nearby vineyard. By 1985, they had managed to rent a total of six hectares and Catherine remembers that they produced 6,000 bottles. At that point, Didier decided to work full-time on their estate. In the course of the last 10 years, the Champalous have managed to put together a 10 ha property and they have built up a solid reputation thanks above all to their unflagging commitment to quality.

Vouvray Cuvée C. C. 1990 ♥♥♥ ③
The sweetest and most concentrated Champalou cuvée with 180 g of residual sugar. Old gold color with a full, complex nose and an intensely honeyed palate that finishes on a fresh note. Will age for half a century.

Vouvray Moelleux 1990 ♥♥♥ ②
From botrytized Chenin grapes. A golden, full-bodied and marvellously balanced wine with exceptional finesse. 90 g. of residual sugar.

Vouvray Pétillant ♥ ①
A dry, refreshing méthode champenoise wine from Chenin grapes. Unlike most Champagne houses, where the remuage is mechanized, here it is Catherine Champalou who patiently carries out the task herself.

TOURAINE/TOURAINE
LOIRE
FRANCE

467

TOURAINE/VOUVRAY
LOIRE
FRANCE

Domaine du Clos Naudin

14, rue de la Croix Buisée
37210 Vouvray
Tel. 47527146

Philippe Foreau grew up during a period of crisis and recession for viticulture. In this area, horses were not replaced by tractors until the mid-1960s and that is one of the reasons why, having qualified in enology, Philippe then enrolled at a business school. Family pressure, gentle though it was, proved too much in the end and he gave up accounts for the vineyard. It was not long before the best restaurateurs in France were taking notice of his exceptional winemaking skills. Philippe's wines have no frills. Their clean aromas blossom into a stupendously complex follow-through. Philippe's number one priority is to bring out the "goût de terroir" and it has to be said that he does so magnificently. The only vintage when there has been an exception to this rule was 1990. Not since 1893 has there been a vintage with such a wealth of sugar and the potential in the more concentrated cuvées to reach 28° alcohol. Philippe Foreau is not in the least worried. The 1990 will age for a century or more and the soil will have all the time it needs to recuperate. Besides, while it is easy to be hypnotized by the great Vouvray vintages (1989 and 1990) one should not forget that Clos Naudin also produces elegant dry white wines, a miracle that Philippe renews year after year.

Vouvray Sec 1991   ℘℘℘ ②
Pale yellow color with an attractive flowery nose of carnations and roses. Clean and racy with surprising power in the finish. A wine of superb quality from a challenging vintage.

Vouvray Moelleux   ℘℘ ④
Goutte d'Or 1990
Faced with an exceptional vintage like 1990, Philippe Foreau decided, more by way of an experiment than anything else, to make the sweetest of all cuvées producing 7,000 bottles under the label Goutte d'Or. The yeasts ceased fermentation at 8.5° alcohol in the presence of a super-abundance of sugar, leaving 320 g of residual sugar. A collector's item, with a honey and apricot palate.

Vouvray   ℘℘℘℘ ④
Réserve Moelleux 1990
The late-harvest botrytized Chenin grapes used for this cuvée contained an incredible quantity of natural sugar. Fermentation, in old wooden barrels, went on for many months before coming to a halt when there were still 200 g. of residual sugar and an alcohol content of only 10.5°. Nevertheless, this wine in no way lacks balance. Golden yellow, the aromas are exquisitely elegant, with spicy notes dominant. The palate is full flavored and highly concentrated, with aromas of outstanding complexity. A wine that bears Philippe Foreau's unmistakeable stamp and one that future generations will be able to enjoy for a very long time to come.

TOURAINE/VOUVRAY
LOIRE
FRANCE

468

TOURAINE/VOUVRAY
LOIRE
FRANCE

Bernard Fouquet

32, rue Gambetta
37210 Vouvray
Tel. 47526155-47526782
Fax 47526781

This bearded young man's frankness wins
you over at once. Bernard Fouquet's only
priority is to bring out the cru and he cannot
understand why Touraine producers strive to
imitate the great wines of Bordeaux or
Burgundy through the widespread use of new
oak. He will tell you all this in no uncertain
terms. Fouquet's first vintage was back in
1983 and in 1993, he gained complete
control over the whole 20 ha family estate.
Much of the property was planted 50 years
ago, on the slopes in the center of the
appellation. Bernard cultivates the land the
way his father and his grandfather did before
him, tilling the soil because he will not hear of
herbicides. In Bernard's opinion, there is no
more aristocratic wine than sweet Vouvray
and the results he obtained in 1989 and 1990
certainly bear him out. Vouvray sparkling
wine, in Bernard's opinion, is a second-string
product or even a mere fall-back solution
when the vintage is only moderate or poor.
An attitude for which he can be proud.

Vouvray Grande Année 1990 🍇🍇 ②
Golden yellow, with discreet aromas of honey.
Full-bodied and firm on the palate. The finish is
clean with a crisp mineral note. A well balanced
Chenin, sweet but not cloying.

Gaston Huet

Le Haut Lieu
37210 Vouvray
Tel. 47527887
Fax 47526651

The soil, the low yields, and the grapes
picked by hand over the course of several
selections have all contributed to make this
estate "the" Vouvray. Famous for many years,
the property received a further stimulus when
Catherine Huet married Noël Pinguet, a
mathematician from Vouvray. Pinguet was
going to move to Paris to work in the
computer industry when his father-in-law
suggested he should take over the family
estate. Although he knew absolutely nothing
about wine, Noël took to the job with a will
and was soon questioning many accepted
practices. In 1976, after a five year
apprenticeship, he produced his first, highly
successful, vintage but it was in 1987 that the
estate took a new direction. Pinguet was tired
of pouring chemicals into the soil and started
to employ biodynamic techniques. The results
have been very convincing for the vines are
thriving and the grapes are even more
delicious. For Noël, biodynamic agriculture
does not mean going back to the Stone Age.
His cellar uses state-of-the-art technology and
he was one of the first to acquire a pneumatic
press. Pinguet is also experimenting with
fermentation in new oak barrels as his wines
seem perfectly capable of standing up to such
a challenging approach.

Vouvray Le Haut Lieu 1990 🍇🍇 ④
Wine from this parcel is usually ready before the
other Huet cuvées but the remarkable 1990
vintage, powerful, sweet and intense, can safely
be laid down for half a century or even longer.

Vouvray Clos du Bourg 1989 🍇🍇 ④
From the part of the estate where biodynamic
methods have been used longest. This sweet
Chenin-based white wine is full bodied and
opulent on the palate with a complex, soft
texture. The nose has the characteristic aromas
of botrytis as well as spices and apricot. An
exceptional wine with a never ending finish.

TOURAINE/VOUVRAY
LOIRE
FRANCE

469

TOURAINE/VOUVRAY
LOIRE
FRANCE

Christophe Pichot

25, rue de la Bonne-Dame
37210 Coteaux de la Biche - Vouvray
Tel. 47526255-47527524

In 1984, Christophe Pichot, a member of the Vouvray young growers' association, inherited 14 ha on the Biche ridge in the heart of Vouvray from his grandparents. He thus became the seventh generation of growers to work in the same village. Christophe's family has never had a low profile in Vouvray. His great grandfather opened the Grand Restaurant, which still flourishes, and above all convinced Hardouin, the great pork-butcher whose rillon and rillettes are legendary, to set up shop next door to him. Christophe, for his part, spent two years studying viticulture at Amboise but his real apprenticeship was served at his father's side on the Peu de la Moriette estate. Today, he has a modern pneumatic press and produces wines which are a perfect expression of delicacy, finesse and flowery aromas. For the 1990 vintage, Christophe did not follow the majority's rush to sugar rich, wildly expensive, micro-cuvées. His aim is always to produce consistent quality wine at a reasonable price. And this old head on young shoulders probably produced in 1990 the most concentrated wine of his entire career.

Vouvray Sec 1990 ℗ ①
One of the few dry white wines produced in Vouvray in 1990 as most growers preferred to harvest the grapes late when their sugar content was highest. Pale color and dry on the palate. A fresh, racy wine to drink now.

Vouvray Demi-Sec 1989 ℗ ②
A very well-made demi-sec. The nose is dominated by flowery aromas with a note of white truffle while the faint hint of sweetness gives the wine a delightful texture. Full-bodied with a crisp, clean finish.

Alain Rohart

85 bis, route de la Monnaie
37210 Vouvray
Tel. 47526370
Fax 47527042

Alain Rohart was brought up on Champagne. This was because his father, a shoemaker, lived 50 km from the district and was unable to imagine a family celebration without bubbly. This early contact with the world of wine must have had an influence on Alain for in 1976 he and a few of his friends decided to spend their holidays discovering French wine. It was a holiday that was to change the course of his life for Alain was soon spending all his weekends in Touraine learning about wine. When he was made redundant in 1987, Alain decided to become a vigneron after twenty years as an industrial designer. There followed a period of searching and moving around during which his family began to have doubts about his sanity but in the end Alain found a small estate in Vouvray with old vines and an apparently even older cellar. Not for a moment did Alain consider producing a méthode champenoise as a last recours. His sparkling wines are made with the painstaking care of a true artisan. In 1989 and 1990, he had the chance to show off his skills as a maker of sweet wine, producing crisp, forthright wines of outstanding finesse. Keep an eye on this shoemaker's son who is on his way to becoming one of the best winemakers in the region.

Vouvray ℗ ③
Cuvée des Loges Vendanges Triées 1990
In comparison with most of the sweet Vouvray wines made in 1990, this cuvée with its 14° of alcohol and 50 g. of residual sugar seems almost like a demi-sec. A powerful, complex wine with a deliciously long finish.

Vouvray Méthode Traditionelle ℗ ①
Alain Rohart does his utmost to produce top-quality sparkling wines, even going to Champagne to acquire the boxes for the harvest. This méthode champenoise is dry and elegant with a personality of its own.

TOURAINE/VOUVRAY
LOIRE
FRANCE

470

TOURAINE/VOUVRAY
LOIRE
FRANCE

Alain Demon

La Perrière
42820 Ambierle
Tel. 7765649

By some bizarre coincidence, two of the producers mentioned in this guide turned to viticulture after being made redundant by the same steel mill in northern France. One is Alain Rohart, who settled in Vouvray, and the other is Alain Demon. Demon will candidly admit to never having been particularly interested in wine and not even drinking very much of it. The first time he held a book on the subject in his hands was in 1979, shortly before he bought a vineyard. This is perhaps not the ideal background for a grower but Demon, who went on to take an eight month course at Mâcon, is something of an exception. In 1980 at the age of 36, Alain bought a three hectare vineyard near Lyon. It did not cost him very much but there again little known growers on the Côtes Roannaises have limited commercial prospects. Alain went to work with a will, trod the grapes himself, regardless of what the neighbors thought and the difficulties he had in selling the wine. His dedication bore fruit and Alain's excellent, moderately-priced wines are now to be found in Paris's best wine bars.

Côtes Roannaises 🍇 ①
Cuvée Reserve 1990
An absolutely unique example of the fruit and velvety softness of which Gamay is capable. Old vines, low yields and an antique vertical press contribute to a deliciously concentrated wine, redolent of cherries.

Maurice Lutz

Domaine du Pavilion
42820 Ambierle
Tel. 77656435

But for a family quarrel, Maurice Lutz would probably be making white wines in Alsace today. In 1951, his father decided to leave the family vineyard and set up on his own. He was toying with the idea of going abroad to run a coffee plantation when an advertisement in the local paper caught his eye. There was a house and a hectare of Gamay vines for sale in Ambierle. Lutz had no notion of where Ambierle was as he had never even been as far south as Lyon but he went to see the house, which is 50 km north-east of Beaujolais, and moved in two months later. Never having made a red wine in his life, Lutz decided to compromise and try a rosé, thus becoming the first producer in the Côtes Roannaises ever to do so. One of the local restaurateurs liked the wine and bought some. The restaurateur's name was Troisgros and after he had become famous, Troisgros continued to keep Lutz wine on his wine list, giving this unknown grower the very best kind of publicity possible. Today the property extends over six hectares, or one twentieth of the total surface area of the Côtes Roannaises. On his granite slopes, Maurice Lutz produces attractive red wines with an exceptional aroma. They bring to mind a good Beaujolais, but at half the price.

Côtes Roannaises 1991 🍇 ①
Gamay grapes at their very best. Ruby red, with aromas of red currants and strawberries. Invitingly light on the palate with lovely aromas and a delicious spicy finish.

VINS DU CENTRE/COTES ROANNAISES
LOIRE
FRANCE

471

VINS DU CENTRE/COTES ROANNAISES
LOIRE
FRANCE

Georges Chavet et fils

Les Brangers
18150 Menetou-Salon
Tel. 48648087
Fax 48648478

Philippe Chavet's family have lived in Menetou-Salon for many generations and have made wine at least since 1710. One ancestor was a "garde vigne", whose job it was to keep an eye on the ripening grapes and make sure that nobody stole them. Today, the grape harvest on this 15 ha estate, a stone's throw from Sancerre, is completely mechanized. As a child, Philippe was always helping his father in the vineyard or the cellar when he was not at school. There was never any doubt about his future profession. Philippe's brother Jean-Michel, on the other hand, was never attracted by wine so he looks after the family orchards and makes apple juice. Philippe went to a school of enology in Mâcon, returning to the family estate in 1976. He grows the same varieties as are grown in Sancerre, as indeed do all the producers in the 300 ha appellation of Menetou-Salon. Half the domaine's vineyard is planted with Sauvignon and the other half Pinot Noir for the production of reds and rosés.

Menetou-Salon Sauvignon 1991   🍇 ①
Pale yellow tinged with green and a nose with the typical Sauvignon aromas of freshly-cut grass. The palate is fresh, racy and well-balanced. Excellent summer drinking.

Didier Dagueneau

Saint-Andelain
58150 Pouilly-sur-Loire
Tel. 86391562
Fax 86390761

Didier Dagueneau is often spoken of as an unusual grower who makes atypical wines. He is not the kind of person who unquestioningly accepts tradition nor is he likely to be influenced by fashion. Unlike most of his colleagues, Didier did not inherit vines from his father, a wine producer in Pouilly-Fumé. He left home at an early age and only made up his mind to return and make wine ten years later. He began in 1982 with one and a half hectares. The tiny vineyard left him with plenty of time to travel and observe what other producers elsewhere were doing. He went to California and to the finest estates in France, making a lot of firm friendships in the process. Didier was not looking for the recipe for instant success but listened instead to what producers had to say about the many problems they faced. Didier, who now has 11 ha, came to an important conclusion. To make first-class wine, care and attention must be devoted to every detail from the soil type to the vines and bottling. Didier's low yield Pouilly-Fumé fermented in wood conceals no tricks of the trade. It is, however, on the wine lists of many of France's three-star restaurants.

Pouilly-Fumé Cuvée Silex 1990   🍇 🍇 ④
A white wine from Sauvignon grapes fermented and aged in oak barrels. But there is much more to this wine than just the aromas of oak and vanilla. Low yields confer a concentrated flavor of raisins and honey with a distinctive flinty flavor.

Le Maudit 1990   🍇 🍇 ④
Didier Dagueneau christened this late-harvest Sauvignon Le Maudit (The Cursed) because it was so unusual that it was refused the Pouilly-Fumé appellation. Botrytized grapes have produced a full-flavored, honeyed wine with 50 g of residual sugar and a well-defined mineral note. A wine for keeping, close in style to a Sauternes.

Michel Redde et fils

La Moynerie - Saint-Andelain
58150 Pouilly-sur-Loire
Tel. 86391472
Fax 86390436

Michel Redde has seen the Pouilly-Fumé vineyard go through some hard times. He took over the small family property in the 1950s, when most producers had abandoned their estates to go and earn a better living elsewhere. Michel, however, has a strong sense of family tradition and for him to break a line of growers that has been uninterrupted for seven generations would have been unthinkable. His son Thierry, who is 34, works alongside him and will inherit the estate. Michel hopes his two grandchildren will also pass on the art of viticulture to future generations when their turn comes. The craftsmanship of the Redde family produces Pouilly-Fumés that are fresh and at the same time have good structure. Michel's grandfather was an innovator, one of the first growers to replace the traditional Chasselas with Sauvignon, and so too is Michel, who has pioneered stainless steel vats. Michel frowns on aging in oak as he thinks the "terroir" is sufficiently noble to speak for itself without interference.

Pouilly-Fumé 1990   🍷 ②
Pale straw-yellow with greenish tints. A full-bodied white wine made from Sauvignon grapes. Mouthfilling flavor with a refreshing note on the finish. The perfect aperitif wine.

Pouilly-Fumé Cuvée Majorum 1989   🍷 ②
A Sauvignon where the characteristic grassy note is dominated by blackcurrant aromas. Bright yellow in color it is a sophisticated wine made from very ripe grapes. It has tremendous length of flavor and finishes on an ample note.

Claude Lafond

Le Bois Saint-Denis
36260 Reuilly
Tel. 54492217

Claude Lafond is one of the most dynamic producers in the sleepy appellation of Reuilly. In 1980, the total area of the appellation was barely 50 ha and the residents of the village of Reuilly were resigned to seeing their winemaking tradition come to an end. By 1992 the vineyard had doubled in size - Claude Lafond had taken things in hand. In partnership with another producer, he found 107 shareholders, including an American astronomer, and had financed the purchase and planting of a 10 ha vineyard, which went into production in 1992. In addition, Lafond has collaborated with the appellation's most committed growers to make a move in the direction of quality, starting with more severe pruning. Claude's own estate comprises 15 ha, more than half of which is planted in Sauvignon. His aim is to give Reuilly's wines the opportunity to express their own characteristics to the full and to shake off the image of being merely second rate Sancerre.

Le Reuilly 1990   🍷 ①
Yellow with greenish tints and an aromatic, flowery nose. An elegant white wine where cru and ripe fruit prevail over the herbaceous notes of Sauvignon. Proof that Reuilly wines can be truly splendid.

Reuilly Rosé 1990   🥂 ①
A sensual rosé obtained from Pinot Gris grapes, full-bodied and with plenty of ripe fruit. Salmon pink with attractively peppery aromas. The full flavored palate finishes on a dry mineral note.

Reuilly Rouge 1990   🍷 ①
Ruby red with purple tinges. A full, spicy wine with the softness of a Rhône and a meaty nose. The texture is invitingly velvety and the nose is dominated by cherry notes. Ready to drink now, this is a wine with the potential to age for several more years.

VINS DU CENTRE/POUILLY-FUME
LOIRE
FRANCE

473

VINS DU CENTRE/REUILLY
LOIRE
FRANCE

Gérard et Jean-Louis Pétillat

Domaine de Bellevue
03500 Meillard
Tel. 70420556
Fax 70420975

This area was renowned for its wines in the Middle Ages but today only 350 ha remain under vine. The Saint-Pourçain appellation might even have disappeared altogether had it not been for the dynamic, innovative local cooperative, which is responsible for putting Saint-Pourçain back on the map. Today, there are also some independent producers who make interesting wines and among these must be included the Pétillats who have been one step ahead of the others for three generations. Grandfather Pétillat was the first grower in the region to bottle the entire production of his three hectare vineyard and the Pétillats have never sold a single drop of wine wholesale since. Gérard, the father, took a course in enology at Beaune long before most growers in the district realized that winemaking could actually be studied. His son, Jean-Louis, has completely renovated the cellar. The traditional Tressalier grape is no longer to be found on the Pétillant estate as it has been replaced by more fashionable varieties; Sauvignon, Chardonnay, Gamay and more recently Pinot Noir.

Saint-Pourçain Grande Reserve 1990 ⚇ ①
A pale yellow dry white wine produced from Sauvignon and Chardonnay grapes. Heady flowery nose and medium texture with an attractively fresh finish.

Saint-Pourçain 1991 ❦ ①
A ruby red Gamay with aromas of strawberries and raspberries. Dry and fruity on the palate. Extremely drinkable.

Domaine Henri Bourgeois

18300 Chavignol - Sancerre
Tel. 48542167
Fax 48541424

The Bourgeois are one of those rare happy families who work together in complete harmony. The two brothers, Rémy and Jean-Marie look after the vineyard and sales respectively. Every day of the year, with the exception of Christmas Day and New Year's Day, their wives sell the wine in their own shop in the charming village of Chavignol, famous both for its Sancerre and its goat's milk cheese, Crottin de Chavignol. The brothers are helped by three of their children, one of whom, Jean-Christophe, is the winemaker. Jean-Christophe's task is by no means easy because the 45 ha property comprises 100 separate parcels on three different soil types, which produce very different wines from the same Sauvignon grapes. The Bourgeois estate produces four distinct cuvées of white Sancerre, a Sancerre rosé, two red Sancerres and two Pouilly-Fumés. Some of the most interesting cuvées are experimental, like the 1989 Sancerre made from two hectares of late harvested grapes which produced an outstandingly robust wine with a natural alcohol content of 15°. Unfortunately, the wine is not for sale as it was made only as an experiment. However, if you visit the shop the ladies will be only too happy to pour you a glass.

Sancerre Le MD de Bourgeois 1991 ⚇ ②
Straw-yellow with cool aromas of fresh-cut grass. Good structure on the palate with elegant aromas of blackcurrant and a racy finish. 5 to 7 years aging potential.

Sancerre Cuvée Etienne Henri 1990 ⚇ ③
After four years of experimental wine-making the Bourgeois were finally able to offer this Sauvignon wine fermented in oak barrels, one-third new. Heady vanilla and fruit aromas. The wood is still dominant on the palate but will mellow out with time. A wine which will easily age for ten years.

Sancerre La Bourgeoise 1990 ❦❦ ②
More color than the average red Sancerre, which is usually nearer to pink than red, but this wine is also fuller in color than many Burgundies. A new style for the region from very ripe Pinot Noir grapes aged in oak barrels. Full-bodied, firm and complex, with a hint of wood on the finish.

VINS DU CENTRE/SAINT-POURÇAIN
LOIRE
FRANCE

474

VINS DU CENTRE /SANCERRE
LOIRE
FRANCE

Paul Cotat

Chavignol
18300 Sancerre
Tel. 48540422

Paul Cotat has never wanted to expand his vineyard. The hectare and a half he has in one of the best locations in Sancerre is quite enough for him. The domaine could be considered a little larger as Paul's brother Francis owns one and a half hectares too and his 28 year-old son François has another hectare. Paul himself was only fourteen when his father was killed in the war and he took over the vineyard in partnership with his brother. The two of them have continued to make wine in almost exactly the same way as their father, doing nearly everything by hand. Until very recently, they even sprayed the vines manually and it is only now that a helicopter has taken over the job. During the harvest, Paul has difficulty in finding workers to help work the grape press, which is naturally manually operated. It is a vertical model dating from the nineteenth century and was left to him by his father. The wine ferments in 600 lt barrels and is racked only twice. It is never filtered or fined and is bottled straight from the barrel. The end product is a superb Sancerre which can safely be aged for 15 to 20 years.

Sancerre 1990   ♟ ♟ ②
Straw-yellow with exquisitely elegant flowery aromas on the nose. One of the noblest expressions of the chalky Chavignol terrain and the Sauvignon variety.

Lucien Crochet

Place de l'Église
18300 Bué - Sancerre
Tel. 48540810
Fax 48542766

Lucien Crochet and his wife come from a long line of growers at Bué, in the heart of Sancerre. The soil at Bué is particularly chalky and produces some of the freshest and liveliest wines in the area. Lucien Crochet's white wines are well known to connoisseurs to the extent that today he has to turn customers away. This was not always the case. When he inherited his father's and father-in-law's vineyards, Lucien had to search out new markets for his 30 ha property and it was then that he visited Paul Bocuse. Since then, France's most celebrated chef has kept Crochet wines on his wine list and offered them to his customers from all over the world. Lucien himself, however, has not changed in any way and goes to Paris regularly to deliver his wine in person. Lucien's son Gilles is a 30 year old enologist who has worked on the family estate all his life, except for his college days in Burgundy and a short stay in Australia. Gilles came back from his travels not with a desire to force new wood on to the family wines but with the determination to make the best Sancerre in the appellation.

Sancerre 1990   ♟ ♟ ②
The secret of this elegant Sancerre is to be found in the chalky soil of the vineyards and the low yields of the vines. Pale yellow with greenish tints, this is a fragrant wine with a firm, chalky flavor. Fresh, racy and with a lingering finish.

Sancerre Cuvée Prestige 1990   ♟ ♟ ③
A wine which shows just what enormous progress Sancerre has made over recent years. It can now compete with the best white Burgundies. This is an elegant wine, beautifully balanced and very generous, with notes of honey and a crisp finish.

Pierre et Alain Dezat

Domaine du Petit Roy
Maimbray
18300 Sury-en-Vaux
Tel. 48793416

Pierre Dezat remembers the day he first started working in his father's one and a half hectare vineyard. It was the day after he finished school, 20th May 1944 and Pierre was 13 years old. His grandparents had spent their entire lives working for other people but they had managed to put together a modest vineyard, which their son inherited. Over the years, the property grew especially after Pierre's son Alain decided to join him. Like most of the older generation of vignerons, Pierre had a grafting diploma and up until a few years ago, used to do all the grafting himself. He uprooted his father's Gamay vines, widely planted after the destruction of the vineyard by phylloxera, and grafted from very old Pinot Noir vines. Today, one third of the property is planted with Pinot Noir from which a red wine partly aged in wood is produced. Pierre Dezat is better known for his white wines. He can point to some extremely famous names on his list of customers, including the legendary Troisgros restaurant, which has been buying Dezat wines for more than thirty years.

Sancerre 1990
Over the last twenty years, winemaking in Sancerre has witnessed a succession of different styles. The Dezat approach is very close to local tradition, even though their cellar is today equipped with the very latest in modern technology. The aromas of this wine are reminiscent of hay and gooseberries while the palate is dominated by a fresh note of acidity.

Alphonse Mellot

Domaine de la Moussière
18300 Sancerre
Tel. 48540741
Fax 48540762

Alphonse Mellot can trace his winemaking roots back to the sixteenth century. Always busy, he manages at the same time not to take himself too seriously and to enjoy life. Having gained his early experience at Beaune, an important period in his life which opened his eyes to different white wine techniques, Alphonse took over his father's vineyard and négociant business. Ten years later in 1980, the Mellot production had reached one and a half million bottles of Sancerre a year. As the years went by, Alphonse realized that the way forward was to aim to improve the quality of the wine from the 45 ha estate and as a result, he ran down the négociant side of the business. Since 1987, the estate has undergone a large number of changes, beginning with an increase in the number of vines per hectare. The 45 year old Alphonse is also carefully studying the geology of his soils and is using chemical sprays much less frequently than before. He is also a man who likes to experiment. He recently tried a late harvest Sauvignon and has also opened a wine bar in the center of Sancerre.

Sancerre 1991
A difficult vintage but a successful wine. The key to the concentrated aromas is partly to be found in the fact that the wine was left on its lees for several months. Pale yellow with light aromas of honey and chalk. Full body and generous texture with a dry finish.

Sancerre Cuvée Edmond 1988
Produced from Sauvignon grapes harvested from old vines with tiny yields, this oak fermented white wine has an intense yellow color with a nutty nose. Good fruit attack but thins out a little on the finish. Drink now.

VINS DU CENTRE /SANCERRE
LOIRE
FRANCE

476

VINS DU CENTRE /SANCERRE
LOIRE
FRANCE

André Vatan

Domaine des P'tits Perriers
18300 Verdigny - Sancerre
Tel. 48793307
Fax 48793630

André Vatan's father Jean was a hard working, traditional winemaker who was widely respected. When his son was not at school, he was expected to help in the vineyard. André became disenchanted with the work until the day in 1980 when he was 16 and his father gave him his first hectare of vines. Since then, André has been totally wrapped up in his work. He studied enology and learnt about the latest production techniques, gradually taking over the family estate. Today, he has 11.5 ha and a well equipped modern cellar. He works in close collaboration with the National Institute for Agricultural Research and is currently carrying out research into selected yeasts. The Vatan estate extends over all three classic Sancerre soil types: flint, clay-limestone and limestone. In addition, André has a parcel of iron rich soil that he has planted with Pinot Noir. From this, he produces a red Sancerre partly aged in wood. The domaine's other noteworthy red wine comes from a vineyard just outside the border of the Sancerre appellation. It is a Vin de Pays, also made from Pinot Noir, which sells for half the price of a Sancerre.

Sancerre La Côte 1991   🍇 ②
A fresh, dry, aromatic Sauvignon from a successful blend of grapes grown on two of the domaine's different soil types. A wine which will need a couple of years to develop and mellow.

Sancerre Moulin Bele 1990   🍇 ②
Ruby red with the typical aromas of the Pinot Noir variety. A hint of wood comes from the 10% aged in oak. The palate is full bodied and fruity with a tannic note on the finish.

Vin de Pays du Cher   🍇 ①
Cuvée La Roncière
A red wine made from Pinot Noir grapes, less complex in structure than a Sancerre. Attractively fresh, fruity and very drinkable.

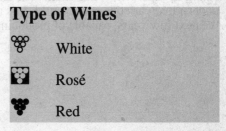

Type of Wines

🍇   White

▦   Rosé

🍇   Red

VINS DU CENTRE /SANCERRE
LOIRE
FRANCE

477

VINS DU CENTRE /SANCERRE
LOIRE
FRANCE

Provence

While many of the wine-growing areas of Provence have traditions that can be traced back to the ancient history of the Mediterranean, today's cellars are the results of the massive investments of the 1960s and 1970s, which aimed to turn Provence into the California of France, a region of sunshine where modern technology would combine with the terroir to produce world-beating results. Unfortunately, despite the endless rows of stainless steel vats, which virtually every cellar boasts, and the great number of new oak barrels sitting in air-conditioned comfort, only a handful of wines actually merit international recognition. The region's rich, spicy reds, refreshing rosés and whites with exotic aromas are generally very well-made, but for the moment at least there are neither real bargains nor truly great wines. The remarkable red Bandols of Domaine de Tempier and Château Pibarnon, like most of the other stars of the region, come from ancient winemaking strongholds like Palette, Cassis, Bandol and Bellet, where tradition has corrected the errors of the recent past.

The "King of Provence" in the production of red wine is Mourvèdre, a difficult variety both to grow and to vinify. Traditionally, Provencal vignerons have always said that Mourvèdre needs a view of the sea as it ripens late and makes unattractive, aggressive wines if harvested too early. It is also an extremely tannic variety, highly resistant to oxidization. Wines with a high Mourvèdre content take many years to soften. An influx of new producers has brought the planting of considerable quantities of Cabernet Sauvignon, with highly variable results which offer no real challenge to Bordeaux. Opinions on what are Provence's most successful wines are as numerous as the wines themselves, but it is significant that all the best products are blends of different varieties. The most active promoters (and consumers) of these wines, which take full advantage of the benefits of modern technology, are the residents of Provence themselves. Recently the biggest surprise has been the progress made by the region's white wines. Individual Appellations have made substantial improvements in quality as producers learn to identify the most suitable varieties for their soils and apply up-to-date technology to monitor vinification and maintain acidity, freshness and aroma.

The next ten years may well witness dramatic developments. The wines from estates such as Domaine de Trévallon at Les Baux and La Courtade on the island of Porquerolles, which are currently beginning to find their form, demonstrate undeniable potential. There is ample evidence in countries like Australia, America and South Africa that the intelligent use of modern technology makes the production of great wines possible in hot climates. Certainly in Provence there is no lack of excellent locations with the right sunlight, superb clay-and-chalk soils and some of the most interesting and under-rated varieties in the world. It is a region worth following closely over the next few years, capable of producing some exciting surprises.

Château de Pibarnon

83740 La Cadière d'Azur
Tel. 94901273
Fax 94901298

Count Henri de Saint-Victor is a former student of the Paris École de Sciences Politiques and a keen collector of Neapolitan temperas. Together with his son, he runs a 49-ha estate which is one of the most distinguished of the Bandol Appellation. The property lies on the edge of the Sainte-Baume massif on Triassic clay-and-chalk, sandstone and green marl terrain. 30 ha had to be broken up with bulldozers before vines, 70% of which are Mourvèdre, could be planted. Grapes are harvested late and yields are very low. White wines are fermented at low temperatures and the reds macerate slowly before aging in wood for two years. Without becoming entrenched in modern dogma,the Saint-Victors keep up-to-date on winemaking technology and recent experiments have included maceration on the skins for white wines, added yeasts, systematic racking and non-filtering. The family is also always willing to take on new ventures and has recently acquired a 20-ha vineyard in a single parcel next to the Pibarnon estate. Prospects here are exciting: soil analysis has revealed the presence of blue clay of exactly the kind found at Pétrus.

Bandol 1990 ②
Inviting, slightly warm nose with a background of peach stone and spices. Considerable finesse on the palate which is kept together by a nicely balanced acidity.

Bandol 1988 ❦❦❦ ③
Intense, bright ruby red. The nose has the characteristic Mourvèdre aroma of seashells, pine resin, tar and wood shavings. On the palate smoothly integrated redcurrant and liquorice flavors come through the massive fullness of the fruit and tannins.

Bandol 1982 ❦❦ ④
Dark red, tending to mahogany, with quite extraordinary luster. The nose has enormous depth of aromas, including treacle with hints of smoke and tar blending with truffles and redcurrant jelly. A wine with already ten years' bottle-age which will last - like its finish - for a very long time to come.

Bandol 1989 ❦❦❦ ③
The latest masterpiece from Counts Saint-Victor which amply demonstrates their intimate familiarity with the Mourvèdre variety. A wine of a deep, inviting, bright ruby red, already with quite exceptional concentration on the nose where cherries, red berries and liquorice dominate while the typical Mourvèdre aromas of tar, tobacco and treacle are less in evidence. They do, however, emerge on the palate where the excellent structure is complemented by the rich intensity of tropical fruit that characterizes all French wines from the fabulous 1989 vintage. At present, it is difficult to predict the evolution of this wine as a Pibarnon has never before had such concentration. If it develops in the same way as its predecessors, the notes of tar, tobacco and warm spices will begin to come through over the rich, sweet berries which prevail at the moment, and in a few years' time it will develop into one of the world's most evocative wines, a symphony of these aromas. The temptation is to drink it now, but the greatest satisfaction will be in handing down a bottle or two to future generations.

BANDOL
PROVENCE
FRANCE

479

BANDOL
PROVENCE
FRANCE

Château Pradeaux

83270 Saint-Cyr-sur-Mer
Tel. 94321021
Fax 94321602

Countess Arlette Portalis, an eccentric lady who is sorely missed, died recently, leaving 26 ha of vineyards, completely replanted after the last war, in the capable hands of her neice Cyrille, who also took her aunt's surname. The vines produce about 28 hl/ha of Mourvèdre on clay-and-chalk soil. The estate also has small quantities of Grenache and Cinsaut to bolster its extremely modest production of rosés. No chemicals are used on the property and grapes are fermented on the stem in the traditional manner in cement containers. Two of these date from the 17th century and cannot be replaced as the entire château rests on them! The wine ages for three to five years in oak barrels which similarly cannot be replaced because the roof of the cellar would have to come off to install new ones. The estate produces about 50,000 bottles of superb red wine a year, the long aging of which means that it goes on the market much later than the majority of Bandols. Despite the prohibitive production costs of the Château Pradeaux style, Cyrille Portalis continues to be faithful to her aunt's winemaking creed.

Bandol 1987 ▼ ③

This wine is always difficult to evaluate. The 1987 Pradeaux is dark ruby with a nose that has faint notes of strawberry jam and tar. The palate is very tannic, with hints of violets and caramel. The finish lacks a little definition, but these wines notoriously take many years to fulfill their huge potential.

Château Vannières

83740 La Cadière d'Azur
Tel. 94900808
Fax 94901598

Château Vannières has been producing wine since the 16th century. The present-day 34-ha vineyard on chalk and clay soil is the work of Lucien Boudot, who previously owned estates in Burgundy and Beaujolais before buying Château Vannières with its sunny Bandol location in 1957. In 1968, Lucien handed over to his daughter Colette Boisseaux who, with her son Eric, is still in charge today and continues to obtain excellent results. Half of the property is planted in Mourvèdre and the other half in equal proportions of Grenache and Cinsaut. Annual production is about 100,000 bottles, half of which is rosé and the majority of the remainder red, with just a small quantity of white wine. Grapes are hand-picked from vines with an average age of 25 years. Rosé wines are vinified in stainless steel at controlled temperatures after soft-pressing designed to extract the desired degree of color. The wine is bottled after six months in the vat. As for the red wines, the grapes are crushed and then ferment for around 20 days in temperature-controlled stainless steel vats. The wine is then aged - unusually for Bandol - in new oak for up to two years. Although Château Vannières does not achieve the levels of concentration of other Bandol wines, it is generally elegant and has distinct personality.

Bandol 1989 ▼ ②

An invitingly deep, dark, rich red wine. Aromas of plain chocolate and ripe fruit. Full-flavored and tannic, a little hard and overpowering but with good length and an elegant finish.

BANDOL
PROVENCE
FRANCE

480

BANDOL
PROVENCE
FRANCE

Domaine de la Tour du Bon

83330 Le Castellet
Tel. 94326162
Fax 94327169

Agnès Hochard manages an estate which is well worth visiting. Her wines get better every year and although her reds are austere Bandols, made for laying down, they win medals even while they are still purple-red and evidently not yet ready for drinking. The Hochards bought their estate in 1968 and built a house on it right in the middle of the vines which they had replanted, with a high proportion of Mourvèdre, on a rocky plateau outside the village of Le Castellet. Annual production is about 50,000 bottles, most of which consists of red and rosé cuvées. There is also a very small amount of white and a similarly small quantity of Cuvée Saint-Ferréol, from monovarietal Mourvèdre. Fermentation of the rosés is at controlled temperatures and the wine is bottled for sale six months after the completion of the malolactic. Grapes for red wines are crushed and fermented in stainless steel containers where the wine undergoes its malolactic before aging for two years in large oak barrels.The Cuvée Saint-Ferréol is aged in pre-used Burgundy barriques and recent vintages will not be ready for drinking before the end of the century.

Bandol 1989
Purple with inky tinges round the edges. A wine with complex aromas of mint, liquorice, cedar and blackcurrant. Blackcurrant returns on the palate together with rich aromas of violet, although the wine is also still intensely tannic and will only become more approachable with time.

Bandol 1990
Deep purple with a still undeveloped nose which suggests leather and liquorice. The palate is full-bodied but also has excellent fruit to balance out the tannins. A wine with superb aging potential.

Domaine Le Galantin

Achille et Liliane Pascal
83330 Le Plan du Castellet
Tel. 94987594
Fax 94902955

Both Achille and Liliane Pascal come from farming backgrounds. Having bought Domaine Le Galantin in 1965, it took them seven years to replant the 20-ha property and bring the proportion of Mourvèdre up to 70%, with 15% of Grenache and Cinsaut. The vines are located on the clay, chalk and sand soils of the Plan du Castellet. The principal wine is Bandol red. About 30% of the total output consists of rosé and there is also a small production of white. The recently extended cellar is clean and well-equipped. Fermentation is in temperature-controlled stainless steel vats. Grapes for red wines (90% Mourvèdre) ferment for 15 days during which the wine is pumped over the cap regularly, a rather unusual practice in Bandol. It ages for 18 to 36 months in oak and then in the bottle for a few months before release. The Pascals aim for a style of wine suitable for laying down, typical of the sub-zone which produces some of the most slow-evolving reds of the Appellation. The rosé is a blend of 70% Cinsaut and 30% Grenache and Mourvèdre.

Bandol 1989
Rich, intense red color and an equally intense nose with notes of peppery fruit. Well-rounded and full-bodied on the palate with aromas of ripe red fruit and unobtrusive tannins. Excellent length. Superb expression of a variety which gives particularly rustic, meaty wines.

Bandol 1986 ♟♟ ④
Lovely intense ruby red in the glass, becoming lighter at the edges. Full, soft, round palate with hints of leaves, good balance and a truly delicious follow-through of herbs and spices. Ready for drinking now. Ideal accompaniment to meat dishes, including those with spicy sauces.

BANDOL
PROVENCE
FRANCE

481

BANDOL
PROVENCE
FRANCE

Les Domaines Ott

Château Romassan
83330 Le Castellet
Tel. 94987191

In 1896, Marcel Ott was all set to go to Morocco to plant vines and seek his fortune. His wife refused to board the ship so Marcel stayed in Provence to create the Ott empire, which today comprises three properties. The Ott company is well-known for the unusual shape of its rosé wine bottles, but it also produces reds, whites and rosés at the former monastery of Château Romassan. Despite being located in an Appellation known above all for red wine, the Otts concentrate on making elegant rosés. Their Coeur de Grain is widely held to be one of the best rosés in the zone. Most of the grapes come from the 50 ha that Marcel supervises personally, and one of the characteristic Ott hallmarks is the "cordon de royat" system of training the vine which is not normally used in Bandol. The Coeur de Grain rosé is obtained from 90% Grenache together with Mourvèdre and Cinsaut. The juice ferments at low temperatures and is then kept in the vat until it is bottled in spring. The Otts also produce an interesting white wine from Sauvignon Blanc and Rolle grapes as well as two reds. The normal cuvée is from 50% Mourvèdre while the Cuvée Longarde has a higher percentage of Mourvèdre and greater concentration.

Bandol Coeur de Grain 1991 ②
Obtained mainly from Grenache grapes together with Mourvèdre and Cinsaut, the 1991 vintage confirms the well-deserved reputation of this wine, considered one of France's best roses.

Bandol Château Romassan ④
Cuvée Longarde 1987
Dark ruby-red shading into apricot round the edges. The nose has rich aromas of ripe redcurrant mingling with tobacco. A soft, fleshy wine with a very long finish. Altogether a superbly made wine.

Domaine Ray-Jane

Raymond Constant et fils
83330 Le Plan du Castellet
Tel. 94986408
Fax 94986408

Raymond Constant is the owner of the world's largest collection of cooper's tools and one of Bandol's most offbeat producers. He will tell you that the estate, the family name and even the vines at Ray-Jane have been the same since the 12th century. It is undoubtedly true that the vines, especially the plants surrounding the house, are very old and that yields are low (32 hl/ha) throughout the 14 ha of the property. Bandol's chalky clay soil varies considerably over the Appellation and at Ray-Jan the unusual terraced vines on compact fossil shell-bearing soil confer a highly distinctive personality to the wine. The estate uses organic methods to produce equal quantities of red and rosé Bandols (about 60,000 bottles a year) with a high proportion of Mourvèdre (circa 80%) plus Grenache and Cinsaut. Rosés are made with 2-5 hours of skin contact. Fermentation is in stainless steel vats and bottling takes place in spring. The red is traditionally made with surprisingly light extract and fresh fruit.

Bandol 1991 ②
One of the most interesting rosés in Bandol, from Grenache and Cinsaut grapes. A wine with a flowery nose - fresh, heady and very inviting.

Bandol 1988 ②
Full, intense, well-developed color. Concentrated notes of leather and balsam on the nose. Rounded on the palate with a soft texture, good length and attractive balance.

BANDOL
PROVENCE
FRANCE

482

BANDOL
PROVENCE
FRANCE

Domaine Tempier

83330 Le Plan du Castellet
Tel. 94987021
Fax 94902165

There is no doubt at all that wine lovers in general, and the Bandol Appellation in particular, owe a debt of gratitude to Lucien Peyraud for the unwavering determination with which he has promoted the name "Bandol". Lucien's philosophy is a simple one: appreciate what the wine itself has to offer and give it sufficient time to do so. According to Peyraud, every wine is unique. With his wife Lulu and their two children, Lucien cultivates 30 ha of vineyards located on clay and chalk soil, including the two parcels of La Migoua below the village of Le Beausset and La Tourtine at Le Castellet. The vines are an average of 40 years old and produce five cuvées of red wine. The Cuvée Classique and the Cuvée Spéciale, which contains a greater proportion of Mourvèdre, are from vineyards all around the estate. The Cuvée Cabassaou is a monovarietal Mourvèdre from the La Tourtine vineyard and is only available in limited quantities. Winemaking techniques are simple: the de-stemmed grapes ferment at controlled temperatures and then age in large oak barrels for a period which varies in accordance with the requirements of each wine. These wines, neither fined nor filtered, are among the very best Bandol reds.

Bandol Cuvée Spéciale 1989   👄👄 ③
Extract-rich purple-and-garnet tones in the glass which open out on the nose after breathing for a few hours to offer well-developed aromas of tar, treacle, tobacco and flint competing with plums and caramel. The structure on the palate derives from solid tannins balanced by attractive fruit. A great wine which demands at least another five years in the cellar.

Bandol Cuvée Spéciale 1988   👄👄 ③
A young, mauve-tinted ruby red. Liquorice, leather and caramel dominate the nose. Velvet-smooth violet, caramel and hints of tar come through on the palate and in the finish. Another Tempier wine with quite stupendous structure.

Bandol   👄👄👄 ③
Cuvée Spéciale La Tourtine 1989
Bright red, with a clean, sweet spicy nose and a very round, smooth palate which highlights flavors of mint, spicy herbs and rich, sweet menthol. Peyraud's outstanding achievement in this wine is the combination of velvet-soft texture with great aromatic complexity : in short, another outstanding wine in the distinctive Domaine Tempier style. Left to breathe for 24 hours, it develops quite extraordinarily, releasing a bouquet of alternating fruit, spices and underlying gamey aromas without a hint of oxidation.

BANDOL
PROVENCE
FRANCE

483

BANDOL
PROVENCE
FRANCE

Domaine de Terrebrune

724, Chemin de la Tourelle
83190 Ollioules
Tel. 94740130
Fax 94746054

Georges Delille used to be a hotelier in Paris until he bought an estate near Les Ollioules in the 1960s which today is by far the most active in Bandol. The 22 ha are planted with 70% Mourvèdre with an average age of 20 years. The soil is reddish-brown clay, not unlike that of Coonawarra in Australia. The superbly equipped cellars are carved out of the rock and designed to minimize the need for pumps; as Delille points out, 'pumps are bad for the wine'. The majority of the production is red, supplemented with a little rosé. The red is made with the conventional slow fermentation at low temperatures followed by aging for two years in large oak barrels, no fining or filtration and two years' aging in the bottle. Georges keeps a stock of more than 200,000 bottles of old vintages, a luxury which few producers could afford, but Delille will not compromise in his crusade to make Terrebrune a "grand cru classé".

Bandol 1987
Ruby red with tinges of opal round the edges. The nose has faint notes of redcurrant and leather while the tannins on the palate are softened by elegant caramel, leather and toasty fruit. Good length.

Bandol 1985
Graded shades of ruby red with aromas of tobacco and leather. The features of the palate are the robust tannins and the underlying notes of violets and cigars.

Château de Bellet

Saint-Roman-de-Bellet
06200 Nice
Tel. 93378157
Fax 93379383

"Bottled by Ghislain de Carnaché, heir of R. de Bellet de Carnaché". These simple words on the label of Château Bellet wines reveal a great deal about the cellar's history. The noble Bellet de Carnaché family has owned the Château for 400 years and has lent its name since 1830 to the wine made in this tiny Appellation perched on the hills behind Nice. Today Château Bellet makes around 30,000 bottles a year. Production is divided between two whites, one traditional and the other a recently introduced barrique-conditioned cuvée, a rosé and a red "vin de garde" aged in the same oak barrels used the year before for the white. On the 12-ha property, Ghislain cultivates the zone's classic varieties with the meticulous care of one who is preserving the heritage of a winegrowing area which runs the risk of being swallowed up by the urban sprawl of nearby Nice. The white Rolle is especially noteworthy among the varieties cultivated at Château Bellet, where it is used to make the estate's monovarietal white wines. The principal variety for red wines is Braquet, used in conjunction with Folle Noir and Grenache.

Bellet Cuvée du Cinquantenaire 1991
Bright straw-yellow with warm, sweet aromas of ripe fruit. Substantial palate with good body, and very firm acidity, light fruit and a slightly bitter flavor in the finish. An honest, well-made wine.

Bellet Cuvée Baron G. 1989
Medium intensity, spicy character on the nose with evidence of respectable alcohol content. Warm on the palate with good balance despite a certain lack of extract. The wood is still very noticeable both on the nose and on the palate, but is not disagreeable. Good clean finish.

BANDOL
PROVENCE
FRANCE

484

BELLET
PROVENCE
FRANCE

Château de Crémat

442 Chemin de Crémat
06200 Nice
Tel. 93378030
Fax 93723333

Château de Crémat was built by Antoine Mari in 1890, two years after the Bellet vineyards had been destroyed in the phylloxera epidemic. Mari's efforts were renewed by the next owner, M. Thome, who is remembered for his work in promoting Bellet wines. Thome's efforts were rewarded in 1941, when Bellet became one of France's first AOCs. Jean Bagnis bought the estate in the 1950s and fought hard to prevent planning permission being given for building development in vineyard locations. Today, Jean's son Charles runs the 12-ha estate on crumbly chalk-and-clay soil. One third is planted to Rolle and a little Chardonnay for white wines, with the other two thirds given over to Folle Noir, Braquet, Grenache and Cinsaut which are used in the production of equal quantities of reds and rosés. Grapes for these wines are crushed and the must separated by natural decantation before filtering and fermentation in temperature-controlled stainless steel vats. The red wine is pumped over the cap twice a day during the early stages. At the end of the fermentation it is fined and goes into oak barrels which have a maximum age of three years. After 12 months in barriques it is transferred into 40 hl oak barrels where it remains for a further year before bottling.

Bellet 1990   ❦ ❦ ③
A wine with the typical opaque pale yellow-gold color of the whites of south-east France. Delicate nose with notes of pine and resin alongside aromas of thyme and wild honey. The palate has cookie aromas and is almost oxidized, although this is in no way a defect. Underpinned by good acidity, the wine is satisfyingly long.

Domaine du Paternel

Route de la Ciotat
13260 Cassis
Tel. 42017703
Fax 42010954

The Cassis AOC zone is located a few kilometers from Marseilles, around the town of the same name and along the bay which forms a kind of natural amphitheater protected to the east by a ring of hills. The unique micro-climate of the Appellation is determined by the mistral which is tempered by sea-breezes as it arrives from the west. Cassis is a little corner of paradise where vines have flourished in an ideal environment for centuries, producing in particular delicately scented, fruity, fresh and well-balanced white wines. Jean-Pierre Santini has been one of the leading producers in this tiny area since he inherited the estate his uncle founded in 1950. Domaine du Paternel produces 60,000 bottles a year, 80% of which are a white wine sold 14-15 months after the harvest, while the remainder is vintage rosé from Grenache with a small quantity of Mourvèdre. The property has a total of 19 ha, 17 of which are currently in production. The south/south-west-facing vineyards are all close to the small cellar and enjoy good sunlight. Yields are low. The varieties cultivated are Marsanne, Clairette, Ugni Blanc, Sauvignon Blanc and Bourboulenc Blanc.

Cassis Blanc de Blancs 1990   ❦ ②
Pale yellow with shades of green and touches of gold. The nose has an aromatic character of medium intensity. Marked acidity gives freshness on the palate, which has good follow-through of the aromas. Dry, clean and lingering finish.

BELLET
PROVENCE
FRANCE

485

CASSIS
PROVENCE
FRANCE

Clos Sainte-Magdeleine

Avenue du Revestel
13620 Cassis
Tel. 42017028
Fax 42011551

Francois Sack is no ordinary vigneron . Steer the conversation as you set out with him along the fabulous Route des Crêtes towards topics such as the syncopation of Roy Eldridge, onomatopoeia in Ella Fitzgerald, American art or the Seven Deadly Sins of Hieronymus Bosch and you will be assured of his full attention. Not least of his passionate interests, however, is the wine of Cassis, whose praises he will remind you were once recited by the poet Mistral. Francois Sack cultivates his beloved vineyards at the magical spot where Cap Canaille plummets into the translucent Mediterranean. His 11 ha of chalk soil on a hillside dominated by dramatic coastal gullies produce exquisite Cassis, above all white, which are among the best of the Appellation.. The aim of François's winemaking is to express the cru to the full. He believes in allowing wines to develop in their own time, leaving Nature to complete the job that he begins. And Mother Nature is usually generous in this part of the world.

Cassis 1991 ②
Bright straw-yellow. Slightly closed on the nose, earthy aromas,very clean palate, smooth, with good body and attractive length. An excellent white wine with carefully measured acidity which guarantees its freshness.

Cassis 1990 ②
Clean straw yellow with notes of fruit and mineral. Well-rounded on the palate where good extract makes up for the slightly low acidity. Honest, immediate and easy to drink.

Château de Beaupré

Les Plantades
13760 Saint-Cannat
Tel. 42573359
Fax 42572740

The lovely 18th-century Château de Beaupré is located in the heart of Provence near Saint-Cannat. In 1890, Baron Emile Double decided to plant vines and today his grandson, the actor Christian Double, makes wine from 40 ha of Cabernet Sauvignon, Syrah, Grenache, Mourvèdre, Sauvignon, Sémillon, Carignan, Clairette, Ugni Blanc and Cinsaut planted on chalk-and-clay soil. The average age of the vines is 15 years. Annual production of AOC Coteaux d'Aix-en-Provence, red, white and rosé amounts to about about 150,000 bottles, including a special selection red and white bottled under the Collection label.The rosé is made from the free-run juice of 60% Cinsaut, 30% Grenache and 10% Cabernet Sauvignon fermented in temperature-controlled stainless steel containers. It is then kept in enameled vats until it is bottled. The basic white is made from Sémillon, Ugni Blanc and Clairette while the Collection has up to 50% Sauvignon Blanc and is aged in new barrique. The red Collection has a Cabernet base with a touch of Syrah and ages in oak barrels, 25% of which are replaced every year. The basic cuvées are always particularly well made for drinking young.

Coteaux d'Aix-en-Provence Cuvée Spéciale 1991 ②
Delicate, bright yellow with broad aromas in which the fruit is enriched by oak. The palate is also rich and clean, with intense notes of wood. Well-rounded fruit and good length. Good acidity maintains freshness despite the round, smooth palate.

Coteaux d'Aix-en-Provence 1989 ①
Deep, intense color and a clean nose with spicy fruit and a note of plums. Fresh and juicy on the palate with plenty of fruit. Easy to drink, stylish and uncomplicated. An ideal wine for a picnic or a barbecue.

Château de Calisanne

13680 Lançon-Provence
Tel. 90426303
Fax 90424000

Château de Calisanne is open for visitors and tastings every single day of the year. The prize-winning products of the Château, which regularly come out top in blind tastings ahead of many French and other wines, are made by a former INAO official from Burgundy, Denis Langue, who conceals his authority behind austere, almost monastic attitudes and devotes body and soul to the estate. The 1,000-ha property has 120 ha of vineyard located on gentle stony, chalk slopes, on the edge of the Berre marsh. Langue avoids any trace of a dogmatic 'Burgundian' approach to winemaking while exploiting the techniques of enological science and his methods are widely respected in Coteaux d'Aix-en-Provence. He grows a wide range of varieties,including eight hectares of newly-planted Syrah, each of which is vinified separately for blending after tasting. The whites and rosés are of an excellent standard (there are prospects for a white aged in new wood), but it is the red wines that attract connoisseurs.

Coteaux d'Aix-en-Provence　　🎴 ①
Cuvée Prestige 1991
A rosé Provence can be proud of. Lovely rich color and a nose which is more fruity than flowery. Full-flavored palate, good body and a clean, youthful finish .

Coteaux d'Aix-en-Provence　　🍇 ②
Clos-Victoire 1989
Almost black in color with an elegant nose of very ripe red berries. Chewy texture on the palate and a long finish with excellent aging potential. A wine with a great future.

Cuvée Prestige 1989　　🍇🍇 ②
Lovely deep color and an inviting nose of truffle, spices and fruit (raspberry and cherry). Full-bodied and velvety on the palate with elegant tannins, magnificent structure and fine balance. The finish has a wealth of aromas.

Domaine de Pont-Royal

13370 Pont-Royal
Tel. 90574015
Fax 90591228

A 40-ha estate with a traditional outlook, the Domaine de Pont-Royal grows traditional local varieties (with the exception of only Cabernet Sauvignon), uses no chemical herbicides or pesticides, and harvests by hand. Each variety is vinified separately and the totally de-stemmed grapes are fermented for a period which varies from 5 to 12 days. Fermentation is concluded in October, but the malolactic for red wines only begins in July because of the low temperatures maintained in the cellar. The Grande Cuvée, obtained from Grenache and Mourvèdre grapes, ages for a minimum of 18 months in wood and then for a further 6 in the bottle before going on sale. It is no surprise that the cuvée's finish is tannic. Rosés are made according to the "saigné" method with a fermentation lasting 20 days and the subsequent addition of grape juice to the vat while fermentation is under way. The Domaine de Pont-Royal also offers an interesting Bouches-du-Rhône Vin de Pays.

Coteaux d'Aix-en-Provence 1990　　🍇 ①
Bright, rich color and a nose of coffee and dark chocolate. The palate is warm and spicy with lots of fruit, and although a little short of extract, is long and has a nice, clean finish.

COTEAUX D'AIX-EN-PROVENCE
PROVENCE
FRANCE

487

COTEAUX D'AIX-EN-PROVENCE
PROVENCE
FRANCE

Domaine de Trévallon

13150 Saint-Étienne-du-Grès
Tel. 90490600
Fax 90490217

At the end of the 1960s, the late, great chef Jacques Manière introduced us to an outstanding personality whose love for wine and love for art were one and the same thing. Georges Brunet, the dynamic owner of the Domaine de Trévallon, demonstrated that Cabernet Sauvignon can adapt superbly to Provencal soil. Georges later sold the property to Eloi Dürbach, the son of a sculptor turned vigneron, who set out to emulate his predecessor. Eloi arrived at the Domaine in the early 1970s and made his first wine in 1977. The 17 ha, entirely organically cultivated, are planted in Cabernet Sauvignon (60%) and Syrah. Eloi's success today is acknowledged by all and envied by many. With his manual harvest, low yields, Burgundy pressing and aging by variety in wood lasting for 18 to 22 months, Eloi Dürbach has created a sophisticated style which puts his products right at the top of the Appellation and indeed on the roll of honor of France's great wines. Time will tell whether his Marsanne- and Roussanne-based white wines will join them, or the results of the typically enterprising and courageous experiments with Viognier and Chardonnay.

Coteaux d'Aix-en-Provence   ♥ ③
Les Baux 1988
Lovely red with more intense shades round the edges. Truly outstanding nose, well-rounded with faint notes of ripe red fruit. Medium body on the palate,with excellent balance. Not quite up to the level of the 1989, but in 3-5 years this will develop into a wine of elegance and style.

Coteaux d'Aix-en-Provence   ♥♥ ③
Les Baux 1985
Full, rich, complex color and a nose in which the full Syrah fruit is dominant. The palate has the style and character of a Bordeaux, with fine length and depth of aromas. Difficult to pin down in blind tasting as it has very little in common with most Provence wines.

DOMAINE de
TRÉVALLON
1989
COTEAUX D'AIX EN PROVENCE
LES BAUX
APPELLATION COTEAUX D'AIX-EN-PROVENCE CONTROLÉE
12% vol.   750 ml
Produce of France
MIS EN BOUTEILLE AU DOMAINE
JACQUELINE DÜRRBACH PROPRIETAIRE A 13150 ST-ETIENNE-DU-GRÈS

Coteaux d'Aix-en-Provence   ♥♥♥ ③
Les Baux 1989
A great, intense, complex red wine. The nose is still a little closed and hard and the palate, too, is undeveloped at the moment. Remarkable fullness of fruit with a Cabernet Sauvignon entry which at present dominates the more subtle, spicy Syrah. A broad-shouldered wine with excellent structure which will need a long time to reach its full potential. Should certainly be decanted as it was bottled after only light fining and no filtration, in accordance with the practice of Dürbach's close friend, Francois Perrin, of Château de Beaucastel at Châteauneuf-du-Pape.

COTEAUX D'AIX-EN-PROVENCE
PROVENCE
FRANCE   488

COTEAUX D'AIX-EN-PROVENCE
PROVENCE
FRANCE

Domaine du Bas Deffens

Le Bas Deffens - Pontèves
83670 Barjols
Tel. 94771036
Fax 94771164

When Jean-Marc Etienne and his wife Brigitte arrived at Domaine du Bas Deffens in January 1977, not only were there very few vines planted on the estate, but there was no water except for that which came from a single well. Life was difficult in those early days, not least because the Etiennes had decided to use organic growing methods. In 1980 the couple bottled their first wine, which they sold unlabeled, in used bottles they had collected from local restaurants and washed themselves. Luckily for the Etiennes the period between 1980 and 1984 was one of expansion in the wine trade and by showing their wines at all the local fairs they slowly built up a loyal clientele, first of private consumers and then of importers in Germany, Switzerland and America. Today, they have 10 ha of Cabernet Sauvignon, Merlot, Syrah, Grenache and a rare variety called Caladoc on well-ventilated chalk and clay slopes. The grapes are hand-picked and fermented slowly in stainless steel. All the wine is aged in 30-hl oak barrels. The Etiennes produce about 35,000 bottles a year of quite delicious red Coteaux Varois.

Coteaux Varois 1988
Exceptionally intense purple-scarlet. The nose is still a little closed, but has well-defined aromas of stewed and spicy red fruit. Rich, ripe red fruit again on the tannic palate, with good body and outstanding length. Peppery aftertaste. Decanted and left to breathe, this wine improves considerably.

Mas de Cadenet

13530 Trets
Tel. 42292159
Fax 42613209

One of the original features of this estate, which has belonged to the same family since 1813, is that it manages to maintain an unusually high degree of self-sufficiency. 55 ha of arable farmland feed a fine herd of sheep which provides the fertilizer necessary for the 60 ha of vineyards. The only non-traditional variety grown is Cabernet Sauvignon which, however, Guy Négrel never allows to mask the strictly local character of his wine. For the same reason, carbonic maceration is not used at Mas de Cadenet. On the other hand the estate has been carrying out rigorous research over a three year period into the use of wood for its cuvées with the aim of introducing controlled oxidation and improved finesse. Finesse is in fact sought above all else, starting with the way the grapes are processed to bring out the maximum concentration, with pumping over the cap and a high (31°C) fermentation temperature. As for the rosés, they are partially fermented in new oak to produce a real food wine and not just an easy-to-drink bottle. Guy believes that discipline in winemaking is absolutely indispensable and that technology should never have the better of terroir. The aging qualities of his wines testify to the validity of the theory.

Côtes de Provence 1990
A blend of Cinsaut, Mourvèdre and Grenache, this is a rosé aged in new wood. Very pale orange with aromas of blackberry and good weight on the palate. The finish is fresh and flowery .

Côtes de Provence 1990
A red wine obtained from Grenache, Syrah and Cabernet with wood well to the front. The palate has alternating red fruit and candied peel flavors on a spicy background and a full and fleshy texture suggesting real aging potential.

COTEAUX VAROIS
PROVENCE
FRANCE

489

COTES DE PROVENCE
PROVENCE
FRANCE

Château Barbeyrolles

Presqu'Ile de Saint-Tropez
83580 Gassin
Tel. 94563358
Fax 94563349

"Rose Petal" is the very pretty name for a rosé with a pale color and delicate aromas which is the premium wine of this 12-ha estate. Pétale de Rose is the result of research by Régine Sumeire, a top-flight winemaker with a number of diplomas and a degree in history to her name. The wine is made from a soft-pressed blend of 90% Grenache and 10% Cinsaut, is certainly original, and reflects the rigor with which Régine approaches all of her production. Yields are limited to 35-48 hl/ha, all fertilizers are organic, no herbicides are used and the harvest is hand-picked over the course of several extremely careful selections. An indication of how different all this is from the mass winemaking which predominates in the Var region is that the black and gold label cuvée aged in new barriques, which delights the world's greatest restaurateurs, is unavailable when the vintage is not up to standard, as was the case in 1984. Another point to note is that Régine prefers to highlight the elegance and balance of her wines rather than systematically attempting to extract maximum color and fruit. A lesson in style and quality.

Côtes de Provence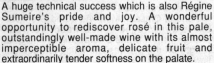
Pétale de Rose 1990
A huge technical success which is also Régine Sumeire's pride and joy. A wonderful opportunity to rediscover rosé in this pale, outstandingly well-made wine with its almost imperceptible aroma, delicate fruit and extraordinarily tender softness on the palate.

Côtes de Provence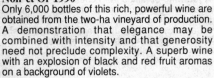
Noir et Or 1990
Only 6,000 bottles of this rich, powerful wine are obtained from the two-ha vineyard of production. A demonstration that elegance may be combined with intensity and that generosity need not preclude complexity. A superb wine with an explosion of black and red fruit aromas on a background of violets.

Château Maravenne

Route de Valcros
83250 La Londe-les-Maures
Tel. 94668020
Fax 94669779

For its owner, Jean-Louis Gourjon, Maravenne is the story of falling in love at first sight with a neo-Provencal house and a superbly-located vineyard on the border of the Maures massif and the Saint-Tropez peninsula. With the foundation of Dionys' Art, an association for the promotion of wine and the creativity it inspires, the location has also become the place where Jean-Louis indulges his passion for the arts. In 1991, the Collection Privée cuvée was graced with a label created by Laure Einaudi, winner of a competition organized for this specific purpose by Dionys' Art. Jean-Louis Gourjon's 62 ha of red clay soil for red varieties, light sandy soil for whites and shale terrain for rosés comprise one of those Provencal estates which are coming strongly back into fashion. Compared to other similar estates, Maravenne is wonderfully sited on south-facing slopes overlooking the sea where each parcel and each variety is harvested separately to capture the maximum ripeness from the grapes. A progressive estate distinguished by its openness to change.

Côtes de Provence 1991
An excellent rosé with intense aromas dominated by red berries in which strawberry predominates. Very juicy on the palate with a lovely fresh and lively finish.

Côtes de Provence
Grand Reserve 1990
Dark color and a nose of candied peel with a background of vanilla and vegetable aromas. A hint of liquorice on the palate, outstanding softness and full body with lovely elegant, well-developed tannins. The finish ends on a note of violets.

COTES DE PROVENCE
PROVENCE
FRANCE

490

COTES DE PROVENCE
PROVENCE
FRANCE

Château Réal-Martin

83143 Le Val
Tel. 94864090
Fax 94863223

Jacques Clotilde's estate is located at a height of 400 m. above sea-level, and spread over many small parcels which once belonged to the château of Miraval. Château Réal-Martin is famous for the consistency of its superb quality wines, as well as for the dynamic marketing of Gilles Meimoun, Jacques' son-in-law, a 'bon viveur' originally from Marseilles who moved to Provence from Africa. The aim of these two very likable individuals is the production of wines of character from the extraordinary vineyards, some of which cling to the sheer rock face on sites that can only be reached by jeep. The harvest in these locations is often late and yields are very low indeed. Réal-Martin reds have an authentic Provencal personality in addition to the varietal character of Cinsaut, Grenache and Syrah (the estate has never grown Cabernet). The whites are monovarietal Ugni, the only grape that Clotilde and Meimoun consider makes wines suitable for aging. The rosés made by the "méthode saignée" are often exceptional, as was the case with the 1991. None of the Réal-Martin wines are aged in wood and as long as Clotilde and Meimoun are around, none will ever be.

Côtes de Provence 1990   🍷 ②
A wine obtained from 100% Ugni grapes, grown on very low-yielding vines. There is a slight hint of super-ripe fruit on the nose with candied aromas of lemon and a note of bergamot, fennel and pear. Refreshing palate and a long, clean finish.

Côtes de Provence 1991   🍷 ②
Made with the "méthode saignée" from black grapes, an elegant wine with a bright, pale pink color reminiscent of rose petals. Fruity nose, with apple and green lemon. Good concentration and a very fresh finish.

Côtes de Provence 1989   🍷🍷 ②
Deep color and a stylish nose of red fruit (wild cherry and kirsch), autumn leaves, spices and mushrooms. Very concentrated and full-flavored on the palate with soft structure and good tannins which, though still a little hard, will integrate well given time. Beautiful balance and a long, lingering finish.

Domaine de l'Ile

Ile de Porquerolles - Ferme de Brégançonnet
83400 Hyères
Tel. 94583160
Fax 94583103

The magical ecosystem of the island of Porquerolles has always particularly favored the production of wine. Ownership of the vineyards today is divided between three estates of different sizes. Sébastien Le Ber, an old sailor who loves both life and wine, is the owner with the longest family association with the island: his grandfather actually bought it at the beginning of the century when he returned from Mexico, where he made his fortune. Today, the French authorities have re-acquired most of the land, but Le Ber still has his estate and his vines, entirely devoted to the production of rosé wine. Le Ber and vigneron friends from as far away as Saint-Barthélémy have launched an original and fun way of promoting their wines through a yacht race which they have named the 'Route du Rose' and which takes place at the beginning of every November, after the famous 'Nioulargue' when 20 or so ships leave Saint-Tropez loaded with cases of rosé wine to arrive a month later at the French islands of the Antilles: a lovely celebration of a wine that is not yet as popular as it deserves to be beyond the shores of the island.

Côtes de Provence 1991   🍷 ①
A thirst-quenching rosé. Bright, clear color and aromatic nose, deliciously tasty palate without the excess alcohol and acidity of many Provencal rosés. Extremely fresh finish. A wine one could go on and on drinking.

COTES DE PROVENCE
PROVENCE
FRANCE

491

COTES DE PROVENCE
PROVENCE
FRANCE

Domaine La Bernarde

83340 Le Luc
Tel. 94607131
Fax 94479604

The 'search for perfection' at the Domaine La Bernarde is more than just a turn of phrase. Forty-year old Guy Meulnart, a graduate of Zurich Polytechnic and his 88 year-old father Roland, who used to manage a precision-tool factory, are only interested in hard facts. At their estate on the stony hills overlooking the plain of the Luc, the commitment to perfection is total. It can be seen in the harvesting of the 33 ha of 40 year-old Cabernet, Cinsaut, Grenache and Syrah vines (still supported by wooden poles) where selection is severe and the fruit is transported to the cellar with meticulous care to ensure the vinification of whole berries. Their involvement with research bring them into close contact with the experts of the Avignon INRA. Other indices of perfectionism are the immaculate cellar hygiene and scrupulous winemaking which includes the use of long maceration to extract the absolute maximum of aromas and fruit.

Côtes de Provence 1990   ♟♟ ②
Obtained from 40% Sémillon from an 80 year-old vineyard and 60% 'ordinary' Sémillon, this wine is made with painstaking care. The grapes are hand-picked over two selections and fermented with selected yeasts at a temperature which never exceeds 16°C. The resulting white wine is deliciously dry with an intense, well-defined nose of apricot, acacia honey and peach, mouthfilling flavor and outstanding length.

Côtes de Provence 1990   ▦ ②
Superb quality rosé with pale pink color, fruity aromas of black berries and flowers over a spicy background. Complex palate with splendid extract, elegance and length.

Côtes de Provence 1989   ♥♥ ③
A blend of Grenache (10%), Cabernet (40%) and Syrah (50%) with a brilliant ruby hue, a nose of almost super-ripe gooseberry and cassis with notes of menthol and a vigorous, extract-rich, palate with elegant tannins. The finish is very long with just a hint of truffle. A great wine with superb aging potential, from an exceptionally warm vintage.

Domaine de la Courtade

83400 Porquerolles
Tel. 94583144
Fax 94583412

Porquerolles is a picture-postcard dream island, a little piece of Paradise broken off the end of the Maures chain where heather and myrtle, pine woods and beaches, undergrowth and vine all happily coexist. The proportion of vines has increased since the arrival eight years ago of a 'wine-nut' who fell in love with this tourist-free island. Henri Vidal, a civil engineer who invented 'reinforced earth', is the owner of this domaine, although the running of the estate is entrusted to Richard Auther, the son of an Alsatian grower. Richard has put together a property of 35 ha spread over several different parcels which nestle snugly in the folds of the island's topography, planted to Mourvèdre (70%), Grenache and Syrah for red wines and equal parts of Rolle and Sémillon for white. Auther has also created a very impressive olive-grove out of nothing. The quality of Courtade wines is due mainly to the terroir, with its stupendous coastal climate and a sub-stratum of metamorphic shale which can only be found on the mainland at an altitude of 600 m.,too high for viticulture. Vidal's investment is amply rewarded by the wines of this estate destined for fame

Côtes de Provence 1990   ♟ ②
Fermented after macerating on the skins for maximum extraction and then stored at low temperatures while the aromas develop,the wine is subsequently aged in new wood. The fleshy, well-rounded palate has a faintly exotic character and a finish which has a light flavor of hazelnut.

Côtes de Provence 1989   ♥♥ ③
A wine dominated by Mouvedre from 100% de-stemmed grapes, fermented at between 28°C and 35°C and macerated for as long as 15 days. The shale soil comes through strongly in the formidable breadth on the palate. Although still a little undeveloped, it will be well worth waiting for.

COTES DE PROVENCE
PROVENCE
FRANCE

492

COTES DE PROVENCE
PROVENCE
FRANCE

Domaine Richeaume

13114 Puyloubier
Tel. 42663226
Fax 42663059

Winemaking at the Domaine Richeaume is characterized by a long list of quality-determining features: modern technology, totally organic cultivation, low yields, aging in Bordeaux barriques and rigorous winemaking techniques. Heating is solar energy-based and a tiny lake keeps the cellar cool. The 22-ha estate is located in the mountainous terrain of La Sainte-Victoire, and area cherished by Cézanne, and the vines are tended by a gentleman-viticulturist from Germany, Henning Hoesch, who has made Richeaume one of the most beautiful properties in France since he took over in 1972. Varieties are fermented separately according to their vineyard of origin and the vintage cuvées are obtained from blends aged in wood for up to 18 months. Thanks to the bitter winter cold and the cool summer nights, Richeaume wines acquire impressive finesse. Following fire damage at La Sainte-Victoire, Hoesch has re-planted some of the vines on terraces; it will be extremely interesting to follow their development..

Côtes de Provence 1990   🍇 ①
Very pale pink with a nose reminiscent of the wines of Burgundy. Aromas of citrus and a soft palate of good depth and length with lots of fruit and great elegance. Longish finish.

Côtes de Provence 1988   🍇🍇 ②
Monovarietal Syrah aged in barriques for 12 months. Dark in appearance with aromas of Provencal "garrigue" vegetation over a background of violets. The tannic entry mellows out attractively into a full, well-rounded palate with plenty of backbone. A fine, vigorous wine destined to age well.

Domaine de Rimauresq

Route de Nôtre-Dame-des-Anges
83790 Pignans
Tel. 94488045
Fax 94332231

Domaine de Rimauresq used to belong to a retired diplomat who made wine of such fine quality that it was often compared to Châteauneuf-du-Pape. The estate, with the ancient cedar tree standing in front of the house, was then acquired by the Wemyss family from Scotland, who having decided to continue their predecessor's policies were rewarded when the domaine was one of the first to be included in the Appellation Côtes de Provence. The vineyard located on the north side of the Maures, almost at the foot of Notre-Dames-des-Anges, is at present being replanted although the very old vines of Cinsaut, Grenache, Mourvèdre and Syrah will not be touched. Plans are to completely modernize the cellar and in the wake of experiments of recent years, to introduce new oak barrels for white wines. Although at present methods are rather artisanal, the estate is clearly working seriously for the future.

Côtes de Provence 1990   🍇 ①
A superb nose of vanilla over notes of pear-drops and ripe banana. The flavors are clean and frank without aggressive alcohol. A wine to drink within three years.

Côtes de Provence 1988   🍇 ②
Full, deep ruby red with a well-rounded palate of exceptional concentration containing hints of "maquis". The complex finish has great finesse and elegance.

COTES DE PROVENCE
PROVENCE
FRANCE

493

COTES DE PROVENCE
PROVENCE
FRANCE

Domaine de Saint-Baillon

Flassons-sur-Issole
83340 Le Luc
Tel. 94697460
Fax 94698029

Hervé Goudard is quite unique. The grandson of the founder of Solex, he used to be a legal consultant, but for the last ten years or so he has preferred the vineyard to his desk. Although an inveterate grumbler, particularly on the subject of taxes, he is also the nicest person in the world to talk to when he is describing his 25-ha estate in the shadow of the fortress of Maunier. Goudard's vines are located on very stony clay-and-chalk soil. He himself is one of the most rigorous winemakers in the Appellation. The Provencal terrain produces marvelous results with varieties ranging from Syrah to the Bordeaux favorite Cabernet Sauvignon. In the Cuvée Roudai, which Goudard does not make every year, Syrah and Cabernet are brought together in new wood to produce a wine of extraordinary complexity. There is also a wine from low-yielding monovarietal Syrah, the ravishingly concentrated Farretier which ages for many years in barriques and is Provence's answer to Côte Rôtie. Goudard, this prince of wine, also vinifies a powerfully aromatic white wine and a rosé, the Cuvée Opale, which is both a thirst-quencher and a versatile food wine.

Côtes de Provence Cuvée Opale 1991

A delightful pale pink shade with a fresh, clean nose containing a hint of spices. Also very clean on the palate with good body and spicy flavors.

Côtes de Provence Cuvée Roudai 1989

Intense red with a toasty, fruit-rich nose. Complex and well-rounded on the palate with fruity notes of jam and resin. Good length. A fine example of quality combined with local character.

Les Maîtres Vignerons de la Presqu'Ile de Saint-Tropez

Carrefour de Provence
83580 Gassin
Tel. 94563204
Fax 94434257

'Les Maître Vignerons...' is the trade name of a giant cellar which selects, blends, bottles and markets (with particular attention to the design of the labels) the wines of ten independent producers from the Saint-Tropez peninsula who combined own 190 ha of vineyard, and those of the 250 ha of the Saint-Roches-les-Vignes Cooperative at Cuers. None of the wines, which are 60% rosé, 35% red and 5% white, are vinified directly by the firm. The fact that the products are distributed by Castel is an indication of the market force of these 'master winemakers' whose rosés are to be found, for example,all over the Far East. Quantity does not appear to be achieved at the expense of quality, to judge by the standards of the red or rosé Carte Noire or the red Château de Pampelonne (partially aged in new wood). While not breathtaking, the cooperative's wines are good, honest products.

Côtes de Provence Carte Noire 1991

Good intensity of color and aromas which are fresh without being sharp. The first impact on the palate is immediate with frank flavors and firm, positive acidity.

Côtes de Provence Carte Noire 1989

Very dark color, tending to black, but lacking in brilliance. The nose has a hint of alcohol and baked aromas in which liquorice and smoky oak dominate. The entry is a little understated but the palate is very well-rounded.

Côtes de Provence Château de Pampelonne 1989

Dark color and a nose with powerful alcohol aroma. The palate is a little weak on entry but the Syrah then emerges very attractively. Although the wood tends to give the palate a vague impression of dryness towards the end, the length is nonetheless good.

COTES DE PROVENCE
PROVENCE
FRANCE

494

COTES DE PROVENCE
PROVENCE
FRANCE

Château Simone

13590 Meyreuil
Tel. 42669258
Fax 42668077

A very rare wine from Palette, one of France's smallest AOCs, which extends over a mere 23 ha .This ancient estate enjoys a majestic location and is noted for its cellars carved out of the hillside and for the crenelated turrets of the 16th-century château which look over its vineyards, terraces and gardens. The Rougier family has been making the traditional wine of the Appellation since 1848. The sun shines warmly during the day but the nights are cold - the frost of 1991 is still clearly remembered. The 17-ha property has chalk and gravel soils and vineyards which date back to the last century. Although they are gradually being replaced, at present the average age of the vines is still in excess of 50 years. The varieties are traditional, with Clairette for white wines and Grenache for reds, but there are also small quantities of Grenache Blanc, Ugni, Picpoul and Muscat. The harvest is manual. White grapes are fermented at low temperatures and rosés are made by the "méthode saignée" after rapid pressing.The reds, on the other hand, ferment slowly for 10-15 days and are aged in wood. The results in each case are splendid.

Palette 1989   ♕ ②
Brilliant straw-yellow color and a delicate nose with mineral notes and a hint of meringue. The palate is soft, clean and balanced with fresh acidity, full flavors and good length. A wine of character and interest.

Palette 1988   ♕ ②
Bright, rich, intense red with aromas which are warm and spicy of jammy fruit. On the palate, softly rounded fruit comes through again with the same spice , good acidity and lightweight, but adequate, structure. Good length in the finish.

Provence Appellations in this Guide

Bandol
Bellet
Cassis
Coteaux d'Aix
Coteaux Varois
Côtes de Provence
Palette

PALETTE
PROVENCE
FRANCE

495

PALETTE
PROVENCE
FRANCE

Savoie

Although better-known for skiing than viticulture, Savoie nevertheless has the significant total of around 1,500 ha of vineyards and produces four AOC wines: Vin de Savoie, Roussette de Savoie, Crepy and Seyssel.

The annual production of Vin de Savoie amounts to around 100,000 bottles. Whites for early drinking are made from Chasselas grapes and reds from Gamay. The Mondeuse variety is the base for the more interesting and personal reds of the Appellation which benefit from moderate bottle aging.

Roussette whites are obtained from monovarietal Altesse, in the case of single cru wines, or from blends of the same grape with varying proportions of Mondeuse.

Crépy is a sub-zone with about 80 ha of vineyards which produces approximately 6,000 bottles a year of a light, monovarietal white from Chasselas, the better examples of which have considerable aging potential. The Chasselas variety also predominates in the 75 ha of vineyard of Seyssel where it is vinified on its own to obtain still white wines or together with Molette and Altesse to produce sparkling wines which receive an obligatory three years aging before release.

Other grape types grown in Savoie include Pinot Noir, Chardonnay and Roussanne (known locally as Bergeron) as well as typically Savoyard varieties like the white Jacquère and Apremont.

The 11 cellars in this Guide are representative of a region which in recent years has witnessed the introduction of interesting innovations by young producers who have developed the ability to exploit to the full the potential of their unique terroir.

Pierre Boniface

Les Rocailles
73800 Saint-André-les-Marches
Tel. 79281450
Fax 79281682

Pierre Boniface is equally at home with all the varieties of the region. He has a very young face for a man of almost 50 with eyes which are never still, but he also has the air of a seasoned grower. His burning ambition is to restore to the wines of Savoie the noble status they enjoyed in the past. The cellar turns out more than 400,000 bottles a year, only a part of which, however, is made from Pierre's own 15-ha estate, the rest of the wine being bought in. He uses limited chaptalization which means that his wines have moderate alcohol content, rarely exceeding 11.5°. Vinification is fairly traditional, although the cellar is currently being re-equipped. A new pneumatic press extracts maximum fruit, aromas and extract and the old wooden vats are gradually being replaced. A new stainless steel container is being added every year until the whole battery is electronically controlled. Pierre obtains excellent results over the complete range of Apremont, Abymes, Mondeuse (aged in wood from Arbin), Chignin-Bergeron, Roussette (from monovarietal Altesse) and a méthode champenoise Brut de Savoie full of character.

Roussette de Savoie 1991 ☙ ①
From monovarietal Altesse, a wine with a brilliant color, floral aromas which are perhaps just a shade artificial and notes of apricot and honey. Good concentration and depth on the palate, very lively with surprising exotic flavors in the finish.

Vin de Savoie Apremont 1991 ☙ ①
Bright yellow and broad on the nose with highlighted aromas of passion fruit. Very full-bodied palate, powerful extract and satisfyingly long fruit flavors. Fresh finish with just a hint of residual sugar. Good length and balance.

Vin de Savoie Mondeuse 1990 ☙ ①
A good vintage for the Appellation. Very aromatic nose with a predominance of red fruit over liquorice. Full, rich texture. The young tannins are well-integrated with fruit, which comes to the fore on the palate, and in the long finish. A wine not to be drunk too young.

Château de Monterminod

Monterminod
73230 Saint-Alban-Leysse
Tel. 79330124

The château of Mons Ermenoldi, known today as Monterminod, stands on the site of a 5th-century Burgundian fortification. Legend has it that the first Savoyard vineyard was planted here in the 17th century with vines imported from Hungary. The present-day vineyard is a single seven-hectare parcel on the terraced lower slopes of Mt. Nivolet, in an exceptional south-facing location where the 50,000 vines of Roussette, Mondeuse and Gamay enjoy marvelous sunlight. Pascal Paget, a graduate of the Beaune college of viticulture, has been in charge of winemaking since 1988. The vineyard has been completely restructured. The outstanding Roussette de Savoie, obtained from two hectares of 40 year-old vines on gravelly chalk-and-clay soil, is the product of yields which never exceed 35 hl/ha. It is a wine that deserves greater respect than it often receives for there is a regrettable tendency to drink it too early. Wines from Mondeuse and Gamay, in contrast, are made to be drunk young. Overall the Chateau produces a very attractive range of wines of which the speciality is the particularly elegant, stylish Roussette.

Roussette de Savoie ☙ ②
Monterminod 1990
Bright, with green tints around the edges and a powerful, intense nose with aromas of dried fruit and lily-of-the-valley. Very soft and vaguely exotic on the palate with a hint of vanilla. Very refreshing, elegant finish. A wine which can be safely laid down for a few more years.

Domaine de l'Idylle

Saint-Laurent
73800 Cruet
Tel. 79843058

The Tiollier brothers Francois and Philippe inherited the firm which has been in their family since 1840 from their father. The 12-ha estate, which surrounds a beautiful great Savoyard mansion, produces about 80,000 bottles a year. Gamay and Pinot are very much in evidence on the chalky soil of the property on the Bauges massif, but the Tiolliers also have a predilection for the region's traditional varieties: Altesse, Mondeuse and Jacquère. Yields are average for the region, 60 hl/ha for example for the delicate Mondeuse which undergoes a relatively long maceration of about twelve days. The Tiollier brothers are particularly successful with soft, seductive whites from the Roussette and Jacquère varieties which confer elegance to wines - a tasting experience not to be missed.

Roussette de Savoie 1991   ⑨ ①
Despite a touch too much residual sugar, this is a cru which deserves serious attention. The nose has attractive apricot and peach aromas, there is good concentration of fruit on the palate and balance is ensured by just the right hint of acidity.

Vin de Savoie Cruet 1991   ⑨ ①
An attractive pale straw-yellow wine obtained from Jacquère grapes. Flowery aromas on the nose with almonds and fresh fruit. Firm body on the palate, a hint of effervescence and a faint note of residual sugar in the finish.

Claude Marandon

116, chemin des Moulins
Saint-Alban-Leysse
73000 Chambéry
Tel. 79331365

To see Claude Marandon, you really have to want to. He will come to collect you at Chambéry station in the early light of dawn and weigh you up with his tired eyes before taking you, glass in hand, into his hills. Marandon is the 'grand old man' of Savoie wine, a former president of the region's masters of wine and a noted enologist. Today he is a dealer and above all producer of wine with some very sound ideas on how to promote local products. Often contested, Marandon is never ignored and not even his strongest opponents would refuse to raise a glass with him. His obsession is quality. His estate has a mere 4,000 vines on four hectares of stony, south-facing morainic soil of glacial origin where yields are limited to 30 hl/ha. Marandon's methods of cultivation are as natural as possible, with manual harvesting and weeding and a total ban on chemical fertilizers. The outcome is a unique Roussette cuvée of 2,000 bottles per year from the renowned Altesse variety which is bottled under the Anne de Chypre label. Maradon ferments the wine for six weeks in barriques and then ages it for a year in oak. It is only with great difficulty that he can be persuaded to part with a few bottles of the resulting wine, an extremely rare, extraordinary late-harvested white which reflects the unique personality of its creator.

Roussette de Savoie   ⑨ ⑨ ③
Anne de Chypre 1990
A reserve from monovarietal Altesse with a pale straw color and a nose which is both flowery and vegetal with hints of asparagus. The palate is rich in extract with exotic flavors, concentrated structure and superb balance. The acidity in the finish is outstanding - the morainic terroir is very much in evidence - and there is only the faintest of vanilla flavors from the oak. A great wine to age, and a credit to a producer who defines himself a "craftsman-winemaker".

Régis Masson

La Monette, Apremont
73190 Challes-les-Eaux
Tel. 79283757

The famous Mont-Granier landslide of 1248 which caused thousands of deaths also created the terrain where the Régis Masson vineyard, south of Chambéry, stands today. The four hectares of vines have an average age of 20 years and are located on a stony chalk sub-soil with heavy white marl on top. They produce Apremont and Abymes crus from the local Jacquère variety as well as wines from Chardonnay and Roussette. Régis Masson has a special soft spot for the Apremont which does particularly well on these soils. Fermentation is unhurried and Masson uses low temperatures to capture maximum aroma and add finesse, and racks only at the end of winter; methods which produce truly excellent results, full of personality and of a quality comparable with many other more famous wines. The Apremont is perfect to start a meal with or, better still - in an ideal world - to sip under the shade of the vines where it is grown.

Vin de Savoie Apremont 1991   ❦ ①
Pale yellow, with strongly characteristic fruit on the nose, a little exotic with vegetal nuances and a note of flint. A delicate effervescence on the palate gives way to a finish with a flavor of bitter almond.

Vin de Savoie Chardonnay 1991   ❦ ①
A shade of yellow tending to gold with green reflections at the edges, attractive aromas of candied citrus and medium depth and intensity on the palate. The structure is solid with a robust finish.

Domaine du Prieuré Saint Christophe

Fréterive
73250 Saint-Pierre-d'Albigny
Tel. 79286210
Fax 79286174

Michel Grissard is a great character and a great winemaker. Modest as he is, many in Savoie consider him to be one of the few people who have contributed to relaunching the region. Michel was one of the first to foresee that the way forward was by limiting yields to a maximum of 30 hl/ha, even if this meant reducing turnover. He makes two wines from his 4.5 ha of difficult-to-cultivate vines on the steep mountain slopes: Roussette de Savoie from Altesse grapes which Grissard coaxes to perform miracles, and Mondeuse which he, unlike others, feels can age successfully. The Roussette spends a month in barriques without any ill effects .The Mondeuse consistently achieves exceptional concentration (Grissard lengthens the maceration every year) and is characterized by an astringency which only time can mellow. Michel is an outstanding vigneron , the epitome of reliability and a credit to his region .

Roussette de Savoie 1990   ❦ ②
From Altesse grapes, a wine with distinct aromas of mirabelle plums on the nose. Full-bodied and concentrated, the finish is dominated by hazelnut. A fine wine.

Mondeuse Cuvée Prestige 1990   ❦ ❦ ②
Very deep color, very concentrated body and aromas of pepper and violet with grassy notes in the background. Vigorous, powerful palate which features noble tannins, without harshness. A well-built wine which opens out beautifully, and with a finish which allows a little of the wood and spices to come through. A wine to lay down.

Les fils de René Quénard

Les Tours
73800 Chignin
Tel. 79280115

It would be difficult to say exactly how many Quénards make wine in Savoie, but there is no doubt that these are among the best producers in the entire region. René Quénard's sons Georges, who looks after the vineyard, and Jacky, in charge of the cellar, set themselves very high quality standards. On their 14 ha they grow all the local varieties: Chignin-Gamay, Jacquère, Pinot, Chignin-Bergeron and Mondeuse. The Quénard wines range from light, subtle Pinots and silky Mondeuses to the delicious products of the incomparable Bergeron variety which are reminiscent of the aristocratic Roussannes of the northern Rhône valley. Bergeron produces wines which are lively when young and which then mature serenely for as much as 10 years, sometimes even longer.

Vin de Savoie Chignin-Bergeron 🍇 ②
Coteaux de Mont-Ronjoux 1990
Peach, apricot and tropical fruit give this wine aromatic complexity and a varietal character typical of Roussanne. Flavorsome palate with a positive finish. A wine which will develop elegance with bottle age.

Vin de Savoie 🍷 ①
Chignin Mondeuse 1990
Good, dense color and complex aromas which combine blackcurrant, vanilla, violet and spices. Meaty palate with well-integrated tannins of unusual elegance. A wine worth seeking out.

Pascal Quénard

Le Villard
73800 Chignin
Tel. 79280901

Standing in front of his huge map of the world, young Pascal Quénard with his film-star looks, might be dreaming of foreign shores many miles from his native Savoie, but he is one of the region's up-and-coming new winemakers. The son of Raymond Quénard, an outstanding figure in Savoie, Pascal has already accumulated more than ten years' experience and is beyond doubt one of the producers Savoie wines need to break out of the stereotype of unpretentious crus to be sipped on a mountain top with a fondue. Pascal's four-hectare estate on clay-and-chalk soil has vines with an average age of 35 years and he uses several different vinification techniques with his unorthodox selection of varieties: 80% Jacquère, 8% Roussanne, 7% Mondeuse and 5% Altesse. His father used to use wood barrels, but Pascal refuses to follow his example. Like his father, he carries out malolactic fermentation but he vinifies separately, parcel by parcel. Pascal show no signs of wanting to expand. Limited quantity, he maintains, is the necessary price of quality.

Roussette de Savoie 🍇 ①
Monterminod 1991
From monovarietal Altesse, a cru which has a fairly exotic initial impact on the nose, with strong notes of citrus and apricot. Lively on the palate with genuine freshness and just the right note of acidity to suggest an aging potential of two years, but no more.

Roussette de Savoie 🍇 ①
Cuvée Annick 1990
Attractive clear pale yellow, a delicate nose with an exotic character, and a well-rounded, fleshy palate finishing on a note of quince, cinnamon and almond. Features of this Roussette are the freshness and fine balance between residual sugar and acidity.

Domaine Raymond Quénard

Le Villard - Les Tours
73800 Chignin
Tel. 79280146
Fax 79281678

The Domaine Raymond Quenard extends for 6.5 ha over clay-and-chalk soils on south-west-facing hillsides in the shadow of the ruined towers of the feudal château of Chignin. The owner, a fourth-generation vigneron , is no ordinary producer. Not content merely to collect awards and medals for his wines, Raymond is also one of the region's great personalities. Despite his many years' experience, he claims never to be satisfied with his work; always full of doubts and reservations, his one aim is quality. He tends his vines of Jacquère (80%), Gamay, Roussanne and Mondeuse, some of which are up to 100 years old, with loving care. Yields are kept low, residual sugar is strictly controlled and all the wines undergo malolactic fermentation. The resulting products are as good to drink as they are well made.

Vin de Savoie
Chignin-Bergeron 1990   🍇 ①
Intense and very attractive floral nose with added aromas of quince and honey. Tropical fruit flavors feature on the well-rounded, fleshy palate which has balance, good texture and a long finish.

Vin de Savoie Gamay 1991   🍇 ①
Slightly pale color and a nose with inviting blackcurrant and wild cherry aromas. A mouthfilling wine which such density and rich, earthy personality that it gives the impression of being chewable. The finish has an interesting peppery note.

Vin de Savoie Mondeuse 1991   🍇 ①
Still undeveloped on the nose, although aromas of raspberry and violet are beginning to emerge. Soft and meaty on the palate with silky tannins. A wine which can happily wait in the cellar for two or three years.

Domaine Bernard Rey

Chemin de Rocheray
Chevigneux
73310 Chindrieux
Tel. 79542758

Bernard Rey was a builder until ten years ago, when he took over a family property that was sliding into decline. Funds for investment were lacking and the modern technology on which Bernard relied in his previous occupation had to remain on the drawing board. The old vats, however, continue to do their job well. His 10 ha of vines, the oldest of which are over 70 years old, are planted in Chautagne Gamay and Pinot Noir. Rey is making efforts to limit yields and hopes to bring them below 70 hl/ha. He ferments whole grapes and allows them to macerate for about ten days to extract maximum fruit. Bernard's goal is to improve quality while keeping his feet firmly on the ground.

Vin de Savoie Chautagne 1991   🍇 ①
Attractive deep red with the meaty aromas fairly typical of the zone, as well as complex red fruit (blackcurrant and raspberry). Delicious on the palate, with faint spice and pepper flavors and elegant texture. The finish is long, although only moderately intense.

Domaine de Ripaille

74200 Thonon-les-Bains
Tel. 50717512-50262119

The Château de Ripaille estate, with its fairy-tale location on the shore of Lake Leman and the temperate climate of the Chablais plain, has traditions rooted firmly in the past. Vines have been cultivated at Ripaille since the time of the Gauls and the Ancient Romans. In the Middle Ages the domaine was occupied first by the Canons Regular and subsequently by the Carthusians of Vallon, who settled here thanks to St. Francis of Sales. In the period from the Revolution up until 1892, the property was owned by General Dupas and his descendants. Since then, it has not left the Engel-Gros family, Alsatian spinning-mill owners whose heirs, the Neckers, themselves descendants of Louis XVI's Minister of Finance, own it today. The buildings of the estate form a little village in the shade of the mulberry trees, cypresses, umbrella pines and almonds which surround the vineyards. The annual production from the 21 ha planted in Chasselas on well-drained gravel soils, amounts to around 160,000 bottles. Grapes on the estate are harvested manually when fully ripe. Since 1985, Claude Guillerez, an agronomist, has taken over the management of the estate and has proven himself to be an expert winemaker.

Vin de Savoie Chasselas 1991
Drought affected the vines less in 1991 than it did in 1990. The nose is rich, with dominant aromas of lemon and a note of petrol reminiscent of Riesling. Good depth on the palate with honey, pineapple and good, chewy extracts. Altogether an extremely attractive wine with an almond flavor in the finish.

Sud-Ouest

No other wine-producing region in France has emerged as quickly over the last ten years as the Sud-Ouest. Despite the fact that it is one of the most ancient wine-growing regions in the country, until recently the Sud-Ouest had slipped quietly into the background. Today, however, a major revival is in progress. In addition to the new blood coming from abroad, including experts like the Englishman Richard Doughty at Saussignac or the Swiss Christian Gerber at Domaine de Ribonnet, serious research and considerable investment are being carried out by local families. The entire region, from Gaillac to Cahors, Jurançon, Bergerac and Irouléguy is humming with activity.

When the price of classic wines sky-rocketed in the early 1980s, many buyers began to take a closer look at what was going on in areas where prices were more accessible. Trade magazines and a number of wine merchants and restaurateurs started promoting alternatives, not only because they offered attractive margins, but also because the wines genuinely met consumer demands. The improvements in technique, both in the vineyard and in the cellar, have allowed an increasing number of producers to opt for quality rather than quantity. A further important factor in the general improvement in standards has been the conscious return to local varieties. In Gaillac, producers like Robert Plageols set the theme for the decade with a return to traditional varieties like Mauzac and Len de l'Ehl, in the same way as Brumont has done in Madiran with Tannat and Henri Ramonteu with the Petit Manseng which he uses to produce glorious sweet white Jurançons.

In Irouléguy, the new policy of the Cave d'Irouléguy at Saint-Etienne-de-Baïgorry to market wine from individual properties, starting with Domaine de Mignaberry and followed by Domaine Etchegaraia, has encouraged Domaine Brana and Domaine Ilarria to produce their own wines. Top local restauranteurs have also played an important part in promoting the wines of the Sud-Ouest by putting the region's products on their wine-lists; people like Michel Guérard at Eugénie-les-Bains (who has even gone so far as to produce his own wines on his property at Tursan), the Château de Bachen and André Daguin of the Hôtel de France at Auch, who enthusiastically sells the wines of Madiran as well as the less expensive and perhaps more commercial wines of the Producteurs de Plaimont. These factors have improved the consumer image of the wines of the Sud-Ouest. Today, it is no longer possible to say, "I don't like Madiran or Irouléguy, they're too rustic" as many outstandingly elegant, stylish wines can be found in the region.

The Sud-Ouest is geographically vast and has a wide variety of climates and soil types. One could say the same about the wines, which go from the lively dry whites of Bergerac, Jurançon and Tursan through a whole range of red wines from Madiran, Cahors, Gaillac, Bergerac, Côtes de Duras and Irouléguy, from the refreshing, tangy, fruity rosés of Irouléguy or Bergerac to the magnificent sweet wines of Jurançon and Saussignac. The only cloud on the horizon concerns prices, for while many Sud-Ouest wines are still excellent value for money, increasing demand has forced the price of some Jurançon, Madiran and Gaillac wines to exorbitant levels.

Henry Ryman

Château de la Jaubertie
24560 Colombier
Tel. 53583211
Fax 53574622

This enchanting estate 8 km south of the town of Bergerac was acquired in 1973 by the British businessman Henry Ryman who extended the original 27 ha and today has 51 ha under vines out of a total of 75 ha. The estate grows eight varieties: Sauvignon Blanc, Sémillon, Chardonnay and Muscat for whites and Merlot, Cabernet Sauvignon, Cabernet Franc and even half a hectare of Malbec for reds. The annual production of about 280,000 bottles consists of seven different wines: three reds, a rosé and three dry whites. Before Charles Martin arrived in 1987 as enologist and partner, the wines were made by Henry's son Hugh, a young man of genuine talent. Hugh learnt much of his trade in Australia and today has his own estate in Bordeaux. Château de la Jaubertie whites are always particularly refreshing and well-made and in recent years the reds have improved enormously, primarily because most of the vines have now matured and considerable investment has been made in equipment for the cellar.

Bergerac 1991
Bright, clear color with pale yellow borders. The aroma is extremely fruity and well-defined while the palate, with all the full-bodied, smooth style of Sémillon, is underpinned by good acidity in the finish.

Bergerac Colombier 1989
Rich, irresistibly attractive color. Fruit and flowers come through on the nose together with a hint of tobacco. The palate has a huge range of ripe fruit flavors with blackcurrant at the front and soft, round, well-balanced tannins.

Domaine de Tourné

47600 Calignac
Tel. 53971500
Fax 53971619

Thierry Schellens looks all set to make his mark in this Appellation which is almost totally controlled by the Cave Coopérative, with only seven independent estates. Since he arrived in 1987, the Belgian has transformed the property, which was in very poor condition when he bought it, into a model estate which produces premium quality wines that set the standards for the region. The Domaine de Tourné estate comprises 15 ha of chalky soil planted in Cabernet Sauvignon, Merlot and Cabernet Franc vines of an average age of 20 years. Christian Gioli, the vineyard manager, has brought a little order on the growing side, while Didier Denat, the enologist, takes care of winemaking. The cellar has been completely rebuilt and equipped with the latest technology. Average yields are 50 hl/ha. The wines are obtained from a blend of equal parts of the three varieties grown on the property. Production of the standard Domaine de Tourné is around 50,000 bottles a year. The wine that has recently attracted most attention is the Cuvée du Vert Galant, first made in 1988 and aged for 6-8 months in oak barrels, one third of which are replaced every year. 20,000 bottles of this cuvée were produced in 1990 and production is destined to increase at the expense of the standard wine.

Buzet
Cuvée du Vert Galant 1990
Good, deep color and a light, clean, fruity, nose with an unobtrusive hint of wood. Stylish flavors of fresh, juicy fruit return on the palate together with pepper and a nicely balanced note of oak. Lots of sweet fruit and good length. Quite delicious.

BERGERAC
SUD-OUEST
FRANCE

504

BUZET
SUD-OUEST
FRANCE

Château Bovila

Boîte Postale 26
46001 Cahors Cedex
Tel. 65369130

Jean-Claude Valière has dedicated over 18 years of his life to the development of this estate. After buying the property in 1974, he completely restructured both house and cellar, increasing the area under vines from 4 ha to the present 20 ha. The vines are located on south-facing slopes on clay soil identical, so it seems, to that of Champagne. 71% of the vineyard is planted in Auxerrois (Malbec) and Merlot with Tannat, Sémillon and Mauzac making up the remainder. The last two varieties, although traditional, are by no means common in Cahors and yield no more than 10-15 hl/ha. Only organic fertilizer is used. Château Bovila releases a single cuvée of Cahors from an average yield of 40 hl/ha, for a total production of around 100,000 bottles a year. Fermentation in enameled vats lasts approximately 12 days during which time the wine is pumped over the cap two or three times a day. The wine ages in the vat for 9 months and in oak barriques (one year old from Château Cheval Blanc at St. Emilion) for a further 6 to 9 months. It is not filtered and only fined with egg-white in some years to leave the wine's characteristic tannins intact.

Cahors 1989   🍇 ②
Medium depth of color, tending to vermilion with shades of purple. The nose has slightly austere fruit with the strawberry typical of the cru and metallic notes which partially mask the primary aromas. The entry is sweet and a little lean. Good fruit and fairly marked acidity. The well-defined, powerful tannins provide good structure. A traditional Cahors, perhaps lacking a little extract but with good balance.

Cahors 1988   🍇 ②
Medium intensity garnet red. A wine to lay down, with a solid tannic structure, a little hard in the finish. Good extracts and concentration, but needs time to develop fully. A well-made wine but not one to drink young.

Château Eugénie

Rivière-Haute
46140 Albas
Tel. 65307351
Fax 65201981

The Czars of Russia held Cahors wine in high esteem and this is commemorated at Château Eugénie by the Cuvée Réservée des Tsars, one of the three cuvées made by brothers Jean and Claude Couture. The Coutures, who come from a family of growers active in Cahors since 1470, have 25 ha of vineyards both in the valley and on the hillsides. The average age of the vines is 20 years, but some plants are as old as 70. The stock consists of 80% Auxerrois, 14% Merlot and 6% Tannat. Winemaking is carried out by traditional methods in stainless steel vats with a fermentation which lasts for about 15 days with the wine being regularly pumped over the cap. The generic Cahors with its black label has an annual production of about 100,000 bottles and is obtained from a blend of grapes from young vines of all the varieties on the estate. The 30,000 bottles of the excellent Cuvée Réservée des Tsars are obtained from 80% Auxerrois and 20% Merlot aged for a year in oak. The most outstanding Château Eugénie product is the Cuvée Réservée de l'Aïeul which is obtained from 95% Auxerrois and aged for 18 months in oak barrels, including a period in new wood.

Cahors 1989   🍇 ②
The style is simple and easy to drink: an elegant ruby color, sweet nose with aromas of cherry and raspberry and smooth, fruity extracts backed up by soft tannins on the palate. The fruit flavors in the finish are satisfyingly long.

Cahors   🍇 ②
Cuvée Réservée de l'Aïeul 1989
A classy, elegant wine with deep color and a nose of ripe cherries and raspberries. Very good structure with nice extracts, although lacks the balance of the Cuvée Réservée des Tsars. The alcohol is also rather more prominent than in the other cuvée.

Cahors   🍇🍇 ②

Cuvée Réservée des Tsars 1989
A very correct and complete wine, elegant and concentrated. Ruby color and well-rounded bouquet with rich, sweet fruit extract and a faintly smoky note. Rich, concentrated extract on the palate, good balance with marked tannins which give a great sensation of depth.

CAHORS
SUD-OUEST
FRANCE

505

CAHORS
SUD-OUEST
FRANCE

Château La Caminade

46140 Parnac
Tel. 65307305
Fax 65201704

Château La Caminade is at Parnac on the banks of the river Lot. Before the Revolution, the château was home to a community of monks, but for the last four generations it has belonged to the Ressès family. The 35 ha of vineyards are managed today by Léonce Ressès and his children Dominique and Richard. The vines are an average of 18 years old and yield 56 hl/ha. The soil is a mixture of chalk and sand which gives the wines a touch of elegance. The blend is a traditional 70% Auxerrois, 25% Merlot and 5% Tannat. Grapes are de-stemmed and ferment in stainless steel containers at controlled temperatures for 12 to 21 days. Up to 10% of second-press wine is used in the final blend. Only one third of the average annual production of 150,000 bottles at Château La Caminade is aged in wood. The special reserve Le Commandery, which has an annual production of 50,000 bottles, uses the same blend of varieties as the basic cuvée but is left to age for 12 to 14 months in Vosges and Allier oak barriques, one third of which are new.

Cahors 1990 ♈ ②
Deep, rich, dark, inviting color. The nose has fairly marked hints of meat extract together with the typical Auxerrois mineral notes. The aromas on the palate are reminiscent of ripe fruit with good concentration and reasonably well-balanced structure, although the finish is a little hard.

Cahors La Commandery 1989 ♈♈ ②
Superb shade of dark red. Here again the nose brings to mind ripe fruit, but with more satisfying definition and greater concentration. A wine with more body and better balance than the straight Cahors 1990. It will age well, thanks both to the tannins and firm acidity which will help the wine's development. One of the finest wines of the Appellation.

Château Lamartine

46700 Soturac
Tel. 65365414
Fax 65246531

Documents dating from the phylloxera epidemic of 1883 reveal that the Gayraud family was already cultivating a five-hectare vineyard at that time. Since then the property, which in 1981 passed into the hands of Alain Gayraud, has grown to its current size of 22 ha. The area around Soturac, at the head of the Lot valley, has a micro-climate with a maritime influence which allows grapes to ripen earlier than in other parts of the Appellation. Auxerrois is by far the most popular variety on these clay, chalk and sand soils, accounting for 90% of the final blend, the remainder consisting of Merlot and Tannat. Alain Gayraud produces an absolutely traditional wine in terms of aging potential, but he also tries to preserve the freshness of the fruit. Fermentation is in temperature-controlled stainless steel vats and lasts 20 days. 20% of Château Lamartine's total production (100,000 bottles a year) is then aged in oak. Since 1986, Alain has been carrying out further experiments with wood and in 1988 he produced, for the first time, 25,000 bottles of a Cuvée Particulière from selected parcels which matures in barrels which are replaced every year.

Cahors Cuvée Particulière 1990 ♈ ②
A massive wine with lots of personality and outstanding aging potential. Deep, concentrated ruby color, ripe fruit extracts and full-bodied tannic structure. In line with the typical rustic Cahors style, whose wines are not at their best young, this will need plenty of time to soften and acquire smoothness.

Cahors Cuvée Particulière 1989 ♈ ②
Intense ruby color with deep fruit and berry aromas. Generous extract on the palate together with a solid yet unaggressive tannic element. Rather closed at the moment, this is a wine for the cellar. Very similar in style and personality to the preceding wine.

CAHORS
SUD-OUEST
FRANCE

506

CAHORS
SUD-OUEST
FRANCE

Château Triguedina

46700 Puy-l'Évêque
Tel. 65213081
Fax 65213928

Jean-Luc Baldes has a very personal way of looking at wine. He maintains that the defining feature of all great wine is the ability to age, a philosophy he applies to all the wines he makes at Château Triguedina. The estate lies to the west of Puy-l'Évêque and has belonged to the same family for eight generations. The 40 ha of vineyard are located on south-facing slopes where the influence of the Mediterranean climate protected the plants from the great frost of 1956. The vines, whose average age is 25 years although some are as old as 100, yield 45-50 hl/ha. The cellars have recently been modernized and equipped with temperature-controlled stainless steel vats and inert-gas technology, used to prevent oxidization. Wine is made traditionally with 70% Auxerrois grapes, 20% Merlot and 10% Tannat. Château Triguedina is bottled at two years and is cellared for six months before release. In outstanding years, the Château bottles a special cuvée, the Prince Probus, a monovarietal Auxerrois obtained from old vines.

Cahors 1990　　　　　🍇🍇 ②
The intense garnet color indicates a very young wine. Stylish spicy fruit aromas of redcurrant, nuts and smooth oak are followed by more sweet and incredibly rich fruit on the palate and up-front spicy flavors. Concentrated and full-bodied but also elegant, especially in the finish.

Cahors Prince Probus 1985　　🍇 ②
Deep ruby color shading into garnet round the edges. A little hard on entry with hints of game, ink and spices. Softish on the palate, where there is a warm flavor of cherry jam and fruit with spices and good tannic structure. Excellent to serve with food now, although it is difficult to predict the development of a wine of such austerity.

Clos de Gamot-Château du Cayrou

46220 Prayssac
Tel. 65224026
Fax 65224544

Clos de Gamot and Château du Cayrou both overlook the river Lot, the former at Prayssac and the latter at Puy-l'Évêque. The exuberant owner-director of the two properties is Jean Jouffreau who is supported in the day-to-day management by daughters Martine and Maryse and son-in-law Yves Hermann. The Joffreaus have been making wine on the 12 ha of Clos de Gamot since 1610. The vineyards, which include parcels more than 100 years old which yield a mere 25 hl/ha, are planted entirely with Auxerrois. Grapes from both young and old vines are harvested together for a production which totals barely 30,000 bottles a year. Château du Cayrou dates from the 12th century and was acquired by the Joffreaus in 1971, when they completely replanted the estate's 35 ha with 70% Auxerrois, 20% Merlot, 7% Tannat and 3% Gamay. The grapes are vinified separately according to variety and vineyard of origin. Annual production is around 200,000 bottles. The wines from both estates ferment for 15-21 days and age for a minimum of 18 months in oak barrels. Clos de Gamot is robust with very good structure while Château du Cayrou is a little softer, due to the Merlot in the blend.

Cahors Château du Cayrou 1989　　🍇 ②
A wine with a decidedly softer and fruitier style than its sibling Clos de Gamot. The difference can be seen in the intense ruby color in the glass. The extracts are rich in fruit with a hint of tannin. Less concentrated than the Gamot, but still vigorous and full-bodied.

Cahors Clos de Gamot 1989　　🍇 ②
Rich purple color tending to garnet, with good depth. The bouquet is still closed but has faint dusty aromas and is powerful, intense and austere. Full-bodied, complex palate with firm tannins and sweet extract – a fine example of a traditional, slightly rustic, Cahors.

Cahors Château du Cayrou 1988　　🍇
②
Slightly harder and more tannic than the 1989. Rich plum aromas stand out in a nose which also has black berries and tobacco leaves and good length and intensity. Slightly overpowering tannins make the finish rather coarse and astringent.

Cahors Clos de Gamot 1988　　🍇 ②
Even this wine has deep color, great texture and solid weight on the palate. It gives the impression of having less fruit and extract than the 1989, but is equally robust.

CAHORS
SUD-OUEST
FRANCE

507

CAHORS
SUD-OUEST
FRANCE

Domaine de Paillas

Floressas
46700 Puy-l'Évêque
Tel. 65213442
Fax 65246130

The 27 ha of Domaine de Paillas are located on a plateau above the valley of the river Lot at Floressas, in the southern half of the Appellation on gentle, south-facing chalk slopes. The Domaine grows 82% Auxerrois, 16% Merlot and the rest Tannat. After partial replanting in 1979 and 1980, the average age of the vines is now 15 years. Germain Lescombes, at present in his forties, took over the estate in 1981, ten years after his father had bought it. He makes only one cuvée, producing about 180,000 bottles from an average yield of 50 hl/ha .His aim is to produce a wine which combines aroma, body and softness uncompromised by tannin. The winemaking is conventional: 8-10 days' fermentation with regular pumping of the must over the cap, aging in the neutral environment of stainless steel vats, and no contribution at all from wood.

Cahors 1989
Young ruby color of medium intensity. The nose has gamey notes with hints of red berries and subtle spices. Complex and full-bodied on the palate with warm mineral fruit flavors in the finish.

Prieuré de Cénac

Château Saint-Didier Parnac
46140 Luzech
Tel. 65307010
Fax 65201624

The Prieuré de Cénac vineyard is situated on a plateau to the south of the river Lot, not far from the village of Albas, where an ancient monastery once stood. Brothers Franck and Jacques Rigal, producers and distributors who own two other properties in Cahors, bought this estate in 1976. Since then, the terrain has been completely reworked with the stony substratum broken up and turned over and 50 tons p/ha of natural fertilizer were dug in. The first vintage was harvested in 1983. The main variety at Prieuré de Cénac is Auxerrois, which accounts for 85% of stock on the 32-ha property, the remainder being Merlot. The ground between the vines is ploughed and the vines are treated exclusively with copper-based products. Grapes are harvested in part mechanically and in part manually, de-stemmed and soft-pressed before fermentation in the modern cellar equipped with temperature-controlled stainless steel vats. Maceration lasts for up to 15 days. Up to 50% of the wine is aged in new wood. The production in 1990 was around 160,000 bottles.

Cahors 1989
Deep ruby red color and an open, well-developed bouquet with notes of blackcurrant jelly and vanilla. The tannins are surprisingly soft on the palate which has juicy, wild-berry fruit. Toasted oak flavors come through strongly in the finish.

CAHORS
SUD-OUEST
FRANCE

508

CAHORS
SUD-OUEST
FRANCE

Château Lafon

Route de Soumensac
47120 Loubès Bernac
Tel. 53947714
Fax 53947316

The origins of Château Lafon date back to the time of the Gauls and the Romans. In the Middle Ages, monks cultivated vineyards here and by the 17th century the estate's wines were already being exported to Holland. The future seems linked to the Loire after the château's acquisition in 1989 by the Gitton family, who have estates at Sancerre, Pouilly-Fumé and Coteaux du Giennois. Château Lafon lies to the south of Saint-Foy-la-Grande and produces a vast range of wines from its 12 ha of vineyards. The soil type, known as "blanc de l'Agenais", is similar to that at Sainte-Croix-du-Mont and Monbazillac. Two hectares of vines, both red and white varieties, have been planted in the last 10 years. The rest of the vines are over 30 years old. The wines,which are all AOC Côtes de Duras, ferment in cement and stainless steel containers. The Gittons produce three whites, a Sauvignon, a monovarietal Sémillon and a Moëlleux blend of Sémillon (70%) Sauvignon and Muscadelle .The reds are a Merlot and a Bordeaux-style cuvée of Cabernet Sauvignon, Merlot and Malbec. Finally, there is a rosé obtained principally from Cabernet Franc. Total production comes to about 70,000 bottles a year.

Côtes de Duras ♈ ②
Sauvignon Blanc 1991
Very pale yellow with greenish edges. The nose has attractive exotic fruit rather than grassy Sauvignon character. The palate is lively although slightly low in acidity.

Côtes de Duras 1990 ▧ ②
Light salmon pink in the glass. The nose is fairly neutral but has hints of delicate red berries. Fresh, medium bodied, easy-drinking, representative of the Appellation.

Château Bellevue La Fôret

Domaine de la Fôret
31620 Fronton
Tel. 61824321
Fax 61823970

No one has done as much for the Appellation Frontonnais and for the Negrette grape grown exclusively in this area as Patrick and Diane Germain of Château Bellevue La Fôret. Most of their 115 ha are located on gravely alluvial terraces above the river Tarn. Half of the estate is planted in Negrette and the remainder in more or less equal parts of Syrah, Cabernet Franc, Cabernet Sauvignon and Gamay. Six wines are made for a total production of 900,000 bottles, the majority (640,000 bottles) of which consists of the basic red and rosé. The most significant of the four special cuvées is a wine called 'Ce Vin', a monovarietal Negrette obtained from grapes from different sites which undergo two kinds of maceration, one at higher temperatures to obtain color and structure, the other at low temperatures to preserve the more delicate fruit character. The resulting wines are blended and aged for 8 to 12 months in vats or barrels. Château Bellevue La Fôret is an interesting estate which has been in operation since 1973 and has proved capable of combining tradition with the best that modern technology has to offer.

Côtes du Frontonnais Ce Vin 1988 ♈ ③
100% Negrette, a rare variety only cultivated in this zone. An interesting wine obtained through painstaking vinification. Good body, fruity aromas and good extract. Well worth discovering.

Côtes du Frontonnais Prestige 1988 ♈ ②
Bright, clear red. Still developing, with a bouquet already tending towards the tertiary aromas of game, leather and smoke. Well-rounded on the palate, complex and sweet, with good balance and inviting length. Quite delicious.

COTES DE DURAS
SUD-OUEST
FRANCE

509

COTES DU FRONTONNAIS
SUD-OUEST
FRANCE

Robert Plageoles et fils

Domaine de Très Cantous
81140 Cahusac-sur-Vère
Tel. 63339040
Fax 63339564

Robert Plageoles is a tireless worker who has been at the forefront of the Gaillac Appellation for some time with a series of wines that are always interesting and in some cases exceptional. Robert, his wife Josiane and their son Bernard manage two properties: the Domaine de Très Cantous, which has been in the family since 1820; and the Domaine Roucou-Cantemerle, bought in 1963. The vineyards have an average age of 20 years. Between them the two properties produce ten different wines. The major part of the 17 ha are planted in white varieties used to make a Sauvignon Blanc and both a dry and a sweet Mauzac fermented at low temperatures in cement containers. There are also two Moelleux, one from Mauzac grapes and the other from Muscadelle, both aged in wood. In addition to these, the family also make a rare and expensive dessert wine from Ondenc Blanc known as Vin d'Autan. Another rarity, the Vin de Voile, is produced with the same traditional methods used for sherry and Jura's Vin Jaune. The delicately sparkling Mauzac Nature is a typical Gaillac. There are also two monovarietal reds from Duras and Gamay grapes vinified with semi-carbonic maceration. Annual production ranges from 2,000 bottles for some of the more exclusive wines, to 25,000 for the Sauvignon Blanc.

Gaillac Doux 1990   🍇 ②
Pale yellow-gold with only moderate clarity. The elegant nose has notes of beeswax and quince in a style that includes an element of oxidation. The palate suffers a little as a result, but nevertheless has rich grapey flavors. Delicately structured but clean and and long in the finish.

Gaillac Vin d'Autan 1990   🍇 🍇 ③
Opaque golden color with an aroma of chopped celery which develops into stewed apple, sultana and cloves. The stewed apple carries over onto the palate with the same slightly bitter note which derives from the grape skins as do the sweet spice and fruit flavors. A completely unique wine.

Rotier et fils

Domaine de Petit Nareye
81600 Cadalen
Tel. 63417514
Fax 63415456

It was only in 1985, when Alain Rotier came home from the University of Toulouse where he had graduated in agricultural engineering and enology, that this cellar began to vinify the grapes it had previously sent to the Cave Coopérative at Técou. Alain is now in charge of winemaking and helps his father Gérard and mother Michèle with the vineyard and administration. Their 27 ha of vineyard are divided into two parcels on the gravely plateau on the left-hand bank of the Tarn. The soils, which in some places are covered by a layer of rocks and pebbles, permit reasonable yields of attractively aromatic wines. The eclectic assortment of varieties includes local reds, like Duras and Braucol, and the white Len de l'Ehl, besides more well-known varieties such as Sauvignon Blanc, Syrah, Cabernet Sauvignon and Gamay. Les Gravels and Les Gravels Renaissance are both interesting red wines. Also worth noting is the Les Gravels white made from mainly Len de l'Ehl grapes, fermented and aged in oak. The Les Gravels red is obtained from 40% Braucol, 40% Cabernet Sauvignon and 20% Syrah. The Renaissance is a blend of 80% Syrah with Braucol and Cabernet Sauvignon aged in barriques for seven months.

Gaillac Les Gravels 1990   🍇 ③
Ruby color of medium intensity, rich fruit extract and a bouquet with aromas of purple plums, mint, eucalyptus and redcurrant. Stylish and full-flavored, a wine with soft tannins that make it surprisingly opulent and almost Californian in style.

Gaillac Les Gravels 1989   🍇 ③
The same dark color and bouquet of mint and eucalyptus as the '90. The fruit is soft and full-bodied on the palate with notes of raspberry. Attractive sweet entry although the finish lacks a little length.

Gaillac Les Gravels   🍇 🍇 ③
Renaissance 1989
A darker purple shade and bigger structure than the Les Gravels '89. The nose is still undeveloped with just a hint of spices and liqueur. The palate is currently dominated by the oak, but the vanilla gives a certain smoothness of texture. Up-front tannins on the palate are followed by a clean finish. Classy.

GAILLAC
SUD-OUEST
FRANCE

510

GAILLAC
SUD-OUEST
FRANCE

Cave de Técou

81600 Gaillac
Tel. 63330080
Fax 63330369

The vineyards of Gaillac, among the oldest in France, are located to the north-west of Toulouse near the towns of Albi and Castres. La Cave de Técou, founded in 1953, today has 300 members who between them cultivate 750 ha of vineyards on soil which is mainly chalk and gravel, with a total production of around a million bottles a year. The range of local red wines is obtained from Fer Servadou, Duras, Syrah, Gamay, Cabernet Sauvignon and Merlot varieties while the whites include the local Len de l'Ehl, Sauvignon Blanc, Muscadelle and Mauzac. The red grapes are soft-pressed and then ferment for 8-15 days depending on the variety with the must pumped over the cap twice a day. Aging is in stainless steel and cement containers. There are several special wines at Cave de Técou, above all the Gaillac Passion obtained mainly from Fer Servadou with the addition of Merlot and Syrah and aged for three months in stainless steel and six in new wood. The Gaillac Séduction series includes a red wine from Syrah, Fer Servadou and Merlot, a dry white from Len de l'Ehl and Sauvignon Blanc and a Moëlleux from old Mauzac and Muscadelle vines.

Gaillac Passion 1990　　　　🍇 ②
Good rich, deep color. Fruity if slightly coarse on the nose. Ripe fruit flavors come back on the palate, which has outstanding texture and balance. A wine with more style than is usual for the Appellation and one which will age better than many more fashionable bottles, thanks in no small part to the very evident tannins.

Domaine Brana

3 bis, avenue du Jaï-Alaï
64220 Saint-Jean-Pied-de-Port
Tel. 59370044
Fax 59371428

The Branas started trading as négociants specializing in the wines of the Sud-Ouest in 1897. In 1974, to diversify the business, Etienne Brana founded a distillery to produce a series of Eaux-de-vie, including Poire William, from the orchards of his own estate. The creation of an AOC Irouléguy vineyard is a further sign of the family's links with the area. The terraced property lies at a height of between 200 and 400 m on hillsides with gradients of as much as two in three. Established in 1986, the vineyard extends over 25 ha planted in Cabernet Franc, Cabernet Sauvignon and Tannat for red wines and Petit Courbu and Gros Manseng for Irouléguy white, a wine which has almost completely disappeared today. Because of the altitude and the sandy, shale-bearing terrain, yields are limited to a mere 15-20 hl/ha. The harvest is manual and vinification, entrusted to Etienne's son Jean, reflects in its modern technology Jean's experience with the enologists Denis Dubourdieu and Jean-Claude Berrouet. The white is obtained from soft-pressed grapes which undergo a brief maceration on the skins and then ferment in stainless steel at controlled temperatures. The de-stemmed red grapes ferment for 10-12 days and then spend a year in oak.

Irouléguy 1991　　　　🍇 ①
A wine with a style to which technology contributes more than varietal character and which could easily come from any one of several other regions. Nonetheless a highly drinkable, well-made product. Very pale and bright color and clean, lively bouquet are the result of modern vinification techniques. Well-defined flavors on the palate backed up by aromas of wild berries give the wine a very refreshing quality.

Irouléguy 1990　　　　🍇 ①
Very deep, rich color and a nose of elegant wood and ripe fruit in the best Médoc style. Ripe fruit comes through again on the palate with a note of mint. The stylish flavors reminiscent of game and rich texture derived from the Tannat in the blend, the variety which also contributes to the clean and positive finish.

GAILLAC
SUD-OUEST
FRANCE

511

IROULEGUY
SUD-OUEST
FRANCE

Domaine Ilarria

64220 Irouléguy
Tel. 59372338-59373367

Domaine Ilarria is the result of the commitment of two young growers, Peio Espil and Michel Riouspeyrous. Their estate was created in 1988 but the two families only joined forces in 1991. Both firmly believe in the potential of the cru and in painstaking attention to detail. At present they have 10 ha of vineyard, 5.5 ha of which are in production. The vines themselves, with ages ranging from 4 to 40 years, are located on terraces set into the shale-bearing slopes of the Basque mountains. The principal variety is Tannat supplemented with Cabernet Franc and Cabernet Sauvignon. Only natural fertilizers are used. Annual production is 10,000 bottles divided between a red, a rosé and a special cuvée known as Bixintxo The grapes are vinified separately according to variety and vineyard of origin in stainless steel containers. The rosé is made using the "méthode saignée" at a controlled temperature of 20°C. The Cuvée Bixintxo is obtained mainly from old Tannat vines and is aged for 14 months in new barriques. Allier oak is currently used, but the discovery of Basque coopers has prompted Peio Espil and Michel Riouspeyrous to consider experimenting with locally made barrels.

Irouléguy 1991 🏆 ①
Magnificent color – a brilliant pink shading into orange. Extremely fruity and fresh, leaving an intense sensation of crunchy, slightly under-ripe, fresh fruit on the palate. The finish is clean with flavors of pear. A unique rosé and a perfect accompaniment for spicy food. Serve chilled.

Irouléguy 1991 🍷 ②
Very well made, but without the concentration of the '90. Given time, this will be a bottle to reckon with. Full, rich, dark red and a surprisingly fruity redcurrant nose, very fresh and juicy. The palate, too, is fruity and well-rounded with background notes of tar and sweet liquorice. Lots of tannins in the finish.

Irouléguy ② 🍷 🍷
Cuvée Spéciale Bixintxo 1990
Fantastically rich, deep and luminous color. Warm, intense, spicy nose. Impressive extracts of black berries followed on the palate by huge tannins from the new oak. A very concentrated red with enough body to take all the wood. A wine to leave in the cellar for at least another five years.

Cave Coopérative d'Irouléguy

64430 Saint-Etienne-de-Baïgorry
Tel. 59374133
Fax 59374176

The Cave Coopérative d'Irouléguy was established in 1953 and today has 60 members. Irouléguy went through a period of decline after the arrival of phylloxera in 1912, but has re-emerged in recent years. The area under vines, which had fallen from 470 ha to just 64 ha in 1980, is steady today at 170 ha and the Cave Coopérative controls 140 of them. Most of the vineyards are located on terraces carved out of the Basque mountains planted in Cabernet Sauvignon and Tannat for red and rosé wines, as well as a small quantity of Petit Courbu and Gros Manseng from which a small amount of Irouléguy white was produced in 1992. Grapes from each parcel are vinified separately, generally after de-stemming. Fermentation lasts for 8-12 days. Irouléguy red is sold under the label Garri d'Ansa ('Garri' means red wine in Basque) and the rosé is labeled Argi d'Ansa. About 120,000 bottles of each are made. Many estates send their grapes to the Coopérative including Domaine de Mignaberry, Domaine Iturritxe, Domaine Mendisokoa and Domaine Les Terrasses de l'Arraday. The most important of these is Domaine de Mignaberry with its 25 ha.

Irouléguy Domaine Mendisokoa 1990 🍷 ②
The dark color is reminiscent of Cabernet as is the nose with its pronounced, characteristic notes of ripe blackcurrant, but the fruit is more elegant on the palate and the tannins a little less aggressive. Good fruit flavor although this wines has less concentration and less structure than the Mignaberry.

Irouléguy 🍷 ②
Domaine de Mignaberry 1990
Very representative of the Appellation but a little lacking in concentration. Intense ruby color and a robust, solid style with a nose of wild berries. Good texture with subtle tannins and fruity extract of moderate concentration, although the finish is a little disappointing.

Irouléguy 🍷 ②
Domaine de Mignaberry 1989
The same rustic style as the '90. A nose of wild berries with just slightly better concentration than the preceding wine and a moderately long, but clean and positive finish. Has all the solid tannic structure of the Appellation with a toasty flavor in the finish.

IROULEGUY
SUD-OUEST
FRANCE

512

IROULEGUY
SUD-OUEST
FRANCE

GAEC Barrère

Clos de la Vierge – Clos Cancaillaü
64150 Lahourcade
Tel. 59600815

Anne-Marie Barrère took over the management of the family estate in 1986, after an apprenticeship as winemaking assistant to her father. The Barrère property produces three wines: Jurançon Sec Clos de la Vierge, Jurançon Clos Cancaillaü and a special selection, Clos Cancaillaü Crème de Tête. In a good year production totals 80,000 bottles, two thirds of which are rich and mellow Jurançon. The three varieties authorized for the Appellation are cultivated on the 16-ha estate of which 10 ha are dedicated to Gros Manseng, 4 ha are planted in Petit Manseng and 2 ha in Courbu. Clos de la Vierge is obtained from monovarietal Gros Manseng, harvested in mid-October. Fermented at low temperatures (15°C-20°C) in stainless steel vats, the wine spends 4-5 days on the skins to extract fruit aromas. The harvest for Clos Cancaillaü, which is made from Gros Manseng and the rare and delicate Courbu variety, takes place at the beginning of November when the grapes are practically sun-dried.(10-25%). Fermentation is in stainless steel containers and aging in large oak barrels. The Crème de Tête is obtained from Petit Manseng with selected lots of Gros Manseng.

Jurançon Clos Cancaillaü ♀ ②
Crème de Tête 1989
Very intense golden color reminiscent of corn. Sweet, rich aroma and a little rustic on the palate but well-rounded and full-flavored. A wine with good body and ripe, succulent aromas of Petit Manseng as well as an exotic touch of pineapple. Good length on the palate.

Domaine Bellegarde

Quartier Coos
64360 Monein
Tel. 59213317
Fax 59214440

After studying at the La Tour Blanche school of viticulture at Sauternes and then working for a time at Domaines Cordier in Bordeaux, Pascal Labasse took over Domaine Bellegarde in 1986. Since then he has made some astounding wines, through rigorous care in the vineyard and in the cellar where he uses new barriques with excellent results. The estate's 11.5 ha include 7.5 ha of Gros Manseng used for the dry Jurançon and 4 ha of Petit Manseng for the sweet version. Yields are low: in 1991, 46 hl/ha were obtained for the Gros Manseng and a mere 20 hl/ha for the Petit Manseng. There are two cuvées of Jurançon sec: one is fermented in temperature-controlled stainless steel vats, the other in oak barrels, one third of which are new. The Jurançon Cuvée Thibault is made from Petit Manseng, 80% fermented in barriques. In 1989, Pascal Labasse produced an intense and opulent Jurançon Sélection DB from Petit Manseng grapes obtained from a vineyard with a yield of only 9 hl/ha. The experiment will be repeated only in other outstanding vintages.

Jurançon Cuvée Thibault 1990 ♀ ♀ ②
A pale gold wine with a brilliant, lively appearance in the glass. At the moment the bouquet is dominated by new wood, but the vanilla is well-integrated with opulent tropical fruit. Good balance on the palate with an abundance of elegant, succulent exotic fruit (pineapple) and a creamy texture. The entry is rich and sweet but there is also fresh acidity which mingles well and provides balance. A fine wine, with excellent body and superb length.

JURANÇON
SUD-OUEST
FRANCE

513

JURANÇON
SUD-OUEST
FRANCE

Domaine Castéra

Quartier Uchaa
64360 Monein
Tel. 59213498

Domaine Castéra is a family-run estate. The
present owner, Christian Lithour, is a
member of a group of young growers
dedicated to the promotion of quality in
Jurançon. After a solid apprenticeship with
his father, Christian started supervising
winemaking personally and has continued to
follow traditional methods, avoiding new
wood. The 7-ha property has around 1.5 ha
of Petit Manseng, the rest being planted in
Gros Manseng. The vine stock, which has
been progressively renewed, today has an
average age of 20 years. There are plans to
add a further three hectares of Petit Manseng
and the terraces, on moist clay soil, have
already been prepared. Christian produces
three wines: a Jurançon sec from Gros
Manseng vinified in stainless steel, and two
versions of sweet Jurançon, one from Gros
Manseng and the other from Petit Manseng.
The former is picked with 15°-16° potential
alcohol, the latter with 20°, towards the end
of November. Both are fermented in stainless
steel and aged for 18 months in oak. Total
production is about 35,000 bottles, one third
of which is Jurançon sec and 10% Jurançon
Petit Manseng.

Jurançon Petit Manseng 1987   ❦ ❦ ②
Deep gold color. The bouquet is an explosion of
sultana, apricots and pineapple. The flavors on
the palate resemble stewed fruit and jam with a
hint of citrus and a rich, sweet finish which
features notes of pine and walnuts.

Sud-Ouest Appellations in this Guide

Bergerac
Buzet
Cahors
Côtes de Duras
Côtes du Frontonnais
Gaillac
Irouléguy
Jurançon
Madiran
Pécharmant
Saussignac
Tursan
Vins de Marcillac
Vins de Pays des Côtes de Gascogne
Vins de Pays de Haute-Garonne

JURANÇON
SUD-OUEST
FRANCE

514

JURANÇON
SUD-OUEST
FRANCE

Domaine Cauhapé

64360 Monein
Tel. 59213302
Fax 59214182

Henri Ramonteau is the brightest star in Jurançon. In 1985, he was voted Grower of the Year for the Sud-Ouest and in 1989 Domaine de Cauhapé wines entered the inner circle of the world's great wines when Quintessence de Petit Manseng 1988 won fifth place out of 70 competitors from 11 countries in an Olympiade des Liquoreux held at Vinexpo (first place went to Château d'Yquem 1983). Domaine Cauhapé has 24 ha of vineyard, 9 ha planted in Petit Manseng, 13 ha in Gros Manseng and a further 2 ha in red varieties. Total production is around 140,000 bottles a year. Since 1975, when Henri Ramonteau inherited Cauhapé, the cellar facilities have been extended and up-graded with increasing use of new oak for fermentation and aging. Both the Jurançon and Jurançon sec are obtained from Gros Manseng. Two styles of dry white are produced: Vieilles Vignes, from 80 year-old vines, and the Cuvée sous Bois, fermented and aged in new wood. The Jurançon Vendages Tardives, Noblesse du Petit Manseng and Quintessence du Petit Manseng (which is fermented and aged for two years in new oak) all achieve the highest levels of excellence. The prize-winning Quintessence is the product of vines which yield a bare 7 hl/ha and a must with 20°- 24° potential alcohol.

Jurançon Vieilles Vignes 1990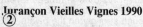
②
Very bright pale yellow and a rich nose with fresh notes of apple subtly laced with wood. Full-bodied, salty palate. Clean with good acidity which gives freshness and length. A very classy wine.

Jurançon Noblesse 1989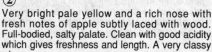
Very attractive, luminous pale gold. Rich nose with hints of butter and opulent fruit. Even more complex and fleshy on the palate than the Vendages Tardives, with a range of mouthfilling flavors of candied peel and pineapple together with exceptional length. The remarkable acidity ensures that the wine does not cloy despite its honeyed sweetness.

Jurançon Quintessence 1989 ④
Extraordinarily rich, deep gold color. Nose of sweet fruit together with cinnamon and honey. Sweetness and outstanding length again on the palate although, as in the case of the Noblesse, good acidity guarantees freshness. For all the dominant concentration of sweet flavors, the final impression is one of exceptional balance.

Jurançon
Vendanges Tardives 1990 ③
A wine which only superlatives can describe. Bright and very pale in the glass with light reflections of gold and green. Complex, headily elegant bouquet and a palate with juicy fruit and vanilla aromas emerging in a perfect balance of fruit and acidity. Wonderful length and stunning style. The great virtue of Petit Manseng is the balance between sweetness and acidity which makes the wine perfect as an aperitif or an end-of-the-meal wine to serve with fresh fruit-salad. The outstanding personality of the variety gives the wine a richness of sensations which puts this Jurançon, although less well-known, on a par with top Sauternes and the great dessert wines of the Loire or Alsace.

JURANÇON
SUD-OUEST
FRANCE

515

JURANÇON
SUD-OUEST
FRANCE

Clos Uroulat

Quartier Trouilh
64360 Monein
Tel. 59214619
Fax 59214690

Charles Hours produces an average of 35,000 bottles a year of sweet and dry Jurançon, but limited quantities are sufficient to demonstrate the superb quality of his wines. After attending the universities of Pau and Bordeaux, where he studied under Professor Ribereau-Gayon, Hours bought the Clos Uroulat estate in 1983 and since then he has produced some of the most interesting wines to be found in this ancient winegrowing zone south-west of Pau. His 7.5 ha property is planted with Petit Manseng, which is used exclusively for the AOC Jurançon, Gros Manseng and Courbu. Yields for the Jurançon from the highly selective late harvest in November are low at about 20-30 hl/ha. Yields for Jurançon sec are between 40 and 45 hl/ha. Both wines ferment and then age for 11 months in barriques, 25% of which are new. The Jurançon Clos Uroulat is complex with good structure, typical aromas of tropical fruit and lively acidity. The Jurançon sec Cuvée Marie, named after Charles Hours' daughter, is well-balanced and full-flavored.

Jurançon 1990   🍇 🍇 ②
Rich straw-gold color with greenish tints. Headily sweet, honeyed nose and complex, powerful and sweet on entry. Superb acidity confers excellent balance and remarkable freshness. It may lack the concentration of a Sauternes but it is still a wine with well-developed character and extraordinary depth of aromas.

Jurançon Cuvée Marie 1991   🍇 🍇 ②
A wine whose density and concentration almost give the impression of sweetness, although in fact this is a very dry Jurançon. Bright, pale color and a well-defined, fresh bouquet with a touch of spicy fruit. Full on the palate but very refreshing with good fruit. Dry and very positive finish.

Domaine Berthoumieu

Viella
32400 Riscle
Tel. 62697405
Fax 62698064

Since 1850, six generations of the Barré family have cultivated the Domaine Berthoumieu. The two youngest members of the family work side by side today, with Louis in charge of the vineyards and Didier looking after winemaking and marketing. 60% of the 24-ha estate is planted in Tannat, 30% in Cabernet Franc and Cabernet Sauvignon and 10% in Fer Servadou, a variety prized for its aromatic qualities. There are also two hectares of Petit Manseng and Courbu which yield a limited quantity of sweet Pacherenc du Vic Bihl. The two main soil types found on the property are silt and gravel, and a stoney mixture of silt and clay. 165,000 bottles a year of the two Madiran cuvées are produced. The Cuvée Tradition from 55% Tannat, 35% Cabernet Franc and Cabernet Sauvignon and 10% Fer Servadou, ferments in vats where the wine then ages for a further 18 months before going into old barriques for 2 to 5 years. The Cuvée Charles de Batz, 90% Tannat and 10% Cabernet Sauvignon obtained from older vines, ferments at 30°C for 21 days. It then ages for a year in oak barrels, one-third new, to finish off with six months in stainless steel.

Madiran   🍇 ②
Cuvée Charles de Batz 1989
Very concentrated garnet-purple. The nose has notes of ink hovering over nutmeg, sweet spices, black cherries and tar. Blackcurrant and apple come through strongly on the palate, but the impressive tannins and acidity dominate. The oak flavors are well integrated and the finish is long, if a little hard.

JURANÇON
SUD-OUEST
FRANCE

516

MADIRAN
SUD-OUEST
FRANCE

Alain Brumont

32400 Maumusson
Tel. 62697467
Fax 62697046

Alain Brumont has climbed his way to the top in less than ten years. He acquired his first property, the 14-ha Domaine Bouscassé, in 1979. Today he owns 80 ha spread over three estates (Château Bouscassé, Château Montus and Domaine Meinjarre) and turns out half a million bottles a year. 80% of the production is Madiran red, a wine which might have disappeared altogether since Tannat is tending to be replaced by Cabernet as producers look to make suppler, more easily marketable wines. Brumont spotted the potential of this variety that is said to have been introduced to the region from Burgundy by monks in the 11th century and today more than three-quarters of his vineyards are planted in Tannat. Besides Madiran, Brumont also produces Pacherenc du Vic Bilh and several sweet white wines from Petit Courbu, Manseng, and Arrufiat. Alain Brumont is known for his in-depth research into the use of oak both for red and for white wines – in 1987 he went so far as to age a small quantity of wine in the mountains of the Pyrenees for 12 months, using helicopters for transport. He may appear an eccentric, but Alain Brumont is responsible for some of the most interesting wines made in France today.

Madiran Château Montus 🍷🍷 ③
Cuvée Prestige 1990
Majestically rich dark color. Complex nose with several layers of ripe fruit over an elegant, clean underlying aroma of new wood. Impressive ripe blackcurrant and tobacco flavor, exquisite balance and excellent length. A wine which will age comfortably well into the next century.

Madiran Château Bouscassé 🍷🍷 ③
Vieilles Vignes 1989
Like the Montus Prestige wines, it is obtained from monovarietal Tannat and aged for 12 months in new wood. Deep, concentrated color and an incredibly rich nose, still a little hard and woody with notes of ripe fruit and a sweet concentration of liquorice. Chewy tannins on the palate together with an intense sensation of ripe fruit. Incredible length of flavor.

Madiran Château Montus 🍷 ③
Cuvée Prestige 1988
Yet another wine with a superbly deep, concentrated appearance. The nose is spicy and complex, redolent of black fruit. Rich and spicy palate, once again with aromas of ripe black fruit. Very good balance and length. A complete wine, though perhaps without the concentration of the '89 or the '90. Will age comfortably for another 8-10 years.

Madiran Château Montus 🍷🍷🍷 ③
Cuvée Prestige 1989
Stunningly deep, dark, intensely concentrated color. Complex on the nose with notes of candied peel and a subtle trace of new wood in the Médoc style. The palate has overwhelming ripe black fruit, liquorice and aniseed with incredible depth and length of flavor. A wine with all the intensity of a great Saint-Julien, and despite its concentration, the wood reveals the skill and sensitivity of this outstanding winemaker. This was the first genuinely great wine from the Appellation Madiran – consequently it has been an inspiration to other producers, proving, once and for all, this variety's true potential. Like the 1985, this wine was made from 100% Tannat. In the past, Tannat was believed to be capable of producing only harsh, rustic wines, but this Cuvée Prestige proves the skeptics wrong.

MADIRAN
SUD-OUEST
FRANCE

517

MADIRAN
SUD-OUEST
FRANCE

Château Barrejat

Maumusson
32400 Riscle
Tel. 62697492
Fax 62697754

Maurice Capmartin is an honest, no-nonsense winemaker with his feet firmly on the ground. His Madiran is robust, compact, vigorous and suited to aging. Château Barrejat is the Capmartin family estate, which Maurice inherited during the 1960s. Since then, he has doubled the area under vines to the present 16 ha. The cellar has also been modernized, but the parcel of ungrafted Tannat vines has been left intact. These vines are more than 200 years old, located on clay-and-silt soil which gives complexity and vigor to Barrejat wines. The estate is planted in 60% Tannat and 40% Cabernet Franc and Sauvignon. The average age of the vines is 40 years. Yields are around 55 hl/ha and total production amounts to 100,000 bottles a year. The grapes are picked by hand after scrupulous selection and fermented up to 21 days in either oak or cement and stainless steel vats. The wine then ages for a minimum 18 months in a combination of barrels and vats. The result is a "vin de garde" with remarkable structure, built to age.

Madiran 1989   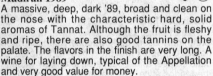

A massive, deep, dark '89, broad and clean on the nose with the characteristic hard, solid aromas of Tannat. Although the fruit is fleshy and ripe, there are also good tannins on the palate. The flavors in the finish are very long. A wine for laying down, typical of the Appellation and very good value for money.

Château d'Aydie

64330 Aydie
Tel. 59040117
Fax 59040153

In the early 1960s, Frédéric Laplace was one of the first Madiran growers to start bottling the wine from his estate, in a drive for quality over quantity. Today the 45-ha property, which is the second most important in the Appellation after Alain Brumont's estate, is run by Laplace's three grandsons, François, Jean-Luc and Bernard together with his only grand-daughter, Marie. A total of 40 ha are planted in Tannat (60%) and equal proportions of Cabernet Franc and Cabernet Sauvignon. A small area of the estate has vines which pre-date phylloxera. Another five hectares grow Arrufiat, Gros and Petit Manseng and Courbu which go into the production of the majestic dry Pacherenc du Vic Bihl. The basic Madiran Liseré Or and the Cuvée Frédéric Laplace, obtained from 50% Tannat plus Cabernet Sauvignon and Cabernet Franc, are both fermented in stainless steel containers, the difference between them being that the Frédéric Laplace ages for 8 months in oak barrels. The cuvée Château d'Aydie (annual production 80,000 bottles) is made from 80% Tannat and 20% Cabernet Sauvignon, and is aged for 14 months in new wood. Production of the two red cuvées totals about 240,000 bottles a year

Madiran Château d'Aydie 1990   🍇 ②

The feature of this wine is its intensity. The color is ink-black shading into purple round the edges. The nose has powerful cassis, black cherries and violets and underlying hints of wood. The tannins on the palate are balanced by the sweet, concentrated fruit which gives the wine its delicious, long finish.

MADIRAN
SUD-OUEST
FRANCE

518

MADIRAN
SUD-OUEST
FRANCE

Château Laffitte-Teston

32400 Maumusson
Tel. 62697458
Fax 62697687

Jean-Marc Laffitte is, together with Alain Brumont and Patrick Ducourmau, one of the vignerons who have set the standards for the new generation of producers in Madiran. Low yields, modern winemaking techniques, traditional varieties and the intelligent use of barriques all contribute to the quality of the wines produced at Château Laffitte-Teston. When Jean-Marc took over the family estate in 1975, there were 12 ha under vines and the wine was sold unbottled. Today he cultivates 27 ha and produces around 145,000 bottles of Madiran a year. Most of the vineyard area is planted with Tannat, Cabernet Sauvignon and Cabernet Franc. Four hectares are planted with white varieties – Petit Manseng, Gros Manseng, Arrufiat and Courbu – which produce limited quantities of a dry Pacherenc du Vic Bihl and a Moëlleux. There are two red wines, a basic Madiran and a special Vieilles Vignes cuvée. The simpler of the two wines is obtained from 70% Tannat and 30% Cabernet Sauvignon and Cabernet Franc, vinified in the traditional manner and aged in vats and oak barrels. The Vieilles Vignes is obtained from 80% Tannat from low-yielding, 70 year-old vines and 20% Cabernet Sauvignon. Fermentation in this case lasts 18-21 days and the wine is aged in oak barriques, 60% of which are replaced new every year.

Madiran 1989 ♥ ①
One of the finest Madirans from the 1989 vintage with just the right fullness of fruit and structure provided by the Tannat. Intense, full color and a bouquet with meaty game aromas and black fruit. Rich, very ripe black fruit dominates on the palate and the wine has good overall balance and a satisfying finish.

Madiran Vieilles Vignes 1989 ♥♥②
Intense, full-bodied color again. The nose is still closed, although very clean and with the fruit already at the fore. The palate has rich flavors of game and fruit and compact texture. The concentration of flavors is much superior to that of standard Madiran.

Domaine Damiens

64330 Aydie
Tel. 59040413

A family-run estate where the work is shared by the athletic André Beheity, his wife Raymonde and their son Pierre-Michel, who has just completed his agronomy studies at Bordeaux Blanquefort. The original property André inherited in the early 1970s had only four hectares, but it has since been extended to the present 14 ha of vines with an average age of 15 years. The blend used for the basic Madiran is 50% Tannat and 50% Cabernet Franc and Cabernet Sauvignon. About 40,000 bottles a year of this wine are produced from an average yield of 45 hl/ha. Fermentation and aging of a minimum 12 months are in stainless steel containers. The Domaine's other wine is the Cuvée Vieillie en Fûts de Chêne, obtained from 70% Tannat and 30% Cabernet Sauvignon and Cabernet Franc selected from the oldest vines on the estate. Production of the Cuvée, which is fermented in stainless steel and aged in new barriques, totals around 10,000 bottles a year. It is a red that needs several years' bottle-age.

Madiran 1990 ♥ ②
A very drinkable Madiran that is ready now. The purple-red color is so concentrated it is almost black. The nose is open and evolved, with well-defined aromas of blackcurrant, eucalyptus and peppery spices. The palate is surprisingly juicy with the initial astringency of the tannins balanced by elegant aromas of ripe fruit.

Madiran ♥ ②
Cuvée Vieillie en Fûts de Chêne 1989
Again, rich, deep, almost opaque, color. Complex nose, still a little hard and closed. The Tannat is very much in evidence on the palate, producing a full-bodied wine with backbone and varietal flavors which include a hint of bitter chocolate. A tannic Madiran in a very rustic style.

MADIRAN
SUD-OUEST
FRANCE

519

MADIRAN
SUD-OUEST
FRANCE

Domaine de Grabieou

32400 Maumusson-Laguian
Tel. 62697462
Fax 62697308

René Dessans' father bought the Domaine de Grabieou in 1974. Originally, there were only three hectares in the Madiran AOC zone, but this was subsequently increased to 12.5 ha in the course of a replanting program initiated in 1973. The red varieties are Tannat (70%) and Cabernet Franc planted on a mixture of chalk clay and gravel soils. René and his son Frédéric produce four different cuvées of Madiran, as well as a limited quantity of sweet Pacherenc du Vic Bihl from monovarietal Petit Manseng fermented in stainless steel containers. The various cuvées of Madiran are obtained from selections of grapes from different lots, the riper and more aromatic of which go into the Cuvée Prestige which is obtained from monovarietal Tannat and has an annual production of 18,000 bottles. There is also a traditional Madiran, from 70% Tannat and 30% Cabernet Franc as well as an experimental cuvée called Vieillie en Fût de Chêne Neuf, with a higher percentage of Tannat. The wines are fermented and aged in stainless steel.

Madiran 1989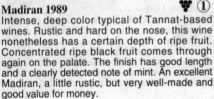
Intense, deep color typical of Tannat-based wines. Rustic and hard on the nose, this wine nonetheless has a certain depth of ripe fruit. Concentrated ripe black fruit comes through again on the palate. The finish has good length and a clearly detected note of mint. An excellent Madiran, a little rustic, but very well-made and good value for money.

Domaine Mouréou

32400 Maumusson-Laguian
Tel. 62697811
Fax 62697587

Madiran has an ancient winemaking tradition, but the story of Domaine Mouréou and Chapelle Lenclos only began in 1986, when Patrick Ducournau returned to his native region after graduating in enology and working in Bordeaux and Burgundy. Patrick rented seven hectares of vineyard from his father and planted a further six hectares, creating two styles of Madiran which he bottles under separate labels. The Domaine Mouréou is the more supple wine made from equal parts of Tannat and Cabernet Franc obtained from vines with an average age of 20 years. After fermenting for 8-12 days, most of the wine is then aged in cement vats for 22 months. The Chapelle Lenclos is a wine with robust structure, almost exclusively obtained from Tannat grown on chalky soil which Patrick considers the best in the Appellation. Fermentation for the Chapelle Lenclos is slower, lasting up to 21 days and it is followed by malolactic fermentation in wood. The wine then ages in 40 hl oak barrels, 50-75% of which are new, and is bottled after a further 10 months in vats. Patrick has planted one hectare in local white varieties – Petit Manseng, Arrufiat and Courbu – and in 1992 produced his first Pacherenc du Vic Bihl, fermented in wood.

Madiran 1990 ♥ ①
A balanced and elegant wine that shatters the "rustic" image of Madiran. Color of medium intensity and depth and a powerful blackcurrant nose. The palate has rich black fruit, backed by superb balance and excellent length.

Madiran Chapelle Lenclos 1989 ♥♥ ②
Rich, dark color with shades of mauve. Oak on the nose over layers of sweet, ripe fruit aromas which come back on the palate. Very good length in the finish. A stylish wine and excellent value for money.

Madiran Chapelle Lenclos 1988 ♥♥ ②
A first-class bottle of wine. Incredibly dark with smoky spice on the nose and a palate with sweet ripe fruit flavors, good extract and great complexity. The new wood is unobtrusive and well-integrated. Full-bodied. Utterly delicious.

MADIRAN
SUD-OUEST
FRANCE

520

MADIRAN
SUD-OUEST
FRANCE

Producteurs Plaimont

32400 Saint-Mont
Tel. 62696287
Fax 62696168

This cooperative was founded by a small group of growers in 1979. Toda it has 1,350 members who between them own 2,260 ha of vineyards and produce 9 million bottles a year, 40% of which are exported. Annual investment is currently running at around FF.15 million. Alongside this picture of impressive growth, the Producteurs have also become famous as the sponsors of the Jazz in Marciac Festival, which attracts the great names of Jazz – in 1992 stars like Dee Dee Bridgewater, Tommy Flanagan, Dizzie Gillespie and Michel Petrucciani performed. The same dynamism is evident in the Plaimont approach to growing and winemaking. Grapes are selected from all over the Appellation for their Madirans and Pacherenc du Vic Bihl, which account for 30% of turnover. Harvesting is in 30-kg baskets. Grapes are partially de-stemmed prior to soft-pressing and a part macerated on the skins before fermentation in barrels, where every effort is made to ensure that the wood aromas are minimized. Through products like these the cooperative is making a significant contribution to the general standards of winemaking in the area.

Pacherenc du Vic Bilh 1989　　🍇🍇 ②
Fermented and aged in wood, this rich sweet wine, known as "de la Saint-Albert", is made from grapes harvested on November 15. Flowers, honey, nuts and gingerbread on the nose. The palate is full, the texture very concentrated and the finish exceptionally long and elegant. A wine for long aging.

Côtes de Saint-Mont 1990　　🍇 ①
Attractive dark ruby color. Very intense nose of ripe fruit, almost of candied peel. The palate is well-rounded and balanced with notes of vanilla and spices. A very well-made wine.

Madiran Collection 1989　　🍇 ②
Aged in new barrels which give elegant hints of oak, this cru is an excellent expression of the Tannat variety, here blended with 30% Cabernet Franc, Cabernet Sauvignon and Pinenc. Well-rounded palate with aromas of vanilla and blackcurrant. Subtle tannins in the long finish. Will age for at least five years.

Château de Tiregand

24100 Creysse
Tel. 53232108
Fax 53225849

Tradition has it that this magnificent château, towering above the right-hand bank of the Dordogne, was established in the 13th century by Edward Tyrgan, one of Henry III of England's sons. The present-day owner, the Countess of Saint-Exupéry, is a descendant of the Count of La Panouse, who bought the château in 1826 and gave it its present appearance. Both the Countess's sons work on the estate: François-Xavier is in charge of winemaking and Pierre is responsible for the vineyards. The property is located to the east of Bergerac and comprises 140 ha, 39 ha of which are planted with local red and white varieties on sand and gravel Périgord soils. The Pécharmant red, which has an annual production of 150,000 bottles, is made from 46% Merlot, 30% Cabernet Sauvignon, 16% Cabernet Franc and 8% Malbec. Fermentation takes place in enameled stainless steel vats followed by 14-month aging in oak barrels, 20% of which are new. 30,000 bottles of white AOC Bergerac sec are also produced from 85% Sauvignon and 15% Sémillon The grapes macerate briefly on the skins, ferment at low temperatures (15°C) and remain on the lees for six weeks.

Pécharmant 1990　　🍇🍇 ②
A well-made wine with great balance and particularly good extract. Bright purple in the glass and an elegant nose of berries, barely veiled by notes of vanilla. Elegant fruit with stylish tannins well integrated on the palate. A very attractive bottle.

Pécharmant 1989　　🍇 ②
The appearance is that of a rich full-bodied red. Blackberries on the nose and a fruity palate in which flavors of plum predominate. A touch of quite harsh tannins and a finish of medium intensity. The classic Pécharmant style, less elegant than the 1990 but more robust.

Pécharmant 1988　　🍇 ②
Full color leading into light fruit aromas on the nose. Elegant tannins and good balance. Slightly less well-rounded than the 1990, but nonetheless complex with lots of body in the finish.

MADIRAN
SUD-OUEST
FRANCE

521

PECHARMANT
SUD-OUEST
FRANCE

Château Richard

La Croix Blanche
24240 Monestier
Tel. 53584913
Fax 53611728

Richard Doughty looks like a typical English – large-framed, tough and in great shape. His mother was in fact a Frenchwoman from Auvergne, not far from the forest of Troncais, and one of his great-uncles was a cooper. Doughty himself is an oceanographer by profession and it was only in 1986 that he discovered a passion for sweet botrytized wines following a course at Château La Tour Blanche. Richard's change of profession has been to the advantage of the Saussignac Appellation. This great, ancient wine, mentioned by Rabelais, had almost disappeared when Doughty started out in 1988. Luck was on his side because his first two vintages were made under ideal conditions for sweet wine. Today the 13.5 ha of clay and chalk terrain produce about 80,000 bottles of red, white and rosé Bergerac as well as another 8,000 of deliciously sweet Saussignac. The Bergeracs are good but the sweet Saussignac, with its 90% Sémillon and 10% Muscadelle grapes harvested over the course of several selections, vinified and aged in wood for 15-24 months, is exceptional and heralds a new, glorious future for the wine.

Saussignac 1990   🍷 ②
Very bright pale yellow. Sweet, creamy aroma with notes of honey. Very soft and full on the palate with flavors of honey and fruit. Long finish. Quite delicious, with its exceptionally clean, well-defined aromas. Well-made, extremely fresh, a classic example of this style of dessert wine.

Saussignac Coup de Coeur 1990   🍷🍷 ②
Another wine with a pale, luminous color. The nose is richer and fuller than that of the basic Saussignac, with a more buttery, creamier flavor. The palate is incredibly complex, weighty, and slightly oily and honeyed. It is so rich that the acidity seems on the low side. When a wine has as much length as this does, it will probably last forever.

Château de Bachen

40800 Duhort-Bachen
Tel. 56508532
Fax 56394999

Château de Bachen belongs to the restaurateur Michel Guérard and his wife Christine. The estate dates from the 13th century, but the château's present aspect is heavily influenced by the architecture of the 17th century. The Guérards bought the property in 1983 and replaced the vines, which had been neglected for 30 years. Enologist Thomas Stonestreet is in charge of winemaking. The Château de Bachen white, an AOC Tursan, is a blend of several varieties including a fairly rare local grape called Barroque which vinified on its own is extremely fresh and lively. Barroque accounts for 50% of the vineyard area of 11 ha. 25% is planted in Gros Manseng and a further 25% in equal proportions of Sémillon and Sauvignon Blanc. The soils have a high proportion of gravel. The estate's most prestigious wine is Baron de Bachen, first made in 1988 from a blend which varies from vintage to vintage. It is fermented and aged on the yeasts for 6-8 months in oak barrels. The second wine, Château de Bachen, is fermented in stainless steel vats. The annual production of Baron de Bachen is 35,000 bottles and that of Château de Bachen 15,000.

Tursan Baron de Bachen 1990   🍷 ②
Clear and bright with a perfectly clean, fruity nose containing a hint of new wood. Round and fresh on the palate. Very clean flavors with lots of oak and moderate length in the finish.

SAUSSIGNAC
SUD-OUEST
FRANCE

522

TURSAN
SUD-OUEST
FRANCE

Domaine du Cros

12390 Goutrens
Tel. 65727177

Credit for the recent promotion of the wines of the Domaine du Cros to AOC status belongs to owner Philippe Teulier, a self-taught producer who studied enology in the past, is one of the most passionate enthusiasts of this fascinating, but difficult winemaking zone. After the death of his mother Adrienne, who had started bottling her wine in the early 1960s, Philippe enlarged the estate to the present size of 12 ha, modernized the cellar and introduced up-to-date winemaking techniques. The vineyards, which have vines of 50-80 years of age, are located on steep red-earth slopes. Harvesting is always manual and the grapes are de-stemmed to give softer tannins. Fermentation is fairly brief after soft-pressing, but aging in oak barrels can last as long as 24 months – intelligent methods which give excellent results.

Vins de Marcillac
Domaine du Cros Cuvée Spéciale 1989
From vines between 50 and 80 years old, this is a cuvée that will age for quite some time. Very bright color and fruity aromas of blackcurrant which develop a more gamey, floral character on the palate. Good structure, rustic but by no means lacking in elegance, with tannins that are not excessively austere.

Jean-Luc Matha

Bruéjouls
12330 Marcillac-Vallon
Tel. 65726329

Marcillac's 99 ha of vineyards could easily have ceased to exist. Most of the production used to go to Decazeville, capital of the coal-fields of Rouergue. After the closure of the open-cast mine at Lassalle, the region seemed to have contracted a kind "coal sickness" which drained the vitality of both the town and the population. There were wine producers, however, who fought to keep the production alive. One of these was Jean-Luc Matha who cultivates 11 ha of terraced vineyard on stony Bruéjouls sandstone north of Rodez. This young man with his unruly mustache, who already has over 20 years' experience in winemaking, created an exceptional monovarietal wine from Fer Servadou, a grape also known locally as Mansois. The harvest is manual and the fruit is de-stemmed before being trodden in the time-honored fashion with bare feet. The wine is aged for 18 months in oak barrels to produce an artisan wine of great interest.

Vins de Marcillac

Cuvée Spéciale 1989
From a selection of grapes from the oldest vines on the estate, a wine with a lovely violet-red color and an intense, rather heady, nose of blackcurrant, mulberry and raspberry. Full-bodied on the palate with closed tannins. A wine which expresses both the character of the cru and the variety.

VINS DE MARCILLAC
SUD-OUEST
FRANCE

523

VINS DE MARCILLAC
SUD-OUEST
FRANCE

Domaine du Tariquet

Le Tariquet
32800 Eauze
Tel. 62098782
Fax 62298949

Armagnac has been going through a recession since the late 1970s, but it does not seem to have affected the winemaking on this estate. The Grassa family cultivate the clay and red sand of the lower Armagnac: father Pierre looks after the vineyards and public relations, daughter Maité is in charge of marketing and son Yves is the winemaker. Together they manage 100 ha planted in Colombard, Ugni Blanc and Gros Manseng to make two unpretentious, but delicious, Côtes de Gascogne wines. The first cuvée is a white sold very young, obtained from the best-positioned, lowest-yielding parcels. In this case slow fermentation at low temperatures aims to bring out the grape aromas. The second cuvée is a more robust white wine with more length which spends some months in new oak. Both are made with an impeccably professional approach and prices are extremely reasonable.

Domaine du Tariquet 1991   🍷 ①
Very elegant on the nose with surprisingly intense aromas, more flowery than fruity in character. Sinewy palate, but not without a touch of softness. The finish is appetizingly fresh.

Domaine du Tariquet   🍷 ①
Cuvée Bois 1990
A cuvée with an inviting note of wood from six months spent in new oak. Full texture, almost fat on the palate, but still very attractively fresh.

Domaine de Ribonnet

31870 Beaumont-sur-Lèze
Tel. 61087102
Fax 61080806

The lovely 15th-century Domaine de Ribonnet is located near Toulouse on a hill overlooking the Lèze. The estate extends over 200 ha of rolling hills, of which 33 ha are planted in vines. At one time, around the turn of the century, the property belonged to Clément Ader, the famous French aviator and engineer. In 1974 it was acquired by Christian Gerber's family, who were farmers from near Lausanne in Switzerland. Young Christian vowed to restore the domaine to its former glory. Today he grows no fewer that 17 grape varieties including internationally-known cultivars such as Pinot Noir, Cabernet Sauvignon, Gamay, Syrah, Chardonnay, Sauvignon, Sémillon and Marsanne and others like Chasselas which are more usually associated with his native Switzerland. All the domaine's wines ferment in stainless steel vats with the exception of a few Chardonnays which are fermented in barriques. Only Vins de Pays are produced, sold under the Domaine de Ribonnet label, despite the fact that the Ribonnet buildings would put many so-called Bordeaux "châteaux" to shame. This is undoubtedly a domaine to watch in the future.

Chardonnay 1990   🍷 ②
Clear, bright pale yellow color. The nose is fruity and fresh with slightly toasted aromas and an exotic touch of honey. The palate is rich and quite buttery, with good length. An easy-drinking wine, to enjoy before it loses its characteristic freshness.

VINS DE PAYS – COTES DE GASCOGNE
SUD-OUEST
FRANCE

524

VINS DE PAYS DE LA HAUTE-GARONNE
SUD-OUEST
FRANCE

GERMANY

In terms of size, Germany is one of the world's smaller wine-growing nations. Its vineyard area (102,000 ha) accounts for only 10% of that of France and produces less wine than the USA (10-15 million hl). Germany is, nevertheless, a very special wine nation. On the one hand, it is one of the few countries in which wine consumption is on the increase; on the other, the northerly position of the growing areas bring forth wines of a style and character rarely found elsewhere in the world. This is due to the fact that the vineyards lie close to the 51st parallel, which is regarded as the absolute climatic limit for grape growing in the northern hemisphere. In the relatively cool continental climate, there are only a few areas where the grapes can accumulate enough sugar to produce wines which meet the legal requirements for quality wine status. It is, therefore, not by chance that European wine legislation places Germany (with the exception of Baden and Württemberg) in wine-growing zone A, which is the lowest classification possible, shared only by England and the Benelux countries. In other words, these are countries in which it is extremely difficult to produce wines due to the restrictions of their cool climates. However, this should not lead to the conclusion that German wines are at the bottom of the quality scale. On the contrary, as the case of Champagne shows, some of the world's finest, most characterful wines come from areas close to the climatic limit for wine-growing.

Altogether Germany's vineyard area is made up of 12 wine producing zones of origin (including the zone in what was formerly Eastern Germany which is not included in this guide). In some cases they are large areas with intensive wine-growing, in others vines can only thrive in 'ecological niches', on steep slopes, in south-facing sites or fragmented vineyards. In terms of the export market the most important wine areas are those of the Rhine and the Mosel. These include the regions of the Rheingau, Rheinhessen, Rheinpfalz (Palatinate), Nahr, Mittelrhein, Ahr, Nahe and the Mosel-Saar-Ruwer. There are also, however, quality wines which have a large domestic following to be found in the regions of Baden, close to the Alsatian border, Franken and the less well-known Württemberg.

The German wine laws date from 1971 and are intrinsically linked to the ripeness of the grape. They are structured and simple to understand up to a point but are restrictive and open to misinterpretation and plans have been set in motion to have them overhauled. At present the laws divide German wines into three categories: Tafelwein which is the lowest level, Qualitätswein bestimmter Anbaugebiete (QbA) and Qualitätswein mit Prädikat (QmP). In order to qualify for Qualitätswein bestimmter Anbaugebiete (QbA) status, or quality wine from a designated region, wines must attain at least 7% natural alcohol and be made from a grape variety which is authorized for the respective area. It is possible to increase the natural sugar content of the grape juice (and thus the potential alcohol of the end wine) by adding sugar (up to 3.5% alcohol in zone A and 2.5% in zone B). Qualitätswein mit Prädikat is the top category and amongst other controls does not allow sugar to be added. SbA wines correspond to the French AOC or Italian DOC classifications. 93% of Germany's wine production is white, made almost entirely from single varieties. A special and unique feature of German white wines is their low alcohol (around 10% by volume) and high acidity (6-10 g/lt). Many wine drinkers find the tart acidity in wines from the Mosel and Rhine rather difficult to cope with. For decades it was common practice to compensate for this by leaving them with a portion of unfermented sugar (often added). During the 1970s and 1980s, new generations of wine-growers changed to making dry wines and now about 70% of Germany's production is dry; in some areas this proportion is as high as 90%. The change over to dry wines has given an unexpected new stimulus to the industry, especially within Germany itself. Many of the best producers, particularily along the Mosel, but also along the Rhine, have increasingly realized that some residual sugar greatly enhances the noble qualities of Riesling. Therefore, styles tend to be 'sweetly fruity' or 'mild' on the Mosel and "halbtrocken" or 'off-dry' along the Rhine. In any case, off-dry and dry wines are given equal status in Germany.

Germany's most noble variety is the Riesling, accounting for 20% of the vineyard area, though in the Rheingau and Mittelrhein areas its share is 75%. It is responsible for virtually all the greatest wines in Germany. The most popular variety, on the other hand, is the Müller-Thurgau (27%). It is easy to cultivate and in all areas produces relatively simple, lightly flowery, though seldom highly prestigious wines. This is followed by Silvaner and Kerner, with 7% each. Scheurebe, Pinot Gris (known in German as Ruländer or Grauburgunder) and Pinot Blanc (Weissburgunder) can produce excellent wines but each accounts for significantly less than 5%. Germany's few red wines are made from Pinot Noir, generally known as Blau- or Spät-Burgunder (around 4%), followed by Portugieser, Trollinger, Schwarzriesling, Samtrot and Lemberger.

The German wine law is unique in that it subdivides the quality wine category into further classifications: "Qualitätswein", or simply quality wines, and "Qualitätswein mit Prädikat" (QmP), or quality wines with special attributes. Whether or not a wine falls into the latter category, and how high up the hierarchy of "Prädikat" it is placed, depends on the natural sugar content of the juice or 'must weight', which in turn expresses the degree of ripeness of the grapes. These wines are not allowed to add sugar, are made from authorized grape varieties and are quality tested. Their classification by natural sugar content is as follows: Kabinett (ripe grapes from a normal harvest), Spätlese (riper grapes, late-harvested), Auslese (selected, very ripe grapes), Beeren-Auslese/Eiswein (individual berry selection for ripeness and concentration) and Trocken-Beeren-Auslese (only grapes attacked by noble rot).

This system of classifying quality exclusively on the basis of sugar content of the juice is often rightly criticised for being one-sided. After all, sweetness is only one of many factors that determine the quality of a wine. Quality minded producers and wine lovers also judge quality equally by the wine's acidity, body and concentration as well as the harmony of all its components.

Auslese, Beeren-Auslese (BA) and Trocken-Beeren-Auslese (TBA) are practically always nobly sweet wines. The residual sugar is nowadays rarely added (Prädikat wines can add unfermented grape juice or "süssreserve" to sweeten dry, fully fermented wines). Therefore, in most cases the sweetness is natural and caused by the inability of the yeasts to turn all the juice's natural sugar into alcohol during fermentation. Other times, the winemaker may deliberately decide to stop the fermentation, to leave residual sugar in the wine. However, dry Auslese wines (labelled as "Auslese trocken") are becoming increasingly common. Another German specialty is Eiswein. In order to produce this wine the grapes are left on the vine until winter (December-January) and must be harvested when the temperature has dropped to below zero degrees centigrade. They are pressed while still frozen and the ice or water content removed to leave a concentrated juice that is high in sugar and acidity. Another popular specialty is the so-called "Weissherbst", which is a rosé wine made from Pinot Noir or other red varieties.

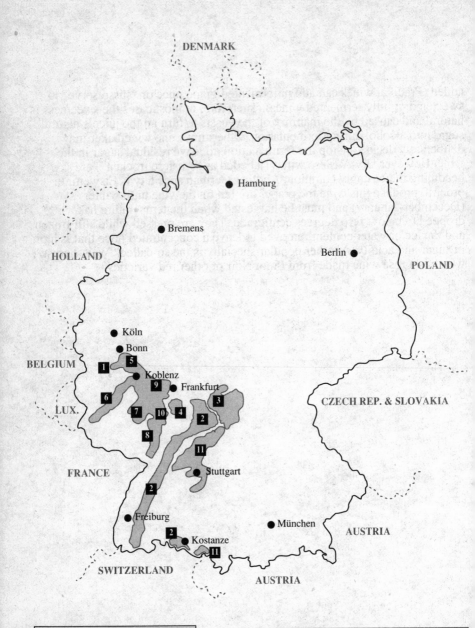

DENMARK

● Hamburg

● Bremens

HOLLAND

● Berlin

POLAND

● Köln

● Bonn

BELGIUM

5

1

Koblenz

9

● Frankfurt

6

3

CZECH REP. & SLOVAKIA

LUX.

7

10

4

2

FRANCE

8

11

2

Stuttgart

2

● Freiburg

● München

2

Kostanze

11

AUSTRIA

SWITZERLAND

AUSTRIA

1	Ahr
2	Baden
3	Franken
4	Hessische Bergstrasse
5	Mittelrhein
6	Mosel - Saar - Ruwer
7	Nahe
8	Pfalz
9	Rheingau
10	Rheinhessen
11	Württemberg

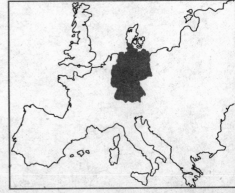

Ahr

The Ahr is a small wine region that is well-known in Germany for its red wines. It lies to the south of Bonn but belongs to the Federal State of Rheinland-Pfalz and is, thus, Germany's most northerly wine-growing area with less than 400 hectares of vineyard. The vines grow on often steep slopes along the Ahr. This small tributary river originates in the Eifel, meanders down through the upper Hohen Venn valley and finally runs into the Rhine river near Remagen. The slatey soils in the sometimes minute terraces are able to accumulate enough warmth to ripen grapes even at this northerly latitude. Pinot Noir (known as Spätburgunder) is the most common variety (40%). The typical Ahr wine from this grape is light red, velvety and low in tannin, often made in an off-dry style with residual sugar. As a red wine model, this type of wine has influenced a whole generation of wine drinkers and is still the dominating style along the Ahr. It is part of the folklore of this beautiful region with its picturesque, timbered buildings, though rather spoilt by tourists who are far from discerning when it comes to wine.

Nevertheless, there are a handful of growers who are determined to show that Ahr Pinot Noir has far greater potential than that which has been realised to date, that it is capable of producing more firmly structured, noble, in short, better wines than in the past (or, for that matter, the present).

Ahr's second most important variety (23%) is the red Portugieser and a little Riesling can also be found.

Weingut Adeneuer

Max-Planck-Strasse 8
Ahrweiler 5483
Tel. (02641) 34473
Fax (02641) 37379

Adeneuer's vineyards produce finely fruity Ahr wines which excel with their fruit and spice even in their youth. Marc Adeneuer justifies the very brief maturation period for his red wines with the comment: "customers snatch the bottles from our hands in spring." The 1991s were already bottled and on sale by March 1992 because all previous vintages were already sold out. Compared to the very good 1990s, as well as to the preceeding good vintages like 1989 and 1988, the 1991s leave much to be desired, being rather light and lacking body and the usual fine fruit which is typical of Adeneuer's vineyards. This 0.75 ha-estate has the exclusive ownership of the best vineyard along the Ahr, the Walporzheimer Gärkammer, an extremely steep terraced site. In 1992 Marc, responsible for sales and wine-making, and Frank Adeneuer, who cares for the vineyards, bought barriques and began experimenting. Perhaps we will soon be able to taste very different Adeneuer wines, ones which are made less for quick sales and consumption and show more clearly the excellent potential of the estate.

Bachemer Karlskopf 🍇 ①
Frühburgunder QbA trocken 1991
Soft, warm climate strawberry fruit, still a little wild; rosé style red wine from an old specialty varietal.

Neuenahrer Spätbugunder 🍇 ①
QbA trocken 1991
An excellent cuvée made of grapes from several small sites; a product with many nuances, body and tight structure - the vintage's best QbA.

Walporzheimer Gärkammer 🍇 ④
Spätburgunder Trockenbeerenauslese 1989
A rarity and specialty: concentrated, raisiny with cocoa and coffee aromas and a very interesting, spicy interplay between sweetness and acidity. An aperitif wine.

Staatliche Weinbaudomäne Marienthal

Walporzheimer Strasse 48
Bad Neuenahr-Ahrweiler 5483
Tel. (02641) 3285
Fax (02641) 4014

Staatliche Weinbaudomäne is the only red wine producer in Rheinland-Pfalz and the largest wine estate in the Ahr. It is part of the experimental research institute for agriculture directed by Wolfgang Frisch who adamantly opposes aging in barrique (and the use of new oak) since he does not consider it "typical of the Ahr region." The wines match this attitude and are generally very traditional: mostly light colored, lacking tannin, often containing residual sugar, exactly as they should be. The vineyards are managed by Karl Peter Böll and the head winemaker is Lorenz Jakoby, originally from Mosel who has helped define the Ahr's typical style of wine, with its characteristically accentuated acidity. The wines only occasionally undergo malolactic fermentation, and in less ripe years they are deacidified with chalk. All wines, among them 62% Spätburgunder (Pinot Noir) as well as much lesser known experimental varieties are matured slowly; up to two years in cask and subsequently several years in bottle. Then they even make us sometimes forget how light weight they are compared to French Burgundies.

Marienthaler Klostergarten 🏵 ①
Spätburgunder Weissherbst trocken 1990
A succulent rosé, with accentuated acidity, not as pure and balanced as other vintages.

Marienthaler Klostergarten 🍇 ②
Spätburgunder Kabinett trocken 1987
A light red wine and thus a typical Ahr specialty; rounded off by light sweetness.

Weingut Meyer-Näkel

Friedensstrasse 15
5487 Dernau
Tel/Fax (02643) 3363

Werner Näkel, formerly a mathematics and physical education teacher, retired over ten years ago to concentrate on his parents small red wine estate. The vineyard modernization or "Flurbereinigung" which took place in Dernau, and the increasing demand for red German wines were two factors which suddenly opened up new economic opportunities. Since then, he has searched for ways to produce alternatives to the typical red wine style with courageous and innovative impartiality. The region's often pale red tending to brown colored wines, lacking in tannin, were not to the taste of this athletically-built youngster, who wanted his wines to have colour and grip. He wanted to prove that the Ahr can produce 'real' red wines. To this end, he has reduced yields in recent years to 30-40 hl/ha and prolonged skin contact during fermentation. "Tannin should be regarded as a spice," he says. He reduced the bitter tannin in his wines by de-stemming a greater percentage of the grape bunches. 25% of the blend has been barrique aged, though the experimentation phase has not been completed. There are still noticeable variations between one wine and another. Nevertheless, there can be no doubt that from the great 1990 vintage and from the Ahr's heat-retaining, slatey soils he has produced one of Germany's most exciting Spätburgunders (Pinot Noir).

Dernauer Pfarrwingert 🍇🍇 ③
Spätburgunder Auslese trocken 1990
Spätburgunder Auslese trocken 1990
Differing from the S cuvée for which ripe and botrytized grapes are used: well-structured and long, ripe but with fine acidity.

Meyer-Näkel S 🍇 ③
Spätburgunder QbA trocken 1990
Aged in Allier oak, half new and half used. Cherry and vanilla aromas, succulent tannin, stylish.

Spätburgunder Sekt Extra Brut 1989 🍇 ③
Although made without dosage this sekt has a pronounced raspberry-cherry fruitiness: as a red Ahr sparkling wine a rarity and specialty at the same time.

Bad Neuenahrer Sonnenberg 1988 🍇 ④
Spätburgunder Beerenauslese trocken
Actually an aperitif wine with 15° alcohol, aged in new barriques, with concentrated raisin aromas and an incredible concentration of spice, chocolate and wild herb aromas.

Baden

Baden, like Württemberg, is a very individual region. Its wine traditions differ sharply from other regions and are often more influenced by Alsace than other parts of Germany. As a result, more dry wines are produced and the tradition of making nobly sweet Beeren-Auslesen is less widespread than elsewhere in Germany.
Red wine is traditionally very important and accounts for 25% of production. Being the most southerly of all German wine regions, it produces relatively full bodied reds, especially from vineyards around the Kaiserstuhl, which are more reminiscent of Burgundy than the reds of the Ahr. The same is also true of the whites. Despite being made from the same varieties found all over Germany, they produce very different wines compared to the Mosel or Rhine. Riesling lacks the high acidity, Pinot Blanc (Weissburgunder) and Pinot Gris (Ruländer or Grauburgunder) are more vigorous than those grown elsewhere, though the latter has lost favor among consumers, being often a very unctuous, 12° alc., lightly sweet wine. The same is true of Sylvaner and Müller-Thurgau, the latter being Baden's most common, though certainly not its most prestigious variety. It is occasionally called Rivaner and, in this case, is usually barrique-aged. Baden also has its own specialties. The white Gutedel, usually labelled as a varietal, is a typical quaffing wine unlikely to be found elsewhere, being confined mainly to Markgräfler Land, which stretches from just south of Freiburg to the Swiss-German border at Basel. Perhaps the region's most popular wine, it is usually served from a pitcher or sold in liter bottles.
As a wine-growing region Baden is far from uniform. It is a vast and scattered region reaching as far as the Tauber, a tributary of the Main, and on down to Lake Constance (or Bodensee). Wines from its most northerly tip are similar to those of Franken (Franconia) and are allowed to be filled in the typical broad-bellied Franconian bottle under the appellation "Badisches Frankenland." The area around Kraichgau to the south of Heidelberg produces light, fresh wines which, in turn, are very different to those of Ortenau and Kaiserstuhl-Tuniberg, often regarded as the best in all Baden. Baden-Baden Ortenau's eroded granite soils produce very delicate Rieslings (known locally as Klingenberger) and soft Pinot Gris (Grauburgunder). Kaiserstuhl's vineyards are the warmest in Germany and Burgundian varieties have become their specialties. Pinots Blanc and Gris are very fine, as is the often rich and deep Pinot Noir (Spätburgunder). Kaiserstuhl is a group of hills which tower above the Rhine with differing soil compositions (black basalt, loess and granite), on which Riesling, Sylvaner and Traminer (known locally as Clevner) excel.
Markgräfler Land adjoins Kaiserstuhl to the south and produces Müller-Thurgau and Gutedel.
The cooperative movement is also a typical, strong Baden tradition although the top wines still come from private wineries. Nevertheless, there are numerous small and medium sized cooperatives, occasionally even better run than private estates. The Central Cellar of Baden Cooperatives (Zentralkellerei der Badischen Winzergenossenschaften) at Breisach is the largest cooperative in Europe and has set very high standards for Baden's premium table wine industry. They fill 50 million bottles of characterful, clean Grauburgunder alone, which has nothing in common with the traditional Ruländer (both synonyms for Pinot Gris).

Weingut Bercher

Mittelstadt 13
Vogtsburg-Burckheim 7818
Tel. (07662) 6066
Fax (07662) 8279

Rainer Bercher is serious, but when it comes to his Spätburgunders (Pinot Noirs), he always utters the same sentiments. "There's music in there." In saying this he is mainly thinking of his excellent Spätburgunder from a low-yielding vineyard, aged in Nevers oak barriques and labelled as Selektionswein. It is a bright red, lightly tannic and fruity-dry wine which lingers long on the palate. His are among the best red wines in Baden. In good vintages he also makes Selektionsweine from Pinot Blanc (Weissburgunder) and Pinot Gris (Grauburgunder) which are matured in small casks. However, their top wines from the superb 1990 vintage were Riesling Spätlese and a very fine Muskateller Spätlese. According to Rainer Bercher (who runs the 17 ha estate together with his brother Eckhardt) the 1991s are "at least a step lower." Nevertheless, the Berchers have made the best of this vintage and produced very nice Kabinett wines from Scheurebe, Gewürztraminer and Spätburgunder, even though, strictly speaking, they are of Spätlese level.

Burkheimer Feuerberg 🍷 ①
Weisser Burgunder Kabinett trocken 1991
Weisser Burgunder Kabinett trocken 1991
This vintage's most concentrated white, with finesse in its soft fruit, and mild acidity.

Burkheimer Schlossgarten 🍷 ①
Riesling Kabinett trocken 1990
Delicate Riesling, with good backbone, delicately spicey bouquet and firm acidity. An extremely successful wine.

Burkheimer Feuerberg 🍷🍷 ③
Spätburgunder Spätlese trocken 1990
The estate's best red (Selection Exclusiv) and one of Baden's best 1990 red. Rich, tannic, matured in barrique and, thus, strongly influenced by new oak.

Weingut Fritz Blankenhorn

Baslerstrasse 2
Schliengen 7846
Tel. (07635) 1092
Fax (07635) 3856

Markgräflerland rarely produces wines as full and complex as those from Kaiserstuhl, situated farther north. They excel more by their soft, elegant aromas, and this is especially true of Blankenhorns' wines, made in a clear, clean style. Some drinkers may find them lacking body and weight, though winemaker Volker Mainz and owner Rosemarie Blankenhorn insist that the character of the wines is determined by nature. They come from 25 ha of vineyard on medium compact loess and clay soils around Schliengen planted with the light Gutedel, the classic Burgundy varieties plus a little Riesling, Muskateller, Gewürztraminer, Nobling and Müller-Thurgau. The excellent 1990 vintage produced unprecedented quality at all levels: a delicious, nutty Gutedel, very nice Spätlesen from Pinots Blanc and Gris, two Spätburgunder (Pinot Noir) Spätlesen from the Römerberg and Sonnenstück sites as well as a very fine Gewürztraminer Auslese. The 1991s are in comparison less impressive, being mainly of Kabinett level though are nevertheless among Markgräflerland's best.

Schliengener Sonnenstück 🍷 ①
Grauer Burgunder Kabinett trocken 1991
Supple and elegant with very fruity acidity though somewhat lacking the complexity and finesse of the Spätlese from the previous vintage.

Schliengener Sonnenstück 🍷 ②
Grauer Burgunder Spätlese trocken 1990
A rich, full-bodied wine with plenty of substance, a light, lemony scent and succulent fruit.

Schliengener Sonnenstück 🍷 ③
Spätburgunder Spätlese trocken 1990
Garnet red, delicately fruity on the nose, good concentration of aromas The best of this vintage's Spätlesen.

Weingut Hermann Dörflinger

Mühlenstrasse 7
Müllheim/Baden 7840
Tel. (07631) 2201
Fax (07631) 4195

At a time when people in Baden were still drinking unctuous, sweetish wines, Hermann Dörflinger was the only salvation for the few existing wine gourmets. As far back as the 1970s, he was already fully fermenting his wines without sweetening them with süssreserve (unfermented grape juice added as a sweetner). By doing so he made a name for himself as an uncompromising, fearless defender of dry wines with accentuated acidity. He still enjoys this reputation today and is now completely dedicated to making moderately modern wines in a Baden, or better still, Markgräfler style. At tastings there are often crowds eager to try his Gutedel, Pinot Blanc and Gris and by spring most of his wines are already sold out. He no longer has the unique status he used to enjoy as there are plenty of ambitious Baden producers making wines in a similar style. Many have become even more interested in new methods while Dörflinger has not changed. The wines are still good but no longer exceptional.

Müllheimer Pfaffenstück   🍇 ①
Gutedel QbA trocken 1991
This vintage's best Gutedel: clean, pure with a delicate peach aroma and mild acidity. A good food wine.

Müllheimer Reggenhegg   🍇 ②
Gewürztraminer Spätlese trocken 1991
Pure elixir to the nose, with the perfume of roses similar to those located at the entrance to the estate's courtyard. Rich in body and long.

Müllheimer Pfaffenstück   🍇 ③
Spätburgunder Auslese trocken 1990
Tartly fruity red, rich and unctuous with a bitter-sweet almond flavor. A well made, traditional style of wine.

Freiherr von und zu Franckenstein'sches Rentamt

Weingartenstrasse 66
Offenburg 7600
Tel. (0781) 34973
Fax (0781) 36046

The vineyard, located on the outskirts of Offenburg, belongs to Freiherr von und zu Franckenstein, and since 1985 has been leased to Hubert Doll, the former administrator. He tends the estate's 14 ha of vineyards, although his best wines all come from the vineyard of Zell-Weierbacher Abtsberg. Riesling, Spätburgunder, Müller-Thurgau, Pinot Gris, Pinot Blanc, Traminer and several other varietals grow in steep vineyards on warm and deep rocky, granite and gneiss soils. The Rieslings and Pinot Gris (Grauburgunder) are among Ortenau's best wines and 90% are vinified dry. Doll produces excellent table wines, especially in the Kabinett and Spätlese categories, characterized by fresh acidity and pure varietal flavors. Even in the great 1990 vintage the red Spätburgunder is a no-frills wine. The fruit dominates the oak, even though Doll cautiously ages a part of the wine in small oak casks (as he also does with the white Rivaner).

Zell-Weierbacher Abtsberg   🍇 ②
Grauburgunder Spätlese trocken 1990
Strong and full-bodied, with a light, almost candy-like fruit sweetness. Quite elegant thanks to its accentuated acidity.

Zell-Weierbacher Abtsberg   🍇 ①
Riesling Kabinett trocken 1990
Full yet light, relatively uncomplicated with a lively acidity.

Spätburgunder Spätlese trocken 1990 🍇 ③
Medium weight, elegant red wine. It has been aged for a while in barrique but is not too dominated by the oak.

Weingut Dr. Heger

Bachenstrasse19-21
Ihringen 7811
Tel. (07668) 205
Fax (07668) 9300

This estate's wines have improved since young Joachim Heger took over the management of the winery in 1981. It is difficult to find a first class German restaurant that does not list on its menu a Pinot Blanc, Pinot Gris, Silvaner or Riesling from the estate's finest vineyard, Winklerberg in Ihringen. The wines are all extremely polished, characterized by an elegant "gout de terroir," acidulously fresh and at the same time rich. Heger places great value on leaving his white wines at length on the lees and subsequent aging in tank rather than in wood. The 1991 vintage was extremely successful for whites. Heger earned his reputation (many consider him Baden's number one) with red Spätburgunder (Pinot Noir). In blind tastings his wines, in terms of finesse and structure, match great Pinot Noirs from Burgundy. In fact, the 1989 Spätburgunder Auslese is considered by some to be better than many famous French Pinots. All wines are aged at length in new or used barrique.

Ihringer Winklerberg 🍇 ②
Silvaner Spätlese trocken 1991
A fine, very distinguished wine with rather neutral fruit, very clean in style with accentuated, at first rather coarse acidity.

Ihringer Winklerberg 🍇🍇 ②
Weissburgunder Spätlese trocken 1991
Supple with a delicate mint bouquet, elegant with the fruit supported by lively acidity.

Ihringer Winklerberg 🍇🍇 ②
Grauburgunder Spätlese trocken 1990
Full and rich with very fine, deep, fruity aromas and supple due to the racy acidity.

Ihringer Winklerberg 🍷🍷 ③
Spätburgunder Rotwein Spätlese trocken 1990
Impressive due to finesse and weight; a wine which can stand up to many French red Burgundies.

Ihringer Winklerberg 🍷🍷🍷 ④
Spätburgunder Auslese* trocken 1990**
In the 1990 vintage, along with the late-harvest, Ihringer's vineyard of Winklerberg also produced two superb Auslesen of a quality not seen in Baden in the last 20 years. With specific must weight reaching the level of a Beeren-Auslese (112° and 115° Öchsle) and very healthy grapes, these wines confirm that Kaiserstuhl is a unique vineyard area capable of producing wines from Pinot Noir grapes which are full-bodied and long lasting as well as being fruity (some traditionally made Kaiserstuhl Spätburgunders from the 1962 vintage are still drinking well). Heger distinguishes the best wine from a selected harvest with three asterisks on the label. Deep red in color due to a 28 day fermentation on the skins and 16 months in French barriques. A wine still heavily masked by the oak that does not hide its fruit potential.

Weingut Albert Heitlinger

Am Mühlberg 1
Tiefenbach 7524
Tel. (07259) 1061
Fax (07259) 1876

In 1972 Eberhard Heitlinger took over the management of this winery from his father, a former butcher and gastronomist. He immediately put into practice the knowledge acquired at viticultural school, and for a few years rode on the so-called 'sweet wave.' He soon realized that this was not the right way forward and, in 1980, started reducing yields drastically and making the wines in a dry style, mainly Riesling, Pinot Blanc and Gris as well as red Spätburgunder (Pinot Noir). Success soon followed. His whites are supple with firm acidity, and he uses barrique for the Spätburgunder. To date, Heitlinger has been one of Baden's most innovative producers with a great love for experimentation and has developed a strong enthusiasm for the development of cuvées. Terms like Phonix, Tantris, Dialog and Allegro continue to replace the names of the vineyards. Tantris is used for particularly successful wines. Heitlinger's philosophy is very much based on that of the best Italian and French producers.

Tantris 🍇 ③
Riesling Spätlese trocken 1991
UConcentrated, racy Baden Riesling relatively light in body which immediately appeals to very demanding palates.

Weingut Albert Heitlinger 🍇 ①
Weissburgunder trocken 1991
Typical Pinot Blanc from Kraichgau's rainbow colored marl soil. It is clear, clean with good varietal flavors and not lacking in finesse.

Tantris 🍇 ③
Spätburgunder 1991
Very surprising depth, a dry red with firm, tightly knit structure and well dosed oak though no match to its predecessor.

Weingut Albert Heitlinger 🍇🍇 ③
Lemberger 1990
Heitlinger's finest red. It is skillfully aged in small oak barrels and bottled in elegant Futura bottles.

Weingut Reichsgraf und Marquis zu Hoensbroech

Hermannsberg
Angelbachtal-Michelfeld 6929
Tel. (07265) 381
Fax (07265) 7998

Rüdiger Graf von und zu Hoensbroech has a weakness for Pinot Blanc, a varietal rarely cultivated in Kraichgau which accounts for 30% of his vineyards (15 ha). The "Wein-Graf" (wine count) took a big risk with this varietal since Pinot Blanc is very sensitive to climate. Nevertheless, the experiment has been successful and his Pinot Blancs rank among the best examples of this variety in Baden. Like most of his wines, they are not light-weight but strong, full-bodied and rich on the palate, especially from the excellent 1990 vintage. After a period of study in Geisenheim, Hoensbroech moved to the Spanish Penedes in 1966 where he worked on two wine estates. He has made it his principle to interfere as little as possible in the wine-making process. He does not centrifuge and is against the practice of heating crushed red grapes before fermentation to extract color, de-acidification and, if possible, even fining. With Müller-Thurgau, Silvaner, Riesling, Gewürztraminer and Ruländer (Pinot Gris), as with Spätburgunder (Pinot Noir), he prefers aging in the bottle to bring forth the varietal character rather than cask aging. Only Schwarzriesling (Pinot Meunier) and Lemberger are aged in barriques.

Michelfelder Himmelberg 🍇 ①
Grauburgunder QbA trocken 1991
A vigorous wine, fruity and mellow with ripe acidity. Rich with plenty of bite and not at all heavy.

Michelfelder Himmelberg 🍇 ④
Weissburgunder Eiswein 1991
In 1991 Hoensbroech was also able to produce a small quantity of Eiswein, from Pinot Blanc, of course. Pure, sweet nectar, with an enormous volume of fruit.

Michelfelder Himmelberg 🍇 ①
Weissburgunder Kabinett trocken 1991
A fresh wine, made in stainless steel with light, candy-like fruit and lively acidity. Easy to drink.

Weingut Bernhard Huber

Heimbacher Weg 6
Malterdingen 7831
Tel. (07644) 1200
Fax (07644) 8222

Breisgau producers are often made fun of by their Kaiserstuhl colleagues. All agree that good sites down towards the Rhine are few and far between, though they forget Bienenberg, close to Malterdingen, with its shell-limestone soil and its wine-growing tradition going back 700 years. In the 14th century Cistercian monks of the Tennenbach Abbey were making red wine famous under the name 'Malterdinger', made primarily from Pinot Noir. Bernhard Huber has kept half his vineyard area planted with Spätburgunder and some Kaiserstuhl producers would lose their smirk if they tasted his concentrated wines with accentuated tannin and finesse. Huber's estate has been worked according to ecological principles since 1990 and produces other varietals such as Riesling, Muskateller, Müller-Thurgau and Auxerrois with excellent results. Huber also distills Schnaps and produces sparkling wines. In a beer factory's former freezer-room he personally carries out remuage for his Pinot Brut Extra.

Malterdinger Bienenberg ❦ ①
Muskateller Kabinett trocken 1991
Concentrated, complex Muskateller due to low yields, characterized by a delicate aroma of roses. Ideal as an aperitif.

Malterdinger Bienenberg ❦ ②
Riesling Spätlese trocken 1990
A very rich wine with delicate, though not racy acidity. A rather soft Baden Riesling but with plenty of substance.

Malterer 1990 ❦ ③
Made from 60% Pinot Blanc and 40% Freisamer, aged for eight months in barrique. A little broad on the palate but otherwise very successful. Rather like a dry Auslese in character..

Malterdinger Bienenberg ❦ ③
Spätburgunder Spätlese trocken 1990
A superb red wine with a very strong berry fruit character and a light aroma of oak on the nose.

Schlossgut Istein

Efringen-Kirchen 7859
Tel. (07628) 1284
Fax (07628) 8632

Schlossgut Istein is the wine estate owned by the district council of Lörrach in Germany's south-westerly corner near the Swiss border. Albert Soder has held the lease on it since 1977 and has since made Istein one of Baden's leading wine estates. However, his aim is not to produce the usual easy drinking wines. Soder is an uncompromising supporter of dry wines. Whether it be the local Gutedel, the typical Baden Burgundy varieties, Riesling, Sylvaner, Nobling or Gewürztraminer, his wines are always full of character, rich and a pleasure to drink. They are made and matured in stainless steel to preserve their freshness and accentuated varietal character. The red Spätburgunder (Pinot Noir) is aged in casks, which have recently been renewed. 1990 produced numerous Spätlesen and Auslesen, among which is a Riesling Auslese of a quality never seen before in these parts, plus an excellent Spätburgunder Auslese. However, 1991 is in some ways the more interesting vintage at Istein, as the wines have turned out more elegant and lighter. Chardonnay is a recent introduction, planted in 1989 to replace Müller-Thurgau and has already produced 1,000 bottles of full, racy wine.

Isteiner Kirchberg ❦ ②
Riesling Kabinett trocken 1991
A rather acidulous, medium-fruity, singular wine which seems to reflect the calcareous soils at Istein.

Isteiner Kirchberg ❦ ②
Weisser Burgunder Kabinett trocken 1991
A pleasant, easy drinking wine with lively acidity and soft aromas of sweet fruit which make up for the lack of depth.

Isteiner Kirchberg 🍇 ④
Spätburgunder Auslese trocken 1990
This vineyard's top red from this vintage. It is a powerful, opulent Pinot Noir with masses of tannin while, at the same time, velvety soft on the palate with good length.

Weingut Karl Heinz Johner

Gartenstrasse 20
Vogtsburg-Bischoffingen 8718
Tel. (07662) 6041
Fax (07662) 8380

These wines have for long been highly regarded in England, though the Germans have only recently discovered them. Everything about Karl Heinz Johner's winery is unique. He is the only German producer who makes a rule of aging all of his wines in barrique and markets them as "tafelwein" without any indication of region of origin. This may explain the publicity Johner has received over the last five years. In 1980 he inherited three ha of vines and began life as a wine-grower. His ascent from nowhere to become one of Baden's main producers is the result of hard work, an iron will to produce top quality, the patient buying up of good vineyards throughout Kaiserstuhl and constant, productive dissatisfaction. Johner endeavours to make contact with top Burgundy producers, travels to Italy and California and is constantly trying out new wine-making methods. His assortment of 1990 wines is impressive, with the two red Spätburgunders (Pinot Noirs) in the lead. 1991 yielded lighter white wines (he rejected Grauburgunder or Pinot Gris). However, the 1991 Spätburgunders are surprisingly good, not far behind the 1990s.

Rivaner Tafelwein trocken 1991 ☸ ②
Fresh, fruity Müller-Thurgau, not too broad nor exuberant in the bouquet, fermented in barrique.

Grauer Burgunder ☸☸ ②
Tafelwein trocken 1990
Johner's first Pinot Gris and an immediate hit. Vigorous and sinewy at the same time, a wine with excellent potential..

Weisser Burgunder ☸☸ ③
Tafelwein trocken 1990
A very stylish wine with delicate fruity aromas that are not overpowered by sweet oak. Great finesse.

Blauer Spätburgunder ♥♥ ③
Tafelwein trocken 1990
One of Baden's finest reds. Medium weight yet very fine with carefully dosed oak, soft tannins and typical Pinot Noir aromas. The subsequent vintage promises even more.

Winzergenossenschaft Königschaffhausen

Kiechlinsberger Strasse 2-6
Endingen-Königschaffhausen 7833
Tel. (07642) 1003
Fax (07642) 2535

This cooperative can look back upon 1,000 years of history. Today, however, under the direction of Willi Merkle, it is focusing more on innovation than on tradition. This entails harvesting the grapes considerably earlier than in the past. The grapes are selected according to acidity and healthiness as well as to the usual sugar level. Then there is wine-making technology which includes maturation in stainless steel for whites to avoid contact with the air on the one hand and cask aging for reds on the other. In this way the Königschaffhausen cooperative has managed to take its place among the elite of Baden's wine producers. The vineyard area of around 160 ha is planted mainly with Müller-Thurgau, Pinot Noir and Pinot Gris while a little Pinot Blanc, Gewürztraminer and Riesling enriches the assortment (altogether 1.2 million bottles). 1990 was a great vintage matched only by 1964 and 1961 for Pinot Noir. "Each single berry was perfectly, deeply colored," says winemaker Helmut Staiblin. Grau- and Weiss-Burgunder (Pinots Gris and Blanc) produced from 20 year old vines and partly matured in barrique are close behind marketed as "Selektionsweine". The 1991s though very good, are well behind the 1990s.

Grauer Burgunder ☸ ②
Tafelwein trocken 1990
The vintage's finest white in terms of richness also outstanding for its finesse. Aged in barrique

Weisser Burgunder ☸ ②
Tafelwein trocken 1990
After the over-oaked 1989 the 1990 was also matured in small oak casks but the results are better, as the oak flavor is much less dominant.

Königschaffhauser Steingrüble ♥ ②
Spätburgunder Spätlese trocken 1990
The more simple version of the red Spätburgunder from the great 1990 vintage matured in traditional casks: excellent quality a a super price.

Königschaffhauser Steingrüble ♥♥ ③
Spätburgunder Spätlese trocken ** 1990
This "Selektionswein" is the best red which has ever left the cooperative's cellar doors. Intense color, masses of tannin with an accentuated oak flavor (barrique) but with plenty of fruit to match

Weingut Heinrich Männle

Sendelbach 16
Durbach 7061
Tel. (0781) 41101
Fax (0781) 440105

Heinrich Männle is no longer the youngest producer in Durbach and certainly not the only one called Männle. To differentiate him from others of the same name, he is known in Durbach as "Rotwein-Männle." Pinot Noir accounts for 38% of his five hectare estate, and the wines it produces are highly regarded as food wines in Baden's restaurants. They are matured in large oak casks as are his Weiss- and Grau-Burgunders (Pinots Blanc and Gris), while the more aromatic varieties are made and matured in stainless steel to preserve their varietal aromas. In addition, only half his production is made in a dry style. Männle aims at wines high up on the 'quality wines of distinction' scale, especially Auslesen and Beeren-Auslesen and his bottles have won numerous medals. He is fully aware of the fact that he missed out on the trend towards dry white wines and barrique-aging for reds. However, it bothers him just as little as the complaints he received after using the tin foil capsules on his bottles for advertising holiday flats that is until a hotel owner threatened to stop selling the wines.

Durbacher Kochberg ♛ ②
Scheurebe Spätlese trocken 1990
A rare wine in Baden, nevertheless of excellent quality, rich with a cassis and paprika flavor, reminiscent of Sauvignon Blanc.

Durbacher Kochberg ♛ ②
Weissburgunder Spätlese trocken 1990
Opulent, almost bursting with fruit and fruity acidity. It has an enormous richness which slightly detracts from its finesse.

Durbacher Kochberg ♛ ②
Spätburgunder Spätlese trocken 1990
Dark colored, meaty red wine with good body and characterised by ripe, warm fruit aromas.

Weingut Emil Marget

Schlossgartenstrasse 4
Müllheim Hügelheim 7840
Tel. (07631) 2354

Emil Marget's Gutedel has been a favorite in Freiburg's wine bars for decades, though the wine still remains a regional insider's tip. This is due to the fact that the name Marget in Baden stands for completely dry wines and he makes a rule of not using "süssreserve" or unfermented grape juice used in Germany for sweetening. His wines are known for their digestibility, as he has always placed importance on using very little sulphur and maturing the wines in cask. Another of Marget's specialties, and of Markgräflerland in general, is the Nobling variety, Freiburg's traditional 'students wine.' The estate has produced it in a good, wine bar quality. He also grows Pinot Blanc and Pinot Noir, all according to ecological principles. The estate is run by Klaus Marget, the administrator, and his nephew, Rheinhard Marget, who is in charge of wine-making. Due to differences of opinion, Rheinhard is unable to introduce the innovations in red wine vinification he would like. Barrique-aging has been only cautiously practiced to date. This is a shame, as Marget's Spätburgunders are rich and have a great concentration of fruit.

Hügelheimer Schlossgarten ♛ ①
Gutedel QbA trocken 1991
Light, moderately fruity with mild acidity, a refreshing and uncomplicated, easy-drinking wine which is extremely popular locally.

Hügelheimer Gottesacker ♛ ②
Ruländer Spätlese trocken 1990
The Margets still call their Pinot Gris "Ruländer" instead of Grauburgunder. This is a selection made from 25 year old vines with lengthy aging in wooden barrels, yielding an old fashioned but interesting wine.

Hügelheimer Höllbergcken ♛ ④
Spätburgunder Auslese trocken 1990
An enormously concentrated wine, having spent a year in large casks plus three weeks in barriques. Already very advanced in maturity.

Weingut Gebrüder Müller

Richard-Müller-Strasse 5
Breisach 7814
Tel. (07667) 7511
Fax (07667) 8370

Since 1825 this estate has exported Kaiserstuhl wines throughout the world, especially to England and the USA. It has been doing well since the early 1980s with some very interesting wines produced from Riesling, Pinot Blanc, Pinot Gris as well as Pinot Noir. The five and a half hectare vineyard is located in Ihringen (Winklerberg) and Breisach (Eckhartsberg). In 1988 the estate was inherited by Peter Bercher. As he was kept very busy by his carpet factory at Breisach, he engaged Hans Jörg Lang as winemaker. Lang is on his way to placing the estate alongside Baden's elite. 1990 is the proof. Pinots Blanc and Gris (Weiss- and Grau-Burgunder) are the highlights, against which the Riesling has no chance of competing. They are opulent and almost bursting with fruit while in 1991 the tables were turned, with elegant, racy Rieslings far outstripping the two Burgundian varieties. The 1990 Pinot Noir (Spätburgunder), aged half in traditional casks and half in barrique, is unbeatable, though the 1991 is also very successful.

Breisacher Eckartsberg 🍇 ①
Grauer Burgunder Kabinett trocken 1990
A delicate wine, almost as if drawn fresh straight from the yeasts with lively, fruity acidity, very full and well balanced..

Breisacher Eckartsberg 🍇 ②
Weisser Burgunder Spätlese trocken 1990
Full and fleshy with ripe fruity aromas, extremely mellow and almost fat in style.

Ihringer Winklerberg 🍇🍇 ③
Spätburgunder Spätlese trocken 1990
Barrel No. 21 is a very meaty wine with deep, berry fruit and soft Burgundian spiciness, medium weight and plenty of soft, warm mellowness.

Weingut Salwey

Hauptstrasse 2
Vogtsburg-Oberrotweil 7818
Tel. (07662) 384
Fax (07634) 6340

Wolf-Dietrich Salwey is one of the Kaiserstuhl producers who in terms of viticulture and wine-making took a new direction long ago when others were still arguing the pros and cons. In doing so, he set high standards. His aim is to produce clean wines with pure varietal flavors that reflect the various soils at Oberrotweil and Glottertal. Pinot Blanc and Gris, ranging from delicate to opulent, depending on vintage and, of course, always vinified dry, are extremely popular classics. The Weissherbst, a rosé from the Glottertal vineyard, can justly be included among Baden's best wines of this kind. A sinewy Riesling, a slim Silvaner, Müller-Thurgau, Muskateller and every now and again a superb Gewürztraminer complete this winery's range. The heart of Salwey's production is, however, red Spätburgunder (Pinot Noir). Conceived as a wine with accentuated tannin, he tries for more volume and weight for balance, while the fruit is supported by the sweet flavor of young Swabian oak (the straight forward Spätburgunder version is matured in traditional oak casks). In addition Salwey distills very fine Schnaps from lees and grapeskins, as well as fruit brandies.

Oberrotweiler Kirchberg 🍇 ②
Riesling Kabinett trocken 1991
Definitely the winery's best white from his 1991 assortment. Racy, rich, fresh and 'spritzig' and very elegant.

Oberrotweiler Henkenberg 🍇 ①
Weissburgunder QbA trocken 1991
Remarkably fresh, with pure varietal flavor and mouth-watering acidity. A masterpiece given such a difficult vintage.

Oberrotweiler Henkenberg 🍇 ③
Grauburgunder Spätlese trocken 1990
Yet another wine of great class from Salwey. The 1990 is truly exquisite, subtly spiced with great richness and a lively acidity.

Oberrotweiler Kirchberg 🍇🍇 ③
Spätburgunder Spätlese trocken 1990
The best red that Salwey has ever made, very rich, full-bodied, not too oaky in spite of barrique-aging but still needs time.

Weingut Hartmut Schlumberger

Weinstrasse 19
Sulzburg-Laufen 7811
Tel. (07634) 8992
Fax (07634) 8255

Hartmut Schlumberger is one of Baden's most unique, single-minded producers. Not only has he managed his vineyards according to ecological principles since the 1950s, but he has managed to maintain a particular, unmistakable character and style. All of his wines are dry with lively acidity, and captivatingly fruity with pure varietal aromas. His most typical wine is the Gutedel, a delicate and light, easy drinking "zechwein" (tavern wine) that is often sold in one liter bottles and accounts for 40% of his total production. The more noble whites are Riesling and Pinots Gris and Blanc (Grau- and Weiss-Burgunder). In 1991 they yielded surprisingly good wines. 1990 was an exceptionally good vintage for the Schlumbergers and produced rich, unctuous Spätlesen. Their top wines are the Spätburgunders (Pinot Noirs), aged partly in traditional casks and partly in barrique and the bottles are decorated with arty labels. The 1991 Spätburgunders are also extremely successful thanks to a scrupulous reduction of yields in the vineyard. Schlumberger is also known in the region for his Pinot Noir marc and brandies made from apple, pear, yellow plum, cherry and blackberry. §

Grauburgunder   ☆ ①
Spätlese trocken 1991
The top white from this vintage. Mouth-filling, almost opulent, scented like a basket full of ripe fruit and very long on the finish.

Gutedel QbA 1991   ☆ ①
Fresh, uncomplicated, with an aroma reminiscent of gooseberry. Mouth-filling with mild acidity. A thirst-quencher.

Spätburgunder Spätlese trocken 1990 ❦ ③
The top red wine of this incredible vintage, very full, laden with aromas. Complex on the nose in spite of barrique aging, long and fruity.

Weingut Reinhold Schneider

Königschaffhausener Strasse 2
Endingen 7833
Tel. (07642) 5278

Reinhold and Cornelia Schneider only became true wine producers at the beginning of the 1980s, when they sold their cattle and gave up fruit growing to grow vines and make wine. The change over was difficult, but they have never regretted it. Today, their seven hectare estate at the foot of the Kaiserstuhl produces very expressive white wines as well as characterful Spätburgunder (Pinot Noir). Although the Schneiders are from an agricultural background, they describe their wines as modern and hardly rustic in character. The whites are made in stainless steel tanks to protect them from oxidation, and the best results are almost always obtained from Pinots Blanc and Gris (Weiss- and Grau-Burgunder) together with Riesling. The red Spätburgunder is matured partly in traditional casks and partly in barriques made of Baden oak from the Wildtal valley. The vineyard is a small, notorious and excellent red wine site with sandy loess soils on the Endinger Engelsberg hill, traditionally known as "Diel". They have also focussed on a new crossing called Dornfelder and would also like to show what can be done with Elbling. They have recently begun making bottle fermented sparkling wine from the Muskateller grape, their six children being in charge of the remuage.

Ruländer Kabinett trocken 1991   ☆ ①
A young wine which still needs time, delicate with firm acidity. Ruländer is the old name for Pinot Gris.

Weisser Burgunder   ☆ ①
Kabinett trocken 1991
A full-bodied, very singular wine with fruit aromas but still has a few rough edges and needs time to develop.

Spätburgunder Spätlese trocken 1990 ❦ ③
Dark ruby-red with an exotic bouquet. Plenty of depth, a complex and muscular red from the Diel site, aged in traditional casks.

Weingut Schwarzer Adler

Badbergstrasse 23
Vogtsburg-Oberbergen 7818
Tel. (07662) 715

Franz Keller, the growling Kaiserstuhl gastronomist, had Germans holding their breath for years with his criticism and controversial views. He had no qualms when it came to defending fully fermented, dry wines at a time when most German wines were made sweet and became a cult figure of the new type of German wine. The fact that he confused Baden's situation with that of other German wine-growing regions, and that in Baden some of his wine-producing colleagues were even less compromising, should not detract from his achievements. The best advertisement for his ideas have always been his own wines. Today, his son, Fritz Keller, runs the estate, and the wines are still among the most widely distributed German wines in restaurants. Under his direction they have improved in finesse and style. The 1990 vintage has yielded their greatest wines since 1959, especially Spätburgunder (Pinot Noir), and also Weiss- and Grau-Burgunder (Pinots Blanc and Gris) which Keller describes as enormously rich, combined with a high acidity. The 1991s are lighter, though not thin, with an appealing fruitiness and fine acidity.

Oberbergener Bassgeige   🍇 ②
Silvaner QbA trocken 1991
Succulent, solid, clean and linear, delicately fruity yet full in body.

Oberbergener Pulverbuck   🍇 ②
Weissburgunder QbA trocken 1991
Extremely delicate and especially appealing due to its racy acidity and accentuated fruit.

Grauburgunder Selektion A 1990 🍇🍇 ④
An excellent Auslese (hence the A) with opulent, fine berry fruit and great richness. Barrique aged.

Weissburgunder Selektion S 1990 🍇🍇 ③
A fabulous Spätlese saturated with complex fruit and accentuated acidity (8.4 g/lt), harmonious with the barrique oak well integrated.

Spätburgunder Rotwein 1990   🍇 ③
This barrique aged Spätburgunder is the estate's best red wine, concentrated with accentuated tannin and very, very refined.

Weingut Rudolf Stigler

Ihringen 7817
Tel. (07668) 297

This is a conservative estate with an unusually high percentage of Riesling. Rudolf Stigler, together with his son and winemaker Andreas, are cautious when it comes to following fashion and are equally cautious in following new trends. They are enthusiastic traditionalists, maturing their wine in large casks. Over two thirds of their wines are given this treatment, especially those of the Qualitätswein mit Prädikat (QmP) category. Only normal QbA or light Kabinett wines are made and matured in stainless steel tanks. The Stiglers are also enthusiasts of long aging and, consequently, their Riesling Spätlesen from the Ihringer Winklerberg vineyard (this estate owns the largest part of this top site) never leave cask until they are at least two years old and are never released until ready for drinking. Their red Spätburgunders (Pinot Noirs) are, of course, always made dry, but their nobly sweet Beeren-Auslesen and Trocken-Beeren-Auslesen are also excellent. For some time now their only concession to modern trends has been the introduction of Chardonnay. As it is not a 'recommended' variety in Baden, only few visitors are privileged to taste it in the cellar - it's delicious!

Ihringer Winklerberg   🍇 ①
Grauburgunder Spätlese trocken 1990
Mellow, very soft, and with great richness which flows over the palate like velvet. Good aging potential.

Ihringer Winklerberg   🍇 ②
Weissburgunder Spätlese trocken 1990
A very rich and complex wine which needs plenty of time to develop. Very impressive.

Ihringer Winklerberg   🍇 ②
Riesling Spätlese trocken 1989
Delicate and very fruity Baden-style Riesling round and ready to drink, though still with great aging potential.

Ihringer Winklerberg   🍇 ③
Spätburgunder Spätlese trocken 1989
Medium-weight, fruity red with fine tannin, aged in the traditional way in large casks.

Gräflich Wolff-Metternich'sches Weingut

Grol 4
Durbach 7601
Tel. (0781) 42779

One of Baden's few Riesling estates with over 36 ha of vineyard, one third of which is planted with Riesling, known locally in the Ortenau district as Klingelberger. Thanks to first class sites at Durbach and Oberkirch this variety, together with Spätburgunder (Pinot Noir), traditionally produce the very best wines. Ottmar Schilli, the administrator, belongs to the 'old guard' among Baden's winemakers. He continues to mature the wine in small casks and indicates cask and bottle numbers on the labels. In addition, 60% of the wines are dry. Schilli aims at a late-harvest and a high proportion of wines are at the Qualitätswein mit Prädikat (QmP) level. Many bottles also bear medals and other awards, though unfortunately their contents do not always live up to the promise on the packaging. The wines are often very broad and obtrusive in bouquet. At least among the lighter wines one could wish for a cleaner, longer lasting style. Nevertheless, the nobly sweet dessert wines are superb.

Durbacher Schloss Grohl ☙ ①
Riesling Kabinett trocken 1991
From the steep slopes at Durbach Castle. A simple, clear Riesling with a lively interplay between fruit and acidity.

Lahrer Herrentisch ☙ ①
Weisser Burgunder QbA trocken 1991
An elegant and delicate wine with good structure and refined, vinous acidity.

Durbacher Schlossberg ☙ ☙ ②
Riesling Spätlese trocken 1990
Excellent Riesling with perfect balance of acidity, very complex and lively.

Durbacher Schloss Grohl ☙ ☙ ④
Weisser Sauvignon Beerenauslese 1990
Rare Beerenauslese in Baden, enormously rich with strong acidity, and fantastic fruit, aged in barrique.

Durbacher Schlossberg ☙ ☙ ④
Spätburgunder Auslese trocken 1990
This vintage's best red, soft and warm on the palate, powerful richness, elegant in style and character.

Franken

Franken's wines were first made famous by the typical broad-bellied "Bocksbeutel" bottle in which they are filled. This unmistakable container first appeared in the 13th century and has become the trademark of Franken's wine industry. Now the region is privileged in being the only one in Germany allowed to use it. Of course the bottle is not the only factor which has contributed to its fame, as Franken's wines are among the absolute best of Germany's elite class. Although they are made from the same varieties found all over Germany, the soils and relatively northerly position of the growing area leave a very strong imprint. 96% of the wines are white, 4% red. Franken lies on the Main river and is fairly fragmented, with wine-growing carried on in special microclimates. The western limits are at Aschaffenburg, only a few kilometres from where the Rheingau begins. In the east, the vineyards penetrate deep into the Steigerwald forest, while its northern limits are on the heights of the Rhön near Hörstein. To the south it adjoins Baden.
The greatly differing geographic characteristics are reflected in the very varying styles of wine. The region's centre in the Main river 'square' at Würzburg has dry, shelly, calcareous soils which produce elegant wines. In the Steigerwald forest heavier, red marl soils are prevalent, and the wines are more vigorous. To the west, the soils consist of colored sandstone which are especially suitable for red wines. Finally, around Aschaffenburg there is a small island of primary rock soils which bring forth soft wines rich in extract. Although Müller Thurgau is the most widely planted vine, Sylvaner is Franken's typical variety. Its earthy, fruity-neutral aroma has made it the emblem of Franken's wine culture. However, the very finest wines come from the Riesling grape, though it can only be grown in very few sites due to its demanding and late-ripening nature. Rieslaner (a Sylvaner-Riesling crossing) produces good quality, though seldom matches Riesling's finesse. Numerous other supplementary varieties are also grown, such as Kerner, Scheurebe, Bacchus and Pinot Gris, while Pinot Blanc and, in places, Chardonnay are also on the increase.
Along with Baden and Württemberg, Franken has a long tradition of making dry wines. Just under 90% of all Bocksbeutel wines are dry, and it is interesting to note that in Franconia 'dry' means less than four grams of residual sugar, while elsewhere in Germany the limit is nine g/lt. Thus, a dry Franken wine has had all its sugar fermented out to dryness. Franconian wine-growers use the term "Fränkisch trocken" with pride.

Bürgerspital zum Heiligen geist

Theaterstrasse 19
Würzburg 8700
Tel. (0931) 35030
Fax (0931) 3503444

If there is one thing the Bürgerspital has not been lacking in recent years it is praise. It is regarded as N° 1 in Franken and its wines as being able to stand on their own on an international level. Be that as it may, they are first and foremost Franken wines. Secondly, they are not the usual light, 'modern' wines but powerful and fat and not immediately appealing, being long-lasting, only justifying their reputation after five or ten years - sometimes never. There is no other wine estate of this size in Germany which, for so many years, has brought forth so many superb wines as the Bürgerspital. They include mouth-filling, neutrally-earthy and, nevertheless, soft Sylvaners as well as superb Rieslings with more meat on their bones than those of the Mosel or Rhine. Especially when made in an off-dry style, they can have the richness of Chardonnay. Then there are deeply fruity Pinot Blancs (Weissburgunder) which, on occasions can even outstrip Riesling. When it comes to nobly sweet Beeren-Auslesen and Trockenbeeren-Auslesen even Chateau d'Yquem has little change of competing, at least not during the first 25 years. And, in spite of all this, a civil servant is in charge, though not the usual kind: Rudolf Freiss.

Würzburger Abtsleite 🍇🍇 ③
Riesling Spätlese trocken 1991
Bürgerspital's class is expressed in the fact that in the difficult 1991 vintage more Spätlese than Kabinett wines were made. Among dry wines this is the absolute top of the 1991s.

Würzburger Stein 🍇 ①
Silvaner QbA trocken 1991
A classic, earthy, acidulous Sylvaner with concentrated fruit in spite of the summer drought and wet autumn - even a little rich, fresh and straightforward.

Randersackerer Teufelkeller 🍇🍇 ③
Silvaner Spätlese trocken 1990
An exceptionally opulent, softly fruity wine, pleasantly full, of a quality only harvested every ten years.

Würzburger Pfaffenberg 🍇 ③
Weissburgunder Spätlese trocken 1990
This wine does not match the finesse of the great 1988s as a hint of botrytis spoils the opulent fruit. The Trockenbeeren-Auslese version of this wine (still in the cellar) is, however, superb.

Würzburger Stein-Harfe 🍇🍇🍇 ④
Riesling Auslese 1990
The most impressive wines of the exceptional 1990 vintage were made from Riesling. It produced a series of superb wines never seen before, beginning with the finest Spätlesen through to Berren-Auslesen and even a Trockenbeeren-Auslese, a small sensation for this variety, as "Riesling gives away nothing" as Freiss knows, at least not in Franken. Between these wines, there are two nobly sweet Auslesen from Abtsberg and from Stein-Harfe, the center of Würzburger Stein: extremely fine nectare harvested as early as mid-October, as botrytis had by that time already infiltrated the vineyards, and weighing in at 115°Oechsle with 40 grams of residual sugar in the finished wine. They are the most noble wines yet to emerge from Bürgerspital's cellars. The last was a 1976, a similarly concentrated Riesling and who knows how it has developed in the meantime. However, it cannot equal this one.

Fürstlich Castellsches Domänenamt

Castell 8711
Tel. (09325) 60170
Fax (09325) 60185

The picturesque village of Castell lies a little off the beaten track in the Steigerwald forest. The wines from this estate profit from the microclimate which exists where the slopes of this chain of hills drop down to the Main plain, and wine-growing has been carried on here since early times The wines of the Princes of Castell are very highly regarded in Franken. They are strong in character, very solid growths of a consistently high level. Although they are very pleasant, easy-drinking wines, what is sometimes lacking is spectacular quality: a refined touch of acidity or the final degree of finesse. One is satisfied with what these excellent sites (ie Casteller Schlossberg) have produced for over 1000 years. However, time does not stand still. Rieslander is no longer given precedence over Riesling. The modern, fresh style has always been pursued and this estate is leader among Franken's large wine producers in changing over from natural to ecological viticulture.

Casteller Schlossberg   🍇🍇 ③
Rieslaner Spätlese 1991
An almost dry Spätlese with accentuated acidity (9.7 g/lt) which makes this top wine from the 1991 vintage seem almost lean.

Casteller Schlossberg   🍇 ②
Silvaner Kabinett trocken 1991
Made from Castell's best site: firm acidity, concentrated with a touch of elegance. A very high standard not only considering the weak vintage.

Casteller Kirchberg   🍇 ②
Silvaner Kabinett trocken 1990
A very vigorous, full-bodied wine with almost the weight but lacking the high acidity of a Spätlese.

Weingut Rudolf Fürst

Hohenlindenweg 46
Bürgstadt 8768
Tel. (09371) 8642
Fax (09371) 69230

Paul Fürst has continuously enlivened the Franken wine scene with new ideas and initiative for several years, ideas which many established producers lack either the courage or imagination to put into action. He is undoubtedly N°1 with red wines and when it comes to barrique-ageing at least one of the leaders. The most impressive thing is his high success rate in everything he does. This is no coincidence: he is a fervent fighter for quality starting from scratch with every vintage. He succeeds with white wines and especially with difficult varieties (Riesling, Rieslaner, Sylvaner), reaching quality levels which nobody else manages to equal on Franken's colored sandstone soils. Even in the difficult 1991 vintage he made excellent dry wines, some of which are spectacular, such as a Rieslaner Auslese and Riesling Spätlese. 1990 was a red wine year which at last produced wines with body, color and sweet tannins. Fürst's Spätburgunders (Pinot Noirs) are also the best which have ever emerged from his barrique cellar. An interesting speciality is a rosé (Weissherbst) Auslese. The grapes had the sugar concentration of a Beeren-Auslese, and the wine was matured in small oak casks, turning out similar to a great Meursault.

Bürgstadter Centgrafenberg   🍇🍇 ②
Riesling Kabinett trocken 1991
Restrained in aroma and only lightly spicy with steely acidity in a style similar to The Rheingau's. Very long.

Bürgstadter Centgrafenberg   🍇🍇 ②
Riesling Spätlese 1990
White wines only grow in islands of fine sand on Bürgstadt's colored sandstone soils and never have the body of their competitors from calcareous and keuper soils around Würzburg and in the Steigerwald forest. This superb Riesling Spätlese is the exception, harvested on 25th of October and intended as a dry Spätlese. However, the fermentation stopped prematurely leaving 12 g/lt of residual sugar, but well-balanced by sensationally high acidity (10.5 g/lt). This wine is difficult to beat for opulence, like a mouthful of the finest fruit. The last Franken Spätlesen in this class were in 1979.

Bürgstadter Centgrafenberg   🍷 ②
Spätburgunder QbA trocken 1991
This winery's classic red: medium-weight, with accentuated tannin and delicate Pinot flavors, aged traditionally in large casks. A wine that goes well with food.

Spätburgunder   ④
Spätlese Franken 1990
A wine like this is only made every ten years in Franken: medium-weight but very polished with elegant oak and all the attributes of a great Burgundy.

Staalicher Hofkeller

Residenzplatz
Würzburg 8700
Tel. (0931) 3050923
Fax (0931) 3050966

The Hofkeller is sometimes jokingly referred to as "Holzkeller" (wood cellar) because it is filled with very large casks. However, the new director, Alfred Schmidt, is not at all happy about this situation, as he would like to reduce the time the white wines spend in cask to a maximum of three months to preserve their aroma and varietal characteristics. This is not the only change he has in mind. He regards temperature-controlled fermentation as absolutely necessary, and in the vineyards he has had more Sylvaner planted at the expense of the Kerner and Müller Thurgau. He has also had vineyard yields reduced, thereby recognizing the mistakes made in the past. Nevertheless, one cannot turn over a new leaf overnight, and the farm-yard style of the Baverian State Wine Estate is also very noticeable in the 1990 and 1991 wines. The Hofkellerei owns very good sites throughout Franken which produce Riesling as high up the quality scale as Trockenbeeren-Auslese. The 1991s are less impressive but make up for this by their appealing fruit.

Randersackerer Pfülben   ❦ ①
Riesling QbA trocken 1991
Clean Riesling with pure varietal flavors and plenty of fruit, bone dry with piercing acidity. Needs plenty of time to develop.

Hörsteiner Abtsberg   ❦ ②
Riesling Spätlese 1990
This Riesling is grown on the primary rock soils around Aschaffenburg and is close to those of the Rheingau in style: not a heavy-weight but elegant with steely acidity.

Würzburger Stein   ❦ ③
Rieslaner Auslese 1990
Although Riesling and Rieslaner Auslesen are rare in Franken the Hofkeller produced large quantities in 1990: very unusual but good wines.

Juliusspital

Klinikstrasse 5
Würzburg 8700
Tel. (0931) 3084147
Fax (0931) 3084340

Horst Kolesch, the young administrator of this estate is sure of one thing: "In Franken much has changed when it comes to wine." Above all the wines of Juliusspital have changed. They are looked upon as modern, if modern means wines with pure varietal flavors, fresh acidity accentuated fruit, richness and a pleasure to drink early, though they age gracefully. The best examples are the 1990s. Such superb quality has not been produced here for years, already showing breed and finesse, but with the potential to last for 20 years or more, especially Sylvaner and Riesling. However, Rieslaner also produces sensational dry Auslesen with 16° alcohol - a monument of a wine to last well into the next century. Sylvaner is not usually as concentrated but spicier, while the Riesling is fruitier. Lesser vintages like 1991 cannot do Juliusspital any harm as long as they own Franken's best sites.

Würzburger Stein ℗ ②
Riesling Kabinett trocken 1991
This wine embodies the characteristics of this vintage: delicate stature, very little bouquet, light fruity sweetness and a dry finish.

Würzburger Stein ℗ ②
Silvaner Kabinett trocken 1991
Not a rich Silvaner, elegant with Riesling-like acidity: an extraordinary high class wine.

Würzburger Stein ℗℗ ③
Riesling Spätlese trocken 1990
The best dry Riesling ever to come from the "im Stein" vineyards: highly concentrated, firm acidity and fruity.

Würzburger Stein ℗℗ ③
Silvaner Spätlese trocken 1990
A rich, concentrated wine almost Auslese though seems supple and slim. A great wine.

Julius-Echter-Berg ℗℗℗ ③
Riesling Spätlese trocken 1990
A wine like this is not produced every day: an absolutely terrific Auslese weighing in at 104° Oechsle. As the grapes were perfectly healthy with no sign of 'noble rot', the wine fermented out to dryness, producing a Riesling of great complexity and crystal clear fruit which was downgraded to Spätlese. Already unctuous, an aroma of green leaves after warm summer rain, fruit aroma of fig, acacia and raisins with pepper and green pepper skin spice supported by fine acidity: an absolutely superb wine, perhaps the greatest Riesling to emerge from Franken in the last ten years. Incidentally, Juliusspital has decided that the proceeds of the sales of this wine will go to help an old people's home and a home for the disabled.

Weingut Furst Löwenstein

Rathausgasse 5
Kreuzwertheim/Main 6983
Tel. (09342) 6505
Fax (09342) 6205

Duke Löwenstein's wines are exotic among Franken wines. Compared to those of Würzburg and Iphofen, they often appear defective, with a smell like dry Madeira or as if a shot of Malaga liqueur had been added to them. The estate's qualified director, Paul Schauber, says that this is nothing new, the cause being that the vineyards, especially the Homburger Kallmuth site, which is a precipitously steep slope, dive straight down to the Main river. It has a partly mediterranean climate and plants that grow there are, otherwise, only found south of the Alps. Inevitably, these unique growing conditions have their effect on Löwenstein wines. They also go heavy on the oak ageing, using many types of traditional casks. The resulting wines are big, with southern, hot-climate nuances on the nose, sometimes broad on the palate, that take a bit to understand and appreciate.

Homburger Kallmuth ♗ ♗ ②
Silvaner Spätlese trocken 1991
This wine proves that even in lesser vintages Kallmuth produces surprisingly good wines, at times better that those of great vintages.

Reichholzheimer Satzenberg ♗ ①
Riesling QbA trocken 1991
A rich Riesling from grapes of one of the estate's best terraced vineyards in Taubertal that are grown on sandstone soil.

Homburger Kallmuth ♗ ♗ ③
Riesling Spätlese trocken 1990
The greatest Spätlese of the last 15 years, it is rich but not over-powering, with fantastic acidity and great potential.

Homburger Kallmuth ♗ ③
Silvaner Spätlese trocken 1990
An old style, lush Franken wine, with pansy and musk aromas, fruity-earthy flavors and strong final sensation. A dinosaur of a wine.

Weingut Johann Ruck

Am Marktplatz 19
Iphofen 8715
Tel. (09323) 3316
Fax (09323) 5035

Johann Ruck demotes his wines to a lower rank than those which would be their birthright. His superb 1990 Spätlese is in reality an Auslese, his 1991 Sylvaner Kabinett a Spätlese. "I'd rather make a decent Kabinett than a small Spätlese" is his motto. The young owner of this estate, located on the Iphofen market square, is also one of the few, new talented producers to come out of the woodwork from Franken in recent years. Wine-making techniques are modern (only stainless steel tanks together with a few barriques); meanwhile, in the vineyard he is a strict conservative: short pruning, plenty of manual work and concentration on classic varieties. Sylvaner has always been his leading variety, and he is focussing increasingly on Riesling, while he would also like to increase the prestige of Müller Thurgau. The best wine from this variety is barrique-aged and sold to restaurants under the name Rivaner with enormous success. 1990 was a great Spätlese year for him, with very impressive Rieslings and Grauburgunders (Pinot Gris). 1991 was excellent for Sylvaner, which is in no way inferior to the 1990.

Iphöfer Julius-Echter-Berg ♗ ②
Riesling QbA trocken 1991
Typical Julius-Echter-Berg Riesling: full-bodied, spicy aroma, captivating acidity. Very successful.

Iphöfer Julius-Echter-Berg ♗ ②
Silvaner Kabinett trocken 1991
The vintage's best Silvaner, higher acidity than the 1990, rich and concentrated: a wine with a long life span.

Iphöfer Kronsberg ♗ ②
Müller-Thurgau Kabinett trocken 1990
Very firm, delicately spiced with mild acidity, full in substance and restrained in bouquet.

Rödelseer Schwanleite ♗ ♗ ③
Grauer Burgunder Spätlese 1990
Demoted from Auslese, having weighed in with 103° on the Öchsle scale: an excellent, almost dry wine, will need many years to develop completely.

Weingut Robert Schmitt

Maingasse 13
Randersacker 8701
Tel. (0931) 708351
Fax (0931) 708352

Young Bruno Schmitt has been running this estate together with his uncle and estate owner Robert Schmitt since the early 1980s and in the meantime holds the reins firmly in his hand. He openly admits: "Others can make polished wines better than us." Both have concentrated on unfined, guaranteed unchaptalised, rough-hewn wines. They are among the few 'natural' producers, even though this expression is forbidden under German wine law. This honest pledge brings with it many challenges: as they refuse to chaptalise grapes must attain at least 71° Oechsle in order to qualify as Qualitätsweine, as only these may be filled in the traditional Bocksbeutel. In unfavourable vintages this is not easy and can only be achieved by severely reducing vineyard yields by short pruning. In 1991 this was no problem, while the 1990s ("best vintage for 20 years") all wines were above 84° Oechsle. However, there was another problem: some wines refused to ferment out to dryness and have retained a small amount of unfermented sugar. At first the Schmitts were concerned about their "trocken" image, although, in the meantime, they have come to find these wines drinkable, if not very good!

Randsackerer Abtsleite
Silvaner QbA trocken 1991
A light, angular wine, with an aroma more of bread than earth. Typical Franken Vesperwein.

Randersackerer Pfülben
Riesling Spätlese trocken 1990
An uncompromisingly dry wine from young vines and its piercing acidity needs rounding off. A good food wine.

Weingut Schmitt's Kinder

Am Sonnenstuhl
Randersacker 8701
Tel/Fax (0931) 708303

Bacchus still plays an important rôle. The reference here is not to the God of Wine but, instead, the grape variety itself. It seems that in Franken this new hybrid is relatively common and produces an easy-drinking, often sweetish tavern-wine that is very popular among young wine drinkers. For Karl Schmitt, it is his main source of income. His heart, however, is more with the classic Franken varieties Sylvaner, Riesling and Rieslaner. The wines from these varieties which leave his cellar make him number one at Randersacker, the small picturesque wine village on the Main. Travels to Italy, Sauternaise and other parts of Europe have sharpened his judgement and his palate, and his wines have been among Franken's most interesting in recent years. His Sylvaners are especially fine, as are his Rieslings, even though Schmitt regards Rieslaner as superior. He also enjoys making wines from mixed varieties and ageing them in barrique: dry Spät- and Auslesen (1989) and nobly sweet Beeren-Auslesen (1990). The varieties which go into the wines are a secret.

Randersackerer Pfülben
Silvaner Kabinett trocken 1991
An earthy, very acidulous wine without the concentration of the 1990 but still with good substance.

Randersackerer Sonnenstuhl
Rieslaner Spätlese 1991
This vintage's best wine, with light residual sugar but fruity and firm thanks to a scrupulous bunch selection at harvest-time.

Weingut Hans Wirsching

Ludwigstrasse 16
Iphofen 8715
Tel. (09323) 3033
Fax (09323) 3090

Wirsching is not only one of Franken's most reliable estates, but his wines are consistently among the region's absolute best. Riesling and Sylvaner, particularly from the excellent Iphofen sites of Kronsberg and Julius Echter-Berg, attain a quality level that is equal to wines from the great Würzburg sites. Scheurebe is also very elegant, more reminiscent of Sauvignon than of a Sylvaner/Riesling crossing. The principles behind their quality policy are reduction of vineyard yields to an average of 55 hl/ha, harvesting completely by hand, natural clearing of the juice prior to fermentation by sedimentation rather than centrifuging, temperature-controlled fermentation and ageing in stainless steel. In addition Heinrich Wirsching, the owner, has cleaned up the assortment of grape varieties by eliminating new crossings and reducing Müller Thurgau's share in the vineyards. The 1990 produced quality wines that were unseen in these parts to date, especially in the Spätlese class together with a great Auslese and a Sylvaner Trockenbeeren-Auslese (which will not be released until 1994). 1991 was also a very good vintage and produced the best Kabinett qualities for years, at the upper limit for the category bordering onto Spätlese.

Iphöfer Kalb ☙ ②
Silvaner Kabinett trocken 1991
Elegant, fresh and solid, wine with accentuated acidity and very pronounced, fruity-earthy spice.

Iphöfer Kronsberg ☙ ②
Riesling Kabinett trocken 1991
A small Spätlese down graded to Kabinet: a very fine Riesling with excellent acidity and very full in body.

Iphöfer Julius-Echter-Berg ☙ ☙ ③
Silvaner Spätlese trocken 1990
Made from grapes harvested at the end of October, yet impressively full with no traces of noble rot: not 'fat' but very concentrated.

Iphöfer Kronsberg ☙ ☙ ③
Scheurebe Spätlese trocken 1990
Extremely refined and delicate wine despite its richness, with flinty and blackberry aromas. Perfectly suited drink with food.

Iphöfer Julius-Echter-Berg ☙ ☙ ☙ ③
Riesling Spätlese 1990
In 1990 Heinrich Wirsching managed to make two Riesling Spätlesen: alongside a dry wine from Kronsberg, which restaurateurs snatched up before it even hit the price list. He made another with very light residual sugar (4 g/lt) which, however, is hardly noticeable on the palate. As has been seen with numerous other Spätlesen, the unfermented sugar enables the wine to keep longer and better. This 1990 is a power pack, harvested at the end of a hot October when the berries were more concentrated as the their water content evaporated. The grapes were, thus, very ripe but not excessively so. The best Wirsching Riesling for over 20 years weighed in at 97° Oechsle with enormous richness and finesse and (for Franken) high 8.5 g/lt acidity. 6,500 bottles were made.

Hessische Bergstrasse

Vines also grow on the side of the Rhine opposite Rheinhessen. Indeed, wine has been made from grapes grown on the west-facing slopes of Odenwald around the towns of Bensheim and Heppenheim since Roman times. There is mainly Riesling (54%) but also a little Müller-Thurgau (17%).

The Hessische Berg-Strasse is known for its mild climate and early spring. Fruit trees blossom earlier here in the area between Darmstadt and Heidelberg than amost anywhere else in Germany. The early vegetation is especially favorable for the late ripening Riesling which has a long vegetative cycle, increasing the probability of grapes ripening in the autumn, before the cold weather sets in. Unfortunately, there are now few vineyards and wineries left along the Berg-Strasse, due more to urbanisation, new road building and the development of small businesses. The wine's quality and wine-making standards were otherwise good.

Thus, the Hessische Berg-Strasse is Germany's smallest wine-growing region with only 390 hectares under vine. Nevertheless, it produces delicate Riesling with accentuated acidity which, at its best, can be very racy and fine.

Staatsweingut Hessische Bergstrasse

Grieselstrasse 34/36
Bensheim 6140
tel. (06251) 3107
Fax (06251) 65706

Although this estate is owned by the state of Hessen and administered from Eltville on the Rhine, it is able to work independently to a large extent. The cellars of the winery, filled one third with wooden casks and two thirds with stainless steel tanks, are situated in the picturesque village of Bensheim. The administrator, Heinrich Hillebrand, is the third generation to run the estate, following in the footsteps of his father and grandfather. His home is located in the middle of the 17.65 ha exclusive site Heppenheimer Centgericht which often produces Eiswein. The estate focuses on Riesling, which accounts for 73% of the vineyard area. The very mild climate (on the Bergstrasse almond trees blossom earlier than anywhere else in Germany) sometimes produces rather soft Rieslings (as in 1989 for example) which lack vitality and race. In other years of high acidity (like in the 1985, 1987 and 1990 vintages) it often yields exceptionally succulent, fine-tuned wines. In addition to Riesling their Spätburgunder (Pinot Noir) and Weiss- and Grauburgunder (Pinots Blanc and Gris) are interesting.

Heppenheimer Steinkopf   🍇 ①
Riesling Kabinett halbtrocken 1991
The best wine of this vintage from the Bergstrasse's top site. Fine, minerally fruit and attractive, soft acidity.

Heppenheimer Steinkopf   🍇🍇 ③
Riesling Auslese 1990
A copy-book Riesling Auslese expressing the unique finesse conferred by the site. Very ripe, succulent fruit and strong botrytis.

Heppenheimer Centgericht   🍇🍇 ④
Riesling Eiswein 1987
Almost creamy, already delicious to drink and with the soft acidity typical of the Bergstrasse. A rather small wine (145° Oechsle) compared to its successors but correspondingly well-priced.

Heppenheimer Centgericht   🍇🍇 ②
Spätburgunder Spätlese trocken 1990
After the very good 1985 wine, at last a great vintage. A red with firm tannin and deep fruit.

Weingut Tobias Seitz

Weidgasse 8
Bensheim-Auerbach 6140
Tel. (06251) 75825

Tobias Seitz built up this estate from a wine tavern after the last war, and today, it is the largest in the northern district of the Hessischer Bergstrasse. With the acidulous, racy style of his wines Seitz has created his own circle of enthusiasts. Son-in-law Peter Schrott took over the estate several years ago and runs it with the active help of its founder. Like most other estates on the Hessischer Bergstrasse, Seitz is dependent on buying in grapes from other growers as his seven hectares of vineyard do not provide sufficient quantities to meet the strong demand for the wines, especially from elsewhere in the region. Riesling dominates with 70%. Spätburgunder (Pinot Noir) and Grauburgunder (Pinot Gris) are specialties though less interesting. 75% of the wines are dry and off-dry. The remainder, made in a fruity, slightly sweet style are never obviously so as the sweetness is cut by sinewy acidity. It is a peculiarity of the estate that they never put the words "trocken" (dry) or "halbtrocken" (off-dry) on the labels but express them through the color of the wine seal (yellow means dry).

Auerbacher Fürstenlager   🍇 ①
Riesling QbA trocken 1991
Hearty, crisp, dry Riesling from soils composed of eroded granite. A very typical and characterful Bergstrasse wine.

Auerbacher Fürstenlager   🍇 ②
Extra Brut 1990
A full sparkling wine with a very fine perlage, produced with the traditional method of bottle fermentation.

Auerbacher Fürstenlager   🍇 ②
Riesling Spätlese trocken 1990
Ripe Riesling fruit with minerally nuances in flavor, steely acidity, very racy and stylish.

Auerbacher Rott   🍇 ①
Riesling Spätlese 1990
Although the label features the general area of Rott, the wine in fact comes from the tiny original Rott site. It is sinewy, sweet and acidulous wine of good quality.

Mittelrhein

Stretching from Lorch to Königswinter on the outskirts of Bonn, the Mittelrhein joins the northern part of the Rheingau and encompasses an area just under 100 km on both banks of the Rhine. However, it is only possible to grow vines on a few slopes alongside the Rhine. They are almost always steep, south-facing, terraced sites with clay and slaty soils and are planted with Riesling (73%).

Vineyards are seldom modernised, or "flurbereinigt," thus mechanisation is seldom possible. The vineyards are cared for and cultivated almost always with the help of winches. For this reason, it is becoming increasingly difficult to find enough laborers willing to work the steep slopes. In recent years a large part of the vineyards have been abandoned and left to run wild. Since 1975 the vineyard area has shrunk from 900 to 750 hectares. This is a shame, as Rieslings from here fear no comparison with those of the more famous Rheingau. The best estates produce lively, very racy wine with much finesse, kept fresh for years by a sharp acidity. Müller-Thurgau (10%) and Kerner (5.6%) are also grown but are not particularly significant in terms of quality or quantity.

Weingut Toni Jost

Hahnenhof
Bacharach 6533
Tel. (06743) 1216
Fax (06743) 1076

Hahnenhof at Bacharach is lucky enough to be able to offer the wines of two wine regions from one single winery. In marrying a Rheingau producer's daughter, Toni Jost acquired land in the Wallufer and Martinsthaler sites. It is very interesting to compare these Rheingau wines with those from classic Bacharach Mittelrhein sites. Even though they are compact and vigorous, especially in the dry wine class, the Rheingau wines are at a disadvantage when it comes to finesse and fine fruit. Jost's special site, Bacharacher Hahn, where he owns the lion's share with 3.5 hectares, produces with great regularity highly subtle and finely fruity Rieslings and above all wines in the nobly sweet wine category which express the peachy character derived from the devonian slate soils. The dry wines are very fresh with a slight sparkle and always have an accentuated acidity, in some years excessively so (as in 1990). In order to balance this, in each vintage Jost produces special selections aged in new casks. Those who do not mind the soft but pleasant oak flavor will find wines with better integrated acidity.

Bacharacher Hahn   ❦ ❦ ③
Riesling Auslese 1991
One of only two Auslesen harvested in Mittelrhein in this vintage, made from a tiny yield more typical of Trocken-Beeren-Auslese. Massive with a very delicate botrytis and peach aroma.

Bacharacher Hahn   ❦ ①
Riesling QbA trocken 1991
In spite of its rather accentuated 11.2° alcohol, this is a finely fruity wine, well-structured, straight forward Riesling.

Bacharacher Schloss Stahleck   ❦ ①
Riesling Spätlese halbtrocken 1991
A wine labelled as coming from an extensive vineyard area though more precisely from the Oberdiebacher Fürstenberg site on clay and slatey soils which leave their strong mark on the wine.

Bacharacher Hahn   ❦ ❦ ③
Riesling Auslese 1990
From this top site with devonian slate soils, Hahn produced a phenomenal 12,000 lt of Auslese of this quality. Very polished and elegant with fantastic concentration of fruit and a fine interplay between acidity and sweetness.

Weingut J. Ratzenberger

Blücherstrasse 167
Bacharach-Steeg 6533
Tel. (06743) 1337
Fax (06743) 2842

Wine-growing is decreasing in this most picturesque and famous stretch of the Rhine due to the very difficult working conditions on steep sites and small terraces. Wines are mainly sold to tourists, as many English, Dutch and Japanese flock to holiday in the Loreley valley, causing prices to drop as a result. The Ratzenberger family are originally from eastern Prussia and started producing wine in the 1950s in the Bacharacher Steeger Tal. More or less with an outsider's view, the present owner, Jochen Ratzenberger, began to produce wine with another dimension to that of the usual 'tourist wine.' The wine is hardly ever de-acidified, is hard and steely, and is 90% made in a dry or off-dry style. Due to the general decrease of wine-growing in the region, this estate has been able to extend its vineyard area and improve the quality. Riesling is the dominant variety covering 80% of the vineyard area, followed by some interesting Spätburgunder (Pinot Noir) with 12% and Müller-Thurgau with 8%. The 1990 vintage from a tiny yield of 30 hl/ha is extremely good. The 1989s are rather unbalanced in flavor. On the whole all the wines, through to the Eiswein, are of a good quality.

Bacharacher Wolfshöhle   ❦ ②
Riesling Kabinett trocken 1991
From a very low 40 hl/ha yield, this wine has turned out rich and full with firm, steely acidity and a very dry finish.

Steeger St. Jost   ❦ ❦ ②
Riesling Spätlese 1990
In 1990 a fat Spätlese with opulent yellow fruit came from the heart of this fabulous vineyard. Its sweetness is well harmonised by racy acidity. It is almost dry on the finish.

Bacharacher Spätburgunder   ❦ ①
Rosé QbA trocken 1991
A well-structured rosé matured in wood with good Pinot Noir fruit and spice.

Bacharacher Wolfshöhle   ❦ ①
Spätburgunder trocken 1990
This is a copy-book example of a very good German Pinot Noir from a once renowned red wine site. Grown on slatey soil with a yield of only 35 hl/ha. Only 400 lt of this cask aged wine were made.

Mosel-Saar-Ruwer

Throughout the world Riesling from the Mosel is looked upon as the epitome of German wine, in good ways and bad. The name of this growing area itself evokes the image of a light, delicate, high quality Riesling alongside that of a thin, made-up, cloyingly sweet grape juice which the Germans describe with the banal expression "lieblich", meaning sweetish. This "lieblich" kind of wine is still around today, though, generally speaking, recent developments have made it less typical of the region's produce in general. Over the last 15 to 20 years, wine prices plummeted as the vineyard area along the Mosel irresponsibly extended itself, encouraging over-production. Also, the practice (which is no longer allowed) of sweetening the wine by adding a mixture of sugar and water has been cleaned up in the region.

These and other factors encouraged growers to rethink their production philosophy, and many are once again trying to focus on the classic style of Mosel Riesling. But what exactly is it? It could be defined as a light coloured, brightly pale wine, gently spiced with high natural acidity, slim-bodied with a slight sparkle when young, though it can also be long-lasting, revealing its true finesse only after several years' bottle age. Today this kind of classic Riesling is often made in a dry and off-dry ("halbtrocken") style, which accounts for 20% of production. However, whether a wine is dry or not is more an indication of personal taste than of quality. There are excellent dry Rieslings as well as equally good, lightly sweet wines, for which producers like to the adjectives "fruchtsüss" or "mild". They often make three styles of the same wine from the same vintage in a dry, off-dry and lightly sweet style. For this reason,they label their drier wines as "trocken" and "halbtrocken". When these words are missing from the label, consumers can expect that the wine will be more or less sweet. In recent years, wine-lovers and connoisseurs have become increasingly convinced that the characteristics of Mosel wines are best expressed when backed by a light degree of sweetness. Due to their high acidity the residual sugar is often hardly noticeable, especially in the "halbtrocken" category. In addition light, fruity sweetness (up to 25 g/lt) makes the wines seem more elegant and contributes to their aging potential. After five or ten years, the sweetness is no longer noticeable, and the wine tastes dry. At this stage, they are the perfect partners for food, even for presumibly more red wine-foods. The fermentation is only halted early with high-quality Auslesen, leaving them with often very accentuated sweetness. However, in this case, the wines are nobly sweet, as the grapes have been shrivelled by noble rot. Botrytis Cinerea, as the noble mould is called in Latin, tends to absorb the water content of the berries, imparting a noble, lightly bitter taste to the end wine. While botrytis is not normally desired in dry wines, it adds an extraordinary touch of class to the nobly sweet wines. They are held in high esteem by wine-lovers all over the world and often fetch stunningly high prices. These kind of Auslese wines (or even more so, Beeren-Auslesen and Trockenbeeren-Auslesen) are not wines for every-day drinking, being regarded as specialities that are only made in exceptionally good years.

The growing area stretches from the border with Luxembourg almost to where the Mosel runs into the Rhine at Koblenz. The Mittelmosel, or mid-Mosel, which runs from Zell to Trier is nowadays thought of as the best part of the region. The very best wines come from vertiginously steep slopes descending down to the river, where vines grow on slatey soils at Bernkastel, Wehlen, Brauneberg, Graach, Erden and Trittenheim. Then there are the Mosel's tributaries, the Saar and Ruwer. Rieslings from these parts are, by no standards, inferior to those of the Mittelmosel. Saar Rieslings are famous for their high acidity, while those from the Ruwer, for their delicate style. On the whole, Riesling accounts for 54% of production, making it the number one growing area for Riesling in Germany. Other varieties such as Müller Thurgau (22%), Elbling (9%) and Kerner (7%) are of secondary importance. The estates that belong to the Association of German Wines of Distinction, which is "Verband der Deutscher Prädikatsweinwinzer" or VPD, hold an auction called "Grosser Ring" to sell their best wines once a year in September, attracting buyers from all over the world.

Bischöfliche Weingüter

Gervasiustrasse 1
Trier 5500
Tel. (0651) 43441
Fax (0651) 40253

With a total of 107 ha of vineyards, the Bischöfliche Weingüter is the largest estate in the Mosel-Saar-Ruwer region. As one would expect of the Church, tradition plays a very important part here. Of the total capacity 500,000 lt are kept in stainless steel tanks, while the main emphasis is on wine matured in the 600 large casks which guarantee optimum vinification and which facilitate the still popular fermentation block process that produces wines with unfermented sugar. The Austrian estate director, Wolfgang Richter, and sales director, Erwin Engel, place great importance on maintaining the identity and character of individual sites. Their regular customers would never accept a simple, standard estate Riesling, in fact, "they would ask us what is really inside." They produce a wide selection of wines typical of their individual sites, which is what makes the estate most interesting: from the Saar (38 ha), to the Ruwer (36 ha), to the Mosel (13 ha) and the Trier (13 ha). Nevertheless, in order to find the really great wines, one must taste one's way through, encountering a few disappointments along the way eventually. The 1989s are rather unharmonious and too tannic, while the 1988s are generally successful, as are the 1990s.

Eitelsbacher Marienholz 🍇 ①
Riesling QbA trocken 1991
This standard dry wine comes from the largest of the estate's vineyards with 19 ha, it is always of good quality.

Kaseler Nies'chen 🍇 ①
Riesling Kabinett 1991
An individual wine with fine fruit, ripe, sinewy acidity and very succulent, coming from perhaps the best Ruwer site.

Ayler Herrenberger 🍇🍇 ②
Riesling Auslese 1990
This relatively good value Auslese is appealing because of its very fine sweetness, piquant acidity and noble grapey aromas.

Ayler Kupp 🍇🍇 ③
Riesling Auslese trocken 1990
A monument of ripe grapey fruit, full, succulent with firm acidity, a very interesting table wine.

Weingut Bollig-Lehnert

Joh.-Trithemius-Strasse 62
Trittenheim 5501
Tel. (06507) 5077

Stefan Bollig is the 31 year-old owner of this estate which used to run under two separate names, even though they were worked together. Since 1991 he has merged the two properties in Trittenheim and Lehnert-Matheus at Piesport and called the estate Bollig Lehnert. In contrast to most newly built wineries, the Bollings built theirs in the center of the Trittenheimer Altärchen site in traditional style, with slate arches which guarantee the perfect level of humidity and temperature due to the typical cellar mold. This is perfect for the estate's classic method of aging the wines 100% in wood. This also goes for the Riesling, while the Müller Thurgau from flat sites is sold exclusively in tanks. In the old tavern of the well-known Lehnert-Matheus estate, a wine bar is open from Easter until the end of October, on weekends from Friday to Monday; light snacks are served to go with the generally solid, dependable wines.

Piesporter Goldtröpfchen 🍇🍇 ③
Riesling Auslese+++1990 **
The three crosses denote the best cask of the 1990 vintage: a very fine, nobly sweet Auslese from a superb vintage.

Trittenheimer Apotheke 🍇🍇 ②
Riesling Auslese 1990
A little lighter and less sweet than the Piesporter Auslese, however an appealing and complex wine from the heart of the Apotheke site.

Trittenheimer Altärchen 🍇 ①
Riesling Spätlese halbtrocken 1988
A very well-balanced, medium-weight wine with a pleasant wood flavor which is subservient to the fruit.

Weingut Joh. Jos. Christoffel Erben

Schanzstrasse 2
Ürzig 5564
Tel. (06532) 2176
Fax (06532) 1471

Hans Leo Christoffel inherited his nickname "Rotbäckchen", or red cheeks, from his father and beams the image of a full-blooded vigneron who grew up in the vineyard and cellar. For decades he has attained top prices for his very characterful Rieslings at the "Bernkasteller Ring" auctions. They all come from the superb, steep sites, Ürziger Würzgarten (1.8 ha) and Erdener Treppchen (0.4 ha), mostly from ungrafted, old vines. In the cellar, wines are matured almost exclusively in classic wood casks called "Holzfudern". The various, very individual Auslesen styles are very appealing and profity given the fact that, in order to produce them, Christoffel has to renounce making Beeren-Auslesen and Trockenbeeren-Auslesen. His strength lies in his sweet wines, though he also excels with dry Rieslings which express the character of the red soils at Ürzig. The 1988s were superb, the 1989s suffer from having been harvested a little too early, though the 1990s are once again excellent.

Ürziger Würzgarten　　　　🍷 ①
Riesling Hochgewächs trocken 1991
A simple but very characterful wine with firm acidity. It fits in well among the estate's regular line.

Ürziger Würzgarten　　　　🍷🍷 ②
Riesling Kabinett 1991
A lighter and more straightforward wine than the Kabinett from the neighboring village of Erden. Succulent, spicy and very sucessful.

Ürziger Würzgarten　　　🍷🍷 ②
Riesling Spätlese 1990
Although 1990 produced excellent Auslesen, this lightly sweet Spätlese is a perfect example of this estate's high standards and is an nnbeatable value for money.

Ürziger Würzgarten　　　🍷🍷 ②
Riesling Auslese trocken 1988
One of the greatest and most concentrated dry 1988 Mosel Auslesen, it has a perfect interplay of highly ripe fruit and acidity.

Weingut-Weinkellerei Jos. Christoffel Jr.

Moselufer 1-3
Ürzig 5564
Tel. (06532) 2113
Fax (06532) 1050

Nobody has such a large assortment of old vintages as Jos. Christoffel Jr. at Ürzig. Apart from this, the estate is largely over-looked by both consumers and wine press alike. The owners, Kurt and Karl-Josef Christoffel are reserved people. Until the 1960s, Christoffel Jr. (not to be confused with Joh. Jos. Christoffel) was basically just a cellar, the vineyard being relatively obscured. Today things have shifted and, although they are no longer so young, the Christoffels also seem to have understood the value of their vineyards, in order to harvest top-grade grapes, as a prerequisite to produce high-quality wines. They bought just under half of a hectare in the heart of the Ürziger Würzgarten and Erdener Prälat sites in 1990 at a time when the price of land there was over DM 50 per m2. They are very passionate wine-lovers whose only weakness has been, perhaps, allowing too much sweetness in their wines. But, this, too, is changing. Slipping by unnoticed even by the local restaurant trade, Karl Josef, the wine-maker, has produced a run of excellent dry wines in recent years.

Erdener Treppchen　　　🍷🍷 ②
Riesling Spätlese 1991
Still with fresh fermentation aromas and very pure fruit with grapefruit and pineapple flavors: one of this vintage's top wines.

Ürziger Würzgarten　　　🍷🍷 ②
Riesling Auslese* 1990**
A very fine, nobly sweet Auslese (denoted by +++ on the label), that is very compact and unctuous.

Ürziger Würzgarten　　　🍷 ②
Riesling Auslese trocken 1990
Still yeasty-fresh and with a fine sparkle, this Riesling has an intense, fine grapey aroma.

Ürziger Würzgarten　　　🍷 ①
Riesling Spätlese trocken 1989
With herbs, mint and aniseed on the nose, plenty of botrytis, fat and sinewy with well-integrated, firm acidity.

Vereinigte Weingüter
J. Dötsch & Haupt
Lennigstrasse 38
Kobern-Gondorf 5401
Tel. (02607) 383

In the Untermosel area, with its spectacular panorama and steep terraced vineyards, much overly sweet, characterless Mosel wine is produced for the tourists. The Mayor of Kobern-Gorndorf, Franz Dötsch, has done his part to counter this by founding the "Deutsches Eck" growers' association, which is quite already unusual for the Mosel. They have made it their principle to reduce yields to a maximum of 80 hl/ha and to adhere to strict self- regulation with quality-oriented production strategies. Dötsch produces even less and prunes the vines back to one shoot. His ideal is to make a full, dry wine with character. He leaves the wine on its lees until spring and bottles without fining two years later. They are wines with clear fruit, richness and plenty of character, dry and off-dry wines in the traditional style which never taste sour.

Koberner Fahrberg   ❦ ②
Riesling Spätlese trocken 1989
Compact, intense fruit, very fresh with accentuated acidity: a very rich wine, acidulous in flavor.

Koberner Schlossberg   ❦ ①
Riesling QbA trocken 1989
Good balance between maturity and acidity, good substance and racy. A good representative of honest, natural Riesling.

Franz Dötsch   ❦ ①
Spätburgunder QbA trocken 1990
Fine, slatey Pinot Noir fruit, a slim and elegant and delicate red wine, made in tank.

Friedrich-Wilhelm-Gymnasium

Weberbach 75
Trier 5500
Tel. (0651) 73849
Fax (0651) 45480

With only 36 ha remaining on the banks of the Mosel and Saar, the FWG foundation's wine estate is the smallest among the large Trier producers. Its aim is to support the needy students attending the Jesuite school (which even Karl Marx attended) with the proceeds of the estate's wine sales. It is managed by Benedikt Engel, who is at the same time the founder and head of the "Riesling-Freundeskreis", a large Riesling wine-appreciation society with headquarters at Trier. The FWG's wines are still matured exclusively in wood casks. They are traditional, fine, fruity wines which retain their freshness thanks to the deep, cool cellar aging. Nevertheless, they often seem light and the sweetness, sometimes artificial, especially in less ripe vintages. Among their assortment, the most impressive are almost always the Trittenheimer Apotheken wines (which are wonderfully succulent and delicately fruity) as well as those from the Graach and Oberemmel sites along with Mehringer Blattenberg and Neumagener Rosengärtchen. As one might expect, due to their delicate, light style, the wines with residual sugar are more impressive than the drier versions.

Trittenheimer Apotheke   ❦ ①
Riesling Kabinett 1991
Once again ,even in the weak 1991 vintage, the Apotheke vineyard has produced a wine with the finest spice and refined interplay between acidity and sweetness.

Dhroner Hofberger   ❦ ①
Riesling Spätlese halbtrocken 1990
A sinewy wine with plenty of bite and appealing acidity and fruit from one of the estate's most reliable vineyards.

Graacher Domprobst   ❦ ③
Riesling Auslese 1990
Opulent, grapey Auslese (105° Oechsle) with an accentuated botrytis flavor. This is the first wine made from a newly-planted vineyard.

Weingut Grans-Fassian

Römer Strasse 28
Leiwen 5501
Tel. (06507) 3170
Fax (06507) 8167

Gerhard Grans could be described as the rising star of the 1980s, ever since he took over the estate in 1982. Until then, a large part of the wine was sold generically in tank. In the Leiwen area, the part of the Mosel where vineyards were first planted on a large scale in flat sites, he soon distinguished himself among the active and quality-oriented Young Wine-Growers' Association. Gran's quality consciousness is very impressive and evident, from the vineyards to the cellar through to his very clever marketing strategy. Wines from the approximately 6 ha of flat vineyards (though still relatively good because they are planted predominantly on gravel) are sold as the estate's standard Riesling and Grans-Fassian-Sekt sparkling wine. He manages to produce highly respectable quality by short pruning and reducing yields still further to a maximum of 80 hl/ha. His Müller Thurgau is reduced in yield to 50 hl/ha to make a barrique wine called Catherina which, however, is still suffering from 'teething problems'. His Rieslings from 4 ha of steep sites, on the other hand, are very fine with brilliant fruit and acidity. The most spectacular among them are the incredibly fine, fruity wines from the top Trittenheim site.

Leiwener Laurentiuslay   ❦ ②
Riesling Kabinett halbtrocken 1991
The Laurentiuslay is a small, steep, finely slatey vineyard which also produced very racy, straightforward Rieslings in 1991.

Trittenheimer Apotheke   ❦ ❦ ③
Riesling Auslese 1990
Although the 'smallest' 1990 Auslese it is also the most delicate and refined, with firm, lemony acidity and good concentration.

Trittenheimer Apotheke   ❦ ❦ ②
Riesling Spätlese trocken 1990
An extremely fresh wine, harvested early, but nevertheless very elegant, with ripe acidity rounded by a fine wood flavor.

Trittenheimer Apotheke   ❦ ❦ ③
Riesling Auslese 1989
It has a fine scent of botrytis and is delicately balanced, with elegant sweetness. Fairly harmonious but with lively acidity.

Weingut Fritz Haag

Dusemonder Hof
Brauneberg 5551
Tel. (06534) 410
Fax (06534) 1347

Wilhelm Haag, owner of the Fritz Haag estate and president of the Grosser Ring of the Mosel-Saar-Ruwer VPD (see introduction) is a very high spirited man. Above all he is a fervent defender of the light, delicate Mosel Riesling style and his wines are genuine prototypes. They are very clean, well-made, fresh and natural with fine sparkle and are the result of careful, reductive oxygen-free vinification. His creations are light-weight, and, while some may be fuller and more suculent in flavor, they are rarely finer. He makes the most of his two top sites, the Brauneberger Juffer Sonnenuhr (1.7 ha) and the Brauneberger Juffer (1.3 ha). Of course, the wines of a light, delicate styled-producer are at their best in a slightly sweet version. His Kabinett and Spätlese wines are impressively gentle and easy to drink, especially at ten or more years. From Auslese upwards they are truly great, and the interplay between body, fruity sweetness and acidity could not be more perfect. Not surprisingly, young producers use Haag wines as models to compare against their own.

Brauneberger Juffer Sonnenuhr 🍷🍷 ②
Riesling Kabinett 1991
Maybe even more appealing than the same wine of the great 1990 vintage. A little lighter but full of finesse and natural fruit sweetness.

Brauneberger Juffer Sonnenuhr 🍷🍷 ③
Riesling Spätlese Nr.03 1991
A very remarkable Spätlese of this vintage: explosive, fruity, unusually piquant and succulent.

Fritz Haag 🍷 ①
Riesling QbA trocken 1991
Wonderful fresh, pure fruit with noble Spätlese components, almost better than the 1990 and extremely delicate. 20,000 bottles were made.

Brauneberger Juffer Sonnenuhr 🍷🍷 ③
Riesling Spätlese trocken 1990
A perfect example of how a dry Mosel can be superbly balanced in good vintages: very firm and fine.

Brauneberger Juffer Sonnenuhr 🍷🍷🍷 ④
Riesling Auslese Lange Goldkapsel 1990
The absolute climax of the superb and unique series of Auslesen. It comes from the center of the Sonnenuhr site planted with old, ungrafted vines and weighed in at 118° Oechsle with 11.8 g/lt acidity. It is enormously concentrated without being fat or cloying, full of Riesling fruit and fantastic sweetness balanced by the steely acidity. In short, it is pure nectare. It was offered at a starting bid of DM 80 at the Grosser Ring auction at Trier in 1991 and went for DM 197.20, a sensational auction price. However, those who know how Haag's nobly sweet wines taste after 10-20 years will find that their money has been well-invested.

Weingut Reinhold Haart

Ausoniusufer 18
Piesport 5555
Tel. (06507) 2015
Fax (06507) 5909

Karl-Theo Haart, the 41 year-old owner of
this traditional Piesport estate, openly admits
that he was far too preoccupied with wine-
growing policies until 1986. The resulting
wines were often inconsistent and
unsatisfactory, especially in 1986, even
though one or two turned out very well,
indeed. In 1987 he made a great leap
forward and with the excellent 1988s he
suddenly rose to take his place among the
Mosel's elite. With 3 ha in the internatonally
acclaimed Goldtröpfen site, 0.4 ha in the
Grafenburg and 0.2 ha in the Domherr sites,
his estate is one of the largest owners in the
Piesporter Hauptberg cru. 1989 and 1990
once again produced very fine, delicate
Riesling collections. 90% of the wines are
exported, mainly to Japan and, for this
reason, among others, the emphasis in both
quality and quantity is on fruity-sweet wines
which are more highly esteemed abroad than
at home.

Piesporter Domherr 🍇 ①
Riesling Kabinett 1991
From the heart of the Goldtröpfchen site: an
extremely elegant wine with lively acidity.

Wintricher Ohligsberg 🍇🍇 ③
Riesling Spätlese 1991
1991 produced the most appealing and
succulent Spätlese from this site which is hardly
known any more.

Piesporter Goldtröpfchen 🍇🍇 ③
Riesling Auslese 1990
The smallest 1990 Auslese with a fascinating,
minerally accent and restrained sweetness: the
most interesting wine of this vintage.

Piesporter Goldtröpfchen 🍇 ②
Riesling Spätlese 1989
Fine, clear and mature nose, rather light, soft,
mild interplay between sweetness and acidity: a
light wine.

Weingut Hauth-Kerpen

Uferallee 9
Bernkastel-Dues 5550
Tel. (06531) 2321

Picture a beautiful, sunny day in November in
1990: the Wehlen hill opposite Bernkastel is
covered with the most sublime autumn
yellow. Gernoth Hauth stood on the bank, his
face beaming with delight and exclaimed, "At
last, a really great vintage". The most
passionate producer among the large estates
at Wehlen, is a man who carries out all the
most important tasks himself, both in the
cellar and in the vineyards. The plots are
situated in the finest parts of the Mittelmosel:
1.9 ha in the best, steep plots of the
Wehlener Sonnenuhr, 0.45 ha in the
Graacher Domprobst site. Without
exaggerating, at that moment, one could
sense the pride of having worked for
something really great flooding out of him. He
defines the greatness of the 1990 vintage as
follows: "When at least 50% of the harvest in
these sites exceeds 90° Oechsle, it is a noble
as well as great vintage." Especially the
sweet 1990 Auslesen prove this, being
incredibly compact and delicate.

Wehlener Sonnenuhr 🍇🍇 ②
Riesling Auslese* 1991
Assembled from 3 casks: nobly sweet, a wine of
94° Oechsle; great complexity, highly piquant,
grapey nuances and fantastic interplay between
the crisp acidity and sweetness.

Wehlener Sonnenuhr 🍇🍇 ③
Riesling Auslese** 1990
Only 1,500 lt of this wine were produced, grown
in the steepest plots on fine slate: lots of fruit
and richness.

Weingut von Hövel

Agritiustrasse 56
Konz-Oberemmel 5503
Tel. (06501) 15384
Fax (06501) 18498

Eberhard von Kunow is the 6th generation to run this estate situated in a side valley of the Saar. Of his 11 ha of vineyard 98% is planted with Riesling, the rest with a little Pinot Blanc. 5 ha are in the exclusive Oberemmeler Hütte site, 2.8 ha in the famous Scharzhofberg. The Hütte wines often turn out as equally noble as those from Scharzhofberg. Since they export 70% of the production, 90% of the wines are made in a lightly sweet style, but yet this corresponds to the owner's preferences. He comments "I want to make wines that I like, too". The sweetness comes from the blocked fermentation. In this way, he also makes high-grade Auslesen and Eisweine. Among recent vintages the 1989s were a little too light. On the other hand, the 1990s have crystal clear fruit and are compact with firm, steely acidity (from a small yield of 30 hl/ha). They are copy-book examples of what makes Saar wines so charming.

Balduin von Hövel   ☙ ①
Riesling QbA halbtrocken 1991
From the very good Rosenberg site a firm, fine wine, perhaps a little too warm in alcohol.

Oberemmeler Hütte   ☙ ①
Riesling Kabinett trocken 1991
Still closed but with noticeable fine grapey fruit, slim and with rather green acidity. This wine comes from a vineyard over 100 years-old.

Oberemmeler Hütte   ☙ ②
Riesling Spätlese 1991
It was only possible to make this racy Spätlese by painstaking selection of single bunches (which were of Auslese level).

Scharzhofberger   ☙☙ ②
Riesling Spätlese 1990
A perfect Saar Spätlese: noble fruit interlaced with piquant but ripe acidity and well-dosed sweetness.

Weingut Immich-Batterieberg

Im Alten Tal 2
Enkirch 5585
Tel. (06541) 9376
Fax (06541) 2790

It is difficult to think of more individual wines than those of Georg Immich. It begins with the color, which is more intense and yellow than those of others even as young wines, though they are not oxidised. At the end of 1989 Immich sold the estate to Sabine Basten, wife of a Munich property dealer, as at 60 he had no successor. The Bastens are distant relations, long-standing friends as well as customers, and in them he found successors willing to carry on his philosophy in wine producing down to the finest details. They even found and bought new wooden containers used by the pickers to carry the grapes on their backs. The harvest is usually not until November. Also, in other respects, the wine is made just as it was a hundred years ago when Immich's great grandfather, a wine-dealer, set the foundations for the present-day winery. He bought the enormous machinery that is still around today. The low-pressure, hydraulic press from those days is still in use and probably explains how Immich managed to make perfectly clean and harmonious wine in the difficult 1989 vintage, including the dry wines.

Enkircher Batterieberg   ☙☙ ③
Riesling Auslese 1990
Real nectare with velvety richness and unobtrusive residual sugar and thus very successful and fine.

Enkircher Batterieberg   ☙☙ ③
Riesling Auslese halbtrocken 1990
A restrained, fruity bouquet rounded off by cask aging: one of this estate's best 1990s

Enkircher Batterieberg   ☙ ②
Riesling Spätlese trocken 1989
A rather old-fashioned wine with an unusual, but not unpleasant, wood flavor, mature, full with a subdued, peachy aroma.

Weingut Karlsmühle

Mühlengrund 1
Mertesdorf-Lorenzhof 5501
Tel. (0651) 5123
Fax (0651) 52016

Although the Karlsmühle family are the exclusive owners of the Lorenzhöfer Felsay and Lorenzhöfer Mäuerchen sites (7 ha altogether), which are among the steepest and best Ruwer vineyards, their clear imprint has been on the wines only since 1987. They had produced the one or two other exciting wines beforehand, however Peter Geiben is a very vital and enthusiastic experimenter. Since then, he has increased his efforts towards attaining high quality, starting from the vineyard through to the cellar. Reduction in yields, better harvesting techniques and stainless steel tanks are the main principles. A cellar built into the hillside in the slatey rock guarantees constant, cool temperatures and is one of the main reasons why Geiben's wines have rich, cassis-like fruit. His 1989s have won several awards in blind tastings and are without doubt among the greatest of all Mosel-Saar-Ruwer wines. With this vintage, along with the equally successful 1990s (the peak is a fantastic, not overly sweet Beeren-Auslese), a third top estate was born on the Ruwer alongside Schubert and Karthäuslerhof.

Lorenzöfer   ℗ ①
Riesling Kabinett trocken 1991
Very sinewy and racy, wonderfully slim and delicate: a perfect example of how a Kabinett can turn out finer than a Spätlese.

Lorenzhöfer Felslay   ℗℗ ③
Riesling Auslese Goldkapsel 1990
An impressive Auslese with a strong Ruwer bite, superb sweetness-acidity interplay, very successful and balanced.

Lorenzhöfer Felslay   ℗℗ ④
Riesling Eiswein 1990
A highly concentrated Eiswein with fantastic acidity and light alcohol (7%). Could hardly be better.

Lorenzhöfer Felslay   ℗ ②
Riesling Spätlese halbtrocken 1990
A very appealing Spätlese, exceedingly fruity, compact and still retains a light sparkle - a wine with plenty of potential for future development.

Weingut Kees-Kieren

Hauptstrasse 22
Graach 5550
Tel. (06531) 3428
Fax (06531) 1593

Since the 1970s Ernst-Josef Kees, now 38, has been one of the best addresses for finely fruity Mittelmosel Rieslings. He is in charge of wine-making and sales, while his younger brother Werner looks after the agricultural side. The vineyards are fragmented, also in lesser-known but interesting sites at Kesten and Kinheim. His Kinheimer Rosenberg vineyard, located directly behind the village church, is thought to be the best plot in the whole village. Along with Kestener Paulinshofberg, it often produces exceptionally delicate wines of great finesse. He produces wines with marked acidity and pure varietal fruit by reductive wine-making, while very strict selection of grapes at harvest is the basis for his success. Occasionally the wines lack richness and could be a little fatter, but this is Kees' style. Apart from the wines, his Riesling 'marc' has become important and comes from an old-fashioned steam distillery.

Graacher Domprobst   ℗ ①
Riesling Kabinett halbtrocken 1991
A delicately, fruity wine with substance and firm, sinewy acidity, still very young but starting to reveal its potential.

Kestener Paulinsberg   ℗ ②
Riesling Auslese trocken 1990
Very clean, clear grapey fruit, made from perfectly healthy grapes, fermented and matured in stainless steel: a wine with future.

Kinheimer Rosenberg   ℗℗ ②
Riesling Auslese 1990
A perfectly made Auslese, very refined, with an excellent balance between sweetness, acidity and botrytis. It comes from a modernized, "flurbereinigt" vineyard right above the church of Kinheim.

Graacher Domprobst   ℗ ①
Riesling Spätlese halbtrocken 1989
A perfectly clean 1989, finely slatey, racy acidity and noble grapey fruit. A very classy, honest wine.

Weingut Heribert Kerpen

Uferallee 6
Bernkastel-Wehlen 5550
Tel. (06531) 6868
Fax (06531) 3464

This most famous Wehlen estate was run by Hane Kerpen until 1987. She was a charming school mistress who was widowed at an early age and taught many famous, and less famous, Mosel producers. Her son, Martin, was already able to handle the wine-making and took over in 1988, contributing substantially towards the estate's fame. Since then, he has continued to increase the vineyard holdings to 4.5 ha. With 3.3 ha, he is already the third largest owner in the Wehlener Sonnenuhr site. Martin Kerpen is also a clever businessman and markets his cousin Gernot Haut-Kerpen's wines. The main thing they have in common are their first class wine-making techniques which perfectly express the elegant style of Wehlener Sonnenuhr wines. Kerpen's wines often seem even clearer, more refined than those of his cousin, though often lack the latter's structure and finesse (as in the 1990 Auslesen for example).

Bernkasteler Bratenhöfchen   🍷 🍷 ④
Riesling Eiswein 1991
This brilliant Eiswein with a fascinating interplay between sweetness and acidity is from a very small but excellent, high altitude vineyard.

Graacher Himmelreich   🍷 ①
Riesling QbA trocken 1991
A fine minerally style with depth, very succulent and with good acidity; Kerpen's best QbA of this vintage.

Wehlener Sonnenuhr   🍷 ①
Riesling Kabinett 1991
A fine, elegant wine from a top site on the Mittelmosel: very gentle and succulent sweetness well-balanced by sinewy acidity.

Wehlener Sonnenuhr   🍷 🍷 ③
Riesling Auslese 1990
A wine almost bursting with fruit while at the same time gentle and elegant; this estate's best 1990 Auslese.

Bernkasteler Mateisbildchen   🍷 🍷 ②
Riesling Auslese trocken 1988
A rich but gentle Auslese. It is delicate and fresh in spite of its weight; dry and excellent with food.

Weingut Reichsgraf von Kesselstatt

Liebfrauenstrasse 9-10
Trier 5500
Tel. (0651) 73316
Fax (0651) 75101

This estate is owned by Günter Reh, who is the main shareholder in an enormous wine concern with an annual turn-over of DM 700 million. The administration and the gourmet restaurant, Palais Kesselstatt, together with a wine-tasting room, are housed in a magnificent barroque palace at Trier. The winery was completely rebuilt in 1988 and is located on the hills above the Ruwer valley at Schloss Marienlay. Considering the size of the estate (65 ha) its standard of quality is exemplary. Wine-maker Bernward Keiper plays a leading rôle. After all, he took the initiative to equip the new winery with stainless steel tanks in order to control fermentation temperatures as well to process grapes with the utmost care. He is helped by the managers Annegret Reh-Gartner and Gert Nussbaum. Wines from the various sites along the Saar (33 ha), Ruwer (12 ha) and the Mosel (20 ha) are made and matured individually. The often explosive fresh fruit of the Kesselstatt Rieslings is striking, just as it is in the dry wines.

Trittenheimer Apotheke   🍷 ②
Riesling Kabinett trocken 1991
A wine with unusual, delicate fruit and spice that is typical of the site - delicate and light, it goes well with food.

Ockfener Bockstein   🍷 🍷 ④
Riesling Auslese Goldkapsel 1990
After the Bernkastler Doktor, this is probably most interesting Auslese of the vintage: lemony sweetness, steely acidity, it is a powerful wine without being unctuous.

Palais Kesselstatt   🍷 ②
Riesling QbA trocken 1990
A high class Riesling, this cuvée has a considerably high percentage of Saar and Ruwer Auslese.

Riesling QbA halbtrocken 1990   🍷 ①
A charming, hearty, crystal clear Riesling with crisp acidity: without doubt, one of the best of the region's wines sold cheaply in liter bottles.

Weingut Peter Lauer

Ayl an der Saar 5511
Tel. (06581) 3031
Fax (06581) 2344

It is not easy to find harmony between food
and wine in the Mosel-Saar-Ruwer region.
However, this is not the case at Peter Lauer's
estate, for his wife, Julia, manages the 26-
bed Hotel Ayler Kupp in the center of Ayl, the
restaurant of the same name, as well as
looking after their three children. The
restaurant is known for its seafood and fish
dishes, and Lauer can play his trump cards
with his Saar Rieslings to accompany them.
Peter Lauer occupies himself first and
foremost with the five ha of vineyard which
offers exclusively wines from one of the Top
Saar sites, the Ayler Kupp. Two thirds of the
vineyard area is in the heart of the site, the
rest in the extended area. He is the second
largest owner in this cru and produces very
individual Saar Rieslings, usually appealingly
slim and fine. Wines from the various plots
are harvested, fermented and aged
separately and carry the cask numbers on
the labels. Single nuances deriving from
within the Ayler Kupp and the various
vintages can be detected. But unfortunately,
the best are quickly sold out to regular
customers.

Ayler Kupp   ⚇ ②
Riesling Kabinett Fass 2 1991
A big wine with appealing acidity and mouthfilling succulence, made from 30 year-old vines
grown in the heart of the Kupp site.

Ayler Kupp   ⚇ ②
Riesling Kabinett Fass 5 1990
A full-bodied wine with lots of soft, rich fruit with
lively acidity and soft, not obtrusive sweetness.

Ayler Kupp   ⚇⚇ ②
Riesling Spätlese Fass 7 1990
A very well-balanced wine with high acidity (11
g/lt) and the weight of an Auslese from one of
the highest, steepest and stoniest parts of the
Kupp site.

Weingut Dr. Loosen

St. Johannishof
Bernkastel-Kues 5550
Tel. (06531) 3426
Fax (06531) 4248

Ernst F. Loosen has enjoyed one of the most
spectacular rises to fame in recent years.
When he was called by his sick father to look
after the estate, the young archaeology
student at first considered it a short break.
Together with the 87 year-old, he ran the
estate and lead the way towards improving
the wine which, until then, had often proved
to be less than exciting. Under the brand
name "Dr. Loosen" the wines improved
enormously in quality, and the level has
stayed the same since. Their best sites are
Wehlener Sonnenuhr (2.2 ha) and the
Erdener Prälat, while the Bernkasteller Lay is
an insider tip, especially for 1989s. The
estate's credo is: "Keep the yields low, as a
wine must have power." With 10,000
ungrafted Riesling vines per hectare as is
usual in the Mittelmosel producing under 60
hl/ha the yields are lower than those of J. J.
Prüm, Loosen's ideal producer.

Dr. Loosen   ⚇ ①
Riesling QbA trocken 1991
The estate's dry Riesling is once again a
classic, following in the footsteps of its
sensational predecessors, with a low 9.5°
alcohol content typical of QbA.

Erdener Prälat   ⚇ ②
Riesling Spätlese 1991
From Ernst Loosen's favorite site: for the
vintage an unusually unctuous, noble,
fantastically fruity Riesling.

Ürziger Würzgarten   ⚇⚇ ③
Riesling Auslese Goldkapsel 1990
From a series of great 1990 Auslesen, this
superbly successful Riesling essence, without
being overly sweet, is remarkable for its great
elegance.

Wehlener Sonnenuhr   ⚇⚇ ③
Riesling Auslese Goldkapsel 1988
One of the best and most elegant Auslesen of
the vintage: classic cask-aging, unobtrusive
sweetness, great aging potential.

Weingut Meulenhof

Zur Kapelle 8
Erden 5553
Tel. (06532) 2267

Meulenhof is one of the oldest estates on the Mosel, first mentioned in 1337, though it is still relatively unknown. Stefan Justen runs it today, together with his father, who also looks after the distillery. With much commitment and meticulous care, Justen has been able to come up with consistently improving quallity, wines which are distinguished by clean and painstaking wine-making. They are fermented with selected yeasts, a practice that is frowned upon by most other top estates in the Mosel-Saar-Ruwer region. They say it produces uniform wines which are rather light and lacking in substance. This assertion cannot be denied when it comes to Justen's wines, though they make up in succulence and concentration, at least this is the result from the excellent plots in the Erdener Prälat and Wehlener Sonnenuhr. The careful harvesting methods also play their part. Both are noticeable in the impressive and otherwise problematic 1991 vintage. In addition to the steep sites they own over two ha in the flat Erdener Flur which produce simple wines usually sold in tank.

Erdener Prälat   🍇 ①
Riesling Spätlese 1991
Even more than in other years this 560-vine vineyard has shown its characteristic stamp of unique fruit and succulence which it imparts to the wines.

Erdener Treppchen   🍇 ①
Riesling Hochgewächs 1991
For a QbA, this wine has excellent fruit and finesse. A perfect example of the inner ripeness of the 1991s after a hot summer.

Wehlener Sonnenuhr   🍇 ①
Riesling Spätlese 1990
This late-harvest Spätlese from the Wehlener Sonnenuhr site is an elegant addition to the Erdener wines, that is more similar to an Auslese.

Weingut Markus Molitor

Klosterberg Wehlen
Bernkastel-Wehlen 5550
Tel. (06532) 3288
Fax (06532) 4225

Since Markus Molitor took over this estate at the age of 20 it has become exemplary and dynamic. Apart from doubling the vineyard area, he has placed the accent on quality by renting a four-hectare vineyard in the Zeltinger Sonnenuhr. With this move the ambitious new-comer, helped on the sales side by his father, seemed unstoppable. Between 1988 and 1990, he produced a series of Beeren-Auslesen, Trockenbeeren-Auslesen and Eisweine unique in the Mosel-Saar-Ruwer, mainly in straightforward style. Apart from J J Prüm hardly anybody else dares risking to extend the harvest date so long, often until December. The wines are traditionally matured, mainly in cask, without using finings. As a result they are robust, sometimes rough-hewn but always concentrated Mosel wines in a very elegant, dry style which are mainly sold in restaurants.

Zeltinger Sonnenuhr   🍇🍇 ②
Riesling Spätlese 1991
A very fine Spätlese from very strictly selected grapes produced by old vines which yielded 3-4 bunches each, at the most. Crystalline elegance.

Trabener Würzgarten   🍇🍇 ②
Riesling Spätlese trocken 1990
A very full wine with power, good acid structure, a light hint of botrytis and opulent fruit.

Zeltinger Sonnenuhr   🍇🍇 ④
Riesling Trockenbeerenauslese 1990
The absolute climax of a high caliber series of nobly sweet wines between '88 and 1990. Harvested at 185° Oechsle.

Wehlener Klosterberg   🍇 ①
Riesling Spätlese trocken 1988
Bone dry wine with good, mature acidity, still perfectly fresh and not at all tired.

Weingut Mönchhof

Robert Eymael
Ürzig 5564
Tel. (06532) 2116
Fax (06532) 1019

The Mönchhof estate, built in 1898, is a testimony to the wealth Mosel producers enjoyed at the turn of the century. Not only the neo-Renaissance building, but also the steep Ürziger Würzgarten and Erdener Treppchen sites planted with ungrafted vines, offer a spectacular panorama of the area. The Eymaels are represented here with 3 and 1 ha of vineyard respectively. The wine is matured in the classic manner, exclusively in the region's typical "Fuder" casks. Their wines have plenty of residual sugar, a style which has, otherwise, gone out of fashion in many estates. Both senior and junior Robert Rymael prefer this style as it tends to enhance their wines' fine fruitiness and makes them seem richer. In turn, the concentrated fruit from the exceptionally favorable vineyards balances out the sweetness. "Our customers insist on nothing else," as both father and son agree. By interrupting the fermentation earlier than their colleagues, they have been producing the best Auslesen available in recent years. They are high grade, elegant wines, the 1990s in some cases proving to be sensational.

Ürziger Würzgarten ❦ ①
Riesling QbA halbtrocken 1991
Among a rather disappointing range of 1991s, this rather cheap wine turned out to be a pleasant surprise: succulent, clean and fresh.

Erdener Treppchen ❦❦ ③
Riesling Auslese Goldkapsel 1990
Neither the richest nor the most expensive Auslese, but it is certainly the best. With great fruit, the wine has a fine, grapey flavor and delicate structure.

Ürziger Würzgarten ❦❦ ③
Riesling Spätlese Goldkapsel 1990
The result of the extreme understated efforts of the Eymael family, as at 92° Oechsle, this clearly belongs in the Auslese category. It has light, noble sweetness and brilliant acidity.

Ürziger Würzgarten ❦ ②
Riesling Spätlese trocken 1990
A 'fat' Spätlese with obvious grapiness and highly ripe fruit, relatively high in alcohol and slightly bitter: an unusual, interesting wine.

Weingut Egon Müller

Scharzhof
Wiltingen-Scharzhof 5511
Tel. (06501) 17232

It is as though Egon Müller's Scharzhofberger wines epitomised the whole drama of the Mosel-Saar-Ruwer, with absolute peaks on the one hand and great failures on the other. Scharzhof holds the world record for the price attained for a young white wine. In 1984 the phenomenally delicious 1983 Eiswein sold for 1,400 DM. Every year his 'fat' Auslesen break new price records at the "Grosser Ring" auctions at Trier. Nobody else has his knack of selecting the grapes or of achieving the perfectly integrated combination of sweetness and acidity which have made Scharzhofberger so notorious. They are wines of voluptuous sweetness, spectacular acidity and perfect harmony. At least as far as wines from Auslese upwards are concerned, and until a few years ago, this was also true of wines from the Spätlese level upwards. In recent years, Egon Müller's lesser wines have too often been characterised by green, apply, coarse acidity which do not fullfil expectations evoked by such a great name and, of course, by the prices. This is especially true when it comes to the old-fashioned woody style, which is otherwise found so appealing in more concentrated wines.

Scharzhofberger Nr.21 ❦❦ ③
Riesling Auslese 1991
Only very few vineyards produced wines of this class in the difficult 1991 vintage: a near perfect wine.

Scharzhofberger ❦❦ ③
Riesling Auslese Goldkapsel 1991
With 125° Oechsle and a quantity of less than 500 lt, this is a true gem for its vintage. Together with the Beeren-Auslese (with 164° Oechsle) which is not finer but fatter, this is a most interesting 1991. A perfect berry and peach essence but with great finesse and lightness. An elegant, nobly sweet wine which is not unctuous; herein lies the strength of the 1991s.

Scharzhofberger Nr.6 ❦ ③
Riesling Spätlese 1991
A delicate Riesling, well made, with crisp acidity: a great, classic Saar wine.

Weingut Dr. Pauly Bergweiler und Weingut Peter Nicolay

Gestade 15
Bernkastel-Kues 5550
Tel. (06531) 2063
Fax (06531) 7201

Two of the Mosel's most interesting wine estates, steeped in tradition and with superb sites, were united by marriage in 1971. By purchasing new vineyards, the Pauly-Nicolay families now own more top sites than any other estate on the Mittelmosel. They stretch from Erden across Ürzig, Zeitingen, Wehlen, Graach, Bernkastel to Braunenberg, totalling 15 ha in all. 75% are steep, 25% sloping vineyards. In 1980 Dr. Peter Pauly solved the problems of space with a radical step which at that time was unusual on the Mittelmosel, by building a very modern winery filled with stainless steel at Bernkastel-Andel on a green meadow. Since then wood casks have only been used for certain wines, especially in lesser vintages. Otherwise, the wines are made in stainless steel. Temperature-controlled fermentation produces extremely fresh wines with intense aromas. As they are not rounded off by wood aging they sometimes seem rather acidic and raw, especially the dry wines. In addition, Pauly's preference for higher alcohol in the wines does not always produce the finesse that is more typical of the Mosel. Thus the estate's strength lies in its off-dry and fruity, sweet style, while they occasionally demote perfect Auslesen to Spätlese.

Bernkasteler Alte Badstube   🍇 🍇 ③
am Doctorberg Riesling Auslese 1990
This polished, fruity wine with a high sugar content is delicately balanced by good acidity and comes from the vineyard close to the famous Doctor vineyard; it was one of the highlights at the 1991 Bernkasteller Ring auction.

Ürziger Goldwingert   🍇 ②
Riesling Spätlese 1990
This very unctuous, fat wine comes from a superb site of only a quarter of a hectare. Round and sweet, and full of complex fruit and a finely balanced by acidity: an Auslese wine in style.

Spätburgunder QbA trocken 1990   🍇 ①
This wine comes from the Graacher Domprobst vineyard, a very steep site renowned for its blue devonian slate. It is a light red wine with good spice and is a rarity on the Mosel.

Weingut Joh. Jos Prüm

Uferallee
Bernkastel-Kues 5550
Tel. (06531) 3091
Fax (06531) 6071

Like Egon Müller on the Saar, Johann Josef Prüm is the number one on the Mosel and a cult estate for Riesling lovers. Its reputation is inseparable from the Wehlener Sonnenuhr site, in which he is the largest landowner with 5-ha of vineyards. Wehlener Sonnenuhr is regarded world-wide as the incarnation of the most finely scented Mosel Riesling. The estate is now run by the lawyer Manfred Prüm. He makes no secret of how seriously commited he feels towards this inheritance from his father, who, in the 1930s established the estate's unique reputation by his exemplary improvement of grape selection techniques. In recent years the top wines as well as normal ones have been excellent, especially in problem vintages like 1982, 1986 and 1989. According to the owner, the excellent 1990s are not yet drinkable. As a result many of the best wines will not be released for sale for some time to come. Who else could get away with forcing this kind for policy on his customers? However, they have got used to the fact and have even learned to appreciate it when suddenly a fantastic 1983 Riesling Eiswein is released or an 1981 Riesling Kabinett, perfectly fresh in spite of having been forgotten in cask.

Graacher Himmelreich 🍇🍇 ③
Riesling Auslese 1990
Noble scent of berries, very ripe acidity, harmonious and elegant, very rich in body: a great Auslese.

Dr. M. Prüm 🍇 ①
Riesling QbA trocken 1989
Manfred Prüm always waits a long time before releasing his wines: the standard estate Riesling is delicately ripe with hearty acidity.

Wehlener Sonnenuhr 🍇 ②
Riesling Kabinett 1989
A wine with piquant, concentrated fruit, very succulent and long-lasting, it is one of the best Mosel Kabinett Rieslings from the 1989 vintage.

Zeltinger Sonnenuhr 🍇🍇 ③
Riesling Auslese 1988
A very young, light-weight but extremely delicate and elegant Auslese with a long life ahead.

Wehlener Sonnenuhr 🍇🍇🍇 ④
Riesling Auslese Lange Goldkapsel 1990
Without doubt, this is one of the half dozen undisputed best wines produced in this exceptional year, even better than the 1988 Auslese. What is special about this wine is the fact that the grapes were harvested in November by techniques normally used to make Beerenauslese. In fact, it was produced using two different types of berries. Some were ripe and healthy, and others overripe, almost raisined, but still not attacked by botrytis. They were cut out from the bunches one by one with scissors, according to an age-old technique that was last used in Prüm's estate in 1959. The end wine is 120° Oechsle, making it, in theory a Beerenauslese. With intense scents of passion fruit and ripe peaches, as well as its fantastic elegance and crisp 9 g/lt acidity, it is certainly a wine to drink in 50 years' time.

Weingut S. A. Prüm

Uferallee 25-26
Bernkastel-Wehlen 5550
Tel. (06531) 3110
Fax (06531) 8555

This estate is no longer the undisputed number two. In the 1970s it fell directly behind Joh. Jos. Prüm. But "roter Raimund" (Prüm's nickname due to his red hair) has been so busy experimenting and rennovating his quality and image, starting with his labels on through to the winery, that today his position is slightly teneble. This wine village has always distinguished itself for its conservatism and traditional style of making wine. Indeed, rather uneven standards have recently become obvious, especially among the simpler wines. His special method of pressing the grapes without previously crushing them seems to increase the gentleness and finesse of the wines while at the same time making them unstable in structure. Nevertheless, time and time again, Raimund Prüm's sensitivity to draw out the finest essence of the single plots of vineyard, together with his harvesting expertise, produces very refined wines from the Wehlener Sonnenuhr, the Graacher Himmelreich and Bernkasteler Lay sites.

S.A. Prüm ♈ ①
Riesling QbA trocken 1991
A QbA with a nice sparkle, characterized by a slatey "gout de terroir", ripe, harmonious and succulent; from the Wehlener Klosterberg vineyard.

Wehlener Sonnenuhr ♈♈ ③
Riesling Auslese (9-91) 1990
The 'fatter', weightier of the two 1990 Sonnenuhr Auslesen with an accentuated grapey flavor, delicate and piquant.

Zeltinger Schlossberg ♈ ②
Riesling Spätlese 1988
With considerable residual sugar (20 g/lt), this is an unusual, easy drinking, fine, top Riesling from very old, ungrafted vines.

Rautenstrauchsche Weingutsverwaltung

Karthäusehof
Trier-Eitelsbach 5500
Tel. (0651) 5121
Fax (0651) 53557

Christoph Tyrell, the present owner of the Karthäuslerhof took over this picturesque estate rich in traditions in 1986 in a very difficult period. His father, Werner Tyrell, had given it a bad reputation, when he was found guilty of illegally adding sugar to QmP wines (quality wines of distinction). Thanks to the energetic 43 year-old Christof Tyrell, a lawyer by profession, who threw himself into the work with tremendous commitment, the winery has now regained its excellent reputation. Together with wine-maker Ludwig Breiling, they decided to shorten the distance the grapes had to travel from vineyard to cellar and to bring in a full selection of new stainless steel tanks. However, it is not true that the wines used to be worse or sweeter than they are today, as one often reads. Their special feature, in comparison to their competitors, was always their wines' understated sweetness. What is new, indeed, is the extreme freshness, fruit and marked acidity. The 1987s and 1988s were and still are wonderful; the 1989s inconsistent, often weighed down by too much botrytis, yet the 1990s are very promising.

Eitelsbacher Karthäuserhofberg ♈ ②
Riesling QbA 1991
As in preceeding vintages, among the simple "Qualitätsweine", the fruity, sweet style is more successful, even though less in demand.

Eitelbacher Karthäuserhofberg ♈ ③
Riesling Spätlese trocken 1991
1991 produced several Spätlesen (and even one Auslese). The dry version is recognizable by its supple elegance and minty aroma.

Eitelsbacher Karthäuserhofberg ♈ ③
Riesling Auslese Nr.23 1990
Perhaps not the Auslese with the highest Oechsle ratings, but it has fantastic acidity and an aroma and flavor reminiscent of a basket full of exotic fruit, especially lychee and pineapple.

Eitelsbacher Karthäuserhofberg ♈ ④
Riesling Auslese Nr.6 Lange Goldkapsel 1990
The top Auslese of a great vintage: with ripe but mild acidity, extremely rich, noblest sweetness and finest grape flavor. It fetched DM136.5 at the auction.

Weingut Max Ferdinand Richter

Hauptstraße 85
Mülheim/Mosel 5556
Tel. (06534) 704
Fax (06534) 1211

Driving from Bernkastel towards Mülheim one sees an imposing, long winery built of the area's typical slate stone. The largest cellars of the Mittelmosel were built here in the 1880s. At that time Max Ferdinand Richter was one of the largest wholesale wine merchants on the Mosel. At first, the vineyards were little more than a plaything for his grandfather, but, in the meantime, they have grew to become the main object of focus. In addition to the famous wines from the well-known sites of Brauneberg, Wehlen and Graach, there are the lesser known but very individual and interesting wines, from Trarbacher Ungsberg and Veldenzer Elisenberg. Almost every year an Eiswein is harvested from the exclusive Mülheimer Helenenkloster site. Often the grapes get eaten up wild boar, as was the case in 1991. The wines are aged in the classic manner, in the many wooden casks which fill the impressive cellars. Although they are rarely delicate, they have good character and are consistent, especially at the medium quality level, which the son, Dirk Richter, has worked hard on in recent years.

Cuvée Constantin 🍇 ①
Rivaner QbA trocken 1991
A good Müller-Thurgau, also called Rivaner, rounded by a small addition of Riesling and aged in oak.

Dr. Richter's 🍇 ①
Riesling QbA halbtrocken 1991
A wine produced exclusively from the free run juice, it is refreshing and sincere. A marvellous Mosel wine for everyday consumption.

Brauneberger Juffer Sonnenuhr 🍇🍇 ③
Riesling Auslese 1990
Only 500 lt were produced in this first harvest from young vines. Weighing in at 105° Oechsle, it is a very creamy and full wine with rich sweetness and good acidity but needs time in the bottle.

Veldenzer Elisenberg 🍇🍇 ②
Riesling Spätlese 1990
This first-class estate-owned vineyard produced an interesting Spätlese for the vintage with piquant, mouth-watering acidity and mature, grapey aromas.

Weingut Schloss Saarstein

Dieter und Christian Ebert
Serrig/Saar 5512
Tel. (06581) 2324

Schloss Saarstein towers high above its own vineyards called Serriger Schloss Saarsteiner. However, it is not a real castle, as the name seems to indicate, but a large estate-house built at the turn of the century when Mosel wine trade was booming. The agriculturalist Dieter Ebert, originally from Mark Brandenburg acquired it in 1956. With much perseverence, he made it once again to what it is today, that is, one of the top names for fresh Saar Rieslings. His son, Christian Ebert, is gradually taking over, while the father is toying with the idea of returning to the old property in eastern Germany. 70% of the wines are made in a dry style, 10% as off-dry (halbtrocken). No other Saar estate can match these percentages. Even in mediocre vintages like 1989, their dry wines are usually very successful. However, this does not mean that fruity-sweet and nobly sweet versions are neglected. Contrary to the philosophy of most of their colleagues on the Mosel-Saar-Ruwer, Schloss Saarstein swears by the addition of clean grape juice (Süssreserve) to sweeten the wines, instead of using the natural residual sugar, retained from the blocked fermentation.

Schloss Saarstein 🍇 ①
Riesling QbA trocken 1991
Lighter in alcohol and in body than the same wine from the 1990 vintage but it makes up in elegance and soft, concentrated fruit thanks to a very low 36 hl/ha yields.

Serriger Schloss Saarsteiner
Riesling Auslese Goldkapsel 1991
Extremely delicate with a clear, grapey flavor and light apricot aroma: one of the Saar's best 1991 nobly sweet dessert wines.

Serriger Schloss Saasteiner 🍇🍇 ④
Riesling Eiswein 1989
After several runs to pick the normal and super-ripe grapes, in the end only those affected by botrytis were left on the vines: a great, extremely concentrated Eiswein which weighed in at 145° Oechsle, 14 g/lt of acidity and 200 g residual sugar. It is undoubtedly the greatest of its kind on the Saar in this vintage; unfortunately, only 100 lt could be made.

Willi Schaefer

Hauptstraße 130
Graach 5550
Tel. (06531) 8041
Fax (06531) 1414

In spite of or, perhaps because of, his small spectacles Willi Schaefer's eyes light up whenever he sees wine. When he tastes it and finds it good, his face melts into a voluptuous smile. He is one of the increasingly rare 'vignerons' who make their wines with the eye of a genuine aficionado and epicure. He has always stood for 100% Riesling. What is most impressive is the way the 43 year-old manages to make the most archetypical, softly fruity, delicate Mosel wines at all levels, from simple, dry QbA through to Beeren-Auslese. However, he only owns 2 ha of vineyard which he regards as his ideal. It is just the right size that he can devote himself to wholeheartedly, from vineyard through to bottle. Although his dry Rieslings are very popular, the most refined wines are those with light sweetness. His small, cool cellar naturally temper and block the fermentation.

Graacher Domprobst   🍇 🍇 ④
Riesling Auslese 1991
An attempt at Beeren-Auslese: 105° Oechsle, a very fine aroma of raisins and apricot, very soft, sugar-sweet fruit and enormous potential for future development.

Graacher Himmelsreich   🍇 ①
Riesling Kabinett 1991
A delicate Riesling, characterised by wood-aging from the oldest plots of the Himmelreich site. A very delicate Kabinett.

Graacher Himmelsreich   🍇 ①
Riesling QbA Hochgewächs 1991
An easy-drinking, inexpensive Mosel Riesling with fine, fruit-sweetness, good acidity and substance from a good site. By the way, it is not a "Hochgewächs" even if it is allowed to be called so.

Graacher Himmelsreich   🍇 🍇 ②
Riesling Auslese halbtrocken 1990
A high-grade Riesling with plenty of substance, refined, soft fruit and the typical Domprobst spiciness: one of the best 1990 Graacher wines.

Weingut Carl Schmitt-Wagner

Longuich 5501
Tel. (06502) 2437

65 year-old Bruno Schmitt is the type of original wine-grower character found in almost every village along the Mosel. He is a walking wine-making encyclopedia full of anecdotes on Mosel and on how he has been one up on the present day accepted theory and can back his stories with old wines which are still super fresh. He is an old-school Mosel producer who takes samples from every cask in half-liter bottles and numbers every single one of them. His father began after the First World War 1, appropriately with bottle N° 1. Bruno Schmitt is now up to N° 1,200. In this way he has a complete museum of his own wines. Thus, practically every cask is bottled individually. In addition to ordinary wines, there are often true gems to be found and often at similarly modest prices. The wines are matured in a damp, arched cellar that is exclusively made out of wood. He still uses an old vacuum press made in 1919 and still makes almost clear juice. This very juice is the prerequisite for the incredible finely scented Rieslings made by this estate.

Longuicher Maximiner Herrenberg 🍇 ①
Riesling Kabinett AP 5/92 1991
A finely fruity wine with gentle acidity with a pronounced, natural sparkle from ungrafted vines planted in 1896.

Longuicher Maximiner Herrenberg 🍇 🍇 ①
Riesling Kabinett Nr. 1143 1990
An unusually intense, finely fruity aroma, nobly grapey; demoted from high quality Auslese - impressive.

Longuicher Maximiner Herrenberg 🍇 🍇 ④
Riesling Trockenbeerenauslese 1989
Selected by hand, berry by berry. Very concentrated, nobly sweet nectare and not at all cloying in spite of its 174° Oechsle.

Longuicher Maximiner Herrenberg 🍇 🍇 ②
Riesling Auslese trocken 1988
Very gentle and elegant, though a rather light Auslese, it comes from an extremely steep vineyard that was planted with ungrafted vines in 1938.

C. von Schubert'sche Gutsverwaltung

Grünhaus 5501
Tel/Fax (0651) 52122

The address already gives an indication as to this winery's special position. Grünhaus, or more precisely, Maximum Grünhaus, is a locality all its own. Even the labels carry the exclusive indication of the three prestigous localities of Maximum Grünhäuser Abtsberg, Maximum Grünhäuser Herrenberg, Maximum Grünhäusler Brudersberg. The present day owner, Carl von Schubert, also categorises the quality of his three sites in this order. Abtsberg produces wines that are rich in finesse; Herrenberg, wines with the highest acidity (especially among dry wines); the Brudersberg; the most straightforward. The large difference in styles between these growths is impressive. Maximum Grünhaus is one of those wines that 'everyone who is anybody must have', being a popular brand among Germany's best restaurants and wine merchants. But the estate also makes a good range of styles, including single cask bottlings. The individuality and quality of each site is noticeable. Before the finesse of a wine goes lost by making a large blend, Carl von Schubert prefers to bottle it individually.

Maximin Grünhäuser Abtsberg ℗ ②
Riesling QbA trocken 1991
An unusually full table wine, the most extrovert of the '91 assortment and also the fruitiest.

Maximin Grünhäuser Herrenberg ℗ ②
Riesling Kabinett trocken 1991
A somewhat bitter wine with very fruity acidity and a minerally flavor. One of the best classic Ruwer Riesling wines.

Maximin Grünhäuser Abtsberg ℗℗ ④
Riesling Auslese trocken 1990
Dry Auslesen are a speciality of Schubert's. This wine was harvested at a high Oechsle level and high acidity and has stayed more or less the same.

Maximin Grünhäuser Herrenberg ℗℗ ②
Riesling Kabinett trocken 1990
Full-bodied, spicy, of noble character, with the typical mineral flavors, it has a strong sense of 'terroir' to be expected from the Herrenberg area from which it comes from. Similar to an Auslese.

Maximin Grünhäuser Abtsberg ℗℗℗ ④
Riesling Auslese Nr. 96 1990
The fact that both the Oechsle rating and the cask number 96 are identical is a mere coincidence. It is significant and unusual to have such a high sugar level from perfectly healthy grapes. The grapes come from old, densely planted vines in the heart of the Abtsberg site. Since the grapes from the 1990 vintage were impeccable and healthy ,without noble rot, the wine is straightforward, powerful and completely lacking in botrytis aromas (which were otherwise plentiful in the 1989s). The pickers selected only the small, seedless, unpollinated berries that had very little liquid content and were highly concentrated. The finished wine has 9.1 g/lt of acidity and 55.4 g residual sugar. In spite of its weight, it has remained light, delicate and fresh. The interplay between sweetness and acidity is fantastic. It will likely retain its youthful spirit for decades to come.

Weingut Selbach-Oster

Uferallee 23
Zeltingen 5553
Tel. (06532) 2081
Fax (06532) 4014

J & J Selbach was formerly one of the last of the smaller wineries, and has now merged to form the Selbach-Oster estate, whose increased holdings are now a respectable 7.2 ha of vineyards. The increase in size has also meant an increase in vineyard quality. The 1.3 ha Zeltinger Sonnenuhr (which is the equal of the neighboring Wehlener Sonnenuhr site) produces some of the Mittelmosel's finest, most gently scented Rieslings. Both father, Hans Selbach, and son, Johannes, are quality-fanatics as producers as well as merchants. The 1989s are very delicate and unusually good for this vintage; among the 1990s, the fruity Kabinett and Spätlese wines are very appealing and their understated sweetness making them very good food-wines. Although the Auslesen are fine, they sometimes seem light. Altogether with its 10 Beeren-Auslesen, Trockenbeeren-Auslesen and Eisweine between 1988 and 1991, Selbach-Oster have managed to produce an impressive collection of nobly sweet wines.

Bernkasteler Badstube
Riesling Kabinett 1991
Firm, succulent Kabinett with typical Selbach austerity (with 20 g/lt residual sugar). An easy-drinking wine.

Zeltinger Schlossberg
Riesling QbA trocken 1991
This wine is almost a classic by now. In blind tastings it often does better than the more prestigious Kabinett wines.

Zeltinger Sonnenuhr
Riesling Auslese 1990
A very mature Auslese with light grapiness and botrytis together with delicate, supple with well-balanced sweetness.

Bert Simon

Weingut Herrenberg
Serrig/Saar 5512
Tel. (06581) 2208
Fax (06581) 2242

Not all wines from this medium-large private estate are convincing. Some seem strange, others faulty. A few wines from the large assortment are undoubtedly superb, especially among the 1991s. This is perhaps partly because Thomas Haag, the eldest son and future successor of Wilhelm Haag at Brauneberg, helped out in this vintage. His commitment seems to have brought about a general improvement in all wines. When it comes to structure, spice, compactness and elegance some of his best Auslesen are only beaten by the great Egon Müller. Unfortunately, although it was not their fault, there were very obvious cork problems, especially in the 1989. All Simon wines show good substance due to the vineyard extension and the intentionally short pruning, aimed to reduce yields to as low as 55 hl/ha. The steep, sloped vineyards on the Saar (19 ha) and Ruwer (19 ha), planted 80% with Riesling, show extraordinary potential

Bert Simon
Riesling Kabinett 1991
A piquant, spicy wine with an accentuated cassis aroma, supple with a very succulent, intense interplay between fruit and acidity.

Bert Simon
Riesling Kabinett trocken 1991
Still rather subdued fruit, but racy, spicy, crisp acidity: a hearty Saar Riesling with substance.

Serriger Würtzberg
Riesling Auslese Goldkapsel 1990
A very fine, nobly sweet wine, it weighed in at 107° Oechsle and has plenty of acidity and delicate fruit. It is a top Auslese of this vintage.

Kaseler Kehrnagel
Riesling Auslese 1989
Strong botrytis scents on the nose, with powerful spice and good length: a small Beeren-Auslese.

Weingut St Urbanshof

Ökonomierat Nic. Weis
Leiwen 5501
Tel. (06507) 3041-2
Fax (06507) 3042

Hermann Weiss owns one of the largest vine nurseries in Europe and yet, for a long time, his wine estate was only of secondary importance in Leiwen. All this changed in 1990, when he bought 15 ha of vineyard with superb sites on the Saar: 3.9 ha in the Ockfener Bockstein site and 9 ha in the best part of the Wiltinger Schlangengraben site An extension of vineyard of these dimensions and quality standards can only matched by Tyrell, von Schubert and the Staatsdomänen. In 1990 Weis became a sudden hit. It started them off by producing such an interesting range of wines, both dry and nobly sweet, that they quickly established a top reputation in the Saar. The proportion of dry (60%) and off-dry (25%) wines is high. Self-assured, he comments: "I make dry wines which also appeal to sweet-wine drinkers." In order to do so, the restrict yields to 70 hl/ha and increase the alcohol content of QbA wines to 11% by chaptalisation. The results are good, even if occasionally the typical finesse of Mosel and Saar wines is smothered in the high alcohol.

Leiwener Laurentiuslay 🍇 ②
Riesling QbA trocken 1991
An explosive wine with fruit and massive acidity and warm alcohol (11.5%), typical of the grape, which comes from a superb site.

Ockfener Bockstein 🍇🍇 ③
Riesling Auslese 14/91 1990
From a newly-acquired and highly productive exceptional vineyard comes an immediate success: a very fine, minerally Auslese.

St. Urbanshof 🍇 ①
Riesling QbA trocken 1990
A fresh wine with slightly hard acidity, very compact and vigorous: a generous Riesling, a little high in alcohol.

Wiltinger Schlangengraben 🍇 ①
Riesling Kabinett 1990
A fine, elegant Saar Riesling with 10.6 g/lt acidity and 32 g/lt residual sugar: a very classy wine.

Leiwener Laurentiuslay 🍇🍇🍇 ③
Riesling Auslese trocken 1990
There are two depressions in the 19 ha steep Leiwener Laurentiuslay, which is a relatively unheardof top site. One of these is owned by Hermann Weis. The soil is composed of oily, finely erroded slate gravel: no single piece is larger than a five mark coin. It is the slate which makes this wine so fine. Its incredible fruitiness balances the piercing acidity, while the high 12° alcohol content, very unusual along the Mosel, is well-integrated and gives additional support to the acidity and fruit structure. According to Weiss all this is further accented by the very low yields. This wine shows how dry Mosel Riesling can be first-class when supported by ripe fruit, as can be the case in great vintages.

Wein-Erbhof Stein

St. Aldegund 5581
Tel. (06542) 2979

"Theory and Practice". These very words could be used as a sub-title for Weingut Stein. Ulrich Stein, who runs the estate together with his brother, Peter, is a scientist, a qualified viticultural engineer and a biologist and wrote his thesis on Botrytis Cinerea (noble rot). His customers are mainly from intellectual circles and the arts. He is always keen to point out to them that since he was 18 he never lost touch with the practical reality of wine production in spite of his intense scientific approach, always practicing what he learned in the vineyard. Involved with the company wholeheartedly since 1985, he has concentrated more on the wine-making, meanwhile his brother is more active in the vineyard. Based on his experience, he aims at producing elegant, delicate and digestible wines with low tannin. When in doubt, he renounces the final degree of richness. By means of vineyard techniques which include the practice of using only ungrafted vines, he keeps botrytis and the problem of grape loss, as they naturally fall to the ground, well under control. His 'credo' in wine-making focusses on harvesting the grapes in small containers, careful destemming and using the very old method of fining with isinglass.

St. Aldegunder Himmelreich 🍇 ①
Riesling QbA halbtrocken 1991
The most straightforward Riesling but superbly successful: fresh, slim, succulent, racy. A serious wine for everyday drinking.

St. Aldegunder Palmberg-Terrassen 🍇 ①
Riesling Kabinett trocken 1991
From a very steep, terraced site comes a dry wine with accentuated acidity, slim and at the same time powerful.

St. Aldegunder Palmberg-Terrassen 🍇 ②
Riesling Spätlese halbtrocken 1990
A complex, finely strung Riesling with a nuance of sweetness, also good with food as it tastes almost dry.

Weingut Studert Prüm

Maximinhof
Bernkastel-Weheln 5550
Tel. (06531) 2487
Fax (06531) 3920

In addition to J. J. Prüm and S. A. Prüm, this is the third estate to emerge from the former Prüm property. With a rich heritage in wine-growing and merchant traditions, Stephan Studert gave this estate its present name and form after marrying one of Peter Prüm's daughters. The 68 year-old still runs the estate together with his sons, Stephan Jr. and Gerhard. The latter is the estate's businessman and speaks of this threesome as a 'triumvate'. Generally speaking, the Studerts aim at producing vigorous wines with more alcohol and considerably less sweetness than the norm, and sweet Spät- and Auslesen are generally drier than those of other producers, especially among the 1989s and 1990s. The 1991s on the other hand are just as successful as the 1990s inspite of the lesser vintage. All their wines have gained in delicacy and elegance. Due to the small quantities produced, they can still be matured in traditional large casks, a method which the Studerts still favor.

Bernkasteler Graben 🍇 ①
Riesling Kabinett halbtrocken 1991
From the neighboring site to the Bernkasteler Doctor, it almost always produces very racy sinewy wines with an accentuated slaty character.

Wehlener Sonnenuhr 🍇🍇 ②
Riesling Spätlese 1991
From the Keller plot, which is an indentation in the hillside that has a constant and abundant water supply, this is a high grade Spätlese with a fine, slatey style wine that is very generous and succulent.

Wehlener Sonnenuhr 🍇🍇 ③
Riesling Auslese 1990
Having weighed in at 95° Oechsle and now with 9 g/lt of acidity, this is a very racy Auslese with a fine sparkle, masses of botrytis and very accentuated fruit.

Wehlener Sonnenuhr 🍇 ①
Riesling Spätlese 1989
An elegant wine with typical Wehlen peachy fruit and a strong grapey aroma - definitely Auslese in style.

Weingut Wwe Dr. H Thanisch

Saarallee 31
Bernkastel-Kues 5550
Tel. (06531) 2282
Fax (06531) 2226

Though only four ha in size, it has four owners who are, as may be expected, very envied in the wine-world. Indeed, they are the proprietors of what is likely to be the world's most expensive vineyard: the Bernkasteler Doktor. However, the most expensive wine is not always the best, as many experts say, and they tend to prize other Mosel sites more highly. The Widow Dr. Thanisch estate (not to be confused with Thanisch Müller Burggraef) at the moment shows what superb wines can emerge from this vineyard, which towers above the rooftops of Bernkastel. With their fresh acidity, they are in a class of their own. Mechtild Thanisch is the principle owner of the estate, while her niece, Sofia Spier, (who, incidentally, married a teacher at the Bernkastel school of wine-growing, Ulrich Spier), is part owner and administrator. Norbert Breit is the wine-maker and matures the wines traditionally in wood casks. Over many years the quality tended to be irregular, but it has increasingly stabilised in recent years. Their best wines, as well as their more simple ones, are appealingly delicate and come not only from the Doktor vineyard but from the Lay, Graben and Badstube sites as well.

Bernkasteler Lay 🍇 ②
Riesling Spätlese 1990
A fine, delicate, slatey wine with apricot and peach aromas; succulent and piquant with a fine balance between sweetness and acidity.

Wwe Dr. Thanisch 🍇 ①
Riesling QbA halbtrocken 1990
Very succulent with crisp acidity and breed and lots of fine grapefruit flavor; explosively fruity.

Bernkasteler Badstube 🍇 ②
Riesling Spätlese halbtrocken 1988
With its subtle, pleasant bouquet and soft cassis nuances, it is fresh and elegant with a fine slatey character.

Berncasteler Doctor 🍇🍇🍇 ④
Riesling Auslese 1989
This Auslese is without doubt one of the absolute great nobly sweet Mosel wines of the 1989 vintage. A sublime, exotic fruit bouquet and an almost creamy essence of honey and melon together with a stunningly refined balance between sweetness and acidity (the acidity is 10.5 g/lt). The harvest took place at the beginning of November and the nobly rotten sprigs of berries had to be broken off the bunches by hand. Only just over 300 lt could be produced. At the traditional "Grosser Ring" auction at Trier, it fetched DM 170. By the way, on the original label dating back to 1901, the name of the village is spelt with a 'c', while other producers spell it in the modern manner with 'k'.

Dr Heinz Wagner

Bahnhofstrasse 3
Saarburg 5510
Tel. (06581) 2457

Tanned and red-cheeked, the profession of wine-producer is written all over Heinz Wagner. Apart from a couple of helpers he works his 10 ha of steep vineyard alone. His attitudes towards wine are correspondingly deep-rooted. For example, grapes which have fallen from the vine never find their way into his wines. A further reason for the crystal clear, Saar Riesling fruit which Wagner is so adept at bringing out in the wines is the cellar, with its gigantic arches, which goes back to the merchant business of his father. His own water source assures continuous humidity and very cool temperatures which naturally stop the wines from fermenting, leaving them with natural residual sugar; meanwhile the air shafts keep the air in the cellar clean. These factors produce perfect conditions for cask aging. Wagner's dry and off-dry styles wines are among the most reliable and are often the best along the Saar. The refined Riesling fruit in his sweet wines is also difficult to beat, especially the QbAs and Kabinetts.

Ockfener Bockstein   ⚇ ①
Riesling Kabinett 1991
Delicate fruit-sweetness, fresh with lively acidity, nuances of grapefruit. A very stylish, light Saar Riesling.

Dr.Wagner   ⚇ ②
Saar Riesling Brut 1990
This sparkling Riesling wine is still very young with hearty, fresh acidity. Wonderfully slim and creamy.

Saarburger Rausch   ⚇⚇ ②
Riesling Spätlese halbtrocken 1990
A very strong, natural sparkle; elegant and ripe with a very fresh balance between acidity and sweetness.

Gutsverwaltung Geheimrat Wegeler-Deinhard

Friedensplatz 9
Oestrich-Winkel 6227
Tel. (06723) 7031
Fax (06723) 1453

The Mosel and Ruwer wines of the Geheimrat Wegeler Deinhard estate are made in the cellars of Germany's largest sekt producer and wine merchant at Koblenz, 100 km away from the vineyards. The 31-ha Mosel and Ruwer estate (95% steep vineyards, 90% Riesling) is managed by Norbert Holderreith, who is also director of the company's headquarters in the Rheingau. The distance from the production area probably expalins why most Deinhard wines are slightly lacking in finesse and complexity, inspite of Norbert Holderreith's diligence. They are very solid and characteristic Mosel and Ruwer wines with firm, hearty Riesling acidity. And yet, apart from a few top wines, they could be better, given the fantastic potential of the sites. 1.3 ha in the Bernkasteler Doktor, 4.9 ha in the Wehlener Sonnenuhr, (second largest owner), plus 7.37 ha in the fantastic Ruwer Kaseler Nies'chen site. In order to tighten the range only the above-mentioned are bottled as cru wines, while all others are marketed anonymously as Geheimrat Wegeler-Deinhard Mosel-Saar-Ruwer.

Wehlener Sonnenuhr   ⚇⚇ ②
Riesling Kabinett 1991
A Spätlese which stopped fermenting with 22 g/lt of residual sugar (hardly noticeable) and, therefore, was declassified to Kabinett. An admirable wine in a difficult vintage.

Bernkasteler Doctor   ⚇⚇ ④
Riesling Auslese 1990
The greatest Auslese from this top site in 20 years (although it produced eight in the 1980s and three in the 1970s). An enormous, nobly sweet wine which was harvested at 102° Oechsle, it needs time to develop.

Bernkasteler Doctor   ⚇ ④
Riesling Spätlese 1990
Restrained fruit with nuances of citrus fruits: the small amount of residual sugar is hardly noticeable. A good food wine.

Bernkasteler Lay   ⚇⚇ ②
Riesling Spätlese trocken 1990
Even those who are not fans of dry Mosel wines will find this one very appealing, having good structure, and plenty of fruity mellowness.

Weingut Dr Weins-Prüm

Uferallee 20
Bernkastel-Wehlen 5550
Tel. (06531) 2270
Fax (06531) 3181

Bert Selbach never learned how to make wine academically. He worked in a few other wineries, but otherwise merely carried on with what he learned from his father. Of course, the fermenation temperatures are controlled naturally in his deep, arched cellars with a small stream running through it which produces constantly cool temperatures and generates humidity. Weins-Prüm is directly next to J. J. Prüm and along with him it has been the best balanced Wehlen estate since the mid 1980s. Selbach concentrates more on Kabinett and Spätlese than on Auslesen. Apart from Wehlener Sonenuhr, the estate owns a property on the Ruwer with one hectare in the Waldracher Sonnenberg site. Ürziger Würzgarten (0.7 ha), Erdener Prälat (0.1 ha), Graacher Himmelreich (0.43 ha and Graacher Domprobst (0.5 ha) complete their range of steep vineyards.

Wehlener Sonnenuhr　　　　🍇 ①
Riesling Kabinett trocken 1991
Soft, delicate fruit; an elegant, high-grade Kabinett of medium structure but plenty of finesse and elegance.

Wehlener Sonnenuhr　　　　🍇 ①
Riesling QbA 1991
The product of a long fermentation, very sweet, charmingly, youthful with plenty of body and almost explosive fruit.

Wehlener Sonnenuhr　　　🍇🍇 ②
Riesling Spätlese 1991
Wonderfully ripe balance between fruity acidity and sweetness, light and elegant. A perfect example of a successful 1991.

Wehlener Sonnenuhr　　🍇🍇 ③

Riesling Auslese 1990
Very delicate fruit nectare; harvested at only 90° Oechsle but very supple with gentle sweetness and ripe acidity.

Weingut Weller-Lehnert

St. Michael Strasse 27-29
Piesport 5555
Tel. (06507) 2498

The second ancient Roman grape press found on location proves that Piesport may be considered the most important wine-growing town north of the Alps in those early times. And oddly enough, Karl Hain, with his black, curly hair and small but powerful stature looks like a typical Roman, as do many other inhabitants of Piesport. He has run the Weller-Lehnert estate for 40 years and its present day reputation is due to him. His wines are classic expressions of the traditional method of maturing the wines in wood cask. The trend towards making over-sweet wines for export has weakened over the last few years and his dry wines are masterpieces of fruit and structure. In 1991 Hain leased the estate to his daughter Petra, who is completely convinced of her father's style and intends to follow in his footsteps. Their more simple wines are sold off in bulk.

Piesporter Goldtröpfchen　🍇🍇 ②
Riesling Spätlese 4/91 1990
With its great length, substance and understated sweetness, it is almost equal to the Auslese. A copy-book example of classic wood aging.

Piesporter Goldtröpfchen　　🍇 ①
Riesling Kabinett 1989
A very fine aroma of cassis and without any of the typical '89 weaknesses: not by chance, this wine ranked in the top five wines in Decanter Magazine's 'Mosel-Saar-Ruwer' top 20 tasting.

Piesporter Goldtröpfchen　　🍇 ①
Riesling Spätlese trocken 1988
Amongst a very impressive series of dry Spätlesen between 1988 and 1990, this is the lightest and, at the same time, finest.

Weingut Zilliken Forstmeister
Geltz Erben

Heckingstrasse 20
Saarsburg 5510
Tel. (06581) 2456
Fax (06581) 6763

Those who follow Hans-Joachim Zilliken down to his cellar and experience with what pride and satisfaction he reaches for 20 year-old bottles, will realise how the heart of his estate is in this three-story winery. It was bought in the 1950s after the original building of the Royal Prussian Forestry Official, Geiz (the great grandfather of "Hajo" Zilliken) had been completely destroyed in World War 2. The raather plain new estate building was constructed above the cellar on the edge of the small, picturesque, medieval town of Saarburg. The cool freshness of the cellar with almost 100% humidity seems to have its effect on the wines. In contrast to the typical freshness and lightness of modern Saar Rieslings, Zilliken makes long lasting wines in the old-fashioned manner using classic 1,000 lt casks. The strength of this estate is in its high caliber Auslesen and especially in its Eisweine. Here is where Zilliken can really flaunt his great skills as a master in the region. Among the lesser products, and especially dry wines, the acidity occasionally seems a little coarse, though with increasing maturity the wines become rounder and harmonious.

Saarburger Rausch
Riesling Kabinett 1991
ɣ ①

This is actually a Spätlese with plenty of fruit, sinewy acidity and relatively high residual sugar. It was the vintage's best Kabinett.

Zilliken
Riesling QbA halbtrocken 1991
ɣ ①

Their standard 'house-estate' wine, it shows good substance and harmonious acidity.

Ockfener Bockstein
Riesling Auslese 1990
ɣ ɣ ③

A superb, harmonious, tightly-knit Auslese with fine sweetness and excellent acidity.

Saarburger Rausch
Riesling Auslese Lange Goldkapsel 1989
ɣ ɣ ④

Made from half Beeren-Auslese and half Eiswein: plenty of botrytis and ripe fruit - almost as great as the Eiswein.

Saarburger Rausch
Riesling Eiswein 1989
ɣ ɣ ɣ ④

Weighing in at 150° Oechsle, this is not the biggest Eiswein of the last ten years, but one with rare characteristics. Over-ripe exotic fruit combine with masses of botrytis along with 15 g/lt acidity, it proves to be a genuine Saar speciality. Perhaps it is what is borne of the green rubble which is deposited between the blue devonian gravel in the Rausch site, or perhaps it is the unique microclimate in the vineyards above Saarburg. Matured in small, old casks, the wine is tightly-knit, its compactness harmonizing the fruit, which shifts from apricot to lemon, the high acidity and massive, natural sweetness. The grapes were harvested the night of November 26th at minus 10°C by 15 pickers (Hajo Zilliken was sound asleep).

Nahe

The Nahe is a small tributary of the Rhine. It rises in the hills of the Hunsrück and runs into the Rhine at Bingen. For over 1,000 years, vines have been grown on the often steep slopes that drop down to the river. The most important varieties are Müller Thurgau and Riesling, each accounting for a quarter of the vineyard area, after which only Sylvaner (12%) is significant from a quality point of view. Kerner and Scheurebe are both well below 10%, while for several years top estates have focussed on Pinot Gris (Grauburgunder) and Pinot Blanc (Weissburgunder) which can produce fine, delicious wines.

The Nahe is a relatively small growing region, accounting for only one fifth of the area covered by the Mosel-Saar-Ruwer. In addition producers here have been (and, to a certain extent, still are) over-shadowed by their more famous colleagues along the Mosel or the illustrious Rheingau. This is unfortunate, as the best Nahe wines are of a similar high standard to those of the neighbouring regions. Riesling, especially, produces excellent wines, both in a dry and off-dry style, as well as in the nobly sweet wine category. In good years the best sites at Schlossböckelheim, Oberhausen, Niederhausen along with others produce very fine Auslesen, Beeren-Auslesen and Trockenbeeren-Auslesen while Eiswein has recently been making a come-back. Nahe Riesling is similarly light, delicate and softly spicy compared to those of the Mittelmosel and has the same high, sinewy acidity which keeps it fresh for years. Average prices are significantly lower than those of other growing areas.

In spite of the relatively limited growing area, which is delineated in part by its geographical position, the Nahe has a variety of different soils that distinguish the end wines. Lying between the Mosel and Rheinhessen, there are blue Devonian slate soils typical of the Mosel as well as the new red sandstone found on the Rhine in Rheinhessen. Soils on the lower Nahe are dominated by loess on top of sand with a high chalk content. Gravel or quarzite deposits are found in other places. Again, each soil leaves its own imprint on the wine.

In recent years the pretty landscape has attracted many tourists who come to explore the area, on foot or by bicycle. Most producers are very accomodating, ever-ready to pull out the glasses and cork their wines for sampling.

Weingut Paul Anheuser

Stromberger Strasse 15-19
Bad. Kreuznach 6550
Tel. (0671) 28748
Fax (0671) 42571

Peter Anheuser is an active man in his
1950s. Due to his various political wine
offices, he is also a rather controversial
figure. He has made his Kreuznach estate
into the largest in the region, and, as a result,
it is represented in a dozen Nahe top sites. In
the Nahe's best known wine-village,
Schlossböckelheim the estate is by far the
largest vineyard owner. Recently Peter
Anheuser bought a part of the world-famous
Kupfergrube site at a very high price. He was
especially successful in the exceptionally
good 1989 vintage, which Anheuser regards
as superior to the 1971s. The basis of his
selection is a range of well-built Spät- and
Auslesen wines, with enormous power as
well as finesse, which follow behind four
superb Beeren-Auslesen and two
Trockenbeeren-Auslesen. Nonetheless, over
half of his wines are dry, and Riesling
dominates with 75%. Up to now, Anheuser
has avoided close encounters with trendy
wine fashions. The wines are inexpensive,
and older vintages can be found in
reasonable quantities at relatively low prices.

Schlossböckelheimer In den Felsen   ☙ ①
Weissburgunder QbA trocken 1991
A fresh Pinot Blanc from an excellent site with
an accentuated sparkle, plenty of substance and
ripeness.

Roxheimer Höllenpfad   ☙ ①
Riesling Spätlese trocken 1990
Rieslings from Roxheim can be just as rich in
body as those from Kreuznach, though they
tend to lack the latters' firm acidity.

Kreuznacher Mollebrunnen   ☙ ☙ ②
Riesling Auslese 1989
One of the truly great nobly sweet Kreuznach
Auslesen from this very ripe vintage with fine
botrytis without being the least bit oily or cloying.

Weingut Crusius

Hauptstrase 2
Traisen 6551
Tel. (0671) 33953
Fax (0671) 282189

This is, without a doubt, the most consistent
estate on the Nahe. Hans Crusius and his
son, Peter, make Rieslings without
embellishments. Their name is a guarantee
for consistently high quality due to their
excellent vineyard sites. The most prestigious
is the unique Traiser Bastei, in which a few
rows of vines are squeezed in between the
Nahe river and the 200 m high Rotfels, or
Red Rock. The unique microclimate
produces unusually ripe wines with a very
accentuated "goût de terroir" flavor. Even in
the cool 1987 vintage, they attained Spätlese
level. They also harvest similarly characterful
Rieslings at Schlossböckelheimer
Felsenberg, as well as in the Norheimer and
Niederhäuser sites. Three-quarters of the
vineyard area is planted with Riesling,
followed by Müller Thurgau and Pinot Blanc
(Weissburgunder). The Crusius family mature
their wines in the traditional manner in wood
casks. Their emphasis is on gentle, fruity
wines with pure varietal flavors and piquant
acidity, though harmonious, nobly sweet
Riesling still has its regular place in the
collection which is often quickly sold out upon
release.

Crusius   ☙ ①
Riesling QbA halbtrocken 1991
A generous, succulent standard 'estate wine', it
is only one wrung down from the cru wines
made.

Schlossböckelheimer Felsenberg   ☙ ①
Riesling Kabinett halbtrocken 1991
The best Kabinett wine of this vintage, it is made
from very young vines which suffered from
drought; still, a round, succulent wine.

Traiser Bastei   ☙ ②
Riesling Spätlese 1991
Their best wine of the vintage from old vines
and a top site; it has a smooth backbone of
acidity and fine fruit.

Traiser Rotenfels   ☙ ①
Riesling QbA trocken 1991
This wine is the epitome of their production
standard in 1991. Crisp, fruity and dry, it has
nuances of citrus fruit and slightly coarse acidity
which needs smoothing with bottle age.

Niederhäuser Felsensteyer   ☙ ☙ ①
Riesling Auslese 1990
The best wine harvested by the estate in 1990,
it is ripe and has grapey aromas and piquant
acidity, with concentrated fruit and richness.
Likely to last a very long time.

Schlossgut Diel

6531 Burg Layen
Tel. (06721) 45045
Fax (06721) 45047

When Amin Diel offered a nobly sweet Spätlese in 1989 for the first time in years, he could hardly believe the success. It was so popular that even the estate's owner grew to like it. After years of concentrating on making dry wines, the acclaim which his 1990 collection received convinced him. Riesling grown in the very north of Germany needs a degree of sweetness to develop perfect harmony and to gain respect as a unique product on world markets. However, as it is difficult to survive with one's eggs-all-in-one-basket, the 39 year-old is now glad to be able to concentrate once again on his well-established dry wines. The traditionally vinified Rieslings develop enormous power without compromising their finesse and freshness. Also a consulting ecologist, Diel has gained special recognition for his achievements in maturing Pinot Gris and Pinot Blanc (Weissburgunder and Grauburgunder) in small barriques. The most successful wine is a blend of the two from the best barrels named Victor. Diel is always good for surprises: among the 1991s the share of nobly sweet wines has increased still further.

Dorsheimer Goldloch ♛ ②
Riesling QbA trocken 1991
By severe short pruning, the yield was reduced to 26 hl/ha. The result is a wine with concentrated aromas and fresh acidity.

Dorsheimer Pittermännchen ♛♛ ③
Riesling Spätlese 1991
An exception to the rule, harvested at the beginning of December. Essentially an Auslese which has been declassified, it is characterised by racy acidity which makes the wine seem slimmer than it really is, plus a light nuance reminiscent of Eiswein.

Schlossgut Diel ♛ ③
Grauburgunder QbA trocken 1991
The experimental phase with barriques got this far on this estate, and the focus is now on combining optimum fruit development with unobtrusive oak. The 1991 has firm acidity, plenty of substance and enormous length.

Schlossgut Diel ♛♛ ④
Riesling Eiswein 1991
A stunning, nobly sweet wine harvested at 135° Oechsle by the whole family at 5 am, though less impressive than its predecessor.

Schlossgut Diel ♛♛♛ ④
Riesling Auslese Goldkapsel No.4 1990
Armin Diel has made it his aim to produce a high calibre nobly sweet wine every year if possible. In 1990 he succeeded in harvesting a sensational Eiswein on 8th December at 170° Oechsle and 10.5 g/lt of acidity. The last time a wine like this was produced was in 1971. It comes from 40 year-old vines which produced only 40 hl/ha. He added 50 lt of it to his Auslese from Dorsheimer Goldloch ("Bad business when you add up the costs - the Eiswein sells at over DM 600 a bottle"). The Auslese only bears the site name on the label but is recognisable by its long 'gold capsule'. It has the fruit of a Beeren-Auslese coupled with fabulous acidity of over 10 g/lt - a wine which will keep endlessly.

Weingut Hermann Dönnhoff

Bahnofstrasse 11
Oberhausen 6551
Tel. (06755) 263
Fax (06755) 1067

Helmut Dönnhoff is now N° 1 on the Nahe.
He is one of the few producers who manage
to make completely dry perfectly balanced
Spätlesen However, he only succeeds in
exceptional vintages, such as 1989, when his
dry Rieslings had opulence, style and
elegance reminiscent of the top wines from
Austria's Wachau region. In autumn the
quality fanatic with 20 years' experience goes
through the vineyards in search of optimum
raw material. Although in a very ripe year like
1989 he has his work cut out to preserve
acidity in the face of rising sugar
concentration, in 1991 he made exceptionally
good specialities by craftily waiting his
moment. The resulting wines are difficult to
match elsewhere and include two generous
Rieslings with biting acidity, one Beeren-
Auslese and a Grauburgunder (Pinot Gris)
Eiswein with great ageing potential. In the
cellar the perfectly skilled wine producer acts
with the wisdom of a true master: as few
technical interventions as possible and the
necessary steps at just the right moment.
This is the basis of his extraordinary success,
not to mention his presence felt in the superb
vineyards of Niederhäusler Hermannshöle,
Schlossböckelheimer Felsenberg and
Oberhäuser Brücke.

Niederhäuser Hermannshöhle   ℬ ①
Riesling Kabinett trocken 1991
The 45 year-old vines withstood the drought and
produced a lightly spicy, fruity Riesling
dominated by acidity which is all but light in this
Kabinett wine.

Oberhäuser Felsenberg   ℬ ①
Riesling QbA trocken 1991
Dönnhoff's dry wines from this site require
patience from wine-lovers. The acidity is often
too racy, as in the 1991. Nevertheless, the
wines usually have substance and show
enormous class when mature.

Niederhäuser Hermannshöhle   ℬ ℬ ②
Riesling Spätlese 1990
This wine from the most highly regarded site on
the Nahe belongs in the Auslese category.
Complex Riesling fruit, spicy maturity, nobly
sweet with accentuated acidity and only just
starting to develop: truly great.

Oberhäuser Brücke   ℬ ℬ ②
Riesling Spätlese 1989
This should also be classified as Auslese: a
generous, rich wine, mellow with concentrated
fruit and brilliant acidity which gives it elegance
and finesse.

Oberhäuser Brücke   ℬ ℬ ℬ ③
Riesling Auslese 1991
Every time Hermann Dönnhoff walked through
this top vineyard in autumn, he snapped a few
bunches off the vines which he did not deem
good enough. Yet a spring frost had already
reduced the yield considerably. And even
though it had rained a lot, he insisted on
producing an Auslese. When he finally went in
to harvest on 30th October 1991, everything
was covered in frost, for there had been a
sudden chill during the night. The berries were
even lightly frozen. He cut them from the vine
and carefully emptied them in the cellar, still ha
frozen, into a basket press so that the juice
would run out without much pressure. He
obtained high grade, very sweet juice which
due to the frost, was practically botrytis-free
with clean, pure fruit. He made 900 lt in this
precise way, producing two spectacula
Auslesen of a type seldom seen even in top
vintages. Both are bursting with fruit and marke
by high acidity (up to 12 g/lt) which is wel
balanced by 100 g/lt residual sugar.

Weingut Emrich Schönleber

Naheweinstrasse 10a
Monzingen 6557
Tel. (06571) 2733
Fax (06571) 4864

This is, by far, the best producer in the Upper Nahe region of Germany. The soils there are mainly light and sandy and Werner Schönleber, who has run this estate for some time, owns the best parts, precisely at Monzingen with the Frühlingsplätchen, Rosenberg and Hallenberg vineyards. The latter is one of the best in Nahe. Schönleber has recently managed to secure the best part, planted 70% with Riesling, with Pinot Gris (Grauburgunder), Müller Thurgau and Kerner completing the assortment. Dry, off-dry ("halbtrocken") and nobly sweet wines each account for one third of the estate's production. According to Schönleber, quality wines start in the vineyard. Last autumn he harvested three times in each site. Temperature-controlled fermentation also helps preserve varietal flavors and Nahe wine-makers have mastered it increasingly over the past ten years. His wine often have the typical Riesling aroma of peaches and citrus fruits together with racy acidity.

Monzinger Frühlingsplätzchen   ꭐ ①
Riesling Kabinett 1991
A very nice, characterful example of this excellent site which has been greatly extended. This wine comes from its classic center.

Monzinger Halenberg   ꭐ ①
Riesling Spätlese trocken 1991
A Spätlese in the classic sense of the word, it was not harvested until November as a preliminary Eiswein harvest. It has ripe fruit, a soft bouquet and firm, lively acidity.

Monzinger Halenberg   ꭐꭐ ①
Riesling Auslese 1990
An Auslese through and through: nobly rotten grapes were carfeully selected by hand and produced a slender wine on the one hand, but with a flavor of ripe, fruity opulence on the other.

Monzinger Frühlingsplätzchen   ꭐ ②
Riesling Spätlese trocken 1990
This estate's most powerful 1990 Spätlese, with understated maturity, great richness and firm acidity which is just starting to mellow.

Weingut Carl Finkenauer

Salinenstrasse 60
Kreuznach 6550
Tel. (0671) 28771
Fax (0671) 35265

This traditional, family-run estate improved significantly when Sabine Trummert took over the cellar. Two thirds of the wines are dry, and are for the most part fresh and rich. Sometimes wines are kept in cask for several years (they have over a hundred wood casks) and then bottled as specialities, often especially for classy restaurants. Sabine Trummert is far from timid when it comes to using the barrique, but only for the reds, to impart structure and roundness to their Pinot Noir (Spätburgunder) and Dornfelder. The 33 ha of vineyard are mainly around Kreuznach and Roxheim. Riesling accounts for 56%: Müller Thurgau, Scheurebe, Burgundy varieties, Traminer and, more recently, Chardonnay (for making sparkling wine) complete the assortment. Yields seldom exceed 60 hl/ha, though in 1991, they were down to 50 hl/ha due to severe spring frost damage, mostly in the Kreuznach sites of St. Martin and Gutental. While the dry wines are quickly sold out upon release, there are good stocks of the superb 1989 noble sweet wines available.

Finkenauer   ꭐ ①
Riesling Hochgewächs trocken 1991
The best QbA wine of each vintage has been characterised by the letters 'cf' since 1937 and mainly sold in restaurants.

Kreuznacher St. Martin   ꭐ ③
Gewürztraminer Auslese trocken 1989
There's lots of Alsace in this glass. In spite of its weight, it has plenty of acidity which gives it a touch of finesse.

Kreuznacher St. Martin   ꭐꭐ ④
Riesling Beerenauslese 1989
An extraordinary speciality for the very deep Kreuznach soils. Despite the warm alcohol, it is still gentle, with the fine acidity making it lean and long-lasting.

Weingut Hahnmühle

6761 Mannweiler-Cölln
Tel. (06362) 2693
Fax (06362) 4466

In a place where local growers find wine-growing difficult to imagine, a group of young producers have been trying to reintroduce it for several years now, in Alsenztal to the south of the Nahe. This new generation is led by Martina and Peter Linxweiler, who because of their convictions, work the vineyards with a more ecological philosophy and have set very high quality standards. In extreme cases this can lead to minute yields of 14 hl/ha as with the 1990 Pinot Noir (Spätburgunder) which, after a year in barrique, is unbelievably rich for such a northerly latitude. Apart from this Riesling, it dominates with 70% and in these parts its steely acidity is reminiscent of the Saar. It is usually made as a dry wine. In recent years the traditional method of harvesting and vinifying together a grape mix of Riesling and Traminer has been successful. Their grandfather's recipe of softening the rather hard Riesling is still valid, and in 1989 a powerful Auslese was made. 1990 once again produced wines with pure varietal flavors, but some of them seem a little too acidulous. What a shame their customers only ask for dry wines, as a little sweetness would make them more harmonious.

Cöllner Rosenberg   ℗ ①
Riesling QbA halbtrocken 1991
A still youthful Riesling which refused to ferment out to dryness, with a strong acid bite and nice fruit.

Cöllner Rosenberg   ℗℗ ①
Riesling QbA trocken 1991
An exceptional wine from 35 year-old vines with an aroma of blackcurrant, tangy fruit, generous with elegant acidity.

Cöllner Rosenberg   ℗℗ ①
Silvaner QbA trocken 1991
This wine carried on fermenting all through the winter. The remaining small amount of residual sugar suits it well and is balanced by the fresh acidity.

Cöllner Rosenberg   ℗℗ ②
Riesling Auslese 1989
This estate's best wine in 1989 with a scent of honey and dried figs that is typical of Beerenauslese, racy acidity and a long finish.

Weingut Kruger-Rumpf

Rheinstrasse 47
Münster-Sarmsheim 6538
Tel. (06721) 43859
Fax (06721) 41882

Stefan Rumpf is fortunate to own large plot in the best sites on the Lower Nahe Colleagues who find work in the stee vineyards too onerous make him more offer to buy their land than he could ever accept In just five years he has increased hi vineyard area from 10 to 15 hectares, buyin into the very best sites, to grow prime rav materials for his dry wines, which account fo 85% of the production. The prerequisite fo pure varietal flavor is healthy grapes. Indeed in autumn Rumpf is often one of the first t start picking. In the cellar his mai preoccupation is to preserve the freshness o the young wines. He already has a mouth watering Müller Thurgau for everyda consumption, bottled before Christmas of th year of production. His main wine is Rieslin and accounts for just under 60% of the vine planted. Rumpf's best can be stunning, rip wines with substance as well as fine fruit. H is also open to new ideas, among which ar a Blanc de Noir made from Pinot Noir and new Chardonnay vineyard. Rumpf intends t mature both in wood, as he already does wit his Sylvaner.

Dorsheimer Burgberg   ℗ ①
Riesling QbA trocken 1991
A typical product from this classic site i Trollbachtal: mouth-watering Riesling fruit wit an aroma of ripe apples and accentuate acidity.

Münsterer Kapellenberg   ℗ ①
Gewürztraminer Spätlese trocken 1991
A soft Traminer, not over-powering in bouquet but with a fine rose scent, discreet acidity and pleasant aftertaste.

Münsterer Pittersberg   ℗ ①
Riesling Kabinett halbtrocken 1991
A wine from one of this village's first class sites with a high slate content in the soil, giving th wine freshness in its balance between fruit an acidity.

Kruger-Rumpf   ℗ ②
Silvaner Tafelwein trocken 1990
Rumpf has been maturing his Sylvaner in new oak for three years. In spite of the accentuate oak, the fruit flavor still comes through.

Weingut Reichsgraf von Plettenberg

Winzenheimer Strasse
5550 Bad Kreuznach
Tel. (0671) 2251
Fax (0671) 45226

There was a time when Plettenberg wines were among the most noble of the Nahe. The great Riesling rarities from the first half of this century were gems, and their 1950s were legendary. The estate still has the potential to do great things, and the counts are still ever-present in the best vienyards at Schlossböckelheim (Kupfergruber and Felsenberg). Out in the vineyards the emphasis is still on quality. Two-thirds are planted with Riesling and 20% with Burgundian varieties. As the proportion destined for export is relatively high (a quarter), numerous nobly sweet wines are produced by late-harvesting. Auslese wines accounted for over 60% in 1989 and, even in less favourable years like 1991, a respectable 69% of production was Spät- and Auslese level. It is only in the cellar that the potential may not have been exploited to the fullest. The dry wines suffer most of all, appearing more rustic in style than noble. However, most of all the nobly sweet wines still justify the once enviable reputation and can still be very powerful and rich.

Kreuznacher St. Martin   🍷 ②
Chardonnay Spätlese trocken 1991
The conservative counts were skeptical when it came to planting Chardonnay but then were convinced: clean, but as often happens with German Chardonnay, it is too acidulous.

Kreuznacher Mollenbrunnen   🍷 ②
Weissburgunder Spätlese trocken 1989
The heavy soils around Kreuznach often bring forth strong varietal flavors as in this fine, ripe Pinot Blanc.

Winzenheimer Rosenheck   🍷🍷 ④
Riesling Trockenbeerenauslese 1989
Great wines have always come from this superb site of a Kreuznach suburb in exceptionally good years. This nobly sweet speciality is characterised by extremely concentrated sweetness and a grapey, raisiny aroma.

Prinz zu Salm-Dalbergsches Weingut

Schloss
6551 Wallhausen
Tel. (06706) 289
Fax (06706) 6017

The oldest document attesting to the existence of this family's wine estate is from 1200. No small wonder, therefore, that tradition dominates among today's generation. That is not to say that they renounce sensible innovations. At the moment the estate is in the middle of changing over to natural, ecological wine-growing, the credit for which goes to Michael Prinz zu Salm. He is also president of the German Association of Producers of Wines of Distinction (VDP). Chemicals are avoided and cover crops are grown between the vines even in steep sites. The extremely low yield of 45 hl/ha in 1991 was also due to this. For instance, the surface weeds left on top prevented the vines from absorbing the excess rainfall that fell just before harvest that would have otherwise diluted the grape juice. Now, as in the past, the aim is to produce natural wines, either dry or with natural sweetness. Hardly a year goes by without a nobly sweet Beeren-Auslese or Eiswein being produced. A 1989 Grauburgunder (Pinot Gris) Trockenbeeren-Auslese, harvested at 240° Oechsle was recently bottled after a two year fermentation. In 1991 a sensational Riesling Eiswein was harvested, but only 120 lt!

Schloss Wallhausen 1991   🍷🍷 ②
Riesling Spätlese
The result of a late-harvest, and careful bunch selection: a finely fruity Riesling Spätlese with a sinewy acid structure and very complex fruit.

Wallhäuser Johannisberg 1991   🍷 ①
Riesling Kabinett
The best Kabinett of this vintage, made from the village's top site planted with 40 year-old vines.

Dalberger Ritterhölle 1990   🍷 ①
Riesling Kabinett halbtrocken
This Riesling's fresh, lively acidity and sparkling freshness comes from the slatey soil. Good ageing potential over several years.

Schloss Wallhausen 1991   🏴 ①
Spätburgunder Roséwein QbA trocken
This has been a much sought-after speciality of the estate for years, very successful in 1991. The Pinot Noir fruit is expressed very well.

Staatliche Weinbaudomänen

Niederhaus-Schlossböckelheim
Oberhausen 6551
Tel. (06758) 6215
Fax (06758) 6303

Founded by the Prussian state at the turn of the century, this estate owns the largest proportion of the best sites on the Nahe. Up until 1987, the Staatsdomänen enjoyed a excellent reputation. They set new standards in the selection of Riesling vines, and especially in wine-making techniques: temperature-controlled fermentation and oxygen-free reductive treatment were perfected here. The superb Rieslings made here express to the full the characteristics imparted by their sites, with a beautiful interplay between the fruit and the acidity, breadth and elegance. To date, the estate's reputation is untarnished, as they still turn out superb wines, not only from the Schlossböckelheimer Kupfergrube and their own Niederhäuser Hermannsberg sites. However, recent staff changes have contributed to the lack-lustre production, leaving customers and colleagues alike are baffled. The pressure from the Rheinland-Pfalz accounting office to cut costs at all expense, risks being detrimental to the quality.

Altenbamberger Rotenberg ℘ ①
Riesling QbA trocken 1991
A very remarkable wine bearing the stamp of eroded volcanic soil in a steep site: at first closed, then becoming very complex.

Ebernburger Schlossberg ℘ ①
Riesling Kabinett trocken 1991
A typical Riesling from volcanic rubble soils in the middle Nahe. It is solid in structure, not too light and will soon be ready to drink.

Niederhäuser Hermannsberg ℘ ℘ ②
Riesling Spätlese 1991
A great wine with spice and depth, the deep soil from which it is made is noticeable in the richness, the slate, in its refined acidity.

Niederhäuser Hermannsberg ℘ ℘ ④
Riesling Trockenbeerenauslese 1989
A speciality more characterised by sweetness (raisins, honey) than fruity acidity. It needs plenty of time to develop.

Erbhof Tesch

An den Naheweisen 24
Langenlonsheim 6536
Tel. (06704) 20404
Fax (06704) 204128

This is one of the Nahe's more modern an best-equipped producers, with the best site in Laubenheim, Langenlonsheim an Dorsheim under their control. Yields ar reduced and the harvest is carried out wit the pickers passing through the vineyards several runs to pick only the ripest grapes Riesling for accounts for 75% of the grapes their vineyards, the remaining area bein planted with Sylvaner, Pinot Blan (Weissburgunder) and Pinot No (Spätburgunder) which is used to make a ful colored, fresh rosé. Hartmut Tesch swears b the exclusive use of stainless steel tanks an comments, "Casks are more appealing to th eye, but less so for the flavor of fine wines He is determined to abide by reductiv principles in wine-making through to bottlin completely oxygen-free conditions t preserve freshness. A unique feature of th estate is 'biological natural acidity regulation At the moment the estate produces 60% dr wines, for the most part with clear variet flavors, positively austere with accentuate acidity. Although grown on deep sites mos wines are not as rich as one might expec and some seem rather slim.

Laubenheimer Karthäuser ℘ ②
Riesling Spätlese 1991
A wine which has profited from the hea retaining effect of the soil, it has clear Rieslin fruit, mouth-watering acidity and good potenti for future development.

Langenlonsheimer Löhrer Berg ℘ ①
Riesling QbA trocken 1991
Firm Riesling from deep soils. It has richnes and is round though not hard in acidity.

Langenlosheimer Steinchen ℘ ℘ ①
Weissburgunder QbA trocken 1990
A very successful QbA of Auslese quality wit clear, elegant fruit and lively fresh acidity.

Laubenheimer St. Remigiusberg ℘ ℘ ①
Riesling QbA trocken 1989
Spicy Riesling fruit strongly marked by the rock soils, it is a full-bodied, powerful wine with th finesse of a high-class Spätlese.

Pfalz

The Pfalz is one of Germany's wine-growing regions which enjoys the influence of a mild continental climate, at least in the south. To the south of Lindau even palm, lemon and fig trees grow in places. Wines from here are correspondingly full and ripe with concentrated flavors, and Rieslings attain alcohol levels closer to those of Alsace than to the same variety from the Mosel. However, Riesling is far from being the only variety. In recent years ambitious growers have focused on Pinot Gris (Grauburgunder) and Pinot Blanc (Weissburgunder) and rightly so, for they occasionally make highly classy wines difficult to match in other German wine-growing areas. In good sites even Scheurebe produces excelent results on a par with Riesling. Pinot Noir (Spätburgunder) is also making a come back. With the help of the warm climate numerous Pfalz producers have managed to make wines which have little in common with the usual pale, thin red wines which have become typical for Germany.

In terms of volume the Pfalz is Germany's second most important wine region and stretches from Worms to the border with Alsace. It can be subdivided into two areas: the Southern Wine Route District (Bereich Südlicher Weinstrasse) on the edge of the Pfalzer Forest around Landau, and the Haart district, a hilly area to the north of Neustadt. The very best Riesling sites are to be found on the slopes of this stretch of hills, especially around romantic wine villages such as Deidesheim and Wachenheim. They produce top quality Spätlesen and Auslesen (in exceptional years also Beeren-Auslesen and Trocken-Beeren-Auslesen). Wines from here are usually dry, as the ripe fruit and mild acidity yield harmonious wines which do not need rounding off with residual sugar. In the southern part of the region white as well as red Burgundian varieties perform well. However, the greater part of Pfalz wine comes from Müller-Thurgau. It is grown in the endless vineyards which extend as far as the eye can see as far as the Rhine plain and usually produces simple, easy-drinking wines which are correspondingly filled into liter bottles, as are a large proportion of the region's wines. It flows in torrents in the numerous wine taverns which are very popular among tourists.

The region also produces red wine though from a quantity point of view it is far from significant (the most widely grown is Blauer Portugieser with 9%). However, when it comes to quality the Pfalz produces some of Germany's best reds, especially from Pinot Noir (Spätburgunder), Dornfelder and the Austrian Blauer Zweigelt - varieties which almost vanished from the vineyards during the 1970s and have recently found favor once again among ambitious growers. Generally speaking, the Pfalz has brought forth numerous new talented producers, of which only the most successful are described in the following pages.

Bassermann-Jordan

Deidesheim 6705
Tel. (06326) 6006
Fax (06326) 6008

Bassermann-Jordan is really the first among
the three 'big B's' together with the Reichsrat
von Buhl and Bürklin-Wolf estates, which
were once the only producers known abroad.
Since 1987 Bassermann-Jordan has been
the first and only winery from the Pfalz to
produce 100% Rieslings from the best
vineyards such as Kirchenstück,
Jesuitengarten, Ungeheuer and Pechstein im
Forst. The 1990 wines from these sites are
the best of the last 20 years, aged exclusively
in large, old oak casks, a further indication of
Bassermann's traditional thinking. They are
ready for drinking at an early age
characterized by accentuated fruit, often with
a strong scent of cassis, racy and refined.
For some time now the Bassermann wines
have become increasingly fruitier due to a
newly introduced high capacity separator
which has set new standards for pure varietal
fruit.

Forster Freundstück   ℞ ①
Riesling Kabinett trocken 1991
A fine, softly fruity Riesling. Due to a light flavor
typical of the vintage it tastes slightly bitter.

Deidesheimer Hohenmorgen   ℞ ③
Riesling Auslese 1990
Finely racy and very classy: an appealing wine
for enthusiasts of sweet Riesling with mild
acidity.

Deidesheimer Leinhöhle   ℞ ①
Riesling Kabinett 1990
A full and muscular Riesling, with a clear peach
aroma and softly mellow on the finish.

Forster Ungeheuer   ℞ ①
Riesling Kabinett 1989
Pleasant mineral substances and a peachy
flavor which add a touch of youthfulness to this
wine. The light petrolly flavor is off-set by light
sweetness.

Weingut Friedrich Becker

Schweigen 6742
Tel. (06342) 290
Fax (06342) 6148

The Fritz Becker estate is in the southern
part of the Pfalz, just a stone's throw from the
French border. Half of his vineyards are in
French territory, in what is called
Sequesterland. For this reason nearly every
morning Fritz Becker crosses the border
which is no longer guarded, to tend his
Spätburgunder vines. This wine should
actually be sold as AOC Pinot Noir d'Alsace,
though to avoid this the French authorities
have declared the viticultural area between
Schweigen and Weissenburg as non AOC.
Therefore Fritz Becker has no other choice
but to take advantage of a special German
regulation, which allows the wines from these
vineyards to be marketed under the name of
Schweigener Sonnenberg. Becker, a
seemingly gruff and reserved person,
continues to age his wine in classic wood
casks. In recent years he has caused a
sensation with his Spätburgunder (Pinot
Noir), especially after winning second prize in
a national red wine competition with his 1989
Spätburgunder Auslese.

Schweigener Sonnenberg   ℞ ②
Grauburgunder Spätlese trocken 1990
A compact, concentrated wine with strong
acidity and a good aging potential, promises to
improve with bottle age.

Schweigener Sonnenberg   ℞ ②
Weissburgunder Spätlese trocken 1990
A nice Burgundian bouquet and discreet lemony
aroma; a clearly structured wine with good
balance between alcohol and acidity.

Spätburgunder   ℞℞ ③
Tafelwein trocken 1990
Concentrated Pinot Noir fruit combined with well
integrated, smoky tannin and oak characterize
this unique Pinot, only at the beginning of its
maturation: a fascinating wine.

F. u. C. Bergdolt

Klostergut St. Lamprecht
Neustadt-Duttweiler 6730
Tel. (06327) 5027
Fax (06327) 1784

The Klostergut St Lamprecht winery, which once belonged to the University of Heidelberg, is an emblem of the historical importance of the wine-growing locality of Duttweiler. This still does not prevent wine-growing colleagues at Deisenheim from dismissing this flat vineyard area as 'turnip land.' However, the limestone soils of Duttweiler are excellent for wine growing, especially for the increasingly popular Pinot Blanc (Weissburgunder). Rainer Bergdolt is completely devoted to this variety and for several years now has produced superb Weissburgunder Spätlesen. He also focuses on Riesling, and his wines have done at least as well as the best wines of Mittelhaardt in blind tastings. Also his first red wines, the 1989 and 1990 Spätburgunder and St Laurent, are surprisingly dense. The Silvaner and Pinot Blanc are barrique aged and have been extremely successful in gastronomic circles. The first Chardonnay to be bottled was the 1990 and is very promising. Characteristic for the unperturbed, self-assured producer is the fact that, while others are throwing out their traditional large casks Bergoldt is buying new ones.

Duttweiler Kalkberg ❦ ③
Riesling Spätlese trocken 1991
This Riesling, grown in the excellent Kalkberg site, is one of the very few successful 1991 Spätlesen.

Kirrweiler Mandelberg ❦❦ ①
Weissburgunder Spätlese trocken 1991
A monumental wine: this exceptional Pinot should be tried with poached Loup de Mer in Burgundian sauce - superb!

Kirrweiler Mandelberg ❦❦ ②
Weissburgunder Auslese trocken 1990
Delicate aromas of late-ripening autumn fruits, blackberries, figs and walnuts: a fantastic wine from a great vintage.

Duttweiler Kalkberg ❦ ②
Spätburgunder Spätlese trocken 1990
A wonderful variety of aromas, including a well integrated hint of oak (barrique-aged) - a wine with great aging potential.

Weingut Josef Biffar

Niederkircher Strasse 13-15
Deidesheim 6705
Tel. (06326) 5028
Fax (06326) 7697

The spectacular and regular success of several Pfalz 'outsiders' has long puzzled the establishment. Gerhard Biffar, himself a long established name in the region was the first to react and engaged Ulrich Mell, a young, newly qualified enologist from the wine-making school at Weinsberg. As a result, after just one year Biffar has become one of the most important estates at Deidesheim. His wines have distinguished themselves time and time again in blind tasting, thanks to temperature controlled fermenation and to a small dose of residual sugar (though the wines are still in the dry category). Biffar's wines are certainly not for dogmatic dry wine freaks, but appeal to those who appreciate fruity white wines and who have difficulty in coming to terms with Riesling's accentuated acidity. In addition to Riesling there are good quality Pinot Blancs which the owner and winemaker intend to concentrate on much more in the future. The first vintages have been aged on their lees, and this has proved a successful experiment.

Wachenheimer Gerümpel ❦ ①
Riesling Kabinett trocken 1991
Full on the palate, very round and appealing with plenty of soft, fruity acidity and seems almost sweet: the new style.

Wachenheimer Goldbächel ❦ ①
Riesling Spätlese trocken 1991
A very full, intensely flavored Riesling with strong acidity but a fascinating interplay of aromas.

Deidesheimer Hergottsacker ❦ ①
Riesling Kabinett trocken 1990
A well built Riesling, with very expressive, almost exotic fruit and a harmonious acid framework - needs time.

Deidesheimer Mäushöhle ❦❦ ②
Riesling Spätlese trocken 1990
One of the best Pfalz Riesling discoveries in 1990, an excellent wine, well rounded, pleasant with a light sparkle on the finish.

Weingut Reichsrat von Buhl

Weinstrasse 16
Deidesheim 6705
Tel. (06326) 96500
Fax (06326) 965024

Bad news had spread through the region: the Reichsrat von Buhl estate was up for sale. Elevated costs due to the estate's enormous size and a down turn in profits had forced the owners to take this spectacular step. Thus the destiny of one of the Pfalz's flagships seemed sealed. All this happened three years ago, but things turned out differently than expected when three wine merchants together with the large Japanese Suntory concern took on the lease for 12 years. In the meantime the locals have got used to the new situation and the German management proudly point out that they are given a completely free hand in all decisions regarding wine production. Thanks to enormous investment the winemaker Udo Loos has managed to give von Buhl Rieslings a new polish. Made in a very reductive manner, they are racy, almost steely, though still lack the personal style which characterized them in earlier times. Sales are also far from satisfactory, a situation which can hopefully be quickly put right.

Deidesheimer Kieselberg 🍇 ②
Riesling Spätlese trocken 1990
An excellent, finely-tuned Riesling (with an arty label) with the scent of a basket full of ripe fruit and very harmonious on the palate.

Deidesheimer Leinhöhle 🍇 ①
Riesling Kabinett halbtrocken 1990
Astonishingly full and still a little undeveloped - perhaps their finest 1990 Kabinett.

Forster Jesuitengarten 🍇 ③
Riesling Auslese trocken 1990
A rich wine, softly mellow with strong acidity. A typical Auslese from a great vintage.

Forster Ungeheuer 🍇🍇 ②
Riesling Spätlese trocken 1990
A fantastic Spätlese, mature with winey acidity and very clear aromas: their best Spätlese of the vintage.

Weingut Dr. Bürklin-Wolf

Wachenheim 6706
Tel. (06322) 8955
Fax (06322) 66557

The generation change at the Bürklin estate was announced officially in March 1992. The daughter, Bettina, and her husband, Christian von Guradze, have taken over the estate and proudly distinguished the first wines produced under their supervision with the initials BB. Since the Bürklin daughter took over the reins of the largest Pfalz estate (110 ha) an era strongly influenced by the personality of former estate administrator Georg Raquet has come to an end. They have 70 ha of Riesling at their disposal, plus a significant amount of Müller-Thurgau along with various secondary varieties and their strength is definitely in the production of nobly sweet Beeren-Auslesen. Apart from this the general progress made in recent years seems to have passed by the prestigious Wachenheim estate. All one can do is wait to see whether the new generation will succeed in bringing this supertanker back on to the right course.

Dr. Bürklin-Wolf 🍇 ③
Weissburgunder Kabinett trocken 1991
With a scent almost like a summer meadow, this is an appealing and delicate wine, very refreshing and thus best drunk while young.

BB Riesling Auslese trocken 1990 🍇🍇 ③
Nice scents of of ripe yellow peach, of elder flowers and red apples with pleasant, lively acidity; early maturing.

Selection Geheimrat Dr. A. Bürklin 🍇 ②
Wachenheimer Goldbächel Spätlese 1990
Very full aromas of mirabelle plums, apricots and banana; a ripe, opulent wine.

Forster Ungeheuer 🍇 ①
Riesling Kabinett trocken 1987
A pleasant aroma of maturity characterizes the rehabilitated 1987 vintage: a very nice drink for enthusiasts of mature wines.

Weingut A. Christmann

Gimmeldingen 6730
Tel. (06321) 66039
Fax (06321) 68762

Steffen Christmann Junior, who succeeded his father in running the estate in 1959, has left his imprint on the style of these wines. His preference is for dry, fresh and fruity wines to go with food. The wines can be best tasted at the Meerspinnkeller, a wine bar situated close to the estate. In addition to their legendary Trocken-Beeren-Auslesen Christmann concentrates above all on Riesling. Their red wines such as Portugieser and Spätburgunder have an intense color, are very expressive in flavor with extraordinary depth. Reduction in yields by thinning out the grapes and removing foliage from around the bunches when the berries begin to ripen, together with fermentation in closed tanks have brought their rewards. Along with the best sites at Gimmeldingen and Königsbach (Ölberg, Iding), since 1990 they have also owned very good sites at Ruppertsberg including a vineyard planted with old Silvaner vines which has enabled them to revive the old, classic Silvaner tradition.

Ruppertsberger Hoheburg   ❦ ①
Riesling Kabinett trocken 1991
A very good, finely fruity Kabinett wine with hearty acidity and clear varietal flavors - very elegant.

Ruppertsberger Linsenbusch   ❦ ①
Silvaner Kabinett trocken 1991
A minerally, smokey, rich and at the same time elegant Sylvaner, well above average for the vintage.

Königsbacher Ölberg   ❦ ②
Riesling Spätlese trocken 1990
Intensely fruity perfumes develop in the glass: yellow peach, nectarine, and plum. A very noble and elegant Spätlese.

Gimmeldinger Bienengarten   ❦ ❦ ③
Riesling Beerenauslese 1989
Wonderful noble sweetness, with fruity aromas and concentrated acidity. With reason a famous Christmann specialty.

Weingut Dr. Deinhard

Deidesheim 6705
Tel. (06326) 221
Fax (06326) 7920

The name Deinhard has been associated with quality wine for generations. It is most famous for the sparkling wine production plant at Koblenz, the descendents of which founded the Deidesheim estate in 1848. Their heyday was under Dr Andreas Deinhard who, as a member of parliament was supposedly involved in the first German wine law of 1901. In 1917 the estate was acquired by the Hoch family. This exemplary Riesling estate is now run by Heinz Bauer. Ecological viticultural methods in the very best Deidesheim sites guarantee constant quality throughout the year. Their main distinguishing feature is their clarity of varietal fruit together with fresh acidity and delicate flavor. Even in the difficult 1991 vintage Deinhard had everything under control.

Deidesheimer Grainhübel   ❦ ②
Riesling Spätlese trocken 1991
A scent of apples and peaches with accentuated acidity, fresh with great aging potential - a superb achievement for this vintage.

Deidesheimer Kieselberg   ❦ ①
Riesling Kabinett trocken 1991
Steely, fresh Riesling in which the 8 g/lt of acidity are well integrated: for enthusiasts of Rieslings with accentuated acidity.

Deidesheimer Mäushöhle   ❦ ①
Riesling Kabinett halbtrocken 1991
A fresh, steely Riesling, finely strung and very delicate in flavor, slightly green with racy acidity.

Deidesheimer Grainhübel   ❦ ❦ ②
Riesling Spätlese trocken 1990
A powerful Riesling aroma jumps out of the glass; an intensely fruity Spätlese with all the characteristics of this fully ripe vintage.

Winfrid Frey u. Söhne

Essingen 6741
Tel. (06347) 8224
Fax (06347) 7290

'The king of dessert wines' or 'the Eiswein king' are among a few titles encountered when reading about Winfrid Frey from the wine growing locality of Essingen near Landshut. Frey's specialties are in fact Beeren-Auslese, Trocken-Beeren-Auslese and Eiswein. In 1979 he made a "Dreikönigswein" (wine of the Three Magi): the grapes for which were harvested on 6th of January, the day of the Epiphany. For these specialties the Freys have already received much acknowledgement, prizes, oscars and trophies, and wine lovers are often left speechless when one or other of his sweet wines are poured. In the meantime, the Freys have also tried their hand at dry QbA and Kabinett wines but with less success, as the wines seem to lack harmony and class. However, Frey and his wife Ursula only started making wine in 1973 and therefore still have plenty of time to catch up.

Essinger Osterberg 🍇🍇 ④
Riesling Beerenauslese 1990
A concentrated aroma of peaches and dried fruits, striking acidity, well balanced - a dream-like dessert wine.

Essinger Osterberg 🍇🍇 ④
Riesling Trockenbeerenauslese 1990
A very dense, liqueur-like wine, with a superb scent of honey and apple and a gentle hint of cumin.

Essinger Osterberg 🍇🍇 ③
Scheurebe Trockenbeerenauslese 1990
A multi-layered aroma of cassis, peach and rhubarb, sweet and refined with balanced acidity, incredibly racy.

Essinger Osterberg 🍇 ④
Ruländer Trockenbeerenauslese 1985
A superb hint of cumin and quinced apples, very full on the palate and already very mature.

Essinger Osterberg 🍇🍇🍇 ④
Grauburgunder Eiswein 1989
In aroma and flavor, this wine is like a stroll through a fruit orchard in late summer: ripe quince, pears, grapes and apples. A wine of the century which, in spite of devastating hail, nature endowed with a must specific gravity of 180°Oechsle, 20 g/lt of acidity and a dry extract level of 53 mg. The harvest took place on 6th December 1989, starting at 4 a.m. at a temperature of minus 4°C. 150 lt were made, bottled in half bottles and sold at DM 250 each. This is expensive but justified by the fantastic, over-powering fruit. In addition, the wine is already very enjoyable and unlike many Mosel Trocken-Beeren-Auslesen and Eiswein, it does not need to be aged for decades.

Weingut Wolfgang Geissler

Am Burggarten 7
Neustadt-Duttweiler 6730
Tel. (06327) 2770
Fax (06327) 1546

The fact that he is relatively unknown is due to his having to survive from the proceeds of six hectares of vineyard, which is just about enough to get by on. In spite of this Wolfgang Geissler has no intention of increasing his holdings as he fears not being able to maintain his standards of quality if he increases production. He works his vineyards on ecological lines and this agreement with nature is reflected in his wines, in which the differences between the various growing seasons are clearly expressed. For example, his Rieslings from lesser vintages are a little too 'honest', in other words acidulous. He is number one in the Pfalz with Silvaner, though Burgundian varieties are his strength. He has also produced very promising red wines. The wines are made mainly in stainless steel tanks and he is regarded as one of Germany's pioneers in the use of barriques. His Pinot Blancs made in this style have attracted international attention.

Duttweiler Kreuzberg 🍇 ①
Silvaner Kabinett 1991
A pleasant scent of clover, hay and nettles, a wine with bite and race.

Duttweiler Kreuzberg 🍇🍇 ②
Weissburgunder Spätlese trocken 1991
Lively acidity and multi-layered aromas make this one of the finest 1991 Pinot Blancs.

Duttweiler Mandelberg 🍇 ②
Gewurztraminer Spätlese trocken 1991
A lively Gewürztraminer with fresh acidity. A good representative of this vintage.

Grauburgunder 🍇🍇 ③
Tafelwein trocken 1990
A very nice hint of honey, quince and oak characterize this superb wine which has excellent aging potential. Needs another 2-3 years bottle age.

Weissburgunder
Tafelwein trocken 1990
Wolfgang Geissler's oldest vines are in the Kreuzberg site and yield his best Pinot Blanc on a regular basis. He fermented and matured this rich 1990 Auslese in Limousin oak barriques (106°Oechsle) for 14 months, the result of which is a wine of the century with an aroma of melon and ripe, sweet pear, with muscle, mellowness and a hint of botrytis. This opulent Pinot Blanc is a perfect match for dishes with cream sauces or with fruity-sweet combinations, and for this reason it is sold almost exclusively to restaurants. It is most likely to be found in top Pfalz restaurants.

Weingut Henninger IV

Weinstrasse 93
Kallstadt 6701
Tel. (06322) 2277
Fax (06322) 8640

Walter Henninger is the 'grand seigneur' among Pfalz producers. He produced dry, acidulous wines at a time when his colleagues still regarded this style as unsalable. Today, his wines enjoy a great reputation among connoisseurs, with the emphasis on his Pinot Gris (Grauburgunder) from the Kallstadter Steinacker site. In recent years his Rieslings and Silvaners have also become very classy. Alongside the four hectare wine estate Henninger, together with his wife, runs a wine merchant business in Munich, as well as a very cosy wine bar in Kallstadt, "Weinhaus Henninger". However, his wine list only contains bought-in wines. Discussing wine with Henninger is not only a pleasure, but a chance to increase one's knowledge about history, wine culture or the latest trends and experiences outside one's own sphere. For the past two years Henninger has made the wines in the cellars of the neighboring Koehler-Ruprecht estate without changing anything of their typical, fresh and acidulous style.

Kallstadter Annaberg ❦ ②
Riesling Kabinett trocken 1991
A typical Henninger Riesling: soft fruit reminiscent of white peach, balm, lemon, lightly grassy with crisp acidity, pleasant to drink and light.

Kallstadter Saumagen ❦ ②
Riesling Kabinett trocken 1991
A rich Riesling aroma, the wine has a lively sparkle and an obvious hint of maturity, racy on the finish.

Kallstadter Steinacker ❦❦ ②
Scheurebe Spätlese trocken 1991
A rich and very fresh aroma of cassis, an intense scent of peach, very aromatic: a classic, noble and elegant Scheurebe, very lively and racy.

Weingut Jul. Ferd. Kimich

Deidesheim 6705
Tel. (06326) 342

The Kimich estate was founded by an Alsatian family, which settled at Deidesheim in 1758. Today, Joachim Arnold runs the estate, with vineyards in the very best positions at Ruppertsberg, Forst and Deidesheim planted over 75% with Riesling on the area's typical sandstone soils. Traditional wood casks still dominate in the cellar and he has dramatically increased the proportion of dry wine to almost 80%. The 1991s are impressively fruity and racy while the 1990s are appealingly opulent and generous, especially from the sites Mäushöhle, Grainhübel, Pechstein, Leinhöhle, Ungeheuer and Kalkofen.

Deidesheimer Grainhübel ❦ ①
Riesling Kabinett trocken 1991
A very rich, spring flower-like aroma with a scent of cumin and firm acidity. A very nice Riesling with a good future ahead, though a little light because of the vintage.

Forster Stift ❦ ①
Gewürztraminer Kabinett trocken 1991
An aroma of rose petals and fresh foliage, fresh grapes on the palate: a noble Gewürztraminer with good acidity..

Deidesheimer Kalkofen ❦ ②
Riesling Auslese trocken 1990
An opulent, fine Auslese with ripe fruit, generous with delicate acid framework.

Weingut Johannes Kleinmann

Birkweiler 6741
Tel. (06345) 3547
Fax (06345) 7777

When the conversation turns to Karl-Heinz Kleinmann the discussion inevitably includes the red variety St Laurent. In 1967 a grower from Siebling recognized a single vine in a nursery at Rhodt which was due to be grubbed up. It turned out to be Germany's last remaining example of the Austrian variety St Laurent. The grower found a fellow supporter in Karl-Heinz Kleinmann and cuttings were taken from this vine, after which the variety was reproduced and tried out on an experimental basis. In the meantime he has almost one hectare planted with St Laurent and it has enjoyed a small renaissance since other estates in the Pfalz have taken an interest in it. Kleinmann, who runs the estate together with his wife Hannelore, has also selected his own Pinot Gris clones, and as a result his Grauburgunders have attained increasingly high quality in recent years and are among the Pfalz's best wines.

Birkweiler Kastanienbusch   🍇 ②
Riesling Spätlese trocken 1990
This firm Riesling grown on primary rock soils is equipped with a light, smoky aroma, crisp acidity and plenty of potential for future development.

Birkweiler Mandelberg   🍇🍇 ②
Grauer Burgunder Auslese trocken 1990
From old vines this is one of the top Pinot Gris from this vintage and very ripe in style.

Weissburgunder   🍇 ③
Tafelwein trocken 1991
This Pinot Blanc was aged for eight weeks in small, new Swabian oak barrels resulting in a generous, almost unctuous wine.

Birkweiler Rosenberg   🍇 ①
St. Laurent QbA 1991
A slight scent of roses and a hint of walnuts: a very compact and dense wine, spicy, meaty and full-bodied. Very successful considering the vintage.

Weingut Knipser

Johannishof
Laumersheim 6711
Tel. (06238) 742
Fax (06238) 4377

At the moment Werner Knipser is the most successful and the most popular Pfalz producer, though he sometimes feels misunderstood, as it is mainly his reds which enjoy popularity among wine enthusiasts and in restaurants. On the other hand he is equally proud of his whites, especially his Rieslings, Pinot Blancs and Pinot Gris fermented and aged in barrique. His barrique fermented Rieslings have proven wrong the assumption that the variety loses its typical fruit when aged in oak. In fact tasting his 1990 Riesling is like biting into a fully ripe peach. He also causes a sensation with his reds. Together with his brothe,r Volker, he has bought hundreds of barriques in which he matures Pinot Noir (Spätburgunder), Portugieser, Dornfelder and St Laurent, all deep red in color and characterized more by fruit than oak. Nevertheless they are unusual and do not always do well in blind tastings when compared with reds from other producers.

Riesling* trocken 1990**   🍇🍇 ③
This is Knipser's best Riesling labelled as 'Tafelwein.' Barrique fermented with a smokey, honeyed aroma and good aging potential.

Weissburgunder   🍇 ③
Tafelwein trocken 1990
Still characterized by a hint of new oak, altogether generous in flavor, reminiscent of quince and cumin, well balanced.

Laumersheimer Kappellenberg   🍇🍇 ②
Schwarzriesling Auslese trocken 1989
A superb aroma of berries, dried figs and cherry along with cedarwood and spices: muscular, and rich with strong acidity, well balanced by high alcohol.

Laumersheimer Mandelberg   🍇 ②
Spätburgunder QbA trocken 1989
A scent of ripe blackberries and figs, a typical Pinot Noir in style, a delicate red wine, concentrated on the finish.

Grosskarlbacher Osterberg   🍇 ②
Portugieser Spätlese trocken 1988
A basket full of aromatic summer berry fruit plus nut and almond, generous, spicy with low acidity.

Weingut Koehler-Ruprecht

Weinstrasse 84
Kallstadt 6701
Tel. (06322) 1829
Fax (06322) 8640

Hats off to Bernd Philippi! He has managed to unite tradition, marketing and innovative trends, adapting them to modern times. 'Wines from the old school' is how his philosophy could be described. Late harvesting, aging in classic wood casks and late bottling are the basis of a style which at the moment may not be very fashionable, but which has the advantage of infinitely prolonging the wines life span. The baroque white wines especially are reminiscent of the good old days. Nevertheless tradition has not prevented Philippi from aging his Spätburgunder in barrique, bottling it in Bordeaux style bottles and calling it Pinot Noir for marketing purposes. He has also planted Chardonnay, made a Pfalz similar in style to the noble French Sauternes and distilled a sensational marc, plus many other novelties. Thus Philippi is a genuine all-rounder. Some regard him as number one in the Pfalz and he is definitely among the region's top twelve. His wines can be tasted in the Weincastell, an excellent restaurant right next to the winery.

Kallstadter Saumagen ♛ ♛ ③
Riesling Auslese trocken 1990
Rather smokey on the palate, clear and streamlined in structure, full with steely acidity - a wine with a great future.

Kallstadter Saumagen ♛ ②
Riesling Spätlese trocken 1990
Still undeveloped on the nose, reminiscent of peach, a nice hint of wood (old casks), long on the finish, a wine for laying down.

Philippi ♛ ③
Riesling Tafelwein trocken 1989
Fermented and matured in barrique, with a hint of walnuts and orange peel it is rich in aroma with understated oak.

Philippi 1990 ♛ ③
Pinot Noir Tafelwein trocken
Aroma of blackberries and figs, a scent of toasted walnuts, fairly full but a little too soft.

Weingut Lingenfelder

Grosskarlbach 6711
Tel. (06238) 754
Fax (06238) 1096

Rainer Lingenfelder worked for years in the wine export business before taking over his father's estate together with his uncle Hermann Lingenfelder. He gathered the latest enological knowledge from all over the world and adapted it to local conditions and this has formed the basis for his philosophy. The tools to accomplish this are closed fermentation tanks for red wines, stainless steel storage tanks, a cellar filled with oak casks, used barriques to age red wine to avoid loss of regional characteristics and new 1,000 liter casks made of Pfalz oak called "Stückfässer." He fermented and matured a 1991 Silvaner in them with sensational results. Rainer Lingenfelder does not wish his wines to be indistinguishable from other international wines and takes pains to express their origin. The solution, of course, is to produce less but better. He offers a clearly structured selection featuring mostly just one wine from each varietal: Scheurebe, Silvaner, Dornfelder and a classy Pinot Noir which journalists have turned into a cult wine, plus a few dessert wines. All this combines to make Lingenfelder the Pfalz's most convincing producer at present.

Freinsheimer Goldberg ♛ ②
Riesling Spätlese trocken 1991
This wine from 30 year-old vines.shows clearly how reducing vineyard yields can intensify flavor.

Grosskarlbacher Burgweg ♛ ♛ ①
Scheurebe Kabinett trocken 1991
A powerful aroma of cassis, fully ripe peaches with delicate fruity acidity: a perfectly balanced, super Scheurebe.

Grosskarlbacher Ostgerberg ♛ ①
Riesling Kabinett trocken 1991
A clear, clean scent of peach, though a little weak on the finish: a very presentable Kabinett which should improve with bottle age.

Silvaner Tafelwein trocken 1991 ♛ ♛ ②
Very nice hints of ripe pear on a smokey background, understated acidity and interesting oak: a highly elegant Silvaner.

Spätburgunder ♛ ③
Tafelwein trocken 1990
A generous red wine with an aroma of plums, a strong hint of caramel, toasty and autumn fruit flavors though a little alcoholic.

Weingut Herbert Messmer

Burrseiler 6741
Tel. (06345) 2770
Fax (06345) 7917

We have to make special efforts to compensate for the lower average temperature of 2°C compared with the Mittelhaardt," says Herbert Messmer. It is not difficult to guess what he means by this - consistently lower vineyard yields. He has an advantage with the geological characteristics of his south facing single vineyard Schäwer, which is the only Pfalz site with slatey soils. The Rieslings it produces are finely structured with soft, peachy fruit, elegant acidity and good concentration which in blind tastings are difficult to tell apart from the renowned top Rieslings of the Mittelhaardt. Herbert Messmer founded this wine estate in 1964 and his son Gregor, who shares responsibility for the estate's fortunes continues in his father's footsteps. Nevertheless the new generation has left its mark with very successful barrique versions of Pinot Noir (Spätburgunder), and St Laurent and an estate bottled sparkling wine is also available. We can expect Messmer wines to find their place among the Pfalz's great classics in the next few years..

Burrweiler Schäwer   🍇 ①
Riesling Kabinett trocken 1991
A Riesling from slatey soils, a unique micro-geological peculiarity in the Pfalz: clear, minerally, slender and racy.

Burrweiler Schlossgarten   🍇 ①
Grauburgunder Kabinett trocken 1991
Very fine, lean Pinot Gris with a light sparkle and a soft almond-like aroma.

Burrweiler Schäwer   🍇 ②
Riesling Spätlese trocken 1990
A very nice top Riesling from the southern Pfalz which is in no way inferior to the more famous versions from the Mittelhaardt.

Burgweiler Altendorf   🍇 ③
Spätburgunder Spätlese trocken 1990
A bouquet of cherry and redcurrant with a light hint of caramel, dense and compact in structure: one of the top Pfalz Pinot Noirs.

Hemlinger Herrenbuckel   🍇 ③
St.Laurent Spätlese trocken 1990
An aroma of cherry and cinamon, compactly structured and firm: shows the class of this variety which has become rare in the Pfalz.

Weingut Georg Mosbacher

Forst 6701
Tel. (06326) 329
Fax (06326) 6774

What emerges when an enologist from southern Baden marries into a Pfalz Riesling estate? It is still early days to tell, as Jürgen Düringer only started work at Weingut Mosbacher in July 1992. His wife Sabine, the owner's daughter had already worked for a year on her parents estate. When asked about the many awards won by Mosbacher wines she alludes to her father's efforts which have strongly shaped the wines for many years. Nevertheless the young couple are bound to introduce a few ideas of their own, perhaps focusing more on Burgundian varieties in future and hopefully the unnessessary added sweetness (süssreserve) will vanish. Up to now even their dry wines have been rounded off in this way. However, the estate's characteristic slender Riesling style will certainly remain and thanks to these wines the Weingut Georg Mosbacher is among the Pfalz's top three most awarded estates.

Forster Stift   🍇 ①
Weissburgunder Kabinett trocken 1991
This wine was harvested very early which gives it a straight forward, slender, elegant style. A typical Riesling producer's Pinot Blanc.

Forster Ungeheuer   🍇 ①
Riesling Kabinett trocken 1991
A light, typical Riesling, discreetly scented with underlying, pleasantly fresh acidity.

Forster Pechstein   🍇 ②
Riesling Spätlese trocken 1990
Minerally aroma and lightly flinty - a super Spätlese with a few grams of residual sugar.

Forster Ungeheuer   🍇🍇 ②
Riesling Auslese trocken 1990
A typical 1990 Auslese, very generous in flavor with plenty of power, volume and firm acidity.

Weingut Müller Catoir

Neustadt-Haardt 6730
Tel. (06321) 2815
Fax (06321) 480014

Alongside the rather reserved owner Heinrich Catoir his very energetic and dynamic winemaker Hans-Günther Schwarz has recently moved into the limelight. He has been very influential in forming the style of Müller-Catoir wines, which are extremely fruity, soft and made in a very reductive manner which preserves the original fruit character. "Tasting wine should be like biting into grapes," he says, and indeed, in blind tastings Müller-Catoir wines regularly excel by their appealing, typically varietal fruit. Schwarz dismisses the assertion that his Rieslings taste more like Scheurebe, insisting that the vines are long established clones. As well as Riesling they produce Pinot Blanc (Weissburgunder), Muskateller and Rieslaner as well as the red Spätburgunder (Pinot Noir) which is a superb wine, deep red, powerful on the palate with extraordinary bite. Unfortunately Müller-Catoir wines do not age well and are at their most appealing in their youth, including the reds.

Mussbacher Eselshaut   ⚇ ②
Rieslaner Spätlese trocken 1991
A speciality of the estate: fully ripe with an Auslese character, accentuated and well integrated acidity, botrytis on the nose and pleasantly mature - a wine to meditate over.

Haardter Herrenletten   ⚇ ②
Gewürztraminer Spätlese trocken 1990
A wine with a fascinating scent of roses, this Gewürztraminer comes from an old vineyard with minute yields. It is fully mature with an especially noble aroma.

Haardter Herrenletten   ⚇⚇ ②
Grauburgunder Auslese trocken 1990
A sensational wine which is fully present on the palate long after tasting with a scent of hay, acacia blossom, a summer meadow full of flowers plus noble hints of botrytis, though it is still linear and fresh.

Gimmeldinger Meerspinne   ⚇⚇ ③
Spätburgunder Spätlese trocken 1990
This is the answer to all German attempts at aging red wines in barrique: deep red with a classic Burgundian nose, dense and complex with a very rich aroma of blackberry, cassis, violets and fig.

Haardter Bürgergarten   ⚇⚇⚇ ②
Riesling Spätlese trocken 1991
Only Müller-Catoir can succeed in making Spätlese of this calibre in such an unreliabl growing season as 1991. It was especiall negative for Riesling after a summer droughu and too much rain in October. A grower need to be almost fanatical to harvest in severa stages and patiently to wait until 28th October tu harvest such a small amount of such a grea wine: absolutely clear and rich with a pure, ripe peachy aroma which jumps out of the glas followed by an endless aftertaste. Apart fron this their achievement in making a wine like thi in such a problem vintage is especiall admirable.

Weingut Münzberg

Godramstein 6740
Tel. (06341) 60935
Fax (06341) 64210

Family father Lothar Kessler only started selling bottled wine 15 years ago. He has recently moved the once small concern in the center of Godramstein to a hilltop above the village with a fantastic view of the neighbouring villages' vineyards. His sons Günther and Rainer Kessler are now in control and have cleaned up the assortment of grape varieties to focus on classic Riesling, Pinots Blanc and Gris, Silvaner along with the reds, Pinot Noir and Dornfelder. The wines are steely, clear as a bell with enlivening freshness. A barrique-aged 1990 Spätburgunder (Pinot Noir) is very promising. Their Pinot Blancs (Weissburgunder) have a gentle aroma of pear and the Silvaner is also excellent, with a light sparkle and discreet but very classy fruit. It goes without saying that their skill and talent are also used to distill Schnaps and make their own bottle-fermented sparkling wine.

Godramsteiner Münzberg 🍷 ②
Silvaner trocken QbA 1991
A typically varietal nose, concentrated and peppery on the palate, rather slender with a light, refreshing sparkle: a very pleasant, uncomplicated Silvaner.

Godramsteiner Münzberg 🍷🍷 ①
Weissburgunder Spätlese trocken 1991
A soft aroma of pear, classy and elegant on the palate and will improve with bottle age: a masterpiece considering the difficult 1991 growing season.

Godramsteiner Münzberg ▦ ②
Spätburgunder Weissherbst
Kabinett trocken 1991
A pale colored rosé with a discreet, clear varietal bouquet: a lively, fine rosé for warm summer evenings.

Godramsteiner Münzberg 🍇 ②
Dornfelder Tafelwein trocken 1990
Lively, bright cassis red in color with a scent of bilberry and equipped with youthful tannins. Its compact, dense structure bodes well for future improvement.

Weingut Pfeffingen

Fuhrmann-Eymael
Bad Dürkheim-Pfeffingen 6702
Tel. (06322) 8605
Fax (06322) 8603

Karl Fuhrmann is regarded locally as one whose engagement and authority have strongly influenced Pfalz wine production in recent years. A personality among wine producers, he has generally influenced developments by his clear and consistent style rather than through his position as president of the wine producers association. Fulmann's wine style may appear rather antiquated to some but he makes exactly the classic type of wine for which the Pfalz used to be famous. His leading products are Riesling and Scheurebe which reflect the power and heaviness of the Pfalz soils. His dry Kabinett wines and Spätlesen and especially his mature Beeren-Auslesen and Trocken-Beeren-Auslesen are legendary and are the wines which established his reputation. His daughter Doris and son-in-law Günther Eymael have been influential in the running of the estate for several years. Their 1989 Scheureben and Rieslings were great, the 1990s sensational, while the 1991s are much better than the vintage's reputation.

Ungsteiner Herrenberg 🍷🍷 ③
Scheurebe Auslese trocken 1991
Scheurebe is a Fuhrmann specialty. This wine has a strong cassis aroma and a gentle scent of rose petal: a noble Auslese.

Ungsteiner Honigsäckel 🍷 ①
Riesling Kabinett trocken 1991
A nice scent of violets, delicate and refined; a wine which is only starting to mature.

Ungsteiner Honigsäckel 🍷 ②
Silvaner Spätlese trocken 1991
A generous wine, very warm, with complex floral aromas: a very mature Spätlese, typical of Fuhrmann's style.

Ungsteiner Weilberg 🍷🍷 ③
Riesling Spätlese trocken 1991
A pleasant Riesling scent jumps out of the glass accompanied by a gentle hint of honey with strong, well integrated ripe acidity: a superb achievement for such an unfavorable growing season.

Weingut Ökonomierat Rebholz

Siebeldingen 6741
Tel. (06345) 5459
Fax (06345) 7954

When Hans Rebholz died suddenly a few years ago, his son, Hans Jörg Rebholz, was suddenly forced to take over the family wine estate. The numerous mistakes which the young and inexperienced producer made in the mid 1980s have now been forgotten. Today, he has not only gained experience but has followed in the steps of his grandfather in championing the cause for producing natural wines. He has renounced chaptalisation, even though he is fully aware that this sometimes sets him very narrow limits and of the need to make up for this by appropriate steps in the vineyard to attain optimum ripeness in a natural way. He is proud of being able to offer deep, dark, very ripe and rich Pinot Noirs as well as the classic white varieties (mainly Riesling plus Pinots Gris and Blanc and a consistently good Müller-Thurgau). He has already concluded his first experiments with barrique-aged Pinot Noir (Spätburgunder), which is not sold under the estate name but independently as 'Hans-Jörg-Rebholz' selections.

Birkweiler Kastanienbusch 🍇🍇 ③
Riesling Auslese trocken 1990
With a very pleasant peachy aroma this is a clear, striking, succulent Auslese. The elegant acidity promises to help it on its way to an even greater future.

Siebeldinger Königsgarten 🍇🍇 ④
Muskateller Beerenauslese 1990
Muscat is a Rebholz speciality. In 1990 he succeeded in making a fantastic Beeren-Auslese with recognizable varietal characteristics, fruity sweetness and hearty, piquant acidity.

Siebeldinger Rosenberg 🍇 ②
Weissburgunder Spätlese trocken 1990
An excellent Pinot Blanc with gentle rose petal and discreet fruit aromas: a wine for laying down.

Spätburgunder 🍇🍇 ③
Tafelwein trocken 1990
Marvelous aroma of violets and berry fruits with a faint hint of vanilla. A still undeveloped Pinot Noir with a great future ahead.

Weingut Karl Schäfer

Bad Dürkheim 6702
Tel. (06322) 2138
Fax (06322) 8729

The rumors would not cease: the Karl Schäfer estate at Bad Dürkheim was up for sale and prices were even mentioned. Dr Wolf Fleischmann, owner of this estate which is perhaps the Pfalz's best Riesling producer catagorically denied this, and the estate is run exactly as before. Hopefully he is right, as Fleischmann's wines are superb and highly regarded both in restaurant circles and among wine enthusiasts. Nevertheless, Fleischmann has always kept his distance from fashion and transitory trends. Under his direction tradition (maturation exclusively in wood) and modern technology (air-conditioning in the cask cellar) are happily combined. The resulting wines are characterful and express the variety of the differing soils in their make-up. Their excellent quality is confirmed in the results of Riesling competitions and comparative tastings.

Dürkheimer Fronhof 🍇 ②
Weissburgunder Spätlese trocken 1990
Great richness of aroma, reminiscent of acacia and lavander: generous Pinot Blanc with great length.

Dürkheimer Pochstein 🍇🍇 ②
Riesling Kabinett trocken 1990
Grown on volcanic soil this Riesling has a gentle aroma of rose and elder flower, linear clean and clear.

Dürkheimer Spielberg 🍇 ①
Riesling Kabinett trocken 1990
A scent of spices and undergrowth and very strong fruit: a wine which is still very discreet but with good potential.

Wachenheimer Gerümpel 🍇 ①
Riesling Spätlese trocken 1990
A very fruity and mature Spätlese, with hints of banana and ripe berry fruits, a succulent Riesling, typical of the Mittelhaardt.

Weingut Georg Siben Erben

Weinstrasse 21
Deidesheim 6705
Tel. (06326)) 214

More than a decade has passed since Wolfgang Georg Siben stirred up a controversy in the press by putting the analytical data of his wines on the labels, a step which was against the law in those days. To the detriment of the authorities this case brought him plenty of publicity and he emerged as a very upright wine producer. Indeed he is one of the few who, years ago, made no secret of what their wines contained, especially residual sugar, which in their case was usually zero. The Sibens have never had anything to do with süssreserve (unfermented grape juice added as a sweetener) a fact which, years ago caused dry wine fans to flock to Deidesheim. The effort seems to have paid off, as the 1991 Rieslings are exceptionally classy, finely-strung, steely, racy - simply successful. The same goes for almost all wines which emerge from this 17 ha estate mainly planted with Riesling, followed by Müller-Thurgau, Silvaner and Pinot Blanc.

Deidesheimer Kieselberg   🍇 ①
Riesling Kabinett trocken 1991
A scent reminiscent of a basket full of melons, grapes and apples: a spicey Riesling aroma interwoven with fresh, steely acidity..

Ruppertsberger Reiterpfad   🍇 ①
Grauburgunder Kabinett trocken 1991
An unusually slender Pinot Gris, with an aroma of green pears and surprisingly strong acidity. Only just starting to mature.

Deidesheimer Kieselberg   🍇 ②
Riesling Spätlese trocken 1990
Scent of exotic fruits (papaya, mango and pineapple), very generous with the fruit well supported by racy acidity.

Weingut Thomas Siegrist

Leinsweiler 6741
Tel. (06345) 1309
Fax (06345) 7542

'The Pfalz rebel' is how the press described Siegrist a few years ago. The wine control officials had confiscated a barrique-aged 1985 Pinot Noir (Spätburgunder) which in tastings had evoked a wave of enthusiasm among restaurant owners and wine lovers. The criminal proceedings which ensued failed miserably and since then he has steadily increased the number of barriques in his cellar and the officially 'regionally typical' red wines are in enormous demand. Prior to this there was no real red wine tradition in the Pfalz which could be used as a model for a typical style. It will take a few years yet to judge the class of Sigrist's Dornfelder and Pinot Noir (Spätburgunder), which will emerge when the excellent 1988, 1989 and 1990 vintages are ready for drinking. He has also made Pinots Blanc and Gris (Weiss- and Grauburgunder) in barrique with some excellent results. Nevertheless, his wines occasionally seem a little thin.

Leinsweiler Sonnenberg   🍇 ②
Riesling Spätlese trocken 1991
A light scent of peaches with a hint of maturity, very succulent and generous, surprisingly dense for this vintage. It should be laid down for a further one to two years..

Leinsweiler Sonnenberg   🍇 ②
Weissburgunder Spätlese trocken 1990
A delicately fruity bouquet, fresh acidity plus understated, well-integrated oak.

Dornfelder Tafelwein trocken 1990   🍇 ③
Very generous and compact with well-integrated oak, long and powerful on the finish, a very well-made Dornfelder.

Spätburgunder   🍇 ③
Tafelwein trocken 1990
An aroma of strawberries, spicey on the palate, medium weight with the oak very much to the fore: good aging potential.

Karl-Heinz Wehrheim

Weingut Hohenberg
6741 Birkweiler
Tel. (06345) 3542
Fax (06345) 3869

Dr. Heinz Wertheim handed over the estate to his son Karl-Heinz in 1990. Since then a red wine fermenting tank, a few barriques and an unsuccessful bottle label have been introduced, though the style of the wine remains unchanged. Apart from several nobly sweet specialties the wines are dry with accentuated acidity and occasionally almost puzzling depth. The reason for this are the deep, heavy and often damp and cool soils of the Südpfalz. Rieslings from there are different from those of the Mittelhaardt, being more discreet, more complex and not always easy to appreciate. However, when they finally open up the wine drinker's patience is rewarded with fantastic taste experiences. On the other hand Wehrheim's Pinot Blancs (Weissburgunder) overflow with charm. The red Pinot Noir and St Laurent are very francophile and tannic in style and are among Germany's best reds. St Laurent is now only found in its Austrian homeland and in the Pfalz where it is increasing in popularity.

Birkweiler Kastanienbusch　🍇 ②
Weissburgunder Spätlese trocken 1991
A mature bouquet and strong acidity, very harmonious, it is a very racy Pinot Blanc, with scents of meadow flowers, walnuts and almonds.

Birkweiler Kastanienbusch　🍇 ①
Riesling Kabinett trocken 1991
A light, acidulous wine for summer drinking with grassy-green aromas together with apricot, and a fresh sparkle combining to make a fresh, lively, light Riesling.

Birkenweiler Mandelberg　🍇 ②
Riesling Spätlese trocken 1990
Slim in body, steely, almost 'crunchy' acidity and a minerally flavor: a wine with great potential for future development..

Birkweiler Kastanienbusch　🍇🍇 ③
Spätburgunder Auslese trocken 1990
A cornucopia of very ripe late summer fruits, with an enormous spectrum of aromas: an exceptional wine of 'grand cru' quality.

Rheingau

The Rheingau is a small wine-growing region situated on the northern bank of the Rhine between Wiesbaden and Lorch (west of Frankfurt). Although it produces only a quarter of the volume of wine grown on the Mosel, German Riesling owes its fame very much to the Rheingau. It is fuller in body and generally richer than that from the Mosel, while Spätlese Auslese wines are especially powerful and are harvested more rarely. On the other hand, they lack the Mosel's delicate structure. Kabinett and simple "Qualitätsweine" are also comparatively full. Compared to other great white wines of the world,they are considerably lower in alcohol (between 10° and 12°/vol) but have excellent keeping qualities. Unlike Mosel Riesling, around 62% of that produced in the Rheingau is either dry (trocken) or off-dry (halbtrocken), and their weightier structure harmonizes well with the high acidity. The Charta Association (Charta-Vereinigung) has done much to promote the Rheingau's dry and off-dry Riesling style. The name stands for a voluntary association of producers who make special selections of their best wines from each quality level and market them in a special bottle, with a special label and back label. Charta wines must be 100% Riesling, the sugar level of the grape juice must be significantly higher than the minimum required by law and the residual sugar must not exceed 18 g/lt (ie, they must taste dry). In short, they should distinguish themselves by the interplay between fine, steely acidity, elegance and body.

88% of the Rheingau's vineyards are planted with Riesling. This variety is responsible for the notoriety which the wine achieved at the turn of the century in England, home of great wine connoisseurs. Among the world's white wines, it enjoyed similar status to Bordeaux's standing among reds and fetched equally high prices. Names like Schloss Johannisberg, Schloss Vollrads and Prinz von Preussen (now Schloss Rheinhartshausen) have made it famous throughout the world. At Kloster Eberbach at Eltville a festive auction is held each year of very fine wines of recent, mature and very old vintages. Great Auslesen and comparatively simple Kabinett wines from good vintages can keep for 20, 30 years and in exceptional cases even longer, kept fresh and intackt by their high acidity.

The second significant Rheingau variety is Pinot Noir (Spätburgunder) accounting for 7%, which produces good quality in and around Rudesheim and Assmannshausen due to the warmer microclimate. Nevertheless, Rheingau Spätburgunder does not achieve the body and depth found in great French Burgundies. It is generally made as a light, fairly pale red, without the tannic backbone found elsewhere. However, in recent years several producers have begun trying to extract more tannin from the grapes by longer fermentation with the skins and occasionally maturing the young wine in barrique with encouraging results.

Due to its vicinity to Frankfurt, the Rheingau has become a popular recreational area for the city's inhabitants. Especially in spring and summer weekends, there numerous festivities and cultural activities held to attract visitors to the cellars and taverns in the small wine villages along the Rhein. A significant part of the region's production is consumed in tavern courtyards (called "Strausswirtschaften") in the open air. Producers have responded to demand by making simple drinking wines which account for a considerable part of their production.

Weingut Fritz Allendorf

Georghof-Kirchstrasse 69
6227 Oestrich-Winkel
Tel. (06723) 51021
Fax (06723) 7699

Fritz Allendorf stands for a part of the Rheingau's popular wine culture as well as for his own estate. He is just as much in his element at open-air festivals as he is at high-class gourmet events which emphasize the connection between wine and food. Allendorf's charm is just as much appreciated by his customers as is his consistently traditional style of wine: plenty of body, succulent and strongly characterized by cask-aging. He took over the estate from his father when it consisted of 2.5 ha - today he owns 36 ha and boasts 150 wines from five vintages on his list, most of which customers can try by the glass in the estate's wine bar. The cellar is no secret either, and is always open to interested visitors, even during the harvest. Allendorf thrives on close contact with his consumers, a fact which in the past often led to the one or other weakness being over-looked. In recent years his rather unpolished, rustic wines have become suppler, a development which his son, Ulrich Allendorf, has probably had a significant influence upon.

Hallgartener Jungfer Riesling QbA 1991   🍇 ①
A very clear Riesling with pure varietal flavor and a fine scent of honey along with very carefully dosed sweetness.

Rüdesheimer Drachenstein Riesling Spätlese 1991   🍇 ②
A full-bodied, rather heavy wine with fascinating fruit. Like all Allendorf wines it is reasonably priced.

Assmannshäuser Hinterkirch Spätburgunder QbA trocken 1990   🍇 ②
A substantial, almost powerful wine with a deep, heavy Pinot Noir bouquet: a warm, mellow red wine matured in traditional casks.

Geheimrat Aschrott'sche Gutsverwaltung

Kirchstrasse 38
6203 Hochheim am Rhein
Tel. (06146) 2207
Fax (06146) 7335

Traditional wood casks play an important part in the philosophy of this estate, and the administrator Holger Schwab regards them as absolutely necessary to smoothen the rough, 'prickly' edges of their rather hard young Rieslings. He likes Riesling to be round and harmonious and tries to achieve this by traditional methods. They include a small amount of residial as well as cask aging to give the impression of ripeness. Their list includes at least five vintages which offer the lover of generous, fruit-sweet wines a good selection of mature bottles. Their best wines are made in this style, while the young, simple dry wines often appear a little hard and brittle. The 1990s are almost all excellent at all quality levels, while 1991 produced several fascinating high grade specialities.

Hochheimer Kirchenstück Riesling Auslese 1991   🍇🍇 ③
One of this vintage's few Auslesen harvested at a fabulous 122° Oechsle. Light botrytis, expressive fruit due to light frost before the harvest - very fine.

Hochheimer Kirchenstück Riesling Eiswein 1991   🍇🍇 ④
Velvety richness of honey and over-ripe fruit, an unusually fine Eiswein which does not stick the mouth together in spite of its sweetness.

Hochheimer Hölle Riesling Kabinett halbtrocken 1990   🍇 ①
An appealingly good Kabinett wine which owes its mildness to the clayey soils at Hochheim as well as to its unobtrusive sweetness.

Hochheimer Hölle Riesling QbA trocken 1990   🍇 ①
Typical of 1990: seems mature, ready for drinking now. The fruit is not as accentuated as the high alcohol.

Staatsweingut Assmannshausen

Höllenbergstrasse 10
Assmannshausen 6220
Tel. (06722) 2273

Times have changed - also at Assmannshausen. A the begining of the 1980s the Staatsweingut made thin, pale red wines while today they are intensely-colored power packs, of a kind seldom found among German Pinot Noirs. The credit goes to Friedrich Dries, who has managed this estate belonging to the Federal State of Hessen since 1988 and their wines have been extremely influential as a style in the Rheingau for years Assmannshausen is regarded as a red wine enclave in the Rheingau. Dries is successful in producing loose-berried, healthy grapes grown on the eroded rock soils by ecological wine-growing methods.and reducing yields to a maximum of 50 hl/ha. The harvest is carried out by hand followed by an eight day fermentation on the skins in open vats and six months maturation in traditional wood casks. Dies has not become a victim of 'barrique mania' but tries to bring forth and preserve the traditional style of Rheingau Spätburgunder (Pinot Noir).

Assmannshäuser Höllenberg 🍷 ②
Spätburgunder QbA trocken 1991
A wine with a powerful red color and good richness, generous, warm and clothed in soft tannin. It has plenty of finesse and a long life expectancy.

Assmannshäuser Höllenberg 🍷 ②
Spätburgunder Weissherbst QbA trocken 1991
A salmon-colored wine with clean, clear varietal fruit; a pleasantly fresh, characterful rosé.

Assmannhäuser Höllenberg 🍷 ③
Spätburgunder Spätlese trocken 1990
Dark red with a full, rich bouquet; generous on the palate, concentrated with strong tannin and a long finish.

Assmannshäuser Höllenberg 🍷🍷 ④
Spätburgunder Auslese trocken 1989
A monumental wine, full red in color, already showing orange reflections, mellow on the palate with soft tannins.

J B Becker

Rheinstrasse 5-6
Walluf 6220
Tel. (06123) 72523
Fax (06123) 75335

Johann Josef Becker is a Rheingau red wine specialist, and his Spätburgunders (Pinot Noirs) are always among the region's most interesting, being concentrated, relatively dark in color with plenty of natural tannin, warm and full of character. Although they are typical Rheingau style reds, they have more body than those of their competitors. Becker is a conservative and no fan of either stainless steel or barriques, being a great upholder of traditional cask aging and even Riesling is matured in this way. He is never in a hurry to bottle his wines and only started filling his 1991 wines in July 1992; Becker's wines excel by virtue of their clarity, their pure varietal flavors and their unbelievably high extract levels due to vines over 40 years-old, an exception in the Rheingau where they are often grubbed up at an age of 18-20 years.

Wallufer Walkenberg 🍇 🍇 ③
Riesling Auslese trocken 1990
Onre of this vintage's top wines with a mouth-filling flavor of apricots, cassis and a nuance of botrytis, with fine, fruity acidity - a great wine.

Wallufer Walkenberg 🍇 ②
Riesling Kabinett trocken 1990
Very rich for a Kabinett, a powerful wine with plenty of fruit and finesse even though made as a dry wine.

Wallufer Berg Bildstock 🍇 ②
Riesling Spätlese trocken 1990
A rich, lemon-colored wine with an opulent bouquet of southern fruits, powerful with highly elegant acidity and length boding well for future development.

Wallufer Oberberg 🍇 🍇 ④
Riesling Beerenauslese 1989
A rarity: almost fermented to dryness and thus an alcohol content of 16%: best drunk with goose liver or lobster in a heavy butter sauce.

Wallufer Walkenberg 🍷 ②
Spätburgunder QbA trocken 1989
Dark red, an aroma of cherry and plum with an underlying oak flavor and soft tannins.

Baron von Brentano

Am Lindenplatz 2
6227 Oestrich-Winkel
Tel. (06723) 2068

Members of the Brentano family, originally
from Lake Como, settled as merchants in
Frankfurt at the end of the 17th century. In
1804 they acquired the Brentanohaus at
Winkel which now has a wine estate and
wine bar. The 9.3 ha of vineyard, planted
almost exclusively with Riesling (apart from
this only the red Pinot Noir is tolerated), are
the main object of focuss and under the
direction of Udo Baron von Brentano
traditional casks have been renounced for
stainless steel. This has not been to the
detriment of quality: on the contrary, the
wines' contours have become much clearer.
Brentano wines can be extraordinarily fine
and delicate, though some appear flabby,
and, in addition, with all respect for the
acidulous Riesling style they are rather
heavy-handed in dosing the residual sugar.
Apart from this, even though they do not
market the wines under cru names (perhaps
with good reason) it should not be necessary
to exploit the name of Goethe for marketing
purposes, who one stayed with the
Brentanos.

Riesling Kabinett trocken 1990   ♥ ①
A very vigorous Kabinett made in a Spätlese
style, high but ripe acidity, relatively high in
alcohol and seems a little clumsy.

Winkeler Hasensprung   ♥ ②
Riesling Kabinett 1990
A fine, elegant wine made especially classy by
the interplay between alcohol, fruity acidity, fruit
sweetness and a nuance of residual sugar.

Winkeler Hasensprung   ♥ ②
Riesling Spätlese 1990
A sweet Spätlese with a strong, grapey flavor
and a shot of Riesling spice together with a soft
aroma indicating early maturity.

Georg Breuer

Geisenheimer Strasse 9
6220 Rüdesheim
Tel. (06722) 1027
Fax (06722) 4531

Bernhard Breuer, the present day owner of
this estate is a man who seems to be driven
by an engine. He is a founder member of the
"Charta" association and an untiring front line
fighter for the Rheingau and its wines, which
have been made respectable once again
both at home and abroad. Of course he
always takes his own wines with him on his
travels and is never afraid to present them
when the situation arises, as Breuer
Rieslings have become noticeably classier in
recent years, being above averaage in both
price and quality. This is especially
noticeable in comarative tastings with other
Charta wines, all of which represent the the
top of their categories. His best wines are
recognizable by their site names which
appear on the labels, especially Rauenthaler
Nonnenberg and Berg Schlossberg at
Rüdesheim, while his normal range is
maketed under the district name
Rüdesheimer. The letters "GB" are used to
denote a full, dry, uncomplicated Riesling for
everyday consumption. His 1991s are at
least a step behind the 1990s.

Rüdesheimer Berg Rottland   ♥♥ ④
Riesling Beerenauslese 1991
One of 1991's best wines, very sweet with
concentrated fruit (maracuja and peach). It has
a long life expectancy.

Rüdesheimer Berg Schlossberg   ♥ ②
Riesling Kabinett 1991
A compact, off-dry wine with elegant acidity, and
strong cassis, peach and apple fruit - a very
successful Charta wine.

Rüdersheimer Berg Schlossberg   ♥ ③
Riesling Kabinett 1990
A very elegant wine, very muscular for a
Kabinett with spice and super fruit, multi-layered
and harmonious in flavor.

Rauenthaler Nonnenberg   ♥♥ ③
Riesling Spätlese 1989
An unusual wine made from very ripe grapes
(vineyard yields kept to 18 hl/ha) with its strong
acidity well-integrated by richness. A Charta
wine.

Weingut Diefenhardt

Hauptstrasse 4
6228 Eltville-Martinsthal
Tel. (06123) 71490
Fax (06123) 64841

Back in 1938, when great-grandfather Diefenhardt gave his friend, airplane captain Löckner a bottle of 1921 Rauenthaler Rothenburg Riesling to take with him on his trip around the world, it must have been a wine from the very best site even then. He could hardly have suspected that his great-grandson would become one of the greatest defenders of the cru philosophy. Peter Seyffardt, the present-day owner regards two things to be essential: individual harvesting and making and maturing the wines separately. He has been working hard to increase the prestige of the top Rauenthaler sites Wülfen and Rothenberg, along with the Martinsthal Langenberg and Martinthaler Wildsau. Of his 16 ha, 87% are planted with Riesling and 13% with Pinot Noir. He is also very fussy when it comes to reducing yields by pruning, resulting in a range of stylish, often very refined wines highly regarded by connoisseurs. Seyffardt, who increased his wine knowledge in South Africa among other places, organizes Charson evenings and other cultural events at his estate several times each year.

Martinsthaler Langenberg   🍇 ①
Riesling QbA 1990
Perhaps the best Diefenhardt QbA in this vintage and definitely a typical Charta wine: finely fruity bouquet, full and softly elegant, made in an off-dry style.

Martinsthaler Langenberg   🍇🍇 ②
Riesling Spätlese trocken 1990
Produced from old vines this wine has race, fruit and finesse due to its high acidity - a very nice Spätlese.

Martinsthaler Wildsau   🍇 ②
Riesling Kabinett trocken 1990
Very fine, ripe Riesling with firm acidity and plenty of substance. At 11% alcohol it should be in the Spätlese category.

Spätburgunder Barrique 1990   🍷 ①
A barrique-aged Pinot Noir. Medium-weight, rich and not over-powered by wood.

Staatsweingut Eltville

Schwalbacher Strasse 56-62
6228 Eltville
Tel. (06123) 61055
Fax (06123) 4366

Rowald Hepp at 30 is thought to be the youngest state domaine director ever. He has run operations at the largest Rheingau estate (850,000 bottles a year) since 1987 Hopefully the fortunes of the 'state wines' (the estate is owned by the regional government of Hessen) will now improve, as in recent years they have seemed old-fashioned and flabby, lacking acidity and freshness, even if some consumers thought they were fantastic. Hepp's first steps, shorter pruning, natural viticultural methods, rigorous grape selections in order to obtain the prime raw materials and de-stemming the bunches even with white grapes are already bearing fruit. Only half the wines are made in a dry or off-dry halbtrocken style. Their mild, nobly sweet wines are increasing their traditional share. Although the Staatsweingut was a founder member of the Charta movement they market their Charta wines without any indication of site in order to concentrate on producing a typical Charta style without alluding to cru characteristics and components.

Erbacher Marcobrunn   🍇 ①
Riesling QbA trocken 1991
Very nice interplay between fruit and acidity, powerful in body, succulent and firm. A fine, characterful table wine, good with food.

Rauenthaler Baiken   🍇 ④
Riesling Auslese** 1990
At last another great Auslese from this superb vintage: strong, noble sweetness, brilliant acidity, opulent fruit right through - a wine to put away for decades.

Rauenthaler Baiken   🍇 ③
Riesling Spätlese trocken 1990
This attractive, full wine with a light nuance of botrytis comes from a superb site above the Rhine: elegant rather than heavy-weight.

Rüdesheimer Berg Schlossberg   🍇 ③
Riesling Spätlese 1990
A successful wine already surprisingly well developed. The light botrytis together with noticeable sweetness gives it a touch of class.

Weingut August Eser

Weinhole 14
Eltville 6228
Tel. (06123) 2858

Joachim Eser was able to carry on in peace for years until a sudden upsurge in demand for his wines occurred, brought about by numerous positive comments in the press. He finds this difficult to comprehend as, apart from the occasional weak vintage little has changed in the quality of his wines. So what brought all this about? It cannot be the combination of wood casks and stainless steel tanks, as others have both as well. Growing cover crops, minimum use of pesticides (ie natural viticulture) cannot be the key either. So perhaps it all comes down to details. Speed and cleanliness are extremely important at harvest time, and Eser has learned to avoid leaving the picked grapes standing around on the trailer. Fast processing in the cellar, careful pressing and slow fermentation are all factors which have led many people to regard Eser to be number one in the Rheingau. He even managed to produce good quality wines in the difficult 1989 and 1991 vintages, and his 1990s are superb.

Hallgartner Schönhell   ℗ ①
Riesling Spätlese trocken 1991
A very successful Spätlese, not at all hard inspite of its dryness, with multi-layered fruit and delicate structure.

Winkeler Hasensprung   ℗ ①
Riesling Kabinett trocken 1991
Slim and plenty of finesse, rich in body with accentuated acidity - a wine with a great future.

Oestricher Lenchen   ℗ ①
Riesling Kabinett 1990
The estate's best 1990 Charta wine, almost dry and, thus, an excellent wine to go with food.

Oestricher Lenchen   ℗ ℗ ①
Riesling Spätlese 1990
The kind of wine which can only be produced in great years: opulent fruit, fruity acidity, obvious sweetness - a great Spätlese.

Weingut J Fischer Erben

Weinhole 14
Eltville 6228
Tel. (06123) 2858

Hanni Fischer is a Rheingau original. She has run this estate at Eltville since 1957 and is still full of energy to combat the unpleasant features of the wine business. She is very competent and experienced in the vineyards, while in the cellar she has engaged a wine technician who has understood how to interpret her ideas of classic Rheingau wines and make them manifest in the final products. In her opinion her own wines are more structured than elegant, and appeal mainly due to their substance and bite. This estimation is not far from the truth. Fischer Erbens' Rieslings are uninimateably rustic, sometimes even coarse, but boss Hanni's endearing nature allows us to forgive the occasional rough attack on our palates. Nevertheless, the best wines are firm and concentrated.

Eltviller Langenstück   ℗ ①
Riesling Kabinett 1990
A generous wine with obvious sweetness and power. It is a good representative of a certain type of Rheingau Riesling - the kind our grandfathers used to drink.

Eltviller Sonnenberg   ℗ ①
Riesling Kabinett trocken 1990
A vigorous wine noticeably rich, from deep soils which yield generous wines by nature: a very traditional Kabinett.

Schloss Groenesteyn

Suttonstrasse 22
Kiedrich 6229
Tel. (06123) 2492

Heinrich Freiherr Ritter zu Groenesteyn, the
present day castle owner does not
particularly care for armour and jousting. His
main interest is wine. Together with the
estate director Franz Heinrich Hubert he
places great importance on working the
vineyards in order to produce the best
possible raw materials to scupture into wine.
Reduced yields and strict grape selections
are a matter of course for them, and they
have set their own Oechsle degree standards
for Kabinett and Spätlese at higher levels
than those required by law. The wines are
made and matured in stainless steel and
fiberglass tanks, while casks are reserved for
their absolute top wines. In this way they
manage to produce very harmonious wines
with elegant, fruity acidity and understated
sweetness, though only 25-30% of their
wines are made in a dry or off-dry
(halbtrocken) style. The estate's proportion of
Prädikatsweine is very high, a phenomenon
which the wine-maker puts down to their
excellent sites and the reduced yields. Even
in the less favourable 1991 vintage, 50% of
the harvest was of Kabinett quality and
above, including high grade Spätlesen and
Auslesen. In the meantime what is lacking
are normal, light, drinking wines.
Unfortunately among the 1991s numerous
wines developed off-flavors and only a few
were successful.

Kiedricher Wasserrose   🍇 ①
Riesling Kabinett 1991
This wine is especially appealing due to its
lightness: multi-layered fruit, winey acidity and
soft, harmonious sweetness.

Kiedricher Gräfenberg   🍇 ②
Riesling Spätlese trocken 1990
A rich wine with a gentle aroma, elegant, fruity
acidity and long finish - needs time to develop.

Rüdesheimer Berg Schlossberg   🍇 ②
Riesling Spätlese 1990
Gently sweet on the palate with a strong aroma
of southern fruits. The fresh acidity adds a touch
of class and a light hint of botrytis is noticeable
on the finish.

Prinz von Hessen

Grund 1
Geisenheim-Johannisberg 6222
Tel. (06722) 8172
Fax (06722) 50588

With 50 ha of vineyard this is one of the
largest Rhingau estates: the Landgräflich
Hessische Weingut, as it was known until
1990. It was then given the shorter name
Prinz von Hessen, though the prince himself
has little or nothing to do with the wine. All he
did was tell the administrator Karl-Hienz
Glock to make him a 'nice wine estate' when
he engaged him back in 1969. Glock did just
that and the owner, the Hessische
Hausstiftung foundation (which owns such
noble properties as the Schlosshotel
Kronberg and the Hotel Hessischer Hof at
Frankfurt) turned out to be far from penny-
pinching when it came to investing large
sums of money in the winery and in buying
new vineyards. Nevertheless, the size of the
estate has often caused problems as the
quality of their wines was often inconsistent
in the past, when obviously harmless 'also-
ran' wines coexisted alongside their good
products. The 1990s and 1991s show an
improvement, though even now a noticably
high number of simple, uncomplicated,
ordinary drinking wines adorn the list. The
present day head of the foundation, Moriz
Landgraf von Hessen has helped them on
their way with a small dedication by using site
names on the labels of their better wines.

Kiedricher Sandgrub   🍇 ①
Riesling Kabinett trocken 1990
A firm, muscular wine with plenty of fruit and
aroma along with high acidity - so high that it is
a match for even the richest foods.

Prinz von Hessen   🍇 ②
Riesling Kabinett trocken 1990
The refined interplay between sweetness and
acidity enlivens this characterful wine, while the
hardly noticeable sweetness makes it an
elegant (Charta) table wine.

Winkeler Hasensprung   🍇 ④
Riesling Auslese 1990
A high grade Auslese with rare finesse, only just
starting to develop. It is nobly sweet with
accentuated,sinewy acidity which has yet to
become integrated.

Winkeler Hasensprung   🍇 ③
Riesling Spätlese 1990
A generous wine with plenty of substance and
ripe acidity which makes it seem powerful and
heavy to the detriment of elegance.

Weingut Hupfeld

Rheinstrasse 113
Oestrich-Winkel 6227
Tel. (06723) 3307
Fax (06723) 4556

This 11 ha estate's moment of glory was
almost 150 years ago when, in 1845 the
English queen Victoria visited a vineyard at
Hochheim. She was so impressed by the
wine that she allowed the owner of the five
ha vineyard to call it "Königin Victoriaberg".
Since then this estate has enjoyed a
monarchistic aura, though its residence is
now at Oestrich-Winkel and the Hochheim
sites came into the Hupfeld family by
inheritance. The present owners are not
completely happy about this situation, though
it has proved far from simple to put their own
name to the fore, as the Hupfelds would
dearly like. Although the Winkeler
Hasensprung and Oestricher Lenchen sites
produce for the most part interesting
Rieslings the Königin Victoriaberg is still their
standard bearer. Very low yields, hand
picking and long maturation of the finished
product have a very positive effect on quality.
Their best wines are bottled as "Charta-
Weine".

Grauer Burgunder 1990 ♀ ②
A lesser-known Hupfeld product, the grapes for
which come from a small Hochheim plot and the
wine is matured in barrique: strong in structure
with depth and plenty of oak.

Hochheimer Königin Victoriaberg ♀ ①
Riesling Kabinett trocken 1990
A very slender wine grown on the Main and not
the Rhine: very successful for a dry Kabinett.

Hupfeld Riesling QbA trocken 1990 ♀ ①
A scented, very ripe wine from the heavy
Oestrich soils, full and long and deserves to be
of Charta status.

Winkeler Jesuitengarten ♀♀ ②
Riesling Spätlese 1990
An Auslese which has been declassified with an
unmistakable bitter-sweet botrytis flavor:
powerful and at the same time fine with plenty of
reserves for future development.

Schloss Johannisberg

Johannisberg 6222
Tel. (06722) 70090
Fax (06722) 700933

This estate has written wine history. They
planted exclusively with Riesling in 1720,
discovered Spätlese in 1775 and produced
the first Eiswein in 1858, all of which led to
Schloss Johanisberg being looked upon
throughout the world as the symbol for
Riesling. Now, after years of sometimes
rather weak products, they have gone back
to making high grade wines with substance,
spice and accentuated, fruity acidity and the
quality trend is still upwards. Nevertheless,
they have lost their unique status. Their
recent success is due to the estate
administrator Wolfgang Schleicher, who has
introduced a maximum yield of 55-60 hl/ha
and severe grape selections at harvest time.
Schleicher has set the estate high standards
in the production of QmP wines, with the
result that Johannisberg wines have average
Oechsle ratings of 5-8° above the limits
prescribed by law. The quality category of the
wines and their style is distinguished by the
color of the capsules.

Schloss Johannisberger Gelblack ♀ ②
Riesling QbA halbtrocken 1991
A wine with compact fruit, astounding richness
and depth: a demoted Spätlese.

Schloss Johannisberger Gelblack ♀ ②
Riesling QbA trocken 1991
A successful wine with piquant acidity and a
spicy note: a hearty, thirst-quenching wine with
finesse.

Schloss Johannisberger Grünlack ♀♀ ③
Riesling Spätlese trocken 1990
Muscular with good spice, at first just a hint of
fruit and rather tart acidity: a wine with
enormous potential.

Schloss Johannisberger Rosalack ♀♀ ④
Riesling Auslese 1990
Concentrated maracuja and peach on the nose,
highly elegant acidity together with powerful
richness and a hint of botrytis: a great Auslese,
harvested at 112° Oechsle.

Weingut Johanishof

Im Grund 63
Johannisberg 6222
Tel. (06722) 8216
Fax (06722) 6387

Together with his cousin, Joachim Eser, from Weingut Eser in Oestrich, Hans-Hermann Eser is top of the hit parade among Rheingau estates. Time and time again he succeeds in adding the final touch of finesse to the strong, sometimes even heavy Rheingau Rieslings, in polishing the fruit, in smoothing the acidity. In short, he creates a high-grade product from the raw material supplied by the vineyard. He has always been the proud owner of excellent sites at Johannisberg and Geisenheim, but that is not the whole story. By reducing yields and by virtue of a large proportion of old vines, his wines become enriched with plenty of body and substance, while fermentation and maturation in stainless steel tanks help preserve primary flavors derived from the grapes. After the excellent 1988 and 1990 vintages as well as botrytis problems with the 1989 dry wines, from 1991 they only offered wines up to Kabinett level. In order to maintain standards and not disappoint customers, they preferred to declassify the wines rather than offer weak Spätlesen. The exception is a stunning Eiswein which weighed in at 173° Oechsle; the finished wine has 23 g/lt of acidity.

Johannisberger Hölle　　　🍇 ①
Riesling Kabinett trocken 1991
Fine fruit together with an earthy character, soft citrus fruit on the nose and very elegant due to its strong acid backbone.

Winkeler Hasensprung　　　🍇 ①
Riesling Kabinett halbtrocken 1991
One of this vintage's finest Kabinett wines: hardly noticeable sweetness but fine harmony between fruit and acidity and good length.

Johannishof　　　🍇🍇 ③
Riesling Auslese 1990
Powerful and at the same time elegant with a super interplay between strong sweetness and accentuated acidity followed by unbelievable length.

Winkeler Hasensprung　　　🍇🍇 ②
Riesling Spätlese trocken 1990
Compact on the palate with mouthwatering, elegant fruit and plenty of substance - a steely wine with great aging potential.

Weingut Jacob Jung

Eberbacher Strasse 22
Erbach 6228
Tel. (06123) 62359
Tel. (06123) 63273

He calls himself a 'small' producer among Rheingau estates, though the owner Ludwig Jung comes up great wines time and time again. For example his 1990 dry Riesling Spätlese from the Erbacher Höhenrain site has beaten just about all other high ranking names in blind tastings. 1990 was altogether a superb vintage for Jung, as the best prerequisite for high quality in the rich, muscular wines produced by the heavy soils at Erbach is perfectly healthy fruit and in this year there was practically no botrytis. His dry Rieslings had never been better, crystal clear and mellow in spite of high acidity. Even his Riesling Auslese (Erbacher Michelmark) has not the slightest hint of botrytis. The only disadvantage is that he could not produce nobly sweet specialities, though in 1989 he made an opulent Riesling Beeren-Auslese, while 1991 produced large quantities, for which reason the simple QbA wines are highly recommended.

Erbacher Hohenrain　　　🍇🍇 ②
Riesling Spätlese 1990
Perhaps the best 1990 Rheingau 'Charta' Spätlese: plenty of power and depth plus highly elegant acidity and excellent fruit.

Kiedricher Sandgrub　　　🍇 ①
Riesling Kabinett halbtrocken 1990
A wine of high Spätlese quality equipped with plenty of fruit, fresh acidity and pleasant, harmonious sweetness.

Erbacher Michelmark　　　🍇🍇 ②
Riesling Auslese 1989
A whole basket of ripe fruit on the nose followed by opulent sweetness on the palate balanced by piquant acidity.

Erbacher Michelmark　　 ①
Spätburgunder QbA trocken 1990
Jung's first attempt at barrique-aging has been successful: very nice harmony between fruit and wood, compact in body with soft tannins.

Weingut Graf von Kanitz

Rheinstrasse 49
Lorch 6223
Tel. (06726) 346

This quiet estate in the northern-most point of the Rheingau is very unique. They have shown that is possible to practise ecological wine-growing and still make highest quality wines. In doing so, they have angered some of their neighbors, who are no longer allowed to fly over the Kanitz vineyards when spraying by helicopter. Together with short pruning the ecological viticultural methods lead to a small production of 55 hl/ha. The heat-retaining slate and eroded quartz soils produce vigorous, rich wines with racy acidity. They are fermented slowly in stainless steel tanks or wood casks without cultured yeasts, and made almost entirely in a dry or off-dry style (nobly sweet wines are only produced from Auslese level upwards) and are filled by the end of April following the vintage, after which they are aged for 18 months in bottle before release. Estate Director, Gernot Boos, who retired in early 1992 always aimed at consistent quality and saw to it that Kanitz wines were among the Rheingau's finest.

Lorcher Bodental-Steinberg 🍇 ①
Riesling QbA trocken 1991
A powerful wine with crisp acidity, plenty of spice, minerally in flavor and good aging potential.

Lorcher Kapellenberg 🍇🍇 ②
Riesling Spätlese trocken 1991
Power and substance on the palate; fruit and very elegant acidity are united to form an astonishingly high class wine.

Lorcher Schlossberg 🍇 ①
Riesling Kabinett trocken 1991
A generous wine, hardly recognizable as Kabinett, with strongly accentuated fruit interwoven with strong acidity: a very individual wine.

Lorcher Bodental-Steinberg 🍇🍇 ③
Riesling Auslese 1990
This wine is dominated by expressive fruit rather than sweetness, with soft, winey acidity: a wine which does not satiate.

Lorcher Pfaffenwies 🍇 ②
Riesling Spätlese halbtrocken 1990
Not excessively compact but elegant with very ripe fruit and gentle sweetness.

Weingut August Kesseler

Lorcher Strasse 16
Assmannshausen 6220
Tel. (06722) 2513
Fax (06722) 46466

A whisper spread through the Rheingau in early 1991: August Kesseler had renounced barriques. The man who had been the first to mature his Spätburgunder (Pinot Noir) in small French oak barrels had gone back to using traditional wood casks. He need not regret it, for his 1990 reds have everything: fine tannins, fantastic pure varietal fruit, power and depth and they do not miss the extra spice given by new oak. It is true that Kesseler has not yet found his ideal style, and trips to California, Oregon, Bordeaux and Tuscany keep renewing his ideas. Nevertheless, he has gone part of the way towards discovering a different, new style of German red wine. His products now serve as an example when it comes to fruit and finesse. In the meantime he has discovered his love for Riesling and Sylvaner, which the 34 year-old has managed to make classy wines from. His 1990 Riesling from simple QbA through to Spätlese (all dry) show how Rheingau Riesling can be gentle, fresh, sinewy and still long-living with plenty of finesse. He sold off most of his 1991s in tank.

Rüdesheimer Berg Schlossberg Riesling Spätlese trocken 1990
A fantastically clean, clear wine, made in stainless steel, light but still bursting with fruit and fruity acidity.

Assmannshäuser Höllenberg Spätburgunder QbA trocken 1990
Ruby red with fine, berry fruit, soft tannins and nice harmony: Kessler's most straightforward red.

Assmannshäuser Höllenberg Spätburgunder Spätlese** trocken 1990
A very full aroma of cherry, cassis, cinnamon and cocoa. It is on the palate that the wine shows its real class: a Pinot Noir of international level.

Assmannshäuser Höllenberg Spätburgunder Spätlese*** trocken 1990
The three crosses denote the estate's best red wine of this vintage, though the wine is more than that. It's the best red he has made to date. It is only medium-weight and unlike many Burgundies, it is not overly alcoholic but makes up by being very refined, with smooth tannins, concentrated fruit, tightly-knit and as firmly built as a Gothic cathedral. This wine's unique class derives from its style rather than weight, which combines finesse and fruit into a harmonious whole. The grapes come from a small plot of the Höllenberg site planted with 60 year-old vines which yielded only 17 hl/ha. They were harvested in a perfectly healthy state on 20th October at 101°Oechsle. The malolactic fermentation took place at the end of a ten-day fermentation with the skins, after which the wine was aged in small, old wood casks - not barriques.

Weingut Hans-Peter Kessler

Imm Messwingert
Martinthal 6229
Tel. (06123) 71235
Fax (06123) 75361

There is only one thing which interests Klaus Peter Kessler as much as wine and that is his family history. With great precision he has managed to trace the Kesslers' family tree back to 1739, when one of his ancestors called Carolus settled in the Rheingau. He is correspondingly keen to refer to tradition, though his wines from the Im Messingert estate are anything but traditional, having the freshness of wines made in the modern manner, with clear varietal fruit and the unbroken acidity typical of Rheingau Rieslings which has only been smoothened a little by aging in traditional casks. In this way he has secured for himself a place among the top Rheingau producers. His 1990s are unusually fruity, characterful and probably long lasting wines (the best are Kabinett and Spätlesen). In 1991 he did not produce any Spätlesen but made very good Kabinett wines plus a small quantity of off-dry Auslese from the Eltviller Taubenberg site and a 138°Oechsle Eiswein, harvested in a cold night on 8th December. Considering the quality, prices are very reasonable.

Eltviller Sonnenberg
Riesling Kabinett 1990
This off-dry Charta wine is a power pack which shows very little of its potential at the moment but promises the finesse and richness only encountered in a great vintage.

Eltviller Sonnenberg
Riesling Spätlese trocken 1990
An enormous wine, compact, muscular with clear, varietal and unbelievably complex fruit through and through with taut acidity which is very well counter-balanced. It is very rare to find a dry Riesling as successful as this.

Eltviller Taubenberg
Riesling Auslese 1989
A super Auslese at an astonishing price, which appeals by its intense bouquet reminiscent of honey and exotic fruit and light hint of botrytis.

Weingut Freiherr zu Knyphausen

Klosterhof Drais
Elville 6228
Tel. (06123) 62177
Fax (06123) 4315

Gerko zu Knyphausen is a patient man. When most Rheingau producers were denouncing the 1991 vintage as only fit to be sold off in tank he waited until all the grapes were in the cellar. Then came the discovery: the wine they produced was not only drinkable but of excellent quality. The rain which fell before the harvest had done little harm to the vines - at least not to his. His trust in nature had been rewarded, though it must be mentioned that Knyphausen is blessed with the best sites, planted with old vines (from 1990 onwards his best five sites appear on the labels). Several Spät- and Auslesen are the fruits of his patience, a virtue he also demands of his consumers as the 1991s were not released until they were a year old. Among the 1990s his cloister cellar (which the traffic on the Eltville by-pass thunders past) offers everything a demanding palate could ask for: superb Kabinett wines, sensational Spätlesen and fantastic Auslesen, many of which are also available in magnums.

Erbacher Marcobrunn ℗℗ ③
Riesling Spätlese 1990
This wine shows what a great Spätlese vintage 1990 was: a dense, powerful wine with plenty of finesse and a super contrast between acidity and sweetness.

Erbacher Riesling Spätlese1990 ℗℗ ③
A muscular wine with elegant acidity, superbly balanced with just a hint of residual sugar and equally impressive due to its gentle fruitiness: a super Charta wine.

Erbacher Steinmorgen ℗ ②
Riesling Kabinett 1990
This estate's best Kabinett (Charta wine) with plenty of finesse, almost dry with bite, muscle, strong fruit and steely acidity.

Hattenheimer Wisselbrunnen ℗ ③
Riesling Spätlese trocken 1990
Their biggest Spätlese from this vintage with 102°Oechsle: a monument to grace every wine list as well as the collector's cellar.

Kiedricher Sandgrub ℗℗ ④
Riesling Auslese 1990
A generous, very fine, nobly sweet Auslese, dense and concentrated in a way not seen for years. A wine for the next century.

Weingut Franz Künstler

Freirr-von-Stein-Ring 3
Hochheim 6203
Tel. (06146) 5666
Fax (06146) 5767

Franz Künstler set up on his own in 1965 with three hectares of vineyard in the best sites at Hochheim. In the meantim,e he and his son Günter (the wine-maker who is gradually taking over the business), have become regarded as the rising stars of the past few years. They owe their high reputation to their ability to make superb wines even in less favorable years like 1991. The reason for this is the fact that at harvest time they place importance on high acidity as well as high Oechsle ratings. According to Günter Künstler, as long as the acidity is balanced by enough alcohol the wine will be harmonious. Depending on the character of the wines they are matured in large casks or stainless steel. Their 1991 whites were bottled very early in contrast to preceeding vintages. The reds are extremely powerful and deep red in color and turned out to be so good that the Künstlers saw no need to make rosé wine. Like every year they have produced two red wines, one made in the traditional manner and a cuvée aged in barrique, though they will only be released after long bottle aging.

Hochheimer Hölle   🍇🍇 ③
Riesling Auslese 1991
The strong, noble sweetness is cut by elegant, fruity acidity. It is a very rich, compact wine with accentuated fruit and all the prerequisites for a long life.

Hochheimer Hölle   🍇 ①
Riesling Kabinett trocken 1991
Like almost all their 1991s this Riesling is very rich with fine, elegant acidity: a wine with class and length.

Hochheimer Kirchenstück   🍇 ②
Riesling Spätlese trocken 1991
An unusually fine Spätlese with plenty of volume, elegance and finesse: pure power on the tongue.

Hochheimer Stielweg   🍇🍇 ③
Riesling Spätlese trocken 1991
Almost oily concentration, enormous extract, opulent fruit: a wine with great potential and super length: their best dry 1991 Spätlese.

Weingut Hans Lang

Rheinallee 6
Hattenheim 6228
Tel. (06723) 2475
Fax (06723) 7963

Hans Lang has been running a wine shop in the Carsch-Haus at Wiesbaden for seven years and this has exposed him to wines from Burgundy, Bordeaux and Italy, enabling him to develop a feeling for international styles, particularly for barriques. He has taken advantage of this experience in making his own wines from Burgundian varieties. His Pinots Gris and Blanc are aged for six months in Allier barriques, Pinot Noir between 12 and 18 months in Limousin and Allier oak. It is only with Riesling that Lang remains faithful to the traditional large oak casks. This enriches his wines with racy acidity and expressive fruitiness. Since he had botrytis problems with his dry wines in 1988, he has been a strong supporter of very selective harvesting by hand. In 1991 he harvested each vineyard three times, selecting only the ripest and healthy grapes. The result is clean wines with clear varietal flavors from a very difficult vintage.

Hattenheimer Hassel   🍇 ④
Riesling Eiswein 1991
Almost oily concentration of acidity, fruit and sweetness with an explosion of exotic fruits on the palate: pure nectare, harvested at 178°Oechsle.

Hattenheimer Wisselbrunnen   🍇 ③
Riesling Auslese trocken 1990
Opulent in body, very ripe, giving the impression of over-ripe fruit balanced by good acidity and a gentle hint of botrytis.

Kiedricher Sandgrub   🍇 ①
Riesling Kabinett 1990
Astonishingly rich for a Kabinett, coupled with elegant acidity and concentrated fruit.

Hattenheimer Spätburgunder   🍇 ②
trocken 1990
A barrique aged wine with mellow, warm fruit with underlying tannin and great depth.

Freiherr Langenwerth

Kirchgasse
Eltville 6228
Tel. (06123) 3007
Fax (06123) 3009

After several years of weak products this estate has been producing superb wines in a traditional style since 1989. Traditional in this sense means generous, ripe Rieslings with winey acidity made round by aging in traditional casks. Their first-class sites are their main advantage, which at Erbach, Rauenthal and Hattenhiem includes almost everything which has a ring to it, from Marcobrunn to Nussbrunnen. After spontaneous fermentation the wines are aged from three to six months in old 1,000 lt casks to give them their traditional Rheingau character. The administrator Helmuth Kranich, a cautious Swabian knows the wines then need two to three years' bottle age to develop and open up, though he is also aware of their superb keeping qualities. By short pruning yields are kept to 60 hl/ha and harvesting is carried out 70% by hand and 30% by machine. In difficult years like 1991, the latter can lead to off-flavors in the must.

Erbacher Marcobrunn   ③
Riesling Auslese 1991
In 1991 they even managed to harvest a nobly sweet wine with a light hint of botrytis: not unctuous, but a very fine Auslese.

Erbacher Marcobrunn   ②
Riesling Kabinett trocken 1991
This Kabinett from the most notorious Rheingau site has fine fruit, round acidity and a unique, candy-like aroma.

Hattenheimer Mannberg   ②
Riesling Spätlese halbtrocken 1991
Obvious sweetness envelops the fruit: together with firm acidity this wine is a very respectable, characterful Spätlese.

Hattenheimer Nussbrunnen   ①
Riesling Kabinett trocken 1991
A very succulent, muscular wine with spice, piquant, dry acidity and a minerally-fruity aroma.

Fürst Löwenstein

Schloss-Vollrads
Oestrich-Winkel 6227
Tel. (06723) 5056
Fax (06723) 1848

In 1979 Erwein Count Matuschka-Greiffenclau rented 17 ha of the Duke Löwenstein vineyards in neighbouring Hallgarten and added them to his 50 ha Schloss Vollrads wine estate. The grapes harvested there are processed in Schloss Vollrads' cellars but vinified completely separately and the wines are sold under a different label. Although the Löwenstein sites are at the most three kilometres away from Vollrads the wines have very different characteristics, appearing rounder, softer and a little fuller, though not as long-lasting. In 1990 they produced several brilliant Rieslings which manifest the richness of this great vintage, just as much in the Kabinett as in the Spätlese category. Even the dry Spätlesen with hardly noticeable botrytis are fruity and soft, full and not at all bitter. The peak is a 138°Oechsle Beerenauslese. In 1991 they produced excellent QbA and Kabinett wines, and the Vollrads wine-maker Senft decided not to make Spätlesen.

Fürst Löwenstein   ②
Riesling QbA trocken 1991
Their simplest 1991 Riesling: light, pleasantly round with delicate, lightly aromatic fruit and the wine is already drinking well.

Fürst Löwenstein   ②
Riesling Kabinett halbtrocken 1990
An almost perfect wine in which the residual sugar is hardly noticeable but gives it great harmony.

Fürst Löwenstein   ③
Riesling Spätlese halbtrocken 1990
Powerful with a hint of botrytis: a multi-layered, ripe Spätlese, rich, very fine with enormous aging potential.

Fürst Löwenstein   ③
Riesling Spätlese trocken 1990
A powerful and smooth wine with a hint of noble rot, a wine which can be drunk like red wine with food.

Georg-Müller-Stiftung

Weingut der Stadt Eltville
Eberbacher Strasse 7
Hattenheim 6228
Tel. (06723) 2020

Those who know the Rheingau scene have only been acquainted with the name Georg-Müller-Stiftung since 1988 at the longest. Since then the quality has continuously improved, helped along of course by three excellent vintages. The 11 ha wine estate with the best sites at Hattenheim, Erbach and Hallgarten has belonged to the town of Eltville since 1972, before which it was part of the commune of Hattenheim. Eltville has not regretted this acquisition as the wines have attracted plenty of attention. In the vineyards the administrator, Roland Brossmann, practices natural, ecological viticulture with strictly limited yields and very selective harvesting by hand which sometimes lasts for weeks. In the cellar the grapes are lightly pressed, after which the juice is fermented slowly in tank or cask, and the young wine is kept on its fine lees until spring and bottled in June. The wines are characterized by plenty of fruit and race with a very impressive fruit-acidity balance and finesse. After the successful 1988s, 1989s and 1990s which included wines through to Beeren-Auslese, in 1991 they produced almost exclusively simple QbA wines, though very high class ones.

Hattenheimer Nussbrunnen   ❦ ①
Riesling Kabinett trocken 1991
A full, rich bouquet, strong, muscular in body with compact fruit and elegant acidity.

Hattenheimer Nussbrunnen   ❦ ②
Riesling Spätlese halbtrocken 1990
Hardly noticeable residual sugar, well supported acidity and very ripe fruit - needs time to mature.

Hattenheimer Wisselbrunnen   ❦❦ ②
Riesling Spätlese 1990
A full bouquet with rich fruit, light botrytis, powerful in body, highly elegant acidity and strong sweetness: a wine of Auslese quality.

G H von Mummsches Weingut

Geisenheim-Johannisberg 6222
Tel. (06722) 70090
Fax (06722) 700933

This estate is directly next to Schloss Johannisberg, and the wines are made in the castle cellar, though by their own wine-maker and according to their own principles as the owner, Rudolf August Oetker (with 53 ha of vineyard, mainly at Assmannshausen) has his own ideas about wine. For this reason the estate is not part of his grocery empire - one of Europe's largest - but a private concern of the owner. Mumm is best known for its dry Rieslings which are often of a very high standard. Above all 1990 produced several excellent dry Spätlesen, though their simple QbA and Kabinett wines are also impressive. Then there are several high grade Auslesen and among reds the Spätburgunder (Pinot Noir), an Assmannshausen speciality, shows that the trend towards richer wines with more tannin is continuing.

Johannisberger Schwarzenstein   ❦ ①
Riesling QbA trocken 1991
One of the first QbA wines to be released from this vintage: a soft, pleasant table wine with typical Mumm charm.

G.H. von Mumm   ❦ ①
Riesling QbA halbtrocken 1990
A very pleasant, round estate wine with mouth-watering acidity and almost commercial smoothness: the off-dry style reinforces this impression.

Johannisberger Klaus   ❦❦ ②
Riesling Spätlese trocken 1990
A compact, very elegant and discreet wine with understated richness and impressive finesse: the best Spätlese of this vintage.

Assmannshäuser Frankenthal   🍇 ①
Spätburgunder QbA trocken 1990
Strong, not too light color, expressive fruity bouquet and noticeable tannin, light in body: a nice, light drinking red.

Dr Heinrich Nägler

Friedrichstrasse 22
Rüdensheim 6220
Tel. (06722) 2835

Even before 1826 the Rüdesheim wine and artisan family Nägler owned vines in the Rüdesheimer Berg site. Their vineyards are 90% in steep sites and almost entirely planted with Riesling. The slatey and eroded quarzite soils produce full, spicy wines with fine, elegant acidity and the quality is continuously improving, as recent vintages have shown. The person behind this success is Dr. Heinrich Nägler, who learned how to make wine from his father. The basis for their excellent quality is the superb raw material which is harvested above all according to ripeness. Botrytis is very desirable, even with dry wines, though it can on occasion produce negative effects. He is also for the addition of unfermented grape juice to to give the wines polish, spice and fruit. They are also long lasting. The Näglers very much enjoy drinking their dry 1983 Riesling Spätlese from the Rüdesheimer Berg Schlossberg which is still astonishingly fresh and fruity.

Dr. Nägler ♗ ①
Rüdesheimer Riesling trocken 1991
A steely Riesling with plenty of fruit and has become elegant due to its gentle acidity: an uncomplicated, easy-drinking wine.

Rüdesheimer Berg Rottland ♗ ②
Riesling Kabinett trocken 1991
Its accentuated fruit and high acidity are appealing, but it appears very light in body.

Rüdesheimer Berg Schlossberg ♗♗ ②
Riesling Spätlese trocken 1990
A big wine dominated by strong acidity with concentrated fruit and a noble bitter hint of botrytis. Very long.

Rüdesheimer Bischofsberg ♗♗ ②
Riesling Spätlese 1990
A typical 1990 fruit bomb which has everything in excess: fruit, spice, richness and volume.

Weingut Eberhard von Oetinger

Maximilianhof - Rheinallee 2
Eltville-Erbach 6228
Tel. (06123) 62648
Fax (06123) 61743

Christoph von Oetinger, son of the owner Eberhard von Oetinger, makes the most acidulous wines at Eltville and in the whole vicinity. They are long-lasting wines which need aging and which have their share of rough edges in their youth. They may not be the Rheingau's most elegant, but are certainly among the most authentic and genuine Rieslings grown on the Rhine. Two-thirds of their production is consumed in their own 'wine garden', one of the most traditional taverns of the area where people from Frankfurt and Wiesbaden enjoy drinking 'a mouthful of wine'. In addition to their easy-drinking wines they have high class, refined products, such as high grade Spätlesen from the great 1990 vintage or a 1991 Eiswein which is so "big breasted" as Oetinger puts it, that even the owner's son is lost for words. The good quality of Oetingers' wines derives from painstaking work in the vineyard and they are working full steam to change over to ecological wine-growing.

Erbacher Hohenrain ♗♗ ④
Riesling Eiswein 1991
In spite of its high residual sugar (230 gr/lt) it is not a sticky, but very elegant wine which explodes with fruit on the palate.

Erbacher Hohenrain ♗♗ ②
Riesling Kabinett 1990
A 'Charta' Kabinett, an off-dry, elegant Riesling with concentrated fruit and ripe acidity - excellent.

Erbacher Michelmark ♗ ①
Riesling Kabinett trocken 1990
On tasting it in its early youth Oetinger's wife insisted on this super wine being made and bottled separately: a very acidulous, racy wine for Riesling enthusiasts.

Weingut Wilfried Querbach

Dr. Rody-Strasse 2
Oestrich 6227
Tel. (06723) 3887
Fax (06723) 87405

Wilfried Querbach describes his philosophy briefly and to the point: his wines must be digestible, have a pleasant aroma and must taste good - and all that at a very high level. This may sound simple, but Querbach wines are significantly above average by Rheingau standards. Many well-known names would lose their smile if they had to compare their wines to those of this small wine estate with less than eight hectares of vineyard. They are in the very best Oestrich sites, mainly in the first class Oestricher Lenchen. 86% are planted with Riesling, the rest with Pinot Noir (Spätburgunder). However, the cellar is also influential for its quality. A small stream flows through it, and the coolness as well as high humidity it produces are important for preserving the wines' freshness, even after bottling. Querbach Rieslings are characterful wines with a discreet bouquet, finely fruity, complex, and, even in ordinary vintages like 1991, it is obvious that they are fighting for quality. Their wines are also good value for money.

Oestricher Lenchen   🍇 ①
Riesling QbA 1991
Their best 1991 QbA, labelled as a Charta wine with a light sparkle, medium weight and off-dry in style.

Oestricher Lenchen   🍇 ①
Riesling Kabinett trocken 1990
A finely fruity, gentle Riesling of the best Kabinett quality, harmonious, clear in aroma and still with a fresh sparkle.

Oestricher Lenchen   🍇 ①
Riesling QbA 1990
An unusually elegant QbA with very light and well-dosed sweetness which expresses well the positive side of the vintage.

Oestricher Lenchen   🍇🍇 ②
Riesling Spätlese trocken 1990
Very similar to the Kabinett wine in character from the same site, though noticeably superior - an excellent, super-fresh Spätlese.

Weingut Schloss Reinhartshausen

Hauptstrasse
Eltville-Erbach 6228
Tel. (06123) 4009
Fax (06123) 4222

This castle overlooking the Rhine was bought by industrialist, Willi Leibbrand, in 1988 and transformed into a luxury hotel with a gourmet restaurant. The wine estate remains intact. Leibbrand's determination and the skill of wine-maker and estate administrator, Karl-Heinz Zerbe, have brought about a new, upward trend in quality after a short period of weakness. Alongside Riesling, Pinot Noir and Chardonnay are given an important place in this estate. Back in 1979, acting on the advice of Robert Mondavi, they planted this noble vine on the Rhine island Mariannenaue - the first estate in Germany to introduce it - and today the wine it produces, made partly in barrique and partly in stainless steel tanks, can stand on its own at international level. The Rieslings are also equipped with plenty of body and strong acidity, especially the 1990s. In 1989, on the other hand, they had problems with botrytis and acidity, defects which become increasingly noticeable with bottle age. Wines from the difficult 1991 vintage excel in the normal QbA and Kabinett categories.

Erbacher Rheinhell Weissburgunder 🍇 ①
und Chardonnay QbA trocken 1991
A full, rich bouquet in which Pinot Blanc dominates. This is a wine with power together with Chardonnay elegance, while spice and compact fruit complete the picture.

Hattenheimer Nussbrunnen   🍇 ③
Riesling Spätlese trocken 1990
A muscular Spätlese with substance and a minerally-fruity aroma, appealing elegance and length.

Hattenheimer Wisselbrunnen   🍇🍇 ④
Riesling Trockenbeerenauslese 1990
A very rare Rheingau speciality: high-grade, concentrated fruit nectare with enormous richness.

Erbacher Marcobrunn   🍇🍇 ④
Riesling Auslese 1989
Fantastic concentration of fruit and body combined with high sugar, fine acidity and strong botrytis.

Erbacher Marcobrunn   🍇 ②
Riesling Kabinett trocken 1989
An unusually compact wine for a Kabinett with succulent fruit, round acidity and finesse.

Weingut Balthasar Ress

Rheinallee 7
Hattenheim 6228
Tel. (06723) 3011
Fax (06723) 1711

"The wine is fine" is written into the coat of arms of this wine-producing Ress family, and Stefan Ress, the present day owner, is intent on making sure it stays that way. He has run the estate since 1979 and, since then, has increased their vineyard holdings to 27 ha with sites all over the Rheingau from Hochheim to Assmannshausen. Since 1979 they have also exclusively owned the vineyards of Schloss Reichartshausen though the wines which originate from there are not quite up to the level of the other Ress products. Ress is not a properly trained wine-maker but listened as a guest at the viticultural school of Geisenheim and worked in Franken as well as for a large wine merchant in France. Now, with the help of the estate director Bruno Klüpfel, he is intent on putting his high quality requirements into action. The wines have improved noticeably since 1988 due to yield reduction by very short pruning (six buds per vine for Pinot Noir and eight for Riesling). In addition they have a good proportion of old vines which will not be grubbed up in the near future, and very strict grape selections at harvest time has always been a matter of course.

Von Unserm　　　　　　🍇 ②
Riesling QbA trocken 1991
The standard Ress estate wine, always a mouth-watering, easy drinking, delicate Riesling with no rough edges.

Hattenheimer Riesling　　🍇🍇 ③
Spätlese trocken 1990
Ress has also made a name for himself with designer labels produced by well-known artists. One of them graces this very interesting Spätlese which is a very good restaurant wine.

Rüdesheimer Berg Schlossberg　🍇🍇 ④
Riesling Auslese 1990
A fruit bomb - highly sweet Auslese with very ripe, almost exotic aromas, of a kind not seen in Ress's collection for years.

Asmmannshäuser Höllenberg　🍇 ②
Spätburgunder QbA trocken 1990
An elegant, compact wine with fine cherry and plum fruit, soft tannins and warm length.

Weingut Jakob Riedel

Taunstrasse 1
6227 Hallgarten
Tel. (06723) 3511

Wolfgang Riedel has run this estate since 1976 and is still helped by his energetic mother, Christine, the soul of the company. This enables Riedel, who completed his practical studies at the nearby Schloss Vollrads, to dedicate time to his hobby, which is religious art history. His other passion is dry Riesling. He loves firm, racy wines with plenty of power, and power for Riedel means high extract levels and fruit as well as alcohol. He needs plenty of extract to balance the strong acidity, often 10 g/lt as in 1990. The 1990s are also excellent, compact wines with intense fruit aromas. He is also happy with the 1991s, which are due for release in summer 1993. Second rate wines are declassified and sold off in bulk. In order to satisfy long-standing customers who appreciate fruit-sweet and off-dry wines, he produces a a small proportion of his Rieslings with residual sugar and is also a great noble sweet wine enthusiast.

Hallgartner Jungfer　　　🍇 ①
Riesling QbA trocken 1990
A rich wine from the Hallgarten top site, with plenty of power, accentuated acidity and a strong, grapey aroma.

Hallgartner Schönhell　　🍇🍇 ①
Riesling Kabinett trocken 1990
Although this is only in the Kabinett category, it is a muscular wine in the best Rheingau off-dry style which will turn out to be an excellent food wine with increasing maturity.

Hallgartner Jungfer　　　🍇 ①
Riesling Spätlese trocken 1988
A very compact wine with fresh acidity which adds a touch of elegance: a very appealing table wine for very demanding palates which is gradually becoming mature.

Schloss Schönborn

Hauptstrasse 53
Hattenheim 6228
Tel. (06723) 2007
Fax (06723) 7961

Karl Count von Schönborn enjoys travelling to places like the USA and Asia and always carries with him a few bottles, usually Riesling. As a result 50% of his production (280,000 bottles) are exported. Also director Robert Englert, who has been running the estate for 34 years, is a widely travelled man with a preference for Burgundy wines. There he obtained many ideas for his own Pinot Noir, and it is very noticeable in the compact, round wines with a hint of tannin and new oak. At the moment, they are experimenting with various casks made of French, Taunus and Hunsrück oak. Nevertheless, Riesling stays Riesling, at least at Schloss Schönborn, where it accounts for 90% of production. It is made in large oak casks, while Englert regards stainless steel tanks as useful only for storage purposes. The high quality of Schönborn wines (among which there are spectacular peaks) has its roots in the vineyard and no other Rheingau estate can boast of owning plots in so many excellent sites, such as 2.2 ha in the famous Erbacher Marcobrunn, where Schönborn is thus the largest owner.

Erbacher Marcobrunn
Riesling Kabinett trocken 1991
A full wine with a strong fruity aroma of peach and pear, piquant acidity and bitter aftertaste - very successful considering the vintage.

Hattenheimer Nussbrunnen
Riesling Spätlese 1991
Very clear Riesling fruit in bouquet together with harmonious sweetness - a Spätlese with richness and power though without the length of Marcobrunn from the previous vintage.

Hattenheimer Pfaffenberg
Riesling Spätlese halbtrocken 1991
Very noticeable sweetness and full fruit together with the acidity give this Spätlese bite and length.

Erbacher Marcobrunn
Riesling Spätlese 1990
A dense, muscular wine with plenty of finesse, multi-layered fruit and strong sweetness - very fine but needs time.

Sektkellerei Schloss Vaux

Kiedricher Strasse 18a
Eltville 6228
Tel. (06123) 4001
Fax (06123) 63339

Schloss Vaux has no vineyards and is not a wine producer, being specialized in buying base wine to transform into sparkling wine, or "Sekt", Riesling Sekt of absolute top quality. It was founded as a company in Berlin in 1868, and the production was located in the historic Schloss Vaux near Metz which at that time belonged to Lothringen and, thus, to the German Reich. After World War 1, the cellars were moved to Eltville on the Rhine where they are still located. No other sparkling wine producer in the Rheingau (and there are very many) have such strict quality standards, especially in their system of selecting the base wines. They make a principle of only using quality wines and not unclassified "Tafelweine", and the second fermentation takes place in bottle according to the méthode champenoise system. Their most impressive products are their Rheingau cru Sekte, sparkling wines made from base wines deriving from the best Rheingau sites. They come from the estates Langwerth von Simmern and the Hessische Staatsweingut at Eltville.

Eltviller Langenstück
Riesling-Sekt Brut 1990
Fine Riesling fruit on the nose, noticeably rich on the palate, gently spicy with a fine sparkle.

Rauenthaler Wülfen
Riesling-Sekt Brut 1990
Another highlight in their assortment: a Spätlese category base wine made by the best Champagne methods, still too young to drink.

Rheingau Riesling-Sekt
Extra trocken 1988
Made from Kabinett wine, a very serious sparkling wine, very appealing due to its softness, elegance and good value for money.

Erbacher Marcobrunn
Riesling-Sekt Brut 1986
The star among Vaux sparkling wines with everything which can be expected from a great Sekt: full aroma, the finest perlage, strong mousse, gentle in body, highly elegant and very rare.

Assmannshäuser Höllenberg
Spätburgunder-Sekt Brut 1989
A deep red Sekt with a very fine Burgundian aroma, muscular with fine, succulent tannin: a very serious food wine.

Schloss Vollrads

Oestrich-Winkel 6227
Tel. (06723) 660
Fax (06723) 1848

Schloss Vollrads is one of the estates to which the Rheingau owes a lot, especially because of the impressive castle vineyards sunk deep into the Oestrich hinterland, its brilliant history and the present day owner Erwein Graf Matuschka-Greiffenclau. An untiring ambasssador for greater appreciation of the uniqueness of German wines, he demonstrates his ideas about the combination between food and wine all over the world, though most stylishly with culinary wine tastings at his own castle. Then there is the wine itself, a fine, often very fine Riesling with its trademark of accentuated acidity. Even if it is sometimes said that the wines lack weight, they more than make up for this by the special polish which wine-maker Georg Senft gives them. They are marketed simply as Schloss Vollrads without any indications of site and are hardly ever matured in wood nowadays, the preference being for stainless steel and they are made almost exclusively in a dry and off-dry style. 1990 produced excellent wines, Spätlesen, one Auslese and one Beeren-Auslese, while in 1991 they limited their production to very good QbA and Kabinett wines, plus one Eiswein.

Schloss Vollrads 🍇 ②
Riesling Kabinett halbtrocken 1991
A very successful wine with accentuated fruit and acidity with all the positive characteristics of the Vollrads style, a light sparkle, elegant and light.

Schloss Vollrads 🍇🍇 ②
Riesling Kabinett trocken 1990
The typical 1990 richness enabled them to produce appealingly dry Kabinett wines which are very pleasant to drink.

Schloss Vollrads 🍇 ③
Riesling Spätlese halbtrocken 1990
Perhaps the finest Spätlese of this vintage: high fruit concentration, superb acidity and (still) dominated by sweetness - who knows if it will become harmonious?

Schloss Vollrads 🍇🍇 ④
Riesling Auslese 1989
Their best Auslese since 1976 with plenty of botrytis, richness, acidity and sweetness, all in perfect harmony.

Geheimrat Wegeler-Deinhard

Friedensplatz 9-11
Ostrich-Winkel 6227
Tel. (06723) 7031
Fax (06723) 1453

Wegeler-Deinhard is the one company among the largest estates which has produced the most reliable quality in recent years. Norbert Holderreith is responsible and has been in the company since 1959, in the meantime becoming director of the whole of their estates, including the companies in Bernkastel and Koblenz. His reputation was established 1983 when he produced a new cuvée called Geheimrat J, a Riesling Spätlese from the best Rheingau sites which is included on just about every top restaurant's wine list. He later developed the Geheimrat Wegeler-Deinhard range (in order to get away from the confusing German site names) and more recently the Geheimrat J Sekt' sprkling wine - all highly successful products. Holderreith likes to make wines which are elegant rather than fat, for which reason he places just as much emphasis on acidity levels as on Oechsle ratings. His wines also shine in lesser vintages. Although he likes to make them in a dry style, he also regards longevity to be very important. 1990 was a super year for him, 1991 a good, average vintage though he still managed to make a hit with two sensational Eisweine, produced in surprisingly large quantities.

Oestricher Doosberg 🍇 ②
Riesling Kabinett halbtrocken 1991
A classic Wegeler-Deinhard wine, also successful in 1991, even though it is suppler and more approachable than the same wine from 1990

Geheimrat J 🍇🍇 ③
Riesling Spätlese trocken 1990
Norbert Holerreith's best Gemeimrat J in over 20 years: a brilliant, distinguished wine which needs time to develop.

Oestricher Rothenberg 🍇 ③
Riesling Spätlese 1990
A striking, almost dry Spätlese bordering on to Auslese, very rich and very ripe (also the acidity), though it does not have the perfection of Geheimrat J.

Rüdesheimer Berg Rottland 🍇🍇 ④
Riesling Auslese 1990
A high grade Auslese with a noble grapey flavor from the best Rheingau vintage of the past 20 years, harvested at 114°Oechsle and with high acidity - a wine of the century.

Weingut Robert Weil

Mülberg 5
Kiedrich 6229
Tel. (06123) 2308
Fax (06123) 1546

This estate caused a lot of excitement in 1988 when it was bought by the Japanese Suntory group. Since then the Dr. Robert Weil estate, founded in 1868, has been enlarged from 18 to 39 ha and is now one of the largest Rheingau estates. The vineyards are planted 97% with Riesling. Wilhelm Weil is estate manager, wine-maker and salesman in one. The wines are appealing due to their full bouquet, concentrated fruit aromas and racy acidity. The high quality is achieved by natural viticultural techniques, strictly limited yields and risky, late-harvesting. As a result they managed to produce three Spätlesen in 1991, which are partly over-lapping into the Auslese category - one of which was harvested mid-November. The estate is especially famous for its exquisite nobly sweet wines. In 1991 the harvest was spread out over eight weeks, though the high gambling stakes brought their reward: four high-grade Auslesen, a superb Eiswein plus a Beeren- and Trockenbeeren-Auslese.

Kiedricher Gräfenberg 🍇 ④
Riesling Auslese Goldkapsel 1991
This vintage's 'simplest' nobly sweet wine, very fine, clean and not unctuous but very concentrated.

Kiedricher Gräfenberg 🍇🍇 ④
Riesling Beerenauslese 1991
A still more concentrated variation of the Auslese: a fine, grapey aroma, refined botrytis and (still) dominating acidity.

Kiedricher Wasserros 🍇🍇 ④
Riesling Eiswein Goldkapsel 1991
A superb Eiswein which weighed in at 160°Oechsle and now with 13 g/lt of acidity, with very successful harmony. Dominated more by fruit than sweetness.

Robert Weil 🍇🍇 ③
Riesling Spätlese halbtrocken 1991
A well-balanced, rich wine with clear, fresh fruit, soft, hardly noticeable sweetness and strong acidity: excellent.

Kiedricher Gräfenberg 🍇🍇🍇 ④
Riesling Trockenbeerenauslese 1991
Although it is not such a high grade wine as the 1990 Trockenbeeren-Auslese which was harvested at 216°Oechsle, it still has enormous richness and impressive acidity. A wine 'harvested with forceps', as Wilhelm Weil explains: pickers went through the vineyards for five days, each with three containers: one for Auslese grapes, the others for lightly shrivelled, 'dry berries' or 'Trocken-Beeren'. With the latter he only managed to harvest 400 ml per day. But what a wine: almost oily with a bouquet of exotic scents and endless flavors with explosive acidity and masses of botrytis on the palate. The potential of this wine, highly concentrated by natural evaporation is enormous and it should continue to develop for decades.

Domdechant Werner'sches Weingut

Rathausstrasse 30
Hochheim 6203
Tel. (06146) 2008
Fax (06146) 61153

Franz-Werner Michel's main job is director of
the German Wine Foundation, though his
heart is in his own wine estate on the eastern
edge of the Rheingau, only a few kilometers
from Frankfurt, where he produces
increasingly rich, long-lived Rieslings. 70%
are made in an either dry or off-dry style and
they are occasionally referred to as
'Fränkisch Rheingauer' due to the calcareous
soils and the vicinity of the area to Franken.
The high extract levels (on average 25 g/lt)
found in Michel's wines derives from the
estate's high proportion of old vines, 50% of
which are more than 20 years-old. The best
wines generally come from the excellent
Hochheimer Domdechaney site (also
reflected in the price). They are usually made
in a fruity-mild style, ie with residual sugar. In
1990 the dry wines ('problem children' in this
estate) were unusually successful, while
1991 produced average quality, though it
also included Spätlesen. Michel also
produces Pinot Noir, but from less than half a
hectare of vineyard. In favourable vintages it
is made as a red wine, in lesser years as a
rosé.

Hochheimer Domdechaney ♀ ②
Riesling Kabinett halbtrocken 1991
An elegant but relatively light wine with
understated sweetness, full of apricot fruit and
minerally flavors: appeals due to finesse rather
than power.

Hochheimer Kirchenstück ♀ ②
Riesling Spätlese halbtrocken 1991
A surprisingly rich Spätlese for this vintage with
delicate sweetness on the tongue and the
acidity has not yet become integrated but
promises well for the future.

Hochheimer Domdechaney ♀ ♀ ③
Riesling Auslese 1990
A super wine from the famous Domdechaney
site. Very elegant due to its opulent,
concentrated fruit and fresh acidity

Hochheimer Kirchenstück ♀ ②
Riesling Spätlese trocken 1990
This wine is more characterized by minerally
aromas than by fruit, which will need time to
develop.

Rheinhessen

Rheinhessen accounts for around a quarter of Germany's wine production, making the region between Bingen, Mainz and Worms the country's largest wine-growing area. It stretches from the Rhine westwards, deep into the area known as Hinterland, where vineyards are often planted alongside corn and turnip fields on heavy, loess soils. Sites like these which are hardly suitable for wine-growing have become the breeding ground for medium quality new crossings such as Bacchus, Perle, Ortega, Optima and Faber. The region's most famous product is Liebfraumilch, originating from vineyards around the city of Worms, which has unfortunately come to epitomise German wine abroad. Among connoisseurs, however, it is seen as the trademark of one of Germany's worst wines. Made from various varieties from Müller-Thurgau through to Riesling it is thin, vulgar and coarsely sweet. As it has become a hit on export markets in recent years its cultivation area has spread beyond Rheinhessen's borders, and it is now produced in almost all German wine-growing regions. In Germany itself, however, it has never been widely popular.

Rheinhessen's leading role in terms of quantity has diverted attention away from the fact that it is the source of some of Germany's best white wines, especially from Riesling and Silvaner. At their best they are equal to those of the Rheingau, but are fuller without the latter's steely acidity. They usually come from the area known as the 'Rheinfront' around the towns of Nackenheim, Nierstein and Oppenheim, though certain sites in the 'Hinterland' area such as Gau-Odernheim and Bingen produce surprisingly fine wines with plenty of character. In these vineyards Riesling is the leading variety, but elsewhere it only accounts for 7% of Rheinhessen's grape varieties.

Almost half the vineyard area is planted with Silvaner, which can make very classy, fine wines especially at the Kabinett and Spätlese levels. In the past they were often made in a sweetish, 'lieblich' style, while recently a campaign has been started to re-establish it as a dry, uncomplicated, easy-drinking wine. Rheinhessen Silvaner, abbreviated to RS, has become a trademark for a light, fresh, occasionally very characterful white wine. Pinot Blanc (Weissburgunder) does not yet play an important role in Rheinhessen and Scheurebe has become completely insignificant. Among reds only Pinot Noir (Spätburgunder) is of minor importance around Ingelheim.

Weingut Bürgermeister Balbach Erben

Mainzer Strasse 64
Nierstein 6505
Tel. (06133) 5585
Fax (06133) 59114

Driving along state route 9 from Mainz towards Worms a wonderful historic building belonging to the Bürgermeister Balbach Erben estate on the bank of the Rhine catches the eye. This family has written wine growing history by clearing the present day Pettenthal site at Nierstein. Balbach's Rieslings and Silvaners are nowadays made in stainless steel tanks and grouped into three categories, with only the very best being sold under site names. Others are labelled under the name of the town, Nierstein, or simply under varietal names. In this way the estate is able to make better selections and emphasise their best sites in a similar way to the Alsace grand cru system. Wines like the dry 1990 Oelberg Riesling Spätlese justify such a system and at the same time reveal the estate's potential. However, it must be said that such wines are not the rule, especially in 1991 and they will have to put in a great deal of effort to maintain such high quality standards.

Niersteiner Spiegelberg   ⚜ ①
Silvaner QbA trocken 1991
A very cleanly made Silvaner with appealingly gentle acidity. Light in style.

Niersteiner Oelberg   ⚜ ②
Riesling Spätlese trocken 1990
A successful wine with a fruity, minerally flavor; already pleasant to drink and with good aging potential.

Niersteiner Spiegelberg   ⚜ ①
Silvaner QbA trocken 1990
Earthy-fruity in flavor, light-weight, smooth with a long finish and a little too mild in acidity. An everyday drinking wine.

Weingut Brüder Dr.Becker

Mainer Strasse 3
Ludwingshöhe 6501
Tel. (06249) 8430
Fax (06249) 7639

Lotte Pfeffer and Hans Müller now run this estate. With their elegant, slender and fruity dry and off-dry white wines they show how products deriving from ecological viticulture can be excellent if cared for professionally both in the vineyard and in the cellar. This is achieved by careful grape selections, the minimum use of wine-making technology and patiently waiting for the wines to mature in cask. The results are delicate, soft Rieslings, slender but muscular Silvaners and piquant Scheureben. Once tasted, these clearly structured wines make it easy to believe in ecological wine-growing. They come from the Ludwigshöher Teufelskopf and Dienheimer Tafelstein and Paterberg sites, grown mainly on sandy soils or a mixture of clay and loess. These soils leave a strong imprint on the wines and by careful vinification their wines are never too broad.

Dienheimer Tafelstein   ⚜ ②
Riesling Auslese trocken 1991
A very successful 1991 and without doubt their best wine of this difficult growing season.

Dienheimer Tafelstein   ⚜ ①
Riesling Kabinett trocken 1991
A scented Riesling with a hint of vanilla on the nose and palate. The accentuated acidity prevents it from seeming broad.

Ludwigshöher Teufelskopf   ⚜ ①
Silvaner Kabinett trocken 1991
An unpretentious but very well made Silvaner, clearly structured, clean on the palate with good length.

Dienheimer Tafelstein   ⚜ ②
Scheurebe Spätlese trocken 1990
A worthy successor to the excellent 1988 Spätlese from the same variety which is little known in Germany.

Weingut Heinrich Braun

Glockengasse 9
Nierstein 6505
Tel. (06133) 5139
Fax (06133) 59877

He insists on pointing out that although from a legal point of view the estate belongs to the Rheinhessen growing region, in reality it is directly on the Rhine in the section known as the Rheinfront. Peter Braun, vineyard manager and winemaker in one, makes this distinction to distance himself from the mass-producing Hinterland area, where vines are planted on heavy arable soils. Of course owning vineyards on the Rhine at Nierstein, Oppenheim and Nackenheim alone is no guarantee of quality. Since he took over the family business in 1964 at the age of 21 Peter Braun has made his name as one of Rheinhessen's top producers. He makes fruity wines with accentuated acidity and experiments with Riesling clones from other German regions. He swears by cask-aging, though still experiments with barriques. His Gourmet Selection is a novelty, whereby ten tasters from various sectors of the wine and restaurant business taste his wines in order to select the best, which are subsequently marketed under a special label. The 1990 wines are excellent while the 1991s are some distance behind.

Niersteiner Pettenthal ♚ ②
Riesling Spätlese trocken 1991
An explosion of fruit along with strong but ripe acidity. A wine with great aging potential.

Niersteiner Ölberg ♚♚ ③
Riesling Auslese trocken 1990
Very fruity and lightly bitter in aroma and flavor; great aging potential and a good example of dry Auslese.

Niersteiner Pettenthal ♚♚ ④
Riesling Trockenbeerenauslese 1989
This TBA is dominated by the aroma of quince and the flavor is enriched by gentle bitterness deriving from botrytis: a superb wine.

Brenner'sches Weingut

Pfandturmstrasse 20
Bechtheim 6521
Tel. (06242) 894
Fax (06242) 874

Christian Brenner is one of Germany's most innovative producers. When he made a dry Silvaner back in 1963 he was thought to be mad as at that time the great majority of consumers drank sweet wines. Although he had some initial success the market still proved too immature for this kind of wine. Nevertheless, Brenner was undeterred and his final success has proven him right. He was equally successful with the method of oxidizing the grape juice prior to fermentation, a practice very much against the accepted teachings and theory of the time, and today he has found recognition in numerous technical publications. He has now started on a new project, that of making an aperitif from wine which has been matured for years according to the sherry method. Along with products like these Brenner also makes classic wines. For example he has produced Pinot Blanc (Weissburgunder) since 1978 which has earned him the title 'Weissburgunder-König.' All his wines are distinguished by a fine bouquet and strong acidity, while his reds are produced according to the barrique philosophy.

Bechtheimer Geyersberg ♚ ①
Weisser Burgunder Kabinett trocken 1991
A succulent, medium-weight Pinot Blanc, already very elegant but still with potential to improve in bottle.

Bechtheimer Geyersberg ♚ ②
Weissburgunder Auslese trocken 1990
An enormous wine though still undeveloped; opulent but not obtrusive, generous fruit and soft, winey acidity.

Bechtheimer Rosengarten ♚ ②
Riesling Spätlese trocken 1990
A good Riesling, muscular and firm with ripe acidity and good bottle-aging potential.

Weisser Burgunder trocken 1990 ♚ ③
Classified as Tafelwein and matured in barrique with plenty of lasting potential to integrate the oak.

Weingut Jean Buscher

Wormser Strasse 4
Bechtheim 6521
Tel. (06242) 872
Fax (06242) 875

Sculptures in the press room of the winery and casks used to stand them on. This is the conception Weingut Jean Buscher gives to visitors to the various wine events organised by the founder's grandson Michael Buscher. Art in the cellar is one of the ideas which Michael Buscher has brought to fruition in recent years in order to draw customers' attention to the combination between wine and culture. Michael Buscher's conviction prevents these things turning into publicity events which ignore the quality produced by the 140 year-old wine estate. "We can only present ourselves to the public when everything in the vineyards and in the cellar is as it should be and the wine quality correct," he insists. The wine quality is correct, with well above average Rieslings, very good Spätburgunders (Pinot Noir) - generally speaking a very consistent assortment with few exceptions. The premium selection is marketed as Edition Jean Buscher as well as special bottlings with designer labels of wines from the best sites with low yields, for which the berries are destalked by hand.

Bechtheimer Geyersberg ☙ ①
Riesling Kabinett trocken 1991
The elegant acidity makes this wine appealing: a long finish, very mouthwatering and racy and not too heavy.

Bechtheimer Geyersberg ☙☙ ②
Riesling Spätlese trocken 1990
A generous, stylish wine with a light grapey flavor, more Auslese than Spätlese in quality.

Bechtheimer Stein ☙☙ ③
Weisser Burgunder Beerenauslese 1989
Very concentrated sweetness and accentuated acidity. A very big and at the same time delicate wine.

Bechtheimer Stein ☙ ②
Schwarzriesling Spätlese trocken 1991
A light, fruity red wine with the interplay of aromas well in harmony with the soft tannin.

Weingut Gunderloch

Carl-Gunderloch-Platz 1
Nackenheim 6506
Tel. (06135) 2341
Fax (06135) 2431

The 1913 wine list of the thermal baths of Wiesbaden proudly refers to the purchase of a cask of 1911 Nackenheimer Rothenberg Riesling Edelbeeren-Auslese from the Gunderloch estate. The 1,200 lt of this noble wine were bought for 24,000 marks and the sale serves as a shining example of Rheinhessen's wine culture. Little has changed since then, except for the fact that the wines no longer fetch top prices. Nevertheless, this estate still produces some of Rheinhessen's best wines; delicate with a very finely tuned balance between fruit, acidity and richness. They are mostly dry but the assortment also includes first class nobly sweet wines through to Trocken-Beeren-Auslese. However, Agness and Friedrich Hasselbar-Usinger have also tried out new methods such as aging their Pinot Gris (Grauburgunder) and Rivaner from the Niersteiner Paterberg site produced from 40 year old vines in barrique. A Gunderlocher Cuvée of Riesling and Silvaner takes us back to the old days when vineyards were planted with mixed varieties - a very pleasant everyday wine.

Gunderloch Cuvée ☙ ①
Riesling und Silvaner QbA trocken 1991
A wine produced according to the old tradition of planting vineyards with mixed varieties and harvesting them together. The Riesling gives it aroma and acidity, the Silvaner its round and mature style, all of which are well integrated.

Gunderloch Jean-Baptiste ☙ ①
Riesling Kabinett 1991
This wine stopped fermenting prematurely leaving 18 g/lt of residual sugar. It is excellently balanced and reminiscent of Kabinett wines of the last century.

Gunderloch Silvaner ☙ ①
QbA trocken 1991
Without exaggeration this is a picturebook Silvaner: mouthwatering, easy to drink and full with round acidity.

Grauburgunder Tafelwein 1990 ☙☙ ③
Power and concentration are already noticeable in this wine, which has been skilfully aged in barrique - a wine which can stand on its own in an international context.

Nackenheimer Rothenberg ☙☙ ③
Riesling Auslese Goldkapsel 1990
Botrytis characterizes the bouquet, enormous concentration the nose and palate: one of this vintage's greatest Auslesen.

Weingut Louis Guntrum

Rheinallee 62
Nierstein 6505
Tel. (06133) 57090
Fax (06133) 570957

Turning the pages of wine magazines it is
hard not to notice regular references to the
Louis Guntrum estate and its wines.
Nevertheless, with all due respect to the
quality of their wines, although they own plots
in all the best Nierstein sites, really great
'grand cru' Rieslings seldom emerge from
their cellars (the last was a dry 1990 Riesling
from Niersteiner Oelberg). Riesling is seldom
found among their Auslesen and Beeren-
Auslese which is due to the fact that Hajo
Guntrum, who runs the estate now in the
tenth generation, focuses more on Silvaner.
This variety produced Beeren-Auslese and
Eiswein in 1989 and 1990 - good but not
great wines (the latter, by the way, is labelled
with unusually bad taste featuring a penguin).
He cannot keep from making off-dry
Silvaners and it is above all the dry style
which shows the variety's potential. This is
also true of the dry Pinot Gris
(Grauburgunder) which are also among his
top wines.

Oppenheimer Sackträger ❦ ②
Gewürztraminer Spätlese trocken 1991
Strongly characterised by its aroma reminiscent
of withering rose petals and exotic fruits. An
opulent wine, almost too obtrusive to drink with
food.

Niersteiner Pettenthal ❦ ①
Riesling Kabinett trocken 1990
Lightly minty on the nose with clear, ripe winey
acidity on the palate. An easy-drinking,
uncomplicated wine.

Oppenheimer Herrenberg ❦❦ ④
Silvaner Eiswein 1990
Very refined in aroma with honeyed sweetness
on the palate. A wine worth laying down but
stops short of perfection because of its mild
acidity.

Oppenheimer Kreuz ❦ ②
Riesling Spätlese trocken 1990
Soft but accentuated bitterness, acidulously
fruity on the palate: a medium length wine which
will peak soon.

Weingut Freiherr Heyl zu Herrnsheim

Mathildenhof
Langgasse 3
Nierstein 6505
Tel. (06133) 5120
Fax (06133) 58921

The old estate building in the center of Nierstein and its English style garden with a view of the falcons nesting in the winery tower evoke an atmosphere of calm and relaxation. However, this idyllic impression is not reflected in the work Peter von Weymarn and his wife Isa have put in over the past 20 years, though it does emerge in the wines. Heyl zu Herrnsheim is by far the best wine estate in Rheinhessen and von Weymarn's wines are among Germany's absolute best Rieslings. They express very impressively the characteristics deriving from the sites on the bank of the Rhine, called the Rheinfront: Pettenthal, Hipping, Auflangen, Oelberg, Orbel, Kranzberg and especially Brudersberg. With its red, rust-colored soils (Rotliegenden), it is owned entirely by the estate. Only their Rheinfront wines are labelled under site names. Below this level a second range was introduced a few years ago under the name Heyl and these 'second' wines are better and cheaper than numerous other producers top wines.

Niersteiner Hipping 🍇 ②
Weissburgunder Spätlese trocken 1991
A very impressive Pinot Blanc from the Hipping site: elegant but concentrated, it will reveal its true potential in two to three years.

Niersteiner Oelberg 🍇 ②
Silvaner Spätlese trocken 1991
A superb wine of great stature thanks to its high acidity and richness. It would be difficult to find a better dry Silvaner.

Niersteiner Oelberg 🍇🍇 ③
Riesling Spätlese trocken 1990
This is the first time Heyl zu Herrnsheim has produced a dry Spätlese which can seriously compete with Brudersberg, and many consider it to be even better.

Niersteiner Oelberg 🍇🍇 ④
Riesling Trockenbeerenauslese 1989
A finely tuned, complex aroma and enormous potential, power, elegance and class and a finish which goes on and on.

Niersteiner Brudersberg 🍇🍇🍇 ③
Riesling Spätlese trocken 1990
For years the Brudersberg vineyard has produced Spätlesen which are among the greatest in Germany in this category. Rieslings from this site are the most unyielding, latest maturing of all Rheinfront wines, though with maturity they usually turn out to be the finest. The Brudersberg 1990 Spätlese is also a sleeping giant and already beats the excellent 1989 Spätlese from the same site. It is also a perfect example of how a dry Riesling with high acidity can be truly fine if the dryness is backed up by richness, alcohol and fruit, as is the case with this 1990.

Weingut Krug'scher Hof

An der Königsmühle 7
Gau-Odernheim 6509
Tel. (06733) 1337
Fax (06733) 1700

Generally speaking great wines are not grown in the Rheinhessen backlands (called Hinterland as it is away from the Rhine). There are of course exceptions, one of which is the Krug'scher Hof estate at Gau Odernheim. Gina and Klaus Menger-Krug are better known for their excellent sparkling wine from Rheinpfalz called Menger-Krug but have developed a wine estate at Gau Odernheim which has come up with some excellent wines. The grape varieties grown are Pinot Blanc, Pinot Gris (Grauburgunder), Chardonnay and Riesling. Their typical varietal flavors and finesse make them very appealing and the wines have been a revelation in numerous blind tastings. The vineyards are worked on ecological principles and they have obtained environmentally friendly pesticides with the help of environmental scientists and biologists. Wine-making is on reductive lines in stainless steel tanks and some wines are later matured in small casks. Alongside their dry wines they produce nobly sweet specialties and their barrique-aged Trocken-Beeren-Auslese cuvée or their first class Eiswein have surprised many critics.

Gau-Odernheimer Herrgottspfad 🍷 ①
Riesling Kabinett trocken 1991
A wine made for early drinking which is already very enjoyable with soft aromas and ripe acidity.

Alzeyer Römerberg 🍷 ④
Chardonnay Spätlese trocken 1990
A supple wine with strong, but not aggressive acidity: the best 1990 Rheinhessen Chardonnay.

Grau-Köngerheimer Voglsang 🍷🍷 ③
Weissburgunder Auslese trocken 1990
Very scented and full without seeming too rich. Delicate on the palate in spite of its power.

Krug'scher Hof 🍷🍷 ④
Trockenbeerenauslese 1989
A cuvée of various grape varieties: an opulent, richly sweet concentration of aromas and flavors with plenty of depth and finesse.

Weingut Kühling-Gillot

Oelmühlstrasse 25
Bodenheim 6501
Tel. (06135) 2333
Fax (06135) 6463

'A young wine estate with old traditions' is the motto chosen by the Kühling-Gillot estate. Young, because the estate was created through a marriage in 1970 and old, because the the two estates Kühling and Gillot can look back on a 200 year old tradition. One might think that Roland Gillot and his wife had woken up to their inheritance from a sleeping beauty-like sleep, as they have repeatedly come up with sensational wines since the merger, especially Beeren-Auslesen and Eiswein. No wonder journalists all over the world praise these wines and place the 1989 Bodenheimer Burgweg Ruländer Trockenbeeren-Auslese among the best 50 wines tasted in 1991. On the one hand the wines have the advantage of coming from excellent sites. Their eight and a half hectares of vineyard include the best sites at Oppenheim and Dienheim. Roland Gillot, who takes care of both the vineyards and wine-making places great importance on preserving the characteristics derived from the single sites and grape varieties. His wines are clear and streamlined.

Oppenheimer Sackträger 🍷 ②
Riesling Spätlese trocken 1991
An opulent Riesling with delicate, fruity aromas and discreet acidity: well made though perhaps a little too smooth.

Bodenheimer Burgweg 🍷🍷 ④
Ruländer Trockenbeerenauslese 1990
Perhaps an even greater sweet wine than the Eiswein: caramel and roasted aromas on the nose with incredible complexity and depth on the palate. Rheinhessen's best 1990 TBA.

Oppenheimer 🍷 ①
Riesling Kabinett trocken 1990
Good acidity, well balanced by the strongly accentuated fruit aromas. Good value for money.

Bodenheimer Kapelle 🍷🍷 ④
Riesling Eiswein 1989
This wine shows Roland Gillot's skill: a superb, nobly sweet wine which needs to be laid down for several years.

Oberstleutnant Liebrecht'sche Weingutsverwaltung

Rheinstrasse 30
Bodenheim 6501
Tel. (06135) 2301
Fax (06135) 8221

This winery, with its military sounding name (it is actually an old convent) was once the model of Rheinhessen's wine-growing culture. The descendents of Liebrecht, a Prussian army officer and wine enthusiast, are still trying hard to live up to the estate's reputation with varying success. Their Pinot Blancs - especially those made in a dry style - are among the region's best and are usually even superior to their Rieslings which, in spite of being high ranking (plenty of Spät- and Auslesen) are a little old fashioned, rather broad due to their being harvested late with correspondingly low acidity. They are often one-dimensional and for the most part made in a sweetish style (which, in accordance with German wine policy earns them many prizes and medals). The estate would be better off producing less and their storerooms, still full of old vintages, would become empty faster. Nevertheless, the wines of Oberstleutnant Liebrecht can still be among Rheinhessen's best.

Bodenheimer Burgweg　　　　🍾 ②
Riesling Spätlese halbtrocken 1991
A wine with a perfect balance between sweetness and acidity, delicate, acidulously fruity, an impression which is reinforced by discreet sweetness.

Bodenheimer Hoch　　　　🍾 ②
Weisser Burgunder Spätlese trocken 1991
Complex aromas on the nose, succulent and not overly aromatic on the palate with an elegant texture and concentration.

Bodenheimer Heitersbrünnchen　🍾 ②
Grauer Burgunder Auslese trocken 1990
A powerful and concentrated Auslese which could have done with more acidity to balance its opulence.

Bodenheimer Silberberg　　　🍾 ②
Riesling Auslese 1989
A classic Auslese with its noticable sweetness well harmonised by acidity. A very well made wine.

Josef Neus

Weingut Sonnengerg - Bahnhofstrasse 96
Ingelheim 6507
Tel. (06132) 73003
Fax (06132) 2690

Nowadays the word conservative usually has a negative ring to it, though applied to the red wine producer Josef Neus it evokes a completely different, positive meaning. The Burchards family, which manage the inheritance of the founder Josef Neus now in the fourth generation, have succeeded in saving the traditional Ingelheim Spätburgunder (Pinot Noir) style. While many wine producers are now concentrating on barrique wines with varying success, at Josef Neus the focus is on tradition and developing it in a meaningful way. This includes classic fermentation on the skins in large oak casks. The result is some impressive Pinot Noirs with very little tannin and fine fruit reminiscent of redcurrant and cherry, together with a fine hint of almond typical of the calcareous soils at Ingelheim. 70% of their vineyard area is planted with Pinot Noir, followed by 20% Portugieser. This variety is scorned for its massive yields and bad quality though the Josef Neus estate produces excellent examples by reducing yields. It is only in this way that Ulrich Burchards, who is now responsible for the wines, sees a future for Portugieser. The top Pinot Noirs are made in a style which will soon have a rarity value.

Ingelheimer Horn　　　　🍇 ①
Spätburgunder Qualitätswein trocken 1991
Not a great wine but still disproves the argument that German reds are only worth taking seriously from Spätlese level upwards.

Ingelheimer Rheinhöhe　　　🍇 ①
Portugieser QbA trocken 1990
A good wine from a discredited grape variety: intense fruit, light tannin and low acidity.

Ingelheimer Sonnenberg　　　🍇 ②
Spätburgunder Kabinett trocken 1990
A classic German Pinot Noir, opulent in bouquet, fruity with a harmonious balance between tannin and acidity.

Ingelheimer Pares　　　　🍇 ③
Spätburgunder Auslese trocken 1989
A discreet toasty aroma and very strong blackberry flavor: a good example of a traditional Pinot Noir made and matured in large casks.

Weingut Rappenhof

Bachstrasse 47-49
Alsheim 6526
Tel. (06249) 4015
Fax (06249) 4729

Rappenhof wines have not always been able to satisfy high expectations in recent years. Perhaps due to the size of the estate, former Wine Growing Association president Reinhard Muth and his son Klaus have missed their chance to make great wines time and time again, especially at the QbA and Kabinett levels, even in superb vintages like 1988, 1989 and 1990. This is caused by careless wine-making, though in spite of this there are some real gems in their large range. The main variety is Riesling (44%), followed by Pinots Blanc and Noir and Chardonnay which together account for 26%. In addition to the large range of dry wines the estate also produces nobly sweet wines, mainly from Riesling and Pinot Blanc which are appealingly rich and unobtrusive. Rappenhof has also made a name for itself with efforts at barrique-aging Chardonnay and Pinot Noir. A short stay in wood is preferred (two months for Chardonnay) as the oak should play a supporting, not dominant role.

Niersteiner Oelberg 🍇 ①
Grauer Burgunder Kabinett trocken 1991
The promise made by the aroma is maintained on the palate. The wine is still a little closed but will develop well in bottle.

Chardonnay Tafelwein trocken 1990 🍇 ②
The relatively short stay in barrique leaves a delicate hint of oak, enriching the wine with light spicey quality.

Guntersblumer Eiserne Hand 🍇 ②
Gewürztraminer Spätlese trocken 1990
Rich and concentrated in flavor without becoming obtrusive, with well integrated aromas.

Weingut Schales

Alzeyer Strasse 160
Flörsheim-Dalsheim 6523
Tel. (06243) 7003
Fax (06243) 5230

As early as 1989 the Schales estate took the very unusual step of deciding to eliminate site names from their labels. Grape variety, rank and style together with the name Schales should suffice in the opinion of owner Arno Schales. It would be wrong to assume that this is done to standardize production by making large blends from various vineyard sites, as the wines are still cleanly made and each has its own distinct character. The three brothers are in full agreement on this policy. Heinrich Schales is responsible for the vineyards, while in the cellar the wines mature under the care of Kurt Schales, who decides on how each variety should be made, whether in stainless steel tanks, cask or fiberglass tanks. He aims at reductive wines which are compact, rich with stable acidity. Arno Schales is responsible for the general running of the estate and public relations. Their specialties are classic Rieslings, which account for the larger part of production as well as nobly sweet wines and older, mature vintages.

Schales Weissburgunder 🍇 ②
Spätlese trocken 1991
One of the finest, most intensely fruity Rheinhessen Pinot Blancs with good concentration, a long finish and good aging potential.

Schales Silvaner QbA trocken 1990 🍇 ①
Rheinhessen's best, most humbly priced Silvaner sold in liter bottles: fresh on the nose, acidulous and excellently balanced. An easy-drinking, honest wine.

Schales Weissburgunder
Spätlese trocken 1989
A nice mature Pinot Blanc, though it does not quite equal the 1990.

Weingut Schlamp-Schätzel

Oberdorfstrasse 34
Nierstein 6505
Tel. (06133) 5512
Fax (06133) 60159

Otto and Nanne Schätzel are at present responsible for this traditional wine estate which they took over from their grandmother 26 years ago. Under their direction its fortunes have enjoyed an upturn and it is now among the most highly respected Rheinhessen estates. Otto Schätzel teaches at the school of viticulture and wine-making at Oppenheim and his Rieslings are very racy wines which are made in a way which strongly expresses their varietal characteristics. The style of the wines is influenced by the way they are aged traditionally in large casks and a good example is the excellent dry 1990 Riesling from the Niersteiner Pettenthal site. Silvaner also profits from this treatment. In comparative tastings with other RS (Rheinhessen Silvaner, a concept introduced a few years ago to market Silvaner from Rheinhessen under a standard label) those of Schlamp-Schätzel always stand out. They own vineyards in the very best sites at Nierstein and Guntersblum, a factor which has enabled them to develop a selection of top wines marketed under the name General von Zastrow consisting of the best Rieslings from the best sites in each respective vintage.

Niersteiner Rehbach
Riesling Kabinett trocken 1991 🍇 ①
A typical Schlamp-Schätzel wine with its concentrated earthy-fruity aroma together with a good acid framework.

Niersteiner Pettenthal
Riesling Spätlese trocken 1991 🍇 ①
This wine bears the distinct imprint of the soil on which it was grown expressed by an aroma of hay and almond. Shows that excellent Rieslings could be made even in 1991.

RS Silvaner QbA trocken 1991 🍇 ①
RS stands for Rheinhessen Silvaner, a trademark for the modern style of easy-drinking, dry Silvaner just like this wine, with its mild acidity.

Niersteiner Pettenthal
Riesling Auslese trocken 1990 🍇🍇 ②
A wine with character and depth: this estate's classiest Riesling from the General von Zastrow selection.

Weingut St. Anthony

Wörrstadter Strasse 22
Nierstein 6505
Tel. (06133) 5482
Fax (06133) 59139

St Anthony can thank its existence to the production of steel. More precisely under the name Stahlwerk (Steelmill) Gutehoffnungshütte it was a quarry supplying chalk for the production of steel and when it was no longer required in 1918 it was transformed into a vineyard. An estate needed to be founded in order to care for the vines, which is the present day St Anthony, now one of Rheinhessen's most prestigious names. The vineyards are planted 60% with Riesling which produces the best quality in the Nierstein grand cru sites Pettenthal, Hipping and Oelberg as well as Orbel. The longevity of the Rieslings is due to strict reductions in vineyard yields, which in the top sites are as low as 45 hl/ha. The wines are matured in traditional casks. At one time they were made exclusively for entertaining guests of the engineering concern MAN (owner of the Gutehoffnungshütte). Unfortunately the wines are no longer a hidden secret.

Niersteiner Ölberg 🍇 ③
Riesling Spätlese trocken 1991
This is proof that it is possible to make excellent quality wines even in unfavorable vintages as long as vineyard yields are drastically reduced.

Niersteiner Pettenthal 🍇🍇 ②
Riesling Spätlese trocken 1991
A very fine fruit aroma, concentrated and rich, muscular in structure with plenty of depth: one of the region's best 1991s.

Niersteiner Ölberg 🍇🍇 ③
Grauburgunder Spätlese trocken 1990
Enormously generous fruit with a fine overlay of honey, at the same time elegant with an underlying aroma reminiscent of roasted nuts - a very typical St Anthony.

Niersteiner 🍇 ①
Riesling QbA trocken 1990
A mouthwatering, racy Riesling with a soft, mature aroma: a very skilfully made wine.

Weingut Stallmann-Hiestand

Eisgasse 15
Uelversheim 6501
Tel. (06249) 8463
Fax (06249) 8614

Stallmann-Hiestand is another estate which has experienced an upturn since the change of generation. Until 1974 it was a mixed farming business in which wine was of secondary importance and sold in bulk. When Werner Hiestand took over all this changed. First of all he converted it completely into a wine estate and marketed the wines in bottles, thereby laying the cornerstone for the present quality. He decided to concentrate on the classic varieties Riesling, Silvaner and Müller-Thurgau and the wines are streamlined with good structure. Even though 80% are made in a dry style they also excel with charming, nobly sweet wines. Barrique aged Chardonnay and Pinot Noir (Spätburgunder) is also an important theme. The vineyards are in excellent sites at Uelversheim, Dienheim and Guntersblum where the soils are mainly calcareous with a mixture of loess and clay.

Dienheimer Kreuz   ℣ ①
Grauburgunder QbA trocken 1991
A rather discreet style of Pinot Gris though still with concentration and depth.

Dienheimer Tafelstein   ℣ ①
Weissburgunder Spätlese trocken 1991
This wine derives its generosity from concentrated fruit and its freshness from lively acidity: a slim, harmonious Pinot Blanc.

Silvaner QbA trocken 1991   ℣ ①
A typical apply aroma with a fresh, fruity flavor on the palate: a mouthwatering, delicate summer wine.

Dienheimer Siliusbrunnen   ℣℣ ④
Riesling Eiswein 1989
A nobly sweet specialty with elegant acidity and a minerally Eiswein aroma: the region's most impressive 1989 Eiswein.

Weingut Villa Sachsen

Mainzer Strasse 184
Bingen 6530
Tel. (06721) 13001
Fax (06721) 10116

This estate has a very complex history when it comes to ownership and wine quality. The most recent chapter began in early 1992 when wine merchant and marketing manager Gerd Schönfelder (together with other shareholders) bought the Villa from the Nestlé group. Schönfelder is a trained enologist and well acquainted with Rheinhessen's wine culture. He is already on course to improve the quality of the estate's wines and especially to re-establish the reputation of Scharlachberg, the only excellent site at Bingen. Over 70% of this steep, south-facing slope is owned by Villa Sachsen and the dry Rieslings derived from there have long enjoyed notoriety. Schönberger insists that the acidity in the wines is completely natural and unaltered and their products are made in a completely traditional manner, aged in large casks for seven months. When it comes to nobly sweet wines the Villa could do better, though their achievement of producing 60,000 bottles a year of simple, mouthwatering, all-purpose QbA Riesling is highly commendable.

Binger Kapellenberg   ℣ ①
Silvaner QbA trocken 1991
A rich Silvaner with understated fruit and mild acidity - a good example of Rheinhessen's uncomplicated, light style of Silvaner.

Binger Scharlachberg   ℣ ①
Riesling Kabinett trocken 1991
A clean aroma, concentrated on the palate with rather coarse, tart acidity: a typical Villa Sachsen wine.

Binger Schlossberg Schwätzchen   ℣ ①
Weissburgunder QbA trocken 1991
An easy-drinking, though at the same time characterful and fresh Pinot Blanc, impressive even in this quality category.

Binger Scharlachberg   ℣ ②
Riesling Spätlese trocken 1990
A successful Riesling which disproves all preconceptions of Rheinhessen wines: multi-layered, complex and clear.

Binger Scharlachberg   ℣℣ ④
Riesling Beerenauslese 1989
Strongly characterised by botrytis with strong, unobtrusive sweetness and good acidity: a very fine nobly sweet wine.

Weingut Eugen Wehrheim

Mühlgasse 30
Nierstein 6505
Tel. (06133) 58125
Fax (06133) 57605

When Eugen Wehrheim speaks about his wines he is unable to hide his pride, as they can easily match the quality of those from estates which are far more famous. The Wehrheim family has owned vineyards at Nierstein since 1693 and for this reason they cannot be described as newcomers. Nevertheless, Wehrheim wines are still recent discoveries and almost all come from famous Nierstein sites on red 'Rotliegend' soils together with loess, clay and chalk, each of which leaves its own individual strong imprint on the wines. They are acidulously fresh, fruity wines which age well and their unique characteristics are strongly shaped by aging in traditional casks. His nobly sweet wines can be really classy and a 1986 Siegerrebe TBA which has just been bottled is an absolute top wine. Although this variety is not exactly highly regarded it can produce very interesting botrytised wines. One sentence of Wehrheim's when answering a question on wine-making embodies his whole attitude towards making natural products. "The wines need time, not chemistry or technology," he says.

Niersteiner Bildstock　　　🍇 ①
Riesling Kabinett trocken 1991
A mouthwatering, firm, fruity-sweet Riesling with a fine aroma of rhubarb, though rustic and not elegant.

Niersteiner Ölberg　　　🍇 ①
Riesling Spätlese trocken 1991
An accentuated aroma of exotic fruits (lychee and mango) and well integrated acidity - a perfectly harmonious wine. Wehrheim's best 1991 Riesling.

Niersteiner Ölberg　　　🍇 ①
Riesling Spätlese trocken 1990
Exotic-minerally fruit, fine acidity and concentrated aromas make this wine Wehrheim's best dry 1990 Spätlese.

Niersteiner Bildstock　　　🍇🍇 ④
Riesling Beerenauslese 1989
A lively aroma of apple with refreshing acidity on the palate: an opulent, concentrated wine with an explosion of fruit aromas in the mouth.

Weingut Schloss Westerhaus

Ingelheim 6507
Tel. (06130) 6674
Fax (06130) 7513

Westerhaus Castle is most probably Germany's oldest wine estate going back to the 15th century. It was bought by the car manufacturer Heinrich von Opel in 1900, who started a stud farm there and enthusiastically continued its wine-growing tradition. It is now owned by his grandson Heinz von Opel. The estate boasts 13 ha of vineyard in the best Ingelheim sites, with Ingelheimer Schloss Westerhaus (in exclusive ownership) and Ingelheimer Sonnenhang forming the nucleus of quality wines. The most important varieties are Riesling (47%) and the red Spätburgunder (Pinot Noir, 26%) plus Pinot Blanc (Weissburgunder). Chardonnay is a rarity and is made in barrique. In addition to their dry, acidulous wines the estate is also famous for its excellent Eiswein, Beeren-Auslesen and Trocken-Beeren-Auslesen which are among Rheinhessen's best noble sweet wines.

Ingelheimer Schloss Westerhaus　🍇 ①
Gewürztraminer Kabinett trocken 1991
At last a Gewürztraminer with delicate structure and gentle aromas, the kind which does not overpower food.

Ingelheimer Schloss Westerhaus　🍇 ①
Riesling Spätlese trocken 1990
This wine embodies the typical Schloss Westerhaus style: delicate, gently fruity with finely dosed residual sugar.

Chardonnay 1989　　　🍇 ①
A fine, barrique-aged Chardonnay classified as Tafelwein, more promising than its sometimes excellent predecessors.

Ingelheimer Schloss Westerhaus　🍷🍷 ④
Spätburgunder Rotwein
Trockenbeerenauslese 1989
A real rarity: dark amber in color with an aroma of honey, blackberry and candy, long on the palate finishing with a hint of coffee - a tremendous noble sweet wine.

Württemberg

Although Württemberg is in south-west Germany it belongs to the EEC Wine
Zone A, as do the northerly regions Mosel-Saar-Ruwer, Rheingau and
Rheinhessen, the reason being that its vineyards reach an altitude of up to 400
metres. The climate is cool, with an average annual temperature of 10°C as
against 10.5°C in neighbouring Baden. Württemberg wines are
correspondingly lighter and the sugar concentration in the grape juice seldom
matches that of Baden. However, this depends on where the grapes come
from, as Württemberg is a very varied region measuring 250 kilometres from
north to south. It stretches from the Tauber river near Bad Mergentheim to
Lake Constance (Bodensee) near Lindau. Soils and grape varieties differ
enormously, as do the wines. In the Remtal valley near Stuttgart, one of the
main Württemberg growing areas, the climate is warmer than around
Heilbronn, Württemberg's real wine-growing center which accounts for
approximately 80% of the region's production.
However, Württemberg differentiates itself from other wine-growing regions
by being a red wine producer, with over half its vineyard area planted with
red varieties. The main red grape is the Trollinger (22%), so-called because of
its Tyrolean origin and is a form of the South Tyrolean (Alto Adige)
Vernatsch or Schiava. The wine it produces is also called Trollinger and is a
kind of obligatory drink among the locals. This light red, easy-drinking wine
is usually consumed in fairly large quantities and Württemberg's per capita
wine consumption is double that of Germany's as a whole. The second most
widely grown variety is the Müllerrebe, also known as Schwarzriesling and
Pinot Meunier. It is a Pinot Noir mutation, though Pinot Noir itself is seldom
found in Württemberg. The third most common red is the Portugieser.
However, all three produce light, commercial wines which evoke little
enthusiasm outside Württemberg. The best reds come undoubtedly from the
Lemberger grape (known as Blaufränkisch in Austria and Franconia in Italy)
and Samtrot (a mutation of Müllerrebe) which make deep red wines with
noticeable tannin and fine fruit. They can easily stand up to Pinot Noirs from
other areas. An interesting specialty is Clevner (as Frühburgunder is known in
Württemberg) which also produces characterful red wines in spite of their
lightness and pale colour. It has won the hearts of numerous producers in
recent years.
The most widely grown vine is nevertheless Riesling which produces
concentrated wines, more vigorous than those of the Rhine and Mosel, even if
they seldom have the same finesse. Müller-Thurgau, Kerner and Silvaner
complete the white wine assortment while Traminer and Muskateller remain
specialities. 'Schillerwein' is an unusual product, being a rosé made by
blending red and white wine.

Weingut Graf Adelmann

Burg Schaubeck
Steinheim-Kleinbottwar 7141
Tel. (07148) 6665

Count Michael Adelmann is well known as an ambassador for Württemberg's wine culture. The region owes much to his commitment in numerous organizations and if it were not for him many things would not be as they are today. However, it is especially in his rôle as an exemplary wine producer that Count Adelmann has remained a reserved and diplomatic Swabian and visitors to his castle are struck by the noble residence's modest and unpretentious aura. Just like his wines, nothing in the whole style of the building is overdone even though everything is agreeably elegant. The clever wine diplomat Count Adelmann is helped in the same Swabian manner by his very energetic winemaker and administrator Peter Albrecht, and for years both have been guarantors for the quality of this famous and highly respected wine estate. Their wines traditionally bear the name 'Brüssele' on the labels, which goes back to the previous owner, and the name 'Brüssele'r Spitze' appears on the labels of their absolute top wines. Adelmann wines are usually regarded as the most elegant in Württemberg. Riesling is a classic, though Traminer and Muskateller are also excellent. Among reds, along with the superb Lemberger, old Württemberg varieties like Clevner (a mutation of Pinot Noir), Urban (a relative of Trollinger) and Samtrot (a mutation of Müllerrebe or Pinot Meunier) are also grown.

Brüssele Kleinbottwarer Oberer Berg 🍇 ②
Muskateller Kabinett trocken 1990
Very expressive and fresh in aroma, sinewy with firm acidity on the palate and a pleasant, strongly fruity aftertaste.

Brüssele'r Spitze Kleinbottwarer 🍇🍇 ③
Riesling Auslese trocken 1989
A Schaubeck classic: enormously generous and sweetly rich, brilliant elegance and finesse. So supple it seems an almost feminine Auslese.

Brüssele'r Spitze Kleinbottwarer 🍷🍷 ③
Lemberger Spätlese trocken 1990
It is difficult to find Lemberger of such elegance and complexity as this Spätlese: a spicy wine which is completely worthy of its 'Spitze' label.

Brüssele'r Spitze Kleinbottwarer 🍷 ③
Samtrot Spätlese trocken 1990
Typical Pinot Noir fruit, full with velvety tannin - a very characterful wine.

Weingut Robert Bauer

Heilbronner Strasse 56
Flein 7107
Tel. (07131) 51662
Fax (07131) 573288

Hardly any other Württemberg producer is talked about as much as Robert Bauer. The controversial loner from Flein has made many adversaries by his bold, uncompromising manner, though his fans are probably in the majority. The reason for this is simple. Bauer does not make wines to please consumers, he makes 'his' wines, and you either like them or you don't. The fact that his supporters are in the majority is proved by the fact that Bauer's wines are usually sold out within a year of being harvested. Those who are put off by Bauer's manner should bear in mind that it derives from his deep-rooted love for wine as a natural product. And Bauer's wines are natural products, in the true sense of the word: genuine and individual. All his wines are consistently dry, he scorns chaptalisation and tries to avoid fining and the use of chemicals. Bauer's wines reflect the nature of their maker; honest, uncompromising and self-assured. He also makes sparkling wines, high quality brandies and vinegar.

Fleiner Sonnenberg 🍇 ②
Riesling Qualitätswein trocken 1991
This Riesling is positively distinctive compared to others of the same variety from Flein: fresh acidity, bone dry and still harmonious.

Méthode Classic Blanc de Blancs 🍇 ③
Extra Brut 1990
Made exclusively from Chardonnay this sparkling wine is immensely rich, assertive and lightly yeasty on the finish. Even without dosage it reflects the richness and complexity of a very good wine.

Trollinger 🍷 ①
Tafelwein trocken 1991
A very unusual Trollinger, discreetly full with a fine tannic framework and exceptionally long. The only thing it has in common with normal wines made from this variety is its light red colour.

Weingut E Dautel

Lauerweg 55
Bönnigheim 7124
Tel. (07143) 21719
Fax (07143) 28537

Ernst Dautel is one of Württemberg's producers with the greatest zeal for experimentation. Each visit to his winery reveals new surprises in wine-making, wine-growing and pest and disease control methods. It is only natural that a 100% success rate is unlikely when trying out new methods, though Daniel makes some of the most interesting wines in his area called Unterland. Nevertheless he is cautious when it comes to innovations and he knows and cares for the roots and traditions of the region's wine-growing culture. His assortment ranges from barrique-aged Chardonnay through to Schillerwein, an old Württemberg specialty made by harvesting red and white grapes together. Dautel's wines always express the typicity of the vintage and region and are usually full with a strong acid backbone and good structure. The estate style has a certain honest rusticity about it, looked upon as typical for the district between Stromberg and Heuchelberg, though sadly this seems to be diminishing. They also make sparkling wine, various brandies and vinegar.

Chardonnay Tafelwein troken 1990 ❦ ③
One of Germany's very rare Chardonnays, though at the same time one of the best, perhaps the absolute best: supple in body, finely fruity, concentrated on the palate with very well dosed oak - a masterpiece.

Kreation Spätlese trocken 1990 ❦ ②
A cuvée of classic white grape varieties. A very rich wine with good aging potential. It is a mix of wines produced by very old vines and harvested with sugar levels in the upper Spätlese category.

Lemberger Tafelwein trocken 1989 ❦ ②
Light vanilla on the nose, a well-structured barrique wine which shows the sensitivity of the producer: not coarsely oaky, the wood is well integrated by succulent richness with velvety tannin and length.

Weingut Drautz-Able

Faiss Strasse 23
Heilbronn 7100
Tel. (07173) 77908
Fax (07173) 61876

Richard Drautz runs this family estate together with his sister Christel Able and is regarded as an innovative and courageous producer who is very tenacious once he has taken a decision. He was the first to produce estate bottled sparkling wine in 1978 and within the HADES group (an association of Württemberg producers who experiment with barriques) he produces excellent barrique aged wines. He is the region's only producer to obtain official permission to try out Sauvignon Blanc and achieves almost sensational results. In 1988 he first presented his Jodokus range. These are wines aged for over 20 months in barrique and not released until at least three years old. These superb wines can lead us to forget that the 'normal' range is also excellent, with good and strong acid structure and pure, clear varietal flavors.

Riesling Tafelwein trocken1990 ❦ ③
Those who assert that Riesling is not suitable for aging in barrique have not tasted this wine. It was harvested at almost 100° Oechsle and is so strong in varietal flavor that the oak has no chance of dominating.

Riesling Composition Extra Brut ❦ ③
A highly interesting sparkling wine, the base wines for which were partially vinified in barrique: an intense, fine mousse with a lightly bitter aroma.

Heilbronner Wartberg ❦ ②
Trollinger Spätlese trocken 1990
Only hand picked grapes with small berries were used for this Trollinger, harvested from almost 30 year old vines to produce a wine seldom encountered using this variety.

Jodokus ❦❦ ③
Dornfelder Tafelwein trocken 1990
Afer 22 months in barrique this wine was offered for sale in autumn 1992 for delivery late 1993. Never before was such a dense, concentrated wine produced in these parts.

Weingut Jürgen Ellwanger

Bach Strasse 21
Winterbach 7065
Tel. (07181) 44525

Even though the modest Swabian does not like hearing it, Jürgen Ellwanger is one of the rising stars among Württemberg's wine producers. The new sales and tasting rooms of this family wine estate and the modern interior design within the old walls show how this company has been able to break away from the accepted values of the region and set new standards. Today, Ellwanger makes wines of a class not seen for years in the upper Remstal valley. He has made a name for himself especially with barrique aged red wines which are among the best made in this style. The classic Rieslings and Spätburgunders (Pinot Noirs) made in a traditional manner are also among the region's most popular. Ellwanger's wines are distinguished by their intense, typically varietal fruit and are rich with a good acid framework. The barrique wines are concentrated, dense with well integrated, spicey oak.

Riesling Tafelwein trocken 1990 🍇 ②
Barrique aging has given this wine enormous richness plus an extra dimension, while the strong but still fresh acidity gives it firmness: a wine for laying down which will develop great complexity with bottle age.

Schnaiter Altenberg 🍇 ①
Riesling Spätlese trocken 1990
A concentrated Riesling with intense fruit of a kind unusual for this region. The firm acidity is well integrated and makes the wine appealingly elegant.

Zweigelt Tafelwein trocken 1990 🍇🍇 ③
The Austrian Zweigelt vine seems to feel very much at home in Remstal. This deep, concentrated wine has rare elegance and great complexity, spice and fruit, all perfectly interwoven with soft, mature tannin.

Güterverwaltung Burg Hornberg

Baron von Gemmingen-Hornberg
Neckarzimmern 6951
Tel. (06261) 5001
Fax (06261) 2348

The imposing castle Hornberg which towers high above Neckarzimmern and once the home of Götz von Berlichingen now houses one of the 'youngest' and at the same time oldest Württemberg wineries. Although the estate is in territory belonging to Baden, in character the wines are typical Württemberg products, for which reason the company became part of the latter wine-growing region in 1986. Vineyards have occupied the steep, terraced slopes with calcareous soils and nine kilometers of terraced walls for over 700 years. The two single sites (Götzhalde and Wallmauer) are owned entirely by the estate but are no longer featured on the labels, which now only bear the estate name 'Burg Hornberger.' The white wines bear the strong imprint of the vineyard site which yields delicate and elegant wines. Due to the soils the reds tend to be light-weight but with clear varietal characteristics. Sparkling wines made from Pinot Blanc, Schwarzriesling (Pinot Meunier) and Pinot Noir are also in production.

Riesling Spätlese trocken 1990 🍇 ②
A surprisingly full, well structured wine. The ripe acidity is well interwoven into the wine's rich texture - very powerful for a wine grown on friable calcareous soils.

Weissburgunder 🍇 ③
Auslese trocken 1990
The typical varietal flavor is not masked by oak and the supple fullness is supported by a spicey background deriving from barrique ageing. Long and promising.

Muskateller Kabinett trocken 1987 🍇 ②
A speciality of this estate, light weight but elegant: a delicious, low alcohol aperitif.

Samtrot Kabinett trocken 1990 🍇 ②
A rare mutation of the Schwarzriesling (Pinot Meunier) vine: very full fruit reminiscent of Pinot Noir, medium weight with good acidity.

Weingärtnergenossenschaft Grantschen

Wimmentaler Strasse 9
Weinsberg-Grantschen 7102
Tel. (07134) 3856
Fax (07134) 980222

The 165 members have good reason to be proud of their Grantschen cooperative as the quality of their wines is in no way inferior to that of private estates. By starting to produce excellent dry Lemberger and Riesling in 1986 which were marketed as a special series with a black label they secured for themselves a place in the quality wine sector of the market which no other cooperative in the region has been able to enter. Their next coup was the red wine cuvée SM in 1988 and finally barrique aged Grandor in 1989 which is seen as a new flagship among Württemberg's red wines. The creators of these successes are managing director Bruno Bolsinger and winemaker Fritz Herold. The greatest achievement of these two innovators has been their ability to transfer their quality-mindedness to the members. Their wines shine by their harmony and the finely tuned balance of all their components.

Grantschener Riesling Spätlese trocken 1990

This wine is almost over-embellished with richness and concentration without appearing fat and clumsy. The well interwoven acidity gives it suppleness.

Grantschener Lemberger Spätlese trocken 1990

An exemplary Lemberger: intense aromas with an underlying hint of oak, well structured, harmonious and long.

Grandor Rotwein QbA trocken 1989

A cuvée of Lemberger and Dornfelder with intense fruit (morello cherry and plum) and pleasantly full. It will probably improve considerably with bottle age.

SM Rotwein QbA trocken 1989

When did a cooperative ever make a wine of this stature? In spite of 11 months in Swabian oak barriques this cuvée of Lemberger and Dornfelder has fruit and richness of such concentration that it has set new standards for Württemberg.

Weinbau Karl Haidle

Hindenburg Strasse 21
Kernen-Stetten 7053
Tel. 07151/42503

The name Haidle is a symbol for quality wine in Remstal like no other. With great regularity this family estate consistently produces wines which show what can be achieved in the region. Nevertheless, Hans Haidle, the present owner, is still not the kind of person to rest on his laurels. For example, although he has become famous as a white wine specialist, recently he has produced more and more superb reds. In true Swabian style he concentrates on constantly improving the quality of his wines rather than boasting and making a noise about them for marketing purposes. The estate's wines are strong in character without being obtrusive. They are clearly structured and their regional identity does not get lost even among high ranking wines. Each of Haidle's wines has character and at the same time bears the producer's fingerprints.

Stettener Pulvermächer Riesling Auslese 1989

This is a rich wine and at the same time classy, supple and racy, mature and clearly expresses the characteristics imparted by the site: one of Württemberg's greatest white wines.

Schnaiter Burghalde Spätburgunder Auslese trocken 1990

Deep and intense purple red with a typical Burgundian aroma, lightly toasty with perfectly integrated acidity, rich but well structured - a small sensation from Remstal.

Stettener Mönchberg Trollinger Kabinett trocken 1990

A fruity-spicey Trollinger which offers plenty of flavor with little alcohol: a very respectable wine.

Württembergische Hofkammer-Kellerei

Schloss Monrepos
Ludwigsberg 7140
Tel. (07141) 31086
Fax (07141) 38385

With 42 ha the Württemberger Hofkammer is the region's largest private wine estate. They are exclusive owners of several of Württemberg's best sites and the winery is highly modern and spacious, while the wines enjoy an excellent reputation far beyond the region's borders. Thus the prerequisites for producing excellent quality seem to be perfect. Sadly though the wines do not live up to their reputation at present, lacking personality, character and balance. The aroma of the whites is often rather fleeting, while the reds are a little loose and short. Wines from chalky marl sites (especially Untertürkheimer Mönchberg) have an unpleasant earthy character. One can only hope that the new generation at this estate will succeed in getting things on the right course and that the Hofkammer's enormous potential will be better exploited.

Maulbronner Eilfingerberg ♆ ②
Klosterstück Riesling Kabinett trocken 1990
The Klosterstück Riesling is still this estate's best white, though it is hardly a great wine. Lightly exotic on the nose reminiscent of citrus fruits, medium weight but well structured.

Stettener Brotwasser ♆ ①
Riesling Auslese trocken 1990
In Remstal's best site 1990 produced a full flavored Auslese with smooth acidity, still restrained and a little vegetal. A rather rustic wine.

Weingut Fürst zu Hohenlose-Oehringen

Im Schloss
Öhringen 7110
Tel. (07941) 609930
Fax (07941) 37349

Even though the most easterly point of the Unterland part of Württemberg is a little off the beaten track there is a famous vineyard there called Verrenberg. The wines from the site Verrenberger Verrenberg which is owned exclusively by this estate are the most widely found Württemberg wines on German and international wine lists. This achievement is completely due to persistent quality oriented work and the guarantor for this is without doubt the administrator and winemaker Siegfried Röll. His perseverence has definitely earned him the title, shared with very few others, of 'one of the great names' on the Württemberg wine scene. His main achievement is the continuation of this hard and consistent work, and the attitude that recognition does not mean renouncing progress. His dynamism becomes evident time and time again in innovative steps such as making wines in barrique, planting Chardonnay - a relatively new variety in the region - plus making a very successful red wine cuvée. The Öhringen vineyards are on the edge of Verrenberg on mainly heavy coloured marl soils on a south-facing slope. The wines are definitely the region's most characterful.

Verrenberger Verrenberg ♆ ②
Riesling Kabinett trocken 1990
This wine already shows the typical characteristics of the estate and region: fresh and vegetal on the nose, lightly bitter with earthy fruit and strong acidity.

Verrenberger Verrenberg 🍇 ②
Lemberger QbA trocken 1991
A very good achievement in this difficult vintage. The accentuated acid-tannin structure gives the wine spice and length.

Verrenberger Verrenberg 🍇 ③
Samtrot Spätlese trocken 1990
This wine unites character and fruity charm in a rarely found way. Deep and finely fruity in aroma, on the palate it is powerfully spicey, cleanly structured with good length.

Cuvée Ex Flammis Orior 🍇🍇 ③
Tafelwein trocken 1989
A finely tuned cuvée of classic red varieties and the barrique character adds an extra dimension: complexity on the nose, fullness on the palate with sweet richness and soft tannins are its distinguishing features.

Schlosskellerei Graf von Neipperg

Im Schloss
Schwaigern 7103
Tel. 07138/5081
Fax 07138/4007

This traditional estate in the heart of Heuchelberg has always been regarded as one of the region's leading wine producers, which makes the enormous improvement in quality over the past few years even more surprising. The Schwaigern estate was long regarded as a red wine specialist (a certain Count Neipperg was the first to introduce Lemberger into the region) until in 1987 the young winemaker Elmar Kalchschmitt showed the quality potential of their white wines. Today the famous Lemberger and Rieslings are their standard-bearers. However, this success is also the result of numerous factors, including the exemplary vineyard management and very intelligent company policy of owner Karl Eugen Erbgraf zu Neipperg. The 1988, 1989 and 1990 wines show by the consistently high quality level that this is one of the absolute best estates in Württemberg. Wines from the very unfavourable 1991 growing season will confirm this.

Neipperger Schlossberg ℗ ②
Muskateller Kabinett trocken 1990
A Muscat with an acid backbone, extraordinary structure and a fine bouquet of blossoms.

Neipperger Schlossberg ℗ ①
Riesling Kabinett trocken 1990
An unusually rich Riesling with strong but ripe acidity and still elegant in spite of its intense fruit.

Neipperger Schlossberg ℗ ℗ ③
Riesling Spätlese trocken 1990
Schlossberg Spätlese is one of the absolute best Rieslings in all Württemberg with concentration, richness, great elegance and complexity.

Neipperger Schlossberg ℗ ②
Schwarzriesling Kabinett trocken 1990
A light-weight red wine but fruity and pleasant to drink, a specialty of the estate.

Schwaigener Ruthe ℗ ℗ ③
Lemberger Spätlese trocken 1990
Definitely one of their really great red wines made in a classic style, well structured, dense and a complex, intense blackberry aroma plus plenty of power and spice.

Staatliche Lehr- und Versuchsanstalt für Wein- und Obstbau

Traubenplatz 5
Weinsberg 7102
Tel. 07134/50467
Fax 07134/50433

The viticultural school at Weinsberg is the oldest teaching and experimental institution in Germany and was founded in 1868 by Karl von Württemberg as a royal viticultural school. It is therefore only right to regard it as the home of Württemberg's wine culture. Generations of wine producers learned their trade here and many of the successful widely diffused new crossings (like Kerner and Dornfelder) are children of the institute's research activities. The director of the school Dr. Gerhard Götz is regarded as one of the leading figures in his sector both at home and abroad. However, the wines from the insitute's 53 ha of vineyard have also contributed to its reputation, under the direction of winemaker Gerhard Wächter. They are typical Württemberg wines, harmonious and round with mild acidity and usually ready for drinking at an early age. The large extent of the vineyard area in five districts of Unterland make the viticultural school the largest estate in Württemberg and it is the exclusive owner of the famous site Abstatter Burg Wildeck.

Grauburgunder ℗ ③
Tafelwein trocken 1989
In spite of barrique aging this Pinot Gris has preserved its accentuated varietal character: lightly toasty, rich in body and supple.

Weinsberger Schemelberg
Lemberger QbA trocken 1991
A richly fruity, cleanly-structured Lemberger with a very accentuated varietal flavor reminiscent of blackberry.

GREAT BRITAIN

England, together with Wales, is the most northerly wine-producing nation in the world, most of her 800 or so hectares of vineyard lying between 50.40° and 52.40° north of the equator. Indeed, the world's northernmost vineyard is in England, near the city of Durham.

Three factors make this unlikely scenario possible. The first is the Gulf Stream, which keeps Britain warmer than many areas further south. The second is the English autumn, which tends to be relatively extended compared with countries having a continental climate. The third is the development, over the past few years, notably in Germany, of grape varieties (crossings) which are capable of giving good fruit quality even at relatively low mean temperatures. These include Müller Thurgau (the most widely planted variety), Reichensteiner, Bacchus, Schonburger, Huxelrebe and Kerner. Other varieties able to succeed in these unlikely conditions are the hybrids Seyval Blanc and Madeleine Angevine. A few French varieties, mainly of the Pinot family, are also attempted, generally with less success.

Wine-grape growing in England is both new and not so new. There is evidence that it flourished in Roman times, 2000 years ago, and in the period following the Norman invasion. On both occasions it died out, to be reinstated in the mid-20th century by Sir Guy Salisbury-Jones at Hambledon in Hampshire.

Today, there are some 400 vineyards in England and South Wales. Most of them are in Kent and Sussex, towards the south-east, but they are dotted over most of the southern half of the country. The average annual production is 1,500,000 liters, which seems very modest, but quality and quantity are improving all the time. The prime character of English wine is fragrance of bouquet and crispness of acidity. The main faults tend to be excessive acidity and lack of body.

All English wines are Table Wines by EC standards, but the best of them recieve the EVA (English Viticultural Association) Seal of Quality, to obtain which the wine has to undergo quite stringent tests. Moves are underway at present to organise an EC approved Quality Wine designation for English wines.

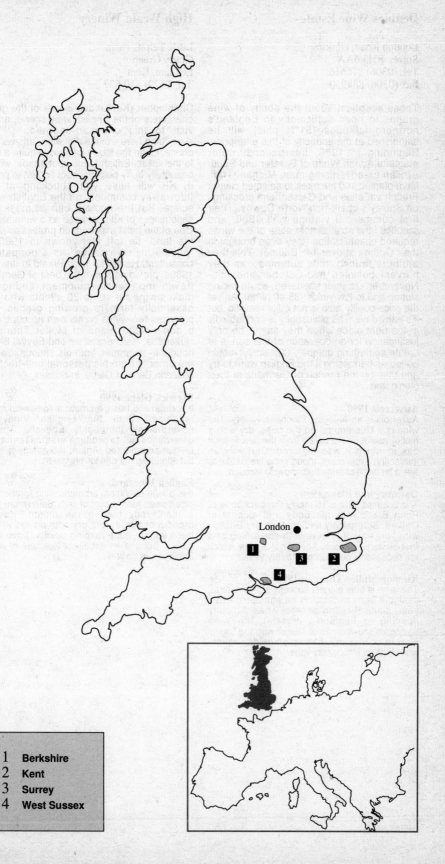

London

1 Berkshire
2 Kent
3 Surrey
4 West Sussex

Denbies Wine Estate

London Road, Dorking
Surrey RH5 6AA
Tel. (0306) 876616
Fax (0306) 888930

Those sceptical about the ability of wine grapes to ripen sufficiently in England's northern latitudes (51°N plus) will be astonished at the audacity of this enterprise. Beginning in 1986, international water magnate Adrian White of Biwater and South African ex-advertising man, Michael Trull, have planted 100 hectares to selected classic French varieties and Geisenheim crossings on Surrey's chalk-rich North Downs. Their first commercial vintage was 1990, and sceptics take note, almost none of the wines required chaptalization (they even brought in their Optima at over 14° Baumé). This they attribute to long, mild autumns - as they harvest between mid-October and mid-November - to their sheltered, south-facing slopes and to low yields (35-40 hl/ha). As yet the price-quality ratio is not quite realistic, but it's early days. The philosophy is undoubtedly in the right place when they say: "The only justification for an operation of this sort is to create something unique". Certainly it would be too embarrassing if the English were to try and take on the French or Germans at their own game.

Auxerrois 1990   ❀ ②
Auxerrois is an Alsatian, Pinot-like variety. The wine is a little neutral on the nose, dry with a hint of vanilla on the palate from the new French oak in which it was matured. Certainly an interesting experiment, though one would like to see a bit more creamy fruit showing through.

Optima/Pinot Blanc 1990   ❀❀ ②
The attempt here is to marry the backbone of Pinot Blanc with the body and alcohol of Optima. Surprisingly mellow for a dry English wine, creamy of texture with something of a fruit-custardy flavour. Again, not a wine which will necessarily be attempted every year.

Riesling/Müller Thurgau 1990   ❀❀ ②
This wine is their biggest success of the vintage, though it won't necessarily be attempted every year, since Riesling generally has difficulty ripening in England's climate. The wine combines the aromas of Müller with the steely finesse of Riesling, having an acidity which, while high, is structurally valid.

High Weald Winery

Little Telpits Farm
Gratty Green
Lenham, Kent
Tel (0622) 850 637

Christopher (Kit) Lindlar is one of the great characters of the English wine scene, and a visit to this one-man-operation ("I do everything here - make the wine, answer the phone, clean the loos") can prove quite a fillip to the spirits. British to his boot-straps, with a beautifully fruity public school accent to prove it, Kit will have you chuckling at his throwaway comments on the English wine scene. But the humour cannot mask the seriousness of Kit's purpose as a winemaker. One of the most experienced professionals in the land, he left Merrydown in 1980 to "paddle his own canoe" as a peripatetic consultant. He set up High Weald in the late 1980s, providing it with the best of German, Italian and French equipment, and today makes wine for some 30 clients who are essentially farmers growing grapes. He produces two wines on his own account: one a non-vintage blend of Müller Thurgau, Huxelrebe, Reichensteiner and Seyval Blanc bought in as grapes from his various clients; the other is from his personal one-hectare estate in Berwick Glebe, in Sussex.

Berwick Glebe 1990   ❀ ①
It is clean and fresh, aromatic if somewhat more restrained than the English Vineyard, nevertheless thoroughly English. "I was determined not to produce ersatz Germans," Lindlar commented. Again, the acidity is high but somehow not offensively green.

English Vineyard   ❀❀ ①
It is a high-definition, aromatic wine (grapefruit, elderflower, reminiscent of catty Sauvignon) with a lean, racy feel in the mouth. Having pronounced fruit, it is dry with an extremely fresh yet not quite rasping acidity. Love it or hate it, but it is an excellent example of what England can do well.

Lamberhurst Vineyards

Ridge Farm
Lamberhurst, Tunbridge Wells
Kent TN3 8ER
Tel. (0892) 890286

Though founded in 1982, Lamberhurst is still the best known if no longer the biggest vineyard in England. This may in part be due to the fact that their winery processes not only the grapes of their own vineyard (presently 22 hectares, planted mainly to German crossings), but also, under their own label, those of a further 40 ha contracted to them, plus those of various growers whose wine they bottle under the producers' labels. It also stems no doubt from their skills in marketing and catering to the tourist trade, operations which are financed by the megabucks of owner Kenneth McAlpine. The present winemaker, Stephen Donnolly, a Northumbrian trained in California, seems to have a good grasp of the problems and opportunities which confront him. The biggest problems consist in a north-facing vineyard and a heavy moisture-retentive soil, not attributes one would consider ideal in England where you need all the help you can get. The opportunites consist in demonstrating you can overcome the difficulties with skillful winemaking. Although he only had total control from the appalling 1991 harvest, the results of Donnolly's improvements are beginning to show.

Bacchus 1991 ❦ ❦ ②
Bacchus has good aroma and is quite rich with a variety of fruit salad flavours, enhanced by 19 grams residual sugar (by stopped fermentation). High acidity gives it a fresh, clean finish. A good "marriage", to use Donnolly's own word.

Müller Thurgau Dry 1990 ❦ ②
With a bit of Huxelrebe blended in, it belies its 10 g/lt acidity with a fairly full, slightly aromatic, fruity palate, helped along a bit by 9 grams of residual sugar. Here Donnolly seems to have got the balance just right. A very drinkable quaffer.

Schönburger 1990 ❦ ②
It has an agreeable aroma reminiscent of lychees. Here the residual sugar (süss reserve) is a bit high, but the wine finishes very clean with good follow-through. A wine of some character despite being somewhat tailored for the mass market.

Nutbourne Vineyards

Nutbourne Manor
Pulborough
West Sussex
Tel/Fax (071) 720 6249

This seven and a half hectare vineyard began life in 1981 as a hobby of the then owner, who thought it might be picturesque to have a few vines surrounding his fine Georgian Manor, with its windmill and trout lakes. The idea was not ill-conceived. The site is on south-facing, chalky slopes, protected from violent sea winds by the nearby South Downs. It has the advantage of regular light breezes, to minimize rot, soil with good drainage ideal for the production of aromatic grapes, and as much warmth as you are likely to find anywhere in the world at 51°N latitude. In 1991 the property was purchased by Peter Gladwin, owner of a successful catering business, and it is now receiving the extra impetus that new brooms are famous for sweeping in with. Not that things were not already going largely in the right direction. With David Shaw as vineyard manager since 1983, and Kit Lindlar as winemaker (the grapes are transported to his High Weald winery at vintage time), Nutbourne had already made a mark for itself with the sheer Englishness of its product. On the basis of our tasting, the ingredients appear to be all there and the party is about to begin.

Sussex Reserve 1990 ❦ ❦ ③
It is a newly released blend of Bacchus, Huxelrebe and Reichensteiner. In fact, the wine is an excellent expression of what is best in English wine, having aroma (catty, gooseberry, elderflower), reasonable body and good balance.

Bacchus 1989 ❦ ②
Another German crossing, having in English conditions, a pronounced floral-catty bouquet, which some say comes more from unique grapes than from grape character. This wine has the cattiness but combined with a certain creaminess of texture and good length.

Huxelrebe 1989 ❦ ④
This is Nutbourne's most expensive wine, though the 1989 fails to prove why. Aromas are good but not exceptional. Huxelrebe, one of Germany's more popular crossings (from Chasselas and Cortillier Musque - hence the Muscat scent) is reputed to be England's answer to Sauvignon; not on this evidence.

Müller Thurgau 1989 ❦ ②
Müller Thurgau is the most planted variety in Britain, managing to ripen most years without too much catty aroma. This wine is a little restrained, the aroma being hinted at rather than clearly stated on the back palate. One for drinking rather, perhaps, than for admiring.

Schönburger 1989 ❦ ②
Schönburger is a Geisenheim crossing, having considerably more success in England than in Germany. This wine has plenty of aroma- too much for some, who think it is hydrogen sulphide (it is not). The palate is quite full, nicely balanced between fruit and acidity, good length.

Thames Valley Vineyard

Stanlake Park
Twyford
Berkshire RG10 OBN
Tel. (0734) 340176
Fax (0734) 320914

In 1979, Jon Leighton returned to his family
estate from Australia, determined to establish
his own vineyard. The first hectare was
planted in 1980, the present count being 10
with a further two and a half to come
(production in 1991 was 90 tons). In the late
1980s he recruited Australian-Ukrainian
winemaker John Worontschak, transformed
his stables into a well equipped winery, signed
up other grape-growers to supply half his
needs (the aim is 500,000 bottles by 1993)
and earned a reputation as one of England's
best, most forward-thinking wine-producers.
While having upwards of 18 varieties in the
vineyards (French, German and hybrid),
Leighton and Worontschak believe that
weather conditions in England are too variable
to make varietal wines except in top years.
The blended wines sell under the Valley
Vineyards label, varietals and top wines as
The Clocktower Selection. Emphasis is given
to fermentation characteristics (yeastiness,
oakiness, absence of H2S and green acidity)
rather than to the primary, sometimes
aggressive fruit and floral aromas typical of
England. Worontschak and Leighton agree
that the aim is to compete in a world market
and not to concentrate on local peculiarities.

Botrytis Clocktower   🍇🍇 ③
Selection 1990
A blend of Scheurebe, Siegerebe, Ehrenfelser
and Kerner, this unashamedly sweet wine, picked
at 13.8° Baumé (botrytised grapes), has all the
style and class of a German Beerenauslese,
being luscious and complex, with firm acidity
providing a clean finish of some length.

Fume 1990   🍇🍇 ②
A dry white wine international-style, this blend of
Seyval Blanc, Scheurebe and Madeleine
Angevine (no Sauvignon), fermented in new
Limousin oak casks, is a touch herbaceous on
the nose, (from the fermentation and the oak)
with a slightly toasty, leesy palate. The acidity is
fresh rather than aggressive.

Regatta 1990   🍇 ①
Made from the German crossing, Bacchus, this is
an attempt to produce a wine of varietal
character, fresh and fragrant, without the
dimension of wood. Clean if somewhat neutral on
the nose, bone dry, almost flinty on the palate,
one recognises the validity of the wine but would
like to see a touch more aromatic character.

Sweet Lee 1990   🍇 ①
A medium-dry white produced from a blend of
Schönburger, Siegerebe, Kerner, Wurtzer and
Gewürztraminer with the popular market in
mind. There is a grassy, aromatic nose, less
sweetness than the name suggests, thanks to
firm acidity on the finish. A well-balanced,
attractive and very English wine.

Key to the symbols

Types of Wines

🍇 White

🌸 Rosé

🍷 Red

Rating System

🍇   An exemplary wine of its
type with outstanding local
character

🌸🍇   An international premium
quality wine

🍷🍷🍇   A Top Wine, considered one
of the 150 best wines in the
world

*The 'grape bunch' symbol is used to
indicate the color of the wine; the
number of bunches represents the quality
rating assigned by the contributor*

Price levels

①   up to $ 9.99

② $ 10.00 - $ 14.99

③ $ 15.00 - $ 24.99

④ $ 25.00 or more

*The 'ex-cellar', or direct from the
producer, bottle prices, are calculated in
US dollars and are intended only as an
approximate guide*

**Entries are arranged in
alphabetical order by country,
region and winery or producer
name.**

GREECE

There is a dynamism about the Greek wine industry today that reminds one of Italy 20 years ago. Greece today has only recently begun hauling herself back from a long dark age in terms of standards and interest in quality. This darkness lasted many centuries began with the Ottoman occupation, or even before. The first step was establishing an Appellation of Origin system (from 1969 on) which links quality grape varieties with particular geographical zones. Today there are eight Controlled Appellations of Origin (the highest qualification, reserved so far for vins de liqueur like Samos and Mavrodaphne of Patros) and 20 or so AO of Superior Quality (such as Naoussa, Nemea, Santorini). The plan is to expand on this base and to develop also a Topikos Oinos, or Country Wines system, similar to France's Vins de Pays.

Half of Greece's 186,000 ha of vines are devoted to wine grapes and half for table and raisin grapes. The most important wine types are red, the principal ones being Agiorgitiko (the grapes of Nemea, generally considered Greece's finest), Xinomavro (Naoussa et al), Mavrodaphne and Limnio. Interesting white varieties include the Assyrtiko of Santorini, Saviatano (base of many resinated wines and the odd quality white, Kantza), the Robola of Cephalonia, the ubiquitous Moscato and the nearly extinct Malagousia being revived at Château Carras. Roditis is a red used for both white (Patras) and light red wines, often resinated. All are of Hellenic origin (in some cases of great antiquity) and remain virtually exclusive to Greece, a major factor in its potential in this era of universal standardisation.

Inevitably, Cabernet & Co. have infiltrated here, too, and with impact indeed. The small estate remains a rare phenomenon. Production is dominated by cooperatives or by large private concerns buying in grapes or wine from co-ops, or from contracted farmers in various parts. But, as the economy improves and demand for quality grows, it is not difficult to envisage a 21st century market blossoming with all kinds of characterful, individual wines of the type that proliferate today in the Italian market across the Ionian Sea. The vine flourishes everywhere, from the islands to the mainland, from sea-level to 1000 m, from south to north. The further north, the less likely the vineyards are to have roots in antiquity. The best are newly planted in line with the cool climate philosophy of other emerging wine-lands of sunny disposition; the best soils are rocky and/or chalky, with marly chalk or friable tufa subsoils. Specialised vineyards are taking over from those in mixed cultivation, but still many linger amongst the olives and tomatoes for home drinking.

In 1990 Greece turned out about 3.5 million hl, which is less than Hungary, Yugoslavia or Romania. Consumption is on the same level. To date little is exported, not only because of the mediocre quality which has prevailed. Until recently, one suspects, non-Greeks have had difficulty in disassociating the concepts of Greek wine and resination. Made in the same way as any other wine, with added pine resin during fermentation, resinated wine is almost as old as wine itself. Very tasty in the right circumstances, with the right foods, it has undeniably caused Greek producers image problems, however. The will and enthusiasm are there and it is only a matter of time before Greece resumes its rightful place among serious wine-producers.

BULGARIA

EX YUGOSLAVIA

TURKEY

ALBANIA

Thessalonica

4

4

TURKEY

2

Pátrai

Mantigna

Athens

1

5

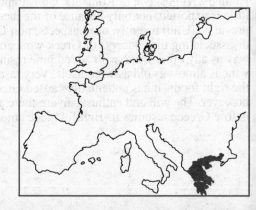

1 **Arcadia**
2 **Attica**
3 **Crete**
4 **Macedonia**
5 **Samos**

Achaia Clauss

P.O. Box 51176
Athinon, Lamais National Rd.
14510 Kifissia, Athens
Tel. (1) 8075312-1
Fax (1) 8077983

Anyone who has ever holidayed in Greece will know the name Achaia Clauss, especially in connection with the brand Demestica (red and white table wine, blends of no particular origin, the first Greek wine to be bottled in 1901) and with Mavrodaphne of Patras and Muscat de Patras, liqueur wines dating back to 1873. This is the oldest winery in Greece, founded in 1861 by the Bavarian expatriot Gustav Clauss. Today the winery is in Greek hands (chairman Achilles Nerotsopoulos owns 51% of the shares) and the main offices are in Athens, but the center of production, as ever, is the huge winery at Patras, northern Peloponnese. Achaia Clauss do own extensive vineyards in the Patras area, but the bulk of their production comes from grapes bought in under contract. Production is in the region of 1.8 million cases annually of which about half is exported to 37 different countries. Presently, the main thrust of their marketing is behind the newly repackaged Appellation d'Origine wines as exemplified by Patras and Mantinia white and Nemea red.They still, however, regard Muscat de Patras as their most prized wine.

Patras 1991 AO
Dry white wine from the Roditis grape, grown at altitude (200-450 m) on the northern slopes of Mount Panachaikon. The wine has a pale straw color and a clean bouquet as of fresh laundry. Creamy, salty-savoury flavours blend with a brisk, almost lemony acidity to achieve an interesting combination of the traditional (hot-climate viticulture) and the modern (thermo-controlled vinification in reductive conditions).

Muscat de Patras AO
Non-vintage vin de liqueur from Muscat grapes grown in the Patras region. This has a palish amber color, a flowery-muscat aroma of no great intensity, perfumed fruit flavors (peaches, dried apricots) and a quite viscous, spirity feel in the mouth. It is very sweet but has reasonable balancing acidity. Needs to be drunk very chilled, in considerable moderation.

Nemea 1988 AO
Dry red wine from the Agiorgitiko grape grown between 300 and 650 m, aged in oak. A wine of intense, surprisingly light ruby hue. There's a whiff of fresh raspberries on the nose and bright, penetrating fruit on the palate.Very supple, with almost no tannin and a fresh acidity. A clean, modern red for summer drinking, scarcely needs food.

Athanase Parparoussis

26500 Patras
Tel. (061) 420334
Fax (061) 420334

The Athanase Parparoussis winery is located in a picture perfect scenario, among the vineyards on the outskirts of Patras. Athanase is undoubtedly one of Greece's foremost producers, having studied oenology at the University of Dijon. Stubborn and determined, he has expanded to eight hectares of vineyards and buys the rest of the grapes needed from local growers with his same quality standard. 80% of his wines are whites, harvested early to ensure a better, crisper acidity. The same goes for the reds, and their natural freshness. The wine ages in stainless-steel vats and goes through as few manipulations as possible in the cellar. One trick that he does use, however, to enhance the acidity backbone, is to use the native Sideritis grape. This is one of the winery's most prized grapes, with two selections made at harvest. In fact, the smaller late-harvested grapes left behind go into the cuvée used to make Dionysos. The Acquavite that he has been making for several years now is also worthy of note.

Dorssalis Patras 1990 AO
A clear, white wine made from the red Rhoditis grape, its aroma is mature but not too much and its bouquet has a faint nuance of tea. On the palate, it is robust, spicy and has refreshing acidity.

Dora tou Dionysou Patras AO
Generally speaking, there are not too many noticeable differences between the vintages of his whites. This is no exception. The Dora usually has an anice nose and is surprisingly lively in freshness and lingering on the palate.

Inari Nemea AO
The grapes to make this wine are bought entirely from Parparoussis in Nemea. Somehow every year he manages to make a wine that is supple, possibly a bit too spritzy, full and with a pleasant bouquet of fresh fruit.

Averof, Metsovo

Karkavitsastr. 12
15452 Paläs Pyckiko-Athens
Tel. (647) 2768-3642117
Fax (647) 3336

Former head of the Neo-Demokratia political party, Evangelos Averof died in 1990 but had been committed to the vine ever since 1961. He began by planting Cabernet Sauvignon and Merlot near the village of Metsovo on the Epiro river. The wooded site at 100 meters above sea level had to be cleared costing him much more than the land itself. He wanted to "make top wines that could demand top dollar," as he gruffed. Without a doubt he has succeeded according to Greek standards at least. Originally, only 2,000 square meters of vineyards were farmed. Gradually that has extended to eight hectares. Grapes are also bought from outside but only under the family's strict quality standards. The wines are sold in restaurants and wine bars in Athens and gradually the family intend testing the waters of the export market. The winery has built somewhat of a reputation for itself, coming in 7th at the major wine show held in Paris in the late 1970s.

Kathogi 1987

Inarguably very good; the maker himself, Averof, has compared this wine to a Médoc. It was aged for a long time (at least two and a half years) in wooden casks. It has a fruity bouquet with hints of wild fruit and of wood. It has an elegant full-body, with some aggressive young tannins.

J. Boutari & Son

6 Aristoteles
54623 Thessaloniki
Tel. (31) 281103
Fax (31) 271606

One of the giants of Greek wine production Boutari has been a family concern for over five generations, since its inception in 1879. They own eight wineries in various parts of Greece the two main ones being at Naoussa in Macedonia in northern Greece, and at Pikerin Attika in central Greece, where all the bottling is done. The wines themselves are made locally, both from grapes of their own vineyards and from fruit bought in under contract. Thei total annual production is about three million cases, of which Lac des Rocs, Greece's most popular white wine (100% from the Savatiano grape grown in various parts of central Greece) accounts for nearly one third. Their philosophy has always been to concentrate on native wines and varieties, though inevitably they too are experimenting with French grapes. They try to stay within Greek appellation parameters as much as possible, maintaining that the best wines come from Greek varieties. They are also equally keen to escape the stereotype of Greek wine (resinated and/or oxidised), using modern technology to achieve well-made, fruity reds and characterful whites.

Kretikos Topikos Oinos 1991

A dry white wine mainly from the native Cretan Vilana grape, this has a hot, slightly pungent nose, with a hint of oranges. Good acidity and extract give it freshness and easy drinkability. It successfully combines originality of character and the cleanness and purity which come from modern vinification.

Santorini 1991 AO

A dry white 12° alc wine entirely from the Assyrtiko grape, one of the world's rarest white grape varieties, grown almost exclusively on this volcanic island, linked by some with Plato's Atlantis. It is, indeed, unusually characterful, having a full, almost salty-savoury style with plenty of body and fresh, fleshy acidity. Not unlike good white Rhône or Piemontese Arneis.

Naoussa 1990 AO

A full-bodied, dry red wine, from 100% Xinomavro grown on the slopes of Mount Vermion in north-west Macedonia and aged one year in oak. Of a deepish ruby color, it has a warm rich bouquet and full, quite muscular fruit, being tannic and robust. Despite a slightly bitter finish it has a certain finesse and character. Needs the right food, like meat, even game or cheese.

Nemea 1990 AO

A medium-bodied dry red wine made from the Agiorgitiki grape in north-eastern Peloponnese, near Corinth. This wine displays a deepish purply-ruby color, a spicy aroma (touch of cinnamon) and a spicy-fruity palate, fairly soft tannins and medium acidity. A rare combination of individual character, technical know-how and drinkability.

Cambas

Kantza-Pallini
10210 Athens
Tel. (1) 6659942
Fax (1) 6658424

This establishment began life as a distillery for the production of brandy. The name derives from that of the founder, Andrew P. Cambas, who beginning in 1882, bought large tracts of land in the Kantza and Yalou regions of Attica, 16 kilometers south-east of Athens, to supply the distillery's needs. With all those grapes (mainly Savatiano) it was inevitable that the company would become involved in winemaking, beginning with Retsina and graduating via dry white, rosé and red wines to more sophisticated levels. Eventually, Kantza even became an Appellation of Origin, principally if not entirely thanks to the prestigious presence of Cambas. The firm, recently purchased from the National Bank of Greece by the Boutari group, also owns extensive vineyards in that part of the Peloponnese known as Arcadia, specifically at Mantinia, known for its delicate, slightly scented, eponymous dry white (also an AOC) from the Moskofilero grape. Indeed, Cambas are the major producers of this wine which unfortunately we did not get to taste. Better luck next year.

Nemea Lion de Nemea 1988 AO   ♥ ①
This dry red wine of the noble Agiorgitiko grape, produced and bottled by Cambas, with its warm, spicy fruit and middle body, its touch of astringency and suggestion of strength (though only 11.5° alc) could put one in mind of a better-than-average Côtes du Rhône. As Cambas' flagship red, however, one feels it ought to be better.

Kantza Château Cambas 1988 AO   ♥ ②
Cambas are more or less the sole producers of this appellation wine (11.5° alc, from the Savatiano grape). However, one cannot help thinking that they should be able to achieve something more than this wine with its neutral bouquet and uneventful palate, clean and fresh as it may be. A touch of interest from a hint of liquorice on the finish, but it's not enough.

Château Carras

Sithonia
63081 Halkidiki
Tel. (0375) 71380
Fax (0375) 71229

Château Carras, Europe's largest privately owned wine estate (385 hectares under vine), was created by the late John Carras who purchased the land in the Sithonian peninsula in Macedonia, northern Greece, in 1963. In 1967 oenologist Emile Peynaud of Bordeaux was called in as consultant and the first experimental vineyards were planted on Mount Meliton, a superb site looming over the sea at Porto Carras (a tourist complex also created by John Carras). By the mid-1970s, under the tutelage of winemaker Evangelos Gerovassiliou, a student of Peynaud's at Bordeaux University, the now famous Château Carras red was on the market and attracting favorable comment. Grape varieties planted on the rolling slopes of Mount Meliton include, for the reds, Cabernet Sauvignon, Cabernet Franc and Merlot as well as the Greek Limnio. White grapes are mainly the native Assyrtiko and Athiri, together with a bit of Sauvignon Blanc. The winery is obviously modern, and includes thermo-controlled oak and bottle cellars, the latter capable of holding up to 3,000,000 bottles at 12°C (very necessary in the white heat of Greece).

Melissanthi 1991   ♥♥ ②
This modern dry white (12°alc) wine is made from the classic Greek varieties Athiri and Aassyrtiko. Its clean, fresh bouquet displays an interesting array of aromas: apricots, melon, even a hint of coffee. Good acid backbone, no residual sugar, considerable concentration and depth on palate.

Château Carras   ♥♥♥ ②
Côtes de Meliton 1990 AO
This 12.5° alc wine is made from the same varieties as the1987 but with a higher percentage of Cabernet Sauvignon and aging in new Limousin casks. Fresh berry fruit on the nose and palate, with soft tannins despite its youth, a whiff of new oak on the finish and a slightly bitter aftertaste. Not quite knit at present but a wine of serious intent and excellent fruit concentration.

Château Carras   ♥ ②
Côtes de Meliton 1987 AO
A blend of Cabernet Sauvignon, Cabernet Franc, Merlot and Limnio aged in barrique for 18-20 months, plus 18-20 months in bottle. It has a surprisingly youthful, deep, vibrant color and a warm, sensuous bouquet, with a savoury-cum-fruity palate. There is a certain heat, but this is a characteristic rather than a defect, there being a nice balance between richness of fruit and restraint of vinification technique.

Kourtakis

19003 Markopoulo
Attica
Tel. (299) 22231
Fax (299) 23301

Kourtakis, with their old winery at Markopoulo, south of Athens, and their new one at Ritsona, 80 kilometers north, are the biggest producers of bottled wines in Greece at about 65,000,000 bottles per annum. This they say exceeds the combined figures for the next three biggest Greek bottlers. The company was founded in 1895 by Vasilis Kourtakis and a Vasilis Kourtakis presides over the family firm today. He is not the world's oldest man (thought wine can have a remarkable effect so they say) but the grandson of the founder. Apart from having extensive vineyards they buy grapes and wine from all parts of Greece and are well known for their red and white Cretan table wines. In addition to which they market a Samos (bought from the Union des Cooperatives), a Mavrodaphne of Patras and Greece's biggest selling Retsina wine. The latter is deservedly so, being much more vinous and more subtly resinated than many found in crown-cap bottles. Recent developments include the importation and plantation in the Ritsona area of a selection of classic French grape varieties and the development of a pair of Greek AOC wines (Patras white and Nemea red) under the Kouros label.

Patras Kouros 1990 AO   ♀ ①
A characterful, dry white from the Rhoditis grape, very nicely balanced with its slightly aromatic nose and its warm and fleshy, herby palate. The fruit reminds one of melons, the style of good quality Lugana. Clean, with a dry finish, which nonetheless hints at sweetness.

Mavrodaphne of Patras   ♀ ①
A sweet, liqueur wine (15° alc and about 8% residual sugar), mainly from the Mavrodaphne grape of Ionian origin, grown in the Akhaia viticultural area, south-west of Patras. A herby nose and a spirity, very sweet impact on the palate. Clean and fragrant, it lacks a bit of subtlety.

Nemea Kouros 1987 AO   ♀ ①
From the Agiorgitiko grape, "the noblest red variety of Greece" according to the back-label (and judging from our tastings it probably is). Of deepish color with a wild cherry bouquet and bilberry flavors on the palate. Robust yet smooth, packed with fruit, with international appeal.

Country Wine of Crete   ♀♀ ①
A dry, red wine, mainly from the native Kotsifali grape, with some Mandilaria, this deep-colored red has a peppery nose and a rich, full palate. Reminiscent of a youthful southern Rhône red, with more power than finesse perhaps but a certain earthy charm.

Union des Cooperatives Vinicoles de Samos

2 Kontaxi Str.
83100 Samos
Tel. (273) 27375-27458
Fax (273) 239

On this beautiful, mountainous, Aegean island, dominated by the 1140 meter high Mount Ambelos (Ambelos meaning vine), the Muscat grape has been grown on sloping, often terraced vineyards and vinified into luscious sweet wine for some 3,000 years. The island is divided into 26 vine-growing areas and, in 1934, rebelling against merchants' exploitation, the Union des Cooperatives was formed. Fortunately, tourism has turned landowners attention at lower levels towards more lucrative matters, and today most vine-growing happens at the cooler, upper altitudes. Being a large mediterranean cooperative, there is ample capital for investment in modern vinification equipment, though there is still a fair amount of old oak around for maturation purposes. A variety of oenological methods are used in producing the range of wines. The most important of these wines is the ancient sun-dried Nectar whose raisined grape sugars are concentrated up to a staggering 500 g/lt. Vin doux naturel and vin de liqueur are also produced, being grapier but less complex. One cannot help feeling that the wines, given such great raw material, could be vastly improved by just a little more care and artistry.

Samena   ♀ ①
A dry, white table wine, 100% Muscat. Pleasant enough, if somewhat lacking in distinction and having disappointingly little fresh varietal perfume, perhaps because it is picked a little too late (the acidity is a bit low). It's probably best consumed in situ and is not presently a competitor on the world market.

Samos Nectar AO   ♀♀ ②
A rich dessert wine of bright caramel color, it has surprisingly little varietal character on the nose. This is confirmed on the palate, which is nonetheless very complex, weighty, and sweet, with various fruit and dried flavors. A very concentrated wine, for sipping not drinking.

Strofilia

Mikras Asias St.
19013 Anvyssos-Attica
Tel. (291) 38 849
Fax (291) 38 850

In the early 1980s, Giannis Maltesos and a friend Achilleas Lampsidis decided to revive an old family tradition by becoming vine farmers again. Both engineers, it wasn't easy getting started, in fact, as Maltesos remembers: "We had no idea that making wine was going to be that hard to do." Today their winery is among the best equipped. Fermentation is temperature-controlled (20°-22°C). Stainless-steel vats are used for the whites and barriques for the reds. Production has inevitably risen from the initial 10,000 bottle level and they continue to be quite successful. Virtually only organic vine training and farming methods are used as the use of chemicals dwindles gradually.

Strofilia
This white wine is a blend of the Greek Savatiano and of a French imported Sauvignon Blanc. It has a spiced aroma, with hints of lychees. On the palate it is compact, supple and has a sufficiently lingering finish.

Strofilia 1985
A Cabernet Sauvignon aged in barrique, so it shows some nice oak. There is also good mint on the bouquet. The flavor is chewy and typical of ripe fruit, almost as if it had some residual sugar left. It is a wine worth laying down for a while.

Tsantalis S.A.

Agios Pavlos
63080 Chalkidiki
Tel. (399) 61394-8
Fax (399) 61466

The name Tsantalis is all over Greece as the company's advertising department has been successful in making it a household name (for its Ouzo and wine) from the north all the way to Crete. All this is due to managing director, Georg Tsantalis, a marketing specialist, who has skillfully improved sales and exports. In fact, he now exports 10,000,000 liters (mainly to Germany) which is about one third of the total product.ion. Like most of the larger Greek wineries, the strongest line of wines are the simple, light-bodied table wines, but Georg is busy planning and improving. The assortment of wines made has in fact been expanded in the past few years, especially with varietal wines like Cabernet Sauvignon, which have been improved by better wine-making and some barrique aging. Tsantalis buys most of the grapes from nearby growers.

Samos AO
This traditional dessert wine comes from the Island of Samos and has 15° alc. With an impressive aroma of Muscat, it is very elegant and full-bodied, almost chewy. As usual with these wines no vintage year is indicated but it can age for a while.

Makedonis
Tsantalis has a series of wines called Makedonis that go from low alcohol wines to fortified sweet wines. Undoubtedly the best of them all, the rosé has a pleasant aroma that tends to be clean but understated considering its chewy fruitiness. Its sweetness is mellowed by a firm acidity.

Cava Tsantalis
This Cava is made from a blend of several red grapes aged in new barriques. It is their first attempt at a new style of wine, one probably worth laying down for a few years. The wine has some good toasty aromas and is medium-bodied and yet thick and very lingering on the palate.

Mavrodaphne AO
A Grecian speciality from Patras, most wineries make their own versions of this red liqueur wine. It is strong in alcohol (15°), and if lacking in extract/complexity, it is round, full and well-balanced on the palate. It has a slightly bitter aroma on the nose.

HUNGARY

Hungary has about 200,000 hectares of vineyard and produces about 5,000,000 hectoliters of wine annually. In terms of vinous reputation among Eastern European countries she has, in recent centuries, stood supreme, not merely because of her one world-class wine, Tokay, but also thanks to the quality and character of her table wines. In the early 1970s Hungarian wines enjoyed an important market in the U.K. and other Western countries, especially the full-bodied red wines like Egri Bikaver or "Bulls Blood" (then from the Kadarka grape, though these days it is a rather lighter blend) and medium-bodied whites like Olasrizling from Pecs and Squrkebarat or Pinot Gris, Furmint and Keknvelu from the north shore of Lake Balaton. There are also the important reds of Villany (Nagyburgundi or Pinot Noir) or, to a lesser extent, of Sopron on the Austrian border (Kekfrankos or Gamay). Alas, the fierce and proud Hungarians gradually lost interest in making wines of character in economic and social conditions of uniformity and centralised control. The insatiable Russian market was willing and able to soak up anything they produced at whatever quality level. As a result, the Western market slipped away. Even Tokay became a pale shadow of its former self, to the extent that it became difficult for Westerners to believe that it has ever been considered one of the wonders of the vinous world.

Hungary is, in fact, ideally placed to produce wine of high quality. On a parallel with the great vineyard areas of France and northern Italy (Bordeaux, Burgundy and Piemonte) she has a temperate climate with generally long fine autumns which favour body, balance and aromatic development in wines. Yields tend to be low and fruit quality good. It was in the winery that things were going wrong as Hugh Ryman found when he literally invaded the country (see Gyongyos Estate). Neither musts nor wines were being handled properly and hygiene was almost nonexistent.

With Western help, there is every reason to believe that Hungary can reclaim its lost heritage in the next few years. Already Western style wines of ethereal character, both white and red, are emerging. Ryman's Sauvignon and Chardonnay are impressive, and his Pinot Noirs from Villany are showing promise. Furthermore, Tokay is on its way back after a long period in the dog-house. It is an exciting time for Hungarian wines.

CZECH REP. & SLOVAKIA

UKRAINE

AUSTRIA

Budapest ●

ROMANIA

EX YUGOSLAVIA

1	**Eger**
2	**Lake Balaton**
3	**Great Plains**
4	**Pecs**
5	**Sopron**
6	**Tokaji**

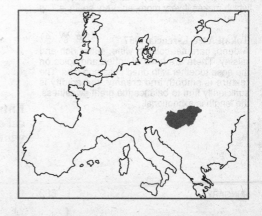

Allaini Gazdagasi Borkombinat/Tolcsva
Tokaj-Hegylja

Tokay was recognised as one of the world's greatest wines until as recently as the mid-20th century when its "bourgeois" image disgraced it in the eyes of political masters now departed. Homogenisation and pasteurisation are processes more associated with milk, yet such was the fate of this unique wine. Tokay was traditionally made from Furmint and Harslevelu grapes grown on volcanic soil in the foothills of the Zemplen range in north-east Hungary, vinified into Szamorodni, meaning "as it comes", or Aszù, which is Szamorodni refermented with 3 to 6 "putts" (multiples of 25 kilos of paste made from botrytised grapes) per 136 liter "gonc" (barrel) or Essencia, which is wine from free run juice from botrytised grapes. In 1989 the German firm, Schlumberger of Meckenheim, following discussions with various state officials, gained control of all stages of viticulture, selection, maturation and bottling, principally for export purposes. The result is a range of wines which permits us to see, at last, what all the fuss was about. It is nice to be able to confirm that Tokay can indeed be great.

Tokaji Szamorodni Edes 1983   ✿ ③
This is more one's idea of Tokay: grapey and nutty on the palate, much more rounded and balanced than the dry. The pains taken in making the wine have paid off, for it lacks the oxidation and attenuation of old-style Tokay, finishing fresh and lively, and not too sweet.

Tokaji Szamorodni Szaraz 1983   ✿ ③
With such an amber color one is expecting a sweet wine, so it comes as quite a shock to find that it is not only bone dry but has quite a searing acidity. This is an aperitif-style wine, with faint hazelnut aromas on nose and palate. Lively and different.

Tokaji Aszú 4 Puttonyos 1981   ✿ ✿ ④
With 13.5° alc and about 75 g/lt residual sugar one might expect a blockbuster, but this wine, with its hints of orange-peel on the nose and of nuts, dried fruits and marmelade on the palate is brilliantly balanced by a zingy acidity, all of which makes it very more-ish. Very nearly a Top Wine.

Tokaji Aszú Eszencia 1957   ✿ ✿ ④
A deep, caramel-colored wine, super rich and raisiny. There are hints of coffee and spice on the nose together with dried fruits and nuts. The texture is smooth and creamy, the acidity is sufficiently firm to balance the great sweetness, the length is exceptional.

Csopakvin Boraszati Kft.

Csopak
Füredi u. 3
Tel. (86) 46390

Hegyközség was one of the first communities of vine-growers to settle in Csopak in 1754. In laying out the rules for wine production, they wrote a detailed 33 point doctrine that is proudly commemorated on their winery label. There is also a reproduction of the old wooden press that historically greeted visitors at the entrance to the winery. Csopakvin crushes grapes that come in from about 500 hectares of vineyards scattered throughout a 25 km radius near the banks of Lake Balaton. Like most Hungarian wineries without a private bottling line, the winery only crushes, vinifies and ages in oak wood. Most of the wine is sold in bulk, while only 5% is bottled for export.

Sauvignon Balaton 1989   ✿ ①
With a marked perfume of geraniums and bell peppers on the nose, it is well-balanced and quite lingering on the finish.

Riesling Balaton 1988   ✿ ①
Made exclusively from free run juice, it has a pleasant, young, greenish color with a delicate, slightly fruity bouquet. On the palate it is well-balanced, round, with a refreshing acidity and good backbone.

Entries are arranged in alphabetical order by country, region and winery or producer name.

Egervin

Eger
Széchenyi u. 1/3
Tel. (36) 12411

One of the most important companies in the region, Egervin is involved in several commercial enterprises ranging from farming equipment to distilled spirits and soft drinks to local vine research. Together with Tokay, Egri Bikavér or Bull's Blood is reputedly one of the world's greatest wines and proof that local vintners can create prized wines. This is undoubtedly the case here although the wine is unfortunately experiencing a setback as hard times hit the country. Nonetheless, there are plans to restore and restructure the whole program. In addition to the aforementioned Bull's Blood, the winery also makes several styles of white wine including Chardonnay, Rizling and Sauvignon. Egervin's quality standard is undoubtedly above average, if not on occasion extraordinary.

Chardonnay 1989   ☗ ①
With a delicate bouquet, this Chardonnay is a prime example of the quality standard throughout. A fine marriage of top quality fruit and skillful wine-making.

Egri Bikavér 1987   ☗ ①
Made from Kadarka, Kékfrankos and Merlot (or Médoc Noir, as it is called here), this wine is dry, very elegant, round, and full bodied. It pairs well with red meats.

Egri Bikavér 1973   ☗☗ ①
20 years old and at its peak. It shows the wonderful aging power that this great red has in store. With a concentrated elegant nose, on the palate it is very well-balanced, full and considerably lingering on the finish.

Gyongyos Domoszloi (Gyongyos Estate)

3200 Gyongyos
Tel. (37) 13096
Fax (37) 11576

The recent success of the Gyongyos wines on the British market is due principally to the efforts of a "flying winemaker," Hugh Ryman. A France-based Englishman trained by Australians, Ryman quickly saw in the spring of 1991 that with the Soviet block breaking asunder and the big freeze destroying the white-wine crop in Francea golden opportunity existed for the resourceful. Having found the capital backing, collected the wine-making team and selected Hungary for its cool climate and long tradition, Ryman mounted a commando operation, selecting Gyongyos as a likely source of fruit. Gyongyos, a typical massive state-controlled operation, had the right varieties, moderate yields, some excellent oenological equipment, but was simply suffering the hangover of Soviet inertia. Ryman and Australian Adrian Wing, who has been left in place, brought their own equipment and introduced temperature control of musts and wines, antioxidative measures in vineyard and winery, regular cleaning of all equipment and a less severe pressing. The results are truly impressive, as is the modesty of the prices.

Chardonnay 1991   ☗☗ ☗ ①
Ryman is looking here for a dry white of European structure combined with New World intensity. For this he gives the must 12 hours skin contact and allows the wine to rest two months on the lees, achieving a distinctive yeasty-leesy Chardonnay character, salt cracker flavour balanced by lively acidity. A good bargain.

Sauvignon Blanc 1991   ☗ ①
12 hours skin contact and a long cool fermentation yields a wine of grassy but not catty aroma, having bright gooseberry fruit and fresh acidity. The body is a little thin but the typicity is that of a good Loire (lean, racy and aromatic) at something like half the price.

Pannonvin Winery

Rokoczi 1
7773 Villany
Tel. (73) 21-344
Fax (73) 11-255

Pannonvin, situated in Pannonia which was famous until the 1970s for her Villany Burgundi wine, is one of many large wineries in Eastern Europe currently on the cusp between state ownership and private control. Recently it was identified by Hugh Ryman as being ideal for the production of red wines for export to the west. It has some excellent equipment and 400 hectares of vineyard attached, with a further 400 from which to purchase fruit. Grapes, a mix of local and international wih the accent on reds, include most of the noble Burgundy and Bordeaux varieties, which it is claimed give wines of outstanding varietal character thanks to a cool climate and exposition on generally south facing limestone slopes. Annual production is in the area of 5,000,000 bottles, most of which are destined for markets which are disappearing or which have disappeared. However, Ryman's resident winemaker, Adrian Wing, is confident that a quick transformation can be achieved based on the fact that the remote Villany managed to miss the worst excesses of the Communist regime and he maintains that the future is very bright.

Cabernet Sauvignon 1991
A pure varietal, having less immediate charm than the Merlot. Nevertheless, a very western approach is evident: clean, considerable depth, lots of berry fruit, avoiding herbaceousness. More structure (firmer acid, harder tannins), less varietal character than the Merlot and built to last.

Merlot 1991
This is a 100% varietal wine which well demonstrates the Ryman/Wing approach of packing into the bottle the maximum amount of fresh fruit with a minimum of hard edges - tannins or acids. It has lots of plummy, berry fruit, is smooth and nicely balanced, with good varietal characteristics.

Tokajihegyaljai Allami

Gazdasaagi Borkombinat
Sataoraljaujhely
Martirol u. 17
Tel. (41) 22133

State-run and founded in 1971, the winery is responsible for coordinating the vine-growing and wine-making activities throughout the region. Inevitably, a number of changes are underway as the departments of finance and agriculture turn private, selling state-owned assets. Proceeds generated are contributing to the erection of private wineries of 30-40 hectares to boost the regional economy and wine trade. Operations are slow moving, but several wineries have indeed changed hands. At present, Borkombinat continues to be a role model, especially for visitors to the area and its facilities. Of particular interest are the cellars which form a series of underground tunnels scooped out of the friable tuff that fan out in all directions for miles and miles. A thick layer of mould covers the walls, casks and bottles, leaving an eerie awe of mystery. Borkombinat makes several styles of wines, ranging from Muscat, a dry and off-dry Furmint to the three Szamorodni, Aszú and Eszencia styles of Tokay.

Tokaji Aszú 6 Puttonyos 1972
Made by adding six doses of botrytized grape pasta (the maximum allowed) to the juice, this Tokay Aszú is already 20 years old but still relatively young. The high sugars ensure a graceful development and long life.

Tokaji Aszú Eszencia 1963
Made from choice botrytized grapes, this rare version of Tokay is made only in exceptional vintages, from the best crus. The fermentation is a matter of several years while the wood aging takes at least a decade. The end wine coincides perfectly with its name: Eszencia.

Tokaji Aszú 6 Puttonyos 1957
A top-quality dessert wine, highly characteristic of its gender, there is no reason why it should not compete with the world's more famed dessert wines. It has a complex nose with great finesse and leaves a good, long-lasting impression on the palate, never tiring or boring.

INDIA

According to the French historian, Fernand Braudel, wine is a European cult that accompanied Europeans wherever they settled. If wine is to be considered part of one's heritage, linked to people's nutritional habits, then this affirmation is undeniable. It was only around tables of some countries in the old continent that fermented grape juice was drunk and for all social classes had a primary role of importance for its nutritional qualities. And yet, even in its ancient, mysterious origins, the vine has infiltrated almost everywhere. In North America the Vikings were the first civilization to set foot on this continent in the year 1000, baptizing it Vinland. Even in the Orient, odd as it may seem, the pre-Islamic languages often have poetry about wine.

The truth is that wine culture in the Orient is of relatively minor importance, with low gross production and low consumption per capita. There are, of course, a few exceptions among the various countries, especially those traditionally geared towards satisfying the demand for sweet wines. In India, where the vine has been cultivated if only for table grapes for over two millenia, there is still very little official or accurate information about wine production or consumption. Basically, there are about 12,500 hectares of vineyards, primarily situated in the hilly areas surrounding Bombay. Since the 1970s, however, a few wineries have been gaining ground, with the help of wine-making equipment and oenologists from the West. The trend is to plant vineyards and make international-style whites and reds from the European, especially French, varietals. One winery that stands out above the rest and which for the moment is almost unique is Champagne India. The méthode champenoise sparkling wine produced does surprisingly well in comparison with its European counterparts. Inevitably, Champagne India has dedicated its product to Omar Khayyam, the famous Persian poet, who celebrated the joys of wine.

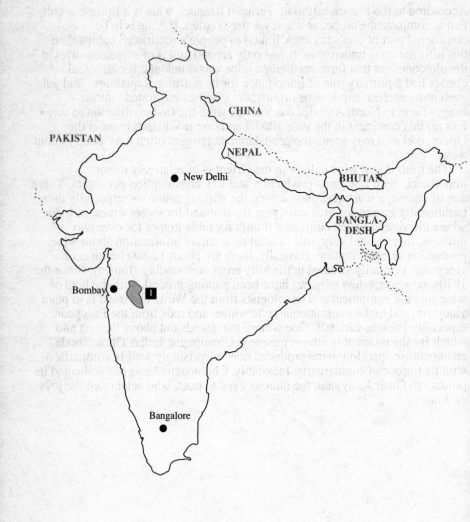

CHINA

PAKISTAN

NEPAL

● New Delhi

BHUTAN

BANGLA-
DESH

Bombay ● 1

Bangalore

1 Maharashtra

Champagne India

Narayangaon
Maharashtra State
Fax 4930036

Champagne India is one of the most unlikely wine estates in the world. It is situated 100 miles or so inland from Bombay where the climate is such as to make possible two vintages a year (though only one is practised), in a region where table grape production is traditional but no one ever dreamt of making wine, let alone high quality sparkling wine. It was the brainchild of Indian tycoon, Sham Chougoule, who, after several abortive attempts at interesting the sceptical Champenois in helping him, finally in the late 1970s managed to persuade Piper Heidsieck to send one of their whiz-kids, Raphael Brisbois, to create from scratch a vineyard and winery. Chougoule's capital ensured that only state-of-the-art equipment was installed, all imported from France. Brisbois has moved on now, but winemaker Abhay Kewadkar carries on the work of confounding the experts with this classy méthode champenoise, one-year-on-yeasts sparkler made from Chardonnay and Ugni Blanc grapes with a touch of Pinot Noir for complexity. To add further dimension, the estate in now experimenting with still wines made from Chardonnay, Cabernet Sauvignon and Syrah.

Omar Khayyam ②

The current commercial vintage is a blend of 1986 with a bit of 1984. The wine is pale with a good persistence mousse. One just catches a whiff of heat on the nose, but it is nicely balanced on the palate with firm, fresh acidity holding the biscuity, almost bready after-taste in place for some time. Not top Champagne level, but as good as many these days.

Rating System

 An exemplary wine of its type with outstanding local character

 An international premium quality wine

 A Top Wine, considered one of the 150 best wines in the world

The 'grape bunch' symbol is used to indicate the color of the wine; the number of bunches represents the quality rating assigned by the contributor

ISRAEL

We know from the Bible that Israel has been a land of vines and wine for thousands of years. On the other hand she might with some justification be thought to be too hot to produce wines of a quality able to compete in this wine-crazed world we live in today. The traditional vine-growing areas have been on the coastal belt where, a century go, Baron Rothschild founded the Carmel Mizrachi Company, planting for the most part varieties derived from southern France, in other words grapes likely to be able to withstand extremes of heat (Carignan, Grenache, Alicante Bouchet, Muscat and Clairette). The result were wines which no one would be likely to drink unless forced to imbibe something kosher and alcoholic.

Since 1948, however, with the expansion (or the occupation, depending on your point of view) into territories like the Golan, winemaking in Israel has taken a qualitative leap. Present production is about 2,000,000 cases a year coming from some 6,000 hectares of vineyard. Grape varieties introduced in recent years include Cabernet Sauvignon, Merlot, Petite Sirah, Chardonnay, Sauvignon, French Colombard, Chenin Blanc and Emerald Riesling.

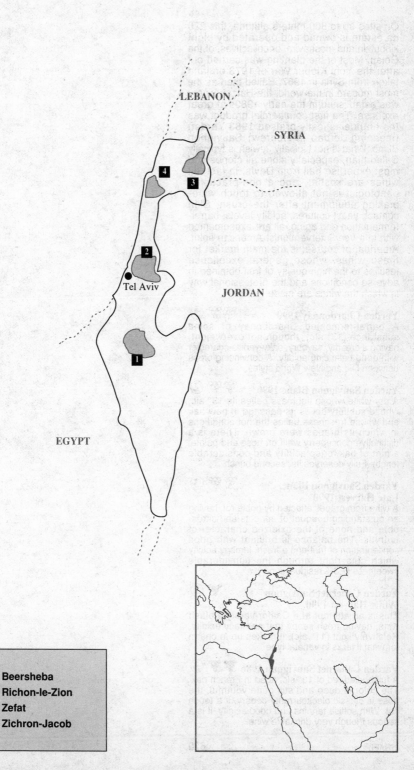

LEBANON

SYRIA

4

3

2

Tel Aviv

JORDAN

1

EGYPT

1 Beersheba
2 Richon-le-Zion
3 Zefat
4 Zichron-Jacob

Golan Heights Winery

P.O. Box 183
Quatzrin 12900
Tel. (972) 6962001

On sites up to 800 meters altitude, this 220 ha estate is owned and operated by eight kibbutzin and moshavim, or collectives, of the Golan. Most of the planting was carried out after the Yom Kippur War of 1973 on land taken from Syria in 1967. Hailed then as the most modern in the world, the Hatzor winery was established in the early 1980s at great expense. The first commercial product was the enthusiastically praised 1983 Yarden (meaning Jordan in Hebrew) Sauvignon Blanc. What is not typically Jewish is typically Californian, especially since all clones and most expertise hail from Davis. In fact, all wines are kosher, and a non-practising oenologist is not allowed to touch wine-making equipment after the crush. Skin contact, yeast cultures, acidity levels, barrel-fermentation and aging, all are experimented with in a very interventionist American spirit. America, of course, is the main market for these wines, whose general excellence testifies to the high quality of fruit obtained in adverse conditions and the professional way in which the wines are made.

Yarden Chardonnay 1990 🍇🍇 ③
A barrel-fermented Chardonnay of some substance (13° alc), though not overweight, having a creamy, savoury, oaky-vanilla character with good balancing acidity. A convincing cross between Old and New World styles.

Yarden Sauvignon Blanc 1990 🍇🍇 ②
A dry white whose lightness belies its 13° alc, whose subtlety belies its passage in new oak and whose freshness belies the hot conditions in which its grapes were grown. There is a distinctive gooseberry whiff on nose and palate, a hint of oak, crisp acidity and considerable length. Fully deserves its "second bunch".

Yarden Sauvignon Blanc 🍇🍇 ③
Late Harvest 1990
A wine from grapes affected by noble rot, having an outstanding bouquet of apricots and citrus-peel and none of the oxidized character of botrytis. The balance is brilliant with good concentration of fruit and a fresh, lemony acidity which cuts right through the considerable sweetness (7.3% residual sugar).

Yarden Cabernet Sauvignon 🍇 ②
White Harvest 1990
This is an attempt at a California-style blush wine, having fresh sappy fruit and racy acidity. Relatively light (11° alc), it makes up in charm for what it lacks in varietal type.

Yarden Cabernet Sauvignon 1986 🍇🍇 ③
A full-bodied red of 13° alc, aged in French oak. The color is deep and still quite youthful, the nose is classic blackcurranty-cedary, if a touch hot. With softish tannins and good acidity, it is a serious though very drinkable wine.

ITALY

Protruding like a 'boot' into the Mediterranean sea, Italy is surprisingly a hilly and mountainous country. Nearly 35% of its territory is montainous as the Alps mark the northern border and the Apennines run north-south the peninsula, like a spinal chord. Hilly strips and foothills form 40% of the territory and design a landscape which for millennium has been the cradle of western civilization. Valleys are few and all densely populated.

From time immemorial vines have found a home in the peninsula thanks to the variable climate due in part to the vicinity of the Mediterranean sea. Vines and wines have always been an important part of Italian history, culture and life. Together with fresh, baked bread and 'liquid-gold' olive oil, not to mention other food staples, wine makes up what has been called the "Santa Trinità mediterraneana".

Historically, the ancient Greeks used to call the Italian Republic "Enotria", the land of wine. Later, the Roman Empire spread its dominion, the Pax Romana, by planting vines in conquered territories. Medieval monasticism and the Catholic church defended and maintained viticultural production for sacramental rites, and the aristocracy and dominant classes in Italy's history have always considered vine cultivation on their lands and vinification in their castle and palace cellars a sign of prestige and something to be proud of. Each and every region and village in all corners of the peninsula proudly lays claim to the birthplace of some wine, the originality of the grapes grown on their territory, or the historical pairing with traditional dishes. The Italians' deep peasant roots turn each and every one of them into proud narrators and presumed connoisseurs of the wines and vineyards that characterize much of Italy's landscape, whit over one million hectares of vineyards.

Italy's ampelographic heritage is extremely rich. Over the centuries many indigenous vines have evolved and improved, but many other vines have arrived from neighboring countries. Whether intentional or not, there has been much experimentation, cross-breeding and cloning, often simply by trial and error.

Over 500 vine varieties are grown in Italy, the majority of which have adapted to the regions where they are grown. For example, Sangiovese (or Sangioveto) is found throughout central Italy but takes on different characteristics in the regions of Romagna and Tuscany, and even within Tuscany itself. Historical and widely planted vines include Barbera, Nebbiolo, the Cabernet, Trebbiano, Malvasia and Moscato families, Lambrusco, Merlot, Montepulciano d'Abruzzo, the Pinots and Rieslings, Tocai Italico, Verdicchio, Vermentino and many, many others. This remarkable heritage enriches and diversifies Italy's own wine scenario, even though France has though time imposed the leadership of its wines and varieties (becoming the international standard of comparison). Italian enology is now rediscovering and re-evaluating the uniqueness of its wines, some still largely unexplored or untapped in terms of potential quality.

Italy produces more wine that any other country in the world and is third, after Spain and the former Soviet Union, in terms of surface planted to vineyards. The wine-making and viticultural geography is, however, more difficult to classify and assess. For the purposes of this guide we have, therefore, chosen to simply subdivide the country alphabetically according to region. Regional prefaces give a prelude to the entries that follow.

Vineyards can be found throughout Italy, as already mentioned, but three regions are unanimously recognized as having the highest wine vocation. Piedmont has a long tradition of making austere and prestigious reds such as Barolo and Barbaresco, both from the Nebbiolo varietal. It is also characterized by a series of mono-varietal wines such as Barbera, Freisa, Grignolino, Gavi and Gattinara. In the dessert wine range, production of Moscato d'Asti and Asti Spumante has deeply marked Piedmontese enology since the beginning of the century. Piedmont is also the birthplace of Vermouth, the most well-known flavored wine. The most prestigious zone in this region is the Langhe of Alba, with its particular microclimates and soils, where the region's wine traditions were born and developed.

Tuscany has different productive patterns, agricultural geography and viticultural heritages. It is now undergoing a production revival and reaching new quality levels which are widely acclaimed, not only in Italy but in many other countries. The most important phenomenon is the authentic rebirth of Chianti wines, and particularly of Chianti Classico. In several stages, Chianti Classico delineated its production s area within reasonable limits and then gradually revised the traditional grape blending, eventually excluding the white Trebbiano variety. Results are clearly evident. Flourishing Tuscan viticulture and winemaking will certainly bring new surprises in the future.

The Chianti area was not the only one involved in this revolution, with Montalcino gaining international fame for its precious Brunello. Other important Tuscan wine zones are Montepulciano, Carmignano, San Gimignano and Montecarlo, and the Tyrrenian coast has recently produced some gems that Italian production can be proud of. In Europe's overall wine scenario, Tuscany is undoubtedly destined to play a leading role.

Whereas Tuscany and Piedmont have been producing high-profile reds for many years, Friuli has gained fame as the region of great whites. Friuli's stubborn viticulturists have succeeded with a range of superb whites, characterized by floral fruity perfumes and good cellaring potential. A border territory often tormented by wars, Friuli has rebuilt its vineyards with both native and imported vines over the last century.

Although these three regions are the most stimulating in terms of quality, worthy also of mention are Trentino and Südtirol's well-priced wines, the good wines of the coastal regions of Liguria, (Le) Marches and Campania, the sun-filled wines of the southern regions and Veneto's great vineyards.

Discovering the 366 wineries listed in this guide will be like taking a long trip to Italy. It is important to keep in mind, however, this is a unique period of legislative transition for the wine sector. Since the beginning of the 1960s, when laws on name and origin control or DOC were enacted, over 240 wines and zones have obtained this status. This maze of DOCs has regulated with appropriate laws and regulations each wine with geographical or historical denominations and the production parameters which refer to the varietal or local customs. It is a complicated puzzle and various forms of self-regulation have developed, in some cases with worthy intentions, at times for speculative

CONSORZIO TRA PRODUTTORI DELL'ACETO BALSAMICO TRADIZIONALE DI MODENA

c/o Camera di Commercio - MODENA - Via Ganaceto, 134

Tel. (059) 208285 - 208298 - Fax (059) 211035 - 208298 - Telex 510589 CAMMO

VINITALY: THE BIGGEST EVERY YEAR

28th INTERNATIONAL WINE EXHIBITION

The biggest world wine event is held every year in April in Verona.

Growers and producers from all over the world meet at the show, which occupies an area of over 150,000 m² (covered), for discussions, negotiations and debates with a truly international flavour.

Every year Vinitaly offers its participants a magnificent opportunity to display their products to their very best advantage.

VINITALY

VERONA APRIL 8 - 12, 1994

VERONAFIERE

VERONAFIERE • For more information: C.P. 525 • I • 37100 VERONA • Tel. +39/45/588111 • Fax +39/45/588288

così MARTINI,
così ROSSO.

INCONFONDIBILE PER LE SUE RARE ERBE ED I SUOI VINI.
MARTINI ROSSO E' TUTTO NATURALE.

MARTINI

reasons, and always a step further from the DOC regulations.

Generally speaking, this confusion and laxity helped to create the so-called Vini da Tavola (table wines) category, a phenomenon which is still relatively incomprehensible to outsiders looking in. Many different types can be found within this 'umbrella' category, from every-day inexpensive wines to wines of international fame. Italian producers wishing to experiment outside rigid regulations have often had no alternative but to find refuge in this category. Most of the so-called 'super Tuscans' went through this phase before attaining the end results which saved the product's image and quality. But understanding Italian production is a not an easy task abroad, often reserved for true specialists. Many foreign consumers do not understand what is hidden in a Vino da Tavola that costs ten, twenty times more than the much vaunted DOC wines.

A new law was passed at the beginning of 1992 which should unequivocally regulate the subject, but the path is still long. Inevitably, numerous, conflicting interests are at stake. If the spirit of this new legislation is understood and its rulings respected, the classification of Italian wines in the main production areas would resemble the Burgundy pyramid-model, with the denomination of single vineyards at the top and regional or main zone denominations at the bottom. Italian wine needs this type of regulation primarily for its image abroad, to help consumers lost in a myriad of labels, denominations and wineries.

The reputation of Italian wines has not always been particularly high. The term 'Italian wine' is often synonymous with inexpensive, medium quality. This concept was fostered by production often more attentive to sales volumes than product quality. Over-production, as in the case of Soave and Lambrusco wines, to name two, has harmed the image of Italian wine, particularly in the eyes of American, English and German consumers.

Today production concepts and philosophies are changing. Quality has already improved enormously over the last ten years and will continue to do so. Italian wine is also able to fly on the wings of the "Cucina Italiana", as fine restaurants gain recognition and respected status worldwide. Yet all this may not be enough to noticeably improve the image of Italian enology. Faced with an unstoppable decrease in consumption as well as EEC rulings, Italy's numerous hectares of vineyard must be drastically reduced, making room for the best and most suitable areas, limiting yields per hectare, making quality the primary objective and exalting the particularities of historical native varietals - just what the international market wants from the ancient "Bel Paese" of wine.

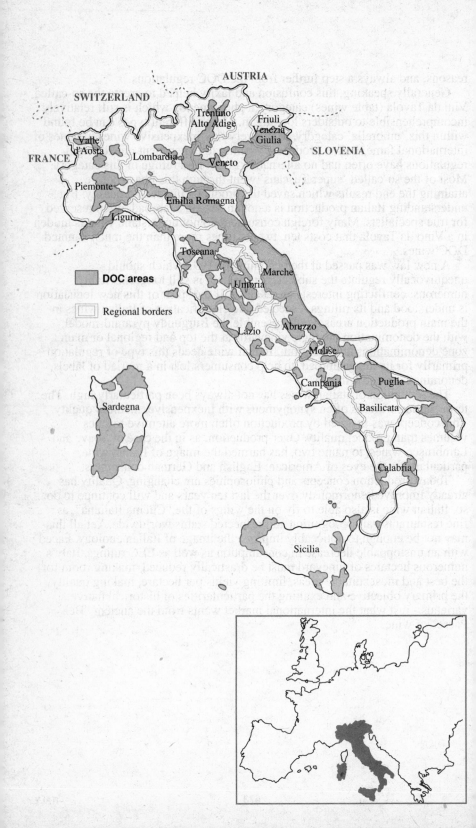

AUSTRIA

SWITZERLAND

Trentino
Alto Adige

Friuli
Venezia
Giulia

Valle
d'Aosta

Lombardia

FRANCE

SLOVENIA

Veneto

Piemonte

Emilia Romagna

Liguria

Toscana

Marche

Umbria

DOC areas

Regional borders

Lazio

Abruzzo

Molise

Campania

Puglia

Sardegna

Basilicata

Calabria

Sicilia

Abruzzo and Molise

Although separate since 1963, these two regions still have much in common, particularly with their mountainous characteristics. Extensive, often impressive mountain ranges generate beneficial day-time wind currents and minor temperature variations; while the nearby seaside creates good ventilation. These two environmental factors make the regions perfectly suit to viticulture.

Ancient Romans much appreciated Abruzzo's wines, especially the Praetutian. The Praetuttii tribe originally inhabited the hilly coastal area between current-day Teramo and Pescara and lent their name to the area, Aprutium, which in turn became the current-day Abruzzo. Other civilizations such as the Parrucini, the Paeligni, the Marsi, the Samnites from Molise and many other tribes also inhabited these lands over the centuries yet maintained their independence and hostile attitude towards invaders. Out of mere necessity, solidarity became a strong common trait.

Wine production averages 4,000,000 hl per year in Abruzzo and 500,000 hl in Molise. Both regions have encountered numerous difficulties this century in rebuilding their vineyards after phylloxera struck, due to the territory's particular soil type. It took years to recuperate, once initial problems were addressed and confronted, and, worse yet, many of the production decisions that followed were shortsightedly aimed at quantity, instead of quality, much like the productive trends in Puglia. Many wines, particularly Montepulciano, were sent north, illegally bottled and labelled as Barolo. Fortunately those days are gone, and Montepulciano's great potential is starting to emerge and to be appreciated. Abruzzo DOC wines are Montepulciano, both red and rosé, or more precisely Cerasuolo (cherry-red), and Trebbiano.

Molise, once in the embarrassing position of being the only region in Italy without a DOC wine, has now been granted Denomination of Origin for its Biferno (in Campobasso) and Pentro (in Isernia) wine areas. Until now the Masseria Di Majo Norante is the only estate to have put them on Molise's winemaking map that is otherwise dotted with cooperatives. Abruzzo's wines are more diversified, with a handful of interesting wineries, each potentially capable of producing attractive prospects, and with a legendary niche reserved for Edoardo Valentini's wines.

Dino Illuminati

Contrada San Biagio, 12
Controguerra (Te) 64010
Tel. (0861) 856631
Fax (0861) 810004

Celebrating the winery's 100th anniversary seems to have rejuvenated its current owner, the dynamic Dino Illuminati. He has brought a new spark of life to the cellar, particularly in the barrel-room, and begun making a new style of wines. Illuminati's vineyards are excellently positioned in the hilly strip between the Tronto river and Val Vibrata (a flourishing new business area). The Montepulciano and Trebbiano d'Abruzzo wines produced from these vineyards are among the region's best. In a vast range of products, recently enriched by Nicò, a sweet wine made from partly dried Montepulciano grapes, and Loré, a "Vino a Meditazione", the most striking are the Montepulciano Zanna Reserves and Ciafré, a white made from Trebbiano, Riesling, Passerina and Chardonnay. The choice of names in dialect reveals Dino's strong ties to the region's traditions and expresses the winery's philosophy; modern interpretations of wines made from native varietals.

Ciafré 1991
Undoubtedly one of the region's best whites, made from a blend of Riesling Italico, Garganega, Passerina, Trebbiano and Malvasia. Good intensity and persistence on the nose, distinguished and balanced on the palate. Will be able to express itself better in the course of 1993 thanks to its good structure.

Montepulciano d'Abruzzo
Cerasuolo 1991 DOC
Rosé version, once again from Montepulciano grapes. Fresh and fruity, a modern than rather than structured version of Cerasuolo wine.

Montepulciano d'Abruzzo
Zanna 1988 DOC
Full-bodied red, variegated perceptions on both nose and palate, firm and polished thanks to well-measured aging, first in oak then in bottle, able to fully reveal itself for several more years.

Masciarelli

Via Gamberale, 1
S. Martino sulle Marrucina (Ch) 66010
Tel. (0871) 85241-82333
Fax (0871) 85330

From small-town Italy to the upbeat Caribbean tropics. Indeed Masciarelli's wines take quite a unique route: from the 1,000 pop. provincial town of San Martino sulla Marruccina (Chieti) across the Atlantic to the Caribbean Sea. His Trebbiano and Montepulciano d'Abruzzo wines have been waving the Italian flag for years in several tropical restaurants on islands in the Greater and Lesser Antilles. For years, and even more so today, Gianni Masciarelli has been one of Abruzzo's leading (and more passionate) wine producers of Trebbiano and Montepulciano wines. The vines are situated at 350 m, on a hilly well-exposed stretch of vineyard, which produces top quality raw material. Vineyard and cellar operations are carefully supervised, with the Villa Gemma label showing particularly interesting results; but all the wines are clean and consistently good.

Trebbiano d'Abruzzo
Villa Gemma 1991 DOC
Made with Trebbiano, it is a well-made wine, fresh and ready to drink, but not necessarily an easy wine. Though the Villa Gemma line generally includes the winery's best, the standard Masciarelli range should not be overlooked, especially its Trebbiano.

Chardonnay Villa Gemma 1990
One of the winery's experimental products, soon to be joined by a barrique-blended Chardonnay and Trebbiano. Balanced and not lacking in elegance, with ample and harmonious bouquet, it was released after careful bottle aging. Refined on the palate and delicate in structure.

Montepulciano d'Abruzzo
Cerasuolo 1991 DOC
From estate-grown Montepulciano grapes, a worthy result even in the rosé version. From a gentle crush and short maceration on skins, it is an interesting Abruzzo rosé.

Montepulciano d'Abruzzo
Villa Gemma 1988 DOC
By far one of the best Montepulciano wines, elegant and complex thanks to meticulous and knowledgeable work in the vineyard and cellar, where it underwent balanced aging in oak. Ready to drink now but could bear pleasant surprises in years to come.

Camillo Montori

Via Piane Tronto, 23
Controguerra (Te) 64010
Tel. (0861) 809900
Fax (0861) 809912

The Tronto river clearly marks the border between the regions of the Marche and Abruzzo, which has been otherwise historically blurred. They both share the area of Piceno, surrounding the Adriatic town of Ascoli Piceno. A grower from the southern bank of the Tronto, Camillo Montori calls this area Marcuzze. He mainly produces Montepulciano and Trebbiano d'Abruzzo, the two regional DOCs, the first made in both red and rosé versions. Camillo often experiments with other varietals such as Cabernet and Chardonnay, respectively used in the Montepulciano and Trebbiano blends, Leneo Moro and Leneo d'Oro, which have captured the attention of wine lovers. Camillo Montori's new tavern-enoteca makes for a pleasant stop-over, and something new is always going on the winery or in its owner's restless creative mind. Forever setting new goals, experimenting with new ideas and new regional styles, Camillo is certainly one of their most inspired protagonists.

Leneo d'Oro 1991
Almost 50/50 Chardonnay and Trebbiano, it has a lively and pleasant nose; fresh and medium-firm on the palate, to be matched preferably with uncomplicated seafood dishes and drunk within the year.

Trebbiano d'Abruzzo Fontecupa 1991 DOC
A correct and enticing interpretation of the white Abruzzo DOC, with a floral spring bouquet and pleasant savoury palate. A good white which is characteristic of its terroir, best with fish or vegetable dishes, to be drunk young.

Leneo Moro 1990
Camillo Montori's most interesting blend, from equal amounts of Cabernet Sauvignon and Montepulciano. Polished red, not particularly demanding, with good balance of fruit and wood; a happy union of the diverse character of the varietals.

Montepulciano d'Abruzzo Fontecupa 1990 DOC
A red made from selected Montepulciano grapes, aged in varying sized oak barrels, it has a pleasant lingering bouquet with notable hints of plum and marasca cherry, soft and smooth on the palate. Ready to drink now but should keep for at least two years.

Bruno Nicodemi

Via Veniglio, 8
Notaresco (Te) 64024
Tel. (085) 895493

Reconstruction of the Nicodemi winery began in 1970. Located in Notaresco, a hilly area traditionally suited to vines and olive-trees, the family-owned winery used the share-cropping system for generations, until Bruno Nicodemi gradually reorganized their 22 ha of mixed properties. He invested in new, specialized vineyards and started producing Abruzzo's DOC wines Trebbiano and Montepulciano (both red and rosé) using modern and selective criteria, especially cutting yields per hectare. Recent vintages constantly rank Nicodemi's Trebbiano among the top, appreciated by both the public and critics. His Montepulciano wines are just as good, especially the Reserves and the better 1985 and 1988 vintages. These wines, with their gradually-attained qualitative regularity, guarantee a bright future for this winery.

Trebbiano d'Abruzzo 1991 DOC
Moderately lingering and refined perfumes, justly sapid and balanced, it confirms Bruno Nicodemi's success in recent vintages in not only making reds but also pleasant and fresh modern-style whites.

Montepulciano d'Abruzzo Cerasuolo 1991 DOC
Its color is clearly cherry; lingering, lively and fruity perfumes are continued on the palate. A well-made rosé which expresses the tradition in the area of this type of wine.

Montepulciano d'Abruzzo 1988 DOC
Remarkable interpretation of Abruzzo's red DOC, entirely from Montepulciano grapes. Oaked then bottle-aged for two years, Bruno Nicodemi's '88 has a harmonious and velvety flavor but has not yet reached its peak.

Edoardo Valentini

Via del Baio, 2
Loreto Aprutino (Pe) 65014
Tel/Fax (085) 826138

When asked the secret of his extraordinary and unique wines, Edoardo Valentini suggests that one read the philosophical works of the era of Socrates. Heated often provincial disputes over the use of oak and barriques do not seem to phase him in the least. He studied them back in the 1950s, deciding then that they did not suit the Trebbiano and Montepulciano d'Abruzzo wines he wanted to produce. Today, he has many followers. Valentini's Trebbiano and Montepulciano d'Abruzzo are unique wines, with good seven to eight year aging potential, even for the whites. (The incredible freshness of one of his 10 year-old Trebbiano whites is still vivid in our minds). A sworn enemy of the early-release wines, Valentini releases his wines only when, and if, he thinks they are ready, which for whites can mean up to four years after harvest, and up to five years for Montepulciano. His wife, Adriana, and son, Francesco, share in this story of wine, one of the most fascinating in Italy.

Montepulciano ③
d'Abruzzo 1987 DOC

Edoardo Valentini's 1987 is yet another great vintage, released only months ago. The potential of Montepulciano grapes is fully expressed, revealing typical aromas of ripe plum and licorice, spicy notes and an obvious hint of coffee. With great character, foreseeably long lasting, yet another confirmation of the excellent quality of Italian wines.

Trebbiano ③
d'Abruzzo 1988 DOC

Given the variety from which it is made, this Trebbiano truly stands apart from the usual easy-drinking versions that are unable to provide exciting or magical moments. A peremptory and authoritative example of unrepeatable personality, even compared to what this wine has achieved in past vintages. Unquestionable quality transcends its geographical origins. In the traditional Valentini style, it was released three years after harvest. Golden yellow, its thick perfumes laden with nuances, it combines an evolved character and surprising freshness, finishing with exuberant, embracing richness.

Ciccio Zaccagnini

Contrada Pozzo
Bolognano (Pe) 65020
Tel. (085) 8880195
Fax (085) 8880288

Abruzzo has only three DOC wines: Trebbiano, Cerasuolo and Montepulciano d'Abruzzo. A small group of enlightened producers must be given credit for improving the region's viticulture, which is often set back by the difficulties in rebuilding its phylloxera-struck vineyards. Also, considerable damage was done by the approach of quantity versus quality. Ciccio and his son, Marcello, are among the protagonists of this rebirth and are somewhat traditionalist (the vine-shoot was chosen as the symbol for the standard range and is hung on the neck of every bottle). They are definitely modern in their wine making philosophy and in the techniques, facilities and equipment used. Helpfulness and friendliness are Marcello's two most distinguishable traits on visiting the winery and the beautiful vineyards. (The Colle Morto vineyard is particularly impressive.) The wines, especially those labelled the Castello di Salle and above all the Montepulcianos, are the result of experimentation including the use of different varietals, as in the unique Capsico made from Nebbiolo grapes.

Montepulciano d'Abruzzo Cuvée dell'Abbate 1990 DOC
The standard version of Montepulciano, easier to drink than the Castello di Salle, but not lightweight. Distinguishing notes on the nose and palate of ripe fruit and vinous suggestions, with good aging potential.

Capsico 1988
A bizarre enological rarity, this red from Nebbiolo grapes delivered by the nursery by mistake. After a few disappointing first vintages, Ciccio Zaccagnini crafted a wine of good personality, tannic and rather warm due to its alcohol level.

Montepulciano d'Abruzzo Castello di Salle 1988 DOC
Austere yet lively depth and appeal achieved with lengthy aging in oak. As in past years this Montepulciano d'Abruzzo 1988 is one of the region's best reds. Already a mature wine but will last for a long time yet.

Di Majo Norante

Contrada Ramitelli, 4
Campomarino (Cb) 86042
Tel. (0875) 57208
Fax (0875) 57379

Luigi Di Majo Norante and his son, Alessio, have been the only notable flagbearers of Molise wines for years. This small, southern region shares the record for being so mountainous (60% of its territory) with Abruzzo. The hilly slopes of the Di Majo Norante estate have the particularly foothill microclimate. Located in Capomarino, a few kilometers from Termoli, this winery has proven that even Molise, with its Biferno and Pentro DOC wines, can produce good quality wines. The Di Majo property dates back to the 18th century, but has taken on its current modern appearance since 1968. It produces a wide range of wines: Sangiovese, Montepulciano, Aglianico, Trebbiano, Malvasia and others like Falanghina, Greco, Fiano as well as Ramitello and Molì, the winery's flagship wines. A new line called "Nuovi vini da antichi vitigni", or new wines from ancient varietals, has been created and the results, with the technical help of Giorgio Grai, are once again impressive.

Greco 1990
Another white from the "Nuovi vini" range, with no inferiority complexes in relation to Campania's Greco wines, it has an impressive fruity character typical of the varietal.

Ramitello Bianco 1990
The Di Majos have made Ramitello into one of their flagship wines. Made from the Falanghina grape, of Samnite origin, this 1990 vintage Ramitello confirms its class. The bouquet is reminiscent of acacia but also of lemon-verbena, with a pleasant almond flavor.

Fiano 1989
It is worthwhile spending the time to appreciate the richness, both on the nose and on the palate, of this white. It is made from Fiano grapes which have found in Campomarino's hot and dry climate conditions as favorable as its native Campania.

Aglianico 1987
100% Aglianico, from the Di Majo's range of "Nuovi vini". Rather intense aromas, soft and well-balanced components, on the palate pleasant, not too demanding.

Ramitello Rosso 1987 ☿ ①
Made from Aglianico and Montepulciano grapes grown in the Ramitello district. It is a mature wine with spicy notes and full harmonious flavors due to careful aging.

Basilicata, Calabria, Campania

First planted on the slopes of Mount Vulture in the Basilicata region by the ancient Greeks, Aglianico is the region's most important grape and is certainly ranked among southern Italy's best. Basilicata's sole DOC wine since 1971, Aglianico del Vulture's production is relatively low compared to the rest, at approximately 1,000,000 bottles per year. D'Angelo and Paternoster, the region's finest Aglianico makers, are also experimenting and researching other styles of wines, particularly among the whites. They promise to change the Aglianico as little as possible; infact, the elegant wines that these producers are making eloquently confirm their efforts.

Being 90% mountainous, Calabria's vine-growing areas are heavily influenced by a number of unique microclimates. Its flagship-wine, the famous Cirò, is produced in all three versions: white, rosé and red. In 1989 there were significant legislative changes to the production methods which should result in a further improvement in its quality. But Calabria is more than Cirò. Besides this wine, which comes from the mid-Ionic coast, worthy of note also are the wines from Aspromonte and from the southern coasts, the Greco di Bianco and Mantonico di Bianco in particular, which are two unique and great dessert wines. Other important wines include those from Pollino and western Sila (Pollino itself, Savuto, Donnici and Lamezia) which use such grapes as Gaglioppo, Greco Nero, Nerello Mascalese and Nerello Capuccio for the reds and Malvasia Bianca, Mantonico Bianco and Guarnaccia Bianca for the whites. Non-native varietals, like Cabernet Sauvignon, Chardonnay and Pinot Blanc are being experimented with, and some leading wineries, such as Odoardi and Fattoria San Francesco are doing extremely important work with Calabria's main wines. Let's hope also that such exciting and exclusive wines from small growers like Ceratti and Messinò are not neglected or, worse yet, destined to become 'endangered species' on a wine equivalent of the WWF list.

With Campania's rich volcanic soils, abundant rainfall and sunshine, even the ancient Romans called the region "Campania felix". The situation changed in 1860, however, with the fall of the Kingdom of the "Due Sicilie". Since then growing areas throughout the country have shifted and changed locations, from the cooler areas around Irpinia to the hilly, coastal strips so dear to the ancient Greeks and Romans. There are, of course, other noteworthy wine zones, around the hills of Falerno to Ischia and the Amalfi coast. There is also Solopaca in the north, where especially in recent decades the Mastroberardino winery has kept the region's winemaking reputation high. The situation seems to be changing thanks to a dynamic group of producers who are proudly reverting to native grapes. Some whose potential should not be overlooked include particularily Aglianico, but also Fiano, Greco di Tufo, Falanghina, Piedirosso, Biancolella, Forastera and Coda di Volpe. The main non-native varietals used in some of Campania's DOC wines or the Vino da Tavola blends are Sangiovese, Trebbiano Toscano, Barbera, Aleatico and Verdeca. At the last harvest wine production reached 2,500 hl.

D'Angelo

Via Provinciale, 8
Rionero in Vulture (Pz) 85028
Tel. (0972) 721517
Fax (08972) 723195

Particularly suited to southern Italy and especially in the Vulture area, Aglianico is the most interesting southern varietal. It has Greek origins, and takes its name from vitis hellenica. Donato and Lucio D'Angelo's winery is based in Rionero in Vulture, a farming town which dates back to the early Middle Ages. Faithful and innovative crafters of Aglianico, they strongly believe in the grape and have yet to realise its full potential in this area of Basilicata, which is as great as that of Taurasi from Campania. They have an innovative approach to wine-making, without shying away from experimentation and the use of new techniques. One up and coming southern red, Canneto, is made with Aglianico grapes from low-yielding and historical vineyards in the zone of Vulture, skillfully aged in Slovenian and Allier oak. There is innovation also with white wines with the introduction of new varietals like Riesling Italico and Malvasia. This winery is definitely on the rise and should be considered a reference point for enology in Basilicata.

Aglianico del Vulture 1988 DOC   🍇 ①
The standard version of Aglianico del Vulture, traditionally aged, is worthy of a mention for its texture, balance and elegance and confirms this varietal's potential and this winery's patience and seriousness.

Aglianico del Vulture   🍇🍇 ②
Canneto 1988 DOC
Deep ruby-red in color, with intense aromas with hints of cherry and red currant. Good concentration and softness on the palate, supported by a good balance between acidity and tannin. An outstanding wine, from Aglianico grown in the province of Potenza.

Paternoster

Via Nazionale, 23
Barile (Pz) 85022
Tel. (0972) 770224
Fax (0972) 770658

Located on the outskirts of Barile (of Albanian origin), the winery of Giuseppe Paternoster ("our Father" in Latin) and his sons, Vito and Sergio, is very beautiful with its cellars carved from the tufa rock. An avant-garde winery for "Lucania", or Basilicata, the vineyards are well-cared for and the cellars, well-equipped with machinery and small oak casks, to age the Aglianico wines. Relatively new grapes, such as Pinot Blanc and Chardonnay, have been introduced to expand on the range of products. Aglianico del Vulture, also made in a sparkling version, will continue to dominate and rightly so: the proof is in a taste of a recent vintage of this generous, warm red. Particularly noteworthy is the Don Anselmo reserve, in fond memory of his grandfather, Anselmo Paternoster, a unique and well-respected restauranteur and wine-grower.

Aglianico del Vulture 1988 DOC   🍇 ①
Inarguably a good vintage for this Aglianico which Giuseppe and sons currently produce in a 'normal' version (the reserve will be released in 1993), with composite and fleshy maturity, good intensity on nose and palate.

Aglianico del Vulture   🍇🍇 ②
Don Anselmo Riserva 1985 DOC
Made from slightly over-ripe Aglianico grapes, elegant, aged in barrique and large oak barrels, it was bottled in 1990 and is currently at peak maturity, with ample, complex aromas.

Librandi

Contrada San Gennaro, S.S. 106
Cirò Marina (Cz) 88072
Tel. (0962) 31518
Fax (0962) 370542

The winery's owners, the Librandi brothers, have always been among the finest producers of Cirò. They recently started upgrading both the cellar and vineyard by introducing new varietals. With an important role in the planning and creation of several great Italian wines from the South, Severino Garofano has strongly backed their moves. Chardonnay and Sauvignon have been introduced and from them they make Critone, an interesting new generation white. More recently, Cabernet Sauvignon and Franc were planted in a 15 ha vineyard and now bottled for the first time as Gravello. Although it was released only a few months ago, it is already surprisingly elegant and individualistic. Other positive results have been obtained with the more traditional Cirò, the winery's flagship wine, especially the selections, characterized by a modern style which does not upset its traditional traits. Librandi's Cirò is characterized by unusually clean and refined notes.

Critone 1991 ♈ ①
A blend of 80% Chardonnay and 20% Sauvignon, recently added to Calabria's wine production. Strong varietal character of Chardonnay, fruity and moderate bouquet, also on the palate, supported by pleasant structure and texture.

Gravello 1988 ♈♈ ②
Already at its first release, to be immediately added to the award winning series of wines made by Severino Garofano. A blend of 40% young Cabernet Sauvignon with 60% Gaglioppo, it has elegant and remarkably intense aromas, fully confirmed on the palate, soft and ample.

Cirò Riserva San Felice 1985 DOC ♈ ②
Royal ruby-red in color with brick orange highlights, of excellent texture, made from Gaglioppo grapes, ample perfumes and equally ample and full-bodied flavors, powerful and more elegant than in past vintages.

Ferdinando Messinò

Via Calvario, 8
Bianco (Rc) 89032
Tel. (0964) 911222

According to historian Fernand Braudel, Calabria's coastline resembles a kind of rocky skeleton along the Mediterranean Sea, a sea which was historically very hostile to this region. For centuries, after the Greek dominion, the area was raided and invaded numerous times. One of southern Italy's most extraordinary grapes, Greco, whose wines are singular and festive yet rare, comes from Greece as its name clearly states. Ferdinando Messinò, a forefather of this white "Vino da Meditazione", prefers to use its original ancient name, Greco di Gerace, even though his vineyards are in the district of Bianco, within the limits of the DOC production zone of Greco di Bianco. Besides the change in names, the wines of this elderly yet youthful and tenacious producer still enchant consumers, thanks to their aromatic richness and sunny warmth. The Mantonico di Bianco, made from dried grapes from the Bruzzano Zeffirio area, is also worth tasting.

Greco di Gerace 1991 ♈ ②
A particularly unique wine, made from Greco grapes. Deep yellow with amber reflections, decidedly Mediterranean perfumes, hints of bergamot, dried figs and apricot. Its full, lengthy palate is equally brilliant.

Mantonico di Bianco 1991 ♈ ②
Messinò's other gem, from reed-dried, Mantonico grapes. A more amber-colored wine, yet bright, with intense, rich perfumes, incense, and a unique sweet-tannic palate.

Odoardi

Contrada Campodorato
Nocera Terinese (Cz) 88047
Tel. (0968) 91159
Fax (0984) 28503

Based in Campodorato, at 400 m above sea level, Giovanbattista Odoardi's winery is one of Calabria's more historical yet avant-garde companies. The Odoardi family has lived in Nocera since the 13th century. Each wine is a single-vineyard wine, made from estate vineyards located either in Nocera Terinese or in the commune of Falerna. The latter produces white Scavigna (Pian della Corte and Est/Ovest) and Valeo, whereas the other vineyards (Mortilla, Vecchia and Chiusa) produce the three Savuto DOC Superiore crus. Dr. Odoardi, chief physician at the hospital of Cosenza, is motivated by pure passion and is determined to improve the already remarkable quality of his products. He is constantly experimenting and renewing the cellar and vineyard. In Falerna he has planted a dozen new varietals, ranging from Gaglioppo and Cabernet Sauvignon to Moscato di Valeo and Gewürtztraminer. Cellar equipment features an array of wood, from the traditional 'double caratello' barrique to larger Slovenian oak barrels. The new labels proudly illustrate a Calabrian harvest scene, showing his deep link with the land.

Pian della Corte 1991 ♈ ①
From a vineyard replanted in 1988 in the Scavigna area, it is a blend of Pinot Blanc, Chardonnay and Riesling Italico grapes, not lacking in perfumes, well structured with good personality.

Valeo 1990 ♈ ②
Absolutely unique, a blend of the native Valeo version of Moscato; on the nose it reveals various fruity notes, dominated by papaya. Ample, aromatic and bone-dry on the palate. Best at the start or the end of a meal.

Savuto Superiore ♈ ①
Vigna Mortilla 1988 DOC
Another cru of Savuto Superiore made by the Odoardis, with grapes from a recently replanted vineyard close to the coast. Deep, bright ruby-red, full nose and palate, which will develop further.

Savuto Superiore ♈ ①
Vigna Vecchia 1988 DOC
Deep ruby-red, with purplish highlights. With a red currant and strawberry jam bouquet, it is made from Gaglioppo grapes, with some Sangiovese, Nerello Cappuccio, Greco Nero and others. A decidely tannic and full character on the palate.

Fattoria San Francesco

Casale San Francesco
Cirò (Cz) 88071
Tel. (0962) 32228
Fax (0962) 32987

Originally a convent in 1578, the hamlet of Casale San Francesco is completely surrounded by olive-groves and vineyards and brings to mind the days of humming farm-activity. Creamy ricotta, fresh mozzarella and extraordinary local cheeses are still made daily. The vineyards of the winery, owned by the Siciliani family, are in the heart of the Cirò Classico production zone, on plots called Vallo, Cognale dei Bovi, Monaco and Artino, where the varietal Gaglioppo, the base of Cirò Rosso wines, is ideally suited to the foot-hill climate. Everything else is a labor of love, made by Francesco Siciliani and his winemaker, Severino Garofano. Garofano recieves credit for making some of Calabria's most exciting wines, such as Ronco dei Quattroventi (a brilliant oak-aged wine, made from Gaglioppo) and Donna Madda, in honor of Francesco Siciliani's wife. The Greco grape is traditionally used to produce one of the winery's most popular wines, the San Francesco Bianco. They also make Greco di Bianco and Mantonico di Bianco, two outstanding dessert wines crafted by Pasquale Ceratti.

Greco di Bianco Ceratti 1991 DOC ♈ ③
Made by Pasquale Ceratti, who is also a skilled grower of Mantonico. This has rich aromas, reminiscent of apricots; it is sweet on the palate but balanced by fresh acidity.

Cirò Rosso Classico Superiore ♈ ②
Donna Madda 1989 DOC
This first vintage is his first try at a barrique-aged style of Cirò and already the results are impressive. It has character and interesting spice and fruit on the nose, while it is soft and lengthy on the palate.

Cirò Rosso Classico ♈♈ ②
Ronco dei Quattro Venti 1988 DOC
A varietal of Greek origins, the Gaglioppo is Calabria's most important varietal, consistently notable in this Cirò cru, which for the last few years has been one of Calabria's best red wines. It has elegant tannins and texture from the oak-aging. The 1988 is the most recent vintage we tasted and although the 1989 is on its way soon this is still drinking well.

D'Ambra Vini d'Ischia

Via Mario D'Ambra
Panza d'Ischia (Na) 80070
Tel. (081) 907210-907246
Fax (081) 908190

The D'Ambra family's first link to wine dates back to the 16th century, when a distant relative loaded wine onto outbound ships in the port of Naples. Gradually wine production on the island of Ischia was pushed aside by a tourism boom, as real-estate speculation set in and highrise buildings quickly cluttered the coast. The D'Ambra winery deserves a special merit for having kept the island's wine tradition alive. Years ago, Mario D'Ambra pulled the winery out of bankruptcy, concentrating on producing quality wines. Though he's no longer there, the winery is now in the hands of his nephews, Andrea and Corrado, who continue to advocate the island's local wines. They have been able to identify some particularly fertile zones, several favorable vineyards carved on the slopes of Mount Epomeo on crumbly tufa soils. From these vineyards they create real jewels.

Biancolella   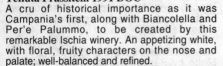
Tenuta Frassitelli 1991 DOC
A cru of historical importance as it was Campania's first, along with Biancolella and Per'e Palummo, to be created by this remarkable Ischia winery. An appetizing white, with floral, fruity characters on the nose and palate; well-balanced and refined.

Per'e Palummo
Tenuta Montecorvo 1990 DOC
A cru wine from this unique DOC area, made from native Per'e Palummo grape. The name is Neapolitan dialect for "pidgeon's foot" and refers to the shape of the grape's stalks and bunches. Considerable aromas of violets, suggests pleasant drinking and fragrant flavor; concentrated and well-structured.

Mastroberardino

Via Manfredi, 89
Atripalda (Av) 80342
Tel. (0825) 626123-626125
Fax (0825) 624154

Irpinia is a relatively untapped wine area which potentially could head the rebirth for premium wine production in southern Italy, and particularly, in Campania. Its climate, soils and special native grapes are the 'building block' elements needed to obtain quality results. The Mastroberardino winery has blazed the trail for years, representing 'an oasis in the desert' and is now starting to illuminate the region's enology and reputation. Although the Mastroberardino family first began producing wine in the 16th century, the business flourished only after World War 2, when Michele and his three sons, Antonio, Valter and Carlo, joined the winery. In fact, these brothers deserve all the credit for bringing back unique wines like Fiano, Greco di Tufo, Lacryma Christi and Taurasi, each the result of the latest cultivation and vinification techniques under the Mastroberardino brand name.

Greco di Tufo
Vignadangelo 1991 DOC
The strong fruity character in wines made from Greco grapes is easily distinguished in this lively, Mastroberardino cru (another remarkable cru is the Nova Serra). It is the result of experiments aimed at improving quality and style.

Fiano di Avellino
Radici di Lapio 1990 DOC
An other cru selection, this time from Fiano grapes, is Radici di Lapio. The 1990 vintage (rather than the 1991) best captures all the flavors and nuances that a wine from Fiano can indeed have.

Taurasi Radici 1988 DOC
The result of a careful selection of Aglianico grapes, it has strong personality and undisputable elegance. Dark and intense color, on the nose obvious spicy tones and fruity characters. Ample, rounded palate, just reaching its peak.

Taurasi 1987 DOC
Mastroberardino produces Taurasi in three versions: a reserve, a standard and the Radici selection. This 1987 standard version confirms the great potential of Aglianico grape, and, in terms of strength and sheer elegance, does not shy away from comparisons to its grander siblings.

Ocone

Via Del Monte
Ponte (Bn) 82030
Tel. (0824) 874040-874576
Fax (0824) 874328

This small winery is located in the heart of the Sannio area, near the city of Benevento. The Ocone family has been producing wine here since 1910, although they initially sold wine in bulk or by the demijohn and little mattered if it was of any great quality. The turning point came a few years ago when Domenico Ocone took matters in his hands. He has made all efforts to successfully improve the quality of the wines: from careful vineyard selections, to restricting vine yields and installing new equipment in the cellar. Of considerable interest, the production philosophy is based on organic methods in the vineyard, completely avoiding the use of harsh chemicals and using only organic fertilizers. The winery also purchases grapes from neighboring growers on contract and has enlarged its own estate vineyards by purchasing premium sites. The changes also being being undergone in the cellar promise a bright future for this winery, which is already one of Campania's finest.

Greco Del Sannio 1991   ☻ ②
From Greco grapes, grown mostly on the hills of Benevento, this is a white with particularly fruity character, partly thanks to short maceration of the must on the skins; it has a good balance of alcohol and acidity.

Piedirosso Del Sannio 1990   ☻ ①
Piedirosso is one of Campania's long-forgotten varietals which the Del Monte winery has brought out back to life, and which gives its name to this wine. To be appreciated for its self-composure and pleasant drinkability.

Vigna di Pezza La Corte 1987   ☻ ②
An Aglianico del Sannio whose grapes come from a particularly well-exposed and ventilated cru which gives its name to the wine. The result is an interesting, well-structured and soft wine, not lacking in perfumes and character.

Vadiaperti

Loc. Vadiaperti
Montefredane (Av) 83030
Tel. (0825) 607270

Owned by Professor Antonio Troisi, this winery is currently putting out some interesting wines, as it concentrates almost exclusively on the production of two white DOC wines, Fiano d'Avellino and Greco di Tufo. Plans are in store to expand on their Taurasi, made from Aglianico grapes, which was recently granted DOCG status. Founded in 1983 with the passionate determination of Troisi, who is first and foremost a history professor. The winery is made up of two different parts. Situated in Montefredano, one vineyard is 4 ha entirely planted to Fiano and makes Vadiaperti's most interesting varietal wine. There are also 4 ha in Montefusco, where the Greco di Tufo grapes are grown. The winery is respectably old-fashioned in terms of both planting and vinification facilities and techniques, with little modern innovations except for skilled aging, particularly in the case of Fiano. With such rich and complex wines to distinguish him, he has established a fine reputation for making white wines in southern Italy.

Fiano di Avellino 1990 DOC   ☻ ☻ ①
Made from Fiano, it has quite a bright yellow color and charming, intense perfumes, with toasted hazelnut and fresh almond scents. Similar aromas also come through on the palate, as it is rich, complex, and lingering with excellent aromas: a wine which can easily stand comparison with other counterparts abroad.

Villa Matilde

S.S. Domitiana, 12
Cellole (Ce) 81030
Tel. (0823) 932088
Fax (0823) 932134

Falanghina, Piedirosso, Coda di Volpe, Abbuoto and Aglianico (also found in Basilicata) are just a few of the native varietals with which several Campania producers are experimenting. These wines would otherwise risk being overshadowed by seasonal vogues or by more fashionable wines and varietals. Francesco Avallone, a lawyer by profession, has always believed in these regional varietals and has grown them for many years. His passion in youth for wine and wine culture has turned out to be a full-fledged winery which is today managed by his two children, Maria Ida and Tani. This philological penchant for ancient varietals is not merely limited to learning about the historical aspects but is carefully put into practice in the vineyard, with selective cloning and re-planting. Thus were born some of Campania's most interesting recent wines, such as the Vigna Camarato, which is made from selected Aglianico grapes, the Vigna Caracci, from Falanghina grapes, or the Paterno. The latter is produced in both a white version (from Falanghina grapes) and a red one (from a blend of Aglianico and Piedirosso grapes).

Falerno del Massico Bianco
Vigna Caracci 1991 DOC   ♈ ①
Made from scrupulously selected Falanghina grapes, using techniques which preserve the ripe aromas of fruit. The result is a fresh, fruity wine with pleasant vanilla and citrus-fruit aromas.

Falerno del Massico Rosso
Riserva 1990 DOC   ♈ ③
An oaked blend of Aglianico (80%) and Campania's native Piedirosso, it is bright garnet-red in color, with rich perfumes and aromas of small berries and moss. A consistently elegant body.

Cecubo 1986   ♈ ③
The interesting range of Villa Matilde products includes, among the reds, this Cecubo is made from a blend of Piedirosso, Coda di Volpe Rosso and Abbuoto grapes. Good body, well-aged, and unique in its perfumes and flavors. Proof that almost-extinct grapes can give give excellent results with the help of proper winemaking techniques.

Vigna Camarato 1985   ♈ ③
Currently the most impressive red wine made by the Avallone family, especially in terms of perfumes and flavor complexity. Fleshy and velvety, it is made from Aglianico grapes grown in one of the winery's best vineyards and is currently at its peak.

Emilia Romagna

Emilia Romagna is actually two distinct regions in one, each being quite different from each other in terms of cultural identity. First of all, both were historically 'marked' by the ancient Romans in their names. "Emilia" was the name of the road they built to link the coast to the hinterland, from Rimini to Piacenza. The name "Romagna" can be traced to when the Romans actually occupied the area for a lengthy period. Wines coming from the two areas are also very different from one another.

Emilia produces much more Lambrusco wine, while Romagna puts out more Sangiovese and Trebbiano. Ten years ago, roughly 3 out of 10 bottles produced for export to the United States were Lambrusco from Emilia. Today, things have changed. The disappearance of this 'American paradise' has luckily encouraged the larger companies to change their production policies and shift their emphasis to quality rather than quantity. Furthermore, the total vineyard surface in Emilia Romagna has been considerably reduced. Hopefully this is only the first step of others to follow in replanning grape-growing production on the flat Po valley, where most of the production is concentrated. Last year's harvest still yielded 8,000,000 hl of wine.

Lambrusco is the most common varietal with sub-species which include Sorbara, Grasparossa and Salamino. The best examples are made by Bellei and Cavicchioli who were selected for this guide. Sangiovese is the other important grape which makes for straightforward, undemanding and honest 'territorial' wines. There are some very powerful wines derived from different clones, that are mostly of Tuscan origin. Most noteworthy are the wines made by Castelluccio, Zebina who also makes an exquisite Albana Passito and a handful of other wineries. Albana, incidentally, is still the only Italian white wine to have been granted DOCG status. To date we feel that the best are the Passito or sweet/semi-sweet versions. The other four native red varietals include Bonarda, Barbera (especially in Piacenza's hills), Barbarossa and Cagnina.

The onslaught of Cabernet Sauvignon, Pinot Noir and Merlot has the captured the attention of several interesting wineries like Vallania in Bologna's hills, La Stoppa and the emerging La Tosa in Piacenza's hills. Among whites, in addition to Trebbiano, native grapes include Ortrugo, Pagadebit, Pignoletto, Verdea and Malvasia but once again Sauvignon, Chardonnay, Riesling, Pinot Blanc and even Sémillon have proved to do remarkably well under the right conditions and in the hands of the right wine makers.

Francesco Bellei

Via per Modena, 80
Bomporto (Mo) 41030
Tel. (059) 909117
Fax (059) 818100

The rich traditional foods of Modena demand an equally traditional wine to match. Even the more skeptical wine drinkers have to tip their hats to a real Lambrusco di Sorbara when they see one. Francesco Bellei's Lambrusco wines are definitely within this category, with wonderful consistency, year in year out. Located between Bomporto and San Prospero, the winery was founded in 1930 and is currently run by Francesco Bellei and his son Giuseppe, who studied in Coneglieno, Italy and in France. The Bellei make two styles of Lambrusco from estate-grown grapes from the zone of Sorbara. One is a vintage wine and made according to traditional standards. It is naturally fermented in the bottle and will have some slight leftover residue. The other, Calle Capsula Oro, is also bottle fermented, but it undergoes a final dégorgement. Bellei devotes special attention to the production of methode champenoise sparkling wines. In the district of Serramazzoni, and more precisely in Località Ricò, Bellei has recently planted Pinot Noir and Chardonnay to strengthen and improve this other side to his production which has already yielded interesting results.

Francesco Bellei Riserva 1987   🍇 ③
Made from equal amounts of Pinot Noir and Chardonnay grapes, a very pleasant methode champenoise sparkling wine. It has lingering and fine bubbles, is elegant, perfumed on the nose with traces of bread crust. Dry, with a pleasant almond finish.

Lambrusco di Sorbara 1991 DOC   🍷 ①
Bright and luminous ruby-red color, exuberant mousse and fairly generous floral perfumes on the nose, confirmed on the palate, sustained by good acidity.

Lambrusco di Sorbara   🍷 ①
Capsula oro DOC
Compared to the more traditional version of Lambrusco di Sorbara, this particular selection is more refined on the nose and palate thanks to the dégorgement which eliminates the deposits left by bottle fermentation, thus softening the wine.

Castelluccio

Corso Matteotti, 25
Faenza (Fo) 48018
Tel. (0546) 663031
Fax (0546) 992106

The vineyards are situated at altitudes which are unusually high for Romagna (over 400 m), on incredibly well-exposed and difficult to manage steep slopes between Brisighella and Pieve del Tho, not far from the Tuscan border. Gian Matteo Baldi, the winery's owner, together with his father Gian Vittorio, a bold movie director and producer, purposely chose a Tuscan Sangiovese purist as their wine consultant. Attilio Pagli was well-taught by the famous Tuscan wine technician, Guilio Gambelli. In operation since 1975, the winery's four main wines come from Sangiovese grapes. There is also a limited supply of Sauvignon and future plans to include a Cabernet Sauvignon. All are labelled Vino da Tavola and made from selected cloned varietals and grapes from single-vineyards such as Ronco dei Ciliegi, Ronco delle Ginestre and Ronco del Casone. Ronco della Scimmia was added in 1990. After several experiments Gian Matteo opted to use small, 350-lt oak barrels. His aging process is exemplary, as the oak never overpowers but actually complements the wine.

Ronco del Re 1990   🍇 ④
With embracing and very particular notes, despite its Sauvignon origin, it reveals personality even on the palate; full with good balance between alcohol and other components. Only limited quantities were produced.

Ronco dei Ciliegi 1988   🍷🍷 ③
Luminous and intense ruby red, elegant and pronounced on the nose, combining vigor and fresh fruit. Ample, lingering, marked by some fine tannins; it will develop, but already reveals its personality.

Ronco delle Ginestre 1988   🍷 ③
Made from selected clones of Sangiovese Grosso. Compared to past vintages, the wine seems more immediate, due in part to a shorter maceration on the skins. Elegant and polished, its expressive structure can improve further.

Cantine Cavicchioli

Piazza Gramsci, 9
San Prospero (Mo) 41030
Tel. (059) 908828
Fax (059) 906163

The towns of Sorbara and San Prospero are somewhat in the heart of the production area of DOC Lambrusco di Sorbara. Founded by Umberto Cavicchioli in the period between the two World Wars, or more precisely in 1928, the winery is located just north of Modena, where the rivers Secchia and Panaro join closest to each other and the climate is rather continental. The winery has always vinified only estate-grown grapes. Market growth in the 1950s allowed the winery to invest in facilities and build a modern vinification cellar, in Cristo di Sorbara adjacent to the 7-ha vineyard which yields the cru Vigna del Cristo. In San Prospero the Cavicchioli brothers, with Sandro as winemaker, own a modern bottling center and the vineyards which yield their other cru, Due Madonne. This, unlike the Vigna del Cristo wine, is re-fermented in bottle for nearly one year and then subject to the classic dégorgement.

Vigna del Cristo 1991 ♈ ①
Mostly made from Lambrusco di Sorbara grapes, with a small amount of Lambrusco Salamino, grown in a low-yielding vineyard. An extremely refined wine, of good structure and pleasant mousse, with penetrating floral notes, especially violets and roses.

Lambrusco di Sorbara ♈ ①
Due Madonne 1990 DOC
This debut of a bottle-fermented cru of Lambrusco di Sorbara passes the test brilliantly; attractive fresh and floral bouquet, with good crisp acidity to support the palate, pinching any excess sweetness.

La Stoppa

Fraz. Ancarano
Rivergaro (Pc) 29029
Tel. (0523) 958159
Fax (0523) 956085

Particularily intrigued by the variety of grapes that were grown on the Piacenza hillside, Raffaele Pantaleoni bought the La Stoppa estate in 1974. Until then he managed his family's art printing company but had always dreamt of producing wine with the strange grapes of those vineyards. From Piacenza's Bonarda and Barbera to Chardonnay, Pinot Noir and Sémillon, each were very different in their type and style. His dream has since come true: indeed Pantaleoni has created one of the region's most interesting wineries, noted for its native varietal wines such as Gutturnio, white and red styles of Ancarano and Macchiona, made from Barbera and Bonarda grapes. He is best known for wines made from other varietals, such as the red Stoppa (a Cabernet/Merlot blend, aged in barrique then, at length, in bottle), the Chardonnay and Alfeo (a surprising Pinot Noir, elegant and well-oaked). Angela Braga assists her husband with enthusiasm and conviction.

Armelio 1990 ♈♈ ②
From Chardonnay grapes, fermented in barrique and aged one year in bottle before being released. Bright yellow-golden color, intensely smokey and ripe fruit perfumes. When tasted it was still in its polishing phase on the palate.

Buca delle Canne 1990 ♈♈ ③
A limited production Vino da Meditazione made from botrytized Sémillon grapes. Marvellously intense and lingering on the nose, with an embracing and ample palate, suggesting pastries and ripe dates.

Alfeo 1990 ♈♈ ③
Probably the most elegant wine of the ample and colorful line of La Stoppa wines. Made from oaked Pinot Noir, its has intense and rich perfumes ranging from toasted bread to vanilla and small fruits, ample and soft on the palate. Skillfully matched freshness and texture.

Colli Piacentini Gutturnio ♈ ②
Macchiona 1988 DOC
Our favorite version of this DOC from Piacenza, made with Bonarda and Barbera grapes. Aged in 10 and 20 hl oak barrels, ruby-red in color with an orange rim; rich warm smells, soft embracing palate.

Stoppa 1988 ♈ ②
Like other La Stoppa reds, this has the winery's unmistakable 'signature' and a personal touch. Made with Merlot and Cabernet grapes, has reached its peak with elegance, although still youthful, with spicy notes and suggestions of licorice and pastries. Good drinkability.

La Tosa

Loc. Casa Bruciata
Vigolzone (Pc) 29090
Tel/Fax (0523) 870727

Beginnings were humble for this winery, with its 8 ha tract of vineyard (with exceptionally good exposure and foot-hill microclimate) particularly suited to the production of semi-sparkling wines. On purchasing the property in 1980, the Pizzamiglio brothers, Stefano and Ferruccio, set their goals to produce still, elegant and possibly long-lasting wines. The grapes used were to be those traditionally grown in Piacenza's hills (including Bonarda, Barbera, Malvasia and Ortrugo) with room left for Cabernet Sauvignon and Sauvignon Blanc. Piedmontese enologist Piero Ballario is a very active and results have not been late in coming. He makes a unique but relatively unheard of white wine, Val Nure dei Colli Piacentini, (a blend of Malvasia, Trebbiano and Ortrugo) that is skillfully crafted both in the vineyard and cellar. The same is true for the Gutturnio, in both the standard and reserve versions, and for the Sauvignon (one of the DOC wines from Piacenza's hills), to date the winery's only real hit. The new wines should prove to be successful, including a limited production Cabernet Sauvignon released this year.

Colli Piacentini La Tosa   ♈ ①
Il Bianco 1991 DOC
50% Malvasia, 35% Ortrugo and 15% Trebbiano: these are the grapes used to make this classy white, rich in perfumes and on the palate, pleasant and fairly full-bodied. We eagerly await the first release of a Malvasia which, upon first tasting, promises to have an extremely great future.

Colli Piacentini Sauvignon 1991 DOC ♈ ①
When tasted comparatively against the 1990, this had less pronounced varietal characters, but instead the greater fullness and maturity of the vintage. Supple and rather fat on the palate.

Luna Selvatica 1989   ♉ ②
1989 was generally on off-vintage for reds in the hills of Piacenza, but strict thinning-out allowed the Pizzamiglio brothers to do wonders with their Cabernet Sauvignon grapes, oak-aged 14 months to soften its accentuated, grassy flavor.

Colli Piacentini Gutturnio   ♉♉ ①
Vigna Morello 1990 DOC
Made with 55% Barbera and 45% Bonarda grapes, a cru produced for the first time in 1987 with the intention to seek unpretentious elegance in a local wine which is generally not much vaunted. The experiment was a success, with appealing aromas softness and a Piedmontese heart.

Vigneto delle Terre Rosse

Via Predosa, 83
Zola Predosa (Bo) 40069
Tel/Fax (051) 755845

This winery went against all odds to establish itself. It was created by Enrico Vallania, a medical doctor but winemaker at heart, who has gone on to become legend in the local wine scenario. When he passed away, his wife, Adriana, and their two children, Maria Elisabetta and Giovanni, took over operations. Surprizingly indeed, they produce great wines from classic varietals but in an unsuitable location, with vineyards on loam-limestone iron-rich soils called "terre rosse", which are especially intense at sunset. The wines are very individualistic and do not touch wood (neither large barrels nor barrique). Instead they age in large stainless steel vats and later in bottle. Wines include Cabernet Sauvignon (outstanding in many vintages), Sauvignon, Pinot Grigio, Chardonnay (elegant and worth cellaring), and Petroso (a classic Bordeaux style Merlot/Cabernet blend and which most clearly shows the high quality levels reached by this estate).

Malagò 1991   ♈ ①
Bright in color, with fragrant perfumes and a good structure, more immediate than other Vallania products. Made from Riesling Italico with some Riesling Renano. The late-harvest version of the 1990 vintage is also worthy of mention.

Chardonnay Cuvée 1989   ♈♈ ②
Lengthy and lively youthfulness is not only a standard virtue of Vallania's reds, but also for its whites. Such is the case with this intensely fruity Chardonnay, just released after three years' aging in steel vats and bottle.

Colli Bolognsi Sauvignon 1991 DOC ♈ ①
At time of tasting, it was still decidedly young but clearly capable of evolving well, thanks to its good backbone. Varietal flavors, particularly sage and hazelnut, seem more pronounced than in the previous year's vintage.

Petroso 1988   ♉ ②
A new style for the Vallania's winery, this Merlot and Cabernet blend will soon be joined by a Pinot Noir. It has good complex aromas and intensity and a robust palate; not yet completely evolved.

Rosso di Enrico Vallania   ♉♉ ③
Cuvée 1987
A Cabernet Sauvignon of rare elegance, one of Italy's best, it is made from clones selected by the late Enrico Vallania and aged in stainless steel and bottle. Intense and elegant perfumes with aging have surpassed the varietal fruit flavor; concentrated and lingering.

Zerbina

Fraz. Marzeno, via Vicchio, 6
Mazzeno (Ra) 48010
Tel. (0546) 40022
Fax (0546) 40275

Both the vineyards and winery are located in the hilly Valle di Marzeno, one of Romagna's areas most suited to viticulture. The owners' passion together with wise investments and good advice have combined to assure this winery a front row seat in the region's winemaking. Vincenzo Geminiani gave impetus to the company in the 1960s and 1970s, while his son, Franco, modernized where needed in the 1980s. His grandaughter, Cristina, joined in the 1990s and commutes between Monza and Marzeno; they rely on the enological advice of Vittorio Fiore and Gianfranco Bolognesi. Zerbina's flagship wine is Albana Passito Scacco Matto, one of the best examples of this particular wine. Always determined to improve, they continue to experiment and innovate, as for example with a particular clone of the white Albana grape called L14. The range of wines also includes Vicchio, from Trebbiano and Chardonnay grapes, a dry white with a very definite personality and, among the reds, Marzeno di Marzeno, Pietramora and Sangiovese Ceregio.

Vicchio 1990   ♀ ②
A convincing white made from Chardonnay grapes with small amounts of Trebbiano, aged in small barrels. Marked by an enticing array of perfumes, it has good concentration and balance on the palate.

Albana di Romagna Passito   ♀ ③
Scacco Matto 1988 DOCG
Quite possibly their flagship wine, and almost certainly the best version of this wine; exuberant richness and aromatic complexity, ripe fruit and vanilla notes and generous lingering palate, without being too sweet.

Marzeno di Marzeno 1988   ♀♀ ②
Made for the first time in 1987, this second vintage was only recently released, after lengthy aging in barrique and bottle; it fully confirms the the successful combination of Sangiovese with some Cabernet Sauvignon. Elegant and firm, will develop with time.

Pietramora 1988   ♀ ②
A Sangiovese reserve made only in better vintages, French oak aged and later bottle-aged for months. Bright and luminous in color, with fruity and ethereal aromas; well-balanced fruit and wood also on the palate; very attractive and quite lingering.

Friuli-Venezia Giulia

It was the Romans who, following the conquest of the region by Julius Caesar, first brought the grape vine to Friuli. Under their empire its ancient capital, Aquilea, became the departure point for the convoys of wine exported to northern Europe (convoys in which, according to historians, the Mediterranean amphora was quickly replaced by the wooden barrel of the Celts which besides being less fragile helped to preserve the wine in the cold climates of the north). For many centuries viticulture was a feature on the plains of Friuli and the coastal areas, which extended into Istria. The Longobards valued the crop so highly that severe penalties were imposed for the theft of a mere bunch of grapes from the vines. In the 15th and 16th centuries the production developed further still and official records of the era testify to the importance of vineyards at Rosazzo and the Collio. The fortunes of Picolit date on the other hand from the 19th century. The dessert wine was made famous by the Counts Asquini in the royal courts of Europe and at the Vatican city. In the period that followed, Friuli-Venezia Giulia was governed in turn by Venice, France and Austria. Each of these countries introduced its own grape varieties, creating the wide spectrum of cultivation which exists in the region today, several of which have mutated in the local conditions to the point that it is difficult to trace their origins.

Current statistics show that Friuli makes 1.6% of the national wine product from 2.2% of its vineyards. These very percentages underline the low yields that are a feature of the region and, in particular, of the hilly zones where harvests of more than 80 Q/ha are extremely rare. 65% of the 70 million bottles produced every year have DOC status, the remainder being officially Vino da Tavola, a category which paradoxically includes many superb wines of outstanding importance. The DOC hill zones are the Collio, Colli Orientali del Friuli and the Carso; Grave del Friuli, Isonzo, Aquilea, Latisana and a small part of Lison-Pramaggiore are all situated on the plains. Soils on the hillsides are mainly a type of flysch known locally as "ponca", while on the plain they consist of alluvial deposits with often shallow top soils. The climate benefits from the cold air of the north by the chain of the Alps and its foothills.

Up until 20 years ago, red wines predominated throughout the region, but the commercial demand for whites has led to widespread conversion of the vineyards. Meanwhile, growers have tended to increase the vine density per hectare and reduce grape yields. In the winery there have been enormous investments in new technology. Stainless steel has, for example, almost universally replaced wooden, cement and fiberglass vats. A growing number of winemakers use oak barriques, while others are again experimenting with the traditional 400-500 lt barrels as well as the use of other wood types like acacia. Friuli gained its international reputation as a producer of fresh, fruity whites to drink young. The modern trend now in the region is to offer a wide selection of wines, both white and red, which begin to show their best from three years onwards. The wines tasted for this guide were the newly released vintages, 1990 and 1991, the former being excellent and the latter considered good.

Abbazia di Rosazzo

Loc. Rosazzo
Manzano (Ud) 33044
Tel. (0432) 759693-759240
Fax (0432) 759884

The agricultural estate of the ancient Monasterium Rosarum is located half-way along the road between Gorizia and Udine. After having passed from the ownership of the Benedictine Order to that of the Domenicans and finally to the Archbishop of Udine, it has been managed since 1981 by the Zamò and Palazzolo families. A number of leading experts have worked on the estate, but credit for the wines currently being made rests with the young enologist Sandro Facca and a winemaker of wide-ranging experience and exceptional ability, Franco Bernabei. Naturally, however, neither their technical expertise, nor the state-of-the-art cellar equipment would be of any avail without the natural resource of 20 ha of prime vineyard planted on eocene marl at 176 m above sea level in one of the best sites in the entire region. Only 30 km from the sea, this zone has a unique micro-climate in which, in past centuries, even olive trees flourished (trees which incidentally are being replanted today). The production strategy of the estate has been to invest in the local grape varieties which have been revitalised through either barrique aging in the historic cellars of the Abbey, or through the creation of carefully judged cuvée.

Colli Orientali del Friuli Chardonnay 1991 DOC   ♟ ①
Intense, stylish, with bread crust aromas on the nose and good strucure and depth of flavor on the palate. Well-balanced acidity gives length and interesting prospects for development.

Colli Orientali del Friuli Tocai Friuliano 1991 DOC   ♟ ①
A wine which shows the quality of which this often under-estimated variety is capable. Intense and well-defined on the nose, on the palate dry, smooth, fruity, long and full of character.

Ronco dell Acacie 1990   ♟♟ ③
A blend mainly of Chardonnay, Pinot Bianco and Tocai aged in barriques which impart elegant vanilla scents. Intense fruit on the nose, balanced, complex, full of flavor. Long-lived.

Ronco dell'Abbazia 1989   ♟ ③
From Verduzzo and Picolit grapes, part late-harvested and part dried in special lofts designed for the purpose, fermented slowly in barriques. The nose has fruit and flowers aromas and the palate is rich, smooth and sweet.

Ronco dei Rosetti 1988   ♥♥ ③
A blend of Cabernet Sauvignon, Cabernet Franc, Merlot and other local red and white grapes. Deep ruby in color, the nose has a gamey but elegant character with underlying spice and rich complexity. Full-bodied with well-balanced tannin and lots of character. Made to age.

Bandut - Colutta

Via Orsaria, 32
Manzano (Ud) 33044
Tel. (0432) 740524-299208
Fax (0432) 506126

Few graduates with degrees in pharmaceutical medicine have taken up winemaking in Friuli, but those who have, have been successful. Probably their intense training and the meticulous attention to detail characteristic of their profession, applied viticulture and the science of vinification, lies behind their achievements. The Colutta family are chemists from Udine who produce wines from their own 70 ha of vineyard and another 25 ha which they rent, all situated in the Colli Orientali zone around Buttrio, Manzano and San Giovani, 18 km south-east of the provincial capital. The vines are planted on sunny slopes where marl alternates with sandier soils. Warm Adriatic winds blow from the south and the range of hills to the north protects from cold air streams. The young Elisabetta and Giorgio Colutta, both of whom graduated with theses in enology, supervize their 200,000 bottle production of the estate, owned by their respective parents, Gianpaolo and Giansandro. The use of modern techniques to control fermentation in white wines are typical of the region in the elegance and intensity of their aromas.

Müller Thurgau 1991   ♟ ②
It is not easy to find a Müller Thurgau in Friuli which turns out so successful, year in year out. The Colutta family produce an elegant white with subtle varietal aromas and good fruit, acidity and balance on the palate.

Nojar 1991   ♟ ②
A blend of Pinot Bianco, Ribolla, Müller Thurgau and Picolit, aged in stainless steel. A wine with intense fruity-floral aromas, still young on the palate but already with good depth of flavor, length and balance.

Selenard 1990   ♥ ②
Refosco, Schioppettino and Cabernet Sauvignon combine with a touch of Pinot Nero to give a wine with a slightly evolved ruby color and good fruit on the nose. Nicely balanced on the palate with the soft oak tannins of barrique aging.

Borgo Conventi

Strada Colombare, 13
Farra d'Isonzo (Go) 34070
Tel. (0481) 88004
Fax (0481) 888510

Gianni Vescovo left his job as technical director at one of the biggest private wineries in Friuli in 1975 in search of new personal rewards and with the aim of building a model estate of his own. Today he works in a newly-constructed winery which he designed himself and is the owner of not one but three estates, with a total of over 90 ha of vineyards in the area where the Collio and Isonzo DOC zones meet. From his first property, Borgo Conventi in the Collio, he makes a range of serious, premium quality wines including the renowned Bordeaux-blend, Braida Nuova. Sharply differentiated by intention is the "Linea Fiori" line launched in 1985 featuring modern easy-drinking varietal wines made from 50 ha on the Isonzo plain. The most recent acquisition, again in the Isonzo, is the Sant'Elena estate where Vescovo is 'revolutionizing', to use his own word, vineyards targeted for the future production of limited quantities of prestige wines. The feeling of having realized his ambition of creating an environment where work is almost a hobby has not lessened this dynamic winemaker's urge to expand, to experiment and, always with a finger on the pulse of the market, to launch new projects.

Collio Sauvignon 1991 DOC   🍇 ②
Broad, very typical varietal aromas (sage and green peppers to the fore; firm, well-structured palate are the main features of this very well-made wine. A serious Sauvignon with lots of personality.

Collio Merlot 1990 DOC   🍇 ②
Fermentation in stainless steel and aging in third-year barrique mean that the varietal character predominates over flavors of oak. The depth of color, concentration of fruit and very respectable body reflect the super vintage.

Braida Nuova 1988   🍇🍇 ③
Vescovo uses all new barriques for this big-scale Cabernet-Merlot blend in which the tannins combine with the ripe fruit to produce aromas of great intensity and a broad 'masculine palate'. Very good aging potential.

Borgo del Tiglio

Via San Giorgio, 71
Brazzano di Cormons (Go) 34070
Tel/Fax (0481) 62166

Nicola Manferrari is one of the producers most respected by fellow winemakers in Friuli, and his estate is often cited as the model of its type. The production is small (a mere 25,000 bottles in 1991) and highly specialized. Manferrari, contrary to more fashionable trends, has dedicated his greatest efforts to demonstrating the value of the traditional varieties of the Collio, the same ones he found planted on the family estate when he took it over in 1981, namely Tocai, Malvasia and Merlot. Tocai Ronco della Chiesa, extracted in tiny quantities from old vines grown on the traditional narrow terraces is the most eloquent statement of Manferrari`s beliefs about wine. It has a richness of texture which is rare in white wines and subtle but highly personal aromas which need bottle age to develop to the full. Manferrari has a stoical dedication to growing and making wines which does not express itself in easy enthusiasm. Like the majority of forward-looking, Italian producers, he is carrying out practical research in the vineyard and the cellar, but the standards he sets himself are such that changes in the production will be gradual and only materialize when this perfectionist winemaker is confident of the long-term benefits.

Collio Tocai Friulano   🍇🍇 ②
Ronco della Chiesa 1990 DOC
This cru from traditionally terraced old vines on a steep south-facing slope lifts Tocai to levels rarely achieved elsewhere. With tightly-packed concentration, it opens slowly to reveal lime blossom, dried apricot, barley sugar and the bitter almonds which is the variety's fingerprint. The follow through on the palate is exemplary. Voluminous and mouth-filling with the stature of serious red wine. For long aging.

Chardonnay 1990   🍇 ③
Complex, subtle and long on the nose with wild flower aromas and a background of buttery Chardonnay and lightly toasted oak. Ample body and a vein of lemony acidity on the palate, finishing with concentrated, fresh grape flavors. Balanced and stylish, will keep well for another couple for years.

Rosso della Centa 1989   🍇🍇 ③
A vineyard selection from 20 to 30 year-old Merlot vines produced in limited quantities, in only the best vintages. Potent, with rare concentration of fruit and, like all Manferrari wines, serious and full of personality.

La Castellada

Loc. Oslavia, 1
Oslavia (Go) 34170
Tel. (0481) 33670

Giorgio and Nicolò Bensa are in the process of converting what was once a family side-line into one of the most interesting small producers to emerge in the province of Gorizia in recent years. The Bensas were primarily Trattoria owners with a few vineyards at Oslavia. They were well-sited but farmed with scant attention to the quality of a wine that was sold locally in demi-johns. The break with the past came in 1985 with the first releases under the Castellada label of a new "azienda agricola" dedicated to the production of limited quantities of premium quality wines. The brothers revolutionized work in the vineyard to reduce yields which had previously topped 130 Q/ha in some vintages to an average 50 Q. They invested in a soft press, stainless steel vats and the French oak which have now become one of their hallmarks. Giorgio and Nicolò are quick to acknowledge the inspiration and support of their neighbor, Josko Gravner. Like Josko, they have a penchant for full-bodied wines that unfold on the palate rather than burst with fresh, immediate aromas. Another similarity is their love for Ribolla, a local variety which, when treated with the respect it deserves, makes wines which are a revelation to the uninitiated.

Collio Ribolla Gialla 1990 DOC   ℱ ②
Ribolla is the great speciality of Oslavia where the grapes ripen very late and, despite exceptional sugar levels, maintain high natural acidity. The Bensa brothers use barrique fermentation for 50% of the final cuvée. The result is a full-bodied wine with broad structure and excellent aging potential. The 1990 has the characteristic slightly honeyed varietal aroma and restrained lemony fruit. Enjoyable now but also worth keeping.

Collio Sauvignon 1990 DOC   ℱℱ ②
A big, muscular Sauvignon with lots of sweet oak and fruit cocktail on the nose. The palate is concentrated and rich an almost oily texture and flavors of soft fruit. There is a slightly intrusive note of green tannin in the finish which suggests the need for bottle age.

Rosso della Castellada 1988   ℱℱ ②
A cuvée of 85% Merlot, 10% Cabernet Sauvignon and 5% Franc which indicates that Oslavia produces splendid reds as well as whites. The color is still very dark with blackcurrant shades in the center; the nose is intense and long. On the palate, there is plummy Merlot, with well-integrated new oak.

Colmello di Grotta

Loc. Villanova
Farra d'Isonzo (Go) 34070
Tel. (0481) 888445
Fax (0481) 888485

This estate, owned by Luciana Benatti and situated at Farra d'Isonzo, produces around 60,000 bottles a year of very fairly-priced wines. It has vineyards both on the plain of the Isonzo DOC zone and on the low hills of the Collio, which protect the estate from the cold, north winds. The estate has a number of pre-requisites for the production of top quality wines: a favorable micro-climate influenced by the warm air from the nearby Adriatic coast, meticulous care of the vineyards, a modern, well-equipped winery and not least the human element, in the person of the talented enologist Fabio Coser. A feature of the wines is their freshness and elegance allied to a structure which comes from the low yields per hectare and which enables them to improve in the bottle over two to three years. The top products are the very consistent whites (in particular the Sauvignon) in which the varietal character brings to mind some of the illustrious wines of France.

Collio Pinot Grigio 1991 DOC   ℱ ①
Bright, pale straw, complex nose with good fruit which returns on the palate. Medium body, good balance and a nice vein of fresh acidity.

Collio Sauvignon 1991 DOC   ℱ ①
Nice straw yellow with hints of green reflection. The varietal aromas of capiscum and tomato leaf jump out of the glass. Good structure and firm acidity, lots of young fruit on the palate and a long finish. Ready now but capable of developing interestingly in the bottle.

Isonzo Sauvignon 1991 DOC   ℱ ①
Pale straw, impressive on the nose with well-defined tomato and capiscum aromas. Complex flavors, good fruit and acidity. An elegant, mid-weight varietal.

Conti d'Attimis Maniago

Via Sottomonte, 21
Buttrio (Ud) 33042
Tel. (0432) 674027
Fax (0432) 674230

The family of the counts Attimis-Maniago
have owned the Sottomonte estate at Buttrio,
10 km south-east of Udine for over 500 years
and have tended vines here since the 17th
century. The vineyards extend for over 70 ha
in a single plot, in part on the south-facing
marl slopes of the Colli Orientali, in part on
the flat clay soils around the village of Buttrio.
Estate bottling began in 1946, the production
having previously been sold in demijohns.
The family winemaking tradition is upheld by
the young Alberto d`Attimis Maniago who
eight years ago abandoned a promising
career in the navy to give all his attention to
the work of the vineyards and cellars. A
feature of the estate is that 70% of the vines
come from selections made from the existing
stock and therefore already acclimatized to
the soils. The continuity of the house style is
assured by the technical expertise of
enologist Antonio Spitaleri. An insight into the
attention given to details which guarantee the
condition of the wines to the consumer is the
practice of leaving bottles upright for three
weeks after corking to ensure a perfect seal
before labeling and release.

Colli Orientali del Friuli
Ramandolo 1990 DOC
Golden straw yellow with full, round aromas.
The palate has the natural sweetness of
interrupted fermentation and long, intense, ripe
fruit flavors.

Colli Orientali del Friuli
Pinot Nero 1991 DOC
Classic pale ruby shade and elegant, lightly
spiced varietal aromas of bitter cherries. Very
correct on the palate with nice balance between
the fruit, the light tannin and the acidity.

Colli Orientali del Friuli
Merlot 1989 DOC
Matured briefly in old barrels, a Merlot with a
good, typical ruby shade of red, intense aromas
of straw and spice and a very long palate with
tasty fruit and moderate tannin.

Girolamo Dorigo

Via del Pozzo, 3
Buttrio (Ud) 33042
Tel. (0432) 674268
Fax (0432) 673373

Rosetta and Girolamo Dorigo founded the
estate in 1966. Men are often thought to be
the practical partner in a marriage, women
more spontaneous and intuitive. In the case
of the Dorigos, who own 27 ha of vineyard in
the Colli Orientali del Friuli, 10 km south-east
of Udine, quite the opposite is true. Girolamo
is forever plunging into new projects, and
Rosetta is the one with her feet on the
ground, who has to restrain her husband`s
unbounded enthusiasm. The couple have
worked for several years now with the
experienced Piemontese enologist, Donato
Lanati. The empathy which has grown
between the Dorigos and Lonati, the soils,
dense planting (up to 8 and 10,000 vines per
ha) low yields, state-of-the-art winemaking
and the ample barrique use in many of their
wines have all helped to make them one of
Friuli`s most important estates. The style is
clearly influenced by French traditions,
although the Dorigos also specialize in local
varieties. Their full range consists of 16
wines, possibly too many for a winery with an
average production of 120,000 bottles a year.

Colli Orientali del Friuli
Chardonnay Ronc di Juri 1990 DOC
Intense yeast/vanilla character both on the nose
and the palate where very well-judged toasty
oak backs up the fruit. Good solid structure
promises long bottle life.

Colli Orientali del Friuli
Picolit Montsclapade 1990 DOC
A mere 225 1t/ha of this great Friuli dessert
wine were produced. Fermentation and aging in
barrique, with a yellow-gold color and a rich,
intense, elegant nose. Good balance on the
palate with delicately sweet fruit, rose petal
flavors and generous alcohol.

Montsclapade 1988
Made from Merlot and Cabernet Franc, the
aggressive character of which is rounded out by
barrique-aging and well-adjusted blend. Intense,
spicy nose, powerful, well-built with good extract
and fruit flavors, not overwhelmed by the oak.
Long bottle potential.

Pignolo 1988
From very low yields of the rare indigenous
variety of the same name comes a deep ruby-
colored wine; an exceptionally complex bouquet
of wild fruit and spices balanced against the
toasted oak of the barrique. Rich, soft and very
long on the palate.

Schioppettino 1988
From another local grape, Schioppettino, aged
at length in barrique. Bright ruby red; intense
spicy nose; full-bodied and long on the palate
where the fruit has a nice underlying nuance of
liquorice.

Livio Felluga

Via Risorgimento, 1
Brazzano di Cormons (Go) 34071
Tel. (0481) 60203
Fax (0481) 630126

Livio Felluga has worked with wine since 1938. He was a wholesaler and later the director of Friuli's most important privately-owned winery. He founded his own estate in 1956, in a period in which the industrial expansion in the region induced numerous small landowners to sell up and move to the towns. Felluga began to purchase vineyards, piece by piece, gradually building up a property which today composes 98 ha in the Colli Orientali del Friuli at Rosazzo and 14 in the Collio. The winery is now run by Livio's children, Maurizio, Elda and Andrea, a friendly and experienced team supported still, although he is approaching his 80th birthday, by their father's vast knowledge and enthusiasm. Despite the production of 600,000 bottles a year with the classic topographical map label which first appeared in 1959, the range of wines is sensibly limited. The strategy of the winery is to produce, in addition to a selection of premium quality varietals, the great wines: a white, a red and a dessert wine. The first objective has been long achieved. Infact, their outstanding Terre Alte, a white cuvée of superb structure and balance, has won major awards both in Italy and abroad.

Colli Orientali del Friuli 🍷 ②
Sauvignon 1991 DOC
Pale straw, a white wine which is beginning to come into it's stride now, although it still has a long way to go. The intense fruit on the nose is faithfully reproduced on the palate. Long and gutsy.

Terre Alte 1990 🍷🍷 ②
A perfect blend of Tocai, Pinot Bianco and Sauvignon. Pale straw, with the faintest pf green reflections and fruit aromas rounded out by the partial malolactic fermentation. Acacia flowers and graceful notes of culinary spices on the nose. Full, rich and velvety fruit flavors. Complex and although already well-balanced, will only reach optimum drinking in another three years, a peak which it will maintain well into the future.

Colli Orientali del Friuli 🍷🍷 ④
Picolit 1988
The story of this wine begins with the selection and re-planting of old virtually abandoned clones of rare native Picolit. Made from late-harvested, botrytis-affected fruit, fermented and aged in wood, a dessert wine of gentle sweetness, enormous complexity with long, lingering fruit and spice.

Price levels

①   up to $ 9.99

② $ 10.00 - $ 14.99

③ $ 15.00 - $ 24.99

④ $ 25.00 or more

The 'ex-cellar', or direct from the producer, bottle prices, are calculated in US dollars and are intended only as an approximate guide

Gravner

Via Lenzuolo Bianco, 9
Oslavia (Go) 34070
Tel/Fax (0481) 30882

Josko Gravner began to make wine at 16, when his father put him in charge of the family farm's cellar at Oslavia north-east of Gorizia, where vineyards straddle the border with Slovenia. Experience has convinced him that the measure of quality in white wines is not primary aroma but structure and longevity. In the determined pursuit of these features, Josko has evolved a personal style which is not always easy to understand at first but which is becoming increasingly influential in Collio and further afield. His own points of reference are trans-alpine. He uses clones selected and grafted in France. The vines are planted at high density, pruned very short and harvested very late to get the maximum sugar. In the cellar he returned to methods which pre-date stainless steel vats and refrigeration. His whites and two reds are fermented on its lees in barrique at natural temperatures, and the red grapes macerate in open wooden barrels. In 1989 he began the policy of only releasing his wines after a minimum 12 months bottle age. Josko makes some of the most important wines of the region. Production is typical of the Collio, small by any other standard. Prices may raise an eyebrow, but they are in line with the costs involved in producing this level of quality.

Bianco Gravner 1990   ♔♔ ③
Cuvée of Pinot Grigio and Riesling Italico: the impact is immediate, with the assertive quality of the Pinot Grigio already showing aromas which need lots of bottle age to reach full potential. A big round mouthful, of rare richness yet complex and balanced.

Collio Ribolla Gialla 1990 DOC   ♔ ③
Amazing how a wine of such body can possess such elegant, refined aromas. Below the smooth, rich texture given by super-selected, late-harvested fruit, there is subtle varietal fascination with the added complexity of new oak.

Chardonnay Selezione 1987   ♔♔ ④
Incredible as it may seem, this special reserve, after almost four years in bottle still has room to development. Massive concentration in the bouquet and enormous weight with nuances (wild herbs, honey and toasted hazel nut). Difficult to place in any established category, with extraordinary richness and personality.

Collio Chardonnay 1990 DOC   ♔♔♔ ③
The perfect expression of the Gravner philosophy. Josko sustains that white wines need to find their depth and complexity, the features which red wines possess by virtue of their tannin, through the long oxidation process of aging. To obtain the extraordinary range of nuances and the structure which are the hallmarks of Gravner's whites, exceptional quality fruit is needed - the result of severe pruning, dense planting and late-harvesting. The transformation takes place in barriques, through spontaneous fermentation, as free of intervention as is humanly possible. There is nothing new about these methods (great French whites are made in a similar way) but for Friuli they represent a revolution. The outcome is this stupendous Chardonnay, intense and aristocratic on the nose with perfect integration of the varietal aromas and the vein of toasted oak. Powerfully full-bodied on the palate, concentrated, long and amazingly complex.

Vinnaioli Jermann

Loc. Villanova, via Monte Fortino, 21
Farra d'Isonzo (Go) 34070
Tel. (0481) 888080
Fax (0481) 888512

Silvio Jermann runs what in California would
be considered a 'boutique winery'. He
cultivates just over 20 ha of vineyard, which
is just enough to allow him to supervise the
production down to the last detail. Every wine
that leaves his cellar bears the stamp of one
of the most accomplished and original
winemakers in the region, including the
choice of names. The boutique style extends
to the winery itself. Good wine can also be
made in an anonymous hangar, but Jermann
has created a work space which besides
being functional is also smartly, aesthetically
designed. It has become a cliché to say that
an estate represents the contemporary re-
interpretation of tradition, but in the case of
Jermann the description has a precise
meaning. From the emblematic tensions
between the generations (father of
conservative farming stock, and un
independent minded son full of enological
science) has grown a style of wine which is
broad-shouldered in an old-fashioned way
yet also fresh, clean and modern in its
aromas. The epitome of this achievement is
Jermann's Vintage Tunina which is a modern
classic of Italian winemaking and possibly the
most important single wine to come out of
Friuli in the present generation

Vinnae 1991   ❦ ②
Vibrant lemon and herbs aromas and forthright
acidity are the features of the exquisitely
Friulan Ribolla which Jermann exalts in his
Vinnae. Possibly linear compared to the grand
wines of the estate but full of personality.

Where the Dreams   ❦ ❦ ③
Have no End 1990
Jermann's only barrique wine, in its first
vintages very faintly oaked but now more self-
confidently "barricato" with complex aromas of
wood aging and discernable toasted note
under the Chardonnay fruit on the palate.
Stylish and full of class.

Vintage Tunina 1990   ❦ ❦ ❦ ③
An inspirational wine, one of the more
monumental in modern quality winemaking in
Friuli. Silvio Jermann ferments late-harvested
Chardonnay and Sauvignon together with
smaller percentages of Ribolla, Malvasia and
Picolit from an old vineyard next to the winery
to produce a wine of great complexity in which
freshness combines with a luscious richness of
texture. The floral aromas are elegant and
elusive. The flavors have exceptional depth
and length. Irresistably racey. Amazingly
consistent from year to year, the 1990
continues a tradition established by a long
sequence of previous vintages.

Edi Kante

Loc. Prepotto
S. Pelagio (Ts) 34011
Tel. (040) 200761

There is a special mystique attached to vineyard areas where the cultivation of vitis vinifera is possible only through the almost super-human efforts of growers to overcome the obstacles of nature. The Carso, a windswept chalk plateau which overlooks the bay of Trieste, is one such area. Edi Kante, pioneer of quality winemaking on the Carso, had to blast through solid rock to build an underground cellar for his barriques. In order to create a top soil on which to plant new vines he had to find the equivalent of 1,200 truck-loads of the local red, ferrous soil for each hectare of vineyard. Kante`s estate is young. The current output is around 15.000 bottles per year, with vineyards just entering or still to come into production. Although Kante also produces Chardonnay and Sauvignon, his personal ambition is to develop wines of quality and style from the rustic local varietes (Vitovska, Malvasia and Terano) through the the drastic limiting of yields, rigid fruit selection and the measured use of oak. Results so far are encouraging, and the prospects for the future are very interesting.

Carso Malvasia 1990 DOC   ♈ ②
After the initial impact of barrique on the nose, the subtle herby aromas of this very interesting variety begin to emerge. Round and full textured, the flavors are still quite closed in; balance and concentration are evident and ensure improvement with bottle age.

Chardonnay 1990   ♈ ♈ ②
Almost aggressive intensity on the nose and sustained power on the palate with all the components (acidity, extract, alcohol and considerable charred new oak) of an impressive wine for the future. Of all Kante wines released in spring 1992, this one develops the slowest but possibly has the most exciting potential.

Vitovska 1990   ♈ ②
This very rare autoctonous variety has a personal character with slightly grassy aromas of wild herbs that marry with the sweet barrique oak. As with all Kante's wines, the palate is smooth and substantial with a long chewy finish; the varietal flavors will shine in due time.

Livon

Via Montarezza, 33
Dolegnano (Ud) 33048
Tel. (0432) 757173
Fax (0432) 757690

The Azienda Agricola Livon is a family-owned estate whose evolution has run parallel to the wine renaissance in Friuli-Venezia Giulia. Founded at the beginning of the 1960s with the acquisition of the first vineyards at the time of the break-up of the share-cropping economy, Livon was one of the small group of producers which established the reputation of the newly-created DOC Collio. The policy of expansion in the years that followed makes Livon today one of the most important owners in the region with 50 ha of prime vineyard in the Collio, 15 in the Colli Orientali and another 25 in the Grave. Sensitive to an emerging trend, the estate began to plan a new range of single vineyard "cru" wines in 1982 to complement the standard lines which continue to make up the bulk of the production. The sheer number of labels in this range (15 counting red and white varietals and various blends) and the unfamiliarity of the dialect names can be confusing, but the overall quality level is high. Continuing investment in vineyard research and the perfecting of barrel fermentation in the state-of-the-art winery reserved for the cru wines promises great things for the future.

Colli Orientali del Friuli   ♈ ②
Verduzzo Casali Godia 1990 DOC
A deep amber gold shade suggests the dimensions of the flavor of this unashamedly sweet dessert wine. A nose of apricot and vanilla precedes a big round palate with lively young fruit and sweet oak blending happily.

Grave del Friuli   ♈ ③
Chardonnay Braida Mate 1990 DOC
A single-vineyard wine from the Grave, it epitomises the Livon philosophy: impeccable winemaking and direct, immediate varietal style. A Chardonnay with intense, distinctly flinty Chablis character. The impact on the palate is fresh, dry and fruity with a long, classic flavor in the finish.

Tiareblù 1989   ♈ ③
From old vines in a small, limited production vineyard in the Collio, this Bordeaux blend ages well, gaining depth and nuance in the bottle. A pale-colored mature wine, the nose is clean and plummy with tertiary aromas of incense. The flavors are dry and well-balanced between fruit and toasted oak. Medium-bodied but firmly structured.

Giovanni Marin

Loc. Fornalis
Cividale del Friuli (Go) 33043
Tel. (0432) 759429
Fax (0432) 759887

Giovanni and Angelo Marin belong to a family active in the construction industry which bought this delightful estate 25 km east of Udine in 1976. The 12 ha of vineyard benefit from the effects of a very particular micro-climate which keeps temperatures relatively cool, despite the south-facing aspect. The nature of the soil (eocene marl), the high density of vines/ha and the low yields combine to produce premium wines of notable structure and unusually complex aroma. Top winemaker, Walter Filiputti, is responsible for the management, and enthusiastic owner, Giovanni Marin, who lives in the midst of the vineyards, is actively involved in the cellar and vineyard work. The winery, which is equipped to the highest modern standards, boasts soft presses, temperature-controlled stainless steel vats and a battery of French barriques reserved for the prestige wines of the estate. Among these are the rare local Verduzzo and Picolit, late-harvested dessert wines which owe their residual sugar to the natural arrest of fermentation, without the slightest manipulation or sugar addition.

Colli Orientali del Friuli
Picolit 1990 DOC
Made in the same way as the Verduzzo, this has a similar golden-yellow color. Intense fruit, flowers and honey aromas on a background of vanilla from the new oak. Generous body, velvety texture and complex flavors. Long and well-balanced.

Colli Orientali del Friuli
Verduzzo 1990 DOC
Late-harvest, cold maceration and aging in barrique give this dessert wine a deep golden color and intense and complex nose with an array of aromas from honey to ripe peaches and spice. The palate is rich and butttery, full-bodied and balanced.

Ronchi di Fornaz 1990
A blend based mainly on Cabernet Sauvignon and Franc, matured over a long period in French oak. Powerul mixture of fruit and spice on the nose followed by a palate which is smooth and full-bodied with nice round tannins. Excellent prospects for the future.

Francesco Pecorari

Via Gavinana, 10
S. Lorenzo (Go) 34070
Tel. (0481) 80105
Fax (0481) 809592

Alvaro Pecorari is one of the new generation of producers who are investing heavily in the Isonzo DOC zone, convinced in its quality and full potential which has been masked in the past by the commercial style of winemaking generally practised here. He makes 110,000 bottles a year, and, although the estate is expanding, he is wary of arriving at the point where he loses control of the vineyard and the cellar. Pecorari`s wines are supple, for young drinking but also improve with age. They have concentration combined with finesse, a most difficult balance to achieve. The credit is shared by the micro-climate and the chalky gravel beds of the zone, very similar in composition to those of Bordeaux and by Alvaro himself who has completely re-organized the family estate over the past decade. The current range of single cru wines, for the most part from new vineyards, only began to appear in 1988. In relatively short time, Alvaro has managed to lay the foundations of a production which bears his own personal stamp, summed up in the exquisite, estate specialty Pinot Grigio which is inspired by the wines of Alsace.

Pinot Grigio Gris 1991
Alsatian clones selected by Pecorari for this cru produce a wine with a charm and finesse rarely found in Italian Pinot Grigio. The 1990 is big and full-bodied, at present more closed than the 1989, but the delicate rose petal aroma is still there. The palate has fruit, acidity and structure; great promise for the future.

Verduzzo Tal Luc 1991
Pale amber with delicate, restrained aromas, fresh and complex (acacia flowers, caramel, vanilla oak aromas). Original with fascinating wild herbs. The palate is smooth, barely sweet and again full of delicate and complex flavor. A subtle, very personal wine, produced in limited quantities; a fine Vino da Meditazione.

Lis Neris 1989
This Merlot-Cabernet blend is a mature garnet red with good depth of color. The nose needs time but with breathing reveals rich ripe aromas with prominent juniper berry and leather. The palate has velvety tannins, good flavor and a dry finish with a hint of liquorice.

Pierpaolo Pecorari

Via Tommaseo, 36/c
San Lorenzo Isontino (Go) 34070
Tel/Fax (0481) 808775

Pierpoalo Pecorari began to revolutionize methods on his 10 ha estate around six years ago. Since then, despite a couple of unfavorable vintages in the region as a whole, the quality of his wines has maintained a steady upward curve. The current output of a mere 50,000 bottles a year is an indication of the low yields which are an essential component in the pursuit of quality, and which have helped transform an honest if rather uninspiring production into a range of wines of outstanding character. Pierpaolo is also at work in the cellar, to develop a style which combines good solid structure with well-defined varietal character. White wines, for instance, are made with brief maceration on the skins and the increasingly well-judged use of 500 lt tonneaux. Alongside the whites there is also now a serious premium quality Merlot, Vieli Baolar, confirming the vocation of the Isonzo for full-bodied, scented reds. Incidentally, his wines represent excellent value for money in a region which had seen a number of recent, unjustified price increases. l

Isonzo Chardonnay 1991 DOC ☆ ①
Pecorari's Chardonnay has the best aging potential. The breadth of the aromas while young, its body and firm acidity all point to long bottle life. Older vintages have honey and almond aromas and the intensity on the palate confirms the impression that Chardonnay is often drunk much too early.

Isonzo Sauvignon 1991 DOC ☆ ①
Sauvignon does well in Isonzo, with yields kept under control. Once they cross a certain threshold, the wines are inevitably bland and unexciting. Quite the opposite with Pecorari, with their complex, varietal aromas; though not particularly full-bodied, equally long and characterful on the palate.

Pratoscuro 1991 ☆ ①
A blend of Müller Thurgau and Rhein Riesling which highlights the fresh aromatic character of the varieties. Easy-drinking weight on the palate with nice acidity and a surprisingly long, intense finish; an ideal match for vegetarian foods.

F.lli Pighin

Fraz. Risano, viale Grado, 1
Pavia di Udine (Ud) 33050
Tel. (0432) 675444
Fax (0432) 609001

The philosophy with which the Pighin brothers founded what is now the largest private wine estate in Friuli-Venezia Giulia is encapsulated in the slogan they painted on the cellar's façade: "Man must never leave the land as he found it." In the late 1960s Pighin converted 160 ha of farmland into vineyard in the Grave DOC zone on the plain south of Udine and completely rebuilt a hillside in order to plant vines at Capriva, in one of the most splendid natural sites in the Collio. They owe their solid commercial success to their reliable, reasonably priced wines, tuned to modern tastes. Pighin exports around 600,000 bottles a year and is one of the architects of the Friuli's reputation for lively, fresh dry whites. The other great strength of the firm is their research and development. Enologist Livio Pighin`s taste for a challenge is currently finding expression in a project which is certainly unique in Italy, involving a 1.5 ha plot of ungrafted vines in the Grave. The risks are enormous since, in theory, a European vine ungrafted onto American rootstock is defenceless against the root-destroying phylloxera. Pighin`s Cassette vineyard, planted in 1986, continues to grow strong and healthy and has started to produce interesting wines. The future looks bright.

Grave Tocai Friuliano ☆ ①
Cassette 1990 DOC
Ungrafted vines impart ample aromas, extract and balance. Open and very typical on the nose with bitter almonds in the background. The palate has a freshness to enjoy now, although it will continue to develop in the bottle.

Sorelli 1990 ☆ ②
An interesting blend of Tocai, Pinot Bianco and Sauvignon from Capriva in the Collio, one of the new generation of Friuli whites which combine fresh fruit aromas with body and aging potential. Melon, tropical fruit and peach kernel on the nose, followed by a long, dry and characterful palate.

Baredo 1986 ♥ ②
A Cabernet Sauvignon, Merlot and Refosco blend which shows Grave's potential for serious, cellarable reds. Still deep and dark on the rim. The nose has well-developed fruit, with cedar and cigar box scents. The Refosco distinguishes it from more conventional Bordeaux blends and gives it a vigorous, slightly rustic character.

Doro Princic

Loc. Pradis, 5
Cormons (Go) 34071
Tel. (0481) 60723

Doro Princic is a sprightly, young gentleman of 81 years who has dedicated his life to vines and wines. It would be permissable to expect from a person of his agea certain attachment to the traditions of the past, but he is so involved that he is able to cheerfully admit that the today winemaking methods produce results far superior to those of his younger days. His son, Sandro, uses what has become known as the 'Friuli' method of vinification of white grapes and, in particular, practises the aroma-enriching control of the temperature of fermentation. The rest is done by the meticulous care of the vineyards and the zone of Pradis itself with its mild, 'air-conditioned' micro-climate and stoney marl soils. The estate has 7 ha of which more than 3/4 is planted with white varieties. New projects are being developed gradually, step by step. The specialities, however, remain Tocai, Pinot Bianco and Malvasia which have the magical balance of fresh, elegant aromas and round, full-bodied palate typical of the regions best wines.

Collio Malvasia 1991 DOC   ℽ ①
Malvasia has fascinating aromas which range from herbal to spicy nutmeg. In lesser examples, the palate can be lean and stretched, but this wine has a rich, silky texture and a long finish. More subtle than the Tocai, in its flavors, it has good balance and good bottle potential, although it also drinks well young.

Collio Pinot Bianco 1991 DOC   ℽ ℽ ①
An outstanding wine with a big, open nose, already hinting at the complexity which can be expected within two years. The apricot fruitiness of young Pinot Bianco emerges from a rich and full-bodied palate of impressive concentration.

Collio Tocai Friulano 1991 DOC   ℽ ①
The deep straw color gives advance notice of the very typical broad and open nose. Soft floral notes predominate, with hints of bitter almonds. The impact on the palate is big and youthful with the very full body balanced by zestful flavor and a long finish.

Puiatti

Via Dante, 69
Farra d'Isonzo (Go) 34070
Tel. (0481) 888304-80158
Fax (0481) 809685

One of the respected senior statesmen of Friuli's young wine industry, Vittorio Piuatti already had 30 vintages behind him when he began selecting grapes in the Collio and making wine at his Eno-Friuli firm in 1976. His ability to produce quality in quantity there made an important contribution to the revitalization of the region's wine trade. The new house founded in 1982 under his own name was set up with the specific intent of making top-class spumante. It has since become the base for the realization of Piuatti's theory that Collio whites should be considered "vins du garde", or wines for aging. He is not alone in Friuli in pursuing this idea, but unlike fellow regional vintners or often wherever mature white wine is made at all, he does not use oak. His wines age some time in stainless-steel vats, are bottled and then cellared for up to 3 years before release. The Archetipi line, Piuatti's most important wines, respond well to this treatment, putting them amongst the most characterful products currently available, truly memorable for their fleshy texture and unbelievably fresh palate.

Collio Chardonnay 1991 DOC   ℽ ②
A confirmation of Puiatti's ability to turn out a line of 'normal' (in the sense of non-reserve) wines of impeccable and consistent quality. Pale straw, classic varietal fruit on the nose, good body and a final note of fresh, dry acidity.

Nuvizial 1990   ℽ ②
A cuvée of Chardonnay and Pinot Nero (the classic Champagne base) with inviting appley fruit, intense and full on the palate with a slightly honeyed finish. More immediate than the grand Archetipi, but equally full of character.

Collio Sauvignon   ℽ ℽ ③
Archetipi 1988 DOC
Ripe, rich varietal aromas softened with bottle age and a full, luscious palate seemingly sweet given the fruit concentration, although the wine is perfectly dry. A very personal expression of a variety, generally quite uniform if not predictable.

Chardonnay Archetipi 1988   ℽ ℽ ③
Extraordinary complexity on the nose, with very personal almost gamey aromas which give a certain austerity, mellow voluptuous texture on the palate backed by firm acidity. A serious Chardonnay of striking individuality and indisputable class.

Radikon

Loc. Tre Buchi, 4
Oslavia (Go) 34070
Tel/Fax (0481) 32804

Like many small vineyard owners in the early 1980s, the Radikon family was faced with the difficult decision of whether to limit themselves to merely growing and selling grapes, or whether to produce and bottle their own wine. The current market in the region guarantees safe returns and profit margins for Chardonnay and Sauvignon growers, per say. Making and selling the wine of a small independent estate, on the other hand, involves on-going investment, long hours of extra work and, in the end, more financial risk. Radikon is one of those who, in spite all the disadvantages, launched himself into producing wines that express their zone of origin and the ability and tastes of their creator. The evolution of the 5-ha estate over the past decade follows a familiar pattern: the re-planting with selected clones, the increased vine density , the severe reduction of yields, the construction of a modern, functional cellar and a gradual approach to barrique. Radikon only makes around 20,000 bottles a year, but should he ever decide to stop, his broad and generous wines would be sadly missed.

Collio Ribolla Gialla 1990 DOC   ♉ ②
A good vintage for the variety, it shows a big, round texture but also firm, lemony acidity. 40% of the final cuvée was aged in new barrique, adding more intensity than oak. The aromas of this top grape are still closed but the typical honeyed floral notes are there with intriguing bitter-sweet fennel and liquorice.

Collio Sauvignon 1990 DOC   ♉ ②
A wine of extraordinary concentration, almost chewy as the flavors linger on the palate. Despite the super ripeness of the fruit, there is a vein of acidty which gives freshness and varietal definition. As with the other 1990s, the best is yet to come.

Slatnik 1990   ♉♉ ②
Chardonnay with some Tocai and Sauvignon, in perfect Radikon style: low yields and late-harvested fruit, it has generous body and great concentration. He is not interested in immediate primary aromas, confident that the nose will come with time. A shame to drink now: wait til they reach this very moment.

Paolo Rodaro

Via Cormons, 8
Spessa di Cividale (Ud) 33040
Tel/Fax (0432) 716066

The property is situated 15 km east of Udine, in the heart of the DOC zone Colli Orientali del Friuli. Gigi and Edo Rodaro may be the owners, but their father Paolo is the leading figure. He is proudly named after their great grandfather, who, in turn, was the estate's original founder. The 20 ha of vineyard are spread out over the surrounding hills of chalk and marl. The annual output comes to just over 100,000 bottles. The estate began bottling in the late 1950s. The quality has been steadily improving over the years, with the refining techniques both in the vineyard and the cellar, although certain traditional habits die harder, including that of producing too many wines. One positive feature which has remained constant is the excellent value for money which Rodaro`s wines represent. The cellars are equipped to modern standards with pneumatic presses and temperature-controlled, stainless steel fermenting vats. Barrique aging is reserved exclusively for the sweet Verduzzo. A special release from the top cru Bosc Romain has been available since 1990, under a separate label.

Colli Orientali del Friuli   ♉ ①
Tocai Friuliano 1991 DOC
A classic white of the region, straw yellow, complex on the nose with attractive fruit and a slightly smoky character. The aromas return on the palate which has a dry, tangy intensity and moderate length.

Colli Orientali del Friuli   ♉ ①
Bosco Romain 1991 DOC
A special selection from a particularly favorable hillside location. Yellow gold with a complex bouquet of ripe, almost raisiny fruit, nicely balanced against the barrique's toasted oak. Good structure, elegantly dry on the palate.

Colli Orientali del Friuli   ♥ ①
Schioppettino 1990 DOC
A brilliant ruby red from the local grape variety of the same name. Rich cherry fruit on the nose and the palate, long and very lively freshness.

ACQUA S. BERNARDO.
Qualità naturali.

From the Land of the Black Rooster

Black Rooster Wines

The land of the Chianti Classico is the oldest officially designated winegrowing area in the world, and the Consorzio del Marchio Storico, which was formed in 1924, is Italy's oldest wine consortium.

The organization's aim has always been the validation, qualification and promotion of the wines produced within the 70,000 hectares of territory between Florence and Siena. From the very beginning the Consortium has used the Black Rooster as its symbol.

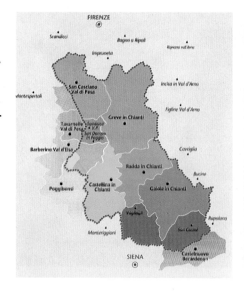

With time, the 33 founding members grew to 606, who represent over 80 percent of the total Chianti Classico production. Only after very vigorous controls, first in the vineyards, then in the wine cellar, and finally in the bottle, are the Consortium's members allowed to decorate their bottles with the prestigious Black Rooster logo.

Throughout the world, the Black Rooster symbolizes to the consumer the high quality of these Chiantis, and serves as a memory of the beautiful Tuscan landscape.

Ronco del Gnemiz

Via Ronchi, 5
San Giovanni al Natisone (Ud) 33048
Tel. (043) 759693-759240-756238
Fax (0432) 759884

The Ronco del Gnemiz estate, which has
been owned by the Palazzolo family since
1964, is located half-way between Udine and
Gorizia in the commune of San Giovanni al
Natisone. The zone is particularly favored by
winds from the nearby Adriatic. Planted at the
relatively high density of 4,000 vines per ha
cover the lower slopes of a hillside of eocene
marl, the vineyards have grown grapes for
centuries. Enzo Palazzolo gave the estate its
present name. "Ronc" in Friulian dialect
means terraced hillside and Gnemiz, in honor
of the Gnemiz family, who were the last to
live and farm there. Serena Palazzolo, the
young, exuberant estate manager, lives in
the midst of the vines. The modern, super-
equipped winery is next to the house, and the
cellars where the top wines mature in
barrique have been built underneath it. The
long-standing enologist at Ronco del Gnemiz,
Sandro Facca, has recently been joined by
one of the country's most widely acclaimed
consulting experts, Franco Bernabei.

Colli Orientali del Friuli Tocai Friuliano 1991 DOC   🍇 ②
Proof of this estate's consistently high
standards. Pale straw, intense fresh and fruity
character on the nose, dry, deep-flavored and
balanced on the palate. Moderate acidity. Good
prospects for the future.

Colli Orientali del Friuli Picolit 1990 DOC   🍇 ④
Golden yellow shade, extraordinarily complex
on the nose with aromas which bring to mind
peach and fig, honey and flowers. Young on the
palate and only moderately sweet. Complex,
elegant and firmly built.

Rosso di Gnemiz 1989   🍷🍷 ③
A blend of Merlot and Cabernet with long oak
aging, still young. Deep ruby red, intense spicy
nose of cherry and ripe plums, full-bodied and
firm on the palate with well-judged extract and
rich fruit on the palate.

Chardonnay 1990   🍇🍇🍇 ④
Chardonnay from a vineyard planted in 1946.
Subsequent expansion has used cuttings from
the original vines to maintain the clone's
homogeneity. Although the wine originates from
the Colli Orientali, the DOC name is not used on
the label, to emphasize the unique personality of
the cru. The grapes were picked in the second
half of September and crushed in soft
pneumatic presses. The free run juice is
separated from the sediment by a brief period in
stainless steel at low temperature and then
racked into barriques (in part new) to ferment. At
the end of the malolactic, the wine is assembled
in stainless steels vats, where it remains until
bottling. The 1990 has the authentic class of this
great variety. Broad aromas of honey and bread
crust just slightly covered by the vanilla of the
barrique. On the palate, very impressive
structure backed up by good acidity and rich,
scented fruit.

Schiopetto

Via Spessa, 20
Capriva del Friuli (Go) 34070
Tel/Fax (0481) 80332

Mario Schiopetto remains faithful to the style of winemaking which he pioneered in the region in the 1970s. It has since become commonly known as the 'Friuli method'. Although he also makes red wine, he has always been associated with whites. He sums up his function as winemaker as that of transferring, with as little human intervention as possible, the varietal character of his raw material to the wine. The basic principles are simple: grapes with natural balance need little adjusting in the cellar, and the vinification and brief maturation introduce no estraneous aromas or flavors. He has an antipathy towards the use of oak barrels and believes that a wine should be ready once it leaves the producer. Historically, he deserves credit for reviving the cruelly mistreated indigenous Tocai, previously the base for the anonymous, often oxidized caraffe wines of the local inns. In his hands, it is a refined, technically-perfect white, fresh, clean and up front. After 20 years of activity, Schiopetto has decided to leave their cramped cellar below the house, rented from the local bishop. The next vintage will come from a new, modern winery, but he promises little or no change in style.

Collio Malvasia 1991 DOC
Open on the nose, delicate but well-defined with the initial aromas of wild herbs giving way to a slightly spicy potpourri. Intense, limey, varietal flavors, dry without harshness, long and savoury finish.

Collio Pinot Bianco 1991 DOC
Immediate, intense, fruity aromas of ripe apricot and mouth-filling flavor. Despite its very respectable body, a wine with the great impact of youthful freshness which is Schiopetto's winemaking trademark.

Collio Pinot Grigio 1991 DOC
Tasted in spring, at only six weeks from bottling, this wine still has a greenness, sure to soften in the coming year. Classic varietal aromas suggest baked pears, cinnamon and just the right grassiness.

Collio Tocai Friulano 1991 DOC
Fine varietal character in this quintessential Friulian classic. Complex nose, still under-developed but with breathing opens into delicate but well-focussed lime blossom, fennel and unmistakeable bitter almonds, typical of Tocai. Excellent structure, dry and firm but well-balanced with restrained flavors on the finish, the sure sign of quality. A serious white with ample margins for evolution.

Leonardo Specogna

Via Rocca Bernarda, 4
Corno di Rosazza (Ud) 33040
Tel/Fax (0432) 759420

In Corno di Rosazzo, half-way between Udine and Gorizia the traditional street names have been joined by those of wines of the world. Thus, the "via Rocca Bernarda" is also "via Barolo". Just below the "Rocca" there are nine hectares owned by Leonardo Specogna, bought in 1963 and today farmed directly by his son Graziano. The rigorously scientific running of this prestigious estate is supervized by Valdino Diust, consulting chemist who is currently turning a number of small traditional wineries into authentic models of enology. Specogna crushes mainly local varieties with Tocai Friuland representing the house speciality. This particular grape, which is almost certainly the result of clonal mutation of Sauvignon Blanc makes completely different wines compared to those of the same name produced in Alsace and Hungary. Here it is intensely perfumed without being aromatic, dry, full bodied and relatively low in acidity Meticulously kept vineyards and modern vinification enable Specogna to turn ou products of considerable interest, despite the number of wines in the range, nine in all each with a production of around 5,000 bottles a year.

Colli Orientali del Friuli Sauvignon 1991 DOC
Intense, complex, slightly grassy aromas with sage leaf scents. Powerful flavors of fruit and capiscum and satisfying length. Lots of character and firm structure. Will continue to improve with bottle age.

Colli Orientali del Friuli Tocai Friuliano 1991 DOC
Their speciality and one of the more consistent Tocai in the region. Pale straw with hints of green, fresh, intense vegetal aromas and the same freshness on the palate with tasty fruit and respectable body.

Coll Orientali del Friuli Cabernet 1990 DOC
Still young, a deep ruby color tinged with purple Intense fruit on the nose with an underlying touch of grassiness which returns on the palate The tannins suggest slow evolution.

Castello di Spessa

Via Spessa, 1
Capriva del Friuli (Go) 34070
Tel. (0481) 759429
Fax (0481) 630161

When the industrialist, Loretto Pali, bought the Castello di Spessa and the wine estate of the same name in 1987, the first thing he did was to bring in top technicians. Alongside those of enologist, Gianni Bignucolo, he secured the services of one of Italy's most talented consultants, a specialist in custom winemaking techniques and cuvées of excellence as well as sales and promotion, Walter Filiputti. Under his direction the vineyards are undergoing modifications which include the elimination of minor varieties and an increase in vine density, up to 5,750 vines, with yields of around 50 Q/ha in the new plots. Other important changes have been made in the aging. The young whites (now only four wines) come out a full year after the vintage. The barrique-fermented Pinot Bianco Riserva is released after two years, after bottle aging during which the body fills out, and the wine develops a complex array of aromas. The classic Bordeaux blends age the longest, maturing in barriques at a constant 12° C, in what used to be a military bunker.

Collio Pinto Bianco 1991 DOC
Very pale straw, intense and complex on the nose with interesting aromas which pass from fruit to acacia flowers to tobacco leaf. On the palate notable body, rich flavors, balance and length.

Collio Pinto Grigio 1991 DOC
Bright and limpid in the glass, dried fruit with a hint of spice on the nose and the palate. The flavors are attactive and the structure is not bad.

Collio Pinot Bianco
Santarosa 1990 DOC
Positive straw color with green reflections. Aged in oak for over a year, it has good balance between the barrique's vanilla and the elegant fruit on the nose. Complex palate. Great structure. Still young.

Collio Sauvignon 1990 DOC
Pale straw with green reflections, impressive intensity on the nose, with the varietal aromas of sage and sambuco. On the palate the flavors are broad and elegant. A vein of acidity gives satisfying length.

Torre Rosazza

Loc. Poggiobello
Manzano (Ud) 33044
Tel. (0432) 750180
Fax (040) 671511

The slopes 20 km east of Udine where the Torre Rosazza estate, currently owned by the Assicurazioni Generali insurance group, have been reknowned for quality wine since the Renaissance. Again, Walter Filiputti is behind their more recent success story, ever able to pull out wines of excellence wherever his talents are employed. The area is mainly of marl, with only small pockets of sandier soils. With over 75 ha of vines and the diverse sites and the homogenous soil types, they can produce a wide selection of varieties. It has also been possible to identify several top-class cru. Separate vinification and aging of these different cru means that the total number of wines exceeds that of the grape varieties on the estate. The drawback of this policy is that, as is the case with many producers in Friuli, it is very difficult to maintain the consistently high standards over the range that one would hope for.

Colli Orientali del Friuli
Sauvignon Silterra 1991 DOC
From the fruit of several vineyard selections, partially aged in barrique, this wine needs at least another two years to show its best. Elegant and stylish, with intense aromas of tomato leaf and capiscum with good acidity.

Collio Orientali del Friuli
L'Altromerlot 1990 DOC
Its name, 'The Other Merlot', aims to distinguish it from the gross production of anonymous Merlot in the region. Aged in barrique for over a year, it has intense cherry, ripe plum aromas with subtle spicy nuances. Great structure on the palate, balanced with good extract and length.

Colli Orientali del Friuli Cabernet
Sauvignon Ronco della Torre 1989 DOC
Even ruby-red, with intense fruit and spice aromas. Good broad tannins on the palate, with body and complex, ripe and slightly vegetal flavors. Matured over 12 months in barrique, sure to improve with time.

Valle

Via Nazionale, 3
Buttrio (Ud) 33042
Tel. (0432) 674289
Fax (0432) 674280

Gigi Valle is one of the leading figures in Friuli wine history, and among the first to qualify in enology back in 1950. Valle has followed the evolution of the region's winemaking, from its high volume phase to that of high-quality. Friuli has been this 'old lion's' stomping ground, letting him prove his talents, above all that of virtuosity. He purchased a number of plots in prime locations at Rosazzo and Prepotto in the Colli Orientali and more recently at Ruttars in the Collio; total vineyard area is now 22 ha. Spacious cellars are equipped with the technology synonmous to top quality wines (soft presses, temperature-controlled stainless steel vats, perfect cellars for barrique and bottle aging). His cellars turn out younger wines of immediate impact but also long-lived reds such as Merlot or Cabernet, still in all fullness at 7-8 years' old. Here, too, production is divided into too many sub-labels (there are four different lines: 'standard', Selezione Araldica, Selezione San Blas and Collezione Gigi Valle): a common feature of estates here that tends to generate a bit of confusion.

Colli Orientali del Friuli   🍷 ②
Riesling Renano Selezione Araldica 1991 DOC
Among the best Rieslings produced in the region, a pale straw color with hints of green, stylish floral-fruit aromas and a distant flavor of green apples on the palate. Long and elegant.

Colli Orientali del Friuli   🍷 ②
Ramandolo San Blâs 1990 DOC
Yellow-gold, with powerful ripe, slightly raisiny fruit aromas. The palate is sweet, rich and fruity with the touch of tannin, a feature of this variety. Will keep for several years yet, though sold in half liter bottles.

L'Araldo 1987   🍷 ②
A Merlot-Cabernet Franc-Refosco blend with a deep ruby shade starting to shade into orange. Surprisingly live and elegant on the nose, with attractive toasted oak. Good balance, a wine at the peak.

Venica & Venica

Loc. Cero, via Mernico, 42
Dolegna (Go) 34070
Tel. (0481) 61264
Fax (0481) 639906

There is probably no other wine region in Europe with the breadth of production of Friuli-Venezia Giulia. Concentrated in this small corner of north-eastern Italy are the classic varieties of Alsace, Burgundy, Bordeaux and the Loire, plus a few from the Rhine, not to mention the gamut of indigenous types which are steadily regaining respect after long neglect. Working with up to a dozen varieties calls for in-depth knowledge of the raw materials and ecclectic repetoires of winemaking techniques. Brothers Gianni and Giorgio Venica, who make 15 wines from this 22 ha property, are examples of the Friuli producers who thrive on this challenge. In addition to the familiar, regional reds and whites, they set aside the cream of the production to make limited quantities of special estate wines. The white Vignis di Dolegna, a blend of local and international varieties, takes the lead and is designed to develop slowly in the bottle. Venica pays great attention to the variations in vinification which differentiate one wine from another. At the same time, they succeed in giving all their wines intense fruit flavors, the distinctive feature of this very efficient estate.

Collio Sauvignon 1991 DOC   🍷🍷 ②
A Venica speciality, here in an explosively intense version with varietal character and aromas, from fragrant ripe gooseberry, sage, yellow peppers and tomato leaf to the unmistakable 'cat's pee'. The palate matches the nose with great concentration and fresh acidity. Made to drink young but intriguing to follow in the bottle for a couple years.

Vignis di Dolegna 1991   🍷 ②
A cuvée of 50% Tocai, 15% Sauvignon and 35% Pinot Bianco with the complexity and the fresh, intense flavor expected of Venica wines. The nose has prominent, grassy Tocai aromas; strong native varietal flavor, with hints of bitter almonds. Slightly nervy, penetrating but also full-bodied with lots of personality.

Cerò 1990   🍷🍷 ③
Another limited production special. 100% Sauvignon with the breadth and complexity of Puilly Fumé. Pale straw, with yellow-gold reflections; an intense, well-defined nose; oak blends perfectly with capiscum and minerally aromas. Long, velvety finish.

Chardonnay Bernizza 1989   🍷🍷 ②
A small percentage of the production is set aside each year for an oaked Riserva released a year later than the rest. A serious wine with a complex nose in which tropical fruit and new oak fight it out for prominence. Dry, powerful and rather austere as concentrated Chardonnay can be.

La Viarte

Via Novacuzzo, 50
Prepotto (Ud) 33040
Tel/Fax (0432) 759458

The Viarte estate is located 30 km east of Udine, on the borders between the DOC zones of Colli Orientali del Friuli and the Collio, and Slovenia. Giuseppe Ceschin, an enologist from the Veneto, is the estate's owner. The full-bodied richness of the wines of Eastern Friuli win over at first impact. After several years of work in some of the most important cellars in the area, Ceschin set up by himself an 1973 with an estate which he called La Viarte, which means "the spring" in Friulan dialect. Ceschin has planted 21 ha of tidily-kept, south-facing vineyards with vines at a density of 2,500 units per ha. If the care lavished on the vineyards is exemplary, that given to the work of the cellar is nothing less. Viarte wines are sometimes criticized, wrongly in our view, for being supposedly 'too technical'. We believe that the finesse which characterizes the whites and the balance, which is the feature of the reds, are indications of their utmost reliability. The hand of the experienced winemaker is evident in the up-lifted varietal character of the varietal wines, but Ceschin's strength lies in the cuvées, the white Liende (legend) and the red Roi (rivulet).

Colli Orientali del Friuli
Ribolla Gialla 1991 Doc
Pale yellow shade, intense aromas tending more towards the floral than the fruity, nice fresh acidity, balance and respectable length on the palate.

Liende 1990
Made from Pinot Bianco, Riesling, and Sauvignon, this wine has fresh floral aromas which are long, stylish and complex with an underlying greenness and a smooth balance on the palate accompanied by good acidity.

Roi 1987
A blend of Cabernet Franc, Refosco and Merlot which after a year in barrique and long bottle age has developed an intense spicy bouquet. Good extract and grassy character on the palate.

Rating System

An exemplary wine of its type with outstanding local character

An international premium quality wine

A Top Wine, considered one of the 150 best wines in the world

The 'grape bunch' symbol is used to indicate the color of the wine; the number of bunches represents the quality rating assigned by the contributor

Vie di Romans

Loc. Vie di Romans, 1
Mariano (Go) 34070
Tel/Fax (0481) 69600

Vie de Romans is a 15-ha estate in the Isonzo owned by father and son, Stelio and Gianfranco Gallo. Despite being relatively young, Gianfranco is an experienced grower and winemaker who has very clear ideas about quality and style having run the family estate the past decade. Since the mid-1980s he has been perfecting a range of wines which reflect his own impatience with the simple, standardized varietals with which this zone is generally associated. The Vie de Romans line mainly consists of single-vineyards selections. Viticulture is aimed at finding the equilibrium between micro-climate, terrain and growth cycle of the vine, resulting in low yields of top-quality fruit. In the handsome, newly-constructed winery, Gianfranco makes wines of concentration and natural balance for aging. The whites are released at the end of the year following the vintage when they drink well but also promise further depth and complexity with time. Gianfranco has recently begun to introduce 500-lt French tonneaux in place of the smaller, more common barrique; the results in terms of texture and finesse show much promise and an exciting future for this interesting estate.

Isonzo Chardonnay Ciampagnis Vieris 1990 DOC 🍇 ②
This vineyard's name in dialect refers to the parcels of land distributed to the local populace by the Empress Maria Teresa in times of famine. Still very closed on the nose but has outstanding structure and rich, satisfying texture. Exciting potential.

Isonzo Chardonnay Vie di Romans 1990 DOC 🍇🍇 ③
Young, pale lemon shade. Intense, faintly smokey, long, ripe and complex. The palate has verve and freshness but also a very solid structure and oaky tannins. Judging by the superb 1989, the flavors here too should blend and impart great depth and harmony.

Isonzo Piere Sauvignon 1990 DOC 🍇🍇 ③
Piere is their non-oaked Sauvignon, that lets the variety speaks for itself. A racy wine with exuberant, pure fruit flavors which are intense without being coarse. The generous 13° alcohol gives body which balances the fruity acidity perfectly.

Isonzo Pinot Grigio Dolee 1990 DOC 🍇 ③
Fermented and aged in 500 lt tonneaux casks, a Pinot Grigio with the classic pale copper reflections of top-class wines from this variety. Broad and soft with aromas of ripe pears, cinnamon and rose petal. The palate is smooth and complex with a long, balanced finish.

Isonzo Sauvignon Vieris 1990 🍇🍇🍇 ③
There are international experts who maintain, despite evidence of old vintages of Sancerre or superb, long-lived dry Bordeaux, that Sauvignon is a wine with little aging potential. The tendency in Italy certainly has been to produce fresh and immediate varietals without great character, incapable of improving with age. Gianfranco Gallo's Vieris is not a part of that trend. This Sauvignon (like all his others) completes a full malolactic fermentation. It is then given prolonged oak-aging. The varietal character on the nose blends perfectly with the stylish oak which, in turn, adds complexity to the tertiary aromas. The extraordinary complexity offers a spectrum of flavor and aroma on which each taster will test his powers of recognition and description. The generous alcohol is balanced by gusty acidity. Although elegant and already open and irresistibly drinkable, the length on the nose and the palate indicate that this is a wine to keep and enjoy well into the future.

Vigne dal Leon

Loc. Rocca Bernarda
Premariacco (Ud) 33040
Tel. (0432) 716083-759693
Fax (0432) 759884

The estate of the Vigne dal Leon is situated in a zone blessed by Bacchus on the hill of Rocca Bernarda. For centuries vines have grown in the soils of eocene marl, on terraces which alternate with woods populated by game. The landscape, which greets the eye from the vineyards or from the villa of the estate, has few equals, as in fact have the quality of the grapes and wines produced here. The seven hectare property was purchased by a person of exceptional cordiality, Tullio Zamò, in 1978. The technical management of the estate, which today is one of the most reliable in the Colli Orientali DOC zone, is in the hands of Sandro Facca and Franco Bernabei. The cellars are equipped to maintain the most rigorous control over the whole winemaking process. The estate's top wines are matured in barrique. Tullio shares a special interest for the indigenous varieties. Even though projects for the future involve a reduction in the number of wines produced, there will always be space for Malvasia Istriana, Tazzelenghe and Schioppettino to ensure the continuity of the region's age-old winemaking traditions.

Colli Orientali del Friuli � 2
Pinot Bianco 1991 DOC
Made exclusively in stainless steel, an elegant white with flowers, fruit and a touch of yeast on the nose. Good structure, balance and length.

Colli Orientali del Friuli 🍇🍇 ②
Sauvignon 1991 DOC
An exemplary varietal made in stainless steel to bring out all the zippy freshness of the grape. Long and elegant on the nose with notes of nettle and tomato leaf. Soft and silky on the palate, although not particularly full-bodied, with a delicious fruit finish.

Tullio Zamo' Bianco 1990 🍇 ③
This estate blend based mainly on Pinot Bianco has been developed over the years. Stylishly fresh and fruity on the nose with understated oak in the background. The palate is rich, smooth, full and firm, with excellent prospects for future development.

Schioppettino 1988 🍇🍇 ③
The great speciality of the estate from a local variety known also as Ribolla Nera. This vintage has an even ruby red color, aromas of cherry and toasted oak on the nose a palate which has intense flavors, good balance and a touch of tannin in the finish.

Vigneti Le Monde

Loc. Le Monde, Via Garibaldi, 2
Prata di Pordenone (Pn) 33080
Tel/Fax (0434) 626096

The DOC Grave del Friuli does not enjoy a particularly high reputation as a result of the policy of many growers to concentrate more on the production of quantity than quality. This general criticism does categorically not apply to Piergiovanni Pistoni's Vigneti Le Monde, situated 60 km north-east of Venezia on the Friuli's western border with Veneto. His 25 ha of vineyard, planted at a density of between 2,400 and 4,000 vines per ha, produce quantities far below the maximum limits of the DOC regulations, which, in part, explains the high quality of his wines. Another reason for the success of the estate, which was founded at the end of the 19th century and has been bottling wines for the last 20 years, is the undivided, day-to-day commitment of 34 year-old Piergiovanni and his charming wife, Antonella. Piergiovanni's great faith in the potential of the zone known in dialect as "Le Monde" has lead him to concentrate his efforts on growing varieties, in particular Cabernet Sauvignon, to produce premium quality wines for medium and long term aging.

Grave 🍇 ②
Refosco del Peduncolo Rosso 1990 DOC
Bright ruby, intense grassy character on the nose with aromas of camomile and a palate which combines fruit, extract and body. Complex and balanced.

Grave 🍇 ②
Cabernet Sauvignon Superiore 1988 DOC
Ruby red with purple edges and an intense bouquet of fruit, leather and spice. The palate has warm, ripe fruit and grass flavors and the tannin and acidity to suggest continuing and very interesting development.

Querceto 1987 🍇🍇 ②
A blend of Cabernet Franc and Sauvignon with a deep ruby color and intense aromas on the nose which range from stewed fruit to bitter oranges, hay and spice. Full and broad on the palate with good balance and a hint of liquorice on the finish.

Villa Russiz

Loc. Russiz Inferiore, 5
Capriva del Friuli (Go) 34070
Tel. (0481) 80047
Fax (0481) 809657

Estates in Friuli are often criticised for producing too many wines. Properties of less that five hectares often grow up to 10 different varieties, each of which is vinified separately. One consequence for the wine-buyer is that the availability of the single wines can be frustratingly limited. The producer has to maintain a constant level of quality over a range of red and white varieties with often widely differing characteristics. Estate manager Gianni Menotti produces a dozen wines from 29 ha at Villa Russiz and is unrepentent about it. He is even experimenting with new varieties. His policy is justified by the results. Menotti consistently extracts the potential from each variety grown. Capriva is known for its rich Tocai, Pinot Bianco and Sauvignon, but alongside these classics at Villa Russiz minor wines such as Sylvaner are also models of their type. As further demonstration of his own versatility and that of the vineyards in this superb cru of the Collio, Menotti is currently giving much attention to two reds, a Pinot Noir and the estate's Rosso de La Tour both of which are destined to further enhance the prestige of this fine estate.

Collio Pinot Bianco 1991 DOC   ♈♈ ②
Delicious to drink now for the open, soft fruity character but also endowed with the balance and concentration to develop very interestingly in the bottle. Exemplary varietal character and generous body.

Collio Sauvignon   ♈♈ ②
de La Tour 1991 DOC
The star of the 1991 vintage, as good if not better than the exceptional 1989. Enormous on the nose, with penetrating gooseberry fruit and a whole range of vegetal nuances matching on the palate; intense, steely and even slightly austere in its raw youth; ample, full body. A Sauvignon with the penetrating aromas of the Loire and the ripeness of Friuli.

Rosso de La Tour 1990   ♈ ②
Depth of fruit and broad, soft tannins reveal the excellent potential of this Bordeaux-blend, autumn 1992 release. It will be tempting to drink young, but the real class of this super vintage will only show in time.

Tenuta Villanova

Via Contessa Beretta, 7
Farra d'Isonzo (Go) 34070
Tel. (0481) 888013
Fax (0481) 888513

The commune of Farra d'Isonzo has a pocket of vineyards which, although separated from the hills which make up the rest of the DOC zone, shares the same soils (marl and sandstone) as the Collio and, as a result, is included in the latter denomination. The Tenuta Villanova, founded in 1499, has part of its 104 ha of vineyard in this zone and part in the DOC Isonzo, a short distance south east of Gorizia. The ancient cellars of the estate, which have been painstakingly restored, have an evocative atmosphere all their own. The winery has an equally impressive array of the equipment that modern technology offers the winemaker intent on extracting optimum quality from his raw materials. The cellars are geared to handle a max of 12,000 hl of wine, including wood aging, and the estate crushes an average 8,500 Q of grapes/year. The talented technical director, Paolo Cora, born in Piemonte and scholared in Veneto, is responsible for identifying the cru such as Monte Cucco and Roncocucco from which, in the best vintages, the Tenuta Villanova produces special selections of great interest.

Collio Monte Cucco 1990 DOC   ♈ ②
The classic white blend of the Collio made from Ribolla, Tocai and Malvasia. Pale straw color refined and elegant on the nose and full but also fresh, stylish and very drinkable on the palate.

Isonzo Chardonnay   ♈♈ ②
Monte Cucco1990 DOC
Mid-depth straw yellow. Barrique aging gives vanilla on the nose which blends well with the fruit. Intense and complex on the palate with a smooth finish. Still improving in the bottle.

Cabernet Sauvignon   ♈ ②
Monte Cucco 1990
Ruby shade with mauve reflections, intense on the nose and full, rich and complex on the palate. Leather and spice aromas hint at the very interesting evolution guaranteed by the structure.

Volpe Pasini

Via Cividale, 16
Togliano di Torreano (Ud) 33040
Tel. (0432) 573864
Fax (0432) 715151

Volpe Pasini is without doubt one of the oldest estates in Friuli. Wine was made in the 17th century, although it was not customary then to bottle any more than limited quantities. The vineyards, 28 ha in all, are situated in three different parts of the DOC zone Colli Orientali del Friuli. The splendid 19th century villa and cellars are at Togliano di Torreano, about 20 km east of Udine. The estate has been managed for several years by Diego Volpe Pasini, who makes a point of personally seeing to the cellar and vineyard work, despite his numerous other commitments in the field of food and wine. Credit for the high standards currently being achieved belongs to enologist-winemaker Giovanni Crosato. Among the measures he has introduced are harvesting in small cases, hyper-oxidation of the white wine must, the technique of partial freeze-drying to obtain the desired alcohol content and barrique aging, all of which have had a determining effect. A final positive note: the estate has decided to cut back the number of varieties it grows, setting an example which unfortunately too few producers in the region seem ready to follow.

Colli Orientali del Friuli Pinot Grigio � ③
Zuc di Volpe 1991 DOC
Rich straw yellow from barrique aging. The toasted oak comes through on the nose, complementing the intense fruit and gunflint aromas. Good balance and structure on the palate promise slow evolution.

Colli Orientali del Friuli Sauvignon ☆ ③
Zuc di Volpe 1990 DOC
Pale straw color with green reflections. Exceptionally fine varietal nose with capiscum and tomato leaf preludes a palate which has fruit and acidity, body and intensity. Can only improve with time.

Chardonnay Zuc di Volpe 1989 ☆☆ ③
One of the winery's best products, the result of successful clonal selection and a carefully studied vinification. Yeast and vanilla on the nose and ripe fruit on the palate. Broad, complex and full of verve.

Le Marne 1988 ♥ ③
A grape blend of Merlot, Cabernet and Refosco, matured in barrique. Deep ruby shade, rich and complex on the nose with aromas of cooked plum and spices. Great structure, fruit and extract on the palate. Made to last.

Lazio

Supplying one fifth of the national produce, the region of Lazio makes an average of 6,000,000 hl per year and has 18 DOC wines. Soils are mostly of volcanic origin, thus rich in potassium which gives the wines a particular maturity for which the Frascati wines and other Latium whites have been renowned since the days of Emperor Augustus. Whites still prevail, in terms of quantity, with two thirds of total production; varietals include Trebbiano Giallo, Trebbiano Toscano, Malvasia del Lazio, Malvasia di Candia, Grechetto, Greco Bianco, Bombino Bianco, Bellone, Moscato, Riesling Italico and others. The main red grapes are Cesanese, Bombino Nero, Cabernet, Merlot, Ciliegiolo, Sangiovese, Montepulciano and Greco Nero. Some of the region's growing areas are located near Rome, the most famous being Marino, Velletri, Frascati, Colli Lanuvini and Zagarolo. Particularly famous and original in its name and history, is Est! Est!! Est!!! di Montefiascone, in the province of Viterbo. Indeed Viterbo's wine areas have been especially active in focusing on quality rather than quantity.

Dubious wine laws in the past, which, to name just two, encouraged the increase of yields per hectare and lowered the minimum alcohol content allowed, inevitably had their impact in standardizing styles and flattening character. There have been many improvements and changes in trends, however, thanks to producers such as Paola Di Mauro, Villa Simone and Fontana Candida near Rome, several wineries around Viterbo and others still. They have supported and advocated their regional DOC wines as flagships while also deftly bringing innovation and experimentation with new blends. In boosting the quality standard, they are also improving Lazio's reputation to make wines that are not merely thirst-quenchers.

Colacicchi

Loc. Romagnano
Anagni (Fr) 03012
Tel. (06) 4469661
Fax (06) 4468351

Founder of this small winery located in the Frosinone wine area, Luigi Colacicchi was one of the most famous music composers of the later 20th century. He was very successful as a musician, and the same can be said of his activity as wine producer. He had the brilliant idea of planting Cabernet and Merlot in Anagni vineyards which were blended with Cesanese, a typical local grape, to make Torre Ercolana, one of Lazio's, if not Italy's, greatest reds. Luigi's nephew, Bruno Colacicchi, directed the winery for a short time, although the winery is now in the hands of Marco Trimani who already sold Colacicchi wines in his famous wine bar in Rome. Together with his children, Paolo, Francesco and Carla, Marco plans to promote the Colacicchi label, ensuring better quality from the vineyard and cellar. With this in mind, he had a 1.5 ha vineyard re-planted, which had been abandoned for quite some time, keeping yields per hectare low (to 50 quintals) and experimenting with the composition of the blends.

Romagnano 1990 ☆ ①
A very original white, a blend of Malvasia Puntinata and Romanesco, it is deep yellow color with delicately mature perfumes, a considerable rich flavor and structure, and a pleasantly bitter finish.

Torre Ercolana 1986 ☆☆ ②
A real gem for Lazio: a blend of Cabernet, Merlot and Cesanese grapes, with a wonderful aroma of spices, marasca cherry and black cherry. Excellent length on the palate, full-bodied with pleasant but not overpowering tannin.

Paola Di Mauro

Via Colle Picchioni di Marino, 46
Frattocchie (Rm) 00040
Tel. (06) 3546329
Fax (06) 7211580

Since the early 1970s, Paola Di Mauro's winery has been the most interesting novelty in the Castelli Romani wine scene and has successfully developed a range of wines relatively unique to the area. Paola Di Mauro is the driving force behind the winery and is assisted by her son, Armando, and Giorgio Grai, the famous and highly competent enologist from Bolzano. This trio has successfully managed to put together a very particular range of wines, from golden-colored classic-style whites with typical perfumes, to extremely soft and complex reds aged in chestnut-wood barrels. More recently they have come out with Vignole, a modern-styled white aged in barrique. Wines are released only after lengthy bottle-aging, a production policy which is not the norm but which enables the drinker to readily appreciate the wine's well-defined and developed organoleptic characteristics.

Le Vignole 1989 ☆ ①
A white made from an interesting blend of Malvasia del Lazio, Trebbiano and Sauvignon, aged in small 500 lt barrels and then at length in bottle. Currently at its peak, with its wealth of perfumes and ample, lingering flavor.

Vigna del Vassallo 1988 ☆☆ ③
Elegance is the distinguishing characteristic of this wine made from Merlot, Cabernet Sauvignon, Sangiovese and Montepulciano grapes. For years, it has been one of central Italy's best; the pleasant red currant, cherry and herbaceous nose comes through on the palate, with a nice balance of tannins, alcohol and acidity.

Falesco

S.S. Cassia, km 94,155
Montefiascone (Vt) 01027
Tel. (0761) 826332
Fax (0761) 66280

Est! Est!! Est!!! di Montefiascone is a wine
with a glorious past, but which has more
recently been damaged by over-production
and the resulting quantity over quality. Over
the last few years, however, things have
improved within the production zone of Est!
Est!! Est!!!, as a handful of wineries opt for
premium wines. Falesco, a recently
established medium-sized winery run by
wine-technician Riccardo Cotarella stands
out. Grapes are purchased from selected
growers who rely on Falesco's constant
technical assistance for their vineyard care
and grape analysis. Close to Lake Bolsena,
the vineyard's soils are of volcanic origin and
enjoy a tempered Mediterranean climate. The
grapes used follow the DOC wine legislation
and include Malvasia Bianca, Trebbiano
Toscano, Rossetto and other local varietals.
Supervision in the vineyard and up-to-date
vinification methods make for medium-bodied
and structured wines, with some agebility.

Est! Est!! Est!!! 🍇 ①
Poggio dei Gelsi 1991 DOC
An interesting cru from a DOC re-discovered
and brought to new heights by Falesco. Yellow
in color with typical greenish highlights, it has
ample and intense perfumes of ripe fruit and
remarkably lengthy, soft flavors.

Villa San Patrizio 1991 🍇 ①
In addition to its styles of Est! Est!! Est!!!, the
Falesco winery also produces a late-harvest
wine from native grapes. Gentle and ample
perfumes, with a well-balanced and supple
palate.

Fontana Candida

Via Fontana Candida, 11
Frascati (Rm) 00040
Tel. (06) 9420066
Fax (06) 9448591

For years the Fontana Candida brand has
been synonymous with Frascati wine both in
Italy and worldwide. It was the first winery to
distribute Frascati in bottles, labelling them
with its own name, and still today exports
about two thirds of its total production. All the
fruit comes from vineyards cultivated by small
growers close to the Tuscolane hills, south of
Rome. The main grapes grown are
Trebbiano Toscano, Trebbiano Giallo,
Malvasia di Candia as well as several natives
such as Bombino and Bellone. A Chardonnay
blend is the backbone of the winery's newest
wine, Villa Fontana Candida. The vast
quantities of wine produced (a little over than
580,000 cases) are impressively matched by
extremely high quality. The credit for this
goes to the wine-technician, Francesco Baldi
who, aided by Narciso Faggia, supervises the
entire production cycle of the winery. He has
recently started to help the estate's 270
grape-growers, giving technical advice on
how to improve their vine-growing practices.
This project which has already proved to be
positive and will inevitably lead to new quality
standards in the wines.

Frascati Superiore 🍇 ①
Santa Teresa 1991 DOC
Though not quite up to the heights of the 1990
vintage, this specially selected Frascati is still
one of the best of its type, marked by pleasant
fruity bouquet with striking apple perfumes and
impressive, lingering aromas.

Villa Fontana Candida 1991 🍇 ①
In addition to its Frascati Superiore (also
available in the standard and Santa Teresa
versions), the winery also makes this blended
wine from Malvasia del Lazio, Trebbiano
Toscano and Chardonnay Trentino. Rich in
bouquet, extremely pleasant on the palate, with
good fresh acidity.

Villa Simone

Via Torricella, 2
Monteporzio Catone (Rm) 00040
Tel/Fax (06) 3213210

Piero Costantini, owner of Villa Simone, is known for the whole-hearted effort and passion he puts into the occupation of wine producer. As well as making local wines, Villa Simone also bottles a Rosso Piceno and a Cabernet that are made from his other winery in the the Marche region called La Torraccia. He is also owner of one of the oldest and most established Roman wine bars and began producing wine in the Castelli Romani area in 1983. Since then he has constantly improved, so much so that today the winery ranks among the best producers of Frascati wine not to mention the very rare Cannellino wine. Costantini wines have strong personality and style and are made using modern cultivation and vinification practices. Vineyards are planted in rows, soils are fertilized organically, no harsh chemicals are used in treating the vines and yields are kept to 90 qu/ha. Alberto Corti is the house wine-technician and is assisted by Piero's nephew, a young enologist Lorenzo Costantini. The winery is a model of its kind, and the greastest care is taken in the vinification and bottling of the wine.

Frascati Superiore ☙☙ ①
Villa Simone 1991 DOC
A perfect example of a Frascati Superiore cru produced by Piero Costantini. Bright straw-yellow in color, it has an appley bouquet and a consistent and savoury flavor. The solid backbone ensures good future development.

Frascati Cannellino 1990 DOC ☙ ①
A modern-day version which easily bears comparison with the off-dry Cannellino wines of the past. Made from late-harvested grapes, this wine stands out with its powerful aromas, soft and full flavors, and aromatic length.

Entries are arranged in alphabetical order by country, region and winery or producer name.

Liguria

Many different varieties of grapes have made up Liguria's vine-growing history. They generally arrived by way of the busy maritime trade and made simple, ready-to-drink styles of wines. Wild vines were cultivated probably since 1000 BC. Centuries later (in 100 AD) Greek geographer, Strabone, complained that the quality of the local wines was poor, being limited, sour and often resinous. The Roman conquest, on the other hand, brought change and perfection. Indeed, Plinio the Elder's testimony is significantly full of praise in saying "Etruriae Luna palman habet, Liguriae Genua." It was not until the Middle Ages, however, that the production and commerce reached a larger scale, and vineyards began to weave beautiful patchworks into the landscape.

A wealth of documents and historical writings chart the history. A land register dated 1420 shows that vines flourished in Albenga in the western Ponente while to the south-east, from Chiavari down to La Spezia, numerous religious documents show the importance of wine. In the centuries to come, the use of crop rotation was established, mainly benefitting both vines and olive-trees.

Liguria's wine history is still rather scanty. With over 18,000 producers, mostly with less than one hectare of vineyard, relatively few wineries are currently producing quality wines. Many have non-specialized vineyards that commonly yield what is affectionately referred to as "nostralini", or local wines. Vineyards are to be found in the most unimaginable places, from the hill-sides to the terraced cliffs by the sea, to those inland. The Ligurians have to admit that the morphological difficulties of the steep and unmanageable land are practically unsurmountable. They are lands which over the centuries have been stolen from the mountain by the tenacity of man who transformed them into steep and narrow terraces, creating winding kilometers of stone-laid walls supporting the terraces and making efficient mechanization practically impossible. As a result, wine-making in Liguria a difficult feat.

According to recent statistics in the agriculture sector, wine represents only 3% of the gross, placing it 11th among the 21 regions in Italy. Approximately 12,000 ha are planted with vines, and total production nears 400,000 hl with DOC wines playing a relatively insignificant part.

Starting from the French border and ending with Cogoleto, near Genova, the Riviera Ligure di Ponente DOC includes the varietal wines of Pigato, Vermentino, Rossese, Ormeasco (a Dolcetto clone with green stalks) and Ormeasco Sciac-trà. Rossese di Dolceacqua DOC is also produced in the western Ponente, in an area around Val Nervia comprising 14 towns. The other two DOCs are in the eastern Levante. Cinque Terre is made from the indigenous Bosco, Vermentino and Albarola grapes; a Passito, raisined-style from those same grapes is called Sciacchetrà. Towards the southern border with Toscana, the Colli di Luni is made in three styles of white, red and varietal Vermentino. The Levante produces the most quantity, immediately followed by the provinces of Genova, Savona and Imperia. Vines are generally limited to the hillsides and trained in the "alberello" form in the Mediterranean coastal tradition. Vines are also trained in the Guyot, Spalliera and Cordone Speronato methods.

Gio Batta Mandino Cane

Via Roma, 21
Dolceacqua (Im) 18035
Tel. (0184) 206120

When "Mandino" Cane decided to combine his profession of olive oil presser with that of vine-grower 20 odd years ago, the foundations were already there: the plots were situated at medium altitude on hills, good sun exposure, an ideal microclimate in an exceptional zone, especially the Arcagna vineyard, which is considered a true cru. A great passion and the gratification from producing his premium quality Dolceacqua Superiore gradually brought "Mandino" Cane to a full-time committment and pushed him even to plant yet another vineyard, in the Morghe area. Though he is no longer a young man (or so his birth certificate has it), he is totally devoted to wine and Ligurian traditions. Amazingly enough, he runs a one-man operation in both vineyard and cellar. Of course, the surface planted to vines and production remain limited, with sales and distribution generally within regional boundaries. The wine is unique, made by traditional vinification of Rossese grapes, first aged in stainless steel then oaked, without capitulation to the siren of barrique aging.

Dolceacqua Superiore Vigneto Arcagna 1990 DOC

A wine with aristocratic character and subtle charm, it has an intense and lengthy bouquet. Smooth yet robust, full depth of palate and a typical bitter finish.

Cascina delle Terre Rosse

Loc. Manie, 3
Finale Ligure (Sv) 17024
Tel. (019) 698782

Located behind the coastal strip which runs from Final Pia to Noli, Le Manie is an interesting high plateau and nature habitat. The native Pigato and Lumassina grapes grown on the plateau's Terre Rosse, or red clay soils, together with Vermentino and Rossese make up the current vine-growing heritage of this 1970-founded winery. Vladimiro Galluzzo had not shown a particular interest in his family's vineyards until he took it over from his father. Self-taught and urged by pure passion, Vladimiro lead the winery to its rebirth in only a few years. He made all the right moves and with successful results. His tenacity, together with considerable financial investments, helped to create a modern winery with a production philosophy aimed at quality. Flagship wines of great character like Pigato and Vermentino serve to enhance the potential of his others such as the nearly-forgotten Lumassina. He also used his personal skills and research in the making of such unique wines as his Passito.

Riviera Ligure di Ponente Pigato 1991 DOC

From the native Pigato varietal, a glorious white with light and delicate aromas on the nose. Pleasantly soft on the palate with lightly fresh acidity, a good body, lingering tastes and typical bitter finish.

Riviera Ligure di Ponente Vermentino 1991 DOC

A wine with a surprisingly intense bouquet, seductive and lingering. On the palate, it is fresh, dry, well-balanced, very drinkable and graceful. Lingering, with a distinctive character.

Passito 1990

Made from Vermentino and Pigato grapes that were raisined at length and then fermented very slowly. This fine Vino da Meditazione is very seductive, suggestive and ample on the nose, with alcohol to impart depth and length. With a complex palate, good balance, soft and outstanding body.

Cascina Feipu

Fraz. Bastia, Loc. Massaretti, 8
Albenga (Sv) 17030
Tel. (0182) 20131

In 1965 Bice and Pippo Parodi, overwhelmed with compliments for a wine that they had made only for their friends and relatives, eventually decided to make a life-long dream come true and planted new vineyards of Pigato in the sunny Massaretti area. Thus Liguria's first important white was born several years later. Well-liked Pippo is an enterprising wine producer with undoubted personal skills who captures audiences with his sheer charm and ability to communicate. In a land where technological innovation is still seen with diffidence and scepticism, Pippo understands the importance of a well-equipped cellar. Together with premium raw material, he can make a good modern product and still maintain its varietal character. It's wines like these that have made Cascina Feipu into a model winery for Liguria's enology, helping to establish a reputation for Pigato nationwide. His daughter, Ivana, and her husband, Gianni, have also fairly recently moved in to the winery, thus ensuring continuity.

Riviera Ligure di Ponente   ☙☙ ①
Pigato 1991 DOC
This Pigato is clearly a quality wine, it has an ample bouquet, and is full-bodied and elegantly textured on the palate; savoury, supple and warm, with a lingering finish.

La Colombiera

Loc. Montecchio, 92
Castelnuovo Magra (Sp) 19030
Tel. (0187) 674265-601206
Fax (0187) 670264

An exhuberant colorful native Sicilian who has long since settled in the Lunigiana area, Francesco Ferro succeeded in creating a solid winery. He is convinced that wine, more than a commercial product, is above all the expression of human skills, ability, passion and direction. A talented and intellectually generous man, he has also made it his duty to relaunch Liguria's Levante viticulture by actively helping to organize the growers and establish an efficient association. He went out of his way to ensure that wines of Colli di Luni could gain DOC status. His son, Piero, a graduate of Alba's school of enology, shares his father's philosophy and determination and is in charge of the cellar. The winery primarily produces whites from Vermentino, Trebbiano and Malvasia Toscana grapes, the only exception being Terrizzo, which is a Ligurian crafted blend of Sangiovese.

Colli di Luni   ☙ ①
Vermentino 1991 DOC
Very refined and extremely pleasant, with marked varietal character, well expressed and delicately lingering bouquet; dry and savoury, medium-bodied, with a light almond finish.

Colli di Luni   ☙ ①
Vermentino Vignale Paterno 1990 DOC
This Paterno cru undergoes an extremely lengthy lees-aging in vats. A successful wine, delicate, elegant and pleasant aromas; well-balanced and soft on the palate.

Colli di Luni   ☙ ①
Rosso Terrizzo 1989 DOC
Made from Sangiovese, Ciliegiolo Nero and Canaiolo grapes, a wine of great class, released after two years' aging. Extremely pleasant and complex bouquet, with good texture on the mouth; full-bodied with a lingering finish.

Forlini e Cappellini

Piazza Duomo, 6
Manarola (Sp) 19010
Tel. (0187) 920496

Viticulture in the Cinque Terre is extremely difficult, if not 'acrobatic' in places due to the steep slopes. What the locals call "pastini", or terraces a few meters wide, have over the centuries transformed Liguria's steep hills into majestic staircases, discouraging more than one farmer from cultivating in this area. Alberto Cappellini and wife, Germana, have long been growers, although for years they also operated a small newsstand at the entry to Manarola. Currently, both are involved in the winery full-time and manage the property which, although limited in surface, is divided into many small plots: Posa, Campu, Traversa and Donega just to mention a few. The vineyards are planted to Bosco, Albarola and Vermentino. With its cellars carved out of the stone cliffs, the winery only makes a few bottles that are of high and uncompromising standards from raw materials of the highest quality. These and other particulars help to place this small Cinque Terre winery at the top of Liguria's production.

Cinque Terre 1991 DOC   🍇 ②
Mainly Bosco grapes with small amounts of Vermentino and Albarola are used. Gentle and typical lingering varietal aromas. Soft, dry and savoury with a salty finish, that makes for pleasant drinkability.

Ottaviano Lambruschi

Via Olmarello, 28
Castelnuovo Magra (Sp) 19030
Tel. (0187) 674261

After many years of working at marble quarries in nearby Carrara, nearly 30 years ago, Ottaviano Lambruschi decided to devote himself to the profession of viticulture. He succeeded thanks to the obstinacy, intolerance and resoluteness he puts into everything he does. At first, there was little room for his able son, Fabio, a young agronomist to assist him. The increasingly successful winery is located on hilly sedimentary soils, facing south in a zone called Costa Marina, carved from the forest by patient and hard work. Production concentrates on Sangiovese varietals (Colli di Luni Rosso) and Vermentino. The Lambruschi only vinify estate-grown grapes and, contrary to some, refuse to use concentrated musts. This is only one of Ottaviani's numerous merits, as a man who has always believed in Lunigiana's wines and in no small way has helped improve them.

Colli di Luni Vermentino   🍇 ①
Vigna Costa Marina 1991 DOC
Unusually rich bodied for a white from Liguria, it combines intense and lengthy floral perfumes with good complexity and structure. Balanced acidity helps to add savour and freshness.

Tommaso and Angelo Lupi

Via Mazzini, 9
Pieve di Teco (Im) 18026
Tel/Fax (0183) 276090

Both father and grandfather were wine merchants, and Tommaso and Angelo followed in their footsteps with managerial dynamism. The opening of an enoteca in the 1960s marked their first bottling of small selections of premium wines. Soon they began purchasing local grapes (Ormeasco, Pigato and Vermentino) and making their own. In 1977, with a substantial capital investment, they restructured an ancient building in Pieve di Teco, transforming it into one of the region's best-equipped wineries. They succeeded in convincing Liguria's stubborn farmers of the importance of basic improvement in the grapes (grafting selected clones, meticulous care, low yields, pruning, etc). Their wines have benefitted from these practices, reaching excellent levels to become flagbearers of the wines of Liguria di Ponente. A second production center was recently purchased in Soldani, in the Valle Crosa, so that the Lupi brothers can make Rossese di Dolceacqua within its DOC production zone. The latest addition is a one ha vineyard of Ormeasco in Pieve.

Riviera Ligure di Ponente 🍇 ②
Pigato Le Pietraie 1991 DOC
Pigato is an ancient varietal which takes its name from the dark stains locally referred to as "pighe" which appear on the ripening berries. Ample and intense perfumes, moderately fruity, balanced taste, soft and savoury, of great charm.

Riviera Ligure di Ponente 🍇 ②
Vermentino Le Serre 1991 DOC
An excellent cru yielding a wine with delicate perfumes of aromatic herbs, slightly floral on the finish. With a caressing palate, fresh and fragrant; the initial off-dry taste of the wine blends into a slightly bitter finish.

Vignamare 1990 🍇 ②
A Pigato and Vermentino blend, in a traditional yet innovative style. A touch of barrique, then aged in stainless steel vats and later in bottle, yields a wine with refined, apply perfumes, good texture, good character and a certain richness of body.

Riviera Ligure di Ponente 🍇🍇 ②
Ormeasco Superiore Le Braje 1990 DOC
Made from the Dolcetto clone with green stalks, brought to Liguria in the early 14th century, this Ormeasco is the best expression of its potential. Refined and lengthy perfumes with aromas of ripe cherries and hints of violets and vanilla. Beautiful lively palate, matched on the nose. Good acidity with fruit notes, and an ample and balanced structure.

Coop. Agricoltura di Riomaggiore, Manarola, Corniglia, Vernazza e Monterosso

Loc. Groppo di Riomaggiore
Manarola (Sp) 19010
Tel. (0187) 920435
Fax (0187) 920076

Agricultural cooperatives in Liguria are usually rather lacklustre and the quality of their products is often questionable. but this Cinque Terre cooperative is different. Created in the 1970s, each farmer consigned his own small lots of wine which were produced in different styles, made with premium grapes and to the best of their personal skills, but rarely with the appropriate technology. Initially the cooperative aimed at marketing the wines, more often striving to improve distribution channels than supervising the quality aspect of production. The turning point took place in 1982 with the construction of the Groppo di Riomaggiore winery, well-furnished with the appropriate vinification equipment. Today the contributing vintners number nearly 400, and all the grapes are vinified separately according to vineyard suitability and location, the maturation calendar and harvest date. Extremely satisfying results have been attained in quality standards, confirmed year after year, to the approval of both Italian and foreign consumers.

Cinque Terre 1991 DOC 🍇 ①
The cooperative's main wine is quite impeccable. It has a good intense bouquet with floral perfumes and a pleasantly full flavor.

Cinque Terre 🍇 ①
Cosat de Sera 1991 DOC
Boccaccio considered it one of the marvels of Bengodi, and it has continued to be an excellent wine. Delicate aroma with floral character, rich in nuances. Balanced on the palate, dry and well-structured.

Lombardia

Lombardia takes its name from "Longobardia", which means land of the Longobards, although its was once much larger in land size. The Longobards reigned over almost the whole current-day Italy during the 13th century. Later, from the 15th to the 19th centuries, Lombardy no longer existed as an independent entity. Valtellina was then part of Switzerland; Bergamo, Brescia and Crema were outposts of the Republic of Venice against the Duchy of Milan which controlled the rest of the region. Mantova remained a separate entity thanks to the Gonzagas.

Lombardy's winemaking history is equally fragmented. Starting from the north, on the Swiss border, there is Valtellina where the main grape Nebbiolo Chiavennasca makes a series of DOC wines including Grumello, Sassella, Inferno, Valgella and the late-harvest Sfursat. West of Lake Iseo, in the province of Brescia, bordering the province of Bergamo, the Franciacorta area grows mainly grapes of French origin. Its red DOCs are Merlot, Cabernet Sauvignon and Franc, Barbera and Pinot Nero based, whereas the still whites are made with Pinot Grigio, Pinot Bianco and Chardonnay; each is often made as single-varietal wines. The méthode champenoise and crémant, or slightly sparkling wines, often of great caliber, complete the picture.

Franciacorta has a kind of annex on the other side of the lake, in Valcalepio, where unpretentious red (Merlot and Cabernet) and white (Pinot) DOC wines are produced. Besides Merlot and Cabernet, several producers are rediscovering the zone's traditional grapes, such as Imberghem (a variant of the Franconia grape), and results are decidedly encouraging.

Another traditional Lombard wine zone is Oltrepò Pavese, the part of the province of Pavia extending south over the Po river. Local Barbera and Bonarda varietals predominate for reds and again Pinot for whites. Chardonnay, Sauvignon and Riesling Renano and Italico are commonly found throughout the area, and méthode champenoise is quite common.

The small strip of land called Lugana, on the Brescia side of Lake Garda, deserves an honorable mention for its Trebbiano, to which the area's particular climate and soils have given an unmistakable perfume and aroma when, of course, skillfully vinified.

Bellavista

Via Case Sparse, 17
Bellavista di Erbusco (Bs) 25030
Tel. (030) 7760276
Fax (030) 7760386

From building constructor to wine producer: Vittorio Moretti is one of many entrepreneurs who started making wine as a passionate hobby. After purchasing a beautiful estate in the countryside near Bellavista di Erbusco, the heart of the Franciacorta area, he decided to test his skills as a professional wine producer. Once an entrepreneur, always an entrepreneur; Moretti did not shy away from investing in both the vineyard and cellar, and hired Mattia Vezzola, a highly respected enologist, as the winery's technical manager. The result is that from 1977 this large winery's production has made enormous leaps in quality, producing excellent quality sparkling and still wines, both white and red. The fact that Franciacorta holds a prestigious position among Italy's wine producing areas is due in no small part to the Bellavista winery and above all to Vittorio Moretti's considerable skills and to the quality of his wines.

Franciacorta ⓓⓓ ④
Pas Operé 1987 DOC
Obtained from a selection of Pinot Nero and Chardonnay grapes, and left on the lees for more than four years. The result is a straw-yellow sparkling wine with fine abundant, white mousse. Dry on the palate, with pleasant aftertaste.

Franciacorte Brut DOC ⓓ ③
A pleasant sparkling wine with medium-fine bubbles and elegant fruity perfumes. On the palate harmonious and well-flavored. Excellent value for money.

Ca' dei Frati

Via Frati, 22
Lugana di Sirmione (Bs) 25010
Tel/Fax (030) 919468

In running their father Pietro's winery, Igino and Franco Dal Cero combine peasant traditions with the most modern enological technology. Granted, Pietro Dal Cero did miracles when running Ca' dei Frati almost single-handedly. In terms of quality, he rose above many other producers in the area of the Brescian shore of Lake Garda, which is more inclined to produce rivers of mediocre tourist-level wine for tourists from the other side of the Alps. The more demanding palates soon learned to distinguish Ca' dei Frati's wines from amongst the scores of other Lugana wines: the standard version, a fresh style of Trebbiano grown in its own particular microclimate, and the crus which also a little time in barrique. As often happens in the best of wineries, the new generation of the Dal Cero family have devoted more attention to, and invested heavily in, both the vineyard and winery, enriching and updating the equipment. The results of their efforts are evident.

Lugana Vigna Il Brolettino 1990 DOC ⓓ ①
This wine, made from Lugana grapes from the Il Brolettino vineyard, stands out foremost for the finesse of its perfumes and flavors. Even after wood-aging, it maintains all of Lugana's varietal character. Fresh and pleasant.

Ca' dei Frati Brut ⓓ ③
Straw-yellow in color, this sparkling wine is made from 100% Chardonnay. Rather intense fruit bouquet with appley aromas; dry on the palate, soft and pleasantly harmonious.

Ca' del Bosco

Via Case Sparse, 11
Erbusco (Bs) 25030
Tel. (030) 7267196-7267311
Fax (030) 7268425

Maurizio Zanella's winery celebrated its 20th anniversary in 1992, while its Ca' del Bosco sparkling wine had its 14th. The winery is rightly proud of the decisive role which it has had in promoting Franciacorta. Traditionally a general farming area, where vines played a secondary role, Franciacorta has now become one of Italy's most interesting wine zones. They took the challenge upon themselves very seriously, hiring top technicians, investing in vineyards and new plantings and stocking a highly equipped state-of-the-art cellar. Results were not been slow in coming and have paid fully off the investment. With total devotion and unyielding professionalism, Maurizio's calling turned out to be anything but passing. With ongoing experimention, verifying, cross-checking and correcting, and the planting of new vineyards, always with quality foremost, Ca' del Bosco has created and aged wines which are now firmly fixed among the excellent wines of Italy, and of the world. A well-equipped laboratory has been installed to back the vineyard and cellar operations. Even top universities would envy its sophisticated technology and computers.

Franciacorta Crémant DOC   ❦ (3)
From Chardonnay and Pinot Bianco grapes, kept on the lees for over 30 months before dégorgement. A Franciacorta with small and lingering bubbles,and a fine and lengthy bouquet. Dry on the palate, with good length and pleasant drinkability.

Franciacorta 1985 DOC   ❦❦ (4)
A sparkling wine of great class, made from Chardonnay (35%), Pinot Bianco (35%) and Pinot Nero (30%). After fermentation in large oak barrels it is left for five years on the lees before dégorgement. A méthode champenoise with rich, white creamy mousse which develops a balanced and complex bouquet, with pleasant yeasty aromas. Soft on the palate, of excellent structure and lingering taste. Undoubtedly one of Italy's best sparkling wines.

Maurizio Zanella 1988   ❦❦ (3)
Ruby-red with garnet highlights, made from Cabernet Franc, Cabernet Sauvignon and Merlot grapes, oak-aged for approximately 15 months. Perfumes are intense and embracing, with vanilla and tobacco aromas. The palate is dry, velvety and of excellent structure. Good aging potential.

Carlozadra

Via Gandossi, 13
Grumello del Monte (Bg) 24064
Tel. (035) 832066-830244

Originally from the town of Tres in Trentino, Carlo Zadra moved to the province of Bergamo as a youngster fresh out of Conegliano's school of enology in 1961. He was eager to get involved in what was then an unquestionably depressed sector. He knew from his textbooks that four centuries ago the province of Bergamo had been famous for its vineyards, but which had since fallen from grace, to become the Cinderella of Lombard viticulture. He tried to fight against the flow, in the name of quality, but came across harsh reality. Finally in 1965 he got his own space, albeit with Bergamesque vineyards and varietals. But Zadra is still closely linked to his city of origin and to Trentino's Pinot and Chardonnay grapes which he carefully selects to produce excellent méthode champenoise sparkling wines (brut, extra dry and pas dosé) with a Carlozadra label. He also makes several thousand bottles of still wines from Pinot Noir which keep on improving each year.

Carlozadra Extra Dry Tradizione   ❦ (3)
From Chardonnay and Pinot Bianco grapes selected in Trentino, this sparkling wine is left for about 30 months on the lees. The result is yellow-colored wine with golden highlights, intense perfumes and a hint of bread crust. Dry and soft, with a good backbone,

Carlozadra Non Dosato   ❦ (3)
The Chardonnay and Pinot Nero grapes used for the production of this sparkling wine are selected by Carlo Zadra himself in Trentino. Straw-yellow in color, with a short frothy mousse, fine and long-lasting bubbles, and afruity bouquet of green apples. Dry, well-balanced.

Cavalleri

Via Provinciale, 74
Erbusco (Bs) 25030
Tel. (030) 7267350
Fax (030) 7760217

Established in 1967, Giovanni Cavalleri's winery was the first of Franciacorta's many wineries to be worthy of consideration. Most importantly it deserves credit for having spurred on radical changes in the vineyard and cellar in a zone which cannot otherwise boast a very glorious wine history. Traditionalist farmers were convinced that the only way to make good wine was to use old grapes and old barrels. A true wine-lover, Giovanni Cavalleri is assisted by his daughters who share his good taste. Together they make premium wines from all parts of the estate and have more recently created two crus, Seradina and Rampaneto. Results are obviously closely linked to the vintage quality, but the overall quality level is always high, where even mediocre vintages are quite respectable while good vintages, stupendous. These wines must be tasted to be believed.

Franciacorta Collezione 1986 DOC 🏵🏵 ③
Made from 100% Chardonnay grapes, with lots of very fine bubbles and perfumes of yeast pleasantly mixed with marked aromas of bread crust; well-balanced, lingering and nicely structured.

Franciacorta Bianco 🏵 ②
Rampaneto 1991 DOC
A straw-yellow in color, a Franciacorta made from 100% Chardonnay with floral perfumes tending to fruity (especially banana); dry and elegant on the palate but could do with further cellaring.

Tajardino 1989 🍇 ③
Made from Cabernet Franc, Cabernet Sauvignon and Merlot grapes, oak-aged for about a year. An ample bouquet which goes from the herbaceous to berry-fruits; full-bodied, supple and embracing.

Cornaleto

Via Cornaleto, 2
Adro (Bs) 25030
Tel. (030) 7450565
Fax (030) 7450552

Son and grandson of farmers and a farmer himself, Luigi Lancini created this winery in 1968 in Adro, on the hills of Franciacorta. His first vineyard was in Poligono in Cornaleto, which yields one of the zone's best red wines. Later he purchased four vineyards, each at different altitudes (reaching 500 m) to grow Cabernet Sauvignon and Merlot as well as Pinot Bianco and Chardonnay. Backed by wine technician Cesare Ferrari, one of the wizards in Franciacorta's winemaking, Lancini has gradually extended his production. In addition to his initial reds-only production, he has also added whites and has been successful with sparkling wines. Cornaleto's range of products and their quality gets better every year. Our hats go off for the outstanding results thus far achieved.

Franciacorta Extra Brut DOC 🏵 ③
A lightly bubbly sparkling wine with an evolved bouquet of quince, well-structured with a savoury, pleasantly bitter aftertaste, made from Chardonnay and Pinot Bianco grapes.

Franciacorta Bianco 🏵 ②
Saline 1990 DOC
Straw-yellow wine made from 70% Chardonnay and 30% Pinot Bianco grapes, it has an ample bouquet with clean aromas ranging from golden delicious apples to geranium blooms. Flavors are fresh, well-structured and lengthy.

Franciacorta Rosso 🍇 ②
Poligono 1990 DOC
Made from selected grapes from the Poligono vineyard (Cabernet Franc, Merlot, Nebbiolo and Barbera), it is one of Franciacorta's reds best suited to aging. Intense red in color, herbaceous bouquet with fruity and marasca cherry aromas; dry, warm and balanced.

Fay

Via Pila Caselli, 1
S. Giacomo di Teglio (So) 23030
Tel. (0342) 786071
Fax (0342) 786058

The Fay winery, founded in 1973, is a small but interesting winery situated a few kilometers from the characteristic town of Teglio. The carefully groomed, high quality and renowned estate-owned vineyards are located in the most northern zone of Valtellina, called Valgella. Wine-technician Sandro Fay skillfully manages the winery, confidently applying the most modern and rigorous vinification and aging methods. His latest wine is a unique Sassella made from grapes grown in a sunny, sloped vineyard near Sondrio. Over 8,000 cases are produced, primarily consisting of Valgella, Valgella Riserva and Ca' Morei, the latter being aged in barrique. All wines are made from Nebbiolo Chiavennasca grapes. The Sforzato is big and well-structured, made with the traditional raisining of grapes on wooden racks.

Valtellina Superiore   🍷 ②
Valgella Riserva Ca' Morei 1989 DOC
This winery's choice single-vineyard wine, obtained from a careful selection of the grapes in the vineyard, has a rich bouquet, with lots of aromas. Just the right amount of oak-aging gives it roundness and elegance on the palate.

Valtellina Sforzato 1988 DOC   🍷 ②
A prime, well-made example of its type, it has a full and long-lasting bouquet. Considerable body and pleasantly tannic flavor in the mouth.

Valtellina Superiore   🍷 ②
Sassella Selezione Il Glicine 1988 DOC
An interesting modern style of Sassella, it has well-blended perfumes and a fresh, firm palate.

Tenuta Mazzolino

Via Mazzolino, 26
Corvino S. Quirico (Pv) 27050
Tel. (0383) 876122
Fax (0383) 896480

Wine-technician Giancarlo Scaglione, a leading figure in Italian enology, found in the Mazzolino winery the ideal place to create his idea of a premium wine. This winery combined a number of practically unrepeatable circumstances. The property was owned by a wealthy financier Enrico Bragiotti, with considerable sums to invest. There was an intelligent and enterprising manager, Roberto Piaggi. There were 14 ha of impeccable vineyards located adjacent to the cellar, which were expressly cultivated to allow low yields and excellent wines, through clonal selection and the organization of the varietals. With all these factors to hand, year after year Mazzolino is reaching increasingly high quality standards, and not only with classic regional Oltrepò reds. The Tenuta is also engaged in more difficult international styles, such as 100% Pinot Nero and also classic whites. Since 1988 each year 5-6000 bottles of méthode champenoise sparkling wine are rested on their lees and will be will aged for at least 8-9 years. It's an ambitious gamble which, given the background, certainly will have some wonderful surprises in store.

Oltrepò Pavese   🍷 ①
Riesling Camarà 1991 DOC
Riesling Italico and a small amount of Riesling Renano team up to form this extremely perfumed white, fruity and refreshing, with surprising aristocratic elegance and rich in extracts.

Oltrepò Pavese   🍷 ①
Bonarda 1991 DOC
A 100% Bonarda wine that proves that this varietal is undervalued. A bouquet of wild berries prevails over the typical herbaceous varietal character. Ample, powerful and lengthy with good backbone and liveliness on the palate. A wine of great character.

Oltrepò Pavese   🍷 ①
Rosso Terrazze 1991 DOC
A typical Oltrepò blend (50% Barbera, 30% Bonarda and 20% Uva Rara), this Terrazze has very agreeable bouquet with hints of "panettone", the Italian Christmas cake, and green herbs. Lovely crisp acidity and slightly astringent; for easy drinking.

Noir 1988   🍷 🍷 ③
The winery's flagship wine, made from Pinot Nero grapes from an old, low-yielding vineyard. Barrique-aging gives the nose austere aromas of wood and tobacco, lengthy and velvety, full-bodied, soft, not very ample but inarguably appealing.

Nino Negri

Via Ghibellini, 3
Chiuro (So) 23030
Tel. (0342) 482521
Fax (0342) 482235

Housed in the ancient, 15th century Castello Quadrio in Chiuro, the 1897-founded Nino Negri winery now belongs to the important Gruppo Italiano Vini. Enologist Casimiro Maule is the key element behind the project and has skillfully helped promote and advocate Valtellina's wines abroad. The extremely large and modern cellars have separate and well-equipped facilities for the various phases of winemaking, from the fermentation, to oak or bottle aging and storage. Production is carefully geared towards market demands, covering the full range of local wine specialties, from the classic DOCs like Sassella, Inferno, Grumello and Valgela to the winery's peculiarities such as Fracia and the noble Riserva Valtellina Superiore Nino Negri. There are also the Nebbiolo-based 'Fantasy' wines with geographical indications like Chiavennasca Bianco, Ca' Brione, Vergiano and Grigioni. The famous Sfursat is truly unique and is made from gently-crushed select Nebbiolo bunches left to raisin on wooden racks.

Valtellina Superiore
Inferno Selezione Botti d'Oro 1989 DOC
As with Sassella, the production regulations call for at least two years' aging. Garnet-red in color with brick reflections, much lingering ripe fruit on the nose; bone-dry on the palate, with good structure and a slightly tannic finish.

Valtellina Superiore
Sassella Selezione Botti d'Oro 1989 DOC
Sassella is the essence of the Valtellina style of wine, and in this case it is also the result of scrupulous selection. Intense bouquet with distinct and lingering flavors, full and warm on the palate and long-lasting.

Valtellina 5 Stelle
Sfursat 1988 DOC
Of classic vinification, with deft use of barrique in aging. Well-balanced bouquet of oak and berries, it has a marvellous structure, with particularly warm, embracing flavors.

Valtellina Superiore ❦ ②
Nino Negri Riserva Oro 1986 DOC
One of the great Valtellina wines made with 100% Nebbiolo-Chiavennasca grape. The oak-aging is just right and exalts the wine's varietal characters. Fine, ample bouquet, well-balanced flavor, good tannin and great texture.

Conti Sertoli Salis

Piazza Salis, 3
Tirano (So) 23037
Tel. (0342) 704533
Fax (0342) 704566

History, tradition, modern outlook and a bright future are the terms which might best sum up the identity of the young but promising Conti Sertoli Salis winery. Housed in the 16th century cellars of the prestigious Palazzo Salis in Tirano, this winery relies on the precious managerial skills of Claudio Introini, a wine technician of undoubted expertise. Recently restored with particular respect for the original architectural style, the cellars are rationally divided into sections for vinification and wood-aging with yet another even more impressive area for the bottle aging. The winery leases nearly six ha of vineyards which supply 40% of the grapes for processing; the remainder is purchased from small local growers. Wines are produced from Nebbiolo Chiavennasca grapes, with careful and modern style crafting. Typical Valtellina grapes such as Rossola and Pignola are use to make the whites.

Il Saloncello 1989
An easy drinking wine yet with some ageability. There is lots of pleasant fruit, harmonious flavors and medium-tannin on the palate, with good aromatic length.

Valtellina Superiore ❦❦ ②
Corte della Meridiana 1989 DOC
Vinified using the ancient method of rinforzo, or "fortification", it is oak-aged and has an intense, complex bouquet, with licorice and light vanilla aromas. With good body and character, it has lots of potential.

Stefano Spezia

Via Matteotti, 9
Mariana Mantovana (Mn) 46010
Tel. (0376) 735012

In northern Italy, wines of the plains are not considered the most popular. Lambrusco particularly fits into this category; many connoisseurs consider it soda pop disguised as wine. So what to do with a few hectares of vineyard in Mariana Mantovana, smack in the middle of the flat Po valley between Lombardy and Emilia? Not able nor willing to betray tradition, all one could do was to re-establish, by creating a worthy version, the reputation and quality of a wine whose name had been tarnished by over-production by scores of producers. Real professionals like Lucio Spezia, who was later joined by Stefano, were the first to attempt this feat. Indeed they made a very good Lambrusco and then went on to experiment with the native Ancellotta varietal wine, which had always been used to add bouquet to Lambrusco-based wines. On its own it turned out to be extremely worthwhile product. Stefano Spezia's wines may be a bit rustic, and peasant-like, but his non-sparkling 1990 Ancellotta can surely capture some positive acclaim, even from serious wine-lovers.

Ancellotta 1990
1988 was the first vintage for this trial at making 100% Ancellotta still wine. And the 1990 proves this varietal's full potential. Beautiful ruby-red in color, it has a floral bouquet and rich fullness of palate, with outstanding texture.

Uberti

Via Fermi, 2
Erbusco (Bs) 25030
Tel. (030) 7267476
Fax (030) 7760455

The Uberti family has been running the family wine business in Franciacorta since 1793. Granted they had a much larger family then, it is still a family-cottage estate. It's hard to say what kind of wine was made then, although reason lead us to believe that it was extremely different. Obviously it is only modern wine-writing that can describe and ably illustrate the wine's color, bouquet, flavor, aftertaste, length and so on. The exceptionally well-exposed 13 ha of vineyards in the Comarì in the area called Salem are cultivated with a passion, and the cellar is equipped to bring out the full potential of prime raw material. In fact, we could say that the grapes carry the blessing of the Priori friars, who were original owners. Agostino Uberti and his wife Eleonora make not only DOC wines able to compete with the area's best, but also other products: various méthode champenoise sparkling wines and varietal Chardonnay and Cabernet Sauvignon wines, the latter fermented and aged in barriques.

Franciacorta Bianco
Maria Medici 1990 DOC
Deep straw-yellow in color, made from Chardonnay, it has a lingering floral and fruity bouquet. Medium-bodied, savoury and soft on the palate.

Franciacorta Spumante
Comarì del Salem 1986 DOC
A cuvée of different wines (Chardonnay and Pinot Bianco) of which the percentages vary year to year, this sparkling wine remains on the lees for nearly four years before the dégorgement. Straw-yellow in color, it has fine and long-lasting bubbles, a balanced bouquet with a light toasty aroma and medium length on the palate.

Rosso dei Frati Priori 1989
Made with a selection of estate-owned grapes from a vineyard planted with Cabernet Sauvignon, fermented in small barrels for at least 20 months before being bottle-aged. Intense ruby-red in color, it has an herbaceous bouquet with vanilla overtones. Dry and warm on the palate.

Marche

According to a recent survey, the Marche region has the record in Italy for the longevity of its inhabitants. This, together with the high per capita wine consumption, clearly indicates a high and healthy standard of living. Perhaps this is reason enough for a just and incontrovertible counterattack on the savage and indiscriminate campaigns against wine drinking.

The precise origins of viticulture in this region are not historically certain, but in the Piceno area fossils of Vitis Vinifera dating back to the Iron Age have been found. Piceno wines were popular among the ancient Romans, just as the ancient Greeks especially favored the wines produced in the hills close to Ancona, a city which they founded. Not by mere chance do the clay amphoras used to transport Marche wines to their Greek homeland resemble the Verdicchio bottle shape centuries later.

The region's climate is very well-suited to the cultivation of vines, with its sea breezes that climb inland through the humid valleys. Landlocked on three sides, smack in the center of Italy, Le Marche is a predominantly mountainous and hilly region with a surface area of about 10,000 square km facing the Adriatic Sea. Numerous short rivers and streams trickle from the Appenines towards the coast, cutting a series of valleys which run perpendicular to the seaside. Over the last 20 years the physical shape of the vineyards has changed remarkably; tree-held vines or lush "pergola" porches surrounding farmhouses or shading courtyards have mostly disappeared to make room for new, more efficient training methods (mainly vertical and double arched).

Currently the region produces approximately 3,000,000 hl of wine per year, with whites making up 70%. Verdicchio, among the whites, plays the leading role. DOC production is substantial, larger than the national average, with 12 classifications and a prevalence of Verdicchio, Trebbiano (in its various forms), Malvasia and Biancone among white grapes and Sangiovese and Montepulciano for the red. There are several other interesting native varietals such as Lacrima di Morro d'Alba and Vernaccia di Serrapetrona. The quality of Marche wine has risen steadily for at least a decade. Also, their affordability has certainly not harmed the curiousity for 'new generation' Verdicchio wines. More complex and unique in character, reds like Montepulciano-based Rosso Conero or Sangiovese-based Rosso Piceno Superiore can also be appealing.

Small producers such as Brunori, Bucci, Cocci Grifoni or Moroder, to mention a few, as well as the larger wineries, who experiment more with the local grapes, such as Garofoli, and last, but not least, the Cantine Sociali and cooperatives, such as Belisario or Colonnara, each make up dynamic points of reference for the production of premium wines in the region.

Cantina Sociale Belisario

Via Merloni, 12
Matelica (Mc) 64024
Tel. (0737) 85730-85122
Fax (0373) 85122

The Cantina Sociale di Matelica e Cerreto d'Esi is otherwise simply referred to as Belisario, which is also the brand name of one of its leading wines. Due to its foot-hill position it is one of the region's more interesting and particular growing areas. Their Verdicchio di Matelica DOC undoubtedly deserves more attention, particularly for its outstanding cellaring potential. The in-house experimentation laboratory, in fact, has already done wonders to improve the Verdicchio in recent years. Practically putting the cooperative on the map, the Belisario flagship wine is an elegant selection of Verdicchio di Matelica. The winery also produces other noteworthy products such as Cerro and particularly Cambrugiano, both created by the young and brilliant enologist Roberto Potentini. The 1988 Cambrugiano is still very good indeed, but try it for yourselves. The two Passiti should not be overlooked either. One is made from Verdicchio grapes. The other, from Vernaccia Cerretana, very nearly an endangered species, has been revived by Belisario.

Verdicchio di Matelica ❦ ①
Belisario 1991 DOC
It was this Verdicchio di Matelica that actually launched the cooperative into its resolute search for quality, and with impressive results. Elegant and already soft, it has a fine bouquet and pleasant flavor of almonds. It is one of the best of its type, even from this vintage.

Verdicchio di Matelica ❦ ❦ ②
Cambrugiano 1990 DOC
Bright straw-yellow in color, fragrant and penetrating bouquet with grassy, floral notes. Full-flavored and long-lasting with an almond finish. Released nearly two years after vintage, it promises to develop with time.

Brunori

Viale della Vittoria, 103
Jesi (An) 60035
Tel/Fax (0731) 207213

Young enologist Carlo Brunori, having recently joined his grandfather Mario and father Giorgio, is the third generation of this winemaking family to make Verdicchio dei Castelli di Jesi. The Brunori name is practically synonymous with the wine, being its most faithful adherents. Inevitably they played a leading role in the rebirth which this 'jug' wine, with its poor quality standards and image, underwent in the 1970s. In over 30 years of winemaking, the Brunoris have consistently upheld the principles which inspired their wine philosophy, paying great attention to each and every phase of production with a balanced use of technology, kept to an extreme minimum. They make very classic yet characteristic Verdicchio wines. This small winery dedicates itself to making above all two styles of Verdicchio, a standard version and the single-vineyard San Nicolò; fairly recently was added Lacrima di Morro d'Alba, a pleasant and easy-drinking red.

Verdicchio dei Castelli di Jesi ❦ ①
San Nicolò 1991 DOC
With a pleasant, intense and lingering nose, it is fresh and rather full flavored and well-balanced; quite obvious cellaring potential, typical of Brunori Verdicchios.

Lacrima di Morro d'Alba 1991 DOC ❦ ①
The Brunoris have always concentrated on Verdicchio wines, but they also make an interesting varietal red which has recently acquired DOC status. A fresh, easy summer-sipper, with a fragrance of violets.

Fratelli Bucci

Loc. Pongelli
Ostra Vetere (An) 60010
Tel/Fax (071) 964179 - (02) 6554470

Milanese manager Ampelio Bucci took part in the 1980s rebirth of Verdicchio dei Castelli di Jesi which is still continues. Moved by a deep love for the Marche hills, he sought out this area to produce premium wines and hired one of Italy's best winemakers, Giorgio Grai. Within a few years, his wines attracted the attention of Robert Parker, the famous American wine-writer, who described his Verdicchio dei Castelli di Jesi reserve as being extremely elegant, long-lived and of all Italian wines most reminded him of white Burgundies. The Bucci winery also presses an excellent extra virgin olive oil. Although Bucci concentrates on its Verdicchio dei Castelli di Jesi, it also makes an interesting blended red from its vineyard in Pongelli.

Verdicchio dei Castelli di Jesi Villa Bucci 1988 DOC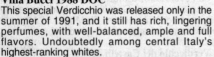
This special Verdicchio was released only in the summer of 1991, and it still has rich, lingering perfumes, with well-balanced, ample and full flavors. Undoubtedly among central Italy's highest-ranking whites.

Pongelli 1987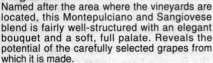
Named after the area where the vineyards are located, this Montepulciano and Sangiovese blend is fairly well-structured with an elegant bouquet and a soft, full palate. Reveals the potential of the carefully selected grapes from which it is made.

Castiglioni-Bisci

Via Fogliano, 120
Matelica (Mc) 62024
Tel. (0373) 86367

It is common knowledge that in domestic and international blind tasting competitions, Castelli di Jesi and Matelica Verdicchio wines are among the wines most easily distinguished. They have an unmistakeable style, unique color (with its greenish highlights), bouquet and flavor. Fortunately, the Bisci brothers, owners of the winery, do little to alter this character, especially nowadays when new styles and imitations are flooding a confused market. The vineyards are located in Fogliano, one of the best DOC areas of the district of Matelica. Available in both the standard version and the Villa Fogliano selection, the wines are elegant and unusually robust for whites, with potential to age and improve for two or three years in the better vintages. Although Matelica is now noted for its whites, until the 1950s it was primarily red wine country. The Bisci brothers have not forgotten and regularly experiment with blends of Cabernet Sauvignon and Barbera with Sangiovese and Montepulciano. The results have been impressive, particularly with the Rosso Fogliano.

Verdicchio di Matelica 1990 DOC
The Biscis have always been among the best makers of this Marche DOC, similar to, yet different from, the Jesi version. Very typical in character, with its young, green leaf bouquet, among other floral notes. Savoury, supple flavor with a slightly bitter finish.

Villa Castiglioni 1990
A new product from the Bisci brothers, from Cabernet Sauvignon and Sangiovese grapes whose rating is above all a sign of our belief in its potential than in the merits of this particular vintage. It has a good backbone but is slightly lacking in balance and finesse.

Cocci Grifoni

Fraz. S. Savino, contrada Messieri, 11
Ripatransone (Ap) 63030
Tel. (0735) 90143
Fax (0735) 90123

Guido Cocci Grifoni's family-run winery was born in the late 1960s when the Piceno district's two main wines, Rosso Piceno Superiore and Falerio dei Colli Ascolani, were granted DOC status. More than anyone else, Guido deserves credit for having believed in and promoted both the Falerio and Rosso Piceno Superiore wines. He has put out some convincing and indeed at times outstanding interpretations of these wines. Interpretation is particularly apt in the case of Falerio where there are many varietals that can be used alongside Trebbiano, making for a wide range of styles. The vineyards are located on a band of medium-high hills bordered to the south and east by the Tronto river and the Adriatic sea. This mountain-like atmosphere is also marked by particular soils and microclimates. Only the red from this zone, from Sangiovese and Montepulciano grapes, can call itself Superiore. For the last few years, Guido has been helped, in addition to his wife, by his young daughters, Paola and Marilena.

Falerio dei Colli Ascolani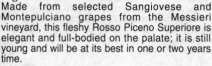
Vigneti San Basso 1991 DOC
A blend of Trebbiano, with Verdicchio and the native Passerina grapes. This selected wine from Cocci Grifoni, for some time the best Falerio DOC, is fresh and delicate; should be drunk within the year.

Podere Colle Vecchio 1991
Made from 100% Pecorino grapes, this admirable wine is the only example of this rediscovered native varietal. A fresh and fruity wine with personality and fragrance, it encapsulates what the territory can offer.

Rosso Piceno Superiore
Vigna Messieri 1990 DOC
Made from selected Sangiovese and Montepulciano grapes from the Messieri vineyard, this fleshy Rosso Piceno Superiore is elegant and full-bodied on the palate; it is still young and will be at its best in one or two years time.

Cooperativa Colonnara

Via Mandriole, 6
Cupramontana (An) 60034
Tel. (0731) 780273
Fax (0731) 789610

Founded in 1959 this cooperative is located in the heart of the Verdicchio dei Castelli di Jesi DOC production zone. Many will be surprised to hear that it has been producing sparkling wines from Verdicchio grapes as early as the mid 19th century. Colonnara's winemaker and devoted maker of sparkling wines, Carlo Pigini Campanari, has traced the origins of this tradition. Apparently, for many years France and the Marche traded in sparkling wines, but this practice came to a dramatic end with the institution of appellation laws. Although primarily renowned for its méthode champenoise and charmat sparkling wines, Colonnara is not all bubbles. More recently, the cooperative's still Verdicchio Riserva, Cuprese, has been ranked among the best, with its superb aging potential and elegance. The cooperative has nearly 200 member-growers, the majority of whom are small local farmers with generations of viticulture in their blood. Some of their vineyards are very ancient. In addition to Verdicchio, there is an interesting oak-aged red called Tornamagno that is made from skillfully blended Sangiovese.

Colonnara Metodo Classico
Straw-yellow in color with greenish highlights, typical of the Verdicchio varietal, it has balance and finesse and confirms the suitability of this varietal for the making of sparkling wines.

Verdicchio dei Castelli di Jesi
Cuprese 1991 DOC
A specially selected Verdicchio that has in recent years shown itself capable of development when aged. When tasted the 1991 was outstandingly youthful, fresh and full on the palate.

Tornamagno 1988
A cuvée of two different Sangiovese clones, mainly oak-aged Sangiovese Piccolo Montanino. Its aromas and flavors bring to mind cherry and licorice. It shows clever use of the common Sangiovese varietal.

Fattoria Coroncino

Contrada Coroncino, 7
Staffolo (An) 60039
Tel. (0731) 779494

The winery and one of its two vineyards are located in the Coroncino district. The other vineyard is in Cupramontana, heart of the Verdicchio dei Castelli di Jesi Classico production zone. A typical family-run winery, both his wife and his father help Lucio Canestrari in the vineyard and cellar. The production is very limited and concentrated on the two styles Verdicchio, a standard version and the single-vineyard Vigna Gaia. The latter especially has enabled Lucio to make a name for himself among the rising Verdicchio producers. If Verdicchio's distinct personality is linked to its place of origin and can be disappointing when made elsewhere; then it is also madness to rob it of its particular character by trying to copy other styles of wine, however good they are in themseves. The result will lack spirit and soul. With this simple philosophy, Canestrari moved to the Marches and started producing powerful wines rich in bouquet and with good cellaring potential. Fattoria Coroncino is now a firmly established quality winemaker. The only problem is meeting the demand.

Le Lame 1991   ♀ ①
A new style of white for Fattoria Coroncino, made from Trebbiano and Verdicchio grapes, admirably true to type and easy drinking. An interesting expression of the two most common white varietals of the Marches.

Verdicchio dei Castelli di Jesi   ♀ ①
Vigna Gaia 1991 DOC
A Verdicchio full of character and backbone, as can be expected from the Coroncino winery. Possibly more upfront than the 1990 vintage. A fresh and ample bouquet, with a balanced rich palate and an almond finish.

Gioacchino Garofoli

Via Arno, 9
Loreto (An) 60025
Tel. (071) 7820163
Fax (071) 7821437

This winery hardly looks 90 years-old and neither is it showing signs of wear and tear. On the contrary it has acquired a rather youthful taste for research and novelty. The Garofoli winery, whose history has reflected that of the evolution of wine in the Marche, today plays a leading role in the region's wine industry. The Garofoli brothers are among the best producers of Verdicchio dei Castelli di Jesi and Rosso Conero, made in various styles, and are probably most appreciated outside the region, if not the country. The most noteworthy are Serra Morese, a long-lived and elegant spicy white which shows déft use of oak, and Agontano, by far one of the region's best reds. They also produce pleasant, more easy and early drinking wines, all of good quality. Winemaker Carlo Garofoli looks after the sparkling wine sector, with results that reveal Verdicchio's suitability for this type of vinification. Finally, there is Brule, a golden Passito of marked personality which is also made from Verdicchio grapes.

Verdicchio dei Castelli di Jesi   ♀ ①
Macrina 1990 DOC
Slightly less structured than the Serra Fiorese, yet fresher and with stronger varietal character. It is ready now but, confirming Verdicchio's ageability, will keep for at least another year.

Verdicchio dei Castelli di Jesi   ♀ ♀ ②
Serra Fiorese 1990 DOC
Among the various types of Verdicchio wines produced by Garofoli, Serra Fiorese is undoubtedly the most elegant and complex. Oak-aged, it has a good balance of fruit and wood, a fine, lingering bouquet and a soft, full flavor and solid backbone.

Rosso Conero   ♥ ♥ ②
Agontano 1988 DOC
Exclusively 100% Montepulciano grapes, aged in small oak casks. With marasca cherry and liquorice on nose and on palate, it is soft and somewhat reminiscent of tar. Has yet to reach its peak.

Rosso Conero   ♥ ①
Vigna Piancarda 1990 DOC
Its bouquet is admirably intense and lingering, with lots of fruit. It has been aged one year in barrel (30% French oak and the rest Slovenian). At present it seems rather closed and tight, which is characteristic of this type of wine.

Fattoria La Monacesca

Via D'Annunzio, 1
Civitanova Marche (Mc) 62012
Tel. (0733) 812602
Fax (0733) 810593

The name La Monacesca is a tribute to the Benedictine monks who grew many different crops in this fertile area, above all wine. Particularly fond of the rolling countryside, Casimiro Cifola was in the shoe business until 1966, when his pastime of wine-making gradually became his main occupation. In the meantime, his son Aldo finished his studies in agriculture and began working full-time at the winery. The soil and particular microclimate of these foothills clearly distinguish Verdicchio di Matelica from its sibling Castelli di Jesi. Fully aware of their wine's keeping potential, the Cifolas prefer to bottle age at length, a usage starkly in contrast to many wineries' rush to release. La Monacesca's Verdicchio wines (standard and single-vineyard versions and, in better vintages, the Riserva Mirus) are always elegant and balanced, and have become classics among the output of Marche wine.

Verdicchio di Matelica Mirus 1990 DOC
Produced for the first time in 1988 and now again in 1990, it is made from choice late-harvested grapes of Verdicchio di Matelica. Only just recently released, its very fresh, lively aromas are already developing and showing elegant notes.

Verdicchio di Matelica La Monacesca 1990 DOC
This is La Monacesca's classic style of the single-vineyard Verdicchio, released a year after harvest. With a refined yet delicate medium intense bouquet, it has well-balanced flavors and a slightly almond finish.

Alessandro Moroder

Loc. Montacuto, 112
Montacuto (An) 60029
Tel/Fax (071) 898232

Although the winery has been in the Moroder family for over a century, Alessandro and Serenella have only taken it to new avantgarde heights in the last ten years. Their Rosso Conero (in the standard version with the Dorico riserva in good vintages), as well as the Rosa di Montacuto, imposed itself on the national scene and substantially helped to alleviate the identity crisis from which this DOC had been suffering for some time. This despite the fact that Rosso Conero had been one of the very first Italian wines to obtain DOC status. Their recipe for success included meticulous selection in the vineyard, modern wine-making equipment, a particularly modern barrel-room (Slovenian oak for the larger barrels, French oak for the smaller ones) and, most importantly, an overwhelming passion. The winery is located in Montacuto near Monte Conero, which is a beautiful natural park facing the Adriatic; yet another reason to get acquainted with Alessandro and Serenella's wines and their warm hospitality.

Candiano 1991
Made from Trebbiano, Malvasia and 20% Moscato grapes, this is the debut of this wine and is already proving admirable in its pleasant drinkability. Its Moscato nose is immediately appealing and captivating, followed by a savoury, bone-dry flavor that may be ephemeral but is extremely clean and polished.

Rosa di Montacuto 1991
Moroder creates this rosé from Montepulciano grapes and a small amount of Sangiovese. Its fruity notes and dry balanced flavor are its best qualities. It's a good, faithful interpretation of a tradiitonal Marche wine.

Rosso Conero Dorico 1990 DOC
A top-ranking Marche wine from selected Montepulciano grapes, made only in better vintages. Luminous color, it has an intense and inviting nose with luscious aromas of marasca cherries, plums and liquorice, with a velvety fullness on the palate.

Umani Ronchi

Osimo Scalo 60028
Tel. (071) 7108019
Fax (071) 7108859

Founded in 1955 by Gino Umani Ronchi, the winery is now actually owned by the Bianchi Bernetti family but has kept the original owner's name. It is one of the region's more substantial wineries, in terms of production quantity. The winery has always been well-known on the export markets especially since Umani Ronchi was a shareholder of the Swiss Wine-Food group in the 1970s. It has consistently improved its quality, particularly in the ample and diverse range of styles such as the Verdicchio dei Castelli di Jesi and Rosso Conero. The Verdicchio is made exclusively in the Castelbellino cellar, while the Rosso Conero comes from Osimo Scalo, and where each is respectively bottled and stored prior to release. The winery's most prestigious products include the single-vineyard San Lorenzo and Cùmaro wines of the Rosso Conero DOC, and the white Le Busche (oak-aged in small casks of Allier and Tronçais). The more traditional single-vineyard Casal di Serra Verdicchio is not to be overlooked either.

Verdicchio dei Castelli di Jesi ☙ ①
Casal di Serra 1991 DOC
A single-vineyard cru from Verdicchio grapes grown in the classic Colli di Jesi zone, it shows the wine's style and elegance, with a good intensity of perfumes, balanced flavor, medium-body and a pleasantly bitter finish.

Le Busche 1990 ☙ ②
Rather deep straw-yellow in color, it has perfumes which maintain the primary varietal character along with graceful vanilla nuances from the oak-aging. Medium bodied, well-balanced and developed, and very drinkable now.

Rosso Conero Cùmaro 1989 DOC ☙ ②
Though not a particularly brilliant vintage for Rosso Conero and not up to the standard set in better years by itself and the San Lorenzo single-vineyard wine, Umani Ronchi's barrique-aged Cùmaro is to be appreciated for its finesse and drinkability.

Fratelli Zaccagnini

Via Salmagina, 9
Staffolo (An) 60039
Tel. (0731) 779892
Fax (0731) 779219

The name of the commune of Staffolo is taken from the words Staphylos and Oenos which are the names the Greek god of wine, Dionysus, gave to the grape bunch and wine. This, indeed, reveals the special relationship this commune has always shared with wine. There was also a legend in which Staphylos, son of Arianna and Theseus, settled here to cultivate the vine and make wine. Legends and tales aside, this link is reconfirmed by the quality of the Staffolo wines in which Zaccagnini play a lead part. Established fairly recently, the winery makes a more than decent Verdicchio dei Castelli di Jesi (the Salmagina single-vineyard is well-known even outside the region). Other wines include sparkling wines, and red wines such as Rosso Conero, made from indigenous varietals, and wines from more recent arrivals varietals, such as Cabernet Sauvignon and Pinot Nero. Factors such as the altitude of the vineyards (440 m), the predominantly limestone soil and the use of carefully selected clones combine to give the wines an excellent structure and character, especially the Verdicchios, which are lively and elegant.

Salmagina ☙ ②
Verdicchio dei Castelli di Jesi 1991 DOC
A cru Verdicchio named after its vineyard. This 1991 vintage is a rather pale straw-yellow in color, with a medium-intense bouquet and refined flavors; less ample and generous than the previous two vintages.

Cesolano 1990 ☙ ③
A new arrival in the Zaccagnini range, it is a wine made from Verdicchio grapes left to over-ripen on the vine, aged in small oak casks and then in bottle. The impressive results prove the extreme versatility of the grape, yielding wines which cannot be repeated elsewhere.

Vigna Vescovi 1990 ☙ ②
The debut of this red blend of Montepulciano, Cabernet Sauvignon and Pinot Nero grapes, the last only recently added to the Zaccagnini estate. Aged in small barrels, very evident at time of tasting, but more bottle-aging should provide a better balance, given its solid structure and complexity.

Rosso Conero 1988 DOC ☙ ①
In anticipation of the Zaccagnini's experimental Cabernet Sauvignon-based wines, reds like this Rosso Conero DOC should certainly not be overlooked. Fruity, marasca-cherry aromas on the nose, it has a soft, full-bodied palate, improving with cellaring.

Piemonte, Valle d'Aosta

With a worldwide reputation founded on its great red wines, Piemonte's history and prestige make it one of Italy's leading wine-growing regions. It is no mere coincidence that Barbaresco and Barolo were among the very first Italian wines to be awarded the DOCG classification. Piemonte's best-known area for winemaking is, in fact, the Langhe district of the Alba region, home of Barbaresco and Barolo. With over 65,000 ha under vine and an annual production of approximately 3,00,000 hl, over 1,200,000 hl of which is DOC wine, the whole of Piemonte can justly be considered a quality wine producing region. Many factors contribute to this situation including the soil types and hillside locations of the vineyards, the sheltering arc of the Alps and even the sea breezes to the south-east. All of these 'accidents of nature' combine to make Piemonte an ideal area for vine cultivation.

It is obvious at first glance that wine-growing in Piemonte is characterized by a wide variety of sub-regions, each unique in its own way. One has only to note the number of DOC wines (43 in all) and the impressive range of styles prouced. It boasts fresh, fruity whites and medium-bodied reds right through to the noble, structured wines. The Langhe, for example, offers an ideal terrain for the Nebbiolo, Dolcetto, Barbera and Freisa varieties. These same grapes also thrive in the adjacent area called Roero, which is on the opposite side of the Tanaro river. The superb white Arneis variety in recent years has contributed substantially to this particular area's success, as well.

There are, however, many other areas which deserve mention. Starting in the north-west, bordering with Valle d'Aosta, we find Carema and the Canavese area. Here, well-established Nebbiolo vineyards produce full-bodied Carema wines with excellent aging potential; Erbaluce is one of Piemonte's increasingly harder to find, indigenous white varieties. Moving eastwards to the hills of Vercelli and Novara, we find Nebbiolo again, here as the backbone of the DOC Lessona, Bramaterra, Gattinara, Boca, Ghemme, Sizzano and Fara wines. Further south, Monferrato was for many years an abundant producer of Barbera and Grignolino table wines but is today making huge progress towards better quality standards. The Monferrato area produces aromatic dessert wines from Moscato grapes in the two styles of Asti Spumante and Moscato d'Asti. The hills of the Chieri district near Turin with their Freisa and Malvasia varieties and the Tortona area, producing Barbera and Cortese, lie respectively to the west and east of Monferrato. Within sight of Liguria's branch of the Apennine mountains towards Piemonte, we find the Gavi area with its Cortese vineyards as well as Dolcetto in the thinner soils of Acqui and Ovada.

Piemontese viticulture has also included a number of minor grape types which have enriched the diversity of the region's wines. More recently, these lesser varieties have become more popular. This is partly in response to the increasing demand for white wines, Arneis being the most striking example of the trend. We should not forget Favorita and the now-rare Timorasso either. Another reason for the renewed interest in these varieties is certainly the increased awareness of the importance of "cru." Bonarda, Pelaverga, Brachetto and Ruché, for instance, have undergone something of a renaissance. They now make some truly unique and highly attractive wines. An overview of Piemontese production shows that reds still account for 70%

of the total but the proportion of white wines seems likely to increase.

Since the 1970s, vine-growing in Piemonte has substantially improved in terms of quality. Once again, the Langhe area has taken the initiative, as the rest followed suit. A large number of small producers have appeared, 'preaching the gospel' of careful vineyard cultivation as a fundamental base to produce premium-quality wines. Cellars have been modernized, and esperience acquired abroad in visiting the world's best producers abroad has been meticulously assimilated. New techniques and enology studies are being promoted and advocated throughout. A run of exceptional vintages, with 1988, 1989 and 1990 being the latest in a long line, has done the rest, providing a well-deserved reward for the growers' labors. Today, historic wines such as Barolo, Barbaresco and Barbera (the three B's) are being reinterpreted and presented in a more contemporary style. Without stripping them of their typicity, as they value the single-vineyard production, they are wines for a more mature, knowledgeable palate and an increasingly international market. Thus, it is in this particular context that we must view the onset of international varieties like Cabernet Sauvignon, Pinot Nero, Chardonnay and Sauvignon Bianco on these sub-Alpine slopes. A handful of forward-looking growers had already been experimenting with them, but today they account for a considerable proportion of the region's wine. The results obtained fully demonstrate the potential of the terrain and the growers' skill. Viticultural regulations cannot continue to ignore them for long.

Wine-growing in Valle d'Aosta, north-west of Piemonte, has always been an arduous enterprise. The varieties that are grown have a strong French influence, due to its proximity across the Alps. The single DOC Valle d'Aosta, with its 19 sub-types, includes varieties such as Gamay, Pinot Nero and Petit Rouge among the wide range of grape types permitted. Müller-Thurgau, Dolcetto, Nebbiolo, Pinot Grigio and Freisa are some of the more important varieties, but we also find indigenous Muscat de Chambave and Malvoisie de Nus. Estates are generally small as growers scale terraced vineyards on the bare, rocky mountainside. One or two cooperative cellars are showing promise, as well. Valle d'Aosta produces a total of only 3,000 hl a year from a mere 300 hectares of vineyards.

Abbazia dell'Annunziata

Fraz. Annunziata, 7
La Morra (Cn) 12064
Tel. (0173) 50185
Fax (0173) 509373

Renato Ratti is one of those enterprising individuals who has turned the old approach to wine-making around and enabled the wines of the Langhe to achieve the solid reputation they currently enjoy. The new philosophy looks beyond the old-fashioned chewy, "mangia e bevi" style Barolo in search of more elegant wines with a more complex bouquet, capable of doing full justice to the varieties used in production. Thus, was born Barolo Marcenasco and a similar approach was taken with other Annunziata wines, all of which have a fresh new identity. After Renato Ratti's death, his son Pietro has continued the search for ever-higher standards of quality with the help of Massimo Martinelli, who has personally overseen production for many years. The Annunziata Barolo consistently displays that depth of aromas which is typical of La Morra wines. The flavors of the fruit blend in well with the wood, producing nuances of great finesse. The palate, while not outstandingly powerful, is lingering and well-balanced with an elegance that has the potential to impress even further with a little bottle-age. The characteristic Dolcettos are also well worth mentioning as are some experimental cuvées of particularly intense Cabernet and Merlot aged in barriques.

Cabernet Sauvignon I Cedri 1990 🍷 ③
From a vineyard in Costigliole d'Asti on the Villa Pattono estate, managed by Ratti. Typical varietal herbaceous notes which dominate the bouquet. Full and well-rounded on the palate, the wine is braced by good acidity and a finish with just the right tannin.

Nebbiolo d'Alba Occhetti 1990 DOC 🍷 ①
Obtained by the Ratti cellar from grapes from one of the most famous crus in the Roero sub-zone, this is a highly characteristic Nebbiolo. The aromas are unobtrusive and the palate is frank and full with an attractive tannic note.

Barolo 🍷🍷 ③
Conca Marcenasco 1988 DOCG
This La Morra Barolo from Conca dell'Annunziata has a little less structure than the preceding wine. The nose offers notes of ripe cherry while the body on the palate is already soft and well-balanced. Discreet tannins.

Barolo 🍷🍷 ③
Rocche Marcenasco 1988 DOCG
The nose with its hints of liquorice and tobacco has yet to develop fully. Good depth on the palate. The tannins are still well to the fore, but the overall texture of this 1988 Rocche di Marcenasco is very acceptably soft.

Lorenzo Accomasso

Fraz. Annunziata, Borgata Pozzo
La Morra (Cn) 12064
Tel. (0173) 50843

Lorenzo Accomasso has been making wine at Borgata Pozzo in La Morra since 1958 and takes lessons on modern methods from no one. He is well-informed on all the latest trends and will listen carefully to opinions and advice, but this eccentric individualist continues to produce his Barolo using the most time-honored and traditional methods with the help of his sister Elena, who looks after the sales and accounting sides of the business. On reflection, though, Accomasso's approach with its emphasis on the cru and the importance of climatic factors and methods of cultivation is as up-to-date a philosophy as one could wish to find. He was limiting yields at a time when everybody thought he was foolish to be doing so. 10 or 20 years ago, he was a firm believer in adapting bottling and marketing schedules to the characteristics of the vintage. As a result, Accomasso's wines are full of character and powerful without being excessively heavy. They are wines which beautifully express the personality of their producer and the excellence of their cru.

Dolcetto d'Alba 1990 DOC 🍷 ①
A Dolcetto with impressive structure. The aromas are elegant, with distinct spicy notes. Intense garnet red color and a palate with wonderful texture. The considerable alcohol is well-blended into the extract and tannins. The piquant finish has good length.

Barbera delle Langhe 🍷 ①
Vigna Pozzo 1989
From Barbera grapes grown in Annunziata (La Morra) in a long-established estate-vineyard, this wine has a nose where the wood of the large cask aging is prominent at first, with fruit emerging through the oak. Powerful, warm and full-bodied while the finish is piquant and lingering.

Barolo Rocche 1985 DOCG 🍷🍷 ②
A Barolo which underlines the style of the Accomasso cellar: wines with excellent texture, made for cellaring, which need to breathe before they give their best. This Barolo is intense in appearance with developed, evocative aromas. The palate is full-bodied, warm and complex. Very satisfying.

Matteo e Claudio Alario

Via Santa Croce, 23
Diano d'Alba (Cn) 12055
Tel. (0173) 231808

When the young Claudio Alario took charge of the family cellar at Diano d'Alba, his thoughts turned first to vineyard cultivation. Unlike the majority of young growers in the Langhe, Claudio has not tried to set himself apart from the older generation by filling his cellar with stainless steel and computer technology. He knows that the first step along the road to a great wine is through the vineyard. His father Matteo fully agrees and still plays an active part in the cellar. They now reduce the chemicals used, prune short and select the grapes at harvest-time. Only after completing these initial stages will he be able to convert the property from being a mixed-produce farm business into a wine producer. In 1988, the cellar produced a mere 3,000 bottles, but by the time of writing, annual production has risen to 20,000 bottles. Naturally, the lion's share is Dolcetto from the small but prestigious Diano d'Alba DOC. The two crus, Montagrillo and Costafiore, come from a total of 4 ha of vineyards. Now, as is inevitable for any cellar in the sub-zone wishing to launch itself onto the international market, the Alarios are also making Barbera and Nebbiolo aged in barriques. This is definitely a cellar to keep an eye on.

Dolcetto di Diano d'Alba
Montagrillo 1991 DOC
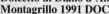
At last a Dolcetto di Diana that does not overwhelm the nose with the powerful herbaceous aromas so often found others. Elegant aromas of cherries and red berries. Remarkable full, ripe but refreshingly acidic fruit. Full-bodied with a liquorice finish and alcohol beautifully balanced by the extracts.

Barbera d'Alba Valletta 1990 DOC
A Barbera whose cru gives it some of the features of a Dolcetto di Diano. Bright with fruity aromas and potent extracts. Barrique aging contributes to the violet-tinged ruby color while the aromas are gentle and alluring, with toasty vanilla oak and mulberry. Fine body and powerful acidity well-balanced by the extract.

Giovanni Almondo

Via S. Rocco, 14
Montà d'Alba (Cn) 12051
Tel. (0173) 9575256

Giovanni Almondo's long-established property in the Roero sub-zone received an invigorating shake-up when Giovanni's son Domenico took the cellar firmly in hand a few years ago and began to make and bottle wine himself from the grapes grown on the four hectares or so the Almondos have under vines. Arneis, the recently successful local white grape, is naturally the main variety grown with smaller amounts of Nebbiolo, Bonarda, Barbera and Freisa. Brachetto, another variety which is also more popular these days, has also been planted. For Arneis, Domenico has chosen to vinify the grapes from the family's various crus separately. The result is Burigot and Bricco delle Ciliegie, year after year among the finest wines of their type. Moving on to reds, we find Roero, as Nebbiolo is called locally in both a standard version and the Burigot selection as well as Valbianchera, a blend of red grapes aged in barriques and finally Freisa.

Roero Arneis
Bricco delle Ciliegie 1991 DOC
An Arneis with elegant, stylish aromas and well-defined notes of fruit. The palate is piquant and dense and the slightly bitter finish is clean and frank.

Roero 1990 DOC
Made from Nebbiolo grapes with a small proportion of Arneis, this wine has good texture, in contrast to many wines of its type. Bright ruby red in color with attractively fruity aromas. Full-bodied and satisfying on the palate.

Elio Altare

Fraz. Annunziata
La Morra (Cn) 12064
Tel/Fax (0173) 50835

Altare's wines have become the standard all young winemakers in the Langhe measure themselves against. As you go around the Altare cellar, you are likely to come across one or two of them sharing their experiences and picking up hints on vineyard techniques. Altare has been successful thanks to painstaking attention to the vineyard in recent years. Careful selection of the grapes is necessary to achieve the texture, intensity and length which are the hallmarks of Altare's wines. Altare Barolos, Dolcettos and Barberas are all attractively mouthfilling and give immense drinking pleasure. Elio knows how to get the best out of his fruit without hi-tech excesses, carefully calculating the potential of each individual vintage. The 1986 Barolo was elegant, with moderate body. Now it is now a beautifully rounded wine free of the aggressive tannins that could easily have overwhelmed such a stylish vintage. Likewise the Vigna Larigi 1988 Barbera blends the unmistakable Langhe style with the international touch added by aging in barriques.

Dolcetto d'Alba La Pria 1991 DOC 🍇 ①
Intense red, shading into purple. A Dolcetto with a full, juicy aroma containing fresh notes of fruit and subtle grassy overtones. Full-bodied and well-balanced on the palate with forthright, young tannins that should mellow out in time.

Vigna Larigi 1989 🍇🍇 ③
A Barbera that transcends its Denominazione to represent the very ideal of what a Barbera should be. Incredible color and concentration, made from two separate grape selections within a week. Unusually rounded on the nose for a Barbera, where subtle vanilla blends with the fragrance of ripe cherries. Impressive, almost meaty, depth and alcohol well balanced by the rich extract.

Barolo Arborina 1988 DOCG 🍇🍇 ③
Attractively intense in the glass with stylish elegant aromas in a complex, fresh bouquet. Mouthfilling, lingering palate. The pleasantly bitter finish is slightly astringent, thanks to the abundance of tannins.

Vigna Arborina 1989 🍇🍇🍇 ③
To describe an Altare wine properly, first you have to establish precisely which experiments were involved in its production. It is obvious at the first swirl in the glass that this is a great wine, but there are many other things to take into account. First of all, there is the territory. Until recently, the Arborina or Arburine cru, in the heart of La Morra, was not considered a major Barolo zone, but its reputation is growing fast. It makes fruitier, less tannic wines than its neighbors, ideal for aging in barriques. Altare makes three separate selections at harvest time over the course of eight days. The first lends acidity, the second aromas and the third extracts. The quality of the harvest is enhanced by low yields (400 kg/ha), 40 year-old vines and merciless thinning out. Fermentation is exclusively in temperature-controlled stainless-steel vats. After fermentation, part of the wine goes into barriques, where it ages for as long as the wine Elio seems fit. This monovarietal Nebbiolo is a deep, violet-tinged ruby color. The nose is rich and intense, with elegant toasty wood and coffee mingling with attractive blackberries and violets. Rich with a slightly alcoholic entry which moves on to a velvet softness. Lively but pleasant tannins and a finish of liquorice and spices.

Antichi Vigneti di Cantalupo

Via Michelangelo Buonarroti, 5
Ghemme (No) 28074
Tel. (0163) 840041
Fax (0163) 841595

Antichi Vigneti di Cantalupo belongs to the Arlunno brothers, builders with a passion for wine. The estate has always made a fine Ghemme and continues to contribute to the reputation of the Denominazione. Since the late 1970s when they built an attractive and efficient cellar, the Arlunnos have been enthusiastically and skillfully modernizing and developing the estate's vineyards. Success soon followed and today the Arlunnos are the leading winemakers in the Ghemme Denominazione. Ghemme is made from Nebbiolo grapes and sold under the name Collis Breclemae or Collis Carellae, according to the hill slopes where the grapes are grown but the estate also grows Vespolina, a very rare local variety. The recent crisis experienced by the market for full-bodied reds has led to the planting of Greco, Arneis and Chardonnay. A new range of wines has been created in response to this development in the market, with Nebbiolo-based Primigenia and Novaria and Villa Horta from monovarietal Vespolina well worth investigating. These are attractive, excellent-value wines with livelier aromas and more modest structure than the Ghemme. The Arlunnos have also recently begun experimenting with Nebbiolo in barriques.

Ghemme Collis Breclemae　　🍷 ②
1986 DOC
A Ghemme to lay down from the sunniest vineyard on the estate. Still fresh on the nose, and rich in extract, with piquant yet unobtrusive tannins. The pleasant, slightly bitter finish is typical of Nebbiolo.

Ghemme Collis Carellae　　🍷🍷 ②
1985 DOC
This Collis Carellae cru is a classic Ghemme wine. A full-bodied monovarietal Nebbiolo which confirms the cellar's premium quality standards. Structure only moderate but an extremely pleasant and very drinkable wine.

Azelia

Via Alba Barolo, 27
Castiglione Falletto (Cn) 12060
Tel/Fax (0173) 62859

Owned by the Scavino family, Azelia is a typical family-run Langhe estate. Luigi Scavino manages the property with the help of his father Lorenzo and his wife Lorella. Most of the 5 ha of vineyards lie around the farmhouse in the Garbelletto area, where they account for almost all of one of the most important Barolo crus, Fiasco. The remaining vineyards are in the commune of Montelupo Albese. The estate is planted in the classic Langhe varieties with Nebbiolo predominant and Barbera and Dolcetto also present. The winemaking style reflects the local tradition of small-cellar craftsmanship, with great pains taken in the vineyard and scrupulous cleanliness in the cellar, where respect for tradition has not prevented the introduction of modern technology. There are two Dolcetto d'Alba wines: Azelia, from Castiglione grapes, and Oriolo da Montelupo. Two Barolo crus, Fiasco and Bricco Punta, are also produced as well as a Barbera d'Alba made from grapes grown in a leased vineyard named Punta.

Dolcetto d'Alba　　🍷 ①
Bricco dell'Oriolo 1990 DOC
A satisfyingly clean, full-bodied Dolcetto with a range of typically spicy aromas. Rich, warm palate and a sufficiently astringent finish to round out the impressive texture.

Barolo Bricco Punta 1988 DOCG　🍷 ③
Garnet red, with intense aromas of mature fruit and autumn leaves. Good structure and smooth on the palate. The unassertive tannins indicate that the wine is already well developed.

Barolo Bricco Fiasco 1988 DOCG　🍷 ②
Fresher than the Bricco Punta with younger aromas and substantial, as yet undeveloped, tannins that augur well for the future. The finish has a pleasant hint of bitterness.

Vini Banfi

Via Vittorio Veneto, 22
Strevi (Al) 15019
Tel. (0144) 363485
Fax (0144) 363777

The headquarters of the Banfi company are in Montalcino, but during the 1980s the Mariani brothers decided to expand into Piemonte. The Bruzzone estate at Strevi in the province of Alessandria was chosen. There are two production centers, one at Gavi, where the vineyards and cellar make the white Gavi wine among others, and at Strevi, where the Acqui wines and spumantes are produced. The management team includes Giuseppina Viglierchio, marketing director for the whole Banfi group, her husband, Attilio, and wine technician, Silvano Marchetti. 35 of the 45 ha are planted in Cortese with the remaining 10 in Acqui at the La Rosa estate, where the grapes for the DOC Brachetto d'Acqui come from. There are also plans to expand the estate in the near future. Some grapes are also bought in from local growers. Banfi is noted above all for its sparkling wines made both from local grapes and, in the case of Tener, from Montalcino-grown Chardonnay and Sauvignon.

Gavi Vigna Regale 1990 DOC ☙ ①
From Banfi's finest Cortese vineyard at Monterotondo, this is an impressive white, released for sale a year later than is normal for Gavi wines. Good personality and intense, frank aromas. The palate is piquant and refreshing, with plenty of acidity.

Banfi Brut 1988 ☙ ③
Obtained from Chardonnay and Pinot Nero grapes together with a small quantity of Pinot Bianco, a méthode champenoise fermented in the bottle for three years. Straw-yellow with flecks of gold, it has lots of firm mousse and a delicate, lingering perlage. Yeasty aromas and fresh, lively acidity.

Brachetto d'Acqui 🍇 ③
Vigneto la Rosa 1991 DOC
From the 15-ha La Rosa estate at Acqui, a Brachetto spumante made in pressurized stainless-steel vats. Pale ruby with attractively well-defined aromas and a distinct hint of roses. Agreeably stylish palate and perhaps rather too much mousse.

Dolcetto d'Acqui Argusto 1988 DOC 🍇 ③
One of very few Dolcettos to age slowly in Slavonian oak barriques. Typical berry and sour-cherry aromas. Elegant body with the tannins from the wood still in evidence. Extremely drinkable, with a finish of cherries and berries.

Key to the symbols

Types of Wines

☙ White

🎴 Rosé

🍇 Red

Rating System

☙   An exemplary wine of its type with outstanding local character

🎴🎴   An international premium quality wine

🍇🍇🍇   A Top Wine, considered one of the 150 best wines in the world

The 'grape bunch' symbol is used to indicate the color of the wine; the number of bunches represents the quality rating assigned by the contributor

Price levels

①   up to $ 9.99

② $ 10.00 - $ 14.99

③ $ 15.00 - $ 24.99

④ $ 25.00 or more

The 'ex-cellar', or direct from the producer, bottle prices, are calculated in US dollars and are intended only as an approximate guide

Entries are arranged in alphabetical order by country, region and winery or producer name.

La Barbatella

Strada Annunziata, 55
Nizza Monferrato (At) 14049
Tel/Fax (0141) 701434

A small estate and a small miracle, one might say to sum up Angelo Sonvico's La Barbatella estate. It stormed into the winemaking élite of Piemonte with three wines of supreme quality. La Barbatella has brought out the full potential of both the Nizza Monferrato area and the noble Barbera grape, which was badly in need of a new, bolder approach. Angelo Sonvico is a Milanese with a passion for winemaking who settled in Monferrato, bought a few hectares in a prime location and equipped his cellar with up-to-the-minute machinery. Sonvico placed himself in the hands of Giuliano Noè, a first-class enologist. Results soon came along and Sonvico's Barberas, both the traditional kind to be drunk young and the barrique-aged Vigna dell'Angelo, reached the top of their category. They are powerful, elegant and austere and extremely satisfying to drink. The estate's latest offering is Vigna di Sonvico from Barbera and Sauvignon grapes. This is yet another extraordinary success story, further confirmation of the huge potential of the area and of the skills of Sonvico and his team.

Barbera d'Asti 1991 DOC   🍷 ①
Incredibly smooth and rounded for a Barbera d'Asti, usually forthright to the point of being aggressive. This 1991 fully reflects all the varietal characteristics. Deep garnet with well-defined, uncomplicated aromas and a full body mingling beautifully on the palate. A wine of outstanding frankness.

Barbera d'Asti Superiore   🍷🍷 ②
Vigna dell'Angelo 1990 DOC
The ideal location, painstaking care in the vineyard, low yields and scrupulous aging in barriques are the secrets behind this Vigna dell'Angelo 1991. The robust, powerful structure is mellowed and enhanced by the oak, which adds elegance and complexity on the nose. Superbly full-bodied but wonderfully easy to drink.

La Vigna di Sonvico 1990   🍷🍷🍷 ③
The aim Angelo Sonvico and Giuliano Noè had in mind when they were making this Vigna di Sonvico was to marry the power of Barbera to the elegance of Cabernet Sauvignon, thus creating a red wine with international appeal. The superb location of the vineyards, very low yields and the skillful use of wood have all contributed to the project's success. The Barbera grapes, which predominate in the coupage, impart strength while the Cabernet adds softness and classy aromas. The result is a deep garnet red wine with a delightfully complex bouquet and a warm, lingering mouthfilling palate. A truly great red wine satisfying to drink today but one which will be a magnificent glass tomorrow.

Beni di Batasiolo

Fraz. Annunziata
La Morra (Cn) 12064
Tel. (0173) 50130
Fax (0173) 509258

The current manager, Mauro Monchiero, has succeeded in the far-from-easy job of turning this mass-production winery into one of Italy's finest premium estates. Monchiero used to be manager of the Bigi property in Orvieto before taking on the task of restructuring and upgrading former Sette Cascine estate, with its 96 ha of excellently located vineyards, perfect for growing Nebbiolo grapes to make Barolo. He also found a capacious, well-equipped cellar and a property willing to make the sacrifices necessary to achieve success. With the help of Giorgio Lavagna and Gian Domenico Negro in the cellar and Sergio Germano and Matteo Monchiero in the vineyard, Mauro enabled the Beni di Batasiolo label to turn the corner. Bottles and labels were redesigned, marketing was improved and, most important of all, new quality standards and experimental programs were introduced into the cellar. The result is a series of excellent crus of Barolo, impressive, noble wines with superb aging potential as well as a fine Chardonnay.

Dolcetto d'Alba ♥ ①
Bricco di Vergne 1991 DOC
A Dolcetto obtained from grapes picked before the autumn rains devastated the Nebbiolo and Barbera harvests. The vintage was unexceptional but the fruity aromas are very attractive. Rich ruby in the glass, with plenty of acidity.

Barolo ♥♥ ③
Corda della Briccolina 1988 DOCG
The grapes come from the property's Serralunga cru, which produces around 10,000 bottles a year. An up-to-the-minute version of Barolo, made without excessive maceration but with long fermentation and aging in barriques. The oak imparts its lingering, stylish aromas and wonderful smoothness while the overall structure is impressive.

Barolo ♥♥ ③
Vigneto Bofani 1988 DOCG
Bofani comes from a cru known as Munie in the Monforte area near Castiglione Falletto and has a more classic style than the two Serralunga Barolos. Still a little closed, with tannins much in evidence but a great future is guaranteed.

Barolo ♥ ③
Vigneto Boscareto 1988 DOCG
Another Barolo from Serralunga, one of the highest-lying crus in the Langhe. Although perhaps less velvety and rich than the Briccolina, it is an elegant wine with an intense bouquet and a excellent length.

Nicola Bergaglio

Fraz. Rovereto, località Pedaggeri, 59
Gavi (Al) 15066
Tel. (0143) 682195

Nicola Bergaglio is one of the most widely respected winemakers in the Gavi area. His vineyards are in the frazione of Rovereto, one of the best zones for Piemonte's premier white wine. Nicola produces exclusively Gavi, from plants with an average age of 25 years and has recently created a special reserve called Minaia from selected grapes grown in the vineyard of that name. Bergaglio's wines are famous not only for their quality but also because they are sold at very attractive prices. The estate's policies include low yields per hectare and rigorous selection of the fruit. Second-choice grapes are used to make an excellent table wine which is sold unbottled to a loyal clientele. All aspects of production, both in the vineyard and in the cellar, are supervised personally by Nicola with the help of his family. The Bergaglios are remarkable not only for their courtesy but also for the scrupulous care with which they look after their vineyards and cellar.

Gavi 1991 DOC ♥ ①
The aromas are a little muted but the balance of acidity and extracts brings out all the typical characteristics of Cortese.

Gavi di Gavi Minaia 1991 DOC ♥ ①
The grapes of this cru come from vineyards of Rovereto in the heart of the Denominazione and express the character of Gavi at its best. 1991 was not the greatest of vintages but this Minaia has good structure and is outstandingly fresh and easy-to-drink.

Bertelli

Fraz. San Carlo
Costigliole d'Asti (At) 14055
Tel. (0141) 966137
Fax (02) 76004311

This young estate was soon noticed by experts attracted by its innovative approach to cultivation methods and winemaking techniques as well as the varieties grown. For all its modern equipment, the cellar has a unique charm thanks to its stunning location and the building where it is housed, which is adorned with a vast and growing range of barriques. Most of the wines sold go for export, including the Barbera d'Asti Giarone (there was no 1989 vintage), Barbera Montetusa, Plissé Traminer Dry Late Harvest, Chardonnay Giarone and Cabernet Sauvignon I Fossaretti. Barbera Giarone in particular is noted for its balance and finesse, the result of painstaking work in the vineyard and careful aging in barriques. Traminer is almost unknown in the region and this example has soft, elegant aromas when young while it becomes decidedly more complex with time, bringing out both the primary aromas of the grape and the stylish contribution of the wood. A constantly improving estate which deserves close attention.

Chardonnay Giarone 1990
The vineyard where the grapes were grown is in part Guyot- and in part lyre-pruned. The wine itself, golden straw-yellow flecked with orange, is aged and fermented in barriques. Aromas of sweet vanilla and acacia-wood, a very complex palate of fruit and oak and a refreshing finish of mint and almond.

Plissé Traminer
Dry Late Harvest 1990
Made from super-ripe grapes fermented in barriques of Limousin and Nevers oak until after the malolactic. Golden yellow color and a nose of oak followed by cakes and apricot. Well-balanced in the mouth. Full, moderately concentrated, structure and good softness. Lively hazelnut-and-mint finish.

Barbera d'Asti
Montetusa 1989 DOC
Deep, intense ruby shading into violet. The nose opens with the austere, concentrated oak of the barriques with strawberry and red berries then emerging. Soft in the mouth with acidity still in evidence, perfectly balanced by the stupendous richness of fruit. The finish is long and piquant, almost salty.

I Fossaretti 1989
Monovarietal Cabernet Sauvignon, aged and fermented in Allier and Nevers oak. Bright, deep ruby in the glass and intense aromas with a strong hint of alcohol which opens out into berries and liquorice. Complex palate dominated by a lingering flavor of liquorice, discreetly tempered by the elegance of the wood.

Gianfranco Bovio

Fraz. Annunziata, borgata Ciotto, 63
La Morra (Cn) 12064
Tel/Fax (0173) 50190

The Bovio estate is located in the heart of the renowned Annunziata frazione of La Morra, at Borgata Ciotto. Gattera and Arborina with their Nebbiolo grapes for Barolo and Firagnetti, planted in Dolcetto, are all outstanding vineyards. Gianfranco Bovio also owns the Belvedere di La Morra restaurant, a veritable institution on the Langhe gastronomic scene, where he encourages his customers to taste other producers wines, especially those of the younger, up-and-coming growers. The Bovio cellar began bottling during the legendary 1978 vintage and since then Gianfranco has devoted an increasing proportion of his time to winemaking, a "hobby" he loves. Assisted by estate manager Walter Porasso, Bovio keeps a watchful eye on quality and experiments with new aging techniques. Bovio's Barolo is a traditional, intense, full-bodied wine, ideal for laying down although rich in aromas even when young. The Dolcetto Firagnetti is in a similar style and Bovio puts it on the market late to allow it to develop to the full.

Dolcetto d'Alba
Vigneto Firagnetti dell'Annunziata 1991 DOC
A Dolcetto which expresses La Morra's main variety perfectly. Deep garnet-red with correspondingly powerful, fresh aromas. Well-rounded on the palate with excellent texture.

Regiaveja 1989
Gian Bovio obtained the grapes for this impressively-structured wine from an long-established Barbera vineyard at Gattera dell'Annunziata. The wood is still a little prominent on the nose with the fruit emerging only in the background. Well-balanced on the palate with good extract and acidity.

Barolo
Vigna Gattera dell'Annunziata 1988 DOCG
Lovely bright red in the glass. Well-defined, intense aromas with pronounced notes of spice and pepper which are still fresh and young. The substantial body and firm tannins are a guarantee of the wine's considerable aging potential

Braida

Via Roma, 94
Rocchetta Tanaro (At) 14030
Tel. (0141) 644113
Fax (0141) 644584

The former owner of the Braida cellar, Giacomo Bologna who died in December 1990, was a great personality on the Italian wine scene and the man who was mainly responsible for the upturn in the fortunes of Barbera. Obtained from the grape of the same name, Barbera accounts for more than 50% of the production of Piemonte, one of Italy's leading wine-growing regions. The huge quantities of Barbera produced have been achieved at the expense of quality although the variety itself has great potential: high acidity, plenty of extract, good structure and an attractive deep ruby red color which shades into violet when the wine is young. It is to Giacomo's credit that he was among the first to understand that Barbera could give excellent results with barrique aging with the result that year after year Bricco dell'Uccellone and Bricco della Bigotta, recently joined by Ai Suma, have won over the most demanding wine-lovers both in Italy and abroad, for the Braida cellar exports to Germany, Switzerland and the United States. In addition to the wines mentioned above, Moscato d'Asti, Brachetto d'Acqui, a good Grignolino and a young Barbera called La Monella are also produced. 1988, 1989 and 1990 were three superb vintages for red Piemontese wines to tuck away in the cellar. The Bologna family's products are no exception.

Barbera d'Asti Ai Suma
1990 DOC   🍷🍷 ③
One of the great Piemontese reds, with stunningly elegant aromas where the frankness of Barbera is barely masked by the aristocratic oak. Quite staggering on the palate, where extract and acidity are in perfect harmony. A complex wine to lay down for a very long time.

Bricco della Bigotta 1989   🍷 ③
Another Barbera from Rocchetta Tanaro with an extrovert personality. Austere aromas with the oak still to the fore. Impressive structure, backed up by typical Barbera acidity.

Bricco dell'Uccellone 1989   🍷🍷 ③
Giacomo Bologna was the first grower to believe that Barbera could compete with the world's great reds and it was the 1982 Bricco dell'Uccellone that proved him right. This premium-quality 1989 vintage has aristocratic vanilla aromas that enhance the floral bouquet and well-defined liquorice that backs up a body of exceptional length and depth.

Carlo e Ermanno Brema

Via Pozzomagna, 7
Incisa Scapaccino (At) 14045
Tel/Fax (0141) 74019

The Brema estate is long established and has always grown the traditional Monferrato varieties. Recently, a new production unit at Bricco di Nizza has been added to the two farmhouse estates of Croce and Giacomina. The Bremas are right in the heart of one of the best areas for Barbera, the estate's mainstay, and the Brema cellar produces wines of outstanding personality. Pride of place must go to the Vigna Donato cru, a Barbera vinified in stainless steel and aged in large oak barrels, while the lively Barbera del Monferrato is a more approachable, easy-drinking wine. In 1991, for the first time Brema produced a small quantity of Brachetto d'Acqui spumante, a dessert wine obtained from recently-planted vines on Giacomina estate. To complete the range, the Bremas offer Dolcetto d'Asti, one of the finest examples of this DOC wine, Grignolino d'Asti Bric le Roche and a classic Moscato d'Asti. Summing up, this is an estate with an individual style, which is not satisfied merely to follow the latest trend but strives carefully to reinterpret tradition.

Brachetto d'Acqui 1991 DOC   🍷 ①
Brachetto is a characteristic aromatic grape from the southern Monferrato sub-zone, well-suited to the production of attractive, lively dessert wines with a good bouquet. The Brema Brachetto is a beautiful deep pink, with characteristic floral aromas. Fresh and clean in the mouth, with just a shade too much sparkle.

Dolcetto d'Asti 1991 DOC   🍷 ①
From a relatively little-known Denominazione, this is a an extremely drinkable Dolcetto d'Asti. Clean and slightly herbaceous on the nose with a frank, dry palate. A pétillant wine that is an ideal accompaniment for Monferrato cold meats and appetizers.

Barbera d'Asti   🍷 ①
Cascina Croce Vigna Donato 1990 DOC
A Barbera d'Asti in the classic mold, vinified and matured in the traditional style with fairly lengthy maceration on the skins and oak aging. A wine to savor for the fullness and power of its structure and the delights it offers nose and palate.

Giacomo Brezza e figli

Via Lomondo, 2
Barolo (Cn) 12060
Tel. (0173) 56191
Fax (0173) 56354

The Brezzas are an institution in Barolo. Winemakers since 1885, the family started bottling their own wine in 1910. The Barolo crus where the Brezzas have parcels are legendary - Cannubi, Sarmassa, S. Lorenzo and Castellero. Almost to underline the historical importance of the family, Giacomo Brezza's sister Franca is married to one of the founding fathers of Langhe enology, Bartolo Mascarello. The Brezzas also run a very well-known restaurant and recently added an attractive little hotel next door to it. For all of these reasons, we can justly affirm that Oreste, Giacomo and Mariuccia Brezza are in the front rank of Barolo winemaking. Their spirit of initiative and thirst for new challenges is as fresh as ever, particularly in wine types, where Oreste wages a one-man war to dispel Barolo's impressive but uncomfortable image as a wine for meditation and to bring it back into the realm of everyday drinking. Oreste will even go so far as to serve it as an aperitif in his restaurant to his surprised and amused customers. Provocative, no doubt, but also a sign of genuine passion - a passion that is rewarded by the superb quality of the Brezza estate's wines.

Dolcetto d'Alba
San Lorenzo 1991 DOC
The harvest was completed before the disastrous rains of 1991. Ruby-red tending to violet with well-defined aromas of moderate intensity. A herbaceous note of green leaves is prominent together with butter and chocolate. Good texture on the palate, with perhaps a little too much tannin but plenty of extract.

Barbera d'Alba
Cannubi Muscatel 1989 DOC
Bright ruby in appearance, a little less full and intense than is usual in a Barbera. Stylish, attractive aromas with notes of spice and violet. Soft entry on the palate, with sugar and alcohol prevalent. Velvet-smooth texture, good length and very drinkable.

Barolo Cannubi 1988 DOCG
From one of Barolo's most legendary crus, the Brezzas produce around 8,000 bottles a year of this bright garnet-red, orange-tinted wine. The aromas are subdued with an impression of alcohol that gradually fades away. Fruit and unassertive tannins are in evidence on the palate, well-balanced by a lively acidity. Lingering finish of cherry and liquorice.

Bricco Mondalino

Regione Mondalino
Vignale Monferrato (Al) 15049
Tel. (0142) 923204
Fax (0142) 923421

The Bricco Mondalino estate owned by the Gaudio family is the leading producer in the Casale Monferrato area, particularly famous for its characteristic traditional Grignolino variety. Since the 1970s, Amilcare Gaudio has made a series of decisive contributions towards the introduction of Grignolino to a wider wine-drinking public. Today his son Mauro continues this work with commitment and foresight. As well as producing traditional Grignolino, he has added the Bricco Mondalino cru, an exacting, complex wine which highlights the potential of an often misunderstood variety. Alongside this top-of-the-range wine, we can find other excellent products such as Barbera del Monferrato, in both classic and modern versions, the commendable Barbera d'Asti Il Bergantino with its superbly-balanced structure and good aging potential, the lively Freisa La Monferrina and the sweet Malvasia di Casorzo, the most recent addition to the Gaudio range and perfect to sip with "petits fours."

Grignolino del Monferrato Casalese
Bricco Mondalino 1991 DOC
Mauro Gaudio selects the best locations on the estate for the grapes which go into this Grignolino cru, delaying the harvest until the fruit is absolutely ripe. The result is unusual for a wine of this type with its deep cherry color, warm aromas with faint hints of spice and its full, velvety texture.

Barbera d'Asti
Bergantino 1990 DOC
A Barbera with remarkable structure and personality, aged in French oak barrels which add softness and balance. Beautiful vivid garnet-red, light aromas typical of the variety and a very satisfying palate.

Gian Piero Broglia

Tenuta La Meirana, località Lomellina, 14
Gavi (Al) 15066
Tel. (0143) 642998
Fax (0143) 78707

Gian Piero Broglia has been in charge of the family estate since 1972, when he took over from his father, who founded the cellar. Although Gian Piero divides his time between the estate and his manufacturing business, he has given a considerable boost to the estate's output. The estate itself comprises 100 ha, 36 of which are planted in vines, situated around the farmhouse with its modern cellar. Gian Piero personally supervises each stage of production and sets great store by vineyard management, having reduced the yield per hectare each year. In the cellar, work is directed by Donato Lanati, a young and already well-established enologist. The range, naturally, is based on Gavi, obtained from Cortese grapes, but also includes Roverello, a sparkling Gavi fermented in the bottle in the manner traditional locally, and Vigna delle Pernici, a Dolcetto-based red wine which the estate had produced in the past. Barrique-aged Gavi Fasciolla is still at the experimental stage with only a very limited number of bottles available for sale.

Gavi di Gavi Villa Broglia 1991 DOC 🍇 ②
Obtained from a vineyard selection of the best Cortese grapes. A wine with a well-defined personality, classy, elegant, fruit aromas, a clean flavor and good length on the palate. Very attractive bitterish hint in the finish.

Gavi La Meirana 1991 DOC 🍇 ①
The basic Broglia wine, from a blend of grapes from different vineyards all located near the cellar. Tasting showed this to be a very correct wine, both in its fruity aromas and in its flavor, with good acidity in a delicately light body.

Gavi di Gavi Bruno Broglia 1990 DOC 🍇 ②
The cellar's premium wine, obtained from its longest-established vineyard. Low yields and careful vinification make this a bottle to lay down for quite a few years. The aromas are complex and developed to just the right degree. On the palate, alcohol and acidity are well backed up by impressive structure.

F.lli Brovia

Via Alba Barolo, 28
Castiglione Falletto (Cn) 12060
Tel. (0173) 62852-62934
Fax c/o Consorzio (0173) 361380

The Brovia family owns ten hectares of superbly located vineyards at Rocche, Monprivato and Codana in Castiglione Falletto. This is terrain that yields imposing wines with good structure and plenty of aging potential. Add to the terrain the Brovia brothers' cellar management philosophy, which aims for extract, alcohol and complexity, and you will have a good idea of what wines to expect. The Brovia Dolcetto Solatio, which in some years can reach as much as 15° alcohol while still maintaining its fresh aromas, is typical. Not even the arrival of new blood with a younger generation has changed the Brovia style for Elena and Cristina, the latter recently qualified at the Alba enological college, continue as before. The cellars have, however, been restructured, a sign that the Brovias are not insensible to change. And if they can manage to round off some of the rough edges that inevitably arrive in the wake of such bursts of energy, Brovia wines will go on to reach new heights.

Dolcetto d'Alba 🍇 ①
Solatio Brovia 1990 DOC
Produced thanks to a special selection of grapes, this is a wine made only in outstanding vintages. Deep garnet-red with elegant, complex aromas and notes of ripe fruit. Warm and mouthfilling with a very dry tannic finish.

Barolo Rocche dei Brovia 🍇 ②
1987 DOCG
Although 1987 is not generally considered a great year, this Barolo demonstrates the Brovias' traditional winemaking skills at their best. A well-balanced wine with plenty of structure, developed but with fresh young tannins.

Barbaresco Rio Sordo 1985 DOCG 🍇 ②
From a small lot of only 2,500 bottles. Lovely garnet-red shading into brick, well-defined aromas with hints of autumn leaves. Full-bodied on the palate with liquorice flavors and tannins still prominent.

Barolo Monprivato 1985 DOCG 🍇🍇 ②
Tasted seven years after the vintage, this Barolo was in tip-top condition. Powerful, well-balanced body, clean, crisp, yet complex aromas with just a hint of tar. Full-bodied, warm and soft on the palate with lingering aromas.

Castello di Verduno

Via Umberto I, 9
Verduno (Cn) 12060
Tel. (0172) 459125 - 459284
Fax (0172) 459298

Gabriella Burlotto, a Verduno winemaker and restaurateur, and her husband, Franco Bianco, a Barbaresco grower, decided in 1989 to bring their various activities together under one label, Castello di Verduno. The couple's main difficulty lay in the very different natures of the wines produced by the two cellars. While the Burlotto family have always been able to count on the unique charms of Pelaverga, their production is based around Barolo Massara, a solid, austere wine for the cellar and since 1988 on Barolo Monvigliero. Bianco, in contrast, produced elegant, attractive wines with good balance. Although the two ranges were complementary in style, it was difficult reconcile them without losing something in terms of clarity of image. Today all wine-making is done at the Barbaresco cellar while storage and bottle-aging is carried out at Verduno. Luckily, Gabriella is able to keep a close eye on quality from a consumer's point of view as she looks after the wines served in the excellent restaurant over her cellar in rooms which once welcomed Carlo Alberto, king of Italy.

Pelaverga di Verduno 1990
Pelaverga is an unusual grape variety of uncertain origin that has recently found a home in the Verduno area. Here at Castello di Verduno, it displays all its characteristic traits with peppery, almost sharp, aromas which open out into flowery notes. The palate is full, aromatic and slightly astringent.

Barbaresco
Vigneto Fascet 1989 DOCG
Good, moderately intense, deep garnet-red. Interesting complexity on the nose, with spices, dried flowers and aromatic herbs mingling in a bouquet of remarkable intensity and length. The tannins still dominate the medium structure. A final balance has yet to be found but prospects for the future are good.

Barolo Vigna Massara 1988 DOCG
Roses, violets and rain-soaked Langhe earth are prominent in the complex bouquet of this Barolo from the Massara di Verduno cru, right opposite Santa Maria di La Morra. Full structure and good complexity. A wine that is still opening out, with the tannins contributing a bitter note in the finish.

Castlèt

Strada Castelletto, 6
Costigliole d'Asti (At) 14055
Tel. (0141) 966651
Fax (0141) 961492

A few years ago, Mariuccia Borio closed her wine merchant's business in Turin and went back to her beautiful family farmhouse estate at Costigliole d'Asti, in the frazione of Castlèt. With her enthusiastic, can-do approach, she wholeheartedly threw herself into wine-making, running the estate personally and getting involved in hundreds of other wine-related projects. She became especially active in the promotion of premium wines, and above all Barbera, the wine that Costigliole d'Asti locals like Mariuccia are weaned on. Cascina Castlèt offers various kinds of Barbera: the classic Barbera d'Asti, a Superiore known as Litina, barrique-aged Policalpo, and the unique Passum, obtained from grapes harvested late and laid out to dry in the sun on trellises before crushing. Another sweet dessert wine that graces the range of this incredible 'lady of wine' is Avié, from Moscato grapes. It is a highly enjoyable dessert wine in the modern idiom and there are certain to be more surprises in store from Castlèt, a cellar as memorable for the exquisite taste of its packaging as it is for the style of its wines.

Avié 1990
A dessert wine from sun-dried Moscato grapes made in the modern style to preserve the freshness of the attractive Moscato aromas without cloying.

Passum 1988
Following a long-established tradition of the Costigliole d'Asti area, Mariuccia Borio obtains this Passum from lightly sun-dried grapes. A special wine with highly individual aromas of stewed fruit, ripe grapes and violet.

Policalpo 1988
From selected Barbera grapes grown in the Costigliole d'Asti area and aged in an assortment of French barriques. Lovely deep garnet-red, frank aromas and agreeable acidity on the palate.

Caudrina

Strada Caudrina, 20
Castiglione Tinella (Cn) 12053
Tel. (0141) 855126
Fax (0173) 855008

The Moscato grape, traditional mainstay of the area between Langhe and Monferrato, has made the fortune of the spumante industry in general and in particular of Canelli, who have exported Asti Spumante all over the world. But these aromatic and fragrant grapes will also yield a naturally-fermented, non-sparkling wine that faithfully brings all the fresh aromas and flavors of the variety to the eyes, nose and palate of the taster. The recent rediscovery of the long unfashionable Moscato d'Asti variety has been to a large extent the work of the Dogliotti family. During the 1960s, Redento and his sons Carlo, Pierfranco and Romano were among the first to see the wine's potential. With the help of modern wine-making techniques, they practically created Moscato d'Asti from scratch, preparing the way for many other producers and gracing Italian enology with an outstanding dessert wine. Today at the Cascina Caudrina, as the Dogliotti property is called, two types of Moscato d'Asti are made. One bears the name of the cellar and the other is called La Galeisa, after one of the estate's vineyards where the variety thrives.

Moscato d'Asti   🍇 ①
La Galeisa 1991 DOC
Obtained from a careful selection of grapes from the property's finest vineyard. A superb expression of the variety with rich aromas where flowers are to the fore. Abundant mousse and a full-flavored palate, sweet on entry with a dry, pleasantly bitter finish.

Moscato d'Asti   🍇🍇 ①
La Caudrina 1991 DOC
Another top-quality Dogliotti product. Moderate intensity on the nose with lemon prominent. The palate has light, pleasant acidity in a well-balanced body. Less structure than the preceding wine but excellent drinking nonetheless.

Cavallotto

Loc. Bricco Boschis
Castiglione Falletto (Cn) 12060
Tel. (0173) 62814
Fax (0173) 62914

Since 1948, the Cavallotto family has lived in the heart of Barolo country, where they own a 20 ha vineyard at Bricco Boschis - practically the entire cru. The estate's great red wines have never received the recognition they deserve owing to poor marketing and the lack of a precise image. The Cavallotti's used to put their wines on the market in rather the same way that Piemontese families once used to send their sons out into the world when they came of age. They instilled them with sound principles, gave them an education if they could and put a (very) little money in their pocket before they let them find their feet on their own. The arrival of Olivio Cavallotti's three sons coincided with the modernization of the cellar and the introduction of a rational approach to organic pesticide techniques, which has always been one of the estate's main experimental concerns. Thanks also to the consultancy of Professor Corino from the Agricultural Institute of Asti, it may truthfully be said that today no chemical pesticides are used in the Cavallotto vineyards. Skeptics have only to taste the results to be convinced of the validity of organic methods.

Barolo Riserva   🍇 ②
Vigna San Giuseppe 1986 DOCG
This vintage cannot be compared to 1985 and the well-developed color is ample proof. Nevertheless the aromas are well-defined and, intense, with notes of coffee and cloves. Velvet-smooth on the palate, where the young tannins contribute frankness and drinkability.

Barolo Riserva   🍇 ②
Vigna Colle Sud-Ovest 1985 DOCG
Cavallotto is one of the few estates in the Langhe to have a certain quantity of wine from this vintage. The aromas are still young and fresh with tar and coffee dominant. Plenty of body and sinew, lots of green tannins and a long life ahead of it.

Barolo Riserva   🍇🍇 ②
Vigna San Giuseppe 1985 DOCG
Still very lively in the glass, with the color just shading into orange. The aromas are spicy and intense, with aristocratic notes of tar. Good concentration on the palate, the slightly alcoholic entry opening magnificently out into noble tannins which support a body of wonderful texture.

F.lli Ceretto

Loc. S. Cassiano, 34
Alba (Cn) 12051
Tel. (0173) 282582
Fax (0173) 282383

To get a good idea of the Ceretto estate, you need to completely unfold the map of the Langhe region. The Ceretto parcels go from Bricco Rocche at Castiglione Falletto, to the seven hectares at Brunate, three hectares at Prapò, one hectare at Bricco Asili and two and a half hectares at Faset, to mention only the great red wines. For Blangé, an Arneis that came out about four years ago which has proved immensely popular, the Cerettos have a total of 15 ha at Vezza d'Alba, Monteu Roero and Canale with eight more at Castellinaldo. Recently, they have also leased the lovely Bernardina estate, once the property of the counts of Mirafiori, with 12 of the 81 hectares planted in vines and a futuristic complex housing all the estate's winemaking cellars. New plantings of Chardonnay, Viognier, Pinot Nero, Cabernet Sauvignon and Syrah (5-6,000 bottles per type) will open up new possibilities for the Cerettos. It is Bruno Ceretto who looks after marketing and public relations while Marcello takes care of wine-making. Always busy, full of energy and always open to new ideas, the Cerettos combine a willingness to take risks with genuine old-fashioned Langhe wisdom.

Blangé Arneis 1991   ❦ ②
A highly successful white, created for summer drinkers. Produced from Arneis grapes vinified in a modern style, a pétillant wine with fruity, captivating aromas. Fresh and easy-to-drink, with good body and modest length.

Barbera d'Alba Piana 1990 DOC   ❦ ①
Intense on the nose with the characteristic Barbera aromas where gamey notes come through. Deep garnet red. Well-rounded on the palate, full-bodied with good texture and well-defined acidity in the finish.

Barolo Brunate 1988 DOCG   ❦❦ ③
Brunate, in the commune of La Morra, is one of the historic Barolo areas. Ceretto's version has complex aromas, with hints of coffee and attractively deep color. The palate is still developing while the body has good texture.

Barolo Prapò 1988 DOCG   ❦ ③
Another Barolo, this time from the commune of Serralunga. Typically for the area, the body is full and the wine needs time to mature. The nose is complex with distinct aromas of autumn leaves while structure of the tannins and acidity can be savored on the palate.

Barbaresco   ❦❦❦ ③
Bricco Asili 1989 DOCG
The vines were planted in 1970 when the Ceretto brothers bought this 1.2 ha lot, a natural continuation of the Martinenga cru which was once a meadow. The point is more than just anecdotal in importance because it gives this Nebbiolo vineyard, planted at 4,500 vines per hectare, such a wealth of surface vegetation that it never has required any chemical or organic soil enrichment. Vinification was traditional, with a 10-15 day submerged-cap maceration, fermentation in stainless steel with the cap broken up and the wine pumped over three or four times. First-racking, racking and the malolactic were carried out immediately after fermentation. The wine went into Slavonian-oak barrels just before Christmas, with around 30% going into barriques. A powerful Barbaresco with rich color and structure. The nose is already open, lingering and rich with spices and tar to the fore, followed by fruity notes of cherry and small berries. The palate has a stunning entry with lively, piquant tannins and great concentration. The body has yet to find a balance but the cellar and the bottle will transform this wine into a masterpiece.

Michele Chiarlo

Strada statale Nizza-Canelli
Calamandrana (At) 14042
Tel. (0141) 75231
Fax (0141) 75284

The Michele Chiarlo estate is one of Piemonte's major producers with an output of over one million bottles a year but it is even more important for other reasons: the constantly improving standard of its research; its series of acquisitions in the region's most select locations, the most recent of these being a vineyard at Cannubi di Barolo; and finally for its rigorous selection of grapes and the careful work in the cellar of its dedicated and skillful young wine technician, Roberto Bezzato. Production covers the entire panorama of Piemontese wines including Cortese di Gavi, Monferrato Grignolino and Barbera and the great Langhe wines, Barbaresco and Barolo. Besides a line of value-for-money wines aimed at the middle of the market, Michele Chiarlo also vinifies the grapes from the estate's vineyards and from trusted local growers to produce a prestigious series of whites (notably the Gavi cru, Fornaci) as well as the austere, elegant reds, Barbaresco Rabajà, Barolo Vigna Rionda, Barbera Vigna del Sole and Barilot, a blend of Barbera and Nebbiolo grapes.

Gavi   🍷🍷 ③
Fornaci di Tassarolo 1989 DOC
The aromas go beyond the usual Gavi range to include mint, grass and above all aniseed. The structure is generous and attractive with aniseed again to the fore while the finish has good length.

Barbera d'Asti   🍷 ②
Vigna del Sole 1988 DOC
The grapes come from Castelboglione, an outstanding Barbera area that produces piquant wines with well-defined aromas and good acidity. Chiarlo has softened this powerfully structured wine with careful use of barriques while preserving all the wine's vigor.

Barilot 1989   🍷🍷 ②
Obtained from Barbera grapes grown in two prestigious areas, Barolo and Vinchio. Very low yields and barrique-aging first, then maturing in the bottle, give the wine rare elegance. Distinct wood and coffee aromas. Impressive texture backed up by the acidity, good concentration and excellent aging potential.

Barolo Vigna Cerequio   🍷🍷 ③
1988 DOCG
The first Barolo from the recently acquired five hectare vineyard on the hill of Cerequio, between the communes of La Morra and Barolo. Bright ruby with very stylish aromas containing hints of wild roses, autumn leaves and vanilla. Magnificent elegance and breadth of body, with well-balanced tannins.

Quinto Chionetti & Figlio

Via S. Luigi, 44
Dogliani (Cn) 12063
Tel/Fax (0173) 71179

It is only over the last twenty years that Dolcetto di Dogliani has achieved success in Italy and abroad. In the past, hardly any estates bottled this wine, which was destined largely for bulk sale in demijohns. The Chionettis proved that a premium-quality product could compete on a par with the already famous Dolcetto d'Alba and as a result of their success, other cellars started to bottle Dolcetto di Dogliani. Chionetti's idea was to concentrate all his efforts on one variety, Dolcetto, vinifying grapes from different vineyards separately in a modern, well-equipped cellar. The wines he produces in this way are Dolcetto di Dogliani Briccolero, Dolcetto di Dogliani San Luigi and Dolcetto di Dogliani Le Coste. Briccolero has always been most popular. A full-bodied wine with plenty of alcohol, it has generous, lingering aromas. A little less powerful, but very elegant nonetheless in many vintages is San Luigi.

Dolcetto di Dogliani   🍷🍷 ①
Briccolero 1991 DOC
A traditional wine from the estate's main cru, as befits the Chionetti style. The aromas are intense, lingering and complex, with almond to the fore. Considerable structure on the palate and a pleasantly bitter finish.

Dolcetto di Dogliani   🍷 ①
San Luigi 1991 DOC
The hill which goes up from Dogliani towards Monforte provides the grapes for this Dolcetto with loads of personality. The 1991 vintage produced a very interesting wine with deep ruby color, rich, spicy aromas, good drinkability and excellent length.

F.lli Cigliuti

Loc. Serra Boella, 17
Neive (Cn) 12057
Tel. (0173) 677185
Fax (0173) 67247

Recently, Barbaresco has risen considerably
in the estimation of consumers all over the
world, yet only a few estates have a solid
track record of quality in the production of this
great wine. Cigliuti is certainly one of these
estates, receiving accolades year after year
as quality continues to improve. The top-of-
the-range product is Barbaresco Serraboella,
a wine with a structure of unvarying
excellence and superb depth of aromas,
where attractive notes of tobacco and leather
emerge over time. The estate's four hectares
also produce a full-bodied Barbera d'Alba
with good acidity and a Dolcetto d'Alba,
particularly pleasing on the nose with its fresh
winey texture. These successes have not
satisfied Renato Cigliuti for he has he
decided to restructure the cellars by adopting
modern technology and gradually introducing
barriques. A cellar which is sure to come up
with a lot of interesting wines in the future.

Dolcetto d'Alba   ♥ ①
Serraboella 1991 DOC
Not the greatest of years for this characteristic
Dolcetto d'Alba. Rich, frank aromas and
unassuming structure on the palate but a very
good glass nonetheless. Finishes on a
herbaceous note.

Barbera d'Alba   ♥ ②
Serraboella 1990 DOC
An absolutely representative Barbera d'Alba
from the superb 1990 vintage. Deep garnet red
with complex aromas where the wood still
dominates. The palate brings out the variety's
strength to the full. Great structure, crisp acidity.
Needs more bottle-age.

Barbaresco   ♥ ♥ ③
Serraboella 1989 DOCG
The nose is still a little closed while the as yet
unintegrated tannins are in evidence on the
palate. Good texture and well-balanced
structure. Elegant with a promising future as
well as being very good value for money.

Antiche Cantine
Francesco Cinzano & C.
Via Statale Cinzano, 63
Santa Vittoria d'Alba (Cn) 12060
Tel. (0172) 478041
Fax (011) 57401

Apart from the big winery at Santa Vittoria
d'Alba extending for almost a whole kilometer
along the road from Alba to Bra, Cinzano has
about thirty other production units scattered
around the world. A veritable colossus in the
world of spumantes and vermouths, the
fortified and flavored wines that have added
luster to an already-famous name, the
Cinzano company was recently taken over by
a British group. Despite the elevated levels of
production, premium quality is guaranteed,
especially in spumantes, where Asti
Spumante takes pride of place. Cinzano is
one of the most important producers of this
wine. Recently, a vintage selection called
Alteluci was created, a refreshing novelty at a
time when innovation is needed. Also worthy
of note is Marone, a champenoise from Pinot
Nero grapes of the Oltrepò Pavese area.

Asti Spumante Alteluci 1991 DOC   ♥ ♥ ①
A vintage Asti Spumante (1990 was the first
year of production) that has yielded wonderful
results and given this wine from Cinzano, the
market's leading brand and largest producer,
the nobility and elegance normally associated
with small growers. Intense, fragrant varietal
aromas, full and lingering on the palate and
altogether a delicious glass.

Asti Spumante DOC   ♥ ①
Known and appreciated all over the world as the
wine to celebrate with. This is certainly one of
the best Astis, with a pleasant flowery nose and
a lively palate, not overwhelmed, as is so often
the case, by the abundant effervescence.

Marone Cinzano Pas Dosé 1987   ♥ ③
The finest reserve of a big-numbers, big-range
spumante producer. The Pinot Bianco, Grigio
and Nero grapes come from the Oltrepò area
and the wine has an elegant perlage, lively
aromas with yeast and crusty bread as well as
good length and texture backed up by fresh
acidity.

Tenute Cisa Asinari
dei Marchesi di Gresy
Via Rabajà, 43
Barbaresco (Cn) 12050
Tel. (0173) 635222
Fax (0173) 635187

The vineyards are located in Martinenga, one of the finest areas to grow Nebbiolo for Barbaresco, on a hill where local growers say the very best grapes can be cultivated. Alberto di Gresy has brought to this territory his strong determination to produce premium-quality wines, a state-of-the-art cellar and the support of skillful wine technicians. His best results are to be found in three different versions of Barbaresco: Gaiun, with its special elegance enhanced by aging in small oak barrels; Camp Gros, generally with more structure and aging potential; and Barbaresco Martinenga, with its stylish, polished aromas and excellent drinkability even when young. Another of the company's successes is Dolcetto d'Alba Monte Aribaldo, another wine with structure but free of the tannins that so often make Dolcetto d'Alba aggressive. New products from unconventional varieties will soon be launched and will doubtless confirm the estate's reputation for quality.

Chardonnay 1991 ❦ ①
From barrique-fermented grapes, a full-bodied Chardonnay with the typical Chardonnay aromas and a full, rich, well-rounded structure. Good balance and length on the palate.

Dolcetto d'Alba ❦ ①
Monte Aribaldo 1991 DOC
A very attractive wine, with heady aromas and notes of fresh fruit. Well-balanced and soft on the palate.

Barbaresco ❦ ❦ ③
Camp Gros 1989 DOCG
Obtained from grapes from the Camp Gros cru. The aromas are subtle with spicy overtones still opening out. Crisp tannins on the palate. Full and well-balanced texture. A wine for the cellar.

Barbaresco Gaiun 1989 DOCG ❦ ❦ ③
Gaiun differs from Camp Gros in that it is only partly aged in barriques. Rather pale in the glass, in the Cisa Asinari style. Elegant aromas of autumn leaves and Morello cherries. Stylish and complex on the palate, where the oak integrates beautifully with the underlying aromas

Domenico Clerico

Loc. Manzoni Cucchi, 67
Monforte d'Alba (Cn) 12065
Tel/Fax (0173) 78171

This winery enjoys such a high reputation that wine merchants and restaurants from all around the world as well as discerning wine-lovers are always on hand to snap up the year's production. This success is entirely due to Clerico's skill as a grower and winemaker. The cellars have recently been restructured and enlarged to make room for the increasing number of new barrels and barriques. Clerico Barolo, particularly Ciabot Mentin Ginestra which has for years been the estate's top-of-the-range product, has rare elegance and style with the body to ensure its aging potential. Arte is another great product of Clerico's skill in the cellar. It is obtained from Nebbiolo with a small proportion of Barbera, and slowly aged in barriques. The aromas have complexity and depth, with Morello cherry and vanilla standing out over a typical Nebbiolo background. The Freisa Ginestrina is also widely appreciated. A fresh, lively, easy-to-drink wine to accompany the uncomplicated cuisine of the Langhe.

Barbera d'Alba 1990 DOC ☙ ①
A very elegant Barbera, soft yet with plenty of structure. Deep garnet red with complex aromas containing well-defined spicy overtones. Good acidity on the palate together with exceptional body. Rich, well-rounded, warm flavors and good length.

Barolo Bricotto Bussia 1988 DOCG ☙ ③
A lovely deep garnet-red wine from one of the best-known Barolo areas. In comparison with Mentin Ginestra, the aromas are more restrained, with autumn leaves to the fore. Stylish on the palate, but with generous tannin structure.

Barolo ☙☙ ③
Ciabot Mentin Ginestra 1988 DOCG
This cru confirms Clerico's vocation for Barolo. Intense aromas of autumn leaves, blackberry and spices with rich color in the glass. Well-balanced on the palate, already opening out although the tannins still need to mellow. Impressive texture and outstanding length.

Arte 1990 ☙☙☙ ③
It was a simple idea that produced this superb result. Clerico used part of the Barolo juice, adding 10% Barbera, to create a wine specifically made to age in barriques. Two days before the grapes from Ginestrina and Cucchi di Monforte finish their fermentation, part of it is drawn from the vat and racked off into barriques. The next step is to heat the cellar to induce malolactic fermentation in both the Nebbiolo and the Barbera, which is also fermented in oak. After blending in stainless-steel vats, the wine is aged in new and one-year-old oak barriques for 17 months. Finally, in order to become the Arte we tasted, the wine matures for nine months in the bottle. The color is intense, concentrated and flecked with blue and aromas of spice and fruit emerge through the still-dominant wood. The palate is mellow and velvety, opening out magnificently after the oak that characterizes the entry. Powerful, elegant structure, lively acidity and crisp tannins. Allow another three years at least before drinking.

Colle Manora

Via Fubine, 133
Quargnento (Al) 15044
Tel. (0131) 769252

Eleonora Limonci had the courage to keep
this estate going in an area where winemaking, once the main occupation, had been
almost completely abandoned. It was not
because the territory had become somehow
unsuitable but simply because growers were
unable to foresee developments in the
market. This charming lady concentrated on
small quantities of premium-quality wine,
entrusting the technical side to a veritable
wizard of wine - Donato Lanati. The
innovative names of the wines, Pais,
Mimosa, Manora and Palo Alto, show that the
estate is not afraid of throwing aside
traditional Denominazione descriptions and
striking out on its own. Colle Manora, for
example, were among the very first in
Piemonte to plant Cabernet Sauvignon. They
have also carefully nurtured the only long-
established vineyard they possess, a
higgledy-piggledy confusion of varieties as
was customary in the Monferrato of
yesteryear and Pais, the wine Eleonora and
Donato obtain from this parcel, is awesome.

Mimosa 1991   🍇 ②
Eleonora Limonci has proved that it is possible
to obtain premium-quality Sauvignon Blanc on
the Monferrato hills. Mimosa is a perfect
expression of the variety, with classy, lingering,
flowery aromas, outstanding freshness and fine
structure. Full-bodied and well-rounded on the
palate.

Pais 1991   🍷 ①
From traditional Monferrato varieties, Barbera in
particular. A particularly fresh red wine with a
bright ruby-red color and soft, frank aromas.
Medium structure and just the right acidity to
ensure attractive drinkability, the wine's most
characteristic feature.

Palo Alto 1990   🍷🍷 ③
From a multifarious blend of Pinot Nero, Merlot,
Cabernet Sauvignon and Barbera, a wine with
very special personality and attractive aromas.
Soft and appealing on the palate with a
herbaceous note to the fore and good acidity. A
wine full of promise for the future.

Manora Collezione 1989   🍷 ③
A Barbera-based red wine with excellent
personality. Aged in barriques and matured in
the bottle for a year, thanks to which the
roughness and aggression of the wood mellow
out. The resulting wine is soft and well-rounded
with warm, intricate sensations both on the nose
and on the full, nicely-balanced palate. Has
quite a few years left ahead of it.

Le Colline

Via Massimo d'Azeglio, 6
Gattinara (Vc) 13045
Tel. (0163) 833000
Fax (0163) 835401

Bruno Cervi's Le Colline estate is located in
the commune of Gattinara with seven
hectares on the Monsecco estate producing
30,000 bottles, but he also has parcels in the
commune of Treiso, with 11 ha on the
Bordino estate turning out a further 50,000
bottles. Both vineyards are largely planted in
Nebbiolo. The Monsecco estate produces
Gattinara and Treiso, in the Langhe,
Barbaresco. Le Colline is famous for its
Gattinara, better known as Monsecco, the
name given to the wine by the previous
owner, Count Ravizza. Great store has
always been set by aging at Le Colline.
Indeed, the finest Monsecco vintages of the
past twenty years can be still found in the
cellars and continue to possess all the
qualities of this often underrated wine. Bruno
Cervi's hard work has brought its rewards
with Barbaresco and other Langhe wines for
the estate's wide range and variety has
assured it a strong market-share.

Gattinara 1986 DOC   🍷 ②
Gattinara is Nebbiolo grown in the Vercelli area.
This Monsecco version is very interesting with
warm aromas in a moderately complex bouquet.
Soft on the palate, the body is well-balanced
with medium structure.

Ghemme 1986 DOC   🍷 ②
A good Ghemme from Nebbiolo grapes grown in
the province of Novara. Moderately intense
color with stylish, lingering aromas. Well-
rounded and full-bodied on the palate with an
astringent finish due to the still-developing
tannins.

Poderi Aldo Conterno

Loc. Bussia, 48
Monforte d'Alba (Cn) 12065
Tel. (0173) 78150
Fax (0173) 787240

The Conternos come from a winemaking dynasty, a genuine star in the firmament of great Barolo producers. The head of the family, Aldo, has a marvelous personality and all the human warmth of the Langhe as well as being one of the masters of Italian enology. The estate's success and the excellence of its wines are in great part due to his foresight and intelligence. He sensed the potential of the Conterno vineyards in the Bussia region as early as 1968 and since then he has continued to invest in parcels located in the same cru to form the solid base on which the property now rests. Later on, his sons Franco and Stefano took charge of modernization, establishing the Conterno image and rationalizing cellar operations. They also convinced their father to experiment with barrique-aged Nebbiolo. Aldo is, however, quite firm when it comes to Barolo. He is not really interested in cutting-edge technology and remains of the opinion that suppleness and fragrance come from the vineyard, not the microchip.

Barbera d'Alba
Conca Tre Pile 1989 DOC 🍇🍇 ②
Usually Barberas and Dolcettos from Monforte tend to be "Barolized", but this Barbera d'Alba combines drinkability with excellent aromas and flavors. The fruit is sweet, ripe and velvet-smooth, backed up by good acidity. Lovely ruby red in the glass, not too intense, and a classy bouquet with distinct notes of cherry and mulberry.

Barolo
Bricco Bussia Vigna Cicala 1988 DOCG 🍇🍇 ③
It was far from easy to decide which of the two Conterno crus was going to be awarded the "Top Wine" accolade. Tasting produced very close results, which were superlative in both cases. In the end, the decision went in favor of the Colonnello (Colonel), a wine with the aging potential to slumber happily away in the cellar well into the next century. But what a great Barolo this is, too! Garnet ruby in the glass, with noble oak aromas, spice and a hint of tar. Imposing structure, great texture, lively notes of fruit rounded off by nicely-balanced tannins.

Il Favot 1988 🍇🍇 ②
The property's only barrique-aged wine, a Nebbiolo from the grapes of Bussia Soprana. Very deep garnet-ruby, and austere aromas with the oak dominant. Wonderful concentration on the palate, while the tannins are still green. Appealing notes of tar, liquorice and wild black cherry in the finish.

Barolo 🍇🍇🍇 ③
Bricco Bussia Vigna Colonnello 1988 DOCG
The Colonnello and Cicala vineyards insist they are part of the Bussia cru, almost entirely owned by the Conterno family, but according to the Atlas of Great Langhe Vineyards (Barolo Zone) published by Arcigola Slow Food, they really ought to be considered separate cru. There is a certain amount of confusion on the subject but Carlo Petrini, who edited the map of historic Barolo vineyards, is convinced that the Bussia cru should be considered a commune or village Denominazione. Individual vineyards, such as Colonnello, should therefore be recognized as crus. They all lie close to one another but there is a world of difference between them. We awarded this Barolo Vigna Colonnello the highest rating although the Cicala is certainly more attractive at the present time. This "Top Wine" is still a little closed, though after it is allowed to breathe, the aromas open out into violets and tar which linger on the palate seemingly for ever. The lively tannins back up magnificent concentration and a sensational liquorice finish. Will be at its best in ten years.

Giacomo Conterno

Loc. Ornati, 2
Monforte d'Alba (Cn) 12065
Tel. (0173) 78221
Fax (0173) 787190

Giovanni Conterno is rightly considered to be one of the most conventional growers in the Barolo area but while he opposes anything that might jeopardize the character of the wine, his cellar is absolutely functional and well-equipped with all that is needed for the production of superb-quality wines. All wines are aged in large oak barrels which seem to fill the cellar and an underground area is being prepared for bottle-aging, especially for Barolo. The international reputation of the Giacomo Conterno label is due in large measure to Monfortino, a Barolo reserve produced only when the vintage is exceptional. It is a wine of heady, triumphant aromas, superb texture and firm alcohol, perfect for laying down. But Giovanni Conterno's skill is also evident in other wines such as Dolcetto d'Alba, the very special Freisa, the Barolo and the delicious Barbera d'Alba.

Barbera d'Alba 1991 DOC
This Barbera, always one of the cellar's most successful products, comes from a vineyard on the Francia estate. The 1991 vintage is no exception to the rule and offers crisp, clean aromas with a faint herbaceous note. Excellent balance on the palate with a very definite personality. Piquant and perfectly delicious.

Dolcetto d'Alba 1991 DOC
A Dolcetto that confirms all Giovanni's winemaking skills, combining structure and drinking pleasure. The nose is clean and characteristic of the variety and the palate is attractive with a bitter, slightly astringent, dry finish.

Freisa delle Langhe 1991
Very characteristic aromas, with the typical spicy hints in a fresh, heady bouquet. Made from monovarietal Freisa, soft and uncomplicated on the palate. Easy-to-drink, with a slightly piquant finish of good length.

Barolo 1988 DOCG
Lovely deep color with hints of orange. The nose is still a little closed with tar coming through strongly, while the fruit is in the background. Attractive on the palate with a tangy entry and finish. Good structure and very lively, almost aggressive tannins. Will improve in the cellar.

Barolo
Riserva Monfortino 1985 DOCG
The term "legendary" for such an ephemeral product as a wine is perhaps excessive and certainly oft-abused but if any Italian wine ever deserved such a description, then that wine is Monfortino. Giovanni's father was already producing it and there are still some fabulous bottles from the 1930s to be found. This explains why it has kept the name under which it became famous even though the grapes are not from Monforte but from the Francia di Serralunga cru. It would be folly to tamper with a legend, a wine with extraordinary aging potential, the result of staggering concentration and winemaking techniques of exceptional audacity. In the finest vintages, part of the Nebbiolo juice for Barolo, after a normal 30-35 day maceration, goes into a separate, slow, submerged-cap fermentation at a temperature of not more than 27°C. It then passes into Slavonian oak barrels, where it is aged for at least seven years. Ruby with bluish, near-purple tints in the glass. The nose is still in the process of opening but already has notes of coffee, tobacco, leather and tar. Time will bring out additional fruit aromas. Awesomely imposing on the palate. The lively tannins are progressing in the right direction and the body is sumptuous with a lingering plum-and-liquorice finish. Come back in the year 2,000.

Conterno-Fantino

Reg. Fracchia, 5
Monforte d'Alba (Cn) 12065
Tel/Fax (0173) 78204

Wine-making in the Langhe is going through a very active, busy period at the moment, with a revolution in cellar techniques under way. The Conterno-Fantino property is one of the foremost examples of this extraordinary vitality and recent vintages confirm this impression. The best results have been obtained with Barolo, particularly Sorì Ginestra, its aromas varying from vintage to vintage but always stylish and elegant. With its firm but unaggressive body and no excess tannin or alcohol, it is ready to drink when it goes on the market. Also much appreciated Monprà, from Barbera and Nebbiolo grapes aged in barriques. Improvement from year to year is tangible with a really outstanding result in 1989, when the oak integrated perfectly with the characteristics of the varieties. Dolcetto d'Alba, Freisa and Barbera d'Alba continue to be produced in a recently acquired cellar and experiments with new grape types have been announced.

Barbera d'Alba Vignota 1990 DOC 🍷 ①
Typical of the variety with its deep garnet-red color and frank, almost rustic, aroma barely mellowed by the oak. Powerful yet soft on the palate with the acidity to age well.

Monprà 1989 🍷🍷 ③
From Nebbiolo and Barbera grapes fermented in barriques. Monprà has intense aromas with a note of smoky oak. Admirably well-rounded structure underpinned by Barbera's acidity. A wine that successfully combines elegance and drinkability.

Barolo Sorì Ginestra 1988 DOCG 🍷🍷 ③
From one of the finest crus in Monforte. Still young and closed but already offering distinctively intense, complex aromas with a note of coffee. Well-balanced strength on the palate. Very drinkable with a promising future.

Barolo Vigna del Gris 1988 DOCG 🍷 ③
Slight lack of balance on the nose, but with plenty of body and a deep color. Tannin still dominates the palate although the wine is well developed.

Luigi Coppo & Figli

Via G.B. Giuliani, 53
Canelli (At) 14053
Tel. (0141) 823146
Fax (0141) 823563

It was far from easy to establish a cellar specializing in small quantities of high-priced noble red wines and serious whites in Canelli, one of the major growing areas for spumantes. The Coppo brothers, Roberto, Piero, Paolo and Gianni, did it. In just a few years, they transformed the estate, founded in 1892, concentrating on quality and reinterpreting some unjustly underrated wines, such as Freisa and Brachetto d'Acqui. They explored avenues that were new for the area, such as technical and commercial cellar management contracts. They have such a contract for the Galleria di Vallarone estate, with its Grignolino, Chardonnay, Sauvignon and Cabernet Sauvignon and the Adriano Vacca's Cascina del Pino, where the Coppos act as managers and marketing consultants for the excellent Dolcetto d'Alba as well as for the Gavi La Rocca. This consultancy work goes hand in hand with restructuring at the Coppo cellar, which has moved into new premises, modernizing its equipment and acquired new properties.

Monteriolo Chardonnay 1990 🍾 ③
Making this wine is very important for the Coppo brothers. Obtained from selected grapes grown in long-established vineyards with very low yields, fermented and aged in barriques and matured for a year in the bottle. The results are remarkable, with elegant aromas of banana and vanilla in a classy, lingering bouquet. Tempting on the palate, with a tangy, fresh finish.

Spumante Classico 🍾 ③
Riserva Coppo 1987
Barrique fermentation gives this spumante great complexity together with a slightly intrusive note of wood on entry. The nose then opens out into noble aromas of crusty bread. The palate is astringent with medium structure. An aristocratic wine.

Mondaccione 🍷🍷 ③
Freisa di Valdivilla 1990
Freisa grapes from the long-established vineyards of Valdivilla are fermented slowly before the wine is aged for 14 months in barriques. The oak aromas do not completely mask the typical strawberry and redcurrant notes in a stupendous bouquet. Good depth and structure, with plenty of acidity and extract.

Barbera d'Asti 🍷🍷 ③
Pomorosso 1989 DOC
Obtained from monovarietal Barbera vinified after long maceration on the skins with a long, slow fermentation. Lovely garnet red in the glass, with typical intense aromas ennobled by the oak and broad structure. Zesty acidity brings the wine to life.

Corino

Fraz. Annunziata, 24
La Morra (Cn) 12064
Tel. (0173) 50715
Fax (0173) 50219

The hallmark of this company is simplicity.
Even after all the praise showered on it from
all around the world, the Corinos continue
modestly and quietly to go about their
exacting self-appointed task of producing
wine, aided only by their own ability and the
helpful advice of friends and other producers
in the area. But simplicity does not
necessarily mean conservatism and over the
last years, various innovations have been
made both in the vineyard and in the cellar.
Selection of the grapes has been made more
severe, entailing a considerable reduction in
yields per hectare, while in the cellars the use
of French barriques has led to better-
balanced and more velvety flavors,
particularly appreciable in the Barbera Vigna
Pozzo and the Barolo. The Corino Barbera
Vigna Pozzo has substantial structure and
acquires particular elegance from the hints of
sweet, new wood while the Barolo has a very
well-balanced and unaggressive body, with
clean aromas reminiscent of leather and
tobacco. The Dolcetto d'Alba is also worthy
of mention as is the Nebbiolo delle Langhe
and the traditional Barbera d'Alba Vigna
Giachini.

Dolcetto d'Alba ♥ ①
Vigna Giachini 1991 DOC
A Dolcetto whose heady aromas have marked
spicy overtones. Good texture on the palate.
Tangy, with a typically bitter finish. A wine that
exalts both the skill of the winemaker and the
potential of the cru.

Barbera d'Alba ♥♥ ②
Vigna Pozzo 1989 DOC
Deep garnet red in the glass, with elegant
aromas of toasty oak well-integrated into the
variety's characteristic nose. Full-bodied, warm
and utterly satisfying. Will be at its best in a year
or two's time when the acidity has softened a
little.

Barolo Vigna Giachini ♥♥ ③
1988 DOCG
A powerfully structured classic Barolo. Still
perfectly fresh and young, as the note of acidity
indicates, with tannins prominent and a
somewhat closed nose. A wine with a great
character and personality, with superb aging
potential.

Correggia

Via Santo Stefano Roero, 124
Canale (Cn) 12043
Tel/Fax (0173) 978009

Matteo Correggia's fledgling estate
discovered its true identity thanks to the
traditional Roero wines reinterpreted in a
thoroughly modern, functional approach.
Arneis, Barbera, Nebbiolo and the very rare
Brachetto are used and the results have
been impressive. The cellar is equipped with
stainless-steel vats for temperature-
controlled fermentation while aging is in
traditional wooden barrels as well as
barriques, which are used only for red wines.
One of the best products is Roero, obtained
from Nebbiolo grapes without the addition of
the percentage of white grapes allowed by
the DOC regulations. The resulting wine is a
ruby red of moderate intensity, with clean
aromas which are fresher and more flowery
than the Langhe Nebbiolo and unassertive
tannins and body. Another well-known wine
is Brachetto, both in the traditional version
and in the version made from late-harvest
grapes sun-dried until Christmas, with
subsequent racking into small barrels. A new
wine, ideal for chocolate-based sweets.

Brachetto delle Langhe ♥ ①
Bric Marun 1991
In the Roero area, it has always been the
custom to plant a few rows of Brachetto to make
a dessert wine. Correggia has reintroduced this
custom to produce a wine with structure,
delicate aromas of roses and wild flowers, a
sweet entry and a long almond finish.

Roero Bricco Anime 1991 DOC ♥ ①
A Roero made in the manner of the great
Langhe reds, vinifying for structure and color,
without the slightly anemic character of Roero
Nebbiolos. Bricco Anime has a superb violet
color and rich, intoxicating aromas. Mellow and
rounded on the palate, with tannins in evidence
but unobtrusively so.

Barbera d'Alba
Bric Marun 1990 DOC
Matteo Correggia surprised us with this Roero
Barbera. Obtained from rigorously selected
grapes and then fermented in small oak barrels
to stupendous effect. Intense aromas, with
discreet oak not overpowering the fruit. The
palate is already well-integrated, the body
generous, warm and mouthfilling.

Carlo Deltetto

Corso Alba, 43
Canale d'Alba (Cn) 12043
Tel. (0173) 979383
Fax (0173) 95710

When young Antonio took over the Deltetto company, he stood everything on its head. He transformed a trading company selling a vast range of mostly bought-in wines into a quality cellar concentrating on Roero products. The mainstay is naturally white Roero Arneis, in two versions: the S. Michele cru, a blend fermented and aged 50% in barriques and 50% in stainless-steel vats; and the normal version. The other white Roero produced, La Favorita (20,000 bottles) is also worthy of mention as is the stunning limited production of oak-aged Roero from Nebbiolo grapes for its wealth of extract and elegance. Antonio concentrated his efforts on cellar equipment at first: rotating containers for cold-maceration, stainless-steel vats and electronic temperature control equipment. Now he has turned his attention to the cellar's image and visitor hospitality A delightful tasting room has already been created among the barriques in the new underground cellars with their attractive brick-faced vaulted reception rooms.

Roero Arneis San Michele 1991 DOC 🍷 ①
Obtained with a 12-hour cold-maceration of destemmed grapes. After soft-pressing, part of the free-run juice goes for barrique-fermentation while the remainder ferments in stainless-steel vats. The aim was to give structure to the wine and this has been successfully achieved. Perhaps some of the liveliness of the aromas, where camomile prevails, was lost in the process.

Bric Tupin 1990 🍷 ②
Carlo Deltetto has created a minor masterpiece with this sweet dessert wine obtained from Arneis. He has managed to impart elegance, structure and depth to a wine usually associated with liveliness and lightness. The quince flavor is surprisingly crisp while the finish is long and lingering.

Roero 🍷🍷 ②
Madonna dei Boschi 90 DOC
An exciting red wine from a white-wine cellar. Prominent but not obtrusive tannins and noble, fresh aromas of cherry and Morello cherry. Powerful on the palate with well-defined liquorice, while maintaining a splendid liveliness.

Poderi Luigi Einaudi

Viale Rimembranza, 1
Dogliani (Cn) 12063
Tel. (0173) 70321
Fax (0173) 70191

Established at the turn of the century by Luigi Einaudi, first president of the Italian Republic, who was born in Dogliani, the Einaudi estate formed part of an economic policy based on agriculture at a time of crisis for viticulture. Einaudi wrote ironically that he had often heard of a crisis in winegrowing and that "he had always lost money making bad wine, never... making good wine." Utterly convinced of the truth of this dictum, Einaudi added hectare to hectare, buying in the Dogliani area as well as in Barolo-growing zones. Today the Poderi Luigi Einaudi have a total of 100 ha, 25 under vine. Wine technician Lorenzo Raimondo runs the estate and has the exacting task of managing a cellar that has always been a bench-mark in the Dogliani area. At present the property is undergoing a gradual transformation and Paola Einaudi, who took her father Roberto's place at the head of the estate is committed to investment. A new cellar is being built next to the Tecc farmhouse, stainless-steel vats will partly replace wood and production is receiving more attention. The results are now being seen.

Dolcetto di Dogliani 🍷 ①
Vigna Tecc 1991 DOC
Traditional methods such as aging in large oak casks are still used for this top-of-the-range cru. The resulting wine is black, full-bodied and a little rustic on the nose but a perfect expression of Dolcetto from this Denominazione.

Barolo Costa Grimaldi 1988 DOCG 🍷 ②
From a vineyard in the commune of Barolo owned by the estate comes this old-fashioned wine, with all the virtues and vices of the past. The body with its powerful extract and tannins produces few rough edges but also guarantees exceptional aging potential.

Luigi Ferrando e figlio

Corso Cavour, 9
Ivrea (To) 10015
Tel/Fax (0125) 422383

Luigi Ferrando, wine producer and owner of a very well-stocked wine merchant's, is one of the most enthusiastic promoters of the Canavese viticultural area. He produces the full range of Canavese DOC wines, including Carema from Nebbiolo grapes grown at Carema, Erbaluce di Caluso and the Passito dessert wine from the same variety. One of Ferrando's great merits is the study of new methods of vinification with the help of the experience and advice of Gaspare Buscemi, an enologist from Friuli. Luigi has worked to reestablish a number of small growers who would otherwise have been doomed to disappear and never to achieve the recognition they deserved. That is how Erbaluce Colombaio, from a vineyard belonging to Dr. Pacchié, Boratto's Passito di Caluso and finally, since only a few years ago, Villa Montodo from grapes grown in the splendid Biglia vineyards, all came to be produced. Luigi does not merely attend to the marketing of these products. He supervises work in the vineyards personally as well as the vintage and wine-making into the bargain. The Carema, which in some years reaches peaks of quality comparable to much more widely known wines obtained from the same grape type is particularly outstanding.

Erbaluce di Caluso   🍇 ①
Vigneto Cariola 1991 DOC
The straw-yellow color with pinkish tints might convey an impression of advanced oxidation, but this is actually a very fresh wine, with sweet aromas of caramel and stewed fruit. Good acidity on the palate, clean fruit and a rich, attractive body. The finish has pineapple and cedar wood.

Solativo 1989   🍇 ③
From late-harvest Erbaluce, Ferrando produces around 3,000 bottles of Solatio. This 1989 vintage is a superb golden yellow with intense, clean aromas of exotic fruit and lilies. Generous, mouthfilling sweetness on the palate with hints of honey. Slightly lacking in acidity.

Carema etichetta bianca 1986 DOC   🍷 ①
Characteristic color of Nebbiolo aged in northern Piemonte, brick-red with streaks of orange. A young, powerful wine with full aromas of clove, cinnamon and coffee. Prominent green tannins and dense extract make this a wine to lay down.

Carema etichetta nera 1985 DOC 🍷🍷 ②
The famous "black label" Carema selection with its breath-takingly intense, bright garnet-red tinted with orange. Well-developed lingering aromas, less spicy than the "etichetta bianca", with tar in the background. Still tannic.

Tenimenti Fontanafredda

Via Alba, 15
Serralunga d'Alba (Cn) 12050
Tel. (0173) 613161
Fax (0173) 613451

When visiting the Langhe, you cannot help but notice a number of lovely farmhouses painted with lengthwise stripes - Fontanafredda estate properties. Scattered over various communes, Serralunga, Diano d'Alba and Barolo, they stand out both for the picturesque color of their buildings and for their well-tended vineyards. All this is a result of substantial investment by the Monte dei Paschi di Siena bank, which bought the properties in 1931 and did everything possible to transform them into the market leaders of Italian wine-making. The previous history of the Tenimenti Fontanafredda is quite well-known. The main villa, today perfectly restored and used for guest accommodation, was donated by king Vittorio Emanuele II to his morganatic wife Rosa of Mirafiori, the famous "Bela Rosin," or "fair Rosy." Later, their illegitimate son, count Emanuele Guerrieri, established the present-day cellar near the villa. After the change of ownership, for many years at Fontanafredda more attention was given to commercial expansion (6,500,000 bottles a year produced) than to quality, which is now the first priority of the new owners.

Asti Spumante DOC   🍇 ①
This spumante is made with slow fermentation at a controlled temperature of 12°. The aromas are satisfying and sweet but not cloying. Lively body without excessive carbon. Fresh with lingering fruity finish and 6° alcohol.

Metodo Classico Brut Gattinera 1986 🍇 ③
Gattinera is an excellent cru for Nebbiolo for Barolo. With this in mind, it is easy to imagine the structure of the Pinot Nero used for this wine. Powerful acidity and extract with abundant mousse that allows the flavor to emerge. Attractive, lingering aroma (the bottle we tasted was degorged on 21st January 1992).

Barolo   🍷🍷🍷 ③
Vigna La Rosa 1985 DOCG
Separate vinification for each vineyard, already adopted in 1982, was employed for another great vintage, 1985. The results are excellent. The La Rosa cru, about seven hectares at Serralunga, offers superbly elegant aromas, with dried roses, liquorice and tar all evident. The dry, mouthfilling palate is still a little tannic.

Barolo   🍷🍷 ③
Vigna Gattinera 1985 DOCG
Another great Barolo, from four and a half south-facing hectares at Serralunga d'Alba. The body is more velvety in comparison with the La Rosa and the aromas are less intense but generous and extremely elegant. More open than the La Rosa but still with quite a few years to go.

Gaja

Via Torino, 36/a
Barbaresco (Cn) 12050
Tel. (0173) 635158
Fax (0173) 635256

Angelo Gaja is well aware of how important the media can be nowadays when you want to reach the top end of the market, now matter what product you are selling. He also knows how to add value to everything that leaves his company, not just the wines but also the other products marketed by Gaja Distribuzione - glasses, carafes and plates for exclusive restaurants as well as mini refrigerators, corkscrews, spirits and foreign wines. This obsession with image only makes sense if we take into account the consistently high quality of the wines Gaja produces. Angelo never forgets that the heart of the Gaja company is its splendid vineyards - 81 ha in the finest Barbaresco and Barolo zones, with 3,500 Guyot-pruned vines per hectare tended as carefully as if they were planted in a garden. To the vineyards, we can add low yields, superb wine-making techniques and painstaking selection of wood for the barriques, seasoned on-site and then sent to France for further processing. The 250,000 bottles a year produced by the Gaja estate, all or nearly all of them perfect, are the best proof there could be of Angel Gaja's management skills.

Chardonnay Gaia & Rey 1990   🍇🍇 ④
This superb monovarietal Chardonnay from a vineyard in Treiso can stand comparison with the best whites in the world. Elegant aromas with a gentle hint of vanilla accompany the magnificently long structure with its powerful extract. Stunningly drinkable.

Barbera d'Alba   🍷🍷 ③
Vignarey 1989 DOC
An absolutely extraordinary Barbera. Deep ruby red shading into garnet, intense nose with violet and berry notes and remarkably full texture. The acidity and extract are perfectly balanced.

Darmagi 1988   🍷🍷 ④
Monovarietal Cabernet from the Barbaresco hills. Achieved worldwide success thanks to the fantastic concentration of fruit, consistent elegance and a particularly stylish bouquet, intense, with splendidly prominent red berries.

Barbaresco Sorì Tildin   🍷🍷 ④
1988 DOCG
This 1988 is at the very top of its cru. Ruby-red in the glass, complex, generous aromas of rose, autumn leaves and the crisp vanilla of the wood. Powerful sinew and concentration as well as marvelous length. Delicious now but with a long way to go.

Barbaresco   🍷🍷🍷 ④
Sorì San Lorenzo 1988 DOCG
As is often the case, it was not easy to decide which of Gaja's wines should receive the maximum accolade. The delightful fruit of Sorì Tildin won us over, as did the imposing structure of the Darmagi but, in the end, San Lorenzo pipped the others at the post. Released onto the market a few months after the other two Sorìs from Gaja but obtained with the same vinification process as all the estate's Barbarescos - long maceration on the skins, the malolactic immediately after alcoholic fermentation and the sudden lowering of the temperature to stabilize the wine. Then eight months in barriques before blended in oak barrels, where the wine remains for eight to ten months, sometimes more, as in the case of this San Lorenzo. Perhaps the fruit is a shade less super-ripe than that of the Tildin but this is a wine with the nobility of a bottle from a great château. Ruby red, with a bouquet that still has living, noble hints of oak which do not mask the autumn leaves and violet. Incredibly rich texture on the palate with sinew, strength and dryness although it is already a delightful glass. A cut above the rest.

F.lli Gancia & C.

Corso Libertà, 16
Canelli (At) 14053
Tel. (0141) 8301
Fax (0141) 835341

Gancia is the leading producer of the Canelli spumante industry, a force that has helped to shape the economy, social structure and rural topography of the entire area. It was Carlo Gancia, founder of the company in the early nineteenth century, who created Asti Spumante, a fun-to-drink dessert wine obtained from Moscato grapes which went on to conquer the markets of the world. Over the years, Gancia grew to become the impressive industrial concern that it is today, with buildings spread over 60,000 sq.m. of land and an annual production of around 15 million bottles. The current owner, Vittorio Vallarino Gancia, is active and innovative, striving to upgrade the image and name of the company through product diversification. The Charmat method and méthode champenoise wines are among the results, as also are some classic Piemontese reds obtained from superior varieties.

Camillo Gancia 1990   ℰ ②
From Moscato grapes grown on the hills of Canelli and vinified after the fashion of the Gancia company's founder after whom it is named. A sweet vintage spumante with lovely straw-yellow color and stylish, long-lasting mousse. The aromas have depth and varietal character while the flavor is full and long.

Vintage dei Gancia 1988   ℰ ③
One of the new products of the historic Gancia cellar. A méthode champenoise spumante from barrique-fermented Chardonnay grapes. Well-defined oak aromas, intense straw-yellow color and good perlage. Palate of medium depth with wood still to the fore.

Gastaldi

Borgata Albesani, 20
Neive (Cn) 12057
Tel. (0173) 677400

This young estate has made a name for itself with its premium-quality Dolcetto d'Alba. The grapes come from Rodello d'Alba, an area traditionally well-suited to the variety. It is an extremely interesting wine with uncommon strength and great depth of flavor combined with unusual elegance for a Dolcetto. The color is deep ruby red with violet tints, the aromas have breadth and depth with well-integrated notes of fresh fruit. On the palate, great body and good alcohol soften the tannic aggressiveness typical of the variety. Bernardino Gastaldi has almost finished restructuring the new cellars where he intends to produce and age Barbaresco, as he owns parcels in good locations. He has obtained fine results from two whites, Chardonnay and Sauvignon, aged exclusively in steel vats. Both are wines with huge structure, which comes from rigorous vineyard selection, and are characterized by their alcohol content and length of flavor and aroma.

Sauvignon 1990   ℰ ③
The very modest production (about 1,000 bottles) of this wine is based on maximum extract and the opulent fruit of super-ripe grapes. Generous aromas of good depth with marked varietal notes. Complex on the palate, with residual sugars that round the wine out and render it even more attractive.

Dolcetto d'Alba
Moriolo 1990 DOC
Gastaldi obtains this wine from Rodello, one of the top Dolcetto zones. Impressive, deep violet-red, with frank, intense aromas and a herbaceous note from the variety which is mellowed by mulberry and plums. Stupendously drinkable, with great texture and lingering liquorice and tannins.

Bruno Giacosa

Via XX Settembre, 52
Neive (Cn) 12057
Tel. (0173) 67027
Fax (0173) 677477

Bruno Giacosa is without doubt one of Italy's greatest wine-makers, with an international record that has seen his wines triumphant at the most exclusive blind tastings. The range of Giacosa wines is large and embraces nearly everything the viticulture of the Langhe has to offer. The most outstanding wines have always been Barolo and Barbaresco, from selected vineyards with good soil and sunlight looked after by expert growers. We must mention first the breadth and elegance of the Barolo Vigna Rionda, produced -like the great Barbaresco Santo Stefano- only during the best vintage years and exported all over the world. Two other excellent locations produce Barolo Rocche di Castiglione Falletto and Barbaresco Gallina di Neive , both exceptionally good. In recent years, Bruno Giacosa has also turned his hand to the production of white wines, with results once again worthy of his skill. The Roero Arneis is usually among the most successful and the vintage spumante, named after the cellarmaster, is one of Italy's top sparkling wines.

Bruno Giacosa Extra Brut 1988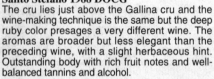
A spumante obtained from Oltrepò Pinot Nero grapes. Lovely straw-yellow, with dense, lingering perlage of medium fineness. Intense aromas of crusty bread, almond and "petits fours." Vigorous on the palate, fruity with a pleasantly bitter finish.

Barbaresco
Gallina di Neive 1988 DOCG
The finesse of this wine hides the fact that it has undergone a typical Giacosa long submerged-cap maceration. The color is bright ruby and the nose intense, with lingering tar and splendid violet. Elegant on the palate, with well-defined lively fruit, only moderately concentrated but very attractive nonetheless. Long finish with good sinew, piquant and still fresh.

Barbaresco
Santo Stefano 1988 DOCG
The cru lies just above the Gallina cru and the wine-making technique is the same but the deep ruby color presages a very different wine. The aromas are broader but less elegant than the preceding wine, with a slight herbaceous hint. Outstanding body with rich fruit notes and well-balanced tannins and alcohol.

Barolo
Le Rocche di Castiglion Falletto 1987
Not a great year, but this is certainly a great interpretation of the cru. Ruby with faint flecks of orange and a lively nose of tar and berries. The powerful alcohol on the palate is balanced by good fruit and lively, lingering tannins.

Giovanni Battista Gillardi

Cascina Corsaletto
Farigliano (Cn) 12060
Tel. (0173) 76306
Fax (0173) 76813

The Gillardis stand out among producers of Dolcetto di Dogliani for a particularly stylish and soft wine, which still preserves the good structure typical of the area. The cellar has recently undergone restructuring and modernization, not so much to increase output as to allow the vinification and storage of the wines in a more modern and functional environment. Only Dolcetto grapes from two estate vineyards located on a steep hillside with excellent sunlight are vinified in the cellar. About 3,000 bottles of the Dolcetto di Dogliani Cursalet are produced. It is a wine with fresh, full aromas, while the typical varietal tannins are delicate on the palate. The Dolcetto di Dogliani Vigna Maestra is normally fuller and more robust with somewhat closed but stylish aromas. About 15,000 bottles a year are produced. The Gillardi family boasts great viticultural and wine-making skills which they have brought to the creation of a new product, made from Syrah and Cabernet. A wine which is sure to attract attention.

Dolcetto di Dogliani
Vigneto Maestra 1991 DOC
A very typical Dolcetto di Dogliani. Fruity aromas, with subtle herbaceous notes. Fresh on the palate, well-balanced and easy to drink.

Dolcetto di Dogliani
Cursalet 1991 DOC
A red with good personality, fresh full aromas and a certain elegance. Full-bodied on the palate, well-balanced with satisfying body and the pleasant characteristic bitterish finish.

Elio Grasso

Via Garibaldi, 17
Monforte d'Alba (Cn) 12064
Tel/Fax (0173) 78491

Elio Grasso decided to start making wine when he was around forty, leaving his bank job to do so. Helped by his wife Marina, he took over management of the family property, with its parcels in good locations in the Monforte area, Gavarini and Ginestra, and its name for structured wines from the typical varieties of the Langhe region - Dolcetto, Barbera and, of course, Nebbiolo for Barolo. In addition, thanks to recent plantings, the estate will soon be able to boast a barrique-aged Chardonnay. Barriques are also used by Elio, who is assisted by wine technician Piero Ballario, to age the powerful, elegant Barbera d'Alba Martina. The estate's leading product naturally Barolo, in two crus, the Casa Maté and the Runcot, while the pleasant Nebbiolo Gavarini and Dolcetto d'Alba complete the range of a cellar which exploits the natural advantages of its vineyards to the full.

Dolcetto d'Alba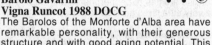
Gavarini Vigna dei Grassi 1991 DOC
A Dolcetto with unusually good structure and intense color, still a little rough on the nose. On the palate, all the potential comes through in the richness of extract. Alcohol and acidity are well-defined and nicely balanced.

Vigna Martina 1989
A table wine from barrique-aged Barbera grapes, this Vigna Martina needs a few moments to breathe before it fully expresses its stylish aromas, where varietal notes are well-integrated with the wood. Soft and well-balanced on the palate, although perhaps lacking in breadth.

Barolo Gavarini
Vigna Runcot 1988 DOCG
The Barolos of the Monforte d'Alba area have remarkable personality, with their generous structure and with good aging potential. This Runcot by Elio Grasso is representative both in its spicy aromas on the nose and on the palate, where tannins and alcohol have still to integrate fully.

Barolo Ginestra
Vigna Casa Maté 1988 DOCG
Perhaps not yet as open as its sister wine, this Casa Maté from the famous Ginestra cru seems to have even more promise. Full texture and flavor characterized by a nice bitterish tannic finish, with mouthfilling aromas and a warm personality.

Silvio Grasso

Fraz. Annunziata, cascina Luciani
La Morra (Cn) 12064
Tel. (0173) 50322
Fax c/o Consorzio (0173) 361380

The passion for Barolo which characterizes the Grasso family is proverbial. It can be best appreciated by tasting their wine and following the evolution of this paragon of longevity. Material evidence of the Grasso obsession can be found in the old bottles in their cellars, still affording great satisfaction to lovers of mature Barolo. Not even the great progress made by the cellar in recent years in the field of technology have changed Grasso's wines, which continue to express all their potency and tannins. These are wines that will live for ever. Today, Silvio has his sons Alessio and Giuseppe working with him but this has not led to a more accommodating approach. Instead, the Grassos have chosen to bottle all of their output and discontinue the policy of selling some unbottled in order to open up new markets. One Barolo with all the above characteristics is Bricco Luciani, a strong, decisive wine which combines typical Barolo intensity with a surprising breadth of aromas. Grasso's Dolcetto d'Alba is sharp and fresh, in no way resembling a Barolo. Stylish fruit combines with a body of considerable length.

Barbera d'Alba Fontanile 1989 DOC
This Barbera is aged in small oak barrels and sold after a period of maturation in the bottle. Deep garnet red and elegant, complex aromas with ripe fruit notes and a prominent hint of alcohol. Powerful acidity and extract on the palate, with a lingering finish and a promising future.

Barolo Bricco Luciani 1988 DOCG
Silvio Grasso obtained this Barolo with its slightly closed nose from one of his La Morra vineyards. On the palate, it reveals good texture, with the acidity and tannins to guarantee aging potential. Perhaps a little "rustic," but only in the positive sense of the term.

Liedholm

Villa Boemia
Cuccaro Monferrato (Al) 15040
Tel/Fax (0131) 771916

Carlo Liedholm, son of the famous soccer player Niels Liedholm who bought this beautiful estate at Cuccaro in 1973, has been working here full time since 1985. He does so with genuine managerial ability but without arrogance. Carlo believes in reasonable prices, honest products, and word-of-mouth marketing. He abhors aggressive advertising and novelty for novelty's sake. The Liedholm range of products reflects this philosophy with an extract-rich Grignolino from the Casalese area, perhaps lacking in aromas but solid and impressive, a vigorous Barbera, softer, chewier and easier to drink than Barbera d'Asti, and a Rosso della Boemia, the result of a more or less random blend of the grapes that were being grown in the vineyards when the Liedholms bought the company. It is a powerful, structured wine with good aging potential but free of excess wood and made without recourse to technological trickery. Much of the credit must go to Donato Lanati, who equipped the cellar with state-of-the-art equipment, brilliantly adapted to the young owner's ultra-relaxed, down-to-earth approach.

Grignolino del Monferrato Casalese 1991 DOC   🍷 ①
Well-defined herbaceous varietal nose opening out into flowery notes. Characterized by light astringency on the palate, making this a wine to serve with traditional Monferrato appetizers.

Rosso della Boemia 1988   🍷🍷 ③
80% Barbera and Nebbiolo-based with the addition of Pinot Nero, Cabernet Franc and Grignolino. An important barrique-aged red with complex aromas including liquorice and tobacco. Good breadth on the palate, mouthfilling and warm with remarkable structure.

Luja

Cascina Rosso, reg. Ronconuovo
Loazzolo (At) 14050
Tel. (0141) 831596
Fax (0141) 831595

Giancarlo Scaglione is a man who loves the land, the rugged, lonely Langhe of Asti. Poor yet fascinating borderland, there is little cultivable soil and viticulture is often a difficult or even almost foolish enterprise. Giancarlo, however, has achieved this goal. He replanted a few Moscato vines and revived the tradition of Passito with new technology, and adapting it to today's tastes. Thanks to Giancarlo's spirit of initiative, Loazzolo, the village where the cellar is located, was able to obtain a Denominazione di Origine Controllata, the smallest in Italy and the most severely disciplined, for the production of a wine from late-harvested Moscato grapes fermented in barriques, which immediately caught the imagination of lovers of dessert wines and, though this is perhaps stretching a point, was compared to the legendary Sauternes. Scaglione used a similar technique with Brachetto grapes -another traditional local variety- adding the Forteto Pian dei Sogni to the Forteto della Luja he was already producing. The latest novelty is the elegant red Le Grive, from a recently successful experiment in which Barbera and Pinot Nero grapes were blended.

Forteto della Luja 1989   🍷🍷🍷 ④
From botrytized or sun-dried grapes, aged for at least 18 months in small barrels then matured for a further year in the bottle. A vintage with fresh mint and acacia-wood aromas and a dense, lingering palate which does not cloy.

Le Grive 1990   🍷🍷 ③
From 80% Barbera and 20% Pinot Nero. Brief aging in barriques lends elegance, balance and drinkability to the piquant, full-bodied structure. Stylish aromas of pepper, herbs and berries on a very attractive vanillaed background.

Forteto Pian dei Sogni 1989   🍷 ③
Brachetto wine has recently enjoyed something of a resurgence in popularity. This Pian dei Sogni, from monovarietal sun-dried Brachetto has the typical green aroma of geraniums mellowed by two years in barriques. Aromatic and seductive on the palate, with good length.

CULTIVATING QUALITY

THE QUEST FOR QUALITY IN PIEDMONT INVOLVES CLOSE COOPERATION BETWEEN THE REGIONAL GOVERNMENT, GROWERS ASSOCIATIONS, WINE CONSORTIUMS, PROFESSIONAL ORGANIZATIONS, AND RESEARCH INSTITUTES.

The charm of a land is at times the magic of a natural landscape molded by the hands of man. Agriculture in Piedmont is this and more.

It is rolling hills between austere mountain ranges and spacious plains that spread to the southeast like an open sea.

Piedmont is also a region of contrasts. But thanks to the hard work of generations of farmers it has many agricultural riches. Learning about the foods a land creates means discovering its innermost secrets. Secrets that reveal its true nature.

And so it is with the wines of Piedmont. Renowned throughout the world, as are many other of its products such as vegetables and fruit; cheese, white truffles, and rice – all of them perfect with the local wines.

Quality products and a long-standing gastronomic tradition are just two of many reasons to come and visit Piedmont. And you'll leave with lasting memories of its landscape and the delightful flavors born there.

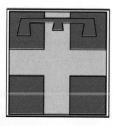

REGIONE PIEMONTE

ASSESSORATO AGRICOLTURA E FORESTE

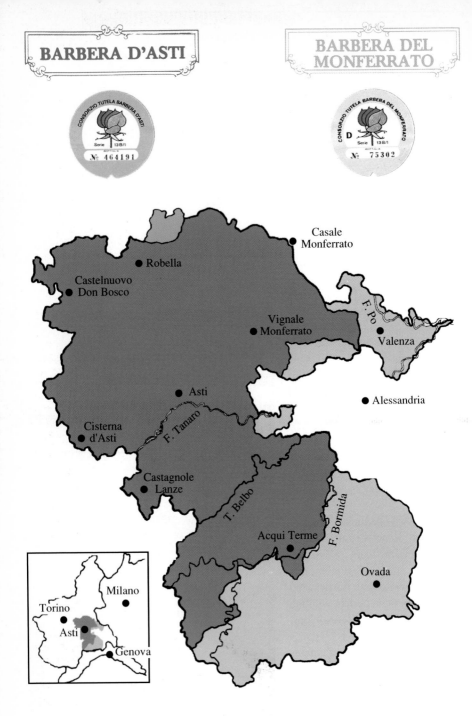

BARBERA D'ASTI

BARBERA DEL MONFERRATO

Barbera is the most widely grown grape variety around the town of Asti and in the Monferrato hills. It can be full-bodied and rustic, or elegant with a long aging potential. The Asti vineyards cross and mingle with those of the Monferrato. In reality, the Monferrato and Asti are virtually synonymous. But there are two distinct geographical denominations. A single grape variety and two DOC wines from the same area: Barbera del Monferrato and Barbera d'Asti.

Consorzio di Tutela Barbera d'Asti e del Monferrato
Galleria Argenta, 2 - 14100 Asti, Telephone and Fax +39/141/598984

Malvirà

Via S. Stefano Roero, 56
Canale (Cn) 12043
Tel. (0173) 978057
Fax (0173) 978145

The Malvirà estate is owned by the Damonte brothers who have for many years been an object lesson in how to promote the wines of Roero. The zone took center stage when the "Arneis phenomenon" took off and the variety's success saw a huge increase in the vines planted and the number of producers involved, with all the deleterious effects on quality standards and prices that entailed. Malvirà was the first company to make a serious attempt to produce the traditional wines of Roero, including the Roero Arneis, Favorita, another white which has been reintroduced to the market, and Roero, from Nebbiolo grapes with a small proportion of Arneis. Renesio, Saglietto and Trinità are the three separately vinified crus of the main Malvirà wine, which the Damontes also make in a base version. Their commitment to the production of red wines is also apparent with, as in addition to Roero, the barrique-aged San Guglielmo, a blend of Barbera, Bonarda, Nebbiolo and Freisa.

Roero Arneis Renesio 1991 DOC   ♈ ①
One of the crus vinified separately by the Damonte brothers. A very successful white, a lovely straw-yellow, with classy, lingering aromas. Well-rounded on the palate with good acidity in the finish.

Roero Arneis Saglietto 1991 DOC   ♈ ①
Saglietto stands out from the other two Arneis wines produced by Malvirà as it comes from a partly barrique-aged blend. Still a little closed on the nose but with good texture on the palate. Well-balanced, with the components already nicely integrated.

Roero Superiore Trinità 1990 DOC   ♈ ①
Obtained from Nebbiolo grapes grown in the DOC zone, this wine is described as "superiore" because it is aged for a year before being released onto the market. Good structure, clean, fruity aromas and fresh on the palate with slight tannic astringency and a good, faintly bitter, finish.

Poderi Marcarini

Piazza Martiri, 2
La Morra (Cn) 12064
Tel/Fax (0173) 50222

The Marcarini estate is justly famous for its Barolo, but all products with the Marcarini label are synonymous with premium quality. Poderi Marcarini is an estate with solid traditions and superb soil, where wine-making is a matter for the heart as well as the head. Production is perfectly organized both overall and in the cellars reserved for individual processes, from traditional aging in oak barrels to bottling and storing. The Barolo comes from several outstanding locations which give their names to the different selections: Barolo Brunate, Barolo La Serra, Barolo Brunate Canun. The Brunate is noted for its breadth of aromas and drinkability when young. The Dolcetto d'Alba Boschi di Berri is consistently among the very best in the area and is characterized by a body and fullness that beautifully complement the traditional freshness and vinosity of Dolcetto. The great Barbera d'Alba Camerano is aged in barriques, its only fault being that it is so difficult to get hold of.

Dolcetto d'Alba   ♈ ②
Boschi di Berri 1991 DOC
From long-established vineyards at La Morra, Poderi Marcarini selects this Dolcetto d'Alba with its unique personality, characterized by intense, spicy aromas, solid structure and good tannins well integrated with the alcohol.

Barbera d'Alba   ♈ ②
Ciabot Camerano 1990 DOC
Not entirely clean on the nose with a hint of oxidation suggesting that it should be allowed to breathe before serving. This Barbera d'Alba expresses its variety to the full on the palate - aggressive but elegant, full-bodied and lingering with a distinct piquancy in the frank, clean finish.

Barolo Brunate 1988 DOCG   ♈ ♈ ③
From Nebbiolo grapes grown in one of the most prestigious Barolo crus, the Marcarini cellar offers an 1988 with very attractive fruity, fresh aromas. The palate is not overwhelming but well-balanced with soft structure and a good tannic finish. An elegant wine with good texture.

Marchesi di Barolo

Via Alba, 12
Barolo (Cn) 12060
Tel. (0173) 56101
Fax (0173) 56320

To tell the story of the Marchesi di Barolo cellar, founded by Marchioness Giulia Falletti di Colbert, one has to go right back to the beginning of the history of Barolo itself. The enological process for making Barolo from Nebbiolo grapes was created here during the first half of the nineteenth century. Thanks to this track record, the estate developed considerably, acquiring more and more vineyards in prestigious positions, such as Cannubi, Valletta, Sarmassa and Brunate to arrive at the present production level of three million bottles a year. But quality has not always kept pace . The Opera Pia di Barolo, as the estate used to be known, went through different phases until it passed into the hands of the Abbona and Scarzello families. The present owners completely reorganized the technical and managerial staff, now led by general manager Roberto Vezza, Flavio Fenocchio in the cellar and Franco Pittatore in the vineyards, thus opening the way to diversification. Alongside current product lines, they have set up a premium-quality range that will ensure excellent wines, particularly Barolo, through separate vinification of crus and rigorous grape selection.

Dolcetto d'Alba   ♥ ①
Madonna di Como 1991 DOC
An utterly typical Dolcetto, both on the nose and on the palate. Especially noteworthy for its drinkability although somewhat lacking in structure. Average for the vintage.

Barolo Brunate 1988 DOCG   ♥ ③
From selected grapes grown in the Brunate cru at La Morra, a Barolo that impresses with its freshness of aroma and characteristic deep color. Full-flavored on the palate and a little astringent with tannins still evolving. Lingering finish.

Barolo Cannubi 1988 DOCG   ♥♥ ③
From the Cannubi cru in Barolo, perhaps the most prestigious Barolo zone of all. A red with loads of personality made from selected grapes. Grape aromas on the nose and a palate with prominent tannins that are bound to evolve in the future.

Barolo Sarmassa 1988 DOCG   ♥♥ ③
Another selection of grapes of the Barolo area. Good structure, mouthfilling, with typical nose and palate backed up by clear tannins.

Marengo-Marenda & C.

Via del Laghetto, 1
La Morra (Cn) 12064
Tel/Fax (0173) 50137

The owners of this company, which was called Vinicola Piemontese until a short time ago, are not professional growers but their love of the land is immense and they consider wine-making their main occupation. Stefano Marenda, although he lives in Rome, follows developments with close attention. Pietro Marengo, who works in a bank, looks after sales and marketing. Wine-making is the responsibility of Marco Ferrero, an experienced enologist and taster. His association with the company started around twenty years ago at the time of the legendary Barolos of 1970, 1971 and 1979, which can still be tasted and purchased today. These are wines with stupendous texture and intense, well-defined personalities as was the 1986 vintage, with its aging potential guaranteed by the richness of its aromas and the length of its palate. It is Marengo-Marenda policy to release Barolo later than is usual and this is all to the good for the consumer purchases a wine that is already well-balanced, even though it is young. Apart from Barolo, the estate produces a Barbera d'Alba and a Dolcetto d'Alba, both full-bodied, and a Langhe Arneis, which has a surprising intensity of aroma.

Barbera d'Alba Cerequio 1989 DOC ♥ ①
A characteristic Barbera d'Alba with well-defined aromas and ruby, almost garnet-red, color. The sharp acid typical of the variety is evident on the palate, but this will soften out with further aging in the bottle.

Barolo Cerequio 1986 DOCG   ♥♥ ②
This Barolo comes from one of the best crus in La Morra and is released only after long, slow aging, as is the policy of the estate. The 1986 has good breadth and complexity of aromas with autumn leaves to the fore. Good balance on the palate, soft and with good length.

Martini & Rossi

Pessione (To) 10020
Tel. (011) 94191
Fax (011) 9419324

The Martini & Rossi company has become famous all over the world for its spumantes and vermouths. The millions and millions of bottles that are sold under the Martini & Rossi label are the reward for the carefully planned efforts of young wine-technician Giuseppe Gabri. He has at his disposal a first-class team of scrupulously competent professionals and a fully equipped, state-of-the-art laboratory at the company headquarters in Pessione. As a result, Martini & Rossi can point to a range of excellent products with the top of the range to be found in the spumante catalogue. Asti Spumante above all is the pride and joy of the house with more than ten million bottles a year turned out. Quality is always high. Then there is the Riesling dell'Oltrepò Pavese, Charmat method, which is very good value for money, and the Montelera, a méthode champenoise also sold in a vintage version, in confirmation of the desire to maintain a distinctively individual Martini style. The Pessione headquarters of Martini & Rossi are well worth a visit for those who are interested in enological history, as is the fascinating Museum of the History of Wine.

Asti Spumante DOC   🍇 ①
Asti Spumante has all the character of Moscato and a very attractive personality, thanks to careful selection of the fruit and tried and trusted vinification techniques. The aromas are intense, aromatic and varietal while the mousse is abundant and the flavor fresh and full-bodied, although a little short.

Riserva Montelera   🍇 ①
Montelera is a méthode champenoise from Pinot grapes of the Oltrepò Pavese. The perlage is delicate and persistent and the color a pale straw-yellow. There is a hint of yeasts on the nose which then gives way to notes of fruit. Dry on the palate dry, well-balanced, with a slightly acid finish.

Montelera Millesimato 1988   🍇 ①
The careful selection of the grapes gives this wine its lovely, warm straw-yellow color. The effervescence is generous and persistent. Crusty bread dominates the nose while the entry on the palate is remarkably full-bodied and rounded, denoting good structure.

Bartolo Mascarello

Via Roma, 15
Barolo (Cn) 12060
Tel. (0173) 56125

Bartolo Mascarello is a patriarch who has known no autumn, despite the title of the novel by Gabriel García Márquez. He rarely goes anywhere, not even to tastings, prize ceremonies or markets and although he has handed over management of the estate to young wine-technician Alessandro Fantino, his reputation as a Barolo producer and an ironic, witty raconteur has remained untarnished and universally acknowledged. Sooner or later, everyone involved in wine-making or just interested in wines stops by to visit the cellars and sit with Bartolo munching nuts, sipping a glass of Barolo, and listening to one of his pessimistic but affectionate tales of the madness of modern times. All this has contributed to making Mascarello Barolo a legend that transcends the passage of time. The family estate has been producing 20,000 bottles of Barolo since 1918 from four and a half hectares of the finest crus. Mascarello is a hard man to convince and continues to vinify without separating the crus, selling all his wine personally from home without agents and most important of all at extremely attractive prices, given the excellent quality of his products.

Dolcetto d'Alba 1990 DOC   🍇 ①
A Dolcetto which is utterly characteristic of the Langhe. Deep ruby red, heady aromas, and full-bodied drinkability. Ideal to drink all the way through any meal based on the local cuisine.

Barolo 1987 DOCG   🍇🍇 ②
A premium-quality Barolo, despite the unexceptional year. Made from a blend of the best grapes from the property's vineyards, a Barolo which has good complexity both on nose and palate, with tannins that give it the typically astringent finish. The body is full and already well-rounded.

Giuseppe Mascarello & Figlio

Via Borgonuovo, 108
Monchiero (Cn) 12060
Tel. (0173) 792126
Fax (0173) 792124

Giuseppe Mascarello set up this estate in 1881 and then his son Maurizio took over, expanding the property which today thanks also to some recent acquisitions has 20 ha of vineyards located in some of the finest positions in the Langhe. The premier cru is Monprivato at Castiglione Falletto, while there are other parcels at Monforte d'Alba, Pianpolvere Soprano, in the Villero area and finally at Santo Stefano di Perno. The cellar is located at Monchiero, in a beautifully restructured 18th century building where Mauro Mascarello works with his father Giuseppe, making a range of wines which are outstanding for their consistency and quality. The estate policy is to encourage the wine to mature without hurry. There is no rush to market the vintage so that the products are sold only when the time is right. A wise decision, prompted by the nature of the Mascarello wines themselves. They are all imposing and full-bodied, not just the Barolo Monprivato but also the two Barbera d'Alba crus, Ginestra and Fasana, and even the Dolcetto d'Alba wines.

Barbera d'Alba Fasana 1990 DOC 🍇 ①
Impressive, sumptuous body with the good acidity typical of the variety softened out by the richness of the fruit. Heady, frank, aromas. Very easy to drink. A wine from a Mascarello vineyard at Novello, a sub-zone that deserves to be more widely known.

Dolcetto d'Alba Bricco 1990 DOC 🍇 ①
Mauro Mascarello produces this Dolcetto from a vineyard in the Monprivato cru at Castiglione Falletto. It has impressive structure and good alcohol in all the complexity of a great red wine. Aromas of nuts and mulberries, warm on the palate but balanced by powerful extract.

Barbera d'Alba Ginestra 1989 DOC 🍇 ①
So intense in the glass that it is almost opaque and the wine has all the consequent characteristics. The herbaceous warmth typical of the Monforte zone with notes of mint and berries on the nose. Good length on the palate with mouthfilling flavor and unusual tannins for a Barbera.

Barolo Monprivato 1986 DOCG 🍇🍇 ③
The estate's premium wine, from one of the best Nebbiolo crus for Barolo, Monprivato at Castiglione Falletto. Bright, deep color, elegant, lingering aromas of tar and truffle and a palate with the typical suppleness of Monprivato. Superb structure and drinkability.

Moccagatta

Via Rabajà, 24
Barbaresco (Cn) 12050
Tel. (0173) 635152-635228

The Minuto brothers believed that instead of being ordinary growers they could become quality winemakers. Their efforts were finally rewarded. Now the number of barriques in the cellar increases each year and extensions are being planned as well as a whole range of improvements. The market has responded extremely favorably to the estate's products and Moccagatta wines can be found in many restaurants and wine merchant's in Italy as well as in the United States, where large quantities are exported. The most outstanding product is the Barbaresco, aged both in traditional oak-barrels and in barriques. The barrique version is particularly attractive with its cherry aromas and vanilla elegantly integrating with the impressive structure of Nebbiolo. The Minuto brothers are making serious efforts to produce premium-quality wines and have achieved good results in a very short time. Apart from the three Barbarescos, attention has also focused on the Barbera d'Alba and the Chardonnay, produced both in traditional and barrique-aged versions.

Barbera d'Alba 🍇 ②
Vigneto Basarin 1990 DOC
Very deep garnet-red shading into violet. Still rich on the nose, a sign of the wine's youth, but the aromas are already complex and well-integrated with the vanillaed note of the wood. Piquant on the palate, full-bodied, and with a structure of remarkable texture.

Barbaresco 🍇🍇 ③
Bric Balin 1989 DOCG
The Moccagatta estate is making constant progress and this Barbaresco is proof of how far it has come. Extremely vivid in the glass, stylish, elegant aromas and good length. Tasting reveals the remarkable texture, crisp tannins and full, complex body.

Monfalletto

Fraz. Annunziata, 67
La Morra (Cn) 12064
Tel. (0173) 50344
Fax (0173) 509235

Monfalletto is one of the leading new-wave producers of Barolo. The founder, Paolo Cordero di Montezemolo, saw many years ago that it was necessary to make Barolo more accessible and better balanced from the moment it went onto the market. The soil of La Morra was well-suited to this production philosophy because it could easily offer a more elegant, aroma-rich wine, in a French style and that is how Barolo Monfalletto was born. Paolo's sons, Gianni and Enrico, continue their father's work and take great pains to impart more and more character into their wine. Cordero's Barolo preserves the wine's legendary finesse and, in more favorable years, the structure, length of flavor and natural fullness are further enhanced. Drinkability is maintained but considerable aging potential is also present. Doubters should sample some of the older vintages to be found in the Monfalletto cellar and find out just how sharp and well-developed the wine's original characteristics still are.

Barbera d'Alba 1991 DOC 🍷 ①
The nose has still not opened fully but this Barbera, produced only in the last two years, has lots of personality on the palate and a full body, backed up by the typical varietal acidity and just the right extract. Piquant finish of medium length.

Dolcetto d'Alba 1991 DOC 🍷 ①
Ruby red, with fresh, alcohol-rich aromas at first which linger and are followed up by faint notes of fruit (wild black cherry and cherry). Medium texture on the palate with a marked note of acidity and a slightly astringent finish.

Barolo Enrico VI 1988 DOCG 🍷🍷 ③
A Barolo from Villero, one of the historic crus of Castiglione Falletto. The color is very fresh and vivid and the aromas are clean and frank, with subtle hints of aromatic herbs. The roughness of the wine's youth is still apparent on the palate. Bottle-age and tannins will smooth this out.

Fiorenzo Nada

Via Ausario, 12/c, loc. Rombone
Treiso (Cn) 12050
Tel. (0173) 638254

Over recent years, Bruno Nada, a schoolteacher who enjoys making premium-quality wines as a hobby, has been managing the family property with the help of his father, Fiorenzo. Their estate is situated in Treiso, a Barbaresco-growing area, and comprises a small parcel planted in Dolcetto, Nebbiolo and Barbera. After obtaining an attractive Dolcetto d'Alba, a full-bodied Barbaresco and an easy-drinking Nebbiolo, in 1988 Bruno started experimenting with barriques. The result is Seifile (Six Rows), a wine that took its name from the six rows planted in Barbera in a forty-year-old vineyard. The Barbera grapes are blended with 40% Nebbiolo selected from the best grown on the estate, after aging in barriques, the wine is matured for a period of time in the bottle and released onto the market three years after the harvest. The first vintage was 1988 and after the huge success it enjoyed, we can look forward to a brilliant future for this Nada wine. In 1990, Bruno opted to have his wine marketed by a firm which brings together some of the best small producers in Italy, Silvano Formigli's Selezione Fattorie.

Barbaresco 1988 DOCG 🍷 ②
Nada's Barbaresco is characterized by fresh aromas that are strongly redolent of Nebbiolo. A wine of moderate structure but with its own personality. Attractive nose, easy to drink and good balance of the components.

Seifile 1989 🍷🍷 ②
Obtained from Barbera grapes grown in a long-established vineyard with the addition of some Nebbiolo. A barrique-aged red with good texture, well-defined oak aromas and good acidity to back it up.

Andrea e Ornella Oberto

Via G. Marconi, 25
La Morra (Cn) 12064
Tel. (0173) 509262

Andrea and Ornella Oberto run a delightful little estate in a very special position right underneath the ramparts of La Morra, sloping down towards Barolo. Their decision to return to work on the land after various other occupations is proving to be a source of great satisfaction. They personally supervise every stage of production, from harvesting to bottling. The estate's vineyards produce excellent grapes which in turn make wines of remarkable structure, like the Barbera Giada 1990. In a superb vintage, the wine retains all its natural exuberance. The Barolo delle Rocche is outstanding even in difficult years and has a full flavor with all the elegance of a La Morra wine. It is a wine that evolves steadily for a very long time and tastings from numerous vintages confirm this. The Dolcetto d'Alba, produced in two crus, is also very interesting, not so much for its rather closed aromas as for its flavor which, like that of the Barbera, is full-bodied and lingering. Andrea Oberto is a small producer but the results he has so far obtained do not satisfy him. Over the past two years, he has been successfully experimenting with barriques.

Dolcetto d'Alba
Vigneto San Francesco 1991 DOC
Lovely deep ruby red, with frank, alcohol-rich, rather spicy aromas. Astringent on the palate, then opening into the typical bitterish flavor of Dolcetto and on to a dry, piquant finish.

Barbera d'Alba Giada 1990 DOC
In this, its second vintage, this Barbera d'Alba from La Morra shows off all Andrea Oberto's skill with barriques. The wine is now correct, with oak rounding out and lending elegance to the power of the basic wine. Gentle on the nose with well-balanced flavor which does not betray the variety. Remarkable texture in a wine which will certainly improve with bottle-age.

Barolo
Vigneto Rocche 1988 DOCG
Bright ruby red in the glass. A Barolo with classy, clean aromas containing herbaceous hints. Well-rounded on the palate, with marked softness and good balance. The slightly tannic finish is pleasantly dry.

F.lli Oddero

Via S. Maria, 28
La Morra (Cn) 12064
Tel. (0173) 50618
Fax (0173) 509377

The Oddero cellar is situated in the midst of a huge historic vineyard. In times gone by, the monastic community of S. Frontiano lived here and the estate was already famous for its wine during the early Christian period. The cellar was established on this excellent location as long ago as 1878 and has lived up to its past reputation for the quality and excellence of its products. Thanks to Luigi's work in the cellar and to his niece Cristina Oddero who looks after sales and administration, the roughly 180,000 bottles produced -half of which are Barolo- are all of exceptional quality. It must also be said that this cellar has always vinified only its own grapes, and it is no easy task to keep an eye on vineyards so far away from each other. We are in complete agreement with the Odderos when they say that the wine is its own best advertisement, even today when so much importance is placed on marginal factors such as the label design, the shape of the bottle, the length of the cork, public relations and the like. Good locations and meticulous work in the vineyards and correct wine-making techniques are all that is needed to produce quality wines.

Barolo
Mondoca di Bussia Soprana 1988 DOCG
In Monforte, the Bussia sub-zone has always produced Barolo with superb texture and Oddero's Barolo is no exception. It has well-defined characteristic aromas of leather and tobacco, softness on the palate good balance and substantial tannins in the finish.

Barolo Vigna Rionda 1988 DOCG
From Vigna Rionda, the finest cru in Serralunga d'Alba. A classic Barolo style for color, garnet red which has already acquired shades of brick-red The nose has wood from the large oak barrels and prominent tannins on the palate. Moderate extract but good balance.

I Paglieri di Alfredo Roagna

Via Rabajà, 8
Barbaresco (Cn) 12050
Tel. (0173) 635109

Alfredo Roagna is a winemaker who knows where he is going. His father Giovanni put the family estate in his hands about ten years ago and he has been following in his footsteps while continuing to improve. Alfredo was dissatisfied with a cellar which only produced Barbaresco and at the end of the 1980s, Alfredo bought a vineyard at Castiglione Falletto, the extraordinary Pira cru, to be precise, a natural continuation of the Rocche di Castiglione Falletto. We shall have to wait for a couple of years to sample the first Barolo vintage but the Paglieri estate is still making its highly successful Barbaresco as well as the Crichet Pajé from Nebbiolo, the Opera Prima from barrique-aged Nebbiolo and Chardonnay. The cellar, while maintaining almost unchanged its traditional features, has boosted its production potential with the acquisition of temperature controlled stainless steel vats and the by now perfected use of barriques. Finally we should also mention the limited but superb-quality production of Dolcetto d'Alba.

Langhe Chardonnay 1990 ③
Vinified in new barriques and then aged for a few months in bottle, a Chardonnay made from top-quality grapes. Bright yellow tending to amber, with broad, intense aromas. The extract-rich body has very good balance.

Barbaresco 1988 DOCG ②
Obtained from Nebbiolo grapes grown in the Pajé sub-zone. A Barbaresco whose superb texture is due in part to the excellent vintage. The tannins are still evolving and the complex, intense aromas have well-defined notes of autumn leaves. A wine which will be at its best in a few years' time.

Crichet Pajé 1985 ③
Crichet Pajé is made from the finest Nebbiolo grapes grown in the cru. It is bottled as a table wine after barrique aging. A wine with all the characteristics of a great Barbaresco, mouthfilling aromas, a full and soft body and excellent length on the palate.

Opera Prima VII ③
From Nebbiolo grapes from several different vintages, in this case the 1987, 1988 and 1989, an impressive barrique-aged red. The blend of these three vintages has produced wonderful results for this wine is powerful yet elegant, with complex, noble aromas and a light herbaceous note.

F.lli Pecchenino

Borgata Valdibà, 41
Dogliani (Cn) 12063
Tel. (0173) 70686
Fax (0173) 721481

An estate that in a short period of time has become widely known among Dolcetto connoisseurs. It has just celebrated its tenth anniversary. The soil in the Dogliani area traditionally produces full-bodied, alcohol-rich wines, characteristics that one associates with Pecchenino wines with the addition of a unique finesse and freshness of aroma. The leading product is Dolcetto di Dogliani Siri d'Yermu, always a very elegant bottle with good texture, without the dominant tannin that often makes this wine rather unapproachable. In blind tastings, it convincingly confirmed a steady year-by-year improvement in quality. The Dolcetto di Dogliani Pizabò is also excellent, almost the twin brother of the Siri d'Yermu but slightly less fruity and fresh on the nose. Freisa and Barbera are also produced by the Pecchenino cellar, the former characterized by attractive flowery aromas and by vinification that gives it outstanding structure, without the effervescence that one normally finds in Freisa.

Dolcetto di Dogliani ①
Siri d'Yermu 1991 DOC
For a difficult vintage, this Dolcetto has good color, alcohol and concentration. The aromas are typically herbaceous, with prominent geranium and liquorice. The palate is agreeable, backed up by considerable acidity and with lingering aromas.

Barbera Langhe Vigna Gildu 1990 ①
Deep ruby red with lovely tints of violet. Elegant and stylish on the nose, with strong notes of fresh-cut grass and geranium. The palate is full and powerful, with its 14% alcohol well-balanced by the extract. Marked acidity will ensure a long future in the cellar.

Pelissero

Via Ferrere, 19
Treiso (Cn) 12050
Tel/Fax (0173) 638136

Originally, the Pelissero estate was a typical Alba farm but in the 1960s it began to produce only wine, exploiting the 11 ha of vineyards situated in the lovely village of Ferrere right in the middle of a huge wine-growing zone that joins Treiso to Barbaresco and Neive. This is an area that is particularly well-suited to Dolcetto, recognized here under the Denominazione Dolcetto d'Alba. Dolcetto di Treiso also deserves its own individual Denominazione for its personality. It is an intense, aromatic, soft wine without the tannic harshness of Monforte Dolcettos or the austere, many-sided structure of La Morra Dolcettos but it is rich in color and extract. The Pelissero family bring out these characteristics with great skill and since Giorgio Pelissero joined the estate after graduating from the Enological School of Alba, the property has started to bottle its entire production of about 75,000 bottles, mainly Barbaresco and Dolcetto. These wines have consolidated their solid reputation as premium-quality wines in the finest restaurants and wine merchant's in Italy.

Dolcetto d'Alba Augenta 1991 DOC 🌱 ①
Deep garnet red, very attractive with frank, alcohol-rich aromas. The palate is soft and full-bodied , with the typical bitterish Dolcetto finish.

Barbera d'Alba Ronchi 1990 DOC 🌱 ①
A wonderful example of a Barbera, traditionally vinified by the skilled hand of Giorgio Pelissero. Gentle, stylish aromas of moderate intensity. Warm on the palate, with good body and a rustic touch typical of the variety.

Barbaresco Vanotu 1989 DOCG 🌱🌱 ②
The estate's top-of-the-range wine. The quality of the Barbaresco from the Pelissero Vanotu cru is once again confirmed in the 1989 vintage. It has a frank "rustic" personality with herbaceous, slightly balsamic aromas. Full-flavored on the palate with marked tannins in the finish.

Pianpolvere Soprano

Loc. Bussia, strada Alba-Monforte, 32
Monforte (Cn) 12065
Tel/Fax (0173) 78335

Barbera has finally achieved international recognition after a number of years during which lackadaisical producers and incompetent civil servants ruined the wine's image. Producers like the Fenocchios of the Pianpolvere Soprano estate have contributed to this, stubbornly maintaining Barbera d'Alba as their leading product. The rewards have followed and foreign markets now buy most of the production of Pianpolvere Soprano Barbera. A particularly stylish, elegant wine with a structure that integrates well with the acidity of the variety, it can be laid down for quite a few years but is already eminently drinkable as soon as it reaches the market, having fermented in oak and stainless steel for more than a year. The estate also produces Barolo, Dolcetto d'Alba and Grignolino, all wines with excellent texture from a zone, Bussia, that is one of the best in the Langhe for premium-quality viticulture. As well as the Barolo, the Grignolino ought to be mentioned, with its extraordinary freshness and wonderful drinkability.

Barbera d'Alba 1989 DOC 🌱 ①
Pianpolvere Soprano has always relied on Barbera. The 1989 vintage confirms the cellar's wine-making capabilities and brings us this deep garnet-red wine with spicy notes dominating on the nose. Full-bodied on the palate, frank and at the same time well-rounded and velvet-smooth.

Barolo 1987 DOCG 🌱 ②
The estate policy is to market its Barolo a year later than the minimum time permitted by the DOCG regulations. This means that today we can savor a 1987 Barolo which is among the best that were made in that far from easy vintage. Already has good breadth and open aromas of well-defined spices. Soft and unaggressive on the palate, a wine that should not be kept for too long in the cellar.

Pio Cesare

Via Balbo, 6
Alba (Cn) 12051
Tel. (0173) 440386
Fax (0173) 363680

Pio Cesare is Barolo! This statement is no exaggeration and not even competitors could deny it. The history of this cellar, founded in 1881 by the legendary Pio, is closely tied to the history of Barolo and to its increasing fame and fortune. Pio's skill contributed in no small measure to this process and the premium-quality Barolos he made won prizes and awards outside Italy as well as at home, the first of these dating from 1898. As a result, new markets were opened up to the wines of the Langhe. The Pio Cesare style did not change as generation succeeded generation. The present manager Pio Boffa is the great-grandson of the founder and with the invaluable contribution of wine-technician Paolo Fenocchio, he has effected innovations the cellar needed, those required by today's market. New wines have been created such as Nebbio, a Nebbiolo vinified with carbonic maceration, to be drunk young as well as Chardonnay. Pio has tried new wine-making techniques, such the use of barriques and temperature control. But Barolo, in the beautiful vaulted rooms of the historic Pio Cesare cellars in the center of Alba, continues to be made the way it was made in the past, the way that made it world-famous.

Barbera d'Alba 1989 DOC   ❦ ①
A Barbera that reflects all the characteristics of this Piemontese wine. Moderately intense ruby red and frank, but unobtrusive, aromas. Full-flavored on the palate, rich and warm with good length.

Barolo 1988 DOCG   ❦ ③
A blend of grapes from different parts of the Barolo area, Barolo is the Pio Cesare estate's number one wine. Good structure, with well-defined tannins and young aromas but autumn leaves and fruit are already coming through. A wine to lay down.

Barolo Ornato 1986 DOCG   ❦❦ ③
Pio Cesare has always used the technique of blending grapes from different vineyards for its wines, but in 1985 it adopted a different method for the Ornato. Obtained from a superb Barolo vineyard in Serralunga, this 1986 vintage has elegant aromas of medium intensity, with notes of autumn leaves and fruit already opening out. Firm on the palate, with good acidity and lively tannins.

Podere Ai Valloni

Via Traversagna
Boca (No) 28010
Tel. (0322) 87332
Fax (011) 502011

Boca is a Denominazione in the province of Novara, where the town to which it owes its name is located. It is home to one of the many variations on the theme of Nebbiolo to be found in Piemonte. Nebbiolo is a vine type with an ancient tradition that seems to lack growers capable of providing a modern interpretation of its potential. One praiseworthy exception is the Podere Ai Valloni. Since 1980, when the estate was acquired by Boca-born, Turin-based lawyer, Guido Sertorio, Ai Valloni has been the most important property in the zone. The vineyard has been replanted, with old vine stock being reestablished and new stock planted and expert wine-technician Armando Cordero has been busy in the cellar. The resulting Boca is made in accordance with the stipulations of the Denominazione regulations from 60 % Nebbiolo together with Vespolina and Bonarda, the last two being local varieties, It is a sturdy, elegant wine which will age well while being at the same time pleasant to drink immediately.

Boca 1986 DOC   ❦ ①
The 1986 vintage produced further confirmation of the estate's potential. Deep ruby red, this is a wine which has fresh aromas on the nose, opening into the characteristic notes of autumn leaves. On the palate, the tannins give way to a bitter flavor which will develop into a greater complexity of flavor.

Boca 1985 DOC   ❦ ①
Lovely ruby red flecked with orange. Classy, elegant aromas of autumn leaves and spices, good structure, warm and full-bodied, with tannins still prominent

Produttori del Barbaresco

Via Torino, 52
Barbaresco (Cn) 12050
Tel. (0173) 635139-635119
Fax (0173) 635130

The Produttori del Barbaresco cooperative was formed by the original twenty founder members in 1958 with the intention of improving the status of some of the best vineyards in the Barbaresco zone and increasing the financial rewards of the growers themselves. At the time, this task looked difficult but the twenty finally pulled it off. Today there are three times as many members and the name Produttori del Barbaresco is synonymous with premium-quality Barbaresco and very competitive prices. Some wise policy decisions have been taken with the aim of adding value to the wines produced from as many as nine different superb crus in the zone, Rabajà, Pora, Moccagatta, Ovello, Montefico, Montestefano, Asili, Pajé and Rio Sordo. In better vintages, the various crus are vinified separately and the name of the grower who supplied the grapes is mentioned on the back label of the bottle. The Produttori cellar is enthusiastically managed by its president, Celestino Vacca, a tireless promoter of Produttori wines, and skilled wine-technician Giovanni Testa.

Barbaresco 1989 DOCG
The Produttori base version of Barbaresco, aged only for the minimum three years required by Denominazione regulations. Moderately deep, brilliant garnet red, with alcohol-rich aromas where fruit and flowers are prominent. Rich palate, with just a touch too much acidity.

Barbaresco
Riserva Asili 1985 DOCG
A superb vintage from one of the great Barbaresco crus. Elegant deep garnet red in the glass with a fine range of stylish aromas including a light tarry note mingling with autumn leaves and mushrooms. Complex in the mouth, where the still-evident noble tannins blend with warm sensations of alcohol.

Barbaresco
Riserva Pajé 1985 DOCG
12,500 bottles a year are produced from this cru, with its garnet-red, orange-tinted color and well-developed, alcohol-rich, nose which opens into autumn leaves and dried roses. Elegant on the palate, with good structure and soft, lively tannins.

Produttori di Nebbiolo di Carema

Via Nazionale, 28
Carema (To) 10010
Tel/Fax (0125) 85256

Carema is in the extreme north-west of Piemonte, on the border with Val d'Aosta. Wine-growing has ancient roots here and is based on the charming traditional pergolas supported by dry-stone walls and pillars which are characteristic features of these hills in the shadow of the Alps. The Cantina di Carema, established in 1960, brings together the small growers of the zone. Today, it has around fifty members and it is a reliable producer of premium-quality Carema. The work of Gaspare Buscemi, the wine-technician responsible for the cellar's excellent results, has been and continues to be fundamental. Life is not easy for the Produttori, who must often come to terms with a wine that is neither famous nor immediately appealing, with a natural tannic roughness that softens only after many years in the cellar. Their Carema is, however, another Nebbiolo-based wine which lovers of austere, slow-aging wines should taste if they can.

Carema 1986 DOC
This Carema, made from Nebbiolo grapes, is a wine with imposing structure that has softened its robust tannins and acidity over the years to develop intense, toasty-warm aromas. Full and lingering on the palate. An austere, value-for-money wine.

Carema di Carema 1986 DOC
Fierce, rigorous selection of the grapes gives this wine a rich concentration of extract. Attractive aromas of Peruvian bark and liquorice on the nose and a warm, mouthfilling palate. An imposing red wine to tuck away in the cellar.

Prunotto

Reg. San Cassiano, 4/g
Alba (Cn) 12051
Tel. (0173) 280017
Fax (0173) 281167

In 1989, the Antinori estate took a majority holding in the Alfredo Prunotto cellar, but everyone knew that the heart and mind of this prestigious producer, wine-technician Beppe Colla, would never allow anyone else to take over. And so it was. There is no one else who can boast Beppe's knowledge of Langhe grape types and winemaking techniques. He has already produced forty vintages since he stepped into the shoes of the legendary Cavalier Prunotto, who bought the property in 1923 and transformed a cooperative winery with financial worries into a leading Italian grower. The estate philosophy has not changed since those early years. Trusted suppliers bring selected grapes from the finest zones, the wine is aged slowly before being released onto the market and barriques are never used. Beppe Colla's extraordinary skill is also demonstrated by the fact that as early as 1961, he understood the importance of separate vinification for each vineyard and he was the very first grower in the Langhe to indicate this on the label.

Barbera d'Alba ❦ ①
Pian Romualdo 1990 DOC
This Barbera comes from the Pian Romualdo cru at Monforte, 550 m above sea-level, where the vine stock is at least 20 years old. A wine with a lovely purple color in glass, rich in spicy aromas and with a faint hint of violet. The body has excellent good texture.

Nebbiolo d'Alba Occhetti 1990 DOC ❦ ①
This splendid Nebbiolo from Roero is a pale ruby red and has intense, very classy aromas of flowers (geranium) and berries. Superb texture on the palate, rich and powerful.

Barbaresco ❦❦ ③
Montestefano 1989 DOCG
Low yields from 22-year-old plants in one of the best Barbaresco crus are the foundation for a wine with absolutely typical characteristics and great elegance. Lovely bright ruby red, with intense aromas of rose and liquorice and a remarkably complex body. Among the best wines of the vintage.

Barolo Bussia 1988 DOCG ❦❦ ③
The Prunotto cellar vinifies Barolo using traditional methods but after the conventional period of aging in large barrels, a few months' evolution in new Slavonian oak casks help to confer a touch of elegance to this full-bodied dry wine, with rich aromas of violet and tar.

Barolo Cannubi 1988 DOCG ❦❦ ③
Cannubi is one of the legendary Barolo crus, famous for its particularly elegant, aroma-rich, slow-aging wines. The 1988 vintage has slightly more subdued aromas than the Bussia, but the body is powerful, full-flavored, long and velvet-smooth.

Francesco Rinaldi e Figli

Via Umberto Sacco, 4
Alba (Cn) 12051
Tel/Fax (0173) 440484

A company founded at Barolo in 1870. During the 1930s, Francesco, the father of the present owner Luciano, moved to Alba to exploit Barolo's commercial potential, and there the winery has remained. Rinaldi wines continue to privilege the aging potential and fullness of body that has always characterized them. The 50,000 bottles of Barolo, of a total production of about 90,000, come from prestigious crus such as Cannubi and Brunate -territories that could justifiably be called "grands crus" - and express all the potential of these sub-zones. Wines are aged slowly at Rinaldi, more slowly than required by the Denominazione regulations. Nevertheless, they are not for drinking immediately after purchase for the nose may still be closed and the tannins aggressive and rough. Further bottle-age will enhance the wine's flavors, aromas and austerity. This is traditional Barolo, then in the best sense of the term and excellent value for money.

Dolcetto d'Alba ❦ ①
Vigneto Roussot 1991 DOC
A typical Dolcetto both in its ruby red color shading into violet and in its fresh, rich aromas with herbaceous notes. Drinkability is confirm on the tangy palate with its pleasantly dry finish.

Barolo Cannubio 1987 DOCG ❦ ②
Garnet tending to brick red and subtle aromas, including the well-defined oak of the large barrels. A Barolo in the mainstream of tradition. Good body on the palate, with a well-defined, attractively bitter, liquorice finish.

Barolo La Brunata 1987 DOCG ❦ ②
Though not exceptionally powerful, this Barolo has intense color, and elegant, clean aromas. Well-balanced on the palate, with marked astringency in the finish.

Rinaldi Giuseppe

Via Monforte, 3
Barolo (Cn) 12060
Tel. (0173) 56156

The Giuseppe Rinaldi estate was managed until not long ago by one of the people who made Barolo's fortune, Battista, who for many years was mayor of the town of Barolo and president of the regional Enoteca, or wine institute, located at the Barolo Castello Comunale. A man of firm moral principles and great technical ability, Battista's efforts over the last years have been directed at the complete renovation of the beautiful cellars, enlarging the rooms and replacing the traditional oak barrels. Battista's son, Citrico, having completed his enology studies, is now manager and is always happy to welcome visitors. The estate owns well-located parcels in the Barolo area, particularly in Brunate. The wine from the beautiful Brunate valley from the few fortunate growers who own parcels there is the most elegant of the entire Barolo zone, uniquely stylish and drinkable. It is company policy to age the most prestigious Barolos slowly before bottling and so the Giuseppe Rinaldi cellar can offer some quite stunning rare vintages.

Barolo 1988 DOCG   🍷 ②
Deep ruby red in the glass, with a lively, bright appearance. The nose still closed as the wine has only recently been bottled but has well-defined hints of coffee, chocolate and still pungent oak. Abundant liquorice on the palate and good concentration with green but not aggressive tannins. Drink after at least another three years in the bottle.

Barolo   🍷🍷 ③
Riserva Brunate 1985 DOCG
A Barolo vinified in exactly the same way as it was a hundred years ago. After three or four years aging in barrels, it goes into large bottles for further evolution before bottling. Garnet red with brick-red streaks and well-defined aromas of spices and chocolate. Velvet-smooth on the palate with well-rounded tannins.

Bruno Rocca - Rabajà

Via Rabajà, 29
Barbaresco (Cn) 12050
Tel/Fax (0173) 635112

In a short period of time, Bruno Rocca has become one of the most interesting producers in the Barbaresco area and has received well-deserved recognition for his dedication, enthusiasm and expertise as a winemaker that has improved steadily over the years. The Barbaresco Rabajà has deep, bright color, remarkable structure, good alcohol content and particularly complex aromas, the aging in new oak adding rich, fresh aromas to the traditional Nebbiolo nose. The excellent 1988 Barbaresco, now impossible to find, was recently replaced by the 1989 version. After the initial tastings, the 1989 looks as if it will be an absolutely staggering wine, with body to equal the great vintages, even though it is already extremely attractive. The cellar, now being restructured and enlarged, also produces a delightful Dolcetto d'Alba and a Langhe Nebbiolo with good structure. New vineyards are being acquired and in a few years' time, this should ensure an increase in production, which now barely exceeds 20,000 bottles.

Dolcetto d'Alba   🍷 ①
Vigna Trifolé 1991 DOC
A Dolcetto that expresses the best of its cru, between Barbaresco and Treiso. Powerful extract combined with tangy, frank drinkability. Bright ruby red with cherry-red tints and alcohol-rich aromas and herbaceous notes to the fore. Good acidity on the palate and a pleasant bitterish finish.

Barbaresco Rabajà 1989 DOCG   🍷🍷 ③
In 1988, this upwardly-mobile young producer surprised everyone with the richness of the extract and the elegance of this wine. The 1989 vintage is on a par, with notes of oak that do not mask the aromas of the variety. Morello cherry and rose are to the fore. The structure is impressive but already has good balance.

Poderi Rocche dei Manzoni

Loc. Manzoni Soprani, 3
Monforte d'Alba (Cn) 12065
Tel. (0173) 78421
Fax (0173) 787161

Valentino Migliorini likes to remind people that he was one of the first 15 years ago to introduce barriques into the Langhe and how the move was derided as being excessively Francophile and alien to the traditions of the zone. Time proved him right and today many other cellars use them. The decision to buy the parcel in front of the cellar also raised an eyebrow or two. That parcel is Rocche Manzoni, a beautiful but hard-to-cultivate vineyard from which Valentino now produces the highly successful Bricco Manzoni. Migliorini started to acquire vineyards to ensure that he would have all the grapes he needs and today the property owns as much as 46 ha of vineyards and has 20 employees, renting a further six hectares. Everything is located in the Monforte area, in line with the policy of producing only Langhe wines. This year's Brut will also be made 100% from Monforte grapes. The restructuring of the beautiful cellars with two floors for temperature controlled aging, the planting of Sauvignon and Sémillon at Castelletto and the creation of the Pinònero are the latest exploits of Migliorini's cellar. "That does it," says Valentino, "I've got enough work to do to keep me going until the year 2020. I think that's about as much job security as I'm going to need."

Pinònero 1990   ♥ ③
The experiment of planting Pinot in one of the leading Barolo zones was certainly a risk. The result is this wine, totally different from the Pinots produced on the other side of the Alps, with its intense, lightly wooded aromas, lovely bright ruby red color and piquant, delightful palate.

Bricco Manzoni 1989   ♥♥ ③
Made from Nebbiolo and Barbera grapes, this was one of the first Langhe wines to be aged in barriques. Vivacious, bright color and rich aromas with a hint of berries and vanilla. Excellent drinking with its long-lasting, powerful body, backed up the acidity of the Barbera variety.

Barolo Vigna Big 1988 DOCG   ♥♥ ③
From a small vineyard at Mosconi di Monforte, Valentino makes around 10,000 bottles of this fine Barolo, a superb expression of the cru. Rich color and well-defined varietal aromas including tar and a faint hint of wood. Powerful and lingering on the palate.

Barolo Vigna d'la Roul 1988 DOCG   ♥ ③
Obtained from a small vineyard on a steep, rocky Migliorini property boasting an ancient oak tree, this Barolo is softer than the Vigna Big. The color and aromas have nobility and elegance but the body has yet to achieve a balance of tannins and acidity.

Josetta Saffirio

Fraz. Castelletto, 32
Monforte d'Alba (Cn) 12065
Tel. (0173) 78660

Josetta Saffirio is a viticulture lecturer at the Enological School of Alba and her husband Roberto Vezza works as wine-technician in a large, well-known Langhe estate. Together they run a small company with a beautiful vineyard in the Castelletto di Monforte d'Alba zone, a superb growing area. Here they cultivate the classic grape types of the zone - Barbera, Dolcetto and Nebbiolo for Barolo. Their painstaking care in the vineyard and the absolutely excellent job they do of wine-making ensure that Josetta and Roberto obtain exceptional results from their grapes. The Dolcetto d'Alba, called Alessio after their son, has quite outstanding body and personality for a wine of this type and may safely be laid down for a few years. The Barbera d'Alba has great structure while the Barolo is extraordinary for its stylish aromas and fullness on the palate, as well as being very easy to drink. A pity that so few bottles are produced.

Barbera d'Alba Sara 1989 DOC   ♥♥ ①
This limited-production Barbera d'Alba comes from the village of Castelletto di Monforte d'Alba. Justly considered something of a minor miracle, it is intense and bright in the glass, with rich aromas well-integrated by aging in small barrels. Full body with good structure and balanced.

Barolo 1988 DOCG   ♥♥ ②
Josetta produces only 1,200 bottles of this Barolo, which is almost a collector's item. Remarkably concentrated color, and rich, intense aromas ennobled by a hint of wood in the background. Slightly sharp on the palate, which is complex and long. A wine destined to age well.

Luciano Sandrone

Via Alba, 57
Barolo (Cn) 12060
Tel/Fax (0173) 56239

Luciano Sandrone's cellar is the biggest thing to happen to Barolo over the last ten years. Luciano's secret lies in his vineyard management and his desire to get the best concentration of Nebbiolo's characteristics by piloting the fermentation process without altering the characteristics of the grape. The final stage for Sandrone Barolo is aging in 600 lt barrels. The wine stays in the wood just the right length of time before its fullness emerges in the bottle, where it continues to evolve slowly. Powerful, with excellent balance and plenty of noble tannins, it is a Barolo with supremely elegant texture. The method may not be very innovative but we share Sandrone's opinion that this is the only way to give a premium-quality wine a personality that is too often neglected. The Sandrone range is now being expanded and includes, as well as the ever-intense Dolcetto d'Alba, a Barbera d'Alba that needs bottle-age to find a balance. The cellar started out by producing a few thousand bottles but output has now reached a level of 30,000 bottles a year, the minimum required for a reasonable network of distributors.

Dolcetto d'Alba 1991 DOC
A Dolcetto that stands out for the balance of its components, both on the nose, where the varietal aromas integrate attractively with the secondary ones and on the palate with its full body, rich, complex flavors and drinkability. Good length in the finish.

Barolo
Cannubi Boschis 1988 DOCG
Sandrone's Barolo is characterized by extraordinary consistency of quality, strongly varietal fruit characteristics and attractive vinification. The fruity aromas of mulberries, wild berries and coffee are elegant and fresh. Attractive length on the palate, where prominent tannins are nicely balanced by the extract and acidity. Long liquorice finish.

Paolo Saracco

Via Circonvallazione, 6
Castiglione Tinella (Cn) 12053
Tel. (0141) 855113
Fax (0141) 855360

The story of the Saracco company is the story of many other family-run cellars in the Castiglione Tinella and Santo Stefano Belbo zones. At first, they were producers of grapes to supply the Canelli spumante industry and then, little by little, with the help of technology and the enthusiasm of the younger generation, estates which were transformed into cellars vinifying and bottling their own Moscato d'Asti. This followed the surge of popularity during the 1980s which established this wine as one of the great partners for desserts. Paolo Saracco, as a young graduate at the Enological School of Alba, was one of the first to carry out this metamorphosis and today he produces around 80,000 bottles of a Moscato d'Asti which is one of the most highly thought of on the market. There are two versions, the standard wine and the one obtained from slightly super-ripe grapes, called Moscato d'Autunno. A superbly-equipped cellar and proven wine-making skills enable Paolo and his father Giovanni to produce a total of 10,000 bottles of two white wines in addition to the spumantes. These are Chardonnay Prasué, with its solid structure, and the lighter easier-to-drink Bianc du Lou from Cortese and Favorita, traditional Piemontese grape types.

Chardonnay Prasué 1991
This Chardonnay proves that Paolo Saracco's skills extend beyond Moscato, generally considered his strong-point. A white with good personality, well-defined varietal aromas and good structure. Moderately full and rounded on the palate.

Moscato d'Asti 1991 DOC
In recent years, Saracco's Moscato d'Asti has gone right to the top of its category. The 1991 vintage confirms this with its fresh, varietal aromas, correct effervescence and fullness on the palate. Pleasantly tart in the finish.

Moscato d'Autunno 1991 DOC
The Moscato d'Autunno is obtained from a rigorous selection of fully ripe grapes. The outstandingly rich, complex aromas and above-average body for the wine type are the result. Fat and full-bodied on the palate.

Antica Casa Vinicola Scarpa

Via Montegrappa, 6
Nizza Monferrato (At) 14049
Tel. (0141) 721331
Fax (0141) 702872

The name Scarpa of Nizza Monferrato is without doubt one of the best-known in Piemontese wine circles, and not just because the Scarpas have been part of the scene for so many years. The quality, the unique style and the extraordinary aging potential of Scarpa wines are instantly recognized by wine professionals and wine-lovers the world over. Scarpa is a cellar that refuses to follow the crowd and has never made bland wines for the undiscriminating mass market. These are wines for serious wine-drinkers to savor at the height of their maturity, including the Grignolino and Brachetto, accompanied by the right food. If you are lucky enough to meet Mario Pesce, who makes these wines and has headed the Scarpa cellar since it was founded, you will notice that his personality reflects that of his wines. On the surface, he is reserved to the point of being rough but he soon reveals an underlying warmth and old-fashioned style. The Scarpa Barbera d'Asti is the flagship wine of the house. Then come the Barbaresco and Barolo crus and the unique Brachetto and Rouchet, to make up a range of premium-quality wines reflecting the expertise of wine-technician Pasquale Castino.

Brachetto Secco
La Selva di Moirano 1990
The supreme expression of the quality of Scarpa's Brachetto is to be found in the aromas. Elegant and complex at the same time, with stylish flowery notes. Bright, pale ruby red in the glass, while on the palate the initial slightly aromatic impact makes way for a dry, lean and thoroughly satisfying finish.

Rouchet Briccorosa 1990
Ruché is a rare, traditional Castagnole Monferrato variety, which probably originally came from France. Scarpa obtains from it a highly individual wine, with intense aromas of violets and spices as well as remarkable structure and elegance. Utterly satisfying. Try it with cheese.

Barbera d'Asti
La Bogliona 1988 DOC
La Bogliona, from grapes grown in superb vineyards, is perhaps the cru that best represents the cellar's philosophy and style. Vinified using traditional techniques, it is an extraordinarily powerful wine that needs time to mellow out into a frank, clean-tasting glass.

Barolo Tetti Morra 1985 DOCG
A Barolo with great aging potential. The developing aromas are already characteristic, while the tannins on the palate are much in evidence but well balanced by the extract and acidity. The entry is warm and the finish full and long.

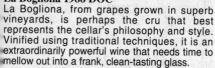

Cascina Scarsi Olive

Loc. San Lorenzo, reg. Scarsi Olive
Rocca Grimalda (Al) 15078
Tel. (0143) 873261

Giuseppe Ratto, winemaker in the town of Rocca Grimalda, has for some time been waging a very personal battle against the modern trend towards emphasizing the superficial aspects of wines - such as nose and drinkability - at the expense of structure, that is to say, body, aging potential and complexity. Ratto believes in what he is doing but he also has good personal motives for the stance. His estate is located in one of the most difficult wine-growing areas of the Piemonte, the Ovada district. The soil here produces a Dolcetto with such a unique purple color and richness of extract as to be one of a kind. Ratto owns two of the best crus in the zone, the Scarsi and Olive vineyards from which the estate takes its name, and his wines are utterly distinctive. He certainly knows his job and how to keep the vinification and barrique-aging processes under control so as not to force the characteristics of his Dolcetto. The aromas are lively, without the herbaceous, medicinal flavor typical of so many products from this area. The body is nonetheless powerful, well-sustained and long-lasting. We would suggest you drink these wines a year or two after they come onto the market to enjoy them at their peak.

Dolcetto d'Ovada Scarsi 1990 DOC
A red with remarkable personality, if slightly rough on the palate owing to the richness of body and extract that give this Dolcetto its aging potential.

Dolcetto d'Ovada
Le Olive 1990 DOC
Ruby red flecked with violet. The typical herbaceous notes of Dolcetto d'Ovada are evident on the nose, ennobled by the flowery hints of the superb cru. Austere and concentrated on the palate with a liquorice finish.

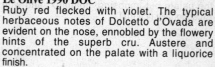

Giorgio Scarzello e Figli

Via Alba, 29
Barolo (Cn) 12060
Tel. (0173) 56170

For two generations, the Scarzello family has been running this small but functional cellar. Today it is Giorgio, with his wife Gemma, who manages the five hectare estate, not all of it under vine. Some of the most important Barolo crus, such as Paiagallo and Sarmassa, are the base for the wines produced by Scarzello. A large proportion of the production is, obviously, of Barolo, from Nebbiolo grapes grown in their Sarmassa parcel, but there is also a Dolcetto d'Alba from the Paiagallo cru and from other areas in the commune of Barolo. A limited quantity of Barbera d'Alba completes the range but this is not bottled every year. The Scarzellos are definitely looking to the Barbera d'Alba to guarantee their future and it has recently had great success. New vineyards entirely replanted in Barbera will soon come onstream and production, restricted at present to about 1,000 bottles, will rise. Another point in favor of this company is the excellent value of their wines.

Dolcetto d'Alba 1990 DOC   🍇 ①
The Dolcettos of Barolo take their very special color and concentration from their zone of origin This wine has a deep ruby, almost black, appearance in the glass, aromas with notes of tar, remarkably powerful extract and rich, juicy fruit, well backed up by acidity and sinew.

Barolo 1988 DOCG   🍇🍇 ②
An old-fashioned wine. Lots of power, perhaps at the expense of finesse and the elegance of the aromas. Deep garnet red, with a typical Barolo bouquet of well-defined tar and tobacco together with vegetal notes. Still a little rough on the palate but imposing, complex, and with exceptionally rich fruit.

Price levels

①   up to $ 9.99

② $ 10.00 - $ 14.99

③ $ 15.00 - $ 24.99

④ $ 25.00 or more

The 'ex-cellar', or direct from the producer, bottle prices, are calculated in US dollars and are intended only as an approximate guide

Paolo Scavino

Via Alba-Barolo, 33
Castiglione Falletto (Cn) 12060
Tel/Fax (0173) 62850

Enrico Scavino is a typical representative of the new generation of winemakers who have carried the reputation of the Langhe and its wines back to the highest levels. A passionate love of the soil together with the careful study of experience elsewhere has led to unforeseen success stories from grape types such as Nebbiolo, Barbera and Dolcetto. Enrico Scavino - the estate is still named after his father - has opted for quality. Vineyard selections are merciless both during the pruning and in summer with the thinning out of the grapes, while the model cellar lets him get the very best from the already carefully selected grapes. A management policy of this kind can only yield superb results and that is exactly what has happened in the case of Enrico's reds, such as Dolcetto d'Alba Vigna del Fiasc, always elegant and well-structured, the Barbera d'Alba softened by barrique-aging and above all the Barolos, particularly the Cannubi and Bric del Fiasc crus, made only in the very best vintages.

Dolcetto d'Alba ♈ ①
Vigneto del Fiasc 1991 DOC
From the Fiasco cru at Castiglione Falletto, where the winery produces 10,500 bottles of Dolcetto. This 1991 vintage is extraordinary, despite the poor year. Deep ruby with violet tints and aromas so intense and so characteristic that they could be used to typify all the Dolcetto produced in the Barolo area - hints of violet, grass and liquorice in perfect harmony. Rich extract on the palate, especially on entry. Attractive tannins dominate the finish, where liquorice is again present.

Barolo Cannubi 1988 DOCG ♈♈ ③
A small lot (3,500 bottles) of Barolo with the name of one of the most prestigious crus on the label, Cannubi di Barolo. These glorious vineyards helped Scavino save the 1987 vintage, which was fairly disastrous in some other areas. The 1988 vintage is all power and texture, almost with an overtone of anger. Great breadth of aroma, but still lacking in elegance. Rich and long on the palate, with lively evolving tannins. Tuck this bottle away in the cellar for a good few years.

Barolo Bric del Fiasc 1988 DOCG ♈♈ ③
Enrico Scavino makes 12,500 bottles of wine from his Fiasco cru (Fiasc in the local dialect) at Castiglione Falletto, all of them expressing the local Barolo at its best. This 1988 is deep ruby red with garnet shades in the glass. The nose is still closed but intense with notes of tobacco and tar. Powerful tannins on the palate, well balanced against the structure. It will start to emerge in three years time.

Barbera d'Alba 1989 DOC ♈♈♈ ②
The decision to give a Barbera the ultimate accolade is only superficially a rash one. Until recently the archetypal cheap table wine from incredibly high yields per hectare and good at best to set alongside anonymous blends for color and acidity, Barbera is today enjoying a reawakening of interest and a quantum leap in quality. It has proved to be an ideal wine for aging in small oak barrels, with excellent cellar potential and a superb range of crus. The 4,500 bottles of this monovarietal Barbera come from the Fiasco and Codana di Castiglione Falletto crus, where yields never exceed 50-55 q/ha. Fermentation is in stainless steel with the malolactic partly in barriques and partly in vats. 70% then goes into small oak barrels while the rest remains in stainless steel. Blending and bottling took place in August 1991. This is a Barbera with a marvelous ruby and violet appearance in the glass. The plums and cherries on the nose are ennobled by a background of oak. Frank and inviting on the palate with perfect acidity on entry. Rounded out by the carefully calculated use of oak over very concentrated fruit that practically explodes on the palate in the finish.

La Scolca

Villa Scolca
Gavi (Al) 15066
Tel. (0143) 682176
Fax (0143) 682197

The Soldati family proudly remembers that the founder of their company, Vittorio, was the man who invented Gavi. In the post-war years, spumante producers bought up much of the Cortese grape harvest. Vittorio Soldati thought that the vines around his lovely La Scolca estate in the Rovereto zone deserved a better fate. In Vittorio's opinion, this was the premier Cortese cru where climate and soil type produce perfect grapes. That was how the idea of making wine directly and make it in a different way from run-of-the-mill Cortese was born. Very low yields - at the time 50 q/ha. as opposed to the permitted 100 q/ha., manual harvesting and meticulous selection were employed. In 1959, Gavi di Gavi was launched and its black label was soon to become renowned. The rest, as they say, is history. The international success of the new wine, the DOC denomination and higher prices for the growers. Throughout this period of whirlwind development and even today, La Scolca has remained aloof from the hurly-burly. They may no longer be right at the top anymore but they have a solid reputation that no one can deny.

Gavi di Gavi   🍇 ③
Etichetta Nera 1991 DOC
This wine's black label made the cellar's fortune and that of Gavi as well, reintroducing the wine to the market as an important white. The 1991 vintage is bright straw-yellow with moderately intense but very fresh aromas. Pleasant acidity on the palate with plenty of fruit but lacking the complexity of past vintages.

Soldati La Scolca Brut Riserva 1986   🍇 ③
A spumante méthode champenoise, obtained mainly from Cortese grapes aged on the yeasts for five years. Straw-yellow with flecks of gold. The perlage is delicate and lingering while the aromas are intense, with a touch of yeast, "petits fours" and rusks. Well-balanced on the palate, with good length.

Sebaste

Loc. San Pietro
Barolo (Cn) 12060
Tel. (0173) 56266
Fax (0173) 56353

Sylla Sebaste, who gave her name to the cellar, created this estate through sheer will power. Today, there is a new owner but the Sebaste winery in the lovely village of Bricco delle Viole is still the same and wine-technician Donato Lanati ensures that quality standards do not waver. The range of Sebaste products includes wines from the property's own vineyards, mostly located in the superbly located Bussia zone. There is a fresh, lively Freisa that others were quick to copy, a classic Dolcetto d'Alba, the Bricco Viole from a blend of Nebbiolo and Barbera grapes, and finally, as far as reds are concerned, a Barolo from the Bussia and Monforte crus. When it comes to whites, the limited production of Arneis is worthy of a mention. The new manager, Eleonora Limonci Pavesi, has added two items to the cellar's range, wines that are certainly new to this area and the result of selections made in other wine-growing areas of Italy: the Blanc de Morgex, a Val d'Aosta wine from the foothills of the Alps; and Moscato Passito from Pantelleria.

Freisa delle Langhe 1991   🍷 ①
Freisa is the most traditional Sebaste product and one that contributed decisively to its success in Piemonte. Characterized by a light, pleasing effervescence, it is clean on the nose and fresh on the palate with seductive fruity aromas.

Bricco Viole 1989   🍷 ②
From Nebbiolo and Barbera grapes, aged in barriques. The aromas are still partly masked by oak and potent alcohol. Stylish and elegant on the palate, with a good acid finish. Well-balanced overall and a wine which will improve in the cellar.

Barolo Bussia 1988 DOCG   🍷🍷 ③
A wine from the Bussia di Monforte cru, a classic Barolo zone. The aromas are slightly toasty, with notes of spices and tobacco. Good structure and a mouthfilling palate with a faintly jarring note of acidity. A wine which will grow over the next few years.

La Spinetta

Via Annunziata, 17
Castagnole Lanze (At) 14044
Tel/Fax (0141) 877396

The name Rivetti is synonymous with Moscato. The La Spinetta label is legendary among lovers of this sweet, aromatic Piemontese wine and production of the wine itself is never enough to fill all the waiting orders. The credit for this goes to the Rivetti family, who chose just the right moment to devote their energies to the vinification of their own grapes and create a Moscato with a freshness, fragrance and drinkability unrivaled by anyone else on the market. The Rivettis are a patriarchal family with head of the family Giuseppe surrounded by his three sons Bruno, Carlo and Giorgio and their respective spouses. Together, they manage about 20 ha of vineyards, most of which is planted in Moscato with the remainder in Grignolino, Dolcetto, Nebbiolo and Barbera. In the cellar, the various different crus of Moscato, San Rumu, Bric Lapasot, Biancospino and Bricco Quaglia, are vinified separately as are smaller quantities of Grignolino, Dolcetto, Barbera and Nebbiolo. From a blend of Barbera and Nebbiolo, La Spinetta produces a fresh, drinkable red called Ca' di Pian as well as, since 1989, the Pin, the leading red wine of the house.

Bricco Quaglia 1991
Obtained from the Moscato grapes of the superb La Spinetta vineyards, Bricco Quaglia is one of the estate's four crus. The 1991 vintage reflects the level quality attained in preceding years. The typically varietal aromas are explosive, the palate fleshy and lingering with the right degree of effervescence and a clean, dry finish.

Dolcetto d'Alba
San Rumu 1991 DOC
While La Spinetta is particularly well-known for its Moscato, the cellar also knows how to handle the traditional local reds. This Dolcetto d'Alba is absolutely typical both on the nose, with a well-defined note of almond, and on the palate where it is frank and deliciously dry.

Pin 1990
The leading Rivetti red comes from a blend of Barbera and Nebbiolo grapes, aged in barriques and French oak barrels. Remarkable structure, with rich, full aromas where the oak is still to the fore. Powerful and extremely elegant on the palate, with well-defined tannins to guarantee a great future.

Tenuta La Tenaglia

Strada Santuario di Crea, 6
Serralunga di Crea (Al) 015020
Tel. (0142) 940252
Fax (0142) 455446

This estate, located on the steep hillside leading up to the Sanctuary of Crea, once belonged to the Governor of Moncalvo and condottiere Giorgio Tenaglia, and the vine has been cultivated here since the Middle Ages. The favorable micro-climate and well-protected location, safe from the ravages of frost and hale, persuaded Turin-born Delfina Quattrocolo to move in with her family about ten years ago and start producing wine commercially. She delegated the task of vinification to one of the best wine-technicians in Piemonte, Donato Lanati, while she looks after the vineyards herself. And Delfina knows exactly what she wants to do. She uses very few chemical-based products and indeed hopes to do without them entirely. Yields are very limited, with separate harvests for each vineyard according to the speed at which the grapes ripen. Monferrato means that the estate's leading product is, obviously, Barbera, which La Tenaglia produces in several versions. These range form barrique-aged, to a livelier version and a traditional wine from long-established vines, which it is no exaggeration to call "sumptuous". Grignolino and Chardonnay complete a range which lovingly highlights the character and personality of local varieties in line with the latest in modern wine-making techniques.

Bricco Crea 1991
From a vineyard located on the hillside from which it takes its name, Bricco Crea is a Barbera-based blend that catches the attention with its clean, fresh aromas and the softness and roundness characteristic of this sub-zone of Monferrato. Full-flavored and frank on the palate, backed up by good texture.

Grignolino
del Monferrato Casalese 1991 DOC
Grignolino is a typical wine of this area of Piemonte and the Grignolino made by Tenuta La Tenaglia has attractive flowery aromas and cherry-red color tending to orange in the glass. Only moderate structure but loads of personality. Drink at once.

Giorgio Tenaglia 1990
This Barbera-based red is Delfina Quattrocolo greatest achievement. Obtained from the grapes of a long-established parcel, it has a deep garnet-red hue and herbaceous aromas followed by an elegant bouquet of ripe fruit and clean spices. Soft and well-balanced on the palate.

Emozioni 1989
Emozioni is a red from Barbera grapes aged in barriques. The oak is well-integrated with complex aromas and notes of ripe fruit. Remarkable color, very deep and intense. The palate warm, full-bodied structure and good length, with a touch of acidity.

Terre del Barolo

Via Alba Barolo, 5
Castiglione Falletto (Cn) 12060
Tel. (0173) 262053
Fax (0173) 231968

The history of the Cooperativa Terre del Barolo is inseparably linked to the name of Arnaldo Rivera, who founded the enterprise and, until his death in 1987, was its unflaggingly enthusiastic president. Rivera was a larger-than-life character who seemed to have come out of a tale by Fenoglio, who wrote about the partisans in the Langhe. A lieutenant in the Italian Alpine troops first and after 1943 a partisan with the Garibaldi Brigade, Rivera became mayor of Castiglione in 1951 and held office until 1987. Despite his many other commitments, he continued to teach until his retirement. The success of the Terre del Barolo cooperative, the only one in the Langhe not to go under ignominiously, is due to Arnaldo's insistence that members should hand over to the cooperative cellar their entire grape harvest and not just second-choice fruit. The policy is still followed today by the 540 members. The current president Matteo Bosco introduced the new strategy of vinifying separately the best crus from each member. Today, alongside the huge output of good everyday wines for the mass market, Terre di Barolo is developing a range of premium-quality wines which is certain to be extremely interesting, given the enormous potential of the cooperative.

Barbera d'Alba Valdisera 1990 DOC 🍷 ①
The policy of separate vinification of the best crus from members of the cooperative has created among others this Barbera. Wonderfully representative of the zone, it is characterized by a moderate structure but exceptional freshness and drinkability.

Diano d'Alba 🍷 ①
Cascinotto Vigneti Colla 1990 DOC
The small town of Diano d'Alba has been awarded a Denominazione di Origine Controllata for its Dolcetto and it is from Diano d'Alba that this Cascinotto comes. Deep ruby red, with intense aromas where spices emerge. Nicely integrated on the palate.

Barolo Rocche 1985 DOCG 🍷 ②
Rocche di Castiglione Falletto is one of the most prestigious Barolo crus. Well-developed aromas, with traces of dried mushrooms and well-rounded on the palate, where the components are already well-integrated. Tangy, clean finish.

Gian Carlo Travaglini

Strada delle Vigne, 36
Gattinara (Vc) 13045
Tel/Fax (0163) 833588

Gattinara is one of Piemonte's finest wine-growing areas with Nebbiolo the most important variety. The wine, aged for five years, has superb structure, remarkable tannins and excellent aging potential. The Travaglini cellar is widely recognized as one of the best producers of this wine, which is made in standard and vintage versions. Travaglini has never suspended production, even during those years when wines of this kind were little appreciated, and thanks to the Travaglinis' name and reputation, stocks have always sold without difficulty. The Travaglini vineyards are scattered all over the slopes of Gattinara so that at harvest time, the best grapes can be selected to make a premium-quality product every year. In contrast to the practice of other cellars, the various crus are not vinified separately. Recently, in response to a market demand for more ready-to-drink wines, Travaglini has produced a Nebbiolo not aged in wood which is sold only a few months after the harvest.

Gattinara 1986 DOC 🍷 ①
From Nebbiolo grapes grown in the Vercelli zone. A Travaglini Gattinara that has good texture in the standard version, deep ruby red color and aromas redolent of ripe fruit. Full-bodied and lingering on the palate.

Gattinara 🍷🍷 ②
Riserva Numerata 1986 DOC
Travaglini's finest selection is this red from a blend of premium-quality grapes from several different vineyards. The result is a wine with remarkable personality, deep ruby-red color and a complex, lingering bouquet. Tremendously satisfying on the palate, where the tannins are already round and well-balanced.

F.lli Trinchero

Loc. Vianoce, 27
Agliano d'Asti (At) 14041
Tel/Fax (0141) 954016

The Trinchero brothers own a cellar that has been active since the 1930s and recently, though continuing to follow tradition, they have initiated a process of renovation and product diversification. This means that the Trinchero flagship continues to be Barbera, the leading grape type in the zone, cultivated on hills that offer ideal conditions for this variety. Trinchero's Barbera Vigna del Noce has a classic personality and firm structure with lots of aging potential. The cellar also proposes a lively, easy-drinking version called Luna di Marzo and goes on to pay the inevitable tribute to current market trends with the barrique-aged La Barslina. The range of reds also features Bonarda, Grignolino, Freisa, a good, dry Brachetto and above all an extremely interesting blend of Dolcetto and Merlot called Le Taragne, with impressive body and elegance. Vignapalmé from Arneis grapes and Malvasia are the whites but Trinchero is at its best with red wines.

Barbera d'Asti Vigna del Noce 1990 DOC

In the traditional style, with a nose that has yet to open fully and impressive structure. More bottle-age is needed to smooth out the rough edges typical of the variety which are still apparent. A wine that time will enhance.

Le Taragne 1990

Le Taragne is the intriguing result of a successful new blend of Dolcetto and Merlot grapes grown on the Trinchero estate. Dolcetto aromas with notes of almond are present and prominent alcohol. Tangy and dry on the palate.

Giuseppe Domenico Vajra

Loc. Vergne, via delle Viole, 25
Barolo (Cn) 12060
Tel. (0173) 56257
Fax (0173) 56345

17 ha. of vineyards in the Vergne zone on the Barolo hills are the excellent credentials of one of the leading companies in the Langhe. Aldo Vajra looks after the estate lovingly coaxing the best grapes possible from the soil for his wines of structure, body and roundness. Despite the great number of parcels, Vajra's production stands at less than 100,000 bottles a year. Both standard and cru wines are produced. Outstanding among the latter are Barbera d'Alba Bricco delle Viole, Dolcetto d'Alba Coste & Fossati and Barolo Bricco delle Viole. This small grower is not a great believer in trends and puts his wines on the market only when he has tasted them and thinks they are ready for sale. Holder of a degree in agriculture, Aldo revived the family estate after it had lain neglected for a generation. With his wife Milena, he devoted himself to the cultivation of vines which would produce the great wines he wanted to make. For Aldo, the first step along the road to a good wine is taken in the vineyard. The Varjas have also built a large, functional, modern cellar divided into three sectors for vinification, fermentation and bottle aging.

Dolcetto d'Alba Coste & Fossati 1990 DOC

Obtained from grapes grown in two different locations, Coste and Fossati, this deep violet and ruby Dolcetto has distinct aromas with a marked herbaceous note. Good structure on the palate with well-balanced components and a tannic, slightly astringent finish.

Barbera d'Alba Bricco delle Viole 1989 DOC

Intense garnet red, a Barbera that although still evolving has great structure and will have much to offer in the future. Frank aromas with prominent fruit. Full on the palate, with good length and sufficient acidity to back up a texture rich in alcohol and extracts.

Barolo 1987 DOCG

A very elegant Barolo, a fine result in a poor vintage. Ruby red with brick-red tints, very stylish aromas and marked flowery notes. Already evolved on the palate, with soft tannins. A Barolo that is now reaching its peak.

G.L. Viarengo e figlio

Via Roma, 88
Castello di Annone (At) 14034
Tel. (0141) 401131
Fax (0141) 401706

This estate is in some ways emblematic of the entire history of Asti wines. It was founded in 1883 by Gian Lorenzo Viarengo, who had returned from a profitable period as an immigrant worker in the United States. It has been in production ever since, enjoying the prosperity that came with the triumph of Barbera wines in the 'osterie', or taverns, of Piemonte and Lombardia. Recently, the estate has had to raise its quality levels to weather a crisis brought on by the demand for better wines. The Viarengo cellar, now run by the fourth generation of the family, took up the challenge and under the enterprising management of Carlo Viarengo and Paolo Dania it is now well on the way to achieve its goal. The product range includes classic Asti wines such as Grignolino and Barbera - always a Viarengo strong point- as well as other Piemontese wines like the white Cortese di Gavi, Dolcetto and Barolo of the Langhe. Most wines are vinified on-site, some of the grapes coming from the few hectares the cellar owns and the remainder from other growers.

Grignolino d'Asti 🍷 ①
Della Tagliata 1991 DOC
Pale cherry red, with flowery, elegant, lingering aromas. A Grignolino d'Asti obtained from a Viarengo vineyard with typical varietal characteristics on the palate. Fresh and clean-tasting, recommended for serving with appetizers.

Barbera d'Asti 🍷 ①
Bricco Morra 1990 DOC
Made with grapes from the Nizza Monferrato zone, a Bricco Morra from the great 1990 vintage. The excellent quality of the grapes has given superb texture and elegant, complex aromas which are unusual for the variety. Warm and lingering on the palate.

Barbera d'Asti Superiore 🍷🍷 ②
Il Falé 1989 DOC
Also obtained from selected Barbera grapes from long-established vineyards and aged two years, first in barriques, then in the bottle. The vanilla wood is unobtrusive on the nose, allowing the varietal aromas to come through. Full-bodied on the palate with good length.

Vietti

Piazza Vittorio Veneto, 5
Castiglione Falletto (Cn) 12060
Tel. (0173) 62825
Fax (0173) 62941

Vietti wines are famous for their consistency and one can be sure of drinking a good product even in years which are less than exciting whether one tastes Dolcetto d'Alba, Barbaresco or Barolo. Underpinning this quality is the serious Vietti approach to grape selection, both in the estate vineyards and when it comes to bought-in fruit. A visit to the cellars will also reveal the care taken over vinification and aging of the traditional Langhe wines with stainless- steel vats for temperature controlled fermentation, traditional wood barrels for aging more important wines, and barriques in which the first Vietti experiments with aging are taking place, for the moment only with reds. The most interesting products are the Barolos, with Riserva Villero, vinified only in outstanding vintages, Rocche and Brunate. We should also point out the Barbera d'Alba Pian Romualdo from Monforte d'Alba and the Scarrone from Castiglione Falletto as well as the crus of Dolcetto d'Alba Sant'Anna and Disa, with their surprisingly full body and structure.

Barbera d'Alba Scarrone 1990 DOC 🍷 ①
From a vineyard below the castle at Castiglione Falletto. An entirely successful Vietti Barbera d'Alba with aromas that after a first impact lacking a little definition open out into a fresh, fruity bouquet. On the palate the remarkable body has well-balanced components and soft, round texture.

Dolcetto d'Alba Disa 1990 DOC 🍷 ①
Lovely ruby red and a herbaceous opening on the nose with strong hints of spices and pepper. Good personality on the palate with rich extract and a tannic, slightly bitter, finish typical of the varietal. Excellent drinking.

Barolo Brunate 1988 DOCG 🍷 ③
The first impression on the nose lacks definition, but then gives way to notes of tar and dried rose. A Barolo with only moderate concentration on the palate, as is already obvious from the color, but with good texture and a very pleasant bitterish finish.

Barolo Rocche 1988 DOCG 🍷🍷 ③
Another Barolo from the Castiglione Falletto zone, from the celebrated Rocche cru. In the modern idiom, with tannins still prominent but already delicious to drink. Full-flavored and lingering on the palate, with subtle, persistent aromas of great elegance. Destined for a very long life.

Villa Fiorita

Via Case Sparse, 2
Castello di Annone (At) 14034
Tel. (0141) 401231-401852
Fax (0141) 401209

Villa Fiorita is a good example of how intelligent investment can transform an old property on the brink of collapse into a model company. The Rondolino brothers, entrepreneurs from Turin, embarked on this project in 1986, when they took over the management of the old Castello di Annone estate. Since then, they have created a cellar equipped with up-to-date equipment and renovated the vineyards. Alongside the traditional local varieties, Barbera, Grignolino, Freisa and Cortese, they have planted international grape types such as Chardonnay, Sauvignon and -a very unusual choice for Monferrato- Gamay. As well as vinification of the traditional Grignolino, Barbera and Freisa, experiments are being carried out with barriques for Giorgione, from Barbera grapes, and for the noble white Sovrano, for which vineyards have recently been established. Rosé wines are also made, Le Corti being the most successful, and carbonic maceration is used for the Abaco "vin nouveau" obtained from Gamay grapes. All in all, a very active company and a stimulating addition to the Asti scene.

Sovrano 1990 ☙ ③
A recent planting (1987) of Sauvignon and Chardonnay vines from France. A serious, barrique-aged white. Elegant aromas with marked varietal notes of Sauvignon. Modest structure on the palate but fresh and well-balanced.

Le Corti di Villa Fiorita 1991 ☙ ②
The best of the rare Piemontese rosés. From Grignolino, Barbera and Freisa grapes made with a brief rosé fermentation after light carbonic maceration of part of the cuvée. A very fresh wine, with aromas of wild rose. Good texture on the palate, slightly tannic.

Grignolino d'Asti ☙ ①
Pian delle Querce 1990 DOC
This 1990 Villa Fiorita vintage proves that Grignolino can give premium-quality wines. Attractive, with good texture and a color already shading into orange. Medium-full palate, with a typically astringent finish.

Il Giorgione 1988 ☙ ③
From Barbera grapes aged in French-oak barriques, this Giorgione has moderately intense ruby color and aromas where the vanilla of the wood dominates the fruit. Soft on the palate, with powerful extract and rather less prominent acidity.

Villa Sparina

Fraz. Monterotondo, 56
Gavi (Al) 15066
Tel. (0143) 634880-634958
Fax (0143) 634895

In the 18th century, the aristocratic families of Genoa built summer residences in the countryside around Gavi, proof that the climate here was considered particularly clement, sunny and warm, but at the same time breezy and invigorating, in short the ideal climate to grow vines and produce good white wines. That is why the Moccagatta family acquired the Villa Sparina estate in 1977, moving into the lovely house right in the middle of the beautiful vine-covered valley that surrounds it. The family intended to work there but also to escape from the city and enjoy a very different life-style. Today the property has 39 ha., of which 30 are planted in Cortese di Gavi, as well as new facilities which permit the storage and vinification of more than 3,500 hl in a recently-built underground cellar. All these were necessary investments, but the Moccagattas know that it is in the vineyard that quality is born. Guyot method short-pruning, very low yields and painstaking care during the manual harvest of the grapes are the secret of Villa Sparina's whites. Fruity and aromatic, pure Gavi in style, but all with great structure and complexity.

Gavi di Gavi 1991 DOC ☙ ①
The vintage and the policy of low yields produced a very limited harvest of only 32 q/ha. The resulting wine is rich in extract and has good density on the palate, while the aromas of almond and acacia-wood are enhanced by the long fermentation - 28 days in stainless-steel vats.

Gavi di Gavi La Villa 1991 DOC ☙ ②
From a selection of the best grapes on the property, the superb condition of the fruit made it possible to macerate on the skins for 18 hours with very little sulphur. Lovely golden straw-yellow color and broad aromas of sage, banana and acacia-wood. The flavor is full and mouthfilling, with noble aromas and good acidity.

Gavi Villa Sparina Brut 1988 DOC ☙ ③
A DOC spumante produced from monovarietal Cortese di Gavi grapes. The 1988 vintage was outstanding for this wine, which has intense perlage, perhaps slightly too much mousse and stylish aromas, delicately balanced between yeasty notes of crusty bread and flowery hints.

Gianni Voerzio

Strada Loreto, 1
La Morra (Cn) 12064
Tel/Fax (0173) 509194

Voerzio makes modern wines in a beautiful modern building with up-to-date equipment. The large wooden barrels that once characterized all the historic cellars of the Langhe region have disappeared and the cellars are now dominated by stainless steel and barriques. The range of wines covers almost all of the local varieties - Dolcetto d'Alba, Barolo, Roero Arneis, Freisa, Nebbiolo, Barbera d'Alba and Moscato d'Asti. All these wines have unassertive body, acidity that is never too sharp, and balance and roundness on the palate, in response to a demand for softness and delicacy as opposed to marked tannin content. The only exception is the Serrapiù, from Nebbiolo and Barbera grapes aged in barriques. In blind tastings, it showed good character, excellent texture and firm body, well integrated by the sweetness of the small French barrels. The Voerzio Barolo is also exceptional, with its breadth of aromas and unaggressive body. Very popular, especially with young people, are the Roero Arneis and the naturally fermented Freisa.

Roero Arneis
Bricco Cappellina 1991 DOC
Gianni Voerzio's Arneis comes from grapes bought in the Roero area and consistently stands out for excellent quality. The 1991 vintage has subtle, sweet aromas, with notes of tropical fruit. Very fresh on the palate, backed up by good acidity.

Serrapiù 1990
Good depth and definition of aroma, where the fruit is evident and not masked by the soft, seductive oak. Correct aging in barrique and bottle allow the wine to develop a complex nose, dominated by notes of spice. Good length and depth on the palate, with well-balanced tannins.

Barolo La Serra 1988 DOCG
From a prestigious vineyard at La Morra on the border with the legendary Brunate cru, this Barolo is beautifully expressed. Moderately deep garnet red, with clean aromas. Full, but not overwhelming, on the palate with good balance of tannins and acidity.

Roberto Voerzio

Loc. Cerreto
La Morra (Cn) 12064
Tel. (0173) 509196-50123
Fax (0173) 509196

Roberto and Pinuccia Voerzio are a couple who share a passion for wine. Together, they carefully manage their vineyards and run their cellar, doing everything with a marvelous "joie de vivre." The cellar has expanded over the past few years as a result. The crus of Barolo, Dolcetto d'Alba and Barbera d'Alba from which the Voerzios obtain their grapes are located in some of the finest spots in the commune of La Morra and this comes through in their wines. The Barolo La Serra is always full-bodied with good length. Even in difficult years like 1987, the structure is not overwhelmed by the well-integrated tannins. The Dolcetto d'Alba Priavino has young, fruity aromas followed by a flavor that is all the more attractive for a few months' bottle-age. Alongside classic Langhe wines, the Voerzio couple has done a good job experimenting with Nebbiolo and Barbera in barriques to explore every possibility that the two classic grape types offer. The Voerios are assured of a bright future, a future they have earned by consolidating the reputation of La Morra wines.

Barbera d'Alba Vignasse 1989 DOC 🍇 ②
Three years after the vintage, this Barbera expresses its potential to the full. A wine with good structure, where fruit is well-integrated with the oak in a full, soft body. Tangy and well-rounded on the palate, with a lingering finish.

Vignaserra 1989 🍇🍇 ③
From a blend of Nebbiolo and Barbera grapes grown in the commune of La Morra, Vignaserra is an excellent example of the new trends in Langhe winemaking. Aged in barriques, it already has complex, stylish aromas. Good structure on the palate in a texture which still has just a hint of acidity.

Barolo Brunate 1988 DOCG 🍇🍇 ③
Obtained from a single hectare in Brunate located in the upper part of the cru, on the border with La Serra. The soil is partly clay-and-chalk and partly tufa-rich, and Roberto Voerzio coaxes from it a cru with lots of personality, complex aromas and a very full body on the palate. Excellent length.

Barolo La Serra 1988 DOCG 🍇 ③
The nose of this cru is still closed. It has remarkable structure on the palate, with alcohol to the fore. Exceptional personality in a wine that will be at its best with a little more time in the cellar.

BAROLO 1988
Denominazione di Origine Controllata e Garantita
Cerequio

Imbottigliato all'origine nell'Azienda Agricola
Roberto Voerzio La Morra - Italia

13,5% vol.   L 07 - 91   e 75 cl.

Barolo Cerequio 1988 DOCG 🍇🍇🍇 ③
Another wine from the magnificent valley, in the commune of La Morra where the Brunate and Serra crus are also to be found. The awesome structure guarantees the future development of this Barolo. Voerzio thins the vineyard very thoroughly, usually in the month of July, when the grapes are still unripe. The rows of 20-30 year-old vines stand in grass and only organic treatments are used. Vinification is traditional, with a 15-day maceration where the cap is left on the surface and regularly broken up. Fermentation is carried out entirely in stainless-steel vats, after which part of the wine goes into barriques while the remainder is transferred into 15 hl vats for about 15-20 months, depending on the vintage. This calculated combination of modern and traditional approaches gives the wine superb personality. Deep garnet-tinted ruby red, with a very fresh nose containing hints of Morello cherry, berries and coffee. Stupendous, concentrated structure, with boisterous fruit. Very drinkable, elegant with a tangy finish. Great cellar potential but already a delight to drink even though it is a little "green."

Costantino Charrère

Rue du Moulin, 33
Aymavilles (Ao) 11010
Tel. (0165) 902135
Fax (0165) 902274

Charrère's vineyards are located on the morainic hills of Aymavilles in a superb wine-growing area. Costantino Charrère continues to experiment with special regard for clones of Petit Rouge, a local variety from the Valle d'Aosta but without neglecting the vinification of minor grapes like Prier Rouge in order to relaunch wines like Premetta. This young grower inherited from his grandparents the passion and tenacity you need to take on the job of wine-making. He left his job as a teacher to be able to look after the vineyards full-time. His wines are already widely appreciated and improve each year thanks to careful selection of the grapes and fermentation in barrels preserved in the family cellars, where one can still see an old-fashioned flour mill.

La Sabla 1989
A blend of Petit Rouge, Fumin and Tinturier that came to the attention of wine-lovers because of a structure that allows it to age much better than other Valle d'Aosta wines. Bright ruby red, with rich wild-berry aromas. Dry on the palate, well-balanced and elegant.

Premetta 1990
One of Prier Rouge's hallmarks is the pink color, shading into cherry red. Subtle aromas and dry, alcohol-rich flavor in a wine that will age well. Will reach its peak in three years.

La Crotta de Vegnerons

Piazza Roncas, 2
Chambave (Ao) 11023
Tel/Fax (0166) 46670

Established in 1980, La Crotta de Vegnerons commenced operations in 1985. Today, there are 135 members working under the careful supervision of Yves Burgay. Chambave was one of the first areas in Valle d'Aosta to witness the renaissance of wine-growing and the credit goes in large measure to Burgay. Under his watchful eye, small growers bring their grapes to the cellar and here, after meticulous selection, the fruit is vinified. Thanks to the results so far obtained and to great demand for Moscato, the area under vine is increasing and now extends over almost the whole of the estate owned by the cooperative. The good fortune of this estate, one of the best equipped, prompted other producers' associations to redouble their own efforts. The most important grape type is Moscato Bianco, from which a dry wine and above all an extraordinary Passito dessert wine are obtained. New experiments have led to the rediscovery of Fumin, an old grape type that had all but disappeared. Fumin is the basis for an impressive red wine.

Valle d'Aosta Chambave
Muscat 1990 DOC
The bright straw-yellow color, the classy, intense aroma and the dry flavor make this Moscato a delight to drink with almost anything.

Valle d'Aosta Chambave
Muscat Flétri 1990 DOC
A wine to sip while meditating. Unique. Golden-yellow color, intense, Moscato aromas and a sweet, seductively harmonious flavor. Obtained from sun-dried grapes, a wine with great cellar potential.

Fernando Grosjean

Fraz. Ollignan, 1
Quart (Ao) 11010
Tel. (0165) 765283

Vincent Grosjean is one of the most representative personalities on the Valle d'Aosta wine scene. He completed a diploma in viticulture and then took over the management of the family company, assisted by his experienced father Delfino and his innovative young brothers The team has enabled the small Grosjean cellar to expand in a very short time. When you are talking about the Grosjeans, it is a good thing to remember just how attached to the land they are. They refuse, for example, to use herbicides or any other chemical products which might upset the balance of the environment. The Grosjean passion for research is also demonstrated by Vincent's hard work in charge of the Enological Service of the regional administration and as consultant to a number of estates. The Grosjean cellar's range is based on red wines such as Torrette, Pinot Noir and Gamay, with some experimentation with the use of barriques but the Blanc d'Ollignan obtained from Moscato and Pinot Grigio grapes is also an eye-catching wine.

Blanc d'Ollignan 1990 ❦ ②
From a blend of Moscato and Pinot Grigio grapes, a highly aromatic, very elegant white wine with a dry, well-balanced, intense flavor. Rather similar to Moscato di Chambave in its intensity of aroma, but with a little more structure on the palate.

Valle d'Aosta Pinot Noir 1990 DOC ❦ ②
Ruby red tending towards garnet. Fruity, lingering aroma and a dry, slightly tannic flavor. A wine to serve with game "ragouts." The intriguing experiment with barrique-aging has produced soft tannins that make this an extremely well-balanced glass.

Valle d'Aosta Torrette 1990 DOC ❦ ②
Alcohol content of between 11.5° and 12.5°. Ruby red in appearance, full, intense aromas and a dry, clean flavor with a faint bitter overtone. From Petit Rouge grapes.

Institut Agricole Regional

Reg. La Rochere 1/a
Aosta (Ao) 11100
Tel. (0165) 553304
Fax (0165) 553297

The Institut Agricole Regional was founded in 1949 as a school for agriculture on the initiative of the regional administration. The institute, managed since its very early days by the Canons of Gran S. Bernardo, has been of vital importance for the economy of the Valle d'Aosta and has been responsible for the education of many generations of breeders and farmers. On the initiative of Canon Vaudan, since 1951 the institute has developed the viticultural and wine-making sector and is now a valuable point of reference for young growers. The grapes from the 5.3 ha of the institute's parcels at Cossan, La Rochere and Moncenis produce a total of around 70,000 bottles, mainly of red wines. The white varieties grown are Pinot Grigio, Petite Arvine and Chardonnay while Gamay, Petit Rouge, Pinot Nero, Grenache and Syrah are the reds under cultivation.

Vin du Conseil 1990 ❦ ②
A premium-class white wine, full-bodied with an elegant bouquet, marked acidity and great aging potential. The Petite Arvine grape, brought to Valle d'Aosta by the Canons of the Gran S. Bernardo, has been welcomed with approval for its well-integrated palate and fine balance.

Torrette 1990 ❦ ②
Bright red in the glass, with intense aromas of autumn leaves. A wine with a frank, dry flavor. Superb served with the cuisine of Valle d'Aosta. From Petit Rouge grapes.

Tresor du Caveau 1990 ❦ ③
An elegant, aristocratic red with intense, subtle aromas. Dry and full-bodied, it accompanies red meat and game perfectly. The Syrah variety must still be considered experimental at the Institut Agricole as it is only recently that barriques have been introduced for aging.

Les Cretes

Rue du Moulin, 33
Aymevilles (Ao) 11010
Tel. (0165) 902274

If the old saying "unity is strength" is true, this enterprise should produce exceptional results. The team is made up of Vincent Grosjean and Costantino Charrère, winemakers and growers of vast experience, together with the Vai brothers, Paolo and Francesco, chefs and owners of the legendary "Cavallo Bianco" restaurant in Aosta taking care of sales and marketing. It sounds like a winner all the way. Their task was not an easy one, for the aim is to promote the premium-quality wines of Valle d'Aosta worldwide. To this end, the four have bought and leased a total of eight hectares of vineyards at Aymavilles and Saint-Christophe. Given the limited area under vine in Valle d'Aosta as a whole, this is in no way a modest undertaking, indeed it is the biggest private estate in the entire region. With a stock including Petit Rouge, Chardonnay, Pinot Noir, Petite Arvine and Syrah, they immediately started experimentation in their brand new Aymavilles cellar. The first wines came onto the market with the 1991 vintage the results look very interesting.

Les Cretes 1991
The variety is Chardonnay while the stainless steel vinification and aging are traditional, that is to say without barriques. The result is a very fresh wine that gets its acidity, clean taste and sinew, hallmarks of all Valle d'Aosta whites, from the cru. Delicious to drink, although a little lacking in breadth.

Torrette Les Toules 1991
A wine dominated by Petit Rouge, a difficult variety which produces uneven results. In this case, Petit Rouge produced one of the most interesting wines of the vintage. Clean, intense aromas with notes of autumn leaves, well-integrated body and decent structure. The faintly gamey finish is characteristic of the variety.

Puglia

According to the statistics compared to Sicily, Puglia has fewer vineyards, and yet it produces more wine, around 10,000,000 hl of wine a year. Yields per hectare are the highest anywhere in Italy, especially in southern Italy. Vineyards are spread almost everywhere but mainly on the south-eastern side in the Salento area, around Bari in the middle and in the Capitanata area of Foggia in the north.

Viticulture in Puglia, like olive-growing, has an ancient and glorious past. Vines thrived not only in the Roman period but also throughout the centuries to follow. The region was occupied by such diverse civilizations as the Saracens, Goths, Bourbons, Normans and the Aragonese. Ancient Puglia was one of the few active vine-growing and wine-making regions of the peninsula.

Today wine production has changed and intensified, especially in terms of quantity. The 24 DOC areas produce 56 different types of wines. The percentage of DOC wine is quite low compared to the total and is even lower in terms of what is bottled versus what is sold in bulk. Negroamaro, Primitivo, Malvasia Nera, l'Uva di Troia, Sangiovese, Barbera, Aleatico and other less widespread native varietals such as Ottavianello and Apulano Rosso are the most commonly used grapes for the red wines. Verdeca, Malvasia Bianca, Trebbiano, Bombino Bianco, Bianco d'Alessano are the most common for whites, although European grapes such as Sauvignon, Chardonnay and Pinot Bianco are now also being grown.

Many of the DOC appellations exist only on paper. Often there are only a few producers who truly believe in the potential quality of the varietals, or they lack the proper winemaking techniques and motivation to experiment. The situation is not necessarily utterly grim, but some aspects and figures of the regional wine industry speak for themselves, and keeping quiet about the need to make important changes certainly will not help the drive to improve quality. Here, as elsewhere, some wineries have made these changes by divorcing themselves from the generally backward looking and desolate picture. There are some elegant and imposing New Generation reds from Puglia. In the development of rosé wines, areas of particular compatibility, such as the Salento, are being discovered. There is serious experimentation on non-native varietals being carried out with rigor and without mere slavish obedience to fashion. These are positive signs of a change of direction, lead above all by the producers selected for this guide.

Michele Calò e figli

Via Masseria Vecchia, 1
Tuglie (Le) 73058
Tel. (0833) 596242

Vigna Spano, like other imposing reds from Puglia, is made mostly from Negroamaro grapes and to a lesser extent from Malvasia Nera. Its distinguishing elegance places it among the aristocratic wines of the region. It bears witness to the quality of wines made by Michele Calò and his sons, who help him in running of the estate. It is a fairly small winery but efficient and well-organized, with a well-equipped cellar. Calò mostly makes the three styles of the Alezio DOC appellation: white, rosé and red. The brand name "Mijere", or Merum in Latin, means a wine that has not been watered down. This expression is still commonly used in the Apulian dialect, to indicate 'pure wines'. The reds and rosé wines are made from Negroamaro and Malvasia Nera grapes, while the white Alezio Bianco uses the native Verdeca. All wines are clean, well-made and have a very drinkable style.

Mijere Bianco del Salento 1991   🍇 ①
If Salento has rightly earned its reputation as an area for rosé wines, one must not underestimate the potential of its whites. This white from 100% Verdeca grapes is fresh and flowery and shows how pleasant a local varietal wine can be.

Mijere Alezio Rosato 1991 DOC   🔲 ①
Made from the same grapes as the red Alezio. Cherry-red in color, with intense, fruity aromas. Savoury and with full flavor, it can accompany a variety of foods.

Mijere Alezio Rosso 1990 DOC   🍇 ①
From 80% Negroamaro and 20% Malvasia Nera of Lecce, it has quite intense and lingering aromas and is ample and velvety on the palate. Certainly not inferior to the cru Vigna Spano, in terms of quality, in any aspect. A good ambassador for the winery.

Vigna Spano 1988   🍇🍇 ①
Deep ruby-red in color, typical of Puglia's bigger reds, it is made from Negroamaro grapes (and 10% Malvasia Nera). With lingering aromas (of cane sugar and liquorice), it has an ample and appealing palate. A very attractive wine to drink, and one of the region's best reds.

Francesco Candido

Via Armando Diaz, 46
Sandonaci (Br) 72025
Tel. (0831) 635674
Fax (0831) 634695

One of Candido's barrique-aged Negroamaro and Malvasia Nera blends won an award during an event held to discuss the direction and future of Puglia's red wines. This was their flagship wine, called Cappello di Prete, literally the Priest's hat. Brothers Giacomo and Sandro Candido are owners of the winery and are assisted by the skillful wine technician Severino Garofano. The winery still carries the name Francesco Candido after the devoted man who deserves the credit for almost completely replanting his phylloxera-struck vineyards as well as expanding the winery. Francesco began selecting the vine-stocks to improve the quality of the local varietals and started to bottle the production around the end of the 1950s. The wines have already been successful and will certainly improve still further in the future. Wines like Aleatico di Puglia, Salice Salentino (especially the Riserva), Duca D'Aragona and Cappello di Prete represent the best in Puglia's regional wine-making.

Cappello di Prete 1988   🍇🍇 ①
Among the 'new generation' reds, it certainly impresses with its elegance and also for the consistency that it has already demonstrated. From Negroamaro grapes, a deep ruby with purple highlights, intense and ample perfumes, warm and velvety on the palate, with a typical bitter finish.

Salice Salentino Riserva 1988 DOC   🍇 ①
Another interesting red from this dynamic winery. With skillfully judged oak-aging, it is an impressive supple, elegant example of the Salice Salentino DOC, which will continue to develop.

Duca D'Aragona 1986   🍇 ②
The Montepulciano grape interrupts and widens the dialogue between Negroamaro and Malvasia Nera grapes which so frequently dominate the blends of wines of Puglia. A more than successful debut for this wine, well balanced and correctly vinified, but we foresee further improvement in the future.

Leone De Castris

Via Senatore De Castris, 50
Salice Salentino (Le) 73015
Tel. (0832) 731112
Fax (0832) 731114

Having bottled and sold its wines as early as 1925, the De Castris winery has been a benchmark winery in the region for rosé wine. In 1943 an American general fell in love with the Rosé Stravecchio del Salento, as it was called, and decided to export it to the United States, where it took on the name Five Roses. In those days, it was released after only two years' aging. Styles of wine and the tastes of wine-drinkers have since evolved, of course. In addition to the Rosé Stravecchio, and the traditional styles of Salice Salentino reds, De Castris is also experimenting with oak-aged selections like Donna Lisa and new wines from European grapes. Particularly interesting are the Vigna Case Alte Sauvignon and the Imago Chardonnay. Leonardo Pintois has been the in-house enologist for the past 20 years and thus he represents an element of continuity in a transitional phase. The owner, Cav. Leon De Castris, is also President of the Unione Italiana Vini.

Vigna Case Alte Sauvignon 1991
A new wine for the De Castris range and made from Sauvignon grapes; if somewhat subtle or lacking in varietal character, it is clean and well-made, with a respectable, refined nose and palate.

Five Roses 1991
Made from Negroamaro, with some Malvasia Nera. One of Italy's historic, benchmark rosés, certainly among the best in its kind. Shrugging off any memories of the odd, recent off vintage, this has decidedly refined fruity aromas and an attractive, well-balanced, savoury flavor.

Salice Salentino
Maiana Riserva 1990 DOC
Deep ruby-red in color, with pleasant and refined, relatively fresh aromas, though not particularly marked. Harmonious on the palate, with notable tannins, likely to improve further.

Salice Salentino
Donna Lisa Riserva 1988 DOC
Our favorite of the wide range of products: an oak-aged Riserva of Salice Salentino which is more balanced than past vintages. With rich aromas and a full and velvety flavor, it is maturing well, with no signs of fatigue.

Rivera

Viale Alto Adige, 139
Andria (Ba) 70037
Tel/Fax (0883) 82862

Owners of Rivera, the De Corato family has been making wine since the beginning of the century. The stages of its history, normally in the vanguard of development, mirror closely the evolution of the region's enology; a history of constant progress and improvements in quality. The winery's restoration after World War 2 marked the beginning of estate-bottling as well as the early experimentats, in the newly planted vineyards, with native and non-native varietals such as Sauvignon and Pinot Bianco. These were the splendidly positioned vineyards near Castel del Monte (with its impressive Swabian architecture). Today the company has a considerable production, mainly from grapes from the original property at Castel del Monte, sold under that name, and also from a newer property, named after the winery's founder, Sebastiano De Corato. The latter supplies the wines for the new Vigna al Monte range of Sauvignon, Pinot Bianco and most recently, Aglianico, which threatens to overshadow Falcone, one of Puglia's best reds in recent years.

Castel del Monte Pinot Bianco
Terre al Monte 1991 DOC
The Terre al Monte range features Rivera's experimental wines, which have recently received DOC status. A Pinot Bianco with good personality, refined fruity aromas, and a well-expressed varietal character.

Castel del Monte Sauvignon
Terre al Monte 1991 DOC
Sauvignon is right at home in this hilly part of Castel del Monte, especially with its tufo-loamy terrain. Bright straw-yellow in color, with fairly intense varietal aromas; savoury and clean on the palate, with lightly tart freshness.

Castel del Monte Rosso
Riserva Il Falcone 1988 DOC
The first of the 'new generation' wines, the 1990 vintage maintains its high standing thanks to its aromatic elegance and flavor. A full-bodied wine, soft and austere, a blend of selected small-berry Uva di Troia and Montepulciano grapes.

Rosa del Golfo

Via Garibaldi, 56
Alezio (Le) 73011
Tel. (0833) 281045
FAx (0331) 992365

Retiring and yet dynamic, Mino Calò has firm ideas on how to achieve and maintain the quality standards that have made his winery one of the most important of the region, if not of all southern Italy. His Rosa del Golfo, a first-press traditional-style blend of Negroamaro and Malvasia Nera, is still one of the best rosés in the country. In addition to this rosé there is the white Bollina (standard version and the special selection Scaliere di Rosa del Golfo), made from Verdeca grapes, and two interesting reds, Portulano and Quarantale. In Salentino dialect the name "Quarantale" refers to the hard work done in the vineyards with a hoe but the true meaning is based on the word quarantum, or the sentence to which the deserters of the Roman army were condemned to serve: "quaranta" (forty) days of hard labor, in the blistering summer heat. This reference to ancient times we do not find empty as all the innovations and progress of this estate seem to come from a true regard for tradition.

Bolina 1991   ♈ ①
For pleasant easy summer sipping, fresh and uncomplicated. Good wine making ensures that this is a clean and attractive wine, made entirely from Verdeca grapes.

Rosa del Golfo 1991   ▦ ①
Easy to spot even in blind tastings, with its unique lively pink color and coral-red highlights. From lightly crushed Negroamaro grapes and a small percentage of Malvasia Nera. Despite the rather unfavorable year, it's still one of the best of its type with its pleasant fruitiness.

Quarantale 1988   ♈♈ ①
Mostly from Negroamaro grapes, with 10% Malvasia Nera, partly aged in small barrels followed by bottle-aging, for a rather long time. Intense aromas, with spicy and vanilla nuances, which translate to the palate; full and well-balanced.

Cosimo Taurino

Via Toselli, 8
Guagnano (Le) 73010
Tel. (0832) 706490
Fax (0832) 706242

With their unusual and unforgettable names, the two vineyards called Patriglione and Notarpanaro produce the grapes and names for the two flagship wines of estate. Other vineyards are for experimental whites, especially Chardonnay, and for the traditional Salice Salentino DOC. Cosimo Taurino abandoned his profession of pharmacist to work as a full-time winemaker. The results, which are certainly impressive and make one hope that more pharmacists become winemakers, have placed Cosimo Taurino wines among the ranks of the best in southern Italy. Enologist Severino Garofano has played a very important part. The winery is located in the heart of Salento, a land traditionally suited for red wines. Even though the winery also produces whites, it is the marvellous reds like Patriglione (mostly Negroamaro with a touch of Malvasia Nera) and Notarpanaro as well as the classic Salice Salentino that have truly established the Taurino reputation.

Salice Salentino Riserva 1986 DOC   ♈ ①
Taurino is particularly well-known for fine reds, such as this one with its impressively ample and complex bouquet, of berries, among other aromas. Supple on the palate, of rather long and pronounced flavors.

Brindisi Patriglione 1983 DOC   ♈♈ ②
From Negroamaro grapes and, in small percentage, Malvasia Nera, it has a distinct color, lively and luminous, with lots of spice, tobacco and fur on the nose and a remarkably concentrated and rewarding flavor. Made only during special vintages such as '83, it is now at its peak.

Notarpanaro 1983   ♈ ①
Another first-class product from Puglia, made from the same grapes as Patriglione but grown in the Notarpanaro vineyard. Again, a Cosimo Taurino wine noticeable for its strength, though not lacking elegance, complexity and lingering aromas.

Vallone

Via XXV Luglio, 5
Lecce (Le) 73100
Tel. (0832) 308041
Fax (0832) 43108

The dynamic and outspoken Vallone sisters, Vittorina and Maria Teresa, together with the winery director, Donato Lazzari, and their enologist, Severino Garofano, have done much to improve wine-making in southern Italy. The diversified range of Vallone wines includes local DOCs as well as the modern experimental wines. The Brindisi DOC is made in both rosè and red styles, particularly successfully in the special selection Vigna Flaminio, and the Salice Salentino DOC, made in various styles, have been produced by Vallone ever since the beginning in 1982. Meanwhile, the Sauvignon grapes come from the Le Viscarde vineyard and are used to make two "new generation" wines: the fresh, young drinking Sauvignon del Salento and the Le Viscarde, more structured and ageable. Also modern is Graticciaia, made from the local Negroamaro grapes, semi-dried on "graticci". Other attractive new products are in the making and will undoubtedly increase the number of wine drinkers already deservedly captured by this estate.

Passo delle Viscarde 1990
Passo is short for Passito, which means a raisined, dessert-style of wine as the Malvasia Bianca and Sauvignon grapes are indeed left to dry for a couple of months. Bright yellow-gold, with fairly ample aromas, a rich flavor and well-balanced acidity and sugar.

Brindisi Rosso
Vigna Flaminio 1989 DOC
Vallone's version of the Brindisi DOC, this Vigna Flaminio '89 single-vineyard wine is from Negroamaro and Malvasia Nera grapes. It combines smoothness with juicy, vinous fruit; for versatile, easy drinking.

Graticciaia 1989
Graticciaia is an exclusive Vallone wine, of Negroamaro grapes, named after the reed mats or "graticci" used for its raisining technique. Released after some barrique-aging and made in the only the best vintages, it has intense mature fruit and a smooth flavor.

Rating System

An exemplary wine of its type with outstanding local character

An international premium quality wine

A Top Wine, considered one of the 150 best wines in the world

The 'grape bunch' symbol is used to indicate the color of the wine; the number of bunches represents the quality rating assigned by the contributor

Sardegna

Sardegna, or Sardinia to English speakers, with its diverse and complex variety of grape types, is a truly singular region. Recently archaeological researchers have discovered that viticulture was practised during prehistoric times (which were associated with the mysterious stone towers called "nuraghi") as well as during the Phoenician-Punic and the Roman periods. In centuries to follow, the island was occupied many civilizations: Byzantines, Muslims, Pisans and Genoese. This resulted in a fractured and stunted viticulture and winemaking tradition. But the arrival of the Spaniards in the 13th century marked a long and successful period of strong Spanish influence on Sardinian wines, which were thus obviously influenced by Sherry, Madeira and Port.

The name Vernaccia di Oristano goes back to Roman times, with "Vernaculum" indicating of native character. Malvasia, whether of Cagliari or of Bosa, apparently dates back to the Byzantine age. The Cannonau grape seems to have been introduced in the Nuraghic age. Some say it is a derivative of a Spanish varietal. The Carignano del Sulcis grape is also probably of Spanish origin, just as is the Torbato di Alghero, from the Catalan word "Tubat". Another ancient Sardinian grape, the Cagnulari, has been recently revitalized by a number of producers. The common white Vermentino is certainly from Liguria, along with Nuragus. The latter became somewhat the symbol of the 1950s cooperative-lead trend. A variety which could too easily produce the light, drinkable wines then in demand, Nuragus was produced in great quantities under DOC regulations which allowed some of the highest yields in Italy. The consequent wine had a more or less anonymous character, in contrast to the present movement, lead mostly by private companies, towards a wine with as much personality as the other native varietals.

The current production, which varies between 2-3,000,000 hl a year, is improving in terms of quality. The viticultural areas can be divided into four, each part with its own distinct style and type of wines: the hot, cork-wooded north with its fresh Torbato and Vermentino (Gallura, Alghero and Anglona); the eastern hills down from Monti del Gennargentu (Cannonau and Mandrolisai); the variable mid-west for its Malvasia di Bosa and Vernaccia di Oristano (Planargia and Oristano); lastly, the warm south (Cagliari, Campidano, Sulcis and the islands). Everywhere there are signs of progress and experimentation from the small producers such as Cherchi, Contini, Argiolas and others, to the larger producers such as Sella & Mosca, to some of the cooperative wineries and the Centro Enologico Sardo which performs valuable research and data-base work. These form the vanguard of a movement which will increasingly interesting to follow.

Antonio Argiolas & C.

Via Roma, 56/58
Serdiana (Ca) 09040
Tel. (070) 740606
Fax (070) 743264

Located about 20 km from Cagliari, the commune of Serdiana (from "Xeridiani", meaning a place with many cedar trees) is renowned for its flourishing grape and olive cultivation thanks to its climate and abundant natural water resources. 80 year-old Antonio Argiolas, now assisted by his sons, Franco and Peppetto, has worked in the ideal conditions of the Serdiana vineyards for over 50 years, bringing to bear the use of modern wine-making equipment. The result is a foremost position in Sardinian enology. His vineyards, situated at 300 m altitude on the hills of Trexenta, grow the native Nuragus and Vermentino grapes for the whites and Cannonau, Monica, Carignano, Pascale and Bovale Sardo for the reds. Less conventional varietals have proved to be successful innovations, especially among Argiola's reds. Turriga (a barrique-aged blend of Cannonau, Carignano, Sangiovese and Malvasia Nera grapes) is a proud example of the Argiola production philosophy and standard.

Nuragus di Cagliari
S'elegas 1991 DOC
A native varietal white wine for pleasant, carefree drinking, delicious with shellfish and seafood, with a well-defined delicate and fruity character from the Nuragus grape.

Vermentino di Sardegna
Costamolino 1991 DOC
Pleasantly fresh, fruity and long-lasting Sardinian DOC white, obtained from 95% Vermentino grapes with the small addition of more recent varietals.

Cannonau di Sardegna
Costera 1990 DOC
Generous and appealingly young varietal wine, very drinkable now due to the ripe vintage but with a good capacity for aging. Plenty of varietal character with soft supple fruit, noticeable tannin and a lingering finish.

Monica di Sardegna
Perdera 1990 DOC
A good year for this Monica DOC (mostly Monica grapes with the local Carignano, Pascale and Bovale grapes). Fairly intense on the nose, soft on the palate with a typically almost sweet finish of the Monica di Alberello grape.

Turriga 1988
A blend of Cannonau, Carignano, Malvasia Nera and Sangiovese grapes, this Turriga is one of the best Sardinian reds of recent years. As attractive for its elegance as it is for its power and body, showing careful use of French oak. An innovative and interesting wine with a local feel.

Cantina Sociale di Dolianova

Località Sant'Esu, S.S. 387, km 17.150
Dolianova (Ca) 09041
Tel. (070) 40643
Fax (070) 740531

The Cantina Sociale di Dolianova had 35 member growers when it first opened in June of 1949. Viticulture in Sardegna is typically patchy, fragmented into many different small plots of land. Producers soon realized that the only way to improve quality standards and benfit from modern methods was through cooperatives. Today the Cantina Sociale di Dolianova has become the largest producer in southern part of the island, with over 1,000 members. Qualitative and quantitative analysis of results of these first 40 years is certainly positive. The large and versatile range of products includes the DOC whites of Vermentino di Sardegna, Nuragus di Cagliari and the special Moscato di Cagliari (a fortified "liquoroso" from selected Moscato grown on the hills of Parteolla). Among the reds, the Cantina makes a Cannonau del Parteolla and the DOC Monica di Sardegna. It is also experimenting with wines like Falconaro (from Cannonau, Sangiovese and Bovale grapes), Dolicante and others. There is also a clean, well-made sparkling wine made.

Moscato di Cagliari 1988
A limited-production fortified wine from Moscato grapes, made with particular care and pride, which shows in the resulting quality. Shiny bright yellow in color, with intense fruit aromas, a generous palate and decidedly sweet.

Falconaro 1990
Their best red, made from Cannonau, Sangiovese and Bovale grapes and aged in wood. With its certain elegance and clearly defined vaaaarietal, this is an interesting and innovative interpretation of what this land can offer.

Cantina Sociale del Mandrolisai

Via IV Novembre, 20
Sorgono (Nu) 08038
Tel/Fax (0784) 60113

The more than 300 vine-growers that form this cooperative winery have vineyards in some of the most beautiful areas on the entire island. They are particularly suitable for viticulture thanks to the nature of the dry and permeable soil. Situtated at varying altitudes and often surrounded by woods, the vineyards grow a remarkable array of grapes, mainly reds, that cover a surface area of about 500 ha. In this context, the Cantina Sociale del Mandrolisai's role is valuable and also critical as much of the vineyard has real potential. They are on the right track, for example, in reducing the amount of wine sold in bulk, and in making good examples of the Mandrolisai DOC wines, in both red and rosé. The Mandrolisai is a blend of Cannonau, Muristellu, Monica, Girò, Pascale, Malaga, Barbera and other local grapes, both for the rosé and interesting red. The red has some aging potential and seems to acquire complexity and character with a few years' aging, as the latest vintages have proved.

Mandrolisai Rosso 1989 DOC   ①
A truly good red, showing the intelligent use of regional grapes, listed above. Ruby-red to garnet-red in color, with medium intense aromas, from spicy to ethereal, with a full, supple flavor. Well-developed.

Cantina Sociale di Santadi

Via Su Pranu, 12
Santadi (Ca) 09010
Tel/Fax (0781) 9500129-950127

One of the best examples of wine cooperatives on the island, the Cantina Sociale was founded in 1960 and has close to 250 members. The 400 ha of vineyards are situated in the area of Sulcis, on the south-western side of the island. The cooperative is currently working to expand the vineyards to the coastal areas, as farmers and inhabitants abandon the harsher hinterland. The production philosophy is geared towards quality although the facilities are capable of handling large volumes in terms of quantity. The range of wines is ample and versatile with wines such as Cala Silente (a successful blend of Nuragus, Vermentino and Pinot Bianco) and Villa Solais (one of the better known Sardinian whites); among the reds, Rocca Rubia and Terre Brune, both from Carignano grapes. The latter, Terre Brune, is oak-aged, a new approach to Carignano, and its character and balance have been important in helping to restore a little of the reputation of this varietal, first imported by the Spanish and planted on the islands of San Pietro and Sant'Antioco, and suffering until recently fom an image as a "Vino da Taglio", or a dense wine used for blending to add body and structure.

Carignano del Sulcis 1989 DOC   ①
From 100% native grapes, originally of French and Spanish origin. This Sardinian DOC has a lively ruby color, fruity aromas and a soft mellow flavor with a medium structure for youthful, pleasant drinking.

Terre Brune 1987   ①
More complex and better structured than the Carignano del Sulcis DOC, though from the same grapes. The wine is aged in small oak barrels and bears a mature, evolved character on both nose and palate, soft and harmonious.

Centro Enologico Sardo

Strada Villasor-Villacidro, km 14.600
Villasor (Ca) 09030
Tel. (070) 9648068
Fax (070) 9648645

Originally founded in 1971 as the experimental branch of the Provincial Fruitgrowing Consortium, the winery has rapidly became an important center for viticulture in the region. With wine-making consultants, Paolo Cardu and Marcello Serra, the well-equipped winery continues to dedicate much of its efforts to selecting vines and nursery clones, whether native or non-native, researching the most suitable growing areas and experimenting with new wine-making techniques. Since the name change to Centro Enologico Sardo, the center has also achieved good results in the sparkling wine sector, making sweet and demi-sec styles of Malvasia. Also of considerable interest are the dessert wines made from Malvasia, Moscato and Nasco grapes. New plantings of Sangiovese, Montepulciano and Cabernet Sauvignon among the reds are also proving to be interesting, as are Sauvignon, Chardonnay and Pinot Bianco for the whites.

Blasco 1991   ♈ ①
Along with Nubia, this is a brand new experimental release from the Centre. Both wines are blends of Chardonnay and Pinot Bianco, but Blasco has more lively, ample fresh fruit, with nuances of flowers and melon or cantalopes. Just as fresh and deep on the palate, dry and well-balanced.

Malvasia Spumante Demi-Sec 1990   ♈ ①
Careful efforts to identify the best growing areas for Moscato, Nasco and Malvasia are proving to have been worthwhile. An interesting off-dry sparkling wine made from Malvasia grapes using the charmat method. Clean and correct.

Sangiovese di Sorres 1990   🍷 ①
Ruby-red in color, it has rather juicy, grapey aromas, a fruity fragrance and pleasant, supple flavors; medium-bodied, youthful easy-drinking but with potential to cellar in a vintage such as 1990.

Giovanni Cherchi

Via Ossi, 12
Usini (Ss) 07049
Tel/Fax (079) 48273

A true vigneron, humble and stubborn. With his few hectares of vineyards (eight to be exact) and Vermentino and Cagnulari grapes, Giovanni Maria Cherchi makes the most of what he has and so join the ranks of Sardinia's top producers, in particular with rich and elegant whites like Vigna Tuvaoes, from Vermintino grapes. Cherchi doesn't have any particular tricks up his sleeve or keep any special secrets, but he does have great patience and devotion. To save time and avoid the recurrent problem of drought, he uses drip irrigation in his vineyards. Cherchi's approach includes careful selection of grapes in the vineyard and wine-making techniques that maintain the fruit aromas and varietal character. Born of such envious and unique simplicity, his Vermentino and the single-vineyard Vigna Tuvaoes still manage to be excellent value for money. As well as these outstanding whites, the winery also produces some red wines made from native varietals including a Cagnulari and a Cannonau as well as Luzzana, the latter being a blended wine from Cagnulari and Cannonau grapes.

Vermentino di Usini 1991   ♈ ♈ ①
Vigna Tuvaoes
Another excellent vintage for the Vermentino cru produced by Cherchi. With a rich array of aromas, both flowery and fruity, it is elegant and well-balanced; perhaps not as exuberant as former vintages but very refined.

Cagnulari 1991   🍷 ①
In addition to Vermentino, Cherchi produces some reds from Cannonau and Cagnulari grapes, either as 100% varietal wines or blends of the two. Pleasant and well-vinified, this is medium-bodied, balanced and fruity, with a notable tannin backbone: a solid effort and example of a wine from the area.

Attilio Contini

Via Genova, 48/50
Cabras (Or) 09072
Tel. (0783) 290806
Fax (0783) 290192

One of the oldest and best wineries of the entire island, it was founded in the later 19th century by Salvatore Contini. His son, Attilio, continued in his steps, and now his two sons, Antonio and Paolo, are the current proprietors. Over the years, the Contini winery has achieved many an important award, both in Italy and abroad. They make a wide range of wines, mainly made from Vernaccia grapes, and other native varietals grown and bought on contract by local growers. In particular, they have managed to improve somewhat the image of Vernaccia di Oristano, a wine had been damaged by unscrupulous producers. The Continis have their own special method production; the wine is aged in chestnut or oak barrels filled only part way and kept in well-ventilated rooms subject to sudden changes in temperature. The presence of air helps the formation of a veil on the top of the wine, created by special yeasts which impart a special character to the wine as it ages.

Antico Gregori ♈♈ ②
The pearl of the winery, it is a blend of various vintages of Vernaccia di Oristano, some of which are very old. Topaz-amber in color, it has intense, almond aromas and flavors; consistently rich, mellow, supple flavors from oak and chestnut-aging. Chock full of personality.

Elibaria 1990 ♈ ①
A white from Vernaccia grapes, grown in the lower valley of the river Tirso, and some Vermentino and Chardonnay grapes. Barrique-aged, it has true character and good structure to guarantee a interesting evolution.

Vernaccia di Oristano 1988 DOC ♈♈ ①
A special wine with very intense, almost penetrating aromas, and distinct nuances of almond flowers. Savoury flavor, soft, consistent with slightly bitterish tones. This vintage is a perfect expression of a fully developed Vernaccia.

Sella & Mosca

Località I Piani
Alchero (Ss) 07041
Tel. (079) 997700
Fax (079) 951279

The company was founded in 1899 by an engineer, Mr. Sella, and a lawyer, Mr. Mosca. Over time it has become the most important Sardinian wine company and among the largest grape growing and wine making complexes in the whole of Europe. All wines are made entirely from estate-grapes and vineyards. The original winery is now used as an aging cellar and has been replaced by a modern and efficient complex, complete with offices, cellars, tasting rooms and a museum illustrating the history of the estate as well as a beautiful private collection of archaeological findings. Mario Consorte arrived in 1961 to head the technical wine-making sector and then later also the viticulture, presiding over the great strides forward in the quality of the Sella & Mosca range. He manages to balance large production with a quality much more than decent, even reaching excellence in some cases. This is only possible due to crucial production strategies both in the vineyard (such as low yieldsand the conversion from "alberello" training to "tendone") and in the cellar (the most modern equipment and practices).

Terre Bianche 1991 ♈ ①
One of the best whites of the Sella & Mosca line, if not of the whole island. From Torbato grapes, straw-yellow in color with greenish highlights, it has impressively fresh, fruity aromas and a creamy, rich flavor. Well-balanced, quite possibly still improving with time.

Oleandro 1991 🍷 ①
A unique and original example of a rosé wine, unusually from Cabernet Sauvignon grapes, successful thanks to the vinification technique that has preserved so well the fruity varietal character.

Tanca Farrà 1987 🍷 ②
A hallmark wine of the company, made from a blend of Cabernet Sauvignon and Cannonau grapes. The considerable structure comes mostly from the Cannonau, and the clear herbaceous nose from the Cabernet. Ample and lingering on the palate, with mature tannins.

Anghelu Ruju Vintage 1981 🍷🍷 ②
A special dessert-wine from sun-raisined Cannonau grapes, oak-aged for several years and then cellared for a long time prior to release. Named after a prehistoric burial site. This may not ever reach the formidable heights of the 1979 but is decidedly intense, with tones of loganberries, plums and very mature fruit; full, sweet and elegant on the palate, with very good length.

Sicilia

Sicilia made more than 9,000,000 hl of wine last year and is largest producer of all Italy's regions. But more important than any of the statistics is that Sicilia's image is slowly changing from that of an area solely capable of producing heavy, unmanageable blending wines. There is a new approach to production in the island now, with a new generation, often quite capable of competing with international standards.

The antiquity of winemaking in Sicilia is shown, among other things, by the fact that the word for wine, "vino", was used for the very first time on the island. The words "vino brtom" can be found in a Indoeuropean inscription, proving the existence of wine in pre-Roman times. There are nine DOC wines in Sicilia, but the only account for only a fraction of the total production. They are: Bianco d'Alcamo, Cerasuolo di Vittoria, Etna, Faro, Malvasia delle Lipari, Marsala (with its Fine, Superiore, Vergine, Soleras types), Moscato di Pantelleria, Moscato di Noto and Moscato di Siracusa. Unfortunately, the last two are DOC wines only on paper since they are still waiting for producers to recreate the ancient glories of these delicious wines. In the meantime, there are also various wines with only the "Indicazione Geografica" status or the Regional Seal of Quality.

With 1,500 km of coastline, Sicilia can be divided into five production zones: the volcanic north-east (Etna, Messina and the islands of Lipari); the arid Monti Ibei slopes of the south-east (towns of Siracusa and Ragusa); the hot, hilly plateau center and southern coast (Caltanissetta and Agrigento); the flourishing low hills of the west (Alcamo, Marsala and Trapani); and the island of Pantelleria, only 70 km across the sea from the Sahara desert.

The history and rebirth of Sicilian wines has many facets and boasts prominent figureheads, as as can be seen in the following pages. In brief, however, we would like spare a few words on behalf of the region's world-class Vini da Meditazione or the luscious dessert wines made from the indigenous Malvasia or Moscato (Zibibbo) grape, or even from Catarratto, Grillo and Inzolia (Ansonica). Sicilia puts out a considerable array of wines of international stature, often quite reasonably priced. The best reds are made from indigenous varietals such as Nero d'Avola (Calabrese), Nerello and Perricone. Elegant, long-lasting whites are made not only from local varietals (which dominate by two-thirds), particularily Catarratto Bianco, Inzolia, Trebbiano, Grillo and others, but also from some Chardonnay and Sauvignon. One possible potential risk is that, in the region's rush to convert from the heavy and the traditional to lighter and brighter styles, the standards could go from one extreme to another. The pendulum might swing from strong and powerful, unbalanced wines suddenly to overly light, completely anonymous, exasperatingly acid wines. These are the risks that change can bring but the signs are the companies in Sicilia are too aware and instead project a signal that is altogether positive.

Vitivinicola Avide

Strada Provinciale 7, km 1.5
Comiso (Rg) 97013
Tel. (0932) 967456-621358
Fax (0932) 967456-961700

The label changes somewhat each year, adding a different architectonic motif from the many proud works of Baroque art in Ragusa. The wine itself has been called Baroque. The two Demostene and Calcaterra founding families have long been making wine, but the new company named Avide was established only in 1984. Long a believer in Cerasuolo di Vittoria wine made from Frappato and cherry-scented Nero d'Avola grapes, Giuseppe Calcaterra has tried to mould a more consistent style and enhance its potential ever since it was granted DOC status in 1975. With the young wine technician Giovanni Rizzo progress has been constant ever since the creation of Avide in 1984 and there are now two styles of Cerasuolo di Vittoria: the barrique-aged Barocco and more traditional Black Label. Avide's Terre di Herea range of wines includes a red, a rosé and a white, made respectively from Frappato, Nero d'Avola and Ansonica grapes..

Cerasuolo di Vittoria
Etichetta Nera 1990 DOC
Made, like Barocco, from Frappato and Nero d'Avola grapes but in this case more of the latter (40%). Intriguingly original in its pleasant aromas and refined, good balance on the palate. An easy, unpretentious drinking wine.

Cerasuolo di Vittoria
Barocco 1989 DOC
An admirable version of this Sicilian DOC with the color and smell of luscious ripe cherries, it is full, elegant, rather spicy and deep on the palate, generous and well-balanced. Clever use of oak-aging in small oak barrels. At its peak of maturity now.

Duca di Salaparuta

Via Nazionale, S.S. 113
Casteldaccia (Pa) 90014
Tel. (091) 953988
Fax (091) 953227

Founded in 1924, the Duca di Salaparuta has been a real institution of Italian enology, attracting over its long history many extraordinary men. One such was the founder, Edoardo Alliata di Villafranca, the Duke of Salaparuta, who was followed by Enrico Alliata. In 1961 the firm was taken over by the Ente Siciliano per la Promozione Industriale, but it was restored to its former splendor by Piedmontese head enologist, Franco Giacosa: not an easy task with an average bottle production of 10,000,000 per year. Above all Duca di Salaparuta has been able to make some wines of real class, especially by Sicilian standards, from exclusively native grapes: Bianca di Valguarnera, Terre d'Agala and Duca Enrico (Nero d'Avola grapes). Each is outstanding in its elegance and strength, especially the latter, a legend among Italy's great reds. The Company is equipped with the most modern and computerized machinery and cellars, and it offers the good quality, value-for-money classics of Corvo Bianco, Rosso, Rosato and a sparkling Brut.

Colomba Platino 1991   ♈ ①
An alternative to the classic, and always good, Corvo Bianco, the Salaparuta range has also been offering for some years this Colomba Platino white made from Inzolia and Grecanico grapes. Fresh, crisp acidity, with flowers and delicate fruit on the nose, of some body and well-balanced flavors.

Bianca di Valguarnera 1989   ♈♈ ③
Proof that the Inzolia grapes are second none when well vinified; this Bianca is made from 100% Inzolia and is fermented in Allier oak. With ample aromas of fruit and almonds, with full and enveloping flavors; excellent backbone; for generous drinking now.

Terre D'Agala 1989   ♈ ②
A blend of 50% Nero d'Avola, with Perricone and Frappato di Vittoria, all vinified separately, with different lengths of maceration and aged for different periods and in different types of wood barrel. Interesting aromas, ranging from spices to fruit, concentrated flavor, though not exceedingly demanding.

Duca Enrico 1987   ♈♈♈ ③
Behind the Duca Enrico label lies years of experimentation, with the identification of eight ancient low-pruned vineyards giving low yields of very concentrated fruit, employing a varietal that had never seemed too ambitious, the Nero d'Avola. Chief enologist, Franco Giacosa, knew how to navigate this obstacle course and can produce, even in a year like 1987, a wine that combines the power of the 1985 with the richness and scent of the 1986. The aromas are intense and complex, from hazelnut to spices to very ripe fruit. The palate is perfectly balanced between fruit and oak: great body and persistence. The fruit of each vineyard has been vinified and aged individually, for a year in Slovenian cask and then for a year in barrique, resulting in a superbly balanced wine.

Vinicola Italiana Florio

Via Vincenzo Florio, 1
Marsala (Tp) 91025
Tel. (0923) 781111
Fax (0923) 982380

Like any self-respecting legend Marsala wine has an intriguing tale of adventurous seafarers and difficult voyages to lands afar. Did John Woodhouse fortify with alcohol the barrels of wines to ensure that they would ship better to Britain, or was he trying to enhance the wine's honey-almond character to make a wine that resembled Spanish Madeira? Though quite likely a combination of the two, the truth may forever remain a mystery. We do know for certain that around the year 1830 there started a company by the name of the Florio that was to become known around the world for its link with Marsala. Now owned by the Cinzano group, Florio is working to regain Marsala's early status and to improve its quality and image after a flood of over-production. With the help of technicians like Carlo Casavecchia and Marco Rabino, the house remains linked to the more traditional Marsalas while making innovative international-style wines. Baglio is one such example, no longer aged in the traditional caratelli but in medium to slightly charred barriques, and Morsi di Luce (bites of sunshine), made from early harvested Zibibbo di Pantelleria grapes and then aged 18 months in French oak.

Marsala Superiore
Riserva Targa 1840 DOC   ℜℜ ②
One of the wines that has signalled the new leap in quality for Florio, this 1989-bottled Marsala was made from Grillo grapes and a small part of Inzoliat. Off-dry and amber colored, it has marked aromas of mature fruit with lots of dates and prunes and generous raisin and honey flavors.

Morsi di Luce 1989   ℜ ③
Interesting and much debated part of the Florio range; made from Zibibbo di Pantelleria grapes it comes from outside the Marsala area. A wine with a more international appeal, it is certainly pleasant, if slightly shy and somewhat unbalanced in its youth.

Marsala Vergine   ℜ ③
Terre Arse 1983 DOC
Deep yellow in color, with golden highlights; clear, almondish aromas with nuances of honey and carob, though liquorice dominates on the palate; dry, harmonious and lingering.

Marsala Soleras   ℜℜ ③
Oro Baglio Florio 1979 DOC
A great Marsala Soleras, made from 100% vine-raisined Grillo grapes and then aged in Slovenian oak. Intense, complex, penetrating aromas of honey and vanilla, it is dry with velvety, warm almond and liquorice flavors.

Carlo Hauner

Fraz. Lingua di Salina
Salina (Me) 98050
Tel/Fax (090) 9843141

Imagine a video (the promotional sort that the Regione Siciliana might commission) of the island's natural beauties and have Carlo Hauner star in it. Indeed a Treasure Island-like story; he spent a holiday in Salina the summer of 1963 and fell in love with the island. Gradually abandoning his successful practise as an architect, Hauner bought a house by the sea, surrounded it with eucalyptus trees and patiently set about restoring the glorious potential of the island's dying Malvasia delle Lipari. He started to buy vineyards in the best areas of the island, in Capo Faro, Malta and Quadrara di Lingua. Within a few years, he managed to raise it to its true stature, one of Italy's Vini da Meditazione or foremost dessert wines. Hauner has since moved to the hills, the vineyards now cover 22 ha and there is a modern, sophisticated winery near Lingua. The Hauner adventure lives on, and he will probably never leave the island.

Malvasia delle Lipari 1990 DOC   ℜ ②
A gem of Sicilian enology, a great dessert wine able to seduce international palates with its luscious, unique character. It even looks sunny and generous, with evocative, full aromas and ample sensations on the palate, without ever overpowering or tiring.

Salvatore Murana

Contrada Khamma, 276
Pantelleria (Tp) 91017
Tel. (0923) 915231

A vine-grower and fireman by profession, Salvatore Murana has been able to join the ranks of Sicilia's top producers in relatively short time. Unique in his logic and production philosophy, compared to other producers, Murana is stubbornly passionate (if not obsessed) and soundly convinced of the benefits of thinning and of selection in the vineyard, as against depending on technology or modern equipment. Given Pantelleria's torrid, North African climate, this is hardly an easy chore. His favorably-exposed vineyards are in Martingana and are trained low, in the traditional alberello-style. Indigenous varietals include Zibibbo, which makes the two styles of Moscato di Pantelleria dessert wine: the Moscato Naturale with an alcohol level of 12.5% and the Passito at !45 minimum. With the help of enologist Antonio D'Aietti, Murana also produces a dry Zibibbo, which has a peculiar though pleasant salty zip. It is the sweet versions however with their sunniness and elegant sweetness that recall the nectar sipped by the Greek gods.

Moscato di Pantelleria   ❦ ②
Mueggen 1991 DOC
Made from Zibibbo grapes that were harvested in the latter half of August and then raisined on reed mats; juice of fresh grapes is also added to the must. Thanks to Salvatore Murana's dedication, even in an off year, the wine has great charm and an ample range of aromas of dates and honey.

Moscato Passito di Pantelleria   ❦ ③
Khamma 1989 DOC
Like the Martingana this also is a 14° alc Moscato Passito, but the grapes come from other vineyards and the characteristics are different. The aromas are not as ample and exuberant, but the wine is certainly no less interesting, and the flavor is well-balanced and with no sign of cloying.

Moscato Passito di Pantelleria   ❦❦ ③
Martingana 1989 DOC
A single-vineyard Moscato, from grapes grown in a soil of lava stone, and with higher alcohol content than average. Oak-aged for two years, it has appealing and marked aromas and flavor, opulent and varied, with lots of aromatic tones.

Regaleali

Contrada Regaleali
Sclafani Bagni (Pa) 90020
Tel. (091) 6371266
Fax (091) 363198

The Count Giuseppe Tasca d'Almerita is the current, third generation star behind a story of wine-making that began in 1834, when Lucio Tasca bought a feudal domain in Sclafani. Today, the Regaleali estate, with its 460 ha of land, half of which is comprised of vineyards, is completely replanted and has restructured its winery. Innovations include improved cellar techniques; vineyards now trained to "spalliera" method; indigenous varietals (Inzolia, Sauvignon Tasca, Nerello Mascalese) mix with Euoropean varietals (Cabernet Sauvignon and Pinot Nero) in the vineyard; fine enologists such as Cavalleri, young Guzzo, and the legendary Curcio have had an important role in building up the house name, from the vineyards on; and the impeccable leadership of Ignazio Miceli, whose level of committment goes beyond sales and marketing. The vineyards are at an altitude between 450 and 650 m above sea level, with their loamy-clay soil and favorable microclimates. Regaleali makes an array of different styles and includes first-class Chardonnay and Cabernet Sauvignon and other classics. One flagship wine, Rosso del Conte, shows the successful use of oak aging in substituting for the traditional chestnut barrels.

Nozze d'Oro 1991   ❦❦ ②
Produced since 1984, it was made to commemorate the 50th wedding anniversary of Count Giuseppe and his wife, Franca. A blend of 75% Sauvignon with Inzolia, released one year after harvest, it has the intense aromas and the ample and generous flavors of a wine with a solid backbone; as in the other vintages, is destined to live on for years.

Chardonnay 1990   ❦❦ ③
With only this second vintage, after the astounding 1989 vintage, the Chardonnay Regaleali can join the ranks of other top Italian whites. Fermented in small 350 lt-barrels, it has rich, fruity complex aromas. Rather ripe and fat on the palate with good structure of extracts and acidity, but is not as fine as the previous release.

Cabernet Sauvignon 1988   ❦ ③
This limited production wine is worth inclusion due to its rich, full-bodied character; the 1990 vintage should be more plentiful.

Rosso del Conte 1988   ❦ ②
One of the best Sicilian reds, from Perricone and Nero d'Avola grapes, with better oak nuances than previous vintages improving the balance of the nose; very fruity, with clear berry and red currant aromas, which are even more pronuonced in the mouth, with round, aristocratic elegance.

Terre di Ginestra

Contrada Piano Piraino
Sancipirello (Pa) 90040
Tel. (091) 8576767-8576802
Fax (091) 8576041

One of the handful of wineries responsible for the rebirth of Sicilian enology during these last years, Terre di Ginestra has surpassed regional borders with its captivating, generally well-priced wines. They are generally made from indigenous grapes such as Catarratto or Nero d'Avola or from 'imported' varietals such as Cabernet Sauvignon and Chardonnay. Law and Medicine school graduates at the University of Padova, the two Micciché brothers, proprietors of the company, decided to abandon the family tradition of joining a profession in order to dedicate themselves wholeheartedly to the production of wine. With such a decisive return to their roots, they were bursting with new ideas and projects in mind for the future. A few of their techniques include: considerable investment in efficient, modern equipment; application of separate vinification of the grapes of the three estates; extensive experimentation in the blending of their wines, whether white and red, to create interesting new styles of good quality wine.

Olmobianco 1991 ♀ ①
The Catarratto, Sauvignon and Chardonnay grapes used for this wine come from the vineyards of the Casalbaio estate, in the upper Belice area. Aged for a short period in small oak-barrels, it reveals an excellent aroma with ample, complex flavors.

Terre di Ginestra Bianco 1991 ♀ ①
With considerably intense aromas, fresh and fruity, fairly rich and not ephemeral on the palate, this white from 100% Catarratto grapes proves the skill of enologist Gianni Zanatta, as well as that of the Micciché brothers, even in off-years.

Rubilio 1990 ♥ ①
An intelligent blend of Sangiovese, Cabernet Sauvignon and Nero d'Avola, the latter being slightly prevalent, made with a 10-day maceration on the skins and temperature-controlled fermentation. Soft, with fruity aromas of berries and marasca cherries, slightly tannic, not too demanding drinking.

Vecchio Samperi

Via Samperi, 292
Marsala (Tp) 91025
Tel. (0923) 962093
Fax (0923) 962910

If any one man may be credited for improving Marsala and tightening its DOC regulations then it must be Marco De Bartoli. Indeed, the new law passed in November 28th, 1984 certainly serves to safeguard better techniques to make Marsala and preserve its quality standard, as its reputation plummeted to record lows. It was among the first of Italy's 230 plus DOC wine areas, although the best production areas had been delineated as early as 1931. Considered the standard for excellence, Marco de Bartoli's winery is certainly worth a visit. Don't worry if you find dozens of cars dating from 1960s parked in front, often in fairly rough shape; they're another hobby of De Bartoli's. Just as he enjoys restoring them in his free time, one might say that he practically does the same with his precious barrels of Marsalas, spread throughout the house and in the cellars. Some are 50 or even more years old. Vecchio Samperi, Solera, Vigna La Miccia, Josephine Doré, Bukkuram and several Vintage-dated Marsala Superiores are some of the outstanding products from De Bartoli.

Il Marsala Superiore ♀♀ ③
Riserva 20 anni Solera DOC
One can sense the passage of time with wines like this Riserva di Marsala, with their extraordinary vitality imparted by the lengthy wood-aging. Luminous, almost penetrating on the nose, it has a dense and opulent flavor and an admirably long finish.

Vecchio Samperi 20 anni Solera ♀ ③
A most extraordinary De Bartoli wine, perhaps it best epitomizes the great turn in quality of the Marsala. Lovely golden amber in color, intense aromas, decisive and fascinating flavor. Made from Grillo, Inzolia, Catarratto and aged at length, according to the Solera method.

Bukkuram ♀ ③
Moscato Passito di Pantelleria 1987 DOC
From sun-raisined Zibibbo grapes. Tawny orange-amber in color, it has distinct mature fruit aromas, sweet and complex flavor, without cloying.

Vigna la Miccia ♀♀ ③
Marsala Superiore Oro 1987 DOC
A single-vineyard Marsala Superiore from early harvested grapes, made with temperature-controlled fermentation and with subsequent addition of "mistella", which is a local mixture of grape juice and distilled wine. Aged in stainless steel and then in oak, it has intense fruity and flowery aromas and a consistent, personalized flavor that is never cloying.

Toscana

Toscana (or Tuscany) is a region with a great natural aptitude for winemaking. On the whole, the hills where viticulture is practised are of Pliocene and Eocene origin, formed millions of years ago leaving rich marine sediments. As a result, the soil is composed of 50% limestone, or "Alberese" and marl-clay, or "Galestro". The climate is mild and sunny throughout spring and summer. Substantial temperature changes between night and day helps to produce grapes rich in sugar and extracts. Ideal growing conditions such as these contributed to the spread of the vine in Tuscany even centuries, or milennia, ago.

Vines were cultivated by the Etruscans who colonized the area in the 8th century BC. Originally from Asia Minor, which is the homeland of "vitis vinifera", the Etruscans were responsible for introducing grape cultivation to central Italy, where it adapted so well that they called the region "Enotria". Since then, the vine and wine have progressively gained importance in the economy and culture of Tuscany. In one of his famous musical poems entitled "Bacco in Toscana" Francesco Redi gave a meticulous account of regional production in the 17th century, listing winemaking areas with a connoisseur's critique of the wines made. At the beginning of the 17th century the Grand Duke officially delineated the limits of the Chianti and Carmignano production zones, creating the first example of Appellation of Origin wine legislation. In the mid-18th century the Baron Bettino Ricasoli laid down new laws for wine production on his Fattoria di Brolio near Siena, thereby establishing the blend of grapes from which Chianti was to be made. That recipe spread throughout Tuscany and beyond and is still followed today.

The vineyard replantings after the phylloxera plague together with the reconversion to monoculture after the fall of the "mezzadria" feudal sharecropping system contributed to the boom of vineyards, especially in the "Chianti" area. The resulting overproduction caused its quality and image to plummet, throwing the entire sector into profound economic repression for almost two decades, between the 1960s and 1970s. As the 1980s neared, courageous quality-oriented winemakers, with the help of skilled enologists and technicians, began turning the tables. With a more serious and selective approach to wine production, Tuscan wines were able to regain their prestige, building an even better image than ever before.

The 72,000 ha of vineyards that cover the region today produce an average 3,000,000 hl of wine. Over 40% of the vineyards are registered under the various DOC appellations districts. Let's begin with a brief overview of the main Tuscan wines. One of four DOCG wines (Chianti, Vino Nobile di Montepulciano and Carmignano), Brunello di Montalcino is made exclusively in the commune of Montalcino from Sangiovese Grosso, which is locally known as Brunello. Regulations set maximum yields at 80 quintals per hectare with an aging period of four years, three and a half of which must be in wooden barrels. 130 wineries produce an average of 40,000 hl Brunello and cover 1,000 ha of vineyard.

Sangiovese is also the backbone of Carmignano DOCG, which is made in the communes of Carmignano and Poggio a Caiano. Other grapes essential in the blend include Canaiolo Nero, Malvasia del Chianti, Trebbiano Toscano, Cabernet Franc and Sauvignon. A mere 100 ha of vineyards are registered to make this DOCG, which by law undergoes a minimum of two years' aging, three for the Riserva.

Chianti on the other hand, is the largest wine region in all of Italy both in terms of surface and production. With production stretching across the five provinces of Arezzo, Florence, Pisa, Pistoia and Siena, the styles and terrains vary enormously; often the only commmon factor is the blend of grapes used, which is generally at least 70% Sangiovese, Canaiolo Nero, Malvasia and Trebbiano. Chianti is divided into seven zones: Chianti Classico, Colli Aretini, Colli Fiorentini, Colline Pisane, Colli Senesi, Montalbano and Rufina. Strictly speaking the term 'Chianti' should refer to the specific Classico area between Florence and Siena, covering the Monti del Chianti and the hills of the Ema, Greve, Pesa and Arbia river valleys. 970 registered wineries here produce 300,000 hl of Chianti Classico. The difference between 'regular' Chianti and the 'Classico' lies in the production methods, which are tighter for the latter. Chianti Classico restrictions include yields set at 75 qu/ha, a minimum natural alcohol content of 12%, longer aging periods and a fewer white grapes in the blend.

Vino Nobile di Montepulciano comes from the hills rolling down from the town of Montepulciano towards the Chiana plain and where 170 wineries grow 800 ha of vineyards. Again Sangiovese Grosso, or more specifically a clone known as Prugnolo Gentile, is the main grape, along with Canaiolo Nero. Per hectare yields are limited to 80 quintals, with minimum two years' wood aging, three for the Riserva. Nearly 600 ha of vineyards are registered to produce the Vernaccia di San Gimignano DOC wine in the hilly tufaceous terrain of the medieval town of San Gimignano. The Vernaccia grape variety grows large bunches and has compact and fine skinned grapes. Vernaccia can, in fact, be aged to make Riserva wines, as part of the DOC production regulations.

Even though controlled appellation wines make up 40% of Tuscan production, there's still room left for quality wines. After the success of legendary benchmark wines like Sassicaia and Tignanello, many producers have planted Cabernet and Merlot for the reds, Chardonnay, Sauvignon, and Pinot for the whites, which have adapted extremely well to many production zones in the region. A combination of factors like the use of modern vinification techniques, French barriques and other oak for aging have brought about a new generation of wines with great character and unquestionable class. They have managed to gain international recognition and prestige despite simply being labelled or classified according to their geografical place of origin. Apart from the occasional successes, sometimes due to fads and trends, it appears evident that a new approach to winemaking has set in, convincing and involving the majority of growers and vintners in Tuscany. Producers are now stimulated to experiment more and improve the quality of their wines. One of the more interesting developments, as a result, has been the considerable progress made in Sangiovese-based wines. After all, Sangiovese is Tuscany's chief variety and will continue to be at the heart of its most authentic winemaking traditions.

Altesino

Loc. Torrenieri
Montalcino (Si) 53028
Tel. (0577) 806208
Fax (0577) 806131

Cypress trees may be quite commonplace in the Tuscan countryside, but Altesino's parkway entering the winery is lined with them. With 22 ha of vineyard and an exceptional staff, boasting such prestigious names as Claudio Basla and Pietro Rivella, this winery has positioned itself on the top end of producers in Montalcino. The estate-vineyards vary in terms of position and elevation, from the Saltennano vineyard at 220 m above sea level to the Due Porte vineyard that almost reaches 500 m. The Montosoli vineyard, which produces the cru Brunello, is quite high at 450 m. Specific varieties are planted to meet the needs of the distinct soil character, growing conditions and climate. In addition to the Sangiovese Grosso grown in the Montosoli, Due Porte and Altesino vineyards, Cabernet Sauvignon is planted at Altesino, Chardonnay at Saltennano, and Trebbiano, Malvasia and Moscadello at Altesino and Montosoli. All of the grapes are processed and vinified in the large, well-equipped facilities at Altesino. The winery boasts an interesting and verstaile line of products.

Rosso di Altesino 1990 🍇 ①
Be sure to sample the unusual aromas of this Rosso 1990, a vino da tavola from 100% Sangiovese Grosso. Irresistably compact, with vibrant fresh fruit and youth and a faint grassy flavor. Good texture on the palate, and balance will come with time.

Alte d'Altesi 1988 🍇🍇 ③
A blend of Sangiovese Grosso and Cabernet Sauvignon, it has delicate aromas, with well-marked red bell peppers and figs. Judging by its mouthfilling flavors, its makers chose to accentuate the elegance and not the strength.

Brunello di Montalcino 1986 DOCG 🍇 🍇 ③
When aged in oak Sangiovese Grosso has its own distinctive bouquet, with a wide range of spices including tobacco. This Brunello is no exception; promises made on the nose come through on the palate. Full, harmonious, with tannins still developing.

Key to the symbols

Types of Wines

🍇 White

🍇 Rosé

🍇 Red

Rating System

🍇 An exemplary wine of its type with outstanding local character

🍇🍇 An international premium quality wine

🍇🍇🍇 A Top Wine, considered one of the 150 best wines in the world

The 'grape bunch' symbol is used to indicate the color of the wine; the number of bunches represents the quality rating assigned by the contributor

Price levels

① up to $ 9.99

② $ 10.00 - $ 14.99

③ $ 15.00 - $ 24.99

④ $ 25.00 or more

The 'ex-cellar', or direct from the producer, bottle prices, are calculated in US dollars and are intended only as an approximate guide

Entries are arranged in alphabetical order by country, region and winery or producer name.

Castello di Ama

Loc. Lecchi
Gaiole in Chianti (Si) 53013
Tel. (0577) 746031
Fax (0577) 746117

In 1773 the Granduca di Toscana, Pietro Leopoldo, described the hills around Castello di Ama as a happy, fertile and prosperous oasis, better cared for than a garden. Two centuries later the hamlet of Ama and its countryside still give an impression of order and harmony, although the geometrical layout of the vineyards has changed considerably. The 75 ha of estate-vineyards are now grouped into the four areas of Bellavista, San Lorenzo, La Casuccia, and La Bertinga and each is further divided into parcels. In addition to the indigenous Chianti varieties, grapes like Merlot, Pinot Nero, Chardonnay, Sauvignon and Pinot Grigio also do well and are vinified separately. High technology in the modern cellars allows fermentation to be controlled step by step. Grapes are hand-picked in several pickings and carried whole to the cellar. The wines are matured in medium-capacity oak casks or in French barriques and bottle age for a long time in large, temperature-controlled areas, with a 500,000-bottle capacity. The wide range of wines produced includes five types of Chianti Classico, five whites, two red table wines and a rosé.

Vigna al Poggio 1990   🍇 ③
Rich straw-yellow in color, this vino da tavola is made from Chardonnay and has a complex bouquet of well-evolved flavors harmonized with hints of toasted oak. Good structure in the mouth, balanced and of remarkable aromatic length.

Chianti Classico 1990 DOCG   🍇 ①
Castello di Ama's first Chianti Classico to be released, it has fresh exuberant flavors, with hints of flowers and fruit. Good structure, full and rich in the mouth, with tannins still well-marked.

Vigna l'Apparita 1989   🍇🍇 ④
Yet again Castello di Ama offers a wine that will be much talked about. Though still young, this premium-quality Merlot has intense fruity aromas and typical herbaceous flavor of the grape, it has the underlying strength and backbone for a promising future.

Chianti Classico   🍇🍇 ④
Vigneto San Lorenzo 1988 DOCG
A typical Chianti Classico, with its fresh and youthful exuberance. Bright ruby-red in color with tinges of violet, fruity flavors and stylish spicy nuances. Full and round in the mouth, savoury, harmonious, very drinkable and long lasting.

Chianti Classico   🍇🍇🍇 ④
Vigneto Bertinga 1988 DOCG
Bertinga is one of four prized single-vineyards owned by the winery. Directed by Lorenza Sebasti, Castello di Ama is a frontrunner in the rebirth of Tuscan wines and of Chianti in particular, and was the first winery to vinify grapes from the cru vineyards separately. This remarkably structured red is aged in French oak, in the winery's traditional style. Chief winemaker Marco Pallanti has a brilliant carreer ahead of him, judging by the outstanding results. Made from grapes grown on the high hills of Lecchi in the commune of Gaiole in Chianti, it has a rich garnet-red color and a refined and stylish bouquet, with hints of fruit and flowers; full, warm and complex in the mouth, with a finish that is still relatively green. Worth cellaring.

Marchesi L. & P. Antinori

Piazza degli Antinori, 3
Firenze (Fi) 50123
Tel. (055) 23595
Fax (055) 2359884-2359883

Modern Tuscan enology owes a great deal to the Antinori family, dedicated to winemaking since the 1365. With their nobile approach to winemaking as well as the 1970s wave of innovation in winemaking inspired by the great enologist Giacomo Tachis, they have set the standards in Tuscany. 330 ha of their 2,000 ha of vineyards are located in the Chianti Classico area, where the estates at Badia a Passignano, Peppoli and Santa Cristina produce the famous wines. In fact, Santa Cristina is home to the legendary vineyards of Tignanello and Solaia, which border one another. Careful experiments and selections of Sangiovese clones have been conducted for some time, as it is rightly considered the most important Tuscan variety. From vine to vinification, extreme care is taken in all aspects of winemaking: not something to be taken lightly for a multi-million bottle winery of this stature. The key to Antinori's success lies in maintaining a consistent quality standard throughout all their wines, whether they be in the 10,000 plus bottle range or, as is generally the case, exceed 500,000 bottles annually.

Chianti Classico Pèppoli 1989 DOCG 🍇 ①
The great winemaking skills of the Antinori house shine through in this Pèppoli. A very likable wine that focuses on elegance since it tends to lacks a solid structure, its fresh aromas of fruit are well blended with the wood notes and turn rich in the mouth, with a fairly harmonious tannin finish.

Chianti Classico Riserva 🍇🍇 ③
Tenuta dei Marchesi Antinori 1988 DOCG
Rich, young ruby-red in color, its fruity bouquet is in full bloom, with pleasant notes of oak. It is full-flavored, intense and concentrated on the mouth and boasts a powerful, round structure.

Chianti Classico Riserva 🍇 ②
Villa Antinori 1988 DOCG
The deep ruby color foretells a highly concentrated wine. Intense and complex on the nose, with hints of mushrooms and toasty aromas, it has harmonious, mouthfilling textures and a soft but firm structure.

Tignanello 1988 🍇🍇 ③
This legendary precursor of the Sangiovese-Cabernet blend is a perfect expression of the favorable 1988 vintage. Somewhat closed on the nose in the beginning, it opens into a rich and complex bouquet. Warm and persuasive in the mouth, extremely soft, with lots of body and length.

Solaia 1988 🍇🍇🍇 ③
The Antinori house could rightly be considered the inspirators of the new generation of Tuscan wines, from the rebirth of the Chianti Classico formula to the celebrated innovative wines like Tignanello and Solaia. Amazingly enough, the Piero Antinori-Giacomo Tachis duo is able to put out substantial quantities of top-quality wines every year. Such is the case with this Solaia, made from Cabernet Sauvignon and Franc, and Sangiovese. From a vintage that many consider to be absolutely extraordinary, it has all the varietal character to be expected (bell peppers and grass) combined with the sweet spiciness of the oak. Its ample and full-bodied structure enables it to withstand the exuberant young tannins and guarantees long cellar life.

Tenuta di Argiano

Sant'Angelo in Colle
Montalcino (Si) 53024
Tel. (0577) 864037
Fax (0577) 864210

One could never get tired of Palazzo Argiano's incredible view of the rolling hills and vineyards of Montalcino. Owners of Argiano (the Gaetani-Lovatelli family and Cinzano) have invested a lot in the 22 ha of vineyards, and the results are proving them right. In no time at all, Argiano has risen to be among the best wines of Montalcino. It probably all started when the high-calibre wine consultant Maurizio Castelli joined, giving a decisive turn about especially in terms of care of the vineyard, reducing yields per hectare by frequent bunch thinning. Even the cellars and winemaking machinery has been brought up to par; beneath the splendid brick vaults rest beautiful oak casks with a total capacity of 3,100 hl of wine. In the future Argiano will produce more Sangiovese Grosso-based reds, as the rough experimental blends have shown impressive results.

Brunello di Montalcino 1987 DOCG ❦ ③
Clean and brilliant ruby-red in color, it has a rich, well-developed bouquet where aromas of ripe fruit merge with leather and spice. Round and soft to the taste, it is well-balanced, its firm tannins carried well by just the right degree of freshness.

Brunello di Montalcino ❦❦ ③
Riserva 1985 DOCG
An extremely exciting wine made in an extraordinary vintage. Deep ruby-red, it has remarkably intense aromas, being clean and well-developed, with a distinct spiciness. A rich and encompassing Brunello, warm, with a robust body and great class.

Avignonesi

Via di Gracciano nel Corso, 91
Montepulciano (Si) 53045
Tel. (0578) 577872

The Avignonesi winery is one of the oldest in Montepulciano and is housed in a splendid palazzo in the historical center of town. But, for several years now, most winemaking operations have been done in the new, more efficient and technologically equipped cellars in Valiano di Montepulciano. As the cellar facilities were improved, so were the vineyards. Of the 84 ha planted to vines, about half make Vino Nobile and Rosso di Montepulciano; the rest are grafted with the French varieties Cabernet Sauvignon, Merlot, Chardonnay and Sauvignon Blanc. Under the knowledgable guidance of the Falvo brothers, the winery has been increasingly successful in producing some interesting, competitive wines. In addition to its flagship Vino Nobile di Montepulciano, Avignonesi makes varietal Vino da Tavola wines called Il Marzocco (100% Chardonnay), Il Vignola (Sauvignon Blanc), I Grifi (Cabernet Sauvignon) and Merlot. Annual production comes to around 300,000 bottles, a third of which is Vino Nobile, vintage and Riserva

Il Marzocco 1990 ❦ ②
This bright straw-yellow wine comes from 100% Chardonnay. Clean, intense well-blended aromas of ripe apples with rich spice from the oak. With just the right touch of acidity, the wine is full-bodied and rich, with a long finish.

Vendemmia Tardiva 1988 ❦❦ ④
There's surely a bit of Bordeaux in this precious, pricey nectar. Sparkling golden yellow, with rich persuasive aromas and strikingly mature notes from the raisiney, botrytized grapes. Fat in the mouth; well-balanced, aromatic and very long lasting.

Merlot 1988 ❦❦ ④
Without a doubt a wine with great structure, able to hold well for years. Though in a blending and ripening stage at present, already one can appreciate the deep ruby-red color and the fine aromas, rich but not too complex. Shows mouthfilling strength on the palate and a long finish.

Vino Nobile di Montepulciano ❦ ②
1988 DOCG
Despite being the product of a great vintage, this Vino Nobile relies more on its elegance than its structure. The aromas, though already harmonious, are not overwhelmingly intense, with a roundness on the palate that prevails over fullness and length.

Badia a Coltibuono

Gaiole in Chianti (Si) 53013
Tel. (0577) 749498
Fax (0577) 749235

Apparently the Benedictine monks that lived
in the Badia a Coltibuono were the first to
grow grapes in this zone as early as the 11th
century. The area does, indeed, have an
ancient viticultural history, of which the
present proprietors, the Stucchi Prinetti family
can be very proud. The winery is situated in
the Badia at an elevation of 600 m, while the
vineyards hover between 300 and 350 m in
Monti di Sotto. All 37 ha of estate-vineyards
(some are considerably old) are planted with
Chianti varieties except for a small area
which is planted with Chardonnay and Pinot
Bianco. In addition to the more traditional
Coltibuono wines, Chianti Classico and Vin
Santo, they produce Sangioveto (an oak-
aged varietal Sangiovese) and a limited
range of white wines made from the non-
indigenous Chardonnay and Pinot Bianco.
The average production capacity of Chianti
Classico, including both vintage and Riserva
styles, is around 12,500 cases a year.

Sella del Boscone 1990 🍇 ②
100% Chardonnay, bright straw-yellow in color,
with a fragrant bouquet. Lots of tropical fruit
well-blended with the oak. Good fatty fullness on
the mouth, too, with a pleasant twist of
freshness on the finish.

Trappoline 1990 🍇 ②
From Trebbiano and Malvasia on a 50% Pinot
Bianco base, it is brilliant straw-yellow. Light and
elegant bouquet, well-balanced on nose and
mouth, showing full and harmonious flavors.
Only in the finish is it less persistent.

Chianti Classico 🍇🍇 ②
Riserva 1987 DOCG
A good Riserva, from a quite difficult year. Deep
in color with a touch of garnet. The well-evolved
ethereal bouquet with its hearthy aromas
doesn't overpower the aromatic fruit flavors;
good impact on the palate with firm tannins.

Sangioveto 1986 🍇🍇 ③
From a selection of Sangiovese grapes, a
mature, deep ruby wine. The aromas are
intense with a fruity note in the rich, refined
bouquet. Rich and full to the taste, with good
structure and remarkable balance.

Banfi

Loc. S. Angelo Scalo
Montalcino (Si) 53024
Tel. (0577) 864111
Fax (0577) 864141

The company owns 2,830 ha, 710 of which are vineyards. These statistics are indicative of the colossal endeavor begun (and now successfully completed) in the mid-1970s by Harry and John Mariani in Montalcino. But, to speak of Banfi only in numerical terms would be missing the point. Thanks to the expertise of Ezio Rivella together with Pablo Harry, the estate-vineyards have gradually been planted not only with Brunello vines, but also with Syrah, Pinot Nero, Cabernet Sauvignon, Merlot, Chardonnay and Sauvignon Blanc. Grown at 180-260 m, these varieties have yielded wines of great complexity and structure, enabling Banfi to establish a world-class reputation in just a few years. But the Brunello di Montalcino is what undoubtedly flies the Banfi flag. It ages in large 60-120 hl oak barrels and ages for years in the state-of-the-art cellars. For the other high quality wines on the other hand, only the small 350 lt French casks are used, and again of top quality wood. After all, big investments give big results, bottle after bottle, year after year.

Serena 1990   ❦ ②
This fine Banfi wine from Sauvignon Blanc is aged a few months in French barrique. A lovely straw color with intense and pleasing grassy nuances on the nose. Full and harmonious, with pleasant, long lasting flavor.

Fontanelle Chardonnay 1989   ❦ ②
It hasn't lost a thing in three year: in fact, it's even more refined on the nose, where nice ripe fruit mixes with the oak. All of the Chardonnay varietal strength comes through in the mouth, harmonized by lively freshness.

Rosso di Montalcino Centine 1990 DOC   ❦ ①
Bright, fairly intense ruby color. Long lasting, complex bouquet, with fruit and refined spice flavors. Good correspondence in the mouth, rich, soft and elegant.

Brunello di Montalcino 1986 DOCG   ❦ ③
Not an exceptional vintage, yet characteristic in its bright garnet color and its ample, complex and fragrant bouquet with nuances of liquorice and spice coming through, it has a firm backbone, with tannins that are still a little rough, moderate length.

Brunello di Montalcino   ❦❦❦ ④
Poggio all'Oro 1985 DOCG
Undoubtedly one of the most important wineries in the Montalcino area, Banfi gave the biggest impulse to rejuvenate the area and its prince of wines, Brunello. With its substantial dimensions, Banfi is able to offer a wide range of wines with remarkably interesting, high quality Riserva selections. This Poggio all'Oro is exemplary; intense, bright garnet in color, it has ample and complex aromas, which have yet to fully develop, with a refined spiciness and hints of fruit and dried grass. With round, velvety, elegant flavors, it shows a remarkable structure and lots of concentration.

Terre di Bindella

Fraz. Argiano, via delle Tre Berte, 10/A
Montepulciano (Si) 53040
Tel. (0578) 767777
Fax (0578) 767255

This medium-sized winery was taken over in 1984 by Rudolf Bindella, a Swiss wine importer-turned producer. The new management added three hectares of experimental plantings to the original 12, and two more are on the drawing board. Since his production philosphy is to improve and enhance Vino Nobile, he aims to single out the best clones, growing techniques and plant density to bring out the maximum potential of the Prugnolo Gentile variety. Bindella plants only indigenous grapes, which accord to the wine laws for Vino Nobile di Montepulciano, nor does he have plans to plant other types. The facilities are among the most modern and well-equipped of the area and are perfectly tuned into the local tradition. Bindella does have a good selection of barriques to oak age his Nobile blend, called Vallocaia, that is classified as a Vino da Tavola. Average annual production is around 3,200 cases for the Vino Nobile and 830 cases for the Vallocaia.

Vino Nobile di Montepulciano 1989 DOCG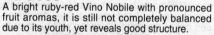
A bright ruby-red Vino Nobile with pronounced fruit aromas, it is still not completely balanced due to its youth, yet reveals good structure.

Vino Nobile di Montepulciano Riserva 1988 DOCG
The Riserva is a more complex and developed wine, as evident by its more garnet hue. With lots of complex, rich fruit on the nose, it opens slowly and shows elegance and harmony in the mouth.

Poderi Boscarelli

Via di Montenero, 24
Montepulciano (Si) 53045
Tel/Fax (0578) 767277

This winery is small and relatively new on the scene. But with such an ideal location and micro-clmiate (perfect for growing Prugnolo Gentile) and such dynamic and enthusiastic owners, it is a rising star in the Montepulciano area. The Marchesi De Ferrari are untiring in improving and enlarging their estate. 11 of their 16 ha are vineyards planted mostly to Prugnolo Gentile, Canaiolo and Mammolo (the main varieties used to make the DOCG wine) but now there's also a healthy amount of Sangiovese and some Cabernet Sauvignon. The vineyards slightly outgrew the cellars which appear a little overloaded and have that "permanently temporary" look. Vinification and aging, on the other hand, are well-kept, both by the owners and by top consultants. Average annual production amounts to 5,000 cases of Vino Nobile, Chianti Colli Senesi and some Vino da Tavola.

Boscarelli 1988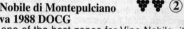
Great freshness in color and aroma. Lots of fruit on the nose, with clean, mossy flavors. This varietal Sangiovese has a warm impact on the palate, slightly warm in alcohol, with a touch of tartness and a hint of grassiness on the finish.

Vino Nobile di Montepulciano Riserva 1988 DOCG
From one of the best zones for Vino Nobile, it has a well-developed, complex bouquet that will refine with time. Well-balanced, with a powerful but harmonious structure, and a full, persistent finish.

Fattoria del Buonamico

Via Provinciale Montecarlo, 43
Montecarlo (Lu) 55015
Tel. (0583) 22038

The Cercatoia area is a sunny, sheltered dell to the south-east side of Montecarlo: what better conditions to grow grapes. The Fattoria del Buonamico lies in the middle with its 15 ha of vineyards planted 60/40 to make classic Montecarlo whites and reds, respectively. The whites have a Trebbiano base, complemented by Pinot, Sauvignon, Sémillon and Roussanne and the reds are based on Sangiovese with Canaiolo, Malvasia Nera, Cabernet, Merlot and Syrah; the average vine age is 15 years. The cellar is modern, roomy and well-organized. Cement and oak dominate throughout, confirming the penchant for red. In addition to Montecarlo Rosso (the most structured and typical available), they make a red geografic appellation called Cercatoia, that is aged like a riserva in good years. With regards to Vino da Tavola wines, they are conducting some interesting research with varietal wines such as Syrah, Cabernet and Merlot. In addition to the Montecarlo DOC, they produce two whites, of which the Vasario (100% Pinot Bianco) is undoubtedly a wine with class.

Vasario 1990 ☙☙ ②
The Bianco di Cercatoia is the winery's most pampered wine, dedicated to Vasari. Straw-yellow, well-developed, with a complex bouquet and rich floral flavors and good alcohol. Full and soft with intense, long-lasting flavors.

Rosso di Cercatoia 1990 ☙ ②
Still relatively young but rich with promise. Intense color, rich, fruity bouquet, with notable aromas from the new oak. Full and highly concentrated on the mouth; already soft and harmonious tannins abound.

Castello di Cacchiano

Fraz. Monti
Gaiole in Chianti (Si) 53010
Tel. (0577) 747018
Fax (0577) 747157

Situated in the southernmost part of the Gaiole district, near the village of Monti, the castle of Cacchiano was an ancient fortress that marked the boundaries of the Republics of Florence and Siena. When it was no longer needed as an outpost, the castle became the country manor of the Ricasoli-Firidolfi family, who have owned it from time immemorial. The 33 ha of vineyards are mostly planted with Sangiovese, with a small percentage of Canaiolo and Malvasia. Traditional winemaking methods (in glass-lined cement tubs, with long skin contact) makes for highly concentrated, rich wines that require lengthy wood aging in different sized casks. The bottles are later stacked in the castle's cool cellars for further aging. Average production is around 8,000 cases of Chianti Classico, one tenth of which is Vino da Tavola (a Sangiovese in barrique) and just over 200 cases of half bottles of an unusually characteristic Vin Santo.

Chianti Classico 1988 DOCG ☙ ①
Clean, bright ruby-red in color, with youthful overtones. This Chianti Classico has characteristic flavors with good fruitiness and a hint of dried fruit and tobacco. Well-developed and rich in the mouth, blessed with good body and texture, evident tannins and a good finish.

Chianti Classico Riserva ☙☙ ②
Il Millennio 1987 DOCG
This prestigious Riserva is intense ruby-red, with characteristic flavors and a well-developed and complex bouquet, ethereal with mossy nuances. Good structure for the vintage, with marked but not aggressive tannins.

Canalicchio di Sotto

Loc. Canalicchio di Sotto, 8
Montalcino (Si) 53024
Tel/Fax (0577) 848476

Maurizio Lambardi, owner of Canalicchio di Sotto, is one of the smaller, passionate Brunello makers that best represent the average quality standard in the Montalcino zone. This standard is maintained both in good years and in less fortunate ones due to thespecial care of the vineyards and the cellar. Like most family-run wineries, who seldom refer to outsiders for help, they make consistently good, robust wines. Maurizio owns three hectares of vineyard from which he makes only Brunello and Rosso di Montalcino, leaving Vino da Tavola wines and experimental wines to the larger, more well-endowed wineries.

Rosso di Montalcino 1990 DOC
From Lambardi's vineyards, that slope down from Montalcino to face Siena, this pleasant Rosso is made in limited quantities. It has fresh and fruity aromas, with great structure and concentration on the palate.

Brunello di Montalcino 1987 DOCG
Its deep ruby-red in color, with violet highlights, gives this wine a youthful aspect. Intense aromas with a clear note of dried fruit, well-harmonized with the spicy flavors from the oak-aging. Well defined tannins on the mouth make it destined to age gracefully.

Podere Capaccia

Loc. Capaccia
Radda in Chianti (Si) 53017
Tel. (0577) 738385 - (0574) 23395
Fax (0574) 606802

A marketing specialist from the industrial town of Prato, in 1975 Giampaolo Pacini bought this farmstead that consisted of 20 ha of property and a medieval hamlet which was beginning to fall to pieces. He was able to recover plots of land not yet completely overtaken by woods and overgrowth and planted three hectares of vineyard on a hill that overlooks the upper section of the Pesa river. The varieties planted are those typical of Chianti (Sangiovese, Canaiolo, Trebbiano and Malvasia) and follw the wine laws governing its production. The small, well-organized and well-equipped cellar holds stainless steel vats, Slovenian oak casks and French barriques. Marketed only in the past few years, (the first bottles were sold in 1986), the Podere Capaccia wines have rapidly won their fame on an international level, thanks not only to the enormous potential of the vineyard, but also to Pacini and consulting enologist Vittorio Fiore, who oversees production. Other than the 830 cases of Chianti Classico a year, they make nearly 1,000 cases of Querciagrande, a varietal barrique-aged Sangiovese.

Chianti Classico

Riserva 1988 DOCG
Deep ruby-red with full aromas of ripe berries and fruits. Rich and pleasant in the mouth, with a good acid-tannin balance and a remarkable aromatic length on the finish.

Querciagrande 1988

A wine that will only be at its best in a few years time. Aromas of vanilla from the barrique-aging are still partly closed, but promise an interesting evolution. Sangiovese in all its crude strength on the palate, still young but already very persistent.

Capannelle

Loc. Capannelle
Gaiole in Chianti (Si) 53013
Tel. (0577) 749691
Fax (0577) 79121

Raffaele Rossetti's rennovated farmhouse lies nestled atop a steep hill overlooking Gaiole. Behind a rustic façade, the sophisticated remodeling work done throughout their beautiful home is carried on next door in the winemaking cellars where modern technology reigns and stainless steel glimmers. With an engineer's penchant for perfection and precision, even Rossetti's drain pipe grills are impeccable. Equal care and generosity were used in rejuvenating and, where necessary replanting, the four hectares of estste vineyard that surround the winery. The superb growing conditions together with the area's blessed climate and several different pickings at harvest, guarantee that only perfectly ripe, healthy grapes are brought in. From then, until labelling and bottling, all operations are rigorously controlled in a completely sterile, sanitized environment. Production is limited to only three wines which are Capannelle (a Sangiovese-Canaiolo blend), Capannelle Barrique (100% Sangiovese) and an oak-aged Chardonnay, totalling approximately 8,300 cases.

Chardonnay 1989 ♛ ③
Bright straw-yellow, intense aromas of honey and vanilla with shining ethereal and toasty overtones. Full-bodied and rich, with good fresh acidity, long lasting with a slightly bitter aftertaste.

Capannelle Barrique 1987 ♛ ④
A good sound product considering it was a less than exceptional year. Medium bright ruby in color, with delicate complex aromas. Full and elegant on the mouth though slightly rough and of medium length.

Tenuta Caparzo

Loc. Torrenieri
Montalcino (Si) 53028
Tel. (0577) 848390
Fax (0577) 849377

When the winery opened in the 1960s, it bought up plots near Torrenieri and substantially invested in its winemaking facilities. Today Tenuta Caparzo is one of Montalcino's most important wineries, with more than 26 ha of vineyard, 15 of which are planted with Sangiovese Grosso. But Caparzo is better known for the sophisticated production level which it has achieved after years of intensive and well-defined experimentation. In addition to regular Brunello di Montalcino DOCG, made in the traditional style, they make an exclusive oak-aged selection called La Casa, that seems to improve each year. French barrique is also used to make two Vino da Tavola: the red Ca' del Pazzo, from a 50/50 Sangiovese Grosso and Cabernet Sauvignon blend, and the white Le Grance, from 75% Chardonnay and the rest Sauvignon Blanc and Traminer fermented in Allier oak. Representing almost half the total production of 10,000 case production, Rosso di Montalcino DOC completes the production list.

Le Grance 1989 ♛ ③
A blend of Chardonnay with a small addition of Sauvignon and Traminer, this white has a rich complex bouquet with great aromas and good oak tones. Fat and harmonious on the mouth, with long-lasting aromas.

Brunello di Montalcino 1987 DOCG ♛ ③
A Brunello that's already very pleasant and soft, and whose aroma shows maturity and drinkability. Lacking in great structure, this off-vintage was enriched with grapes normally used for the La Casa selection.

Brunello di Montalcino ♛♛ ③
La Casa 1986 DOCG
The single-vineyard Caparzo rarely disappoints: even in 1986 this is a well-developed, complex and aromatic wine, with fruity nuances evolving into leather and vanilla. Round, with wonderful long-lasting flavors. Intense color, very harmonious and full.

Tenuta di Capezzana

Loc. Seano, via Capezzana, 100
Carmignano (Fi) 50042
Tel. (055) 8706091-8706005
Fax (055) 8706673

Likely the most famous estate in Carmignano, Capezzana is a family owned and operated winery, headed by the serene patriarch-figure of the Count, Ugo Contini. Wine production here has had a remarkable impetus especially ever since Carmignano wines were granted the DOC and then DOCG status. Estate vineyards are spread over 30 ha on the slopes of Montalbano west of Florence and undergo continuous rennovation. The varieties planted are those called for by the Carmignano wine regulations, with the addition of Merlot and Chardonnay. Large underground cellars, equipped with the most modern technology, create an ideal setting to age their wine. Production (around 42,000 cases a year) includes three styles of Carmignano DOCG including a vintage, a Riserva and a Villa di Trefiano selection; others include Ghiae della Furba, Barco Reale (a young version of Carmignano) and three whites made from Trebbiano, Chardonnay and Malvasia. Last but not least, Capezzana's traditional style Vin Santo rightfully has many a faithful follower.

Vin Santo 1987
Undoubtedly a good year for this product. A fascinating wine at first sight, with its luminous, golden color. The rich and refined bouquet is reminiscent of dried fruit and almonds. Intense aromas accompany a full body and a perfect balance.

Ghiaie della Furba 1989
Ruby colored already tending towards garnet, this wine has a crisp herbaceous touch, with clear varietal reference to the Cabernet Sauvignon and Merlot base-blend. Soft on the palate with an elegant impact and a long finish.

Carmignano
Villa di Trefiano 1988 DOCG
Ruby-red with garnet highlights, intense and typical aromas appear still slightly out of balance, with a bit too much oak. Rich in the mouth, round and balanced with good texture and a pleasant bitter aftertaste.

Casale - Falchini

Via di Casale, 40
San Gimignano (Si) 53037
Tel. (0574) 28123 - (0577) 941305
Fax (0574) 37204

Ever since Riccardo Falchini, an established industrialist, bought Il Casale in 1964, it has slowly but surely come to be one of San Gimignano's leading wineries. Year after year, the company has remodernized, updated and expanded and today they own 32 hectares of vineyard and a modern, well-equipped cellar. But to Riccardo Falchini, San Gimignano's lush hills can offer more than the typical Vernaccia wine; in fact, he also produces other top-level wines such as the Il Campora, which is a Cabernet Sauvignon that spends 24 months in barrrique and 24 more in the bottle before release. Always a very busy man, Falchini handles all cellar and vineyard operations. Most vineyards are situated at 300 m altitude and have a splendid view of the Tuscan countryside as well as the world famous towers of San Gimignano.

Chianti Colli Senesi 1990 DOCG
A typical Chianti from the Colli Senesi, with young fruity aromas of currents and cherry. Clean and full flavored with a remarkable structure in the mouth and a lingering finish.

Campora 1988
Their best wine, this remarkable 100% Cabernet wine has an intense, deep ruby color with ample aromas, with lots of red bell peppers. Despite being quite soft in the mouth, a slight acid-tannin unbalance gives away its perky youthfulness.

Fattoria Le Casalte

Via del Termine, 2
Montepulciano (Si) 53045
Tel. (0578) 799138
Fax (06) 9306988

The Silvestri-Barioffi family deserves all the credit for having redeemed this cellar from ruin. Armed with lots of patience and love, they began restoration in the 1970s, starting with the vineyards up. Eight of 39 hectares of the estate are planted to well-exposed vineyards on the hills of Sant'Albino at around 400 m altitude. Today the vines are fully mature and express the best characteristics of the terrain and varieties planted there. Aside from a few hectares of white grapes, production is mainly centered around the Vino Nobile di Montepulciano. The cellar is well-equipped and well-fitted to the needs and dimensions of the winery. Owner Guido Barioffi personally oversees the vineyards and has an expert enologist help out in the cellar and winemaking. Average production reaches 1,700 cases of Vino Nobile DOCG, 660 of Rosso di Montepulciano DOC and around 1,000 of white and rosé table wines.

Vino Nobile di Montepulciano 1989 DOCG
Despite being considered an off year, this wine has a nice nose, with its clear aromas of ripe fruit, and makes up for a light body with its pleasant grace and charm on the palate.

Vino Nobile di Montepulciano Riserva 1988 DOCG
Good texture and softness are what make this deep, ruby-red Nobile from Casalte so appealing. Lots of youthfulness on the nose with a wide range of aromas such as coffee and vanilla, that have yet to harmonize.

Casanova di Neri

Torrenieri
Montalcino (Si) 53028
Tel. (0577) 834029
Fax (0577) 834455

Casanova is a great example of a family-run business, as parents and children alike work together to achieve an even better product. Nestled among the hills that rise from Torrenieri to Montalcino, the winery has already gained recognition abroad especially thanks to Giacomo Neri. One of the most promising among young Brunello makers, he personally sees to the enological and viticultural sides of the business. The 15 ha of vineyard are divided in three parts: vines from the Grosseto and Cerreto Alto plots are over 20 years old, while those from Fiesole are only five years old. All are planted to the Brunello clone of Sangiovese Grosso, with a plant density varying from 3,300 to 3,700 vines per hectare. The efficient cellar has all it takes to make good wine, including cement and stainless steel vats for vinification as well as good Slovenian and French oak barrels for aging and a temperature-controlled area for cellaring prior to release. Production reaches 4,200 cases per year, evenly split between Brunello and Rosso di Montalcino. The new 1987 Brunello selection called Cerreto Alto could prove to be interesting.

Rosso di Montalcino 1990 DOC
Giacomo Neri has always made very drinkable, pleasant wines. This 1990 Rosso fully confirms the Casanova house style with an even more complex bouquet, with aromas ranging from cherries to peppers.

Brunello di Montalcino Riserva 1986 DOCG
To produce a wine this good, with such ample, elegant fruit aromas, in an off year is quite an achievement. In its rounding and mellowing phase, the solid tannin backbone perfectly balances with the fresh acidity.

Case Basse

Loc. Vila Santa Restituta
Montalcino (Si) 53024
Tel. (0577) 848567 - (02) 4697934
Fax (02) 48195341

Originally from Milan, Gianfranco Soldera has done wonders with the estate he bought in the 1970s, proving his skills as a master wine-grower in Montalcino. He has 25 hectares of land, six planted to vineyard, which are situated on a hillside at 350 m above sea level with good south-west exposure and grows only Sangiovese Grosso. Soldera could make Brunello and Rosso di Montalcino, but chooses not to make the Rosso. Instead he makes a Vino da Tavola called Intistieti, which is aged for three years before being marketed. Low-yielding, scrupulously cared-for vines and selective bunch picking provide for perfectly ripe, healthy grapes. Maceration and fermentation are controlled step by step to preserve the primary aromas and fruit flavors, meanwhile skillful aging in oak and bottle do the rest. Almost 3,000 cases of Brunello, Riserva and Intistieti are produced annually which, though not cheap, regularly sell out.

Intistieti 1988
The Case Basse's flagship wine from 100% Sangiovese is noted for its refined bouquet, to which aging in small oak barrels confers elegance and fullness. Full-bodied and well-balanced.

Brunello di Montalcino 1986 DOCG
Surely one of the best Brunellos of the vintage. Intense ruby-red, with a rich, well-developed bouquet with hints of cherries, peaches, black pepper and coffee. Though not excessively long lasting in the mouth, it is elegant, refined and harmonious and has a good structure.

Castell'in Villa

Loc. Castell'in Villa
Castelnuovo Berardenga (Si) 53019
Tel. (0577) 359074
Fax (0577) 359222

Having left the harsh white limestone outcroppings just to the north, imagine the gentle, opulent hills dropping slowly down from Siena in the southernmost leg of the Chianti production area. This is where the noble Castell'in Villa farmstead is located. It is also where the old and new blend in harmony, thanks to the distinctive sensibility and good taste of the estate's proprietor-manager Coralia Pignatelli. A splendid, flower-filled terrace over the wine cellar gazes across an amphitheater of estate vineyards and olive groves. Of great power and character, the wines are the essence of tradition and sophisted technique. The grapes, mostly Sangiovese, come from mature vineyards of which is demanded little in quantity but much in quality. Only the most modern technology is used and the wine is matured at length in oak. Average production is made up of 30% Chianti Classico, 60% Chianti Classico Riserva and the remaining 10% of Santacroce (a Vino da Tavola blend of Sangiovese and Cabernet) plus a small bottling of precious Vin Santo.

Chianti Classico 1988 DOCG
Powerful and yet elegant. It has clear, intense aromas, first of raspberry then of spice, creating a rich and persuasive bouquet with great texture.

Chianti Classico Riserva 1986 DOCG
The Riserva is already well-developed and very drinkable now. Intense and bright garnet in color, its intense, mature evolved aromas reveal the typical Chianti fruitiness. Firm and long lasting on the palate.

Castelli del Grevepesa

Loc. Mercatale, via Grevigiana, 34
S. Casciano in Val di Pesa (Fi) 50024
Tel. (055) 821101-821196
Fax (055) 8217920

This large co-operative cellar brings together 170 growers of the Chianti Classico area and controls approximately 850 ha of vineyard. Its' directors persevered in stimulating growers along the road to quality even in hard years when Chianti production was in crisis. They began making selections of grapes as they arrived for crushing, using new enological techniques and adopting a marketing strategy aimed to increase the bottled-wine market. Encouraged by the first commercial results, they continued to select the grapes from specific areas, and then went on to produce single-vineyard wines. The latter have now joined the ranks of the élite in Chianti, but the entire line of Grevepesa wines has actually reached a very acceptable level, especially given the volumes involved. While the vintage Chianti Classico production looms at an impressive 125,000 cases, the selections (Panzano, Lamole and Montefiridolfi) average around 3,500 cases each and the single-vineyard wines Sant'Angiolo and Vigna Elisa respectively at 1,000 cases and 1,300.

Chianti Classico Riserva 1988 DOCG 🍇 ②
Bright ruby-red with garnet edges, it has intense, slightly dry aromas with notes of development. Highly strung and tight to the taste, but rich and appealing. A medium-structured wine that goes well with stewed meat dishes.

Chianti Classico 🍇 ②
Sant'Angiolo Vico l'Abate 1988 DOCG
Another impressive wine, with its complex, well-developed bouquet of mature fruit, dried mushrooms and truffles. Supple in the mouth, of medium structure, with a long finish and a pleasant bitter aftertaste.

Chianti Classico 🍇 ②
Selezione Panzano 1988 DOCG
Interesting on the nose, typical of the area from which the grapes are grown, with intense fruit and mushroom flavors. It should have a bright future, judging by the vibrant young color. Dry, with stiff tannins but rich and long lasting.

Predicato di Biturica Magliolo 1988 🍇 ②
A Sangiovese-Cabernet blend named after the area where it comes from, this well-structured wine, with firm tannins that have yet to soften, has a good nose-palate link, with rich, harmonious aromas of fruit and spices.

Luigi Cecchi & Figli

Loc. Casina dei Ponti
Castellina inChianti (Si) 53011
Tel. (0577) 743020
Fax (0577) 743057

Fortunately time has healed memories of when the Cecchi brand name was synonmous to cheap, jug wines. Today, thanks to Commendatore Luigi and his two young sons, Cesare and Andrea, the Cecchi winery does, indeed, produce a lot of wine but now most is of good, solid quality and some of which have real appeal. The Villa Cerna estate has always belonged to the family, together with the modern winemaking facilities below at Casina dei Ponti. In both rest aging big red wines with a great future ahead thanks to improved vineyard care and high technology in the winery. Andrea and Cesare have no doubt: "quality is the only way to win the market over". In fact, wines like Spargolo (a barrique-aged Sangiovese) and their Chianti Classico have gained national and international praise.

Chianti Classico 🍇 ①
Villa Cerna 1990 DOCG
A Chianti Classico with good aromas from the historic Cecchi estate. Aromas of fruit and good oak are clear and intense, accompanied by strong alcohol. Rich and robust in the mouth, already quite harmonious.

Chianti Classico 🍇 ②
Messer Pietro di Teuzzo 1988 DOCG
Good aromas of spice and soft impact in the mouth are the primary characteristics of this Chianti. Fine texture and elegance, with a long and pleasant finish.

Chianti Classico Riserva 🍇🍇 ②
Villa Cerna 1988 DOCG
From an important vintage comes an equally important Riserva, with interesting and variegated aromas that range from coffee to cloves. Full, with good texture in the mouth and nobile tannins destined to round out and mellow.

Cerbaiola

Piazza Cavour, 19
Montalcino (Si) 53024
Tel. (0577) 848499
Fax c/o Consorzio (0577) 849425

Generally wineries in Montalcino are small, but Cerbaiola is truly microscopic. With less than two ha of vineyard at 420 m above sea level, Mirella and Giulio Salvioni produce one of the area's best Brunello's and modestly continue to be as surprised now at the success of their wines, as they were with their first bottlings. When talking about the legendary 1985 vintage Giulio candidly recalls, "we were so doubtful about it that I wanted to give it away to the first person that came along". Fortunately for us, there are 20 hl barrels of the precious wine still carefully aging in the winery's cellar, that risk being sold before going to bottle. The vineyard from which it is made is unusual primarily due to its high altitude; secondly because it is completely on the flat. The resulting Brunello di Montalcino, however, is hardly unusual: with its great velvety and soft texture, it can easily stand up to the bigger local brand names.

Brunello di Montalcino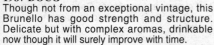
1987 DOCG
Though not from an exceptional vintage, this Brunello has good strength and structure. Delicate but with complex aromas, drinkable now though it will surely improve with time.

Cerbaiona

Loc. Cerbaiona
Montalcino (Si) 53024
Tel. (0577) 848660

Diego Molinare hung up his Alitalia pilot's uniform in 1977 in order to buy Cerbaiona and begin making Brunello. Much of his wines' success is due to his impeccably cared for vineyards, situated at 400 m above sea level. To Molinare, a cellar should be able to make great wines with only the bare essentials if the work has been done well in the vineyard. In fact, his cellar only has nine 20 hl barrels. He also choses to move his wine as little as possible, according to golden rule that he explains further, "Four rackings are necessary in the first year, two in the second and third years, none in the fourth." With these simple but well-focused ideas on winemaking, he makes well-structured Brunello wines that need at least a year of bottle aging to bring out its best. Molinari makes a Rosso di Montalcino with the same care and love. Here, too, the results are evident, as orders pile in from every corner of the world.

Brunello di Montalcino
1987 DOCG
The 1987 Cerbaiona Brunello shows great promise in a few years' time though its ripe fruit and pleasant oak bouquet might already appeal to early drinkers. Rich and long-lasting, a note of tannin still in development lingers on the finish.

Fattoria del Cerro

Via della Graziella, 5
Montepulciano (Si) 53040
Tel. (0578) 767722-767700
Fax (0578) 768040

A large firm with substantial financial backing, Fattoria del Cerro has risen in the past decade thanks to considerable investments aimed at improving the quality of the wines produced. It is owned by an important Italian insurance company, Sai. In addition to building a spacious, well-equipped cellar, extensive work has been done in the vineyard. An experimental vineyard was created to study the Prugnolo Gentile biotypes found on location as well as compiling an impressive selection of other indigenous vines. Aside from the experimental aspect, the genetic material generated represents a precious source for future plantings. Of the nearly 120 ha of vineyard, 83 are registered to produce Vino Nobile di Montepulciano. The vineyards are trained to Cordone Speronato on gently rolling hills at altitudes varying between 350 and 450 m, with a plant density of 2,700 vines per hectare for the old plantings to 4,200 for the newer. Despite the 3,000 hl total capacity of the aging cellars, they seldom produce that much (only in exceptional years) what with the careful selection at harvest and in the cellar.

Vino Nobile di Montepulciano 1989 DOCG 🍇 ①
Its lovely ruby color could denote freshness but also simplicity. In truth, judging from its well-evolved, almost austere bouquet one can see that it is very complex wine. This same complexity, together with texture and noble tannins, also comes through on the palate.

Vino Nobile di Montepulciano 1988 DOCG 🍇 ②
A wine that unites harmony and power and will surely give great satisfaction for many more years. Rich and harmonious bouquet, with delicate flavors of spice and fruit. Resolute and clean in the mouth, with great texture and persistence.

Vino Nobile di Montepulciano Riserva 1988 DOCG 🍇🍇 ②
Lovely garnet-red in color with ruby reflections, a wine that will improve with time, as is often the case with Fattoria del Cerro's wines. Ample tannins in the mouth but still young with good strength.

Agricoltori del Chianti Geografico

Via Mulinaccio, 10
Gaiole in Chianti (Si) 53013
Tel. (0577) 749451
Fax (0577) 749223

Located in the heart of Chianti Classico, this cooperative cellar was borne in the late 1950s out of the need of many local growers often lacked the equipment and means necessary to bring out the best from their splendid grapes. Thanks to modern vinification facilities, efficient marketing operations and an able administration department, the cooperative has done very well and has slowly but steadily expanded. Today, they supervise 375 ha of DOCG registered vineyards and give the growers helpful suggestions as to how to achieve maximum quality. Having recently purchased a cellar and attracted new member growers in the San Gimignano area, Agricoltori will be able to widen its range of products. Their clean, well-priced Chianti Classico remains the flagship wine with production averaging 100,000 cases a year, but the Tenuta Montegiachi and the Contessa di Radda selections also do well.

Chianti Classico 1990 DOCG 🍇 ①
Rich ruby colored, this Chianti has an ample and elegant fruity bouquet. Good structure in the mouth, with a remarkable freshness and harmony.

Chianti Classico Contessa di Radda 1988 DOCG 🍇 ①
This full-bodied, soft and velvety wine is bursting with flavor. Its aromas are intense, with mature fruit and refined spiciness, and the bright color still has its luscious violet highlights.

Predicato di Biturica Vigneti del Geografico 1987 🍇 ②
A Sangiovese-Cabernet blend, this bright, evolved ruby wine with sophisticated bouquet of well-blended aromas of fruit, grass and mushrooms. Round and endowed with good strength, it is quite an elegant wine with a long-lasting finish.

Ciacci Piccolomini D'Aragona

Fraz. Castelnuovo dell'Abate, Borgo di Mezzo, 62
Montalcino (Si) 53020
Tel. (0577) 835616
Fax (0577) 835785

Winemaking at Castelnuovo dell'Abate
winery began in the early 1980s when it was
bought by Giuseppe Bianchini. Until then the
Ciacci Piccolomini d'Aragona dynasty had
owned it for generations. For a start, he
doubled the original vineyard surface of nine
hectares and restored and updated the brick-
vaulted winemaking cellar, which is housed in
a splendid antique villa. Results were quick in
coming thanks to the impetus of the
winemaker Roberto Cipresso. Even the
newly planted vineyards were designed
according to the most modern criteria
viticulture has to offer, including clonal
selection while still fully respecting tradition.
Both normal and Riserva Brunello is made,
as well as Rosso di Montalcino, with a total of
3,000 cases a year. When the new vineyards
come on stream, production should push to
over 4,200 cases.

Rosso di Montalcino 1990 DOC   ♥ ①
A powerful Rosso, at first sight of its deep ruby-
red color and violet highlights. The bouquet is
intense with ripe fruit well-blended with the oak.
Rich and concentrated in the mouth, with texture
and a solid backbone.

Brunello di Montalcino 1986 DOCG ♥ ③
Brilliant garnet red in color, it has a typical range
of aromas, with strong hints of spice.
Harmonious in the mouth with discreet long-
lasting flavors. Barrel tastings of the 1988, 1989
and 1990 vintages all show fine quality.

Tenuta Col d'Orcia

Loc. Sant'Angelo in Colle
Montalcino (Si) 53020
Tel. (0577) 808004
Fax (0577) 864018

Owned by the Marone Cinzano family of Piemonte, Col d'Orcia's property extends for more than 500 hectares across the hills of Sant'Angelo near Montalcino. 30 ha of estate-vineyards are planted with Brunello and are split into different parcels according to the varying altitudes and sun exposures. Poggio al Vento is the prized vineyard from which the winery's flagship cru wine is made. Another 10 ha of vineyards are planted to Moscadello, Cabernet Sauvignon and Chardonnay. More Brunello vineyards will be planted, however, in order to meet the growing demand for Brunello di Montalcino wine without having to pressure the present low-yields that guarantee the label's constant quality level. The cellar is well-equipped for vinification, meanwhile they are presently making more room for the barrel and bottle aging. In addition to vintage and Riserva Brunello di Montalcino, they also make Rosso di Montalcino, Moscadello di Montalcino and several Vino da Tavola, with a total of nearly 42,000 cases per year.

Moscadello di Montalcino Pascena 1987 DOC
Slightly more raisined than the classic Moscadello, Pascena is a luscious, seductive wine that many sweet wine lovers would enjoy. Brilliant straw yellow with golden highlights, it has the typical, slightly evolved aromas of super-mature grapes and is fat, rich and well-balanced on the palate.

Rosso di Montalcino 1990 DOC

Lively and full-bodied, this Rosso is appealingly full-flavored, long-lasting and harmonious and very, very drinkable.

Brunello di Montalcino 1985 DOCG

Even though it was an exceptional vintage for Brunello, the intense, variegated and refined aromas found in this wine are the results of careful vinification and perfect wood aging. Furthermore, it has a wonderful texture and is remarkablly long-lasting.

Brunello di Montalcino Riserva Poggio al Vento 1985
This grand old Brunello is indicative of what can come from selected bunches picked, from the prized single-vineyard, in the hands of such expert winemakers as Alberto Antonini and Maurizio Castelli. At seven years from harvest, it is almost at its peak maturity but still promises wonders for at least ten more years. With an extraordinary full and complex bouquet, it has well-developed flavors of ripe fruit, spice and coffee. Extremely young in color, being intense ruby-red with a slight garnet hue. Mouthfilling and velvety on the palate, with good textur; harmonious, with a good acid and tannin balance.

POGGIO AL VENTO®

1985

RISERVA
BRUNELLO
DI MONTALCINO
DENOMINAZIONE DI ORIGINE
CONTROLLATA E GARANTITA

TENUTA COL D'ORCIA
IMBOTTIGLIATO DA TENUTA COL D'ORCIA S.P.A - MONTALCINO - ITALIA

750 ml ℮   13,5% vol. ITALIA

And now Cinzano.

the wines of tuscany

Tuscany. A rich tradition of grape growing. An extraordinary artistic heritage. A region with boundless cultural treasures including some of the most delicious wines known to man. It is a land of rolling hills and magical panoramas where a multitude of civilizations left their indelible mark. A tradition which has created 21 DOC and 4 DOCG wines. Four factors contribute to making great wines: soil, grape varieties, climate, and man.

Here in Tuscany, the four ideally combine creating a myriad of distinctive wines. The tradition all started in the region's rolling vineyards where dedicated growers still tend the vines with loving care. These are great wines that deserve your undivided attention. They should not be merely consumed, but tasted, contemplated and discussed. Create an ongoing relationship with them and you'll find you too, will appreciate and enjoy the wines of Tuscany for many years to come.

REGIONE TOSCANA
Assessorato dell'Agricoltura e Foreste

Colle Bereto

Loc. Colle Bereto
Radda in Chianti (Si) 53017
Tel/Fax (0577) 738083

The vineyards of Colle Bereto are on the outskirts of Radda in Chianti in a south-facing valley. Everything from the rennovated farmhouses to the invitingly antiquated rows of vineyards is stamped and sealed with respect for the Chianti tradition. In fact, the vineyards share comon ground with olives and other crops and grow only local grapes, as prescribed by centuries of experience. Yields are kept low and the bunches carefully selected at harvest, for fermentation and prolonged maceration in stainless steel tanks. The wine is aged in small Slovenian oak casks, before being bottled and laid to rest for cellaring. In excellent years the best Sangiovese bunches from the oldest vines are vinified separately to make a special, barrique-aged wine called Il Tocco. Colle Bereto's main wine is Chianti Classico, averaging 2,500 cases per year. Except for a modest supply of white table wine, the bottled wines are generally released after four to five years of cellaring, ready for drinking.

Chianti Classico 1987 DOCG   🍇 ②
The slightly dull ruby color, with a garnet edge betrays an unexceptional vintage. Nevertheless, the aromas are exuberant, not pin sharp, but complex and evolved, with considerable spice on the nose. Elegant, rich, round and balanced on the palate.

Il Tocco 1986   🍇🍇 ③
Though not as good as earlier vintages, such as the legendary '83 or the excellent '85, this Tocco is a fair expression of Colle Bereto's well-known wine. Brilliant garnet-red, it has the elegance and the velvety, harmonious flavors that one expects after such an intense, rich and well-developed nose.

Colombaio di Montosoli

Loc. Colombaio di Montosoli
Mntalcino (Si) 53024
Tel. (0577) 848109

"My land is a land of vines": this is how Nello Baricci's proudly responds when asked about his property. Behind these few words lies all the civilization and country culture that allow Nello to make great, traditional-style wines year after year. He ages his full-bodied reds in 20 to 40 hl oak casks, in accordance with the DOCG regulations. The best parcels of wine age longer in wood and become prestigious Brunello di Montalcino. Baricci's special Rosso di Montalcino has basically the same characteristics as a young Brunello but only is bottled earlier, as insistent buyers urge him to release. The 4.5 ha of vineyards are situated at altitudes varying from 180 to 250 m and are well-exposed to the sun. Consequently, he often picks early to avoid excess ripening.

Rosso di Montalcino 1990 DOC   🍇 ①
From a great vintage, this Rosso shows medium intensity and complexity on the nose. The taste reveals good body and a fairly good structure.

Brunello di Montalcino 1987 DOCG   🍇 ②
A high class Brunello; one can tell by the rich, brilliant ruby-red color that is acknowledged by the powerful bouquet, with generous hints of fruit well-blended with the nuances of the oak aging. It's a surprizingly good wine given the mediocre 1987 vintage.

Contucci

Via del Teatro, 1
Montepulciano (Si) 53045
Tel/Fax (0578) 757006

The 17th century cellars winding underneath Palazzo Contucci have now witnessed three generations of winemaking in the Contucci family. Today, the winery has four vineyards, each favorably exposed and situated at high elevations varying from 350 to 480 m. They are planted with typical Montepulciano grapes such as Prugnolo Gentile, Canaiolo and Mammolo, along with a small amount of Trebbiano and Malvasia del Chianti. Of the 21 ha of vineyard, 13 are registered to produce Vino Nobile di Montepulciano DOCG and two are registered to make the Rosso. They are trained to the traditional Guyot system at a density of 3,000 plants per ha. The grapes are fermented in the cool underground cellars, where the best technology further helps to guarantee maximum expression of premium grapes. Over half the wine made is Vino Nobile di Montepulciano DOCG, and the Contucci brothers would not have it any other way. Long-time president of the local Consorzio del Vino Nobile, Alamanno Contucci has helped to rekindle an enthusiasm for the wine.

Vin Santo 1985   🍇 ③
Bright golden-yellow and sparkling clean, its heavenly bouquet is well-developed, with characteristic raisined notes. Quite dry and warm in alcohol on the palate but mouth-filling and rewarding with intense and complex flavors that make it a pleasant and not too sweet Vin Santo.

Rosso di Montepulciano 1990 DOC   🍇 ①
The Rosso di Montepulciano DOC has not yet found its own personality or niche in the market. For the time being, it is comparable to the Contucci Rosso: very balanced, with firm, pleasant tannins and fine aromas of fruit and spices.

Nobile di Montepulciano   🍇🍇 ②
Vigna Pietra Rossa 1988 DOCG
This Contucci single-vineyard is truly an exceptional wine. Full, ample and even rich, despite its gripping tannins, still in evolution. Brilliant ruby-red in color, with warm, spicy aromas of good intensity.

Andrea Costanti

Loc. Colle al Matrichese
Montalcino (Si) 53024
Tel. (0577) 848195
Fax (0577) 849349

It would be safe to say that the Costanti family's winemaking history is firmly established in Colle al Matrichese. After all, they have owned the winery, adjacent to their homestead, since the 16th century. The youngest heir, Andrea, has been running the estate for several years and with excellent results thus far. Located at an average altitude of 400 m, the vineyards have been replanted in stages, beginning in 1965. Sangiovese Grosso is the main variety grown, but recently Cabernet Sauvignon has also been planted. Andrea is particularly fond of Brunello and Rosso di Montalcino and is an active chairman of the Consortium which safeguards and promotes the two in Italy and abroad. The cellar alone, with its 30 hl oak barrels, proves that tradition is the guiding inspiration for this skilled viticulturist. Judging from a 1987 barrel-sampling of Brunello di Montalcino, it will be extremely refined and pleasant wine.

Rosso di Montalcino 1990 DOC   🍇 ①
Andrea Costanti was able to make this pleasing wine in a great vintage, by succeeding in softening the tannins without emasculating them. An interesting wine also due to its fruity aromas which blend well with the spicy oak flavors.

Brunello di Montalcino   🍇🍇 ③
Riserva 1985 DOCG
This 1985 Riserva has been designated for elegance. Fairly deep garnet-red, it has refined complexity and developed perfumes with aromas of jam, spices and tabacco. Rich, warm and embracing flavors, with good backbone and length.

Fattoria di Felsina

S.S. Chiantigiana, 484
Castelnuovo Berardenga (Si) 53019
Tel. (0577) 355117
Fax (0577) 355651

Fattoria di Felsina is located between one of the southern-most tips of the Chianti mountains and the vast Ombrone river valley. Originally an ancient borough along the road to Siena from Arezzo, today it is a well-organized farming estate with 350 ha of land, 52 of which are planted with vines. The soil composition in this area between the Chianti and the "crete senesi" (the beautiful clay-soiled hills) is rather mixed and variable, and imparts a unique and unmistakable character and a penetrating earthy bouquet of smoke and tobacco to the wines, particularily the Sangiovese. The vineyards are well exposed on slopes which range from 300 to 400 m and are mostly devoted to the production of Chianti Classico. There are two recent plantings of Chardonnay and Cabernet Sauvignon, respectively of five and two ha. Two long-established Sangiovese vineyards, Fontalloro and Rancia, are worthy of special mention as they produce the estate's best cru wines. On average 10,000 cases of normal and Riserva Chianti Classico are produced; a Riserva Rancia and Fontalloro are also produced in better years. Still other products include a Bianco Val d'Arbia DOC and a Chardonnay VdT I Sistri.

I Sistri 1990   ⚇ ②

Deep, bright straw-yellow and made from barrique-aged Chardonnay. Intense and complex, its clean, ethereal perfumes reveal a subtle use of oak. Full-flavored, fat, well-balanced and long-lasting.

Chianti Classico 1990 DOCG   ⚇ ①

A very typical and particularly pleasant Chianti, it has intense clean aromas of marasca cherry and black pepper. Very powerful on the palate with great backbone which does not compromise its overall balance.

Fontalloro 1987   ⚇⚇ ③

Normally powerful and robust in other vintages, this 1987 straight Sangiovese is elegant, ripe and extremely enjoyable. Medium-deep ruby red, it has a rich and refined bouquet with a pleasant fruity-sweet spiciness. Harmonious and well-rounded, of great length.

Chianti Classico Riserva   ⚇⚇⚇ ③
Vigneto Rancia 1988 DOCG

In only a few years' time, Fattoria di Felsina has shot to the top of premium wine production. A winning combination; the skilled enologist Franco Bernabei and by Giuseppe Mazzocolin, the estate's dynamic managing director. This Chianti Classico cru of great character is the result of a rigorous selection of the best bunches picked from the Rancia vineyard. Its structure is truly impressive and only lengthy cellar aging in bottle will soften and enhance it. Aromas are complex, as the vanilla from oak aging gracefully blends in with the fruit. The flavor is embracing, warm and very lengthy. A textbook example of modern Chianti Classico.

Le Filigare

Via Sicelle, 37
S. Donato in Poggio (Fi) 50020
Tel. (055) 8072796
Fax (055) 755766

To honor the local patron saint, the local inhabitants used to decorate the old manor-house high on the hill with torches and celebrate the "fiaccola di sopra" torchlight procession. Although torches are no longer lit at Filigare, some good wines are now being produced, thanks to the impetus of Carlo Burchi and consulting enologist Vittorio Fiore. The estate vineyards range in altitudes from 400 to 500 m above sea level and they particularily concentrate on Chianti Classico production, aging it in 30 hl oak barrels. Only the Riserva and the Vino da Tavola Le Rocce wines are barrique-aged in 225 lt casks for about 10 months.

Chianti Classico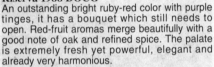
Riserva 1988 DOCG
An outstanding bright ruby-red color with purple tinges, it has a bouquet which still needs to open. Red-fruit aromas merge beautifully with a good note of oak and refined spice. The palate is extremely fresh yet powerful, elegant and already very harmonious.

Podere Le Rocce 1988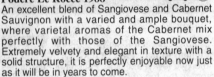
An excellent blend of Sangiovese and Cabernet Sauvignon with a varied and ample bouquet, where varietal aromas of the Cabernet mix perfectly with those of the Sangiovese. Extremely velvety and elegant in texture with a solid structure, it is perfectly enjoyable now just as it will be in years to come.

Castello di Fonterutoli

Loc. Fonterutoli
Castellina in Chianti (Si) 53011
Tel. (0577) 740476-740522
Fax (0577) 741070

Fonterutoli was once an ancient military fortification situated along the Roman road which linked Florence to Siena. Though all traces of the stronghold have since disappeared, the stone hamlet hums with agricultural and artisan activities connected to the estate's winemaking heritage. For centuries it has been owned by the noble Mazzei family of Florence. Located at altitudes which range from 250 to 500 m, 50 of the estate's 66 ha of vineyards are planted with Sangiovese and are divided into three plots (Siepi, Fonterutoli and Badiola). The other varietals grown include Cabernet Sauvignon, Canaiolo, Merlot, Trebbiano and Malvasia. The winery is well-organized and efficient with its modern winemaking equipment and layout in the cellar. Product yields are kept low by the very nature of the poor soil composition and the rigorous bunch selection during the different pickings at harvest time and rarely exceed 40 hl/ha in wine. In better vintages about 12,500 cases of Chianti Classico are produced in addition to 3,300 of Riserva Ser Lapo and 3,300 of Concerto, a fine Vino da Tavola made from Sangiovese and Cabernet Sauvignon.

Chianti Classico 1990 DOCG
Fonterutoli wines need lengthy aging, particularly in exceptional vintages; such is the case with this Chianti Classico. Slightly lacking in complexity on the nose despite the intense fruity, spicy aromas. Rich, warm in alcohol, firmly structured; likely to become more harmonious in due time.

Chianti Classico Riserva
Ser Lapo 1988 DOCG
This Riserva is maturing well, with its rich, spicy perfumes and hints of truffles to match the refined and not so intense fruit aromas. Dry and tight on the palate, warm and very considerably long-lasting.

Concerto 1988
Powerful Sangiovese is well counter-balanced with the 20% Cabernet Sauvignon. Still young with intense perfumes and good fruit merging with the vanilla scents from the oak aging. The palate shows good structure, with tannins that still need to develop; good intensity and long lasting flavors.

Fontodi

Via San Leonino, 87
Panzano in Chianti (Fi) 50020
Tel. (055) 852005
Fax (055) 852537

During the first 'International Convention on the Wines of Tuscany' organized by Arcigola Slow Food, Fontodi's owner, Giovanni Manetti appropriately described his wines as being the "the result of my friendship with Franco Bernabei". Indeed, much of the success of this estate can be attributed to this winning combination: a young and passionate owner guided by a master winemaker. Together they have succeeded in drawing the best from the vineyards located in the famed "Conca d'Oro" vineyard in Panzano in Chianti. Having a high-tech cellar also helps to guarantee consistent, top-quality wines. But Chianti is not the only wine made at Fontodi, as they are keen to experiment with and improve their wines made with non-native varietals, such as Cabernet Sauvignon or Syrah. This is the one of the area's hottest, trend setters to watch for in the future.

Meriggio 1990 ⅋ ②
A special blend of Pinot Bianco, Sauvignon and Traminer Rosa, it is a good wine with ample, convincing aromas. Very pleasant and fresh on the palate, with good length, just as one would expect from such a distinctive nose.

Chianti Classico 1990 DOCG ⅋ ①
A good example of the style of the Panzano area, powerful and with aging potential. Clean aromas of maraschino cherries and currants with good oak notes lead into a firm, youthful and robust body, which although rough, will surely mellow with time. Rich and lingering on the finish.

Flaccianello della Pieve 1988 ⅋⅋ ③
A very young wine which will undoubtedly benefit from further aging although it already seems to stand up to the fame of its predecessors. Rich and intense, with oaky aromas, that accompany a powerful, concentrated body and firm tannins which still need to be tamed.

Chianti Classico Riserva ⅋⅋ ③
Vigna il Sorbo 1987 DOCG
Bright, deep ruby-red; rich, fruity and slightly herbaceous but harmonious aromas from the skilled oak aging. Rich and full-bodied on the palate with good structure and firm tannins which could soften further.

Podere La Fortuna

Loc. La Fortuna
Montalcino (Si) 53024
Tel/Fax (0577) 848308

La Fortuna is located north-east of Montalcino on the slopes facing Siena and the "crete senesi". The Zannoni husband-wife team has owned the estate since 1985 and have run it with the single-handed help of the wine technician, Paolo Vagaggini. Fortunately, the estate is small, with only three hectares of vineyards. As a result they are able to take great care of the vineyard and personally follow through with each operation. The vinification and aging cellar has vats which hold a maximum of 540 hl of wine and they have oak barrels which vary in size, from 25 to 30 hl. Annual production averages over 800 cases. With such a limited size, they choose to focus on the classic Montalcino wines, Brunello and Rosso di Montalcino.

Brunello di Montalcino 1987 DOCG ⅋ ③
Bright, clean garnet-red. If slightly lacking in intensity, the aromas are rather fine, ethereal and complex, with a pleasant almond scent. Full-flavored, medium-structured but quite long-lasting with pronounced yet refined tannins.

Marchesi de' Frescobaldi

Via S. Spirito, 11
Firenze 50125
Tel. (055) 218751

Famous worldwide, Frescobaldi is one of Tuscany's oldest family-run houses. Even considering the large volumes, all the wines are made from estate vineyards (an impressive 725 hectares) which are divided among eight estates strategically positioned in the region's best wine areas. Three estates deserve special mention, starting with the one closest to home, Tenuta di Pomino, an area recently granted DOC status. The vineyards here are located at different altitudes: Sangiovese, Canaiolo, Merlot and Cabernet are planted at 400 to 600 m; Pinot Nero, Pinot Bianco, Pinot Grigio and Chardonnay are planted at even higher altitudes, with the Benefizio vineyard reaching 750 m. The latter makes a prized Chardonnay cru wine of the same name. The Castello di Nipozzano estate, in the Chianti Rufina zone, produces typical DOCG wines and Mormoreto Vino da Tavola from Cabernet Sauvignon. The Tenuta di Castelgiocondo in Montalcino boasts the largest area planted with Brunello, but other varietals are grown, too, such as Sauvignon Blanc in the Vergena vineyard. The group's seven vinification cellars produce about 450,000 cases a year. All are top-quality but Frescobaldi's most prestigious labels come from the above-mentioned estates.

Pomino Il Benefizio 1989 DOC ℘ ②
From Chardonnay, shiny straw yellow in color, with a refined fruity bouquet with well-balanced scents from the new oak-aging. Fresh and full-bodied on the palate, marked with a certain finesse.

Mormoreto 1988 ❦ ②
Vino da Tavola made from Cabernet Sauvignon. It has a deep ruby-red color and an intense fruity bouquet with a light herbaceous note and good harmony thanks to the skilled use of oak. A rich, powerful palate with outstanding balance and a pleasant finish.

Chianti Rufina ❦❦ ③
Montesodi 1986 DOCG
A Chianti Rufina of great class, it is still youthful in color, with its rich ruby-red color and purplish highlights. Rich and spicy, nutty aromas and pleasant gamey scents. The palate is round with ample texture, balance and considerable length.

Brunello di Montalcino Riserva ❦❦ ③
Castelgiocondo 1985 DOCG
A Riserva wine from a legendary vintage. Intense ruby-red tending to garnet, rather gripping aromas. Mature, complex perfumes with notes of leather, dried fruit and mushrooms. Ample and rich, revealing good body and structure.

Tenuta di Ghizzano

Via della Chiesa, 1
Ghizzano (Pi) 56030
Tel. (0587) 630096 - (050) 20596

Ghizzano is a perfect example the so-called Tuscan wine renaissance of the 1980s, when the pressure was on to make increasingly better wines. Veneroso, a barrique-aged blend of Sangiovese and Cabernet Sauvignon, was the first wine to launch the estate to international fame. It was the brainchild of Pierfrancesco Venerosi Pesciolini and Pier Mario Meletti Cavallari, a young but established viticulturist in the Bolgheri area. The Venerosi Pesciolini family has been cultivating vines and olives here for over six centuries. The estate's 12 ha of vineyards are located on the gentle hillsides surrounding Pisa and enjoy favorable sun exposures at 200 m elevations. Bordered by woodlands and olive groves, they are sectioned into six plots, each being planted at different times. The typical Chianti varieties do very well, as well as Cabernet Sauvignon, naturally. For experimental purposes, Merlot and Petit Verdot have recently been planted. In the cellar, a good selection of barriques and medium-sized barrels are used to age small batches of wine after careful selection in the vineyard. Production is evenly split between the VdT Veneroso and Chianti Colline Pisane DOCG.

Veneroso 1988 ❦❦ ③
A blend of Sangiovese and Cabernet Sauvignon, this is an extremely elegant wine. Its impressive structure strikes immediately on the nose, with a defined and incredibly ample bouquet. Soft and velvety on the palate, most persuasive and harmonious.

Podere Grattamacco

Loc. Grattamacco
Castagneto Carduci (Li) 57022
Tel. (0578) 763840

Recently, the lush hilly coastal area called the Alta Maremma, between Cecina and Cornia, has experienced a rapid and exciting wine revolution. Many factors have concurred in order to create this situation, but the guiding light behind it all has been Pier Mario Meletti Cavallari. He simply fell in love with the Grattamacco estate and its remote location in the Castagneto bushland. He began crafting wines which have surprised many an Italian and international wine lover. Grattamacco wines rank among Tuscany's best. The estate only has 7.5 ha of vineyards, but they are blessed with an exceptional climate and rich soils. Two thirds are planted to Sangiovese and Cabernet and one third to Trebbiano and Vermentino. The cellar, efficient and well-equipped, perfectly depicts the owner's pragmatic nature. After rigorous selection both at harvest-time and in the cellar, the winery averages 1,250 cases of Rosso and 1,000 of Bianco. A very decent white table wine is made and sold locally.

Grattamacco Rosso 1989 🍇🍇 ③
Even with such an off-vintage, Pier Mario Meletti Cavallari has succeeded in sculpting an excellent product. An outstanding bouquet with defined bell-pepper and spice aromas and very fine fruit. Still very young, with lively, fresh tannins which promise great cellaring potential.

Il Greppo Biondi-Santi

Località Il Greppo
Montalcino (Si) 53024
Tel. (0577) 848087
Fax (0577) 849396

The saga behind the Biondi Santi family history is part of the rich heritage of Brunello di Montalcino. In fact, it was a Biondi Santi who first discovered that the Sangiovese Grosso grape that grew on the hills was able to give a wine of such robust character one hundred years ago. Through patient experimentation in both the vineyard and cellar, he explored all aspects of the grape that was locally referred to as Brunello. With the right vinification and aging, it became King of all Italian wines. Tancredi Biondi Santi deserves the credit for having laid the foundations for this wine, which today claims international fame. Upon his death, Franco Biondi Santi took the lead, carrying on the family tradition with professionalism and style. The estates' 14 ha of vineyards at Il Greppo are planted with Sangiovese Grosso, but nine more will soon be planted. Except for a small production of Rosso di Montalcino, most of the grapes are processed to produce Brunello and Brunello Riserva, the latter made with grapes from the older, lower-yielding vineyards. These wines age an exceptionally long time, as proven by the vertical tastings periodically carried out at the estate.

Brunello di Montalcino 1986 DOCG 🍇 ④
Rich, brilliant ruby-red with light garnet highlights. Its bouquet may not be particularly intense, but the aromas are well-defined. Somewhat unbalanced on the palate, for now, since its high acidity seems to lack the backbone of a firm structure.

Brunello di Montalcino 🍇🍇 ④
Riserva 1985 DOCG
Franco Biondi Santi believes that his best vintages nearly always end with the digit 5. Indeed this 1985 Riserva has charming and elegant aromas, with a fine bouquet of outstanding length, and the palate has good backbone and persuasive elegance which compensates for a medium structure.

Isole e Olena

Via Olena, 15
Barberino Val d'Elsa (Fi) 50021
Tel. (055) 8072763
Fax (055) 8072236

For years, Isole e Olena has been a point of reference in the Tuscan cult for wine lovers. Many remain sound in their conviction that this area makes the best wines in the world. The estate is owned and managed by Paolo De Marchi, who is 'Piemontese by birth but Tuscan by adoption'. He was determined to make a Chianti that would rank among the best. To this end, his vineyards are trained low, periodically thinning shoots and bunches during the growing season. His quest for excellence does not stop here: he studies his own soil, its composition and nature, experimenting along the way with clones of both Chianti and non-Chianti varieties on particularly versatile and suitable trial plots of land. His wines are the direct results of these experiments and others being conducted regularily. Scrupulous care in the vineyards and a conscientious and technologically-advanced management of the cellar also help considerably. His wines have great character, body and aging potential. Not only do the Chianti wines fit this description but so do the other great wines such as the barrique-aged Sangiovese Cepparello and the recent varietal wines based on Syrah, Cabernet and Chardonnay.

Chardonnay
Collezione De Marchi 1990
This wines has a very interesting, distinctive bouquet. In addition to the typical varietal aromas, there are notes of peach and white melon, all harmoniously blended with pleasant oak notes.

Chianti Classico 1990 DOCG
An excellent Chianti, with a beautiful bright and vibrant ruby-red color, and a remarkable range of fruity aromas, still slightly held back by the oak. Big, round, well-balanced and smooth with the structure of a great wine.

Cabernet Sauvignon
Collezione De Marchi 1989
Even this wine suffered the effects of a poor vintage. The aromas are typical of the varietal and rather elegant, but lacking in intensity. There's a good backbone on the mouth but it lacks the texture and fullness of better vintages.

Cepparello 1989
Probably the estate's most famous wine, made from 100% Sangiovese. It has a refined bouquet with leather and berry-fruit perfumes. Ample, well-structured and long-lasting.

Cabernet Sauvignon
Collezione De Marchi 1988
With this Private Collection Cabernet Sauvignon, Paolo De Marchi practiced what he has learned in years of experience, having visited some of the world's most famous wine regions. The wine, which is already excellent and pleasant, will reach its peak in a few years. Deep purple-red, it has the typical varietal aromas but is particularily elegant and ample. In addition to the typical bell pepper aromas, there is lots of red ripe fruit and spice. It will surely develop a very complex bouquet. Powerful, full, warm and balanced on the palate, although the tannins still need to soften.

Tenuta di Lilliano

Località Lilliano
Castellina in Chianti (Si) 53011
Tel. (0577) 743070
Fax (0577) 743036

The fortified "borgo" of Lilliano near Castellina in Chianti was brought under siege and destroyed several times during the Medieval age as the Republics of Siena and Florence fought each other. Since 1920 it has belonged to the Ruspoli family. The Princess Eleonora Ruspoli Berlingeri is responsible for the jump in quality seen in the past two decades. The vineyards are planted on marly-clay-calcareous soils and on the sunny hilly slopes at 280-380 m elevations. Only indigenous grapes are grown except for some Merlot. The winemaking is the essence of tradition: rigorous bunch selection at harvest, hand-picking only, long maceration on skins, the must ages in cement vats until spring then gets pumped into small and medium-sized oak barrels where it ages for about a year, once bottled it ages for at least six more months. The result of this process (which is as ancient as Chianti itself) are powerful wines of great breadth. Average production is around 17,000 cases of vintage Chianti Classico, 1,650 of the Riserva and 1,000 of Anagallis, a barrique-aged Sangiovese.

Chianti Classico 1990 DOCG ♈ ①

An excellent vintage for Chianti, this one is powerful and extremely fruity on the nose, with fine aromas that make up a complex bouquet which has not yet fully blossomed.

Anagallis 1988 ♈ ③

Deep ruby-red in color and made from Sangiovese and Colorino grapes. Complex, ethereal aromas with pronounced oak which needs to blend with the delicate fruit base. Powerful and rich on the palate, it is sure to improve with further aging.

Chianti Classico ♈♈ ③
Riserva 1988 DOCG

Lilliano wines usually need take time to express themselves fully and this 1988 Riserva is no exception. Deep ruby-red with a youthful, ethereal and rich bouquet and a lively palate of great texture and considerable length.

Lisini

Sant'Angelo in Colle
Montalcino (Si) 53020
Tel. (0577) 864040
Fax (0577) 864219

The Lisini brand name is undoubtedly one of prime importance in the heritage of Brunello di Montalcino. Wines like their 1975 Riserva have literally gone down in history. The estate is currently managed by Elina Lisini, a gentle and refined businesswoman with a stubborn, resolute character. After all these years, of course, consulting enologist Franco Bernabei has learned how to work with her. Despite their amicable ups and downs, there have been some excellent results. The estate's flagship wine is undoubetdly the Brunello di Montalcino, made from grapes grown on eight hectares of vineyards. It ages four years in oak and chestnut barrels for six months in the bottle before release. This final step is indispensable to fully appreciate this wine.

Brunello di Montalcino 1987 DOCG ♈♈ ③

A very well-balanced Brunello, with a composite and ample bouquet with leather, berry fruit and black pepper aromas. The palate has good texture, elegance and length. A wine where aromas and flavors are well matched.

Brunello di Montalcino ♈♈ ③
Riserva 1986 DOCG

A big, powerful wine with texture and good body. The palate is ample and lingering, whereas on the nose the bouquet still needs to develop, although it is clean and correct. Deep and rather bright ruby red in color.

Niccolò Machiavelli

Località S. Andrea in Percussina
S. Casciano Val di Pesa (Fi) 50026
Tel. (0577) 989001
Fax (0577) 989002

One of the most prestigious wineries of the Gruppo Italiano Vini, the Antica Fattoria Niccolò Machiavelli boasts an illustrious winemaking heritage. Its cellar and estate-vineyards (notably Fontalle and Il Piano) have always provided a high-quality level which one always came to expect of Machiavelli wines. Only the grapes grown on the estate's 22 ha are used to produce the wines marketed under the Machiavelli label.The Sangiovese is at the heart of the Chianti Classico single-vineyard Vigna di Fontalle, whereas the Cabernet Sauvignon is for Ser Niccolò. The white grapes go into the Vin Santo. Dr. Nunzio Capurso is managing director at this estate as well as the other GIV properties in the region. He is an extremely skilled enologist originally from Veneto but long since established in Tuscany.

Chianti Classico Riserva 🍇 ②
Vigna di Fontalle 1987 DOCG
Even in unexciting 1987, this Riserva Vigna di Fontalle does not disappoint. It has a rich, complex bouquet where spicy aromas of herbs combine with good fruit. Full, generous and well-structured on the palate and long-lasting.

Ser Niccolò 1985 🍇🍇 ③
An extremely concentrated and powerful wine, as evident at first sight. From 100% Cabernet Sauvignon grapes, it has intense and lingering aromas with typical bell-pepper aromas accompanied by good, sweet and ripe fruit.

Ezio Mantellassi

Fattoria S. Giuseppe, 16
Magliano in Toscana (Gr) 58051
Tel/Fax (0564) 592037

Ezio Mantellassi's large estate is located in the heart of beautiful Maremma and is run with the help of his son, Giuseppe. One tenth of the property's 400 ha are monoculture vineyards. In recent years the quality of his wines has risen sharply, especially since they decided to dedicate more attention to the winemaking cellar. They now have a beautiful set of 15 hl oak casks as well as 40 barriques sitting in the cool cellars, where Giuseppe practically lives year-round. Consulting technician Stefanini has also his part in the rennovation. Morellino di Scansano is their best and most important wine, naturally, since it's the area's most interesting DOC wine. They make two styles, a vintage and a Riserva. More recently, the winery has spotted a perfect location for a single-vineyard, which is sure to become the Mantellassi flagship wine.

Alicante Querciolaia 1990 🍇 ①
This wine strikes you immediately with the fruity varietal aromas of the Alicante grape. Ample and well-structured, with slightly rough but not pungent tannins, it has a pleasant finish with long-lasting aromas.

Morellino di Scansano 🍇 ①
Le Sentinelle 1989 DOC
This Mantellassi cru wine is deep ruby-red with ripe fruit and liquorice aromas and spicy notes. Rich and well-structured, with a velvety texture and good length.

Melini

Località Gaggiano
Poggibonsi (Si) 53036
Tel. (0577) 939667

Years and years ago, the Melini company was a wine négociant. Today it is one of the major producers and bottlers in the Chianti area, with over 100 ha of vineyards subdivided into three properties: Selvanella, Terrarossa and Granaio, all in the Classico zone. Its headquarters and winemaking cellar facilities in Gaggiano are among the best equipped of the region. Melini is owned by the Gruppo Italiano Vini, a major producer and distributor in the European wine industry. Nunzio Capurso was appointed as managing director of the estate. An experienced enologist with great managerial skills, he is responsible for improving the quality of Melini wines. By limiting yields, scrupolously selecting bunches at harvest and concentrating on better vinification methods, separating the vineyards and varieties where possible, the quality has noticeably increased. The efficient cellar is designed to cope with both the industrial and more selective production styles. In fact, Melini bottles three different styles of Chianti Classico that are made from estate vineyards including the vintage I Sassi and the Selvanella Riserva. The third, called Chianti Classico Laborel, is a Riserva but aged longer and was named in honor of the winery's founder.

Chianti Classico Riserva Laborel 1987 DOCG
Despite the vintage, which was not one of the best, this wine has intense, refined aromas of red fruits, with spicy notes. Fat and embracing on the palate with good texture and a full-body.

Chianti Classico Riserva La Selvanella 1987 DOCG
Even in such a mediocre year, wines like this prove that La Selvanella is one of the best examples of its type. Bright ruby-red with garnet highlights, complex with clean fruity aromas. Warm and full with ample texture and a good solid backbone.

Castello di Monsanto

Via Monsanto, 16
Barberino Val d'Elsa (Fi) 50021
Tel. (055) 8059000
Fax (055) 8059049

The range of hills between the Pesa and Elsa river beds is the easternmost slice of the Chianti Classico production zone. The most interesting, elegant wines of the whole Chianti area come from here, with its unique south-westerly slopes and clayey schists called Galestri. Monsanto, with its 50 ha of vineyards, is one of the area's most important wineries. Since the early 1960s it has been run by Fabrizio Bianchi, an industrialist from Milan who brought upbeat proficiency and drive to this sleepy corner of Tuscany. A well-organized and equipped estate, it tends to focus on obtaining the best results directly in the cellar. Though all improve with cellaring, the Chianti Classico is made in several styles including a vintage, a Riserva and a single-vineyard called Il Poggio. Production averages 120,000 bottles for the Riserva compared to 60,000 for the more drinkable vintage and only 35,000 bottles for the special Poggio. In addition to the DOCG wines, they also make 70,000 bottles of Vino da Tavola including three reds (a Sangiovese, a Cabernet and a blend of the two) and a Chardonnay.

Nemo 1988
Made from Cabernet Sauvignon, it is ample, elegant and well-balanced. One of the few Tuscan Cabernets without obvious bell-pepper aromas, a characteristic not to be overlooked. The bouquet is complex, intense, very individual and extremely pleasant.

Tinscvil 1988
A blend of mostly Sangiovese with some Cabernet. Rich and lingering on the palate with intense aromas of mushrooms and berry-fruits. Good texture and balance, elegant, ideal for early drinking.

Chianti Classico Riserva Il Poggio 1986 DOCG
Bright garnet-red, with a complex, developed bouquet with ripe fruit aromas which are not overwhelmed by a toasty note of oak. Intense and rich on the palate; rough but ample and persistent.

Fabrizio Bianchi 1986
A good Sangiovese wine with an extremely refined, complex bouquet with notes of tobacco and leather. Soft and velvety, harmonious and of good aromatic length.

Fattoria Montellori

Via Pistoiese, 5
Fucecchio (Fi) 50054
Tel. (0571) 260641
Fax (0571) 592003

The Nieri family have been the proud owners
of Fattoria Montellori for more than a hundred
years. Giuseppe Nieri and his son
Alessandro run all operations. In an area with
little or no quality winemaking heritage,
surprizingly enough, this estate has always
managed to produce noticeably good wines.
They make a traditional Sangiovese and
have recently planted 'alternative' varieties
like Cabernet Sauvignon, Chardonnay,
Sauvignon and, more recently, Merlot. The
winery's two best wines are Castelrapiti
Rosso (a blend of Sangiovese and Cabernet)
and Castelrapiti Bianco (a barrique-aged
Chardonnay). The cellar, too, has also
received a facelift, with the acquisition of
temperature-controlled fermentation vats,
new barrels and barriques. All these factors
have combined to improve the quality and
image of Montellori wines.

Castelrapiti Bianco 1990 ※ ②
A Chardonnay aged in barrique, it has refined
and elegant yet not extremely powerful aromas.
On the palate it shows good texture, elegant
and rich yet still very refreshing.

Vin Santo 1985 ※ ③
An elegant and velvety Vin Santo made only
with Trebbiano grapes. Crystal clear amber in
color with typical aromas of candied fruit. But it
gives its best on the palate, with its soft,
luscious, seductive and harmonious flavors.
Certainly one of the best Vin Santo wines
available.

Castelrapiti Rosso 1988 ※※ ②
A blend of Sangiovese and Cabernet. On the
nose, it shows good, refined spices with the
typical varietal character of Cabernet, with a
rather ample and complex bouquet. Strikingly
elegant and soft with good structure in the
mouth.

Price levels

①   up to $ 9.99

② $ 10.00 - $ 14.99

③ $ 15.00 - $ 24.99

④ $ 25.00 or more

*The 'ex-cellar', or direct from the
producer, bottle prices, are calculated in
US dollars and are intended only as an
approximate guide*

Fattoria di Montevertine

Località Monte Vertine
Radda in Chianti (Si) 53017
Tel. (0577) 738009
Fax (0577) 738265

Several of the most famous Chianti Classico vineyards face the upper Pesa valley where vines have flourished since Etrucan times. One of these happen to belong to Montevertine. The estate's owner, Sergio Manetti, fell in love with the area and brought it back to life in the early 1970s. Today prized single-vineyards surround the perfectly restored Tuscan hamlet of Montevertine where this wonderful family lives and works. Under the undisputed guidance of Sergio, every year they put out oustanding wines. The vineyards include Le Pergole Torte, with 3 hectares of 22 year-old Sangiovese vines, and Il Sodaccio, with 1.5 ha of 16 year-old Sangiovese and Canaiolo vines. The cellars are laid out according to the traditional style out are very well-equipped and ensure perfect vinification; the wines are wood and bottle-aged at length in the cool cellars underground. Production is around 20,000 bottles of Le Pergole Torte, 12,000 of Montevertine and 10,000 of Sodaccio, in addition to a small quantity of a white called M and a very individual "Passito" or raisined wine called Il Maggio.

LE PERGOLE TORTE 1988

L'89 di Sergio Manetti 🍇 ③
The name itself is already provocative and enticing: it singles out a poor vintage and the name of the man who had the 'courage' to bottle it all. It shows his self-confidence, despite the elements. From 100% Sangiovese, it is actually quite good, being ready and pleasant on both the nose and the palate, with the classic elegance of Montevertine wines.

Montevertine 1989 🍇🍇 ③
Bright yet medium-light ruby colored, its aromas may not be intense but rather elegant with rich spices and good complexity. Full flavored, round with a certain bite. Balanced, with an elegant finish.

Le Pergole Torte 1988 🍇🍇🍇 ④
With the help of famed enologist Giulio Gambelli, Sergio Manetti has crafted a red of legendary character. The Sangiovese grapes, the base of the wine, were grown in a single-vineyard named Le Pergole Torte located in Radda in Chianti, which lends its name to the wine. An excellent vintage, this Pergole Torte is aged 18 months in French barrique and a year in bottle. Intense bright ruby-red, very intense and complex on the nose with light vanilla scents from the oak-aging; well-blended with the aromas of mature fruit, violets and spices. Warm and persistent, with a well-balanced nose and palate and an exceptional, full-bodied texture, with a firm backbone of tannins. It's already soft and round enough to drink now but further cellaring would do no harm.

Bruno Moos

Via Pier Capponi, 98
Soiana (Pi) 56030
Tel/Fax (0587) 654180

Originally from Canada, years ago Elyane and Bruno Moos decided to move and settle in the tiny provincial village of Soiana, near Pisa. The local farmers affectionately nicknamed them "i Canadesi". They raised a few eyebrows as the newcomers immediately took to growing vines and making their own wines. Even more to their surprise, the wines were very good. Since then, Moos' wines have constantly and consistently improved. Wines like their Chianti from the Colline Pisane DOCG area or their barrique-aged Vino da Tavola Fontestina, or their fresh Vermentino are all top-level. Quality is achieved through attentive management in both the vineyard and particularly in the cellar, with ongoing renovation from year to year.

Soianello 1991 🍇 ①
Although extremely young, it already shows pleasant aromas and a strong typical vinous character. Lots of young fruit flavors hardly compromise the overall result but instead guarantee a good future. A blend of Sangiovese (80%), Canaiolo, Malvasia Nera and Ciliegiolo.

Chianti Colline Pisane 🍇 ②
Riserva 1988 DOCG
A strikingly powerful and full-bodied wine, perfect for a few years' aging thanks to its solid backbone. With fine, mature aromas and well-defined and elegant notes of spice. Bright ruby-red with purplish tinges.

Tenuta di Nozzole

Località Passo dei Pecorai
Greve in Chianti (Fi) 50020
Tel. (055) 858018
Fax (055) 850737

The Nozzole farmstead is located on the hilly slopes to the right of the Greve river in the northernmost part of the Chianti Classico production zone. It has been in on the upswing ever since it became part of the Ruffino group, what with the substantial experimental plantings, grafting, restructuring and new cellar building. Although the innovations have not been completed, today the estate has taken on a completely new appearance. The 85 ha of vineyards are separated from one another by dense pine forests. Sangiovese, Canaiolo and Colorino are the main varieties grown to produce Chianti Classico wines. The Il Pareto vineyard is entirely planted with Cabernet Sauvignon whereas the Chardonnay is planted in the Le Bruneche plot. These specific grapes have proven to be particularly successful here, as they shine in well-defined, varietal character. The Cabernet Sauvignon resonates with a certain power and richness found in few other parts of the world. Attention to the non-traditional styles, however, does not distract the winery from the more typical but ever improving wines like the Chianti Classico La Forra.

Chianti Classico Riserva 🍇🍇 ④
La Forra 1988 DOCG
With enough bottle-aging, this wine provides enormous drinking pleasure. Extremely intense and concentrated, with rich aromas and a powerful structure which need time to blend and fully mature.

Il Pareto 1988 🍇🍇 ④
100% Cabernet Sauvignon, its aromas are rich and complex, brimming with varietal aromas of good fruit and a typical herbaceous note. Despite its powerful structure, it is soft and seductive, with intense, concentrated and long-lasting flavors.

Tenuta dell'Ornellaia

Via Bolgherese, 191
Bolgheri (Li) 57020
Tel. (0586) 762140

Ornellaia's extremely beautiful and well-equipped cellar mirrors the rare passion and considerable investments put forth by the Marquis Ludovico Antinori. In very little time, he created an estate that established itself at the top of Tuscan wine production. The estate's 56 ha of vineyard are located at varying elevations (60-120 m) and are planted separately to Cabernet, Merlot and Sauvignon Blanc. The cellar houses oak casks with a total capacity of 870 hl and French barriques for an additional 950 hl. These incredible assets, among others, are entrusted to the famed enologists Dr Dupond and Tibor G'Al. Ornellaia's most important wines are undoubtedly the Poggio alle Gazze, made with Sauvignon grapes, and Ornellaia, a Bordeaux blend, both of which have taken little time to become world famous.

Ornellaia 1989 🍇🍇 ③
A blend of Cabernet and Merlot, it shows full character at immediately with its rich ruby color and its interesting, intense varietal aromas which build into a rich and full bouquet. Bold, powerful and ample on the mouth though further cellaring would refine some sharp points for rewarding drinkability.

Masseto 1988 🍇🍇 ④
This varietal Merlot is sure to be talked about, although only a lucky few will be able to do so first-hand: indeed, only 2,000 bottles were produced. It is nonetheless amazingly elegant, supple and pleasant on the palate.

Podere Il Palazzino

Monti in Chianti (Si) 53010
Tel. (0577) 747008

Situated in one of the most typical Chianti areas, with its harsh and stony landscape so admired by tourists from all over the world, Palazzino is one of few that has always belonged to a local family. Even during the bleak years of the Chianti farming and wine crisis, the Sderci family held tight and resisted the temptation to sell their farm. Years of sacrifice and determination have paid off, as their small production of premium wines becomes successful. Five ha of traditional vineyards are trained in the alberese system on the pebbly-galestro soil and yield a small but extremely concentrated crop of grapes. The tiny, efficient cellar, located inside their beautiful stone home, has cement and stainless steel vats where the must ferments on the skins. The wine is then aged in Slovenian oak casks or French barriques. Besides Chianti Classico and Riserva they also make in the best vintages a varietal Sangiovese called Grosso Sanese. Generally total production stays within 2,000 cases.

Chianti Classico 1990 DOCG 🍇 ①
This wine's intense color with purplish highlights shines bright with youth. The bouquet itself is vinous with fruit and spices which with time will develop and blend. On the palate it is already rather harmonious, although lacking aromas.

Chianti Classico 🍇🍇 ②
Riserva 1988 DOCG
This Riserva, in comparison, seemed mature, with a nice clean and bright ruby-red color and intense aromas of ripe fruit in full maturity. Rich, concentrated and well-structured on the palate, with a pleasant, long finish.

Castello della Paneretta

Via Monsanto
Barberino Val d'Elsa (Fi) 50021
Tel. (055) 8075577

The hills of Barberino Val d'Elsa, which divide the Pesa and Elsa river valleys, make up the westernmost corner of the Chianti Classico zone. The medieval Castello looms up amidst cypress trees in a remote but easily accessible area. Wine has been produced here since the late 16th century, given the ideal growing conditions, such as the well-exposed, hilly slopes with particularly fertile soils. The vineyards are 4 to 20 years old and cover a surface area of 14 ha and the vines are densely planted (circa 3,000 vines per ha) at elevations of over 300 m. By choice, production concentrates exclusively on Chianti Classico and they grow only those grapes in compliance with the DOCG wine laws. The age-old cellars have recently been perfectly restored and can now house the modern stainless steel vats and small casks made of Italian oak. Average annual production is circa 5,000 cases of vintage and Riserva Chianti Classico.

Chianti Classico 1990 DOCG   🍷🍷 ①
In comparative tastings featuring 1990 Chianti Classico wines, Paneretta always ranks among the best, thanks to its beautiful deep ruby color and the exuberant fruity scents of maraschino cherry, currant and jam. Incredibly full and long-lasting finish.

Chianti Classico   🍷🍷 ②
Riserva 1988 DOCG
Deep ruby red, clean and bright, very intense aromas and toasty and caramel notes. The flavors match the aromas in that it has a mature and pleasant body, good texture and is long-lasting.

Giovanni Panizzi

Località Racciano, Santa Margherita, 34
San Gimignano (Si) 530378
Tel. (0577) 941576-(02) 90938796
Ffax (02) 9090729

This small estate shows just how much San Gimignano's generous soil and its Vernaccia grape can give those who tackle them with the right approach, passion and skill. Giovanni Panizzi chose a hilltop of Pliocene origin to plant 2.5 ha of Vernaccia. He also has 7,000 m of Sangiovese vineyards. To meet the increasing market demands, a new vineyard is being planted which will double the production of Vernaccia. Panizzi wines continue to improve in terms of quality, due to the estate's fully-equipped vinification cellar and the temperature-controlled stainless steel vats and a barrel-room dug into the tufa walls. There's an ongoing search for quality revolving around Vernaccia, with special attention devoted to a barrique-aged selection. Average production is 22,000 bottles of Vernaccia and 7,000 bottles of red wine, split into Chianti Colli Senese and a Vino da Tavola called Ceraso.

Vernaccia di San Gimignano   🍷 ①
1991 DOC
In recent years we have grown accustomed to Giovanni Panizzi's good Vernaccia wines; this one is a nice, clean straw-yellow color, with typical varietal aromas and a light fruity note. Refreshing and pleasant, it will surely improve with some light aging.

Vernaccia di San Gimignano   🍷 ②
Riserva 1990 DOC
His first attempt at a Riserva, Panizzi offers a pleasant, somewhat balanced wine. Aromas are still developing and will reach full maturity after several months in bottle.

Fattoria Petrolo

Località Galtrona
Mercatale Valdarno (Ar) 52020
Tel. (055) 992022
Fax (055) 992749

The border of the Chianti Classico production zone runs along the watershed of the Monti del Chianti hills, at times reaching the slope which faces the Arno valley. Fattoria Petrolo is located on this precise ridge, just over the enological border. As a result, its wines can not be labelled Chianti Classico but, in terms of richness and structure, they can easily compete with its more famously named cousins. Lucia Bazzocchi Saint Just is the estate's owner who passionately seeks to improve the quality of Petrolo wines. With the same determination, she is fighting to have the Medieval tower of Galatrona brought to its original splendor. It dominates the vineyards and the valley and practically symbolizes estate itself. 27 of the estate's 31 ha of vineyards produce grapes, mainly Sangiovese and other complimenting varieties to make Chianti. Merlot is gaining ground, though, as well. The best bunches from the oldest Sangiovese vineyards (more than 40 years-old) are selected to make Torrione, a Vino da Tavola made only in better vintages. Chianti remains the estate's main production with nearly 4,200 cases produced, evenly split between vintage and Riserva.

Chianti 1990 DOCG   🍇 ①
This Chianti has a great nose, with rich fruit and good complexity. The palate shows excellent drinkability and body impressive for a Chianti which is not Classico. Has great potential and can only get better with further aging.

Chianti Riserva 1988 DOCG   🍇🍇 ①
The deep ruby red color is bursting youth, with a fresh and exuberant bouquet where fruit combines with spicy aromas. Rich and soft with an ample texture that gives it overall balance and wholeness.

Torrione 1988   🍇 ②
This wine's rich and complex aromas are proof of the great potential of Sangiovese grown at Petrolo. It has a powerful backbone, with marked tannins which need to mellow with age. But the wine is still young, young even in its color, which is very rich and lively.

Podere Pian di Conte - Talenti

Fraz. Sant'Angelo in Colle
Montalcino (Si) 53020
Tel. (0577) 864029
Fax (0577) 864165

Pian di Conte is located towards the entrance of the town of Sant'Angelo in Colle. When Pierluigi Talenti bought the estate ten years ago, it was like a dream had come true for him. Finally he had the chance to practice what he had learned in more than 30 years of management of a nearby estate. With 7 ha of vineyard planted entirely with Sangiovese Grosso (and lots of willpower and determination), he has attained excellent results in a relatively short time. He dedicates much effort in both vine cultivation and in the winemaking, which is kept traditional but no less skillful nor discriminatory. The bunches are carefully selected and vinified separately, depending on how ripe and healthy they are. The best wine is aged at length in wood and becomes Brunello, the remainder being classified Rosso di Montalcino. On average around 40,000 bottles of wine are produced, divided fairly equally among the two.

Rosso di Montalcino 1990 DOC   🍇 ①
Pierluigi Talenti's excellent winemaking skills shine through with this solid, pleasant Rosso. The aromas are still very young and fruity, and the tannins are rather marked but well-balanced by the warm alcohol and the fresh acidity.

Brunello di Montalcino 1987 DOCG 🍇 ③
A wine with a substantial impact, with a nice deep and bright ruby-red color. A rich bouquet of well-developed fruity aromas and fine spicy scents. The aromas are fully confirmed and convincing on the palate, with its robust, full body and firm texture.

Poggio Antico

Località Poggio antico
Montalcino (Si) 53024
Tel/Fax (0577) 848044

This large, 200-ha estate has a winemaking heritage that many would envy. It owns 20 ha of vineyards planted with Brunello, sitting on one of the best-exposed, highest zones in Montalcino. Outstanding altitudes and poor soils naturally limit vine yields and assure healthy, sun-drenched, rich grapes. The beautiful underground cellar is well-equipped with stainless steel and cement vats and a large barrel-room with a capacity of circa 5,000 hl of oak casks. They only grow Sangiovese Grosso, which is the heart of their Brunello and Rosso di Montalcino. Brunello represents over 60% of the total production. In better vintages they also produce one or two barrels of a wine called Poggio Antico, which does not qualify as Brunello since it is not aged as long (two years less). For years, enologists and producers have been split, and often end up in heated arguments, about the current regulations governing the length of time necessary for wood aging. In times like these, of reformation, many are demanding modifications.

Rosso di Montalcino 1990 DOC 🍇 ①
Pleasant fruity aromas predominate at first impact. Soft and elegant on the palate, despite a slight over-acidity. Pleasant and very enjoyable now, as it will be in years to come.

Altero 1987 🍇🍇 ③
A wine of unique character both in terms of aromas, where berry-fruits and truffles merge into a harmonious and complex bouquet, and on the palate, which reveals the wine's great texture, balance and elegance.

Brunello di Montalcino 🍇🍇 ③
1987 DOCG
Well-balanced in its components and rather complex aromas, quite oaky. The flavor keeps the promise made by the bouquet: it is full and balanced with young but not aggressive tannins.

Il Poggiolo

Via Pistoiese, 76
Carmignano (Fi) 50042
Tel. (055) 8711242
Fax (055) 8711252

Founder and chairman of the Congregation of the Carmignano Wines, Giovanni Cianchi Baldazzi runs the family estate with the help of his son, Giuseppe. It is one of the area's most substantial in terms of quality and bottle production and is consistently improving. Half of the estate's 32 ha of vineyards are registered to produce Carmignano DOCG and the remaining land will soon be since new vineyards are currently being planted at high density (8,000 vines per hectare) with Sangiovese, Canaiolo and Cabernet, the varieties blended to make Carmignano according to the appellation rulings. They have begun using temperature-controlled vats for the fermentation, chestnut wood is being progressively replaced with oak and new rooms are being finished for bottling and temperature-controlled storage. One objective is to double the current production of Carmignano (50,000 bottles). Other wines include Barco Reale (Carmignano's other rosso, recently granted DOC status), a rosé Vin Ruspo (bled off from Carmignano in fermentation), Lacrime di Cantina (a Trebbiano-based white) and a traditional Vin Santo.

Carmignano 1989 DOCG 🍇 ①
Bright ruby red, it has a fruity bouquet with red currants backed by aromas of fresh herbs, well-balanced with oak. Round, full-bodied, persistent and well-balanced, it is surprisingly well structured for such a mediocre vintage.

Carmignano Riserva 1988 DOCG 🍇🍇 ②
This Riserva has all the characteristics of a wine destined to improve with cellaring: deep ruby, an intense and complex bouquet with clean, fruity scents; a good structure with marked but balanced tannins. A wine of great impact and excellent potential.

Il Poggione

Località Sant'Angelo in Colle
Montalcino (Si) 53024
Tel. (0577) 864029
Fax (0577) 864165

Undoubtedly one of Montalcino's more famous wineries, il Poggione is owned by the Franceschi brothers, Clemente and Roberto. For years it was managed by Fabrizio Bindocci and by Pierluigi Talenti, who now also owns a winery of his own. With a large area planted with vines, Poggione can produce considerable quantities of Brunello and Rosso di Montalcino, besides several Vino da Tavola and Moscadello di Montalcino. Their beautiful vineyards are located in the Sant'Angelo in Colle zone at 200 to 350 m elevations, with south to south-west exposures. Their well-structured wines are often purchased by Montalcino producers to add character and blend into their own. Poggione's large cellars have a notable selection of barrels, with circa 70 barrels of various sizes (10-131 hl). French barrique also has an important, though limited role. There are about 20 in the cellar, but they are literally shadowed by the large, traditional casks brimming with good Brunello.

Rosso di Montalcino 1990 DOC   ☘ ①
This wine is the essence of youth; purple rims on a dark ruby base. Intense spicy bouquet with hints of aromatic herbs and a rich and full-bodied palate with good balance, as to be expected of Poggione wines.

Brunello di Montalcino 1987 DOCG ☘☘ ②
Deep ruby red, its perfumes show that it is maturing, with gamey scents a on good ripe and intense fruit background. It has backbone and good texture, length and balance.

Poliziano

Via Fontago, 11
Montepulciano (Si) 53040
Tel/Fax (0578) 738171

Federico Carletti is a vigneron who manages one of the most interesting Montepulciano estates with extraordinary professionalism and skill. 85 ha of estate-vineyards are situated in the fertile growing zones of Caggiole, Gracciano and Pietrose. Nearly half of the vineyards' crop goes into their Chianti Colli Senesi, the estate's biggest product. In recent years, however, Carletti has devoted much time and effort to the production of the zone's quality, native wines (Vino Nobile and Rosso di Montepulciano), with some outstanding results. Very successful is the cru Vigna Asinone, made from careful bunch selection in the vineyard bearing the same name, on the Caggiole hill in Montepulciano. In addition to the typical Montepulciano varieties, small quantities of Chardonnay and Cabernet Sauvignon are also grown and experimented with. Interesting results include a barrique-aged red called Elegia. Vin Santo has also tested Carletti's talent. It's a touchy, difficult wine to make but very fascinating and rewarding, especially in good vintages.

Vino Nobile di Montepulciano 1989 DOCG   ☘ ①

In the various tastings held, this Nobile has always been among the best in its vintage, thanks to its refined aromas which are already almost mature in terms of overall bouquet and its outstanding texture, hard to come by in this vintage.

Vino Nobile di Montepulciano Riserva Vigna Asinone 1988 DOCG ☘☘ ②
A Vino Nobile which, in such an exceptional vintage, reaches remarkable heights. Sure to bring joy in the years ahead. Both its aromas, which span a wide range but are beginning to mature, and its flavors, with its big and ample, maturing structure, show that it is a 'wine for the future'.

Vino Nobile di Montepulciano Riserva Vigneto Le Caggiole 1988 DOCG ☘☘ ②
Together with Vigna Asinone, this wine ranks among Tuscany's best. It has great structure mellowed by a certain harmony and softness which make it pleasant now, although a long future is guaranteed.

Fattoria Ponte a Rondolino

Località Ponte a Rondolino
San Gimignano (Si) 53037
Tel. (0577) 940143
Fax (0577) 942016

As owner of Fattoria Ponte a Rondolino, Enrico Teruzzi broke important ground in San Gimignano. He was the first to make new, modern styles of Vernaccia di San Gimignano. Made from 40 ha of estate-vineyards located at 200-250 m, Teruzzi's wines are known and appreciated all over the world. His Terre di Tufi, 100% Vernaccia aged for 4-5 months in barrique, is one of most famous Italian whites, but even his more traditional Vernaccia di San Gimignano helps to keep the standards high in this famous but limited production DOC area. He personally takes care of the technical aspects and prides himself on having one of the best equipped cellars in Italy. This farsighted viticulturist understood that by using modern techniques he would be able to bring out this wine's full potential and join the ranks of other great international whites.

Vernaccia di San Gimignano   ❦ ①
1991 DOC
Rather pale straw yellow in color, its has fairly ample and fine floral scents. Firm acidity makes it fresh and very drinkable, with a typical aromatic aftertaste.

Carmen 1990   ❦ ②
Made from a complex and unique blend of grapes which includes Sangiovese vinified off the skins, this wine is pale straw yellow in color with a fairly complex bouquet of floral and herbaceous aromas. Solid structured with a rather pleasant touch of acidity on the finish.

Vernaccia di San Gimignano   ❦❦ ②
Terre di Tufi 1990 DOC
This Vernaccia aged for 4-5 months in barrique is undoubtedly Teruzzis' leading wine. It is an excellent white with its fine floral aromas and remarkably fresh backbone and balance on the palate.

Peperino 1988   ❦ ③
Made with Sangiovese grapes, this Vino da Tavola is pleasant and easy-drinking. Its intense, fresh and fruity aromas are soft and balanced on the palate although not extremely full bodied.

Pruneto

Podere Pruneto, 37
Radda in Chianti (Si) 53017
Tel. (0577) 738535

Riccardo Lanza is the owner of this small hilltop estate in Chianti. Of 20 ha of land, only two are planted with vines and are located at nearly 700 m, which is the maximum elevation limit set for Chianti production. Such altitudes have in no way disturbed the quality of the product. To the contrary, in relatively short time Pruneto wines have come to be as good as those from the best wineries nearby. The cellar is among the most modernly equipped, however this success is in part due to the young and spirited enologist, Giovanna Morganti, who carries on the family tradition of winemakers. The winery mainly produces Chianti Classico, available in both vintage and Riserva styles.

Chianti Classico   ❦❦ ②
Riserva 1988 DOCG
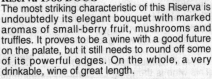
The most striking characteristic of this Riserva is undoubtedly its elegant bouquet with marked aromas of small-berry fruit, mushrooms and truffles. It proves to be a wine with a good future on the palate, but it still needs to round off some of its powerful edges. On the whole, a very drinkable, wine of great length.

Fattoria Le Pupille

Località Pereta
Magliano in Toscana (Gr) 58051
Tel/Fax (0564) 505129

Flourishing in the hilly hinterland behind the coastal town of Grosseto between the Ombrone and Albegna rivers, the Morellino di Scansano grape, or the local Sangiovese clone, is vinified on its own to make a wine of the same name. Le Pupille's vineyards are located in the Peretaarea at an altitude of 250 m. Ten hectares are devoted to the production of Morellino, with small amounts of Alicante, Ciliegiolo and Canaiolo; four more hectares have recently been planted with more Alicante and some Cabernet and Merlot. With such sun-drenched, concentrated grapes, they have to vinify in a temperature-controlled environment and as a result, the cellar is well-equipped with modern technology. Afterwards, the wine is put aside to wood age in their ancient cellar located in the old part of the town of Scansano until it is fine enough for bottling and release. Morellino di Scansano is mainly produced in a Riserva style, with 40,000 bottles produced compared to 20,000 for the normal vintage. They also make 6,000 bottles of a Vino da Tavola called Saffredi from the new vineyards.

Morellino di Scansano Riserva 1988 DOC

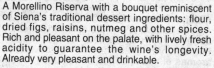

A Morellino Riserva with a bouquet reminiscent of Siena's traditional dessert ingredients: flour, dried figs, raisins, nutmeg and other spices. Rich and pleasant on the palate, with lively fresh acidity to guarantee the wine's longevity. Already very pleasant and drinkable.

Saffredi 1988

A very particular blend of Cabernet, Merlot and Alicante, with pronounced, nearly pungent aromas of spices and well-defined scents of vanilla. Outstanding in structure, already soft which makes it very pleasant to drink even now.

Castello di Querceto

Località Dudda
Lucolena (Fi) 50020
Tel. (055) 8549064
Fax (055) 854963

The castle of Querceto is situated at the eastern border of the Chianti Classico district. This border not only delineates a geographic area but a physiological one too, due to the different growing conditions here, specifically in terms of climate and altitude. Only great passion and strong determination can help producers to overcome difficulties in these growing conditions. Alessandro François has both of these qualities as proven by the results he has so far obtained. The estate's 45 ha of vineyards are subdivided into a dozen plots, all at 400 m elevation and primarily planted with varieties blended to make Chianti (Sangiovese, Canaiolo and Malvasia) with a notable selection of old indigenous grapes such as Ciliegiolo, Colorino and Mammolo. More recently, Cabernet Sauvignon, Sangiovese Grosso and Chardonnay have also been planted. The grapes from each vineyard are picked and vinified separately; after wood-aging, it is either blended or, if the vintage is good enough, bottled as single-vineyard, varietal wine. Querceto wines are generally very individual, elegant and often medium-bodied, at times slightly unpolished, and almost always in need of lengthy bottle aging.

Chianti Classico Riserva Il Picchio 1988 DOCG

Among Castello di Querceto's 1988 Riserva wines, this cru definitely seemed the best to us because of its great character and complexity and unique perfumes. Bright ruby red in color, with ample body, texture and length.

Querciolaia 1988

The still rather vinous aromas of this Sangiovese and Cabernet blend give way to full flavors and the firm, marked tannins, in turn, foretell a long cellar life. The color's purplish highlights confirm both.

Cignale 1987

Sparkling bright ruby-red, this Bordeaux blend has a rich, well-bred bouquet with marked aromas of dried cherries. Fat and sensuous, it is as well-balanced and full-bodied as you would expect on the palate.

Fattoria Querciabella

Località Ruffoli
Greve in Chianti (Fi) 50022
Tel. (055) 853494-853307
Fax (055) 8544657

Located on a hilltop south-west of Greve in Chianti, the Fattoria Querciabella is a promising, new winery among the top Chianti Classico wineries, especially considering how young its plantings are and how increasingly successful its wines have already been. 19 of the estate's 25 ha of vineyards are producing grapes, on good limestone soils at 350 to 580 m. These figures convert to an average production of circa 90,000 bottles with a potential for over 120,000. Sangiovese is the main variety, but they also grow Cabernet Sauvignon and, at higher altitudes, Pinot Bianco and Pinot Nero. The modern and completely temperature-controlled cellars are not lacking in stainless steel and wood of the finest oak, both medium-sized casks and barriques. Current production is circa 65,000 bottles of Chianti Classico, 10,000 bottles of Camartina (a Sangiovese and Cabernet blend) and circa 2,500 of Bâtard-Pinot, an oak fermented Pinot Bianco.

Bâtard-Pinot 1990   ❦ ②
A white with an outstanding personality which should be even more enjoyable with further bottle aging. Currently the aromas have a marked scent of good oak, sure to help it develop into a more complex wine; meanwhile, it is very elegant on the palate.

Chianti Classico 1990 DOCG   ❦ ①
An excellent Chianti, nice deep ruby in color with clear cut notes of berry fruit and maraschino cherry on the nose. Mellow and full on the palate, youthful with its slight imbalance of acidity and tannins which will mature with time.

Camartina 1988   ❦❦ ③
A very intense bouquet with clear bell-pepper and bread crust aromas. The palate is super powerful but juxtaposed by great elegance and balance. Fully enjoyable and drinkable now, but it can only get better with aging.

Chianti Classico Riserva 1988 DOCG   ❦❦ ②
Bright ruby colored, it has a complex bouquet with aromas of vanilla, black pepper, peach jam and, faintly, green pepper. Full, with a good backbone and excellent texture of outstanding aromatic length.

Castello di Rampolla

Località Santa Lucia in Faulle
Panzano (Fi) 50020
Tel. (055) 852001
Fax (055) 854291

This estate is fortunate enough to cover the largest portion of the fertile territory known as the Conca d'Oro of Panzano in Chianti. It boasts 50 ha of vineyards, 10 of which are new plantings. The main grapes grown include Sangiovese and Cabernet for reds and Chardonnay, Traminer and Sauvignon for whites. True to the zone, there is a clear prevalence of red vines (85% of the total) which are destined to produce big, powerful wines. Whites are planted almost "for show" as they are of minor importance. The ancient yet most functional cellars are housed in the castle itself, which is located at the center of the vineyard. The grapes are temperature-control fermented, and the wine is wood-aged and cellared in large, naturally climatized rooms. Matteo Di Napoli, the estate's amicable and unconventional owner, personally supervises all activities in the vineyards and in the cellar. He also promotes his products in a rather blatant, outspoken manner, but he has every reason to be proud of his wines. Average production is broken down into 80,000 bottles of Chianti Classico, 2,000 of Riserva, 40,000 of Sammarco (a rightfully famous Sangiovese-Cabernet blend) and circa 10,000 of Trebianco, a white Vino da Tavola.

Chianti Classico 1989 DOCG   ❦ ①
A good Chianti, showing a solid structure and better body than others of its vintage. Furthermore, it has fine and well-developed aromas of spice, coffee and nutmeg. Deep, sparkling clean ruby-red in color.

Chianti Classico Riserva 1988 DOCG   ❦❦ ②
The deep ruby color fortells a wine of great texture and strength. Sure enough, ample and powerful perfumes with balanced mature fruit and spices on the nose. Velvety and persuasive, with a structure that guarantees a good future.

Sammarco 1988   ❦❦ ③
The 1988 Sammarco is certainly just as good as the exceptional '85 and '86 vintages. Extremely complex and refined aromas, ample and intense, matched by roundness and softness and blended with great elegance. It captures the best of the Sangiovese and Cabernet grapes from which it is made.

Riecine

Località Riecine
Gaiole in Chianti (Si) 53013
Tel/Fax (0577) 749527

Like many other properties in the upper
Chianti area, Riecine was completely
abandoned from the late 1950s to early
1970s. Under the rocky and hostile growing
conditions, the sharecropping families who
had worked and lived on the land had barely
managed to scrape a living. Gradually
economic interest was brought back in the
area as Chianti Classico regained its former
reputation and the demand for the wine grew
again. In the meantime, John Dunkley, who
had purchased and completely restored
Riecine with the aim of producing great wines
just out of interest, soon found himself caught
in all the excitement. Suddenly his wines
were being praised by connoisseurs and
winning awards at major wine-tastings and
events. Everything at Riecine is very
traditional and very Italian, from the 2.5 ha of
Chianti vineyards to the cellars with its
cement vats and oak and chestnut casks.
There are some French barriques, however,
used to age a special Sangiovese called La
Gioia di Riecine. Most of the production,
some 15,000 bottles, is made into Chianti
Classico, plus 5,000 of Riserva. La Gioia di
Riecine, when it is produced, doesn't account
more than 3,500 bottles.

Chianti Classico 1990 DOCG   🍇 ①
A good example of the successful 1990 vintage.
Intense and already complex bouquet with good
fruit and fine spice scents. Rich and harmonious
on the palate, it shows great texture and
longevity.

Chianti Classico   🍇🍇 ③
Riserva 1988 DOCG
Intense, deep ruby in color, with a medium-
intense bouquet and well-balanced, mature fruit
and spice aromas. Full-flavored and well-
structured on the palate, with a long-lasting
finish.

La Gioia di Riecine 1988   🍇🍇 ③
This Sangiovese Vino da Tavola is extremely
powerful and already harmonious on the palate.
The bouquet could benefit from longer bottle
aging to fully develop its rich bouquet, which is
quite characteristic of the upper Chianti area.

Rocca delle Macìe

Località Macìe
Castellina in Chianti (Si) 53011
Tel. (0577) 741220
Fax (0577) 741150

Italo Zingarelli began his enological
adventure in 1973 with the acquisition of
Macìe, a small, semi-abandoned winery with
only one hectare of vineyards. After building
new winemaking cellars, restoring those
already existing, and planting new vineyards,
Rocca delle Macìe is now one of the
foremost wineries in Chianti. The numbers
speak for themselves: three properties (Le
Macìe, Sant'Alfonso and Fizzano), with a
total of 124 ha of vines, while 100 more are
leased, 18 different types of wine with a total
of 15,000 hl, including 7,000 hl of Chianti
Classico. At the heart of this industrial-size
winery are its spacious, state-of-the-art
winemaking facilities where particular
attention is devoted to preserving the varietal
and the vineyard character. With this
approach, the winery is able to produce large
amounts of very good wines. The Chianti
Classico, especially the Riserva, are gaining
increasing attention and praise, as are the
Sangiovese and Cabernet Sauvignon Vino
da Tavola wines, respectively called Ser
Gioveto and Roccato.

Chianti Classico   🍇 ①
Tenuta Sant'Alfonso 1989 DOCG
Pleasant and balanced, it is best drunk young
as it is not meant to age at length. Furthermore,
it was an off year in Chianti, nevertheless, it has
beautiful fruity bouquet with soft and long-lasting
flavors.

Chianti Classico   🍇 ②
Riserva di Fizzano 1987 DOCG
With its pleasant fruity aromas and scents of
peaches, this wine is generally placed high in its
type in winetasting competitions. Fresh and soft
on the palate, very elegant and long.

Rocca di Castagnoli

Località Castagnoli
Gaiole in Chianti (Si) 53013
Tel. (0577) 731004
Fax (0577) 731050

One of the giants of Chianti, Rocca di Castagnoli owns a total of 1,600 ha of property, 260 of which are planted to vineyards. This substantial legacy, together with solid financial foundations, has a well-trained management which operates with a quality-oriented production philosophy. The three estates of Castagnoli and Sansano in Gaiole in Chianti and Capraia in Castellina in Chianti, each different according to its origin, provide the raw materials that are directed to the two vinification sites in Capraia and Rocca. The latter, one of the most beautiful and characteristic wineries in the world, has a capacity of over 5,000 hl, stored in small and medium French and Slovenian oak casks. Production includes 200,000 bottles of Chianti Classico, 30,000 each of Chianti Classico Capraia and Poggio ai Frati and a range of single cru, Vino da Tavola wines including 25,000 bottles of Stielle (a Sangiovese base with Cabernet Sauvignon), 13,000 of Molino delle Balze (an oak-aged Chardonnay) and 7,000 of Montornello, a varietal Cabernet Sauvignon.

Molino delle Balze 1990   ☆ ③
A surprizngly good Chardonnay in terms of its pure and ample floral bouquet, with its vanilla and sweet almond scents, but above all for its impact on the palate, being fat, harmonious and elegantly balanced.

Chianti Classico 1990 DOCG   ☆ ①
Intense and harmonious aromas of fruit and spices, it is full-bodied and shows well-structured tannins that need more time to age, even though they already impart an interesting roundness to the wine.

Chianti Classico Riserva   ☆☆ ②
Capraia 1988 DOCG
Decidedly a good vintage judging by its vibrant ruby color and its intense and complex, maturing aromas with scents of dried fruit and truffles; full and rich, well-structured for lengthy aging.

Montornello 1988   ☆ ③
Lively ruby-red with rather young tinges, it has good fruit and a distinctive fumé character on the nose. Well-structured and full on the palate; sufficiently well-balanced.

Rodano

Località Rodano
Castellina in Chianti (Si) 53011
Tel/Fax (0577) 743107

Rodano's 20 ha of vineyards glide across rolling hills just west of Castellina in Chianti, towards the Elsa valley. One part is situated in the lower 200 m, clay and sand floodlands. Sangiovese does well in the warm and sunny microclimate that is found here. Higher up on the more calcareous terrain, Sangiovese is accompanied by the white Chianti grapes, as well as Merlot and Cabernet Sauvignon, all destined to become refined, elegant and aromatic wines. More recently, Rodano has been concentrating on rejuvenating the old vineyards, planting selective clones at a higher density. Vinification is traditional as bunches and types are carefully chosen at harvest and vinified separately, with long skin contact (up to 25 days in some vintages) and French and Slovenian oak aging. Besides Chianti Classico, Rodano produces two Vino da Tavola wines from Sangiovese and Cabernet Sauvignon, both barrique-aged as is the fashion in Tuscany these days.

Monna Claudia 1988   ☆ ③
Intense and still youthfully ruby-red in color, it is a beautiful expression of Sangiovese. A rich and well-matured fruitiness mixes well with the fine spice aromas. Full and generous in flavor, being balanced and long-lasting; it should round out with further bottle aging.

Chianti Classico Riserva   ☆☆ ②
Viacosta 1986 DOCG
This great Riserva will have much more to say in coming years. Intense ruby-red with garnet highlights, it is extremely rich and sophisticated bouquet features scents of maraschino cherries, aromatic herbs and apricots. Rich and seductive on the palate, too, with a firm body and tannins that still need to mellow.

Tenimenti Ruffino

Via Aretina, 42/44
Pontassieve (Fi) 50065
Tel. (055) 8368307
Fax (055) 40889

Ever since the winery has belonged to the Folonari family, one of the main points of Ruffino's production philosophy was to expand the vineyard area. It now owns 1,500 ha of property or "tenimenti", 450 ha of which grow grapes and are situated in the region's best areas. The production trend now is to improve the quality standard of this legacy through extensive experimentation and clonal selection and grafting of the best traditional and non-traditional varieties. In the latter case, the focus is on Cabernet and Pinot Nero for the reds and Sauvignon and Chardonnay for the whites. This approach, together with the substantial technical resources on hand, has made Ruffino a leader and model winery in the so-called rebirth of Tuscan wine in the past decade. But, Ruffino is also an innovator, having created Cabreo la Pietra, Tuscany's first oak-aged Chardonnay. It is proof that this land can boast of more than just great reds. Meanwhile, year by year, the entire range of Ruffino's traditional wines have continued to improve, especially their famed Chianti Classico Reserva Ducale with the Etichetta Oro gold label.

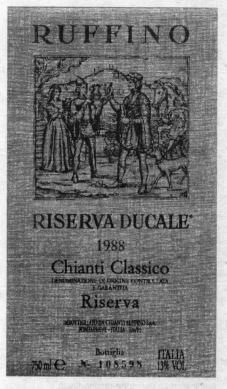

Chianti Classico   ①
Santedame 1990 DOCG
Bright ruby-red in color, at tasting it was bursting with exuberant youth both on the nose and in the mouth. The lively, intense fruit was accompanied by hints of complexity and maturity; full and well-structured on the palate.

Chianti Classico   ②
Riserva Ducale 1988 DOCG
Beautiful ruby-red, clean and bright. Its intense and penetrating bouquet features scents of aromatic herbs and spices that enhance the mature fruit aromas. With its rich and concentrated flavors, it is well-structured and balanced and very long-lasting.

Predicato di Biturica   ③
Cabreo Il Borgo 1988
An excellent Cabernet, very soft and persuasive on the palate, showing elegance and notable aromatic length. The bouquet is complex and ample, with liquorice and spice scents that chime with the mature fruit and wood and berry aromas.

Brunello di Montalcino Riserva   ③
Greppone Mazzi 1986 DOCG
A good example of a modern style of Brunello made at Ruffino's estate in Montalcino. Bright garnet-red in color, it has an intense bouquet where the fruit is well-blended with the rich and refined spicy aromas. Rich and long-lasting on the palate, harmonious and medium-bodied.

Chianti Classico Riserva   ④
Riserva Ducale 1988
A majestic red in the greatest of Italian traditions. This is the most appropriate definition of Ruffino's Chianti Classico Riserva Ducale 1988, proudly distinguished by its gold label. The aromas are already complex and seductive, with extremely fine scents of violets and marked aromas of red currants. It is silky smooth and already harmonious, as over three years of bottle-aging have proven their worth. Sure to reach its apex around the year 2000, it already shows strikingly complex elegance, concentration and balance in its aromas and flavors. In short, it is one of those wines that reminds us that Italian winemaking is second to none.

San Fabiano in Calcinaia

Località Cellole
Castellina in Chianti (Si) 53011
Tel. (0577) 979232
Fax (0577) 979455

The winery is nestled in the hills beneath Castellina in Chianti that slope down towards the Elsa river valley. This particular area is proving to be one of the most favorable (and underestimated) growing areas for Chianti Classico. Some of the estate vineyards are situated in San Fabiano, while the rest can be found near Cellole at over 500 m; in either case, the label will proudly specify the place of origin. Production focusses on Chianti Classico, which is made in the extremely well-equipped cellars and aged in 25-40 hl oak casks. In the last few years, director Giorgio Rocco along with enologist Giuseppe Bassi have made special efforts to craft quality Vino da Tavola wines. The new styles of Cerviolo Bianco (a Chardonnay and Sauvignon blend) and the Cerviolo Rosso (a Sangiovese and Cabernet blend) are distinctively elegant and easy-drinking wines.

Cerviolo Bianco 1991
An impressive and interesting blend. Bright straw-yellow, with fine floral aromas well-blended with the toasty scents from the oak-aging. Equally pleasant aromas on the palate, showing lean body, freshness and exceptional length.

Chianti Classico 1990 DOCG
Though it may seem very young judging by its color, it is already very drinkable. With lots of intense, fresh fruit on the nose, it is rich, full and well-structured on the palate with elegant tannins and a very long-lasting finish.

Chianti Classico Riserva Cellole 1988 DOCG
Again, all the elegance and refined character to be expected. Sparkling clean medium ruby-red in color, it has ample and refined aromas with scents of strawberry, rasberry and spices. Rich in flavor with body and good structure and a long-lasting finish.

Agricola San Felice

Località San Felice
Castelnuovo Berardenga (Si) 53010
Tel. (0577) 359087
Fax (0577) 359223

An ancient, farming hamlet on the southernmost hills of Chianti near San Gusmè, San Felice was given a complete facelift when an important insurance group invested substantially. Spacious, modern cellars were built, farmhouses renovated and the surrounding landscape redesigned with newly planted vineyards, gardens and greenery. Even the most humble and dilapidated barns were carefully restored to new splendor. Looking back ten years later, the benefits of those considerable efforts and investments can be seen and admired; indeed, San Felice acted as a role model for many wineries in Chianti. Of the winery's 220 ha of vineyards, an impressive 118 are devoted to Chianti production while the few remaining grow Cabernet, Chardonnay, Riesling, Pinot Bianco and Vermentino. Most importantly, San Felice is very proud of its collection of vines and varieties found on location and in the surrounding area. This precious library of genetic materials helps to preserve a rich heritage that might otherwise have been lost forever. The extensive line of wines includes wines for everyday drinking on up to big, structured wines of great class. All are made with great precision and integrity.

Predicato del Muschio 1989
A Chardonnay with intense aromas, with pungent, but appealing, tropical fruit scents. Savoury and harmonious on the palate, it has a certain elegance and a long-lasting aromatic finish.

Chianti Classico Riserva Il Grigio 1988 DOCG
Intense ruby-red with violet highlights, it is rich and fruity with lots of spice aromas and a warm sensation on the nose. Very nice on the palate, too, with a firm texture and a balanced, medium-full body.

Brunello di Montalcino Campogiovanni 1987 DOCG
Still quite young, it has a lively, intense ruby-red color. Rather vinous aromas at first impact develop in complexity, with penetrating, spicy scents. Rich on the palate, it has a firm texture and solid structure, with a pleasant sensation of softness on the finish.

Vigorello 1986
Despite its age, surprizingly enough it has yet to fully express its balance and complexity. Still very young in color, with young rough tannins on the mouth. Only the nose shows a certain evolution in maturity as the herbaceous aromas mingle with the fruit and wood scents.

San Filippo

Podere S. Filippo dei Comunali
Montalcino (Si) 53024
Tel/Fax (0577) 848705

Owner and jack-of-all-trades in the winery, Ermanno Rosi does not know the meaning of the word relax. It's not unusual to catch him at three in the morning doing office work or taking care of something in the cellar. His son, Stefano, is just like his father although he directs his energy partly in other fields. With their own five ha of vineyards (and others that are rented), these two have turned San Filippo into one of the best medium-small wineries in Montalcino. The vineyards face easterly at an altitude of 300 m. The cellars are not only beautiful but well-equipped. Like other vintners in the area, they prefer to use 20-22 hl casks made of Slovenian oak. San Filippo has just finished a new building, where the bottling and bottle aging will take place and which will hold up to 180,000 bottles.

Rosso di Montalcino 1990 DOC
The aromas are rather complex and rich, but not yet completely harmonious with the wood accents; potent and rich on the palate, with good, long-lasting flavors. A full-bodied red with many years of life ahead.

Brunello di Montalcino 1987 DOCG
The beautiful and intense ruby-red color opens the way for ample and complex aromas featuring maturing scents of spices and wildberries. Already pleasant to drink now, although the tannin is still evolving and promises greater satisfaction in future years.

Brunello di Montalcino Riserva 1985 DOCG
Certainly one of San Filippo's best wines. At first impact, it has an impressive, extremely wide range of aromas, all most refined and elegant. On the palate, it shows a firm backbone and structure and is still very soft and harmonious.

Fattoria di San Giusto a Rentennano

Località S. Giusto a Rentennano
Monti in Chianti (Si) 53010
Tel. (0577) 747121
Fax (0577) 747109

This winery has been the Martini family since the turn of the century and is now skillfully and passionately managed by Francesco, a member of the new generation. There are 28 ha of estate-vineyards, which have a fertile soil composition of "alberese" with a fair amount of clay. Sangiovese accounts for 75% of the grapes grown, followed by Canaiolo Nero and white Trebbiano and Malvasia. Most of the vines are over 20 years-old, the oldest being 36; as a result, new vineyards are constantly being replanted. The newer and highly select Sangiovese clones are planted to a higher density: up to 5,000 rootstocks per ha instead of the current 3,000. Gradually innovation has also found its way into the winemaking, as well, as stainless steel vats and oak casks line the thick brick walls. 80% of the 60,000 bottle production is Chianti Classico, both vintage and Riserva; the remainder includes wines like Percarlo (a oak-aged Sangiovese) and 2,500 half-bottles of a classic, precious Vin Santo.

Percarlo 1988
Its exuberant strength blends with fullness with such rare elegance, that it is undoubtedly one of Tuscany's best Vino da Tavola wines. Sangiovese provides the backbone for the noticeably deep and vibrant ruby-red color. Equally robust on the palate, with a refined bouquet showing vinous aromas and scents of spices, mushrooms and underbrush.

Tenuta San Guido

Località Capanne, 27
Bolgheri (Li) 57020
Tel. (0565) 762003
Fax (0565) 762017

Probably Italy's most famous wine, Sassicaia was conceived in 1944 as part of an experiment conducted by the Marquis Mario Incisa della Rocchetta. He planted some Cabernet taken from Château Lafite in his coastal estate in Bolgheri. Grapes grown at the foot of the white cliffs of Castiglioncello were vinified according to a mixture of Bordeaux and traditional local methods, with truly disappointing results. Niccolò Antinori came along and encouraged his brother-in-law to try again. In 1965 the vines were replanted at Sassicaia, which had a similar terrain but was lower in elevation and closer to the sea. This time Giacomo Tachis, Antinori's in-house enologist, supervised production. Results were quick in coming, particularily due to the use of fine casks made of Tronçais and Slovenian oak in fermenting and aging the precious Sassicaia wine. 1968 was the first vintage to be released, with a production of 7,300 bottles. Since then, Sassicaia has been the quintessential success story; inevitably, the vineyards have now expanded to cover 40 ha, 32 of which planted to Cabernet Sauvignon and the remainder to Cabernet Franc. Production is stable at 100,000 bottles.

Sassicaia 1989 🍇🍇 ④

An excellent Cabernet Sauvignon, already harmonious and beginning to mature. Intense ruby-red with youthful tones on the rim, it has rich, exuberant aromas, with scents of pepper and spices mixed with wood tones, already appealing and complex. It tastes as good as it smells: rich and ample, with a velvety texture, grand elegance and balance.

Sassicaia 1988 🍇🍇🍇 ④

The Marquis Incisa della Rocchetta, along with enologist Giacomo Tachis, is celebrating this wine's 20th anniversary with yet another fine vintage, possibly the best. Sassicaia has carved an important chunk in the history of winemaking in Italy. After many years, its vinification technique is now stabilized and represents an intelligent marriage between tradition and innovation. Carefully tended vines, low yields per hectare, temperature-controlled fermentation and skillful wood-aging are but a few of the underlying factors. This '88 is very young but well-marked with softness and extraordinary concentration; intense garnet-red in color, with elegant, ample and complex aromas ranging from wildberries to jam to tobacco, to finish with spice. Absolutely sensational on the palate, it is velvety and soft, with a sumptuous body and a perfect acidity/tannin balance. Extremely long-lasting on the finish, with noticeable flavors of liquorice and maraschino cherry.

Castello di San Polo in Rosso

Località S. Polo in Rosso
Gaiole in Chianti (Si) 53013
Tel. (0577) 746045-746070
Fax (0577) 746153

Crowned in vineyards, the hilltop castle of San Polo in Rosso is located near Gaiole and overlooks the upper Arbia river valley. Despite the rather high 400 m altitude, the favorable, sunny exposure and quality soils ensure ripe, concentrated grapes. Sangiovese accounts for 85% of the vineyards, followed by Canaiolo and the white Chianti varieties; the latter are gradually being replaced by more noble vines. Minimal use of fertilizers, low vine training and shoot thinning add to the high quality; meanwhile the grapes are harvested in several pickings and vinified under temperature-controlled conditions. Long maceration on the skins for the reds and taking some free-run off for rosé guarantees structured and concentrated Chianti Classico wines. In addition to the vintage and Riserva Chianti Classico, they make a barrique-aged Sangiovese called Cetinaia in better years. The small range of wines is completed by the small production of rosés and whites, the best of which is a fine Sauvignon called Le Coccole.

Le Coccole 1990
A Sauvignon Blanc with a bright straw yellow color and a rich aromatic and complex bouquet, with refined spices. Fresh and balanced on the palate, with a wealth of great and long-lasting aromas.

Chianti Classico Riserva 1988 DOCG
A high class Chianti Classico; here a legendary vintage enhances the typical characteristics of its place of origin. Intense ruby with violet highlights, it has rich and complex aromas, with evident notes of fruit and spices. Well-structured with a good backbone on the palate and refined tannins.

Fattoria Selvapiana

Via Selvapiana, 3
Pontassieve (Fi) 50065
Tel. (055) 8369848
Fax (055) 8316840

The long and narrow valley formed by the Sieve river has long since been acnowledged for its vineyards and its big, generous wines. Indeed, the valley is worthy of its own particular sub-zone appellation, which is Chianti Rufina. Located in the heart of this area, Fattoria di Selvapiana cultivates 35 ha of vineyards on its 400-ha holding. Selvapiana has gradually begun upgrading and remodernizing its traditional vineyards and its vinification facilities. Adjacent to the oldest Sangiovese vineyard, Bucerchiale, they have planted new varieties and clones, experimenting with different training systems and vine densities. Likewise in the cellars, stainless steel vats with computer controls have appeared next to their older, cement counterparts, and the old chestnut barrels are giving way to new oak and French barrique. Production includes Chianti Rufina, both vintage and Riserva, Riserva Bucerchiale (made only in favorable years), a Trebbiano-based white and Borro Lastricato, a modern white blend of Pinot Bianco and Pinot Grigio. A traditional Vin Santo tops the list.

Vin Santo 1985
Appealing, star bright amber with golden reflections, this 100% Trebbiano sweet wine has strikingly ample and harmonious aromas of raisined fruit and resin. Soft and silky on the palate, it shows good backbone and texture.

Chianti Rufina Riserva 1988 DOCG
Good fruity aromas lead-off in the tasting of this optimal '88. Notably well-structured, it will round out over time. Though already quite interesting, its aromas still need to evolve and mature to form the refined bouquet normally expected of the Selvapiana label.

Chianti Rufina Riserva Bucerchiale 1986 DOCG
Amazingly young despite its age, it is still extremely fresh on the palate, with soft tannins that still have a lot to offer. A really interesting bouquet, with ample and harmonious aromas, with good spice and earthy, wood scents.

La Stellata

Via Fornacina, 18
Manciano (Gr) 58014
Tel. (0564) 620190

Located in the Tuscany's rural Maremma, La Stellata is a small winery with only 4.5 hectares of vineyards. Clara Divizia and Manlio Giorni are the enthusiastic owners who almost ten years ago abandoned the city life and chaos of Rome to settle in the country. They began to make an exclusive white Pitigliano DOC wine called Lunaia. Still today this is the only wine they make, from a blend of Procanico (as the Trebbiano is called here), Malvasia, Grechetto and Verdello indigenous white grapes. The efficient cellar has glass-lined cement and stainless steel vats for vinifying this white and the second, slightly spritzy version called Doccio. Lunaia is Clara and Manlio's best and most successful wine.

Bianco di Pitigliano
Lunaia 1991 DOC
This vintage confirms the level of excellence attained by La Stellata. Bright straw-yellow, it has an elegant nose with clean, appley aromas, floral fragrances and a refined and well-balanced body.

Tenuta Valdipiatta

Via della Ciarliana, 25/a
Montepulciano (Si) 53045
Tel/Fax (0578) 757930

The latest arrival on Montepulciano's high quality wine scene, Tenuta Valdipiatta is a good example of how much change can take place in a short time when a winery has clear ideas, determination and financial means. Until 1989 Valdipiatta was a modest winery geared towards mass production; today it is an orderly and bright holding where every activity is part of an ambitious plan. Of 31 total ha of property, there are 13 ha of vines, most around 20 years old. The 2,200 rootstocks per hectare feature Prugnolo Gentile, Canaiolo, and Mammolo, as well as small quantities of white vines like Trebbiano, Malvasia and Grachetto. Almost half a hectare has been overgrafted with Cabernet Sauvignon, while another hectare is being densely planted for experiments on new clones of Prugnolo Gentile. The winery uses advanced technology and has created a cellar for aging by hollowing out the side of a hill. The first wines released on the market are well-made and have a distinct personality. Production averages about 50,000 bottles of Vino Nobile di Montepulciano, 5,000 di Rosso di Montepulciano and 10,000 of white table wine.

Vino Nobile di Montepulciano
1988 DOCG
Extremely balanced; maintains on the palate what it promises on the nose; refined, medium-intensity fruity perfumes; elegance and roundness compensate for a less than exceptional structure.

Vino Nobile di Montepulciano
Riserva 1988 DOCG
A complex and harmonious bouquet is this wine's most important feature; well-structured on the palate and, above all, balanced and elegant. Can only improve with time.

Fattoria Valtellina

Località Riecine
Gaiole in Chianti (Si) 53013
Tel. (0577) 731005

Situated along the sloping Chianti mountains, this winery once took part in an attempt to acclimatize Valtellinese cattle; hence the name. In the 1970s it was reconverted to its true wine vocation by then owner Giorgio Regni, whose name still appears on the label. Today Valtellina is directed by a young and dynamic German technician, Christoph Schneider, whose presence attests to the Chianti region's growing cosmopolitan nature. The classic Chianti vines are cultivated on four hectares, at over 400 m. Although severe climatic conditions often put these vines to the test, attentive care and careful selection during the harvest has nevertheless produced surprising results. The vinification process, characterized by long maceration, is conducted with the help of the most modern enological techniques, and the use of small wine containers ensure maximum control of every phase of the process. The production of vintage and reserve Chianti Classico oscillates around 12,000 bottles per year. Approximately 3-4,000 bottles of table wine, both white and red, are also produced.

Chianti Classico 1989 DOCG   ♥ ①
Despite the mediocre vintage, it has pure and well-harmonized perfumes, though not particularly intense. Soft and rich on the palate, with a pleasant finish, revealing superior quality and confirming this winery's elevated standards.

Convivio 1988   ♥ ♥ ③
Color denotes a pure and still quite youthful Sangiovese. Palate confirms a concentrated, still untamed tannic element and a rather powerful body of great character. Intense and rich perfumes, as normal for this wine, have a fruity exuberance and good complexity.

Chianti Classico Riserva 1987 DOCG ♥ ②
Great impact on the nose is this wine's most important quality; ample and refined fruity perfumes with a noticeable black cherry scent; well harmonized with good spices. Body is apparent on the palate; tannins are present, but it is fresh and persistent.

Key to the symbols

Types of Wines

♣ White

♦ Rosé

♥ Red

Rating System

♣   An exemplary wine of its type with outstanding local character

♦♦   An international premium quality wine

♥♥♥   A Top Wine, considered one of the 150 best wines in the world

The 'grape bunch' symbol is used to indicate the color of the wine; the number of bunches represents the quality rating assigned by the contributor

Price levels

① up to $ 9.99

② $ 10.00 - $ 14.99

③ $ 15.00 - $ 24.99

④ $ 25.00 or more

The 'ex-cellar', or direct from the producer, bottle prices, are calculated in US dollars and are intended only as an approximate guide

Entries are arranged in alphabetical order by country, region and winery or producer name.

Vecchie Terre di Montefili

Via S. Cresci, 45
Greve in Chianti (Fi) 50022
Tel/Fax (055) 853739

This winery may be considered emblematic of the agricultural revolution that took place in the Chianti region in the '70s. Many estates like this one, abandoned following the collapse of the "Mezzadria" or share-cropping system, were bought at this time and, thanks to an influx of new capital, were given the tools to show off their natural talents. Roccaldo Acuti, an industrialist from Prato, believed in this land and, with the help of enologist Vittorio Fiore, he proved to be right. Sangiovese grapes prevail on the 8.5 ha of vineyards, followed by Cabernet Sauvignon and Chardonnay. The modernly equipped facility has all it needs for the production of high quality wines: stainless steel, good small-sized barrels, barriques, and ample space for aging in bottle. The attentive and rigorous management concentrates on scrupulous selection and low output, producing only 28,000 bottles of Chianti Classico, 4,500 of Riserva Anfiteatro, 6,000 bottles of the Vino da Tavola Bruno di Rocca made only in the best years, and less than 1,000 bottles of an extremely special white fermented in barrique and called Vigna Regis.

Bruno di Rocca 1989

The difficult 1989 year produced surprising results with this wine, based on Cabernet Sauvignon and Sangiovese. Intense ruby, bright and pure; perfumes are rich, long-lasting and well-evolved. Displays backbone and a decisive structure on the palate; rich and lengthy.

Chianti Classico Riserva Anfiteatro 1988 DOCG

Choosing between Bruno di Rocca and this Riserva Anfiteatro which should receive our highest honor was an extremely difficult choice. In the end we opted for this one, which has striking concentration and complexity. A just award for owner Riccardo Acuti's stubbornness and for the highly ranked capabilities of enologist Vittorio Fiore. Already well-evolved, though further refinement could only render it more complex and pleasing. Rich, fresh and ample bouquet features toasted tones, while those of vanilla still slightly overpower good mature fruit. Ample, rounded and well-structured on the palate; good alcohol level.

Castello di Verrazzano

Località Greti
Greve in Chianti (Fi) 50022
Tel. (055) 854243
Fax (055) 852533

The medieval castle of Verrazzano, set in the northern territory of Chianti Classico on a hill dominating a bend in the Greve river, was the birthplace of Giovanni di Verrazzano, explorer of the New World and discoverer of the Bay of New York. Today this winery makes some interesting products, well-consolidated in quality. The most suitable Sangiovese clones for this 40-ha territory are chosen and carefully tended to regulate quantity. The winery is set in the middle of the vineyards, ready to receive the flow of selectively harvested grapes which are then immediately crushed. This is the beginning of the rigorously controlled vinification process, whose products are then sent to mature in the underground castle cellars. Annual production features 120,000 bottles of Chianti Classico, 45,000 bottles of reserve, 10,000 bottles of a white with geographical origins, and 4,000 half-liter bottles of Vin Santo. 30,000 bottles of a red table wine, obtained from Sangiovese and called either Sassello or Botiglia Particolare, are also produced in the best harvest years.

Vin Santo 1985
Extremely typical, made according to tradition like all Verrazzano's wines. Strawish yellow with golden highlights; intense ethereal perfumes; pure scents of semi-dried fruits and oxidation. Dry and generous on the palate, with a light tannic note.

Chianti Classico 1989 DOCG
Verrazzano has passed the difficult test of 1989 with honors. Refined, pure perfumes, not overly intense but well-balanced. Savoury on the palate with good backbone and length.

Chianti Classico
Riserva 1988 DOCG
Optimal bouquet with pure perfumes of wildberries and liquorice. Slightly stringent tannic note does not disturb the well-developed body; excellently aromatic and long sensation in the finish.

Tenuta Vicchiomaggio

Via Vicchiomaggio, 4
Greve in Chianti (Fi) 50022
Tel. (055) 854079
Fax (055) 853911

The Chianti area is famous for beautiful castles crowning green rolling hills: Vicchiomaggio certainly stands out among these, both from a historical and enological point of view. The first document mentioning the fabulous castle dates from 957 AD; about 1000 years later, it became the property of John Matta and his family. It was actually in 1964 that John began to plant vineyards, which now extend over 25 ha. All the Chianti Classico products made here are born from rigorously selected vines, chosen for their suitability for the terrain and microclimate. Wines are aged in oak barrels with 50-85 hl capacities and then, after a few months of bottle aging, they are released on the market. This is the common procedure for Chianti Classico, while the reserves and crus spend a much longer time in the cellars. Vicchiomaggio is known for creating well-structured wines that also have an innate softness.

Chianti Classico
San Iacopo 1990 DOCG
A fragrant and unusually drinkable Chianti Classico; uncommon for '90, but equally pleasing. Light ruby; fresh and refined perfumes of Marasca cherry and spices. Rich, harmonious and elegant flavor.

Chianti Classico
Riserva Petri 1988 DOCG
Bright ruby tending towards garnet on the rim. Intense and penetrating perfumes, with fruit scents that shine through the spices. Rich and long flavor, moderately well-structured, balanced and long-lasting.

Villa Cafaggio

Località Panzano
Greve in Chianti (Fi) 50020
Tel. (055) 852200

Panzano, a small village in the commune of Greve in Chianti, sits on a ridge dominating the passage route from the Greve valley to the Pesa valley. This area is considered to be the center of the most northerly part of Chianti Classico that produces the finest wines. Villa Cafaggio occupies the northwest part of these fortunate hills, with a dozen separate vineyards meandering at an altitude of 450 m. Although almost entirely planted with Sangiovese, save for a few rows of Cabernet Sauvignon, each vineyard has its own peculiar character; some sparse rootstocks in Solatio Basilica are over 50 years-old, while Vigne Nuove has only just been planted at high density. Grapes are vinified separately and, only after maturation, are mixed together. In particular good years the wines from San Martino and Solatio Basilica are bottled separately and sold as Vini da Tavola. The vinification process is still extremely traditional; only in the aging phase has the innovation of barrique been recently introduced. An average production consists of 120,000 bottles of Chianti Classico, 30,000 of reserve and just over 1,000 bottles of Cabernet Sauvignon.

Chianti Classico
Riserva 1988 DOCG
Refined and intense perfumes were a pleasant surprise; pleasing scents of elegant and fruity spices, all well-evolved. Well-structured and elegant; pleasant almond finish.

San Martino 1988
Bright and clear ruby; pure Sangiovese; somewhat meek but refined bouquet, complex and well-evolved. Full and soft on the palate; well-structured, long, with a light, bitter aftertaste.

Villa Cilnia

Località Montoncello, 27
Pieve a Bagnoro (Ar) 52040
Tel. (0575) 365017
Fax (0575) 365639

In 1974 Giovanni Bianchi moved down from Milan to Arezzo to begin his very successful venture with Villa Cilnia. He owns part and rents part of the 30 ha of vines that he plants and carefully tends himself. His results have been a big surprise to those who thought this area was little suited to making high quality wines. The secret of his success is an extremely limited production of grapes and meticulous attention given to both the vinification and aging processes. This is especially true for the Chianti Colli Aretini and other wines made from varietals like Cabernet Sauvignon, Montepulciano d'Abruzzo, Müller Thurgau, Chardonnay and Sauvignon, which he planted from scratch. Special mention must also go to Giovanni's patented idea of a 'revolving vine', a new system he developed after researching possible improvements in viticulture. This revolutionary technique consists of a mechanism set amidst the vines, permitting maximum exposure to the sun; the vines are actually attached to a revolving support that orients itself in the direction of the sun.

Campo del Sasso 1990
Rather unusual mixture of Chardonnay and Malvasia Nera vinified into a white wine. On the nose, the pure fruit scents are still somewhat masked by new wood. Dry on the palate, with light, woody notes; good aromatic length.

Le Vignacce 1988
A blend of Cabernet Sauvignon, Sangiovese Grosso and Montepulciano d'Abruzzo. Intense color; complex and harmonious perfumes, with a good balance between scents of mature fruit and spices. On the palate, good core and notable body; extremely long-lasting. Will improve even more with time.

Vocato 1988
Potent, strong character; mixture of Sangiovese and Cabernet; dry and pure on the palate; perfumes lean towards mature fruit, displaying refinement and harmony.

Chianti Colli Aretini 1987 DOCG
Ruby with a brick rim; well-evolved; ethereal perfumes are not intense but pure, with meaty scents. On the palate, good core, sustaining an extremely soft and coaxing body.

Castello di Volpaia

Località Volpaia
Radda in Chianti (Si) 53017
Tel. (0577) 38066
Fax (0577) 38619

There isn't much left of the castle that once reigned at the summit of this hill, only a few reminders in the slanting curves of the walls and the layout of the streets that follow the old footpaths. The arms once used here have been laid down for centuries, the castle having been long since transformed into a tranquil agricultural hamlet. The quiet and harmonious simplicity of this atmosphere is enriched by owner Giovanella Stianti's collection of modern art and by the recently restored church. One may not suspect that behind these stone walls and underneath the pavement worn away by time there lies hidden the modern equipment of a perfectly organized winery. And yet Volpaia is centered around agriculture, especially wine and extra virgin olive oil. The 37 ha of vineyards, well-exposed at altitudes between 400m and 600m, are planted mostly with Sangiovese, but there is still space left for Chianti's other complementary vines and for Cabernet Sauvignon. Production includes Chianti Classico and two Vini da Tavola: Coltassala, made from Sangiovese, and Balifico, comprised of Sangiovese and Cabernet. Total production reaches an average of 200,000 bottles per year.

Torniello 1990   🍇 ②
Full strawish yellow; made from 80% Sauvignon and the rest Sémillon. Fruity perfumes in the bouquet are well-harmonized with oak elements from the aging in barrique. Full and well-structured taste; good acidity.

Chianti Classico Riserva 1988 DOCG 🍇 ②
A good year and a great success; pleasant bouquet features pepper and cloves, with a noticeable softness on the palate; great harmony among elements and good length.

Coltassala 1988   🍇🍇 ③
Derived mostly from Sangiovese; beautiful, bright ruby. On the nose, perfumes of mature fruit, still evolving. On the palate, good body, with notable aromatic length.

Rating System

🍇   An exemplary wine of its type with outstanding local character

🍇🍇   An international premium quality wine

🍇🍇🍇   A Top Wine, considered one of the 150 best wines in the world

The 'grape bunch' symbol is used to indicate the color of the wine; the number of bunches represents the quality rating assigned by the contributor

Trentino-Alto Adige

Spit into two distinct provinces, Trentino-Alto Adige's landscape is extremely varied. Vineyards range from 200 m altitudes near Lake Garda to nearly 1,000 m in the Cembra valley; as a result, a number of different wine types and styles are produced. In Trentino, to the south around the city of Trento, 90% of wine production is 'controlled' by approximately 20 large cooperative wineries, with a total of 5,000 contributing growers. In Alto Adige, or Südtirol, around the northern city of Bolzano at the foot of the Dolomite mountains, large coops here too harvest and vinify most of the fruit grown. However, there is no shortage of small producers who often lead the way, forcing cooperatives to institute new quality-oriented production techniques. Such was the case with sparkling wines made from new plantings of Chardonnay at the beginning of the century. Rightfully considered the father of Italian sparkling wine-making, Giulio Ferrari was, and remains, the undisputed leader among other skilled cellarmen.

In addition to the production of sparkling wines, the average 1,000,000 quintals of the grapes harvested each year in Trentino mainly goes to the production of reds, notably Teroldego and Marzemino. Teroldego reigns in the Campo Rotaliano plains area north of Trento, whereas Marzemino predominates in Vallagarina. The main white grapes and wines grown are Nosiola, which is native of the Valle dei Laghi lake area, and Müller-Thurgau, more typical of Alpine foothills.

Nature is particularly respected and protected in the region. The grower's association and the Instituto Agrario of San Michele all'Adige are especially concerned with environment-friendly techniques to improve quality, with positive results so far.

Although more famous for its fruity and spicy whites (one in particular says it all: Traminer Aromatico), Alto Adige produces more red, generally Schiava-based, wines with 65% of its 1,000,000 hl annual production. Although wine culture in Alto Adige has ancient origins, the turning-point in production came in the 1960s. An uncompromising search for quality, inspired even the smallest of farmers to improve their production methods and invest in their vineyards. In addition to Traminer, which was actually born in Alto Adige (from the town of Termeno or Tramin, in German), other varietals grown include Chardonnay and Pinot Bianco, as well as some Cabernet Sauvignon. Pinot Nero seems to be very suitable, especially in the lower hills of Mazzon in Bassa Atesina. The wine producers are almost always of German origin, consequently most make wine in an Alto Adige or Südtirol-style. It seems there's a penchant for the peculiar in the Alto Adige, as witnessed in the recent rediscovery of Moscato Rosa (the region's flagship wine, together with Traminer) or by the protection of Lagrein, whose vineyards cradle the city of Bolzano, making it a true "città del vino".

Abate Nero Spumanti

Loc. San Lazzaro di Gardolo
Trento (Tn) 38100
Tel/Fax (0461) 46566

This winery's main product, a sparkling wine, steadily improves each year and is made from carefully selected Chardonnay and Pinot Nero grapes after being patiently aged for three years before release. With its fine bubbles and character, this sparkling wine confirms Trentino's suitability to sparkling wine production. Abate Nero is crafted with the best technology available, but without forgetting the importance of the human touch. First and foremost they are wine-growers rather than wine technicians... a considerable asset for the company. Their wines are aged in modern-designed cellars on the shores of the river Avisio, towards the valley of Cembra, where the happy union of nature and culture can be seen and admired.

Abate Nero Extra Brut 1989   �☐ ③
Totally brut as no dosage is added at dégorgement, it maintains all its beautiful fruitiness and has aromas that recall the fragrances of the base-wines, Chardonnay and Pinot Nero, from which it was made.

Abate Nero Riserva 1987   ☐ ③
One of Trentino's most prestigious méthode champenoise sparkling wines, this is this small winery's best. As mature as it is fragrant, it has very lively bubbles and is complex and enjoyable with a slightly toasty flavor.

Bolognani

Via Stazione, 19
Lavis (Tn) 38015
Tel. (0461) 46354
Fax (0461) 46240

To young Diego Bolognani, the password to success is 'selection'. In charge of the family winery for the past five years, he is particularly skilled at selecting the grapes to make precious limited release wines from amongst the hundreds and hundreds of tractor-loads of grapes conferred to his winery by various growers. Few wines will bear the Bolognani family name, distinguishing themselves from the massive quantities of wines made on behalf of large wineries of other regions. To improve the quality of his wine, Diego has stocked his cellar with the best equipment and, a couple of years ago, began focussing on careful selection in the vineyards as well. As a result, he is able to pick the best at their source to make his own wines labelled Müller-Thurgau, Moscato Giallo, Chardonnay, Nosiola and Pinot Grigio and, more recently, Cabernet Sauvignon. All are wines of an undisputed quality, continuously on the rise, year in year out.

Chardonnay   ☐ ①
della Valle di Cembra 1991
Perfectly in line with the current production trend, this Chardonnay has balanced perfumes and flavors and is crafted with exceptional winemaking skills. Most inviting and rewarding in its drinking pleasure.

Moscato Giallo 1991   ☐ ①
Dry and appealing at start or finish, when served as an aperitif or to accompany certain desserts. An extremely stimulating Moscato Giallo using clean and skillful vinification. Intense on the nose and palate and considerably lingering.

Müller Thurgau   ☐ ①
della Valle di Cembra 1991
Intense on the nose and full in the mouth, this is a mountain-style wine that successfully exalts the underlying varietal strength, which is a cross between Riesling and Sylvaner. Dry and bold and ready to drink now.

Cantina Produttori Colterenzio Schreckbichl

Strada del Vino, 8
Cornaiano (Bz) 39050
Tel. (0471) 51246
Fax (0471) 660633

The Cantina Produttori di Colterenzio continues to hold its firm position among the larger premium DOC wine producers, with its uncompromising and determined efforts. Member growers are paid according to the quality of their grapes, with grape selections aimed at safeguarding the pecularities of each single-vineyard's harvest. Despite its location in the best Austro-Hungarian production zone, Colterenzio's wines are considerably more 'Latin', as the best wines are personally selected by Luis Raifer. Raifer is the Managing Director and is also an expert of the international wine world. The Praedium ('vineyard') range is the pride of the house. There is also a substantial range of well-priced wines. These two ranges work well together thanks to a production philosophy based on years of business experience and a modern marketing policy.

Alto Adige Gewürztraminer   ☙ ②
Cornell 1991 DOC
It has an unforgettable aroma, with enough spice to place it amongst the best aromatic wines. Its mature fruit flavors and unique acidity make it delicious with seafood dishes or as a Vino da Meditazione, when aged.

Alto Adige Pinot Grigio   ☙ ②
Praedium Puiten 1991 DOC
Bright, sparkling clean yellow in color with greenish highlights, richer than others of its type. Intense perfumes, slightly herbaceous and fruity. Rewarding and savoury on the mouth and long lasting.

Alto Adige Merlot   ☙☙ ②
Praedium Siebenech 1990 DOC
Intense in its very color, bouquet and flavor. It tastes grassy and earthy and has beautiful acidity and convincing roundness. Soft and well-structured, it will undoubtedly improve with bottle aging.

Cornelius 1989   ☙ ③
A classic Bordeaux-blend produced by Colterenzio as its highest achievement in quality. Fleshy and delicate, with a complex range of aromas and flavors. Pleasant, with an extremely lengthy finish.

Cantina Sociale di Cornaiano

Via S. Martino, 24
Cornaiano (Bz) 39050
Tel. (0471) 52403
Fax (0471) 52654

Cornaiano is in the middle of Alto Adige's most substantial wine zone; 2,600 ha of vineyards gently curl down from the hills to Lake Caldaro. Schiava, the most common grape, takes on different forms and is the basis of wines like Lago di Caldaro, Schiava and Schiava Grigia. Easy-drinking, appetizing wines, each with fresh and elegant varietal aromas and soft body. Wines like these have helped to establish Alto Adige's reputation for wine-making, particularily in the German-speaking areas. Mr. Spittaler is at the root of the winery's passion and potential. In better vintages, the Cantina makes a special line that can be distinguished by the letterings "botte no. 9". Also of interest is the selection from the old vines of Gschleier, with its extremely low yields and significantly richer taste sensations. Hardly a conservative winery as the quest for quality improvement goes on, always with respect to the Südtirol-style of wine-making. Indeed, Spittaler's passion for Pinot Nero is to be interpreted in these precise terms, bursting with potential among the reds, and for Traminer Aromatico, as mature and well-structured as it is perfumed.

Alto Adige Pinot Bianco   ☙ ①
Plattenriegel 1991 DOC
This Plattenriegel selection seeks to express the full potential of Pinot Bianco in Alto Adige. Deep straw-yellow in color, it is well-structured, bone-dry, with an ample, elegant body and a lingering finish.

Alto Adige Traminer   ☙ ①
Aromatico 191 DOC
Balance is this Traminer's strong-point. Its aromas are not overpowering but harmoniously blended with the other components. The result is a fresh wine, pleasant as an aperitif or in-between meals; always appetizing, never cloying.

Alto Adige Pinot Nero   ☙ ②
Trattmannhof Linea Optimum 1990 DOC
Produced with the best grapes of the Colterenzio zone and aged at length in wood, it embodies the best characteristics of Alto Adige's Pinot Nero. Bright in color with garnet-red tinges, it is almost pungent on the nose; rich and long-lasting, soft and full-bodied, with delicate wood aromas.

Cantina Sociale Lavis

Via del Carmine, 2
Lavis (Tn) 38015
Tel. (0461) 46325
Fax (0461) 40718

This Cantina Sociale in Trentino has best epitomized the concept of quality. It induced its members to upgrade their growing methods, yielding less quantity but better quality wines. The managers at Lavis go to all lengths in their constant search for quality. The cantina was founded in 1948 by the growers from the neighboring towns of Lavis, Sorni and Salorno. All fruit is carefully selected from the various zones, bottling only small batches of quality wine. Rigorous selection in the vineyard inevitably improves the rest of the winery's production as well, just as efficient cellars and wine-making technology enable the premium raw materials to express their full potential.

Trentino Müller Thurgau
I Ritratti 1990 DOC
This white attains peak levels in Trentino, possibly because it is made from grapes from vineyards situated at high altitudes. It has greenish highlights, beautiful acidity, and a rather fleshy flavor. The typical, ample bouquet comes from the Riesling Renano and Sylvaner grapes, crossed to create Müller Thurgau.

Trentino Pinot Nero
I Ritratti 1990 DOC
Bright ruby red in color, it has a classic Pinot Noir bouquet, very fruity and appetizing. Just as fruity in the mouth as on the nose, with aromas of small wood berries and hints of liquorice and cocoa.

Trentino Cabernet
I Ritratti 1988 DOC
Pleasant, well-structured; an easy match for other big reds, powerful and yet immediate and frank. Currants and berries on the nose, with good fruit on the palate, too, with an ample and lengthy finish.

Cantina Sociale di Terlano

Via Colline d'Argento, 7
Terlano (Bz) 39018
Tel/Fax (0471) 257135

The town of Terlano, about 10 km from Bolzano, is at the center of a clearly defined micro-zone with a specific DOC area. The cantina has been processing the grapes from local growers since 1893. As the untiring, driving force for the past 40 years, Managing Director Sebastian Stocker based the company policy on quality through careful selection of the grapes delivered, backed by prizes and other incentives, and bought at prices that discourage excessive production. Needless to say, the cellar is equipped with medium to small barrels in which batches of wine are kept separate to retain their special character. Only a careful cuvée will then give the final quality product. Because of the estate's wonderful southerly exposure, the white grapes are particularily well-structured, at times slightly over-ripe. Stocker is a stickler for temperature-controlled fermentation; wines are traditionally wood aged (in 50 and 100 hl oak barrels) to attain considerable longevity. Indeed, his whites often maintain a perfect balance and extraordinary richness of taste even after 20 years of cellaring.

Terlano Sauvignon 1991 DOC
Remarkably robust, as forthright as its 13° alc content on the label. From vineyards that directly overlook the town of Terlano, its unique vinification includes some aging in large oak barrels, which impart an intense color and a soft, round impact.

Alto Adige Pinot Bianco
Selezione 990 DOC
This particular still selection of Pinot Bianco is released only after sufficient aging in large oak barrels. Pleasant, with delicate perfumes and ample body; time will tell of its great texture.

Cantina Castello Schwanburg

Via Schwanburg, 16
Nalles (Bz) 39010
Tel. (0471) 678622
Fax (0471) 678430

The impressive medieval castle of Schwanburg in Nalles looms to the right of the Adige river, between the towns of Merano and Bolzano. The site's charm has certainly helped to make the winery named after it famous also. Indeed, many tourists instinctively link the pleasant, fresh wines to the unique beauty of the site. Dieter Rudolph, the winery's owner and manager prefers to highlight the favorable growing conditions of the site which his ancestors chose centuries earlier. The area is shielded from the wind yet exposed to the sunshine, ideal for viticulture. A wood-aged Cabernet, the cru Castel Schwanburg wine is produced from new plantings in the vineyards surrounding the castle and is exemplary in expressing this land's potential. As is customary among Alto Adige's commercial wineries, the winery produces an extremely wide range of wines made from grapes grown on the estate's own 26 ha of vineyards as well as grapes from growers on contract. All wines are of a good quality level, enologically correct and well-made thanks to modern cellar equipment.

Alto Adige Cabernet ♟ ①
Riserva 1988 DOC
From low-yielding vineyards in Nalles, aged at length in large wood barrels, released 3-4 years after harvest. Intense and bright in color, it has an elegant varietal nose, with good fullness on the palate matched by persuasive, velvety softness.

Alto Adige Castel Schwanburg ♟ ②
Cabernet 1988 DOC
The winery's leading wine, from vineyards surrounding the castle, aged at length in oak barriques. The vineyard's strong character merges with complex wood aromas giving an harmonious balanced wine of great elegance and length. Good now, but further bottle aging would do no harm.

Cavit

Loc. Ravina di Trento, via del Ponte, 31
Trento 38100
Tel. (0461) 922055
Fax (0461) 912700

For the past 25 years, Cavit has grown to be a giant active in improving Trentino enology and grouping together 14 large cooperatives with over 5,000 growers. The house continuously varies its styles and wine making techniques to keep abreast of changing market trends. More recently Cavit has invested in upgrading its commercial image by building new and improved wine-making structures and business offices. In particular, much focus is being put on the méthode champenoise sparkling wine made with choice bunch selection in its cooperative wineries that are located in the various DOC zones of the province of Trento. This is hardly a superficial face-lift and is now bearing its fruits as thousands of member growers are making respectable wines of solid character for more today's diverse and demanding palates.

Trentino Chardonnay ♟ ②
Maso Toresella 1990 DOC
Made only in better vintages, it maximizes the fruit from an extremely favorable vineyards and growing conditions in the Valle dei Laghi lake area. New training methods are being tested there to yield small, prestigious batches of grapes to make premium wines.

Graal Spumante Riserva 1987 ♟ ③
This wine is part of the exclusive selection of the best sparkling wines produced by the member cooperatives. With extremely refined bouquet flavors and lingering complex aromas, it will cellar gracefully for a few more years.

Trentino Marzemino ♟ ②
Maso Romani 1991 DOC
Delicate on the nose, full and ready to drink now, this is an exemplar style of Marzemino (a red varietal indigenous to Trentino). Grapey purple in color, with unmistakable fresh fruit, above all most loved for its easy drinkability.

Ferrari

Loc. Ravina di Trento, via del Ponte, 15
Trento (Tn) 38100
Tel. (0461) 922500
Fax (0461) 903008

For some Ferrari is a legend, for others it's living proof that Italian sparkling wine-making has indeed attained international stature. For others, still, it a role model of how to produce wines of undisputed quality combined with efficient use of market and business research. The Lunelli brothers have been in charge of the winery since the 1950s and continue to produce new and exciting styles of wines. They also own a mineral-water bottling plant called Surgiva, a distillery called Segnana and a small winery where they produce a single white wine called Villa Margon. The 'futuristic' cellar, in construction until now, was recently completed. Meanwhile, the estate continues to select the very best fruit the region has to offer. In light of the 90th anniversary of the winery's foundation by Giulio Ferrari, the 'father of Italian sparkling wines', the Lunellis plan to challenge the international market of quality wines by further emphasizing the Trentino character of their sparkling wines, particularly their distinct alpine-fresh character.

Villa Margon 1990   🍇 ③
The only white produced by the Lunelli brothers under the Ferrari brand name. Incredibly supple and fruity. Aged exclusively in stainless steel vats (no wood) and released after a few years of bottle aging.

Ferrari Perlé 1988   🍇 🍇 ③
A sparkling wine of great class and finesse, certainly one of Italy's best méthode champenoise sparkling wines. Full, of great structure, it makes for a perfect companion to the Riserva Giulio Ferrari sparkler. Made only in exceptional vintages.

Foradori

Via Chiesa, 1
Mezzolombardo (Tn) 38017
Tel. (0461) 601046
Fax (0461) 603447

This winery is one few to be run entirely by women in Italy. Mother and daughter, Gabriella and Elisabetta, are well-skilled and passionate about their wines and have managed to keep the winery at peak levels despite the painful loss of the head of the family. In the Rotaliano plains the name Foradori is synonymous with wine, particularly of Teroldego. More recently, Elisabetta's husband, Reiner Zierock, has brought new ideas to the winery, especially in planting rare varietals and vinifying small batches of grapes for experimental wines. Nevertheless, Teroldego Rotaliano remains the winery's benchmark product. The vineyard plots have been rearranged and delineated, now allocating the less fertile soils to other types of crops. Production is kept limited, as traditional as possible, but there's an elegant women's touch and originality, thanks to Gabriella and Elisabetta.

Trentino Chardonnay 1991 DOC   🍇 ①
From vines planted on Campo Rotaliano's alluvial flood soils, an area devoted to viticulture since the Middle Ages, it is intense in its color and aromas. All the varietal's elegance unfurl in the glass.

Granato 1990   🍇 🍇 ②
This Teroldego-based wine is vinified exclusively in wood to fully exalt its varietal strength. Garnet-red in color (hence the name), it has a spicy vanilla-nose and complexity and will undoubtedly improve with age.

Teroldego Rotaliano
Vigneto Morei 1990 DOC
From grapes grown in the valley between the Adige river and one of its tributaries, the Noce. Robust rich red, at first impact it is rough and coarse on the palate but then it unfolds a generous, embracing drinkability. A solid structure foretells considerable longevity.

Franz Gojer - Glögglhof

Loc. Santa Maddalena
Via Rivellone, 1
Bolzano 39100
Tel/Fax (0471) 978775

Some say that Alto Adige's truest wines come from the hills surrounding Bolzano. For centuries farmers have grown vigorous Schiava grapes to produce their typically smooth, often quite elegant Santa Maddalena red wine. Saint Maddalena also lends her name to the small church that overlooks the vineyards of the classic production area, from Bolzano to the Renon high plain. Franz Gojer is the probably the best Schiava grower and, indeed, he makes some very full and incredibly long lasting wines. He is traditionalist at heart, in his wine styles and practices; in fact, the barrel-room dates to 1450 where iron-ore bells were orginally cast, and where the name Glögglhof comes from. But his continuous interest in the experiences of other Italian and foreign wineries has enabled this winery to produce wines of international appeal. Gojer aims to add more prestige to the Santa Maddalena label, to bring it to the stature of other more noble reds.

Alto Adige
Santa Maddalena 1991 DOC
An easy-drinking red, which is proof of the area's devotion to quality vine-growing and wine-making. Ruby-red with garnet highlights, it has a mature fruit bouquet and good lingering aromas; ample and appealing.

Franz Haas

Via Villa, 5/6
Montagan-Egna (Bz) 39040
Tel. (0471) 812280-820300
Fax (0471) 812280

The hill called Montagna, just above Egna towards the Val di Fiemme, has already been included in viticultural handbooks printed in the 19th century in Südtirol. The founder of the first Middle European school for enology in 1870, Edmondo Mach applauded the viticultural suitability of the Mazzon and Montagna soils. Today Franz Haas, the fifth generation of family cellarmasters, reaps the benefits of the past and grows beautiful grapes in an unique micro-climate. The perfectionist in him is forever working at experimental laboratory testing, transplanting and grafting with international varietals. Of considerable interest are his achievements with the rare Moscato Rosa grape, indigenous to Alto Adige, and with the late-harvest wines. Admitedly, Franz has a special penchant for Pinot Nero, quite possibly as a homage to the original wine scientists who called this area the Burgundian grape's second home.

Alto Adige Moscato Rosa 1990 DOC ④
Deep cherry-red colored dessert wine with sumptuous aromas of rose petals, cinnamon and spices. Mouthfilling and ample, immediate and unmistakeable. Perfect with desserts now, a pleasant sipper with cellaring potential.

Alto Adige Pinot Nero 1990 DOC ②
A curious bitter edge on the palate exalts the personality of this rich, plummy red wine. Elegant with complex aromas, pleasantly tannic, grapey flavors. One of Alto Adige's best examples of Pinot Nero.

Hofstätter

Piazza Municipio, 5
Termeno (Bz) 39040
Tel. (0471) 860161
Fax (0471) 860789

The Hofstätter winery is a benchmark brand for quality Alto Adige wines. Created in 1907 by Josef Hofstätter, it has always been family-run and is currently managed by Paolo Foradori. The huge 600 hl wooden barrel is not only a tourist attraction but is an unmistakeable sign of tradition. Symbolic of Südtirol's role as the cradle of wine during the Austro-Hungaric empire, it is still used today to age the Kolbenhofer wine. The winery deserves full credit for having revived the quality of two typical wines: Blauburgunder (Pinot Nero) and Gewürztraminer (Traminer Aromatico). The estate-owned vineyards planted with Pinot Nero in Mazzon area are in one of Alto Adige's best wine zones. After careful selection at harvest, Hofstätter makes three varietal styles including the fresh and fruity Barthenau, the more structured yet surprizingly supple Riserva Villa Barthenau and, in recent years, the oak-aged Vigneto San Urbano. Of course, Traminer vines grow adjacent to the winery; indeed, the village is named after the grape, which is called Tramin in German. The Riserva Kolbenhof is the best expression of the aromatic and structural richness of this type of wine.

De Vitae 1991 ☕ ①
Paolo Foradori strongly believes in this varietal wine, made from a cross of Schiava and Rheinriesling (Kerner in German). Moderately aromatic, fresh and pleasant.

Alto Adige Gewürztraminer ☕ ② Kilbenhof 1990 DOC
From the Termeno zone traditionally suited to growing Gewürztraminer, and made with careful bunch selection, it is very rich and ample, with intense aromas and a lengthy finish. Bottle aging will fully bring out its character.

Alto Adige Pinot Nero ☕ ② Vigneto S. Urbano 1989 DOC
Three years from its first release, it already ranks among the region's best wines in terms of quality. Bright in color, it has an intense and full bouquet and is refined and elegant on the palate, thanks to oak-aging.

Alto Adige Pinot Nero ☕☕ ② Villa Barthenau Riserva 1989 DOC
From the Mazzon vineyards, it is oak-aged in large casks for 24 months. Slightly garnet red in color, well-balanced with elegant and lingering perfumes and a velvety, supple body. One of Italy's best Pinot Nero wines.

Istituto Agrario Provinciale

Via Edmondo Mach, 1
San Michele all'Adige (Tn) 38010
Tel. (0461) 650108
Fax (0461) 650872

An enological laboratory in the true sense of the word; all that is vinous is studiously elaborated, admired and made public. Housed in a beautiful Benedictine convent, it began piloting the enological revolution as early as 1874. Thousands of trained growers have since graduated from the institute, which also boasts a few of Italy's most prestigious enologists and cellar-masters. Directed and managed by the independent Provincial administration of Trento, the Instituto Agrario sets a high standard for numerous other international research centers, particularly because of its in-depth specialization program. The nearby San Michele all'Adige research center bases its intense program on tree sciences and winemaking experimentation. The Institute has always been at the disposal of quality-oriented wine producers in Trentino (and abroad) in its goal to advocate better wine production worldwide. In truth, much innovation and guidance has come from decades of experience here at the feet of the Dolomite mountains.

Trentino Chardonnay 1990 DOC ☕☕ ②
It is not always easy to find such strength and elegance in a white wine. Aromas and flavors are well-blended in this Chardonnay, which is nurtured with care is and the result of constant research the agricultural institute.

Trentino Merlot 1990 DOC ☕ ②
Here's proof that Merlot can do wonderful things even in Italy. Perfectly balanced and quite convincing, with delicate spice aromas and rich fruit on the palate. A wine which can easily be aged.

Castel San Michele 1988 ☕ ②
This classic Burgundy blend (Cabernet Sauvignon and Merlot) was the first of its type to be made in Trentino in 1960. It boasts all the best characteristics, with pleasant spicy notes from the wood aging.

Alois Lageder

Via Druso, 235
Bolzano 39100
Tel. (0471) 920164
Fax (0471) 931577

Alois Lageder caused quite a stir in the Alto Adige wine scenario when he bought the Hirsprumm estate, with its 100 ha of vineyards and orchards. Having done that, not only did he move the winery offices from Bolzano to Magré, where most of the wines were already being made, but did he also confirmed his production philosophy. He firmly believes that quality wines start in the vineyard and that grapes should be vinified separately according to grape origin. The Löwengang cabernet is a prime example: made from a vineyard replanted to 8,000 vines/ha, severely limited yields, long maturation in wood to buff any unpolished Cabernet edges. Elegant whites such as Benefizium Porer Pinot Grigio or Terlano Sauvignon Lehenhof are treated little differently. The success obtained in recent years is surely rewarding and encourages Lageder to continue in his campaign to tap Südtirol's enological potential. He favors white grapes andalso advocates the use of grapes that have been relatively unexploited so far in Alto Adige, such as Cabernet and Chardonnay.

Alto Adige Pinot Grigio
Benefizium Porer 1990 DOC
Rather deep yellow in color, it has great personality and character, with intense green-apple aromas and a structure that would rival many red wines.

Terlaner Sauvignon
Lehenhof 1990 DOC
Terlano has always been considered the best valley in Alto Adige for Sauvignon; the Lageder's Lehenhof vineyard is no exception. Intense and typical varietal on the nose, with pineapple, sage, bell-pepper and mint aromas. Elegant with pleasant, fresh acidity on the palate; of good character.

Alto Adige Chardonnay
Löwengang 1989 DOC
Of the prestigious Lageder range of wines, this white best represents the international style. Special vinification in small oak casks enhances the Chardonnay character. Deep golden yellow in color, with intense complex perfumes. Sapid, elegant and well-structured, with a lingering aromatic finish.

Alto Adige Cabernet Sauvignon
Löwengang 1989 DOC
Made only in exceptional vintages. Clean garnet-red in color, with a compact, herbaceous bouquet. Warm, embracing, with a solid backbone.

Laimburg
Scuola Fruttivinicola Provinciale

Loc. Vadena
Ora (Bz) 39040
Tel. (0471) 960193
Fax (0471) 960016

Active for 20 years, the school is a true laboratory. All that is agriculture or food related in Alto Adige eventually goes through the Stazione Sperimentale in Laimburg. Flanked by fruit orchards and vineyards, apples and grapes for wine, it is situated in a picturesque area along the banks of the Adige, between Ora and Lake Caldaro. The research program is especially geared towards training growers from the province of Bolzano. Through numerous experiments and trials, the school has been able to achieve considerable results with limited batches of red wines, especially with its Cabernet but also with its good whites. Without a shadow of a doubt, it can be said that, with scrupulous studies and new wine-making techniques, vineyards and grapes are once again the building blocks for each and every grower, and not only on a local level.

Alto Adige Lagrein 1990 DOC
Made from indigenous grapes from plains of Bolzano, it has a very intense red color, with fruity notes on the nose and the typically 'earthy' Lagrein backbone.

Alto Adige Cabernet
Riserva 1988 DOC
Wood aged, garnet red in color with purplish highlights. Complex vanilla aromas on the nose, it is well-balanced and has an excellent structure and beautiful elegance on the palate; good aging potential.

Letrari

Palazzo Lodron
Nogaredo di Rovereto (Tn) 38060
Tel. (0464) 411093-432587
Fax (0464) 414147

The Letraris are agricultural entrepreneurs who have been active in the wine sector for many years. The venture started with the father, Lionello, who even 40 years ago was toying with barrique-aging, then considered a transgression and contrary to the winemaking philosophy of Trentino wineries. Today Lionello's children, Lucia and Paolo Emilio, specialized wine-technicians, help in the winery and are improving and innovating the winmaking. Mixed batches of grapes, nearly all estate-grown, are processed in the beautiful cellars of Palazzo Lodron, which once hosted the young Mozart. Particular care is taken in the selection of Cabernet and Marzemino, a varietal wine made from the native Marzemino grape, which is widely grown in Vallagarina. Impressive whites include Chardonnay-based, refined and elegant méthode champenoise sparkling wines, which are all too familiar to Lionello since he was one of the first to apply French techniques to making sparkling wines in Italy. They have recently begun to produce a Riserva Cabernet Sauvignon which is proving to be a wine of great class.

Spumante Letrari Riserva
Left to age for nearly four years on the lees, this méthod champenoise sparkling wine epitomizes the production philosophy of Trentino sparklers. Of impressive finesse and elegance, its structure will enable improvement with age.

Trentino Marzemino 1991 DOC
Intense violet in color, on the nose ripe cherry aromas, on the palate easy-drinking yet rewarding, full, rounded.

Trentino Cabernet Sauvignon Riserva 1989 DOC
Intense in color, with exciting perfumes and distinctively spicy, variegated flavors that emphasize its true vigour and varietal character.

Maso Cantanghel

Loc. Forti, 33
Civezzano (Tn) 38045
Tel. (0461) 858714
Fax (0461) 859050

The Maso Cantanghel winery draws its name from an old toll-house and border checkpoint, high on the hills between Trento and Val Sugana. Owners Piero Zabini and his wife, Lucia Gius, primarily run their own restaurant but, for the last ten years, have been producing great wine as a challenge. They do it with winning spirit and rewarding results have proven them right. Their range of wines (Pinot Nero and Chardonnay as well as new Cabernet Sauvignon and a rare Moscato Rosa) continues to reap success as does their restaurant, conveniently located next door to the winery. The fare served is extremely simple but very original, carefully matching and exhalting the flavors of local raw materials. The husband-wife team has learned how to take advantage of an unexploited vine-growing corner of Trentino, blazing the way for new styles of wines. All in all, they are examplary in their dedication and commitment to the vineyard, the winery and the kitchen; unique and hard to find not only in Trentino but also abroad.

Chardonnay Vigna Piccola 1991
This white wine goes wonderfully with the cuisine served at Piero and Lucia's restaurant. Slightly aromatic, intense, full-bodied and structured thanks to its wood-aging, it is already pleasant and quite drinkable now, despite its youthfulness.

Moscato Rosa Pregiato 1990
Undoubtedly Trentino's best Moscato Rosa. Refined and captivating in its highlights and aromas, it needs to be sipped to be appreciated and to understand its full potential. A fashionable varietal wine which rarely attains this level of quality.

Pinot Nero Riserva Piero Zabini 1990
Chef and winemaker Piero is proud to have this limited-production Riserva carry his name and bear the winery's reputation. Well-structured, oak-aged, it has a unique appeal and is extremely rich, ample and elegant on nose and palate.

Thomas Mayr e figli

Via Mendola, 56
Bolzano, 39100
Tel. (0471) 281030

The small but extremely active Thomas Mayr winery lies in the green wedge which cuts into the city limits of Bolzano, in the Gries area. The alluvial soils of the plain are historically home to Lagrein (here called Lagrein di Greis), which makes a dark colored wine, rich in extracts and low in acidity. When vinified off the skins, the grape produces an extremely fresh and pleasant rosé wine called Lagrein Kretze. Mayr and others passionately believe in this wine's potential and are determined to fend off local residential construction which threaten to encroach upon his vineyards. Traditionally they used nothing but small 5-10 hl barrels anyway, due to the small quantities of wine made; consequently, the use of the barrique only further improved the aging techniques already applied. More recently they have improved their packaging, which certainly can't hurt their image nor that of their wines.

Alto Adige Lagrein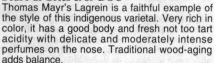
Scuro di Gries 1989 DOC
Thomas Mayr's Lagrein is a faithful example of the style of this indigenous varietal. Very rich in color, it has a good body and fresh not too tart acidity with delicate and moderately intense perfumes on the nose. Traditional wood-aging adds balance.

Pojer & Sandri

Loc. Molini
Faedo (Tn) 38010
Tel. (0461) 650342
Fax (0461) 651100

Pioneers for the last two decades in wine researching, Mario Pojer and Fiorentino Sandri are considered the "nouvelle vague" of Trentino enology. They were the first to strike out to make wines that accentuated the fruity fragrance of the grapes grown of the hilly Faedo zone, and more sceptical growers, not only in Trentino, have eventually followed in their foot steps. Their passion to produce extremely valid wines is still very much alive today. All vineyards are planted with varietals which are relatively new to Trentino and are meticulously cared for, as in gardens. They fully exploit the aptitude of the high-altitude soils to obtain top-quality Müller Thurgau, Chardonnay and Sauvignon Blanc fruit. The skins are distilled to make robust yet delicately perfumed grappas and some fascinating Acqueviti. Though further details are jealously kept secret, we do know that the cellars are being expanded to make room for a new range of sparkling wines. Above all, they maintain their solid conviction in making world-class wines that know no borders.

Chardonnay di Faedo 1991
Aged exclusively in stainless steel, this wine is a perfect expression of Trentino's suitability to Chardonnay. Straw yellow with golden highlights, it has aromas of green apples and is long-lasting on the palate. Probably the winery's best wine.

Müller Thurgau di Faedo 1991
The grapes from these high vineyards, at nearly 800 m altitude, ripen well and evenly but have slightly more acidity. The resulting full-bodied wine positively shows the unique combination: pleasant and yet serious drinking, with lots of fresh fruit.

Spumante Pojer & Sandri 1985
Produced only in better vintages, from selected Chardonnay and Pinot Nero grapes which give extremely different base-wines. Aged on the yeasts for several years, it has an intense bouquet and surprizingly fine, lingering bubbles.

Schiava di Faedo 1991
Made from Schiava, the most popular grape grown in the hilly vineyards along the Adige river, and which is vinified by rapidly separating the juice from skins. A tart easy-drinking rosé with good texture, it goes well with food, for every-day drinking.

Pravis

Via Lagolo, 28
Lasino (Tn) 38076
Tel. (0461) 564305
Fax (0461) 564565

Pravis is a Rhaeto-Romanic place-name which means the 'strength of the vined field'. The three young partners who own this modern winery chose it to emphasize the characteristic landscape of small plots of vineyard dotting the hillsides from Lake Cavedine to the peaks of Mount Bondone, from 150 m to over 600 m. Gianni Chisté, Domenico Pedrini and Mario Zambarda handle the vineyards, cellar operations and sales, respectively. Grapes are vinified separately according to their vineyard of origin, to distinguish the various styles made. Technology or human intervention is kept to a minimum in order to respect the harvest's style. As a result, their wines tend to be simple, almost understated, though quite personable. Vineyards planted with Chardonnay, Sauvignon and Müller Thurgau are wedged between the rocky mountainsides. The indigenous Nosiola grape does well here, however. Used to make distinctive dry whites, it is apparently native to the Valle dei Laghi lake area. This wine best epitomizes the Pravis production philosophy: to make wine from choice grapes only, preserving varietal character, and to maintain the utmost respect for the fine balance between man and nature. In the end, the wine must pay homage to the 'strength of the vined field'.

Trentino Müller Thurgau ☙ ① San Thomà 1991 DOC
The wines has considerable varietal character both in its greenish hue and its grassy-green aroma and flavors. As lively and fresh as it is aromatic and lingering, with a pleasant aftertaste.

Trentino Nosiola Le Frate 1991 DOC ☙ ①
From the native grape of the same name comes a dry white wine, with lean perfumes and a typical flavor of freshly-picked wild hazelnuts. Mouthfilling and appetizing.

Stravino di Stravino 1990 ☙ ①
From old vines of Chardonnay on the hills that overlook the small borough of Stravino, towards Lake Garda and the Dolomite mountains near the town of Brenta. Oak-aged and made only in the very best vintages, it has a distinct personality.

Fratagranda 1988 ☙ ①
Classic Bordeaux blend of Cabernet and Merlot, brilliant vivid red in color, it has a complex range of aromas due in part to its wood-aging. Excellent structure, soft, very appealing, with generous tannins.

Tenuta San Leonardo

Loc. San Leonardo
Borghetto all'Adige (Tn) 38060
Tel. (0464) 689004-689000
Fax (0464) 461236

According to historical findings and the writings of the Cruciferi priests, vines have been cultivated in San Leonardo since the 10th century. The religious sect chose this fascinating corner bordering the Veneto and Trentino to explore vine-growing in the valley. Owned since 1870 by the noble vigneron Guerrieri-Gonzaga family, the winery has been lead by the Marquis Carlo Guerrieri-Gonzaga for the last 20 years. In his youth, he studied wine in exclusive colleges abroad and passed on much of what he had learned to the Incisa della Rochetta's estate. Indeed, he had a key part in creation of the legendary Sassicaia wine. Needless to say, he also concentrates on red grapes and wines in Trentino, with a penchant for Cabernet Sauvignon. The Marquis is particularly proud of the special blend used to make San Leonardo, the winery's flagship wine, which first came out in 1982. Lots of work in the vineyard together with top cellar equipment combine to improve the overall quality standards. Only the best wood is used to age these aristocratic reds (no stainless steel vats). The estate's small ethnographic museum is also worth visiting.

Trentino Cabernet 1990 DOC ☙ ①
Traditionally vinified wine which respects the house rules that favor the use of wood. With its intense bouquet and savoury flavor, it is a very well-made wine. Pleasant with good structure, that enables it to improve with age.

Trentino Merlot 1990 DOC ☙ ①
Carlo Guerrieri-Gonzaga is busy working to improve this wine of noble character obtained from extremely low-yielding vineyards. At present, it is typically herbaceous, slightly tannic, warm and harmonious.

Villa Gresti 1990 ☙ ①
A Burgundian blend, it has a beautiful garnet-red color with a purplish rim and highlights. Fragrant fruit aromas on the nose; pleasant and very satisfying drinking.

San Leonardo 1988 ☙☙ ③
One of Trentino's most prestigious reds. A classic skillful blend of Cabernet Sauvignon, Franc and Merlot grapes, it is bright ruby-red and has a complex range of flavors thanks to correct wood-aging. Its great aromatic charm is matched by rich velvety, elegance on the palate.

Turmhof Tiefenbrunner

Via Castello, 4
Cortaccia (Bz) 39040
Tel. (0471) 880122
Fax (0471) 880433

By restoring farm houses and mountain tool sheds, the family has gradually turned their country retreat into what resembles a fairy-tale castle from the 19th century. Handed down from father to son, the winery is now directed by Herbert who works side by side with his son, Christof. The estate vineyards are among the most picturesque in all of Alto Adige, especially the high plot of Müller Thurgau at over 1000 m at Favogna. This vineyard is called Feldmarschall in honor of the great Marshall Franz von Pfenner, a commander of the Kaiser's bodyguards and who came originally from the town. As well as making a few more innovative wines, the Tiefenbrunner winery has established a solid reputation for its Traminer Aromatico, Pinot Bianco, Sylvaner and Cabernet.

Alto Adige Müller Thurgau Feldmarschall 1991 DOC
This wine is made from grapes grown at over 1000 m altitude and, therefore, has an unmistakable character and potential. Intense on the nose, with well-defined flavors, it reaches its peak after a few years in bottle and has a structure rarely found in wine of this type.

Alto Adige Chardonnay Linticlarus 1990 DOC
Straw yellow with golden highlights, it has well-defined perfumes with a faint scent of vanilla and fruit. Vigorous on the palate, with somewhat lingering aromas and lively, crisp acidity on the finish, it will improve with age in bottle.

Alto Adige Gewürztraminer Schloss Turmhof 1990 DOC
From estate-grown grapes, this is one of the benchmark varietal wines not only of this estate, but also of all Alto Adige. Golden yellow in color, it has intense aromas and bouquet; fresh, with considerable extracts, it has a supple, generous finish.

Alto Adige Lagrein
Schloss Turmhof 1990 DOC
Produced from estate-grown grapes of the prized Lagrein grape indigenous to Alto Adige. With an intense bouquet reminiscent of violets, plums and spices, it is clean-cut and well-rounded, with lots of fresh fruit flavor.

Vallarom

Loc. Masi di Vò Sinistro, 21
Avio (Tn) 38063
Tel. (0464) 684297

The Scienza family has always been as strongly tied to the vineyard and wine as it is today. They grow grapes on the low hilly vineyards which the Romans called Vallarom, making the most of the fertile soils of lower Vallagarina production zone, where the Adige river widens to the south towards the province of Verona. The whole family is involved in the operation; Attilio (a university lecturer and viticulturist) began in 1972 followed by his brother Renato, a neurosurgeon by profession. Both wholeheartedly devote their efforts to the winery, owned by their parents, Giuseppina and Ezio. Two other young sons, Filippo and Michele, also show much promise and dedication. They only grow a few varietals and yields per hectare are held back to a minimum, to assure extremely personal wines. Their wines are targeted at the international palate but continue to be very characteristic as little heed is paid to rollercoaster trends. Wines of special interest include their late-harvest Chardonnay, an excellent Cabernet, a typical Marzemino and a Pinot Nero.

Sauvignon Atesino 1990
Absolutely splendid, fanning green highlights like a color chart. With faint vanilla scents from the oak-aging, it has a supple, seductive palate, being full and harmonious, and a considerable structure, of great class, with captivating personality.

Trentino Chardonnay 1990 DOC
In addition to an aromatic version and the late-harvest, they produce a barrique-fermented Chardonnay. The two distinct clones from which it is made impart complex perfumes, where vanilla and spice scents blend well with fresh fruit and ripe apples. Full-bodied, still young but in time will take on any competition.

Trentino Marzemino 1991 DOC
Even Mozart was charmed and fascinated by Marzemino to the point of mentioning it in his Don Giovanni. Vallagarina's red symbol-wine, it is best drunk young to capture all its luscious fresh fruit and has marked aromas of violets and well-defined jam and berry flavors.

Trentino Pinot Nero 1990 DOC
Aged exclusively in small barrels made of different types of oak, its intense and complex bouquet is supported by a robust structure. Pleasant on nose and palate, with the typical Pinot Nero elegance; should age for a few more years before being decidedly convincing.

Vivaldi - Arunda

Numero civico 53
Meltina (Bz) 39010
Tel. (0471) 998033
Fax (0471) 998266

The idea of a sparkling wine winery situated at 1,200 m in Meltine, above the vine's survival point, seemed a bit strange to us. All doubts vanished, however, upon meeting the man behind it all. Joseph Reiterer is, indeed, one of Südtirol's prime authorities on enology, as we had to admit on tasting his excellent sparkling wines. From high above in his 'nest', Reiterer literally reigns over the entire Alto Adige wine production, selecting only the best Chardonnay, Pinot Bianco and Pinot Nero to make his sparkling wines. His refined techniques permit him to make wonderful method champenoise sparkling wines: Brut, Extra Brut and, in better years, an elegant vintage wine. As of this year, he will also make a promising selection called Cuvée Marianne. The winery's production potential is about 60,000 bottles per year, evenly split among the two labels, Vivaldi and Arunda, respectively for national and local distribution.

Arunda Extra Brut
Cuvée Marianne Metodo Classico
From a blend of Pinot Nero, Pinot Bianco and Chardonnay grapes grown in Alto Adige's best zones. Lack of dosage gives it an austere character and a well-defined flavor. Faint scents of yeast contribute to overall elegance. Elegant and lingering bubbles.

Umbria

The green hills of Umbria very much resemble those of Tuscany. With such
similar climates and terrains, they have many viticultural aspects in common.
But the comparison does not hold; Umbria's wine history has hardly been as
decisive or fortunate as its neighbor. Historically, wines from towns like Città
di Castello, Todi and Orvieto were praised as early as the late 16th century
when Andrea Bacci wrote the "Storia Naturale dei Vini d'Italia". Numerous
other historical sources can testify to Umbria's aptitude for wine, but progress
here has traditionally been sporadic and slow moving, as if it was weighted
down. The region was divided in two; most wine came from small estates and
was not destined to leave the region, while the wine of Orvieto, the one wine
known not only in the rest of Italy but throughout the world, suffered from
virtual enological colonialism. Ironically if colonialism it was, it was Tuscany
that perpetrated it.

In the last few decades, however, a handful of producers have come to
realize the importance of winemaking in the region and tap into its potential.
Among these, the Lungarotti winery deserves much credit for creating a new
stimulus and generating a new mentality in Umbria. Wines like Torgiano,
which attracted international acclaim and approval, blazed the trail for many
other wines from the region, each with no less potential. The introduction of
DOC legislation also helped boost production standards in the region, which
now has eight viticultural zones. The winds of change also brought new
techniques in the vineyards, including monoculture and vertical vine training.
Furthermore, in proportion, the region of Umbria produces more DOC wine
than any other region, today exceeding 15% of the region's total wine
production.

The most common varieties, and now subject to clonal selection, include:
Trebbiano Toscano, Procanico (a scion of Trebbiano commonly grown around
Orvieto), Grechetto and Malvasia for whites, and Sagrantino, Sangiovese,
Ciliegiolo, Canaiolo and Montepulciano for reds. As in other regions, many
experiments are being conducted and non-native varieties are being
introduced into Umbrian vineyards, such as: Chardonnay, Cabernet
Sauvignon, Garganega, Sauvignon Blanc, Pinot Nero, Merlot, Gamay and
Barbera. The recent DOCG seal attributed to Sagrantino di Montefalco
(which will soon be referred to as Montefalco Sagrantino), makes for a
prestigious match with Torgiano Rosso Riserva, Umbria's first DOCG wine,
which is aged for at least three years. Together, they ensure a future that
quality-oriented producers can bank on. Viticulture in the area would benefit
even more if only DOC wine legislation could take a more decisive stance on
quality standards and reduce yields, especially in Orvieto for instance. On the
whole, signs of improvement are stronger and stronger, as witnessed by the
wineries listed in the following pages that focus on Montefalco, Orvieto and
Torgiano. In the 'green' region with its strong farming economy, not everyone
is standing back 'shooting the breeze', so to speak.

F.lli Adanti

Loc. Arquata
Bevagna (Pg) 60031
Tel. (0742) 360295
Fax (0742) 361013

Owners of this winery since 1960, Domenico and Piero Adanti have earned international acclaim for their dry red Sagrantino di Montefalco. Also produced in a sweet version, until recently it was considered little more than an enological whim outside its own area. In all truth, the winery's successful track record is also due to the devoted cellarmaster, Alvaro Palini, who is forever researching and improving the quality of Adanti wines, especially the reds. Alongside the Sagrantino and the Rosso di Montefalco, some interesting varietal blends have resulted in wines like Bianco d'Arquata, derived from Chardonnay, Malvasia, Trebbiano and Grechetto. Rosso d'Arquata is surely the winery's most important wine. Originally made from Barbera and Merlot, since 1988 it has been enriched by the addition of Cabernet Sauvignon, and it soon joined the ranks of Italy's noble red wines, at least those of Central Italy. Located near the beautiful town of Montefalco, the winery is worth a visit, even if just for the warmth and hospitality of the Adanti family.

Grechetto 1990 DOC   ♈ ①
Even though it might be hard to find anymore of the 1990, except possibly in restaurants or wine-shops, we thought it deserved a few kind words, in anticipation of the release of the 1991. A fresh and elegant white, it gets better and better with aging.

Rosso d'Arquata 1988   ♈♈ ②
A truly outstanding wine and exceptional value for the money. A blend of Cabernet, Barbera and Merlot, it is bright and intense, with suggestive perfumes and a full palate. Highly concentrated with complex fruit and coffee aromas.

Sagrantino di Montefalco 1988 DOC ♈ ①
A good example, packed with concentration and texture and marked with distinctive tannins and robustness, but also with a noble character. Intense and austere on the nose, it is full-bodied and should achieve greater character and softness in time.

Barberani-Vallesanta

Loc. Cerreto
Baschi (Tr) 05023
Tel. (0744) 950113 - (0763) 41820
Fax (0763) 40773

The classic production area of Orvieto lies just across the way from Orvieto, in a hilly area overlooking Lake Corbara and running along the Tiber river. Despite a period of decline and overproduction, it is central Italy's most important wine. A group of quality-oriented producers have taken the lead as in the success stories of Chianti and Verdicchio, and Orvieto is now making a dignified comeback. Luigi Barberani, owner of Vallesanta, is one of the new generation supporters of the wines of Orvieto. The winery's ancient history dates back to medieval times when it was the castle of Monticello, an agricultural center and a strategic defense post for Orvieto and Todi. In recent years it has undergone extensive restoration and is now home to the winery. Production is mostly centered on dry and sweet Orvieto, but other interesting wines are also made from Sauvignon, Sémillon, Cabernet Sauvignon, Pinot Nero and others varieties. Maurizio Castelli is Luigi Barberani's consulting enologist.

Orvieto Classico Castagnolo 1991 ♈ ①
This is modern style does not sway too far from the more typical Orvieto DOC. Pale straw-yellow in color, with good intensity, it is not particularly deep in its flavors but has pleasant clean aromas of Trebbiano Procanico.

Pomaio 1990   ♈ ①
Though a blend of French and Umbrian grapes of Sauvignon, Sémillon and Grechetto, the former is definitely more pronounced on the nose. Refined and long-lasting on the palate, thanks to an considerable structure.

Orvieto Muffa Nobile   ♈ ②
Calcaia 1989 DOC
This noble rot-influenced Orvieto is one of Vallesanta's most impressive experimental wines. Vibrant gold and very seductive on the nose while pronounced, mouthfilling and synchronized on the palate, with sweet tones. A worthy effort to revive an Orvietan tradition.

Foresco 1990   ♈♈ ②
Obtained from Sangiovese, Cabernet Sauvignon and Franc, each vinified separately and refined in small casks, and then assembled to create an undoubtedly elegant wine of intense and still youthful aromas and of concentrated taste, with good texture and balance.

Cantine Lungarotti

Via Mario Angeloni, 16
Torgiano (Pg) 06089
Tel. (075) 982384
Fax (075) 9880294

One of the nation's most illustrious houses, Lungarotti is synonymous with quality wines. Founder Giorgio Lungarotti did much ground-breaking and pioneering to achieve international recognition for this ancient and traditional wine region. Among his many contributions, he opened a Wine Museum as well as the Tre Vaselle hotel and restaurant and still today organizes the Banco di Assaggio di Torgiano annual tasting seminar. Thanks to his determination, the Torgiano Rosso Riserva wine was recently attributed DOCG status. Other wines produced include Torgiano DOC Rubesco which is probably the most emblematic of the wide range made. Vigna Monticchio, a riserva made only in the best years, is one of central Italy's greatest reds and has been compared to the great wines of Burgundy. Of equal prestige are San Giorgio (Cabernet Sauvignon and Sangiovese) and an interesting series of whites such as Torre di Giano Riserva Vigna II Pino and Chardonnay Vigna I Palazzi. Giorgio's daughter, Maria Teresa, is determined to maintain the quality standards already achieved by the winery, currently under the direction of Angelo Valentini.

Torgiano Torre di Giano Vigna II Pino 1989 DOC
This wine has already proven it can age well and this vintage is no exception. Elegant and balanced, made from Trebbiano and Grechetto, it is refined blend of wines from small casks, made with years of experience.

Cabernet Sauvignon di Miralduolo 1986
Fresh on the nose with hints of herbs and vanilla and an herbaceous-peppery character on the palate, it still shows good structure and backbone, thus leaving promise of further development.

San Giorgio 1982
A wine at its peak of enjoyment, worth drinking now for its exceptional balance and texture. It is a blend of Cabernet Sauvignon and Sangiovese, that has mellowed with time, and gained softness and seductiveness

Torgiano Rubesco Riserva Vigna Monticchio 1982 DOC
The most precious wine of this winery's full range. From Sangiovese and Canaiolo, it is aged in oak and released only after ten years of bottle aging in the Lungarotti cellars. Very fresh and well-balanced after all these years.

Castello della Sala

Loc. Sala
Ficulle (Tr) 05016
Tel. (0763) 86051
Fax (0763) 86491

This exemplary winery, owned by the Marchesi Antinori, is largely responsible for the rebirth of Orvieto's production. Many experiments have been conducted to research new types and vinification techniques, especially in perfecting the whites. Orvieto's wines have a long tradition and have always been popular; Chianti-based wineries never stopped offering it as a white that would fit nicely into their preponderantly red line of wines. However there came a moment when the fashionable Galestro seemed to come close to threatening Orvieto's production and reputation. Luckily Castello della Sala and other wineries then stepped in, with a new wave of polished Orvieto wines and reversed the trend. Under the guidance of enologist Renzo Cotarella, the Antinori winery looks more like a laboratory specialized in viticultural experimentation. Prestigious results have been achieved not only with Orvieto, but above all with the Vino da Tavola wines like Cervaro della Sala (a Chardonnay and Grechetto blend which was recently placed among Italy's best whites), Muffato (a botrytized blend of Sauvignon, Grechetto and Traminer) and Borro della Sala Fumé (Sauvignon Blanc and Procanico).

Borro della Sala 1991
A successful blend of French Sauvignon Blanc and Umbrian Procanico, it has a decisive impact on the nose, with clearly marked Sauvignon aromas; there's a perfect balance on the palate, with medium length on the finish.

Orvieto Classico 1991 DOC
Straw yellow, it has pleasant floral and fruity perfumes and a moderately intense flavor. An admirably clean and well-made modern interpretation of this historical DOC.

Cervaro della Sala 1990
From grapes harvested and transported with extreme care, Cervaro is a blend of mainly Chardonnay with some Grechetto, fermented and matured in barriques. Rich and long-lasting on the nose, with joyous, lively sensations on the palate, with an uncanny harmony of the elements.

Muffato della Sala 1989
A fine dessert wine made of Sauvignon, Grechetto and Traminer grapes, affected by noble rot, it has a distinctive elegance as a result, with an intense and ample bouquet and harmonious and complex flavors.

Val di Maggio - Caprai

Loc. Torre
Montefalco (Pg) 06036
Tel. (0742) 378802
Fax (0742) 378422

Arnaldo Caprai's winery is situated in one of the oldest wine areas in Umbria. Pliny the Elder once cited the Itriola grape, describing it as typical of the area of nearby Bevagna. Further on, in the 15th century, documents housed in the Archives of Montefalco testify to the existence of strict laws protecting the 'fields planted with vines.' Year after year, Val di Maggio has proven itself capable of carrying on this important heritage, having achieved a happy medium between the modern and traditional. The dynamic team behind the brandname is comprised of young Marco Caprai, his father Arnaldo and enologist Attilo Pagli. Among the whites the oak-aged Grecante stands out, as an intelligent rendition of the Grechetto DOC. Notable reds include Sagrantino di Montefalco, now known as Montefalco Sagrantino, Umbria's second DOCG wine, and Montefalco Rosso, a blend of mostly Sangiovese with small amounts of Montepulciano, Barbera, Sagrantino and Merlot. Marco Caprai also works with other varieties such as Syrah and Sémillon and has high hopes for the Cabernet Sauvignon he planted this year.

Grechetto dei Colli Martani ☙ ①
Grecante 1990 DOC
As impressive and particularly well-made as it is, this fine Umbrian wine is in no hurry to unfurl its best characteristics. With its rather intense and individual aromas on the nose, it is harmonious on the palate, reflecting its clean, well-made origins.

Montefalco Rosso 1990 DOC ☙ ①
Not to be confused with the Sagrantino di Montefalco DOCG , this Montefalco Rosso is made from Sangiovese grapes with some Sagrantino. More garnet than ruby in color, its bouquet is brimming with subtle spices. Despite the notable tannin, it is sufficiently harmonious.

Sagrantino di Montefalco 1988 DOC ☙ ②
Bright rich garnet in color, it has somewhat austere perfumes with tones of berries and is full-bodied but rather soft on the palate, with solid tannins. There's still some room for improvement with bottle aging, which should mellow its sharpness some.

Entries are arranged in alphabetical order by country, region and winery or producer name.

Veneto

Veneto lies third in Italy, after Puglia and Sicily, in terms of the quantity of wine produced but first in terms of DOC production. One-fifth of the total 8,000,000 hl annual production (1,700,000 hl) is DOC. Wine-growing in the Venetian hills, especially near Verona, was practiced as early as the Etruscan times and was especially flourishing around the year 1000 BC, with the settlement of peoples from Venice.

In the last few decades, regional wine production has soared. In fact, more wine is produced in the province of Verona alone than in all of Piedmont. DOC wine legislation condoning the highest yields per hectare in all of northern Italy seemingly encouraged the spread of vineyards across the plains of the fertile river valleys. By the 1970s, production was booming and big firms and cooperative wineries were conquering foreign markets everywhere. In the last few years, however, trends have begun to reverse and the focus has turned to quality-oriented production.

Aside from the overwhelming figures and statistics, Veneto's importance may also be measured in terms of the complexity, number and variety of styles of wine produced from the different growing areas. The Brenta river roughly splits the region into two large areas: the eastern side, with four zones lying between the Brenta river and the Friuli-Venezia Giulia region, and the western side, which reaches across to Lake Garda, making a number of different types. For example, wines from the province of Verona differ from those of Padova and Vicenza due to the climate, growing conditions and native varieties. The Instituto Sperimentale in Conegliano Veneto has had a fundamental role in conducting extensive research on indigenous grapes, particularily the red Corvina Veronese (used for Bardolino, Valpolicella, Amarone and Recioto), the red Rondinella (also for Bardolino and Valpolicella), Garganega (used for Soave) and Trebbiano di Soave for light whites. Other important varieties include Prosecco, Tocai, Verduzzo, Trevigiano, Vespaiola, Molinara, Durella, two mixed types of Manzoni, Raboso and many others, for a total of over 80 authorized varietals.

European grapes like Merlot and Cabernet are now commonly grown, along with lots of Chardonnay, Sauvignon and Pinot, dominating indigenous types like Bianchetta Trevigiana, Pavana and Trevisana Nera. Medium to small family wineries are putting out some very impressive new styles and interpretations of the major DOC wines of the region, often trying to refine Amarone's strength or to add complexity to Valpolicella, for example. The wineries and wines listed in this guide, some worthy of Top Wine status, are indicative of the progress being achieved.

Adriano Adami & C.

Via Rovede, 17
Vidor (Tv) 31020
Tel. (0423) 980410
Fax (00423) 981311

Colbertaldo di Vidor is a tiny village nestled between the towns of Valdobbiadene and Conegliano. Owner Adriano Adami and his sons, Franco and Armando, are part of a family winemaking tradition that dates back to the 15th century, when the first written documents cite the winery's most famous single-vineyard, Giardino. Bordering on the famous Cartizze production zone, the Giardino vineyard makes a highly reputed Prosecco, with fragrant, refined aromas. Adami's Extra Dry may be a touch better than the vintage Prosecco Giardino, in 1991 as it was a slightly off year. The reason is this is that the higher sugar of the former helps to round out the wine and fill in the hole that would normally be filled by a better level of extract. Few producers of Prosecco are able to offer a selection of wines at this level.

Prosecco di Valdobbiadene
Vigneto Giardino 1991 DOC
From Adami's most famous vineyard, this wine is extremely fragrant, with beautiful perfumes, and is clean and fresh on the palate.

Prosecco di Valdobbiadene
Extra Dry DOC
Adami makes the best Extra Dry in the Prosecco area. Produced by the Charmat method, that is with a second fermentation in vats, not in the bottle, it shows good aromatic length on the palate.

Prosecco di Valdobbiadene
Superiore di Cartizze Dry DOC
Excellent bubbles, clean perfumes and fruity character on the palate are but a few of the assets of this Prosecco, which comes from the most prestigious subzone in Valdobbiadene.

Allegrini

Loc. Corte Giara
Fumane di Valpolicella (Vr) 37022
Tel. (045) 7701138
Fax (045) 7701774

The Allegrini family winery has been progressively gaining ground since 1983 when siblings Franco, Walter and Marisa Allegrini took over. Founded by their late father, Giovanni, it is located in Fumane, in the most westerly valley of the classic Valpolicella area. The noticeable changes start in the vineyard where the oldest son, Walter, is in charge. The most extraordinary vineyards are found high up on the Grola hill, at 310 m between Lake Garda and the Adige valley. Made of almost pure limestone and planted solely to Corvina, the vineyard produces Allegrini's famous La Poja Vino da Tavola. The youngest son, Franco, is definitely responsible for the improvements in the cellar and wine-making, including the skillful use of the barrique as well as keeping a watchful eye on Amarone's common problem with oxidation. These are only two of the significant steps which have helped to distinguish Allegrini wines, today ranked among Verona's best. The La Poja in particular is first-rate, by any international standard.

Recioto della Valpolicella
Classico 1990 DOC
This sweet Recioto is one of Allegrini's best products. Its enormously ample perfumes and impressive flavors would appeal even to those who are not even familiar with this type of wine.

Valpolicella Classico Superiore
La Grola 1990 DOC
One of the best Valpolicellas of the vintage, La Grola is intense red in color, with a warm sensation. Complex and full-bodied, with wood tones and hints of overripe grapes, it has great aromatic persistence.

Valpolicella Classico Superiore
Palazzo della Torre 1988 DOC
This second single-vineyard Valpolicella is more classic and typical than La Grola. Supple and rounded, slightly lacking in power and structure compared to its more famous relative.

Amarone della Valpolicella
1985 DOC
The regular 1985 Amarone seems better than the single-vineyard Amarone, Fieramonte. Dense and well-structured on the palate, it shows good aromatic complexity.

La Poja 1985
Allegrini's flagship wine, it shows the full potential of the Corvina grape, here vinified as a single variety and then refined in barrique. It has great structure and generous, captivating aromas.

Roberto Anselmi

Via San Carlo, 46
Monteforte d'Alpone (Vr) 37032
Tel. (045) 7611488
Fax (045) 7611490

With unprecedented efforts and in relatively little time, Roberto Anselmi has turned his father's 15 million-bottle winery into a gem of Italian enology. Situated in one of the most beautiful areas, it has very low-yielding, densely planted vineyards (10,000 plants per ha). He practices controlled-temperature fermentation and matures some of the wine in barrique. To further improve his Soave, Anselmi is experimenting with new clones and rootstocks and different systems for caring for the vines. A steep, new estate vineyard capping the top of the Foscarino hill, at 330 m altitude, will soon go into production. Anselmi makes whites that are easily distinguishable from other producers because he blocks the malolactic fermentation and adds a small part of Chardonnay to the classic recipe. In favorable years, the white oak-aged Capitel Croce and the sweet Recioto dei Capitelli are truly exceptional; complex, aromatically rich and flavorful.

Soave Classico   🍇 ②
Capitel Foscarino 1990 DOC
Foscarino is the most famous cru in the classic Soave area. This vintage is well-structured, spicy and long, but it still needs some time to fully express itself.

Recioto di Soave   🍇 ③
I Capitelli 1989 DOC
Aged in barrique, for years this Recioto was a benchmark wine for producers in the area. With already mature aromas, it is sweet and dense on the palate. Moderately complex and intense in aromas, it may still improve with time.

Soave Classico   🍇🍇 ②
Capitel Croce 1988 DOC
Definitely an unusual Soave Classico, with its California-style twist. This vintage is better balanced than its predecessors and easily stands up well to the so-called 'international' wines. It is about to reach its peak in flavors and aromas.

Realda 1989   🍇🍇 ③
A Cabernet from very young vines, this 1989 is the first vintage that lives up to the high quality standards set by the Anselmi label and reputation.

Bertani

Loc. Novare
Arbizzano (Vr) 37020
Tel. (045) 7513999
Fax (045) 7513305

One of the giants of the Veronese wine industry, Bertani was founded in 1857 by Giovanni Battista Bertani, who was a deputy in Italy's first parliament. Unlike many fellow growers in the area, he has always resisted the tendency to overproduce and make lean, low quality wines. Surprizingly enough, a winery of this size, and with such a large commercial impact, is able to put wines on the market with over ten years of aging. Only a quarter of the grapes are bought in to achieve the 250,000-case production, all of which is made in Bertani's three wineries in Novare, Monteforte and Grezzana. These figures are even more impressive given the consistently high quality of the wine even in times of turmoil, when other large Veronese wineries tended to abandon their vineyards. One of the most emblematic personalities in Valpolicella, Nino Franceschetti joined the team last year and already has great plans for the future, including the restoration of the beautiful villa in Novare into a true Bordeaux-style château.

Soave Classico 1991 DOC   🍇 ①
In our comparative tastings, this regular Soave Classico ranked high for its vintage. With lots of pleasant, floral aromas, it has medium body and good aromatic length.

Catullo Bianco 1988   🍇 ②
Produced from the local Garganega variety and the more international Chardonnay and Pinot Bianco grapes, the resulting cuvée is fresh and elegant, but also well-structured and dense.

Soave Classico Superiore   🍇🍇 ①
Le Lave 1988 DOC
This vintage has been on the market for some time and continues to improve. Its petrol-like aromas actually recall the great whites of northern Europe and it still has the capacity for improvement.

Fratelli Bolla

Piazza Cittadella, 3
Verona (Vr) 37122
Tel. (045) 594055
Fax (045) 592198

Much of the fame earned world-wide by
Veronese wines, particularily Soave, is owed
to one, single brand; Bolla, practically
synonymous with Veneto and a house-hold
name in the United States. The story of this
famous family of businessmen dates back to
1883 when a certain Abele Bolla, owner of
the hotel Gambero of Soave, founded his
winery. For far too long, Bolla rolled out very
low-priced wines, still of decent quality but
never outstanding. The winds of change have
struck here, too. The large numbers still
linger, but now there are some exciting
jewels to be discovered among the house
wines, starting with the Vino da Tavola Creso
Rosso. Another is Creso Bianco (100%
Chardonnay) which certainly merits the great
tradition carried on by the heirs of Abele
Bolla.

Creso Bianco 1990
Straw yellow in color with wood scents and
extremely refined aromas, it is very drinkable
even though, unfortunately, its character doesn't
yet seem sufficiently focused yet.

Recioto Classico 1990 DOC
Since the sugars that accumulated during the
raisining phase have not completely developed
into alcohol, there's always a risk that the wine
could continue to ferment. As a result, this
Recioto has a dry, spritzy, easy-drinking
character.

Creso Rosso 1988
The most interesting Creso blend that Bolla has
to propose to date. A strong Cabernet base
together with other native grapes, it is what
convinced us to place Bolla back in the
prestigious circle of Veneto's best wineries.

Paolo Boscaini e Figli

Loc. Marano
Valgatara di Marano (Vr) 37020
Tel. (045) 6800840
Fax (045) 6800837

If the Boscaini family from Valgatara weren't
direct cousins of the Boscaini family behind
Masi Agricola, one of the more famous
Veronese wineries, one might think they were
the younger siblings as they have always
remained almost completely unknown. But,
this is hardly the case. Not only is Paolo
Boscaini & Sons the bigger winery of the two,
but they also own almost all of the vineyards
held by the two families. They have produced
some wines, especially in recent years, that
are fully capable of competing with those of
their more famous cousins. For obvious
business reasons, Boscaini continues to
produce large quantities of simple,
supermarket wines, readily available around
the globe, but with the Vigneti range they
have a range of top quality wines. Wines like
the Amarone Ca' de Loi and Marano, the
Vino da Tavola Santo Stefano de Le Cane
and even the Soave Classico Monteleone get
the front row among wines made in the hills
surrounding Verona.

Recioto della Valpolicella Classico
Ca' Nicolis 1990 DOC
The difference between Recioto and Amarone
can sometimes be very subtle: such is the case
with this Ca' Nicolis, which has converted most
of its sugar and shows dryness and severity on
the palate, while attractive fruity perfumes
prevail on the nose.

Santo Stefano de Le Cane 1988
A typical "Ripasso" wine or wine enriched by
using the rich lees of Recioto: it's already quite
mature though the aromas may seem to lag.
This small defect is promptly compensated by
fullness and great concentration on the palate.

Cavalchina

Loc. Cavalchina
Custoza (Vr) 37066
Tel. (045) 516002
Fax (045) 516257

Cavalchina is an old family winery that, way back in 1962, was the first to bottle Bianco di Custoza, which was then called Soave dei Colli Morenici. Young Luciano Piona, grandson of the founder, is one of the most highly respected producers of Custoza. Most of the vineyards can be found in the nearby province of Mantova where Piona owns another winery, La Prendina, where his most famous wines are made: Rosso il Falcone and the two simpler Colli Morenici del Mantovano wines, available in white or red. All grapes are vinified at Cavalchina. Having recently renewed the winery's structure, Luciano has been conducting extensive experiments in an area where top-level wines were relatively few and far between. Almost every year is filled with little surprises: a late-harvest wine, a new style of white oaked in barrique or possibly some early vintages held back in the cellar just waiting to be discovered and tasted.

La Prendina Sauvignon Blanc 1991 ①
Many years of experimentation have gone into the making of this Sauvignon, with its full expression and distinctive character. The floral perfumes, full body and good length amply compensate for the slight absence of varietal character.

Le Pergole del Sole ②
Müller Thurgau Passito 1990
Bright yellow in color, it has fruity aromas that are almost sweet, especially after a few swirls in the glass. It's a pleasant dessert wine and relatively unusual for this part of Verona.

La Prendina Il Falcone 1989 ②
"One of Italy's best Cabernets" according to many who have tasted it. The vineyards are located in Lombardy, but the wine is made in Veneto. Intense ruby, its fruity scents are well-blended with the wood tones; complex, with a long finish.

Corte Gardoni

Loc. Gardoni
Valeggio sul Mincio (Vr) 37067
Tel. (045) 7950382
Fax (045) 6370270

Dynamic vintner, Gianni Piccoli, cultivates over 20 ha of vines on his 62-ha holding and grows delicious apples on the rest. Located on the border between the Veronese and Mantovan regions along the Morenic hills of Lake Garda, Corte Gardoni is one of the most important wineries of the area. The Piccoli family happened to find refuge here from the phylloxera that was devastating the Valpolicella area. This misfortune gave birth to a winery that mixes excellent wines of unusually consistent quality. Gardoni's Bardolino and Bianco di Custoza are usually a cut above the rest and, more recently, the winery has been conducting numerous experiments with different wines: late-harvests, Chardonnay and Riesling for white Vini da Tavola and DOCs, stylish red wines from typical Bordeaux mixtures, and wines made from a Corvina base, a classic Veronese varietal that is matured in barrique.

Bardolino Le Fontane 1991 DOC ①
The best of the young Bardolino wines tasted this year carries the Gardoni label. With an incredibly distinctive color compared to others of its type, it is fruity, intense and full on the palate.

Bardolini Superiore 1990 DOC ①
Once the slight notes of reduction disappear, the aromas unfurl their peppery fruit. This sublte wine is full-bodied and quite lingering on the finish.

Rosso di Corte 1988 ②
If Piccoli wines are known for their extraordinary drinkability, this Rosso di Corte is no exception; dense in color, with extremely clean aromas though a bit closed and very elegant on the palate.

Villa Dal Ferro - Lazzarini

Fraz. Villa Dal Ferro
S. Germano dei Berici (Vi) 36040
Tel. (0444) 868025
Fax (049) 8759032

Almost a generation ago, Alfredo Lazzarini
bought the beautiful 16th century Villa Dal
Ferro di San Germano (designed by Venetian
Michele Sanmichele), with little or no
intention of producing wine there. But once
he visited the beautiful underground cellars,
he was enthralled by the idea of planting
vineyards. He immediately set to work and
very soon his wines gained international
recognition. His selection of varietals is
extremely interesting and includes Riesling
Renano, Sauvignon Blanc, Pinot Bianco,
Merlot, Cabernet and Pinot Nero. We tasted
a number of Lazzarini's mature wines which,
for the most part, showed great aging
potential. In anticipation of the new Riservas
of Cabernet and Merlot which are produced
only in the best years, such as the 1985 and
1986 Merlots, we can at present only
highlight two solid whites and the traditional
house Cabernet, Rive Rosse.

Colli Berici Pinot Bianco   🍇 ①
del Rocolo 1991 DOC
Villa Dal Ferro's best white of the year. Fresh,
aromatic and full-bodied: a good, solid product.

Riesling Renano Busa Calcara 1991   🍇 ①
A Riesling Renano from the Colli Berici hillside:
this may seem a bit extravagant, but it is truly a
beautiful white wine, refined and well-structured
on the palate.

Colli Berici Cabernet   🍇 ①
Le Rive Rosse 1989 DOC
In the absence of Lazzarini's great reserves, we
present this Cabernet which, despite the burden
of coming from a slightly off year, has good
regional character and is very drinkable.

Romano Dal Forno

Via Capovilla, 35
Illasi (Vr) 37031
Tel. (045) 7834923

Romano Dal Forno vinifies only the best
bunches picked from his small vineyards; the
rest is sold wholesale. Located outside the
so-called classic Valpolicella area in the
valley of Illasi, the vines are cultivated on
poor rocky and gravely floodsoils. They are
trained low using the Guyot system, in order
to reduce the yield per hectare as much as
possible. These conditions, as well as the
use of barrique, are only a few of the many
little secrets that give Dal Forno's wine
enough complexity and concentration to
render it victorious in numerous recent wine-
tastings. It's no secret that Dal Forno has
followed in the footsteps of the great master
Quintarelli of Negrar, but only recently have
we discovered that he is about to surpass
him. Furthermore, the new winery Dal Forno
has just finished building can only help to
improve his wines.

Amarone 1987 DOC   🍇🍇🍇 ②
Absoultely fantastic! This was the tasters'
unanimous exclamation after sampling this
excellent barrique-aged vintage, even after
trying the equally exciting 1986. Clearly
international in style, it is one of the best
Amarone wines of the vintage.

Valpolicella Superiore 1987 DOC 🍇🍇🍇 ②
To produce such an intensely perfumed,
flavorful, powerful and tannic Valpolicella from
the disappointing 1987 harvest is no small
endeavor. Even though it's missing some length
on the finish, we cannot withhold our words of
praise for this excellent wine.

Nino Franco

Via Garibaldi, 167
Valdobbiadene (Tv) 31049
Tel. (0423) 972051
Fax (0423) 975977

Primo Franco's winery is bound to be one of the most beautiful, modern and functional wineries in Italy. For the past two years Franco has begun to grow his own vines and not just make the wines, as previously, entirely from grapes bought in from growers in the area of Valdobbiadene and the fascinating subzone Cartizze. Located just outside the town of Valdobbiadene, the vineyards are surrounded by walls, just like a French clos, and enjoy a beautiful view of the Piave river and the hills of Montello. Even the most sceptical Prosecco-drinkers have to admit that the sparkling wines from this house are top of the line. But Franco doesn't stop there; he is determined to continue experimenting and make new and better styles of wines. His latest creation is a still, late-harvest Prosecco, that is fermented in oak: definitely uncanny for this area, but with plenty of room for development.

Prosecco di Valdobbiadene Brut DOC 🍷 ①
The same quality level as the Primo Franco below, but this brut stands out for its full and fresh aromas and for its very pleasant drinkability.

Prosecco di Valdobbiadene 🍷 ①
Primo Franco DOC
A normal Prosecco perfectly capable of competing with all the DOC Superiore di Cartizze wines. With lively fruit on the nose, it has a light tinge of sweetness on the palate that makes it mouthwateringly appetizing.

Conti Guerrieri Rizzardi

Piazza Guerrieri, 1
Bardolino (Vr) 37011
Tel. (045) 7210028
Fax (045) 7210704

Amidst other fascinating villas of the Veneto, each with lots of well-positioned vineyards, the large Rizzardi estate is in Bardolino in the middle of a tiny, beautiful area off Lake Garda. Operating 140 ha of estate vineyards is no small feat. With this potential, and its 150 year-old winemaking history, the winery could be in a position to rule the regional wine industry but the Rizzardi family seems to content itself with much less. They certainly produce a solid line of wines, but not one that particularly stands out, a benchmark wine against which all the others producers would have to measure themselves by. Among their whites and reds, the most interesting are the Amarone Le Calcarole (released only after considerable cellaring) and the Soave Classico Costeggiola.

Soave Classico Costeggiola 1991 DOC 🍷 ①
A single-vineyard Soave made by the Bardolino-based estate the way it should be: soft, flavorful and full on the palate.

Amarone Le Calcarole 1985 DOC 🍷🍷 ②
Made from Corvina grapes grown on loamy terrain in the Negrar valley, this traditional Amarone is already very mature showing great softness on the palate and a long-lasting finish.

Maculan

Via Castelletto, 3
Breganze (Vi) 36042
Tel. (0445) 873733
Fax (0445) 300149

Visiting Fausto Maculan's vineyards and extremely modern winery really gave us a sense of his dynamic charisma. Determined to give traditional winemaking techniques a face lift, he has turned his vineyards into super-vineyards, that seem to belong to another world. Both vineyards and vinification are modeled after the French, as are most of the wines. He makes lots of wines; some good, some a bit controversial, and some truly outstanding. The best wines come from a new vineyard called the Ferrata, named after the railroad tracks that used to pass through. Even the regular Chardonnay is superb. Maculan's penchant, however, surely lies in the two internationally-styled sweet wines, obtained from raisined grapes and aged in barrique.

Sauvignon Blanc Ferrata 1991 ☸ ②
Though the weakest of the Ferrata line, it is still a beautiful wine that may improve in the bottle and fully revealing its clean aromas and soft body.

Chardonnay Ferrata 1990 ☸☸ ②
This is the first time that Chardonnay Ferrata has surpassed the regular Chardonnay; proof that the vines are coming of age and beginning to produce great wines. Dense and still a bit young, there's a correct balance between fruit and wood.

Torcolato 1990 ☸☸ ③
We thought nothing could beat the excellent 1989 vintage, but with the use of dried grapes in a temperature-controlled environment, Maculan has succeeded again.

Cabernet Sauvignon Ferrata 1989 ☸☸ ③
One look at the vineyards reveals all of Ferrata's potential: densely planted, low-yielding vines provide an excellent base for refined, well-structured and powerful Cabernets.

Acini Nobili 1989 ☸☸☸ ④
Fausto Maculan has succeeded in crafting a dessert wine capable of competing with the world's best. The grapes are the same as the ones used to make Torcolato, but he only selects those affected by noblr rot. Acini Nobili is made from indigenous grapes that no one would have ever guessed capable of such superb results: Vespaiola, Garganega and Tocai Nostrano team up to rival any Riesling or Sémillon or Sauternes. Matured in small oak casks, the wine is luninous gold in color with green highlights. With pleasant aromas on the nose from the botrytis cinerea and the wood-aging, with accents of exotic fruit, apple and flowers, it is full, almost fat on the palate. With due bottle aging, it should develop a grand bouquet.

Masi

Loc. Gargagnago
S. Ambrogio di Valpolicella (Vr) 37020
Tel. (045) 6800588
Fax (045) 598066

In the 1970s Masi Agricola made a decisive contribution to the improving the reputation of Valpolicella wines, going to great lengths to restore its dignity and prestige. Until then it had flooded Pizzerias and supermarkets all over the world at rock-bottom prices. First of all, Masi conducted experiments in cooperation with the San Floriano School of Viticulture. The recent plantings which resulted presage a bright future with even better quality wines. Specific experiments done on almost-extinct varieties indigenous to the Valpolicella (like Dindarella, Oseleta, Forsellina and possibly clones of Corvina) may well help to tone down overproductive varieties traditionally used for the reds. Besides vinifying and distributing their own brandname wines, Masi also handles the notable Count Serègo Alighieri range.

Recioto della Valpolicella Classico Degli Angeli 1990 DOC
This sweet red wine is slightly anonymous but has clean aromas and good texture.

Amarone della Valpolicella 1988 DOC
This vintage is still quite young and may seem slightly unbalanced, but good positive flavors foretell a promising development in time.

Amarone della Valpolicella Mazzano 1986 DOC
It was difficult to reproduce the perfection of the legendary '85 vintage, a truly great year, especially since the time and conditions necessary for raisining are critical and difficult to assess. This 1986 Mazzano is still very good and very well made.

Amarone della Valpolicella Mazzano 1985 DOC
The most prestigious wine of the house, made from grapes from the newest vineyards in the Marano valley. A top level Amarone, wih elegance and great fullness from the bouquet on through to the palate.

Leonildo Pieropan

Via Camuzzoni, 3
Soave (Vr) 37038
Tel. (045) 7680044
Fax (045) 6190040

As a small grower in the center of the town of Soave, Leonildo Pieropan has always made some of the best DOC Soave, a wine abused by the larger houses. Not only does Pieropan have to contend with growing conditions and all the problems of vinification, but it seems that he is also forced to take on the might ot industrial and commercial interests which even dominate the local consorzio which is in charge of policing the laws protecting this Veronese wine, one of the best known in italy. Pieropan's refined and clean wines are surprisingly harmonious and have the potential to age well, something quite unusual for this area. In fact, we tasted 12 year-old bottles of the regular Soave Classico as well as the single-vineyards, La Rocca and Calvarino, that had not only maintained their freshness but even improved in complexity and character.

Soave Classico 1991 DOC
In a year when many producers had grapes with low levels of extract and alcohol, a Soave of this caliber is truly exceptional. Aromas of apples and flowers, it is well-structured and has a long aftertaste.

Riesling Italico 1990
It may seem strange to find a Riesling Italico from this area, but Pieropan's is a solid product that can stand its own against the newer styles of barrique-aged Chardonnays currently made here in Verona, too.

Soave Classico La Rocca 1990 DOC
Pieropan's La Rocca cru has always been the slowest to mature. It has clean, varietal perfumes; with its elegance and finesse and good structure, it is an excellent wine with good cellar life.

Fratelli Prà

Via Fontana, 31
Monforte d'Alpone (Vr) 37032
Tel. (045) 7612125

Graziano and Sergio Prà are the vintners behind their own winery in Monteforte, which concentrates on making the area's two classics, Soave Classico and Recioto di Soave. Their 10 ha of rolling hillside vineyards provide all the fruit they need to make 5,000 cases each year. Thanks to the new and spacious cellar facilities inaugurated in 1990, they were able to vinify and bottle the entire harvest. Despite the small, family-run dimensions, Prà wines, together with Graziano's charisma, have conquered many fans both in Italy and abroad, particularily in Germany. Sergio's hard work in the vineyard has paid off, keeping yields per hectare considerably lower than the wine laws indicate and vinification tends to improve noticeably each year. Today Prà wines are among the best in the Soave area.

Soave Classico 1991 DOC ℗ ①
This is a good example of Soave, with its fresh, fruity bouquet. Savoury on the palate, with medium intensity, and lovely fresh acidity on the finish.

Soave Classico ℗ ①
Monte Grande 1991 DOC
Prà's cru Monte Grande is better structured and composed than the regular Soave. It has refined and long-lasting perfumes with evident floral and fruity tones and its texture reveals the underlying high fruit quality. A wine in full evolution.

Recioto di Soave ℗ ③
delle Fontane 1989 DOC
This sweet version of Soave is now at its peak, three years after bottling. Complex with scents of dried fruit and light tones of apple; it is soft on the palate, fleshy; finishes dry and is hardly boring.

Giuseppe Quintarelli

Via Cerà, 1
Negrar di Valpolicella (Vr) 37024
Tel. (045) 7500016

Giuseppe Quintarelli is, by far, the most admired and beloved "vignaiolo" in all of Valpolicella. Some say that he is so attached to his vineyards that he lovingly calls them each by their own name. In the winery, however, he is the quintessential traditionalist, the like of whom the Italian wine world has not seen for at least a generation. His dense, robust wines with their complex and appealing aromas, are made the old-fashioned way, without the use of modern technology. To prove his unique production philosophy, he still goes so far as to bottle by hand, but this often results in uneven quality. There have been rumours in the past few months that Giuseppe wanted to sell his business since he had no heirs. It's hard to say, but it will certainly be difficult for Giuseppe to give up his cherished winery.

Alzero Cabernet Franc ♟♟ ③
Monte Paletta 1987
Relatively subtle raisined-grape aromas, clearly varietal in origin, with great fruit, dense, fat, silky and long-lasting. These are but a few of the enthusiastic comments after a taste of Quintarelli's best.

Valpolicella Classico Superiore ♟ ②
Monte Ca' Paletta 1987 DOC
This particular wine falls slightly short of our expectations, though it is still very elegant and pleasant; a typical Quintarelli wine.

Amarone della Valpolicella ♟♟ ③
1984 DOC
This vintage has been on sale for some time but at the time of writing the 1985 had not yet been bottled. Although not considered a great year, this 1984 is truly exceptional and is now maturing to its fullest.

Russolo & C.

Via LIbertà, 13
Pramaggiore (Ve) 30020
Tel. (0431) 79087

Iginio Russolo's winery has an unusual set-up. Not only is it on the border of two regions, Veneto and Friuli, but it also produces DOC wines from three distinct and far away zones, namely Lison-Pramaggiore in Veneto and Collio and Grave del Fruili in Friuli. So far, the best wines seem to come from Grave in Friuli where, not by chance, the winery has its largest vineyard. Of Russolo's large selection of wines produced each year, the Ronco Calaj series is undoubtedly the best, named after the newly purchased vineyards from which it is made. For years they were forced to buy grapes from outside. The new "I Legni" (the woods) range is interesting, but so far only the Refosco has made a good impression; oddly enough, the others seem to suffer from too much oak and are not harmonious, as a result.

Grave del Friuli Sauvignon   ①
Ronco Calaj 1991 DOC
What a pleasant surprise; this Sauvignon Blanc managed to outshine much bigger names in a recent blind tasting. Refined, lightly herbaceous and floral, it is well-structured, fleshy and long-lasting.

Müller Thurgau Mussignaz 1991   ①
Judging from its aromas, typical of a very early harvest, this Müller could easily pass for a Moscato or a Gewürztraminer. Unusual and successful, especially given its place of origin.

Grave del Friuli   ②
Merlot Massarac 1990 DOC
It is rather unsual for a Merlot wine from Fruili to have an herbaceous and somewhat buttery nature. On the other hand, its soft structure and body testify to this area's natural suitability for producing great red wines.

Grave del Friuli Refosco   ②
I Legni 1989 DOC
On the whole, the Legni series has suffered from mediocre wood and barrels; this Refosco, however, has managed to develop rather well. It has warm, spicy aromas and is very drinkable.

Santi

Via Ungheria, 33
Illasi (Vr) 37031
Tel. (045) 7834008-480469
Fax (045) 6520044

Located on the border of the Soave and Valpolicella regions, Illasi was founded by Carlo Santi back in 1848. One of the most celebrated wineries in the province of Verona, Santi is part of the giant Gruppo Italiano Vini wine group, one of the most important wine producers in the world, which produces a impressive 5,000,000 annual cases, mostly exported worldwide. The more modest dimensions of Santi, about 170,000 cases per year, enable it to maintain a quality-oriented production philosophy. Santi's leading wine is undoubtedly hte exclusive Amarone, Botte Regina, although there are plenty of other high quality wines. Among the many fine wines made, a few of special interest include the Bardolino Ca' Bordenis, made from Santi's estate-vineyards (located right in front of GIV international headquarters in Calmasino), and the Le Solane, the new Valpolicella wine recently tasted for the first time.

Chardonnay Trentino I Piovi 1991   ①
A Chardonnay from grapes from the Adige river valley, just across the border from Veneto. Extremely attractive in color, with lightly spiced aromas, full on the palate.

Bardolino Ca' Bordenis 1991 DOC   ①
From grapes picked right in front of the Gruppo Italiano Vini's beautiful villa in Calmasino, off the shores of Lake Garda. Fresh, typical and very drinkable.

Valpolicella   ①
Castello d'Illasi 1990 DOC
A blend of Corvina, Molinara and Rondinella grapes from the Castello d'Illasi vineyards. Granite red in color, it has clean aromas and is pure, with scents of mature fruits. Medium-bodied on the palate; round and refreshingly dry on the finish.

Valpolicella Le Solane 1990 DOC   ①
Garnet red in color, mature and dense though not particularily spectacular, it has wonderful aromas, typical of extra-ripe or raisined grapes, together with nice vanilla. Full-bodied and captivating.

Amarone della Valpolicella   ②
Botte Regina 1985 DOC
Santi's pride and joy: produced only in outstanding years and from choice barrels. Rich garnet in color, it maintains its freshness and intense and complex rasberry scented bouquet. Harmonious, austere and long-lasting on the palate.

Slow Food Manifesto

International Movement for the Defense of and the Right to Pleasure

Born and nurtured under the sign of Industrialization, this century first invented the machine and then modelled its lifestyle after it. Speed became our shackles. We fell prey to the same virus: 'the fast life' that fractures our customs and assails us even in our own homes, forcing us to ingest "fast- food".

Homo sapiens must regain wisdom and liberate itself from the 'velocity' that is propelling it on the road to extinction. Let us defend ourselves against the universal madness of 'the fast life' with tranquil material pleasure. Against those - or, rather, the vast majority - who confuse efficiency with frenzy, we propose the vaccine of an adequate portion of sensual gourmandise pleasures, to be taken with slow and prolonged enjoyment.

Appropriately, we will start in the kitchen, with Slow Food. To escape the tediousness of "fast-food", let us rediscover the rich varieties and aromas of local cuisines.

In the name of productivity, the 'fast life' has changed our lifestyle and now threatens our environment and our land (and city) scapes. Slow Food is the alternative, the avant-garde's riposte.

Real culture is here to be found. First of all, we can begin by cultivating taste, rather than impoverishing it, by stimulating progress, by encouraging international exchange programs, by endorsing worthwhile projects, by advocating historical food culture and by defending old-fashioned food traditions.

Slow Food assures us of a better quality lifestyle. With a snail purposely chosen as its patron and symbol, it is an idea and a way of life that needs much sure but steady support.

Arcigola Slow Food
via della Mendicità Istruita, 14
12042 Bra (Cn) - Italy
Tel. 0039 (172) 41 12 73 - 41 75 19 Fax 42 12 93

OSTERIE
D'ITALIA

Sussidiario del
mangiarbere all' italiana **1993**

Slow Food Editore

F.lli Speri

Via Fontana, 14
S. Pietro in Cariano (Vr) 37020
Tel. (045) 7701154
Fax (045) 770494

Owned by the Speri brothers Giuseppe, Benedetto, Eliseo and Carlo, it is one of the most renowned wineries in Valpolicella. The four brothers and their children continue the family wine-making tradition which originated in the early 19th century in Pedemonte where their ancestors made wine. The current-day winery was founded in 1874 and bottling began in the 1950s, much sooner than most neighboring growers. Tradition is the rule in the Speri house: they stopped using harsh chemical fertilizers over 15 years ago and continue to till the vineyards by machine and tractor and avoid the use of weed killers in between the vineyard rows. Speri also goes by the book when it comes to which indigenous types of grapes to grow and remains unconvinced by the fashions for international varieties. This continuity is carried over into the vinification where, despite having stainless steel vats for fermentation, the brothers still choose to keep the larger Slovenian oak barrels, which have until now kept the smaller barrique.

Valpolicella Classico 1991 DOC   🍇 ①
It's quite rare to taste a young Valpolicella this good: intense in color, it has typical aromas, with some pepper and hints of cherry.

Recioto della Valpolicella Classico   🍇 ②
I Comunai 1990 DOC
Sweet Recioto from the Valpolicella area is always drunk young. But sometimes it's worth waiting for, as in this case. With lots of clear aromas of grape must and fermentation, it still has room for improvement with time.

Valpolicella Classico Superiore   🍇 ①
La Roverina 1990 DOC
A quintessential Valpolicella wine, it has extremely mature fruit aromas and is rich and soft on the palate, for very pleasant drinkability.

Amarone della Valpolicella   🍇🍇🍇 ②
1986 DOC
Intense ruby red in color, it has refined and deep smokey, grapey aromas and is fat, rich, powerful and long-lasting on the palate. Certainly one of the best Amarone wines on the market.

F.lli Tedeschi

Fraz. Pedemonte, via Verdi, 4/a
S. Pietro in Cariano (Vr) 37020
Tel. (045) 7701487
Fax (045) 7704239

The Tedeschi brothers have found a happy balance: Renzo Tedeschi buys all of his grapes from his brother who owns 12 ha of vineyards in the growing areas of Monte Olmi, Monte Fontana and Capitel delle Lucchine, and which provide nearly all the grapes the winery needs. As a result, one brother tends the vines and supplies the raw materials, while the other dedicates himself to the vinification and commercialization. Only the Soave is made from bought-in grapes, purchased from the former cellarmaster at Anselmi in Monteforte, who owns of 12 ha of prime vineyards. In recent years, Renzo has made an incredible effort to modernize the winery, above all replacing those barrels which have given him preoccupations. Since then, Tedeschi wines have been considered among the best in the area. The vino da tavola Capitel San Rocco delle Lucchine is particularly notable, as well are the three Amarone wines: the regular, the Capitel Monte Olmi and the Fabriseria.

Valpolicella Classico   🍇 ①
Capitel delle Lucchine 1991 DOC
The "little brother" of the great red San Rocco turned out particularly well this year. Somewhat rustic in character, though well-structured and full-bodied enough, it may still improve with aging.

Amarone della Fabriseria   🍇🍇 ②
1988 DOC
Of Tedeschi's three Amarone wines, all of a par qualitatively, La Fabriseria is the most interesting this year. A well-orchestrated cuvée of grapes from different vineyards, it shows lots of freshness and fullness and a firm tannin backbone.

Capitel San Rocco   🍇🍇🍇 ②
delle Lucchine 1988
For years a "Vino di Ripasso", or wine made by passing over the still rich lees of a recioto, one of Tedeschi's best wines. Made with the same grapes as Valpolicella, it has considerable complexity and depth of flavor.

Recioto Classico   🍇 ②
Monte Fontane 1988 DOC
Tedeschi's sweet, but not too sweet, red wine is practically a monument in Valpolicella. Surely it is one of the most 'international' Recioto wines made.

Valpolicella Classico Superiore   🍇 ②
Capitel dei Nicalò 1988 DOC
A wonderful wine to match with food: garnet red in color, with clean and already mature aromas and a firm, pleasant taste texture. The breadth ot flavours make this a wine for all foods.

Vignalta e Ca' Lustra

Via S. Pietro, 50, loc. Faedo
Cinto Euganeo (Pd) 35030
Tel. (0429) 94128
Fax (0429) 644111

Vignalta and Ca'Lustra are actually two distinct wineries, whose respective owners decided to join forces a few years ago, to make and sell their wines. The two, Lucio Gomiero and Franco Zanovello, between them produce a very interesting selection of wines; the whites are made from Chardonnay and Sauvignon, while the reds are based on Cabernet Sauvignon and Merlot, in addition to small quantities of a prized Moscato-based wine. By far their strongpoint, their reds are surprizingly good, especially for an area that is otherwise unheard of for great wines. The grapes are harvested from the vulcanic soils of the Colli Euganei hills and are known for their elegance and vigour, especially in outstanding years like 1990. At present their whites have shown to be slightly inferior to their siblings.

Colli Euganei Cabernet 1990 DOC 🍇 ①
Ca' Lustra's 'little brother' is a great example of this winery's noble efforts. Though the Vigneto Ca' Lustra may have more appeal on the palate, this regular Cabernet still has an attractive price.

Colli Euganei Cabernet 🍇🍇 ①
Vigneti Ca' Lustra 1990 DOC
1990 was a great year for reds and this area was no exception. This Cabernet Vigneti Ca' Lustra recieves top honors for its color, body, texture and length.

Gemova 1988 🍇 ②
Vignalta's best red: warm with good fruit aromas, soft and very drinkable. An excellent, medium-bodied wine with a good potential for further development.

Le Vigne di San Pietro

Via S. Pietro, 23
Sommacampagna (Vr) 37066
Tel. (045) 510016
Fax (045) 8960701

Sergio and Carlo Nerozzi's winery has long since been considered one of Verona's most serious and dedicated producers. The estate vineyards, located within the DOC production zones of Bardolino and Bianco di Custoza, year in year out, produce wines which are consistently among the best of their types. The classic Bianco di Custoza especially lofts on high; meanwhile the house's best Vino da Tavola is Refolà, made from slightly raisined Cabernet Sauvignon grapes, similar to the way Amarone or Recioto is made locally. Both have been waning in recent years due to particularly unfavorable growing conditions, but, given the vintage years and the average quality level of the area, they still confirm San Pietro's top ranking. The two Rosso and Chiaretto styles of DOC Bardolino have maintained their indigenous character and continue to be good, solid buys; the new I Balconi Rossi is a more recent experiment with an interesting twist.

Bardolino Chiaretto 1991 DOC 🏵 ①
Similar in structure and drinkability to the Bardolino red, the Chiaretto has lots of fruity aromas and light scents of walnuts and hazelnuts, Among the best of its type for the vintage.

Bardolino 1991 DOC 🍇 ①
One of San Pietro's most succesful wines this year, it is fresh, fruity and clean, both on the nose and on the palate. Very good natured and easy to drink.

I Balconi Rossi 1990 🍇 ②
San Pietro's newest product, this blend of Bardolino and Cabernet has a fresh, fruity bouquet with lively green notes; full and savoury on the palate with an attractive bitter aftertaste.

Refolà 1988 🍇🍇 ③
95% Cabernet Sauvignon with a small addition of Cabernet Franc. Well-structured and refined in French oak casks; complex bouquet with clear tones of dried fruit. Body based on good material; long-lasting on the palate.

Zenato

Via S. Benedetto, 8
Peschiera del Garda (Vr) 37010
Tel. (045) 7550300
Fax (045) 6400449

The Zenato family of Peschiera have a long, family tradition of winemaking in the Lake Garda countryside, where they are currently active as winemakers and négociants. The Santa Cristina estate boasts 20 ha of vineyards on clay-loamish terrain, which is the best-suited soil to guarantee high quality wines in the Lugano area. For several years now, their Massoni wine has been their benchmark wine, consistently placed high among the best DOCs. Other top level products include their Amarone, their Bianco di Custoza Sole del Benaco and, above all, their wonderful Cabernet Sauvignon Santa Cristina. This latter wine particularily shows a capacity to reach even greater heights.

Bianco di Custoza ☙ ①
Sole del Benaco 1991 DOC
Brightly colored, with a light twist of carbon dioxide, it has fruity aromas and is clean, full-bodied and soft. It's a good ticket to success for the Zenato brand name.

Lugana Santa Cristina ☙☙ ①
Vigneto Massoni 1991 DOC
This single-yard Lugana wine is probably what made this winery famous. Extremely attractive in color, it has lots of fruit and spice, particularly of apples. Round and almost fat on the palate, it is very lingering.

Cabernet Sauvignon ☙ ②
Santa Cristina 1988
What a pleasant surprise to find such an excellent Cabernet Sauvignon in the Verona region. A harmonious ensemble of fruit and wood with creamy vanilla, it is full-bodied with some herbaceous tones.

Amarone 1986 DOC ☙☙ ①
This Zenato Amarone needs time to breathe before it opens up in the glass. But then it shows, as well as its bright intense color, beautiful aromas and a body both dense and soft. It persists well on the mouth.

Key to the symbols

Types of Wines

☙ White

🍇 Rosé

🍇 Red

Rating System

☙ An exemplary wine of its type with outstanding local character

🍇🍇 An international premium quality wine

🍇🍇🍇 A Top Wine, considered one of the 150 best wines in the world

The 'grape bunch' symbol is used to indicate the color of the wine; the number of bunches represents the quality rating assigned by the contributor

Price levels

① up to $ 9.99

② $ 10.00 - $ 14.99

③ $ 15.00 - $ 24.99

④ $ 25.00 or more

The 'ex-cellar', or direct from the producer, bottle prices, are calculated in US dollars and are intended only as an approximate guide

Entries are arranged in alphabetical order by country, region and winery or producer name.

LEBANON

The Middle East, we are often told, is the cradle of wine. In what is today Lebanon, wine production goes back to the time of the Phoenicians, who are said to have introduced the practise to Europe. One sure sign that wine stood in high regard for the ancients of this region is the existence of the Temple of Bacchus in the Bekaa Valley.

The Bekaa Valley remains today the source of most if not all of Lebanon's wine. The valley is at an altitude of about 1,000 meters, lying between two mountain ranges, and its soil (gravelly with a limestone base) and climate (summer temperatures average around 25°C) are well suited to the vine's growth. What is not so suitable are war and shifting boundaries, which have made life for the sole Lebanese representative of the international wine community, Château Musar, exceedingly difficult over the past ten years.

Principal grape varieties are Cabernet Sauvignon, Cinsault and Syrah for red wines, Chardonnay and Sauvignon for whites. Vine diseases are almost non-existent, so if one could only eradicate the disease of the human mind this would be a viticultural paradise.

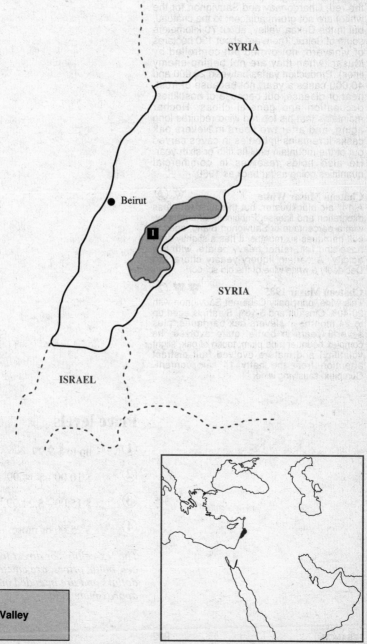

SYRIA

● Beirut

1

SYRIA

ISRAEL

1   Bekaa Valley

Château Musar

Ghazir
U.K.office
Tel. (081) 941 8311
Fax (081) 941 7843

Gaston Hochar founded this winery in 1930, in an early 18th century castle 20 kilometers north of Beirut at the foot of Mt. Lebanon. Today it is run by his sons, Serge and Ronald, the elder of whom, Serge, studied oenology at the University of Bordeaux and has travelled the wine world. The grapes (Cabernet Sauvignon, Cinsault and Syrah for the red, Chardonnay and Sauvignon for the white) are not grown adjacent to the château, but in the Bekaa Valley, about 70 kilometers south of Beirut. There are about 130 hectares of vineyard, not owned but controlled by Musar (when they are not behind enemy lines). Production varies between 20,000 and 40,000 cases a year, not because of frost, heat or disease, but because of hostilities, occupation and general choas. Hochar maintains that his top red wine requires long aging, and after two years in Nevers oak casks it remains in bottles in caves carved out of the mountain until its fifth or sixth year. He also holds reserves in commercial quantities going as far back as 1960.

Château Musar White   🍇 ②
A 14° alc blockbuster, but this time with less integration and finesse. Principally Chardonnay, with a percentage of Sauvignon Blanc, aged in oak barriques six months, it has a slightly tired nose and full, rather heavy palate, with low acidity. A certain liquory-yeasty character. Decidedly a white wine of the old school.

Château Musar 1985   🍇🍇 ②
This wine, principally Cabernet Sauvignon with 20-40% Cinsault and 5-10% Syrah, is aged up to 24 months in Nevers oak barriques, plus several years in bottle; quite evolved. Its complex bouquet (ripe plum, touch of oak, slight volatility) and mature evolved fruit distract attention from the hefty 14° alc content. Complex, satisfying wine.

Price levels

①	up to $ 9.99
②	$ 10.00 - $ 14.99
③	$ 15.00 - $ 24.99
④	$ 25.00 or more

The 'ex-cellar', or direct from the producer, bottle prices, are calculated in US dollars and are intended only as an approximate guide

MEXICO

Until just recently, Mexican wines were little more than a whim for pioneers, or a curiosity for wine collectors, and were regarded with skepticism in terms of quality. Today experts must admit that the quality is there and improving. Wine consumption is low, but is consistently increasing, especially in restaurants. Ordering a bottle of Mexican wine was once considered a pompous thing to do, now they are looked upon with due reverence and elegance.

The Conquistadores that landed in America found that many different types of vines grew in the wild but none actually produced grapes. Of course, there could be no Catholic mass without wine, nor could they drink plain water with their meals, so they began planting vines in addition to growing wheat and raising hogs as their main food staples. They eventually got carried away in their enthusiasm, however. In fact, on March 20th, 1524, Fernando Cortés ruled that all Spanish who had been assigned indigenous workers (in other words, slaves) had to plant one thousand vines for every one hundred slaves they had, planting up to 5,000 vines. Few actually abided by the rule, but, it did, after all, mark the start of a flourishing if not fluctuating vine-growing history. After this initial boom, another ruling arrived from Madrid in 1610 that in practise, ordered all further production to cease in order to protect and defend Spanish wines. Furthermore, given the economy's ups and downs throughout the colonization period, production was haphazard and irregular and technically antiquated. Political instability during the Revolution did not help matters, inevitably. Thus, during the peaceful Porfirian era, from 1877 to 1911, French wines had gained in popularity. With new domestic political stability found in 1940, as well as strict protectionist program, viticulture was finally able to develop in the country. More recently, however, free importation of the wines from other countries in 1982 and competition from neighboring countries, shipping across cheaply priced bulk wines, created a difficult situation. Many wineries went under, but for those who survived it served as a hard learnt lesson. Indeed, quality is at the heart of successful winemaking.

National wine production was approximately 25 million lt in 1982 and in ten years fell to 21 million. The most important wine zones are the northern part of Baja California, along the border with the US, and the states of Durango, Zacatecas, Coahuila, Aguascalientes and Quereato to the south. There have been considerable financial investments and many foreign wine technicians brought in, many of which are Italian or who have studied enology there or other world-wine regions elsewhere. More and more consumers are learning about wine and are encouraged to try different styles of wines. Mexicans are building a certain confidence and pride in their domestic wines and products, which are better today than ever before. Mexican food is already very popular in the United States, and now it is beginning to catch in other countries. With the cuisine, new channels for wine exportation are opening, as well. These are just a few of the conditions that have helped to set the stage for Mexico's wines and the promising future of wine-growing ahead. As progress sets in, however, so does the need for wine-making legislation. In fact, the laws regarding name and origin for wine areas and production methods and quality standards in general are not very clear and need redefinition.

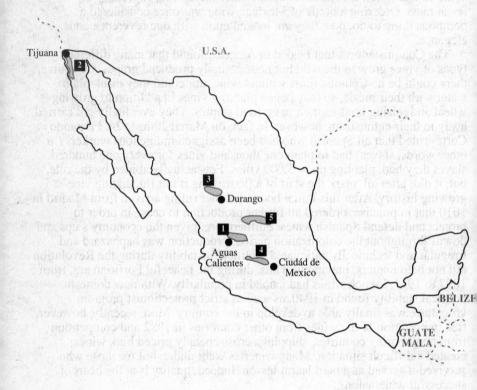

Tijuana

U.S.A.

3

Durango

5

1

Aguas
Calientes

4

Ciudád de
Mexico

BELIZE

GUATE
MALA

1	Aguas Calientes
2	Baja California
3	Durango
4	Queretaros
5	Zocateca

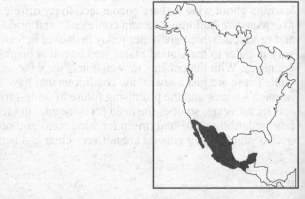

L.A. Cetto Productos de Uva

Ave. Constitucion sur s/n
Tijuana, B.C. 2200
Tel. (85) 7014-3031
Fax (85) 3552

Cetto is a winery with a rich wine-making heritage. The founding grandfather, Angelo, left Italy to settle in Mexico in 1926. Today his son, Luis, manages the firm together with his 24-year old grandson, also Luis. They have always produced for some of the better known Mexican wineries but began bottling their own in 1983. LA Cetto owns and operates 1,230 ha of vineyards in Baja California, 800 of which are in the Gaudalupe valley, 300 in the San Vincent region, 70 in Tecate and 60 in Santa Rosa. The modern cellar equipment includes a centrifuge which can handle 40 tons of grapes an hour. They produce a remarkable variety of products, from sparkling wines to Cinzano Vermouth, under license of Marone Cinzano in Italy, which also licenses them to handle the Dubonnet, Gilbey's Gin and Long John Whiskey brands. In the past few years, the firm has taken over other smaller vineyards and today produces more than 50% of all the wines in Mexico, not to mention a substantial amount of other alcholic beverages. Milanese enologist Camillo Magoni has been the director since 1965.

Fumé blanc   🍷 ①
This style of wine is very popular in California with its pale, cheerful, "alegro" style and easy drinkability. In fact, it is one of Mexico's best-selling young-drinking wines.

Chardonnay Réserve 1986   🍷 ②
This classic Chardonnay from a particularly favorable vintage has been fermented and aged at length in oak casks. It has a distinctive flavor of dried fruits, spice and the typical spicy, vanilla aromas.

Nebbiolo Riserva 1986   🍷 ②
It is interesting to notice how the change in environments affects this wine, here made from the best vines imported from Piemonte. Bright, clean garnet color, it may lack the typical aroma of violets, but it is rich with other delicate floral aromas. Dry and intense, it should cellar and drink well in years to come.

Cabernet Sauvignon   🍷 ①
A non-vintage wine, its style has remained consistent in the past few years. 10 days' fermentation in 400-hl temperature controlled vats, it is aged 18 months in oak casks and bottle ages for one year before release. With an intense varietal aroma, it is mellow, chewy and fairly long-lasting on the finish.

Petite Syrah   🍷 ①
As in California, the grapes are left to macerate briefly (5 days) before fermentation and aging for 6 months in oak casks and 3 months' fining in the bottle. The end result is a pleasant, crisp wine, if not too grapey, that has a good, rich color and lots of freshness.

Casa Pedro Domecq

Avenida Mexico 337
Coyoaca
Tel. 5 (325) 9292
Fax 5 (554) 4432

The fifth generation of the famous Domecq family in Spain, Pedro Domecq Gonzàles settled in Mexico in 1925 and founded what was to become a benchmark winery for the nation. The economic base of Domecq is inarguably their impressive Brandy industry (including the famous Presidente and Don Pedro brands). But Domecq also deserves credit for the leaps and bounds made in winemaking progress. With Spanish technicians and considerable investments, they were able to increase the area planted to vine from 2,000 hectares in 1958 to the present 60,000. Although considered the most important estate in Mexico, it does not own immeasurable tracts of vineyards and grows relatively little fruit itself. In fact, each year they purchase grapes from many small and medium-sized growers and process the grapes in their modern facilities located in the beautiful Calafia valley. 36% of the grapes are white, mainly Chenin Blanc and Chardonnay, and the rest are red, including Petite Syrah, Cabernet Sauvignon, Ruby Cabernet Zinfandel and others in lesser quantities. Antonio Ariza Canadilla, the company's outgoing president, is originally from Andalucia; Mexican technical director and cellarmaster, Eustaquio Ibarra, works together with Italian enologist, Camillo Magoni, whose services are also employed at Productos de Uva.

Blanc de Blancs 1991   🍷 ①
Bright, very pale yellow, it has the typical appley, lemon varietal aromas from the Chenin Blanc. Refreshing and pleasant to drink.

Château Domecq 1991   🍷 ②
A pleasant off-dry Chardonnay with lots of fresh fruit and a long, lingering finish on the palate.

Los Reyes 1989   🍷 ①
The country's most popular red wine, it is lively in color, fresh, light, and a bit astringent on the palate. Historically, it was the Domecq house's first sample of success, selling 50 cases of the 1955 vintage.

Cabernet Sauvignon 1988   🍷 ①
Very appealing and drinkable, this wine has great character, with a solid, round bouquet. It spends two years in 110 lt barrels and oak cask before bottle aging for two more.

Château Domecq 1987   🍷 ②
A Cabernet Sauvignon with some Merlot and Ruby Cabernet. After fermenting in stainless steel vats, the wine ages three years in cask and another three in bottle, in climatized cellars kept at 12-15°C. Full-bodied, with a fruity, oaky bouquet that is still slightly closed. Sure to age well, as the 1972 is very drinkable now.

Monte Xanic

Av. Marina 10
Ensenada, Baja California
Tel. (667) 83146
Fax (667) 40028

The youngest winery in the country, Monte Xanic was founded in 1988 by five Mexican wine-lovers with a quest for quality. With 60-ha of vineyards in the Guadalupe valley, the winery uses only the finest wine-making eqipmente, most of which is imported from Italy. Their first investment is still far from rendering a proft, but the partners are in no hurrty. They are busy trying to produce the best wines in Mexico. The well-trained enologist and director Hans Backhoff, first chose to focus on making a fine Chardonnay aged in new oak casks. Next came the first red which was a convincing Cabernet Sauvignon 1988 which has already sold out. Next still came two whites, the Chenin Blanc and a little Savignon Blanc, both fermented temperature-controlled stainless steel vats. The managing director and partner Tomas Fernandez hopes to achieve a 360,000 annual bottle production. A Merlot is on its way and Malbec has been planted.

Chardonnay 1991   🍇 ③
Made from eight acres of low-yielding vineyards, this wine has a complex bouquet with buttery aromas of almonds and chocolate, along with flowers and fruit. Well-balanced and well-made, with a drylingering finish, sure to cellar several years.

Chenin Blanc 1991   🍇 ①
Pale, clean yellow, with greenish highlights, it has the classic floral, fruity aromas. More full-bodied, round and slightly sweet than normally expected of this grape and type of wine. It has a glorious finish with a hint of bitterness.

Sauvignon Blanc 1991   🍇 ②
Bright straw-yellow with amber reflections, the intense bouquet has distinct floral notes with a tropical twist. Bone dry on the palate, with a pleasant oakiness from the long aging in cask.

Cabernet Sauvignon 1989   🍇 ③
With exceptional maturity for such a young wine, it shows backbone and a firm structure, good aromatic complexity and great drinkability. Though excellent now, it promises to be extraordinary in a few years.

MOROCCO

The Romans were the first to introduce the vine to Morocco. The conquering legionnaires (and heavy-tipplers they were) were eager to plant vine stakes as their flag was hoisted in the name of colonization. Vines thrived in the ideal climate and soil conditions and spread rapidly until the fall of the Roman Empire. With the rise of Islam, however, wine became taboo and cultivation ceased. As the 20th century approached, the French and Spanish began their imperialistic colonization, enabling the vine to return to its once-prestigious place. When Morocco gained its independence in 1956 the government instituted a quality-control system based on the French system. Neighboring Algeria and Tunisia followed close behind. Within 15 years, the surface area of vineyard had stretched to over 80,000 hectares and in 1973 the wine industry was officially recognised as a national industry. Muslim prohibition has since reduced the vineyard area to 20,000 hectares distributed throughout the four provinces of Meknès-Fès, Rabat-Casablanca, Oujda-Berkane and Marrakech.

Although accounting for a mere fraction of the total production, still dominated by bulk wines for blending, premium-quality Moroccan wines carry the Appellation d'Origine Garantie seal (AOG). The main grape varieties include the traditional North African classics of French origin, like Carignan, Cinsault and Grenache or those of Spanish origin, like Alicante. Other international-style grapes are also taking well. The latter are used to make the local rosé wines, or vins gris as they are referred to here, and some promising red wines.

MOROCCO

Rabat

Fes

Meknès

1

2

Marakech

3

4

ALGERIA

MAURITANIA

1 Oujda
2 Meknès-Fes
3 Rabat-Casablanca
4 Marakech

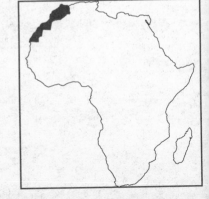

Meknès Vins

11 rue Ibn Khaldoun
Meknes
Tel. (212) 522052
Fax (212) 527506

Created in 1976 and owned by Mr. Brahin Zniber, a successful Moroccan businessman, this is a large, impressively equipped winery with refrigeration and centrifuges in both the production plants, as well as a modern bottling line and storage capacity for well over 200,000 hectoliters. The winery owns 500 hectares of vineyard in the Guerrouane and Beni M'tir appellation regions and has access to the fruit from a further 450 hectares. Meknès Vins are probably the most active producers in Morocco in respect of seeking exports, selling over 1,000,000 of their 13,000,000 bottle production abroad (about 50% of the national total). With a 20 million bottle capacity Meknès Vins has the potential for considerable further growth, providing they can find the markets. The grape varieties for the present remain those traditional in North Africa (Carignan, Cinsault, Alicante and Grenache) although they are in the early stages of experimenting with Chardonnay, Syrah, Merlot and Cabernet.

Guerrouane 1989 ♥ ①
This appellation or AOG red wine is a blend of Carignan, Cinsault, Alicante and Grenache, in the traditional style of North Africa and southern France, though vinification is according to modern principles. Medium-depth purply-ruby color and as pleasant if somewhat understated bouquet. Easy, jammy fruit, very soft in terms of tannin and acid, puts it in the pleasant quaffing class.

NEW ZEALAND

A journey by car from New Zealand's most northerly wine region to the most southerly would take over 24 hours, including three hours by boat between the islands. It is quicker to travel the length of France.

Despite the moderating influence of a maritime climate there is a considerable difference between the wines produced in the North Island (who's principal zones are Auckland, Hawke's Bay, Waikato, Wairarapa, Bay of Plenty and Poverty Bay) and those made in the South (Nelson, Marlborough, Canterbury and Central Otago). Later ripening varieties such as Cabernet Sauvignon thrive in the north, while the earlier ripening Gewürztraminer, Pinot Noir and Chardonnay respond well to the cool southerly growing conditions. In the North Island Sauvignon Blanc tends to produce ripe, luscious wine while in the south it is aromatic, zestier and more herbaceous.

Although vines were planted in New Zealand as long ago as 1831 the modern wine industry really only began its rapid evolution 20 years ago. In that time the national vineyard has expanded fourfold to over 6000 hectares and the quality of New Zealand wine has gained international respect. Exports which were non existent two decades ago now account for over 15% of total production.

New Zealand has nearly 150 winemakers although 90% of the country's wine is made by just three companies; Montana (includes Penfolds and the McDonalds Winery), Corbans (includes Cooks) and the Villa Maria group (includes Vidals and Esk Valley). The rest are mostly small family-owned wineries. Although there are a growing number of wineries which specialize in one wine style most offer a range of wines made from several grape varieties which are sometimes grown in different wine regions. During the vintage grape must is often transported many hundreds of kilometers from vineyard to winery in large tankers. Most of the country's wine is produced from grapes grown by independent growers who sell their harvest to wineries, usually under a long term contract. A number of small wineries make wine only from their own vineyard.

Irrigation is permitted although its use is limited to a few areas of low rainfall. New Zealand has no restriction on chaptalisation although the practise is little used in premium wines.

New Zealand labelling laws require that wines must comprise at least 85% of the grape variety, vintage and region, district or vineyard indicated on the label. The alcohol and volume of each wine must also be shown. It is now quite common for winemakers to show a wide range of technical information including grape sugar at harvest, grape acid, date of harvest, plus the wine acid, sugar and pH. Generic terms such as "claret" or "Chablis" are now seldom used and may be outlawed very soon. The term Champagne has already been outlawed on New Zealand wine labels.

The most commonly planted variety is the Müller-Thurgau, a high cropping variety which sustains an active winecask industry. The second most popular variety is Chardonnay (10%), followed by Sauvignon Blanc (8.5%), Cabernet Sauvignon (5%) and Chenin Blanc (4.8%).

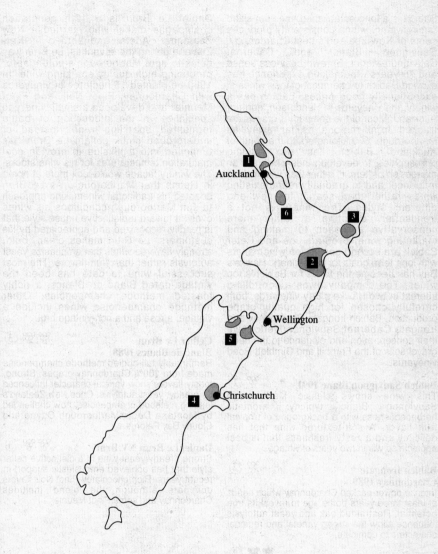

Auckland

3

6

2

Wellington

5

Christchurch

4

1	Auckland
2	Hawke's Bay
3	Poverty Bay
4	Canterbury
5	Marlborough
6	Waikato

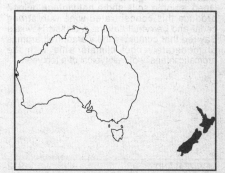

Babich

Babich Road
Henderson, Auckland
Tel. (09) 8337859
Fax (09) 8339929

Babich is a long established, medium sized family winery which consistently produces some of New Zealand's best Chardonnay, Sauvignon Blanc and Cabernet Sauvignon/Merlot. Shrewd business sense and 75 years winemaking experience has allowed Babich to offer most of their wines at exceptionally good prices. Babich has a winery and vineyards in Henderson, north of Auckland. Most of the company's grapes are trucked from regions as far away as Marlborough, 600 kilometers to the south of Auckland. Babich has two guiding philosophies; to develop wines which are an expression of "terroir" rather than winemaking influence, and to gradually refine existing wines rather than search for new and different styles. The winery is not a trendsetter, adopting a rather more conservative approach to making and marketing wine. Brothers Joe and Peter Babich are second generation winemakers with long term goals for their winery. Hawke's Bay has become the focus for Babich's top wines. The company owns a controlling interest in two Hawke's Bay vineyards, both carefully chosen for high quality grape production. Babich Irongate Chardonnay and Irongate Cabernet Sauvignon/Merlot owe their concentration and elegance to the deep gravel soils of the Fernhill and Gimblett Road vineyards.

Babich Sauvignon Blanc 1991
This wine shows classic Marlborough Sauvignon Blanc typicity; aromatic herbaceousness with a background of tropical fruit flavor. A soft-textured wine that has delicacy and a zesty freshness that is best appreciated within two years of vintage.

Babich Irongate
Chardonnay 1989
Intense power-packed Chardonnay which needs at least three years bottle age to reveal its true potential. Restrained oak and yeast autolysis influence allow the strong varietal and regional characters to dominate.

Irongate
Cabernet Sauvignon/Merlot 1989
Deep, shingle soils and a hot vintage helped produce this concentrated wine with strong cedar and berryfruit flavors. A classic Hawke's Bay red that combines the vibrant fruit aromas of moderately cool climate wine with the aromatic intensity of fruit typical of a top year.

Cellier Le Brun

Terrace Road
Renwick, Marlborough
Tel. (03) 5728859
Fax (03) 5728814

Daniel Le Brun is a 12th generation champagne maker who married a New Zealander, Adele, and settled in New Zealand during the seventies. Le Brun was quick to spot Marlborough's potential for producing high quality sparkling wine. In 1980 he planted 15 hectares of vineyards with Chardonnay, Pinot Noir, and Pinot Meunier and developed a small winery to specialize in the production of bottle fermented sparkling wine. Instead of underground chalk cellars Le Brun has tunnelled into a hillside to provide cool maturation temperatures for his wine stocks. The winery facade would look more at home in Reims that Marlborough. As Le Brun adapted his traditional winemaking approach to suit Marlborough conditions his wines evolved toward a distinctive house style that is readily recognized and appreciated by his customers. Le Brun makes clean, bold, strongly flavored wines that emphasize yeast autolysis rather than fruit flavors. The most successful wine to date has been the vintage-dated Blanc de Blancs, a richly toasted methode champenoise. Other méthode champenoise wines include a vintage, a rosé and a non-vintage brut.

Cellier Le Brun
Blanc de Blancs 1988
Remarkably full-bodied methode champenoise made from 100% Chardonnay grapes. Strong, toasty flavors show varietal character influenced by bready, yeast autolysis. Once New Zealand's leading methode champenoise, now challenged by Montana Deutz Marlborough Cuvee and Cloudy Bay Pelorus.

Daniel Le Brun NV Brut
Strong bready/yeast wine in a distinctive cellar style that has achieved enthusiastic support in recent years. Rich chocolatey Pinot Noir flavors dominate although the blend includes Chardonnay and some Pinot Meunier.

Cloudy Bay

Jacksons Road
Blenheim, Marlborough
Tel. (03) 5728914
Fax (03) 5728065

When David Hohnen, Cape Mentelle's owner and winemaker, tasted a New Zealand Sauvignon Blanc for the first time in 1984, he immediately realized the enormous potential that this country had for producing rich, aromatic whites. In 1985 he visited the region and rented a winery to make the first vintage of Cloudy Bay Sauvignon Blanc. The following year he had already built his winery to satisfy numerous requests from Australian, British and New Zealand merchants. This exceptional Sauvignon Blanc is still so popular that it is often sold out before having finished fermentation. Capitalizing on the success of it's Sauvignon Blanc, Cloudy Bay produces a high quality Chardonnay, Cabernet Sauvignon/Merlot and a methode champenoise sparkling wine from Marlborough region grapes. In 1990 French champagne house Veuve Clicquot joined Cape Mentelle and Cloudy Bay allowing a program of expansion.The amazing success of Cloudy Bay has surely contributed to raise the image of Marlborough as a great wine region and at the same time bring attention to the excellence and high quality of New Zealand's wines.

Chardonnay 1990 ♟♟ ③
Powerful, complex Chardonnay, with a firm backbone of acidity balanced by richness in extracts and alcohol. Tight, integrated wine with the potential to age very well indeed.

Pelorus Methode Champenoise 1988 ♟ ③
The second vintage of Cloudy Bay's highly acclaimed methode champenoise wine has as much strength and character as the first but offers broader, softer flavors with obvious malolactic influence. A blend of Chardonnay and Pinot Noir in approximately equal proportions.

Cabernet Merlot 1990 ♟ ③
Cloudy Bay has a strong reputation for its whites though founder, David Hohnen, first gained fame for the reds of his family winery Cape Mentelle, in Western Australia. Cool growing conditions have produced an elegant, supple wine with notable herbaceous influence behind strong berry-fruit characters. Moderately complex wine which demands several years bottle age.

Cloudy Bay ♟♟♟ ②
Sauvignon Blanc 1991
The best ever vintage of the best New Zealand Sauvignon Blanc. A strong flavored wine with typical aromatic herbaceousness and red capsicum/gooseberry characters contrasting with a riper tropical fruit influence. A 15% blend of Sémillon adds a subtle fresh cut grass flavor to make the wine more assertive but less varietal than examples from other Marlborough producers. Approximately 20% of the wine was fermented in new oak barriques, an influence that is barely discernible but adds to the wine's overall complexity. Cloudy Bay helped put New Zealand Sauvignon Blanc on the world wine map. Other winemakers have capitalized on Cloudy Bay's phenomenal success by planting Sauvignon Blanc vines in the Marlborough region and yet none have duplicated this understated and stylishly complex wine. Although Cloudy Bay Sauvignon has only been made since 1985 the style has already demonstrated an ability to develop well with bottle age. The strong fruit flavors are very attractive in youth but after five years the wine becomes finer, more integrated and complex.

Collards

303 Lincoln Road
Henderson, Auckland
Tel. (09) 8388341
Fax (09) 8375840

Collards is a small Auckland-based family winery operated by father Lionel, and his two sons, Bruce and Geoffrey. Their meticulous attention to detail and almost fanatical pursuit of quality has produced a series of very successful varietal wines. In addition to their own Auckland vineyards, Collards buy grapes from all the main areas. A close relationship with contract growers and care of their own vineyard provides high quality grapes. Chardonnay is their most successful wine. Collards produce Chardonnay from each of the country's four major viticultural regions: Auckland, Gisborne, Hawke's Bay and Marlborough. They have won top awards with all four wines, a remarkable feat which probably qualifies them for the title of the country's best Chardonnay maker. The Collards formula is simplicity itself; provide minimal winemaking influence and allow the regional and varietal fruit flavors to dominate. When other winemakers were producing heavily oaked wine with strong yeast autolysis and malolactic influence the Collards wines tasted of Chardonnay and not oak barrels. Heavily oaked wines have fallen from favor and the Collards style now reigns supreme. Collards other significant success has been with the more humble Chenin Blanc grape.

Collards Dry Chenin Blanc 1991   🍇 ①
Full-flavored varietal wine with crisp acidity. Un-oaked, with intriguing aromas and flavors and good potential for bottle development.

Collards Hawke's Bay   🍇🍇 ②
Chardonnay 1991
Strong fruit flavors, with hints of peach, apple and tropical fruit, are flattered by the subtle use of sweet, spicy oak. Ripe Chardonnay with style and cellaring potential.

Rothesay Chardonnay 1991   🍇 ③
Collards Rothesay vineyard, north of the city of Auckland, produces several top wine styles, the best of which is Rothesay Chardonnay. A strong-flavored and complex wine, it is Collards best of four regional Chardonnay styles.

Coopers Creek

Main Road, State Highway 16
Huapai, Auckland
Tel. (09) 4128560
Fax (09) 4128375

Coopers Creek was established in 1982 to produce high quality wines for a growing market. The winery achieved rapid recognition for its wines by winning many top awards at local wine competitions. Owner Andrew Hendry chooses to make wines that he likes to drink in styles that suit food. Apart from an occasional botrytized Riesling all Coopers Creek wines are dry. Most are made from one grape variety. Quality is achieved through grape and wine selection. Coopers Creek has a policy of growing grapes in the region where they perform best. After extensive research Hendry chose Huapai as the source of Cabernet Sauvignon and Merlot; Gisborne for Chardonnay, Gewürztraminer and Chenin Blanc; Hawke's Bay for Cabernet Franc, Cabernet Sauvignon, Riesling and Pinot Noir, and Marlborough for Sauvignon Blanc. Hendry and his winemaker, Kym Crawford, try to emphasize the regional characteristics of their wines and are careful not to mask fruit flavors with excessive oak, malolactic or yeast influence. The wines of Coopers Creek are always good, and often excellent.

Coopers Creek   🍇 ②
Rhine Riesling 1991
Hawke's Bay's finest Rhine Riesling with strong fruit flavors that show a touch of honeyed complexity from botrytis influence. Past vintages clearly demonstrate an ability to improve with at least five year's bottle age.

Fumé Blanc 1991   🍇 ②
Oak matured Sauvignon Blanc from the Hawke's Bay region. A lush, North Island wine with hints of honeysuckle and melon with typical Sauvignon herbaceousness. Oak influence offers complexity without dominating fruit flavors.

Swamp Reserve   🍇🍇 ③
Chardonnay 1990
Coopers Creek's most successful label with a history of top awards for past vintages. A stylish Hawke's Bay Chardonnay showing the benefit of long oak maturation and good fruit concentration. Classic Hawke's Bay style with strength and elegance.

Corbans

Great North Road
Henderson, Auckland
Tel. (09) 8373390
Fax (09) 8360005.

Established in 1902 by a Lebanese winemaking family, Corbans is now a division of Magnum Corporation and the second largest winery in the country. Corbans make a wide range of wines to suit all tastes and market segments, from low-priced three-liter winecasks to expensive small production wines with single vineyard labels. The company's brands include the widely exported Cooks label and Robard & Butler, a premium brand which enjoys strong support from the domestic market. Corbans entered the Marlborough region a decade after Montana planted the first vines there in 1973. The company has established a solid reputation with it's Stoneleigh Vineyard label and other Private Bin wines made from Marlborough grapes. Corbans 1986 Private Bin Noble Rhine Riesling is the only wine ever to have won New Zealand's most prestigious wine award, the THC Trophy, on two occasions. Corbans was New Zealand's first wine exporter, beginning with a small shipment to Canada in 1961. Export markets now include Britain, USA, Sweden, Japan and Australia. Corbans crushes about 30% of the country's grape crop. From that large base it is possible to select premium grapes for small scale, high quality wine production.

Stoneleigh Sauvignon Blanc 1992   ☙ ①
A cool 1992 vintage produced this lighter, leaner and more herbaceous wine than in previous years. An aromatic wine with strong varietal flavor that shows pronounced grassiness and muted tropical fruit flavors.

Corbans Stoneleigh Vineyards   ☙ ①
Rhine Riesling 1991
Zesty, cool-climate Reisling with a hint of botrytis influence for extra complexity. A medium dry wine in a "Spätlese" style but with more weight and flavor than the German equivalent.

Corbans Private Bin   ☙ ②
Chardonnay 1989
Full-bodied Chardonnay from the Marlborough region with more flesh and flavor than is typically found in wines from this area. Strong oak, yeast autolysis and malolactic influence add further complexity.

Delegat's

Hepburn Road
Henderson, Auckland
Tel. (09) 8360129
Fax (09) 8363282

Delegat's is one of New Zealand's larger family-owned wineries. In response to the growing demand for premium New Zealand wines Delegat's have gradually rationalised their once large product range to focus on premium varietals from two of the country's top regions, Hawke's Bay and Marlborough. By New Zealand standards Delegat's is a medium sized winery. Their larger than average production has helped reduce prices and allowed the company to develop a buoyant export market. The Hawke's Bay wines are marketed under two labels. The premium Winemakers Reserve label is a selection of the best wines produced in limited quantities. All are matured in small oak barriques. Winemakers Reserve wines include Sauvignon Blanc, Chardonnay, Cabernet Sauvignon and Merlot. Most of the Hawke's Bay wine is bottled under a regional varietal label; Sauvignon Blanc, Chardonnay and Cabernet Sauvignon/Merlot. All are lower priced wines made for early consumption. Delegat's market their Marlborough wines under the Oyster Bay label. A zesty Sauvignon Blanc and mellow, oak-matured Oyster Bay Chardonnay were enthusiastically received on the domestic and export market after their launch in 1991.

Delegat's Proprietor's Reserve   ☙ ②
Chardonnay 1990
Big luscious Chardonnay with peach and nectarine fruit flavors supported by savory toasty oak. Seductively drinkable now but will age well for up to five years.

Proprietors Reserve   ☙ ②
Late Harvest Rhine Riesling 1989
Some botrytis influence provides a rich, honeyed background to luscious Rhine Riesling varietal character. Heavy, concentrated wine with an almost syrupy texture.

Proprietors Reserve   ❦ ②
Cabernet Sauvignon 1990
Savory, developed wine with firm tannins and some herbal influence which adds complexity to berryfruit flavors. A rather green, cool climate style that reflects cool ripening conditions in Hawke's Bay, one of the countries best red wine districts.

Hunter's

Raupara Road
Blenheim, Marlborough
Tel. (03) 5728489
Fax (03) 5728457

Hunter's is one of Marlborough's star wineries with an outstanding record of medal awards at local and international wine competitions. They boast super-stylish Sauvignon Blanc, lean and elegant Chardonnay, vibrant Riesling, and even a luscious botrytized Chardonnay, New Zealand's most expensive wine. Credit for Hunter's wine quality must go to the late Ernie Hunter for having the vision to establish the winery and vineyards on their present site; his widow Jane Hunter whose viticultural training provides meticulous vine management; Australian wine consultant Tony Jordan who has supervised the development of Hunter's wines; and the winemaking team. They make two styles: one is fermented and matured in oak barriques and another, bottled without any oak contact. Both are distinguished by riper fruit flavors and less herbaceousness than is typically found in other examples of Marlborough Sauvignon Blanc. Hunter's may be better known for Sauvignon Blanc, but their flagship wine is certainly Chardonnay, a wine of real strength, style and longevity, a consistent winner at local and international wine competitions.

Hunter's 🍇🍇 ②
Sauvignon Blanc Oak Aged 1991
An impressive wine with true Marlborough style only slightly more complex with a nuance between grassy and aromatic. Oak influence flatters the strong fruit flavors and adds an extra dimension to match with food than the non-oaked version.

Hunter's Chardonnay 1990 🍇 ②
Fine-flavored Marlborough Chardonnay with good mealy complexity and an aromatic herbaceous influence. Truly elegant wine with subtle oak and impeccable balance. A wine with obvious cellaring potential.

Cabernet Sauvignon 1991 🍷 ②
Cool climate Cabernet Sauvignon with a minty, herbaceous influence behind strong berryfruit flavors. Rich, moderately complex wine that deserves to be enjoyed within three to four years of vintage.

Kumeu River

2 Highway 16
Kumeu, Auckland
Tel. (09) 4128415
Fax (09) 4127627

Heavy clay soil and hard summer rains do not make the Kumeu region ideal for producing high quality wines. In spite of this, Kumeu River makes some of New Zealand's finest Chardonnay, Cabernet Sauvignon/Merlot and high class Sauvignon Blanc. Credit for the success of this small family-run winery goes to the creativity of winemaker-grape grower Michael Brajkovich, a second generation New Zealander of Yugoslavian origin. He links his scientific background with European winemaking experience to create surprisingly high quality wines. Brajkovich holds a degree from Roseworthy Agricultural College where he graduated at the top of his class. He also has the privilege of being New Zealand's first Master of Wine. With unusual vine support and pruning techniques he is able to reduce the exuberant leaf growth, typical of Kumeu River vineyards, leaving his grapes with more concentrated flavors. Harvesting is done by hand, whites are crushed in whole bunches and fermentation is by natural yeasts only. Not following the typical New Zealand style the Kumeu River winemaking techniques are more European than New World.

Sauvignon 1991 🍇 ②
Not a typical New Zealand Sauvignon but a very stylish dry white with individual style. Oak fermentation has blurred varietal intensity but added complexity and richness to produce a wine that in some respects is more like a Chardonnay.

Kumeu River Chardonnay 1990 🍇🍇 ③
The excellent 1989 Chardonnay won a trophy at the International Wine Challenge in London in 1991. The 1990 is similar to the previous vintage, has a high concentration of fruit, an elegant toasted oak influence and supple creamy body.

Merlot/Cabernet Sauvignon 1990 🍷 ③
Deep, complex wine with hints of cherry, chocolate, leather and coffee indicating Merlot dominance. Integrated spicy oak flavors add character and further complexity. A mellow, sophisticated wine that will improve well with bottle age.

Martinborough Vineyards

Princess Street
Martinborough
Tel. (06) 3069955
Fax (06) 3069217

Martinborough is a tiny wine region near the southern tip of the North Island. Established a decade ago the region today supports a little over 100 hectares of vineyards which supply about a dozen winemakers. The most famous of these is the winery which bears the region's name. Martinborough Vineyards is a small producer with a big reputation for making the country's finest Pinot Noir. Winemaker Larry McKenna, has made wine in Burgundy, attended international Pinot Noir conferences and studied every work on the subject in an attempt to understand wine's most fickle and challenging grape variety. The results speak for themselves. In 1988, 1989 and 1990 Martinborough Vineyards won the prize for making New Zealand's top Pinot Noir (they have not entered the competition since 1990). McKenna has also won the country's top trophy for Chardonnay and Riesling despite the fact that Pinot Noir gets his attention ahead of every other wine during vintage. An expanded vineyard with new clones and refined winemaking techniques will help to maintain McKenna's reputation as the "King of New Zealand Pinot Noir".

Riesling 1992   ❦ ②
The cool conditions of 1992 produced high levels of acidity, moderated in this case by the malolactic fermentation. The result is a broad and delicate wine, with blurred varietal character. An unusual example from this highly respected winery.

Chardonnay 1991   ❦❦ ③
The best ever example of a consistently top New Zealand Chardonnay label. Soft-textured and complex with subtle, mealy flavors. Burgundian styled wine that promises to cellar well.

martinborough Vineyard

PINOT NOIR

1990

11.5% VOL ℮ 750ml

PRODUCED AND BOTTLED BY MARTINBOROUGH VINEYARD LTD,
PRINCESS STREET, MARTINBOROUGH, NEW ZEALAND.

PRODUCE OF NEW ZEALAND

Martinborough Vineyards   ❦❦❦ ③
Pinot Noir 1990
Martinborough is probably the driest viticultural region in New Zealand's North Island with an annual rainfall of 700 ml per year, most of which falls in winter and spring. Free draining soils of alluvial loam over deep alluvial gravel further reduces the available moisture. Although many vineyards in the region are irrigated, the vines that produced this Pinot Noir are not. 1990 was a particularly dry year with drought stressed vines that provided lower that usual levels of sugar and acid in the grapes although flavors showed good concentration. The grapes were hand-harvested. About half were whole bunch fermented on the stems while the remainder were destemmed, crushed and fermented in the conventional manner. After three weeks fermentation and maceration the wine was pressed into a mixture of 25% new and the rest one or two-year-old Tronçais barriques. Oak maturation lasted 12 months. An intense purple-rimmed color characterises this and previous vintages which have demonstrated the wine's ability to maintain its youthful appearance for several years. The wine has the intense ripe fruit aroma of plums and cherries with a background of more herbaceous characters. A smooth-textured palate with a soft finish and great length.

Matua Valley

Box 100
Kumeu, Auckland
Tel. (09) 4118301
Fax (09)4117982

Matua Valley made their first wine 20 years ago. The birth of this Auckland based family winery coincided with the start of the modern New Zealand wine industry. Brothers Ross and Bill Spence, were able to meet the new demand for high quality table wines as others struggled to adapt their vineyards and winemaking techniques from fortified wine production. Matua Valley helped lead the wine industry through a period of very rapid growth by their innovative approach to viticulture and winemaking. Sauvignon Blanc, Sémillon, Shiraz and Malbec were all pioneered by Matua Valley in their search to find grape varieties which suited New Zealand growing conditions. To maintain their position as premium winemakers Matua Valley soon found it necessary to look beyond their own Auckland vineyards to other regions. Grapes are now shipped from as far away as Amberley, 800 kilometers south of Auckland. Matua Valley has an annual production of over 1,000,000 bottles with a wide range of wine styles from all major wine regions. Their reputation as quality winemakers was not built on one wine style. Wines which have won top awards include Cabernet Sauvignon, Merlot, Chardonnay, Sauvignon Blanc, Gewürztraminer, botrytized Riesling and even vintage Port.

Matua Valley Judd Estate Chardonnay 1991 ♀ ②
Single vineyard Chardonnay from the Gisborne region. Soft, almost luscious, ripe melon and peach flavors flattered by subtle toasty oak. A consistent and very successful style with typical regional characters.

Shingle Peak Botrytis Riesling 1991 ♀♀ ③
One of New Zealand's best ever Botrytis wines with intense and very luscious flavors that give equal emphasis to varietal flavor and botrytis influence. A harmonious and complex wine that shows much potential for bottle development.

Shingle Peak Sauvignon Blanc 1991 ♀ ①
A soft and gently aromatic Sauvignon Blanc with lush ripe fruit flavor. Passionfruit, red currant and capsicum flavors dominate this luscious Marlborough wine.

Matua Valley Merlot 1989 ♀ ②
Merlot mostly blended with Cabernet Sauvignon to soften this normally tannic variety and add extra complexity to the wine. Mutua Valley produced one of the country's first and finest examples of the single variety. This rich plummy wine has caused many to wonder whether New Zealand might not have been wiser to focus more attention on the variety.

The Millton Vineyard

Papatu Road
Manutuke, Gisborne
Tel. (06) 8628680
Fax (08) 9628680

Millton Vineyards is New Zealand's first organic winemaker. Owners James and Annie Millton have pursued a policy of no chemical sprays, except sulphur and Bordeaux mixture. They use only natural fertilizers and interplant the vines with plants that help repel harmful insects and disease. Millton grow vines under biodynamics, a Rudolph Steiner method of horticulture that is now employed by several New Zealand vineyards. Millton is based in the Gisborne region where they produce wine only from their own vineyards. Millton Vineyards makes a high quality range of very individual wines. Winemaker James Millton's specialty is Chenin Blanc. It is his ambition to make wine in the Vouvray style. To achieve maximum concentration and complexity the Chenin Blanc vines are pruned to yield three different crop levels. The grapes are picked at three stages of ripeness, the last of which usually achieves extra concentration through botrytis. After fermentation in oak the wines are blended. One of Millton's best known wines is Opou Vineyard Rhine Riesling, a luscious wine of auslese sweetness made from botrytis affected grapes. From 1992 they will separate the Riesling grapes into two batches to make one dry and one very sweet wine.

Millton Barrel Fermented Chenin Blanc 1991 ♀ ②
Concentrated fruit flavors, subtle oak and a honeyed botrytis influence combine to produce a wine of great complexity and intensity. An individual style which promises benefit from several years bottle age.

Opou Vineyard Riesling 1991 ♀ ②
Lush botrytis influenced wine with good fruit flavor concentration and length. The grapes from three vineyards with different pruning methods and picking dates have been blended for greater complexity. A consistently successful label.

Gisborne Cabernet Sauvignon 1989 ♀ ②
A hot, ripe vintage produced this moderately intense wine from a region that is not renowned for the quality of its reds. A hint of peppery herbaceousness adds complexity and character to intense berryfruit flavors. A strong Bordeaux style red.

Montana

171 Pilkington Road
Glen Innes, Auckland
Tel. (09) 5705549
Fax (09) 5271113

Montana crushes nearly 45% of New Zealand's grape crop making it the country's largest winemaker. The company has steadfastly clung to a policy of making large quantities of the best wines possible. But in the late 1980s Montana purchased a small winery in Hawke's Bay to make smaller quantities of top quality wines. A large investment in vineyards and new equipment has made the McDonald Winery into a showpiece for the production of top Chardonnay and Cabernet Sauvignon. At the same time Montana retained the services of Champagne Deutz to help develop a top quality New Zealand méthode champenoise sparkling wine. The Deutz project has been very successful with the release in 1991 of Montana Deutz Marlborough Cuvee, a bottle-fermented sparkling wine which has been acclaimed as the country's finest. Managing Director, Peter Hubscher, is determined that Montana will be the best as well as the biggest New Zealand winemaker. The company certainly has the grape supply, financial backing and commitment to achieve that goal. The first releases from the McDonald Winery are excellent wines with better yet to come.

Montana Marlborough   ❦❦ ①
Sauvignon Blanc 1991
The inaugural 1980 vintage of this wine is still in remarkably good condition although the zesty, gooseberry/tropical fruit flavors are probably best appreciated within a year or two of the vintage as shown by the quality of this '91, with its typical varietal characteristics.

Montana Estates   ❦ ③
O Ormond Chardonnay 1990
This small production Chardonnay by New Zealand's largest winery demonstrates that big can also be best. It is one of the country's most expensive wines but justifies its price with seductively soft and stylish ripe fruit flavors supported by strong toasty oak. Intense and luscious wine from the Gisborne region.

Montana Deutz Marlborough   ❦❦ ③
Cuvee NV Brut
Methode champenoise made with the technical assistance of Champagne Deutz. Soft-textured fruity wine with creamy yeast autolysis character.

Morton Estate

State Highway 2
Katikati
Tel. (07) 5520795
Fax (07) 5520651

The winemaking skills of John Hancock and marketing abilities of Morton Brown proved a devastating combination in the first few years of Morton Estate's existence. The wines of this small winery rapidly attained cult-like status soon after the first release of their first vintage in 1983. In 1988 Morton Estate, then a mid-sized winery by New Zealand standards, was purchased by the Australian winemaker Mildara. The takeover resulted in the purchase of sizeable new vineyards in Hawke's Bay to expand the production of Morton Estate's premium wine range. Chardonnay is undoubtedly the star of Morton Estate's product range. Hancock pioneered the technique of barrique fermented Chardonnay in New Zealand during the early 1980s and introduced strong flavored and often very oaky wines to a receptive market. Morton Estate's latest Chardonnays still have plenty of flavor but today their strength is derived from fruit intensity rather than oak. While other New Zealand wineries have turned to Marlborough for Sauvignon Blanc grapes, Morton Estate remains loyal to Hawke's Bay with a big, ripe oak fermented wine, a non-oaked version and even a sweet late harvest style.

Morton Estate   ❦❦ ③
Black Label Reserve Chardonnay 1991
Barrel fermentation and yeast autolysis have contributed to the flavor of this big, buttery Chardonnay but do not threaten the intense fruit character of the wine. A classic Hawke's Bay Chardonnay that offers excellent cellaring potential.

Sauvignon Blanc 1991   ❦ ①
Sauvignon Blanc from the North Island region of Hawke's Bay. Lush, ripe wine with strong stone nectarine flavors. A style that contrasts markedly to the normally aromatic, herbaceous wines of Marlborough.

Methode Champenoise 1989   ❦ ②
Clean, soft methode champenoise that reflects an even balance between the Pinot Noir and Chardonnay components without either variety dominating. Attractive, full-bodied wine with moderately ripe fruit flavors.

Nobilo Vintners

Station Road
Huapai, Auckland
Tel. (09) 4129148
Fax (09) 4127124

As with a number of wineries in New Zealand Nobilos was established after World War II by an immigrant family from Yugoslavia. A large part of their production consisted of fortified wines until the end of the sixties when the market began demanding table wines. Soon after, Gilbeys the British wine and spirits chain bought 50% of Nobilos and introduced classic European varietals like Chardonnay, Cabernet Sauvignon and Gewürztraminer plus the South African cross Pinotage. In 1975 Gilbeys sold its half of the share in the winery which returned to the hands of the founding family. In the early 1970s Nobilos was the first winery in New Zealand to buy American and French oak barrels for aging Chardonnay and red wines. The winery remains a great experimenter, still trying different varieties of grapes and new viticultural and winemaking techniques to produce an array of often very unusual wines. Commercially enterprising Nobilos exports about 65% of its wines to Great Britain, Sweden, Japan and Australia.

Nobilo Marlborough   ℘ ①
Sauvignon Blanc 1991
A wine that has gained praise; in classic Marlborough style with varietal flavors, intense aroma and a sharp note. The fresh fruity taste reaches its peak within two years of aging.

Marlborough Chardonnay 1991   ℘℘ ②
Soft-textured wine with peachy ripe fruit flavors that are unusual for this cool, southerly wine region. A rich, almost luscious wine supported by firm acidity and strong alcohol. Integrated oak adds a spicy, nutty element.

Nobilo Dixon Chardonnay 1989   ℘ ②
Three Gisborne vineyards furnish Chardonnay grapes, the best of which are from Dixon. This 1989 vintage was selected as New Zealand's top export wine. It is a fat buttery Chardonnay, with strong hints of oak.

Huapai Pinotage 1988   ♥ ②
Pinotage is a South African cross between the Pinot Noir and Cinsault grape varieties. It produces a soft, fruity wine that clearly shows its Pinot Noir lineage. This example has rich earthy flavors and strong oak influence.

Selaks

Box 34
Kumeu, Auckland
Tel. (09) 4128609
Fax (09) 4127254

Selaks have followed the world and national trend of drinking less but better by reducing their total wine production to focus only on premium varietals. At the same time they have expanded their vineyards to maintain tight control over grape quality. Selaks have their own vineyards in Auckland and Marlborough. They also buy grapes from contracted growers in Gisborne and Hawke's Bay. This extra emphasis on quality appears to have paid off. The winery has enhanced its reputation locally and has expanded export sales. Selaks have consistently made New Zealand's best Sauvignon Blanc/Sémillon blend since they first launched the style in 1983. The strong herbal/grassy character of Sémillon adds weight and flavor to the aromatic Sauvignon Blanc component. Oak aged Sauvignon Blanc is another Selaks speciality. Deft oak influence adds spice and subtle complexity to delicate Sauvignon Blanc flavors. Selaks market their "super-premium" wines under the Founders label. Oak-aged Marlborough Sauvignon Blanc, a powerful Cabernet Sauvignon/Merlot from Hawke's Bay, and a lush Marlborough Chardonnay are the company's finest wines.

Sauvignon Blanc/Semillon 1991   ℘ ②
Selaks pioneered this blended style which introduces a strong, grassy flavor to the normally delicately herbaceous Marlborough Sauvignon Blanc. This top vintage produced Selaks most successful example to date. Flavorsome wine with crisp acidity and a lingering finish.

Selaks Founders Chardonnay 1990   ℘ ②
A mouthwateringly lush wine that shows the benefit of careful grape selection. Flavors of quince and tropical fruit abound in this oppulent wine. It is unusual to find such generous and apparently ripe fruit flavors in normally austere Marlborough Chardonnay.

Stonyridge

Onetangi Road
Ostend, Waiheke Island, Auckland
Tel/Fax (09) 728822

Stonyridge was the second winery to be
established on Waiheke Island, about 35
minutes by boat from Auckland, New
Zealand's largest city. The island has a
moderate maritime climate, warmer and dryer
than the mainland. An olive orchard grows
alongside the vineyard, a common sight in
the Mediterranean, but unique in cool New
Zealand. Owner Stephen White learned
winemaking in South Africa and Europe, his
vineyard and cellar methods reflect his
European experience. Stonyridge specializes
in red wines. The two hectare vineyard is
planted to Cabernet Sauvignon (78%), Merlot
(18%), Cabernet Franc (2%), and Malbec
(2%). The best barrels are labled Larose,
second selections are labeled Airfield. The
low yield, north facing vineyard, is protected
by a rocky outcrop which inspired the
winery's name. Due to high demand and
limited production most of Stonyridge's wines
are sold "en primeur". In any case,
Stonyridge deserves to be counted among
the top three red wine producers in New
Zealand. Their wines reflect a search for
quality without compromise.

Stonyridge Larose 1990   ♥ ♥ ♥ ③
This blend of various Bordeaux varieties could
be mistaken for a Médoc cru classé. The wine
has an intense fruity aroma, perked up by strong
hints of spicy oak. A high class red that, with
care, could age for ten years.

Te Mata Estate

Te Mata Road, Havelock North
Hawke's Bay
Tel/Fax (06) 8774399

Te Mata, New Zealand's oldest winery, produces some of the country's best wines. Its success can be attributed to two factors: a motivated dynamic owner, John Buck, and the favorable Hawke's Bay climate and terrain. At the end of the 1970s Buck bought the old Te Mata winery. He modernized the facility and planted new vineyards. In 1981 a Cabernet Sauvignon/Merlot blend appeared that won New Zealand's most prestigious prize, while Te Mata's 1982 and 1983 reds are still considered among the country's best ever. Coleraine, the winery's best Cabernet Sauvignon/Merlot shows well even after a decade. L'Awatea, their second label for reds, can hold up well to bottle aging, but is better young. Te Mata offers one of the best whites in the country, Elston Chardonnay. The 1989 was voted top white wine at the 1991 International Wine Challenge in London, beating off strong competition at an international level. In the 1980s, Te Mata lead the quality evolution of New Zealand's wines, surprising consumers and inspiring other winemakers.

Elston Chardonnay 1991
The product of very favorable vintage conditions, this wine shows great fruit strength supported by strong oak and firm acidity. An impressively complex wine which will certainly improve for at least five years.

Awatea
Cabernet Sauvignon/Merlot 1990
The Coleraine label represents a selection of the best grapes from two vineyards, while Awatea is the second label. Nevertheless Awatea stands out as one of New Zealand's best reds, meatier and more aromatic than the Coleraine, though lacking a bit of elegance.

Te Mata Estate Coleraine
Cabernet/Merlot 1990
Coleraine is a blend of 54% Cabernet Sauvignon, 36% Merlot and 10% Cabernet Franc. The grapes are not neccesarily grown in a single vineyard. They represent the finest selection of a harvest intended for three Te Mata reds; Coleraine, Awatea and Te Mata Cabernet/Merlot. The grapes are hand-picked, de-stemmed and crushed before a traditional fermentation which involves both plunging and pumping over to extract color, tannin and flavor from the skins. The wine matured in 80% new French oak barriques for 18 months. Coleraine has strong, savoury ceder/oak flavors supported by ripe blackberry and cassis. It is a tight and stylish wine which can appear rather restrained in youth but will develop great complexity and elegance within five to ten years of vintage. Coleraine's first release, from the 1982 vintage, stood head and shoulders above the red wines of the day, providing other winemakers with a useful benchmark. A decade later Coleraine still manages to maintain a slender lead ahead of several worthy challengers.

Vavasour

Redwood Pass Road
Awatere, Marlborough
Tel. (03) 5727481
Fax (03) 5727240

For several generations the Vavasour family have been landowners in the Awatere Valley, a viticultural satellite of the main Marlborough wine region 25 kilometers away. Talented viticulturalist, Richard Bowling, spotted the valley's potential and persuaded Peter Vavasour to establish a 12.5 hectare vineyard on his property. A small but highly efficient winery was built in 1989 for the first vintage. Vavasour has been developed to exploit the potential which the winemaking team passionately believe exists in this scenic cool-climate wine region. Everything, from low yielding vines to designer Italian bottles, has been carefully chosen to produce and present quality without compromise. Only Sauvignon Blanc, Chardonnay, Cabernet Sauvignon and Cabernet Franc have been planted, along with a tiny plot of Merlot and Shiraz. Vavasour market their wines under two labels. The top label, Vavasour Reserve, includes a Sauvignon, Chardonnay, Cabernet Sauvignon/Cabernet Franc and Shiraz. Reserve wines require several years bottle aging to reach their full potential. Dashwood, the second label, includes a Sauvignon and Cabernet Sauvignon/Merlot which are intended for early consumption.

Vavasour Reserve 🍇🍇 ③
Chardonnay 1991
This stylish Chardonnay was awarded the trophy for top overall wine at a New Zealand competition in 1992. A truly stylish wine with real flavor concentration which includes hazelnuts, wholemeal, toast and vanilla.

Vavasour Reserve Sauvignon 1991 🍇 ②
A powerful, aromatic Marlborough style Sauvignon with extra depth and complexity from barrel fermentation and maturation which adds subtle flavors without masking varietal definition.

Vavasour Reserve 🍇🍇 ③
Cabernet Sauvignon/Cabernet Franc 1990
One of the best reds ever made from Marlborough grapes. Concentrated berryfruit flavors with a fine, peppery/minty herbaceousness as evidence of cool-climate viticulture. Supple, elegant red with good cellaring potential.

Villa Maria

5 Kirkbride Road
Mangere, Auckland
Tel. (09) 2756119
Fax (09) 2756618

Villa Maria, New Zealand's third largest winery, is a tribute to the entrepreneurial skills of founder and chief executive, George Fistonich. He sustained a rapid and at times perilous expansion almost since the company began in 1961, and has successfully achieved the goal of becoming the leading producer of high quality wines. Villa Maria's record at both local and overseas wine competitions is impressive. Villa Maria is based in Auckland, a few kilometers from the city's main airport. Most of Villa Maria's grapes, however, are purchased from contract grapegrowers in Hawke's Bay where Fistonich owns two other prestigious wineries; Vidals and Esk Valley. More recently the company has begun to buy white grapes from Marlborough where they are pressed and the juice trucked 18 hours to Auckland. Perhaps Villa Maria's greatest strength is in red wine making. By carefully selecting vineyard sites in Hawke's Bay and closely supervising the efforts of contract growers, Fistonich is able to produce concentrated reds with real ripe fruit intensity. The best have more weight and flavor than all others from the Hawke's Bay region.

Barrique Fermented 🍇 ③
Chardonnay 1991
Ripe melon flavors with a strong hint of oak, good length in the finish. A creamy wine that needs another year or two to integrate the oak and develop more complexity.

Marlborough Reserve 🍇🍇 ②
Chardonnay 1991
This new wine made from Marlborough grapes, shows their ability to make top wine with grapes from any region. Mature, with hints of fruit, combining strength with softness. Soft-textured with a solid backbone of alcohol that emphasizes the fruit sweetness.

Villa Maria Reserve Noble 🍇🍇 ③
Rhine Riesling 1991
A stunning sweet white with strong botrytis influence that still allows floral varietal characters to emerge. A tight wine with firm acidity and great cellaring potential.

Villa Maria Reserve 🍇🍇 ③
Cabernet Sauvignon/Merlot 1989
This successful red shows all the concentration and flavor which has made the Villa Maria label famous. Suppported by strong savory oak, it promises long life for a decade or more.

PORTUGAL

Portugal produces an average of 9.5 million hl of wine per year, equivalent to 20% of the gross agricultural product, which puts it at sixth place in the world for percentage of territory dedicated to growing grapes (9%). Portuguese wines, in particular the red table wines, Port and Madiera, are of high quality and individual style. Wines produced in "area demarcada", or the top quality controlled zones of origin, together with fortified dessert wines from "determinada" regions represent 46% of total production, while table wines account for the remaining 53%. Of these, 43% are white and the rest, reds and rosés. Among the wines made in Demarcada regions worthy of mention are the so called Vinhos Verdes (annual production 2,000,000 hl) and those of the Douro region which produces more than 1 million hl a year.

The history of Portuguese wine up to the 12th century, to the period when the country won its independence from Spain, diverges little from that of the Iberian Peninsola as a whole. Vine cultivation, probably introduced by the Phoenicians, was developed considerably by the Romans and Greeks, especially in the eastern regions. Strabone documents the presence of vines in the areas today known as Portugal and Galicia. Though mentions of trade start from much earlier times, it is only towards the end of the 17th century, in the period when trade between France and England was broken off, that Portuguese wines began to gain ground on the English market. It was the needs of this new market together with the prevailing socio-economic conditions that modified the style of wines arriving in ever greater quantities from Lusitania and Galicia. The origins of British interest in Port can be traced to 1678 when two English gentlemen visiting Portugal for business were put up by the Abbot of Lamego, who had them taste his wine. They found it sweet, very soft and quite different from others in the region. The Abbot confessed that he usually added a bit of spirits to the wine, thus revealing the secret of a wine, the popularity of which was consolidated in Great Britian through a treaty of1703 that granted Port particularly favorable rates of import duty.

Port gradually gained a footing in the rest of the world as well. The increase in trade however led to fraud and the adulteration of wines. In response, in 1756, the Marquis of Pombal demarcated the geographic region allowed to produce Port wine, prohibited the use of colorants, laid down grape yields per hectare and reduced the power of the British commercial companies. Thanks to this key figure in the history of Port, the wine went on to establish a prestige which has never declined.

Vinification techniques are still virtually those of the Marquis' time. The only significant innovation is the introduction of closed fermentation vats which use the carbon dioxide released by the fermenting must to keep the juice percolating over the cap, a system which obtains the same extraction results as treading the grapes, which is still done in some wineries. Other phases are perfectly traditional. The moment that residual sugar in the must gets to 90 g/lt, brandy is added at 77° proof in the measure of 110 l per 440 l of wine. Two years of aging in oak precede bottling, which up until1986 had by law to take place at Vila Nova de Gaia. Today bottling is also permitted on the various individual estates or "quintas". This is the procedure followed to make Vintage, the superior quality of Port. Vintages are wines made only in the best years from the grapes of a single vintage. From this peak the quality pyramid broadens down to the basic commercial Ports made from a blend of wines of various types and origins (White, Ruby, Tawny, etc.). The quintas, which are classified on a scale from A to F on the basis of quality factors such as location, terrain, and yields are in effect crus within the delimited zones. Today in Portugal there are nine Demarcada regions, and 33 wine zones differentiated by type of production. In the first category are the regions: Vinho Verde, Douro, Dão, Bairrada, Bucelas, Colares, Carcavelos, Moscatel de Setúbal and Madeira. The 33 zones are: Cartaxo, Palmela, Arrábida, Borba, Redonda, Portalegre, Almeirín, Arruda, Chaves, Tomar, Valpaços, Planalto, Mirandés, Reguenogos, Vidigueira, Encostas de Nave, Varosa, Santarén, Castelo Rodrigo, Cova da Beira, Lafoes, Encostas da Aire, Alcobaça, Obidos, Alenquer, Torres and A Graciosa and O Pico in the Açores zone. The delimited region of Vinhos Verdes is situated in the north west of the country in an area bordered on one side by the Miño river at the frontier with and and on the other by the Atlantic coast. Immediately south is the Douro region which includes the Port production zone. Further south still, in the center of the country, are the Dão and Bairrada zones. Bucelas, Colares, Caravelos, and Muscatel de Setúbalare are located around Lisbon. Madiera, Portugal's best known wine after Port, is produced on the island of the same name north of the Canaries.

A total of approximately 100 cooperatives, individual wineries and merchant houses operate in the production and bottling of wine in Portugal today. The biggest of these, most of which are funded by foreign investment, are located in Porto and Madiera.

There have been considerable recent developments in enology in the country, although the Portugese themselves, who are rather conservative on the subject, remain atttached to deeply colored wines with high alcoholic content. The basic choice in Portuguese wine is between the youthful "verde" style and the austere, mature reservas. The most consistent quality wine is without doubt Port. It is worth remembering that Portugal also produces excellent brandies, the most famous of which are aged in oak.

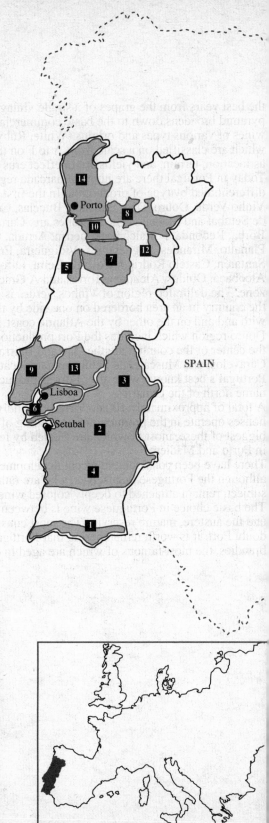

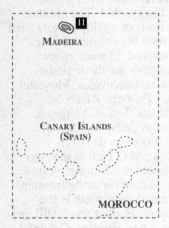

1	**Algarve**
2	**Alentejo**
3	**Upper Alentejo**
4	**Lower Alentejo**
5	**Bairrada**
6	**Bucelas**
7	**Dão**
8	**Douro**
9	**Estremadura**
10	**Lafões**
11	**Madeira**
12	**Pinhel**
13	**Ribatejo**
14	**Vinho Verde**

Caves Aliança

Apartado 6, Sangalhos
Anadia Codex 3783
Tel. (034) 743160
Fax (034) 743008

Second only to Sogrape on the Portuguese market, Caves Aliança, founded in 1920 by the Neves family, is the main winery in the Bairrada area. Though they also own vineyards, most of their grapes are bought in. This large winery makes a wide range of products, of generally sound quality, amongst which the cellarable red from Bairrada has been the country's best seller. Both the whites and the reds are aged in the traditional way in Limousin or local oak. The firm, whose name ends with the phrase "Vinicola de Sangalhos", also makes rosés as well as wines from the Dão, Douro and Vinhos Verdes regions. Their Reserva Antiquissima brandy is worth looking out for.

Dão Vintage 1989   ①
A good, representative white Dão. Pale straw yellow, young both on the nose and on the palate which has fresh, intense fruit.

Garrafeira 1982   ②
Bright, deep golden straw color. Nice oak in the bouquet and on the palate, which has a just the right amount of lively acidity.

Angelus Reserva 1984 ❦ ①
An excellent Bairrada selection, deep ruby color, with typical oak aromas and good development. Light tannins on the palate.

Gran Escolha 1984 ❦ ①
An outstanding Douro. The color is light garnet with chestnut shades around the edges. Tannins on the nose, elegant and satisfying palate with well-judged oak.

Garrafeira 1980 ❦ ②
Medium ruby-red, delicate but stylish on the nose. The slightly toasty character on the palate does not overpower the fruit. Long with clean, fresh fruit in the finish.

Quinta do Barao

Carcavelos
Tel. (01) 4570380

The Quinta do Barao is the only winery in the Carcavelos region, one of Portugal's new delimited areas. It specializes in the production of sweet wines, produced by a two-stage process: one part of the grapes are fermented off the skins in the usual way while fermentation of the second part of the must is interrupted with the addition of brandy. The two parts are blended and aged from one to four years in oak. Another long period in the bottle completes the aging. This mellow wine, sold in two styles (sweet and dry, with 18° to 22° alcohol) is made from Galego Dourado, Boal, Arinto, Trincadeira, Torneira Negra Mole and Espadeiro grapes. It is best served as an aperitif or with desserts. The proximity of this Demarcada region to the tourist and residential zones of Estoril and Cascais now undergoing heavy urban development, has resulted in land being lost to building sites, which in turn means that production from the Ferreira family winery can no longer expand beyond the current output of barely 400 hl a year.

Quinta do Barao ❦ ②
A beautiful topaz color with flavors that faintly recall almond, both sweet and bitter. Powerful on the palate, with good length.

Artur Barros & Sousa

Rua dos Ferreiros, 109
Funchal 9000
Tel. (091) 20622

This small family-run producer makes one of Portugal's best Madeiras using Boal, the noble grape variety indigenous to the island, and a traditional aging process known as "canteiro". This lengthy method requires meticulous care in the beginning phases which last no less than five years. With around 1,500 hl of wine in the cellar in various stages of aging, the company continues to make wines according to strictly artisan traditions. Casks are over 100 years old, only noble grape varieties are used (in addition to Boal, Malvasia, Verdelho, Sercial, Listrão and Terrantez) fining is done exclusively with egg whites no pumps are used in racking the wines. Artur Sousa's reserves, which have a minimum ten years' barrel age, are checked personally by him up until their fifth year, for as long as the quality of each lot can be determined by tasting. The results of these methods are honest, full-bodied wines which bear the personal stamp of their producer.

Terrantez 1965   ℘ ③
A wine that has reached its optimum drinking age, with an elegance which comes from not having been treated to "estufagem" or heating. Clear deep-yellow color, with dried fruit flavors. Best to drink now as it is unlikely to improve further.

Madeira Doce   ℘ ①
Clear, bright, shade of gold, with aromas that reveal careful and intelligent winemaking. Good Muscatel varietal character and a finish which leaves hints of flowers and almond on the palate.

Reserva Malvazia   ℘ ②
This variety, which appears in many other versions (the English Malmsey, for example) makes whites of rich sweetness and length. This reserva is clear and bright in color and stylish on the nose and the palate.

Boal Reserva   ℘℘ ②
A brilliant, clear topaz color, slightly resinous on the nose with hints of walnut. Very respectable structure. Round and elegant with perfect balance between the acidity and the semi-sweet fruit flavors. A wine destined for long life which can only improve with further bottle age.

Borges & Irmão

Avenida de Republica, 796
Vila Nova de Gaia 4400
Tel. (02) 305002-305027
Fax (02) 304985

Antonio Borges and his brother, Francisco, were successful merchants in tobacco, foreign currency and matches who in 1884 decided to diversify by opening a Port wine export business. Their enterprise and initiative helped the new winery they founded establish itself firmly in the luxury wine market by the end of the last century. Today they make a wide range of products, from Vinhos Verdes to all types of Port, Douros and sparkling wines. Among the Ports, the Vintage, the Character and the 10 and 20 year reserves are of especially high quality. Also well known are their Tawny, Ruby, White and Lácrima Ports which are aimed at a broader market and can be found for sale in many distribution points. It is no surprise that their Vinho Verde, Gatão, is one of Portugal's best sellers. The company has modern wineries at Lixa and Vila Real, while bottling and storage take place at Olival, in a high-tech plant.

Pérola Garrafeira 1980   ℘℘ ④
One of the best Douro wines produced in the region. A pale, aromatic, flavorful table wine, from Arinto and Cercial grapes.

Roncao 20 años   ℘ ②
A blend of grapes of different origins, aged in barrique. By now the color has become pale red. Aromatic nose and good value for money.

Vintage Port 1985   ♥♥ ③
Bright garnet-red with hints of chestnut. The alcohol is still very obvious but should settle down with aging. A light, sweet wine.

Quinta do Junco 1977   ♥♥ ④
Rich in personality, made from the local grapes of the region: French and Portuguese Touriga, Tinta Roriz and Tinta Cão. Well-balanced.

Vintage Port 1970   ♥♥ ④
Clean and bright, with toasty aromas on the nose. Round and full-bodied on the palate. A wine from a good year at the peak of its development.

Palacio da Brejoeira

Quinta Brejoeira
Monção 4950
Tel. (051) 666129
Fax (02) 300550

A walled vineyard with a production of 2,000 quintals of Albariño grapes surrounds the splendid neoclassical residence that houses the headquarters of the Monção region's most important winery. Both the house and the grounds of this beautiful estate, complete with rich woods and parkland are well worth a visit. Built near the end of the 18th century, Palacio da Brejoeira vinifies only Albariño, the most prestigious variety of the Vinhos Verdes, obtaining flavorful whites with good balance between the acidity and an alcohol content of around 12. These are fresh, stylish products that rival those from the far shore of the Miño in Galicia. Unlike most Portuguese wines, these are best drunk within their first two years, as they peak early and tend to fade quite quickly. Sold mainly locally, they are superb with fish.

Palacio da Brejoeira 1991   🍷 ②
Elegant straw-gold color with green reflections and intense floral aromas. Fresh, light and dry on the palate with a long finish.

Buçaco Palace Hotel

Parque Nacional de Buçaco
Tel (031) 930101-930466

The Bucao Palace Hotel has aged its own special reserves for many years, creating over the decades what José A. Salvador described as 'a priceless heritage'. Here tradition takes precedence over fashion or personal whim. The Hotel ages the best wines of the Sierra in the Bairrada zone, north of Coimbra, following a tradition begun in the 12th century by the Barefoot Carmelites, without worrying too much about sophisticated enological technology. They obtain great wines which, besides their intrinsic value have an ethnographic interest, which can only be fully appreciated through a visit to the sumptous Hotel. The Buçaco Palace was begun near the end of the last century by the Italian Luigi Manini. Though slightly rundown, the unusual building is one of Portugal's most interesting pieces of architecture, built in an impressive Baroque style and set in the middle of a 450 ha national park.

Colheita 1977   🍷 ②
Splendid antique-gold color, with topaz reflections. Complex on the nose with broad flavors of very ripe fruit, rounded out with a hint of resinous oak.

Colheita 1968   🍷 ③
Elegant flashes of gold in the color and delicate aromas. Not a wine with great structure, so even the restrained oak comes through quite strongly.

Colheita 1960   🍷 ③
A blend of Baga, Trincadeira, Castelhão and Tinta Pinheira which produces a wine with an intense color, powerful nose and complex palate.

Colheita 1953   🍷 ④
Pale color that tends toward orange. The fruit still comes through both on the nose and the palate, which has exceptional elegance and supple balance.

J.W. Burmester

Rua de Belmonte, 39
Porto
Tel. (02) 321274
Fax (02) 314331

The name of this winery refers to the title of "Burgermeister" which several members of the family who founded the firm held in their native town of Moellen in Germany. Established in 1730, a mere 20 years later the company was already specializing in the sale of Port wine, exporting throughout Europe the popular Ruby and Tawny styles, prestigious Vintage Ports and also various dry, barrel-aged whites. In 1984 brothers Federico and Eduardo Burmester, lacking descendents, brought into the company their nephew Johan W. Burmester from Hamburg, who shortly after became the sole proprietor. The winery does not own vineyards, though they are negotiating the acquisition of a quinta in the Douro valley. Even so, some of the most respected wines of the denomination lie aging in the cellars of the Vila Nova de Gaia, wines it is worth recalling which belong to one of the world's oldest enological traditions, based on knowledge and experience handed down from generation to generation.

Jockey Club
Clear, grain-colored wine obtained from white varieties fermented completely dry. Intense and very personal aromas on the nose and dry on the palate. Not exceptional but, nevertheless, an original aperitif.

Late Bottled Vintage
Extra Selected 1985
A Port from grapes harvested from a number of different vineyards, aged in oak for five years. Elegant and well-balanced, very live on the palate with good texture.

Vintage Port 1985
Bright, with attractive chestnut hues. The ongoing evolution is balanced by very respectable alcohol, the sensation of which comes through on the palate along with a touch of astringent tannin.

Vintage Port 1984
A wine which has developed surprisingly quickly. Deep cherry-red with a stylish nose, though a little weak on the palate. Probably at its best now.

Vintage Port 1948
Seppia tones prevail in the color, while the nose has almonds and dried fruit aromas. Round, nice to drink now, but will not keep for much longer.

Cockburn Smithes

Rua das Coradas, 13
Vila Nova de Gaia 4400
Tel. (02) 3794031
Fax (02) 300550

Controlled by Harvey's of Bristol, Cockburn is one of the big wineries which select the best barrels from their various estates with extreme severity, and blend them with other mature wines in stainless steel vats to obtain high quality Vintage Ports. Cockburn was in fact out of the Vintage market for quite a few years, and only started production again in 1983, a great year. Quality since has remained at the same high level. The firm's own estates, Quinta dos Canais, Quinta do Tua and Cachao da Valeira, guarantee a constant supply of top quality fruit from the local varieties; Portuguese and French Touriga, Tinta Barroca and Tinta Roriz. Cockburn make a complete range of Ports, following traditional methods. The wines are matured in used barrels (preferable because they allow greater control over the aging process) for two years, after which they are bottled and released.

Vintage Port 1985
1985 was the first year that Cockburn experimented with blending. This Vintage promises much. Deep red color, at the moment the alcohol still predominates on the nose and the palate, but this is obviously a premium quality wine.

Late Bottled Vintage 1982
A Late Bottled Vintage from a blend of different wines. The nose is broad and warm. Clean-cut and very drinkable on the palate.

Vintage Port 1967
A polished, cherry-red color of medium intensity. Powerful nose, good texture, elegant with a long, lingering finish.

Vintage Port 1963
Color and finish very similar to the 1967 but with more fruit and an extra velvety texture. Superb palate; a wine that will continue to improve.

Vintage Port 1955
Splendid well-defined ruby-red color, potent and elegant nose with hints of fruit. Great body and concentration. Still very alive, fresh and flavorful.

Adega Regional de Colares

Banzao, Colares
Tel. (01) 9291210

The Adega Regional de Colares, with its beautiful façade in blue ceramic tiles lies on the road that leads to the beach of Maças. Founded in 1931, the association already had 507 members by 1935, although it took government regulations (currently being revised) to impose adequate quality controls. The Adega makes all of the wines of the region. The majority of the production is distributed by merchants, although the association sells the wines of smaller producers directly. They also control the production of a small area near Cintra, not far from Lisbon. Their main vineyards are in San Joao das Lampas and Terrugem, where vines are planted in sand dunes, using a method called "punción", to reach the clay layer below where the roots take hold. Fortunately the difficult soil conditions are counter balanced by the micro climate which benefits from the influence of Atlantic breezes. Among the reds made by the ARC those from the local Remisco variety are particularly interesting. In the case of these wines the must is first held in cement vats for a few days, then filtered and racked into large oak barrels, where it ferments for about a month. In March the wine is put into new barriques, where it remains for two years before bottling and further long aging.

Colheita 1984
Though Portuguese whites may not have the personality of the reds, this is still a good quality wine. Pale straw-yellow color, very correct on the palate with light-medium body and lowish acidity.

Colheita 1979
A reserve with a bright ruby color and shades of chestnut. It has remarkable tannin and good acidity which should ensure that it ages well in the bottle.

Colheita 1973
Bright, deep ruby-red color, intense bouquet and a powerful palate which is smooth and silky despite the touch of tannin. Very long finish.

Colheita 1953
Transparent, dark ruby-red, touched with orange. Ripe fruit on the nose, powerful, full-bodied and long with more fruit on the palate.

Croft

Largo Joaquim Magalhaes, 23 - Apartado 6
Vila Nova de Gaia 4400
Tel. (02) 305539
Fax (02) 300642

Founded in 1678, Croft is the second oldest exporter of Vintage Port. Only Warre (today owned by the Symington family) who began shipping their wines eight years earlier have a longer tradition. The first Croft landed in Lisbon in 1730 and quickly took control of the firm. The event signalled the beginning of a true dynasty in Porto, although with a touch of British national pride the Crofts continued to write on their letterhead 'Merchants of York', their birthplace. At the beginning of the 20th century Croft was bought by Gilbey's, the well-known Gin producer (which today is one of the three major firms owned by International Distillers & Vintners, together with JM Fonseca and Delaforce). Croft makes the true fortified wines of Porto, first aged in oak and then in the bottle. The Croft Vintages are made from selected fruit of exceptional quality. The Late Bottled Vintages (LBV) are similar to the above, but slightly less grand. The range is completed by the delicate dry, white Port.

Vintage Port 1985
Cherry-red color, very young on the nose with marked alcohol aromas. Lightly built on the palate with a touch of green tannin.

Quinta da Roeda
Vintage Port 1980
A wine which has all the character of the firm's best vineyard. A relatively light weight Vintage, aromatic and flavorful.

Tawny 20 Years Old
A color commonly described as onion skin. Enticing on the nose with aromas of tropical fruit, apricots and dried figs. Substantial but at the same time supple and elegant.

Dow's Port - Silva & Cosens Lds.

Travessa do Barão de Forrester. Ap. 14
Vila Nova de Gaia 4400
Tel. (02) 396063

James Dow entered the world of Port in
1832, by marrying the granddaughter of
Samuel Weaver, an important merchant of
the City. At his father-in-law's death, he found
himself running the business that was to take
his name. James Dow's son, James Ramsay,
continued the job, developing his father's
business with intelligence and initiative. To
define this James as a character would be an
understatement: his passion was the flute (in
his spare time he played in a symphony
orchestra), but his gutsy, competitive spirit
led him to fall in love with the wine business,
with great results. His rages in the presence
of clients and suppliers remain famous (if
angered, he was liable to slam the door and
throw away the key until he got satisfaction),
but so was the sincere human sympathy that
he was able to communicate. In 1912 the firm
was taken over by Warre, though maintaining
its autonomy on the winemaking side. Today
both are part of the Symington group within
which the Dow label continues to enjoy
remarkable respect in particular for the
quality of its prestigious Vintages.

Late Bottled Vintage 1981   🍇 ③
Attractive, lively garnet color, and a ripe,
complex nose with hints of cooked fruit, cocoa
and toast. Long on the palate, elegant, softened
by four years in oak.

Vintage Port 1977   🍇🍇 ②
Still not perfectly mature. The color, in fact,
remains a very deep, full ruby and the warm,
alcoholic nose has underlying spices waiting to
come out. Good structure, excellent
concentration, long and powerful on the palate.

Key to the symbols

Types of Wines

🍇 White

🍇 Rosé

🍇 Red

Rating System

🍇 An exemplary wine of its
type with outstanding local
character

🍇🍇 An international premium
quality wine

🍇🍇🍇 A Top Wine, considered one
of the 150 best wines in the
world

*The 'grape bunch' symbol is used to
indicate the color of the wine; the
number of bunches represents the quality
rating assigned by the contributor*

Price levels

① up to $ 9.99

② $ 10.00 - $ 14.99

③ $ 15.00 - $ 24.99

④ $ 25.00 or more

*The 'ex-cellar', or direct from the
producer, bottle prices, are calculated in
US dollars and are intended only as an
approximate guide*

**Entries are arranged in
alphabetical order by country,
region and winery or producer
name.**

A.A. Ferreira

Rua da Carvalhosa, 19/103
Vila Nova da Gaia 4400
Tel/Fax (02) 309732

The Douro Barca Velha made by this important producer is considered the best wine of the region and Portugal's most aristocratic red, comparable to the legendary Vega Sicilia, made on the Spanish side of the river. Barca Velha was the brain child of Fernando Nicolau de Almeida who, in 1953, took the decision to start production of a red different to the traditional fortified wines of Porto. The history of this prestigious house goes back to the time of the famous Antonia Adelaide Ferreira, a member of the fourth generation of a winemaking family who was a major landowner in the Douro region, and known as the 'Queen without a crown'. The low, solidly-built Ferreira winery, dates from 1892. It is typically Victorian in style although it incorporates a number of quite advance features for the time such as the large main staircase which leads to the fermentation area or the intelligent and functional lay out of the vats. Today the company is owned by Sogrape and run by Fernando Nicolau de Almeida. It produces mainly Port and Douro wines.

Vintage Port 1985　　　🍇🍇 ③
Still young, but with great structure. Bright, intense garnet, with rosy nuances around the edges and a powerful nose. The elegance of fruit and light tannins are evident in spite of the vigorous alcoholic content which will ensure long life and excellent evolution in the bottle.

Reserva Especial Ferreirinha 1980　🍇 ④
Wines that don't reach the high standards necessary to become Barca Velha are bottled under this label. The 1980 is outstanding: a mature and balanced red ready to drink now. A top quality Douro with both structure and bouquet.

Barca Velha 1981　　　🍇🍇🍇 ④
An exceptional wine. Intense cherry-red with shades of chestnut around the edges. The nose has clean, well-defined tertiary aromas developed during the lengthy aging. The palate is dominated by the slightly tannic oak but has good fruit, elegance and smooth balance. The intelligently blended Touriga and Tinta Roriz grapes give a mouthfull of great roundness, texture and body. The 50,000 bottles of this vintage will undoubtedly have long life. This legendary Portuguese red is fermented in stainless steel vats at controlled temperatures, left 18 months in oak and then aged at least ten years in the bottle. Rigorous selection has meant that since it was first made only a dozen vintages of this outstanding wine have been bottled.

José Maria da Fonseca Succs.

Rua José Augusto Coelho, 11/13-Apartado 8
Azeitao 2925
Tel. (01) 2191500-2080002
Fax (01) 2191560

W. & J. Graham

Rua Rei Ramiro 514 - Apartado 19
Vila Nova da Gaia 4400
Tel. (02) 396063
Fax (02) 3703642

In 1834 José Maria da Fonseca founded a company with the intention of specialising in Moscatel de Setúbal. Fifteen years later he won the first of 191 medals, amongst the most important of which was that of the World Trade Fair of Paris in 1889. Fonseca remains the largest producer of this denomination, although they do not only make Moscatel but also wines from the nearby area of Arrábida and from other regions of the country including the Dão. Moscatel de Setúbal is vinified in cement vats. After the addition of alcohol the wine is racked into 120 hl vats and then one year later transferred to smaller 6 hl barriques where it ages for at least five years until bottling. The special reserves are marked with codes corresponding to the provenence of the wine or to specific techniques used in the winemaking or aging. The top "garrafeira" or reserve wines are made at controlled temperatures and aged in oak and their progress rigorously checked at every stage of the production. The firm owns more than 500 ha of vineyard, part of which is in the nearby region of Palmela.

Quinta do Camarate 1986   🍇🍇 ①
Made in Arrábida on an estate that mainly grows Arinto, Moscatel, Fernao Pires and Roupeiro grapes. Aromatic, full-bodied and very dry.

Moscatel 1968   🍇🍇 ③
Clean and bright amber color. The powerful nose still has fresh aromas of fruit and hints of toast and acquavite. Produced exclusively with Setúbal variety Moscatel. pag 934

Moscatel Roxo 1969   🍇🍇 ④
A rosé only in color. This is a Moscatel made from red grapes, in a style exclusive to Fonseca. Dark, aromatic, intensly flavored with up-front fruit on the mouth.

Terras Altas 1980   🍇🍇 ①
A red from the Dão region, realm of the Touriga Nazionale, Afrocheiro and Tinta Roriz varieties. Ruby-red with orange reflections. Top quality oak on the nose, long and full on the palate with light, dry acidity.

The founders of the house, William and John Graham, originally from Glasgow, established their firm in Porto in 1820, the year they bought their first 27 barrels. The business began almost by accident as a result of agreeing to pay a debt with Port wine. Exports, especially to Britain, developed hand in hand with the prestige of the company, which has been headed by the Symington family since 1970. Graham own a prestigious property, the Quinta dos Malvedos, in Alto Douro, the wine region in the center of the country where, spread along the banks of the Douro river, the grapes which become Port are grown. The wine takes its name from the city around whose port were established the great export houses and where (at Vila Nova da Gaia, across the river) the main wineries are located. Here Graham make exquisite sweet vintage wines, fortified in the traditional manner, which are among the best in the region.

Vintage Port 1983   🍇🍇 ④
Intense, bright red. The alcohol predominates slightly in the nose, a sign of youth apparent on the palate, too, which has young tannins and acidity, that are already however beginning to soften.

Malvedos Vintage Port 1979   🍇🍇 ④
Bordeaux red with chestnut shades around the edges. Complex on the nose. Polished, balanced, fleshy and rich on the palate. A round, balanced and velvety Vintage at the peak of its evolution. To be drunk now, with enormous enjoyment.

Old Tawny 20 años   🍇🍇 ④
The result of a blend of different harvest selections aged for 20 years. Toasty character both on the nose and the palate, with a touch of honey.

Cooperativa Agraria da Granja

Baldio - Granja
Mourão 7240
Tel. (01) 57119

This co-operative, which specializes in the wines of Alentejo from the zones of Borba, Reguengos de Monsaraz and Redondo, is known for its well-built reds. The success of the co-op dates back to the great response from critics and consumers alike to the 1984 vintage. In this vintage one lot of 250 hl was selected from the total of 4,000 produced that year and fermented at high temperatures in cement, where it remained to mature for two years, before being transferred to 300 lt oak barriques for a further 12 months. The whites are quite pleasant, especially while young, but the Cooperativa Agraria da Granxa's best products are its well-known reds, which unlike others made in the country do not need long aging.

Garrafeira 1984
A splendid purple-red color. The wine is made from the Afrochiero variety which gives an intense, elegant nose and a velvety palate rich in extract. Good balance and structure.

Madeira Wine

Rua dios GFerreiros, 191 - Apartado 295
Funchal Codex 9003
Tel. (091) 20121
Fax (091) 22925

The Madeira Wine society was founded by a small group of growers in 1913. With time, the group has grown to include some of the most famous companies on the island: Blandy's (founded in 1811), Cossart Gordon (in 1745), Leacock and Co. and Mails. Today Madeira Wine is the oldest house operating in the production and export of Madeira wines. The ancient cellers of the company, which is famous for its long-lived Vintages, have seen some of the best Madiera ever produced. Malvasia is the main grape on the island, together with Boal, Sercial, Verdelho and Terantez. The cellars are equipped with old oak barrels for the fermentation and maceration of the wines which are bottled with between three and twenty years of wood aging. It is possible to find Vintages in perfect condition even after 200 years.

Miles Verdelho
Inviting appearance, delicate varietal aromas and nice freshness on the palate, with a clean dry finish.

Blandy's Malmsey
A classy wine made exclusively from Malvasia. Deep and complex color, concentrated bouquet, good body, sweet and flavorsome on the palate with an intense finish.

Cossart Gordon Sercial
A medium amber color, elegant and concentrated on the nose. Quite dry. Excellent as an aperitif.

Garrafeira CO
The initials CO refer to fining with egg whites or "Clara de Ovo". A 100% varietal from the Castelhão Frances grape of Periquita. Deep color, a vigorous toasty nose and smooth balanced palate.

Leacock Boal
A style of wine somewhere between the two previous ones. The slightly aggressive acidity on the palate is well balanced by the stylish sweet finish. A versatile wine, matchable with a wide variety of foods.

Niepoort

Rua Infante D. Henrique, 39-2°
Porto 4000
Tel. (02) 2080473
Fax (02) 320209

This winery has been in the van der Niepoort family since 1848, when it was bought from Eduard Krebe who had founded it six years earlier. Today the company, which is directed by Rolf van der Niepoort and his son, Dirk, is highly esteemed both for its high quality standards (in 60 years only 16 Vintages have been declared), and for the great personality and the inimitable style of its wines. Niepoort are particularly well-known for their outstanding range of Colheitas, wines made for long aging which are capable of maintaining their impressive structure after a century in the bottle. Another speciality are the Late Bottled Vintages first introduced in the early 1980s which attain such high standards that they are hard to distinguish from the excellent Vintages. The winery owns the Quinta do Carril and the Quinta de Napoles, a 45 ha estate acquired in 1988 but nontheless still needs to buy in grapes. The majority of the supply comes from the same group of ten small growers in the Pinhão Valley, which guarantees the consistency of the fruit.

Late Bottled Vintage 1988 🍇🍇 ③
The most recent LBV bottled by the winery. A wine to buy and put away. Still young, but one can already see in its great structure future complexity and outstanding development. Deep color, big, aromatic and fruity.

Vintage Port 1985 🍇🍇 ④
Bottled in 1987, still very deep in color and flavor. A wine that will live long and develop considerably with time.

Late Bottled Vintage 1981 🍇🍇 ③
Clear and bright, peppery on the nose and lingering flavors on the palate. Balanced and well-built.

Colheita 1977 🍇🍇 ④
An elegant, beautiful topaz color wine with complex flavors of fruit and oak which have knitted together with time. In the mouth it is extremely long and stylish. Full-bodied with very good balance.

Vintage Port 1945 🍇🍇 ④
From one of the greatest vintages of this century, a wine which demonstrates both the stature and the style this producer. Elegant ruby red, subtle yet quite powerful flavors. Smooth and well-balanced with an elegant and silky finish.

Quinta do Noval-Vinhos

Rua Candido dos Reis, 575 - Apartado 57
Vila Nova de Gaia Codex 4401
Tel. (02) 302020
Fax (02) 300365

The Quinta do Noval name appeared for the first time on commercial registers in 1715. In 1784 the estate was bought by Antonio José de Silva, who found himself almost immediately in the middle of a phylloxera epidemic. In 1981 a fire destroyed the winery and with it important stocks of premium wines. Despite the many set backs the Quinta do Noval has always bounced back to become one of the few Portuguese houses to earn the universal acclaim of British experts. The firm which has been active in Porto since1780 was bought by the famous Flemish van Zeller family in1930. The winery works with the traditional varieties: French and Portugese Touriga , Sousão, Tinta Cão, Malvasia, Cunifesco and Mourisco Rosso and indulges in the luxury of traditional methods like crushing the grapes by foot. The company also owns a small plot of vines that escaped the phylloxera, from which they eke out a few bottles labeled with the name of the vineyard, Nacional. Hardly ever sold, these bottles are generally offered to priviledged clients. When they do appear at auction, they achieve record prices.

Solar das Boucas 🍇🍇 ①
A white made in the Vinhos Verdes region. Bright straw yellow, with good fruit on the nose and the palate and all the personality of the Albariña grape.

White Extra Dry 🍇🍇 ②
One of Portugal's best aperitif whites, from a blend of the most popular varieties of the region. Elegant, silky and uncomplicatedly refreshing.

Quinta Do Noval
Vintage Port 1970 🍇🍇 ④
Bright, very attractive ruby-red. Warm and powerful on the nose, with excellent development on the palate.

Quinta do Noval
Vintage Nacional Port 1964 🍇🍇 ④
Beautiful color, subtle on the nose and elegant on the palate. From ungrafted Touriga and Sousão grapes, aged in oak. Full of personality, an exceptional quality Port which would certainly have won a Top Wine award were it not for its extreme rarity.

Noval Late Bottled Vintage 🍇🍇 ③
A mature, high quality Port from an unspecified vintage but with a nose and palate which reveals long wood aging.

Ramos Pinto

Avenida Ramos Pinto, 380 - Apartado 65
Vila Nova da Gaia Codex 4401
Tel. (02) 300716
Fax (02) 3793121

The Adriano Ramos Pinto company was founded in 1880 and quickly gained a reputation for its high quality products. Today the house is controlled by French investors, but continues to maintain impeccable standards, standards which begin, quite rightly, in the vineyard. Ramos Pinto have invested heavily in viticulture on the estate and when, in the near future, the new vineyards of Bons-Ares, Bom-Retiro, Ervamoira, Santo-Domingos and Urtiga enter full production they will supply the winery with all the fruit for its needs. Low yields and scrupulous selection ensure the necessary base to obtain the excellent Vintages which, especially in the last decade, have earned this company its excellent reputation. The Vintage Ports, made from the best French and Portuguese Touriga and Tinta Roriz grapes, spend two years in wood before bottling. For the newcomer to Port, the name Ramos may be unfamiliar compared to those of the world-famous brands, but Portuguese connoisseurs and the best wine critics consider this winery's Port a real gem, an authentic elite product that still has not obtained the recognition that it deserves.

Vintage Port 1985   🍇🍇 ④
Bright, intense cherry-red color, rich fruit on the nose,sweet and fleshy on the palate. Extremely well-rounded and already very drinkable.

Vintage Port 1983   🍇🍇 ④
Transparent despite its deep color, powerful on the nose, still young and alcoholic. Slightly astringent in the mouth now but guaranteed to age well.

Colheita Ramos Pinto 1937   🍇🍇 ④
An excellent Tawny, which after long aging has now reached its peak in the bottle. Aromatic and superbly balanced. Lingers on the palate.

Quinta Ervamoira   🍇 ④
A ten year old Tawny, intense cherry-red color, assertive on the nose, full-bodied and powerful in the mouth.

Caves San João

San João da Anadia
Anadia 3780
Tel. (034) 741118
Fax (034) 741895

The owner of this winery, Luis Costa, is an important personality in the region being the leading figure in of the Cofradía de Enófilos de A Bairrada, an association that works for the promotion of the local wines. The Caves San João is located between Port and Coimbra, in the province of Beira Litoral, a "demarcada" region. The majority of the production is based on a popular local red variety called Baga. White grapes are mostly used for sparkling wines, and come mainly from the Maria-Gomez variety, though some vineyards are planted in Pinot and Chardonnay. The medium-sized winery produces some of the region's best reds, which are initially tough on the palate, a feature of Baga wines, but soften with time. Their capacity for bottle age is considerable, and the wines will keep for 20 or 30 years without fading.

Caves San Joao Seco 1987   🍇 ①
Straw-yellow, clear and bright, this wine shows its youthfulness both on the nose and the palate. Delicate flavors with a nice touch of acidity.

Bruto 1985   🍇 ②
A sparkling wine with a long and well-defined perlage. Slightly unformed on the nose, dry on the palate. The structure promises great development with time.

Quinta do Poço do Lobo 1988   🍇 ①
1988 was a great year for the wines of A Bairrada. This example is an elegant ruby-red color with an intense aromatic nose and good structure although the balance is slightly upset by some astringent tannin. It should, however, soften with time.

Porta dos Cavaleiros 1983   🍇 ②
A typical Dão red, a denomination also produced by this winery. Cherry-red color, good body and up-front tannins.

Frei Joao 1980   🍇 ①
Ruby-red with chestnut edges. Very evident oak on the nose, which also comes through on the palate. Powerful, good structure, should develop well.

Sandeman

Largo Miguel Bombarda, 3 - Apartado 2
Vila Nova da Gaia Codex 4401
Tel. (02) 3706807
Fax (02) 3706816

This winery, which belongs to Seagrams, has had fabulous commercial success with an excellent table wine made from the top grape varieties of the region: French and Portuguese Touriga, Tinta Cão and Tinta Roriz. George Sandeman, founder of the company, settled in Porto in 1809 and became a respected merchant not only of the local wine, but also Sherry and Madeira - so respected in fact that he received the honor of supplying the Duke of Wellington and his troops. If table wine has proved a good commercial option, the speciality of this great house is and always has been Port. Amongst these Sandeman produce a very interesting cold-fermented dry white from Malvasia, Gouveio and Moscatel grown on the well-known Sabrosa Estate on the left bank of the Douro, a quite unusual wine for this appellation but one of the best of its type in the country.

Apitiv   ❦❦ ②
A dry white, excellent as an aperitif and best served cold. It has fresh intense aromas of Moscatel and a stylish palate full of character.

Quinta do Confradeiro 1986   ❦❦ ③
This wine is fermented on the skins at controlled temperatures, a technique which brings out the grape character. Good impact on the nose and the palate and reasonable balance which will improve in the bottle.

Vintage Port 1982   ❦❦ ④
Intense garnet color, lively and elegant, with a predominance of alcohol on the nose that isn't felt on the palate, which is mature and slightly tannic.

Sogrape

Avenida da Boavista, 1163 - Apartado 70
Porto Cedex 4001
Tel. (02) 695751
Fax (02) 293504

This winery was founded in 1942 by Fernando van Zeller Guedes, an enologist who had been responsible for the winemaking in a number of firms in the region. Profiting from this experience, when the economic problems of World War 2, obliged wineries to forego his services, he decided to found his own company. It was then that he created Mateus Rosé. The first production of this wine made from the Alvarelho variety was a mere 100 hl, a production which has grown since to make Mateus the world's best selling wine (thanks mainly to demand from Brazil). Sogrape is one of Portugal's biggest producers. It exports throughout the world - from the United States to Japan - a rosé that has become a symbol of Portugal. In the same sector, a recent pink wine from Bairrada is an interesting novelty. Its sparkling wines are among Portugal's best. Sogrape could become, for Portugal, what Torres is for Spain, Mondavi for the Untied States and Antinori for Italy.

Reserva Bairrada 1989   ❦❦ ②
A white of exceptional quality. Yellow with lemon reflections. Good acidity adds a touch of liveliness to the broad and robust texture on the palate.

Reserva Douro 1987   ❦❦ ③
A mature white, of surprising quality. Golden-yellow color. Light hints of oak on the nose do not cover the aromatic varietal character of the Malvasia, Gouveio and Viosinho. Fleshy and well-balanced in the mouth.

Nobilis 1990   ❦❦ ②
A dry rosé, very aromatic, made from Baga and Moreto grapes of the Bairrada region. Extremely fresh and well-balanced.

Reserva Dão 1980   ❦❦ ③
Intense ruby-red, with chestnut reflections. A mature wine which shows good development on the palate, held together by moderate acidity. Overall well-balanced.

Taylor, Fladgate & Yeatman

Rua Choupelo, 250 - Apartado 24
Vila Nova da Gaia Codex 4401
Tel. (02) 304505-304555
Fax (02) 304655

This firm arguably produces the best Vintages Ports. It was founded in1692 by the English Bearsley family, following the example of Christian Kopke, a pioneer who half a century earlier had created the first company to produce Port. Job Bearsley was a wool merchant, who marked his bales of raw material with "4XX", the logo which still today we find on the Port label of this house. Taylor have become leaders in Porto thanks to the consistently high standards of production: between 1870 and 1985, (an exceptional year) they have decalred only 30 Vintages. The firm owns two important estates: Quinta das Vargellas and Quinta de Terra Feita, with respectively 41 and 50 ha of vineyards planted in Tinta Roriz, Tinta Barroca, Tinta Cão and Touriga (Portuguese and French). The wines are complex and destined for lengthy bottle aging and long life.

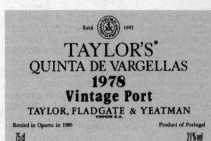

Taylor Fladgate Vintage Port 1985 🍇 ④
Lively garnet-red with hints of chestnut. Powerful on the nose where the alcohol dominates the tertiary aromas. The sweet flavor is balanced well by light acidity. The slightly astringent tannin and the alcohol, which nevertheless give the wine punch, vigor and flavor, will mellow with time.

Taylor Fladgate Vintage Port 1980 🍇 ④
This is a Vintage that will reach its peak within a few years. Clean and intense on the nose, year by year it gains greater elegance and balance between the tannin and the fruit. Well-balanced and full of personality.

Special Ruby 🍇 ①
To be recommended among the Ports in the medium price range. A sweet wine with medium color, vigorous and aromatic.

Tawny 20 años 🍇 ④
Bright, ruby color with brown reflections. Great structure with intense and elegant flavors heightened by the alcohol content. Pure and sweet in the mouth with elegant notes of oak.

Quinta de Vargellas 🍇🍇🍇 ④
Vintage Port 1978

The dry soils of the Quinta de Vargellas give wines of exceptional power and vitality. Brilliant clean color, intense garnet with shades of bordeaux and cherry. A combination of vigor and elegance on the nose with its aroma of violets, and perhaps over-evident alcohol. This wine is dominated by the personality of the Touriga grape, which makes up 50% of the blend. Wines from this Quinta have been botttled with the single vineyard label since the beginning of the 1800s. This 1978 had splendid youthfulness, its structure, and length undiminished by the years. Will continue its progress towards the sublime for some time to come.

Casal de Valle Pradinhos

Macedo de Cavaleiros 5340
Tel. (078) 421716

Macedo de Cavaleiros, owner of this 35 ha
estate, crafts wines with great personality,
representative of the province of Tras Os
Montes. The zone is generally considered a
part of the Douro, although it has a different
VQPRD because it produces wines without
the sugar (or the polished elegance) of its
western neighbors. The vineyards in question
belong to the communes of Chaves,
Valpaços (where a cooperative produces
very interesting wines) Vila Pouca de Aguiar
and Bragança on the Spanish border. Both
whites and reds are made in the area,
including several with deep color, full-body
and high alcohol content. The Bodega Casal
de Valle Pradinhos bases their production on
regional varieties like Tinta Barroca and Tinta
Roriz, but lately Cabernet Sauvignon has
entered the composition of the reds, adding
structure and class. Enologist Joao Nicolau
de Almeida oversees the winemaking.

Porta Velha 1987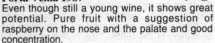
Even though still a young wine, it shows great
potential. Pure fruit with a suggestion of
raspberry on the nose and the palate and good
concentration.

Reserva 1985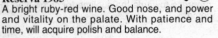
A bright ruby-red wine. Good nose, and power
and vitality on the palate. With patience and
time, will acquire polish and balance.

Caves Velhas - Camilo Alves

Rua Fernão Lopes, 9
Lisbona 1000
Tel. (01) 533031-4
Fax (01) 563397

The Camilo Alves winery was founded in
1881 at Bucelas and later taken over by
Caves Velhas, a company that also sells
Dão, Estremadura, Ribatejo and a series of
wines, some of very high quality, outside the
appellation system. 50% of the grapes
handled come from the winery's own
vineyards. The must is first held in cement
containers, fermentation takes place in 30 hl
vats, and the wine is then matured in 150 hl
Austrian or Brazilian oak barrels. All of the
winemaking and storage operations take
place in a beautiful Victorian stone building
with grand roof tiles supported by wooden
beams, overlooking the Bucelas, a
winemaking area where white wines are of
better quality than reds. The company's other
properties are not worth mentioning.

Bucelas Velho 1985 🍇 ①
A bright, intense straw color. Oak flavors stand
out on the palate, nicely poised against the
characteristic acidity.

Garrafeira 1983 🍇 ①
Bright straw-yellow, subtle and refined on the
nose, with hints of banana which are also
present on the palate. Still in a period of positive
evolution.

Garrafeira 1982 🍇 ①
A limpid pale straw color. Quite evolved yet
polished flavors, delicate texture underlined by a
touch of acidity. Still improving in the bottle.

Dão Caves Velhas 1985 🍷 ①
Intense ruby-red. Mature both on the nose and
the palate, which has marked acidity.
Flavorsome finish.

Bairrada Caves Velhas 1984 🍷 ①
Bright ruby-red color, with chestnut shades at
the edges and an aroma that recalls Soleras.
Light-weight with slightly green tannin in the
finish.

Vercoope

Gandra-Agrela
Santo Tirso 4780
Tel. (02) 9681512
Fax (02) 9680739

This is the brand name of a consortium of 13 cooperatives based in the Vinhos Verdes area of the northern Miño region. They belong to the Associazione Productores-Engarrafadores de Vinho Verde, a group whose membership has grown from the original 17 to today's total of 40. The regulations of the association state that all wines must be made in the producer's own cellars, from grapes grown on the property. Standards of viticulture within the group are high, and the products have consistent quality and style. Wines for the Consorzio, which is directed by the owner of the Brejoeira Winery, are made on the member estates and labelled with the name of the individual producer. The main varieties are Albariño and Loureiro, used by themselves or in blends. Other grapes include Trajadura, Pederñao, Asal and Avesso for the whites and Brancelho, Pedral, Vinhão, Borraçal and Espadeiro for the reds.

Blanco Verde Vercoope 1991   ᵛ ①
Clean lemon-yellow with green reflections. A definite prickle of CO_2 adds intensity to the nose. Fresh and fruity on the palate.

Casa de Compostela 1991   ᵛ ①
Clear, straw-yellow with hints of green. Very fruity to the nose and the palate, with good acidity and a touch of spritzy CO_2.

Quinta de San Claudio 1991   ᵛ ①
Brilliant, lemon-yellow. Very clean and fruity both in the aromas and the flavor, moderate acidity and again a light prickle on the palate.

Quinta do Tamariz 1991   ᵛ ①
Made from 100% Loureiro grapes, lemon-yellow, clean, with the ever present light carbon dioxide sparkle. Intense aromas characteristic of the variety. Fruity on the palate. Drink the youngest vintage available.

Tinto Verde Vercoope 1991   ᵛ ①
Good positive color, with a slight sparkle in the glass. Young, fruity aromas, fresh and dry on the palate.

Vimompor

Sociedade Vinícola de Monção, Lda.
Monção 4950
Tel/Fax (051) 653001

This is probably the best winery in the Vinhos Verdes region. It belongs to the RAR group and owns two properties that give their names to its two best wines: La Quinta da Pedra in Monçao, where there is also a modern winery, and La Quinta do Convento de Fanfei, near Valenca do Miño. The winery has embarked on a large scale project to renew vineyards and renovate cellars throughout the region. Fortunately, properties here have remained modest in size, so that the vineyards receive great care and attention. The quality and selection of the grapes guarantee excellent, fresh, fruity wines. Although they may have a somewhat lower alcohol content than is usual for the country, these are extremely pleasant wines, made to drink young and an excellent accompaniment to seafood. The Vinhos Verdes are a result of a blend of wines from local varieties such as Loureiro, Azal, Avesso, and Albariño, to which a small amount of CO_2 is added. The Quinta da Pedra merits special mention, a more expensive white wine obtained exclusively from top quality Albariño grapes and produced in limited quantities.

Quinta da Pedra 1991   ᵛ ②
A mono-varietal Albariño, not particularly full-bodied, yet elegant on the nose. Attractive straw color with green reflections, fruity and intense on the palate.

ROMANIA

With 2.5 million hectares under vine and a production of around 6,000,000 hectoliters per annum, Romania is one of the world's top ten wine producing countries. Conversely, Romania is one of the least well-known since national consumption more or less equals production, so the bulk of it remains within national borders. Wine that has travelled in recent decades has almost all gone north-east. Romania, therefore, remains something of a vinous enigma in the West.

Romania has some impressive credentials as a wine-producing nation. The vine has been cultivated there for 6000 years or more and internationally famous wines made for over 2000 years (the Dacian, beloved of Romans). The country lies on roughly the same latitude as the great vineyards of France and northern Italy. Climatic and microclimatic conditions are in many parts ideal for making quality wines. The topography helps too, with its mainly south-facing sub-Carpathian foothill expositions, its proximity, in Dobrudja, to the Black Sea, and its hilly Transylvanian Plateau. The established vine varieties are a useful blend of the best from France, Germany and home: Cabernet Sauvignon, Merlot, Pinot Noir, Chardonnay, Pinots Blanc and Gris, Gewürztraminer, Italian Riesling, Silvaner, Muscat, Fetascu, Tamiiosa and Grasa. There is an established quality control system using the initials VSO and VSOC roughly equivalent to the German QbA and QmP categories.

Despite Ceaucescu and state terror, the controls and depreciation of the currency, Romanians have consistently turned out some wines of quality, notably the classic sweet wines of Cotnari and Murfatlar in the east. Other important growing areas include Tirnave in the center of the country (light, dry whites), Minisi-Arad and Recas-Tirol in the west. An Italian Riesling, once marketed as Banat Riesling, is a speciality here, as is a deep, gutsy red from the Cadarka or Hungary's Kadarka grape. Also worthy of note is the Dragasani area, for its red and white table wines of native and imported varieties. The Focsani region, east of the Carpathians, is a source of large volumes of very ordinary wine.

While her potential is excellent, Romania's table wines are of unacceptably low often faulty quality for Western markets. It is only a matter of time before Westerners descend to exploit the wide open situation, as they have in Hungary, Czechoslovakia and the erstwhile USSR. It would be wise to arrive with a large check-book.

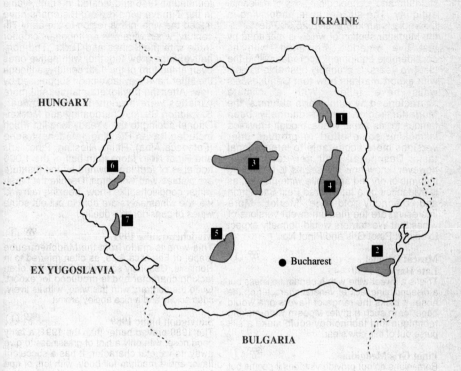

UKRAINE

HUNGARY

EX YUGOSLAVIA

● Bucharest

BULGARIA

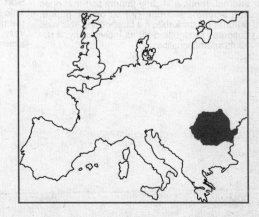

1	Cotnari
2	Murfatlar
3	Tìrnave
4	Focsani
5	Dragasani
6	Minis - Arad
7	Recas - Tirol

S. C. Fruvimed F.A.

Medgidia, Murfatlar
Dobrudja
Tel. 918 10235
Fax 918 11982

The history of vine-growing and wine-making in this gifted zone near the Black Sea is as long as that of any viticultural area in the world, as testified in Greek and Roman literature and archeological finds of millennial antiquity. The current area under vine in Dobrudja is an impressive 25,000 hectares, the Murfatlar section of which is managed by just five wineries. Fruvimed, with its considerable equipment upgraded within the last two years, is probably best able to deal with export markets now that Ceaucescu's walls have fallen. With a climate characterised by long, warm autumns, the Murfatlar region has traditionally been famous for its sweet wines, though Fruvimed is making some effort to produce drier versions more acceptable to international taste. Despite all their new technology, however, know-how still seems to be lacking in terms of dry red and white wine-making, as is evidenced by a rather tired Petit Sauvignon and distinctly old-style Merlot. More interesting are the medium-sweet versions of wines that Westerners would normally expect to be dry: Pinot Gris and Pinot Noir.

Muscat Ottonel
Late Harvest 1990
This is a sweet wine with a certain fruitiness but a disappointing lack of varietal character on the nose. It lacks the range of flavors one would hope for in such a style. Modern wine-making technique and technology could make a silk purse out of this sow's ear.

Pinot Gris Medgidia
Romanians do not provide vintages it seems but tell you that the bottle contains Vin Vechi sub 2 ani or is less than two years old. This 1991 is a sweet white wine of considerable weight but balanced by good acidity. Despite its 35 g/lt residual sugar it finishes fairly dry. Something of a late-picked Alsace style without the finesse.

Pinot Noir Fruvimed 1990
Sweet reds are a rarity these days, which explains why this wine is of considerable interest. It has a slightly jammy soft-fruit nose and smooth, wild-cherry fruit on the palate. Surprisingly drinkable, if a bit shocking, this wine deserves recognition for its individuality, if not for its internationality.

Statiunea de cercetari viti-vinicole - Blaj

Str. Ghearoghe Baritiu Nr. 2
3175 Blaj
Tel. (4067) 1075
Fax (4067) 10620

There are a handful of experimental oenological institutions in Romania, but seldom do they emphasise quality in their codes. One exception to this rule is Blaj, founded in 1946 and located in Transylvania in the Tîrnave wine region. Historians have traced the vine in this region to the early 7th century, when wine was an important crop for trade with the Sciites and Turks. The non-native vines grew together with native ones even at the turn of the 19th century, although the latter have inevitably been suppressed by now. After the phylloxera plague, still more varieties were brought in, like Traminer, Sauvignon Blanc, Chardonnay and Muskat-Ottonel adding to the already long list which included Italian Riesling , Mädchentraube (Feteasca Alba), Rhine Riesling, Pinot Gris and Pinot Noir. More than half of the 1,000 hectares of farmland owned by the Institute are planted with vineyards. Despite the harsh winter conditions, like snow, freezing rain and ice, the winemakers are able to put out some wines of considerable quality.

Mädchentraube 1991
This wine is made from the Mädchentraube grape, or Feteasca Alba, as often referred to in Romania. Generally somewhat flabby it is often lacking character and is produced for export. Quite the contrary with this wine, with its lively, crisp acidity and a nice appley-aroma.

Sauvignon blanc 1989
The 1989 proved better than the 1991; a fairly good nose, with only a hint of grassiness to give away its varietal character. It has a succulent flavor and a medium-full body, with lots of ripe fruit.

Muskat-Ottonel
Here is proof that the Romanians can indeed make some notable wines showing good ripe fruit. Even after several years of aging, this wine seems to hold very well. A subtle and pleasant degree of residual sugar has helped to maintain its freshness.

Sekt 'Tirnavelle'
This is a non-vintage sparkling wine made by the méthode champenoise technique. It has very fine bubbles and a surprisingly crisp, almost gripping acidity.

Vinia Iassy S.A.

4 Meturgiei Sreet
6000 Iasi, Moldavia
Fax 35382

Vinia Iassy is a typical example of one of Eastern Europe's massive state-controlled wine operations emerging into the blinding sunlight of international commerce. Vinia Iassy deal with grapes and wines from various viticultural zones of Moldavia, of which the most important historically is Cotnari. There is abundant evidence stretching back centuries if not millenia to suggest that Cotnari, with its characterful native grape varieties (Grasa, Feteasca Alba, Tamiioasa, Romanea and Frincusa), is among the select few regions of the world for the production of sweet wines. Its mild, long autumns are ideal for late-harvested grapes, with or without noble rot, and the vintage often takes place late in October with sugar levels at the time of picking as high as 300 g/lt. Less dependent on technology, sweet wines seem to have survived the Soviet years better than their dry counterparts. The re-equipping program which winemaker Nicolae Bolohan says will be imminent will be useful more for putting a final polish on, rather than for totally transforming, the products presently made.

Grasa de Cotnar   ☙ ☙ ②
This is a sweet white wine of 12° alc and 60 g/lt residual sugar, aged three to five years in 500 to 5000 liter barrels of Romanian oak. It is yellow gold in color, rich and rather heavy, with a slightly petrolly nose, reminiscent of old Riesling, with an almost medicinal finish.

Tamiioasa Romaneasca 1988   ☙ ②
A rich, sweet if rather bland wine of 12° alc and 80 g/lt residual sugar. Wood aged less than Grasa, it is less aromatic, while having good acid-fruit balance and an intrinsic interest which cries out for a modern winemaking approach.

SLOVENIA

Slovenia is a young country, having gained its independence only in 1991, but its wine history goes back many centuries. The Maribor cellars for instance were built in the 15th century. Wine is made almost everywhere but the best comes from the Podravje region to the north (along the Drava river and bordering the Austrian side of Istria), the Collio region (as in the neighboring Friuli), the Vipacco area (to the south-east of Collio) and lastly the southern-most strip facing the Adriatic Sea, the Istrian horn. The Podravje region or Padravski rajon is the area where the damp, sub-alpine currents clash with the warm Mediterranean climate. The soil composition is mixed (clay, limestone, chalk) and the vine-training generally "a ritocchino" with a vine density of 2,000-4,000 vines per hectare.

Most of the production is in the hands of large public cooperatives, but more recently two dozen or so small but courageous vintners have joined forces and begun bottling on their own. As the quality standards rise, inevitably so do the prices. However, the tragic political situation, as former Yugoslavia is torn apart, caused prices to plummet again and balance out in line with a depressed and difficult economy.

As in neighboring Istria, the main varieties are Rhine Riesling, Italian Riesling, Pinot Gris and Pinot Blanc. Purely native vines include the Sipon, which makes a light-bodied white wine. The Sauvignon grape, or Silvaner Muscat as it is known here, is usually late-harvested to make semi-sweet and off-dry versions with aromas vastly different from its French counterpart. The Collio or Goriska Brda is an interesting area and its wines have come in for recent praise. Dozens of small growers, some having vineyards that dip into nearby Italy, compare the results of their vineyard and cellar experiments with Friulian colleagues. The wines are often made from the same grapes such as Tocai, Chardonnay, Sauvignon, Pinot Blanc and Gris, Merlot and Cabernet. Vine densities average 2,000-4,000 vines per hectare using terraced rows for a marly soil composition. If vintners in Maribor prefer to pick later to make sweet or semi-sweet wines then here in Collio they prefer to pick earlier to preserve the fresh acidity and the rich concentrated fruit that the favorable growing conditions impart. The Vipacco or Vipava is similar to the Collio area in its soil composition but few enterprising producers have ventured into the area so far. Even the Carso or Kras could use a push in the right direction in order to explore alternatives to the Terrano red wine which many consumers across the border find too tart to be drinkable. Slovenia's largest cooperative winery, Vinakopern, is located in the Capodistria region or Koprski Vinorodni okolis. Malvasia Istriana is the best known grape although Chardonnay is taking on well for obvious commercial reasons. Reds range from Merlot and Cabernet Franc to Sauvignon Terrano, known as Refosco, which is not as bitter as Carso's Terrano. The wines are generally very good buys, as in all of Slovenia, and there is certainly no lack of enthusiasm or will to improve. Slovenia's entire production covers only 45-50% of domestic consumption. As a result cheaper wines are generally imported from neighboring countries especially as the best Slovenian wines are exported.

AUSTRIA

HUNGARY

● Ljubljana

ITALY

CROATIA

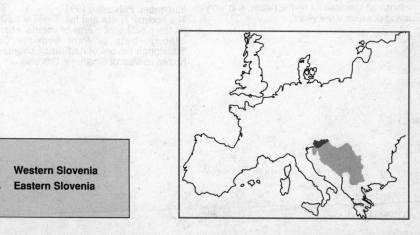

1 **Western Slovenia**
2 **Eastern Slovenia**

Ivan Batic

Sempas 130
Sempas 65621
Tel. (065) 48676

44 year-old Ivan Batic has kept his family's 300 year-old wine business alive while also cattle breeding and tending to his fruit orchards. He is committed to researching new training techniques and up-dating wine-making techniques in the cellar. The eight hectares of vineyards in the Vipava valley, or Vipacco in Italian, have a marly soil and an excellent sunny exposure. Vine density is about 4,000 plants per hectare and the yields are kept to 60 hl/ha. A spring frost in 1991 considerably limited the crop. In imitation of nearby Italian producers like Gravner, Radikon and Bensa, he tends to limit production, trying for a higher quality standard. He takes pride in using special cone-shaped bottles, symbolic of the Slovenian Republic. Better known for his red wines than his whites, Ivan bottles the wines in the August following the vintage and likes to put aside the best crop (about 260 hl) to bottle-age and mature in the cellars which were built in 1717.

Chardonnay 1990   🍇 ①
Pale straw yellow in color, it has been partly aged six months in new barriques and shows a typical toasty character. In the mouth it is full, long-lasting, with hints of bread and yeast.

Sauvignon 1990   🍇 ①
Having fermented and aged for six months in used barriques it has acquired complex aromas and a firm structure. Elegant and lingering.

Zelen 1990   🍇 ①
Straw yellow with green highlights, it is made from the native Zelen grape. Its bouquet gives off lots of fresh fruit but leaves a riper, more mature flavor in the mouth. Despite the low yields in the vineyard it is low in alcohol and lacks complexity.

Rosso Batic 1990   🍷 ①
A blend of Merlot, Cabernet Franc and Cabernet Sauvignon, this red has been aged in oak barriques. As well-structured, full, spiced and intense on the nose as on the palate. It is worth laying down for a few years.

Ivan Borko in Marija

Partizananska c. 47
69250 Gornja Radgona
Tel. (069) 61394

Ivan Borko's impressive winery is located 40 km east of Maribor below a majestic villa regretfully on the verge of crumbling down any day now. Built in 1428, its arches and brick walls caked with centuries of blackened mould and foamy white brick rot, the Borko winery neatly lines up its medium-capacity wood casks, where the wines ferment and mature. A youthful 72 year-old, Borko has a right to be proud when showing off the wines that he has been bottling since 1986. The four hectares of well kept and positioned vineyards are located on the hillsides surrounding the winery and another one-hectare vineyard is nearby. Daniela, Borko's 30 year-old daughter, a graduate in agriculture, assists in operations helping to boost production to an average 20,000 bottles each year. The wines are clean, honest, often elegant, and among the best made in Slovenia. No small wonder, in fact, that Borko manages to keep an empty cellar. It would have been nice to taste some of the older vintages, to see how they age and to follow their surely promising evolution.

Laski Rizling Pozna Trgatev 1991 🍇 🍇 ①
This late-harvest Italian Riesling ages for nine months prior to bottling. It is striking for its impressive elegance and complexity, rich aroma, and underlying balance due to a good firm acidity.

Renski Rizling Polsuho 1991   🍇 ①
Semi-dry due to a fermentation block, on the nose this Rhine Riesling is intense, complex, rich with fruit and lingering. On the palate it shows a good structure and fresh acidity, with a hint of aromatic sweetness.

Renski Rizling Pozna   🍇 ①
Trgatev Polsuho 1991
Harvested on 31 October, the wine has a good structure together with rich and well balanced flavor and a nose of fresh flowers and other aromas. It is moderately semi-sweet.

Sauvignon Polsladko 1991   🍇 ①
The bouquet is rich and full. There is freshness on the palate with plenty of varietal character although quite different from the classic Sauvignon flavors of its French counterpart. Known as Muscat Silvaner in Slovenia.

Stanko Curin

62276 Kog 15
Tel. (062) 716046-717039
Fax (062) 717037

The witty and well-versed 63 year-old Stanko Curin has been a pioneer for wine growers in Slovenia for years. Initial production and bottling began in 1971, and this in a country that mainly operated under collective organizations or the State. At the Ljubljana Wine Show, the most important wine competition in what used to be Yugoslavia, Curin used to cause acute embarrassment by winning numerous awards. Today this winery has 10 ha of vineyards (1,500-4,500 vines per hectare) planted on slopes in the Podravje region which lies between the Drava and the Mura rivers between the Austrian and Croatian borders. Most of the 70,000 bottle production is of white wine and includes a Laski Rizling (made from Italian Riesling), Sipon (a close relative of the Furmint Sipon grape), a Renski Rizling or Rhine Riesling, Rulandec Sivi Pinot (made from Pinot Gris) and a Sauvignon (otherwise known as Muscat Silvaner). As often done in neighboring Austria, Curin likes to make late-harvested wines made from carefully selected grapes that on occasion are raisined or have been affected by botrytis.

Laski Rizling 1991   ⴼ ①
Its bouquet at first seems closed, but then it slowly opens to reveal an uncommon freshness and typicity. On the palate it has a certain elegance, with a solid roundness and a fruity acidity that will enable it to age well.

Laski Rizling Izbor 1991   ⴼ ④
Made from botrytised grapes that were harvested on 29 October, this wine is incredibly full-bodied and intensely aromatic despite the poor quality of the 1991 vintage compared with the previous year. Yields were kept low to 4 hl/ha.

Renski Rizling 1991   ⴼ ①
This wine shows the potential of the Slovenian Rizling. Fruity, with a pleasant aromatic quality it is rich and balanced on the nose and is counterbalanced by a refreshingly lingering acidity. It holds much promise for the future.

Lanski Rizling Izbor 1990   ⴼ ⴼ ④
Made from botrytised and raisined grapes that ripened on the vine until 13 January, this wine has only 7.5° alc and 255 gr/lt of residual sugar. The unique aromas of wet leather, tobacco and spices make this "trockenbeerenauslese" truly exceptional excusing its high price tag.

Jurij Hlupic

Kamniska 9a
62000 Maribor
Tel.(062) 25979

Jurij Hlupic, a polite and good natured 42 year-old, has vineyards that are situated close to the border with Austria just 20 kilometers north-east of Maribor, at the foot of a peak that carries his name. Ideal conditions which include the sandy-clay soil and favorable microclimate which shelters the vineyard from strong northerly winds, enables Hlupic to harvest the grapes three weeks later than other producers in the Podravje region. Bottling since 1981, Hlupic has 11 hectares of vineyards and likes to keep yields around 40 hl/ha contributing in part to his 40,000 bottle production. Of the wines produced, he makes more Riesling (both the Italian and Rhine) and some late-harvest Riesling, Pinot Bianco and Traminer in various vintages and with differing degrees of botrytis which have proven to be particularly successful. More for the fun he produced an Eiswein in 1991 extracting a mere 80 liters of juice from 600 kilos of grapes. The high production costs means the wine is reserved only for friends. On the whole Hlupic's wines are very honest and typical often having a good structure and potential for bottle aging.

Beli Burgundec 1991   ⴼ ①
An elegant Pinot Blanc with a floral-fruity bouquet. Like all Hlupic's wines it is full on the palate with a fresh acidity and long persistent finish..

Jurija Vina 1991   ⴼ ①
A blend of Rhine Riesling, Italian Riesling, Pinot Bianco and Müller Thurgau, this wine has maintained intense, fruity, well-balanced aromas with a concentrated structure for potential bottle aging. A well made wine.

Laski Rizling Pozna Trgatev 1991   ⴼ ①
This late-harvested or Pozna Trgatev wine made from Italian Riesling is the ultimate proof that this grape has adapted well to its environment. It has a freshness that complements the underlying sweetness. The 1983 vintage still has a good acidity to it as well as aromas of tobacco and leather, proof of its aging capabilities.

Beli Burgundec Pozna Trgatev 1986   ⴼ ②
This late-harvest 1986 has won many an award in London for its intense honey bouquet, rich almond flavor on the palate, and its excellent firmness.

Kogl di Franci Cvetko

Velika Nedelja, 23
62274 V. Nedelja
Tel. (062) 718301
Fax (062) 718302

At 31, Franci Cvetko is a young producer of rare profiency and skill. After graduating from the school of oenology in Maribor, he decided to work for himself and bought a hilltop vineyard in Velika Nedelja (40 km south-east of Maribor). A stone inscription commemorates the fact that the vine once thrived there as far back as 1482. The south-facing vineyard has a friable clay and sandy soil composition and as of 1984 covers four hectares with a vine-density of 4,000 plants per hectare. On the opposite slope is a fruit orchard. The brick vaulted cellar built in 1825 houses wooden casks of different sizes (20-38 hl) used to age the wines for a few months. Since his first bottling experiences in 1987 Franci has improved the cellar operations and learned to keep the fruit yields modest in the vineyard. Today he is one of the most interesting producers in the area. His only possible weakness is the large range of 12 wines that are produced. As a result bottle production per type of wine (5,000-7,000 for the Sipon and for the Laski Rizling) is relatively low for a market that is destined to expand.

Laski Rizling 1991　　　　　　♈ ①
The grape (Italian Riesling) shows itself very well in these climatic and geographical conditions giving good fruit and intensity in both the bouquet and on the palate. Fresh in acidity, it has a typical and lingering finish. All the right components for a longish period of bottle aging.

Muskat Otonel 1991　　　　　　♈ ①
Intense straw yellow in color with the aroma of the Muscat grape. It is agreeable, sweet, balanced and very persistent on the palate.

Sauvignon 1991　　　　　　♈♈ ①
At long last a good Sauvignon that you can recognize at first sight, with its herbaceous bouquet. Franci differs in his way of making Sauvignon by harvesting later. Its flavor is complex, full bodied and lingering.

Sipon 1991　　　　　　♈ ①
Pale straw yellow with green highlights, this light-bodied white has a floral bouquet. On the palate it is dry and shows good acidity, with a slightly bitter aftertaste. It is fairly widespread throughout the Maribor region.

Kerner Izbor 1990　　　　　　♈ ④
Made from selected grapes of a new hybrid, produced from a cross between Rhine Riesling and Trollinger, this is a complex wine, elegant, intense with a bouquet of ripe fruit. On the palate it is sweet and fresh with a pronounced acidity.

Kristancic Silvio/Dusan

Medana, 29
65212 Dobrovo
Slovenia
Tel/Fax(065) 45088

Medana is located on the border between Slovenia and Italy in the Goriska Brda and has a soil and climatic conditions similar to those of the Collio Goriziano in Italy. The only minor difference is in the temperature which here is slightly cooler causing harvest times to be put back a few days. Dusan Kristancic, 37 years-old, is not affected by this much since only 10% of his eight hectare vineyard is in Slovenia with the rest in Ruttars in the Collio DOC area. Dusan is a prime example of the caliber of youth operating in the wine world today. Ever since his first bottlings in 1989 he has been set on making premium quality wine and knows what is required. He has a fully equipped cellar with modern press, cooling equipment and stainless steel vats (together with cement ones). The bottling line (production is at around 40,000 bottles) is shared with other small producers in the area. All this ironically contrasts with Dusan's inexperience in the vineyard and reluctance to reduce the vine yield. The results, in terms of the wine quality, vary from a low yielding vintage like the 1990 to a more abundant harvest in 1991. Nonetheless, the average quality standard remains high.

Chardonnay 1991　　　　　　♈ ①
Straw yellow with greenish highlights, it has that varietal character on the nose (with bread crust and yeast notes) a good structure on the palate, with a refreshing acidity to enhance its lingering finish and a certain complexity. It is the best wine of the vintage.

Rumena Rebula 1991　　　　　　♈ ①
This is a good example of the Ribolla Gialla grape. Straw yellow in color, it has lots of young fruit on the nose. On the palate it is supple, lingering and shows good balance, with a slightly bitter aftertaste.

Sivi Pinot 1991　　　　　　♈ ①
This Pinot Gris has a rich fruit and mineral bouquet. Medium-bodied, on the palate it has complex flavors reminiscent of dry hay and fruit.

Joze Kupljen

Jeruzalem-Svetinje
Velicane 59 - 62259 Jvanikvoci
Tel. (062) 714128
Fax (062) 714015

Joze Kupljen is a good oenologist, but he tends to spread himself too thin while trying to manage two different establishments. He has a restaurant presently under renovation in Mainz, Germany, and his hillside-winery in Jeruzalem, once an important cross roads for Pilgrims on their journey to the Holy Land. With its clay-sand soil composition and well-exposed hillside vineyards, this area is among the best for wine production. Kupljen has upgraded much of his machinery, although he refuses to let go of his beautiful wooden barrels that impart a unique flavor. In his absence the jovial Alojz Cedula lends a hand. He owns a tavern located near to Kupljen's main cellars. There are 11 ha of vineyards although only six are actually under production. To maintain his 100,000 bottle production Kupljen buys and vinifies the best grapes available from the local farmers. Three years from now the new five hectare vineyard planted mainly with Pinot Gris, Rhine Riesling and Chardonnay will be under production.

Renski Rizling 1991　　　　🍇 ①
Pale straw yellow with nice green highlights, it has a fine bouquet. Its flavor is characteristic, having a firm acidity, the right grapey aroma, with a lingering and intense finish.

Kerner Pol-Suho 1990　　　🍇 ①
This wine is a perfect expression of the hybrid Kerner grape, a cross between Rhine Riesling and Trollinger. It has an intense fruity nose and on the palate a refreshing acidity, complex backbone and good balance, being faintly off-dry on the finish.

Rumeni Muskat 1990　　　　🍇 ①
This is the last of the old yellow Muscat vines. The new ones will be planted in two or three years. Showing great typical character and complexity, the aroma is fair and the finish, lingering. A real pleasure to taste.

Sauvignon Pol-Suho 1990　　🍇 ①
Pol-Suho means semi-dry but due to its firm acidity this wine doesn't show any noticeable traces of residual sugar. Instead, it has harmonious aromas, with a hint of elder flowers, and a clean finish.

Mlecnik Andrej in Valter

Bukovica, 31
65293 Volcja draga
Tel. (065) 53031

The colossal state-run cooperatives have completely dominated wine production in the Vipava Valley until now so recently there has been a real awakening among the smaller estates, especially those who have maintained contact with neighboring Collio producers in Italy. It was only in 1989 that Andrej and his 33 year-old son Valter began bottling on their own, urged on by the Oslavian "guru" Josko Gravenr. The Mlecnik family settled in Bukovic in 1946 and began producing bulk wines, sold by the demi-john, from its vineyard which was planted to a density of 3000 vines per hectare. Since then thanks to Valter's enthusiasm and dedication they have planted new vines and doubled the density to 6000 vines per hectare. The soil composition is prevalently marl and all the vineyards are south facing. Of all his wines Valter Mlecnik pays most attention to the Tocai, blending grapes from vines that are more than 45 years-old with grapes from younger vines, and the Chardonnay which has a yearly production of 10,000 bottles. Both are imported into Italy by the famous restaurateur Josko Sirk in Cormons.

Chardonnay 1990　　　　🍇🍇 ①
The extreme vine density, harvest ing at peak ripeness and the oak barrel fermentation are all contributing factors to its high alcohol content, notable structure and balance which make this a very promising wine.

Furlanski Tokaj 1990　　　🍇 ①
Pale straw yellow in color, this wine has a sharp freshness with a complex bouquet and an equally pleasant richness on the palate with grassy fruit flavors.

Movia di Kristancic Mirko in Ales

Ceglo, 18
Loc. Medana
65121 Dobrovo Slovenja
Tel. (065) 55103

Italy's borders have shifted more than once since the Kristancic family settled in Ceglo di Medana in 1820 planting vineyards that once-upon-a-time belonged to the Movia family. This explains why part of the 13 hectare vineyard is in the Goriska Brda and another part, about eight hectares, in the Collio Friuliano DOC area. The soil composition is the same on both sides (oceanic marl, particularly favorable to vine-growing) and the nearby seaside imparts a maritime micro-climate. Mirko Kristancic was in 1986 one of the first producers to bottle his own wines privately withdrawing from the Dobrovo cooperative (Castel Dobra). Today Mirko produces 100,000 bottles under his Movia label which are mainly sold to the restaurant trade in Slovenia and in smaller quantities exported to Belgium, Germany and Japan. At his side since early times has been the renowned Italian oenologist, Giovanni Crosato, whose underlying skill shines through especially when supplied with top quality fruit. Another important point is the dedication of Mirko's 27 year-old son Ales who helps out with all cellar operations and promises continuity and progress in the family business.

Goriska Brda Tokaj 1991　　🍇 ①
Pale straw yellow, this Tocai has an intense bouquet, with fresh fruit aromas, maybe a shade grassy. It comes through well on the palate, being intense, lingering and full-bodied.

Goriska Brda　　🍇🍇 ②
Chardonnay Barrique 1990
Following the first fermentation the wine has been aged for six months in Slovenian oak barriques and then bottle aged. Full-bodied, it is drinkable now while also showing good promise for the future.

Goriska Brda Izbrani Plodovi 1990　🍇 ②
This wine is made from selected grapes of Pinot Grigio, Pinot Bianco, Chardonnay and Ribolla, vinified on 10 January 1991. The resulting wine is intensely rich, with notes of dried figs closely bound with the scent of acacia wood.

Goriska Brda Merlot 1990　　🍇 ①
Brilliant, intense ruby in color, it has a refreshing acidity on the nose. Young but no less intense for that reason, it shows a good structure, with decent tannins and well-balanced fruit.

Goriska Brda Merlot Barrique 1990　🍇 ②
Rich ruby red in color, indicating that the grapes were harvested when very ripe. With its intense, well-balanced bouquet, it comes through well on the palate with tannins that are not too aggressive.

Vinakoper

Smarska 1
66000 Koper - Slovenia
Tel. (066) 31161
Fax (066) 33733

The Vinakoper winery is the fourth largest producer in Slovenia, with its 2000 hectares of vines (400 owned directly) and a production capacity of 86,000 hl. Founded in 1953, it is one of the wineries to watch for in the future due to recent modernisation of equipment and the skills of Iztok Klenar, a Ljubljana graduate, who has been managing the winery for the last seven years. Next to the larger wooden casks, used for red wines, are stainless-steel vats for temperature-controlled fermentation, hydraulic presses, modern crushers and the old-fashioned cement and fiberglass tanks. Apart from the bulk wines, there are approximately 800,000 bottles of better quality wines, specially selected at the cellars, which are insufficient to cover a demand which in Slovenia is nearly double the national production. Reds represent 75% of the production at Vinakoper the largest portion being made from Refosco which is relatively similiar to Terrano with its high acidity and tannin. Among the whites Malvazija (Malvasia) is the most classic. There have also been some interesting results from Chardonnay and the new red and white Capris.

Malvazija 1991　　🍇 ①
Pale straw yellow in color, it has an intense, fresh and fruity bouquet that delivers even more on the palate. Medium-bodied, it has good varietal character and a delicate finesse that should make it pair well with fish.

Capris Beli 1990　　🍇 ①
A late-harvest wine made from a blend of Malvasia and Chardonnay with some Moscato Bianco and Pinot Grigio. It has full fruit flavors.

Cabernet Sauvignon 1989　　🍇 ①
Rich ruby red in color, it has an excellent bouquet of wild-berries and maraschino cherries; velvety, full, robust on the palate, with ripe fruit. Drinks well now although will age for a few years.

Capris 1989　　🍇 ①
A cuvée of Cabernet Sauvignon, Cabernet Franc and Merlot with a touch of Refosco. It has a garnet ruby color and a herbaceous, grassy bouquet, slightly wild, due to the Cabernet Franc and Refosco. Well-balanced, medium tannin on the palate, with a hint of jam. Its lingering finish promises an interesting evolution.

SOUTH AFRICA

South Africa's wine producing history began in 1652 when the Dutch East India Company, led by Jan van Riebeeck, settled in the Cape. The first vine cuttings were imported from Europe, and in 1659 the first harvest took place. Cape wines have had a long and at times glorious history with the wonderful Constantia wines gracing the tables of European nobility, but the development of the industry was actually rather problematic. The original settlers knew little about vine cultivation, but the arrival of a new Commander of the Cape, Simon van der Stel, in 1679 set off a series of important changes. A cultured and well-travelled man, he immediately set about improving wine quality and established Stellenbosch, the country's first wine center. Then, in 1688, the arrival of the first Huguenots gave the industry the much needed injection of expertise.

The first notable exports of red and white Constantia wines took place in 1761 and following the purchase of Groot Constantia by the Cloete family in 1778, production of the great, sweet Constantia wines began. The situation improved enormously after the first British occupation of the Cape (1795-1802), and particularly after the second, more permanent occupation with the introduction of quality control on exports in 1811. The Cape depended greatly on the British market and on Great Britain's relationship with France. Initially the situation ran in favor of the Cape with high tariffs being imposed on French wines in 1825 but in 1861 the situation was reversed, with disastrous consequences for South African wines. In the mean time the emancipation of slaves in 1834 had an even deeper effect since it struck at the very heart of the colonial system. The result was the Great Trek inland (thousand of settlers decided to abandon their lands) and a total change in the social system.

The country's viticulture did not escape the ravages of phylloxera which first struck in 1885 and was only overcome at the turn of the century with the help of grafting on to American rootstocks. In 1909 over-production caused a major slump in prices. From the beginning a substantial amount of production was of poor quality and over-production and falling markets soon became the norm. This led in 1918 to the formation of the KWV (Kooperatieve Wijnbouwers Vereniging), which in 1924 was given power to fix the minimum price of distilling wine and so, in effect, control of the industry which it has had to the present. Its control grew significantly in 1940 when it was empowered to regulate the entire wine sector and then again in the late 1950s, with the introduction of a quota system and more controls over all members of the industry.

The KWV has been both a blessing and a curse. Without it the majority of grape growers and wine producers would not have been able to profit from their endeavors given the increase in over-production. But although the KWV has been highly successful in regulating the industry, the quota system benefitted the more numerous grape farmers and prevented the more enterprising producers from planting new vineyards and introducing certain new grape varieties. There are still less than 100 estates compared to around 6,000 grape growers. Fortunately this situation came to end in 1992 with the demise of the quota system.

South Africa's wine industry was largely based on fortified and dessert wines, but this is currently changing with the production of premium whites and reds, although over half the total production of grapes is still for table consumption or for distilling. Cold fermentation techniques were employed only after the Second World War, a development initiated in the 1920s by Professor Perold and later advanced by the early German immigrants. During the 1950s the German style dominated, but by the 1970s it had moved towards a more French approach, and this has continued to gain ground.

The Wine of Origin legislation was introduced in 1973 and remains much the same today. The use of a multi-colored label affixed to the capsule certifies the statements on the label regarding origin, vintage and grape variety. It is illegal to specify a vineyard site but an increasing number of estates are doing so without being prosecuted. The system of defined origin, at times rather confusing, is based on regions, districts and wards. Currently, however, only a very small proportion of South African wines carry the Wine of Origin sticker, since many of the more popular brands do not bother to go through the rather troublesome and expensive process of certification. The legislation has however helped to encourage the production of quality wine and to increment consumer awareness.

In terms of quality much has been accomplished in recent years. Barriques and Bordeaux blends were unheard of until the 1980s, but today many of the estates are technically up-to-date with young qualified winemakers who combine talent with experience gained traveling and working in wineries around the world. One of the factors which has held the industry back, the lack of virus-free clones, has been overcome in recent years; consequently many of the vineyards have young vines. When these mature there is little doubt that quality levels will rise higher and, with the increasing experience of the winemakers and the increasing flexibility of the KWV, the future of South African wines looks bright.

The first vineyards in the country emerged in the Coastal region, whose inland districts still benefit from coastal breezes, whereas those in other regions face much more difficult climatic conditions and require irrigation, mainly for young vines and at times of severe drought. The most important region continues to be the Coastal region which covers Constantia, Durbanville, Swartland, Stellenbosch, Paarl with its ward Franschhoek and Tulbagh. Nearly every estate located in these districts can claim special micro-climates, soils or other factors that makes them unique. Paarl and Stellenbosch are considered the country's largest wine districts. In more recent years the Breede River Valley region has gained importance, particularly with the district of Robertson, and even the region-less district of Overberg, with its ward of Walker Bay, has seen some exciting developments.

Port-style fortified wines remain an important part of South Africa's wine production along with dessert wines often made from botrytized grapes (Gewürztraminer), and reds produced uniquely from Cabernet Sauvignon, Cabernet Franc, Merlot, Shiraz, Cinsaut or used in a blend. The production of whites (Chardonnay, Sauvignon Blanc, Chenin Blanc and Rhine Riesling) and méthode champenoise sparkling wines is extremely encouraging.

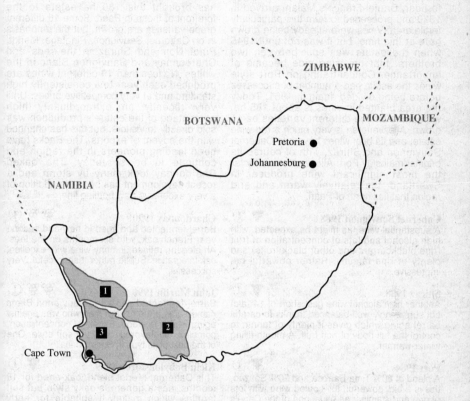

ZIMBABWE

BOTSWANA

MOZAMBIQUE

Pretoria ●

Johannesburg ●

NAMIBIA

Cape Town ●

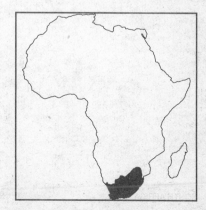

1 **Boberg**
2 **Breede River Valley**
3 **Coastal Region**

Allesverloren

Riebeck West 6800
Swartland
Tel. (02246) 320

Granted in 1704 by Willem van der Stel to one of the Cloete family, this estate took its name after an incident in the 18th century when the then owner returned from Stellenbosch to find that the farm had been totally destroyed in an attack by bushmen. Allesverloren literally means "all is lost." The present owners are the Malan family, whose forbear, Daniel François Malan, arrived in 1870 and proceeded to farm this particularly fertile area. Vines were already being grown here at this time, but it was not until 1945 when the estate was split between two brothers, that the wine side became of importance. Concentrating on Port style wines the estate had a number of successes before being divided again in 1961. Today the area planted in vines is about 185 ha, with some twelve different varieties being grown. Allesverloren is very much a red wine estate, and its best wines have ben Cabernet Sauvignon and Shiraz, with of course its original mainstay Port. Allesverloren is by far the most significant wine producer in Swartland, the relatively warm and arid region that lies north of Paarl.

Cabernet Sauvignon 1988   🍷 ①
A substantial wine, as might be expected, with high alcohol and lots of concentration of fruit (ripe blackcurrant and other black fruits) and plenty of ripe tannins. Rather powerful but impressive.

Shiraz 1988   🍷 ①
Another high alcohol wine (just short of 14° alc) but surprisingly well-balanced thanks to careful barrel aging which gives it plenty of tannin to control the full body of rich fruit. A mouth-filling winter-warmer.

Port 1984   🍷 ①
A blend of 80% Tinta Barroca and 20% Souzao, this is a big, powerful, full-bodied wine with lots of grip and stamina; as usual one of the Cape's best Ports.

Backsberg

Box 1, Klapmuts 7625
Paarl
Tel. (02211) 5141
Fax (02211) 5144

Originally called Klein Babylonstoren, this estate was purchased in 1916 by Charles Back, a Lithuanian immigrant, and has remained in the family ever since. Today it is ably run by Sydney Back, his son Michael and winemaker Hardy Laubscher. Sydney has twice been honored with the Winemaker of the Year award, in 1978 and 1982, and has brought this 180 ha estate to the forefront of those in Paarl. Some 16 different grape varieties are grown, but the emphasis in on Cabernet Sauvignon, Pinotage, Merlot, Pinot Noir and Shiraz in the reds and Chardonnay and Sauvignon Blanc in the whites. No less than 19 different wines are produced each year to a consistently high standard and at very competitive prices. Until very recently an extraordinarily high percentage of the estate's production was sold directly to visitors, but this has changed with the advent of exports. The Backs have been leading pioneers in the region and continue to be so today. The oaked Chardonnay took many by storm and a recent development has been the addition of a very expensive new bottling line.

Chardonnay 1990   🍷🍷 ①
Barrel-fermented and aged in new and second year French oak, with six months on the lees. An elegant, refined, lemony wine with excellent oak integration. Subtle rather than forceful. Very successful.

John Martin 1990   🍷🍷 ①
Barrel-fermented and aged Sauvignon Blanc named after a member of staff who was against aging whites in wood. Excellent concentration, complex, full-flavored, oaky yet soft style. One of the best of its type in South Africa.

Klein Babylonstoren 1989   🍷 ①
This Cabernet-Merlot blend, oak-aged for 18 months, has a generous oaky style but soft tannins which makes it suitable for early drinking. It will develop over many years.

Shiraz 1989   🍷 ①
A classic Cape Shiraz with deep, smoky, full-bodied flavor and supple tannins, suitable for early drinking but will keep.

The Bergkelder

Box 5001
Stellenbosch
Tel. (02231) 73480
Fax (02231) 99533

The Bergkelder is a major force in the South African wine industry. It is affiliated to Stellenbosch Farmers' Winery, Gilbeys and KWV and is a sister company to the Distillers Company under the umbrella of the Rembrant Group. In effect the Bergkelder does a bit of everything, acting as large cooperative, owner, wholesaler and retailer. Besides its own large range of wines, it looks after the marketing of 19 of the Cape's leading estates, and for the majority of them bottles their wines in a purpose-built cellar. This estate has undoubtedly made a major contribution to the Cape wine industry, although it has come in for regular criticism, largely because of the sheer influence that it wields. Gerhard Hofmann is production director and cellarmaster is Dr. Julius Laszlo, who having escaped from Hungary in 1975 joined the Bergkelder a year later and will soon be retiring. His contribution in the intervening years has been immense.

Here XVII Grande Cuvée 1987   ❦ ❦ ①
Traditional méthode champenoise sparkling wine made from Pinot Noir. Excellent mousse and impressive yeasty bouquet and flavor from four years on yeasts. This is an outstanding wine.

J C Le Roux Pinot Noir 1986   ❦ ❦ ①
Another top quality traditional méthode champenoise sparkling wine made from grapes grown on Meerlust estate. Winner of the Schramsberg trophy for best bottle-fermented wine in the 1991 International Wine & Spirit Competition, it reveals a full, deep yeasty character and is well balanced.

Fleur du Cap   ❦ ①
Cabernet Sauvignon 1987
This is part of a range of over a dozen wines. It is a well oaked wine showing excellent fruit concentration backed by good ripe tannins. Lovely deep color.

Stellenryck collection,   ❦ ❦ ❦ ①
Cabernet Sauvignon 1987
Winner of the Dave Hughes Trophy for best Cape red in the 1991 International Wine & Spirit Competition. Superb Cabernet with ripples of ripe blackcurrant and mulberry fruit underpined by excellent tannin structure from two years in new oak. This outstanding wine is made from carefully selected grapes grown on the perimeter of Cape Town in the Durbanville area which is a relatively cool region because of its proximity to the sea. Critical factors such as perfect ripeness of grapes at harvest, location of vineyard site, the choice of French oak (Nevers) and yeast strains have been learnt over many years. It will be interesting to see whether winemaker Julius Laszlo's successor will have the same touch.

Beyerskloof

Box 107, Keolenhof 7605
Stellenbosch
Tel. (02231) 92376

It may seem strange to list a winery that produced its first bottling in 1990 (Cabernet Sauvignon 1989), but not when you know the enigmatic Beyers Truter. For ten years the extraordinary winemaker at Kanonkop, now fabled as "Winemaker of the Year," having won the Robert Mondavi Trophy in the 1991 International Wine & Spirit Competition, Beyers is one of South Africa's most dedicated red winemakers and undisputed champion of the Pinotage grape. With more than a little help from wife Esme, he manages a part-time farm on land that once belonged to the Beyers family. The estate is small, but the results speak for themselves. A single red wine is produced, sadly in very small quantities, but the three vintages so far have been remarkable. Although pricey and very much a cult wine, this is nevertheless a development to watch closely.

Cabernet Sauvignon 1990   ❦❦ ②
A firm Cabernet Sauvignon, deep colored, concentrated yet well-balanced. Aged one year in new Nevers oak, it has ample depth and length for further development. Still very closed and tannic, but shows the true class that will reward patience.

Blaauwklippen Agricultural Estate

Box 54
Stellenbosch 7600
Tel. (02231) 900133
Fax (02231) 98562

Located at the foot of the Stellenbosch mountains on the Blaauwklip river after which it is named, this estate was first granted by Simon van der Stel in 1692. Although it has a long history of wine production, it was not producing any in 1971 when it was bought, in a run-down condition, by Graham Boonzaier. Today over 90 of its 220 ha are planted with some 14 different grape varieties. Its reputation is largely based on the achievements of Walter Finlayson and his wife who joined in 1975 and produced a succession of award-winning wines throughout the 1980s. The Finlaysons have recently departed to develop their new estate Glen Carlou and another talented winemaker, Jacques Kruger, Walter's assistant who is also a member of the Cape Independent Winemakers' Guild, has taken over the reins. The soil seems particularly suited to red wines and the estate specializes in Cabernet Sauvignon and, surprisingly, Zinfandel. In total the estate produces 17 wines.

Zinfandel 1989   ❦ ①
A powerful alcoholic but very fruity wine of intense color, well-balanced helped by careful barrel aging. Only four wines of this type are produced in the Cape, and this one is the best.

Cabernet Sauvignon 1988   ❦ ①
A deep-colored, highly distinctive flavory wine with real depth and length. Slightly rounder berry flavor than usual owing to vintage characteristics. Well balanced.

Cabernet Sauvignon Reserve 1988 ❦ ❦ ①
Usually sold at the Cape Independent Winemakers' Guild annual auction. A selection of the best grapes aged in better and newer French oak. A concentrated fruity wine of some class.

Boplaas

Klein Karoo, Box 156, 2 Saayman Street
Calitzdorp 6660
Tel. (04437) 33326
Fax (04437) 33750

Die Krans, an estate purchased in 1890 by the Nel family, was subdivided in 1980 to form Boplaas which was then given to Danie Nel and his son Carel, who today runs it. Located in Calitzdorp in the Klein Karoo, which is generally considered to be a hot and arid region, the estate benefits from cool nights and cool southerly winds from the sea. A new fermentation cellar was built in 1981 to complement the original barrel aging one. The estate has 60 ha of vines and produces a number of quality wines, but it is best known for its Port and dessert wines. Linked with Boplaas is another property, Ruiterbosch Mountain Vineyards, which was purchased in 1986 and overlooks the sea at Mossel Bay. Ruiterbosch is believed to have the coolest climate of any vineyard in South Africa and its first wines are remarkably European in style.

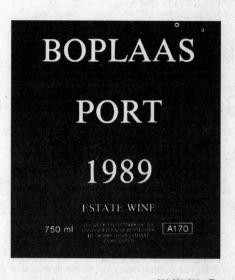

Bonaparte Red Dessert 1989   🍇 ①
A deliciously rich blend of Tinta Barroca and Muscadel this is an unctuous rather than cloying wine for sipping on lazy afternoons.

Grand Vin Rouge 1989   🍇 ①
An attractive 50% Cabernet Sauvignon, Merlot and Cabernet Franc, blend matured in French oak barriques. Surprisingly elegant for this region it should develop well.

Vintage port 1989   🍇 ①
This latest vintage, more alcoholic and drier than previous Ports, is the result of the Symington family influence which makes it more Portuguese in style. Made from Tinta Barroca grapes and wood-aged for two years, it needs time to attain perfect balance. It will benefit from extended bottle aging.

Vintage Reserve Port 1989   🍇🍇🍇 ①
This top of the range Port is only produced in the finest years and can only be purchased direct from the cellar on a futures basis (both the 1986 and 1987 are already sold out). An outstanding wine of great concentration and depth, rich in tannins, crafted very much in the Portuguese fashion which tends to dryness rather than overt sweetness. The best Port from the New World that Peter Symington, with whom Carel Nel has established an exchange working system, has tasted, and destined to improve further once the new plantings of Touriga Nacional are added to the blend.

Boschendal

Groot Drakenstein 7680
Paarl
Tel. (02211) 41031
Fax (02211) 41864

This huge estate, owned by Anglo-American since 1969, was first granted to Jean de Long, a Huguenot immigrant, in 1685. Although it had a long and illustrious wine history, the decline of the industry in the 19th century resulted in its sale and later conversion to a fruit farm by Cecil Rhodes. Today, with nearly 400 ha of vines of which 40 were planted in 1991, it has the largest plantings of Chardonnay in the Cape (over 80 ha). The quality of its wines has been rapidly improving, first under the direction of Achim von Arnim and more recently under Hilko Hegewisch. A broad range of 16 wines is produced with a strong emphasis on white and sparkling wines. However the most recent plantings have been of classic red varietals which will strengthen their position in the marketplace. Boschendal was the first estate to produce single vineyard wines to be sold under the vineyard name, and in so doing tested South African law which to date does not permit indication of the vineyard or place name.

Chardonnay 1991
A fairly restrained, elegant and fruity wine, lightly oaked by aging in Nevers and Vosges barrels. Shows none of the over-oaking so prevalent in some New World wines.

Grand Vin Blanc 1990
A blend of 75% Sauvignon Blanc and 25% Riesling, oak-aged and just off-dry. Excellent acid and fruit balance gives it freshness and character.

Jean Garde Vineyard Gewurztraminer 1990
One of the three single-vineyard wines produced by this winery. It is a good example of dry Gewürztraminer made in the European style without the bitterness on the finish which many Cape dry Gewürztraminers display.

Brut 1989
A 50% blend of Pinot Noir and Chardonnay produced this classic méthode champenoise sparkling wine with a fine bead and elegant style, displaying some yeast autolysis character which will develop further in bottle.

Buitenverwachting

Klein Constantia Road
Constantia 7800
Tel. (021) 7945190-1
Fax (021) 7941351

Originally part of Groot Constantia, it was subdivided in 1712 and again in 1793 to form what is now known as Buitenverwachting, which literally means "beyond expectations." Although it has had a long line of owners, many of whom were not the most successful, today it is one of the finest estates in the country. In 1981 Richard Mueller bought the estate and set about completely renovating it and replanting the vineyards. The only vines he retained are some 100 plus year-old ungrafted Hanepoot which are a reminder of how vines were grown prior to the outbreak of phylloxera last century. Approximately 70 of the 105 ha are now planted with seven different grape varieties and to date 13 different wines are made. Initial successes were with white wines, but a series of outstanding reds are now appearing. Cellarmaster Jean Daneel is a member of the Cape Independent Winemakers' Guild.

Blanc Fumé 1991
One of the wines that made the estate's reputation. A big, powerful, full-flavored barrel-fermented Sauvignon Blanc with pronounced grassiness married to fullness and complexity provided by the oak. This is a wine to keep.

Sauvignon Blanc 1991
Excellent example of un-wooded Sauvignon Blanc showing the classic hallmarks of the varietal: gooseberries, lively acidity and a degree of flintiness even though it has substantial alcohol (over 13° alc).

Chardonnay 1990
Oak fermented and matured in a wide variety of mainly new oak barrels. It has a full-flavored, toasty character, yet retains an attractive lemony zest. A big mouth-filling white.

Grand Vin 1988
This is the first release of this 70% Cabernet Sauvignon, 20% Merlot and 10% Cabernet Franc blend. Stylishly oaked, it is a ripe yet elegant wine with depth and good length. Reflects the excellent Constantia climate.

Clos Cabrière

Box 245
Franschhoek 7690
Tel. (02212) 2630
Fax (02212) 3390

In 1694 Pierre Jourdan, a Huguenot immigrant and one of the first 53 to arrive in the Cape, was granted land in the beautiful Olifantshoek Valley, which later became known as Franschhoek. He came from Cabrière d'Aigues, south-east of Avignon, and therefore called his new estate Clos Cabrière. The present Clos Cabrière is part of the original estate and is now a specialist producer of quality sparkling wines made by the classic méthode champenoise. In fact the first sparkling wine made exclusively from Pinot Noir and Chardonnay was made here by Achim von Arnim, the colorful owner and at the time winemaker at Boschendal, and his assistant Pieter Ferreira, who has now moved on to a major new estate. In the short time that Achim has been at Cabrière, the first release was the 1984 vintage, he has achieved remarkable success. The 12 ha of vines are planted exclusively with Pinot Noir and Chardonnay and the wines, all truly brut in style, are barrel fermented to increase complexity.

Pierre Jourdan brut   ☙ ①
This is a cuvée of 60% Chardonnay and 40% Pinot Noir from the 1989 vintage, although it is sold as a non-vintage wine. Fine, lively, persistent bead and dry, elegant palate it requires another year or two to develop the classic yeasty/toasty flavors.

Pierre Jourdan   ☙ ①
Blanc de Blanc brut
Another 1989 sold as non-vintage from barrel-fermented Chardonnay grapes. It has a persistent bubble, long flavor with just a twist of lemon to it and nice crisp finish.

Pierre Jourdan brut Sauvage   ☙☙ ②
Made only from the first pressing this is totally dry and requires a couple of years to soften. Exquisite flavor for those who like this type of sparkling wine.

Pierre Jourdan   ☙☙ ②
Cuvée Belle Rose brut
A sparkling wine made from 100% Pinot Noir grapes from a single vintage, although sold as a non-vintage wine. Extremely subtle aromas, top of the range in quality thanks to a complex bouquet and refined flavor of ripe strawberries. Persistent rather than forceful, it has a refined mousse, long clean finish with a very delicate, elegant aftertaste. Subtle yet particularly intense palate.

De Wetshof

Box 31
Robertson 6705
Tel. (0234) 51857
Fax (0234) 51915

Located in Robertson, a hot and arid inland region, De Wetshof would not seem to be capable of producing top quality wine, but there are several factors that make it possible. First, it boasts the highest soil lime content in the country and it has a constant supply of water from the Breede river. Danie de Wet went to Geisenheim in 1968 to learn modern winemaking methods and on his return installed cold fermentation equipment and planted new grape varieties. The results have been spectacular. De Wetshof was the first in the area to be granted Estate status, the first inland estate to gain a Superior rating, and with its wood-matured Chardonnay 1985 made history when it won the Best Wine award at Vinexpo in Bordeaux in 1987. There are 165 ha planted with 12 predominately white, grape varieties. De Wetshof wines are marketed by the Bergkelder.

Chardonnay Reserve 1990   ☙ ①
Oak fermented, it is big, mouth-filling and fully flavored. Retains its firmness and at under 13° alc is not overly alcoholic.

Rhine Riesling 1990   ☙ ①
A bone-dry wine with surprising elegance and the typical fruit acidity balance of the varietal. Develops well in bottle.

Delheim Wines

Box 10, Koelenhof 7605
Stellenbosch - Simonsberg
Tel. (02231) 92033
Fax (02231) 92036

Grapes grown in Driesprongh, a territory originally granted to Lourens Campher by Willem Adriaan van der Stel in 1699, and Veracruz go into the making of Delheim wines. But Delheim's fine reputation came about more recently with the purchase of the estate by Mr. Hoheisen in 1938 from Charles Nelson, a descendant of Admiral Lord Nelson of Trafalgar, and the arrival of his wife's nephew "Spatz" Sperling from Poland. Spatz is one of the most colorful and irrepressible characters in the industry and over the years has brought Delheim to its present eminent position. The estate's 188 ha are planted with 16 different grape varieties which produce an array of 19 wines. Until recently Spatz was aided by the talented winemaker Kevin Arnold who has now taken up a position at Rust en Vrede. He has been replaced by the more reserved but equally capable Philip Constandius. Driesprongh lies in the shadow of the Simonsberg mountain and is more suited to the production of white wines whereas Veracruz is the source of the outstanding Grand Reserve red.

Edelspatz Noble Late Harvest 1991   🍷 ①
Full golden hue, intensely sweet yet not cloying, more honeyed because of noble rot. It is made from Riesling and Bukettraube with elements of Sauvignon, Chenin and Muscat. Delicious.

Spécial Late Harvest 1991   🍷 ①
Usually made with Bukettraube and Chenin Blanc grapes although often made from only Chenin. Sweet and alcoholic, the style of wine Delheim excels in. Lovely sweet and sour flavors with clean, lingering finish.

Grand Reserve 1989   🍷🍷 ①
Delheim's finest wine made from 75% Cabernet Sauvignon and 25% Merlot aged in new Nevers oak barrels for up to 14 months. Deeply concentrated with a complex and totally individual palate of ripe berry fruits and spicy cedar tones.

Neil Ellis Wines

Box 917
Stellenbosch 7600
Tel. (02231) 92960
Fax (02231) 92644

A former winemaker at Groot Constantia and then at Zevenwacht, Neil Ellis was the first in South Africa to make the bold decision to set up his own winery without any vineyards. This has permitted him to source top quality grapes from a number of the best areas, often widely spread, and indeed a number of different vineyards within one area, a situation that is not permitted under the restrictive Estate laws. The experiment has been highly successful with the result that Neil has had to reduce his rapidly growing range of wines to manageable levels. He also makes wines under contract for one of the large retailers in South Africa. Neil's cellar is located in the Devon Valley on the Louisvale Estate, for whom he makes excellent Chardonnay.

Chardonnay 1991   🍷 ①
From four Stellenbosch vineyards this is a big, barrel fermented Chardonnay with lemony aromas, intense yet still quite elegant. Very individual.

Whitehall Sauvignon Blanc 1991   🍷🍷 ①
In 1990 Neil was the first to release a wine from the cool climate area of Elgin. This 1991 has true varietal style with a herbaceous character, refined and elegant.

Cabernet Sauvignon 1990   🍷🍷 ①
Oak aged, intense ripe berries on the bouquet and lovely ripe, elegant fruit on the palate. The style of wine only Neil knows how to make.

Fairview

Box 583
Suider-Paarl 7625
Tel. (02211) 632450
Fax (02211) 632591

The estate was purchased in 1937 by a Lithuanian immigrant, Charles Back, on the death of the previous owner who had owned a substantial part of Paarl mountain. This smaller part of what was Bloemkoolfontein farm became known as Fairview. Most of the 200-odd ha have such poor soil that they are given over to sheep, goats and cows. They not only produce some of the finest cheese in the country but also substantial quantities of natural manure which is used on the 130 ha of vines. Still very much a family estate, it was taken over in 1954 by Charles' son Cyril who won a string of awards in the 1970s, but today the winemaking is the responsibility of his son Charles. Some 16 grape varieties are planted and produce a range of over 20 competitively priced wines, mainly red. Because of the relatively poor soils yields are low giving good concentration to the wines.

Charles Gerard Reserve 1990
A 60% Cabernet Franc, 30% Merlot and 10% Cabernet Sauvignon blend. Deep plum color with lovely ripe berry aroma and stylish, well-balanced palate which will develop fairly quickly.

Shiraz Reserve 1990
Aged for one year in small barrels, it has a deep purple color with an almost exotic bouquet of berries, oak and cedarwood with a chocolatey richness on the palate and good underlying tannins. Should develop well.

Pinotage Reserve 1989
Barrel-aged for over one year, it has a lovely sweet ripe fruit aroma. Mouth-filling with a soft, slightly tannic finish. Very individual.

Glen Carlou

Box 23, Klapmuts 7625
Paarl
Tel. (02211) 5528
Fax (02211) 5314

Ths is a relatively new property, set up in the 1980s by Walter Finlayson and his wife. Previously, Walter had worked on the Montagne family estate, now known as Hartenberg, and then became the talented winemaker at Blaauwklippen. In just five vintages at Glen Carlou some exceptional wines have appeared and now that the cellar is fully equipped and the vines have aged one can expect further achievements. The farm's name has nothing to do with Walter's Scottish ancestry but is the result of putting the first three letters of each of the previous owners' daughters names together (Lena, Carol and Louise) and then adding a G to facilitate pronunciation. Of the estates108 ha, 38 are planted with eight different vine types with the emphasis on Bordeaux and Burgundy varietals. Recently some Port grapes were added. The cellar has a large array of different types of oak barrels, mainly from the François Frères cooperage in Burgundy, France.

Chardonnay 1990
A highly acclaimed wine which showed well in London at the inaugural South African tasting in May 1991. Positively oaked; citrusy (lemon and lime) with a lingering flavor and crisp finish. Excellent aftertaste.

Merlot 1991
Only the third vintage for this beautifully oaked exciting wine with lovely fruit flavors. Should develop well.

Classique 1990
A blend of 70% Cabernet Sauvignon, 22% Merlot, 3% Cabernet Franc and 5% Petit Verdot aged 18 months in barrel. Ripe, fruity wine with lots of supple tannins and good depth. It is made for long-term aging but is accessible now.

Les Trois 1990
This is a blend of 30% Petit Verdot, 55% Cabernet Sauvignon and 15% Merlot. A well balanced and attractive wine made for early drinking. It is full flavored, rounded, with a supple fruity style but with sufficient tannins for aging.

Pinot Noir 1990
Only the second vintage but a true rendition of this fickle grape. Nice toasty oak complexity, clean, positive fruit flavor and attractive acid which gives it lift.

Groot Constantia

Private Bag
Constantia 7848
Tel. (021) 7945128
Fax (021) 7941999

Granted in 1685, this is South Africa's, and possibly the New World's, most famous estate and the source of great dessert wines that once graced the tables of European nobility. In 1791 Constantia already had the prestige it is trying to regain today, but like many government-owned properties, it became a slumbering giant and standards fell to disappointing levels. However, the giant has awoken and a remarkable transformation is now well under way. The vineyards are being re-organized, the cellars updated and the old large barrels are being replaced with smaller ones. There is a general air of excitement. The results are immediately visible and the winemaker Pieter du Toit has been elected to the Cape Independent Winemakers Guild, a sure sign of great progress. None of this could have been achieved without the necessary changes to the board of governors and the helpful consultancy of other winemakers. Danie Appel, the general manager, has been responsible for overseeing these changes. 16 different wines are produced from 18 different vine varieties grown on the estate's 150 ha of vineyards.

Chardonnay 1991   ❦ ①
Good depth, strength and complexity with nice subtle oak from barrel fermentation. Good acidity and fairly high alcohol.

Weisser riesling 1991   ❦ ①
Beautiful, delicate, flowery bouquet. Low alcohol palate with lovely fruit acid balance. Reflects Constantia's cool climate.

Gouverneurs Reserve 1988   ❦❦ ①
A blend of 80% Cabernet Sauvignon and 20% Merlot aged in small oak casks for 18 months. Top of the range, this is a well balanced, stylish wine with positive oak characters, lean and flavory rather than big and bold.

Hamilton Russell

Walker Bay, Box 158, Hermanus 7200
Overberg
Tel. (0283) 23595
Fax (0283) 21797

Few have done as much as Tim Hamilton Russell to improve the quality of South African wines. He has questioned everything and refused to submit to what he sees as the oppression of the authorities. He has also convinced consumers, used to low prices, that they would have to pay more if they wanted better quality wines. Tim purchased land in 1974 in the Hemel-en-Aarde valley, which he had carefully selected because of its cool climate, and planted Pinot Noir, Chardonnay, a little Sauvignon Blanc and a very small quantity of Gewürztraminer. Pioneers in the production of Pinot Noir, he and previous winemaker Peter Finlayson, who recently left to set up his own venture, have had some remarkable successes with this varietal, but the quest for perfection goes on. Peter Finlayson has been replaced by Gail "Storm" Kreusch-Dau.

Chardonnay Reserve 1990   ❦❦ ①
Longer oak aging than the regular Chardonnay, a refined example with a good deal of complexity, understated rather than forceful, with attractive nuances of oak and citrus. This was the last wine made by Peter Finlayson.

Pinot Noir 1990   ❦❦ ①
This is still the top Pinot Noir in South Africa and a wine that ages well. Up to 18 months in oak, it displays a pronounced perfume and has multiple layers of flavor on the palate. A textbook example.

Hartenberg

Box 69, Koelenhof 7605
Stellenbosch
Tel. (02231) 92541
Fax (02231) 92268

This property was granted in 1704, but it was not until its purchase in 1949 by Maurice Finlayson, and more particularly upon the arrival of his son Walter ten years later, that the wine side took on any real significance. It was renamed Montagne but reverted back to Hartenberg upon its sale to Gilbeys in the late 1970s. Since 1986 it has been owned by Ken Mackenzie. A substantial investment in new cellars and a lot of new small oak barrels has given the present winemaker, Danie Truter, the opportunity of showing exactly what this estate can produce. The initial results already look very promising. Sixteen grape varieties are planted on 98 ha with the emphasis on Cabernet Sauvignon and Shiraz for the reds and Rhine Riesling, Sauvignon Blanc and Chardonnay for the whites. Red wines are always released late when they show some bottle development and are ready for drinking.

Sauvignon Blanc 1991   🍇 ①
A marvelous rendition of this varietal. Dry and direct with excellent refreshing acidity, although high in alcohol.

Cabernet Sauvignon 1986   🍷 ①
Produced in large barrels, it is a flavory yet roundly fruity wine which still needs a couple of years to ripen. Reminds one of Bordeaux in the 1960s. New editions will be made in small oak barrels.

Shiraz 1986   🍷🍷 ①
A classic old-style, big, gutsy, smokey Shiraz. Certainly very impressive and one of the finest made that year. Now ripe but will continue to give great pleasure for years.

Kanonkop

Box 19, Muldersvlei 7606
Stellenbosch
Tel. (02231) 94656-7
Fax (02231) 94719

Originally part of Uitkyk, which was granted in 1712 but divided in 1929 when the larger part was sold to Baron von Carlowitz by the owner Senator J. H. Sauer. The retained portion was named Kanonkop after the site of a nearby hill from where cannons were fired to announce the arrival of approaching ships. Senator Sauer's son, The Hon. Paul began making wine shortly after and on his death the estate passed to his son-in-law Jannie Krige whose two sons Johann and Paul are involved today. The responsibility for winemaking fell first to Jan "Boland" Coetzee, now at Vriesenhof, and then Beyers Truter, whose forbears were once proud owners of Uitkyk. Beyers recently shot to fame when he won the Robert Mondavi Winemaker of the Year Award in the 1991 International Wine & Spirit Competition. The estate is particularly suited to red wines and is the country's leading exponent of South Africa's own grape variety, Pinotage. Kanonkop was one of the first estates to plant this varietal and has since remained loyal to it. By careful husbandry and judicious use of wood aging Kanonkop has introduced Pinotage to the world stage. The other important variety is Cabernet Sauvignon which has the largest plantings on the estate's 140 hectare vineyard.

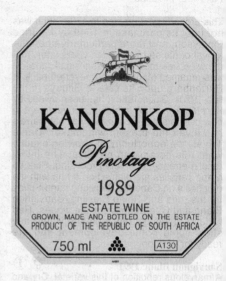

Cabernet Sauvignon 1988   🍇 ①
100% Cabernet grapes aged in new oak barrels. An individual, long-lived wine which takes some time to show itself. It has good concentration, a firm backbone and long finish.

Paul Sauer 1988   🍇🍇 ①
A top of the range blend of 75% Cabernet Sauvignon, 10% Merlot and 15% Cabernet Franc, aged up to 22 months in new or second-year wood. Dry, tightly packed and full flavored with excellent harmony and balance. Plenty of ripe tannins promise long life.

Pinotage 1989   🍇🍇🍇 ①
This barrel-aged Pinotage is the yardstick for this typically South African varietal. It has a deep, concentrated flavor with firm backbone and plenty of fruit for long life. The alcohol content is high (over 13° alc) but it still retains elegance and crisp aromas and flavors. Only surpassed by the Auction Reserve, made in limited quantities from a specially selected cask and given longer barrel aging and produced for the annual Cape Independent Winemakers' Guild auction. Pinotage can behave in an almost schizophrenic manner, in some years resembling Pinot Noir and in others Cinsaut, which is not surprising as Pinotage is a cross between these two varietals. Kanonkop's Pinotage is more typically Pinot Noir in style.

Klein Constantia

Box 375
Constantia 7848
Tel. (021) 7945188
Fax (021) 7942464

It is hard to believe that this model estate with such an outstanding reputation for wine was brought by the present owner in 1989 in such poor condition. No wine had been made for some 50 years and most of the vineyard was completely overgrown. But enormous determination, careful planning and a lot of good advice and hard work have brought this estate to its present pinnacle of success. Originally part of Groot Constantia until subdivided in 1819, it may well have been responsible for the production of some of the great Constantia wines of the past. The estate's brilliant winemaker Ross Gower shot to fame with the release of his first wine, a 1986 Sauvignon Blanc, and has hardly looked back since. Now that all 80 ha of vineyard are planted with eight varietals one can expect further success. Credit for the vineyard layout is due to Ernst le Roux, once chief viticulturist at Nederburg and later general manager at Klein Constantia who has since returned to Nederburg.

Chardonnay 1990   🍇 🍇 ①
This is a big yet fairly elegant oak-aged wine with a clean, dry citrus finish. Very impressive.

Sauvignon Blanc 1990   🍇 🍇 ①
Outstanding and now "classic" Constantia unwooded Sauvignon. Big but true to type with lively gooseberry character and fresh acidity.

Rhine Riesling 1989   🍇 ①
Off-dry but not sweet, the wine is fruity but with an excellent lively acid finish. Long bottle development seems assured.

Vin de Constance 1987   🍇 ①
An interesting attempt to duplicate the great Constantia dessert wines of the 18th century. Unfortified and aged in small barrels, it is intensely sweet and made from very ripe rather than botrytized Muscat de Frontignan grapes.

Cabernet Sauvignon 1987   🍇 ①
Excellent follow-up to the first vintage in 1986. It is big and alcoholic, over 13.5° alc, with heaps of fruit and a complexity derived from aging in 500-lt barrels. Plenty of tannin and acidity for long-term aging.

KWV (Kooperatieve Wijnbouwers Vereniging Van Zuid-Afrika)

Box 528, Suider-Paarl
Paarl
Tel. (02211) 631001
Fax (02211) 633440

Founded in 1918 to overcome the serious problem of over-production within the grape-growing industry, and ratified by the government in 1924, the KWV is a growers' cooperative which now has nearly 5,000 members and in one way or another accounts for around 80% of all wine and spirit sales in South Africa. Given near-legal powers to regulate the industry, it is seen by some as a monster that impedes progress and by others as a life-support system. It has been remarkably successful in stabilizing the market, but in recent years this appears to have taken place at the expense of quality. There are signs, however, of significant changes taking place. The majority of the grapes that the KWV deals with are of low quality and are converted into brandy or industrial alcohol. Nevertheless it is the source of a substantial volume of well-made, inexpensive wines which were for many years about the only wines to be found on the world market. The KWV takes up a large area in Paarl where its offices and wineries are located in addition to the 45 ha which make up its own estate Laborie, also in Paarl. The KWV's range is substantial and covers the entire spectrum of low strength, fortified and sparkling wines as well as spirits.

Noble Late Harvest 1987   🍇 🍇 ①
Outstanding example of this distinctive Cape style with brilliant pale gold color and enticing apricot and ripe peach nose and flavor, beautifully balanced with refreshing acidity.

Roodeberg 1988   🍇 ①
Cabernet, Pinotage, Shiraz and Tinta Barroca in roughly even quantities blend to form this long-lived, full-bodied red which every year reaches consistent standards. Good value for money.

Laborie Taillefert 1987   🍇 ①
A blend of Cabernet Sauvignon, Cabernet Franc, Shiraz and Merlot matured in small barrels. The increasing use of new small oak improves this medium-bodied, yet quite elegant, ripe, rounded, fruity wine. Newer vintages will no doubt be even better. A white wine is also sold under this label.

L'Orm... Estate

Fran...
Privat... ...uder-Paarl 7624
Tel. (02211) 41024-41026
Fax (02211) 41361

Granted in 1694 to Jean Roi, a Huguenot immigrant, it was purchased by Dr. Anton Rupert in 1969 and is now the home of his youngest son Anthonij. This beautiful yet substantial estate with its impressive cellar which was completed in 1981, continues to produce wines of the highest quality. The most recent development has been the introduction of an excellent sparkling wine made by the méthode champenoise and some very individual Ports which are fermented in small oak barrels, a technique practiced by few, which show a marked oakiness and a dry finish. With almost 200 ha of vines and with 15 different varietals producing some 15 different wines the future potential of this estate looks particularly exciting. Nico Vermeulen is the winemaker responsible for all the activities except bottling which is carried out by the Bergkelder.

Blanc Fumé 1990   ❦ ①
Typical oak-aged Sauvignon Blanc, fairly alcoholic yet fresh with good keeping qualities. It has been consistently good since its first release in 1983.

Chardonnay 1989   ❦ ①
A very successful wine and gold-medal winner at the 1991 International Wine & Spirit Competition. Pleasant lemon and lime flavor with excellent toasty character from new oak.

Cabernet Sauvignon 1987   ❦ ①
A well structured Cabernet with noticeable oak character and ripe fruit. The tannins are already relatively supple but the wine will age further in bottle.

La Motte

Franschhoek
Box 45, La Motte 7691
Tel. (02212) 3119
Fax (02212) 3446

This estate was first granted in 1695 to a German, Hans Heinrich Hattingh, who later sold it to Pierre Joubert, a Huguenot from La Motte d'Aigues in France. Following a succession of owners, some of whom were engaged in wine production, it was purchased by Cecil Rhodes in 1897 to become part of Rhodes Fruit Farms. Another change of ownership took place in 1970 when it was bought by the Rupert family and since then the real changes have taken place. After substantial renovation and a massive planting program, a new pressing cellar was built in 1985. Jacques Borman is the cellarmaster and Paul Neethling manages the estate. The latter managed to convince the Bergkelder to allow bottling on the premises. This is definitely out of character as the Bergkelder, which handles and markets a substantial number of wines from leading estates; normally insists on taking the wines for further maturation and bottling at their purpose-built cellars. La Motte has over 80 ha planted with vines with red varietals in the ascendency, although a large parcel of Sauvignon Blanc has produced some excellent results.

Blanc Fumé 1990   ❦ ①
A well made lightly oaked wine, elegant rather than overpowering, refined and refreshing with good varietal character.

Sauvignon Blanc 1990   ❦ ①
Rather alcoholic but vigorous and refreshing. Another good rendition of this varietal which should develop well.

Cabernet Sauvignon 1987   ❦ ①
Typical dry, lean style of the estate but still flavory and ripe with rather high alcohol. Plentiful oak on the palate which suggests a long life.

Le Bonheur

Klapmuts 7625
Stellenbosch
Tel. (02211) 5432

When Lord Charles Somerset granted this land to Jacob de Villiers it was still called Oude Weltevreden. It was renamed Le Bonheur (Happiness) and later purchased in a run-down state by Mike Woodhead in the early 1970s. Today this 160 ha estate has been completely renovated and replanted with over 70 ha of quality vines of which Chardonnay, Sauvignon Blanc, Cabernet Sauvignon, Shiraz and Merlot are the most important. Mike Woodhead, a reserved yet talented viticulturist and winemaker, shot to fame when he won the Warren Winiarski Trophy for the best Cabernet Sauvignon in the International Wine & Spirit Competition with his 1984 vintage against an impressive array of wines from around the world. The vineyards are worked by Xhosas and managed by Louis Tshambu, both of whom have been with the estate for many years creating an excellent working partnership. The first bottlings from the estate took place in 1981 and have since been marketed by the Bergkelder.

Blanc Fumé 1990 🍇 ①
This is an unwooded Sauvignon Blanc with high alcohol and acidity. It has a pronounced style with a leafy, almost green nose and fairly substantial palate. Should develop well.

Cabernet Sauvignon 1986 🍷🍷 ①
A very complex wine, deep colored and intensely tannic, closed yet deeply concentrated needing many years to develop. Noticeable oaking gives added complexity to compliment the interesting berry-fruit flavors. It has a long finish.

Lievland

Box 66, Klapmuts 7625
Stellenbosch
Tel. (02211) 5226
Fax (02211) 5213

Known as Beyers Kloof since 1820, although originally part of Natte Valley, this estate was purchased by Baron von Stiernheilm of Lievland, a small eastern European state which was swallowed up during the Second World War. The Baron died before his wife and family could join him, and upon her arrival in the Cape in 1936 she renamed the estate Lievland in his honor. Today it is owned by Paul Benade, whose father and a partner bought the estate in 1973. A program of replanting and a new cellar, completed in 1982, have brought the estate right up to date. At this time Janey Muller, one of the few women involved in winemaking, joined the team while she was in the process of setting up her own estate in Tulbach, Lemberg. The present winemaker is Abraham Beukes who is producing some exciting reds, many of them award-winning wines although the estate's earliest successes were with whites and in particular Late Harvest wines.

Weisser Riesling 1990 🍇 ①
An outstanding example of just off-dry Riesling with low alcohol and classic character. One of the wines that has put Lievland on the map.

Noble Late Harvest 1989 🍇🍇 ①
This blend of Bukettraube, Riesling and Chenin Blanc was the gold medal winner and top scorer at the 1991 International Wine & Spirit Competition. It is intensely concentrated yet retains a beautiful freshness aided by the effect of noble rot and enhanced by peach and apricot aromas.

Cabernet Sauvignon 1989 🍷 ①
Fifteen months in barrel and a good amount of Merlot have resulted in the best Cabernet to date. Excellent structure, with good aging potential but round enough to attempt now.

Shiraz 1989 🍷🍷 ①
Perhaps the Cape's finest Shiraz, beautifully oaked, elegant, with low alcohol and a subtle style that makes it so appealing.

Meerlust

Box 15, Faure 7131
Stellenbosch
Tel. (024) 43587
Fax (024) 43513

Meerlust was purchased at the start of the 18th century by Henning Huysing, a very wealthy Free Burgher. He had the monopoly of supplying meat to the Dutch East India Company's ships on their way to the Orient. After his death in 1713 a succession of owners followed until it was purchased in 1756 by Johannes Myburgh. It is currently run by Hannes Myburgh, the ninth generation Myburgh to own Meerlust. It was his father Nico who was responsible for the substantial improvements since his inheritance in 1950. He replaced the old varietals with Cabernet Sauvignon, Merlot, Cabernet Franc and Pinot Noir, upgraded the winemaking facilities and built a large dam to supply irrigation. These improvements took many years to be completed, but by 1980 Meerlust took the market by storm with Rubicon, the first Bordeaux blend to be produced in South Africa. Nico's helping hand was the talented and experienced winemaker Giorgio Dalla Cia, a native of Friuli in north-east Italy. Although predominantly a red wine estate, there have been recent planting of Chardonnay but these account for less than 10% of the 235 ha planted with vines. Another recent development has been the introduction of a second wine, thus permitting a rigorous selection. The wines are bottled and marketed by the Bergkelder.

Cabernet Sauvignon 1987 ♥ ①
A big, powerful wine with lots of concentration, rather more forceful than usual. It has an individual character and should keep.

Merlot 1987 R*1
An exciting, densely packed, deeply fruity wine with excellent mineral tones. Full, balanced, soft and elegant.

Pinot Noir 1987 ♥ ①
Another excellent 1987 with heaps of slightly jammy fruit, true and ample if not generous Pinot bouquet and long, silky finish.

Rubicon 1987 ♥♥ ①
A 65% Cabernet Sauvignon, 25% Merlot, 10% Cabernet Franc blend. After some slightly middle-of-the-road examples, the wine has returned to top form with this vintage with the help of better barrel aging. A concentrated but still typical, understated style with subtle use of oak and fine, dry palate.

Key to the symbols

Types of Wines

🍇 White

🍇 Rosé

🍇 Red

Rating System

🍇 An exemplary wine of its type with outstanding local character

 An international premium quality wine

 A Top Wine, considered one of the 150 best wines in the world

The 'grape bunch' symbol is used to indicate the color of the wine; the number of bunches represents the quality rating assigned by the contributor

Price levels

① up to $ 9.99

② $ 10.00 - $ 14.99

③ $ 15.00 - $ 24.99

④ $ 25.00 or more

The 'ex-cellar', or direct from the producer, bottle prices, are calculated in US dollars and are intended only as an approximate guide

Entries are arranged in alphabetical order by country, region and winery or producer name.

Nederburg Wines

Box 46, Huguenot 7645
Paarl
Tel. (0221) 623104
Fax (0221) 623320

Named after the Commissioner-General of the Dutch East India Company Sebastian Nederburg who in 1792 granted some land to a German immigrant, Philip Wolvaart. The estate did not become truly significant until 1937 when Johann Graue, also a German immigrant, bought the property of some 93 ha of vines. Shortly after the Second World War Johann developed cold fermentation which was a major step forward and by 1952 had won a spectacular array of awards at the annual Cape Wine Show. Sadly, Johann's son Arnold was tragically killed the following year; the shock proved to be too great for Johann, who merged his business with Monis. Fortunately Günter Brözel, another German immigrant, had joined the company in 1956 and picked up where the Graues had left off. Further important developments took place and in 1966 the much expanded company was merged with the giant Stellenbosch Farmers' Winery, which more recently has been absorbed into the monolithic Cape Wine & Distillers Group. Today the vineyard area stands at over 1,000 ha. It is impossible to explain in a few words the important role Nederburg and Günter Brözel in particular have played in developing South Africa's modern wine industry - undoubtedly they are owed an enormous debt. On Günter's departure to Neethlingshof, Newald Marais took over the important position of cellarmaster. Nederburg produces a vast array of wines of which the following are only a small sample.

Chardonnay 1990 ☙ ①
Partly barrel-fermented and partly barrel-matured. A substantial wine with citrus fruit palate, plenty of flavor and requiring another year or two to reach its zenith.

Elgin Weisser Riesling 1990 ☙☙ ①
Exciting new development from Elgin's cool climate. Pronounced bouquet and palate, intensely fresh with attractive low alcohol.

Prélude 1990 ☙ ①
A fascinating blend of 75% Sauvignon Blanc and 25% Chardonnay, partly barrel-fermented and partly barrel-matured. Substantial, multi-faceted, mouth-filling, dry wine. This is the third vintage.

Private Bin S354 1990 ☙ ①
Interesting Late Harvest Riesling and Gewürztraminer blend. Highly fragrant, intense, yet not overly sweet with lovely balance of vibrant fruit acids. Long follow through and aftertaste.

Edelkeur 1988 ☙☙☙ ②
This spectacular creation of Günter Brözel is a highly complex botrytized wine with multitudinous honeyed ripe fruit flavors (apricot, peach, exotic fruits). Made from Chenin Blanc harvested at approximately 70-80% botrytis, it is deep golden in color with very positive botrytis character on both nose and palate. Even with its very high level of residual sugar, around 160 gm/lt, it still retains an excellent lively clean finish with no cloying. Sold in half bottles, it is pure nectar.

Neethlingshof

Box 104
Stellenbosch 7600
Tel/Fax (02231) 76832

Granted by Simon van der Stel in 1699 to Willem Lubbe, the estate was originally called De Wolwedans or "the dance of wolves." It took its present name in 1816 when the estate was purchased by Johannes Neethling, an eccentric dandy who was referred to as "Lord Neethling." The estate was extended at this time by a further 200 ha. More recently, in 1985, it was bought by Hans-Joachim Schreiber, an international financier of German origin based in Singapore, who immediately set about completely reorganizing the estate with a comprehensive program of building which included staff accommodation and the most up-to-date winemaking facilities. The vineyards were also replanted after a careful survey had been carried out. Some 150 ha are now planted with the best varietals and just three years ago Günter Brözel, Nederburg's near-legendary cellarmaster, was brought in to head up the operation. Günter has wasted no time in stamping his authority on the organization and has already shown some of his old magic.

Gewurztraminer 1991　　🍷 ①
More than just off-dry, this wine displays an outstanding perfume and excellently balanced full-flavored palate.

Noble Late Harvest　　🍷🍷 ①
Sauvignon Blanc 1991
Outstanding botrytized dessert wine with seductive opulence matched by lively acidity. A Günter Brözel special.

Cabernet Sauvignon 1987　　🍷🍷 ①
Outstanding, deep colored, spicy, subtly oaked wine with multiple layers of finely packed fruit and substantial reserves of ripe tannins which will give long life.

Overgaauw

Box 3, Vlottenburg 7604
Stellenbosch
Tel. (02231) 93815
Fax (02231) 93436

Overgaauw received its name in 1906 upon its purchase by Abraham van Velden from his maternal grandfather Willem Joubert who was the fifth generation to own this property. By-den-Weg, as it was originally named, had been a grant of land in 1704 by Simon van der Stel to Hendrik Elbertz. Overgaauw was only part of the original estate and was the maiden name of the wife of the first van Velden to arrive in the Cape from Holland. Abraham built the wine cellar in 1909 and his home the following year. His son David took over in 1945 and together with his son Braam run Overgaauw today. Although traditionalists the van Veldens are always in the vanguard of change and can probably claim to be the first to have matured a Cabernet in new French oak barriques in 1970 and the first to offer a Merlot in bottle in commercial quantities. They are also the only estate to produce a Sylvaner which grows very successfully in this area. A large new underground maturation cellar capable of holding more than 100,000 bottles was built in the 1970s and with it a wine center.

Chardonnay 1990　　🍷 ①
Low alcohol and gentle oaking make this a most attractive Chardonnay in the Cote d'Or style. Interesting toasty note and refined palate with a twist of lemon.

DC Classic 1988　　🍷🍷 ①
Available only through the annual Cape Independent Winemakers' Guild auction, this 100% Merlot, oak-matured wine has a beautiful perfume and attractive fruit balanced by soft tannins.

Merlot 1988　　🍷 ①
Medium-bodied but deep colored wine with soft berry fruit and attractive gentle elegance, this is a charming wine.

Cabernet Sauvignon 1987　　🍷 ①
Medium-bodied, nice herbal character, elegant rather than showy style with good acid and tannin balance. Quite European in style.

Tria Corda 1987　　🍷 ①
A blend of 65% Cabernet Sauvignon, 20% Merlot and 15% Cabernet Franc. Restrained, fairly lean but flavory with good fruit. Clever use of oak promises long life. Confirms the estate's European style.

Rozendal Farm

Box 160
Stellenbosch 7600
Tel. (02231) 76855

Originally part of the famous Lanzerac estate, this 25 ha farm with its homestead and cellar, built in 1864, was purchased in 1981 by Kurt Ammann. Kurt, a talented chef, born and trained in Switzerland, had originally come to South Africa to improve his English but liked the country so much he decided to stay. After a highly successful career running his own restaurants and building up one of the most impressive cellars in the country, he was forced to leave his last restaurant at the top of Hertzog Tower which had become a security risk. This led directly to the development of Rozendal. Kurt's first vintage was the 1983 made partly from grapes picked from very old vines at Lanzerac and although this was a moderate vintage the wine was highly successful. The estate only makes a single red wine although there is a second label, Val de Lyn, named after his wife, which permits a stringent selection. In the last few years five ha of Merlot and Cabernet Franc have been planted to supplement the existing vines.

Rozendal 1989   🍇🍇 ①
An unfiltered blend of 80% Merlot and 20% Cabernet Sauvignon. A very individual wine, deep colored, medium-bodied but richly flavored. Good tannin balance promising good future development. Softer and more approachable than the 1987 which is just beginning to open.

Ruiterbosch Mountain Vineyards

Box 156, Calitzdorp 6660
Mossel Bay
Tel. (04437) 33326
Fax (04437) 33750

This viticultural region, which overlooks the Indian Ocean from the lower slopes of the Outeniqua Mountains, is one of South Africa's newest developments. It has the coolest climate in South Africa, even cooler than Hamilton Russell Vineyards at Hermanus even though it is not as far south. Perhaps more significant is the poor soil which is extremely gravelly and produces very small yields. During wetter growing periods the resultant wines are much more similar to those of Europe than any other produced in the Cape. The plantings are still quite small, especially since current yields are not competitively priced, but quality-wise they are very interesting and show enormous promise. Over the next few years many new ventures will probably be set up in this potentially superb area. Plantings, which are based on the European high-density system (7,000 vines/ha) are at the moment restricted to Pinot Noir, Chardonnay, Sauvignon Blanc and Riesling. The wines will continue to be made by Carel Nel at Boplaas until it becomes worthwhile to establish new cellars in the immediate area. The first bottling took place in 1988.

Sauvignon Blanc 1991   🍇🍇 ①
Unwooded and very European in style, this could almost be mistaken for a top-quality Sancerre. Flinty, with a lovely gooseberry freshness and a matching lively acidity. Good intensity and ripeness with quite an individual character.

Chardonnay Mountain Cuvée 1990   🍇 ①
Barrel fermented and quite similar to Chablis in style. Fresh, dry and elegant with cool-climate characteristics. Has lovely length for such a young wine. Needs two years to develop.

Riesling 1990   🍇 ①
Off-dry yet surprisingly dry on the finish. Fine Riesling fruit and perfume on the bouquet, now developing well. Fairly full-bodied and fruity, yet shows none of the weight of most South African Rieslings.

Rust en Vrede

Box 473
Stellenbosch 7600
Tel. (02231) 93881
Fax (02231) 93000

In 1694 Simon van der Stel granted to Willem van der Wereld a property known as Bonte Rivier which was subdivided in the mid-19th century to form Rust-en-Vrede. Vines were first planted in 1730 and the wine cellar, which still exists, was completed in 1790. However, by 1920 winemaking had ceased, although vine cultivation continued, and it was not until 1978 when the celebrated rugby Springbok Jannie Engelbrecht bought the estate that matters were put in order again. The soils at Rust-en-Vrede, ideal for red varietals, were planted with Cabernet Sauvignon and Shiraz, but also produced Pinot Noir, Merlot, Tinta Barroca and Cabernet Franc. It was decided that the estate should concentrate on producing a single top-quality red blend, so the Pinot Noir was replaced with more Cabernet, Merlot and Shiraz. In 1987 the talented Kevin Arnold joined the estate from Delheim and with Jannie has produced some innovative wines which could easily change the direction of blended red winemaking in South Africa. Only five varietals are now planted on the estate's 40 ha.

Shiraz 1988
One of the leading Cape Shiraz wines. Substantial, mouthfilling thanks to the robust house style with plenty of fruit and a slightly smokey character.

Cabernet Sauvignon 1987
Produced principally for the home market. Good deep color and ripe berry fruit, leaner and more elegant than the norm. It has good oak complexity.

Rust en Vrede 1988 ②
An exciting blend of 75% Cabernet Sauvignon, 10% Merlot and 15% Shiraz. It is matured in thinner, and much more expensive Bordeaux barriques and was produced only after a long series of trial blends using only the finest casks. Compact, multi-dimensional, ripe, deep flavored wine with additional oak complexity and long finish. The Shiraz gives a touch of extra richness and at the same time exotic elegance. The oak has now combining nicely with the wine which still needs many years to evolve and reach its peak. A wine able to last 10 to 20 years.

Rustenberg Wines-Schoongezicht

Box 33
Stellenbosch 7600
Tel. (02231) 73153
Fax (02231) 78466

The estate, one of the greatest in the Cape,
dates back to 1682 when Willem Adrian van
der Stel made a grant of land to Roelof
Pasman. In 1810 the property was divided
and the two farms were united again only in
1945 when Peter Barlow bought
Schoongezicht having purchased Rustenberg
five years earlier. Today his widow Pamela
and their son Simon run the reunited estate.
Wine production was restarted by one of the
previous owners John Merriman who was the
last prime minister of the old Cape Colony.
Rustenberg has bottled wine on the estate
since 1900 and in many ways should be
considered a First Growth of South Africa.
Technically though this is not true as the
winery, built in 1770, is on Schoongezicht
and not Rustenberg land. In the future, for
marketing purposes, all wines will be sold as
Rustenberg. There is a tremendous sense of
tradition on this estate and changes happen
only slowly and only after careful thought.
Even the winemakers seem to stay for life:
The latest is the quietly spoken but highly
talented Etienne le Riche who joined in 1974
taking over from the legendary traditionalist
Reg Nicholson. The estate has some 80 ha
planted with 10 different grape varieties
which produce around eight different wines
each year.

Chardonnay Reserve 1990   ❦ ①
Barrel fermented, toasty and lemony with some
slightly burnt notes. Well structured, this will
develop well. The first vintage was 1986.

Rustenberg Dry Red 1990   ❦ ①
Highly successful blend of 60% Cabernet
Sauvignon, 10% Cabernet Franc, 10% Merlot
and 20% Cinsaut crushed together rather than
blended later. Well structured, fruity wine with
ample body. A wine that matures relatively
early.

Cabernet Sauvignon 1989   ❦ ❦ ①
Usually restrained and European in style, this
1989 has greater weight than normal. Full, ripe
fruit with excellent tannin back-up, nicely oaked
and promising a good, long life.

Pinot noir 1989   ❦ ①
Rustenberg was one of the first successful
producers of this varietal. Relatively light but
true-to-form Pinot with pleasant fruit and
sufficient structure for aging. The 1986 is still
going strong.

Rustenberg Gold 1989   ❦ ❦ ①
The blend is 60% Cabernet Sauvignon, 30%
Merlot and 10% Cabernet Franc. Outstanding,
richly fruity wine - blackberries, blackcurrants -
with cedar-wood topping and underlying firm but
ripe tannins. This is to date the best vintage.

**Entries are arranged in
alphabetical order by country,
region and winery or producer
name.**

Simonsig

Box 6, Koelenhof 7605
Stellenbosch
Tel. (02231) 92044
Fax (02231) 92545

The wines of Simonsig come from two farms, Simonsig and De Hoop. Both were parts of other estates, the oldest being Koelenhof, which was a land grant in 1682 to Simon de Groot. Today Simonsig is one of the biggest of the privately owned wine estates with 260 ha of vineyards planted with some 20 varieties which are constantly being upgraded. Simonsig is a family affair with Frans Malan, a former director of the KWV at the helm and sons Pieter, François and Johan respectively responsible for marketing, viticulture and winemaking. Johan is a member of the Cape Independent Winemakers' Guild and has been responsible for the exciting array of wines produced in recent years. The estate has excellent facilities and has been a pioneer in the field of South African wines. It was the first to re-introduce méthode champenoise sparkling wine (Kaapse Vonkel) and the first to grow Chardonnay. In 1990 Simonsig almost swept the board of awards at the International Wine & Spirit Competition. Further expansion in the vineyards with top quality varieties and in the cellar with even more oak barriques looks inevitable .

Chardonnay 1990 ⅋ ⅋ ①
Outstanding barrel-fermented wine with lemon/lime flavour and interesting ripe tropical fruit bouquet. They also produce a reserve wine.

Gewurztraminer ⅋ ①
Special Late Harvest 1990
Consistently one of the finest Special Late Harvest wines. Exciting floral bouquet matched by beautifully balanced rich, ripe fruit flavour with refreshing acidity. Some botrytis.

Kaapse Vonkel Brut 1989 ⅋ ①
66% Pinot Noir, 33% Chardonnay. Fine bubble and refreshing young palate, needs a couple more years to broaden its flavour. Good length.

Pinotage Reserve 1989 ⅋ ⅋ ①
Outstanding, oaked Pinotage. Quite easily the best in the Cape except for Kanonkop. Much more perfumed/fruity style. Very attractive but has structure for aging. Grapes come from land once belonging to Kanonkop.

Cabernet Sauvignon 1987 ⅋ ①
Well-coloured, oaky, fairly deep wine with good berry fruit flavour and balancing tannin. Needs time.

Stellenbosch Farmers' Winery

Box 46
Stellenbosch 7600
Tel. (02231) 73400
Fax (02231) 71335

Better-known as SFW, this enormous organization is South Africa's largest wholesaler and accounts for almost two thirds of the total South African consumption. With headquarters on the historic Oude Libertas estate, it has a long and complex history. Once part of the Cape Wine & Distillers Group, although it operated independently, it is now separately listed on the Johannesburg stock exchange. Among the many things under its control is the annual Nederburg auction, first held in 1975, which has had a major impact on the domestic scene and to a lesser extent the international market. SFW has also greatly contributed to plant and clone improvements. Duimpie Bayly is production director and Wouter Pienaar is cellarmaster. In recent years Paul Pontallier, the régisseur of Château Margaux, has been consultant to the group. A major new investment in oak barriques and the upgrading of the red fermentation facilities should further improve the extensive range of wines and in particular the top of the line Zonnebloem label.

Zonnebloem Chardonnay 1990 ⅋ ①
The second vintage for this wine which will improve as vintages progress. Very open, pronounced lemon bouquet, attractive fruity palate.

Zonnebloem Merlot 1988 ⅋ ①
Matured in new oak and obviously oaky. Medium to full depth with excellent fruity palate and good tannin structure. Should develop well.

Thelema Mountain Vineyards

Box 2234
Stellenbosch 7601
Tel. (02231) 91924
Fax (02231) 91800

Purchased in 1983 as a run-down fruit farm, Thelema has since shot to national and now international acclaim. It is very much a family-run business with Gyles Webb, wife Barbara and her mother all playing a significant part. The winery was completed in time for the 1988 vintage and the vineyards, which cover over 30 hectares, some perched high up on the Simonsberg mountain, are a textbook example of what viticulture is all about. Gyles strongly believes that quality starts in the vineyard, therefore the layout and choice of vine variety and clonal selection have been very important. Initial success was attained with white wines, particularly the Sauvignon Blanc, which has no difficulty in finding eager buyers, but now a series of very distinctive reds have begun to emerge. Varietals grown now include Cabernet Sauvignon, Merlot, Chardonnay, Sauvignon Blanc, Riesling and Muscat de Frontignan.

Chardonnay 1991 ♀♀ ①
This wine's fourth vintage and the best to date. Barrel-fermented, limey and well structured with medium alcohol and a touch of elegance. Very attractive.

Sauvignon Blanc 1991 ♀ ①
Lovely crisp, classic gooseberry style with a full-bodied, lengthy palate and refreshing finish.

Cabernet Sauvignon 1990 ♀♀ ①
A very individual red wine with deep almost opaque purple color and mouth-filling consitency with mint and eucalyptus flavors. It has a very concentrated fruit and oak complexity. Can the Blue Gums that surround the farm have anything to do with it?

Villiera

Box 66, Koelenhof 7605
Paarl
Tel. (02231) 92002-3
Fax (02231) 92314

The estate, named after the De Villiers family who were once owners, was purchased in 1975 by Helmut Ratz, an Austrian, at a time when wine production had ceased completely. Accompanied by the experienced viticulturist Josef Krammer he planted a range of quality grape varieties and refurbished and extended the original cellar. In 1983 he sold the thriving winery to the Grier family who are the present owners. One of the estate's specialities is méthode champenoise sparkling wine, aptly called Tradition de Charles de Fere after a chance meeting in 1984 with Jean-Louis Denois, a Champagne producer from near Epernay who has advised Jeff Grier ever since. Jeff's responsibilities lie in the cellar and his cousin Simon looks after the vineyards. Together this young team has produced some outstanding results and recent innovations suggest that more are to follow. About 15 different wines are produced from 16 vine varieties planted on over 120 hectares. Insecticides have not been used for many years.

Rhine riesling 1991 ♀ ①
A lovely off-dry version with almost spicy character which develops well with bottle age. This wine is consistently good.

Sauvignon Blanc 1991 ♀♀ ①
This is an unwooded but remarkable, full bodied, steely, clean and penetrating Sauvignon. Ages extremely well, keeping its freshness and character for many years.

Tradition de Charles de Fere ♀ ①
Carte Rouge brut
Made from a blend of Pinot Noir, Pinotage, Chenin Blanc and Chardonnay. Slightly fuller and rounder than in previous vintages due to riper grapes and an increase in the percentages of Pinot Noir and Chardonnay. Excellent bubble and good long, clean flavor.

Cru Monro 1988 ♀♀ ①
One of South Africa's best 60% Cabernet Sauvignon, 40% Merlot blends. It is beautifully balanced with a blackcurrants and cedar-wood palate and with depth and length. Improves every year.

Merlot 1989 ♀ ①
The grapes come from very low yielding vines and the wine was aged one year in new French oak barrels. A ripe, deep, concentrated red with complexity of fruit and mineral flavors. Outstanding but in short supply.

Vriesenhof

Box 155
Stellenbosch 7600
Tel. (02231) 900214
Fax (02231) 601503

Little is known of the early history of Vriesenhof but all one really needs to know is that it was purchased by Jan "Boland" Coetzee in 1980. Jan, a well-known rugby Springbok, started his wine career with a ten-year stint at Kanonkop. Today he is one of the industry's foremost consultants, a grower and winemaker of his own wines and for the neighboring farm, a rugby coach and a ceaseless worker for the Rural Foundation. A man of his own convictions, he seems capable of meeting any challenge. True to form his order of priorities when setting up Vriesenhof were workers first, cellar second and homestead last. The cellar was completed last year, so we might expect work to start on the homestead soon. The 15 hectares of vineyards are planted with Cabernet Sauvignon, Merlot, Pinot Noir and Chardonnay. Vriesenhof also has a second label, Paradyskloof, for the lesser wines which are supplemented with bought-in grapes.

Chardonnay 1990   ❦ ❦ ①
A regular winner and European in style (Jan spent some time at Joseph Drouhin in Burgundy). Reserved yet complex, needs time to open up. Cleverly oaked.

Cabernet Sauvignon 1989   ❦ ①
A typically elegant, refined, almost restrained style that needs several years to develop. Plenty of sweet fruit but well integrated. It needs to age for at least 10 years.

Kallista 1989   ❦ ❦ ①
A 65% Cabernet Sauvignon, 35% Merlot blend, aged in new oak for two years. Multi-dimensional fruit palate, tightly packed with firm tannins for long aging. Elegant rather than forceful.

Warwick

Box 2, Muldersvlei 7602
Stellenbosch
Tel. (02231) 94410
Fax (02231) 94025

Once part of a substantial 17th century farm called Good Success, Warwick was given its name when purchased by Colonel William Alexander Gordon in honor of the Warwickshire Regiment which he commanded during the South African War. Although wine was probably originally made here it was not until 1964 when Stan Ratcliffe became the new owner, to be joined by his wife Norma in 1971, that the seeds were sown for what is now a rapidly rising star. Norma, a native of Canada and presently the only woman member of the Cape Independent Winemakers' Guild, had no formal training in wine production but this has certainly not prevented her from making some truly fine, individual wines. She is helped in the cellar by Lola Hunting. The vineyards, which lie close to those of Kanonkop and Lievland, cover around 70 hectares and are planted with Cabernet Sauvignon, Cabernet Franc, Merlot and Chardonnay. This area seems to give a special, distinct quality to red wines.

Chardonnay 1991   ❦ ①
A new arrival to the range, it is barrel-fermented, with attractive peach flavor, combining elegance with some weight. Available in very limited quantities.

Cabernet Franc 1989   ❦ ①
A lovely example of this grape variety, intensely fruity (raspberries and red currants). Fresh and quite distinctive.

Cabernet Sauvignon 1989   ❦ ❦ ①
Fruity Cabernet, beautifully aged in new oak; on the palate rich and juicy with good underpinning tannin. On the nose complex with an initial impression of ripe fruit.

Trilogy 1989   ❦ ❦ ①
A 70% Cabernet Sauvignon, 23% Merlot and 7% Cabernet Franc blend. A beautiful rendition of ripe fruit with almost exotic complexity from new oak aging, giving a hint of liquorice. Full, rich palate and a highly individual character.

Welgemeend

Box 69, Klapmuts 7625
Paarl
Tel. (02211) 5210

Welgemeend is a small estate of 16 hectares of which nearly 14 are planted to vines. Despite its small size it has, since 1974, made a large contribution to the evolution of the South African wine industry. Originally known as Monte Video, it was renamed upon its purchase by Billy Hofmeyer after the last vineyard owned by his family in Cape Town before it was overtaken by development. Billy, who had a passion for Bordeaux wines, particularly those from Pomerol and St Emilion, replanted the estate with Cabernet Sauvignon, Merlot, Cabernet Franc, Petit Verdot and Malbec and by 1979 had produced the first "Bordeaux blend". Welgemeend is strictly a red wine estate, and today there are additional plantings of Grenache, Shiraz and Pinotage. Billy was also in large part responsible for the creation of the Cape Independent Winemakers' Guild, a body set up to help the leading winemakers from independent estates study wine and compare notes. Little could he have known what a contribution this would make to the improvement of the Cape's wines in such a short period of time. Sadly Billy has recently been incapacitated by illness, but his wife Ursula and daughter Louise continue to produce excellent wines.

Amade 1990   ❦ ①
This is an elegant and fruity wine made from Shiraz, Grenache and a little Pinotage. Very smooth and easy to drink.

Estate Wine 1990   ❦ ①
A blend of 50% Cabernet Sauvignon, 30% Merlot and 20% Cabernet Franc with some Petit Verdot. Aged in new and second-year barriques, good deep color, with plenty of fruit, positive oak tones and intensity. It will develop well.

Zevenwacht Wines

Box 387, Kuils River 7580
Stellenbosch
Tel. (021) 9035123
Fax (021) 9033373

This large 353 hectare estate which lies on the Bottelary hills is the result of the joining of two properties, Zevenfontein and Langvewacht - hence the name Zevenwacht. It was purchased by Gilbert Colyn, a Cape Town architect, in 1978. Gilbert descends from the Colijn family who were once connected with Groot Constantia, the cellar of which he more recently designed. This experience came in handy for the cellar he was to build on Zevenwacht and with the help of Neil Ellis as winemaker he set about making a range of quality wines. There will be over 220 hectares of vines when planting is completed but parts of the estate will be kept as a nature reserve with rare flora and fauna. There is a significant range of different soils which permits a wide variety of vines to be planted with success. Following Neil Ellis's departure to set up his own venture, Eric Saayman took over as winemaker and has already produced a number of very good wines. One of the estate's specialities is its Blanc de Blanc which ranks among the finest in the Cape and is its most popular wine.

Blanc de Blanc 1991   ❦ ①
A blend of Sauvignon, Chenin and Cape Riesling which has a depth and complexity that sets it apart from others. Although light and fresh in youth, it improves with a few years in bottle.

Sauvignon Blanc 1991   ❦ ①
Excellent, intense gooseberry and nettle aroma with well balanced, clean palate and fresh aftertaste.

Cabernet Sauvignon 1988   ❦❦ ①
An oak aged, individual style of Cabernet with firm tannins which contrasts with the lovely red fruit (blackberries and blackcurrants). As with previous vintages it will need time to develop.

Shiraz 1988   ❦ ①
Matured in large wooden barrels. Pepper and leather aromas with ample sweet fruit and length on the palate. It is more European in style than South African.

SPAIN

With 1,700,000 hectares of vineyard, 17% of the world total and 22% of that of Europe, Spain is the nation with the largest surface area dedicated to vines in the world. The extent of this vast vineyard is not reflected in the amount of wine produced, which rarely exceeds 33 million hectoliters, barely half that of France or Italy. The majority of this production, about 20 million hl, remains at home, eagerly consumed by the Spanish, despite the recent slight reduction in favor of lighter beverages, such as beer. 80% of the families in the Iberian peninsula drink wine daily, mostly during meals, with the healthy social tradition of the "chateo". Although the Roman emperor Diocletion banned the planting of new vineyards in Spain to avoid damaging competition for the rest of the Empire, today Spain's wines are diverse, abundant and good. And the Spanish, as a result, delight in drinking them.

Spain is a privileged country for wine production. Its climate and soils produce an incredible variety and quantity of wine. Each town or village has its own local wine; and in Spain there is not only quantity, but also quality. In an enological expanse that embraces practically the entire nation there are excellent areas, including (La) Rioja, Jerez, Penedés, Ribera del Duero, Rias Baixas and La Mancha. Yet despite the excellent quality of the fruit, which gives the winemaker an excellent starting point, it is not always treated with the necessary respect at the processing stage. Winemaking often comes up against an old prejudice: that wine must be 'pure', that modern winemaking techniques are clinical and unnecessary. There is nothing further from the truth. Pure wines, made without the necessary treatment or selection, turn out rather badly, although with luck a good year may produce a better wine. The modern argument aims to revolutionize winemaking in Spain, by adopting modern viticultural, vinification and aging techniques.

Due to the fragmentation of the Spanish wine industry it is very much at odds with this objective. With more than 10,000 large wineries each producing over 100 hl of wine, the problem of widespread inferior technology will be hard to address. It is not unusual to find antiquated equipment, which undoubtedly influences the quality of the wine. All of these factors mean that very low quality, rustic wines, highly appreciated by local consumers, are being produced in Spain.

During the last ten years, the outlook has changed, but a decade is nothing in terms of winemaking evolution. In this short time, many favorable circumstances have contributed to a nationwide enological explosion of exceptional vintages such as: 1981, 1982, 1983, 1984, 1986, 1988 and 1989 in Spain's major DOs, that is, Alella, Ampurdán-Costa Brava, Campo de Borja, Conca de Barberá, La Mancha, Montilla-Moriles, Méntrida, Navarra, Ribera del Duero, Rioja, Tarragona, Terra Alta, Valdepeñas and Yecla; some areas have even enjoyed exceptional consecutive vintages. In the 1980s, blessed with good weather, Spain's largest wineries upgraded and modernized their cellars and equipment. Enological research centers have been increased along with the number of qualified technicians. Wine knowledge is spreading to the consumer, resulting in a more selective market, and thanks to the more stringent DO policies of the Consejos Reguladores is on its way to quality wine production.

Spain can now face the 1993 Common Market with confidence, and, due to an excellent quality/price ratio, almost unbeatable in the European community, is hot competition. Spain has already earned its niche in the market thanks to some of its most prestigious wine-producers, such as Torres, Cune, Magaña, Marqués de Murrieta, Marqués de Riscal, Muga, Pesquera, Raimat, La Rioja Alta, Vega Sicilia, and the list grows longer every year.

Continuing on this path, Spain is sure to recover its rightful position of great prestige among the world's winepowers.

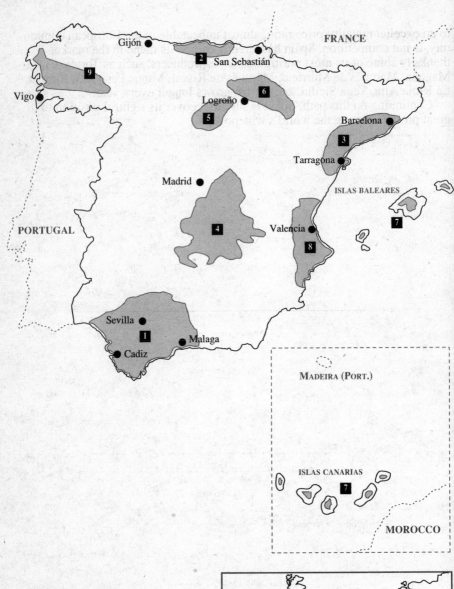

Gijón

FRANCE

San Sebastián

2

9

Vigo

Logroño

6

5

Barcelona

3

Tarragona

Madrid

ISLAS BALEARES

PORTUGAL

Valencia

4

7

8

Sevilla

Malaga

1

Cadiz

MADEIRA (PORT.)

ISLAS CANARIAS

7

MOROCCO

1	**Andalucía**
2	**Cantábrica**
3	**Cataluña**
4	**Centro**
5	**Cuenca del Duero**
6	**Cuenca del Ebro**
7	**Islas**
8	**Levante**
9	**Noroeste**

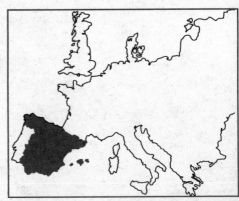

Andalucia

The province of Andalucia boasts over 71,000 ha of vineyards. The most prominent varieties are: Pedro Ximénez, Palomino, Zalema and Moscatel. A total of 3,000,000 hl of wine is produced, about 10% of Spain's total production. Undoubtedly the specialty of Andalucia is its vino Generoso or fortified wine, produced mostly in the DOs of Jerez, Manzanilla and Montilla-Moriles. Their uniqueness lies in their special aging system. The wine is vinified traditionally but then racked into oak barrels. At this point the terms "flor" and "solera" come into play. Flor is the particular yeast covering that forms over the wine, preventing air contact and oxidation. The particular micro-climatic conditions of this part of Andalucia cause the yeast to be especially abundant in certain seasons, thus performing the fundamental task essential to the success of these wines. In Sanlúcar de Barrameda, located in the western part of Jerez on an estuary along the Guadalquivir river, temperatures are lower and humidity is higher due to the proximity of the sea. These conditions favor the development of flor and result in a thicker, more active layer of yeast, greatly influencing the wine's evolution. For this reason, the Jerez or Sherry from Sanlúcar de Barrameda has its own DO Manzanilla. The aging of the wines brings us to the solera system. Barrels are stacked in "criaderas" or rows sometimes up to 40 high, with the oldest wines on the bottom layer and the youngest at the top. A carefully regulated amount of wine for bottling is drawn from the oldest barrels. These barrels are in turn topped up with the younger wines from above. In this continuous cycle the younger wines take on the characteristics of the maturer wines. As flor prevents oxidation, the thicker it is the more delicate the wine. Wines which have little flor are, therefore, more oxidised and tend to be fuller and nuttier.

Andalucia's other DOs are Condado de Huelva, an area producing good white wines with the native Zalema grape, and Malaga, famous for its unctuous wines made from Moscatel (Muscat) and Pedro Ximénez. As Spain's second largest wine producing area, it is also beginning to diversify from its traditional fortified wines to younger, fresher style whites which are currently in demand on the domestic market. Andalucia is an area with a bright future.

Bodegas Andrade

Av. Coronación, 35
Bollullos del Condado (Huelva)
Tel. (955) 410506

No need to trace back to the wine-loving Greeks to see that quality wine has been produced here for years. Despite their similarity in style to their neighbors in Jerez, these wines have their own special character. Bodegas Andrade was founded in 1942 and has remained faithful to tradition throughout. Its 200 ha of vineyards are planted with native Zalema and Palomino varietals. The property also buys in grapes from local producers. The winery is well-equipped and able to produce many different kinds of wine. For example, for the production of the white wines made from Zalema (a wine with DO status), temperature-controlled stainless steel tanks have been installed. The winery also has approximately 1,000 American oak barrels in which the more traditional wines are aged.

Castillo de Andrade 1991 ①
Light, fresh and fruity, a delightful modern style wine made from Zalema. Smooth, pleasant with low alcohol content.

Doceañero ①
Pungent nose and full in the mouth mainly due to its 20° alc, which is not, however, overpowering. The wine is 100% Palomino.

Vinícola del Condado

San José, 2
Bollullos del Condado (Huelva)
Tel. (955) 410261
Fax (955) 410171

After a period of crisis in the 19th century, the historic vineyards of the Condado underwent a revival with the arrival of families from the winemaking area of La Rioja in Old Castille. In 1983, their descendants founded this cooperative, and repeated history by once again giving a new and important impetus to the area's wines. Backed by 1,800 member growers and 4,500 ha of vineyards, the cooperative is equipped with the most modern technology and latest winemaking equipment. The Vinícola del Condado have an interesting white wine production made mainly from Zalema grapes, and an excellent Pálido wine, which is aged similarly to the wines of Jerez, that is using the traditional Criadera and Solera systems.

Privilegio del Condado 1991 ①
Pale yellow with delicate primary fruit aromas of the Zalema grape. Smooth and pleasant in the mouth.

Condado Pálido Mioro ①
Delicate and pleasing bouquet, typical of Solera aging. Well-structured, rich and long on the palate. An interesting blend of Zalema, Palomino and Garrido Fino.

Bodegas Sauci

Dr. Fleming, 1 e 11
Bollullos del Condado (Huelva)
Tel. (955) 410524

Tradition has it that wine from Condado de Huelva was loaded by Columbus onto his three ships before setting sail for the Indies. Today, centuries later, it is found in the modern-day wineries such as Manuel Sauci's. For 70 years this winery has produced typical generoso or fortified wines from native grapes, mainly from Zalema, a variety also ideal for making young and fruity white wines. In 1958 they started to produce wines with the Palomino grape, originally from the Jerez area. In 1965, American oak barrels were brought in for the "Espinapura", inarguably one of the most representative wines from this DO as well as being excellent value for money. Production, however, is still mostly in bulk wines made in barrel. In short, Manuel Sauci has overcome many initial difficulties and has succeeded in producing a generoso wine easily comparable to that of his neighbours in Jerez.

Fino Espinapura
Rich, dried fruit aromas due to solera aging. Attractive pale yellow. A perfect example of the Palomino's extraordinary capabilities.

Oloroso Riodiel
Lighter on the nose than its highly perfumed Jerez counterparts, though it is made from the same Palomino grapes. Rich and harmonious flavors on the palate.

CONDADO DE HUELVA
ANDALUCIA
SPAIN

985

CONDADO DE HUELVA
ANDALUCIA
SPAIN

Herederos de Argüeso

Mar, 8
Sanlúcar de Barrameda (Cadiz)
Tel. (956) 360112
Fax (956) 368169

Nature has been exceptionally generous to Cádiz. The proof is in its vivacious and warm-hearted inhabitants who do not blow hot and cold, like the two contrasting, complementary winds which breeze through the town: the dry, warm easterly Levante and the cool, humid westerly Ponente. In the area of Marco de Jerez, the people, the winds and the terrain have produced a unique combination, which makes one of the best wines in the world, and means Sanlúcar de Barrameda cannot go wrong. Here Don León de Argüeso y Argüeso initially set himself up in business in 1822, gradually branching out into his own wine production. The Manzanilla is aged in 20,000 m2 of cellars located in the center of Sanlúcar. The winery has installed some of the most modern and technologically advanced equipment for stabilizing and filtering the wines, plus steel fermentation tanks and a bottling line, even though Argüeso's heirs believe that retaining artisanal, traditional winemaking methods is fundamental for the production of their excellent Manzanillas.

Amontillado Viejo Argüeso   ♕♕ ③
Beautiful, brilliant topaz color. Refined but pungent aromas accompany a persistent and balanced flavor. The wine is made from the Palomino varietal.

Manzanilla Viruta   ♕♕ ①
Pale but brilliant yellow, delicate but vivid secondary aromas of dried fruit. Decisive character on the palate, delicate and elegant with a bitter Palomino varietal finish.

Manzanilla Pasada San León   ♕♕♕ ①
Manzanilla is an enigma which escapes traditional enological guidelines. The special method of vinification uses Soleras, Criaderas and Bajo Flor methods. These wines usually age for more than 15 years and maintain their vibrant color. A perfect example is "San León" which is pale, limpid yellow with golden tones and a pronounced rim. Intense aromas of lengthy aging with fresh and dried fruits. Dry and complex on the mouth, with well-balanced distinguishable flavors. Lingering, sophisticated, delicate: undoubtedly a very special wine.

JEREZ
ANDALUCIA
SPAIN

986

JEREZ
ANDALUCIA
SPAIN

Antonio Barbadillo

.. Eguilaz, 11
Sanlúcar de Barrameda (Cadiz)
Tel. (956) 360241
Fax (956) 365103

Born in Covarrubias, Spain, Don Benigno Barbadillo emigrated to Mexico as a very young man at the beginning of the 1800s. Years after the American states had won their independence, he returned to Spain to start his successful wine business in Sanlúcar. On his death in 1837, the branch of the business dealing in the production and sale of wine and brandy was still growing. Always image and quality conscious, the winery has not surprisingly kept growing and is now considered one of the largest producers in Sanlúcar. The huge cellars contain over 60,000 oak barrels for aging their famous and excellent Manzanillas and sweet-perfumed Amontillados. The brandy from Barbadillo is also outstanding. Stainless steel vats hold young, dry white wine made from Palamino, currently a stylish grape in Andalucia which alone does not yet have DO status. The winery owns 460 ha of vineyards in the best areas of the region, planted mostly with Palomino grapes.

Amontillado Principe   ℗ ℗ ②
Topaz, packed with complex and potent secondary aromas; profound lingering sensations. The Palomino varietal's potential is fully expressed.

Manzanilla Eva   ℗ ℗ ①
Beautiful, light yellow, brilliant and clear. Loaded with aromas from solera aging. Fat, refined and potent on the palate.

Manzanilla Solear   ℗ ℗ ①
Extremely refined, concentrated with flavor and aromas, pungent but delicate. Powerful and elegant on the palate. In short, a great Palomino varietal wine.

Hijos de Agustín Blázquez

Ctra. Jerez-Algeciras
Jerez de la Frontera (Cadiz)
Tel. (956) 348250

Like most other wineries in Jerez, this winery has British ancestry. It was founded in 1795 by the Scottish family, Paul, which continued to manage it through the 19th century. The winery changed to its present name after a marriage into the Blázquez family. In 1973, the winery passed to the Domecq group, though remaining completely independent. Its wine cellars in El Puerto de Santa Maria use state-of-the-art equipment and have space for 15,000 Jerez-type barrels. Thanks to the Domecq distribution network, its wine can be found virtually everywhere. The name Hijos de Agustín de Blázquez is recognized largely due to its 'Fino Carta Blanca' wine, which, since its debut a few years ago, has won over many a taster in wine tastings and events.

Dulce Medal Cream   ℗ ℗ ①
Made from the extremely rare blend of Pedro Ximénez and Oloroso, the latter made from the Palomino grape. Complexity on the nose and in the mouth forgive any unpleasantness left by its sweetish character.

Fino Carta Blanca   ℗ ①
Pleasant looking, not very intense yellow. Notable, delicate secondary perfumes that actually tend to be rather pronounced. Smooth and elegant, with a notably bitter aftertaste.

Oloroso Carta Roja   ℗ ②
Vigorous and potent, well-balanced and ample in the mouth. Of good Palomino varietal character, with complex sensations in its aftertaste.

JEREZ
ANDALUCIA
SPAIN

987

JEREZ
ANDALUCIA
SPAIN

Bodegas Bobadilla

Ctra. Circunvalación, s/n
Jerez de la Frontera (Cadiz)
Tel. (956) 348600
Fax (956) 320856

Rioja-born Don Manuel Fernández de Boba-dilla and the Marquis of Bertemati, a great farmland owner from Jerez, founded this winery in 1882. Later the Marquis of Berte-mati sold his share to the Marquis of Misa. The ancient buildings housing the winecellars were to be found in the monastery of the Fathers of the Order of the Mercede in Jerez. Bobadilla's Bodegas or cellars occupy 10,000 square meters and produce 14,000 hl of wine annually. The two famous regional aging processes of Criaderas and Soleras are carried out with 14,000 barrels from Jerez. Excellent aging gives the classic Bobadilla wine its pronounced aroma. The winery's 40 ha of Palomino vineyards are located in famous Macharnudo. The property was recently acquired by Osborne, one of Spain's largest brandy producers, giving rise to fears that the future emphasis of the winery may shift away from Jerez to brandy, although Bobadillo brandy is already fairly widespread.

Fino Victoria ✿ ①
Golden yellow, clean, presenting secondary floral aromas with medium intensity salty tones. Fat and savory on the palate, but a bit short. Produced from the reigning variety of the area, Palomino.

Oloroso Capitán ✿✿ ②
Mahogany with ruby highlights; crystal clear, with a sensation of thickness. From intense and complex aromas emerges a rich and extraordinary woody scent. Balanced and lengthy on the palate, elegant sensations on the finish, with strong Palomino character.

Pedro Ximénez Romántico ✿ ②
This is a sweet, aromatic and complex dessert wine, with typical scents of semi-dried fruits. Smooth and sweet in the mouth, but a bit short.

Croft Jerez

Ctra. Jerez-Cadiz, s/n
Jerez de la Frontera (Cadiz)
Tel. (956) 306600
Fax (956) 303707

Croft Jerez is a young winery with an old name. Originally founded in Oporto in the 17th century, the winery was later acquired by Gilbey, which then had close business ties to Jerez. Then, in 1962, the group merged with an English multinational, boosting quality considerably when, in 1970, Croft Jerez was established. Production facilities were enlarged, with modern, new additions built to the Rancho Croft, overlooking 350 ha of estate-owned Palomino vineyards. Production of these vines is still insufficient to satisfy the needs of the winery, which must then buy grapes from nearby growers. The equipment is state-of-the-art technology, preserving very little of the traditional wine-making process. Nevertheless, the quality of the wine is unquestionable. The winecellars use 50,000 American oak barrels to produce 40 million lt of wine, seven of which are exported each year.

Amontillado Croft Classic ✿ ②
Topaz with copper highlights, it has refined wood tones that are accompanied by a sweetish aroma, especially on the palate. 100% Palomino.

Fino Croft Delicado ✿ ①
A clean-cut wine, pure and light yellow in color with golden highlights. Its secondary aromas are not very strong, showing traces of dried fruit. Full-bodied on the palate, with a bitter finish, typical of the Palomino varietal.

Palo Cortado Croft ✿ ②
Sparkling topaz in color, with good aromatic evolution and intensity, it has especially nice quality wood and sweet tones. Smooth, rich and slightly sweet on the palate, it is made with Pedro Ximénez along with the classic Palomino.

JEREZ
ANDALUCIA
SPAIN

988

JEREZ
ANDALUCIA
SPAIN

Delgado Zuleta

Ctra. Sanlúcar-Chipiona, km 15
Sanlúcar de Barrameda (Cadiz)
Tel. (956) 360133
Fax (956) 370780

The small, Atlantic coastal town of Sanlúcar de Barrameda is the homeland of Manzanilla wine, the queen of Generoso wines and Sorceress of sea breezes. The name Manzanilla, meaning camomile in Spanish, comes from the very time when the beneficial effects of camomile on the stomach were discovered. Manzanilla (a DO wine) can be produced only in Sanlúcar de Barrameda, where Delgado Zuleta established his winery as far back as 1745. Production philosophy is so dedicated to tradition that not much has changed in the last two and a half centuries. Here, the use of time-tested techniques are deemed essential in maintaining Manzanilla's exclusive reputation and prestige. Delgado Zuleta's wines are of medium quality, although no effort is spared in preparing top Generoso wines. Furthermore, in-house experimentation has also brought to light a pleasant, new style of white wine from Palomino that is lighter in alcohol.

Amontillado Quo Vadis B*2
Extremely complex and well-structured, it has all the qualities of skillfully-aged great wine; from the Palomino varietal.

Manzanilla Barbiana   ♔ ♔ ①
Pure, bright, light yellow with golden highlights. Refined secondary floral aromas, tossed with honey, wood and hazelnut scents. Well-balanced and flavorful, with considerable salty tones and a slightly bitter aftertaste, with lingering full aromas, clean and potent.

Manzanilla La Goya   ♔ ♔ ①
Light yellow in color, with pungent aromas and very elegant scents of dried fruit. It develops and unfolds nicely on the palate, with a light, bitter aftertaste from the Palomino.

Díez-Mérito

Cervantes, 3
Jerez de la Frontera (Cadiz)
Tel. (956) 330700

The 1976 merging of two traditional Jerez wineries, Díez Hermanos (founded in 1876) and Marquéz del Mérito (founded in 1895) gave rise to Díez-Mérito, which has been managed since 1983 by the Rumasa construction firm. Headed by José María Ruiz Mateos, the group had an outstanding role in Jerez in the 1960s and 1970s until 1983, when it was reclaimed by the government. The state-controlled winery then acquired another famous winemaker, Zoilo Ruiz Mateos. A year later, in 1984, Rioja native Marcos Eguizábal bought the entire winery. The scattered vineyards, sufficient for current production, are concentrated in the El Carrascal, a renowned vineyard area. Despite the numerous trials and tribulations and economic/political upheavals, Díez-Mérito manages to distinguish itself for the high quality of its wines.

Amontillado Fino Imperial   ♔ ♔ ④
The epitome of good intensity and balance, from its beautiful, brilliant topaz color to its lingering aromas of refined wood and the salty scents; all in all, a fine delicate Palomino wine.

Fino Don Zoilo   ♔ ①
Brilliant golden yellow in color, emitting potent and pungent aromas due to solera aging. A dry and somewhat powerful approach on the palate, probably due to its high alcohol content.

Pedro Ximénez Don Zoilo XXX   ♔ ③
Classic mahogany in color, although not very intense. Made from the Pedro Ximénez grape, with sea scents that accompany rather pure, sweet aromas.

JEREZ
ANDALUCIA
SPAIN

989

JEREZ
ANDALUCIA
SPAIN

Pedro Domecq

San Ildefonso, 3
Jerez de la Frontera (Cadiz)
Tel. (956) 331800
Fax (956) 349966

Patrick Murphy left his beloved Irish homeland to make wine in Jerez in 1725. In 1791, his business passed into the hands of a man named Juan Hurie, whose heir later married Juan Domecq. The new Domecq name brought good fortune to the winery, which began its formidable climb to success. Pedro Domecq owns one of the most beautiful properties in Marco del Jerez, in the locality of Macharnudo, where the Palomino grape reaches its full potential. A castle lies at the center where all the vineyards converge. These and other scattered tracts constitute a total of 800 ha of vineyards. The gigantic facilities have numerous kinds of cellars for vinification and aging. Some, such as the more famous Mezquita, are authentic tributes to wine culture. Pedro Domecq has financial interests in Rioja, Brazil, Argentina, Mexico and Colombia, reaching an annual gross of 75,000 million pesetas. Regardless of these mind-boggling quantities and figures, there is something special about PD, which nonetheless gives the impression of a small, handcrafted masterpiece.

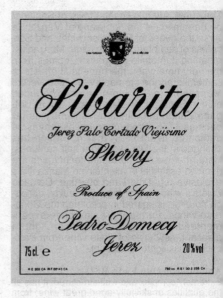

Fino La Ina   🍇 ①
Slightly lacking in intensity but brilliant yellow in color, emanating powerful and acute aromas. Refined and elegant, revealing salty traces and a light bitter aftertaste, typical of the Palomino grape.

Pedro Ximénez Venerable   🍇🍇 ③
Fruit of an aging process that has transformed a high quality wine into something truly exceptional. Thanks goes to the slow passage of time, concentrating color, aroma and taste.

Palo Cortado Sibarita   🍇🍇🍇 ④
Sibarita is an authentic work of art created by exemplary enological technology. The Palomino varietal realizes its full potential in this infinitely flavored wine. Mahogany with iodized highlights; extremely seductive; displays proof of a special aging process. Complex and intense on the nose, with aromas of fine wood, dried fruit and compôte. Smooth approach, perfect and splendid development in all corners of the mouth, revealing itself to be well-structured and elegant. Extremely long and fat with powerful lingering sensations, and traces of mature fruit to complete the grand finale.

JEREZ
ANDALUCIA
SPAIN

990

JEREZ
ANDALUCIA
SPAIN

Garvey

Divina Pastora, 3
Jerez de la Frontera (Cadiz)
Tel. (956) 330500

Sir William Garvey, born in the Castle of
Annagh, Ireland, was among the earliest
winery founders in Marco de Jerez to specialize in exportation. In the last decades, Garvey has suffered a drop in quality of its own
production, followed by a Rumasa group
takeover. The history and great fortune of this
winery has allowed it to recover its lost lands.
The vineyards are all of Albariza (the white,
chalky terrain), that gives the wine an extremely delicate character. Each year, the
vineyards yield grapes for 3,700,000 liters of
wine which is aged in extremely beautiful cellars, known as 'cathedrals'. In another building, there are vats for the fermentation and
aging of brandy and a bottling line. 32,000
oak barrels age the wine, each containing
550 lt. As one of the most historical vineyards
in Jerez, Garvey refuses to adapt to modern
methods of vinification. This has not stopped
it from producing some notable and well-
distributed wines, such as Fino San Patricio
(owing its name to Ireland's patron saint).

Amontillado Tío Guillermo   ❦ ②
Delicate aromas are attributed to aging in wood.
Well-structured and potent, producing long, lingering sensations, most prominently those from
the Palomino varietal and the bajo flor aging
process.

Fino San Patricio   ❦ ①
Golden yellow with a dense rim. The perfume
due to its aging process is particularly outstanding. A traditional product, typical of Garvey.

Oloroso Ochavico   ❦ ②
Pure and brilliant topaz/amber with iodized
tones. Potent complex of aromas, featuring traces of extended aging. Long and rich on the
palate; lingering sensations instantly recall Palomino.

JEREZ
ANDALUCIA
SPAIN

991

JEREZ
ANDALUCIA
SPAIN

González Byass

Manuel María González, 12
Jerez de la Frontera (Cadiz)
Tel. (956) 340000
Fax (956) 349985

González Byass is one of the few wineries in Jerez to remain in the hands of the same quality-driven family. This family trait is reflected in their generous wines: some masterly and others truly exceptional, deserving a place on the list of the best wines in the world. Particularly noteworthy is the superb Noé, unsurpassed in its category, and Fino Tío Pepe, the biggest selling Spanish wine in the world, available practically everywhere and renowned as the classic Fino of Jerez. Don José María González established the winery in 1835 and, after adding the wineries of Los Apostoles and La Cuadrada in 1858, he reached an export capacity of 1,000,000 bottles. Expansion continued at a strong rhythm and, in 1963, Tío Pepe was constructed to house 30,000 barrels, yielding 15,000,000 lt of wine. A few years later the even larger Las Copas was realized, holding 60,000 barrels. The immense properties of the winery are in Balbaina and Macharnudo, considered the best territories in the so-called 'Jerez Superior', an irregular triangular-shaped area that includes the towns of Jerez de la Frontera, El Puerto de Santa María and Sanlúcar de Barrameda.

Fino Tío Pepe   ♟♟ ①
Brilliant golden yellow. Complex secondary aromas from natural aging, with acute and powerful traces of dried fruit. Intense and well-balanced on the palate, with a bitter aftertaste. Lingering sensations emphasize primary aromas.

Oloroso Matusalem   ♟♟ ④
Clear and elegant; pleasant mahogany with orange tones. Powerful perfumes set the tone for an ample aromatic circulation. After a smooth approach on the palate, the wine is potent, fat and rather long.

Pedro Ximénez Noé   ♟♟♟ ④
A rare example of a very old wine which disproves the theories of traditional vinification of sweet wines. Obtained from naturally faded Pedro Ximénez grapes and fermented to a 10° alc content, it is aged many years through the process of Soleras and Criaderas. Opaque, dense, almost black, and crowned by amber and orange highlights. Aromatic and elegant with tones of sweet dried grapes, dried figs and wood. Delicate on the palate, velvety and extremely intense. High Baumé, though not at all distasteful; leaving a light, sweet sensation in the mouth.

JEREZ
ANDALUCIA
SPAIN

992

JEREZ
ANDALUCIA
SPAIN

Grupo Harvey

Colón, 2
Jerez de la Frontera (Cadiz)
Tel. (956) 330950
Fax (956) 341255

Harvey was already bottling and labeling Jerez wines before 1970, even though it owned neither vineyards nor a winery. In order to make a better and more quality consistent production, in 1970 Harvey formed a partnership with Terry, a long-standing winery in the Jerez area. The group merged with various other wineries such as Palomino and Vergara, maker of the famous Fino Tio Mateo. Their cellars may be described as nothing less than grandiose: they hold 110,000,000 lt and house 120,000 oak barrels for a total production of 31,000,000 bottles annually. The winery controls 1,300 ha of Palomino-dominated vineyards in the Jerez DO. With such an efficient London-based distribution network, Harvey's wine may be found practically worldwide. Their most famous products are surely their Cream Sherries, as well as their highly appraised Finos.

Fino Tío Mateo　　　　　　🍷 ①
Brilliant, golden yellow; acute and powerful aromas resulting from long maturation. Well-balanced flavors in the mouth with a long, complex finish. Produced from Palomino grapes.

Oloroso Bristol Cream　　　🍷 ②
A typically Anglosaxon-tasting wine. Aromas of ripe grapes. Rich and pleasant on the palate with a sweet mellow finish. The wine is made by a curious blend of two wines: one made from Palomino, the other from Pedro Ximénez.

Vinícola Hidalgo y Cía

Banda de la Playa, 24
Sanlúcar de Barrameda (Cadiz)
Tel. (956) 341597

Manzanilla is the quintessential wine produced from Solera aging, a strict process which calculates everything down to the last mm. The result is a miracle in vinification achieved only in this small area of the Atlantic coast near the mouth of the Guadalquivir river. The Hidalgo family, whose emphasis has always been on quality, produces one of Spain's best Manzanillas. This is mainly due to their superb, perfectly tended vineyards which are planted on Albariza terrain. The 180 ha area of vines, situated near the towns of Balbaina and Miraflores, are, of course, planted with the Palomino grape varietal. The Hidalgo family is also known for their use of traditional vinification methods, and aging in criadera and solera. The production of nearly 20,000 hl comes entirely from the family's own vineyards, which is rare in an area where grapes are often brought in from outside growers.

Amontillado Napoleón　　　🍷 ②
Attractive mid-amber color; pure aromas of dried fruit, more profound than those normally found in Amontillados. Rich on the palate; flavorful and elegant, with a delicate, long finish.

Manzanilla La Gitana　　　🍷🍷 ①
Bright medium yellow. Elegant, dried fruit and hints of sea-salt on the nose. Light, balanced and flavorful in the mouth. Bitter overtones tell us this is a typical Palamino.

JEREZ
ANDALUCIA
SPAIN

993

JEREZ
ANDALUCIA
SPAIN

Bodegas de los Infantes de Orléans

Baños, 1
Sanlúcar de Barrameda (Cadiz)
Tel. (956) 360241

In contrast to the older wineries in the region, Bodegas de los Infantes de Orléans was founded in only 1943 by the Infante de Orléans-Bourbon family. The family also owns the vineyards of Torre Breva, a magnificent estate containing large areas of Albariza terrain. The area's abundance of limestone contributes to the wines' superior quality and finesse. Settled in the 19th century by the Duke of Montpensier, the property was first used as a hunting reserve until the Infanta Donna Beatrice of Sassonia founded, with the help of the Barbadillo, her own winery. Today the property is still divided equally between Barbadillo and the Infante family, but it is Barbadillo who has always been responsible for the making and distribution of the wine. In only 50 years, Bodegas de los Infantes de Orléans has succeeded in producing important, high quality wines, fully capable of competing with their more famous neighbors.

Amontillado Botánico   🍇 🍇 ②
Rich and powerful, having all the qualities of a great wine. Well-balanced flavors harmonize perfectly together on the palate. Crafted from 100% Palomino.

Manzanilla Torre Breva   🍇 ①
Light yellow; secondary aromas include toast and hints of honey. Balanced and dry with a bitter aftertaste, typical of Palomino's traditional aging process.

Price levels

①   up to $ 9.99

② $ 10.00 - $ 14.99

③ $ 15.00 - $ 24.99

④ $ 25.00 or more

The 'ex-cellar', or direct from the producer, bottle prices, are calculated in US dollars and are intended only as an approximate guide

JEREZ
ANDALUCIA
SPAIN

994

JEREZ
ANDALUCIA
SPAIN

Emilio Lustau

Plaza del Cubo, 4
Jerez de la Frontera (Cadiz)
Tel. (956) 348946

Some wineries, despite expansion and modernization, remain typically family-oriented in character. Even outside Spain, Emilio Lustau's winery is a shining example of this. In 1896 the winery was founded as a hobby by a wine-crazed lawyer. The wine was not in fact marketed until many years later by Emilio Lustau, the lawyer's son-in-law. Today the winery is known and praised throughout the world for its high quality wines, so much so that Richard Ford, writer and expert on the Jerez region, often quotes Lustau's 'Cruz de Husillo' vineyard as a model example. A new winery called Pinfiel, built along the same lines as the old premises, has been established on the Nuestra Señora de la Esperanza estate, and nestles against the ancient city walls. Both facilities have the most up-to-date equipment and together use 20,000 barrels from Jerez for vinification and aging.

Moscatel Emilín 🍷🍷🍷 ④
Simply the quintessential Moscatel. Attractive color, perfume; a synthesis of richness and delicacy, along with the dry extracts on the palate, make it unforgettable.

Oloroso Emperatriz Eugenia 🍷🍷 ③
Brilliant mahogany with amber and copper highlights. Pure and powerful aromas from the long aging process. Full and silky, but also powerful in the mouth. The lingering intensity of the wine emanates scents of dried fruit and subtle wood.

Amontillado Escuadrilla 🍷🍷🍷 ③
Amontillado wine is undoubtedly a fascinating example of a fortified wine characterized as always by solera aging. They are among some of Andalucia's most complete wines. Amontillado Escuadrilla is noted especially for its perfect balance and harmony. It is refined yet delicate, with powerful structure due to its aging process. Brilliant ambered topaz with copper highlights. Elegant aromas of wood, with pure, pungent traces of the bajo flor aging. Soft, full and perfectly balanced on the palate. Long, even finish. In short, an unforgettable wine.

ANDALUCIA
SPAIN

995

JEREZ
ANDALUCIA
SPAIN

Herederos del Marqués del Real Tesoro

Ctra. Nacional IV, km 640
Jerez de la Frontera (Cadiz)
Tel. (956) 321004
Fax (956) 340829

The prestigious Herederos del Marqués del Real Tesoro winery has a colorful history, recovering recently from a dark unhappy period to become a success story. Established by the noble heirs who gave it its name, the winery was a great success, but, after a severe crisis in the 1960s, it went into decline. Saving it from almost certain failure, José Estevez, enterprising and resolved, set out on a mission to revolutionize the winery and make quality wines. More recently, José has been concentrating on his latest problem: the demand for less alcoholic, young, fruity wines, which he has succeeded in producing. The investment and effort made to the property has been substantial and although the fruits of José's labour may be long-coming, his deserved reputation is already firmly established.

Amontillado Del Príncipe
Attractive, bright topaz, powerful on the nose, with faint aromas of dried fruit and those typical of the long aging process. Full and complex on the palate.

Oloroso Almirante
Powerful and complex example of Oloroso. Perfection has been reached after years of aging in oak barrels. Like most of these wines, it is produced solely from Palomino grapes.

Oloroso Covadonga
This winery's best wines are their Olorosos, aged extensively in wood. Such is Covadonga, rich, complex and complete in flavor and aroma.

Rating System

🍇 An exemplary wine of its type with outstanding local character

🍇🍇 An international premium quality wine

🍇🍇🍇 A Top Wine, considered one of the 150 best wines in the world

The 'grape bunch' symbol is used to indicate the color of the wine; the number of bunches represents the quality rating assigned by the contributor

*JEREZ
ANDALUCIA
SPAIN*

996

*JEREZ
ANDALUCIA
SPAIN*

Osborne y Cía

Fernán Caballero, 3
Puerto de Santa María (Cadiz)
Tel. (956) 855211
Fax (956) 853063

Thomas Osborne, an Englishman in love with Jerez wines, founded his winery in El Puerto de Santa Maria in 1792, giving life to one of the first and most traditional Jerez labels. With a 40,000,000 bottle output, Osborne has become the region's largest producer and its leader in turnover. Despite the huge quantity, these wines have not lost the traditional, handmade character of the Marco de Jerez area and are often considered real pearls of winemaking. The immense, 300,000 m2 cathedral-like winery uses 30,000 oak barrels for aging. The mere 167 ha of vineyards owned by the winery are obviously insufficient to satisfy the enormous demand, resulting in the acquisition of large quantities of grapes from nearby growers. The name Osborne is known in Spain and throughout the world not only for its Jerez wines, but also for being one of Spain's largest producers of brandy.

Amontillado Coquinero　　🍇🍇 ②
Attractive, bright amber with golden tones. Delightful nuances of long maturation on the nose, together with intense aromas of subtle oak. Obtained from Palomino.

Fino Quinta　　🍇🍇 ①
Lighter than most classic Finos. Seductive secondary aromas, elegant and delicate on the palate; bitter aftertaste.

Oloroso Bailén　　🍇🍇🍇 ③
Because of a special vinification process, it has a higher alc content than other Jerez wines. A perfect example of an Oloroso wine. Palomino grapes undergo the traditional oxygen-reduced aging process of the soleras and criaderas. Maturation takes place in 550 lt barrels and may last up to thirty years. Amber and topaz in color, with pretty, bright orange tones. Aromatically complex and powerful with refined scents of varnished wood, dried and passita fruit. Full, powerful, and extremely rich on the palate. Balanced alc level gives it great structure. Long finish of dried fruit. Aromas, due to long aging, are complex and elegant.

JEREZ
ANDALUCIA
SPAIN

997

JEREZ
ANDALUCIA
SPAIN

Hijos de Rainiera Perez Marín

Misericordia, 1
Sanlúcar de Barrameda (Cadiz)
Tel. (956) 361940
Fax (956) 182820

This winery is a work of art and its 'Manzanilla La Guita' too; together they are known and highly praised throughout Spain. Founded in 1825, Hijos de Rainiera Perez Marín focuses its expertise on the celebrated Manzanillas of Sanlúcar. Remarkably, La Guita is aged in a solera with eight rows of barrels. The winery and its production may be defined as modest in relation to its gigantic neighbors. 1,300 Jerez-type barrels, each with a 550 lt capacity, are used in the traditional, organic vinification process. The winery's over 200 ha of vineyards are situated in the center of beautiful Marco de Jerez, on the calcareous Albariza terrain, clayey and rich in salt carbonate. This land produces the best Palomino grapes, the essential ingredient in these superb wines.

Manzanilla La Guita   ♈♈ ①
Bright, golden yellow, forward aromas of top class Palomino. Extremely tasty in the mouth; four distinct fundamental flavors; very well-balanced.

The House of Sandeman

Pizarro, 10
Jerez de la Frontera (Cadiz)
Tel. (956) 301100

In the 1700s, a merchant from London named Sandeman began to import Oporto wine and Sherry. Towards the end of the century, his colleague, J. Gordon, representing the firm Duff, transferred to Cadiz to export Jerez wine using the label Sandeman. For many years Sandeman was known as a Jerez label, despite its lack of vineyards and winecellars. The actual winery was established many years later by the acquisition of winemaking facilities from the Pemartin family and of some criaderas from the Bernaldo de Quiros family. Sandeman now produces 110,000 hl of wine, obtained from 400 ha of vineyard mostly planted with Palomino. The enormous winery spans an area of 55,000 m2 and houses 50,000 oak barrels used in its traditional winemaking techniques. The House of Sandeman sells mostly abroad, above all in the United Kingdom. Its interest in the Spanish market came about in the 1960s, when flocks of Sandeman-drinking British tourists came on vacation to Spain and demanded the wine there as well!

Amontillado Royal Esmeralda   ♈ ③
Brilliant, golden amber color. Aromas alluding to Fino, but with stronger woody accents. Soft and rich in the mouth, with a slightly bitter aftertaste common to the Palomino varietal.

Fino Don Fino   ♈ ①
Beautiful bright golden yellow in color. Secondary aromas with some notes of honey. Rich but delicate in the mouth with a medium, balanced finish.

Oloroso Imperial Corregidor   ♈ ③
Aromatically intense, full and rich on the palate. Flavorful and long in the mouth with a slightly honied aftertaste. Long and complex finish. The blend of Palomino and Pedro Ximénez wines makes a perfect marriage.

JEREZ
ANDALUCIA
SPAIN

998

JEREZ
ANDALUCIA
SPAIN

Fernando A. de Terry

Santísima Trinidad, 2-4
Puerto de Santa María (Cadiz)
Tel. (956) 867700

The colorful Terry family from Ireland, apart from its reputation for producing Spanish military heroes, has for years been closely associated with wine. Residing in Puerto de Santa Maria since the 17th century, they have given the town a certain cultural resonance, above all by virtue of their beautiful family palace, which contains a money museum and important art collections. Don Santiago, a member of the Court of Cadiz, was the first Terry to enter the wine business. The winery was later founded by one of Don Santiago's descendants and soon became a booming success, receiving notoriety in Spain and abroad. In 1981, the Terry family sold the winery and the famous Cartujanos horse stables. In the following four years, the property changed hands numerous times until 1985, when the British holding company, Harvey, intervened to become the sole proprietor. Today the bodega possesses vineyards in the best areas of Marco de Jerez, but large production means buying in fruit from selected outside growers.

Amontillado Camborio   ☙ ②
Noted for its Fino-like aromatic qualities, it is made exclusively from Palomino grapes. Rather good value for money.

Fino Camborio   ☙ ①
Golden yellow, pure and pungent perfume. Rich on the palate, with classic Bajo Flor aging character. An unmistakable work of the Palomino.

Williams & Humbert

Nuño de Cañas, 1
Jerez de la Frontera (Cadiz)
Tel. (956) 331300
Fax (956) 326536

Like many of their peers, Alexander Williams and his brother-in-law, Arthur Humbert, came to Jerez de la Frontera in 1887 to export local wine to their native England. A few years later they began their own production, gathering praise for their soleras. Today the winery still traditionally ages its wines in these impressive old soleras. Still, however, their greatest source of pride is the vineyards, which claim some of the best Albariza terrain in Marco de Jerez. Añina, Balbaina, Macharnudo, El Carrascal, all rich in limestone, are perfect for growing Palamino vines, and give the wine great finesse. It is the knowledgeable heirs of Williams and Humbert who are in charge of making the wine, most of which is still exported.

Amontillado Dry Sack   ☙☙ ①
A firm favorite of the Anglo-Saxons. Attractive amber with copper highlights. Honied fruit on the nose and a supple finish compliment its robust character. Produced with Pedro Ximénez and Palomino.

Fino Pando   ☙ ①
Pale, bright yellow colour. Clean, and delicate bouquet. Smooth and light on the palate. A well-structured wine made exclusively from Palomino.

Oloroso Dos Cortados   ☙ ②
Mahogany with amber tones. Pungent, rich aromas. Initially full on the palate developing into interesting and complex flavours. Long, lingering finish. Also made from Palomino.

JEREZ
ANDALUCIA
SPAIN

999

JEREZ
ANDALUCIA
SPAIN

Larios

Av. La Aurora, 33
Málaga
Tel. (952) 241100
Fax (952) 240382

For many years phylloxera plagued the vines of the Málaga region, causing a severe crisis in its wine industry. Recently, wineries like Larios have been trying to restore Málaga wine to its ancient splendor. Larios is well-known for its wonderful brandy and for certain spirits. Its sweet wines, however, do not receive the attention they deserve, despite their high quality. This is probably due to inadequate publicity, plus the current lack of public interest in sweet wines: a big problem in the Iberian Peninsula. The winery makes a total of 500,000 lt of wine, all carrying the Málaga DO. Most of the production is of the classic Málaga, a rich, sweet wine made from Moscatel and Pedro Ximénez, but there is also a very interesting dry, white wine. Having no vineyards of its own, Larios has for many years bought its Pedro Ximénez and Moscatel grapes from independent growers.

Malaga Larios 🍇 ②
Classic sweet wine of this DO. Rich, honied dried fruit on the nose backed by more delicate secondary aromas. Hefty and warm on the palate. Long honey and nuts finish. Produced from Pedro Ximénez and Moscatel grapes, typical of the Sierra Malagueña.

Moscatel Larios 🍇 ②
Classic Moscatel of the area. Aromas are dominated by wood scents and a little alc. Delicate and gratifyingly long on the palate. Pleasant lingering sensations. Overpowering smell of Moscatel.

Oloroso Benefique 🍇 ②
Beautiful deep yellow, with golden highlights. Its rich flavors are balanced and rounded. Made from Pedro Ximénez.

López Hermanos

Canadá, 10 Pol. Industrial El Viso
Málaga
Tel. (952) 241100
Fax (956) 359819

The most outstanding Spanish sweet wines are those made in Málaga. The winemakers of the region are almost all located in or near the city of Málaga, whereas most of the vineyards are many km away in the heart of the Sierra. Some of these vineyards, planted with Moscatel and Pedro Ximénez vines, belong to López Hermanos, who turn the grapes into well-made, modern wines that are light and balanced. However, they are still one of the most traditional wineries in the area, operating since 1885. Since then, production has diversified from sweet wines to dry, all of which come under the Málaga DO. 4,000,000 lt of wine is produced annually to be sold in Spain and for export. The most famous López Hermanos product is the 'Málaga Virgen', an intense, rich, sweet wine that does not qualify for DO status as it is made differently. It is obtained from Moscatel and Pedro Ximénez.

Moscatel Cartojal 🍇 ①
Outstanding Moscatel from this area, intense varietal aromas and a rich, mellow palate.

Oloroso Trajinero 🍇 ②
Amber with orange highlights. Dried fruit on the nose harmonize with underlying aromas of nuts. Big and slightly alcoholic on the palate. Long, almondy finish. Moscatel and Pedro Ximénez grapes produce this quality wine.

MALAGA
ANDALUCIA
SPAIN

1000

MALAGA
ANDALUCIA
SPAIN

Alvear

Av. María Auxiliadora, 1
Montilla (Cordova)
Tel. (957) 650100
Fax (957) 650135

It is wonderful to come across a family that has been making wine for 260 years. They have kept the business going non-stop since Don Diego de Alvear came to Córdoba in 1729. The members of this family, noblemen, philanthropists and military leaders, have always managed to combine their passion for the wine of this region with their expert wine-making. They have achieved a constant growth in their business keeping a keen eye on future possibilities. This may explain why Alvear was the first to adopt American root-stock and also why they have always invested such a large part of their earnings in the most advanced equipment for their winery. With the help of 20,000 oak barrels, approximately 140,000 ha of wine is produced annually. Their latest product, Marqués de la Sierra, is a light, fresh, young wine made from Pedro Ximénez.

Amontillado Carlos VII   ⚇⚇ ②
Clear topaz with nuances of mahogany. Intense aromas of dried fruit and refined wood. Rich flavor, balanced and long in the mouth. Like most of the wines from this denomination of origin, it is made with Pedro Ximénez.

Amontillado Solera Fundación   ⚇⚇ ②
Brilliant ruby red tones shine from the bottom of the glass. Harmonious and powerful on the nose; pleasing, full-bodied and rich on the palate. Long, complex finish.

Marqués De La Sierra   ⚇ ①
Excellent example of a young, fresh white wine made from Pedro Ximénez.

Gracia Hermanos

Av. Marqués Vega de Armijo, 4
Montilla (Cordova)
Tel. (957) 650162
Fax (957) 650208

Don José Gracia, who began his wine career by taking care of his father-in-law's soleras, is a real character in Montilla, a place where personality is quite rightly considered a very important part of winemaking. In the 50 years since its foundation, Gracia's winery has progressively become the best equipped in the area. 18,000 m2 of cellars house the latest in technology as well as the long-standing tradition of the solera and the criadera, located in special thermically-sealed naves de crianza. The 100 ha of vineyards are almost exclusively planted with Pedro Ximénez. These grapes are almost enough to make the winery self-sufficient, but in order to achieve their average yearly production of 6,000,000 lt of wine, a certain amount of grapes must be obtained from selected growers.

Viña Verde 1991   ⚇ ①
Clear, straw yellow with fruity and grassy aromas deriving from the Pedro Ximénez. Light and extremely fresh, but a short finish.

Amontillado Montearruit   ⚇ ②
Beautiful, bright amber colour. Powerful and perfectly integrated aromas; good development on the palate, revealing softness and strength. Results from a special mixed aging (bajo flor and oak) of Pedro Ximénez grapes.

Fino María Del Valle   ⚇ ①
Clear, golden yellow, with pungent overtones and dried fruit on the nose. Flavorful, full-bodied and long on the palate.

MONTILLA-MORILES
ANDALUCIA
SPAIN

1001

MONTILLA-MORILES
ANDALUCIA
SPAIN

Perez Barquero

Av. Andalucía, 27
Montilla (Cordova)
Tel. (957) 650500
Fax (957) 650208

The Perez Barquero brothers, sons of a Castillian who emigrated to Andalusia, founded their winery in Córdoba at the beginning of the century. By 1917 they were producing wines from their own vineyards in Montilla, an area extremely well-suited for growing Pedro Ximénez. The property expanded and consequently underwent slight changes; it was later sold to the Rumasa group. However, these changes did not affect the outstanding value for money of the wines produced. Perez Barquero now forms part of Vinícola del Sur, a group controlling 120 ha of vineyards in Sierra de Montilla. Since its requirements outweigh the harvest from its own vineyards, the winery has to acquire extra fruit from outside growers.

Amontillado Gran Barquero   🍇🍇 ②
Intense, clear amber; strong aromas of fruit, dried figs and refined wood. Long and full on the palate, rich with complex, lingering flavors.

Gran Barquero Pedro Ximénez   🍇🍇 ②
Pedro Ximénez, relative of the aromatic vines of Reno, excels in this area. This is a perfect example of what it can achieve.

Oloroso Gran Barquero   🍇🍇 ②
Aromatically complex, rich but delicate on the nose, lightly warm and powerful in the mouth. Long, slightly honied, nutty finish.

Bodegas Víbora

Av. José Solís, 2
Lucena (Cordova)
Tel. (957) 500207

Unlike the large producers of Jerez, the Montilla-Moriles DO comprises mostly small, family-run wineries that produce fortified wines and unique Finos using long-tried, traditional methods. The 100 year-old Bodegas Víbora who still make wine in their original building, is one such winery. Traditional vinification methods, experience and the love of these wines have been passed down from father to son. Pedro Ximénez, because of its high tolerance for heat, is the choice grape for this winery and the entire Montilla-Moriles area. Typically, the equipment includes 2,500 barrels for the special aging process, resulting in excellent quality Finos. An annual total of 25,000 hl of wine is produced, 80% of which is bottled; the remainder is sold in bulk.

Fino Ana María   🍇 ①
Not very intense yellow; rich aromas from bajo flor aging. Delicate and light on the palate, with elegant lingering flavors of dried fruit. Pedro Ximénez grapes realize their full aromatic potential in this wine.

MONTILLA-MORILES
ANDALUCIA
SPAIN

1002

MONTILLA-MORILES
ANDALUCIA
SPAIN

Cordillera Cantábrica

The Asturians, Santanderins and Basques, all inhabitants of the regions along the Bay of Biscay framed by the Cantabrian mountains, love to drink wine and eat good food. Working with very little vineyard space, the wine production of this area is concentrated almost exclusively on Txacolí, which is produced in the areas of Zarautz, Getaria and Dia in the province of Vizcaya. These brilliant, fresh, low alc wines are mostly destined for consumption in the bars and households of the Basque Country. For a long time, however, the great demand placed upon the short supply of vineyards in this picturesque market scenario opened the way to fraud.

Today, the best Txacolí is made under the Chacolí de Guetaria DO, which in just two years has achieved remarkable results. It is worth noting that vine-growing in these regions is the outcome of the Basque people's obstinate striving for centuries to come to terms with their rather cool climate and the annual 1,500mm precipitation that are anything but ideal. The Chacolí de Guetaria DO, easily the smallest in Spain, counts on little more than 50 ha of vineyards producing around 250,000 bottles per year, almost all of which is consumed here. The diverse selection of products ranges from whites to reds and rosés. All the wines, however, are made using the two native varietals: the white Hondarribi Zuri, which covers over 80% of the vineyards, and the red Hondarribi Beltza.

Gorrondona

Caserío Gorrondona
Baquio (Biscaglia)
Tel. (94) 6194795
Fax (94) 6740018

Some areas of Cantábrica are known for their original wines, low in alc yet with highly accentuated acidity. The most famous are the wines of Baquio and Guetaria, the latter having only obtained DO status in 1990. Baquio's wines differ from those of the Basque Country's third province, Guipuzcoa, mainly in the method of vinification used: Baquio wine is not fermented on the skins and seeds, and is also influenced by the French varietal, Folle Blanche. The Gorrondona family has taken on the important task of restoring the area's vineyards, once heading gradually towards extinction. Their work is yielding good results, and it seems this wine with a long tradition is making a slow but steady comeback. Currently the company produces 25,000 bottles annually.

Gorrondona 1991　🍇 ①
Obtained from Hondarribi Zuri. Light yellow; clean; light and a bit tart. Fruity aromas recall rennet apples.

Txacolí Aretxaga

Barrio Aretxaga, 26
Zalla (Biscaglia)
Tel. (94) 6390899

If it were not for the family traditions in wineries like Aretxaga, Chakolí wine, spelt Txacolí in Basque, would be destined to a slow but inexorable decline. Highly traditional, even symbolic, this wine represents another face of Spanish winemaking, resulting as it does from different climatic conditions that provide less body and a lower alc content. The mere five ha of vineyards grown on well-exposed slopes are unable to provide enough grapes to fill the 150,000 bottles demanded by the market each year. The wine is made from the native varietals, Hondarribi Zuri and the red Hondarribi Beltza, similar to Bordeaux's Cabernet Franc. Hondarribi Beltza has been used less recently due to the need for off skins fermentation, and another great traditional varietal in the Biscay wine region, the Guascone Folle Blanch, which gives wines extremely fine aromas, is currently making a comeback from the verge of extinction.

Txakolí Aretxaga 1991　🍇 ①
Undoubtedly one of the Iberian Peninsula's most original wines. Extremely aromatic, with perfumes of apples and compote. Not very alcoholic; vivacious effervescence. Obtained from the above-mentioned grapes.

C. V. TXAKOLI DE BAKIO
CANTABRICA
SPAIN

1004

C.V. VALMASEDA
CANTABRICA
SPAIN

Txomín Etxaniz

Caserío Gurutze Aldamar, 33
Getaria (Guipuzcoa)
Tel. (943) 832702

Chacolí de Guetaria (Getariako txakolina in Basque), with a production area of only 48 ha, is Spain's smallest and most recent DO. The climatic conditions brought on by the Cantábrica Cordillera result in a low alc content wine, which was drunk more for sentimental reasons than for the quality of its out-dated and not always sterile production techniques. Certainly these circumstances were no guarantee for success: someone was needed who would put aside their sentimental feelings and work seriously to save the wine. Iñaki Chueca and his three sons, Ernesto, Iñaki and Andrés, arrived just in time, modernizing their winery to introduce a few simple measures (sterile fermentation, temperature control), which proved sufficient to bring about a sensational success that has spread beyond the local setting these wines had previously been limited to. The extensive modernization has included not only the facilities, but also the 12 ha of vineyards, newly replanted with the native Hondarribi Zuri and Hondarribi Beltza varietals that have adapted over centuries to this particular climate and terrain. Traditionally, these wines have always undergone refermentation, providing them with an attractive, fresh liveliness.

Txakolí Txomin Etxaniz 1991   ①
A very particular wine; potent and clean; nose of apples and wild herbs. Smooth and fat on the palate; slight fizziness makes it lively. Extremely fresh, with the right acidity for balance. Made from the classic varietals, Hondarribi Zuri and Hondarribi Beltza.

CHACOLI DE GUETARIA
CANTABRICA
SPAIN

1005

CHACOLI DE GUETARIA
CANTABRICA
SPAIN

Cataluña

Catalonian vineyards, extending over 90,000 ha, are some of the most dynamic in Spain. They are cultivated with the traditional grape varietals of Macabeo, Parellada, Xarel-lo and Garnacha Blanca for white wines, and Cariñena and Ull de Llebre for most of the reds. Some noble French varietals like Cabernet Sauvignon, Merlot, Pinot Noir and Chardonnay have adapted perfectly to the climate and are growing steadily in use.

Catalonian wineries have made great efforts to export, sending abroad 25% of their total production, or 3,000,000 hl of wine. The unique wines from the Cava region constitute an important part of these exports. Over the last 100 years, Cava has won the reputation as the best Spanish sparkling wine, save a few remarkable exceptions.

The "Consejo Regulador de Vinos Espumosos Naturales" recognizes 161 municipalities, including 67 in Barcelona, 42 in Tarragon, 12 in Lérida and five in Gerona. Besides the Cava DO, which does not correspond to any particular region, there are eight other delineated DOs. relating to specific geographical areas. Penedés, probably the best known, is famous for its young whites and recently for some new reds. The Priorato DO has undergone a recent revolution, and is becoming one of the leading lights in Spanish winemaking. By updating traditional methods for its red wines, they have made them some of the best in the country. Other interesting DOs are Alella, a small but dynamic area specializing in intense, peculiarly perfumed whites, and Costers del Segre, one of Catalonia's most vibrant areas, which includes the sub-DO of Raimat, an area almost entirely monopolized by a single winery. Ampurdán-Costa Brava and Tarragona are more modest in size and importance, producing luscious, sweet wines that traditionally age for 12 years in oak. Conca de Barberá, with its high-quality production of light whites and rosés, was used for a long time by Penedés producers but is now earning its own reputation. Finally there is Terra Alta, an ever-developing DO, striving to learn the great traditions of ancient, sweet, aromatic wines.

Alella Vinícola

Angel Guimerá, 70
Alella (Barcelona)
Tel. (93) 5403842
Fax (93) 5401648

Heir to an ancient wine tradition, this tiny region was a favorite of the Greeks and Romans. The bourgeosie of Barcelona have appreciated the vivacious and fruity wines from this miniscule enclave since the 19th century. The Alella Co-operative, the direct descendant of this tradition, established itself and its reputation in the 1960s, and now seems able to overcome the temporary decline which began several years ago. With 400 ha of vineyards, the co-operative controls 80% of the vines in Spain's smallest DO. The winery is excellently decked out with the latest stainless steel vats and refrigeration systems. The predominantly white (with some rosé and red) wine production reaches 500,000 bottles annually.

Alella Marfil Blanco 1991   ℗ ①
Impeccable example of Spanish winemaking. Fresh, fruity with good balance and acidity. Produced with the native Pansa Blanca.

Marfil Chardonnay 1991   ℗ ①
Aromatically representative of the varietal, firm acidity on the palate gives it a clean freshness.

Parxet S.A.

Mas Parxet
Tiana (Barcelona)
Tel. (93) 3950811
Fax (93) 3955500

This establishment is made up of two wineries that share the same DO, but are located in different places. This diversity is reflected in the respective productions of tranquil wines and Cava wines. The older one, founded in 1920, is situated along the Mediterranean Sea in La Tiana. Its solid and perfectly equipped facilities have won it a special place amongst Spanish sparkling wine producers. Native Pansa Blanca, Chenin and Chardonnay are blended to make this unique sparkling wine, helped along by the particular local 'sauló' terrain. The other winery, located in Santa María de Martorellas (Alella), was built near a beautiful 18th century farmhouse. The vinification facilities include the latest advances: a pneumatic press and refrigeration systems. The impeccably tended vines, surrounded by a forest, are planted with Pansa Blanca, Macabeo, Parellada, Chenin and Chardonnay. Parxet S.A. produces exclusively white wines. Finally, praise must go to Dr Juan Peláez, the Marqués de Alella, and Dr. Ismael Manaut, all founders of the winery, who were instrumental in saving this land from serious threats of urbanization.

Marqués de Alella   ℗ ℗ ②
Chardonnay 1991
Superb example of Chardonnay's best qualities. Pale, bright yellow with lemony highlights; intense aromas of fat, buttery fruit and honey (common to this varietal). Elegant, round and fresh on the palate. Long, balanced finish with clean acidity.

Marqués de Alella Seco 1991   ℗ ①
Its character and elegance result from a clever blending of Pansa Blanca, Macabeo and Chenin which together make an excellent final product.

Parxet Brut Nature Chardonnay   ℗ ℗ ②
Pale, straw yellow, crowned with a fine mousse. Fresh primary aromas are followed by more intense secondary ones. Initially light, it becomes full on the palate, with a slightly bitter aftertaste.

ALELLA
CATALUÑA
SPAIN

1007

ALELLA/CAVA
CATALUÑA
SPAIN

Caves Roura

Vall de Rials, s/n
Alella (Barcelona)
Tel. (93) 5557148
Fax (93) 3524339

Roura is Spain's avant-garde leader in still and sparkling wines. Officially founded in 1987, the winery began experimenting in 1981 with grape varietals from Europe's best winemaking regions. Chosen for the red wines were Cabernet, Tempranillo and Merlot. Selected for the whites were Sauvignon and Chenin Blanc, which now occupy 20 ha of property along with native Pansa Blanca. The property also buys in grapes from 40 ha belonging to outside growers, who all work under supervision of the winery's own experts. The results of this well-organized set-up are top-class, skillfully made wines. Here we are witnessing the introduction of the most advanced technology into a region which was already known for its winemaking 2,000 years ago when Pliny said, "If there were less wine in the world, Alella would cease to exist".

Roura Blanco 1991   🍷 ①
Produced with Chardonnay and Pansa Blanca. Notably aromatic with a light acidity, making it pleasant and fresh.

Roura Brut Nature   🍷 ②
An aromatic wine with a fine mousse; well-balanced and long on the palate. Distinct secondary flavors. Fresh, lingering finish. Produced with Pansa Blanca and Chardonnay.

Roura Rosado 1991   🍇 ①
Produced with Merlot, which truly characterizes the palate. Up front fresh fruit with pleasant lingering finish.

Cavas del Ampurdán

Ctra. Figueras, s/n
Perelada (Gerona)
Tel. (972) 538011

Progress is slow in coming to the stagnant Ampurdán-Costa Brava DO. Despite the potential to produce high quality wines, bulk wine is more common. Therefore this well-known Spanish winery, together with a sporadic few others, are the only positive signs in the area. Ironically, Perelada was the first Catalonian home to the Carmelite monks, known for their winemaking. The winery, established in a 14th century castle in Perelada, produces wine that has always been well-represented in the market, especially in the restaurant sector. The reds are typical of the area: well structured, full-bodied and warm. The only exception is their latest 'Vi Novell', a lighter, younger style wine. Some well-made sparkling wines are also produced.

Gran Claustro Perelada 1986   🍷 ③
A characterful Brut Extra Sec obtained from Xarel-lo, Parellada and Macabeo varietals. Dry, powerful and elegant; distinct from the winery's other Cavas.

Blanc de Blancs   🍷 ①
Fruity, forward bouquet, fat fruit and a fresh, persistent acidity. Based upon Parellada, Macabeo and Xarel-lo varietals.

Vi Novell Tinto 1991   🍇 ①
Youthful bright ruby color, bouquet of 'hard-candy' fruit. Light tannins and supple fruit in the mouth. Delicious to drink now.

ALELLA
CATALUÑA
SPAIN

1008

AMPURDAN-COSTA BRAVA/CAVA
CATALUÑA
SPAIN

Can Feixes

Can Feixes, 1
Cabrera d'Anoia (Barcelona)
Tel. (93) 7718227

This beautiful winery is lucky enough to occupy an old 16th century farmhouse. Dr José Huguet, backed by centuries of family experience, began to make wine in 1946. His purely traditional methods produce 120,000 bottles per year. His top wine is an excellent Cava aged under perfect conditions in his underground cellars. This he makes as Brut and Brut Nature. The winery's 120 ha are planted with Chardonnay and the classic Penedés whites: Macabeo, Parellada and Xarel-lo. Cabernet Sauvignon and Tempranillo are cultivated on a smaller scale, producing some interesting still red wines.

Huguet Brut ❦ ②
Clean, straw yellow with greenish tones. Made from Chardonnay, Macabeo and Parellada; clean, fruity nose. with fresh, fat fruit on the palate; well balanced. Slightly tart finish.

Huguet Brut Nature ❦❦ ③
Chardonnay, Macabeo and Parellada varietals give this pale, straw yellow sparkling wine its character. Abundance of tiny pin-prick bubbles. Forward, fresh, toasty bouquet. Balanced and elegant on the palate, with a clean, long finish.

Codorniú

Gran Vía, 644
Barcelona
Tel. (93) 3014600
Fax (93) 3186651

This gigantic winery was, in many respects, a precursor of Cava production. The first sparkling wine in Penedés was created by Codorniú in 1872, under the direction of Josep Raventós, whose son had learned the secrets of the méthode champenoise at Champagne Mercier. Father and son were also descendents of Don Jaime Codorniú, who was making wine in 1551. After rapid growth at the beginning of the century, the famous architect, J. Puig y Cadafalc, was commissioned to build the premises which are now considered national monuments. During the First World War, the winery sold 300,000 bottles a year. Today they sell the most sparkling wine in Spain and are one of the top five producers in the world. The huge winery, probably the largest in the world, produces millions of bottles, refined in kilometre-long tunnels. The wine is sold worldwide and the stress is on quality. This is certainly the case with their top wine 'Jaume de Codorniú'.

Anna De Codorniu ❦ ③
A fine, delicate sparkling wine, with a flowery, fruity bouquet. Balanced, but a bit short on the palate. Made from Macabeo, Parellada, Xarel-lo and Chardonnay.

Gran Codorniu ❦ ③
Bright, straw color, with a fine mousse of tiny bubbles. Clean, dry light fruit on the palate; very pleasant. Made from the same grapes as Anna de Codorniu.

Jaume De Codorniu ❦❦ ③
Produced from the traditional Champagne varietals, Chardonnay and Pinot Noir. One of the most outstanding, well-made wines of Spain.

CAVA
CATALUÑA
SPAIN

1009

CAVA
CATALUÑA
SPAIN

Cavas Ferret

Av. Cataluña, s/n
Guardiola de Font Rubí (Barcelona)
Tel. (93) 8978054
Fax (93) 8978362

This winery makes an outstanding product that is capable of satisfying even the most demanding palates, who are often dissatisfied with this DO's occasional shortfalls in careful winemaking. Ever since Ezequiel Ferret acquired the property in 1941 from his relative Domingo, a still wine producer, the property has remained in the family. Located in the small, Penedés town of Guardiola de Font Rubí, Cavas Ferret was completely renovated in 1986, adding spacious cellars capable of holding 450,000 lt of sparkling wine. Athough sparkling wines are considered their strongest product, they also make some very interesting still wines.

Ferret Brut Nature 1987   ❦ ❦ ③
Abundance of fine mousse. Fresh, clean toasty fruit on the nose, flavorful, balanced and rich in the mouth, it leaves a pleasant aftertaste.

Ferret Brut   ❦ ②
Straw yellow with bright green highlights; abundant mousse of slightly larger bubbles. Fresh, clean bouquet. Smooth and well-balanced in the mouth, with a slight sweetness on the finish. A blend of Macabeo, Parellada and Xarel-lo varietals.

Ferret Brut Rosado   🍇 ②
Delicate, bright rosy pink, abundant mousse of medium-sized bubbles, faint fruity nose, light fresh, raspberry flavours on the palate. Made from Ull de Llebre and Garnacha varietals.

Freixenet

Joan Sala, 2
Sant Sadurní d'Anoia (Barcelona)
Tel.(93) 8910700
Fax (93) 8183095

Freixenet, another historic name in Catalán sparkling wine, has evolved from very modest beginnings to become a giant in its field. At the end of the last century, Felix Ferrer joined a family of wine-makers whose production was sold, not only nationwide, but also to the Americas. His sparkling wine was so successful that Ferrer decided to devote all his efforts to its production. At first sold without a label, the wine later acquired several, one of which was Freixenet, a name which was to gain great notoriety. With these promising beginnings, his successor, José Ferrer, built a veritable sparkling wine empire. His winery, installed with the most up-to-date equipment, produces 50,000,000 bottles which are exported to 70 countries. In the mid-1980s, Freixenet triumphed by selling 1,000,000 cases in the U.S. Since then, the Ferrer family has acquired more property and more facilities, including a winery in the Champagne region. The winery's 350 ha of vineyards are insufficient to supply such a huge quantity of wine, so the Ferrers buy in extra grapes from outside growers. Regardless of its mass production, Freixenet still makes high-quality wines highly regarded by wine connoisseurs.

Freixenet Brut Nature 1988   ❦ ②
Healthy mousse with medium-size bubbles. Smooth, clean and flavorsome on the palate. Here, Macabeo, Xarel-Lo and Parellada come together to give this wine its unique character.

Cuvée 1985   ❦ ③
Light yellow in color with a fine mousse. Clean fruity, and yeasty nose. Smooth and fat on the palate, quite a short finish. Made from the classic Penedés blend.

CAVA
CATALUÑA
SPAIN

1010

CAVA
CATALUÑA
SPAIN

Gramona

Industria, 36
Sant Sadurní d' Anoia (Barcelona)
Tel. (93) 8910119
Fax (93) 8183284

Since the Gramona family, already involved in wine, founded their winery in 1921, their traditionally made Cava has always been the most typical example. 15 ha of carefully tended vineyards are planted with the classic white Penedés varietals, with the recent additions of Chardonnay and Pinot Noir. This small, yet modern winery uses the most advanced equipment to produce its prized Cava, as well as other wines. Compared to other wineries in the region, its 170,000 bottle production could be called limited. 'Gamona Tres Lustros' is one of the best Cavas in Penedés. Gamona also vinifies some very interesting still and pétillant wines.

Celler Battle Extra Brut 🍷 ④
Golden yellow; fine and abundant mousse. Slighty dumb fruit on the nose, but a good toasty, yeasty character. Rich and powerful on the palate. Made from Macabeo, Xarel-Lo and Parellada.

Gramona Imperial 🍷 ③
Bright straw yellow; persistent mousse with medium-size bubbles. Bouquet is clean and fresh with strong notes of yeast and toast. Clean and balanced on the palate. Made from the three classic varietals.

Gramona Tres Lustros 🍷🍷 ③
Straw yellow with golden highlights; fine and abundant persistent mousse. Intense, mature, rich aromas; buttery and full on the palate with a lingering, herbaceous finish.

Cava Llopart

Industria, 46
Sant Sadurní d'Anoia (Barcelona)
Tel. (93) 8910410
Fax (93) 8911648

The earliest document pertaining to the Llopart family's wine activities dates back to the 14th century, when Leopardi Llopart inherited a vineyard. Much later, in 1881, the family built a winery and began making mostly still wines. Pere Llopart was determined to achieve quality using traditional methods. The winery is located in the ancient winemaking area of San Sadurní d'Anoia, the capital of Cava wines, and is very well-equipped. The sparkling wine has an interesting character due to long aging in underground cellars. The 30 ha property is planted with the classic Penedés varietals: Macabeo, Parellada and Xarel-Lo. The Lloparts use only their own grapes to ensure that the quality of the wine begins with the vine.

Llopart Leopardi 1986 🍷🍷 ③
Light, bright yellow; rich persistent mousse with tiny bubbles. Intense and elegant bouquet. Dry on the palate; but rich and flavorsome. Made from Xarel-Lo, Macabeo and Parellada.

Castell De Subirats R. Familia 🍷 ③
Straw yellow with bright golden highlights. A fine mousse of slightly bigger bubbles. A rather faint bouquet, but a well-structured, flavorful palate, with a satisfactory finish.

Reserva Brut Natural 🍷 ②
Bright, straw yellow; abundant mousse. Bouquet is fresh, with a slightly toasty/yeasty character due to bottle-aging. On the palate, rich with a crisp acidity.

CAVA
CATALUÑA
SPAIN

1011

CAVA
CATALUÑA
SPAIN

Cavas Masachs

Ponent, 20
Vilafranca del Penedés (Barcelona)
tel. (93) 8900593
Fax (93) 8901218

The winery dates to the beginning of this century, when an ancestor of the current owner decided to make his own Cava. The experiment was a big success and encouraged him to sell his wine. Still family owned, the winery has barely expanded, retaining its original, traditional character. In 1987 a new winery was built, but Cavas Masachs' real asset is its 55 ha of vineyards. Here, the 'A-team' of varietals are planted: Macabeo, Parellada and Xarel-Lo, plus a little Chardonnay; its aromatic quality gives elegance to the wine. The common factor to all these sparkling wines is their high quality level, for which the winery is undoubtedly reputed. Cavas Masachs makes two types of Cava: one a high quality, vintage wine, and another more favored for its excellent value for money.

Brut Josep Masachs ☍ ②
Fresh, pungent, aromatic nose; typical of the Parellada, Macabeo and Xarel-Lo blend. Nose show signs of bottle-aging. Clean and fresh on the palate with a mouth-cleansing acidity on the finish.

Carolina de Masachs ☍ ②
Golden yellow with a superb mousse. Rich and long on the palate with great finesse due to the addition of Chardonnay to the traditional Macabeo and Parellada blend.

Louis de Vernier Brut Nature ☍ ②
Lighter than the other two Cavas; delightful light, flowery bouquet. Clean and most refreshing.

Mestres

Plaza del Ayuntamineto, 8
Sant Sadurní d'Anoia (Barcelona)
Tel. (93) 8910043
Fax (93) 8911611

With 19 generations of wine-makers, few families rival the great Mestres family tradition. Despite their long-standing fame in the area, the Mestres only began bottling their wine at the beginning of the century. The winery was completed in 1928, thanks to the enterprising Josep Mestres, head of the sparkling wine division. However it was Antoni Mestres, then head of the winery, who pushed it to the forefront of this highly competitive, sparkling wine region. Mestres' 80 ha of vineyards produce all the grapes needed for production. The typical Penedés varietals are cultivated along with the red Monastrell and Ull de Llebre (the Catalán name for Tempranillo), the latter two constituting the rosé wine. The most important characteristic of this particular Cava is its long aging in bottle: the youngest wine aging at least three years, and the reserves from four to five.

Clos Nostre Senyor 1988 ☍☍ ③
Slowly rising, pin-prick bubbles define the mousse. Complex and powerful aromas of bottle aging; initially dry, with a rich, round middle palate. Clean, crisp finish.

Mestres Mas Vía 1987 ☍☍ ③
After four years of aging in bottle, this Cava presents a perfect mousse; refined, subtle aromas, rich and buttery in the mouth with a delicious, long-lasting finish. A blend of Xarel-Lo, Macabeo and Parellada.

Rosado Brut Nature ▨ ②
Bright rosy pink, healthy mousse with medium-sized bubbles. Refined bouquet with slightly honied aromas. Balanced on the palate. Made from the three classic white varietals and a little Monastrell.

CAVA
CATALUÑA
SPAIN

1012

CAVA
CATALUÑA
SPAIN

Cavas Nadal

Can Nadal, s/n
El Plá del Penedés (Barcelona)
Tel. (93) 8988011
Fax (93) 8988443

Cavas Nadal is recognised for its careful efforts to preserve the traditional production methods and quality of its Cava wines, which date back to the 1500s. Faithful to the land and proud of their property, the Nadals produce sparkling wine only with grapes from their own excellent, carefully tended vineyards planted with Xarel-Lo, Macabeo and Parellada. 110 ha provide enviable autonomy to these sparkling wine specialists who, drawing on 500 years of family expertise, began producing sparkling wine in 1943. Their most prized wines are the Brut Naturals, although their whole range of DO wines are carefully made and of the highest quality. Production reaches 700,000 bottles annually, showing the family's commitment to the name of Cava.

Nadal Brut Especial 1988   🍷 🍷 ③
Balance is the principal feature of this sparkling wine, demonstrating fresh fruit and toasty aromas on the nose.

Nadal Brut Salvatge 1987   🍷 🍷 ③
Traditional Cava with no modern adjustments. Long aging gives it outstanding structure. Like all Nadal sparkling wines it comes from the classic Penedés trio: Macabeo, Parellada and Xarel-Lo.

Brut Nadal   🍷 ②
Pale straw yellow. Fresh acidity and simple structure make this Brut totally approachable.

Puig Munt

Revall, 38
Martorell (Barcelona)
Tel. (93) 89030756

Juan Sigüenza directs a modern, well-equipped and recently renovated (1984) winery in Martorell. The great character of his Cavas results from the native Macabeo, Parellada and Xarel-Lo fruit, of which Sigüenza is the perfect advocate. The winery owns 210 ha of property, but as the vineyards are too young to achieve full production, Juan buys in most of his grapes from the local co-operative. One of the most outstanding characteristics of his Cava Reservas is its long aging. This process is carried out in a maze of underground tunnels capable of housing 2,000,000 bottles, "only" 600,000 of which are produced each year. Besides the various kinds of sparkling wines (Demi-Sec, Sec, Brut and Nature), he also produces a still white and rosé.

Brut Reserva Puig Munt   🍷 ③
Bright pale yellow; moderate abundance of mousse of miniscule bubbles. Interesting pungent bouquet. Elegant and full on the palate, with a fine acidity. Produced from the classic Penedés trio.

Puig Munt Brut Nature   🍷 ②
Golden yellow with greenish highlights; persistant mousse of medium-sized bubbles. Distinct secondary aromas, well integrated with floral notes. Clean and well-structured, elegant, unctuous and long on the palate. Made from the typical Penedés varietals.

CAVA
CATALUÑA
SPAIN

1013

CAVA
CATALUÑA
SPAIN

Cavas Recaredo

Tamarit, 7-12
Sant Sadurní d'Anoia (Barcelona)
Tel. (93) 8910214
Fax (93) 8911697

Antoni Mata has opted for traditional methods to produce his Cava, believing this to result in a truly 'sublime' wine. Founded by his father, Josep Mata, in 1924, the winery has grown slowly and steadily under family reign. The only modern touch is the technologically advanced equipment, which, under sterile conditions, annually produces 180,000 bottles. Over the years the traditional Cava method, which makes this wine so special, has been carefully preserved. Most of the wine is aged in oak; all the bottles are sealed with special corks before they undergo a second fermentation and remuage en pupitre. The property comprises 30 ha of vineyards of the classical Cava varietals: Xarel-Lo, Parellada and Macabeo. These are accompanied by Chardonnay that is not, however, used in the sparkling wines. For this reason, Recaredo wines have a distinctive, Spanish flavour.

Recaredo Gran Riserva 1988   🍇 🍇 ③
Initial fresh, forward bouquet and fat secondary aromas fill the glass; very seductive. Full-bodied, fleshy in the mouth. Long, clean finish.

Recaredo Brut Nature 1987   🍇 🍇 ③
Very pale yellow; fine mousse. Fresh, floral perfumes mixed with subtle secondary aromas. Long and well-structured on the palate. Antoni Mata's sparkling wines are produced solely from the traditional varietals.

Cavas Rovellats

Finca Rovellats, La Bleda
Sant Sadurní d'Anoia (Barcelona)
Tel. (93) 8980131
Fax (93) 2414001

Generation after generation, Rovellats' gradual introduction of modern technology has allowed their deep, traditional roots to remain firmly in the ground. The winery's own 210 ha of vineyards provide all the fruit needed to produce méthode champenoise sparkling wine. This is rare in Penedés, as most Cava producers buy in grapes or wine from independent growers. All the wines produced at Rovellats have the hallmark of its winery character due to the extended aging in underground cellars. These are regulated to keep a constant humidity and temperature of 15°C, essential for this type of production. In the constant effort to improve their products, Rovellats have recently introduced a small percentage of Chardonnay grapes to some of their sparkling wines.

Rovellats Brut Imperial 1988   🍇 ③
Truly characteristic of this winery. Extended aging results in harmony and a sumptuous bouquet. Well-structured on the palate; intense, lingering flavors. Unmistakable example of the classic varietals of the region.

Rovellats Gran Cru   🍇 🍇 ②
Here classic Penedés varietals unite with Chardonnay providing fatter, forward aromas and fuller taste sensations.

CAVA
CATALUÑA
SPAIN

1014

CAVA
CATALUÑA
SPAIN

Segura Viudas

Ctra. de Sadurní-Igualada, s/n
Sant Sadurní d'Anoia (Barcelona)
Tel. (93) 8995111
Fax (93) 8996006

This imposing winery runs its enterprise out of a splendid, 11th century residence called La Heredad. Belonging to Freixenet, Viudas' products are well-known in many countries throughout the world. Modern vinification equipment is used in conjunction with the méthode champenoise to yield up to 12,000,000 bottles annually, which are aged in immense underground cellars. Director Augustí Torelló is a true authority in the difficult world of Cava and an expert in blending the Macabeo, Parellada and Xarel-Lo varietals. The 50 ha of vineyards under direct ownership are matched with advanced equipment to produce high quality sparkling wines. Besides the more commercial wines, there is a high quality range featuring the truly exceptional Aria.

Segura Viudas Brut Vintage 1988   ❦ ③
Bright straw yellow; abundant mousse. Fresh, almondy nose, clean refreshing palate with crisp acidity. Well-made.

Aria Brut   ❦❦ ③
Obtained from the classic Penedés varietals; straw yellow with greenish highlights. Clean and bright, with a mousse of miniscule bubbles with a beautiful crown. Notably elegant secondary perfumes with toasted tones.

Segura Viudas Reserva Heredad   ❦ ②
Clean, clear straw yellow; less abundant mousse. Fresh and buttery with toasty, almond aromas. Developed palate with crisp acidity. A very enjoyable mouthful.

Augustí Torello

Industria, 6
Sant Sadurní d'Anoia (Barcelona)
Tel. (93) 9810315

Finally Cava production reaches its greatest heights. D. Augustí Torello, an authentic sparkling wine genius, manages his winery guided by the highest principles of morality. In fact, his harvest from vineyards undergoes such a ruthless selection process that only 5,000 lt of wine may have the honor of the Kripta label. Born and raised in the Cava region, founder Augustí Torello learned his craft in the family winery, studying intensely each phase of production. After receiving his degree in enology from the Enological School of Requeña and Vilafranca and having held responsible positions with other Cava producers, Augustí set out to realize his lifetime dream: this outstanding Cava.

Kripta   ❦❦ ④
Highest quality sparkling wine. Every detail, from the elegant label to the eye-catching bottles, has been given the utmost attention. Complex and refined; delicate and elegant. Here the three classic varietals: Macabeo, Parellada and Xarel-Lo reach their full potential.

CAVA
CATALUÑA
SPAIN

1015

CAVA
CATALUÑA
SPAIN

Celler Cooperativa de Villafranca del Penedés

Bisbe Morgades, 18
Villafrance del Penedés (Barcelona)
Tel. (93) 8901049
Fax (93) 8900418

Most of the wineries specializing in Cava, the Spanish sparkling wine par excellence, buy their wine from private viticulturalists, who are often part of co-operatives like Villafranca. This cooperative, one of the largest in Penedés, is the leading producer of a very respectable quality Cava. Founded in 1933, the group's 410 members pool together grapes from 1,100 ha of vineyards planted with the classic Macabeo, Parellada and Xarel-Lo varietals, as well as the latest fashionable Cabernet Sauvignon and Chardonnay. Each year the 7,000,000 lt production is selected and then made into one of the Cooperative's many wines and sparkling wines.

Els Castellers Brut ℗ ①
Pale straw yellow; rich mousse. Distinct but faint fruity aromas. Light and pleasing with a clean acidity. Made from the above classic varietals.

Els Castellers Brut Nature ℗ ②
Straw yellow with golden highlights; long-lasting mousse of medium-sized bubbles. Secondary aromas are simple, but pleasant. Straightforward and clean on the palate with a medium length fruit-dominated finish.

Castell de Vilarnau

Vilarnau, 34
Sant sadurní d'Anoia (Barcelona)
Tel. (93) 8912361
Fax (93) 8912931

Castell de Vilarnau is a modern winery belonging to the González Byass group. The group's continual expansion in the most prestigous wine areas of Spain is seen here, just as it is in the Rioja region with their Beronia winery. Faithful to its high-quality ideals, the group has equipped itself with the latest technology so it may move even closer to perfecting the art of the méthode champenoise. In only a short time, Castell de Vilarnau Brut has become one of the most perfected Cavas. The group's main interest in sparkling wine production is supported by 15 ha of vineyards planted with the three classic varietals. This insufficient grape production is supplemented with grapes bought in from nearby viticulturalists. The latest in winemaking equipment is used along with the underground cellars for aging the wine.

Castell de Vilarnau 1987 ℗ ②
Extremely long-lasting on the palate; balanced, with light traces of a long aging in the bottle, resulting in a long, complex finish. Made from the classic Penedés varietals: Macabeo, Xarel-Lo and Parellada.

Castell de Vilarnau Brut ℗ ①
Clear, straw yellow, delicate mousse. Zesty fruit bouquet, and light ripe fruit extract on the palate. Clean, simple finish. Produced from the same varietals as its older brother.

CAVA
CATALUÑA
SPAIN

1016

CAVA
CATALUÑA
SPAIN

Raimat

Afueras, s/n
Raimat (Gerona)
Tel. (973) 724000

The owners of Codorniú, the Raventos family, have owned this property since 1918. Together with Raimat, they deserve the credit for developing the Costers del Segre DO. The winery, in the heart of this DO, is a 'whim' of Codorniu's and can be described as Californian in design. To achieve this, a high desert plane was transformed into a vast, purpose-built property. The vineyards, perfect examples of modern viticulture, cover 1,000 ha and are mostly planted with French varietals: Cabernet Sauvignon, Merlot, Pinot Noir and Chardonnay, together with the native Tempranillo, Garnacha, Macabeo and Parellada grapes. Raimat's cellars contain 8,000 French and American oak barrels, and their most famous wines are those slowly and carefully produced with foreign varietals. Top sparkling wines are also produced, consisting mostly of Chardonnay. The modern facilities and avant-garde agricultural techniques have provided this winery with the essential tools for achieving, in a very short time, its well-deserved reputation.

Raimat Chardonnay 1990 ☙ ②
Beautiful white wine; fermented in oak barrels, where the varietal's honey/butter aromas combine perfectly with the spicey new oak.

Raimat Brut Nature ☙ ②
Pale golden yellow with greenish highlights. Lasting fine mousse. The distinctive Chardonnay perfumes marry perfectly with those of Parellada and Macabeo. Slight smokiness. Full rich flavors on the palate.

Raimat Cabernet Sauvignon 1981 ♥ ♥ ②
Attractive ruby-red, orange rim. Ripe Cabernet fruit in harmony with tobacco of oak aging. Well-integrated tannins. Long, but a little tart on the finish.

Castell del Remei

Ctra. de Tárrega Balaguer, s/n
La Fuliola (Lérida)
Tel. (973) 580200
Fax (973) 750511

Constantly stimulated by the powerful and older Raimat, Castell del Remei, with its vineyards that stretch over 100 ha, has made a tremendous investment to guarantee the quality of its wines. In the early 1980s the Cusiné family became owners of the property and initiated an intense operation to replant the vineyards. The property is situated in Piana de Urgell and enjoys a micro-climate suited to French grapes and the production of high quality Bordeaux-style wines. 1988 was the first Cabernet harvest, featuring the wines listed below, and more recently, Merlot, Chardonnay and Sauvignon Blanc have been produced. The winery is technologically well-equipped and the first results are encouraging. Here, they expect an extremely bright future.

Castell del Remei Cabernet 1988 ♥ ②
Based on Cabernet Sauvignon (85%) and a small part of Tempranillo, this wine has a warm stalky, cassis nose. It is velvety on the palate with round tannins and good fruit extract. Oak aging is apparent.

Gotim Bru 1986 ♥ ②
Garnet hue; soft bouquet; ripe tobacco/cassis flavors on the palate, soft tannins. Supple finish leaving oaky flavours. Made from Tempranillo and Cabernet Sauvignon.

COSTERS DEL SEGRE
CATALUÑA
SPAIN

1017

COSTERS DEL SEGRE
CATALUÑA
SPAIN

Masía Bach

Ctra. Capellades, km 20.5
S. Esteve Sesrovires (Barcelona)
Tel. (93) 7714052

Don Josep Bach, owner of a farm in San Esteve, dreamed for a long time of having a Bordeaux-like winery in the region. The perfect opportunity came along when he was able to extend his property by buying some land from a neighbor. Accompanied by architect Josep Sola, he immediately began to tour the wine regions of France, learning everything he possibly could so as to return to Spain with the necessary inspiration. Thus, in the 1920s, his dream came true. Masía Bach now belongs to Codorniú and has 8,000 m2 of facilities, including two kilometers of underground cellars. Here, 10,000 barriques carry out the important task of aging. The winery's 8,000,000 lt production is obviously not covered by its mere 15 ha of vineyards and must buy in great quantities of grapes. Masía Bach's most famous wines are its whites, especially the sweet ones aged in oak. Just for the record, the term 'extrísimo', which appears on some of their labels, comes from the best type of cotton that the Bach family's textile factory imports from India.

Extrísimo Bach Blanco 1987 ❦ ②
Vibrant, bright golden yellow; compound aromas of resin and exotic fruit. Complex on the palate, with a full wack of flavor and just the right amount of sweet oak. Produced from Macabeo and Xarel-Lo; aged in barriques and in the bottle.

Bach Cabernet Sauvignon 1985 ❦ ②
Garnet with brick-red highlights. Ripe red fruit, tobacco, pepper and all-spice; vanillin notes. Soft and balanced in the mouth. Drink now.

Celler Ramón Balada

Av. J.A. Clavé, 7
Sant Martí Sarroca (Barcelona)
Tel. (93) 8991356
Fax (93) 8991028

Ramón Balada is a dynamic and enterprising businessman who takes wine and the need to continuously update his products very seriously. His concept of wine differs from the Penedés tradition, which has always respected the classic blend of regional whites. Ramón, on the other hand, is inspired by the vinification process in Alsace, land of great white wines par excellence, and has tried to replicate the process at home. Experience and capability have turned into positive results. Ramón also produces some very interesting, fruity Cavas that are balanced and perfectly aged. Grapes are harvested from 20 ha of vineyards, planted with white varietals Xarel-Lo, Macabeo, Parellada and Chardonnay, and the red varietal Cabernet Sauvignon. The recently acquired facility was inaugurated in 1985 and furnished with all the latest advances that contribute to great and distinctive wines.

Balada Chardonnay 1991 ❦ ②
Powerful aroma, forward and fleshy typical of the varietal. Elegant on the palate, with a good acidity that adds freshness.

Viña Toña Parellada 1991 ❦ ①
Bright shade of yellow. Wafting delicate floral bouquet (typical Parellada) perfectly combines with its sappy qualities. Developed Parellada fruit in the mouth, plus clean acidity make this an all-round winner.

Vinya Sibilla 1989 ❦ ①
Unique treatment of Cabernet Sauvignon, without aging in wood. Up front fleshy candied fruit nose. Supple, approachable palate, little tannin due to vinification method used. Very easily drinkable.

PENEDES
CATALUÑA
SPAIN

1018

PENEDES/CAVA
CATALUÑA
SPAIN

René Barbier

Ctra. Sant Sadurní-Igualada
Sant Sadurní d'Anoia (Barcelona)
Tel. (93) 8995111
Fax (93) 9886006

Going back to 1880, René Barbier was founded by a French businessman and became famous right away. Its wines were popular in the 1960s, when the tourist boom was just hitting Spain. In those days it was rare to find a restaurant that did not have Barbier on its wine-list. Above all, the wines were noted for their careful production and high quality. Now a part of Freixenet, its production is geared more towards mass consumption: Barbier can be found in every supermarket, thanks to the support of a powerful distribution network. Nevertheless, it still produces some high quality wines, especially some well-aged reds. For this phase of production the winery uses 1,000 oak barrels, in which the wine enjoys the best conditions for aging. Barbier's best known products are their whites and rosés, the latter ranging from low to high quality. The vineyards cover 250 ha.

René Barbier Cabernet 1986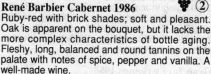
Ruby-red with brick shades; soft and pleasant. Oak is apparent on the bouquet, but it lacks the more complex characteristics of bottle aging. Fleshy, long, balanced and round tannins on the palate with notes of spice, pepper and vanilla. A well-made wine.

Cellers Grimau Gol

Norte, 8
Villafranca del Penedés (Barcelona)
Tel. (93) 8920372
Fax (93) 8920812

This winery has been in business only seven years, but its wines have already reached absolutely outstanding heights. Such quick and optimal results have not, however, affected the relentless quest to further raise the level of quality. The winery's winning cards are the 35 ha of perfectly tended vineyards, where the classic Penedés varietals can be found alongside the native Ull de Llebre (Tempranillo in Rioja) and the increasingly popular French Cabernet Sauvignon and Chardonnay. Grimau Gol utilizes the most avant-garde technology, appropriate for this winery's desire to produce an ample range of wines and, above all, to achieve the ultimate in good quality whites, rosés, young reds, aged reds and even sparkling wines. Underground cellars serve to refine the sparkling wines, and approximately 400 oak barrels are used to age the reds, which are undoubtedly among the best in Penedés.

Rosat Floral 1991
Harmonious and balanced rosé; obtained from Cariñena and Ull de Llebre. Light rosy-pink with peachy highlights. Ripe and pure fruity aromas, especially apricots. Well-structured, refreshing and simple on the palate. Roll on Summer!

Duart de Sió Negre Grana 1986

Great 50/50 blend of Cabernet Sauvignon and Tempranillo. Perfect aging in oak; spicy and oaky/vanilla aromas well-integrated with fruit. Drink now or wait a while.

PENEDES
CATALUÑA
SPAIN

1019

PENEDES
CATALUÑA
SPAIN

Cavas Hill

Bonavista, 2
Moja (Barcelona)
Tel. (93) 8900588
Fax (93) 8170246

In the second half of the 17th century an English immigrant named Hill settled in the tiny town of Moja, heart of the Penedés, and began to cultivate vines on his property, El Maset. In the generations to follow, his descendants carried on the family tradition until, at the end of last century, everything passed into the hands of Don Josep Hill i Ros. His study of other countries' vinification techniques and continuous activity not only permitted him to improve his own production, but also brought new technology to all of Spain. For example, Don Josep Hill was one of the first to introduce the rootstock system in the fight against phylloxera. In 1918, with extremely far-sighted vision, he began to produce the first sparkling wines with the métode champenoise. Since then, the winery has always researched and kept itself up-to-date in order to remain ahead. This creativity is apparent in the original design of almost all the Cavas Hill bottles.

Brut Brutísimo 1988   ❦ ③
This vintage Cava made with the traditional varietals is guaranteed by the producer Hill's decision to put the year on the label, thus proving his blind faith in the product. Pale greenish yellow. Light, clean, and dry; a very refreshing version of Cava. Clean-cut perfect finish. Makes a great 'Kir Royale'.

Cabernet Sauvignon Hill 1988   ❦ ②
Spain is in a constant boom with its high quality single varietal wines. Among these, Cabernet Sauvignon Hill has the personality of a great Bordeaux, with the exotic warmth and spice of Spain.

Gran Toc Hill 1987   ❦ ②
Made the old-fashioned way with Tempranillo, Garnacha and Cariñena: full and mellow. Soft vanilla oak, ripe red fruits and tobacco dominate the bouquet and palate. Almost Rioja in style. One of the region's finest reds. Perfect for aging.

Juvé y Camps

Sant Venat, 1
Sant Sadurní d'Anoia (Barcelona)
Tel. (93) 8911000
Fax (93) 8912100

Founded at the beginning of the century by Juan Juvé Baqués, this winery's continual growth has earned it one of the most notable reputations in Spain for its 'hand-made' cava. Its secret lies in hard work, continuous production and continuous activity not only of the best vineyards in all of Penedés. Juvé y Camps wisely adapted its antique artisanal spirit to meet the needs of the exigent and dynamic Cava market, under constant pressure from French Champagne makers. The vineyards, located on the Espiells estate, are bordered by the holdings of Monserrat, which protect them from the northern winds. Two other vineyards contribute to Espiells' production, allowing Juvé y Camps to enjoy an exceptional position of self-sufficiency. Extended aging in its cellars is yet another reason for this winery's individualism.

Ermita d'Espiells 1990   ❦ ②
Brief aging in stainless steel vats and in bottle add complexity and elegance. Composed of Xarel-Lo, Parellada and Macabeo varietals. According to wide opinion, this vineyard is one of the best in Penedés.

Gran Juvé y Camps 1986   ❦ ③
A great sparkling wine, and not simply because of its name. Optimal development of effervescence, dry on the palate, full, and well-structured. A top-class, noble wine.

Juvé y Camps R. de la Familia   ❦ ②
Elegant and light, but sufficiently balanced to make it very drinkable. It is the winery's most famous product. Produced from the typical Penedés varietals: Macabeo, Parellada and Xarel-Lo.

PENEDES/CAVA
CATALUÑA
SPAIN

1020

PENEDES/CAVA
CATALUÑA
SPAIN

Jean León

Afueras, s/n
Torrelavit (Barcelona)
Tel/Fax (93) 8995033

Jean León had an almost prophetic vision of the future. Originally from Cantabrica, he had been living in California with his parents for many years (doing various jobs, and later owning a number of restaurants), when he decided to do in Penedés what would surely have been much easier to do at his home: produce wine from popular American varietals, practically unknown in Spain. Thus, in the 1960s, he bought 160 ha of land in Torrelavit and planted the French varietals Chardonnay, Cabernet Sauvignon and Cabernet Franc. Some years later the winery was founded and immediately furnished with the most modern equipment. The first harvest to be vinified in the cellars was in 1969. Today the winery uses 1,000 barriques to produce 725,000 lt of wine annually. Given that the French varietals are perfectly suited to the area, Jean León still yields some of the best oak-aged Cabernet and Chardonnay in the whole Iberian Peninsula.

Jean León Chardonnay 1988   ♟ ♟ ②
Intense golden yellow with green highlights. Toasted, oaky aromas and vanilla going towards fruit and honey. Well-balanced on the palate; fat, fresh, perhaps too oaky, but fresh acidity.

Jean León Cabernet 1987   ♟ ③
Deep cherry-red with orange highlights. Pleasant secondary aromas with definite spicy, fruity notes. Succulent cassis fruit, big oaky factor, round tannins; sits well on the palate. Elegant long finish.

Marqués de Monistrol

Pl. de la Iglesia, s/n Monistrol d'Anoia
Sant Sadurní d'Anoia (Barcelona)
Tel. (93) 5932400
Fax (93) 5935855

Both the winery and the town, Marchesato de Monistrol (near San Sadurni d'Anoia), get their names from an ancient monastery built on the banks of the river Noya. The Marquis of Monistrol founded their winery in 1882, and the family has remained owners of this enormous property, which consists of 60% of all the vineyards in San Sadurni d'Anoia. In all, the winery's holding extends 450 ha, 300 of which are fully planted and harvested. The white varietals cultivated here are very similar to those of this region's vineyards, while the reds are more diverse: varietals range from Tempranillo to Garnacha to Monastrell, with three ha of experimental Cabernet and Merlot. The winery's huge production guarantees a certain level of raw materials, and allows for an ample line of products with varying qualities. This wide spectrum comprises some very high quality products: from Gran Reserva reds, very similar to Rioja, to fruity, fresh rosés, whites, and excellent Cavas.

Marqués de Monistrol   ♟ ①
Blanc en Noir.
This still wine is one of the best. Mouthfilling fruit with balance of fresh acidity. Elegant with a long finish. Produced from mainly Xarel-Lo, the skins are left in the must for 12-18 hours and only the 'vin de goutte' is used..

Marqués de Monistrol   ②
Gran Tradición
Fruity, full-bodied Cava, lasting, fine mousse; redolent aromas from bottle aging. Broad and pleasing on the palate; great balance with crisp acidity.

Cava Marqués de Monistrol   ②
Rosado
Meticulously made rosé, pale onion-skin colored. Clearly marked fruity aromas, backed with honey. Light, fresh, strawberry fruit. Delicious and crisp. Produced solely from Garnacha.

PENEDES
CATALUÑA
SPAIN

1021

PENEDES/CAVA
CATALUÑA
SPAIN

Cavas Naverán

Can Parellada, San Martín de Sadevesa
Torrelavit (Barcelona)
Tel/Fax (93) 8988274

Local evidence shows us that wine has been made in this region since Greek and Roman times, giving Cavas Naverán a strong tradition to uphold. Towards the second half of the 19th century, Don Pablo Parellada bought some property once owned by the monks of Montserrat and, after the phylloxera plague, he replanted it with the white varietal Montonec, grafted onto American rootstock. Since then, this varietal, known for its delicate and elegant contributions to the traditional Penedés blend, has been called by the family name, Parellada. Another Parellada, son of the founder, later installed vinification and aging equipment in the winery, whilst other descendants have since introduced the French varietals Merlot and Cabernet Sauvignon and Chardonnay for sparkling wine. The property extends over 110 ha in the northern Penedés, and from these vineyards 500,000 bottles are produced each year. A strict selection process applies to all the wines, especially the Cavas.

Naverán Brut Nature 1987 ℗ ②
Straw yellow with golden tones; fine, healthy mousse. Fresh fruit and yeasty aging aromas on the nose, smooth approach that delicately opens out on the palate. Produced from Xarel-Lo, Macabeo and Parellada.

Naverán Tinto 1988 ♥ ①
Excellent bouquet, marked by the warm red fruits of Cabernet, Merlot Tempranillo, and vanilla oak. Rather soft for its age, but well-defined flavors.

Naverán Cabernet Sauvignon 1987 ♥ ②
Deep garnet with cherry-red hues. Bouquet of warm cassis with spiced tones. Smooth approach, deliciously light and balanced on the palate.

Olivella Sadurni

Can Bas de Lavern
Lavern-Subirats (Barcelona)
Tel. (93) 8993351
Fax (93) 8031011

The Olivella family history has for centuries been intertwined with wine-making, and their various properties, as proven by numerous archeological findings, witnessed the arrival of the Romans. Having always made wine, the Olivellas have helped and advised many of the area's producers to make their wine. In 1984 (the unofficial founding date of the winery), Salvador Olivella and his two dynamic sons, Francesco and Raimón, began their own bottling and production. The traditional Penedés varietals of Xarel-Lo and Parellada, along with the recent additions of Cabernet Sauvignon and Chazan, are cultivated on more than 100 ha of property. The winery has remained unchanged, but is very well equipped: it uses modern feeders and crushers and temperature-controlled fermentation systems. The winery, situated in the Subirats area, is right alongside a fabulous Can Bas mansion dating from the beginning of the century.

Prima Juventa 1991 ℗ ①
Bright straw yellow with silvery highlights. Pungent on the nose, with typical aromas of Xarel-Lo. Silky and full-bodied on the palate, with a fresh acidity. Clean, long, balanced finish.

Prima Lux 1991 ℗ ①
Clear, bright straw yellow with golden highlights. Full, silky and well-structured on the palate; balanced acidity gives freshness. Clean, lingering finish. Good Xarel-Lo character.

Prima Juventa Rosado 1991 ▨ ①
Made from Cabernet Sauvignon and Merlot; attractive, vibrant candy-pink with violet highlights. Fresh, 'tea-rose' bouquet. Simple, light red-fruit on the palate, balanced acidity. Fruit dominates a crisp, short finish.

*PENEDES/CAVA
CATALUÑA
SPAIN*

1022

*PENEDES
CATALUÑA
SPAIN*

Pinord

Pasteur, 6
Villafranca del Penedés (Barcelona)
Tel/Fax (93) 8900793

Pinord is a classic Penedés winery whose wide range of products have been well-marketed on the Spanish and international markets, thanks to its thorough distribution network. With 150 years of wine tradition, Pinord has made its niche in commercial winemaking, producing wines for large distribution. Naturally, the direct consequence of this is prevalent in most of Pinord's products, which, despite being well-made and correctly aged, show an average level of quality. Still, the winery has far from given up on quality, as demonstrated by their wide range of top-notch wines. Some of these exude Pinord's full capacity and potential and deserve to be included among Penedés' most outstanding wines. These include the Cava and some of the sweet wines, produced from native varietals, and the Cabernet Sauvignon (used for the reds), all from the property's own vineyards.

La Nansa 1991 ❦ ①
A superb example of the Macabeo variety. Very pale yellow; healthy, fine mousse and crisp freshness give a light bite to the palate.

Marrugat Extra Brut ❦ ②
Obtained from Macabeo, Xarel-Lo and Parellada. Fine abundant mousse and a fresh bouquet. Clean and refreshing on the palate, with mouth-cleansing acidity and good balance.

Can Ràfols dels Caus

Can Ràfols dels Caus, s/n
Avinyonet del Penedés (Barcelona)
Tel. (93) 8970013
Fax (93) 8970370

Can Ráfols, situated along the ancient Roman road to Narbonne, is believed to have been built over a pre-existing winery in the 16th century. Recently, this venerable winery has been modernized and equipped with the latest technology, enabling it to produce some of the most surprising wines in the area. The hacienda owns over 450 ha, but only 30 have been designated for vineyards, as they are surrounded by a typical Mediterranean pine and oak forest. In addition to the vines, they also grow almonds and olives. The terrain is situated 300 m above sea-level, has a sub-soil of calcareous rock, and a clayey top-soil. The obvious Penedés varietals are present: Macabeo, Xarel-Lo and Parellada, as well as the French Cabernet Sauvignon, Cabernet Franc, Merlot, Chardonnay and Chenin, which have adapted perfectly to the soil and have added a distinct character to the wines.

Gran Caus Blanco 1989 ❦ ②
Fresh bouquet with hints of oak aging. Fatness on the palate, backed with lemony acidity. Quite a big wine, to drink now or keep for a few years. Made from Xarel-Lo and Chardonnay.

Gran Caus Rosado 1991 ❦❦ ②
This wine is full of surprises. Light, fresh, plummy bouquet. Dry, round, 'fruit cordial' palate, with perfect clean acidity. Very gluggable, it is produced solely from Merlot.

Gran Caus Tinto 1987 ❦❦ ③
Ripe red fruit aromas are well-integrated with soft oak. In the mouth, it has an exotic Bordeaux aspect and a solid structure. Will keep a little while longer. A fine blend of Cabernet Sauvignon, Cabernet Franc and Merlot.

PENEDES/CAVA
CATALUÑA
SPAIN

1023

PENEDES
CATALUÑA
SPAIN

Raventós i Blanc

Placa del Roure, s/n
Sant Sadurní d'Anoia (Barcelona)
Tel. (93) 8910602
Fax (93) 8912500

The innovative Josep María Raventós i Blanc finds himself in the delicate position of wanting to develop his winery into the most traditional in Cataluña. The decision to completely change its style, go for quality and be the most outstanding in all respects (starting with a new label design and presentation), means the winery now only ages its Cava in the best years, like vintage Champagne. The dynamic Josep Raventós has also taken over a winery in the Saint-Emilion area of Bordeaux, on which he concentrates a great deal of energy and places great hopes. On the surrounding 130 ha of vineyards, some extremely old, the winery cultivates the classic Penedés varietals. The use of Chardonnay adds elegance and complexity to the wines. Raventós i Blanc has the advantage of the latest technology, such as modern presses and stainless steel vats. Only 60% of the fruit produced is used for the wine.

Raventós i Blanc Brut 1987 ℗ ③
Well-made and carefully aged. Produced from the classic Penedés varietals with the addition of Chardonnay grapes, which help provide a complex bouquet and richness on the palate. Attractive presentation.

Raventós i Blanc Chardonnay ℗ ①
Josep Raventós uses this still wine as a base for his Cavas. It is redolent of Chardonnay's unstoppable capabilities in the Penedés soil and microclimate.

PENEDES/CAVA
CATALUÑA
SPAIN

1024

PENEDES
CATALUÑA
SPAIN

Miguel Torres

Comercio, 22
Villafrana del Penedés (Barcelona)
Tel. (93) 8900100
Fax (93) 8170703

Miguel Torres succeeded in bringing prestige and recognition to Penedés by insisting on employing the same sales and enological techniques as the French. This explains why Torres wines have acquired a harmonious flavor with those over the border, without renouncing the tradition of a land undoubtedly capable of producing great wines. The Torres family owns almost 900 ha of vineyards in the Penedés area, guaranteeing the continuity of their large range of wines. It is hard to believe that the Torres empire (they also have properties in Chile and California) cares for its vines with the same meticulous care and love as a small producer, yet each year Miguel Torres proves this to be true. Nothing is left to chance; the right terrain and appropriate microclimate is researched for each varietal. Founded in 1870, today the winery enjoys the latest in ultra modern equipment, such as refrigeration systems and stainless steel vats. There is also an enormous cellar for aging, containing an impressive 12,000 French barriques.

Waltraud 1991   ③
Highly aromatic, with a fresh and balanced palate. Proof that the Riesling is becoming more and more at home in the high Penedés. Intended for early drinking. Thanks to its wonderful drinkability, it is instantly absorbed by the market.

Milmanda 1990   ③
LThe bouquet is a perfect balance of vanilla oak and Chardonnay fruit. Dry, buttery, honied and rich on the palate. Long harmonized finish.

Gran Coronas Mas La Plana ③
Etiqueta Negra 1983
This exceptional wine has been shown on numerous occasions, sharing the limelight with the world's best wines. Produced entirely from the Cabernet Sauvignon varietal, it is gently aged for six months in new Limousin or American barriques and, since 1985, also in bottle. Beautiful dark cherry-red with a brick-red rim. Complex bouquet of ripe cassis, truffle and mint, in harmony with scents of toast and tobacco. In the mouth, delicate at first, dry with warm, ripe fruit and spicey molasses; firm tannins. Long, elegant, complete finish.

PENEDES
CATALUÑA
SPAIN

1025

PENEDES
CATALUÑA
SPAIN

Masía Vallformosa

La Sala, 45
Vilobí del Penedés (Barcelona)
Tel. (93) 8978286
Fax (93) 8978355

Masía Vallformosa is situated in a splendid valley of the same name, that in Catalán means 'beautiful, marvelous valley'. It was given to the area after a gracious 10th century Romanesque chapel; since then, the valley has been associated with viticulture, experiencing good and bad times. In 1987, for example, phylloxera completely destroyed the vines of this region, and Masía Vallformosa was one of the first to replant using American rootstock. The winery currently owns 360 ha of vineyards planted with the native Xarel-Lo, Macabeo and Parellada, alongside the French varietals Muscat and Chardonnay. The red grapes range from Ull de Llebre, Garnacha and Cariñena to Cabernet Sauvignon and Merlot. The varied, perfected vinification processes produce whites, rosés, reds and Cavas, all of extremely high quality. It must certainly be the Doménech family trait of tenacity that made their dream of Vallformosa into a splendid reality.

Brut Reserva Vallformosa 1987 🍇 ②
Un des meilleurs bruts millésimés, généreux, avec de bons arômes primaires et un intéressant rapport qualité/prix. Un "cava" dans lequel les cépages parellada, macabeo et xarel-lo s'épanouissent totalement.

Brut Nature Vallformosa 🍇 ②
Very pale, clear yellow, fine mousse of tiny bubbles. Fresh and light on the palate; crisp finish. Made solely from Macabeo.

Vall Reserva 1982 🍇 ③
Ruby-red with tawny tones; developed bouquet of vanilla, tobacco and soft red fruits. Soft and round, 'Rioja' style palate. Produced from Cabernet Sauvignon, Tempranillo and Cariñena.

Jané Ventura

Carretera de Calafell 2
El Vendrell (Tarragona)
Tel. (977) 660118
Fax (977) 661239

Jané Ventura was a family-owned business that was once dedicated to selling wine. Some ten years ago, Benjamín Jané sensed the need to vinify his own wine and converted his old warehouses into a modern winery capable of offering quality wines under the Penedés DO. Located in the town of El Vendrell, in the south of Penedés, the modern and well-equipped winery offers sterile and temperature controlled winemaking conditions. For his whites, rosés and sparkling wines, Benjamín Jané buys in a large part of the grapes and carefully selects the wine to be bottled, selling the rest as bulk. The winery recently acquired 11 ha of vineyards in the area of the commune of La Bisbal and has planted mostly red varietals, especially Cabernet Sauvignon and Ull de Llebre, which are vinified on-site in a typical Catalunian 'masía'. The house speciality is rosé and recently Jané Ventura has begun experimenting for the production of a rosé Cava.

Brut Reserva Jané Ventura 1987 🍇🍇 ②
High quality sparkling wine produced in limited quantities. Fine fresh aromas, elegance and depth in the mouth. Made from the classical native varieties.

Jané Ventura Rosado 1991 🍇🍇 ①
Beautiful clear, rose-pink with orangey highlights. Packed with seductive floral scent; delicate strawberry fruit with crisp acidity. Regularly finishes among the best in annual wine-tasting events. Produced from Garnacha and Tempranillo.

Jané Ventura Cabernet 1989 🍇 ①
Typical varietal character, very French in style. Fresh blackcurrant, leafy fruit bouquet. Firm tannins and clever oak integration. Makes a balanced mouthful. Will improve on a few years keeping.

PENEDES/CAVA
CATALUÑA
SPAIN

1026

PENEDES/CAVA
CATALUÑA
SPAIN

Masía Barril

Masía Barril
Bellmunt del Priorato (Tarragona)
Tel. (977) 830192

Despite this family's activity in wine production since 1895, the Barril brothers have been bottling their own wine only for a short time. It was a happy step forward, as their 1982 harvest was greeted with much enthusiasm among experts and wine-lovers. The beautiful old winery is in an old farmhouse, but equipped with the latest technology. The family carefully follows each phase of production, making 100,000 bottles each year of various types of wine. Most outstanding are the whites, and then the fabulous rancios (typical of the region); but the true gems of this producer are the reds, carefully made from Garnacha and Cariñena, which, along with the white Garnacha and Macabeo, are harvested from the winery's 20 ha of vineyards. Here, in this gently rocky rural landscape, the peninsula's oldest style wines are produced.

Barril Clásico 1988
Cariñena and Garnacha grapes; quite intense cherry-red, with brick highlights. Potent fruity perfumes and scents of new oak. Pleasant, soft attack but powerful and warm on the palate, with firm tannin. Balanced, pleasant finish.

Barril Especial 1986
Well-structured; forward and refined aromas of mature fruit deriving from the Garnacha grapes. 16° alc content, though fairly imposing, is well-supported by the fruit.

Entries are arranged in alphabetical order by country, region and winery or producer name.

PRIORATO
CATALUÑA
SPAIN

1027

PRIORATO
CATALUÑA
SPAIN

Clos de L'Obac

Camí Manyetes, s/n Pol. 11
Gratallops (Tarragona)
Tel. (977) 839276
Fax (977) 839371

Clos de L'Obac is undoubtedly the most modern and innovative winery under the Priorato denomination of origin: here everything is minutely controlled. Vinification is set at a constant temperature of 22 degrees with macerations that sometimes take an entire month. Aging is in barriques, built from four different qualities of American and French oak, thus giving flexibility. Another important innovation has been the planting of different varietals, Cabernet, Merlot, Syrah and Pinot Noir, which are planted alongside the native Garnacha and Cariñena varietals. The vineyards are situated on the banks of the Siurana, the principal river of the area, on slate slopes dating from the Carboniferous period, at an altitude of roughly 450 m. Besides the high quality terrain, viticulture in this region benefits from the unique micro-climate, noted for its evening Summer thermal. The policy that Carles Pastrana, creator of this superb winery and renowned wine-lover, would like to develop here is one that produces wines along the lines of a Bordeaux Chateau, without the sense of the rigid boundaries that apply to the French DO.

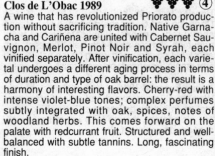

Clos de L'Obac 1990   ④

Plum red with intense, violet-blue tones; fruit and leather perfumes, notes of butterscotch. Pleasing, new oak aromas. Smooth approach on the palate; full-bodied and noticeably tannic, though not unpleasantly so.

Clos de L'Obac 1989   🍇🍇🍇 ④

A wine that has revolutionized Priorato production without sacrificing tradition. Native Garnacha and Cariñena are united with Cabernet Sauvignon, Merlot, Pinot Noir and Syrah, each vinified separately. After vinification, each varietal undergoes a different aging process in terms of duration and type of oak barrel: the result is a harmony of interesting flavors. Cherry-red with intense violet-blue tones; complex perfumes subtly integrated with oak, spices, notes of woodland herbs. This comes forward on the palate with redcurrant fruit. Structured and well-balanced with subtle tannins. Long, fascinating finish.

PRIORATO
CATALUÑA
SPAIN

1028

PRIORATO
CATALUÑA
SPAIN

De Muller

Real, 38
Tarragona
Tel. (977) 210220
Fax (977) 210400

Solitary landscapes of steep slate slopes are home to De Muller's vineyards, mainly planted with Garnacha and Cariñena. Here viticulture is a challenging exercise, as slopes may reach up to 30%, which means terracing. De Muller has been operating in Priorato since 1831, when Augusto De Muller y Ruinart, one of a colorful family with a great wine tradition (one of his ancestors was the first wine merchant in Champagne), decided to settle in Tarragona. In no time, his products became extremely famous in and out of Spain, so much so that he opened a branch in London. His successor, Don Joaquin De Muller y Abadal, is a 'tour de force' in the winery, maintaining the constant search for quality in what are difficult times for this blended, out-of-vogue wine. In addition to the original property, the winery also owns Terra Alta and Tarragona, which produce the celebrated 'Vinos de Misa'. De Muller's latest creation is a sparkling wine produced from traditional methods and belonging to the Cava DO.

De Muller Legítimo Priorato 1986   🍇 ②
Clear cherry-red with brick highlights; strong mineral aromas, with fruit and balsamic scents make a grand bouquet. The combination of Garnacha and Carinena make it liquorice-like on the palate. Brief aging in barrique adds an extra dimension.

Cellers Scala Dei

Rambla de la Cartoixa, s/n
Scala Dei (Tarragona)
Tel. (977) 827027
Fax (977) 827044

The town of Scala Dei, in the heart of Priorato, owes its name to the ancient and currently ruined Certosa, founded by monks from Grenoble in 1163. Legend has it that these monks were looking for a place to settle in the countryside, and, on asking a shepherd, were told this story: on certain afternoons in the area a great ladder appeared, reaching right up to the heavens. The monks interpreted this as a divine message and without futher delay, began to build the Certosa. They were the first in the region to plant vineyards on the difficult slate terrain. Despite having the lowest yields per ha in Spain, the fruit produced is truly the best, turning into one of the greatest wines of the Iberian Peninsula. Only fruit from the winery's 60 ha of vineyards is used: the native Garnacha and Cariñena together with French Cabernet Sauvignon, and the white Garnacha Blanca and Chenin grapes.

Novell Scala Dei 1991   🍇 ②
Gives new meaning to Priorato; soft fruit with very interesting characteristics due to the Garnacha being cultivated on slate terrain.

Negre Scala Dei 1988   🍇 ②
Cherry-red; soft, fruity bouquet produced from aging in the bottle. Full of character on the palate due to the strange marriage of the Garnacha and Cabernet Sauvignon varietals.

Cartoixa de Scala Dei   🍇🍇 ③
Reserva 1987
Classic example of this DO. Produced from Garnacha and Cariñena, resulting perfectly in powerful and intense aroma. Intense and fat due to 14° alc content which is sufficiently supported by wood aging.

PRIORATO
CATALUÑA
SPAIN

1029

PRIORATO
CATALUÑA
SPAIN

Josep Anguera Beyme

Mayor, s/n Dalmós
Tivisa (Tarragona)
Tel. (977) 418302

The Tarragona DO, though rather widespread, is experiencing such difficulties that it is rare to find this region's wine in bottle. Something positive, however, is happening in Josep Anguera Beyme's cellars. Founded some 160 years ago, the family-run enterprise has given Josep some good ideas: to produce, for example, a bold, original red apart from the region's traditional wines, often associated with ancient production methods used to make bulk wine which is sold or used to beef up other European wines. In the hope of improving the quality of his primary materials, Josep has planted his 25 ha of vineyards with the French varietals Cabernet Sauvignon and Syrah, along with the local Garnacha. The winery has been modernized and technologically updated. The 'Negre Novell' is a young, complex and subtle red that may easily compete with most of Rioja's wines, equalling them in body and aging.

Joan D'Anguera Tinto 1991   🍷 ①
Cherry-red with violet-blue tones; aromas are fairly intense; ample and harmonious on the palate. A well-aged and characterful wine due to the Cabernet Sauvignon, Garnacha and Syrah combination.

Pedro Rovira

Av. Carrilet, 257
Gandesa (Barcelona)
Tel. (93) 3371812
Fax (93) 3389587

The name Terra Alta denotes a stretch of land surrounded by the last length of the Ebro river, just a few km from the sea. It is blessed with a climate heavily influenced by the Mediterranean. Since 1982, this wine sub-zone of Catalonia has been able to produce wines with a denomination of origin. The winery that best represents this change is Pedro Rovira, located in the vicinity of Gandesa, Terra Alta's capital. In 1980, in the light of the new DO status, Rovira completely renovated his winery. The varietals used for this winery's production are the red Cariñena, Ull de Llebre, Garnacha Peluda, and the white Parellada, Garnacha Blanca, Xarel-Lo and Macabeo. These grapes, almost entirely obtained from nearby growers and cooperatives, are turned into wine under the direction of Pedro Rovira Solé. In his modern winery, Rovira's best products are the whites, the only wines which stand out from the otherwise average products.

Blanc de Belart 1989   🍷 ①
Dry, slight acidity and quite aromatic. Clear, defined characters in the mouth benefit from bottle aging. Made of Garnacha Blanca and Macabeo.

Altamar 1988   🍷 ①
Delicate and light; just about the right amount of sweet fruit is balanced with a good acidity. Produced from Macabeo and Garnacha Peluda.

Centro

This large territory is host to the world's largest vineyard: in Castile La Mancha alone there are over 700,000 ha, on top of the 25,000 ha in the Autonomous Community of Madrid and the 82,000 ha in Estremadura. In all, these areas make up 52% of Spain's vineyards, translating into an annual production of over 1,700,000,000 lt. The productivity per ha is extremely low, due to severe climatic conditions and a ban on vine irrigation. Despite this, the whole area has gone in for mass production of bulk wine, though to the evident detriment of quality, and only now is a tendency to specialization starting to spread amongst producers.

Without forgoing the bulk marketing that unloads the enormous surpluses, they are now offering quality products, including some aged wines together with reserves refined in stores fitted out with oak barriques.

Moreover, the proliferation of Cabernet Sauvignon has led to the appearance of reds with a bright future, though they tend at times to be rather unrefined. The Almansa DO, which boasts several Rioja-producing wineries of the highest quality, lies within the Castile La Mancha region, although it is actually closer to the Levantine area than to the Centre. Another DO is La Mancha, Spain's winegrowing giant that is caught up in a great struggle between the search for higher quality and the need for quantity, though the scales are tipping in favor of the former. The Mentrida DO is known for its intensely colored, robust red wines that are somewhat antiquated, while the Valdepeñas DO is a great supplier of light wines that are excellent served with meals. Recently a new DO, Vinos de Madrid, has been created in the community of Madrid with the aim of stimulating technological modernization and vineyard classification; still in its early days, this DO has had varying results. Finally, there is Estremadura, an unjustly forgotten region despite its being one of the most important due to its production of over 260 million lt. Most of its wine, however, is sold in bulk, with the exception of a few wineries which bottle their products. White varietals, mainly Airén, prevail in the whole of central Spain, but there are also some red varietals such as Cencibel, Garnacha, Monastrell and Bobal.

Bodega Inviosa

Av. de la Paz, 19
Almendralejo (Badajoz)
Tel. (924) 660977

Marcelino Díaz was a godsend to the Tierra de Barros, where bulk wines and wines used for distillation predominate, with Almendralejo, the area's main town, having one of the three highest concentrations of distilleries in Spain. Within this setting, Marcelino has managed to come up with certain wines that can be considered as ranking among the best in the Iberian Peninsula and even appear in the directories of famous North American wine magazines. Inviosa has 400 ha of vines planted with varietals suited to this soil and microclimate: red Tempranillo, Graciano and Garnacha, and white Cayetana, Macabeo and Chardonnay. The vinification cellars are traditional but well-equipped with, for example, 1,500 oak barrels. For a number of years Marcelino Díaz has been making a traditional method sparkling wine with splendid results. He produces an average of 500,000 bottles a year: the most prestigious in Estremadura.

Brut Bonaval　　　　　　　🍾 ②
Golden yellow; brilliant and packed with a foam of medium-sized bubbles. Elegant primary and secondary aromas, the first featuring fruity Viura varietal tones. Ample and complex on the palate, though light and well-balanced. Good sparkling wine made by the Champenoise method.

Lar de Barros 1987　　　　　🍷 ①
Refined in wood and well-suited to modern tastes. Red with garnet highlights; complex secondary aromas with tones of old wood. Ample and slightly astringent on the palate.

Lar de Lares 1982　　　　　　🍷 ②
Made from the same varietals and in the same proportions as Lar de Barros, but the refinement in wood and bottle is more noticeable. Smoother and more rounded; well-balanced, though a little short.

Fermín Ayuso Roig

Miguél Caro, 4
Villarrobledo (Albacete)
Tel. (967) 140458
Fax (967) 144925

Fermín Ayuso Roig founded this winery in Villarrobledo, in the province of Albacete. At first he sold his wines in bulk, but after a few years, in 1961, he began bottling his products and distributing them on the domestic market. Continuous commitment and a constant search for quality have helped to create a winery that can take advantage of the most advanced winemaking techniques to produce wines with one of the best quality/price ratios in the whole of Spain. Wines are refined in 8,000 oak barriques housed in an underground cellar, while the facility has a total storage capacity of 400,000 hectolitres. The entire production of over 13 million lt, almost half of it red, is bottled. Fermín Ayusa Roig was actually the first in the area to produce red wine, and pride of place among the winery's wide range of products now goes by right to the red Estola Tinto.

Viña Q Tinto 1991　　　　　🍷 ①
Young and fruity; attractive color and pure aromas. Light and unpretentious, but very pleasing. Produced from Cencibel and Airén.

Estola Tinto 1985　　　　　　🍷 ①
Best in Spain in quality/price terms. The Cencibel varietal matured in oak gives it unquestionable character.

Estola Gran Reserva 1978　　🍷 ②
Fruit of the celebrated Cencibel varietal; exquisite refinement in barrique makes it round with an extremely interesting bouquet.

D.O.P. TIERRA DE BARROS
CENTRO
SPAIN
　　　　1032　　　　
LA MANCHA
CENTRO
SPAIN

Vinícola de Castilla

Polígono Industrial, s/n
Manzanares (Ciudad Real)
Tel. (926) 610450
Fax (926) 610466

Until recently, Vinícola de Castilla's enormous production and traditionally bulk sales made it just one of the many wineries in the La Mancha DO, known as the world's largest bulk production area. Then a well-chosen winemaking policy turnaround led to the winery modernizing its facilities to start using temperature controlled vinification and market young, flavorful and richly aromatic wines at extremely competitive prices. An average 17 million lt of wine is produced each year with a wide range of products; these include really excellent young wines made using carbonic maceration - which can also count on a fair number of enthusiasts among wine connoisseurs - and wines made from Cabernet Sauvignon and aged in oak barriques, as well as the first sparkling wine in Castile and La Mancha.

Señorío de Guadianeja Blanco 1991
Extremely light, aromatic, delicate and well-balanced. Pleasing wine made from the Airén varietal; fresh and savory.

Castillo de Alhambra Tinto 1991
Obtained from Cencibel and vinified using carbonic maceration; extremely clean, fruity and floral. Attractive wine with an excellent quality/price ratio.

Señorío de Guadianeja
Cabernet 1985
Brilliant cherry-color with brick shades; outstanding aromas of refinement in barrique and black pepper. Delicate approach on the palate with highly positive development.

Cueva del Granero

Extrarradio, s/n
Los Hinojosos (Cuenca)
Tel. (925) 280285
Fax (925) 180008

Cueva del Granero was built to resemble a Bordeaux château in many ways, although the estate is much smaller. 450 ha of vineyards surround the winery in a fine setting of lightly rolling hills, pine trees, fields of grain and, of course, vineyards featuring the classic Airén and Cencibel varietals, together with Cabernet Sauvignon. The winery has opted to concentrate on various young wines (whites, reds, rosés and single varietals), though it also produces an aging red that is one of the best in the DO. All the wines stand out for their model vinification, and the so-called top-range production is of proven quality. Currently less than half Cueva del Granero's average annual production of 22,000 hectolitres - 30% of which is sold abroad - is bottled, though this is likely to change considerably in the future.

Cueva del Granero
Cabernet Sauvignon 1991
Young, long and deep; fairly brilliant for a Cabernet. Perfumes and flavors of noteworthy quality.

Cueva del Granero 1988
All the fragrance of a young wine, accompanied though by reduced and refinement notes that add a certain complexity. Made from Cencibel.

LA MANCHA
CENTRO
SPAIN

1033

LA MANCHA
CENTRO
SPAIN

Cooperativa Nuestra Señora de Manjavacas

Felix Palacios, 14
Mota del Cuervo (Cuenca)
Tel. (966) 180025
Fax (966) 181120

In the 1980s, La Mancha surprised winemaking circles by starting to produce pleasantly savory wines with clean-cut primary aromas and truly well-balanced acidity. Founded in 1948, the Cooperativa Nuestra Señora de Manjavacas was one of the region's first wineries to equip itself for producing this type of wine, converting all its vinification facilities and installing systems for temperature-control, refrigeration, etc. That it was a co-operative to make such an adventurous move is particularly commendable, given that this kind of set-up is generally not very dynamic when rapid decision-making is involved. Located right in the middle of La Mancha of Cervantes, in the center of Mota del Cuervo at the foot of a hill dominated by windmills, the co-operative collects all the grapes picked by its members each year from over 8,000 ha of vineyards.

Zagarrón Blanco 1991　　　　🍇 ①
Light, fresh and truly well-crafted. Obtained from Airén; aromatic character is influenced by vinification with selected yeasts.

Zagarrón Tinto Joven 1991　　🍷 ①
Clear cherry with violet-blue highlights; fruity perfumes are clean and potent. Slightly sweet, mouth-filling and well-structured. Pure and fruity lingering aromas are derived from Cencibel.

Julián Santos Aguado y Cía

Ctra. Madrid-Alicante, km 121
Quintanar de la Orden (Toledo)
Tel. (925) 181964
Fax (925) 195650

La Mancha, as is well-known, is dominated by white grapevines, with 90% of its vineyards given over to the Airén varietal. Aguado, though, is quite original, being probably the only winery in this DO to produce more red wine than white. The company's 1,000 ha of vineyards are planted largely with Cencibel, along with the white varietals Viura and Airén. All the vineyards are located between the villages of La Villa de Don Fadrique and Quintanar de la Orden, home to Aguado's headquarters. There are two, excellently equipped vinification facilities, one at La Villa and the other at Quintanar. Most of the 174,000 hectolitre production is destined for immediate consumption, while a small part is selected for higher quality whites, reds and rosés. The winery's pride and joy are its reds, refined in new oak barriques: these truly interesting wines attest to the major advances made in this area in the production of this kind of wine.

Don Fadrique Blanco 1991　　🍇 ①
Lightly acidulous and very aromatic; produced from Viura; maintains great cleanliness throughout tasting.

Don Fadrique Tinto 1985　　🍷 ②
Noteworthy wine of this area. Despite the winery's having little experience in maturing, this wine's stay in wood is perfectly timed, resulting in a very pleasant bouquet.

LA MANCHA
CENTRO
SPAIN

1034

LA MANCHA
CENTRO
SPAIN

Vinícola de Tomelloso

Ctra. Toledo-Albacete, km 230
Tomelloso (Ciudad Real)
Tel. (926) 513004

Tomelloso, one of the most dynamic and modern wineries in the world's largest DO, La Mancha, was formed in 1988 by 50 vinegrowers who had decided to renew their vineyards. The members' property covers 2,200 ha of vineyards dominated by the white Airén varietal, though it is slowly being replaced by red Cabernet Sauvignon and Cencibel, and white Macabeo. Macabeo is used to produce one of La Mancha's most pleasant and famous wines, the white Añil. When this masterpiece of enologists Felipe Blanco and Francisco Granados first appeared on the market, it created a sensation and was greeted by enthusiasm throughout the region. The large facility, which is fitted out with the latest technology, is perfectly capable of vinifying the four million kg of grapes provided annually by its members. Their short term goal is to bottle the entire production.

Añil Blanco 1991 ❦ ①
Light and fresh; traces of exotic fruits (pineapple, mango and banana) and a hint of carbon dioxide. Clear, lingering sensations of Viura, an uncommon varietal in this area.

Abrego Tinto 1991 ❦ ①
Intense, pure scents of small wild berries; full-bodied, ample, and long on the palate. Produced from Cencibel grapes.

Bodegas Torres Filoso

Nueva, 9
Villarrobledo (Albacete)
Tel/Fax (967) 140090

This winery, founded almost 80 years ago, has kept a low profile as the quality of its products has gradually become more apparent. Expansion over the years culminated in 1988 with the inauguration of a new, modern and efficient facility that houses all the latest technology and an underground cellar for the barriques. Annual production approaches one million lt, a modest quantity for the La Mancha area. Torres Filoso has also updated its vineyards, planting French Cabernet Sauvignon and Merlot along with white Airén and Macabeo, and red Cencibel (the local name for Tempranillo). The entire production is interesting and the wines are generally of good quality: the best are the fruity reds, whose aging in wood provides elegance and a refined bouquet. Torres Filoso also exports and its products are distributed to a surprisingly wide market.

Torres Filoso Tinto 1988 ❦ ①
Well-evolved, with frank perfumes of mature fruit on the nose; sweet and well-structured approach on the palate. Made from Cencibel, Garnacha and Airén.

Arboles de Castillejo 1986 ❦ ①
Excellent aging; unusually delicate; completely different from the typical products of this area. Obtained from Cencibel with a small percentage of Airén.

LA MANCHA
CENTRO
SPAIN

1035

LA MANCHA
CENTRO
SPAIN

Cooperativa Nuestra Señora de las Viñas

Ctra. de Argamasilla, s/n
Tomelloso (Ciudad Real)
Tel. (926) 510865
Fax (926) 510851

La Mancha's capacity for wine production is quite awesome: its 160,000 ha planted with vines constitutes the largest vineyard in Europe. The white Airén varietal, the base-wine for many Jerez de la Frontera brandies, holds sway, and Tomelloso is one of the two main wine-distilling localities in the Iberian Peninsula. Most of the Cooperativa Nuestra Señora de las Viñas' enormous output is sent on to distilleries for the production of famous brandies. Members pool together the fruit harvested from 22,000 ha of vineyards, planted 95% with white Airén and 5% with red varietals like Cencibel. A small portion of this huge mass of grapes is selected for the production of some aging reds and highly likeable young wines, both white and red, that have met with considerable success on the home market.

Tomillar Tinto Reserva 1988 🍇 ①
Medium-intensity, extremely clear brick-red. Typical Cencibel perfumes, with touches of secondary aromas; well-structured on the palate.

Don Eugenio 5° año 🍇 ①
Classic wine of this area; aged in wood for a certain number of years. Moderately well-structured; made from Cencibel and Airén.

Casa de la Viña

La Solana (Ciudad Real)
Tel/Fax (926) 631419

Casa de la Viña is a good point reference, due both to the quality of its wines and its role in the area's winemaking history. Its original owner was the Count of Casavaliente, who planted the first vines in 1875. Today, the estate covers over 2,800 ha, 840 of which are grown with Cencibel, one of the many names Tempranillo is known by. Only a very small number of white Airén vines are planted, and around 40 ha are currently being switched to Merlot, Cabernet Sauvignon and Pinot Noir. This outstanding real estate was recently acquired by Bodegas y Bebidas, which took over Casa de la Viña in 1983 and has invested not only in the vineyards, but also in the winery facilities, production plant and automatic refrigeration systems. Over 1000 French barriques have been installed in the cellars for the aging of red wines which can rightfully be considered the most interesting in Valdepeñas. The wines are marketed under three labels: Vega de Moriz, Casa de la Viña and Señorío de Val.

Casa de la Viña Cencibel 1985 🍇🍇 ①
Fine example of what the Valdepeñas DO has to offer when crafted with care and high standard equipment. Perfect expression of the grape, both on the nose and on the palate.

Vega de Moriz Reserva 1985 🍇 ①
Garnet-red with shades of brick; fine appearance. Typical varietal nose, with aging features. Delicate and full-bodied on the palate.

LA MANCHA
CENTRO
SPAIN

1036

VALDEPEÑAS
CENTRO
SPAIN

Bodegas Félix Solís

Ctra. N IV, km 200
Valdepeñas (Ciudad Real)
Tel. (926) 322400
Fax (926) 322417

This is the Valdepeñas DO's largest winery and undoubtedly one of the biggest wine companies in the whole country. Bodegas Félix Solís' output of 47 million lt makes it a genuine example of remarkable company expansion, considering it was founded in the 1940s. At that time, the whole area produced mainly in bulk, and this winery was the first to bottle its production. The winery's vineyards provide only a minimal part of production needs; the remainder is bought in from other growers and winemakers in the area. A small amount of high quality product is then selected out of this vast sea of grapes: we mention here a white, a rosé and an excellent reserve red, aged in underground cellars that hold 5,000 American oak barriques. These high quality selections bear the Viña Albali label and are crafted from the classic Cencibel and Airén varietals.

Viña Albali Blanco 1991 ❦ ①
Beautiful aromatic expression of Airén; clean in all tasting stages, with a carbon residue that adds cheerfulness.

Viña Albali Rosado 1991 ▨ ①
Brilliant, extremely attractive pink with shades of raspberry. Light and fresh on the palate; produced from Cencibel and Airén.

Viña Albali Reserva 1984 ❦ ②
Pretty cherry-red with brick highlights; silky and balanced on the palate; a good example of aging in wood. Obtained from Cencibel and a small amount of Airén.

Luís Mejía

Salida del Peral, 1
Valdepeñas (Ciudad Real)
Tel. (926) 320600
Fax (926) 325356

Ever since its founding in 1947, the large Luís Mejía winery has been a model of efficiency and, above-all, continual growth. It was, in fact, one of the first wineries in the area to update its antiquated techniques, enabling it to launch some simple but honest wines with an excellent quality/price ratio. This policy led to Mejía's selling millions of lt of wine (it has a present capacity of 80,000 hectolitres), reaching the markets of countless countries throughout the world. This company's greatest merit lies in its not having rested on the laurels of easy commercial success: instead, it has created a range of fine wines, featuring some excellent young reds produced using a higher percentage of Cencibel than most other local producers. Also featured, rather unusually for Valdepeñas, are some reds aged in wood in a cellar holding 3,000 oak barriques.

Marqués de Gastañada 1990 Tinto ❦ ①
Cherry-red with a tinge of ruby; extremely clean. Pure primary aromas recall aniseed; good development on the palate; light and well-balanced, though not long-lasting. Cencibel grapes provide the base for this red, with a small addition of Airén.

Duque de Estrada 1985 Tinto ❦ ①
Not very intense, but clean cherry-red with shades of brick. Perfumes from aging in bottle together with some subtle wood tones; medium intensity and well-balanced on the palate, with good lingering sensations that highlight wood more clearly. Also made from Cencibel with a small percentage of Airén.

VALDEPENAS
CENTRO
SPAIN

1037

VALDEPENAS
CENTRO
SPAIN

Aigaco

Juan de Austria, 1
Villarejo de Salvanés (Madrid)
Tel. (91) 8744033

Converting a winery specialized in table
wines into a producer of high quality, well-
crafted wines can sometimes prove harder
than starting from scratch. Owner Felix
Martinez and talented winemaker José Casal
del Rey may take some well-deserved credit
for doing just that: they succeeded in placing
their Jeromín among the most prestigious
wines of the Vinos de Madrid DO. Aigaco's
60 ha of vineyards in Villarejo de Salvanés, in
the subzone of Arganda, are cultivated with
the most common local varietals. Their wines
are mostly fresh and for early consumption,
but recently Aigaco has brought out the
area's first reserve, with the support of this
DO's regulatory agency, the Consejo
Regulador. The Vinos de Madrid DO is,
incidentally, one of Spain's most recent, even
though this area can lay claim to a very old
winemaking tradition. Indeed, Madrilena
region wine was already known in the 15th
century as the wine of kings and has had
several literary mentions.

Jeromín Blanco 1991   ⚇ ①
Extremely pale yellow; primary perfumes are
slightly overpowered by exotic fruit aromas;
well-crafted, packed with freshness and
lightness. The main ingredient is Malvar.

Jeromín Rosado 1991   🏵 ①
Currently the best rosé in the Vinos de Madrid
DO. Beautiful color, fragrant perfumes and well-
structured. Produced from Garnacha and
Tempranillo.

Jesús Díaz e hijos

Convento, 38
Colmenar de Oreja (Madrid)
Tel. (91) 8943243

Jesús Díaz is one of the people who was
most convinced of the potential of the Madrid
wine region for producing quality wines, and
it thus fell to him to take on the commendable
task of saving Madrid from anonymous bulk
production by promoting the bottling of its
wines. Today the Díaz winery enjoys a fine
reputation throughout Spain and owns 60 ha
of vineyards in the Arganda subzone.
Alongside the native Malvar and Tinto de
Madrid some French vines, such as Cabernet
Sauvignon and Syrah, are grown. Juan José
Díaz is the resident wine technician who
closely follows these experiments that have
already produced most interesting results as
is borne out by the continually higher quality
of their wines over the last few years.
Although most of the production is still sold
on the domestic market, as is the case with
all Spanish wines increasingly encouraging
signs are being received from abroad.

Colmenar Tinto 1990   ⚇ ①
Tinto Fino and Malvar grapes team up to make
a wine that can be appreciated for its pleasant
balance of acidity and tannins, full and lasting
fruitiness and good dryness in the finish.

VINO DE MADRID
CENTRO
SPAIN

1038

VINO DE MADRID
CENTRO
SPAIN

Bodegas Orusco

Alcalá, 24
Valdilecha (Madrid)
Tel. (91) 8738006

The Vinos de Madrid DO includes three
subzones: Arganda, Navalcarnero and San
Martín de Valdeiglesias. Arganda, in the
East, is undoubtedly the most important of
these, owing not only to the size of its
vineyards, but also to the quality of its wines.
All three wineries reviewed here belong to
this subzone, and Bodegas Orusco is located
right in the village of Valdilecha. The winery,
which has been entirely rebuilt, is nearly one
hundred years old, and its present owner,
Juan Orusco, is responsible for the new,
interesting quality of the house wines.
Orusco's most important product is Viña
Main, which is matured in wood barrels and
is based on a coupage of Tempranillo (80%)
and Malvar. These wines generally stand out
for their clarity and balance. Annual
production surpasses two million lt, supplied
only in part by the winery's 20 ha of vines;
most of the grapes are bought in from
growers in the area.

Viña Main Tinto 1990 🍇 ①
Well-structured, complex and rich; probably this
DO's best red. Fat and harmonious on the
palate.

VINO DE MADRID
CENTRO
SPAIN

1039

VINO DE MADRID
CENTRO
SPAIN

Cuenca del Duero

Throughout the whole Iberian Peninsula, the Duero is the river most associated with viticulture. In a long course that begins in Spain and ends in Portugal (the Douro), it creates ideal conditions for the cultivation of great quality vines. These vines extend across the provinces of Castigliane di Burgos, Valladolid and Zamora, continuing to Portugal, where wines like Porto begin life along the high banks of the Duoro.

The Cuenca del Duero region has made a great impact on Spanish winemaking in recent years with the unstoppable rise of wines from the Ribera del Duero DO, the cradle of the mythical Vega Sicilia Unica. Ribera del Duero is the great alternative to Rioja wines, though its market price is decisively higher (Reservas now easily reach 1,500 pesetas).

The Ribera del Duero DO incorporates 9,000 ha of vineyards, mostly dedicated to the Tinta del País variety (also known as Tinto Fino), one of many versions of the Tempranillo. Production reaches approximately 55,000 hl each year. Besides Ribera's great reds, some very successful whites are also found in the area, especially in Rueda. Here the base varietal is native Verdejo, a grape with great personality, and production is estimated at 39,000 hl. In recent years this DO has undergone an important transformation of its traditional vinification methods, abandoning the Jerez-style production for that of modern, young, fruity whites. This change-over has allowed the area to maintain its outstanding position on the national wine scene. Cuenca del Duero's other DOs include Cigales and the newcomer Toro. Formerly signifying aged, highy alcoholic robust reds, Toro now, after a small revolution, proposes modern, tannic, rich wines that are steadily increasing their national and international market-share. This DOs modest production barely surpasses 10,000 hl annually.

Bodega Cooperativa de Cigales

Las Fábricas, s/n
Cigales (Valladolid)
Tel. (983) 570135

The Cigales' clairettes were so prized at the court of Valladolid that it is believed they were forbidden to be sold elsewhere. These wines, made with traditional methods that combine different varietals, were aged in old wooden barrels, explaining their imperfect nature. This area, to the north of Valladolid, was granted its own DO in 1991, which contributed to the modernization of its vinification techniques. The Cigales Cooperative was one of the first wineries to update its facilities and, thanks to that smart move, has created suitable conditions for producing an excellent rosé. 600 ha of vineyards, planted with red Garnacha and Tempranillo and white Albillo and Verdejo, yield 2,000,000 lt of wine annually. 30% of this mostly rosé production is sold in bulk. The lion's share of vines are given over to Tinta del País (Tempranillo) and are cultivated on over 60% of the entire vineyard area of the DO.

Viña Torondos 1991　　　🍇 ①
Cherry-pink with copper highlights, unlike traditional Cigales. Light red fruit on the palate, slightly flabby acidity. Made of Tempranillo, Garnacha, Albillo and Verdejo.

Bodegas Ismael Arroyo

Los Lagares, 71
Sotillo de la Ribera (Burgos)
Tel/Fax (974) 545109

In only 12 years, Ismael Arroyo has become one of the most classic signatures in the Ribera de Duero DO. The secret to his rise lies in his serious and continuous work, always geared towards the improvement of quality. The winery is small, sensibly equipped, modern and clean, and providing enough space for stainless steel tanks. However, the most unique and characteristic element of this winery is its cellar for aging. More specifically, there is a cluster of many smaller traditional cellars, carved out of a hill near the winery that Ismael and his sons have gradually transformed into a labyrinth of tunnels that houses 600 barriques and roughly 400,000 bottles of reserve wine. The winery's six hectares of vineyards, all cultivated with Tinto Fino, are on the outer limits of the town of Sotillo de la Ribera. Here the mountainous topography makes viticulture unusually difficult. On these steep slopes, wild herbs grow alongside the vines.

Mesoneros de Castilla Tinto 1989　🍇 ①
Bright, deep cherry-red; forward aromas with wild berry character. Full-body and round tannins on the palate. Soft, easy finish.

Valsotillo Gran Reserva 1986　🍇🍇 ②
Same quality and attributes of its older brother (mentioned below), only a bit more tannic and dense. Liquorice and coffee present. Almost a chewy wine. Like all Arroyo wines, produced solely from Tinto Fino grapes. Excellently aged.

Valsotillo Gran Reserva 1985　🍇🍇 ③
Among the best Reservas of the area. Deep, dark, rich, mature red fruit, coffee and tobacco. Very well integrated flavors, great tannic backbone. Ready for immediate drinking, or to keep for a few years.

CIGALES
CUENCA DEL DUERO
SPAIN

1041

RIBERA DE DUERO
CUENCA DEL DUERO
SPAIN

Bodegas Balbás

La Majada, s/n
La Horra (Burgos)
Tel. (974) 541052
Fax (974) 541278

Just being a part of this rising DO may guarantee good sales, though not necessarily good quality. Keeping this in mind, Bodegas Balbás has opted for slow growth and has gradually quietly stepped into the market. In fact, they are almost totally unknown in Spain; the 4,000 hl production is practically all sold abroad, where the winery has earned its reputation for quality wines at extremely reasonable prices. Situated in the heart of the Ribera and equipped with modern technology producing superbly made wines, modest Balbás (founded in 1977) currently has no plans to compete in the national market. Thanks to its great leader, Juan José Balbás, the winery took a giant qualitative step forward at the end of the 1980s. The small, carefully overseen production, moderate prices and the individual production style of the wines are good signs that this discrete and serious winery will have a successful future.

Balbás Rosado
Pleasant pale orange-pink; rather aromatic, with notable fruity perfumes. Light and fresh on the palate, with the unmistakable stamp of Tinto Fino.

Balbás Tinto 1988
Fruity and well-dosed aging in wood; respects the characteristic expressions of Tinto Fino. Medium intensity cherry-red with some violet-blue nuances; balanced and flavorful on the palate, though not excessively long.

Bodegas Famoro

Cantarranas, 7
Pesquera (Valladolid)
Tel. (983) 472852
Fax (983) 472872

The rise of this little winery has been truly astounding, considering that only a few years ago Famoro's wines were sold in bottles without labels or by the glass in nearby Valladolid. In only a few years it has reached excellent qualitative summits and gained notable prestige. The young and dynamic equipe guiding the winery has cultivated a modern and personal image for its wines, benefiting from the fortunate red wine market of the Ribera de Duero denomination of origin, unquestionably with full merit. Famoro is small, and likewise its production, although the vinification process is carried out in a highly original manner: the resulting wines have a totally personal character, with many extracts and a touch of new wood that completes them and enriches their bouquet. The winery possesses some equipment for a reasonably modern vinification that is on par with the 30,000 bottle-production, offered at accessible prices.

Emilio Moro 1990
Original and young; brief passage in wood (three months in barrique), rendering intense and complex aromas. Good tannic expression, as is often the case with Tinto Fino wines from this area.

Emilio Moro 1989
Classic of the Ribera de Duero zone, where Tinto Fino's vigorous nature is almost 'insolent'. Aging in barrique adds aromatic complexity.

RIBERA DE DUERO
CUENCA DEL DUERO
SPAIN

1042

RIBERA DE DUERO
CUENCA DEL DUERO
SPAIN

Alejandro Fernández

Los Lagares, s/n
Pesquera (Valladolid)
Tel. (983) 870039
Fax (983) 870088

In the Ribera del Duero, under the uncontested reign of the fabulous Vega Sicilia winery, the most promising winemaking revolution in the whole Iberian Peninsula has taken place. In less than 15 years this denomination of origin has transformed an area of good, but common wines to the cradle of the best red wines in Spain. The credit goes to a small group of producers who unashamedly and respectfully studied their 'king'. Today, these wineries have converted this monarchistic enological region into a 'democracy'. Of particular note in the group is a very unique man by the name of Alejandro Fernández, creator of the red wine masterpiece, Pesquera. Born between vines and fermentation vats, Alejandro has focused his work on the realization of a dream that is cherished by all viticulturists: to own vineyards and create one's own winery. This became a reality for Alejandro in 1972. Now the winery possesses 100 ha of vineyards, located on the strip of land between Roa and Pesquera, and produces 500,000 bottles of its own red Pesquera each year.

Pesquera Reserva 1987 ♟ ③
Cherry-red with brick highlights; clean and rather intense; good bouquet. Spiced scents of vanilla, pepper and cloves, and notes of butter. Primary perfumes of wild berries. Ample and powerful on the palate, displaying the characteristic stamp of the grape and special terrain of this area.

Pesquera Gran Reserva 1986 ♟♟ ③
Conspicuous, cherry-red; clear and intense. Optimal quality perfumes from aging in oak accompanied by fruity aromas, characteristic of Tinto Fino. Smooth entrance on the palate; develops splendidly with a rich array of extracts; long-lasting.

Pesquera Janus 1982 ♟♟♟ ④
Reserva Especial
The carefully selected grapes are placed under the charms of the expert Alejandro, who has already formulated a strict profile in his head of the wine he wants to produce. The achievement is a marvelous, compact, dense wine with an intense bouquet, resulting from 28 months in barrique followed by a long maturation in the bottle. Produced exclusively from Tinto Fino. Beautiful cherry-red with brick highlights; perfectly harmonized perfumes with notes of bread, a bit of cocoa, and refined and elegant wood. Well-structured and tannic on the palate. Solid acidity, a wide array of lingering aromas and a splendidly flavorful finale.

RIBERA DE DUERO
CUENCA DEL DUERO
SPAIN

1043

RIBERA DE DUERO
CUENCA DEL DUERO
SPAIN

Hermanos Pérez Pascuas

Las Heras, s/n
Prdrosa de Duero (Burgos)
Tel. (947) 540499
Fax (947) 541100

The Pérez Pascuas brothers, in business only 12 years, have charged to the forefront of the Ribera del Duero, a region riding high on the wave of producing the most chic red wines of the Iberian Peninsula. The story of the winery began in 1980, when brothers Alfo, Manuel and Benjamín, longtime viticulturalists, decided to make their own wine with the grapes they had, until then, always sold to other prestigious wineries. The almost immediate positive results were not a miraculous event: the brothers already had impeccable vineyards (owing to their great love of the land), and when they decided to vinify, they sought the advice of respected enologists and equipped their small and spotless winery as advised. The results have been the prize for a job well-done. Inaugurated in 1989, the winery is situated in a pinery that dominates a large part of the nearby valley; it is an attractive building that houses modern and practical vinification equipment. The well-adapted aging rooms contain 1,000 barriques and complete the production process of 450,000 bottles. The winery's 69 ha of vineyards are planted with Tinto Fino and 10% of Cabernet Sauvignon.

Viña Pedrosa Joven 1991 🍷 🍷 ①
Dark, raspberry-red with shades of violet-blue. Intense fruity aromas are followed by remarkable body and a good tannic element. Produced from Tinto Fino; most representative young wine of the Ribera.

Viña Pedrosa Reserva 1989 🍷 🍷 ②
Cherry-red with violet shades; medium intensity, distinct fruity and spicy aromas, the latter from aging in wood. It has many years of life left.

Viña Pedrosa Gran Reserva 1985 🍷 🍷 ③
Ruby-red with brick highlights; elegant bouquet from aging; marked potency and complexity in the mouth. Smooth and rounded on the palate; develops ample lingering aromas, full of subtle and elegant nuances. Also portrays the personality of the Tinto Fino varietal.

Bodegas Señorío de Nava

Ctra. Valladolid-Soria
Nava de Roa (Burgos)
Tel. (987) 550003
Fax (987) 209800

Señorío de Nava is located in the locality of Nava de Roa, along the banks of the Duero river. Built on 7,000 m2 of land, the facilities have been furnished with the most modern and technologically advanced equipment. Its stainless steel vats have a total capacity for storing 2,000,000 lt of wine. A large portion of this production is destined to carry on to age in one of 2,000 barriques, located in underground cellars. The terrain of this area is characterized by rolling, calcareous hills. The 145 ha of Señorío de Nava's vineyards are planted with the native Tinto Fino (which is, as already noted, the Ribera de Duero's name for Tempranillo), Cabernet Sauvignon and Merlot, the last two providing insurance for the product's final quality. The results of these efforts are certain reds and a few rosés with character, fine craftsmanship and a formula that follows today's preferences, while retaining some of the traditional qualities of this outstanding denomination of origin.

Señorío de Nava Rosado 1991 🏵 ①
Smooth and fruity, unlike other classic Ribera rosés. Fresh, light and pleasing. Produced with Ribera's native Tinto Fino.

Señorío de Nava 1991 🍷 🍷 ①
A full expression of the Tinto Fino personality. Beautiful tannin element; profound and vibrant.

Señorío de Nava Crianza 1986 🍷 ②
Aging in oak for two years confers strength and sprightliness. Smelling stages clearly reveal a strong and possibly excessive aroma of new wood, though accompanied by important fruity nuances. Smooth on the palate, with full-bodied development, light astringency and a considerable chance for improvement in the bottle.

RIBERA DE DUERO
CUENCA DEL DUERO
SPAIN

1044

RIBERA DE DUERO
CUENCA DEL DUERO
SPAIN

Vega Sicilia

Ctra. Valladolid-Soria, km 40.2
Valbuena de Duero (Valladolid)
Tel. (983) 689147
Fax (983) 650263

When Eloy Lacanda y Chaves founded Vega Sicilia in 1864, not in his wildest dreams did he imagine to be setting the foundations for a legend. This brand name is now a status symbol for the most refined international wine drinker. But getting one's hands on a bottle of Vega Sicilia can be difficult for a number of reasons: not for the high price (due to the enormous demand and short supply), but especially for the extremely limited, almost rationed, commercial volumes available. Production currently amounts to 350,000 bottles annually, which has, nonetheless, greatly increased from the 1960s level of only 40,000 bottles. Since its foundation, this winery has crafted wine from noble Bordeaux vines like Cabernet Sauvignon and Merlot, raising the aged reds to a Spanish masterpiece with a touch of French nostalgia. The 965 ha holding, 125 of which are cultivated with vineyards, is situated on the left banks of the Duero river, between the towns of Valbuena and Quintanilla. The rolling hills surrounded by two small sierras that protect the valley from the harsh Castilian climate,together with the Atlantic precipitation conditions, combine to form an ideal microclimate for viticulture. The area's soil is loam-calcareous and dry, of mycenic origin and marked by dark transversal strips with alluvial traces. These are the unique conditions behind the inimitable character of Vega Sicilia's wines.

Valbuena 5° Año 1986   🍇🍇 ④
Produced from the same grape combination as Vega Sicilia Unico, this represents the winery's youngest line of products. Aged in barrique for two years and then in the bottle at length. Beautiful, deep red with shades of brick; intense and bright. Ample array of aromas, not well-blended but of extremely high quality. Powerful and full on the palate, with firm tannin expression.

Vega Sicilia Unico 1964   🍇🍇 ④
Light, clear, cherry-red with brick touches. Grand bouquet with spiced, fruity and jam-like nuances. Rounded, velvety, extremely long and powerful on the palate. Despite its 30-year life, it is vibrant and full of energy.

Vega Sicilia Unico 1982   🍇🍇🍇 ④
A universal projection of undisputable quality. Since the last century, varietals infrequently used in Spain have been cultivated to perfect acclimatization: Cabernet Sauvignon, Merlot and Malbec prosper alongside native Tinto Fino. The grapes are aged in barriques for 30 months. Garnet-red with shades of ruby, very intense with a brick-colored rim. Intense, extremely elegant aromas of wild fruit and spices; accompanied by toasted notes and hints of tobacco. Potent, glycerous and pleasant on the palate. Good tannic expression and well-structured. Extremely refined lingering vapors, recalling the same ones of the bouquet, though more refined.

RIBERA DE DUERO
CUENCA DEL DUERO
SPAIN

1045

RIBERA DE DUERO
CUENCA DEL DUERO
SPAIN

Alvarez y Díez

Juan Antonio Carmona, 16
Nava del Rey (Valladolid)
Tel. (983) 850136

Alvarez y Díez deserves credit for being one of the first wineries of the Rueda DO to have renovate its facilities. Modernization has not, however, altered their traditionally long aging period in wood, for the native Verdejo varietal wines. The winery vinifies only those grapes harvested from its 75 ha of vineyards, located near Nava del Rey. Also known in the area as Tierra del Vino, this city has an age-old wine heritage. Since 1922, four generations of Alvarez y Díez family have produced some extremely fine, classic whites of Rueda. Under the present leadership of Etelvino Sánchez, considered a great sage of Spanish enology, this winery has become one of the most technically well-equipped facilities in all of Spain. Great attention is paid to the vinification process, avoiding the addition of sulphurs or other preservatives. Among the different wines produced, they also make a "Generoso" wine, similar to that of the Jerez and biologically aged.

Mantel Nuevo 1991   🍇 ①
An ecological wine, is there ever was one. Carefully crafted, from start to finish; a Verdejo varietal wine without added sulphur or other preservatives.

Mantel Blanco 1988   🍇 ①
Original, though the Verdejo varietal falls short of its potential expression, remaining a bit suffocated by the wood.

Mantel Pálido   🍇 ①
Among the best examples of biological aging outside of Andalusia. Delicate Verdejo aromas combine with those from aging; powerful and glycerous.

Lorenzo Cachazo

Estación, s/n
Pozáldez (Valladolid)
Tel. (983) 822012

The greatest Spanish innovations, in terms of technology and modern-style wines, have been felt most strongly in white wine producing areas. The Rueda DO is no exception to this rule: its whites have rapidly evolved to become more complete and balanced. Angel Lorenzo's winery is a good example of this positive evolution, along with a very important human element. Angel and his son, Javier, make an extremely harmonious team: the first has produced wine his entire life, the second is a professional enologist. Angel and Javier agree that great wines may come from small wineries, but only if they are well-managed and fully equipped. In this respect, Lorenzo Cachazo is a perfect model of neatness and order, where the fruits of 20 ha of vineyards are vinified. The predominant varietal is Verdejo, but there is also a recent planting of Sauvignon Blanc.

Lorenzo Cachazo 1991   🍇 ①
Straw yellow; very clean, a powerful, complex bouquet and well-structured on the palate. Good quality/price ratio. Made from Verdejo, along with Viura and Palomino.

Martivillí 1991   🍇 🍇 ①
Complex and splendid: one of the better expressions of Verdejo on the palate. Glycerous and persistent on the palate; elegant and bitter aftertaste.

RUEDA
CUENCA DEL DUERO
SPAIN

1046

RUEDA
CUENCA DEL DUERO
SPAIN

B. de Crianza Castilla la Vieja

Ctra. Madrid-La Coruña, km 170
Rueda (Valladolid)
Tel. (983) 868116
Fax (983) 868336

This winery can be found along the road that leads from Madrid to La Coruña, just before the city of Medina del Campo. Medina del Campo was once a royal city. In fact, Isabel the Catholic spent her last years here until she died in 1504. The presence of the royal house lent enough prestige to Rueda wines to favor them in later centuries with London importers. La Bodegas de Crianza Castilla la Vieja is the result of Antonio Sanz's strong will and determination. Part of a long line of growers and wine-makers in the family, Antonio finally realized his dream of building his own winery in 1976, after years of working in his family's winery. The various wines are obtained from grapes bought from other growers, as well as from the winery's own 25 ha of vineyards. The white varietals cultivated include Verdejo, Viura, Sauvignon and Chenin; amongst the reds, there are Tempranillo and Pinot Noir. The house's best whites are those made from Verdejo, which is the star grape of the area and surely one of Antonio's favorite subjects.

Colagón 1991   🍷 ①
Clean, straw yellow, typical of Verdejo. Clear, though not intense, primary aromas; delicate approach on the palate. Light, pleasant with lingering scents, not too long-lasting.

Almirante de Castilla 1985   🍷 ②
Cherry-red with shades of brick. Clean; pure and intense scents from aging. There is going through an interesting phase on the palate, showing clean and powerful lingering scents. It is made with Tempranillo, which is somewhat unusual for the area, thus, can not be a Rueda DO wine.

Bodegas y Viñedos de Malpica

Finca Valdepusa
Malpica de Tajo (Toledo)
Tel. (925) 877170
Fax (91) 4577153

Don Carlos Falcó, Marqués de Griñón, has long been determined to produce a European-class wine. One of the biggest obstacles he has had to overcome is the difficult microclimate of the area, which is hardly suited for this type of wine. He has managed with great success, however, with a little help from modern technology and the latest winemaking equipment. Founded in 1982, he began importing Cabernet Sauvignon, Merlot and Malbec from Bordeaux and hired the world's 'god-father' of modern enology, Emile Peynaud, to oversee production. Just recently, another of Don Carlos's long-time aspiration has come true. His air-conditioned, underground aging cellars are ready finally. Painstaking efforts have amply been recompensed given the quality of the wines, which is constantly rising. Indeed, one is lead to think that best has yet to come. The great, world-class Cabernet is flanked by two excellent whites from the indigenous and worthy Verdejo grape.

Marqués de Griñón Blanco 1991   🍷 ①
Attractive, extremely bright straw-yellow; good intensity of aromas and well-balanced on the palate. Produced exclusively from Verdejo.

Marqués de Griñón   🍷🍷 ②
S. Especial 1990
A Verdejo varietal wine fermented in barrique, it has full, complex smokey aromas to be expected from aging. Ample, glycerous and flavorful on the palate.

Marqués de Griñón   🍇🍇 ③
Cabernet 1986
This wines has a very original bouquet, highlighted by distinct aromas from skillful oak-aging. Well-structured and tannic, it is extremely intense in its aftertaste and finish.

RUEDA
CUENCA DEL DUERO
SPAIN

1047

RUEDA/VINO DE LA TIERRA
CUENCA DEL DUERO
SPAIN

Vinos Blancos de Castilla

Ctra. Madrid-La Coruña, km 172
Rueda (Valladolid)
Tel. (983) 868083
Fax (983) 868563

Marqués de Riscal of Rioja has been producing world-class red wines for almost a century. In 1972 they decided to open another winery in Rueda, thus leading blazing the trail to the production of excellent white wines to compliment Riscal's great Rioja reds. Unfortunately, Vinos Blancos de Castilla was founded in a time when winemaking in Rueda was noticeably lacking in enthusiasm. The wines were not meeting new qualitative expectations (not only on the world scale), and the vineyards were being overtaken by imported varietals that were easier to work with. The native Verdejo almost completely slipped away, until the winery brought it back as their first great investment (planting 86 ha of it). Verdejo has made an enormous comeback and is now one of the most noble grapes in the country. Today, some everyone will agree that if Rueda's wines are a success much is due to the Verdejo. In later years, 60 ha were planted with Sauvignon, which took well and has since made exceptional wines. Annual production exceeds 125,000 cases of all white wine, with a good following both on the domestic market as well as beyond the borders.

Marqués de Riscal 1991   ♥ ①
Clean and sincere in all three phases of the tasting: well-structured, with an elegant, bitter note in the finish, typical of the Verdejo grape.

Marqués de Riscal Sauvignon 1991   ♥ ①
Pale yellow with bright, with silvery highlights; floral aromas of acacia and sambuco flowers; a smooth initial approach on the palate, light and extremely delicate as it opens.

Marqués de Riscal   ♥♥ ②
Limousin 1990
One of the best whites with solid aging potential made in the country. With good aromas from the new barrique, it shows green fruit undertones and a lightly bitter aftertaste as to be expected from the Verdejo.

Vinos Sanz

Ctra. Madrid-La Coruña, km 170
Rueda (Valladolid)
Tel. (983) 868100

This prestigious winery began its long family history of wine-making in 1870. It is situated along the life-giving banks of the Duero, in its most enologically important white wine area. There are a total of 70 ha of proprietor vineyards, planted mostly with the noble Verdejo grape with some room left for Viura and Sauvignon Blanc. Enologist Juan Carlos Ayala oversees the modernly-equipped, 700,000-lt capacity winery. In order to fulfil the exclusively white wine production of 600,000 lt annually, the winery is forced to buy grapes from area growers, although there are plans to become completely self-sufficient and purchase choice vineyards nearby. Several years ago, the largest wine club in the country, "Vinoselección", bought controlling stock in the winery. Luckily the move has not jeopardized Sanz's quality standards and upward direction as marked out by the Sanz family.

Sauvignon 1991   ♥ ①
Unmistakably Sauvignon, with its elegant and intense floral bouquet of acacia and elderflowers. There's just the right amount of unctuousness and acidity on the palate for balance and fullness.

Rueda Superior 1991   ♥ ①
Made from mostly Verdejo with small amounts of Viura, it is extremely aromatic, with floral tones; exceptionally clean. Glycerous and flavorful on the palate; lightly bitter and quite elegant on the finish.

Bodegas Fariña

Ctra. Moraleja, s/n
Casaseca de las Chanas (Zamora)
Tel. (988) 571173
Fax (988) 690898

Extremely warm and high in alcohol with their heady long, traditional aging process, Toro DO wines were slowly disappearing and were ill-fated to become blending wines, as a crutch for the more fashionable, light to medium-bodied wines. Don Manuel Fariña was firmly convinced of the area's potential and began to produce wine with a new concept: lower alcohol and shorter aging in wood (more importantly, new wood), thus allowing primary aromas to more fully express themselves. The soon to be seen results were encouraging; the wines were the surprise hit on every winetasting event they entered and even became model wines for the area's wine-makers. Don Manuel Fariña deserves the credit for believing in and demonstrating the immense capabiilities of the local Tinta de Toro grape. After all, it is similar to Tempranillo in fruitiness, color intensity and fullness. Bodegas Fariña's Gran Colegiata is an extremely modern wine but borne in a wine region with a very ancient tradition.

Colegiata 1989
Cherry-red with shades of violet-blue; intense and warm bouquet, ample on the palate. Produced from the local Tinta de Toro; skillful aging in barrique imparts good body and firm tannin.

Gran Colegiata 1986
Deep, clean cherry-red in color; intense and fruity with good secondary aromas, too, from the fermentation. Powerful with lots of firm tannin on the palate, thanks to the Tinta de Toro.

J. M. Fermoselle

Av. de Galicia, 129
Zamora
Tel. (988) 525573
Fax (988) 512829

Despite the current crisis, the Toro DO wines have such qualitative potential that, as soon as they become slightly better adapted to the ways of the marketplace, they will surely rise to immortal heights. Many coinciding factors are present for the making of great wines, most importantly a microclimate and terrain perfectly adapted to vine-growing. The grape of choice here is inarguably Tinta de Toro, which is, in fact, the close relative of Rioja's Tempranillo grape. Fermoselle is one of the wineries at the root of the area's rebirth in winemaking. Having realized the need to upgrade production technology, it created and launched new styles of younger, more modern wines, something that would have been unheard of before. The winery owns 50 ha of vineyards that are mainly planted with Tinta de Toro. Enviously independent, Fermoselle is not obliged to buy all the grapes needed from other growers. The underground cellars are especially beautiful and are well-suited to age their wines.

Novíssimo de Toro Rosado 1991
Lovely strawberry-pink in color; medium-intense fruity aromas; powerful on the palate, with distinct personality. Rather long-lasting. A convincing blend of Tinta de Toro and Malvasia.

Catedral de Zamora 1988
A classic in the area, it reminds one of how the traditional Toro wines used to be; full-bodied and slightly oxidized. A very typical Spanish blend of Tinta de Toro, Tinta de Madrid, Verdejo and Mencía.

Señorío de Toro Etiqueta Negra 1988
Rather intense cherry-red colored, with marked aromas from the wood aging, with a slight reduction. Powerful and big in alcohol; well-structured on the palate and rather long-lasting. 100% Tinta de Toro.

TORO
CUENCA DEL DUERO
SPAIN

1049

TORO
CUENCA DEL DUERO
SPAIN

P. P. Cistercienses

Monasterio de San Pedro de Cardeña
Castrillo del Val (Burgos)
Tel/Fax (947) 290033

On occasion, a wine can reflect the surroundings from which it is borne and take on more spiritual qualities. Such must be the affect of the ancient Romanesque stones as well as the meditative silences and murmurs of Gregorian chants on Valdevegón wine, still today made by the Cistercense monks. Although probably destined for more commercial or frivolous functions, it certainly exudes an overwhelming aura of peace when corked. As for the wine's pedigree, we only know for sure that the high-priests used to buy it young directly in the Rioja, from a prestigious winery, and that Father Marcos, the abbot and cellarman of the monastery, oversees the patient and well-crafted transformation of it into good reserve wine. Despite the short distance from the Ribera del Duero wine region, the monastery does not own vineyards. Vineyards did exist at one time but were later neglected and abbandoned. Today the whole area is being replanted with more common grapes. The Monastery of San Pedro de Cardeña is in the territory of Burgos, which is also the famous birthplace of Rodrigo Díaz, otherwise better known as El Cid, the legendary 11th century hero.

Valdevegón 1987 ☙ ②
Ruby-red with brick highlights, characteristic aromas from the wood aging, good impact on the palate and excellent lingering aromas. Made from a blend of Tempranillo, Garnacha and Mazuelo.

Valdevegón Reserva 1982 ☙ ③
Though made from wine brought in from another region, this wine develops its own most original character with master fining and aging. Produced from the same grapes as regular Valdevegòn.

Mauro

Cervantes, 12
Tudela de Duero (Valladolid)
Tel. (983) 521439
Fax (983) 392844

Housed in a beautiful 16th-century building, Mauro produces some of the best, characterful wines in this prestigious area. Tinto Fino (also known as Tinta del País though it is very similar to Tempranillo), Garnacha and Albillo are the varietals cultivated on the winery's ten hectares of vineyards. These vines, along with other grapes purchased from other trustworthy growers, provide the base for extremely interesting wines that have been a commercial success since their first year of production in 1979. The aging cellars boast 300 Nevers French barriques, which are largely responsible for Mauro wines' distinctive bouquet. Founded by Luciano Suárez, Mauro is located just outside the Ribera del Duero DO border. Consequently, its wines do not fall within this DO's limits; instead they are considered "Vinos de la Tierra", meaning they are produced with more than 60% of grapes from one specifc region. They fall in the middle, being classified between "Vinos de mesa" table wines and DO name and origin wines.

Mauro 1987 ☙ ☙ ②
Medium intense, clear brick-red in color. Secondary perfumes are well-integrated with the primary ones; well-balanced and full-bodied on the palate, perfect lingering scents, full of refined wood and spices. Made with Fino, Garnacha and a small part of the white Albillo.

VINOS DE LE TIERRA
CUENCA DEL DUERO
SPAIN

1050

VINOS DE LE TIERRA
CUENCA DEL DUERO
SPAIN

Cuenca del Ebro

The Ebro river is considered Spain's great 'wine river,' and its banks are home to the country's most prestigious Denomination of Origin zone, La Rioja. The main grapes cultivated on the 30,000 hectares of vineyards include the indigenous Tempranillo, Graciano, Garnacha, Mazuela and Viura. By carefully adjusting the percentages, they are blended into "coupages" and are at the heart of Spain's best-quality aged reds. This DO comprises the whole independent community of the same name, as well as some communities bordering Alava and Navarra.

Rioja is subdivided into three zones: Rioja Alavesa, Rioja Alta and Rioja Baja. The first belongs to the Basque province of Alava; here the terrain is terraced and the altitudes vary from 400 m to almost 800 m above sea level. Rioja Alta, with a similar microclimate and vineyards between 600 m and 700 m above sea level, covers the western border of the DO area. On the eastern front, Rioja Baja is lower than the others and has a hotter, drier climate. Rioja is the first Spanish DO to have been elevated to the "Calificada" status, the exclusive category reserved for regions producing superior quality wines. This status was attributed on April 3, 1991, but the work leading up to it began in the 1970s. It was made effective only years later, due to trouble encountered in establishing fundamental requirements at the base of the DO's legislation. More specifically, there was a need to set a threshold for the price of the grapes that was higher than the national average as well as the obligatory practise of having to sell all bottled product.

Along its journey, the Ebro flows through other wine regions that are currently undergoing profound technological renewal. One of these is the Navarra. With over 27,000 ha of vineyards, it is planted with the same grapes as the Rioja in addition to some white Malvasía and Moscatell. The principal DO in this area is likewise called Navarra, and it covers six communities along the banks of the Ebro within the Rioja. The Navarra DO is most famous for its Garnacha-based rosé. More recently, French red grapes are doing well, the best, more convincing results coming from the Cabernet and Merlot.

The last region, Aragona, has over 100,000 ha of vineyards and includes the Campo de Borja DO, Cariñena DO and, most importantly, the Somontano DO, in the province of Huesca. Already quite distant from the river, Somontano grows nobile varietals like Cabernet Sauvignon, Merlot, Chardonnay, Riesling and Gewürztraminer with surprisingly excellent results. It is one of the most up and coming regions in Spain.

Coop. Comarcal San Alejandro

Ctra. Calatayud, s/n
Miedes de Aragón (Saragozza)
Tel. (976) 892205

The DO Calatayud, the youngest in Aragona and almost unknown in the rest of the country, covers 14,000 ha of vineyards in the province of Saragozza. Almost all the wineries here are cooperatives that, until recently, sold their products in bulk and weren't overly concerned about receiving recognition for the quality of their wine. San Alejandro, one of the best known in the area, has 600 member growers that each year contribute to a total production of 4,000,000 kg of grapes, harvested from 1,400 ha of vineyards. Garnacha is the most common varietal, together with Tempranillo and the other white varietals, Viura, Malvasía and Moscatel. There are also some experimental vines of Cabernet Sauvignon. However, their jump in quality is relatively new, having begun only three years ago, which is long enough to fully develop or judge its qualitative potential. Only 5% of the grapes harvested go to make San Alejandro's most prestigious line of young-drinking whites, reds and rosés.

Marqués de Nombrevilla Rosado 1991
Garnacha's fruity quality results in a delicious bouquet. Very distinct strawberry pink; flavorful and full-bodied on the palate. Lingering aromas are intense, clean and very fruity.

Sociedad Coop. Agrícola de Borja

Capuchinos, 10
Borja (Saragozza)
Tel. (976) 867116

Established in 1958, Borja is one of the more recent cooperatives in Aragona. Modern and dynamic, it is rather out of place among the panorama of generally stagnant associations. The enologists seek to produce a modern-tasting wine, trying to eliminate certain defects which prevent wines from this part of Aragon from being entirely acceptable to the modern-day palate. The techniques are rather advanced, and the equipment modern, including stainless steel vats, refrigeration systems and underground cellars furnished with 200 barriques. The members of the cooperative own a total of 1,600 ha of vineyards planted with the red varietals Garnacha, Tempranillo, Cariñena and Cabernet and the white Macabeo.

Gran Campellas Tinto 1991
Beautiful ruby red with shades of brick. Primary aromas of mature fruit blend with secondary ones resulting in a medium intensity. Clean and potent on the palate, with good lingering aromas featuring scents from aging in wood. Produced from Garnacha and Tempranillo.

Borsao Tinto 1990
Cherry red with shades of violet-blue; extremely clean with intense and pure aromas of fruit. Smooth impact amplifies on the palate, becoming flavorful, potent and full-bodied. Delicate lingering scents.

CALATAYUD
CUENCA DEL EBRO
SPAIN

1052

CAMPO DE BORJA
CUENCA DEL EBRO
SPAIN

San Valero

Ctra. Saragozza-Valencia, km 46
Cariñena (Saragozza)
Tel. (976) 640425
Fax (976) 620425

There have been vines in this region for two centuries, and for almost as long, the wines from the area have been among the most respected in Spain. The robust reds, however, are no longer in-keeping with modern tastes. San Valero, a cooperative, deserves credit for wisely adapting its outstanding wines to the times. Lighter, more aromatic and lower in alcohol, these products have still kept their distinctive character. The principal varietals used in the production of these wine are Garnacha, Tempranillo and Mazuelo. Raw materials are never scarce, as between them the members own 5,000 ha of vineyards which yield 160,000 hl of wine. Despite such large figures and mass production, the cooperative manages to offer some very interesting wines.

Monte Ducay Tinto 1986
From Garnacha, Tempranillo and Mazuelo. Delicious, clear, ruby red with shades of brick. Secondary perfumes feature wood and fruity aromas. Balanced and long-lasting on the palate.

Marqués de Tosos 1985
Clear, ruby red with shades of brick; secondary perfumes emphasize wood with fruity notes. Balanced and long-lasting on the palate.

Viuda de Luís Gasca

Ctra. Saragozza-Valencia, km 37
Longares (Saragozza)
Tel. (976) 377242

Established in Longares in 1983, this winery is housed in an attractive modern designed building. The techniques used in wine production are also modern. The company manages to balance the conflicting concepts and ideals of making wines that are suited to current tastes while also preserving the ancient tradition of the Cariñena DO, an area once known for its particularly robust and highly alcoholic wines. The well-tended vines feature a high proportion of red grapes like Garnacha, Tempranillo and Cabernet Sauvignon. The future is still open, however, to the production of good white wine: some experimental plots have been reserved for the more famous European varietals like Riesling, Gewürztraminer and Chardonnay, which will share space in the vineyard with the already established Macabeo grape. Production is approximately 240,000 bottles per year.

Señorío Gasca Gimeno 1983
Obtained from Garnacha and Tempranillo grapes; cherry red with shades of brick. Aromas from aging in wood with traces of overripe grapes. Smooth approach on the palate; a bit warm and not long-lasting.

Selección Luis Gasca Cabernet
With perfect aging in barrique, it has all the right characteristics for improvement with more bottle aging over the next five years.

CARIÑENA
CUENCA DEL EBRO
SPAIN

1053

CARIÑENA
CUENCA DEL EBRO
SPAIN

Bodegas Cenalsa

Ciudadela, 5
Pamplona
Tel. (948) 227294
Fax (948) 229999

Cenalsa was established in 1983 by a consortium that involved private wineries, the local savings and loan bank and the Regional Government of Navarra and is represented by EVENA (Estación de Viticultura y Enología de Navarra, an agency specialized in the study of the terrain and vines of Navarra). The vineyards used for production lie between the dry and humid areas of Navarra. Planted here are the classic regional varietals: mostly Garnacha, but also Tempranillo and Cabernet Sauvignon (currently in vogue throughout Spain). The white varietals Viura, Malvasía and Moscatel are used to produce a very fine, balanced white. In recent years a concentrated effort to improve quality has incited the winery to upgrade its vinification cellars with better, technologically-advanced equipment. As a result, increased winemaking capacity has brought production up to 5,000,000 bottles a year, a third of which is exported. The winery also provides an important incentive for other producers in the area, by encouraging research and greater initiative.

Príncipe de Viana Rosado 1991
Distinct and pretty raspberry, not very intense but particularly clear. Fruity notes of medium intensity from the Garnacha varietal. Light and fresh on the palate; not very full-bodied but frank and pleasant.

Agramont Tinto 1989
An excellent blend of Garnacha, Tempranillo and Cabernet Sauvignon (as well as light aging in wood) renders the wine full-bodied, flavorful and long-lasting. Distinct tannins assure a few years' life ahead.

Julián Chivite Marco

Ribera, s/n
Cintruénigo (Navarra)
Tel. (948) 110000
Fax (948) 811407

The revival of Navarra's wines began with the rosé, which brings out Garnacha's excellent delicate, fruity qualities beautifully. But, in all truth, Julián Chivite is largely responsible what with his famous rosé Gran Feudo, highly acclaimed throughout Spain and beyond for years and years. His success is not altogether surprising, considering he comes from a family which boasts a tradition of wine-making dating back to 1647. The harvest from 200 ha of estate-vineyards is still not sufficient to meet the huge demand for his wine, and he is obliged to buy grapes from local growers. The winery is furnished with the latest equipment and has all it takes to produce high quality wines. Also interesting are the reds, for which there is a specially built, underground cellar with over 10,000 barriques.

Gran Feudo Rosado 1991
Typical characteristics of a Navarra rosé; seductive color, fruity and unmistakable aromas, light and delicate on the palate. Produced with Garnacha, it is unbeatable in its type.

Chivite 1987
Clear cherry red with shades of brick; secondary aromas are strong on the nose. Tannic and long, it is in-keeping with modern wines. Obtained from Tempranillo and Garnacha grapes.

125° Aniversario 1985
High quality though rather unusual for Navarra. Outstanding secondary aromas; lots of flavor, long and lingering on the palate. Slightly sweet aftertaste. A coupage of Tempranillo and Garnacha.

NAVARRA
CUENCA DEL EBRO
SPAIN

1054

NAVARRA
CUENCA DEL EBRO
SPAIN

Bodegas Guelbenzu

Calle San Juan, 14
Cascante (Navarra)
Tel. (948) 850055

This winery began to make its mark in the first half of last century when it attended the World Exposition in London. After a period of success (which lasted until the end of the century), the wines slowly fell in terms of quality until they were finally sold off in bulk to the Cooperative of Cascante. In 1980 the current owners, the Guelbenzu brothers, completely replanted the winery's 38 ha of vineyards with the noble varietals of Bordeaux, Cabernet and Merlot, adding force to the native Tempranillo. Every phase of cultivation was scrupulously and meticulously overseen: heavy pruning in order to control fruit production, careful use of fertilizers, etc. The well-equipped facilities feature cellars for aging, known as "naves de crianza", which utilize well-selected Allier, Limousin and Nevers barriques. In short, having survived the rough 'white waters', Bodegas Guelbenzu is now making every effort to produce good wine.

Guelbenzu Evo 1988   🍇 ②
Extremely aromatic, well-structured with a good tannin. Will certainly improve in the next ten years. A blend of Tempranillo and Cabernet Sauvignon.

Bodegas Irache

Irache, 1
Ayegui (Navarra)
Tel. (948) 551932

The name Bodegas Irache comes from a monastery dating back to the Gothic period, which served as a gathering place for pilgrims in the 11th century. Surrounded by many wonderful places of historic interest, the winery is situated along the legendary road that leads to Santiago de Compostela and the ranges of Montejurra. Bodegas Irache, now nearing its 100th birthday, has preserved its name and prestige, despite a change of ownership in the 1960s. Thanks to the well-equipped cellars, the winery has been able to create a wide range of products without jeapordizing quality. The vineyards are planted with the classic varietals of the area which include Garnacha, Tempranillo, Graciano and Mazuelo amongst the reds and Malvasía and Viura for the whites. Harvests are insufficient to satisfy production needs, so grapes have to bought from other growers in Tierra Estella, still within the Navarra's DO area.

Gran Irache Tinto 1986   🍇 ②
Striking coupage of Garnacha, Tempranillo and Graciano; beautiful cherry red with slight tinges of brick. Bouquet is complex but not very powerful, with pleasant scents from aging in barrique. Well-structured, flavorful and long on the palate.

Castillo Irache Tinto 1982   🍇 ②
From the same varietals as above; rubyish with distinct shades of brick. Hints of reduction on the nose; soft and rounded on the palate though not very long.

NAVARRA
CUENCA DEL EBRO
SPAIN

1055

NAVARRA
CUENCA DEL EBRO
SPAIN

Bodegas Magaña

San Miguel, 3
Barillas (Navarra)
Tel. (948) 850034
Fax (948) 826517

One of the most extraordinary phenomena of the last ten years in the world of wine, has been provided by the Magaña brothers, who, having established their winery in 1969, set out to produce high quality wines that were different from the norm in Navarra. The brothers chose the Bordeaux varietals (Cabernet Sauvignon, Cabernet Franc, Merlot and Malbec) and also the reigning Côtes de Rhone grape, Syrah. These vines have adapted rapidly to the terrain, thanks in part to a technologically advanced system of cultivation. In addition, an experimental nursery has also been created to select not only the different varietals but also the strains that are most suited to the area's terrain and climate. Surprisingly enought, the result was a model wine that went against the then-accepted tastes but is now heavily imitated. The true pioneers, in their aim to keep a step ahead of the rest, in the avant-garde, have now recently built a new and remarkable winery that was designed by the brilliant architect Rafael Moneo.

Viña Magaña Reserva 1983 🍇🍇 ②
Pleasant cherry red with some medium-intense shades of brick. Elegant, spicy, green pepper and mint aromas; soft and full on the palate, long and flavorful. Obtained from the same coupage as the Viña Magaña 1982.

Viña Magaña Gran Reserva 1982 🍇🍇 ③
Excellent blend of the varietals Cabernet, Merlot, Malbec and Syrah. Hardly an easy wine both to make and to drink, it is slightly closed at first, it crescendos to a grand finish. Before drinking, allow to breathe for a while.

Viña Magaña Merlot 🍇🍇🍇 ③
Reserva 1985
This wine is full of great sensations. Beautiful cherry red tends towards shades of brick, assuring a good future. Complex on the nose, with spicy tones that feature green pepper, then a refreshing peak of balsamic herbs and roasted coffee aromas. Well-structured, ample and long on the palate; pleasant and lightly tannic, it clearly brings to mind all the features of the varietal. Initial perfumes are echoed in lingering aromas that are, however, cleaner and more elegant. Viña Magaña Merlot 1985 is one of the three or four best wines in Spain, and has an authentic European dimension.

NAVARRA
CUENCA DEL EBRO
SPAIN

1056

NAVARRA
CUENCA DEL EBRO
SPAIN

Vinícola Navarra

Ctra. Pamplona-Zaragoza, km 14
Campanas (Navarra)
Tel. (948) 360131
Fax (948) 360275

This winery lies just minutes away from the city of Pamplona, home of the best and most authentic festivals in Europe. It seems there are few festivals where as much wine is drunk in such a happy and carefree (and relatively accident-free) atmosphere, as during the feast days of San Fermin of Pamplona. The great tradition of Navarran wine and a strong work ethic go hand in hand in this winery, bringing them recognition for their classic rosés. But instead of resting on their laurels and contenting themselves with the past successes, the owners of Vinícola Navarra are constantly modernizing their facilities. The rosé Las Campanas is one of the winery's classics, appreciated by wine-drinkers for its freshness and its extremely pleasant aroma. This important winery's production reaches 70,000 hl annually: it is mostly rosé of a very high standard although a few aged reds and some reserve wines are also produced. For the aging of these reds, there are cellars containing almost 2,000 oak casks. The vinification facilities are modern and efficient.

Las Campanas Rosado 1991　🍶 ①
A pleasant, unpretentious rosé wine, which really makes the most of everything the Garnacha varietal has to offer for this type of wine.

Castillo de Tiebas 1982　🍷 ②
A classic red from Navarra. Ruby red with brick highlights; moderately well-structured and rather aromatic with smooth and rounded flavors. Produced from Tempranillo (80%) and Garnacha (20%).

Bodegas Ochoa

Ctra. de Zaragoza, 21
Olite (Navarra)
Tel. (948) 740006
Fax (948) 740048

If the Navarran community of Olite, with its long wine-making tradition, has achieved a certain degree fame in the wine world, it is thanks to a man whose dire passion for wine has been a constant driving force in his quest for quality and innovation. Javier Ochoa's wines carry the unmistakable stamp of products made conscientiously and lovingly. In his old cellars, dating back to 1845 and situated in the town center, French and American barriques are used to perfect wines and to age reserves. The growth in business has obliged Ochoa to build another new facility where wines may be easily vinified using the most up-to-date techniques, techniques which he has adopted in a highly professional manner. Ochoa's 15 ha of vineyards are insufficient to cover production, forcing him to carefully select and buy additional grapes elsewhere. His wife, Mariví Alemán, handles the administration and public relations for their winery.

Ochoa Cabernet Sauvignon 1987　🍷 ②
Here this grape seems to have found its second great home, giving birth to a richly tannic wine of great character. Here is proof that this varietal is very suitable to and successful in the Navarran soil.

Ochoa Tempranillo 1986　🍷 ②
Refined to perfection in barrique, this wine has achieved perfect harmony and balance.

Ochoa Reserva 1985　🍷 ②
A typical coupage of the area: Tempranillo and Garnacha. Delicately aromatic and extremely soft on the palate.

NAVARRA
CUENCA DEL EBRO
SPAIN

1057

NAVARRA
CUENCA DEL EBRO
SPAIN

Bodega Coop.
Nuestra Señora del Romero
Ctra. Tarazona, 33
Cascante (Navarra)
Tel. (948) 851411

Cascante is in the heart of Ribera Baja, characterized as the driest area in the whole Navarra DO. For this precise reason, its wines have a tendency to be full-bodied, concentrated and high in alcohol. The cooperative Nuestra Señora del Romero, almost 40 years-old, represents almost all the viticulturalists in the community. More than 1,200 growers pool their production from 1,500 ha of vineyards planted with Garnacha, Tempranillo and Viura varietals. The vinification facilities, recently redesigned, are capable of holding up to 12 million lt of wine. This huge quantity does not always make for high quality wines. The Coop.'s rosés, however, produced by means of a highly prized vinification process, have achieved great success. This is especially true for Malón de Echaide, which is an outstanding, highly traditional wine through and through. It is one of the most successful rosés in Navarra.

Malón de Echaide Rosado 1991
Produced fom Garnacha; pale pink with extremely light shades of violet. Fruity aromas are not very intense but are pure and natural. Delicate, light and fresh on the palate though not very long-lasting.

Nuevo Vino Tinto 1991
Clear cherry red with shades of violet-blue. Intense fruity aromas. Well-structured, full-bodied and slightly tannic on the palate. 100% Garnacha.

Bodega Coop. Virgen Blanca
Ctra. Calahorra, s/n
Lerín (Navarra)
Tel. (948) 530076
Fax (948) 530589

Over the years the town of Lerín has achieved well-deserved recognition for its excellent wines. It must be said that in this part of Ribera (in western Navarra), there are some truly noble and full-bodied rosés. Rosé wine has been made in this area since when the roads of the region were filled with thousands of pilgrims heading for Santiago de Compostela. The Cooperative Virgen Blanca, established in 1956, fully deserves its outstanding reputation for producing one of the best rosés in the whole Navarra DO. For its own production, it utilizes grapes harvested from the members' 450 ha of vineyards, where there are numerous varietals: the most important, or the 'alma mater' of these wines, is Garnacha. There are also Tempranillo and Mazuelo grapes for reds, and Malvasía and Viura for the whites. Vinification cellars are furnished with modern equipment and an underground cellar containing 300 barriques.

Viña Sardasol Rosado 1991
Bright blackcurrant with copper highlights. Remarkable fruit aromas (peach and apricot) from the Garnacha varietal, with intense traces of lemon peel. Smooth approach and satisfactory development with pure lingering scents displaying clean floral aromas.

Viña Sardasol Tinto 1987
Clear cherry red with brick shades. Secondary aromas are not very intense but clean and pleasant. Smooth, full-bodied and flavorful on the palate, though not very long. Produced from Tempranillo, Garnacha and Viura.

NAVARRA
CUENCA DEL EBRO
SPAIN

1058

NAVARRA
CUENCA DEL EBRO
SPAIN

Cosecheros Alaveses

Ctra. de Logroño, s/n
Laguardia (Alava)
Tel. (941) 100119
Fax (941) 100850

In 1985 Juan Carlos López launched Cosecheros Alaveses when he joined the forces of ten producers from the highly renowned wine-producing towns of Elvillar, Elciego and Leza. The objective was to unite their production and marketing efforts. The winery owns a total of 125 ha of vineyards, almost entirely planted with Tempranillo, and production reaches 600,000 lt each year. The rules governing vinification are rather unusual: members vinify part of their harvest in their own individual wineries, according to the traditional Rioja method, which is similar to carbonic maceration style. Each phase of production is carefully overseen by enologists from the central winery, located in Laguardia, where the rest of the harvest is vinified. The enologists of Cosecheros Alaveses have some of the newest technology for vinification at their finger tips, as well as some 500 French and American barriques, now containing some of the best, modern-style Rioja wines.

Artadi 1991   🍇 ①
Rioja's best "cosechero": s high quality, traditionally vinified and aged wine. Intense and extremely aromatic with plenty of tannin. Made from Tempranillo and 10% white Viura.

Viñas de Gaín 1987   🍇 ①
One of the biggest advantages of the wood aging is that it allows the allows full expression of the fruit. A modern-style wine, well-structured and flavorful. Produced from Tempranillo.

Amézola de la Mora

Paraje Viejo, s/n
Torremontalvo (La Rioja)
Tel. (941) 454532
Fax (941) 363476

During the last century, a high proportion of Riojan producers were noble aristocrats. Some have maintained the same ownership and still carry the names of their noble pioneers, such as Murrieta and Riscal. Others, on the other hand, abandoned their ruined vineyards during the difficult years of phylloxera and turned instead to grain cultivation or other occupations still. One such producer was the Count of Hervia, the great-grandfather of Iñigo Amézola de la Mora who, 135 years later, took on the responsibility of rebuilding his family's winery. The restoration of the old stone walls, ruined by mold and humidity, the repristination of the old vineyards (and the planting of new ones) and the creation of a technologically advanced winery with over 2000 barriques has set the stage for a happy combination of events. The harvests and careful vinification are producing all the hoped-for results, and enologists are predicting even better results from the most recent years (1989 and 1990 in particular).

Viña Amézola Crianza 1987   🍇 ②
Well-produced according to the latest Riojan style, with less wood and more fruity accents. The aromatic potential of Tempranillo is clearly expressed.

Amézola Reserva 1986
Deep cherry/red currant-red with light brick highlights; the fruity aromas (from the grape) and the spicy tones from aging in wood are well-balanced. Light on the palate; produced from Tempranillo and Mazuelo.

RIOJA
CUENCA DEL EBRO
SPAIN

1059

RIOJA
CUENCA DEL EBRO
SPAIN

Bodegas Barón de Ley

Mendavia (Navarra)
Tel. (941) 122216
Fax (941) 111015

The recently established Barón de Ley, closely linked to the El Coto winery in Rioja Alavesa, was created with the intention of making wines like a Bordeaux château would. The vinification site, equipped with the most advanced technology, is located in a beautiful, antique stone building surrounded by gardens. From here emerge some very interesting, newly-conceived wine; with less emphasis on wood aging. Some 3,000 mostly new barriques can be found in the cellars of the winery, set up in 1985 and considered one of the most modern establishments in the Rioja DO. The 100 ha of vineyards, planted almost entirely with Tempranillo, surround the solitary headquarters and extend all the way down to the banks of the Ebro. The enchanting beauty of the winery and its surrounding landscape mark the place where Navarra blurs into the Rioja.

Barón de Ley Reserva 1985 ❦ ②
Intense, cherry red with brick highlights. Clear wood aromas accompanied by strong fruity tones. Slightly sweet, well-structured and full-bodied on the palate. Produced from Tempranillo and aged in oak for two years.

Barón de Ley Reserva 1982 ❦ ③
Dark cherry red with slight tinges of brick; quite clear. Good, strong aromas from aging. Silky, ample and long on the palate. Pleasant and generous lingering aromas with fruity and toasted tones. Also made entirely from Tempranillo.

Bodegas Beronia

Ctra. Ollauri-Nájera, s/n
Ollauri (La Rioja)
Tel. (941) 338000
Fax (941) 338266

Established in the 1970s, Bodegas Beronia was inspired by a dream common to many of the wineries which started up around then in this prestigious wine-making region of Spain: to create a wine along the lines of the wines of the great French châteaux across the border. The first location was in the cellars of Ollauri, in Churrumendi, using the name Bodegas Ollauri. Later, in 1978, the winery was moved to the slopes of Mount Mendiguerra, just a few minutes from the city of Ollauri but still in the midst of vineyards. The unusual character of the wine from this cellar is a result of the long period of aging in wood, as well as refining in the bottle for the reserve wines, in fact, the wine remains in the cellars, to age in the bottle, until it has acquired all the desired features which make up its unique character. Beronia also has a policy of not releasing his reserve vintages until at least five years after harvest. The winery is actually part of a powerful group that also controls González Byass of Jerez; Beronia's principal market is abroad, where it sells 75% of its produce.

Beronia Blanco 1991 ❦ ①
Fresh and natural expression of Viura, accompanied on the nose by some truly interesting fig aromas.

Beronia Reserva 1985 ❦ ③
A fine example of wine made by the book: it ages 22 months in barrique and 20 months in bottle and is a blend of the four classic Rioja grapes, Tempranillo, Garnacha, Mazuelo and Graciano.

Beronia Reserva 1982 ❦ ③
Complex and honest with fruity and spicy nuances; balanced and generous. Similar in character to the above and equally satisfying.

RIOJA
CUENCA DEL EBRO
SPAIN

1060

RIOJA
CUENCA DEL EBRO
SPAIN

Bodegas Bilbaínas

Particular del Norte, 2
Bilbao (Vizcaya)
Tel. (94) 4152815
Fax (94) 4150059

The story of this winery begins in the town of Bilbao, a most unusual setting for wine-making. Strange not because this port-town doesn't appreciate wine (quite the contrary, indeed), but because there isn't a single vine in the whole area. Bilbaínas was established in 1901 by Santiago Ugarte, who soon after bought up wineries in the Riojan villages of Haro and Elciego and in other regions like Valdepeñas (home of another large Bilbaínas winery). Headquarters still remained in Bilbao even when, in 1925, a branch office was opened in London. The equipment in the vinification sites is typical of Rioja: there is ample space for 14,000 barriques and for the storage of 1,000,000 bottles. Proprietors of the winery own a total of 250 ha of vineyards planted with the typical Riojan varietals, guaranteeing 80% of the grapes needed for production, while the remaining 20% is provided by nearby viticulturalists.

Viña Zaco Reserva 1985 ☙ ②
Complex and clear aromas from lengthy aging in oak, smooth and balanced on the palate. A coupage of Tempranillo, Garnacha and Graciano.

Viña Pomal Reserva 1982 ☙ ③
Medium intensity and clear ruby red; a Rioja Alta classic. Rounded and ample on the palate, with two full years of oak-aging. This is the winery's benchmark wine.

Gran Zaco 1976 ☙ ③
The best feature of this wine is its impressive bouquet: complex, intense and characteristic of Rioja. Result of Tempranillo, Garnacha and Graciano; well-aged, with long periods both in wood and in the bottle.

Bodegas Campillo

Ctra. Logroño, s/n
Laguardia (Alava)
Tel. (941) 100826
Fax (941) 100837

Situated right in the middle of the beautiful Santa Lucia estate, the brand new Campillo is the result of a long-time aspiration of the Martinéz family. Also owners of the Faustino Martínez winery, the Martínez family cultivates 24 ha of vineyards on this estate (out of a total of 45 owned by the winery), almost exclusively planted with Tempranillo. The estate is located in the vine-covered area of Languardia, a town famous for its great wine tradition. Since its establishment in 1990, new vinification facilities have been built, completely furnished with modern equipment and advanced technology, such as oxidation-proof steel vats with a capacity of 1,500,000 lt. Campillo produces only aged wines, reserve or great reserve, taking advantage of the 8,000 barriques in its precious cellars. The area available for bottle storage is also vast, and can, in fact, hold up to two million. The most of the wines made by this Bodega are for export.

Campillo Crianza 1987 ☙ ②
An attractive, intense ruby red; pleasant aromas with tones of fruit and wood. Smooth on the palate, with good development, slightly tannic. 100% Tempranillo, it will improve with bottle aging.

Campillo Reserva 1985 ☙ ③
Cherry red with a ruby background; good, strong aromas, good body and a remarkable character on the palate, with a slightly tannic quality and good lingering aromas. Here, Tempranillo benefits from two years of oak-aging and two years in the bottle.

Campillo Gran Reserva 1978 ☙ ③
Beautiful ruby red, with good aromas; velvety and round on the palate; it has the qualities most characteristic of the old Rioja Alavesa wines. 100% Tempranillo.

RIOJA
CUENCA DEL EBRO
SPAIN

1061

RIOJA
CUENCA DEL EBRO
SPAIN

Coop. Vinícola de Cenicero

Ctra. de Logroño, s/n
Cenicero (La Rioja)
Tel. (941) 454110
Fax (941) 454618

Cenicero, a town historically linked to wine-making, is one of Rioja's great wine centers. During the last century, some of the first French-style wineries were established here on a model that later became an enormous success. Established in 1963 and originally called Cooperativa Santa Daría, the organization was set up by a group of local farmers hoping to free themselves from their dependency on the large wineries which, at harvest-time, always took advantage of their powerful positions at the negotiating table. Today the Cooperative counts 585 members who cultivate 1,000 ha of vineyards (an impressive 80% of the region's vineyards). The vines spread out across rolling hills, somewhere between 450 and 600 m above sea level. The terrain is loamy, calcareous and with a tendency to flood. The vine 'par excellence' is Tempranillo. Annual production hovers at around 3.5 million lt, over half of which are bottled. The 2,000 barriques in the cellars produce high quality reserve wines. This winery is privileged, however, in that it is able to select the best raw material used for its bottled wines.

Santa Daría Tinto Joven 1990   🍇 ①
A highly original wine, perhaps more so than the young Rioja wines. Fruit and wild berry aromas; pleasant and well-structured. Crafted entirely from Tempranillo.

Santa Daría Crianza 1988   🍇 ①
Ruby red with brick shades; good, clean aromatic intensity with scents of fruit and oak-aging. Lots of fruit flavor on the first impact, remarkably well-structured and savoury. Also made from 100% Tempranillo.

Bodegas Corral

Ctra. Logroño, km 10
Navarrete (La Rioja)
Tel. (941) 440193
Fax (941) 440195

The Corral family boasts a tradition of wine-making dating back to the last century. In fact, the winery was established in 1898 by the present owners. Today Corral wines appear on the wine lists of first-class restaurants and in prestigious wine stores. The 1970s was a particularly successful period and helped to reinforce their already well-known and respected reputation. The family owns 40 ha of vineyards that are planted with the classic Riojan varietals. The estate is located in Navarrete, which is a famous wine village in the middle of Rioja Alta, along the path to Santiago. The vineyards supply just 40% of the necessary raw material, obliging Bodegas Corral to purchase from local growers. (each year at harvest time) The finished product is typical of the Riojan DO, the traditional aging process is completed in 5,000 barriques, adding their own personal touch to the Rioja wines.

Corral Gran Reserva 1982   🍇 ③
Cherry red with a ruby backround and brick highlights. The perfumes from aging are strong mix well with the spices, cedar wood and fruit scents. Elegant but powerful, ample and round on the palate.

Don Jacobo Gran Reserva 1981   🍇 ③
Ruby red with brick highlights; clear and attractive. Complex and extremely powerful bouquet that opens gradually. Slightly sweet approach on the palate; balanced with good acidity; full with a powerful and clean aftertaste. Lengthy aging in wood.

RIOJA
CUENCA DEL EBRO
SPAIN

1062

RIOJA
CUENCA DEL EBRO
SPAIN

Bodegas El Coto

Camino Viejo de Logroño, s/n
Oyón (Alava)
Tel. (941) 110216
Fax (941) 111015

Operating in the name of purest tradition, the relatively new Bodegas El Coto produces one of the most classically wines in Rioja Alavesa. Since establishment in 1970, the winery has already been expanded twice, giving a clear idea of the commercial success of its products. The modernly furnished vinification site has at its disposal aging cellars equipped with 12,000 barriques. The 100 ha of vineyards are situated in Oyón, one of the most wine-oriented towns in Rioja. Plentiful harvests enable the winery to mantain its self-sufficiency, which is a true luxury in this region. Tempranillo, Garnacha, Graciano and Mazuelo are among the red varietals cultivated; Viura and Malvasía among the white. Production ranges from whites to rosés and reds, the latter being the most successful among consumers.

El Coto Crianza 1987 ❦ ②
Clean, black cherry red with brick shades; aromas from aging in oak with lightly fruity scents. Slightly sweet approach on the palate, sufficiently tannic and classic-tasting. Aged in oak and in bottle. Produced from Tempranillo.

Coto de Imaz Gran Reserva 1982 ❦ ③
Beautiful cherry red with brick, not completely open. Intense aromas from aging in barrique, with spicy tones and a lightly fruity background. Pleasant, full-bodied and extremely clean approach on the palate: Drink now while it is at its peak.

RIOJA
CUENCA DEL EBRO
SPAIN

1063

RIOJA
CUENCA DEL EBRO
SPAIN

Compañia Vinicola del Norte de España

Av. Costa del Vino, 21
Haro (La Rioja)
Tel. (941) 310660
Fax (941) 312819

The Compañia Vitivinícola del Norte de España was established by the Real de Asúa brothers and by Isidro Corcuera in 1879. Their aim was to age Riojan wines of suitable quality and to export them under a full quality guarantee. Since then, the winery has maintained its high standards, taking great care to produce honest wines, some of which are of inimitable quality. In order to achieve this status, The CVNE processes grapes from its own 550 ha of vineyards, planted with the typical Riojan varietals and situated in and around the community of Haro. The demand for its wines is so strong that the Cooperative is constantly acquiring new vineyards. The building used for vinification is simple and impressive: the entirely renovated area of 7,000 m2 features cellars containing 25,000 oak barriques. The CVNE has always been recognized for its classic products, in perfect Riojan style. Lately, however, greater emphasis has been given to their bottle aging, reducing their time in barrique and, consequently, keeping in stept with the current market trends.

Monopole 1988   🍇 ②
An aged white; glycerous, with body and flavor. Good lingering bouquet, produced with Viura and Malvasía.

Viña Real Oro 1982   🍇🍇 ③
Clear cherry red with brick nuances of medium intensity; strong and well-blended perfumes from aging. Ample on the palate and full-bodied with a fairly long-lasting aftertaste. Lengthy aging in wood; obtained from Tempranillo, Mazuelo and Garnacha.

Imperial Gran Reserva 1981   🍇🍇🍇 ③
This wine belongs to another enological dimension, a privileged place reserved for only the best wines in the world. Based on Tempranillo with help from Garnacha, Mazuelo and Graciano, this wine undergoes 36 months of aging in American barriques and is then bottled and set to rest in the cellars for another 18 months. Beautiful ruby red in color with brick on the rim; bright with medium intensity. Perfumes from long aging, marked metallic tones from the Tempranillo, mixed with pepper, leather and balsamic scents. Intense, flavorful and balanced on the palate, with a good degree of development, even though it already expresses full maturity. An intense and elegant finish.

RIOJA
CUENCA DEL EBRO
SPAIN

1064

RIOJA
CUENCA DEL EBRO
SPAIN

Bodegas Domecq

Ctra. Villabuena, s/n
Elciego (Alava)
Tel. (941) 106001
Fax (941) 106235

When the proprietors of the great Jerez winery, Pedro Domecq, began to look for a place to produce quality red wines, to expand their range of products, they found this winery in Elciego suited perfectly. Production began almost immediately, having already gained expertise in many years of winemaking in Andalusia. After an shakey and unfortunate beginning, when the wines had trouble catching on (except for Privilegio del Rey Sancho), a new line of extremely delicate, well-crafted wines with great character was released. Only 40% of the raw material necessary is harvested from the estate's 350 ha: the rest is purchased from local growers. The modern and well-kept winery vinifies 45,000 hl of must each year, mostly destined for aging in one of the 20,000 barriques located in underground cellars. The highly efficient distribution network enables 4,000,000 bottles to be marketed annually.

Marqués de Arienzo Crianza 1985
Clear ruby red with some brick highlights. Pleasant aromas from aging, leaving space for fruity scents from Tempranillo, which are more distinct than those from the Mazuelo and Graciano, also present. Full-bodied, ample and slightly tannic on the palate.

Marqués de Arienzo
Gran Reserva 1981
One of the best reserves in Rioja. Splendid cherry red with brick highlights; perfumes from fine aging and spices. Full and balanced on the palate; strong lingering aromas. Produced solely from Tempranillo.

Marqués de Arienzo
Gran Reserva 1978
Cherry red tending towards brick. Intense aromas from aging, clearly marked by spicy and toasted tones. Extremely pleasant approach on the palate which continues in the development. Magnificent lingering bouquet in which the vanilla of new wood can be distinguished. Also 100% Tempranillo.

Bodegas Lagunilla

Ctra. de Victoria, km 182
Fuenmayor (La Rioja)
Tel. (941) 450100

In 1885 Don Felipe Lagunilla settled in Cenicero, a small village less than 10 km from Fuenmayor along the banks of the Ebro, and established La Rioja Vinícola, with the intention of producing wines for aging. Very soon, however, he found himself caught up in a fierce battle against phylloxera, which was destroying everything that crossed its path. In response, Don Felipe introduced American roostock to the area: the only weapon capable of standing up to the terrible louse. This succesful operation won him the title of "Comendador," awarded to him by the King of Spain himself. The winery remained in the family's hands for a few generations before being sold to the powerful Croft group. The best enological conditions and the best grapes give rise to 20,000 hl of wine each year, some of which is refined in the 10,000 barriques and considered a classic product of Rioja. It is worth noting that this winery's entire production is based on raw material purchased from local growers.

Viña Herminia Reserva 1985
Ruby red with brick shades, its aromas are typical of the aging in older barriques; rather tannic and long. Produced from Tempranillo and Garnacha.

Lagunilla Gran Reserva 1982
Lovely deep ruby red with remarkable brick highlights. Classic aromas of aged Riojan wine. Balanced and long on the palate, with complex lingering scents. From Tempranillo and Garnacha and oak-aged at length.

RIOJA
CUENCA DEL EBRO
SPAIN

1065

RIOJA
CUENCA DEL EBRO
SPAIN

Bodegas Lan

Paraje del Buicio, s/n
Fuenmayor (La Rioja)
Tel. (941) 450050
Fax (941) 4505

Coming out of a series of problems, Bodegas Lan is now heavily relying on the quality of its wines in order to regain the commercial success it once enjoyed. Established in 1973 by a group of shareholders from the winery La Rioja Alta, in Haro, it spent its first two years in business acquiring and aging wines according to instructions from the head-office. The first harvest was vinified in the newly built Fuenmayor winery in 1974. More harvests followed, and the Bodegas Lan rapidly achieved commercial success, gaining in popularity also with wine-experts, thanks in part to their excellent quality/price ratio. In the early 1980s, the winery became an object of envy for many large companies; it was then that the holding company Rumasa took over 76% of the shares. Following the eviction from Rumasa by the government, under guidance from Felipe González, in 1983, the shares changed hands once again, until finally control was returned to the original share-holders. The winery is now focusing on reviving and maintaining the same production techniques that once made Bodegas Lan a successful producer.

Lander Blanco 1988   ℘ ②
Surprisingly well-aged for only six months in barrique and a year in the bottle. Based on the Viura grape; appealing in color, with complex aromas of new wood, fumé and fruit. Savoury and balanced on the palate; ample lingering aromas.

Viña Lanciano 1987   ❦ ②
Produced with the classic varietals of the area; shows good aging; clear cherry red with brick highlights; fruity perfumes with tones of the aging; ample with a certain tannic quality on the palate.

Viña Lanciano 1983   ❦ ③
A Rioja coupage of Mazuelo, Garnacha, Tempranillo and Graciano, this classic reserve wine ages over two years in barrique. Ruby red with remarkable brick highlights; its secondary perfumes are complex and the whole is balanced and ample on the palate.

R. López de Heredia Viña Tondonia

Av. Costa del Vino
Haro (La Rioja)
Tel. (941) 310244

Ever since Ramón López de Heredia established his winery in 1877, he has remained faithful to tradition and relatively uninterested in commercially, fickle fashion whims. Still run by the López family, the winery upholds the Riojan tradition that places great importance on the use of wood. 100 ha of vineyards, situated in the best areas of Rioja Alta along the right bank of the Ebro, have provided a certain constance for quality over the years. The superior-sounding names of these vineyards are reflected in the names on the wine labels. Standing out among the wide array of products is the eternal red Grande Reserva, with a surprising aging potential. López de Heredia's best known wine, however, is its 6° Año. The whites and rosés also undergo varying periods of aging in wood before their commercial release. Particularly fascinating are the winery's ancient cellars, where extremely old vintages produced by the owner's grandparents are still tucked away for safe keeping.

Viña Tondonia Blanco 1987   ℘ ②
Golden, opaque yellow with signs of great aging. Rather characteristic aroma, with elements from long aging in wood. Glycerous and full-bodied; from Viura and Malvasía varietals.

Viña Bosconia 1985   ❦ ②
Clear cherry red with a ruby background; intense perfumes from aging in barrique. Full-bodied and slightly tannic on the palate; pleasant lingering aromas.

Viña Tondonia
Gran Reserva 1982   ❦❦ ④
This wine's best qualities are without a doubt its intense and refined perfumes, the fruit of aging in barrique and in the bottle. Produced with the classic Riojan varietals; well-balanced on the palate.

RIOJA
CUENCA DEL EBRO
SPAIN

1066

RIOJA
CUENCA DEL EBRO
SPAIN

Bodegas Marqués de Murrieta

Ctra. Logroño-Zaragoza, km 5
Ygay (Logroño)
Tel. (941) 258321
Fax (941) 251606

Between 1840 and 1850 Don Luciano Murrieta, Marqués de Murrieta, established on Generale Espartero's Estate, the first Riojan winery dedicated to the production of 'claret' wines in the Bordeaux style. Within a few years, these wines began to prove their value on the international scale when they were exported to Cuba and Central and South America. This commercial success encouraged Don Luciano to buy the Ygay estate in 1870, where the current winery was built and becoming a symbol of Riojan winemaking. Marqués de Murrieta is owned by the avant-garde and enterprising Vicente Cebrián, Conde de Creixell, who may be thanked for pulling the winery out of a dangerous lethargy. He has given it new life without sacrificing its historic value, which is the most valuable heritage of this century-old winery, that is famous the world over for its extremely old vintages which are nevertheless still chock full of life. In taking advantage of this fine reputation, Cebrián released the great Castillo de Ygay reserves, made from wines that demonstrate the winery's talent for traditional aging in wood. Of the winery's total of 290 ha of vineyards, only 180 are currently producing. As harvests are insufficient to supply the amount of raw material needed, the remaining will soon be planted, mainly with Tempranillo. Both the reds and the whites have a distinictive character and all the qualities to last in time.

El Dorado de Murrieta 1987
A reserve white with a shorter aging period than usual, according to a more modern design. From Viura and Malvasía.

Marqués de Murrieta
Gran Reserva 1985
All the qualities of this wine seem to be tightly under wraps ready to emerge within a few years. Raw material provided by Tempranillo, Graciano, Garnacha and Mazuelo.

Castillo de Ygay   🍇🍇 ④
Gran Reserva 1959
Yes, Reserva 1959! A survival story that demostrates the almost magical element of enological science. Aging in barrique lasts no less than 25 years! From Tempranillo, Graciano, Mazuelo and Garnacha grapes.

Bodegas Marqués del Puerto

Ctra. de Logroño, s/n
Fuenmayor (La Rioja)
Tel. (941) 450001

In 1972 a group of farmers and cellarmasters established a winery by the name of López Agós. The founders decided to build a facility in Fuenmayor, in Rioja Alta, where they also bought some vineyards. The project was supported by Don Rafael Martínez, Marqués del Puerto, who also lent his title to the label. Some years later in 1986, the powerful group, Bodegas y Bebidas, took over the winery, which resulted in a dramatic improvement in quality. An area of 9,500 m2 houses the equipment currently used by this winery, which is among the most modern available. As much as a 1,000,000 kilos of grapes can be vinified, and the warehouses can hold up to 3,500,000 lt of wine. Bodegas Marqués del Puerto also uses temperature-controlled cellars to age their wine in 2,000 barriques. The 20 ha of vineyards are insufficient to meet production needs, so they must purchase from other vine-growers.

Marqués del Puerto 1987
Extremely vibrant and intense; attractive color and good aromatic development. Ample and flavorful on the palate. Produced with Tempranillo, Graciano and Mazuelo.

Marqués del Puerto
Reserva 1985
Successful combination of fruitiness from the grape and secondary aromas from the aging. Flavorful, ample and balanced on the palate; obtained from the same varietals as above, with a two year's aging in oak.

Marqués del Puerto   🍇 ③
Gran Reserva 1982
Many years of aging in wood; clean and round on the palate; intense and complex aftertastes. Also based on the classic coupage of Rioja.

RIOJA
CUENCA DEL EBRO
SPAIN

1067

RIOJA
CUENCA DEL EBRO
SPAIN

Herederos del Marqués de Riscal

Torrea, 1
Elciego (Alava)
Tel. (941) 106023
Fax (941) 106000

Established in 1860, this historic, and extremely old-fashioned, Riojan winery prides itself on an enological heritage that for decades has represented the very best of the region. The great vintages from this winery, owned by the heirs of the Marqués de Riscal, are so well-structured and powerful that they seem immune to the passage of time. The winery has its foundations firmly embedded in its own splendid vineyards: the calcareous terrain is positioned in the most desirable areas of Rioja Alavesa (DO found in the Basque province of Alava) and is planted principally with Tempranillo, along with Mazuelo and Graciano. The last two come from old rootstocks from Médoc brought here in the 19th century, when relations with Bordeaux were still very close because phylloxera had mercilessly destroyed most of the French region's vines, forcing many wine-traders to turn their attention to Riojan wines. Besides the classic equipment, it is interesting to note their in-house workshop that makes, repairs and dismantles the 32,000 barriques to be found in the characteristic underground cellars.

Marqués de Riscal 1982 ❦ ③
Attractive dark cherry-red with with brick shades of medium intensity; extremely aromatic on the palate; well-structured and long-lasting. Classic wine aged in barrique and produced from Tempranillo, Graciano and Mazuelo.

Marqués de Riscal 1976 ❦ ④
This wine seems to enjoy the gift of eternal youth: vigorous, fleshy, long-lasting and with an ample aftertaste. Long aging in barrique; from Tempranillo, Mazuelo and Graciano.

Barón de Chirel Tinto ❦❦❦ ④
Reserva 1986
This winery never lost its great reputation for fine wines, even during the years when it produced some rather mediocre ones. One of the latest creations is Barón de Chirel, modern and completely different from Riscal's traditional output. It is possibly the only wine in Rioja that combines Cabernet Sauvignon with Tempranillo and Graciano. The 26 month aging period takes place in 2 to 3 year-old barriques, followed by an appropriate period in the bottle. Cherry red with violet-blue shades; well-covered. Elegant bouquet with tobacco and refined wood tones. Ample on the palate with good acidity and tannin. Smooth and rounded development; intense and long-lasting aftertaste. It definitely has a long life ahead.

RIOJA
CUENCA DEL EBRO
SPAIN

1068

RIOJA
CUENCA DEL EBRO
SPAIN

Bodegas Martinez Bujanda

Camino Viejo de Logroño, s/n
Oyón (Alava)
Tel. (941) 122172
Fax (941) 122111

Frenetic activity and constant renovation seem to be the outstanding characteristics unique to Bodegas Martinez Bujanda. It was established last century and handed down from father to son until 1890, when Don Joaquin Martinez Bujanda built the first family winery. Bodegas' 280 ha of vineyards are dedicated to the classic Riojan varietals, particularly Malvasía and Mazuelo, which are often given little or no consideration. Great efforts are also made to experiment, including the planting of Cabernet Sauvignon and Riesling. Increasing demand for their products forced the Martinez Bujanda family to expand the winery in 1984. The new facilities are among the best in Europe. The temperature-controlled "naves de crianza" house 10,000 French and American oak barriques. One of the winery's strongest points is the almost obsessive attention to detail in the creation and presentation of the wide range of products.

Conde de Valdemar Blanco 1990
A Viura-based wine, fermented in oak barrique. Perfectly balanced, it has extremely refined perfumes of new wood with sweet and smoky tones. Ample and glycerous on the palate.

Conde de Valdemar Tinto 1988
From Tempranillo and Mazuelo; clear cherry red tending towards amarelle; medium intensity. Complex fruity perfumes deriving from aging in wood; well-structured and full-bodied; strong lingering aromas.

Conde de Valdemar
Gran Reserva 1981
Bright, intense ruby red with brick highlights; distinctly closed secondary perfumes due to its two years' aging in barrique and three years in bottle. Balanced, a bit warm, with a pleasant aftertaste on the palate. A product of the Tempranillo and Mazuelo grapes.

Bodegas Faustino Martínez

Ctra. de Logroño, s/n
Oyón (Alava)
Tel. (941) 122100
Fax (941) 122106

Now nearing its 140th birthday, Bodegas Faustino Martínez, was established and is still owned by the family of the same name. It has now become the largest producing Alavesan winery. The continous growth in production was accelerated when the present owner, Julio Faustino Martínez, took charge. He began the restoration and extension of the vineyards, furnished the winery with the latest technology and advanced equipment and personally oversaw all the marketing. The 500 ha of vineyards are planted with the red Tempranillo, Garnacha and Mazuelo, and the white Malvasía and Viura. A large vinification cellar allows for a wide range of products, ranging from differing degrees of wood-aged whites, to Cavas, rosés and reds on up to a great and prestigious reserve. Faustino V Reserva and Faustino I Gran Reserva, the winery's top products, have catapulted Bodegas Faustino Martínez to the top of the world market.

Faustino V Rosado 1991
Clear, strawberry pink with shades of violet; fruity aromas are not overly intense. Smooth and balanced on the palate, with body but not very ample. Produced solely from Tempranillo.

Faustino V Reserva 1985
Ruby red with cherry nuances and some brick shades; clean perfumes from aging ring clear with vanilla and strong tobacco. Sweet entrance on the palate; balanced, if a bit short. From Tempranillo, Graciano and Garnacha.

Faustino I Gran Reserva 1982
Ruby red with brick highlights; clear, elegant and complex aromas from aging and the slight reduction. Flavorful on the palate, with well-balanced body; finishes with ample, lingering aromas. Extended aging in oak; produced from Tempranillo and Graciano.

RIOJA
CUENCA DEL EBRO
SPAIN

1069

RIOJA
CUENCA DEL EBRO
SPAIN

Bodegas Martínez Lacuesta

La Ventilla, 71
Haro (La Rioja)
Tel. (941) 310050
Fax (941) 310050

The Martínez Lacuesta family has owned this winery since it was established in 1895 by Don Félix Martínez Lacuesta. True to its principals, this antique and classic winery has become an institution in Haro, which is the capital of Rioja Alta. Largely dedicated to the aging of wines, the winery hasn't owned vineyards for many years and no longer vinifies its own grapes or wines. Every year, finished wine is bought from the same communities and from the same producers, ready to undergo aging for long periods in barrique, in strict accordance with to the winery's traditional philosophy. Martínez Lacuesta's most distinctive products are the great red and white reserves, that are full of life and rich in character. Besides specializing in wine, the family also keeps a workshop where it customs design and repairs its own barriques. The fact that these wines are generally very highly praised and in great demand has contributed to the owners' indifference to the new wave of modern-style wines geared towards current tastes.

Campeador Reserva 1982　　🍇 ②
Warm, full-bodied and potent; Garnacha achieves its full ampleness. Scents of over ripeness on the nose; remarkable well-structured on the palate.

Martínez Lacuesta　　🍇🍇 ③
Reserva Especial 1981
Ruby red with noticeable brick highlights; extremely complex secondary aromas of spiced tones, refined wood and reduction aromas. Ample and balanced on the palate, with intense lingering perfumes. Fruit of the classic Riojan coupage: Tempranillo, Garnacha, Mazuelo and Graciano.

Bodegas Montecillo

San Cristobal, 34
Fuenmayor (La Rioja)
Tel. (941) 440125
Fax (941) 440663

Bodegas Montecillo was established in 1874 by the Navajas family which maintained the ownership for many years. The high quality of its products immediately won the winery a great reputation for honesty. This reputation stuck for many decades until in 1974, on its 100th birthday, Montecillo was bought by a gigantic company from Osborne that was looking for a good quality red wine to complete its line of products. Indeed, Montecillo places emphasis on aged reds and great reserve wines, which together make up 85% of total production. The other 15% consists of some very interesting young wines, both whites and rosés. One that stands out is Logrado Blanco, a wine whose aroma expresses the full frankness of the Viura varietal. Oddly, the winery doesn't own any vineyards and must buy all its grapes from local growers. The large facilities are classically equipped, with 14,000 barriques and a wine cellar capable of storing over 5,000,000 bottles.

Viña Cumbrero Tinto 1987　　🍇 ②
Medium intensity cherry red; clear with pleasant aromas characteristic of Tempranillo, which are accompanied by less intense aromas of Graciano and Mazuelo; good aging in barrique.

Viña Monty Gran Reserva 1982　　🍇 ③
Beautiful bright brick-red; intense bouquet; extremely silky on the palate. Possibly at its best now, it is made solely from Tempranillo.

Montecillo Gran Reserva 1973　　🍇 ③
Limited production wine, with lengthy aging in barrique; wonderful intense and complex perfumes with a perfect structure on the palate. Also produced entirely from Tempranillo.

RIOJA
CUENCA DEL EBRO
SPAIN

1070

RIOJA
CUENCA DEL EBRO
SPAIN

Bodegas Muga

Barrio de la Estación, s/n
Haro (La Rioja)
Tel. (941) 310498
Fax (941) 312867

Muga is one of the few wineries deeply
rooted in the solid Riojan tradition, as proven
by its inimitable aged reds. The products are
the result of classic methods that are well-
refined over the years, yet still remaining
faithful to a style that has immortalized the
best Spanish wines (along with Jerez) and
keeping abreast of changing tastes. Without
this winery, Rioja would be swallowed up by
the common denominator that has already
destroyed a large part of its viticulture. Here,
the personality of the producer, (a direct
descendent of the founder, Isaac Muga), is
reflected in the character of his wines. They
are masterpieces in flavor and glow with
passion. Muga wines are characterized by
the superb craftsmanship used in their aging,
which calls exclusively for French and
American barriques in every phase. This
procedure also demands the control of
temperature, density and other variables, that
require extreme care and years of
experience. The winery owns 33 ha of
vineyards in Rioja Alta with an annual harvest
of 172,000 kg of Tempranillo, Graciano,
Garnacha and Mazuelo grapes.

Muga Crianza 1985 🍇 ②
One of the best made aged wines in all of Rioja.
It has the Muga stamp and is sufficiently clean.

Prado Enea Reserva 1982 🍇🍇 ③
Slighty more tannic than the Gran Reserva
1981; tasty and ample on the palate. Given its
qualities, It is a wine which may easily keep for
another ten years.

Prado Enea 🍇🍇🍇 ③
Reserva 1981
Even though Isaac Muga has already led us to
expect excellent products, with this vintage he
has outdone himself. Classically produced from
Tempranillo, Garnacha, Graciano, Mazuelo and
a small proportion of the white Viura, the wine is
aged 48 months in oak and 24 months in the
bottle. Extremely beautiful dark cherry red with
ample shades of brick; bright, but not too
intense. Good bouquet from aging,
accompanied by scents from the reduction but
also good leather and tobacco. Smooth, flavorful
and long on the palate; extremely well-balanced,
with an excellent development. Elegant and
complex aftertaste featuring tones of refined
wood, spices and strong tobacco.

RIOJA
CUENCA DEL EBRO
SPAIN

1071

RIOJA
CUENCA DEL EBRO
SPAIN

Bodegas Murua

Ctra. Laguardia, s/n
Elciego (Alava)
Tel/Fax (941) 106260

Another classic winery of the Rioja Alavesa
DO, in this area of the Basque province of
Alava. Murua has been producing high
quality, successful wines since the beginning
of the century. A recent change of
management has brought new youth to the
label, thanks chiefly to the construction of a
new facility just outside the wine producing
town of Elciego. The brand new equipment is
certainly technologically advanced, although
it is used to craft a fairly classic wine. The
2,500 barriques used for aging the reserve
wines are kept in a beautiful, temperature-
controlled cellar. The classic Riojan varietals
are grown in 50 ha of vineyards: Tempranillo,
Garnacha, Mazuelo, Viura and Malvasía.
Murua annually produces 1,500 hl of juice, a
modest quantity when compared to the
extent of the vineyards.

Murúa Tinto Crianza 1986 ❦ ②
Ruby red with brick shades; extremely clean.
Both primary perfumes and those from the aging
are good. Full-bodied, tannic and rather long on
the palate. Produced from Tempranillo and
Graciano.

Bodegas Olarra

Polígono de Cantabria, s/n
Logroño
Tel. (941) 235299
Fax (941) 253703

This great winery, named after one of its
original founder-members, was established in
1972 by a group of wine-loving businessmen
from Rioja and the Basque region. Here
everything has been done in a grand style:
the famous architect, Riduejo, designed such
a modern, dynamic and eye-catching building
that Olarra's headquarters is known as "the
cathedral of Rioja." The 54,000 m2 building is
in the shape of a 'Y', representing the three
zones of Rioja (Rioja Alavesa, Rioja Alta and
Rioja Baja), and is located in the vicinity of
Logroño. The winery's highly esteemed
enologist, Ezequiel García, is nicknamed "el
brujo" (the wizard) in recognition of the
perfection of his wines. The spacious, and
pristine, vinification facility is constantly being
updated with every kind of new technology
possible. The vast range of products includes
young whites, rosés and reds, as well as
aged reserve wines and even a Cava, which
is included under the same DO heading.

Añares Crianza 1988 ❦ ②
A typical, aged Riojan wine; aromas from aging
in used barriques; rather full-bodied with a
pleasant aftertaste. Noble characteristics are
derived from the Tempranillo, Garnacha and
Mazuelo blend.

Cerro Añón 1985 ❦ ③
Ruby red with brick shades; medium intensity.
Complex perfumes in which hints of aging are
accompanied by fruity tones. Flavorful approach
on the palate, powerful development and an
excellent and rather long-lasting woody finish.
Produced from Tempranillo, Garnacha, Mazuelo
and Graciano.

Añares Gran Reserva 1981 ❦ ②
Ruby red with brick nuances; not very
developed ; clean, though not overly intense,
perfumes from aging featuring a tinge of alcohol.
Soft and silky approach on the palate followed
by a moderate tannic expression. From the
classic Riojan coupage.

Bodegas Palacio

San Lázaro, 1
Laguardia (Alava)
Tel. (941) 100057

The Bodega Palacio was established at the end of the last century as the result of an idea which Don Cosme Palacio y Bermejillo had long since been hoping to put into practice. A great lover of Riojan wine, Don Cosme created the first company organized to promote the region's products. He proved his talent and good business sense when challenged by the plague of phylloxera in the Riojan area, by renting an estate along the banks of the Duero so that he could supply himself with the grapes necessary for his wine production: this estate was called Vega Sicilia. Revived by a burst of enthusiasm and a change of ownership in the 1980s, the winery modernized all the vinification equipment. Besides the classic Glorioso and Palacio lines, it began to produce some newly designed whites and reds, aged in new French and American oak. The wine is sold 'in primeur', like the wines of the great châteaux of Bordeaux. This, too, lends credibility to the image of this winery, which is still as swift as ever at keeping with the times.

Cosme Palacio Blanco 1989　　🍇 ②
Beautiful golden yellow; clear, with well-blended perfumes from aging and fruit. Good balance on the palate; pleasant aftertaste with scents of new wood. Vuira is only grape used in this excellent wine.

Cosme Palacio Tinto 1988　　🍇🍇 ②
Clear cherry red with shades of ruby and slight tinges of violet. Intense perfumes of new wood with fruity and toasted tones; delicate approach on the palate; powerful development; full-bodied, slighty tannic and long-lasting. Produced from Tempranillo.

Glorioso Gran Reserva 1982　　🍇 ③
Ruby red with brick tinges; good intensity; perfumes from aging with spiced and toasted tones; extremely intense on the palate; distinctly well-balanced. Riojan classic coupage: Tempranillo, Graciano, Garnacha and Mazuelo.

Bodegas Palacios Remondo

Ctra. Mendavia, km 3
Logroño
Tel. (941) 237177
Fax (941) 183622

The Palacios family links with wine-making can be traced back centuries. Some old parchments found in one of the estates show evidence of wine-related activities as far back as 1651. José Palacios Remondo built the present winery in 1948, and it is still run by his children. The vines are cultivated with the classic Riojan varietals: mainly with Tempranillo, followed by Garnacha, Mazuelo, Graciano and the whites Viura and Malvasía, for a total of 150 ha (including some experimental plots planted with foreign grapes in order to assess their quality/production ratio). The winery is well-equipped for production and aging with the most advanced technology, and yields 4,000,000 lt annually. The aging process uses 1,200 French and American barriques. Furthermore, a project which envisages the construction of a new winery in Haro, dedicated exclusively to producing reserve wines, is nearing completion. And there are plans in the not too distant future to buy several properties in the very best wine-growing areas. Palacios Remondo offers a wide choice of products that range from young wines to aged reds, to reserves and gran reserves.

Herencia Remondo Reserva 1986　🍇 ②
Tempranillo and Garnacha are used in this wine, aged in American barrique for 12 months. Clear, ruby red with brick nuances. Full-bodied fruit perfumes of plum and wild berry; flavorful and powerful on the palate.

Herencia Remondo　　🍇 ③
Gran Reserva 1982
Two years in barrique add and enhance its character. Obtained from the classic Riojan coupage and bottled in 1987. Cherry red with brick nuances, good bouquet from aging; silky and ample on the palate.

RIOJA
CUENCA DEL EBRO
SPAIN

1073

RIOJA
CUENCA DEL EBRO
SPAIN

Granja Nuestra Señora de Remelluri

Ctra. Labastida-Ribas de Tereso
Labastida (Alava)
Tel. (941) 671710
Fax (941) 630874

This beautiful, and modern, winery is nestled in the midst of a spectacular panorama at the foot of the Sierra de Cantabria, on an estate dominated by a 10th-century Romanesque church and surrounded by 60 ha of vineyards. It looks similar to a Bordeaux châteaux, and the winery's terrain is particularly well-suited for viticultur. The largest proportion is dedicated to Tempranillo, followed by the white Viura and the red Graciano.. The members of the Rodríguez family, who own this winery and who also built San Sebastían, originally set it up in the 1970s as a kind of pastime. However, they quickly became aware of the area's potential, and invested heavily in the enterprise. As a result, Granja Nuestra Señora is now blessed with extremely modern vinification equipment, including 3,500 barriques (mostly from the French Médoc region) for aging. The production of 35,000 bottles annually emphasizes aged reds that, thanks to their fruity aromas that are even better compared to those of other similarly refined wines, constitute an important turning-point in the wine-making history of the area.

Remelluri Reserva 1987 🍇 ②
Bright red with abundant fruity shades. Consistent and refined on the palate; good balance; perfect acidity and tannin. Produced from the same varietals as below; a wine for keeping.

Remelluri Gran Reserva 1985 🍇🍇 ③
This was the winery's first harvest made into Gran Reserva. Only 30,000 bottles of this great vintage were made. Elegant and round; from Tempranillo and a small proportion of Viura.

Price levels

①	up to $ 9.99
②	$ 10.00 - $ 14.99
③	$ 15.00 - $ 24.99
④	$ 25.00 or more

The 'ex-cellar', or direct from the producer, bottle prices, are calculated in US dollars and are intended only as an approximate guide

RIOJA
CUENCA DEL EBRO
SPAIN

1074

RIOJA
CUENCA DEL EBRO
SPAIN

La Rioja Alta

Av. de Vizcaya, s/n
Haro (La Rioja)
Tel. (941) 310346
Fax (941) 312854

La Rioja Alta, one of the most prestigious wineries of the area, has always been a favorite amongst true Riojan wine lovers. The winery was established in 1890, when five Riojan families went together to a notary in the town of Haro, to found the "Sociedad de Cosecheros de la Rioja Alta." Barrio de la Estacíon was the neighborhood chosen for the winery's location. This same area is now home to the most famous and the best wineries in Rioja. Guided by French technicians (who held the reins for the first few years, dictating the 'modus operandi' to get producers on their feet), the winery was dedicated immediately to production and aging. Soon afterwards, the wines were winning national and international acclaim. Rioja Alta has grown over the years to become a veritable empire: it possesses 340 ha of vineyards that are pitifully insufficient to cover production demands. This means that over half of the raw material needed must be bought from other growers. The prestigious reserve wines, refined in 32,000 barriques in spacious underground cellars, receive praise from innumerable experts and restaurateurs.

Viña Ardanza 1982 ③
This wine, and particularly this vintage, has a well-deserved reputation. Ruby red with brick shades; extremely clean. Strong and complex perfumes from aging in barrique and in bottle; on the palate it is round, balanced and long with intense, lingering wood aromas.

Marqués de Haro ④
Gran Reserva 1981
Aged for 54 months in barrique; complex perfumes of spices and mature fruit. Round, full-bodied, well-structured and elegant on the palate. Produced from Tempranillo, Graciano, Mazuelo and Viura.

Reserva 904 Tinto 1981 ④
This wine, with no less than 60 months in barrique, is racked by hand ten times and epitomizes the classic production methods used in the area. Produced from 85% Tempranillo grapes, with the addition of Viura, Mazuelo and Graciano. Red with a brick background; not overly intense; bright. Seductive minty and animal-like aromas. Big and powerful on the palate, with the typical flavor and texture of a great Rioja reserva that is already quite evolved. It has a good aftertaste with licorice nuances and an unforgettable finish.

RIOJA
CUENCA DEL EBRO
SPAIN

1075

RIOJA
CUENCA DEL EBRO
SPAIN

Bodegas Riojanas

Estación, 1
Cenicero (La Rioja)
Tel. (941) 454050
Fax (941) 454529

With its long wine-making tradition running in the family blood lines, the Artacho family has been producing well-known "vinos de cosecheros," or wines vinified in the Riojan tradition, similar to carbonic maceration since the end of the 19th century. In 1980, a number of other families joined the Artachos to create Bodegas Riojanas. The owners' unrelenting quest for quality led them to hire more knowledgeable French technicians, to oversee the the winery's construction as well as the initial vinification and aging processes. This management lasted 50 years, and some of its methods are still used today. Bodegas Riojanas has recently celebrated its 100th year of producing finely-crafted, distinctive and traditional-style wines. They started out with 500 barriques and 50,000 bottles. Now this ambitious winery counts 30,000 barriques and produces 10 million bottles, having invested the substantial sum of 3,000 million pesetas to boost production. Bodegas Riojanas has a brilliant future ahead as one of the soundest and most representative wineries in Spain.

Monte Real Gran Reserva 1981 🍇 ③
Cherry red with brick nuances; good bouquet from aging; well-structured, powerful and ample on the palate.

Viña Albina Gran Reserva 1978 🍇 ③
Deep, vibrant color, rich in aromas and a remarkable pleasant approach on the palate are the principle characteristics of this wine that was chosen to celebrate the winery's 100th birthday. Long aging in oak; made from Tempranillo, Graciano and Mazuelo grapes.

Monte Real Gran Reserva 1964 🍇🍇 ③
A splendid, timeless wine with character. Ruby red with distinctive brick highlights. Pleasant intense and complex bouquet, based on the classic Riojan varietals enhanced by lengthy oak-aging.

Viña Salceda

Ctra. de Cenicero, km 3
Elciego (Alava)
Tel. (941) 106125
Fax (941) 106069

Along the way from Elciego to Cenicero, Viña Salceda is situated on a bend in the road that plunges down to the Ebro river. The building's Basque architecture hardly gives the impression that it might be a classic Riojan winery. Salceda's 30 ha of highly suitable, sloping vineyards are planted with Rioja's classic grapes. However, they are still not enough to meet the winery's production needs and, like many other wineries of the area, Salceda must rely on local viticulturalists for the rest of its grapes. Although it is a rather young winery, founded in 1973, Salceda uses the characteristic vinification methods of the area and is equipped to vinify over a million kilos of grapes each year. More importantly, Salceda concentrates exclusively on producing red wines, with real aging potential. To do so, they have and use an impressive range of 7,500 barriques. Viña Salceda's wines are among the most classic in Rioja; they are aged at length in wood, have characteristic aromas and beautiful rich hues and are delicate and rounded on the palate.

Viña Salceda 1987 🍇 ②
Clear, brick red, bright with medium intensity; not excessively woody from the aging; delicate and rounded on the palate, with a light, almost sweetish aftertaste. From a base of Tempranillo base, with a small amount of Viura.

Conde de la Salceda 1982 🍇 ③
Ruby red in color of medium intensity; sufficiently aromatic and well-structured on the palate. Drink now, as it is probably at its peak. Also made from Tempranillo and Viura.

RIOJA
CUENCA DEL EBRO
SPAIN

1076

RIOJA
CUENCA DEL EBRO
SPAIN

Bodegas Carlos Serres

Av. Santo Domingo, 40
Haro (La Rioja)
Tel. (941) 310279

Here is another winery born and raised under the supervision of French negociànts who, at the end of last century, took refuge en masse in Rioja from the phylloxera-devastated vineyards of Bordeaux. Bodegas Carlos Serres was established nearly a century ago by Frenchmen Carlos Serres and Cipriano Roig, with the intent of exporting wines to France. Over the years, the winery has kept to its original policy of producing great quality, well-aged red wines that leave a lasting memory on tasting. These precise characteristics have thrown open the gates of the international market for Serres' wines, especially for the Onomástica reserve, which is the best example of this dedicated, traditional winery's standard. Lying within the Rioja DO, Carlos Serres is one of those wineries with an important historic heritage and image. Nowadays, its production is of medium-level in terms of quantity and quality.

Onomástica 1983 🍇 ③
Dark cherry red with brick shades; round and already well-matured: now is the best moment for drinking. Long aging in oak. Produced from Garnacha, Tempranillo and Mazuelo.

Carlos Serres Gran Reserva 1981 🍇 ③
Classicly design and crafted, with a refined bouquet; silky on the palate. A classic Riojan coupage that undergoes lengthy aging in wood and that many wine-drinkers fancy.

Sierra Cantabria

Amorebieta, 3
S. Vincente de la Sonsierra (La Rioja)
Tel. (941) 334080
Fax (941) 334371

It may seem unusual for a Riojan winery to achieve success with young-drinking wines, and yet, still today, over half of the small producers in the Rioja Alavesa region are now committed to make young wines using very traditional techniques. Sierra Cantabria has risen to the top of this category, with its great quality reds, rich in fruity aromas. The traditional vinification process (as mentioned earlier) is similar to carbonic maceration. The winery's 240 ha of vineyards, situated in the privileged growing area of Sierra Cantabria, are planted mostly with Tempranillo, along with lesser percentages of Garnacha, Graciano, Mazuelo and the white Viura grape. Production, nearly 170,000 lt annually, is somewhat modest compared to the property's potential. Amongst the wide range of products, the best and most successful are the young wines. They are much better known within the production area than outside Rioja Alavesa, being referred to locally as "vinos de cosechero," or the wine-maker's wines.

Murmurón 1991 🍇🍇 ①
Bright and intense cherry red with shades of violet-blue; fragrant perfumes distinctly feature fruit, blackcurrants and flowers. Lightly tannic, full-bodied and intense. Produced from Tempranillo, Garnacha and Viura.

Sierra Cantabria 1991 🍇 ①
Typical of carbonic maceration, extremely aromatic with fruity tones. Full-bodied and long on the palate with a good aftertaste, featuring the strong primary, varietal aromas, typical of Tempranillo.

RIOJA
CUENCA DEL EBRO
SPAIN

1077

RIOJA
CUENCA DEL EBRO
SPAIN

Unión Vitivinícola

Ctra. de Logroño, s/n
Cenicero (La Rioja)
Tel. (941) 454000
Fax (941) 454400

With its revolutionary and classic, if short, history, the Unión Vitivinícola was established in the 1970s by Enrique Forner. As a Spaniard long-established in Bordeaux, he brought a world of experience of his own numerous French châteaux when he finally settled in Rioja. He began to adopt a different method of refining his wines: using little wood and allowing the primary aromas to predominate. The Marqués de Cáceres lent his own title to the new wine which resulted, which became an almost overnight success. As the winery owns only a few vineyards, the winery buys its supply of Tempranillo grapes in the local village of Cenicero, where it grows well. Many factors have contributed to this wine's popularity: it is very drinkable, lacks that heavy woodiness, and is aestically appealing in its presentation and packaging not to mention the excellent marketing backbone. Unión Vitivinícola's annual production surpasses 5,000,000 lt and includes a good range of whites, reds and rosé wines.

Marqués de Cáceres Blanco 1989 � ②
This 100% Viura wine, fermented in Limousin oak, strikes us as a surprise, coming as it does from a winery which has pioneered young and fruity Riojan whites. Extremely aromatic, balanced and flavorful.

Marqués de Cáceres Reserva 1982 ④
Bright cherry red with red currant and some brick highlights; intense perfumes from aging, with vanilla and toasted scents. Slightly sweet approach on the palate with a good evolution; silky. Shows good aging and the classic Tempranillo qualities.

Marqués de Cáceres ③
Gran Reserva 1981
Cherry red with red currant highlights; extremely clean. Medium intense aromas from aging with fruit scents. Slightly sweet and rounded on the palate, though not very long-lasting. Primarily made from Tempranillo.

Viñedos del Contino

Finca de San Gregorio, Laserna
Laguardia (Alava)
Tel. (941) 100201

The land and vines which now belong to this winery have always had strong links with the history and tradition of farming and wine-making. As early as 1034, for instance, the Pope pleaded with Saint Gregory Ostiense to fight the terrible plague of grasshoppers that was destroying the vines. Centuries later, the Catholic kings gave this land to Don Pedro de Samaniego, known as the "Contino" (thus, the present-day name). These stories, however, narrate a history that has little to do with the wine currently produced in the modern and well-equipped facility, which has totally branched away from the antiquated methods of wine-making. The wines of Viñedos del Contino are undoubtedly amongst the best new-style products in Rioja. Conceived along the lines of a French château, this winery vinifies only the grapes harvested from its 62 ha of vineyards. Moreover, they only make and bottle wine in top years, when they are sure that the grapes are top quality and capable of producing the precious gems which have always distinguished the Viñedos del Contino brand.

Contino 1986 ③
Of the three vintages tasted, this one showed the most delicacy and finesse. A pleasant bouquet of harmonious primary and tertiary aromas, rich in fruit, thanks to the skillful aging.

Contino 1985 ③
Still has good chance for improvement with cellaring; characterized by its strength and finesse. Well-aged in wood, it is a magnificent expression of Tempranillo, Graciano and Mazuelo.

Contino 1982 ④
Magnificent structure, it has highly complex perfumes and a fine balance. Truly an unforgettable wine.

RIOJA
CUENCA DEL EBRO
SPAIN

1078

RIOJA
CUENCA DEL EBRO
SPAIN

Bodegas Viñegra

Coscojal, s/n
Elvillar (Alava)
Tel. (941) 104024

In the world of wine, tradition doesn't always represent an advantage; often it becomes a weight to have to bear, forever linking wineries to their pasts, however glorious they might be. Wine-making in Rioja dates from the Middle Ages and experienced its golden era just last century. According to many of the region's wineries, this tradition is a 'double-edged sword.' Such is the case for Bodegas Viñegra, whose owners' ancestors were already in the wine-business as early as the 16th century. Fortunately, tradition has not blinded this particular winery in completely renewing its production philosophy. Techniques that were once considered tabú, such as the use of carbonic maceration for wines that were lightly aged in wood, have now been engaged. With such ideal growing conditions, rich, top-quality Tempranillo, Graciano and Viura grapes and a completely updated vinification facility, they have been able to make aromatic, modern-tasting wines with extraordinary character.

Teófilo I 1989
A pleasant surprise, packed with fruit and grace, it is the result of carbonic maceration and four months in Limousin oak. A new interpretation of Tempranillo with a small percentage of Viura that makes for an original product.

Teófilo I Reserva 1987
In step with modern Riojan wines; beautiful rich color; well-structured. Produced with the same grape combination as above, but ages for 18 months in oak.

Heredad Viñegra
Gran Reserva 1985
A classic Rioja style wine; pleasant and complex perfumes are its most distinctive features. Lengthy aging in barrique; again, made with Tempranillo and Viura.

Coop. Comarcal Somontano

Ctra. Naval, km 3.800
Barbastro (Huesca)
Tel/Fax (974) 311289

The 540 members of this cooperative own 50% of the 2,000 ha of vineyards registered as the Somontano DO. Over 900 ha are dedicated to the red varietals Moristell, Garnacha and Tempranillo, which are flanked by the white Alcañón, Macabeo and Garnacha Blanca grapes. The Somontano region's success has been a source of encouragement to spur on the recent experimentation with French Cabernet Sauvignon and Chardonnay vines, both of which showing convincing results. Established in 1969, the co-op uses a modern, well-equipped vinification facility with a capacity for producing 4,000,000 lt of wine annually, although actual production stands at half that. The cool, climatized aging cellars have been well-stocked with 500 barriques. As a result, the cooperative is able to offer a wide selection of wines, ranging from interesting young wines to aged reds.

Montesierra Rosado 1991
Produced fom Moristell, Tempranillo and Cabernet Sauvignon; one of Spain's most original and fresh rosés. Attractive pale, rasberry-pink; extremely fruity on the nose; light and fresh on the palate, with clean and fruity lingering aromas.

Villa de Alquezar 1990
Produced from Tempranillo; cherry red tending towards violet-blue; quite clean; pure primary aromas of medium intensity. Light, delicate and long-lasting on the palate.

Señorío de Lazán 1987
Produced from Moristell and Tempranillo, with two years' aging in oak, it has a lovely cherry red color with brick shades; strong, spicey aromas. Ample and long-lasting on the palate, with remarkable consistency.

RIOJA
CUENCA DEL EBRO
SPAIN

1079

SOMONTANO
CUENCA DEL EBRO
SPAIN

Cía. Vitivinícola de Somontano

Ctra. Barbastro-Naval, km 3.700
Salas Bajas (Huesca)
Tel. (974) 302323
Fax (941) 302098

Wedged between the outcrops of the Aragon Pyrenees, the new Somontano DO is a wonderful asset to Spanish wine. With its ideal microclimate for vine-growing, the area's new wineries have decided to entrust their fate to hands of advanced wine-making technology. Without ignoring their fine indigenous varietals, these wineries are experimenting with new, imported vines, sometimes with great success. Established in the 1980s, the extremely active Compañía Vitivinícola de Somontano has had two outstanding harvests. 600 ha of vineyards contribute to a potential production of a few million bottles. The winery's highest quality line, Viñas del Vero, offers products to satisfy both traditional and modern tastes. More 'exotic' European grapes such as Cabernet, Merlot and Gewürztraminer flank the local ones like Tempranillo and Moristell; all help to build to a sound, promising future for these enterprising young wine-growers.

Viñas del Vero Chardonnay 1991 🍇 ①
Elegant varietal aromas; a slightly sweet approach on the palate with a lively carbonic peak; extremely fresh, delicate and long-lasting, with a clean, varietal aftertaste on the finish.

Viñas del Vero Tinto 1990 🍇 ①
A red from Tempranillo and Moristell; beautiful cherry red with pleasant, fruity intense nose. Delicate at first impact on the palate followed by a well-structured development, as it unfolds with powerful elegance.

Duque de Azara 1987 🍇 ②
The qualities of the Tempranillo and Moristell grapes are enhanced by the skillful, balanced aging in Bordeaux barriques, thus helping to preserve the primary fruity aromas. Well-structured and full-bodied with firm tannins on the palate.

SOMONTANO
CUENCA DEL EBRO
SPAIN

1080

SOMONTANO
CUENCA DEL EBRO
SPAIN

Islas

The perfect complement to mainland viticulture is to be found on the islands: the Balearic islands are an extension of Catalonian vineyards, while the Canary's unique vines have a personality all of their own. The Balearic vineyards stretch across 2,589 ha of land, although the current decline this area is experiencing may soon reduce this winemaking tradition to only two areas: Benissalem, the latest DO with 500 ha, and Comarca Vitivinícola di Felanitx, where the Cabernet Sauvignon varietal has acclimatized well to its adopted home. Both these areas are located in inland Majorca. The principal red varietals cultivated are Manto Negro, Callet, Monastrell, Tempranillo, Fogoneu, Gueferro and Calop. White varietals include Moll, Parellada, Macabeo and, most recently, Chardonnay.

The self-governing community of the Canary Islands has 14,547 ha of vineyards grown with Listán Blanca, Listán Negra, Vijiriego and Malvasía. Only one of the Canary's wines, Tacoronte-Acentejo on the island of Tenerife has been awarded DO status, but both of the islands' provinces produce high quality whites, as well as excellent red at Santa Cruz de Tenerife. The most original wines of the Canary Islands are probably still those made with Malvasía grapes, which brought great honor to the production on the islands in past centuries, when they were some of the best known and praised whites in the world. They are now making a slow, but steady comeback.

José Luis Ferrer Franja Roja

Conquistador, 75
Benissalem (Baleari)
Tel. (971) 511050
Fax (971) 711623

The Benissalem area is situated in an idyllic spot on the island of Majorca: sitting at the foot of the Sierra de Alfabia, the vines are protected against the cold winds and enjoy an extremely favorable climate, with relatively high rainfall. Thanks to these conditions, José Luis Ferrer is able to take full advantage of his 70 ha of vineyards, on which he has planted the native Moll, Manto Negro and Callet, along with the usual Tempranillo and Monastrell. This variety allows José to produce a number of different wines, some of which - above-al the reds - are of outstanding quality. Founded in 1931, this winery is one of the oldest here and has certainly contributed more than any other to securing DO status for the local wines. 600 barriques in underground cellars are employed for maturing Ferrer's wines.

Viña Veritas Blanco 1991   ℣ ①
Obtained from white Moll and Parellada; extremely fresh and pleasant on the palate.

José Luis Ferrer Tinto 1987   ℣ ①
Lively and full-bodied; not too long, but well-structured. Tannic qualities guarantee good development. Made from Manto Negro and Callet.

José Luis Ferrer Reserva 1985   ℣ ②
Refined in oak for two years and at length in the bottle; displays the personalities of the Manto Negro and Callet varietals.

Bodegas Miguel Oliver

Font, 26
Petra (Maiorca)
Tel. (971) 561117

Majorca, the largest Balearic Island, boasts an ancient winemaking tradition: the island was mentioned by Pliny the Elder on account of its wine, and following the defeat of Moors the wine became the favorite of the Catalonian court. The Oliver family also prides itself on its long tradition: it has been almost a century since Miguel Oliver's grandfather began to cultivate the 40 ha in San Caló he inherited from his own grandfather. Later, the Olivers moved the winery near Petra, making it into one of the most beautiful in Spain. Miguel Oliver began his work in the 1950s, with lots of new ideas and high hopes. His first objective was to bring out the best in the native varietals and to bottle his entire production. Highly satisfying results feature wines with their own distinctive personality, especially those obtained from Majorcan varieties. Each year, 250 barrels are used to refine 2,500 hectolitres of wine.

Muscat 1990   ℣ ①
Delicate and bright; powerful varietal perfumes. Glycerous on the palate, with an extremely aromatic aftertaste.

Mont Ferrutx 1984   ℣ ②
Native Manto Negro, Callet and Guerrafó contribute distinct aromas and little-known flavors. Very original.

BENISSALEM
ISLAS
SPAIN

1082

C.V. FELANITX
ISLAS
SPAIN

Bodegas Monje

Cno. Cruz de Leandro, 32
El Sauzal (Tenerife)
Tel. (922) 561287
Fax (922) 300903

The Canary Islands, and in particular the great vineyards of Tenerife, have recently begun the slow, but steady process of complete renewal, in search of their lost prestige. Furthermore, the vineyards located some 25 km west of Santa Cruz de Tenerife are now included in the Tacoronte-Acentejo DO. One of the most prominent wineries in this greatly improving area is the Bodegas Monje, led for three generations by the same family, a symbol for the people of this land, carefully tending the vines and transforming the precious fruit into wine. Now renovated and modernized, the antique winery offers the best of the island's production, and the Monjes certainly have the skill and know-how needed to exploit the raw materials and facilities to the utmost. The winery's 14 ha lie on the edge of the Sauzal, and are planted with local grapes that are well-acclimatized to the island: Listán Blanco, Listán Negro, and, above-all, Negramoll, which will be much spoken of in the future.

Drago Blanco 1991 ℗ ①
Clean, unique nose; fresh and smooth; differs from the whites produced in this area up to only a few years ago.

Bibiana Rosado 1991 ℗ ①
Same quality standard and cleanliness as its siblings; undoubtedly the best rosé in this denomination of origin. Produced from Listán Negro and Negramoll.

Monje 1991 ℗ ①
Extremely aromatic, tenuous, fleshy and with correct acidity. Recalls Central-European wines produced with Burgunder, even though made from Listán Negro, Listán Blanco and Negramoll.

S.A.T. Viticultores del Norte de Tenerife

Del Medio, s/n
Tacoronte (Tenerife)
Tel. (922) 560107
Fax (922) 562590

This winery is a perfect example of both co-operation and independence at the same time. Founded in 1987, when a group of producers decided to join together for the purchasing of supplies, and the bottling and marketing of their wines, the co-operative currently has 95 members, with 200 ha of vineyards. Each vine-grower processes his grapes in his own facilities under the supervision of S.A.T. technicians and, after the wine has passed several tests, is given the right to use the remarkably successful Viña Norte label. Each Viña Norte label also specifies the individual grower-producer. The members of S.A.T. were responsible for the recent creation of the Tacoronte-Acentejo DO, and their products are extremely interesting, although they should not be kept beyond a year. The vines grown are local: Listán Blanco, Listán Negro and Negramoll are joined by Vijariego, Malvasía and Moscatell.

Viña Norte Blanco ℗ ①
Marcos Guimerá 1991
Fruity, clean and attractive nose; fresh and flavorful on the palate, medium intensity. Derived solely from Negramoll.

Viña Norte Tinto ℗ ①
J. F. Izquierdo 1991
Fruity primary aromas with raisiny scents; smooth and well-structured on the palate, with a touch of acidity. Made from Listán Negro, Listán Blanco and Negramoll grapes.

Viña Norte Tinto ℗ ①
Manuel Barrios 1991
Wild cherry-red with violet-blue shades; open and clean; fruity nose with a tinge of strawberry. Slightly sweet and glycerous on the palate, with a light acidity. Produced from Listán Negro and Negramoll.

TACORONTE-ACENTEJO
ISLAS
SPAIN

1083

TACORONTE-ACENTEJO
ISLAS
SPAIN

Bodegas El Grifo

El Islote, 121
S. Bartolomé de Lanzarote (Las Palmas)
Tel. (928) 812500

In the 16th century the wines of these islands were already popular with the English. Lanzarote's particular climatic conditions, the volcanic soil and the Malvasía varietal all play an integral part in the quality and fame of these wines, which are as original in their taste as they are difficult to grow. Bodegas El Grifo was founded in 1780, as the inscription over the entrance reads. Gería area wines are traditionally highly alcoholic, oxidized and not very clear. A few years ago El Grifo decided to change style, adopting more modern winemaking techniques. The winery enlisted the experienced help of the enologist, Felipe Blanco, and provided him with technologically advanced equipment; the wines immediately gained a new dimension compared to the typical local product, demonstrating the potential of the area's best wines to compete on both the Spanish and international markets with other, better-known labels. Today, as in the past, the main feature of these wines is their distinctive personality.

Malvasía El Grifo   ☷ ①
Strong character; well-balanced and with good aromatic intensity, highlighting exotic fruit and a long-lasting flavor.

VINOS DE LA TIERRA
ISLAS
SPAIN

1084

VINOS DE LA TIERRA
ISLAS
SPAIN

Levante

A vast Mediterranean vineyard stretches out over around 170,000 ha running from the province of Castellon, in the Valencia region, as far as Murcia. This is an extremely important area for Spanish wine-making, as most of its production is exported to other European countries. The warmth, color and body that this Levantine vineyard confers on its wines make many of them more highly appreciated abroad than at home. The Valencia region stands out for its competitively-priced, quality wines. There are other wineries, equally worthy of mention, to be found outside this region, but the best are concentrated in the Alicante DO, home to intensely colored, highly alcoholic red wines that are macerated at length and easily oxidizable. In the Utiel-Requena DO, made mostly from the red Bobal grape, a great, though as yet unsuccessful effort has been made to adjust production to changing tastes; indeed, the area's wines are now lighter and more delicate, with the rosés being particularly attractive. The Valencia DO makes fresh, light Merseguera-based whites, though the area's best products are the Moscateles. The Murcian region includes the Jumilla, Yecla, and Bullas DOs. Now undergoing a complete revolution, Jumilla is still, however, dominated by highly alcoholic, coarse, Mediterranean-style wines. Yecla is in a similar situation, though probably further behind in its renewal process; the climatic conditions are certainly harsher, though there are some wineries with very high-quality young reds.

The most common varietals in the whole of the Spanish Levante, besides Moscateles, Merseguersa and Bobal, are Monastrell (with great potential), Garnacha, Macabeo and Malvasía. Cabernet Sauvignon has also been planted in some areas, though with poor results.

Bodegas Brotons

Partida del Culebrón, s/n
Monovar (Alicante)
Tel. (96) 5477267

The Brotons family, which has been making wine in this picturesque area since the 19th century, can count on 45 ha of top quality, Monastrell vines, the Partida Culebrón being located right in the center of the area where this native Levantine grape flourishes. The winery produces some wonderfully hand-crafted wines; most notably Fondillón, an original, long-aging wine that is produced in small quantities from grapes dried on the vine and is then stored in large barrels for no less than eight years. In the 18th century, this potent wine, which reaches 18° alc naturally, was so fashionable that the vineyards began to invade the town of Alicante, but today its presence in the DO is strictly symbolic. The winery has a capacity of 500,000 lt, 100,000 of which are set aside for the great reserves.

Caserío Culebrón Tinto 1982   🍇 ①
Typical of the area and produced according to traditional methods: very oxidized and highly alcoholic. Produced from 100% Monastrell.

Fondillón Cosecha 1957   🍇🍇 ④
A great wine obtained from overripe Monastrell grapes aged eight years in wood. Ample and unctuous; unforgettable.

Eval

Ctra. de Villena a Yecla, km 58
Villena (Alicante)
Tel. (965) 808483
Fax (965) 808483

Alicante's proud wine tradition reached its peak in the years when its port supplied much of the world with excellent wines. The heirs to this tradition are the vineyards of Villena, an area that most strongly displays the typical characteristics of La Mancha and is home to full-bodied wines of great extract and with a good alc content. Eval, founded some years ago near the historical town of Villena, was originally called Prestige, after a company, run by people of Spanish origins, which owned other firms in Algeria. Gérard Gendrot, a winemaker at the Bordeaux Oenology University, was enlisted to apply the techniques he had learned in France. The current owners acquired the winery in 1987. 350,000 Monastrell vines ensure constant, high quality raw materials to produce wines which are unquestionably the region's most far-reaching.

Brut López de la Torre   🍇🍇 ②
Undoubtedly the best champénoise method sparkling wine made in this DO. Interesting, fruity aromas; produced 100% from Macabeo grapes.

López de la Torre Tinto 1990   🍇 ①
Pure, clean primary Monastrell aromas following carbonic maceration. Light and pleasant on the palate.

López de la Torre Reserva 1982   🍇 ②
Coupage of Monastrell and Tempranillo, which adds sufficient structure for this reserve to mature unhurriedly.

ALICANTE
LEVANTE
SPAIN

1086

ALICANTE
LEVANTE
SPAIN

Gutierrez de la Vega

Canalejas, 4
Parcent (Alicante)
Tel. (96) 5581266

The Moscatel varietal is grown in many areas of the Mediterranean, where it brings out the best of the qualities that made it shine in other, illustrious localities: Samo, where it originated, Alessandria, from which it takes one of its names, and Jávea, where it arrived almost 3000 years ago on Phoenician ships and has adapted perfectly. In this mini-paradise of fertile valleys and whitened landscapes which call to mind the Moriscos, Felipe Gutierrez de la Vega runs the small, artisanal winery where he produces his masterpieces, exploiting the latest technological advances: refrigeration systems, nitrogen-saturated vinification equipment and stainless steel; all limited in quantity, but of the highest quality. The diversified production includes young reds, long-lasting wines and reserves, crafted from the native varietals, Gallata, Giró and Argerina, and from Cabernet Sauvignon; an original rosé; and, above-all, unbeatable whites made from Moscatel grapes picked at different heights, which explains their great character and rare beauty.

Casta Diva Tender 1990 ♉♉ ③
Attractive and original; 100% Moscatel. Aromatically perfect, with its nose of fresh grapes, rose petals, new wood and a tinge of musk. Sweet approach on the palate; develops with great potency.

Casta Diva Cosecha Miel 1989 ♉♉ ④
Gold with amber highlights; glycerous and shiny in the glass. Extremely pure and intense aroma featuring essences of Moscatel, new wood, flowers and honey. Its enveloping taste and intense, lingering aromas make this wine unforgettable and worthy of its name.

Viña Alejandría Rosado 1991 🍇 ①
Unusually designed rosé. Aromatically complex: light, with slight nuances of oak and berries, and traces of Moscatel. Lightly tannic on the palate.

Salvador Poveda

Benjamin Palencia, 19
Monovar (Alicante)
Tel. (96) 5473389
Fax (96) 5470180

Ever since the first Phoenicians brought their native vine shoots here, this warm, mysterious land has always been ideally-suited to wine, although it has never been produced, as in other regions, merely for economic reasons. Salvador Poveda has faithfully taken up the winemaking tradition of this area, but is producing very different, though equally attractive wines by also paying heed to market trends. The winery thus offers some traditional, non-commercial wines that bear no relation to modern tastes, like Fondillón, made from dried bunches and aged up to 12 years in wood, and Doble Capa, a red vinified with a double dose of pomace. Yet right alongside these is Viña Vermeta, the region's most well-known and most popular wine. Located in Monovar, the center of this DO, the company has 250 ha of vineyards planted mostly with Monastrell, the base varietal for reds and rosés in the whole south-eastern part of the peninsula. The wineries are distributed in villages neighboring on Monovar and Pinoso, and they produce an annual total of seven million It covering a really vast range of products.

Fondillón Salvador Poveda 1964 🍇 ①
Vigorous and tannic; vinified with a double amount of Monastrell pomace and aged in barrique for two years. Warm and slightly astringent; fruity aromas; wood residues and good alcohol.

Viña Vermeta Tinto Reserva 1985 🍇 ①
Refined for a year and a half in barrique; obtained from Monastrell; well-known in the area. Updated, with a shorter stay in old wood and a lower alc content; Mediterranean wine personality.

Tinto Doble Capa 1987 🍇 ③
Traditional, long aging; produced from overripe Monastrell grapes and refined for a minimum of eight years in wood barrels. Extremely aromatic and complex; ample and potent on the palate; intense lingering aromas.

ALICANTE
LEVANTE
SPAIN

1087

ALICANTE
LEVANTE
SPAIN

Bodegas Piqueras

Juan Ramón Jiménez, 3
Almansa (Albacete)
Tel. (967) 341482
Fax (967) 345480

Director Mario Bonete's many years of hard, expert work have undoubtedly proven that this transitional DO located between Levante and the Castillian "meseta", or Almansa, with all its cross varietals and microclimate conditions, is in a privileged position for offering high quality wines. As for the magnificent local Monastrell varietal, there is no one in the entire country who can better bring out all its qualities; and if the skillful treatment given to Tempranillo, an increasingly popular varietal in the Almansa DO, is added to this, it becomes easier to understand how this winery is able to offer some unique, full-bodied, sensual, velvety wines that also feature traces of animal and dried fruit. Most of Piqueras' reds are aged in their 2000 barriques, and 80% of the production is exported, though while traditionally the wines of this area were once mostly exported to fortify the wines of other regions, today it is all already bottled.

Castillo de Almansa 1987 ♥ ①
Typical product of this region; obtained from Monastrell, red Garnacha and Tempranillo; privileged by expert aging.

Marius 1985 ♥ ②
Pleasant cherry-red with brick nuances; good secondary aromas; traces of dried figs; harmonious on the palate. Produced from Monastrell and Tempranillo.

Castillo de Almansa Reserva 1982 ♥ ②
Attractive and elegant; traces left from Monastrell and Tempranillo. Good aromatic potency reveals maturation in oak. Ample, well-structured and velvety on the palate.

Bodega Cooperativa San Isidro

Ctra. Murcia, s/n
Jumilla (Murcia)
Tel. (968) 780700
Fax (968) 782351

This cooperative was established in 1934, during the years of the Spanish Republic. Its original name was "Sindicato Agrícola de Progreso", and its cellars were located in the center of Jumilla. Some years later, the current name was adopted in commemoration of the patron saint of farmers, San Isidro. In the 1960s, new facilities were built in the outskirts of town. Today, San Isidro brings together over half of Jumilla's growers and counts a total of 20,000 ha of vineyards. These are planted mostly with Monastrell, which is the most common grape in the south-eastern part of the Iberian Peninsula. The typical wines of this vast region that includes the Alicante, Yecla and Jumilla DOs are produced here: they have low acidity, high alcohol and are slightly oxidized. The co-operative also produces some very interesting, sweet wines. San Isidro produces a total of 150,000 lt of wine annually, half of which is sold in bulk. Credit goes to the co-operative for its progressive philosophy that keeps very much in-tune with consumer tastes. Thus, in response to the current trend toward young, fruity wines, San Isidro is using carbonic maceration to produce some attractive, extremely aromatic wines.

San Isidro 1991 ♥ ①
A unique wine, made from Monastrell with carbonic maceration; robust and very fruity. Fully-developed primary varietal aromas.

ALMANSA
LEVANTE
SPAIN

1088

JUMILLA
LEVANTE
SPAIN

Viña Umbría

Vereda Real, s/n
Jumilla (Murcia)
Tel. (968) 781112

This corporation, founded in 1983, has considerable wine-producing potential, as it brings together over 50 vine-growers in the area for a total of 1,000 ha distributed throughout the Jumilla DO. The vast facilities are capable of holding an impressive 5,000,000 lt of wine and use a refrigeration system to maintain temperature-controlled fermentation. Although most of the wine is sold in bulk, some is selected to produce very attractive, fragrant young reds and rosés. The winery also uses a large, underground cellar where reds and clarets age in 600 oak barrels at a stable temperature. In order to guarantee its production, the co-operative also buys in from other growers in the area. 90% of the grapes are Monastrell owing to the vine's robustness, and its ability to stand the harsh Jumilla climate and resist disease.

Umbría Novel Rosado 1991   🏆 ①
Intense cherry-red; clear and long-lasting on the palate; characteristic Monastrell aromas.

Umbría Novel Tinto 1991   🍇 ①
Intense carmine-red; primary Monastrell aromas; considerable alcohol; long on the palate, with good backbone.

Vitivino

Cañada de Albatana, s/n
Jumilla (Murcia)
Tel. (968) 782854
Fax (968) 782603

Foreign, especially French, entrepreneurs have been attracted by the great potential of certain Spanish wine regions, long underestimated and often given to selling their products in bulk. This region had a lot going for it with its reasonably-priced vineyards which, with the input of modern equipment and technology, offered a profitable return on investment. The recently founded Vitivino in Cañada de Albatana, a small village near Jumilla, has capitalized on this situation with 320 ha of Monastrell vineyards. The company was started by a group from Bordeaux, and is headed by Jacques Germain. The French were lured to Levante, above-all, by the enormous potential of the Monastrell varietal, and since the very first year of production they have revolutionized its identity, revealing its capacity for fruitiness; a complete turnaround from the oxidized and highly alcoholic vinification that was once typical of this area. Attempts are now being made to mature this wine in oak, although the outcome is not yet known.

Altos de Pío Blanco 1991   🍇 ①
Light; perfumes of exotic fruit, bananas and mango, typical when working with selected yeasts that temper the Airén and Verdil varietal aromas.

Altos de Pío 1989   🍇 ①
Aromatic; dried fruit and fig tones; especially robust and warming. Modern product of Monastrell: a varietal of great potential.

JUMILLA
LEVANTE
SPAIN

1089

JUMILLA
LEVANTE
SPAIN

Augusto Egli

Maderas, 21
Valencia
Tel. (96) 3230950
Fax (96) 3234158

The Utiel-Requena DO is not very well-known and seemingly not very active, yet it has long been one of the country's leading exporters. The Augusto Egli winery testifies to this tradition: its parent company was founded in Switzerland in 1895 and was originally only involved in the commercialization of wine. Then, around the turn of the century, a company was started in Valencia's port town of Grao, where the present winery is located. The 10,000 m2 facility has a capacity of 8,000,000 lt and is equipped with up-to-date technology. The winery's 130 ha of vineyards are to be found on an estate called Casa lo Alto in the commune of Venta del Moro, some 100 km inland from Valencia. Besides the area's classic varietals, the estate's vineyards have also been planted with some new, experimental varietals. Augusto Egli currently produces wines belonging to two DOs, Utiel-Requena and Valencia, and exports 20 million lt each year.

Rey Don Jaime Tinto 1986 🍷 ②
Typical of this area; medium intense bitter cherry-red; reduction aromas, with light, fruity scents. Pleasant on the palate, though not very full-bodied. Produced from Tempranillo and Garnacha.

Torre Oria

Ctra. Pontón-Utiel, km 3
El Derramador, Requena (Valencia)
Tel. (96) 2320289
Fax (96) 2320311

The Torre Oria winery is based in the splendid Villa Iñigo, near Requena, which until recently belonged to one of the families that dominated Spain's wine industry. The building was acquired and restored by a group of six local families. Since its foundation in 1982, this winery has gone decidely for quality, also being the first in the area to produce Cava. Over 100 ha of estate-vineyards are currently in production, evenly divided between the varietals used in the wines: the native Planta Nova and Bobal, the most common Utiel-Requena DO varietal, together with Macabeo, planted to be used with Planta Nova in the base wines used to produce the sparkling wine. Torre Oria has been outfitted with the latest technology and possesses beautiful underground cellars for the aging of sparkling wines.

Brut Torre Oria 🍷 ②
A sparkling wine that shows its aging; sufficiently well-structured and balanced. Planta Nova provides it with a pleasant, particular flavor.

Viña Iñigo Rosado 1991 🍇 ①
An original rosé made from Bobal; vibrant pink with orange highlights; shiny; full and fresh.

Baronía de Turís

Ctra. de Godelleta, 20
Turís (Valencia)
Tel. (96) 2526011
Fax (96) 2527282

The best Muscat of the Spanish Levante (where 90% of this grape is grown) comes from the tight area wedged the Valencia DO between Valencia and Valentino. The Turís co-operative is strong here, as its members count a total of 1,400 ha of vineyards. They mostly concentrate on growing white Malvasía, Merseguera, Planta Nova and Roman Moscatel but there is also room for red Garnacha and Bobal, too. Only a small quantity of wine is selected for bottling from the immense harvest, usually weighing in at 11 million kg of grapes, while the rest is sold in bulk. The most notable of the selected products are the single variety Moscatel and Malvasía, magnificent sweet wines with the singular, unfortunate fault of currently being out-of-fashion.

Cañamar 1988　　　　　　　　　 ♉ ①
Produced from Malvasía and aged in oak. Aromatic; scents of dried fruit, figs and grapes; extremely delicate and gratifying on the palate; a pleasant though not very long aftertaste.

Moscatel de Turís　　　　　　　 ♉ ①
Beautiful golden yellow with copper highlights; pure varietal perfumes; clean and potent; smooth and glycerous on the palate, with a sweetness that is not sticky. Intense aftertaste featuring the aromatic Moscatel.

Bodegas Castaño

Ctra. Funenteálamo, 3
Yecla (Murcia)
Tel. (968) 791115
Fax (968) 791900

Yecla DOs, with their robust character and warm alcohol, certainly have a hard time competing against today's lighter styles of wines. More importantly, in this area, which includes Bodegas Castaño, it is vital for wineries to understand the enormous risk they take in continuing to use traditional vinification methods. This problem is much more on a larger scale, affectinh the whole Spanish Levante area, but particularly the Yecla region with a subdesert climate, sun parched soils and little precipitation. Amongst the many wineries that are forced to switch to selling in bulk (which is the last step before 'the grave'), Ramón Castaño rises up as a man who is capable of producing modern wines that make the most of the area's resources, native varietals and terrain. Another important step towards quality was taken when he completely upgraded the vinification facilities and began using new methods to garantee a better harvest and controlled vinification.

Castaño Tinto 1991　　　　　　　 ♈ ①
This wine is made by carbonic maceration, letting the Monastrell grape express all its fruitiness. Attractive ruby red in color with shades of violet-blue.

Pozuelo Crianza 1985　　　　　　 ♈ ①
Ruby red with brick nuances, it is aged in American oak. Dried fruit scents on the nose; well-structured, sufficiently ample on the palate, with warm, generous notes.

VALENCIA
LEVANTE
SPAIN

1091

YECLA
LEVANTE
SPAIN

Noroeste

This northwesterly tip of Spain, which covers the autonomous region of Galicia and the wine area of Bierzo, in Léon, has recently experienced a large-scale enological boom. Galicia's white wines, especially those produced from Albariño, are now considered among the best wines. The reds, on the other hand, from the Valdeorras and Bierzo DO (made from Mencía grapes), have begun to take important steps of improvement towards progress and are on their way to fullfilling their potential.

Such progress has caused the North-West to become the focal point of increasing attention. This wine-making region includes the four DO areas of Rías Baixas, Ribeiro, Valdeorras and Bierzo. The leading DO Rías Baixas covers about 1,500 ha of vineyards which mostly grow Albariño grapes. Indeed, the recent success of its white wines in Spain has given an important impetus to the whole area. Growers are making efforts to recuperate long-since abandoned vineyards just as new ones are being planted and new wineries are opening. The Ribeiro DO produces more wine in Galicia than the other DO areas, averaging 150,000 hl yearly. The Valdeorras DO is undergoing a complete transformation, including the replanting of noble, native varieties like the white Godello grape. Meanwhile, the Bierzo DO, with its 3,000 ha of Mencía-planted vineyards, is the northwestern DO with the greatest forthcoming expectations for improvement.

Viñas y Bodegas del Bierzo

Ribadeo, 21
Villafranca del Bierzo (Léon)
Tel/Fax (987) 540531

Viñas y Bodegas del Bierzo replaced an old winery on the same site and has worked intensely, since its establishement in 1986, to achieve quality production. One of few wineries privileged enough to work with its own vineyards, this winery begins its quality control right in the vineyard. The 30 ha of vineyards are cultivated with Bierzo's most common varietals: Palomino, Doña Blanca, Malvasía and red Mencía, which are all native to Galicia and Léon. These musts are vinified in a well-kept facility which features 300 Bordeaux-type barriques for its reds aging. Viñas y Bodegas del Bierzo, though relatively new on the market, is quickly gaining a reputation as one of the best wineries in the Bierzo DO.

Valdeobispo Blanco 1990 ℗ ①
Made from Malvasia, Doña Blanca and 70% Palomino. Straw yellow with golden highlights; primary aromas of herbs and fennel; traces of yeast. Well-structured and glycerous on the palate though not very long-lasting.

Valdeobispo Tinto 1982 ℗ ①
From native Mencía; ruby-red with brick traces; clear and medium well-structured. The secondary aromas are refined, well-blended and not overpowering. Delicate, full-bodied, silky and rounded on the palate. Good lingering aromas.

Comercial Vinícola Villafranquina

Ctra. Madrid-La Coruña, s/n
Villafranca del Bierzo (Léon)
Tel. (987) 540237
Fax (987) 542364

The El Bierzo valley was already a fountain of great wine and food as early as the 11th century, as it lied on the pilgrimage path to Santiago de Compostela. Cluny and Benedictine monks, who were from there, more great wine lovers and avid viticulturalists. This tradition has carried on into the present, as proven by this region's dominating role in food production all the way to Castille and Léon. In 1962, the wine-growers of the area celebrated this tradition by forming a wine cooperative and becoming the exclusive guardians of these high quality and indigeneous varietals. Mencía, the main red of the Bierzo DO and close-relative of the Cabernet Franc, is a primary example. In 1990 the cooperative passed into private hands and took on its present name. Comercial Vinícola Villafranquina groups together 800 growers from the area who produce 10-12 million kilos of grapes each year.

Don Mariano Tinto 1985 ℗ ①
Cherry-red with brick highlights made from 100% Mencía, one of the most noble Spanish grapes; aromatic and well-structured on the palate; tannic and well-aged in oak.

Padorniña Crianza 1981 ℗ ②
100% Mencía, one of the most noble Spanish grapes; it stands out for its correct aging and delicate bouquet.

BIERZO
NOROESTE
SPAIN

1093

BIERZO
NOROESTE
SPAIN

Agro de Bazán

Tremoedo
Villanueva de Arousa (Pontevedra)
Tel. (986) 555562
Fax (986) 543227

Manuelo Otero Candeira loves the fine things in life and has learned that it takes a great deal of patience to appreciate them. In fact, it took him over ten years to rebuild his winery. The project was not an easy one. On one hand he wanted to save the ill-fated Albariño grapes and wines, on the other hand, his love for the old, noble Galician country estates to an extreme. Indeed he insisted on visiting every single one, even those in Portugal, to obtain a precise idea for the style of his own project. He meticulously studied the plans for his family's winery in Tremoedo and carefully choose the building materials which include stone, curved tiles, noble woods and polychrome glass. The estate is surrounded by 15 ha of Albariño vines; the first harvests served as experiments to find the best type of vinification. The expert wine-making team is headed by enologists José A. Iglesias and Valencian Requena, the latter being the most knowledgeable technician in Albariño vinification responsible for putting the first vintages of Gran Bazán on the market in 1987. He reflected on the accomplishment by saying, "after much hard work, it is very rewarding to make an exciting wine that pills the spirit with optimism."

Gran Bazán Ambar 1991   ♈♈ ②
Albariño expresses its full potential in this splendid wine. Produced from free-run juces; refined and delicate aromas; amply-structured and persuasive.

Gran Bazán Verde 1991   ♈ ②
Traditional vinification; this Albariño is not released on the market until the summer after its harvest. Strong and generous, with all the characteristics of Albariño of times gone by.

Gran Bazán Limousin 1990   ♈ ③
First Albariño on the market after fining in new Limousin barriques. This magnificent variety makes great young-drinking wines but, as in this case, it can last in bottle somewhat.

Bouza do Rei

Puxafeita
Ribadumia (Pontevedra)
Tel. (986) 710257

Bouza do Rei is the brand name used to bottle the Sociedad Agraria de Trasormación's Albariño wine. The winery was built a few years ago by some Salnés valley winemakers, who until then, had sold their grapes to local wineries. The winery's 20 ha of Albariño vines are situated in a beautiful part of the Salnés valley, which is an area designated as one of three subzones of the Rías Baixas DO just north of Pontevedra. Until recently, this was the most prestigious area in the denomination, thanks in part to the cooling effect of sea ocean breezes. Today the most successful wineries are in Condado de Tea which, like the O Rosal DO, is located along the Miño river. Bouza do Rei is an extremely functional and advanced-technology winery where 150,000 bottles of the area's most characteristic Albariño wines are vinified each year.

Bouza do Rei 1991   ♈ ②
A modern style of Albariño; aromatic and fragrant; tasty impact on the palate, balanced with a slightly bitter finish. Shows the good elegance from a well-refined grape.

RIAS BAIXAS
NOROESTE
SPAIN

1094

RIAS BAIXAS
NOROESTE
SPAIN

Condesat

Meder
Salvaterre do Miño (Pontevedra)
Tel. (981) 182928

The Condesat winery is situated in the village of Meder (near Condado), amidst a picturesque landscape along the Miño river. The winery was recently built and is run by an association of vine-growers who altogether own 20 ha of vineyards on flooded terrain that extends all the way down to the stone river banks. The various native varietals include: Treixadura, Loureiro and Albariño. Condesat is one of only two or three wineries in this DO to produce e red wine called Tinto, made from the indigenous Brancellao, Pedral, Caiño and Espadeiro grapes. Although the region is more specialized in whites, growers have high hopes for some of these red native vines. Ideal technological conditions set the stage for the production of three different types of wines: Condado (obtained from a coupage of various whites), Albariño, made solely from this grape, and Tinto. Condesat's total production reaches a level of 200,000 bottles each vintage.

Bouza Grande 1991   ❦ ②
From a type called Condado, it is made of Albariño and Loureiro; pale yellow with greenish highlights; pure primary aromas but low intensity; tasty and glycerous on the palate, with good acidity, if a bit short.

Don Pedro de Soutomaior 1991   ❦ ②
100% Albariño; bright pale yellow with greenish highlights; subtle and delicate fruity aromas of apple. Smooth on the palate; balanced and elegant; lingering aromas of flowers and fruit.

Señorio de Rubios 1991   ❦ ②
Red Caiño, Brancellao, Espadeiro and Pedral grapes make up this pleasant and aromatic wine, with waifs from the Atlantic ocean. Attractive color; full-bodied and flavorful on the palate; extremely fruity aftertaste. Almost too much acidity.

Adegas das Eiras

Goian, s/n
Tomiño (Pontevedra)
Tel. (986) 621001
Fax (986) 621084

Adegas das Eiras is located in the Rosal valley near the estuary of the Río Miño, which is the river that traces the northen border between Spain and Portugal. The area's wines are well-known throughout Spain but especially in Galicia. In order to maintain the special character of Rosal wines, the owners of this winery believe it is fundamental to follow the traditional methods of the area. For example, here the fermentation is primed with yeast from their own grapes. What is radically different from the past is the vinification site, which is technically avant-garde. They grow all varieties that are typical to this denomination or rather, Albariño, Treixadura, Caiño Branco and Loureiro. Adegas das Eiras has not yet decided to follow the trend to produce varietal wines.

Abadía de San Campio 1991   ❦ ②
A typical well-made wine from the Rosal area. Pure fruity aromas; fresh with lots of glycerous on the palate. Not very full-bodied, with marked acidity on the finish.

Terras Gauda 1991   ❦ ②
Bright straw yellow with green highlights; extremely aromatic; refined and long-lasting aromas; clean, lingering finish.

RIAS BAIXAS
NOROESTE
SPAIN

1095

RIAS BAIXAS
NOROESTE
SPAIN

Granxa Fillaboa

Plaza Compostela, 6
Vigo (Pontevedra)
Tel. (986) 437000

The Albariño wine is increasingly more popular, both in Spain and abroad. As a result, the number of wineries, in the Rías Baixas DO, grows each year and more importantly, vinification techniques are being constantly revised and improved. With only a few exceptions, the older Albariño producers that have been in business just a few years are already doing very well. Fillaboa, run by the Barrera family, is a perfect example of this region's young and dynamic wine-making. The 30 ha of Albariño vineyards, in the delineated Condado subzone, have excellent southernly exposure on a hill that slopes down towards the Miño river. Annual production is estimated at 60,000 bottles. Like its neighboring wineries, Granxa Fillaboa (Galician name for the Spanish Granja Fillaboa) looks out onto the Atlantic Ocean and is just a stone's throw away from the Portugese border. The winery also produces fruit, mainly kiwi.

Fillaboa 1991　　　　　　🍇🍇 ②
Rather bright pale yellow with lemon highlights. Simultaneously potent and delicate perfumes, with noteworthy floral and fruit scents, especially yellow apple. Smooth, elegant and well-structured on the palate, with a slight bitter note in the finish accompanied by clean lingering aromas. Very well made.

Lagar de Fornelos

B. de Cruces Fornelos
El Rosal (Pontevedra)
Tel. (986) 625865
Fax (986) 625011

The Northwestern coast of Spain is geographically split into the two subzones, Rías Altas and Rías Baixas, the names of which are both taken from the rivers formed by Galician coastal fjords. The centuries-old craft of wine-making is said to have been brought here by German Cistercian monks on their pilgrimage to Santiago de Compostela. Founded in 1982, Lagar de Fornelos makes its Albariño wine along the estuary of the Miño river in the Rosal valley. The Rosal climate is not as misty and damp as other neighboring zones, consequently grapes are ripier and healthier. Lagar de Fornelos was purchased just after its establishment by the Riojan winery, La Rioja Alta, who was interested by this area's whites. The winery's 22 ha of excellent Albariño vines and its use of advanced enological techniques both insure top production towards 150,000 bottles of Albariño produced. The proof lies in the bottle, however, as attested by the numerous awards they win each year.

Lagar de Cervera 1991　　　　🍇 ②
Straw yellow with lime-green highlights; bright, powerful floral and green apple aromas. Approach is full in extracts on the palate, fullness with a well-defined balance between sugar and acidity. Pleasant and intense aftertastes crown the elegant finish.

RIAS BAIXAS
NOROESTE
SPAIN

1096

RIAS BAIXAS
NOROESTE
SPAIN

Adegas Mar de Frares

Rubians
Vilagarcía de Arousa (Pontevedra)
Tel. (986) 500913
Fax (986) 507006

Founded in the 1970s in Rubíans, near Vilagarcia de Arousa, Adegas Mar de Frares is one of the oldest wineries belonging to the Rías Baixas DO. It is also one of the few wineries who buys its own grapes from other growers as it owns only one hectare of vineyards. This situation has not inhibited them from producing notable quality and unique Albariño wines, however. To set themselves apart from other wineries' products and asserting a desire for renewal, they use an unusual blue-colored bottle. In truth, however, the use of more updated production approach is quite common throughout the entire DO area. Adegas Mar de Frares is furnished with excellent quality vinification equipment: steel vats, electronic controls and temperature-control systems. 400 hl of Albariño wine is produced each year, basically in two styles. The Mar de Frares is light and elegant, the Casabella is more aromatic and concentrated due to longer skin contact.

Mar de Frares 1991   🍇 ②
Golden yellow with green highlights, extremely clean; fresh fruit aromas accompanied by floral tones. Good impact on the palate, showing subtlety and fullness. A bit short on the finish but pleasant. 100% Albariño.

Bodegas Marqués de Vizhoja

Finca la Moreira
Cequeliños-Arbo (Pontevedra)
Tel. (986) 236964

The vitality and creative Mariano Peláez behind Marqués de Vizhoja has helped Rías Baixas' to become an important wine today. The winery is located in a restored, 18th century palace which overlooks the terraced vineyards above the Miño river, in the Condado subzone. The cellars are stocked with the latest technology including small stainless steel vats, grape crushers presses, etc. All the equipment has been custom-made for the annual 100,000 bottle production. Mariano Peláez has launched two types of wine on the market: Condado, a coupage of Albariño and Loureiro, and the monovarietal Albariño. The estate's 15 ha of vineyards are surrounded by lush vegetation.

Torre la Moreira 1991   🍇 ②
Bright straw yellow with lemon highlights; it is made from 100% Albariño, pleasant on the nose, featuring apple and floral scents. Subtle and elegant on the palate, accompanied by powerful and long-lasting aftertastes.

RIAS BAIXAS
NOROESTE
SPAIN

1097

RIAS BAIXAS
NOROESTE
SPAIN

Morgadío-Agromiño

Albeos Creciente
Creciente (Pontevedra)
Tel. (986) 434233
Fax (986) 436229

Wouldn't it be wonderful if such enthusiastic people like Antonio López could miraculously appear to save every declining wine area, region, denomination or nation like 'Superman'. In only a few years, this dynamic man has practically taken over the the entire Rías Baixas DO. The winery was established in 1984, when López and four associates started cultivating vines on suitable plots. Morgadio's wines have impressed wine-lovers and consumers since its very first vintage, reaping awards in every contest it entered. Designed to make wines from its own raw materials, this modern-equipped winery is a perfect example of efficiency and aesthetics. The sloping terrain of extremely well-tended vineyards have a southern exposure, enhancing the Albariño's distinct character and strength. The complementary Loureiro and Treixadura wines are also grown, as well as some highly regarded experimental tracts of red Espadeiro.

Carballo do Rei   🍇🍇 ①
A Condado blend of Albariño, Treixadura and Loureiro. Balanced acidity, powerful, full-bodied and extremely clean in all phases. An excellent match for tasty seafood dishes.

Morgadío 1991   🍇🍇 ②
Pale yellow with greenish and golden highlights; bright and quite attractive. Potent and delicate fruity aromas, with floral notes. Rich, well-structured and long-lasting on the palate. Slightly bitter aftertaste, closing with powerful and pure lingering perfumes. Certainly the best Albariño on the market.

Torre Fornelos 1991   🍇 ②
Golden yellow with greenish highlights; extremely clear and shiny; potent and elegant perfumes characteristic of Albariño. Flavorful approach on the palate, well-structured, ample and full. Bitter aftertaste and clean lingering aromas.

Pazo de Señoras

Vilanoviña
Meis (Pontevedra)
Tel. (986) 548654

Marisol Bueno, owner of Pazo de Señoras, is also the current president of the "Consejo Regulador de la Denominación de Origen Rías Baixas", the local consortium founded in 1988 to promote one of Spain's newest DO wines. Marisol has a very special personality: the calm and peaceful image outside hides a dynamic and enterprising business woman inside. If it's true that hand-crafted wines take on the personality of their creator, then this is exactly what has happened in this winery. With the added use of the most modern enological techniques, they obtain excellent results. The ancient stone "pazo" , or palace in Galician, housing the vinification facilities, is small but well-equipped and very modern. Pazo de Señoras vinifies only the Albariño grapes grown in its own vineyards.

Pazo de Señorans 1991   🍇 ②
Flavorful, smooth, ample, delicate; an uncomplicated Albariño showing great finesse. Beautiful pale yellow with greenish shades; shiny; clean and intense fruity perfumes. A smooth approach on the palate, with good gylcerin and long-lasting flavors.

Bodegas Salnesur

Bouza, s/n Castrello
Cambados (Pontevedra)
Tel. (986) 543535

The abundant Salnés valley grows so much native Albariño that it often has problems in dealing with the entire harvest. Cooperative organizations that group together many growers have proven very important in this respect, and Bodegas Salnesur is no exception. The 100+ member association accounts for a total of 62 ha, almost all planted with Albariño. Some of the vines in these vineyards have been producing grapes for over 100 years, contributing to the excellent quality musts and wines. Salnesur can be found in the little town of Castrello, near the district capital of Cambados. The 1,200 square meter facility is technically well-equipped and produces 500,000 bottles of Albariño wine each year, all carrying the prize-winning label Condes de Albarei.

Condes de Albarei 1991   🍇 ②
Good mono-varietal wine, proudly displaying Albariño's best features. Vibrant, ample and satisfying on the palate.

Santiago Ruiz

San Miguel de Tabagón, s/n
El Rosal (Pontevedra)
Tel. (986) 610568
Fax (986) 614142

Angel Martínez, the founder of this winery, was one of Galicia's pioneer winegrowers who began selling bottles and labeled wines in the late 1800s. His grandson and heir, Santiago Ruiz, revived this illustrious tradition and was also a pioneer when it came to improving the quality of Galician wines. "I could foretell," Santiago Ruiz often said, "Rosal's great potential for quality wines and was attracted by this little area's unique character." Ironically, when Santiago retired in 1987, the gastronomical and enological newspapers finally began to praise him and his winery, applauding the great wave he created in the whole province, which later became the Rías Baixas DO. Today Rías Baixas has bright prospects for the future. And yet no other Galician wine resembles the wines of Santiago Ruiz.

Santiago Ruiz 1991   🍇 ②
Extremely unique and classic, this was the first modern product to provoke the Galician wine revolution. Fom Albariño, Treixadura and Loureiro, perfectly blended and well-balanced. One of few wines made from a blend of grapes and not just Albariño.

RIAS BAIXAS
NOROESTE
SPAIN

1099

RIAS BAIXAS
NOROESTE
SPAIN

Benito Vazquez

Carballal, 3
Ribadumia Barrantes (Pontevedra)
Tel. (986) 710318

Benito Vazquez is an extraordinary man so totally obsessed by wine that when he is working as an advisory judge, he often debates his neighbor's quarrels in his favorite chambers: his own wine cellar! Almost single-handedly in the small but well-furnished winery, Benito produces no more than 10,000 bottles per year. He keeps the vinification as natural as possible, briefly chilling the grapes in a refrigerated cellar and using only small amounts of sulphur. Amidst neighboring wineries that own hundreds of hectares and buy enormous quanties of grapes, Benito vinifies his wine from his own three ha of Albariño vineyards. This classic and unquestionably personal Albariño grape from Carballal is refined in cellars for seven months and released on the market the summer after harvest.

Carballal 1990   𝖄 𝖄 ②
A classic style Albariño with distinct personality; released on the market the summer after harvest and after seven months of refinement on the less. Golden yellow with green highlights; pleasant scents of apple; vigorous and glycerous on the palate; extremely long-lasting.

Bodegas de Vilariño-Cambados

Burgans, s/n Vilariño
Cambados (Pontevedra)
Tel. (986) 542735
Fax (986) 520875

A celebrated poet-lyricist from the 12th century, Martín Códax, left a legacy of written hymns while most of his other contemporaries have slipped away relatively unnoticed. By naming its wine after this very poet, Vilariño-Cambados hopes to marry the image of one of the best-known, modern Albariño wines to that of an equally famous and historic Galician personality. 140 members make up this cooperative, which pools together 100 ha of vineyards. This enormous wine potential translates into 500,000 bottles of Albariño wine, which is a colossal figure when compared to the 100,000-piece average of other wineries. The vinification facility is set on different levels to insure the most natural filtering and pumping possible. Grapes are first brought to the upper level of the winery and slowly descend, thus no need for mechanical pumps.

Martín Códax 1991   𝖄 ②
An Albariño characterized by a great qualitative constancy over the years. Delicate, light and greatly balanced vintage.

RIAS BAIXAS
NOROESTE
SPAIN

1100

RIAS BAIXAS
NOROESTE
SPAIN

Bodegas Campante

Finca Reboreda
Puga (Orense)
Tel. (988) 261212

In the last few years, the Ribeiro DO, like many other wine-growing areas, has been been revolutionized by an enterprising team of producers whose enthusiasm and dedication to their work has earned them top spots in Ribeiro. Inevitably the whole denomination has experienced a big leap in quality. Manuel Mendez and his sons have an ideal workplace, producing clean, fragrant, high quality wines that have won their fair share of awards. Six hectares of vineyards are not enough to cover the family's production needs, obliging the winery to adopt the common area practice of acquiring grapes from area growers. Bodegas Campante uses a number of different grapes, such as white Godello, Treixadura and Torrontés and red Alicante and Mencía. The annual yield fluctuates around a million bottles, 80% of which is white.

Gran Reboreda 1991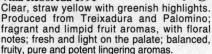
Extremely refined; produced from Treixadura, Torrotés and Godello; potent primary aromas; glycerous on the palate, with the right amount of acidity and freshness.

Viña Reboreda 1991
Clear, straw yellow with greenish highlights. Produced from Treixadura and Palomino; fragrant and limpid fruit aromas, with floral notes; fresh and light on the palate; balanced, fruity, pure and potent lingering aromas.

B. Lapatena-Caves do Ribeiro

Santa Cruz de Arrabaldo (Orense)
Tel. (988) 384200
Fax (988) 384068

This winery is the latest ambitious project of the Arnoya group, which is a large holding company with five members in this region. Arnoya also controls the Caves do Ribeiro label and the Cosecheros de Vino del Ribeiro winery. This facility is the most spectacular in all of Galicia: the huge, 15,000 square meter building of avant-garde design houses the most advanced techniques used in vinification. At each harvest, this winery is able to process up to ten million kg of grapes. Lapatena offers whites, reds and even the first Galician sparkling wine made from a traditional method. Having no vineyards of its own, Lapatena is completely reliant on area viticulturalists. Interestingly enough, the winery has such a large number of suppliers that it has established a service department for area farmers that assists and advises them in the best varietals to plant according to the various types of terrain. This is also helping them to revive their native varieties.

Fin de Siglo 1991
Infinitely clear to the eye, on the nose and on the palate. Comprised of Treixadura, Torrontés and Lado; quite balanced and fruity.

Fin de Siglo Brut
The first Galician sparkling wine; made from Torrontés, Lado and Treixadura. Pale yellow with consistent, medium-fine perlage; bright and sparkling clean. Fruity aromas are not very intense; a light bite on the palate develops pleasantly, though not very long-lasting.

RIBEIRO
NOROESTE
SPAIN

1101

RIBEIRO
NOROESTE
SPAIN

Coop. Vitivinícola del Ribeiro

Valdepereira, s/n
Ribadavia (Orense)
Tel. (988) 470175

Some area viticulturalists joined together in the 1960s to create this cooperative. Their main goal was to be able to bottle their own wine with a guarantee of quality. As a result, the noble vines along the Miño and Avia rivers, once neglected and nearing extinction, were completely revitalized to provide the co-op with its excellent fruit. Today membership has grown to over 800 farmers, who have come to rely on the co-op for its instructive courses relative to their field, information on priming and advice on the correct selection of varieties and rootstocks. It also offers economic incentives to the grower of the best quality raw materials. The members' 500 ha of vineyards are planted with an array of different varieties, including white Treixadura, Torrontés, Palomino and Caíño Blanco, and red Brancellao, Mencía, Souson and Alicante. Vitivinícola del Ribeiro prides itself on having one of Spain's best vinification facilities, capable of reaching worthy levels with its most common wines and touching the stars with its top products.

Amadeus 1991　　　　🍇 🍇 ②
Light yellow with slight shades of green; fruity and floral aromas are intense and pure. Biting entrance on the palate; displays balance and length. 100% Godello.

Pazos de Ullos 1991　　　🍇 ②
Beautiful pale yellow with mother-of-pearl highlights; shiny and crystal-like. Delicate floral perfumes are followed by lightness and freshness on the palate. Produced from two of this area's top varietals, Godello and Treixadura.

Viña Costeira 1991　　　🍇 ①
When released onto the market, it acted as a cure-all for the entire denomination. Year after year, it maintains its limpidness and balance. Produced from Torrontés, Treixadura and Palomino.

Bodegas Senen Guitián Velasco

La Tapada, s/n
Rubiá de Valdeorras (Orense)
Tel. (988) 324195

The Guitián brothers made a big splash on the wine scene when they first arrived, quickly establishing themselves in an area with great, untapped potential. Despite the numerous admirers of the Valdeorras DO (and especially of the native white Godello variety) this wine area is finding success hard to come by. Nine out of the winery's ten hectares of vines are cultivated with Godello. Senen Guitián cultivates his terraced vineyards along the Sil river so well, the Agricultural Committee of the Xunta de Galicia considers them model vines. This is a great honor, considering there are 2,500 ha of vines in this DO and only 3% are planted with Godello. Senen Gutián Velasco is not very big, but it is technically well-equipped and has 65,000 bottle capacity for Godello wine each harvest.

Viña Guitián 1991　　　　🍇 ②
A powerful, clean-cut interpretation of the Godello variety. Well-balanced on the palate, fruity lingering aromas are intense and pure.

RIBEIRO
NOROESTE
SPAIN

1102

VALDEORRAS
NOROESTE
SPAIN

Bodega Coop. Jesus Nazareno

Av. 18 de Julio, 92
El Barco (Orense)
Tel. (988) 320262

Jesus Nazareno has worked for years with driving intensity to do something new and important in Vladeorras, often considered the 'Cinderella' of Galicia's DO wine areas. Founded in 1963, the co-op now counts 500 members and 200 ha of quality grapes-producing property. The vineyards' most important varietal is Godello, which was rediscovered in the 1970s. Other varietals include Moza Fresca, Jerez (or Palomino), Doña Blanca, and red Garnacha, Grao Negro and Mencía. Ever since the facilities were renovated, the quality of Nazareno's wines have improved considerably. Among the five million lt of wine offered each year, there are some interesting products. The Godello, for example, has been the Coop.'s standard quality white for years. Also noteworthy is the red Menciño, made from Mencía grapes, a varietal used by almost all of the area's wineries to produce quality reds.

Godello 1990   ②
Strawish yellow with greenish highlights; clean; intense floral perfumes develop on the nose; balanced and glycerous on the palate. Typical lingering aromas of the varietal.

Menciño Tinto 1990   ①
Young wine; attractive cherry red with shades of violet-blue and vibrant granite highlights. Red fruit perfumes and hints of fermentation on the nose; meaty and flavorful on the palate.

Rectoral Amandi

Amandi
Sober (Lugo)
Tel. (988) 384200
Fax (988) 384068

Great wines are often surrounded by mysteries and legends about their origins. One such story tells of how the wines from the small and beautiful provinces of Lugo and Orense were once tasted by the Romans from Caesar's tima. One of them in particular, Aurelius, preferred the wine above all others. Many centuries later the powerful Arnoya group has come to rescue and renew this downtrodden area, suffering from the slow disapprearance of its varietals and the systematic blending of its grapes and wines with those from the Castille area. Arnoya chose the town of Sber to build its small but technologically-advanced winery, honored with the legendary name Armandi; also the name of the Galicia district famous for its high concentration of monasteries with centuries-old traditions of vinification. The winery's vineyards produce only a minimum percentage of the red Mencía grapes needed for the annual 100,000 bottle production; the rest come from area growers.

Rectoral de Amandi 1990   ②
Coupage of mostly Mencía and a smaller part of Garnacha; handsome cherry red with ruby shades. Fruity aromas are Sylvan and clean; full-bodied and balanced on the palate.

VALDEORRAS
NOROESTE
SPAIN

1103

VINO DE LA TIERRA
NOROESTE
SPAIN

SWITZERLAND

Literally surrounded by the most important wine-producing regions, Switzerland has, in a sense, tried to close itself off in an effort to advocate its own wine culture. On the other hand, it has inevitably welcomed, or rather been subject to, many different influences.

The Ancient Romans were the first to cultivate vines in what was then their Helvetic province. By the early Middle Ages, little wine was drunk compared to beer consumption. In those times, Monasteries were appointed as viticultural centers and helped to spread wine culture. In 1442, a group of Cistercense monks terraced vineyards which still produce the most famous Swiss whites. In the centuries that followed, Switzerland's vineyards underwent considerable changes. Those that weren't profitable were abbandoned during the Plague and during the rural crisis in the late Middle Ages. Further on, more vineyards were created; during this century, vine diseases and industrialization have gradually reduced the area planted to vine, to the present figure of 15,000 hectares.

The most important wine areas are in the west, particularly in the cantons of Wallis (or Valais, in French), Waadtland (Vaud), Genf (Genève) and Neuenburg (Neuchâtel). Roughly 8% of the total vined area is in Italian Switzerland, mainly in the canton of Tessin (Ticino, in Italian). Eastern, German-speaking Switzerland more or less forms an indipendent unit. Wine-growing in the more French-speaking west is characterized by small companies, as only a handful of families manage to earn a living from their harvest. The few who vinify their own produce can be considered the pioneers of modern Valais viticulture, noted for its more organic growing methods and the quality of the wines produced. Other, larger wineries, and the provincial viticultural union itself, are now beginning to follow the same policies, often with remarkably good results. Some from Vaud are very popular, and tend to sell more quickly than the Valais wines, while Neuchâtel is has the lowest yields per hectare despite its ideal climate. In fact, Neuchâtel sets a fine example, as vine-growers are allowed to pick one kg of Chasselas for each square meter of vines. The white Chasselas and the Pinot Noir are the most common varietals in west, the latter doing particularly well in Valais.

In Eastern Switzerland, vines grow only where the terrain is particularly favorable, in tiny pockets of land here and there; the best are around Lake Zurich, in the wine-producing region between Winterthur and Schaffhausen, in Limmattal and in Unteren Tosstal. 70% of the total vined area is planted to Pinot Noir, the remaining 30% for white grapes; mainly Müller Thurgau, with some crispy fresh Raucshling.

Ticinese viticulture, on the other hand, is characterized by two large viticultural unions, a few fairly large wineries, a few dozen self-sufficient wineries and a number of small vine-growers. A group of young German viticulturalists settled in Ticino about ten years ago, intent on producing a rich, worthy Merlot. With considerable skill and commitment, they have done much to improve the quality of Ticinese wines. Lately, the Merlot produced here has given some particularly interesting results, lending a certain credibility to this wine which, after all, represents two thirds of the total in Ticino.

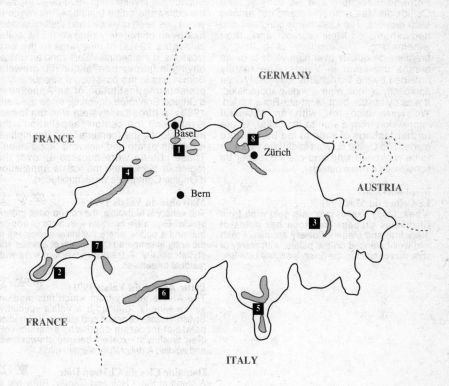

GERMANY

FRANCE

Basel

Zürich

AUSTRIA

Bern

FRANCE

ITALY

1	Aargaud
2	Genève
3	Graubun
4	Neuchâtel
5	Ticino
6	Valais
7	Vaud
8	Zürich

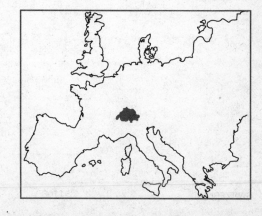

Fernand Blanchard

Le Cellier du Mas
1801 Mont-sur-Rolle
Tel. (021) 8251922

Unlike nearby Féchy, the Mont-sur-Rolle zone features a large number of family-run vineyards. It was above all the noble families of Bern who, more than anyone else, established substantial vineyards here centuries ago but even small-scale producers can manage to produce a good Mont. Fernand Blanchard and his sons at their Cellier du Mas property stand out among such growers. The Blanchards bring skill and dedication to their estate and their winemaking. Their policy of putting a premium on quality over high yelds is by no means universal in Valais. The results obtained by the Blanchards fully justify their approach, as their wine is widely appreciated. It was by far the best Mont-sur-Rolle tasted. We were also left with an excellent impression from a visit to the cellar, where further tastings of wine in the barrel were made. The Cellier du Mas is definitely a cellar to be reckoned with and can no longer be considered a mere outsider.

Mont-sur-Rolle   ♈ ①
Le Cellier du Mas 1991
A beautifully expressive pale gold wine from Chasselas grapes. The nose has notes of grapefruit and elegant flowery aromas. Fresh and well-balanced on the palate, with plenty of style and character, the finish is slightly bitterish.

Charles Bonvin fils

1950 Sion
Tel. (027) 314131
Fax (027) 314707

Charles Bonvin fils is firmly entrenched in what one might call the Sion 'wine establishment' for the cellar, founded in 1858, is the oldest in Valais. Of course, a venerable history is not by itself a guarantee of success, and the new manager has kept this in mind when implementing his new ideas. Substantial investments have been made in the cellar and office buildings, the range of wines has been reviewed and the bottle stock has been completely renewed. The cellar cultivates 22 ha. of vineyards in the best locations in the central Valais zone as well as buying in grapes from about 200 growers. Bonvin has in the past fought strenuously to promote the institution of an Appellation d'Origine Contrôlée, favoring, since the early 1980s, a three-tier system with the lowest level being the canton "appellation", the middle level, the "comune" and the highest level, the estate and vineyard "appellation". These criteria were adopted all over the region in 1991 when the Valais Appellation d'Origine Contrôlées were introduced.

Malvoisie du Valais 1991   ♈ ♈ ②
The variety is Malvoisie, the color a pale, greeny yellow. Evocative bouquet with hints of tropical fruit and a palate where the initial sweetness of the entry is tempered by a wealth of aromas and stylish acidity. A treat for lovers of wine with residual sweetness.

Petite Arvine du Valais 1991   ♈ ♈ ②
The Arvine variety from which this medium yellow wine is obtained is a Valais specialty. Stylish aromas of peach and apricot. Full-bodied palate of moderate depth and a seductively lively finish with excellent balance of sweetness and acidity. A delightfully elegant glass.

Domaine Clos du Château Dôle   ♈ ②
A blend of Pinot Noir and Gamay. Ruby red in the glass with a nose where plum is to the fore. The palate, though still rather hard, has plenty of structure, body and bite. The finish is perhaps a little too warm. A frank, attractive wine, to drink in a mountain refuge.

Jean-Michel Conne

1605 Chexbres
Tel. (021) 9462686
Fax (021) 9463218

Jean-Michel Conne looks and acts younger than 45 years-old. He is passionately dedicated to his work and has fun with it, which is what keeps him young. In 1986 he won an international gold medal at Lubiana with his Oeil-de-Perdrix in the Rosé category. All things considered, however, his favorite wine is not Rosé nor Pinot Noir, aged at length in oak barrels, and not even Chardonnay (with which he is experimenting at the moment) but St. Saphorin Le Semillant, which comes from the Chasselas variety that is typical of this region. Jean-Michel Conne knows that what is on the vine, ends up in the glass. He spends much time in the vineyard itself, harvesting and processing separately only the most ripe clusters of grapes growing in the rows along the supporting walls which retain the sun's heat. Only these grapes are worthy of the appellation of St. Saphorin, which is, by chance, also Conne's birthplace. The result is an elegant, robust wine full of character and anything but bulky. Altogether approximately six hectares are cultivated, three of which are in Bonvillars at the entrance to the canton of Neuenburg. Jean-Michel Conne mostly grows Pinot Noir and Gamay. From the strong limestone in the soil of Giura come firmly-built, robust red wines. Neurenburg Red is considered one of the finest of all Swiss wines.

Dézaley Plan Perdu 1991   ℬ ②
Made from the Chasselas grape, light-yellow in color with greenish traces. On the nose, hints of toasted bread, rich but restrained. A wine with character, fresh, lively and delicately seasoned.

St. Saphorin Le Sémillant 1991   ℬ ②
Also made from Chasselas, slightly aged, pale yellow in color, pure and refined bouquet. Intense, with hints of yeast, lemon and bread; fruity and lively on the palate. A refreshing wine with a pleasing aftertaste of bitter almonds.

Aigle Les Touraises 1991   🍇 ②
Clear in color and transparent, made from Pinot Noir and Oberlin, a bit closed on the nose, pleasing but slight of taste, with a finish that calls to mind cooked fruit. Already aged enough.

Thomas Donatsch

Zum Ochsen
7208 Malans
Tel. (081) 511117

An artist, Thomas Donatsch of Malans is a true wine enthusiast: he painted the label of his wines (all oak-aged) himself. He also loves jazz music and, in fact, plays the saxophone and the piano. He likes to cook, but hardly gets a chance as he and his family are too busy running their winery. Thomas has little time for anything else except wine, his greatest passion. Malans, his home-town, is one of the warmest villages in Switzerland. Hidden in a valley hollow, it is protected from the cold winds and not threatened by hail. The land is perfectly suited to grow grapes. Not being too high in altitude, it insures a good acidity level: the conditions are perfect for producing excellent wine. Thomas makes his reds using the French method (long fermentation, aging in wooden barrels, oak for the better lots, up to 18 months). Together with the Pinot Noir, small quantities of Chardonnay and Cabernet Sauvignon are cultivated. As with Toni Meier of Zum Sternen, Thomas Donatsch's wines can be enjoyed at reasonable prices at the Zum Ochsen.

Malanser Crémant   ℬ ③
Aged in bottle in the traditional méthod champenoise, pale straw-yellow, bright pearly, rich, with medium grain bubbles; vigorous on the nose, hints of fruit and red currant and sambuca leaves. A simple, fruity, supple wine, persistent on the palate; pleasant as an aperitif.

Malanser Blauburgunder   🍇🍇 ③
Réserve Barrique 1988
Ruby red color of medium intensity, a fruity bouquet, intense with toasty hints and traces of oak; clean and linear at first, soft with few yet marked tannins. A smokey aroma with light oakiness, slightly bitter but also fruity on the finish.

Melanser Cabernet   🍇🍇 ③
Réserve Barrique 1988
Also aged in oak: purple-ruby in color, delicate bouquet; with breathing it reveals the more woody taste with traces of mineral and cherry jam; full of surprise, savoury, soft, with tannins present yet well-balanced. A bit warm on the finish.

Pierre Dupraz

Domaine Les Curiades
1233 Lully
Tel. (022) 7572815
Fax (022) 7574785

In Geneva, Pierre Dupraz is considered King of the Aligoté. His grandfather had already begun to cultivate this white grape, with its robust and strong character, from Burgundy which is certainly better than his fame. It makes an aromatic, vigorous wine, fairly acidic by Swiss standards. The 10 ha vineyard is, however, as in the past, planted mainly to Chasselas. On grape varieties, Dupraz doesn't follow the politics of many of his colleagues who tend to replace the Chasselas with red grapes. In all truth, Dupraz did, in fact, end up reducing the amount of Chasselas from 70% to 40%, replacing them with Chardonny, Pinot Noir, Gamay, Aligoté and even Cabernet and Merlot. Pulling any more Chasselas up would not have been wise in the long-run, according to Dupraz. Furthermore, he is not convinced of using only Chardonnay that would produce a better wine. Pierre Dupraz is a realist. He does not consider himself invincible just because he has a range of excellent wines and is able to offer a oak-fermented Chardonnay. At a time when the competition among wine producers is on the rise and the atmosphere of the marketplace is becoming more and more aggressive, one must learn to be prudent and watchful.

Aligoté Domaine Les Curiades 1991 �†† ①
Light yellow, a restrained floral bouquet, buttery and seasoned; vigorous on the palate, with a robust and lively acidity. A fairly acidulous wine, goes well with fish and shellfish.

Chasselas �†† ①
Domaine Les Curiades 1991
Light yellow with green highlights, a bouquet with a slight hint of fermentation, yeast, bread and bitter almonds; effervescent and light in the mouth, savoury, with a notable presence of carbonic acid; delicately fruity, a bit weak. Almost milky on the finish. A pleasant Chasselas.

Pinot Noir ☙ ①
Domaine Les Curiades 1991
Strong ruby in color, rich and variegated bouquet, medium-bodied, velvety on the palate, firmly-built with well-balanced tannin; very harmonious.

Etienne Fonjallaz

Le Crêt
1098 Epesses
Tel. (021) 7991016

The wines of the well-respected Dézaley appellation, in the region of Lavaux on Lake Geneva, have for many years met with the taste of consumers. This certainly explains their fame and, however, has its affect on the price. Dézaley wines are so rare that vintage wine cellars, restaurant owners and wine drinkers must make due with a few precious bottles. For this reason, Etienne Fonjallaz, a wine producer who has always opted for quality over quantity, is forced to repeat the same 'rigamorol'. It is important to note that he does not do so out of vanity. In his words, in fact, one can note a sense of regret when he must turn away clients. "I'm sorry, but that's all I have". In this way, by choosing to limit production less wine is made but what little there is, has a strong character. On the other hand, with more work and more harvest, a wine of mediocre quality is obtained and the demand eventually decreases.

Dézalay Les Grandins 1991 �†† ②
Made from Chasselas grapes, a spicy wine with an unmistakable smokey aroma. It presents a true richness of body. It is round and rich to the taste; in short, an excellent wine and without a doubt very harmonious.

Rosé de Pinot Amadou ▨ ①
Made from Pinot Noir and processed into a rosé which is also called Oeil-de-Perdrix in Switzerland. Orange in color, with a bouquet a bit aggressive, spritzy and lively on the palate. An uncomplicated, easy-drinking wine.

Pinot Epine Noire 1991 ☙ ②
A nice red characterized by its ruby color, delicate bouquet, elegant and harmonious, easy on the palate, refined and full aromatic nuances.

Jean-René Germanier

1963 Vétroz
Tel. (027) 361216
Fax (027) 365132

The Germanier family is known in Vétroz for their Bon Père William, which was the first Swiss grappa made from William's pears. 34 year-old Jean-René, who has been running the business for four years, has become, in the meantime, the mainstay of the vineyard and the cellars. His favorite variety is the older Amigne that, even though it is of Italian origin, is counted among the more traditional Swiss varieties and makes up more than 75% of the varieties cultivated in Vétroz. Germanier reminds us wittily, "Our firm produces almost 6% of the worldwide production of Amigne, 10,000-12,000 lt each year." He claims to be in favor of a precise hierarchy on his 7.5 ha of vineyard, half of which is on a steep incline and half on a flat plain. The wines from the plain are sold under the label of the wine, or with an appellation of origin, while the wines from the hilly area are sold as Grands Crus with the appellation of the vineyard. This priority results not so much from the alcohol content as from the extracts and the balance. "In a good year, from a favorable position and with the right pruning, we always obtain a high enough percentage of natural sugar in the grapes. In Switzerland we are spoiled in that we don't have to tremble in fear as we wait for the grapes to ripen. We can easily choose the havest date."

Fendant Les Terrasses 1991   ℱ ②
Made from Chasselas grapes, straw-yellow color with green reflections, lightly effervescent; rich in body, with aromas of green bananas and grapefruit. A vigorous and substantial wine, with a bitter aftertaste. A typical Chasselas.

Amigne de Vétroz 1990   ℱ ②
A golden hue; on the nose presents a delicate varietal scent and floral perfumes; it is a round wine, harmonious and well-balanced to the taste, On the finish there is a hint of sweet residue. A decidedly good Amigne.

Dôle Balavaud 1990   ♥ ②
The color tends toward red; ripe perfumes, with an aroma of wilted almond flowers, pink and smoky. Made from Pinot Noir and Gamay, it is round and soft on the palate. One appreciates its pleasant and inviting drinkablity.

Domaine de l'Hôpital Pourtalès

Cave de Troub - Route de Troub 4
2088 Cressier
Tel. (038) 471151
Fax (038) 472605

Situated in the gracious town of Cressier on Lake Neuchâtel, the Domaine de l'Hôpital Pourtalès boasts a long history. As far back as the Middle Ages, the monks of the monastery Trub, in Emmenthal, produced what was called Truberwein. The holding was later sold to the Public Hospital of Bern, and subsequently fell into the hands of the French merchant, Jacques-Louis de Pourtalès, who, at the beginning of the 14th century, founded a hospital for the needy of the city. He sought out the financial backing of various businesses, one of which was the Domaine de Troub. Today the Cave de Troub still belongs to the foundation of the Hôpital Pourtalès. Under the direction of the enologist and administrator, Jean-Paul Ruedin, and the head cellarmaster, Hans Maurer, this vineyard produces (from its 11.6 ha) a spicy Pinot Noir and a sparkling and light Chasselas, which are always put up for auction in February. The object of the foundation is to produce the best wines of Neuchâtel and to be, in a certain sense, the ambassador of this small but refined canton. The prices reached at the auction of the Hôpital Pourtalès set the prices for the entire region.

Hôpital Pourtalès 1991   ℱ ①
The Chasselas of Neuchatel are always a bit lighter and more fizzy than the same wines of other regions of western Switzerland. This wine is no exception; it presents a light yellow hue, a flowery perfume and is lively and refined on the palate with an elegant acidity.

Hôpital Pourtalès 1990   ♥♥ ②
In the canton of Neuchâtel, only a special clone of Pinot Noir called Cortaillod can be used. From 100% Cortaillod, it has a beautiful ruby-red hue and a very ample bouquet with hints of bread crust, smoke and cherry; harmonious flavor, well-balanced, lively and very expressive.

Daniel Huber

Ronco di Persico
6998 Monteggio
Tel/Fax (091) 731754

With his doctorate in forestry, Daniel Huber struck out to plant the vineyard of Ronco di Persico, at Monteggio, to cultivate Merlot and some Pinot Noir in 1980. Another small plot nearby has been added to the original vineyard in recent years. By 1984 his Merlot Ronco di Persico was already a success, which is very surprising, given the age of the vines and the mediocrity of the harvest that year. In the following years, this wine maintained the high standard set in the year of its debut. Daniel Huber's wine is distinguished by its rather light texture, with harmonious, well-integrated tannins. It is not intense and robust like the Merlots of other areas of Ticino, but its elegance makes it appealing. At times a certain aggressiveness is apparent in these wines, a feature typical of the Merlots of this region, the Melcanton, where we find lesser values on the Oeschsle scale and rather high in acidity.

Fusto 4/90 1990 ♟♟ ②
Strong purple-red; intense and concentrated, a rich and extremely fruity bouquet with hints of chocolate, sweet wood and orange peel. Still a bit hard and reluctant on the palate, very tannic and in need of further bottle aging. A wine for the connoisseur, made from Pinot Noir and Merlot, fermented and aged in oak barrique.

Montagna Magica 1990 ♟ ③
Dark purple-red; intense bouquet with hints of vanilla, smoke and, after breathing some, blackberries; a clean-cut wine; harmonious and round, of medium length, still a bit aggressive in tannin. Made from Merlot and with a little Cabernet Sauvignon and Syrah. Aged in barrique.

Ronco di Persico ♟ ②
Merlot del Ticino 1990
Young and intense in color, with aromas of very ripe fruit, on the palate it presents an aroma of chocolate; a fruity wine, rather simple, lacking a bit in character and expressiveness.

Caves Imesch

3960 Sierre
Tel. (027) 551065
Fax (027) 561371

In 1990 Caves Imesch produced the finest Swiss white wine ever made from Chasselas grapes. In 1991 this Valais vineyard received the Chasselas Cup for its Fendant Soleil de Sierre, and with the 1991 harvest, Soleil de Sierre has a good chance of a repeat performance. Fruity, lightly sparkling and not too heavy, it is just what one would expect from a Swiss white wine made from Chasselas, a grape known in Germany as Gutedel. The young director, Yves Roduit, is proud of his Fendant but certainly is not one to rest on his laurels. With a little help from the enologist Pierre-Antoine Héritier, Roduit wants to continue his search for greater quality, to improve his Fendant as well as the other wines peculiar to Valais like Petite Arvine, Cornalino and Malvasia. The latter in particularly dear to Valais and has been since the end of the last century. Imesch has himself made two unforgettable interpretations of it. There is good reason to expect that the other wines will eventually reach the same standard as the Fendant, and we are certain that in future this vineyard will offer us some wonderful surprises.

Fendant Soleil de Sierre 1991 ♟♟ ②
The 1991 vintage is pale yellow in color, with green highlights and a fruity perfume, particularly lemon and melon: full-bodied, lively on the palate and lightly sparkling with a wonderful finish. An excellent Fendant.

Fendant Soleil de Sierre 1990 ♟♟ ②
Made from Chasselas, fairly typical, with a delicate and refined aroma. Robust and lively taste, harmonious and very pleasant. Truly a worthy interpretation of the variety.

Pierre-Alain Indermühle

Caves des Cimes
1880 Bex
Tel. (025) 631486
Fax (025) 633529

Bex is located in Chablais, where Vaud borders Valais, just before the point where the Rhône flows into the extreme eastern edge of Lake Geneva. The region of Chablais is home to the most famous wine-making villages of Bex, with such celebrated names as Yvorne and Aigle. The people of Bex hardly lack inventive, however, and Pierre-Alain Indermühle is living proof. No other Valais wine-maker of recent years has been able to generate as much publicity as this young man, who personally tends to his five hectares of property as well as another three belonging to the abbey of St. Maurice. He caused a great scandal in the past with a new system for drying the grapes: "Whatever the Föhn can do, I can do too!" And, with that, he built a sort of tunnel in which the grape, just after being picked, was ventilated with hot air allowing for slight raisining. This process was used only for certain wines, such as Pinot Noir and Pinot Gris. Indermühle has rejuvenated his vines and places strong emphasis on the ecological aspect of his work. In fact, one franc of his bottle price is refundable on bottle return.

Doré de Cimes Bex AC 1991
Light golden in hue, a clean yet restrained bouquet; in the mouth this white made from the Chasselas varietal is lively, fizzy and harmonious. A refreshing and fun wine.

Yvorne 1990
Light gold; an aroma of gooseberry and ripe melon; pleasing to the taste with a lightly smoky aroma; full and well-built. A rarity unfortunately; they produce only 2,000 bottles a year. The varietal is Pinot Gris.

Le Solitaire Pinot Noir de Bex 1989
The ruby red color indicates maturity; a fairly intense bouquet, characterized by the scent of oak from the barrel, with traces of vanilla; full and well-built on the palate, with aromatic nuances. A wine with a strong hallmark of the barrel, for Pinot Noir lovers.

Geri Lienhard

Dorfstrasse 1
8428 Teufen
Tel. (01) 8650214

With a degree in agriculture, Geri Lienhard started out with three hectares of vineyards at the beginning of the 1980s. These days, all the different varieties that one could possibly grow are featured in those same vineyards: Riesling/Sylvaner, Rauschling, Blauburgunder, Pinot Gris and Gewürztraminer. Needless to say, Lienhard is a firm believer in the varietal richness of wine. He personally cultivates his vines according to the integrated production principle that he feels is the best compromise between traditional and biological viticulture. It guarantees the best treatment possible for the earth and the plants, as well as steady earnings. In the cellar, Geri Leinhard lets his passion for experimentation run wild; the must gives rise to all kinds of crazy ideas and new ambitions emerge. The result of his innovation is an aromatic and tannic Auslese of Blauburgunder. He later created, under the name Kristall, an unusual cuvée of Rauschling, Riesling/Sylvaner and Pinot Gris, aged in oak barrel.

Teufener Gewürztraminer 1990
Golden yellow hue; a clean and very expressive bouquet with an aroma of honey and blooming flowers; a fairly light wine but spicy and aromatic, delicate and of medium persistence. Elegant finish, typically bitter; a perfectly executed white.

Teufener Riesling x Sylvaner 1990
Light yellow with green highlights; intense and floral bouquet with delicate, spicy nuances; juicy and round on the palate, semi-sweet and soft with a faintly accentuated acidity and a lightly bitter finish: a pleasant wine to drink.

Teufener Blauburgunder Auslese 1990

Made from Pinot Noir and partly aged in oak barrique: the color is a young purple-red, of medium intensity. On the nose it reveals a strong aroma of dark grapes with a slight trace of oak; delicate and very refined to the taste. The tannins are harmonious but evident and lend this rather soft, light wine a certain character.

Adrian Mathier & Co.

Nouveau Salquenen
3970 Salgesch
Tel. (027) 556028
Fax (027) 562413

Adrian Mathier and his sons deserve to be counted among the enological pioneers of Valais. Dynamic and innovative, they stimulated this region in a big way. They not only do they know how to make good wine, they also know how to market it. Mathier's business is one of the largest in the area; besides managing his own considerably sized 14 ha-property, he also vinifies the harvest of 200 other local growers. The name of the winery, Nouveau Salquenen, is a classic example of the owners' weakness for sophisticated-sounding labels. Here we find a Dôle Sang de l'Enfer, a line of white wines called Terre Promise, a wine aged in oak barrique, called Ambassadeur, (and not only its name makes it worthy of being served to ambassadors) and a Pinot Noir grand cru ambitiously called Pyramides. Why not suggest elegance if the wine is worthy? Even in the traditional canton of Valais, there is room for these linguistic frivolities, as long as the quality is there.

Ambassadeur Fumé Gros ♀♀ ③
Rhin de Chamoson 1990
The varietal is Gros Rhin, aged in oak barrels. A pale yellow; pleasantly fruity on the nose but a bit too woody. On the palate the same aromas dominate. This cannot be called a lingering wine; it can, however, be considered an interesting experiment.

Terre Promise Chamoson 1991 ♀ ②
Light yellow hue with greenish reflections; a fruity bouquet with slight hints of aldehyde, of organic and yeast substances. Made from Chasselas, this white is robust and has a well-defined finish.

Ambassadeur des Domaines ♀♀ ③
Adrian Mathier 1990
A Pinot Noir aged in oak barrel; ruby-red; a bouquet typical of this varietal, although contrasted by a strong aroma of oak which almost seems to dominate. Harmonious and rich in body, without roughness; could be defined as a wine marked by the spirit of the times.

Simon Maye & fils

1956 Saint-Pierre-de-Clages
Tel. (027) 864181

In general a lot is expected from children of a famous person, and Axel Maye has to live with the fact that his father is as much a star of the wine-world as Freddy Girardet is of Swiss cuisine. Maye's wines are regularly awarded first prize in wine-tasting events; so what's their secret? Hard work in both the vineyard and the cellar is the priority of this viticultural family, constantly reinforcing their prestige. The two sons, Axel and Jean-François, are the founders of the association VITI 2000, which brings together young winemakers in favor of a higher degree of professionalism and high quality products. Their daily routine for a long time now has included careful soil analysis, ecologically and organically sound viticultural practices, crop production control and the use of modern vinification techniques. All of this has contributed to the strong character of their wines and a particularly fruity and decidedly elegant bouquet.

Fendant Trémazières 1991 ♀♀♀ ②
Light yellow with greenish reflections, the bouquet is fresh and fruity with hints of blossoming flowers. Made from Chasselas, it is light and fruity on the palate, lively and sparkling, with a pleasant and fruity finish and a refined touch of sweet residue. A very well-made Fendant.

Chardonnay 1990 ♀♀♀ ③
Aged in oak barrels, a lemon yellow hue; the bouquet is intense and fruity with a hint of vanilla mixed with a slightly smoky tone. On the palate the acidity is in perfect harmony with the body, of medium fullness; the result is an elegant and lively wine. Certainly a fine example of a Chardonnay; very well-made.

Pinot Noir 1990 ♀ ②
Medium-intense ruby-red; a bit closed on the nose at first, revealing typical Pinot aromas; on the palate still a bit rough, very tannic with a body of medium consistency. Still a young wine which will improve with bottle aging.

Andreas und Toni Meier

Endingerstr. 7
5303 Würenlingen
Tel. (056) 981413
Fax (056) 982902

The Meiers are perhaps more famous for their viticultural school than for their wines, which are nevertheless rich in character. Albert, the father of Toni, created the clone of the Pinot Noir 10, the oldest example of Pinot Noir in German Switzerland. Toni and his son, Andreas Meier, work their seven hectares of estate-vineyards chiefly with this very refined clone, which provides a harvest of average quantity high Öechsle value and a strong acidity, although it is fairly prone to disease. This is why many grape growers of eastern Switzerland, an area with frequent autumn fog, prefer the Mariafeld clone, which is less refined but more resistent. Even Toni Meier has often wished for warmer and drier autumns for his best vines, planted on two hectares of what used to be the Sion monastery. In Aargau, it is possible to achieve a high Öechsle value: temperatures of 90° are not uncommon, and when the sun beats down, as in 1989 and 1990, even a sweet Pinot Noir and a Beerenauslese can be made. For some time Andreas Meier, always eager to experiment, has also produced an excellent dry Spumante from the Riesling/Sylvaner varietal. The Meier wines may be sampled in the warm, friendly atmosphere of the family's restaurant, Zum Sternen.

Klingnauer Kloster Sion ⚜ ②
Pinot Gris 1990
Delicately fruity, it comes from their favorite vineyard, Kloster Sion. As it ages it becomes more and more complex: the bouquet shows hints of quince, honey and apricot. Soft on the palate and mellow; a lingering wine.

Opus N° 4 Crémant ⚜ ③
A brut Spumante pas dosé made from Riesling/Sylvaner in the traditional méthode champenoise; not too frothy but rather lively and refreshing, with aromas typical of this varietal; slightly spicy with floral tones. A lively texture and pleasantly dry.

Klingnauer Kloster Sion ⚜⚜ ②
Eichenfässli 1990
A bright ruby-red hue, made from Pinot Noir grapes; pleasant on the nose, the aroma one would expect from Pinot Noir mixed with a toasted scent of new wood; full on the palate, semi-sweet, soft and lingering.

Domaine du Mont d'Or

1962 Pont-de-la-Morge
Tel. (027) 362032

"We're looking for richness" is the philosophy of this super-vineyard which produces wine from an area of 21 ha at Mont d'Or. They are wines which regularly achieve a higher grade on the Öechsle scale than any other wine in the canton. The most important varietal is certainly the Johannesberg, which covers almost half of the planted land. This varietal was brought to Valais from the Rhine during the 1870s by George Masson, son of the founder of the Mont d'Or winery. The grape probably originally came from the castle of Johannesberg, hence its name. The late-harvest version of the Johannesberg, like the St Martin (picked no earlier than November 11th) or like 1er Décembre, is certainly able to hold its own among the great German Trockenbeerenauslese wines and the French Sauternes. The late-harvesters come from varieties that are specialities of Valais like Malvasia, Ermitage and Petite Arvine. They make concentrated and delicately sweet wines and are without a doubt the hallmark of Mont d'Or. The Öechsle degree is given great importance in the production of these wines; we could tell this not only by the taste but also from the fact that, as soon as we arrived, the previous year's degrees were read out to us in tones of fully justifiable pride.

Johannisberg doux 1991 ⚜⚜ ③
Made from Sylvaner; straw-yellow color with grayish reflections; fruity on the nose, rich and delicate with hints of cooked fruit. Medium-bodied and nicely sweet, with a slightly bitter finish. In our opinion, this is the best result that could possibly come from a Sylvaner.

Petite Arvine du Valais 1991 ⚜⚜ ③
Lemon yellow in color; a delicate floral bouquet; on the palate presents a flavor of grapefruit, peach and apricot; full, robust, the sweet finish is well-integrated with the acidity. Extremely pleasant on the nose and palate.

Cornalin du Valais 1991 ⚜⚜ ②
Intense dark red with violet highlights; bouquet also intense and spicy, rich with still dominant tannins. Solid texture for this excellent red of Valais, it is not difficult to predict a grand future.

Charles and Jean-Michel Novelle

Le Gran Clos
1242 Satigny
Tel. (022) 7531598

Satigny is the town in Switzerland with the greatest area of vineyards, but is also a place full of contrasts. Next-door to the important organization, Vin Union, which runs three local cooperatives, a young viticulturalist works in his father's vineyard and never fails to surprise his colleagues, even those most open to change and innovation. Jean-Michel Novelle is a perfectionist. His winery is more like a laboratory: steel vats line the walls in an orderly fashion. Father, Charles Novelle, and son, Jean-Michel, cultivate more grape varietals on their 7 ha-plot than any other viticulturalist in Geneva. Jean-Michel, having studying enology at Chagrins, is a true fountain of ideas. He wants to make wine that is true, one that is rich in aroma and flavor, that comes as close as possible to that of the grape of origin, that would shine through in a blind tasting. For this reason, Novelle makes most of his wine straight, with two different styles of refining; he offers a young version refined in small barrels and a barrique-aged version, which featured the typical toasted and vanilla aromas. Novelle also makes an excellent sparkling wine and is at present experimenting with the production of sweet wines, typically French in flavor.

Gewurztraminer 1990   ❦ ②
Straw-yellow in color, with a bouquet that is very pronounced and intense; on the palate it is full-bodied and spicy yet at the same time delicate and elegant; lightly bitter on the finish.

Sauvignon 1990   ❦ ❦ ③
Light yellow with greenish reflections; a seductive bouquet with hints of strawberry and melon; in the mouth characterized by vegetive aromas (green tomatoes and olives in particular); aging in barrique is perfect for this fruity wine; elegant and well-vinified.

Merlot 1990   ❦ ❦ ③
Deep purple-red; vinified only from selected grapes, it has an intense bouquet with hints of vanilla and red grapes which make for a concentrated wine. Perfect balance of tastes, if not a bit heavy on the aromas. Aged in barrique, it is certainly a wine that merits attention.

Jacques Pelichet

1173 Féchy
Tel. (021) 8085141

Féchy, a wine-producing village above Lake Geneva, is truly something out of a story-book. In the upper part of the village, a cluster of a dozen farmhouses surrounds a 13th-century church, with its bell tower and steeple. It is an almost fairytale-like picture of rural life. Of the 490 inhabitants, 28 families earn their living from the yearly harvest. Jacques Pelichet is your typical small wine-maker of Féchy; his family enterprise, which relies on seasonal workers, consists of three hectares of land, with 95% planted to Chasselas, the most common varietal in western Switzerland. Pelichet also experiments with Pinot Gris, Chardonnay, and Gewürztraminer. Chasselas 1989 sold for 7.9 Swiss francs a bottle and the special selections for 9 francs: truly excellent value for money, proving that the wine-maker is not always responsible for the high prices of his wines.

Chardonnay 1990   ❦ ①
Pale yellow-gold ; a pure and fruity bouquet and pleasantly alive and light in the mouth; not lacking in refinement.

Féchy Mon Pichet 1990   ❦ ①
Made from Chasselas, light yellow with the usual greenish reflections. The bouquet is lightly floral, with easily distinguishable fern and honeysuckle. Fruity and round on the palate. A simple wine and pleasant to drink.

Gewurztraminer 1990   ❦ ①
The bouquet is perhaps a bit overbearing but, besides that, it is quite typical and fruity on the palate: a light, pleasant Gewürtraminer, all things considered, and certainly well-made.

Porret et fils

Domaine des Cèdres
Goutte-d'Or 20
2016 Cortaillod
Tel. (038) 421052

When one talks of Pinot Noir of Neuchâtel as being one of the best Swiss wines, the name Albert Porret inevitably crops up. His vineyard, situated in the village of Cortaillod, above Lake Neuchâtel, has been in the Porret family since 1858. The Porrets, who have become famous largely for their Cortaillod clones, stand for tradition with a capital T. Their Pinot Noir, cultivated using exclusively the very costly method of the low culture, is grown mostly in their vineyards of Cortaillod and also in the nearby Boudry. The union of the refined grapes of Boudry together with the more robust grapes of Cortaillod gives a new version of Pinot Noir, aged in oak barrique and bottled only after 11 months of aging. The red wines, (along with the Pinot Noir there is also the rosé, Oeil-de-Perdrix, typical of Neuchâtel) make up, however, only one third of the total production, since two-thirds is devoted to white wine made from white Chasselas, very widespread in western Switzerland. The white Cortaillod is a fruity wine, light and fresh, with the typical bubbles of carbonic acid.

Cortaillod 1991   🍇 🍇 ②
Light yellow in color, it is delicately sparkling with a lean, fruity bouquet. An acidity from the must comes forth on the palate; can be defined as a true Neuchatel Chasselas.

Oeil-de-Perdrix 1991   ②
Made from Pinot Noir, it has good color and is delicately fruity with a slight hint of fermentation on the nose; carbonic acid is also in evidence. An elegant wine with a long finish.

Pinot Noir 1990   🍇 🍇 ②
An intense sparkling violet color; a bit restrained but pleasant on the nose with hints of red and blackberry fruit. Truly a fine wine; very rich and concentrated as well as tannic. On the finish it presents a slight aroma of oak. Still aging.

Bernard and Brigitte Rochaix

Domaine Les Perrières
1242 Peissy
Tel. (022) 7531598
Fax (022) 7531928

That Brigitte and Bernard Rochaix are completely absorbed in their work is obvious from the moment one arrives at their vineyard, Les Perrières. With 15 ha planted to vine, this is certainly not one of the smallest vineyards, but the Rochaix can rely on a small group of experts who work exceptionally well both in the vineyard and in the cellar. Brigitte Rochaix herself handles the marketing and very well: she has great conviction in her products and makes no attempt to hide her enthusiasm, which, inevitably, is contagious. Her husband Bernard, responsible for the administration of the firm, is no less active no exuberant. When he talks his eyes light up and his words express his ambition and desire for action: Bernard Rochaix knows what he wants and how to get it. His cellar is full of extremely modern vinification equipment, with oak barriques from France for refining Chardonnay, Pinot Noir and Gamay. The other areas of the business, such as the aging process and sales are also very up-to-date, completing the modern image of this vineyard, always looking to the future. All of this has naturally resulted in a certain notoriety, and there is a constant flow of visitors to Les Perrières.

Chasselas de Peissy 1991   🍇 ①
Greenish yellow in color; still a young bouquet with aromas of bread and yeast; very vivid and full on the palate; a wine with bite. A Chasselas wine made in the original way, probably without the biological reduction of acidity.

Riesling x Sylvaner de Peissy 1991   🍇 ①
Light straw hue with typical greenish highlights; a floral bouquet, delicately spicy with hints of blossom; elegant body, with a slightly bitter finish. Truly a good wine.

Pinot Noir de Peissy 1991   🍇 🍇 ②
Purple-red, intense and young; this wine displays a complex bouquet, with mixed oak and fruit nuances; full-bodied and concentrated, spicy, backed up by a good acidity. A lingering finish; worthy of attention.

Jean-Bernard
et Dominique Rouvinez
3960 Sierre
Tel. (027) 556661

Werner Stucky

Casa del Portico
6802 Rivera-Capidogno
Tel. (091) 951282

The solitary and picturesque Rouvinez vineyard is situated in the hills of Géronde, between Sierre and Chippis. Its wines enjoy a well-deserved fame. The two Rouvinez brothers, owners of the firm, are both rather reserved; extravagance and extrovert behavior is not their style. They prefer to let the wine and the cellar (modern and extremely clean) speak for themselves. Anyone visiting the vineyard can tell immediately that only fine wines are produced, and that quality is a high priority. Their wines, produced from the harvest of their 15 ha of vineyards, win over for their freshness, fruitiness finesse and elegance. The Rouvinez brothers have devoted themselves to changing the image that the Fendant has had to put up with for a long time (heavy and clumsy, in other words). Fendant has changed, crop production control and vinification have altered the balance of alcohol content to acidity in favor of the latter, and they have become more fruity, lean, and elegant. The modern presentation of the wine-bottles os also in-keeping with the Rouvinez brother's new interpretation of this product.

The head cellarman Werner Stucky, who has a degree in viticulture from Wädenswil, has been devoted to making Ticino Merlot since 1981. The light and pleasant Pinot Noir of eastern Switzerland didn't correspond with his idea of a red wine; robust, and rich in tannins. A native of Zurich, Stucky immediately fell in love with the region of Ticino and its Merlot, a variety that has all the potential for making a firmly-built wine. As soon as the opportunity presented itself, he rented a good vineyard. Today he manages an area of 3.2 ha, as well as acting as spokesman for the young, up-and-coming wine-makers of Ticino, who have begun to shake things up, slowly bringing viticulture back to life in their region. They have been concentrating on the cultivation and aging of the Merlot, using the Bordeaux wines as a model. Stucky's goal was to make wines rich in extracts, which could be aged for long period, coming as possible to the Bordeaux style: few Swiss wine-makers so consistently question their methods and take such risks. Stucky is always experimenting and studying new ways to produce his Merlot, already considered among the best in Ticino.

Fendant de Sierre 1991   🍇 ②
Made from Chasselas grapes; a light yellow hue with green reflections; a bit restrained and floral on the nose. Quite full-bodied and lively; a firmly-built, vigorous and well-structured Fendant.

La Tremaille 1990   🍇🍇 ③
An interesting innovation: a white wine made from Chaselas and Petite Arvine aged in barrique; golden in color, with a bouquet which is fruity, but also vaguely woody. Well-structured body with a fine balance of fruit and acidity, although the tannin is not yet harmonious. Promising wine, which in a few years time will show its true worth.

Pinot Noir de Sierre 1990   🍇 ②
An intense purple-red; fruity, spicy and round with a strong, lingering aftertaste. A harmonious Pinot Noir loaded with extracts, which has a great deal of potential.

Conte di Luna 1990   🍇 ③
Made from Merlot and Cabernet Sauvignon; after a well-balanced aging in barrique, it presents a good purple-red color; fruity tones very rich on the nose, with hints of blackcurrant and notes of oak; harmonious on the palate with a fine balance of fruit and oak; a well-made wine with a straightforward drinkability. Still room for growth.

Merlot del Portico 1990   🍇 ②
An intense purple-red; the bouquet is true to Merlot: plums and violets with herbal notes; harmonic and round on the palate; of medium consistency with a lingering finish.

Merlot del Portico   🍇 ②
Vigneto Casa Cimagudo 1990
A true Merlot cru wine, purple-red color indicates ripeness; maybe a bit aggressive on the nose, but spicy and fruity in the mouth, with notes of chocolate. Moderately long finish.

Eredi Carlo Tamborini

6814 Lamone
Tel. (091) 933434
Fax (091) 932833

The Tamborini vineyard produces about 135,000 lt of Merlot each year, partly from grapes bought elsewhere and partly from their own vines or from those they rent which are cultivated autonomously (a practice that is certainly becoming more common). Claudio Tamborini has been the director of this firm since the beginning of the 1980s when he discovered his passion for Merlot. Whenever he gets a chance, he spends time in Bordeaux, taking specialization courses and visiting producers. Tamborini is very proud of his San Zeno which has considerable body and intensity. The grapes come from seven viticulturalists of Lugano who are supervised throughout the year by experts from the firm. The fermentation period and maceration are adjusted according to the quality of the harvest, which is certainly a time-consuming operation. Vinification takes place in steel vats because Tamborini claims that oak is not right for the Ticinese Merlot; the climate and terrain are, after all, different from those of Bordeaux. Tamborini basically opposes the current boom of barrique-aging and considers his own use of barrique as just an experiment within his vast production.

Collivo Ticino 🍇 ②
Tenuta Colle degli Ulivi 1990
Made from Merlot, from vines planted in 1978 on a hill where there once was an olive grove. The grapes were, naturally, processed in the Tamborini winery. Ruby-red, the bouquet is fairly simple and fruity. Pleasing on the palate; a straighforward wine.

Comano Vigneto ai Brughi 1990 🍇 ③
Aged in barrique, this Merlot has an intense ruby-red color; still a bit closed on the nose with clear notes of vanilla. Robust, fruity, harmonious, tannic enough and savoury on the palate, still softening. Will improve with cellaring.

San Zeno 1990 🍇 ②
Made from Merlot grapes from the San Zeno vineyard, this reserve was made from a select harvest. The wine is a bright ruby-red; the bouquet is intense with hints of cherry; the taste is sincere and full, with the right amount of tannin which gives the wine a good texture and the backbone. A truly fine wine.

Waldemar Zahner

Im Bächi
8467 Truttikon
Tel. (052) 411949
Fax (052) 412095

Waldemar Zahner hates complicated experiments in the wine cellar: for him a well-made wine is one that has been left alone as much as possible in the aging and vinification processes, a wine that, if given enough time, 'makes itself. Impatient handling would detract from its character. Zahner is a man who has changed his life's course. With a degree in agriculture, he worked for Nestlé in Argentina where he was the director of a food company, but he missed agriculture so much that, at the beginning of 1960s, he bought a vineyard in the canton of Zurich at Truttikon and became a wine-maker. Today he cultivates six hectares and has never regreted his decision to change careers. The oldest of his three children unfortunately died in 1990 in a work-related accident, but the other two are following in their father's footsteps. In the cellar, the youngest, Niklaus, continues to use traditional methods which include long fermentation and oak-aging in barriques, which he changes frequently, and bottling without filtering. What then ends up in the glass is a dark, ruby-red and transparent wine: the natural product of an art which is in itself very simple.

Langenmooser 🍇 ②
Gewurztraminer 1991
A yellow color of medium intensity; a fairly refined bouquet, full-bodied without being heavy, a lightly bitter tone in the finish. Unquestionably well-vinified.

Langenmooser 🍇🍇 ②
Riesling x Sylvaner Spätlese 1991
Vinified from a particularly mature harvest; a nice fruity perfume of the Riesling/Sylvaner; compact and refined body, dense and juicy yet very delicate and elegant. An extremely successful wine.

Langenmooser Rot 1991 🍇 ②
Light ruby color; a rather simple bouquet, robust, acidulous and a bit rough given its distinct tannin. A vigorous wine made from Pinot Noir.

Langenmooser Dunkelrot 🍇 ②
Spätlese 1989
Also made from Pinot Noir grapes particularly ripe and select; aged in barrique, the color reveals clear signs of maturity, the bouquet is intense, and the taste is dominated by the flavor of oak. Best drunk now.

Maurice Zufferey

3964 Muraz-Sur-Sierre
Tel. (027) 554716

The vineyard of Maurice Zufferey, viewed from the nearby hills, seems green in autumn because grass is left between the rows. It's important to emphasize that for Maurice Zufferey, his work in the vineyard (always respecting nature as much as possible), is the most important part of producing a fine wine. "Fine wines are made in the vineyard" is his motto. He certainly has all the elements needed: four hectares of dry terrain with a high limestone content, which are situated in the sunniest areas of Sierre, the sunniest and least rainy region of Switzerland. Zufferey produces an average of 40,000 lt of wine a year, 70% made into Pinot Noir, 20% Fendant and 10% into traditional speciality wines of Valais, from varietals like Cornalin, Malvasia, and Humagne Rouge. In the cellar, Zufferey will under no circumstances add saccharose to his must. He is determined that each one of his creations should clearly express its own unmistakable character, and it must be said that he is thus far successful in his endeavors. His wines are characterized by their simplicity, correctness and trueness to the palate.

Chardonnay Les Glarières 1990 ❦ ❦ ③
Made from Chardonnay, aged in barrique: good color; shows vanilla and grapefruit on the nose. Good body which on the palate, with flavors of apple and hazelnut and a hint of caramel on the finish. Result of a truly exemplary vinification.

Pinot Noir Tzanio 1990 ❦ ③
This wine has a well-developed color and a very advanced bouquet. Mature and spicy on the palate, with firm tannin on the finish. A good wine that lovers of Pinot Noir will appreciate. Aged in barrique.

Humagne Rouge de Sierre 1990 ❦ ②
A deep and intense color; a good, fruity perfume with aromas of leather, soot and pepper; on the palate reveals a typical light rose flavor with just the right amount of tannin on the finish. Extraordinary and very fine.

TURKEY

Wine must have originated in or around what today is called Turkey and enjoyed a glorious presence there for literally thousands of years (excavations have uncovered wine containers over 5,000 years old). Taking this into consideration and Turkey's size, population, latitude, geography and even the inspired poetry in praise of wine written in these lands, it is somewhat of a shock to note to what parlous depths wine has sunk in Turkey. What explains this phenomenon is the fact that alcohol consumption was deeply frowned upon, if not forbidden, for 700 years. Even today, with the secular state over half a century old, and tourism thriving, there is precious little activity on the wine production front, in sharp contrast with neighboring Greece, where abstinence was a foreign (indeed Turkish) imposition and not a home-grown habit.

Turkey, however, remains the 6th largest grower of grapes in the world although 96-97% are table grapes or grapes used for raisins. If 3-4% of the crop today goes into wine production, it is purely because the grapes were capable in the centuries of prohibition of doubling up as table-grapes, not normally a qualification for the production of fine wine. Indeed, no fewer than 1,200 different varieties are said to exist in Turkey, a fact which leads one to suspect that bootlegging must have been a thriving trade in the days of dryness. We will never know.

Present wine production is somewhere in the region of 250,000 hectoliters a year, which is actually about half of what it was 20 years ago. Consumption has also fallen by about one third and is running roughly neck and neck with production. Certainly no one would find compelling reasons to import Turkish wine at present, unless they were nostalgic, ex-patriate, free-thinking Turks. The white Narince grape is one of the great neutrals of the wine-world, and while the red Bogazkere and Okuzgozu varieties may have colorful, if unpronounceable names, their wines lack the character to justify an export drive.

One senses that Turkey has a potential in respect of wine production. But the treasure is buried deep, and will probably only emerge when and if Turkey develops the home market which it patently lacks today.

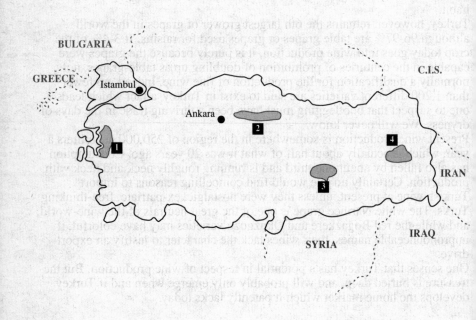

TURKEY

BULGARIA

GREECE

Istanbul

Ankara

1

2

3

4

C.I.S.

IRAN

IRAQ

SYRIA

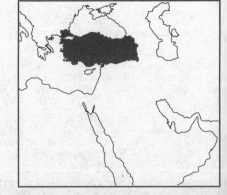

1	Aegean Coast
2	Ankara
3	Central Anatolia
4	Eastern Anatolia

Diren Wines

Tokat, Central Anatolia
c/o World-wide distributors: Ogan
International
16 Meadow Rise, Blackmore, Ingatestone
Essex, England
Tel. 0277 823638
Fax 0277 822668

Mr. Vasfi Diren established this firm in Tokat
in north central Turkey in 1940, and the
business is still run by his six children. The
current chairman, Mr. Orhan Diren, is
apparently the only fully qualified oenologist
in Turkey. The winery is a sort of privately-
run cooperative, with the grapes being grown
by the farmers of a small cluster of villages -
organically, it transpires, in other words with
no use of artificial fertilizers or pesticides. All
fruit is processed at the Diren winery which
from the 1990 vintage on has had
refrigerated fermentation equipment, while
facilities for storage in stainless steel are
currently being installed. Until now, storage
has been effected in large, underground
glass-lined concrete tanks. Production
capacity is scheduled to hit 500,000 cases
annually over the next few years. Five wines
are produced, all vintaged and branded, all
Vins de Qualité, Turkey's rudimentary control
system. They are all made from native
Turkish varieties although, with over 1,000
native grape varieties to choose from, this is
hardly surprising.

Dortnal 1990 ♀ ①
Made from the Narince grape of the Tokat
region, this is a dry white whose somewhat
cooked bouquet and fullness of flavor, rather in
the traditional Greek/Turkish style, do not quite
square with the assurance that temperature-
controlled equipment was used for the 1990
vintage.

Vadi 1990 ♀ ①
Medium-dry white, also of the Narince grape of
Tokat. This one has better balance, the savoury,
slightly medicinal flavors being matched by the
fruitiness of the sweet-acid combination. The
residual sugar is natural, not by addition of
must.

Karmen 1987 ♀ ①
Dry red wine from the Bogazkere and Okuzgozu
grapes, grown in the Elazig region, in the
Euphrates valley. An eminently drinkable if far
from exciting red wine, having good fruit of
somewhat imprecise character on a not-
excessively tannic base, with sufficient acidity to
give it some zing.

Karmen Reserve 1987 ♀♀ ①
This wine has a similar style to the above (not
surprisingly being of the same grape,
provenance and vintage) only more
concentration of fruit and a greater structure in
terms of tannin. Not a heavy wine, indeed, it has
a certain elegance and promise.

Key to the symbols

Types of Wines

♀ White

🂠 Rosé

♀ Red

Rating System

♀   An exemplary wine of its
type with outstanding local
character

🂠🂠   An international premium
quality wine

♀♀♀   A Top Wine, considered one
of the 150 best wines in the
world

*The 'grape bunch' symbol is used to
indicate the color of the wine; the
number of bunches represents the quality
rating assigned by the contributor*

Price levels

①   up to $ 9.99

② $ 10.00 - $ 14.99

③ $ 15.00 - $ 24.99

④ $ 25.00 or more

*The 'ex-cellar', or direct from the
producer, bottle prices, are calculated in
US dollars and are intended only as an
approximate guide*

**Entries are arranged in
alphabetical order by country,
region and winery or producer
name.**

UNITED STATES OF AMERICA

The history of wine in the United States essentially began when vine cultivation and grape growing spread throughout California. Up until the late 1960s, 90% of all American wine came from California, where the Franciscan missionaries planted vines as early as 1778, in their settlements at San Juan Capistrano. Only one varietal was planted, called "criolla", which they had grown then in their missions in Central and South America. European colonizers further widened the selection until 1825 when Jean-Louis Vignes, of Bordeaux, planted the first vineyard in what is today the center of Los Angeles. By 1885, the University of California was already experimenting on the 320 types grown throughout the state. Most of them came from Germany, Italy, Spain and the Slavic countries. Agoston Harazasthy, a Hungarian immigrant, had a major role in introducing hundreds of new varietals not to mention precious technical skills and knowledge. Between 1880 and 1890, Californian grape growers began carefully selecting the types best suited for cultivation, narrowing the selection to the most significant 94 varietals used still today. Of these, 54 are used for wine-grapes and the remaining 40 are table-grapes. After Prohibition, grape-growers and vintners began calling their wines under generic names like Chablis, Xérès or Sauternes. In 1939, however, the situation changed notably as writer and wine importer, Frank Schoonmaker, anxious to increase his line of wines, demanded that all American wines carry the name of the main grape used on the labels. With a keen eye for quality to maintain his exclusive wine selection, Schoonmaker undoubtedly encouraged many producers to improve their wines. Up until the 1940s, most of the estates were run by the large distilleries. But, by the 1960s, things had changed dramatically when an array of people discovered their passion for the sophisticated country-life and the pleasures of wine. Hundreds of small family-run wineries soon popped up everywhere. Still today, in fact, they make up the bulk of California's most interesting wine production. More recently, in the 1970s and 1980s, foreigners have literally invaded the vineyards in the form of large, mainly French corporations, but also Spanish and Italians, bringing Old World experience and technology to exploit the new wine-making opportunities that had opened up.

Throughout the U.S., even as early as the year 1000 when the Vikings set foot in North America, we know that the vine in its most natural and wild state, or "vitis labrusca", has flourished everywhere. Only until more recently has "vitis vinifera" been cultivated, and with quite impressive results, as the entries prove here to follow.

Nonetheless, wine in the United States remains two kinds of an enigma for non-Americans. First, what would seem to be one marketplace is fragmented into 50, with each state free to pursue its own plan for taxation, licensing and every other aspect of commerce. Second, every wine region in the country tries to grow Chardonnay and Cabernet Sauvignon, no matter how ill advised either variety or both might be for a particular soil and climate. Outsiders continually point out that one unified market and 50 distinctive industries would seem wiser, but to no avail. In a nation with little history of wine consumption, the populace will keep wine names simple if the producers do not. At the end of prohibition, when the United States had no wine regions of great fame, marketers hit upon the scheme of naming wines after the grapes that went into them. In the mid-1970s American consumers seized upon Cabernet Sauvignon and Chardonnay as the names to remember.

Little has changed since. In becoming the chocolate and vanilla of American wine, Cabernet Sauvignon and Chardonnay left at least a score of other varietal wine types to fight for the leftovers. For the diligent, they offer most of the hopes for outstanding value. Among varietal white wines, Sauvignon Blanc is Chardonnay's closest rival in quality. Like Chardonnay, it is widely planted among districts, though total area devoted to it is less than a fifth as much. An alternative name to Sauvignon Blanc is Fumé Blanc. Sémillon is something of a rarity on its own, but often seen blended with Sauvignon. Chenin Blanc commands almost as much acreage as Chardonnay. However, much of it goes into indistinct white blends, only a modest amount into varietals, most of them off-dry and meant for everyday use. Once-favored, Riesling has fallen upon very hard times with American consumers; its acreage has dwindled to a tiny fraction of the total in white grapes. Gewürztraminer is planted in about the same amounts. Among reds, the battle for second place behind Cabernet is much more even, and more vigorously fought. Pinot Noir, Merlot and Zinfandel all have sizeable loyal followings. Gamay and Petite Sirah (Duriff in the Rhône) are planted in fewer regions and in smaller amounts.

A few hardy souls are struggling to break the strangleholds of Cabernet and Chardonnay, or, at least, broaden the choices for those who might be tempted an entirely new name. Pinot Gris, Viognier, Marsanne, Roussane, Syrah, Sangiovese, Nebbiolo, and a handful of others are to be had in slightly larger than experimental volumes. However, plantings of all these varieties can still be measured in the 10s of acres or the 100s at best. A separate group of varietal wines is being grown to admirable effect in states other than California, most of them east of the Mississippi River. These are what Americans call French-American hybrids, or what the French call "producteurs directs." The names most frequently seen are the whites Seyval Blanc, Vidal Blanc and Vignoles, and the reds Marechal Foch and Chelois. American law governing varietal and other label information is straightforward, even simple. It requires a minimum 75% of any varietal wine to have been made from the named grape. To be labelled with the name of a county or other political unit, a minimum 75% of a wine must have been grown in the named unit. To be labelled with the name of an American Viticultural Area (AVA), the minimum requirement is 85%. If an AVA-labelled wine is varietal, 75% of it must be made from the named variety grown in the named district. To bear the name of an individual vineyard, a minimum 95% of the wine must come from the named property, which in turn must lie within an approved AVA. To bear a vintage date, a minimum 95% of the grapes used must have grown within the year stated. AVAs are based in relatively homogenous climates and soils. The first one was approved only in 1980, the second in 1982. By 1992 California had more than 60, the nation as a whole more than 115 of them. This still-nascent system is as close as US wine can now come to having AOC or DOC status. AVAs place no requirement limiting varieties, yields, or other viticultural practices. Perhaps the vagueness is correct for the near term. A few districts can be measured by reasonably long histories of making wine, but many others are almost entirely speculative for lack, not only of history, but of current plantings. Obviously, much remains to be learned about how to train vines and manage yields before regulations of the European type could be justified, let alone written. Most fine wines presently are varietals from AVAs, but some important exceptions exist. A class beginning to be known as "Meritage" comes from blends of the Bordeaux varieties in which no one variety need reach a 75% minimum. There are both red and white Meritage types. The finest of American sparkling wines do not necessarily qualify as varietals. In fact, a majority of those made by Méthode Champenoise come from French-owned firms using only chardonnay and pinot noir in their cuvees. Some of these still carry the word Champagne on the labels, though most do not. Because the U.S. is not a signatory to the Madrid Convention or others governing European appellations of origin, American wineries may use the names of such traditional wine regions as Champagne, Chablis, Burgundy and Champagne without any restriction as to content. These so-called generic wine names must also show a statement of origin that is either an AVA or a political unit to reduce possible consumer confusion over the true source of the wine.

Individual states can impose stricter standards than the federal ones for their own production. Although the system of names and other regulations helps keep United States wine names far simpler than their counterparts from France and Italy, many Americans remain cowed by the intricacies of the subject and refuse to venture into wine-drinking. Wine has never been an integral part of the American, more specifically the Anglo-Saxon culture. Quite the contrary, it is that element of the American populace that provides most of a vigorous anti-alcohol constituency that frowns upon wine every bit as much as whiskey and beer. Between a lack of tradition for wine and an emphatic ethical bias against it, consumption has languished around eight bottles per head per year. Since 1986 the trend has been toward seven bottles, not nine.

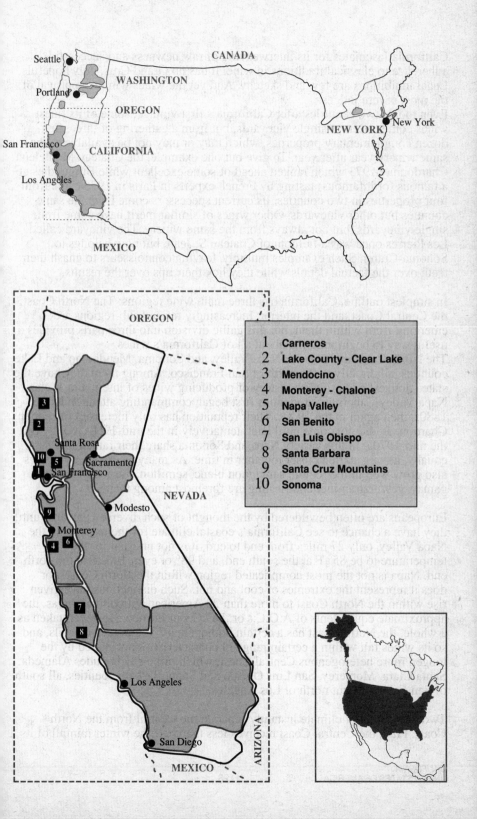

1	**Carneros**
2	**Lake County - Clear Lake**
3	**Mendocino**
4	**Monterey - Chalone**
5	**Napa Valley**
6	**San Benito**
7	**San Luis Obispo**
8	**Santa Barbara**
9	**Santa Cruz Mountains**
10	**Sonoma**

California

California fascinates for its interweaving of raw newness and successful
adherence to classical traditions in wine. It has no Grand Crus, only hopefuls.
Legal inhibitions are few and sketchy. And yet the wines win the approval of
the most severe judges.

Even today, two centuries after California's first vintage, some of its finest
wines come not from single vineyards, but from a gathering of three, four, a
dozen complementary properties, which may or may not be available to the
same winery year after year. To give but one example, the Chateau Montelena
Chardonnay 1973 which ranked ahead of some excellent white Burgundies at
a famous (or infamous) tasting by French experts in Paris in 1976 came from
four properties in two counties. Its current successors come from the same
counties but other vineyards. Other wines of similar merit have come from
single vineyards, but not always from the same winery. The vineyard called
Les Pierres once was a fiefdom of Chateau St Jean, but now belongs to
Sonoma-Cutrer. Such examples multiply, leaving connoisseurs to gnash their
teeth over the factual details while they lick their lips over the results.

In simplest outline, California has three main wine regions: The North Coast,
the Central Coast, and the interior. Increasingly refined sub-regions are
emerging from within them, but this gallic division into three parts provides a
useful way to begin thinking about all of California's wines.

The North Coast includes the Napa Valley, and Sonoma, Mendocino and Lake
counties, all directly to the north of San Francisco. Among them they have the
state's longest and proudest history of producing wines of international class.
Napa Valley Cabernet Sauvignons first began commanding attention in the
1880s, then again in the 1940s. Their reputation has only increased since then.
Chardonnay did not come until later, tentatively in the mid-1960s, boldly by
the mid-1970s. In this variety Napa and Sonoma share their fame more
equally, having started closer together in time. As many as 20 other varieties
also grow well in the region: sauvignon blanc, sémillon, merlot, pinot noir,
gamay, gewürztraminer and riesling are foremost among them.

Europeans are often bewildered by the thought of such diverse vineyards until
they have a chance to see California's coastal climate for themselves. In the
Napa Valley, only 27 miles from end to end, it is not unusual for the
temperature to be 85° F at the south end, and 98° or even 100° F at the north
end. Napa is not the most complicated region within the North Coast, nor
does it represent the extremes of cool and hot. Such distinctions have given
rise within the North Coast to more than 20 American Viticultural Areas, the
approximate equivalents of A.O.C.s or .DO.C.s in Europe. However, taken as
a whole, the North Coast has a certain homogeneity of climate and soils, and
so its wines fall within a certain range of characteristics not shared by the
longer, more heterogenous Central Coast, which primarily includes Alameda,
Santa Clara, Monterey, San Luis Obispo and Santa Barbara counties, all south
of San Francisco but north of Los Angeles.

Two particulars of climate instantly separate the Central from the North
Coast. First, the Central Coast receives less than half the winter rainfall of its

more northerly neighbor. Second, its frost-free season is far longer, ending earlier in spring and beginning later in autumn. Other, subtler aspects of soil and climate contribute still more variations to its wines. The most pronounced differences come to the Bordeaux varieties, which taste noticeably more herbaceous coming from Central Coast vineyards than they do from North Coast properties. At times, Central Coast Cabernets and Sauvignon Blancs become outright vegetative in flavor. Comforting as they seem, these generalities hold less firmly in the Central than in the North Coast. Anyone who cares to make a test can see the narrow range of flavors in Cabernet Sauvignon from Ukiah in Mendocino County to Dry Creek Valley in Sonoma County to Rutherford in the Napa Valley versus the broader range of character in Cabernets from Arroyo Seco in Monterey County, Paso Robles in San Luis Obispo County and anywhere in Santa Barbara County.

However easily flavor distinctions between North and Central Coast may be noted, the questions that separate these two regions are less of quality than of preference, and less pronounced than the differences between coastal and interior wines.
The interior produces 70- 80% of California's wine, compared to 20-30% from the coast. Optimists call it the United States's Midi. Pessimists call it Algeria. Whichever, it is the source of a huge proportion of faceless but usually sound everyday drinking wine, almost all of it unspecified as to origin. A narrow band of tiny vineyards in the Sierra Nevada Mountain foothills give distinctly regional character, especially Zinfandel. Two islands in the San Joquin River delta between Sacramento and San Francisco Bay produce Chenin Blancs of identifiable profile. Between these two, Lodi can produce Zinfandel of individual character. Otherwise, the interior is largely a source of generic Burgundy/Chianti or Chablis/Rhine styled to go with MacBurgers and to be sought by price.

Acacia

2750 Las Amigas Road
Napa, CA. 94559
Tel. (707) 226-9991
Fax (707) 226-1685

Acacia's model is Burgundian - several Carneros Chardonnays and Pinot Noirs each year, as Laboure-Roi offers more than one Meursault or Nuits St Georges from differing properties - but the execution of both red and white is inescapably true to Carneros. The program began when the winery did, in 1979, and held fast through a 1986 change of ownership from the original partners to Chalone, Inc. Some of the consistency owes to the continued presence of Larry Brooks as winemaker since the early days. Much more stems from a stable group of vineyard sources ringing the winery site overlooking San Francisco Bay in the heart of the Carneros AVA. Included among them is the estate Marina Vineyard, planted all to Chardonnay. Brooks, like many in California, uses new French oak as a generous spice for wines made to be full-bodied, firmly built, capable of improving with age in bottle.

Carneros Chardonnay   ♚♚ ③
Marina 1989
A rich, golden hue promises ripe Chardonnay and the wine delivers exactly that. Oak is but a subtle spice. Polished yet firm, promising a life yet to be lived.

Carneros Pinot Noir St Clair 1988   ♚ ④
A certain tannic firmness is, as always, the signature of Acacia, especially this vineyard. Appealingly fresh flavors of Pinot Noir are well spiced by new French oak barrels in a wine that should improve with four to five years in bottle.

Buena Vista Winery

27000 Ramal Road
Sonoma, CA. 95476
Tel. (707) 938-8504
Fax (707) 252-0392

One of California's oldest names had a long, rather wayward career from the turn of the century all the way to the 1980s, when a German firm, A. Racke, bought it and installed Jill Davis as winemaker. The course has been upward ever since. In fact the seeds had been sown by an earlier owner, who began planting what has become 1,100 acres of vineyard on slopes facing straight across the bay to San Francisco. But it has been the Moller-Racke family and Ms. Davis who capitalized fully. Shifting elevations and exposures within the long, narrow vineyard make it uncommonly versatile. The part of it in Napa County favors Cabernet Sauvignon and Merlot, the part in Sonoma County does better with Chardonnay and Pinot Noir. Somewhere in it, Gewürztraminer prospers as well. One variety Carneros does not grow well, Sauvignon Blanc, Buena Vista buys from elsewhere.

Carneros Gewurztraminer 1991   ♚ ②
Made in the off-dry style, but so deftly balanced that it refreshes in that sense as well as with flavors that come as close to grapefruit as they do to lychee.

Carneros Chardonnay 1990   ♚ ②
For all who rejoice in the flavor of Chardonnay perfectly rendered, vintage, vineyard and style come together in rare harmony. With that, a delicacy, a finesse make the wine far from simple.

Lake Country Sauvignon Blanc 1990 ♚ ②
As Lake County so often produces, a Sauvignon far more reminiscent of melons than herbs. As Buena Vista so often produces, a round, polished, just off-dry Sauvignon easy to sip for itself.

Carneros Pinot Noir 1989   ♚ ③
The wine competes favorably with far costlier examples with bright, cherry-like flavors of Pinot Noir set off by deft use of oak. Firm and refreshing in texture, it drinks well young.

Carneros Creek Winery

1285 Dealy Lane
Napa, CA. 94559
Tel. (707) 253-9463

Francis Mahoney and partners began Carneros Creek in 1972 as a cellar making many types of wine from scattered regions of origin. But their location in Carneros slowly captured their attention until, by 1987, all of the grapes came from there. Chardonnay is of interest. Pinot Noir has become close to an obsession. At present, Mahoney makes Pinot Noir in three styles: light and fresh, conventional, and as rich as he can get it. The approach rather echoes that of the Burgundy negociant who offers a passe-tous-grains, a village, and a cru bottling, but only as a step-ladder of quality. Carneros Creek does not mean to imitate Burgundy, but rather to find the truest expression it can of Carneros. Each lesson learned transfers quickly to vineyard, then cellar, then bottle. Thus, following a succession of vintages gives the redoubled pleasure of good drink and new truth revealed.

Carneros Chardonnay 1990   ❦ ②
An appetizing flavor of baked apples comes from the Chardonnay. Deft use of oak adds the spices. Carneros's firmness hides beneath a skillfully polished surface.

Carneros Pinot Noir   ❦ ②
Fleur de Carneros 1990
Lively, fresh, appealing in the full flower of its youth when a meal calls for indelible flavors of Pinot Noir but not much formality and no reverence at all.

Carneros Pinot Noir Reserve 1989   ❦ ④
From the shiest-bearing part of the vineyard come powerful flavors of Carneros Pinot Noir. From the cellar comes a silky polish and a subtle kiss of toasty oak.

Gloria Ferrer

23444 Highway 121
Sonoma, CA. 95476
Tel. (707) 966-7256
Fax (707) 996-0720

No few Californians thought the owners of Spain's bargain-priced Freixenet sparkling wines were more than a little bit crazy to come into the state in the wake of a veritable invasion of Champagne firms, and crazier yet to challenge them head-on with sparkling wines made by the classic method. Crazy they may have been, but Jose Ferrer and family have found success in both cellar and marketplace. In 1991, with x vintages behind them, they have the satisfaction of seeing their wines ranked with the very best California has to offer. Their 120-acre vineyard of Pinot Noir and Chardonnay in Carneros gives winemaker Robert Iantosca an impeccable base for the three cuvees presently offered under the Gloria Ferrer label. Purchased grapes from complementary Sonoma vineyards broaden his palette.
The name Gloria Ferrer honors Jose's wife.

Carneros Brut Royal Cuvée 1987   ❦ ③
Rides the crest of an emerging stylistic wave in California: toasty notes broad enough to overshadow the taste of grapes, plus a certain cleansing briskness of texture.

Carneros brut Carneros Cuvée 1985   ❦ ③
Longer on tirage than the Royal Cuvee, hence even richer in suggestions of toasted nuts, and less fruity. A gratifying, creamy smoothness makes it a wine for wintry eves.

Carneros Brut NV   ❦ ③
Understated but far from blank, impeccably polished. Among non-vintage Bruts, one of the premiers, and decidedly among the price-worthy.

Mac Rostie Steven

17246 Woodland Avenue
Sonoma, CA. 95476
Tel. (707) 996-4480

More often than not it is a wrong idea to
imbue a wine with the personality traits of the
person who made it. Not so with Mac Rostie
Chardonnay, which exactly reflects the calm,
measured style of Steven Mac Rostie. The
Mac Rostie label is one of many belonging to
entrepreneurial winemakers without wineries
to call their own. In addition to producing
wine under his own name, Mac Rostie
currently serves as winemaker for a start-up
Carneros estate called Roche. Before that he
was the long-time winemaker at nearby
Hacienda. The geographic focus of his career
in Carneros may have begun by chance, but
is purposeful now. Chardonnay, similarly, has
become the wine of his primary focus in an
evolutionary way.
Mac Rostie buys grapes from the same
grower, the well-regarded Sangiacomo
Vineyard, each year.

Carneros Chardonnay 1990   🍇🍇 ③
The first note is of toasty oak, then, steadily, the
apple-like aromas of Chardonnay join the
chorus until the flavors are complete and in fine
harmony. Rather full as Carneros whites go.

Saintsbury

1500 Los Carneros Ave.
Napa, CA. 95449
Tel. (707) 252-0592
Fax (707) 252-0595

Owners David Graves and Richard Ward are
two who kept their faith in the possibilities of
Pinot Noir in California through a long, lean
search. When the time came to found their
own winery, they opted for Los Carneros as a
growing region based on the best they had
seen, and they opted for a style based on
what the vineyards gave them, not on hopes
that they had found another Cote d'Or. Both
their patience and approach have been
rewarded. Among other decisions, they
elected to make Pinot Noir in two styles, but
always by blending the fruit from several
vineyards rather than attempting to force
greatness upon one in a region still largely
untested by time. In something of a reversal
of tradition, they give an extra name to the
lighter, more accessible example, and let the
grander wine go forth without extra identity.
Chardonnay is secondary here, but not to be
overlooked.

Carneros Chardonnay 1990   🍇🍇 ③
Saintsbury has pursued the buttery-toasty style
insistently since its first vintage. The results are
now a distinctive and harmonious balancing of
Chardonnay with winemaking technique.

Carneros Pinot Noir Garnet 1990   🍇 ③
Fresh, lively flavors suggest now berries, now
cherries. The textures of Garnet are every bit as
lively as its flavors. If the invitation is to drink it
young, waiting seldom does harm.

Carneros Pinot Noir 1989   🍇🍇 ③
All of the expected spicy tone from Carneros
complicates a wine built upon meaty-rich flavors
of Pinot Noir at its purest. Velvety, decadent
richness puts it in contention for Top Wine.

Schug Cellars

602 Bonneau Road
Sonoma ,CA. 95476
Tel. (707) 939-9363

Walter Schug is a perfect example of the stubborness that can lead to individualistic wines. German-born and trained, he made his first reputation in California with Riesling and Gewürztraminer for Joseph Phelps Vineyard. When he set out on his own, in 1980, he turned his back on those varieties to make only Chardonnay and Pinot Noir. Not only that, he elected to make them in his idea of a purely French style rather than one aimed at the American taste. His idea of French taste includes closed, firm wines that evolve slowly in bottle, sometimes needing several years. Schug made his first wines in leased space in another winery, then in a leased cellar. Only in 1991 did he move his winery into its permanent home. The estate vineyard is just beginning to bear; purchased grapes still dominate Schug's production.

Carneros Chardonnay 1989   ❦ ③
The lean, fim, dry feel of Carneros is everywhere in a Chardonnay built upon not just grapes and oak, but subtler tricks of winemaking until its complexities defy easy description.

Carneros Pinot Noir   ❦ ③
Beckstoffer 1989
The first Schug Pinot Noir to have the velvety, lush tactile for which the variety is known. It carries a definite flavor of oak, but a ripe taste of Pinot carries into a long finish.

Guenoc Winery

21000 Butts Canyon Road
Middletown, CA. 95461
Tel. (707) 987-2385
Fax (707) 987-9351

The Guenoc Winery is one of those brilliant examples of how concentrated time and space can be in California's winemaking history. The property was first planted to vines in 1888 when the British actress Lily Langtry hired a Frenchman vigneron to do the job. A few years later Prohibition wiped out both winery and vineyards. Neither returned until the 1970s when Hawaiian owners named William and Orville Magoon hired a veteran Napa Valley grapegrowing and winemaking family to revitalize the place. It is a case of a circle coming full in two ways; William Magoon is deeply involved in London theater. Winemaker Derek Holstein has developed a solid list of wines, many from vines within the original Langtry estate, some from Magoon-owned grapes nearby in Napa County, some purchased from outside sources. Domaine Breton is a second label.

Guenoc Valley Petite Sirah 1988   ❦ ③
Petite Sirah is by nature dark and hard, but it can be tamed. Here it has been. A deft touch of oak, refined use of tannins, understated fruit flavors bring rare harmony.

Guenoc Valley Zinfandel 1988   ❦ ②
Zinfandel's berry flavors are present, but in company with several grace notes evoking time in both oak and bottle. A firm core promises longer life, yet the wine is supple, polished.

Kendall-Jackson

500 Mathews Road
Lakeport, CA. 95453
Tel. (415) 398-7727
Fax (415) 263-5299

There may be no better insight into the American palate for wine than Kendall-Jackson's, which exactly caught the desire for high profile flavors and marketed the well realized results by calling almost every wine a Reserve of some sort. Americans, wine drinkers or no, love fizz and sweet and the taste of butterscotch. K-J parlayed a shrewd perception of this American taste and an ability to capture the essences of it in white wines that have become one of the fastest-growing labels in the nation. The reds are more traditional in dryness, but they, too, are particularly American in offering unmistakeable flavors of new oak that sometimes dominate more than any taste of grapes. The firm draws upon many vineyard sources, but especially Mendocino, Lake, Sonoma and Santa Barbara counties, in all of which proprietor Jesse Jackson has vineyard holdings.

California Sauvignon Blanc
Vintner's reserve 1990
The herbaceous flavors of Sauvignon well tempered by oak in one of its sweetest evocations spring out of a round, almost fat wine lifted by an easy-to-notice petillance.

California Zinfandel 1990 🍇 ②
Vinter's Reserve 1990
In keeping with the house style oak is a prominent contributor to theflavors, but Zinafndel manages to stay close to the limelight. The wine is fat, almost chewy.

Konocti Cellars

P.O. Box 890
Kelseyville, CA. 95451
Tel. (707) 279-8861
Fax (707) 279-9633

Konocti is an odd partnership of a small cooperative of growers in Lake County and John Parducci, who anchored Mendocino County winemaking for decades before people began to realize its value. In essence, Parducci has undertaken on behalf of Lake County much of what he did for Mendocino twenty years earlier. That is to say, he is working at the long, slow, painful process of building the reputation of a region at a time when people are looking elsewhere, even looking at varieties better suited to those elsewheres. What Konocti in particular and Lake County in general do as well as any winery and region is Sauvignon Blanc, which, unhappily, lags far behind Chardonnay in the market. Cabernet Sauvignon and Zinfandel from this cellar are worth some notice, and are the two reds well adapted to Lake County.

Lake County Grand Fume 1991 🍇 ②
Fermentation in heavily toasted oak barrels adds an unmistakeable note of charred wood to distinct flavors of melon-like Sauvignon in a wine as caressing as silk.

Clear Lake Sauvignon Blanc 1990 🍇 ①
Sauvignon flavors in all their fullness, reaching close to the pipi du chat sometimes remarked in Sancerres of France, make this a wine for the initiated. Crisp and refreshing on the palate.

LAKE COUNTY
CALIFORNIA
UNITED STATES OF AMERICA   1132

LAKE COUNTY
CALIFORNIA
UNITED STATES OF AMERICA

Fetzer Vineyards

P.O. Box 227
Redwood Valley, CA. 95470
Tel. (707) 485-7634
Fax (707) 485-0340

Fetzer Vineyards started very small in 1968, then grew swiftly. It had to do so, because nine of founder Bernard Fetzer's children fell in love with grapes and wine, and wished to take their places in the family business. Their success since Bernard's death has been brilliant as well as heart-warming. Few California wineries can be relied upon so thoroughly for well-made, agreeable-tasting wines across a broad range. Even as the original dependence on Mendocino vineyards yielded to much broader sources, chief winemaker Paul Dolan has kept style and technique in harmony from the early days, with increasing help from Kathleen Fetzer. Other Fetzers run vineyards, sales, administration with a degree of cooperation rarely found in any kind of business. Fetzer produces and sells a second label, Bel Arbors.

Mendocino Chardonnay
Barrel Select 1990
Epitomizes Fetzer. Well selected grapes properly handled in the cellars result in a wine well able to challenge others of twice its price with enjoyable balance and appetizing flavors.

Gamay Beaujolais 1991
Almost unchallenged in California. In fact, few capture the vital textures and fresh flavors of Gamay half as well. Not a wine for contemplation, but rather for casual enjoyment.

Mendocino Zinfandel
Barrel Select 1988
Intense, lingering notes of wild blackberries mark the beginning and the finish of this round, richly textured, handsomely polished wine. And yet, it leaves a sense of complexity.

Greenwood Ridge Vineyards

24555 Greenwood Ridge Road
Philo, CA. 95466
Tel. (707) 877-3262

Greenwood Ridge is one of California's remotest wineries, perched in a small vineyard atop a high ridge between the sparsely settled Anderson Valley to the east and the sparsely settled Mendocino County coast to the west. In spite of that a certain urbanity prevails, for its owner is a San Francisco graphic designer named Allan Green, while the winemaker behind all the vintages noted is a former Napa Valley hand. In its early days, from 1980 through 1987, Greenwood Ridge focussed on estate-grown Cabernet Sauvignon and Riesling. In more recent times it has expanded its horizons to other varieties, other vineyards, even other grape-growing districts, all to positive effect. The signal additions have been Sauvignon Blanc from Anderson Valley and Zinfandel from Sonoma's Alexander Valley. Now an Anderson Valley Pinot Noir also begins to clamor for attention.

Anderson Valley
Sauvignon Blanc 1990
A faint spritz adds crisp textures to an amply tart, well-structured Sauvignon that, in flavor, remains poised between melon and one of the sweeter herbs, evoking an appetite for fish.

Anderson Valley Pinot Noir 1990
What begins to seem typical of Anderson Valley Pinot Noir: a wine of gentle charms and pure but not profound Pinot flavors. Perfect, thus, for its approachability.

Alexander Valley Zinfandel
Scherrer 1990
Mature vines give wonderful flavors of berries without the weight and alcoholicity that sometimes afflict Zinfandel. A middleweight. To try with light tomato sauces.

MENDOCINO
CALIFORNIA
UNITED STATES OF AMERICA

1133

MENDOCINO
CALIFORNIA
UNITED STATES OF AMERICA

Handley Cellars

3151 Highway 128
Philo, CA. 95466
Tel. (707) 895-3876
Fax (707) 895-2603

Milla Handley comes from a grape-growing family in Sonoma. She started her winemaking career at Chateau St Jean, but launched her own small cellar at the earliest moment she could afford equipment and a small building to house it. The original idea was classic method sparkling wines, and it was that plan that led her to the Anderson Valley with its cool growing season and proven suitability to Chardonnay and Pinot Noir ripened expressly for sparklings. Her vintage-dated Bruts remain a part of the program, but have been joined by several still wines from her family's vineyard near the Sonoma County town of Healdsburg, from her own vines in Anderson Valley, and from those of near neighbors. Handley showed a sure sense of style in her earliest vintage, 1978, and has gone from strength to strength since then. Production remains tightly limited.

Anderson Valley ♥ ②
Gewurztraminer 1991
Catches every atom of the lichee-like flavors of Gewurztraminer from its region. Has just enough sweetness to temper but not hide all of the variety's typical suggestion of bitter at the finish.

Dry Creek Valley ♥ ②
Sauvignon Blanc 1990
Bulls-eye Dry Creek Sauvignon flavors leaned more to herb than melon linger and linger in a solidly built wine. Drinking well young but promises to age in bottle for two years or more.

Anderson Valley ♥♥ ③
Chardonnay 1989
Perfect apple-like Chardonnay flavors, a deft spice from oak, and all firm and fresh in a way particular to the cool district in which the grapes grow. Lingers beautifully.

Anderson Valley Brut 1987 ♥ ③
From the next door neighbor to Roederer Estates comes a Brut every bit as close in character as geography suggests: well marked by a flavor of toasted nuts, even more by creamy textures.

Husch Vineyards

P.O. Box 157
Talmage, CA. 95481
Tel. (707) 895-3216
Fax (707) 462-5374

Husch Vineyards, now more than 20 years old, remains one of California's hidden small treasures. The winery is based in two well-proven vineyards. One in the Anderson Valley is devoted mostly to Pinot Noir, Chardonnay and Gewürztraminer, the other in a warmer climate near Ukiah largely given over to Cabernet Sauvignon and Sauvignon Blanc. The name is a relic of the original ownership, which planted the Anderson Valley vineyard and built a tiny winery on it in the early 1970s. Since 1979 these have belonged to the Hugo Oswald family, which already owned La Ribera vineyard near Ukiah. The Oswalds added a winery on their original property in order to be able to make wine from all of their grapes. Although all of their wines often perform very well against established names, their fame remains modest, as do the prices.

Anderson Valley ♥ ②
Gewurztraminer 1990
Less bold of lichee than some of its peers from the Anderson Valley, but the flavor is still there to perfection. Somehow a shade drier than most, though not quite bone dry.

Mendocino Cabernet Sauvignon ♥ ③
North Field Select 1989
The most favored blocks of a substantial vineyard go into this special bottling, and prove their worth with flavors absolutely true to both variety and region. Accessible, yet may age well.

Anderson Valley Pinot Noir 1989 ♥ ③
The aroma is everything one hopes from California Pinot Noir. Behind it comes a well-balanced wine still straightforward and youthful, perhaps at its best in that vein.

MENDOCINO
CALIFORNIA
UNITED STATES OF AMERICA

1134

MENDOCINO
CALIFORNIA
UNITED STATES OF AMERICA

Lazy Creek

4610 Highway 128
Philo, CA. 95466
Tel. (707) 895-3623

Johann (Hans) Kobler spent a long career as a waiter in Jack's, one of San Francisco's great traditional restaurants, the sort in which staff help teach succeeding generations how to eat wisely and well. So, when he retired to his country place in Mendocino County, he knew what sort of wines he liked and what sort of wines thoughtful diners liked. Happily for him, the two tastes coincide neatly.

Kobler's retirement has turned out to be busier than what he had thought of as his working life, not least because his wines have succeeded so well. A few of his early efforts were patchy, but he quickly found his stride with Gewürztraminer, and not long after that settled into a comfortable style for Pinot Noir as well. Though he makes other wines from grapes he grows in his scenic vineyard, these two more than the others keep his clientele loyal in an era when Chardonnay and Cabernet are far easier to sell. The totale production of this small,welcoming cellar ranges around 4,000 cases. The winery, midway between the villages of Navarro and Philo, is surrounded by an estate vineyard ofabout 20 acres at the heart of the Anderson Valley, a region with a distinctive micro-climate much influenced by the nearby Pacific Ocean. The whole valley has about 700 acres in vines.

Anderson Valley Pinot Noir 1989 🍇 ③
Kobler approaches Pinot Noir cautiously. Not to much press. Not too much wood. The program is exactly suited to the gentle flavors Anderson Valley confers on the variety.

Anderson Valley Gewurztraminer 1990
From California's finest region for Gewürztraminer, in a superior vintage, Lazy Creek produced a Gewürztraminer of such memorable flavors, such impeccable balance, such perfect fidelity to type and place that it must be ranked among the best America has to offer, well ahead Chardonnays and Cabernets of great quality but many rivals. It is, in short, one of those wines that reduces one to silent admiration for its nearness to perfection. One can anticipate rewards for cellaring the wine for the next year , two, perhaps even five. It would not be the first Gewurtztraminer from Anderson Valley to improve over such a span of time.

MENDOCINO
CALIFORNIA
UNITED STATES OF AMERICA

1135

MENDOCINO
CALIFORNIA
UNITED STATES OF AMERICA

Navarro Vineyards

5601 Highway 128
Philo, CA. 95466
Tel. (707) 895-3686

Scores of California wineries belong to
gentlemen farmers who made their money in
other callings and retired to the country life.
Few such men dress vines, shovel pomace,
haul hoses, or do the other hard work of
winemaking, but Navarro Vineyards owner
Ted Bennett does, and with inexhaustible
glee. Upon his early withdrawal from the
world of consumer electronics in 1972, he
and wife Deborah Cahn moved to Mendocino
County's Anderson Valley, their first goal to
make dry Gewürztraminer of unforgettable
character from that chilly coastal climate.
Time has proven them right. However,
Navarro has earned greater fame with lean,
understated Chardonnays of the kind that call
for heroic sacrifices by oysters, halibut, and
dozens of their kin. Fine vineyards and skilled
winemaking make all Navarro wines worthy
of consideration.

Anderson Valley   🍇🍇 ②
Gewurztraminer Estate 1990
The 1990, with the most generous taste of
lichee since 1975, promises to complicate itself
with time in bottle until it ranks as one of
Navarro's finest vintages.

Anderson Valley   🍇🍇 ②
Chardonnay Estate 1989
Leaner than most of its forerunners after a one
of California's coolest years on record. It will
always be tart, but the flavors have a depth and
intensity that cry out for seafood.

Parducci Wine Cellars

501 Parducci Road
Ukiah, CA. 95482
Tel. (707) 462-3828
Fax (707) 462-7260

Although the winery and vineyards no longer
belong to the founding family, John Parducci
continues to oversee both, and to keep his
long-standing preference for the flavors of
well-ripened grapes foremost over those of
oak in all of the wines, white and red alike.
The Parducci family almost single-handed
kept winemaking alive in and around Ukiah
during and after Prohibition. Thus they were
able to identify and buy up much of the finest
vineyard land in the region at a time when
others did not see its value. Living in the lean
times, meanwhile, gave them a strong sense
of offering excellent value for price paid. The
result is enormously drinkable wine under
this label, and, in many cases, far greater
depth and interest than is perceived by those
critics who look first for lofty prices.

North Coast Merlot 1989   🍇 ②
Pleasing aromas of ripe Merlot complicated by
notes reminiscent of fresh-brewed coffee lead to
a supple, polished wine that gives pleasure now
even as it promises to keep well.

North Coast   🍇 ②
Cabernet Sauvignon 1987
Textbook flavors of herbs come quickly, then
stay, growing deeper as they do. There is a hint
of coffee here, too. Oak shows how it can stay
in the background and still contribute to style.

MENDOCINO
CALIFORNIA
UNITED STATES OF AMERICA   1136

MENDOCINO
CALIFORNIA
UNITED STATES OF AMERICA

Roederer Estate

4501 Highway 128
Philo, CA. 95466
Tel. (707) 8952-288
Fax (707) 8952-120

According to long-time California winemaker Henry Bugatto, who coordinated the project, the principals of Louis Roederer searched throughout California for a climate as chilly and wet and bleak as the one at Reims, and were satisifed only when they came to the Anderson Valley, the short and remarkably beautiful drainage of the Navarro River, which has its headwaters just a few miles inland from the Pacific Ocean shore. Between the villages of Navarro and Philo they settled down in 1985 to plant vines and build a cellar for sparkling wines to be made in the best traditions of their home province of Champagne. They sent one of their best, Dr. Michel Salgues, to oversee the vineyards and winemaking. The results of his work swiftly changed the face of a district earlier devoted more to Riesling and Gewürztraminer than Chardonnay and Pinot Noir.

Mendocino Brut NV ❦ ❦ ③
One cuvee has been atypical, but most show the hallmarks of the parent: a rosy glow from Pinot Noir, a rich to outright creamy texture, and distinct flavors akin to roasted nuts.

Scharffenberger Cellars

8501 Highway 128
Philo, CA. 95466
Tel. (707) 895-2065
Fax (707) 895-2758

John Scharffenberger describes himself as a bio-geographer. The French might more simply call him a "terroiriste". They have their chance. Champagne Pommery bought a major interest in the firm in 1989. Scharffenberger grew up in a Mendocino County vineyard belonging to his parents, then studied biology at university. On graduation, he became fascinated with the possibilities of classic method sparkling wines in Mendocino. With the founding of his winery in 1981, he set about a systematic study of Mendocino soils and climates in a search for the elements of a superior cuvee. He carried on single-handed until Pommery came into the picture. By that time he had settled on the Anderson Valley as the primary source. The new partners financed a major vineyard property there, built a new cellar, and brought added technical skills as well.

Mendocino Blanc De Blancs 1987 ❦ ③
Entirely from Chardonnay, it is rather the green apple of classic method sparkling wines. That is, lean and tart and so crisp it is almost crunchy. The technique is impeccable.

Mendocino Brut NV ❦ ③
A pale hint of salmon reveals Pinot Noir before the taste can, but Pinot is prominent as a flavor, too. This wine has all the crisp freshness for which California classic method sparklers are known.

MENDOCINO
CALIFORNIA
UNITED STATES OF AMERICA

1137

MENDOCINO
CALIFORNIA
UNITED STATES OF AMERICA

Chalone

P.O. Box 855
Soledad, CA. 93960
Tel. (408) 678-1717
Fax (415) 546-9473

Some California wineries turn away from Europe to seek a path all their own. Some pay homage, but accept inevitable differences. A few attempt, outright, to outperform a European counterpart on the original's terms. Chalone is one of the latter, a house that spares no effort in trying to make Chardonnays and Pinot Noirs that can be, not only mistaken for Burgundies, but preferred to them in the process. Rich deposits of quartz crystals at an isolated site high in hills east of the Salinas Valley governed its selection by Richard Graff as the place in which to make the noble experiment. Every aspect of vineyard and winery is bent to that end, even to the degree of humidifying the cellar to the exact degree of the ancient caves under the walls at Beaune. Rarely does Chalone make a Burgundy, but always it achieves fascinating results.

Chalone Chardonnay 1990   ♈ ③
As always, something of an enigma, seeming sometimes intensely flavored, sometimes closed, sometimes fresh, sometimes fading, but never bland, never ordinary.

Chalone Pinot Blanc 1990   ♈ ③
Though similar to the Chardonnay in many respects, Chalone Pinot Blanc manages against all odds to have distinctive character and a greater depth of flavor.

Stanley Anderson

1473 Yountville Crossroad
Yountville, CA. 94599
Tel. (707) 944-8642
Fax (707) 944-8020

Dr. Stanley Anderson retired from dentistry in Los Angeles in stages, beginning in 1981, so his cellars in the Napa Valley would be in full activity when he was ready to give them his complete attention in 1984. During the same years his wife, Carol, studied enology in both classroom and cellar so she could step in as winemaker. Their passion for wine has led from a modest prefabricated winery building to romantic caves dug into a grassy hill, and from one vineyard to two. The bottled results have earned praise from a champenois who visited them in 1989 and reported back to his colleagues that the wines "etaient plus fruites et plus secs que les notres, mais en tous points remarquables." That and other accolades are leading to ever-growing emphasis on classic method sparkling wines. However, a still Chardonnay remains important to the winemaker.

Napa Valley Brut   ♈ ③
Blanc de Noirs 1987
Creamy rich textures carry the day in a wine with no hint of color that betrays the Pinot Noir, and none of the almost candied flavor the variety often imparts to California sparkling wines.

Napa Valley Brut "Tivoli" NV   ♈ ③
When Carol Anderson has finished assembling the cuvees for Brut and Blanc de Noirs, what is left goes into bold, bright Tivoli, which more than makes up in exuberance anything it might lack in refinement.

Napa Valley Cabernet Sauvignon
1989 Stag's Leap District
In a stunning debut, the winery's first Cabernet showed supple polish and a whole galaxy of interwoven, underplayed flavors ranging from dried herbs to berries to sweet tobacco.

MONTEREY
CALIFORNIA
UNITED STATES OF AMERICA
     1138
NAPA VALLEY
CALIFORNIA
UNITED STATES OF AMERICA

Atlas Peak Vineyard

3700 Soda Canyon Road
Napa, CA. 94581-0660
Tel. (707) 252-7971
Fax (707) 252-7974

Only with difficulty could one imagine a more
international enterprise, begun jointly by
Great Britain's Whitbread, Italy's Antinori and
France's Bollinger, designed and built by an
American of Swedish ancestry, and run now
by two young Italian-Americans. Its first wine,
a type destined to become its signature, was
a Sangiovese 1989. It is to be joined by
others, perhaps including a Cabernet-
Sangiovese blend, certainly a Chardonnay.
All will come from the estate, cupped in high
hills in the southeastern quarter of the Napa
Valley, above Stags Leap District. Dr.
Richard Peterson laid out the vineyards and
engineered the deep tunnels in which will age
the wines made by Glen Salva and Marco Di
Giulio. While the grand venture has only just
begun, already it has caused Piero Antinori to
say, "I believe Sangiovese likes the Napa
Valley."

Napa Valley Sangiovese 1989   🍇 ③
Admirers of Brunello di Montalcino may
recognize a familiar hint of flowers in the nose,
but the rest of the wine is pure Napa: juicy
rather than austere, fresh rather than long-aged
in oak.

Beaucanon

1695 St Helena Hwy
St Helena, CA. 94574
Tel. (707) 963-1896
Fax (707) 963-5961

Although its history is short even by the lax
standards of California, Beaucanon, has
begun to establish a reputation for polished,
intriguingly flavorful Cabernet Sauvignon and
Merlot. And this in spite of keeping almost
total silence about its presence in the
marketplace. Owned and directed by
Jacques de Coninck and family, better known
as the proprietors of Lebegue in France,
Beaucanon began to make wine only in
1986. In the brief time since, winemaker
Louis de Coninck has found the crucial
balance points in grapes from the firm's two
established vineyards. Of the two producing
vineyards, one adjoins the winery in
Rutherford; the other lies some miles south
near the city of Napa. Beaucanon is just now
developing its third and largest property
about eight miles north of the winery.

Napa Valley Merlot 1989   🍇 ③
As polished as the Cabernet is, the Merlot is
fuller and rounder on the palate, even from as
testy a vintage as 1989. The taste of Merlot is
unmistakeable from start to finish.

Napa Valley   🍇 ③
Cabernet Sauvignon 1988
As in earlier vintages, a silky polish made this
wine drinkable from its earliest days. The flavors
of Cabernet are irreproachable, and deftly
seasoned by time in oak barrel.

Beaulieu Vineyard

c/o Heublein Fine Wine Group - P.O. Box 391
St. Helena, CA. 94574
Tel. (707) 963-4480
Fax (707) 967-3190

Once upon a time Beaulieu Vineyard defined what was Napa Valley Cabernet Sauvignon with its Georges de Latour Private Reserves. Now the old beacon is something of an eccentricity. However, in an era populated by scores of me-too winemakers, what B-V began and still does has a sharply defined character, and a great history at table. American wine is much richer because the winery has had the courage to stay with the style that made it an icon: 100% Cabernet, fully ripened grapes, and three years or more in American oak barrels of several differing ages. Beginning in 1936 it was the great Andre Tchelistcheff who undertook the task of producing the finest wines from the central Napa Valley. The wine has seen some ups and downs since, but three of the five oldest vintages remain in excellent form today. It can truthfully be said that no other American wine has been admired for so long a time by skillful tasters. Heublein, Inc.-owned since 1974, Beaulieu Vineyard produces other wines of uncommon quality, but Cabernet remains its yardstick.

Napa Valley Sauvignon Blanc 1990
No hint of oak clouds the melon-like flavors of Sauvignon from a perfect vintage. No trace of sweet diminishes its freshness. No rival does so much for fish.

Napa Valley Cabernet Sauvignon "Rutherford" 1989
The Rutherford bottling of Beaulieu Cabernet spend much less time in oak than the Private Reserve, so emerges fresher and livelier. It is the epitome of a five-year wine.

Napa Valley Cabernet Sauvignon "Georges de Latour Private Reserve" 1987
The trademark note of American oak is not at all hard to find, but neither is the berry side of Cabernet. As always, polished and supple even in youth. History and vintage both say it will age.

Beringer Vineyards

P.O. Box
St. Helena, CA. 94574
Tel. (707) 963-7115
Fax (707) 963-5054

One of the grand old names of the Napa Valley fell to a low state under its original family ownership, then was brought back by a determined effort of corporate proprietors, Nestle, Inc. Early in Nestle's ownership, beginning in 1969, Beringer began acquiring vineyards at a furious pace. For the next ten years, the company bought and sold vineyards swiftly as the late Myron Nightingale conducted a ruthlessly Darwinian search for grapes that would make distinctive wines. Nightingale's successor, Edward Sbragia, reaps the rewards of that search. His penchant for ample use of new oak barrels is greater than his mentor's was, and still Beringer wines are rich with flavors from the vineyards. Cabernet Sauvignon, one from Sonoma's Knights Valley, another from the upper Napa Valley, and Chardonnay from lower Napa are the big three. Fume Blanc, Gewürztraminer and Zinfandel all succeed.

Napa Valley Chardonnay Estate 1990
It marries a toasty note from oak, a honeyed one from ripe grapes, and some bouquets that fall between the two. Rather well structured, as most 1990 California Chardonnays are.

Napa Valley Fume Blanc Estate 1990
Like many 1990s from the southern half of Napa Valley, bold with the herbaceous side of Sauvignon. That and a firm, cleansing tactile make a perfect wine for fish.

Napa Valley Cabernet Sauvignon Reserve 1987
Has all of the intensity of Cabernet flavors of its vintage and vineyards, plus yet more powerful perfumes from fresh oak barrels. It also has enough tannins for purists.

Cain Cellars

P.O. Box 509
St. Helena, CA. 94574
Tel. (707) 963-616
Fax (707) 963-7952

The flagship wine of Cain Cellars is an estate-grown red called Cain Five. The "Cain" pays tribute to the winery's founder. The "Five" recognizes the presence in the wine of all five principal varieties of red Bordeaux: cabernet sauvignon, cabernet franc, merlot, petit verdot and malbec. Such blends are beginning to be known categorically as Meritages, though the name legally belongs to an association of producers of the type. Cain Five and its rivals began as an effort to add dimension to varietal Cabernet Sauvignons. Not many of them truly succeed yet, blending being a more difficult art than some of its newer practitioners understand. However, Cain has hit the bullseye, mainly by limiting itself to estate-grown grapes from a mature mountain vineyard. The winery also produces small lots of Chardonnay and Sauvignon from purchased grapes.

Cain Five Napa Valley 1987 🍇🍇 ④
Dark but not exaggerated ruby hues promise depths of flavor and firm structure. The 1987 declares its foundation in Cabernet Sauvignon with a chorus of herbs, then heaps on the grace notes.

Cakebread Cellars

8300 St. Helena Hwy
Rutherford, CA. 94573
Tel. (707) 963-5221
Fax (707) 963-1067

The winery is a tale of a bold father and more cautious son finding a balance at a most agreeable point somewhere between them. Founder-owner Jack Cakebread made the first wines of 1973 through 1977 with all his heart. From 1978, son Bruce has tempered the style, not much, but enough to move Cakebread from boldest of the bold to one among the bold. This subtle shift, it must be said, seems more befitting of the vineyards upon which the winery draws. Like many California wineries of its size, Cakebread is based in owned vineyard (26 acres at the winery, the rest in hills just west) but each year buys grapes from the same few independent growers to fill out its needs. Unlike most, it does not grow one variety and buy others, but rather blends its own and other grapes to achieve complexity and balance in all its wines, save sauvignon blanc, the only estate-grown type on Cakebread's list.

Napa Valley 🍇🍇 ③
Sauvignon Blanc 1990
The interplay between full body and firm texture say Cakebread in an instant. With that comes the other trademark, a rich flavor hovering between musky melon and delicate herb.

Napa Valley Chardonnay 1989 🍇 ④
From a difficult vintage, the very prototype of Cakebread: intense flavors of both Chardonnay and oak embodied in a wine that somehow manages to be both powerful and balanced.

NAPA VALLEY
CALIFORNIA
UNITED STATES OF AMERICA
1141
NAPA VALLEY
CALIFORNIA
UNITED STATES OF AMERICA

Caymus Vineyard

8700 Conn Creek Road
Rutherford, CA. 94573
Tel. (707) 9634-204
Fax (707) 963-5958

Only with the third generation of Wagners did a winery spring out of the family vineyard east of Rutherford, the most famous part of the Napa Valley for Cabernet Sauvignon. When one did, its immediate and still greatest fame was, no surprise, for Cabernet. Charley Wagner, the second generation, knew the promise of his property. Chuck Wagner, the third generation, knew how to capitalize on it, and has done so with growing success since the first vintage, in 1972. When it comes to Cabernet Sauvignon, Caymus is synonymous with intense, somewhat herbaceous flavors from the grapes, daring amounts of oak, and textures aimed more at sturdiness than refinement, and yet the wine is far from simple or rustic, even when it is rather new in bottle. The same can be said of its other red wines, especially Zinfandel. A second range of wines from Caymus appears under the Liberty School label. Its average annual volume is about 50,000 cases.

Napa Valley　　　　　　　　🍇🍇 ③
Cabernet Sauvignon "Napa Cuvée" 1989
Plenty of oak, part of it American, but even more Cabernet flavors. The fruit must hold on; if it does, bold balance once again promises a wine worth keeping for the gifts of time.

Napa Valley Zinfandel 1989　　　🍇 ②
The owners make Zinfandel in much the same dark, firm, oak-tinted style as their Cabernets. Also like the Cabernets, Caymus Zinfandels trumpet the flavors of their hillside-grown grapes.

Napa Valley Cabernet Sauvignon 🍇🍇 ④
Reserve "Special Selection" 1988
From estate grapes, Caymus Reserve is a wonder of intensity in color, in flavor, in everything. The taste of oak is strong to begin, but slowly marries with that of Cabernet.

Chappellet Vineyard

1581 Sage Canyon Road
St. Helena, CA. 94574
Tel. (707) 963-7136
Fax (707) 963-7445

Chappellet's greatest reputation is with European critics and connoisseurs rather than home-grown ones, because the wines trade on understated flavors that must be savoured to be noticed, and on firm, even austere textures best polished by patient cellaring. That is, the wines have not shown well to those who believe that blind tasting and wine drinking are synonymous, but reserved their best for the table, a statement perhaps truer of the whites than the reds. In this situation, proprietor Donn Chappellet has yielded somewhat on the whites since 1989, but kept the reds in their traditional style. In this he is much aided by lean soils and steep hills in his vineyards to the east of the main Napa Valley, surely for the best. Here, Cabernet Sauvignon has an impeccable history over the vintages since 1969, and Merlot seems to have found one of its most congenial homes in all of California. The more than 100 acres of terraced vine overlooking Lake Hennessey represent the important foundation-stone of this winery, which produced more than 180,000 bottles. But Chappellet Vineyard sells limited numbers of wines from the older vintages to vistors to the cellars; these wines, in making the best case for the positive evolution of Donn Chappellet's production, earn our recognition of its quality.

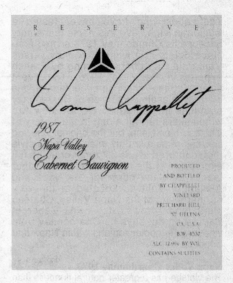

Napa Valley Merlot Estate 1988   🍇🍇 ③
The firmness and depth of flavor so often lacking in California Merlots are here in abundance, in a wine that cries out to be aged in bottle for at least five years.

Napa Valley Cabernet   🍇🍇🍇 ③
Sauvignon Estate 1987
Here is a Napa Valley vintage to keep. Here is a wine to prove why: Deep Cabernet flavors perfectly married to subtle ones of oak, with firm structures to keep all in harmony. As always, the Chappellet is more closed now than many others of its vintage because the nutrient-poor soils and steep slopes from which it sprang impose their own austerity on every wine they yield. History says the 1987 will develop for at least five more years, than linger at or near the top of its form for as many as a dozen more. As evidence, the 1969, from a similar sseason, remains an inviting bottle little weakened by its age.

Chateau Montelena

1429 Tubbs Lane
Calistoga, CA. 94515
Tel. (707) 942-5105
Fax (707) 942-4221

Thousands who have never tasted a California wine have this name in memory because its Chardonnay 1973 scored first-place points in a white Burgundy versus California Chardonnay tasting by French experts in Paris, in 1976. The event celebrated the American bi-centennial, and led to wholesale expansion of Chardonnay plantings in California. We are now two winemakers farther along in the history of Chateau Montelena, but the original vineyard sources remain largely intact, and the style that captured Paris is untouchable: full expression of the fruit, and textures rather leaner than the norm for the Napa and Alexander Valleys. Located at the very northern limit of the Napa Valley, Chateau Montelena grows its own Cabernet Sauvignon but buys its Chardonnay from vineyards in cooler regions within Napa and Sonoma.

Napa Valley Chardonnay 1990   ❦ ❦ ③
The vintage has a greater natural firmness than most, leading to an epitome of the Chateau Montelena style. Fine now, it is a leading candidate for cellaring.

Napa Valley   ❦ ③
Cabernet Sauvignon 1989
The old dense flavors and gripping tannins have given way to a more approachable style, but this remains a wine for the lover of reds that remain dark and stern years after the vintage.

Chateau Potelle

3875 Mount Veeder Road
Napa, CA. 94558
Tel. (707) 255-9440
Fax (707) 255-9444

The paradisiacal side of California has lured millions to move to the state, but Jean-Noel and Marketta Fourmeaux du Sartel are unique in having been sent by the French government to report back on the state of grape-growing and winemaking only to throw in their lot with the people they were sent to study. Their first wines were made with purchased Napa and Sonoma grapes using leased space. Within five years they had purchased two Napa vineyards, one with a small winery on it, and were fully launched as proprietors of a substantial business. What they kept from their homeland was a sense of style that puts completeness of flavor and balance ahead of dramatic flavors of the grape variety. In reds and whites alike, the first impression is of polish and harmony more than of straightforward fruit. The approach has worked well for them.

Napa Valley Sauvignon Blanc 1990   ❦ ②
Haunting scents of ripe melon promise much. The wine delivers even more. A firm, refreshing texture makes a harmonious whole that rouses thoughts of a poached fish with herbs for a garnish.

Napa Valley Chardonnay 1989   ❦ ❦ ③
French owners look for bouquet first, fruit second, and succeed in a cool, long vintage designed to suit their purposes. A silken surface hides a firm core.

Alexander Valley   ❦ ③
Cabernet Sauvignon 1987
Last in a series before estate Napa vineyards take over, it is prototypical Alexander Valley: intense in herb-like flavors but soft and approachable in tactile.

Chimney Rock Winery

5340 Silverado Trail
Napa, CA. 94558
Tel. (707) 257-2641
Fax (707) 257-2036

The ownership of Chimney Rock made its money selling soda pop and beer in South Africa. In repairing to the Napa Valley in 1981, the proprietors raised their sights from soda and beer to wine, and removed half a golf course to plant vines, both deeds sure to count in their favor when their final scorecard is written. They planted Chardonnay, Sauvignon Blanc, Cabernet Sauvignon and bits of Merlot and Cabernet Franc on a property immediately adjoining the well-established Clos du Val. The early results have validated what Clos du Val already had learned: that the Bordelais varieties are the ones for the Stags Leap District. Winemaker Doug Fletcher began doing well with Sauvignon Blanc, even better with Cabernet Sauvignon in the debut vintage of 1986, and has gained ground since. The Chardonnays are agreeable, but seemingly limited by a terroir better suited to other types.

Napa Valley ③
Cabernet Sauvignon 1988
A supple, polished epitome of the Stags Leap District, delicately flavored by Cabernet in its most berryish form, even more subtly marked by time in new French oak. Accessible now.

Price levels

① up to $ 9.99

② $ 10.00 - $ 14.99

③ $ 15.00 - $ 24.99

④ $ 25.00 or more

The 'ex-cellar', or direct from the producer, bottle prices, are calculated in US dollars and are intended only as an approximate guide

NAPA VALLEY
CALIFORNIA
UNITED STATES OF AMERICA

1145

NAPA VALLEY
CALIFORNIA
UNITED STATES OF AMERICA

Clos Du Val

5330 Silverado Trail
Napa, CA. 94558
Tel. (707) 252-6711
Fax (707) 252-6125

Our collected tasting notes on Clos du Val wines run into the hundreds by now, and virtually every one remarks upon the wonderful balance and polish of the wine in question. These qualities, even more than reliably admirable flavors, have been the hallmark of the house since its founding in 1972. Bernard Portet developed his sense of style in his native Bordeaux, and has found little need to amend his original ideas about Cabernet Sauvignon, Merlot, and Semillon since his arrival in the Napa Valley's Stag's Leap District. He and his long-time lieutenant, Krimo Souilah, have had to search longer and harder to find a footing with Pinot Noir and Chardonnay. The winery's second major vineyard, in Carneros, has helped them to do so in recent years. The other Clos du Val wine, Zinfandel, came naturally to Portet, though he sees it differently than native producers do. Proprietor John Goelet, a New York businessman whose family is of French origin, can tale justifiable pride in the work of his winemakers. Their skills have brought annual production at Clos du Val to nearly 600,000 bottles.

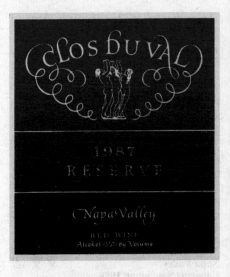

Joli Val California Semillon 1989   🍇 ②
Silken, supple, caressing at every sip. Dictionary perfect flavors of Semillon given extra depth by time in oak barrel and more time in bottle. A small treasure known to too few.

Napa Valley Cabernet Sauvignon 🍇🍇 ③ Estate 1988
Where many make Cabernets rough as wool, Portet makes his with the feel of silk. The 1988 demonstrates the point perfectly, yet promises more for later, and this from a forward vintage.

Napa Valley Merlot Estate 1988   🍇🍇 ③
Understatement, understatement, understatement. In true but subtle Merlot flavors, in admirably restrained use of oak, in the silken polish that hides a firmer than typical core.

Napa Valley Reserve 1987   🍇🍇🍇 ④
Bernard Portet celebrates superior vintages and the very finest blocks of Cabernet and Merlot in his vineyard with the name "Reserve." His caution in using a word much-overworked by others in California is reflected by the fact that only 1978 and 1985 earned the honor before 1987. As do other outstanding Cabernets from vineyards in the Stag's Leap District, this one has understated but indelible flavors, and a remarkable silkiness of texture in a wine so young. Its quiet charms do not mean it must be drunk up swiftly. Quite the contrary, most of is forebears have given their best to the patient, and it promises to outlive all of its older siblings.

NAPA VALLEY
CALIFORNIA
UNITED STATES OF AMERICA
1146
NAPA VALLEY
CALIFORNIA
UNITED STATES OF AMERICA

Corison

P.O. Box 344
Oakville, CA. 94562
Tel. (707) 963-7357

Corison is one of many winemakers labels in California, but one of few belonging to a woman. Cathy Corison elected to establish her own label using leased space and purchased grapes only after she had succeeded in making some of the grandest wines in the history of Chappellet Vineyards, notably including the 1987 Cabernet Sauvignon that has won top wine honors in this edition of the Guide. Under her own label, Corison makes only Cabernet Sauvignon from a selection of vineyards stretching along Napa's highly regarded west side, from Rutherford to the south to Yountville. Though these properties yield very different grapes from the hillside fruit she used at Chappellet during her decade there, the wines under her own label show the same adept balancing of passion for what she does with cool appraisal of the results.

Napa Valley   ❦ ❦ ③
Cabernet Sauvignon 1988
Polish refinement, understatement. Such are the words that come to mind first in tasting this wine. But with the lingering finish comes a realization of how indelibly one tastes Cabernet.

Crichton Hall

P.O. Box 187
Rutherford, CA. 94573
Tel. (707) 963-8524

Richard Crichton, a strayed Brit banker, settled in the Napa Valley in 1979 with the avowed intent of bringing a more restained sense of Chardonnay to what was, then, beyond question a region where, at the time, alcoholic power counted for more than finesse. His credentials were largely as a seasoned admirer of classic white Burgundies. He and wife Judith acquired a vineyard property near Yountville, and leased space in an existing winery for the winemaking. That remains the arrangement. Crichton Hall's first vintage, 1985, was more experiment than achievement, the next rather more polished. The course continues upward, but in unexpected directions, for each succeeding wine has seemed more purely Californian than its predecessor. This on-going shift would appear to be a tribute both to the indelible character of Napa Chardonnay and Mr. Crichton's sensible response to it.

Napa Valley Chardonnay   ❦ ❦ ③
Estate 1990
After a triumph in difficult 1989, Crichton repeats in amenable 1990 with a wine of riches and depths in its flavors, and a memorable firmness of texture. A candidate for Top Wine.

Cuvaison

4550 Silverado Trail
Calistoga, CA. 94515
Tel. (707) 942-6266
Fax (707) 942-5732

Two turning points changed Cuvaison from an ordinary winery into one to be watched. The first was purchase of the winery by the Swiss banking family of Alexander Schmidheiny in 1986. The second was the purchase and planting by the Schmidheinys of a 400-acre vineyard in the Carneros district at Napa County's southern tip. As that vineyard has developed, so, too, have Cuvaison Chardonnay and Merlot. A Pinot Noir with promise is in the wings. Winemaker John Thacher was on hand already when the current owners took control, and making good wines. However, Cuvaison, founded in 1972, had old reputations to put to rest, and it took a patient marketing program to make the public aware of the root changes in vineyard and cellar that began to take serious shape with the vintage of 1985. The course has been steadily upward since then, with Chardonnay always the leader.

Carneros Chardonnay 1990 🍷🍷 ③
Once again Thacher captures the textbook Carneros Chardonnay flavor of ripe apple peels, and spices it with oak. The perfect harmony of fresh flavor and polished tactile beg to be savored immediately.

Carneros Chardonnay 🍷🍷 ③
Reserve 1990
Here "Reserve" means an extra depth of fruit flavors offset by an extra measure of oak, the two balanced to produce a longer-lived wine than the regular Carneros bottling, an idea rewarded by 1990.

Carneros Merlot 1988 🍷🍷 ③
Awkward but likeable in youth, with berry-like Merlot and vanilla-like wood flavors separate rather than joined. However, history says excellent balance will allow time to harmonize the elements.

Napa Valley 🍷 ③
Cabernet Sauvignon 1988
The flavors of Cabernet come close to archetypal for the Napa Valley, yet show a welcome restraint at the same time. Already the wine feels supple from skillful polishing in the cellar.

Domaine Chandon

P.O. Box 2470
Yountville, CA. 94599
Tel. (707) 944-8844
Fax (707) 944-1123

In 1973 Moët et Chandon was the first of what has since become a wave of investors from Champagne in California sparkling wines. Its progress since has been brilliant on both the business and technical fronts. The company began by establishing Brut and Blanc de Noirs as basic, non-vintage cuvees. At its tenth anniversary, it added a more prestigious cuvee, Reserve. In 1991 it introduced what is effectively its luxury cuvee, Etoile. And thus it now participates well at several price levels. Simultaneously, under the direction of Edmund Maudiere of the parent company and resident winemaker Dawnine Dyer, Domaine Chandon has steadily expanded its vineyard holdings in Carneros, and refined its plantings of chardonnay, pinot blanc, pinot noir, pinot meunier within those and its other Napa Valley holdings.

Napa Valley Brut Blanc de Noirs NV 🍷 ③
In young sparkling wines, Pinot Noir gives almost a fruit candy flavor, exactly the case in Chandon's partridge-eye example. Those who wish can outwait it in a year or so.

Napa Valley Brut "Etoile" NV 🍷🍷 ③
This is the Reserve made one shade deeper in the flavors time on yeast imparts, and at the same time one scintilla more delicate and airy on the palate.

Napa Valley Brut "Reserve" NV 🍷🍷 ③
One of the first California sparklers to achieve a personality so specific that one does not even need the label to know its faintly austere melange of flavors and firm textures.

NAPA VALLEY
CALIFORNIA
UNITED STATES OF AMERICA   1148

NAPA VALLEY
CALIFORNIA
UNITED STATES OF AMERICA

Domaine Napa

1155 Mee Lane
St. Helena, CA. 94574
Tel. (707) 963-1666
Fax (707) 963-5471

One struggles to imagine a more international firm: French owner, New Zealander winemaker, California location. With every chance for chaos to rule, instead there prevails an almost uncanny harmony of spirit and purpose. Michel Perret is a professional vineyard manager as well as proprietor of Domaine Napa, and directs his energies to growing fine grapes. Winemaker Grant Taylor pays homage to his boss's work by making wines with strong personalities of the vineyards from which they come, all owned or managed by Perret. Though the winery is young, dating only from 1985, its critical reputation is growing steadily. As for the name, "It's bad French," Perret says with a shrug, "but Americans do not know how to pronounce 'de'."

Napa Valley   ②
Sauvignon Blanc 1990
Pungent with the aromas of melon, typical of Sauvignon from the upper half of Napa Valley, but somehow more complicated and elusive than just melon. Firm and cleansing tactile.

Napa Valley   ③
Cabernet Sauvignon 1988
Between them Perret and Taylor have found a way to get a leaner, drier, more claret-like texture than most Napa Cabernets at no sacrifice of the valley's typical flavors.

NAPA VALLEY
CALIFORNIA
UNITED STATES OF AMERICA

1149

NAPA VALLEY
CALIFORNIA
UNITED STATES OF AMERICA

Etude

P.O. Box 344
Oakville, CA. 94562
Tel. (707) 963-7357

Winemaking in the United States has attracted, more than any other class, entrepreneurs, not all of them with the capital required to acquire vineyards and build wineries. This has given rise to a substantial number of "winemaker labels," labels belonging to professional winemakers who use hard-earned knowledge to buy grapes from vineyards they admire, rent or lease space in their employer's or some other winery, and make wine to their personal ideals. Tony Soter's Etude is one such label, and one of the most admired by critics. Soter earned his first reputation at Chappellet Vineyards, and has enlarged it since, especially at Spottswoode. As the most recent result, movie mogul Francis Ford Coppola chose him to revitalize the flagging Niebaum-Coppola winery. And still, Etude strikes a chord all its own. All the while, Etude continues along its own path with an average annual production of about 2,000 cases equally divided between Pinot Noir and Cabernet Sauvignon. All the grapes are bought from a variety of independent growers. Tony Suter's abilities are revealed both in his selection of grapes and the winemaking that follows. Our maximum recognition goes, thus to this gifted and sensitive artisan.

Napa Valley
Cabernet Sauvignon 1988
🍇🍇 ③

It is no surprise to come across velvety Pinot Noir, but velvety Cabernet is a rare achievement. The soft, richly fruity vintage of 1988 helped Soter to do so in this wine.

Napac Valley Pinot Noir 1989
🍇🍇🍇 ③

A long, cool growing season allowed Soter to capture exactly the moment when his Pinot Noir was ripe, giving wonderful flavors of the vineyard, and caressing textures of velvet. It needed all of its charms to win out over a splendid group of Carneros 1989s, but so it has done, more with subtlety than power. Like many of the other memorable wines of the vintage it is a product of more than one vineyard, wise in face of the youthfulness of the Carneros district as a source of Pinot Noir. The only thing that might be said against this 1989 is that its producer thinks more highly of his 1990.

NAPA VALLEY
CALIFORNIA
UNITED STATES OF AMERICA
1150
NAPA VALLEY
CALIFORNIA
UNITED STATES OF AMERICA

Flora Springs Wine

1978 West Zinfandel Lane
St. Helena, CA. 94574
Tel. (707) 963-5711
Fax (707) 963-7518

As many others in the California of the 1960s
and 1970s, the Komes family, two
generations of it, began with vineyards
located throughout Napa, and moved into
winemaking only after their vines produced
grapes of uncommon quality and character.
In 1992, after developing a name with
considerable critical success, they took the
unprecedented step of changing the label of
their bread and butter wines from Flora
Springs to Floreal (after one of the spring
months in the Napoleonic calendar),
reserving the Flora Springs name for three
luxury wines costing twice or more the price
of Floreal bottlings from the same vineyards.
Time will judge that business decision.
Meanwhile, winemaker Ken Deis continues to
produce wines under each label that merit
close scrutiny and, better yet, grace the table
with well harmonized flavors and deft
balance.

Napa Valley Chardonnay   ℜ ②
"Floreal" 1990
One seldom thinks of Chardonnay as having
intense flavors of apples, but this one does. A
deft touch of oak adds depth. Lustrously
polished on the palate.

Napa Valley Sauvignon Blanc   ℜ ②
"Floreal" 1990
"Floreal" strikes exactly the right image for a
wine that approaches floral flavors, and
combines richness without weight in its tactile
qualities. Lingers on the palate then in memory.

Napa Valley Cabernet Sauvignon   ℜ ②
"Floreal" 1989
Refined cassis from Cabernet joins with a
distinct note from new oak barrels. The tannins
are beautifully reined in. At the finish, fruit and
wood have already achieved synthesis.

Folie A Deux

3070 St. Helena Highway
St. Helena, CA. 94574
Tel. (707) 963-1160
Fax (707) 963-9223

Chardonnay propelled Folie a Deux to the
attention of collectors and connoisseurs with
the very first vintage, 1981. Chardonnay
remains the brightest beacon of this small
winery, though it has changed its spots from
a remarkably true-to-the-grape original
edition to a more distinctively oak-spiced new
style. Some of Folie a Deux's other wines
have reached the same quality level without
achieving quite the same fame, perhaps
because one such is lightly regarded Chenin
Blanc. Most of the grapes come from the
estate vineyard just north of St Helena and
an affiliated property near Yountville. The
curious name comes from the fact that the
winery was founded by a husband-wife team
of mental health professionals who have
since divorced, leaving the winery in the
hands of one of them, Dr. Larry Dizmang.

Napa Valley Chenin Blanc 1991   ℜ ①
Too many Napa Valley Chenin Blancs cloy with
their soft sweetness. This one keeps a crisp
enough edge for the variety's blowsy fruit flavors
to remain fresh and charming.

Napa Valley Chardonnay 1990   ℜ ③
Folie a Deux achieves a gentle flavor between
pear and apple in the vineyard, and leaves it
alone in the cellar. The balance of an estimably
refreshing wine is toward tart.

NAPA VALLEY
CALIFORNIA
UNITED STATES OF AMERICA
   1151
NAPA VALLEY
CALIFORNIA
UNITED STATES OF AMERICA

Forman Winery

P.O. Box 343
St. Helena, CA. 94574
Tel. (707) 963-0234

Ric Forman has a long string of distinguished wines in his past. They come under several labels, for he served as winemaker at Sterling, Newton and Charles F. Shaw before establishing his own winery and vineyards in hills just above the Napa Valley floor east of St Helena, starting in 1986. His Cabernet Sauvignons and Merlots at Sterling, and his Chardonnays at each of the wineries named above all have drawn favorable attention from knowledgeable wine drinkers. It is no surprise, then, that he has focussed on Cabernet and Chardonnay in his own winery. Forman brings great intellectual discipline and on-going curiosity to his winemaking, a fact reflected in a subtle evolution of style down the years since his first vintage, 1969. In all, the trend is ever more to let the vineyard speak.

Napa Valley Chardonnay 1990　🍇🍇 ③
Though the wine tastes abundantly of Chardonnay, the toasty taste of oak is not a shy part of it, either. As always, the wine is structured to endure well in the cellar.

Napa Valley　🍇🍇 ④
Cabernet Sauvignon 1987
Rather fuller and richer than typical of its vintage, but hardly overweight, or over bold. Indeed, some of the richness comes from restrained tannins, the rest from fully realized Cabernet.

Franciscan Vineyards

P.O. Box 407
Rutherford, CA .94573
Tel. (707) 963-7111
Fax (707) 963-7867

Dozens of California wineries have stumbled and lurched their ways from uncertain beginnings to solid, even star status, but Franciscan may hold the record for dimmest beginnings and grandest endings. The first owners had no idea what they were doing, to the point they hired an architect who did not even know to build slope into the cellar floors for drainage. However, when Agustin Huneeus and the Peter Eckes Company of Germany joined forces in 1985, Franciscan transformed itself into a source for accomplished wines at modest prices. Winemaker Greg Upton has shown a particular touch with Cabernet Sauvignon, Zinfandel and Chardonnay from the winery's large vineyard at Oakville, in the mid-Napa Valley. Upton is also in charge of winemaking for the firm's equally priceworthy Sonoma label, Estancia.

Napa Valley Chardonnay Oakville　🍇 ②
Estate 1991
The winemaking, as always, focusses on the apple-like flavors of Napa Chardonnay. This is a wine for fish, crisper and more tart on the tongue than most from the vintage.

Napa Valley Zinfandel Oakville　🍇🍇 ②
Estate 1990
Zinfandel confers a liveliness to wines not kept too long in oak. This is one such. And yet it plays distinct vanilla-like notes from oak against rich berry flavors of Zinfandel.

Napa Valley Cabernet Sauvignon　 ②
Estate 1988
Typical of both vineyard and house style, the polished, supple 1988 manages to play impressive depths of Cabernet flavors against an almost airy lightness of texture. Oak is used with restraint.

Freemark Abbey

P.O. Box 410
St. Helena, CA. 94574
Tel. (707) 963-9694
Fax (707) 963-0554

Freemark Abbey partners Charles Carpy,
William Jaeger, Laurie Wood and John Bryan
are important vineyardists in the Napa Valley,
but a crucial part-owner is Bradford Webb, an
enologist with a passion for refining his craft.
It was Webb who brought French oak barrels
to the forefront in California Chardonnay
during his long-ago tenure at Hanzell
Vineyard in Sonoma, and it is he who has
harmonized Freemark Abbey's Napa Valley
Chardonnay and Cabernet Sauvignon grape
flavors with those from barrels to such
memorable effect.
Freemark Abbey does not refer to an abbey,
but is an assemblage of fragments of three
names of partners who gave it to their winery
in 1937. That firm closed its doors in 1960.
Upon starting their winery at the same site in
1967, the current owners could think of no
better name, so kept the original.

Napa Valley Chardonnay 1990 ❦ ❦ ③
Every vintage has flavors of a stature to call for
salmon, and textures of a richness to
accompany lobster. The 1990 has extra
endowments in both departments.

Napa Valley ❦ ❦ ③
Cabernet Sauvignon 1988
Consistently intense flavors from grapes
combine with gentle tannins in a wine
demanding less patience than most vintages,
and yet one with ample substance to last well.

Napa Valley ❦ ❦ ③
Cabernet Sauvignon "Sycamore" 1988
From a single vineyard at the foot of Napa
Valley's west hills, this is the Napa Valley, only
moreso. With a fillip of Cabernet Franc, it
achieves deeper flavors without adding weight.

NAPA VALLEY
CALIFORNIA
UNITED STATES OF AMERICA

1153

NAPA VALLEY
CALIFORNIA
UNITED STATES OF AMERICA

Frog's Leap Winery

3358 St. Helena Highway
St. Helena, CA 94574
Tel. (707) 963-4704
Fax (707) 963-0242

Frog's Leap is the only winery in the history of the United States that once had its own Minister of Fun, the only one that celebrates Leap Year with epic dinner-dances, the only one that uses its name to poke fun at an appellation (Stags Leap), and the only one named after a farm devoted to growing leggy frogs for San Francisco restaurants. However, fun is fun and wine is wine, and Frog's Leap wines consistently offer character and quality by the most serious of measuring sticks. Physician Larry Turley and winemaker John Williams are partners in a small cellar that has offered memorably true-to-the-variety Sauvignon Blancs and Zinfandels, and much better than average Cabernet Sauvignons and Chardonnays from a region where the standards are among the highest in California and, one could believe, the world. All grapes are bought within the Napa Valley, save for a small proportion harvested from a 10-acre vineyardowned by John Williams and his wife, Julie. It is in the town of Rutherford.

Napa Valley Sauvignon Blanc 1991   🍇 ②
Some Sauvignons suggest herbs, some melon. This one suggest both, now one, now the other, always in subtle whispers. It is firm texture that gives it a cerain boldness and flair.

Napa Valley   🍇 ③
Cabernet Sauvignon 1989
The wine is a veritable walk through a sumer garden, giving here aromas or fruit, there of flowers, still elsewhere of herbs. Its firmness and balance promise a good future.

Napa Valley Zinfandel 1989   🍇🍇🍇 ③
A most intriguing paradox of a wine: richly fruity with the almost tart, berry-like tastes of Zinfandel, and beautifully balanced in a firm style. Yet all is delicacy, wanting far milder food than the hearty, tomato-rich sauces that automatically come to mind in the same instant as Zinfandel. Such delicacy is a rare achievement in a variety that easily goes overripe, one that will probably confuse more Americans than Europeans since the latter are seldom familiar with wines from a grape that seems to have disappeared from its continent of origin, but still deserves to be considered seriously for its contributions to the table.

Grgich Hills

1829 St Helena Highway
Rutherford, CA 94573
Tel. 707/9632784
Fax 707/9638725

An unlikely partnership of a coffee heir and a Croatian emigrant lend their names to a winery solidly planted on flat ground. Austin Hills, the coffee heir, owns the vineyards from which Grgich Hills makes most of its wines, and is a partner in the winery, founded in 1977. Miljenko (Mike) Grgich co-owns the winery and is the winemaker. Grgich won substantial fame for producing the 1972 Chardonnay of Chateau Montelena that placed first in a blind tasting of French and California wines by French authorities in 1976, and has continued to justify his prominence ever since. Grgich stubbornly insists on making wines that will age well in a market where immediate consumption is the norm. His Cabernet Sauvignons, Zinfandels and Chardonnays all start closed and evolve slowly compared to many of their peers. His answer: maintain style and hold the wines in a cellar enlarged for that sole purpose.

Napa Valley Fume Blanc 1990   🍇 ②
Understated but unalloyed herbaceous Sauvignon flavors pair with a tactile polished as smooth as silk in a wine with just a hint of weight. For now, for foods of gentle flavor.

Napa Valley Chardonnay 1989   🍇 🍇 ③
From a difficult, rain-besieged harvest, Mike Grgich produced a beautifully balanced, elegantly understated Chardonnay with years of development still before it.

Napa Valley   🍇 🍇 ③
Cabernet Sauvignon 1985
The reason for waiting is everywhere evident in a wine of intense but still masked Cabernet flavors and stern textures, but all history says patience will be rewarded.

Groth Vineyards & Winery

750 Oakville Crossroad
Oakville, CA. 94562
Tel. (707) 944-0290
Fax (707) 944-8932

Several California winery owners abandoned high-tech electronics for, if not low-tech, at least traditional forms of winemaking. Dennis Groth is one of those. He left the presidency of Atari in order to pursue wine. Groth founded the winery bearing his name in 1982, having purchased two vineyards a year earlier. The larger vineyard at Oakville is also the site of a winery built in 1989, ending a period of making wine in leased space. The second vineyard is some miles south. The list of Groth wines is a short one: Cabernet Sauvignon, Sauvignon Blanc and Chardonnay, all estate-grown. The Cabernet in particular has been well received from the first vintages onward, but all of the wines have earned favorable notice, a testimonial to Groth's adroitness in spotting superior vineyard potential and to winemaker Nils Venge.

Napa Valley Chardonnay 1990   🍇 ③
Absolutely typical of Napa Chardonnay from a sunny growing season, this Groth has ripe, honeyed fruit flavors and rich to outright bold textures. Its time is now.

Napa Valley   🍇 🍇 ③
Cabernet Sauvignon 1987
A cool growing season can still be seen in flavors that lean toward the herbaceous, even more in a tactile quality that manages to be firm at the core yet honed smooth at the surface.

NAPA VALLEY
CALIFORNIA
UNITED STATES OF AMERICA

1155

NAPA VALLEY
CALIFORNIA
UNITED STATES OF AMERICA

Hess Collection Winery

4411 Redwood Road
Napa, CA. 94558
Tel. (707) 255-1144
Fax (707) 253-1682

The word "collection" signals a fact: Swiss businessman Donald Hess uses his winery as a gallery for much of the modern art he has collected over the years, some of it doubtless puzzling stuff to The Christian Brothers from whose order he has leased the winery building they long used to make sacramental and commercial wines. Hess wines surely puzzle the brothers far less, for they are classically styled Cabernet Sauvignon and Chardonnay from Hess's own vineyards in the surrounding Mayacamas Mountains. As winemaker Randle Johnson has settled into his surroundings, quality and reputation have gained with each passing year. Hess Collection wines are not to be confused with Hess Select wines. Though both come from the same cellars, the Hess Select bottlings are from another Hess vineyard in Monterey County and/or from purchased grapes.

Napa Valley Chardonnay 1989   ❦ ❦ ③
The flavors of Chardonnay are beautifully defined, but the even more striking quality of this wine is its vitality, achieved in a harvest when rains made any richness hard to win.

Napa Valley   ❦ ③
Cabernet Sauvignon 1987
The first note is all herbs, then the rest of a grand summer garden crowds in. The wine manages, as Napa often does in its best years, to hide a firm core with a supple, polished surface.

Inglenook - Napa Valley

P.O. Box 391
St. Helena, CA. 94574
Tel. (707) 963-4480
Fax (707) 967-3190

What was from the 1930S through the 1960s the chief rival to Beaulieu Vineyard now is its sister winery in the Heublein Fine Wine Group. And still something remains of the old competition between John Daniel's Inglenook and the De Latour family's Beaulieu. The current winemakers of both houses continue to use the vineyards on which the earlier rivalry was built to make much better than average Cabernet Sauvignons in two different styles.
Inglenook, in fact, gets double mileage from its historic properties. A Cabernet-based wine called Reunion is made from the original two properties (now three), and Inglenook Cabernet Sauvignon Cask Reserve is dominated by grapes from them. The winery has had some ups and downs since Heublein assumed ownership, the downs largely when it abandoned making wines of such particular provenance in favor of mere volume.

Napa Valley "Gravion" 1990   ❦ ②
A marriage of sauvignon blanc and sémillon takes the strengths of each, capturing the firm edge and pointed flavors of sauvignon, then offsetting them with richer, rounder sémillon.

Napa Valley Merlot Reserve 1988   ❦ ②
An abundance of herbaceous merlot, and just a suggestion of mint. Lean, light, firmly structured, the wine leaves an impression of depth on the one hand, and delicacy or finesse on the other.

Napa Valley Cabernet Sauvignon   ❦ ③
Cask Reserve 1987
Dark, as always. Firmly tannic, as always. Well wooded, as always. Richer in the flavors of cabernet of the 1940's and 1950's. It is, as they were, memorably stern and slow to age in bottle.

Napa Valley Reunion 1986   ❦ ③
Reunion brings together the three vineyards that, together, made the grandest Inglenook Cabernets of the 1940's and 1950's. It is, as they were, memorable stern and slow to age in bottle.

Johnson-Turnbull Vineyards

9210 St. Helena Highway
Oakville, CA. 94562
Tel. (707) 963-3859
Fax (707) 982-4608

Some would regard an architect and a lawyer as an unholy alliance. In the case of Johnson-Turnbull, the partnership of architect William Turnbull and lawyer Reverdy Johnson has been a source of consistently impressive Cabernet Sauvignons in the minty-ripe, full-bodied style first popularized in California by the Martha's Vineyard bottlings of Heitz Wine Cellars.

The first vintage was 1979. Later, in 1987, the partners added a typically Californian, toasty Chardonnay from grapes grown in a vineyard Turnbull owns in Sonoma County. Aside from dividing their Cabernet into two lots, they have not been tempted to elaborate on that list.

Their small, impeccably designed and legally correct winery and vineyard look obliquely across Napa's Highway 29 to Robert Mondavi, and are only a few hundred meters north of Opus One.

Napa Valley ③
Cabernet Sauvignon 1988
From a vintage that encouraged full ripeness comes a Johnson-Turnbull that suggests not just mint, but a whole chest full of spices. As always, the wine is fleshy and round.

Charles Krug Winery

P.O. Box
St. Helena, CA. 94574
Tel. (707) 963-2761
Fax (707) 963-7913

Charles Krug Winery has absorbed a fair share of critical rejection in recent years, some of it perhaps deserved, especially when it referred to white wines that fell well short of earlier efforts. However, Peter Mondavi and family have been in Napa since Prohibition ended, and they have gathered as impressive an array of vineyards as any company in the valley. Their Pinot Noir, for example, comes from holdings in Carneros, while their Cabernet is anchored in properties on the same gentle slope as Martha's Vineyard and many other famous properties. Indeed the Cabernet they identify as Vintage Select has come from a single vineyard there in every vintage since 1985. These two wine types are the ones that should lead Krug back toward the high esteem it enjoyed in an earlier time. Others should not be overlooked. The Chardonnay, once a flagship, is returning to the form that made it a leader.

Carneros Pinot Noir 1989 ❦ ②
Has the wonderfully velvety texture of well ripened Carneros Pinot Noir, and all of the flavors that go with that. Its lingering finish is attractive in every way.

Napa Valley Cabernet Sauvignon ❦ ④
"Vintage Select" 1986
These wines focus on, even concentrate the flavors of Cabernet, and they go to bottle hard, even a bit rough. The prospects of greatness are in them, but need 10 years or more to emerge.

NAPA VALLEY
CALIFORNIA
UNITED STATES OF AMERICA

1157

NAPA VALLEY
CALIFORNIA
UNITED STATES OF AMERICA

Markham Winery

2812 St. Helena Highway North
St. Helena, CA. 94574
Tel. (707) 963-5292
Fax (707) 963-4616

Ironically, Markham was founded in 1978 by an advertising executive who never quite figured out how to sell a good product, and ended by selling the whole winery to a Japanese firm, Sanraku, in 1988. The new owners forthwith rehabilitated Markham's three promising vineyards, greatly enlarged the historic but small cellar buildings, and began carving out a market. Through all the changes, Bob Foley has remained the winemaker. Skill got him through the undercapitalized early years with a fair reputation. With better-equipped cellars the wines have taken real strides forward in recent seasons. Well located vineyards are the true key to Markham's prospects for the long term. Most of the winery's Chardonnay is in a cool area south of Yountville while its Cabernet Sauvignon and related varieties are farther north, in Rutherford and warm Calistoga.

Napa Valley Chardonnay 1989   ❦ ③
Well marked by the hint of asparagus that characterizes cool vintages, but what sets it apart is its supple, polished, balanced texture. Overlooked after critics prematurely savaged the vintage.

Napa Valley Merlot 1989   ❦ ③
Markham has home of Napa's most flavorful Merlot vineyards, and puts them to good use vintage after vintage in wines of surprising intensity, given their airy lightness on the palate.

Louis M. Martini

P.O. Box 112
St. Helena, CA. 94574
Tel. (707) 963-2736
Fax (707) 963-8750

One can always spot an inexperienced student of California wine by the phrase, "Martini wines used to age very well, but they don't make them that way any more". The fact is, the Martinis always made their red wines very much as they make them now: balanced, and with the tannins carefully honed smooth before bottling. The other ingredients of Martini excellence are a group of superior vineyards spread throughout Napa and Sonoma counties, and a steadfast devotion to the craft of making wine now embodied in the third generation of the family, Michael Martini. He follows paths laid down from 1933 through 1957 by his Ligurian-born grandfather, Louis M., and by his father, Louis P., who held the reins from 1957 through 1977. Michael also follows ideas of his own, most notably including a greater (but still judicious) use of oak. Under his direction, the white wines have been much improved.

Russian River Valley   ❦ ①
Gewurztraminer 1990
From a vintage which gave great depth of Gewurztraminer flavor, one of the richest of them all in typical Russian River lichee-like flavors. Quite dry, though not absolutely so.

Napa Valley   ❦❦ ③
Cabernet Sauvignon Reserve 1987
Again, textbook Cabernet Sauvignon flavors. Napa, characteristically, confers firmer tannins than Monte Rosso. Oak flavors show slightly more at the outset, but remain subtle even so.

Sonoma Valley   ❦❦ ③
Cabernet Sauvignon "Monte Rosso" 1988
New students of the flavor of Cabernet Sauvignon could go to school on this wine, which has depth without exaggeration. Its polished tannins invite early drinking, but here is a wine to cellar.

Napa Valley Petite Sirah   ❦ ③
Reserve 1987
Cabernet's distinctive flavors are too much for some people, but they like the tannins. Here is the perfect compromise, with the faintly peppery taste of Petite Sirah foremost.

Robert Mondavi Winery

P.O. Box 106
Oakville, CA. 94562
Tel. (707) 963-9611
Fax (707) 963-1007

Mention Robert Mondavi in an obscure corner of Australia, or Italy, or Yugoslavia, and almost surely someone will know that he is famous owner of the Napa Valley winery bearing his name, and most likely will have met him. Only a handful of other men in the world of wine are as well-known to such a broad public. Mondavi has acquired his fame through relentless travel, but he earned it by driving himself and his employees to make wine at the peak of their abilities, and then to make it better by learning something new. He has somehow sustained that driving pace in every year since 1966, which saw the first vintage of the Robert Mondavi label. What is most impressive is that he has won, in addition to the admiration of his peers, a huge popular following with wines that are uncompromising but far from unchanging in style, as the Mondavis stay abreast of technical developments around the globe.

Napa Valley Chardonnay 🍇🍇 ④
Reserve 1990
Often overdone, but in this vintage a splendid synthesis of flavors from ripe grapes and well-toasted oak barrels, all embodied in a wine with unusual firmness and vitality.

Napa Valley Fume Blanc 1990 🍇 ②
Not a Sauvignon for the faint-hearted who run from the fully developed smack of herbs and grasses, nor for those who shy away from lean, dry, almost tart balance. For the fearless, aha!

Napa Valley Pinot Noir 1990 🍇🍇 ③
One could bet on the future, but there is little need. The 1990 already is such a smooth, close marriage of Pinot and toasty wood that one cannot tell where one begins and the other leaves off.

Napa Valley Cabernet Sauvignon 🍇🍇 ④
Reserve 1988
The perfumes of new oak barrels spring out, to be followed by fine flavors of Cabernet until, finally, Cabernet rules a long finish. Firm. History says to age the wine for at least eight years.

Monticello Cellars

4242 Big Ranch Road
Napa, CA. 94558
Tel. (707) 253-2802
Fax (707) 253-1019

When a proprietor with a deep admiration for Thomas Jefferson bought property only a stone's throw from the end of Monticello Road, a name for his winery was not hard to imagine. He followed up on the name by building a scale model of Jefferson's Monticello, and a winery that pays further architectural tribute to the Jefferson style. It is only fitting that the most appetizing of the wines should be the Cabernet Sauvignon "Jefferson Cuvée," but curious that it should come from purchased Napa Valley grapes when proprietor Jay Corley owns so extensive a vineyard of his own. The situation arises because Monticello's vineyard is in a soil at Napa's southern end where cabernet will not ripen fully while chardonnay does, and Corley sensibly accepts the fact, though his Chardonnays have never equalled the Jefferson Cabernets.

Napa Valley Cabernet Sauvignon 🍇 ③
"Jefferson Cuvee" 1988
The 1988 does one of wine's nicest tricks, starting shyly, then building layer upon layer as it goes. Long, beautifully polished, with early charm and all the signs of staying power

Cabernet Sauvignon 🍇 ③
"Corley Reserve" 1989
The word Reserve on a California Cabernet Sauvignon virtually guarantees more oak and tannin, hence less fruit, than a wine not so designated. This Monticello delivers on the promise.

NAPA VALLEY
CALIFORNIA
UNITED STATES OF AMERICA
1159
NAPA VALLEY
CALIFORNIA
UNITED STATES OF AMERICA

Mt Veeder Winery

1999 Mt Veeder Road
Napa, CA. 94558
Tel. (707) 963-7111
Fax (707) 963-7867

Much argument goes on in California about the relative virtues of mountain vineyards versus those on lower ground. In fact the argument is about steep versus shallower slopes. Whatever the terms, Mt Veeder is a compelling argument for growing at least some Cabernet Sauvignon on the steep upper slopes of the Mayacamas Range. Year in, year out, the Cabernet from this property shows depth, structure, and balance without being in any way overdrawn. Like many others, winemaker Peter Franus incorporates percentages of cabernet franc and merlot in the wine. Unlike many others, he also has petit verdot and malbec at his disposal. The label also goes on a Chardonnay. Founded in 1973 by the Michael Bernstein family, the property now belongs to Agustin Huneeus and the Peter Eckes family, also the owners of Franciscan. Vineyards and winemaking remain separate. In spite of the changes of ownership of the property, the quality of Mt Veeder's wines has not suffered. Rather, it has steadily improved. The goal of the current owners is to increase production to 200,000 bottles, from estate grapes and those of near neighbors.

Napa Valley Chardonnay 1990 ❦ ❦ ③
Spicy flavors from oak barrels are abundant, but so are apple-like ones from Chardonnay. Depth and balance should allow them time to marry, which they still need to do.

Napy Valley ❦ ❦ ❦ ③
Cabernet Sauvignon 1987
Because of its origins in a shy-bearing mountain vineyard in Napa's west hills, this estate-grown Cabernet could be broodingly tannic. One would even expect it to be so from other wines of the region. But it is not at al brooding, and not especially tannic. Quite the contrary, it is a stirring demonstration that more is not always better, however much many California winemakers wish to believe that of mountain grapes. In this superior vintage a vitality and a rich blend of Cabernet Sauvignon and its cousins give the wine brilliant depths but no excess weight. Its age-worthiness is all but guaranteed by forerunners from less flavored vintages.

Mumm Napa Valley

8445 Silverado Trail
Napa, CA. 94558
Tel. (707) 9631-133
Fax (707) 963-5160

The joint venture of Seagrams Inc, the Canadian distiller-merchant company, and G.H. Mumm of Reims, France, is the end product of a search that produced experimental classic method sparkling wines from as far east as New York and as far north as Oregon before finally settling on the Napa Valley as the best of all possible worlds for what the partners wished to achieve. First labelled Domaine Mumm, but quickly renamed Mumm Napa Valley, the company made its first commercial wines in 1985. A goal-oriented search for vineyards led quickly to wines of individual character, and sometimes surprising provenance. A major involvement in Carneros was predictable given the success of other sparkling wine producers there. Committing to a smaller but still important source in Franz Valley, to the north of Calistoga, was a surprise, but it contibutes admirable dimensions to the cuvees.

Napa Valley Brut   ☙☙ ③
"Winery Lake" 1988
Rarity of rarities, a fine sparkling wine from a single property, one that endows it with fruit flavors as mystifying as they are pleasing, especially during the first year under cork.

Napa Valley Brut   ☙ ③
"Vintage Reserve" 1987
A more forceful note of toasted nuts from time on tirage than most Californians, but still marked by a typically clear note of fruit and a refreshingly lively texture.

Napa Valley Brut Prestige NV   ☙ ③
The airiest and freshest of Mumm-Napa Valley's lineup of cuvées lives by neatly harmonized, perfectly understated flavors of chardonnay and pinot noir.

Gustave Niebaum Collection

P.O. Box 391
St. Helena, CA. 94574
Tel. (707) 963-4480
Fax (707) 967-3190

Heublein has done a fascinating job of fragmenting its Napa Valley holdings, which otherwise include Beaulieu Vineyard, The Christian Brothers, Inglenook-Napa Valley and Quail Ridge. The particular niche of the Gustave Niebaum Collection is single-vineyard Chardonnays, Cabernet Sauvignons and a Semillon. "Reference" bottlings come as blends from the same vineyards. Winemaker Judy Matulich-Weitz works within the buildings of Inglenook, but is free to follow her own sense of style. The label began with 1985 reds and 1988 whites. To date, the whites have led the way, but that is to be expected, for they can be developed far more quickly than Napa Valley Cabernet Sauvignons. Matulich-Weitz has chosen her sources well: Carneros for three Chardonnays, and mid-valley for the Semillon (called Chevrier) and three Cabernets.

Carneros Chardonnay   ☙ ②
"Reference" 1990
An almost dusty note from new oak precedes the taste of Chardonnay, then gracefully bows out to let the vineyard shine through.

Napa Valley Chevrier "Herrick" 1989 ☙ ②
All of the herbs and almost minty tones that come from the cooler south end of Napa, especially in cool vintages, are present here, summoning up comparisons with Sancerres as they go.

Napa Valley Cabernet Sauvignon   ③
Mast 1987
A skillful use of oak heightens attractive Cabernet flavors in a wine of perfect proportions, with everything in the middle range. Its balance and long finish say it has some future.

NAPA VALLEY
CALIFORNIA
UNITED STATES OF AMERICA
      1161
NAPA VALLEY
CALIFORNIA
UNITED STATES OF AMERICA

Opus One

P.O. Box 6
Oakville, CA. 94562
Tel. (707) 963-1979

Robert Mondavi has had more strokes of
genius than most of his peers in the wine
business. Not the least of them was
convincing the owner of First Growth
Chateau Mouton Rothschild to buy into the
Napa Valley as his partner in Opus One in
1979. Having the Baron Philippe Rothschild
involved in Napa lent instant credibility to
Mondavi's long-standing claim that the valley
is a region fit to play on the world stage of
wine. The Baroness Philippine de Rothschild
succeeded her father as partner on his death
in 1988, in time to help Opus One depart the
Mondavi winery for its own, architecturally
grandiose home. There is only one wine, in
essence a Cabernet Sauvignon but not
identified as such. Its style is the joint product
of the Mondavis and the winemakers of
Mouton. Its price, once startling, is now
merely in the upper tier of Californians.

Opus One Napa Valley 1988   🍇🍇 ④
A typical Opus, matching appetizing fruit flavors
with deceptively gentle textures. It might not
seem an ager after the uncommonly firm 1987,
but is sure to do well in the cellar.

Robert Pepi Winery

7585 St. Helena Highway
Oakville, CA. 94562
Tel. (707) 944-2807
Fax (707) 944-5628

San Francisco furrier Robert Pepi began
purely as a grapegrower at Oakville in 1966,
almost as a hobby to distract him from his
main business. He built a winery 15 years
later for the sole purpose of making estate-
grown Sauvignon Blanc, well established as
the finest of the varieties growing on his
property. By 1988 the Lucca-born Pepi had
added Chardonnay, Cabernet Sauvignon,
and a Sangiovese called "Colline di Sassi"
after the rocky knoll on which it grows rather
like a collar around the stone winery building
at its crown. It is hard to pick one wine over
any other as most successful, so well has
Pepi chosen his vineyards, and so skillful has
been the winemaking. However, it is not
difficult at all to name his sentimental favorite.
That is Sangiovese, even though he
continues to refine its style.

Napa Valley Sauvignon Blanc 1991 🍇🍇 ②
Melon-like flavors stay close to typical Napa
Sauvignon, but rich textures reveal the presence
of Semillon. On the palate all is harmony and
balance and polish.

Napa Valley Sangiovese   🍇 ③
"Colline Di Sassi" 1989
In its second vintage, Pepi Sangiovese shows a
more restrained, yet richer character than did
the 1988. Still it seems a wine that may be
giving its best in the freshness of youth.

Napa Valley Cabernet Sauvignon 🍇🍇 ③
"Vine Hill" 1987
Reflects a highly regarded vineyard in a vintage
that produced remarkable depths of flavor
together with firm, but not hard textures. A
considerable contender for a Top Wine spot.

NAPA VALLEY
CALIFORNIA
UNITED STATES OF AMERICA   1162

NAPA VALLEY
CALIFORNIA
UNITED STATES OF AMERICA

Joseph Phelps Vineyards

200 Taplin Road
St. Helena, CA. 94574
Tel. (707) 963-2745
Fax (707) 963-4831

Joseph Phelps came into the wine business in 1973 largely because his construction firm had built a winery for another producer and he had succumbed to the charms of the Napa Valley. He has stayed in it because his restless search for excellence at whatever he does has put his label into the upper ranks on several fronts. Among other abilities, Phelps has a keen eye for good vineyard land which allowed him to piece together a complex, ranging domain of one large ranch, plus four smaller ones, each chosen to suit a particular variety. He has also has a keen sense of where the market is going. It allowed him to pioneer Botrytis-affected Rieslings, a Bordeaux-style blend called Insignia, and, more recently, several wines styled after those of the Rhone, another category just beginning to come into its own. These and other Phelps wines are worth a look.

Napa Valley Sauvignon Blanc 1990 ②
The winery is not known foremost for its Sauvignon, but the appealingly dry, firm 1990 ranks high in its vintage. Its subtle but indelibly herb-like flavors are archetypal of Napa.

Napa Valley Grenache Rosé Vin du Mistral 1990 ②
At last, all too rare in California, a truly dry rose with the flavors of fully developed Grenache, a wine to savor in the warm days of summer.

Napa Valley Cabernet Sauvignon 1989 ③
A faint whiff of the barnyard hovers about this firmly structured, richly flavored wine, one of few Californians that might rouse thoughts of Bordeaux even in a francophile.

Pine Ridge Winery

5901 Silverado Trail
Napa, CA. 94558
Tel. (707) 253-7500
Fax (707) 253-1493

Gary Andrus followed a circuitous route to winermaking and winery ownership. In youth, he was a first-alternate skier on the U.S. Olympic team. And he is, as he loves to say, the only graduate winemaker from Mormon Brigham Young University. However he came to the Napa Valley, he arrived with a lively curiosity about wine in general, Cabernet Sauvignon, in particular. Since the winery started in 1981, Andrus has acquired cabernet vineyards in Stags Leap and on the Rutherford Bench, and takes grapes from a grower-owned property on Diamond Mountain, toward the top end of Napa. In some years he bottles wines from the separate properties to demonstrate how diverse is Napa at growing cabernet. The Pine Ridge label is also well regarded for its Chardonnays. There are often two of these as well, with the one sub-titled Knollside the better known of the two.

Napa Valley Chardonnay "Knollside Cuvée" 1990 ②
The house style calls for all the round riches Napa Chardonnay can bring, plus a generous dash of perfume from new oak. The proprietor's capitalized completely on made-to-order 1990.

Napa Valley Cabernet Sauvignon Stags Leap Cuvée 1989 ③
The soft, rounded feel and gentle flavors are a textbook lesson in how the Stags Leap District grows Cabernet. The healthy dollop of oak is Pine Ridge's house style.

Napa Valley Cabernet Sauvignon "Rutherford" 1988 ③
A note of fresh oakwood comes first, soon to be succeded by a pure, even driving now-herbaceous, now-cassis-like taste of Rutherford Cabernet. Flesh hides firm tannic structure.

Quail Ridge

P.O. Box 391
St. Helena, CA. 94574
Tel. (707) 963-4480
Fax (707) 967-3190

Quail Ridge is one of many demonstrations of how much California can compact its history. The winery was founded in 1978 by a couple, Jesse Corallo and Elaine Wellesley. Corallo died soon after, leaving his wife to continue, which she did, first alone, then with a partner. After several years they sold the business to The Christian Brothers, with Wellesley again continuing alone as winemaker. Little more than a year later, Heublein, Inc., bought The Christian Brothers, and folded that label and Quail Ridge into its Fine Wine Group.
Corallo had launched Quail Ridge as a showcase for Chardonnay, his special favorite. Wellesley has kept that wine an important part of the production. However, as the years have gone on, Sauvignon Blanc and Merlot have become the most distinctive wines produced under this label.

Napa Valley Sauvignon Blanc 1989 🍇 ②
For the third straight vintage, a Sauvignon of substance and style. Well used oak gives both depth and breadth to the flavors, but understatement and harmony are the watchwords.

Napa Valley Merlot 1988 🍇🍇 ③
Here, in a variety all too often lacking depth, is a wine of excellent character. It needed and got only a hint of oak. Polished textures hide a firm core that promises for the future.

Raymond Vineyards & Cellars

849 Zinfandel Lane
St. Helena, CA. 94574
Tel. (707) 963-3141
Fax (707) 963-8498

Although its own history is short, and although a Japanese brewer, Kirin, has a major financial stake in the business, Raymond Vineyards & Cellars sends roots deeper into the Napa Valley than almost any other firm there, and produces wines that epitomize its sun and soil more than all but a handful. Roy Raymond, Sr., married Martha Beringer, the daughter of a pioneer Napa winemaker, soon after the repeal of America's national Prohibition. Their sons, Walter and Roy, Jr., grew up working in the caves at Beringer. In 1974, not long after the Beringer family sold its winery to Nestle, Inc., the three Raymonds bought a property no more than two miles away, built their own cellar, and and set about making wines from ground they know better than their own thumbprints. The results consistently show off the virtues of the vineyards, and enhance well-laid tables in the process.

Napa Valley Chardonnay 1990 🍇 ③
Remarkable concentrations of the apple-like flavors of its grape variety. After an unusually lean 1989, the 1990 has been aided toward more typical roundness by its ideal growing season.

Napa Valley Sauvignon Blanc 1990 🍇 ②
Clear flavors of the Sauvignon grape caught in a deftly balanced wine. From the superior growing season of 1990 has come perhaps the finest in the series to date.

Napa Valley
Cabernet Sauvignon 1987 🍇🍇 ③
The 1987, from a superior vintage, is already well-knit and gracefully proportioned. Assembled from several Napa vineyards, it exemplifies Napa Cabernet flavors. A candidate for Top Wine.

Rutherford Hill

P.O. Box 410
S. Helena, CA. 94574
Tel. (707) 963-1871
Fax (707) 963-1904

Rutherford Hill has set itself the difficult task of making Merlot its signature wine in the real sense of giving over slightly more than half its considerable capacity to that one variety.
In fact, the task is twice difficult. First, Merlot appears to be extremely sensitive to climate and soil. Second, it is, in all practical senses, a new grape variety in California winemaking. Sparse pre-Prohibition plantings disappeared. Only in 1969 did a new era start. The result is that much California Merlot to this point has been undistinguished at best. There has been just enough promise to justify the adventure. Few wineries are better financed, or better equipped for the role than this sister firm to Freemark Abbey. Its owning partners have vineyards throughout Napa, some apparently well adapted to the chosen variety. They have kept ample acreage in chardonnay and cabernet as fallbacks.

Napa Valley   🍷 ③
Cabernet Sauvignon XVS 1989
From vineyards near Rutherford comes a wine of remarkably intense Cabernet flavors, yet no exaggeration in the wine making. Five to eight years in bottle should add grace notes worth having.

Napa Valley Merlot 1988   🍷 ③
Characteristic of the house, good tannic grip pushes the 1988 toward firm, even lean textures. A suggestion of coffee complicates solid flavors of Merlot.

Schramsberg

1400 Schramsberg Road
Calistoga, CA. 94515
Tel. (707) 942-4558
Fax (707) 942-5943

When Jack and Jamie Davies restored a nineteenth century wine property in 1965, California sparkling wine had strayed far from the style and standards of Champagne. The Davies quickly proved that such did not have to be the case, that California sparkling wine could challenge the original, though not necessarily by attempting to imitate it. By reverting to the traditional grape varieties and by extending the typical time on tirage, Schramsberg soon began producing inimitably Californian sparkling wines of substance and style. With longer experience, the firm has developed vineyard sources that give still richer character than early vintages showed. However, even those earliest wines were enough to attract the attention first of Moet et Chandon, then the other Champagne producers who have entered California since 1973.

Napa Valley Reserve 1985   🍾 🍾 ③
In essence the best of Schramsberg's Blanc de Noirs, the Reserve has rich flavors and rich textures to carry them. Long aging on the yeast assures a polished maturity of character.

Napa Valley Blanc de Noirs   🍾 ③
Late Disgorded 1982
Another long-term Davies goal is satisfied here with a wine that rested nearly a decade on tirage, gaining depth seldom found in sparkling wine from anywhere, yet at no loss in vitality.

NAPA VALLEY
CALIFORNIA
UNITED STATES OF AMERICA

1165

NAPA VALLEY
CALIFORNIA
UNITED STATES OF AMERICA

Sequoia Grove

8338 St. Helena Highway
Napa, CA. 945558
Tel. (707) 944-2945

Two escaped Colorado brothers named
James and Steven Allen founded Sequoia
Grove in 1981 with the idea to make only the
two wines for which Napa was - and is - best
known: Chardonnay and Cabernet
Sauvignon. It was a sound business decision
from the start. Sequoia Grove has prospered
from its early years onward. With their own
and purchased grapes at their disposal, the
Allens opted to make both estate-bottled and
non-estate wines of each type. That program
remains in effect. The ongoing, almost
annual argument is over which bottling is the
better one in each category. For the most
part, the Oakville district estate Cabernet
wins that contest. The Chardonnay question
has proven harder to resolve, partly because
the sources of the non-estate have shifted at
times. In recent years both the Estate and
Carneros bottlings have come from vineyards
owned whole or part by the winery.

Carneros Chardonnay Estate 1990 🍇 ③
The vintage was particularly good in Carneros
and this subtle Chardonnay is in every way
typical Chardonnay of this cool, fog-shrouded
region; it promises to develop well in bottle.

Napa Valley Chardonnay Estate 1990 🍇 ③
Growing conditions typically warmer than those
of Carneros give a rounder, fuller wine, one
more forward than its companion from the same
grape variety. The vintage demonstrates
perfectly the style for which Sequoia Grove is
known.

Napa Valley 🍇 ③
Cabernet Sauvignon 1988 Estate
The owners of Sequoia Grove like a good deal
of flesh on the bones of their Cabernets, and a
generous seasoning of oak to go with the berry-
like flavors from their vineyards in Oakville.

**Entries are arranged in
alphabetical order by country,
region and winery or producer
name.**

NAPA VALLEY
CALIFORNIA
UNITED STATES OF AMERICA   1166

NAPA VALLEY
CALIFORNIA
UNITED STATES OF AMERICA

Shafer Vineyards

6154 Silverado Trail
Napa, CA. 94558
Tel. (707) 944-2877
Fax (707) 944-9454

Appropriately for a family that came to the Napa Valley to grow grapes six years before it began making wine, in 1978, grower John Shafer and his winemaker son, Doug, pay detailed attention to the capacities of their two vineyards. From the main property in the Stags Leap District comes a pure Cabernet called Hillside Select. A second, identified only as Napa Valley Cabernet, has Merlot and grapes from neighbors. Both are the result of strict observation of the vines within different areas of a vineyard of many gradients and exposures. In recent seasons, as the vineyard has matured, the Shafers have added a Merlot to their list of red wines, again because they found particularly rewarding vines to serve as its core. Conversely there is but one Chardonnay from two complementary properties about three miles apart. The annual production at Shafer ranges around 16,000 cases. To sum up, the level of quality achieved by the wines of this cellar is among the loftiest in California; the Cabernet to which we have awarded three clusters merits inclusion among the great wines of the world.

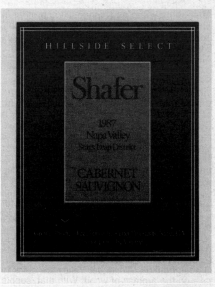

Napa Valley Merlot 1989　🍇🍇 ③
Grapes and French oak barrels join to produce real depths of flavor. The wine distinguishes itself even more by having a firmer core than many California Merlots.

Napa Valley　🍇🍇 ③
Cabernet Sauvignon 1988
Released a year earlier than Hillside Select, the Napa Valley bottling is, curious though it may seem, more flavorful of Cabernet. Vintage and style make it softer and rounder as well.

Napa Valley　🍇🍇🍇 ④
Cabernet Sauvignon "Hillside Select" 1987
The vintage gave wonderful depths of flavor at the same time it produced an equally wonderful lightness of weight. If the proportions are exquisite, so its polishing given the wine by Doug Shafer during its long career in oak barrels. The gentleness imparted by Stags Leap District vines only enhances the style. So accessible is the wine right now that it is hard to recommend long cellaring, this in spite of the fact that several forerunner vintages are holding quite well in bottle. In truth, the Shafers themselves release the wine only when they believe it has achieved its finest hour.

NAPA VALLEY
CALIFORNIA
UNITED STATES OF AMERICA

1167

NAPA VALLEY
CALIFORNIA
UNITED STATES OF AMERICA

Silver Oak Wine Cellars

915 Oakville Cross Road
Oakville, CA. 94562
Tel. (707) 944-8808
Fax (707) 944-2817

After some years as a winemaking brother in
The Christian Brothers (Order of LaSalle),
Justin Meyer learned that his calling was
Cabernet Sauvignon rather than the cloth.
After several years in another winery with an
extensive range of wines, he and partner
Raymond Duncan launched Silver Oak as a
label. Shortly thereafter they found
themselves able to build a winery and
concentrate exclusively on Silver Oak as a
Cabernet-only property. The partners have
their largest vineyard in Sonoma's Alexander
Valley plus a smaller one in Napa. Meyer
separately owns the tiny Bonny's Vineyard,
named after his wife. The winery produces
wines under these three identities. Meyer is a
confirmed believer in using American oak
barrels rather than ones from French oak for
Cabernet. The result is readily tasteable to all
who know the differences in oak flavors.

Alexander Valley　　　　　　🍷 ④
Cabernet Sauvignon 1988
Grapes from the Alexander Valley are quick to
take on the aromas of wood. With that, supple
tannins make this a wine quicker to mature than
its companion from the Napa Valley.

Napa Valley　　　　　　🍷 ④
Cabernet Sauvignon 1988
Fully ripened grapes and long aging in American
oak barrels transform the wines of Silver Oak
into veritable monuments to the style that Andre
Tchelistcheff created in his early days at
Beaulieu Vineyard.

Silverado Vineyards

6121 Silverado Trail
Napa, CA. 94558
Tel. (707) 257-1770
Fax (707) 257-1538

An unfailing sense of harmony has made all
Silverado Vineyards wines sought-after in
every vintage since the beginning, in 1981.
Lillian Disney, widow of the famous cartoonist
Walt Disney, her daughter and son-in-law are
the owner-operators of Silverado Vineyards.
They and winemaker Jack Stuart continue to
build upon reputations that had become solid
before the end of the winery's first decade.
Silverado's continues to climb in critical
esteem even as new vineyards expand its
volume in its second decade. Following a
program ever more typical of the Napa
Valley, the proprietors have developed
several small vineyards scattered throughout
the valley in order to capitalize on differences
in sun, soil and exposure so that each grape
variety has ideal growing conditions. They
have wisely limited the number of wines to
types that their vineyards grow well.

Napa Valley Chardonnay 1990　　🍷 ③
The kiss of oak is a hearty one, but Chardonnay
gains steadily until it dominates the finish of a
wine that, like all its stable mates, is subtle, and
polished to perfect smoothness.

Napa Valley　　　　　　🍷🍷 ②
Sauvignon Blanc 1990
A perfectly polished, textbook expression of
Sauvignon from the cooler southern half of the
Napa Valley, where the flavors somehow evoke
thoughts of a sweet or succulent herb.

Napa Valley　　　　　　🍷 ③
Cabernet Sauvignon 1988
Characteristic of the vintage, the wine is supple,
almost fleshy. With that it is perfectly
proportioned as a middleweight, its melange of
cassis and herb nicely tinted by time in oak.

NAPA VALLEY
CALIFORNIA
UNITED STATES OF AMERICA　　1168

NAPA VALLEY
CALIFORNIA
UNITED STATES OF AMERICA

Spottswoode

1401 Hudson Street
St. Helena, CA. 94574
Tel. (707) 963-0134
Fax (707) 963-2886

When the Spottswoode label reappeared in the Napa Valley with the vintage of 1987, one saw the rebirth of a treasured name from before Prohibition. The winery has been evolving ever since, always in admirable directions. The vineyard nestles in between two residential quarters of St Helena, rather isolated from the main body of plantings. In spite of that, it produces what can only be called mainstream Napa Valley Cabernet Sauvignon grapes. The first planting in the modern era included a substantial proportion of Sauvignon Blanc and some Semillon, but those varieties have given way to the better-adapted Cabernet. White grapes are now purchased from an independent grower near the town of Yountville. Tony Soter, Spottswoode's second winemaker, set a polished, subtle tone for the wines. Now Pamela Starr continues on that path.

Napa valley   ☙☙ ②
Sauvignon Blanc 1990
A faint spritz adds to an already lean, cleansing tactile, which may be the greatest virtue of the wine. However, the melon-like flavors of ripe Sauvignon cannot but be admired.

Napa valley   ☙ ④
Cabernet Sauvignon 1988
Spottswoode's vineyard gives a fleshy fullness to Cabernet in any vintage. In soft, forward 1988 the tendency has produced a wine that is already agreeable to drink, but far from its finest hour.

St. Andrews Winery

2921 Silverado Trail
Napa, CA. 94558
Tel. (707) 252-6748
Fax (707) 252-0220

Though St Andrews offers other wines, the vineyard is all Chardonnay and the dominant wine of the house is the same. It is the correct idea. A long stretch of properties on both sides of the Napa River from the city of Napa north to the boundaries of the Stags Leap District have yielded memorable Chardonnays for just more than a decade, with St Andrews one of the less celebrated but more distinctive among them both as a young wine and one with some age in bottle. The style consistently leans on barrel fermentation, malo-lactic, and all the other tricks of the cellar, but the vineyard has remained triumphant in vintage after vintage, in spite of three changes of winemaker. A Hungarian emigrant, Imre Viskelety, founded the vineyard and, in 1981, the winery, but is has been owned since 1989 by the proprietors of Clos du Val.

Napa Valley   ☙ ③
Chardonnay Estate 1990
As always, a style for those who love the somber depths of flavor that come from fermentation and aging in toasty wood rather than fresh fruit. The balance is impeccable.

St. Clement Vineyard

2867 St. Helena Highway North
St. Helena, CA. 94574
Tel. (707) 963-7221
Fax (707) 963-9174

In a state dominated by enologists with degrees from the University of California at Davis, Dennis Johns is one of several self-taught winemakers who have succeeded well.

While his red wines have won plaudits from important critics, his whites seem to have a surer touch. Certainly they have more immediate appeal. St. Clement Chardonnay and Sauvignon Blanc differ markedly in style, both show a rare consistency, even given the steady climate of the Napa Valley. St. Clement started small, and family-owned, in 1976. Johns took the helm four years later. After a Japanese brewing firm, Sapporo, Inc., purchased the property, the new owner strengthened Johns's hand with a large infusion of capital that improved the cellars and brought the first substantial vineyard into the fold. In Carneros, it is planted primarily to Chardonnay.

Napa Valley   ❦❦ ②
Sauvignon Blanc 1991
The use of oak is quickly evident in a 1991 that is less firm or hard in youth than most St. Clements, still wanting a year or two to harmonize. The Sauvignon flavors are melony, and run deep.

Napa Valley Chardonnay 1990   ❦❦ ③
A real contender for Top Wine honors owes its subtle but specific taste of Chardonnay and its firm structure to Carneros grapes. Its depth and richness come from a sunnier vineyard.

St. Supery Vineyards & Winery

8440 St. Helena Highway
Rutherford, CA. 94573
Tel. (707) 963-4507
Fax (707) 963-4526

St. Supery belongs to a French family with ranging agricultural interests in the Midi. Its name, however, comes from the first developer of the property on which the winery is located, not from the current owners, who are Skallis. Except for one small patch at the winery, all of their vineyards are several miles distant in an upland area called Pope Valley, which had been lightly regarded for grapes until the Skallis developed their sizeable Dollarhide Ranch there. (Dollarhide, like St. Supery, was a nineteenth century settler.) From all early signs, Pope Valley grows grapes that make accessible wines. Winemaker Robert Broman does not fight the tendency, but does not give in altogether, either. His approach does capitalize on the taste of grapes more than oak, but also captures some depth. Further, the wines are resolutely dry.

Napa Valley   ❦ ②
Sauvignon Blanc "Dollarhide" 1990
The warm, upland Pope Valley grows Sauvignon with flavors all to the melon-like rather than herbaceous side of the variety. The balance is pleasantly firm.

Napa Valley Merlot "Dollarhide" 1989 ❦ ③
Warm Pope Valley coaxes Merlot into the taste of cassis more than herb. A restrained use of oak gives complexity to a wine that shows structure beneath its polished coat.

NAPA VALLEY
CALIFORNIA
UNITED STATES OF AMERICA   1170

NAPA VALLEY
CALIFORNIA
UNITED STATES OF AMERICA

Stag's Leap Wine Cellars

5766 Silverado Trail
Napa, CA. 94558
Tel. (707) 944-2020
Fax (707) 257-7501

Warren Winiarski must be the Napa Valley's only winemaker who can rattle off ancient Greek and write passable Latin. A one-time academic who felt a need to get closer to the soil, he founded his winery at the very beginnings of Stag's Leap as a modern vineyard district, and won instant fame when his 1973 Cabernet Sauvignon placed first in a French-American tasting in Paris in 1976. Though he has been making wine since the mid-1960s, Winiarski remains professorial in mien and method. Every Stag's Leap Wine Cellars wine comes as a result of long, painstaking thought. Some of them, some critics contend, have shown rather too much thought and not quite enough of their natural endowments. The winery grows nearly all of its cabernet sauvignon and merlot in a vineyard ideally suited to them, but buys the grapes for its several white wines from elsewhere in the Napa Valley.

Napa valley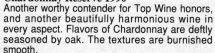
Chardonnay Reserve 1990
Another worthy contender for Top Wine honors, and another beautifully harmonious wine in every aspect. Flavors of Chardonnay are deftly seasoned by oak. The textures are burnished smooth.

Napa Valley Cabernet Sauvignon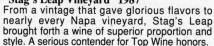
"Stag's Leap Vineyard" 1987
From a vintage that gave glorious flavors to nearly every Napa vineyard, Stag's Leap brought forth a wine of superior proportion and style. A serious contender for Top Wine honors.

Stags' Leap Winery

6150 Silverado Trail
Napa, CA. 94558
Tel. (707) 944-1303

There are two producers called Stags Leap in the Napa Valley district of the same name, all called after a promontory rising high above both properties. This winery belongs to Carl Doumani, who made tiny first lots wines in leased space in 1973, and has built slowly in the years since. Stags' Leap Winery went along well enough in its earlier years, famous mostly for a dark, hearty Petite Sirah. However, it found a new vitality in 1989 when Robert Brittan became the winemaker for Doumani. Brittan, who made some impressive Chardonnays for S. Andrews between 1985 and 1988, now promises a string of memorable Cabernet Sauvignons and Merlots in his new position. At least if his first efforts are any indication, the property has every opporunity to become a major factor in a district most famous for these two varietal wine types.

Napa Valley
Cabernet Sauvignon 1989
The essence of the Stags Leap District is supple tannins coupled with berry-like rather than herbaceous flavors from cabernet. Here is a wine firmer than most, but otherwise absolutely typical.

Napa valley Merlot 1989
Early after bottling flavors from oak dominated, but with each passing month Merlot thrusts itself forward. Uncommon depth of flavor and firmness of texture promise further gains.

NAPA VALLEY
CALIFORNIA
UNITED STATES OF AMERICA

1171

NAPA VALLEY
CALIFORNIA
UNITED STATES OF AMERICA

Sterling Vineyards

1111 Dunaweal Lane
Calistoga, CA. 94515
Tel. (707) 942-5151
Fax (707) 942-0129

Three owners and four winemakers after its
founding in 1969, once-erratic Sterling now
appears set on a course that will last for a
while. Under the ownership of Seagrams,
Inc., the winery is capitalizing on extensive
vineyard holdings from the northernmost end
of Napa to its southernmost by making wines
from individual properties. It is further
capitalizing with a Reserve red that makes
the most of several of its properties.
Winemaker Bill Dyer is seeing to it that the
vines are given full voice in those wines,
though not without substantial countermelody
from oak barrels. One result for serious
students is the opportunity to contrast
Chardonnays from mountainous and flat
vineyards, Cabernet Sauvignons from the
same two situations, and also Cabernet and
Merlot in several different proportions or
combinations. The results give as much
pleasure as they do instruction.

Napa valley　　　　　　　　🍇 ③
Cabernet Sauvignon 1988
Ostensibly the smaller brother of "Diamond
Mountain," yet it manages to be both fuller and
firmer in texture, and richer in the herbaceous
flavors of true Napa Cabernet.

Napa Valley Cabernet Sauvignon　🍇 ③
"Diamond Mountain" 1988
A surprisingly gentle wine more reflective of an
accessible vintage than of the steep slopes of its
vineyard. As are its running mates, it is supple
and polished in texture.

Napa valley "Reserve" 1987　　🍇 ④
Assembled from several vineyards and the
traditional varieties of Bordeaux, still it is a wine
that comes close to being the dream of Napa
Valley Cabernet. Worthy of Top Wine honors.

Trefethen Vineyards

1160 Oak Knoll Avenue
Napa, CA. 94558
Tel. (707) 255-7700
Fax (707) 255-0793

A few large vineyard owners in California have the luxury of taking the best few blocks of grapes for their own use and selling the rest to a clamoring list of competitors. Trefethen is one of these. The family-owned winery uses only about 40% of the grapes it grows for its own label; the rest go to others in the Napa Valley. Since the winery's founding in 1963, its three great successes have been Chardonnay, White Riesling and a proprietary blend called Eschol White. The hidden treasure is its Cabernet Sauvignon. The reason these wines succeed, one suspects, is diligent attention to expressing the vineyard rather than an exaggerated attention to oak or other technical aspects. Even though the winery is barely 20 years old, already in the 1980s its vines, which extend for almost 600 acres in a cool region between the towns of Napa and Yountville, were among the most apreciated in the Napa Valley. Winery production for the Trefethen label approaches 700,000 bottles. A good part of Trefethen's crop goes to Domain Chandon as a result of long cooperation between the two firms.

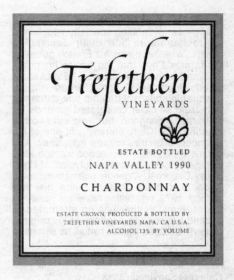

Napa Valley Withe Riesling 1991   🍇 ②
Trefethen has found a particularly Californian balance, at once crisp and lean. With that comes an equally Californian flavor, more suggestive of pear than grapefruity Mosels or Rheins.

Napa valley Eschol White NV   🍇 ②
The name is meant to give Trefethen's winemaker freedom to make a good daily wine. In practice, he uses it to make a fresh, approachable wine that tastes exactly like Chardonnay.

Napa Valley
Cabernet Sauvignon 1987   🍇🍇 ③
From what looks ever more like the vintage of the decade, Trefethen has caught a dozen subtle shadings of Cabernet, of vineyard, of time in oak, all in a wine that can please now or wait.

Napa Valley Chardonnay 1990 🍇 🍇 🍇 ③
In an era when too much is not enough for many Americans, this is a wine one might serve to the most delicate princess in the realm, a wine that speaks clearly of its origins and its breeding. The Trefethen family decided at the very outset to make Chardonnays that would age with distinction. To that end they have resisted the swift rewards of barrel fermentation, malo-lactic, and other sources of instant identity in favor of the 1979 and 1983 still attest, they have found the path they sought. The 1990 shows every sign of equalling or surpassing its predecessors.

NAPA VALLEY
CALIFORNIA
UNITED STATES OF AMERICA

1173

NAPA VALLEY
CALIFORNIA
UNITED STATES OF AMERICA

Tudal Winery

1015 Big Tree Road
St. Helena, CA. 94574
Tel. (707) 963-3947

Arnold Tudal came to grapegrowing after a long career of farming specialty vegetables for restaurateurs and other demanding clients. Whether it was his French genes or his farmer's eye that led him to his small vineyard, he had to know what he was about when he chose it, for a broad ring of unsuitable soils isolates his tiny patch not only from all other celebrated grounds for Cabernet Sauvignon, but from every other planting of it. Quite literally, not one of his neighbors even tries to grow the variety. And yet his wines have succeeded vintage after vintage by being almost prototypical of Napa Valley Cabernet. A gentle, unassuming man, Tudal has been content since his first vintage, 1979, with letting his wines speak for themselves. Neither has he attempted to expand beyond the capacity of his original property because it gives him all he wishes to do.

Napa valley   🍇 ③
Cabernet Sauvignon 1988
The isolation of Tudal's vineyard has its reflection in Cabernet tasting at once typical of Napa and yet distinctively true to its soil. The winemaking is understated but careful.

Vichon

1595 Oakville Grade
Oakville, CA. 94562
Tel. (707) 944-2811
Fax (707) 944-9224

Vichon started well under a partnership formed in 1981, staggered a bit as the original owners began to disagree, then has prospered again since 1985, when the Robert Mondavi family bought it. The motor that got it started and has kept it going is an intriguingly complex, long-lived Sauvignon Blanc-Sémillon blend given ample exposure to oak barrels. First called Chevrier, the wine had to be renamed after the American federal government ruled that Chevrier was a synyonym for Sémillon and thus could apply only to a varietal wine (containing 75%t or more of the named grape). Chevrignon, the somewhat tuneless replacement name, has not harmed the wine inside the bottles. Since the Mondavis acquired Vichon its Cabernets have come up in the world to match their white cousin. In particular the bottling from the Stags Leap District has proven itself worthy against well-known names.

Napa Valley Chevrignon 1990   🍇🍇 ②
Distinctive with the herbaceous flavors of Sauvignon Blanc from the cooler southern half of Napa, yet, in this season, Semillon seems ascendant in a 50:50 blend. Firm, as the vintage demands.

Napa valley   🍇 ③
Cabernet Sauvignon SLD 1989
Vicon manages to coax an extra tannic firmness out of its Stags Leap Cabernet. With that comes a perfectly harmonized duet of hers from Cabernet and floral perfumes from oak.

Villa Mt. Eden

620 Oakville Crossroad
Napa, CA. 94558
Tel. (707) 944-2414

Villa Mt Eden is yet another of the California
wineries that has made slow, steady
progress rather than bursting on the scene
with one grand coup. In its case, two signal
events have added much to its reputation in
recent years. The first was the coming of
Michael McGrath as winemaker in 1982. The
second was the winery's purchase by a
Washington State-based wine group called
Stimson Lane in 1986. McGrath refined a
once ultra-bold style. Stimson Lane gave him
an expanded roster of vineyards from which
to draw grapes. Under the original ownership
of James and Anne McWilliams, Villa Mt
Eden made six unrelated wines
(Chardonnay, Chenin Blanc,
Gewürztraminer, Cabernet Sauvignon, and
Pinot Noir) from the estate vineyard. Under
the new regime there are fewer wines, and
the sources have been diversified to obtain
better suited growing conditions.

Napa Valley　　　　　　　🍇 ②
Chardonnay Grand Reserve 1990
Winemaker Michael McGrath presided over a
perfect marriage of rich Chardonnay and subtle
oak to achieve a wine of great depth and
harmony. Typical of the vintage it is firm enough
to cellar.

Napa Valley　　　　　　🍇🍇 ③
Cabernet Sauvignon "Grand Reserve" 1988
Classical herbaceous Napa Cabernet flavors set
themselves off neatly against an underplayed
note from oak. Typical of the vintage, all is
suppleness and polish already.

Z D

8383 Silverado Trail
Napa, CA. 94558
Tel. (707) 963-5188
Fax (707) 963-2640

Stubborness is a virtue in winemaking, and Z
D's proprietors have their fair share of it. In
an era when others are abandoning
American oak barrels in favor of French, they
insist upon, even trumpet their loyalty to the
forests of Kentucky and Ohio for all their
wines, Chardonnay included. The results are
distinctive. The winery started in Sonoma
County in 1969, and moved to Napa in 1979.
However, for so small a cellar in so famous a
place, it is curiously unattached
geographically speaking. In addition to Napa
and Sonoma, it draws also upon the Central
Coast for grapes, especially Santa Barbara
County. Thus some of its labels give only
"California" as the appellation of origin. The
name comes from the initials of founders
Gino Zepponi and Norman De Leuze. After
Zepponi died in an auto crash, the De Leuze
family bought out Zepponi's heirs.

California Chardonnay 1990　　🍇 ③
This is wine on a scale to bring admiration from
a Texan: bold flavors, rich textures, a hearthy
smack of American oak, and, however it comes
about, a sweetness all its own.

Carneros Pinot Noir 1989　　🍇 ③
Perhaps too specific of American oak for those
bred on Burgundy, this is nonetheless a wine of
pronounced Pinot Noir character and an
indisputably decadent richness of texture.

NAPA VALLEY
CALIFORNIA
UNITED STATES OF AMERICA
　　　　　1175　　　　　
NAPA VALLEY
CALIFORNIA
UNITED STATES OF AMERICA

Calera Wine Company

11300 Cienega Road
Hollister, CA. 93950
Tel. (408) 637-9170
Fax (408) 637-9070

Joshua Jensen is one of perhaps a score of Californians who set out with the same, single, shining goal: to find a place where pinot noir will grow with at least some of the success it finds in Burgundy. He is the only one of that band who settled upon San Benito County as The Place. He believes in it to the degree that he has won A.V.A. status for his patch, under the name Mt. Harlan. Limestone led him there. If limestone mattered so much in Burgundy, he reasoned in 1972, it must matter in California, too. And so he built his cellars in an abandoned lime kiln several miles south of Hollister, and planted pinot noir vines on steep slopes rich in lime. Limestone aside, this is a far sunnier and much less rainy place than the Cote d'Or. However, 22 of 24 acres divided into three blocks remain devoted to pinot noir. Only recently has he hedged his bet with a single acre of Viognier.

Mt Harlan Pinot Noir "Mills" 1989 🍇 🍇 ④
Of three blocks in Calera's vineyard, the Mills somehow seems to produce the softest, roundest wines without any loss of flavor. No exception in this vintage.

Mt Harlan Pinot Noir "Reed" 1989 🍇 🍇 ④
Follows its own tradition of tasting strongly of oak early, then ever more of Pinot Noir with age. And age is a good idea in a wine of unusually firm tannins.

Corbett Canyon

2195 Corbett Canyon Road
Arroyo Grande, CA. 93420
Tel. (805) 544-5800
Fax (805) 544-7205

The crucial moment for Corbett Canyon came when the winery decided in 1989 to buy a major vineyard in neighboring Santa Barbara County for its pinot noir and chardonnay, and to look to the North Coast for grapes for its cabernet sauvignon. With those decisions it solidified its program for finding superior grapes to make its admirably inexpensive "reserve" quality wines. Prior to that the company had already secured a position as a producer of remarkably price-worthy varietal wine types in a series it calls Coastal Classic, which are assembled wines rather than distinctively regional ones. The winemaker at Corbett Canyon, John Clarke, has rung up an impressive record for consistent quality at all levels and in all varieties, but his crowning achievement in most vintages is Pinot Noir that manages to reflect region and variety in equal parts.

Central Coast 🍇 ①
Merlot "Coastal Classic" 1989
Unabashedly inexpensive, straightforwardly fruity in flavor, and yet more than a wine for everyday because of impeccable balance and a certain, solid core.

Central Coast 🍇 ①
Pinot Noir Reserve 1989
The region betrays its presence in a polite, quiet way in a wine otherwise surprising for its intensity of Pinot flavors. All is round and polished. Nothing held back. No need to wait.

SAN BENITO
CALIFORNIA
UNITED STATES OF AMERICA

1176

SAN LUIS OBISPO
CALIFORNIA
UNITED STATES OF AMERICA

Eberle Winery

P.O. Box 2459
Paso Robles, CA. 93447
Tel. (805) 238-9607
Fax (805) 237-0344

In a country with little winemaking history, many winemakers come from unexpected backgrounds. Thus far, Gary Eberle remains the only ex-American footballer who trained in molecular biology before turning his attention to the cellar. After a substantial career experimenting with many grape varieties at the now defunct Estrella River winery, Eberle chose cabernet sauvignon as the centerpiece of his own vineyard in rolling grasslands not far east of Paso Robles town. The series of wines he has produced from it show a restless but reasoned evolution toward richer flavors and firmer textures, in the end toward a balance that promises some age-worthiness in many years, most especially the cool ones. This is not the general pattern in Paso Robles. One of Eberle's fundamental tenets is to keep the flavors of Cabernet lively and fresh all the way to bottle.

Paso Robles
Cabernet Sauvignon 1988
In the way of its region, a wine soft for tannins, faintly warm with alcohol, and richly endowed with the herbaceous (but not vegetative) side of Cabernet. An easy, early drinker.

Edna Valley Vineyard

2585 Biddle Ranch Road
San Luis Obispo, CA. 93401
Tel. (805) 544-9594
Fax (805) 544-0112

The winery at Edna Valley looks eerily like the one at Chalone for good reason. Edna Valley Vineyard is a partnership of Chalone, which provides the winemaking team, and Paragon Vineyard, which provides the grapes from its region-dominating property. Originally the intent was to split production more or less equally between Chardonnay and Pinot Noir. However, not only does Chardonnay sell better in the American market, it appears to grow better in the Edna Valley. And, thus, far the greatest emphasis is now on the white, which is made in exactly the same barrel-fermented, aged-in-damp-cellars style as the more famous Chalone. Comparing the two wines to understand regional as opposed to stylistic differences is one of the on-going amusements of collectors in California.

Edna Valley
Chardonnay 1990
A lovely blending of toasty notes from oak and ripe fruit from chardonnay come together in a wine of finesse and balance, and a slightly greater freshness than the winery's Reserve.

Edna Valley
Chardonnay "Reserve" 1990
The 1990 catches Edna Valley's apple-like flavors of chardonnay deftly, adds a delicate overtone of butterscotch from well toasted oak barrels, and still manages to be a rich wine.

SAN LUIS OBISPO
CALIFORNIA
UNITED STATES OF AMERICA

1177

SAN LUIS OBISPO
CALIFORNIA
UNITED STATES OF AMERICA

Meridian Vineyards

7000 Highway 46 East
Paso Robles, CA. 93447
Tel. (805) 239-5711
Fax (805) 239-5715

Though the address is Paso Robles, and the winery has a 210-acre vineyard there, Meridian has more than twice the vineyard resources farther south, in Santa Barbara County, and buys a small lot of grapes each year from Edna Valley. It is a rather extreme case of a typical practice in California of locating vineyards in several areas in order to make a broad range of wines well. The Santa Barbara vineyards are planted primarily to chardonnay, somewhat to pinot noir. Edna Valley is a source of chardonnay much favored by winemaker Charles Ortman. The home vineyard, in much warmer Paso Robles, is devoted mainly to cabernet sauvignon and syrah. The presence of syrah in the mix would tip off people who know California well that the Paso Robles property originally was the Estrella River Winery.

Santa Barbara Chardonnay 1990 🍇 ②
Stronger in the flavors of oak than earlier vintages, and less powerful of chardonnay, but appealing in that style. Slightly spritzy to start, then acidity keeps it crisp.

Paso Robles Syrah 1989 🍇 ②
Winemaker Charles Ortman dotes on syrah from a mature planting because it gives rich flavors of dark berries without becoming harsh or overbearing. The 1989 soars above earlier vintages.

Wild Horse Winery

P.O. Box 638
Templeton, CA. 93465
Tel. (805) 434-2541
Fax (805) 434-3516

Owner-winemaker Ken Volk burst upon the scene in California with his first wines, most especially with Pinot Noir and Chardonnay. He has followed his successes of 1982 with ever more impressive wines, in both favorable vintages and difficult ones. He is one of those gifted winemakers who has excellent technical credentials, but does not allow himself to be inhibited by them. Wines that seem right must, in his eyes, be right. This free-wheeling spirit sometimes yields results that are not quite typical, but nonetheless remain both fascinating and drinkable. In his search for grapes that produce the flavors he wants, Volk does not limit himself to his home district, or even to his home county. However, as time has worn on, he has become increasingly loyal to a few select vineyards in San Luis Obispo and Santa Barbara counties.

Central Coast Merlot 1989 🍇 ③
Strong of its region, stronger of its variety, hence powerfully evocative of herbs until aromas of berry come to dominate a long finish. Dances a lively dance on the palate.

Santa Barbara Pinot Noir 1989 🍇 ③
A curious interplay between delicate pinot noir and almost eccentric regional or vintage flavors (the harvest was rainy), yet classically proportioned, perfectly polished, wholly pleasing.

Au Bon Climat

Route 1, Santa Maria Mesa Road
Santa Maria, CA. 93454
Tel. (805) 688-8630

Jim Clendenen and Adam Tolmach shared Burgundian dreams when they joined forces to found Au Bon Climat in 1979, and still do. On grounds that sun and soil are everything to these two varieties, especially pinot noir, they keep the best lots from each of several vineyards separate in every vintage. A.B.C., as the winery is known to its loyal audience, has become a benchmark label in its region.Much as the two partners admire the contributions of individual vineyards, nothing keeps them from fairly lavish use of new French oak barrels in the making and aging of their wines. Au Bon Climat began in an old, rented dairy building on a vineyard near the town of Alamo. Exactly ten years later, in 1989, it moved to the more appropriately designed new cellar it shares with several related firms. This home is on the Bien Nacido Vineyard, one of their principal sources of grapes.

Santa Barbara Chardonnay 1990   🍇 ④
An untrammelled enthusiasm for the effects of barrel fermentation and malo-lactic remains in effect at A.B.C. The predictable result, a bold, almost butterscotch-rich Chardonnay.

Santo Barbara   🍇🍇 ④
Pinot Noir "Benedict" 1989
A strong note of oak tolls as steadily as a church bell, leaving more elusive hints of Pinot Noir to provide a counterpoint. Though tannins suggest waiting, this vintage may be best in its youth.

Babcock Vineyards

5176 Highway 246
Lompoc, CA. 93436
Tel. (805) 736-1455
Fax (805) 736-886

Brian Babcock came out of Occidental College with a degree in chemistry in 1982, not long after his parents bought vineyard land in the lower Santa Ynez Valley, and just in time for him to step in as winemaker under the watchful eye of a local veteran. He has, as is now evident, a natural talent for wine. Like many of his age and era, he has no fear of experimenting, a useful bent in a region with little or no tradition to provide guideposts. Babcock has produced barrel-fermented Rieslings and Gewürztraminers, techniques usually reserved for Chardonnay in his part of the world. But no matter what path he takes, he keeps a healthy respect for what the vineyard has given him. It shows in wines from the family property, but also in ones made from the grapes of independent growers. Even his first try with a few rows of young pinot noir was memorable for fidelity to its source.

Santa Ynez Valley   🍇 ③
Sauvignon Blanc "Eleven Oaks"
A popular American expression for something powerful is "in your face". Here is a heady, woody, in-your-face rendition of Sauvignon Blanc that somehow works with Mexican-spiced foods.

Santa Barbara Pinot Noir 1989   🍇 ③
Textbook flavors of variety and region seem bold on the nose, then fall more subtly on the palate. The finish is long in a wine of mouth-watering tartness.

SANTA BARBARA
CALIFORNIA
UNITED STATES OF AMERICA

1179

SANTA BARBARA
CALIFORNIA
UNITED STATES OF AMERICA

The Brander Vineyard

2401 Refugio Road
Los Olivos, CA. 93441
Tel. (805) 688-2455

The more Santa Barbara County's vinicultural fame rests upon its Chardonnays and Pinot Noirs, the more owner-winemaker C. Frederic Brander digs in his heels on behalf of Sauvignon Blanc, Cabernet Sauvignon, and their Bordelais cousins. Brander is not without reason. His part of the Santa Ynez Valley is nearly free of the seafogs that keep vineyards closer to the Pacific shore cool and shaded throughout the growing season. Graves is the model for the Sauvignon Blancs Brander blends from sauvignon blanc and sémillon. (However, as the proprietor readily admits, some vintages remind him more of a Pouilly Fumé). Bordeaux, more broadly, is where Brander aims with the cabernet sauvignon-cabernet franc-merlot blend he calls Bouchet. Early vintages made without cabernet sauvignon, especially 1984 and 1985, seemed more successful than later ones with it.

Santa Ynes Valley   ❦ ②
Sauvignon Blanc "Tete De Cuvee" 1989
As usual, out later than most Sauvignons, and more fully developed because of the fact. A distinct note of oak and other bouquets push otherwise strong notes of Sauvignon toward the background.

Santa Ynez Valley Bouchet 1989   ❦ ③
Cabernet Franc and Merlot notwithstanding, the 1989 tastes as Santa Barbara Cabernet Sauvignon is wont to do: pungently herbaceous. The balance is as delicate as the flavor is strong.

Byron Vineyard

5230 Tepusquet Canyon Road
Santa Maria, CA. 93454
Tel. (805) 937-7288
Fax (805) 937-1246

Byron Kenneth Brown, Ken to all who know him, came to Santa Barbara County in the 1970s, when its vines were just getting started. His depth of experience with its vineyards and his increasingly refined sense of style have made him one of the leading presences in the region, perhaps the one winemaker who has done the most to define its character and style. After leaving Zaca Mesa winery to found his own cellars in 1984, Brown redoubled his emphasis on pinot noir, which appears to have found an especially congenial home in the Santa Maria Valley, yet one that gives the variety flavors quite unlike those of its native Burgundy. His touch with other varieties is no less sure. Brown and his original partners sold the winery to Robert Mondavi Winery, of the Napa Valley, in 1989, with Brown remaining as manager and winemaker.

Santa Barbara Chardonnay 1990   ❦ ②
On occasion Santa Barbara Chardonnay will ripen with aromas not unlike those of Chablis. This is one of those vintages. Ken Brown has framed the fruit handsomely with oak.

Santa Barbara   ❦❦ ②
Sauvignon Blanc 1990
Indisputably Santa Barbara for a flavor not unlike fresh-cut asparagus, which Brown plays beautifully against an elusive note of oak. It feels rich, almost juicy.

Santa Barbara Pinot Noir 1990   ❦❦ ③
The defining flavor is pure Santa Barbara in a year which seems bent in that direction, but Pinot Noir stands squarely behind. Lighter bodied than several earlier vintages, but not light.

Carey Cellars

1711 Alamo Pintado Road
Solvang, CA. 93463
Tel. (805) 688-8554
Fax (805) 686-1256

The winery started out in 1978 as the hobby of three physicians, a father and two sons, whose family name it still bears. Since 198 it has been owned by the same Brooks and Kate Firestone who own Firestone Vineyard. Kate is its driving force. The Careys gave the place a good start, planting a rolling vineyard they named La Cuesta primarily to Sauvignon Blanc and Merlot, and hiring a talented winemaker. The enterprise became too big to be a hobby, and lost headway. Under the vigorous direction of Kate Firestone, the trend at a renewed property is toward greater emphasis on the estate vines through increased plantings on the one hand and narrowed production on the other. Though non-estate Chardonnay remains something of a flagship, Sauvignon Blanc, Merlot and Cabernet Sauvignon are receiving greater attention not only from the proprietor, but also from knowledgeable wine drinkers.

Santa Ynez Valley Sauvignon Blanc 1990
What can be overpowering regional flavors get a downplaying from Sémillon. Most Sauvignons are almost as light as water; this one is as rich and lively as fresh fruit juice.

Santa Ynez Valley Merlot 1989
The flowers flicker between mint and more typical Central Coast Dill. As always, a certain rich, juicy texture gives the wine immediate appeal. It seems as its best in youth.

Firestone Vineyards

5017 Zaca Station Road
Los Olivos, CA. 93441
Tel. (805) 688-3940
Fax (805) 686-1256

Two major vineyards came to Santa Barbara earlier, but Firestone was the first major wine-producing estate in the county when it crushed its first grapes in 1975. It remains a force, partly because owners Brooks and Kate Firestone hit upon a rewarding site for their vineyards, partly because they found an adept winemaker in Alison Green, but primarily because the proprietors are completely committed to quality. The vineyards sit atop a flattened hill, one of half a dozen mesas in the region, in one of the most benign climates on earth. It is cool enough for riesling, warm enough for merlot, and dry enough to produce healthy fruit year after year, no matter what the grape variety. Green's versatility in the cellar means all of the wines are good, but Merlot is a particular star in Firestone's vineyards. Chardonnay is not far behind.

Santa Ynez Valley Gewurztraminer 1991
Though quite dry, the wine has a characteristic regional softness that suits it to summer sipping. So do unmistakeable flavors of the variety at full ripeness.

Santa Ynez Valley Chardonnay 1990
Continues the evolution from straightforwardly fruity to predominantly toasty, even butterscotch-like flavors. With that comes fuller body than an era when the wine was fruity to taste.

Santa Ynez Valley Merlot 1989
A delicate but firm grip from tannin lends depth to a wine that deftly highlights full-flavored Merlot with a distinct note from American oak. Another success in a lengthening string of them.

SANTA BARBARA
CALIFORNIA
UNITED STATES OF AMERICA

1181

SANTA BARBARA
CALIFORNIA
UNITED STATES OF AMERICA

Foxen Vineyard

Route 1, Box 144-A
Santa Maria, CA. 93454
Tel. (805) 937-4251

The latest generation of an old Santa
Barbara County ranching family and a career
vineyard manager joined as partners to found
Foxen Vineyard in 1987. The results of their
collaboration were immediately striking.
Richard Dore is a member of the Foxen
family, longtime cattle ranchers whose name
appears on many local landscape features.
Bill Walthen had managed the vineyards of
Rancho Sisquoc, among others, before
teaming up with Dore. Their winery and 10
acres of wines are at the inner end of the
Santa Maria Valley. They grow their own
cabernet (and blending varieties) and part of
the chardonnay they use. They buy all of the
pinot noir. As location and plantings suggest,
they meant to focus on Cabernet as their red,
but Santa Barbara's vocation for Pinot Noir is
almost impossible to resist.

Santa Maria Valley
Pinot Noir 1989
Pinot Noir in its distinctive, almost herbal
regional character, plus a suggestion of dusty
perfume from roses. Velvety, even in youth,
yet with enough acidity to give counterpoint.

Santa Barbara
Cabernet-Sauvignon 1988
Foxen's Cabernet Sauvignon is as stern from
tannin as the Pinot Noir is velvety for its lack, yet
the house style is constant in flavors too
complex to be described in a word, or several.

SANTA BARBARA
CALIFORNIA
UNITED STATES OF AMERICA

1182

SANTA BARBARA
CALIFORNIA
UNITED STATES OF AMERICA

Sanford Wines

7250 Santa Rosa Road
Buellton, CA. 93427
Tel. (805) 688-3300
Fax (805) 688-7381

A handful of winery owners foreshadow by force of personality the style of their wines. Richard Sanford is one of those. Booming bass voice, steady gaze, kingly gait and other, less tangible expressions of great confidence have their echoes in wines of quite remarkable powers, not the least of them intense varietal flavors played off against forceful contributions from oak. Such was the style of Sanford's first wine, under the Sanford & Benedict label in 1976; such has been the style since he launched his own winery with a set of 1981s. One way and another, Pinot Noir seems best suited to his approach, but all his wines are fascinating. Sanford has recently regained control of the vineyard that first made him famous for Pinot Noir. In the interim he has done much to establish the credentials of several other plantings of that variety in Santa Barbara County. Purchased grapes come in great part from the Santa Maria Valley while the winery's own vineyards are in the Santa Ynez Valley. Total production has reached the goal of 350,000 bottles, of which 50,000 are of Pinot Noir. It is to be expected that Richard Sanford still has pleasant surprises up his sleeve for the future with this variety.

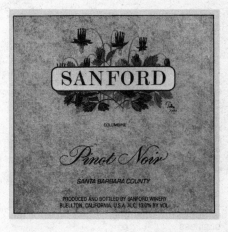

Santa Barbara
Sauvignon Blanc 1990 ☙ ②
The Sanford penchant for richness extends even to normally lean Sauvignon, in which barrel fermentation and malo-lactic combine to give depth of flavors and rounded richness of texture.

Santa Barbara
Pinot Noir Reserve 1989 ❦ ❦ ③
Everything that might be said about the flavors in the regular bottling can be said about this one, but with added emphasis. The added volume is admirable, yet not quite so versatile.

Santa Barbara Pinot Noir 1990 ❦ ❦ ❦ ④
No recipe holds all the flavors (a hint of strawberry, a regional suggestion of mint, something of meat, a scrap of toast from the oak) and yet all is proportion and harmony. This is the first Sanford wine to come from the original Sanford & Benedict vineyard since Richard Sanford established his own cellars. It hearkens back to the 1976 that made his first fame not only for the flavors, but for the tannic grip that has marked every Pinot Noir from its north-sloping site, not far up the Santa Ynez River Valley from the Pacific Ocean shore. Whether it is the tannin or some other quality, these are Pinot Noirs to lay down.

SANTA BARBARA
CALIFORNIA
UNITED STATES OF AMERICA

1183

SANTA BARBARA
CALIFORNIA
UNITED STATES OF AMERICA

Santa Barbara Winery

202 Anacapa Street
Santa Barbara, CA. 93101
Tel. (805) 963-3633
Fax (805) 962-4981

The emergence of Santa Barbara Winery is a story of what a vineyard can do. Pierre Lafond started the firm in 1962 as a glorified retail store for local customers in downtown Santa Barbara. Most of the wines were bought in bulk, bottled, and sold cheaply for everyday use. The vineyard, some 40 miles to the north, in the lower reaches of the Santa Ynez Valley, came in 1972. From that time forward, the list of wines has become more and more refined and, commensurately more expensive. Winemaker Bruce Maguire's arrival in 1982 brought the Santa Barbara label to its current high level, especially for Pinot Noir and Chardonnay.
Lafond has kept the winery in its original quarters, in a converted warehouse not far from the Santa Barbara beachfront, but that is about the only unchanged facet of the business.

Santa Barbara Chardonnay 1990   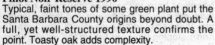 ②
As fleshy as Pinot Noirs are from Santa Barbara, so are its Chardonnays lean, even tart. This texture combines with faintly tropical fruit flavors in a wine perfectly suited to fish.

Santa Barbara   ③
Pinot Noir Reserve 1990
Typical, faint tones of some green plant put the Santa Barbara County origins beyond doubt. A full, yet well-structured texture confirms the point. Toasty oak adds complexity.

Zaca Mesa Winery

6905 Foxen Canyon Road
Los Olivos, CA. 93441
Tel. (805) 688-9339
Fax (805) 688-8796

Zaca Mesa started small, grew, and deliberately shrank back to one of its intermediate sizes. Its original intent was to offer a broad line of wines, but it ended up focussing on Chardonnay and Pinot Noir even though this meant reaching beyond its own extensive vineyards to properties where those varieties fared better. The winery's founder had ambitious plans when he started in 1976 and did much to carry them out with the skilled help from the same Ken Brown who now is the manager-winemaker of nearby Byron Vineyards. However, the costs led his successors to change course during the mid-1980s. After Brown left to found Byron, the new managers found an able replacement winemaker in Gale Sysock. It is Sysock who has found the sources of superior Chardonnay and Pinot Noir, and established the house style. Other wines remain in Zaca Mesa's portfolio, but they take a back seat.

Santa Barbara Chardonnay 1990   ②
The winemaker caught every atom of the apple-skin-like flavors Chardonnay can have, then deepened them with well chosen oak. Refined textures and a lingering finish add yet more pleasure.

Santa Barbara   ③
Pinot Noir Reserve 1989
Sysock is not shy about adding the taste of oak to his wines, but he has abundant regional Pinot flavors to build on. The 1989 is nicely firm beneath its polished surface.

Bonny Doon

10 Pine Flat Road
Santa Cruz, CA. 95060
Tel. (408) 425-3625
Fax (408) 425-3856

Randall Grahm, proprietor of Bonny Doon, is in certain senses a success in spite of himself. Having set the task of making excellent wines in the style of the Rhone in a state where such had seldom been attempted, never with success, Grahm inspired a whole crew of imitators. Try as they have, they have failed to equal his achievements. All the more reason to applaud his singular wines. Having more or less conquered the Rhone, Grahm has now turned his attention to Italy. Some of the whimsically named wines come from his own vineyard near the Pacific Ocean shore north of Santa Cruz, but the larger proportion come from vineyards well to the east, some from Gilroy in Santa Clara County, others from Contra Costa County, where warmer, sunnier weather prevails. In every case the style is bold, and the flavor of grapes foremost.

Clos de Gilroy California 1991   ②
All grenache, and as light and fresh as a red wine can be, yet intensely flavored. Does as well lightly chilled on warm summer evenings as warmer in wintrier weathers.

Le Sophiste California 1991   ③
Grahm achieves a stunningly aromatic blend of marsanne and rousanne in spite of having few vineyards upon which to draw. Like its forerunners, is to grow richer in the bottle for several years.

Le Cigare Volant California 1989   ③
A blend of grenache, mourvedre and syrah catches much of the headiness of the Châteaunef-du-Pape' son which it is modelled, but comes closer to Côte du Rhônes in its frisky fruit flavors.

Thomas Fogarty Winery

19501 Skyline Boulevard
Woodside, CA. 94062
Tel. (415) 851-1946

The Santa Cruz Mountains A.V.A. is one of California's most curious regions of origin for wine, a sprawling territory with only a handful of vineyards to call its own. Thomas Fogarty Winery is there because the locale is convenient to the headquarters in which Dr. Thomas Fogarty conducts his inventive medical research. He has vineyards at the winery, but, like many others in the Santa Cruz Mountains, he reaches elsewhere for the grapes that dominate production. Though winemaker Michael Martella is sure-handed throughout the list, the one wine that has swept this winery into critical focus is, rather amazingly, a Gewürztrmaniner from Monterey County's Ventana vineyard. Hardly a commercial favorite of the moment, Gewurztraminer nonetheless has a loyal following among writers and merchants, and the 1989 was too striking to ignore.

Monterey Gewurztraminer
"Ventana" 1991
A delicate but indelible perfume of carnations wafted on spring breezes. Gentle textures made softer by a trace of sweet. A wine for quaffing under a gentle sun.

Santa Cruz Mountains   ③
Pinot Noir 1989
From a superior year for Pinot Noir in the high hills south of San Francisco comes this Fogarty, vital on the palate, and strong with a flavor not unlike raspberry.

SANTA CRUZ MOUNTAINS
CALIFORNIA
UNITED STATES OF AMERICA

1185

SANTA CRUZ MOUNTAINS
CALIFORNIA
UNITED STATES OF AMERICA

Ridge

17100 Montebello Road
Cupertino, CA. 95015
Tel. (408) 867-3233
Fax (408) 867-2986

Since its inception in 1962 Ridge has been both a business and an unofficial agricultural experiment station. In a state where winegrowing remains a very young, sometimes dimly understood activity, the proprietors of this winery have tested dozens if not scores of vineyards for their capacities to grow memorable Cabernet Sauvignon, Zinfandel and Petite Sirah. One has only to look through a collection of old labels to see which have succeeded and which have fallen by the wayside. Fortunately most of the decisions on vineyards awaited the 1969 arrival of Paul Draper as winemaker. The founders had boundless enthusiasm, but not a firm command of the skills of the cellar. These Draper brought. After time thinned the ranks of original partners, the survivors sold Ridge to Otsuka Pharmaceuticals in 1986. Otsuka had the sense to keep Draper.

Sonoma Zinfandel "Geyserville" 1989 🍇 ③
Though the style of all Ridge reds is consistent, Zinfandel lends a brighter, more accessible character than Cabernet. In this among several bottlings that fact is most evident.

Santa Cruz Mountains 🍇🍇 ④
Cabernet Sauvignon "Montebello" 1987
From steep, west-facing slopes comes a Cabernet of almost epic proportions, even after Draper's taming of it. As always, the flavors are dense, the textures firm and needing time on bottle.

Alderbrook Vineyards

2306 Magnolia Drive
Healdsburg, CA. 95448
Tel. (707) 433-9154
Fax (707) 433-1862

Alderbrook's modest, gray-painted winery buildings sit within a few dozen meters of the point where the Russian River Valley, Dry Creek Valley and Alexander Valley A.V.A.s come together near Healdsburg. Those not familiar with California cannot imagine what differences of climate and soil are thereby immediately at hand. Cool fogs regularly sweep across the Russian River bottomlands where sits an estate vineyard of chardonnay, but seldom do they intrude four miles into the Dry Creek Valley to Alderbrook's source of sémillon. The location is, thus, perfect for a winery founded to make white wines that grow hundreds of miles apart in France. Because winemaker Phillip Staley believes in vines before barrels, vineyard character shines clearly in all his wines. Alderbrook began in 1982 as a producer only of white wines. In 1990 the firm added its first red, a Petite Sirah.

Dry Creek Valley Sémillon 1990 🍇🍇 ②
In temperate years Alderbrook Sémillon surpasses the taste of figs to achieve a delicate floral perfume, as the 1990 has done better than any forerunner, even 1987. Dry and firm in texture.

Sonoma County Chardonnay 1990 🍇 ②
At its best in Sonoma, Chardonnay offers ringingly clear flavors of apples, especially the skins. These Staley loves to preserve in flinty-firm wines, a style perfectly rewarded in 1990.

Sonoma County 🍇 ②
Sauvignon Blanc 1990
As all Alderbrooks are, well structured wine with pure flavors of both grape variety and region. Of the three whites, this one is ready to drink first.

SANTA CRUZ MOUNTAINS
CALIFORNIA
UNITED STATES OF AMERICA   1186

SONOMA COUNTY
CALIFORNIA
UNITED STATES OF AMERICA

Alexander Valley Vineyards

8644 Highway 128
Healdsburg, CA. 95448
Tel. (707) 433-7209
Fax (707) 431-2556

To the pioneer in a young region goes the good fortune of writing the first definitions of its wines. Hank Wetzel had that opportunity with his family's estate beginning in 1975, and seized it, most especially with Cabernet Sauvignon. Wetzel, then a freshly minted graduate of the University of California-Davis, let his hilly vineyard have its head. The resulting Cabernet Sauvignons have consistently shown such depths of character that he has not yet felt a need to change his ideas of putting grapes foremost. Alexander Valley Vineyard white wines have been more problematic, or at least success has come more erratically. For a brief time the owners thought they had outgrown their vineyard, and bought grapes, but quickly decided against making any more wine than their estate could produce.

Alexander Valley 🍇 ②
Cabernet Sauvignon 1989
The epitome of vineyard and style. Darker colors, firmer tannins, and more berry-like fruit flavors than typical of a district where Cabernet persists in showing soft textures and herbaceous flavors.

Alexander Valley Merlot Estate 1989 🍇 ③
Achieving a wine that is both firm and polished is a difficult trick with California Merlot, but Wetzel has done it here. The Merlot is deftly complicated by toasty wood and a hint of coffee.

Benziger Of Glen Ellen

1883 Jack London Road
Glen Ellen, CA. 95442
Tel. (707) 935-3000
Fax (707) 935-3023

In a curious way Benziger of Glen Ellen is a triumph of integrity over marketing success. Bruno Benziger and family began with a small winery called Glen Ellen and used it to sell small lots of wines made mainly from Sonoma Valley grapes. After several years they added several inexpensive wines under the name of Private Reserve. Boom! Sales of nearly four million cases. And so they started their small winery all over again under the family name. With the rapid success of Benziger, they may have to do it again. The supple, accessible wines labeled Benziger of Glen Ellen come from the estate vineyard and others in Sonoma County, especially the Sonoma Valley. Most are varietals, but two are blended on the Bordeaux model and called Meritages. Their first great success was a Sauvignon Blanc 1981. That variety remains one of their crowning achievements.

Sonoma County Fumé Blanc 1990 🍇 ②
Enough true Sonoma Sauvignon aromas form the base to make this a wine for the true believer, but hints of Sémillon and fresh oak barrels add welcome grace notes and some body.

Sonoma Montain 🍇 ②
Sémillon Estate 1990
Like other Sonoma Sémillons from this superior vintage its perfumes range beyond fig-like to floral. With that it is impeccably balanced, firm and refreshing on the palate.

Sonoma County 🍇 ②
Cabernet Sauvignon 1989
The herbaceous side of Cabernet is abundantly present, and so is the taste of oak. But it is a Cabernet for Pinot Noir lovers, set apart because its flesh and polish make it almost velvet-soft.

SONOMA COUNTY
CALIFORNIA
UNITED STATES OF AMERICA

1187

SONOMA COUNTY
CALIFORNIA
UNITED STATES OF AMERICA

Chateau De Baun

1160 Hopper Avenue
Santa Rosa, CA. 95406
Tel. (707) 544-1600
Fax (707) 546-9221

The story of Chateau de Baun comes very close to being a fable to explain a young wine industry. It was founded in 1985 as a showcase for a grape variety called "Symphony," developed at the University of California for use in making light Muscat wines, and grown in Kenneth De Baun's estate vineyard. In the early years, the winery made only Symphony, but offered as many as four sparkling Symphonies and six still Symphonies of differing sweetnesses from none to overpowering, all from its own vineyard near Santa Rosa.
In 1988, de Baun added Chardonnay and Pinot Noir to the lists. In one year, Pinot Noir made a greater impression than all of the Symphonies that went before. The vineyard has yet to be rebalanced, but the die appears to have been cast for once and for all in favor of a well-adapted variety with great tradition.

Russian River Valley   🍇 ②
Chardonnay 1990
The flavor of Chardonnay is here rendered with perfect fidelity, as the region so often does. The almost honeyed richness of texture is another frequent gift from this valley.

Russian River Valley   🍷 ②
"Chateau Rouge" 1989
Cautious after a difficult, rainy harvest, the proprietors elected a proprietary rather than a varietal name. No need. This is a superior Pinot Noir by taste, by balance, by any measure.

Chateau Souverain

P.O. Box 528
Geyserville, CA. 95441
Tel. (707) 433-8281
Fax (707) 433-5174

When Pillsbury built Chateau Souverain in the early 1970s, they made their winery much too large for its markets. A succession of owners found themselves in the same trouble until Nestle, Inc., also owner of Napa's Beringer Vineyards, saw an opportunity to offer wines with distinct appellations at moderate prices. It began with cautious efforts, but is now pursuing such a program vigorously, and with success. Nearly all Chateau Souverain wines now compete above their price level, some well above it, owing to the energy and skill of winemaker Tom Peterson. Peterson, having sought out vineyards that reflect their appellations, is now taking the next step and producing wines from outstanding individual properties. The first of these are a Zinfandel from 1989 and two Chardonnays from the vintage of 1990.

Russian River Valley   🍇 ②
Chardonnay "Allen" 1990
In much-blessed 1990 the Allen ranch delivered indelible apple-like flavors of chardonnay that seem to last forever. A flickering suggestion of spice from oak adds depth. Lean and lively.

Alexander Valley   🍷 ②
Cabernet Sauvignon 1988
It may not be the grandest Cabernet of 1988, but is one of the finest values. Clear cabernet flavors and deft balance make it a wise choice for early drinking, but not a bad bet for some aging.

Dry Creek Valley Zinfandel 1988   🍷 ①
From California's greatest home for zinfandel, an example to drink rather than chew, but still a wine that can hold its own with tomato sauces, ginger, and other powerful flavors.

SONOMA COUNTY
CALIFORNIA
UNITED STATES OF AMERICA   1188

SONOMA COUNTY
CALIFORNIA
UNITED STATES OF AMERICA

Chateau St. Jean

8555 Sonoma Highway
Kenwood, CA. 95452
Tel. (707) 833-4134
Fax (707) 833-4700

Chateau St. Jean established a glowing reputation in its first vintages, starting with 1974, by making as many as six Chardonnays a vintage from individually identified vineyards. Following on that success it began offering Botrytis-concentrated Rieslings and Gewürztraminers of such heroic sweetness that even Trockenbeerenausleses were left far behind. By 1984, when Japan's Suntory bought the winery from its three founding partners, both efforts had bogged down because the competition in both arenas had become much sterner, and also because California's wineries were responding to customer demands for refined rather than heroic proportions, and Chateau St. Jean's vineyards were inclined to the bold. In recent vintages, it has responded to the changing challenges with increasing success. Meanwhile, Methode Champenois sparkling wine has become important.

Russian River Valley   🍇 ②
Fume Blanc "Petite Etoile" 1990
An unmistakeable flash of oak comes quickly from the glass, to be followed by understated aromas of Sauvignon. Only slowly does the true depth of Sauvignon flavor in this sturdy wine reveal itself.

Alexander Valley   🍇 ③
Chatdonnay "Belle Terre" 1990
Robert Young is the nominal king of St. Jean Chardonnays, but in 1990 the Belle Terre vineyard gave more of itself in both ripe flavor and firm, even austere structure in the wine.

Sonoma Country Brut   🍇 ③
Blanc de Blancs NV
Extremely subtle fruit flavors flicker in and out while firmer notes of toasted nuts, perhaps caramel, play a bolder role. The wine has balance, with some depth and length.

Clos Du Bois

P.O. Box 339
Healdsburg, CA. 95448
Tel. (707) 433-8268
Fax (707) 433-5067

Clos du Bois' original owner took the somewhat unusual step of amassing a number of sizeable vineyards without giving much, if any thought to a cellar in which to make the wine. The second owner made do with a converted warehouse for several years to be certain the label was no flash in the pan. Only after annual sales exceeded four million bottles did the company take the plunge and build a permanent home near Geyserville, close to Clos du Bois's main vineyards in the Alexander Valley. Well chosen vineyards and steady winemaking assure quality. Wines from individual vineyards carry the flag, two of them chardonnays (Calcaire, Flintwood), one a cabernet (Briarcrest), one a merlot-based blend (Marlstone). Chardonnay in four, sometimes five different styles, is by a wide margin the mainstay of Clos du Bois, and yet the reds often times attract greater attention.

Alexander Valley   🍇 ③
Chardonnay "Calcaire" 1989
The 1989 "Calcaire" is one of a cool vintage's fatter, richer expressions of Chardonnay. Its first note is all toasty wood, then the vineyard bursts through with nearly tropical fruit flavors.

Sonoma County Merlot 1989   🍇 ②
One expects strong flavors of herbs reinforced by dill-like American oak. The 1989 underplays both, and also is fleshier, less dryingly tannic than recent predecessors.

Sonoma County Pinot Noir 1989   🍇 ③
After years of stumbling with this variety Clos du Bois has brought forth a Pinot with meaty flavors and silken textures that would not shock Burgundian sensibilities.

Dehlinger Winery

6300 Guerneville Road
Sebastopol, CA. 95472
Tel. (707) 823-2378

Tom Dehlinger goes about his work with a quiet, serious air, looking exactly like the sort of schoolteacher who strikes terror into the hearts of children who have not learned their lessons.

He began as a grower and winemaker in 1976. As the years have passed, he has become ever more impassioned by Pinot Noir from his vineyard near the small town of Forestville. To cope with a series of knolls, Dehlinger has kept detailed annual records of the wines from each of several blocks within 20 acres, and adapted the vine training almost row by row to get the finest possible result from each block. The vines continue to show a colorful display of ribbons, indicating just what system is being used where. At the same time Dehlinger has adjusted methods of fermentation and barrel-aging to fit the demands of differing parts of the vineyard. All of the results go into a single blend which, year by year, gains depth, durability, individuality. Total annual production has surpassed 100,000 bottles. An excellent quality level is well demonstrated by our maximum recognition of the 1989 Pinot Noir.

Russian River Valley　　　　🍇 ③
Chardonnay 1990
As opulent as is the Pinot Noir, just that lean and austere is an estate Chardonnay that begs to be held in the cellar for at least three years, better five.

Russian River Valley　　　　🍇 ②
Cabernet Franc 1989
In most of California, Cabernet Franc smacks of berries. In Dehlinger's cool vineyard, the flavors are more herbaceous, closer to Cabernet Sauvignon. The texture is firm, not harsh.

1989

DEHLINGER

Pinot Noir

RUSSIAN RIVER VALLEY
ESTATE BOTTLED

A Vineyard & Cellar Selection of our Best from the Vintage.
PRODUCED AND BOTTLED BY THE DEHLINGER WINERY,
SEBASTOPOL, CA. CONTAINS SULFITES. ALC. 13.4% BY VOL.

Russian River Valley　　🍇🍇🍇 ③
Pinot Noir 1989
Flavors of Pinot Noir weave together with those of well toasted oak puncheons in the tradition of the house until the last, triumphant note of a rich, round young wine is all Pinot, pure Pinot. With age that balance will shift, atom by atom, in favor of bouquets too dense and tangled to give a name. Both evocations are the result of Dehlinger's learning every lesson Burgundy has to teach, and then rethinking them all in order to produce something utterly Californian. One curious upshot is wine better mated to meats grilled and sauced in northern Italian styles than any of the taditional dishes of France.

SONOMA COUNTY
CALIFORNIA
UNITED STATES OF AMERICA
1190
SONOMA COUNTY
CALIFORNIA
UNITED STATES OF AMERICA

De Loach Vineyards

1791 Olivet Lane
Santa Rosa, CA. 95401
Tel. (707) 526-9111
Fax (707) 526-4151

Cecil De Loach looks like he could be the Sheriff of Bowie County, Texas, especially when he wears his cowboy hat, which he does often. Looks are not altogether deceiving, for his approach to making wine is purely American: vineyards that give abundant flavor, modest use of oak as a flavoring, and no hesitation to leave a hint of sweet in the whites, even Chardonnay. Such has been the program from a tiny start in 1983 until now, and it has won his winery a loyal and large following, as well as a favorable reputation among critics.

The cornerstone is attention to vineyards. All of his several properties are in the Russian River Valley, all but one between Santa Rosa and a small town called Forestville. The newest one is at the eastern edge of the valley near Windsor. All have well-known, highly-regarded neighbors.

Russian River Valley 🍇 ②
Gewurztraminer 1991
A delicate perfume of sweet pea blossoms typical of gewürztraminer from the Russian River Valley, an appetizing interplay of tart and sweet, a wine for the open air.

Russian River Valley 🍇🍇 ③
Chardonnay 1990
In spite of being off-dry and honey-rich, De Loach Chardonnays virtually vibrate with varietal character, so intense are the flavors of the grape. No exception the 1990.

Russian River Valley 🍇🍇 ②
Fume Blanc 1990
Pure, bold, uncompromising Sonoma Sauvignon, between a bouquet of herbs and, perhaps, fresh young asparagus. A certain roundness on the palate betrays, what? a hint of unfermented sugar?

Russian River Valley 🍇🍇 ②
Zinfandel Estate 1990
A faint thread of oak adds its note, but ripe, almost floral zinfandel dominates through and through. In texture, the wine approaches chewy in the best tradition of the variety.

De Lorimier Winery

2001 Highway 128
Geyserville, CA. 95441
Tel. (707) 433-7718
Fax (707) 857-3262

Typical of an era in California, the Alfred de Lorimier family found a vineyard in gravelley soils east of Geyserville first, and only later turned to making wine from their property. After purchasing the vineyard in 1963, they paid careful heed to the wines from it made by others. Once satisfied that their grapes had some distinction, they built a small cellar on the property and launched the de Lorimier label in 1985. In two of three dry wines, their goal is not traditional California varietals, but rather blends based on the model of Bordeaux. This approach they signal with fantasy names - "Spectrum" for a pairing of Sémillon and Sauvignon Blanc and "Mosaic" for as assemblage of Cabernet Sauvignon, Cabernet Franc and Merlot. With that, the de Lorimiers elected to give their Chardonnay a name as well, it being "Prism."

Alexander Valley 🍇 ③
Chardonnay "Prism" 1990
With a new winemaker comes a slightly toastier, riper style, but enough of the original lean texture and pure taste of chardonnay remains to make this one of the more refined wines of its type.

Alexander Valley 🍇🍇 ③
Cabernet-Merlot "Mosaic" 1987
Dark, lustrous ruby hues promise a wine of deep and intense flavors, and just such flavors arrive in a still-youthful, vital wine with plenty of flesh on its bones.

SONOMA COUNTY
CALIFORNIA
UNITED STATES OF AMERICA

1191

SONOMA COUNTY
CALIFORNIA
UNITED STATES OF AMERICA

Dry Creek Vineyard

3770 Lambert Bridge Road
Healdsburg, CA. 94558
Tel. (707) 433-1000
Fax (707) 433-5329

Almost 20 years ago I described Dry Creek Vineyard proprietor David Stare as brash. He reminds me of it almost every time we meet, and looks at me as if all my hinges had been loose. Maybe he was just bold, but whatever he was, he still is, and it has worked to his advantage. A winery that was tiny then is substantial now, and wines that were good then are better now, with greater depth, finer polish, more defined personalities. Stare has achieved all this by taking heroic leaps, sometimes into the unknown. Vineyards in the Dry Creek Valley provide the heart of all his wines, but he reaches throughout Sonoma County to buy grapes that will add dimension to them. Fumé Blanc was his first ticket to renown, and it remains one of the most reliable Dry Creek wines. Chenin Blanc is his most surprising success.

Yolo County Chenin Blanc 1991   ❦ ①
David Stare has a knack for giving Chenin Blanc greater depth of flavor than most, and he exercised it to perfection in a barely off-dry 1991.

Sonoma County Chardonnay 1990   ❦ ③
Uncommonly fat for a 1990, but not for a Dry Creek Vineyards Chardonnay. Apple-like fruit flavors predominate, with deft spice from time in oak.

Sonoma County Fume Blanc 1990   ❦ ②
Hints of melon lurk but the grand theme is Sonoma's characterstic smack of herbs. Well polished textures do not hide an underlying firmness. Surely it will age as well as its forerunners.

Sonoma County   ❦❦ ③
Cabernet Sauvignon 1989
A distinct, dill-like note from American oak plays well against the cassis of Cabernet in a wine that is released early, but kept firm in any case. History says it will age to silken smoothness.

Gary Farrell Wines

8075 West Side Road
Healdsburg, CA. 95448
Tel. (707) 433-5852

Gary Farrell is one of many talented, entreprenurial young winemakers who labors days as the employee of another's winery and nights for his own label. In this case, Farrell manages to condense his day somewhat by working as the winemaker for the increasingly well-regarded Davis Bynum Winery, and leasing space from his boss for his own wines. Not only that, he buys grapes from many of the same vineyards. The major difference is that his lots are enough smaller for him to be one extra bit selective, resulting in wines with one or two more layers of flavor to engage the attention, and prices to match. Farrell seeks grapes widely in Sonoma County, but seems to have a particular affinity for his home appellation, the Russian River Valley, and for Pinot Noir and Chardonnay. This should not be taken as an invitation to ignore his Cabernet Sauvignons.

Russian River Valley   ❦ ③
Chardonnay 1990
A burst of ripe apple is quickly joined by one of sweet new French oak, resulting in a wine of bold flavors. Balance and body follow in proportion.

Russian River Valley
Pinot Noir "Allen" 1989
In youth, the fresh taste of pinot noir reigns, as does a lively tactile, but there is depth here, and balance, in a wine sure to benefit by four or five years in bottle.

Ferrari-Carano

8761 Dry Creek Road
Healdsburg, CA. 95448
Tel. (707) 433-6700
Fax (707) 431-1742

"Food is our Frank Sinatra," Don Carano says in explaining why restaurants and not show rooms occupy such an important part of El Dorado, the Reno, Nevada, hotel-casino of which he and wife Rhonda are owner-operators. Their luxuriously appointed winery in Dry Creek Valley is an extension of the Carano love of good food and wine, to the point of having a full-scale teaching kitchen as one of its amenities. Rather than one huge vineyard, Ferrari-Carano draws upon twelve small ones purchased to take advantage of Sonoma's broad range of soils and climates; one of Carano's firm beliefs is that blending grapes from several properties builds greater wines than working with only one vineyard. If the rare exception comes along, he is willing to take advantage. Meanwhile, the wines have been skillfully composed and finished since the debut vintage of 1986.

Sonoma County Fume Blanc 1991 ☙ ☙ ②
Wonderfully ripe, lengthy Sauvignon faintly sweetened by toasty oak. The wine has almost a honeyed feel rather than the brisk one of many California Sauvignons. Close to a Top Wine.

Sonoma County Chardonnay 1990 ☙ ③
Winemaker George Bursick captured precisely the taste of chardonnay, then elaborated on it to just the right degree with oak. Balanced to be enjoyed in youth.

California Chardonnay Reserve 1989 ☙ ④
Much toastier and more buttery than its Sonoma County sibling as a result of malo-lactic fermentation, time on lees and time in oak, the essence of "Reserve" in contemporary California.

Alexander Valley ☙ ③
Cabernet Sauvignon 1988
Ferrari-Carano has begun to find a real delicacy of both texture and flavor in its cabernet sauvignons as its vineyards mature and as cabernet franc comes into play in the blend.

Louis J. Foppiano

12707 Old Redwood Highway
Healdsburg, CA. 95448
Tel. (707) 433-7272
Fax (707) 433-0565

Italian names grace several durable wineries in Sonoma County's Russian River watershed, all of them dating back to Prohibition, some to the 19th century. Their labels are rarely that old. Virtually every one participated for years in the bulk trade, that is, sold wine to other wineries. And virtually every one of them elected to charge modest prices when they turned to bottling their own wines under family names. The secret behind their subsequent success lies partly with price, more with the fact that the founders knew where to buy land for vineyards. Louis J. Foppiano wins on both scores, in fact would win even if their prices were higher than they are for solidly made, reliably age-worthy reds. Proof of that claim comes often in their prestige bottling of Cabernet Sauvignon, labelled Fox Mountain.

Russian River Valley
Petite Sirah 1990
Against the variety's insistence on tannic roughness, Foppiano achieves a certain fleshy texture that haromonizes perfectly with fully-developed ripe fruit flavors. These wines age well.

Fox Mountain Russian River Valley
Cabernet Sauvignon 1986
The 1986 not only recalls the perfect expression of Cabernet from the 1985, but adds another layer or two. It is slightly richer in texture as well, yet retains a welcome delicacy, or lightness.

SONOMA COUNTY
CALIFORNIA
UNITED STATES OF AMERICA

1193

SONOMA COUNTY
CALIFORNIA
UNITED STATES OF AMERICA

Fritz Cellars

24691 Dutcher Creek Road
Cloverdale, CA. 95425
Tel. (707) 771-1900
Fax (415) 771-9398

Dozens of small wineries in California plug along for years, like rising young movie actors waiting for their first big break. Fritz is one of those. Founded in 1979, it did not begin to win critical praise until the end of the 1980s, when three vintages of Chardonnay in succession won favorable notice. The whites of Fritz Cellars are its most consistent successes. The reds, especially the Cabernet Sauvignons, have had more ups and downs, though the best of the winery's Zinfandels have matched its Sauvignon Blanc and both its Russian River and Dry Creek Valley Chardonnays in public esteem. San Franciscan businessman Donald Fritz owns the winery and a vineyard in Dry Creek Valley, and is a partner in a second vineyard in the Russian River Valley. By a quirk of American law, the second vineyard does not qualify for "estate" status.

Dry Creek Valley   🍇 ②
Sauvignon Blanc 1991
This is a wine that does not want a great deal of explanation. It is just good, solid, representative Sauvignon Blanc from one of Sonoma's best districts for the variety.

Dry Creek Valley Chardonnay 1990   🍇 ②
As in the Russian River Valley, it is fruit, fruit, fruit, but of a more restrained character. The same pillow-soft quality is in it, which goes rather against the grain of the vintage.

Russian River Valley   🍇 ②
Chardonnay 1990
Fruit, fruit, fruit, then a complicating hint of toast from time in oak barrels. Soft as a pillow at first glance, the wine firms as it goes. To be enjoyed for the freshness of youth.

Grand Cru

One Vintage Lane
Glen Ellen, CA. 95442
Tel. (707) 996-8100
Fax (707) 996-0336

Like many another California winery, Grand Cru is a story of shifting goals. When two young partners founded it in 1970, their purpose was to make Zinfandel in as many styles as they could imagine, from austere and age-worthy to frivolously fruity. Not too many years later the label no longer offered Zinfandel, but continued to resist Chardonnay. Now, under its second ownership, Zinfandel is coming back and Chardonnay is a mainstay. Current owners Walt and Bettina Dreyer brought new capital and new energy to the winery in 1981, and a new winemaker in Barbara Lindblom in 1988. Lindblom, formed partly by her association with Zelma Long at Simi and partly by two years in France, is subtly altering the Grand Cru style in Cabernet Sauvignon and Sauvignon Blanc, forging its style in Chardonnay, and keeping a popular Chenin Blanc exactly as she found it.

Alexander Valley   🍇 ②
Gewurztraminer 1990
California's long, warm, dry summer evenings invite off-dry wines for outdoor sipping. This one starts out all flowery (sweet peas), then quickly goes to refreshing grapefruit flavors.

Carneros Chardonnay 1990   🍇 ③
Lindblom plays nearly tropical-ripe fruit flavors against sweet ones from oak to achieve a boldness fairly typical of California. The balance is in proportion with those flavors.

Sonoma County   🍇 ②
Sauvignon Blanc 1990
Most of the flavors lean to melon, but the wine hints at fig as well. A touch of oak adds another dimension. It has slightly greater richness or roundness than a typical Sauvignon.

Sonoma County
Cabernet Sauvignon 1988
Some wines begin modestly, then continue to blossom right to the last sip from the bottle. This one does just that, with ever more expansive flavors of cabernet.

SONOMA COUNTY
CALIFORNIA
UNITED STATES OF AMERICA

1194

SONOMA COUNTY
CALIFORNIA
UNITED STATES OF AMERICA

Gundlach-Bundschu

P.O. Box 1
Vineburg, CA. 95487
Tel. (707) 938-5277
Fax (707) 938-9460

Among all of California's winemaking families, Bundschu is one of the oldest. Their Rhinefarm Vineyard in the Sonoma Valley is, beyond doubt, "the" oldest one farmed continuously by one owning family anywhere in the state. Carl Bundschu entered the wine business in California in 1858 as a partner of Jacob Gundlach. Bundschu established a producing cellar on his Rhinefarm vineyard in 1858. Prohibition interrupted the winemaking. However, the family continued to grow grapes. When James Bundschu, thrice-great-grandson of the founder, resumed winemaking in 1973 he had the shell of a building in which to work, and two mature, well-understood vineyards upon which to draw. After some years of pursuing a bold, sometimes outright heady style, Gundlach-Bundschu began shifting gears in 1990 with the arrival of Linda Trotta as winemaker.

Sonoma Valley   ☙ ②
Chardonnay "Sangiacomo" 1990
New winemaker, brilliant new style. The smack of new oak is the here, Chardonnay fruit the tortoise in a well-staged race. The firmness of the vintage is evident all through.

Sonoma Valley   ☙ ③
Cabernet Franc "Rhinefarm" 1989
The winemaker has freighted this Cabernet Franc with plenty of oak, yet the fruit flavors survive intact. An almost silky texture gives it its most pleasing dimensions.

Sonoma Valley   ☙ ②
Merlot "Rhinefarm" 1989
All of the old firmness of texture is still here, but everything is carefully proportionate, allowing well realized Merlot flavors to linger clearly on the palate.

Iron Horse Vineyards

9786 Ross Station Road
Sebastopol, CA. 95472
Tel. (707) 887-1507
Fax (707) 887-1337

When the winery started in 1978, the guiding idea was to produce memorable Pinot Noir and Chardonnay from the often foggy Iron Horse vineyard of Barry and Audrey Sterling, plus smaller amounts of Cabernet Sauvignon and Sauvignon Blanc from the sunnier Alexander Valley property of partner-winemaker Forrest Tancer. Methode Champenois sparkling wines were meant to be a minor aspect of the business. Sparklers have turned into the tail that wags the dog. French consultants helped Iron Horse establish itself as a serious label in classic method sparklers. That the Iron Horse vineyard seems adapted more to that end than to great Chardonnay or Pinot Noir speeded progress in that direction. Still wines remain part of the roster, but, the Bordelais-types from Alexander Valley draw more attention now than the Burgundian types from Sonoma-Green Valley.

Sonoma Green Valley   ☙ ③
Blanc de Blancs 1987
The leanest and most closed of Iron Horse's sparkling wines needs two or three years on the cork to blossom in most years and may need more in this firm vintage.

Sonoma Green Valley   ☙ ③
Blanc De Noirs "Wedding Cuvée" 1987
The Blanc de Noirs plays yin to the Blanc de Blanc's yang, with immediately appealing flavors and textures that begin to be creamy right at the outset.

SONOMA COUNTY
CALIFORNIA
UNITED STATES OF AMERICA

1195

SONOMA COUNTY
CALIFORNIA
UNITED STATES OF AMERICA

Jordan Vineyard & Winery

1474 Alexander Valley Road
Healdsburg, CA. 95448
Tel. (707) 433-6955
Fax (707) 433-0255

Thomas Jordan's first thought was to buy in
Bordeaux, but the cost of that and his warm
response to Beaulieu Vineyards Cabernet
Sauvignon, Georges De Latour Private
Reserve, convinced him to seek vineyard
land in California. The upshot of that decision
is a dramatic wine estate, with a chateau-like
winery high above the Alexander Valley and
a substantial vineyard directly downhill, on
the right bank of the Russian River as it
pursues its drowsy course toward the town of
Healdsburg. Cabernet was in 1976 and
remains today the main event, one which
moves ever closer to classical proportions.
The sparkling wine beautifully made and
dashingly packaged as "J" is, technically,
made by a separate company. However, all
of the winemaking is done at Jordan and the
owners are Tom Jordan and daughter Judy.
The debut vintage was 1987.

Sonoma County Brut "J" 1987   White (3)
A truly memorable debut seduces in part with
understated flavors, but principally with tactile
qualities that somehow manage to be as rich as
cream without having any weight.

Alexander Valley   Red Red (3)
Cabernet Sauvignon 1989
Ever true to the herbaceous taste of Alexander
Valley Cabernet, but has gained yet another
layer of flavor, and yet another degree of polish.
Among earlier vintages only 1985 rivals it.

Key to the symbols

Types of Wines

White

Rosé

Red

Rating System

An exemplary wine of its
type with outstanding local
character

An international premium
quality wine

A Top Wine, considered one
of the 150 best wines in the
world

*The 'grape bunch' symbol is used to
indicate the color of the wine; the
number of bunches represents the quality
rating assigned by the contributor*

Price levels

①   up to $ 9.99

② $ 10.00 - $ 14.99

③ $ 15.00 - $ 24.99

④ $ 25.00 or more

*The 'ex-cellar', or direct from the
producer, bottle prices, are calculated in
US dollars and are intended only as an
approximate guide*

**Entries are arranged in
alphabetical order by country,
region and winery or producer
name.**

Kenwood Winery

P.O. Box 447
Kenwood, CA. 95452
Tel. (707) 883-5891
Fax (707) 833-1146

Although the winery reaches into other parts of Sonoma County for grapes, it devotes uncommon amounts of energy to exploring its home Sonoma Valley as a locale of memorable vineyards and wines. Within and without that context, it has had its greatest successes in varieties other than chocolate-and-vanilla / Cabernet-and-Chardonnay. The Sauvignon Blancs under this label, though blended from many parts of Sonoma, have been some of California's finest and most distinctive. Among reds, it has had equal success with Zinfandel entirely from the home valley. This is not to say that its Cabernets and Chardonnays are less than good, but rather to say that it has come nearer the pinnacle with the other two wines. It seems quite possible the winery, owned and directed by a San Francisco family named Lee, has measured Sonoma Valley better than any of its peers in all four regards. Kenwood has slightly more than 100 ha. of vineyard under cultivation and produces 2 million bottles annually.

Sonoma County 🍇 ②
Sauvignon Blanc 1990
Though assembled from the usual 60 vineyards, forcefully flavorful as always of the herbaceous to grassy notes for which Sonoma is famous. Balance and polish, as always, are impeccable.

Sonoma Valley Zinfandel 1989 🍇 ②
It takes a keen palate to notice that Kenwood's "regular" Zinfandel has a fresher mien and lighter step than its more celebrated and costlier sibling.

Sonoma Valley 🍇 ②
Cabernet Sauvignon 1988
A ringingly clear taste of fully ripe Cabernet leads to a wine of surprisingly gentle charcter, one that calls for immediate use with pork loin, or perhaps a game bird.

Sonoma Valley
Zinfandel "Jack London" 1989
The essence of hearty Zinfandel is in it, but almost miraculously restrained, even deepened by a shadowy seasoning from oak. On the palate it is firm and dry enough, but never aggressive or chewy. Few Zinfandels can be called elegant. This one can. And it is the elegance that recommends it as a top wine, one to be brought out for memorable meals, if not quite for state dinners. The elegance is an irony, for the vineyard lies within a craggy ranch firts developed by the blood-and-guts writer whose name it bears. The property is west of a village called Glen Ellen in the northern Sonoma Valley.

SONOMA COUNTY
CALIFORNIA
UNITED STATES OF AMERICA

1197

SONOMA COUNTY
CALIFORNIA
UNITED STATES OF AMERICA

Kistler Vineyards

997 Madrone Road
Glen Ellen, CA. 95442
Tel. (707) 996-5117
Fax (707) 996-7061

Kistler has had the kind of ups and downs that drive a business owner crazy. The first year's Chardonnay, a 1978, saw critical hosannas far from fully earned (any fool can make a dramatic wine if he can afford enough new oak). Its successor suffered unparalleled scorn (a real flaw diminished itself with time in bottle, too late to recover a reputation). Ever since the proprietors have been wary of critics to the point that one hears less about the wines than they deserve. In truth, Kistler Chardonnays are steadily among the most praiseworthy California offers in the toasty, buttery style. Chardonnays, plural, is correct, for Kistler's partners make several each year from their own and well chosen purchased grapes, each identified as to source vineyard. There are other wines, but Chardonnays are the strength of the house. The architects of these beautiful wines are Steve and John Kistler, with the assistance of winemaker Mark Bixler. Their cellars are located in the Mayacamas Mountains at an elevation of almost 800 m.. Production is about 150,000 bottles per year.

Russian River Valley   ❦❦ ③
Chardonnay "Vine Hill Road Vineyard" 1990
Many would argue that this is the Kistler of the vintage. It has a shade fresher taste of Chardonnay, yet is rounder, more open already than the Estate.

Sonoma Valley   ❦ ③
Cabernet Sauvignon 1987
From vines on a high range of hills that often give Cabernet a soft, round quality, Kistler has somehow learned to strip away the weight without compromising distinctive flavors of cassis.

Sonoma Valley   ❦❦❦ ③
Chardonnay "Estate Vineyard" 1990
No other Chardonnay among Kistler's five single-vineyard bottlings from 1990 shows off so well the winery's mastery of the toasty, buttery style, for the Estate wine keeps both the taste of its grapes and a afirm texture as companions to all of the riches that come from malo-lactic fermentation followed by long aging in oak. Clearly, the model lies somewhere along the Côte d' Or, probably very closed to Le Montrachet. Happily, the exact expression is no mere copy, but rather a heartfelt tribute to a titan. The Estate vineyard, which crowns a high ridge in the northern Sonoma Valley, has somehow escaped the poetic name it deserves.

SONOMA COUNTY
CALIFORNIA
UNITED STATES OF AMERICA

1198

SONOMA COUNTY
CALIFORNIA
UNITED STATES OF AMERICA

Lambert Bridge

4085 West Dry Creek Road
Healdsburg, CA. 95448
Tel. (707) 433-5855
Fax (707) 433-3215

As of this writing, founder Jerry Lambert has placed his vineyard and winery in Dry Creek Valley up for sale after 20 years of ownership. An unsuccessful lawsuit growing out of an unhappy business relationship appears to be the root cause of his decision. One can only hope the new proprietor will have the same devotion to making excellent wine from a proven vineyard. Although the course has not been perfectly level for Lambert, his winery has produced memorable vintages of both Chardonnay and Cabernet Sauvignon, its two principal wine types. The Chardonnay, as happens in this and other parts of California, sometimes has an aroma that can be mistaken for Sauvignon Blanc, especially in cool years. The Cabernet never can be taken for anything other than what it is. The mature vineyard of recent years has given the label its finest wines.

Sonoma County Chardonnay 1989 ❦ ③
Exactly the sort of big, open-hearted Chardonnay many expect from California in spite of its coming from a vintage that pushed in the opposite direction. Well-wooded yet richly fruity too.

Sonoma County Merlot 1989 ❦ ③
A subtle seasoning from oak adds depth to enticing flavors of Merlot. Rather atypically for California, the wine has tannic firmness to equal a Cabernet Sauvignon.

Landmark Vineyards

101 Adobe Canyon Road
Kenwood, CA. 95452
Tel. (707) 838-9708
Fax (707) 833-1164

Only a handful of California wineries have settled down to make one type of wine. Landmark is one. Chardonnay is the type. Owner-winemaker William Mabry currently offers two single-vineyard wines each year, plus a third assembled from several sources. When Mabry started, in 1974, he was not so closely focussed. The early years saw Cabernet Sauvignon, Pinot Noir, Gewürztraminer, and other varieties. But Chardonnay alone truly caught his interest, and, as the winery's growth permitted, he replanted the vineyards best suited to that grape, and ceased using the others. Though he has had to relocate the winery owing to urban expansion around the original site, he has kept his prized vineyards intact. Each year he has become surer in his understanding of how to manage them, and surer in dealing with the vagaries of vintage once the grapes arrive in his cellars.

Sonoma County Chardonnay 1990 ❦ ②
Mabry seeks to keep more of Chardonnay and instill less of oak in this lowest-priced of his wines, and succeeds. A superior vintage gives it admirable depth and balance.

Alexander Valley ❦ ③
Chardonnay "Damaris" 1989
True to the Alexander Valley, a wine of size and intense flavors, nearly all of them from grapes but some from a proportionate use of well-toasted oak.

Sonoma Valley ❦ ③
Chardonnay "Two Williams" 1989
A cool year and a vineyard on the edge of Carneros would foretell a lean, firm Chardonnay. Such is exactly what this is, deeply flavored by grapes, lightly seasoned by oak.

SONOMA COUNTY
CALIFORNIA
UNITED STATES OF AMERICA

1199

SONOMA COUNTY
CALIFORNIA
UNITED STATES OF AMERICA

Laurel Glen

P.O. Box 548
Glen Ellen, CA. 95442
Tel. (707) 526-3914
Fax (707) 526-9801

Patrick Campbell is intensely wedded to his vineyard and even more to his winery. Once a career classical violist, he now gives his vines and wines the kind of attention only a perfectionist can bring to his work, as he has done since 1978. There is, for all practical purposes, only one wine, Cabernet Sauvignon. But Campbell manages to make fugues out of that. He has tried and abandoned cabernet franc in his steep vineyard, and is now experimenting with tempranillo on the simple grounds that Sonoma Mountain is not climatically, geologically or historically part of Bordeaux. If tempranillo does not work out, perhaps he will turn to sangiovese, or syrah. Meanwhile, bibbers do not have to worry about eccentricities in these wines; they hew close to the round, polished, subtly varietal style that has marked them from the outset.

Sonoma Mountain 🍇 🍇 ③
Cabernet Sauvignon 1988
So rich in the berry-like tones of vabernet that it smells as if it will feel juicy once tasted. The promise is kept. The ripe roundness masks firm tannins neatly.

Matanzas Creek Winery

6097 Bennett Valley Road
Santa Rosa, CA. 95404
Tel. (707) 528-6464
Fax (707) 571-0156

Owner Sandra Mac Iver now wryly confesses that she founded Matanzas Creek with the sole idea of making the greatest wine in the world. It is not a bad idea to aim high, as the increasingly lustrous record of the label since 1977 attests. It is also not a bad idea to keep an open mind about what might constitute a great wine. Early Matanzas Creek reds were made to such a heroic scale that few mortals had enough strength and courage to drink them. Sandra and Bill Mac Iver noticed, and shifted the direction of their Merlot toward accessibility. It now ranks toward the top with many critics. The whites did not suffer so much from gigantism, and it was thus the Chardonnay and Sauvignon Blanc that carried the winery to its present reputation. Though both Merlot and Chardonnay are anchored in estate grapes, the winery buys from independent growers throughout Sonoma for its Sauvignon Blanc.

Sonoma County 🍇 🍇 ②
Chardonnay 1990
The pattern is consistent: from bold, even slightly rough beginnins come wines that grow ever deeper and smoother as the months romm by. The perfectly balanced 1990 is right on schedule.

Sonoma County Merlot 1989 🍇 🍇 ④
Herbaceous Merlot and spicy oak interweave as flavors in a wine of near unctuous richness, one that sets off dreams of game or other lean, flavorful meats.

SONOMA COUNTY
CALIFORNIA
UNITED STATES OF AMERICA
1200
SONOMA COUNTY
CALIFORNIA
UNITED STATES OF AMERICA

Nalle Winery

P.O. Box 454
Healdsburg, CA. 95448
Tel. (707) 433-1040

Doug Nalle loves the physical business of winemaking, the hard work in vineyards and cellar. His enthusiasm for it reaches its peak during the grindingly long days of harvest, when he can sense subtle signals from wine in its formative stages, changes as small and slow as the rising and dropping temperature of fermenting juice while he pumps it over the cap, changes as swift and dramatic as the drop in sugar and rise in alcohol. The wine that gives him his greatest pleasure both in the making and the drinking is Zinfandel from benchland vineyards in Dry Creek Valley. He abandoned making wine for larger firms in order to concentrate his efforts on a wine of exactly that definition in a small cellar not far west of Healdsburg. In its first vintage, 1985, the wine won plaudits. The chorus of praise grows year by year. Nalle also produces a Cabernet Sauvignon, which deserves notice for its style and elegnce. As often happens in the world of wine, the passion and strong personality of producers, whereever, reflect themselves in their wines. This is exactly the case with Doug Nalle, among whose excellent wines a Zinfandel of the highest level permits this tiny cellar, with its 25,000 bottles a year, to take a place among the great names of international winemaking.

Dry Creek Valley 🍷 ③
Cabernet Sauvignon 1987
Doug Nalle's fondness for adding a sweet note of vanilla from oak to ripe flavors of garpes gets its full expression in a wine that otherwise covers a firm spine with just enough flesh.

Dry Creek Valley Zinfandel 1990 🍷🍷🍷 ③
The temtation in selecting Top Wines is to shrink into the safety of Cabernet Sauvignon and Chardonnay. No one will argue, as some surely will over the inclusion of Zinfandel, which is regarded somewhat as a bumpkin variety by some. But this is Zinfandel in full cry, the essence of wild blackberries perfumed with a careful suggestion of vanille-sweet oak, the flavors embodied in a hearty, almost chewy wine. And so it is for dinners where meat can be chewed from the bone with friends who do not mind if some of the sauce gets on one' s chin. Life cannot be fully lived unless it has such dinners and such friends, and the wines to go with them, hence top marks for this one.

SONOMA COUNTY
CALIFORNIA
UNITED STATES OF AMERICA

1201

SONOMA COUNTY
CALIFORNIA
UNITED STATES OF AMERICA

J. Pedroncelli Winery

1220 Canyon Road
Geyserville, CA. 95441
Tel. (707) 857-3531
Fax (707) 857-3812

A half-dozen or so of the old bulk wine producers of Sonoma County successfully made the transition to selling bottled wines under the family name, but, of these, only J. Pedroncelli has emerged stronger in white wines than red. Winemaker John Pedroncelli has a sure touch all across the board, not least in Zinfandel, but his Chardonnays and Sauvignon Blancs are often the grandest successes of the house. The Sauvignon Blanc is no surprise, given how well it performs in Dry Creek Valley, where all of the Pedroncelli vineyards are. The Chardonnay is a more surprising achievement for the same reason of vineyard location, Dry Creek being spotty at best with the great white grape from Burgundy. The Pedroncelli family bought land and began making wine in the 1920s. It began serious work under its own label by 1961.

Dry Creek Valley Fume Blanc 1991 ①
The flavors waver between succulent herbs and musty melons. On the palate it is slightly fuller than most California Sauvignons without being at all soft or lacking in structure.

Dry Creek Valley Chardonnay 1990 ①
Admirable understatement of chardonnay flavors that somehow remain indelibly true in spite of ample oak. The textures and balance are leaner and crisper than most from this vintage.

Dry Creek Valley Merlot 1989 ②
The first notes of cedar have crept into a beautifully balanced, polished yet firmly structured wine. The note of maturity is a welcome addition to an already stylish Merlot.

Dry Creek Valley Zinfandel 1989 ①
Many producers now lean to fleshy Zinfandels highly perfumed by oak. Pedroncelli stays with understated flavors of both fruit and oak, and achieves the vinosity many red drinkers seek.

Piper Sonoma

11447 Old Redwood Highway
Healdsburg, CA. 95448
Tel. (707) 433-8843
Fax (707) 433-4134

Piper-Heideseick was one of the first Champagne houses to buy into California after Moet et Chandon. Once in, it became one of the most cautious of the French firms operating in the state. At the outset, in 1980, Piper was a joint venturist with Sonoma Vineyards (now Rodney Strong), but bought out its partner in 1988. As with most of the French-owned, classic-method sparkling wine producers, style very much reflects that of the parent, but the expression of vineyard is purely Californian. Piper gets most of its fruit from the cool, often foggy Russian River Valley, but reaches into other parts of Sonoma County for grapes that add dimensions to the cuvees. Of these there are several, the Blanc de Noirs based in grape variety, the Tete de Cuvée and Vintage Reserve owing much more to blending and prolonged time on tirage.

Sonoma County Brut Tete de Cuvee 1987 ③
In essence the Brut, but from carefully selected lots given extra years on tirage to develop creamier riches of texture and flavor. It is still lean by California standards.

Sonoma County Brut NV ③
The most austere, most closed of California sparklers blossoms only after it has been under the cork for a year, better two. Then it continues to refresh but shows its depths of flavor.

Preston Vineyards

9282 West Dry Creek Road
Healdsburg, CA. 94558
Tel. (707) 433-3372
Fax (707) 433-5307

Lou Preston would seem to have a mild but persistent contrarian streak in him. When others sought exact imitations of French blends, he put chenin blanc rather than sémillon into his Sauvignon Blanc. When others succumbed to the market dictatorship of Cabernet Sauvignon and Chardonnay, he eschewed Chardonnay. Now, perhaps to his surprise, his abiding interest in Rhône varieties places him near the head of a parade, but not quite in front of it. In fact, Preston does what he does because of his firm belief in obeying the dictates of sun and soil. The vineyard he has owned since 1973 sits in the middle reaches of Dry Creek Valley. It grows superior sauvignon blanc, chenin blanc, petite syrah, and syrah, and shows promise with viognier, so he sees no reason to force middling good crops from less adapted varieties.

Dry Creek Valley   🍇 ②
Cuvee de Fumé 1990
Impeccably made, as always, with a deft seasoning from oak to broaden and deepen restrained flavors of sauvignon. The vintage gave admirable balance.

Dry Creek Valley Zinfandel 1990   🍇 ②
Where others give Dry Creek Zinfandel every chance to show its powerful perfumes, Preston reins in that side of the wine in favor of greater vinosity, thus more versatility at table.

Dry Creek Valley Sirah-Syrah 1989   🍇 ③
On its own, Petite Sirah performs much better in California than it does in the Rhône. In the company of true Syrah it produces for Preston a well-structured, deeply flavored, age-worthy red.

Quivira

4900 West Dry Creek Road
Healdsburg, CA. 95448
Tel. (707) 431-8333
Fax (707) 431-1664

Sixteenth century Spanish seafarers believed that an earthly paradise called Quivira was hidden where Sonoma County now lies. Henry and Holly Wendt named their winery Quivira, on grounds that Dry Creek Valley comes close to being the new Elysium envisioned by those explorers. After purchasing an existing vineyard in 1981, the Wendts started making wine in 1983. They decided then to ignore cabernet sauvignon and chardonnay because zinfandel grows best on the hills and sauvignon blanc excels on the flats of their 73-acre vineyard. They have since added cabernet sauvignon to both vineyard and cellar. They also have planted grapes for a Rhône-inspired blend they call "Regnum". However, thus far, the wines they made at the outset remain the ones that most often make their label one to remember.

Dry Creek Valley   🍇🍇 ②
Sauvignon Blanc 1990
Quivira opted for oak-tinted melon-like flavors in its dry, firmly structured 1990 Sauvignon. History says the wine will revert to typical regional herbaceous flavors if left to age.

Dry Creek Valley Zinfandel 1990   🍇 ②
An intense taste of wild blackberries heartily seasoned by French oak barrels mark a wine that may best be opened in its youth for fresh fruit flavors and ripe, even juicy textures.

SONOMA COUNTY
CALIFORNIA
UNITED STATES OF AMERICA
    1203
SONOMA COUNTY
CALIFORNIA
UNITED STATES OF AMERICA

Rochioli

6192 Westside Road
Healdsburg, CA. 95448
Tel. (707) 433-2305

The fame of this vineyard came well after its
first wines, 1982s, for the simple reason that
they were rustic experiments. In fact fame
came on the heels of memorable Pinot Noirs
from Williams & Selyem in 1985 and later.
But now, after some tutelage by Gary Farrell
(q.v.), the Rochioli brothers, Gary and Tom,
have taken hold firmly and are producing
wines of stature. Pinot Noir, not surprisingly,
leads their list. The surprising entrant is
Sauvignon Blanc grown in the same
gravelley riverside soils, under the same
foggy skies, to the vexation of those raised
on European regions where climate tends to
separate varieties far more neatly than it
does in California. As if this pairing were not
enough, the property also grows superior
Gewürztraminer, but one must visit the
winery to find a bottle of it, so small are the
quantities.

Russian River Valley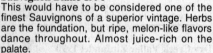
Sauvignon Blanc 1990
This would have to be considered one of the
finest Sauvignons of a superior vintage. Herbs
are the foundation, but ripe, melon-like flavors
dance throughout. Almost juice-rich on the
palate.

Russian River Pinot Noir 1989
The estate-bottled version drives straighter
toward the flavors of Pinot Noir than some of the
celebrated wines made from Rochioli grapes by
others. The effects are just as dazzling.

Seghesio Winery

14730 Grove Street
Healdsburg, CA. 95448
Tel. (707) 433-3579
Fax (707) 433-0545

Italian immigrants provided the backbone of
winemaking in California for years following
Prohibition. A few among scores sold wine
under their own labels. Most sold their
products in bulk to larger companies that
blended them into anonymous commodity
wines. As commodity wines have lost favor
and hand-crafted ones have gained ground
with the United States' wine-drinking public,
old bulk producers have had to shift gears or
go out of business. One that has shifted
those gears with growing success is
Seghesio. [] bought vineyard land in
Sonoma's Alexander Valley in 1894, and
founded the winery on his home property. His
sons, Peter and Edward, continued in the old
tradition, buying a larger winery in
Healdsburg in 1940 and adding further
vineyards in later years. The third generation,
Ted and Peter, Jr., began the transformation
from bulk winery to skillful producer of bottled
wines in 1980.

Alexander Valley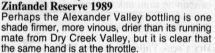
Zinfandel Reserve 1989
Perhaps the Alexander Valley bottling is one
shade firmer, more vinous, drier than its running
mate from Dry Creek Valley, but it is clear that
the same hand is at the throttle.

Dry Creek Valley
Zinfandel "Reserve" 1989
Dry Creek Zinfandels often have a flavor
reminiscent of wild blackberries. This one tastes
of a tamer, lightly spicy fruit. Balance and
texture make it pleasing for now.

Russian River Valley Pinot Noir 1989
After a first impression of oak, excellent flavors
of fully ripe Pinot Noir gain the upper hand in a
supple, polished wine that gives nothing but
pleasure.

SONOMA COUNTY
CALIFORNIA
UNITED STATES OF AMERICA

1204

SONOMA COUNTY
CALIFORNIA
UNITED STATES OF AMERICA

Simi Winery

16275 Healdsburg Avenue
Healdsburg, CA. 95448
Tel. (707) 433-6981
Fax (707) 433-6253

Much of the restless search for perfection
that characterizes the Robert Mondavi
Winery is also to be found at Simi, and for a
straightforward reason. Simi's longtime
winemaker and now its president is Zelma
Long, who was a major contributor to
Mondavi's success during the decade she
was a winemaker there. If the winery is
forever alive with experiments, little of the
turmoil shows in the wines, which are among
the steadiest in style in all of California. Its
steadiness even grows while the experiments
multiply, because it is relying more each year
on its own vineyards and less on purchased
grapes. Cabernet Sauvignon is farthest along
that road, with Chardonnay now beginning to
catch up. One is never left in doubt about the
grape varieties behind Simi wines, and yet
they are never simple or straightforward,
more because of adroit blending than a
heavy hand in the cellar.

Sonoma County   🍇 ②
Sauvignon Blanc 1990
Simi Sauvignons do not spring boldly from the
glass, but lurk quietly, revealing the
undercurrents to their melon-like flavors bit by
bit as a meal unfolds.

Sonoma Mendocino Napa   🍇🍇 ③
Chardonnay 1990
A wonderfully rich marriage of ripe Chardonnay,
vanilla-sweet French oak, and time shows its
distinction from first sip through lingering finish.
Earnest contender for Top Wine honors.

Alexander Valley   🍇 ③
Cabernet Sauvignon 1988
Almost pungent with the berry or cassis-like
flavors of Cabernet, and firmer than many
1988s, this has all the earmarks of being a
benchmark for both vintage and appellation.

Sonoma-Cutrer Vineyards

4401 Slusser Road
Windsor, CA. 95492
Tel. (707) 528-1181
Fax (707) 528-1561

Sonoma-Cutrer is very much the
collaboration of owner-grower Brice Jones
and winemaker Bill Bonetti. Jones had the
courage in the early 1970s, when few
vineyards existed in the Russian River
Valley, to invest heavily there, and to plant
the properties he had purchased. Bonetti was
the master enologist with a passion for
Chardonnay who designed an ultra-modern
winery and established fully traditional styles
for the three markedly different Chardonnays
for which the label has become well-known.
Two of the wines have the personality of their
vineyards. The third is the sum of three parts,
or, rather, three ranches.
Though his mark is sure to linger, these are
the last wines completely Bonetti's. He retired
after the 1991 harvest, his 11th at Sonoma-
Cutrer and 32d in California.

Russian River Valley   🍇🍇 ③
Chardonnay "Cutrer" 1990
In the case of this Cutrer, vineyard and vintage
joined forces to make a wine opposite of the
1989 Les Pierres, a riper tasting, rounder feeling
sibling with greater early charm.

Russian River Valley   🍇 ③
Chardonnay "Russian River Ranches" 1990
Made to be the most accessible of the annual
trio, it succeeds in every way: pleasing flavors of
chardonnay only lightly scented by oak, and a
round fullness of body.

Sonoma Valley   🍇🍇 ③
Chardonnay "Les Pierres" 1989
As is habitual from this vineyard, fruit was much
masked by wood until after a year in bottle, then
Chardonnay sprang forth. Vineyard and vintage
gave a firmness that promises grandeur in age.

SONOMA COUNTY
CALIFORNIA
UNITED STATES OF AMERICA

1205

SONOMA COUNTY
CALIFORNIA
UNITED STATES OF AMERICA

St. Francis Vineyards

8450 Sonoma Highway
Kenwood, CA. 95452
Tel. (707) 833-4666
Fax (707) 833-6534

St. Francis is one of many wineries that is gaining stature slowly by California standards. No grand triumph in an international tasting, no publicity coups following service at a political summit. Just a steadily expanding awareness that the wines taste good and offer value. The heart of them is the estate vineyard adjoining the winery at Kenwood. It provides all of the grapes for several well-regarded wines, though demand for Chardonnay outstripped its capacity several years ago. Merlot is the star among St. Francis reds, Chardonnay among the whites. Winemaker Tom Mackey carries a strong conviction that California red wine requires time in American oak barrels, a belief swiftly revealed by the wines themselves. The whites, contrarily, spend their formative time in French oak.

Sonoma County Chardonnay 1990 ❦ ②
Well-toasted oak is a forceful aspect of the wine, but bold, apple-like Chardonnay flavors refuse to be pushed into the background. Good bones hide beneath ample flesh.

Sonoma Valley Merlot 1989 ❦ ②
The winemaker's fondness for American oak as a spice in reds reveals itself quickly. For all that, berry-like flavors of Merlot remain at the forefront of a sturdy, ripe wine.

Taft Street

2030 Barlow Lane
Sebastopol, CA. 95472
Tel. (707) 887-2801
Fax (707) 823-8622

A few California wineries have caught lightning, as the old expression goes, in their first vintage or two. That is, they have hit upon a superior vineyard and an appropriate style right at the beginning. Most have had to stumble forward, learning by trial and error where their strengths might lie. Taft Street is one of the latter. Its early lists had wines long since dropped, probably for the best. Only in the last few seasons have the owners adopted Sonoma-grown Chardonnay as their focal point even though they have made excellent ones almost from the outset, always with an emphasis on flavors from the vineyard. The owning Tierney family started the label in 1982 as little more than a hobby. Once it began to succeed as a business they moved to larger quarters and began to refine their sources of purchased grapes.

Sonoma County Chardonnay 1990 ❦ ②
The wine assembled from the widest sources is, as always, a forceful demonstration of well-ripened chardonnay grapes only lightly perfumed by time in oak. Perhaps just less than dry.

Russian River Valley Chardonnay 1989 ❦ ②
Of more particular provenance than the Sonoma County, this example from a cool growing year somehow manages to be richer and riper than most from its vintage. Resolutely fruity flavors approach pineapple.

Sonoma County Merlot 1989 ❦ ②
An indelible flavor of merlot comes first, supple polish next. Appetizing as these are, it is an elusive note of coffee that makes the wine rich, and fully satisfying.

William Wheeler Winery

130 Plaza Street
Healdsburg, CA. 95448
Tel. (707) 433-8786
Fax (707) 431-8040

William and Ingrid Wheeler came to the wine
business armed more with dreams than skill,
but they also brought the other vital
ingredient, persistence. Before coming to
wine, Bill Wheeler had been in the U.S.
foreign service, in fact met his Norwegian-
born wife while posted in Rio de Janeiro, then
married her in London. They bought their
vineyard in Dry Creek Valley in 1970, and
started the winery in 1981. By 1989 the
business had grown to the point the
Wheelers needed financial partners. In that
year the American arm of France's Paribas
acquired a majority ownership, keeping the
Wheelers as managers and Julia Iantosca as
winemaker. William Wheeler Winery has
contributed to the reputation of its home
county for Chardonnay since the outset. Its
Rhône-inspired R.S. Reserve, begun in 1988,
carries promise.

Sonoma County Chardonnay 1990   ❦ ③
A few intensely perfumey varieties of apple
faintly suggest bananas. With a hint of help from
oak, that is the aroma of this juicy-rich, firmly
structured 1990.

Sonoma County R.S. Reserve 1989   ❦ ②
Good, hearty, straightforward red wine at a fair
price. The well-harmonized flavors of several
grape varieties are appealing, and sensibly
spiced with oak.

White Oak Vineyards

208 Haydon Street
Healdsburg, CA. 95448
Tel. (707) 433-8429

Founder-owner of White Oak, Bill Myers, was
a fisherman in Alaska in the 1970s, when he
felt an urgent need to change careers. At the
same time winemaker, Paul Brasset, was a
young, but nonetheless experienced hand
who had worked in several Sonoma wineries
and who had a restless urge to develop his
own sense of style. Chance got them
together in 1981. The story since then has
provided bibbers with a steady stream of
intriguing wines. In all, it is the whites, and
above all the Chardonnays, that pushed the
name White Oak forward in the early years.
However, Brasset's deepest affection is for
deeply flavored, long-lasting reds. With time
he and Myers have managed to develop
access to vineyards that give the sort of ripe
fruit Brasset seeks. Already recent vintages
of Cabernet Sauvignon have begun to
command respectful attention.

Sonoma County Chardonnay 1991   ❦ ③
An absolutely pure expression of the apple-like
flavors chardonnay often shows, plus deft
spices from oak. Somehow the wine manages
to be both full and lively in texture.

Sonoma County   ❦ ②
Sauvignon Blanc 1991
Traditional Sonoma herbaceous qualities offset
by the melon-like note of perfectly ripened
grapes. Sturdy textures promise benefits from
several years of bottle age to those with a taste
for it.

Alexander Valley   ❦ ③
Cabernet Sauvignon 1987
Dark ruby color promises rich flavors of
cabernet sauvignon. They are there, but must
compete with a smack of new oak. Like other
White Oak whites, this red is full and round.

SONOMA COUNTY
CALIFORNIA
UNITED STATES OF AMERICA

1207

SONOMA COUNTY
CALIFORNIA
UNITED STATES OF AMERICA

Williams & Selyem Winery

6575 Westside Road
Healdsburg, CA. 95448
Tel. (707) 887-7480

Burt Williams and Ed Selyem look plain, dress plain, and talk plain. Their winery reflects them exactly. But the wines are something else. Somehow, like the best of Burgundian peasants, they know how to treat pinot noir to bring out every bit of the nobility in it. As in Burgundy, that means giving both grapes and wine the tenderest treatment they know. The two got their start in 1979 while Selyem was still working as a printer for a San Francisco newspaper, the Examiner. After only one or two false starts they hit upon the style that has carried them to the forefront of California Pinot Noir producers. Their approach is to seek out the finest blocks within the finest vineyards and then keep only the most promising wines separate from picking basket to bottle. The strength of their conviction is to be seen in the "regular" blended bottling each year. Annual production is limited, barely reaching 2,000 cases; yet, in 1988, the winery made seven distinct lots of pinot noir and one of zinfandel. Since 1981, when this small winery was still known as Hacienda del Rio, it has followed several different paths. Today it has earned the right to be appreciated and evaluated at the international level.

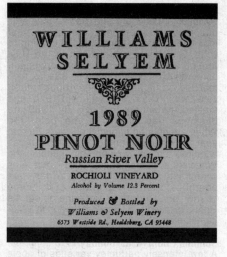

Russian River Valley 🍇 ③
Pinot Noir 1989
Assembled from the above two and two or three other vineyards in near proximity, this wine regularly shows the house style to splendid advantage at less than half the cost.

Russian River Valley 🍇🍇 ④
Pinot Noir "Allen" 1989
The distance from the Rochioli to the Allen vineyard is the width of a country road, and that is the degree of difference, this wine grand in itself but condemned to the shadow of its sibling.

Russian River Valley 🍇🍇🍇 ④
Pinot Noir "Rochioli" 1989
The very greatest of Pinot Noirs are so rich they suggest meat rather than fruit. This is one of those, its powers redoubled by a smoky tone from long slumbers in new, well-toasted oak barrels. The flavors of grape and wood begin separately, but forge and unbreakable bond after a year or so in bottle, with pinot noir consistently at the forefront. The vines that produce such indelibly flavored fruit grow only a few above the Russian River, which can rise to their height in winter, but shrinks to a wan trickle during the growing season, almost as if it understood what was wanted of it.

SONOMA COUNTY
CALIFORNIA
UNITED STATES OF AMERICA   1208

SONOMA COUNTY
CALIFORNIA
UNITED STATES OF AMERICA

New York, Oregon, Washington

Perhaps due to Califonia's success, serious winegrowing spread rapidly across the face of the country during the 1980s. The volumes remain tiny (the rest of the US makes less than 10% as much wine as California), but the achievements begin to loom large. Washington and Oregon states have lead the others since the 1970s, and still do. New York has been their closest rival, and still is. Since 1985, the first remarkable wines have begun to come from such unforeseen sources as Virginia, Arkansas, Texas and even frosty Michigan.

Washington and Oregon, though side by side, are worlds apart when it comes to wine. Nearly all of Washington's grapes grow in the eastern half, in a rain shadow cast by two parallel ranges of mountains, the Olympics and the Cascades. Volcanic soils east of the Cascades are rich, but so arid vines will not survive without irrigation water from the great Columbia River and its tributaries. Oregon's vineyards lie almost entirely west of the Cascades, in a region of year-around rains brought by Pacific storms that are not even slowed by a low range of coastal hills. Western Oregon's Willamette Valley is as cool, damp and green as eastern Washington's Yakima Valley is warm, dry and brown. Neither region is truly versatile for winegrowing, though eastern Washington is more so. The two young industries found their callings quickly after serious winemaking began early in the 1970s. Oregon first cast its lot with Pinot Noir and, to a lesser degree, Chardonnay. The latter begins to give way to the rising Pinot Gris. Eastern Washington looks to Sauvignon Blanc, Semillon, Merlot and Cabernet Sauvignon. Washington also grows Chenin Blanc well but has yet to find a perfect style for it. Both states have produced Riesling to challenge some of Germany's best, but that variety's virtual disappearance from the American wine market has caused its rapid decline in vineyard acreage.

Idaho extends eastern Washington as a growing region, in a tiny way. New York State is the other well defined source of quality wines. Its long tradition of using native and French-American hybrid varieties has not disappeared but is yielding steadily to a new wave of vinifera producers. The traditional heart of New York winemaking nestles among the Finger Lakes. Though winters are forbiddingly cold, the lake waters moderate the weather just enough for vinifera vines to survive in well-chosen sites. Viniferas dominate in the newer, smaller Hudson River and Long Island regions, both tempered by warm Atlantic Ocean waters. Long Island's Chardonnay is popular and increasingly so is its Merlot. Again, Riesling has done well in the bottle but not on the market.

As of 1992, Washington is second behind California in the production of vinifera wines. New York ranks second in all wines, but third if one counts only viniferas. Each state has about 12,000 acres in vinifera vineyards (one-third as much as the Napa Valley) and fewer than 100 wineries. Oregon has barely more than 2,000 acres but almost as many cellars as Washington. Texas, Virginia, and Pennsylvania all have small but vital, vinifera-based wine industries. More and more wineries are establishing firm styles through greater maturity in the vineyards and increased understanding of vinegrowing. None of these last-named states are to be found in this edition of the Guide, but they are unlikely to remain missing for long.

Glenora Wine Cellars

5435 Route 14
Dundee, N.Y. 14837
Tel. (607) 243-5511

Glenora has risen swiftly since its founding in 1977, having set itself the goal of producing sparkling wines styled closely upon Champagnes just at a time when New York's Finger Lakes wine region was shifting from its traditional emphasis on American native grape species and French-American hybrids to the classic vinifera varieties of Europe.

As planned, Chardonnay-based sparkling wines have been Glenora's mainstays from the beginning. The cellar's leading still wine to this point also comes from Chardonnay, though Riesling and Gewurztraminer challenge it. More surprisingly, Cabernet Sauvignon and Merlot show promise.

The winery nestles among vines on steep slopes rising from the shores of Seneca Lake, in some of the most beautiful scenery in all of America's winegrowing regions.

Finger Lakes 🍇 ③
Chardonnay "Sur Lie" 1989
A pale green tint and enticing aromas of ripe apple promise much. The wine gives more, managing to be both comfortingly rich and tartly refreshing as well as deep with flavor.

Finger Lakes Brut NV 🍇 ③
Creamy textures and enticing notes of toasted biscuit mark a sparkling wine made by someone who has paid close, effective attention to Champagne.

Palmer Vineyards

108 Sound Avenue
Riverhead, N.Y. 11901
Tel. (516) 722-9463

Long Island, most particularly the area called North Fork, blossomed quickly as a region for growing fine wines after a small, hesitant start in the mid- and late-1970s. Of the score of wineries now producing on the island, four or five seem to take vintage-by-vintage turns in leading the way for the rest. Palmer has shown enough quality and consistency to become one of those leaders in surprisingly short time, Robert Palmer having produced his first vintage only in 1986. The cellars, modelled on traditional houses and barns of New England, fit right into the farm-dominated North Fork of Long Island. Indeed Palmer's vineyard replaced a potato patch with Chardonnay, Gewürztraminer, Merlot, Cabernet Franc and Cabernet Sauvignon. The varieties from Bordeaux have been the grand market successes to date, but Chardonnay does well here.

North Fork Long Island Chardonnay 🍇 ③
"Barrel Fermented Selection" 1990
More and deeper flavors of toasty, buttery oak mark the wine than Chardonnay, but there is enough of the latter to make an appealing synthesis. Firm structure is another hallmark.

North Fork Long Island Merlot 1989 🍷 ③
The aromas are Merlot, but on the palate a taste of charred wood from time in oak comes first, last, and strongest. Exaggerated style aside, an underlying balance affirms the vineyard's promise.

Adelsheim Vineyard

22150 NE Quarter-Mile Lane
Newberg, OR. 97132
Tel. (503) 538-3652
Fax (503) 538-2248

Quiet, methodical David Adelsheim has been one of the premier figures in Oregon winemaking for most of his career there exactly because he moves carefully when chaos and confusion invite dramatic responses. Rarely have his wines been held up as icons when they first appear in the market. Rarely do they make a loud first impression. However, when showier stuff begins to fade (and all too much of it has), his wines are still on point, exemplary company at the dinner table as well as instructive demonstrations at the tasting bench. Adelsheim launched his winery early in the Willamette Valley's second wave of development, the first vintage being 1978. Like most of his peers, he pinned his major hopes on Pinot Noir, but also continued to explore other varieties to see how they would do in the cool, often rainy climate near Portland.

Willamette Valley Pinot Gris 1990 ⊛ ③
All is understatement, until one cannot know whether the fruit flavors are an obbligato to those of oak, or vice versa. Firm and dry on the palate, in the prevailing style.

Willamette Valley ❦ ③
Pinot Noir "Seven Springs" 1989
The flavors are a hard-fought tennis match between fresh oak and intensely berry-like Pinot Noir. Typical of Adelsheims, it needs age to bring itself into harmony.

Bethel Heights Vineyard

6060 Bethel Heights Road NW
Salem, OR. 97304
Tel. (503) 581-2262

Bethel Heights did much to break the iron grip of Washington County and northern Yamhill County when its first Pinot Noirs, from the vintage of 1984, commanded critical attention.
Once Pinot Noir had its pioneering successes from vineyards in the two named counties, adjacent to each other in the lower reaches of the Willamette Valley, other growers found it difficult to work back upstream. However, once Ted and Terry Casteel found a richly endowed patch near the Oregon State Capitol at Salem, the district known as the Eola Hills began to excite interest as well. Ever since the beginning the course has been an upward one for Bethel Heights, lucky, perhaps, in catching two of Oregon's best vintages early in its career. All of the wines are soundly made, but Pinot Noir remains the dominant factor in the firm's reputation.

Willamette Valley ❦ ③
Pinot Noir Reserve 1989
Dark-hued, and full flavored to match. The Pinot has a faint but persistent peppery tone to enliven it. Silken textures reveal a skilled hand in the cellar. One of the best of a fine vintage.

Domaine Drouhin

P.O. Box 700
Dundee, OR. 97115
Tel. (503) 864-2700

What the Baron Philippe de Rothschild's investment in Opus One did for the Napa Valley almost pales compared to the shot in the arm Oregon received when Robert Drouhin of the esteemed Burgundian house of Joseph Drouhin acquired property near Dundee in northern Yamhill County, and straightaway began planting vineyards and building a winery. Drouhin installed daughter Veronique as winemaker in time to make a debut Pinot Noir from the much trumpeted vintage of 1989. The name alone revived a flagging interest on the part of critics everywhere, too many earlier wines from this initially self-elected New Burgundy having tended to fade in bottle rather than improve. If Veronique's first results provided a boost, they are only a hint of the future. The wine came from purchased grapes, the family's own vineyards not yet being in production.

Willamette Valley Pinot Noir 1989 ♥ ♥ ④
From a brand new cellar there comes first a strong smack of new oak. But, memorable flavors of black cherries swiftly seize the foreground. Time should smooth away a faint youthful roughness.

Elk Cove Vineyards

27751 NW Olseon Road
Gaston, OR. 97119
Tel. (503) 538-0911

Proprietors Joe and Pat Campbell stumbled more often than not with their early wines, and not unexpectedly, for they are self-taught winemakers in a region that not only was a new place for wine grapes in 1974, but one possessed of a climate that would try the patience of Job. Perseverance has begun to pay off. Recent vintages of Elk Cove have produced some of Oregon's shiniest stars, especially when the question has been the two single-vineyard Pinot Noirs in their roster of four. Their own estate, high in hills above the weary-looking old lumber town of Gaston is one of the sources. The other, called Wind Hill, is farther north near the town of Forest Grove. Both are made according to traditional methods of Burgundy. The Campbells produce several other wines including Pinot Gris and Botrytised Rieslings.

Willamette Valley
Pinot Noir "Wind Hill" 1989
Ripe Pinot flavors suggest one of the wild berries that abound in western Oregon. This extra ripeness and a hint of wood add depth and length. The wine is already round and velvety enough.

Eyrie Vineyards

P.O. Box 697
Dundee, OR. 97115
Tel. (503) 472-6315

It is dangerous, as always, to make wine answer to an image of its producer, but David Lett and Eyrie wines are such highly defined individuals they will not let such thoughts slip away. Lett can be dour, but more often gives in to a sometimes sly, occasionally acerbic wit. More than that, he holds himself to high standards with never a thought of compromise, and does not suffer foolishness in others any more gladly than in himself. No doubt you have begun to form a picture of his wines, and you will be correct. They have been like that since Lett started in 1972, one of three durable pioneers in the Willamette Valley and the first of them to seize and hold a style. He did so against all odds, including a lack of capital that forced him to fit a winery inside an old poultry processing plant, and equip it in large part with leftovers from dairies and soft drink bottling works.

Willamette Valley Pinot Gris 1990
Eyrie Pinot Gris is meant to accompany Pacific salmon to the dinner table, and thus its fruity side is tempered by oak but not entirely lost, and it is balanced to cut through the fish's oils.

Willamette Valley Pinot Noir 1989
As always, Lett has pared away all of the fat until one has the sense of looking straight into the soul of Pinot Noir as it grows in this cool, damp climate.

Chateau Ste Michelle - Columbia Crest

P.O. Box 1976
Woodinville, WA. 98072
Tel. (206) 488-1133
Fax (206) 488-4687

Chateau Ste Michelle is Washington State's all everything winery. It was a pioneer in varietal wines in the state in the late 1960s. Combined with Columbia Crest, Snoqualmie, Fallon Ridge and other labels owned by the parent company, Stimson Lane, it is far and away the largest producer in the state, though that does not make it large by world standards. With 2,000 of the state's 12,000 acres of vines, is much the largest grower. Not least, Chateau Ste Michelle is Washington's most aggressive wine exporter. The wines have been reliably good from the beginning, but they jumped up several notches in 1990 with the arrival of Mike Januik as winemaker. Outstanding wine seems to follow him wherever he goes, as evidenced by the impressive reputations he built earlier for Stewart and Snoqualmie before the latter became part of the Stimson Lane group.

Chateau Ste Michelle Columbia Valley Sauvignon Blanc 1990
A faint hint of gold announces a wine with oak aging in its history. It is a promise adroitly kept, with oak a flickering presence while Sauvignon is persistent though understated.

Chateau Ste Michelle Columbia Valley Semillon 1990
At its best Semillon in Washington faintly suggests sweet grasses rather than figs or other, riper aromas. Bullseye! Silky smooth, and saturated with flavor through its long, cleansing finish.

Columbia Crest Merlot Barrel Select 1990
Lovely Merlot flavors in the variety's weedy vein combine with understated notes of oak, of coffee, and the beginnings of bottle bouquet. Lean, firm, but ready now.

Columbia Winery

14030 NE 145th
Woodinville, WA. 98072
Tel. (206) 488-2776

The firm now known as Columbia Winery produced Washington State's first critically acclaimed vinifera varietal, a Gewürztraminer, in the late 1960s. Originally called Associated Vintners because it was an association of home winemakers turned commercial, its wines were hit and miss until Master of Wine David Lake came aboard as winemaker in time to produce a memorable 1980 Semillon, from what is arguably the state's finest white grape variety. An expanded ownership changed the name to Columbia Winery in 1984. Since then Lake's particular triumphs have been with Merlot, the ranking red. Lake has not only made superior wines, he has done much to identify what Washington grows well, and where, through a long series of bottlings from individual, identified vineyards. The reigning champion among locals is Red Willow, but Otis and other properties have staked claims of their own.

Columbia Valley Chevrier   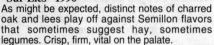 ②
"Sur Lies" 1990
As might be expected, distinct notes of charred oak and lees play off against Semillon flavors that sometimes suggest hay, sometimes legumes. Crisp, firm, vital on the palate.

Yakima Valley   ③
Cabernet Sauvignon "Red Willow" 1988
No fluke, the Merlot. From the same vineyard but a different vintage and variety, another firmly built red of indelible and precisely correct flavors, all in impeccable balance.

Yakima Valley   ③
Merlot "Milestone"1989
Milestone comes from a single and singular Yakima Valley vineyard called Red Willow, literally carved into volcanic soils where the last irrigated greenery gives way to desolate, dry scrub in what must be America' s harshest successful environment for grape vines. A miracle, then, that so special a place could be found so early in the infancy of wine in Washington State. But special it is, as the firmly-structured, richly flavored Milestone proves again with the 1989. Winemaker David Lake elects to add a proportion of Cabernet Franc, not for added firmness - none needed - but rather to give greater depth of flavor.

Gordon Brothers

531 Levey Road
Pasco, WA. 99301
Tel. (509) 547-6224

Growers forced to become wine producers in
an era of oversupply, the brothers Jeff and
Bill Gordon have hurried into the front ranks
of Washington producers. Their first crop
came from 1980, their first wine from 1983.
Their first rave reviews immediately followed
that Merlot's appearance in the marketplace.
The Gordons are making their wines in
consultation with Hogue Cellars from grapes
they grow on a bluff above the Snake River
some miles east of its confluence with the
Columbia, in country that looks impossibly
dry and hot where irrigation waters do not
reach, but incredibly green and fertile where
they do. The Gordon vineyard, like many
others in Washington, appears especially
well adapted to Merlot. It has been their
greatest and most reliable success. However,
their other wines beg thoughtful attention
from the knowledgeable.

Columbia Valley Merlot 1989 🍇 ②
Fat, round, happy textures match perfectly with
ripe, fruity, almost floral flavors from Merlot in a
complex wine needing no prolonged time in
cellar to give pleasure.

The Hogue Cellars

P.O. Box 31
Prosser, WA. 99350
Tel. (509) 786-4557
Fax (509) 786-4580

A long-time farming family in Eastern
Washington, the Hogues almost drifted into
wine. The public reception area of their
winery still has impressive displays of
specialty spiced and pickled asparagus and
other vegetables, crops they have been
growing since the 1940s. Their oldest
vineyards are native Concords grown to
make grape juice. However, once they
planted wine grapes in the early 1970s, they
put their formidable farming and marketing
skills into a winery that has, as a result,
grown by leaps and bounds. The Hogue
Cellars first set the tone for Washington
whites with stunningly fresh, off-dry Chenin
Blancs and Rieslings, then turned to reds and
repeated their original success by adroit
balancing of American oak against the
distinctive regional flavors of Merlot and
Cabernet Sauvignon. With the reds they have
turned increasing attention upon Semillon.

Washington State 🍇 ②
Sauvignon Blanc 1991
There is something unshakeably light-hearted
and fresh about this Hogue Sauvignon Blanc
that balks thoughts of waiting for a special meal.
Yet it has a strong personality.

Washington State Semillon 1991 🍇 ②
Semillon is the Washington white wine that has
depth and holds promise for development in
bottle. This vintage seems especially rich in
flavor and firm in balance.

Washington State Merlot 1989 🍇 ②
In comparison with a far oakier Reserve bottling,
this effort focusses clearly on Merlot. That is not
to say it is without a contribution from time in
barrel. Lean, lightsome.

Leonetti Cellar

1231 School Avenue
Walla Walla, WA. 99362
Tel. (509) 525-1428

Leonetti's limited production, highly individual
wines are particular prizes in the cellars of
local collectors, and have been from the
winery's first vintage in 1978. Owner-
winemaker Gary Figgins started with a single
model, the Martha's Vineyard Cabernet
Sauvignons of Heitz Cellars in California.
Figgins caught the style to perfection, from
the mint of ultra-ripe grapes to the spicy
notes of long aging in various types of oak.
He stayed true to it for a number of vintages,
then slowly began backing away from the
extremes until he has now established a style
that is still distinctive, but clearly his own.
Like many of the small, family-owned
wineries in the state, Leonetti has bought
most of its grapes from independent growers.
However, the sources have narrowed until
their contribution is as consistent as any
estate-grown grapes could be.

Washington State Merlot 1989   ❦ ③
Oak contributes a great deal to the sum of this
wine while the Merlot is almost curiously fruity. It
has similarly lush textures to the Cabernet.

Washington State   ❦ ❦ ③
Cabernet Sauvignon 1988
Figgins has coaxed the cassis side of Cabernet
where herbs usually surface, and sweetened
that note with the perfumes of new oak barrels.
The textures are full, almost lush.

URUGUAY

Wine in Uruguay is of considerable importance both in terms of quantities produced and domestic consumption. Indeed, it has a strong cultural element which is part of the national identity. Uruguay is the fourth largest producer of wine in South America and, with a surface area of only 176,000 square kilometers, produces 90 million liters a year for a pro capita consumption of 34 lt.

Even though the vine arrived by way of the early Spanish colonizers, as one of the staples that they carried and planted along their travels, the evolution of vine-growing and wine-making in Uruguay is much more recent. Italian and Spanish imigrants developed a modest, 'home-grown' wine culture as they settled in the country a century ago. Viticulture is now paradoxically similar in that it is practiced by a number of small private producers.

The wine regions are predominantly in the south, the most important both for quality and quantity being Canelones and Montevideo. The most common varieties planted are Cabernet Sauvignon, Cabernet Franc, Merlot, Syrah, Chardonnay, Riesling, Sauvignon Blanc, Gewürztraminer and Sémillon as well as the little known Vidiella grape. Other grapes like Tannat (here called Harriague), Alicante, Grenache, Cinsaut, Folle Blanche and a run of northern Italian grapes, namely Barbera, Nebbiolo, Lambrusco and Grignolino, have also been successful.

Established in 1987, the "Instituto Nacional de Vitivinicultura" aims to promote and develop a strategy and standard for wine production in the country. In setting the guide-lines for wine production and quality-oriented programs, it efficiently addresses producers' queries, enabling them to better respond to consumer demands and changing markets. As a result, amongst the South American producing countries, Uruguay's mandatory label information system forces producers to provide the consumer with all the information necessary to make an intelligent choice.

To date, Uruguayan wines have not entered the international export circuit, but this will certainly not last long. Some of the bigger names to watch for include Monsieur Gilbert, Faraut, Calvinor and Juan Carrau. Needless to say, Chile and Argentina are Uruguay's stiffest competitors in their ascent to international recognition. But as in the story of 'David and Goliath," intelligence can help win the day. Quality remains the password in Uruguay, but, in the end, the consumer will have the final say.

BRAZIL

ARGENTINA

Montevideo

Vinos Finos Juan Carrau

César Mayo Gutiérrez 2556
Montevideo
Tel. (2) 300238
Fax (2) 308221

This winery is part new, part old, part Catalan, part Uruguayan. Carrau's origins date from 1752 when Francisco Carrau purchased and planted his first vines in Vilasar del Mar in the Catalonia region of Spain. Wine-making flourished for 150 years until 1930 when Juan Carrau Sust built a winery in Uruguay and began to make one of South America's first méthode champenoise sparkling wines. In 1976 his son, Juan Carrau Puhol, moved north to the 31° parallel along the Brazilian border and founded a new wine-making zone in Cerro Chapeau in Rivera. In chosing to plant French varieties such as Cabernet Sauvignon, Merlot, Chardonnay and Sauvignon, he gave the Uruguayan wine industry a new impetus to quality-oriented production. Under the guidance of the in-house enologist Francisco M. Carraus, the winery now makes one third of all premium domestic wines produced. Furthermore, in the past six years, with its numbered bottle, certificate of origin line, Castel Pujol, it has also become a top exporter, shipping to northern Europe, Canada and Japan. Carrau also makes a line of wines called Chateau Lacave In the south of Brazil, in Caixas do Sul.

Castel Pujol
Sauvignon Blanc Rivera 1990
In a country where good white wines are hard to come by this is one of the best. Made according to the most modern parameters of technology, it has typical, intense fruity varietal character on the nose. Well-balanced, supple, fresh and soft on the palate, with a nice finish.

Castel Pujol
Cabernet Sauvignon Rivera 1989
A good red, certainly among the best in the country. Medium intense, ruby-red color, with defined varietal aromas. Soft on the palate with crisp fresh acidity and a pleasant tannic finish and good length.

Castel Pujol Merlot Rivera 1985
A typical example of a Uruguayan red that is a cut above the norm. Lively ruby-red with brick highlights, it has fairly intense aromas with scents of red fruit and spice. Round, full and well-structured on the palate with forward tannins.

Los Cerros de San Juan

Arenal Grande 1360 Bis
Montevideo
Tel. (2) 499763
Fax (2) 499764

One of the oldest viticultural estates in Uruguay, it is located along the banks of the San Juan river in the Colonia region where the Jesuits first grew vines and made wine. Founded in 1854 by the Lahusen family, of German origin, the wines perfectly mirror the nature and characteristics of their origin. White wines have an uncommonly important role here. In a nostalgic effort to make white wines even at these latitudes, the founders planted Rhine and Italian Riesling as well as Gewürztraminer from Alsace. Later these were joined by the more classic Cabernet Sauvignon, Merlot, Tannat and Pinot Noir. The winery is now owned by a large national food manufacturing group and ranks high on the domestic market. Exporting so far is more a question of prestige than a commercial need for the house. Enologist Cayetano Cano is the director. Los Cerros de San Juan can certainly be considered among the country's top three wineries. Its flagship wine, the Riesling, beats the competition hands down.

Los Cerros de San Juan
Riesling Colonia 1991
A truly fine expression of Riesling made in Uruguay. Limited production, rarely found abroad. Straw-yellow with greenish highlights, it it bright, with fruity aromas and floral scents. Harmonious, balanced, with a pleasant finish.

San Juan Fiesta
Vino Tinto Fino 1985
A typical Uruguayan red, made according to the local tastes. Clean, mature aromas, a red fruit background, with herbaceous scents. Full, slightly astringent, with a clean, lingering finish.

ZIMBABWE

Vine and wine culture in Zimbabwe began fairly recently in the 1960s but continues to grow stronger. Approximately 600 hectares of vineyards stretching across the border from South Africa are planted mainly to French varietals. The reds include Cabernet Sauvignon, Cinsault (referred to here as Hermitage) and Pinotage and the whites Colombard, Chenin Blanc, Muscatel, Riesling, Sémillon and Sauvignon.

To date there are only three producers who combined own almost all the vineyard area but in addition buy in grapes from smaller growers. The still whites and reds, as well as some sparkling wines, are produced mainly for domestic consumption but are also exported to neighboring countries.

Vineyards are situated in different areas of the country. Principally in the vicinities of the cities of Bulawayo, Mutare, Gweru Harare and Odzi where growing conditions are favorable with rich alluvial soils and for such a hot climate year round there is a decent annual rainfall.

The quality level of the wines is steadily increasing, thanks to the efforts made by these producers and their commitment to upgrade the wineries and bring in foreign winemakers.

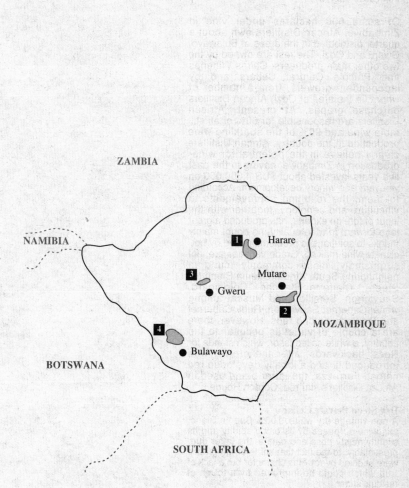

ZAMBIA

NAMIBIA

1 ● Harare

3 Mutare
Gweru ● ● 2

MOZAMBIQUE

4 ● Bulawayo

BOTSWANA

SOUTH AFRICA

1 Harare
2 Mutare
3 Gweru
4 Bulawayo

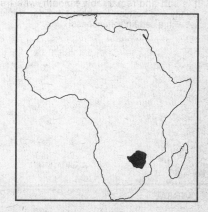

African Distillers

P.O. Box 2346
Harare
Tel. (263) 4 32901
Fax (263) 4 33909

Of some 600 hectares under vine in
Zimbabwe, African Distillers own about a
quarter distributed in the areas of Bulawayo,
Gweru and Odzi. The rest are owned by the
two other main producers, Cairns Wineries
and Philip's Central Cellars and by
independent growers, from a number of
whom (in the area of Odzi) African Distillers
purchase grapes. At present, African
Distillers are responsible for 60% of all still
table wine and 90% of the sparkling wine
production in the country. African Distillers
clearly believe in the potential for wine-
production in Zimbabwe, having in the past
five years invested about $US 4,000,000 on
vineyard and winery development. According
to them, the resulting improvements in
viticulture and oenology, together with the
input of foreign experts, has produced a great
leap forward in wine quality, no doubt mainly
thanks to solutions to problems posed by hot-
climate wine-making. Grape varieties are, not
surprisingly, those commonly found in
neighboring South Africa: Chenin Blanc (or
Steen), Clairette Blanche, Colombard,
Sauvignon, Sémillon and Muscat among
white; Cabernet Sauvignon, Ruby Cabernet
and Pinotage among reds. However, there
are a couple of varieties peculiar to the
country, a white called Issor, which stands for
Rossi backwards, after the grower who
introduced it, and a locally developed red
named Ferrazza, the latter being used in
African Distiller's star red, Cordon Rouge.

Dry Steen Private Cellar   🍇 ①
A non-vintage dry white, 100% Chenin Blanc,
this wine surprises by its biting acidity and its
slightly musty nose and palate, the latter due,
presumably, to the fact that some of the grapes
were affected by rot. Has character but a lack of
fruit which could be improved by a touch of
residual sugar.

Cordon Rouge Private Cellar 1991   🍷 ①
A youthful, purple-hued wine, 85% Ferrazza
blended with Cabernet Sauvignon and other
varieties. There is some berry fruit on the nose,
it is soft and remarkably smooth, with fresh
acidity and nothing hot about it. Easy-drinking
yet with a certain seriousness.

Index of Producers

Emilio **Lustau**, Spain	995
Maurice **Lutz**, France	471

M

Steven **Mac Rostie**, USA	1130
Niccolò **Machiavelli**, Italy	842
Jean **Macle**, France	414
Maculan, Italy	893
J. et H. **Madalle**, France	425
Madeira Wine, Portugal	935
Bodegas **Magaña**, Spain	1056
Jean-Paul **Magnien**, France	328
Domaine Michel **Mallard** et fils, France	301
Bodegas y Viñedos de **Malpica**, Spain	1047
Kommende Mailberg des **Malteser** Ritterordens, Austria	78
Malvirà, Italy	769
Jean **Manciat**, France	338
Weingut Heinrich **Männle**, Germany	539
Ezio **Mantellassi**, Italy	842
Weingut **Mantlerhof**, Austria	78
Adegas **Mar de Frares**, Spain	1097
Claude **Marandon**, France	498
Poderi **Marcarini**, Italy	769
Marchesi di Barolo, Italy	770
Domaine de **Marcoux**, France	394
Marengo-Marenda, Italy	770
Weingut Emil **Marget**, Germany	539
Staatliche Weinbaudomänen **Marienthal**, Germany	530
Giovanni **Marin**, Italy	701
Markham Winery, USA	1158
Marqués de Monistrol, Spain	1021
Bodegas **Marqués de Murrieta**, Spain	1067
Herederos del **Marqués de Riscal**, Spain	1068
Bodegas **Marqués de Vizhoja**, Spain	1097
Bodegas **Marqués del Puerto**, Spain	1067
Herederos del **Marqués del Real Tesoro**, Spain	996
Marquise de Laguiche - Maison Joseph Drouhin, France	298
Martinborough Vineyards, New Zealand	917
Bodegas **Martínez** Bujanda, Spain	1069
Bodegas **Martínez** Lacuesta, Spain	1070
Bodegas Faustino **Martínez**, Spain	1069
Louis M. **Martini**, USA	1158
Martini & Rossi, Italy	771
Mas Amiel, France	431
Domaine du **Mas Blanc**, France	427
Domaine du **Mas Crémat**, France	430
Mas de Daumas Gassac, France	426
Mas Jullien, France	421
Cavas **Masachs**, Spain	1012
Giuseppe **Mascarello** e figlio, Italy	772
Bartolo **Mascarello**, Italy	771
Masciarelli, Italy	676
Masi, Italy	894
Maso Cantanghel, Italy	877
Massandra, Conf. Ind. States	112
Régis **Masson**, France	499
Mastroberardino, Italy	684
Matanzas Creek Winery, USA	1200
Jean-Luc **Matha**, France	523
Adrian **Mathier**, Switzerland	1112
Domaine Joseph **Matrot**, France	297
Matua Valley, New Zealand	918
Mauro, Spain	1050
Simon **Maye** et fils, Switzerland	1112
Franz **Mayer**, Austria	79
Thomas **Mayr** e figli, Italy	878
Tenuta **Mazzolino**, Italy	727
McWilliam's, Australia	18
Meerlust, South Africa	970
Andreas und Toni **Meier**, Switzerland	1113
Luís **Mejía**, Spain	1037
Meknes Vins, Morocco	909
Melini, Italy	843
Alphonse **Mellot**, France	476
Charles **Melton**, Australia	29
Meridian Vineyards, USA	1178
Geoff **Merrill**, Australia	29
Ferdinando **Messinò**, Italy	682
Weingut Herbert **Meßmer**, Germany	601
Mestres, Spain	1012
Louis **Métaireau**, France	454
André **Métrat**, France	286
Hubert **Metz**, France	143
Weingut **Meulenhof**, Germany	568
Jean-Marc **Meunier**, France	284
Jos **Meyer** et fils, France	143
Weingut **Meyer-Näkel**, Germany	531
Louis **Michel** et fils, France	281
Domaine **Michel** René et ses fils, France	339
Robert **Michel**, France	373
Alain **Michelot**, France	332
Domaine **Michelot**, France	306
Mildara, Australia	30
The **Millton** Vineyard, New Zealand	918
Mitchell, Australia	30
Mitchelton, Australia	62
Mitjans, Chile	104
Mittnacht-Klack, France	144
Andrej in Valter **Mlecnik**, Slovenia	951
Moccagatta, Italy	772
Frédéric **Mochel**, France	144
Moët et Chandon, France	353
Weingut Markus **Molitor**, Germany	568
Fattoria La **Monacesca**, Italy	735
Weingut **Mönchhof**, Germany	569
Moncuit, France	354
Robert **Mondavi** Winery, USA	1159
Monfalletto, Italy	773
Bodegas **Monje**, Spain	1083
Domaine Jean **Monnier** et fils, France	311
Castello di **Monsanto**, Italy	843
Domaine du **Mont d'Or**, Switzerland	1113
Clos **Mont-Olivet**, France	395
Montana, New Zealand	919
Domaine de **Montbourgeau**, France	415
Monte Xanic, Mexico	906
Bodegas **Montecillo**, Spain	1070
Fattoria **Montellori**, Italy	844
Viña **Montes** - Discovery Wines, Chile	105
Fattoria di **Montevertine**, Italy	845
Monticello Cellars, USA	1159
Domaine de **Montille**, France	319
Camillo **Montori**, Italy	677
Bruno **Moos**, Italy	846
Domaine de la **Mordorée**, France	407
Bernard **Morey et fils**, France	298
Domaine Marc **Morey** et fils, France	299
Morgadío - Agromiño, Spain	1098
Gilbert **Mornand**, France	339
Alessandro **Moroder**, Italy	735

W

Y

Z

National Coordinators of the Guide

EDITOR-IN-CHIEF
Carlo Petrini, Bra (Cuneo), Italy
A highly esteemed figure in the gourmandise world, Carlo has a long history of wine journalism starting with the *Guida ai Ristoranti dell'Espresso* restaurant guide, the *L'Espresso* weekly review and the original *Gambero Rosso* supplement to the *Manifesto* newspaper. A contributor to many Italian and international publications, he is a founding co-editor-in-chief of the *Guida ai Vini d'Italia* (Gambero Rosso & Slow Food ed.). President and Chairman of the Arcigola *Slow Food* association, Carlo laid the foundations for the international *Slow Food* movement and the *Slow Food* publishing house which, respectively, today boasts over 20,000 members worldwide and a dozen successful books including the *Osterie d'Italia*.

NATIONAL COORDINATORS, LISTED BY COUNTRY
ARGENTINA, CHILE, URUGUAY
Miro Popic, Caracas, Venezuela
Freelance columnist for *El Nacionàl* and a number of international publications, food and wine writer Miro calls himself a "Periodista-Publicista-Panadero" and, in fact, helped to establish the epicurean circle in Caracas. Author of *El Libro del Pan de Jamòn* and the *Guìa Gastronomica de Caracas*, he is a founding delegate of the international *Slow Food* movement.

AUSTRALIA
Huon Hooke, Sydney
A native expert on Australian wines, Huon is a wine educator, cellar consultant and frequently a judge in wine competitions. He freelances for the *Sydney Morning Herald* and *Gourmet Traveller* among other publications and is presently writing a book on Australia's most famous wine, Penfolds Grange Hermitage, featuring its history and creator, Max Schubert.

AUSTRIA
Wolfgang Obermaier, Vienna
Co-founder of *Vinaria* wine magazine and its editor-in-chief for a decade, Wolfgang contributes to several wine publications and work with Hallwag editors for production of the German-language wine guides. A national *Slow Food* delegate, he also owns and runs a food and wine promotion agency in Vienna.

CONFEDERATION OF INDEPENDENT STATES, SOUTH AFRICA
David Molyneux-Berry, MW, London
David's three decades of experience in international wine trade began with Harvey and Sons Ltd. and continued at Sotheby's, where he authored the *Sotheby's Guide to Classic Wines and their Labels*, 1990, D. Kindersley. An active wine writer and lecturer specializing in South African wines, David recently also been an advisor for the ex-Soviet Union republics.

FRANCE
Roger Feuilly, Paris
An experienced, award-winning food and wine journalist, Roger is a regular contributor to *Paris-Capitale, Cuisine et Vins de France* wine magazine and the *Guide Pudlowski de Paris Gourmand*. He also contributes on occasion to the *Slow Food* monthly newsletter and had a major role in the realization of the French edition of the *Guide de Vins du Monde*.

Tim Johnston, Paris

British restaurateur and wine merchant, Tim Johnston has years of trade and cellar experience in California and France as well as in the European capital cities. Founder of several popular establishments including "Willi's Wine Bar", he contributed to *Decanter, Wine* and *The Wine Spectator* and researched for the book *The Wines of the Rhone* (Faber and Faber).

GERMANY

Jens Priewe, München

Journalist of economics and prominent wine writer, specialized in Italian and German wines, Jens regularily contributes to wine publications including *Alles Über Wein, Feinschmecker* and *Falstaff*. He is editor of the world-wine travel book series, "Reisen in die Welt des Weins", (pub. Zabert Sandmann, 1992), the first of which is based on *Toscana*, followed by *Piemont* and is author of *Italiens Grosse Weine*.

ITALY

Antonio Attorre, Grottammare (Ancona)

A regular contributor to the *Guida ai Vini d'Italia* (Gambero Rosso & Slow Food ed.), Antonio is a founding chairperson and regional chapter leader of Arcigola Slow Food association. Based in central Italy, he is a prominent food & wine writer as well as a passionate 'musicologist' and author of several books, his latest being *Nel Cuore delle Marche* (Slow Food Editore).

Gigi Piumatti, Bra (Cuneo)

Long-since employed at Arcigola Slow Food as one of the association's original founders, Gigi is a wine-taster and senior-editor for the *Guida ai Vini d'Italia* (Gambero Rosso & Slow Food ed.). He is also in charge of organizing the association's renowned wine Conventions and numerous other food and wine events held throughout the year.

Giovanni Ruffa, Asti

A contributor to the *Guida ai Vini d'Italia*, Giovanni was senior-editor of Slow Food's *Guida al Vino Quotidiano '92* daily wine guide and is a senior-editor of the *Slow Food* members' monthly newsletter. Editor-in-chief of *Slow Food*'s latest book, *Il Piacere del Vino: a handbook to wine-tasting*, he also writes for *La Stampa* and is a *Slow Food* chapter leader as well as Governor.

MEXICO

Giorgio De'Angeli, Ciudad de México

A Roman-born economist and award-winning food and wine journalist and educator, Giorgio contributes to dozens of international publications (*El Universal, Club de Gourmets*). Together with his wife, Alicia, of the famous "Los Naranjos" restaurant, he advocates fine Mexican cuisine and has written *Comer como Dios manda-good dining in Mexico*, as one of four books to date.

SLOVENIA

Giulio Colomba, Udine, Italy

A full-time Biology teacher, based on the Friulian border of Italy with Austria and Slovenia, Giulio is a regular contributor to the *Guida ai Vini d'Italia* (Gambero Rosso & Slow Food ed) and those publishers' respective magazines and newsletters. Nicknamed the "Tsar of

Friuli", he is an active, founding member of *Slow Food* and a Governor on the board of Directors.

SPAIN
Carlos Delgado, Madrid
The wine columnist for years at Spain's *El Pais*, Carlos contributed to consumer reviews and programs such as *Pueblo e Informaciones, Ciudano* and *Consumo* (TVE). A senior-editor of *Vino y Gastronomia*, he is an award-winning author (*El Libro del Vino, Diccionario Gastronomico, Comer en Madrid*, to name a few) and President of the *Slow Food* in Spain and co-founder of the international movement.

NEW ZEALAND
Bob Campbell, MW, Auckland
A director of Auckland-based wine school, "the Wine Gallery", Bob is the food and wine editor for *Cuisine*, author of *The New Zealand Wine Annual*, a contributor to the *Australian Winestate* and the English magazine, *Wine*. A Master of Wine since 1990, he also judges at competitions in Great Britain as well as in New Zealand and Australia.

PORTUGAL
Guillermo Campos, Pontevedra, Spain
Journalist, professor and food and wine critic, Guillermo writes for consumer publications and programs in Galicia and Madrid (*Voz de Galicia, Vino y Gastronomia, Club de Gourmets*) and is Director of *Consumidores*. An award-winning food & wine and travel journalist, he has helped to establish the European agency *Información al Consumidor*, soon to air.

SWITZERLAND
Peter Osterwalder, Zürich
A collaborator of *Vinum* since 1986 and editor since 1989, Peter is a co-author of the *Welt des Weine-Weine des Welt* (1992) and is a regular contributor to *Hotel- and Touristik-Revue* as well as *Expression* (American Express). With numerous stages abroad, he has extensive wine advertising and cellar experience for Swiss and German wineries.

USA
Bob Thompson, St. Helena, California
A judge in over 80 major wine competions since 1976, author Bob Thompson specializes in California and other American wines. The most recent of nine books are *The Wine Atlas of California/with Oregon and Washington* (1994), *Pocket Guide to California Wine* (1989) and *Notes on a California Cellar Book* (1982). His column "On Wine" began in the *San Francisco Examiner* in 1969.

BULGARIA, CZECH REP. & SLOVAKIA, CYPRUS, GREECE, HUNGARY, INDIA, GB, ISRAEL, LEBANON, MOROCCO, ROMANIA, TURKEY, ZIMBABWE
Nicolas Belfrage, MW, London, England
Born in California and educated in New York, Paris, London and Siena, Nic is a founding director of "Wine Cellars", the London-based merchants. A certified Master of Wine since 1980, he contributes to various wine publications, lectures at international events and is author of *Life Beyond Lambusco* (1985), an award-winning book on fine Italian wines.

Table of Weights and Measures

The most common metric weights and measures used in the European sections of the guide are listed in the following table together with British and American equivalents.

kilometer (km)	=	1.000 meters	= 0.621	miles
meter (m)	=	3.281 feet		
hectare (ha)	=	10.000 square meters =	2.471	acres
kilogram (kg)	=	1.000 grams	= 2.2046	pounds
quintal (Q)	=	100 kilograms	= 220.46	pounds
liter (l or lt)	=	1.76 UK pints/ 1.057 US quarts		
hectoliter (hl)	=	100 liters		

Yields are expressed as either Q/ha (quintals per hectare) or hl/ha (hectoliters per hectare).

Notes

Notes

To know more about Slow Food

I am interested in hearing more about *Slow Food*, the international movement and the catalog of books published.

(please print or type)

❏ Mr. ❏ Mrs. ❏ Ms. _____

street address _____

city _____ state/province _____

postal code _____

country _____

Tel. (_____) _____ Fax (_____) _____

occupation and business address, if preferable _____

_____

_____

_____

my age is ❏ 18-24, ❏ 25-35, ❏ 36-50, ❏ 51-60, ❏ over 60

my impressions of the *Slow Food Guide to the Wines of the World*:

_____

_____

_____

_____

_____

from: